Jane's

MERCHANT SHIPS

Edited by David Greenman

First Edition

1996-97

ISBN 0 7106 1388 1
"Jane's" is a registered trade mark

In the USA and its dependencies
Jane's Information Group Inc, 1340 Braddock Place, Suite 300, Alexandria, VA 22314-1651, USA

British Library Cataloguing-in-Publication Data.
A catalogue record for this book is available from the British Library.

Printed and bound in Great Britain by Biddles Limited, Guildford and King's Lynn

ADMINISTRATION

Publishing Director: Robert Hutchinson

Managing Editor: Keith Faulkner

Production Database Manager: Ruth Simmance

Editorial Services Manager: Sulann Staniford

Production Editor: Nicola Wells

EDITORIAL OFFICES

Jane's Information Group Limited, Sentinel House,
163 Brighton Road, Coulsdon, Surrey CR5 2NH, UK

Tel: +44 181 700 3700
Telex: 916907 Janes G
Fax: +44 181 700 3900
e-mail: yearbook@janes.co.uk

SALES OFFICES

Send enquiries to International Sales Manager:
Tony Kingham (Europe, CIS, Africa, Middle East)
David Eaton-Jones (Scandinavia, Far East, UK)
Jane's Information Group Limited, UK address as above

Tel Enquiries: +44 181 700 3759
Fax Enquiries: +44 181 763 1006
Fax Orders: +44 181 763 1005

Send USA enquiries to:
Joe McHale, Senior Vice-President Product Sales,
Jane's Information Group Inc, 1340 Braddock Place, Suite 300,
Alexandria, VA 22314-1651

Tel: +1 703 683 3700
Telex: 6819193
Fax: +1 703 836 0029

Contents

Introduction V

The Recognition System VI

How to use this book XVII

Flag and Country of Build Abbreviations XVIII

Abbreviations of Ship Types XIX

Abbreviations of Shipbuilders' Titles XX

Abbreviations of Engine Builders/Designers XXXIII

Alphabets XXXVII

Glossary XXXVIII

1 Tankers and Combination Carriers with Cranes 1
2 Tankers and Combination Carriers with Derrick Posts 27
3 Liquefied Gas Carriers with Tanks on Deck 73
4 Liquefied Gas Carriers without Deck Tanks 85
5 Gearless Dry Cargo Vessels (over 83.82 m (275 ft) overall) 105
6 Gearless Dry Cargo Vessels (83.82 m (275 ft) and under) 139
7 Dry Cargo Ships with Deck Cranes 155
8 Dry Cargo Ships with Derrick Posts 201
9 Dry Cargo Ships with Mixed Cargo Gear 261
10 Dry Cargo Ships with Travelling Cranes and Self-unloading gear 285
11 Refrigerated Cargo Ships (Reefers) 299
12 Gearless Container Ships 323
13 Geared Container Ships 347
14 Small Gearless Container Ships (ten 20 ft stacks or less) 363
15 Low-airdraught Ships (Sea/River) 375
16 RO-RO/Container (Gearless) 389
17 RO-RO/LO-LO 403
18 RO-RO Cargo 419
19 Vehicle Carriers 443
20 Passenger Ships (including Ferries) 457
21 Specialised Cargo Ships 497

Index 513

Alphabetical list of advertisers

I

International Maritime Organization
4 Albert Embankment,
London SE1 7SR, UK .... *index*

K

Kelvin Hughes Limited
New North Road, Hainault,
Ilford, Essex IG6 2UR, UK .... *index*

Introduction

Jane's Merchant Ships is, principally, a recognition handbook. It contains drawings and photographs of most of the world's major merchant ships. These are limited to trading ships, that is vessels that are employed as cargo or passenger carriers. Service craft, such as dredgers, research ships and trawlers, do not appear unless they double as cargo carriers. Another qualification for entry is an overall length of 70 m (230 ft) or more. There are a few exceptions to this rule but all for logical reasons which will be apparent.

This edition of *Jane's Merchant Ships* is, rightly, regarded as a new title, despite there having been three previous editions. There are so many changes in the 1996-97 book that it bears only a superficial resemblance to the last edition. Not the least of these changes is to the recognition system around which the book is arranged. The 'Talbot-Booth' system was devised in the 1930s and, despite certain changes, had not had a radical revision since its inception. Such a revision has taken place for this new edition. Although the new system will be seen to be built around the framework of the original, the modifications will be immediately apparent. The system is best suited to 'live' sightings of ships, where they can be viewed from various angles. For those who are familiar with the old system, the new one may seem a little complex. It is important to bear in mind, however, that the recognition system is meant to be used solely in conjunction with *Jane's Merchant Ships* and therefore there is no need to commit it to memory. Regular use will quickly increase its familiarity.

Ship recognition, particularly of merchant ships, has been a contentious issue for many years. In certain circles, the need for visual identification is not accepted. This view was prevalent 30 or more years ago and now, with the sophistication of modern technology, these same sceptics assume that all ships are fitted with foolproof identification instruments, such as transponders. This is clearly incorrect; very many ships do not have automatic identification systems and there is a clear need for a manual system both in the book and CD-ROM formats.

The importance of ships as the key element in world trade is acknowledged universally, although an exception to this is the sad decline of the British-flag merchant fleet in recent years showing that this confidence is not reflected domestically. A record year for shipping was 1995, with a 3.8 per cent rise in the volume of world trade carried by the merchant marine. There was also a 2.2 per cent growth in the size of the world fleet. Perhaps it is not quite so encouraging that the figures are affected by a decrease in the number of scrappings. An ageing fleet does not bode well for either shipbuilding or maritime safety. Nevertheless, with the volume of seaborne trade set to increase again next year, it must be good news for the future of shipping.

As well as for trade, the military importance of merchant shipping has been demonstrated many times in recent years. It has too often been a controversial subject in the UK but it would appear that shortcomings in this area are being addressed with the setting up of a Joint Rapid Deployment Force. It was recently announced that two roll-on-roll-off ferries would be acquired for the force. It is this type of vessel that is essential when personnel and equipment have to be moved rapidly to trouble spots. The USA has had a Ready Reserve Force for some years now and a number of these vessels appear in this volume.

These days, quite rightly, the protection of the environment has an almost equal status with political security. One of the marked features of merchant ship design over the past few years has been the emphasis on improving the environmental friendliness of oil tankers. The tanker incident which did so much damage to the South Wales coast earlier this year, although justifiably highlighted by the media, is not common when considered in the context of the huge volume of oil transported worldwide. It can only be hoped that the lessons learned from such incidents will lead to greater improvements, retrospectively in this case, and will encourage forward planning in the future. Perhaps one area that should be addressed is the extremely complicated multinational nature of some of the merchant marine ownerships and management.

Acknowledgments

With the large selection of new photographs appearing in *Jane's Merchant Ships* I am particularly indebted to Philip Neumann of FotoFlite and Tony Smith of the World Ship Society's World Ship Photo Library who have provided invaluable assistance in this area. My thanks also go to Norman Thomson and John Freestone for the use of their photographs, as well as Lisa Bompasso and Mr Atsushi Taira of the Japan Ship Centre who have been a great help in this area.

Keith Faulkner, Managing Editor, and the long-suffering editorial team at Jane's, led by Ruth Simmance, have shown fortitude and forbearance in equal measures. My thanks also go to Nicola Wells who has painstakingly read all the galley and page proofs. Allan Wyatt and his staff at BPC Whitefriars also deserve congratulations for completing an onerous task in a very short time.

The Recognition System

The recognition system used in this book is the 'Revised Talbot-Booth' system. Those familiar with the original 'Talbot-Booth' system, used in all previous editions of *Jane's Merchant Ships*, will see that the main elements of the revised system are based on those used in the original. To avoid further confusion, no further references to, or comparison with, the original system will be given in this explanation.

The basic principle of the system is to describe a merchant vessel using certain features which should be visible from a distance at which the name cannot be read. The descriptions are in the form of certain letters and numerals. The way in which this system is actually used in this book is described in the section on how to use the book.

The three elements used, in classification order, are:

1) SHIP TYPE
2) SEQUENCE
3) HULL FORM

(1) SHIP TYPE

There are 21 types used. They are based on external appearance and do not take into account the area of operation or size of ship (with one exception). Inevitably, there is some interchangeability between the types and it may be necessary to go to more than one section when using the system. This will be further explained later.

The basic descriptions of the types are as follows:

(1) Tankers and combination carriers with cranes
(2) Tankers and combination carriers with derrick posts
(3) Liquefied gas carriers with tanks on deck
(4) Liquefied gas carriers without deck tanks
(5) Gearless dry cargo vessels (over 83.82 m (275 ft) overall)
(6) Gearless dry cargo vessels (83.82 m (275 ft) and under)
(7) Dry cargo ships with deck cranes
(8) Dry cargo ships with derrick posts
(9) Dry cargo ships with mixed cargo gear
(10) Dry cargo ships with travelling cranes and self-unloading gear
(11) Refrigerated cargo ships (Reefers)
(12) Gearless container ships
(13) Geared container ships
(14) Small gearless container ships (ten 20 ft stacks or less)
(15) Low-airdraught ships (sea/river)
(16) Ro-Ro/Container (gearless)
(17) Ro-Ro/Lo-Lo
(18) Ro-Ro cargo
(19) Vehicle carriers
(20) Passenger ships (including ferries)
(21) Specialised cargo ships

IDENTIFICATION OF TYPES

(1) **Tankers and combination carriers with cranes**

Hose-handling crane, or cranes, amidships. The crane may be difficult to spot on some vessels, particularly chemical tankers where there can be considerable deck clutter with pipework, and so on. This section includes all types of tanker apart from gas carriers; including asphalt, bitumen, chemicals, oil products, vegetable oils and fruit juice. Combination carriers (OBOs (Ore/Bulk/Oil) and so on) are included because it is very difficult to distinguish them from tankers at a distant, sea level view.

(2) **Tankers and combination carriers with derrick posts**

Hose-handling derricks amidships. Some smaller tankers have no hose-handling gear but they have been put in this section. All the other information given for Section 1 applies to Section 2.

(3) **Liquefied gas carriers with tanks on deck**

Hulls built around large spherical or prismatic tanks, the tops of which appear above the upper deck. Some vessels will have longer tanks with rounded or sloping ends and others may have one long tank filling most of the well-deck. The latter could appear to be trunk-decked but the ends of the tank should be clearly seen. Many chemical and product tankers will have tanks of various sizes on deck for the carriage of certain chemicals or liquefied gases. This should not cause confusion as it can clearly be seen that they are not an integral part of the structure.

(4) Liquefied gas carriers without deck tanks

The tanks in these ships are either completely beneath the upper deck or, if they are above, covered by trunking. Can be very similar in appearance to chemical tankers and there are many examples of combination gas/chemical carriers. LGCs can usually be distinguished by large housings on the upper deck. Although chemical tankers will have similar housings, they will be smaller and fewer. LGCs with tanks raised above the upper deck are usually LNG (Liquefied Natural Gas) carriers. The other type of gas is LPG (Liquefied Petroleum Gas). Most of the ships under Section 3 are LNG carriers. Some gas carriers are combination LNG/LPG.

(5) Gearless dry cargo vessels (over 83.82 m (275 ft) overall length)

The larger vessels in this section, and many smaller ones, will be bulk carriers and most of the very largest, ore carriers. Some of the smaller general cargo vessels in this section are able to carry containers on the hatch covers. When seen in this condition, it is virtually impossible to distinguish them from full-container ships. Cross-checking with Section 12 (Container Ships) may be necessary. As deck containers are stacked across the full beam of the ship, beyond the hatch combings posts or some 'piggyback' arrangement, are fitted to support the outer edge of the container.

(6) Gearless dry cargo vessels (83.82 m (275 ft) and under)

Sections 5 and 6 are the only sections which differentiate vessels by size rather than intrinsic features. Cross-checking will probably be necessary for ships around the length limit. The remarks concerning containers on deck under Section 5 also apply to this section.

(7) Dry cargo ships with deck cranes

Deck cranes, in this context, refers to cranes which are used solely for cargo handling. Most modern cargo ships have cranes abaft the superstructure for stores and engine room servicing. These are not considered as part of the ship's gear for recognition purposes. Most of the vessels in this section will be small or medium-sized bulk carriers but some will be general cargo or multipurpose. The latter will have container capacity and will, therefore, be virtually indistinguishable from a geared container ship (Section 13). Pedestal cranes could be a feature of some of these ships. The recognition differences between cranes and derrick posts (or kingposts) are explained on a later page but there may be some examples which are difficult to classify. Again, cross-checking is the only solution.

(8) **Dry cargo ships with derrick posts**

Although derricks have been almost entirely superseded by cranes, there are still many ships in service, so fitted. In 'all-aft' ships, that is, those having no hatches aft, any derrick posts aft of the superstructure will not be considered as part of the ship's gear. If all derricks are removed but the posts remain, the vessel will be regarded as gearless. Some vessels will be multipurpose, with container capacity, and could be confused with geared container ships (Section 13).

(9) **Dry cargo ships with mixed gear**

General cargo ships and bulk carriers with a combination of different types of cargo gear (cranes, derrick posts, gantries and so on). Careful observation is required. One crane may be fitted on a vessel with a large number of derrick posts. Also, a vessel having one hatch aft, while having all the forward hatches served by cranes, may have derrick posts at the after end of the superstructure to serve this hatch. These could be easily overlooked. Some of these vessels may carry containers on deck.

(10) **Dry cargo ships with travelling cranes and self-unloading gear**

Some smaller, travelling cranes may be difficult to identify as such. This is particularly so if they are conventional cranes attached to a small gantry. Excavator cranes also come into this category although they may not always travel. Container ships with travelling cranes appear in Section 13.

(11) **Refrigerated cargo ships (reefers)**

The main distinguishing feature from general cargo ships is the presence of large housings on which the cargo gear is usually mounted. These housings contain refrigerating machinery. Invariably geared, this can be obscured by containers, which are often carried on larger examples. Although cranes have become increasingly popular, there are many with derrick posts. Multipurpose ships, combining container ship, reefer and ro-ro ship, have started to appear. They can be fitted with large, angled stern ramps. Most reefers have side doors to give access to pallet trucks. These are usually quite small and flush with the hull, so they are not visible at sea, but some smaller ships have large side doors amidships which come above the upper deck. Refrigerated fish carriers also appear in this section and they have much the same features as other reefers. Reefer ships have to be versatile due to the seasonal nature of their trade.

(12) **Gearless container ships**

It is very unlikely that one would see a full-container ship without some containers on deck. The latter, therefore, have to be the most significant recognition feature. General cargo ships (Sections 5 and 6) will be indistinguishable when they have containers stowed on deck. Superstructure is usually noticeably tall. This is for visibility above the deck stacks, which can be 12 to 15 m (40 to 50 ft) high. There are many variations in the position of the superstructure: amidships, three-quarters aft, aft and forward. In the latter case, the funnel is usually aft and rises directly from the upper deck. It can be obscured by deck containers. Full-container ships have cell guides in the holds into which the containers are stowed. Some vessels also have these above the upper deck but it will be difficult to appreciate this when fully loaded. A recent development is the 'hatchless' container ship. These have no hatch covers and the cell guides are extended above the upper deck. Container ships have a large size range, from short sea feeder ships to huge deep sea vessels nearly as large as some of the largest tankers and ore carriers. Container capacity is expressed in TEUs (Twenty-foot Equivalent Units) and the largest vessels in service now have a capacity of 6,000 TEUs. Another feature which can distinguish container ships from general cargo is the presence of a large breakwater forward in many ships.

(14) **Small gearless container ships**

Distinguished by the number of fore-and-aft container stacks on the foredeck. Ten stacks or less puts a vessel into this section. Vessels with container stacks aft, as well as forward, of the superstructure, will be in Section 12. Most of the ships in this section will be feeder ships. These are small ships which transport containers from small ports to large, deep sea ports. As this can be an unreliable trade, the vessels are often general cargo ships with facilities for deck loading of containers. This can mean that some will appear in Section 6 and others, possibly, in Section 5, although few will be large enough for the latter section.

(13) **Geared container Ships**

The description of gearless container ships will also apply to geared examples but the latter will generally not be larger than around 1,800 TEUs. Can have any type of cargo gear, including cranes, derrick posts, gantries and jib gantries. Cranes are usually of the pedestal type, to raise them above the container stacks. They can also be fitted to one side, in order to maximise the upper deck space. Many geared bulk carriers and general cargo ships can carry containers on deck to increase their flexibility and some of these can be fitted with the types of crane described above.

(15) **Low-airdraught ships**

Can also be described as LOW-PROFILE or SEA/RIVER ships. A ship's draught is the depth of the hull from waterline to keel. Therefore, the airdraught is measured from the waterline upwards, to the highest point on the ship. Masts, and other uprights, are either telescopic or hinged and the wheelhouse can often be lowered hydraulically. Most sea/river ships are operationally flexible and have large, unobstructed holds. Containers can often be stowed in the holds and on deck. Some are fitted with 'low-profile' deck cranes. There are also some tankers of sea/river design and they are also included in this section.

(16) **Ro-Ro/Container (gearless)**

Will not always be seen with containers on deck, so cross-checking with Section 18 (ro-ro cargo) might be necessary. A lot of the vessels in this section will have a large angled-ramp aft (sometimes referred to as a quarter ramp). These are immediately obvious, but smaller, 'in-line' ramps may require careful observation, particularly if they do not rise far above the upper deck.

(17) **Ro-Ro/Lo-Lo**

A vessel combining ro-ro and lo-lo (lift-on-lift-off) facilities. Many will be ro-ro/container ships and will, therefore, have cranes suitable for container handling (for example pedestal cranes). Some will be very versatile and the cargo gear could include a heavy-lift derrick. A stern view might be required if an 'in-line' stern ramp is to be observed.

(18) **Ro-Ro cargo**

A glance through the drawings in this section will reveal the variety of designs. Some will have a lot more superstructure than others and may start to be confused with ro-ro passenger ships. Clues such as numbers of lifeboats and liferafts will help identification. A high freeboard (which, for recognition purposes only, is regarded as the depth of the hull from the waterline to the upper deck) is always a significant feature of a ro-ro ship. None of the ships in this section will have any type of cargo handling gear.

(19) **Vehicle carriers**

Most of the vessels in this section are large, specialised car carriers. They give a very 'slab-sided' impression as the numerous car decks are plated flush to the sides of the hull. Many modern examples have the upper decks extended to the stem, emphasising the box-like shape. Some earlier vessels had side doors only but these are rapidly disappearing. Stern angled ramps are now popular and are often paired. There are smaller vehicle carriers trading on short sea routes. Some of the latter have features in common with ro-ro cargo ships (Section 18).

(20) **Passenger Ships (including ferries)**

Covers the whole range of passenger vessels from the largest cruise liners to short sea ferries. Numerous, long decks (many of them open) and many lifeboats and liferafts are the most significant features. Some of the cruise ships will have larger landing boats for shore excursions. Ro-ro passenger ships are included in this section and their 'in-line' stern ramps are not always easily appreciated at a distance. Passenger-cargo ships are also included. Although not as numerous as they once were, they seem to be making a 'come back' in some parts of the world. Cargo gear on the latter will be deck cranes or mixed and there will be container capacity. Some training/cargo ships will appear if they have a significantly large superstructure but some cross-checking may be necessary.

(21) **Specialised cargo ships**

This is, essentially, a miscellaneous section for types which fall within the scope of the book but have features which keep them out of other sections. The following types appear in this section:

Heavy-lift ships. Immediately distinguished by very heavy lifting gear, most of these vessels are multipurpose, having capacity for general cargo and/or containers. They also often have ro-ro capability. If their cargo gear clearly indicates that they are designed for general cargo/containers, they may appear in earlier appropriate sections.

Semi-submersible heavy-lift ships. Differ from the above by absence of lifting gear. They load their cargo, usually consisting of very large, indivisible items such as dredgers and drilling rigs, by submerging their barge-like hulls, allowing the cargo to be floated over the deck. The hull is then refloated. A tall forecastle and housings aft remain above the water during the operation. A variation on this type is the dock ship, which is, in effect, a self-propelled floating dock. Cargo is floated on through a stern door. These ships are more versatile than the semi-submersibles, often being able to carry containers on deck and having lift-on-lift-off capability. Neither of these types are particularly numerous.

Barge carriers. Despite having appeared more than 25 years ago, there are not many examples of these in service today. The original versions, LASH and SEABEE, lifted the barges at the stern by gantry and elevator, respectively. Later versions used the dock ship method. Most vessels can also carry containers and can be difficult to distinguish from container ships when carrying a deck cargo of boxes. The USA built a fleet of LASH (Lighter Aboard SHip) vessels, some of which have now been converted to container ships.

Livestock carriers. Easily recognised by the livestock pens running most of the ship's length. Most were converted from general cargo ships or tankers and still have features which betray their origins. A large number of prominent ventilators mounted on the pens can be a feature.

Cement carriers. Although bulk or bagged cement can be carried in conventional cargo ships or bulk carriers, there are many purpose-built vessels with specialised cargo pumping equipment. This equipment gives the vessels a very distinctive profile. Others have systems which are fitted in the holds with little evidence above the upper deck apart from large housings in the well. They may also have conventional derricks for handling bags of cement or hoses.

2) SEQUENCE

After the ship type, the second element in the system is the SEQUENCE. This can be defined as 'the noting of certain, prescribed features on the ship in the order in which they occur (working forward to aft)'.

The features are denoted by 23 letters and one symbol, in order to make the sequence as short as possible.

Here is a list of the initial letters, in alphabetical order, and the basic names of the features they are used for. More detailed descriptions of these features are given later:

A angled (or side) ramp
B paired angled ramps
C crane (conventional)
D paired cranes (conventional)
E cluster vents
F funnel
G paired funnels
H goalpost mast
J jib gantry crane
K gantry crane
L lifeboat, free-fall
M mast or pole
N paired mast
O offloader
P tandem cranes
R ram-luffing crane
S paired ram-luffing cranes
T cross-tree mast

U paired cross-tree masts
V bipod mast
X unclassified feature
Y stern ramp
Z paired stern ramp
— combined or adjacent features

This is a large number of letters and features to become familiar with but many will be used infrequently. Also, many of them are the initial letter of the name of the feature.

Mnemonics have been employed wherever possible to assist the observer in ascertaining the correct sequence letter. There are two types:

a) Letters which resemble the shape of the feature they stand for, that is, H (goalpost), V (bipod), T (cross-tree mast).
b) Consecutive letters for single and paired features. Certain features often occur in adjacent pairs and consecutive letters of the alphabet are used to identify these. The following are the paired features and their letters: A (single angled ramp) and B (paired angled ramps), C (single crane) and D (paired cranes), F (single funnel) and G (paired funnels), M (single mast) and N (paired masts), R (single ram-luffing crane) and S (paired ram-luffing crane), T (single cross-tree mast) and U (paired cross-tree masts), Y (single stern ramp) and Z (paired stern ramp).

BROADSIDE AND ANGLED SEQUENCES

Because many of the features recorded in the sequence can only be classified when the ship is seen at an angle, a problem arises. Many of the sequences given in the drawings sections of this book have been worked out from broadside illustrations only. This means that features such as goalposts, paired features, cross-tree masts, and so on, have not been identifiable. This could also happen on live sightings, although it is unlikely. The effect that this problem has in the drawings sections of this book is explained in the section on how to use the book.

NOTES ON SEQUENCE FEATURES

In these notes, the features are not listed alphabetically but are grouped as follows:

a) cargo handling gear
b) ro-ro equipment
c) all other features.

a) CARGO HANDLING GEAR

Consists of: C (conventional crane), R (ram-luffing crane), P (tandem cranes), M (mast), H (goalpost), T (cross-tree mast), V (bipod mast), K (gantry crane), J (jib gantry crane), O (offloader).

C (conventional crane). The term 'conventional' is only used to distinguish this crane from the later, 'ram-luffing' type (described later). The jib is at the base of the crane and is luffed either by wires from the top of the crane body or occasionally pistons at the base. The difference between a derrick post and a crane is principally that a derrick post is basically a vertical pole with far less width than height, while a crane body has a greater width in relation to its height. Inevitably, there are areas where the two features overlap and the only rule which can be applied is a simple 'try in both places'. (The latter rule applies throughout the system and, although it may seem obvious, it is a very important principle. Although there may appear to be many elements in the system, they will not cover every variation and further difficulties can arise due to weather conditions and distance, for example.) The letter D, as previously stated, is used for a paired C crane. These should not be confused with tandem cranes (described later), which have a single base.

R (ram-luffing crane). The differences in appearance between these and the conventional cranes are immediately apparent if the drawings are compared. The distinctive jib shape and small crane body are very distinctive. The rams which luff the crane are sometimes seen on cranes of the conventional type, so they are certainly not the main recognition feature. The fact that the jib is mounted at the top of the crane body is the most important feature of the ram-luffing crane. Smaller cranes, such as those used for handling small lifeboats, and so on, often have a fixed jib at an angle of around 45°. They are coded R, as their shape is very similar to this type. Hinged or telescopic ram-luffing cranes are also used for various service functions, such as stores or boat handling. S is used for an adjacent pair of ram-luffing cranes.

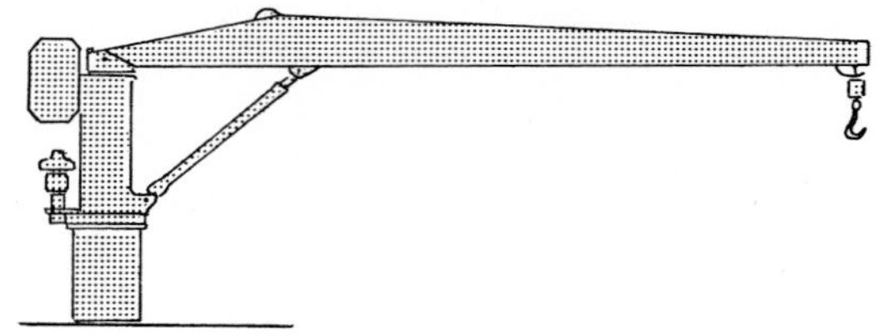

Typical ram-luffing crane. This is not a large version but has the typical features of all these cranes.

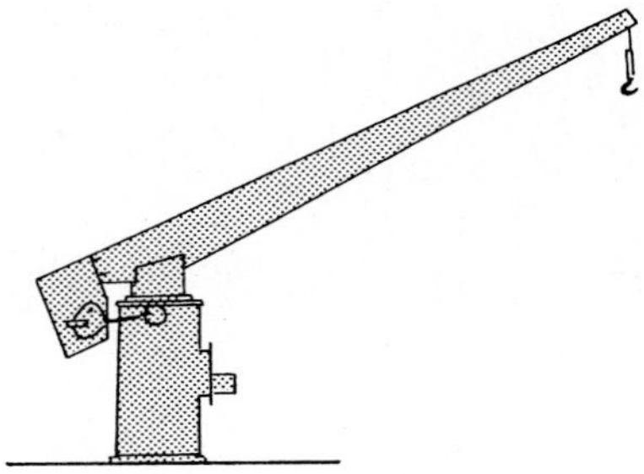

A small hydraulic crane. These would be used for handling liferafts or light stores, and so on. Although it does not have all the features of the ram-luffing crane, it is coded as R.

P (tandem cranes). A pair of cranes, either conventional or ram-luffing, mounted on one base and able to operate in tandem, doubling their lifting capacity. Usually stowed athwartships but may be seen fore-and-aft.

M (mast). Any upright pole or mast (including derrick posts and radar masts) falls into this category. Crane jib or derrick crutches (that is, the uprights on which they are stowed) are not coded unless they clearly double as a mast. Satcom aerials are often raised on fairly tall uprights and these can be coded M. N is used for an adjacent pair of masts. Single masts need not be on the centre-line. All multileg masts, other than bipods and goalposts, are also coded M. Tall ventilators, identified by a prominent cowl at the top, can be coded M or N if sufficiently tall.

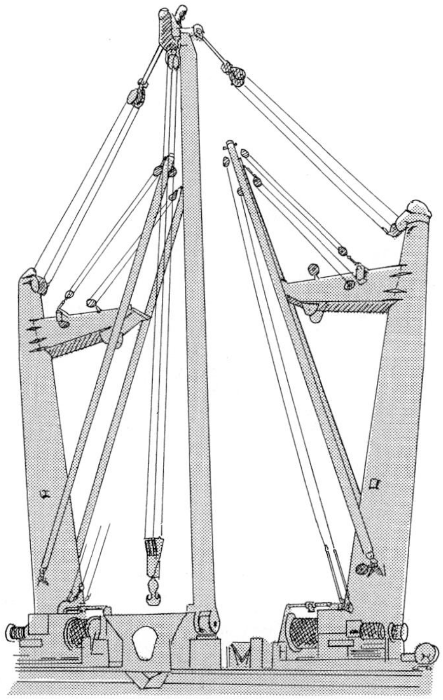

A Stülcken heavy-lift derrick. Although distinctive, these are coded as a paired mast (N). In some versions, the uprights could almost meet at the base, suggesting an inverted bi-pod. Another confusion could arise if the platform near the top of the uprights almost meet. This could resemble a goalpost. There are several variants on these masts, some of the lighter versions being designed for container handling. Although not often fitted on newbuildings these days, there are still a number of older ships so fitted.

H (goalpost mast). Occasionally, particularly with radar masts, the goalpost will be very low with a taller topmast, requiring careful observation. All goalposts are coded H, whether they have a topmast or not. The legs can be vertical or angled inboard. The latter could be confused with a bipod if the angle brings the legs close together. On some goalposts, the legs may have supporting arms. This should not cause confusion with a multileg mast as the latter would have equally spaced legs.

T (cross-tree mast). Usually seen on a mast fitted with a derrick. The size of the cross-tree can vary considerably. Some examples have the cross-tree at an angle to athwartships making them identifiable from either a broadside or angled view. U is used for a pair of these masts.

V (bipod mast). With or without topmast. A supporting leg would not make it a multileg mast. A 'V'-shaped mast (an inverted bipod) appeared in the 1960s but there are probably very few, if any, examples remaining. It is not to be confused with a bipod mast and should not be coded as one.

K (gantry crane). Four- or two-legged versions can be seen.

J (jib gantry). Any design of crane or jib mounted on a travelling gantry. A large crane mounted on a low gantry requires careful observation to classify correctly.

O (offloader). Main feature is a long boom attached to a structure which is integral with the bridgefront. The boom has a conveyor and is either of a girder-type construction or a solid outer casing. It can be swung over the side of the ship. Originating on the Great Lakes, ships of this type can now be seen worldwide.

b) RO-RO EQUIPMENT

Consists of: A (angled ramp) and Y (stern ramp)

A (angled ramp): The development of deep sea ro-ro ships gave rise to the angled stern ramp. These large ramps are often referred to as quarter ramps but this is now misleading, as they are often fitted at the forward end of a vessel. For recognition purposes, the term is also applied to side ramps if these are large and rise above the upper deck. Angled ramps are now common on vehicle carriers and they often have an adjacent pair of them at the stern. The latter feature is coded B.

Y (stern ramp). An in-line ramp in the stern counter. They are normally only coded if they come above deck level. Particularly heavy and tall ones may have equipment on deck for raising and lowering and slewing ramps will have a distinctive post. The latter may be stowed in-line or on the quarter which could, obviously, lead to confusion. Double stern ramps are coded Z. There are some large ships with three stern doors but they are rare and should also be coded Z.

c) OTHER FEATURES

Consists of: F (funnel), E (cluster vents), L (free-fall lifeboat), X (unclassified feature) and — (combined or adjacent feature).

F (funnel). Still, usually, the most significant feature of a ship but this is often due to paintwork on some modern ships. A single funnel on the port or starboard side is coded F but an adjacent pair of funnels is G.

E (cluster vents). These are common features on chemical tankers, where various chemicals are often carried in segregated tanks. Ventilators from these tanks are either brought together as a column on the upperdeck or incorporated into a type of platform. The former arrangement could give the impression of a conventional mast, so careful observation is required. Cluster vents is a descriptive term for recognition purposes and is not the correct technical term for these features. Although E may not be considered an appropriate letter for these vents, it could be viewed as a stylistic representation of them if turned 90° anti-clockwise. Cluster vents may be seen in adjacent pairs but will still be coded E.

L (lifeboat, free-fall). These have become increasingly numerous over the past 10 years. Although usually a large and significant feature, there can be problems with their observation. Some smaller vessels have their superstructure so far aft that there is little deck space abaft it. This usually means that the lifeboat is placed to one side of the superstructure with only the forepart of the lifeboat extending beyond it. This can be further obscured by a large crane which is often situated on the after deck. The latter is for recovery of the lifeboat and probably doubles as a stores/engine room crane. An alternative arrangement is to have a gantry incorporated at the top of the ramp.

X (unclassified feature). This is used for any feature which cannot be placed in one of the other categories. These must be seen to be an additional fitting rather than an integral part of the superstructure or hull, or a deck housing of some description. Purpose-built discharging equipment on a cement carrier would be a good example.

— (combined or adjacent features). The most common feature this applies to is a mast attached to a funnel (M-F). It is used where any feature is superimposed on any other. As previously stated, the sequence not only indicates certain fittings on a ship, it also shows the forward-to-aft order of these fittings. This, obviously, cannot be applied to superimposed features and the rule to be followed here is that the superimposed feature comes before the feature it is superimposed upon, therefore a mast superimposed on a funnel is coded M-F. Adjacent, paired features have already been mentioned (masts, cranes, funnels and so on) but a problem arises if two different features are arranged adjacently (for example crane adjacent to lifeboat). Clearly, one does not precede the other, either horizontally or vertically. In these cases, alphabetical order is used (for example conventional crane (C) adjacent to lifeboat (L) is coded C-L. Ram crane (R) adjacent to lifeboat (L) is coded L-R). Note: a mast would be considered adjacent to a funnel, for example, if it were in line with the centre, forward end or after end of the latter. The comparative for-and-aft lengths of the two features are irrelevant.

3) HULL FORM

The hull form is the final element in the recognition system and can simply be defined as: 'The arrangement of islands, or castles, on the hull'. An island is a superstructure which is attached to the upper deck but is integral to the structure and shape of the hull. There are three islands and these are each given a number, as follows: 1-forecastle, 2-midcastle, 3-poop (or aftercastle). When coding the hull form, the islands observed on the ship are denoted by their respective number and the prefix, H, is added, therefore a vessel with three islands would be coded H123. A vessel with no islands, that is flush-decked, would be coded as H.

The following drawings show the principal arrangements of islands:

It will be seen from the above drawings that the length or exact position of the island is, usually, less important than where it begins and/or ends. A very important rule, which must always be borne in mind when deciding on a hull form is: 'The forward end of a forecastle must be at the stem and the after end of a poop must be right at the stern'. Within this rule, the islands can be of any length, as the drawings above show. This rule should be taken literally, for example if an island ends just a few feet from the stern, it cannot be coded as a poop, even if it begins well aft.

HEIGHT OF ISLANDS

Islands are usually the height of one deck but if several decks are plated flush to the hull sides, they are considered as islands for recognition purposes. Vehicle carriers usually have their many decks plated in this fashion and are a good example of this point.

OTHER CONFUSIONS IN HULL FORMS

a) Bulwark plating could be confused with an island but is only about half the height and should be easily distinguished.
b) Long, curved hances (see Glossary for definition) can disguise an island and give the impression of slightly exaggerated sheer.
c) A trunk-deck can confuse as it can fill the well-deck between two islands and is usually the same height as the islands. This could give the impression of a flush-decked vessel if seen in silhouette.
d) An island can have small windows or portholes but no larger openings.

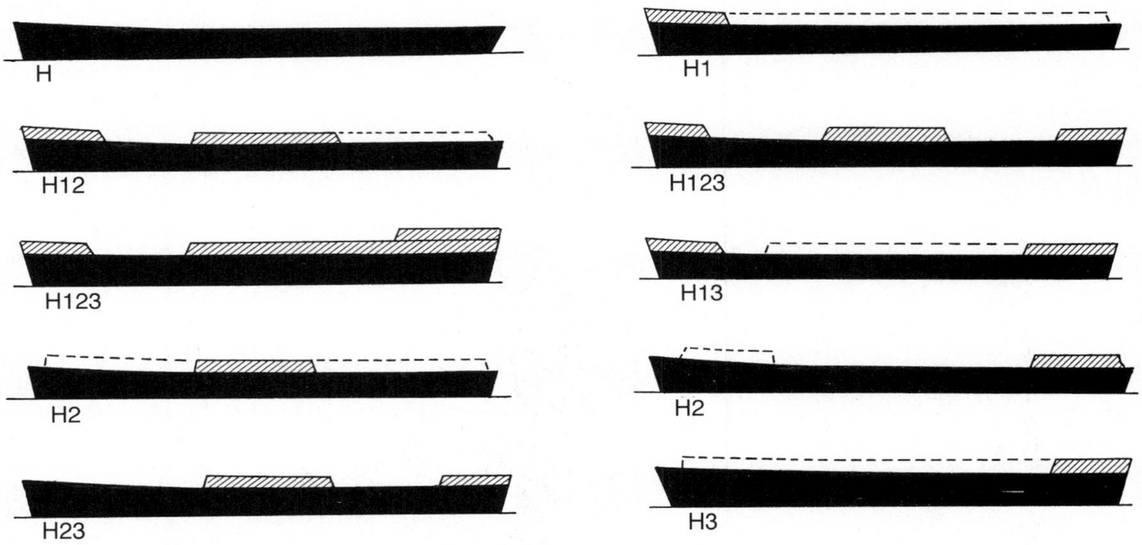

BASIC HULL FORMS AND COMMON VARIATIONS
The dotted lines represent variations in length or positioning of islands.

How to use this book

The book is divided into 21 sections which correspond to the ship types described in the previous section on the recognition system.

APPLICATION OF THE RECOGNITION SYSTEM

The first part of each section consists of drawings of ships in an order which is based on the recognition system. Initially, the drawings are in an order dictated by the sequence. The sequence, as described earlier, lists certain features on the ship, as they occur forward-to-aft, using a single letter for each feature. If MCCMFN is given as a typical sequence, it can be seen that it could be treated like a word in a dictionary and put into alphabetical order with other sequences. It will be noted that a hyphen is also one of the elements that can be used in the sequence. In the hierarchy of the system, it comes after all the letters, therefore MF comes before M-F, and so on. In some sequences, a letter may be repeated several times, for example MCCCCCMF. To make the latter easier to read, it is rendered as MC^{5}MF.

After the sequence, the hull form is given. Should there be one ship only in the particular sequence under which you are looking, the hull form has no relevance in recognition terms. If, however, as often happens, there are many ships with the same sequence, the hull forms can be used to further subdivide the drawings. There are eight possible hull forms and they fall into a numerical order, thus: H, H1, H12, H123, H13, H2, H23, H3. There will be groups of drawings with the same sequence and hull form but there are no further sub-divisions. It is then a matter of comparing the drawings.

There is a very important principle to remember when using the recognition system. Although there are 24 elements in the sequence and eight possible hull forms, there can be no guarantee that every feature seen on a ship will automatically fit one of these. A ship's appearance can be complex and complications such as distance and weather conditions also play a part. The system must be used flexibly and the observer should be prepared to try alternative ship type, sequence or hull form in order to make an identification.

Note: the drawings used in this book are not to scale.

Underlined Sequences

As stated earlier in the section describing the recognition system, there are several features in the sequence which cannot be identified when seen broadside (for example goalpost and bipod). Unfortunately, some of the sequences given to the drawings in this book have had to be ascertained from broadside sources. Paired features (masts, funnels, cranes and so on) will have been coded as single and goalposts and bipods will be coded as single masts (M). All sequences based on a broadside sighting are indicated in the book by being underlined. They are integrated with the angled sequences so that they all follow the strict alphabetical order. Sometimes an angled sequence is also given (for example MCFM/HCGN) as it is strongly suspected, but not confirmed, that the vessel has these features. In this case, only the broadside sequence is used to position the drawing. It is quite likely, of course, that the broadside sequence may be the same as the angled.

DATA WITHOUT DRAWINGS

There are a number of entries throughout the book where it has not been possible to supply a drawing. This is due to a lack of available information. Complete data is provided, including sequence, hull form and reference number. Although it will probably not be possible to make an identification from these entries, it is felt that the information provided could still be of value. In some cases, there is a photograph to cover a 'data only' entry. Where this occurs, a cross-reference is given.

DATA BENEATH DRAWINGS

Information is listed under the following fields (note: a semi-colon separates these fields in the data):

Consecutive number: Drawings are numbered from one onwards in each section. However, they can be easily distinguished in the index, where the section number and page number are also given.

Sequence/hull form: Explained earlier, qv.

Name: Names which have been transliterated, for example Russian and Chinese, use the spellings given in Lloyd's Register. See page xxxvii for transliterations of Greek and Cyrillic alphabets.

Flag/country of build: In abbreviated form (see list on page xviii). For the country of build, the title used is that which was current at the time of building (for example USSR and East Germany).

Shipbuilder: Given in brackets after country of build and not a separate field. Given in abbreviated form (see list on page xx onwards). The title is that which the builder had at the time the ship was built but sometimes the same abbreviation may be used for subsequent titles, if they are not significantly altered. All these titles are listed under the abbreviation.

Year of build/major alterations: Example—1975/80/92 (completed 1975, rebuilt 1980, further rebuilding 1992). Not a separate field.

Type of vessel: In abbreviated form (see list on page xix). The types are more specific than the section title (for example the tanker sections include chemical tankers, bitumen tankers, asphalt tankers, and so on). Where a vessel has more than one function, a combination of abbreviations is used (eg RoC/Con—ro-ro cargo and container carrier).

Tonnages: Two types of tonnage are usually given: *Gross tonnage* (the internal capacity of most of the enclosed space within a vessel. 100 cubic feet = one ton) and *deadweight* (the weight of cargo, stores, fuel, and so on, that can be carried). Gross tonnage presents certain problems these days. The International Convention on Tonnage Measurement (1969) came into force on 18 July 1982. Any vessel laid down after that date has been measured according to the new rules and all earlier vessels were given 12 years to comply (by 1994). Vessels were also remeasured after a major rebuild, such as lengthening. The new rules can increase the gross tonnage considerably, particularly in ro-ro ships and other multideck vessels such as car carriers. The gross tonnages given in this book a mixture of post- and pre-convention. They are all given as 'grt' but this is not strictly correct for ships measured under the convention. There are still many cases where it has not been reported that they have complied to the new rules. Before the convention, shelter deck vessels could alter their tonnage by being 'Open Shelter Deck' (OSD) or 'Closed Shelter Deck' (CSD). This gave the ships two sets of tonnages and draughts (larger for CSD). The establishment of the new rules has done away with this system. Where it is not known that a shelter decker has been remeasured, the old CSD tonnages and draught are given. As most passenger ships have little deadweight capacity, the gross tonnage only is given in most cases.

Dimensions: Length overall x maximum draught in both metric and imperial units. Length between perpendiculars (bp) is given if the overall length is not available.

Machinery/screws: In abbreviated form (see page xix).

Design of main machinery: In most cases this is the design of the machinery but, where this is not known, the builder is given. The design and builder are sometimes the same. A list of the abbreviations used is given on pages xxxiii to xxxvi (note—some abbreviations may appear in the builders section of this list).

Speed: Service speed, unless indicated, in knots.

Ex-names: Only the original name is given. It is omitted if it is the same as the current name.

Notes: Special features, details of rebuilding, and so on. The container capacity, where known, is given in TEU (see definition in glossary). In some cases, there will be facilities for stowing containers on the hatch covers only. If an entry is not illustrated because it is very similar to another vessel, but has to be separated due to having a different coding, this is noted in this section and the basic differences described.

Sister ships: Vessels built to the same design as the name ship. They will not, of course, comply exactly with the particulars given for the name ship. Some differences, such as builders, will sometimes be noted.

Similar ships: Vessels similar enough to the vessel drawn not to warrant a separate drawing.

PHOTOGRAPHS

Several pages of photographs have been included at the end of each 'vessel type' section. These photographs are numbered sequentially carrying on from the last drawing in that section. Each photograph has a caption containing the following information: Name (flag), date of build (see note above) and credit. Indication will be made where a photograph shows the ship under a previous name. The credit WSPL refers to the World Ship Photo Library of the World Ship Society.

Abbreviations

Flag and Country of Build Abbreviations
These indicate the ensign worn at the time of compilation of the book, and country of build. It is not necessarily the same as nationality of owners.

Ab	Abu Dhabi
Ag	Algeria
Al	Albania
An	Angola
Ar	Argentina
As	Austria
At	Antigua and Barbuda
Au	Australia
Az	Azerbaijan (or Azerdaydzhan)
Bb	Barbados
Be	Belgium
Bh	Bangladesh
Bi	Benin
Bl	Belize
Bm	Burma (later Mr—qv)
Bn	Bahrain
Bo	Bolivia
Br	Britain and British Dependencies
Bs	Bahamas
Bu	Bulgaria
Bx	Burundi
Bz	Brazil
Ca	Canada
Cb	Cambodia
Ch	Chile
Cm	Comoro Islands
Cn	Cameroon
Co	Colombia
CR	Costa Rica
Cro	Croatia
Cu	Cuba
CV	Cape Verde
Cy	Cyprus
Cz	Czech Republic
Db	Dubai
DDR	German Democratic Republic (East)
De	Denmark
DIS	Danish International Register
Do	Dominican Republic
Ea	Estonia
Ec	Ecuador
Eg	Egypt
ES	El Salvador
Et	Ethiopia
Fa	Faroes
Fi	Finland
Fj	Fiji
Fr	France
FRG	Federal Republic of Germany (before reunification)
Ga	Gabon
Gd	Greenland
Ge	Germany (after reunification or pre-1945)
Gh	Ghana
Gi	Georgia
Gm	Gambia
Gn	Guinea
Gr	Greece
Gu	Guatemala
Gy	Guyana
Ha	Haiti
HK	Hong Kong
Ho	Honduras
Hu	Hungary
Ia	Indonesia
Ic	Iceland
Ih	Ireland
In	India
Iq	Iraq
Ir	Iran
Is	Israel
It	Italy
Iv	Ivory Coast
Ja	Japan
Jm	Jamaica
Jo	Jordan
Ke	Kenya
Kh	Ra's al Khaymah
Kn	Kerguelen (French Antarctic Territories)
Ko	Republic of Korea (South)
Ku	Kuwait
La	Latvia
Le	Lebanon

Vessels may change their flag from time to time without changing ownership. This particularly applies to US or Greek owned tonnage which is frequently registered under Flags of Convenience such as Liberia, Cyprus, Panama.

Li	Liberia
Lt	Lithuania
Lu	Luxembourg
Ly	Libya
Ma	Malta
Mb	Mozambique
Me	Mexico
Mg	Madagascar
MI	Marshall Islands
Mn	Monaco
Mo	Morocco
Mr	Myanmar (formerly Bm—qv)
Ms	Mauritius
Mt	Mauritania
Mv	Maldives
My	Malaysia
Na	Nauru
NA	Netherlands Antilles
Ne	Netherlands
Ng	Nigeria
Ni	Nicaragua
NIS	Norwegian International Register
No	Norway
NZ	New Zealand
Om	Oman
Pa	Panama
Pd	Poland
Pe	Peru
Pi	Philippines
Pk	Pakistan
Po	Portugal
Pp	Papua/New Guinea
Py	Paraguay
Qt	Qatar
RC	People's Republic of China
RK	Democratic People's Republic of Korea (North)
Rm	Romania
Ru	Russia
SA	South Africa
Sao	Sâo Tomé e Principe
Sc	Seychelles
Sd	Switzerland
Se	Senegambia
Sg	Singapore
Sh	Sharjah
Si	Saudi Arabia
Sk	Slovak Republic
SL	Sierra Leone
Sn	Surinam
So	Somalia
Sp	Spain
Sr	Sri Lanka (Ceylon)
St	St Lucia
Su	Sudan
SV	St Vincent and the Grenadines
Sw	Sweden
Sy	Syria
Ta	Tanzania
Tg	Togo
Th	Thailand
Tk	Turkmenistan
Tn	Tunisia
To	Tonga
Tr	Trinidad and Tobago
Tu	Turkey
Tv	Tuvalu
Tw	Taiwan
UAE	United Arab Emirates
Ug	Uganda
Uk	Ukraine
Ur	Uruguay
US	United States of America
USSR	USSR and CIS (to 1991)
Va	Vanuatu
Ve	Venezuela
Vn	Vietnam
WS	Western Samoa
Ye	Republic of Yemen
Ys	Yugoslavia
Za	Zambia
Zr	Zaire

Abbreviations of Ship Types

Vessels of more than one function will have a combination of abbreviations from this list separated by an oblique stroke (for example, C/HL).

AT	Asphalt Tanker
B	Bulk Carrier
BC	Bulk/Car Carrier
BC/O	Bulk/Car/Ore
Bg	Barge Carrier
BO	Bulk/Oil Carrier
BWC	Bulk Carrier—Wood Chip
C	General Dry Cargo Ship
Cem	Cement Carrier
Ch	Chemical Tanker
Con	Container Ship
Con R	Container Ship with Refrigerated Capacity
CP	Cargo Passenger Ship (up to 12 passengers)
CTS	Cargo/Training Ship
DC	Deck Cargo Ship
Dk	Dock Ship
F	Ferry (probably carrying unberthed passengers)
FC	Fish Carrier
FF	Fish Factory
FFMS	Fishery Mother Ship
Fru	Fruit Ship
HL	Heavy Lift Vessel
IB	Ice Breaker
LGC	Liquefied Gas Carrier
Log	Log Carrier
LS	Livestock Carrier
MT	Molasses Tanker
NP	Newsprint Carrier
O	Ore Carrier
OBO	Ore/Bulk/Oil
OO	Ore/Oil
P	Passenger Ship
Pal	Pallets Carrier
Pap	Paper Carrier
PC	Passenger Cargo Ship (over 12 passengers)
PCTF	Passenger, Cargo and Train Ferry
PR	Passenger Refrigerated Vessel
PRiv	Passenger (River)
PtCon	Part Container Ship
PTF	Passenger/Train Ferry
R	Cargo Vessel with large Refrigerated Capacity
Riv	River Craft
RoC	Ro/Ro Cargo Ship
RoCF	Ro/Ro Cargo Ferry
RoPCF	Ro/Ro Passenger Car Ferry
RoPF	Ro/Ro Passenger Ferry
RoRo	Roll-on/Roll-off (specific function unknown)
RoVC	Ro/Ro Vehicle Carrier
Sal	Salvage Vessel
SCon	Semi-Container Ship
SDT	Slop Disposal Tanker
Slu	Sludge Carrier
Sply	Supply Ship
SSDC	Semi-Submersible Deck Cargo Ship
TB	Bitumen Tanker
TC	Timber Carrier
TF	Train Ferry
Tk	Oil and Oil Products Tanker
TPu	Tanker Pulp
TS	Training Ship
V	Vehicle Carrier (other than Ro/Ro)
VO	Vegetable Oil Tanker
Wa	Water Carrier
WT	Wine Tanker

Abbreviations of Engine Types

D-E	Diesel Electric
GT	Gas Turbine
M	Motor Vessel
N	Nuclear Power
Pdl	Paddle
R	Reciprocating
R & LPT	Reciprocating and Low-Pressure Turbine
T	Turbine
T-E	Turbo Electric

All vessels are single screw unless otherwise stated:

TS	Twin Screw
TrS	Triple Screw
QS	Quadruple Screw

ABBREVIATIONS OF SHIPBUILDERS' TITLES

NOTE: The use of names of 'former' countries (for example, Russia, Yugoslavia) is intentional and is to indicate where that company originally traded. The abbreviations are in alphabetical order, ignoring all punctuation marks.

Aalborg	Aalborg Vaerft A/S (now part of Danyard—qv)	*Denmark*
Aarhus	Aarhus Flydedok	*Denmark*
Abeking	Abeking & Rasmussen, Yacht u Bootswerf (no longer builders)	*W Germany*
ACH	same as Havre—qv	*France*
Adelaide	Adelaide Ship Construction (a division of Adelaide S.S. Industries Pty Ltd)	*Australia*
Adler	Adler Werft, GmbH (later Stephani Werft—qv)	*Germany*
Admiralteiskiy	Admiralteiskiy Shipyard (no longer builders)	*USSR*
Adriatico	Cantieri Riuniti dell'Adriatico (no longer builders) (later Italcantieri—qv)	*Italy*
AESA	Astilleros Espanoles SA (Consortium)	*Spain*
AFNE	Astilleros y Fabricas Navales del Estado SA	*Argentina*
AG "Weser"	Aktien Gesellschaft "Weser" (including AG "Weser" Seebeckwerft) (now Seebock—qv)	*Germany*
A. Hall	Alexander Hall & Co Ltd (no longer builders)	*UK*
Ailsa	Ailsa Shipbuilding Co Ltd (later Ailsa-Perth Shipbuilders)	*UK*
Akers	Akers Mek Verksted A/S (Aker Group) (no longer builders)	*Norway*
Alabama	Alabama Dry Dock and Shipbuilding Co (no longer builders)	*USA*
Alberti	Cantiere Navale Alberti	*Italy*
Alexandria	Alexandria Shipyard	*Egypt*
Alfeite	Arsenal do Alfeite	*Portugal*
Alianza	Astilleros Alianza SA	*Argentina*
Allied	Allied Shipbuilders Ltd	*Canada*
Alto Adriatico	Cantieri dell'Alto Adriatico SpA (no longer builders)	*Italy*
Amels	Amels BV (formerly C. Amels & Zoon and Scheepswerf & Mfbk "Welgelegen")	*Netherlands*
Amship	The American Ship Building Co (Amship Division) (no longer builders)	*USA*
Amsterdamsche D	Amsterdamsche Droogdok Mij NV (no longer builders)	*Netherlands*
Angyalfold	Angyalfold Shipyard, Hungarian Ship & Crane Works	*Hungary*
Ankerlokken	Ankerlokken Group (yards at Floro, Forde and Glommen) (no longer builders)	*Norway*
A. Normand	Ch et At Augustin Normand (later part of Havre—qv)	*France*
Ansaldo	Società per Azioni Ansaldo (later Italcantieri and Muggiano—qv)	*Italy*
A & P	Austin & Pickersgill Ltd (later part of North East Shipbuilders—qv)	*UK*
A. Pahl	Schiffswerft August Pahl (no longer builders)	*W Germany*
A & P Appledore (A)	A & P Appledore (Aberdeen) Ltd (now shiprepairers only)	*UK*
"Appingedam"	Scheepswerf "Appingedam" NV (see also Gebr Niestern) (now merged to form Niestern Sander—qv)	*Netherlands*
Appledore	Appledore Shipbuilders Ltd	*UK*
Appledore Ferguson	Appledore Ferguson Shipbuilders Ltd	*UK*
Apuania	Nuovi Cantieri Apuania	*Italy*
Ardrossan	Ardrossan Dockyard Ltd (no longer builders)	*UK*
Argo	Argo Shipbuilding & Shiprepairing Co (no longer builders)	*Greece*
Argos	Argos Engineering Co (now UDL Shipbuilding & Eng)	*Singapore*
Arminius	Arminius-Werke GmbH	*Germany*
Arnhemsche	Arnhemsche Scheepsbouw Maatschappij NV (no longer builders)	*Netherlands*
Asakawa	Asakawa Zosen KK	*Japan*
"Astano"	Astilleros y Talleres del Noroeste ("ASTANO")	*Spain*
Astarsa	Astilleros Argentinos Rio de la Plata (ASTARSA)	*Argentina*
Astrakhan	Astrakhan Shipyard (no longer builders)	*USSR*
Atlantico	Astilleros del Atlantico SA (see Corcho and "Corbasa") (no longer builders)	*Spain*
Atlantic SB	Atlantic Shipbuilding Co Ltd (later Newport Shipbuilding and Engineering—no longer builders)	*UK*
Atlantis	Atlantis Engineering & Construction Pte	*Singapore*
Atlas-MaK	Atlas-MaK Maschinenbau GmbH (no longer builders)	*W Germany*
Atlas-Werke	Atlas-Werke AG (later Atlas-MaK—qv)	*W Germany*
Aukra	Aukra Bruk A/S (later Aukra Industrier—qv)	*Norway*
Aukra I	Aukra Industrier A/S	*Norway*
Australian Commonwealth	Australian Commonwealth Shipping Board (no longer builders)	*Australia*
Australian SBI	Australian Shipbuilding Industries (WA) Pty Ltd	*Australia*
"Auver"	Astilleros Unidos de Veracruz SA de C V (AUVER)	*Mexico*
Avondale	Avondale Shipyards Inc	*USA*
Axpe	Maritima de Axpe SA	*Spain*
Balenciaga	Balenciaga SA	*Spain*
Baltic	Baltic Shipbuilding and Engineering Works (no longer builders)	*USSR*
Baltiya	Baltiya Shipyard (no longer builders)	*USSR*
Barclay, Curle	Barclay, Curle & Co Ltd (no longer builders)	*UK*
Barens	Barens Shipbuilding & Engineering Corp Ltd (later Sandock-Austral Ltd)	*S Africa*
Barkmeijer	Scheepswerf Barkmeijer NV (no longer builders)	*Netherlands*
Barreras	Hijos de J. Barreras SA	*Spain*
Bartram	Bartram & Sons Ltd (no longer builders) (later part of Austin & Pickersgill—see under A & P)	*UK*
Bath	Bath Iron Works Corp	*USA*
Batservice	Batservice Verft A/S	*Norway*
Bay	Bay Shipbuilding and Dry Dock Co	*USA*
Bayerische	Bayerische Schiffbau GmbH, Vorm A. Schellenberger	*Germany*
"Bazan"	Empresa Nacional "Bazan" de Construcciones Navales Militares SA	*Spain*
Belgian SB	Belgian Shipbuilders Corp	*Belgium*
Beliard, Crichton	Beliard, Crichton & Cie SA (later Beliard Oostende)	*Belgium*

Beliard-Murdoch	Beliard-Murdoch SA (later Beliard Oostende)	*Belgium*
Beliard Oostende	Scheepswerven Beliard Oostende NV (no longer builders)	*Belgium*
Benetti	Cantieri Navali M & B Benetti	*Italy*
Bergens	Bergens Mekaniske Verksteder A/S (no longer builders)	*Norway*
Bethlehem	Bethlehem Shipbuilding Corp (no longer builders)	*USA*
Bethlehem PC	Bethlehem Pacific Coast Steel Corp, Shipbuilding Division (no longer builders)	*USA*
Bethlehem Steel	Bethlehem Steel Corp (previously Bethlehem Steel Co Inc (no longer builders)	*USA*
Beykoz	Denizcilik Anonium Sirketi Beykoz Tersanesi (later Meltem—qv)	*Turkey*
Bijlholt	Scheepswerf Bijlholt BV	*Netherlands*
Bijlsma	Scheepswerf G. Bijlsma & Zonen BV	*Netherlands*
Blyth	Blyth Dry Docks & Shipbuilding Co Ltd (no longer builders)	*UK*
Bodewes Bergum	Scheepswerf Bodewes Bergum BV (no longer builders)	*Netherlands*
Bodewes BV	Scheepswerven v/h H. H. Bodewes BV	*Netherlands*
Bodewes NV	Scheepswerven Bodewes NV (later Scheepswerven Bodewes BV)	*Netherlands*
Bodo	Bodo M/V A/S (no longer builders)	*Norway*
Boel	NV Jos Boel & Zonen (J. Boel et Fils) SA (later Boelwerf—qv)	*Belgium*
Boele's Sch	Boele's Scheepswerven & Machinenfabriek BV	*Netherlands*
Boelwerf	NV Boelwerf SA (later Boelwerf Vlaanderen)	*Belgium*
Bolson	J. Bolson & Son Ltd (no longer builders)	*UK*
Bolsones	Bolsones Verft (no longer builders)	*Norway*
Boot	NV Scheepswerf "de Vooruitgang" v/h D. Boot (later Duijvendijk's—qv)	*Netherlands*
Braila	Santierul Naval Braila	*Romania*
Brand	Heinrich Brand Schiffswerft GmbH & Co KG (no longer builders)	*W Germany*
Brand W	Brand Werft GmbH & Co KG	*Germany*
Brattvag	Brattvag Skipsinnredning A/S	*Norway*
Breda	Cantiere Navale Breda SpA (now part of FCNI—qv)	*Italy*
Bremer V	Bremer Vulkan, Schiffbau und Maschinenfabrik (no longer builders)	*W Germany*
Bremer VW	Bremer Vulkan Werft und Maschinenfabrik GmbH	*Germany*
Bretagne	Ateliers et Chantiers de Bretagne (no longer builders)	*France*
Broken H	Broken Hill Proprietary Co Ltd (see Whyalla)	*Australia*
Brooke	Brooke Marine Ltd (no longer builders)	*UK*
Brown & H	James Brown & Hamer Ltd (no longer builders)	*S Africa*
Bruces	Bruces Shipyard AB	*Sweden*
Bruges	Chantiers Navals de Bruges SPRL (later Ch Navals Flandres SA—no longer builders)	*Belgium*
Buesumer	Buesumer Werft GmbH (no longer builders)	*W Germany*
Burntisland	Burntisland Shipbuilding Co Ltd (no longer builders)	*UK*
Burrard DD	Burrard Dry Dock Co Ltd (later part of Burrard Yarrows Corp)	*Canada*
Burrard Y	Burrard Yarrows Corp (now known as Versatile Pacific Shipyards Inc)	*Canada*
Buschmann	Theodor Buschmann Schiffswerft (no longer builders)	*W Germany*
Butler	Walter Butler Shipbuilders Inc (no longer builders)	*USA*
B + V	Blohm + Voss AG (no longer builders)	*W Germany*
B & W	B & W Skibsvaerft (formerly Burmeister & Wain's Skibsbyggeri A/S; previously Burmeister & Wain's Maskin-og Skibsbyggeri)	*Denmark*
Cadagua	Astilleros del Cadagua, W. Emilio Gonzalez SA (no longer builders)	*Spain*
Cadiz	Astilleros de Cadiz (later part of AESA—qv)	*Spain*
Caen	Chantiers Navals de Caen (no longer builders)	*France*
Caledon	Caledon Shipbuilding & Engineering Co Ltd (later Robb Caledon—qv)	*UK*
Cammell Laird	Cammell Laird Shipbuilders Ltd (no longer builders)	*UK*
Camper & Nicholsons	Camper & Nicholsons Ltd (no longer builders)	*UK*
Canadian Vickers	Canadian Vickers Shipyards Ltd (no longer builders)	*Canada*
Caneco	Industrias Reunidas Caneco SA	*Brazil*
Cantabrico	Astilleros Cantabrico y de Riera SA (no longer builders)	*Spain*
Cargill	Cargill Inc	*USA*
Carrington	Carrington Slipways Proprietary Ltd (later Australian Submarine Corp)	*Australia*
Cassaro	Cantiere Navale Cassaro (no longer builders)	*Italy*
Cassens	C. Cassens Schiffswerft (no longer builders—later Cassens GmbH—qv)	*W Germany*
Cassens GmbH	Schiffswerft u Maschinenfabrik Cassens GmbH (part of Werftunion—qv. Previously C. Cassens Schiffswerft)	*Germany*
CCN	Companhia Comercio e Navegacao. Also CCN Estaleiro Maua (see under Maua)	*Brazil*
C D Tirreno	Cantieri del Tirreno (later part of Riuniti—qv)	*Italy*
Celaya	Astilleros y Talleres Celaya SA (no longer builders)	*Spain*
Ch de France	Chantiers de France (no longer builders—later became Dunkerque-Normandie—qv)	*France*
Ch Dubigeon	Chantiers Dubigeon SA (formerly Dubigeon-Normandie—qv) (no longer builders)	*France*
"Chernomorskiy"	"Chernomorskiy" Shipyard (formerly Nosenko—qv)	*Russian Federation*
China SB	China Shipbuilding Corp	*Taiwan*
Chongjin	Chongjin Shipyard	*N Korea*
Christy	Christy Corp	*USA*
Chung Hua	Chung Hua Shipbuilding and Engineering Co Ltd (no longer builders. Later Zhong Hua—qv)	*China*
Chung Wah	Chung Wah Shipbuilding & Engineering Co Ltd	*Hong Kong*
Clelands	Clelands Shipbuilders Ltd	*UK*
CLEMNA	Società Cooperativa Responsabilita Limitata Lavaratori Edili, Meccanici, Navali Affini	*Italy*
CNIM	Constructions Navales et Industrielles de la Méditerranée (see also Méditerranée) (now part of Nord Med—qv)	*France*
Coaster Const	Coaster Construction Co (1928) Ltd (no longer builders)	*UK*

Cochin	Cochin Shipyard Ltd	*India*
Cochrane	Cochrane Shipbuilders Ltd (no longer builders)	*UK*
Cockatoo	Cockatoo Docks and Engineering Co Pty Ltd (later Vickers Cockatoo Dockyard) (no longer builders)	*Australia*
Cockerill	NV Cockerill Yards Hoboken (now part of Boelwerf)	*Belgium*
Cockerill-Ougrée	NV Cockerill-Ougrée (later Cockerill Yards Hoboken)	*Belgium*
Collingwood	Collingwood Shipyards (Div of Canadian Shipbuilding & Engineering Ltd) (no longer builders)	*Canada*
"Combiship"	"Combiship" BV (no longer builders)	*Netherlands*
Connell	Charles Connell & Co (Shipbuilders) Ltd (no longer builders—became Govan Shipbuilders)	*UK*
Consolidated Steel	Consolidated Steel Corp (no longer builders)	*USA*
Constanta	Santierul Naval Constanta S/A	*Romania*
'Construcciones' SA	Astilleros Construcciones SA (no longer builders)	*Spain*
Coops	Scheepswerf Gebr Coops BV	*Netherlands*
"Corbasa"	Basse Sambre Corch SA "Corbasa" (later became Atlantico—qv)	*Spain*
Corcho	Corcho Hijos SA (later became "Corbasa"—qv)	*Spain*
Crichton-Vulcan	Wärtsilä Koncernen AB Crichton-Vulcan Oy (later became Wärtsilä AB—qv)	*Finland*
Dae Dong	Dae Dong Shipbuilding Co	*S Korea*
Dae Sun	Dae Sun Shipbuilding & Engineering Co Ltd	*S Korea*
Daewoo	Daewoo Shipbuilding & Heavy Machinery Ltd	*S Korea*
Dairen	Dairen Dockyard (later called Dalian Shipyard)	*China*
Dalian	Dalian Shipyard (formerly Dairen Dockyard)	*China*
Damen	Scheepswerf Damen BV	*Netherlands*
Dannebrog	Dannebrog Vaerft A/S (now Aarhus—qv)	*Denmark*
Danyard	Danyard A/S (amalgamation of several Danish yards)	*Denmark*
Davie SB	Davie Shipbuilding Ltd (later known as Versatile Davie Inc)	*Canada*
Davie & Sons	G. T. Davie & Sons Ltd (no longer builders)	*Canada*
DCAN	Direction des Constructions et Armes Navales (formerly Arsenal de la Marine National Française)	*France*
"De Beer"	Scheepswerf "De Beer" NV (no longer builders)	*Netherlands*
"De Biesbosch"	NV Scheepswerf en Machinefabriek "De Biesbosch" NV (later "De Biesbosch-Dordrecht—qv)	*Netherlands*
"De Biesbosch-Dordrecht"	Scheepswerf en Machinefabriek "De Biesbosch-Dordrecht" BV	*Netherlands*
"De Dollard"	Scheepswerf "De Dollard" (no longer builders)	*Netherlands*
"De Gideon"	Scheepswerf "De Gideon" v/h J. Koster Hzn (no longer builders)	*Netherlands*
De Haan & O	Scheepswerf De Haan & Oerlemans (later Verolme Scheepswerf Heusden—qv)	*Netherlands*
"De Hoop"	Scheepswerf "De Hoop" BV (now "De Hoop" L—qv)	*Netherlands*
"De Hoop" L	Scheepswerf "De Hoop" Lobith BV	*Netherlands*
"De Klop"	NV Scheepsbouwwerf en Machinefabriek "De Klop" (later IHC Van Rees De Klop)	*Netherlands*
"De Merwede"	BV Scheepswerf & Machinefabriek "De Merwede" v/h Van Vliet & Co	*Netherlands*
Denizcilik	Denizcilik Bankasi TAO (later Turkiye Gemi Sanayii)	*Turkey*
Denny	William Denny & Bros Ltd (no longer builders)	*UK*
"De Noord"	Werf "De Noord" NV (later Giessen-De Noord—qv)	*Netherlands*
"De Schelde"	BV Koninklijke Mij Scheeps & Maschinefabriek "De Schelde" (later part of Scheldegroep—qv)	*Netherlands*
Deutsche S und M	Deutsche Schiff und Maschinebau AG Werk Seebeck (later A G "Weser")	*W Germany*
Deutsche Werft	Deutsche Werft Aktiengesellschaft (later Howaldts DW—qv)	*W Germany*
Deutsche Werft Reihers	Deutsche Werft AG Betrieb Reiherstiegwerft (later Howaldts DW—qv)	*W Germany*
"De Waal"	Scheepswerf "De Waal" BV (no longer builders)	*Netherlands*
Diedrich	Schiffswerft Julius Diedrich	*Germany*
Dong Hae	Dong Hae Shipbuilding Co Ltd (later Hanjin SB—qv)	*S Korea*
Dorbyl	Dorbyl Marine Pty Ltd (formerly Dorman Long—qv)	*S Africa*
Dorman Long	Dorman Long Vanderbijl Corp (Dorbyl) Ltd (now Dorbyl—qv)	*S Africa*
Dorman Long (A)	Dorman Long (Africa) Ltd (no longer builders)	*S Africa*
Dorman Long SH	Dorman Long Swan Hunter (Pty) Ltd (now part of Dorbyl—qv)	*S Africa*
Doxford	William Doxford & Sons (Shipbuilders) Ltd (later Doxford & Sunderland—qv)	*UK*
Doxford & S	Doxford & Sunderland Ltd (later Sunderland Shipbuilders—qv)	*UK*
Drammen	Drammen Slip & Verksted (no longer builders)	*Norway*
Drypool	Drypool Engineering & Dry Dock Co Ltd (no longer builders but still exist as part of Drypool Group)	*UK*
Dubigeon	Soc Anon des Anciens Chantiers Dubigeon (later called Dubigeon-Normandie—qv)	*France*
Dubigeon-Normandie SA	(see also La Loire) (now Ch Dubigeon—qv)	*France*
Duchesne & B	Ateliers de Duchesne & Bossiere SA (later part of Havre—qv)	*France*
Duijvendijk's	T. van Duijvendijk's Scheepswerf BV (no longer builders)	*Netherlands*
Dunkerque-Normandie	Division Constructions Navales de la Société Métallurgique et Navale Dunkerque-Normandie (later became Société Industrielle et Financière des Chantiers de France-Dunkerque. Now Part of Normed—qv)	*France*
Dunston	Richard Dunston Ltd	*UK*
Duro Felguera	Soc Metalurgica Duro Felguera (no longer builders)	*Spain*
Earle's	Earle's Shipbuilding & Engineering Co Ltd (no longer builders)	*UK*
Ebin/So	Estaleiros Ebin/So SA	*Brazil*
Echevarrieta y Larrinaga	Echevarrieta y Larrinaga (now part of AESA—qv)	*Spain*
"Edgar Andre"	VEB Schiffswerft "Edgar Andre" (no longer builders)	*E Germany*
Eides	G. Eides Sonner A/S	*Norway*
E. J. Smit	E. J. Smit & Zoon's Scheepswerven (no longer builders)	*Netherlands*
Ekensbergs	Ekensbergs Varv AB (no longer builders)	*Sweden*
Elbe B/R	same as Elbewerften—qv	*E Germany*

Elbewerft	VEB Elbewerft (later Elbewerften—qv)	*E Germany*
Elbewerften	VEB Elbewerften Boizenburg/Rosslau (no longer builders)	*E Germany*
"Elcano"	Empresa Nacional "Elcano", Astilleros de Sevilla (now part of AESA—qv)	*Spain*
Eleusis	Eleusis Shipyards SA	*Greece*
Elling	Elling Engineering Co Ltd (no longer builders)	*Hong Kong*
Elsflether	Elsflether Werft AG (no longer builders)	*W Germany*
Emaq	Emaq-Engenharia e Maquinas SA (no longer builders)	*Brazil*
EMAQ Verolme	Emaq-Verolme Estaleiros SA (later IVI—qv)	*Brazil*
Emden	Nordseewerke Emden GmbH (no longer builders—now Thyssen—qv)	*W Germany*
Equitable	Equitable Shipyards Inc (no longer builders)	*USA*
Eriksbergs	Eriksbergs Mekaniska Verkstads AB (no longer builders, now part of Svenska Varv)	*Sweden*
Erste Donau	Erste Donau Dampfschiffahrtgesellschaft, Schiffswerft Korneuburg (now Korneuburg—qv)	*Austria*
Esercizio	Società Cantieri Esercizio	*Italy*
Española	Soc Española de Construccion Naval (now part of AESA—qv)	*Spain*
Euskalduna	Compania Euskalduna de Construction y Reparacion de Buques SA (now part of AESA—qv)	*Spain*
Evans Deakin	Evans Deakin Industries Ltd (no longer builders)	*Australia*
Fairfields	Fairfields (Glasgow) Ltd (no longer builders)	*UK*
Fairfield SB	Fairfield Shipbuilding & Engineering Co Ltd (later Fairfields (Glasgow) Ltd—qv)	*UK*
Falkenbergs	Falkenbergs Varv AB (later Falkvarv AB) (no longer builders)	*Sweden*
Far East-Levingston	Far East-Levingston Shipbuilding Ltd	*Singapore*
FCNI	Fincantieri-Cantieri Navali Italiani (formerly Italcantieri—qv)	*Italy*
Federal SB & DD	Federal Shipbuilding & Dry Dock Co (no longer builders)	*USA*
Fellows & Co	Fellows & Co Ltd (no longer builders)	*UK*
Felszegi	Cantiere Felszegi (later Alto Adriatico—qv)	*Italy*
Ferguson-Ailsa	Ferguson-Ailsa Ltd (formerly Ferguson Bros) (no longer builders)	*UK*
Ferguson Bros	Ferguson Bros (Port Glasgow) Ltd (no longer builders)	*UK*
Ferguson Indust	Ferguson Industries Ltd (no longer builders)	*Canada*
Ferrari	Cantieri Navale "Ferrari" SpA	*Italy*
Ferus Smit	BV Scheepswerf "Ferus Smit"	*Netherlands*
Ferus Smit H	Ferus Smit Hoogezand BV (formerly "Hoogezand" JB—qv)	*Netherlands*
Finnboda	Finnboda Varf AB (later Götaverken Finnboda) (no longer builders)	*Sweden*
Flandre	Chantiers Navals de Flandre SA (no longer builders)	*Belgium*
Fleming & Ferguson	Fleming & Ferguson Ltd (no longer builders)	*UK*
Flender	Flender Werft Aktiengesellschaft (formerly Luebecker Flender-Werke)	*W Germany*
Flensburger	Flensburger Schiffsbau-Gesellschaft (no longer builders)	*W Germany*
FMC	FMC Corp (now Gunderson Inc)	*USA*
Fosen	Fosen Mek Verksteder	*Norway*
Foundation Mar	Foundation Maritime Ltd (no longer builders)	*Canada*
"Foxhol"	Scheepswerf "Foxhol" NV (v/h Gebr Muller) (no longer builders)	*Netherlands*
Framnaes	Framnaes Mek Verksted A/S (no longer builders)	*Norway*
France-Gironde	At et Ch de Dunkerque et Bordeaux (France-Gironde) (later Ch de France)	*France*
Frederikshavn	Frederikshavn Vaerft A/S (now Danyard—qv)	*Denmark*
Fredriksstad	A/S Fredriksstad Mek Verksted (later A/S Nye Fredriksstad Mek Verksted—qv)	*Norway*
Freire	Construcciones Navales P. Freire SA	*Spain*
"Friesland"	Scheepswerf "Friesland" BV (no longer builders)	*Netherlands*
F. Schichau	F. Schichau GmbH (no longer builders, later became part of Schichau-Unterweser)	*Germany*
Fujinagata	Fujinagata Zosensho KK (no longer builders, later became part of Mitsui)	*Japan*
Fukuoka	Fukuoka Zosen (subsidiary of Usuki Tekkosho)	*Japan*
Fukushima	Fukushima Zosen Tekko KK	*Japan*
Furness	Furness Shipbuilding Co Ltd (eventually became Smith's Dock Co—qv)	*UK*
Galatz	Santierul Naval Galatz	*Romania*
Garden Reach	Garden Reach Shipbuilders & Engineers Ltd (formerly Garden Reach Workshops Private Ltd)	*India*
Gavle	A/B Gavle Varv (no longer builders)	*Sweden*
Gaye	Gaye Ltd (no longer builders)	*Turkey*
G. Brown	George Brown & Co (Marine) Ltd (no longer builders)	*UK*
Gdanska	Stocznia Gdanska im Lenina (later Stocznia Gdanska SA)	*Poland*
Gdanska	Stocznia Gdanska im Lenina	*Poland*
G. Dimitrov	Georgi Dimitrov Shipyard (later Varna Shipyard)	*Bulgaria*
Gdynia	Stocznia Gdynia (formerly 'Komuny Paryskiej'—qv)	*Poland*
Gdynska	Stocznia Gdynska im Komuny Paryskiej (see under 'Komuny Paryskiej')	*Poland*
Gebr Niestern	Scheepswerven Gebroeders Niestern BV (later "Appingedam"—qv)	*Netherlands*
Geibi	Geibi Zosen Kogyo (no longer builders)	*Japan*
General Dynamics	General Dynamics Corp	*USA*
"Gheorghiu Dej"	"Gheorghiu Dej" Shipyard (later Angyalfold—qv)	*Hungary*
Giessen	C. van de Giessen & Zonen's Scheepswerven NV (later Giessen-De Noord)	*Netherlands*
Giessen-De Noord	van der Giessen-De Noord NV (formed by Giessen & "De Noord"—qv)	*Netherlands*
Gironde	Forges et Chantiers de la Gironde (later part of Ch de France—qv)	*France*
Giuliano	Cantiere Navale Giuliano (later Alto Adriatico—qv)	*Italy*
Gleue	Interessengemeinschaft Gleue Reederei EGS (formerly Renck—qv) (no longer builders)	*W Germany*
Globe	Globe Engineering Works Ltd (no longer builders)	*S Africa*
Glommens	A/S Glommens Mek Verksted (later part of Ankerlokken—qv)	*Norway*
Goole	Goole Shipbuilders Ltd (no longer builders)	*UK*
Gotav	Götaverken Arendal AB (previously AB Götaverken and other titles. Now incorporated in Svenska Varv)	*Sweden*

Gotav Solvesborg	Götaverken Solvesborg AB (formerly Solvesborg Varvs and so on—qv) (no longer builders)	*Sweden*
Govan	Govan Shipbuilders Ltd (later K Govan—qv)	*UK*
Grangemouth	Grangemouth Dockyard Co Ltd	*UK*
Gravdal	Gravdal Skipsbyggeri (no longer builders)	*Norway*
Graville	Société Chantiers de Graville (no longer builders)	*France*
Gray	William Gray & Co Ltd (no longer builders)	*UK*
Greenock D	Greenock Dockyard Co Ltd (incorporated with Scotts' SB—qv)	*UK*
Groot & VV	Scheepswerf en Machinefabriek De Groot & Van Vliet BV (later YVC Bolnes)	*Netherlands*
Gruno	Scheepswerf Bodewes Gruno NV (no longer builders)	*Netherlands*
Guanzhou	Guanzhou Shipyard	*China*
Gulfport	Gulfport Shipbuilding Corp (subsidiary of Levingston—qv) (no longer builders)	*USA*
Gusto	NV Werf Gusto (later IHC Gusto—qv)	*Netherlands*
Haarlemsche	Haarlemsche Scheepsbouw Maatschappij NV (no longer builders)	*Netherlands*
Hagelstein	Alfred Hagelstein Maschinenfabrik-Schiffswerft (no longer builders)	*W Germany*
Hakata Z	Hakata Zosen KK	*Japan*
Hakodate	Hakodate Dock Co Ltd	*Japan*
Halifax	Halifax Shipyards Ltd	*Canada*
Halla	Halla Engineering & Heavy Industries Co Ltd	*S Korea*
Hall, Russell	Hall, Russell & Co Ltd (later A & P Appledore (A)—qv)	*UK*
Halter	Halter Marine Inc	*USA*
Hamilton	William Hamilton & Co Ltd (no longer builders)	*UK*
Hancocks	Hancocks Shipbuilding Co Ltd (no longer builders)	*UK*
Hanjin HI	Hanjin Heavy Industries	*S Korea*
Hanjin SB	Hanjin Shipbuilding Co Ltd (no longer builders)	*S Korea*
Hanseatische	Hanseatische Werft GmbH (no longer builders)	*W Germany*
Hapag-Lloyd	Hapag-Lloyd Werft GmbH (no longer builders)	*W Germany*
Harima	Harima Zosensho KK (later IHI—qv)	*Japan*
"Harlingen"	Scheepswerf en Reparatiebedrijf "Harlingen" BV	*Netherlands*
Harms	Norderwerf Ulrich Harms GmbH (later Norderwerft—qv)	*W Germany*
Harris & Sons	P. K. Harris & Sons Ltd (no longer builders—became Appledore—qv)	*UK*
Hashihama	Hashihama Zosen KK (now Hashihama Shipbuilding Co Ltd)	*Japan*
Hashimoto	Hashimoto Zosensho	*Japan*
Hasund	Hasund Mek Verksted A/S (no longer builders)	*Norway*
Hatlo	Hatlo Verksted A/S (later Ulstein Hatlo—qv)	*Norway*
Haugesund	Haugesund M/V A/S	*Norway*
Havre	Société Nouvelle de At et Ch du Havre (incorporates A. Normand & Duchesne & B—qv)	*France*
Hawthorn, L	Hawthorn, Leslie (Shipbuilders) Ltd (no longer builders—later Swan Hunter)	*UK*
Hayashikane	Hayashikane Shipbuilding & Engineering Co Ltd (Hayashikane Zosen KK) (now called Hayashikane Dockyard Co Ltd)	*Japan*
Hayes	R. S. Hayes (Pembroke Dock) Ltd (no longer builders)	*UK*
Hegemann	Detlef Hegemann Rolandwerft GmbH	*Germany*
Hellenic	Hellenic Shipyards Co	*Greece*
Helsingborgs	Helsingborgs Varfs Aktiebolag (no longer builders)	*Sweden*
Helsingor	Helsingor Vaerft A/S (two previous titles) (now Danyard—qv)	*Denmark*
Hidrodinamik	Hidrodinamik Gemi Sanayi Ve Tikaret AS	*Turkey*
Higaki Z	Higaki Zosen KK	*Japan*
Highfield	Highfield Sea-Land Development Ltd (no longer builders)	*Hong Kong*
Hill	Charles Hill & Sons Ltd (no longer builders)	*UK*
Hindustan	Hindustan Shipyard Ltd	*India*
Hitachi	Hitachi Zosen (Hitachi Zosen Corporation)	*Japan*
Hitzler	J G Hitzler Schiffswerft u Maschinenfabrik, Inhaber Franz Hitzler (later Schiffswerft u Maschinenfabrik J G Hitzler)	*Germany*
Hjorungavaag	Hjorungavaag Verksted A/S	*Norway*
"Holland"	BV Scheepswerf en Machinefabriek "Holland" (M. Calje) (no longer builders)	*Netherlands*
Hollming	Hollming Oy (later Finnyards Oy)	*Finland*
Holst	Schiffswerft W. Holst (no longer builders)	*W Germany*
Honda	Honda Zosen KK	*Japan*
Hong Kong U	Hong Kong United Dockyards Ltd (merger of Hong Kong & Whampoa and Taikoo—qv)	*Hong Kong*
Hong Kong & W	Hong Kong & Whampoa Dock Co Ltd (see Hong Kong United)	*Hong Kong*
Hong Leong	Hong Leong-Luerssen Shipyard Berhad	*Malaysia*
"Hoogezand" JB	Scheepswerf "Hoogezand" J Bodewes (later Scheepswerf Hoogezand BV, which became Ferus Smit Hoogezand—qv)	*Netherlands*
Horten	Horten Verft A/S	*Norway*
Howaldts	Howaldtswerke (later Howaldtswerke Hamburg AG, subsequently Howaldtswerke-Deutsche Werft—qv)	*W Germany*
Howaldts DW	Howaldtswerke-Deutsche Werft AG (incorporates Deutsche Werft, Howaldtswerke and Kieler Howaldtswerke)	*Germany*
H Peters	Schiffswerft Hugo Peters (later Schiffswerft Hugo Peters Wewelsfleth)	*Germany*
H. Robb	Henry Robb Ltd (later Robb Caledon—qv)	*UK*
Hudong	Hudong Shipyard (formerly Hu Tung—qv)	*China*
Huelva	Astilleros de Huelva	*Spain*
Hung Chi	Hung Chi Shipyard	*China*
Husumer	Husumer Schiffswerft (later Husumer K—qv)	*W Germany*
Husumer K	Husumer Schiffswerft Ihn Gebr Kroeger GmbH & Co KG (formerly Husumer Schiffswerft)	*Germany*
Hu Tung	Hu Tung Shipyard (later Hudong—qv)	*China*
H & W	Harland & Wolff Ltd (later H & W S & H—qv)	*UK*

H&W S&H	Harland and Wolff Shipbuilding and Heavy Industries Ltd (formerly Harland and Wolff Ltd)	*UK*
Hyundai	Hyundai Heavy Industries (formerly Hyundai Shipbuilding & Heavy Industries Ltd)	*S Korea*
Hyundai Mipo	Hyundai Mipo Dockyard Co Ltd (part of Hyundai—qv)	*S Korea*
IFC	Integrated Ferry Constructors Ltd (IFC) (no longer builders)	*Canada*
IHC Gusto	IHC Gusto Staalouw BV (see also Gusto) (later C & I Holland BV)	*Netherlands*
IHC Smit	IHC Smit BV (previously L. Smit & Smit Kinderdijk—qv)	*Netherlands*
IHC Verschure	IHC Verschure BV (see Verschure) (no longer builders)	*Netherlands*
IHI	Ishikawajima Harima Heavy Industries (amalgamation of Ishikawajima Jukogyo, Harima, Ishikawajima Zosensho, Harima Zosensho and others. Associated yards in Brazil and SIngapore (Jurong))	*Japan*
Iino	Iino Shipbuilding and Engineering Co (later Maizuru Jukogyo, now part of Hitachi—qv)	*Japan*
"Ijssel"	Bijker's Aannemingsbedrijf "Ijssel" Werf (no longer builders)	*Netherlands*
Ijsselwerf	NV Ijsselwerf (later Ysselwerf—qv)	*Netherlands*
'Ilya Boyadzhiyev'	'Ilya Boyadzhiyev' Shipyard (later Bourgas Shipyards)	*Bulgaria*
Imabari	Imabari Zosen KK (Imabari Shipbuilding Co Ltd)	*Japan*
Imai S	Imai Seisakusho (Imai Shipyard Co Ltd)	*Japan*
Imai Z	Imai Zosen KK	*Japan*
Imamura	Imamura Zosen (Imamura Shipbuilding Co Ltd)	*Japan*
Inchon	Inchon Engineering and Shipbuilding Corp (later Halla—qv)	*S Korea*
Ingalls	Ingalls Iron Works Co (previously Ingalls SB—qv) (later Ingalls Marine)	*USA*
Ingalls SB	Ingalls Shipbuilding Corp (now Litton Systems)	*USA*
Inglis	A. & J. Inglis Ltd (no longer builders)	*UK*
INMA	Cantiere Navale Industrie Navali Meccaniche Affini SpA	*Italy*
Ish do Brasil	Ishikawajima do Brasil Estaleiros SA ("Ishibras") (later IVI—qv)	*Brazil*
Ishikawajima J	Ishikawajima Jukogyo KK (now part of IHI)	*Japan*
Ishikawajima S & C	Ishikawajima Ship & Chemical Plant Co Ltd	*Japan*
Israel Spyds	Israel Shipyards Ltd	*Israel*
Italcantieri	Italcantieri SpA (later FCNI—qv)	*Italy*
"Ivan Cetenic"	Brodogradiliste "Ivan Cetenic" (later "Inkobrod"—no longer builders)	*Yugoslavia*
Ivan Dimitrov	Ivan Dimitrov Shipyard (later Rousse Shipyard)	*Bulgaria*
IVI	IVI-Industrias Verolme-Ishibras SA (merger between EMAQ Verolme and Ish do Brasil—qv)	*Brazil*
Jadewerft	Jadewerft Wilhelmshaven GmbH (now Jadewerft GmbH)	*Germany*
Jan Smit	Werf Jan Smit Czn (later Verolme Scheepswerf—qv)	*Netherlands*
Janson BV	Scheepswerf Janson BV (later Janson Bridging BV)	*Netherlands*
J. Brown	John Brown & Co (Clydebank) Ltd (no longer builders—became Upper Clyde—qv)	*UK*
Jeffboat	Jeffboat Inc (formerly Jeffersonville Boat & Machine Co) (no longer builders)	*USA*
Jiangnan	Jiangnan Shipyard (previously spelt Kiangnan—qv)	*China*
J & K Smit	J & K Smit's Scheepswerven NV (later IHC Smit—qv)	*Netherlands*
J. L. Thompson	Joseph L. Thompson & Sons Ltd (later Doxford & Sunderland—qv)	*UK*
Jones	J. A. Jones Construction Co (no longer builders)	*USA*
Jonker	Scheepswerf en Gashouderbouw v/h Jonker & Stans BV (no longer builders)	*Netherlands*
"Jozo Lozovina-Mosor"	Brodogradiliste "Jozo Lozovina-Mosor" (no longer builders)	*Yugoslavia*
J. S. White	J. Samuel White and Co Ltd (no longer builders)	*UK*
Juliana	Juliana Constructora Gijonesa SA (no longer builders)	*Spain*
Jurong Spyd	Jurong Shipyard Ltd (affiliated with IHI—qv)	*Singapore*
J. W. Cook	James W. Cook (Wivenhoe) Ltd (no longer builders)	*UK*
Kaarbos	Kaarbos Mek Verksted A/S (later Kaarboverkstedet A/S)	*Norway*
Kagoshima	Kagoshima Dock & Iron Works Co Ltd (no longer builders)	*Japan*
Kaiser Co	Kaiser Co Inc (no longer builders)	*USA*
Kaldnes	Kaldnes Mek Verksted A/S (no longer builders)	*Norway*
Kalmar	Kalmar Varv AB (no longer builders)	*Sweden*
Kama	Kama Shipyard (no longer builders)	*Russia*
Kambara	Kambara Marine Development and Shipbuilding Co Ltd	*Japan*
Kanasashi	Kanasashi Co Ltd (later K K Kanasashi)	*Japan*
Kanawa	Kanawa Dockyard Co Ltd	*Japan*
Kanda	Kanda Zosensho KK (Kanda Shipbuilding Co Ltd)	*Japan*
Kanrei	Kanrei Zosen KK (Kanrei Shipbuilding Co Ltd)	*Japan*
Karachi	Karachi Shipyard & Engineering Works Ltd	*Japan*
Karlskrona	Karlskronavarvet AB (incorporated in Svenska Varv. See Orlogs)	*Sweden*
Karlstads	Karlstads Varv A/B (later Karlstadsverken A/B)	*Sweden*
Karmsund	Karmsund Verft & Mek Verksted A/S (no longer builders)	*Norway*
Kasado	Kasado Dockyard Co Ltd (no longer builders—shiprepairers only)	*Japan*
Kawasaki	Kawasaki Heavy Industries Ltd (previously Kawasaki Dockyard and Kawasaki Jukogyo—qv)	*Japan*
Kawasaki D	Kawasaki Dockyard Co Ltd (later Kawasaki HI—qv)	*Japan*
Kawasaki J.	Kawasaki Jukogyo KK (later Kawasaki HI—qv)	*Japan*
Kegoya	Kegoya Dock KK	*Japan*
Keppel Shipyard	Keppel Shipyard (Pte) Ltd	*Singapore*
K Floro	Kvaerner Floro (formerly Kvaerner Kleven Floro)	*Norway*
K Govan	Kvaerner Govan Ltd (formerly Govan Shipbuilders)	*UK*
Khabarovsk	Khabarovsk Shipyard "Osipovskiy Kirov" (no longer builders)	*USSR*
Khalkis	Khalkis Shipyard SA (no longer builders)	*Greece*
Kherson	Kherson Shipyard (no longer builders)	*USSR*
Kiangnan	Kiangnan Dockyard & Engineering Works (later spelt Jiangnan—qv)	*China*
Kieler H	Kieler Howaldtswerke AG (later Howaldtswerke-Deutsche Werft—qv)	*W Germany*

Kishigami	Kishigami Zosen KK (no longer builders)	*Japan*
Kishimoto	Kishimoto Zosen KK (formerly Setouchi—qv) (no longer builders)	*Japan*
Kitanihon	Kitanihon Zosen KK	*Japan*
Kjobenhavns	Kjobenhavns Flydedok & Skibsvaerft (no longer builders)	*Denmark*
K Kleven F	Kvaerner Kleven Floro (formerly Kleven Floro. Later Kvaerner Floro)	*Norway*
K Kleven Forde	Kvaerner Kleven Forde	*Norway*
K Kleven L	Kvaerner Kleven Leirvik A/S (formerly Kleven Loland A/S, which was previously Lolan Verft A/S)	*Norway*
K Kleven U	Kvaerner Kleven Ulsteinvik (formerly Kleven M/V A/S)	*Norway*
Kleven	Kleven M/V A/S (later K Kleven U—qv)	*Norway*
Kleven	M. Kleven M/V	*Norway*
Kochi Jukogyo	Kochi Jukogyo (Kaisei Zosen) KK (subsidiary of Kurushima—qv) (no longer builders)	*Japan*
Kochiken	Kochiken Zosen KK (no longer builders)	*Japan*
Kockums	Kockums AB (incorporated in Svenska Varv) (no longer builders)	*Sweden*
Koetter	Schiffswerft Gebrueder Koetter (later Koetter Werft GmbH)	*W Germany*
'Komuny Paryskiej'	Stocznia im 'Komuny Paryskiej' (formerly Gdynska—qv) (later Gdynia—qv)	*Poland*
Korea SB	Korea Shipbuilding and Engineering Corp (later HANJIN HI—qv)	*S Korea*
Korneuburg	Schiffswerft Korneuburg AG (incorporated in Osterreichische—qv. Originally Erste Donau—qv)	*Austria*
Koyo	Koyo Dockyard Co Ltd	*Japan*
Kramer & Booy	Handel & Scheepsbouw Maatschappij Kramer & Booy BV (See Tille)	*Netherlands*
Krasnoyarsk	Krasnoyarsk Shipyard (no longer builders)	*USSR*
"Krasnoye S"	"Krasnoye Sormovo" Shipyard	*Russia*
'Krasnoye Sormovo'	Same as "Krasnoye S"—qv	*Russia*
Kremer	D. W. Kremer Sohn GmbH & Co KG (no longer builders)	*W Germany*
Kristiansands	Kristiansands Mek Verksted A/S (no longer builders)	*Norway*
Kroegerw	Kroegerwerft GmbH & Co KG (later Kroeger Werft GmbH & Co KG)	*Germany*
Krupp	Friedrich Krupp Germaniawerft AG (no longer builders)	*Germany*
Kure	Kure Zosensho KK (now part of IHI—qv)	*Japan*
Kurinoura	Kurinoura Dock KK (Kurinoura Dockyard Co Ltd)	*Japan*
Kurushima	Kurushima Dockyard Co Ltd (see Kochi Jukogyo)	*Japan*
Kvaerner Masa	Kvaerner Masa Yards Inc (formerly Masa—qv)	*Finland*
Kvaerner Warnow	Kvaerner Warnow-Werft GmbH (formerly Neptun-Warnow—qv)	*Germany*
Kynossura	Kynossura Dockyard Co (no longer builders)	*Greece*
Kyokuyo	Kyokuyo Zosen Tekko KK (Kyokuyo Shipbuilding and Iron Works Co Ltd). (Later Kyokuyo Zosen KK (Kyokuyo Shipyard Corporation)	*Japan*
La Ciotat	Chantiers Navals de la Ciotat (now part of Nord Med—qv)	*France*
Laing	Sir James Laing & Sons Ltd (no longer builders, became part of Doxford & Sunderland)	*UK*
Laiva	Oy Laivateollisuus AB (later Valmetin Laivateollisuus—qv)	*Finland*
Lake Washington	Lake Washington Shipyards (no longer builders)	*USA*
La Loire	Ateliers et Chantiers de La Loire (subsequently part of Dubigeon-Normandie—qv)	*France*
La Manche	Ateliers et Chantiers de la Manche (later Manche Industrie Marine)	*France*
La Marina	Servicio Industrial de la Marina	*Peru*
Lamont	James Lamont & Co Ltd (no longer builders)	*UK*
Langesunds	Langesunds Mek Verksted A/S (no longer builders)	*Norway*
Langvik	Langvik Sarpsborg M/V (no longer builders)	*Norway*
Lanser	BV Scheepswerf Lanser	*Netherlands*
La Pallice	Chantiers Navals de la Pallice (now part of La Rochelle-Pallice)	*France*
La Rochelle	Société Nouvelle des Ateliers et Chantiers de La Rochelle-Pallice (amalgamation of La Rochelle and La Pallice yards)	*France*
Larvik	Larvik Slip & Verksted A/S (no longer builders)	*Norway*
La Seine	Ateliers et Chantiers de la Seine Maritime (no longer builders)	*France*
L'Atlantique	Chantiers de L'Atlantique (formerly Saint Nazaire—qv) (a Division of Alsthom-Atlantique)	*France*
Leninskaya	Leninskaya Kuznitsa (no longer builders)	*USSR*
Leninskogo	Leninskogo Komsomola Shipyard (no longer builders)	*USSR*
Levingston	Levingston Shipbuilding Co (see Gulfport) (no longer builders)	*USA*
Lewis	John Lewis & Sons Ltd (no longer builders)	*UK*
LF-W	Luebecker Flender-Werke AG (no longer builders—became Flender Werft—qv)	*W Germany*
Liaaen	A. M. Liaaen A/S (now shiprepairers only)	*Norway*
Liffey	Liffey Dockyard Ltd (no longer builders)	*Ireland*
Liguri	Nuovi Cantieri Liguri SpA (formerly Pietra Ligure—qv) (no longer builders)	*Italy*
Lindenau	Schiffswerft u Maschinenfabrik Paul Lindenau GmbH	*Germany*
Lindenau GmbH	same as Lindenau—qv	*Germany*
Lindholmens	Lindholmens Varv AB (later Eriksbergs—no longer builders)	*Sweden*
Lisnave	Lisnave Estaleiros Navais de Lisboa SARL (formerly Navalis—qv, which was formerly Uniao—qv) (no longer builders)	*Portugal*
Lithgows	Lithgows Ltd (no longer builders—later Scott Lithgow—qv)	*UK*
Litton	Litton Systems Inc—see Ingalls SB	*USA*
Lobnitz	Lobnitz & Co Ltd (later Simons-Lobnitz—no longer builders)	*UK*
Lockheed	Lockheed Shipbuilding & Construction Co (formerly Puget Sound Bridge & Dry Dock—qv) (no longer builders)	*USA*
Lodose	Lodose Varv AB (no longer builders)	*Sweden*
Loire	Ateliers et Chantiers de La Loire—see under La Loire	*France*
Loire-Normandie	Société des Chantiers Reunis Loire-Normandie (the two yards in this group were split between Bretagne & Dubigeon-Normandie—qv)	*France*
Lorenzo	Enrique Lorenzo y Cia SA (later Factorias Vulcano SA)	*Spain*

"L. Orlando"	Cantieri Nav "Luigi Orlando" (later part of FCNI—qv)	*Italy*
"Losinj"	Brodogradiliste "Losinj" (no longer builders)	*Yugoslavia*
Lothe	Brodrene Lothe A/S Flytedokken (no longer builders)	*Norway*
L'Ouest	Société des Ateliers Français de l'Ouest (no longer builders)	*France*
L. Smit	L. Smit & Zoon NV (later IHC Smit—qv)	*Netherlands*
Luebecker F-W	same as LF-W—qv	*W Germany*
Luehring	Schiffswerft C. Luehring (no longer builders)	*W Germany*
Luerssen	Fr Luerssen Werft (no longer builders)	*W Germany*
Luzuriaga	Astilleros Luzuriaga SA	*Spain*
Maizuru	Maizuru Jukogyo KK (now part of Hitachi—qv)	*Japan*
Malaysia S&E	Malaysia Shipyard and Engineering Sdn Bhd	*Malaysia*
Mallorca	Astilleros de Mallorca SA (previously Ast de Palma SA)	*Spain*
Malta DD	Malta Drydocks	*Malta*
Malta SB	Malta Shipbuilding Co Ltd	*Malta*
Mandal	Mandals Slip and Mek Verksted A/S (no longer builders—now incorporated in Batservice—qv)	*Norway*
Mangalia	Santierul Naval Mangalia	*Romania*
Manitowoc	Manitowoc Shipbuilding Inc (no longer builders)	*USA*
M.A.N. U	M.A.N. Unternehmensbereich GHH Sterkrade (formerly Sterkrade—qv) (no longer builders)	*W Germany*
Marine Indust	Marine Industrie Ltée	*Canada*
Marinens	Marinens Hovedverft (now Horten Verft—qv)	*Norway*
Marinship	Marinship Corp (no longer builders)	*USA*
Marmara	Marmara Tersanesi (Marmara Transport, Shipbuilding & Construction Inc)	*Turkey*
Marstrands	FEAB Marstrandsverken (no longer builders)	*Sweden*
Maryland SB & DD	Maryland Shipbuilding & Drydock Co (no longer builders)	*USA*
Marynarki	Stocznia Marynarki Wojennej	*Poland*
Masa	Masa Yards Inc (formerly Wärtsilä Marine, originally Oy Wärtsilä. Now Kvaerner Masa)	*Finland*
Mathias-Thesen	VEB Mathias-Thesen-Werft (later MTW—qv)	*E Germany*
Mathis	John H. Mathis Co (no longer builders)	*USA*
Maua	Estaleiro Maua (part of CCN—qv)	*Brazil*
Mazagon	Mazagon Dock Ltd (no longer builders)	*India*
McDermott	McDermott Shipyards	*USA*
Mediterranee	Société des Forges et Chantiers de la Méditerranée (later CNIM—qv)	*France*
Mediterraneo	Cantieri del Mediterraneo SpA (no longer builders)	*Italy*
Meltem	Meltem Beykoz Tersanesi (formerly Beykoz—qv) (no longer builders)	*Turkey*
Menzer	Schiffswerft Ernst Menzer OHG (no longer builders)	*W Germany*
Meyer	Jos L. Meyer GmbH & Co	*Germany*
Middle Docks	Middle Docks & Engineering Co (not shipbuilders)	*UK*
Mie	Mie Zosen KK (Mie Shipyard Co Ltd) (no longer builders)	*Japan*
Mihanovich	Cia Argentinos de Nav Mihanovich (no longer builders)	*Argentina*
Miho	Miho Zosensho KK	*Japan*
Minami	Minami-Nippon Zosen KK	*Japan*
Mitchison	T. Mitchison Ltd (no longer builders)	*UK*
Mitsubishi HI	Mitsubishi Heavy Industries Ltd (amalgamation of Shin Mitsubishi HI (formerly Mitsubishi HI Reorganised), Mitsubishi Nippon HI and Mitsubishi Zosen). The abbreviation Mitsubishi HI also covers vessels built by Mitsubishi HI Reorganised	*Japan*
Mitsubishi J	Mitsubishi Jukogyo (no longer builders—now part of Mitsubishi HI)	*Japan*
Mitsubishi N	Mitsubishi Nippon Heavy Industries Ltd (no longer builders—now part of Mitsubishi HI)	*Japan*
Mitsubishi Z	Mitsubishi Zosen KK (formerly Nishi Nippon Jukogyo—qv) (no longer builders—now part of Mitsubishi HI)	*Japan*
Mitsui	Mitsui Engineering & Shipbuilding Co Ltd (formerly Mitsui Shipbuilding & Engineering) (see Fujinagata & Shikoku)	*Japan*
Miyoshi	Miyoshi Zosen KK (Miyoshi Shipbuilding Co Ltd)	*Japan*
M. Jansen	Schiffswerft u Maschinenfabrik Martin Jansen GmbH & Co KG (no longer builders)	*W Germany*
Mjellum & K	Mjellum & Karlsen A/S	*Norway*
Molde	Molde Verft A/S	*Norway*
Mondego	Estaleros Navais do Mondego SARL	*Portugal*
Morini	Cantiere Navale Mario Morini SpA	*Italy*
Morton	Morton Engineering & Dry Dock Co Ltd (no longer builders—later St Lawrence M & M—qv)	*Canada*
Mort's Dock	Mort's Dock & Engineering Co Ltd (no longer builders)	*Australia*
Moss R	Moss Rosenberg Verft A/S (incorporates Moss Vaerft and Rosenberg—qv) (no longer builders)	*Norway*
Moss V	Moss Vaerft & Dokk A/S (no longer builders—later part of Moss Rosenberg)	*Norway*
MTW	MTW Schiffswerft GmbH (formerly Mathias-Thesen—qv)	*Germany*
Muggiano	Cantieri Navale Muggiani SpA (see Ansaldo and Riuniti) (now part of FCNI—qv)	*Italy*
Murakami	Murakami Hide Zosen KK	*Japan*
Murueta	Astilleros de Murueta SA	*Spain*
Musel	Maritima del Musel SA (no longer builders)	*Spain*
Mutzelfeldt	Mutzelfeldtwerft GmbH (no longer builders)	*W Germany*
Nagoya	Nagoya Zosen KK (now part of IHI)	*Japan*
Naikai	Naikai Shipbuilding & Engineering Co Ltd (an amalgamation of Setoda & Taguma—qv. An affiliate of Hitachi) (later named Naikai Zosen Corp)	*Japan*
Nakamura	Nakamura Zosen Tekkosho KK (Nakamura Shipbuilding & Engines Works Co Ltd)	*Japan*

Naka Nippon	Naka Nippon Jukogyo KK (now part of Mitsubishi HI)	*Japan*
Nakskov	Nakskov Skibsvaerft A/S (no longer builders)	*Denmark*
Namura	Namura Zosensho KK (Namura Shipbuilding Co Ltd)	*Japan*
Nantes	Chantiers de Nantes (Bretagne-Loire) (later Bretagne—qv)	*France*
Narasaki	Narasaki Zosen KK (Narasaki Shipbuilding Co)	*Japan*
National S & S	National Shipyards & Steel Corp	*Philippines*
National Steel	National Steel & Shipbuilding Co	*USA*
Navalis	Navalis Sociedade de Construcao e Reparacao Naval SARL (later Lisnave—qv)	*Portugal*
"Navalmeccanica"	Cantieri Navali "Navalmeccanica" SA (no longer builders—later Italcantieri—qv)	*Italy*
Navashinskiy	Navashinskiy Shipyard	*Russia*
Navire	Oy Navire AB (no longer builders)	*Finland*
Nederlandsche	Nederlandsche Scheepsbouw Maatschappij BV (formerly Nederlandsche Dok en Scheepsbouw) (no longer builders)	*Netherlands*
"Neptun"	VEB Schiffswerft "Neptun" Rostock (formerly Neptunwerft—qv, later Neptun-Warnow—qv)	*E Germany*
Neptun GmbH	Neptun Industrie Rostock GmbH (formerly Neptun-Warnow—qv)	*Germany*
Neptun-Warnow	Neptun Warnow-Werft GmbH (formerly "Neptun"—qv. Later "Neptun" GmbH—qv)	*Germany*
Neptunwerft	Neptunwerft Rostock GmbH (no longer builders)—later "Neptun"—qv)	*E Germany*
Nervion	Astilleros Reunidos del Nervion SA (ARN, SA)	*Spain*
Newport News	Newport News Shipbuilding & Dry Dock Co	*USA*
Newport SB	Newport Shipbuilding & Engineering Co Ltd (formerly Atlantic Shipbuilding Co—qv) (no longer builders)	*UK*
New York SB	The New York Shipbuilding Corporation (no longer builders)	*USA*
Nichiro	Nichiro Zosen KK (Nichiro Shipbuilding Co Ltd)	*Japan*
Niestern Sander	Niestern-Sander BV (formed by merger of 'Appingedam' and Sander—qv)	*Netherlands*
Nieuwe Noord	Nieuwe Noord Nederlandse Scheepswerven BV (previously Noord Nederlandse—qv) (no longer builders)	*Netherlands*
Niigata	Niigata Engineering Co Ltd	*Japan*
Nipponkai	Nipponkai Heavy Industries Co Ltd (later NHI Co Ltd)	*Japan*
Nishii	Nishii Dock Co Ltd (no longer builders)	*Japan*
Nishi Nippon J	Nishi Nippon Jukogyo KK (no longer builders—later Mitsubishi Z—qv)	*Japan*
Nishi Z	Nishi Zosen KK (Nishi Shipbuilding Co Ltd)	*Japan*
Nitchitsu	Nitchitsu Co Ltd	*Japan*
NKK	Nippon Kokan KK (Tohoku Shipbuilding is an affiliate) (later NKK Corp—qv)	*Japan*
NKK Corp	NKK Corporation (Nippon Kokan KK). (formerly Nippon Kokan KK—qv)	*Japan*
Nobiskrug	Werft Nobiskrug GmbH (later HDW-Nobiskrug GmbH)	*Germany*
Noord	Noorde Nederlandse Scheepswerven NV (later Nieuwe Noord Nederlandse—qv)	*Netherlands*
Norderwerft	KG Norderwerft GmbH & Co (see also Harms. Previously Norderwerft Johann Rathje Koser. Originally Norderwerft Koser u Meyer—now part of Sietas group)	*W Germany*
Nordfjord	Nordfjord Verft A/S (formerly Eid Verft)	*Norway*
Nord Med	Chantiers du Nord et de la Méditerranée (formed by merger of Dunkerque-Normandie, La Ciotat and CNIM—qv) (see NORMED)	*France*
Nordso	A/S Nordsovaerftet	*Denmark*
NORMED	correct title for Nord Med—qv	*France*
Norrkoping	Norrkoping Varv & Verksted A/B (later Broderna Ekeroths Metallkonstruktioner—no longer builders)	*Sweden*
North East	North East Shipbuilders Ltd (part of British Shipbuilders) (Formed by merger of A & P (qv) and Sunderland (qv))	*UK*
Nosenko	Nosenko Shipyard (later Chernomorskiy—qv)	*USSR*
NSW Govt	NSW Govt Engineering & Shipbuilding Undertaking (State Dockyard) (no longer builders)	*Australia*
Nya Solvesborgs	AB Nya Solvesborgs Varvs (previously Solvesborgs; subsequently Götaverken Solvesborgs—no longer builders)	*Sweden*
Nya Varv	Nya Varvsaktiebolaget Oresund (later Oresundsvarvet—qv)	*Sweden*
Nye Fredriksstad	A/S Nye Fredriksstad Mek Verksted (formerly A/S Fredriksstad Mek Verksted—qv) (no longer builders)	*Norway*
Nylands	Nylands Verksted (no longer builders) (became part of Aker Group)	*Norway*
Nymo	A/S Nymo Mek Verksted (no longer builders)	*Norway*
Nystads	Nystads Varv Ab/Uudenkaupungin Telakka Oy (later Rauma-Repola—qv)	*Finland*
Oberwinter	Schiffswerft Oberwinter GmbH (no longer builders)	*W Germany*
Odense	Odense Staalskibsvaerft A/S	*Denmark*
Odero	Odero-Terni-Orlando Societa per Azioni, per la Costruzione di Navi, Macchine ed Artiglerie (no longer builders)	*Italy*
Oderwerke	Oderwerke Maschinenfabrik u Schiffsbauwerft AG (later Stettiner Oderwerke—no longer builders)	*Germany*
O & K	Orenstein & Koppel AG (previously Orenstein-Koppel & Luebecker Maschinenbau AG) later O & K Tagebau und Schiffstechnik—no longer builders)	*W Germany*
Okayama	Okayama Zosen KK (no longer builders)	*Japan*
Okean	Okean Shipyard (previously Oktyabrskoye Shipyard) (no longer builders)	*USSR*
Oltenitsa	Santierul Naval Oltenitsa (probably no longer builders)	*Romania*
Omishima	Omishima Dock KK (no longer builders)	*Japan*
Onomichi	Onomichi Zosen (Onomichi Dockyard Co Ltd) (affiliated with Hitachi)	*Japan*
Orens	Orens M/V (no longer builders)	*Norway*
Oresunds	Oresundsvarvet AB (later Götaverken Oresundsvarvet—incorporated in Svenska Varv) (no longer builders)	*Sweden*
Orlogs	Marinverkstaderna Orlogsvarvet (later Karlskronavarvet—qv)	*Sweden*
Orskov C	Orskov Christensens Staalskibsvaerft A/S (formerly Orskovs—qv)	*Denmark*
Orskovs	Orskovs Staalskibsvaerft I/S (later Orskov C—qv)	*Denmark*
Osaka	Osaka Zosensho KK (Osaka Shipbuilding Co Ltd)	*Japan*

Oshima Dock	Oshima Dock KK (no longer builders)	*Japan*
Oshima Z	Oshima Zosensho (Oshima Shipbuilding Co Ltd)	*Japan*
Oskarshamns	Oskarshamns Varv AB (formerly AB Nya Oskarshamns VARV)	*Sweden*
Osterreichische	Osterreichische Schiffswerften AG Linz-Korneuburg (Korneuburg)	*Austria*
Ottensener	Ottensener Eisenwerk GmbH (no longer builders—later Schlieker-Werft—qv)	*W Germany*
Palma	Astilleros de Palma SA (later Mallorca—qv)	*Spain*
Pattje	Scheepswerf "Waterhuizen" NV J. Pattje (later BV Scheepswerf "Waterhuizen" J. Pattje)	*Netherlands*
Peene	VEB Peene-Werft (no longer builders) (see Peene-Werft)	*E Germany*
Peene Werft	Peene Werft GmbH (formerly the East German yard of VEB Peene-Werft before reunification)	*Germany*
Pellegrino	Cantieri Navali Pellegrino (later Esercizio—qv)	*Italy*
Pennsylvania	Pennsylvania Shipyards Inc (no longer builders—later part of Bethlehem Steel)	*USA*
Pennsylvania SB	Pennsylvania Shipbuilding Co (no longer builders)	*USA*
Perriere	Chantiers et Ateliers de la Perriere (later Lorient-Naval-Industrie)	*France*
Peterson	Peterson Builders Inc	*USA*
Peter's Schpsbw	Peter's Scheepsbouw BV (later Peters-Ysselmeer)	*Netherlands*
Philip	Philip & Son Ltd (no longer builders)	*UK*
Pickersgill	William Pickersgill & Sons Ltd (later Austin & Pickersgill—see under A & P)	*UK*
Pietra Ligure	Cantieri Navali de Pietra Ligure (later Liguri—qv)	*Italy*
Pollock	James Pollock, Sons & Co Ltd (no longer builders)	*UK*
Polnocna	Stocznia Polnocna in Bohaterow Westerplatte (later Stocznia Polnocna SA)	*Poland*
Porsgrunds	A/S Porsgrunds M/V (later Porsgrunn—qv)	*Norway*
Porsgrunn	Porsgrunn Verft A/S (formerly Porsgrunds) (part of Trosvik Group)	*Norway*
Port Weller	Port Weller Dry Docks Ltd	*Canada*
Pot	NV Scheepsbouwerf Gebroeders Pot (no longer builders)	*Netherlands*
Provence	Société Anonyme des Chantiers et Ateliers de Provence (no longer builders)	*France*
P. Smit	BV Machinefabriek en Scheepswerven van P. Smit, Jr (no longer builders)	*Netherlands*
Puget Sound	Puget Sound Bridge & Drydock Co (later Lockheed—qv)	*USA*
Puget Sound ND	Puget Sound Naval Dockyard	*USA*
Pullman	Pullman Standard Car Manufacturing Co (no longer builders)	*USA*
Pusey & Jones	The Pusey & Jones Corp (no longer builders)	*USA*
Pusnaes	Pusnaes Mek Verksted A/S (no longer builders)	*Norway*
Rauma OS	Rauma Offshore Works Oy	*Finland*
Rauma-Repola	Rauma-Repola Oy (formed from Nystads (qv) and Reposaaren (qv)) (no longer builders)	*Finland*
Rauma Yards	Rauma Yards Oy (formerly Rauma-Repola—qv)	*Finland*
Readhead	John Readhead & Sons Ltd (no longer builders—became part of Swan Hunter—qv)	*UK*
Redfern	Redfern Construction Co Ltd (no longer builders)	*Canada*
Renck	Komm Ges G. Renck, Jr (no longer builders—later Gleue—qv)	*W Germany*
Reposaaren	Reposaaren Konepaja Oy (no longer builders—later part of Rauma-Repola)	*Finland*
Reunis	Ateliers Reunis du Nord et de l'Ouest (ARNO) (shiprepairers)	*France*
Rhein Nordseew	Rheinstahl Nordseewerke GmbH (later Thyssen Nordseewerke—qv)	*W Germany*
Rhin	Société des Chantiers et Ateliers du Rhin (no longer builders)	*France*
Richards	Richards (Shipbuilders) Ltd (no longer builders)	*UK*
Rickmers	Rickmers Werft (no longer builders)	*W Germany*
Riga	Riga Shipbuilding and Shiprepair Yard (no longer builders)	*USSR*
Rinkai	Rinkai Kogyo KK (no longer builders)	*Japan*
Riuniti	Cantieri Navali Riuniti SpA (formerly Cantieri Navali del Tirreno & Riuniti—see also under CD Tirreno) (later FCNI—qv)	*Italy*
Robb Caledon	Robb Caledon Shipbuilders Ltd (amalgamation of Henry Robb & Caledon) (part of British Shipbuilders) (no longer builders)	*UK*
Rolandwerft	Rolandwerft GmbH (no longer builders)	*W Germany*
Rosenberg	Rosenberg Vaerft A/S (no longer builders—now Moss Rosenberg)	*Norway*
Rosslauer	Rosslauer Schiffswerft GmbH (formerly part of Elbewerften—qv)	*Germany (previously E Germany)*
Rotterdamsche	Rotterdamsche Droogdok Mij BV (no longer builders)	*Netherlands*
Royal Danish Dkyd	Royal Danish Dockyard	*Denmark*
Ruiz	T. Ruiz de Velasco SA (formerly Astilleros de T. Ruiz de Velasco) (no longer builders)	*Spain*
Ruscador	Ruscador Ltd (no longer builders. Shiprepairers and engineers only. Part of Drypool Group)	*UK*
Sabah	Sabah Shipyard Sendirian Berhad (formerly Sabah Shipbuilding Repairing and Engineering Sdn Bhd)	*Malaysia*
SABARN	SA Brugeoise d'Arrimage et de Reparations de Navires (SABARN) (no longer builders)	*Belgium*
Saiki	Saiki Jukogyo KK (previously part of Usuki—qv)	*Japan*
Saint John SB	Saint John Shipbuilding & Dry Dock Co Ltd	*Canada*
Saint Nazaire	Société Anonyme des Chantiers et Ateliers de Saint Nazaire (Penhoet) (later L'Atlantique—qv)	*France*
Salamis	Salamis Shipyard Ltd (no longer builders)	*Greece*
Samsung	Samsung Shipbuilding and Heavy Industries Co Ltd (formerly Samsung Shipbuilding Co Ltd until amalgamation with Daesung Heavy Industries Co Ltd)	*S Korea*
Sander	Scheepsbouw & Reparatiebedrijf Gebroeders Sander BV (no longer builders—now amalgamated with Gebr Niestern—qv—to form Niestern-Sander—qv)	*Netherlands*
Sandvikens	Wärtsilä-Koncernen Ab Sandvikens Skeppsdocka (now part of Wärtsilä—qv)	*Finland*
Sanoyas Corp	Sanoyas Corporation (formerly Sanoyasu—qv. Later Sanoyas Hishino Meisho Corp)	*Japan*

Sanoyas HM	Sanoyas Hishino Meisho Corporation (formerly Sanoyas Corporation—qv)	*Japan*
Sanoyasu	Sanoyasu Dockyard Co Ltd (later Sanoyas HM—qv)	*Japan*
Santander	Astilleros de Santander SA (no longer builders. Shiprepairers only)	*Spain*
Sanuki	Sanuki Zosen Tekkosho KK (Sanuki Shipbuilding and Iron Works Co Ltd)	*Japan*
Sanyo Z	Sanyo Zosen KK (no longer builders)	*Japan*
Sarpsborg	Sarpsborg Mek Verksted A/S K/S (later Marcraft A/S—no longer builders)	*Norway*
Sasebo	Sasebo Heavy Industries Co Ltd (SSK)	*Japan*
'Sava'	Brodogradiliste 'Sava'	*Yugoslavia*
S & B	Abteilung Werft- und Dockbetrieb Schulte & Bruns (no longer builders)	*W Germany*
Scarr	Henry Scarr Ltd (later Dunston—qv)	*UK*
Scheldegroep	Koninklijke Scheldegroep BV (formerly BV Koninklijke Mij Scheepswerf & Machinefabriek "De Schelde". Originally NV Koninklijke Maats "De Schelde")	*Netherlands*
Schichau	Same as F. Schichau—qv	*W Germany*
Schichau See	Schichau Seebeckwerft AG (Formed by merger of Schichau-Unterweser and Seebeckwerft AG)	*Germany*
Schichau-U	Schichau-Unterweser Aktiengesellschaft (amalgamation of F. Schichau and Unterweser—qv) (later Schichau See—qv)	*W Germany*
Schiedamsche	Schiedamsche Scheepswerf (no longer builders)	*Netherlands*
Schlichting	Schlichting Werft GmbH (no longer builders)	*W Germany*
Schlieker	Schlieker-Werft, Willy H. Schlieker KG (no longer builders, formerly Ottensener Eisenwerk—qv)	*W Germany*
Schloemer	Schiffswerft Gebroeder Schloemer (later Schloemer GmbH & Co)	*W Germany*
Schuerenstedt	Gebrueder Schuerenstedt KG (later Berner Schiffswerft GmbH & Co KG—no longer builders)	*W Germany*
Scotstoun	Scotstoun Marine Ltd (part of British Shipbuilders) (no longer builders)	*UK*
Scott Lithgow	Scott Lithgow Ltd (see Lithgow and Scotts' SB. Now owned by Trafalgar House)	*UK*
Scott & Sons	Scott & Sons (Bowling) Ltd (part of British Shipbuilders) (no longer builders)	*UK*
Seatrain	Seatrain Shipbuilding Corp (no longer builders)	*USA*
Sedef	Sedef Gemi Endustrisi AS	*Turkey*
Seebeck	Seebeckwerft AG (formerly A G 'Weser'—qv)	*W Germany*
Setenave	SETENAVE—Estaleiros Navais de Setubal SARL (later Solisnor—Estaleiros Navais SA)	*Portugal*
Setoda	Setoda Shipbuilding Co Ltd (Setoda Zosensho) (later Naikai—qv)	*Japan*
Setouchi	Setouchi Zosen KK (later Kishimoto—qv)	*Japan*
Seutelvens	Seutelvens Verksted (no longer builders)	*Norway*
Severney	Severney Ship Building Yard (also known as Northern Shipyard (Severnaya Verf). Renamed "A Zhdanov" Shipbuilding Yard but reverted to Severny)	*Russia*
Shanghai SY	Shanghai Shipyard	*China*
Shikoku	Shikoku Dockyard Co Ltd (now affiliated with Mitsui)	*Japan*
Shimoda	Shimoda Dockyard Co Ltd (no longer builders)	*Japan*
Shin-A	Shin-A Shipbuilding Co Ltd (formerly Shin Ah Shipbuilding Co. A subsidiary of Daewoo—qv)	*S Korea*
Shinhama	Shinhama Dockyard Co Ltd (also called Niihama Dockyard Co Ltd)	*Japan*
Shin Kurushima	Shin Kurushima Dockyard Co Ltd (formerly Kurushima—qv and Taihei (qv))	*Japan*
Shin Naniwa	Shin Naniwa Dock Co Ltd (no longer builders)	*Japan*
Shin Yamamoto	Shin Yamamoto Zosen KK (formerly Yamamoto Zosen)	*Japan*
Shioyama	Shioyama Dockyard Co Ltd (no longer builders)	*Japan*
Shirahama	Shirahama Zosen KK (Shirahama Shipbuilding Co Ltd)	*Japan*
Short Bros	Short Bros Ltd (no longer builders)	*UK*
Sieghold	Schiffswerft u Maschinenfabrik Max Sieghold (later Siegholdwerft Bremerhaven GmbH & Co—no longer builders)	*W Germany*
Sietas	J. J. Sietas KG Schiffswerft GmbH & Co	*Germany*
Simons	William Simons & Co Ltd (later Simons-Lobnitz—qv)	*UK*
Simons-Lobnitz	Simons-Lobnitz-Ltd (no longer builders. An amalgamation of Lobnitz & Simons—qv)	*UK*
Singapore SB	Singapore Shipbuilding & Engineering (later became Singapore T—qv)	*Singapore*
Singapore Slip	Singapore Slipway & Engineering Pte Ltd (no longer builders. Became part of Singmarine—qv)	*Singapore*
Singapore T	Singapore Technologies Shipbuilding and Engineering Ltd (formerly Singapore SB—qv)	*Singapore*
Singmarine	Singmarine Dockyard & Engineering Pte Ltd (Singapore Slip became part of this company)	*Singapore*
Skala	P/F Skala Skipasmidja	*Faroes*
Slob	Scheepswerf Slob BV (formerly Scheepsbouwwerf Slob BV)	*Netherlands*
Slovenske	Slovenske Lodenice AG (also known as Slovak Shipyard. Formerly Zavody Tazkeho Strojarstva) (no longer builders)	*Czechoslovakia*
Smith's D	Smith's Dock Co Ltd (part of British Shipbuilders) (no longer builders)	*UK*
Smit K	Smit Kinderdijk VOF (later IHC Smit—qv)	*Netherlands*
Solimano	Cantieri Navali Solimano (no longer builders)	*Italy*
Solvesborgs	Solvesborgs Varvs AB (subsequently Gotav Solvesborgs—qv)	*Sweden*
Sonderborg	Sonderborg Skibsvaerft A/S (no longer builders)	*Denmark*
Sorviks	Sorviksvarvet AB (later Uddevallavarvet—qv)	*Sweden*
Southeastern	Southeastern Shipbuilding Corp (no longer builders)	*USA*
Soviknes	Soviknes Verft A/S	*Norway*
"Split"	Brodogradiliste i Tvornica Dizel Motora "Split" (later Brodogradiliste "Split")	*Yugoslavia/ Croatia*
Stabilimenti	Stabilimenti Navali SpA (formerly Raranto—qv) (later part of FCNI—qv)	*Italy*
Stader	Stader Schiffswerft GmbH (no longer builders)	*W Germany*
Stami	Scheepsbouw Stami BV (no longer builders)	*Netherlands*
Stavanger S & D	Stavanger Stob & Dok (no longer builders)	*Norway*

Steinwerder	Steinwerder Industrie AG (later B + V—qv)	*W Germany*
Stephani	Stephani Werft (no longer builders—later Adler—qv)	*W Germany*
Stephen	Alexander Stephen & Sons Ltd (no longer builders—became part of Upper Clyde Shipbuilders—qv)	*UK*
Sterkoder	Sterkoder Mek Verksted A/S (later Sterkoder A/S)	*Norway*
Sterkrade	Gutehoffnungshuette Sterkrade AG (later M.A.N. Unternehmensbereich—qv)	*W Germany*
St Johns River	St Johns River Shipbuilding Co (no longer builders)	*USA*
St Lawrence M & M	St Lawrence Metal and Marine Works Inc (no longer builders)	*Canada*
Stord	Stord Verft A/S (part of Aker Group. Renamed Aker Stord A/S)	*Norway*
Storviks	Storviks Mek Verksted A/S	*Norway*
St Pieter	Scheepswerven St Pieter NV (Chantier Naval St Pieter) (no longer builders)	*Belgium*
Straits SS	Straits Steamship Co Ltd (no longer builders)	*Malaysia*
Stralsund	VEB Volkswerft Stralsund (later Volkswerft—qv)	*E Germany*
Stroobos	Scheepswerf & Machinefabriek Barkmeijer Stroobos BV (formerly Scheepswerf & Machinefabriek Barkmeijer Fa Tj)	*Netherlands*
Stuelcken	(or Stulcken) H. C. Stuelcken Sohn (no longer builders—now incorporated in Blohm + Voss—see under B + V)	*W Germany*
Suerken	Hermann Suerken Stahlbau Schiffbau Maschinenbau GmbH & Co KG (no longer builders)	*Germany*
Suez	Suez Canal Authority (Port Said Shipyard)	*Egypt*
Sumitomo	Sumitomo Heavy Industries Ltd (amalgamation of Sumitomo Mach Co & Uraga HI—qv) (affiliated companies: Nipponkai—qv; Oshima—qv)	*Japan*
Sunderland	Sunderland Shipbuilders Ltd (part of British Shipbuilders) (previously Doxford & Sunderland—qv. Now part of North East Shipbuilders—qv)	*UK*
Sun SB	Sun Ship Inc (formerly Sun Shipbuilding & Dry Dock Co. Later became Pennsylvania Shipbuilding Co—no longer builders)	*USA*
Suurmeyer	Scheepswerf Gebr Suurmeyer BV (no longer builders—previously "Vorruitgang—qv)	*Netherlands*
Svendborg	Svendborg Skibsvaerft A/S (formerly A/S Svendborg Skibsvaerft og Maskinbyggeri. Later Svendborg Vaerft A/S)	*Denmark*
Swan Hunter	Swan Hunter Shipbuilders Ltd (see Swan Hunter & T. Swan Hunter & WR, Readhead, Hawthorn, L and Vickers-Armstrong)	*UK*
Swan Hunter & T	Swan Hunter & Tyne Shipbuilders Ltd (formerly Hawthorn, Lesley now part of Swan Hunter)	*UK*
Swan Hunter & WR	Swan Hunter & Wigham Richardson Ltd (now part of Swan Hunter)	*UK*
Szczecin	Stocznia Szczecinska SA (formerly Stocznia Szczecinska im A. Warskiego)	*Poland*
Szczecinska	Stocznia Szczecinska im A. Warskiego (later Szczecin—qv)	*Poland*
Taguma	Taguma Zosen KK (now amalgamated with Setoda to form Naikai—qv)	*Japan*
Taihei	Taihei Kogyo KK (now part of Shin Kurushima—qv)	*Japan*
Taikoo	The Taikoo Dockyard & Engineering Co of Hong Kong Ltd (no longer builders—see under Hong Kong (U))	*Hong Kong*
Taiwan SB	Taiwan Shipbuilding Corp (no longer builders—formerly Ingalls-Taiwan SB & DD Co, later part of China SB—qv)	*Taiwan*
Taiyo	Taiyo Zosen KK (Taiyo Shipbuilding Co) (no longer builders—taken over by Hayashikane—qv)	*Japan*
Tampa	Tampa Shipbuilding & Engineering Co (no longer builders)	*USA*
Tangen	Tangen Verft A/S (later Tangen Verft Kragero)	*Norway*
Taranto	Cantieri Navali di Taranto (later Stabilimenti—qv)	*Italy*
Taskizak	Taskizak Naval Shipyard (Government owned)	*Turkey*
Teraoka	Teraoka Zosensho (Teraoka Shipyard Co Ltd)	*Japan*
Terneuzensche	Terneuzensche Scheepsbouw Maatschappij BV (no longer builders)	*Netherlands*
Thornycroft	John I. Thornycroft & Co Ltd (later Vosper Thornycroft Ltd)	*UK*
Thyssen	Thyssen Nordseewerke GmbH (see under Emden & Rhein Nordseew)	*Germany*
Tille	Tille Scheepsbouw BV (later Tille Shipyards BV. Formerly Kramer & Booy—qv)	*Netherlands*
Tirreno	Cantieri Navali del Tirreno e Riuniti (later Riuniti—qv)	*Italy*
"Titovo"	"Titovo Brodogradiliste" (later Brodogradiliste "Kraljevica")	*Yugoslavia*
Todd	Todd Shipyards Corp (various titles)	*USA*
Todd-Bath	Todd-Bath Iron Shipbuilding Co (later New UK SB Corp—no longer builders)	*USA*
Tohoku	Tohoku Shipbuilding Co Ltd (formerly Tohoku Dockyard Co Ltd. Later Tohoku Dock Tekko KK) (affiliated to NKK—qv)	*Japan*
Tokushima ZS	Tokushima Zosen Sangyo (now incorporated into Shin Kurushima)	*Japan*
Ton	Scheepswerf Ton Bodewes BV	*Netherlands*
Towa	Towa Zosen KK (Towa Shipbuilding Co Ltd)	*Japan*
Travewerft	Travewerft GmbH (later R. Harmstorf Wasserbau u Travewerft GmbH—no longer builders)	*W Germany*
Triestino SM	Arsenale Triestino-San Marco SpA (later part of FCNI—qv)	*Italy*
Tronder	Tronderverftet A/S	*Norway*
Trondhjems	Trondhjems Mek Verksted A/S (later part of Aker Group as Aker Trondelag A/S—no longer builders)	*Norway*
Trosvik	Trosvik Verksted A/S (Trosvik Group) (no longer builders)	*Norway*
Tsuneishi	Tsuneishi Zosen KK (Tsuneishi Shipbuilding Co Ltd)	*Japan*
Tulcea	Santierul Naval Tulcea	*Romania*
Turnu-Severin	Santierul Naval Turnu-Severin	*Romania*
Ube Dock	Ube Dock (no longer builders)	*Japan*
Uddevalla	Uddevallavarvet AB (part of Svenska Varv) (formerly Sorviks—qv) (no longer builders)	*Sweden*
Ujina	Ujina Zosensho KK (no longer builders—affiliated to Kanawa & Hitachi)	*Japan*
"Uljanik"	Brodogradiliste "Uljanik" (formerly Brodogradiliste i Tvornica Dizel Motora "Uljanik". Renamed Brodogradiliste "Uljanik" dd, after Croatian independence)	*Yugoslavia/ Croatia*
Ulstein	Ulstein Mek Verksted A/S (see Ulstein H)	*Norway*

Ulstein H	Ulstein Hatio A/S (amalgamation of Hatlo (qv) and Ulstein (qv). Later Ulstein Verft A/S)	*Norway*
UN de Levante	Union Naval de Levante SA	*Spain*
Uniao	Companhia Uniao Fabril (later Lisnave—qv)	*Portugal*
United Spyds	United Shipyards Ltd (no longer builders)	*Canada*
United SY	United Shipping Yard Co SA (no longer builders)	*Greece*
Unterweser	Schiffbau-Gesellschaft Unterweser AG (later Schichau-Unterweser—qv)	*W Germany*
Upper Clyde	Upper Clyde Shipbuilders Ltd (consortium of Fairfields, Connell, Stephen and J. Brown—qv. Most of the yards became Govan Shipbuilders—qv)	*UK*
Uraga Dock	Uraga Dock Co Ltd (later Uraga HI—qv)	*Japan*
Uraga HI	Uraga Heavy Industries Ltd (formerly Uraga Dock—qv. Later Sumitomo—qv)	*Japan*
US Naval SY	US Naval Shipyards (United States Navy Yards) (The New York yard became Seatrain—qv)	*USA*
Usuki	Usuki Zosensho KK (Usuki Shipyard Co Ltd)	*Japan*
Uwajima	KK Uwajima Zosensho (Uwajima Shipbuilding Co Ltd. Part of Shin Kurushima—qv)	*Japan*
Vaagen	Vaagen Werft A/S (Formerly Grotvaagens Verft. Later Vaagen Verft Engineering A/S)	*Norway*
Valmet	Valmet Oy, Helsingin Telakka (Helsinki Shipyard) (see Valmetin)	*Finland*
Valmetin	Valmetin Laivateollisuus Oy (formed by merger of Valmet's Pansio Shipyard and Laivateollisuus Oy. When Valmet and Wärtsilä joined, to form Wärtsilä Marine Industries, the yard was named Oy Laivateollisuus AB. It closed in 1988)	*Finland*
Valmet P	Valmet Oy, Pansion Tehdas (Pansio Shipyard) (see Valmetin for later history)	*Finland*
Vancouver	Vancouver Shipyards Co Ltd (renamed Genstar Shipyards Ltd but later reverted to original name)	*Canada*
van der Werf	Scheepswerf Gebroeders van der Werf BV (later Scheepswerf Ravenstein)	*Netherlands*
Van Diepen	BV Scheepswerven Gebr van Diepen	*Netherlands*
Van Lent	Jacht-en Scheepswerf C. van Lent & Zonen BV	*Netherlands*
Varna	Varna Shipyard (see under "Georgo Dimitrov")	*Bulgaria*
Verolme Cork	Verolme Cork Dockyard Ltd (closed in November 1984)	*Ireland*
Verolme Dok	Verolme Dok-en Scheepsbouw Mij BV (incorporated in Verolme United—qv)	*Netherlands*
Verolme ER do Brazil	Verolme Estaleiros Reunidos do Brazil SA	*Brazil*
Verolme Scheeps	Verolme Scheepswerf Alblasserdam BV (no longer builders—now Glessen-De Noord. Originally Jan Smit—qv)	*Netherlands*
Verolme SH	Verolme Scheepswerf Heusden BV (incorporated in Verolme United. See De Haan & O)	*Netherlands*
Verolme U	Verolme United Shipyards (see Verolme Cork, Verolme Dok, Verolme ER do Brazil and Verolme SH)	*Netherlands*
Verschure	Verschure & Co's Scheepswerf en Machinefabriek NV (Later IHC Verschure—no longer builders)	*Netherlands*
Vervako	Vervako Heusden BV (formerly Mach en Schps Vervako BV)	*Netherlands*
Viana	Estaleiros Navais de Viana do Castelo SA	*Portugal*
Vickers-Armstrongs	Vickers-Armstrongs (Shipbuilders) Ltd (Previously Vickers-Armstrong Ltd. Now Vickers SB—qv)	*UK*
Vickers Ltd	Vickers Ltd (now Vickers SB—qv)	*UK*
Vickers SB	Vickers Shipbuilding & Engineering Ltd (see Vickers-Armstrongs and Vickers Ltd)	*UK*
Victoria Mach	Victoria Machinery Depot Co Ltd (no longer builders)	*Canada*
"Visentini"	Cantiere Navale "Visentini" SAS de Visentini Francesco & C	*Italy*
Volgograd	Volgograd Shipyard (no longer builders)	*USSR*
"Volharding"	Bodewes Scheepswerf "Volharding" BV	*Netherlands*
Volkswerft	Volkswerft GmbH (formerly Stralsund—qv)	*Germany*
Volodarskiy	Volodarskiy Shipyard (no longer builders)	*USSR*
"Vooruitgang"	NV Scheepswerf "Vooruitgang" (Gebr Suurmeyer) (later Suurmeyer—qv)	*Netherlands*
"Voorwaarts"	Scheepswerf "Voorwaarts" BV (no longer builders)	*Netherlands*
Vuyk	A. Vuyk & Zonen's Scheepswerven BV (no longer builders)	*Netherlands*
Vyborg	Vyborg Shipyard (no longer builders)	*USSR*
Wakamatsu	Wakamatsu Zosen KK (Wakamatsu Shipbuilding Co Ltd)	*Japan*
Walkers Ltd	Walkers Ltd (no longer builders)	*Australia*
Warnow	VEB Warnowwerft (later Kvaerner Warnow—qv)	*E Germany*
Wärtsilä	Oy Wärtsilä AB (and Oy Wärtsilä AB Helsinki Yard. Previously Crichton-Vulcan (qv) and Sandvikens (qv). Later became Masa Yards Inc and then Kvaerner Masa Yards Inc. See under Valmetin for further history)	*Finland*
Wärtsilä MI	Wärtsilä Marine Industries Inc (see details under Valmetin and Wärtsilä)	*Finland*
Watanabe	KK Watanabe Zosensho (Watanabe Shipbuilding Co Ltd)	*Japan*
'Welgelegen'	"Welgelegen" Scheepswerf & Machinefabriek BV	*Netherlands*
Wenchong	Wenchong Shipyard (later Guangzhou Wenchong Shipyard)	*China*
Werftunion	Werftunion GmbH & Co (amalgamation of three yards)	*Germany*
"Westerbroek"	NV Scheepswerf "Westerbroek" (no longer builders)	*Netherlands*
Whyalla	Whyalla Shipbuilding & Engineering Works (no longer builders—previously Broken Hill—qv) (no longer builders)	*Australia*
Wiley	Wiley Manufacturing Co (no longer builders)	*USA*
Willamette	Willamette Iron & Steel Co (no longer builders)	*USA*
Wilton-Fije	Dok-en Werf Mij Wilton-Fijenoord BV	*Netherlands*
Wisla	Stocznia Wisla	*Poland*
Worms	Ateliers et Chantiers de la Seine Maritime (Worms & Cie (later La Seine—qv)	*France*
Xingang	Xingang Shipyard	*China*
Yamanaka	Yamanaka Zosen KK (Yamanaka Shipbuilding Co Ltd)	*Japan*
Yamanishi	Yamanishi Zosen KK (Yamanishi Shipbuilding & Iron Works Inc)	*Japan*
"Yantar"	"Yantar" Shipyard (formerly Kaliningrad State Shipyard) (no longer builders)	*USSR*

Yarrow & Co	Yarrow & Co Ltd (later Yarrow Shipbuilders Ltd)	*UK*
Yarrows Ltd	Yarrows Ltd (formerly Burrard Yarrows—qv. Became Versatile Pacific Shipyards at one time but reverted to Yarrows Ltd) (no longer builders)	*Canada*
Yorkshire DD	Yorkshire Dry Dock Co Ltd	*UK*
Ysselwerf	Scheepswerf en Machinefabriek Ysselwerf (later YVC Ysselwerf BV)	*Netherlands*
Zaanlandsche	Zaanlandsche Scheepsbouw Maatschappij NV (no longer builders)	*Netherlands*
Zaliv	Zaliv Shipyard (also known as Kerch Shipyard) (no longer builders)	*USSR*
Zavody	Zavody Tazkeho Strojarstva (later Slovenske—qv)	*Czechoslovakia*
Zelendolskiy	Zelenodolskiy Shipyard (or Zelenodolsk Shipyard) (no longer builders)	*USSR*
"Zhdanov"	"A. Zhdanov" Shipbuilding Yard (previously Severney—qv)	*USSR*
Zhong Hua	Zhong Hua Shipyard (formerly Chung Hua—qv)	*China*
"3 Maj"	Brodogradiliste "3 Maj" (formerly Poduzece "3 Maj")	*Croatia*
"61 Kommunar"	"61 Kommunar" Shipbuilding Yard (no longer builders)	*USSR*

Abbreviations of Engine Builders/Designers

Some of these companies are out of existence now or amalgamated with other companies.

ABC	Anglo-Belgian Corporation NV	*Belgium*
ABO	Associated British Oil Engines	*UK*
Adriatico	Cantieri Riuniti dell'Adriatico (see GMT)	*Italy*
AEG	Allgemaine Elektricitats-Ges (AEG) (also AEG-Telefunken)	*W Germany*
AEI	Associated Electric Industries Ltd	*UK*
A G "Weser"	Aktien-Gesellschaft "Weser"	*W Germany*
Ailsa	Ailsa Shipbuilding Co Ltd	*UK*
Aitchison, Blair	Aitchison, Blair Ltd	*UK*
Ajax Unaflow	Ajax Unaflow Co (see also Unaflow)	*USA*
Akasaka	Akasaka Tekkosho KK (Akasaka Diesels Ltd)	*Japan*
Alco	Alco Power Inc	*USA*
Allgemeine	See AEG	
Alpha	same as Alpha-Diesel qv	
Alpha-Diesel	Alpha-Diesel A/S (now part of B & W—see B & W Alpha)	*Denmark*
Alsthom	Alsthom-Atlantique (shipbuilding division is Ch de l'Atlantique)	*France*
Amos & Smith	Amos & Smith Ltd	*UK*
Ansaldo	Ansaldo SpA (see GMT)	*Italy*
APE Allen	A. P. E. Allen Ltd (previously W. H. Allen—qv)	*UK*
Appingedammer Brons	see under Brons	
Associated Electric	see under AEI	
Atlas-Diesel	Atlas-Diesel	*Sweden*
Atlas-MaK	Atlas-MaK Maschinenbau GmbH (see also MaK)	*W Germany*
Australian Commonwealth	Australian Commonwealth Shipping Board	*Australia*
Baltic	Baltic Shipbuilding & Engineering Works	*USSR*
Baudouin	Soc des Moteurs Baudouin	*France*
Belliss & Morcom	Belliss & Morcom Ltd	*UK*
Bergens	Bergens Lekaniske Verksteder A/S	*Norway*
Bergius Kelvin	Bergius Kelvin Co Ltd (English Electric group)	*UK*
Bethlehem	Bethlehem Shipbuilding Corp Ltd	*USA*
Bethlehem Steel	Bethlehem Steel Corp	*USA*
Blackstone	Blackstone & Co Ltd (see later Blackstone and Mirrlees Blackstone)	*UK*
Bofors	A/B Bofors Nohab	*Sweden*
"Bolnes"	NV Machinefabriek "Bolnes"	*Netherlands*
Borsig	Borsig GmbH	*W Germany*
B. Polar	see British Polar	
Bremer V	Schiffbau und Maschinenfabrik Bremer Vulkan	*W Germany*
Bretagne	Ateliers et Chantiers de Bretagne	*France*
British Auxiliaries	British-Auxiliaries Ltd	*UK*
British Polar	British Polar Engines Ltd (part of Associated British Engineering)	*UK*
Brons	Brons Industrie NV (formerly Appingedammer Brons)	*Netherlands*
Brown, Boveri	Brown, Boveri & Co Ltd	*Switzerland*
BTH	B.T.H. Co Ltd	*UK*
B + V	Blohm + Voss AG	*W Germany*
B & W	Burmeister & Wain's Maskin-og Skibsbyggeri (later B & W Diesel A/S—a subsidiary of MAN—qv)	*Denmark*
B & W Alpha	B & W Alpha Division of B & W Diesel A/S	*Denmark*
Cammell Laird	Cammell Laird & Co (Shipbuilders & Engineers) Ltd	*UK*
Canadian Allis-Chalmers	Canadian Allis-Chalmers Ltd	*Canada*
Canadian GEC	Canadian General Electric Co Ltd (see GEC)	*Canada*
Canadian Iron Foundries	Canada Iron Foundries Ltd	*Canada*
Canadian Locomotive	Canadian Locomotive Co Ltd	*Canada*
Caterpillar	Caterpillar Tractor Co	*USA*
CCM	Compagnie de Construction Mécanique (subsidiary of Sulzer—qv)	*France*
CEM-Parsons	CEM-Parsons (Compagnie Electro-Mécanique)	*France*
Central Marine	Central Marine Engineering Works	*UK*
Christiansen & Meyer	Christiansen & Meyer	*W Germany*
CKD Praha	CKD Praha (see Škoda)	*Czechoslovakia*
Cockerill-Ougrée	Société Anonyme Cockerill-Ougrée	*Belgium*
Collingwood	Collingwood Shipyards	*Canada*
Cooper-Bessemer	Cooper-Bessemer Corp	*USA*
Crepelle	Crepelle et Compagnie (later Moteurs Crepelle)	*France*

Creusot	Société des Forges et Atelier du Creusot (later Creusot-Loire)	*France*
Crichton-Vulcan	Wärtsilä Concernen A/B Crichton-Vulcan	*Finland*
Crossley	Crossley Bros Ltd (later Crossley-Premier Engines Ltd)	*UK*
Daihatsu	Daihatsu Diesel Manufacturing Co Ltd	*Japan*
Darmstadt	Motorenfabriek Darmstadt GmbH (Modag)	*W Germany*
Davey, Paxman	Davey, Paxman & Co Ltd (later Paxman Diesel—qv)	*UK*
"De Industrie"	D. & J. Boot "De Industrie"	*Netherlands*
De Laval	De Laval Turbine Inc (later Transamerica De Laval Inc)	*USA*
Deltic	Deltic diesels built by D. Napier & Son Ltd (subsidiary of English Electric)	*UK*
Denny	William Denny & Bros Ltd	*UK*
"De Schelde"	NV Koninklijke Maatschappij "De Schelde"	*Netherlands*
Deutz	Deutz design diesels built under licence (see KHD)	
Dieselmotorenwerk Rostock	VEB Dieselmotorenwerk Rostock	*E Germany*
DMR	Same as Dieselmotorenwerk Rostock—qv	*E Germany*
Dominion	Dominion Bridge Co Ltd	*Canada*
Doxford	Doxford Engines Ltd	*UK*
Dresdner	Dresdner Masch u Schiffs	*Germany*
Duncan Stewart	Duncan Stewart & Co Ltd	*UK*
Duvant	Moteurs Duvant	*France*
Earle's	Earle's Shipbuilding & Engineering Co	*UK*
English Electric	English Electric Co Ltd (later GEC)	*UK*
Enterprise Eng	Enterprise Engine & Machinery Co	*USA*
Espanola	Soc Espanola de Construccion Naval	*Spain*
Euskalduna	Cia Euskalduna de Construccion y Reparacion de Buques	*Spain*
Fairbanks, Morse	Fairbanks, Morse & Co (a division of Colt Industries). Also covers Fairbanks Morse (Canada) Ltd	*USA*
Fairfield	Fairfield Shipbuilding & Engineering Co Ltd	*UK*
Fairfield-Rowan	see under Fairfield; see under Rowan	
Fiat	Soc per Azioni "Fiat" Sezione Grandi Motori (now GMT—qv)	*Italy*
Fiat-Borsig	see Borsig	
Fleming & Ferguson	Fleming & Ferguson Ltd	*UK*
France	Ateliers et Chantiers de France (later Dunkerque-Normandie)	*France*
Franco Tosi	Franco Tosi Industriale SpA	*Italy*
Frederiksstad	Frederiksstad Mek Verksted A/S	*Norway*
Frichs	Aktieselskabet Frichs	*Denmark*
Friedrichshafen	Zahnradfabrik Friedrichshafen AG (later MTU—qv)	*W Germany*
Fuji	Fuji Diesel Co Ltd	*Japan*
Ganz	Ganz Hungarian Shipyards & Crane Works (later "Gheorghiu Dej" Shipyard)	*Hungary*
G. Clark	G. Clark (1938) Ltd (later George Clark & NEM Ltd—part of Richardsons, Westgarth group)	*UK*
GEC	The General Electric Co Ltd (also GEC Diesels, incorporating many diesel engine manufacturing companies)	*UK*
General Metals	General Metals Corp	*USA*
General Motors	General Motors Corp	*USA*
GMT	Grandi Motori Trieste SpA (amalgamation of Ansaldo, Fiat and Cantieri Riuniti dell'Adriatico)	*Italy*
Goerlitzer	Goerlitzer Maschinenbau	*E Germany*
Gotaverken	AB Götaverken (later Götaverken Angteknik AB and Götaverken Motor AB)	*Sweden*
Halberstadt	VEB Maschinenbau Halberstadt	*E Germany*
Hanshin	Hanshin Nainenki Kogyo (Hanshin Diesel Works) Ltd	*Japan*
Harima	Harima Zosensho KK (later IHI—qv)	*Japan*
Hawthorn, L	Hawthorn, Leslie (Engineers) Ltd (later Clark Hawthorn Ltd)	*UK*
Hayashikane	Hayashikane Zosen KK	*Japan*
Hedemora	AB Hedemora Verstader	*Sweden*
Hendy	Joshua Hendy Iron Works	*USA*
Henschel	Henschel-Maschb	*W Germany*
Hitachi	Hitachi Shipbuilding & Engineering Co Ltd (Hitachi Zosen)	*Japan*
Holeby	Holeby Dieselmotor Fabrik A/S (later B & W Holeby Diesel A/S)	*Denmark*
Howaldts	Howaldtswerke Hamburg AG (see Howaldts DW)	*W Germany*
Howaldts DW	Howaldtswerke-Deutsche Werft AG (previously Howaldtswerke Hamburg—qv)	*W Germany*
Hudong	Hudong Shipyard	*China*
Humboldt-Deutz	Humboldt-Deutzmotoren (later KHD—qv)	*Germany*
H & W	Harland & Wolff Ltd	*UK*
IHI	Ishikawajima-Harima Heavy Industries Co Ltd (see also Harima)	*Japan*
Inglis	The John Inglis Co Ltd	*Canada*
Ishikawajima J	Ishikawajima Jukogyo KK (later IHI—qv)	*Japan*
Ito Tekkosho	Ito Tekkosho (Ito Engineering Co Ltd)	*Japan*
J. Brown	John Brown & Co (Clydebank) Ltd (now John Brown Engineering (Clydebank) Ltd)	*UK*
Jonkopings	Jonkopings Motorfabriek Aktiebolaget. Also Jonkopings Mekaniska Verkstads AB	*Sweden*
J. S. White	J. Samuel White & Co Ltd	*UK*
Kaldnes	Kaldnes Mek Verksted	*Norway*
Kawasaki	Kawasaki Heavy Industries Ltd	*Japan*
KHD	Klockner-Humboldt-Deutz AG (see Deutz and Humboldt-Deutz)	*W Germany*
Kieler H	Kieler Howaldtswerke AG (later Howaldtswerke-Deutsche Werft)—qv)	*W Germany*
Kincaid	John G. Kincaid & Co Ltd	*UK*
Kirov	Kirov Works	*USSR*
Kjobenhavns	Kjobenhavns Flydedok & Skibsvaerft	*Denmark*
Kobe	Kobe Hatsuidoki KK (later Kobe Diesel Co Ltd)	*Japan*

Kockums	Kockums Mekaniska Verkstads AB (now Kockums AB)	*Sweden*
Krupp	Fried Krupp Dieselmotoren GmbH. Formerly Fried Krupp Germaniawerft AG (see Krupp-MaK)	*W Germany*
Krupp-MaK	Krupp-MaK Maschinenbau GmbH (formerly MaK—qv)	*W Germany*
Kvaerner	Kvaerner Brug A/S	*Norway*
La Loire	Ateliers et Chantiers de La Loire	*France*
Langesunds	Langesunds Mek Verksted A/S	*Norway*
Lang Gepgyar	Lang Gepgyar	*Hungary*
Larvik	Larvik Slip & Verksted A/S	*Norway*
Lewis	John Lewis & Sons Ltd	*UK*
LF-W	Luebecker Flender-Werke	*W Germany*
Liebknecht	VEB Schwermaschinenbau "Karl Liebknecht" (SKL) (SKL Motoren-und Systemtechnik is new title after reunification)	*E Germany/ Germany*
Lindholmens	A/B Lindholmens Varv	*Sweden*
Lister Blackstone	Lister Blackstone Marine Ltd (later R.A. Lister & Co Ltd. See also Blackstone and Mirrlees Blackstone)	*UK*
Lister Blackstone Mirrlees	Lister Blackstone Mirrlees Marine Ltd	*UK*
Lobnitz	Lobnitz & Co Ltd (later Simons-Lobnitz Ltd)	*UK*
L. Smit	L. Smit & Zoon NV (later IHC Smit)	*Netherlands*
MaK	Maschinenbau Kiel GmbH (formerly Atlas-MaK—qv; now Krupp-MaK—qv)	*W Germany*
Makita	Makita Tekkosho KK	*Japan*
MAN	Maschinenfabrik Augsburg-Nurnberg AG (also own B & W Diesel A/S—qv)	*W Germany*
MAN-Sulzer	see MAN and Sulzer	*W Germany*
Maybach	Maybach Motorenbau GmbH	*W Germany*
Mediterranee	Société Anonyme des Forges et Chantiers de la Méditerranée	*France*
Mirrlees	Mirrlees National Ltd (now Mirrlees Blackstone—qv)	*UK*
Mirrlees, Bickerton & Day	Mirrlees, Bickerton & Day Ltd (later Mirrlees National Ltd, now Mirrlees Blackstone—qv)	*UK*
Mirrlees Blackstone	Mirrlees Blackstone Ltd (formerly Mirrlees National—qv)	*UK*
Mitsubishi	Mitsubishi Heavy Industries Ltd	*Japan*
Mitsui	Mitsui Engineering & Shipbuilding Co Ltd (B & W design engines)	*Japan*
Moss	Moss Vaerft & Dokk A/S (later Moss Rosenberg Verft)	*Norway*
MTM	La Maquinista Terrestre y Maritima SA	*Spain*
MTU	Motoren- und Turbinen-Union Friedrichshafen GmbH	*W Germany*
MWM	Motorenwerke Mannheim AG	*W Germany*
Nagasaki	Nagasaki Shipbuilding & Engineering Works (Mitsubishi)	*Japan*
National Gas & O	National Gas & Oil Engine Co Ltd	*UK*
Nederland	Schps Inst Nederland (later Verolme Machinefabriek Ijsselmonde NV (Verolme United group)	*Netherlands*
Nederlandsche	Nederlandsche Dok en Scheepsbouw Mij vof	*Netherlands*
N.E. Marine	North-Eastern Marine Engineering Co Ltd (see G. Clark)	*UK*
Newbury	Newbury Diesel Co Ltd	*UK*
Newport News	Newport News Shipbuilding & Dry Dock Co	*USA*
N & H	see under Nydqvist & Holm	*Sweden*
Niigata	Niigata Engineering Co Ltd	*Japan*
Nippon Hatsudoki	Nippon Hatsudoki Co Ltd	*Japan*
Nishi Nippon J	Nishi Nippon Jukogyo KK (later Mitsubishi—qv)	*Japan*
NKK	Nippon Kokan KK (build Pielstick design diesels)	*Japan*
Nordberg	Nordberg Manufacturing Co	*USA*
Normo	Normo Gruppen A/S	*Norway*
Nydqvist & Holm	Nydqvist & Holm Aktiebolag	*Sweden*
Osaka Kiko	Osaka Kiko	*Japan*
Oskarshamns	A/B Oskarshamns Varv	*Sweden*
Ottensener	Ottensener Eisenwerft GmbH (later Schlieker-Werft—qv)	*W Germany*
Pametrada	Parsons Marine Engineering Turbine Research & Development Association (warship engine)	*UK*
Parsons	Parsons Marine Steam Turbine Co	*UK*
Paxman	Paxman Diesels Ltd (previously Davey, Paxman—qv)	*UK*
Penta	Volvo Penta A/B	*Sweden*
Pielstick	SEMT Pielstick (Alsthom-Atlantique group)	*France*
Praha	same as CKD Praha—qv	
Pratt & Whitney	Pratt & Whitney	*USA*
Prescott	Prescott Co	*USA*
Rankin & Blackmore	Rankin & Blackmore Ltd	*UK*
Readhead	John Readhead & Sons Ltd	*UK*
Rheinmetall-Borsig	Rheinmetall-Borsig	*Germany*
Richardsons, Westgarth	Richardsons, Westgarth & Co Ltd	*UK*
Riuniti	Cantieri Navali Riuniti	*Italy*
Rotterdamsche	Rotterdamsche Droogdok Mij NV	*Netherlands*
Rowan	David Rowan & Co Ltd	*UK*
Russkiy	Russkiy-Diesel Works	*USSR*
Ruston	Ruston Diesels Ltd (previously Ruston & Hornsby—qv)	*UK*
Ruston & Hornsby	Ruston & Hornsby Ltd (English Electric Group—later Ruston Diesels—qv)	*UK*
Ruston Paxman	Ruston Paxman Diesels Ltd	*UK*
SACM	Société Alsacienne de Constructions Mécaniques	*France*
Scania	A/B Scania Vabis (later Saab-Scania)	*Sweden*
Schlieker	Schlieker-Werft, Willy H. Schlieker KG (formerly Ottensener Eisenwerk—qv)	*W Germany*
Scotts' SB	Scotts' Shipbuilding & Engineering Co Ltd (later Scott Lithgow Ltd)	*UK*
SEM	Société d'Electricité et de Mécanique	*France*
SGCM	Société Générale de Constructions Mécaniques	*Belgium*

SIGMA	Société Industrielle Générale de Mécanique Appliquée "SIGMA"	*France*
SKL	same as Liebknecht—qv	
Škoda	Škoda design engines built by CKD Praha—qv—and under licence	
Smit & Bolnes	Motorenfabriek NV Smit & Bolnes	*Netherlands*
Smith's D	Smith's Dock Co Ltd	*UK*
Stal-Laval	Stal-Laval Turbin AB	*Sweden*
Stephen	Alexander Stephen & Sons Ltd	*UK*
Stork	NV Koninklijke Machinefabriek Gebr Stork & Co	*Netherlands*
Stork-Werkspoor	Stork-Werkspoor Diesel BV (also Spanish subsidiary Naval-Stork-Werkspoor SA)	*Netherlands*
Sulzer	Sulzer Brothers Ltd (subsidiaries include Compagnie de Construction Mécanique Sulzer (France))	*Switzerland*
Swan Hunter & WR	Swan Hunter & Wigham Richardson Ltd	*UK*
Swiss Locomotive	Swiss Locomotive & Machine Works Ltd	*Switzerland*
Thornycroft	John I. Thornycroft & Co Ltd	*UK*
Toyo	Toyo Turbine Manufacturing Co	*Japan*
Turbinfabrik	Turbinfabrik	*E Germany*
Uddevalla	Uddevallavarvet AB	*Sweden*
Unaflow	Unaflow design engines built by Skinner Engine Co and licensees in several countries (also known as Uniflow)	*USA*
Uraga	Uraga Tamashima Diesel Kogyo Works Ltd	*Japan*
Verschure	NV Verschure & Co's Scheepswerf en Machinefabriek	*Netherlands*
Vickers-Armstrongs	Vickers-Armstrongs (Engineers) Ltd	*UK*
Volund	A/S Volund	*Denmark*
Volvo-Penta	Volvo-Penta A/B	*Sweden*
Vulcan	Vulcan Iron Works	*USA*
Waggon	Waggon u Maschinenbau	*W Germany*
Wallsend	Wallsend Slipway & Engineering Co Ltd	*UK*
Wärtsilä	Oy Wärtsilä Ab (engines built by Wärtsilä Vasa factory)	*Finland*
Werkspoor	NV Werkspoor (now Stork-Werkspoor—qv)	*Netherlands*
Westinghouse	Westinghouse Electric Corp	*USA*
W. H. Allen	W. H. Allen Sons & Co Ltd (later APE Allen—qv)	*UK*
White Fuel	White Fuel Oil Eng Co	*USA*
Wichmann	Wichmann Motorfabrikk A/S	*Norway*
Wilton-Fije	NV Wilton-Fijenoord dok-en Werf Maatschappij	*Netherlands*
Yanmar	Yanmar Diesel Engine Co Ltd	*Japan*
Yarwood	W. J. Yarwood & Sons Ltd	*UK*
"Zgoda"	Zaklady Urzadzen Techniczynch "Zgoda" (ZUT "Zgoda")	*Poland*

Alphabets

The English letters following the symbols are transliterations. Other sources, for example Lloyds Register, may use different equivalents.

GREEK

Α	α	alpha	a
Β	β	beta	v
Γ	γ	gamma	j
Δ	δ	delta	th
Ε	ε	epsilon	e
Ζ	ζ	zeta	z
Η	η	eta	e
Ι	ι	iota	e
Κ	κ	kappa	k
Λ	λ	lambda	l
Μ	μ	mu	m
Ν	ν	nu	n
Ξ	ξ	xi	x
Ο	ο	omicron	o
Π	π	pi	p
Ρ	ρ	rho	r
Σς	σς	sigma	s
Τ	τ	tau	t
Υ	υ	upsilon	e or v
Φ	φ	phi	f
Χ	χ	chi	kh
Ψ	ψ	psi	ps
Ω	ω	omega	o

CYRILLIC

Аа	a
Бб	b
Вв	v
Гг	g
Дд	d
Ее	e
Ёё	e
Жж	zh
Зз	z
Ии	i
Йй	y
Кк	k
Лл	l
Мм	m
Нн	n
Оо	o
Пп	p
Рр	r
Сс	s
Тт	t
Уу	u
Фф	f
Хх	kh
Цц	ts
Чч	ch
Шш	sh
Щщ	shch
Ъъ	*hard sign*
Ыы	i
Ьь	*soft sign*
Ээ	e
Юю	yu
Яя	ya

Glossary
(including abbreviations and acronyms)

Abaft Behind an object.
ABS American Bureau of Shipping.
AFRAMAX An oil tanker designed with the cargo capacity optimised to suit the scales of AFRA (American Freight Association). They have a maximum deadweight of around 100,000 tonnes.
Aft Towards the stern.
Aftercastle Raised portion or Island at aft end of a vessel. Also termed the Poop.
Ahead Directly in advance.
Amidships Midway between stem and stern.
AMVER Automated Merchant Vessel Reporting.
Angled Ramp See Quarter Ramp.
ASEAN Association of South East Asian Nations. Treaty organisation comprising Malaysia, Singapore, Thailand, Indonesia and the Philippines.
Astern Directly to the rear or behind a vessel.
Athwartships Across a vessel: at right angles to centre line.
Ballast Water, sand, and so on to give stability when ship is 'light' or empty of cargo.
Beam Greatest width of vessel.
BIBO Bulk-In, Bag-Out (ship type).
BIMCO Baltic International Maritime Council.
Boom Same as Derrick.
Boot-Topping Colour of paint along the waterline, between topsides and underwater surface.
Bow Wave Wave formed under or near the bows when under way.
Bows Adjacent to the stem: either side near front.
Breakbulk A term which has appeared since the advent of container ships to describe a general cargo ship. The cargo is loaded into and broken out of the piece by piece.
Bridge Navigating platform running athwartships high up on front part of superstructure.
Bridge Deck Mid-castle or Island approximately amidships.
Broadside Complete view of a ship from stem to stern—not foreshortened.
Bulk Cargo Heavy dry cargo such as ore or coal or bulky like grain or timber.
Bulkhead Watertight walls which subdivide the hull. Usually transverse.
Bulwark Plating on deck at side to give shelter or protection in place of railings.
Bunkers Fuel capacity or space in which fuel is carried.
Capesize Vessels which are too large for the Panama Canal and are, therefore, routed via the Cape of Good Hope. Particularly applies to bulk carriers.
Castle Raised portion or Island above upper deck.
Catwalk Raised gangway connecting castles, above the upper deck, especially in tankers.
Cellular Describes a container ship with guides in the holds for container storage.
Centre Line Imaginary line drawn on deck from stem to stern.
CMPC Container/ Multi-Purpose Carrier.
CNIS Channel Navigation Information Service (Dover Strait).
Cob Container/ Ore/ Bulk carrier.
Combination Carrier A large vessel suitable for the carriage of either bulk or liquid cargoes, but not simultaneously (for example OBO—Ore/Bulk/Oil and OO—Ore/Oil).
Counter Extreme stern of a ship. Sloping portion of a cutaway stern.
COW Crude Oil Washing (oil tankers).
Crosstrees Platform on top of lower mast or kingpost to which lifting gear is rigged. Also known as Table Tops.
Davits Curved fittings for supporting and handling boats.
Derrick Long spar attached to foot of mast or kingpost for cargo handling.
Derrick post Vertical post to which derricks are fixed but shorter than a mast. Also known as Kingpost.
Draught Depth from waterline to keel. Marked in feet or metres at stem and stern.
DWAT Deadweight All Total.
DWT Deadweight tonnes.
Ensign Flag denoting nationality but not always the same as National Flag.
Ensign Staff Flagstaff right aft from which ensign may be worn.
Flag of Convenience A flag under which a ship is registered but is not the country of ownership. 'Flagging out', as it is often called, is usually practised to gain financial or legal advantages.
Flare Slope outwards of a ship's hull from waterline to upper deck, particularly at bows and stern.
Flush Deck Uninterrupted top line without islands.
Flying Bridge Another name for a Catwalk.
Fore-and-Aft Along the length of a vessel.
Forecastle Raised portion or island at foreward end.
Foreward Towards the fore part—towards the stem.
FPC Forest Products Carrier.
FPSO Floating Production, Storage and Offloading (oil industry).
Freeboard Depth of hull from waterline to upper deck.
Freeing Ports Openings in ship's side or bulwarks to allow water to run off. Also known as Scuppers.
FSO Floating Storage and Offloading facility.
FSU Floating Storage Unit. Usually a converted tanker (North Sea).
Gaff Light fore and aft spar sometimes fitted to aft mast from which ensigns are worn at sea.
GCBS General Council of British Shipping. Merger in 1974 of Chamber of Shipping of the UK and the British Shipping Federation.
Geared A description of a cargo vessel with cargo-handling gear (cranes, derricks and so on).
GmbH Gesellschaft mit beschränkter Haftung (German limited liability company).
GMDSS Global Maritime Distress and Safety System.
Hance Curved or sloping portion of side plating at breaks of castles or islands.
Handy Size Commercial term to describe bulk carriers in the 25,000–40,000 dwt range.
Hatch Opening in deck to give access to cargo holds.
Hatch Covers Steel coverings to hatch.
Hatch Gear Short vertical posts between hatches for working covers. If very prominent should be coded as Kingposts.
Heavy Derrick Particularly heavy derrick usually stowed against mast when at sea.
Hold Compartment for cargo stowage below deck.
ICS International Chamber of Shipping.
IGS Inert Gas System (oil tankers—tank cleaning).
IMB International Maritime Bureau (a division of the **ICS** (qv), dealing with the investigation of maritime crime).
IMCO Inter-governmental Maritime Consultative Organization. A United Nations agency principally concerned with safety and anti-pollution (now **IMO**—qv).
IMO International Maritime Organization (see **IMCO**).
INMARSAT International Maritime Satellite System.
INTELSAT International Telecommunications Satellite Organization.
INTERTANKO International Association of Independent Tanker Owners.
Island Same as Castle. A raised portion of hull above upper deck.
ISO International Standards Organization.
ITOPF International Tanker Owners Pollution Federation.
Jack Staff Small flagstaff in stem at which 'Jack' is worn.
Kingpost Same as Derrick post.
Laden A vessel with full cargo. Down to her load marks.
LCL Less than Container Load.
Light A vessel riding light without cargo. 'In Ballast'.
LNG Liquefied Natural Gas.
Load Line Horizontal lines painted on hull amidships to indicate depth to which vessel may be loaded under varying conditions.
LO/LO Lift On/ Lift Off.
LPG Liquefied Petroleum Gas.
MARPOL The International Convention on prevention of pollution from ships (1983).
Mast House Large deck house at base of mast or kingpost.
Midcastle Raised portion or island amidships. Same as Bridge Deck.
MPS Maritime Prepositioning Ship. Vessel employed by the US Navy as part of the Rapid Deployment Force of the US Services.
MRCC Maritime Rescue Co-ordination Centre.
MSC Military Sealift Command. A US Navy Command with the responsibility of providing sealift of dry cargo and petroleum for all components of the Department of Defense.
Navigating Bridge A term covering wheel house, chart room and athwartships platform high up on foreward part of superstructure.
NOSAC Norwegian Specialised Auto Carriers (ship operator).
NUMAST National Union of Marine, Aviation and Shipping Transport officers.
OECD Organization for Economic Co-operation and Development.
OPEC Organization of Petroleum Exporting Countries.
Open Registry A country's shipping Register which is open to any shipowner, regardless of nationality, who can meet the conditions set by the Registry.
PANAMAX A vessel built to the maximum dimensions which enable it to use the Panama Canal. They have a standard beam of around 32 m (105 ft) and a full load draught of approximately 12.4 m (40.68 ft).
PCC Pure Car Carrier. As distinct from vessels which can carry cars and other cargo.
Peak Extreme outward end of Gaff.
Plimsoll Line Same as Load Line.
Poop Raised castle at stern; same as Aftercastle.
Port Side That side of the vessel which is on the left when facing foreward. Indicated by RED.
PROBO Products/ Oil/ Bulk/Ore carrier.
Quarter Adjacent to stern at either side.
Quarter Ramp A large ramp set in the quarter of a vessel's hull (usually starboard) which lowers at an angle enabling its use on a conventional quay when the vessel is alongside. Also known as an Angled Ramp.
Rake Slope or inclination of mast or funnel.
RINA Royal Institution of Naval Architects.
RO/LO A vessel which has both roll-on/roll-off and lift-on/lift-off capability.
RRF Ready Reserve Force. A pool of dry cargo ships, tankers and so on, operated by the US Navy, that can be made available for sealift operations on five to ten days notice. Also RRS—Ready Reserve Ship.

Rubbing Strake Heavy permanent wood, metal or rubber guard along the Hull to protect plating when going alongside. Prominent feature in coasters or small ships.

SAR Search And Rescue.

SBT Segregated Ballast Tanks (oil tankers).

Scuppers Same as Freeing Ports.

Sheer Slope upwards of hull at foreward and after ends.

Signal Letters A group of four letters of International Code allocated to a vessel for identification. The same as her radio call sign.

Slewing Ramp A ramp which can be swung in a horizontal plane.

SOLAS International Convention on Safety of Life at Sea (1980).

Spirket Plate Raised plating or screen above the upper deck at the stem: varies in length.

Starboard Side That side of a vessel which is on the right hand when facing foreward. Indicated by GREEN.

Stem Extreme foreward part of ship's hull. The cut-water.

Stern Extreme after part of a ship.

STUFT Ships Taken Up From Trade. Refers to merchant ships chartered by the UK Ministry of Defence in times of emergency.

SUEZMAX A vessel of the maximum size, by draught, able to navigate the Suez Canal.

Superstructure Upperworks. Deckhouses, and so on, on upper deck.

SWATH Small Waterplane Area Twin Hull.

TEU Twenty-foot Equivalent Units. A method of expressing the container capacity of a vessel.

Trunk Deck Enclosed structure about two-thirds of the width of a ship joining the islands. Particularly in coastal tankers.

ULCC Ultra Large Crude Carrier.

UNCTAD United Nations Code on Trade And Development.

Ungeared A description of a cargo vessel which has no cargo-handling gear (such as cranes, derricks and so on).

VLBC Very Large Bulk Carrier.

VLCC Very Large Crude Carrier.

Wake Disturbed water left astern.

Washports Same as Freeing Ports or Scuppers.

Waterline Line formed on hull by surface of water.

Weather Deck A technical term for a light deck enclosed by plating. Frequently same as upper deck.

Well Deck Portion of hull between castles or islands and approximately 7 to 8 ft lower.

Winch House Same as Mast or Deckhouse.

Yard A light spar rigged athwart a mast for signal purposes.

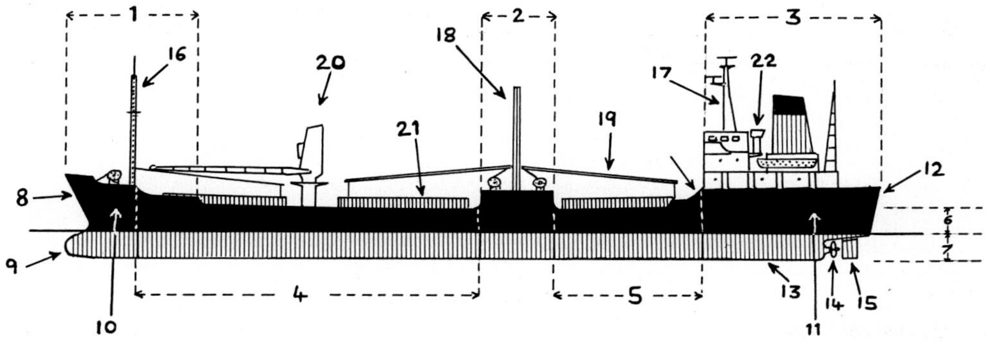

RS 1 **PARTS OF A SHIP**

1. Forecastle
2. Midcastle
3. Poop
4. & 5. Well Decks
6. Freeboard
7. Draught
8. Stem
9. Bulb
10. Port Row
11. Port Quarter
12. Stern
13. Keel
14. Screw
15. Rudder
16. Foremast
17. Mainmast
18. Kingpost
19. Derrick
20. Deck Crane
21. Hatch Combing

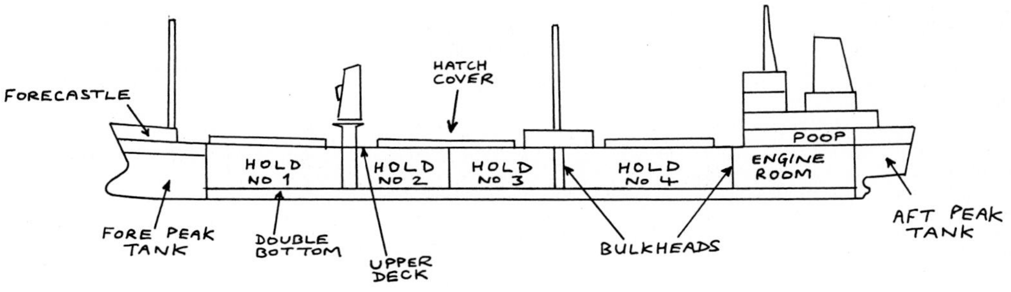

DIAGRAMMATIC SECTION

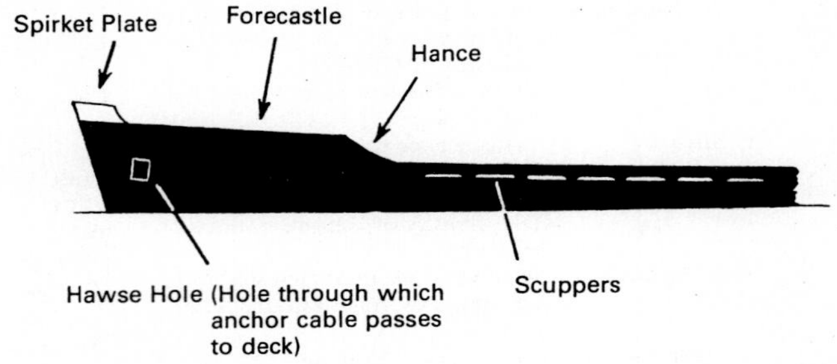
Spirket Plate
Forecastle
Hance
Hawse Hole (Hole through which anchor cable passes to deck)
Scuppers

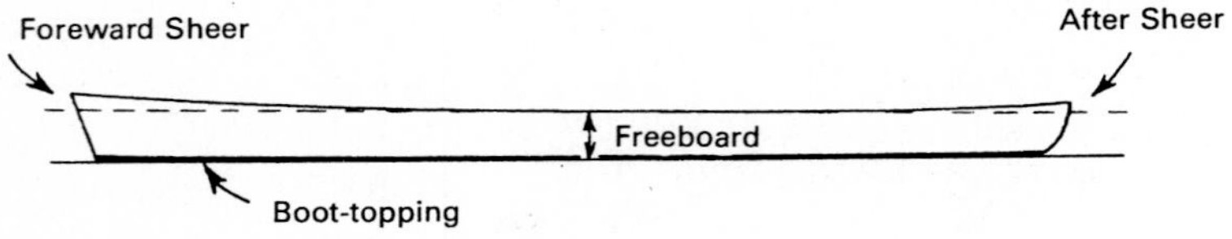
Foreward Sheer
After Sheer
Freeboard
Boot-topping

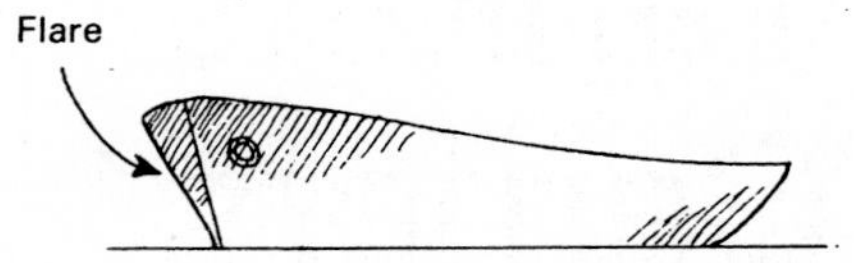
Flare

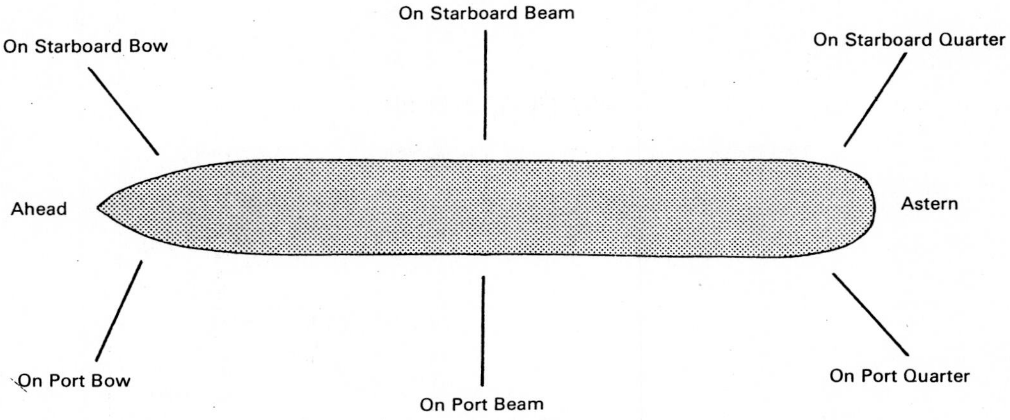
On Starboard Beam
On Starboard Bow
On Starboard Quarter
Ahead
Astern
On Port Bow
On Port Quarter
On Port Beam

1 Tankers and Combination Carriers with Cranes

1 Tankers and Combination Carriers with Cranes

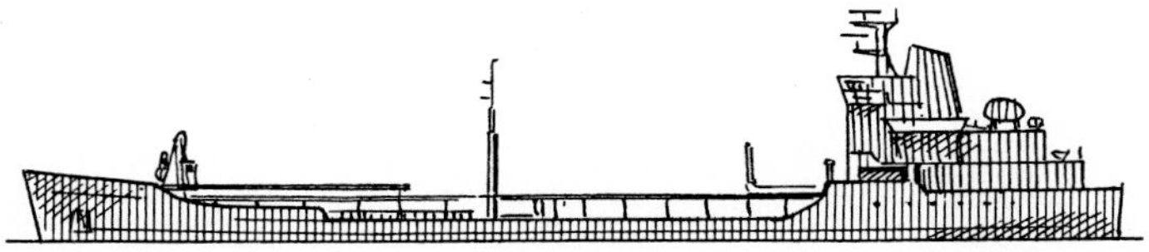

1 *CM³F H13*
IMPERIAL SKEENA Ca/Ca (Burrard DD) 1970; Tk; 3,047 grt/4,856 dwt; 91.45 × 5.56 m *(300.03 × 18.24 ft)*; TSM (British Polar); 12.5 kts

2 *MC²MF H13*
QUINTINO Bz/Fr (Nord Med) 1983; Tk/Ch; 15,163 grt/23,745 dwt; 170.92 × 10.02 m *(560.76 × 32.87 ft)*; M (Sulzer); 15.5 kts; Four tanks on deck
Sisters: **QUINCA** (Bz); **LACERTA** (Ma) ex-*Jacuhy*; **TAMARA 1** (Ma) ex-*Jutahy*

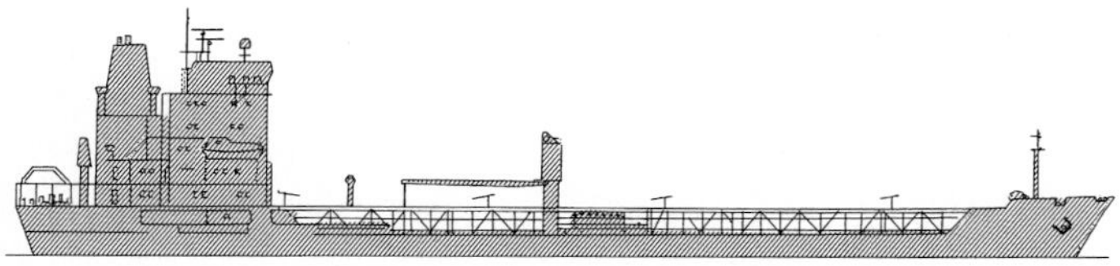

3 *MCHFR H13*
RATHCARRA Ih/Ys ('Uljunik') 1988; Tk/Ch; 6,506 grt/9,939 dwt; 119.82 × 8.00 m *(393.11 × 26.25 ft)*; M (B&W); 12.5 kts; ex-*Vinjerac*
Probable sister: **RAVA** (Li)

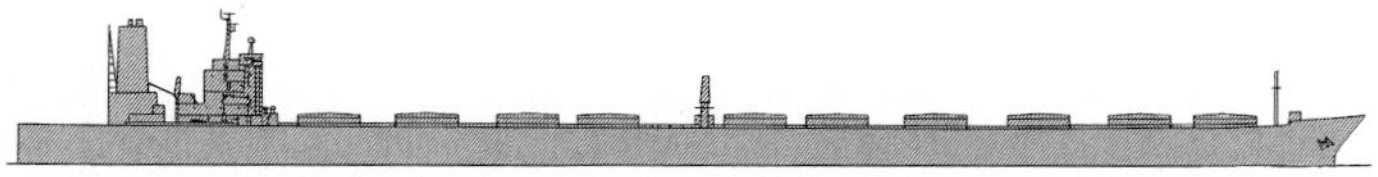

4 *MCMCFM/MDMCFN H*
TIJUCA Li/Bz (Ish do Brasil) 1987; OO; 159,534 grt/310,700 dwt; 332.01 × 23.03 m *(1,089.27 × 75.56 ft)*; M (Sulzer); 13.5 kts
Probable sister: **DOCEFJORD** (Li)

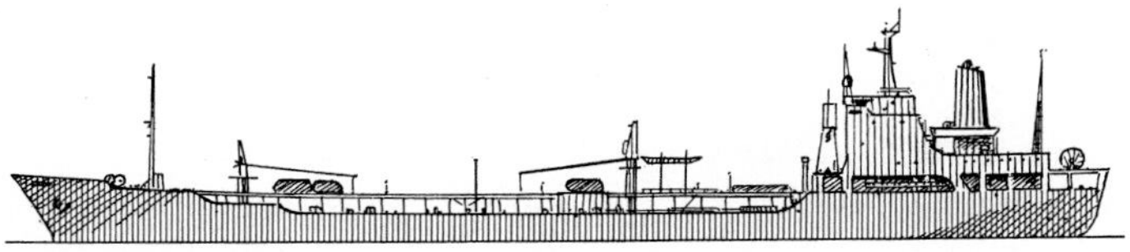

5 *MCMCKNMFN H13*
JAPAN TUNA No 2 Pa/Ja (Hitachi) 1979; Tk; 8,156 grt/10,624 dwt; 128.38 × 8.2 m *(421.19 × 26.9 ft)*; M (Mitsubishi); 13.5 kts

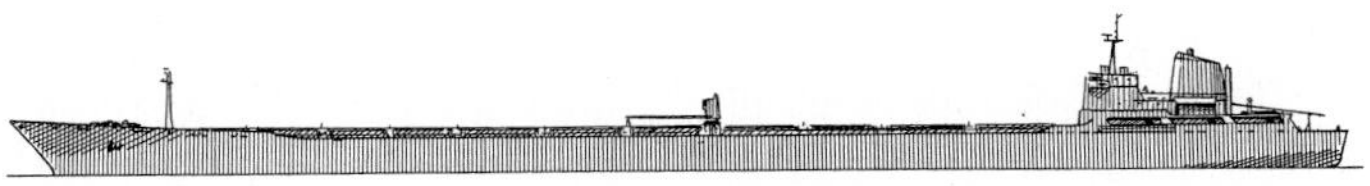

6 *MCMF H*
OAKWELL Ma/It (Breda) 1969; Tk; 28,782 grt/51,540 dwt; 216.42 × 12.45 m *(710 × 40.85 ft)*; M (Fiat); 15.5 kts; ex-*Luisa Lolli Ghetti*; Converted from OBO carrier 1985—drawing shows vessel before conversion

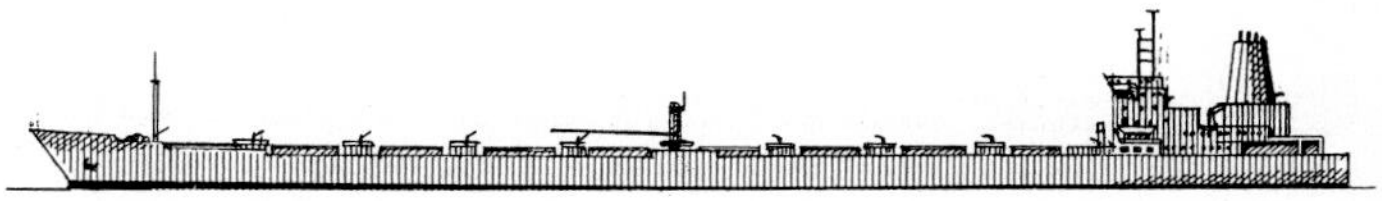

7 *MCMF H1*
SHAWNEE HK/FRG (Thyssen) 1977; BO; 68,778 grt/122,266 dwt; 273.26 × 16.38 m *(896.52 × 53.74 ft)*; M (B&W); 15.75 kts; ex-*Saggat*
Sister: **PAWNEE** (HK) ex-*Suorva*

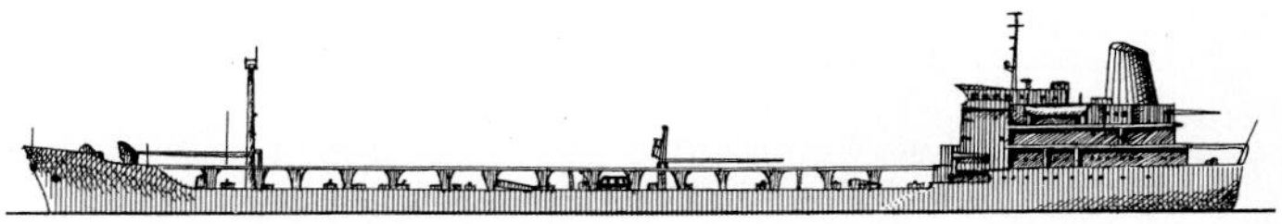

8 *MCMF H13*
FOLGOET Fr/Sw (Eriksbergs) 1968; Tk; 15,115 grt/24,391 dwt; 169.93 × 9.55 m *(556.52 × 31.33 ft)*; M (B&W); 16 kts; ex-*British Liberty*
Similar: **SEA HORSE** (Ma) ex-*British Security*; **BLUE SEA** (Ma) ex-*British Tenacity*; **PORTORIA** (It) ex-*British Fidelity*

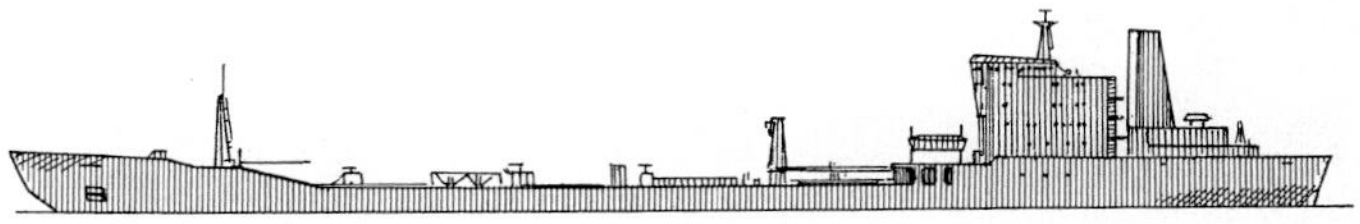

9 *MCMF H13*
LUNNI Fi/FRG (Nobiskrug) 1976; Tk/IB; 11,290 grt/16,420 dwt; 162.01 × 9.5 m *(531.52 × 31.16 ft)*; M (Atlas-MaK); 14.5 kts
Sisters: **SOTKA** (Fi); **TIIRA** (Fi); **UIKKU** (Fi)

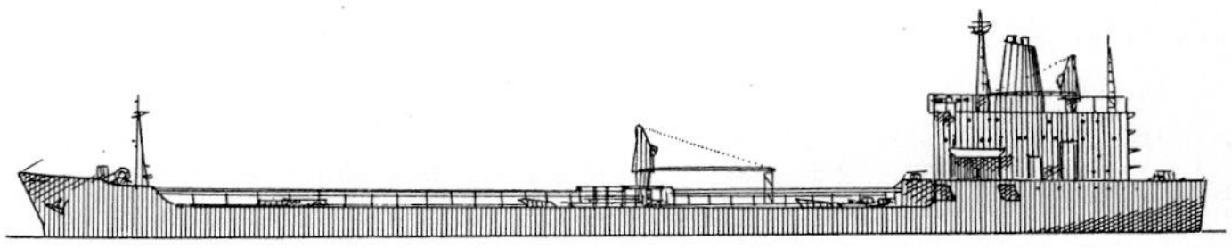

10 *MCMFCM H13*
EBURNA Br/Ja (Mitsui) 1979; Tk; 18,654 grt/31,374 dwt; 170 × 11.04 m *(557.74 × 36.22 ft)*; M (B&W); 14.1 kts
Sisters: **ERVILIA** (Br); **EUPLECTA** (Br); **EBALINA** (Br)

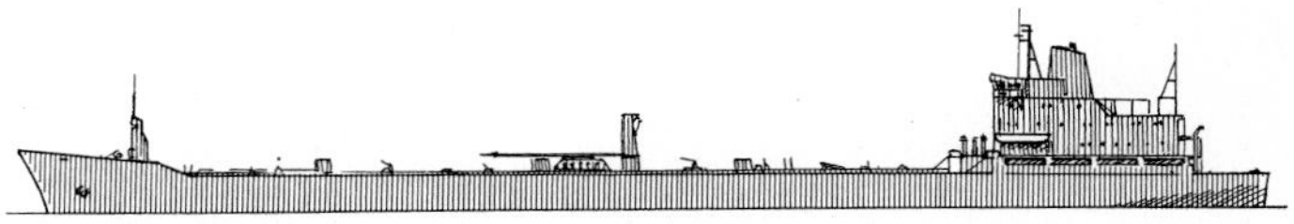

11 *MCMFM H1*
DA QING 87 RC/Fi (Wärtsilä) 1977; Tk; 18,708 grt/32,389 dwt; 171.35 × 11.38 m *(562.17 × 37.34 ft)*; M (Sulzer); 16.25 kts; ex-*Messiniaki Akti*
Sisters: **MAERSK GANNET** (Br) ex-*Messiniaki Anatoli*; **SONIA** (Ma) ex-*Messiniaki Avgi*; **CARUAO** (Ve) Launched as *Messiniaki Avra*; **PARIATA** (Ve) Launched as *Messiniaki Aktida*

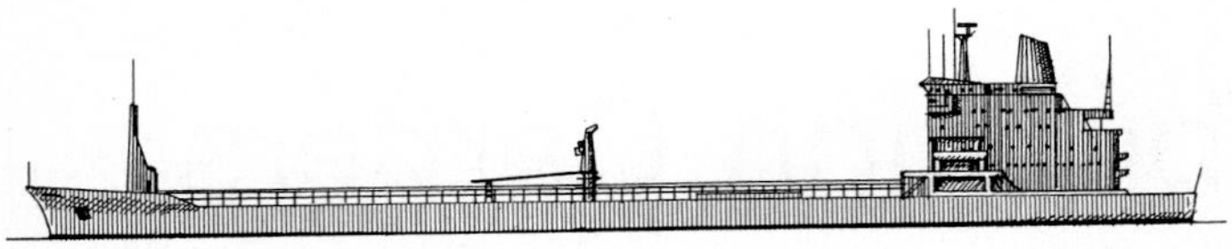

12 MCMFM *H1*

OCEAN PEARL Sg/No (Haugesund) 1974; Tk; 18,672 grt/32,229 dwt; 170.69 × 11.37 m *(560 × 37.3 ft)*; M (MAN); 15.5 kts; ex-*Fulgur*
Sisters: **OCEAN AMBER** (Sg) ex-*Felania*; **OCEAN ONYX** (Sg) ex-*Felipes*; **SEA ANGEL** (NIS) ex-*Ficus*; **OCEAN OPAL** (Sg) ex-*Flammulina*; **OCEAN JEWEL** (Sg) ex-*Fossarus*; **OCEAN TOPAZ** (Sg) ex-Fusus; **OCEAN SAPPHIRE** (Sg) ex-*Fossarina*

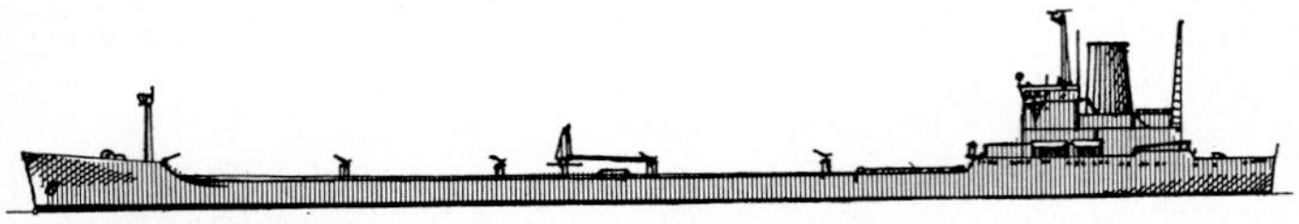

13 MCMFM *H13*

KHAN ASPARUKH Bu/Bu (G Dimitrov) 1978; Tk; 57,079 grt/96,795 dwt; 244.48 × 15.5 m *(802.1 × 50.85 ft)*; M (Sulzer); 14 kts
Sister: **ARETUSA** (Ma) ex-*Olympic Star*

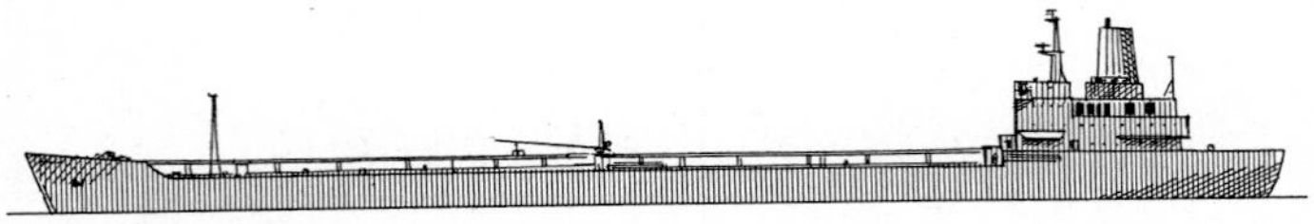

14 MCMFN *H13*
VIVALDI Ma/Au (Whyalla) 1968; Tk; 14,790 grt/25,170 dwt; 171.02 × 9.78 m *(561.09 × 32.08 ft)*; M (Sulzer); 14.5 kts; ex-*Cellana*

15 MCMFRM *H*

CONUS Au/Ja (Mitsubishi HI) 1981; Tk/Ch; 26,324 grt/37,784 dwt; 177.71 × 12.02 m *(583 × 39.44 ft)*; M (Sulzer); 14.5 kts

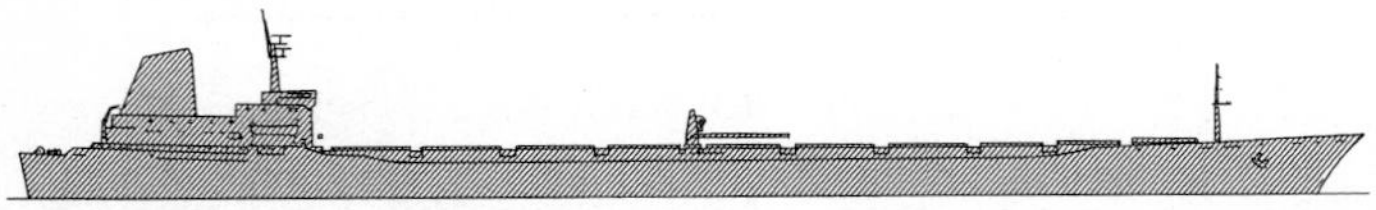

16 MCMFS *H*
ROSEBUD Ma/It (Breda) 1973; OBO; 30,291 grt/44,990 dwt; 215.42 × 12.47 m *(706.76 × 40.91 ft)*; M (GMT); 16 kts; ex-*Elba Lolli Ghetti*
Probable sister: **MARY D** (Cy) ex-*Sardinia Iglesias*

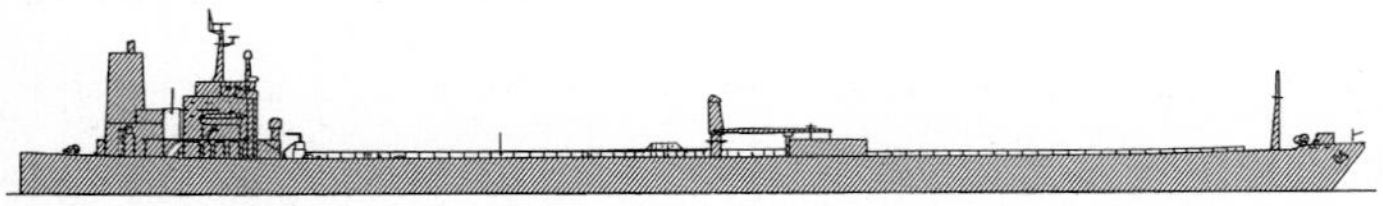

17 MCM^{2}F *H*

SENTINEL Li/Ja (IHI) 1986; Tk; 60,339 grt/106,722 dwt; 235.29 × 14.65 m *(771.95 × 48.06 ft)*; M (Sulzer); 14.1 kts; ex-*Pacific Energy*

See photo number 1/259

18 MCM^{2}F *H1*

SAINT VASSILIOS Bs/Sp (AESA) 1981; Tk; 33,471 grt/67,031 dwt; 224.01 × 14 m *(734.94 × 45.93 ft)*; M (Sulzer); 14.5 kts; ex-*Castillo De Ricote*
Sister: **KADMOS** (Gr) ex-*Castillo De San Marcos*

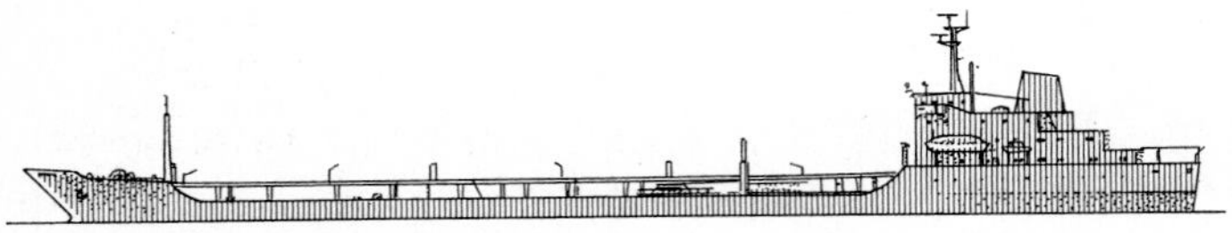

19 MCM^{2}F/HCM^{2}F *H13*

LIBERTADOR SAN MARTIN Pa/Ar (Alianza) 1979; Tk; 9,121 grt/15,261 dwt; 153 × 8.24 m *(501.97 × 27.03 ft)*; M (Sulzer); 15 kts
Sisters: **COMANDANTE TOMAS ESPORA** (Pa) ex-*Ingeniero Villa*; **MINISTRO EZCURRA** (Ar)

See photo number 1/257

20 MCM^{2}FC

BULDURI Cy/Ru (Kherson) 1983; Tk; 18,625 grt/28,750 dwt; 178.52 × 10.4 m *(585.7 × 34.12 ft)*; M (B&W); 15 kts; ex-*Dmitriy Medvedyev*
Sisters: **ASARI** (Cy) ex-*Georgiy Kholostyakov*; **N DUMBADZE** (Ma) ex-*Nodar Dumbadze*; **MOSKOVSKIY FESTIVAL** (Ru); **GRIGORIY NESTERENKO** (Ru); **GELOVANI** (Ma) ex-*Marshal Gelovani*; **VLADIMIR KOKKINAKI** (Ru); **PYOTR SHMIDT** (Ru) (or **PETR SHMIDT**); **PUMPURI** (Cy) ex-*Mikhail Gromov*; **YEVGENIY TITOV** (Ru) (or **EVGENIY TITOV**); **VALERIY CHKALOV** (Ru)

21 MCM^{2}FM

C V RAMAN In/Ja (Mitsubishi HI) 1981; Tk; 27,484 grt/41,123 dwt; 179.51 × 11.6 m *(588.94 × 38.06 ft)*; M (Sulzer); 13.25 kts
Sister: **HOMI BHABHA** (In)

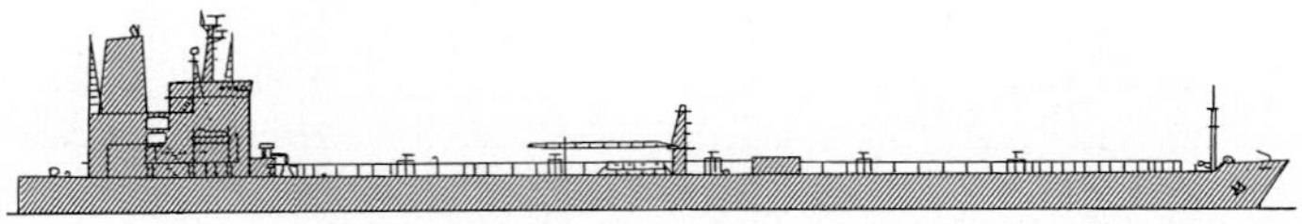

22 MCM^{2}FM *H*

BUNGA ANGGEREK Sg/Ja (Namura) 1988; Tk; 35,375 grt/60,959 dwt; 214.78 × 12.94 m *(704.66 × 42.45 ft)*; M (Sulzer); 15 kts
Probable sister: **GREEN VALLEY** (Li)

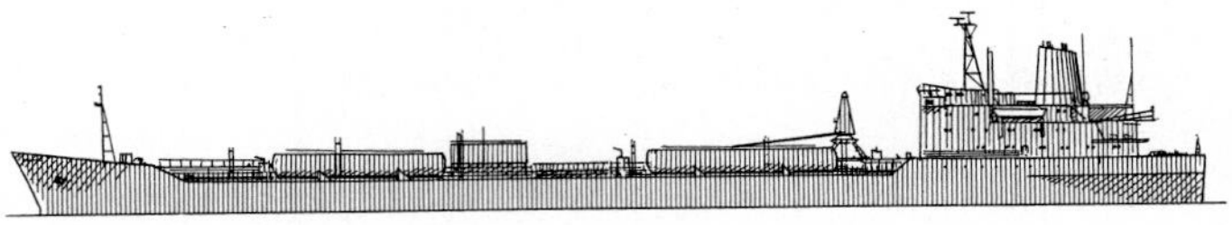

23 MCM^{2}FM *H13*

LANCER Bs/Be (Boelwerf) 1975; Ch; 14,697 grt/23,470 dwt; 170.72 × 10.21 m *(560.1 × 33.49 ft)*; M (MAN); 16 kts; ex-*Quitauna*; Travelling crane
Sister: **QUIXADA** (Bz)

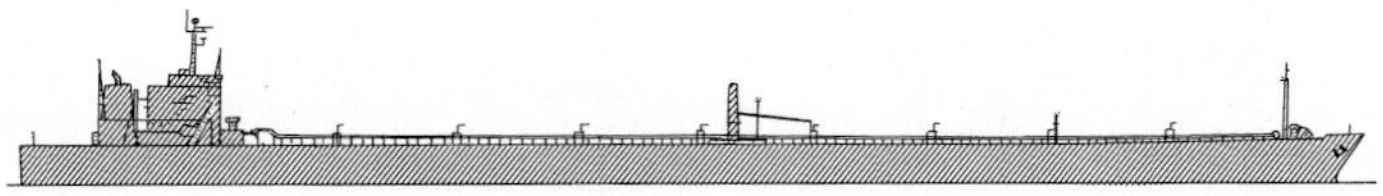

24 MCM^{2}GM *H*
DIAMOND ACE Pa/Ja (Mitsubishi HI) 1988; Tk; 137,728 grt/248,049 dwt; 315.50 × 18.76 m *(1,035.10 × 61.55 ft)*; M (Mitsubishi); 14.5 kts
Possible sisters: **DIAMOND BELL** (Pa); **NAVIX SEIBU** (Ja)

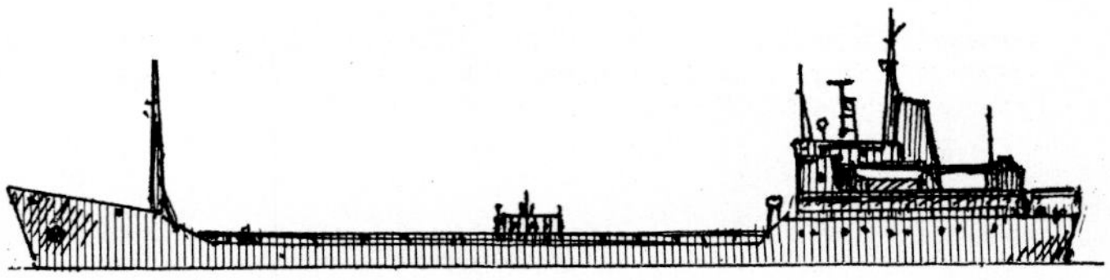

25 MDM-F *H13*
DA QING 216 RC/Ma (Malta DD) 1978; Tk; 3,504 grt/5,943 dwt; 106.28 × 6.88 m *(348.69 × 22.57 ft)*; M (B&W); 13 kts
Sisters: **DA QING 422** (RC) ex-*Da Qing No 217*; **DA QING 218** (RC)

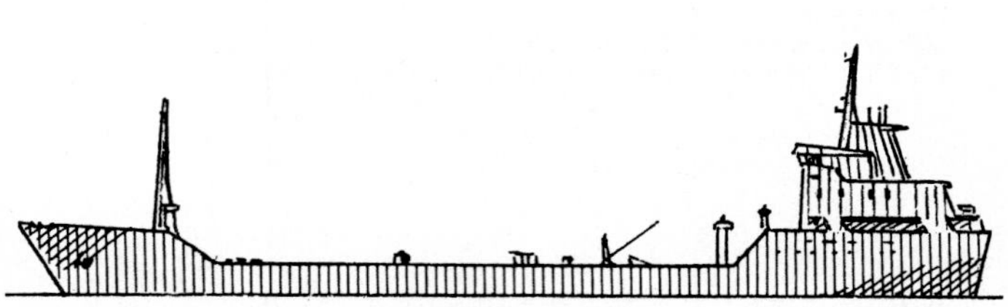

26 MDM-F *H13*
QUALITY I Pa/De (Frederikshavn) 1970; Tk/AT; 993 grt/1,010 dwt; 70.67 × 3.39 m *(231.86 × 11.12 ft)*; M (KHD); 11.5 kts; ex-*Charlottenborg*
Sister: **QUALITY II** (Cu) ex-*Christiansborg*; Similar: **ISLAND KING** (Pa) ex-*Aggersborg*

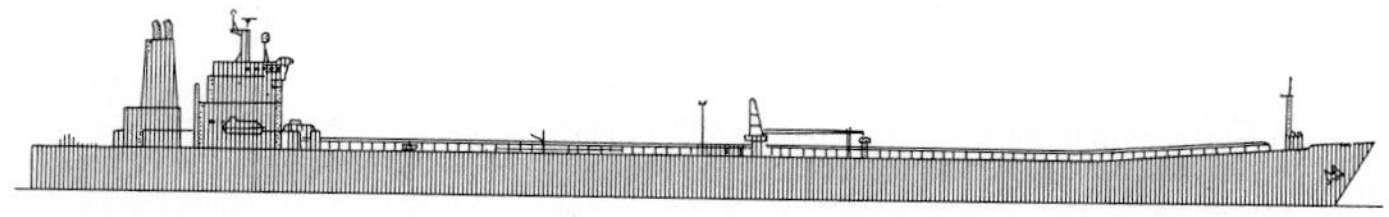

27 *MDNMF H*
GEORGE SHULTZ Li/Bz (Ish do Brazil) 1993; Tk; 80,914 grt/136,055 dwt; 258.90 × 16.79 m *(849.41 × 55.08 ft)*; M (Sulzer); 15 kts
Probable sisters: **CONDOLEEZZA RICE** (Li); **JAMES N SULLIVAN** (Li)

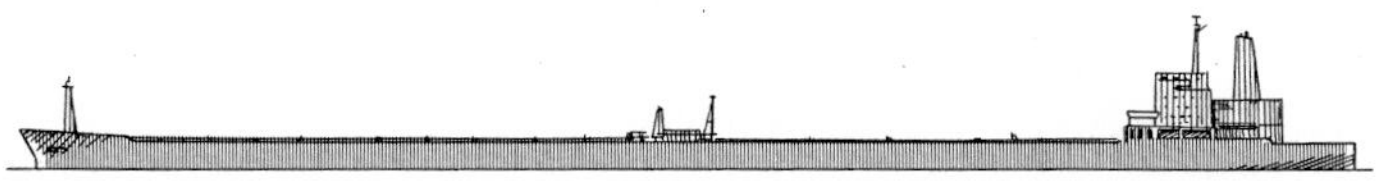

28 *MDNMF H*
LIOTINA Li/FRG (Bremer V) 1974; Tk; 153,809 grt/317,588 dwt; 351.44 × 22.35 m *(1,153.02 × 73.33 ft)*; T (Stal-Laval); 15.25 kts
Similar: **ALAMOOT** (Ir) ex-*Ajdabya*

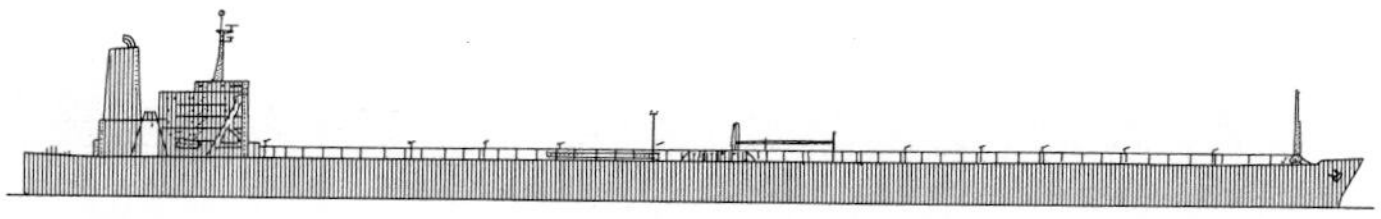

29 *MDNMF H*
T S PROSPERITY Li/Ja (NKK) 1991; Tk; 151,591 grt/258,080 dwt; 338.00 × 18.48 m *(1,108.92 × 60.63 ft)*; M (Sulzer); 16 kts

30 *MECMF H13*
SIBARDE NIS/No (Horten) 1976; Tk; 17,487 grt/31,955 dwt; 168.76 × 11.16 m *(553.67 × 36.61 ft)*; M (Sulzer); 16 kts; ex-*Norsk Barde*

31 *MEDEMF H13*
KIISLA Ru/Fi (Valmet) 1974/79; Tk/Ch; 4,681 grt/6,863 dwt; 130.33 × 6.28 m *(428 × 20.6 ft)*; M (Stork-Werkspoor); 14 kts; Lengthened 1979

See photo number 1/273

32 *ME^{2}CEMF H13*
BITUMA Sw/FRG (Nobiskrug) 1981; Tk/AT/TB; 1,900 grt/2,770 dwt; 86.98 × 5.04 m *(285.37 × 16.54 ft)*; M (Krupp-MaK); 12.5 kts

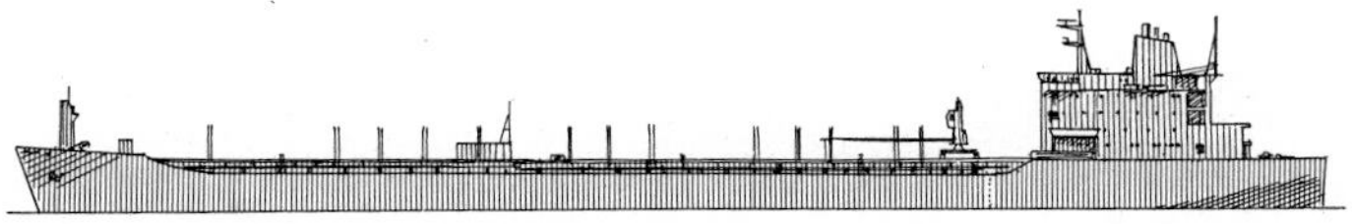

33 *ME^{4}M^{4}E^{6}CMFM H13*
STOLT PRIDE Li/Fr (Dubigeon-Normandie) 1976; Tk; 20,013 grt/31,438 dwt; 176.82 × 11.58 m *(580 × 37.99 ft)*; M (Sulzer); 17 kts; Travelling crane
Sisters: **STOLT SPIRIT** (Li); **STOLT SINCERITY** (Li); **STOLT INTEGRITY** (Li); **STOLT TENACITY** (Li); **STOLT LOYALTY** (Li); **STOLT EXCELLENCE** (Li)

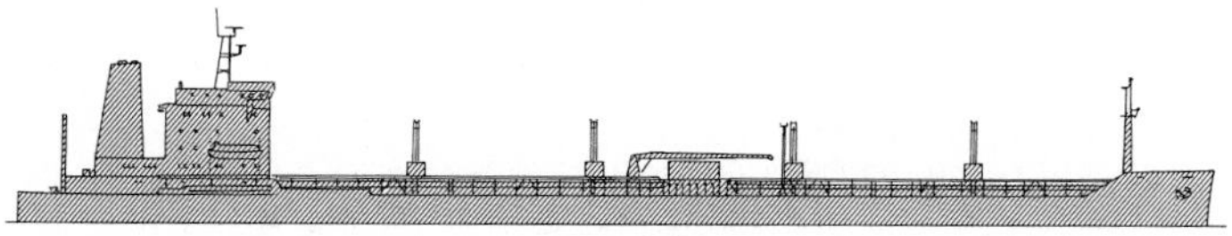

34 *ME^{2}NRE^{2}MFM H1*
SELENDANG SUTERA My/Ys ('3 Maj') 1981; Tk/Ch; 22,683 grt/39,702 dwt; 173.79 × 11.22 m *(570.18 × 36.81 ft)*; M (Sulzer); 12.5 kts; ex-*Atlas Challenger*
Sisters: **SELENDANG DELIMA** (My) ex-*Arabian Trader*; **STOLT PROTECTOR** (Li) ex-*Atlas Exporter*; **BOW MARINER** (Li) ex-*Atlas Mariner*; **TROMS PRODUCER** (NIS) ex-*Atlas Producer*; **BOW TRANSPORTER** (Li) ex-*Atlas Transporter*; **BOW PETROS** (Li) ex-*Atlas Petros*; **SYLVAN ARROW** (Li) ex-*Mobil Challenge*; **ROYAL ARROW** (Li) ex-*Mobil Courage*

See photo number 1/272

35 *ME^{2}REMF H13*
BOW PIONEER NIS/Ko (Daewoo) 1982; Ch; 14,627 grt/23,016 dwt; 158.02 × 9.8 m *(518 × 32.15 ft)*; M (B&W); 15.5 kts
Sisters: **BOW HUNTER** (NIS); **NCC ARAR** (NIS) ex-*Austanger*; **NCC ASIR** (NIS) ex-*Grenanger*

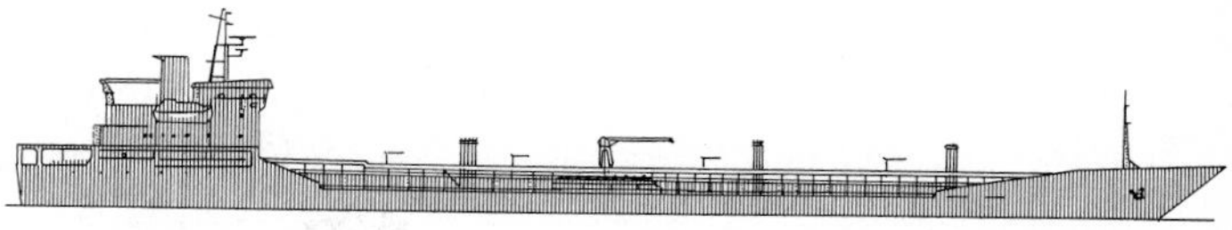

36 *ME^{2}REMFR H13*
JO ALDER Li/It (Esercizio) 1992; Tk/Ch; 7,884 grt/12,400 dwt; 139.00 × 8.00 m *(456.03 × 26.25 ft)*; M (Wärtsilä); 15 kts
Sister: **JO ASPEN** (Li)

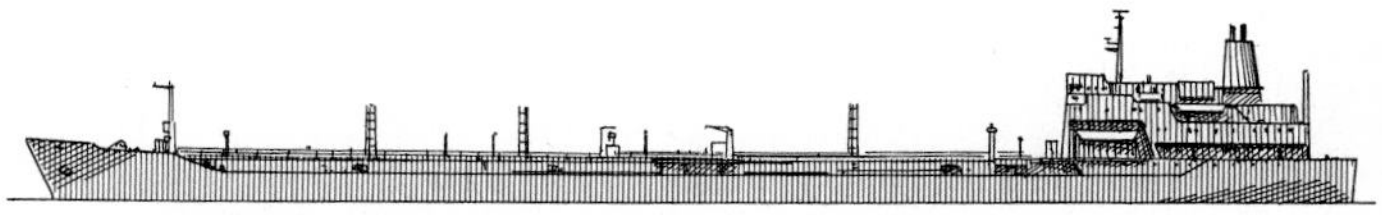

37 *ME^{2}REM^{2}FN H13*
CHOPIN Bs/Sw (Eriksbergs) 1975; Ch; 20,170 grt/33,950 dwt; 171.81 × 11.85 m *(563.68 × 38.88 ft)*; M (B&W); 16 kts; ex-*Osco Sailor*
Sisters: **LADY JANNICKE** (NIS) ex-*Osco Spirit*; **LADY HELENE** (NIS) ex-*Carbo Sierra*; **LADY BENEDIKTE** (NIS) ex-*Carbo Stripe*

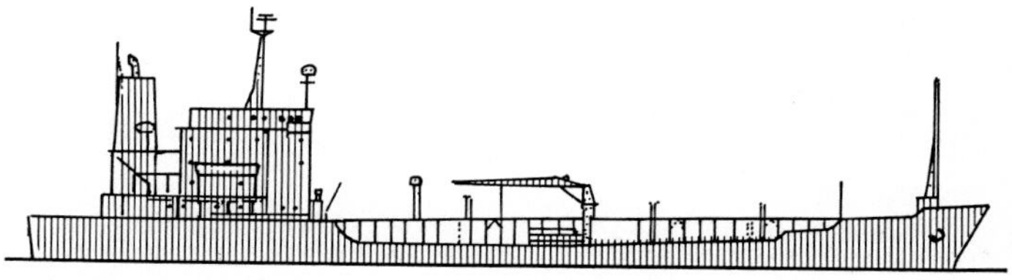

38 *ME^{2}REM^{2}FN H13*
JO HEGG Li/Ja (Mitsubishi HI) 1985; Tk/Ch; 5,357 grt/7,918 dwt; 108.50 × 8.02 m *(355.97 × 26.31 ft)*; M (Mitsubishi); 13.7 kts; ex-*Golden Queen*
Possible sister: **JO HASSEL** (SV) ex-*Golden Princess*; Similar (longer): **JO EBONY** (Li) ex-*Golden Venus*

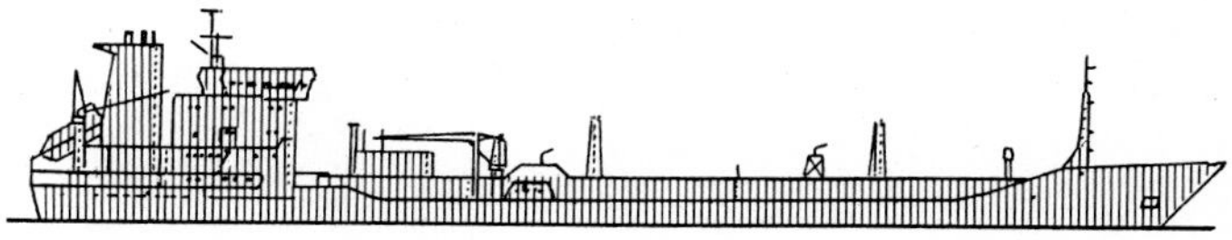

39 *ME^{2}RMFCL* H1
OTTOMAN Tu/FRG (Lindenau) 1985; Tk/Ch; 4,320 grt/6,400 dwt; 115.00 × 7.15 m *(377.30 × 23.46 ft)*; M (MaK); 14 kts; ex-*Manitou*

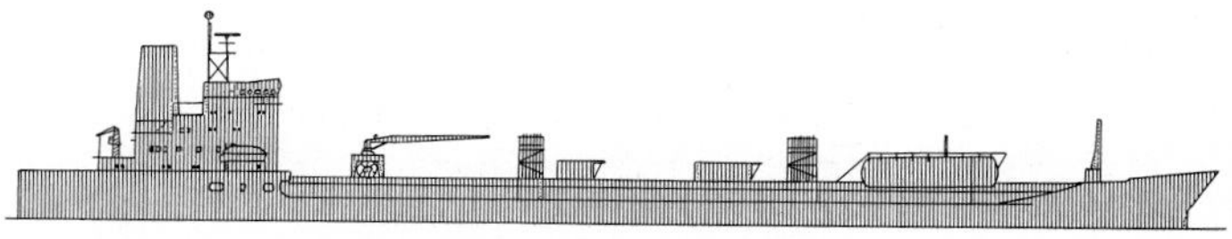

40 *ME^{2}RMFR H13*
STOLT MARKLAND Li/No (K Kleven F) 1991; Tk/Ch; 18,994 grt/29,999 dwt; 174.70 × 9.80 m *(573.16 × 32.15 ft)*; M (B&W); 13.5 kts; Travelling crane
Sisters: **STOLT HELLULAND** (Li); **STOLT VESTLAND** (Li); **STOLT VINLAND** (Li)

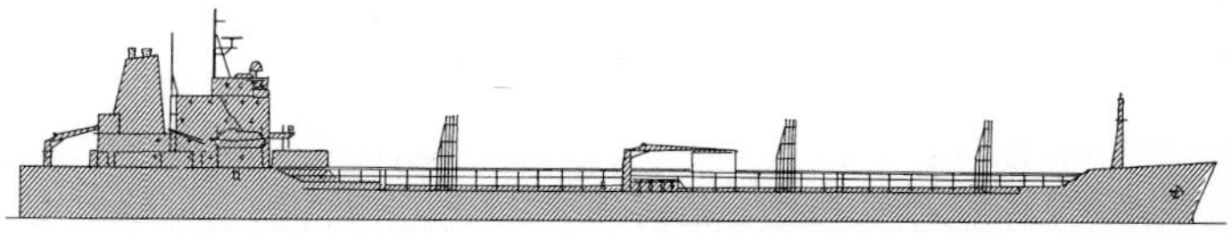

41 *ME^{2}SEMNFR H13*
JO ELM NA/Ys ('Split') 1981; Ch; 15,200 grt/26,328 dwt; 173.43 × 10.66 m *(569.00 × 34.97 ft)*; M (MAN); 15 kts; ex-*Lake Anne*
Sister: **JO BREID** (NIS) ex-*Lake Anina*

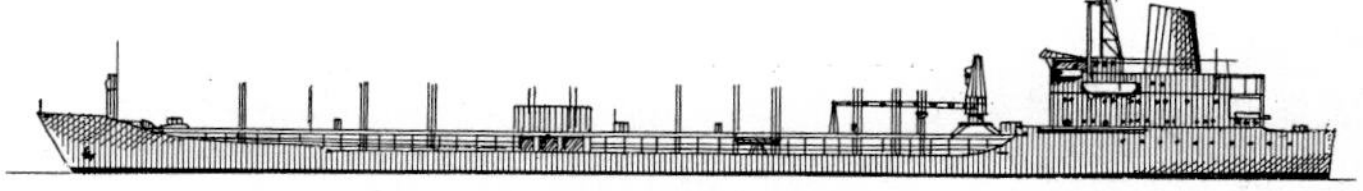

42 *MEME^{10}CMF H13*
STOLT LLANDAFF Li/Be (Boelwerf) 1971; Tk/Ch; 15,121 grt/25,060 dwt; 170.72 × 10.54 m *(560.1 × 34.58 ft)*; M (MAN); 15.75 kts; ex-*Stolt Sheaf*; Travelling crane

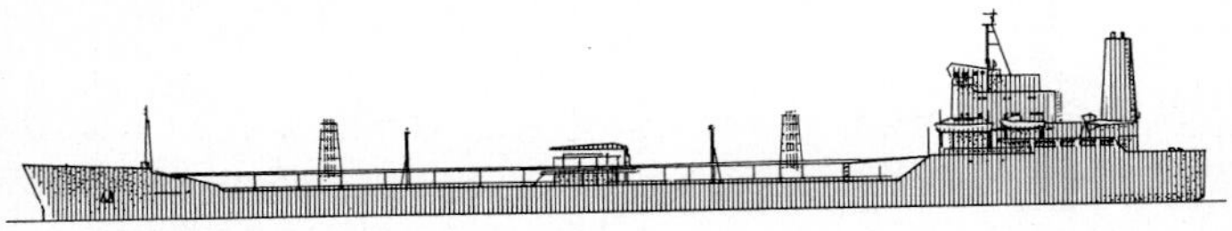

43 *MEMRMEMF H13*
BOW HERON NIS/No (Sarpsborg) 1979; Ch; 20,362 grt/35,210 dwt; 173.7 × 10.5 m *(569.88 × 34.45 ft)*; M (B&W); 15.5 kts; ex-*Iver Heron*
Similar: **BOW FIGHTER** (NIS); **BOW LANCER** (NIS) ex-*Berganger*

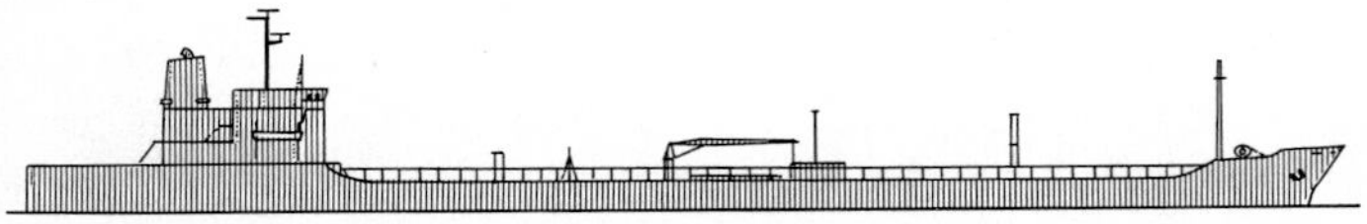

44 *MEMRNMF H13*
FORMOSA ONE Li/Ja (Shin Kurushima) 1981; Ch; 17,560 grt/31,378 dwt; 176.79 × 10.52 m *(580.02 × 34.51 ft)*; M (B&W); 15.5 kts
Sister (builder-NKK): **FORMOSA TWO** (Li)

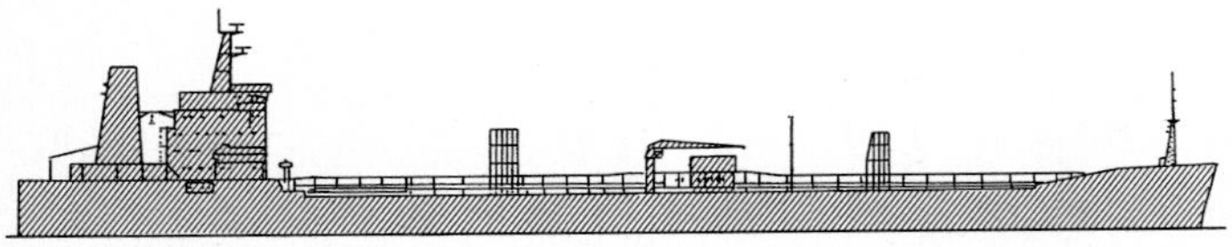

45 *MENSEMF H1*
STOLT GUARDIAN Li/Ys ('Split') 1983; Tk/Ch; 22,904 grt/39,723 dwt; 175.01 × 11.22 m *(574.18 × 36.81 ft)*; M (MAN); 13.5 kts; ex-*Iver Swift*

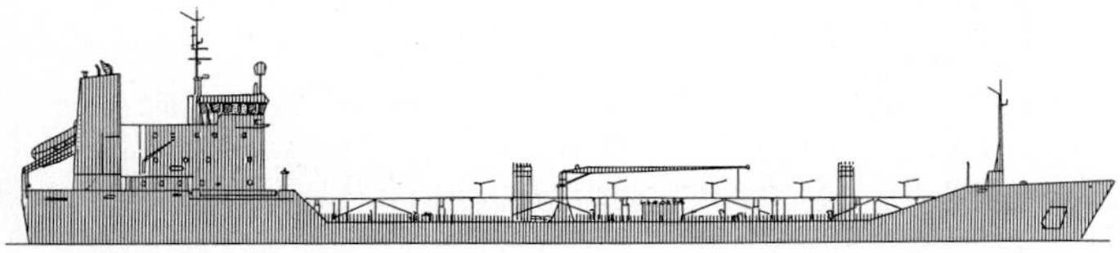

46 *MEREHFL H13*
MARINOR Bs/Ne ('Welgelegen') 1992; Ch; 4,950 grt/7,930 dwt; 112.20 × 7.50 m *(368.11 × 24.61 ft)*; M (MaK); 14.4 kts

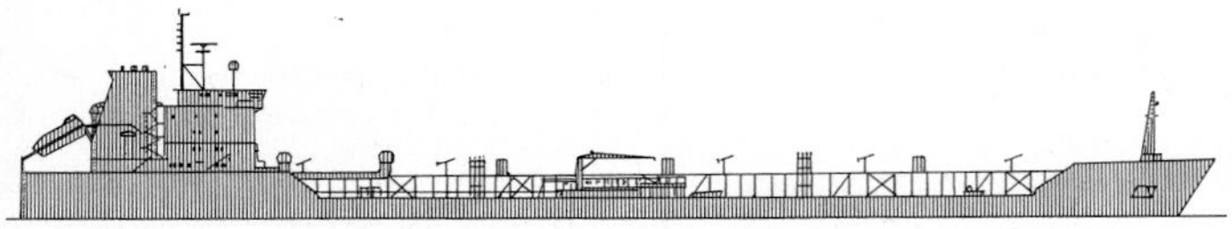

47 *MEREHFRL H13*
CONGER Ge/Ge (Lindenau GmbH) 1991; Tk/Ch; 14,332 grt/24,740 dwt; 169.93 × 10.33 m *(557.51 × 33.89 ft)*; M (MAN); 14.5 kts
Probable sisters: **WELS** (Ge); **DORSCH** (Ge)

See photo number 1/266

48 *MEREMF H13*
EKFJORD AF DONSO Sw/FRG (Schichau-U) 1981; Tk/Ch; 6,823 grt/10,700 dwt; 131.53 × 8.4 m *(432 × 27.56 ft)*; M (Krupp-MaK); 14.75 kts; ex-*Cortina*

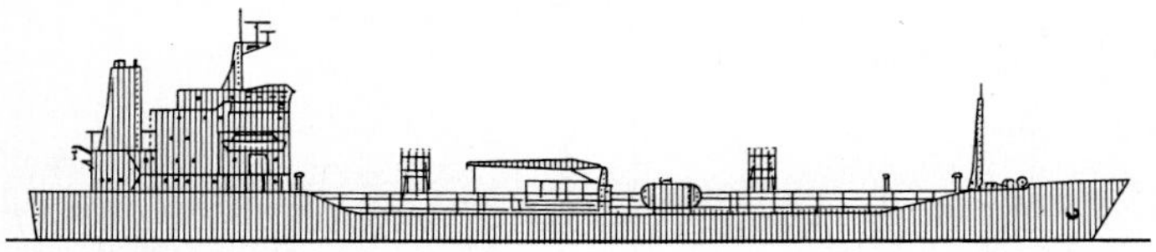

49 *MEREMF H13*
GLOBAL RIO Bz/Po (Viana) 1985; Ch; 11,249 grt/15,089 dwt; 147.00 × 8.50 m *(482.28 × 27.89 ft)*; M (Sulzer); 14 kts
Sister: **GLOBAL MACEIO** (Bz)

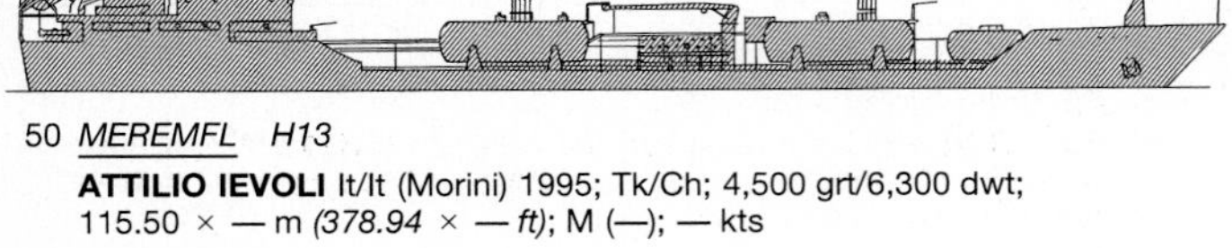

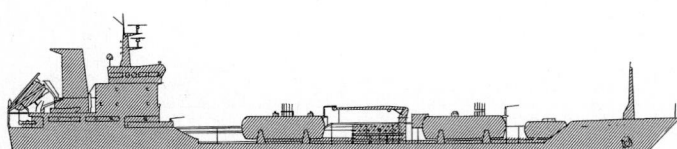

50 *MEREMFL H13*
ATTILIO IEVOLI It/It (Morini) 1995; Tk/Ch; 4,500 grt/6,300 dwt; 115.50 × — m *(378.94 × — ft)*; M (—); — kts

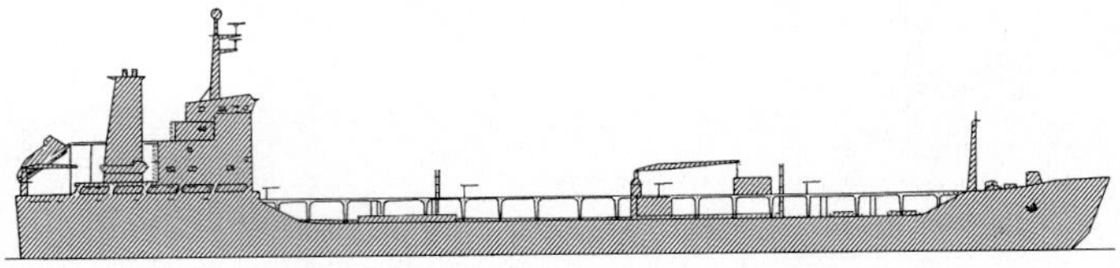

51 *MEREMFLR H13*
TORILL KNUTSEN NIS/Sp (Juliana) 1990; Tk/Ch; 11,425 grt/14,910 dwt; 141.64 × 8.01 m *(464.70 × 26.28 ft)*; M (B&W); 13.5 kts
Sister: **HILDA KNUTSEN** (NIS)

See photo number 1/264

52 *MEREMFMR H13*
VENTSPILS Li/Fi (Rauma-Repola) 1983; Tk; 5,154 grt/6,297 dwt; 113.01 × 7.2 m *(370.77 × 23.62 ft)*; M (B&W); 14 kts; Icebreaking
Sisters: **VANINO** (Ru); **TAGANROGA** (La) ex-*Taganrog*; **RAZNA** (Li) ex-*Razdolnoye*; **KASIRA** (Li) ex-*Kashira*; **ALEISKA** (La) ex-*Aleysk*; **DAUGAVA** (Ru); **DALNERECHENSK** (Ru); **NAGAYEVO** (Ru); **USSURIYSK** (Ru)

See photo numbers 1/235 and 1/267

53 *MEREMFR H13*
BOW VIKING NIS/No (Ankerlokken) 1981; Tk/Ch; 19,639 grt/33,695 dwt; 182.79 × 10.07 m *(600 × 33.04 ft)*; M (B&W); 16 kts; Launched as *Kaupanger*
Sister: **JO CLIPPER** (NA) Launched as *Polux*; Sister (quadpod radar mast and other small differences): **JO BREVIK** (NIS)

54 *MEREMFR H13*
JO LIND NA/No (Ankerlokken) 1983; Tk/Ch; 18,943 grt/33,532 dwt; 182.71 × 10.06 m *(599 × 33.01 ft)*; M (B&W); 15.5 kts; ex-*Johnson Chemspan*

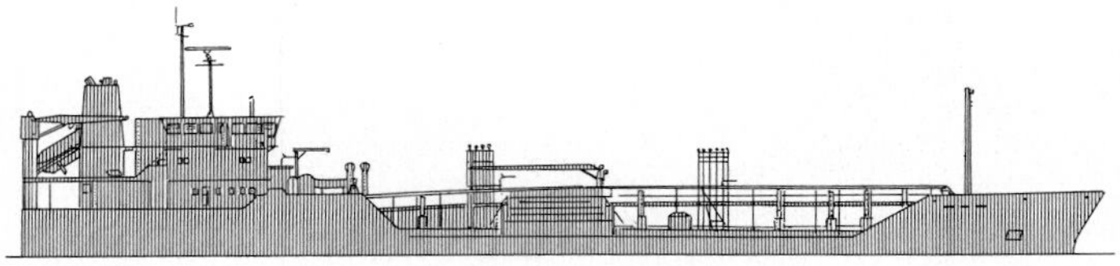

55 *MEREM²FLR H13*
LISELOTTE ESSBERGER Ge/Ge (Sietas) 1992; Tk/Ch; 2,634 grt/3,687 dwt; 90.00 × 6.15 m *(295.27 × 20.18 ft)*; M (MaK); 14.2 kts
Sisters: **ANNETTE ESSBERGER** (Ge); **JOHN AUGUSTUS ESSBERGER** (Ge); **ROLAND ESSBERGER** (Ge)

56 *MEREM-FMR H13*
JACARANDA Bz/No (Ankerlokken) 1978; Ch; 5,805 grt/9,770 dwt; 136.99 × 7.83 m *(449.44 × 25.69 ft)*; M (B&W); 14.5 kts

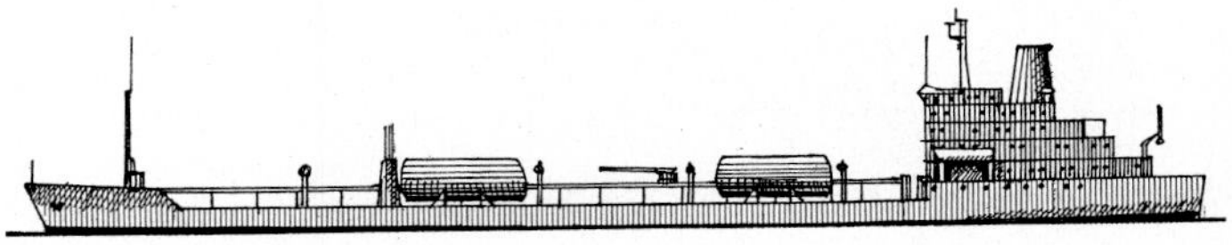

57 *MERMF H13*
PAMELA Li/No (Horten) 1972; Tk/Ch; 15,380 grt/25,300 dwt; 165.08 × 9.94 m *(541.6 × 32.61 ft)*; M (Sulzer); 15.5 kts; ex-*Post Challenger*
Sisters: **KIMBERLEY** (Li) ex-*Post Charger*; **CHARIOT** (Ma) ex-*Post Endeavour*; **CHAMPION** (NIS) ex-*Post Enterprise*; **STOLT STREAM** (Li) ex-*Post Entente*; **STOLT SPRAY** (Li) ex-*Post Energie*

See photo number 1/261

58 *MERMF H13*
SUULA Ge/FRG (Husumer) 1980; Ch; 4,462 grt/6,679 dwt; 112.4 × 7 m *(369 × 22.97 ft)*; M (KHD); 15 kts; ex-*Bomin Emden*

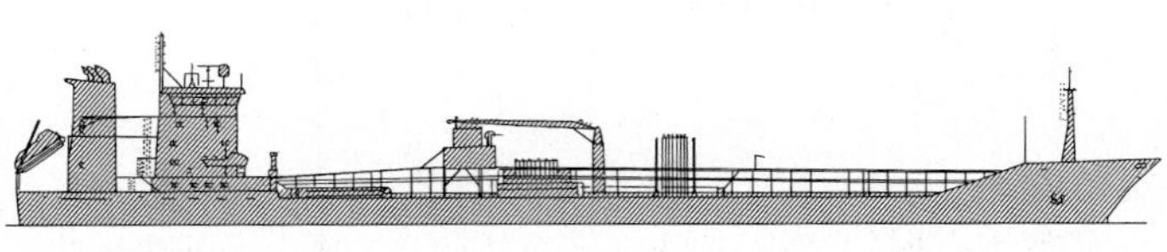

59 *MERMFL H1*
BRAGE ATLANTIC NIS/No (K Kleven U) 1995; Tk/Ch; 10,369 grt/17,460 dwt; 142.44 × 9.20 m *(467.32 × 30.18 ft)*; M (MaK); — kts

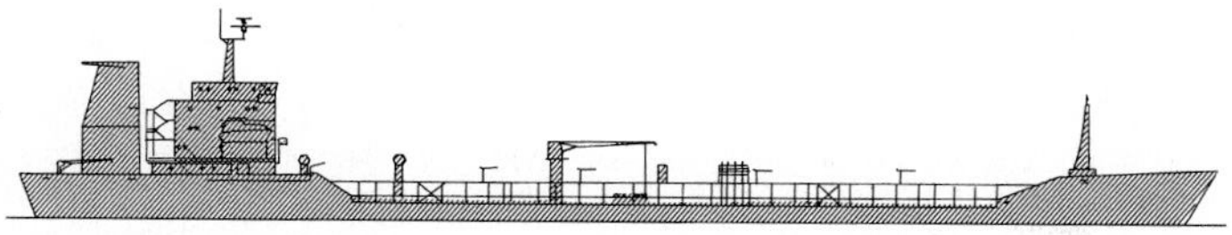

60 MERMFR H13
HUMMEL Ge/Ge (Lindenau GmbH); Tk/Ch; 7,421 grt/12,325 dwt; 145.35 × 8.35 m *(476.87 × 27.40 ft)*; M (MaK); 14 kts

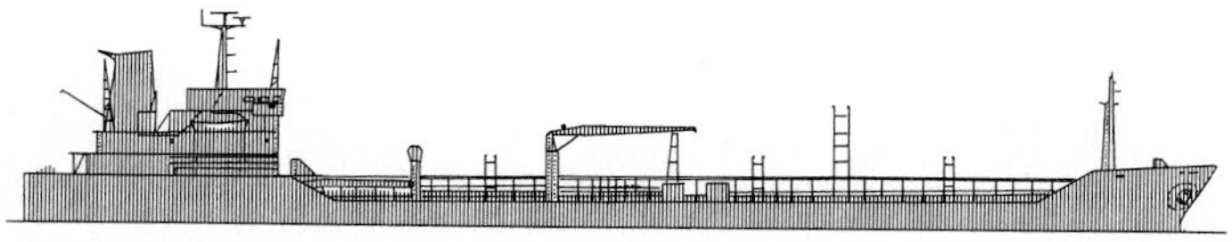

61 MERM^{2}FM H13
BUNGA SIANTAN My/My (Sabah) 1991; Ch; 9,951 grt/16,924 dwt; 143.03 × 9.12 m *(469.26 × 29.92 ft)*; M (Mitsubishi); 13.5 kts
Sister: **BUNGA SEMARAK** (My)

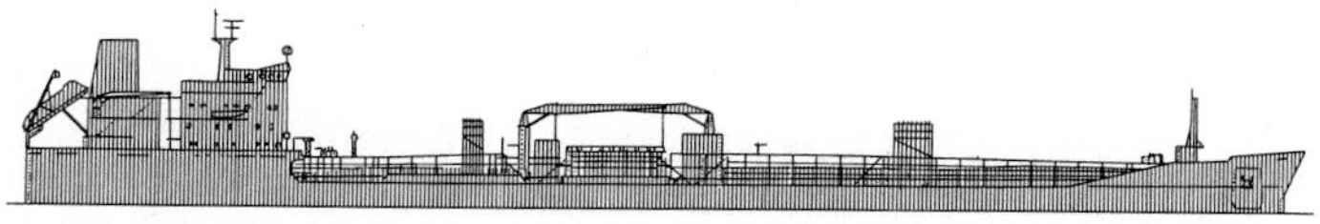

62 MER^{2}EMFL H13
JO SELJE Ne/Br (K Govan) 1993; Ch; 22,380 grt/36,800 dwt; 182.30 × 10.72 m *(598.10 × 35.17 ft)*; M (B&W); 15.5 kts
Sisters (Norwegian built—K Floro/K Kleven Forde): **JO CEDAR** (Ne); **JO SPRUCE** (Ne)

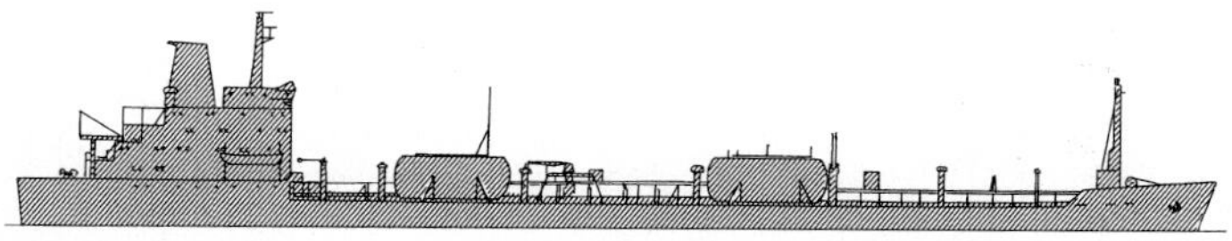

63 MERVMF H13
VINCITA NIS/NO (Horten) 1973; Ch; 15,380 grt/25,300 dwt; 165.08 × 9.94 m *(541.60 × 32.61 ft)*; M (Sulzer); 15.5 kts; ex-*Post Chaser*
Sister: **VENTURA** (NIS) ex-*Post Champion*

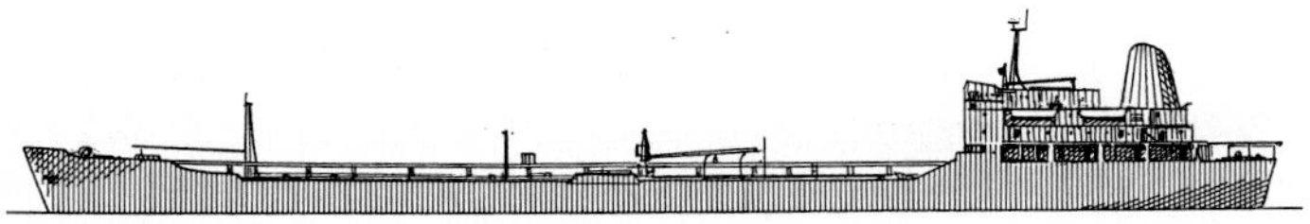

64 M^{2}C^{2}MF H13
PARA Tu/Br (Lithgows) 1965; Tk; 12,938 grt/20,977 dwt; 171 × 9.47 m *(561 × 31.07 ft)*; M (B&W); 14.5 kts; ex-*British Holly*
Similar: **SEA WIND** (Pa) ex-*British Beech*; **MARE EQUATORIALE** (It) ex-*British Hawthorn*; **FAL XVIII** (UAE) ex-*British Hazel*; **MOUG AL BAHR** (Si) ex-*British Laurel*; **VINE** (Cy) ex-*British Vine*

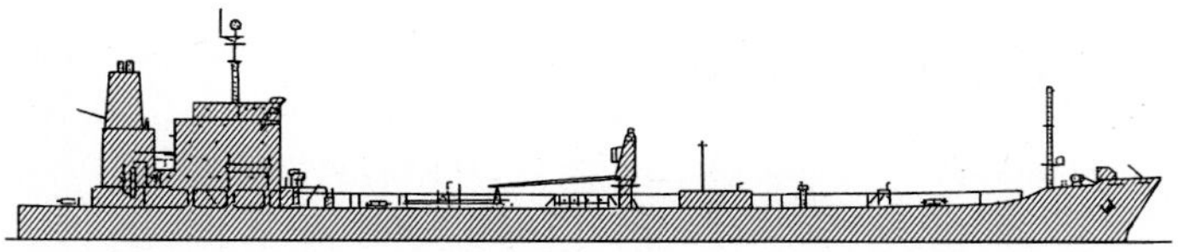

65 M^{2}CMCF H1
NEPTUNE ARIES Sg/Ja (IHI) 1985; Tk; 19,832 grt/29,998 dwt; 173.56 × 9.92 m *(569.42 × 32.55 ft)*; M (Pielstick); 14.75 kts

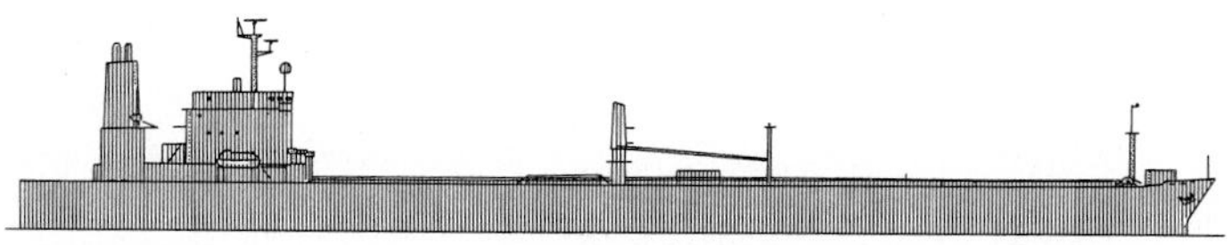

66 M^{2}CMF H
BRITISH ADMIRAL Br/Ja (Mitsubishi HI) 1990; Tk; 23,967 grt/41,100 dwt; 176.20 × 11.53 m *(578.08 × 37.83 ft)*; M (Mitsubishi); 14 kts; ex-*BP Admiral*
Sisters: **BRITISH ADVENTURE** (Br) ex-*BP Adventure*; **BRITISH ARGOSY** (Br) ex-*BP Argosy*

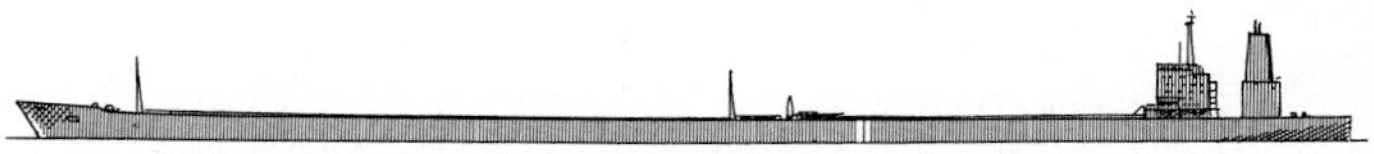

67 M^{2}CMF H
MARE CHAMPION Li/De (Odense) 1975; Tk; 150,960 grt/315,695 dwt; 354.57 × 23.83 m *(1,163.29 × 78.18 ft)*; T (Stal-Laval); 15.75 kts; ex-*Linga*
Sisters: **MARE DISCOVERY** (Li) ex-*Limatula*; **HELLESPONT PARADISE** (Gr) ex-*Liparus*; **HELLESPONT ORPHEUM** (MI) ex-*Limnea*; **BERGE BORG** (NIS) ex-*Limopsis*; **BERGE BOSS** (NIS) ex-*Lyria*

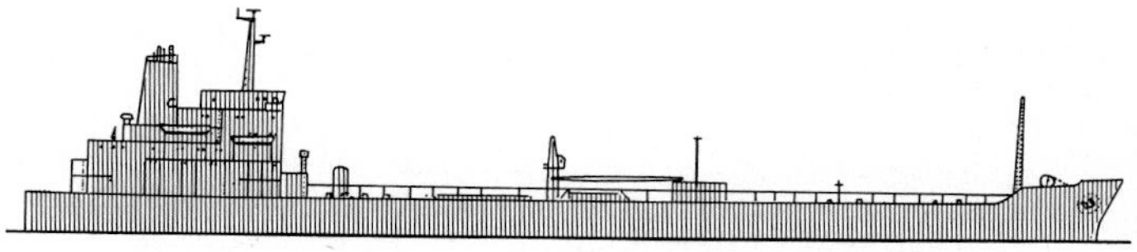

68 M^{2}CMF H1
JAG PREETI In/Ja (NKK) 1981; Tk; 20,302 grt/28,679 dwt; 170.69 × 11.63 m *(560.01 × 38.16 ft)*; M (B&W); 14.5 kts
Sister: **JAG PARI** (In)

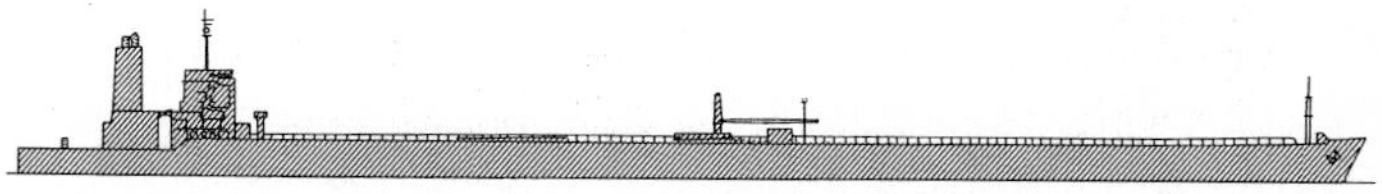

69 M^{2}CMF H1
SUMIDAGAWA Pa/Ja (Kawasaki) 1992; Tk; 145,227 grt/259,988 dwt; 338.00 × 19.27 m *(1,108.92 × 63.22 ft)*; M (B&W); 15.4 kts
Possible sister: **SUZUKA** (Pa)

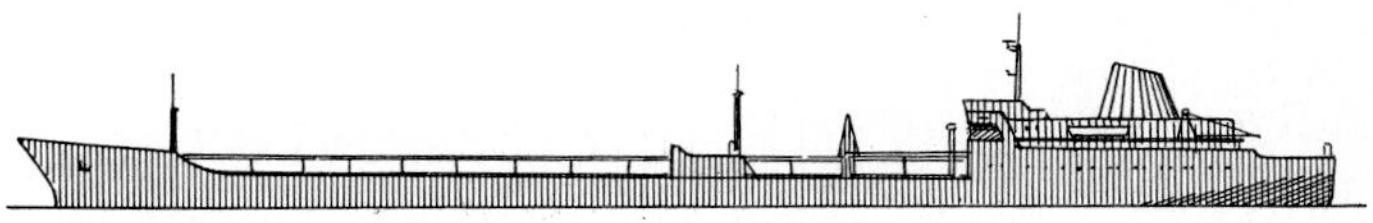

70 M^{2}CMF H13
GENERAL ASLANOV Az/Ru (Astrakhan) 1974; Tk; 8,353 grt/12,334 dwt; 150.02 × 8 m *(492 × 26.25 ft)*; TSM (Skoda); 13.25 kts
Sisters: **SHAMHOR** (Az) ex-*General Babayan*; **KAFUR MAMEDOV** (Az); **NIKIFOR ROGOV** (Ru); **RUKHULLA AKHUNDOV** (—)

71 M^{2}CMF H13
TEAM TROMA NIS/Ja (Sanoyasu) 1982; Tk/Ch; 24,330 grt/42,010 dwt; 184.5 × 11.99 m *(605 × 39.34 ft)*; M (B&W); 14.8 kts; ex-*Troma*
Sister: **TEAM FROSTA** (NIS) ex-*Frosta*

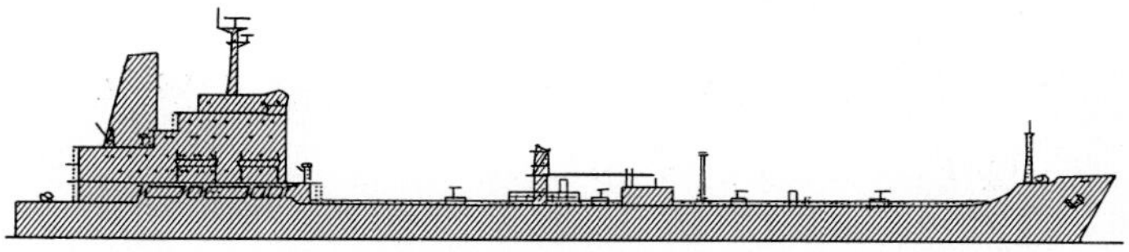

72 M^{2}CMFC H1
JAG PRAGATI In/Ko (Korea SB) 1985; Tk; 18,542 grt/27,402 dwt; 170.11 × 10.11 m *(558.10 × 33.17 ft)*; M (B&W); 15 kts
Sisters: **JAG PALAK** (In); **JAG PRABHAT** (In)

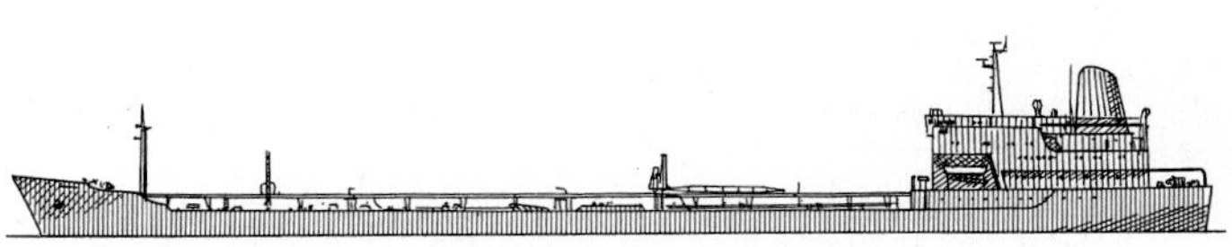

73 M^{2}CMFC H13
KUAKA NZ/Sw (Eriksbergs) 1975; Tk; 15,215 grt/25,097 dwt; 171.46 × 9.58 m *(562.53 × 31.43 ft)*; M (B&W); 16 kts
Sister: **KOTUKU** (NZ)

See photo number 1/271

74 M^{2}CMFM H
LEPETA Br/Br (H&W) 1976; Tk; 153,687 grt/317,996 dwt; 351.42 × 22.38 m *(1,153 × 73.43 ft)*; T (Stal-Laval); 15.25 kts
Sisters: **LAMPAS** (Br); **LEONIA** (Br); **LIMA** (Br); Similar (solid kingpost in focsle): **OLYMPIC ARMOUR II** (Gr) ex-*Lotorium*; Similar (longer): **MAXUS WIDURI** (Cy) ex-*Coastal Corpus Christi*

See photo number 1/268

75 M^2CMFR *H1*
MAASSLOT L Gr/Ne (Giessen-De Noord) 1982; Tk/Ch; 24,794 grt/38,039 dwt; 172.22 × 11.62 m *(565.03 × 38.12 ft)*; M (B&W); 15 kts; ex-*Maassluis*
Sisters: **MAASSTAD L** (Gr) ex-*Maasstad*; **MAASSTROOM L** (Gr) ex-*Maasstroom*

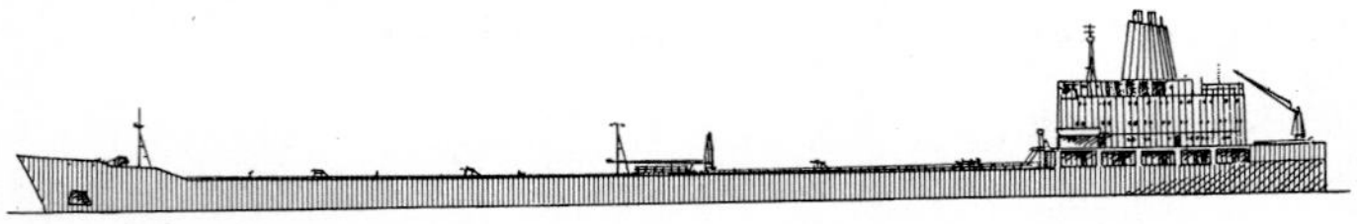

76 M^2CMFR *H13*
COLUMBUS Bs/No (Kaldnes) 1976; Tk; 32,689 grt/59,650 dwt; 211.82 × 12.78 m *(694.95 × 41.93 ft)*; M (B&W); 17 kts; ex-*Jakob Maersk*
Sisters: **RED TEAL** (Li) ex-*Jane Maersk*; **MAERSK ASCENSION** (Br) ex-*Jessie Maersk*; **CLEMENT** (Bs) ex-*Jeppesen Maersk*; **DUBHE** (Ma) ex-*Jesper Maersk*

See photo number 1/270

77 $M^2CMHFMC$ *H1*
CARLA A HILLS Li/Ja (Mitsubishi HI) 1981; Tk; 23,709 grt/35,596 dwt; 179.20 × 10.95 m *(588 × 35.93 ft)*; M (Sulzer); 14.9 kts
Sisters: **ALDEN W CLAUSEN** (Li); **GEORGE H WEYERHAUSER** (Bs); **KENNETH T DERR** (Bs); Probable sister: **CHEVRON PACIFIC** (Li)

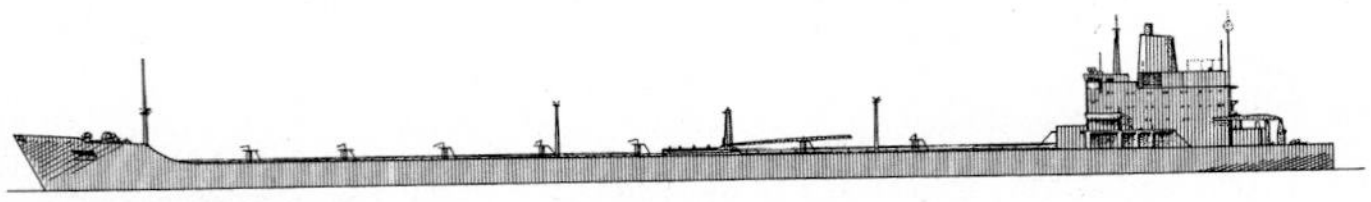

78 $M^2CMHFMR$ *H1*
BT NAVARIN HK/De (Odense) 1977; Tk; 36,376 grt/64,900 dwt; 247.25 × 25 × 13.17 m *(811.2 × 43.21 ft)*; M (Sulzer); 16.5 kts; ex-*Nora Maersk*
Sisters: **BT NAUTILUS** (HK) ex-*Nele Maersk*; **BT NIMROD** (HK) ex-*Nelly Maersk*; **BT NESTOR** (HK) ex-*Nicolai Maersk*; **BT NAVIGATOR** (HK) ex-*Nicoline Maersk*; **BT NEPTUNE** (HK) ex-*Niels Maersk*

79 M^2CM^2F *H1*
KORIANA Gr/Ja (Hitachi) 1985; Tk; 38,629 grt/63,736 dwt; 228.61 × 12.83 m *(750.03 × 42.09 ft)*; M (B&W); 15.5 kts
Sisters: **FLAMINIA** (Gr); **ANDROMEDA** (Gr)

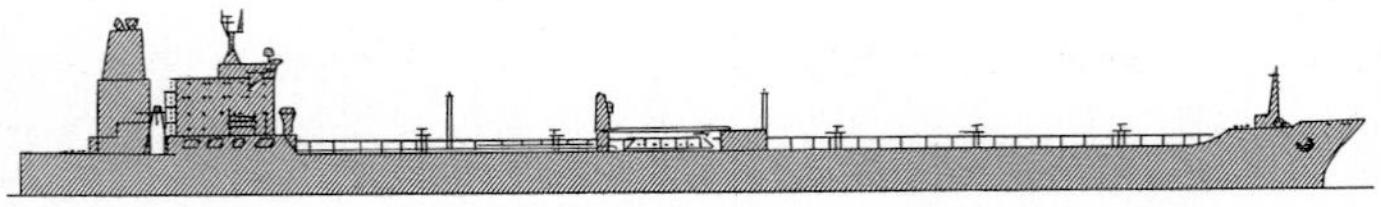

80 M^2CM^2F *H1*
VOO SHEE II Tw/Tw (China SB) 1986; Tk; 59,893 grt/104,882 dwt; 247.58 × 15.87 m *(812.27 × 52.07 ft)*; M (Sulzer); 14.5 kts
Sister: **YU TSAO II** (Tw)

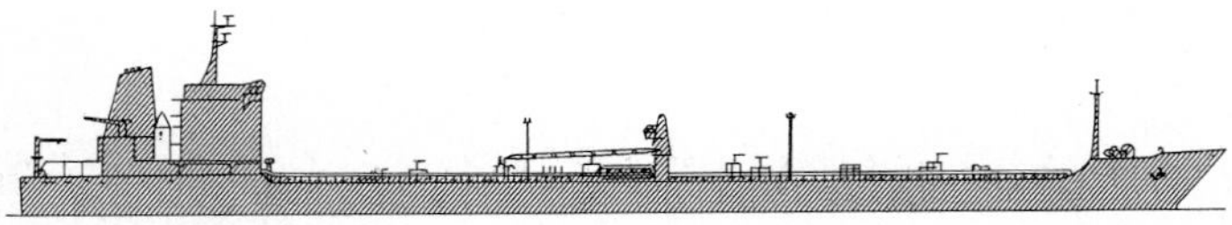

81 M^2CM^2FM *H1*
GUADELUPE VICTORIA II Me/Sp (AESA) 1983; Tk; 26,660 grt/44,653 dwt; 202.01 × 12.45 m *(662.76 × 40.85 ft)*; M (Sulzer); 16 kts
Sister: **LAZARO CARDENAS II** (Pa)

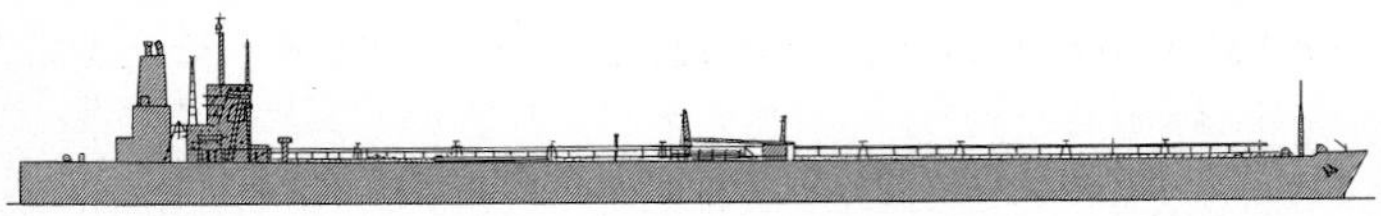

82 M^2CM^3F *H*
KAKUHO Pa/Ja (Kawasaki) 1986; Tk; 150,479 grt/258,084 dwt; 332.01 × 19.11 m *(1,089.27 × 62.70 ft)*; M (B&W); 14.75 kts

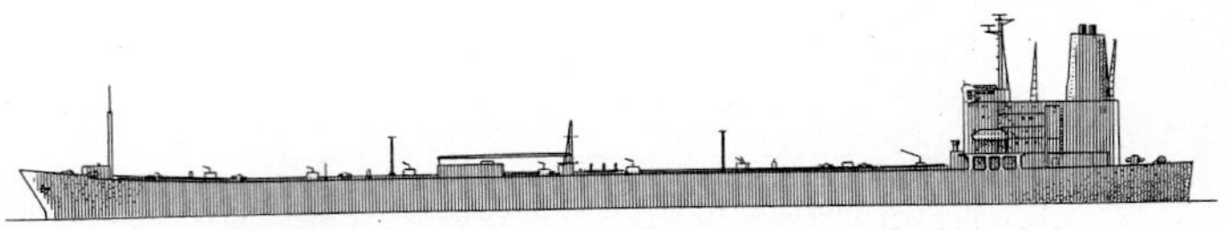

83 M^2CM^3FM *H*
AMPOL SAREL Au/Ja (Mitsubishi HI) 1979; Tk; 65,094 grt/101,609 dwt; 243 × 13.74 m *(797.24 × 45.08 ft)*; M (Sulzer); 15.6 kts

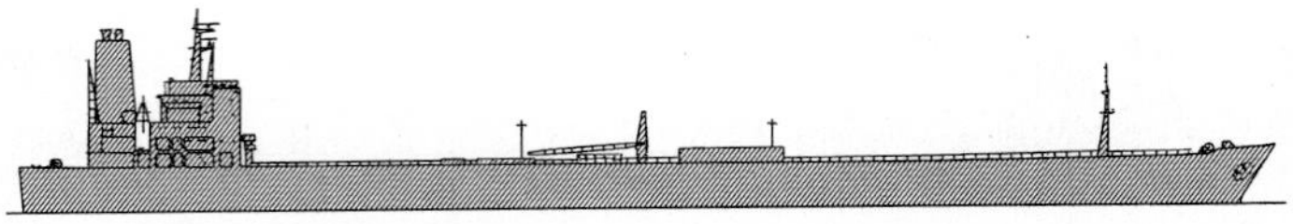

84 $M^2CMNMFN$ *H*
VOLGA Li/Ja (Sumitomo) 1981; Tk; 41,471 grt/59,998 dwt; 228.61 × 11.96 m *(750.03 × 39.24 ft)*; M (Sulzer); 15.25 kts; ex-*Ogden Volga*
Sister: **NILE** (Li) ex-*Ogden Nile*

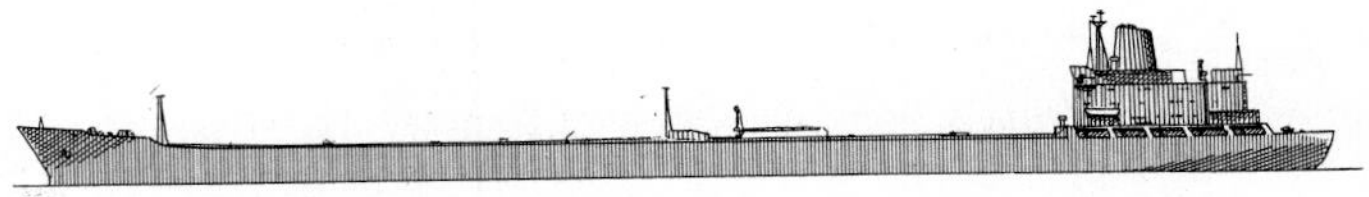

85 M^2DM^2FCM *H1*
ONDA AZZURRA It/Au (Evans Deakin) 1974; Tk; 37,016 grt/66,660 dwt; 239.28 × 13.14 m *(785.04 × 43.11 ft)*; M (Sulzer); 16.5 kts; ex-*Robert Miller*

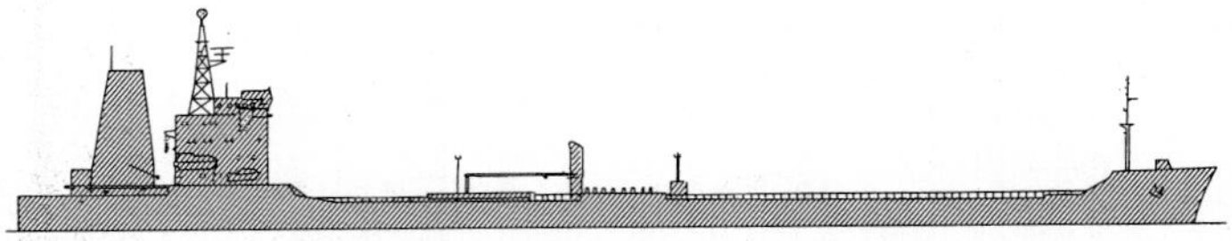

86 M^2DNMF *H1*
OSCO STAR Au/Ys ('Uljanik') 1989; Tk/Ch; 22,572 grt/40,503 dwt; 176.00 × 11.22 m *(577.43 × 36.81 ft)*; M (B&W); 14.3 kts
Sisters: **OSCO STRIPE** (NIS); **FARANDOLE** (Bs) ex-*Osco Sky*

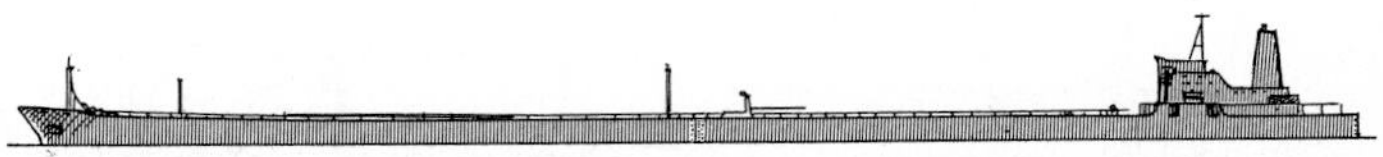

87 M^3CMF *H*
AUTAN Kn/Fr (L'Atlantique) 1975; Tk; 134,523 grt/278,220 dwt; 342.98 × 21.35 m *(1,125.26 × 70.05 ft)*; T (Stal-Laval); 15 kts; ex-*Labiosa*

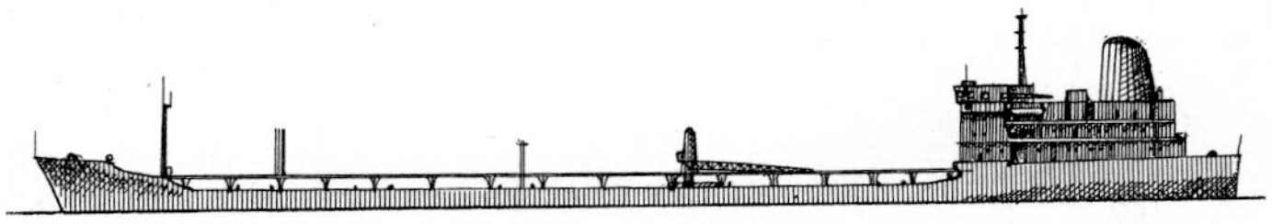

88 M^3CMF *H13*
MINAB 3 Ir/Sw (Eriksbergs) 1972; Tk; 14,947 grt/25,651 dwt; 171.46 × 9.58 m *(562.53 × 31.43 ft)*; M (B&W); 15.5 kts; ex-*British Dart*
Similar (some have foremast set aft of the focsle): **BRITISH ESK** (Br); **CAMARGUE** (Bs) ex-*British Forth*; **MINAB 2** (Ir) ex-*British Kennet*; **BRITISH TAMAR** (Br); **SOUTH WIND 1** (Pa) ex-*British Tay*; **MINAB 4** (Ir) ex-*British Test*; **SEA CASTLE** (Ma) ex-*British Wye*; **MARUN** (Ir) ex-*British Severn* 1976; **MOKRAN** (Ir) ex-*British Neath* 1976; **CARNIA** (Cy) ex-*British Avon*; **TANK PROGRESS** (Cy) ex-*British Spey*; **AKRADINA** (It) ex-*British Humber*; **AZNA** (Ir) ex-*British Tweed*

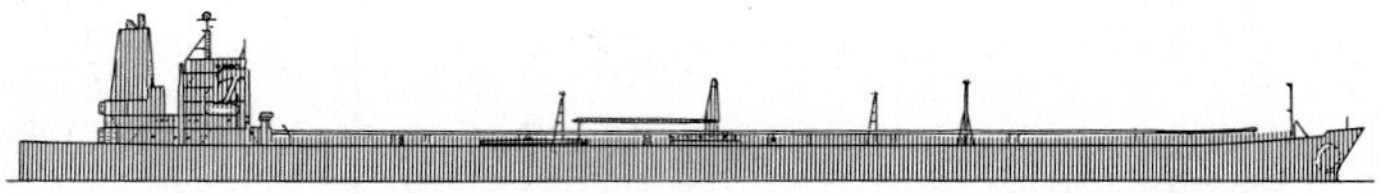

89 M^3CM^2F *H*
CHEVRON ATLANTIC Bs/Ja (Mitsui) 1992; Tk; 80,130 grt/149,748 dwt; 269.00 × 16.86 m *(882.55 × 55.31 ft)*; M (B&W); 15.11 kts

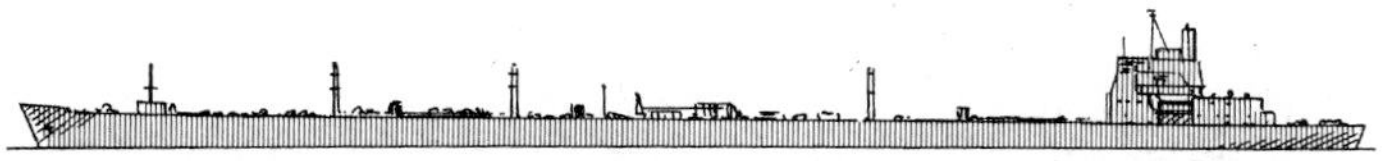

90 M^3CM^2F *H*
S/R SAN FRANCISCO US/US (Avondale) 1969; Tk; 34,266 grt/78,093 dwt; 246.84 × 12.6 m *(809.84 × 41.34 ft)*; T (GEC); 17.5 kts; ex-*Esso San Francisco*
Sisters: **S/R BATON ROUGE** (US) ex-*Esso Baton Rouge*; **S/R PHILADELPHIA** (US) ex-*Esso Philadelphia*

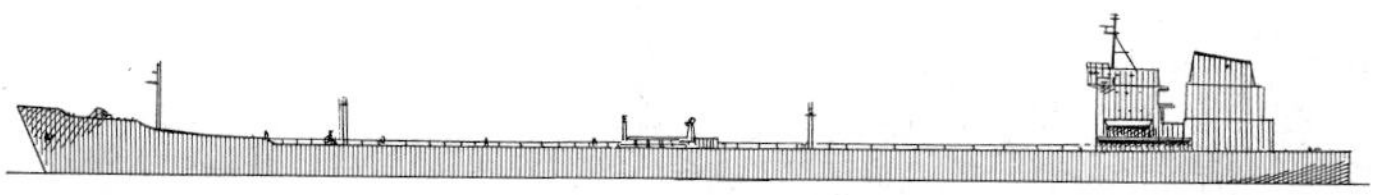

91 M^3CM^2F *H1*
CHEVRON WASHINGTON US/US (FMC) 1976; Tk; 22,761 grt/39,796 dwt; 198.13 × 11.35 m *(650.03 × 37.24 ft)*; GT (GEC); 14.5 kts
Sisters: **CHEVRON COLORADO** (US); **CHEVRON LOUISIANA** (US): **CHEVRON OREGON** (US); **CHEVRON ARIZONA** (US)

See photo number 1/274

92 M^3CM^4F *H1*
PETROTROLL NIS/Ja (Tsuneishi) 1981; Tk; 38,406 grt/58,327 dwt; 228.00 × 13.43 m *(748 × 44.06 ft)*; M (B&W); 14.5 kts; ex-*Jaguar*; Fenders on port side
Sister: **CABO DE HORNOS** (Li) ex-*Janus*

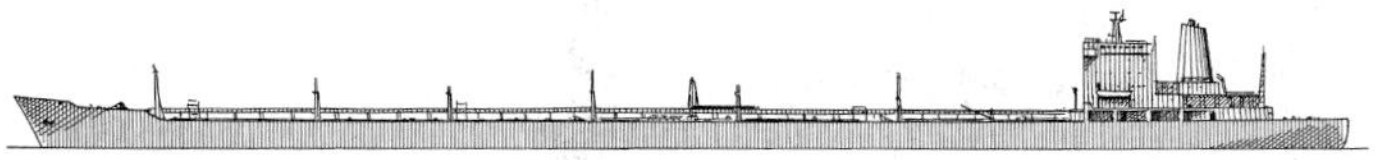

93 M^4CM^3FM *H1*
AL SHARIFA II Eg/Au (Whyalla) 1974; Tk; 37,195 grt/66,700 dwt; 239.28 × 13.16 m *(785.04 × 43.18 ft)*; M (Sulzer); 16 kts; ex-*Arthur Phillip*

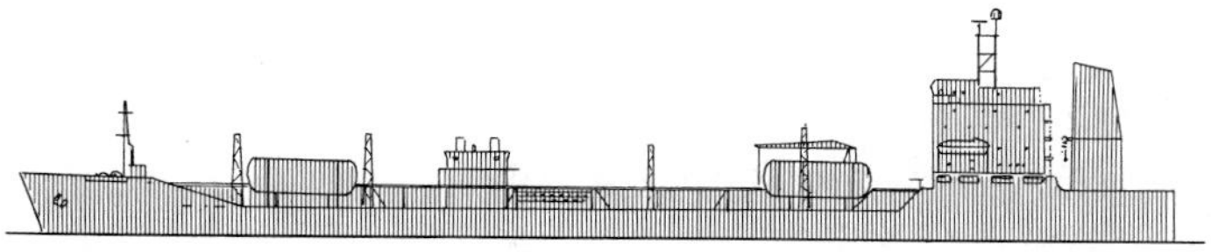

94 M^5RMF *H13*
STOLT SAPPHIRE Li/Ko (Daewoo) 1986; Ch; 23,964 grt/38,746 dwt; 176.80 × 11.42 m *(580.05 × 37.47 ft)*; M (B&W); 15 kts; Travelling crane
Sisters: **STOLT AQUAMARINE** (Li); **STOLT EMERALD** (Li); **STOLT JADE** (Li); **STOLT TOPAZ** (Li)

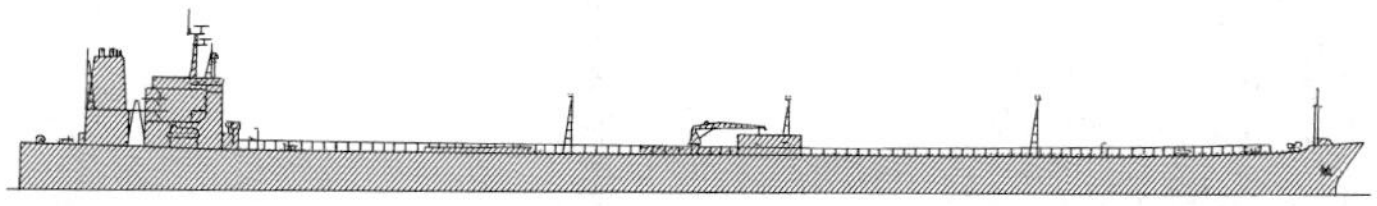

95 M^3SMM-NFN *H*
GENERAL MONARCH Pa/Ja (Hitachi) 1990; Tk; 144,567 grt/275,993 dwt; 326.18 × 20.48 m *(1,070.14 × 67.19 ft)*; M (B&W); 14 kts; ex-*Sea Duke*
Sister: **SEA PRINCE** (Cy); Possible sisters: **NICHIYO** (Pa) ex-*Goho*; **GENERAL ACE** (Pa) ex-*Sea Princess*

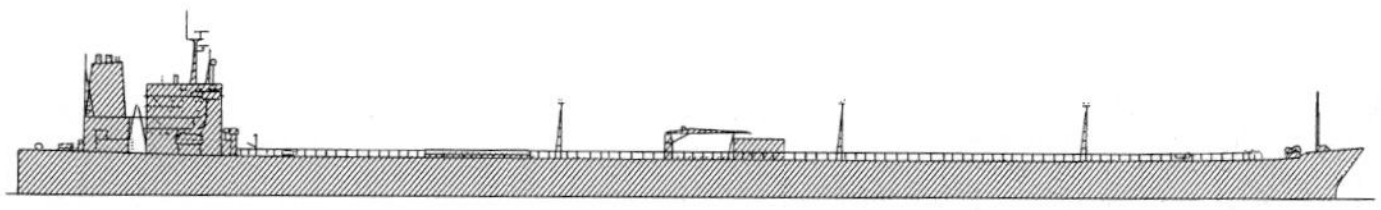

96 M^3SN^2MFN *H*
COLUMBIA Li/Ja (Hitachi) 1989; Tk; 144,139 grt/258,076 dwt; 326.18 × 19.44 m *(1,070.14 × 63.78 ft)*; M (B&W); 14 kts
Possible sister: **OLYMPIA** (Li)

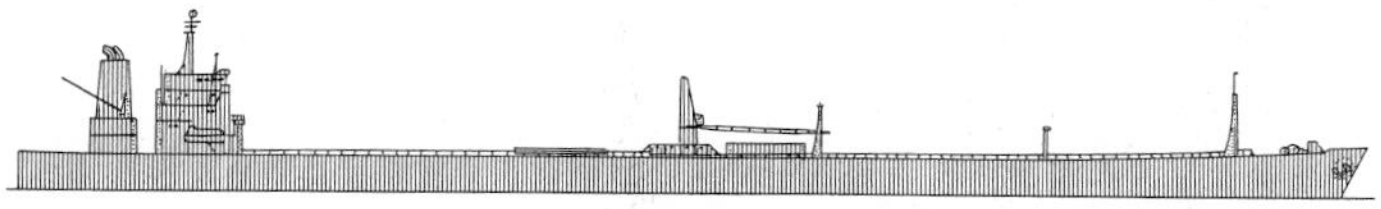

97 M^2NCHF *H*
OLYMPIC SERENITY Gr/Ja (Sumitomo) 1991; Tk; 52,127 grt/96,733 dwt; 232.04 × 14.23 m *(761.29 × 46.69 ft)*; M (Sulzer); 13.9 kts
Sisters: **OLYMPIC SPONSOR** (Gr); **OLYMPIC SYMPHONY** (Gr); **LOUL'WAT QATAR** (Qt) ex-*Olympic Spirit*

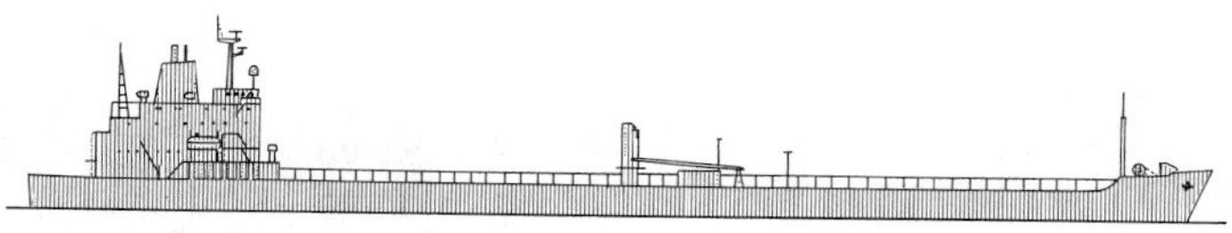

98 M^2NCMFN *H1*
SCOTLAND Bs/Ja (Mitsubishi HI) 1982; Tk; 25,593 grt/40,792 dwt; 204.20 × 10.97 m *(669.95 × 35.99 ft)*; M (Sulzer); 15.5 kts; ex-*Philmac Venturer*

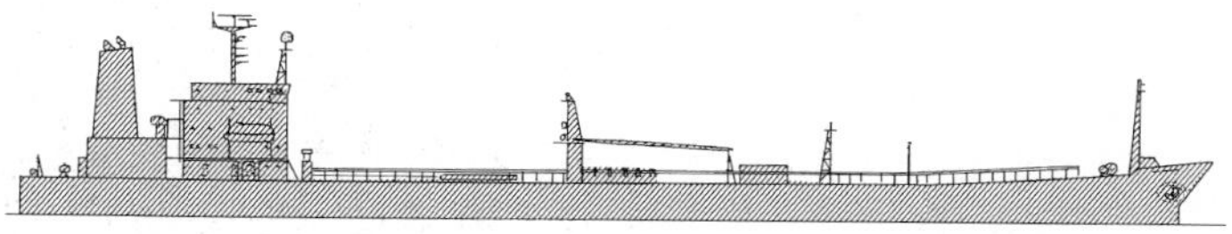

99 M^2NCNMF *H*
PAGODA Li/Ja (Kanasashi) 1988; Tk; 18,055 grt/29,996 dwt; 165.80 × 10.38 m *(543.96 × 34.06 ft)*; M (B&W); 14.3 kts
Sisters: **NORDFARER** (Bs) ex-*Dan Freya*; **NORDFAST** (Bs) ex-*Dan Frigg*

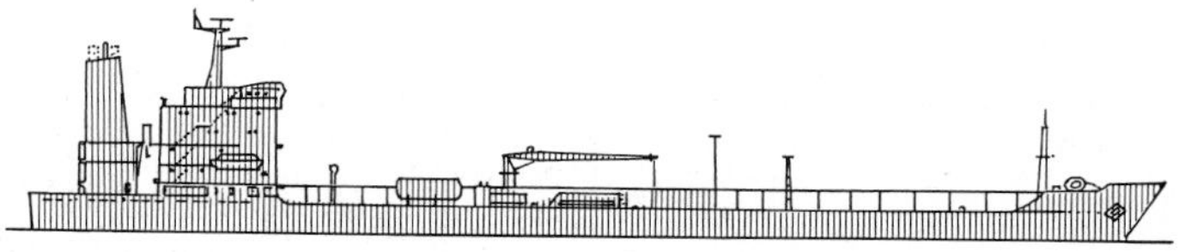

100 M^2NRMF *H1*
GULF OF PARIA Li/Ja (Sasebo) 1984; Ch; 8,823 grt/14,326 dwt; 140.37 × 8.62 m *(460.53 × 28.28 ft)*; M (MaK); — kts; ex-*Trinidad and Tobago*
Sister: **GOODRICH BAY** (Li) ex-*Harold la Borde*

101 $M^2NRNMRF$ *H*
SKS TRUST Li/Ko (Hyundai) 1992; OBO; 57,082 grt/96,002 dwt; 242.76 × 14.52 m *(796.46 × 47.64 ft)*; M (B&W); 14.5 kts; ex-*Scanobo Trust*
Probable sisters: **SKS BANNER** (Li) ex-*Scanobo Banner*; **SKS BREEZE** (Li) ex-*Scanobo Breeze*; **SKS CHALLENGER** (Li) ex-*Scanobo Challenger*; **SKS CHAMPION** ((Li); **SKS ENDURANCE** (Li) ex-*Scanobo Endurance*; **SKS HORIZON** (Li) ex-*Scanobo Horizon*; **SKS SPIRIT** (Li) ex-*Scanobo Spirit*; **SKS STAR** (Li); **SKS TRADER** (Li) ex-*Scanobo Trader*

102 M^2NSMDF *H*
YUHSEI MARU Ja/Ko (Samsung S) 1994; Tk; 53,773 grt/96,101 dwt; 243.50 × 13.96 m *(798.88 × 45.80 ft)*; M (B&W); 14.2 kts

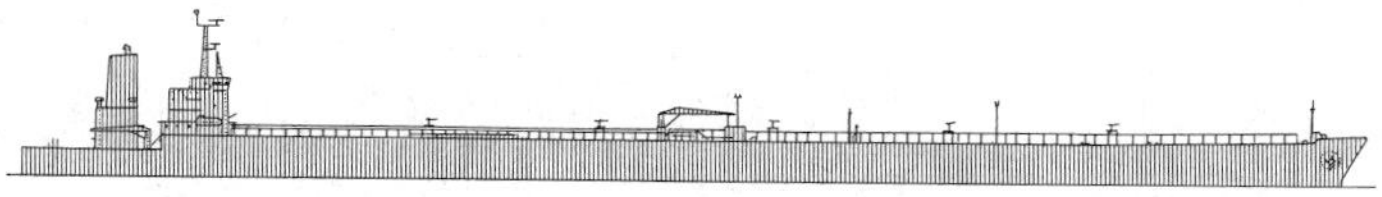

103 M^2NSMRF *H1*
SIAM Pa/Ko (Daewoo) 1993; Tk; 156,539 grt/299,999 dwt; 332.00 × 22.02 m *(1,089.24 × 72.24 ft)*; M (B&W); 15.75 kts
Sister: **SORO** (Pa); Probable sisters: **SALA** (Pa); **SEBU** (Pa) ex-*Seki*; **SUVA** (Pa); **SYLT** (Pa)

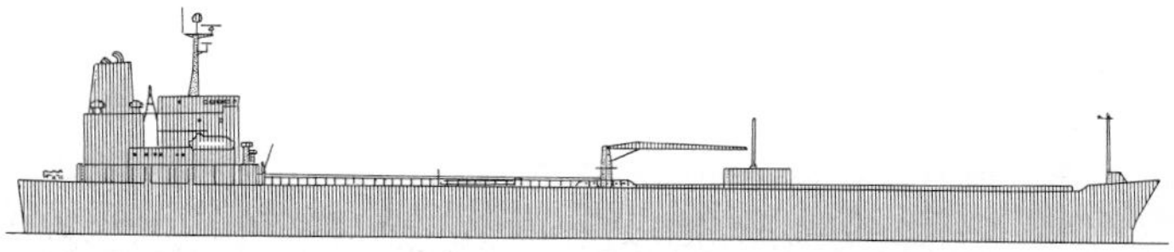

104 M^2RMF *H*
SALAMINA Gr/Ja (Hitachi) 1991; Tk; 29,506 grt/45,425 dwt; 183.00 × 12.00 m *(600.39 × 39.37 ft)*; M (B&W); 14 kts; 'Epoch Mk 2' type
Sisters: **KASTELORIZO** (Gr); **ARGIRONISSOS** (Gr); **FOLEGANDROS** (Gr)

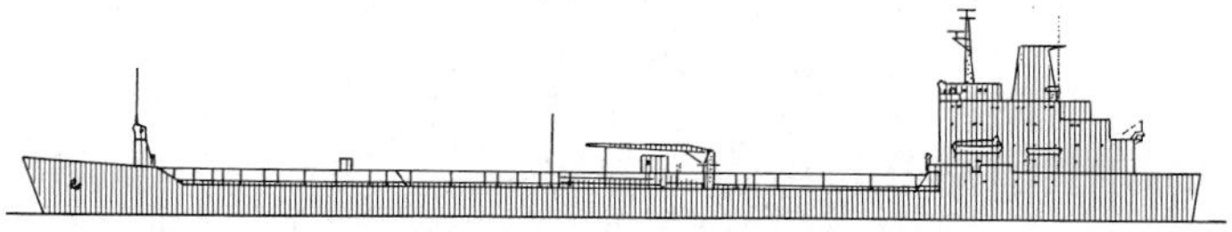

105 M^2RMF *H13*
STAR BERGEN Bs/No (Horten) 1977; Tk; 17,679 grt/31,502 dwt; 168.79 × 11.16 m *(553.77 × 36.61 ft)*; M (Sulzer); 16 kts; ex-*Texaco Bergen*
Sister: **SAN CARLOS** (Ma) ex-*Texaco Stockholm;* Probable sister: **STAR BALTIC** (Bs) ex-*Texaco Baltic*

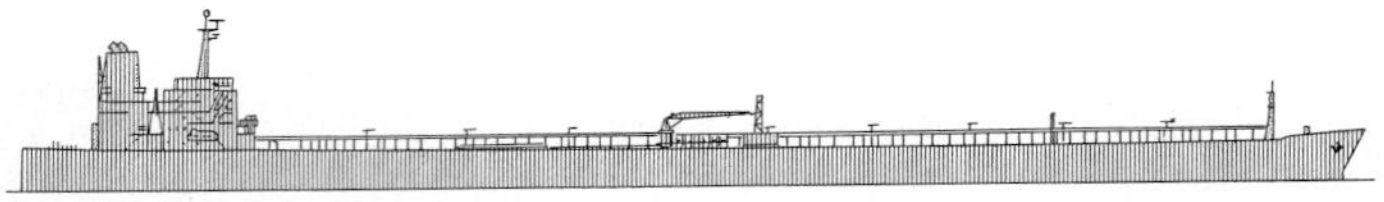

106 *M^{2}RMFM/MNSMFM H*
NEW VITALITY Li/Ja (Sasebo) 1993; Tk; 153,808 grt/290,691 dwt; 330.25 × 21.52 m *(1,083.50 × 70.60 ft)*; M (B&W); 15.4 kts
Probable sister: **MUSASHI SPIRIT** (Bs)

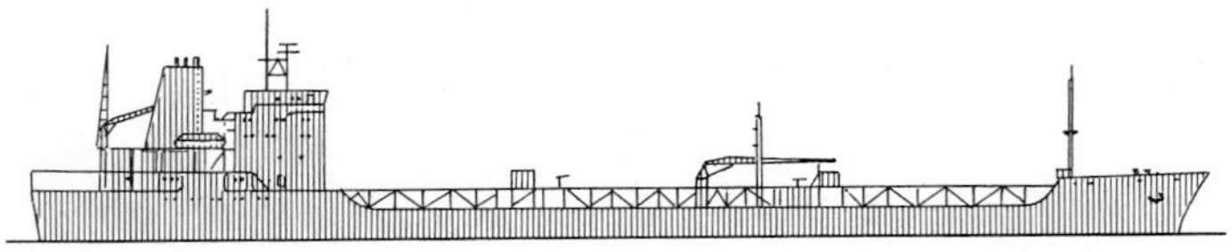

107 *M^{2}RMFMR H13*
VEKUA Ma/Ys ('Split') 1987; Tk; 10,948 grt/16,231 dwt; 151.30 × 9.00 m *(496.39 × 29.53 ft)*; M (B&W); 15.1 kts; ex-*Akademik Vekua*; Mast aft is on starboard side. Ice strengthened
Sisters (Some built by '3 Maj' and some by 'Uljanik'): **UZNADZE** (Ma) ex-*Akademik Uznadze*; **AKADEMIK SEMENOV** (Cy); **LEONID UTESOV** (Ru); **YAKOV SVERDLOV** (Cy); **CHAVCHAVADZE** (Ma) ex-*Ilya Chavchavadze*; **VLADIMIR VYSOTSKIY** (Ru); **G. ORDZHONIKIDZE** (Ma) ex-*Grigoriy Ordzhonikidze*; **KHIRURG VISHNEVSKIY** (Ru): Possible sisters: **KAPITAN KOROTAYEV** (Cy); **KAPITAN RUDNYEV** (Cy)

See photo number 1/269

108 *M^{2}RMFR H*
TORM THYRA DIS/De (Odense) 1985; Ch; 28,017 grt/50,600 dwt; 182.58 × 13.29 m *(599.05 × 43.60 ft)*; M (B&W); 16 kts
Sisters: **A P MOLLER** (DIS); **ODENSE MAERSK** (DIS) ex-*Emma Maersk*; **OLIVIA MAERSK** (DIS) ex-*Evelyn Maersk*; **OLGA MAERSK** (DIS) ex-*Eleo Maersk*; **OLUF MAERSK** (DIS) ex-*Estelle Maersk;* **TORM GUNHILD** (DIS)

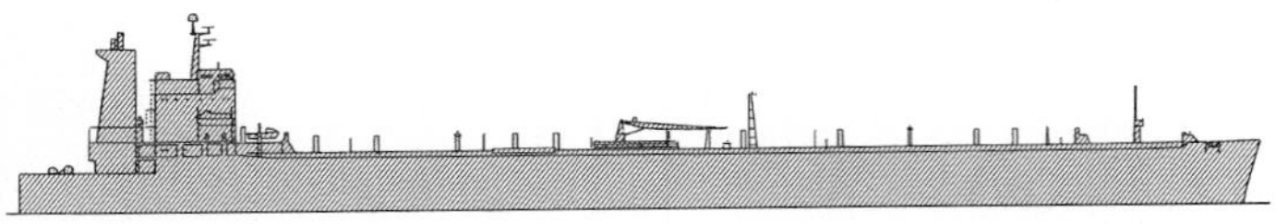

109 *M^{2}RMFR H1*
LOYALTY Pa/Sw (Uddevalla) 1985; Tk; 43,363 grt/75,992 dwt; 228.60 × 14.30 m *(750.00 × 46.92 ft)*; M (B&W); 15.75 kts; ex-*Toluma*
Sister: **VENTURE** (Sg) ex-*Wilanna*

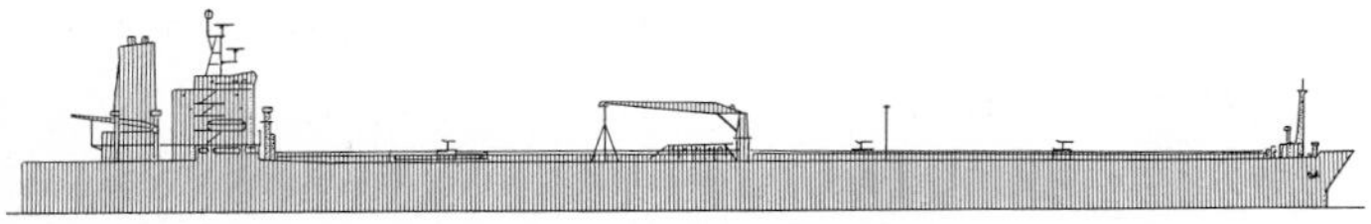

110 *M^{2}RM^{2}F H*
DICTO No/Sp (AESA) 1990; Tk; 60,866 grt/113,131 dwt; 243.01 × 15.00 m *(797.28 × 49.21 ft)*; M (B&W); 14.24 kts; ex-*Dicto Knutsen*; Fitted for offshore-loading
Sister: **TOVE KNUTSEN** (No)

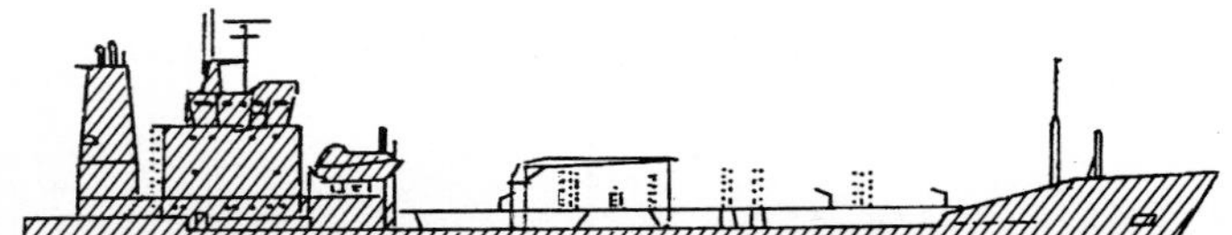

111 *M^{2}RM^{2}F H1*
NORDSTRAUM No/No (Aukra I) 1988; Tk/Ch; 2,894 grt/4,165 dwt; 85.70 × 6.17 m *(281.17 × 20.24 ft)*; M (Wärtsilä); 12.5 kts
Similar (lifeboats by superstructure): **KILSTRAUM** (No)

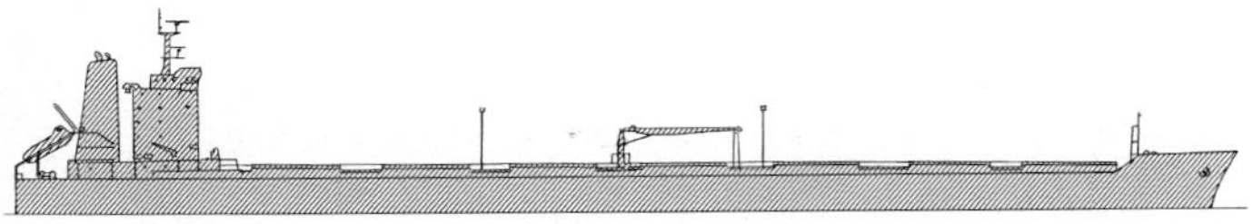

112 *M^{2}RM^{2}FL H1*
3 MAJ Ma/Ys ('3 Maj') 1988; OBO; 39,836 grt/64,850 dwt; 224.65 × 13.37 m *(737.04 × 43.86 ft)*; M (Sulzer); 13.1 kts
Sister: **MARA** (Ma) ex-*Mara Lolli-Ghetti*

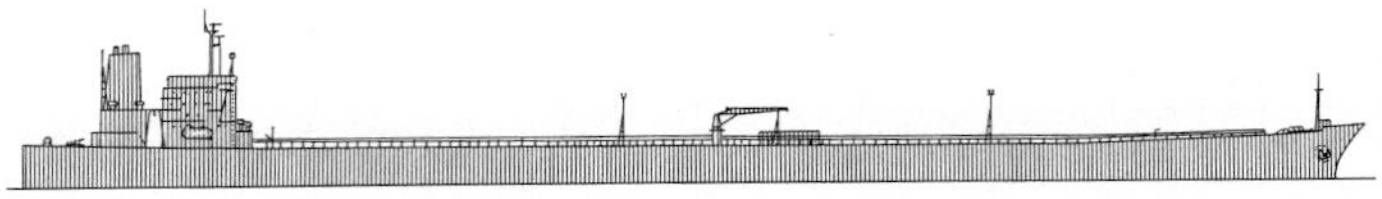

113 *M^{2}RM^{2}FM/M^{2}SNMFM H*
AROSA Gr/Ja (Hitachi) 1993; Tk; 156,336 grt/291,381 dwt; 328.16 × 21.64 m *(1,076.64 × 71.00 ft)*; M (B&W); 15.5 kts

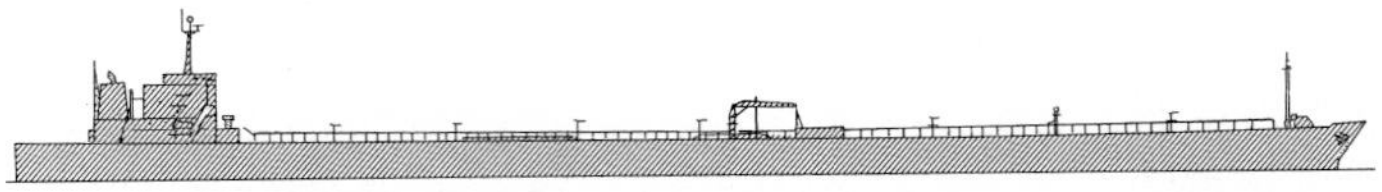

114 *M^{2}RM^{2}FM/M^{2}SM^{2}GN H*
DIAMOND DREAM Pa/Ja (Mitsubishi HI) 1990; Tk; 137,712 grt/243,850 dwt; 315.50 × 18.76 m *(1,035.10 × 61.55 ft)*; M (Mitsubishi); 14.5 kts
Probable sister: **DIAMOND ECHO** (Pa)

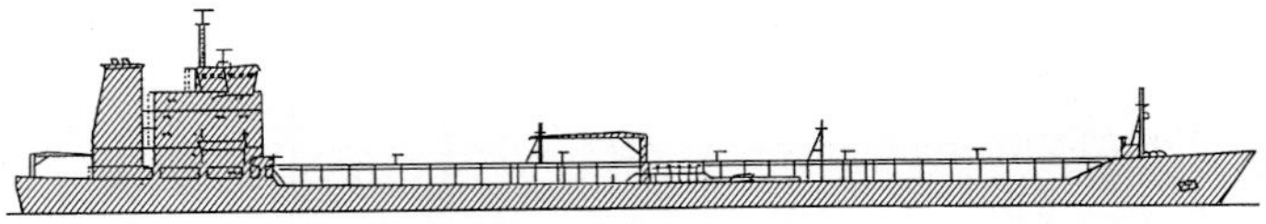

115 *M^{2}RM^{2}FR H1*
TARNFJORD Sw/No (Kaldnes) 1984; Tk/Ch; 12,926 grt/19,561 dwt; 164.50 × 9.80 m *(539.70 × 32.15 ft)*; M (MaK); 14.5 kts

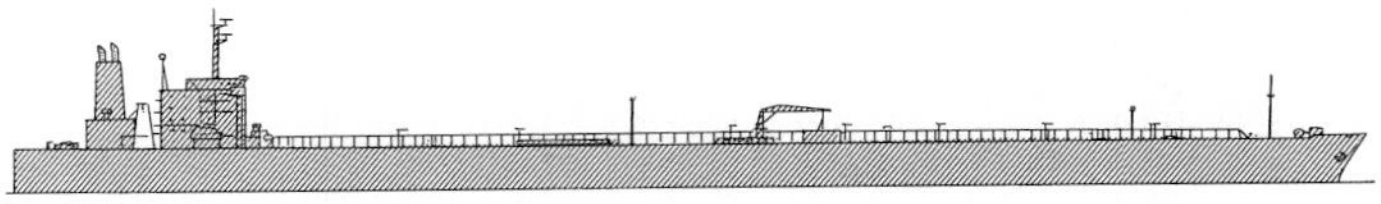

116 *M^{2}RM^{3}F/M^{2}SNM^{2}F H*
HAN-EI Pa/Ja (IHI) 1994; Tk; 147,580 grt/259,999 dwt; 333.00 × 19.06 m *(1,092.52 × 62.53 ft)*; M (Sulzer); 15.35 kts

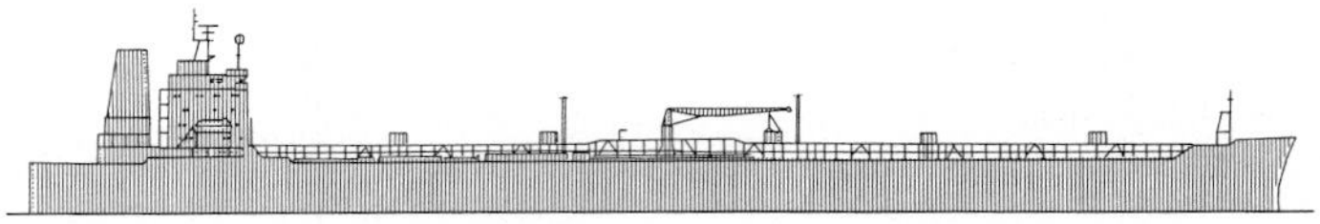

117 *M^{2}RM^{3}F H1*
PANDA Li/Ys ('3 Maj') 1987; Tk; 44,322 grt/83,651 dwt; 228.20 × 12.50 m *(748.69 × 41.01 ft)*; M (Sulzer); 14 kts

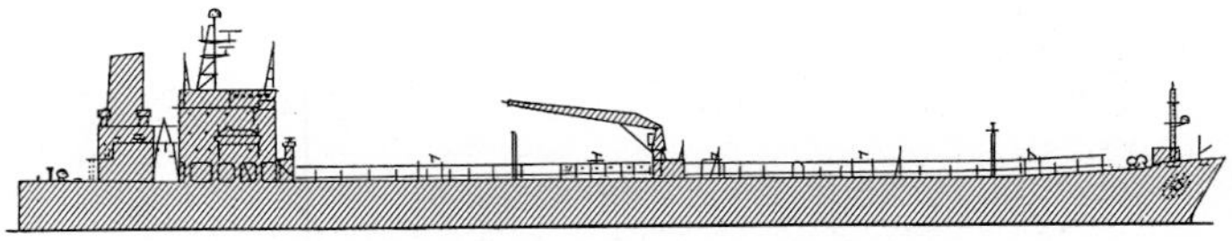

118 *M^{2}RM^{4}F H*
NEPTUNE CRUX Sg/Ja (Hashihama) 1987; Tk; 23,926 grt/40,156 dwt; 172.19 × 11.20 m *(564.93 × 36.75 ft)*; M (B&W); 14.5 kts
Probable sister: **NEPTUNE LIBRA** (Sg)

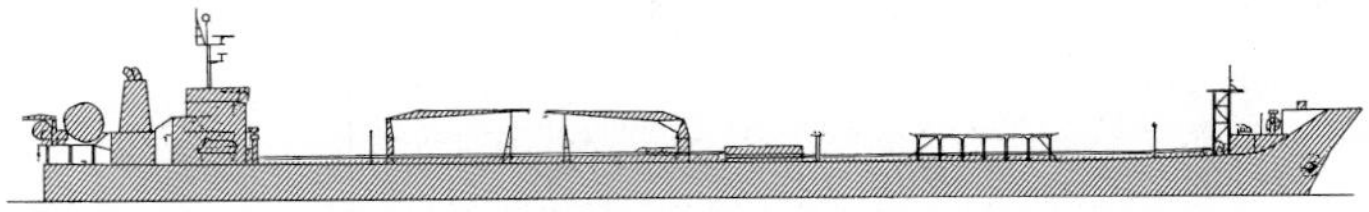

119 *M^{2}R^{2}MFR H1*
VINGA NIS/Ja (Sanoyas HM) 1993; Tk; 52,348 grt/95,029 dwt; 238.24 × 14.23 m *(781.63 × 46.69 ft)*; M (Sulzer); 14.25 kts; Fitted for offshore-loading

120 *M^{2}SMF H*
COSMO DELPHINUS Ja/Ja (Mitsubishi HI) 1993; Tk; 146,527 grt/258,095 dwt; 321.95 × 19.50 m *(1,056.27 × 63.98 ft)*; M (Mitsubishi); 15.25 kts

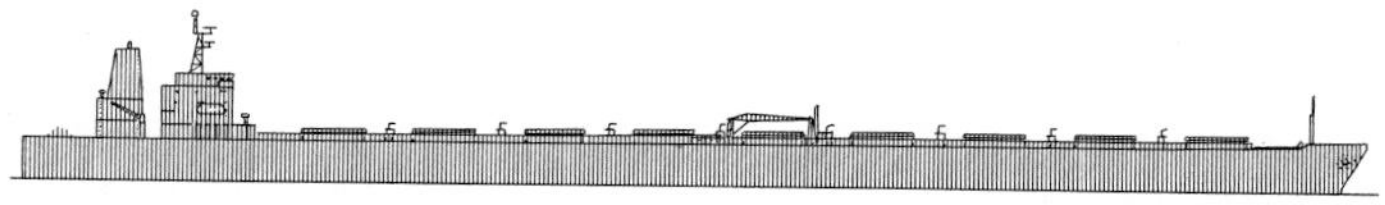

121 M^2SMF *H*
FRONT DRIVER Li/Ko (Hyundai) 1991; OBO; 89,004 grt/134,999 dwt; 284.97 × 15.51 m *(934.94 × 50.89 ft)*; M (B&W); 14.7 kts
Sisters: **FRONT CLIMBER** (Li); **FRONT RIDER** (Sg); Sisters (builder-Daewoo): **FRONT BREAKER** (Li); **FRONT GUIDER** (Sg); **FRONT LEADER** (Bs); **FRONT STRIVER** (Sg); **FRONT VIEWER** (Sg)

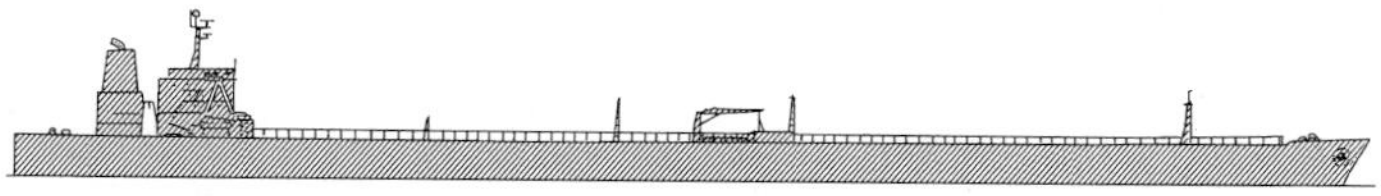

122 M^2SM^2F *H*
EAGLE MI/Ja (Sumitomo) 1993; Tk; 160,347 grt/284,493 dwt; 332.04 × 20.45 m *(1,089.37 × 67.09 ft)*; M (Sulzer); 16 kts

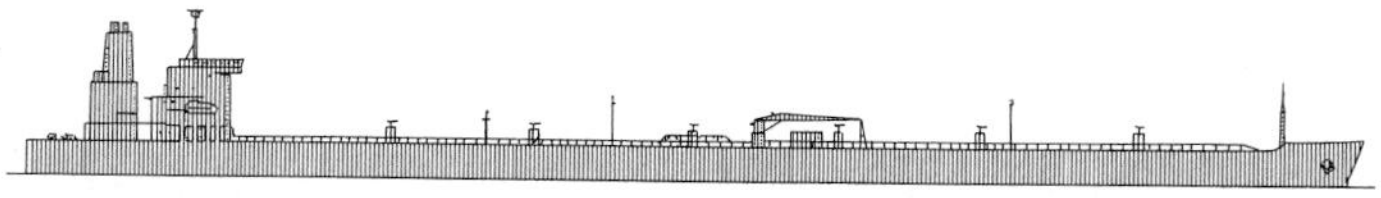

123 M^2SNHF *H*
KNOCK CLUNE Li/Br (H&W S&H) 1993; Tk; 78,843 grt/147,048 dwt; 274.00 × 16.20 m *(898.95 × 53.15 ft)*; M (B&W); 14.4 kts
Sister: **KNOCK DUN** (Li); Probable sister: **KNOCK MUIR** (Li)

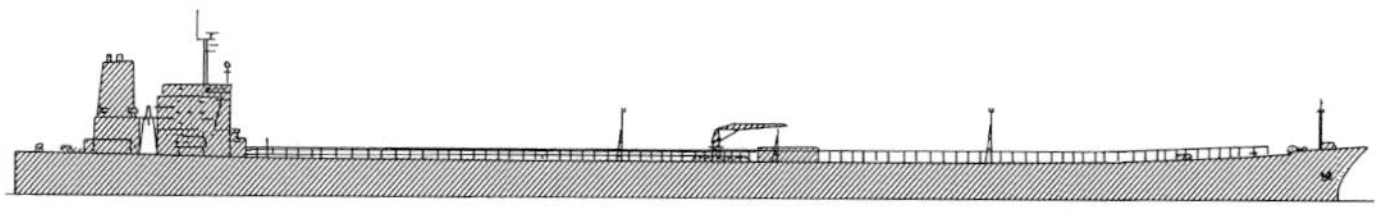

124 M^2SNMF *H*
TARIM NIS/Ja (Hitachi) 1993; Tk; 156,837 grt/280,954 dwt; 328.00 × 22.15 m *(1,076.11 × 72.67 ft)*; M (B&W); 15 kts

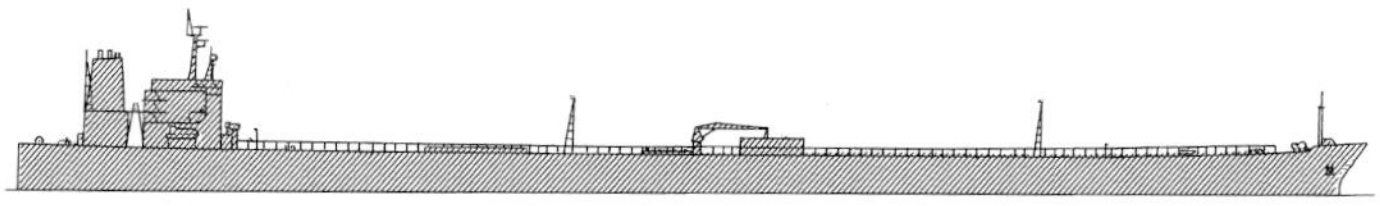

125 M^2SNMFN *H*
GOLDEN FOUNTAIN Pa/Ja (Hitachi) 1995; Tk; 156,303 grt/301,665 dwt; 328.04 × 22.18 m *(1,076.25 × 72.77 ft)*; M (B&W); 15 kts
Probable sister: **GOLDEN STREAM** (Pa)

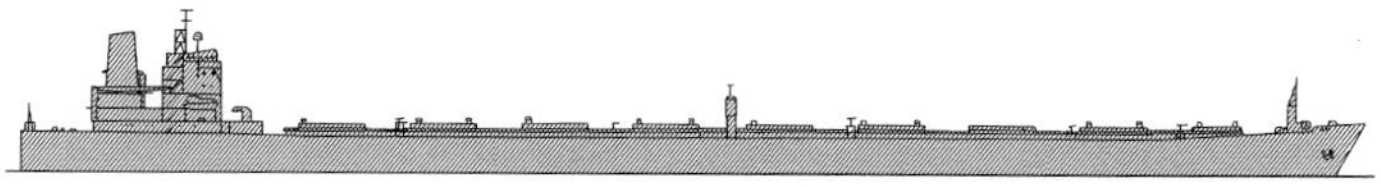

126 *MM-SMRFR H*
WAASLAND Lu/Be (Boelwerf) 1986; OBO; 86,374 grt/164,100 dwt; 274.91 × 18.50 m *(901.94 × 60.70 ft)*; M (B&W); 13 kts

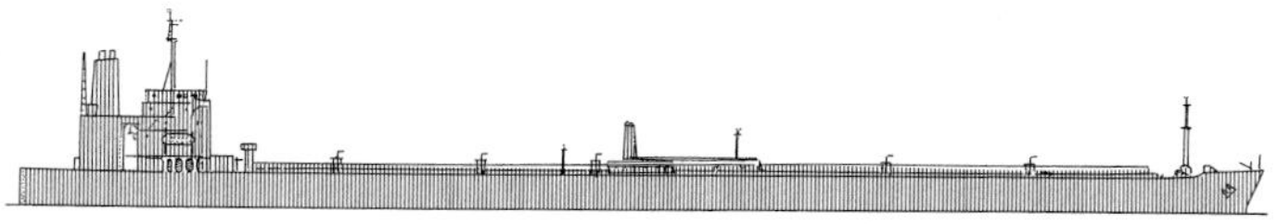

127 *MNCHFN H*
NEW FORTUNER Li/Ja (Kawasaki) 1992; Tk; 78,958 grt/146,041 dwt; 277.00 × 16.53 m *(908.80 × 54.23 ft)*; M (B&W); 14.5 kts
Sister: **ANTINEA** (Bs); Possible sister: **NAUSICAA** (Bs)

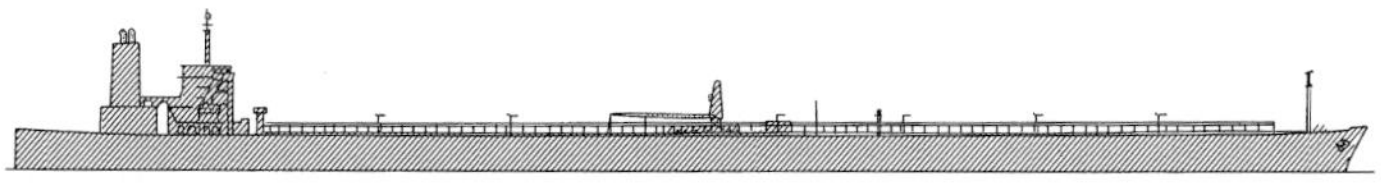

128 *MNDHF H*
APOLLO AKAMA Pa/Ja (Kawasaki) 1994; Tk; 146,849 grt/258,068 dwt; 338.00 × 19.16 m *(1,108.92 × 62.86 ft)*; M (B&W); 16 kts
Sister: **APOLLO OHSHIMA** (Pa)

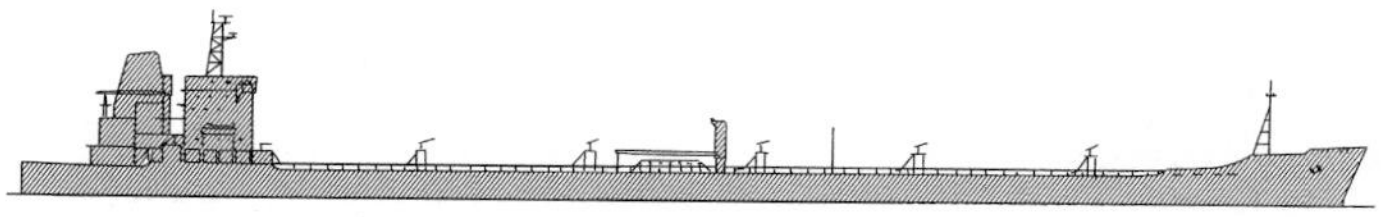

129 *MNDMDF H1*
AGIP LOMBARDIA It/It (FCNI) 1984; Tk; 60,099 grt/113,957 dwt; 257.51 × 15.63 m *(844.85 × 51.28 ft)*; M (GMT); 14.25 kts
Sisters: **AGIP LIGURIA** (It) Sister (taller funnel): **AGIP PIEMONTE** (It)

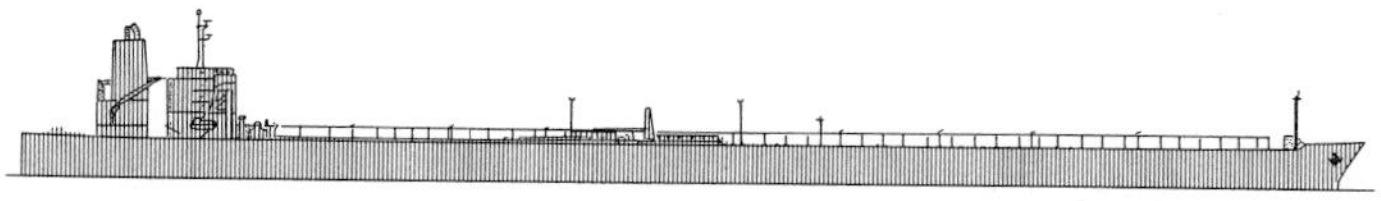

130 $MNDM^2FR$ *H*
BERGE SIGVAL NIS/Ja (NKK Corp) 1993; Tk; 160,214 grt/306,430 dwt; 331.45 × 21.20 m *(1,087.43 × 69.55 ft)*; M (Sulzer); 16.1 kts
Sister: **BERGE STAVANGER** (NIS)

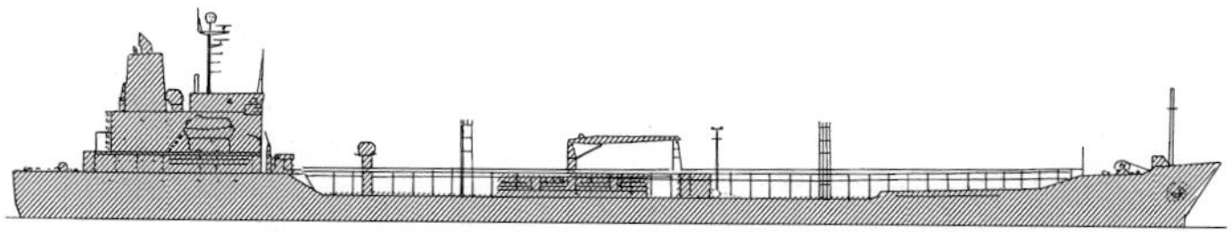

131 $MNENREM^2FR$ *H13*
KAMOGAWA Pa/Ja (Shin Kurushima) 1993; Tk/Ch; 10,829 grt/17,712 dwt; 149.02 × 9.00 m *(488.91 × 29.53 ft)*; M (Mitsubishi); 15.4 kts

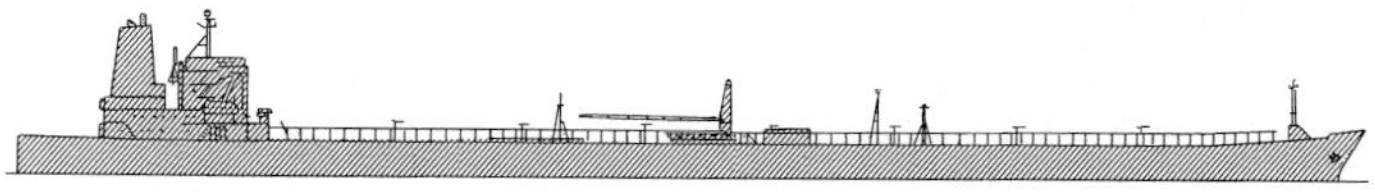

132 *MNMCNHF H*
LONDON PRIDE Br/Ja (Mitsui) 1993; Tk; 79,978 grt/149,686 dwt; 269.00 × 16.84 m *(882.55 × 55.25 ft)*; M (B&W); 14.99 kts
Sister: **LONDON GLORY** (Br)

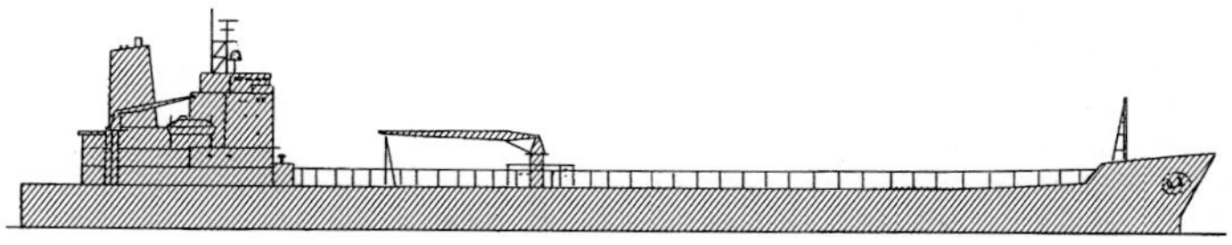

133 *MNMFS H1*
PETROBULK LEOPARD Lu/Be (Boelwerf) 1985; Tk/Ch; 26,113 grt/46,100 dwt; 171.81 × 13.40 m *(563.68 × 43.96 ft)*; M (Sulzer); 14 kts; ex-*Naess Leopard*
Sisters: **PETROBULK LION** (Lu) ex-*Jahre Lion*; **PETROBULK PANTHER** (Lu) ex-*Naess Panther*; **PETROBULK TIGER** (Lu) ex-*Jahre Tiger*; **PETROBULK COUGAR** (Lu); **PETROBULK JAGUAR** (Lu)

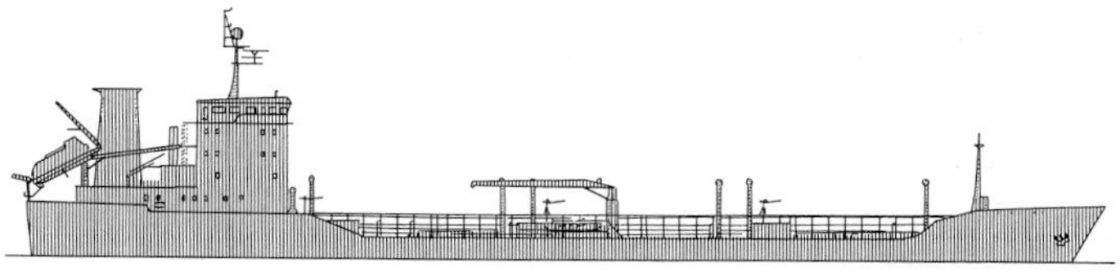

134 MN^3RN^2MFL *H13*
JANANA UAE/Sg (Singmarine) 1993; Tk/Ch; 6,796 grt/9,365 dwt; 127.00 × 7.87 m *(416.67 × 25.82 ft)*; M (MAN); 14.83 kts

135 *MNRMF H*
NAMSAM SPIRIT Li/Ko (Hyundai) 1988; Tk; 59,289 grt/106,666 dwt; 244.08 × 14.66 m *(800.79 × 48.10 ft)*; M (B&W); 14 kts
Probable sisters: **FRONTIER SPIRIT** (Li); **PIONEER SPIRIT** (Li); Similar: **JAHRE PRINCE** (NIS) ex-*Friendship Venture*; Possibly similar: **BONA SPARROW** (Bs) ex-*Golden Fleece*

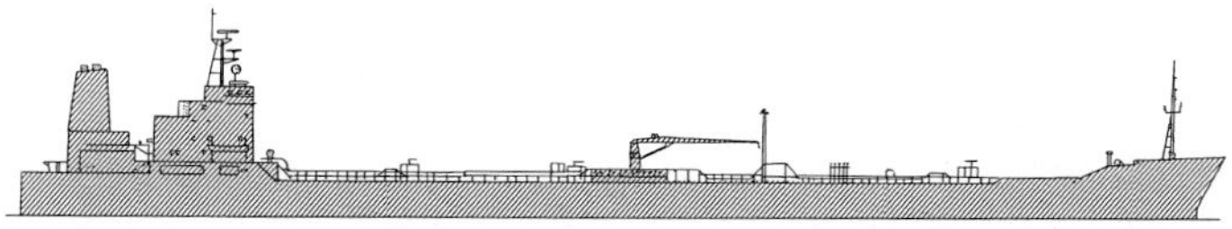

136 *MNRMF H1*
KRITI FILOXENIA Gr/Ys ('Split') 1986; Tk; 26,874 grt/45,243 dwt; 194.50 × 11.40 m *(638.12 × 37.40 ft)*; M (B&W); 14.8 kts
Sisters: **KRITI COLOR** (Gr); **KRITI CHAMPION** (Gr); **KRITI PALM** (Gr); **ZADAR** (Li)

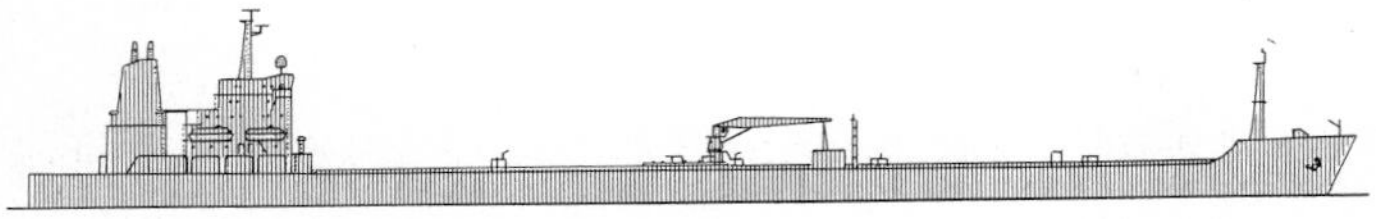

137 *MNRMF H1*
SUBEDAR JOGINDER SINGH PVC In/Ko (Hyundai) 1984; Tk; 37,855 grt/67,137 dwt; 228.61 × 13.60 m *(750.03 × 44.62 ft)*; M (Sulzer); 12.75 kts
Sisters: **CAPTAIN GURBACHAN SINGH SALARIA PVC** (In); **HAVILDAR ABDUL HAMID PVC** (In); **COMPANY HAVILDAR MAJOR PIRU SINGH PVC** (In); **LANCE NAIK KARAM SINGH PVC** (In); **LIEUTENANT RAMA RAGHOBA RANE PVC** (In); **MAJOR DHAN SINGH THAPA PVC** (In); **MAJOR SHAITAN SINGH PVC** (In); **MAJOR SOMNATH SHARMA PVC** (In); **NAIK JADUNATH SINGH PVC** (In); Similar (smaller): **LANCE NAIK ALBERT EKKA PVC** (In): **FLYING OFFICER NIRMAL JIT SEKHON PVC** (In); **LIEUTENANT ARUN KHETARPAL PVC** (In); **MAJOR HOSHIAR SINGH PVC** (In)

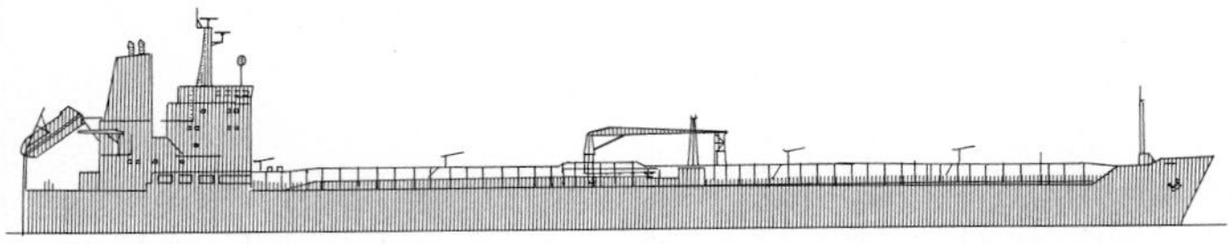

138 *MNRMFL H1*
ARBAT Li/Ko (Halla) 1991; Tk; 28,223 grt/47,083 dwt; 183.20 × 12.21 m *(601.05 × 40.06 ft)*; M (B&W); 14.5 kts
Sisters: **FILI** (Cy); **IZMAYLOVO** (Li); **NAGATINO** (Li); **OSTANKINO** (Cy); **POLYANKA** (Cy); **PRESNYA** (Cy); **SOKOLNIKI** (Cy); **HADRA** (Ne); **HALIA** (Ne); **HAMINEA** (Li); **HASTULA** (Ne); **HATASIA** (Li); Possible sisters: **PORT ALEXANDRE** (Kn); **PORT ARTHUR** (Kn)

139 *MNRMFN H*
BONA SPRING Bs/Ko (Hyundai) 1986; Tk; 52,862 grt/94,752 dwt; 243.87 × 13.62 m *(800.10 × 44.69 ft)*; M (B&W); — kts; ex-*Fortune*

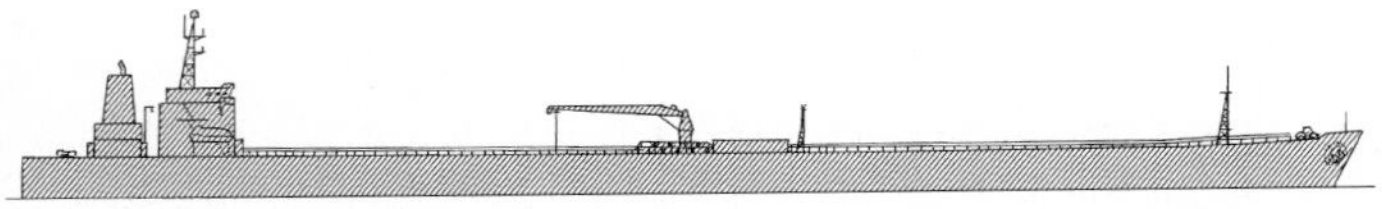

140 *MNRM²F H*
AMERICAN PEGASUS Sg/Ja (Sumitomo) 1988; Tk; 52,159 grt/91,680 dwt; 232.04 × 12.27 m *(761.29 × 40.26 ft)*; M (Sulzer); 15.5 kts; ex-*Caribbean First*
Possible sisters: **NORD-JAHRE PRESIDENT** (NIS) ex-*Jahre President*; **NORD-JAHRE PRINCESS** (NIS) ex-*Jahre Princess*; **NORD-JAHRE PROGRESS** (NIS) ex-*Jahre Progress*; **TROMAAS** (NIS)

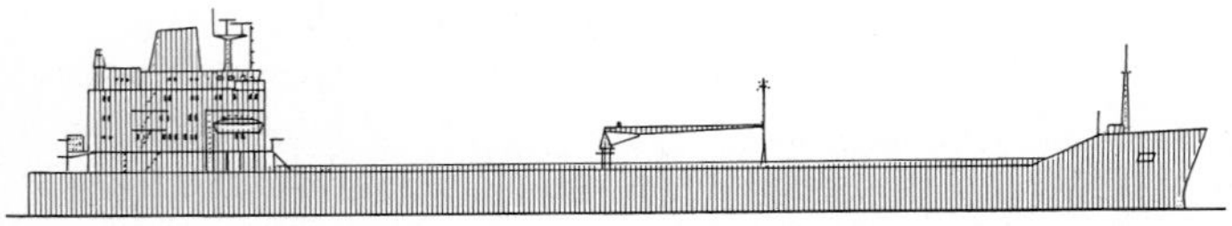

141 *MNRNMFR H1*
ROBERT MAERSK DIS/De (Odense) 1986; Tk/Ch; 16,282 grt/27,350 dwt; 170.01 × 11.41 m *(557.78 × 37.43 ft)*; M (B&W); 15 kts
Sisters: **RAS MAERSK** (DIS); **RASMINE MAERSK** (DIS): **RITA MAERSK** (DIS); **ROMO MAERSK** (DIS)

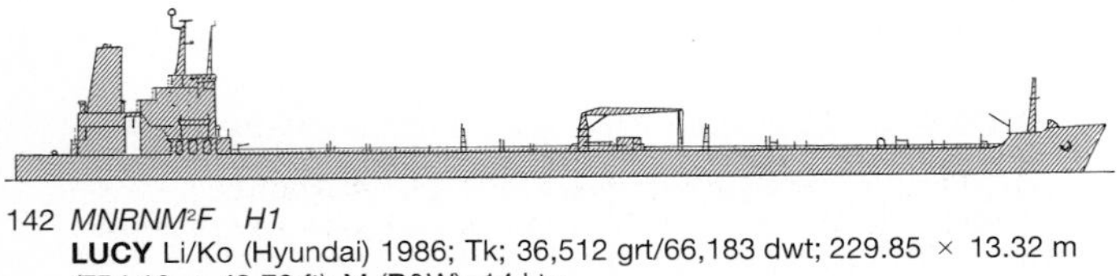

142 *MNRNM²F H1*
LUCY Li/Ko (Hyundai) 1986; Tk; 36,512 grt/66,183 dwt; 229.85 × 13.32 m *(754.10 × 43.70 ft)*; M (B&W); 14 kts
Sister: **SUZANNE** (Li)

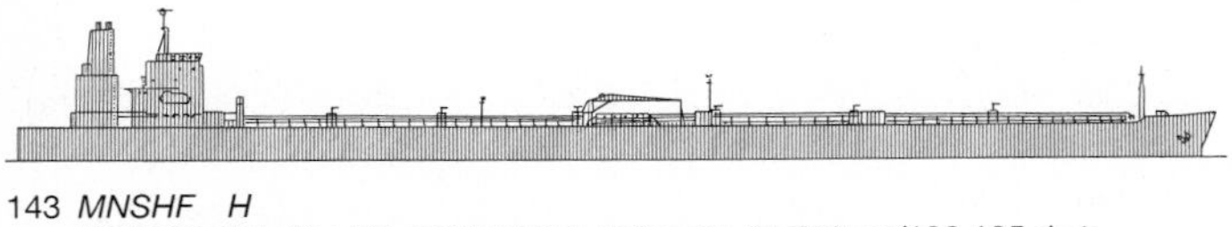

143 *MNSHF H*
KNOCK ALLAN Li/Br (H&W S&H) 1992; Tk; 78,710 grt/138,105 dwt; 274.00 × 15.90 m *(898.95 × 52.17 ft)*; M (B&W); 14.4 kts
Sisters: **KNOCK STOCKS** (Li); **JAG LAADKI** (In) ex-*Knock Adoon*

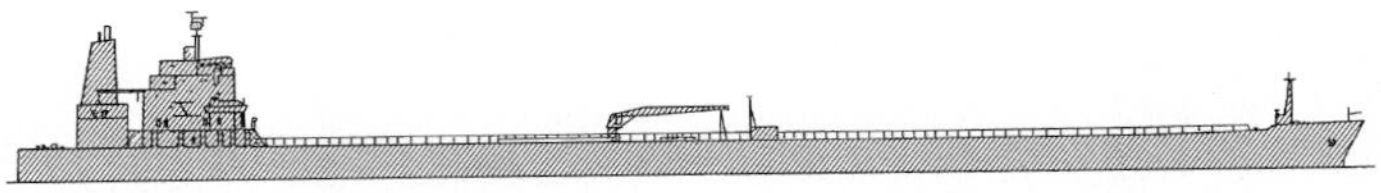

144 *MNSHF H*
SOLARIS Ne/Ko (Hyundai) 1985; Tk; 56,456 grt/83,701 dwt; 244.51 × 14.60 m *(802.20 × 47.90 ft)*; M (B&W); 15 kts
Sisters: **SERICATA** (Ne); **SPECTRUM** (Ne); **SPONSALIS** (Ne); **STELLATA** (Ne)

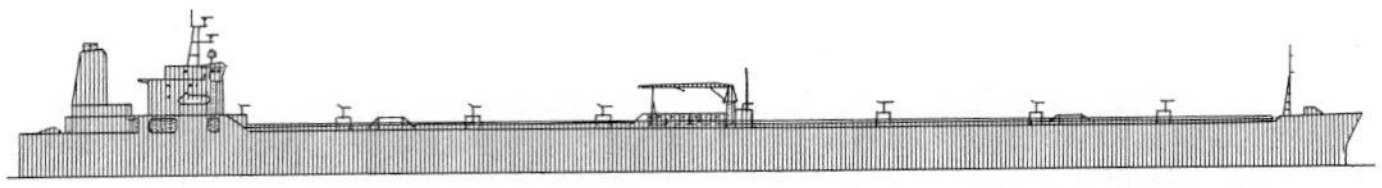

145 *MNSMF H*
NORD-JAHRE TRAVELLER NIS/Ys ('Split') 1990; Tk; 77,931 grt/142,031 dwt; 269.02 × 15.95 m *(882.61 × 52.33 ft)*; M (B&W); 14 kts; ex-*Jahre Traveller*
Sisters: **NORD-JAHRE TARGET** (NIS) ex-*Jahre Target*; **NORD-JAHRE TRANSPORTER** (NIS) ex-*Jahre Transporter*; **GRANITE** (Bs); **JAHRE TRADER** (NIS)

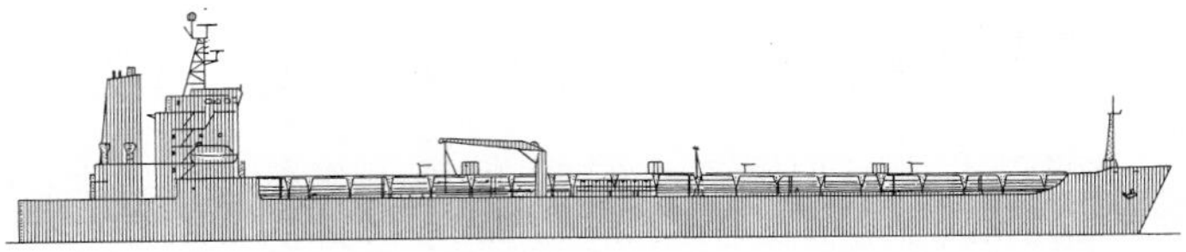

146 *MNSMF H1*
FANDANGO Pa/Sp (AESA) 1991; Tk/Ch; 28,256 grt/46,118 dwt; 182.85 × 12.25 m *(599.90 × 40.19 ft)*; M (B&W); 14 kts
Sister: **FLAMENCO** (Sw)

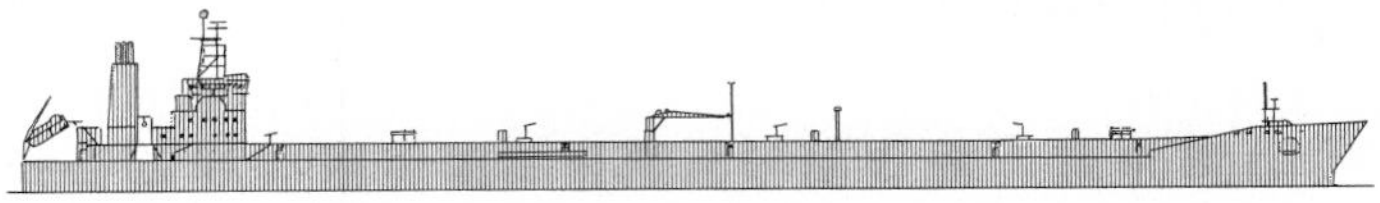

147 *MNSMFL H1*
FUTURA Fi/Fi (Kvaerner Masa) 1992; Tk; 50,907 grt/96,059 dwt; 241.00 × 14.50 m *(790.68 × 47.57 ft)*; M (Wärtsilä); 14 kts; Fitted for offshore-loading

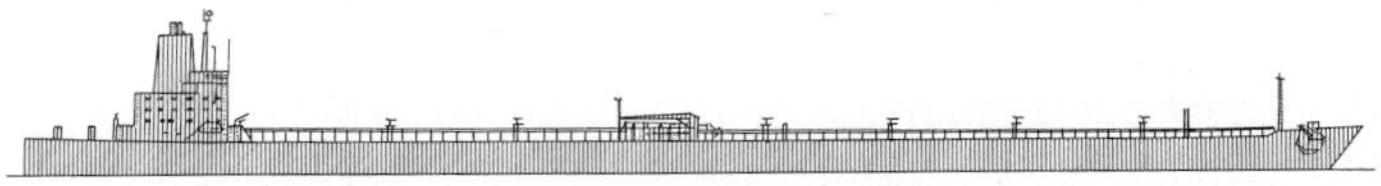

148 *MNSMFR H*
ELEO MAERSK DIS/De (Odense) 1992; Tk; 158,475 grt/298,900 dwt; 343.71 × 21.53 m *(1,127.66 × 70.64 ft)*; M (Mitsubishi); 14 kts
Sisters: **ELISABETH MAERSK** (DIS); **EMMA MAERSK** (DIS); **ESTELLE MAERSK** (DIS)

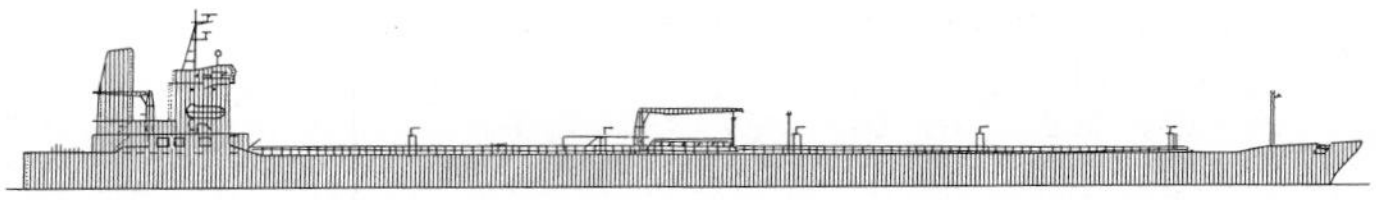

149 *MNSMRF H*
ECO EUROPA It/It (FCNI) 1994; Tk; 79,516 grt/146,698 dwt; 275.72 × 16.12 m *(904.59 × 52.89 ft)*; M (Sulzer); 14 kts
Sister: **ECO AFRICA** (It)

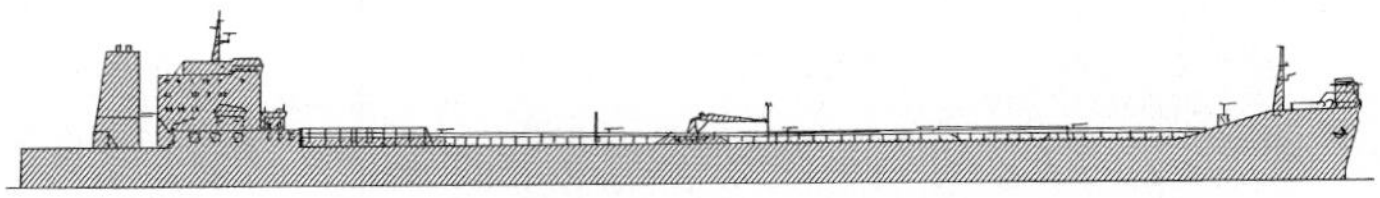

150 *MNSNMF H1*
BERGINA No/Ko (Daewoo) 1982; Tk; 77,704 grt/134,089 dwt; 265.01 × 15.02 m *(869.46 × 49.28 ft)*; M (B&W); 14 kts; ex-*Jarena*; Equipped for offshore-loading

See photo number 1/256

151 *MRERERMF H13*
JO LONN NA/No (Bergens) 1982; Tk/Ch; 21,568 grt/39,273 dwt; 175.01 × 10.74 m *(574 × 35.24 ft)*; M (B&W); 15.5 kts
Sisters: **JO BIRK** (NA); **JO OAK** (NA)

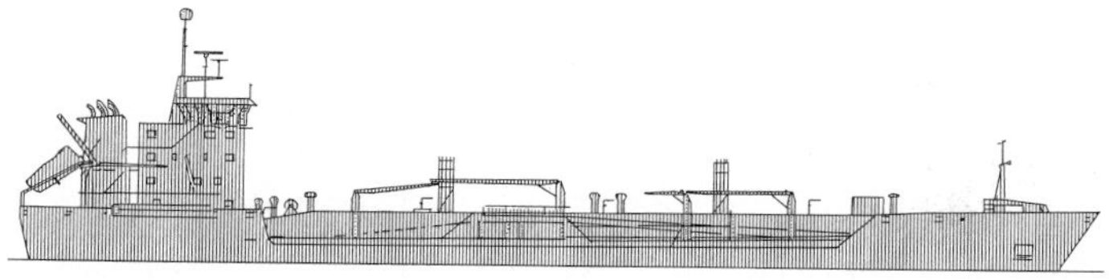

152 *MRER^{2}EMFL H13*
TRANS ARCTIC NIS/Ge (Suerken) 1991; Tk/Ch; 4,712 grt/6,930 dwt; 116.80 × 7.70 m *(383.20 × 25.26 ft)*; M (Normo); 15 kts
Sister: **TRANS SCANDIC** (NIS)

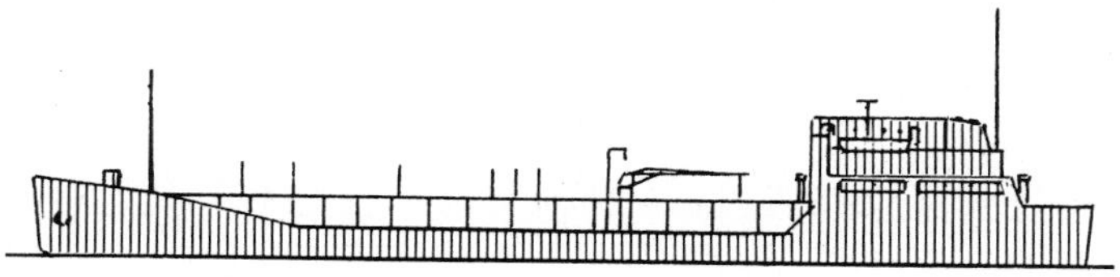

153 *MRFM H13*
BELYAYEVKA Uk/Sw (Lodose) 1971; Tk; 1,599 grt/3,362 dwt; 87.00 × 4.85 m *(285.43 × 15.91 ft)*; M (Ruston); 10.5 kts; ex-*Venern*; Ice strengthened
Sister: **BEREZINO** (Uk) ex-*Melaren*

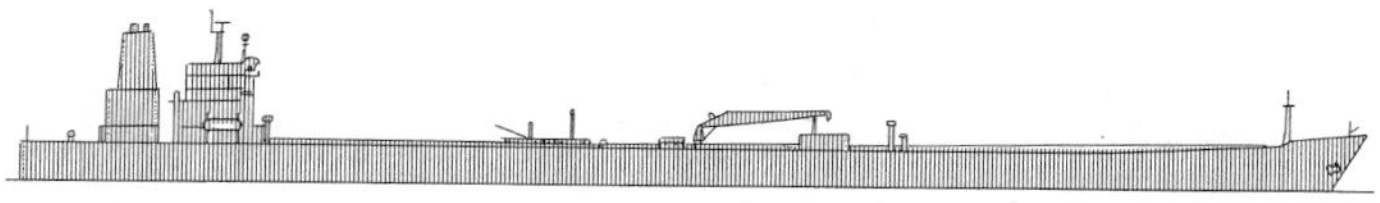

154 *MRHF H*
NISYROS Li/Ja (IHI) 1992; Tk; 81,110 grt/143,932 dwt; 274.30 × 16.93 m *(899.93 × 55.54 ft)*; M (Sulzer); 14.3 kts
Sister: **NAROVA** (Li)

See photo number 1/262

155 *MRMF*
KIHU Fi/Fi (Wärtsilä) 1984; Tk/Ch; 13,974 grt/19,999 dwt; 160.92 × 10.11 m *(527.95 × 33.2 ft)*; M (Pielstick); 14.5 kts
Sister: **TAVI** (Fi)

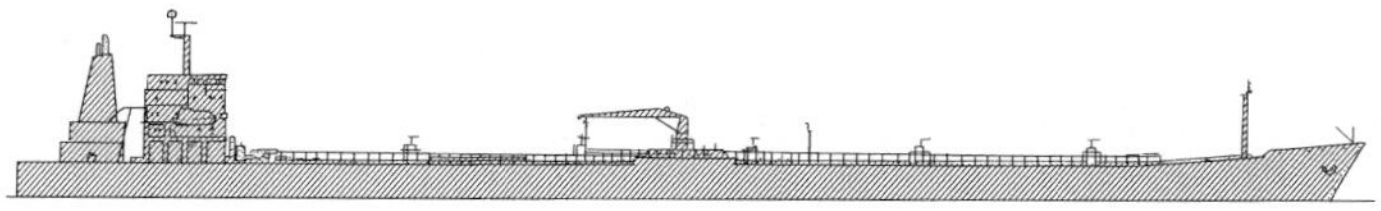

156 *MRMF H*
BURWAIN ADRIATIC Li/De (B&W) 1990; Tk; 43,398 grt/84,000 dwt; 228.60 × 13.89 m *(750.00 × 45.57 ft)*; M (B&W); 15.75 kts; ex-*Zafra*; 'CPT54E' Type
Sisters: **SITACAMILLA** (—) ex-*Chrisholm*; **SITAMARIE** (—) ex-*Fredholm*; **PETROBULK MARS** (Va); **PETROBULK JUPITER** (Li); **BURWAIN TORM** (Li) ex-*Zaria*; **NORTHSEA ANVIL** (Li) ex-*Zaphon*; **BURWAIN ARCTIC** (Li) ex-*Zidona*; Probable sister: **TORM MARGRETHE** (Li)

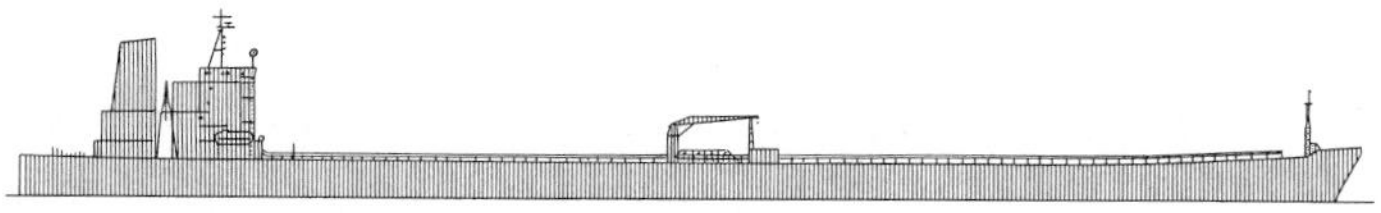

157 *MRMF/MSMF H*
EOS Pa/Ko (Hyundai) 1993; Tk; 54,827 grt/99,440 dwt; 243.97 × 12.95 m *(800.43 × 42.49 ft)*; M (B&W); 16 kts
Sisters: **NEREO** (Pa); **TESEO** (Pa); **PARNASO** (Pa); **PROTEO** (Pa); **ICARO** (Pa); **HERO** (Pa)

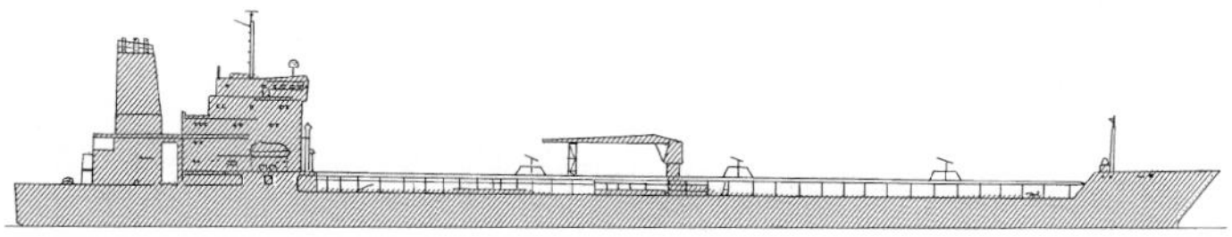

158 *MRMF H1*
ANAHUAC Me/Fr (L'Atlantique) 1986; Tk; 18,960 grt/32,148 dwt; 178.19 × 11.38 m *(584.61 × 37.34 ft)*; M (B&W); 14 kts; ex-*Penhors*
Sisters: **AL DHABBIYYAH** (UAE); **ARZANAH** (UAE); **YAMILAH** (UAE)

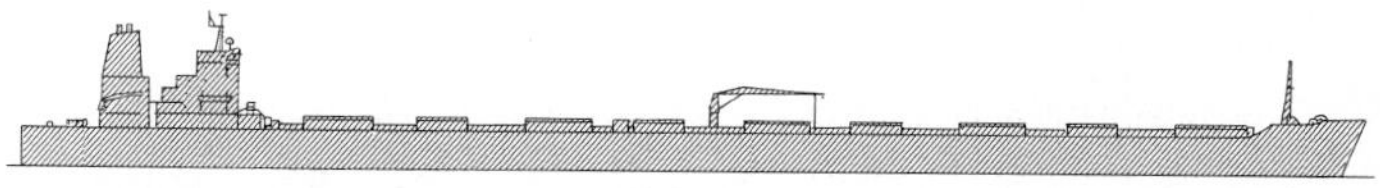

159 *MRMF H1*
CHOCTAW HK/Ko (Hyundai) 1986; OBO; 84,788 grt/152,329 dwt; 280.14 × 17.02 m *(919.09 × 55.84 ft)*; M (Sulzer); 14.5 kts
Probable sister: **CHICKASAW** (HK)

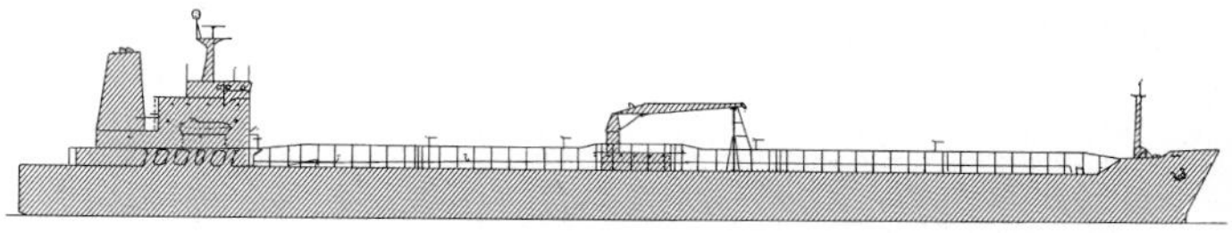

160 *MRMF H1*
SAMOTHRAKI Gr/Ko (Korea SB) 1989; Tk; 27,793 grt/46,538 dwt; 182.88 × 12.20 m *(600.00 × 40.03 ft)*; M (B&W); 14.62 kts
Sisters: **HALKI** (Gr); **PSARA** (Gr); **SHINOUSSA** (Gr)

161 *MRMF H1*
STAPAFELL Ic/FRG (Hitzler) 1979; Tk; 1,432 grt/2,038 dwt; 75.74 × 4.79 m *(248.49 × 15.72 ft)*; M (KHD); 13.5 kts

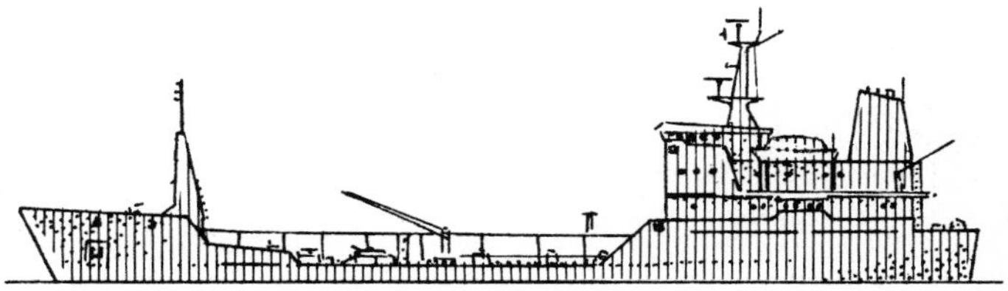

162 *MRMF H13*
BUNA Pa/Ne (Vuyk) 1979; Ch; 1,561 grt/1,760 dwt; 73.46 × 4.91 m *(241 × 16.11 ft)*; M (Atlas-MaK); 13 kts
Sister: **ECOMAR II** (Cro) ex-*Schkopau*

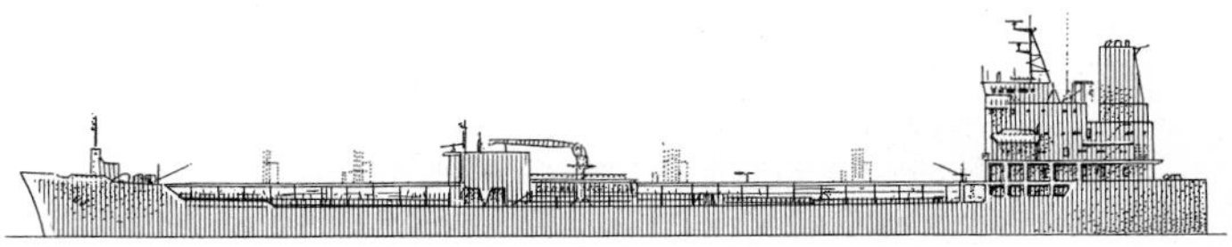

163 *MRMF H13*
JO GRAN NIS/Sw (Kockums) 1980; Ch; 23,194 grt/37,532 dwt; 175.01 × 10.7 m *(574.18 × 35.1 ft)*; TSM (Pielstick); 16.25 kts; ex-*Johnson Chemstar*
Sister: **JO ROGN** (NIS) ex-*Johnson Chemsun*

164 *MRMF H13*
MOSTRAUM NIS/Sw (Oskarshamns) 1981; Ch; 5,973 grt/8,661 dwt; 129.65 × 6.97 m *(425.36 × 22.87 ft)*; M (Sulzer); 14.25 kts; ex-*OT-Phosphorus*
Sisters: **VIKSTRAUM** (NIS) ex-*Ot-Acid*; **CT STAR** (Br) ex-*OT-Sulphur*; Similar: **AURUM** (Sw); **ARGENTUM** (—)

165 *MRMF H13*
PORT ROYAL Tu/Fi (Wärtsilä) 1982; Tk; 26,450 grt/44,993 dwt; 187.64 × 11.62 m *(616 × 38.12 ft)*; M (Sulzer); 14 kts; ex-*Parita*

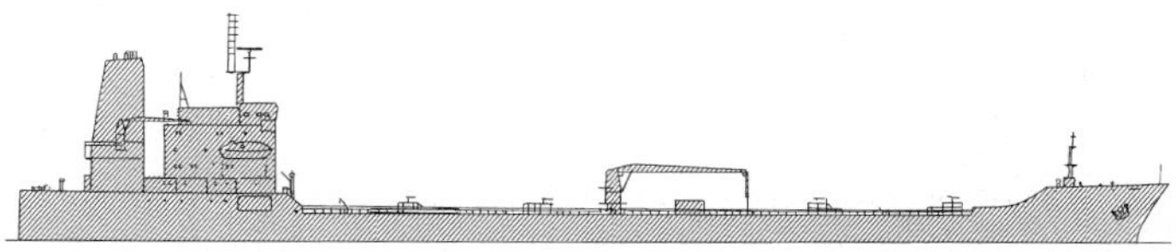

166 *MRMF H13*
REBOUCAS Bz/Bz (Caneco) 1989; Tk; 20,180 grt/30,650 dwt; 175.46 × 10.30 m *(575.66 × 33.79 ft)*; M (B&W); 13.8 kts
Sister: **RODEIO** (Bz)

See photo number 1/263

167 *MRMF H13*
TEBO OLYMPIA Fi/Fi (Valmet) 1980; Tk; 8,825 grt/11,474 dwt; 140.93 × 7.3 m *(462 × 23.95 ft)*; M (Wärtsilä); 15 kts
Sisters: **ACILA** (Ne) ex-*Shelltrans*; **MELKKI** (Fi) ex-*Polar Scan*; **RANKKI** (Sw) ex-*Arctic Scan*

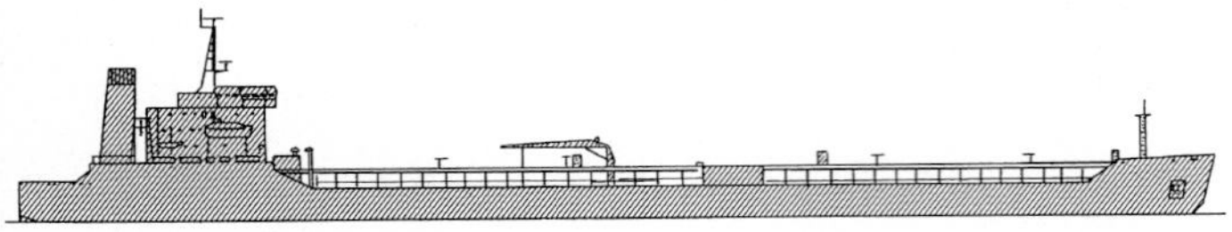

168 *MRMF H13*
TERVI Fi/Fi (Rauma-Repola) 1986; Tk; 28,292 grt/48,375 dwt; 202.11 × 12.50 m *(663.09 × 41.01 ft)*; M (Sulzer); 14 kts; Ice strengthened
Sister: **PALVA** (Fi)

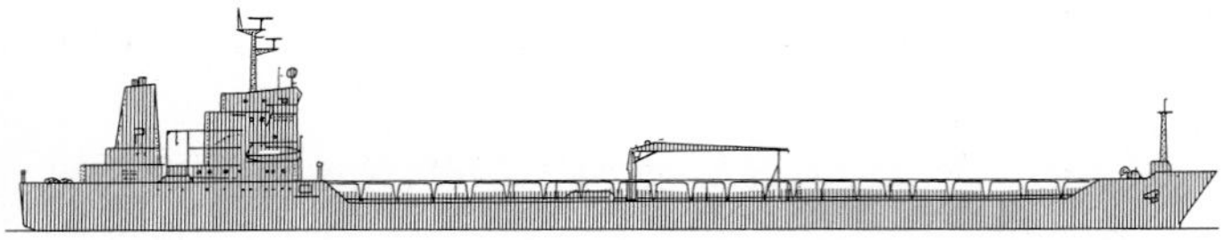

169 *MRMF H13*
TIRUMALAI In/Sp (AESA) 1991; Ch; 21,035 grt/31,004 dwt; 175.25 × 9.12 m *(574.97 × 29.92 ft)*; M (B&W); 15 kts
Sisters: **PALANIMALAI** (In); **SABARIMELAI** (In)

See photo number 1/260

170 *MRMF H13*
VIKLA Fi/Fi (Valmet) 1982; Ch; 6,763 grt/8,388 dwt; 133.31 × 7.22 m *(437 × 23.69 ft)*; M (Pielstick); 15 kts

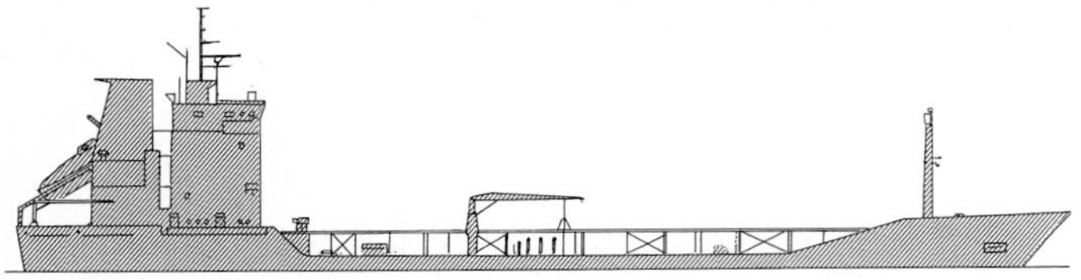

171 *MRMFL H13*
AWASH Et/FRG (Lindenau) 1989; Tk; 2,492 grt/3,618 dwt; 94.50 × 5.41 m *(310.04 × 17.75 ft)*; M (MaK); 12.6 kts

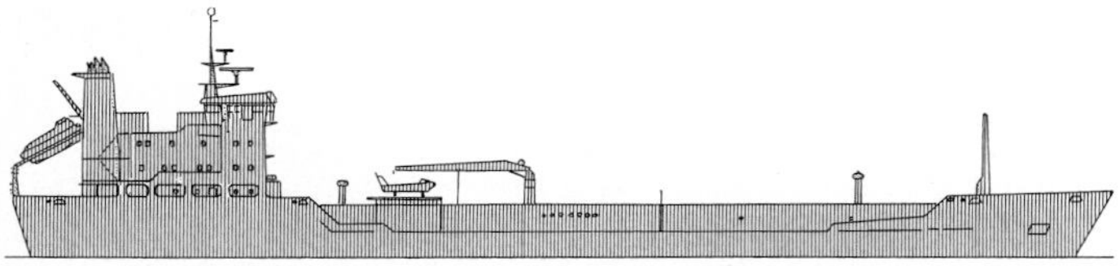

172 *MRMFL H13*
FUREVIK Sw/Sw (Marstrands) 1990; Tk/Ch; 5,774 grt/8,490 dwt; 120.30 × 7.83 m *(394.69 × 25.69 ft)*; M (MaK); 14.7 kts

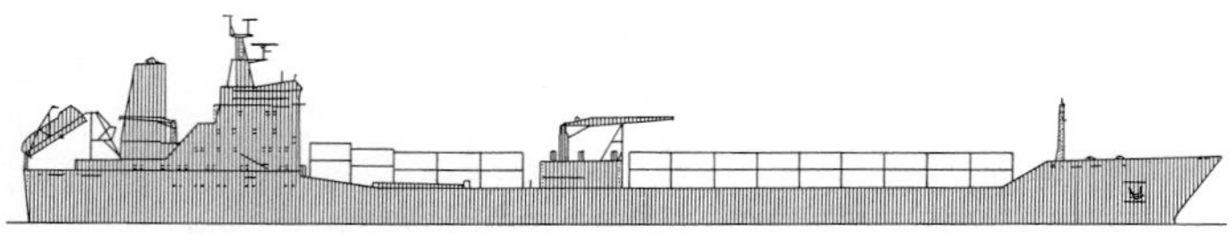

173 *MRMFL H13*
OURO DO BRASIL Li/No (K Kleven F) 1993; FJ; 15,218 grt/18,600 dwt; 173.00 × 9.50 m *(567.59 × 31.17 ft)*; M (Sulzer); 20 kts

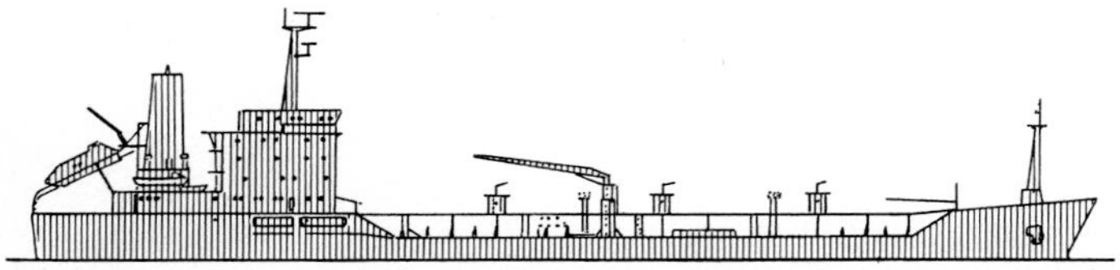

174 *MRMFL H13*
SAN GIOVANNI Gr/Sp (AESA) 1987; Ch; 8,003 grt/9,999 dwt; 126.45 × 7.20 m *(414.86 × 23.62 ft)*; M (B&W); 13.75 kts; ex-*Vasiliy Merkuryev*
Sisters: **SAN MARINO** (Gr) ex-*Ivan Pyrev*; **SAN MATEO** (Gr) ex-*Mikhail Romm*; **SAN PEDRO** (Gr) ex-*Mikhail Kalatozov*

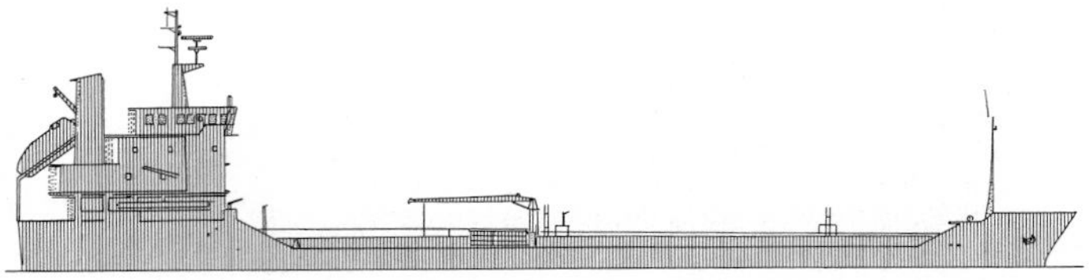

175 *MRMFL H13*
STENA BARBADOS Bs/Sg (Argos) 1991; Tk/Ch; 4,094 grt/6,330 dwt; 101.52 × 6.07 m *(333.07 × 19.91 ft)*; M (Normo); 10.2 kts; ex-*Katarina*
Sister: **AMBROISE** (Fr) ex-*Kristina*

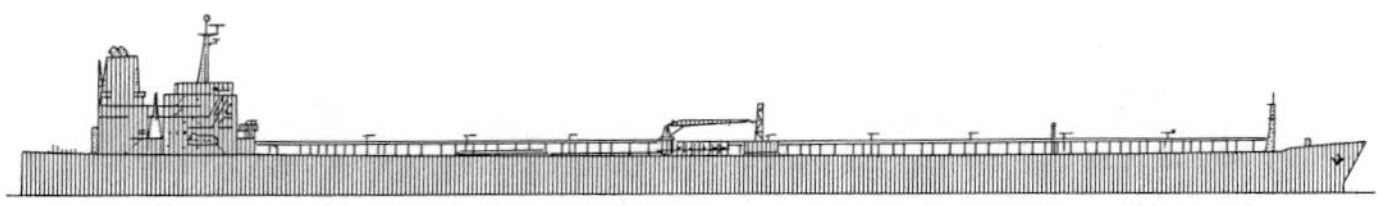

176 *MRMFLR H13*
AGILITY Br/Br (Richards) 1990; Tk; 1,930 grt/3,144 dwt; 70.95 × 5.60 m *(232.78 × 18.37 ft)*; M (Ruston); 11.5 kts
Sister: **ALACRITY** (Br)

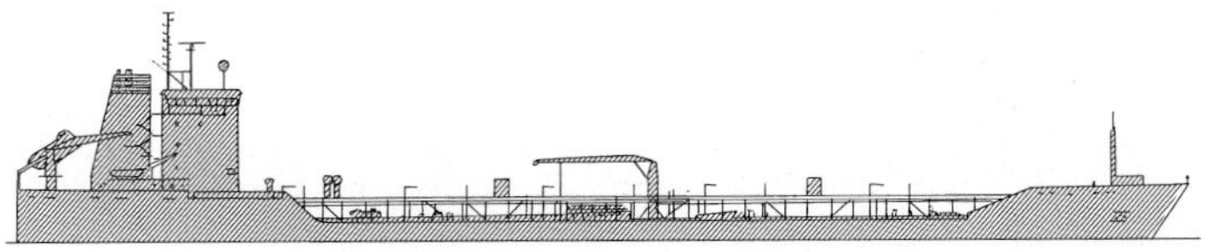

177 *MRMFLR H13*
JIAN SHE 51 RC/Ge (Lindenau) 1995; Tk; 7,894 grt/13,144 dwt; 142.85 × 8.37 m *(468.67 × 27.46 ft)*; M (MaK); 14 kts
Sister: **JIAN SHE 52** (RC)

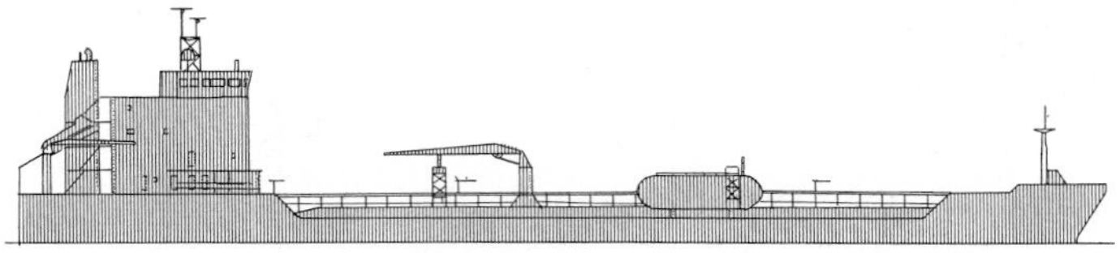

178 *MRMFLR H13*
NATHALIE SIF DIS/Ko (Hyundai) 1993; Tk/Ch; 6,544 grt/9,176 dwt; 116.59 × 7.81 m *(382.51 × 25.62 ft)*; M (MaK); 14.1 kts; Funnel is on port side and forward tanks are on port and starboard. Crane aft is on starboard side
Sisters: **MALENE SIF** (DIS); **ANN SIF** (DIS)

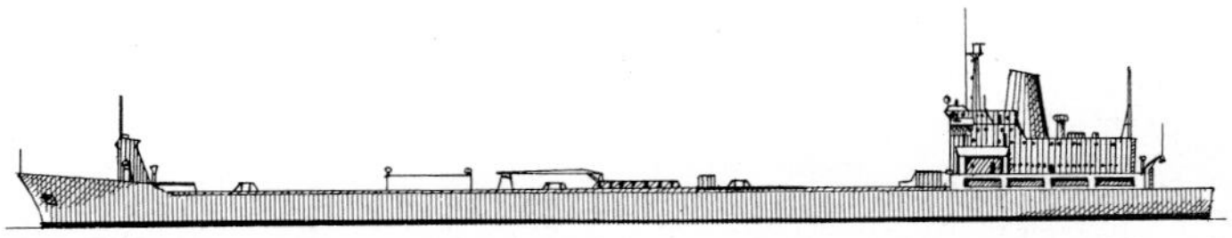

179 *MRMFM H1*
FJORDSHELL No/No (Haugesund) 1974; Tk; 17,966 grt/32,477 dwt; 170.69 × 11.37 m *(560 × 37.3 ft)*; M (Sulzer); 16 kts

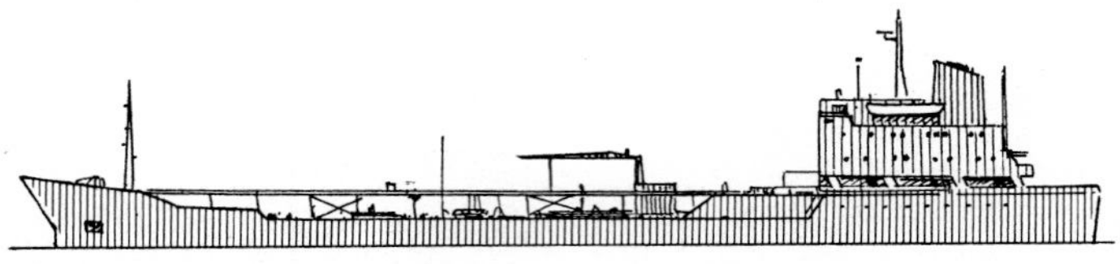

180 *MRMFM H13*
ETTORE It/No (Ankerlokken) 1974; Tk; 4,454 grt/7,250 dwt; 107.93 × 8.08 m *(354.1 × 26.51 ft)*; M (B&W); 14 kts; ex-*Joarctic*
Sisters: **SAN NICOLAS** (Fr) ex-*Joalaska* 1978; **CROMA** (Sw) ex-*Joatlantic*

See photo number 1/265

181 *MRMFMR H13*

GONIO Ma/Ys ('Split') 1984; Tk; 10,937 grt/16,421 dwt; 151.31 × 8.50 m *(496.42 × 27.89 ft)*; M (MAN); 15 kts; ex-*J Broz Tito*
Sisters (some may have modified appearance -see *Vekua*): **KAPITAN NAGONYUK** (Ru); **VACHNADZE** (Ma) ex-*Nata Vachnadze*; **YUSUP K** (Ru) ex-*Yusup Kobaladze*; **KACHARAVA** (Ma) ex-*Kapitan A Kacharava*; **MAKATSARIA** (Ma) ex-*Kapitan Makatsariya*; **BAKRADZE** (Ma) ex-*David Bakradze*; **KOBULETI** (Ma) ex-*Bolshevik Kamo*; **KAPITAN YERSHOV** (Ru) (builder—'3 Maj'); **DZINTARI** (Li) ex-*Moris Bishop*; **ROPAZI** (La) ex-*Panteleymon Ponomarenko*; **OJARS VACIETIS** (Cy) ex-*Oyar Vatsietis*; **ZANIS GRIVA** (Li) ex-*Zhan Griva*; **KEMERI** (Li) ex-*Yuliy Danishevskiy*; **ILYA ERENBURG** (Ru)

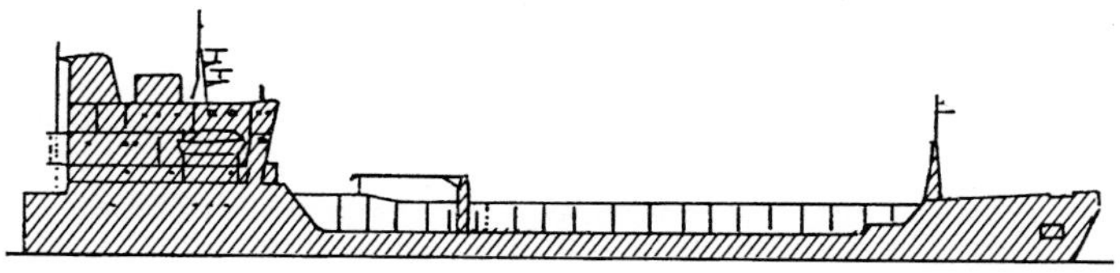

182 *MRMFN H13*

UNITED TONY Sw/Sw (Falkenbergs) 1982; Ch; 2,593 grt/4,165 dwt; 88.02 × 6.40 m *(288.78 × 21.00 ft)*; M (Nohab); 13.5 kts; ex-*Lecko av Lidkoping*

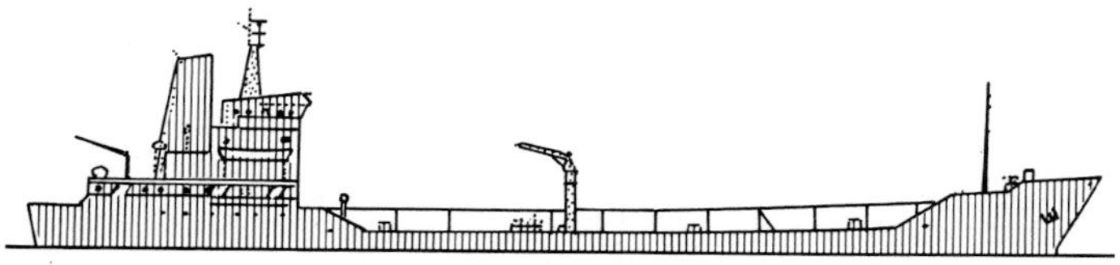

183 *MRMFR H13*

AMPURIAS Sp/Sp (UN de Levante) 1985; AT; 3,931 grt/6,089 dwt; 106.51 × 7.70 m *(349.44 × 25.26 ft)*; M (MAN); 15.25 kts; ex-*Proas Dos*

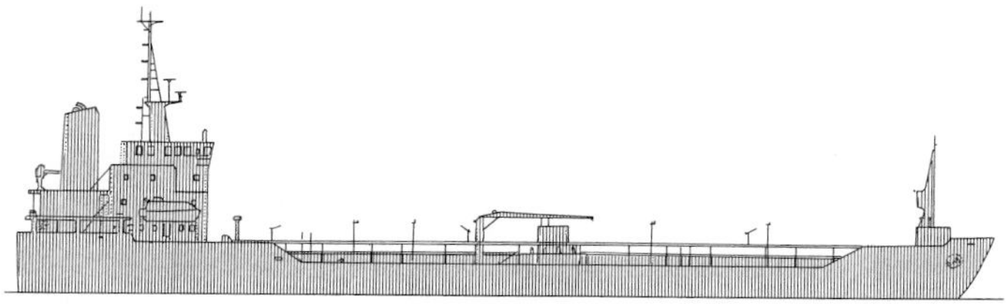

184 *MRMFR H13*

ANCHORMAN Li/My (Malaysia S&E) 1993; Tk; 4,842 grt/6,417 dwt; 101.60 × 6.85 m *(333.33 × 22.47 ft)*; M (Blackstone); 12.5 kts
Sisters: **CHARTSMAN** (Li); **RUDDERMAN** (Li); **STEERSMAN** (Li)

185 *MRMG H13*

FINJA Fi/Fi (Navire) 1981; Ch; 4,468 grt/6,954 dwt; 107.02 × 7.3 m *(351 × 23.95 ft)*; TSM (Wärtsilä); 13.5 kts; ex-*Esso Finlandia*

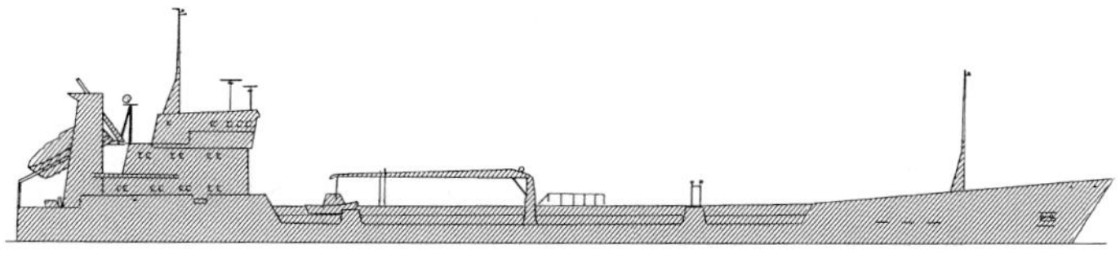

186 *MRMGL H13*

ELLA TERKOL DIS/De (Nordso) 1990; Ch; 1,711 grt/3,294 dwt; 83.50 × 5.46 m *(273.95 × 17.91 ft)*; M (MaK); 10.5 kts
Sisters: **ELSE TERKOL** (DIS); **GRETE TERKOL** (DIS); **HELLE TERKOL** (DIS); **INGRID TERKOL** (DIS); **LEA TERKOL** (DIS); **LONE TERKOL** (DIS); **ANNUITY** (Br) ex-*Janne Terkol*

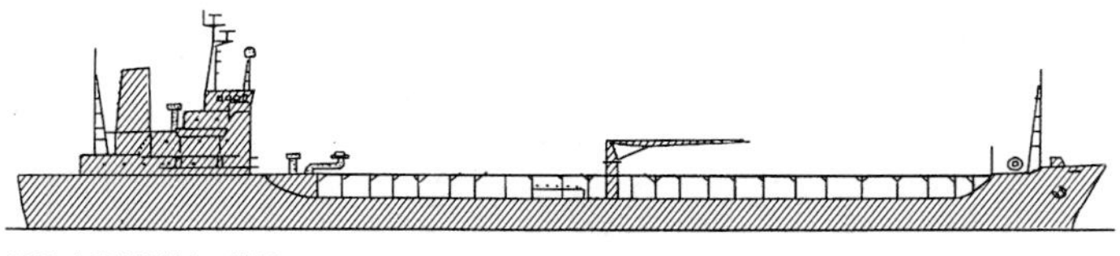

187 *MRM²FM H13*

TOMIWAKA Pa/Ja (Shikoku) 1986; Tk/Ch/MT; 9,792 × 16,933 dwt; 143.03 × 9.02 m *(469.26 × 29.59 ft)*; M (B&W); 13.5 kts
Similar (Funnel shape differs. After masts nearer funnel): **ASUKA ROAD** (Sg)

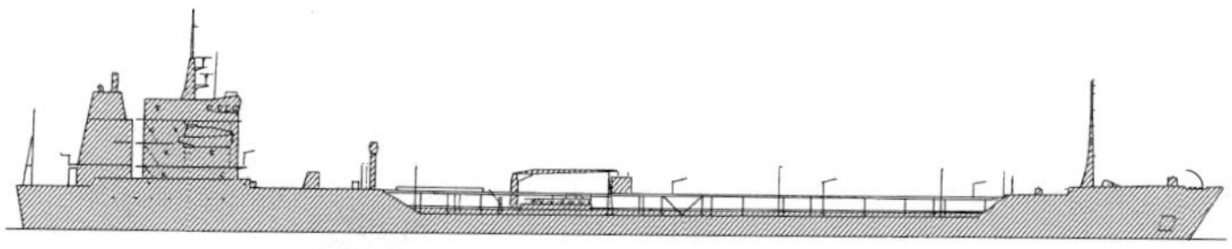

188 *MRM²FM H13*

UNITED TRADER Sw/Ko (Inchon) 1988; Ch; 7,973 grt/14,402 dwt; 143.00 × 9.02 m *(469.16 × 29.59 ft)*; M (Wärtsilä); 14.8 kts; ex-*Thuntank 11*
Sisters: **UNITED TRANSPORTER** (Sw) ex-*Thuntank 12*; **UNITED TRAVELLER** (Sw) ex-*Thuntank 9*; Similar (Sw built-Falkenbergs): **UNITED TRAPPER** (Sw) ex-*Thuntank 8*

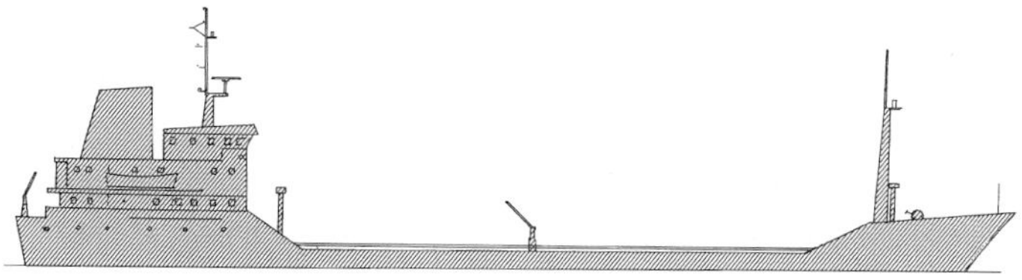

189 *MRM²FR H13*

MITHAT VARDAL Tu/Tu (Hidrodinamik) 1986; Ch; 997 grt/2,356 dwt; 77.32 × 4.89 m *(253.67 × 16.04 ft)*; M (Liebknecht); 11.5 kts

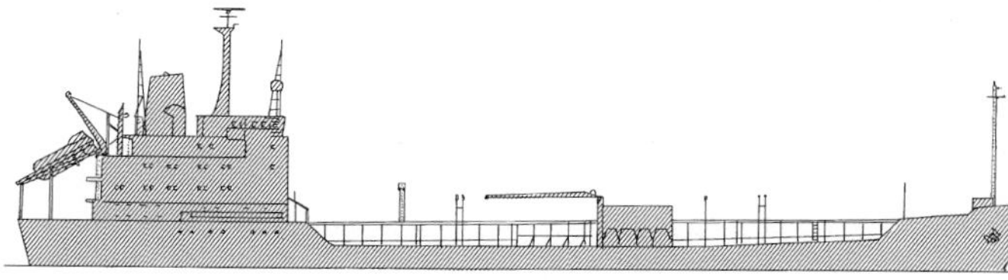

190 *MRM³FMCL H13*

STOLT AUSTRALIA Au/Ja (Mitsubishi HI) 1986; Ch; 6,895 grt/9,939 dwt; 119.56 × 8.32 m *(392.26 × 27.30 ft)*; M (Mitsubishi); 13.5 kts

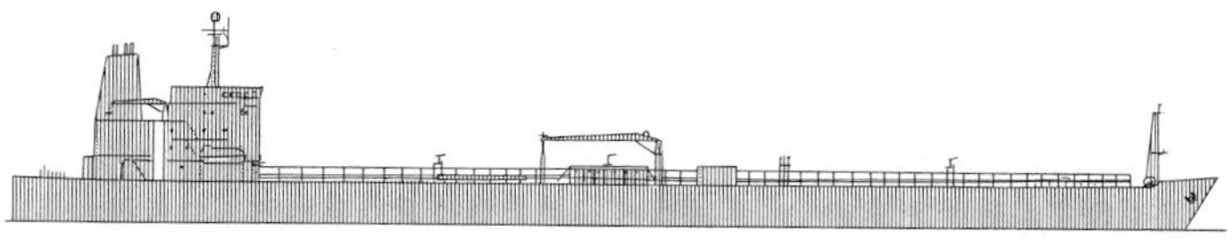

191 *MRM²RF H*

KANDILOUSA Gr/Ko (Hyundai) 1995; Tk; 28,507 grt/45,962 dwt; 182.76 × 12.22 m *(599.61 × 40.09 ft)*; M (B&W); 14 kts

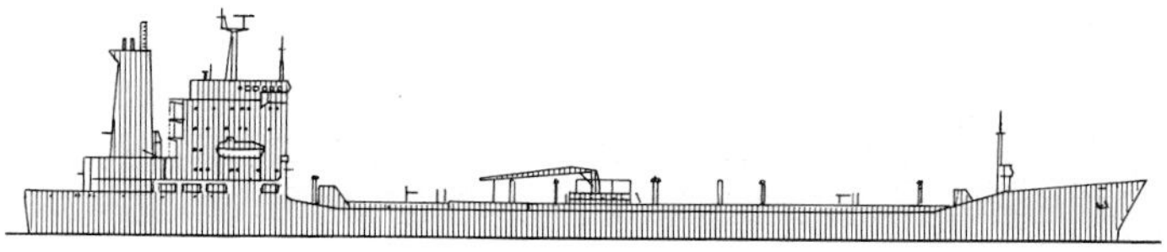

192 *MRM²RF H1*

BAUSKA Cy/Sw (Kockums) 1987; Tk; 14,937 grt/23,050 dwt; 158.30 × 10.00 m *(519.36 × 32.81 ft)*; M (B&W); 15.7 kts; ex-*Nord Skagerrak*
Sisters: **EKTURUS** (Sw) ex-*Okturus*; **OKTAVIUS** (Sw)

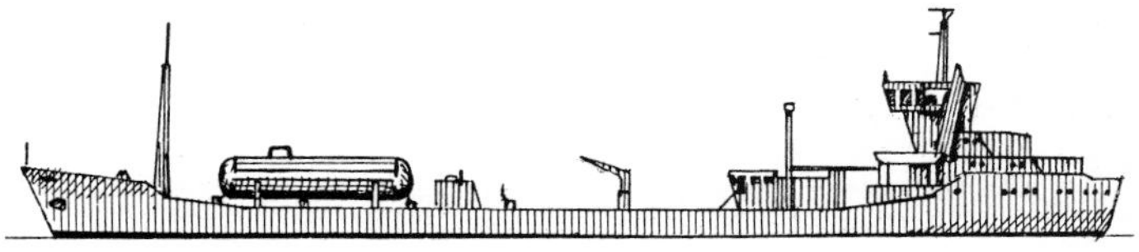

193 *MRMM-G H13*

SUVARNABHUMI Th/Br (Robb Caledon) 1969; Ch/LPG/Tk; 2,963 grt/ 3,749 dwt; 106.13 × 4.65 m *(348.19 × 15.26 ft)*; TSM (Ruston); 11 kts

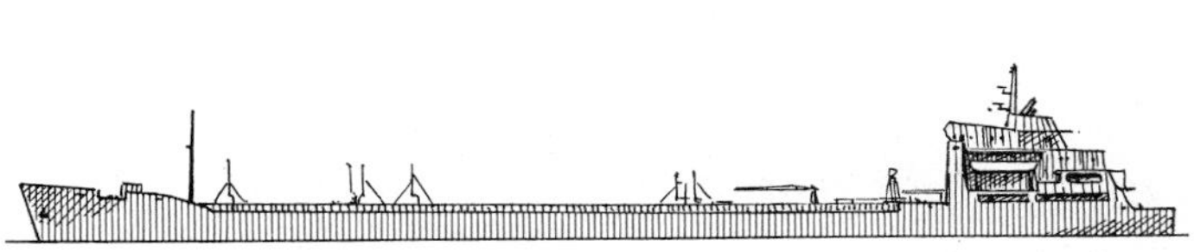

194 *MRM-F H1*

ENERCHEM ASPHALT Ca/Sw (Oskarshamns) 1972; Tk/AT; 5,512 grt/ 9,415 dwt; 126.12 × 7.2 m *(413.78 × 23.6 ft)*; M (Ruston, Paxman); 14.25 kts; ex-*Marina*

195 *MRM-F H1*
LEPTIS MAGNA Ma/Sw (Oskarshamns) 1973/77; Tk; 5,538 grt/9,552 dwt; 126.68 × 7.9 m *(415.62 × 25.92 ft)*; M (MWM); 14.5 kts; ex-*Mariann*; Converted from oil/chemical tanker 1977

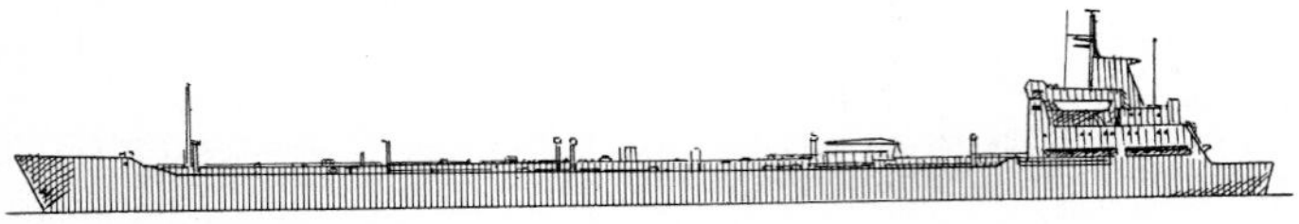

196 *MRM-F H1*
TARNOBRZEG Pd/Sw (Lodose/Oskarshamns) 1973; Ch; 6,650 grt/9,814 dwt; 146.11 × 7.61 m *(479.36 × 24.97 ft)*; M (Ruston, Paxman); 14.5 kts; Launched by Lodose, lengthened and completed by Oskarshamns
Sisters: **PROFESSOR K BOHDANOWICZ** (Pd); **SIARKOPOL** (Pd); **ZAGLEBIE SIARKOWE** (Pd)

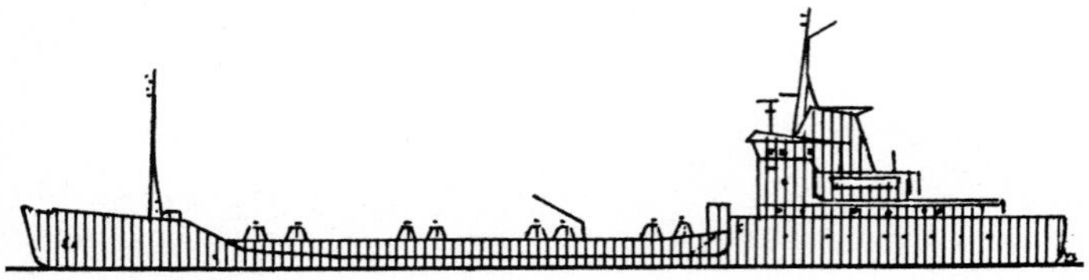

197 *MRM-F H13*
ZANETA Li/Fi (Reposaaren) 1970; Tk; 1,141 grt/2,193 dwt; 78.39 × 4.91 m *(257.19 × 16.11 ft)*; M (Nydqvist & Holm); 12 kts; ex-*Esso Saimaa*

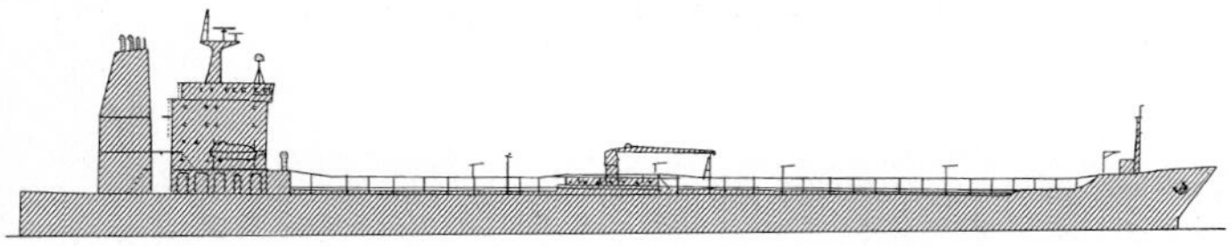

198 *MRNMF H1*
AL KUWAITIAH Ku/Ko (Samsung) 1988; Tk; 26,351 grt/35,643 dwt; 182.88 × 9.77 m *(600.00 × 32.05 ft)*; M (B&W); 13.5 kts
Sisters: **AL BADIYAH** (Ku); **AL DEERAH** (Ku); **AL SABIYAH** (Ku)

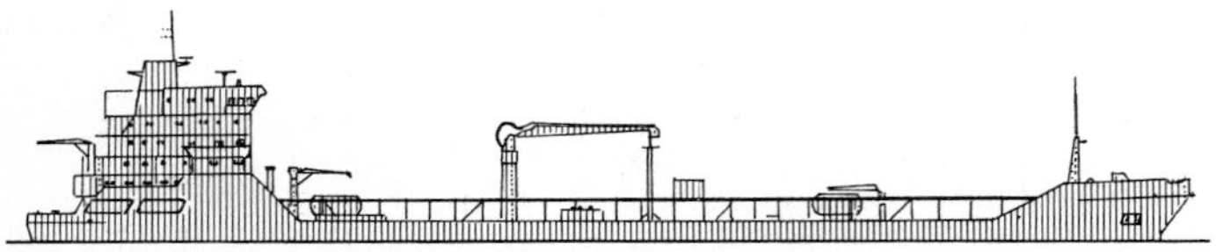

199 *MR^3M-FR H1*
BANGLAR JYOTI Bh/De (Orskov C) 1987; Tk; 8,672 grt/14,541 dwt; 138.03 × 7.25 m *(452.85 × 23.79 ft)*; TSM (Alpha); 11 kts; Small cranes near Focsle and bridgefront are on starboard side
Sister: **BANGLAR SHOURABH** (Bh)

See photo number 1/258

200 *MSHF H*
DANITA Pa/De (B&W) 1985; Tk; 43,733 grt/69,999 dwt; 228.61 × 12.47 m *(750.03 × 40.91 ft)*; M (B&W); 14.6 kts; 'CPT 54E' type
Sisters (some may have pole mast from bridge): **NORITA** (Pa); **NORDTRAMP** (DIS); **SITALOUISE** (DIS) ex-*NordFarer*; **SITALENE** (DIS) ex-*Nordkap*; **SITAKATRINE** (Li) ex-*Nordflex*; **TORM MARGRETHE** (Li) (may have pole mast from bridge)

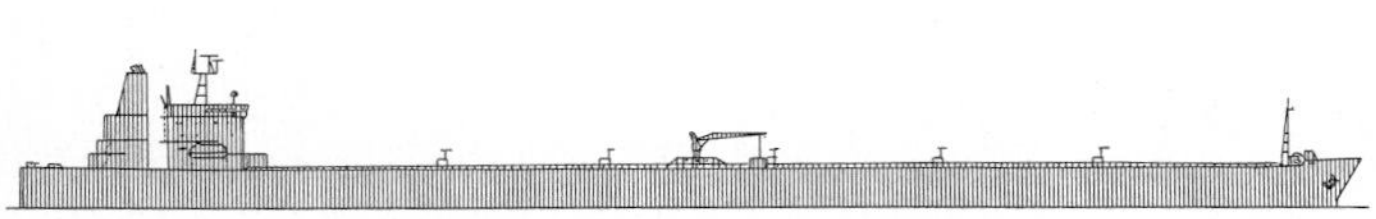

201 *MSMDF H*
ANKLESHWAR In/Ko (Samsung S) 1994; Tk; 80,130 grt/147,563 dwt; 274.03 × 16.62 m *(899.05 × 54.53 ft)*; M (B&W); 14 kts

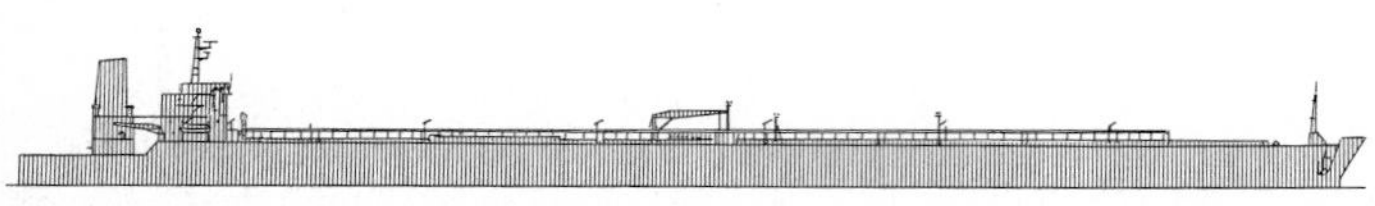

202 *MSMF H*
GOLAR STIRLING Li/Ko (Daewoo) 1992; Tk; 156,408 grt/302,440 dwt; 332.00 × 22.02 m *(1,089.24 × 72.24 ft)*; M (Sulzer); 15.5 kts
Sisters: **GOLAR DUNDEE** (Li); **GOLAR EDINBURGH** (Li); **GOLAR GLASGOW** (Li)

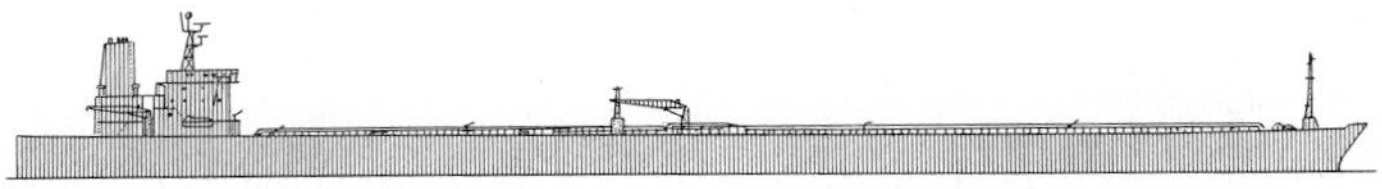

203 *MSMF H*
LANDSORT Sw/Ko (Daewoo) 1991; Tk; 81,135 grt/139,990 dwt; 274.00 × 15.22 m *(898.95 × 49.93 ft)*; M (B&W); 14.7 kts
Sister: **MASTERA** (Fi)

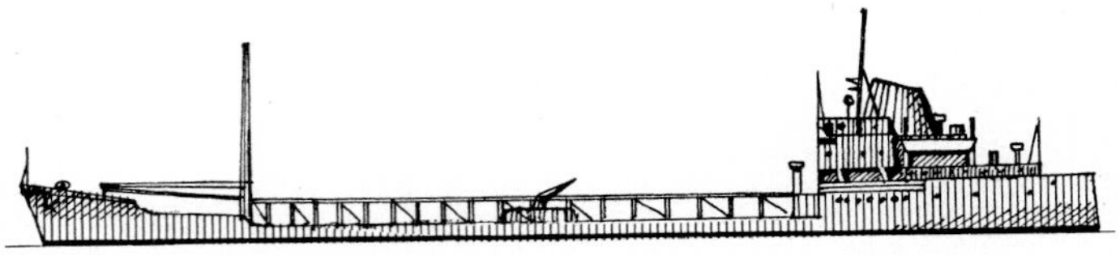

204 *MSMF H13*
POWE Ng/Br (Clelands) 1967; Tk; 2,677 grt/4,648 dwt; 98.3 × 6.08 m *(322.51 × 19.95 ft)*; M (Ruston & Hornsby); 11.5 kts; ex-*Wheelsman*

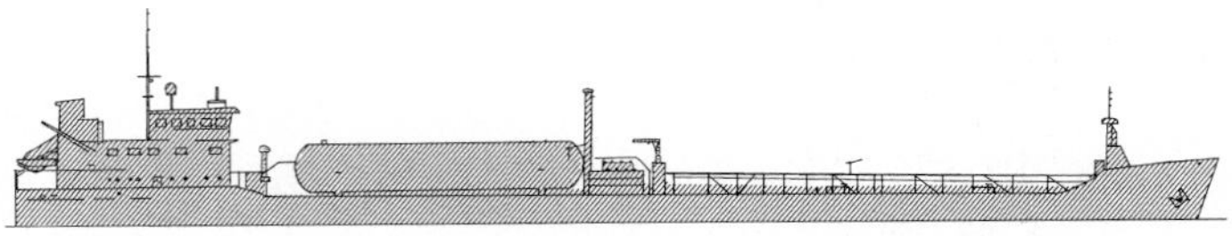

205 *MSMHFL H1*
POINTE CLAIRETTE SV/Ne ('De Biesbosch-Dordrecht') 1994; Tk/LGC; 3,239 grt/5,278 dwt; 103.55 × 5.55 m *(339.73 × 18.21 ft)*; M (Caterpillar); 12.36 kts; LPG tanks on deck

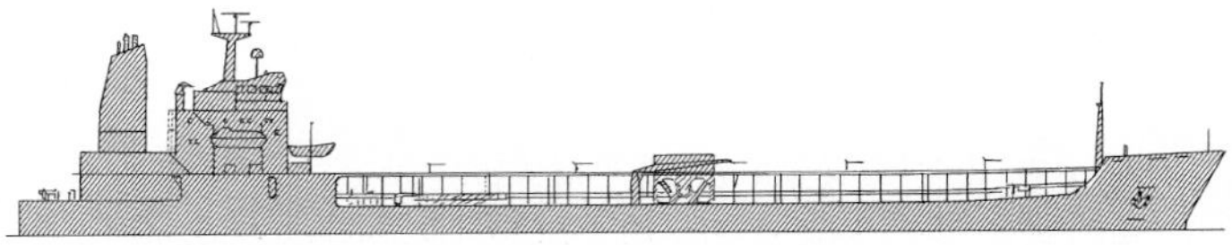

206 *MSMRF H1*
UNITED TINA NIS/Ko (Samsung) 1987; Tk/Ch/MT; 16,555 grt/27,821 dwt; 154.67 × 11.02 m *(507.45 × 36.15 ft)*; M (B&W); 14.25 kts; ex-*Staland*

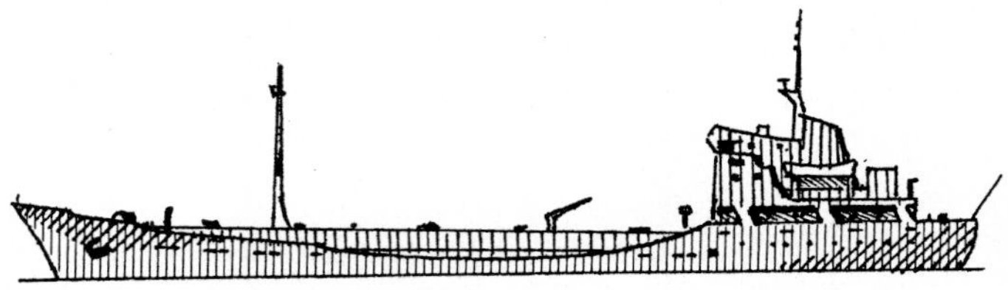

207 *MSM-F H13*
NAXOS It/Fr (France-Gironde) 1969; Ch; 1,429 grt/2,176 dwt; 79.53 × 5.11 m *(260.93 × 16.77 ft)*; M (Atlas-MaK); 13.75 kts; ex-*Casimir Le Quellec*

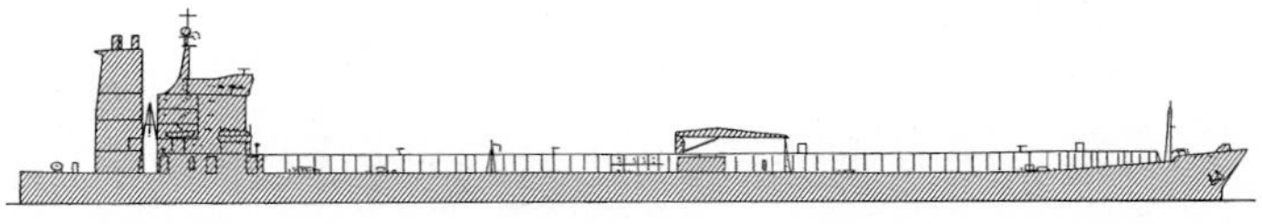

208 *MSNHF H*
CANOPUS Au/Ko (Samsung) 1986; Tk; 54,880 grt/94,347 dwt; 230.03 × 13.62 m *(754.69 × 44.69 ft)*; M (B&W); 14.75 kts
Probable sister: **ERA** (Au); Possible sister: **AUSTRALIA STAR** (Au)

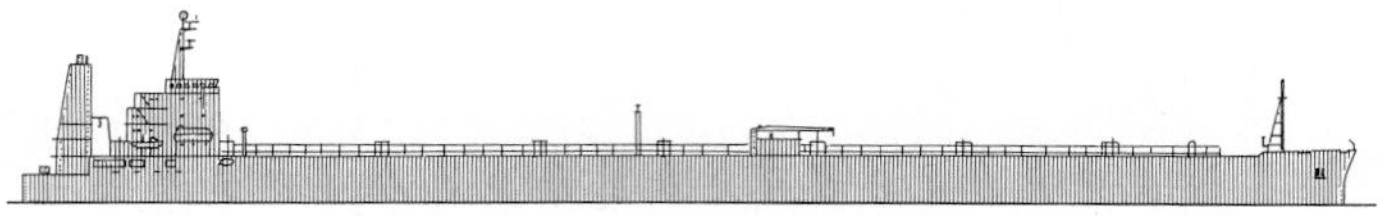

209 *MSNMF H1*
UNITED SELMA NIS/RC (Dalian) 1987; Tk/Ch; 45,140 grt/81,351 dwt; 228.61 × 15.75 m *(750.03 × 51.67 ft)*; M (B&W); 13 kts; ex-*Osco Bellona*
Sister: **PRIMO** (Li) ex-*Osco Beduin*

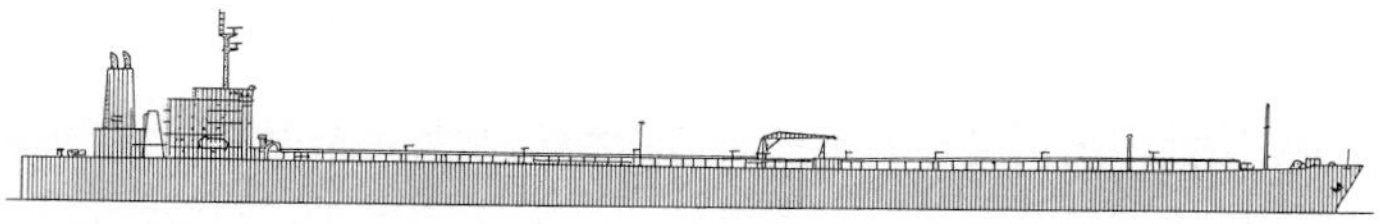

210 MSN^2F *H*
OKINOSHIMA MARU Ja/Ja (IHI) 1993; Tk; 147,665 grt/258,079 dwt; 333.00 × 18.94 m *(1,092.52 × 62.14 ft)*; M (Sulzer); 15.7 kts
Sister: **TOBA** (Li)

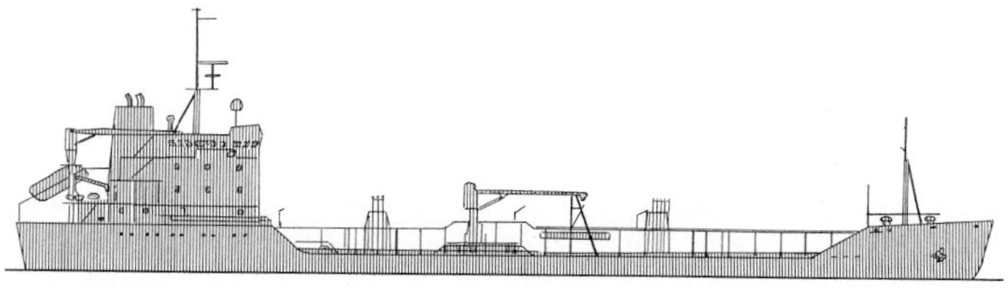

211 *M-NEREMFRL H13*
WESERSTERN Br/Ge (MTW) 1992; Tk/Ch; 5,480 grt/9,028 dwt; 109.72 × 8.54 m *(359.97 × 28.02 ft)*; M (B&W); 12.5 kts
Sister: **ODERSTERN** (Br); Probable sisters (longer—123 m (403 ft)): **DIAMOND STAR** (Ca) ex-*Elbestern*; **EMERALD STAR** (Ca) ex-*Emsstern*; **JADE STAR** (Ca) ex-*Jadestern*; **LEDASTERN** (Ge)

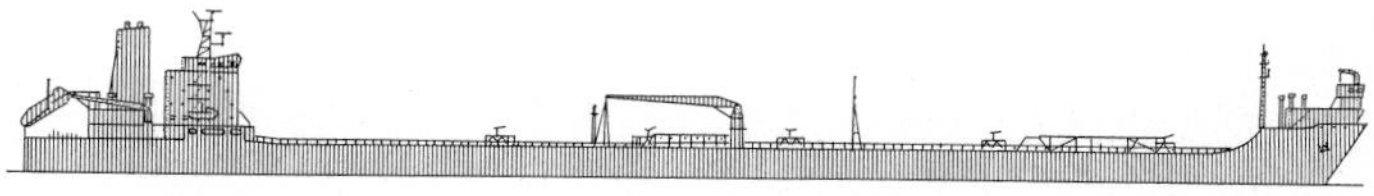

212 RM^2RM^2FL *H1*
TORDIS KNUTSEN No/Sp (AESA) 1993; Tk; 66,671 grt/123,848 dwt; 265.30 × 15.22 m *(870.41 × 49.93 ft)*; M (B&W); 14.75 kts; Fitted for offshore-loading
Sister: **VIGDIS KNUTSEN** (No)

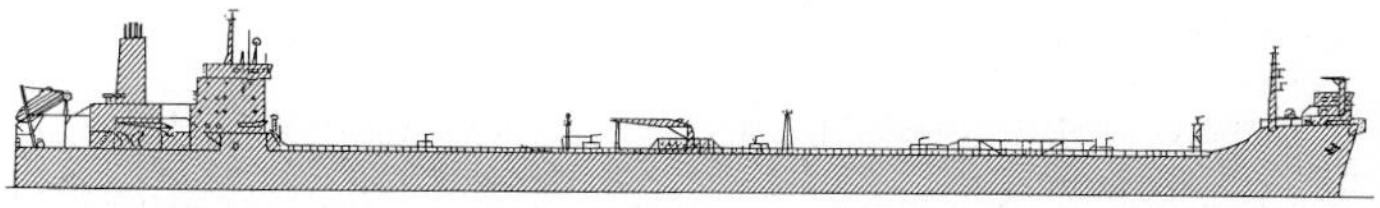

213 $RMNSM^2FL$ *H1*
JUANITA No/Ko (Daewoo) 1988; Tk; 72,129 grt/126,491 dwt; 260.00 × 15.50 m *(853.02 × 50.85 ft)*; TSM (B&W); 14.6 kts; ex-*Lisita*; Fitted for offshore-loading
Similar: **SARITA** (No)

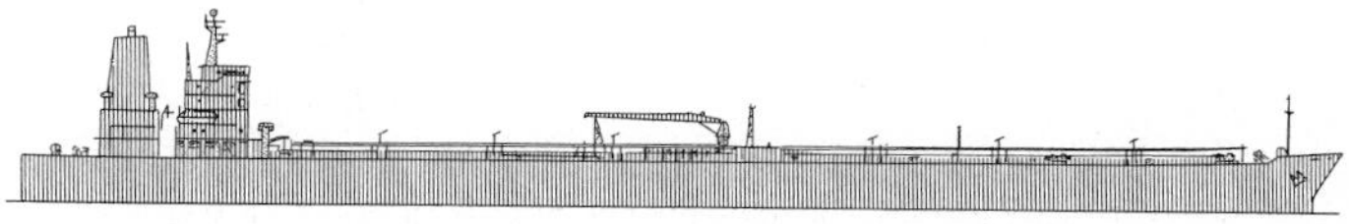

214 *VNRMF H*
MAYON SPIRIT Bs/Ja (Onomichi) 1992; Tk; 57,448 grt/98,507 dwt; 244.80 × 14.42 m *(803.15 × 47.31 ft)*; M (B&W); 14.8 kts
Sisters: **TORBEN SPIRIT** (Bs); **ONOZO SPIRIT** (Bs); **SAMAR SPIRIT** (Bs); **LEYTE SPIRIT** (Bs); **LUZON SPIRIT** (Bs); **TEEKAY SPIRIT** (Bs); **PALMSTAR POPPY** (Bs); Probable sisters: **PALMSTAR CHERRY** (Bs); **PALMSTAR LOTUS** (Bs); **PALMSTAR ORCHID** (Bs); **PALMSTAR ROSE** (Bs); **PALMSTAR THISTLE** (Bs); **MORNING GLORY II** (Li)

215 Satsuma *(Bs); 1993* *"Sea-Japan" Japan Ship Exporters' Association*

216 Tohzan *(Pa); 1995* *"Sea-Japan" Japan Ship Exporters' Association*

217 Navix Azalea *(Pa); 1995* *"Sea-Japan" Japan Ship Exporters' Association*

218 Navix Adventure *(Pa); 1993* *"Sea-Japan" Japan Ship Exporters' Association*

219 Ocean Guardian *(Li); 1993* *"Sea-Japan" Japan Ship Exporters' Association*

220 Berge Stadt *(NIS); 1994* *"Sea-Japan" Japan Ship Exporters' Association*

221 Diamond Grace *(Pa); 1994* *"Sea-Japan" Japan Ship Exporters' Association*

222 Takayama *(Li); 1994* *"Sea-Japan" Japan Ship Exporters' Association*

223 Tartar *(NIS); 1993* *"Sea-Japan" Japan Ship Exporters' Association*

224 Bona Sailor *(Bs); 1994 sister: Bona Spray* *"Sea-Japan" Japan Ship Exporters' Association*

225 Samuel Ginn *(Bs); 1993* *"Sea-Japan" Japan Ship Exporters' Association*

226 Gran Esperanza *(Pa); 1993* *"Sea-Japan" Japan Ship Exporters' Association*

227 Katja *(Bs); 1995* *"Sea-Japan" Japan Ship Exporters' Association*

228 Fosna *(NIS); 1992; sister: Molda* *"Sea-Japan" Japan Ship Exporters' Association*

229 Frontier Express *(Pa); 1993; sister: Challenge Express* *"Sea-Japan" Japan Ship Exporters' Association*

230 Polyclipper *(NIS); 1993; (offshore loading tanker)* *"Sea-Japan" Japan Ship Exporters' Association*

231 Bow Heron *(NIS); 1979; (as Ivor Heron)* *WSPL*

232 Orange Wave *(Li); 1993; (fruit juice tanker)* *WSPL*

233 Hitra *(NIS); 1984* *WSPL*

234 Hightide *(Li); 1989* *WSPL*

235 Jo Clipper *(NA); 1981* *WSPL*

236 Chembulk Rotterdam *(Li); 1993; (as Fifi)* *WSPL*

237 Nand Shivchand *(In); 1982* *WSPL*

238 Jo Calluna *(Ne); 1986; (as Calluna)* *FotoFlite*

239 Sunny Blossom *(Bs); 1986* *FotoFlite*

240 Stolt Alliance *(Li); 1985* *FotoFlite*

241 Eternity *(Sg); 1988* *FotoFlite*

242 Sienna *(Gr); 1986* *FotoFlite*

243 Samco Europe *(Bs); 1988; (as Fina Europe)* *FotoFlite*

244 Eagle *(Gr); 1979; (as Phillips Oklahoma)* *FotoFlite*

245 Stolt Resolute *(Li); 1982* *FotoFlite*

246 Al Dhibyaniyyah *(UAE); 1984* *FotoFlite*

247 Peaceventure L *(Gr); 1987* *FotoFlite*

248 Turchese *(Ma); 1988* *FotoFlite*

249 Maribel *(NIS); 1985; (as Ferncourt)* *FotoFlite*

250 Brage Nordic *(NIS); 1981* *FotoFlite*

251 Eken *(Sw); 1980* *FotoFlite*

252 Petro Avon *(Br); 1981; (as Esso Avon)* *FotoFlite*

253 Galp Leixoes *(Po); 1983* *FotoFlite*

254 Hydro *(NIS); 1980* *FotoFlite*

255 Spic Emerald *(In); 1983* *FotoFlite*

256 Jo Lonn *(NA); 1982* *FotoFlite*

257 Bulduri *(Cy); 1983* *FotoFlite*

258 Danita *(Pa); 1985* *FotoFlite*

259 Saint Vassilios *(Bs); 1981* *FotoFlite*

260 Vikla *(Fi); 1982* *FotoFlite*

261 Suula *(Lu); 1980* *FotoFlite*

262 Kihu *(Fi); 1984* *FotoFlite*

263 Tebo Olympia *(Fi); 1980* *FotoFlite*

264 Ventspils *(Li); 1983* *FotoFlite*

265 Gonio *(Ma); 1984* *FotoFlite*

266 Ekfjord Af Donso *(Sw); 1981* *FotoFlite*

267 Bow Viking *(NIS); 1981* *FotoFlite*

268 Maasstad L *(Gr); 1983* *FotoFlite*

269 Torm Thyra *(DIS); 1985* *FotoFlite*

270 Carla A Hills *(Li); 1981* *FotoFlite*

271 Lepeta *(Br); 1976* *FotoFlite*

272 Bow Pioneer *(NIS); 1982* *FotoFlite*

273 Bituma *(Sw); 1981* *FotoFlite*

274 Petrotroll *(NIS); 1981* *FotoFlite*

275 Evita *(No); 1989; (offshore loading tanker)* *FotoFlite*

276 Cardissa *(Ne); 1983/93; (offshore loading tanker)* *FotoFlite*

277 Dala Corona *(Sw); 1976/78* *FotoFlite*

278 Dutch Mariner *(Ne); 1986* *FotoFlite*

2 Tankers and Combination Carriers with Derrick Posts

2 Tankers and Combination Carriers with Derrick Posts

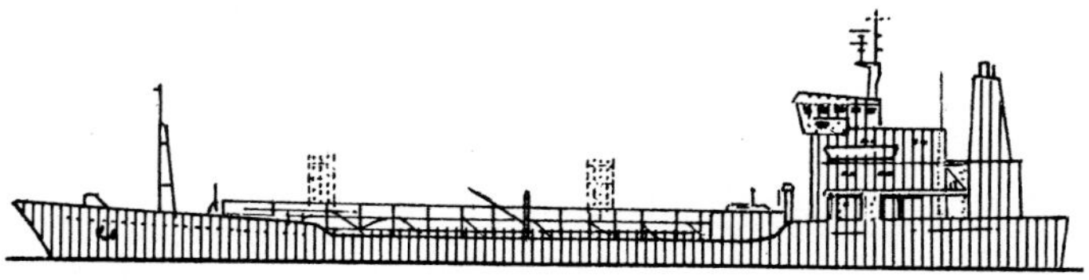

1 *HENEMF H3*
CORAL ESSBERGER Ge/FRG (Buesumer) 1981; Ch; 1,941 grt/2,894 dwt; 81.31 × 5.34 m *(267 × 17.52 ft)*; M (Krupp-MaK); 12.5 kts
Sisters: **TOM ELBA** (Po) ex-*Helga Essberger*; **TOM LIS** (Po) ex-*Liesel Essberger*

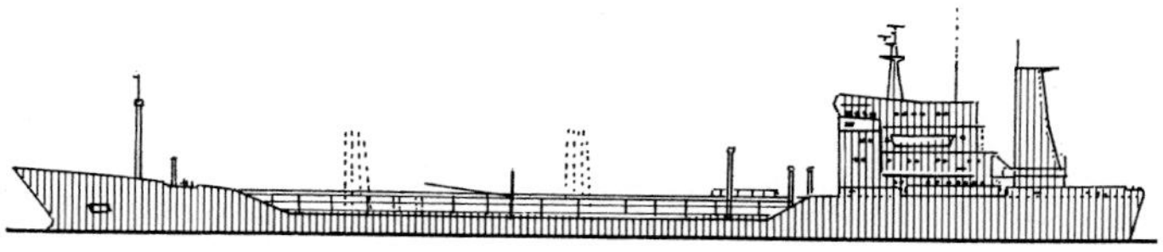

2 *HENEM^{2}G H13*
TOL RUNNER Pa/FRG (Kroegerw) 1976; Ch; 5,054 grt/8,041 dwt; 114.03 × 7.34 m *(374 × 24.08 ft)*; M (MaK); 15.75 kts; ex-*Chemtrans Sirius*

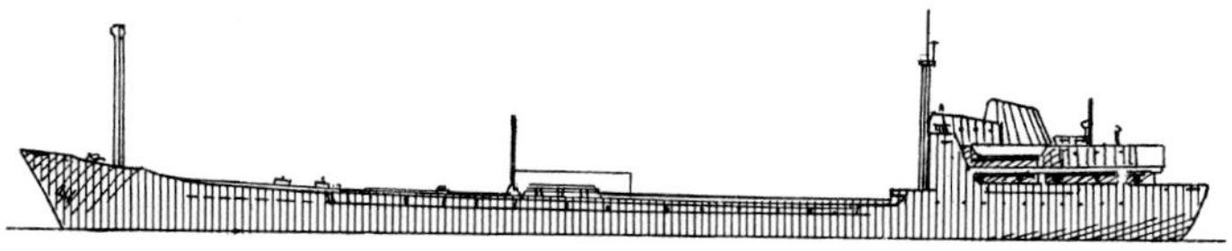

3 *H^{3}F H13*
ASMA SV/Sp (Euskalduna) 1964/72; Tk; 3,451 grt/5,416 dwt; 102.49 × 6.29 m *(336.25 × 20.64 ft)*; M (MAN); 12.5 kts; ex-*Finse*; Converted from cargo 1972 (Smith's D)

4 *HMHF H123*
ENALIOS PROTEUS Gr/Ja (Hitachi) 1965; Tk; 12,079 grt/20,766 dwt; 170.69 × 9.34 m *(560 × 30.64 ft)*; M (B&W); 15 kts; ex-*Tuborg*
Sister: **DA QING 52** (RC) ex-*Viborg*

5 *HMHFN H13*
TRUD Ru/Ys ('3 Maj') 1960; Tk; 17,861 grt/26,874 dwt; 192.36 × 10.24 m *(631.1 × 33.59 ft)*; T (De Laval); 17 kts; ex-*Fraternity*

6 *HMHMNF H1*
PRESIDENTE DEODORO Bz/Ja (NKK) 1960/67; Tk; 30,729 grt/52,989 dwt; 241.05 × 12.26 m *(790.85 × 40.22 ft)*; T (Ishikawajima J); — kts; Lengthened and deepened 1967 (Mitsubishi HI)
Sister: **PRESIDENTE FLORIANO** (Bz)

7 *HMNF H123*
DA QING 16 RC/De (Odense) 1960; Tk; 16,425 grt/28,378 dwt; 194.24 × 10.67 m *(637.27 × 35.01)* ; M (B&W); X kts; ex-*Gjertrud Maersk*

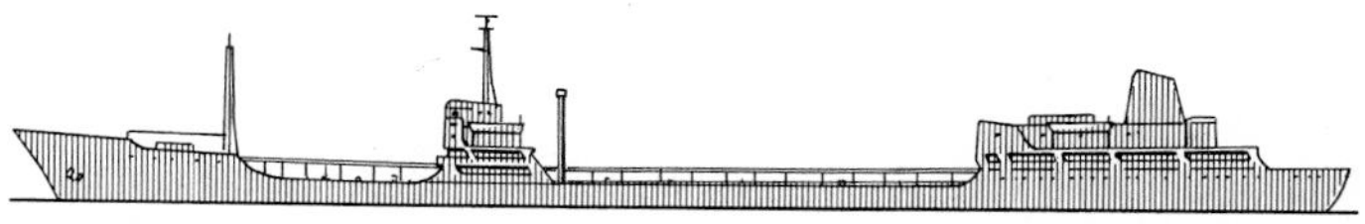

8 *HMNF H13*
DA QING No 232 RC/RC (Dalian) 1974; Tk; 10,532 grt/15,356 dwt; 163 × 9.4 m *(535 × 30.84 ft)*; M (MAN); 15 kts
Sister: **DA QING 231** (RC); Possible sisters: **DA QING 45** (RC); **DA QING 46** (RC); **DA QING 47** (RC); **DA QING 48** (RC); **DA QING 49** (RC); **DA QING 50** (RC); **DA QING 234**

9 *HMNFN H13*
FLORENCE US/US (Newport News) 1954; Tk; 17,378 grt/28,976 dwt; 191.42 × 10.23 m *(628.02 × 33.56 ft)*; T (Newport News); 16 kts; ex-*Esso Florence*; US Government owned

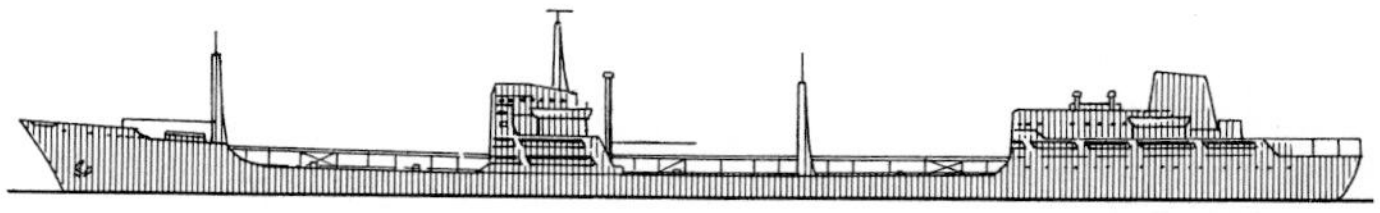

10 *HMNHF H13*
DA QING No 29 RC/RC (Dalian) 1971; Tk; 10,494 grt/15,786 dwt; 163.4 × 8.97 m *(536 × 29.43 ft)*; M (Hudong); 16 kts
Sisters: **DA QING 30** (RC); **DA QING 31**

11 *HMNMFN H123*
DA QING 235 RC/Br (Lithgows) 1959; Tk; 10,655 grt/15,913 dwt; 152.2 × 9.16 m *(499.3 × 30.05 ft)*; M (B&W); 14 kts; ex-*British Trust*
Similar: **NOAH VI** (Ir) ex-*British Swift*

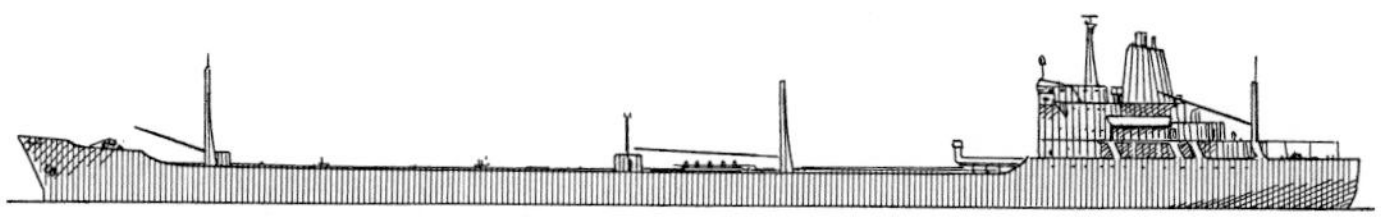

12 *HMNMFN H123*
ATHENIAN HARMONY Cy/Ja (IHI) 1970; Tk; 17,485 grt/30,320 dwt; 170.82 × 11.01 m *(560.43 × 36.12 ft)*; M (Sulzer); 16 kts; ex-*Messiniaki Avra* 1982; ex-*Stakara* 1981
Sisters: **MATHRAKI** (Gr) ex-*Stabenko*; **ASTIPALEA** (Gr) ex-*Stawanda*; **NORTH WIND** (Ma) ex-*Messiniaki Aigli*; **PUPPY F** (Ma) ex-*Messiniaki Anagennisis*; **PUPPY P** (Ma) ex-*Messiniaki Bergen*; **OTHONI** (Gr) ex-*Messiniaki Minde*; **WAWASAN MEGAH** (My) ex-*Messiniaki Ormi*; **KITHNOS** (Gr) ex-*Messiniaki Paradis*; **SAN GIORGIO** (Ma) ex-*Messiniaki Timi*; **AL NABILA 3** (Eg) ex-*Messiniaki Chara*; **MIN RAN GONG No 7** (RC) ex-*Stamenis*; **OTTAVIANO** (It) ex-*Messiniaki Gi*; **GHAZI** (SV) ex-*Messiniaki Thea*

13 *HMN^{2}F H123*
CAROLINE SV/Sw (Eriksbergs) 1962; Tk; 12,303 grt/21,649 dwt; 170.67 × 9.74 m *(559.94 × 31.96 ft)*; M (B&W); 14.5 kts; ex-*Polystar*

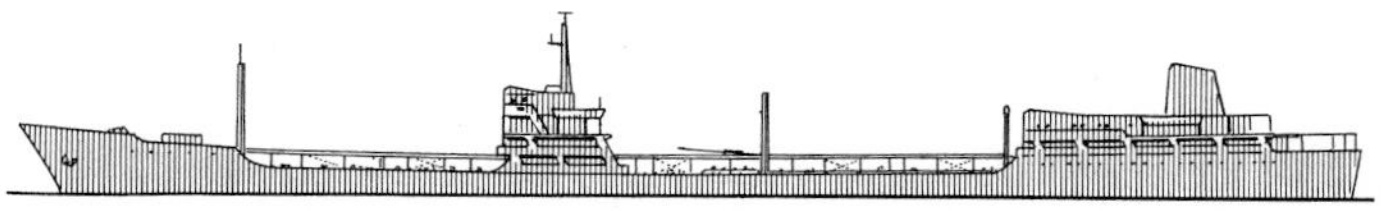

14 *HMN^{2}F H13*
DA QING 240 RC/RC (Dalian) 1975; Tk; 16,729 grt/26,089 dwt; 178 × 9.5 m *(584 × 31.17 ft)*; M (Sulzer); 15 kts
Sisters: **DA QING 241** (RC); **DA QING 42** (RC); **DA QING 44** (RC)

15 *HMN^{2}MFN H123*
GETTYSBURG US/US (Newport News) 1957; Tk; 23,665 grt/41,529 dwt; 217.94 × 11.84 m *(715.03 × 38.85 ft)*; T (Newport News); 18.25 kts; ex-*Esso Gettysberg*; US Government owned
Sisters: **JAMESTOWN** (US) ex-*Esso Jamestown*; **LEXINGTON** (US) ex-*Esso Lexington*

16 *HMN^{3}FN H123*
AL MORGAN Eg/No (Rosenberg) 1959; Tk; 20,449 grt/35,429 dwt; 200.95 × 11.51 m *(659.28 × 37.76 ft)*; M (B&W); 14 kts; ex-*Bergesund*

17 *HMN^{3}FN H123*
WANDERBASS Pa/Sp (AESA) 1962; Tk; 4,316 grt/9,655 dwt; 139.05 × 7.76 m *(456.2 × 25.46 ft)*; M (B&W); 14 kts; ex-*Camporraso*

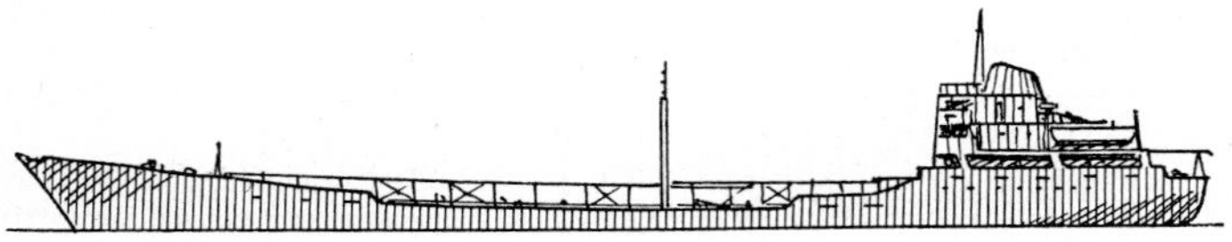

18 *HM-F H13*
MAZAL II Gr/It (Pellegrino) 1965; Tk; 2,676 grt/3,970 dwt; 99.57 × 6.07 m *(326.67 × 19.91 ft)*; M (Fiat); — kts; Launched as *Sisina Pellegrino*

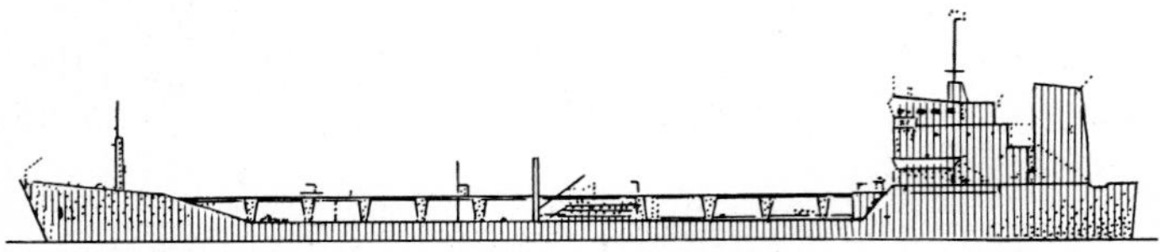

19 *HNMF H13*
CABLEMAN Br/Br (Appledore) 1980; Tk; 4,777 grt/8,496 dwt; 116.52 × 7.2 m *(382.28 × 23.62 ft)*; M (Ruston); 13 kts
Sister: **ECHOMAN** (Hk); Similar (larger): **TANKERMAN** (Br)

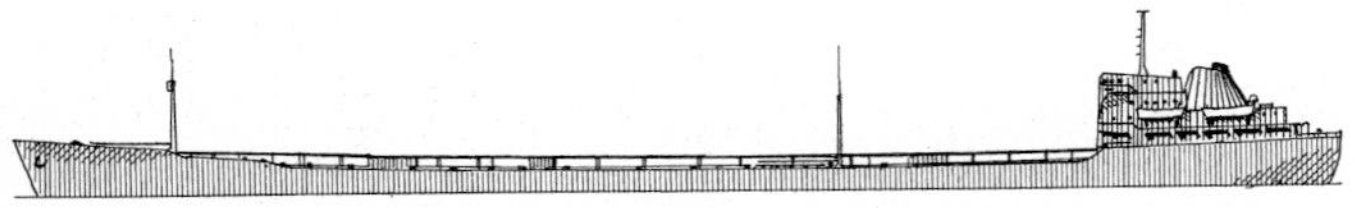

20 *HNMF H13*
LACONIA It/Sw (Eriksbergs) 1960/68; Tk; 13,227 grt/22,455 dwt; 181.67 × 9.57 m *(596.03 × 31.38 ft)*; M (B&W); 14.5 kts; ex-*Texaco Bogota*; Lengthened and converted 1968 (Eriksbergs)

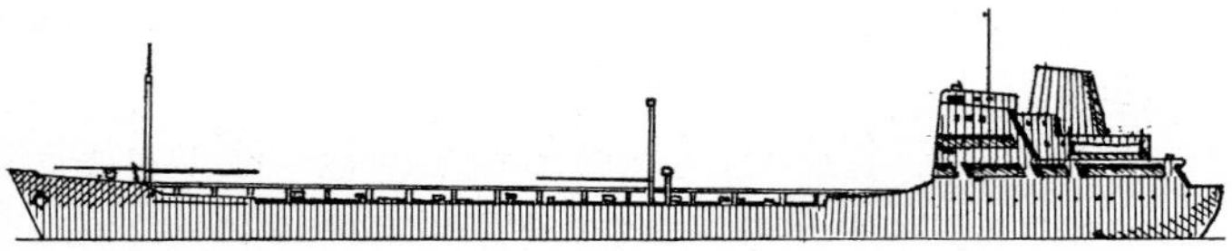

21 *HNMF H13*
LE CHENE NO 1 Ca/Ca (Marine Indust) 1961/78; Tk; 5,065 grt/7,809 dwt; 131.07 × 6.85 m *(430.02 × 22.47 ft)*; M (B&W); 12 kts; ex-*J Edouard Simard*; New forward section added 1978 (Marine Indust); Lengthened 1979

22 *HNMF H13*
VOLGONEFT Type Ru/Ru & Rm (Volgograd/Ivan Dimitrov) —; Tk; 3519-3627 grt/5,067-6,096 dwt; 132.50 × 3.60 m *(434.71 × 11.81 ft)*; TSM (SKL); 10.5 kts; Sea/river ships; A class of around 70; Many will have this sequence; Most names are 'VOLGONEFT' suffixed with a number

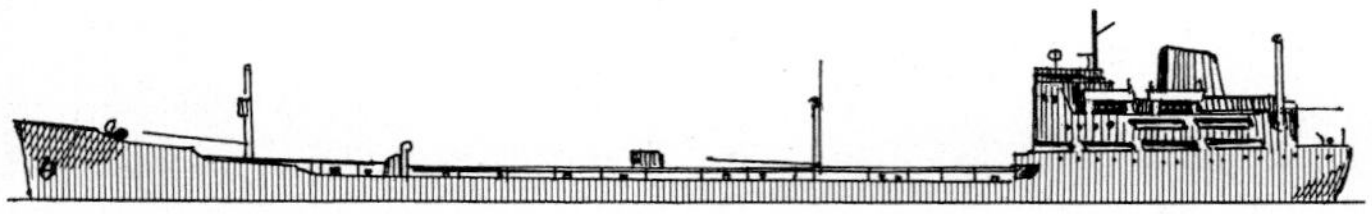

23 *HNMFN H13*
DA QING 38 RC/No (Moss V) 1962; Tk; 8,759 grt/13,643 dwt; 152.41 × 8.46 m *(500.03 × 27.76 ft)*; M (B&W); 14 kts; ex-*Kindvik*

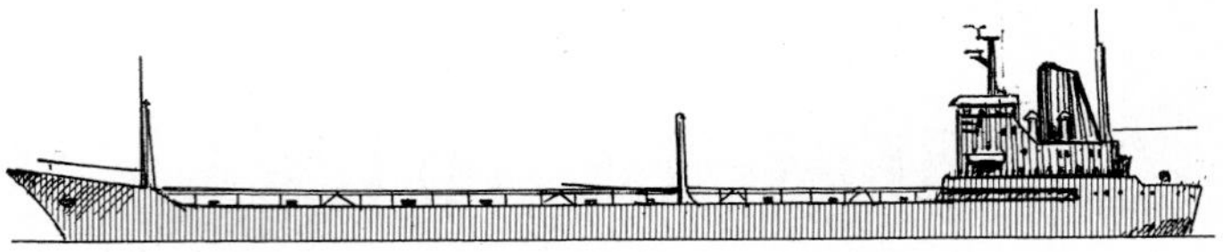

24 *HNMFN H13*
IRATI Bz/Ys ('3 Maj') 1970; Tk; 10,402 grt/14,805 dwt; 142.53 × 7.32 m *(467.62 × 24.02 ft)*; M (Sulzer); 13.5 kts
Sisters: **XIAO WANG II** (Pa) ex-*Ipanema*; **ITORORO** (Bz)

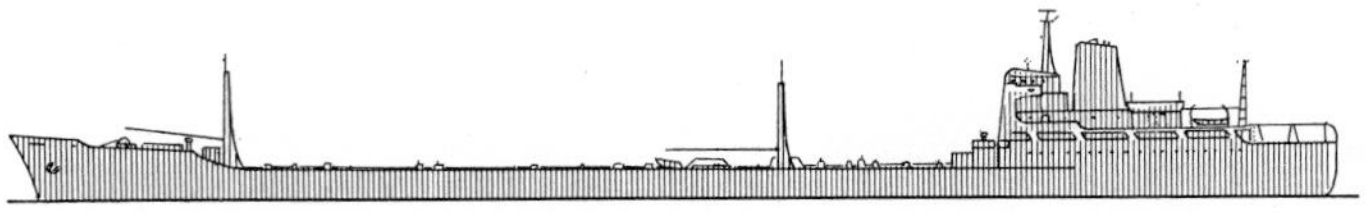

25 *HNMFN H13*
OGOSTA Ja (Osaka) 1966; Tk; 14,518 grt/25,399 dwt; 174.91 × 10.06 m *(573.85 × 33.01 ft)*; M (B&W); 13.5 kts

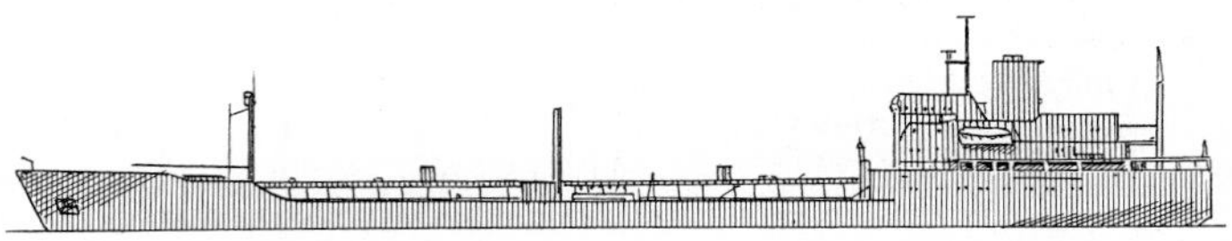

26 *HNMFN H13*
SAMOTLOR Ru/Fi (Rauma-Repola) 1975; Tk/IB; 13,173 grt/17,800 dwt; 160 × 9.17 m *(524.93 × 30.09 ft)*; M (B&W); 16.25 kts
Sisters: **URENGOY** (Ru); **BEREZOVO** (Ru); **GORNOPRAVDINSK** (Ru); **NADYM** (Ru); **NIZHNEVARTOVSK** (Ru); **SAMBURGA** (La) ex-*Samburg*; **USINSK** (Ru); **BAM** (Ru); **VILYUYSK** (Ru); **RUNDALE** (La) ex-*Leninsk-Kuznetskiy*; **KAMENSK-URALSKIY** (Ru); **YENISEYSK** (Ru); **IGRIM** (Ru)

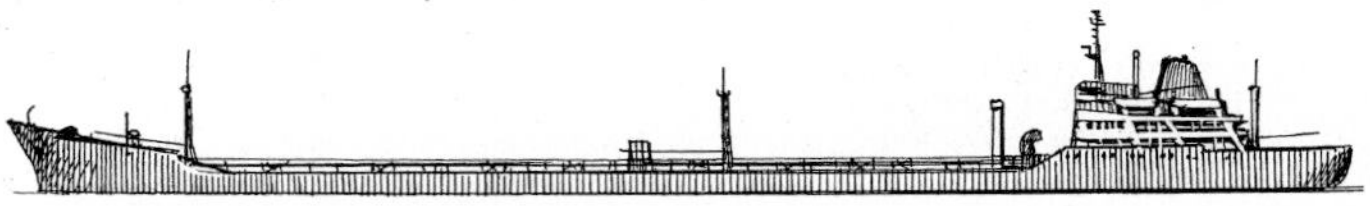

27 *HN^{2}MNFN H13*
NOVOCENTROL 1 Ru/Ja (Mitsubishi Z) 1962; Tk; 22,075 grt/36,767 dwt; 207.02 × 11.08 m *(679.2 × 36.35 ft)*; M (Sulzer); 16.5 kts; ex-*Lenino*
Sister: **NOVOCENTROL 2** (Ru) ex-*Lyublino*

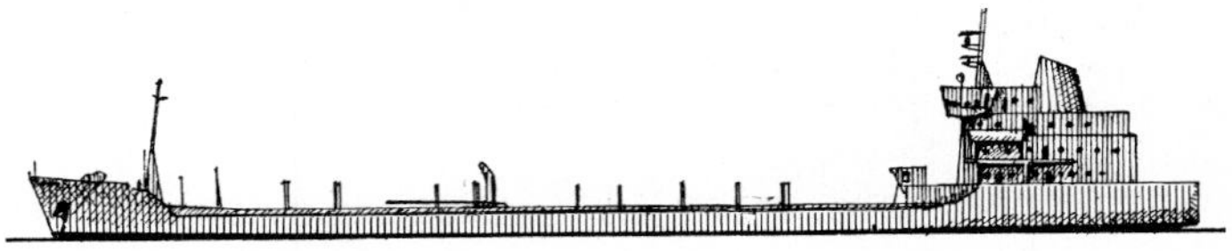

28 *MCSMF H13*
W M VACY ASH Pa/Ca (Marine Indust) 1969; Tk; 5,134 grt/8,697 dwt; 121.93 × 7.1 m *(400 × 23.29 ft)*; M (Ruston & Hornsby); 13 kts; ex-*Lakeshell*

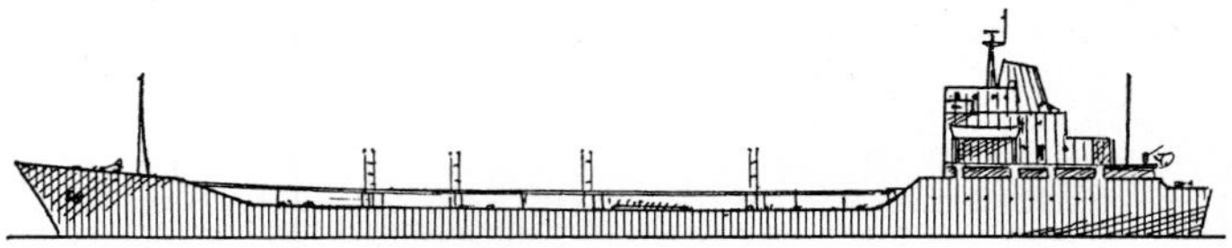

29 *ME^{4}MFM H13*
NIVARIA Sp/Sp (Cantabrico) 1977; Tk/Ch; 3,867 grt/6,352 dwt; 111.92 × 6.73 m *(367.19 × 22.08 ft)*; M (Werkspoor); 15 kts; ex-*Tudela*

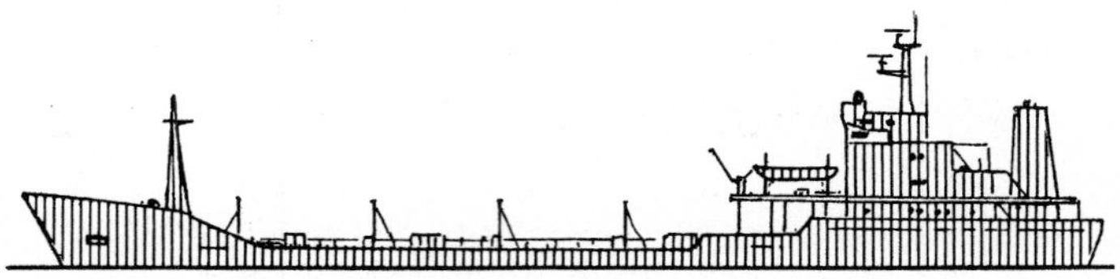

30 *ME^{4}M^{2}F H13*
OUED NOUMER Ag/FRG (Nobiskrug) 1981; AT/Ch; 1,746 grt/2,865 dwt; 86.01 × 5.04 m *(282 × 16.54 ft)*; M (KHD); 11.75 kts; ex-*Hanne Lupe*

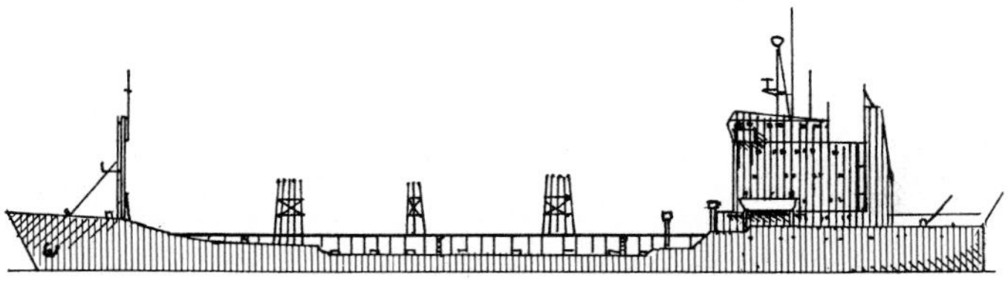

31 *ME^3MG H13*
CAPE HOPE Pa/FRG (O&K) 1974; Ch; 3,976 grt/6,478 dwt; 109 × 8.54 m *(357.61 × 28.02 ft)*; M (Atlas-MaK); 14.5 kts; ex-*Alchimist Lausanne*
Sisters: **MELIS** (Tu) ex-*Chemist Lutetia*; **ALPINE GIRL** (Bs) ex-*Quimico Lisboa*; **ALPINE LADY** (Bs) ex-*Quimico Leixoes*; **RYSTRAUM** (NIS) ex-*Chimiste Sayid*

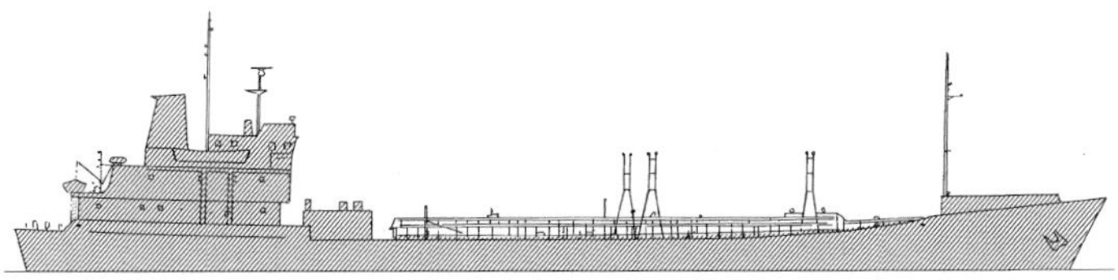

32 *ME^3M^2F H1*
ESSBERGER PILOT Sg/FRG (Hitzler) 1974; Ch; 1,616 grt/2,456 dwt; 77.12 × 4.78 m *(253.02 × 15.68 ft)*; M (Atlas-MaK); 12 kts
Sister: **ESSBERGER PIONEER** (Sg)

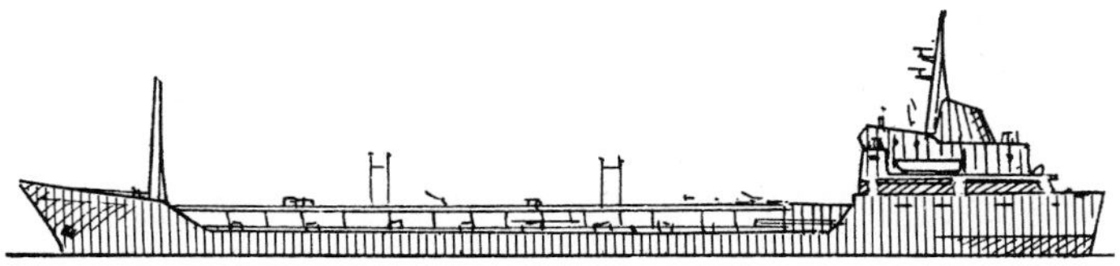

33 *ME^3M-F H13*
MULTITANK FRISIA Li/Sw (Kalmar) 1972; Ch; 1,533 grt/3,005 dwt; 85.86 × 5.4 m *(281.69 × 17.72 ft)*; M (Alpha-Diesel); 14.5 kts; ex-*Monsun*
Sister: **NORTHERN SPIRIT** (Li) ex-*Holsatia*; Similar: **POINTE DU ROC'H** (Bs); **POINTE DU VAN** (Kn) ex-*Pointe De Penharn*

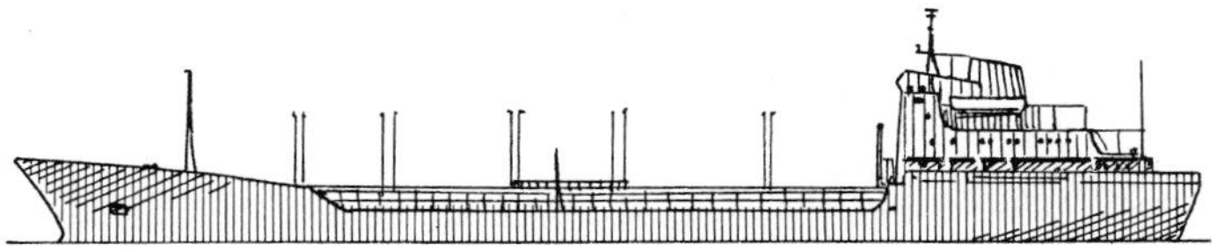

34 *ME^3NE^2NMF H13*
STAINLESS QUEEN Pa/FRG (Kroegerw) 1971; Ch; 2,726 grt/4,925 dwt; 106.03 × 6.43 m *(347.87 × 21.1 ft)*; M (Alpha-Diesel); 14.5 kts; ex-*Terkol*

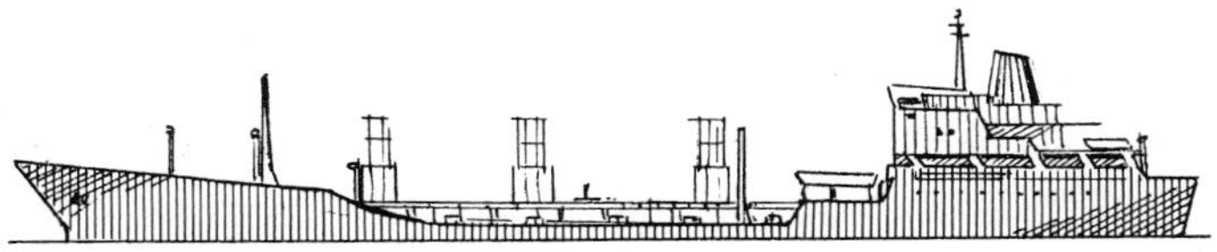

35 *ME^3NMF H13*
CHAMPA STAR Mv/No (Ankerlokken) 1972; Ch; 2,380 grt/3,439 dwt; 100.72 × 5.89 m *(330.45 × 19.32 ft)*; M (Nydqvist & Holm); 16 kts; ex-*Sunmark*

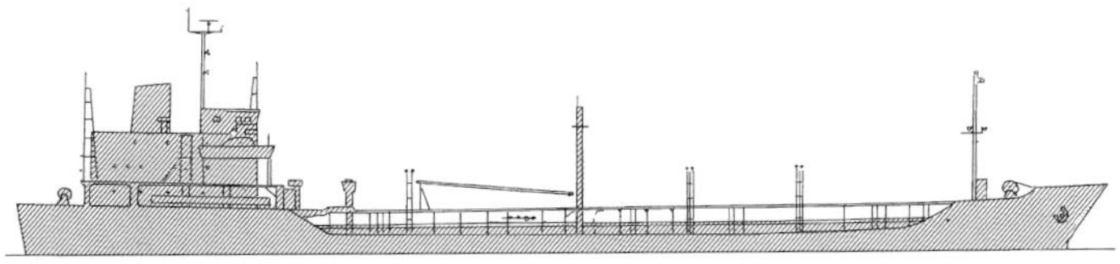

36 *ME^2MEM^2FM H13*
SHIN YANG Ko/Ja (Fukuoka) 1985; Tk/Ch/MT; 4,206 grt/7,199 dwt; 106.51 × 6.71 m *(349.44 × 22.01 ft)*; M (Mitsubishi); 12.25 kts; ex-*Global Mercury*
Sister: **TRADEWIND RIVER** (Pa) ex-*Malaysian Pride*; Possible sisters: **GLOBAL MARS** (Pa); **ANDHIKA ADHITSATYA** (Sg) ex-*Global Venus*; **TRADEWIND STAR** (Pa) ex-*Global Uranus*; **ANDHIKA ARYANDHI** (Sg); **ANDHIKA ADIPARWA** (Pa); **ANDHIKA ASHURA** (Ia); **OCEAN MEG** (Pa) ex-*Andhika Anuraga*; **SAN ANTONIO** (Bl) ex-*Panam Clipper*; Similar: **MARTIN SIF** (Bs) ex-*White Atlas*; **KILCHEM BALTIC** (Bs) ex-*Golden Arrow*

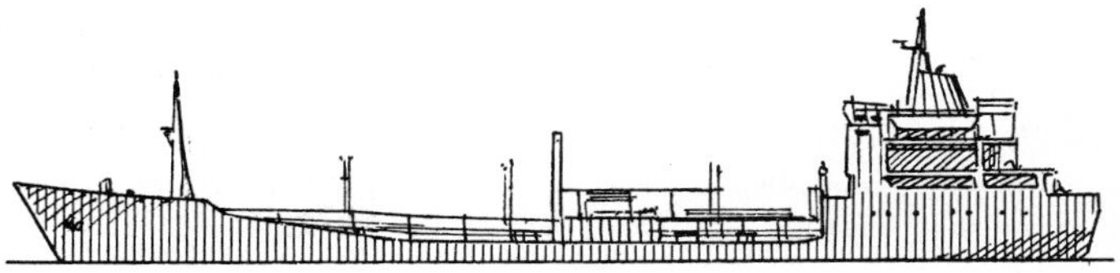

37 *ME^2MEM-F H13*
GUN Tu/No (Karmsund) 1973; Ch; 1,749 grt/3,195 dwt; 82.76 × 6.06 m *(271.52 × 19.88 ft)*; M (MWM); 13 kts; ex-*Bow Saphir*
Sister: **LIVIA** (Pa) ex-*Bow Alecto*; Possibly similar: **TAUFIQ** (SV) ex-*Bow Sailor*

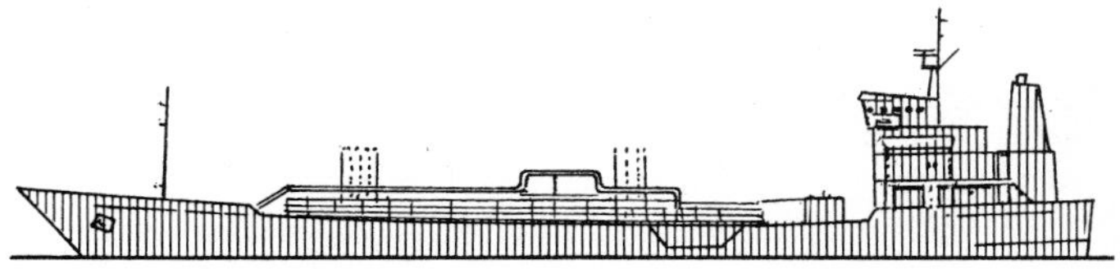

38 *ME^2MF H*
RODENBEK At/FRG (Buesumer) 1981; Ch; 1,599 grt/3,914 dwt; 91.72 × 6.22 m *(301 × 20.41 ft)*; M (MaK); 12.5 kts; Sisters: **FLOTTBEK** (At); **REINBEK** (At); **LAUENBURG** (At); **JERSBEK** (Li) ex-*Cape Island*; **MULTITANK CATANIA** (Li) ex-*Crest Island*; **MULTITANK CALABRIA** (Li) ex-*Southern Island*; **LASBEK** (Li) ex-*Sandy Island*

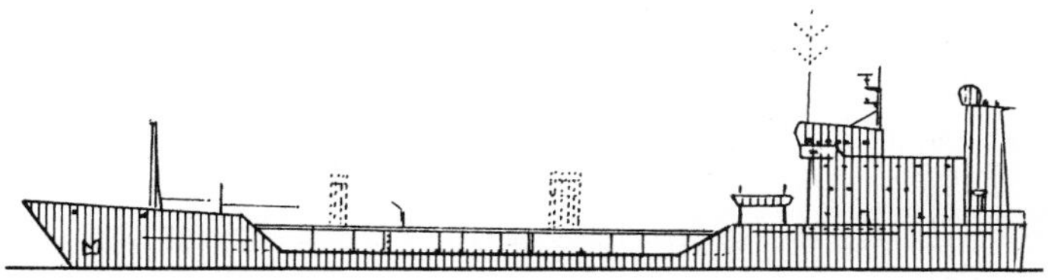

39 *ME^2MF H13*
ANTIGUA Cy/FRG (Menzer) 1981; Tk/Ch; 3,253 grt/4,613 dwt; 99.12 × 6.01 m *(325 × 19.72 ft)*; M (Mitsubishi); 14 kts
Sister: **BONAIRE** (Cy)

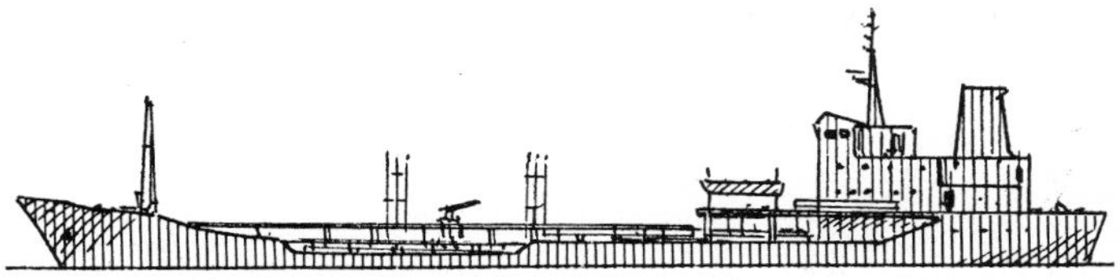

40 *ME^2MF H13*
KEREM KA Tu/Br (Cochrane) 1976; Ch; 1,513 grt/2,324 dwt; 79.51 × 5.27 m *(260.86 × 17.29 ft)*; M (WH Allen); 13.75 kts; ex-*Stellaman*
Sister: **OCEEANA KAREEMATA** (Pa) ex-*Marsman*

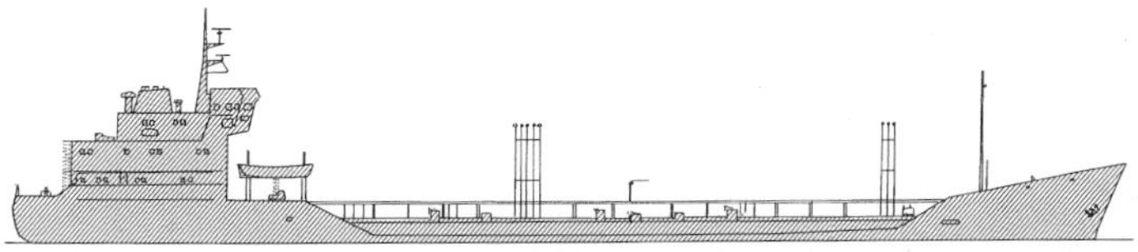

41 *ME^2MF H13*
PUNTA ALA It/FRG (Menzer) 1968; Ch; 1,530 grt/2,273 dwt; 85.43 × 4.36 m *(280.28 × 14.30 ft)*; M (MaK); 12 kts; ex-*Alchimist Hamburg*; Lengthened 1979

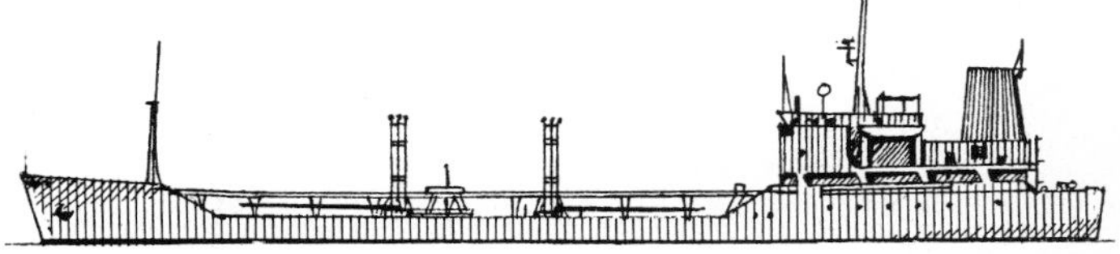

42 *ME^2MF H13*
STOLT MAPLEWOOD NIS/Br (Hall, Russell) 1976; Ch; 2,564 grt/3,560 dwt; 89.18 × 5.9 m *(292.59 × 19.36 ft)*; M (Mirrlees Blackstone); 13.5 kts; ex-*Centaurman*
Sister: **STOLT OAKWOOD** (NIS) ex-*Vegaman*

43 *ME^2MFR H13*
KWAN SIU Li/FRG (Menzer) 1976; Ch; 1,686 grt/2,493 dwt; 80.73 × 5.48 m *(264.86 × 17.98 ft)*; M (MaK); 12 kts; ex-*Solvent Challenger*
Sister: **RAINBOW CHASER** (Li) ex-*Solvent Discoverer*

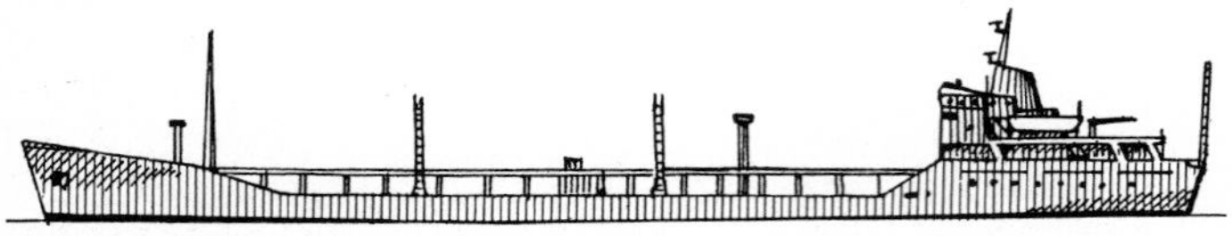

44 *ME^{2}MM-FN H13*
CONCORDE SV/Br (Dunston) 1975; Ch; 2,380 grt/2,700 dwt; 97.52 × 6.2 m *(319.95 × 20.35 ft)*; M (Mirrlees Blackstone); 15 kts; ex-*Pass of Balmaha*
Similar: **NING HUA 404** (RC) ex-*Pass of Brander*

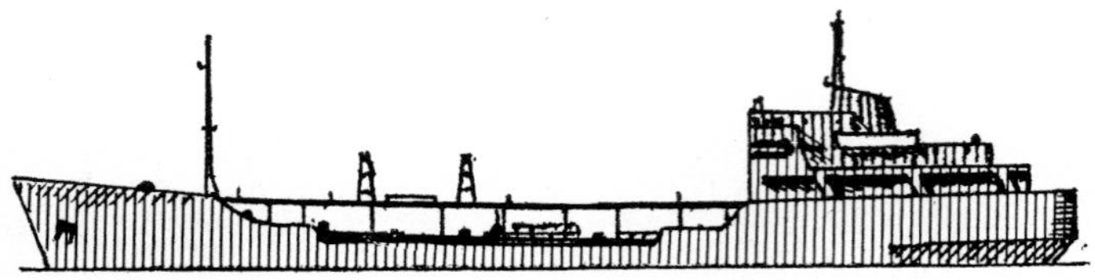

45 *ME^{2}M-F H13*
ARUN Ma/Sw (Lodose) 1968; Tk/Ch; 1,249 grt/1,901 dwt; 77.32 × 4.8 m *(253.67 × 15.75 ft)*; M (MWM); 12 kts; ex-*Silvermerlin*
Similar: **DIDI** (Ma) ex-*Silverfalcon*

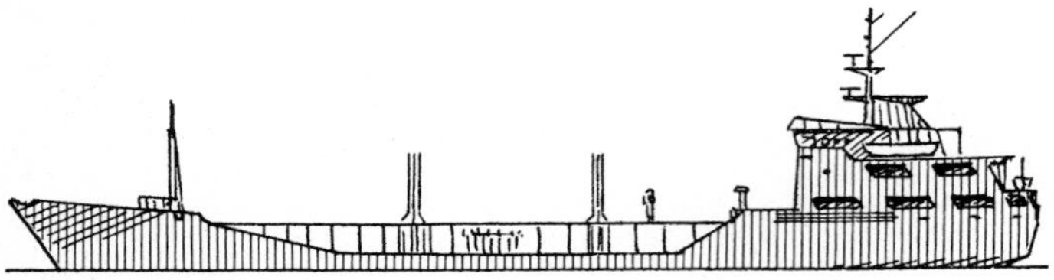

46 *ME^{2}M-F H13*
MARE AURUM Cy/No (Karmsund) 1977; Ch; 2,002 grt/3,153 dwt; 83.01 × 5.91 m *(272.34 × 19.4 ft)*; M (Smit & Bolnes); 13 kts; ex-*Mare Novum*
Sisters: **BREEZE** (Bs) ex-*Mare Bonum*; **MARE ARGENTUM** (Cy) ex-*Mare Magnum*

47 *ME^{2}M-F H13*
ODET Kn/FRG (Buesumer) 1975; WT; 1,599 grt/3,641 dwt; 90.1 × 5.72 m *(295.6 × 18.77 ft)*; M (Atlas-MaK); 13.5 kts
Sister: **RHONE** (Sd)

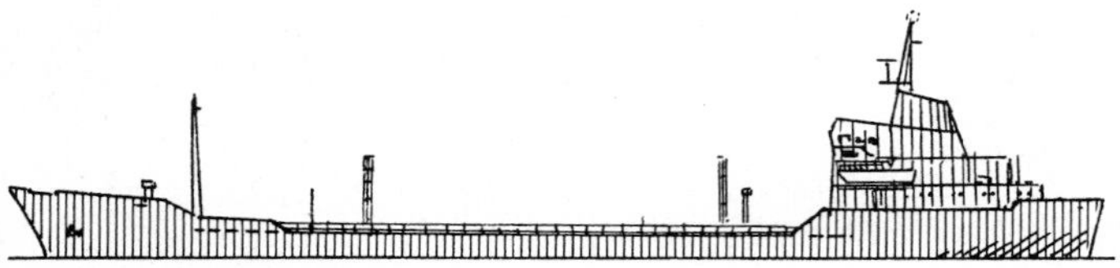

48 *ME^{2}M-F H13*
RHIN SV/Ne (Groot & VV) 1974; WT/Ch; 1,843 grt/3,141 dwt; 90.76 × 5.49 m *(297.77 × 18.01 ft)*; M (Atlas-MaK); 14 kts

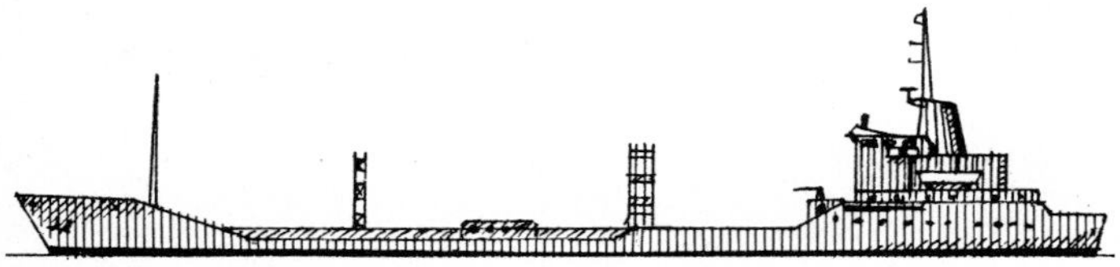

49 *ME^{2}M-F H13*
STRAMAN HK/Br (Cochrane) 1973; Ch; 1,969 grt/3,202 dwt; 87.41 × 5.5 m *(286.78 × 18.04 ft)*; M (Ruston Paxman); 14 kts; ex-*Astraman*
Sister: **GOD PRESTIGE** (SV) ex-*Polarisman*

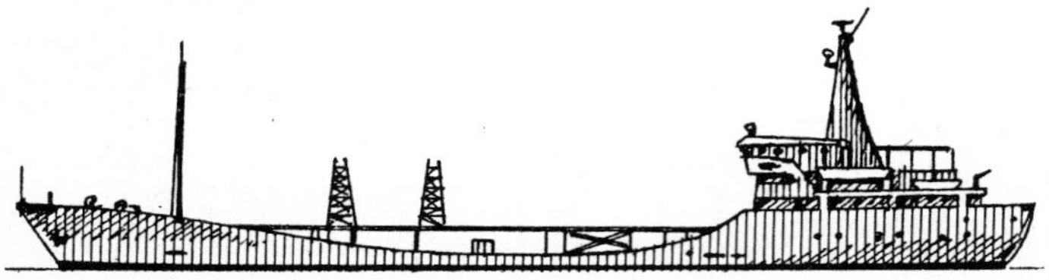

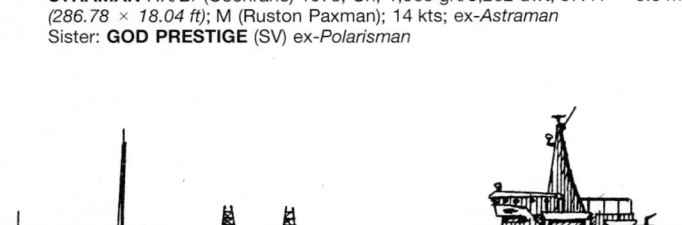

50 *ME^{2}M-F H13*
SULFURICO Sp/Sp (Ruiz) 1969; Ch; 1,174 grt/1,940 dwt; 77.32 × 4.76 m *(253.67 × 15.62 ft)*; M (Stork-Werkspoor); 12 kts
Sisters: **FOSFORICO** (Sp); **CAPITAN ALBERTO FERNANDEZ** (Cu); **VEGLIO** (Ma) ex-*Nitrico*

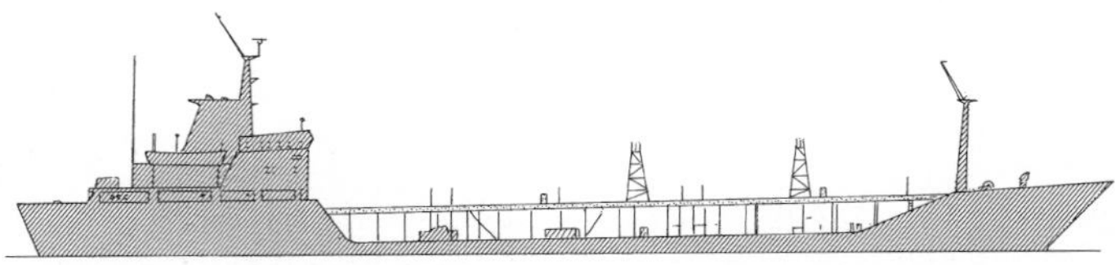

51 *ME^{2}M-FM/ME^{2}M-FN H13*
ESTIRENO Br/Sp (Ruiz) 1977; Ch; 2,612 grt/3,970 dwt; 101.02 × 6.41 m *(331.43 × 21.03 ft)*; M (Werkspoor); 15 kts
Sister: **BENCENO** (Br); Similar: **SANDGROUSE** (Bs) (Tk/Ch) ex-*Xileno*; **TOLUENO** (Sp)

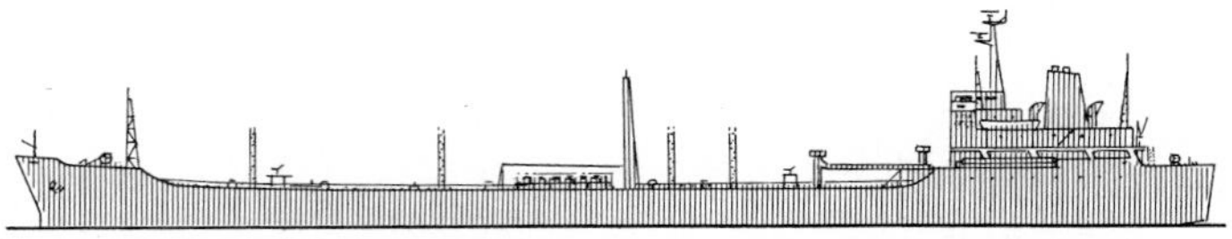

52 *ME^{2}NE^{2}MFN H13*
ORI A Pa/Ja (Koyo) 1978; Tk/Ch; 14,741 grt/21,495 dwt; 163 × 9.22 m *(535 × 30.25 ft)*; M (B&W); 14.75 kts; ex-*Terutoku Maru*

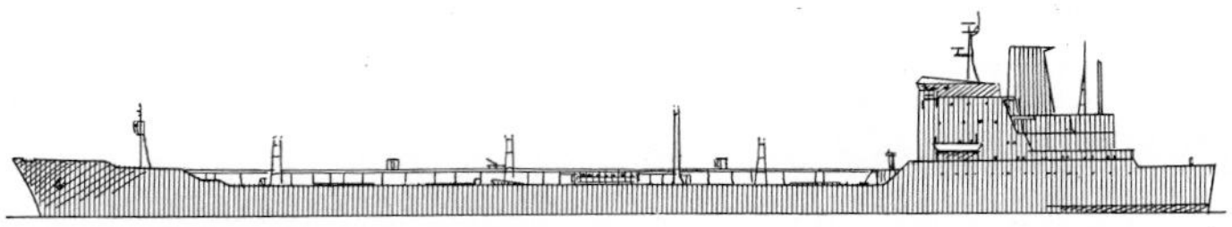

53 *ME^{2}NEMFM^2 H13*
NAFTI Li/Sw (Oskarshamns) 1974; Tk; 17,955 grt/31,241 dwt; 170.77 × 10.97 m *(560.27 × 35.99 ft)*; M (Gotaverken); 15.5 kts; ex-*Sofie*
Sisters: **NORMAR SPIRIT** (Li) ex-*Sonja*; **RABIGH BAY 1** (Gr) ex-*Susanne*;
Similar: **FEARLESS** (Cy) Launched as *Messiniaki Proodos*; **MARINER LT** (Cy) Launched as *Messiniaki Doxa*

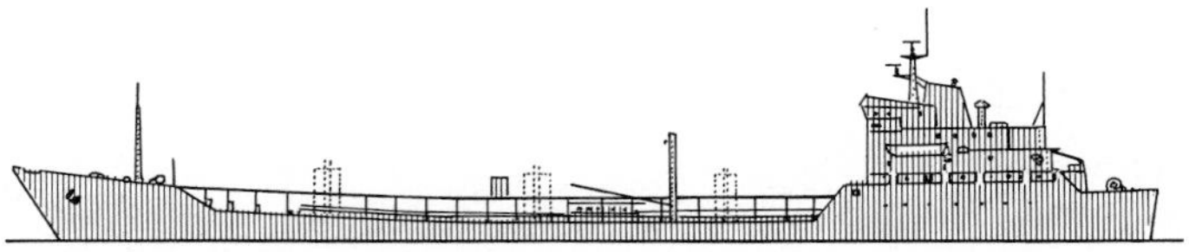

54 *ME^{2}NEMFNR H13*
KAPITAN RADIONOV Uk/Sp (Cantabrico) 1981; Tk/Ch; 5,512 grt/10,079 dwt; 133.03 × 7.95 m *(436.45 × 26.08 ft)*; M (Deutz); 13.50 kts; ex-*Marmara*
Sister: **PROFESSOR NEBESNOV** (Uk) ex-*Cantabrico*

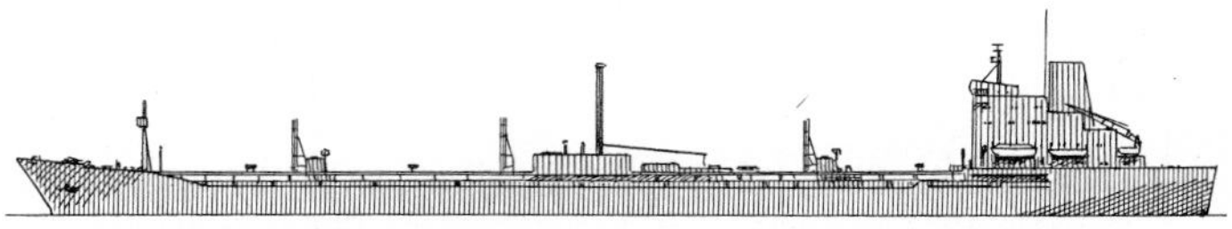

55 *ME^{2}NEMFR H13*
CHAC Me/No (Ankerlokken) 1976; Ch; 17,626 grt/29,500 dwt; 170.69 × 13.25 m *(560 × 43.47 ft)*; M (B&W); 15.5 kts; ex-*Fossanger*
Sister: **BACAB** (Me) ex-*Bow Clipper*

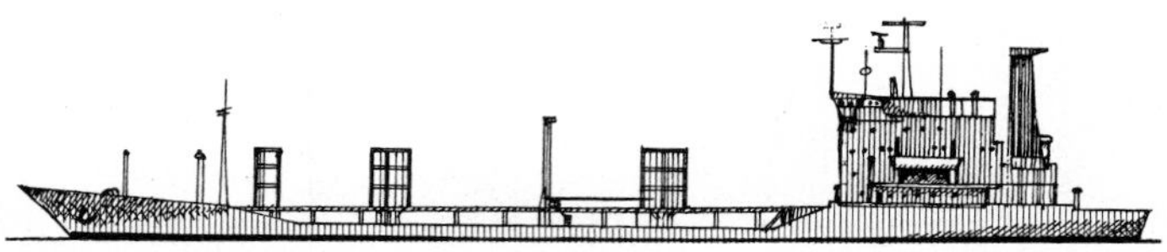

56 *ME^{2}NEMG H13*
BETACRUX It/No (Langvik) 1973; Ch; 5,077 grt/7,751 dwt; 129.85 × 7 m *(426.01 × 22.97 ft)*; M (Wichmann); 16 kts; ex-*Thoralbe*
Sisters: **BAKRI VOYAGER** (Pa) ex-*Thorheide*; **RYKA** (Pa) ex-*Thordrache*; **ALTAIR** (It) ex-*Thorodland*; Possibly similar: **KIRA** (Pa) ex-*Thorhamer*; **HATAN** (Pa) ex-*Thorhaven*

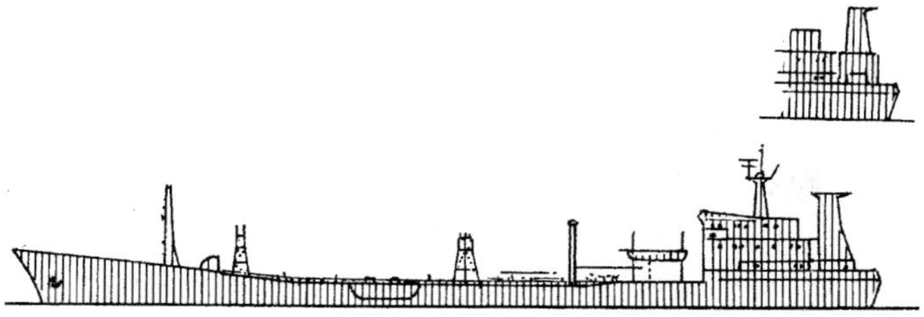

57 *ME^{2}NMF H*
STELLAMAN HK/FRG (Kroegerw) 1980; Ch/Tk; 2,804 grt/3,680 dwt; 97.80 × 5.81 m *(320.87 × 19.06 ft)*; M (MaK); 12.75 kts
Sisters (both lengthened to approximately 1.051m (3.441ft): **WILLY** (Cy) ex-*Gerhard*; **PAUL** (Cy); Similar (also lengthened to 1.051m) (see inset): **EBERHARD** (Ge)

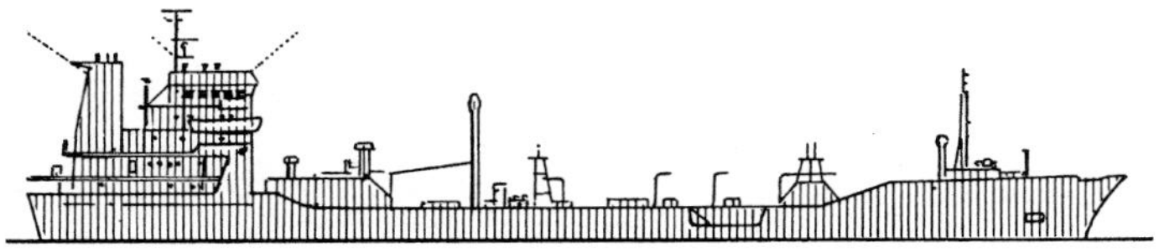

58 *ME^{2}NMF H1*
ROBERT At/FRG (Lindenau) 1979; Ch; 2,830 grt/3,679 dwt; 97.80 × 5.80 m *(320.87 × 19.03 ft)*; M (MaK); 13 kts
Sisters: **AZTEK** (Li); **APACHE** (Li); **SARIBAY** (Tu) ex-*Comanche*; **OSCONA** (Cy) ex-*Seneca*

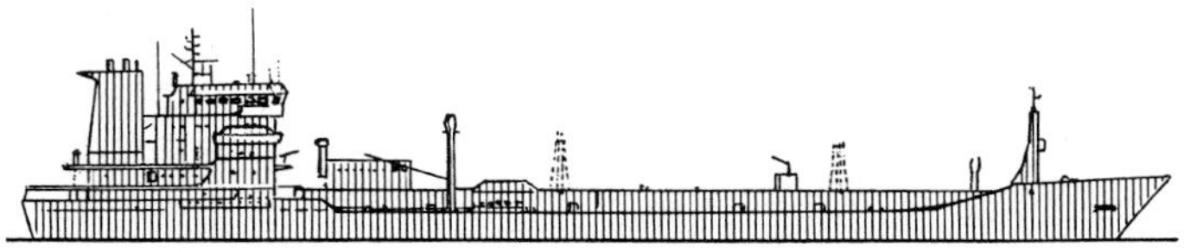

59 *ME^{2}NMF H1*
SIOUX Li/FRG (Lindenau) 1981; Tk/Ch; 4,270 grt/6,400 dwt; 115.02 × 7.3 m *(377 × 23.95 ft)*; M (Krupp-MaK); 14 kts
Sisters: **CHAGALL** (Sw) ex-*Indio*; **UNKAS** (Li)

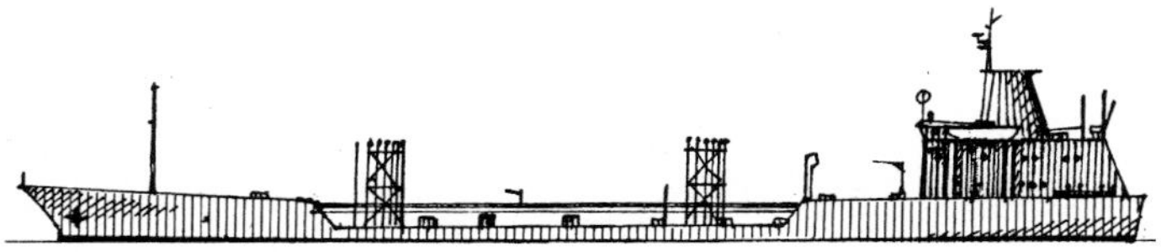

60 *ME^{2}NM-F H13*
ODET Kn/FRG (Buesumer) 1975; WT; 1,599 grt/3,641 dwt; 90.1 × 5.72 m *(295.6 × 18.77 ft)*; M (Atlas-MaK); 13.5 kts
Sister: **RHONE** (Sd)

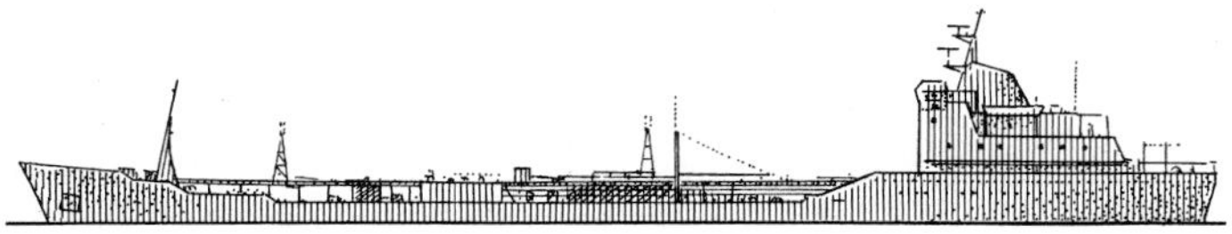

61 *ME^{2}NM-F H13*
STAINLESS DUKE Pa/Br (Cammell Laird) 1969; Tk/Ch; 6,183 grt/ 10,563 dwt; 130.21 × 7.53 m *(427.2 × 24.7 ft)*; M (Pielstick); 14.5 kts; ex-*Silverhawk*

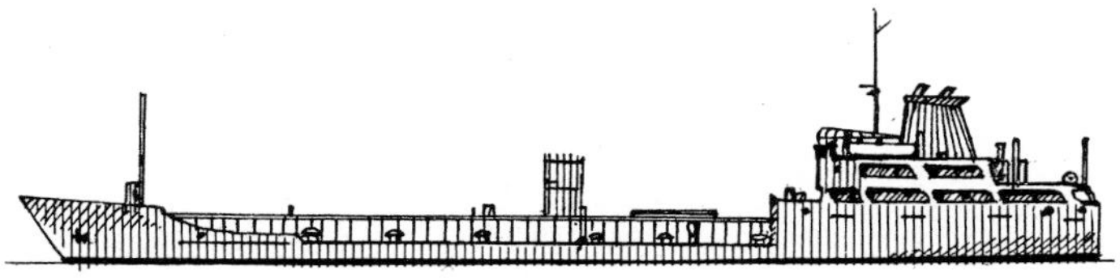

62 *MEHF H13*
MOPA WONSILD DIS/Ne (Nieuwe Noord) 1974; Ch; 1,780 grt/2,581 dwt; 80.78 × 5.38 m *(265.02 × 17.65 ft)*; M (Smit & Bolnes); 12.75 kts; ex-*Benvenue*
Sisters: **MERETE WONSILD** (DIS) ex-*Bencleuch*; **IRENE WONSILD** (DIS) ex-*Benmacdhui*

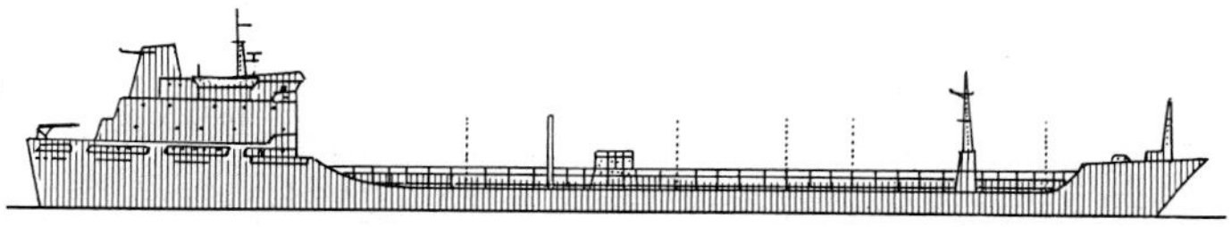

63 *MEME^{3}NEHFR H13*
MARIGOLA It/It (Benetti) 1981; Ch; 7,350 grt/11,815 dwt; 142.25 × 8.09 m *(466.70 × 26.54 ft)*; M (GMT); 16 kts
Sister: **ALESSANDRO VOLTA** (It); Probable sister: **VERAZZANO** (It) ex-*Maramozza*

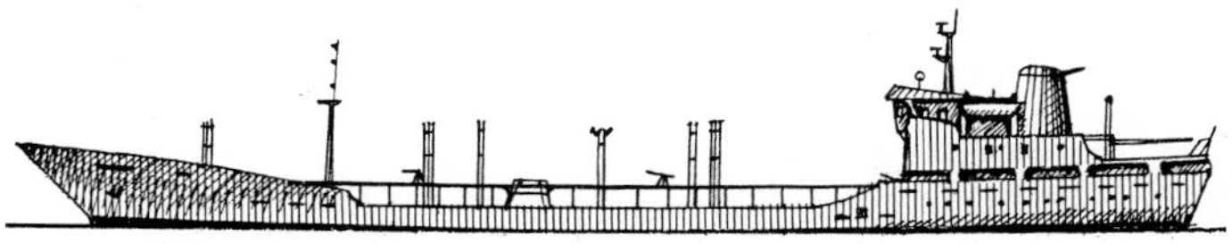

64 *MEME^{2}NE^{2}MFN H13*
TUS Ma/It (Benetti) 1975; Tk; 4,182 grt/7,154 dwt; 117.66 × 7.32 m *(386.02 × 24.02 ft)*; M (GMT); 15.5 kts; ex-*Pertusola*
Sister: **LUBA** (Ma) ex-*Pugiola*

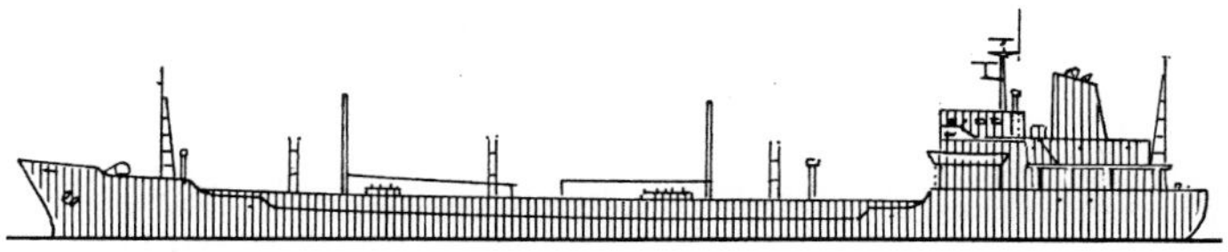

65 *MEMEMEMFN H13*
ROBELA Cy/Ja (Higaki Z) 1978; Tk/Ch; 3,902 grt/6,902 dwt; 105.57 × 7.07 m *(346.36 × 23.2 ft)*; M (Hanshin); 13 kts; ex-*Rich Crane*
Probable sister: **ELFATEH** (Ly) ex-*Silver Crane*; Possible sister: **KILCHEM OCEANIA** (Bs) ex-*Oceania Glory*

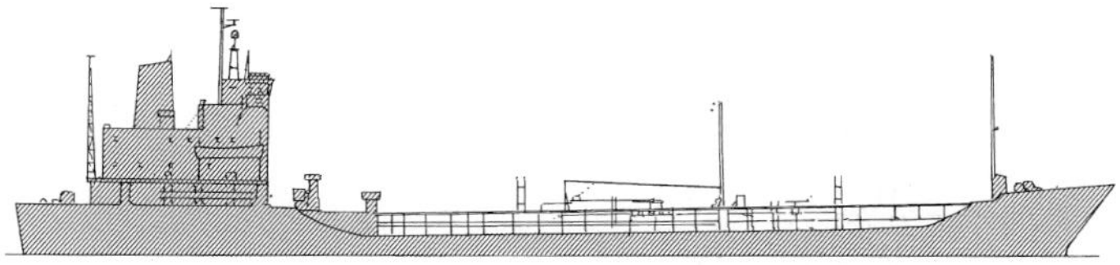

66 *MEMEM^{2}FM H13*
BRAGE SUPPLIER NIS/Ja (Towa) 1985; Tk/Ch/MT; 4,839 grt/7,287 dwt; 114.51 × 6.73 m *(375.69 × 22.08 ft)*; M (MaK); 11.75 kts
Sister: **PACIFIC SPIRIT** (Fj) ex-*Brage Trader*

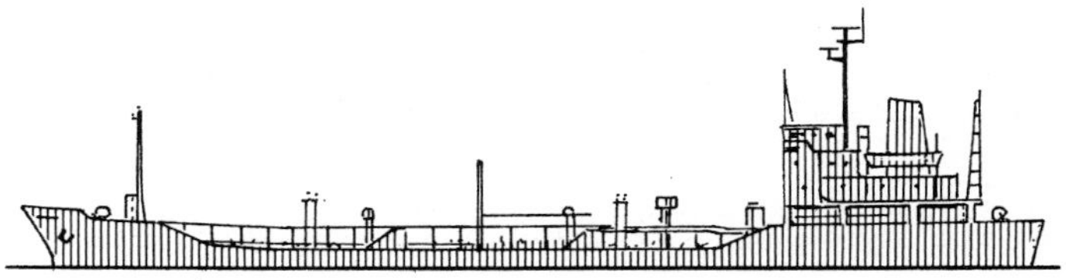

67 *MEMEM^{2}FM H13*
UNIX JAWA Pa/Ja (Towa) 1984; Ch; 2,759 grt/4,201 dwt; 94.01 × 6.27 m *(308.43 × 20.57 ft)*; M (Hanshin); 13.25 kts; ex-*Southern Cross 8*

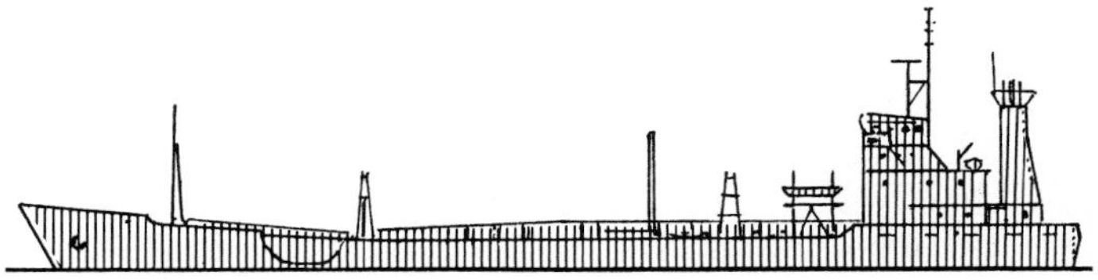

68 *MEMEMM-F H*
STOR Ge/FRG (Schichau-U) 1981; Ch; 2,510 grt/4,040 dwt; 89.08 × 5.6 m *(292.26 × 18.37 ft)*; M (Krupp-MaK); 12 kts

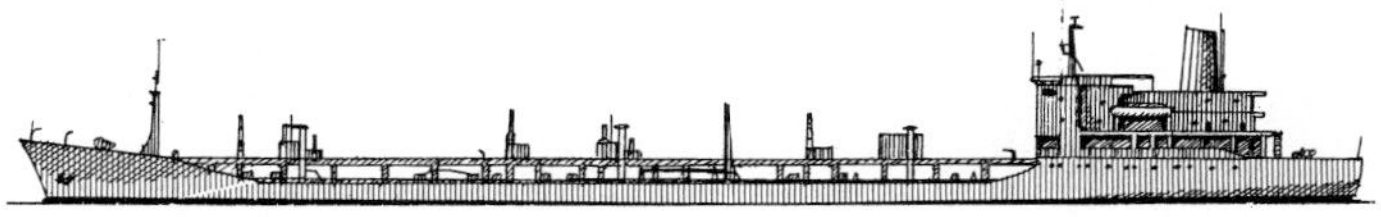

69 *MEMEMNEM^{2}FN H13*
NEW EMPRESS Li/Sw (Uddevalla) 1971; Tk; 14,780 grt/24,222 dwt; 169.7 × 9.69 m *(556.76 × 31.79 ft)*; M (B&W); 16 kts; ex-*Anco Empress*; May have been converted to a liquefied gas carrier
Sister: **LADY SOVEREIGN** (Li) ex-*Anco Sovereign*

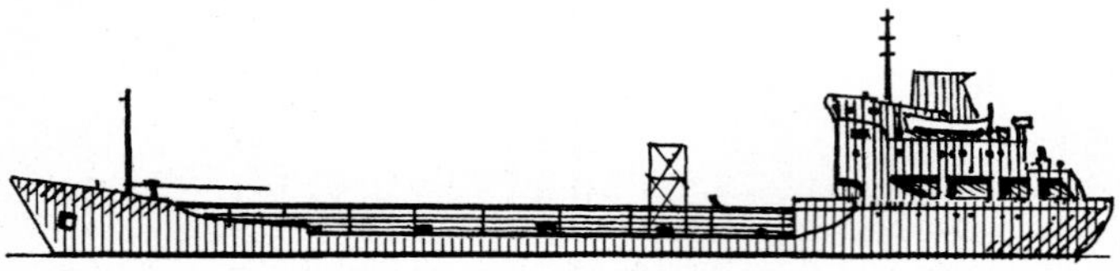

70 *MEMF H13*
DUTCH GLORY Ne/Ne (Nieuwe Noord) 1975; Tk/Ch; 1,640 grt/2,321 dwt; 80.24 × 5.42 m *(263.25 × 17.78 ft)*; M (KHD); 13.5 kts
Sister: **DUTCH MASTER** (Ne); Similar (superstructure more open): **LUCY PG** (Bs) ex-*Corrie Broere* (lengthened 1983 - now 1,031m (3,381ft))

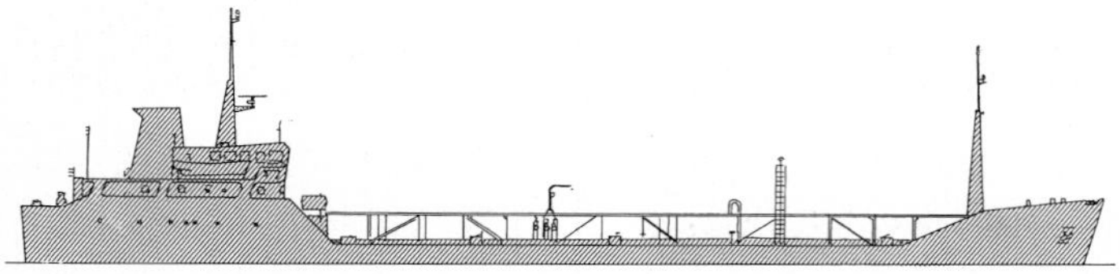

71 *MEMF H13*
OARSMAN Br/Br (Dunston) 1980; Tk; 1,449 grt/2,547 dwt; 76.13 × 4.86 m *(249.77 × 15.94 ft)*; M (Ruston); 10.5 kts

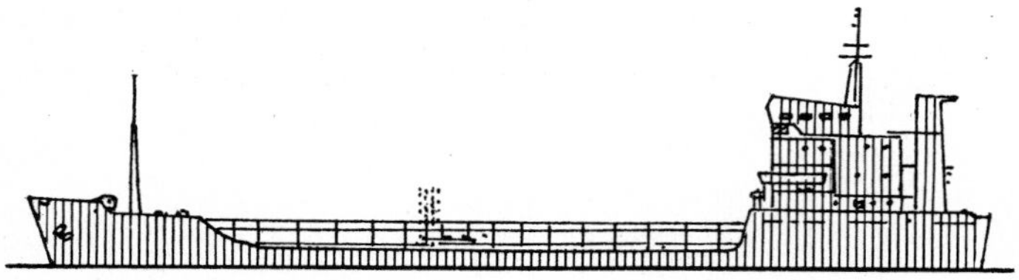

72 *MEMG H13*
AMORIA Br/Br (Clelands) 1981; Tk; 1,926 grt/3,027 dwt; 79.25 × 5.03 m *(260 × 16.5 ft)*; M (Mirrlees Blackstone); 12 kts; ex-*Shell Marketer*
Sisters: **ASPRELLA** (Br) ex-*Shell Seafarer*; **ARIANTA** (Br) ex-*Shell Technician*

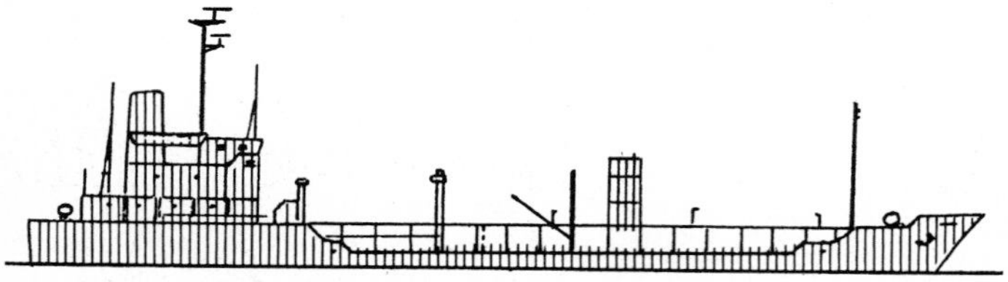

73 *MEM^{4}FM H13*
JI HUA RC/Ja (Sanuki) 1985; Tk/Ch/MT; 1,389 grt/2,206 dwt; 75.95 × 5.06 m *(249.18 × 16.60 ft)*; M (Akasaka); 11 kts; ex-*Day Crux*

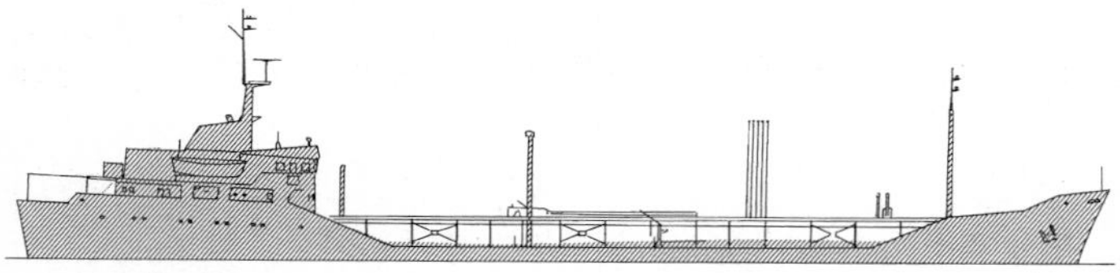

74 *MEMM-F H13*
DANYANNE Ma/Ne (Wilton-Fije) 1969; Tk/Ch; 1,388 grt/2,256 dwt; 80.52 × 5.20 m *(264.17 × 17.06 ft)*; M (English Electric); 13.5 kts; ex-*La Quinta*

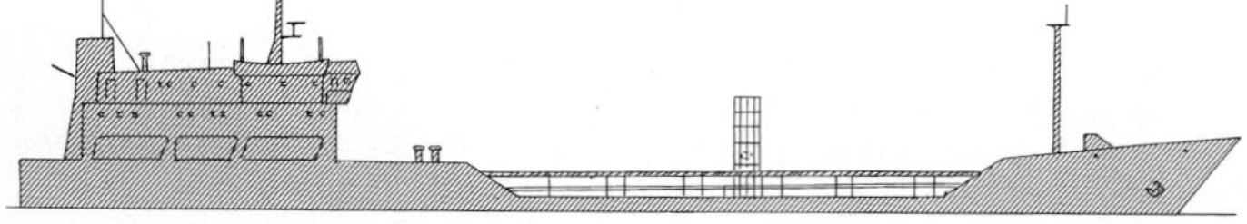

75 *MEMM-F H13*
NANDO It/FRG (Menzer) 1979; Ch/WT/VO; 2,520 grt/3,461 dwt; 94.42 × 5.54 m *(309.78 × 18.18 ft)*; M (MaK); 13.75 kts; ex-*Nabeul*

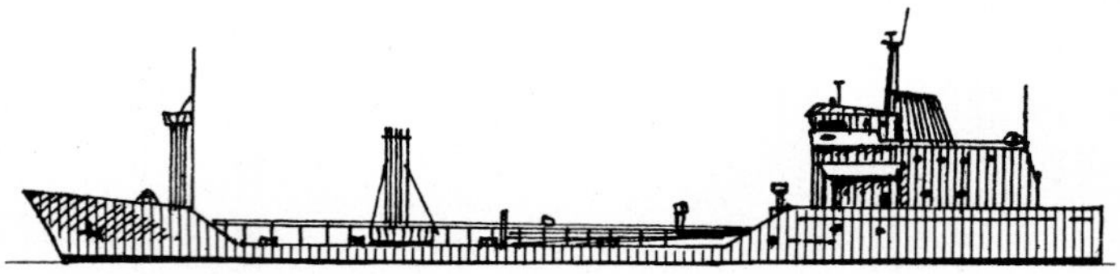

76 *MEM-F H13*
MARE ALTUM At/Ne (Ysselwerf) 1974; Ch; 1,597 grt/2,678 dwt; 80.75 × 5.56 m *(264.93 × 18.24 ft)*; M (Mirrlees Blackstone); 13.5 kts; ex-*Pass of Drumochter*
Sister: **MARE IRATUM** (At) ex-*Pass of Dirriemore*

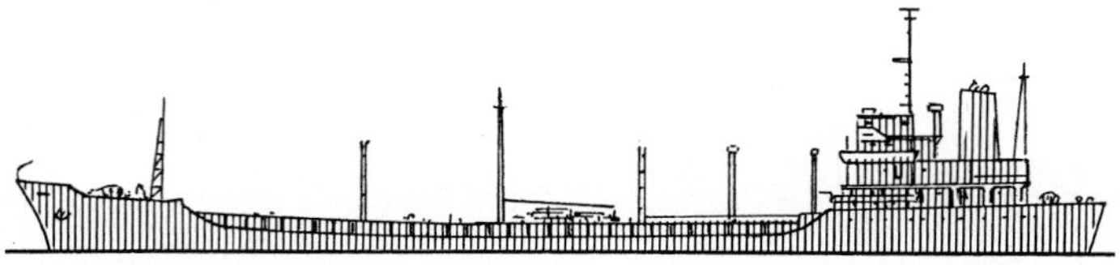

77 *MENE^{2}NMFN H13*
DADES Mo/Ja (Miyoshi) 1977; Tk; 3,694 grt/6,211 dwt; 106.03 × 6.80 m *(348 × 22.31 ft)*; M (Akasaka); 13.5 kts; ex-*Fujiaki Maru*
Possibly similar: **SULU SEA** (Pa) ex-*Dae Won*; **TELLI-1** (Tu) ex-*Blue Sky*; **C P 26** (Th) ex-*Fujiaki Maru*

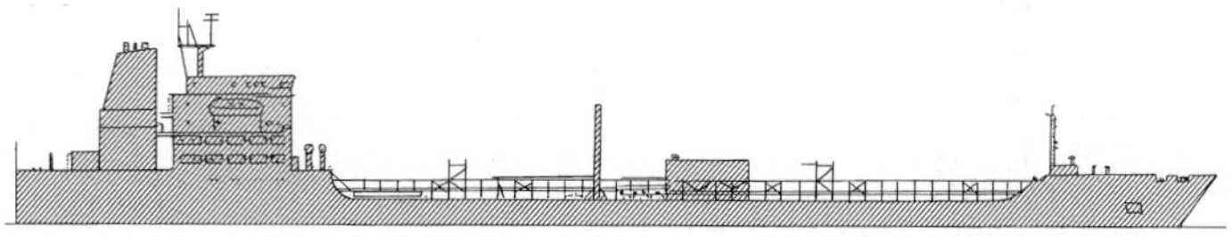

78 *MENEMF H13*
BEN AICHA Mo/Fr (Nord Med) 1987; Ch; 16,477 grt/24,210 dwt; 173.01 × 9.85 m *(567.62 × 32.32 ft)*; M (Sulzer); — kts
Sister: **AL KORTOUBI** (Mo); Similar (without large housing in foreward section of well): **AL FARABI** (Mo); **ADDARRAQ** (Mo); Similar: **CHUY** (Bz); **MERITY** (Bz)

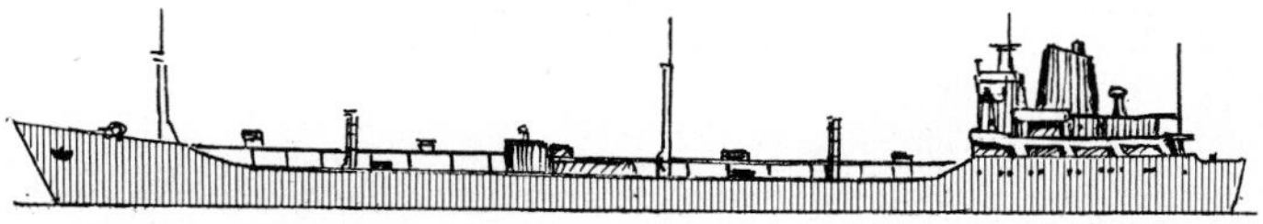

79 *MENEMFN H13*
ENERCHEM CATALYST Ca/Br (Robb Caledon) 1972; Tk; 6,159 grt/10,730 dwt; 131.37 × 8.39 m *(431 × 27.53 ft)*; M (Pielstick); 15 kts; ex-*Jon Ramsoy*

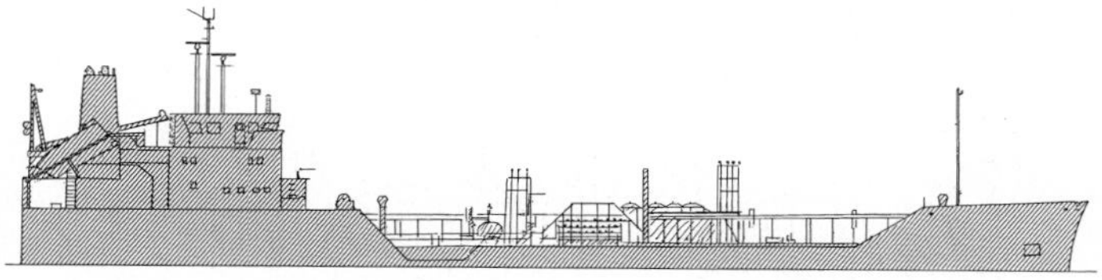

80 *MENEM^{3}FCL H13*
RENO Po/FRG (Sietas) 1986; Ch; 2,238 grt/2,903 dwt; 81.01 × 5.53 m *(265.78 × 18.14 ft)*; M (Wärtsilä); 13 kts; ex-*Heinrich Essberger*; Free-fall lifeboat on starboard side and crane on port side
Sister: **EBRO** (Po) ex-*Eberhart Essberger*

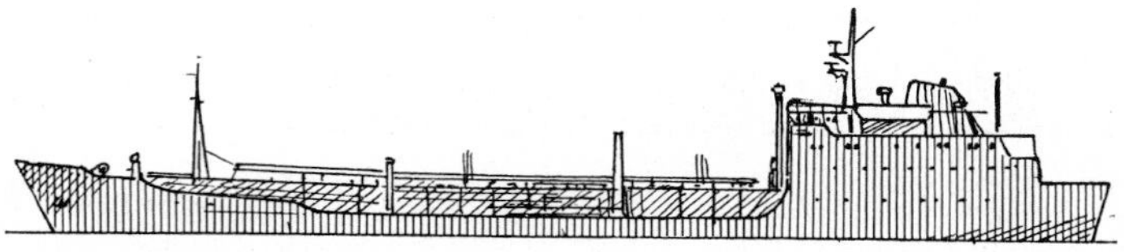

81 *MENENMFN H13*
BABUR KAPTAN Tu/No (Akers) 1965; Tk; 2,847 grt/4,142 dwt; 100.87 × 6.1 m *(330.94 × 19.95 ft)*; M (B&W); 12 kts; ex-*Hassel*

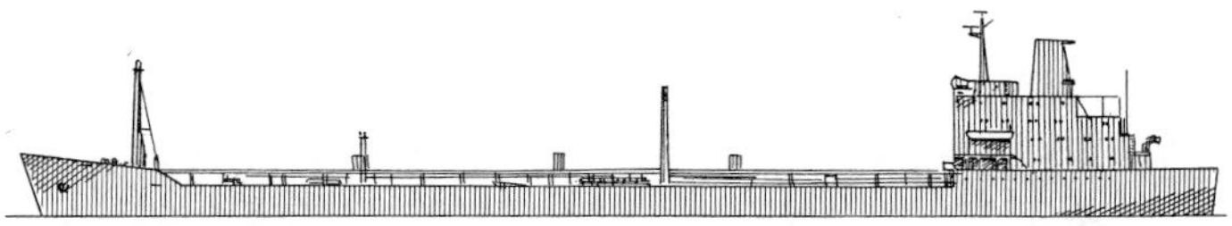

82 *MENMF H13*
CARRIER LT Cy/No (Horten) 1975; Tk; 17,363 grt/31,600 dwt; 168.76 × 10.9 m *(553.67 × 36.76 ft)*; M (Sulzer); 16 kts; ex-*Ardmay*
Sister: **ASEAN PROMOTER** (Sg); ex-*Ardmore*

83 *MENMF H13*
ARCTIC STAR SV/FRG (Kroegerw) 1973; Ch; 4,599 grt/6,720 dwt; 113.14 × 7.41 m *(371.19 × 24.31 ft)*; M (Mirrlees Blackstone); 14 kts; ex-*Silverpelerin*

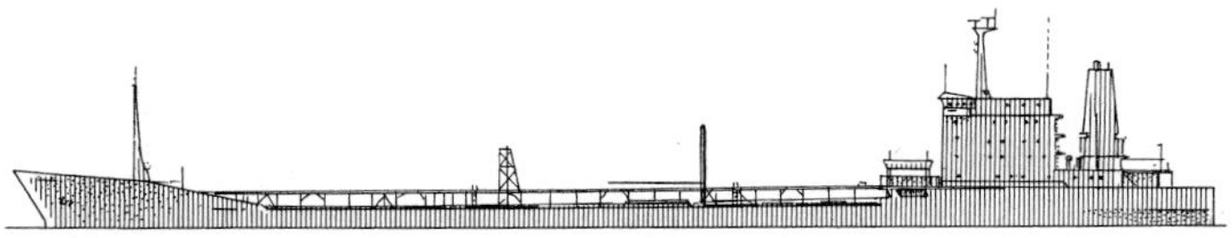

84 *MENMF H13*
IBN ROCHD Mo/Ne ('De Hoop') 1977; Ch; 13,514 grt/21,900 dwt; 172.29 × 10.5 m *(565.26 × 34.45 ft)*; M (Pielstick); 17 kts
Sisters: **SPIC PEARL** (In) ex-*Ibn Albanna* (Norwegian built); **UNITANK** (Pa) ex-*Ibn Otman*

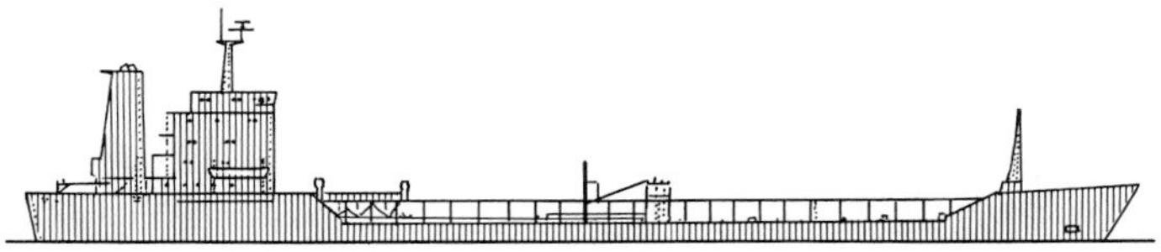

85 *MENMFR H13*
BUTT Ge/FRG (Schuerenstedt) 1980; Ch; 6,689 grt/10,507 dwt; 130.82 × 8.30 m *(429.20 × 27.23 ft)*; M (MaK); 15 kts
Probable sister: **MIRO** (Sw) ex-*Dorsch*

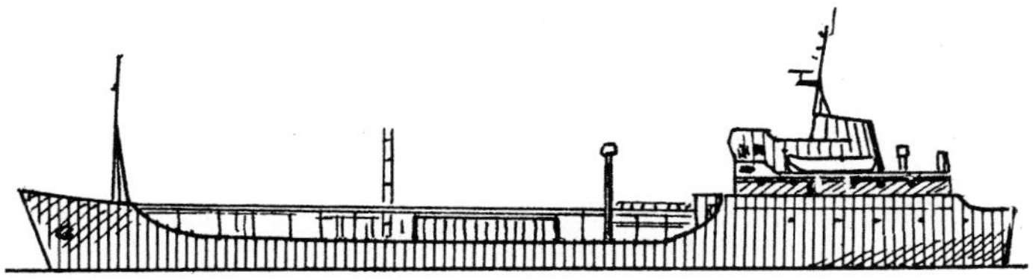

86 *MENM-F H13*
CAPETAN MICHALIS Gr/Br (Appledore) 1970; Tk/Ch; 918 grt/1,650 dwt; 70.16 × 4.19 m *(230.18 × 13.75 ft)*; M (English Electric); 11 kts; ex-*Cordale*; Lengthened 1972
Sister: **DOVERIAN** (Br) ex-*Cordene*

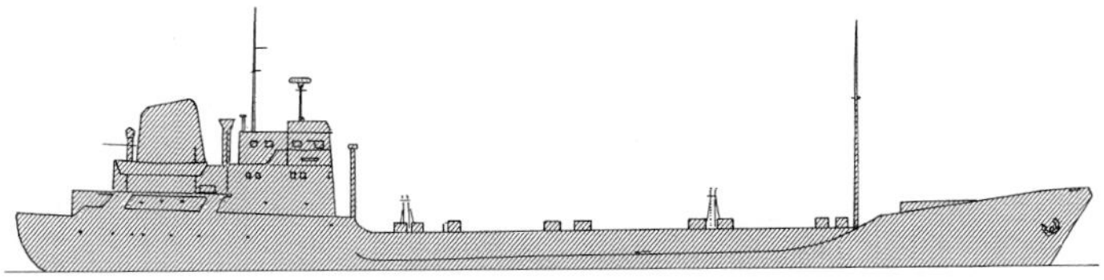

87 *MENVMFLR H1*
KEITUM Cy/FRG (Sietas) 1978/88; Ch; 3,370 grt/4,935 dwt; 105.47 × 6.15 m *(346.03 × 20.18 ft)*; M (Deutz); 13.5 kts; ex-*Hever*; Lengthened and converted from general cargo 1988
Sister: **RANTUM** (Cy) ex-*Eider*

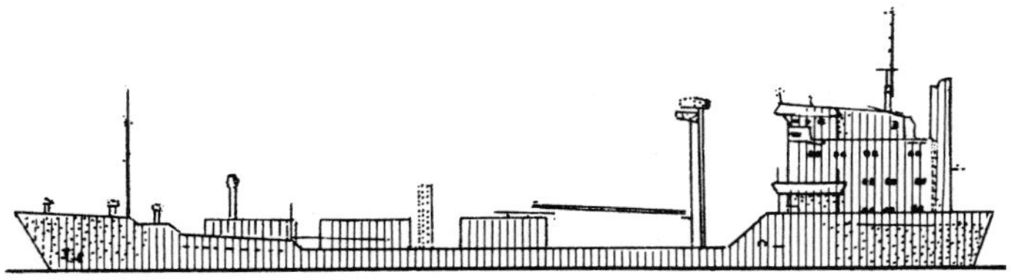

88 *METMG H13*
PROOF GALLANT Li/Ne (Groot & VV) 1980; Ch/WT; 2,783 grt/3,726 dwt; 89.52 × 6.16 m *(294 × 20.21 ft)*; M (Atlas-MaK); — kts

89 *MHF H123*
SHIRAZ Ma/Fi (Rauma-Repola) 1959; Tk; 2,915 grt/4,340 dwt; 105.11 × 6.13 m *(344.85 × 10.1 ft)*; M (B&W); 13.5 kts; ex-*Ventspils*
Sister: **PIRYATIN** (Ru)

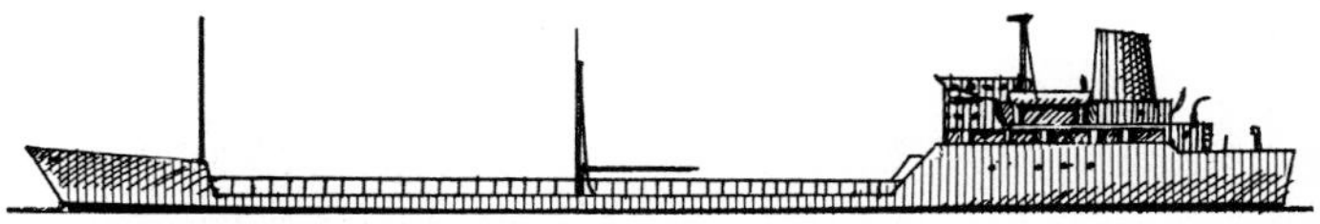

90 *MHMF H13*
POSSIDONIA Ma/Br (Robb Caledon) 1969; Tk; 3,009 grt/5,112 dwt; 101.73 × 6.57 m *(333.76 × 21.56 ft)*; M (English Electric); 14 kts; ex-*Port Tudy*

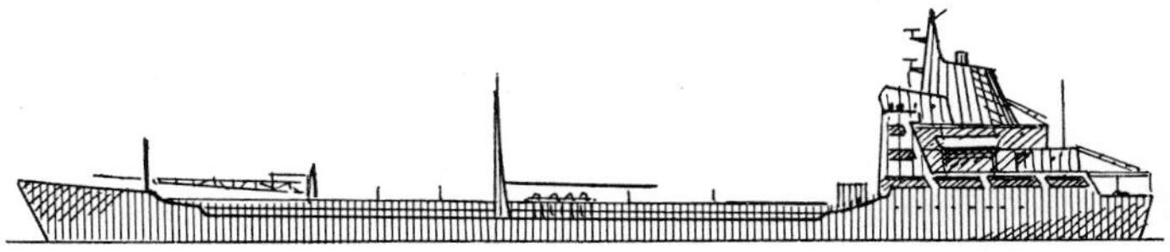

91 *MHM-F H13*
PYTHEAS Fr/It (INMA) 1972; Tk; 3,268 grt/4,959 dwt; 107.12 × 4.70 m *(351.44 × 15.42 ft)*; TSM (KHD); 11.5 kts
Sister: **EUTHYMENES** (Bl)

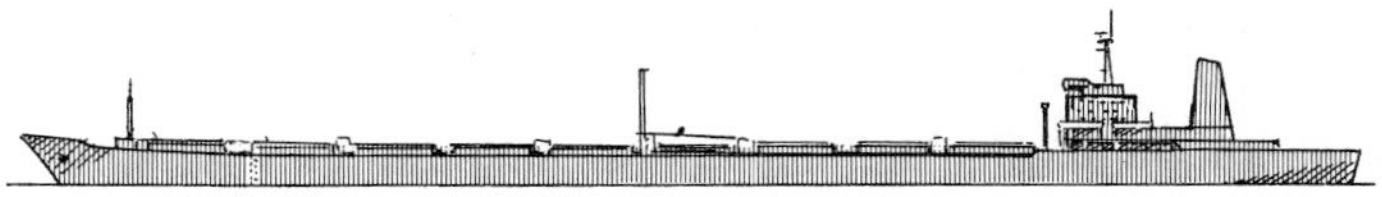

92 *MHNMG H*
BORIS BUTOMA Ru/Ru (Okean) 1978; BO; 63,180 grt/109,640 dwt; 258.22 × 15.65 m *(847.17 × 51.34 ft)*; M (B&W); 15 kts; ex-*Oktyabrsk*
Sisters: **AKADEMIK SECHENOV** (Ru); **GAMAL ABDEL NASER** (Ru); **IVAN TEVOSYAN** (Ru)

93 *MH-F H13*
ORATECA DIS/Tu (Meltem) 1982; VO; 1,733 grt/2,650 dwt; 84.84 × 4.74 m *(278.35 × 15.55 ft)*; M (Deutz); 11.5 kts; ex-*Tecumseh*; **SIMILAR TO DRAWING NUMBER 2/290**
Similar (tripod mast on Focsle): **CHEYENNE** (Li) ex-*Regina*

94 *M^2CF H123*
JUSSARA Ma/Fi (Rauma-Repola) 1963; Tk; 9,143 grt/16,320 dwt; 164.83 × 9.2 m *(540.78 × 30.18 ft)*; M (Gotaverken); 14.5 kts; ex-*Tervi*

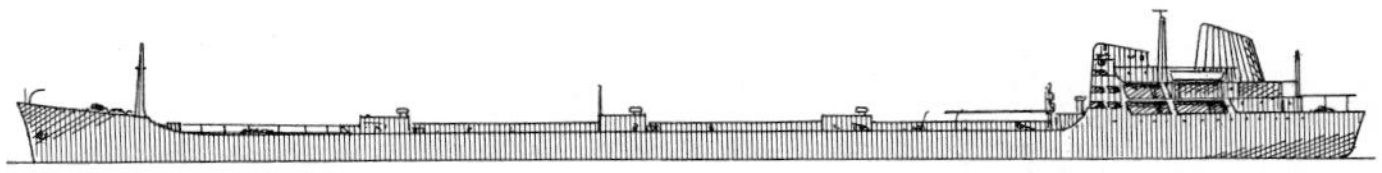

95 *M^2DHFN H13*
NORDIC LOUISIANA Va/Br (Furness) 1964; Sulphur Carrier; 18,589 grt/26,930 dwt; 188.98 × 10.35 m *(620.01 × 33.96 ft)*; M (Sulzer); 16 kts; ex-*Naess Louisiana*

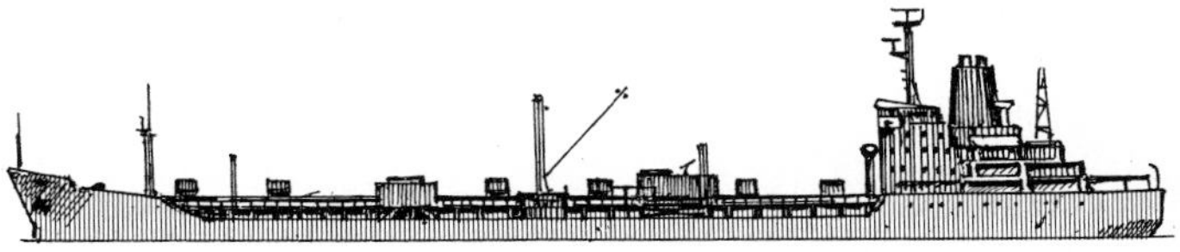

96 *M^2ENEMFN H13*
BUNGA KESUMBA My/Ja (Mitsubishi HI) 1975; Ch; 17,779 grt/29,956 dwt; 170.01 × 11.15 m *(557.78 × 36.58 ft)*; M (Sulzer); 15.25 kts
Sisters: **BUNGA SELASIH** (My); **BUNGA SEPANG** (My)

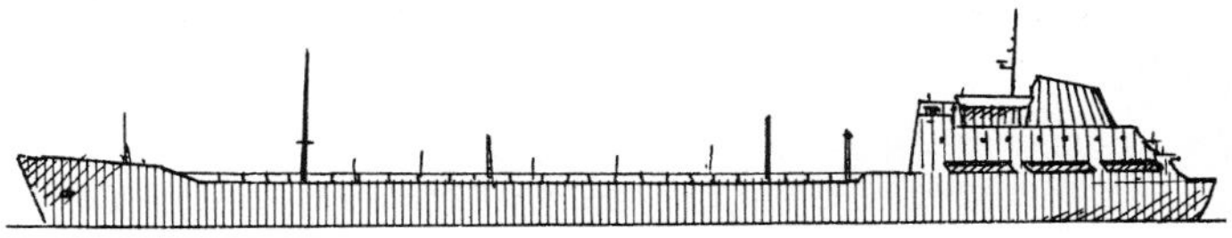

97 *M^2EN^{2}MF H1*
ARCTICA Br/Sw (Lodose) 1969; Tk; 2,671 grt/4,232 dwt; 98.94 × 6.43 m *(324.61 × 21.1 ft)*; M (MWM); 12 kts; ex-*Otelia*
Similar: **NORDSTAR** (Pa) ex-*Ottawa*; **KAPPA 1** (Ma) ex-*Otello*; **MOON TRADER** (NIS) ex-*Otaru*; **KARIM 1** (Pa) ex-*Otoni*

98 *M^2F H123*
EL PETROLERO Sp/Sp (Corcho) 1955; Tk; 1,911 grt/2,388 dwt; 83.39 × 5.14 (273.59 × 16.86) m; M (B&W); 9.5 kts; ex-*Campoo*

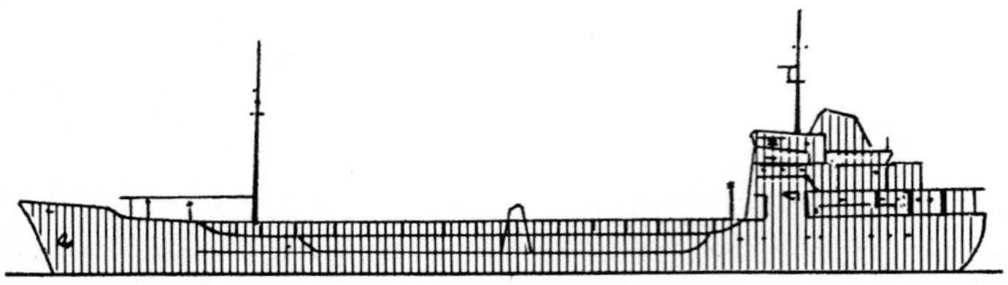

99 M^{2}F H13
AFRICAN QUEEN SV/It (Felszegi) 1967; Tk; 1,865 grt/3,035 dwt; 82.71 × 5.67 m *(271.36 × 18.60 ft)*; M (MWM); 11 kts; ex-*Rositza*

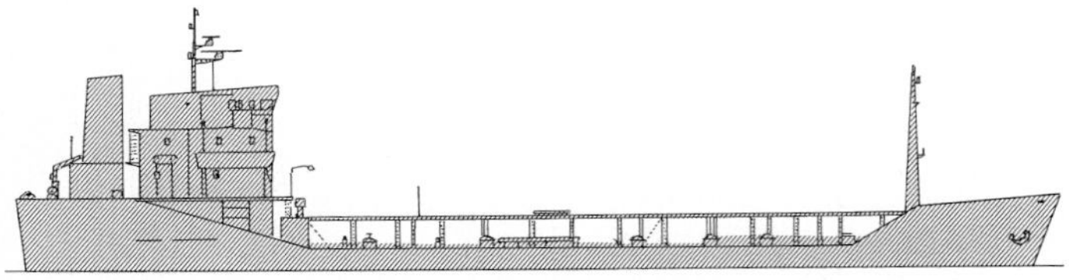

100 M^{2}F H13
BERJAYA DUA Sg/Br (Cochrane) 1980; Tk; 1,405 grt/2,162 dwt; 70.82 × 4.71 m *(232.35 × 15.45 ft)*; M (APE Allen); 11.75 kts; ex-*Esso Plymouth*

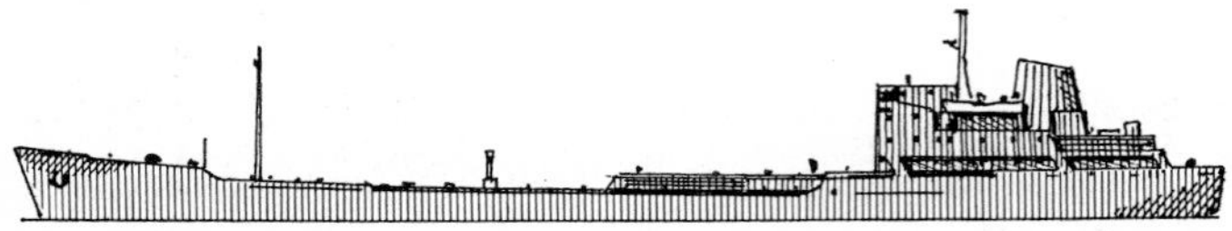

101 M^{2}F H13
EL MORO Ar/Sw (Ekensbergs) 1962; Tk; 4,467 grt/6,451 dwt; 118.78 × 6.86 m *(389.7 × 22.5 ft)*; M (Uddevalla); 14 kts; ex-*Rogn*

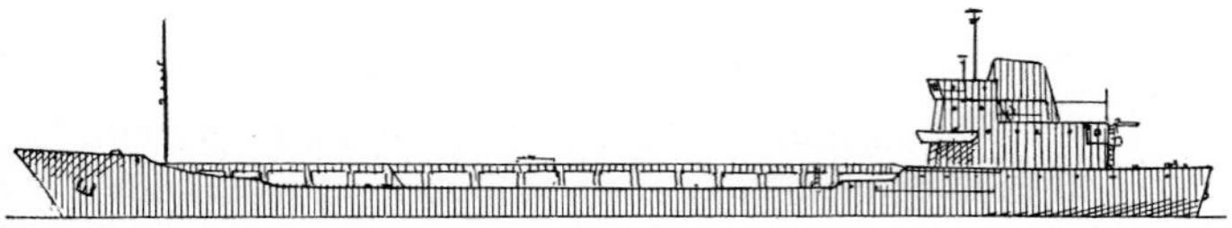

102 M^{2}F H13
J C PHILLIPS Ca/Ca (Marine Indust) 1976; Tk; 5,924 grt/8,703 dwt; 131.93 × 6.84 m *(432.84 × 22.44 ft)*; M (MAN); 13.5 kts; ex-*Gulf Gatineau*
Sisters: **L ROCHETTE** (Ca) ex-*Gulf Mackenzie*; **LEONA II** (Li) ex-*Arsene Simard*; **CAM ETINDE** (Bs) ex-*Arthur Simard*; **L'ORME NO 1** (Ca) ex-*Leon Simard*; Similar: **CORAL REEF** (Cu) ex-*5 de Septiembre*; **BROOSE** (Cy) ex-*Primero de Mayo*

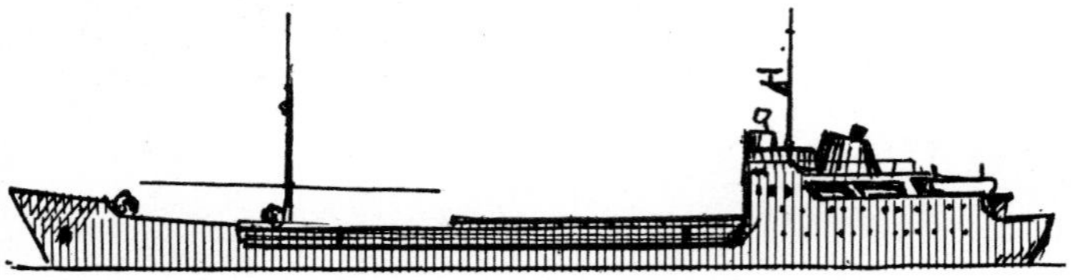

103 M^{2}F H13
JET II Gr/Ys ('Jozo Lozovina-Mosor') 1962; Tk; 1,591 grt/2,100 dwt; 84.89 × 5.23 m *(278.51 × 17.19 ft)*; M (Sulzer); 12 kts; ex-*Olib*

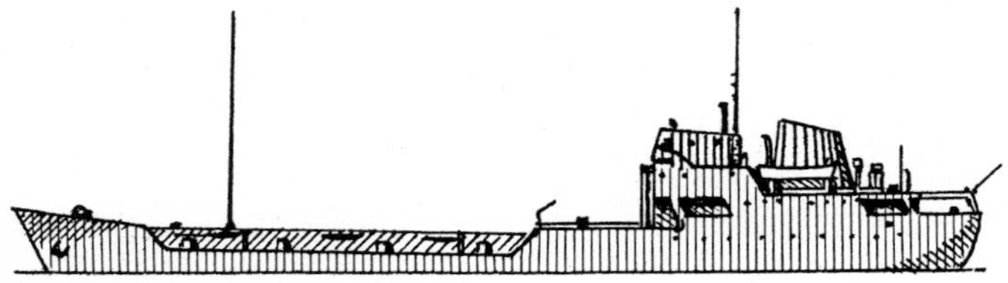

104 M^{2}F H13
JET IV Gr/FRG (Bayerische) 1954; Tk; 1,299 grt/1,875 dwt; 77.09 × 4.48 m *(252.92 × 14.7 ft)*; M (MAN); 12 kts; ex-*Marie Boettger*

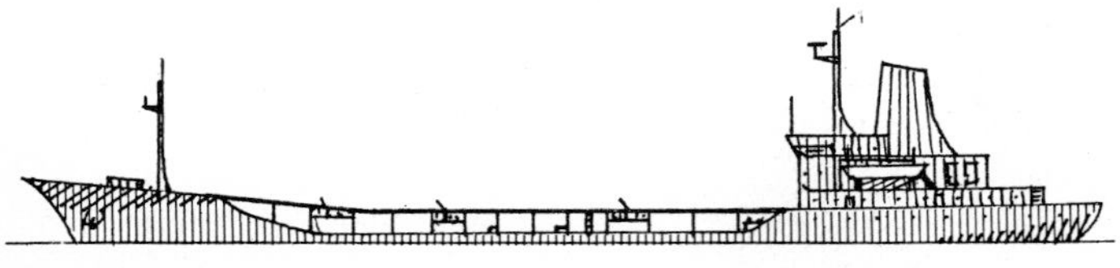

105 M^{2}F H13
ORWEIKUMOR Ng/FRG (Nobiskrug) 1968; Ch; 1,593 grt/3,350 dwt; 94.32 × 5.3 m *(309.45 × 17.39 ft)*; M (MAN); 15 kts; ex-*Thorhagen*

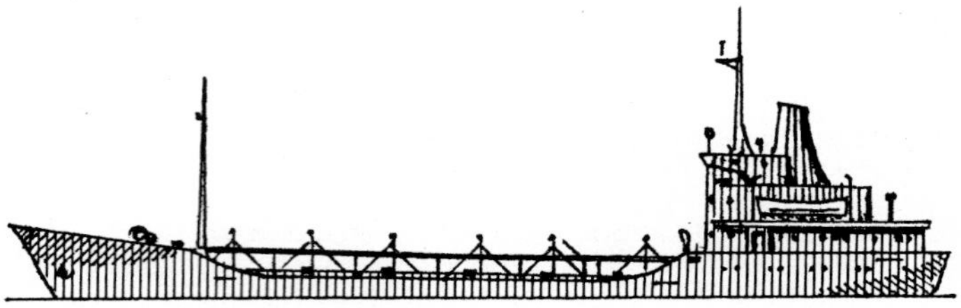

106 M^{2}F H13
POS II Pa/FRG (Nobiskrug) 1965; Tk/Ch; 1,409 grt/2,245 dwt; 77.09 × 5.6 m *(252.92 × 18.37 ft)*; M (MAN); — kts; ex-*Mikhal*
Similar: **ETRUSCO** (It) ex-*Thoralbe*

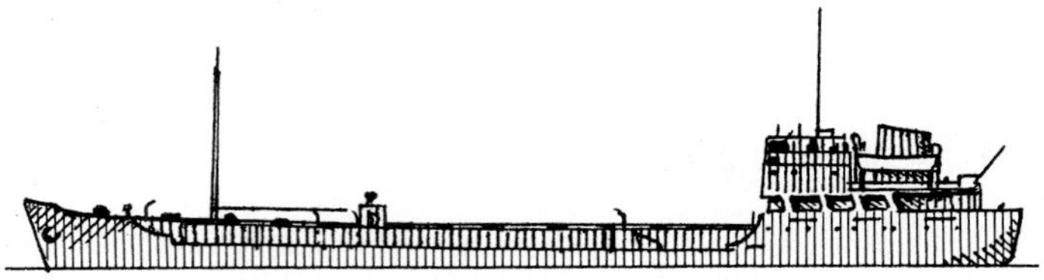

107 M^{2}F H13
PROMETHEUS Gr/Br (Goole) 1961; Tk; 1,683 grt/2,388 dwt; 81.16 × 4.83 m *(266.27 × 15.85 ft)*; M (Mirrlees Blackstone); 10 kts; ex-*Annuity*

108 M^{2}F H13
PROVMAR TERMINAL II Ca/Br (Collingwood) 1948/54; Tk; 4,947 grt/6,832 dwt; 124.54 × 6.67 m *(408.6 × 21.88 ft)*; T (Inglis); 12.5 kts; ex-*Imperial Sarnia*

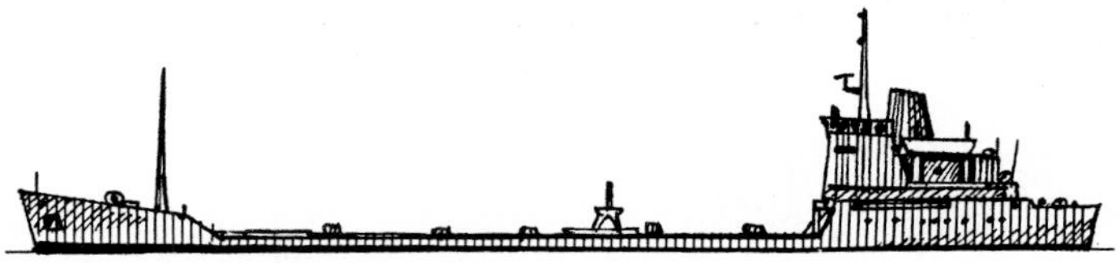

109 M^{2}F H13
RAMA J Tr/Br (Cochrane) 1968; Tk; 1,675 grt/3,004 dwt; 83.52 × 5.15 m *(274.02 × 16.9 ft)*; M (Brons); 12 kts; ex-*Rudderman*

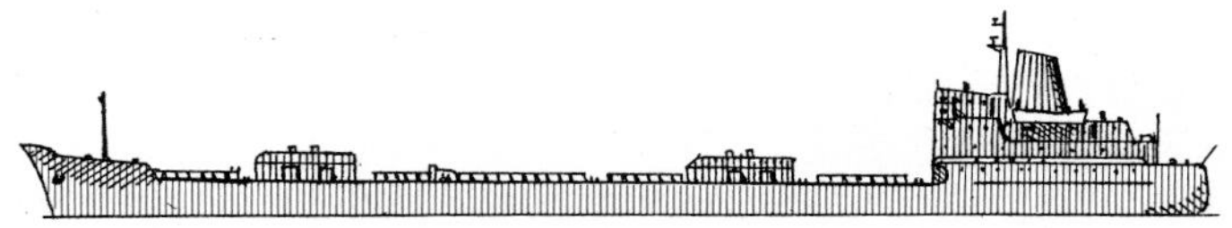

110 M^{2}F H13
SEARAIDER Pa/Br (Vickers Ltd) 1968; Ch; 6,459 grt/10,469 dwt; 125.81 × 8.88 m *(412.76 × 29.13 ft)*; M; 14.5 kts; ex-*Albright Pioneer*

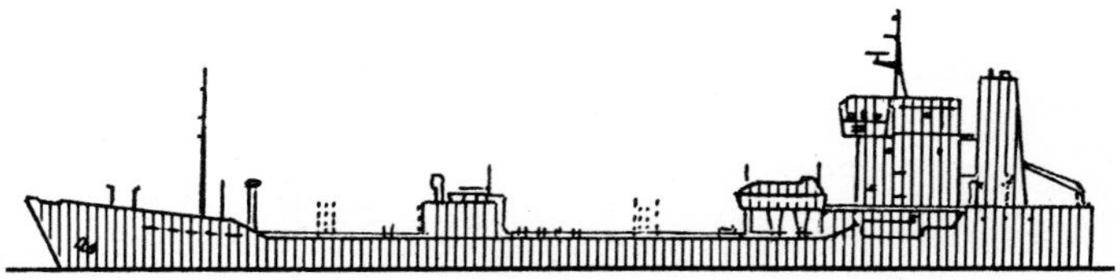

111 M^{2}F H13
STAR TRADER Ma/No (Mandal) 1980; Ch; 1,192 grt/2,710 dwt; 79.15 × 5.02 m *(259.68 × 16.47 ft)*; M (Bergens); 12.5 kts; ex-*Alk*
Sister: **SUN TRADER** (Ma) ex-*Aun*

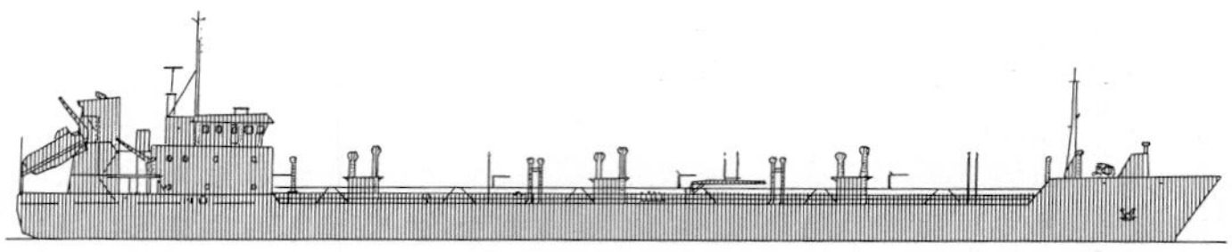

112 M^{2}FL H1
THEODORA Ne/Ne ('De Merwede') 1991; Tk/AT/TB; 4,098 grt/6,616 dwt; 110.60 × 7.05 m *(362.86 × 23.13 ft)*; M (Wärtsilä); 14.5 kts

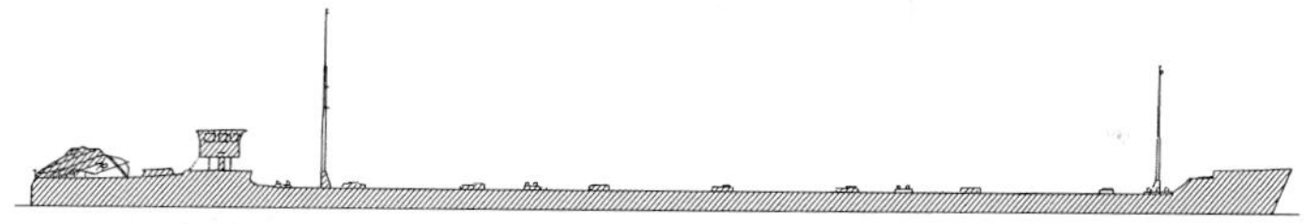

113 $M^{2}FL$ *H13*
MANUELLA Cy/Ne (Lanser) 1988; Ch; 1,853 grt/3,200 dwt; 109.70 × 3.90 m *(359.91 × 12.80 ft)*; M (Wärtsilä); 11 kts; Sea/river design

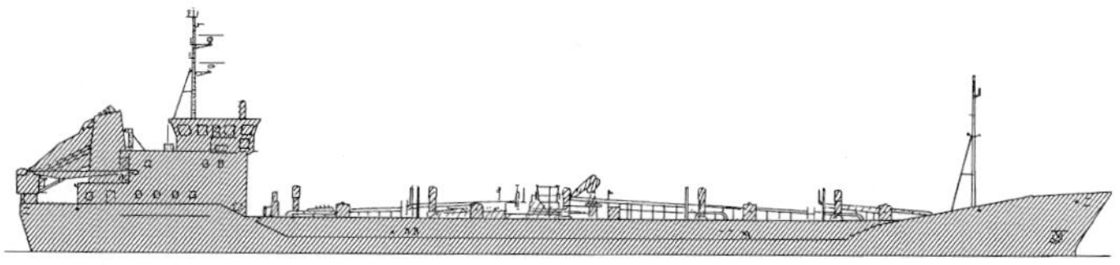

114 $M^{2}FLR$ *H13*
BRABOURNE Br/Br (Cochrane) 1989; Tk; 1,646 grt/2,675 dwt; 78.50 × 4.86 m *(257.55 × 15.94 ft)*; M (MaK); 10 kts
Sister: **BLACKROCK** (Br)

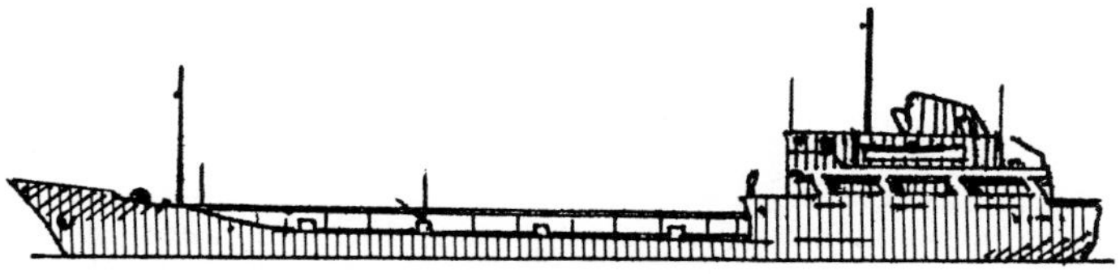

115 $M^{2}FM$ *H13*
CASTOR Gr/Ne (Nieuwe Noord) 1967; Tk/Ch; 642 grt/1,326 dwt; 71.86 × 3.84 m *(235.76 × 12.6 ft)*; M (KHD); 12 kts; ex-*Asperity*

116 $M^{2}FN$ *H*
MARLIN Li/Ja (Hitachi) 1977; OO; 9,792 grt/15,022 dwt; 155.15 × 6.86 m *(509.02 × 22.51 ft)*; TSM (Polar); 13 kts
Sister: **TARPON** (Li)

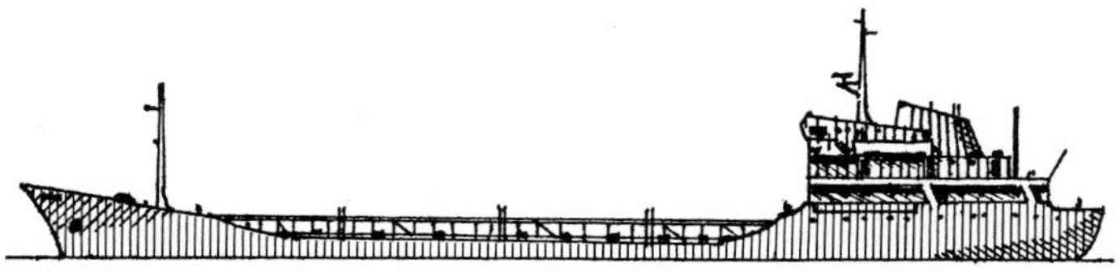

117 $M^{2}FN$ *H13*
POINTE DE MORGAT Pa/Fr (La Rochelle) 1975; WT/Ch; 2,128 grt/3,200 dwt; 90.99 × 5.52 m *(289.52 × 18.11 ft)*; M (Atlas-MaK); 13 kts; ex-*Commandant Henry*
Sister: **POINTE DE LESVEN** (Pa)

118 $M^{2}FN$ *H13*
RTC-1 Pi/Ja (Nipponkai) 1966; Tk; 2,621 grt/4,260 dwt; 92.79 × 6.3 m *(304.43 × 20.67 ft)*; M (Nippon Hatsudoki); 11.75 kts; ex-*Nichiyo Maru*
Possibly similar: **ARAK** (Ir) ex-*Nisshin Maru*

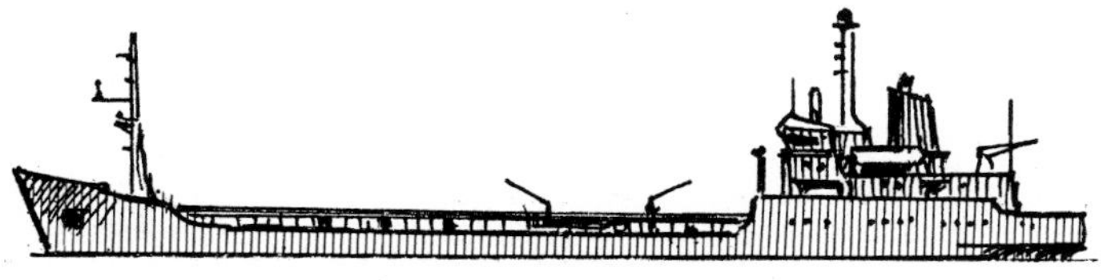

119 $M^{2}FR$ *H13*
APRICITY Br/Br (Appledore) 1971; Tk; 2,144 grt/3,365 dwt; 91.42 × 5.9 m *(299.93 × 19.36 ft)*; M (English Electric); 13 kts; ex-*Esso Inverness*
Sister: **ASSURITY** (Br) ex-*Esso Penzance*; **WHITCREST** (Br) ex-*Esso Tenby*

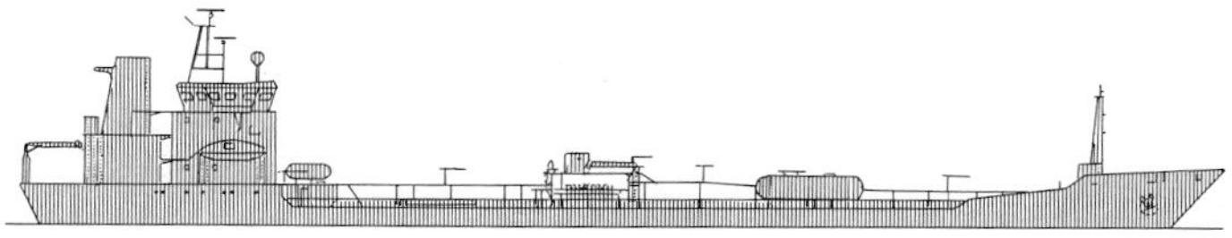

120 $M^{2}FR$ *H13*
CRISTALLO Br/It (Apuania) 1991; Ch; 5,038 grt/8,000 dwt; 125.16 × 7.12 m *(410.63 × 23.36 ft)*; M (Wärtsilä); 14 kts

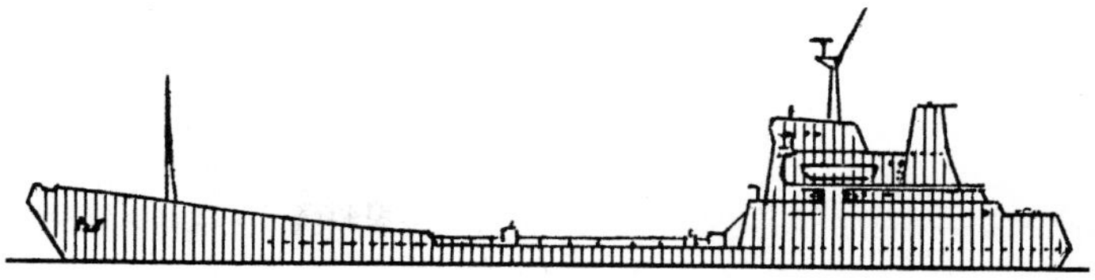

121 $M^{2}G$ *H13*
VALIO Gr/FRG (Buesumer) 1969; Tk/MT; 806 grt/1,306 dwt; 73.73 × 3.65 m *(241.93 × 11.98 ft)*; M (Atlas-MaK); 11.5 kts; ex-*Victoriasand*
Sister: **NAPETCO I** (SL) ex-*Dieksand*

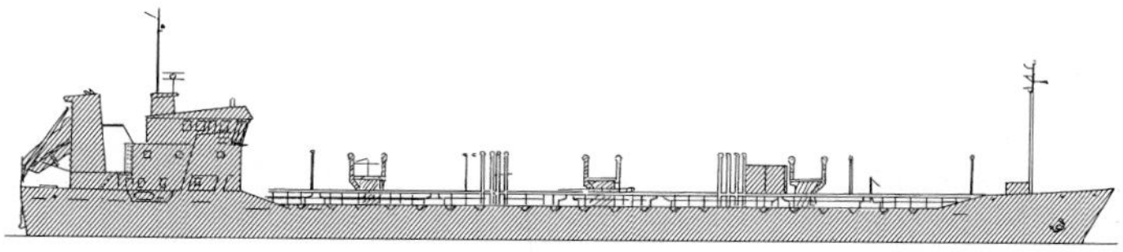

122 $M^{2}GL$ *H13*
STELLA LYRA Ne/Ne (Tille) 1989; Tk/Ch/TB; 2,874 grt/3,480 dwt; 95.75 × 5.71 m *(314.14 × 18.73 ft)*; M (Wärtsilä); 12.5 kts

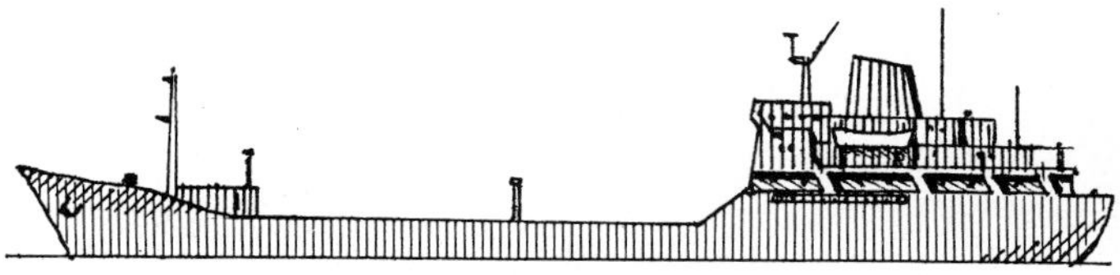

123 $M^{2}HG$ *H13*
S M SPIRIDON Li/Fr (Havre) 1967; Ch; 1,920 grt/2,730 dwt; 87 × 5.97 m *(285.43 × 19.59 ft)*; M (Werkspoor); 13.75 kts; ex-*Tyysterniemi*

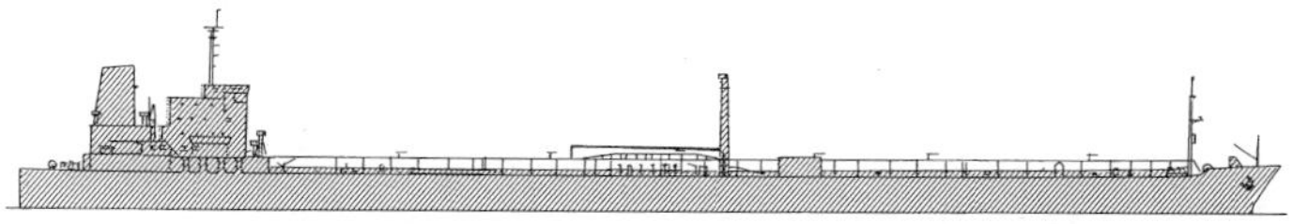

124 $M^{3}CF$ *H*
FAITH IV Sg/Ja (Koyo) 1987; Tk; 39,131 grt/63,765 dwt; 228.61 × 12.19 m *(750.03 × 39.99 ft)*; M (Sulzer); 14.25 kts; ex-*Argo Asia*
Sister: **ACE TRADER** (Pa)

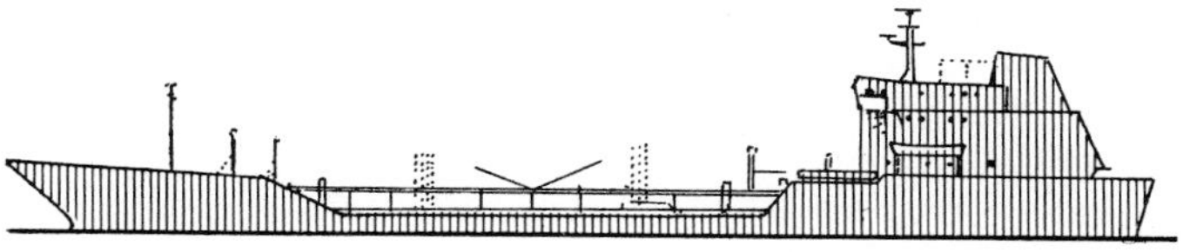

125 $M^{3}E^{2}MF$ *H13*
STOLT COLINA NIS/No (B↓tservice) 1976; Ch; 2,295 grt/3,455 dwt; 96.02 × 5.47 m *(315.03 × 17.95 ft)*; M (KHD); 13.75 kts; ex-*La Colina*
Sisters: **STOLT PRADERA** (NIS) ex-*La Pradera*; **POLISAN 1** (Tu) ex-*Stainless Patriot*

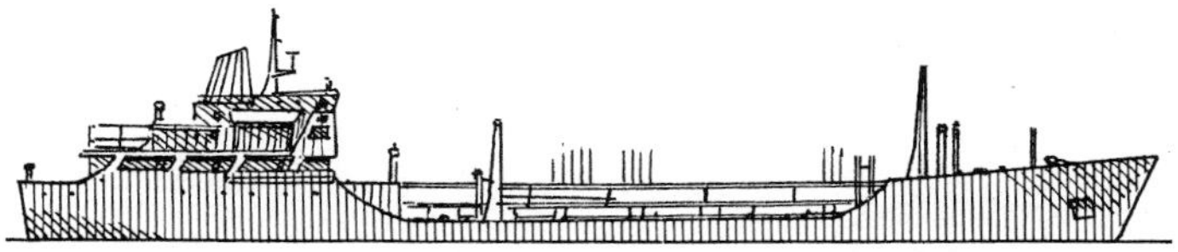

126 $M^{3}EM^{3}F$ *H13*
RIFAT Tu/No (Båtservice) 1971; Tk; 2,318 grt/3,515 dwt; 91.22 × 5.53 m *(299.28 × 18.14 ft)*; M (Alpha); 13 kts; ex-*Multitank Rhenania*
Sister (may have been rebuilt, altering appearance): **ETA** (Tu) ex-*Seamark*

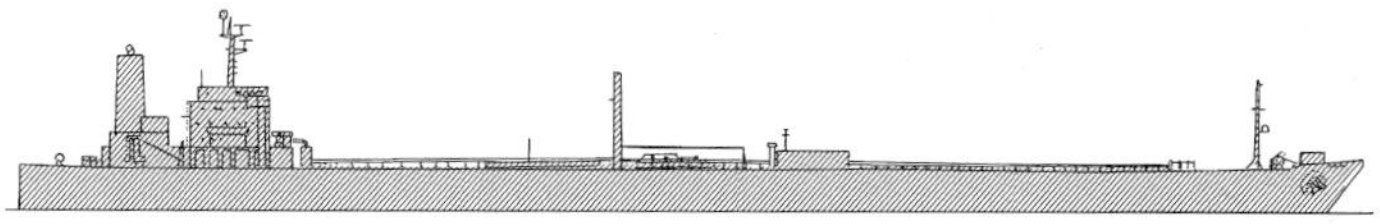

127 $M^{3}F$ *H*
MELOR My/Ja (IHI) 1986; Tk; 51,894 grt/87,768 dwt; 233.03 × 12.97 m *(764.53 × 42.55 ft)*; M (Sulzer); 14 kts; ex-*Neptune Subaru*

128 $M^{3}F$ *H123*
DA QING 247 RC/Sw (Kockums) 1960; Tk; 12,899 grt/20,840 dwt; 170.06 × 10.60 m *(557.9 × 34.78 ft)*; M (Gotaverken); 15.5 kts; ex-*Gunilla Billner*

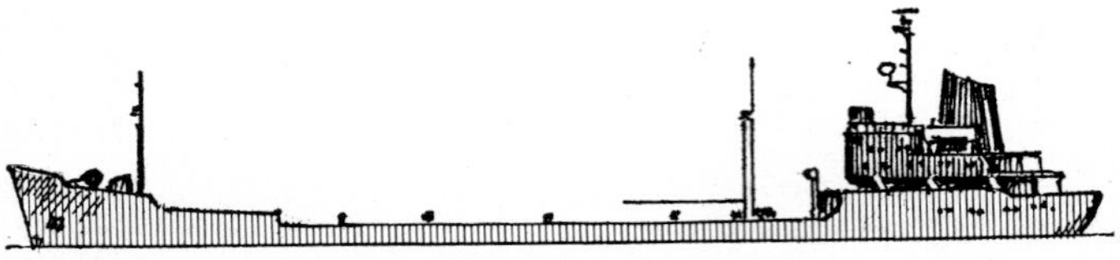

129 M^{3}F *H13*
AFRICAN PRIDE SV/De (Odense) 1965; Tk; 3,536 grt/5,390 dwt; 112.68 × 6.1 m *(369.68 × 20.01 ft)*; M (B&W); 13.5 kts; ex-*Dangulf Maersk*
Sister: **PETRO PYLA** (SV) ex-*Svengulf Maersk*

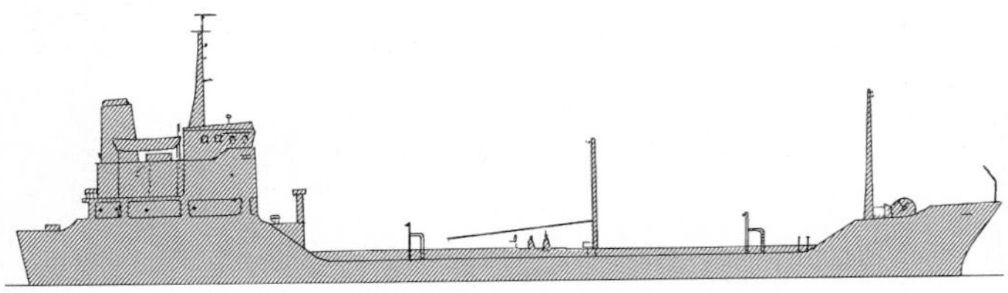

130 M^{3}F *H13*
BARDSEY Br/Ja (Kitanihon) 1981; Tk; 1,144 grt/1,767 dwt; 69.53 × 4.31 m *(228.12 × 14.14 ft)*; M (Yanmar); 10.5 kts; ex-*Sten*
Sisters: **BARMOUTH** (Br) ex-*Per*; **AMITY** (Bs) ex-*Christian*; **AVERITY** (Bs) ex-*Natalie* (bulwark plating on poop)

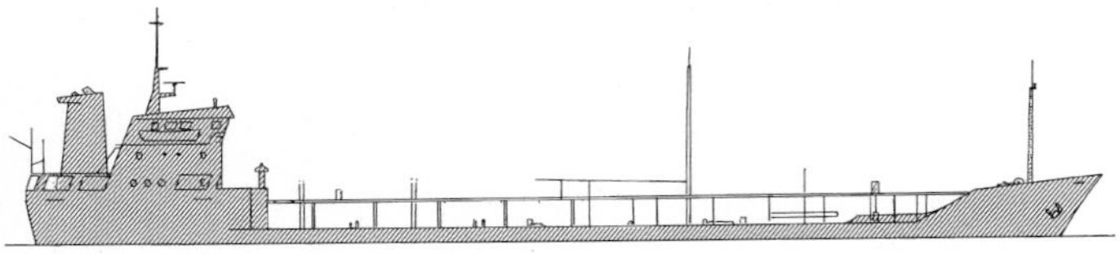

131 M^{3}F *H13*
BITUMA It/Ne (Nieuwe Noord) 1980; Tk/TB; 2,391 grt/3,894 dwt; 93.05 × 5.65 m *(305.28 × 18.54 ft)*; M (Wärtsilä); 11.5 kts; ex-*Stella Castor*; Lengthened 1984
Sister: **STELLA POLLUX** (Ne)

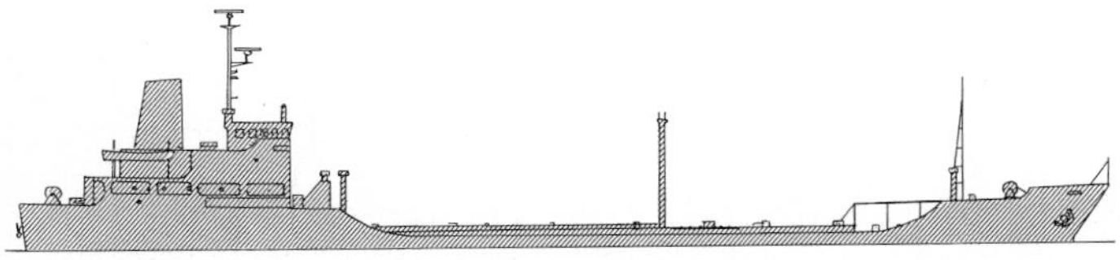

132 M^{3}F *H13*
COSMO MARU Ja/Ja (Teraoka) 1985; Tk; 1,590 grt/3,356 dwt; 88.02 × 5.61 m *(288.78 × 18.41 ft)*; M (Hanshin); 12 kts

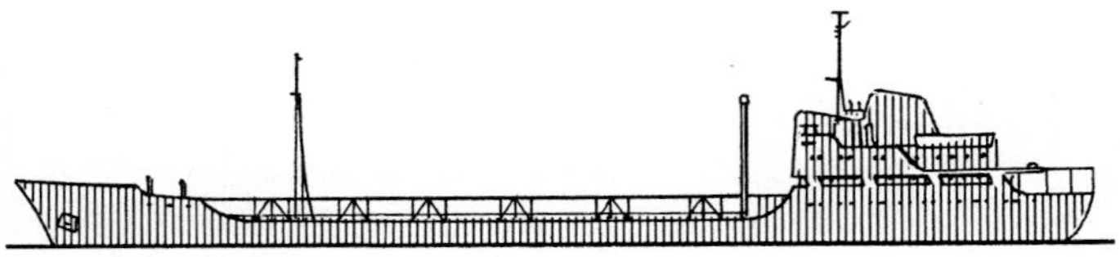

133 M^{3}F *H13*
DA QING 18 RC/RC (Hu Tung) 1965; Tk; 2,419 grt/3,512 dwt; 96 × 5.65 m *(315 × 18.54 ft)*; M (Hudong); 11.5 kts; ex-*Chien She 18*
Sisters: **DA QING 19** (RC); **DA QING 20** (RC); **DA QING 21** (RC); **DA QING 22** (RC); **DA QING 23** (RC)

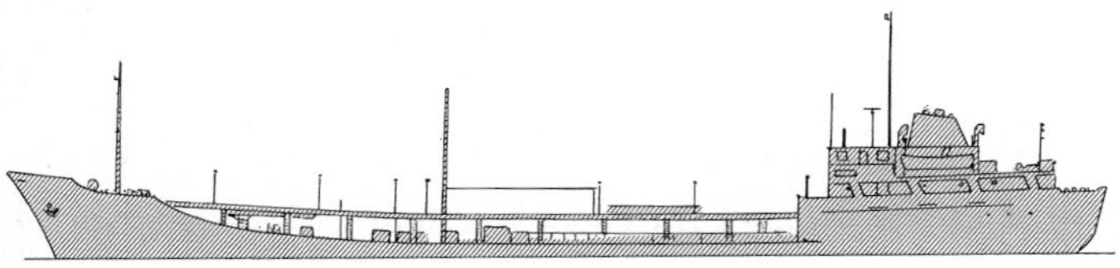

134 M^{3}F *H13*
MARIA Gr/Ne (Nieuwe Noord) 1969; Tk; 890 grt/1,356 dwt; 73.97 × 3.96 m *(242.68 × 12.99 ft)*; M (KHD); 12 kts; ex-*Allurity*
Sister: **VASILIOS XIV** (Gr) ex-*Activity*

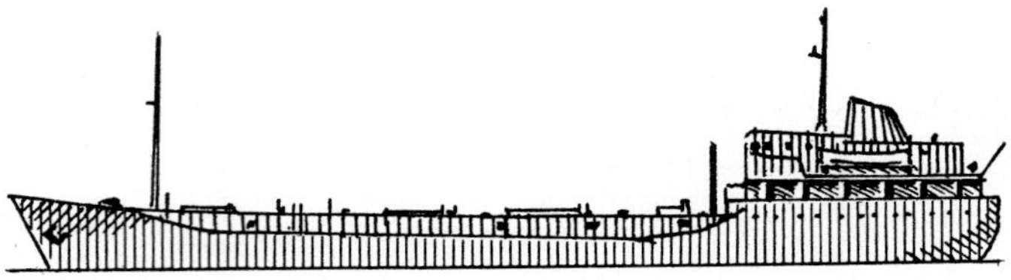

135 M^{3}F *H13*
REDO Sw/FRG (Kremer) 1963; TB; 1,302 grt/1,656 dwt; 72.95 × 4.64 m *(239.34 × 15.22 ft)*; M (KHD); 11 kts; ex-*Nynas*

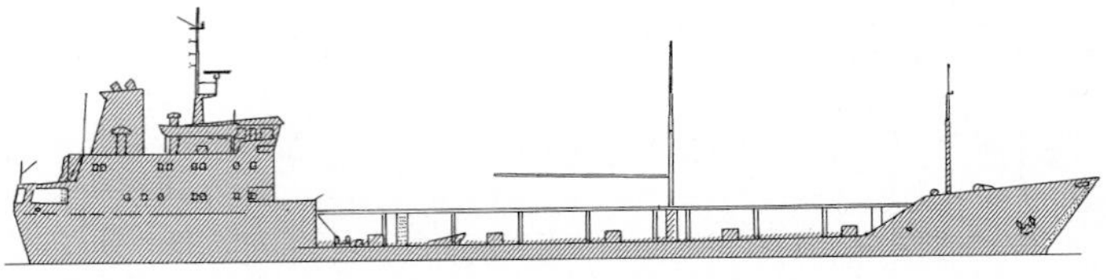

136 M^{3}F *H13*
STELLA PROCYON Ne/Ne (Tille) 1978; TB; 2,697 grt/4,520 dwt; 83.62 × 6.61 m *(274.34 × 21.69 ft)*; M (KHD); 11.75 kts

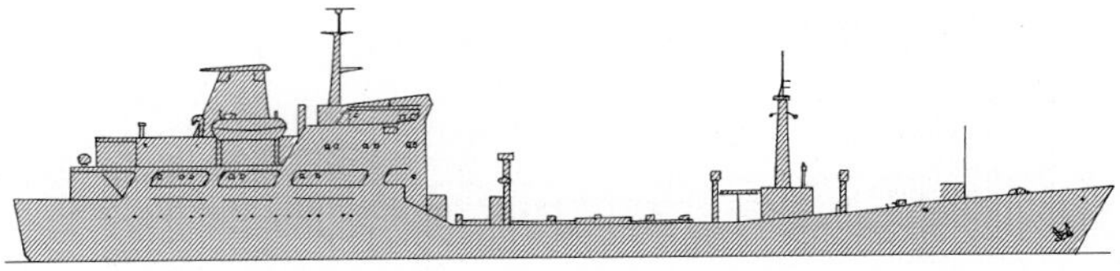

137 M^{3}F *H3*
ALIOT Ru/Fi (Rauma-Repola) 1970; WT/Ch; 3,115 grt/3,319 dwt; 93.88 × 6.5 m *(308.01 × 21.33 ft)*; M (B&W); 14 kts
Sisters: **POLLUKS** (Ru); **PROTSION** (Ru)

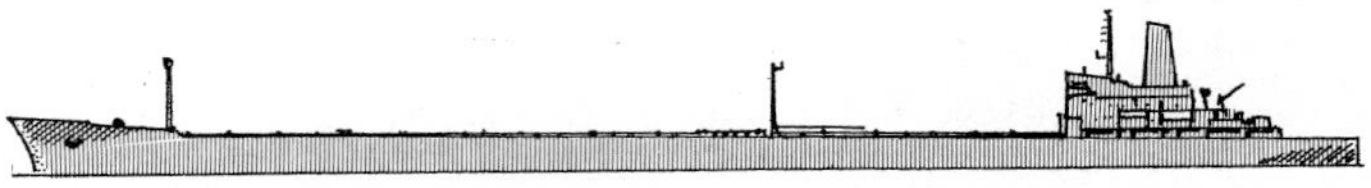

138 M^{3}FC *H1*
AVIN OIL TRADER Gr/Sw (Eriksbergs) 1968; Tk; 50,023 grt/108,550 dwt; 277.05 × 14.72 m *(908.95 × 48.29 ft)*; M (B&W); 16 kts; ex-*Solstad*

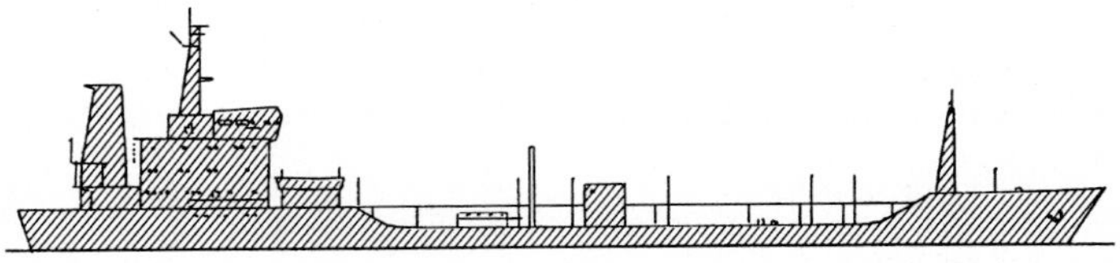

139 M^{3}FC *H13*
MARIA LAURA It/FRG (Lindenau) 1976; Tk/Ch; 5,106 grt/8,000 dwt; 118.45 × 7.26 m *(388.62 × 23.82 ft)*; M (MaK); 14 kts; ex-*Mandan*
Sister: **BREZZA** (It) ex-*Dakota*

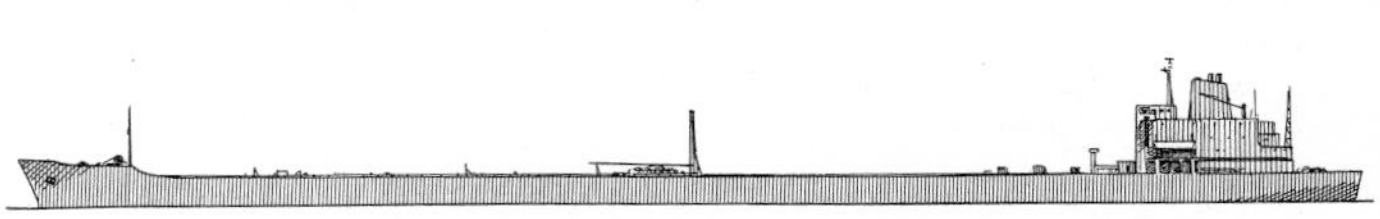

140 M^{3}FCM *H1*
SEAWIND II Ma/Ja (Kawasaki) 1978; Tk; 35,760 grt/66,728 dwt; 238.01 × 12.16 m *(780.87 × 39.9 ft)*; M (MAN); 15 kts; ex-*Alamo*

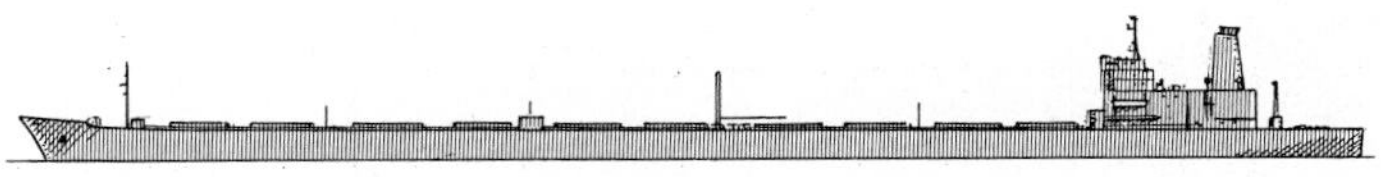

141 M^{3}FM *H*
ARCADIA 1 Pa/Ja (Hitachi) 1973; OO; 89,556 grt/165,037 dwt; 300.01 × 16.99 m *(984.28 × 55.74 ft)*; M (B&W); 16 kts; ex-*Sanko Robin*
Sister: **EPTANISSA** (MI) ex-*Tripharos*; Similar: **AMBER** (Pa) ex-*Zuiho Maru*; **LARINA** (NIS) (converted to ore carrier. Hose-handling derricks may be removed)

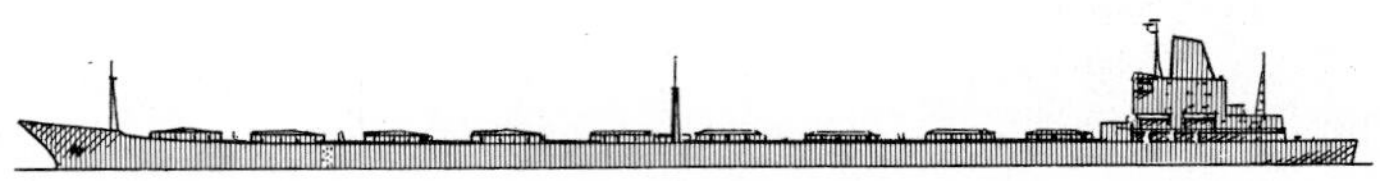

142 M^{3}FM *H*
ASIA ANGEL SV/FRG (Bremer V) 1973; OBO; 42,519 grt/78,130 dwt; 253.68 × 14.23 m *(832.28 × 46.69 ft)*; M (MAN); 15.25 kts; ex-*Mercedes*

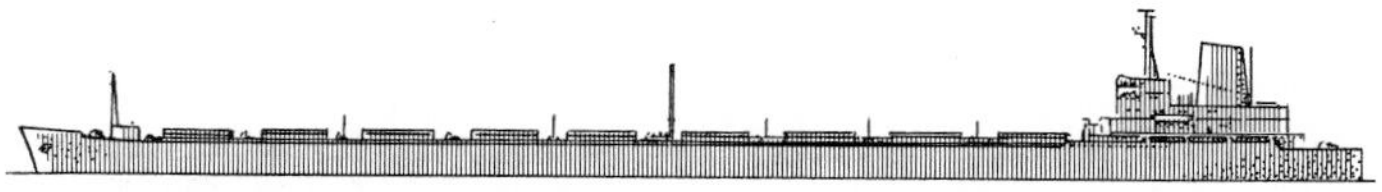

143 M^3FM *H*

IOLCOS FLAME Gr/Ja (Sumitomo) 1971; OBO; 79,279 grt/145,057 dwt; 266.02 × 18.1 m *(872.77 × 59.38 ft)*; M (Sulzer); 15.5 kts; ex-*Avon Bridge*
Sister: **LEON** (Gr) ex-*Australian Bridge*

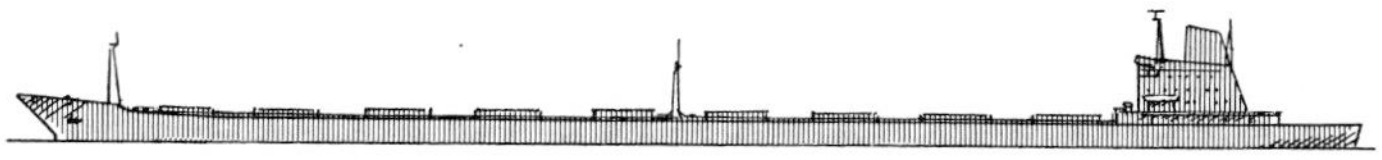

144 $M^3FM/MNMFN$ *H*

OBO ENGIN Tu/FRG (Bremer V) 1974; OBO; 43,386 grt/78,075 dwt; 253.63 × 14.24 m *(832.12 × 46.72 ft)*; M (MAN); 15 kts; ex-*Belobo*
Sisters: **FOREST HILLS** (Bs) ex-*Obo Duke*; **MONTEREY** (Gr) ex-*Jarmina*; Possible sister: **HERMES** (Cy) ex-*Arica*

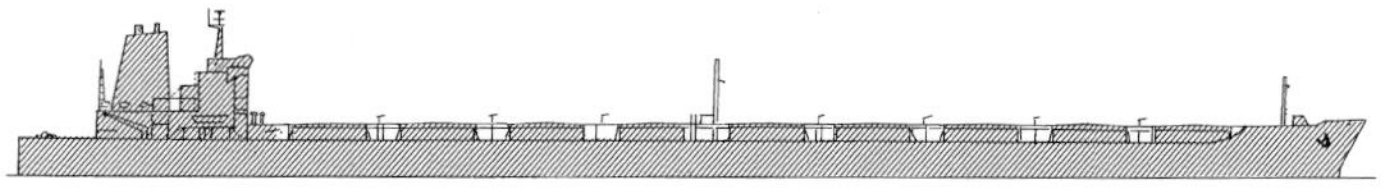

145 M^3FM *H1*

ALGARROBO NIS/Ko (Hyundai) 1984; OBO; 90,747 grt/149,864 dwt; 281.16 × 15.27 m *(922.44 × 50.10 ft)*; M (B&W); — kts; ex-*Cast Orca*
Sister: **EIRINI L** (Gr) ex-*Cast Bluewhale*

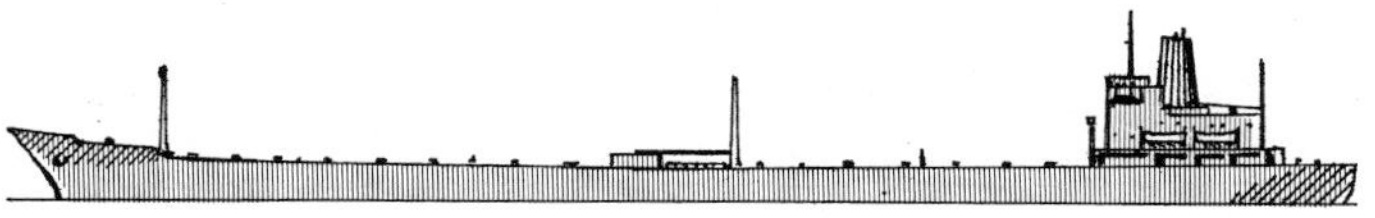

146 M^3FM *H1*

FLORES SEA Pa/Tw (Taiwan SB) 1970; Tk; 50,618 grt/97,372 dwt; 253.04 × 15.58 m *(830.18 × 51.08 ft)*; M (Sulzer); 15.5 kts; ex-*Glory*

147 M^3FM *H123*

PAYASAN SV/No (Stord) 1962; Tk; 20,376 grt/35,415 dwt; 202.7 × 11.15 m *(665.03 × 36.58 ft)*; M (B&W); 15.5 kts; ex-*Thorstrand*

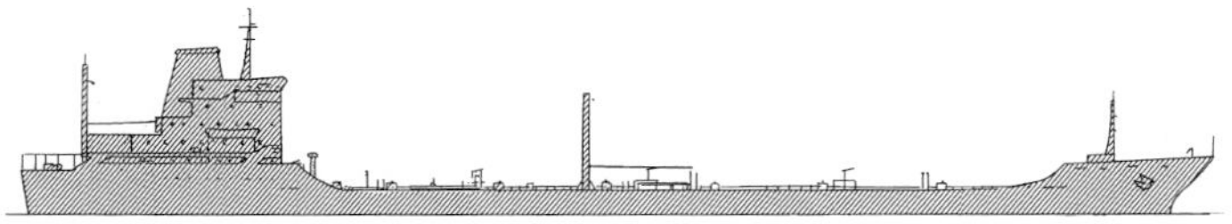

148 M^3FM *H13*

MADDALENA D'AMATO It/It (Apuania) 1984; Tk; 12,509 grt/19,990 dwt; 161.47 × 8.45 m *(529.76 × 27.72 ft)*; M (Sulzer); 14.75 kts; ex-*Mare del Nord*
Possible sister: **STELLA AZZURRA** (It) ex-*Baltico*

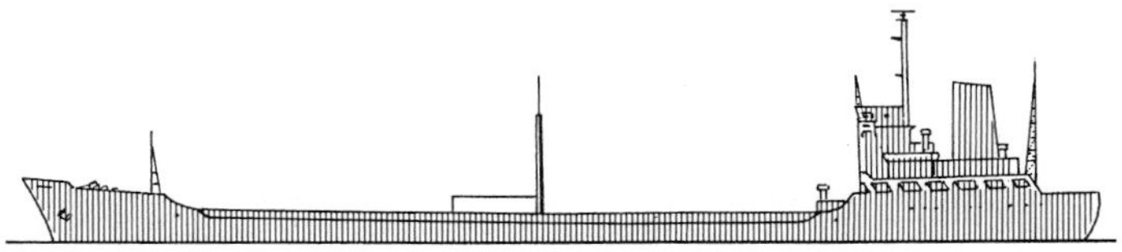

149 M^3FM *H13*

PATRIA 38 Sg/Ja (Ujina) 1973; Tk; 9,838 grt/16,801 dwt; 153.7 × 9.37 m *(504 × 30.74 ft)*; M (Mitsubishi); 15 kts; ex-*Akitsushima Maru*

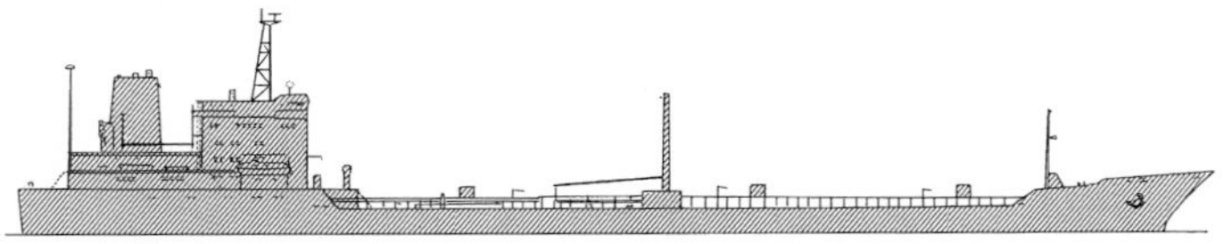

150 $M^3FM/MNMFN$ *H13*

ZINA Li/Bu (G Dimitrov) 1989; Tk; 18,094 grt/29,490 dwt; 175.06 × 11 m *(574.34 × 36.09 ft)*; M (Sulzer); 14.8 kts
Sisters: **NIDIA** (NIS); Probable sisters: **ANDREA** (Ma); **DANILA** (Ma); **PARNAR** (Ma)

151 M^3FMM *H1*

BRAZIL VITORIA Li/Ja (Kawasaki) 1977; OO; 74,139 grt/139,774 dwt; 273.24 × 16.39 m *(896.46 × 53.77 ft)*; M (MAN); 15.25 kts; ex-*Brazilian Vitoria*
Probable sister: **RHODOS** (Gr) ex-*Brazilian Trader*

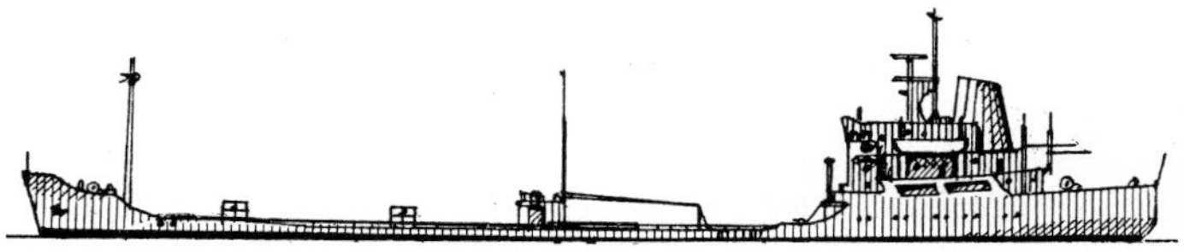

152 M^3FM^2 *H13*

AFRICA SV/Br (Furness) 1967; Tk; 2,538 grt/4,502 dwt; 98.61 × 5.87 m *(323.52 × 19.26 ft)*; M (English Electric); 12 kts; ex-*Esso Purfleet*

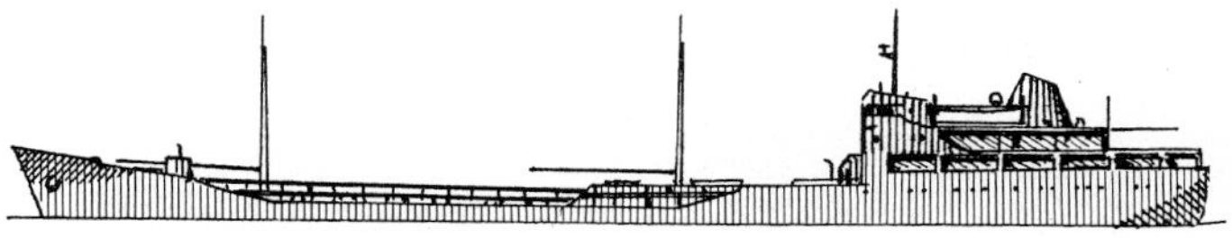

153 M^3FN *H13*

MONTROSE Ke/No (Stord) 1962; Tk; 3,737 grt/5,558 dwt; 114.28 × 6.54 m *(374.93 × 21.46 ft)*; M (B&W); 13.25 kts; ex-*Saphir*

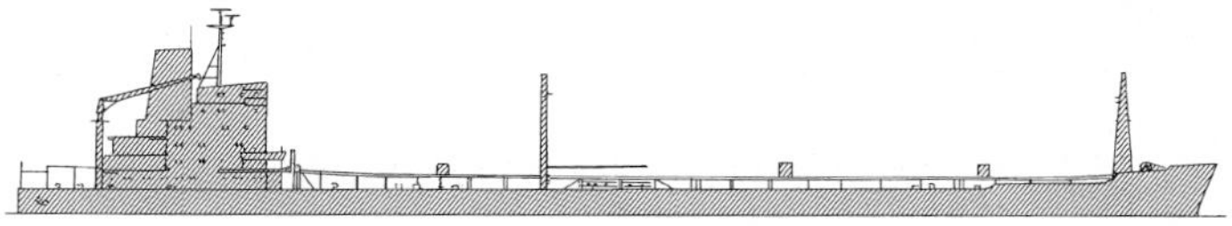

154 M^3FR *H1*

HORIZON IX UAE/FRG (AG 'Weser') 1975; Tk; 22,553 grt/39,998 dwt; 193.02 × 11.65 m *(633.27 × 38.22 ft)*; M (MAN); 15 kts; ex-*St Clemens*; 'Key 40' type

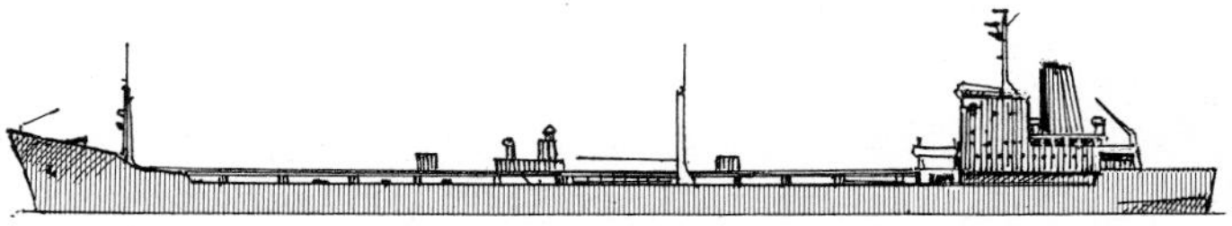

155 $M^3FR/MNMFS$ *H13*

HUA HAI 2 RC/Sw (Oresunds) 1971; Tk; 16,400 grt/28,317 dwt; 170.97 × 10.21 m *(560.93 × 33.5 ft)*; M (Gotaverken); 15.25 kts; ex-*Nitsa*
Sisters: **XIA CHI** (RC) ex-*Cygnus*; **ASPHALT LEADER** (Gr) ex-*Libra*

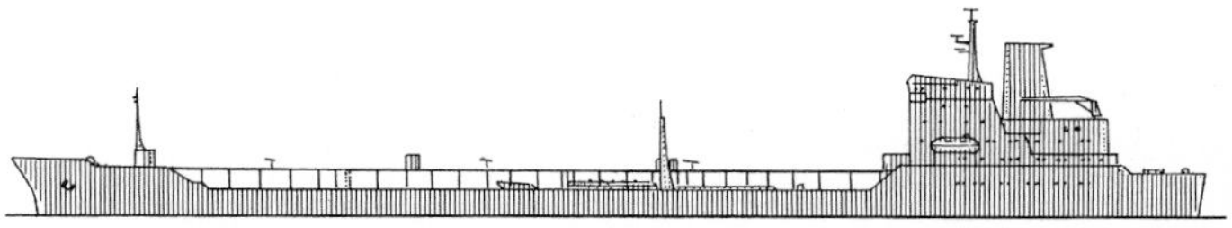

156 M^3FR *H13*

PACIFIC DIAMOND Pa/Sw (Oskarshamns) 1975; Tk; 17,877 grt/31,016 dwt; 170.71 × 11.07 m *(560.07 × 36.32 ft)*; M (Sulzer); 15 kts; ex-*Tatry*; Ice strengthened
Sister: **PACIFIC OPAL** (Pa) ex-*Pieniny II*

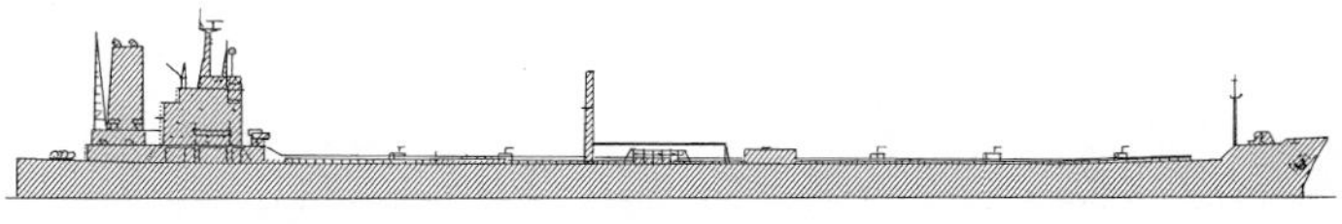

157 M^4CFM/MN^2MCFM *H1*

RICH DUCHESS Bs/Ja (Kasado) 1986; Tk; 50,285 grt/81,279 dwt; 243.85 × 12.19 m *(800.03 × 39.99 ft)*; M (Sulzer); 14.25 kts
Sister: **RICH DUKE** (Bs)

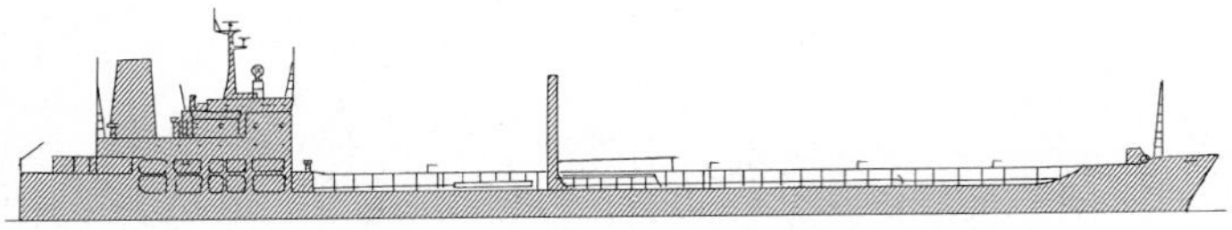

158 M^4CFM *H13*

MEKHANIK KHMELEVSKIY Ma/Ja (Kanda) 1986; Tk; 17,612 grt/29,990 dwt; 170.01 × 10.81 m *(557.78 × 35.47 ft)*; M (Sulzer); 13.2 kts; ex-*Antiparos*
Sisters: **MEKHANIK GAROVNIK** (Ru) ex-*Sporades*; **MEKHANIK ILCHENKO** (Ma) ex-*Velopoula*; **MEKHANIK VRASKOV** (Ma) ex-*Parapola*; **MEKHANIK YURYEV** (Ma) ex-*Alkyonis*

159 M^4F *H1*

BALTIMORE TRADER US/US (Bethlehem Steel) 1955/71; Tk; 27,269 grt/58,813 dwt; 243.85 × 12.16 m *(800 × 39.9 ft)*; T (Bethlehem Steel); 17.5 kts; ex-*P W Thirtle*; Aft section built 1955; Forward and cargo sections built 1971 (Newport News)

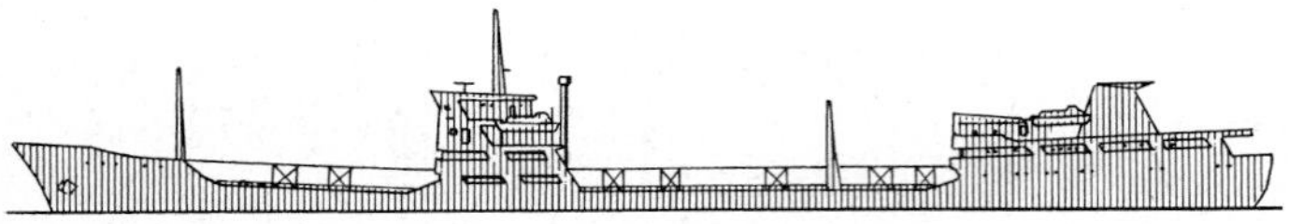

160 M^4F *H13*

DA QING 212 RC/Rm (Turnu-Severin) 1974; Tk; 4,491 grt/5,237 dwt; 128.89 × 4.20 m *(423 × 13.78 ft)*; TSM (Liebknecht); 11 kts
Sisters: **DA QIANG 213** (RC); **DA QING 214** (RC); **DA QING 215** (RC); **DA QING 412** (RC); **DA QING 413** (RC); **DA QING 414** (RC); **DA QING 415** (RC); **DA QING 416** (RC); **DA QING 417** (RC)

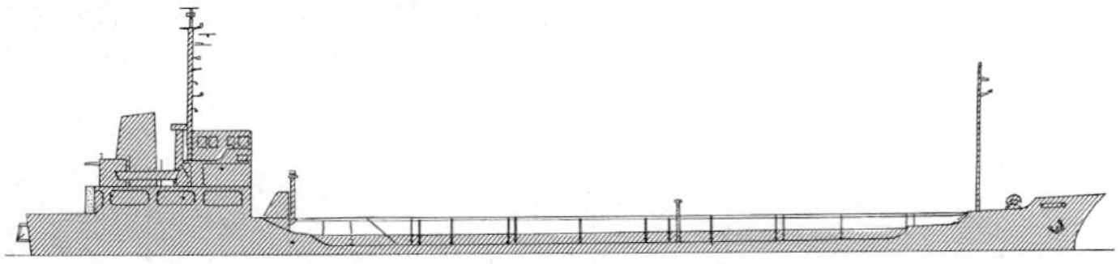

161 M^4F *H13*

KOUYO MARU Ja/Ja (Sanyo Z) 1984; Tk; 993 grt/2,623 dwt; 81.01 × 5.10 m *(266.08 × 16.73 ft)*; M (Akasaka); 11.50 kts

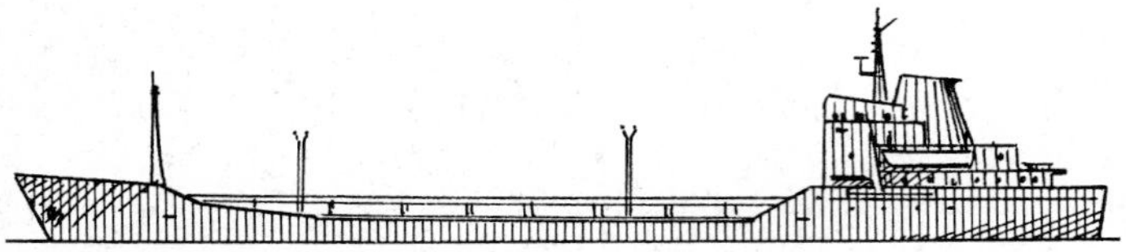

162 M^4F *H13*

YESIM 1 Tu/FRG (Menzer) 1970; Ch; 1,599 grt/3,290 dwt; 87.03 × 5.1 m *(285.53 × 16.73 ft)*; M (Atlas-MaK); 12.5 kts; ex-*Alchimist Lubeck*
Possible sister: **MARGITA** (Sw) ex-*Alchimist Flensburg*

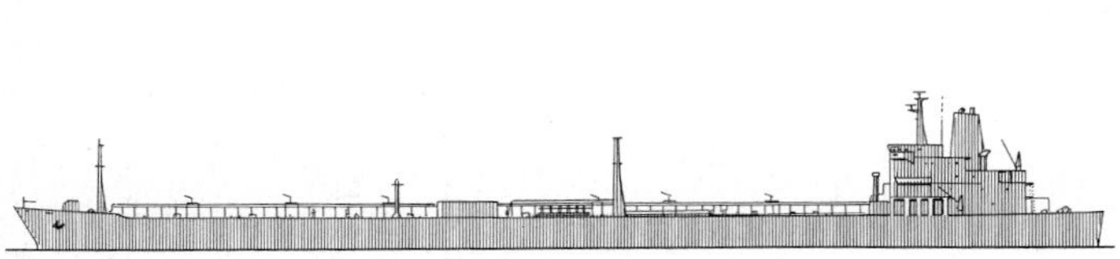

163 M^4FC *H*

PEGASUS ERRE It/Ja (Koyo) 1981; Tk; 37,758 grt/65,779 dwt; 228.73 × 13.22 m *(750.43 × 43.37 ft)*; M (B&W); 14.25 kts; ex-*Fairfield Venture*
Probable sister: **ANMAJ** (Li) ex-*Buena Ventura*

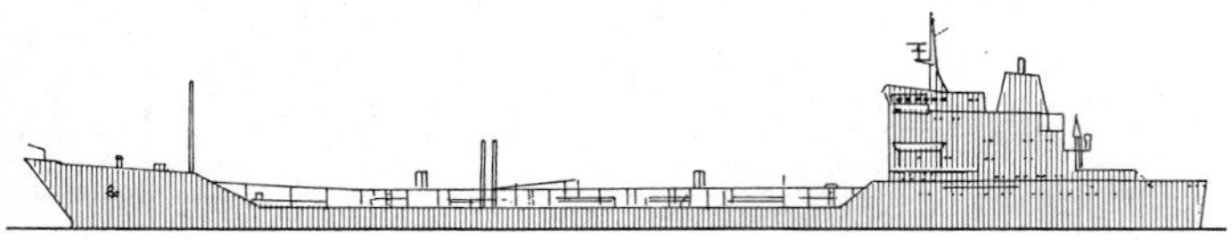

164 M^4FC *H13*

ASDRUBAL Tn/FRG (O&K) 1982; Ch; 11,536 grt/18,771 dwt; 158 × 9.22 m *(518 × 30.25 ft)*; M (MaK); 16 kts; ex-*Maknassy*

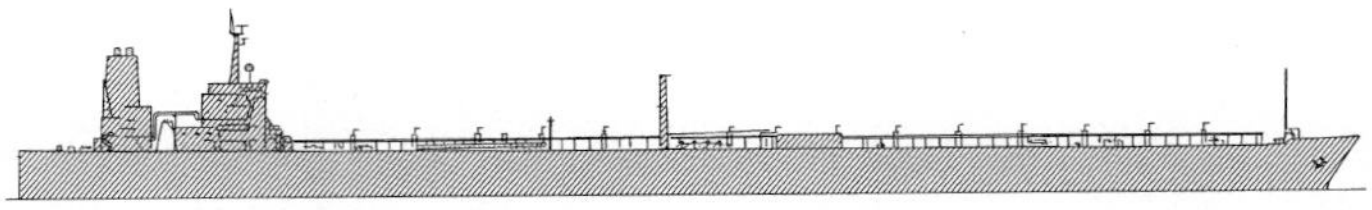

165 M^4FM/MNM^2FM *H*

COSMO ANDROMEDA Ja/Ja; Tk; 140,272 grt/238,465 dwt; 315.48 × 19.65 m *(1,035.04 × 64.47 ft)*; M (Pielstick); 14.01 kts; ex-*Tohkai Maru*

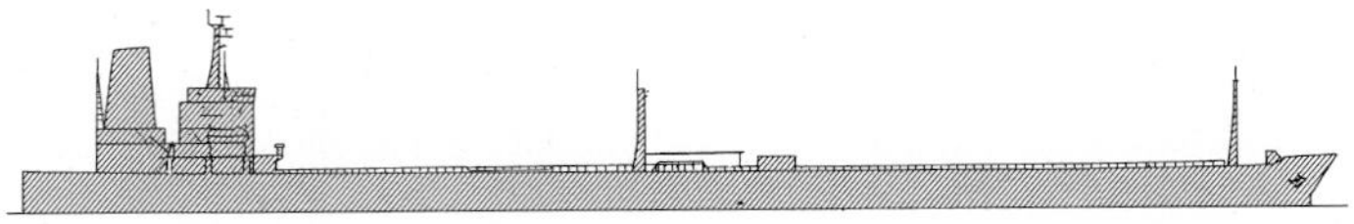

166 M^4FM *H*

GEBANG/PERTAMINA 8002 Pa/Ja (Namura) 1986; Tk; 54,152 grt/85,593 dwt; 241.51 × 12.77 m *(792.36 × 41.90 ft)*; M (Sulzer); 15.75 kts

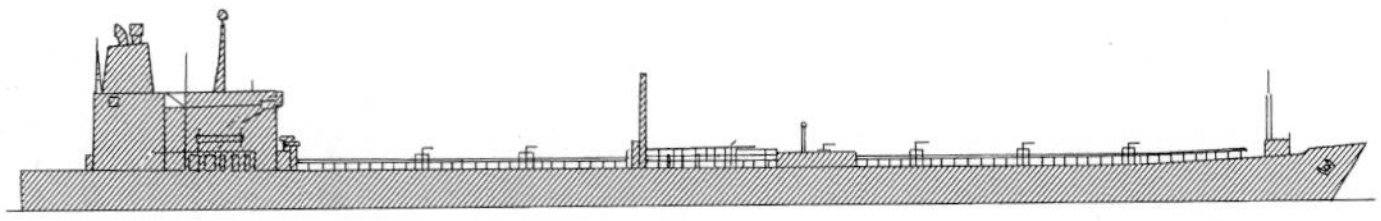

167 M^4FM *H*

IONIKOS Gr/Ja (Mitsubishi HI); Tk; 67,864 grt/119,990 dwt; 241.03 × 15.90 m *(790.78 × 52.17 ft)*; M (Sulzer); 15.8 kts; ex-*Kyokuwa Maru*

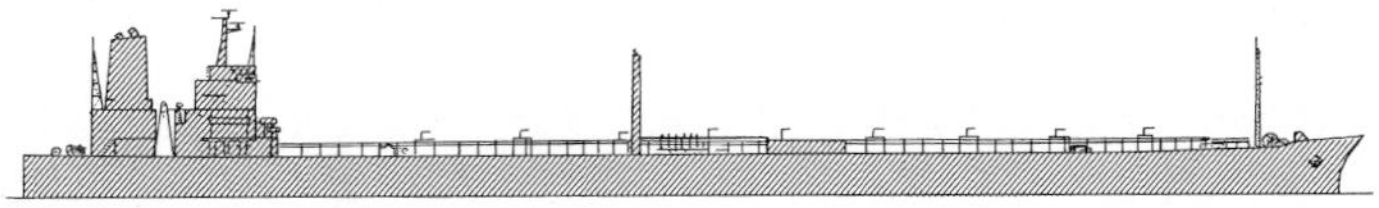

168 M^4FM/MNM^2FN *H*

SANKO EXPRESS Li/Ja; Tk; 52,123 grt/81,275 dwt; 243.01 × 12.13 m *(797.28 × 39.80 ft)*; M (B&W); 15 kts

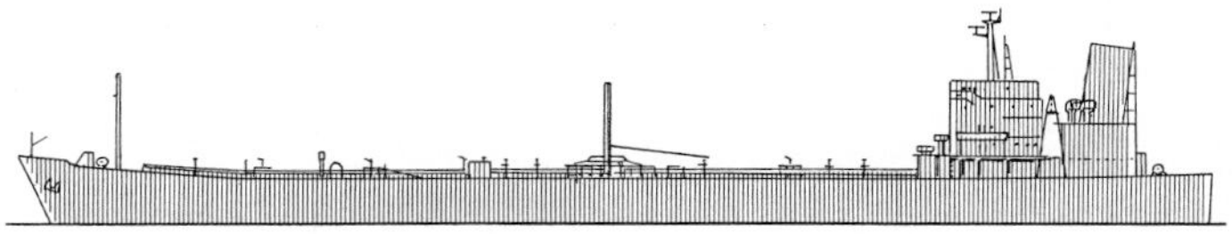

169 M^4FM *H*

WORLD CASTLE Pa/Ja (Kanasashi) 1982; Tk; 29,864 grt/48,532 dwt; 177.22 × 12.77 m *(581.43 × 41.9 ft)*; M (B&W); 14 kts; ex-*World Cosmos*
Sisters: **CABO NEGRO** (Li) ex-*Celchem Catalyst*; **AL MAHAD** (Si) ex-*World Crane*; **AL SAFANIYA** (Si) ex-*World Athenian*; **ALPHA INTELLIGENCE** (Gr) ex-*Crown Award*; **WORLD BRIDGE** (Pa)

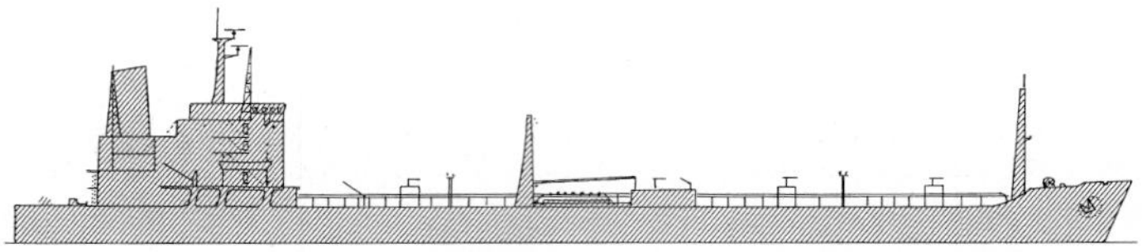

170 M^4FM *H1*

DESTINY Sg/Ja (Tsuneishi) 1980; Tk; 23,333 grt/36,384 dwt; 170.52 × 11.03 m *(559.45 × 36.19 ft)*; M (Pielstick); 15.1 kts; ex-*Cys Mariner*

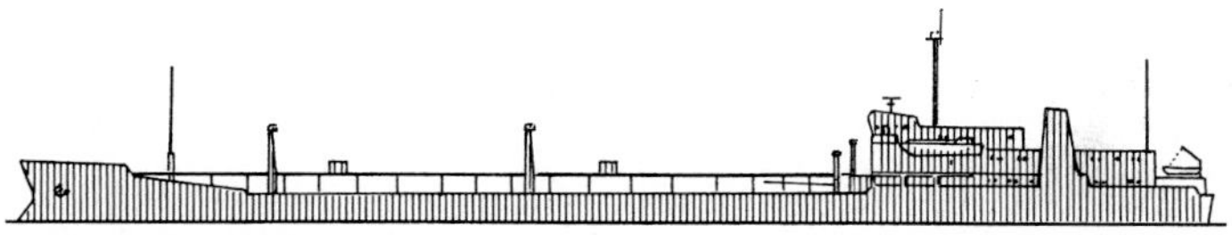

171 M^4FM/M^4GM *H1*

GENERAL SHIKHLINSKJ Az/Ru (Volgograd) 1980; Tk; 4,136 grt/4,987 dwt; 125.61 × 4.2 m *(412.11 × 13.78 ft)*; TSM (Russkiy); — kts; ex-*Oleg Koshevoy*; Sea/river service; Some sisters are Bu built ('Ilya Boyadzhiyev')
Sisters: **GENERAL SELIMOV** (Az) ex-*Sergey Tyulenin*; **GEHREMAN ESEDOV** (Az) ex-*Geroy Asadov*; **GEHREMAN I MAMEDOV** (Az) ex-*Geroy I Mamedov*; **GENERAL MAHMANDAROV** (Az) ex-*General Sabir Rakhimov*; **GENERAL GEYDAROV** (Az); **ORDUBAD** (Az) ex-*Pavlik Morozov*; **GEHREMAN HESENOV** (Az) ex-*Liza Chaykina*; **NAFTALAN** (Az) ex-*Ivan Zemnukhov*; **ISLAM SAFARLI** (Az) ex-*Mirzo Tursun-Zade*; **ZANGELAN** (Az) ex-*Grigoriy Kalustov*; **NARIMAN NARIMANOV** (Az); **GEHREMAN GUSEYNOV** (Az) ex-*Geroy Guseynov*; **GEHREMAN OSIPOV** (Az) ex-*Geroy Osipov*; **NIGAR REFIBEYLI** (Az) ex-*Lyubov Shevtsova*; **GEHREMAN HADJIEV** (Az) ex-*Viktor Tarasov*; **GEHREMAN KHELILBEYLI** (Az) ex-*Nikolay Kobzev;* **VIKTOR KIBENOK** (Uk); **VLADIMIR PRAVIK** (Uk); **GOBUSTAN** (Az) ex-*Klavdiya Nazarova*; **GENERAL ABBASOV** (Az) ex-*Ulyana Gromova*; **GEROY VOLKOV** (Ru); **SAMED VURGUN** (Az)

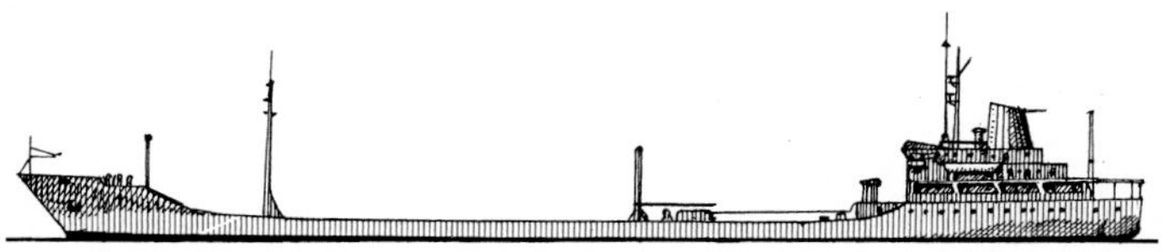

172 M^4FM *H13*

OCEAN STAR UAE/It (Adriatico) 1973; Tk; 7,769 grt/12,342 dwt; 140.21 × 8.50 m *(460.01 × 27.88 ft)*; M (Stork-Werkspoor); 15 kts; ex-*Donna Gabriella*
Sister: **ELISA d'ALESIO** (It) ex-*Donna Mariella*

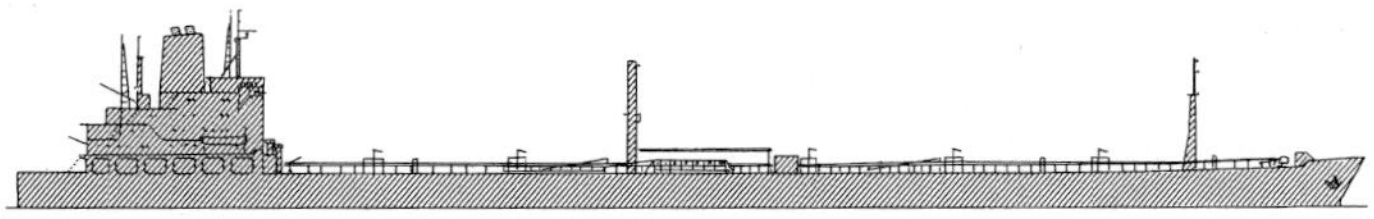

173 $M^4FM^2/MNHNFM^2$ *H*

SAN SEBASTIAN Li/Ja (Oshima Z) 1981; Tk; 37,288 grt/63,795 dwt; 228.60 × 12.79 m *(750 × 41.96 ft)*; M (Sulzer); 14.9 kts; ex-*Methoni*

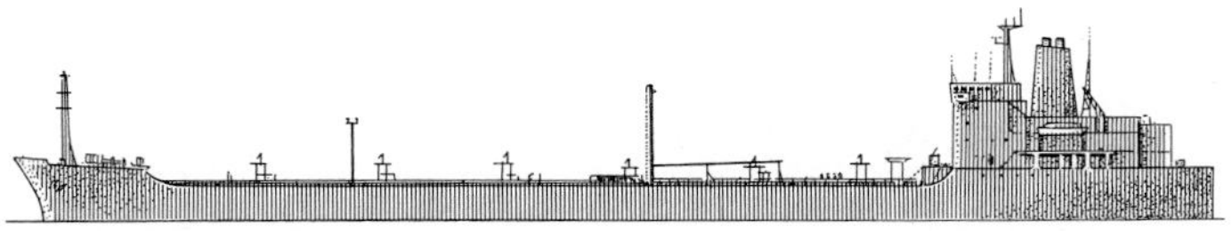

174 M^4FMR/M^2NMFMR *H13*

PALM BEACH Li/Ja (Kawasaki) 1978; Tk; 31,677 grt/50,802 dwt; 196.53 × 11.28 m *(644.78 × 37.01 ft)*; M (MAN); 16.25 kts
Sisters: **BAYWAY** (Li); **ROMITO** (NA) ex-*Esso Portland*

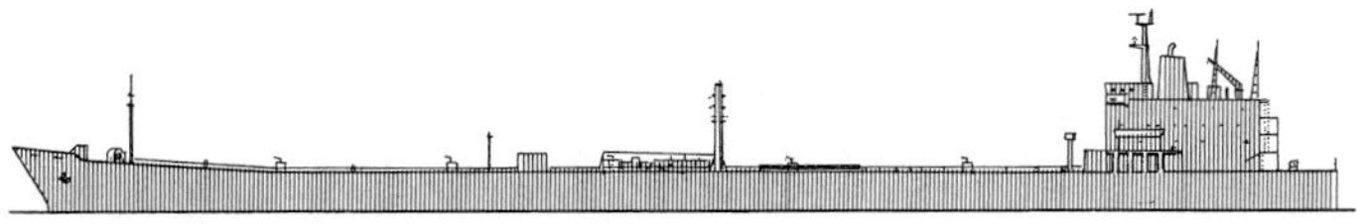

175 $M^4FMRM/M^2NMFMRM$ *H*

MARE QUEEN Pa/Ja (Kawasaki) 1979; Tk; 33,157 grt/55,144 dwt; 208.01 × 11.95 m *(682 × 39.21 ft)*; M (MAN); 15 kts; ex-*Goho Maru*

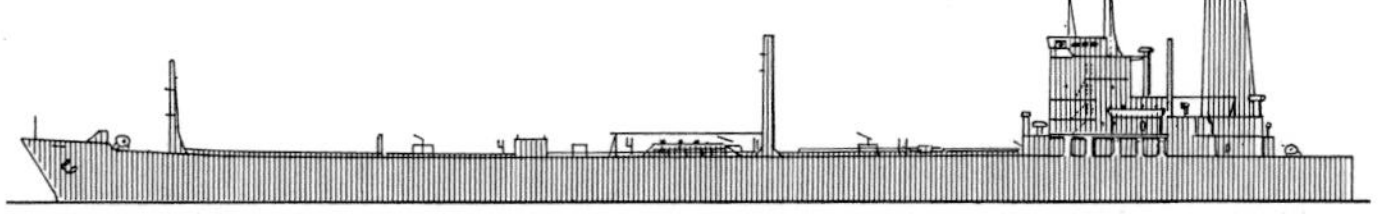

176 M^5F *H*

PLUMERIA Pa/Ja (Onomichi) 1982; Tk; 25,574 grt/38,620 dwt; 183.22 × 10.97 m *(601 × 35.99 ft)*; M (B&W); 14.5 kts; Launched as *Orchid*
Sisters: **OHIO** (Cy) ex-*Jasmine B*; **EXCEL** (NIS) ex-*Blue Excelsior*; **PACIFIC CRYSTAL** (Pa) ex-*White Excelsior*

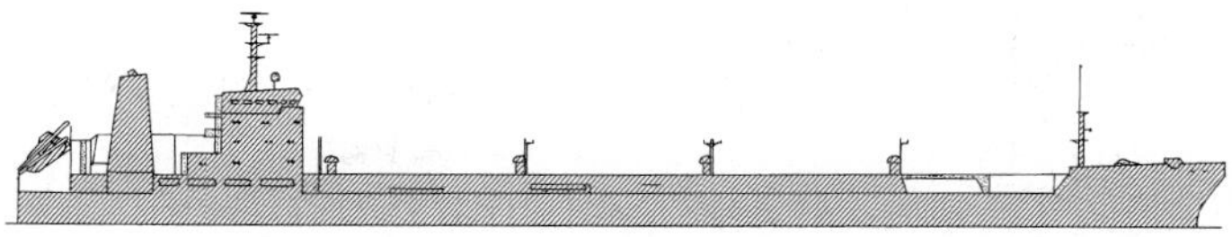

177 M^5FL *H1*

SULPHUR ENTERPRISE US/US (McDermott) 1994; Ch; 16,617 grt/ 21,649 dwt; 159.72 × 10.05 m *(524.02 × 32.97 ft)*; M (Wärtsilä); 15 kts; Free-fall lifeboat on port side

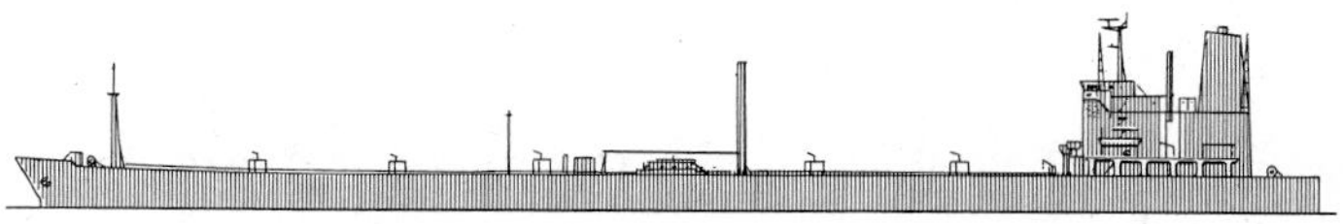

178 M^5FM *H*

LIBERTY Cy/Ja (Oshima Z) 1981; Tk; 36,657 grt/61,375 dwt; 225.03 × 12.52 m *(738 × 41.08 ft)*; M (Sulzer); 15 kts; ex-*Liberty Bell Venture*
Sisters: **AN FU** (RC) ex-*Eastern Ranger*; **ADYGEJA** (Ru) ex-*Norse Venture*; **OCEAN SPIRIT** (Li) Launched as *Asian Thistle*

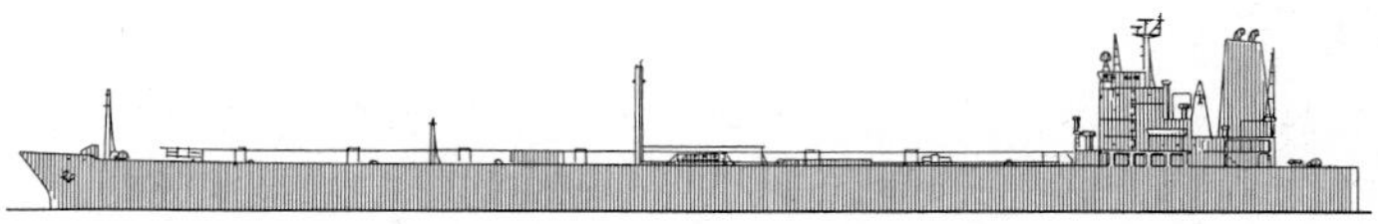

179 M^5FM *H*

SANKO HERON Pa/Ja (Onomichi) 1982; Tk; 39,964 grt/61,540 dwt; 235.8 × 12.23 m *(774 × 40.12 ft)*; M (B&W); 14.5 kts
Sister: **BERTINA** (NIS) ex-*Koyo Maru*

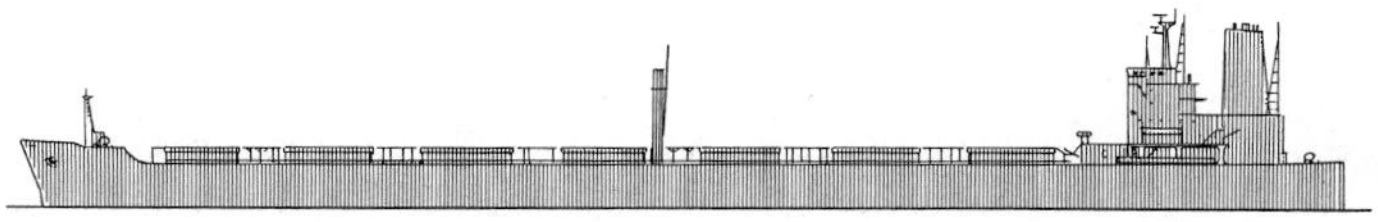

180 M^5FM *H1*

FRONT HARRIER NIS/Ja (Namura) 1985; OBO; 41,181 grt/66,234 dwt; 225.41 × 13.42 m *(739.53 × 44.03 ft)*; M (Sulzer); 13.25 kts; ex-*Cougar*
Sister: **FRONT HAWK** (NIS) ex-*Jaguar*

181 M^5FM/M^2N^2MFN *H1*

SANKO HOPE Li/Ja (Tsuneishi) 1981; Tk; 37,708 grt/60,392 dwt; 225.51 × 12.22 m *(740 × 40.09 ft)*; M (B&W); 14.75 kts; ex-*Sunny Hope*

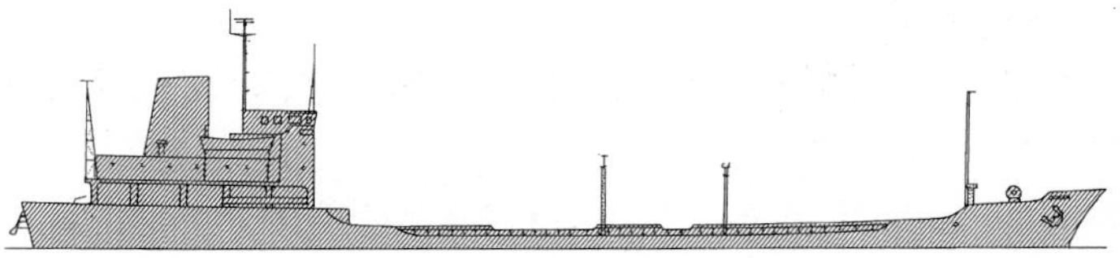

182 M^5FM *H13*

EIYU MARU Ja/Ja (Fukuoka) 1986; Tk; 3,507 grt/5,233 dwt; 107.85 × 6.29 m *(353.84 × 20.64 ft)*; M (Mitsubishi); 12.5 kts
Possible sisters: **OHMINESAN MARU** (Ja); **TOBA MARU** (Ja)

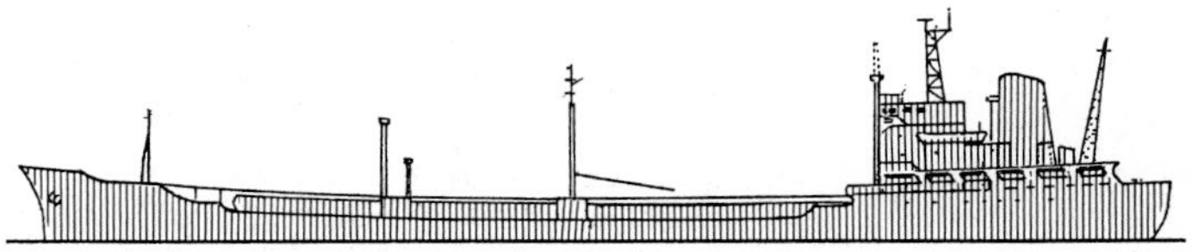

183 M^5FM *H13*

YAN HU RC/Ja (Imai Z) 1972; Tk; 5,166 grt/8,748 dwt; 122.36 × 7.95 m *(401 × 26.08 ft)*; M (Mitubishi); 15 kts; ex-*Ocean Trader*

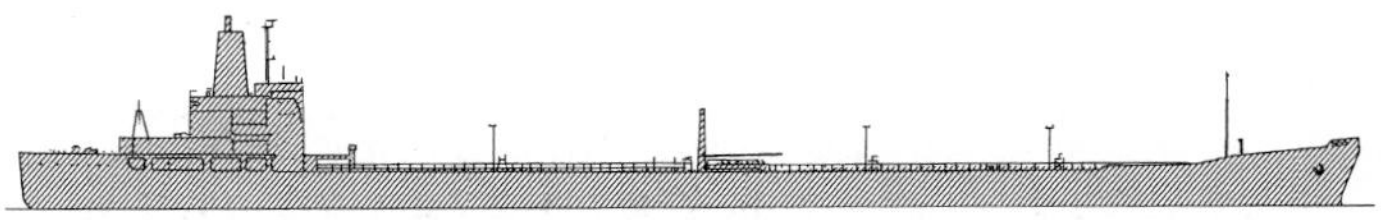

184 M^6F *H13*

PETRO ABERDEEN Br/Ja (Kawasaki D) 1967; Tk; 58,394 grt/110,862 dwt; 276.51 × 14.87 m *(907.19 × 48.79 ft)*; T (Kawasaki); 17 kts; ex-*Imperial Ottawa*; Offshore-loading tanker

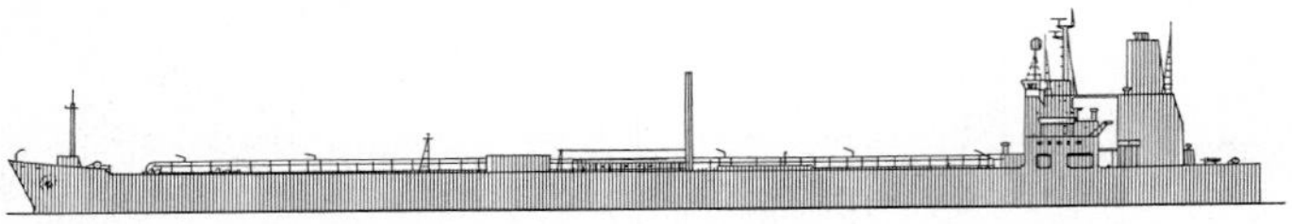

185 M^6FM *H*
SAIRYU MARU NO 2 Ja/Ja (Kasado) 1982; Tk; 40,707 grt/60,960 dwt; 229.06 × 11.64 m *(752 × 38.19 ft)*; M (Mitsubishi); 14.5 kts

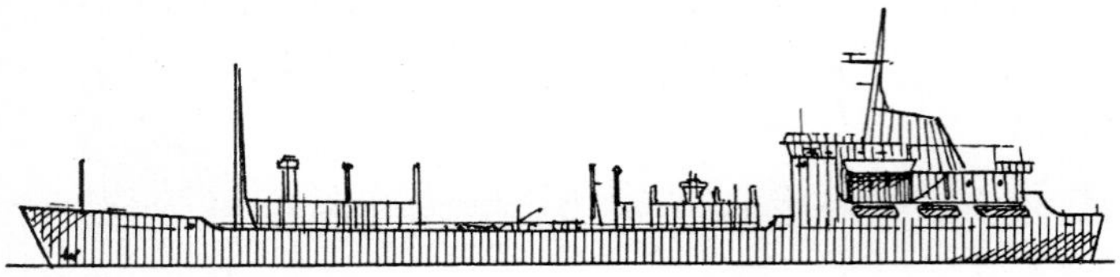

186 M^7F *H*
AMPILLA Bl/No (Trosvik) 1970; Ch; 1,398 grt/3,099 dwt; 87.74 × 5.51 m *(287.86 × 18.08 ft)*; M (Sulzer); 12.5 kts; ex-*Hoegh Vedette*

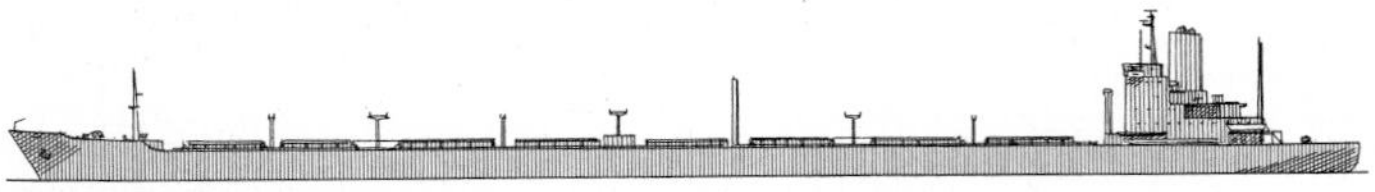

187 M^5NM^4FN *H1*
DONAU Li/Ja (Mitsubishi HI) 1969; OO; 52,740 grt/92,603 dwt; 239.02 × 13.34 m *(784.19 × 43.77 ft)*; M (MAN); 14.25 kts; *ex-Donau Maru*; Converted to bulk carrier 1982 and lengthened to 258 m (846 ft); Drawing shows vessel to original appearance
Sister (still ore/oil): **ELISA F** (It) ex-*Odessa Maru*; Similar (still ore/oil): **DIMITRIS N** (Gr) ex-*Caucasus Maru*; Similar (bulk carrier): **CASPIAN TRADER** (Li) ex-*Caspi Maru*

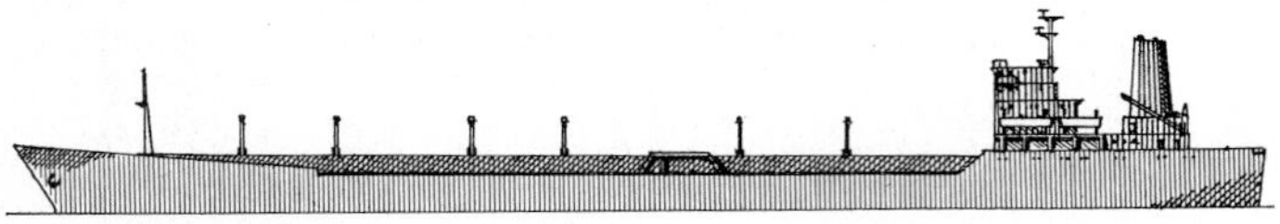

188 M^4NM^3F *H13*
STOLT FALCON Li/Ko (Korea SB) 1978; Ch; 21,043 grt/37,201 dwt; 173.64 × 11.58 m *(569.69 × 37.99 ft)*; M (Sulzer); 15.5 kts; ex-*Stolt Seoul*
Probable sisters: **STOLT OSPREY** (Li) ex-*Stolt Busan*; **STOLT HAWK** (Li) ex-*Stolt Inchon*; **STOLT HERON** (Li) ex-*Stolt Yosu*; **STOLT CONDOR** (Li) ex-*Stolt Okpo*; **STOLT EAGLE** (Li) ex-*Stolt Ulsan*

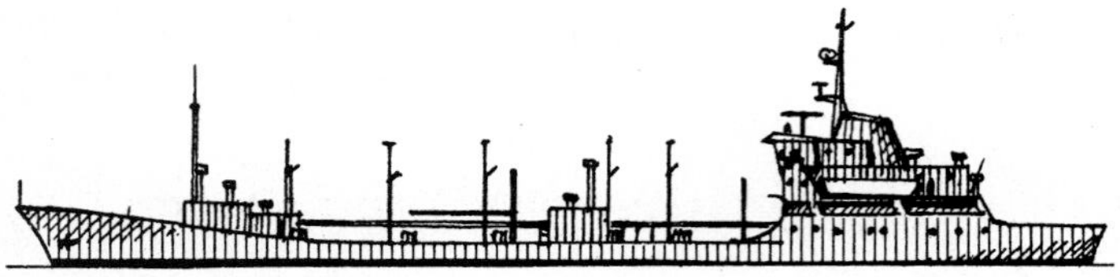

189 M^4NM^2NM-F *H13*
CHEMSKY Gr/Sw (Falkenbergs) 1967; Ch; 1,323 grt/2,006 dwt; 72.95 × 5.17 m *(239.34 × 16.96 ft)*; M (KHD); 12.5 kts; ex-*Porsgrunn*

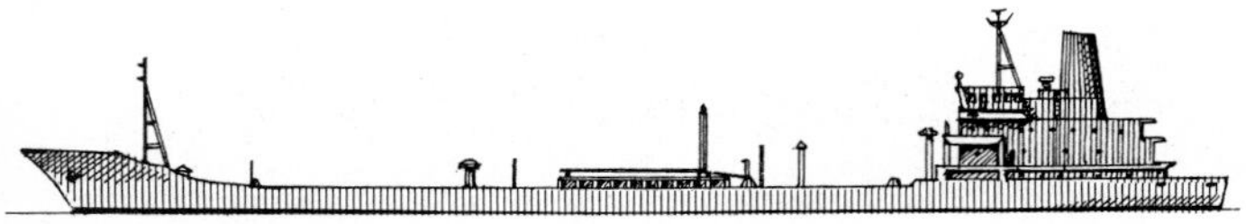

190 M^3NMF *H1*
FRAMNAS Sw/Sw (Nya Solvesborgs) 1972/73; Bitumen/Oil Carrier; 4,230 grt/5,061 dwt; 122.84 × 5.74 m *(403.02 × 18.83 ft)*; M (Pielstick); 14.25 kts; Launched 1972; Lengthened and completed 1973 (Nya Solvesborgs)

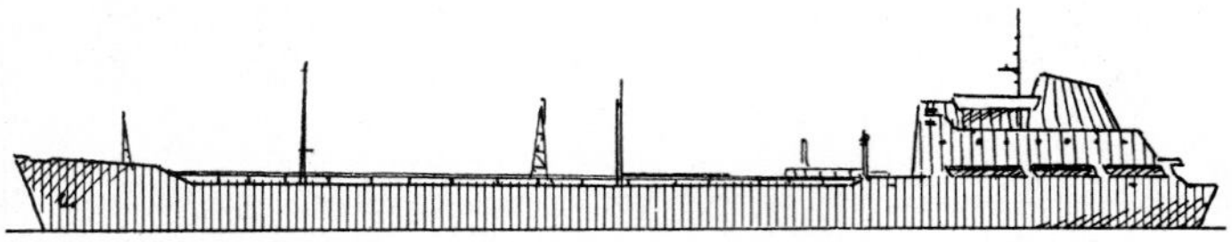

191 M^3NMF *H1*
MOON TRADER NIS/Sw (Lodose) 1969; Tk/Ch; 2,555 grt/4,196 dwt; 99.01 × 9.36 m *(324.84 × 30.71 ft)*; M (MWM); 12.5 kts; ex-*Otaru*

192 M^3NMF *H1*
SHARDA Bs/Ja (Mitsui) 1976; B; 43,393 grt/77,827 dwt; 239.05 × 14 m *(784.28 × 45.93 ft)*; M (B&W); 15.2 kts; ex-*Thorsdrake*

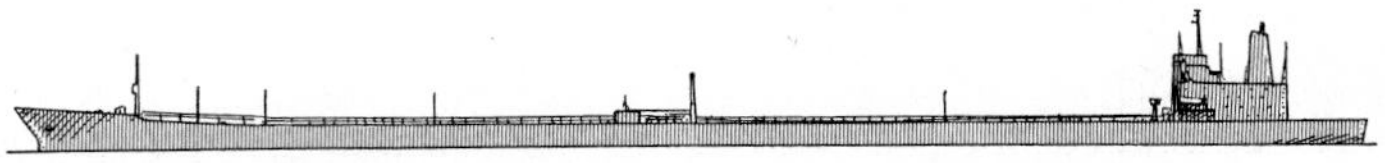

193 M^3NMFN *H*
NOURA Cy/Ja (Kawasaki) 1976; Tk; 114,458 grt/234,202 dwt; 319.95 × 19.74 m *(1,049.7 × 64.76 ft)*; M (Pielstick); 15.5 kts; ex-*Takasaka Maru*

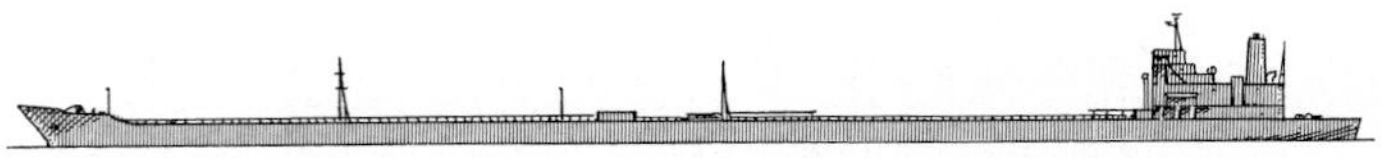

194 M^3NMFN *H1*
FORTUNESHIP L —/Ja (Mitsubishi HI) 1975; Tk; 118,215 grt/264,198 dwt; 338.62 × 20.4 m *(1,110.96 × 67.25 ft)*; T (Mitsubishi); 15 kts; ex-*Grand Brilliance*; Now broken up
Sister: **FELLOWSHIP L** (Gr) ex-*Grand Alliance*; Possible sister: **FRIENDSHIP L** (Gr) ex-*Grand Concordance*

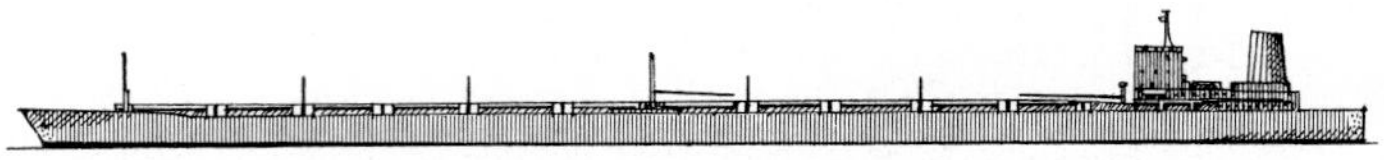

195 M^3NM^2CMG *H*
MOUNT ATHOS Cy/Br (Sunderland) 1973; OBO; 72,343 grt/161,805 dwt; 291.85 × 18.22 m *(975.51 × 59.78 ft)*; M (B&W); 15.5 kts; ex-*Naess Crusader*

196 M^3NM^2F *H*
KHARK 4 Ir/Ja (Mitsui) 1973; Tk; 138,276 grt/284,299 dwt; 342.91 × 21.78 m *(1,125.03 × 71.46 ft)*; M (B&W); 14.75 kts; ex-*Thorsaga*

197 M^3NM^2F *H*
KIRSTEN Gr/De (Odense) 1975; Tk; 158,475 grt/339,005 dwt; 370.47 × 22.46 m *(1,215.45 × 73.69 ft)*; T (Stal-Laval); 15.75 kts; ex-*Kirsten Maersk*
Similar: **CONCORDIA I** (Ma) ex-*Karama Maersk*; **ARCADIA** (Ma) ex-*Karen Maersk*; **KAROLINE** (Gr) ex-*Karoline Maersk*; **LACONIA** (Gr) ex-*Kate Maersk*; **METROTANK** (Ma) ex-*Katrine Maersk*

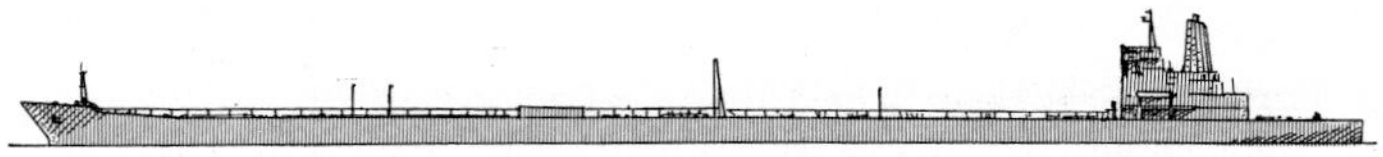

198 M^3NM^2F *H*
LOURDAS Pa/Ja (Mitsui) 1975; Tk; 122,062 grt/238,760 dwt; 324.01 × 20.03 m *(1,063.03 × 65.68 ft)*; T (Stal-Laval); 17 kts; ex-*World Duke*

199 M^3NM^2F *H*
TSURU ORIENT Pa/Ja (Kawasaki) 1974; Tk; 114,174 grt/233,478 dwt; 319.31 × 19.53 m *(1,047.6 × 64.07 ft)*; T (Kawasaki); 16.5 kts; ex-*Manhattan King*

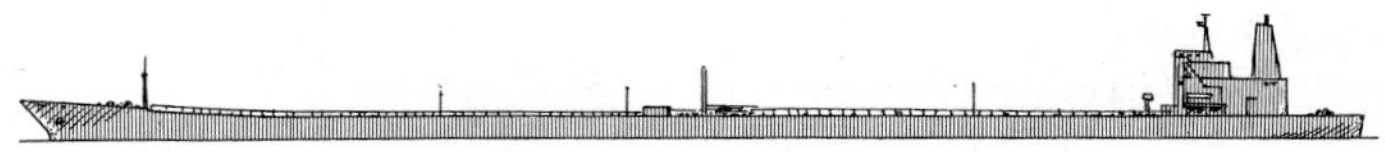

200 M^3NM^2F *H*
VIOLET Ma/Ja (Kawasaki) 1974; Tk; 114,233 grt/232,323 dwt; 319.95 × 19.66 m *(1,049.7 × 64.5 ft)*; T (Kawasaki); 16.25 kts; Launched as *World Consul*

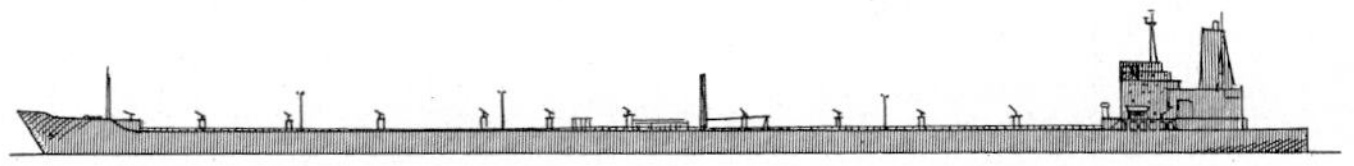

201 M^3NM^2F *H1*
HELLESPONT GRAND Ml/Ja (Kawasaki) 1976; Tk; 201,658 grt/421,681 dwt; 378.01 × 22.98 m *(1,240.19 × 75.39 ft)*; T (Kawasaki); 15.75 kts; ex-*Esso Deutschland*
Probable sister: **MIRA STAR** (Li) ex-*Hilda Knudsen*; Possibly similar: **AURIGA** (Li) ex-*Golar Patricia*

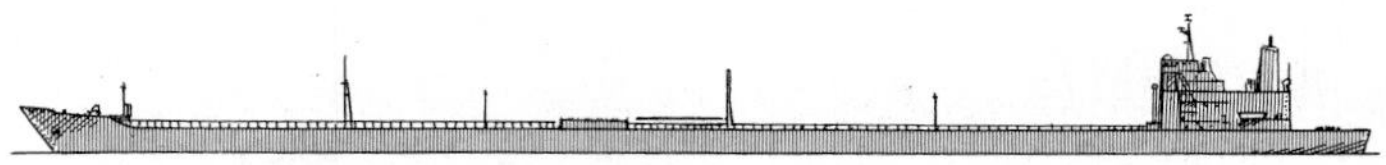

202 M^3NM^2F *H1*
WORLD PROGRESS Pa/Ja (Mitsubishi HI) 1973; Tk; 115,822 grt/237,276 dwt; 320.90 × 19.85 m *(1,053 × 65.12 ft)*; T (Mitsubishi); 15.75 kts
Possibly similar: **CALI** (Li) ex-*World City*

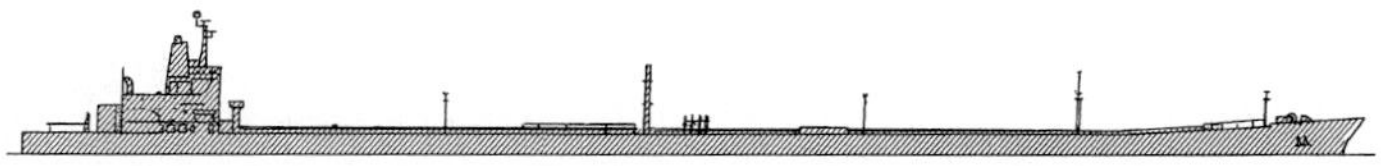

203 $M^{3}NM^{2}FC$ *H*
KAPETAN MICHALIS Gr/Ja (Hitachi) 1977; Tk; 247,160 grt/516,895 dwt; 406.59 × 25.29 m *(1,333.96 × 82.97 ft)*; T (Hitachi); 14.75 kts; ex-*Esso Pacific*; Crane aft is on starboard side
Sister: **KAPETAN GIANNIS** (Gr) ex-*Esso Atlantic*

204 $M^{3}NM^{2}FN$
HONOLULU Bs/Ja (Hitachi) 1974; Tk; 139,150 grt/283,399 dwt; 343.01 × 22.05 m *(1,125.36 × 72.34 ft)*; T (Hitachi); 16.25 kts; ex-*Esso Honolulu*
Sister: **FREEDOMSHIP L** (—) ex-*Esso Bilbao*

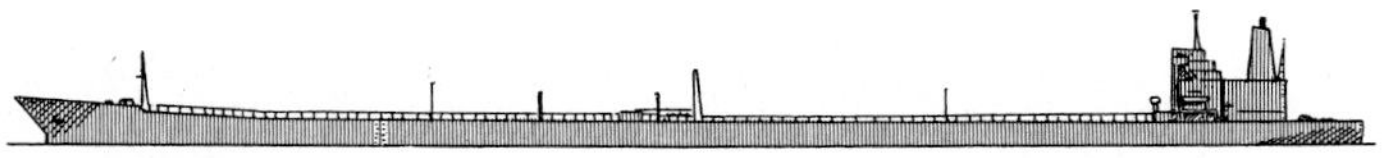

205 $M^{3}NM^{2}FN$ *H*
KUDOS Pa/Ja (Kawasaki) 1975; Tk; 114,446 grt/228,857 dwt; 319.92 × 19.66 m *(1,049.61 × 64.5 ft)*; T (Kawasaki); 16.5 kts; ex-*Wako Maru*

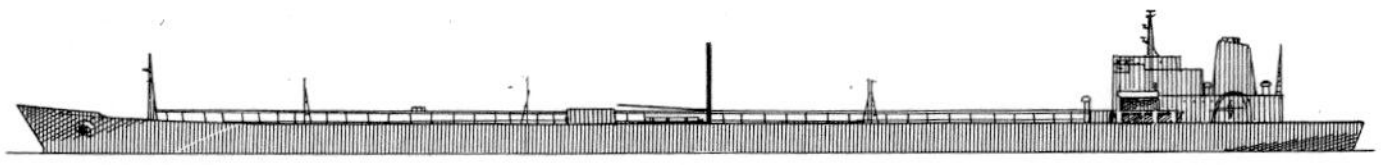

206 $M^{3}NM^{2}FN$ *H*
MESTA Bu/Ja (Kasado) 1974; Tk; 46,774 grt/75,274 dwt; 237.01 × 12.92 m *(777.59 × 42.39 ft)*; M (Sulzer); 16.5 kts
Sister: **OSAM** (Bu)

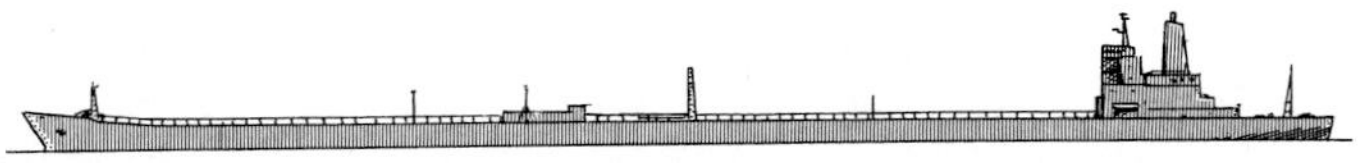

207 $M^{3}NM^{2}FN$ *H*
OCEAN JEWEL Pa/Ja (Mitsui) 1975; Tk; 132,608 grt/273,711 dwt; 331.5 × 20.55 m *(1,087.6 × 67.42 ft)*; T (Stal-Laval); 16.25 kts; ex-*Barbara T Shaheen*
Similar: **SWIFT** (Li) ex-*Takakurasan Maru*

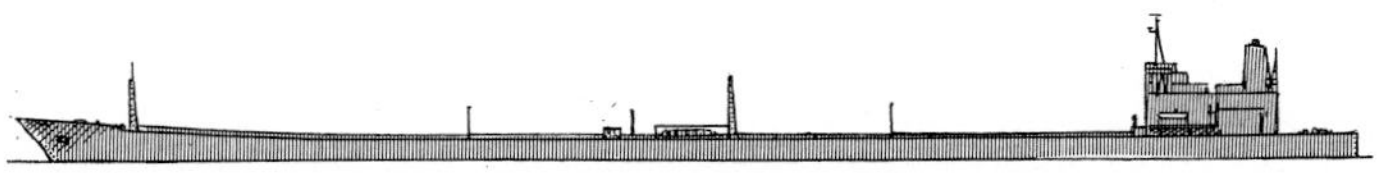

208 $M^{3}NM^{2}FN$ *H*
PISA Pa/Ja (Sumitomo) 1976/78; Tk; 133,822 grt/276,422 dwt; 340.83 × 20.98 m *(1,118.21 × 68.83 ft)*; T (Stal-Laval); 16.5 kts; ex-*Primrose*; Launched 1976; Completed 1978
Sister: **SVELVIK** (Bs) ex-*Conoco Europe*; Possible sister: **WORLD XANADU** (Li) ex-*World Canada*

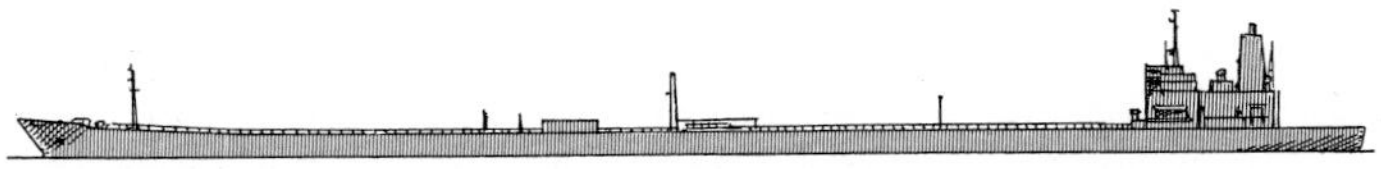

209 $M^{3}NM^{2}FN$ *H*
WORLD BERMUDA Pa/Ja (IHI) 1974; Tk; 131,304 grt/271,580 dwt; 336.99 × 21.05 m *(1,105.61 × 69.06 ft)*; T (IHI); 16 kts; Launched as *World Monarch*
Probably similar: **ROME** (Pa) ex-*Rosebay*

210 $M^{3}NM^{2}FN$ *H1*
HELLESPONT EMBASSY MI/Ja (Mitsubishi) 1976; Tk; 209,788 grt/ 406,490 dwt; 365.87 × 22.9 m *(1,200.36 × 75.13 ft)*; T (Mitsubishi); 15.75 kts; ex-*Aiko Maru*
Sisters: **BRIDGETON** (US) ex-*Al Rekkah*; **CHEVRON SOUTH AMERICA** (Br); **KAPETAN HATZIS** (Gr) ex-*Chevron North America*; **KAPETAN HIOTIS** (Gr) ex-*David Packard*

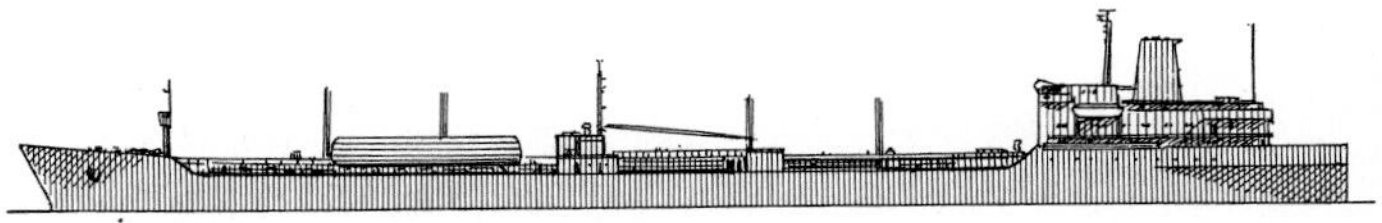

211 $M^{3}NM^{3}FM$ *H13*
BOW FORTUNE NIS/Pd (Szczecinska) 1975; Ch; 17,561 grt/27,954 dwt; 170.52 × 11.08 m *(559.45 × 36.35 ft)*; M (Sulzer); 17 kts; 'B-76' type
Sisters (at least one has large pipes and a platform on funnel): **BOW SPRING** (NIS); **BOW STAR** (NIS); **BOW SUN** (NIS); **BOW SEA** (NIS); **BOW SKY** (NIS); **NCC TIHAMAH** (NIS) ex-*Brimanger*; **NCC MADINAH** (NIS) ex-*Nordanger;* **NCC JOUF** (NIS) ex-*Porsanger*; **NCC NAJRAN** (NIS) ex-*Risanger*; **NCC YAMAMAH** (NIS) ex-*Spinanger*; **NCC JIZAN** (NIS) ex-*Torvanger*

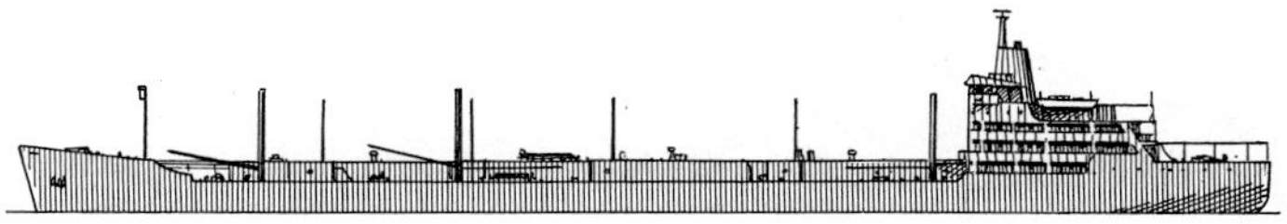

212 $M^{3}NM^{3}NM\text{-}F$ *H13*
OTAPAN Me/Ne (Verolme Dok) 1965; Tk/Ch; 11,867 grt/23,420 dwt; 167.65 × 9.52 m *(550 × 31.24 ft)*; T (GEC); 16.5 kts; ex-*Harry C Webb*

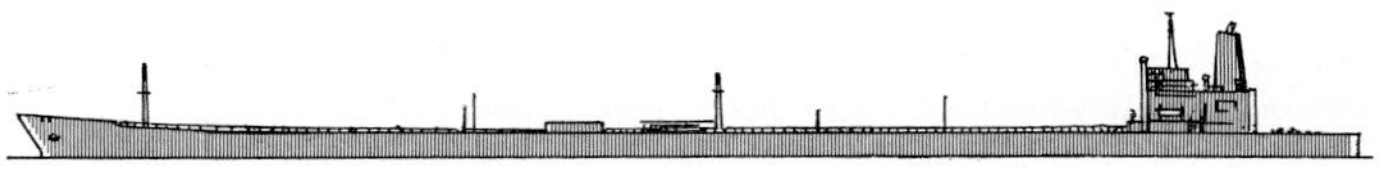

213 $M^{3}NM^{2}NMF$ *H*
STENA CONVOY Li/Ja (IHI) 1972; Tk; 127,535 grt/262,631 dwt; 336.36 × 20.29 (1,103.54 × 66.57) m; T (IHI); 16.75 kts; ex-*Universe Pioneer*
Similar: **STENA CONCORDIA** (Li) ex-*Universe Burmah*; **STENA CONDUCTOR** (Li) ex-*Universe Explorer*; **STENA CONTINENT** (Li) ex-*Universe Guardian*; **STENA CONGRESS** (Li) ex-*Universe Mariner*; **STENA CONCEPT** (Li) ex-*Universe Monitor*; **STENA CONTENDER** (Li) ex-*Universe Ranger*; **STAR CARIBBEAN** (Pa) ex-*Texaco Caribbean*; **STAR VERAGUAS** (Pa) ex-*Texaco Veraguas*; **STENA CONSTELLATION** (Li) ex-*Universe Sentinel*; **LUCINA** (Li) ex-*Universe Frontier*

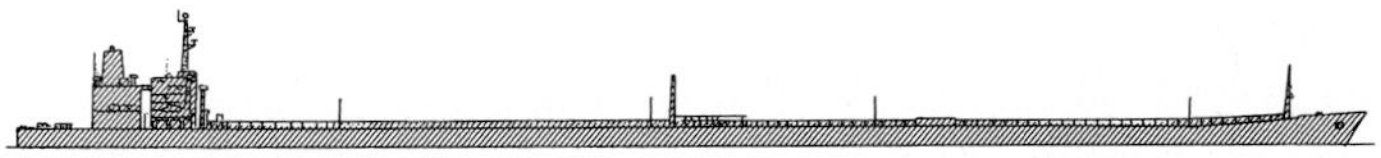

214 $M^{3}NM^{2}N^{2}FN$ *H*
JAHRE VIKING NIS/Ja (Sumitomo) 1976/79/80; Tk; 260,851 grt/ 564,763 dwt; 458.45 × 24.61 m *(1,504 × 80.74 ft)*; T (Stal-Laval); 15.5 kts; ex-*Seawise Giant*; Launched as *Oppama*; Lengthened 1980 (NKK)

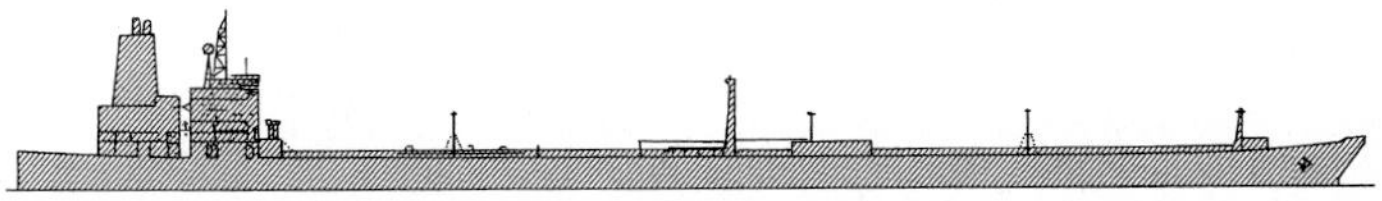

215 $M^{3}NMNM^{2}F$ *H*
BERGE ENTERPRISE NIS/Ja (Mitsui) 1981; Tk; 188,728 grt/360,700 dwt; 340.52 × 23.23 m *(1,117.19 × 76.21 ft)*; M (B&W); 15.25 kts
Sister: **BERGE PIONEER** (NIS)

216 $M^{3}NM\text{-}F$ *H13*
STAINLESS DUKE Pa/Br (Cammell Laird) 1969; Tk/Ch; 6,183 grt/ 10,563 dwt; 130.21 × 7.53 m *(427.2 × 24.7 ft)*; M (Pielstick); 14.5 kts; ex-*Silverhawk*

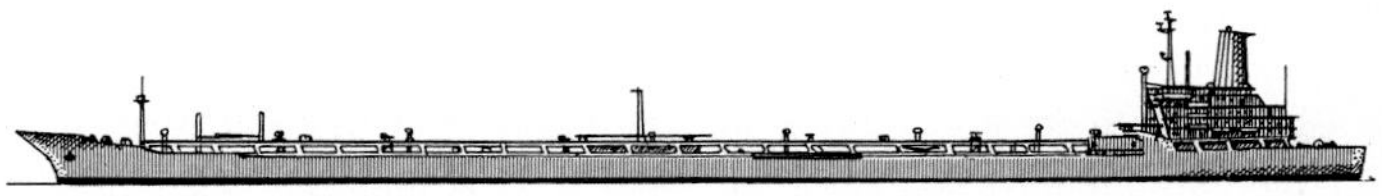

217 $M^{3}N^{2}M^{2}G$ *H1*
SAINT CONSTANTINOS Li/Sp ('Astano') 1974; Tk; 151,221 grt/323,094 dwt; 347.94 × 24.83 m *(1,141 × 81.43 ft)*; TST (Kawasaki); 14.5 kts; ex-*Ocean Park*

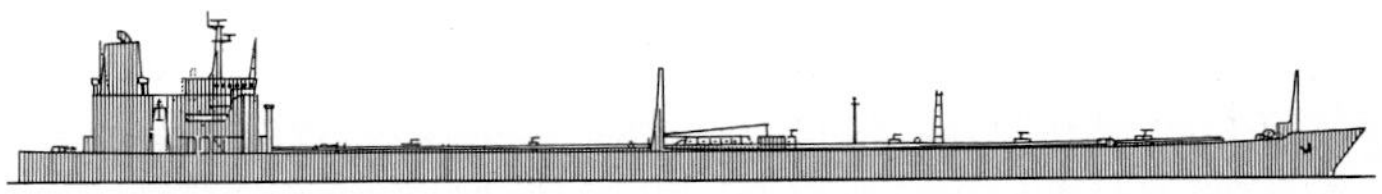

218 $M^{3}N^{3}MFN$ *H*
BILLYJEANNE A HK/Ja (Sanoyasu) 1981; Tk; 51,057 grt/81,282 dwt; 245.04 × 12.20 m *(803.94 × 40.03 ft)*; M (B&W); 16 kts
Sister (12.19 m (40 ft) longer-between second and third uprights): **NEW IDEAL** (Li)

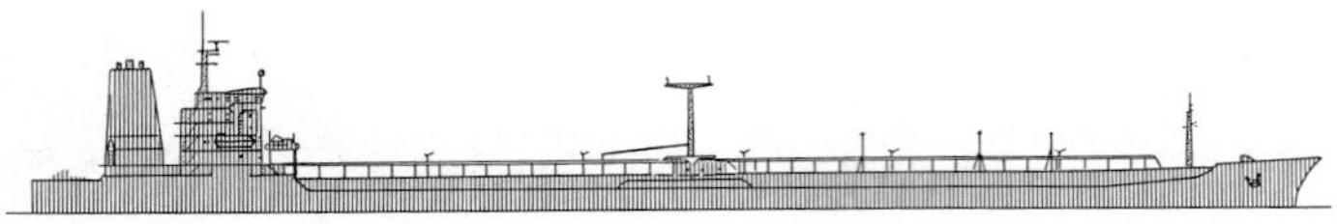

219 *$M^3TMF/MUMF$ H13*
GLENROSS Li/Pd (Gdynia) 1993; Tk; 53,315 grt/89,249 dwt; 247.20 × 13.10 m *(811.02 × 42.97 ft)*; M (Sulzer); 14.3 kts; 'B563' type
Sister: **LOCHNESS** (Li)

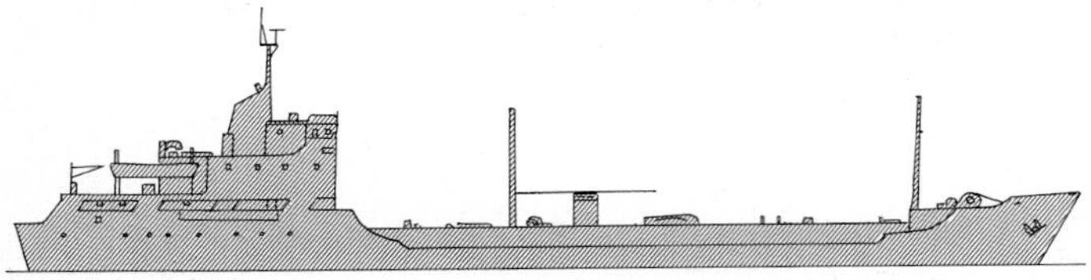

220 *M^2M-F H13*
CAMPOTEJAR Sp/Sp (Cadagua) 1967; Tk; 1,834 grt/2,487 dwt; 79.61 × 5.14 m *(261.19 × 16.86 ft)*; M (Stork-Werkspoor); 14 kts
Sister: **VASILIOS XIII** (Gr) ex-*Campolongo*

221 *M^2NF H123*
ALSAD ALAALY Eg/FRG (Deutsche Werft) 1960; Tk; 13,235 grt/20,110 dwt; 170.69 × 9.4 m *(560 × 30.84 ft)*; M (MAN); 15 kts

222 *M^2NF H123*
EVENSK Ru/Fi (Rauma-Repola) 1963; Tk; 3,360 grt/4,399 dwt; 105.39 × 6.22 m *(345.77 × 20.42 ft)*; M (B&W); 14 kts
Sisters: **NOOREEN** (Pa) ex-*Aluksne*; **APE** (—) ex-*Appe*; **AKTASH** (Gi); **APSHERONSK** (Ru); **ALEKSEYEVKA** (Uk); **ALEKSEYEVSK** (Ru); **DARNITSA** (Ru); **EREBUS** (Ru); **YUGLA** (Ru); **CUBA** (Cu) ex-*Artsyz*

223 *M^2NF H123*
MOUNT WASHINGTON US/US (Bethlehem) 1963; Tk; 27,797 grt/47,941 dwt; 222.44 × 12.26 m *(736.35 × 39.81 ft)*; T (Bethlehem Steel); 17.5 kts; US Government owned
Sisters: **MOUNT VERNON** (US) ex-*Mount Vernon Victory*; **COVE TRADER** (US) ex-*Transeastern*

224 *M^2NF H123*
STAR GEORGIA US/US (Bethlehem Steel) 1964; Tk; 15,633 grt/26,755 dwt; 184.31 × 10.64 m *(604.69 × 34.9 ft)*; T (Bethlehem Steel); 17.5 kts; ex-*Texaco Georgia*
Sisters: **MARYLAND** (US) ex-*Texaco Maryland*; **STAR RHODE ISLAND** (US) ex-*Texaco Rhode Island*

225 *M^2NFN H123*
DA QING 66 RC/Sw (Uddevalla) 1964; Tk; 34,966 grt/59,494 dwt; 235.87 × 12.21 m *(773.85 × 40.06 ft)*; M (MAN); 15.5 kts; ex-*Harwi*

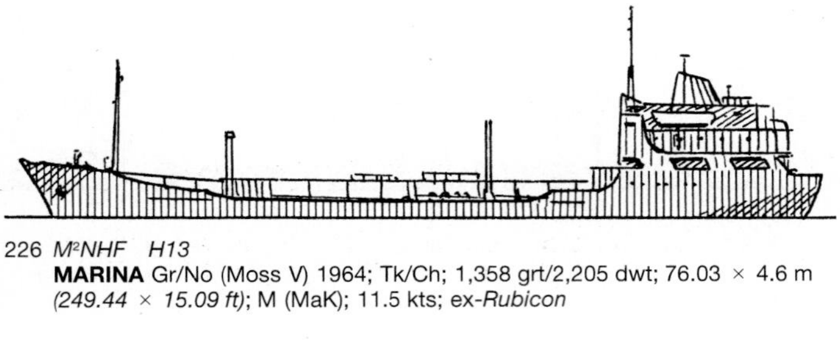

226 *M^2NHF H13*
MARINA Gr/No (Moss V) 1964; Tk/Ch; 1,358 grt/2,205 dwt; 76.03 × 4.6 m *(249.44 × 15.09 ft)*; M (MaK); 11.5 kts; ex-*Rubicon*

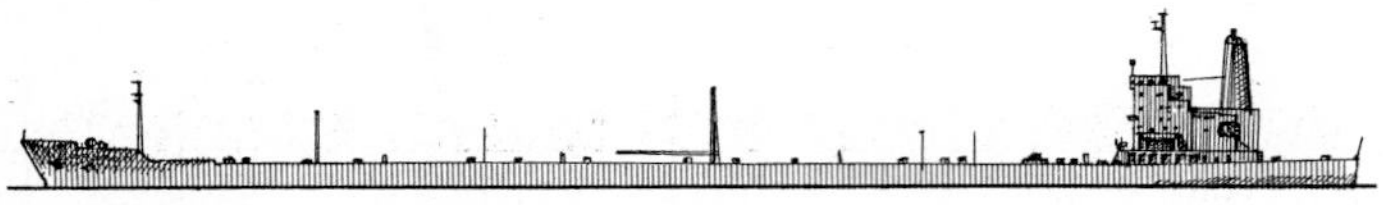

227 *M^2NMF*
DELOS Gr/Ja (Kawasaki) 1974; Tk; 135,940 grt/277,748 dwt; 336.03 × 21.21 m *(1,102.5 × 69.6 ft)*; T (Kawasaki); 17 kts; ex-*British Respect*

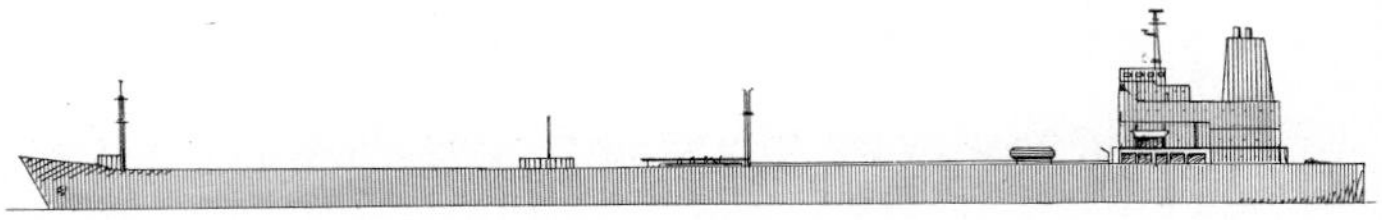

228 *M^2NMF H*
ALFA AMERICA Br/Ja (Mitsubishi HI) 1978; Tk; 51,474 grt/87,368 dwt; 231 × 12.11 m *(757.87 × 39.73 ft)*; M (Sulzer); 16.5 kts; ex-*Nordic Faith*
Sister: **CONSTITUTION** (Li) ex-*Nordic Spirit*

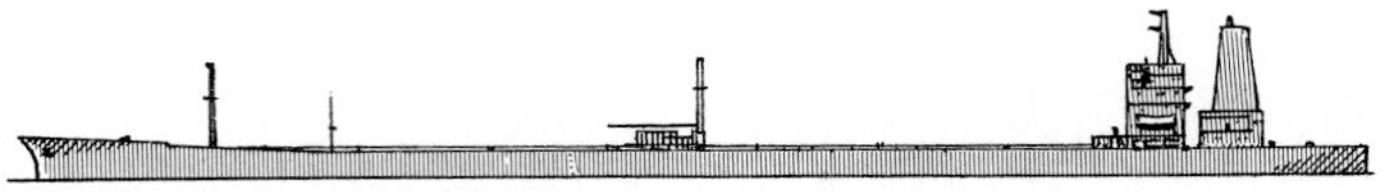

229 *M^2NMF H*
ATIGUN PASS US/US (Avondale) 1977; Tk; 74,250 grt/152,405 dwt; 276.16 × 17.47 m *(906.04 × 57.32 ft)*; T (GEC); 14 kts
Sisters: **BROOKS RANGE** (US); **KEYSTONE CANYON** (US); **THOMPSON PASS** (US); Probable sisters: **S/R BENICIA** (US); **S/R NORTH SLOPE** (US)

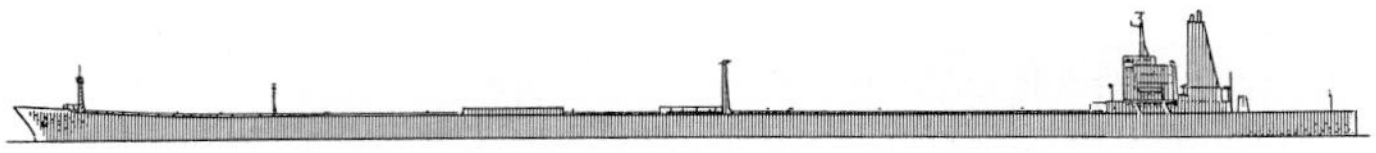

230 *M^2NMF H*
BERGE DUKE NIS/Ja (Mitsui) 1973; Tk; 138,009 grt/284,004 dwt; 342.91 × 21.78 m *(1,125.03 × 71.8 ft)*; M (B&W); 15.5 kts
Sisters: **BERGE SEPTIMUS** (NIS); **BERGE LORD** (NIS)

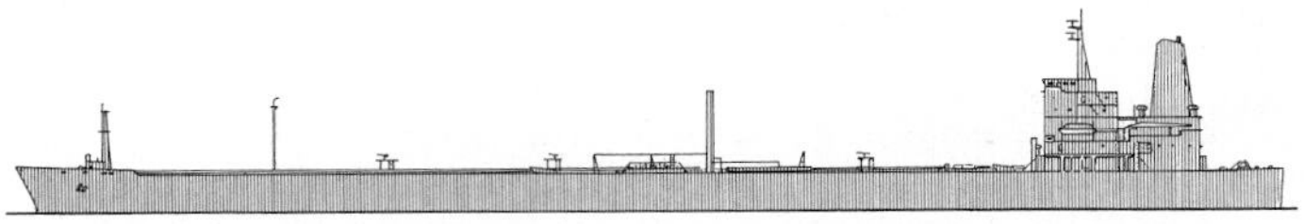

231 *M^2NMF H*
BRITISH SKILL Br/Br (H&W) 1983; Tk; 66,034 grt/117,353 dwt; 261.32 × 17.33 m *(857 × 56.86 ft)*; M (B&W); 13.5 kts
Sisters: **BRITISH SUCCESS** (Br); **BRITISH SPIRIT** (Br) (builder Scott Lithgow); **AUSTRALIAN ACHIEVER** (Au) ex-*BP Achiever* (builder Swan Hunter)

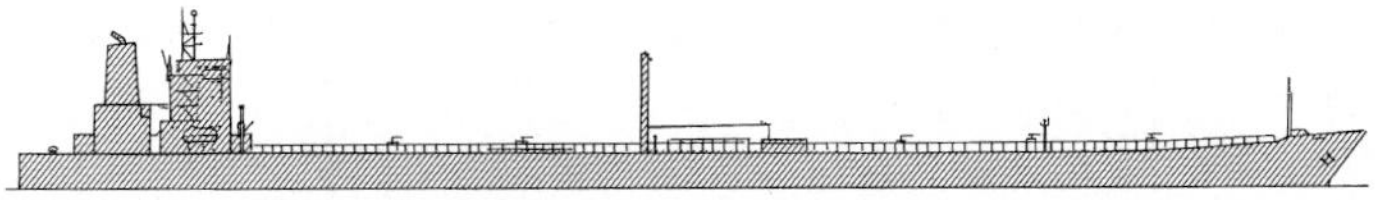

232 *M^2NMF H*
EAGLE AURIGA Sg/Ja (Shin Kurushima) 1993; Tk; 55,962 grt/102,352 dwt; 241.42 × 14.57 m *(792.06 × 47.80 ft)*; M (B&W); 15.26 kts; ex-*Neptune Auriga*

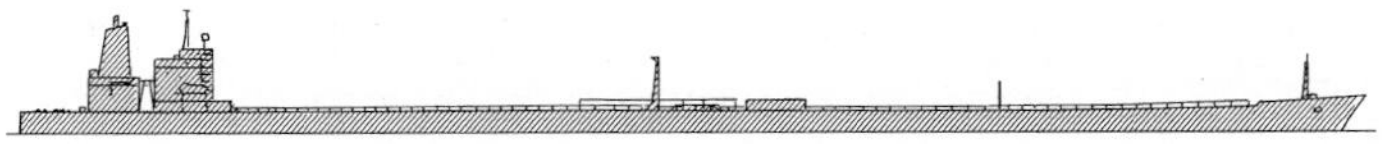

233 *M^2NMF H*
LANISTES Kn/Ja (Mitsui) 1975; Tk; 150,806 grt/311,883 dwt; 343.62 × 22.37 m *(1,127.36 × 73.39 ft)*; T (Kawasaki); 15.25 kts; ex-*Lanistes*
Sister: **BERGE BRAGD** (NIS) ex-*Litiopa*

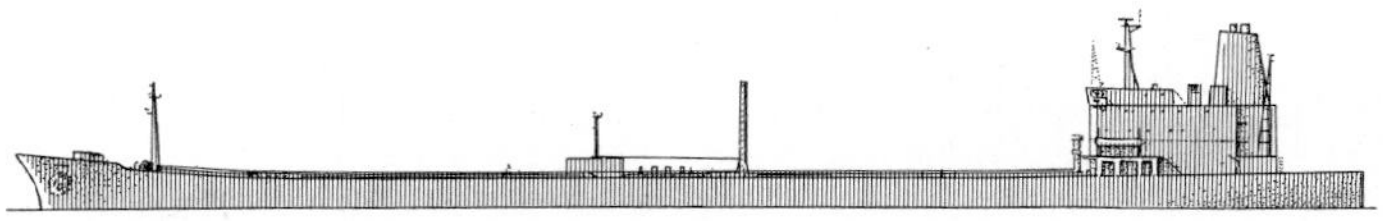

234 *M^2NMF H*
SEAEXPRESS II Ma/Ja (Hitachi) 1978; Tk; 32,641 grt/60,962 dwt; 209.51 × 12.08 m *(687.37 × 39.63 ft)*; M (Pielstick); 15 kts; ex-*Sairyu Maru*

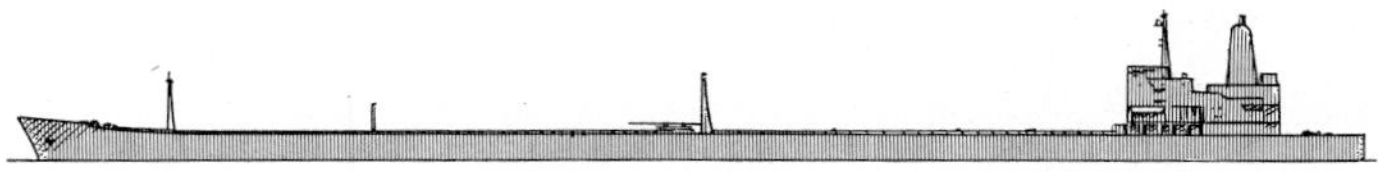

235 *M^2NMF H*
SYMI Gr/Ja (Mitsubishi HI) 1973; Tk; 130,145 grt/269,349 dwt; 338.64 × 20.66 m *(1,111.02 × 67.78 ft)*; T (Nagasaki); 14.5 kts; ex-*British Norness*
Possible sisters: **BRITISH RANGER** (Br); **BRITISH RELIANCE** (Br); **BRITISH RESOLUTION** (Br); **BRITISH RESOURCE** (Br) (motor ship); **ASSOS BAY** (Pa) ex-*British Trident*; Similar: **KNOCK MORE** (Li) ex-*Chambord*; **CHAUMONT** (Kn); **ONCE** (Kn) ex-*Chenonceaux*

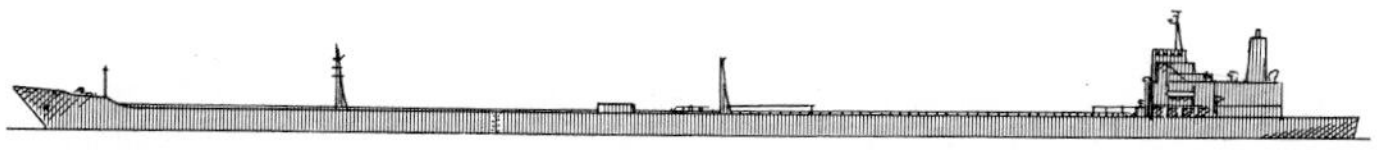

236 *M²NMF H1*
CHEVRON NAGASAKI Li/Ja (Mitsubishi HI) 1974; Tk; 126,723 grt/268,244 dwt; 338.64 × 20.56 m *(1,111.1 × 67.4 ft)*; T (Mitsubishi); 15.25 kts
Sisters: **CHEVRON PERTH** (Bs); **CHEVRON FELUY** (Li); **CHARLES PIGOTT**; Possible sisters: **CHEVRON COPENHAGEN** (Li); **CHEVRON EDINBURGH** (Br) ex-*Chevron Edinburgh*; **MARE ASIA** (Li) ex-*Otto N Miller*; **STAR JAPAN** (Li) ex-*Texaco Japan*

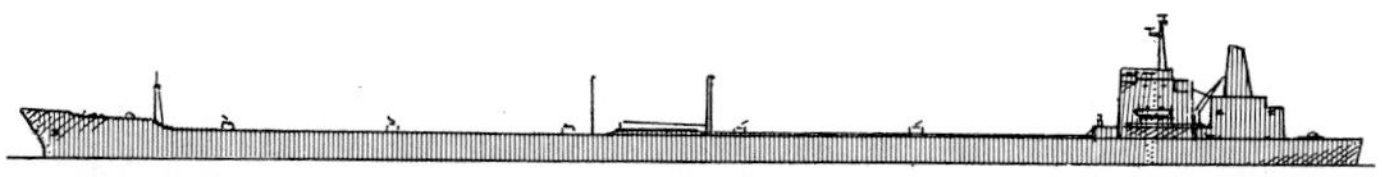

237 *M²NMF H1*
SPLENDOUR Ma/Br (Swan Hunter) 1976; Tk; 57,211 grt/112,745 dwt; 260.33 × 15.18 m *(854.1 × 49.8 ft)*; M (Sulzer); 16 kts; ex-*Geroi Sevastopolya*; Launched as *Kyra Lynn*
Sisters: **ARTEMIS GAROFALIDIS** (Gr); Launched as *Interoceanic I*; **EQUATOR** (Ma) Launched as *Robcap VI*

238 *M²NMF H123*
TEXAS SUN US/US (Sun SB) 1960; Tk; 26,281 grt/54,311 dwt; 229.22 × 12.37 m *(752.03 × 40.58 ft)*; T (Westinghouse); 17 kts

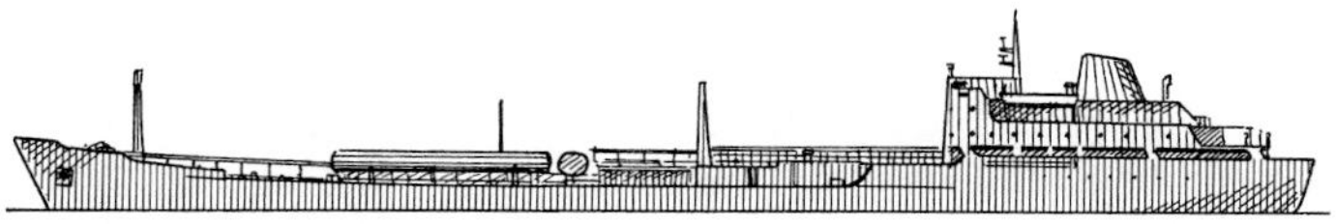

239 *M²NMF H13*
ADA EZE Ng/Sw (Ekensbergs) 1963; LGC/Tk; 6,070 grt/8,335 dwt; 134.73 × 6.97 m *(442.03 × 22.87 ft)*; M (B&W); 14 kts; ex-*Selje*

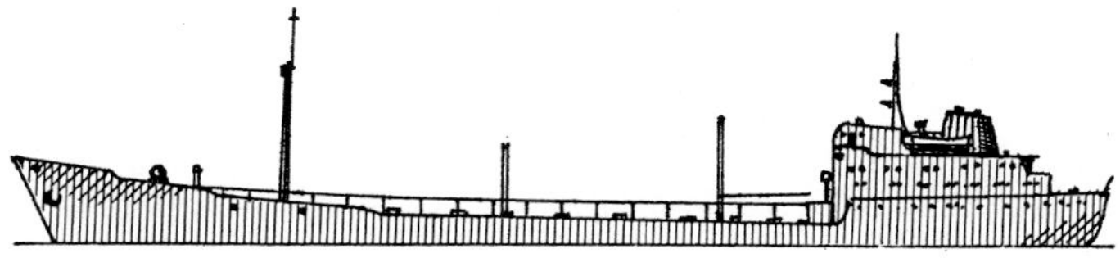

240 *M²NMF H13*
CHIQUITA Ec/No (Trondhjems) 1963; Tk/Ch; 2,688 grt/4,014 dwt; 101.45 × 5.81 m *(332.84 × 19.06 ft)*; M (Werkspoor); 11 kts; ex-*Ek*

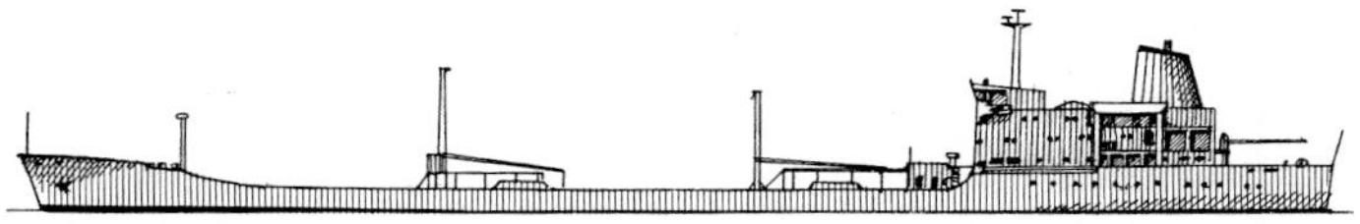

241 *M²NMF H13*
LIAN Ir/BR (Swan Hunter) 1970; Tk; 8,870 grt/14,001 dwt; 147.83 × 8.55 m *(485 × 28.05 ft)*; M (Doxford); 15 kts; ex-*Matadi Palm*

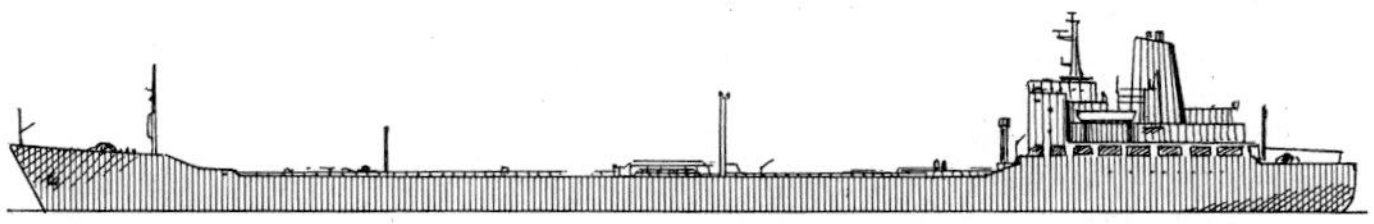

242 *M²NMFM H13*
ESSO PORT JEROME Fr/Ja (Hitachi) 1972; Tk; 13,151 grt/22,726 dwt; 161.02 × 9.76 m *(528.28 × 32.02 ft)*; M (B&W); 15 kts; ex-*Esso Kumamoto*; '22 Type'; Some others in this class may have this sequence

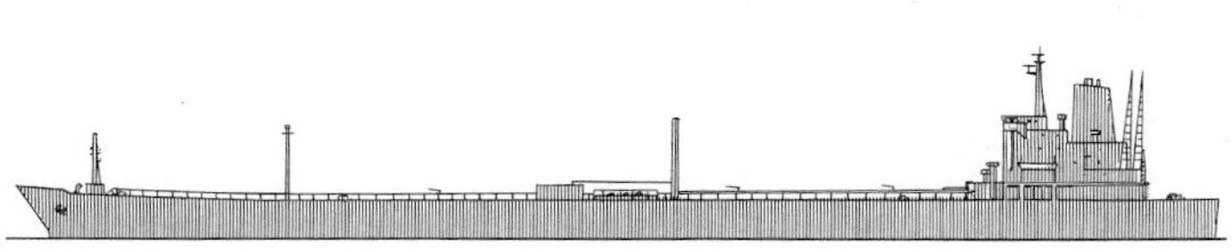

243 *M²NMFM² H*
CANADIAN LIBERTY Li/Ja (Sasebo) 1980; Tk; 53,944 grt/87,542 dwt; 243.01 × 12.73 m *(797 × 41.77 ft)*; M (MAN); 14.5 kts; ex-*Columbia Liberty*
Possible sister: **VENITA** (NIS) ex-*Diana*

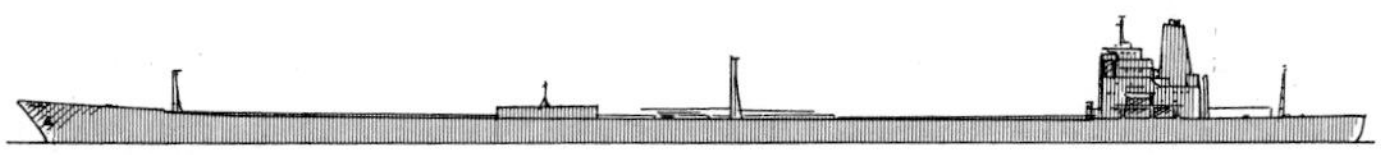

244 *M²NMFMN H*
T M REGULUS Sg/Ja (Mitsui) 1974; Tk; 122,088 grt/234,210 dwt; 324.01 × 19.51 m *(1,063 × 64.01 ft)*; M (B&W); 16 kts; ex-*Meitai Maru*

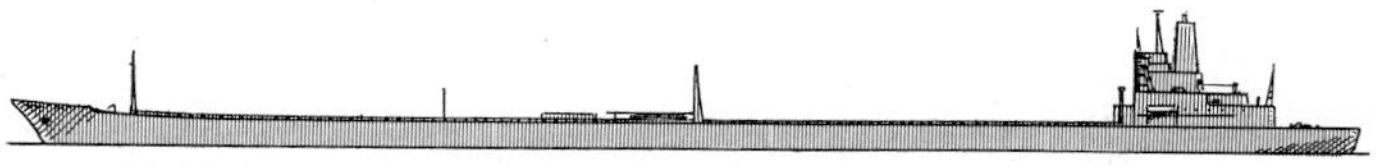

245 *M²NMFN H*
ANCORA NIS/Ja (Hitachi) 1974; Tk; 116,629 grt/238,058 dwt; 324.01 × 19.43 m *(1,063.02 × 63.75 ft)*; T (Kawasaki); 15.75 kts; ex-*Shunko Maru*

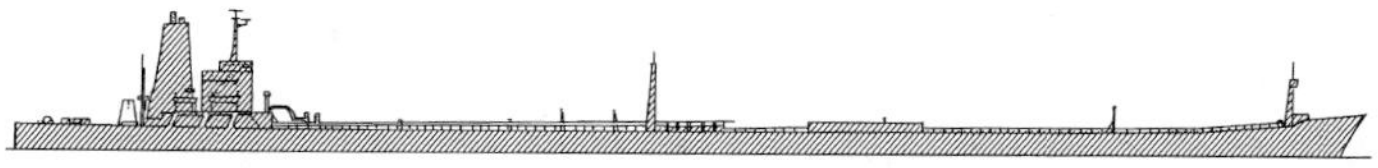

246 *M²NMFN H*
BERGE PRINCE NIS/Ja (Mitsui) 1973; Tk; 138,008 grt/284,522 dwt; 342.91 × 21.78 m *(1,125.03 × 71.46 ft)*; M (B&W); 15.5 kts

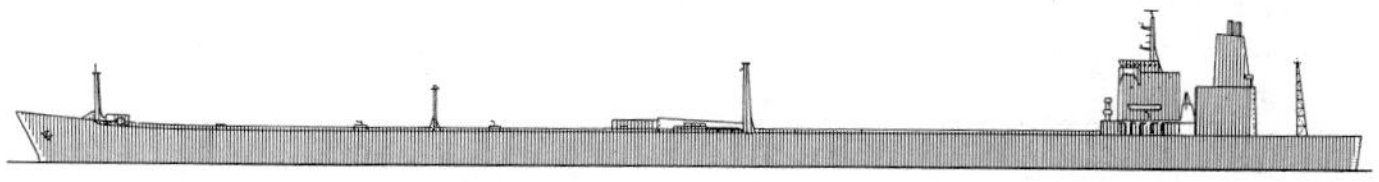

247 *M²NMFN H*
KERKYRA Gr/Ja (Mitsui) 1973; Tk; 70,304 grt/140,462 dwt; 270.52 × 17.04 (887.53 × 55.91) m; M (B&W); 16 kts; ex-*Burmah Pearl*
Sister: **KYTHIRA** (Gr) ex-*Burmah Peridot*

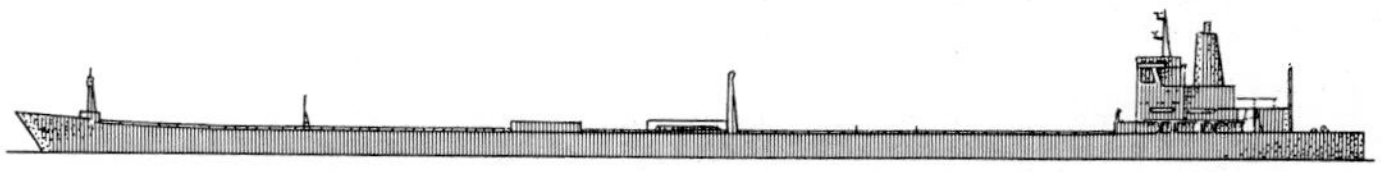

248 *M²NMFN H*
LEONIDAS SV/Ja (Mitsui) 1974; Tk; 126,193 grt/263,372 dwt; 331.53 × 20.6 m *(1,087.7 × 67.59 ft)*; M (B&W); 16 kts; ex-*Polybritannia*
Similar: **BISOTOON** (Ir) ex-*Polynesia*

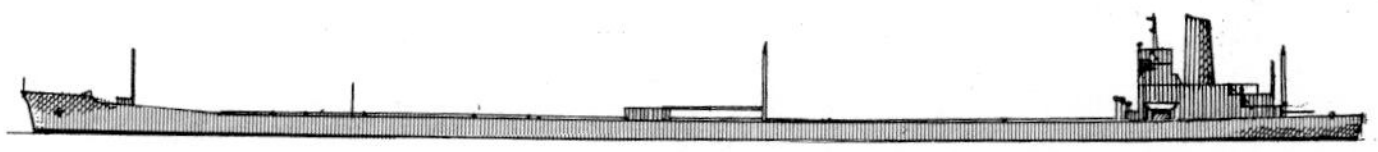

249 *M²NMFN H*
WESTERN LION Li/Ja (Hitachi) 1974; Tk; 130,539 grt/269,117 dwt; 331 × 22.01 m *(1,085.96 × 72.21 ft)*; T (Hitachi); 15.5 kts
Sisters: **SOUTHERN LION** (Li); **NORTHERN LION** (Li); **EASTERN LION** (Li)

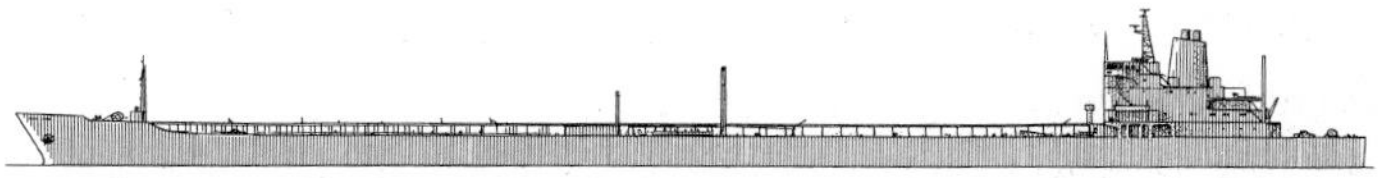

250 *M²NMFN H1*
EDINBURGH FRUID Br/Ja (Mitsubishi HI) 1976; Tk; 79,860 grt/134,996 dwt; 280.42 × 15.24 m *(920.01 × 50 ft)*; M (Sulzer); 15.25 kts; ex-*Grey Warrior*

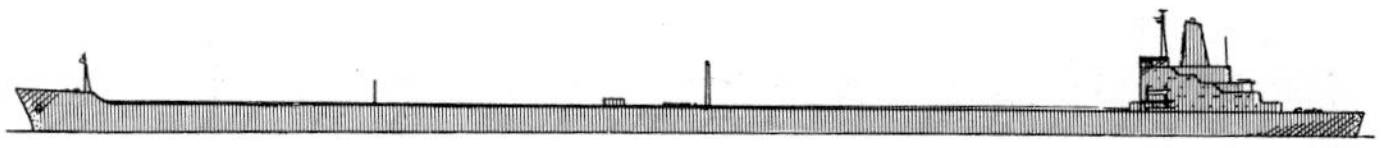

251 *M²NMFN H1*
LIWA UAE/Br (Swan Hunter) 1972; Tk; 122,376 grt/256,390 dwt; 345.5 × 20.07 m *(1,133.5 × 65.85 ft)*; T (AEI); 15.5 kts; ex-*London Lion*
Sisters: **AVAJ 2** (Ir) ex-*Windsor Lion*; **THAI RESOURCE** (Li) Launched as *Tyne Pride*

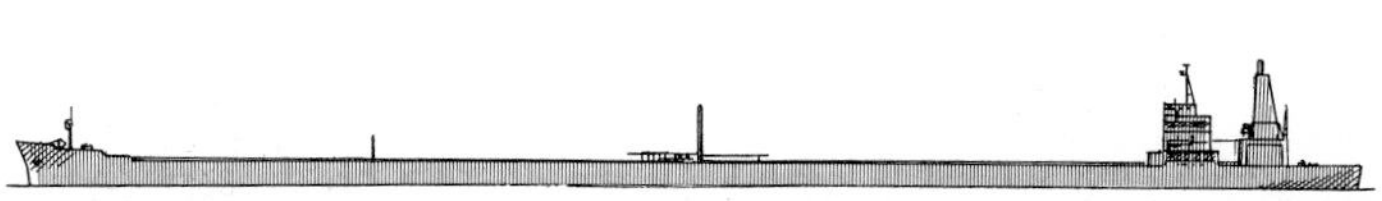

252 *M²NMFN H1*
SERENITY Bs/FRG (A G 'Weser') 1975; Tk; 185,398 grt/392,802 dwt; 370.24 × 22.6 m *(1,214.74 × 74.15 ft)*; T (GEC); 16 kts; ex-*Ioannis Colocotronis*; 'Europa' type
Sisters: **WHITE ROSE** (Cy); ex-*Vassiliki Colocotronis* (in use as a storage vessel)

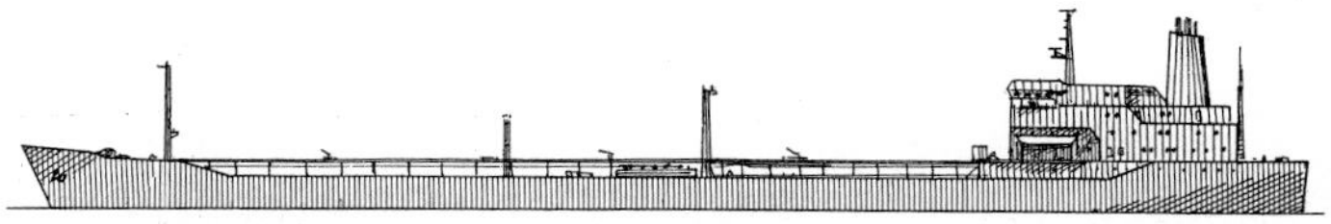

253 *M²NMFN H13*
ITER Li/Sw (Eriksbergs) 1975; Tk; 18,719 grt/31,793 dwt; 170.77 × 11.35 m *(560.27 × 37.24 ft)*; M (B&W); 16 kts; ex-*Jupiter*
Sisters: **CURY** (Li) ex-*Mercury*; **SEAPROMISE** (Ma) ex-*Scaptrust*; **SEAMERIT** (Ma) ex-*Scapmariner*

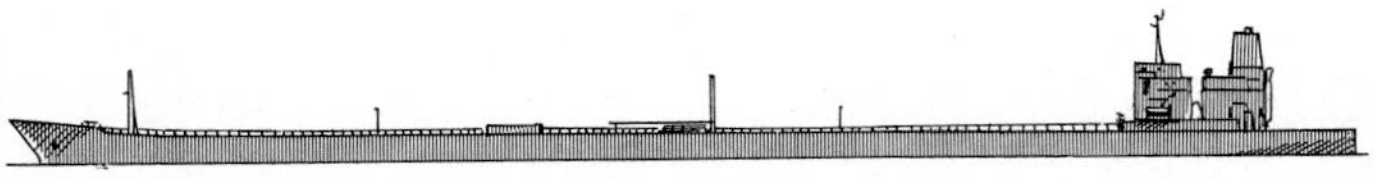

254 *M^2NM^2F H*
CAIRU Bz/Ja (IHI) 1974; Tk; 135,283 grt/282,750 dwt; 337.09 × 21.62 m *(1,105.94 × 70.93 ft)*; T (IHI); 15.75 kts
Sister: **VIDAL DE NEGREIROS** (Bz); Sisters (Bz built—Ish do Brazil): **FELIPE CAMARAO** (Bz); **HENRIQUE DIAS** (Bz); **JOSE DO PATROCINIO** (Bz)

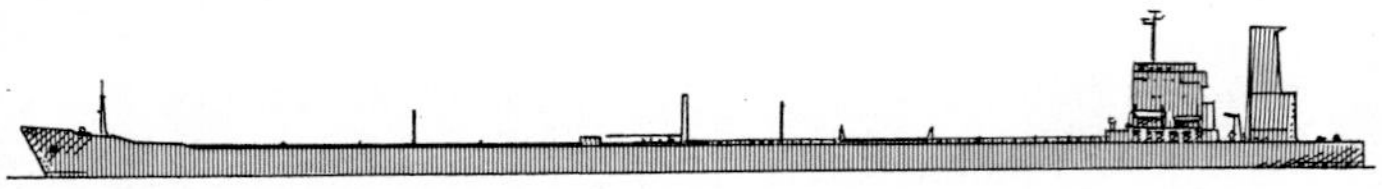

255 *M^2NM^2F H1*
KNOCK TAGGART Pa/Sw (Gotav) 1974; Tk; 69,183 grt/140,905 dwt; 270.01 × 17.07 m *(885.86 × 56 ft)*; M (B&W); 16.25 kts; ex-*London Enterprise*
Sister: **ANASTASIS** (Gr) ex-*Overseas Argonaut*

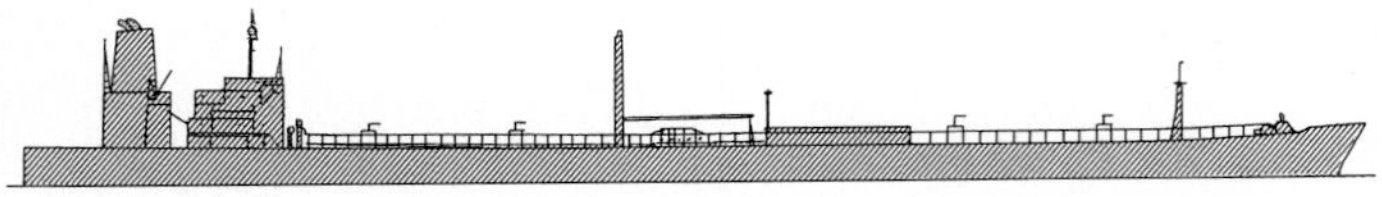

256 *M^2NM^2FM H*
TAGASAN Pa/Ja (Oshima Z) 1980; Tk; 53,350 grt/92,715 dwt; 242.98 × 12.16 m *(797.18 × 39.89 ft)*; M (Sulzer); 15.5 kts; ex-*Tagasan Maru*
Sister: **ANDAMAN SEA** (Pa) ex-*Tenryusan Maru*

257 *M^2NM^2FN H*
RAFIO Li/No (Stord) 1974; Tk; 138,251 grt/290,271 dwt; 347.84 × 22.14 m *(1,114.21 × 72.64 ft)*; T (GEC); 15.5 kts; ex-*Vespasian*
Similar (no short uprights on weather deck): **BERGE CHIEF** (NIS) ex-*Beaumont*; Similar: **BERGE BIG** (NIS) ex-*Cyprian*

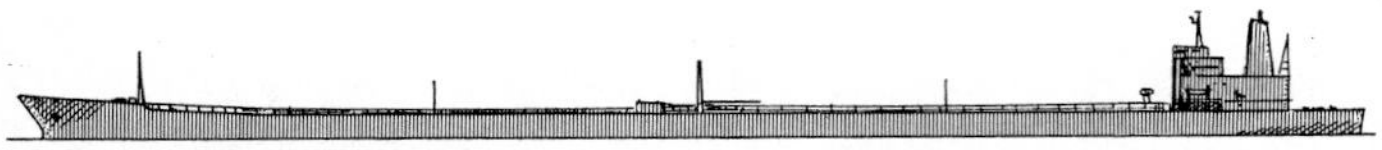

258 *M^2NM^2FN H*
SEAMASTER Ma/Ja (Kawasaki) 1975; Tk; 106,274 grt/234,925 dwt; 319.95 × 19.66 m *(1,049.7 × 64.5 ft)*; M (B&W); 13.6 kts; ex-*Fujikawa Maru*

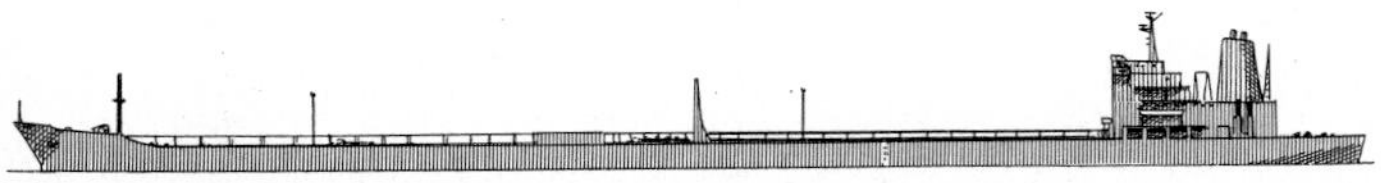

259 *M^2NM^2FN H1*
BANAT Rm/Ja (IHI) 1975; Tk; 46,889 grt/86,093 dwt; 242.12 × 13.61 m *(794.36 × 44.65 ft)*; M (Sulzer); 15.75 kts
Sisters: **CRISANA** (Rm); **DACIA** (Rm); **HISTRIA MOON** (Rm) ex-*Muntenia*

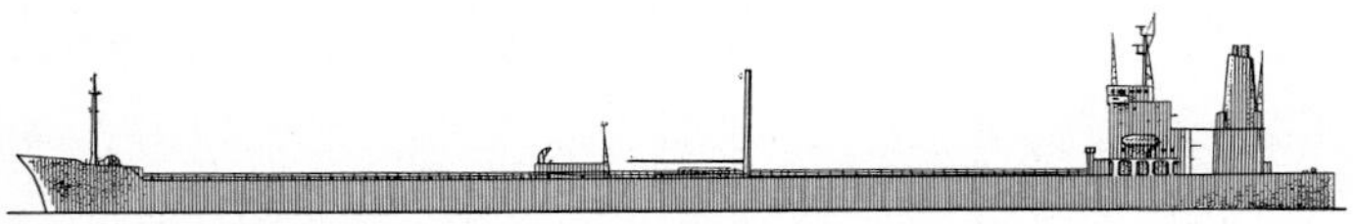

260 *M^2NM^2FN H1*
COLORADO Li/Ja (Hitachi) 1980; Tk; 51,932 grt/86,648 dwt; 243.52 × 12.07 m *(799 × 39.6 ft)*; M (B&W); 14.75 kts; ex-*Globtik Britain*

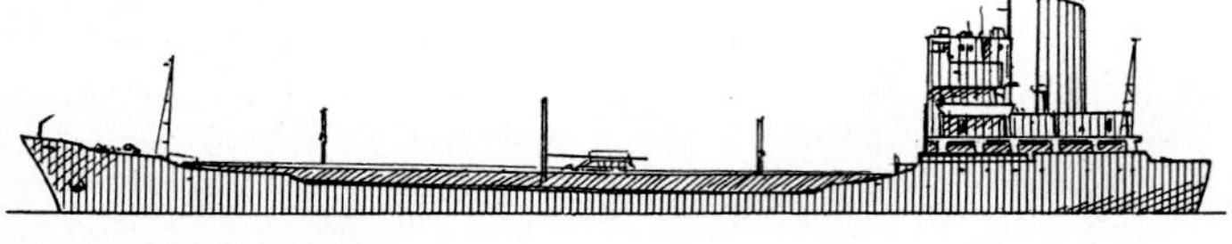

261 *M^2NM^2FN H13*
BLUETANK LANCER Pa/Ja (Taihei) 1974; Tk; 5,096 grt/8,470 dwt; 110.24 × 7.88 m *(361.68 × 25.85 ft)*; M (Mitsubishi); 13.5 kts; ex-*Olau Thor*

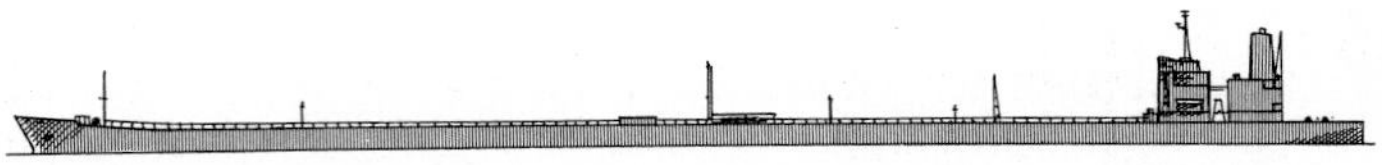

262 *M^2NM^3FN H*
KAPETAN GIORGIS Gr/Ja (IHI) 1976; Tk; 218,447 grt/456,368 dwt; 378.39 × 22.27 m *(1,241.44 × 73.06 ft)*; T (IHI); 15.25 kts; ex-*Andros Petros*
Sisters: **STENA QUEEN** (Br) ex-*Burmah Endeavour*; **STENA KING** (Br) ex-*Burmah Enterprise*; **KAPETAN PANAGIOTIS** (Gr) ex-*Homeric*; Similar: **ANDROS CHRYSSI** (Li); **MYRTOS BAY** (Pa) ex-*Akama Maru* (Ja); **SOMERSET** (Li) ex-*Ise Maru* (Motor ship); **DORSET** (Li) ex-*Shuho Maru* (Motor ship)

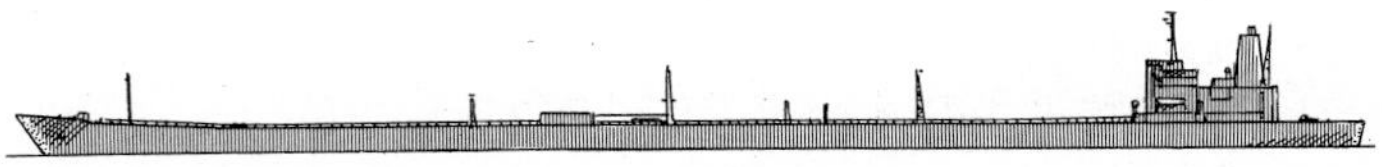

263 *M^2NM^3FN H*
ZANTE Gr/Ja (IHI) 1975; Tk; 132,798 grt/256,797 dwt; 337.07 × 19.94 m *(1,105.87 × 65.42 ft)*; T (IHI); 16.25 kts; ex-*Tokuyama Maru*

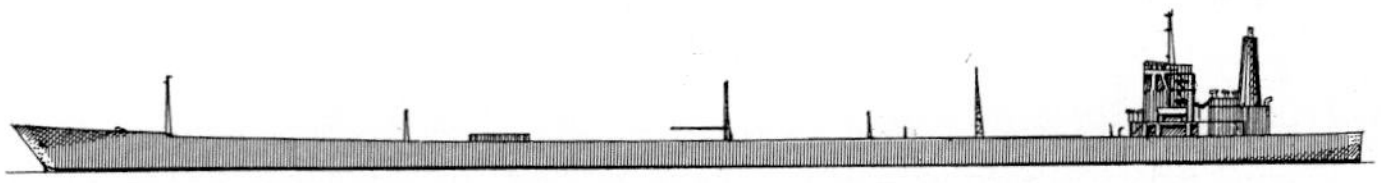

264 *M^2NM^3G H*
NISSEI MARU Ja/Ja (IHI) 1975; Tk; 234,287 grt/484,276 dwt; 378.85 × 28.2 m *(1,242.95 × 92.52 ft)*; T (IHI); 14.25 kts

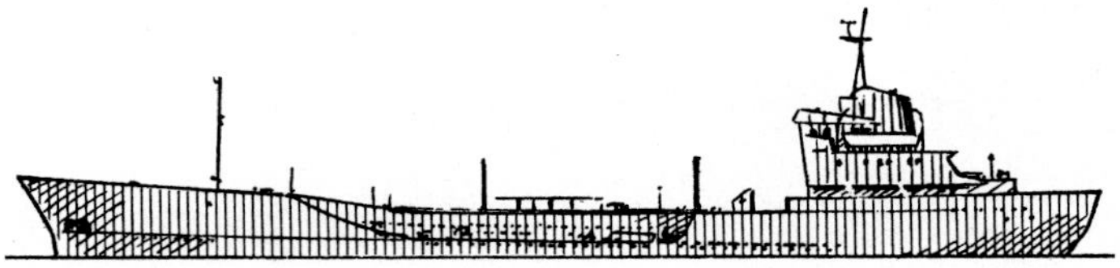

265 *M^2NM-F H13*
LUDWIG Cy/FRG (Kroegerw) 1969; Tk; 1,906 grt/3,114 dwt; 81.11 × 4.97 m *(266.11 × 16.3 ft)*; M (MWM); 12 kts

266 *M^2N^2F H123*
MEACHAM US/US (Bethlehem Steel) 1957; Tk; 18,669 grt/31,645 dwt; 196.5 × 10.55 m *(644.68 × 34.61 ft)*; T (Parsons); 16.5 kts; ex-*Mobil Fuel*
Sister: **NAECO** (US) ex-*Mobil Power*

267 *M^2N^2F H123*
MERSIN Tu/FRG (Bremer V) 1955; Tk; 11,312 grt/17,408 dwt; 165.18 × 9.17 m *(541.93 × 30.09 ft)*; M (Bremer V); 14.5 kts; ex-*Faust*

268 *M^2N^2F H123*
NECHES US/US (Bethlehem PC) 1958; Tk; 20,066 grt/34,930 dwt; 201.48 × 10.87 m *(690.55 × 36.66 ft)*; T (Bethlehem Steel); 16.5 kts; ex-*Hans Isbrandtsen*

269 *M^2N^2F H123*
PRIDE II US/US (Bethlehem Steel) 1959; Tk; 16,913 grt/30,845 dwt; 196.55 × 10.56 m *(644.85 × 34.64 ft)*; T (Bethlehem Steel); 16.75 kts; ex-*Gulfpride*; US Government owned
Sisters: **SOLAR** (US) ex-*Gulfsolar*; **COASTAL MANATEE** (US) ex-*Gulfsupreme*; **SPRAY** (US) ex-*Gulfspray*

270 *M^2N^2FN H123*
AFRICAN EXPRESS SV/Sp (UN de Levante) 1959; Tk; 6,152 grt/9,287 dwt; 139.05 × 7.76 m *(456.2 × 25.46 ft)*; M (Espanola); 13.75 kts; ex-*Campogris*

271 *M^2N^2FN H123*
FAIR DELTA Gr/Ne (Nederlandsche) 1959; Tk; 10,913 grt/20,953 dwt; 170.69 × 9.67 m *(560.01 × 31.73 ft)*; M (Stork); 14.5 kts; ex-*Eidsfoss*

272 *M^2N^2FN H123*
PAMPERO SV/Sp (UN de Levante) 1963; Tk; 6,294 grt/9,100 dwt; 141.79 × 7.76 m *(465.2 × 25.46 ft)*; M (B&W); 13.7 kts; ex-*Campogules*
Possible sister: **NEJMAT EL PETROL XXIII** (Si) ex-*Campoazur*

273 *M^2N^2FN H123*
VALMIERA La/Pd (Gdynska) 1967; Tk; 12,309 grt/19,353 dwt; 176.89 × 9.5 m *(580.35 × 31.17 ft)*; M (Sulzer); 16.25 kts; 'B70' type
Sisters: **VARKIZA** (Gr) ex-*Talsy*; **TSESIS** (Tu)

274 *M²N²MF H123*
COASTAL CORPUS CHRISTI US/US (Newport News) 1960; Tk; 23,299 grt/52,800 dwt; 225.56 × 12.02 m *(740.03 × 39.42 ft)*; T (Newport News); 16 kts; ex-*Esso Boston*
Sister: **COASTAL EAGLE POINT** (US) ex-*Esso Baltimore*

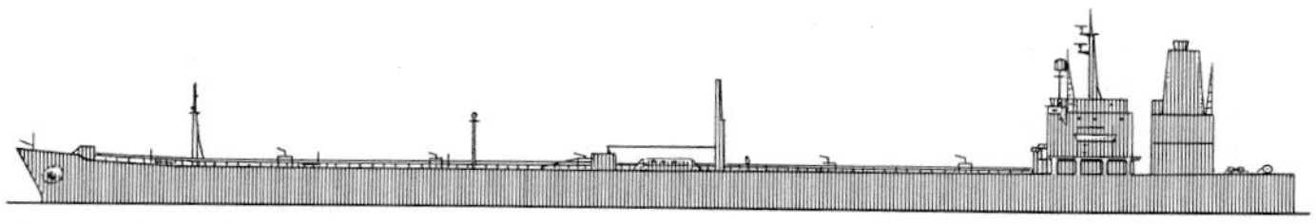

275 *M²N²MFM H*
YUHO MARU I Pa/Ja (Hitachi) 1980; Tk; 49,880 grt/81,278 dwt; 233 × 12.77 m *(764 × 42 ft)*; M (Sulzer); 15.75 kts; ex-*Yuho Maru*

276 *M²N²MFN H*
ANCORA NIS/Ja (Hitachi) 1974; Tk; 116,629 grt/238,058 dwt; 324.01 × 19.43 m *(1,063.02 × 63.73 ft)*; T (Kawasaki); 15.75 kts; ex-*Shunko Maru*

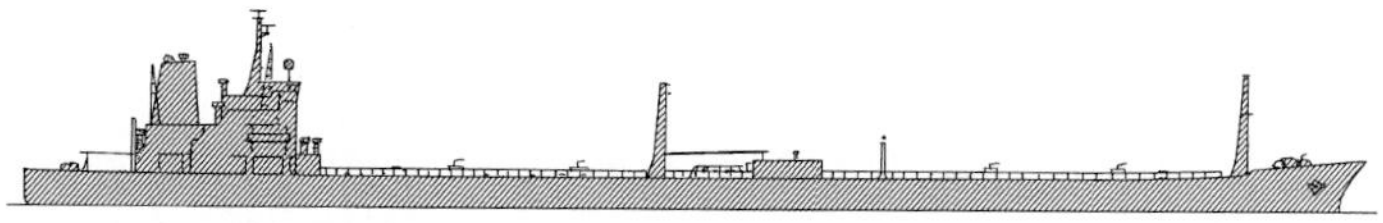

277 *M²N²MFNM H*
SINGA STAR Sg/Ja (Koyo) 1975; Tk; 48,459 grt/87,281 dwt; 245.37 × 13.56 m *(805.02 × 44.49 ft)*; M (Sulzer); 15.5 kts; ex-*Holy Queen*
Probable sisters: **SHOKO** (Ma) ex-*Pan Alliance*; **AL HIJRA** (Pa) ex-*Keiyoh Maru*; **AMBER** (Ma) ex-*Asia Alliance*; **VIGOUR** (Ma) ex-*Prosperity Queen*; **MANHATTAN** (Bs) ex-*Grand Victoria*; **OCEANUS** (Ma) ex-*Japan Peony*; **WARDA** (Ma) ex-*Itel Odyssey*

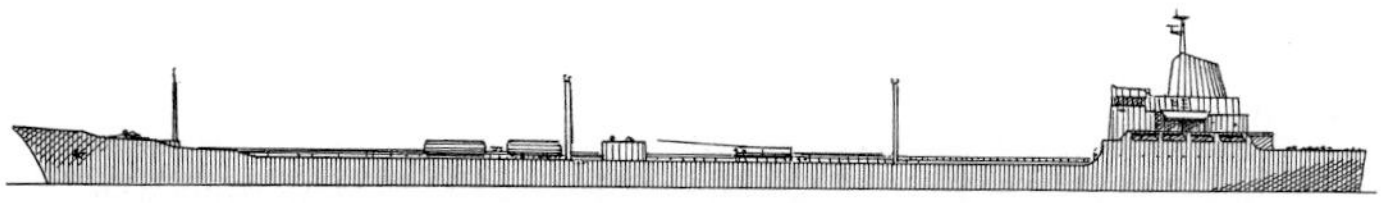

278 *M²N²M-F H13*
MARINE CHEMIST US/US (Ingalls) 1970; Tk/Ch; 20,237 grt/35,949 dwt; 204.93 × 11.05 m *(672.34 × 36.25 ft)*; T (GEC); 16.5 kts

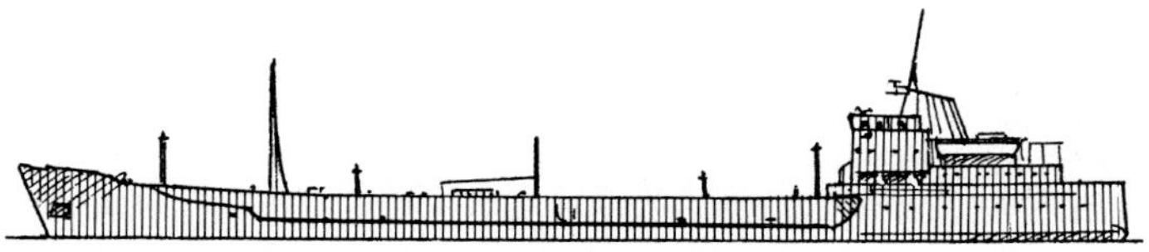

279 *M²N²M-F H13*
STELLA ORION It/Br (Clelands) 1970; Tk; 3,052 grt/5,093 dwt; 98.3 × 6.55 m *(322.51 × 21.49 ft)*; M (English Electric); 12.75 kts; ex-*Thuntank 6*
Sister: **BONITO** (Sw) ex-*Thuntank 5*; Similar: **SEVERYANIN** (Ru) ex-*Alk*

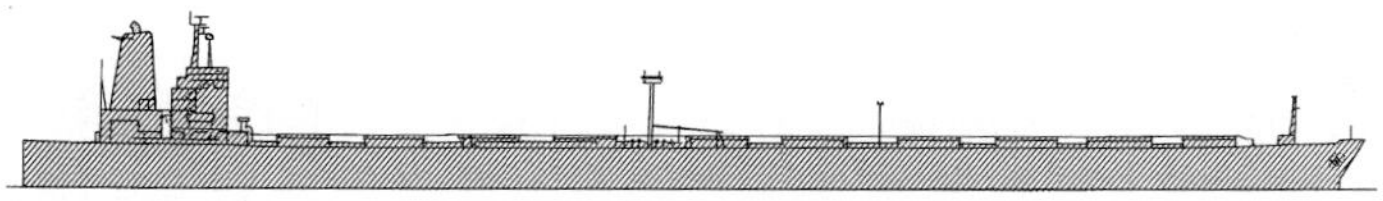

280 *M²TM²FM H*
ALSTER ORE Pa/Tw (China SB) 1988; OO; 171,924 grt/305,893 dwt; 340.01 × 22.03 m *(1,115.52 × 72.28 ft)*; M (Sulzer); 13.5 kts
Sister: **RUHR ORE** (Pa)

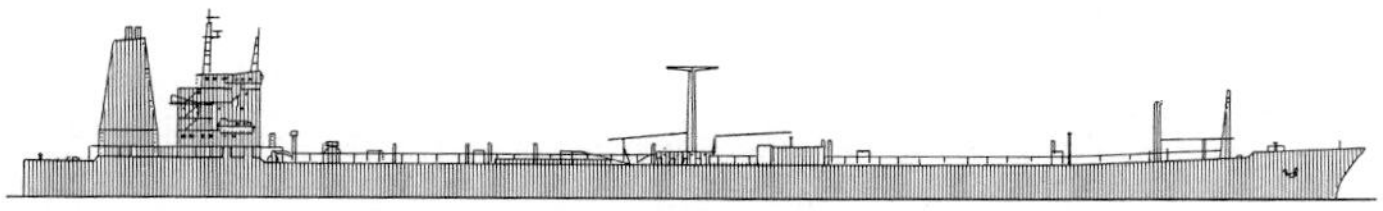

281 *M²UNMF H*
VENLIZA Li/Pd ('Komuny Parysiej') 1986; Tk; 52,518 grt/99,344 dwt; 247.07 × 12.47 m *(810.60 × 40.91 ft)*; M (Sulzer); 15.5 kts; ex-*Colorado*; 'B557' Type
Sister (first and second uprights may be abreast): **VENTARES** (Li) ex-*Eliane*; Possible sister: **SERENO** (Gr) ex-*World Eagle*

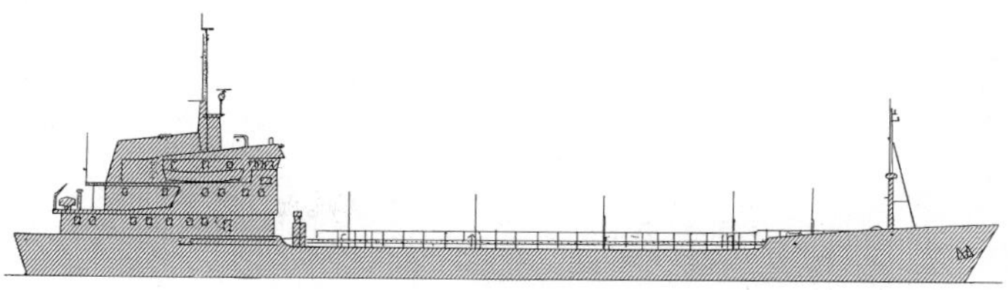

282 *MM-F H*
ANETTE THERESA DIS/FRG (Bayerische) 1976; Tk; 1,440 grt/1,850 dwt; 73.61 × 4.62 m *(241.51 × 15.16 ft)*; M (MaK); 12 kts; ex-*Birgitta*

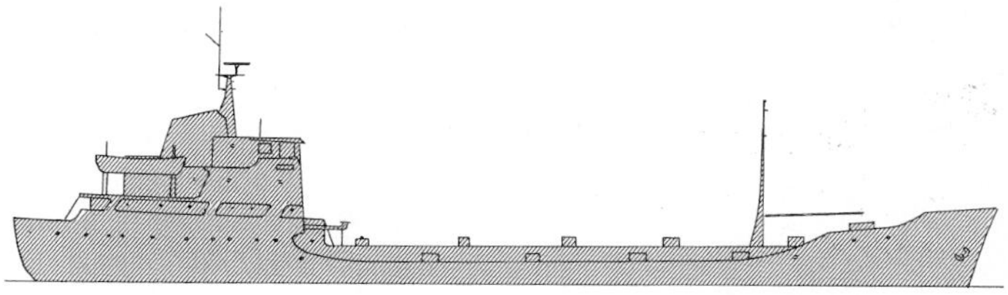

283 *MM-F H13*
ARISTON It/It (Solimano) 1970; Tk/WT; 1,104 grt/1,800 dwt; 68.92 × 4.6 m *(226.12 × 15.09 ft)*; M (MWM); 12 kts; ex-*Altair*
Sister: **CESARE** (It) ex-*Arktur*

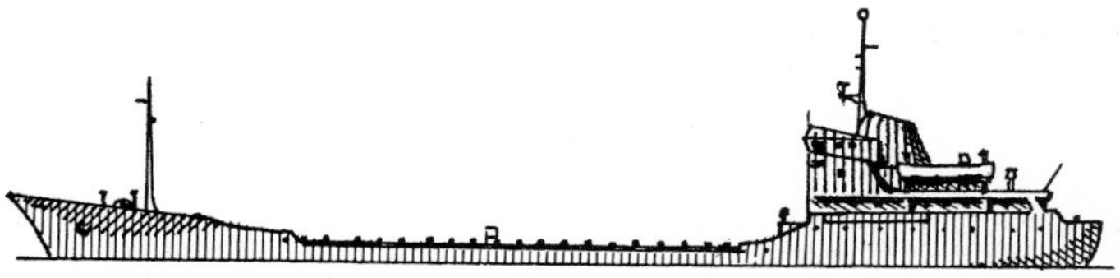

284 *MM-F H13*
CLERVILLE It/Fr (La Rochelle) 1975; Tk/WT; 1,990 grt/3,150 dwt; 91.01 × 5.39 m *(298.6 × 17.68 ft)*; M (Atlas-MaK); 14.5 kts

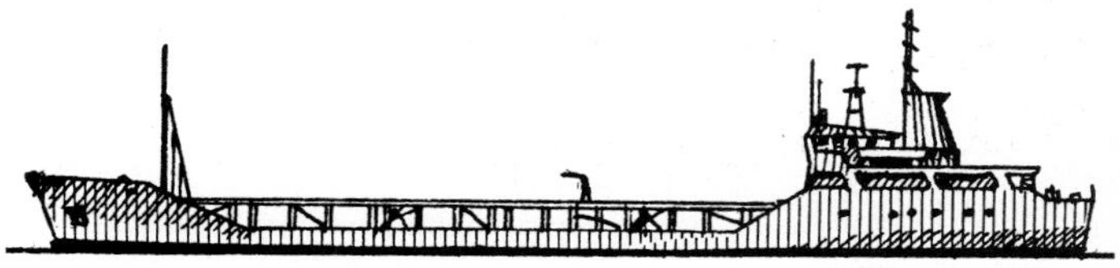

285 *MM-F H13*
DK II SV/Br (Dunston) 1973; Tk; 1,226 grt/2,083 dwt; 72.85 × 4.92 m *(239 × 16.14 ft)*; M (English Electric); 11.5 kts; ex-*Quarterman*

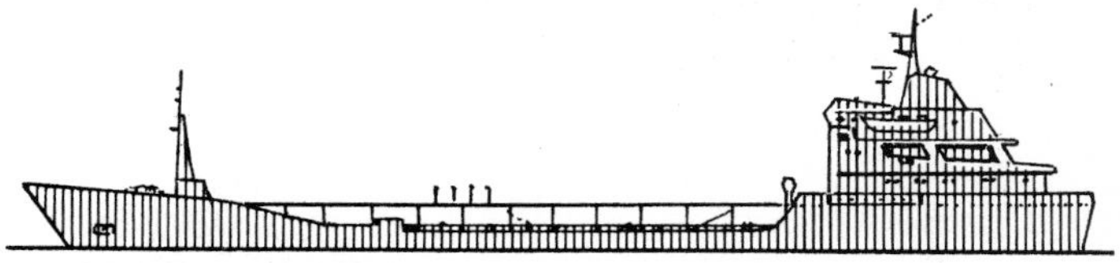

286 *MM-F H13*
HAI FRG/FRG (Sieghold) 1981; Tk; 2,025 grt/3,150 dwt; 86.7 × 5.76 m *(284 × 18.9 ft)*; M (MaK); 12.5 kts
Sisters: **BELLI** (Tn) ex-*Lachs*; **BEILUL** (Ho) ex-*Stint*; **POLLUX A** (Pa) ex-*Wels*

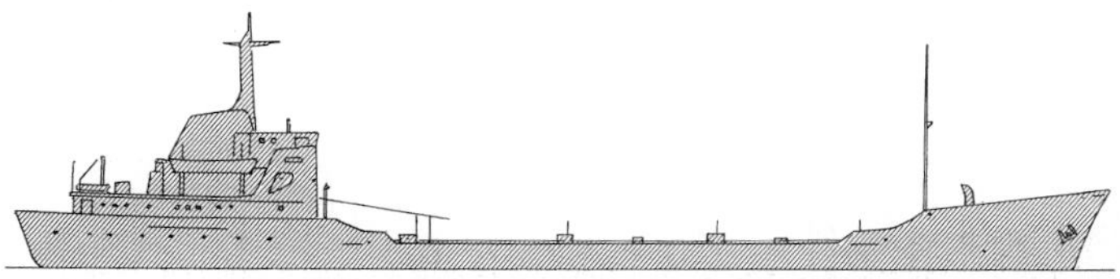

287 *MM-F H13*
IONION Gr/FRG (Nobiskrug) 1964; AT; 1,140 grt/1,890 dwt; 73.72 × 4.8 m *(241.86 × 15.75 ft)*; M (MaK); 11 kts; ex-*Spiekeroog*
Sister: **YESILKOY 1** (Tu) ex-*Wangeroog*

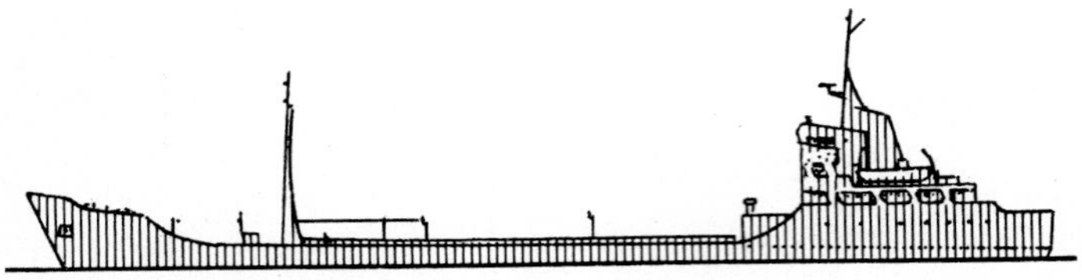

288 *MM-F H13*
KORINTHIA Gr/Br (Dunston) 1969; Tk; 1,607 grt/2,907 dwt; 84.66 × 4.9 m *(277.76 × 16.08 ft)*; M (Ruston); 10.5 kts; ex-*Humbergate*

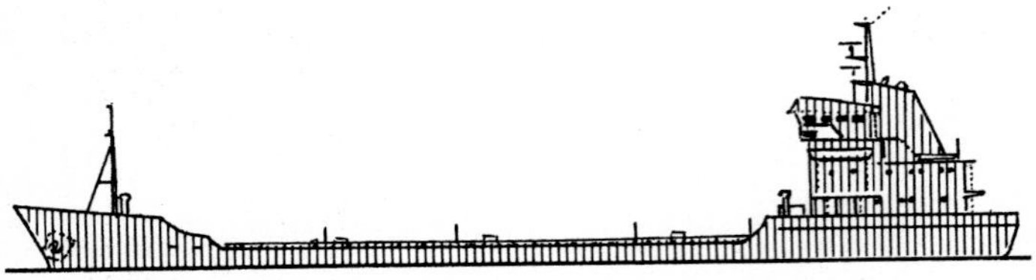

289 *MM-F H13*
ORAKOTA DIS/Tu (Meltem) 1980; Tk/VO; 1,727 grt/2,578 dwt; 84.99 × 4.85 m *(278.84 × 15.91 ft)*; M (MaK); 12 kts; ex-*Doris*

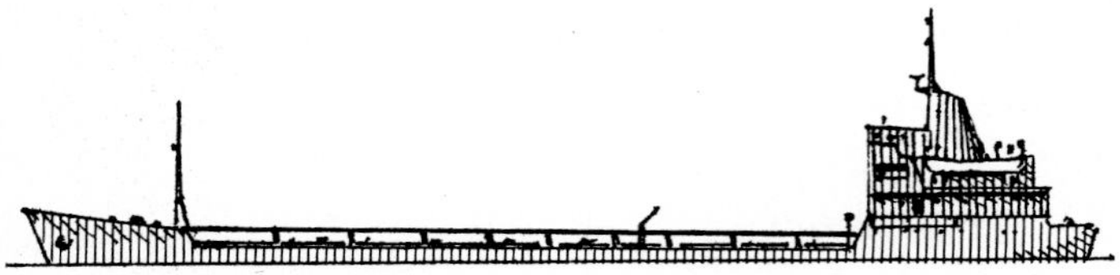

290 *MM-F H13*
SKOPELOS Gr/Br (Cochrane) 1970; Tk; 1,672 grt/2,979 dwt; 83.52 × 5.13 m *(274.02 × 16.83 ft)*; M (Appinge-dammer Brons); 12 kts; ex-*Steersman*

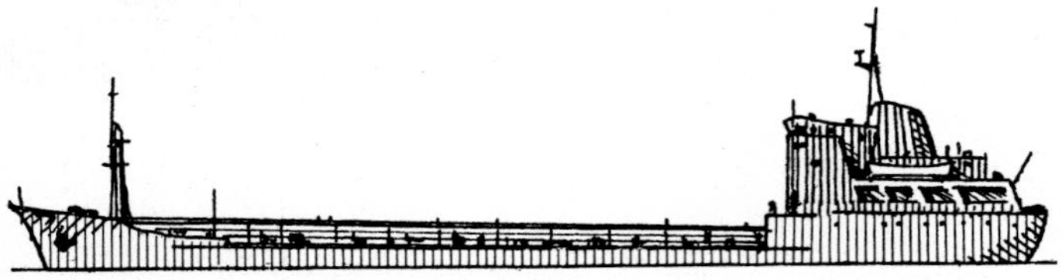

291 *MM-F H13*
SUPERBA It/Ne (Groot & VV) 1971; Tk/Ch; 1,405 grt/2,164 dwt; 81.11 × 4.97 m *(266.11 × 16.31 ft)*; M ('De Industrie'); 13 kts; ex-*Philip Broere*

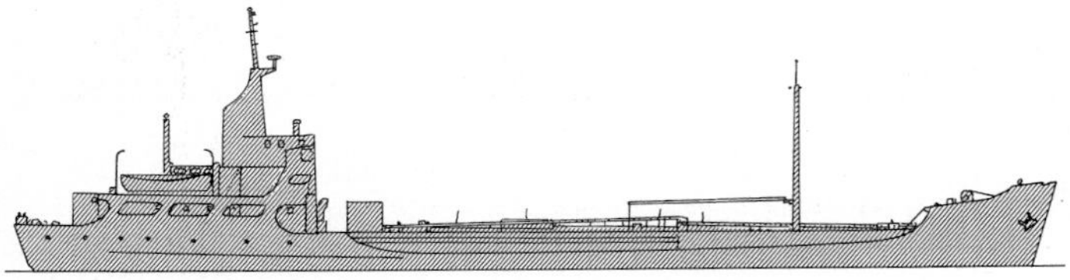

292 *MM-FM H13*
JOHN M Br/Br (Burntisland) 1963; Tk; 1,251 grt/1,839 dwt; 70.11 × 4.83 m *(230 × 15.85 ft)*; M (Lister Blackstone); — kts

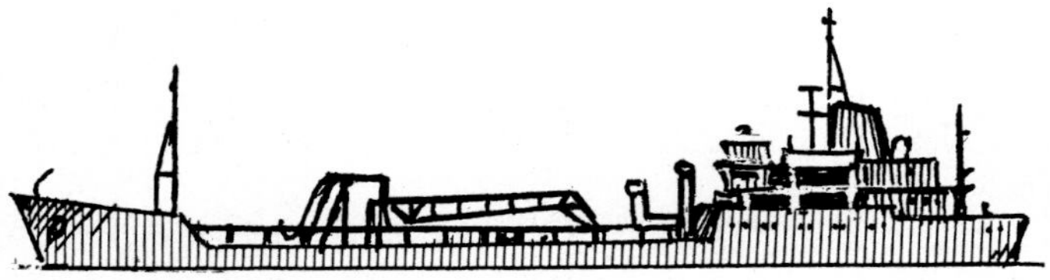

293 *MM-FN H13*
BP JOUSTER Br/Br (Appledore) 1972; Tk; 1,568 grt/2,734 dwt; 78.95 × 4.74 m *(259.02 × 15.55 ft)*; M (Alpha-Diesel); 12 kts; ex-*Swansea*
Sister: **AL KARNAK III** (Pa) ex-*Dundee*; Similar: **CHIOS I** (Gr) ex-*Caernarvon*; **MODERN SUPPLIER** (Ma) ex-*Plymouth*

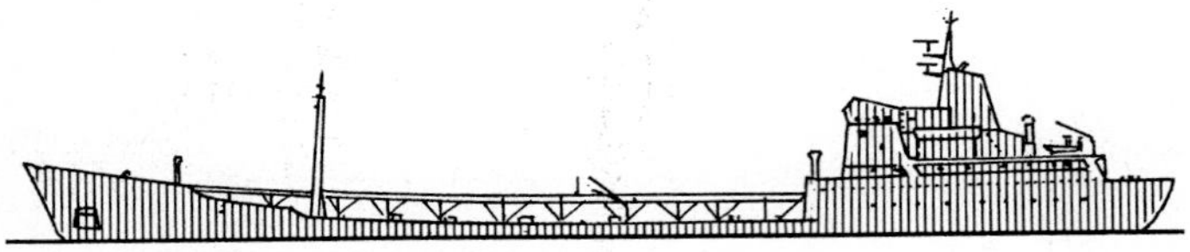

294 *MM-FR H13*
MALIK II Va/Fi (Valmet) 1970; Tk; 2,621 grt/4,168 dwt; 98.35 × 6.05 m *(322.67 × 19.85 ft)*; M (B&W); 14.25 kts; ex-*Tebonia*

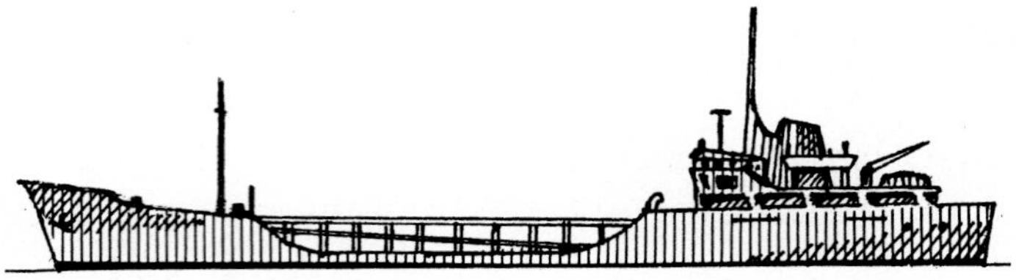

295 *MM-FR H13*
PHOENIX Ma/Br (Goole) 1968; Tk; 699 grt/1,616 dwt; 72.6 × 4.4 m *(238.19 × 14.44 ft)*; M (KHD); 11 kts; ex-*Audacity*

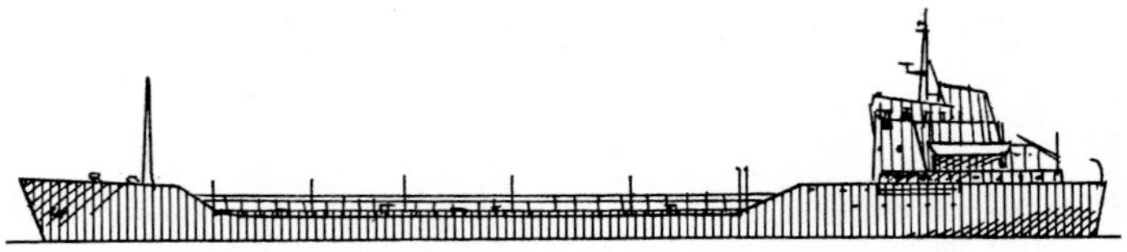

296 *MM-FR H13*
PIC ST LOUP Kn/FRG (Menzer) 1974; WT; 1,599 grt/3,182 dwt; 89.24 × 5.26 m *(192.78 × 17.26 ft)*; M (Atlas-MaK); — kts

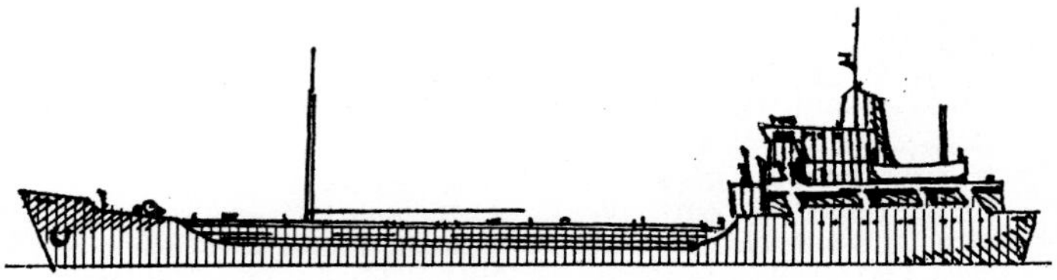

297 *MM-GM H13*
FRANK M Br/Br (Burntisland) 1965; Tk; 1,251 grt/1,803 dwt; 70.72 × 4.83 m *(232 × 15.85 ft)*; M (Blackstone); — kts
Sister: **NICHOLAS M** (Br)

298 *MNEN²MFN H13*
RELCHEM ARJUN Li/Sw (Eriksbergs) 1970; Tk; 15,007 grt/23,928 dwt; 169.6 × 9.56 m *(556.4 × 31.4 ft)*; M (B&W); 16.25 kts; ex-*Anco Sea*
Sisters: **STOLT SPAN** (Li) ex-*Arco Span*; **STOLT SURF** (Li) ex-*Anco Ville*

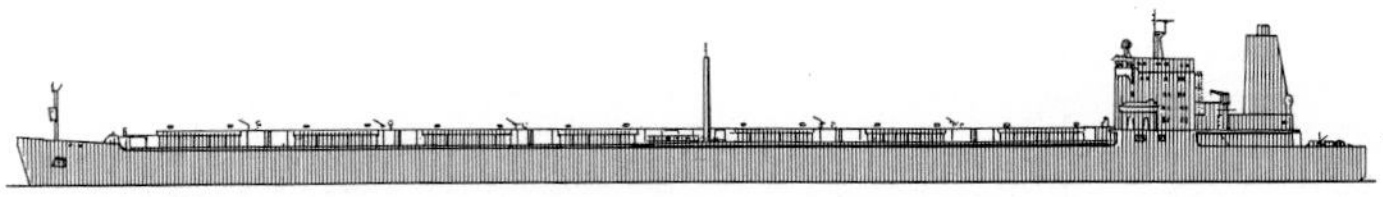

299 *MNHF H*
BONA FALCON Bs/FRG (Howaldts DW) 1981; OBO; 46,801 grt/82,462 dwt; 246.95 × 14.95 m *(810 × 49.05 ft)*; M (B&W); 15 kts; ex-*Hoegh Falcon*
Sister (satcom aerial on radar mast): **BONA FAVOUR** (Bs) ex-*Hoegh Favour*

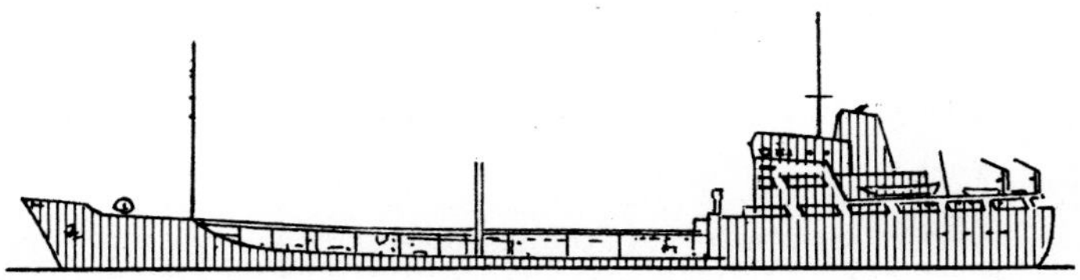

300 *MNHF H13*
FRANCIS It/Ne (Nieuwe Noord) 1968; Tk/Ch; 1,441 grt/2,303 dwt; 82.3 × 5 m *(270 × 16.4 ft)*; M ('De Industrie'); 12.5 kts; ex-*Bastiaan Broere*
Sister: **WINE TRADER** (It) ex-*Jacobus Broere*

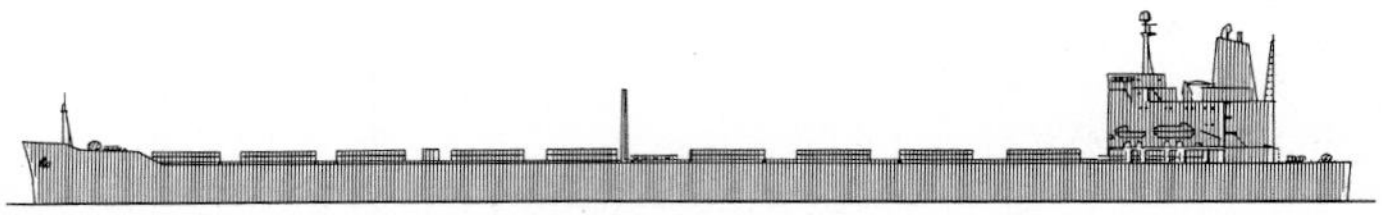

301 *MNHFN H1*
ATLANTIC PRESTIGE Ma/Ko (Hyundai) 1981; OBO; 45,780 grt/78,507 dwt; 243.01 × 14.48 m *(797.27 × 47.51 ft)*; M (B&W); 14.75 kts; ex-*Ambia Fair*
Sister: **ATLANTIC PRIDE** (Ma) ex-*Ambia Finjo*; Probable sisters: **BONA FOAM** (Bs) ex-*Hoegh Foam*; **BONA FORUM** (Bs) ex-*Hoegh Forum*; **BONA FULMAR** (Bs) ex-*Hoegh Fulmar*; **BONA FORTUNA** (NIS) ex-*Hoegh Fortuna*

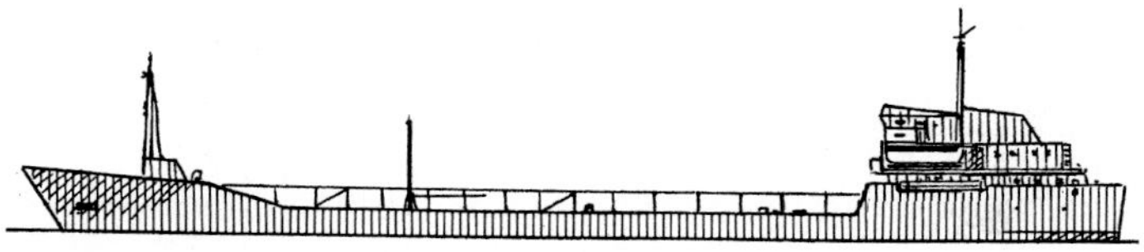

302 *MNH-F H13*
VINGASJO Sw/FRG (Luehring) 1972; Tk; 1,999 grt/3,890 dwt; 96.12 × 5.96 m *(315.35 × 19.55 ft)*; M (Atlas-MaK); 12 kts; ex-*Tarnsjo*

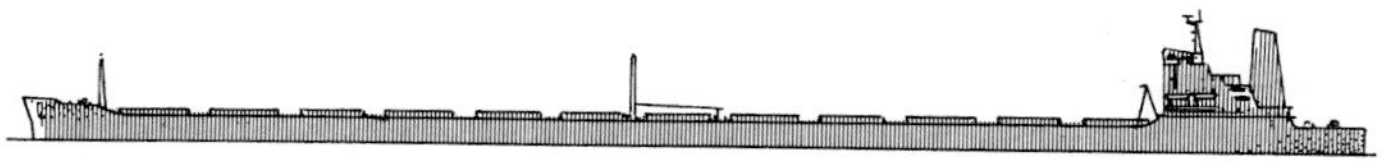

303 *MNKMF H12*
SKRIM Li/Fr (France-Gironde) 1972; OO; 86,093 grt/170,414 dwt; 299.27 × 18.31 m *(981.86 × 60.07 ft)*; M (B&W); 15 kts; ex-*Cetra Centaurus*

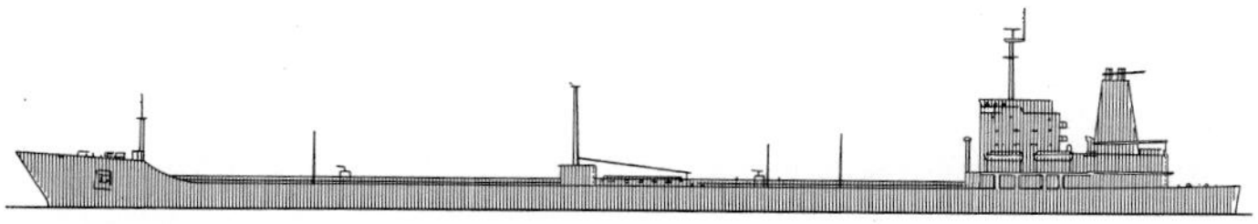

304 *MNMDF H1*
POBYEDA Ru/Ru (Zaliv) 1981; Tk; 37,409 grt/67,980 dwt; 242.81 × 13.6 m *(796.62 × 44.62 ft)*; M (B&W); 15.75 kts; May be spelt **POBEDA**
Sisters: **MARSHAL BAGRAMYAN** (Ru); **MARSHAL CHUYKOV** (Ru); **MARSHAL VASILYEVSKIY** (Ru); **GENERAL TYULENEV** (Ru); **ALEKSANDR POKRYSHKIN** (Ru); **SOROKALETIYE POBEDA** (Ru)

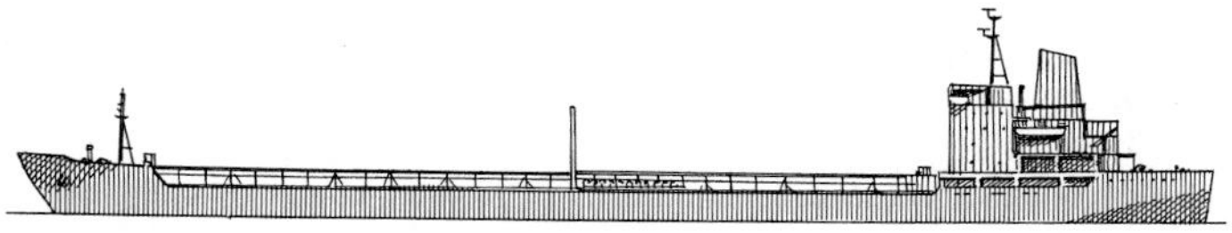

305 *MNMDF H13*
FOUR WINDS Ma/It (Italcantieri) 1974/76; Tk; 18,000 grt/30,475 dwt; 170.69 × 10.95 m *(560 × 35.95 ft)*; M (GMT); 16.5 kts; ex-*Premuda Rosa*; Launched 1974; Completed 1976
Sisters: **FOUR SKIES** (Ma) ex-*Premuda Bianca*; **CIELO DI MILANO** (It) ex-*Buffalo*; **CAMPO DURAN** (Ar); **ARIETE** (Ma) ex-*Canadon Seco*; **SCORPIONE** (It) ex-*Medanito*; **TORO** (Ma) ex-*Puerto Rosales*; Possibly similar: **AGIP GELA** (It); **ELBA** (—) ex-*Agip Ravenna*; **CIELO DI ROMA** (It); **CIELO DI SALERNO** (It)

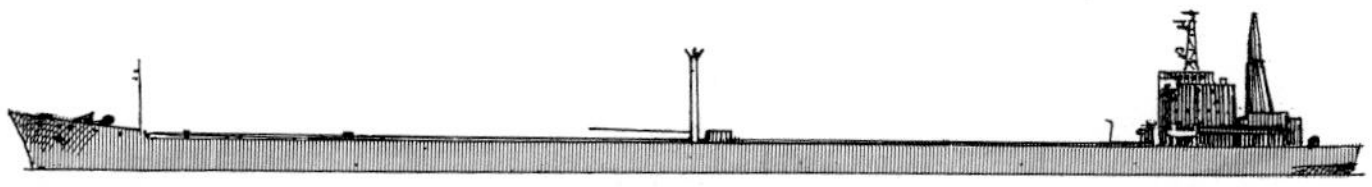

306 *MNMF H*
ADMIRALTY BAY US/US (Sun SB) 1971; Tk; 37,784 grt/82,069 dwt; 247.20 × 13.29 m *(811.02 × 43.60 ft)*; T (GEC); 16.5 kts; ex-*Sohio Intrepid*

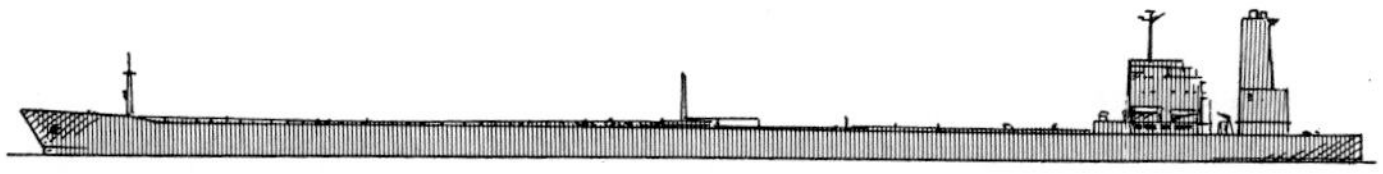

307 *MNMF H*
AMURIYAH Iq/Sw (Gotav) 1977; Tk; 81,228 grt/155,211 dwt; 285.02 × 17.15 m *(935.11 × 56.27 ft)*; M (B&W); 16.25 kts
Sisters: **ALMUSTANSIRIYAH** (Iq); **ALQADISIYAH** (Iq); **HITTIN** (Iq); **ALANDIA BAY** (Bs) ex-*Messiniaki Fisis*; **EVOIKOS** (Cy) ex-*Messiniaki Frontis*; **ELFWAIHAT** (Ly); **ELGURDABIA** (Ly); **ELHANI** (Ly); **BA VI** (Vn) ex-*Bralanta*; **SIR JOHN** (Gr) ex-*Esthel*; **PALLAS ATHINA** (Gr) ex-*Limousin*; **ENDO STAR** (Tu) ex-*Thalassini Doxa*; **PETRO FIFE** (Br) ex-*Thalassini Niki* (converted to offshore loading-small housing, and so on, on focsle); Probable sister: **ARGONAFTIS** (Gr) ex-*Caledonia Team*; Sisters (shortened by 301m (981ft)): **STAR KANSAS** (Bs) ex-*Malmros Merrimac*; **NEW LOUISIANA** (Pa) ex-*Malmros Monitor*

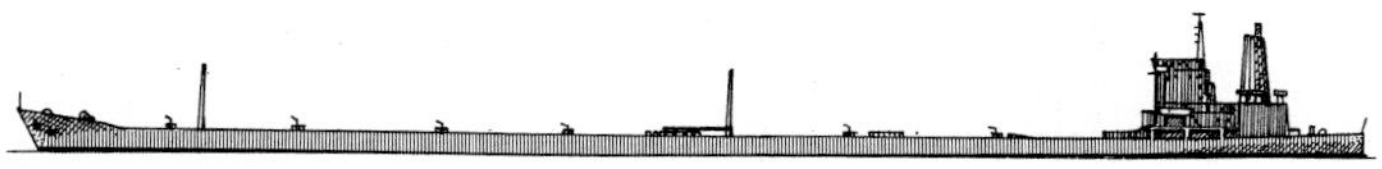

308 *MNMF H*
BERGE FISTER NIS/Br (Lithgows) 1979; Tk; 129,576 grt/267,390 dwt; 344.43 × 20.68 m *(1,130 × 68.1 ft)*; M (B&W); 14 kts; ex-*World Scholar*
Sister: **BERGE FOREST** (NIS) Aft section launched as *Cartsdyke Glen*

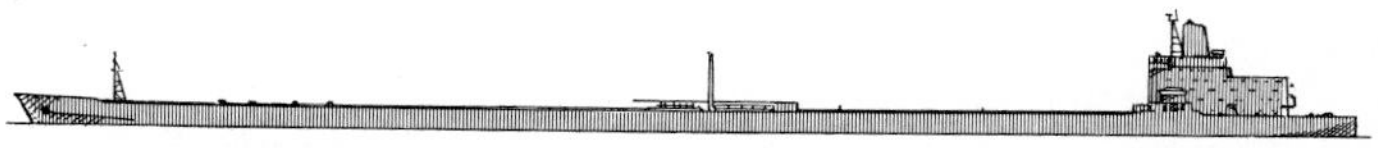

309 *MNMF H*
ESSO NORMANDIE Kn/Fr (L'Atlantique) 1974; Tk; 130,000 grt/274,333 dwt; 343.04 × 21.06 m *(1,125.46 × 69.09 ft)*; T (Stal-Laval); 16 kts
Sisters: **ESSO PICARDIE** (Kn); **AFRICA** (Bs) ex-*Esso Africa*

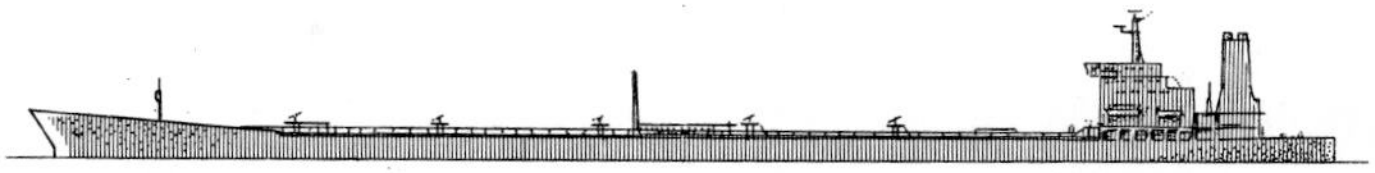

310 *MNMF H*
GOKTURK Tu/Fi (Valmet) 1977; Tk; 75,603 grt/136,000 dwt; 285.02 × 15.5 m *(935.1 × 50.85 ft)*; M (B&W); 16.5 kts; ex-*Sommerstad*
Sisters: **AVAR** (Tu) ex-*Sangstad*; **BUYUK TIMUR** (Tu) ex-*Siljestad*

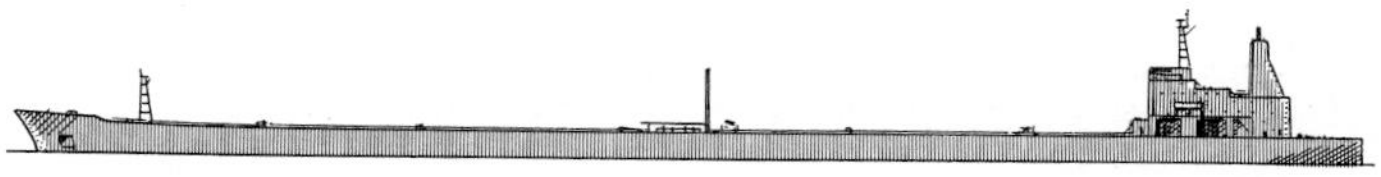

311 *MNMF H*
ISEULT Li/Fr (L'Atlantique) 1974; Tk; 134,778 grt/28,086 dwt; 343.01 × 21.35 m *(1,125.36 × 70.05 ft)*; T (Stal-Laval); 15 kts
Sister: **TORINO** (NIS) ex-*Opale*

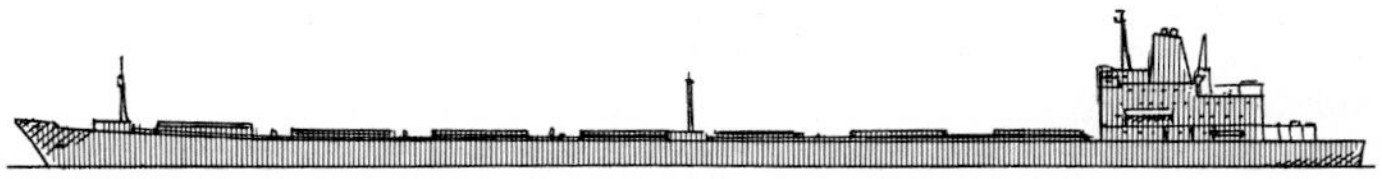

312 *MNMF H*
KANDILLI 1 Tu/Ja (Kawasaki) 1970; OBO; 57,465 grt/102,816 dwt; 250.05 × 15.52 m *(820.37 × 50.92 ft)*; M (MAN); 15.5 kts; ex-*Hoegh Rainbow*

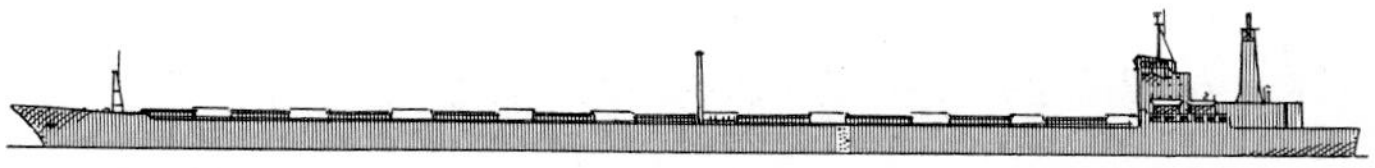

313 *MNMF H*
KONKAR ALPIN Gr/FRG (Howaldts DW) 1973; OO; 118,915 grt/234,752 dwt; 327.74 × 20.5 m *(1,075.26 × 67.26 ft)*; T (GEC); 15.5 kts; ex-*Falkefjell*
Sister: **KONKAR DINOS** (Gr) ex-*Falkefjell*

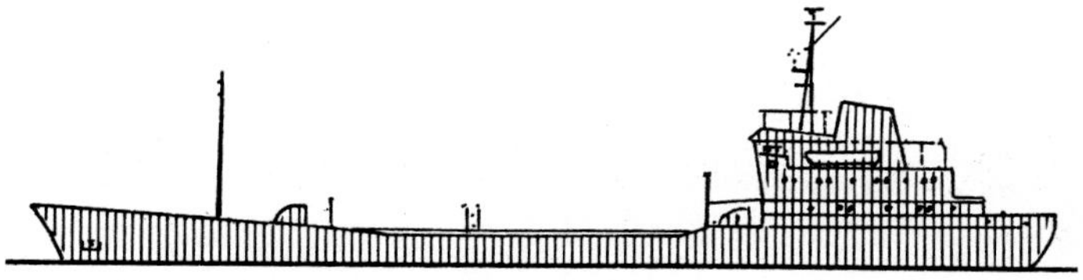

314 *MNMF H*
RIGEL A —/FRG (Kroegerw) 1972; Tk; 1,338 grt/2,855 dwt; 81.01 × 5.27 m *(265.78 × 17.29 ft)*; M (MWM); 12 kts; ex-*Lone Terkol*

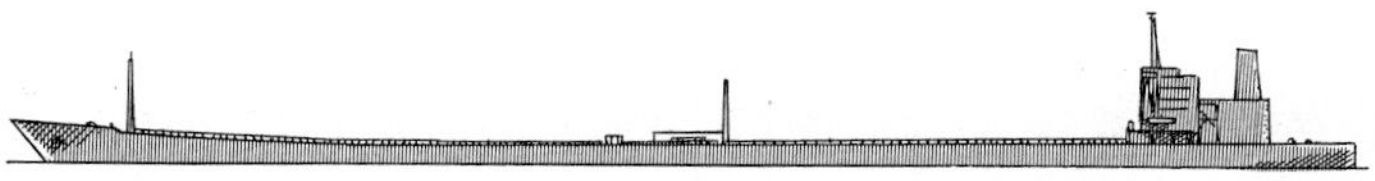

315 *MNMF H*
SAUDI GLORY Li/Ja (Sumitomo) 1974; Tk; 134,514 grt/276,368 dwt; 340.8 × 21.07 m *(1,118.11 × 69.13 ft)*; T (Stal-Laval); 16.25 kts; ex-*Mobil Mariner*
Sisters: **SAUDI SPLENDOUR** (Li) Launched as *Mobil Supplier*; **ATHOS** (Fr); **D'ARTAGNAN** (Fr); **HARRIER** (Ml) ex-*Mobil Falcon*

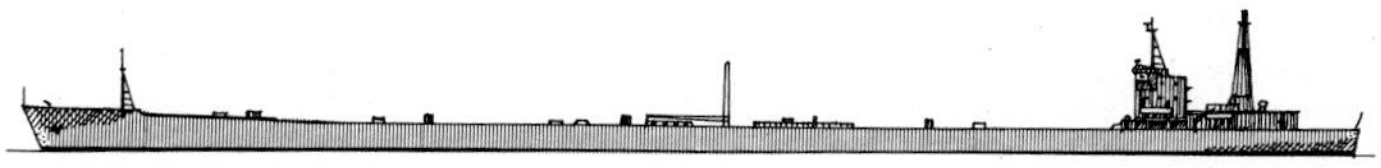

316 *MNMF H*
STRESA Li/FRG (Howaldts DW) 1975; Tk; 113,560 grt/241,199 dwt; 326.02 × 20.65 m *(1,070 × 67.75 ft)*; T (Allgemeine); 15.25 kts; ex-*Sanko Stresa*
Sister: **NEW RENOWN** (Li) ex-*Schleswig-Holstein*

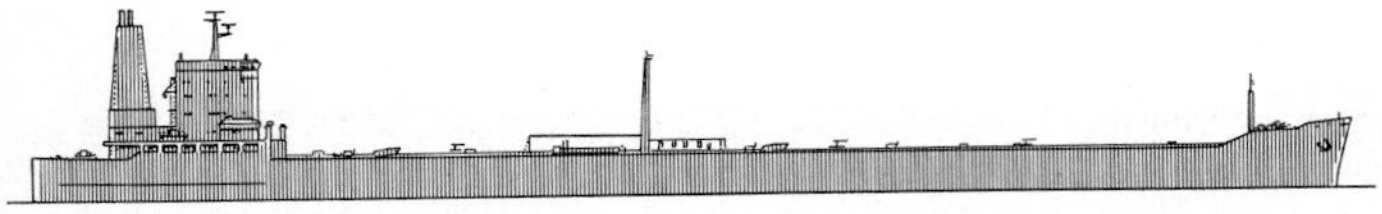

317 *MNMF H1*
AKADEMIK PUSTOVOY Ru/Sw (Uddevalla) 1980; Tk; 42,236 grt/83,723 dwt; 228.48 × 12.66 m *(749.61 × 41.54 ft)*; M (B&W); 15 kts; ex-*Viking Eagle*
Sisters: **THORSAGA** (NIS) ex-*Viking Falcon*; **PRESIDENTE RIVERA** (Ur) ex-*Viking Harrier*; **PARIS II** (Gr) ex-*Viking Hawk*; **VICKY I** (Bs) ex-*Viking Merlin*; **GORBEIA** (Li) ex-*Viking Osprey*; **ONDA BIANCA** (It) ex-*Norse Falcon*

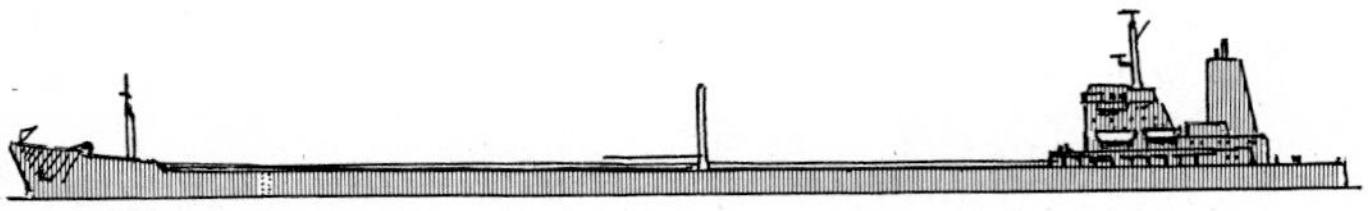

318 *MNMF H1*
AL-AIN UAE/Sw (Eriksbergs) 1974; Tk; 66,852 grt/135,900 dwt; 280.07 × 16.71 m *(918.86 × 54.82 ft)*; M (B&W); 16 kts; ex-*Orator*
Sisters: **NOGA** (Li) ex-*Ibnu*; **MEGA SUN** (NIS) ex-*Evita*; **MARIANNA VII** (Gr) ex-*Kollskeg*; **JOHS STOVE** (NIS) ex-*Gorm*; **TUMA** (Ng) ex-*Sea Breeze* (Now used as storage ship); **JEROM** (Li) ex-*Gina*; **RIZA** (Ma) ex-*Jonny*; **CORCO RADO** (—) ex-*Camargue*; **RABIGH BAY 3** (Gr) ex-*Erika*; **POITOU** (Bs); **SOLOGNE** (Bs)

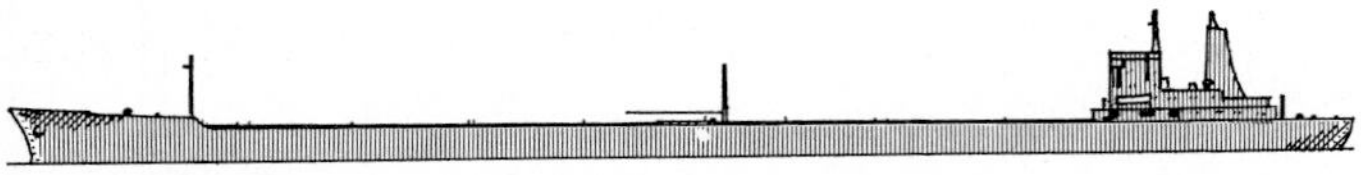

319 *MNMF H1*
ARCO JUNEAU US/US (Bethlehem Steel) 1974; Tk; 57,692 grt/122,196 dwt; 269.15 × 15.77 m *(883.03 × 51.73 ft)*; T (GEC); 16.75 kts
Sisters: **ARCO ANCHORAGE** (US); **ARCO FAIRBANKS** (US); **OVERSEAS JUNEAU** (US)

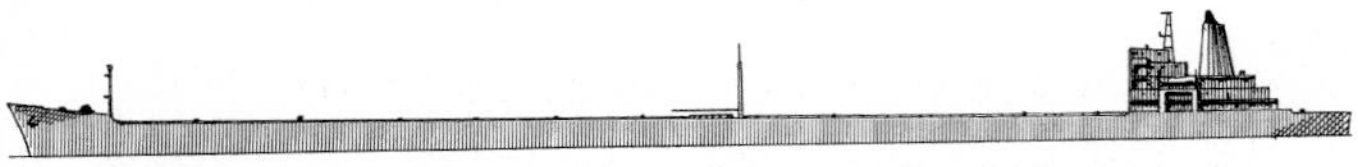

320 *MNMF H1*
ARCO PRUDHOE BAY US/US (Bethlehem Steel) 1971; Tk; 31,487 grt/71,873 dwt; 246.9 × 13.18 m *(810.04 × 43.24 ft)*; T (GEC); 15.5 kts
Sister: **ARCO SAG RIVER** (US); Probable sister: **COVE ENDEAVOUR** (US) ex-*Sansinena II*; Similar: **CHEVRON CALIFORNIA** (US); **CHEVRON MISSISSIPPI** (US); **ARCO TEXAS** (US) ex-*Chevron Hawaii* (lengthened to 2741m (8991ft); Probably similar: **OVERSEAS ALASKA** (US); **OVERSEAS ARCTIC** (US)

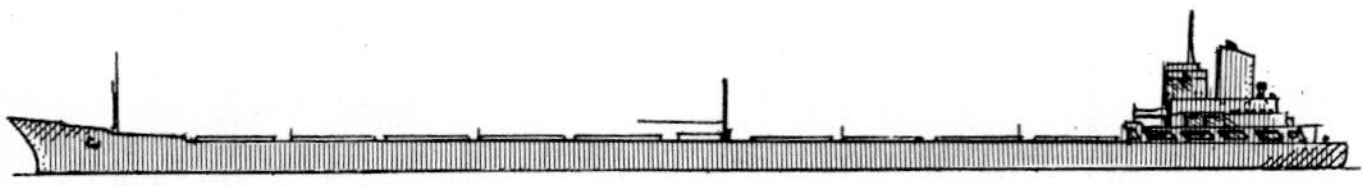

321 *MNMF H1*
ASHEYRA Li/Sw (Oresunds) 1972; OBO; 51,403 grt/103,429 dwt; 256.52 × 15.11 m *(841.6 × 49.57 ft)*; M (Gotaverken); 15.75 kts; ex-*Dagfred*
Similar: **OBO DENIZ** (Tu) ex-*Varvara*; **OBO BASAK** (Tu) ex-*Viscaya*

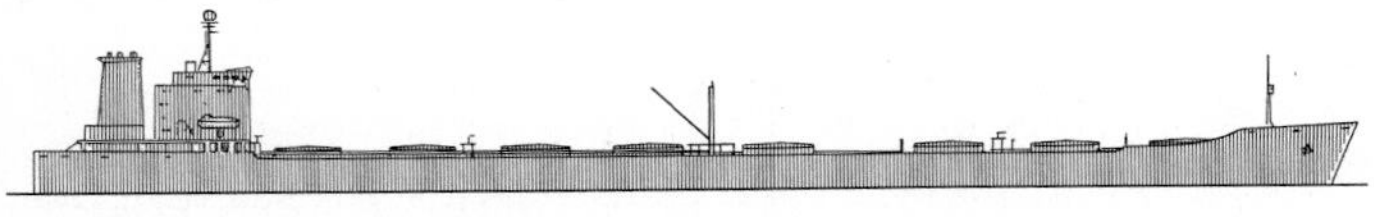

322 *MNMF H1*
BALLERINA NIS/No (Fredriksstad) 1981; OBO; 43,576 grt/77,673 dwt; 243.82 × 14.34 m *(799.93 × 47.05 ft)*; M (B&W); 15.25 kts; ex-*Jarama*
Sister: **BEAR G** (Bs) ex-*Jarmina*

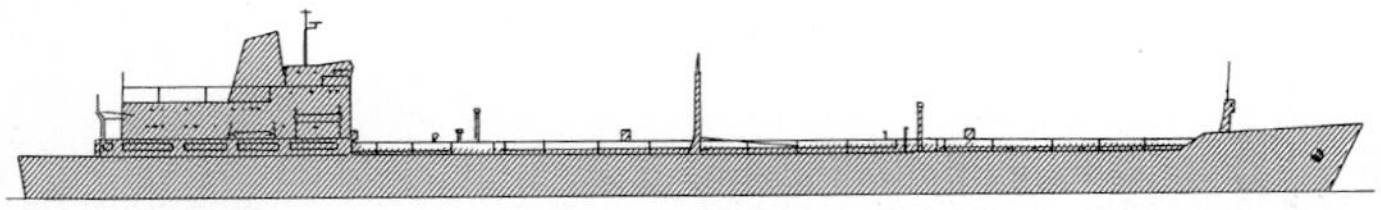

323 *MNMF H1*
BLUE LIGHT Ma/No (Horten) 1970; Ch; 17,851 grt/29,990 dwt; 170.67 × 11.37 m *(559.94 × 37.3 ft)*; M (Sulzer); 15.5 kts; Launched as *Astwi*
Sisters: **RAY** (Ir) ex-*Team Castor*; **ATHOS** (Gr) ex-*Team Pollux*; **AL ZAINAB** (SV) ex-*Team Augwi*; **SUN ROSE** (Ma) ex-*Team Hilwi*

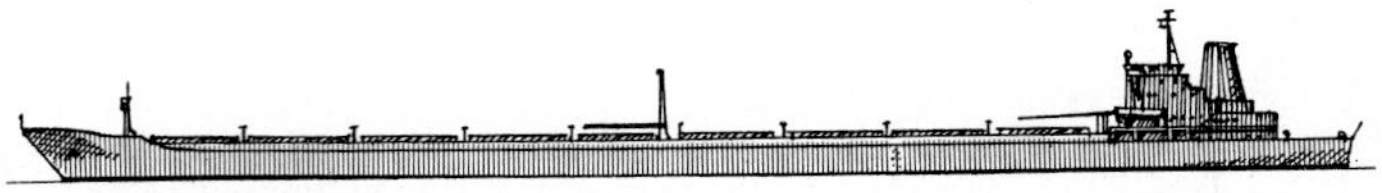

324 *MNMF H1*
BLUE LIGHT Li/Sp ('Bazan') 1972; OBO; 59,783 grt/117,600 dwt; 263.99 × 16.68 m *(866.1 × 54.72 ft)*; M (Sulzer); 16 kts; ex-*Paloma Del Mar*
Sisters: **NIKI** (Cy) launched as *Spirit of Phoenix*; **MURANO** (Bs) ex-*Snestad*

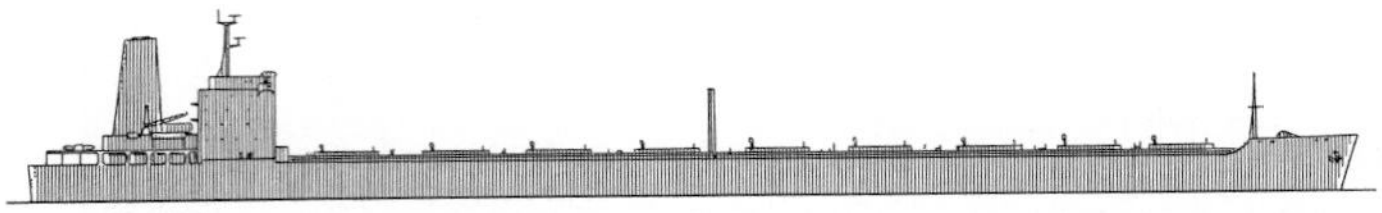

325 *MNMF H1*
BOGA 1 Li/It (Breda) 1980; OBO; 62,031 grt/99,496 dwt; 253.96 × 15.75 m *(833.2 × 51.67 ft)*; M (GMT); 16.5 kts; ex-*Almare Settima*
Sisters: **CERDA** (Li) ex-*Almare Quarta*; **LULA 1** (Li) ex-*Almare Quinta*; **ELLI** (Bs) ex-*Almare Seconda*; **RAYA** (Li) ex-*Almare Sesta*; **KLEON** (Gr) ex-*Almare Terza*

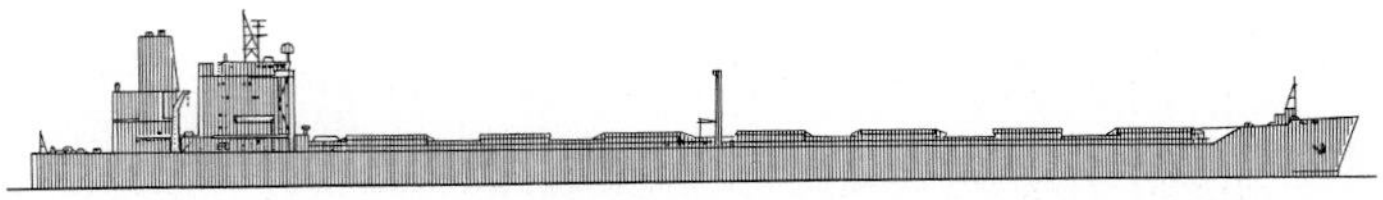

326 *MNMF H1*
HASSBAT QATAR Qt/Be (Boelwerf) 1982; OBO; 70,803 grt/135,169 dwt; 249.1 × 16.8 m *(817 × 55.12 ft)*; M (MAN); 13.5 kts; ex-*Permeke*
Sisters: **DANAT QATAR** (Qt) ex-*Ensor*; **BAOTRANS** (Sg) ex-*Vesalius*

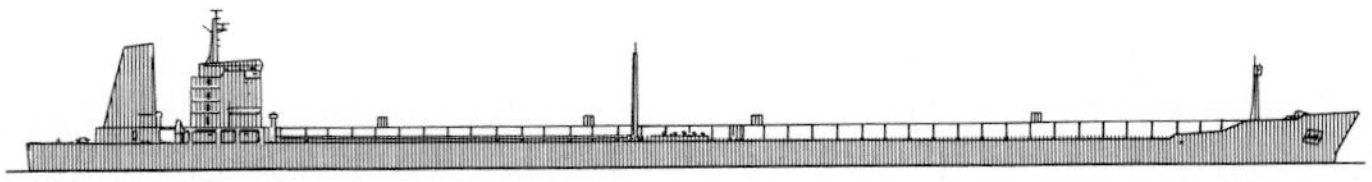

327 *MNMF H1*
KHANIA Gr/Sp (AESA) 1978; Tk; 65,549 grt/132,285 dwt; 279.51 × 16.9 m *(917 × 55.45 ft)*; M (B&W); 15.25 kts; ex-*Cerro Colorado*
Sisters: **SARABAND** (Cy) ex-*Beatriz Maria*; **ROMINA G** (Ma) ex-*Corta Atalaya*; **ISPASTER** (Po) ex-*Iranzu*; **MONTANA** (Gr) ex-*Astrapesa Uno*

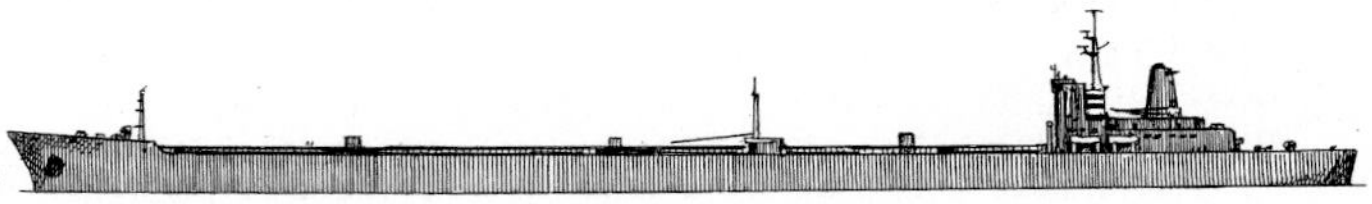

328 *MNMF H1*
KUBAN Ru/Ru (Zaliv) 1976; Tk; 88,692 grt/150,500 dwt; 295.05 × 17 m *(968.01 × 55.77 ft)*; T (Kirov); 17 kts
Similar (converted to processing tanker for offshore installations): **CHI LINH** (Vn) ex-*Krym*

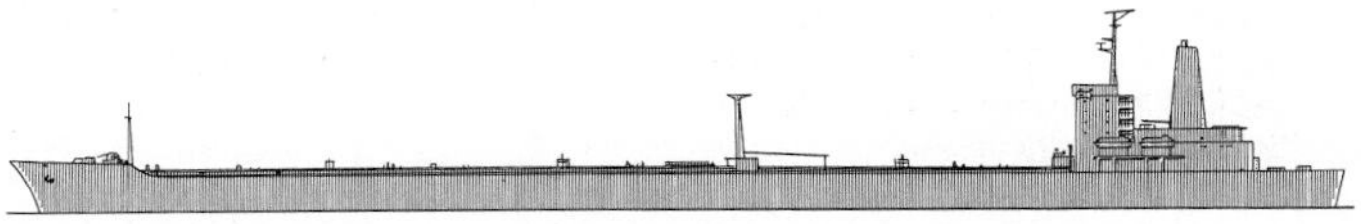

329 *MNMF H1*
KUZBASS Ru/Ru (Zaliv) 1977; Tk; 88,692 grt/150,500 dwt; 295.21 × 17 m *(968.54 × 55.77)*; T (Kirov); 15.5 kts
Sister: **SOVIETSKAYA NEFT** (Ru)

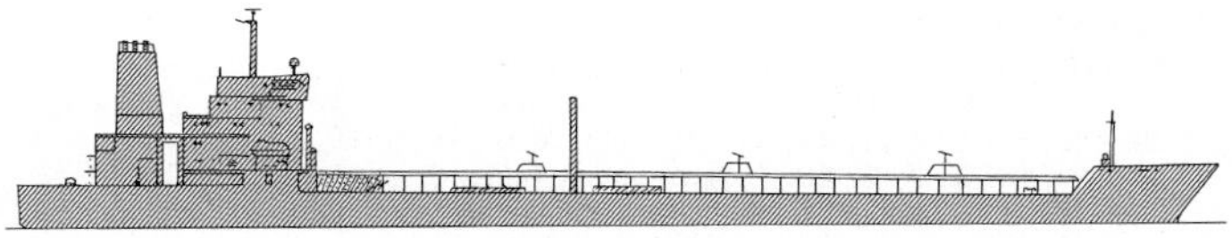

330 *MNMF H1*
MASCARIN Fr/Fr (L'Atlantique) 1986; Tk; 18,956 grt/31,952 dwt; 178.19 × 11.38 m *(584.61 × 37.34 ft)*; M (B&W); 14 kts

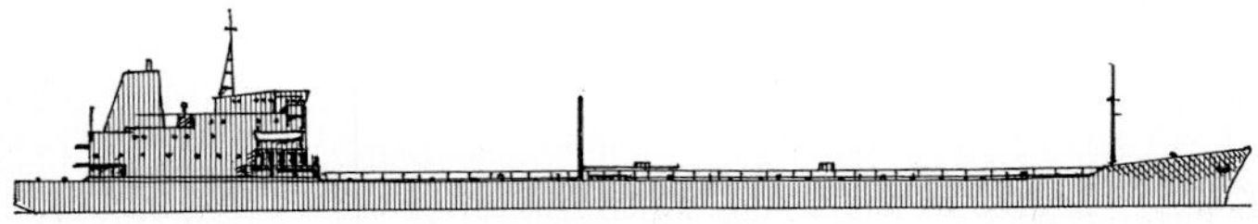

331 *MNMF H1*
MONTE BERICO It/FRG (Howaldts DW) 1971; Tk; 17,805 grt/29,680 dwt; 170.69 × 10.82 m *(560.01 × 35.5 ft)*; M (MAN); 15.5 kts; ex-*Roland Essberger*

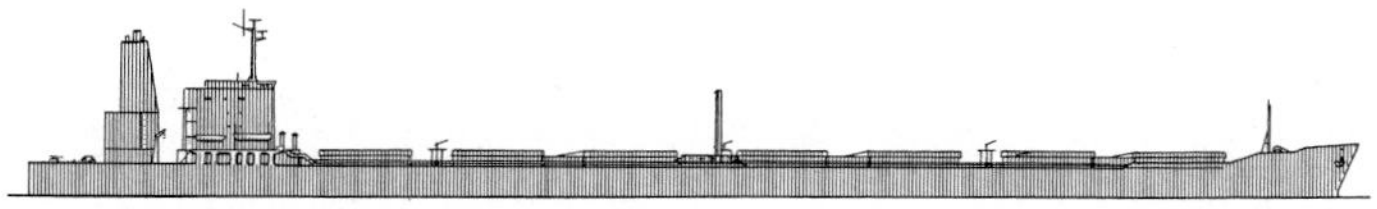

332 *MNMF H1*
OCEAN CENTURION Cy/Sw (Gotav) 1979; OBO; 70,283 grt/128,320 dwt; 250.02 × 16.11 m *(820 × 52.85 ft)*; M (B&W); 15.25 kts; ex-*Norrland*; Now converted to a bulk carrier. Hose-handling derricks probably removed

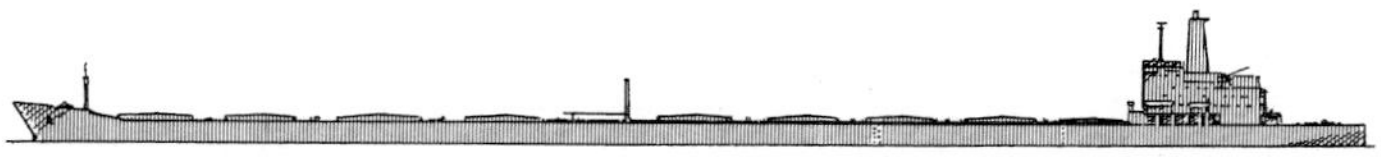

333 *MNMF H1*
ODYSSEA Gr/Sw (Gotav) 1974; OO; 114,685 grt/227,412 dwt; 332.77 × 20.51 m *(1,091.76 × 67.29 ft)*; T (Stal-Laval); 16 kts; ex-*Rinda*
Sister: **OMIROS** (Cy) ex-*Runa*

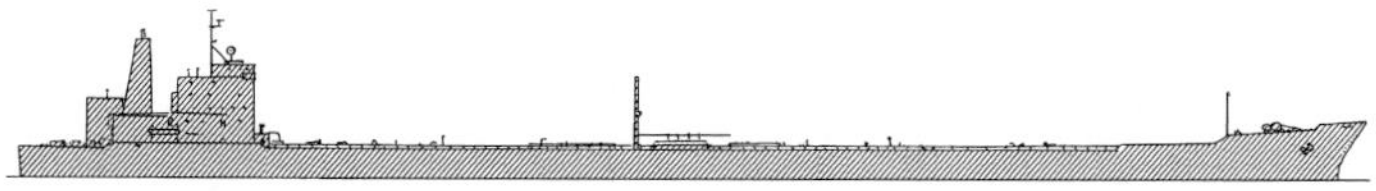

334 *MNMF H1*
OVERSEAS CHICAGO US/US (National Steel) 1977; Tk; 44,869 grt/ 90,638 dwt; 272.50 × 14.96 m *(894.03 × 49.08 ft)*; T (GEC); 16 kts; 'San Clemente' class
Sisters: **OVERSEAS OHIO** (US); **OVERSEAS NEW YORK** (US); **OVERSEAS WASHINGTON** (US); **CHESTNUT HILL** (US); **KITTANNING** (US)

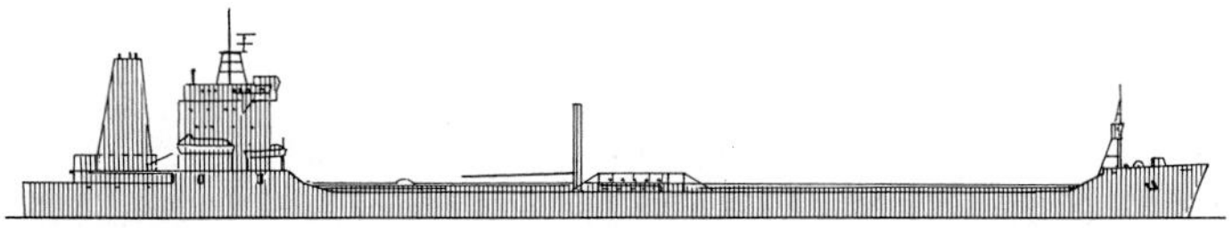

335 *MNMF H1*
PELLA Gr/Ys ('Uljanik') 1984; Tk; 22,102 grt/40,231 dwt; 176 × 11.22 m *(577.43 × 36.81 ft)*; M (B&W); 14.5 kts; ex-*Riaki*
Possible sisters: **LEADER LT** (Pa) ex-*Mosor Carrier*; **STATRADER** (NIS) launched as *Mosor Trader*; **EXPLORER LT** (Cy) ex-*Balder Uljanik*; **DION** (Gr) ex-*Black Marlin*; Similar (separate crowsnest on focsle): **IRAN RAJAI** (Ir) ex-*Ferncraig*

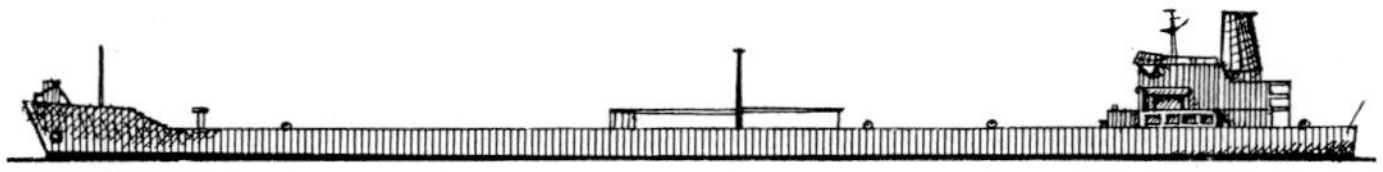

336 *MNMF H1*
POLYTRADER No/Sw (Uddevalla) 1978; Tk (offshore loading); 63,248 grt/ 125,690 dwt; 263.71 × 16.77 m *(865.19 × 55.02 ft)*; M (B&W); 16 kts
Sister: **POLYTRAVELLER** (No); Similar: **NIKI** (Gr) ex-*Hervang*; **TRANS ARGO** (Bs) ex-*Georgia*; **TRANS MINERVA** (Li) ex-*Wangkoll*; **KALAMOS** (Gr) ex-*Fagerjell*; **TRANS HERA** (Li) ex-*Ronacastle*; **KNOCK DEE** (Li) ex-*Wind Endeavour*; **NORRISIA** (Br) ex-*Gerina* (now converted to bow loading - similar to *Polytrader*)

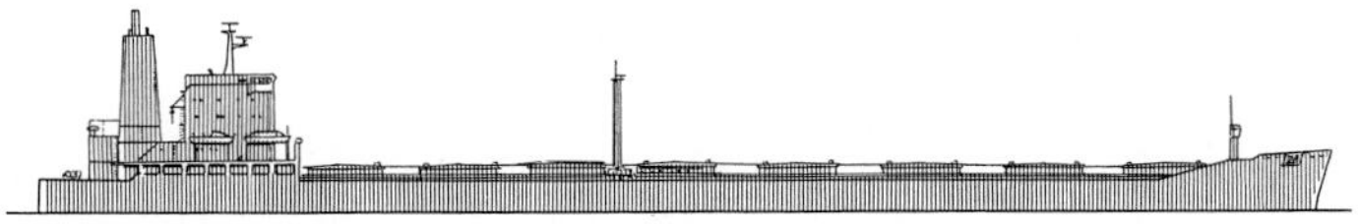

337 *MNMF H1*
RABIGH BAY-2 Gr/Sw (Uddevalla) 1979; OBO; 32,371 grt/54,600 dwt; 206.86 × 12.65 m *(679 × 41.5 ft)*; M (B&W); 16.75 kts; ex-*Sibofir*
Sisters: **BYZANTION** (Gr) ex-*Thorhild*; **KAPITAN E EGOROV** (Ru) ex-*Thorgull*; **SCF VLADIMIR** (Cy) ex-*Viking Head*; **KAPITAN POMERANTS** (Cy) ex-*Viking Cape*; **KAPITAN V IVANOV** (Ru) ex-*Geranta*; **PROTANK MERSEY** (Bs) ex-*Vardaas*; **PROTANK CONDOR** (Bs) ex-*Philippine Obo 2*; **SILVER EAGLE** (Bs) ex-*Philippine Obo 3*; **PROTANK MEDWAY** (Bs) ex-*Philippine Obo 4*; **KAPITAN SOKOLOV** (Cy) ex-*Kollbjorg*; **OBO VICTORY** (Cy) ex-*Ugland Obo One*; **PINDAR** (Gr) ex-*Ugland Obo 5*; **KAPITAN BOEV** (Cy) ex-*Tromaas*

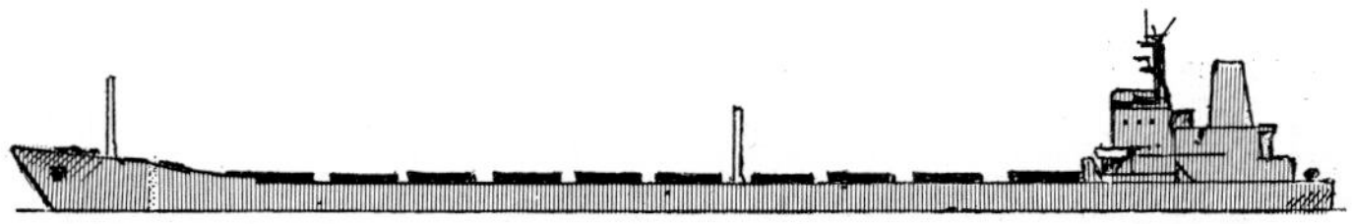

338 *MNMF H1*
ROKKO SAN Pa/Sw (Eriksbergs) 1970; OBO; 71,877 grt/150,900 dwt; 302.98 × 16.94 m *(994.02 × 55.57 ft)*; M (B&W); 16.5 kts; ex-*Turcoman*

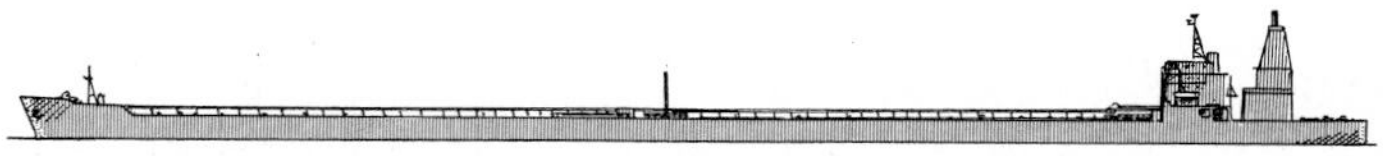

339 *MNMF H1*
SAHARA Li/Sw (Kockums) 1974; Tk; 168,524 grt/356,400 dwt; 362.75 × 22.32 m *(1,190.1 × 73.22 ft)*; T (Stal-Laval); 15.5 kts; ex-*Sea Saint*
Sisters: **OLYMPIAN SPIRIT** (Gr) ex-*Sea Saga*; **PARIS** (Gr) ex-*Sea Scape*; **COMPANION** (Bs) ex-*Sea Song*; **WYOMING** (Li) ex-*Sea Symphony*; **VOLANS** (Li) ex-*Sea Stratus*; **TINA** (Gr); **STAVROS G L** (Gr); **JUNO** (Bs) ex-*Velma*; **MIMOSA** (NIS) ex-*Wind Eagle*; **BERGE BROKER** (NIS) ex-*Wind Escort*; **KRAKA** (Bs) ex-*Vanja*; **JAHRE POLLUX** (NIS) ex-*Wind Enterprise* (fitted with new stern section, 1987, so appearance may differ)

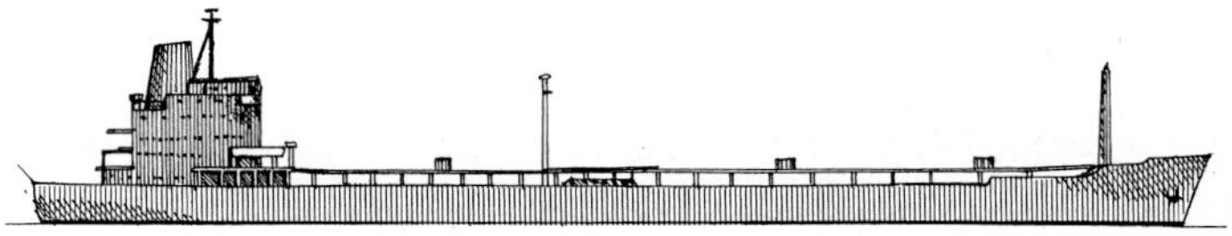

340 *MNMF H1*
SAHARA It/FRG (A G 'Weser') 1976; Tk; 22,806 grt/39,953 dwt; 193.02 × 11.65 m *(633.26 × 38.22 ft)*; M (MAN); 16 kts; ex-*Taifun*; 'Key 40' type

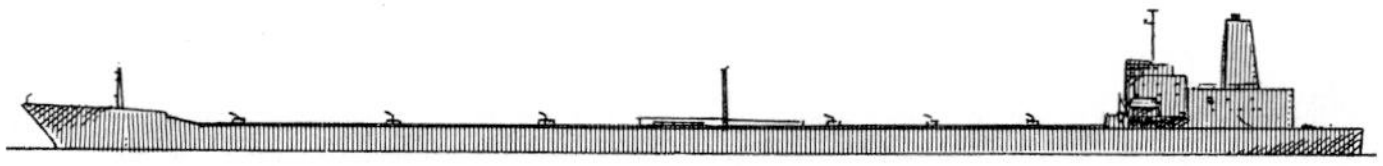

341 *MNMF H1*
SPIROS Li/Bz (Verolme ER do Brazil) 1977; Tk; 59,353 grt/116,783 dwt; 271.74 × 11.60 m *(891.54 × 38.06 ft)*; M (B&W); — kts; ex-*Bocaina*
Sisters: **ASPILOS** (Gr) ex-*Beberibe*; **BAURU** (Bz) ex-*Braganca*

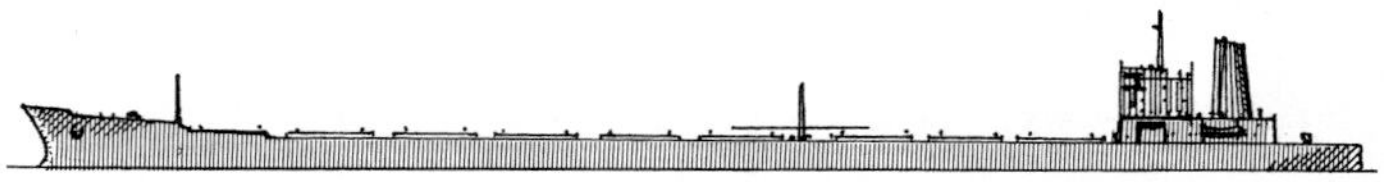

342 *MNMF H1*
ULTRASEA US/US (National Steel) 1973; OBO; 39,827 grt/83,437 dwt; 272.04 × 12.19 m *(892.52 × 39.99 ft)*; T (GEC); 16.5 kts
Sister: **ULTRAMAX** (US) ex-*Ultramar*

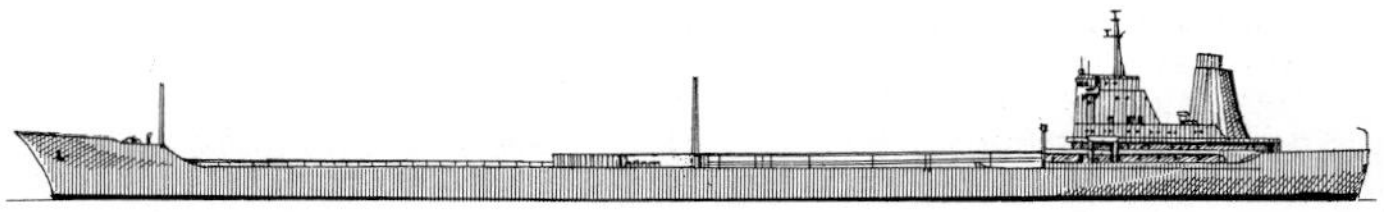

343 *MNMF H123*
ADONIS US/FRG (A G 'Weser') 1966; Tk; 38,297 grt/81,469 dwt; 250.55 × 12.87 m *(822 × 42.22 ft)*; M (B&W); 15.5 kts; ex-*St Petri*; US Government owned

344 *MNMF H13*
ACHATINA Br/Br (Hall, Russell) 1968; Tk; 1,580 grt/2,654 dwt; 75.95 × 4.67 m *(249.18 × 15.32 ft)*; M (Nydqvist & Holm); 14.5 kts; ex-*Ardrossan*

345 *MNMF H13*
AEGEAN V Gr/Ne (Arnhemsche) 1958; Tk; 1,544 grt/2,216 dwt; 83.57 × 5.24 m *(274.18 × 17.19 ft)*; M (Werkspoor); 12 kts; ex-*Airismaa*

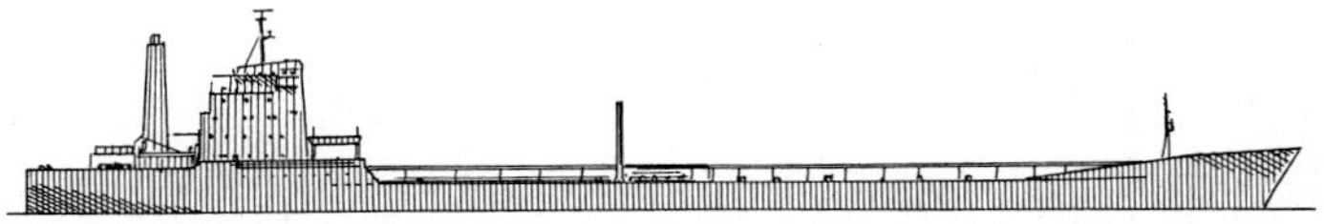

346 *MNMF H13*
AMERICAN CHEMIST Pa/No (Sarpsborg) 1975; Tk/Ch; 9,631 grt/ 16,900 dwt; 152.3 × 8.97 m *(499.67 × 29.43 ft)*; M (Pielstick); 16.5 kts; ex-*Sangatta/Permina 1015*

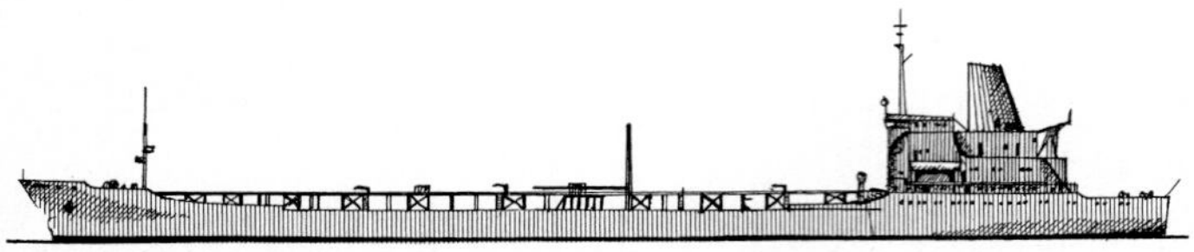

347 *MNMF H13*
ANTEA It/FRG (Rhein Nordseew) 1972; Tk; 16,689 grt/29,752 dwt; 172.04 × 10.68 m *(564.43 × 35.04 ft)*; M (Fiat); 15.5 kts; ex-*Thor Asgard*
Sisters: **SALLY I** (Ia) launched as *P.C. 1*; **SALLY II** (Ia)

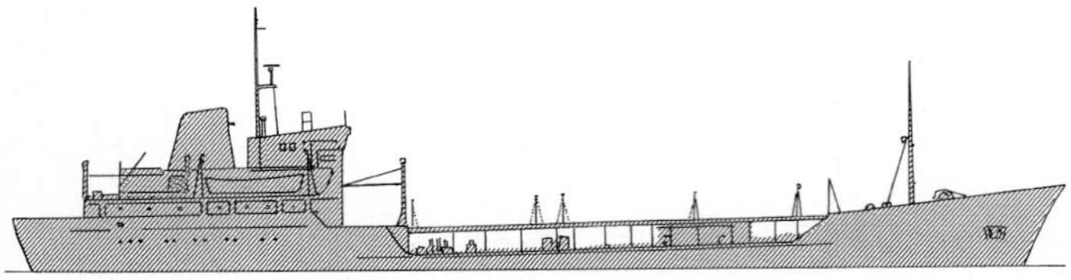

348 *MNMF H13*
BEA 1 Pa/FRG (Lindenau) 1968; Tk/VO/MT; 996 grt/2,200 dwt; 76.92 × 4.67 m *(252.36 × 15.32 ft)*; M (Atlas-MaK); 12 kts; ex-*Manitou*
Sisters: **JOHANGELA** (SV) ex-*Winnetou*; **JOHANNA** (SV) ex-*Yuma*

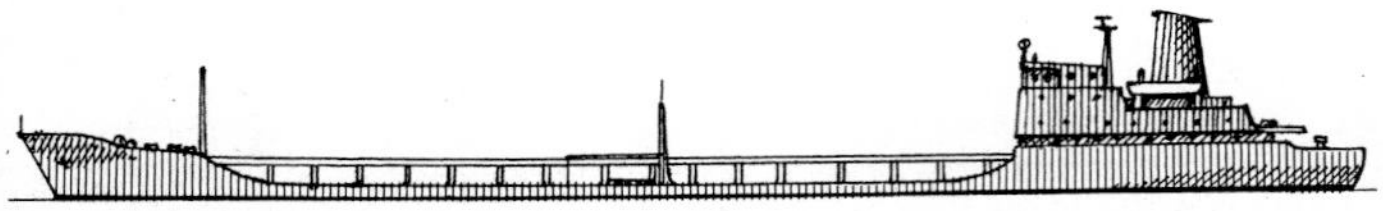

349 *MNMF H13*
CAMPOMINO Sp/Sp (Juliana) 1973; Tk; 4,222 grt/6,452 dwt; 123.68 × 6.03 m *(405.77 × 19.78 ft)*; M (B&W); 13 kts

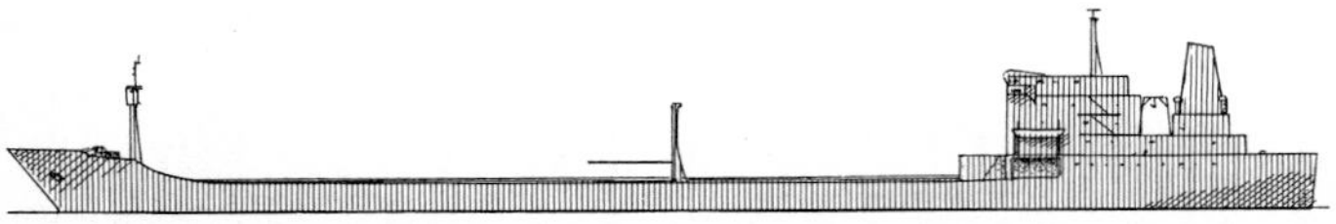

350 *MNMF H13*
CAMPONUBLA Sp/Sp (AESA) 1979; Tk; 14,089 grt/22,227 dwt; 166 × 9.25 m *(544.62 × 30.35 ft)*; M (Sulzer); 14.87 kts
Sister: **CAMPEON** (Sp)

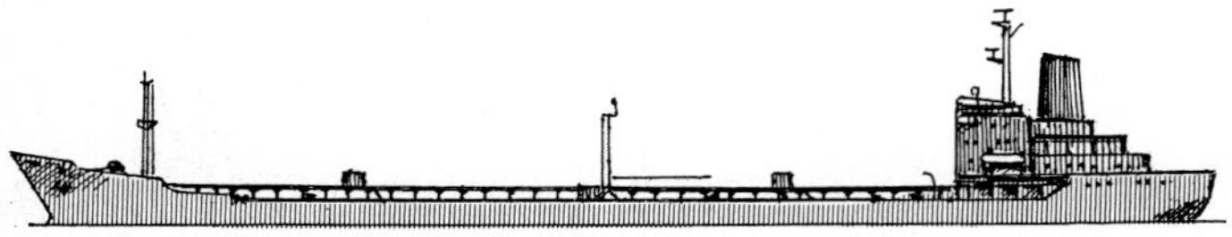

351 *MNMF H13*
CORSICA Ma/It (Italcantieri) 1973; Tk; 17,429 grt/29,960 dwt; 171.61 × 10.93 m *(563.02 × 35.86 ft)*; M (Fiat); 16 kts; ex-*Corsicana*
Sisters: **KRITI GOLD** (Gr) ex-*Conastoga*; **SATUCKET** (Li); Possible sisters: **INDEPENDENCIA 1** (Ve) launched as *Independencia*

352 *MNMF H13*
DA QING 256 RC/Sw (Oresunds) 1965; Tk; 28,891 grt/50,920 dwt; 221.14 × 12.05 m *(725.52 × 39.53 ft)*; M (Gotaverken); 15 kts; ex-*Acina*

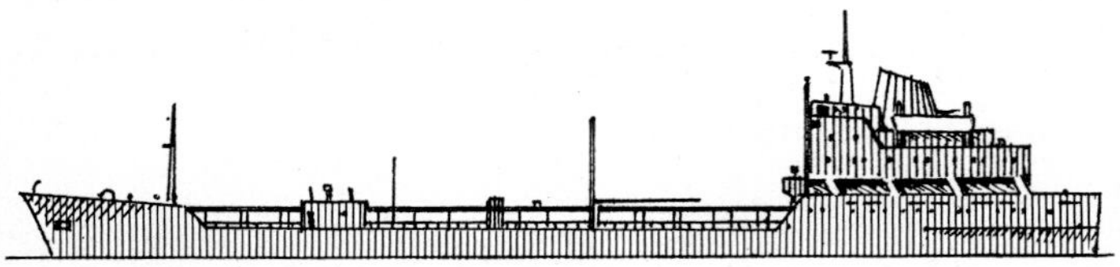

353 *MNMF H13*
DENIZ AY Tu/Br (Hall, Russell) 1970; Ch/Tk; 4,616 grt/6,261 dwt; 106.99 × 7.34 m *(351.02 × 24.08 ft)*; M (Mirrlees Blackstone); 14 kts; ex-*Silverharrier*

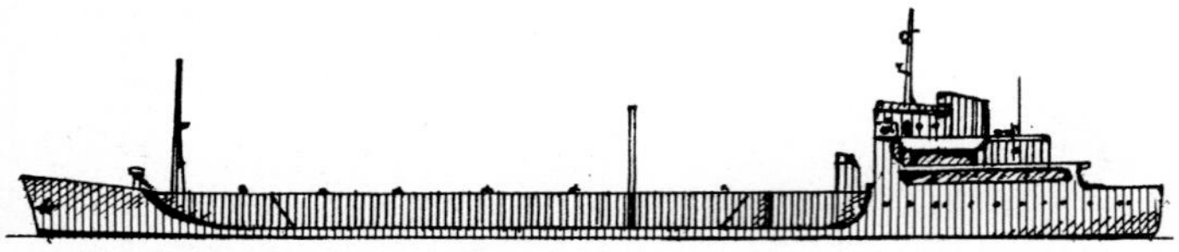

354 *MNMF H13*
GIMONE Sv/Fr (La Rochelle) 1969; Tk/LGC; 3,320 grt/5,270 dwt; 100.03 × 5.61 m *(328.18 × 18.41 ft)*; TSM (Werkspoor); 11.75 kts; Now fitted with liquefied gas tanks on deck—not shown on drawing

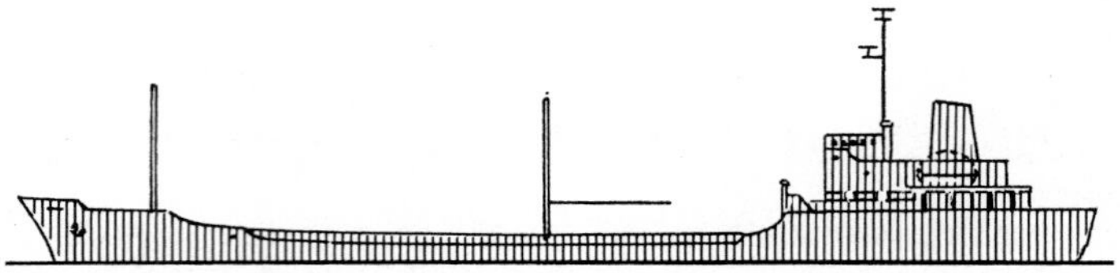

355 *MNMF H13*
GOLDEN OCEAN Sg/Ja (Imamura) 1977; Tk; 2,487 grt/4,232 dwt; 93.35 × 6.6 m *(306.27 × 21.65 ft)*; M (Hanshin); 13 kts; ex-*Sakura Maru*

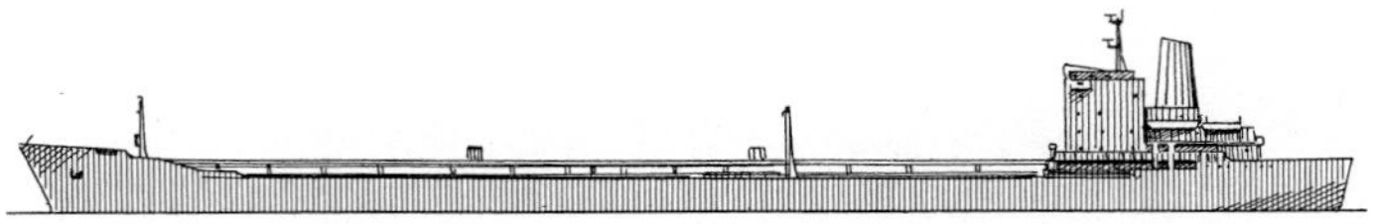

356 *MNMF H13*
LADY EMA Gr/Sw (Gotav) 1977; Tk; 18,189 grt/32,368 dwt; 170.97 × 11.36 m *(560.93 × 37.27 ft)*; M (B&W); 15 kts; ex-*Nordic Breeze*

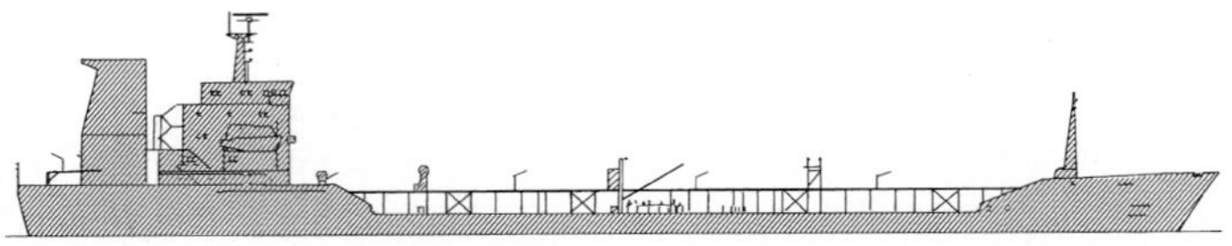

357 *MNMF H13*
LENG Ge/FRG (Lindenau) 1986; Tk/Ch; 7,090 grt/10,628 dwt; 134.65 × 8.26 m *(441.77 × 27.10 ft)*; M (MaK); 14 kts
Similar: **CHESS** (Sw) ex-*Rochen*

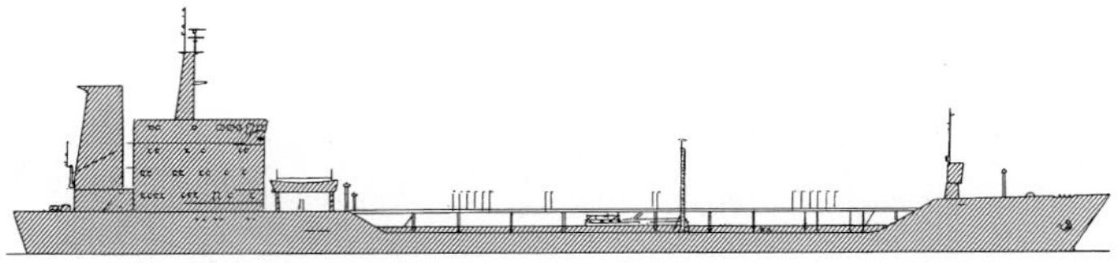

358 *MNMF H13*
LEO It/FRG (Lindenau) 1976; Ch; 4,753 grt/7,420 dwt; 112.86 × 7.36 m *(370.28 × 24.15 ft)*; M (MaK); 13.75 kts; ex-*Mongstadfjord*

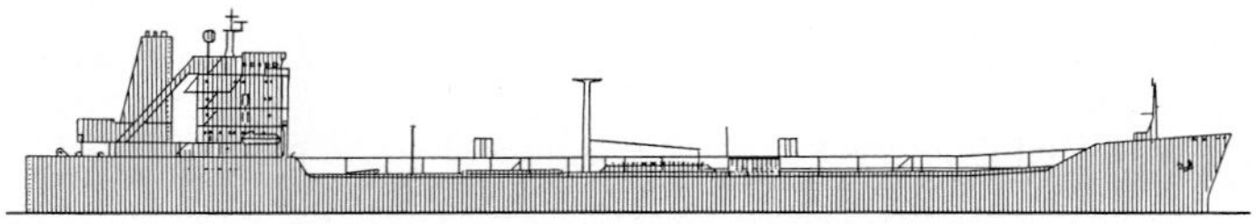

359 *MNMF H13*
LIEPAYA Cy/Pd (Gdanska) 1986; Tk; 27,001 grt/46,825 dwt; 192.21 × 11.83 m *(630.61 × 38.81 ft)*; M (Sulzer); 13 kts; ex-*Miletos 1*; 'B552' Type
Sister: **LIMBAZHI** (Cy) ex-*Marathon*; Probable sister: **RIKHARD ZORGE** (Cy) ex-*Mukale*; Possible sister (may not have the 'supports' at after end of superstructure): **SELENDANG BAIDURU** (My) ex-*Mary*; Sisters (do not have 'supports' aft): **PRODICOS** (Li); **PROTEUS** (Li)

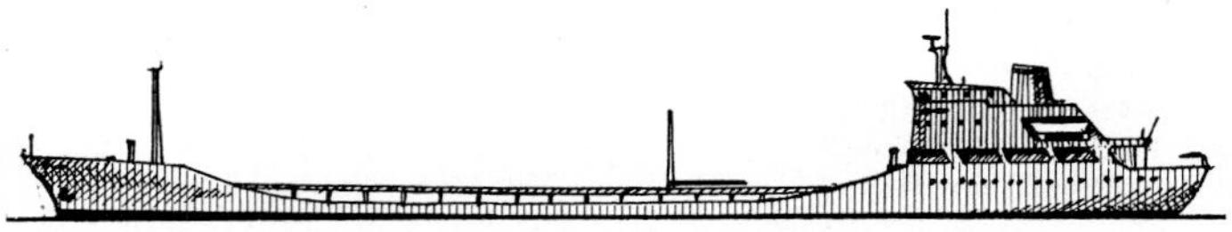

360 *MNMF H13*
ONCU Tu/Tu (Denizcilik) 1969; Tk; 3,297 grt/5,250 dwt; 111.56 × 5.88 m *(366.01 × 19.29 ft)*; M (Sulzer); 11 kts; Lengthened 1971

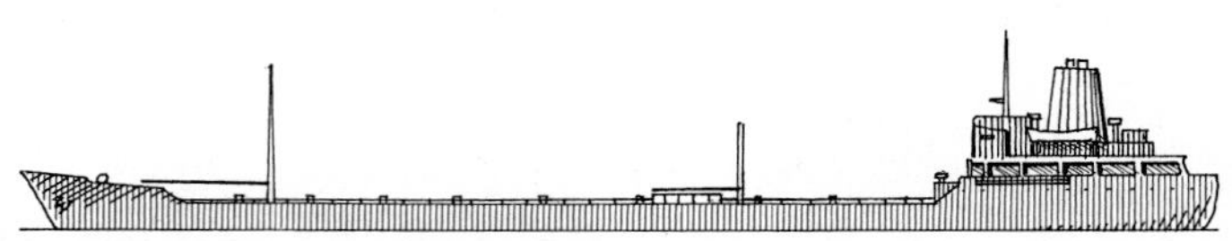

361 *MNMF H13*
PERMINA XXVII Ia/Ja (Hitachi) 1971; Tk; 9,227 grt/15,792 dwt; 141.26 × 9 m *(463.45 × 29.53 ft)*; M (B&W); 15 kts; ex-*Golar Bawgan*
Sisters: **GOLAR XXVIII** ex-*Golar Sabang*; **PERMINA XXX** (Ia) ex-*Golar Sigli*; **PERMINA XXXI** (Ia) ex-*Indotank*

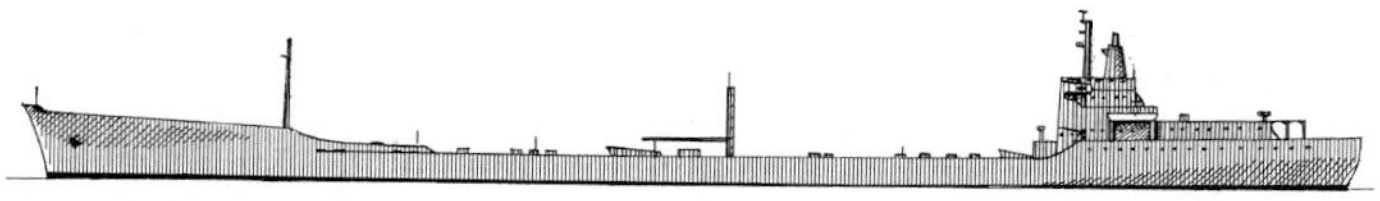

362 *MNMF H13*
PETERSBURG Li/US (Bethlehem Steel) 1963; Tk; 27,469 grt/50,702 dwt; 224.44 × 12.13 m *(735.69 × 39.79 ft)*; T (Bethlehem Steel); 16.5 kts; ex-*Sinclair Texas*; US Government owned

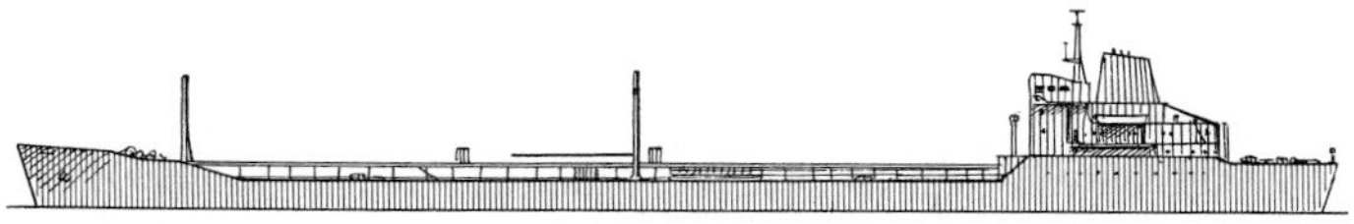

363 *MNMF H13*
PETRO MERSEY Br/Br (Cammell Laird) 1972; Tk; 11,898 grt/20,510 dwt; 166.5 × 9.21 m *(546.26 × 30.22 ft)*; M (Pielstick); 15.5 kts; ex-*Esso Mersey*
Sisters: **PETRO CLYDE** (Br) ex-*Esso Clyde;* **PETRO SEVERN** (Br) ex-*Esso Severn*

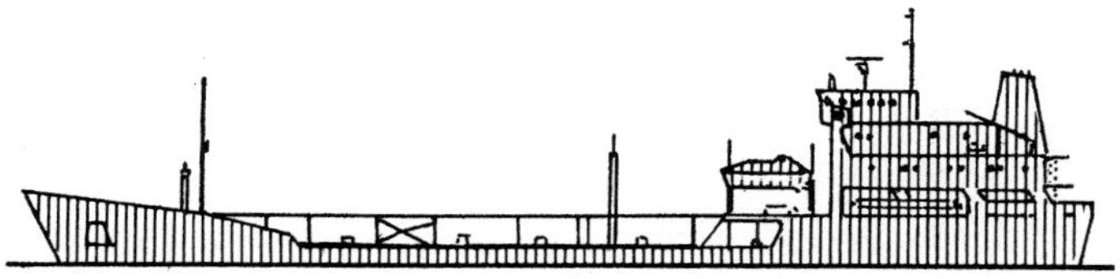

364 *MNMF H13*
REDONIA Sw/No (Aukra) 1981; Ch/AT; 1,838 grt/2,950 dwt; 76.92 × 5.76 m *(252.36 × 18.9 ft)*; M (MWM); 12.5 kts; ex-*Sletfjord*
Sister: **OUED GUETERENI** (Ag) ex-*Sletholm*

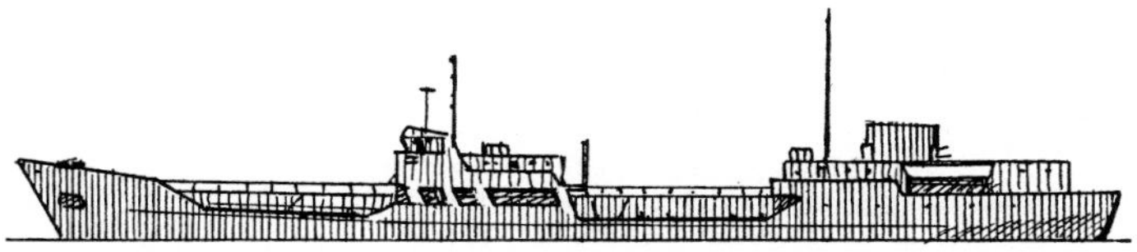

365 *MNMF H13*
ROBERT M Br/HK (Hong Kong & W) 1970; Tk/TB; 1,675 grt/2,449 dwt; 85.04 × 4.44 (279 × 14.75) m; M (MAN); 11.75 kts; ex-*Cree*

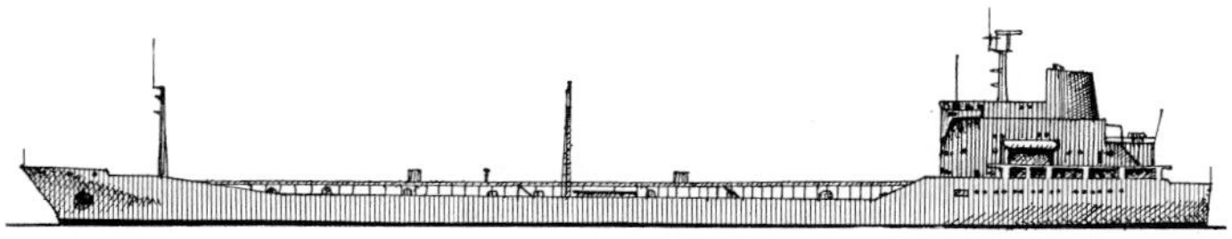

366 *MNMF H13*
SACHEM Li/Fi (Rauma-Repola) 1974; Tk; 18,235 grt/31,102 dwt; 170.49 × 11.06 m *(559.35 × 36.29 ft)*; M (Sulzer); 15 kts; ex-*Mobil Marketer*; Kingpost abreast funnel on port side
Sisters: **SHABONEE** (Li) ex-*Mobil Producer*; **ENERGOS** (Sv) ex-*Mobil Refiner*; **PAOLA D'ALESIO** (It) ex-*Paola*

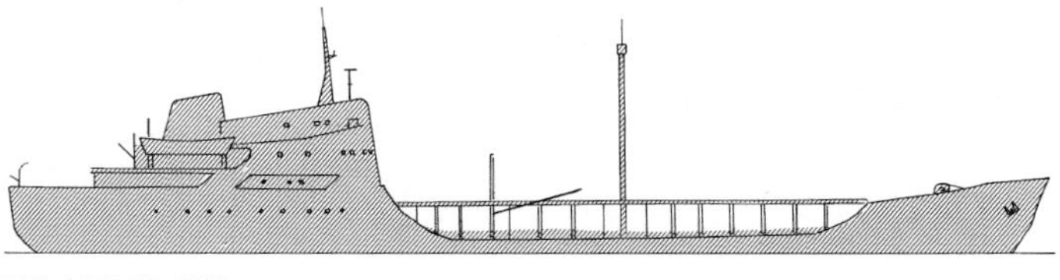

367 *MNMF H13*
UKHTA Ru/Ru (Zaliv) 1964; Tk; 1,769 grt/1,660 dwt; 83.67 × 4.6 m *(274.51 × 15.09 ft)*; M (Skoda); 12.5 kts
Sisters (some have taller funnels): **CUU LONG** (Vn) ex-*Abakan*; **AKADEMIK MAMEDALIEV** (Az); **VASILIOS D** (Gr) ex-*Evensk*; **KEKUR** (Ru); **ROCIO STAR** (Pa) ex-*Narva*; **NIVA** (Ru); **IMANT SUDMALIS** (Ru); **NIKOPOL** (Ru); **ODESSA** (SV) ex-*Sevan*; **FIORD** (Ru); **NOVIK** (Ru); **HA LONG 5** (Vn) ex-*Khrustalnyy*; **SILUET** (Ru); **BERDSK** (Ru); **SOLNECHNYY** (Ru); **ANDROMEDA** (La) ex-*Stepanakert*; **BALADZHARY** (Uk); **BELOYARSK** (Ru); **BORISOGLEBSK** (Ru); **KARAKUMNEFT** (Ru); **NARYMNEFT** (Ru); **BEREZOVNEFT** (Ru); **ICHA** (Ru); **ELTIGEN** (Uk); **ARCHANGELOS** (Pa) ex-*Kumbysh*; **PHEMIUS** (SV) ex-*Nadezhda Kurchyenko*; **KERCHENSKIY KOMMUNIST** (Az); **TITIKA** (Gr) ex-*Bellatrix*

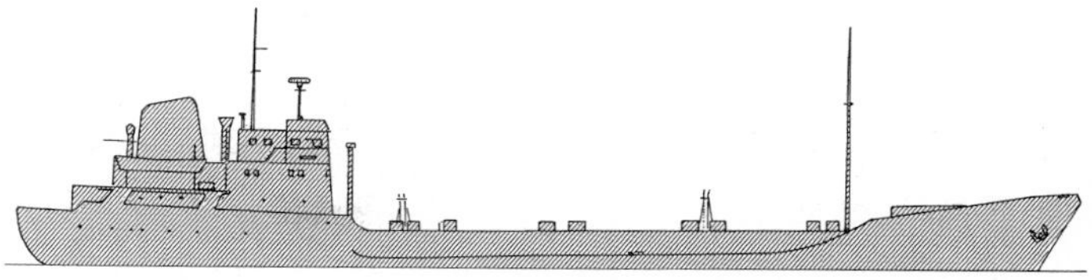

368 *MNMF H13*
VASILIOS VII Gr/FRG (Hitzler) 1959; Tk; 1,545 grt/2,180 dwt; 85.55 × 4.67 m *(280.68 × 15.32 ft)*; M (KHD); 11.5 kts; ex-*Josef Joham*; Lengthened 1968

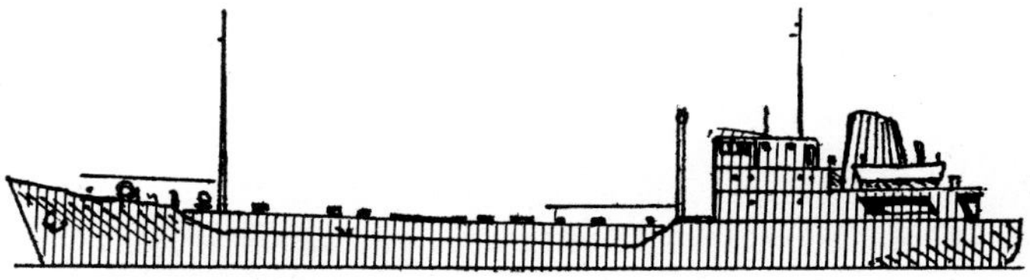

369 *MNMF H13*
VASILIOS X Gr/Po (Viana) 1965; Tk; 1,361 grt/1,890 dwt; 76.51 × 4.73 m *(251 × 15.52 ft)*; TSM (MWM); 12 kts; ex-*Rocas*

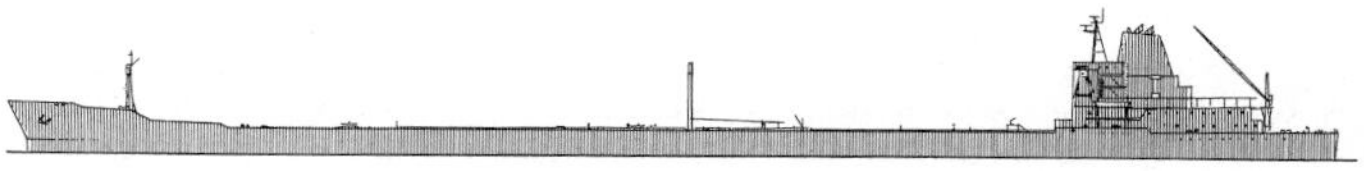

370 *MNMFC H1*
VALENCIA STAR Bs/Sp ('Bazan') 1977; Tk; 69,975 grt/151,805 dwt; 287.66 × 18.62 m *(944 × 61.09 ft)*; M (MAN); 14.25 kts; ex-*Valencia*
Sister: **GERONA STAR** (Bs) ex-*Gerona*; Probable sisters: **SAINT DIMITRIOS** (Bs) ex-*Lerida*; **ENALIOS ETHRA** (Cy) ex-*Puertollano*

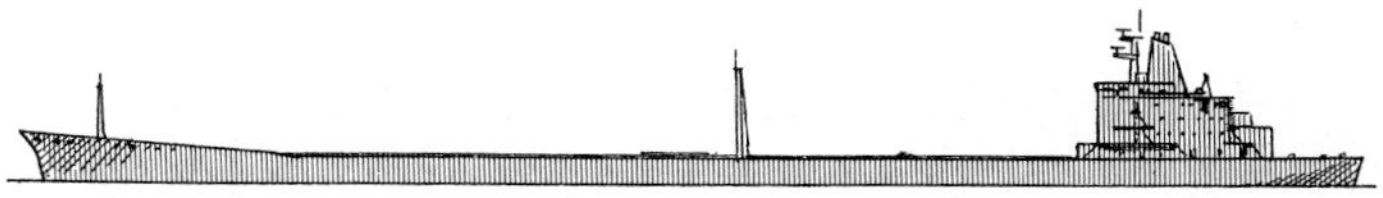

371 *MNMFD H*
BAYOVAR Pe/Fr (La Ciotat) 1976; Tk; 44,489 grt/92,145 dwt; 250.53 × 14.25 m *(820.96 × 46.75 ft)*; M (CCM); 16 kts; ex-*St Vincent*
Sisters: **KOS** (Gr) ex-*Dominant*; **KINGFISHER** (Ma) ex-*Adamant*

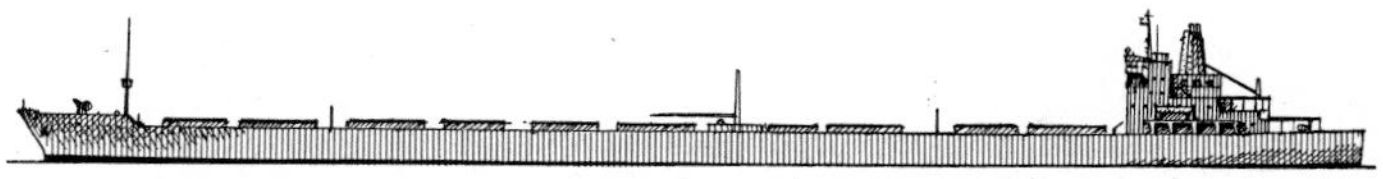

372 *MNMFD H1*
MARE BRAZIL Li/Ja (Kawasaki) 1973; OO; 128,760 grt/248,604 dwt; 326.04 × 20.49 m *(1,069.68 × 67.22 ft)*; T (Kawasaki); 15.5 kts; ex-*Hoegh Hood*
Sister: **TRADE FORTITUDE** (Li) ex-*La Loma*

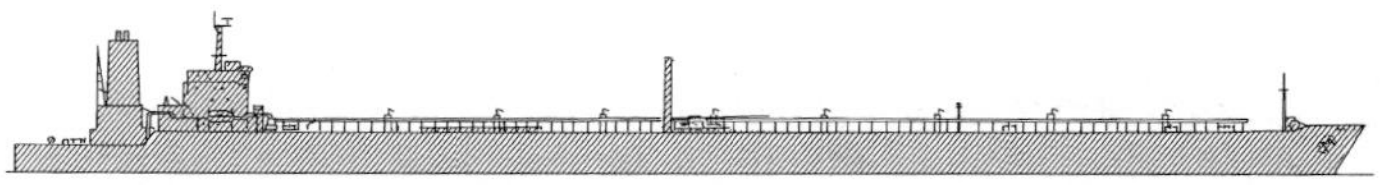

373 *MNMFM H*
COSMO NEPTUNE Ja/Ja (IHI) 1987; Tk; 136,711 grt/238,770 dwt; 319.00 × 19.14 m *(1,046.59 × 62.80 ft)*; M (Sulzer); 14.4 kts
Probable sisters: **COSMO GALAXY** (Ja); **COSMO VENUS** (Ja)

374 *MNMFM H1*
ALANDIA BREEZE Bs/Sw (Uddevalla) 1973; Tk; 62,824 grt/128,358 dwt; 281.39 × 16.70 m *(923.20 × 54.79 ft)*; M (B&W); 16 kts; ex-*Juanita*; 'M' aft is on port side

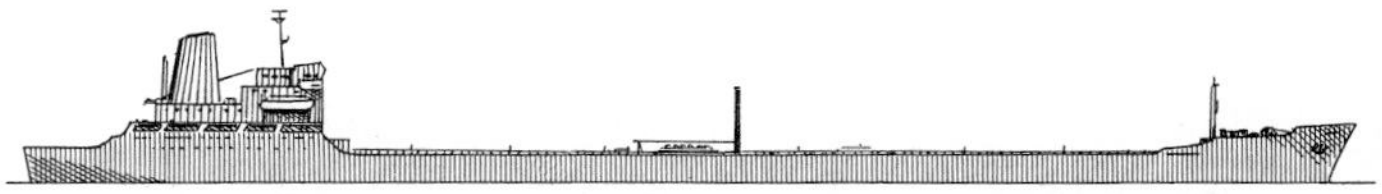

375 *MNMFM H13*
AL WATANIAH Ku/Ca (Saint John SB) 1973; Tk; 17,382 grt/32,250 dwt; 187.76 × 10.42 m *(616 × 34.19 ft)*; M (B&W); 15 kts; ex-*Esso Halifax*; 'M' aft is on starboard side
Sisters: **UMBERTO D'AMATO** (It) ex-*Esso Montreal*; **CAPO NORD** (It) ex-*Esso Saint John*

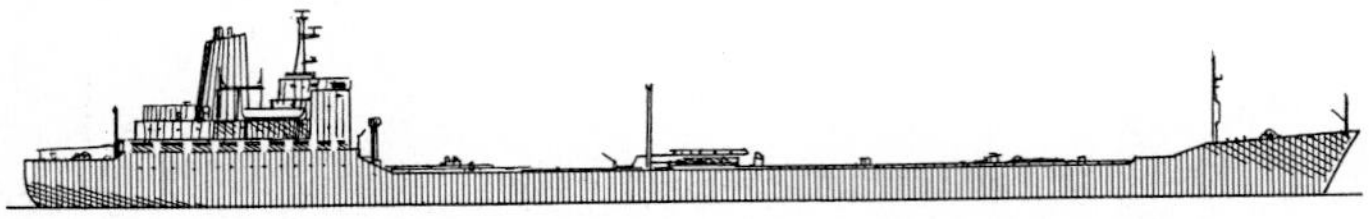

376 *MNMFM H13*
ESSO BAHIA BLANCA Li/Ja (Hitachi) 1974; Tk; 12,806 grt/22,861 dwt; 161.02 × 9.81 m *(528.28 × 32.19 ft)*; M (B&W); 15 kts; ex-*Esso Mukaishima*; 'M' aft is on port side
Sisters: **OCEAN VENTURE** (UAE) ex-*Esso Bayway*; **ASEAN PRESTIGE** (Sg) ex-*Esso Nagoya*; **ISOLA TURCHESE** (It) ex-*Esso Brisbane*; **ESSO PARENTIS** (Kn) ex-*Esso Guam*; **FRANCA D'ALESIO** (It) ex-*Esso Albany*; **PETRO TYNE** (Br) ex-*Esso Callunda*; **ASEAN PROVIDENCE** (Sg) ex-*Esso Hafnia*; Similar: **ESSO PORT JEROME** (Fr) ex-*Esso Kumamoto*

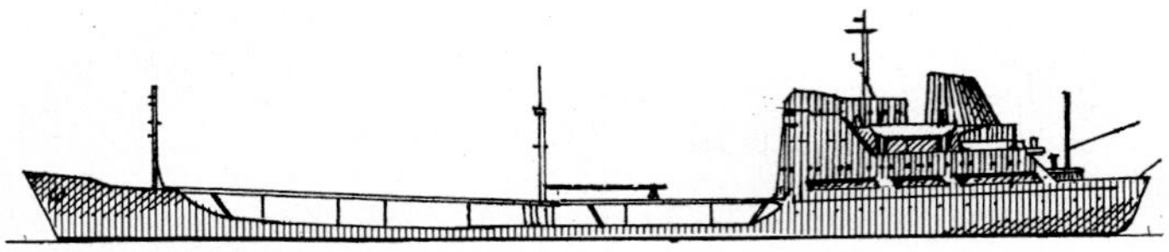

377 *MNMFM H13*
KAPITAN SHVETSOV Ru/Bu (G. Dimitrov) 1973; Tk; 4,198 grt/5,780 dwt; 116.08 × 6.69 m *(381 × 21.95 ft)*; M (B&W); 13 kts
Sisters: **OCEAN A** (SV) ex-*Drogobych*; **LAGEDI** (Ea) ex-*Kapitan Izotov*; **INZHEHIER AGEYEV** (Ru); **KAPITAN GRIBIN** (Ru); **GEORGIOS K** (Ma) ex-*Fore Mosulishvili*; **KAPITAN DYACHUK** (Ru); **KAPITAN DOTSYENKO** (Ru); **KAPITAN KOBETS** (Ru); **KAPITAN NEVEZHKIN** (Ru); Sisters (taller funnels): **BEKASAP/PERMINA 54** (Ia) ex-*Slora*; **BESITANG/PERMINA 53** (Ia) ex-*Slagen*; Similar (larger and with taller funnels): **BEKAPAI/PERMINA 56** (Ia) ex-*Sletta*; **BETUNG/PERMINA 55** (Ia) ex-*Slitan*; **BENAKAT/PERMINA 57** (Ia) ex-*Slensvik*

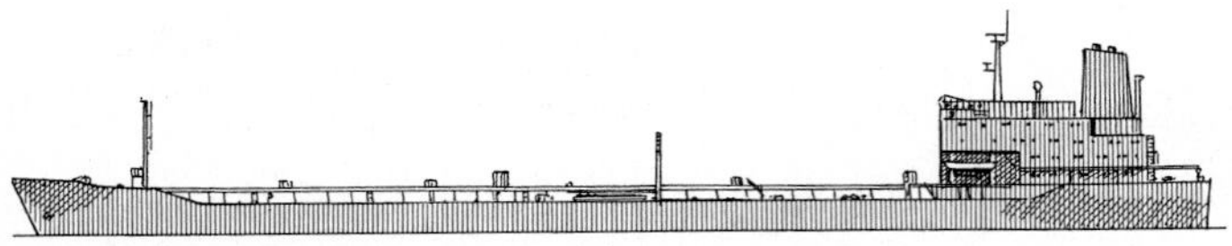

378 *MNMFM H13*
LIAN CHI RC/Sw (Eriksbergs) 1977; Tk/Ch; 17,880 grt/31,600 dwt; 170.72 × 11.33 m *(560.1 × 37.17 ft)*; M (B&W); 16 kts; ex-*Inland*; 'M' aft is on port side
Sisters: **SEAFORD** (Gr) ex-*Broland*; **SINGA WILRIVER** (Bs) ex-*Atland*

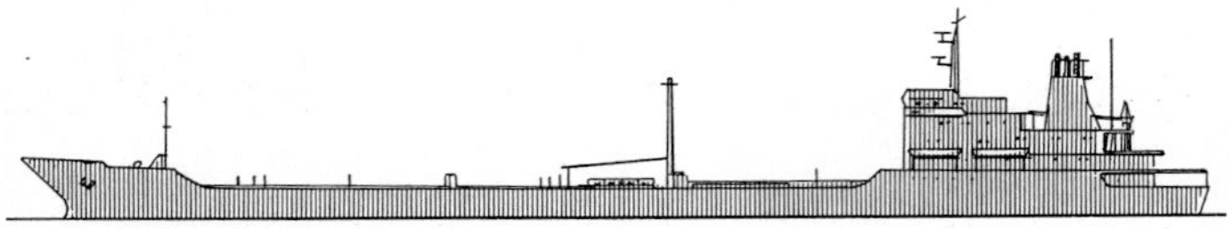

379 *MNMFMC H13*
ALEKSANDR TSULUKIDZE Gi/Ru (Kherson) 1978; Tk; 17,824 grt/ 27,360 dwt; 178.49 × 10.4 m *(586 × 34.12 ft)*; M (B&W); 15.25 kts; May be several in this class with this appearance -see No 67680. 'M' aft is on port side and 'C' on starboard
Sisters: **MAJORI** (La) ex-*Grigoriy Nikolayev*; **JANIS SUDRABKALNS** (Cy) ex-*Yan Sudrabkaln*

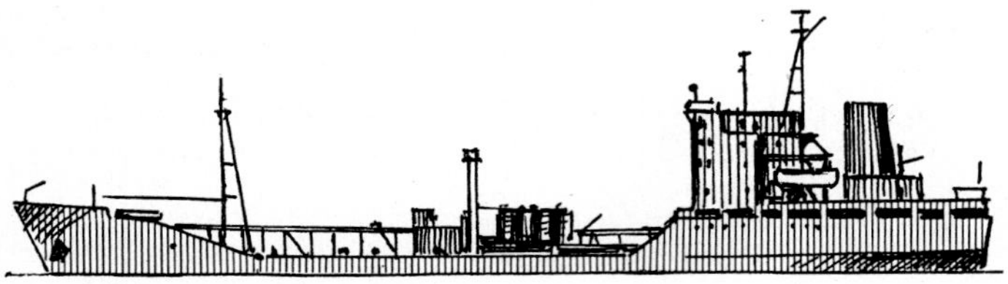

380 *MNMFM² H13*
ANN Li/Fi (Rauma-Repola) 1978; RT/Tk; 4,539 grt/5,873 dwt; 115.53 × 6.5 m *(379.04 × 21.33 ft)*; M (B&W); 16 kts; ex-*Kaliningradneft*
Sisters: **OKHANEFT** (Ru); **GALVYE** (Ru); **KATIE** (Li) ex-*Kaliningradskiy-Neftyanik*; **MYS SARYCH** (Uk); **UST-KARSK** (Ru); **UST-KUT** (Ru); **VESYEGONSK** (Ru); **VIDNOYE** (Ru); **LINKUVA** (Lt); **DELEGAT** (Ru); **KROPOTKIN** (Ru); **INKERMAN** (Uk) ex-*Mys Khrustalnyy*; **UST-ILIMSK** (Ru); **UST-KAN** (Ru); **MYS KODOSH** (Ru); **LUKOMORYE** (Ru); Probable sisters: **GEOLOG YURIY BILIBIN** (Ru); **MINUSINSK** (Ru); **MYS PAVLOVSKIY** (Uk); **SHUYA** (Ru); **UST-IZHMA** (Ru); **UST-LABINSK** (Ru)

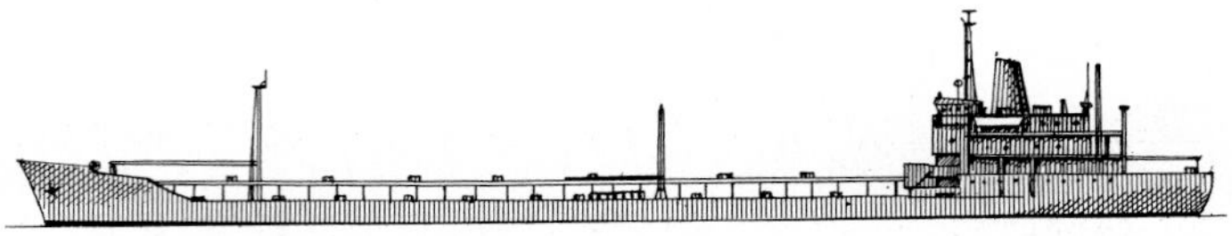

381 *MNMFM² H13*
KRITI GERANI Gr/Sw (Eriksbergs) 1968; Tk; 14,166 grt/24,900 dwt; 169.63 × 9.55 m *(556.53 × 31.33 ft)*; M (Pielstick); 14.75 kts; ex-*Lustrous*
Sisters: **KRITI EPISKOPI** (Gr) ex-*Luminous*; **EGNAZIA** (It) ex-*Lumen*; **ENOTRIA** (It) ex-*Luminetta*

382 *MNMFMN H*
LONG CHALLENGER Li/Ja (Hitachi) 1973; OO; 85,737 grt/164,338 dwt; 313.93 × 17 m *(1,030 × 55.77 ft)*; M (B&W); 16 kts; ex-*World Challenger*

383 *MNMFMN H13*
STAR BALTIC Bs/No (Horten) 1976; Tk; 17,679 grt/31,502 dwt; 168.76 × 11.15 m *(553.67 × 36.58 ft)*; M (Sulzer); 16 kts; ex-*Texaco Baltic*
Similar: **PROGRESSWIND** (Cy) ex-*Balder Horten*

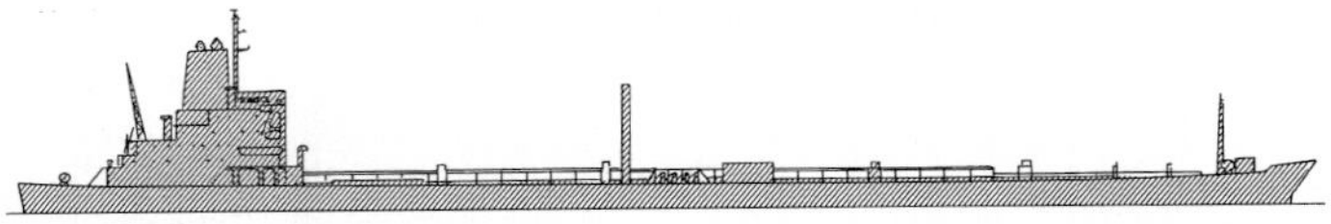

384 *MNMFN H*
ASTRO PEGASUS Ko/Ja (Imbari) 1975; Tk; 42,510 grt/81,272 dwt; 236.81 × 12.94 m *(776.94 × 42.45 ft)*; M (Sulzer); 15 kts
Probable sister: **OCEAN LEO** (Sg) ex-*Astro Leo*; Similar: **CHARISMA** (Cy) ex-*Jadecorn*; **ARCHIA** (Ma) ex-*Tricorn*

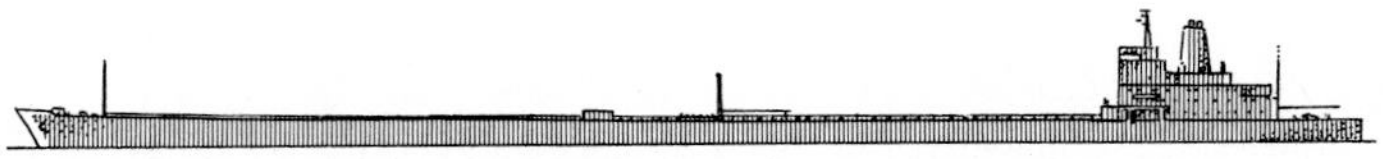

385 *MNMFN H*
CONCORDIA C Pa/Ja (Hitachi) 1976; Tk; 65,938 grt/130,500 dwt; 265.62 × 16.78 m *(871.46 × 55.05 ft)*; M (B&W); 15.5 kts; ex-*Corcordia*
Sisters: **ANIARA** (Bs) ex-*Ania*; **RUTH M** (Pa) ex-*Ruth*; **SHIRLEY** (Pa); Similar: **MARY STOVE** (NIS) ex-*Mesologi*; **MONEMVASIA** (Li); **DOLICHA BAY** (Pa) ex-*Mantinia*; **SEADANCER** (Ma) ex-*Ariela G*

386 *MNMFN H*
GAZIANTEP Tu/Ja (IHI) 1974; Tk; 73,665 grt/146,230 dwt; 286.52 × 16.84 m *(940.03 × 55.25 ft)*; M (Sulzer); 15.5 kts

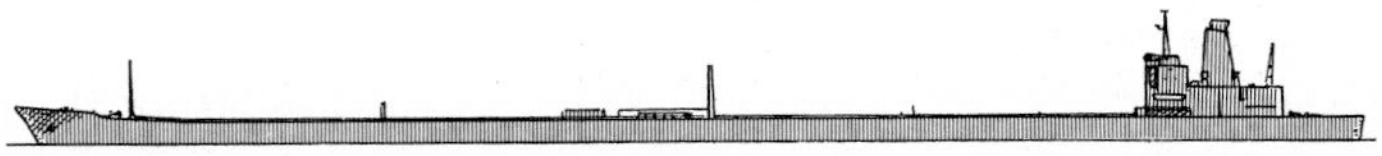

387 *MNMFN H*
HONAM PEARL Ko/Ja (Hitachi) 1974; Tk; 91,608 grt/186,508 dwt; 314.99 × 18.91 m *(1,033.43 × 62.04 ft)*; M (B&W); 15.5 kts
Possible sister: **HONAM JADE** (Ko)

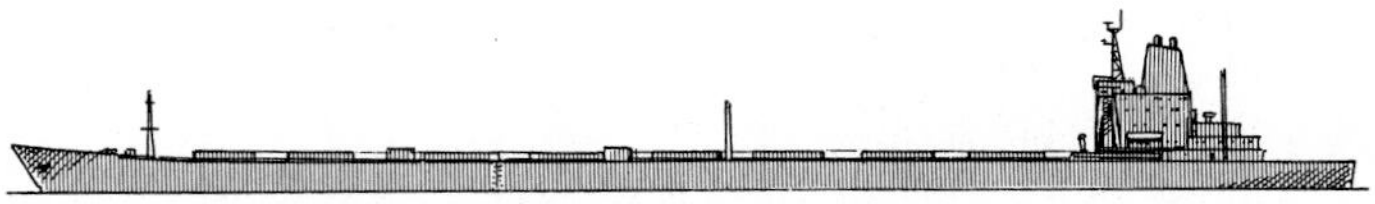

388 *MNMFN H*
HYDRA Li/Ja (Mitsubishi HI) 1975; OO; 89,468 grt/168,937 dwt; 295.03 × 17.9 m *(967.95 × 58.72 ft)*; M (Sulzer); 16.5 kts; ex-*Champagne*
Similar: **SGC MACEDONIA** (Gr) ex-*Cetra Vela*; **KIHO** (Pi) ex-*Cosmic Jupiter* (converted to ore carrier)

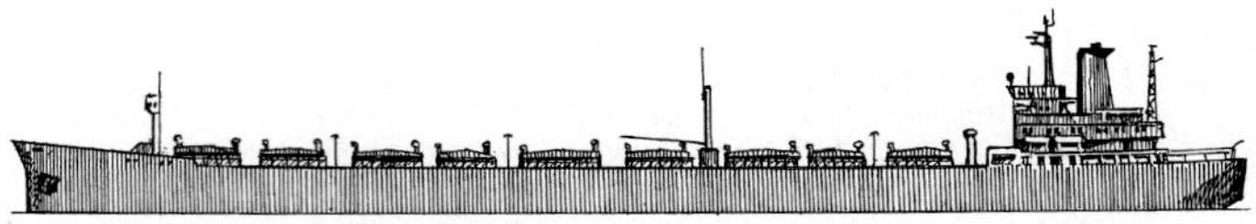

389 *MNMFN H*
MARSHAL BUDYONNYY Ru/Pd ('Komuny Paryskiej') 1975; OBO; 60,482 grt/101,877 dwt; 245.52 × 16 m *(805.51 × 52.49 ft)*; M (Sulzer); 16 kts; 'B-524' type; May be spelt **MARSHAL BUDENNYY**
Sisters: **MARSHAL KONYEV** (Ru); **MARSHAL ROKOSSOVSKIY** (Ru); **MARSHAL ZHUKOV** (Ru)

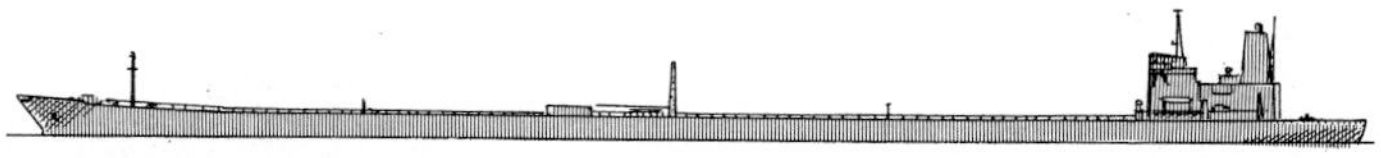

390 *MNMFN H*
WORLD CHAMPION Li/Ja (IHI) 1974; Tk; 131,842 grt/273,117 dwt; 337.02 × 21.03 m *(1,105.7 × 68.1 ft)*; T (IHI); 16 kts; ex-*Andes Maru*

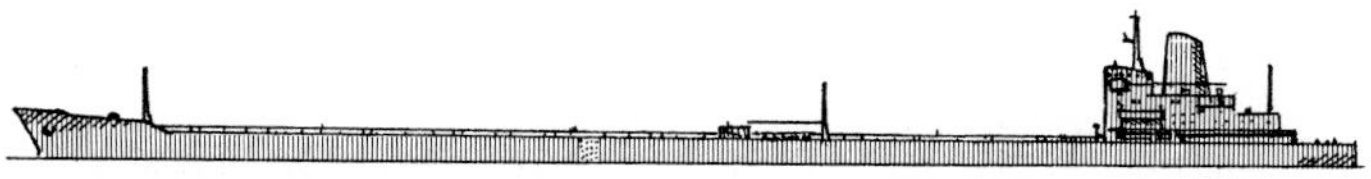

391 *MNMFN H1*
AL FAO Iq/Ja (Mitsui) 1969; Tk; 41,477 grt/89,180 dwt; 257.49 × 13.37 m *(844.78 × 43.86 ft)*; M (B&W); 15.25 kts; ex-*World Knowledge*

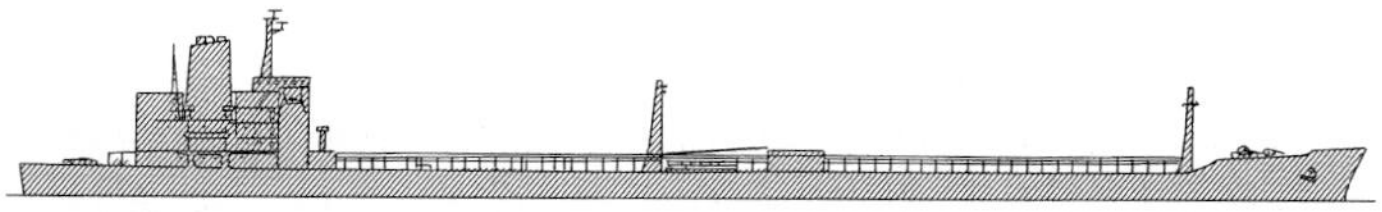

392 *MNMFN H1*
ALANDIA ORIENT Bs/Ja (Tsuneishi) 1976; Tk; 48,710 grt/89,583 dwt; 246.59 × 13.50 m *(809.02 × 44.29 ft)*; M (B&W); 16 kts; ex-*Grand Universe*

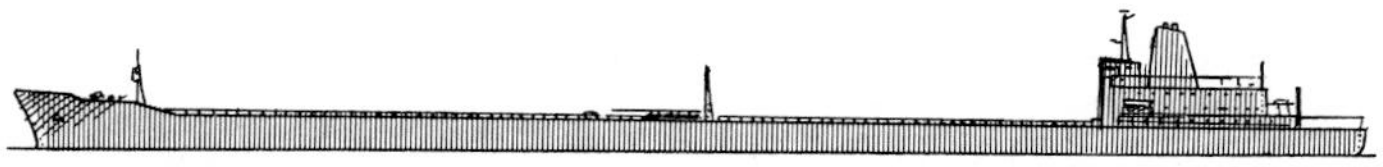

393 *MNMFN H1*
ALANDIA WAVE Bs/Sw (Uddevalla) 1972; Tk; 49,658 grt/97,693 dwt; 255.25 × 14.38 m *(837.46 × 47.18 ft)*; M (B&W); 16.5 kts; ex-*Evina*

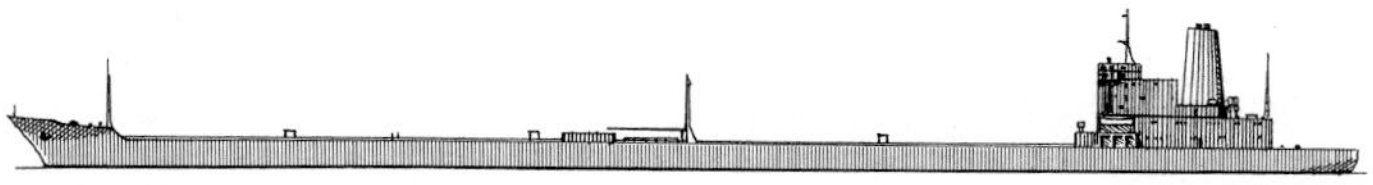

394 *MNMFN H1*
AMINA Eg/Ja (Hitachi) 1973; Tk; 38,929 grt/71,200 dwt; 239.3 × 13.24 m *(785.1 × 43.44 ft)*; M (Sulzer); 16 kts; ex-*Navarchos Miaoulis*

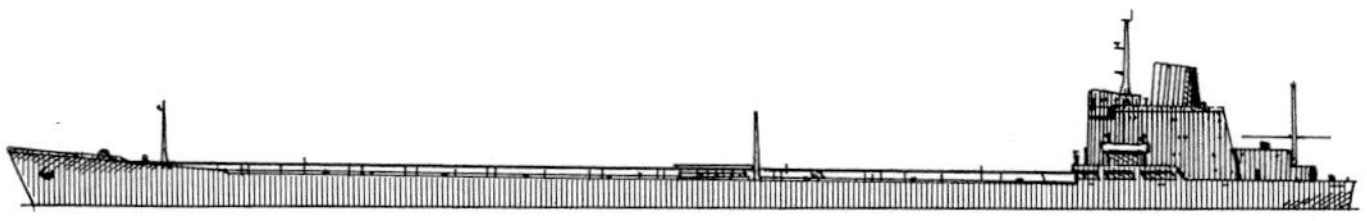

395 *MNMFN H1*
ATLANTIC SEA Ma/Ca (Davie SB) 1975; Tk; 22,126 grt/39,865 dwt; 182.89 × 11.42 m *(600.03 × 37.47 ft)*; M (Sulzer); 15 kts; ex-*Lucellum*
Sister: **SITAXA** (NIS) ex-*Lucerna*; Possibly similar: **SEAEXPLORER** (Ma) ex-*Ogden Ottawa*; **OCEAN QUEEN** (Sg) ex-*Ogden Saguenay*

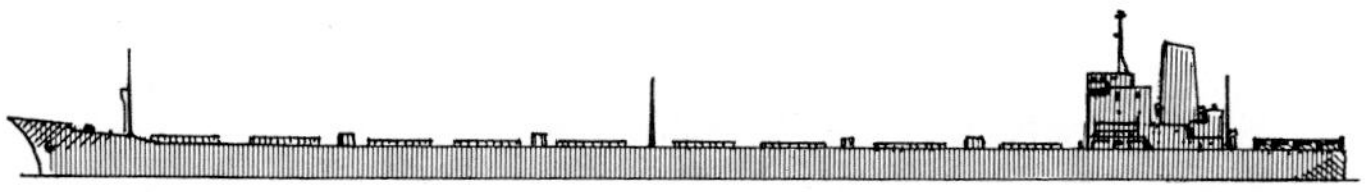

396 *MNMFN H1*
CARAVOS STAR Cy/Ja (NKK) 1972; OBO; 61,218 grt/113,826 dwt; 264.35 × 14.63 m *(867.29 × 48 ft)*; M (Sulzer); 16 kts; ex-*Point Clear*; Helicopter deck aft. Now converted to bulk carrier, so hose-handling derricks may be removed
Similar (also converted to bulk): **CARAVOS SPIRIT** (Cy) ex-*Vergo*

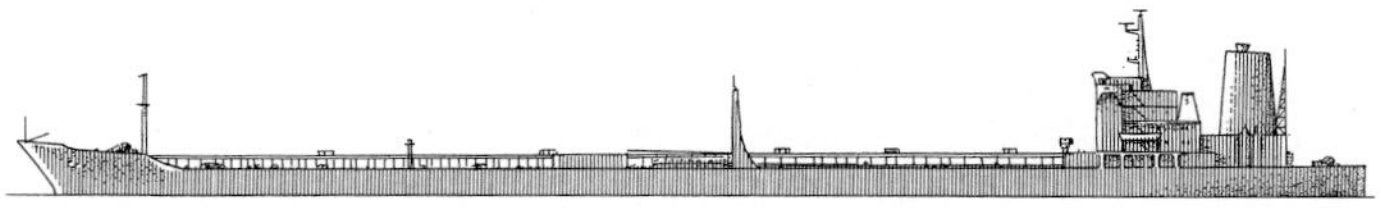

397 *MNMFN H1*
ENDEAVOR II Ma/Ja (Hashihama) 1976; Tk; 47,309 grt/84,000 dwt; 242.98 × 14.5 m *(797.18 × 47.57 ft)*; M (Sulzer); 16 kts; ex-*Cumberlandia*
Similar (some Sg built—Jurong Spyd): **HAWAIIAN KING** (Pa) ex-*Moorfields Monarch*; **NORMAN KING** (Li) ex-*Euroasia Monarch*; **ENALIOS TRITON** (Gr) ex-*Neptune Leo*; **MINT PROSPERITY** (Li) ex-*Northern Victory*; **WABASHA** (Li) ex-*Oceanic Erin*; **ZEINAT** (Eg) ex-*Sanko Honour*; **NP TATINA** (Sg) ex-*Noga*; **NISSOS KYTHNOS** (Gr) ex-*Pageantry*; **STAR CHERRY** (Sg) ex-*Palmstar Cherry*; **STAR ORCHID** (Sg) ex-*Palmstar Orchid*; **BRILLIANCY** (Li); **GYOKO** (Ma) ex-*Bruce Ruthi II*; **HAWAIIAN MONARCH** (Li) ex-*Continental Monarch*; **KIKU PACIFIC** (Cy) ex-*Oceanic Kristin*; **HELLESPONT ENERGY** (Li) ex-*Western Energy*

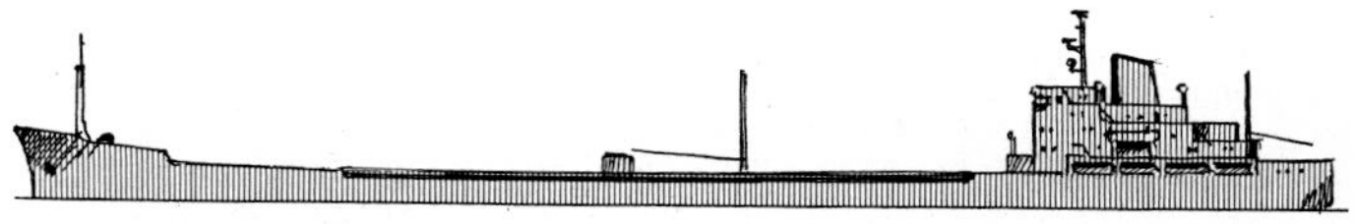

398 *MNMFN H1*
GREEN STAR Ma/Ja (Namura) 1973; Tk; 16,706 grt/30,170 dwt; 171.02 × 10.71 m *(561.09 × 35.14 ft)*; M (Sulzer); 15 kts; ex-*Seaborne*
Sisters: **BLUE STAR** (Ma) ex-*Seaservice*; **QING LONG NO 1** (RC) ex-*Seastar*; Possibly similar: **ORENSE** (Pa) ex-*Cys Integrity*; **KOREA SUNNYHILL** (Ko) ex-*Cys Hope*

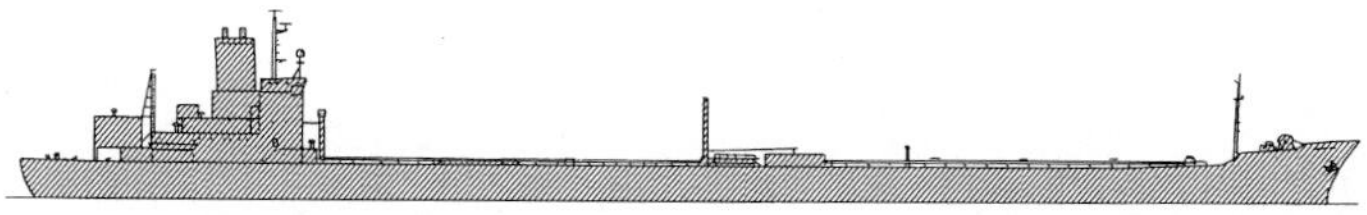

399 *MNMFN H1*
HELLESPONT FAITH Li/Ja (Mitsubishi HI) 1968/81; Tk; 52,550 grt/83,983 dwt; 250.02 × 13.01 m *(820.28 × 42.68 ft)*; M (Mitsubishi); 15 kts; ex-*Kaiko Maru*; Rebuilt from ore/oil carrier 1981 (Kawasaki)

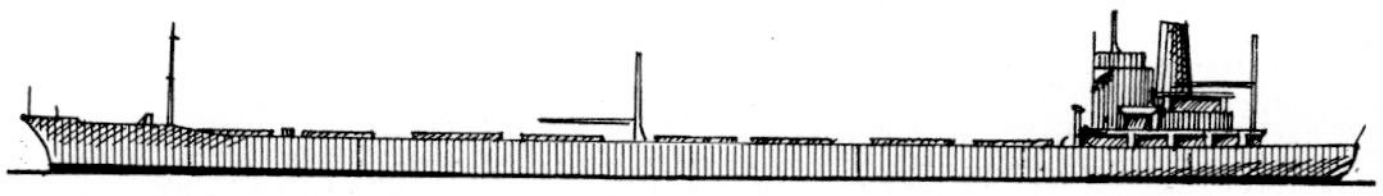

400 *MNMFN H1*
IOLCOS SPIRIT Cy/Tw (Taiwan SB) 1977; OO; 53,029 grt/93,070 dwt; 253.02 × 15.15 m *(830.12 × 49.7 ft)*; M (Sulzer); 15.5 kts; ex-*Brazilian Friendship*

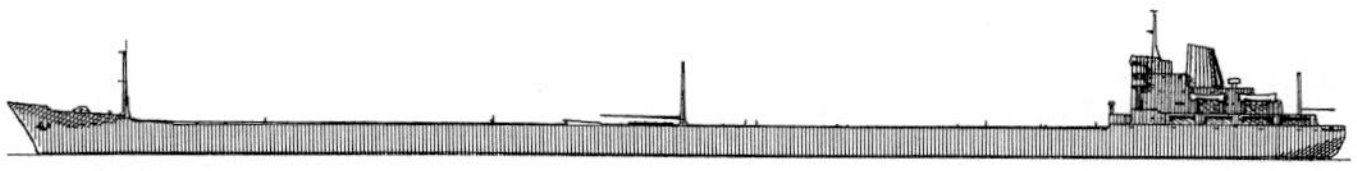

401 *MNMFN H1*
KRITI STAR Gr/Ca (Davie SB) 1973; Tk; 42,567 grt/81,212 dwt; 239.25 × 13 m *(784.94 × 43.77 ft)*; M (Sulzer); 16 kts
Sisters: **KRITI LAND** (Gr); **KRITI WAVE** (Gr)

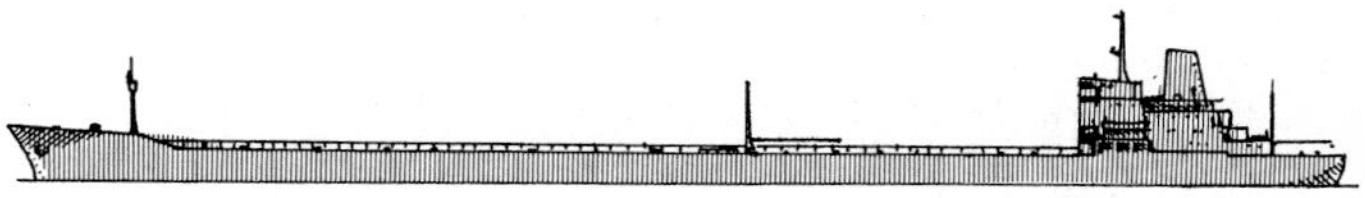

402 *MNMFN H1*
NISI Pa/Sw (Eriksbergs) 1968; Tk; 50,300 grt/98,151 dwt; 255.33 × 14.38 m *(837.7 × 47.18 ft)*; M (B&W); 16 kts; ex-*Artemis*

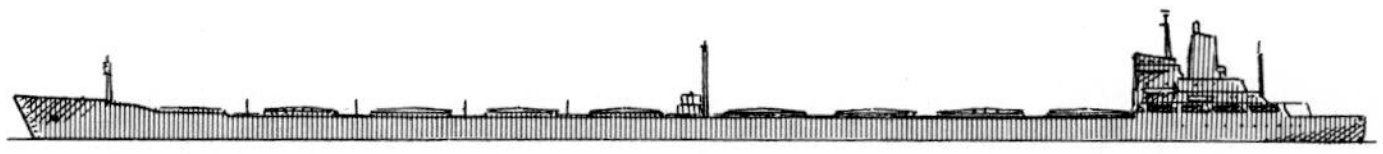

403 *MNMFN H1*
OBO ELIF Tu/Sw (Oresunds) 1973; OBO; 56,232 grt/103,434 dwt; 256.47 × 15.11 m *(841.44 × 49.57 ft)*; M (Gotaverken); X kts; ex-*Aphrodite*
Similar: **OBO SELIM** (Tu) ex-*Kongshav*

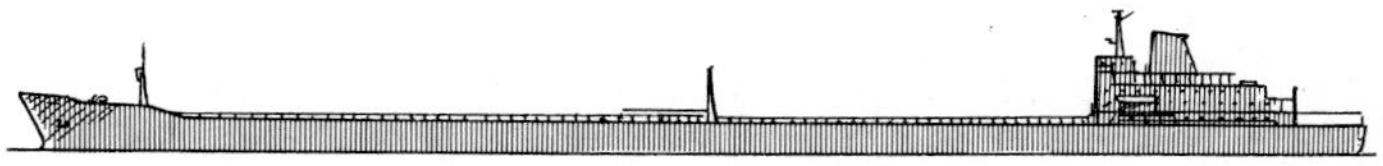

404 *MNMFN H1*
PEGGY Bs/Sw (Uddevalla) 1970; Tk; 49,898 grt/97,672 dwt; 255.25 × 14.38 m *(837.43 × 47.18 ft)*; M (B&W); 16 kts; ex-*Pegny*

405 *MNMFN H1*
PETROSHIP A Si/Ys ('3 Maj') 1975; Tk; 23,598 grt/39,115 dwt; 197.64 × 11.7 m *(648.43 × 38.39 ft)*; M (Sulzer); 16.5 kts
Sister: **PETROSHIP B** (Si)

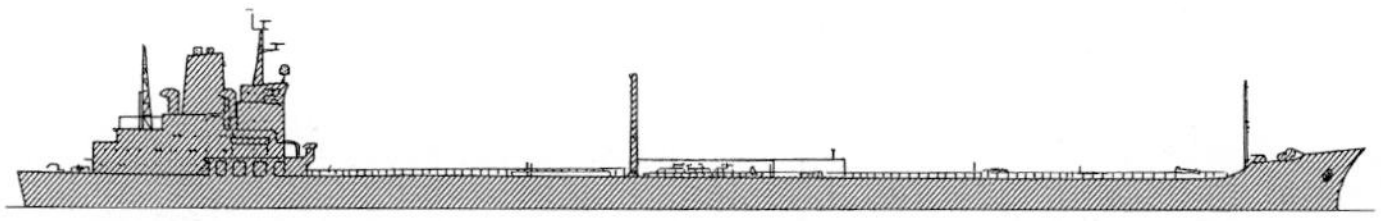

406 *MNMFN H1*
PRESTIGE Bs/Ja (Hitachi) 1976; Tk; 39,920 grt/81,564 dwt; 243.49 × 14.07 m *(798.85 × 46.16 ft)*; M (B&W); 15 kts; ex-*Gladys*; 'N' aft consists of lattice tripod on port side and pole on starboard side
Probable sisters: **APANEMO** (Gr) ex-*Lissa*; **CENTAUR** (Gr) ex-*Majestic Pride*; **ALEXANDROS** (Gr) ex-*Corolla*

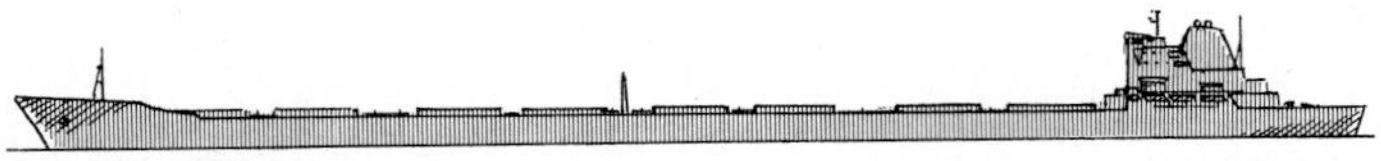

407 *MNMFN H1*
PROSPERITY No 1 Bs/No 1973; OO; 68,493 grt/127,203 dwt; 282 × 17 m *(925.19 × 55.77 ft)*; M; 16 kts; ex-*Acina*
Sister: **FOLEGANDROS** (Gr) ex-*Sandefjord*

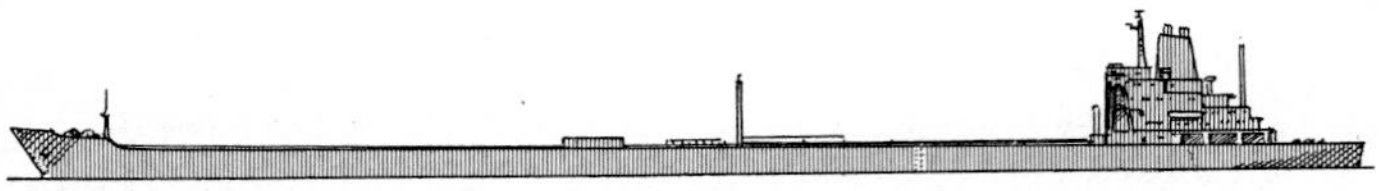

408 *MNMFN H1*
ZAWRAT Pd/Ja (Mitsubishi HI) 1975; Tk; 81,195 grt/145,680 dwt; 293 × 15.29 m *(961.29 × 50.16 ft)*; M (Sulzer); 16.25 kts
Sisters: **CZANTORIA** (Li); **SOKOLICA** (Li)

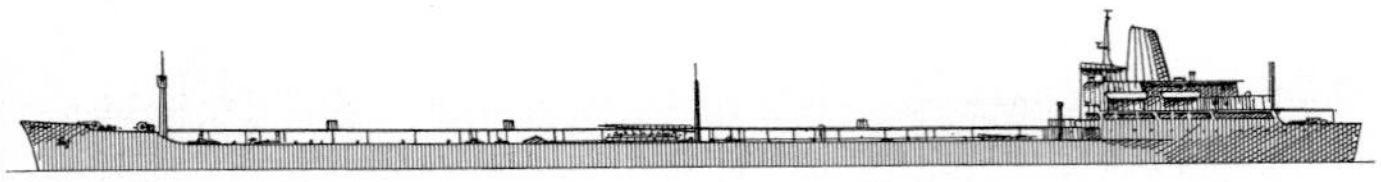

409 *MNMFN H13*
AL MADIHA Eg/Sw (Eriksbergs) 1966; Tk; 27,984 grt/51,200 dwt; 217.81 × 12.16 m *(714.6 × 39.9 ft)*; M (B&W); 13 kts; ex-*Sea Breeze*

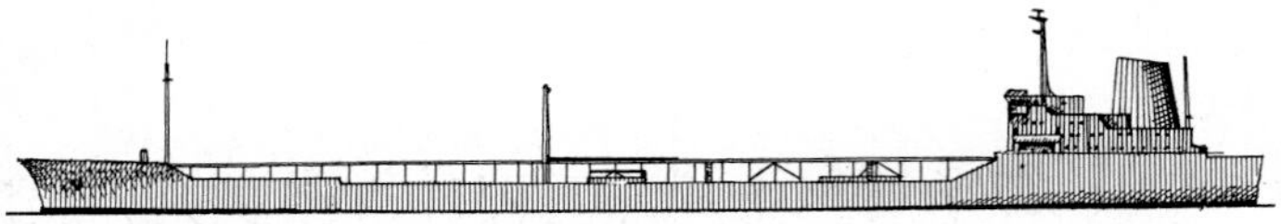

410 *MNMFN H13*
ALEX Li/Ne (Giessen-De Noord) 1973; Tk; 17,123 grt/30,607 dwt; 170.69 × 11 m *(560.01 × 36.09 ft)*; M (B&W); 15 kts; ex-*G. A. Walker*
Sisters: **STRENGTH** (Pa) ex-*R A Emerson*; **ARMA** (Li) ex-*W. A. Mather*; **ULAN** (Li) ex-*Fort Coulogne*; **EDMO** (Li) ex-*Fort Edmonton*; **NIKE** (Li) ex-*Fort Kipp*; **MACLE** (Li) ex-*Fort Macleod*; **COURAGE** (Pa) ex-*Fort Steele*

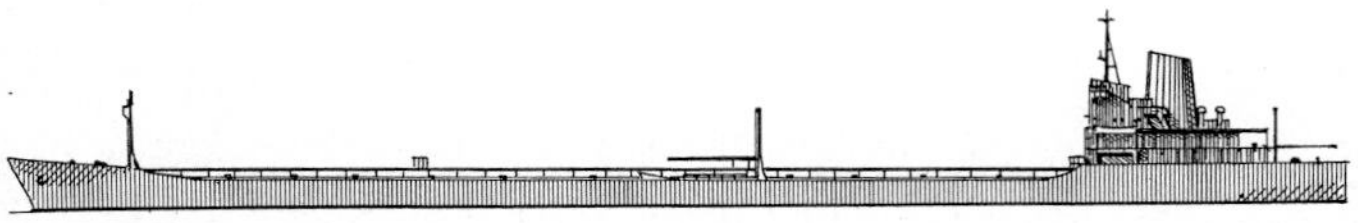

411 *MNMFN H13*
BABA GURGUR Iq/Sp (AESA) 1973; Tk; 21,375 grt/36,397 dwt; 201.02 × 10.96 m *(659.51 × 35.96 ft)*; M (Sulzer); 16 kts
Sisters: **BUZURGAN** (Iq); **JAMBUR** (Iq); **KIRKUK** (Iq); **RUMAILA** (Iq)

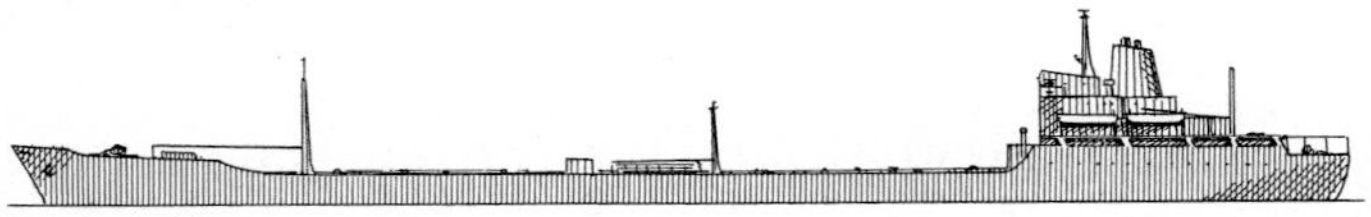

412 *MNMFN H13*
BENITO JUAREZ Me/Ja (IHI) 1968; Tk; 12,761 grt/21,823 dwt; 170.75 × 9.47 m *(560.2 × 31.07 ft)*; M (Sulzer); 15.5 kts
Sisters: **MELCHOR OCAMPO** (Me); **POTRERO DEL LLANO** (Me) ex-*Plan De Ayala*; **PLAN DE GUADELUPE** (Me)

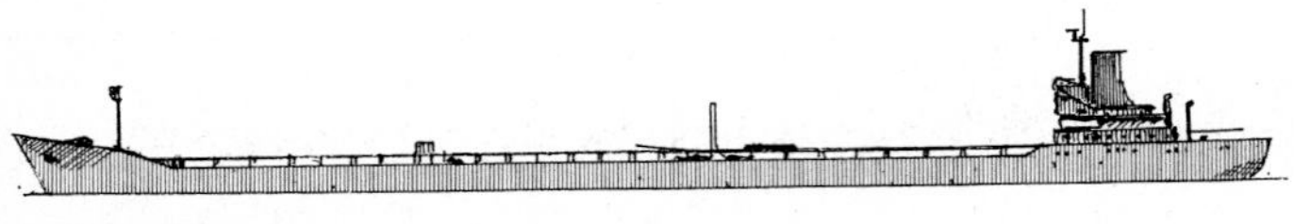

413 *MNMFN H13*
CAMPOMAYOR Sp/Sp (AESA) 1969; Tk; 19,379 grt/35,470 dwt; 209.02 × 10.73 m *(685.76 × 35.2 ft)*; M (B&W); 16.5 kts

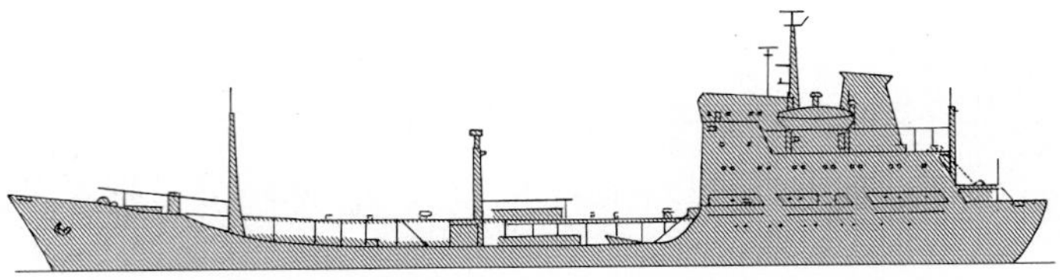

414 *MNMFN H13*
CAPARELI Ma/Fi (Rauma-Repola) 1967; Tk; 3,468 grt/5,042 dwt; 106.15 × 6.74 m *(348.26 × 22.11 ft)*; M (B&W); 13.25 kts; ex-*Aktau*
Sisters (some have a bipod mast foreward and some have a modified funnel with deflector - see number 2/417): **AKTYUBINSK** (Ru); **AMGUN** (Ru); **ADIGENI** (Uk); **ARLET** (Ma) ex-*Anakliya*; **AKHALTSIKHE** (Gi); **ARARAT** (Ru); **AINAZI** (La) ex-*Aynazhi*; **AYON** (Ru); **ANTARES** (Ru); **ABAVA** (La); **ANYUY** (Ru); **ARIAN** (Ma) ex-*Aspindza*; **RAUMA** (Ru); **ZALGIRIS** (Pa) ex-*Zhalgiris*; **ZUGDIDI** (Ho); **NEFTEGORSK** (Ru); **DEBRECENAS** (Lt) ex-*Debretsen*; **NEFTEKAMSK** (Ru); **RUMBULA** (La); **SAKHALINNEFT** (Ru)

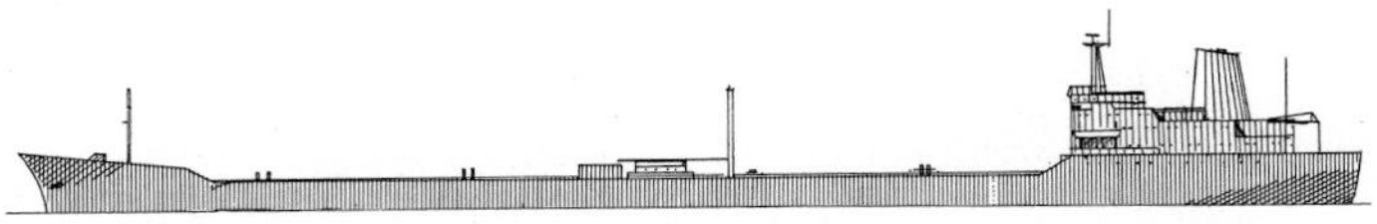

415 *MNMFN H13*
DEMOS Pa/Ne (Giessen-De Noord) 1975; Tk; 30,694 grt/56,050 dwt; 210.32 × 12.41 m *(690.01 × 40.71 ft)*; M (B&W); 16.75 kts; ex-*Cyclops*
Sister: **NUNKI** (It) ex-*Clytoneus*; Probable sister: **ASCOT** (Li) launched as *Hellespont Argosy*

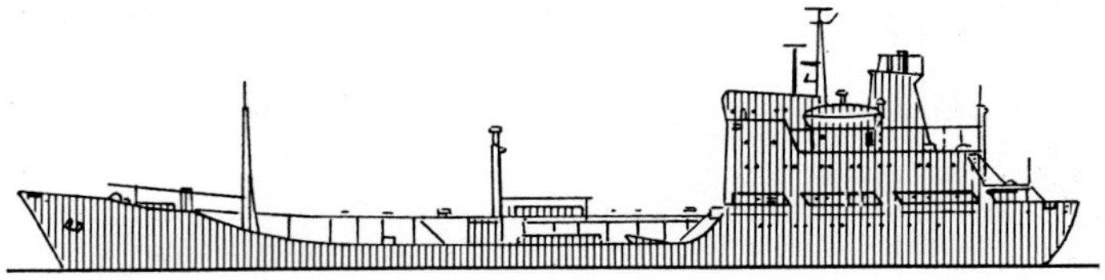

416 *MNMFN H13*
DIANA SV/Fi (Rauma-Repola) 1970; Tk; 3,585 grt/4,976 dwt; 106.15 × 6.74 m *(348.26 × 22.11 ft)*; M (B&W); 13.50 kts; ex-*Auseklis*; Ice strengthened; May be others in this class with modified funnel—see entry number 2/415
Sister: **SIRENE** (SV) ex-*Autse*

417 *MNMFN H13*
DITAS Tu/Tu (Sedef); Tk; 8,763 grt/15,092 dwt; 143.11 × 7.34 m *(469.52 × 24.08 ft)*; M (Sulzer); 13.50 kts

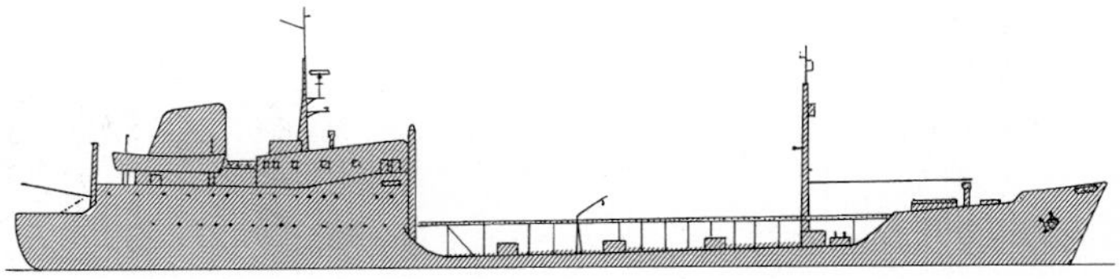

418 *MNMFN H13*
DIVNOGORSK Ru/Pd ('Komuny Paryskiej') 1962; Tk; 1,333 grt/1,344 dwt; 75.62 × 4.74 m *(248.1 × 15.55 ft)*; M (Sulzer); 12.5 kts; 'B-74' type
Sister: **PLAYA DUABA** (Cu) ex-*Ogre*

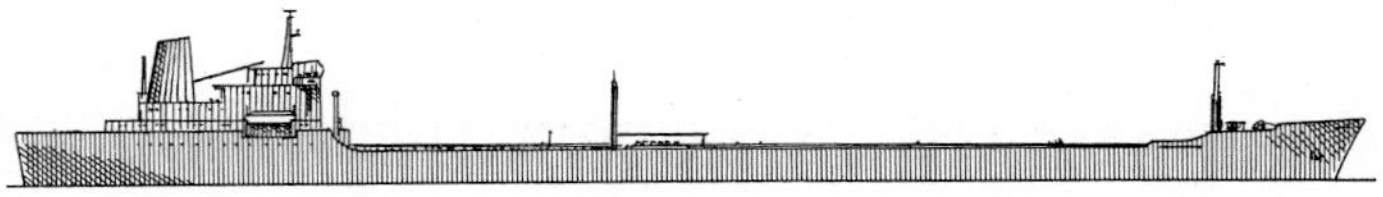

419 *MNMFN H13*
GEBZE Tu/Ca (Saint John SB) 1975; Tk; 20,940 grt/38,987 dwt; 191.57 × 11.25 m *(628.51 × 36.91 ft)*; M (Sulzer); 15.5 kts; ex-*Esso Everett*; 'M' aft is on starboard side
Sisters: **ENIAS** (Cy) ex-*Esso Providence*; **ARISTON** (Cy) ex-*Esso Saint Petersburg*; **ESSO SANTA CRUZ** (Li) ex-*Esso Toronto*; **IRVING ARCTIC** (Ca); Possible sisters: **IRVING ESKIMO** (Ca); **IRVING OCEAN** (Bb)

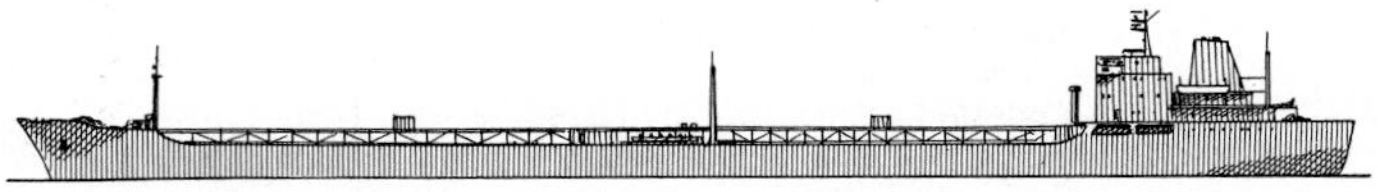

420 *MNMFN H13*
KUTAISI Gi/Ys ('Split') 1976; Tk; 13,598 grt/24,000 dwt; 182.99 × 10 m *(600.36 × 32.81 ft)*; M (MAN); 17 kts; ex-*Kutaisi*
Sister: **SUKHUMI** (Ma)

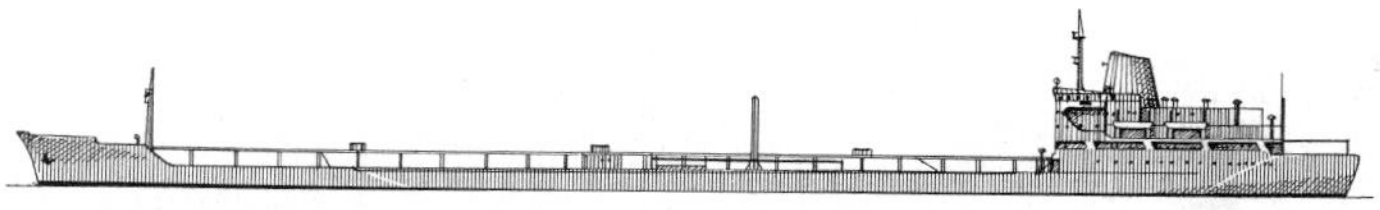

421 *MNMFN H13*
LING HU RC/Sw (Sorviks) 1965; Tk; 36,547 grt/64,719 dwt; 236.1 × 12.68 m *(774.61 × 41.6 ft)*; M (B&W); 16 kts; ex-*Minoru*

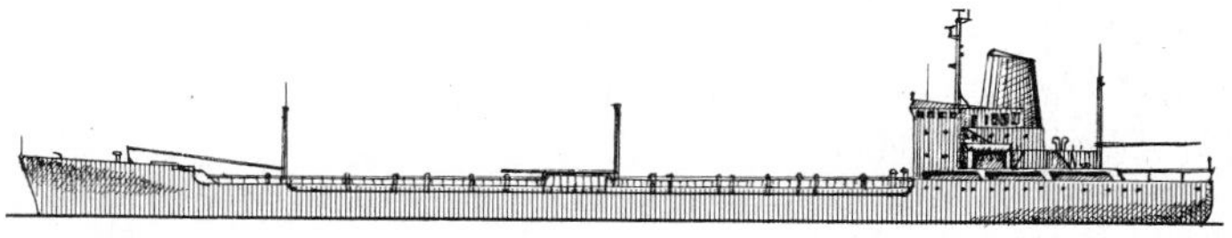

422 *MNMFN H13*
MANUEL AVILA COMACHO Me/Ne ('De Hoop') 1973; Tk; 14,750 grt/21,705 dwt; 170.69 × 9.48 m *(560.01 × 31.1 ft)*; M (Sulzer); — kts
Sisters: **INDEPENDENCIA** (Me); **REFORMA** (Me); **REVOLUCION** (Me); **MARIANO MOCTEZUMA** (Me); **FRANCISCO J MUGICA** (Me)

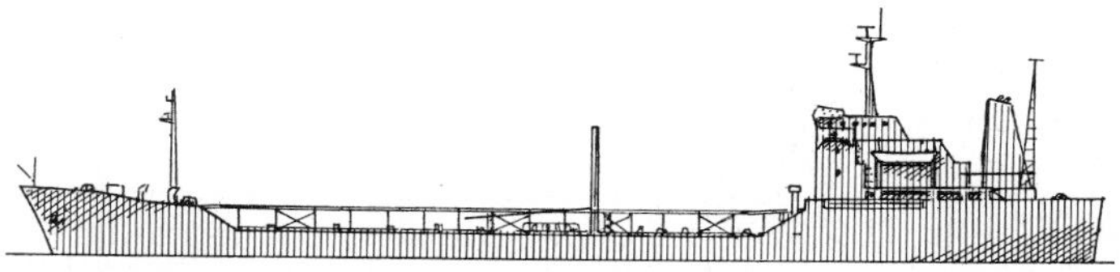

423 *MNMFN H13*
MASSA Mo/Ja (Naikai) 1978; Tk; 4,485 grt/7,538 dwt; 114.8 × 6.6 m *(376.64 × 21.65 ft)*; M (Daihatsu); 13 kts

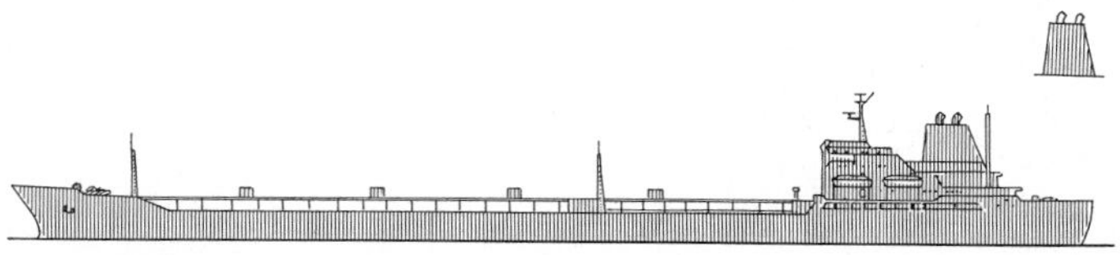

424 *MNMFN H13*
MATE ZALKA Cy/Ys ('3 Maj') 1976; Tk; 25,679 grt/40,030 dwt; 195 × 12.2 m *(639.76 × 40.03 ft)*; M (Sulzer); 17 kts
Sisters (some have taller funnel): **ANTONIO GRAMSI** (La) ex-*Antonio Gramsci*; **PABLO NERUDA** (La); **DAVIDS SIKEIROSS** (La) ex-*David Siqueiros*; **VIKTORIO KODOVILJA** (La) ex-*Viktorio Codovilla*; **ZAKS DIKLO** (La) ex-*Jaques Duclos*; **DZONS RIDS** (La) ex-*John Reed*; **HOSE MARTI** (La) ex-*Jose Marti*; **POLS ROBSONS** (La) ex-*Paul Robeson*; **KLEMENTS GOTVALDS** (La) ex-*Klement Gottwald*; **LIELUPE** (La) ex-*Sukhe Bator*

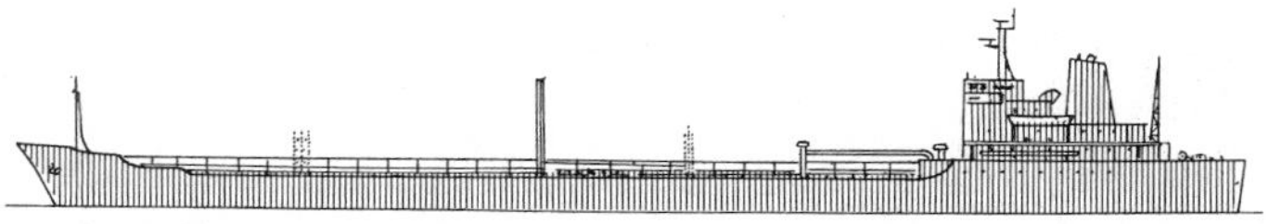

425 *MNMFN H13*
MATSUKAZE Ja/Ja (Mie) 1981; Tk/Ch; 10,795 grt/17,676 dwt; 149.61 × 8.65 m *(491 × 28.38 ft)*; M (Mitsubishi); 13.5 kts

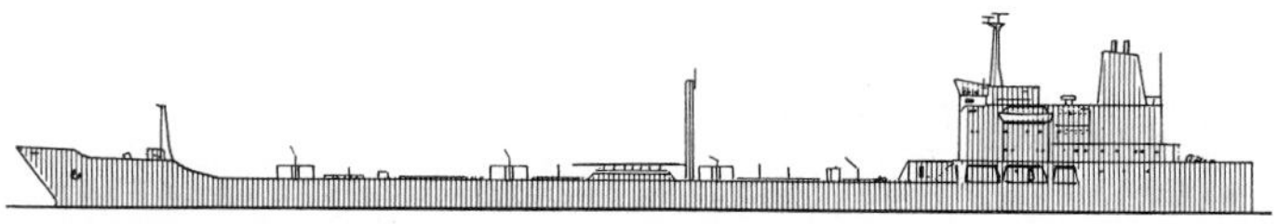

426 *MNMFN H13*
MAYKOP Ma/Br (Swan Hunter) 1975; Tk; 17,824 grt/32,039 dwt; 171 × 11.3 m *(561 × 37.07 ft)*; M (Sulzer); 15 kts; Launched as *Helena K*
Sisters: **APSHERON** (Ma) Launched as *Robkap II*; **GROZNY** (Ma) Launched as *Robkap 1*; **GUDERMES** (Ma) Launched as *Robkap IV*; **MAKHACHKALA** (Ma) Launched as *Robkap III*; **QUIRIQUIRE** (Ve) ex-*Lagoven Quiriquire*; **SANTA RITA** (Ve) ex-*Lagoven Santa Rita*; Similar (lifeboat lower and further aft and so on): **VISHWADOOT** (In) Launched as *Ingram Osprey*

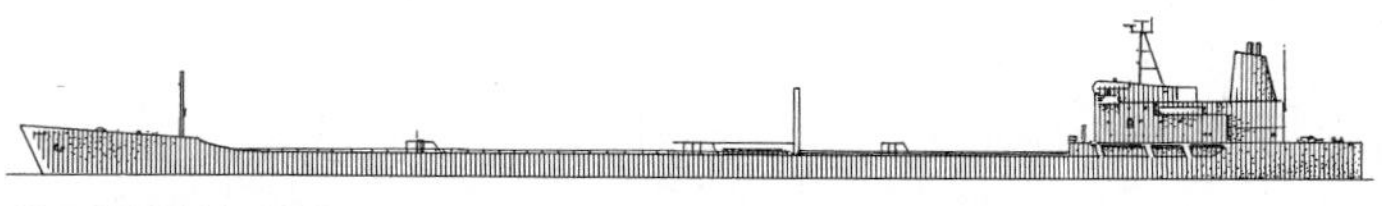

427 *MNMFN H13*
MONTE CHIARO It/Br (Swan Hunter) 1972; Tk; 19,083 grt/32,531 dwt; 192.01 × 10.38 m *(629.95 × 34.05 ft)*; M (Sulzer); 16 kts; ex-*Joseph R Smallwood*
Sisters: **XIANG HAI** (RC) ex-*Strait of Canso*; **SEABRAVERY** (Ma) ex-*Kurdistan*; ex-*Frank D Moores*; Probable sister: **TRANSPORTER LT** (Cy) ex-*Hindustan*

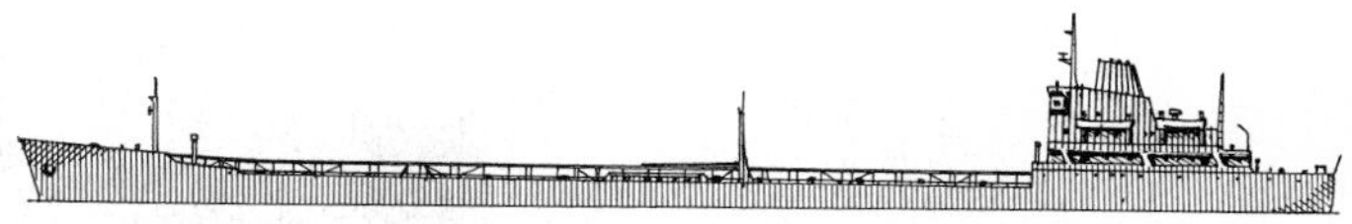

428 *MNMFN H13*
NORDIC VOYAGER NIS/Sw (Lindholmens) 1968; Tk; 10,504 grt/18,797 dwt; 162.67 × 8.87 m *(533.69 × 29.1 ft)*; M (Pielstick); 16.25 kts; ex-*Esso Slagen*

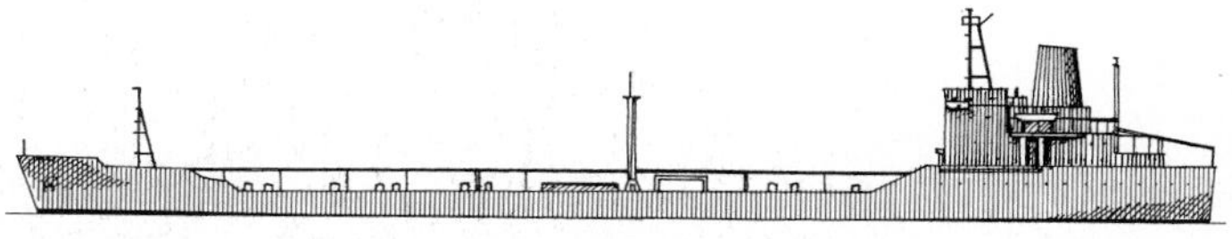

429 *MNMFN H13*
OCEAN TRADER Sg/De (Nakskov) 1974; Tk; 15,162 grt/26,908 dwt; 170.69 × 10.42 m *(560.01 × 34.19 ft)*; M (B&W); 15 kts; ex-*Neptune Aries*
Sister: **OCEAN CORAL** (Sg) ex-*Neptune Orion*

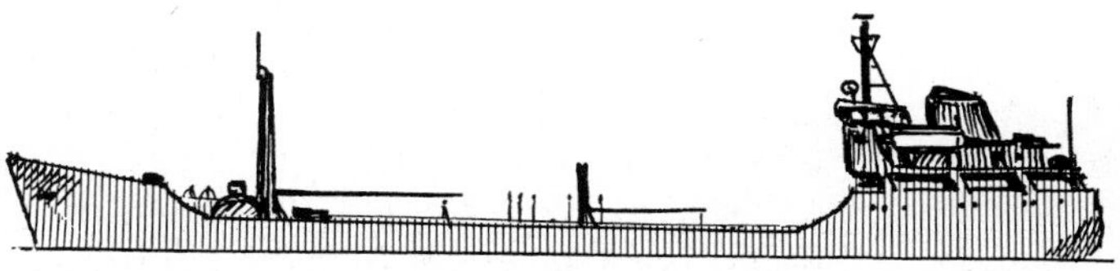

430 *MNMFN H13*
RADWAH Si/No (Fredriksstad) 1966; Tk/LGC; 3,392 grt/5,131 dwt; 103.66 × 5.93 m *(340.09 × 19.49 ft)*; TSM (Sulzer); — kts; ex-*Texaco Puerto Rico*

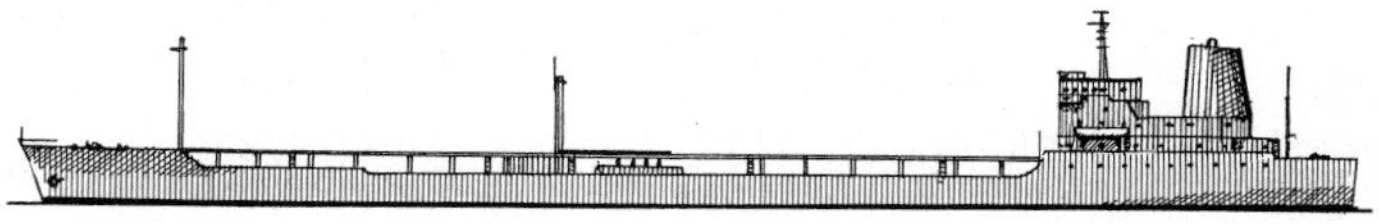

431 *MNMFN H13*
SANTA BARBARA Ma/Gr (Hellenic) 1974; Tk; 17,211 grt/31,127 dwt; 170.62 × 11.02 m *(559.78 × 36.15 ft)*; M (Sulzer); 15 kts; ex-*World Promise*
Sisters: **SEACAPTAIN** (Ma) ex-*World Prospector*; **CAPRICORN** (Ma) ex-*World Provider*; **GIOVANNA** (Ma) ex-*World Prospect*; **NAND PRAKRITI** (In) ex-*Team Gerwi*

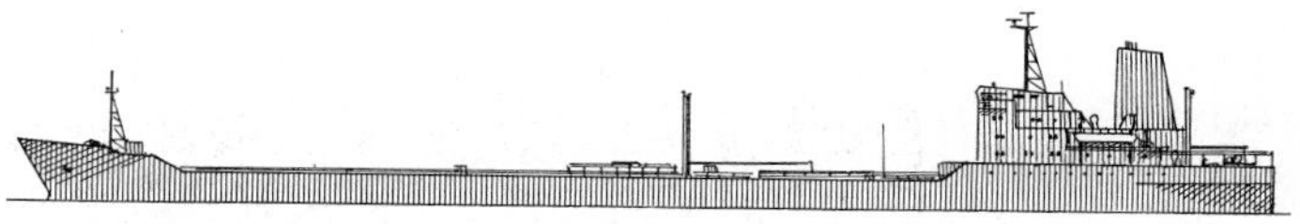

432 *MNMFN H13*
SEAFORTUNE Ma/Be (Boelwerf) 1975; Tk/Ch; 17,841 grt/32,214 dwt; 170.69 × 11.41 m *(560 × 37.43 ft)*; M (B&W); 15.75 kts; ex-*Maaskade*
Sisters: **VERDI** (Ma) ex-*Maaskant*; **SANTA ESMERALDA** (Ma) ex-*Maaskerk*; **SAINT NICHOLAS** (Ma) ex-*Maaskroon*

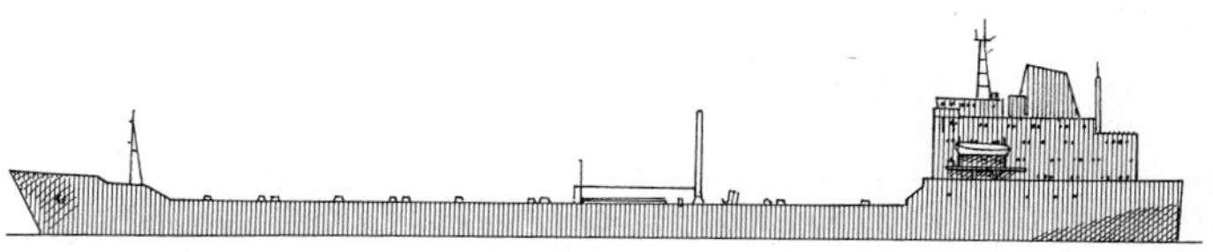

433 *MNMFN H13*
SILINA NIS/De (Nakskov) 1977; Tk; 19,462 grt/33,401 dwt; 170.69 × 11.59 m *(560 × 38.02 ft)*; M (B&W); 15.25 kts; ex-*Panama*
Sisters: **SILVERA** (NIS) ex-*Paranagua*; **OCEAN SAPPHIRE** (Sg) ex-*Pattaya*

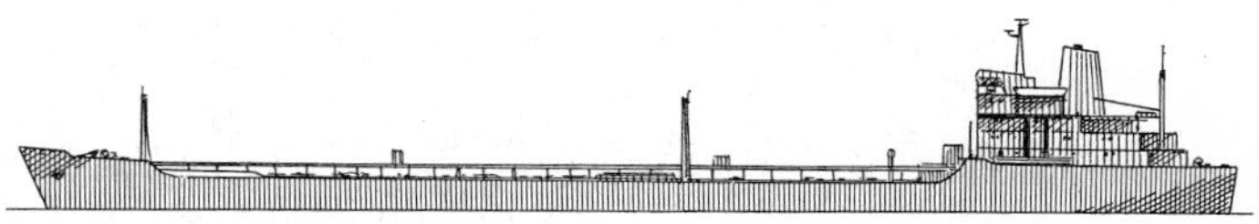

434 *MNMFN H13*
TIMUR MERCURY Bs/Ko (Korea SB) 1974; Tk; 13,439 grt/21,216 dwt; 171.05 × 9.99 m *(561.19 × 32.78 ft)*; M (GMT); 15.5 kts; ex-*Afran Mercury*
Sister: **THORSTREAM** (Li) ex-*Afran Venus*; Probably similar (larger): **OCEAN JUPITER** (Sg) ex-*Afran Jupiter*; **JIAN CHI** (RC) ex-*Golden Crane*; **DIAN CHI** (RC) Launched as *Sweet Briar*; Similar (lower boat deck and so on): **CASTOR** (Cy) ex-*Prima*

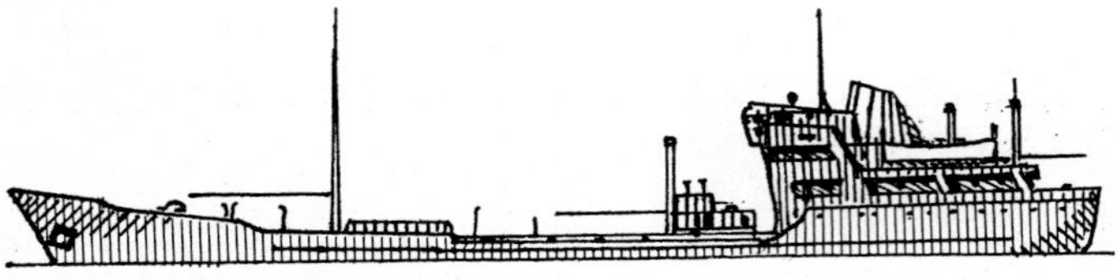

435 *MNMFN H13*
TSIMISARAKA Mg/It (INMA) 1966; Tk; 1,599 grt/2,337 dwt; 84.49 × 4.78 m *(277.2 × 15.68 ft)*; TSM (Deutz); 12 kts

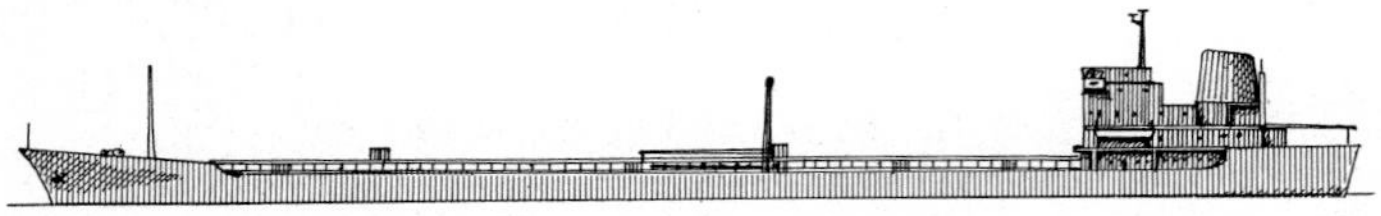

436 *MNMFN H13*
TUSCANIA It/Br (Doxford & S) 1969; Tk; 14,057 grt/25,380 dwt; 169.78 × 9.75 m *(557.02 × 31.99 ft)*; M (Doxford); 15.5 kts; ex-*Laurelwood*

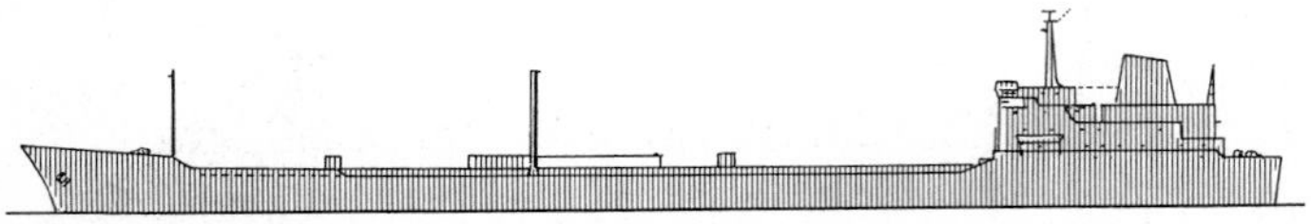

437 *MNMFN H13*
URZHUM Cy/Gr (Hellenic) 1983; Tk; 17,199 grt/29,990 dwt; 170.69 × 10.76 m *(560 × 35.3 ft)*; M (B&W); 16 kts
Sisters: **DZERZHINSK** (Cy); **JAG PRAJA** (In) Launched as *World Product*; **JAG PRAYOG** (In) ex-*Stavropol*; **ULYANOVSK** (Cy); **WORLD PROCESS** (Gr); **WORLD PRODUCE** (Gr); **WORLD PROLOGUE** (Gr); **WORLD PROPHET** (Gr); **WORLD PRODIGY** (Gr)

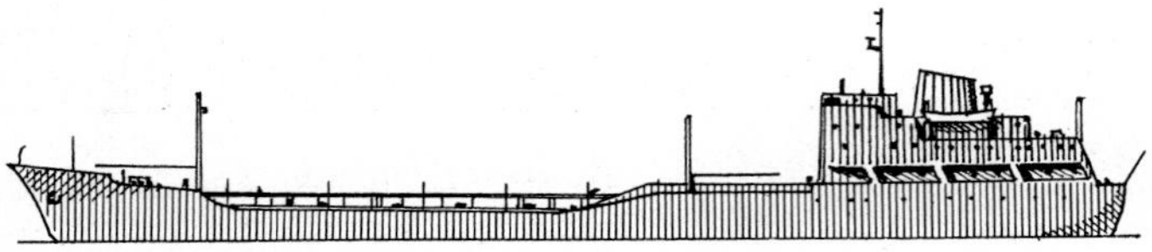

438 *MNMFN H13*
WAN TAI RC/Br (Burntisland) 1966; Tk; 3,721 grt/5,334 dwt; 111.74 × 7.32 m *(366.6 × 24.02 ft)*; M (B&W); 15.5 kts; ex-*Olau Leif*

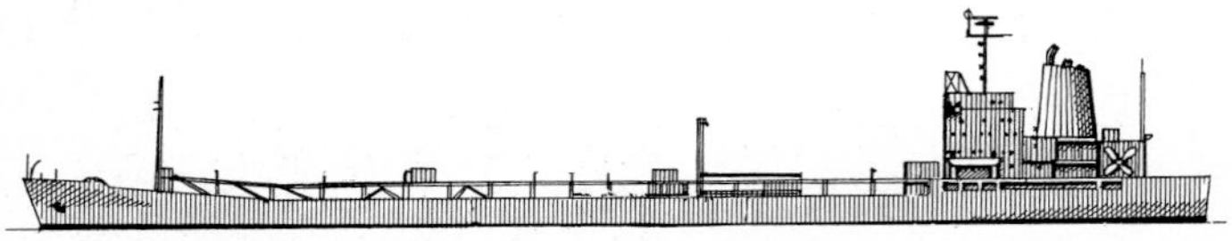

439 *MNMFN H3*
DIRK JACOB Pa/Ne (Verolme Scheeps) 1976; Tk; 18,302 grt/33,788 dwt; 170.69 × 11.85 m *(560.06 × 38.88 ft)*; M (Sulzer); 16 kts
Sisters: **ORANGE STAR** (NIS) ex-*Gertrud Jacob*; **ERIKA JACOB** (Pa) Launched as *Protan Maas*

440 *MNMFNM H1*
KNOCK BUIE Li/Ja (NKK) 1975; Tk; 71,176 grt/135,015 dwt; 266 × 16.99 m *(872.7 × 55.74 ft)*; M (Sulzer); 15.75 kts; ex-*Polartank*; 'M' aft is on port side
Possibly similar: **HALUL** (Qt) Launched as *North Monarch*; **JANE STOVE** (NIS)

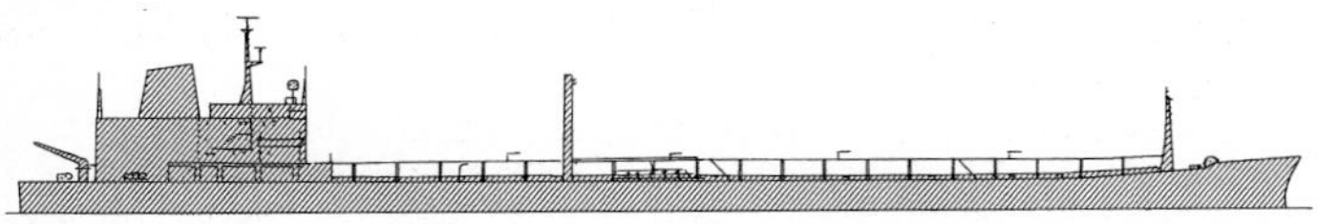

441 *MNMFNR H*
KESTREL Li/Br (Cammell Laird); Tk; 32,995 grt/56,963 dwt; 210 × 12.36 m *(688.98 × 40.55 ft)*; M (Sulzer); 15 kts; ex-*Scottish Lion*; 'StaT 55' type
Sister: **GUI HE** (RC) ex-*Scottish Eagle*

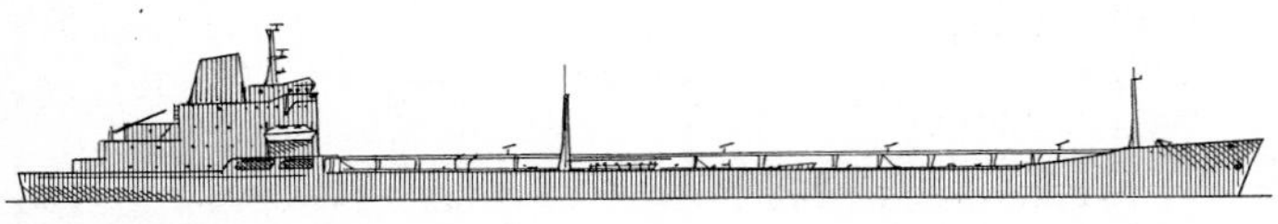

442 *MNMFNR H1*
QUEBEC Bs/Ca (Davie SB) 1977; Tk; 22,138 grt/39,728 dwt; 182.81 × 11.42 m *(599.77 × 37.47 ft)*; M (Sulzer); 15.5 kts; ex-*Athelmonarch*

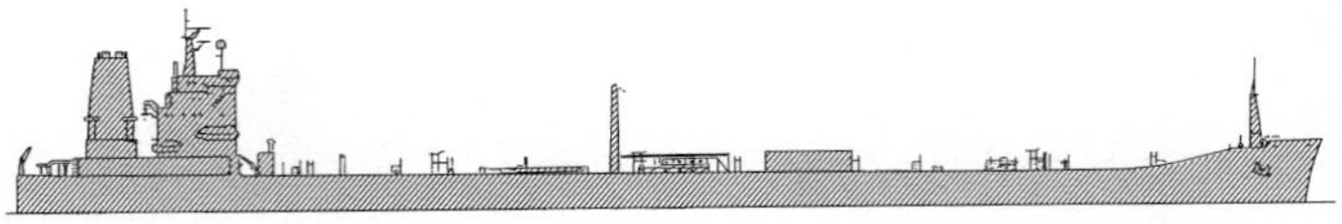

443 *MNMFR H*
IST Li/Ys ('Uljanik') 1986; Tk; 46,632 grt/82,252 dwt; 210.50 × 12.65 m *(690.62 × 41.50 ft)*; M (B&W); 14.5 kts
Sister: **SILBA** (Li)

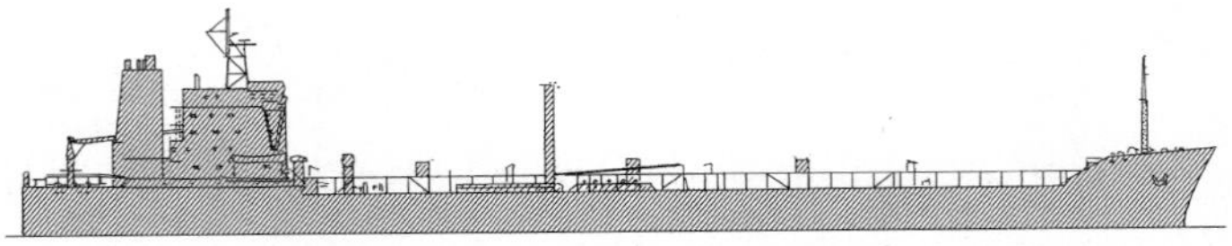

444 *MNMFR H1*
COUNT Bs/FRG (Flender) 1980; Tk/Ch; 24,574 grt/42,861 dwt; 176.18 × 12.02 m *(578.02 × 39.44 ft)*; M (MAN); 15 kts; ex-*Brigitte Jacob*
Sister: **TANJA JACOB** (Tv)

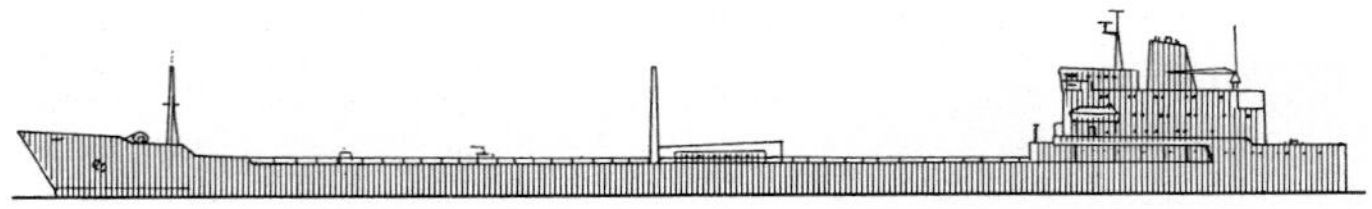

445 *MNMFR H13*
ARALDA It/No (Ankerlokken) 1976; Tk; 17,709 grt/31,543 dwt; 170.31 × 10.08 m *(558.76 × 33.07 ft)*; M (B&W); 14 kts; ex-*Sagona*

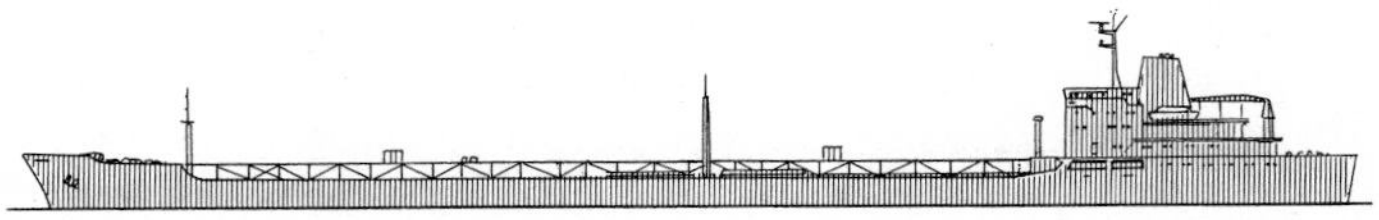

446 *MNMFR H13*
ASHKHABAD Ru/Ys ('Split') 1978; Tk; 15,591 grt/23,900 dwt; 183.01 × 10 m *(601 × 32.81 ft)*; M (B&W); 16.75 kts
Sisters: **TUAPSE** (Ru); **LIPETSK** (Ru)

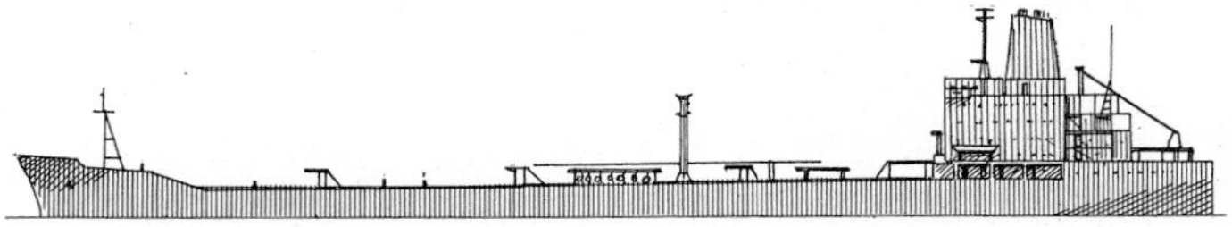

447 *MNMFR H13*
ROBERTA D'ALESIO It/No (Kaldnes) 1973; Tk; 19,113 grt/32,056 dwt; 170.54 × 11.75 m *(559.51 × 38.55 ft)*; M (B&W); 15.5 kts; ex-*Gudrun Maersk*
Sisters: **SEALORD** (Ma) ex-*Gjertrud Maersk*; **MERIOM STAR** (Ma) ex-*Grete Maersk*; **ASPHALT CHAMPION** (Gr) ex-*Gunvor Maersk*

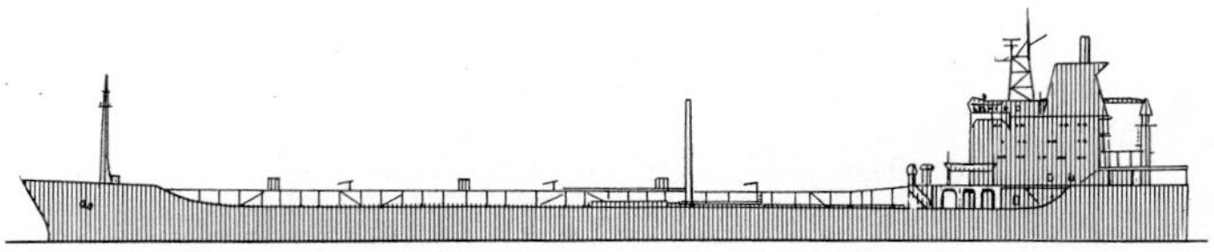

448 *MNMFR H13*
ST MICHAELIS Gr/FRG (A G 'Weser') 1981; Tk; 25,117 grt/45,574 dwt; 182.96 × 12.09 m *(600 × 39.67 ft)*; M (MAN); 14.5 kts; 'R' aft is on starboard side
Sisters: **ST NIKOLAI** (Gr); **MARIETTA C** (Gr) ex-*St Petri*

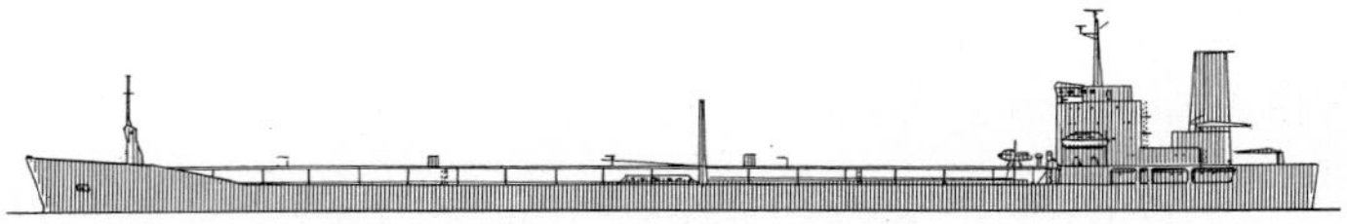

449 *MNMFR H13*
UNITED TRITON NIS/No (Horten) 1981; Tk; 29,874 grt/55,406 dwt; 207.42 × 12.6 m *(681 × 41.34 ft)*; M (Sulzer); 15.5 kts; ex-*Ragnhild Brovig*
Sisters: **UNITED SUNRISE** (NIS) ex-*Barbara Brovig*; **UNITED MOONLIGHT** (Sw) ex-*Randi Brovig*

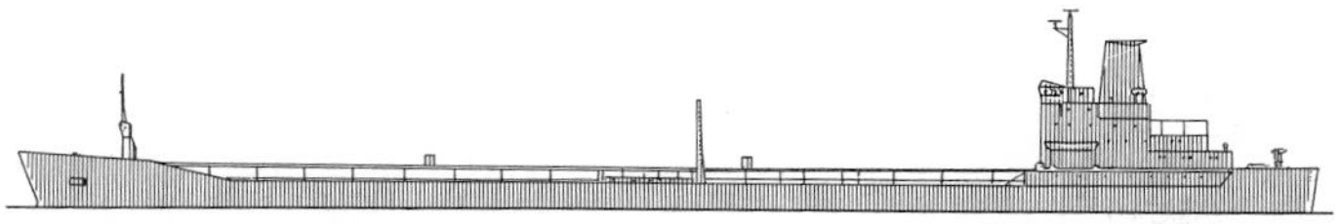

450 *MNMFS*
GEROI SEVASTOPOLYA Ru/No (Horten) 1979; Tk; 28,259 grt/55,870 dwt; 207.43 × 12.65 m *(680.54 × 41.50 ft)*; M (Sulzer); 15.20 kts; ex-*Viking Gull*
Sisters: **GEROI CHERNOMORYA** (Ru) ex-*Viking Tern*; **GEROI NOVOROSSIYSKA** (Ru) ex-*Viking Snipe*; Similar: **SEBASTIAN LERDO DE TEJADA** (Me) ex-*Viken Vest*; **18 DE MARZO** (Me)

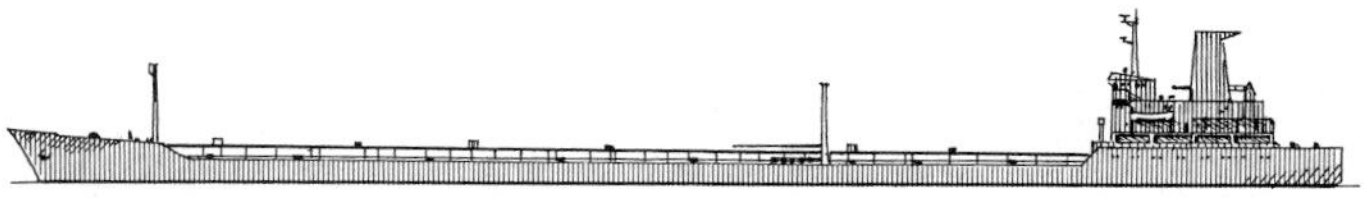

451 *MNMFS H13*
DAN Ma/Ne (Wilton-Fije) 1973; Tk; 17,252 grt/30,615 dwt; 188.2 × 10.36 m *(617.45 × 33.99 ft)*; M (Gotaverken); 14.5 kts; ex-*Okturus*
Sister: **FLORIDA EXPRESS** (Bs) ex-*Oktavius*

452 *MNMFS H13*
PETRO MERSEY Br/Br (Cammell Laird) 1972; Tk; 11,898 grt/20,510 dwt; 166.5 × 9.21 m *(546.26 × 30.22 ft)*; M (Pielstick); 15.5 kts; ex-*Esso Mersey*
Sisters: **PETRO CLYDE** (Br) ex-*Esso Clyde*; **PETRO SEVERN** (Br) ex-*Esso Severn*

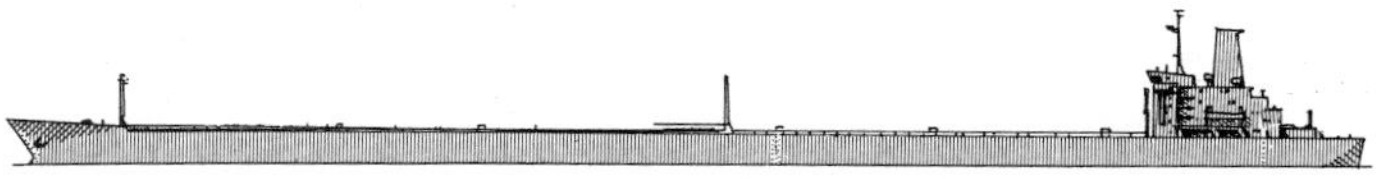

453 *MNMG H*
ISABELLA Gr/Sp ('Astano') 1976; Tk; 132,107 grt/272,495 dwt; 344.33 × 20.1 m *(1,129.69 × 65.94 ft)*; T (Kawasaki); 15.5 kts; ex-*Carthago-Nova*
Similar: **GALP FUNCHAL** (Bs) ex-*Munguia*

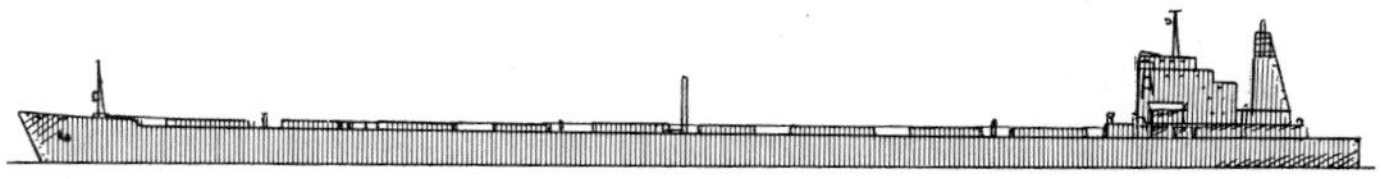

454 *MNMG H*
KLEOVOULOS OF RHODES Cy/Sw (Gotav) 1974; OBO; 60,169 grt/123,768 dwt; 256.85 × 17.07 m *(842.68 × 56 ft)*; M (B&W); 15.25 kts; ex-*Oslo*; Has now been converted to a bulk carrier, so hose-handling derricks may have been removed
Sisters: **JAHRE ROSE** (NIS) ex-*Angelic Blessing*; **GOLDEN CAPE** (—) ex-*Angelic Harmony*; **AKOVA** (Tu) ex-*Bjorgholm*; **ADALYA** (Tu) ex-*Havprins*; **TAHIR KAPTAN** (Tu) ex-*Jag Laxmi*; **JAG LEELA** (In); **MAHARISHI DAYANAND** (In); **MAHARISHI KARVE** (In)

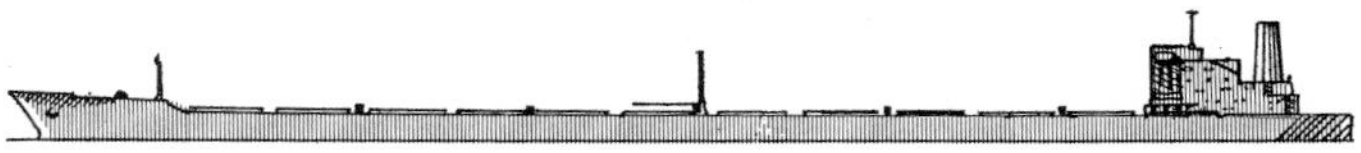

455 *MNMG H1*
ACHILEUS Ma/Sw and Po (Eriksbergs/Lisnave) 1973; OBO; 75,614 grt/156,720 dwt; 291.68 × 17.01 m *(956.96 × 55.77 ft)*; M (B&W); 16.5 kts; ex-*Atland*; Aft section built Sweden; Forward section built Portugal. Now broken up
Sister: **KADIRGA-5** (Tu) ex-*Lappland* (converted to bulk carrier. Hose-handling derricks may be removed)

456 *MNMG H1*
KING ALEXANDER Gr/Sw (Uddevalla) 1978; Tk; 237,768 grt/491,120 dwt; 364.02 × 25.07 m *(1,194.29 × 82.25 ft)*; TST (GEC); 16 kts; ex-*Nanny*

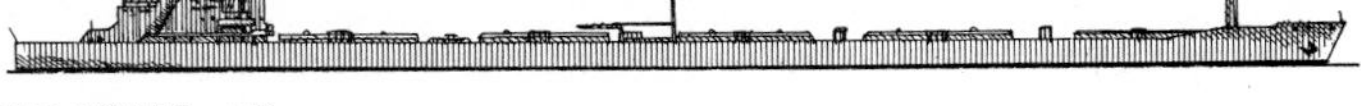

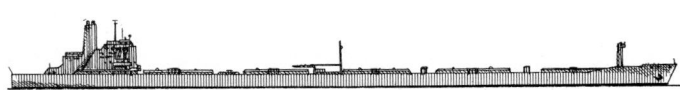

457 *MNMG H1*
NECKAR ORE Li/Sw (Eriksbergs) 1973; OO; 142,543 grt/282,462 dwt; 338.16 × 21.69 m *(1,109.44 × 71.16 ft)*; M (B&W); 15.25 kts; ex-*Svealand*; May have been converted to an ore carrier

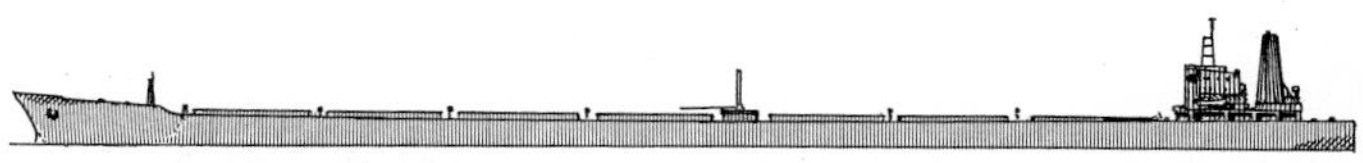

458 *MNMG H1*
WESER ORE Li/Ys ('Uljanik') 1973; OO; 134,366 grt/278,734 dwt; 335.03 × 21.99 m *(1,099.17 × 72.14 ft)*; TSM (B&W); 16.5 kts; ex-*Tarfala*; May have been converted to an ore carrier
Sister: **RHINE ORE** (Li) ex-*Torne*; Similar: **MAIN ORE** (Li) ex-*Mary R Koch*

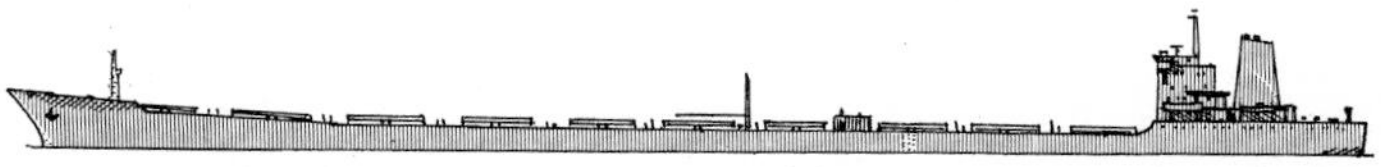

459 *MNMG H13*
BERGE ADRIA NIS/Ys ('Uljanik') 1972; OO; 113,050 grt/227,687 dwt; 314 × 20.42 m *(1,030.18 × 66.99 ft)*; TSM (B&W); 16 kts; Now converted to ore carrier. Hose-handling derricks probably removed

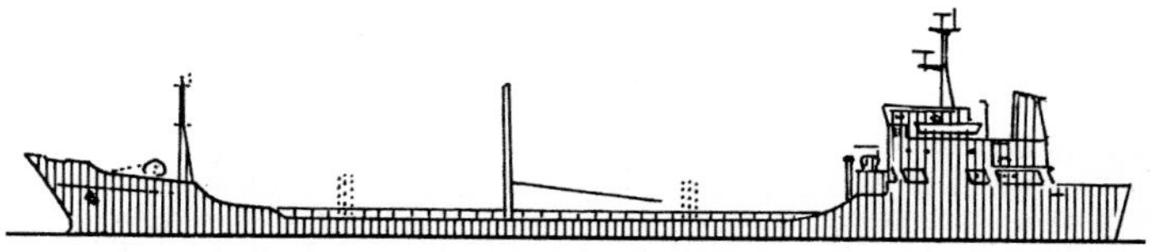

460 *MNMG H13*
IRISHGATE Br/Ja (Kanrei) 1981; Tk; 2,071 grt/3,284 dwt; 93.17 × 5.27 m *(305.68 × 17.29 ft)*; M (MaK); 12.5 kts
Sisters: **EASTGATE** (Br); **NORTHGATE** (Br); **WESTGATE** (Br)

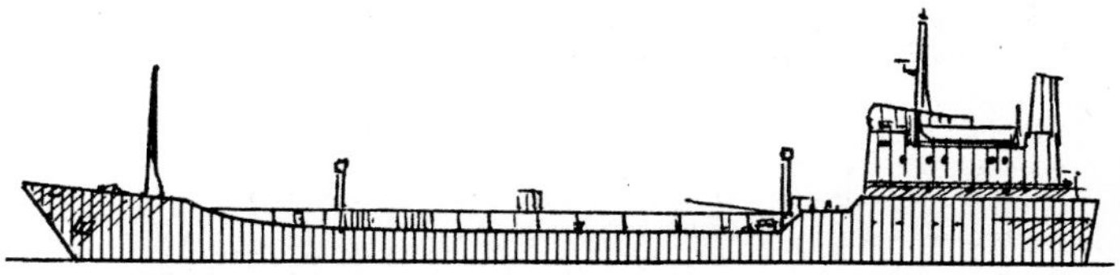

461 *MNMG H13*
MAYONAMI Kn/Sw (Solvesborgs) 1970; Tk; 1,268 grt/2,060 dwt; 75.29 × 3.51 m *(247.01 × 11.52 ft)*; M (Alpha-Diesel); 12.5 kts; ex-*Contank Lubeck*
Similar: **SKY TRADER** (NIS) ex-*Credo*

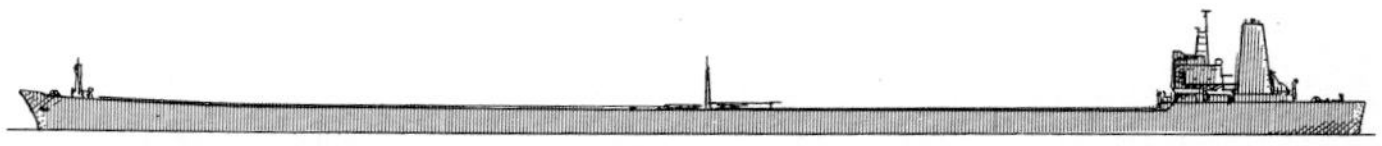

462 *MNMG H3*
KANCHENJUNGA In/Ys ('Uljanik') 1975; Tk; 139,820 grt/276,755 dwt; 332.39 × 21.79 m *(1,090.52 × 71.49 ft)*; TSM (B&W); 17 kts
Sister: **KOYALI** (In); Probable sister: **OLOIBIRI** (Ng)

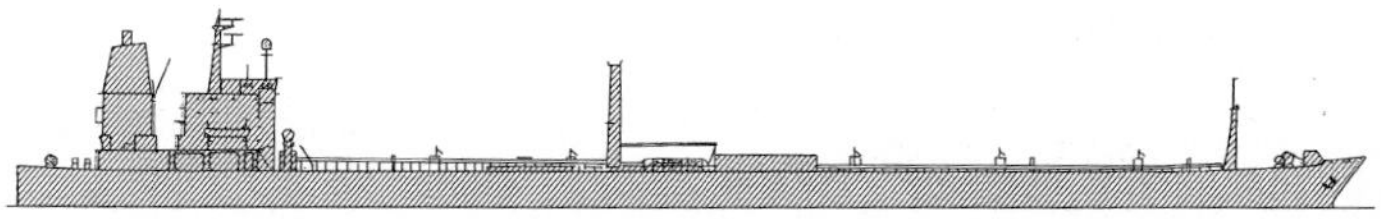

463 *MNM²CF H*
WAPELLO Li/Ja (Sumitomo) 1982; Tk; 41,135 grt/81,283 dwt; 243.21 × 12.16 m *(797.93 × 39.90 ft)*; M (Sulzer); — kts; ex-*Mobil Vanguard*
Sister: **WANETA** (Li) ex-*Mobil Valiant*

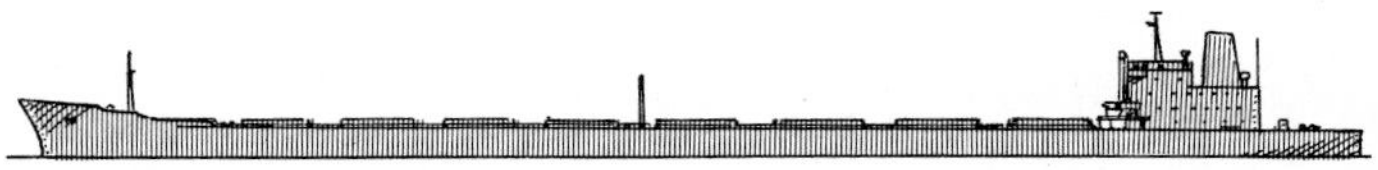

464 *MNM²F H1*
ABANT Tu/Sw (Gotaverken) 1972; OBO; 55,843 grt/105,550 dwt; 256.04 × 15.08 m *(840.03 × 49.48 ft)*; M (B&W); 15.75 kts; ex-*Scandia Team*
Sisters: **LONDON** (Pa) ex-*London Team*; **DIAPOROS** (Gr) ex-*Sevonia Team*; **AGIA THALASSINI** (Ma) ex-*Suecia Team*

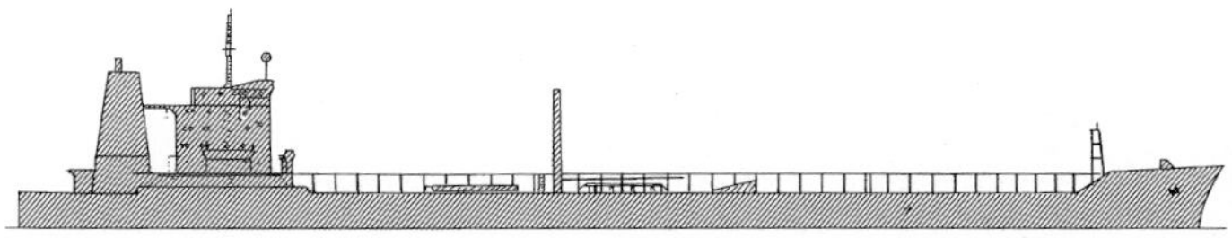

465 *MNM²F H1*
LAMA Ch/Ys ('Jozo Lozovina-Mosor') 1987; Tk; 19,867 grt/40,439 dwt; 175.80 × 11.19 m *(576.77 × 36.71 ft)*; M (B&W); 14.5 kts; ex-*Mosor Challenger*
Probable sister: **AZIJA** (Cy) ex-*Adriatic Star*

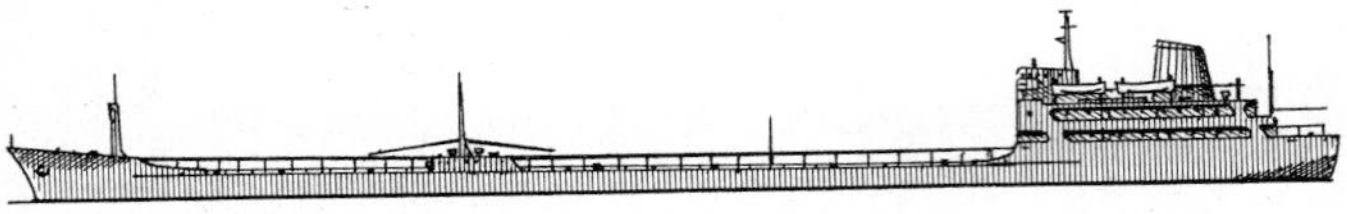

466 *MNM²FM H1*
OKRIKA SUN Li/No (Fredriksstad) 1964; Tk/LGC; 13,034 grt/21,550 dwt; 169.78 × 9.6 m *(557.02 × 31.5 ft)*; M (Gotaverken); 15.75 kts; ex-*Granheim*

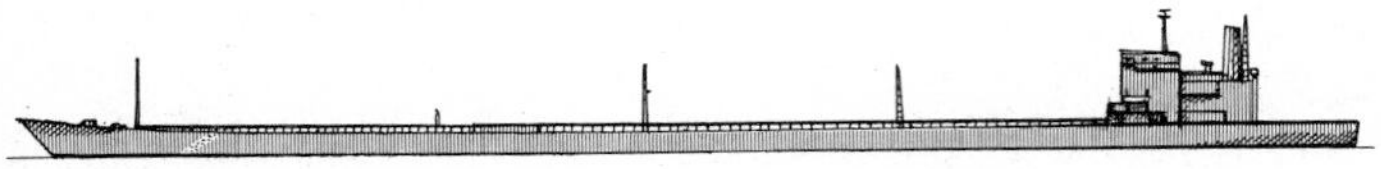

467 *MNM²FN H*
INDEPENDENCE Li/Ja (IHI) 1976; Tk; 132,995 grt/274,774 dwt; 337.02 × 21 m *(1,105.71 × 68.9 ft)*; T (IHI); 16 kts; ex-*Conoco Independence*

468 *MNM²FN H1*
SHIBUMI Ma/Ja (Sumitomo) 1974; Tk; 46,458 grt/89,665 dwt; 241.51 × 14.14 m *(792.35 × 46.39 ft)*; M (Sulzer); 16.5 kts; ex-*Golden Sunray*; Mast between superstructure and funnel is on port side
Sisters: **HELLESPONT COURAGE** (Li) ex-*Canadian Owl*; Sisters (builder-Oshima Z): **ERISSOS** (Cy) ex-*Diana Prosperity*; **PROSPERITY** (Ma) ex-*Judith Prosperity*; **ARAB WANDERER** (Cy) ex-*Hellespont Glory*

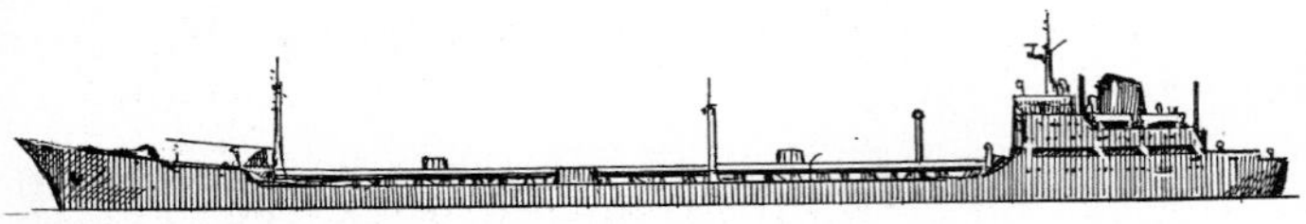

469 *MNM²FN H13*
NOVOKLAV 3 Ru/Ys ('Split') 1965; Tk; 14,286 grt/22,568 dwt; 186.21 × 9.84 m *(610.93 × 32.28 ft)*; M (B&W); 17 kts; ex-*Gori*
Sisters: **NOVOKLAV 4** (Ru) ex-*General Zhdanov*; **NOVOTSAK 2** (Ru) ex-*Marshal Biryuzov*; **NOVOMIR 3** (Ma) ex-*General Karbyshev*; **DMITRIY ZHLOBA** (Ru); **YEPIFAN KOVTYUKH** (Ru); **MITROFAN SEDIN** (Ru); **STEPAN VOSTRETSOV** (Ru); **PYATIDYESYATILYETIYE SOVIETSKOY GRUZII** (also known as **50 LETIYE SOVIETSKOY GRUZII**); **NOVOKLAV 2** (Ru) ex-*Rezekne;* **NOVOMIR 2** (Ru) ex-*General Bocharov*; **NOVOTSAK 1** (Ru) ex-*General Kravtsov*; **NOVOMIR 1** (Ma) ex-*Nikolay Podvoskiy*; **SKIKDA** ex-*Kutaisi* (Ag); **SAETTA** (Ma) ex-*Batumi*

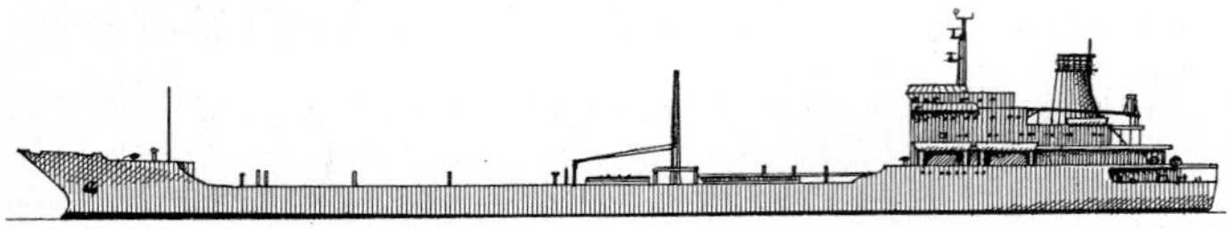

470 *MNMM-FC H12*
KOMANDARM FEDKO Gi/Ru (Kherson) 1976; Tk; 17,824 grt/27,480 dwt; 178.49 × 10.4 m *(585.6 × 34.12 ft)*; M (B&W); 15.25 kts
Sisters: **GENERAL MERKVILADZE** (Gi); **DUBULTI** (La) ex-*General Pliyev*; **KHERSON** (Gi); **TALAVA** (La) ex-*Vsevelod Kochetov*; **ALEKSANDR KORNEYCHUK** (Gi); Probable sisters: **ATHENIAN OLYMPICS** (Cy) ex-*Moscow Olympics*; **ATHENIAN VICTORY** (Cy); **ATHENIAN XENOPHON** (Cy); **CAPTAIN X KYRIAKOU** (Cy); **ATHENIAN THEODORE** (Cy); **ATHENIAN FIDELITY** (Cy); **ATHENIAN BEAUTY** (Cy); **ATHENIAN CHARM** (Cy)

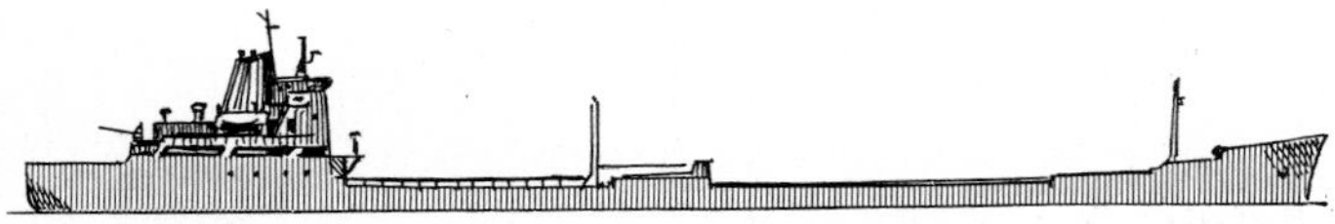

471 *MNMM-FS H13*
PETRO MILFORD HAVEN Br/Sw (Lindholmens) 1968; Tk; 10,631 grt/18,377 dwt; 162.67 × 8.54 m *(533.69 × 28.02 ft)*; M (Pielstick); 16.75 kts; ex-*Esso Milford Haven*
Sister: **PETRO FAWLEY** (Br) ex-*Esso Fawley*

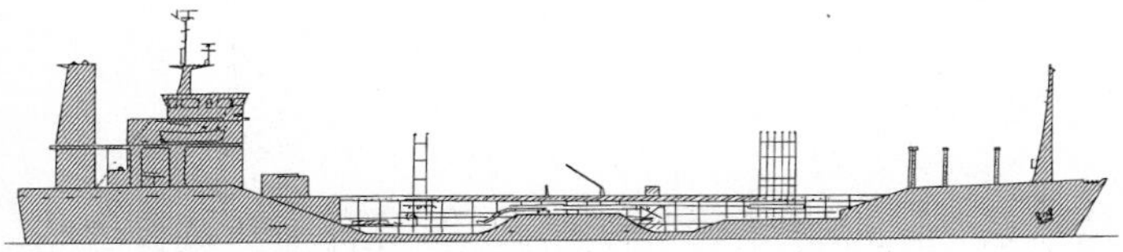

472 *MNMNE²MF H123*
MULTITANK ARMENIA Tv/FRG (Sietas) 1981/86; Ch; 2,780 grt/4,051 dwt; 102.85 × 5.45 m *(337.43 × 17.88 ft)*; M (Alpha); 13.5 kts; Lengthened 1986
Sisters: **MULTITANK ADRIA** (Tv); **MULTITANK ARCADIA** (Tv); **MULTITANK ASCANIA** (Tv)

473 *MNMNF H*
PIVOT Cy/Sp (AESA) 1973; Tk; 109,700 grt/232,104 dwt; 334.02 × 19.94 m *(1,095.87 × 65.42 ft)*; M (B&W); 14 kts; ex-*Amoco Europa*

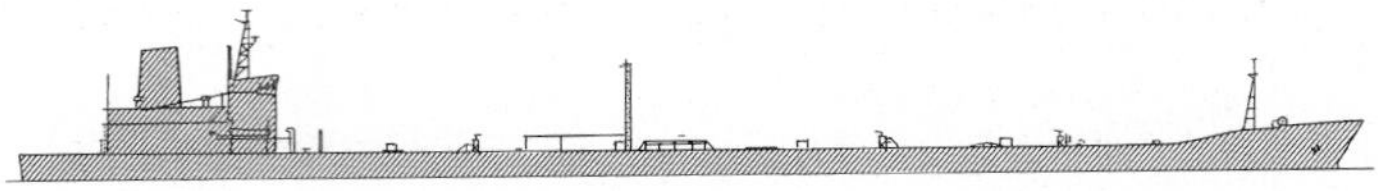

474 *MNMNF H1*
ALANDIA PRIDE Bs/Be (Boelwerf) 1974; Tk; 42,516 grt/83,982 dwt; 253.75 × 13.99 m *(832.51 × 45.90 ft)*; M (MAN); 15.5 kts; ex-*E R Limburgia*
Sisters: **ALANDIA PEARL** (Bs) ex-*E. R. Wallonia*; **YAYA** (Cy) ex-*E R Legia*

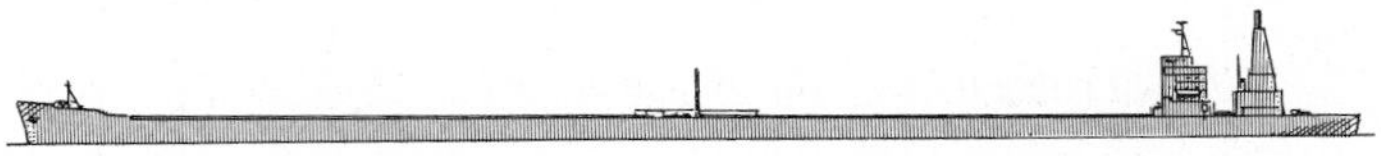

475 *MNMNF H1*
MT. CABRITE Li/Sw (Kockums) 1971; Tk; 122,960 grt/259,447 dwt; 340.52 × 20.07 m *(1,117.1 × 65.8 ft)*; T (Stal-Laval); 16 kts; ex-*Sea Serpent*
Similar: **SAINT LUCIA** (Li) ex-*Sea Swan*

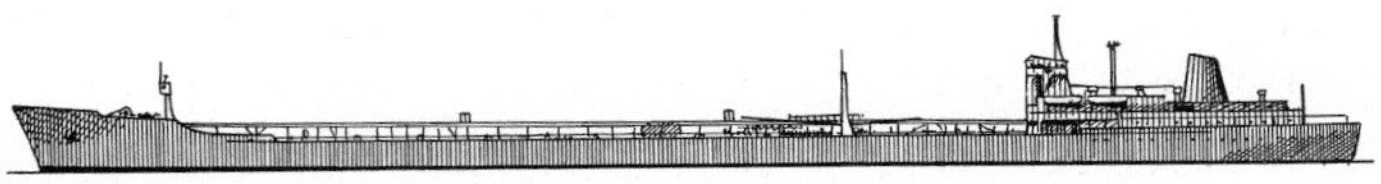

476 *MNMNFN H1*
DA QING 255 RC/Sw (Gotav) 1965; Tk; 29,856 grt/52,525 dwt; 223.45 × 12.64 m *(733.1 × 41.47 ft)*; M (Gotaverken); 15 kts; ex-*Bralinda*

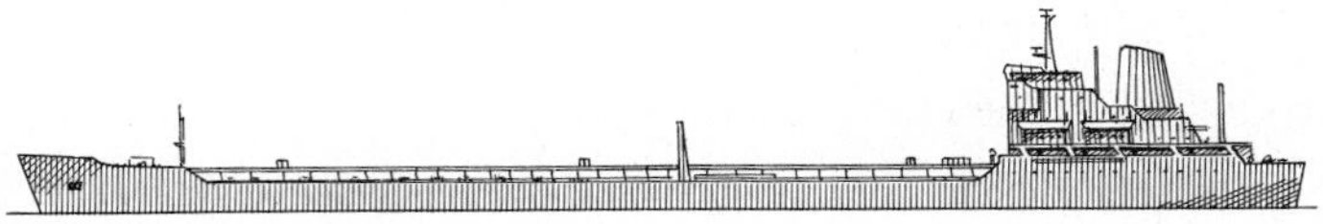

477 *MNMNFN H13*
KOLANDIA In/Ys ('Jozo Lozovina-Mosor') 1976; Tk; 15,045 grt/24,490 dwt; 159.75 × 10.79 m *(524.11 × 35.4 ft)*; M (Sulzer); 15 kts
Sisters: **AUROBINDO** (In); **DADABHAI NAOROJI** (In); **JAINARAYAN VYAS** (In); **RAFI AHMED KIDWAI** (In)

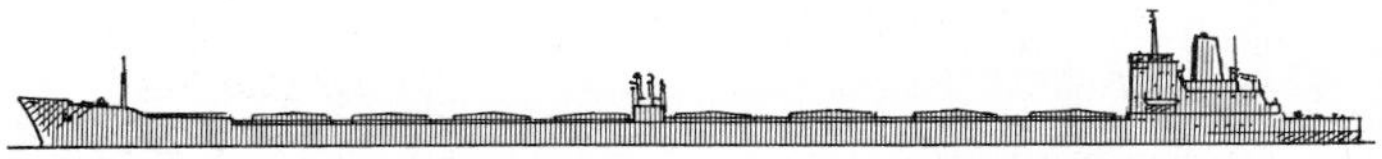

478 *MNMNMFR H1*
ARROW NIKI NIS/Sw (Gotav) 1971; OBO; 56,600 grt/103,739 dwt; 256.55 × 15.11 m *(841.7 × 49.57 ft)*; M (Gotaverken); 16 kts; ex-*A K Fernstrom*

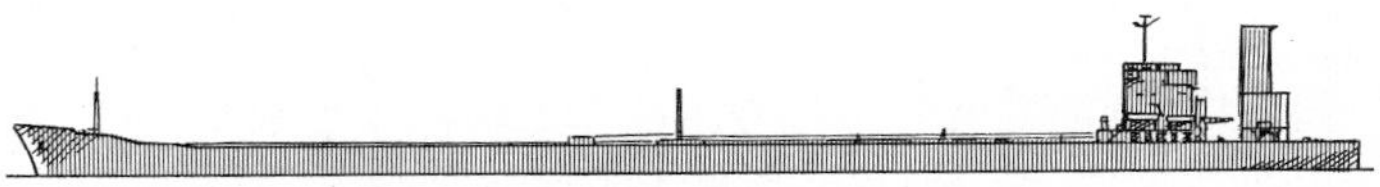

479 *MNMSF H1*
ALADDIN Li/Sw (Gotav) 1974; Tk; 68,885 grt/140,803 dwt; 270.09 × 17.06 m *(886.12 × 55.97 ft)*; M (B&W); 16 kts; ex-*Sydhav*
Sisters: **MEGA POINT** (NIS) ex-*Aino*; **KNOCK DAVIE** (Pa) ex-*Teakwood*; **INTISAR** (Ly) launched as *Mistral*; Similar (larger): **GOLE** (Tu) ex-*Messiniaki Filia*; **ALANDIA FORCE** (Bs) ex-*Messiniaki Floga*; Similar (shortened by 25.51m and other conversion work, may be considerably altered in appearance): **PRINCESS PHAEDRA** (Ma) ex-*Wisa*

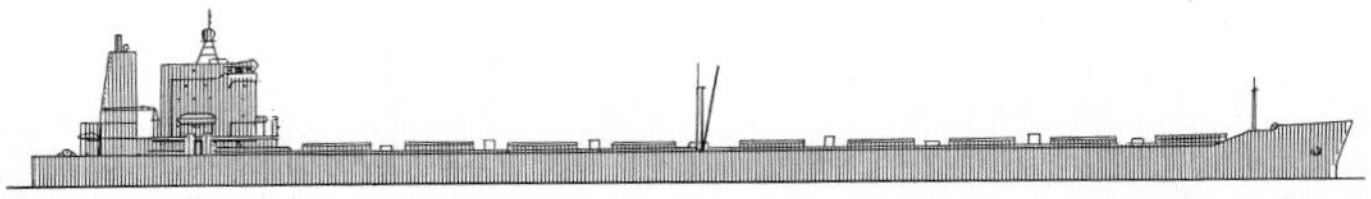

480 *MNMSF H1*
BALEARES NIS/FRG (Bremer V) 1981; OBO; 44,887 grt/75,714 dwt; 240.72 × 14.34 m *(790 × 47.05 ft)*; M (MAN); 15 kts; ex-*Alexander*
Sisters: **BALLENITA** (NIS) ex-*August Thyssen*; **MOSTOLES** (Sp) ex-*Viator*; **BONA FREIGHTER** (NIS) ex-*Siboseven*; **ACINA** (NIS) ex-*Kaszony* (shorter funnel); Possible sisters: **ARIEL** (NIS); **CHEMTRANS BELOCEAN** (Ge) ex-*Belocean*; **HYPHESTOS** (Gr) ex-*Konkar Hyphestos*; **PHAROS** (Ge)

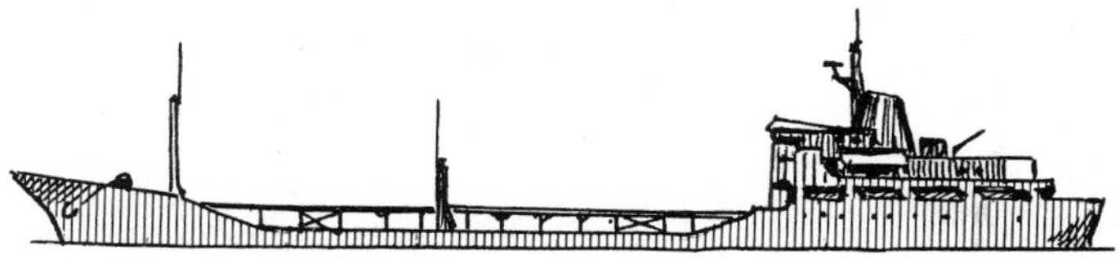

481 *MNM-F*
STAR V SV/FRG (Lindenau) 1969; Tk; 2,211 grt/3,501 dwt; 93.91 × 5.68 m *(308.1 × 18.64 ft)*; M (MAN); 12.5 kts; ex-*Solstreif*

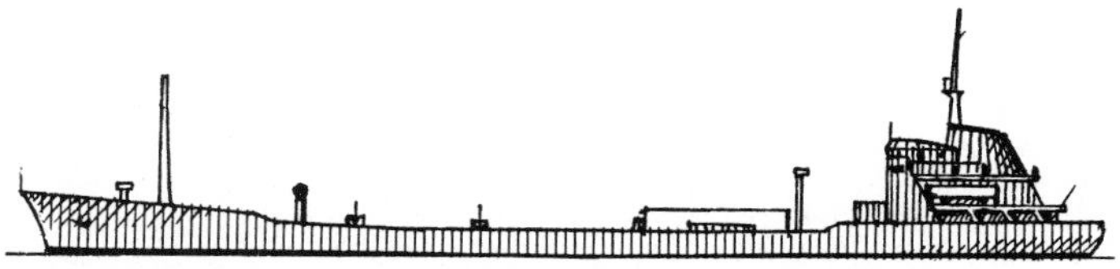

482 *MNM-F H*
AFRICAN HYACINTH SV/FRG (Elsflether) 1970/77; Tk; 1,320 grt/3,191 dwt; 91.17 × 5.2 m *(299.11 × 17.06 ft)*; M (KHD); 12.5 kts; ex-*Oliver*; Lengthened 1977
Sister: **EBELLA** (Ge) ex-*Erik*

483 *MNM-F H123*
NALON SV/Sp (Juliana) 1969; Tk; 4,602 grt/6,574 dwt; 123.68 × 6.04 m *(405.77 × 19.82 ft)*; M (Espanola); 16 kts; ex-*Camponalon*
Sisters: **OCEAN KNIGHT** (SV) ex-*Campodarro;* **DOLPHIN V** (or **DOLPHIN 5**) (Pa) ex-*Campogenil*

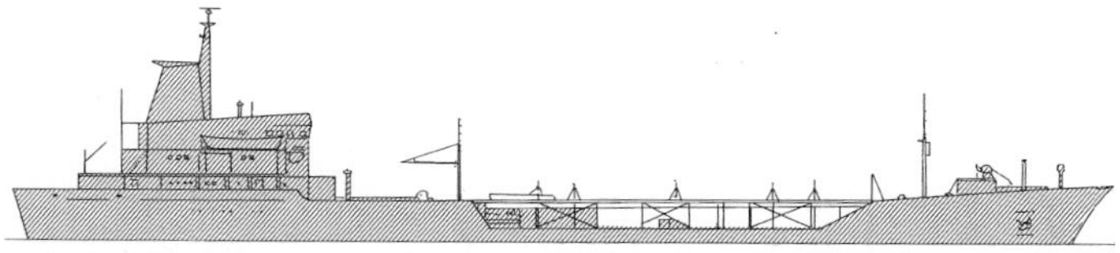

484 *MNM-F H13*
ALFA 1 Ma/FRG (Lindenau) 1971; Tk; 2,091 grt/3,200 dwt; 91.32 × 5.32 m *(299.61 × 17.45 ft)*; M (MaK); 13.5 kts; ex-*Toltek*
Sister: **TINKA** (Pa) ex-*Inka*

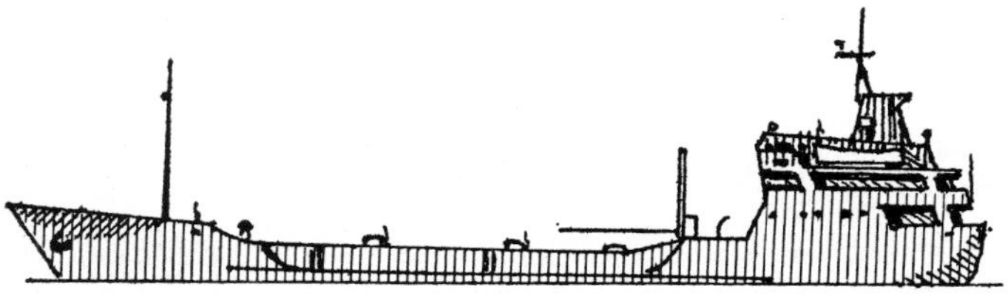

485 *MNM-F H13*
BILALI Gr/Ne (Pattje) 1968; Tk; 494 grt/1,415 dwt; 72.98 × 3.57 m *(239.44 × 11.71 ft)*; M (Atlas-MaK); 12 kts; ex-*Tora*

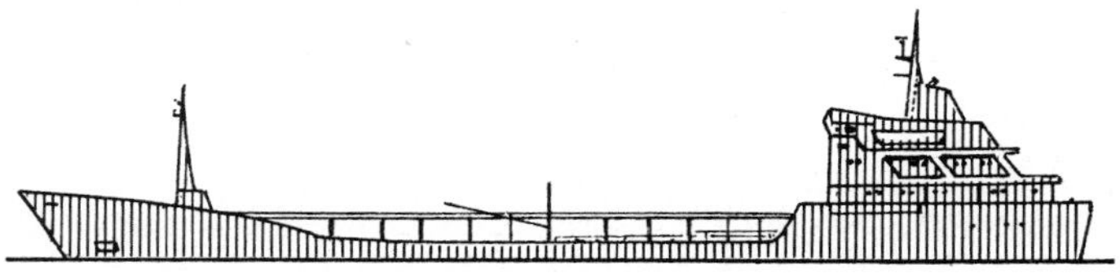

486 *MNM-F H13*
LINDFJORD Sw/FRG (Luehring) 1972; Tk; 2,026 grt/3,184 dwt; 86.72 × 5.63 m *(284.51 × 18.47 ft)*; M (Atlas-MaK); 12 kts; ex-*Stor*
Sisters (lengthened -110.39 m (362 ft) -and deepened): **DALANAS** (Sw) ex-*Hai*; **FURETANK** (Sw) ex-*Tarntank* (1051m (3441ft))

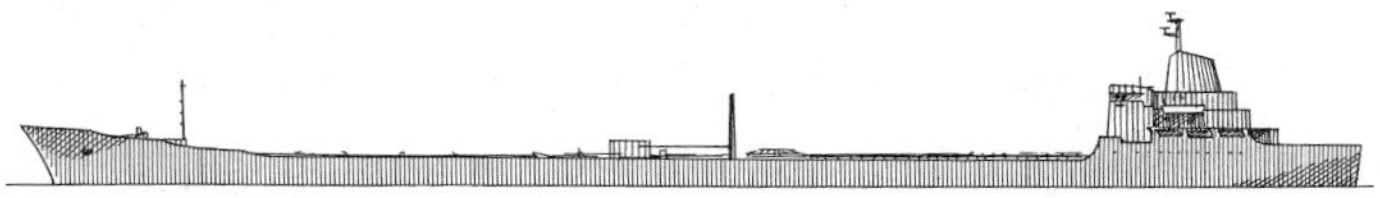

487 *MNM-F H13*
MISSION CAPISTRANO US/US (Ingalls SB) 1971; Tk; 20,751 grt/ 37,874 dwt; 204.93 × 11.04 m *(672.34 × 36.22 ft)*; M (Pielstick); 16.25 kts; ex-*Falcon Lady*; US Government owned
Sisters: **SEA PRINCESS** (US) ex-*Falcon Princess* (privately owned); **DUCHESS** (US) ex-*Falcon Duchess* (privately owned)

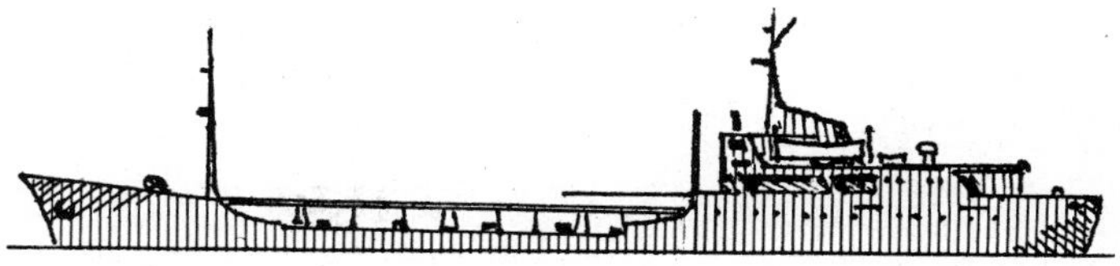

488 *MNM-F H13*
SAINT RAPHAEL II Li/Sw (Karlstads) 1966; Tk; 970 grt/2,097 dwt; 78.09 × 4.64 m *(256.2 × 15.22 ft)*; M (KHD); — kts; ex-*Dalavik*; Lengthened and deepened 1972

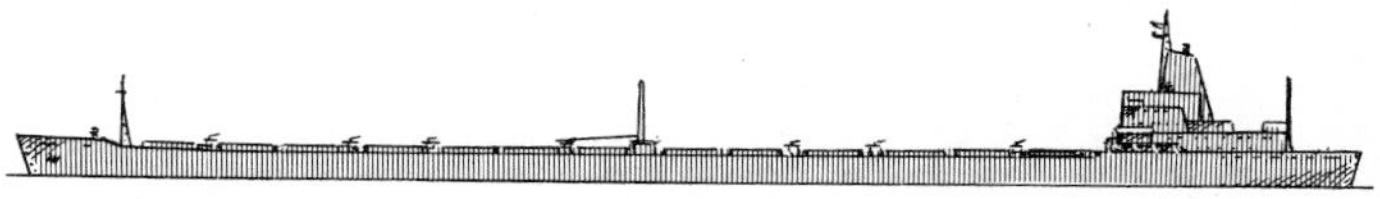

489 *MNM-FN H*
ARISTIDIS Cy/Ys ('Split') 1975; OBO; 47,087 grt/84,790 dwt; 252.86 × 14.81 m *(829.59 × 48.59 ft)*; M (MAN); 14.5 kts; ex-*Excomm Merchant*
Sisters: **SHADOWDANCE** (Ma) ex-*Excomm Mariner*; **JAVA SEA** (Pa) ex-*Pericles Halcoussis*; Possible sister: **ARARAT** (Pa) ex-*Yatia Halcoussi*; Similar: **SONATA 1** (Ma) ex-*Carbay*; Similar (radar mast from bridge): **PENG CHENG** (SV) ex-*Carisle*

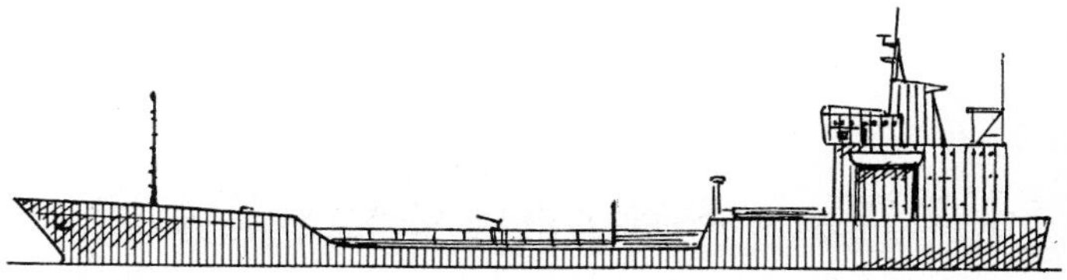

490 *MNM-FN H13*
ISMARA Ag/FRG (Schlichting) 1978; Tk/WT; 2,361 grt/3,601 dwt; 87.76 × 5.72 m *(287.93 × 18.77 ft)*; M (Atlas-MaK); 13.5 kts
Sisters: **DAHRA** (Ag); **ZACCAR** (Ag)

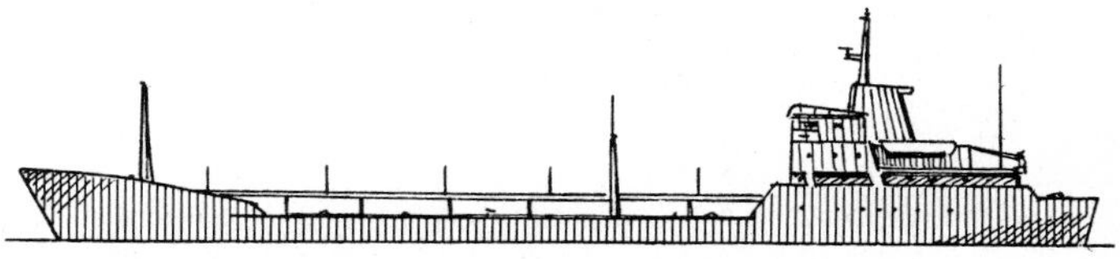

491 *MNM-FN H13*
LUBCHEM Br/Sp (Cantabrico) 1973; Tk/Ch; 1,999 grt/3,310 dwt; 93.33 × 5.36 m *(306.2 × 17.59 ft)*; M (Deutz); 12.75 kts; ex-*Mobil Lubchem*

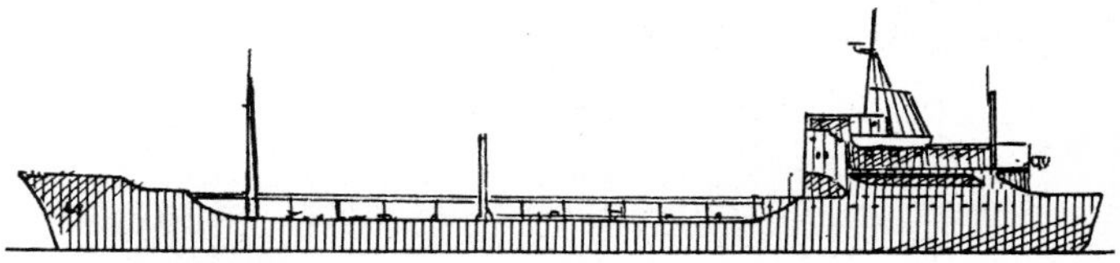

492 *MNM-FN H13*
PETROS A Ma/Br (Smith's D) 1968; Tk; 1,938 grt/3,146 dwt; 86.21 × 5.67 m *(282.84 × 18.6 ft)*; M (Smit & Bolnes); 12 kts; ex-*Preciosa*

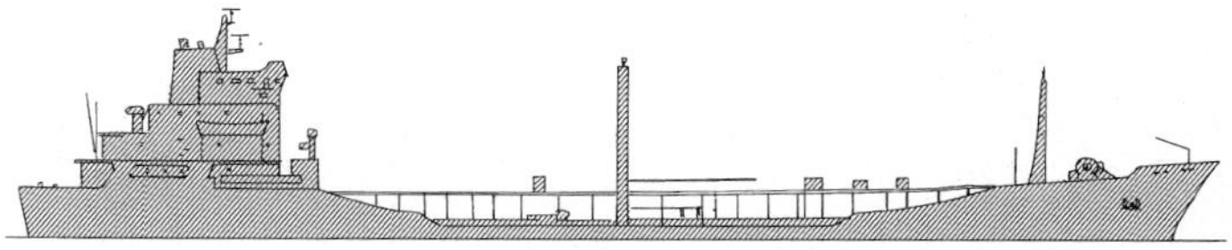

493 *MNM-FN H13*
RATHNEW Ih/Ja (Kagoshima) 1978; Tk/TB; 2,080 grt/3,165 dwt; 93.22 × 5.27 m *(305.84 × 17.29 ft)*; M (MaK); 13 kts

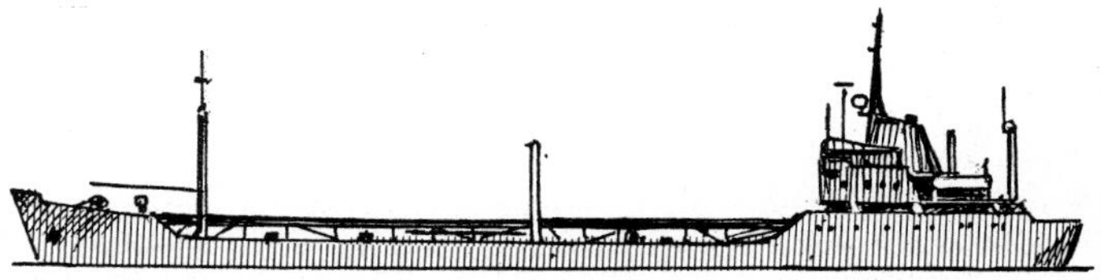

494 *MNM-FN H13*
ROCO Ma/Ys ('Jozo Lozovina-Mosor') 1967; Tk; 2,758 grt/3,790 dwt; 98.53 × 6.23 m *(323.26 × 20.44 ft)*; M (B&W); 14.25 kts; ex-*Pomoravlje*
Sister: **PODUNAVLJE** (Cro); Similar (larger): **CSP 1** (Th) ex-*Podravina*; **GOOD CARRIER** (Pa) ex-*Posavina*

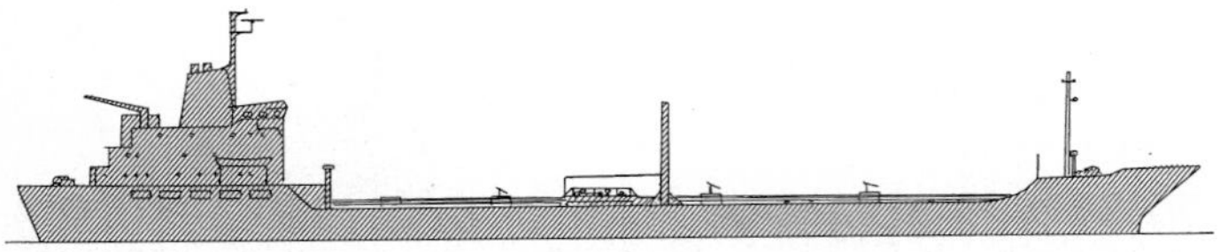

495 *MNM-FS H13*
MAR SOFIA Sp/Sp (AESA) 1979; Tk/Ch; 9,891 grt/15,456 dwt; 149.59 × 9.02 m *(490.78 × 29.59 ft)*; M (B&W); 14.5 kts; ex-*Maria Sofia*
Sisters (converted to Tk/AT/TB): **MAR CATERINA** (Sp) ex-*Caterina*; Sister (lengthened-now 182.611m (599.111ft): **MAR PATRICIA** (Sp) ex-*Albuera*; Possible sister: **ALCUDIA** (Sp) ex-*Julia Rose*

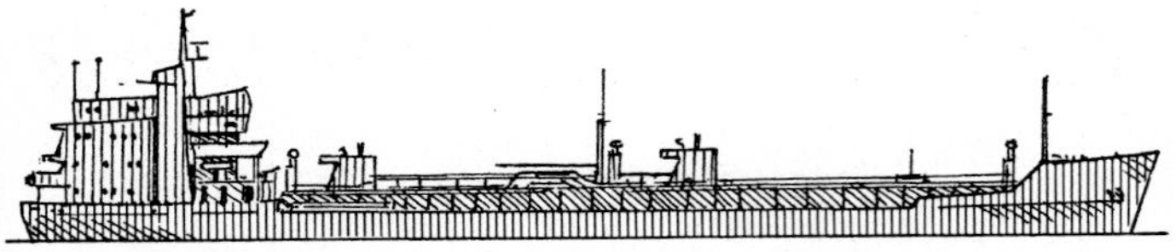

496 *MNM-G H1*
NANCY G Li/Ne (Zaanlandsche) 1972; Ch; 3,902 grt/5,520 dwt; 96.88 × 7.49 m *(317.84 × 24.57 ft)*; M (Werkspoor); 13 kts; ex-*Silver Eirik*; Now has two long tanks (301m) on deck and some alteration to superstructure (not shown on drawing)

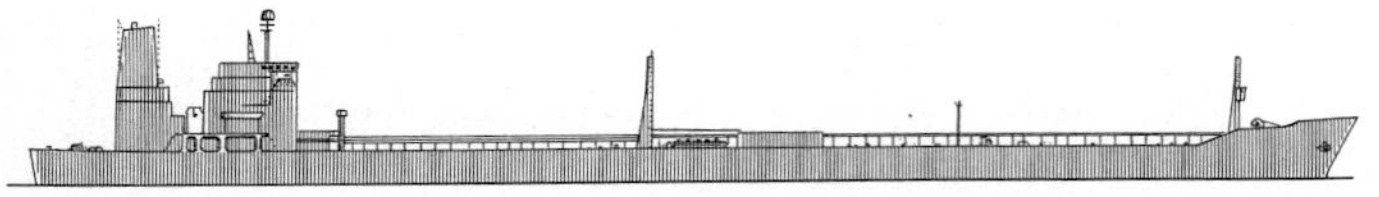

497 *MN²HNMFM H1*
SEA SALVIA Pa/Ja (Tsuneishi) 1979; Tk; 52,853 grt/88,396 dwt; 247.91 × 12.56 m *(813.35 × 41.21 ft)*; M (B&W); 15 kts; ex-*Tamba Maru*
Sisters: **SILVER IRIS** (Pa) ex-*Tajima Maru*; **HONSHU SPIRIT** (Bs) ex-*Tango Maru*

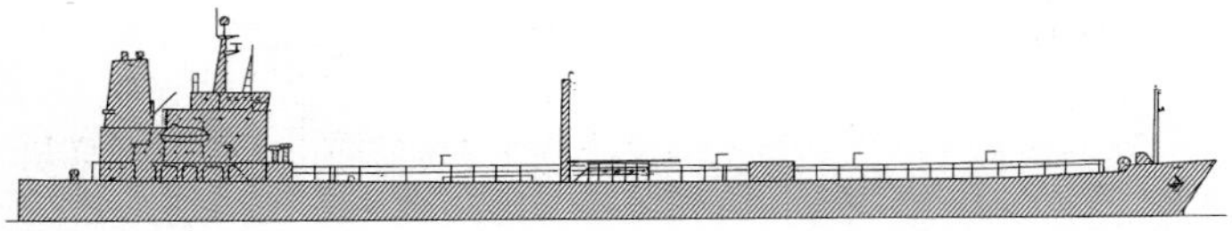

498 *MN²MF H*
PRIMAR Gr/Ja (Onomichi) 1988; Tk; 25,368 grt/39,538 dwt; 182.30 × 10.95 m *(598.10 × 35.93 ft)*; M (B&W); 14.5 kts; ex-*Onomichi Spirit*
Sister: **KOREA VENUS** (Pa) ex-*Nakata Spirit*; Probable sisters: **FULMAR** (Gr) ex-*Kobe Spirit*; **CAPETAN COSTIS** (Gr) ex-*Tokyo Spirit*; **YUYO BREEZE** (Li) ex-*Nakata Breeze*; **SEACROWN** (Ma) ex-*Petrobulk Pilot*

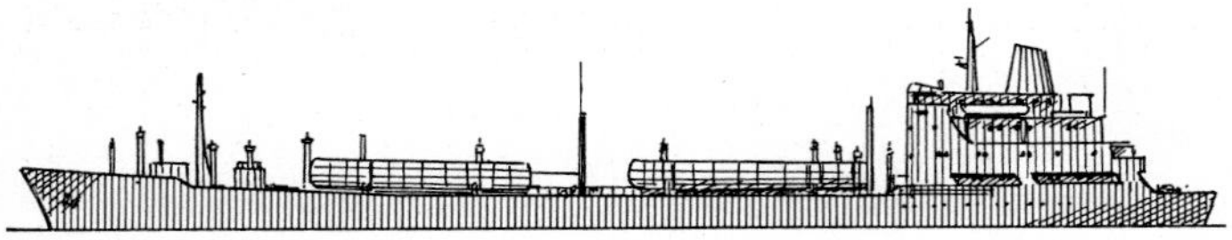

499 *MN²MF H1*
AGIOS NIKOLAOS SV/No (Moss V) 1970; Ch; 6,300 grt/9,813 dwt; 120.83 × 9.06 m *(396.42 × 29.72 ft)*; M (B&W); 14 kts; ex-*Bow Gran*

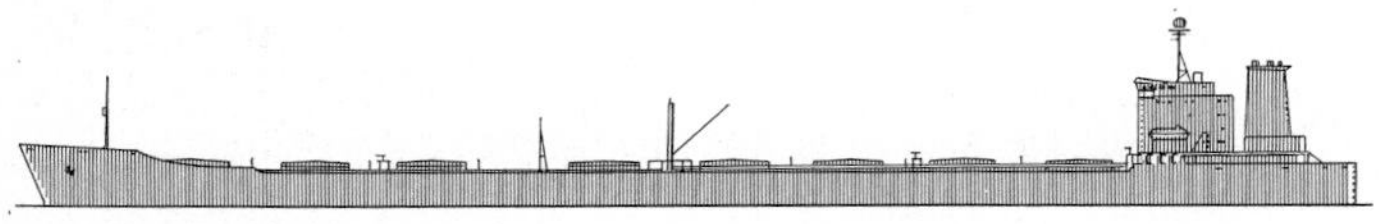

500 *MN²MF H1*
BEAR G Bs/No (Nye Fredriksstad) 1981; OBO; 43,487 grt/77,673 dwt; 243.82 × 14.34 m *(799.93 × 47.05 ft)*; M (B&W); 15.25 kts; ex-*Jarmina*

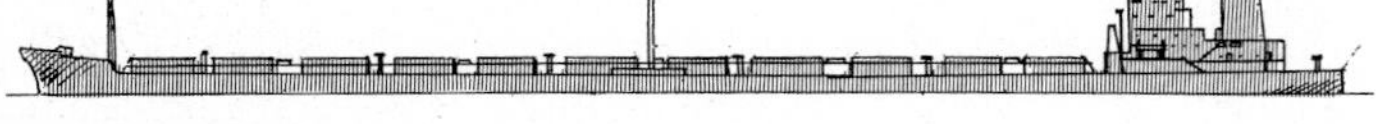

501 *MN²MF H1*
HUDSON BAY 1 Pa/Fr (France-Gironde) 1974; OBO; 90,871 grt/ 152,396 dwt; 299.25 × 17.6 m *(981.79 × 57.74 ft)*; M (Sulzer); 16 kts; ex-*Yemanja*; Modified for ice service - helo pad aft

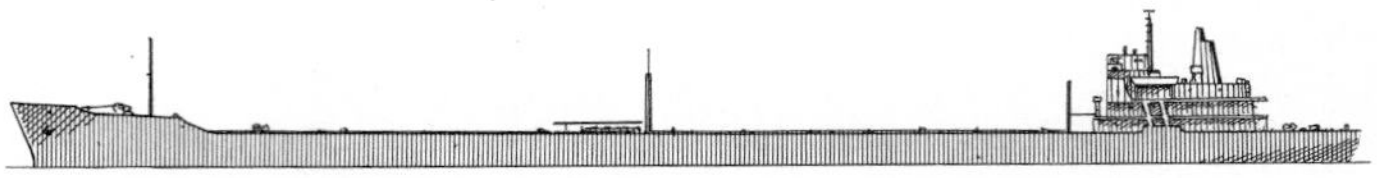

502 *MN²MF H1*
LEADER US/US (Bethlehem Steel) 1969; Tk; 20,877 grt/38,414 dwt; 201.23 × 11.17 m *(660.2 × 36.65 ft)*; T (GEC); 16 kts; ex-*Eagle Leader*
Sisters: **OVERSEAS ALICE** (US); **OVERSEAS VALDEZ** (US) ex-*Overseas Audrey*; **OVERSEAS VIVIAN** (US); **CHAMPION** (US) ex-*Penn Champion*; **WILLAMETTE** (US) ex-*Ogden Willamette*

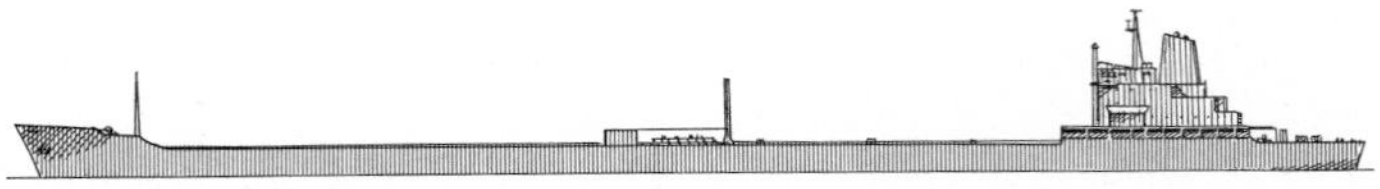

503 *MN²MF H1*
PATRIOT US/US (Todd) 1975; Tk; 21,572 grt/35,662 dwt; 216.8 × 10.52 m *(711.29 × 34.51 ft)*; M (Pielstick); 16 kts; ex-*Zapata Patriot*
Sisters: **COURIER** (US) ex-*Zapata Courier*; **RANGER** (US) ex-*Zapata Ranger*; **ROVER** (US) ex-*Zapata Rover*

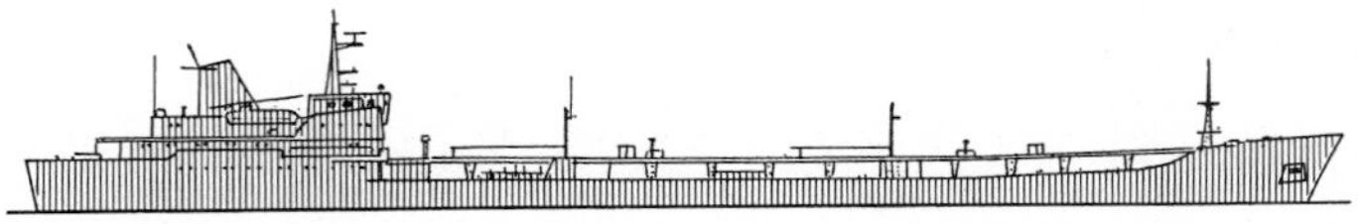

504 *MN²MF H13*
APSHERON Az/Rm (Turnu-Severin) 1983; Tk; 5,944 grt/7,410 dwt; 147.02 × 5.30 m *(482.35 × 17.39 ft)*; TSM (Sulzer); 12.50 kts; ex-*Sergey Kirov*
Sisters: **MESHEDI EZIZBEYOV** (Az) ex-*Meshadi Azizbekov*; **ALI BAYRAMOV** (Az); **ASTARA** (Az) ex-*Alesha Dzhaparidze*; **KHEZER** (Az) ex-*Bolshevik B Aliyev*; **ARAZ** (Az) ex-*Ivan Fioletov*; **SHEMAKHA** (Az) ex-*Stepan Shaumyan*

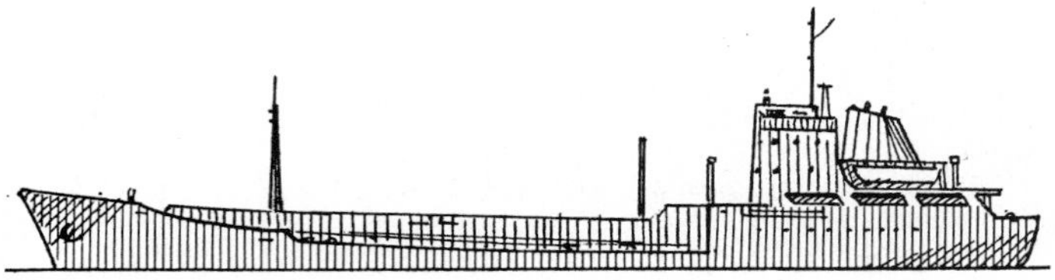

505 *MNNMF H13*
BALTIC PROSPERITY Pa/Sw (Lodose) 1965; Tk; 2,202 grt/3,186 dwt; 86.75 × 5.79 m *(284.6 × 19 ft)*; M (MWM); 12 kts; ex-*Luna*
Similar: **LISA** (—); Possibly similar: **BELLONA** (Sw) ex-*Stella Atlantic*

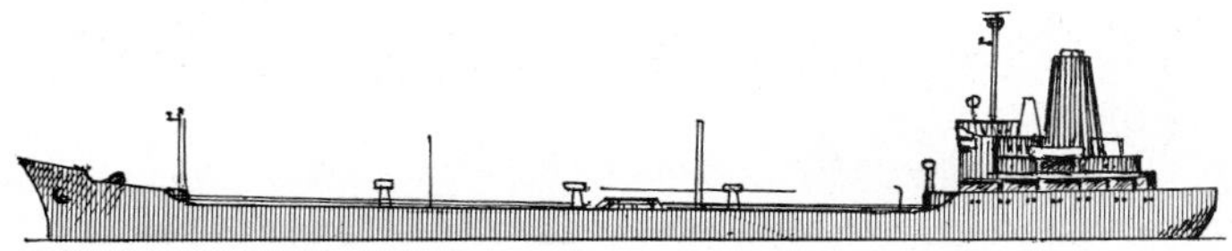

506 *MN²MF H13*
NEW WIND Pa/Ja (IHI) 1968; Tk; 12,994 grt/19,683 dwt; 170.08 × 9.40 m *(558 × 30.87 ft)*; M (Sulzer); 14.5 kts; ex-*Esso Bombay*
Sisters: **MARE ADRIATICO** (It) ex-*Esso Interamerica 1982*; **GEYVE** (Tu) ex-*Esso Nagasaki 1983*; **VARANO** (It) ex-*Esso Penang 1978*; **SEALION** (Ma) ex-*Esso Chittagong*; **ESRAM** (Tu) ex-*Esso Goa*

507 *MN²MFC H*
AMAZON GLORY Gr/FRG (A G 'Weser') 1974; Tk; 123,126 grt/256,715 dwt; 347.81 × 20.05 m *(1,141 × 65.78 ft)*; T (GEC); 15.5 kts; Launched as *Esso Bilbao*
Similar: **MOSCLIFF** (Bs) ex-*Esso Saba*

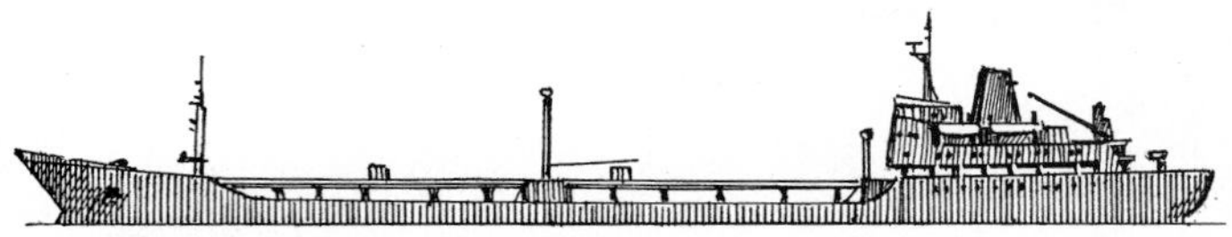

508 *MN²MFC H13*
KONSTANTINOS D Ma/Ru (Baltic) 1971; Tk; 10,232 grt/16,540 dwt; 162.31 × 8.93 m *(532.51 × 29.3 ft)*; M (B&W); 16.25 kts; ex-*Eyzhen Berg*
Sisters: **KONSTANTINS CIOLKOVSKIS** (La) ex-*Konstantin Tsiolkovskiy*; **DAVID GURAMISHVILI** (Gi); **FRIDRIHS CANDERS** (La) ex-*Fridrikh Tsander*; **VASILIY KIKVIDZE** (Gi); **MARITZA** (Bu); **REZVAYA** (Bu): **KAMCHIA** (Bu); **SEA WEED** (—) ex-*9 De Abril*; **GOLD SAND** (Cu) ex-*7 De Noviembre*; **SAROJINI NAIDU** (In); **VISVESVARAYA** (In)

509 MN^2MFDM *H1*
LIDO II Ma/Au (Whyalla) 1971; Tk; 38,216 grt/66,803 dwt; 239.28 × 13.17 m *(785.04 × 43.21 ft)*; M (Sulzer); 16.5 kts; ex-*Amanda Miller*

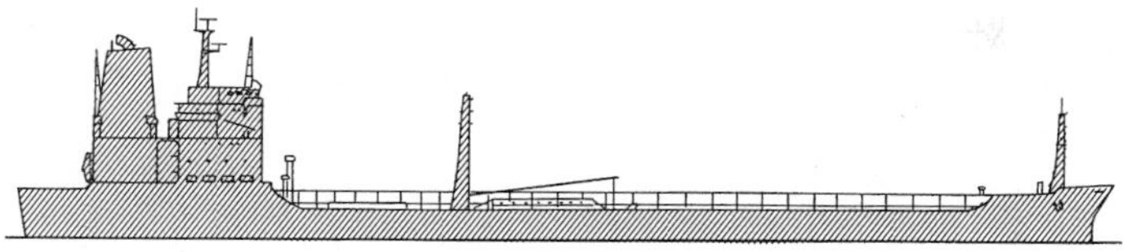

510 MN^2MFM *H13*
CRYSTALVENTURE L Gr/Ja (Sanoyasu) 1980; Tk; 18,812 grt/31,676 dwt; 169.55 × 11.21 m *(556.27 × 36.78 ft)*; M (B&W); 15 kts; ex-*Fort Garry*; Mast aft of funnel is on port side
Sisters: **CLIPPERVENTURE L** (Gr) ex-*Fort Toronto*; **CONQUESTVENTURE L** (Gr) ex-*Fort Assiniboine*; **COURAGEVENTURE L** (Gr) ex-*Fort Rouge*

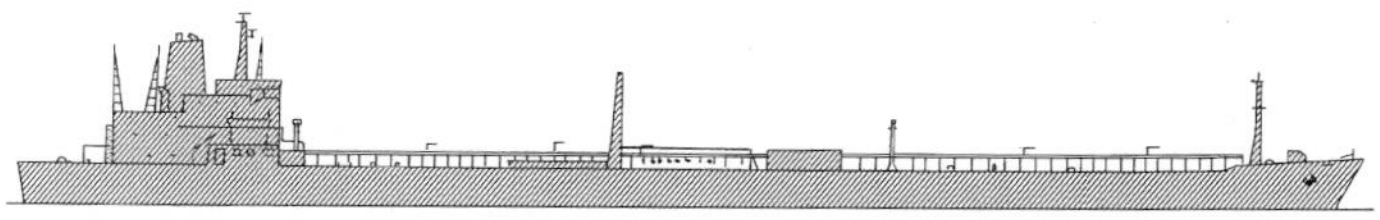

511 MN^2MFM^2 *H*
ZENATIA HK/Ja; Tk; 37,685 grt/57,741 dwt; 228.63 × 11.92 m *(750.10 × 39.11 ft)*; M (B&W); 14.5 kts; ex-*Salena*

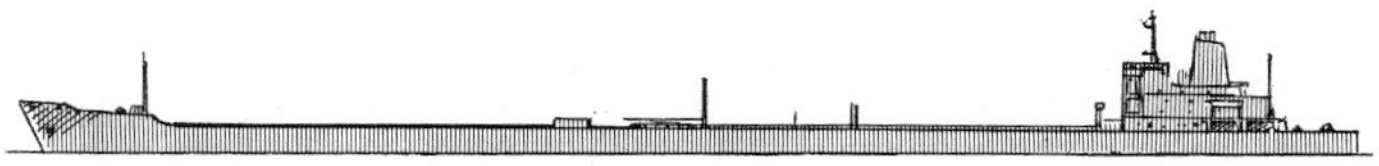

512 MN^2MFN *H1*
CAIRO SEA Li/Ja (Mitsubishi HI) 1975; Tk; 77,648 grt/134,999 dwt; 280.02 × 15.24 m *(918.7 × 50 ft)*; M (Sulzer); 15.25 kts; ex-*Amoco Cairo*
Sisters: **WHITE SEA** (Li) ex-*Amoco Tehran*; **TRINIDAD SEA** (Li) ex-*Amoco Trinidad*

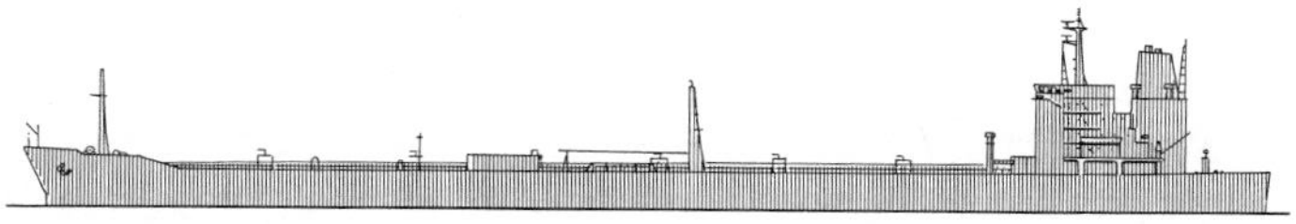

513 MN^2MFN *H1*
COLUMBIA NEPTUNE Li/Ja (Tsuneishi) 1981; Tk; 37,949 grt/60,068 dwt; 225.51 × 12.22 m *(739.86 × 40.09 ft)*; M (B&W); 14.75 kts
Similar: **NORDIC CHALLENGER** (NIS) ex-*Houston Accord*

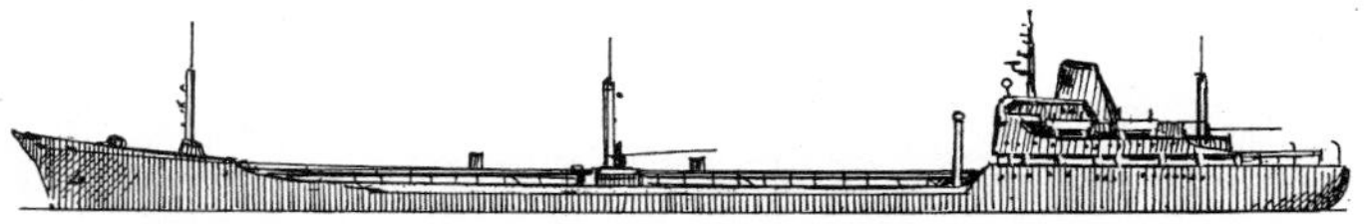

514 MN^2MFN *H13*
NAKHODKA Ru/Pd ('Komuny Paryskiej') 1968; Tk; 13,733 grt/19,986 dwt; 177.27 × 9.37 m *(581.59 × 30.74 ft)*; M (Sulzer); 16 kts; 'B72' type
Sisters: **PAMYAT LENINA** (Ru); **HORIZON III** (Pa) ex-*Pyotr Stuchka*; **ZAVYETY ILYICHA** (Ru)

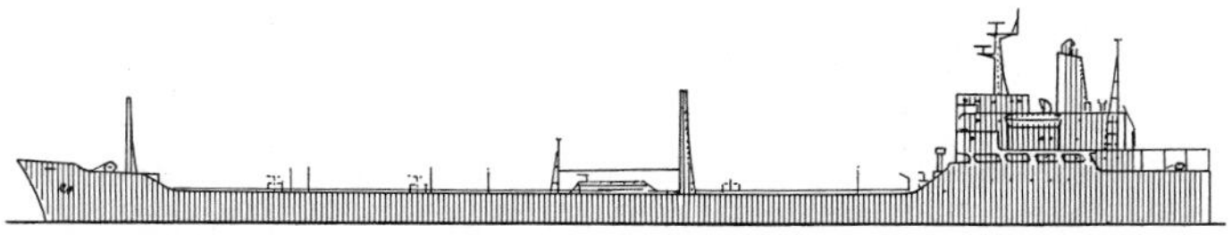

515 MN^2MFN *H13*
PELITA/PERTAMINA 1023 Ia/Ja (Hitachi) 1981; Tk; 12,450 grt/18,065 dwt; 157.99 × 7.02 m *(518.34 × 23.03 ft)*; M (B&W); 13.25 kts; Launched as *Pranedya Tritya*
Sisters: **PERTAMINA 1020** (Ia); **PEMATANG/PERTAMINA 1021** (Ia) ex-*Pertamina 1021*; **PRANEDYA TRITYA** (Pa) (builder—Naikai); **PRANEDYA DWITYA** (Li); **PRANEDYA PRATAMA** (Li); **PRANEDYA QUARTYA** (Pa) (Ko built—Daewoo); **SETCO GAJAH MADA** (Pa); **SETCO MAMMOTH** (Pa)

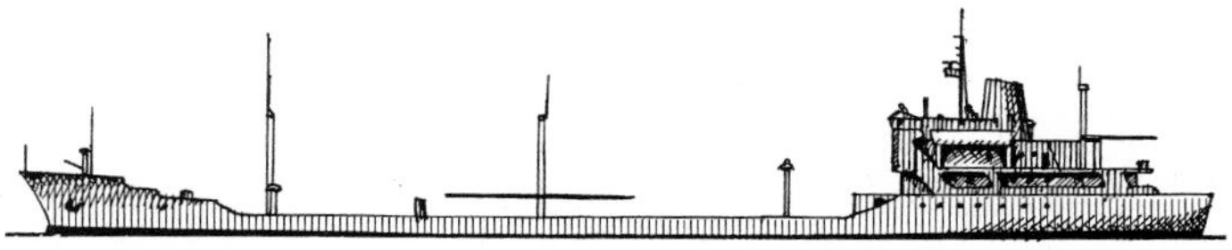

516 MN^2MFN *H13*
UM EL FAROUD Ly/Br (Smith's D) 1969; Ch; 3,273 grt/5,390 dwt; 109.56 × 6.41 m *(359.45 × 21.03 ft)*; M (Smit & Bolnes); 14 kts; ex-*Seafalcon*
Sister: **RED IBIS** (Bs) ex-*Seatern*

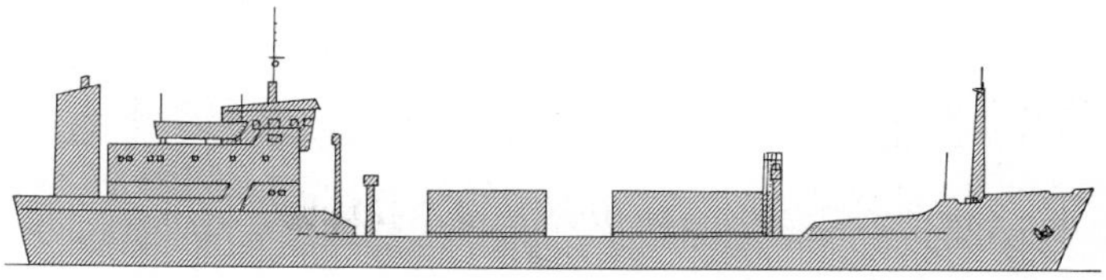

517 MN^2MHG *H13*
HATNYANAWATI Ia/Ne (Groot & VV) 1975; Ch; 1,534 grt/2,650 dwt; 73.46 × 6.15 m *(241.01 × 20.18 ft)*; M ('Bolnes'); 12.5 kts; ex-*Proof Spirit*

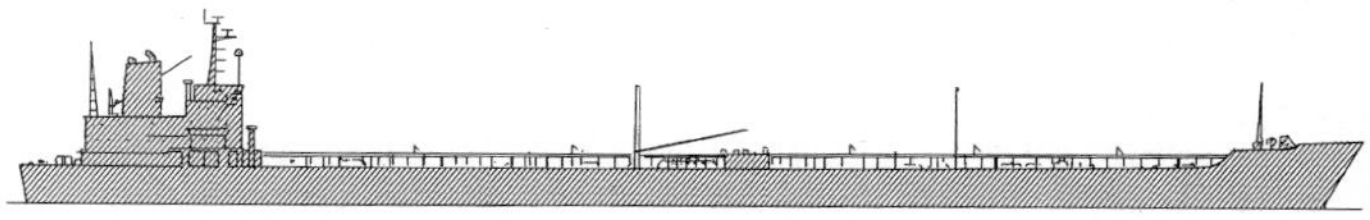

518 MN^2M^2FCN *H1*
BURGAS Ru/Ja (Kurushima) 1981; Tk; 26,540 grt/54,589 dwt; 226.50 × 12.31 m *(743.11 × 40.39 ft)*; M (B&W); 14.8 kts; ex-*Toko Maru*
Possible sister: **OCEAN SWALLOW** (Ja)

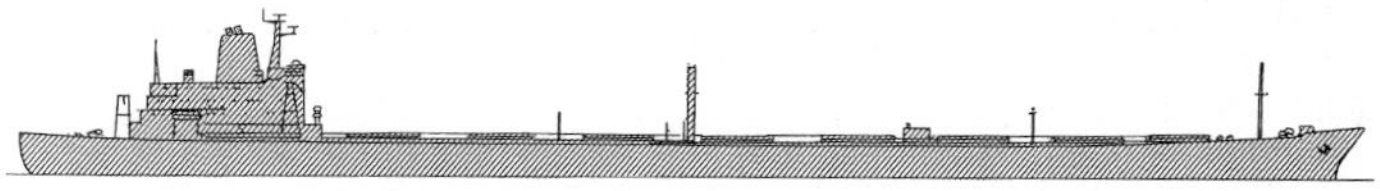

519 MN^2M^2FN *H*
POLO Li/Bz (Ish do Brasil); OO; 73,688 grt/131,423 dwt; 273.52 × 16.18 m *(897.38 × 53.08 ft)*; M (Sulzer); 16 kts; ex-*Docepolo*
Sisters: **CORAL** (Li) ex-*Docecoral*; **JOINVILLE** (Bz); **JURUA** (Bz); **JURUPEMA** (Bz); **JAPURA** (Bz); **JACUI** (Bz)

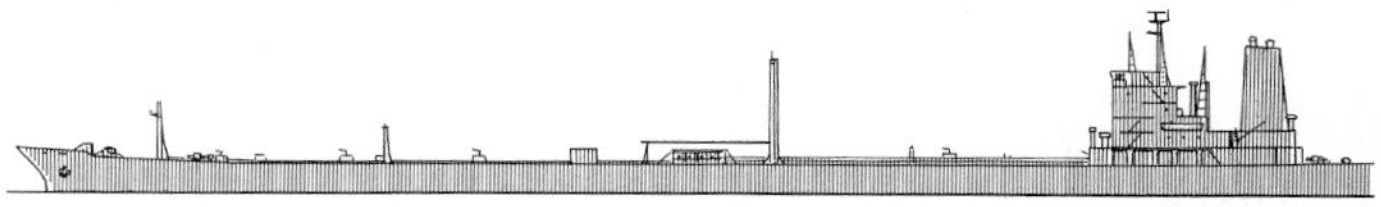

520 MN^2MNF *H*
URIMARE Ve/Ja (Onomichi) 1981; Tk; 33,100 grt/60,598 dwt; 235.8 × 12.22 m *(773.62 × 40.09 ft)*; M (B&W); 14.5 kts; ex-*Caribbean Shoot*
Sister: **MURACHI** (Ve) ex-*Caribbean Sprout*; Possible sister: **STELLA MAR** (It) ex-*Caribbean Sprout II*

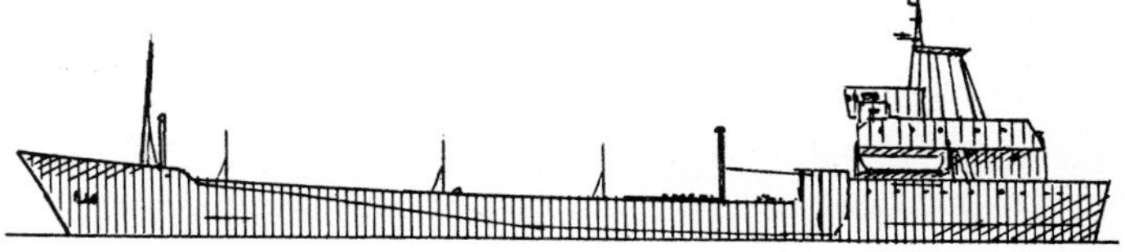

521 MN^2M-F *H13*
ASTRA Pa/No (Vaagen) 1972; Ch; 1,597 grt/3,475 dwt; 82.71 × 6.37 m *(271.36 × 20.9 ft)*; M (Atlas-MaK); 12.5 kts; ex-*Bras*
Similar: **BRAVUR** (Pa); **SARA THERESA** (DIS) ex-*Bragd*

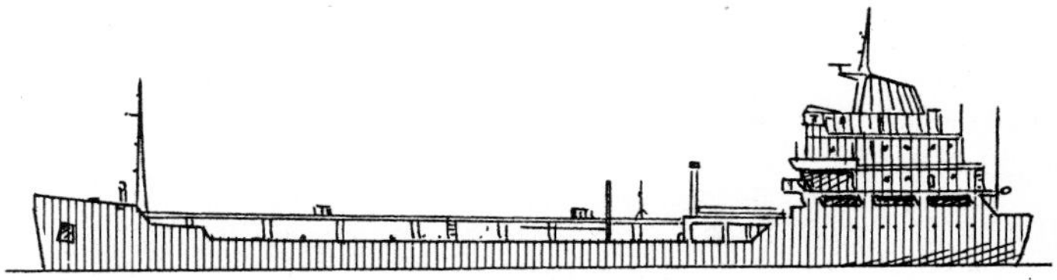

522 MN^2M-F *H13*
UNITED THULE Sw/Sw (Falkenbergs) 1973; Ch; 3,384 grt/6,097 dwt; 107.19 × 6.7 m *(351.67 × 21.98 ft)*; M (Polar); 12 kts; ex-*Thuntank 1*

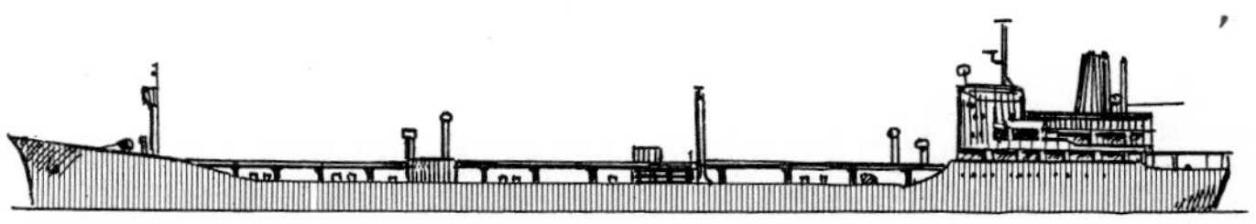

523 MN^3MFN *H13*
EVE SV/Sw (Uddevalla) 1968; Tk; 10,683 grt/17,901 dwt; 160.13 × 9.15 m *(525.36 × 30.02 ft)*; M (B&W); 16 kts; ex-*Atherduchess*

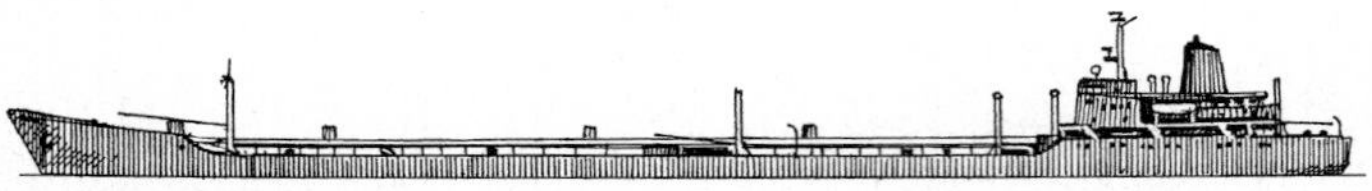

524 *MN^3MFN H13*
NOVOCENTROL 3 Ru/Ja (IHI) 1963; Tk; 23,110 grt/37,012 dwt; 207.04 × 11.11 m *(679.27 × 36.45 ft)*; M (Sulzer); 17.25 kts; ex-*Lyudinovo*
Sister: **NOVOCENTROL 4** (Ru) ex-*Leninakan*

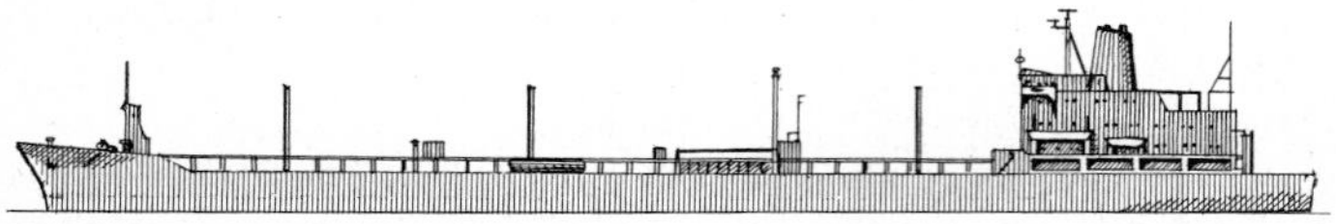

525 *MN^4MFN H1*
BOW EXPLORER Li/Fi (Wärtsilä) 1975; Ch; 17,958 grt/31,510 dwt; 170.72 × 11.37 m *(560.1 × 37.3 ft)*; M (Sulzer); 16.25 kts; ex-*Nyholt*
Sisters: **LADY INA** (NIS) ex-*Nyhorn*; **BOW GERD** (NIS) ex-*Bow Flower*

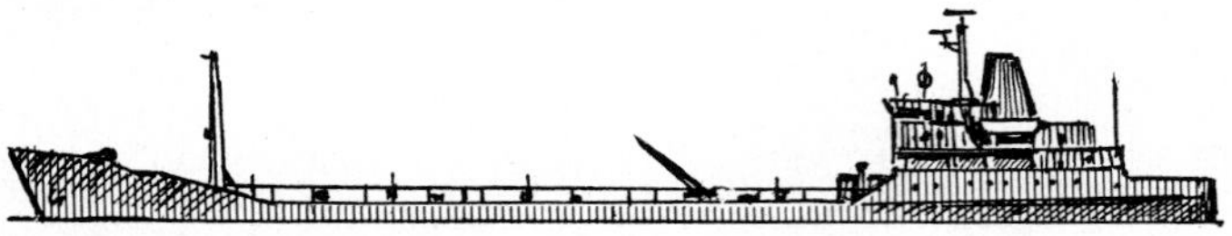

526 *MSMFN H13*
ARGOAT Fr/Fi (Valmet) 1973; Tk; 4,521 grt/7,414 dwt; 107.32 × 6.62 m *(352.1 × 21.72 ft)*; M (Stork-Werkspoor); 14 kts; ex-*Vuosaari*
Probably similar: **AZEROT** (Kn) ex-*Tebostar*

527 *MSMM-FN H13*
NEJMAT EL PETROL XXV Si/Br (Hall, Russell) 1972; Tk; 3,700 grt/6,210 dwt; 103.64 × 6.99 m *(340.03 × 22.93 ft)*; M (Ruston Paxman); 12.5 kts; ex-*Bridgeman*
Similar: **RUFIJI** (Br) ex-*Helmsman*

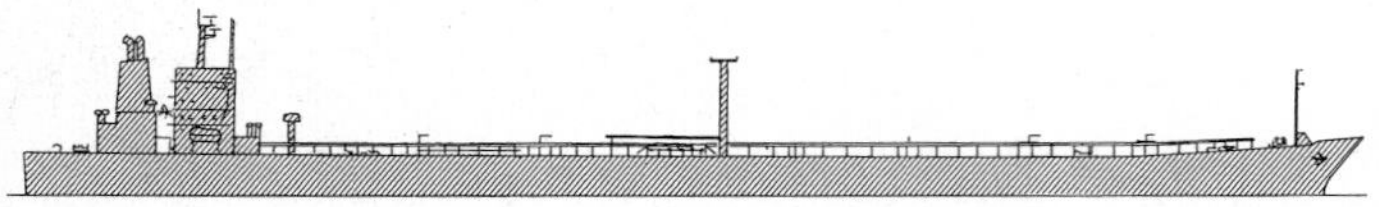

528 *MTMF H*
NISSOS AMORGOS Gr/Ja (Koyo) 1988; Tk; 52,484 grt/98,731 dwt; 246.84 × 12.21 m *(809.84 × 40.06 ft)*; M (B&W); 14 kts; ex-*Seto Breeze*
Possible sisters: **NEW ACE** (Li) ex-*Atlantic Ace*; **NEW ARGOSY** (Li) ex-*Atlantic Argosy*; **SUDONG SPIRIT** (Li) ex-*Full Moon River*; **PACIFIC MERCURY** (Pa)

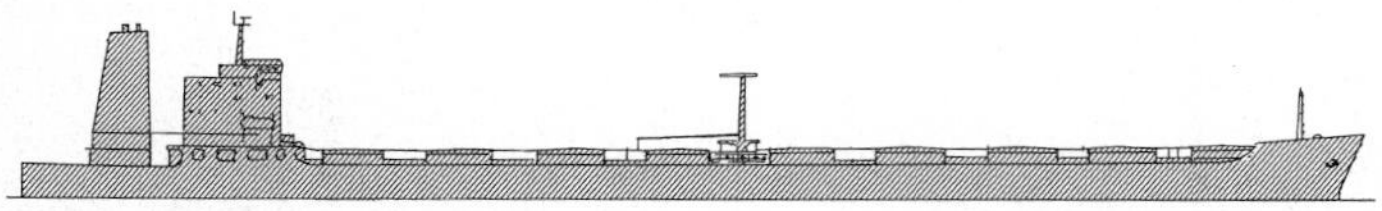

529 *MTMF H1*
OMEGAVENTURE L Gr/Pd ('Komuny Paryskiej') 1986; OBO; 59,850 grt/98,358 dwt; 249.97 × 11.41 m *(820.11 × 37.43 ft)*; M (Sulzer); 14 kts; ex-*Berge Gdynia*; 'B536' type
Sister: **OMIKRONVENTURE L** (Gr) ex-*Arrow Gdansk*

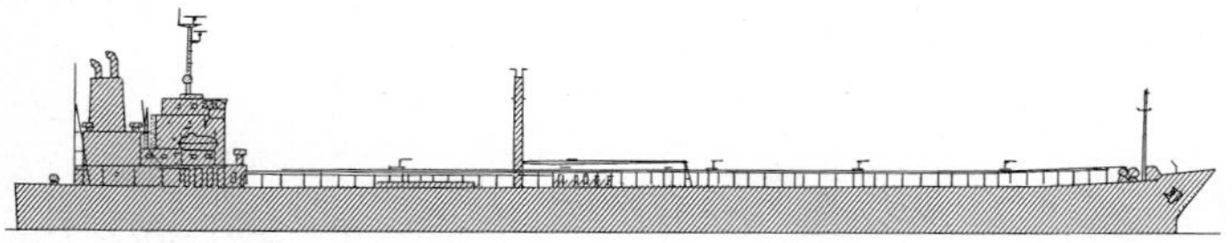

530 *MTMFM H*
OSPREY CHALLENGER Sg/Ja (Koyo) 1988; Tk; 25,740 grt/41,750 dwt; 181.61 × 11.77 m *(595.83 × 38.62 ft)*; M (B&W); 14.2 kts; ex-*Pacific Challenger*
Sister: **WORLD SEA** (Pa)

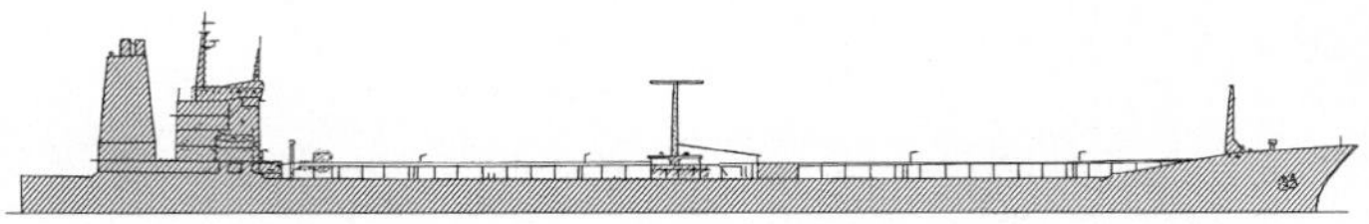

531 *MTM^2F H1*
NEPTUNE DORADO Sg/Pd ('Komuny Paryskiej') 1985; Tk; 53,014 grt/84,711 dwt; 248.50 × 12.47 m *(815.29 × 40.91 ft)*; M (Sulzer); — kts; ex-*Cys Pride*; 'B555' type
Sister: **SKAUBAY** (NIS) ex-*Cys Olympia*

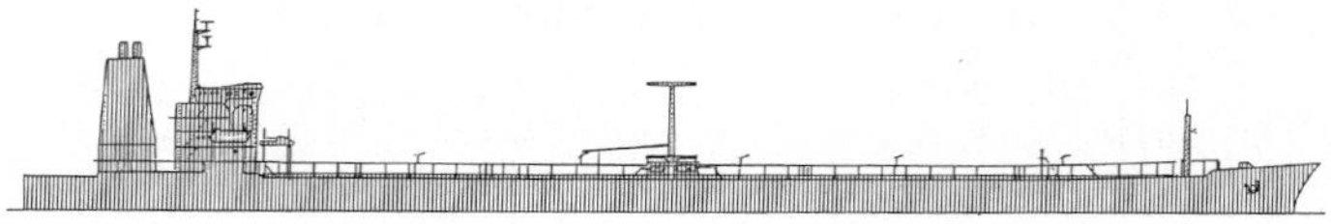

532 *MUMF H*
LARK LAKE Li/Pd ('Komuny Paryskiej') 1991; Tk; 53,569 grt/90,916 dwt; 247.20 × 12.20 m *(811.02 × 40.03 ft)*; M (Sulzer); 14.3 kts; 'B563' type

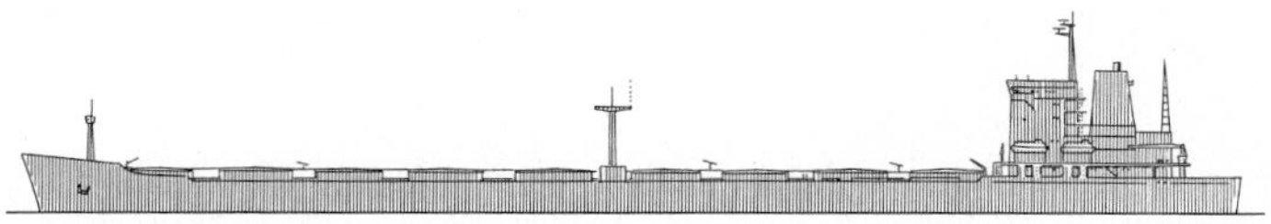

533 *MUMFMS H1*
MARSHAL GRECHKO Ru/Pd ('Komuny Pariskiej') 1978; OBO; 65,763 grt/116,283 dwt; 245.5 × 17.5 m *(805.45 × 57.41 ft)*; M (Sulzer); 14.5 kts; 'B527' type; 'M' aft is on starboard side
Sisters: **MARSHAL GOVOROV** (Ru); **MARSHAL ZAKHAROV** (Ru)

534 *MUNMF H*
SKAUFJORD NIS/Pd ('Komuny Paryskiej') 1983; Tk; 52,509 grt/84,656 dwt; 247.20 × 12.45 m *(811.02 × 40.85 ft)*; M (Sulzer); — kts; ex-*World Falcon*; 'B557' type; Rebuilt 1991

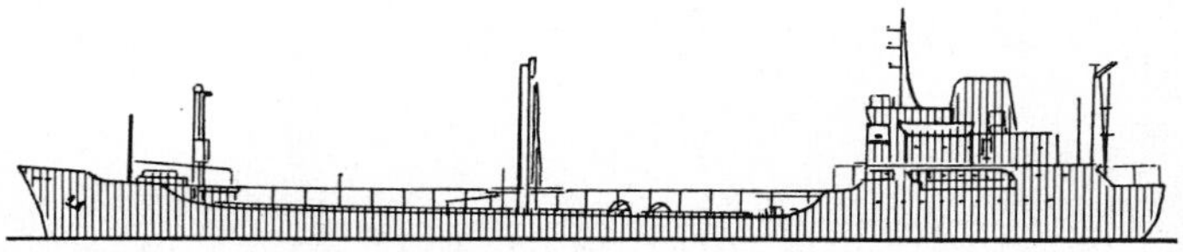

535 *NH^2MFN H13*
ARGUS Cu/Ja (Niigata) 1976; RT; 3,420 grt/5,631 dwt; 106.99 × 6.99 m *(351 × 22.93 ft)*; M (Niigata); 12.75 kts; ex-*Las Guasimas*; Operated by State Fishing Fleet

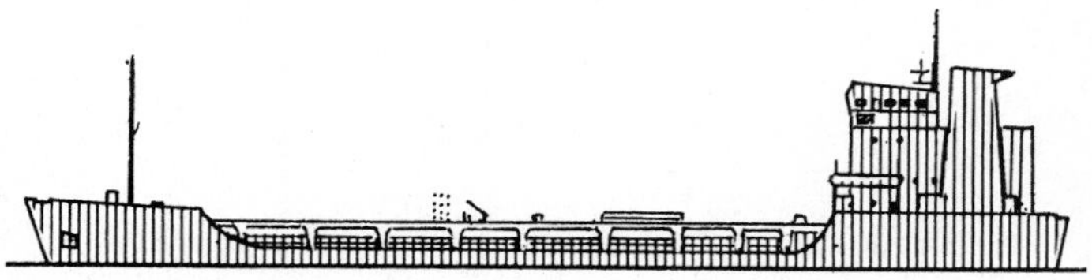

536 *VMG H13*
ABILITY Br/Br (Goole) 1979; Tk; 1,696 grt/2,550 dwt; 79.25 × 4.97 m *(260 × 16.31 ft)*; M (Ruston); 13 kts
Sisters: **AMENITY** (Br); **AUTHENTICITY** (Br)

537 Sealord *(Ma); 1974* *WSPL*

538 Hawaii *(Bs); 1975; (as Esso Hawaii)* *WSPL*

539 Ghazvin *(Cy); 1975; (as Golden Portsmouth)* *WSPL*

540 Chryssi *(Gr); 1973; (as George F Getty II)* *WSPL*

541 Niaga Energi 1 *(Ia); 1979; (as Hassho Maru)* *WSPL*

542 Epic *(Ma); 1975; (as Industrial Prosperity)* *WSPL*

543 Vitoria *(Ma); 1977; (as Fountain Venture)* *WSPL*

544 Salina *(Bs); 1975; (as Michael C)* *WSPL*

545 Norrisia *(Br); 1980; (offshore loading tanker)* *WSPL*

546 Mare Queen *(Pa); 1979; (as Goho Maru)* *WSPL*

547 Jahre Spray *(NIS); 1975; (as Hellespont Splendour)* *WSPL*

548 Honam Pearl *(Ko); 1974* *WSPL*

549 Armata *(Gr); 1980; (as Kikuwa Maru No 2)* *WSPL*

550 Product King *(Bs); 1973; (as Kingfisher)* *WSPL*

551 Aire *(Po); 1976; (as Lilac)* *WSPL*

552 Seaoath *(Ma); 1976; (as Mikata Maru)* *WSPL*

553 Seacross *(Ma); 1974; (as Carina 1)* *WSPL*

554 Menado *(Ho); 1974; (as Tentaku Maru)* *WSPL*

555 Flandre *(Li); 1977; (as Captain John G P Livanos)* *WSPL*

556 Niki *(Cy); 1975; (as Filiatra Legacy)* *WSPL*

557 Jin You 6 *(RC); 1978; (as Botany Treasure)* *WSPL*

558 Mormacsun *(US); 1976* *FotoFlite*

559 Leticia *(Sp); 1978* *FotoFlite*

560 London Spirit *(Br); 1982* *FotoFlite*

561 Wilomi Tanana *(Li); 1992* *FotoFlite*

562 Akebono *(Pa); 1988; (as Akebono Maru)* *FotoFlite*

563 Alandia Tide *(Bs); 1975* *FotoFlite*

564 Lofoten *(Bs); 1977* *FotoFlite*

565 Mar Lucia *(Sp); 1989* *FotoFlite*

566 Freja Svea *(Bs); 1989* *FotoFlite*

567 Isola Bianca *(It); 1980* *FotoFlite*

568 Nan Yang No 8 *(RC); 1984; (as Jahore Express)* *FotoFlite*

569 Chemi Crest *(Pa); 1979; (as Norchem)* *FotoFlite*

570 Stolt Kingfisher *(NIS); 1986* *FotoFlite*

571 Cervin *(Sd); 1982* *FotoFlite*

572 Frederick M *(Br); 1980* *FotoFlite*

573 Mauro D'Alesio *(Ne); 1981* *FotoFlite*

574 Nissos Amorgos *(Gr); 1988; (as Seto Breeze)* *FotoFlite*

575 Ante Banina *(SV); 1980* *FotoFlite*

576 Coronado *(US); 1973* *FotoFlite*

577 Red Seagull *(Br); 1976* *FotoFlite*

578 Biruinta *(Rm); 1984* *FotoFlite*

579 Nand Kishore *(In); 1981* *FotoFlite*

580 New York Sun *(US); 1980* *FotoFlite*

581 Seiko Maru *(Ja); 1977* *FotoFlite*

582 Ionian Jade *(Pa); 1975; (as Jade)* *FotoFlite*

583 Arrazi *(Mo); 1982* *FotoFlite*

584 Thebro *(Cy); 1978; (as Ebro)* *FotoFlite*

585 Coastal Golden *(Li); 1976/83* *Norman Thomson*

586 Nissos Thera *(Gr); 1978* *Norman Thomson*

587 Rhodos *(Gr); 1977* *Norman Thomson*

588 Enalios Thetis *(Cy); 1979; (as Buyuk Timur)* *Norman Thomson*

589 Elfwaihat *(Ly); 1976* *Norman Thomson*

590 Athenian Fidelity *(Cy); 1984* *Norman Thomson*

591 Torino *(NIS); 1975* *Norman Thomson*

592 Crisana *(Rm); 1974* *Norman Thomson*

593 Z-Adalet *(Tu); 1976; (as Tiger Cat)* *FotoFlite*

594 Alandia Nord *(Bs); 1973* *FotoFlite*

595 Poti *(Ma); 1981* *FotoFlite*

596 Pacific Pride *(Li); 1980; (as Pride)* *FotoFlite*

597 Petrobulk Radiance *(Li); 1990* *FotoFlite*

598 Eliza PG *(Bs); 1992* *FotoFlite*

599 Canopus *(Li); 1981* *FotoFlite*

600 Rathmoy *(Ih); 1982* *FotoFlite*

3 Liquefied Gas Carriers with Tanks on Deck

3 Liquefied Gas Carriers with Tanks on Deck

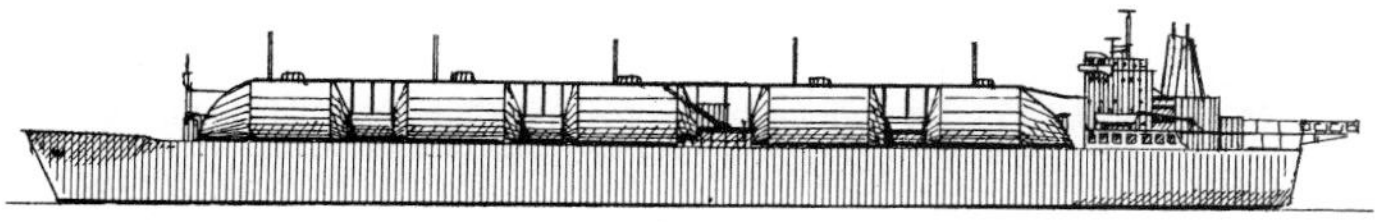

1 *HM^6F H*
ASAKE MARU Ja/No (Moss R) 1974; LGC; 71,822 grt/50,746 dwt; 249.54 × 10.64 m *(818.70 × 34.91 ft)*; T (GEC); 19.5 kts; ex-*LNG Challenger*

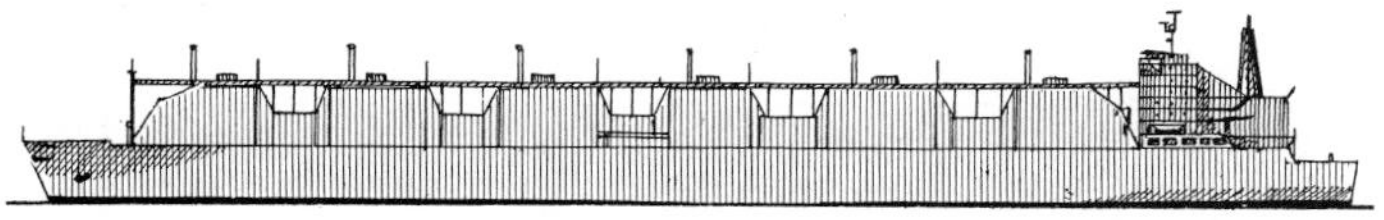

2 *HM^6MG H1*
KHANNUR Li/No (Moss R) 1977; LGC; 96,235 grt/73,074 dwt; 293.76 × 11.7 m *(963.78 × 38.39 ft)*; T (GEC); 19.75 kts
Similar: **HILLI** (Li); **GIMI** (Li)

3 *HM^3NM^3F H*
NORMAN LADY Li/No (Moss R) 1973; LGC; 71,469 grt/50,922 dwt; 249.51 × 10.62 m *(818.6 × 34.84 ft)*; T (GEC); 19 kts

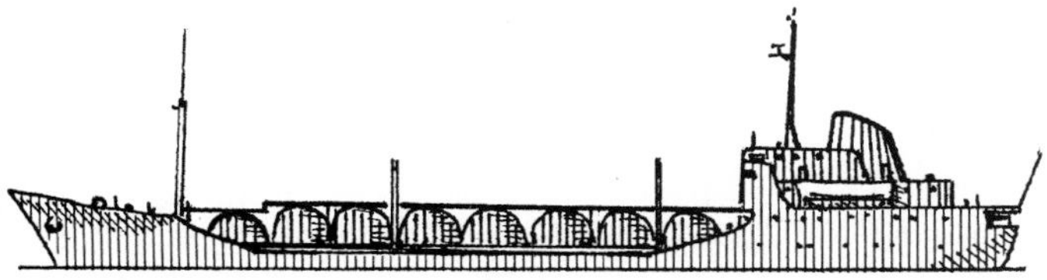

4 *HN^2MF H13*
CAP PHAISTOS Gr/Fr (Dubigeon) 1962; LGC; 1,562 grt/1,610 dwt; 74.68 × 4.99 m *(245 × 16.37 ft)*; M (Werkspoor); 14 kts; ex-*Cap Frehel*

5 *M^2F H*
LNG AQUARIUS US/US (General Dynamics) 1977; LGC; 95,084 grt/71,475 dwt; 285.3 × 11.51 m *(936.02 × 37.76 ft)*; T (GEC); 20.5 kts
Sisters: **LNG ARIES** (US); **LNG CAPRICORN** (US); **LNG GEMINI** (US); **LNG LEO** (US); **LNG LIBRA** (US); **LNG TAURUS** (US); **LNG VIRGO** (US); **LAKE CHARLES** (US); **LOUISIANA** (US)

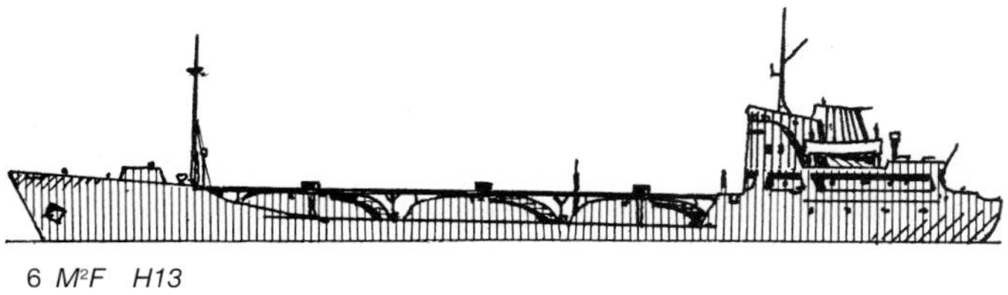

6 *M^2F H13*
BAY ISLAND EXPRESS Ho/Fi (Valmet) 1966; LGC; 1,003 grt/1,114 dwt; 74.53 × 4.08 m *(244.52 × 13.39 ft)*; M (KHD); 12 kts; ex-*Esso Flame*

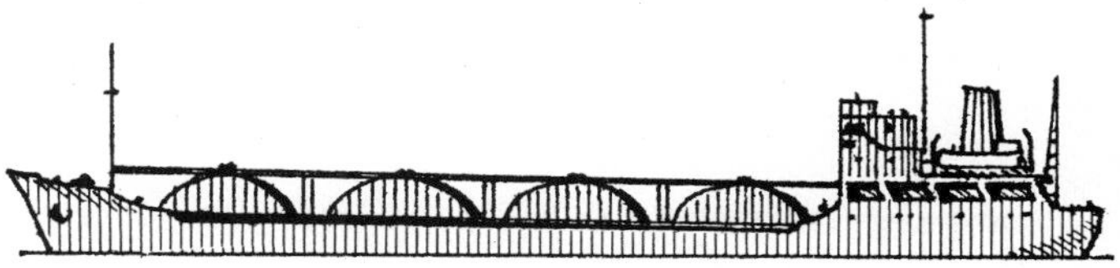

7 *M^2FN H13*
CASTOR GAS Pa/Ja (Tokushima ZS) 1974; LGC; 1,419 grt/1,412 dwt; 73.18 × 4.62 m *(240.09 × 15.16 ft)*; M (Akasaka); 12 kts; ex-*Green Sea*

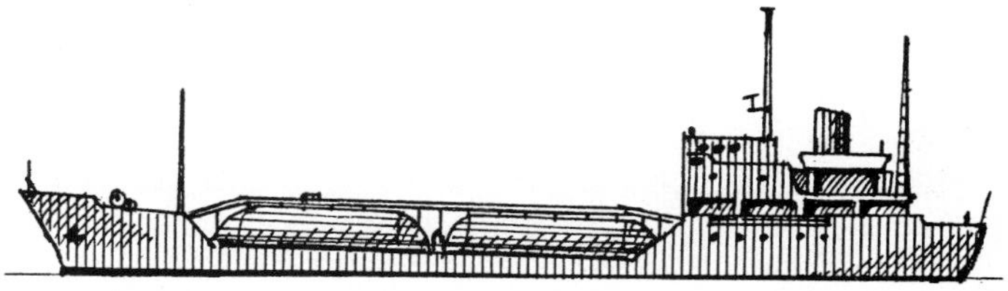

8 *M^2FN H13*
MARCELLE Pa/Ja (Naikai) 1976; LGC; 1,495 grt/1,748 dwt; 75.16 × 5.17 m *(246.6 × 16.96 ft)*; M (Yanmar); 12 kts; ex-*Kokushu Maru No 2*

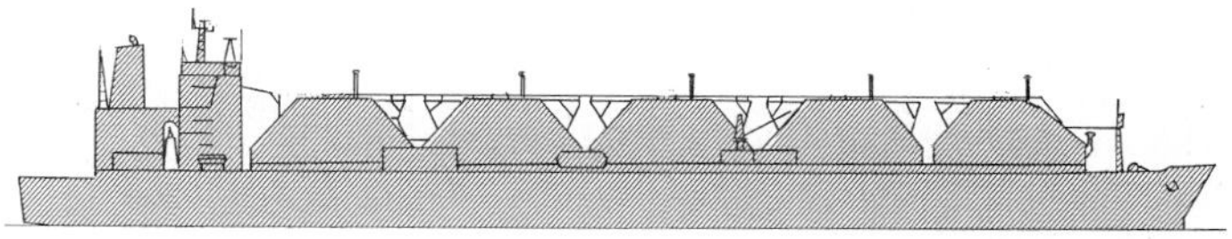

9 *M^3DM^3NMFM H1*
SENSHU MARU Ja/Ja (Mitsui) 1984; LGC; 102,330 grt/69,594 dwt; 283.01 × 11.50 m *(928.51 × 37.73 ft)*; T (Stal-Laval); 19.25 kts
Possible sister: **WAKABA MARU** (Ja)

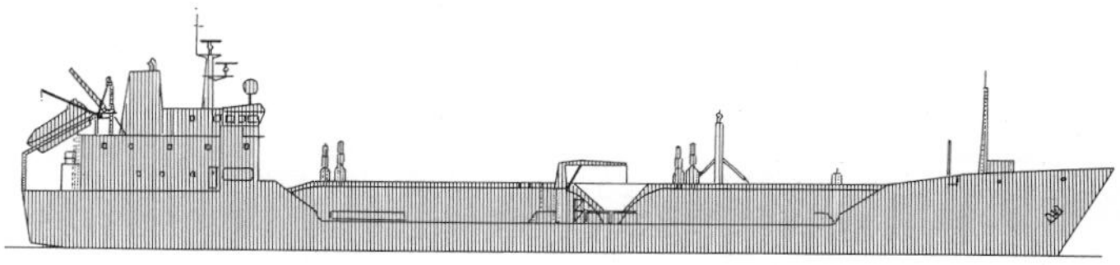

10 *M^3FCL H13*
GAMMAGAS Li/Br (Dunston) 1992; LGC; 3,703 grt/4,447 dwt; 99.35 × 6.47 m *(325.95 × 21.23 ft)*; M (MaK); 14.8 kts
Possible sister: **HAPPY FELLOW** (Pi) ex-*Sunny Fellow*

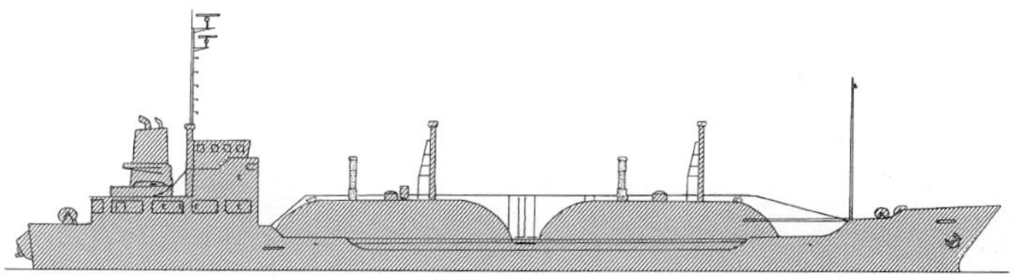

11 *M^4F H13*
YUTOKU MARU Ja/Ja (Narasaki) 1992; LGC; 998 grt/1,390 dwt; 71.98 × 4.37 m *(236.15 × 14.34 ft)*; M (Akasaka); 11.5 kts

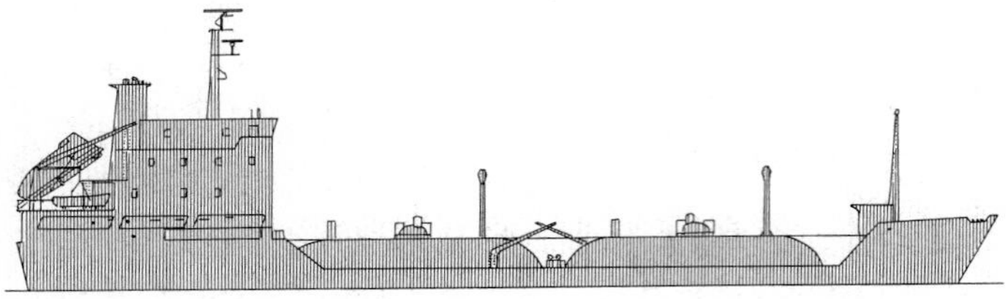

12 $M^{4}FL$ *H13*
MARIA CHRISTINA GIRALT Cu/Sp (Juliana) 1990; LGC; 1,973 grt/ 1,165 dwt; 79.80 × 4.10 m *(261.81 × 13.45 ft)*; M (B&W); 13 kts
Sister: **LOURDES GIRALT** (Cu)

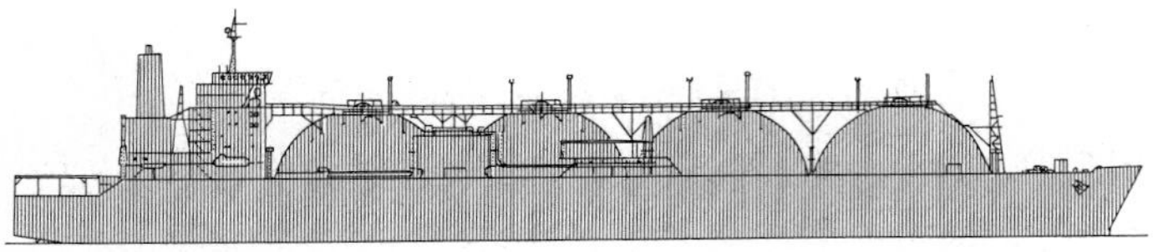

13 $M^{5}DM^{3}HF$ *H1*
NORTHWEST SNIPE Au/Ja (Mitsui) 1990; LGC; 105,010 grt/66,695 dwt; 272 × 11.38 m *(892.39 × 37.34 ft)*; T (Mitsubishi); 18.51 kts
Sisters: **NORTHWEST SANDPIPER** (Au); **NORTHWEST SWALLOW** (Ja); Similar (builder—Mitsubishi HI): **NORTHWEST SANDERLING** (Au); **NORTHWEST SEAEAGLE** (Br); **NORTHWEST STORMPETREL** (Au); **NORTHWEST SWIFT** (Ja); Similar (builder—Kawasaki): **NORTHWEST SHEARWATER** (Br)

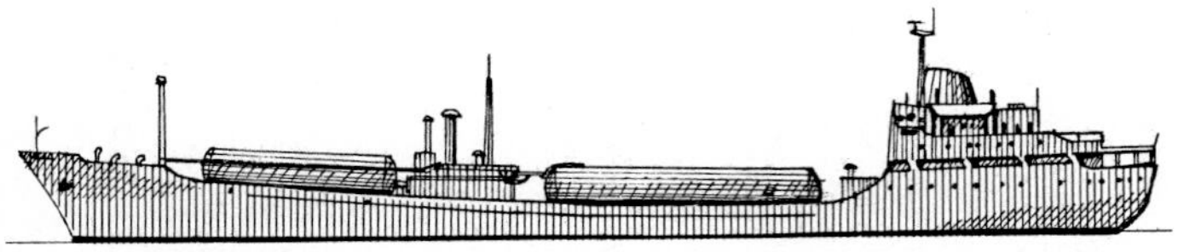

14 $M^{5}F$ *H13*
PAULINE Pa/Fr (La Ciotat) 1965; LGC; 5,312 grt/7,517 dwt; 110.85 × 6.67 m *(363.68 × 21.88 ft)*; M (B&W); 13.5 kts; ex-*Frostfonn*

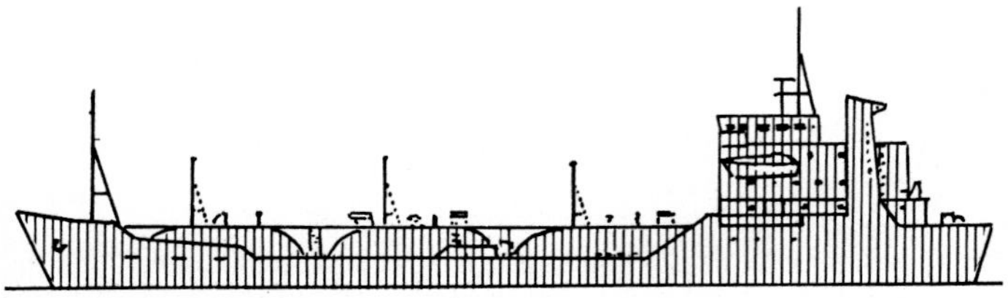

15 $M^{5}G$ *H13*
TARIHIKO NZ/Br (Ferguson-Ailsa) 1984; LGC; 2,169 grt/1,872 dwt; 81.11 × 4.88 m *(266.11 × 16.01 ft)*; M (MaK); 12.5 kts

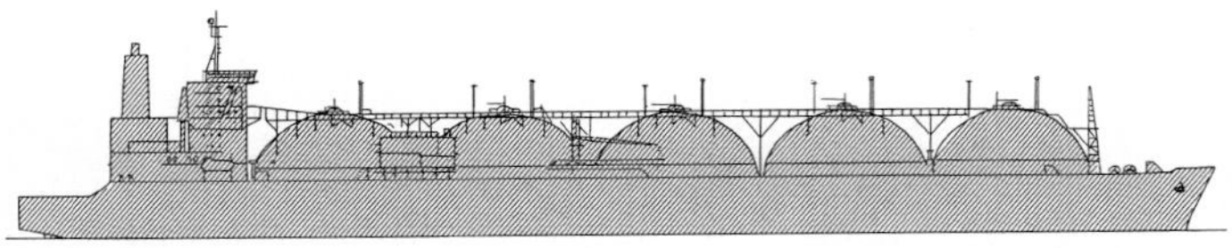

16 $M^{7}DM^{3}HDF$ *H1*
GHASHA Li/Ja (Mitsui) 1995; LGC; 110,895 grt/71,931 dwt; 293.00 × 11.27 m *(961.29 × 36.98 ft)*; T (Kawasaki); 19.70 kts
Sister: **AL KHAZNAH** (Li); Probable sister (builder Kawasaki); **SHAHAMAH** (Li)

See photo number 3/32 and 3/61

17 $M^{7}F$ *H1*
HOEGH GANDRIA NIS/FRG (Howaldts DW) 1977; LGC; 96,011 grt/ 71,630 dwt; 287.54 × 11.52 m *(943.37 × 37.8 ft)*; T (AG 'Weser'); 20 kts
Sister: **GOLAR FREEZE** (Li)

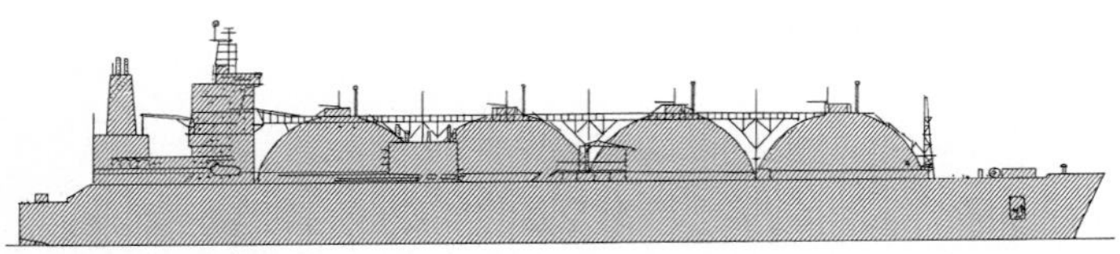

18 $M^{9}SF$ *H1*
MUBARAZ UAE/Fi (Kvaerner Masa) 1996; LGC; 116,700 grt/72,950 dwt; 290.00 × 11.80 m *(951.44 × 38.71 ft)*; T (—); 19.5 kts; Three sisters (1996/ 97 delivery)

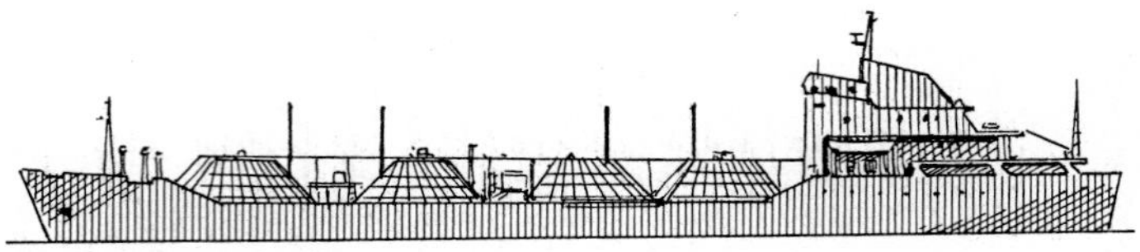

19 $M^{5}M\text{-}FN$ *H13*
CHEM UNITY Pa/Fr (Havre) 1971; LGC; 4,697 grt/3,260 dwt; 107.02 × 6.09 m *(351.12 × 19.98 ft)*; M (Sulzer); 15.5 kts; ex-*Euclides*

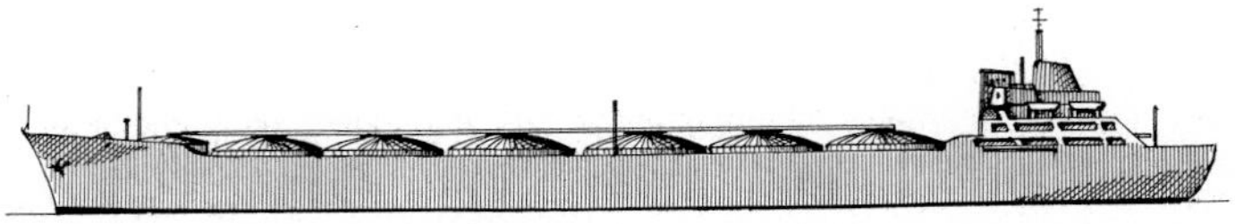

20 $M^{5}M\text{-}FM$ *H1*
JULES VERNE SV/Fr (La Seine) 1965; LGC; 22,062 grt/14,066 dwt; 201.02 × 7.53 m *(659.51 × 24.7 ft)*; T (Parsons); 17 kts

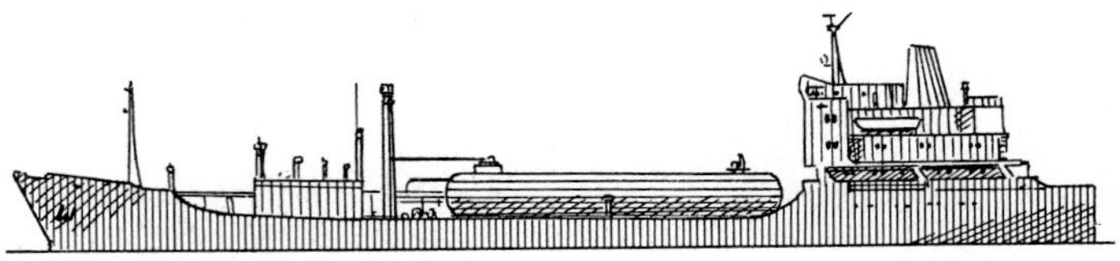

21 $M^{3}NMF$ *H13*
ADELIA Pa/No (Moss R) 1971; LGC; 3,790 grt/4,205 dwt; 106.05 × 6.45 m *(347.93 × 21.16 ft)*; M (Stork-Werkspoor); 14.75 kts; ex-*Tordenskiold*
Similar: **AMAZONIA** (Pa) ex-*Roald Amundsen*

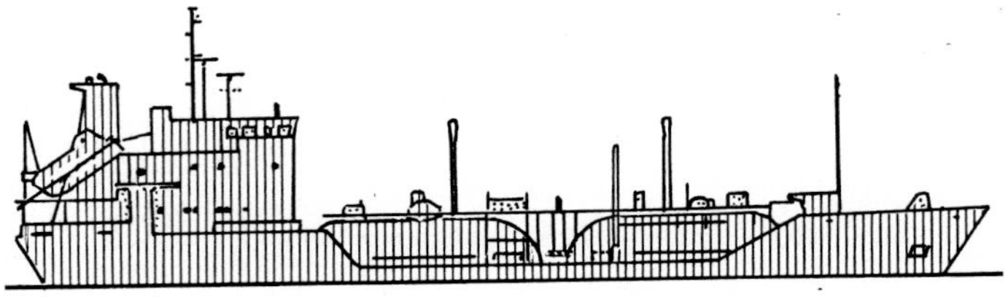

22 $M^{3}NMFLC$ *H13*
NP ENTERPRISE Bs/FRG (Sietas) 1986; LGC; 1,332 grt/1,060 dwt; 69.19 × 4.30 m *(227.00 × 14.11 ft)*; M (Yanmar); 13 kts; ex-*Scott Enterprise*

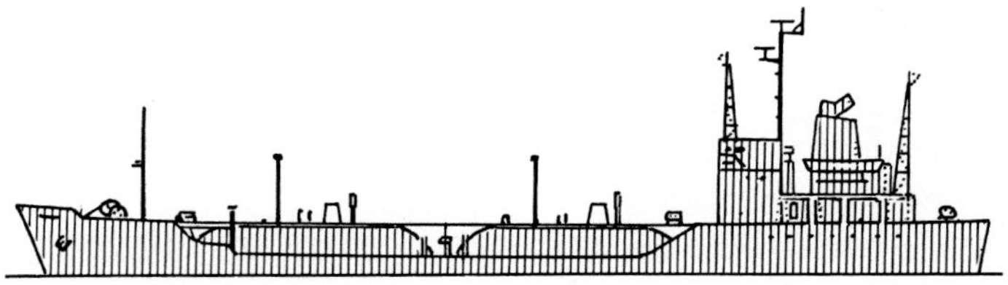

23 $M^{3}NMFN$ *H13*
SIRIUS GAS Pa/Ja (Tokushima ZS) 1980; LGC; 2,688 grt/3,070 dwt; 93.35 × 5.27 m *(306.27 × 17.29 ft)*; M (Akasaka); 13.25 kts; ex-*Vitolla*
Sisters: **ARIES GAS** (Pa) ex-*Helios Gas*; **EVERDINA** (Bs); **BAYSTAR** (Pa) ex-*Fuji Gas*

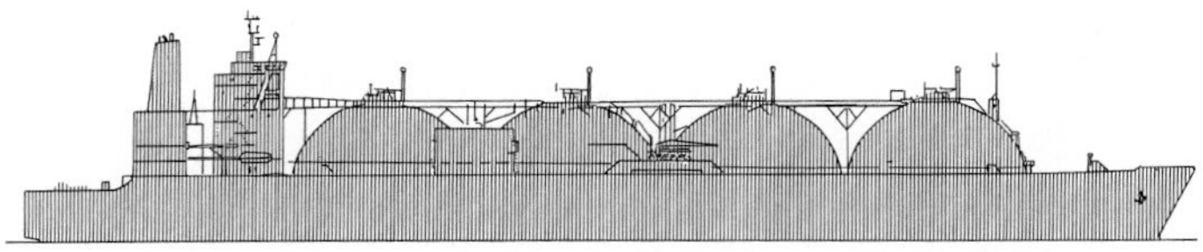

24 $M^{3}RM^{3}HF$ *H1*
HYUNDAI UTOPIA Pa/Ko (Hyundai) 1994; LGC; 103,764 grt/71,909 dwt; 274 × 11.77 m *(898.95 × 38.62 ft)*; T (Mitsubishi); 18.5 kts

25 $M^{2}NMF$ *H123*
CARIGAS Pa/No (Moss V) 1967; LGC; 2,638 grt/3,238 dwt; 90.56 × 6.1 m *(297.11 × 20.01 ft)*; M (Sulzer); 12.5 kts; ex-*Janegaz*
Sister: **CAP AKRITAS** (Gr) ex-*Fridtjof Nansen*

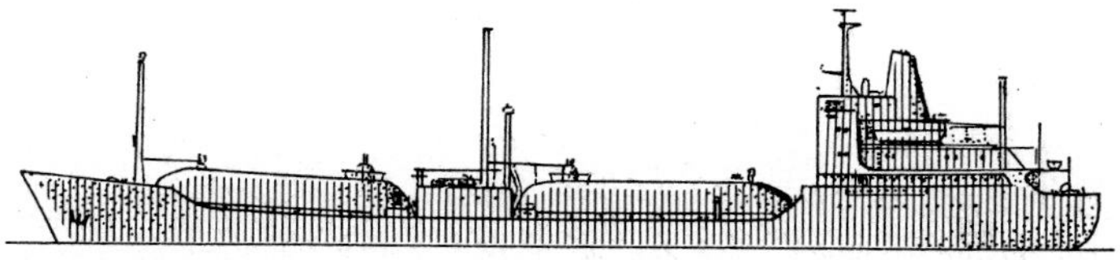

26 *M²NMFN H13*
ANCON Ec/No (Kristiansands) 1969; LGC; 3,194 grt/3,637 dwt; 101.94 × 6.06 m *(334.45 × 19.88 ft)*; M (Sulzer); 13.75 kts; ex-*Cabo Tres Montes*
Sisters: **AYANGUE** (SV) Launched as *Rita*; **CARIBGAS 3** (Pa) ex-*Troika*;
Similar: **MUNDOGAS PIONEER** (Va) ex-*Thor Heyerdahl*

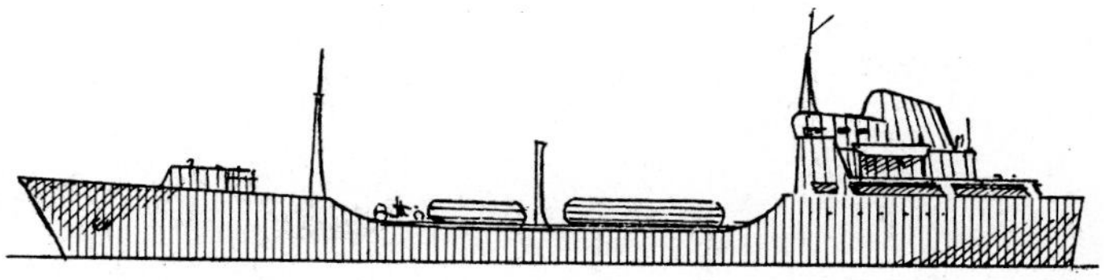

28 *MNHF H13*
MELROSE Bs/FRG (Brand) 1971; LGC; 1,999 grt/2,713 dwt; 86.95 × 6.12 m *(285.27 × 20.08 ft)*; M (MWM); 14 kts; ex-*Melrose*

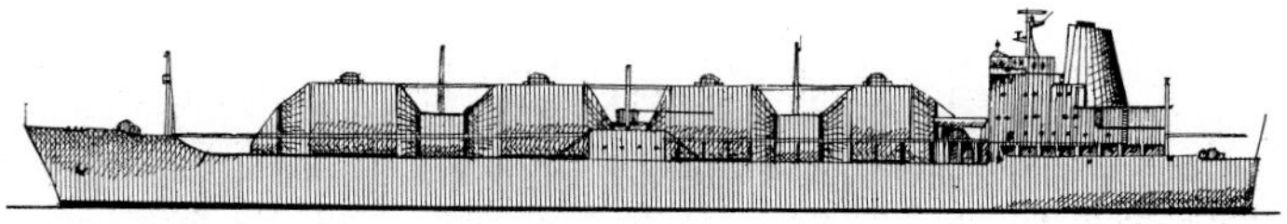

27 *M²NM²FMS H1*
CENTURY NIS/No (Moss R) 1974; 26,097 grt/22,036 dwt; 181.54 × 9.42 m *(595.6 × 30.91 ft)*; M (Sulzer); 19 kts; ex-*Lucian*; Converted from Gas Turbine 1980
Similar: **HAVFRU** (NIS) ex-*Venator*

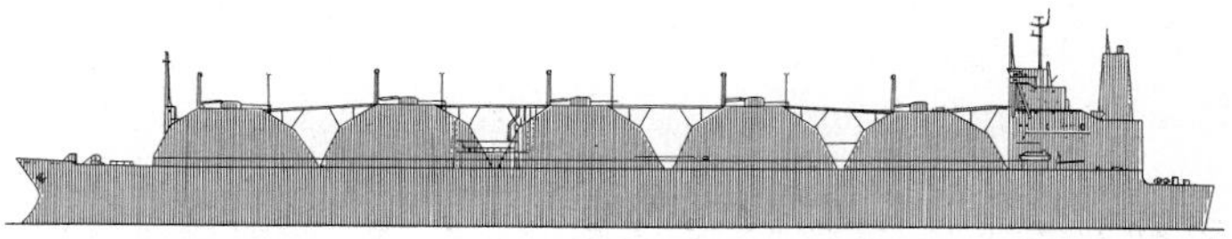

29 *M¹⁰NMF H1*
BISHU MARU Ja/Ja (Kawasaki) 1983; LGC; 100,296 grt/69,991 dwt; 281.01 × 11.47 m *(921.95 × 37.63 ft)*; T (Kawasaki); 19.25 kts
Possible sister: **KOTOWAKA MARU** (Ja)

30 Lng Flora *(Ja); 1993* *"Sea Japan"—Japan Ship Exporters' Association*

31 Northwest Sandpiper *(Au); 1993* *"Sea Japan" —Japan Ship Exporters' Association*

32 Golar Freeze *(Li); 1977* *FotoFlite*

33 Cheltenham *(Bs); 1990; (builder—Kanrei Shipbuilding Co)*

34 Cheltenham *(Bs); 1990* *FotoFlite*

35 Chem Unity *(Pa); 1971* *FotoFlite*

36 Century *(NIS); 1975* *FotoFlite*

37 Adelia *(Pa); 1971* *FotoFlite*

38 Amazonia *(Pa); 1971* *FotoFlite*

39 Norman Lady *(Li); 1973* *FotoFlite*

40 Mundogas Pioneer *(Va); 1969* *FotoFlite*

41 Melrose *(Bs); 1971* *FotoFlite*

42 Everdina *(Bs); 1981* *FotoFlite*

43 Khannur *(Li); 1977* *FotoFlite*

44 Queeny Margaret *(Cy); 1974* *FotoFlite*

45 Golden Crux No 8 *(Pa); 1981* *FotoFlite*

46 Lanrick *(Li); 1992* *FotoFlite*

47 Ruby Star *(It); 1990* *FotoFlite*

48 Silver Coral *(Bs); 1970; (as Helen)* *WSPL*

49 Red Dragon *(It); 1989* *WSPL*

50 Gaz Sun *(Pa); 1977; (as Sunny Duke)* *WSPL*

51 Happy Fellow *(Pi); 1992; (as Sunny Fellow)* *G V Smith*

52 Australgas *(Ch); 1968; (as Happy Bird)* *WSPL*

53 Astra IV *(Pa); 1969; (as Mundogas Atlantic)* *WSPL*

54 Cinderella *(SV); 1965; (as Jules Verne)* *WSPL*

55 LNG Libra *(US); 1979* *WSPL*

56 LNG Aquarius *(US); 1977* *WSPL*

57 Mubaraz *(Li); 1995* *FotoFlite/Kvaerner Masa-Yards*

58 Snowdon *(Sg); 1989* *WSPL*

59 Gimi *(Li); 1976* *WSPL*

60 Sirius Gas *(Pa); 1980* *WSPL*

61 Hoegh Gandria *(NIS); 1977* *WSPL*

62 Hanyang Gas *(Ko); 1973; (as Mercury Gas)* *WSPL*

63 Sargasso *(Pa); 1981* *FotoFlite*

64 Umm Shaif *(UAE); 1991* *FotoFlite*

65 Derwent *(Sg); 1990* *FotoFlite*

66 Marianne Kosan *(DIS); 1968* *FotoFlite*

67 Pauline *(Pa); 1977; (as Enrico Fermi)* *FotoFlite*

68 Prins William II *(Ne); 1985* *FotoFlite*

69 Prins Phillips Willem *(Ne); 1985* *WSPL*

70 Cap Elene *(Li); 1982; (as Capo Amaranto)* *FotoFlite*

71 Henrik Kosan *(DIS); 1984; (as Henrik Tholstrup)* *WSPL*

72 Gaz Coral *(Pa); 1981* *FotoFlite*

73 Santong *(Pa); 1981* *FotoFlite*

74 Fortunato *(Pa); 1980* *FotoFlite*

75 White Star *(It); 1981; (as Calderon)* *FotoFlite*

76 Viking Star *(Pa); 1976* *FotoFlite*

77 Sunshine II *(Pi); 1971* *FotoFlite*

78 Norgas Pilot *(NIS); 1977* *FotoFlite*

79 NP Enterprise *(Bs); 1986; (as Scott Enterprise)* *FotoFlite*

80 Wilson Ruby *(Pa); 1972; (as Joule)* *FotoFlite*

81 Golar Spirit *(Li); 1981* *FotoFlite*

82 Gaz Polaris *(Pa); 1983; (as Polaris Gas)* *FotoFlite*

83 Balder Phenix *(Pa); 1982* *FotoFlite*

84 Silver Pride *(Bs); 1990; (builder—Teraoka Shipyard Co)*

85 Dwiputra *(Bs); 1994; (builder—Mitsubishi Heavy Industries)*

4 Liquefied Gas Carriers without Deck Tanks

4 Liquefied Gas Carriers without Deck Tanks

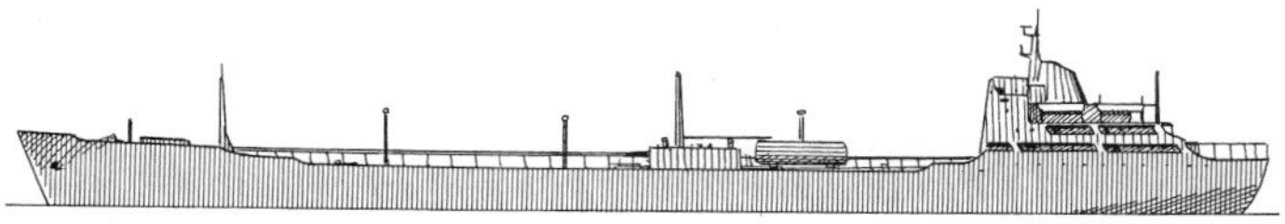

1 *HM^{2}NMM-FN H13*
EXCEL Li/Fr (La Ciotat) 1967; LGC; 14,869 grt/14,982 dwt; 177.2 × 7.72 m *(581.36 × 25.33 ft)*; M (Sulzer); 16 kts; ex-*Isfonn*

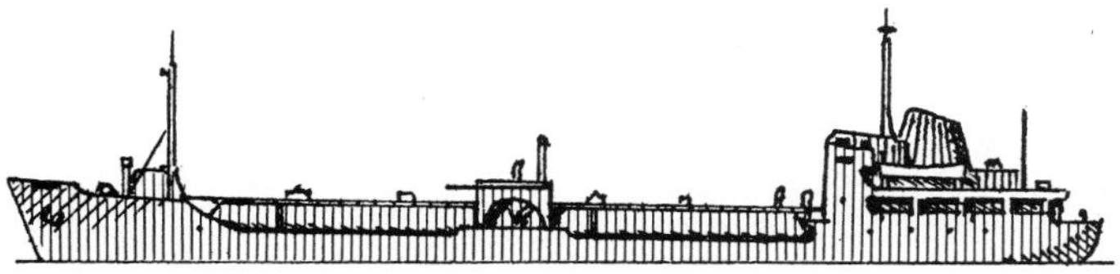

2 *HNHFN H13*
JAVA RAINBOW Li/Sp (Euskalduna) 1965; LGC; 1,970 grt/1,543 dwt; 80.8 × 4.93 m *(265.09 × 16.17 ft)*; M (Gotaverken); 14 kts; ex-*Butatres*

3 *K^{10}G H*
MOSTEFA BEN BOULAID Ag/Fr (La Ciotat) 1976; LGC; 81,548 grt/62,675 dwt; 278.82 × 12.2 m *(914.76 × 40.03 ft)*; T (Stal-Laval); 18.5 kts

See photo number 4/175

4 *ME^{3}NEMF H2*
METHANIA Lu/Be (Boelwerf) 1978; LGC; 81,792 grt/67,879 dwt; 280.02 × 11.23 m *(918.7 × 36.84 ft)*; T (Deutz); 19 kts

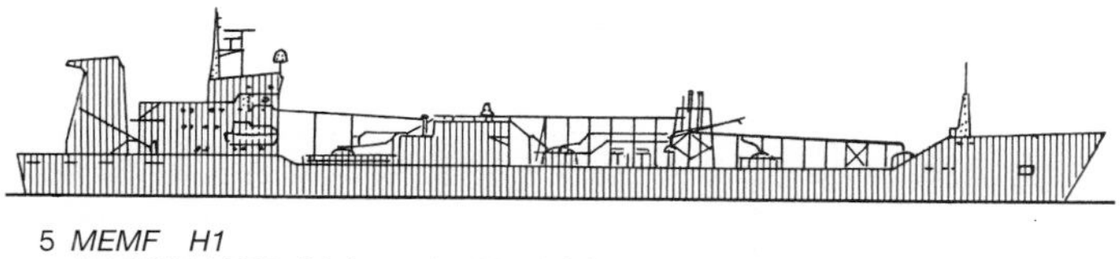

5 *MEMF H1*
ATRICE Li/FRG (M Jansen) 1984; LGC; 6,755 grt/8,711 dwt; 126.06 × 8.06 m *(413.58 × 26.44 ft)*; M (MaK); 15.5 kts; ex-*Beatrice*

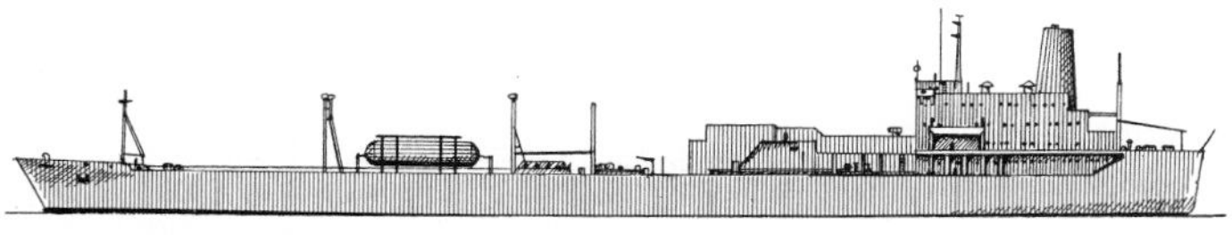

6 *MEMNM^{2}FN H3*
DAVID GAS Li/Sw (Kockums) 1969; LGC; 19,466 grt/21,380 dwt; 184.74 × 9.7 m *(606.1 × 31.82 ft)*; M (MAN); 17 kts; ex-*Phillips Arkansas*

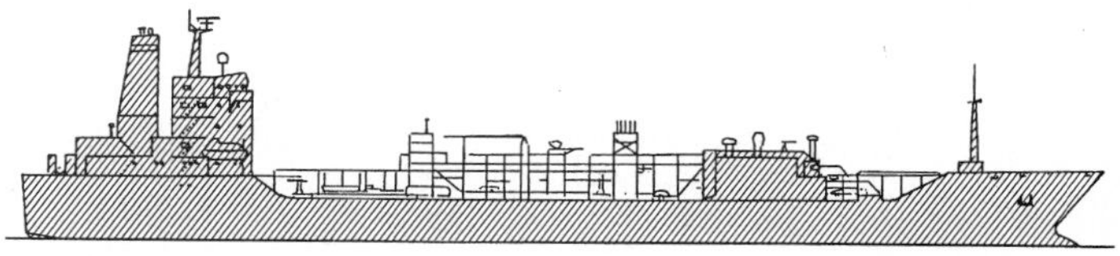

7 *MEREMF H13*
IGLOO MOON Ge/FRG (Thyssen) 1987; LGC/Ch; 10,195 grt/13,125 dwt; 141.81 × 9.00 m *(465.26 × 29.53 ft)*; M (MAN); 16.15 kts; ex-*Gaschem Moon*
Sister: **IGLOO STAR** (Ge) ex-*Gaschem Star*; Similar (10 m (32.8 ft) longer): **GJERTRUD MAERSK** (DIS); **IGLOO HAV** (NIS) ex-*Gudrun Maersk*

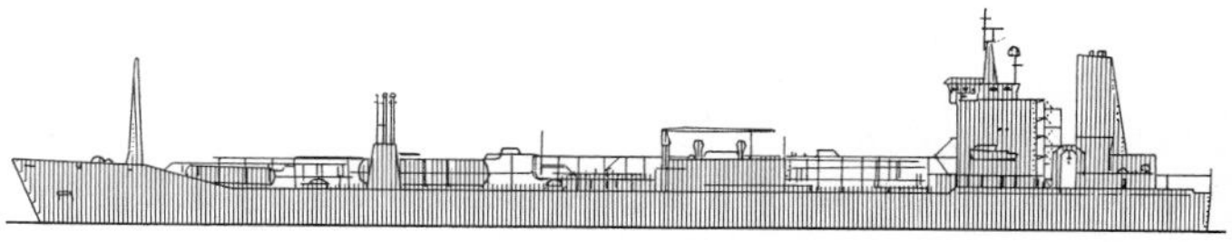

8 *MERMF H1*
GAZ NORDSEE Pa/FRG (Meyer) 1985; LGC; 23,508 grt/32,339 dwt; 183.01 × 11.87 m *(600.43 × 38.94 ft)*; M (Sulzer); 15 kts; ex-*Donau*

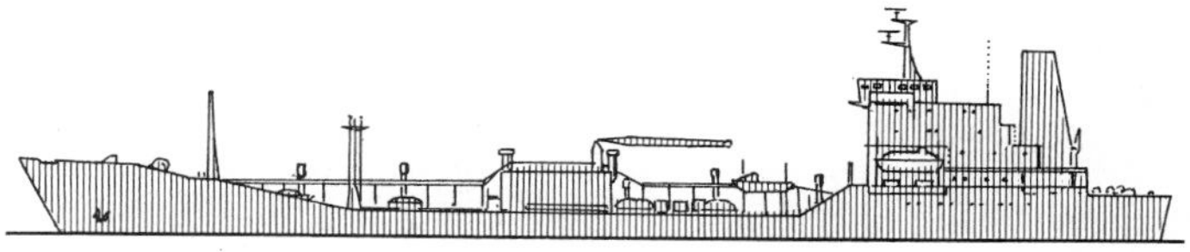

9 *MERMF H13*
IGLOO FINN NIS/No (Moss R) 1981; LGC/Ch; 8,630 grt/11,665 dwt; 127.82 × 9.45 m *(419 × 31 ft)*; M (Sulzer); 16 kts
Sisters: **IGLOO NORSE** (Fi); **IGLOO POLAR** (NIS); **NORGAS VICTORY** (NIS) ex-*Havlyn* (Builder—Drammen); Similar (135.751 m *(445.371 ft)* long): **IGLOO ESPOO** (NIS); **IGLOO MOSS** (NIS)

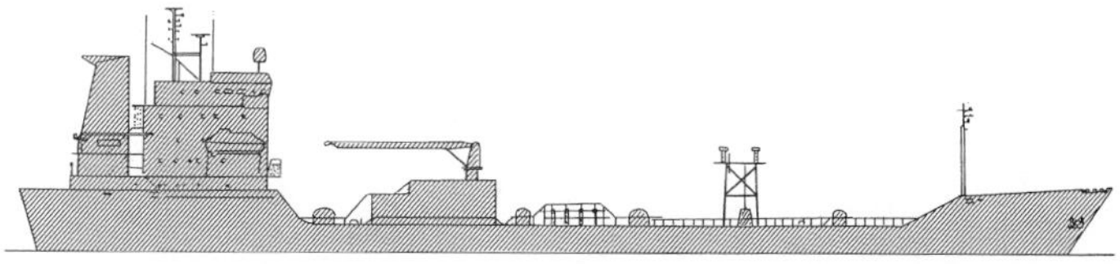

10 *MERMF H13*
LEDAGAS Li/FRG (Lindenau) 1984; LGC; 5,284 grt/5,686 dwt; 114.81 × 6.70 m *(376.67 × 21.98 ft)*; M (MaK); 14 kts
Sister: **EMSGAS** (Li)

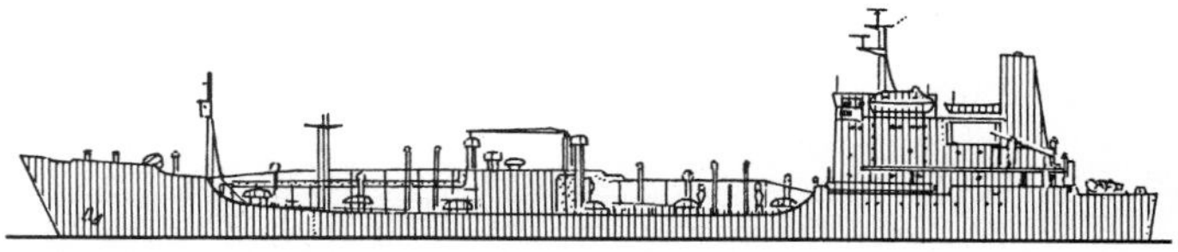

11 *MERMF H13*
NORGAS ENERGY NIS/No (Moss R) 1979; LGC/Ch; 6,521 grt/8,920 dwt; 116.57 × 8.6 m *(382.45 × 28.22 ft)*; M (Sulzer); 15.75 kts; ex-*Helice*
Sister: **NORGAS PIONEER** (NIS) ex-*Admiral Cabral*

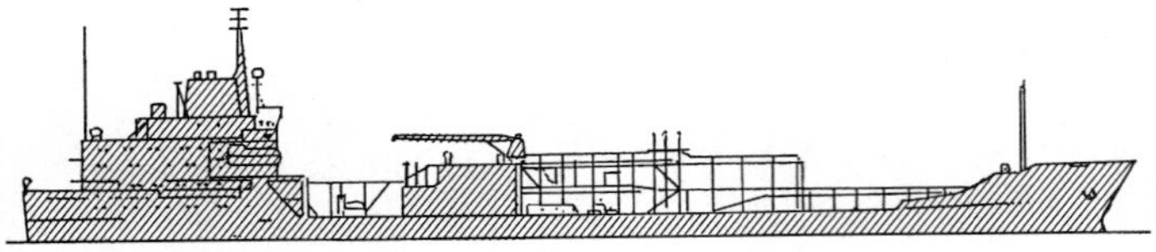

12 *MERMM-FN H13*
NORGAS TRAVELLER Li/DDR ('Neptun') 1980/1987; LGC; 6,684 grt/7,770 dwt; 130.00 × 7.59 m *(426.51 × 24.90 ft)*; M (MAN); 14.50 kts; ex-*Beate*; Lengthened and converted from cargo vessel of 'NEPTUN 471' type 1987 (Sietas)

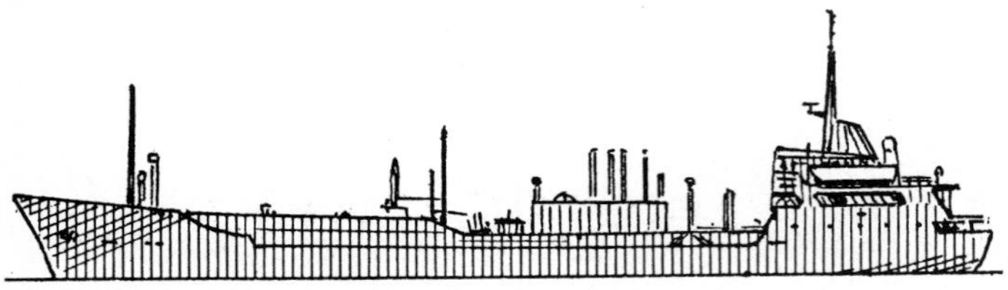

13 $M^{14}F$ *H13*
KILGAS DISCOVERY Bs/No (Kleven) 1965; LGC; 1,403 grt/2,266 dwt; 71.18 × 5.51 m *(233.53 × 18.08 ft)*; M (MaK); 12.5 kts; ex-*Kings Star*; Converted cargo ship 1971
Sister: **ASTRALGAS** (Ch) ex-*Teresa*

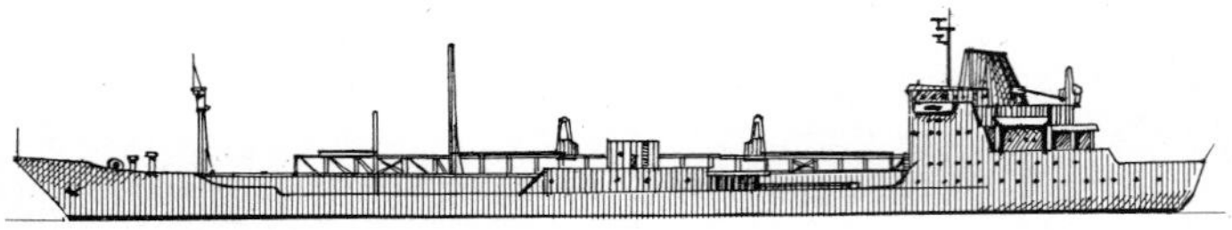

14 $M^{2}C^{2}MFC$ *H13*
KAPITAN LUCA Ma/Sp (Cadiz) 1969; LGC; 10,909 grt/11,470 dwt; 153.2 × 8.52 m *(502.69 × 27.96 ft)*; M (Sulzer); 16.5 kts; ex-*Butanueve*

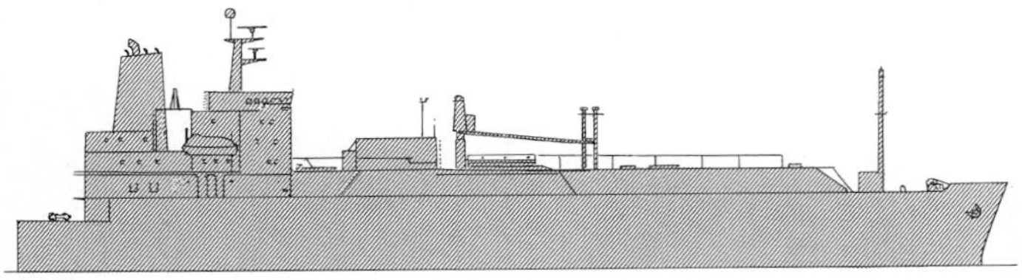

15 $M^{2}DMF$ *H1*
AMAN BINTULU My/Ja (NKK Corp) 1993; LGC; 16,399 grt/11,001 dwt; 130 × 7.12 m *(426.51 × 23.36 ft)*; T (Mitsubishi); 15 kts

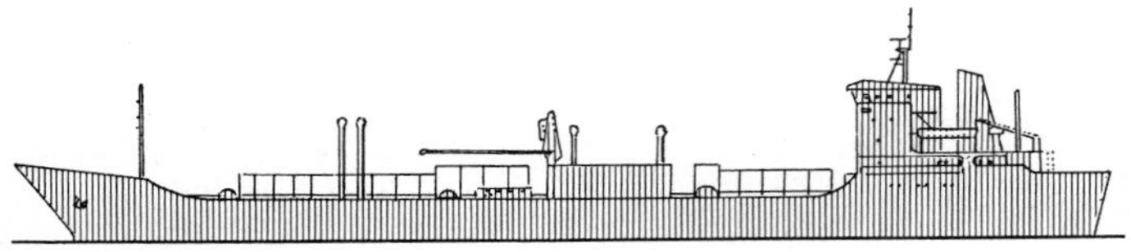

16 $M^{3}CMFM$ *H13*
JAPERI Bz/Sp (UN de Levante) 1983; LGC; 7,724 grt/10,310 dwt; 128.61 × 8.52 m *(421.95 × 27.95 ft)*; M (B&W); 15.25 kts

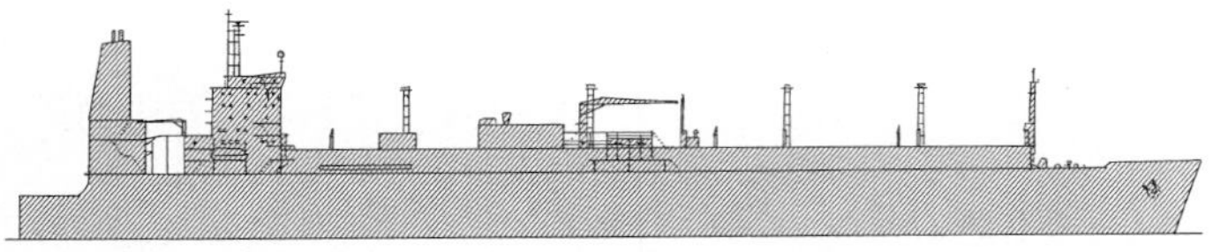

17 $M^{3}DSM^{2}RF$ *H1*
HANJIN PYEONG TAEK Pa/Ko (Hanjin HI) 1995; LGC; 90,004 grt/61,436 dwt; 268.50 × 11.00 m *(880.91 × 36.09 ft)*; T (Mitsubishi); 19 kts

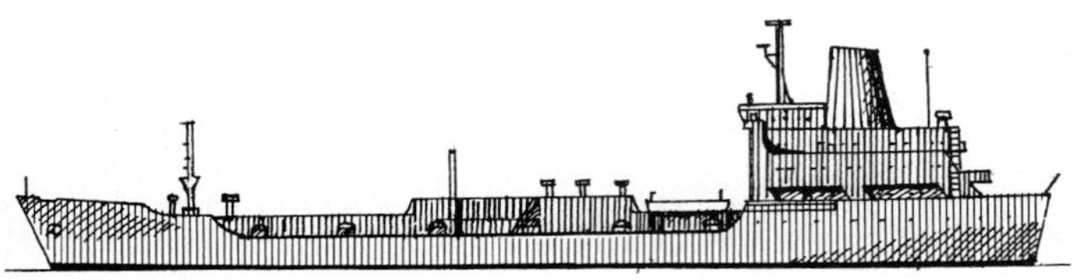

18 $M^{3}F$ *H13*
SAMARGAS Cy/No (Moss R) 1973; LGC; 4,779 grt/4,507 dwt; 105.01 × 7.06 m *(344.52 × 23.16 ft)*; M (Wärtsilä); 14.75 kts; ex-*Nestegas*

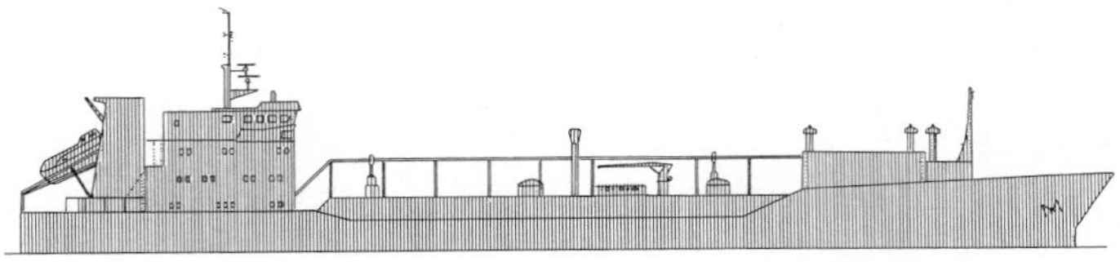

19 $M^{3}FL$ *H1*
ALSTERGAS Li/Ne (Pattje) 1991; LGC; 4,200 grt/5,688 dwt; 99.97 × 7.20 m *(327.99 × 23.62 ft)*; M (MaK); 14 kts
Sister: **DOLLART GAS** (Ge)

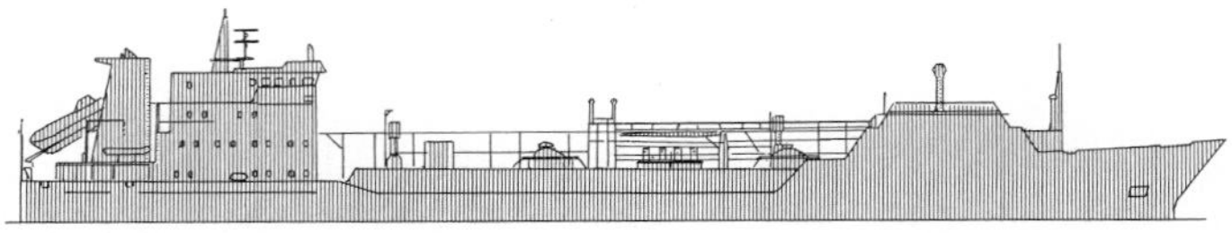

20 $M^{3}FL$ *H1*
RHEINGAS Li/Ne (Pattje) 1992; LGC; 4,200 grt/5,688 dwt; 99.97 × 7.20 m *(327.99 × 23.62 ft)*; M (MaK); 14 kts
Sister: **ISARGAS** (At)

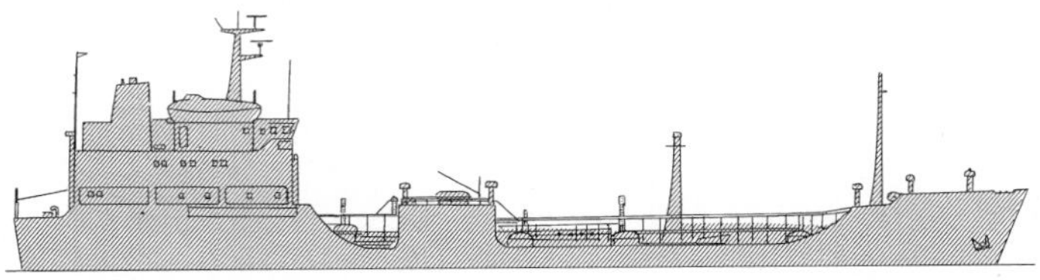

21 $M^{3}GM$ *H123*
NEW PROVIDENCE Li/No (Moss R) 1978; LGC; 2,313 grt/3,092 dwt; 75.72 × 6.81 m *(248.43 × 22.34 ft)*; M (Wichmann); 13 kts; ex-*Hestia*
Sisters: **PETROMAR I** (Pa) ex-*Hermina*; **ERIK KOSAN** (DIS) ex-*Francis Drake*

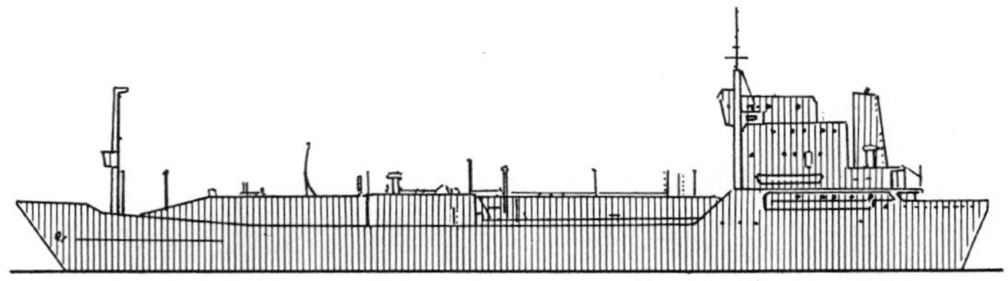

22 $M^{3}HF$ *H13*
SELMA KOSAN Bs/No (Sterkoder) 1976/81; LGC; 5,807 grt/6,680 dwt; 110.78 × 7.66 m *(363.45 × 25.13 ft)*; M (MWM); X kts; ex-*Leikvin*; Converted from general cargo 1981 (Howaldts DW)

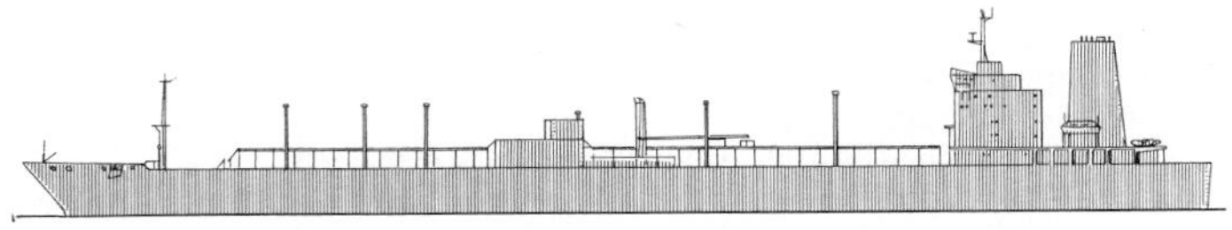

23 $M^{4}CM^{3}F$ *H*
GAZ ATLANTIC Pa/It (Breda) 1980; LGC; 51,039 grt/55,728 dwt; 234.02 × 12 m *(768 × 39.37 ft)*; M (B&W); 16.5 kts; ex-*Lensovet*
Sister: **GAZ PROGRESS** (Pa) ex-*Mossovet*

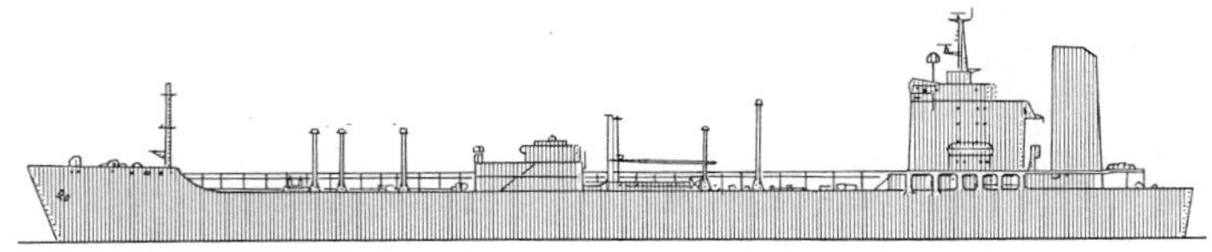

24 $M^{4}CM^{3}F$ *H1*
HAVRIM NIS/It (Breda) 1980; LGC; 26,207 grt/25,663 dwt; 197.42 × 10.10 m *(647.70 × 33.14 ft)*; M (B&W); — kts; ex-*Smolnyy*

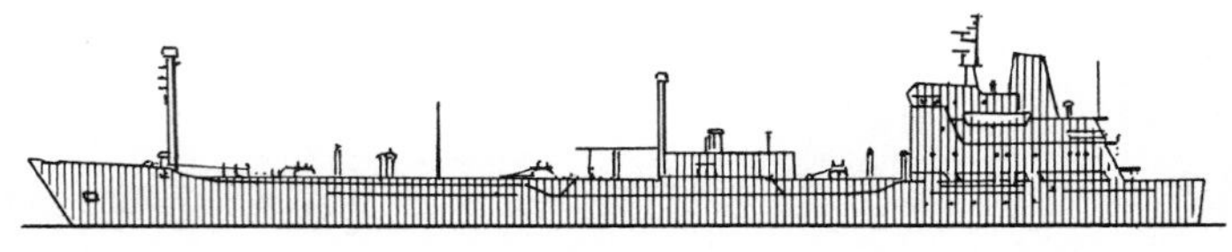

25 $M^{4}F$ *H1*
BALINA NIS/FRG (Meyer) 1975; LGC; 4,226 grt/6,153 dwt; 106.61 × 7.54 m *(349.77 × 24.74 ft)*; M (KHD); 16.5 kts; ex-*Deltagas*

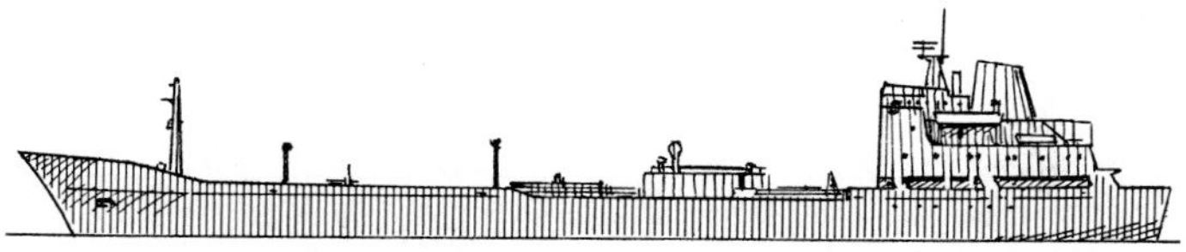

26 M^4F *H1*

BENGHAZI Ag/FRG (Meyer) 1978; LGC; 4,612 grt/5,961 dwt; 108.8 × 7.5 m *(356.96 × 24.61 ft)*; M (KHD); 15 kts

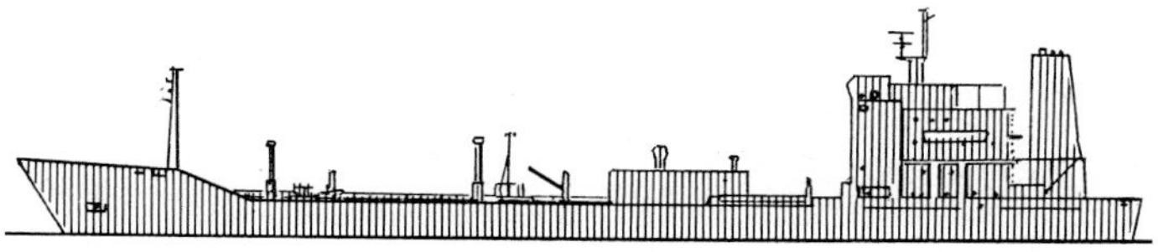

27 M^4F *H1*

DOROTHEA SCHULTE NIS/FRG (Meyer) 1981; LGC/Ch; 4,884 grt/6,118 dwt; 111.03 × 7.51 m *(364 × 24.64 ft)*; M (B&W); 14.25 kts
Sisters: **HERMANN SCHULTE** (NIS); **GALP FARO** (Po) ex-*Gaz Nordsee; GAZ PACIFIC* (Pa)

28 M^4F *H13*

CLIPPER GAS NIS/No (Moss V) 1971; LGC; 9,351 grt/11,745 dwt; 138.72 × 9.23 m *(455.12 × 30.28 ft)*; M (Sulzer); 17 kts; ex-*Vestri*

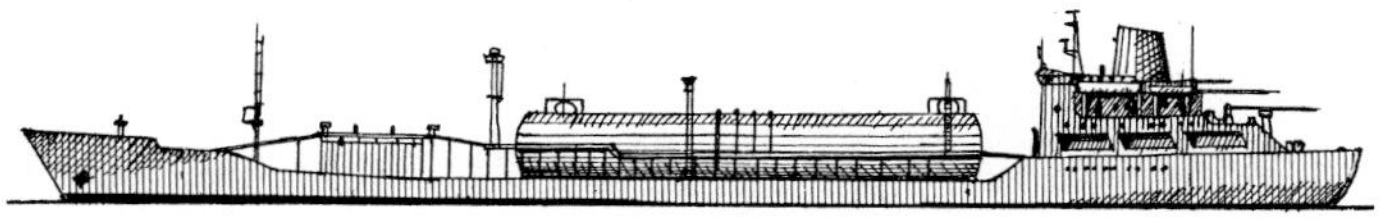

29 M^4F *H13*

HERA NIS/No (Moss R) 1977; LGC; 9,576 grt/11,365 dwt; 138.72 × 11.04 m *(455.12 × 36.22 ft)*; M (Sulzer); 17.75 kts
Sister: **HEROS** (NIS)

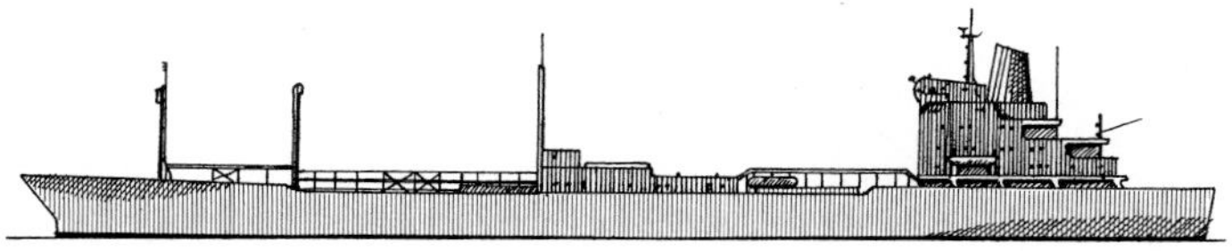

30 M^4FMC *H*

HESIOD Br/Br (Cammell Laird) 1973; LGC; 20,684 grt/23,869 dwt; 177.86 × 10.02 m *(583.5 × 32.9 ft)*; M (B&W); 16.25 kts; ex-*Gambada*
Sister: **HAVJARL** (Br) ex-*Gazana*

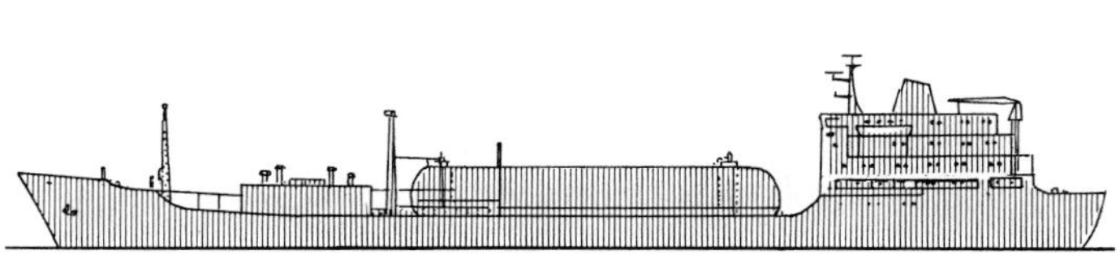

31 M^4FR *H13*

GAZ BALTIC Pa/No (Kristiansands) 1976; LGC; 9,445 grt/11,630 dwt; 138.72 × 9.20 m *(455.12 × 30.18 ft)*; TSM (Sulzer); 17.5 kts; ex-*Sine Maersk*
Sister: **HAVPIL** (NIS) ex-*Sofie Maersk*

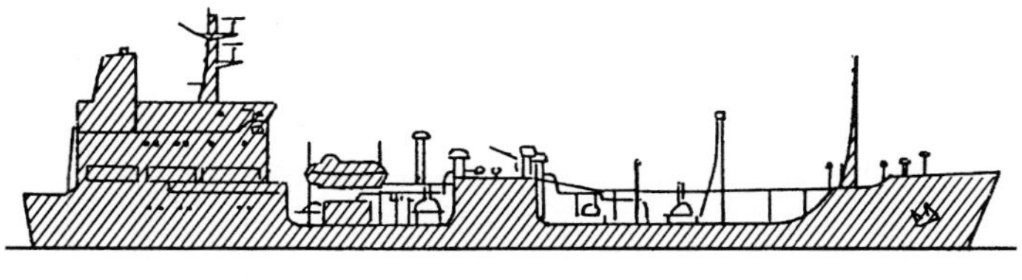

32 M^4GC *H13*

HEBE To/No (Moss R) 1981; LGC; 2,273 grt/2,950 dwt; 76.74 × 6.77 m *(251.77 × 22.21 ft)*; M (Nohab); 13.75 kts
Sister (extra lifeboat on housing amidships—port side): **HELEN** (To); Similar: **LAURITS KOSAN** (DIS) ex-*Traenafjell*; **KNUD KOSAN** (DIS) ex-*Traenafjord*

33 $M^5C^2M^4F$ *H*

BEBATIK Bx/Fr (L'Atlantique) 1972; LGC; 48,612 grt/51,579 dwt; 256.7 × 11.53 m *(842.2 × 37.83 ft)*; T (Stal-Laval); 18.25 kts; ex-*Gadinia*
Sisters: **BEKALANG** (Bx) ex-*Gadila*; **BEKULAN** (Bx) ex-*Gari*; **BELAIS** (Bx) ex-*Gastrana*; **BELANAK** (Bx) ex-*Gouldia*

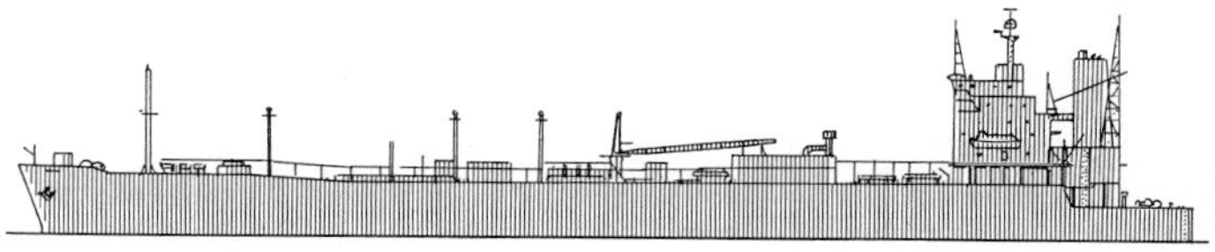

34 M^5CM^2CFM/M^5CNHFM *H1*

TOYOSU Pa/Ja (IHI) 1984; LGC; 24,387 grt/24,947 dwt; 176.71 × 9.2 m *(579.76 × 30.18 ft)*; M (Sulzer); 14.5 kts; ex-*Toyosu Maru*

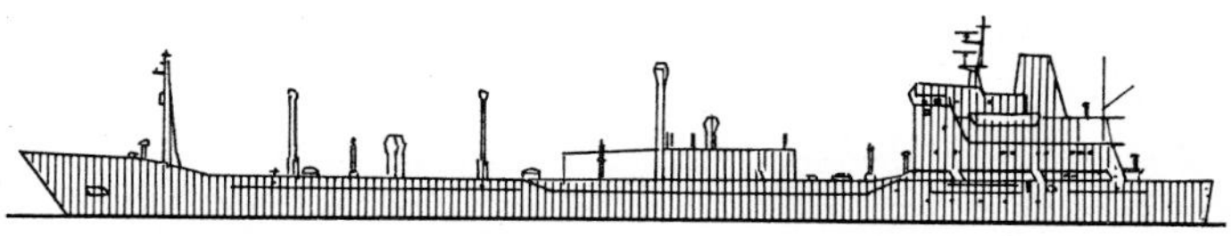

35 M^5F *H1*

EPSILONGAS NIS/FRG (Meyer) 1977; LGC; 4,407 grt/5,961 dwt; 107.7 × 7.46 m *(353.35 × 24.48 ft)*; M (KHD); 17 kts

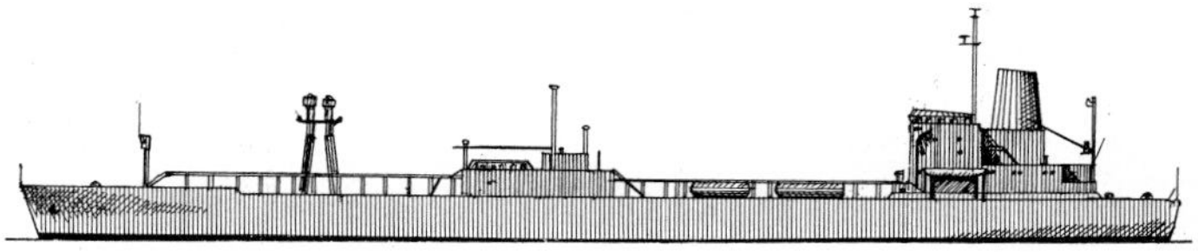

36 M^5FM

GAS GLORIA Ko/FRG (A G 'Weser') 1968; LGC; 19,355 grt/23,300 dwt; 173.84 × 10.26 m *(570.34 × 33.66 ft)*; M (Sulzer); 17.5 kts; ex-*Antilla Cape*

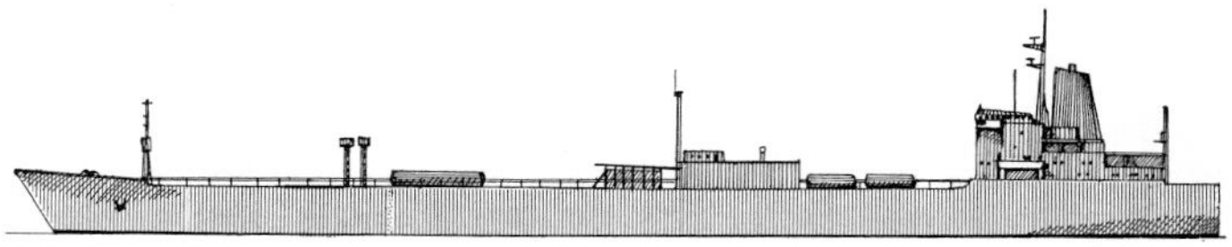

37 M^5FM *H*

HAVMANN NIS/Fr (CNIM) 1973; LGC; 33,288 grt/39,931 dwt; 216.47 × 11.02 m *(710.2 × 36.15 ft)*; M (Sulzer); 17.5 kts; ex-*Antilla Bay*
Similar (after posts nearer funnel—possibly abreast): **HESPERUS** (NIS) ex-*Dorsetown; **HAVPRINS*** (NIS) ex-*Dovertown*; Similar: **REYNOSA** (Me); **MONTERREY** (Me)

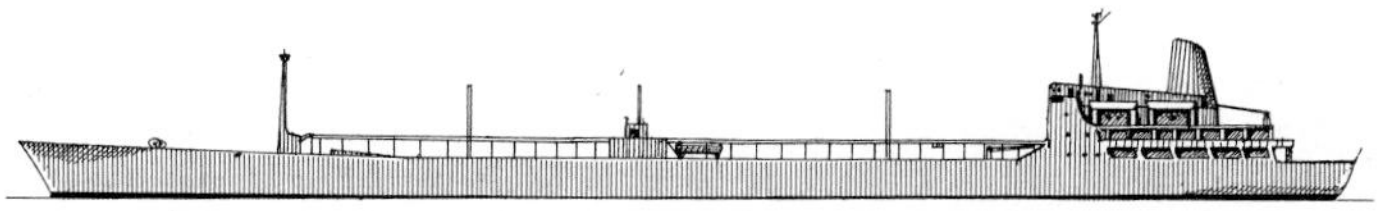

38 M^5FS *H*

METHANE PRINCESS Br/Br (Vickers-Armstrongs) 1964; LGC; 20,653 grt/24,608 dwt; 189.31 × 10.7 m *(621.1 × 35.1 ft)*; T (Pametrada); 17.25 kts

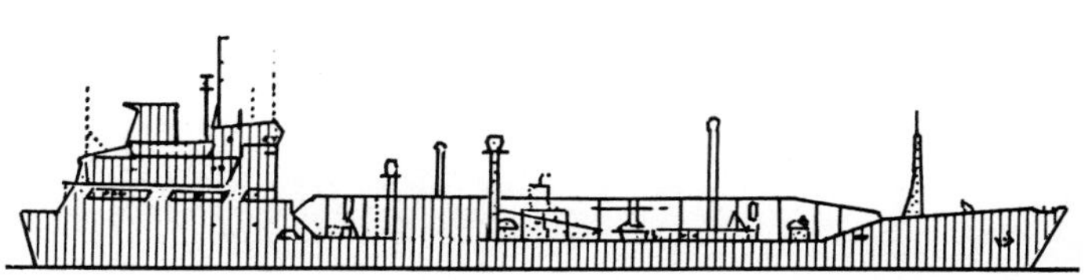

39 M^6FM *H123*

BECQUER Sp/Sp (Nervion) 1987; LGC; 2,795 grt/3,659 dwt; 84.61 × 6.60 m *(277.59 × 21.65 ft)*; M (Alpha); 14 kts; Second upright is on port side
Sister: **GONGORA** (Sp)

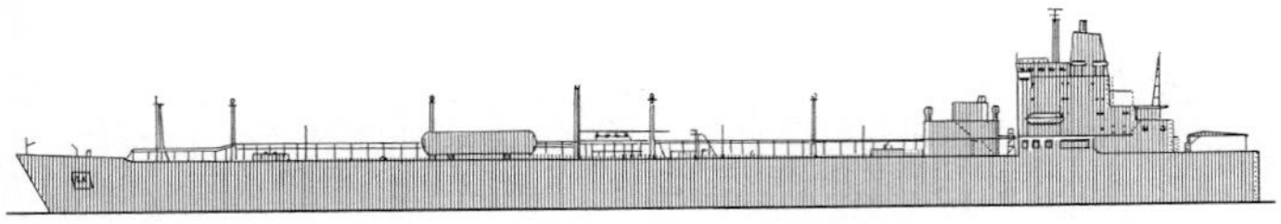

40 M^7FMR H
AL BERRY Si/Fr (L'Atlantique) 1979; LGC; 47,934 grt/59,942 dwt; 222.10 × 13.52 m *(729 × 44.36 ft)*; M (Pielstick); 19.5 kts
Sister: **AL BIDA** (Ku)

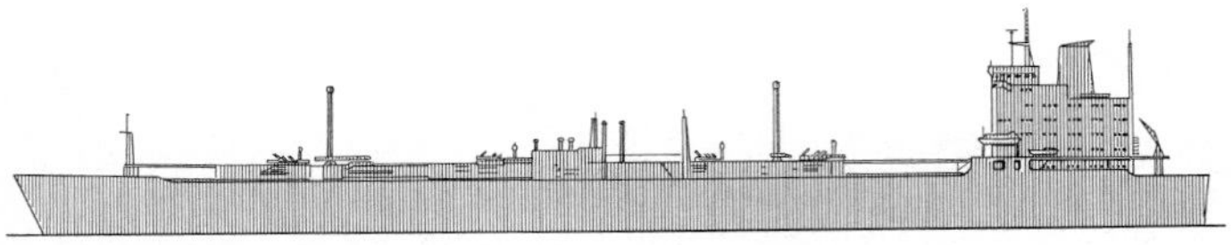

41 M^7FMR H
BERGE ARROW NIS/Pd (Gdynska) 1977; LGC; 44,502 grt/48,821 dwt; 229.32 × 12.90 m *(752 × 42.32 ft)*; M (Sulzer); 17.5 kts; ex-*Northern Arrow*; 'B551' type
Sister: **BERGE EAGLE** (NIS) ex-*Northern Eagle 1*

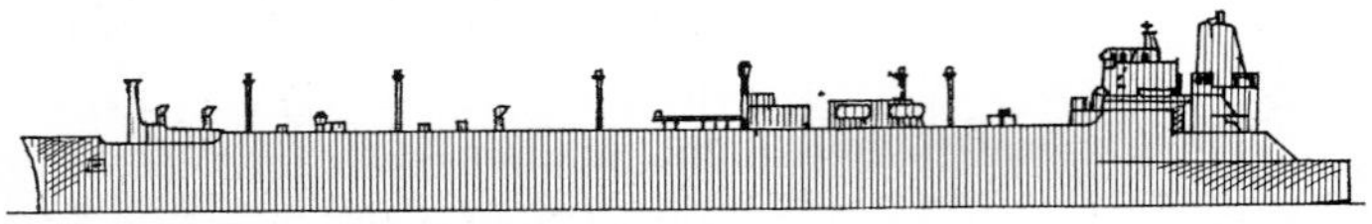

42 M^8F H1
LNG PORT HARCOURT Br/Fr (L'Atlantique) 1976; LGC; 81,472 grt/ 68,122 dwt; 275.01 × 12.9 m *(902.26 × 42.32 ft)*; T (Stal-Laval); 19.75 kts; ex-*Gastor*
Sister: **LNG LAGOS** (Br) ex-*Nestor*

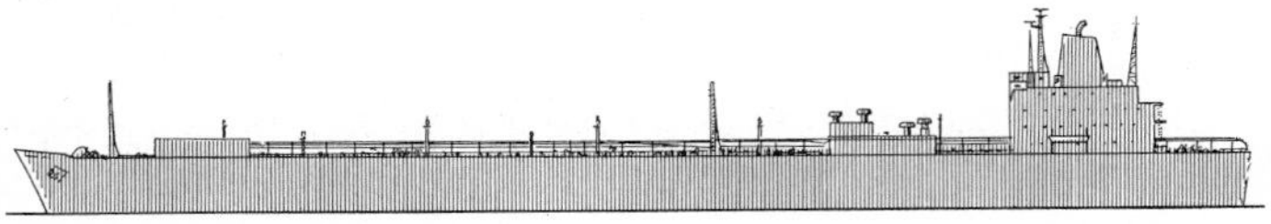

43 M^8FM H
MUNDOGAS ORINOCO Pa/Ja (Kawasaki) 1973; LGC; 39,931 grt/ 50,584 dwt; 210.50 × 12.53 m *(691 × 41.11 ft)*; M (MAN); 15.5 kts; ex-*Ogden Bridgestone*
Sister: **WORLD SKY** (Pa) ex-*World Bridgestone*

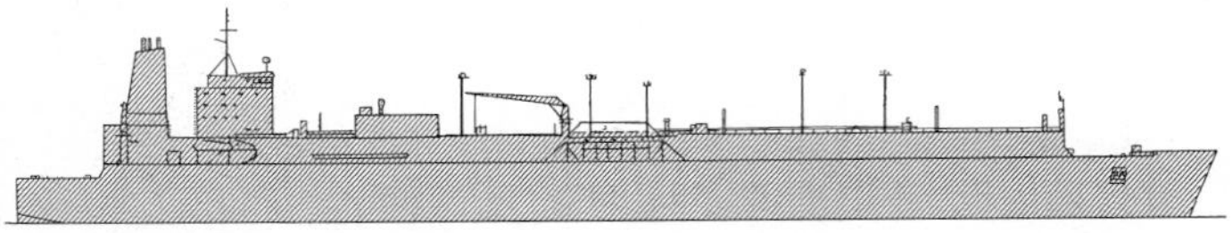

44 M^5RMFS H1
PUTERI INTAN My/Fr (L'Atlantique) 1994; LGC; 86,205 grt/73,519 dwt; 274.30 × 12 m *(899.93 × 39.37 ft)*; T (Kawasaki); 21 kts
Sisters: **PUTERI DELIMA** (My); **PUTERI NILAM** (My)

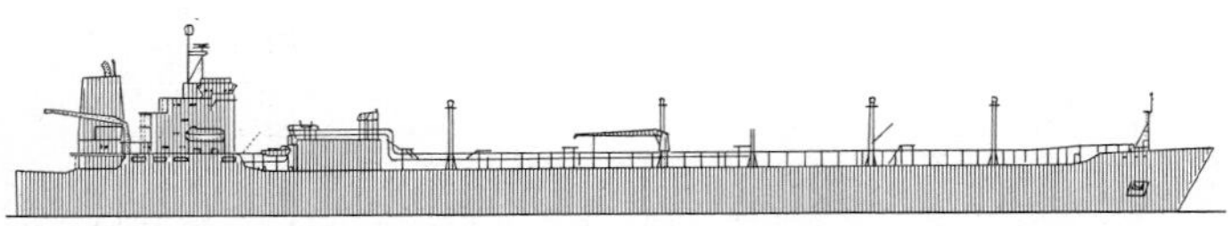

45 $M^4M\text{-}SM^2RF$ H
BERGE RACINE NIS/Fr (Nord Med) 1985; LGC; 49,130 grt/63,296 dwt; 228.61 × 13.68 m *(750.03 × 44.88 ft)*; M (Sulzer); 14.5 kts
Sisters: **BERGE RACHEL** (NIS); **BERGE RAGNHILD** (NIS)

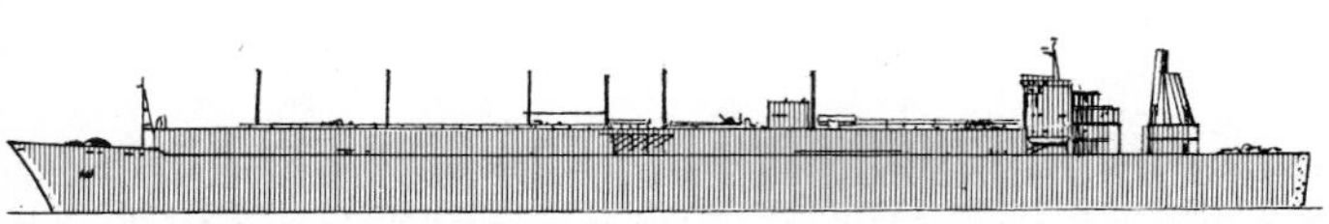

46 M^4NM^3F H
METHANE POLAR Li/Sw (Kockums) 1969; LGC; 48,454 grt/36,896 dwt; 243.34 × 10.04 m *(798.36 × 32.94 ft)*; T (Kockums); 18.25 kts; ex-*Polar Alaska*
Sister: **METHANE ARCTIC** (Li) ex-*Arctic Tokyo*

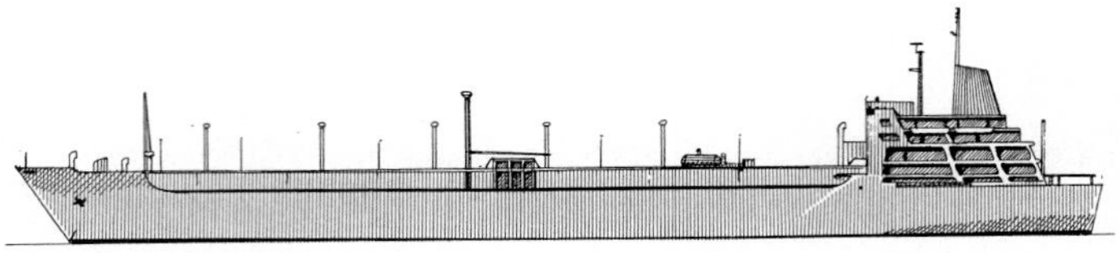

47 $M^4NM^3M\text{-}F$ H1
HASSI R'MEL Ag/Fr (CNIM) 1971; LGC; 31,420 grt/21,175 dwt; 200.01 × 8.5 m *(656.2 × 27.89 ft)*; T (Stal-Laval); 16 kts

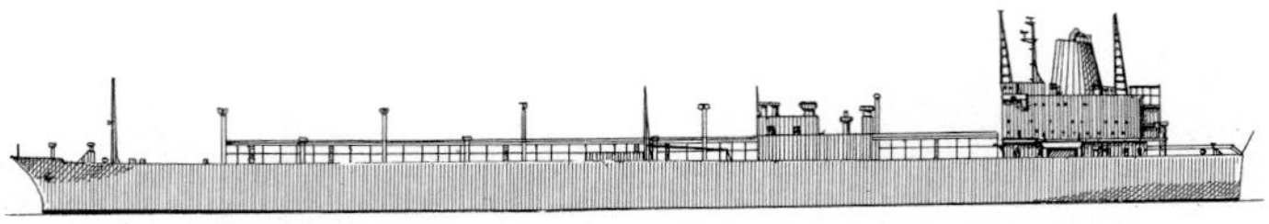

48 $M^4N^2MN^2MFNR$ H
SUN RIVER Pa/Ja (Kawasaki) 1974; LGC; 43,810 grt/51,821 dwt; 224.01 × 11.89 m *(734.94 × 39.01 ft)*; M (MAN); 16 kts
Similar: **GAZ CONCORD** (Pa) ex-*World Concord;* **WORLD CREATION** (Li); **WORLD VIGOUR** (Li)

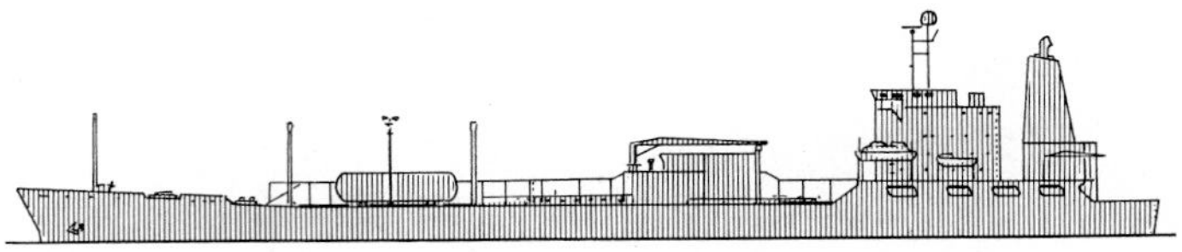

49 M^4RMF H
HERAKLES NIS/No (Moss R) 1982; LGC; 20,531 grt/31,485 dwt; 158.25 × 13.5 m *(519 × 44.29 ft)*; M (Sulzer); 16.8 kts; ex-*Berge Fister*

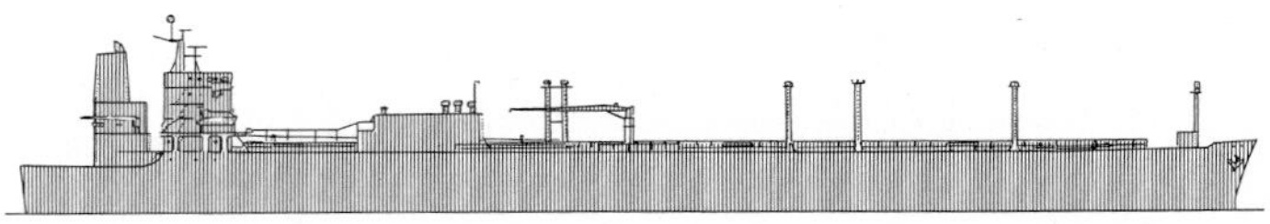

50 M^4RXM^2F H1
BERGE CLIPPER NIS/Ja (NKK Corp) 1992; LGC; 45,302 grt/56,864 dwt; 223.99 × 12.40 m *(734.88 × 40.68 ft)*; M (Sulzer); 16.75 kts
Sisters: **BERGE CAPTAIN** (NIS); **BERGE CHALLENGER** (NIS); **BERGE COMMANDER** (NIS)

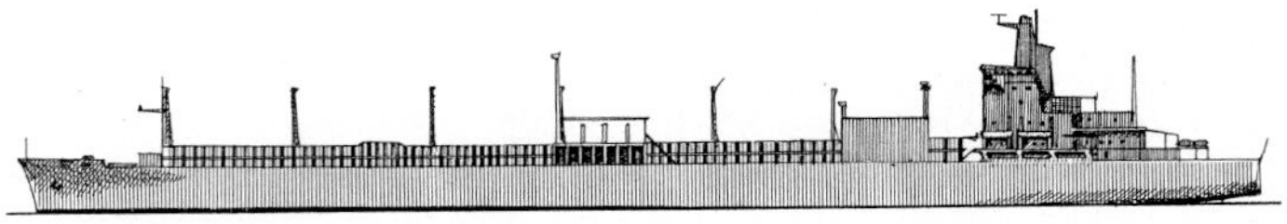

51 $M^3M\text{-}NM^2M\text{-}F$
DESCARTES Fr/Fr (L'Atlantique) 1971; LGC; 32,702 grt/32,634 dwt; 220.02 × 9.2 m *(721.85 × 30.18 ft)*; T (Stal-Laval); 17 kts

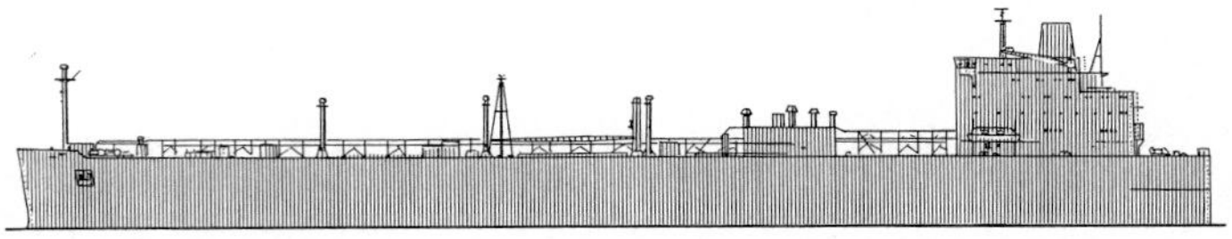

52 M^3NCM^2FM H
ISOMERIA Br/Br (H&W) 1982; LGC; 39,932 grt/47,594 dwt; 210 × 12.45 m *(688.98 × 40.85 ft)*; M (B&W); 17 kts
Sister: **ISOCARDIA** (Br)

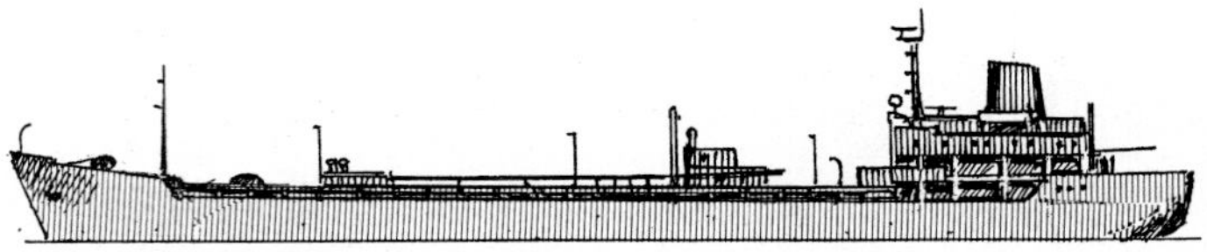

53 M^3NMHFN H13
MARIANO ESCOBEDO Me/Br (Hawthorn, L) 1967; LGC; 7,992 grt/ 9,480 dwt; 140.67 × 8.02 m *(461.52 × 27.07 ft)*; M (Sulzer); 17 kts

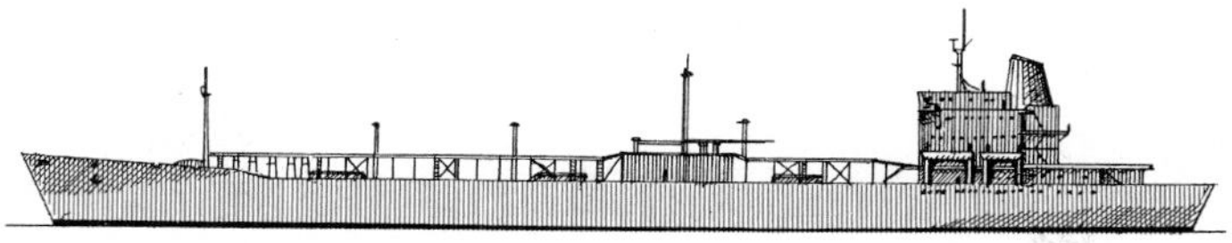

54 *M^3NM^2F H*
MUNDOGAS EUROPE Li/Fr (La Ciotat) 1968; LGC; 16,093 grt/17,667 dwt; 171.1 × 9.03 m *(561.35 × 29.63 ft)*; M (Fiat); 17 kts; ex-*Kristian Birkland*
Sisters: **MUNDOGAS ATLANTIC** (Li) ex-*Cypress;* **CLYDE RIVER** (Li) ex-*Gas Master*

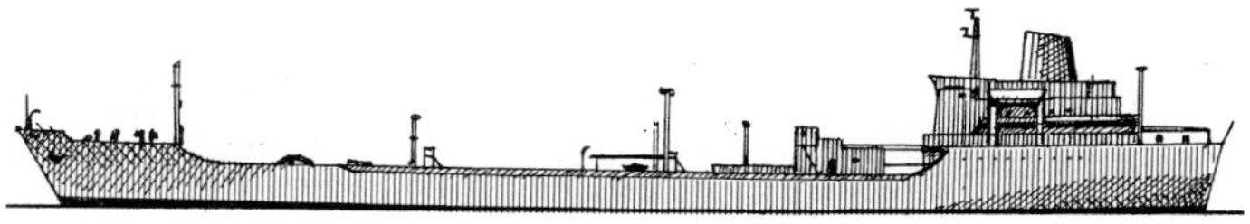

55 *M^3NM^2FN H13*
ZALLAQ Bn/Br (Swan Hunter & T) 1968; LGC; 10,327 grt/12,518 dwt; 151.7 × 8.23 m *(497.7 × 27 ft)*; M (Doxford); 16 kts; ex-*Wiltshire*

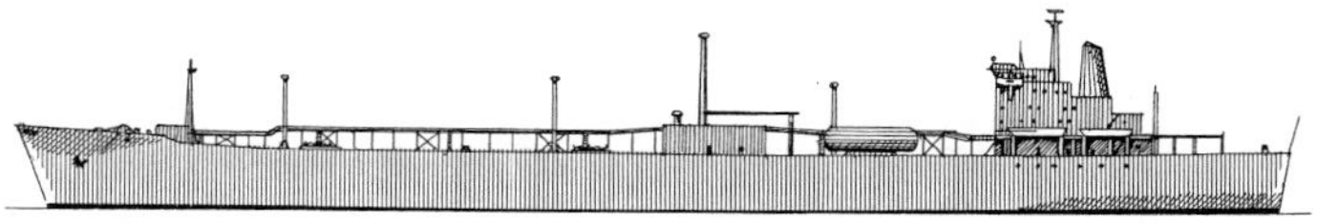

56 *M^3NM^2GN H*
GAZ SUPPLIER Pa/Fr (La Ciotat) 1971; LGC; 26,043 grt/29,528 dwt; 194.27 × 9.91 m *(637.37 × 32.51 ft)*; M (Fiat); 17.25 kts; ex-*Cavendish*

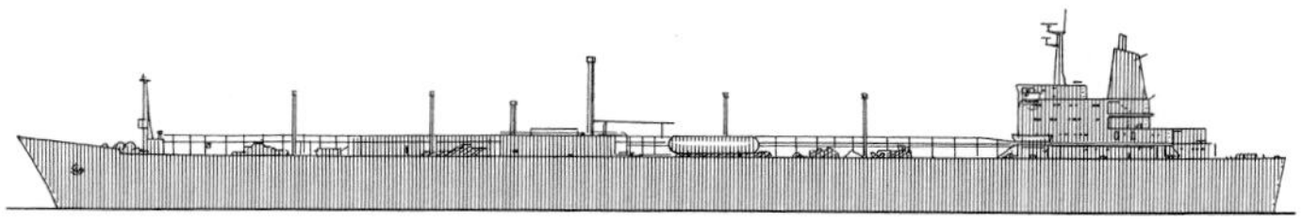

57 *M^3NM^3F H*
MUNDOGAS ENERGY Va/Fr (La Ciotat) 1975; LGC; 39,770 grt/48,772 dwt; 230.89 × 12.62 m *(758 × 41.40 ft)*; M (Sulzer); 18 kts; ex-*Nyhammer*

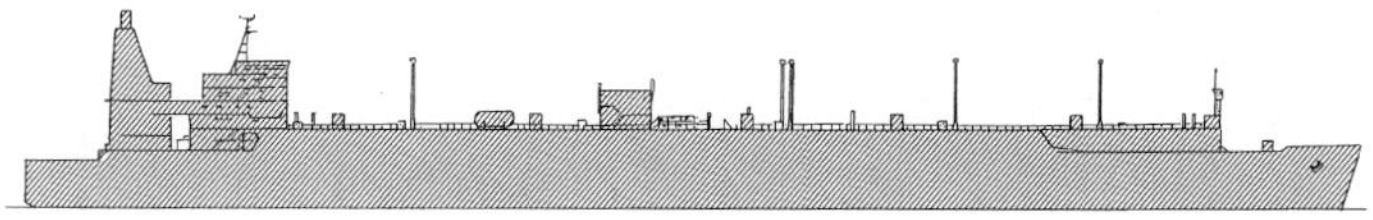

58 *M^3NM^3F H2*
LNG BONNY Br/Sw (Kockums) 1981; LGC; 85,616 grt/89,654 dwt; 286.85 × 13.50 m *(941.11 × 44.29 ft)*; T (Stal-Laval); 20 kts; ex-*Rhenania*
Sister: **LNG FINIMA** (Br) ex-*LNG 564*

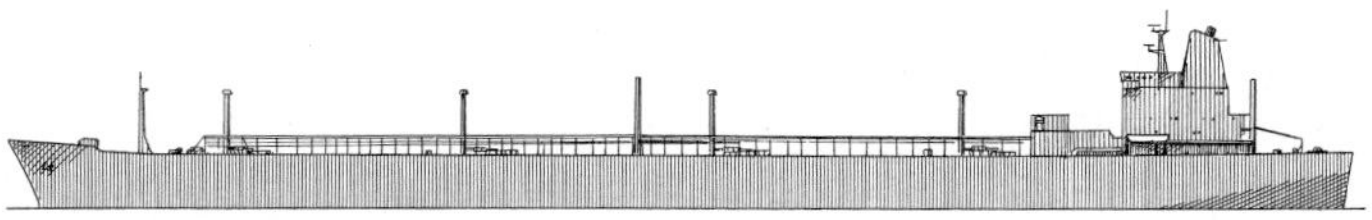

59 *M^3NM^3FN H*
WESTERNPORT Bs/Fr (La Ciotat) 1977; LGC; 57,830 grt/66,769 dwt; 255.13 × 12.6 m *(837.04 × 41.34 ft)*; M (Sulzer); 16.75 kts; ex-*Esso Westernport*

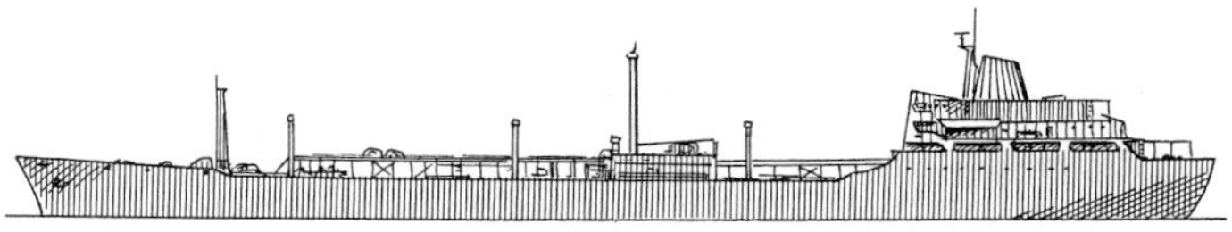

60 *M^3NMM-F H3*
NORDIC RAINBOW Br/It (La Ciotat) 1967; LGC; 10,387 grt/13,157 dwt; 150.48 × 8.86 m *(493.7 × 29.06 ft)*; M (Sulzer); 16 kts; Launched as *Benjamin Franklin*

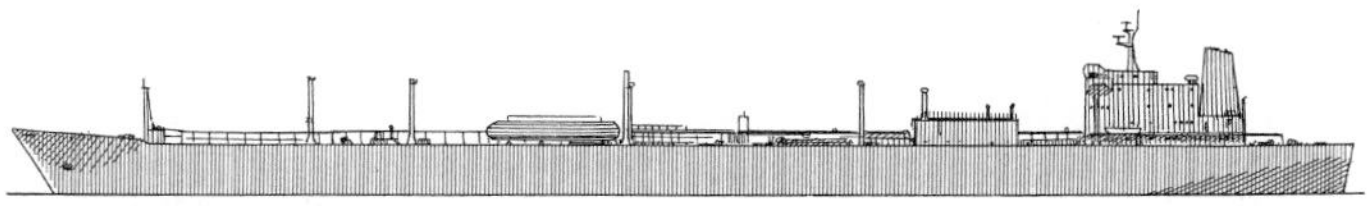

61 *M^3NMNMF H*
BERGE TROLL NIS/Fr (La Ciotat) 1977; LGC; 42,698 grt/54,158 dwt; 231.12 × 13.55 m *(758.27 × 44.46 ft)*; M (Pielstick); 20 kts; ex-*Monge*
Probable sister: **DARWIN** (Br) ex-*Razi*; Similar: **GAS AL AHMADI** (Ku); **GAS AL BURGAN** (Ku); **GAS AL KUWAIT** (Ku); **GAS AL MINAGISH** (Ku)

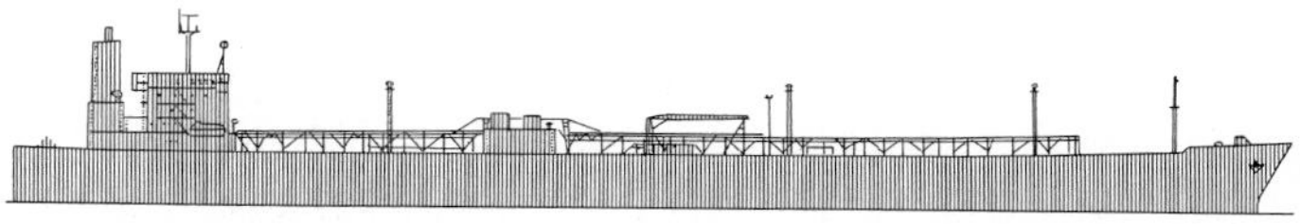

62 *M^3NRM^3F H*
GAS AL GURAIN Ku/Ja (Mitsubishi HI) 1993; LGC; 44,868 grt/49,874 dwt; 230 × 10.84 m *(754.59 × 35.56 ft)*; M (Mitsubishi); 16.5 kts
Sister: **GAS AL MUTLAA** (Ku)

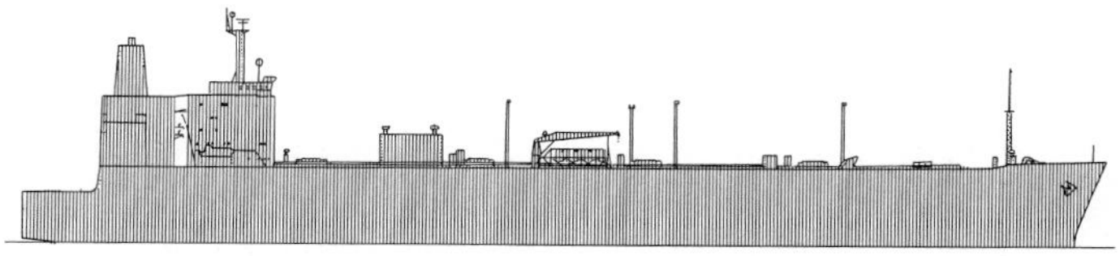

63 *M^3NSM^2F H1*
POLAR EAGLE Li/Ja (IHI) 1993; LGC; 66,174 grt/48,817 dwt; 239 × 11.03 m *(784.12 × 36.19 ft)*; T (Mitsubishi); 18.5 kts
Sister: **ARCTIC SUN** (Li)

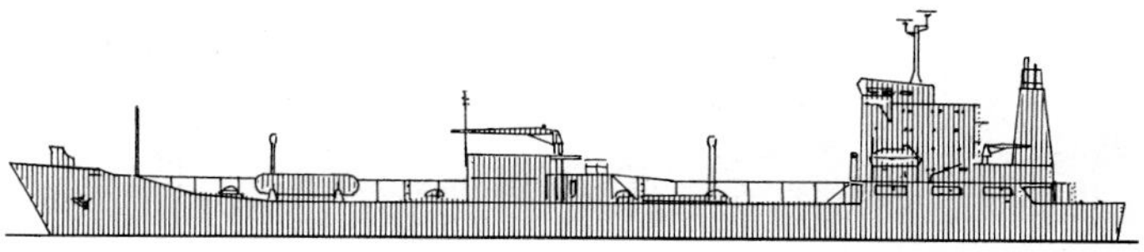

64 *M^3RM^2RF H1*
GAZ MAJOR Pa/No (Moss R) 1979; LGC; 13,760 grt/17,157 dwt; 150.91 × 9.62 m *(495.11 × 31.56 ft)*; M (Sulzer); 16.75 kts; ex-*Celsius*

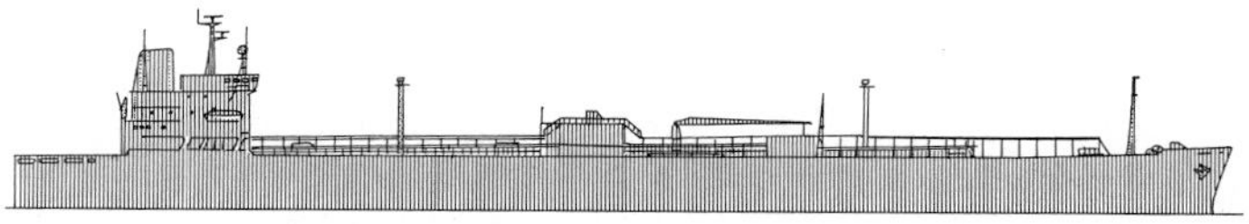

65 *$M^3RMNMFN$ H*
CO-OP SUNRISE Sg/Ja (Hitachi) 1987; LGC; 47,249 grt/51,446 dwt; 219.74 × 11.02 m *(720.93 × 36.15 ft)*; M (B&W); 14.7 kts

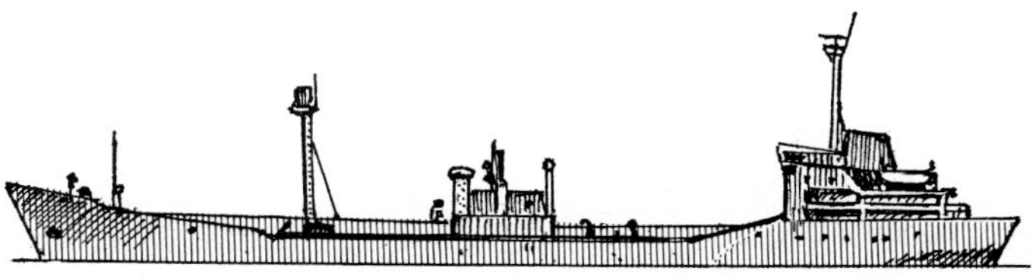

66 *M^2M-F H13*
RELCHEM ISHA Li/Ne ('De Waal') 1969; LGC; 3,846 grt/4,206 dwt; 103.21 × 6.35 m *(338.61 × 20.83 ft)*; M (Smit & Bolnes); 15.75 kts; ex-*Coral Maeandra*

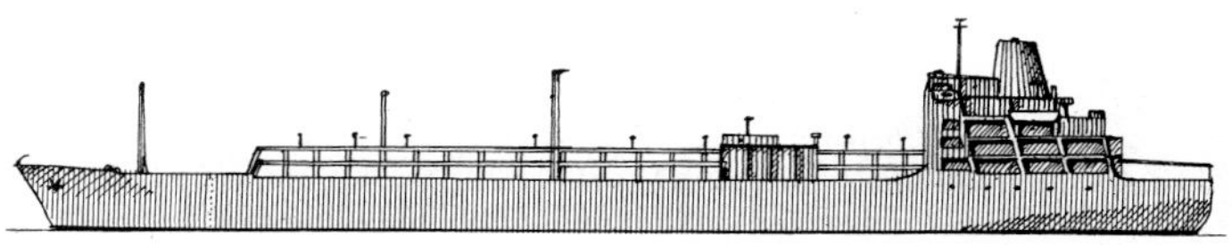

67 *M^2NMF H*
CALINA Li/Ja (IHI) 1967; LGC; 14,388 grt/15,661 dwt; 162.8 × 8.4 m *(534.12 × 27.56 ft)*; M (Sulzer); 16 kts; ex-*M P Grace*

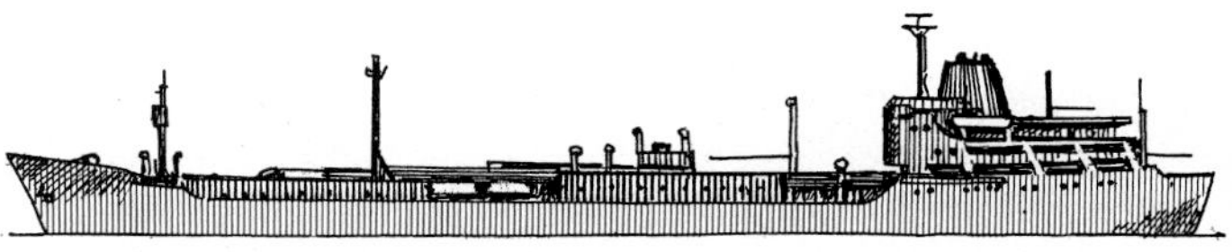

68 *M^2NMFN^2 H123*
GAZ CHANNEL Pa/No (Moss V) 1966; LGC; 8,790 grt/11,532 dwt; 141.33 × 9.52 m *(463.68 × 31.23 ft)*; M (MAN); 17 kts; ex-*Havfrost*

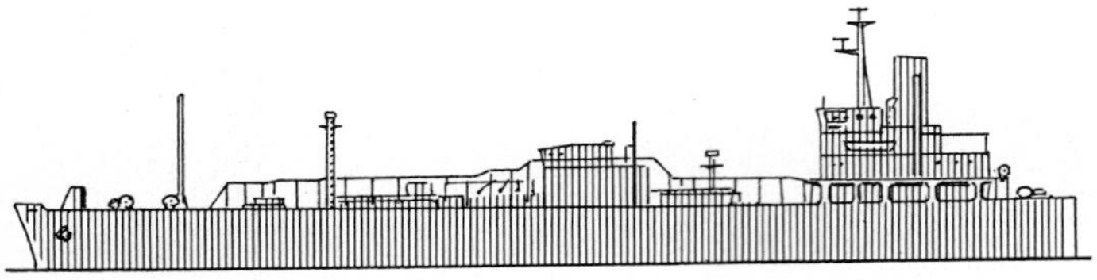

69 *M^2NMF-N H*
ISLE HOPE Pa/Ja (Hitachi) 1981; LGC; 6,411 grt/4,998 dwt; 109.89 × 5.9 m *(360.53 × 19.36 ft)*; M (Mitsubishi); 13.5 kts; ex-*Iwakuni Maru*

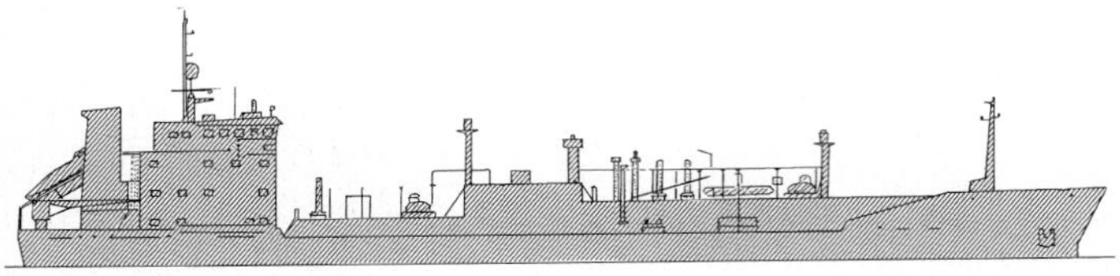

70 *$M^2NMHMFLR$ H1*
PRINS JOHAN WILLEM FRISO Ne/Ne (Stroobos) 1989; LGC; 3,862 grt/4,905 dwt; 97.39 × 6.02 m *(319.52 × 19.75 ft)*; M (Sulzer); 14.1 kts

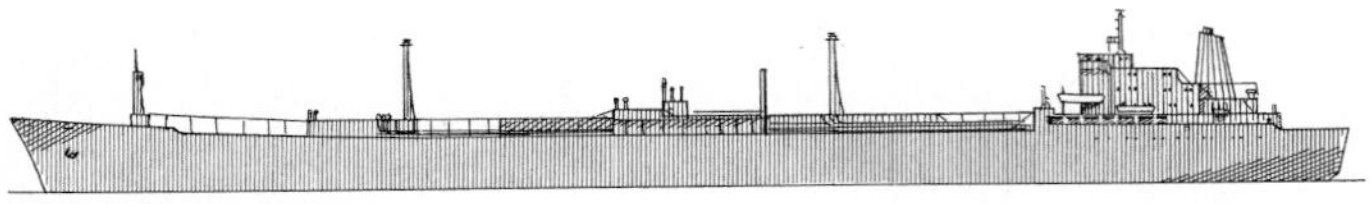

71 *M^2NM^2F H*
HAVGAST NIS/No (Moss R) 1971; LGC; 31,254 grt/38,930 dwt; 207.07 × 11.32 m *(679.36 × 37.14 ft)*; M (Sulzer); 16.5 kts; ex-*Hoegh Multina*

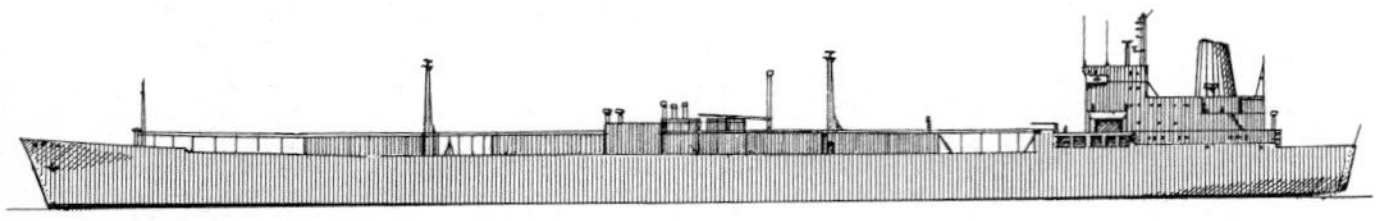

72 *M^2NM^2F H*
HERMES NIS/Fr (France-Gironde) 1974; LGC; 31,222 grt/38,678 dwt; 207.08 × 11.28 m *(679.43 × 37.01 ft)*; M (Sulzer); 17.5 kts; ex-*Hampshire*
Sister: **HEMERA** (NIS) ex-*Devonshire*

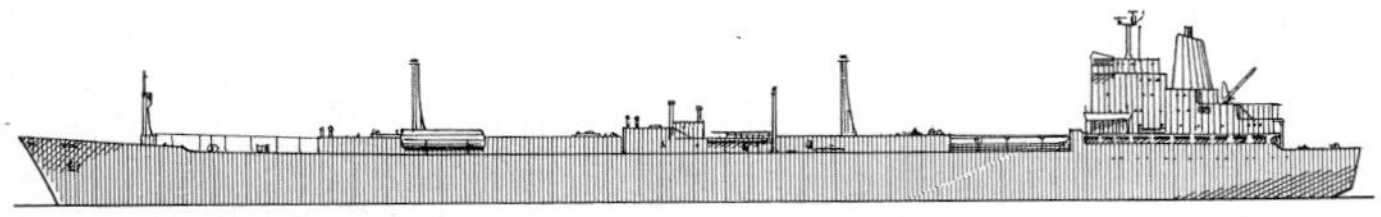

73 *M^2NM^2F H*
MUNDOGAS AMERICA Li/No (Moss R) 1972; LGC; 31,717 grt/38,820 dwt; 207.07 × 11.32 m *(679.36 × 37.14 ft)*; M (Sulzer); 17.5 kts; ex-*Garmula*

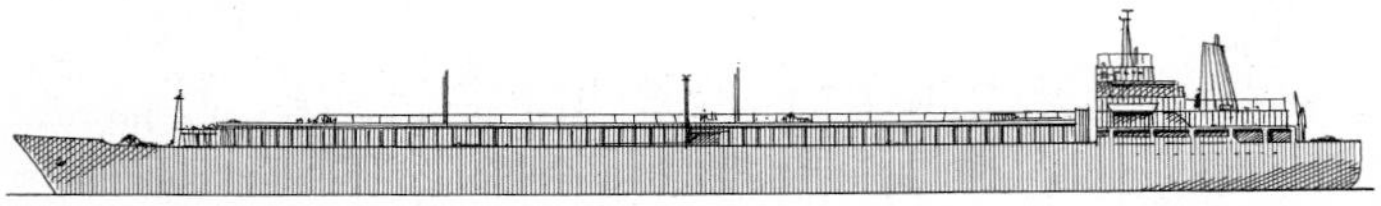

74 *M^2NM^2F H*
SNAM PALMARIA It/It (Italcantieri) 1969; LGC; 29,264 grt/25,397 dwt; 207.73 × 9.17 m *(681.53 × 30.09 ft)*; T (De Laval); 18 kts; ex-*Esso Brega*
Sisters: **SNAM ELBA** (It) ex-*Esso Liguria;* **LAIETA** (Pa) (builder—'Astano')

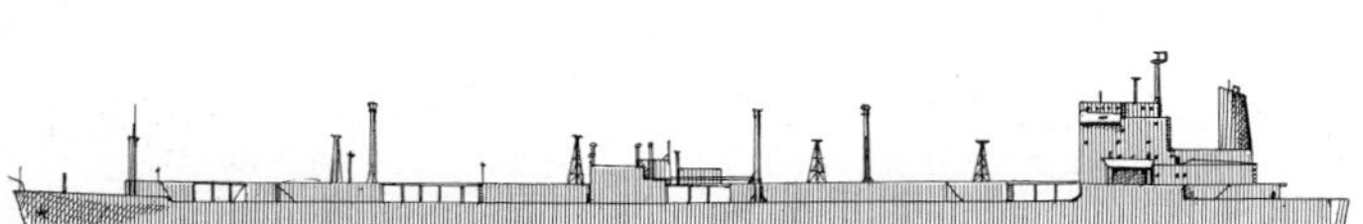

75 *M^2NM^2F H*
STAFFORDSHIRE HK/Fr (France-Gironde) 1977; LGC; 40,281 grt/56,188 dwt; 226.32 × 13.03 m *(742.52 × 42.75 ft)*; M (Sulzer); 17 kts

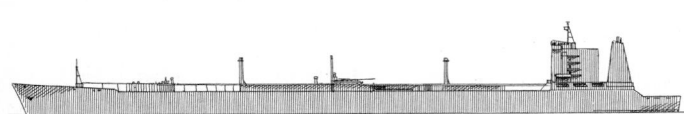

76 *M^2NM^2F H1*
GAS RISING SUN Li/Fi (Wärtsilä) 1978; LGC; 44,076 grt/46,258 dwt; 223 × 13 m *(731.63 × 42.65 ft)*; M (Sulzer); 16.7 kts
Sisters: **BERGE SISU** (NIS); **BERGE SISAR** (NIS); **BERGE SAGA** (NIS); **BERGE STRAND** (NIS); **BERGE SUND** (NIS); **BERGE SPIRIT** (NIS) ex-*Golar Frost*

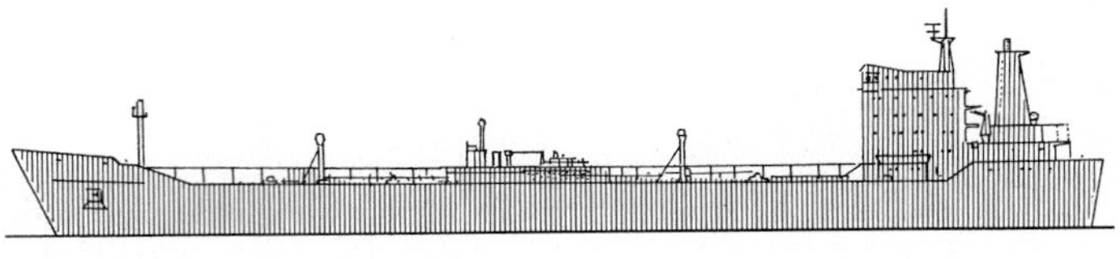

77 *M^2NM^2F H13*
BUSSEWITZ Ge/FRG(Howaldts DW) 1983; LGC; 14,377 grt/13,935 dwt; 157.27 × 8.45 m *(515.98 × 27.72 ft)*; M (MAN); 12.80 kts

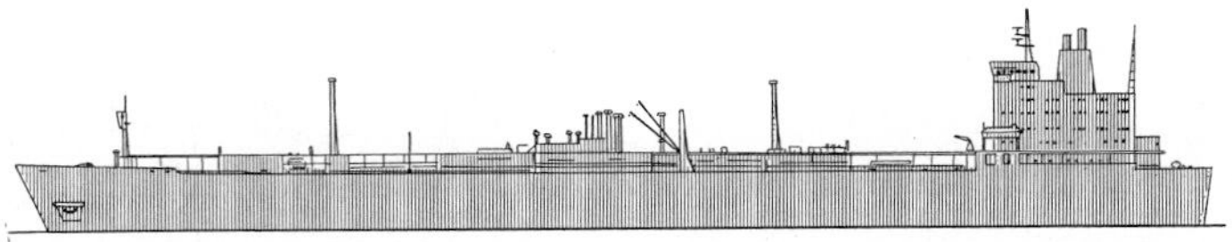

78 *M^2NM^2FN H*
BLUE OCEAN Li/Pd (Gdynska) 1976; LGC; 44,180 grt/49,092 dwt; 229.32 × 12.7 m *(752.36 × 41.67 ft)*; M (Sulzer); 17.25 kts; ex-*Hoegh Swallow*; 'B-550' type
Sisters: **PETROLAGAS 2** (Gr) ex-*Hoegh Swift*; **BERGE SWORD** (NIS) ex-*Hoegh Sword*

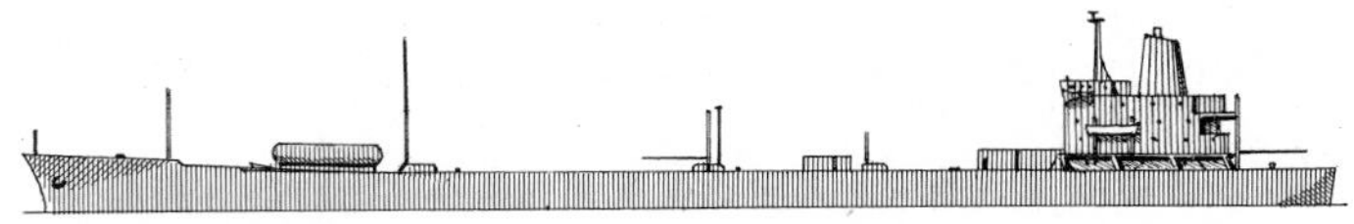

79 *M^2NM^3FN H*
LINCOLNSHIRE Bs/Br (Swan Hunter) 1971; LGC; 19,799 grt/24,950 dwt; 186.85 × 9.75 m *(613.02 × 31.99 ft)*; M (Doxford); 17.25 kts

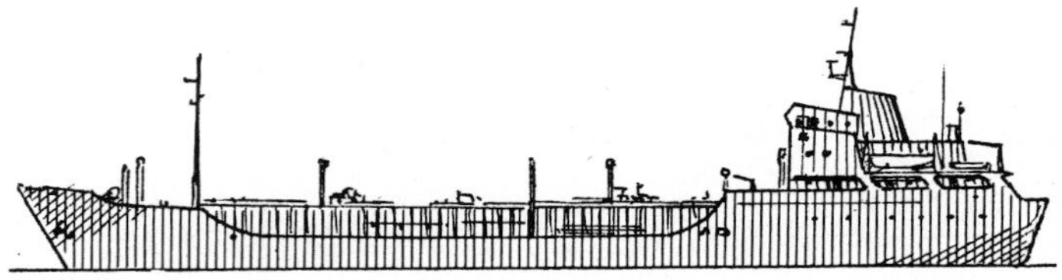

80 *M^2NMM-F H13*
GREEN STAR It/Fr (Havre) 1967; LGC; 1,596 grt/1,546 dwt; 80.98 × 4.62 m *(265.68 × 15.16 ft)*; M (MAN); 13 kts; ex-*Talete*; ex-*Thales*

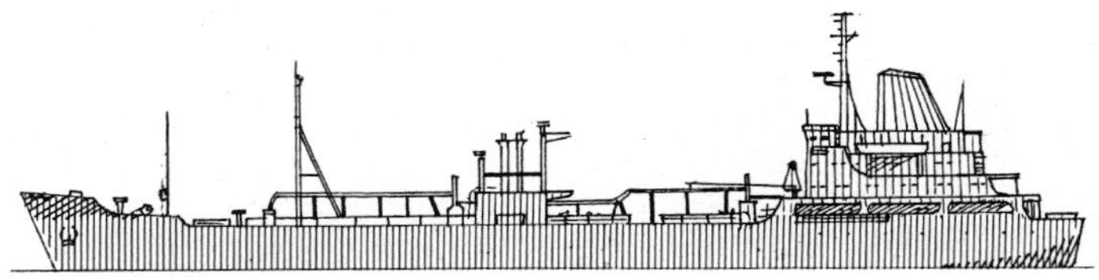

81 *M^2N^2DMF H1*
ATLANTIC STAR Ma/FRG (A G 'Weser') 1967; LGC; 5,923 grt/7,014 dwt; 116.31 × 7.77 m *(381.59 × 25.49 ft)*; M (MAN); 15 kts; ex-*Mundogas Bermuda*

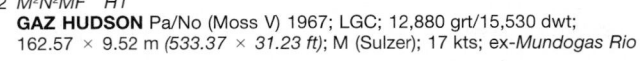

82 *M^2N^2MF H1*
GAZ HUDSON Pa/No (Moss V) 1967; LGC; 12,880 grt/15,530 dwt; 162.57 × 9.52 m *(533.37 × 31.23 ft)*; M (Sulzer); 17 kts; ex-*Mundogas Rio*

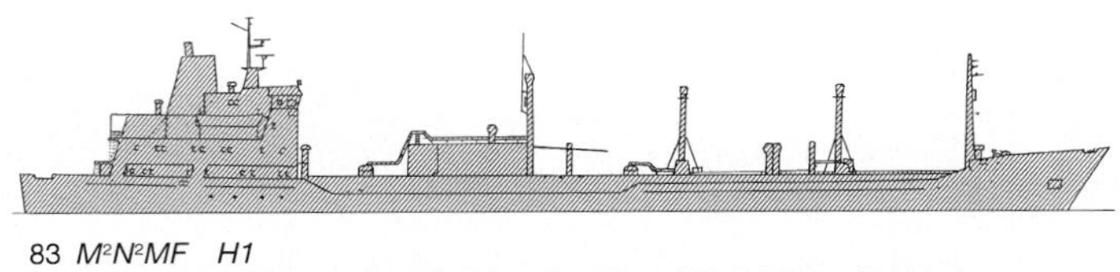

83 *M^2N^2MF H1*
SUNNY CLIPPER NIS/FRG (Meyer) 1976; LGC; 4,326 grt/6,080 dwt; 108.01 × 7.45 m *(354.36 × 24.44 ft)*; M (Deutz); 16.25 kts; ex-*Coral Isis*

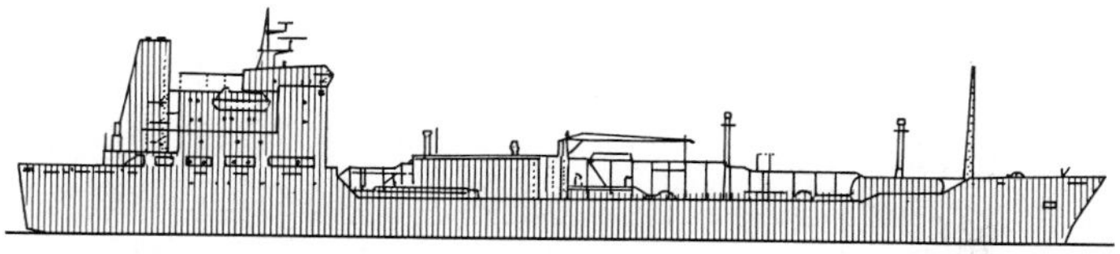

84 M^2NRMF H13
GRAJAU Bz/FRG (Meyer) 1987; LGC; 8,075 grt/8,875 dwt; 134.02 × 8.40 m *(439.70 × 27.56 ft)*; M (B&W); 14 kts
Sisters: **GURUPA** (Bz); **GURUPI** (Bz)

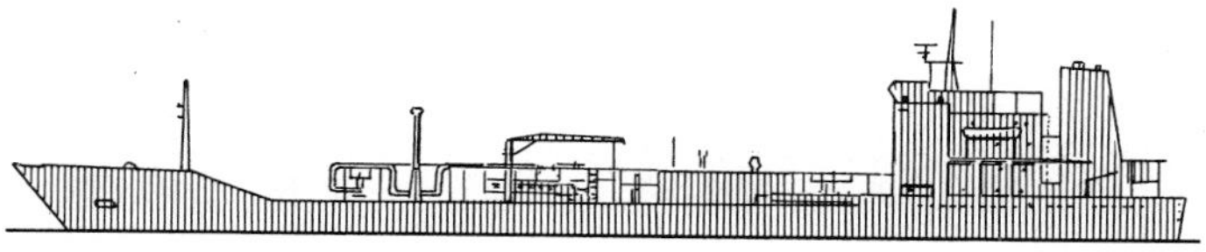

85 M^2RMF H1
CHRISTOPH SCHULTE SV/FRG (Meyer) 1982; LGC; 5,804 grt/7,113 dwt; 122.61 × 7.52 m *(402 × 24.67 ft)*; M (B&W); 14 kts; ex-*Kurt Illies*

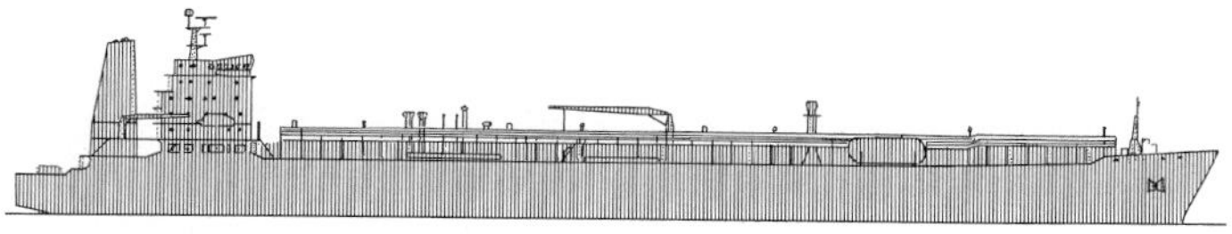

86 M^2RMF H1
HELIOS NIS/Br (K Govan) 1992; LGC; 34,974 grt/49,513 dwt; 205 × 13.02 m *(672.57 × 42.72 ft)*; M (Sulzer); 16 kts
Sisters: **HELICE** (NIS); **HAVIS** (NIS); **HAVFROST** (NIS) (extension to funnel-top and probable variations in superstructure. Others may also be like this)

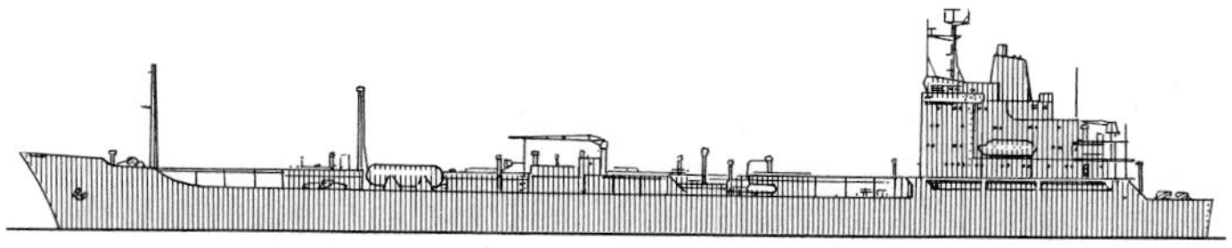

87 M^2RMF H1
HERMOD Br/No (Moss R) 1975; LGC; 15,092 grt/18,165 dwt; 166.07 × 10.32 m *(545 × 33.86 ft)*; M (B&W); 16.5 kts; ex-*Garbeta*

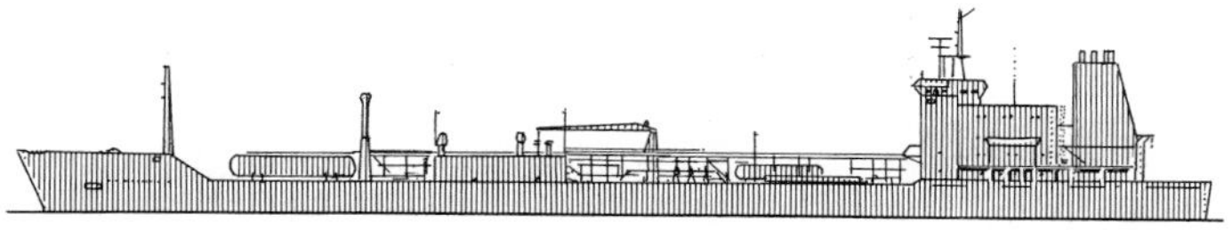

88 M^2RMF H1
TYCHO BRAHE HK/FRG (Meyer) 1982; LGC/Ch; 12,183 grt/16,225 dwt; 159.01 × 9.82 m *(522 × 32.22 ft)*; M (B&W); 14 kts
Sister: **IMMANUEL KANT** (Ge)

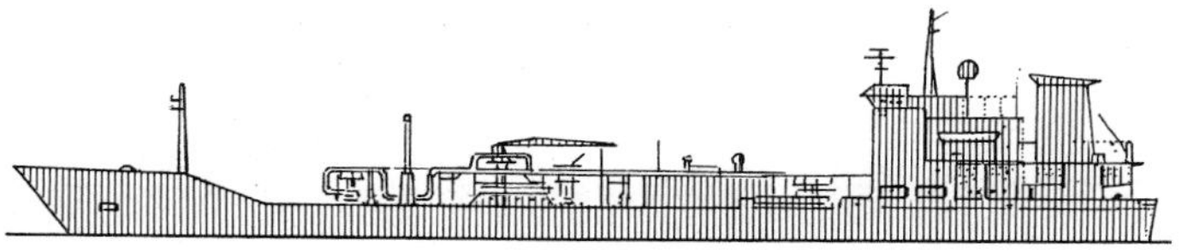

89 M^2RMF H1
ZETAGAS NA/FRG (Meyer) 1982; LGC; 5,643 grt/6,975 dwt; 122.61 × 7.53 m *(402 × 24.7 ft)*; M (B&W); 15.25 kts

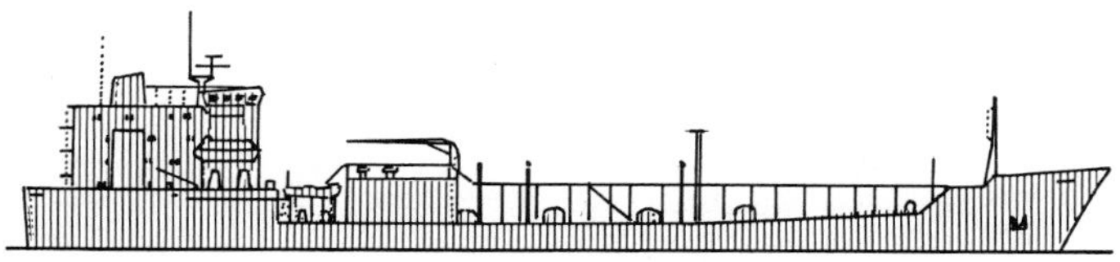

90 M^2RMF H13
NORGAS CHALLENGER NIS/No (Kleven) 1984; LGC; 5,739 grt/7,492 dwt; 115.12 × 7.90 m *(377.69 × 25.92 ft)*; M (Wärtsilä); 14.50 kts; ex-*San Francisco*; Funnel is on port side

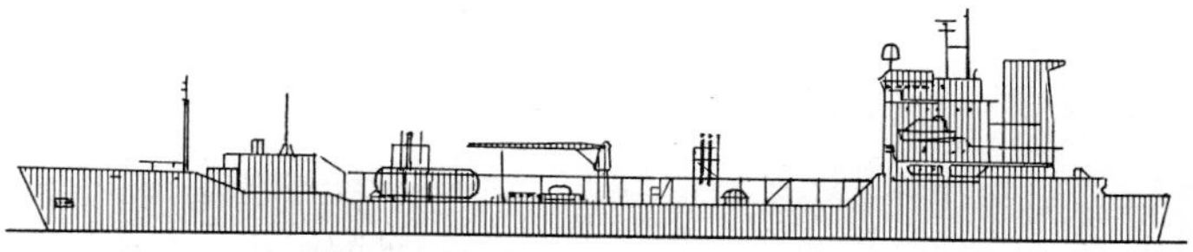

91 M^2RMF H13
SANTA CLARA Li/FRG (Lindenau) 1985; LGC; 7,581 grt/7,850 dwt; 136.25 × 6.75 m *(447.01 × 22.15 ft)*; M (MAN); 15 kts
Sister: **RIO GAS** (Li)

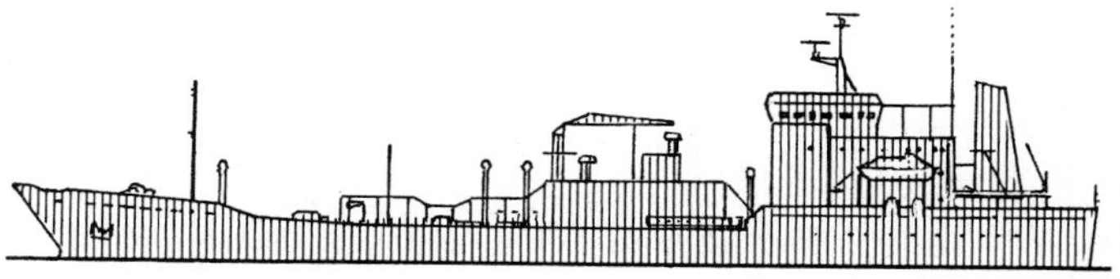

92 M^2RMF H3
ARAGO Bs/No (Kristiansands) 1982; LGC; 4,165 grt/4,852 dwt; 95.66 × 7.12 m *(314 × 23.36 ft)*; M (Wichmann); 13 kts; ex-*Marco Polo*

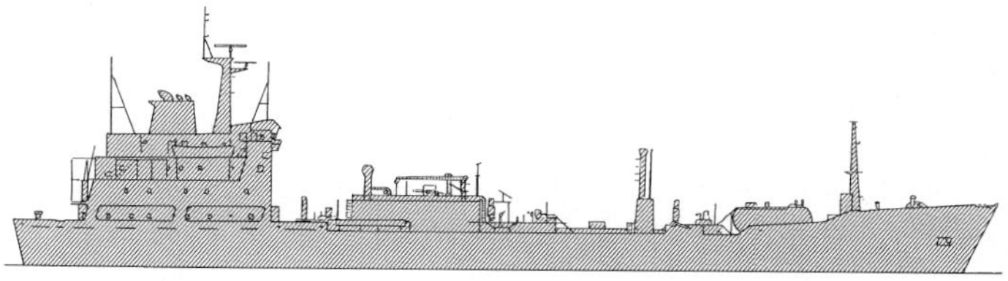

93 M^2RMFNS H1
SULTAN MAHMUD BADARUDDIN II Ia/FRG (Meyer) 1984; LGC; 6,946 grt/9,131 dwt; 113.50 × 6.78 m *(372.38 × 22.24 ft)*; M (MaK); 15 kts; Lengthened to 1,441m (4,721ft) 1990—drawing shows appearance prior to this

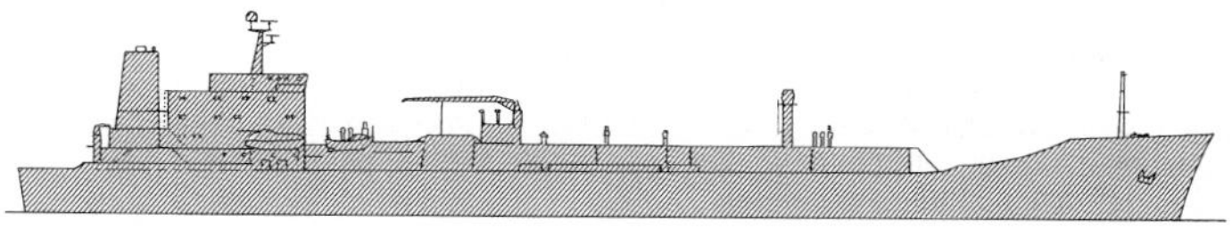

94 M^2RMFR H1
NYHOLM NIS/No (Moss R) 1983; LGC; 15,709 grt/24,470 dwt; 159.32 × 11.97 m *(522.70 × 39.27 ft)*; M (Sulzer); 17.5 kts; ex-*Concordia Fjord*

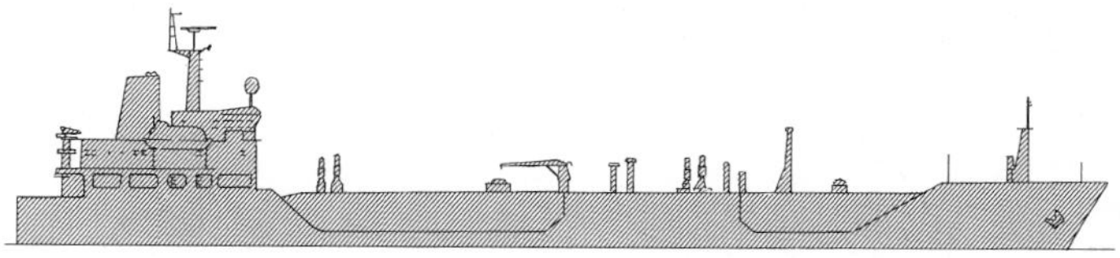

95 M^2RMFR H13
HAPPY GIRL Pi/Ko (Hyundai) 1989; LGC; 3,643 grt/4,247 dwt; 98.30 × 6.27 m *(322.51 × 20.57 ft)*; M (MaK); 15.1 kts; ex-*Sunny Girl*

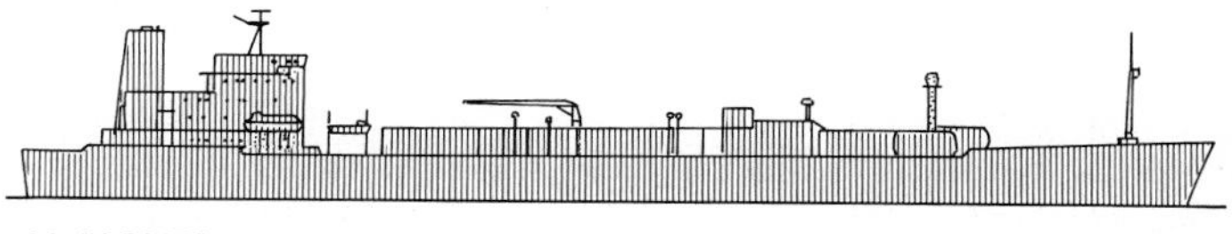

96 M^2RMFS H
HEKTOR NIS/No (Nye Fredriksstad) 1982; LGC; 15,405 grt/28,827 dwt; 157.79 × 10.72 m *(517.68 × 35.17 ft)*; M (Sulzer); 17 kts; Drawing is approximate
Sister: **HEBRIS** (NIS); Similar: **HERMION** (NIS)

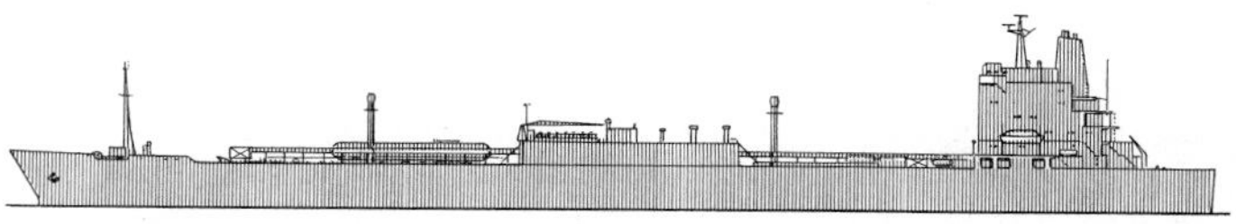

97 M^2RM^2F H
HEKABE Br/FRG (Thyssen) 1977; LGC; 34,572 grt/41,683 dwt; 219.51 × 11.80 m *(720 × 38.71 ft)*; M (MAN); 16.75 kts; ex-*Garinda*
Sisters: **HAVKONG** (Br) ex-*Galconda*; **HAVDROTT** (Br) ex-*Galpara*; **HEMINA** (Br) ex-*Garala*

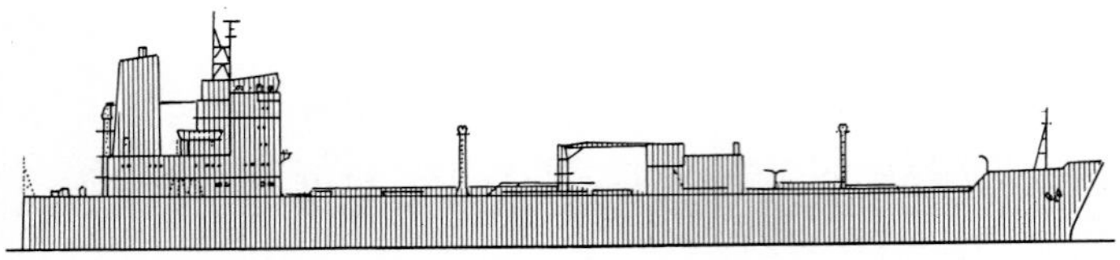

98 *M^2RM^2FR H1*
GENT Lu/Be (Boelwerf) 1985; LGC; 18,155 grt/26,820 dwt; 155.43 × 11.74 m *(509.94 × 38.52 ft)*; M (Sulzer); 16.50 kts; Second upright is on port side
Sister: **OSCAR GAS** (NIS) ex-*Tielrode*; Possible sisters: **CHESHIRE** (Br); **CHACONIA** (Lu); **NYHALL** (Lu); **SOMBEKE** (Lu)

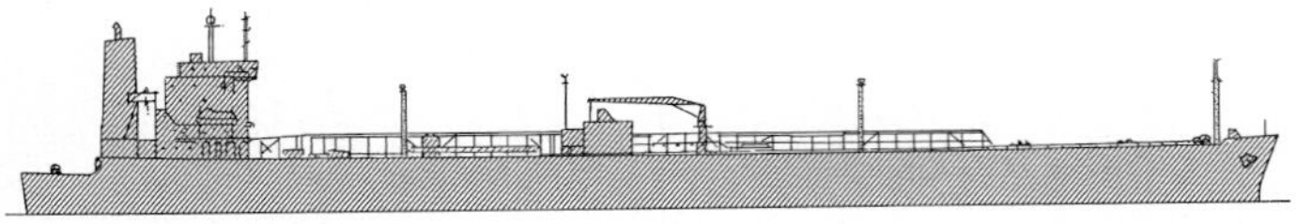

99 *M^2RM^3HF H1*
JA SUNSHINE Ja/Ja (Kawasaki) 1994; LGC; 42,551 grt/49,353 dwt; 224.05 × 11.02 m *(735.07 × 36.15 ft)*; M (B&W); 15.5 kts

100 *M^2RNMG H13*
GAZ SAINT DENIS Kn/No (Kleven) 1977; LGC; 3,999 grt/5,396 dwt; 102.06 × 7.4 m *(334.84 × 24.27 ft)*; M (Atlas-MaK); 14.75 kts; ex-*Al Ghassani*

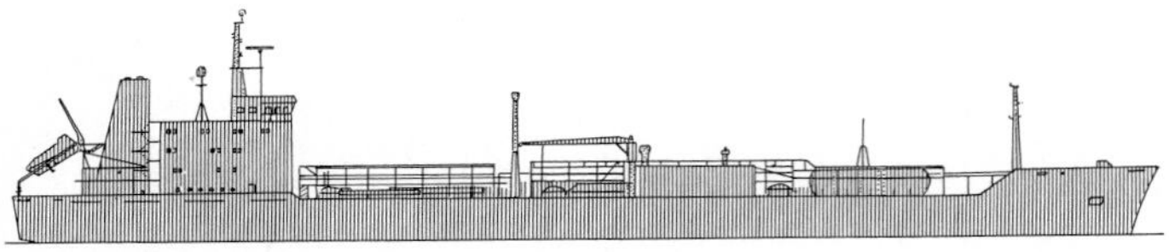

101 *M^2RNM^2FCL H1*
HAI GAS NIS/Ge (Meyer) 1991; LGC; 11,821 grt/11,906 dwt; 158.02 × 9.76 m *(518.44 × 32.02 ft)*; M (B&W); 15 kts; ex-*Skulte*
Sisters: **HAVKATT** (NIS) ex-*Sigulda*; **ANNE-LAURE** (Li) ex-*Sloka*; **RAVNANGER** (NIS) ex-*Salacgriva*; **RISANGER** (NIS) ex-*Saulkrasti*; **POLARGAS** (Pa) ex-*Skriveri*

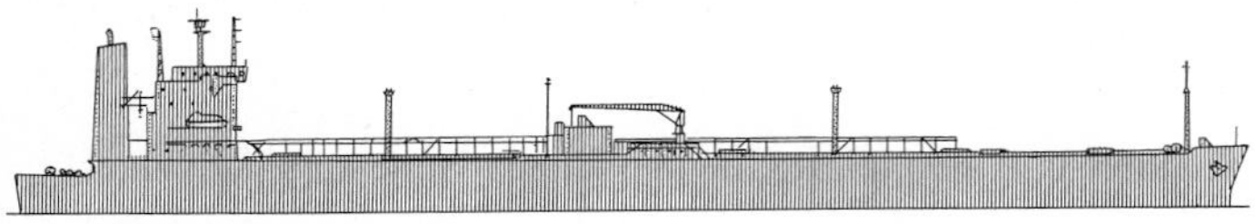

102 *$M^2RNMNHNF$ H1*
PACIFIC HARMONY Sg/Ja (Kawasaki) 1990; LGC; 42,465 grt/49,701 dwt; 224.05 × 11.02 m *(735.07 × 36.15 ft)*; M (B&W); 16 kts
Probable sister: **CRYSTAL MERMAID** (Ja)

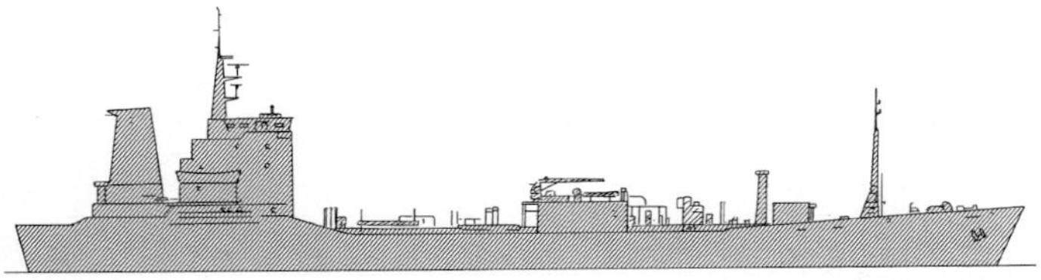

103 *M^2SMF H3*
TRAQUAIR Li/Br (Ailsa/Ferguson Bros) 1982; LGC; 5,992 grt/7,230 dwt; 113.82 × 5.01 m *(373.43 × 16.44 ft)*; M (Sulzer); 16 kts; Aft section built by Ailsa and foreward section by Ferguson Bros

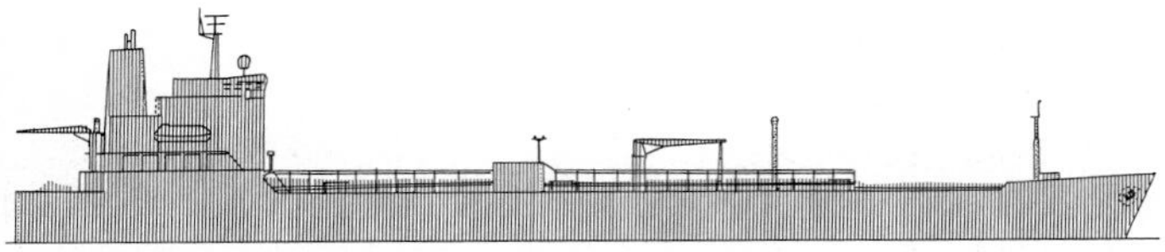

104 *M^2SMFR H2*
ANNAPURNA In/Ko (Hyundai) 1991; LGC; 17,778 grt/17,601 dwt; 159.97 × 8.31 m *(524.84 × 27.26 ft)*; M (B&W); 15 kts
Sister: **NANGA PARBAT** (In)

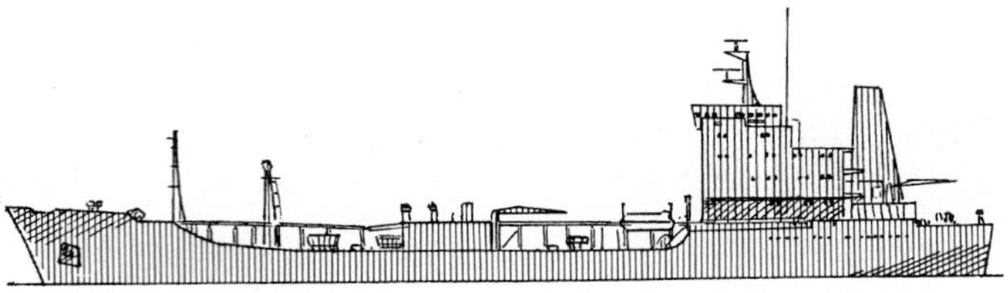

105 *M^2SMF-S H13*
AINO NIS/No (Moss R) 1977; LGC; 6,726 grt/6,830 dwt; 116.54 × 7.81 m *(382.35 × 25.62 ft)*; M (Lindholmens); 14.5 kts; ex-*Nestefox*

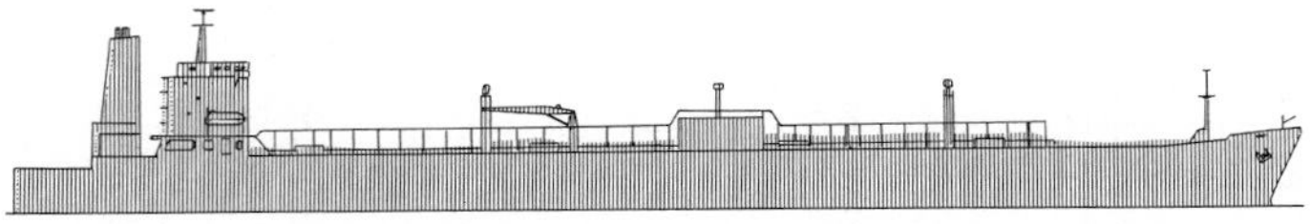

106 *M^2SM^2F H1*
BALTIC FLAME Li/Ko (Hyundai) 1992; LGC; 43,635 grt/59,421 dwt; 219.89 × 13.40 m *(721.42 × 43.96 ft)*; M (B&W); 16 kts

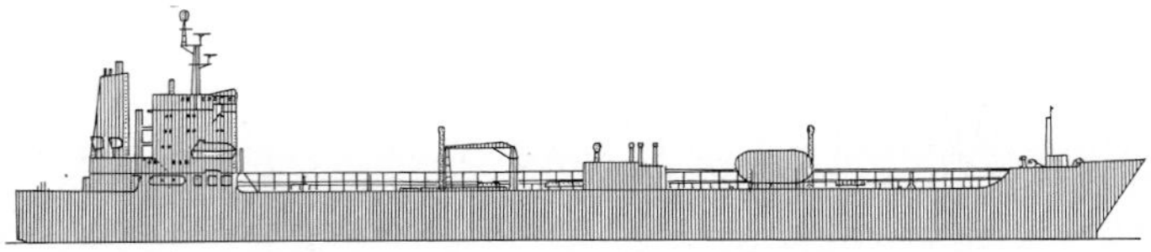

107 *M^2SM^2F H1*
JAKOB MAERSK DIS/Ko (Hyundai) 1991; LGC; 23,878 grt/25,999 dwt; 185 × 10.14 m *(606.96 × 33.27 ft)*; M (B&W); 17.3 kts
Sisters: **JANE MAERSK** (DIS); **JESPER MAERSK** (DIS); **JESSIE MAERSK** (DIS)

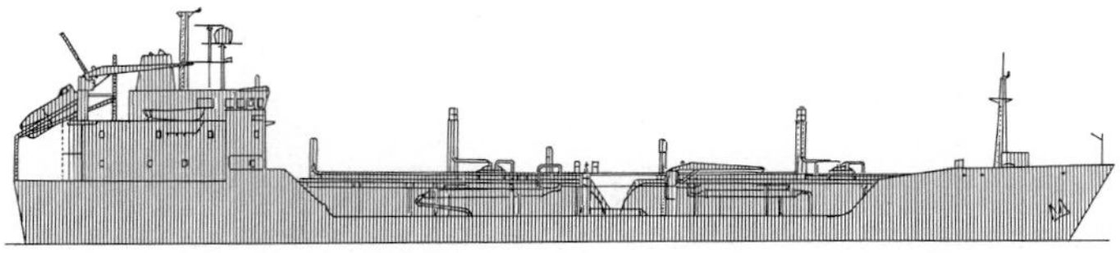

108 *M^2SM^2FRL H13*
DELTAGAS Li/Br (Appledore) 1992; LGC; 3,011 grt/3,582 dwt; 88.35 × 6.21 m *(289.86 × 20.37 ft)*; M (MaK); 14.5 kts
Sisters: **TARQUIN GLEN** (Li); **TARQUIN GROVE** (Li); Similar (larger): **TARQUIN RANGER** (Li); **TARQUIN MARINER** (Li) (builder—Dunston)

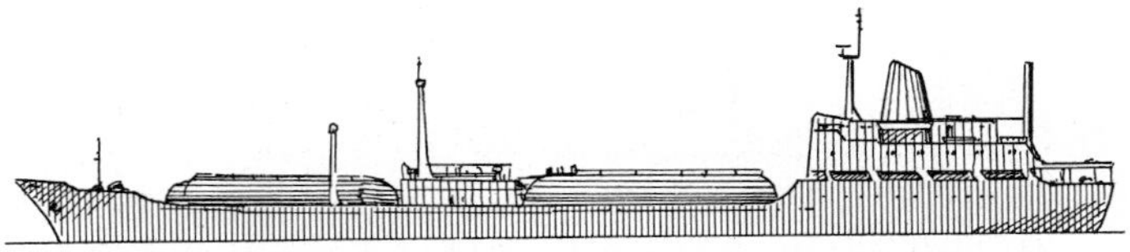

109 *MNHMFN H13*
MANUEL BELGRANO Ar/Fr (La Ciotat) 1969; LGC; 6,733 grt/7,062 dwt; 126.22 × 7.32 m *(414.11 × 24.02 ft)*; M (Sulzer); 16 kts; ex-*Barfonn*

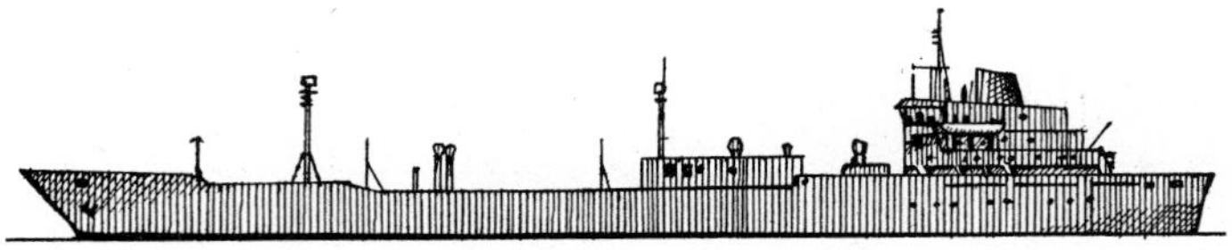

110 *MNMF H*
HAVSOL NIS/FRG (Meyer) 1976; LGC; 9,367 grt/9,551 dwt; 139.71 × 8.22 m *(458.37 × 26.97 ft)*; M (B&W); 16.25 kts; ex-*Yurmala*
Sisters: **HAVLYS** (NIS) ex-*Bolduri*; **HAVBRIS** (NIS) ex-*Dubulty*; **HAVVIND** (NIS) ex-*Dzintari*; **CLIPPER SEA** (NIS) ex-*Lielupe*; **HAVLUR** (NIS) ex-*Mayori*

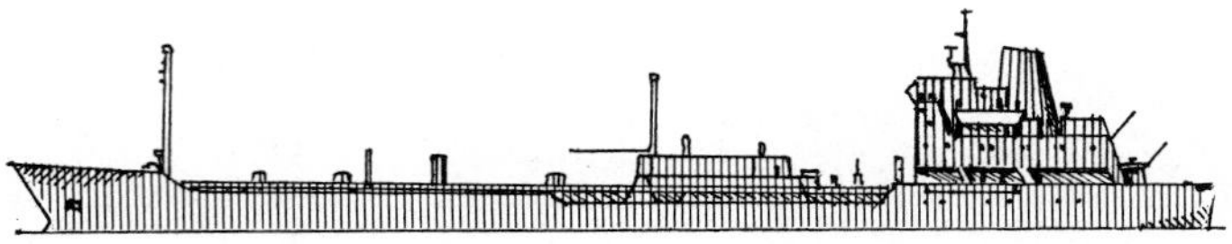

111 *MNMF H1*
ARCADIA Pa/FRG (Meyer) 1972; LGC; 4,216 grt/5,794 dwt; 106.41 × 7.26 m *(349.11 × 23.8 ft)*; M (KHD); 15.5 kts; ex-*Gammagas*
Possibly similar: **SUNNY CLIPPER** (NIS) ex-*Coral Isis*

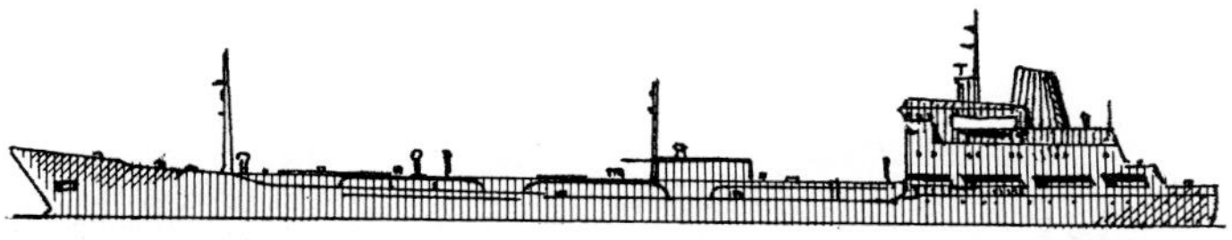

112 *MNMF H1*
JUAN B AZOPARDO Li/FRG (Meyer) 1971; LGC; 4,226 grt/5,810 dwt; 106.41 × 7.27 m *(349.11 × 23.85 ft)*; M (Smit & Bolnes); 16 kts; ex-*Irene*

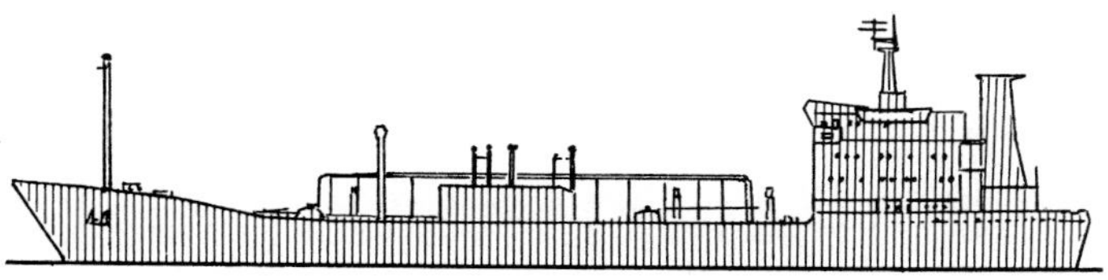

113 *MNMF H1*
POUL KOSAN DIS/FRG (Kroegerw) 1978; LGC; 3,063 grt/3,883 dwt; 92.72 × 6.5 m *(304.2 × 21.33 ft)*; M (MaK); 13.25 kts; ex-*Chemtrans Capella*

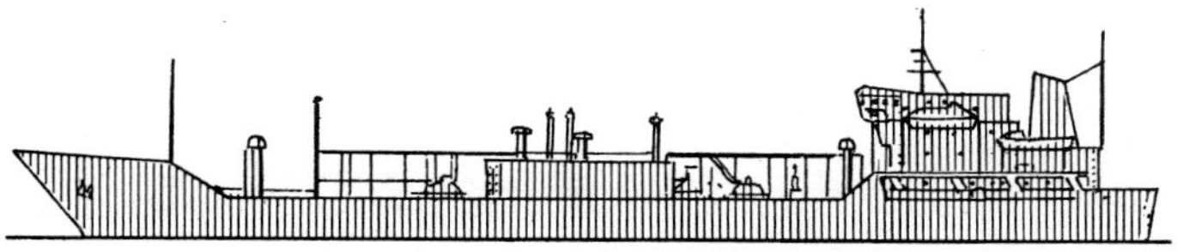

114 *MNMFM H1*
SILVER STAR I Pa/No (Aukra) 1979; Tk/LGC; 4,448 grt/7,035 dwt; 103.54 × 8.43 m *(339.7 × 27.66 ft)*; M (Stork-Werkspoor); 14.5 kts; ex-*Osco Beduin*
Sister: **GOLDEN STAR I** (Pa) ex-*Osco Bellona*

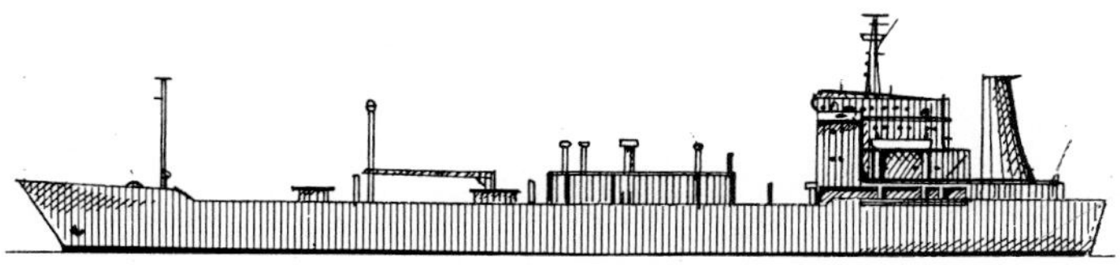

115 *MNMG H*
NORGAS NAVIGATOR NIS/FRG (Kroegerw) 1977; LGC; 6,848 grt/7,154 dwt; 112.76 × 7.5 m *(369.59 × 24.61 ft)*; M (Atlas-MaK); 15 kts; ex-*Bavaria Multina*

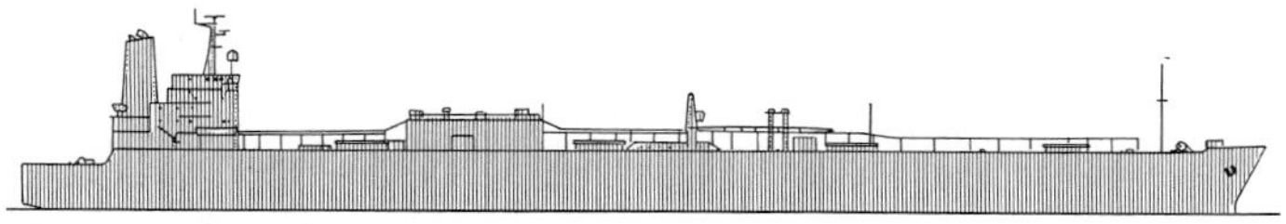

116 *MNM^{2}CNMF H1*
BENNY QUEEN Bs/Ja (NKK) 1981; LGC; 42,501 grt/45,562 dwt; 224.52 × 10.98 m *(736.61 × 36.02 ft)*; M (B&W); 15.50 kts

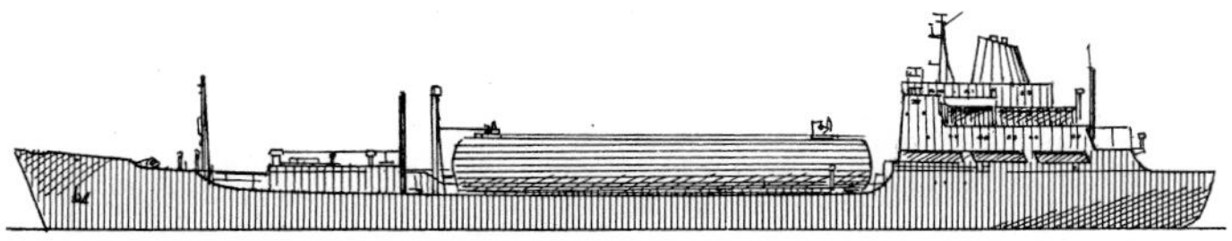

117 *MNM^{2}FN H13*
GAZ LION Pa/No (Moss V) 1972; LGC/Ch; 9,327 grt/11,835 dwt; 138.74 × 9.21 m *(455.18 × 30.22 ft)*; M (Sulzer); 17 kts; ex-*Inge Maersk*
Sister: **IRAN GAZ** (Ir) ex-*Fernwave*; Similar (smaller): **NORGAS DISCOVERER** (NIS) ex-*Bow Elm* **NORGAS VOYAGER** (NIS) ex-*Hardanger*;

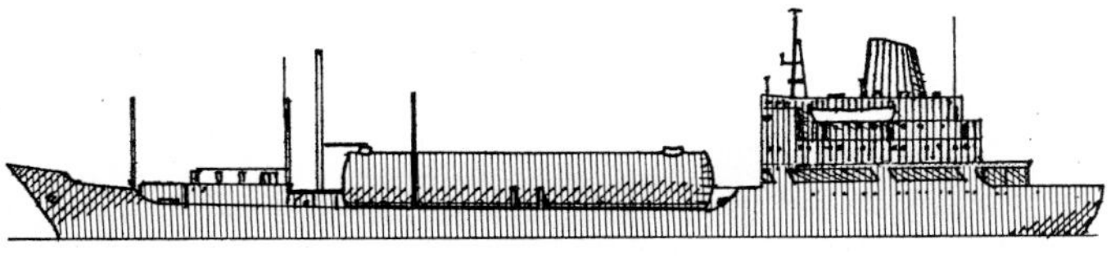

118 *MNMNMF H13*
ASTRA IV Pa/No (Framnaes) 1969; LGC; 6,546 grt/8,784 dwt; 112.89 × 8.79 m *(403.18 × 28.84 ft)*; M (B&W); 16 kts; ex-*Mundogas Atlantic*

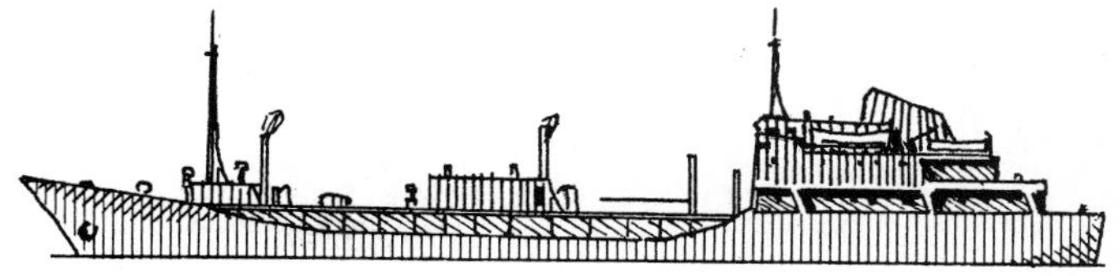

119 *MN^{3}HF H13*
SERENAGAS It/FRG (Brand) 1972; LGC; 1,922 grt/2,462 dwt; 78.49 × 6.20 m *(257.51 × 20.34 ft)*; M (MWM); 12 kts; ex-*Anna Schulte*
Sister: **CAPO MANUELA** (It) ex-*Alexander Schulte*; Similar: **CORAL STAR** (Pa) ex-*Sophie Schulte*; **YASEMIN S** (Tu) ex-*Lissy Schulte*

120 *MN^{3}MF H13*
LIBRAGAS I Ch/FRG (Meyer) 1967; LGC; 1,358 grt/1,622 dwt; 71.2 × 4.52 m *(233.6 × 14.83 ft)*; M (KHD); 12 kts; ex-*Tine Tholstrup*

121 *MN^{3}M-F H13*
CARIBGAS 7 Pa/Sp (UN de Levante) 1965; LGC; 1,469 grt/1,126 dwt; 75.72 × 5.25 m *(248.43 × 17.22 ft)*; M (Werkspoor); 12.5 kts; ex-*Tamames*

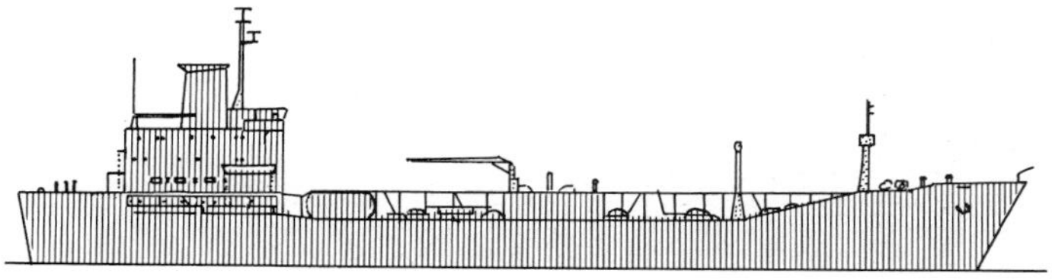

122 *MNRMFN-S H13*
JEMILA Bs/Sp (AESA) 1982; LGC; 8,184 grt/6,909 dwt; 127.26 × 7.00 m *(417.52 × 22.97 ft)*; M (B&W); 15 kts; ex-*Butadiez*

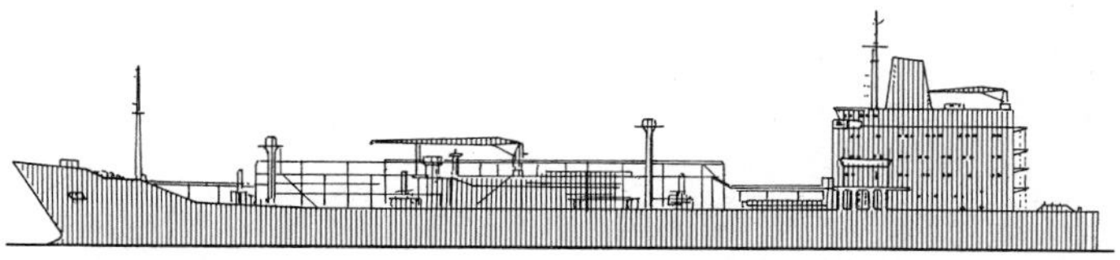

123 *MNRNHFR H1*
MAERSK SUFFOLK Br/De (Odense) 1981; LGC; 14,102 grt/18,270 dwt; 153.12 × 9.93 m *(502.36 × 32.58 ft)*; M (B&W); 17 kts; ex-*Oluf Maersk*
Sisters: **MAERSK STAFFORD** (Br) ex-*Olga Maersk*; **MAERSK SUSSEX** (Br) ex-*Susan Maersk*; **MAERSK SURREY** (Br) ex-*Svend Maersk*; **MAERSK SHETLAND** (Br) ex-*Svendborg Maersk*; **MAERSK SOMERSET** (Br) ex-*Sally Maersk*

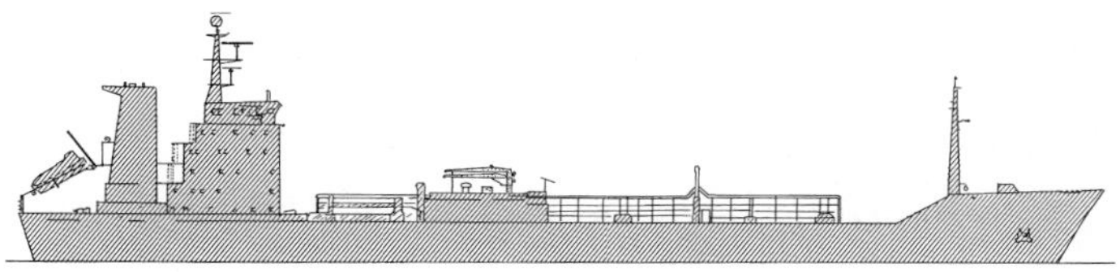

124 *MNSMFL H1*
ETAGAS At/FRG (Schichau) 1988; LGC; 7,314 grt/9,384 dwt; 134.70 × 8.30 m *(441.93 × 27.23 ft)*; M (MAN); 16.5 kts

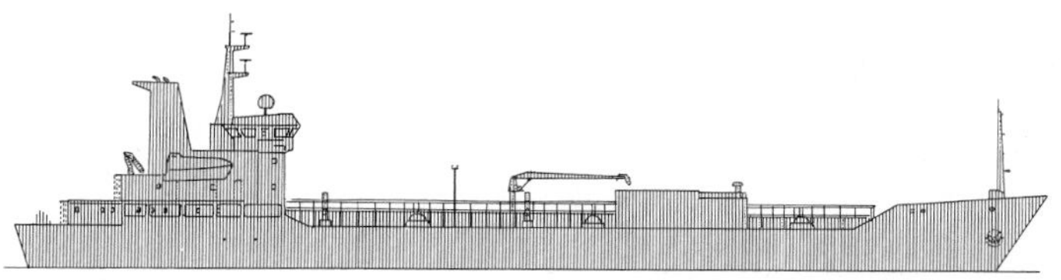

125 *MRMF H1*
VALLESINA It/It (Morini) 1992; LGC; 5,303 grt/6,396 dwt; 106 × 7.80 m *(347.77 × 25.59 ft)*; M (Wärtsilä); 14.2 kts

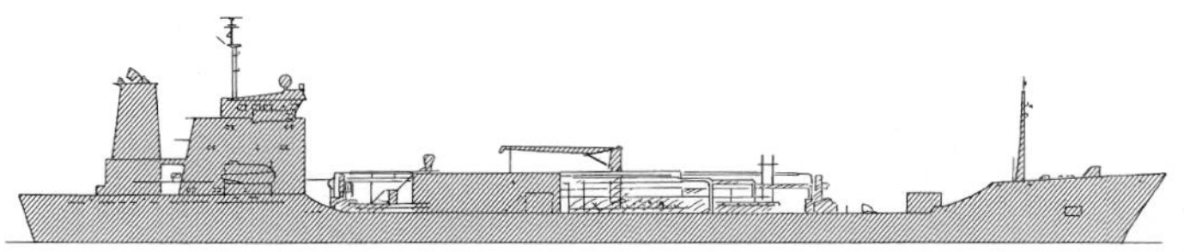

126 *MRMF H13*
TEVIOT Li/FRG (Brand) 1989; LGC; 7,260 grt/9,259 dwt; 132.20 × 8.61 m *(433.73 × 28.25 ft)*; M (Sulzer); 17 kts

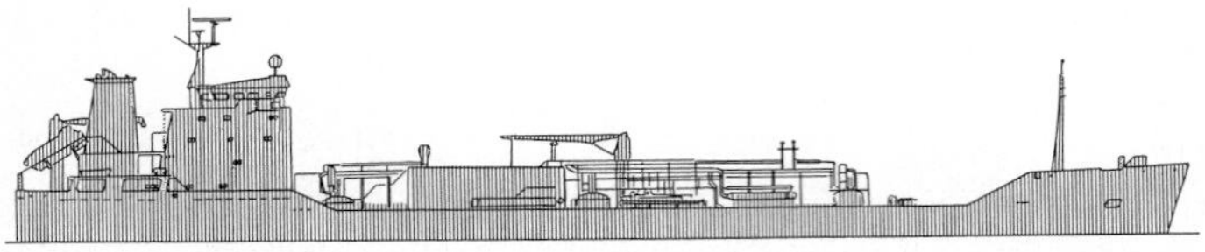

127 *MRMFLR H13*
NORGAS CHRISTIAN Ge/FRG (Brand) 1990; LGC; 7,083 grt/9,490 dwt; 126.20 × 8.40 m *(414.04 × 27.56 ft)*; M (MAN); 16.25 kts
Sisters: **NORGAS PATRICIA** (NIS); **IGLOO BERGEN** (Ge); **IGLOO TANA** (Ge)

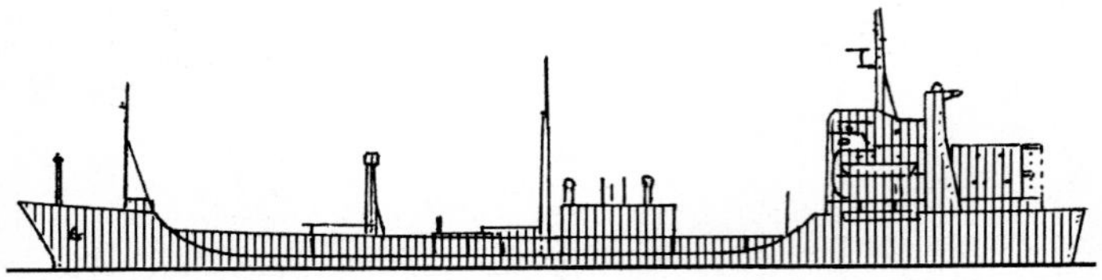

128 *NM²NMG H13*
NEWMARKET Pa/FRG (Werftunion) 1976; LGC; 2,451 grt/3,402 dwt; 89.21 × 6.28 m *(292.68 × 20.6 ft)*; M (MaK); 15 kts; ex-*Sunny Queen*
Possible sister: **NEWBURY** (Pa) ex-*Pentland Brae*; Similar (sister but has shorter kingposts amidships): **GAZ SUN** (Pa) ex-*Sunny Duke*

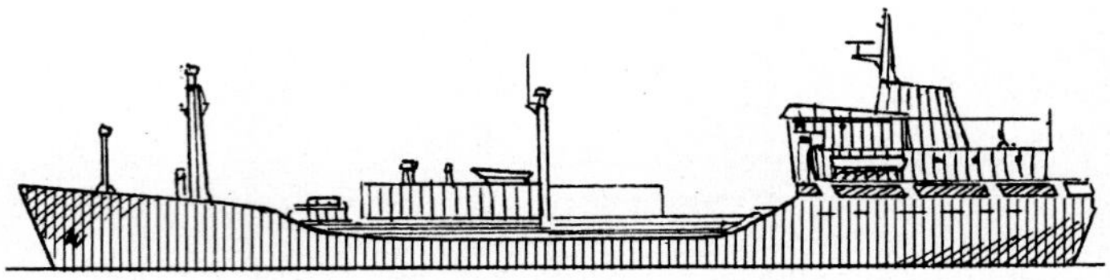

129 *NMNM-F H13*
LADY ROWENA Li/Ne (Pattje) 1973; LGC; 2,024 grt/2,489 dwt; 79.48 × 6.04 m *(260.76 × 19.82 ft)*; M (Atlas-MaK); 13.5 kts; Launched as *Anita*
Sister: **HAUGVIK** (NIS) ex-*Sigurd Jorsalfar*

130 *N²HMF H13*
BERGA Ag/Fr (La Ciotat) 1968; LGC; 5,137 grt/5,290 dwt; 116.9 × 6.5 m *(383.53 × 21.33 ft)*; M (Sulzer); 16.5 kts; ex-*Pascal*
Similar: **MARTINA PRIMA** (Li) ex-*Lavoisier*

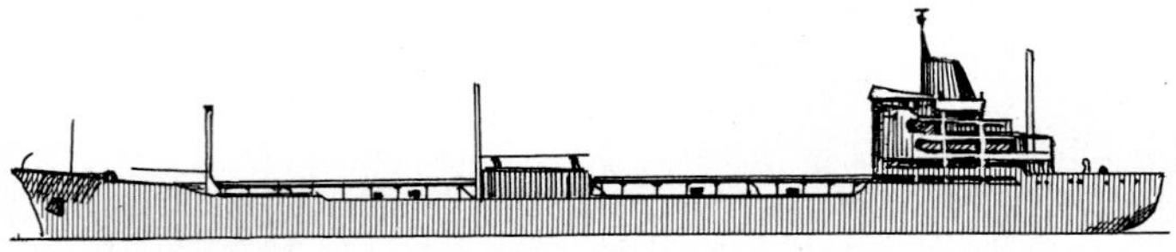

131 *N²M-FN H13*
AMELINA Li/Ne (Verolme Dok) 1964; LGC; 10,343 grt/10,922 dwt; 156.47 × 7.51 m *(513.35 × 24.64 ft)*; M (MAN); 17 kts; ex-*William R Grace*
Sister: **SAVONETTA** (Li) ex-*Joseph P Grace*

132 Havis *(NIS); 1993* *Norman Thomson*

133 Havfrost *(HIS); 1991* *Norman Thomson*

134 Gas Diana *(Li); 1977* *WSPL*

135 Dorothea Schulte *(NIS); 1981* *WSPL*

136 Tarquin Trader *(Li); 1988* *WSPL*

137 Alessandro Volta *(It); 1982* *WSPL*

138 Berge Sisar *(NIS); 1979* *WSPL*

139 Genkai Maru *(Ja); 1980* *WSPL*

140 Balina *(NIS); 1975; (as Tarquin Ranger)* *WSPL*

141 Libra Gas 1 *(Pa); 1967; (as Tine Kosan)* *WSPL*

142 Gaz Supplier *(Pa); 1971; (as Cavendish)* *WSPL*

143 Tarquin Mariner *(Li); 1992* *WSPL*

144 Teviot *(Li); 1989* *WSPL*

145 Hydrogas *(NIS); 1977/89* *WSPL*

146 Eeklo *(Lu); 1995* *FotoFlite*

147 Bussewitz *(Ge); 1983* *FotoFlite*

148 Larbi Ben M'Hidi *(Ag); 1977* *FotoFlite*

149 Sturgeon *(Ne); 1988* *FotoFlite*

150 Cantarell *(Me); 1980* *FotoFlite*

151 Nejma *(Bs); 1983; (as Eupen)* *FotoFlite*

152 Havglimt *(NIS); 1978* *FotoFlite*

153 Helikon *(Br); 1976* *FotoFlite*

154 Annabella *(Li); 1975* *FotoFlite*

155 Borthwick *(Bs); 1977* *FotoFlite*

156 Asterix I *(Pa); 1983; (as Asterix)* *FotoFlite*

157 Luigi Lagrange *(It); 1977* *FotoFlite*

158 Artesia *(Pa); 1975; (as Norgas Commander)* *FotoFlite*

159 Norgas Trader *(NIS); 1981* *FotoFlite*

160 Norgas Mariner *(NIS); 1982* *FotoFlite*

161 Mette Kosan *(DIS); 1981* *FotoFlite*

162 Ben Flor *(Ge); 1985* *FotoFlite*

163 Val Misa *(It); 1981* *FotoFlite*

164 Quentin *(Li); 1977* *FotoFlite*

165 Anna Kosan *(DIS); 1976* *FotoFlite*

166 Merwegas *(Ne); 1981* *FotoFlite*

167 Lingegas *(NA); 1981* *FotoFlite*

168 Berge Frost *(NIS); 1983* *FotoFlite*

169 Lily Pacific *(Sg); 1982* *FotoFlite*

170 Polar Belgica *(It); 1991* *FotoFlite*

171 Hydrogas II *(NIS); 1977/92* *FotoFlite*

172 Hedda *(NIS); 1993* *FotoFlite*

173 Tsugaru Gloria *(Pa); 1991* *FotoFlite*

174 Gitta Kosan *(DIS); 1990* *FotoFlite*

175 Methania *(Lu); 1978* *FotoFlite*

176 Igloo Star *(Ge); 1987* *Norman Thomson*

177 Hemina *(Br); 1979* *Norman Thomson*

178 Hesperus *(NIS); 1973* *Norman Thomson*

179 Havgast *(NIS); 1971* *Norman Thomson*

180 Gas Leo *(Li); 1990* *FotoFlite*

181 Havjarl *(Br); 1972* *FotoFlite*

182 Helios *(NIS); 1992* *FotoFlite*

183 Coral Antillarum *(Ne); 1982; (as Quevedo)* *FotoFlite*

184 Alstergas *(Li); 1991* *FotoFlite*

185 Jean Alleaume *(Kn); 1982* *WSPL*

5 Gearless Dry Cargo Vessels (over 83.82 m (275 ft) overall)

5 Gearless Dry Cargo Vessels (over 83.82 m (275 ft) overall)

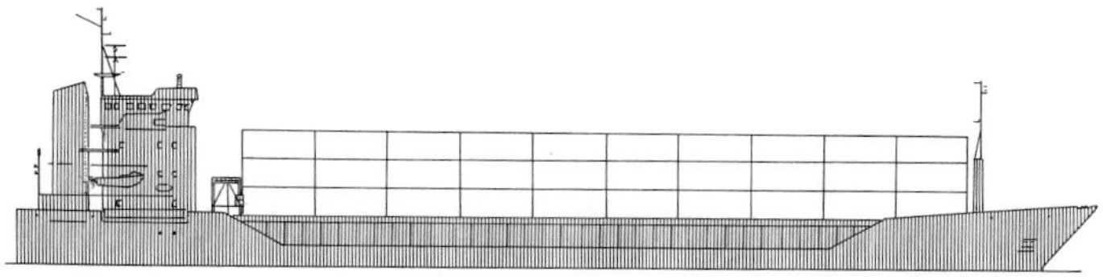

1 *HKMF H13*
LEKNES Cy/Ne (Pattje) 1994; C; 2,901 grt/4,223 dwt; 91.20 × 5.75 m *(299.21 × 18.86 ft)*; M (MaK); 13.5 kts; 188 TEU
Possible sisters: **HAUGO** (Cy); **LAURA HELENA** (Cy)

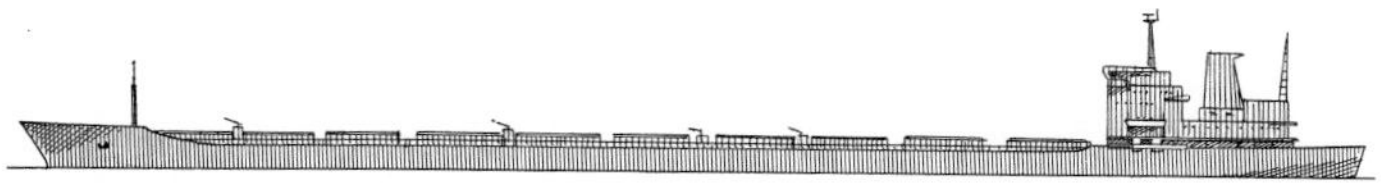

2 *HMFN H1*
AGGELIKI P Cy/Pd ('Komuny Paryskiej') 1975; B; 33,057 grt/54,611 dwt; 221.47 × 12.4 m *(726.61 × 40.68 ft)*; M (Sulzer); 16.5 kts; Launched as *Politechnika Gdanska*; 'B-521' type
Sisters: **XING CHANG** (Pa) ex-*Politechnika Gliwicka*; **HEAVY METAL** (Cy) Launched as *Politechnika Gdanska*

3 *HMFN H123*
ALDO CECCONI It/Br (Lithgows) 1953; O; 6,602 grt/9,297 dwt; 130.16 × 7.95 m *(427.03 × 26.08 ft)*; R (Rankin & Blackmore); 11 kts; ex-*Gleddoch*

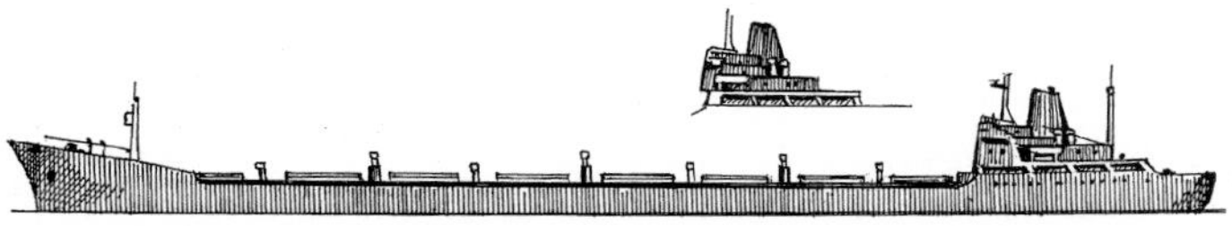

4 *HMFN H13*
DELTA TRIDENT Va/Ys ('3 Maj') 1967; B; 26,130 grt/44,470 dwt; 211.41 × 11.79 m *(693.6 × 36.68 ft)*; M (Sulzer); 16 kts; ex-*Saara Aarnio*
Similar (see inset): **PACIFIC TRIDENT** (Va) ex-*Annukka Arnio*

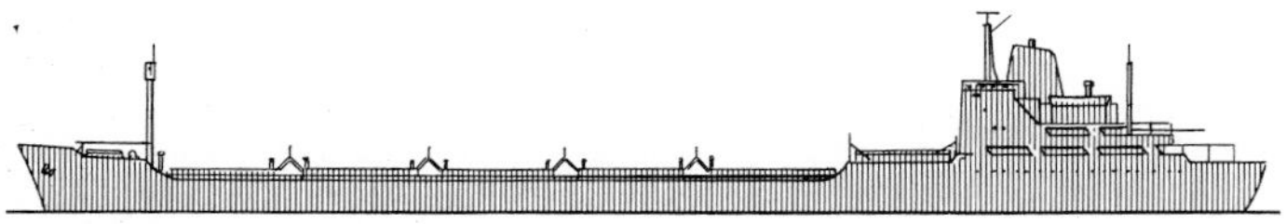

5 *HMFN H13*
JI HAI 9 RC/Sw (Oskarshamns) 1960; B; 12,091 grt/17,374 dwt; 161.19 × 9.9 m *(528.84 × 32.48 ft)*; M (Gotaverken); 12.5 kts; ex-*Sea Master*

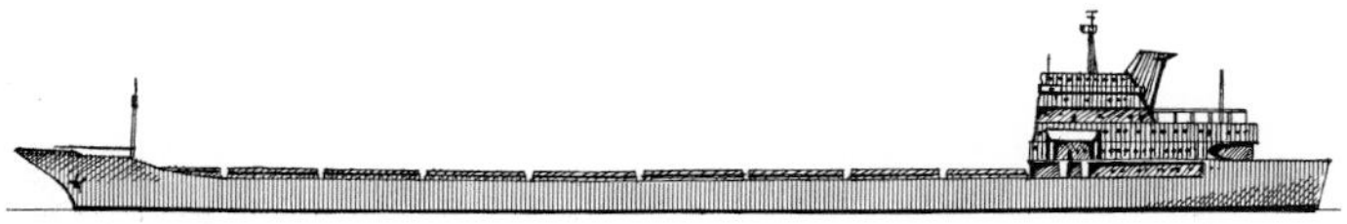

6 *HMFN H13*
LUCKY STAR Li/Pd (Szczecinska) 1971; B; 20,051 grt/32,512 dwt; 202.34 × 10.71 m *(663.85 × 35.14 ft)*; M (Sulzer); 15 kts; ex-*Glyntawe*; 'B447' type

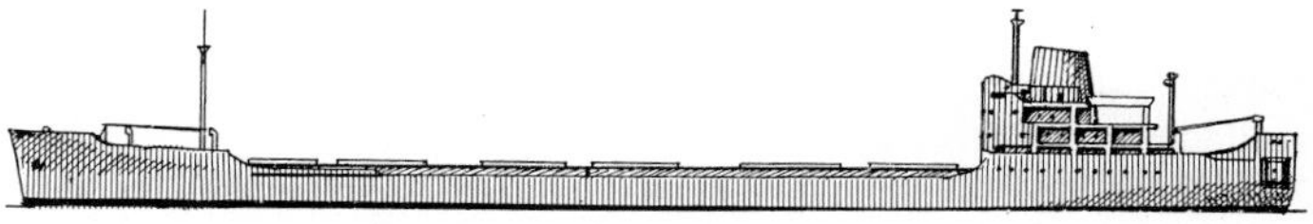

7 *HMFN H13*
MELVIN H BAKER Li/FRG (A G 'Weser') 1956; O; 12,258 grt/17,940 dwt; 159.95 × 9.46 m *(524.77 × 31.04 ft)*; M (Polar); 15 kts

8 *HMG H1*
DESPINA Cy/Pd (Gdynska) 1970; B; 32,757 grt/55,596 dwt; 218.42 × 12.4 m *(716.6 × 40.68 ft)*; M (Sulzer); 15.25 kts; ex-*Manifest Lipcowy*; 'B-521' type

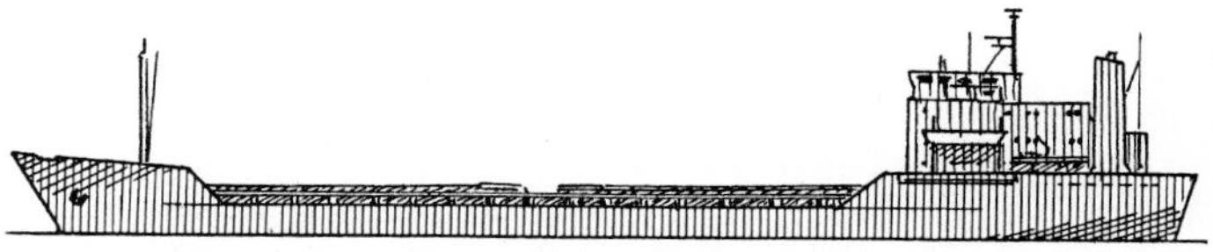

9 *HMG H13*
SELNES Cy/Br (Appledore) 1975; C/B; 3,658 grt/5,790 dwt; 102.01 × 6.83 m *(334.68 × 22.41 ft)*; M (Pielstick); 14 kts; ex-*Risnes*
Sisters: **MARMON** (Cy) ex-*Ringnes*; **ALEXIS** (Cy) ex-*Rocknes*; **ROLLNES** (Pa)

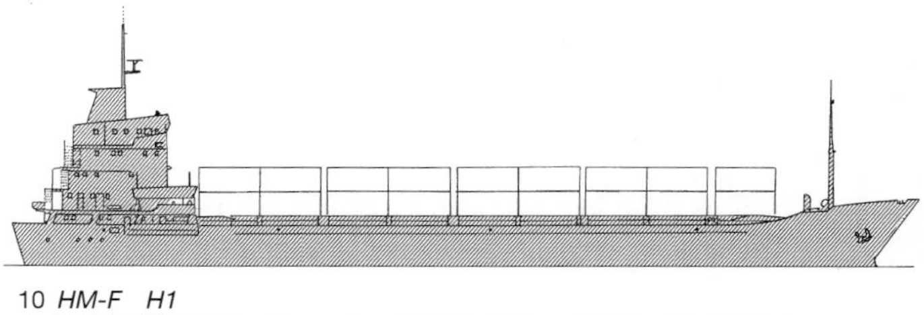

10 *HM-F H1*
NORUNN NIS/As (Korneuburg) 1972; C/Con; 2,586 grt/3,150 dwt; 90.4 × 4.64 m *(296.59 × 15.22 ft)*; M (MWM); 14.5 kts; ex-*Korneuburg*; 183 TEU
Sisters: **ODYSSEY** (At) ex-*Salzburg*; **ARGOSY** (At) ex-*Katharina*; **OLGA I** (Pa) ex-*Joachim*

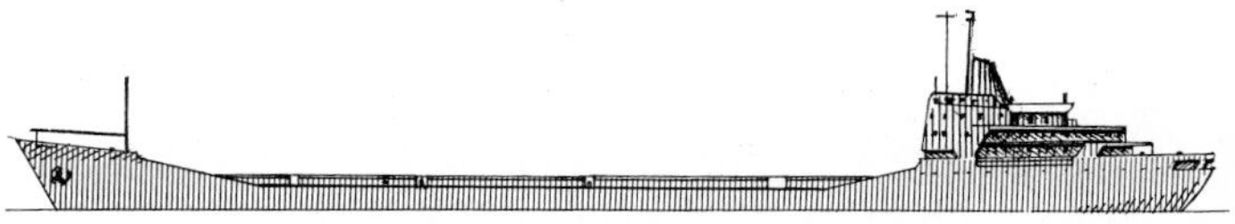

11 *HM-F H13*
HUNG NAM RK/Pd (Szczecinska) 1967; B; 11,010 grt/15,688 dwt; 156.37 × 9.51 m *(513.02 × 31.2 ft)*; M (Sulzer); 15.5 kts; ex-*Zaglebie Dabrowskie*; 'B-520' type
Sister: **CHANG SONG** (RK) ex-*Podhale*

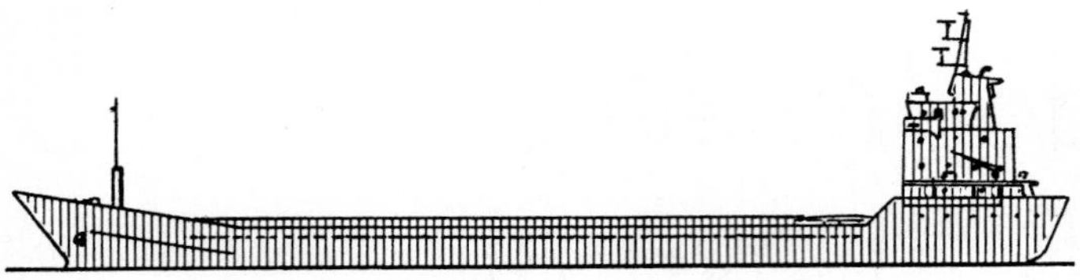

12 *HM-F H13*
MANGO Ma/Sp (Balenciaga) 1981; C; 2,693 grt/4,706 dwt; 89.01 × 6.16 m *(292.03 × 20.21 ft)*; M (Deutz); 13 kts; ex-*Sota Arritokieta*; 178 TEU
Sister: **MINGO** (Ma) ex-*Sota Begona*

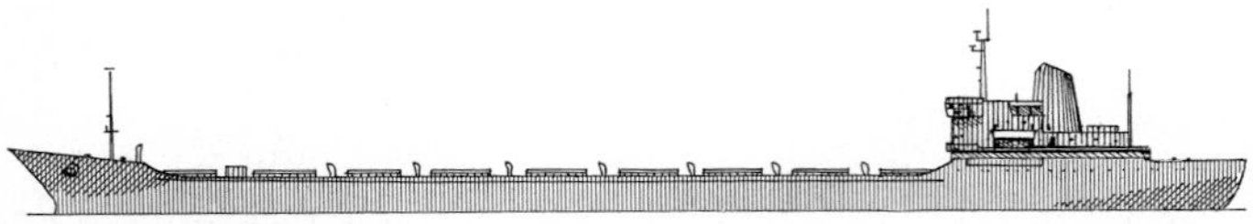

13 *HM-FH H13*
GORLITZ Ge/Ru (Baltic) 1974; B; 23,235 grt/38,250 dwt; 201.38 × 11.21 m *(660.7 × 36.78 ft)*; M (B&W); 15.75 kts; 'Baltika' type
Sister: **THEO C** (SV) ex-*Groditz*; Similar: **MEMED ABASHIDZE** (Gi) ex-*Nikolay Voznesenskiy*; **CAPTAIN B. ATAMAN** (Cy) ex-*Luis Banchero*; **AMAMI** (Cy) Launched as *Renate*

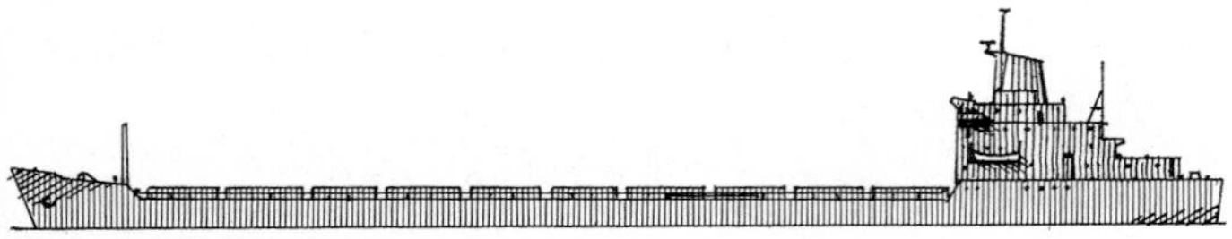

14 *HM-FN H13*
GYPSUM KING Br/Ca (Collingwood) 1975; B; 12,272 grt/18,314 dwt; 150.81 × 9.25 m *(494.78 × 30.35 ft)*; T (GEC); 15 kts
Sister: **GYPSUM BARON** (Br)

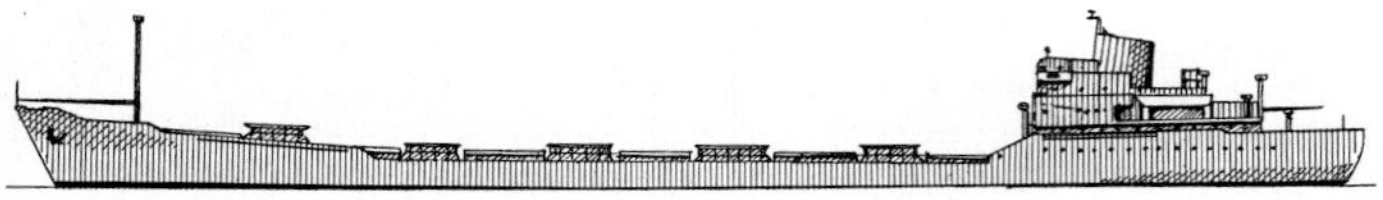

15 *HM-FN H13*
HONG QI 301 RC/FRG (B+V) 1958; B; 10,402 grt/17,151 dwt; 165 × 9.59 m *(541.34 × 31.46 ft)*; M (MAN); 14 kts; ex-*Asmidiske*

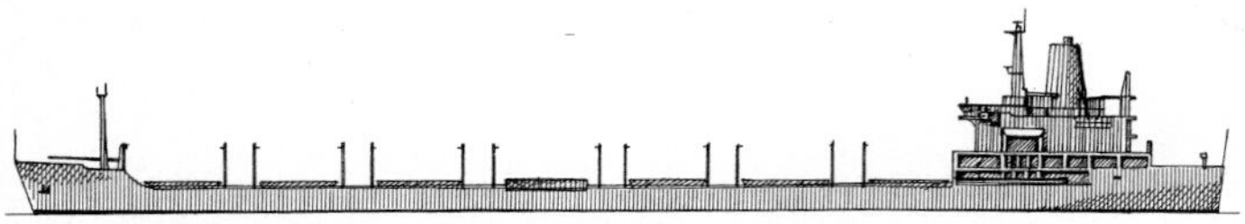

16 *MCM^{13}FC H13*
IRON CARPENTARIA Au/Au (Whyalla) 1977; B; 25,853 grt/45,432 dwt; 202.72 × 12.52 m *(665.09 × 41.07 ft)*; M (Wärtsilä); — kts; New engines 1984
Sister: **IRON CURTIS** (Au)

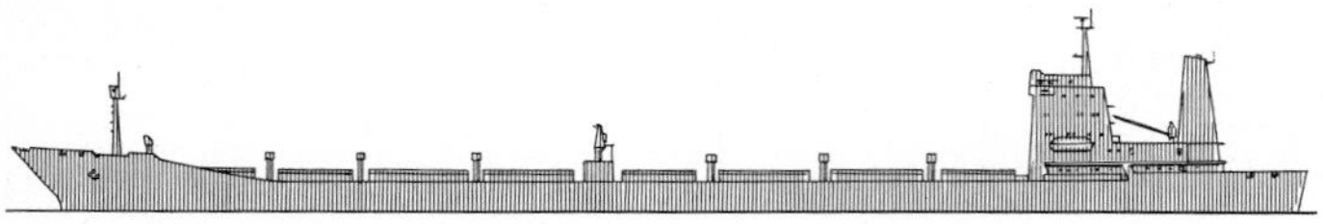

17 *MCMG H1*
ION SOLTYS Uk/Ru (Okean) 1976; B; 30,072 grt/52,975 dwt; 215.37 × 12.22 m *(706.59 × 40.09 ft)*; M (B&W); 14.75 kts; Some other vessels in this class may also have a crane amidships
Sisters: **UNAN AVETISYAN** (Uk); **RODINA** (Bu); Similar (modified superstructure and kingpost between bridge and funnel): **AKADEMIK BAKULEV** (Uk); **GEROI STALINGRADA** (Uk); **KHARITON GREKU** (Uk); **NIKOLAY KUZNETSOV** (Uk); **MIKOLA BAZHAN** (Uk); **ALEKSEY DANCHENKO** (Uk); **AKADEMIK BLAGONRAVOV** (Uk); **DEPUTAT LUTSKIY** (Uk); **ALEKSANDER ABERG** (Ea) ex-*70 Letiye Oktyabrya*; **PAUL KERES** (Ea) ex-*Viktor Bakayev*; **KRISTIAN PALUSALU** (Ea) (or **KRISTJAN PALUSALU**); **ELMAR KIVISTIK** (Ea) ex-*Ivan Babushkin*; **BORIS GORDEYEV** (Li)

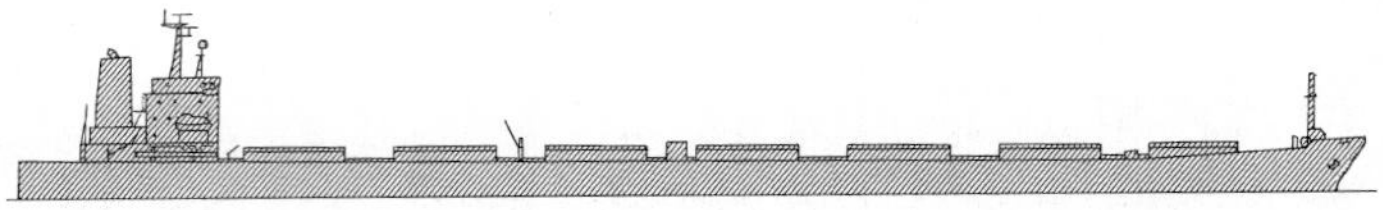

18 *MCM^{2}FC H*
MERCHANT PRIDE HK/Ja (NKK) 1990; B; 36,725 grt/69,458 dwt; 225 × 13.27 m *(738.19 × 45.37 ft)*; M (Sulzer); — kts; 988 TEU

19 *M^{10}F H*
ARNAKI Ma/It (Italcantieri) 1974; B; 46,172 grt/81,881 dwt; 259.01 × 14.05 m *(849.77 × 46.1 ft)*; M (GMT); 16 kts; ex-*Italmere*
Sisters: **AGRARI** (Cy) ex-*Mare Ligure*; **MARE TIRRENO** (It); **URSA MAJOR** (It); **ANTHIA** (Ma) ex-*Capricornus*; **JUNIPER** (Li) ex-*Draco*; **IRENE V** (Gr) ex-*Delphinus*; **PERSEUS** (It); **SOLON OF ATHENS** (Cy) ex-*Sextum*; Probable sister: **ORISSA** (In) ex-*Lupus*

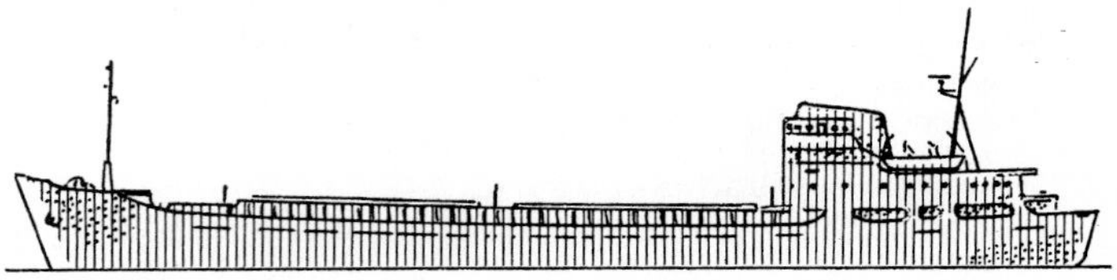

20 *MFM H1*
PAULEMOSE R SV/Br (Hill) 1954/68; C; 1,230 grt/1,504 dwt; 84.82 × 4.17 m *(278.28 × 13.68 ft)*; M (British Polar); 10.5 kts; ex-*Apollo*; Lengthened 1968
Sister: **SEA LORD** (SV) ex-*Echo*

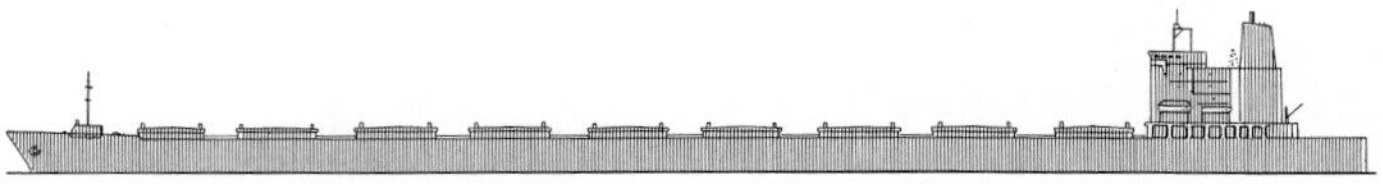

21 *MHF H*
BERGE MASTER NIS/Ja (Mitsubishi HI) 1982; B; 76,594 grt/143,745 dwt; 270 × 17.33 m *(886 × 56.86 ft)*; M (Sulzer); 15 kts
Sister: **OCEAN CONQUEROR** (Cy) ex-*Berge Captain*

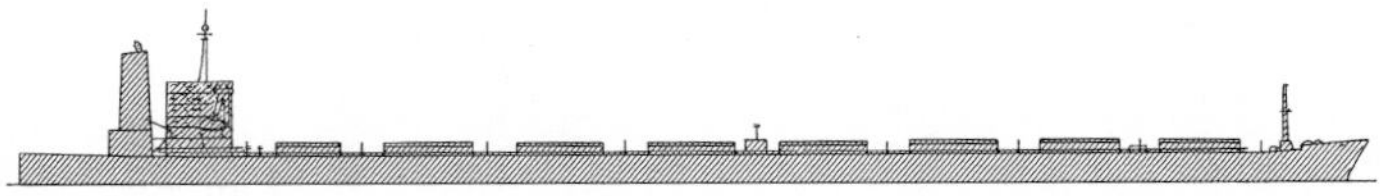

22 *MHF H*
ONOE MARU Ja/Ja; O; 116,427 × 229,334 dwt; 315 × 18.32 m *(1,033.46 × 60.10 ft)*; M (Sulzer); 14 kts

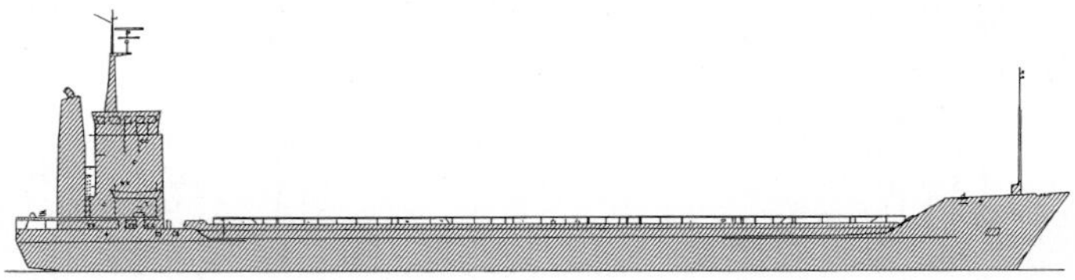

23 *MHF H1*
EMILY BORCHARD At/FRG (Sietas) 1978; C/Con; 4,867 grt/6,811 dwt; 118.42 × 6.51 m *(388.52 × 21.36 ft)*; M (MWM); 17 kts; ex-*Baltic*; 429 TEU

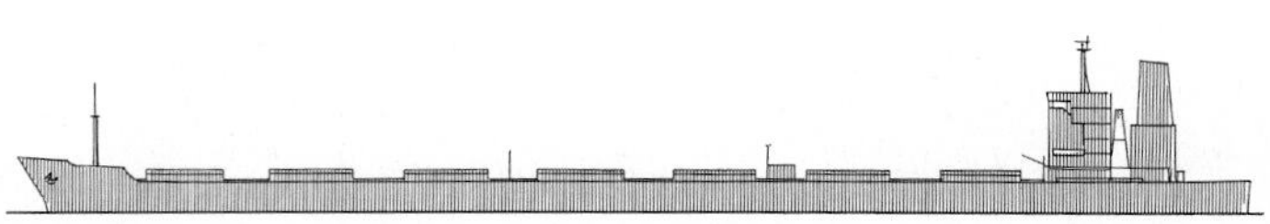

24 *MHF H1*
GOLDEN SEA Pa/Ja (NKK) 1982; B; 49,938 grt/89,127 dwt; 241.1 × 14 m *(791 × 45.93 ft)*; M (Pielstick); 14 kts; ex-*Shogo Maru*; Drawing is approximate

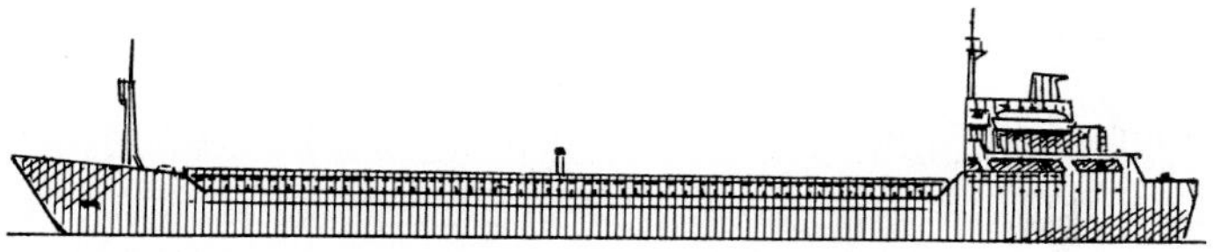

25 *MHF H13*
BERGON Sw/No (Ulstein H) 1978; C; 3,700 grt/5,449 dwt; 100.83 × 6.20 m *(330.81 × 20.34 ft)*; M (Atlas-MaK); 13.5 kts; ex-*Mini Star*; Deck is strengthened to allow a gantry crane to be fitted; 220 TEU

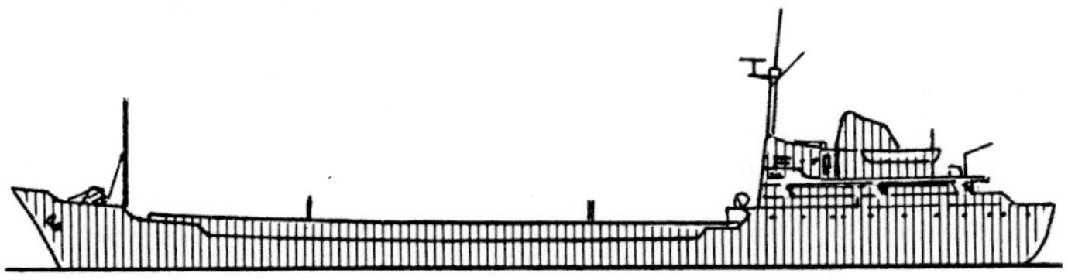

26 *MHF H13*
HIBAT ALLAH Sy/Hu (Angyalfold) 1964; C; 1,596 grt/2,359 dwt; 84.44 × 4.93 m *(277.03 × 16.17 ft)*; M (SKL); 10.75 kts; ex-*Sagahorn*

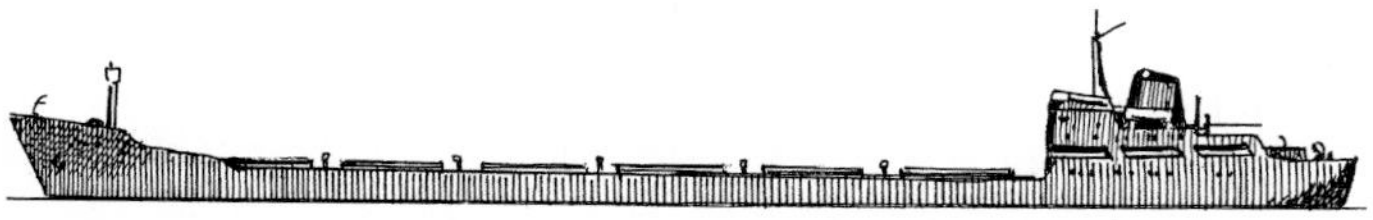

27 *MHF H13*
HUAI HAI RC/FRG (Kieler H) 1962; B; 14,847 grt/26,331 dwt; 179.38 × 10.92 m *(588.52 × 35.83 ft)*; M (MAN); 14 kts; ex-*Benedicte*
Similar: **HUANG HAI** (RC) ex-*Beatrice*

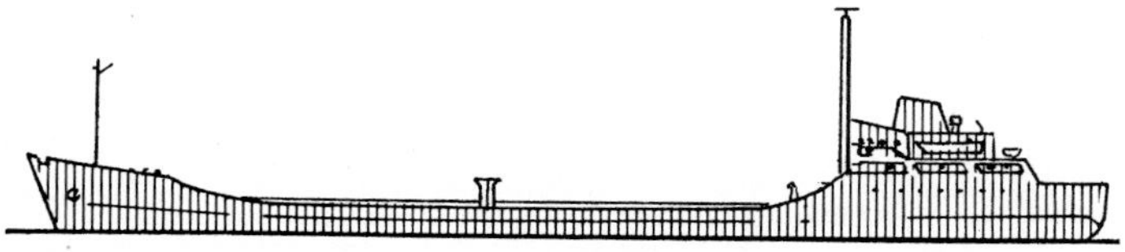

28 *MHF H13*
ORLAN SV/Br (Hall, Russell) 1969; C; 1,978 grt/2,878 dwt; 85.91 × 5.31 m *(281.86 × 17.42 ft)*; M (Mirrlees Blackstone); 10.5 kts; ex-*Malling*

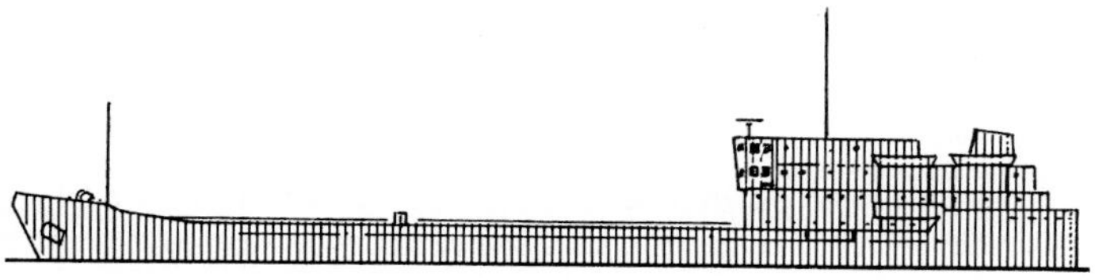

29 *MHF H13*
PAVEL YABLOCHKOV Ru/Fi (Laiva) 1980; C/TS; 2,233 grt/2,554 dwt; 95 × 4 m *(311.68 × 13.12 ft)*; TSM (SKL); 12.5 kts; ex-*Baltiyskiy 112*
Sisters: **ALEKSANDR POPOV** (Ru); **IVAN KULIBIN** (Ru); **IVAN POLZUNOV** (Ru); **VASILIY KALASHNIKOV** (Ru)

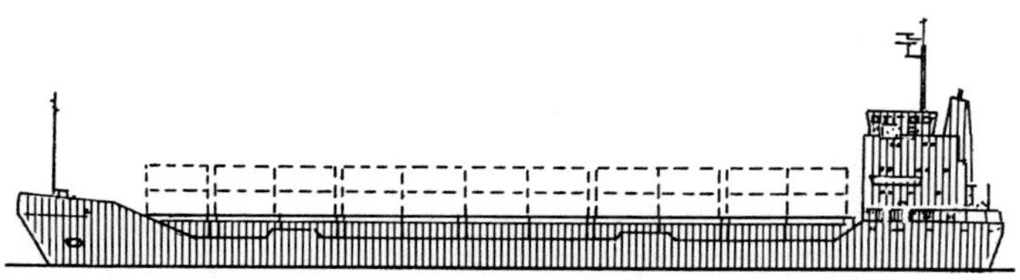

30 *MHF H13*
UB PANTHER NIS/FRG (Sietas) 1977; C/Con; 3,622 grt/4,449 dwt; 97.54 × 5.72 m *(320.01 × 18.77 ft)*; M (MaK); 14 kts; ex-*Karen Oltmann*; 'Type 94'; 348 TEU
Sisters: **OLE** (Ge) ex-*Planet*; **PETER KNUPPEL** (Ge)

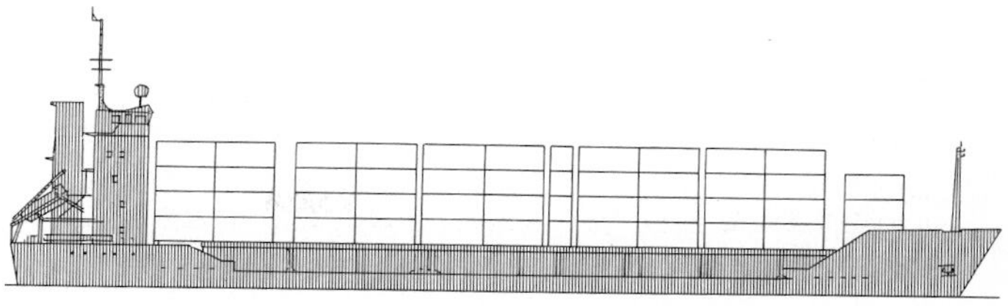

31 *MHFL H13*
VANGUARD At/Po (Viana) 1994; C; 3,806 grt/4,766 dwt; 100.63 × 5.91 m *(330.15 × 19.39 ft)*; M (MaK); 15 kts; ex-*Angela J*; Free-fall lifeboat on port side
Possible sister: **REGINA J** (At)

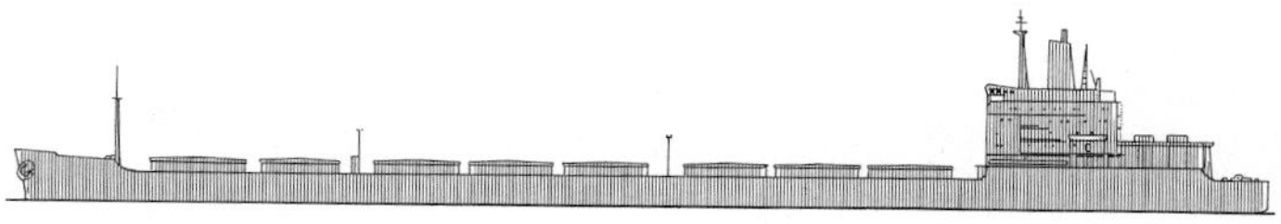

32 *MHFNC H12*
RIVER BOYNE Au/Ja (Mitsubishi HI) 1982; B; 51,035 grt/76,355 dwt; 255 × 12.82 m *(837 × 42.06 ft)*; T (Mitsubishi); 16 kts; Coal-fired
Sister: **RIVER EMBLEY** (Au)

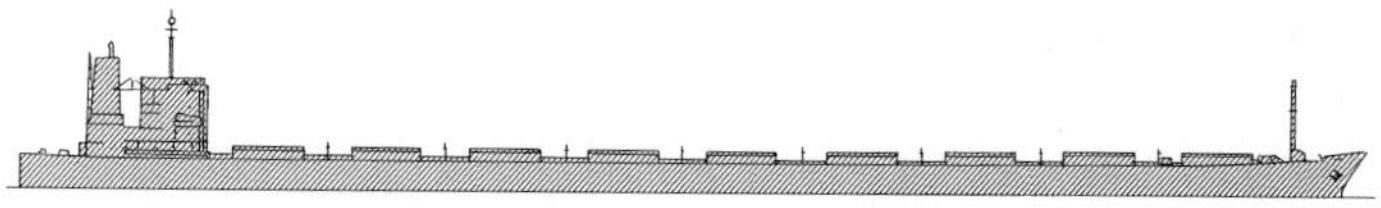

33 *MHMFM H*
CHITA MARU Ja/Ja (Kawasaki) 1989; B; 93,310 grt/179,133 dwt; 290.03 × 18.23 m *(951.54 × 59.81 ft)*; M (B&W); 14.05 kts

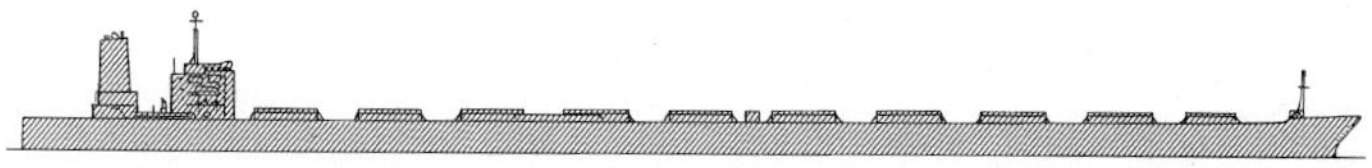

34 *MHSF H*
BERGE STAHL NIS/Ko (Hyundai) 1986; O; 175,720 grt/364,767 dwt; 343.01 × 23.04 m *(1,125.36 × 75.59 ft)*; M (B&W); 13.5 kts

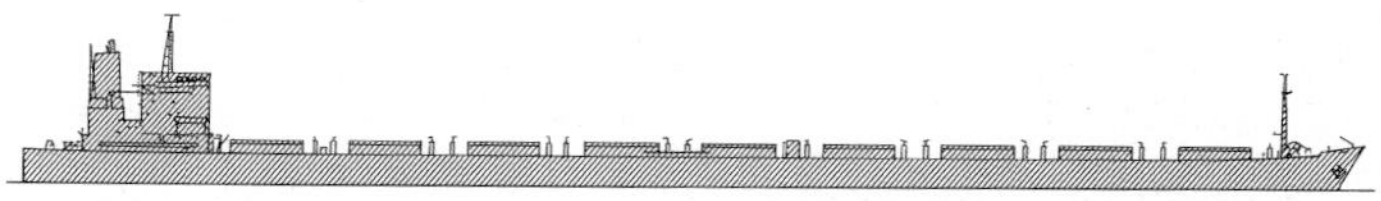

35 *MH-NFM H*
CONCORDE SPIRIT Pi/Ja (Kawasaki) 1986; B; 93,509 grt/181,884 dwt; 290.05 × 18.23 m *(951.61 × 59.81 ft)*; M (B&W); 13.5 kts; ex-*Concorde Maru*
Similar: **TATEKAWA MARU** (Ja); **KYOMI** (Pa) ex-*Kyomi Maru*

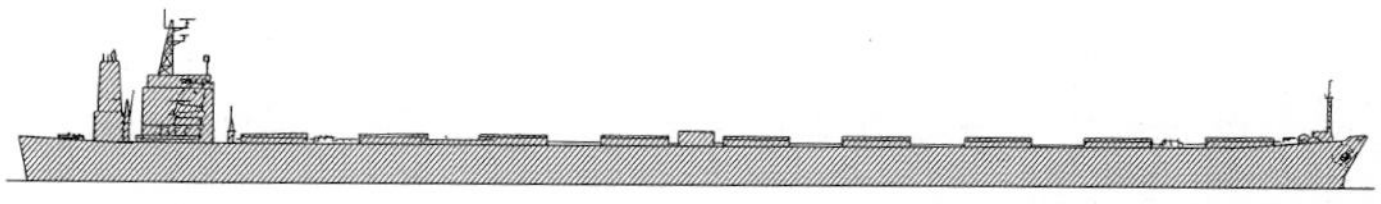

36 *M^2CF H*
FORTROSE HK/Ja (Sanoyas HM) 1994; B; 75,254 grt/150,877 dwt; 270.05 × 17.47 m *(885.99 × 57.32 ft)*; M (Sulzer); — kts
Possible sister: **CHIKUZEN MARU** (Ja)

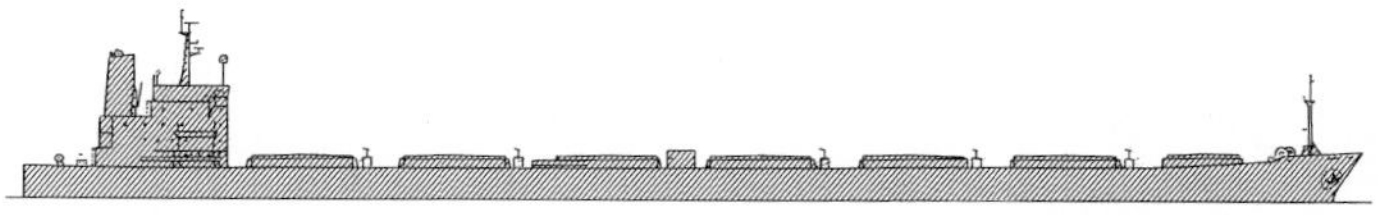

37 *M^2CF H*
NORA NIS/Ja (Kasado) 1986; B; 36,294 grt/68,255 dwt; 225.00 × 13.22 m *(738.19 × 43.37 ft)*; M (B&W); 13 kts; ex-*Polestar Maru*

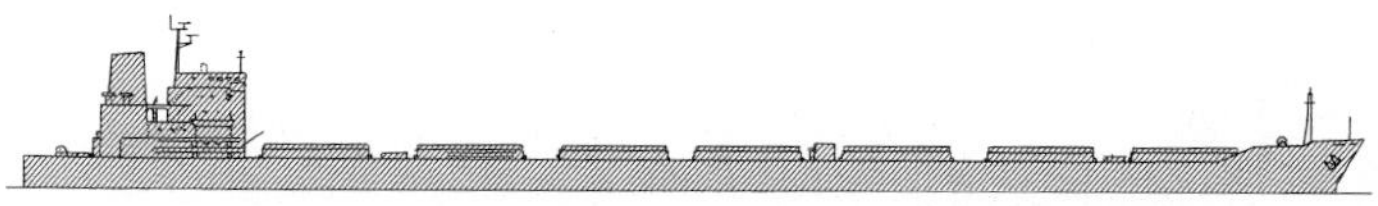

38 *M^2CF H1*
GLORY HOPE Pi/Ja (Koyo) 1987; B; 37,052 grt/68,158 dwt; 224.54 × 13.22 m *(736.68 × 43.37 ft)*; M (B&W); 14 kts
Sister: **NEW AMITY** (Pa) ex-*Hokoku Maru*; Possible sister: **FAR EASTERN EXPRESS** (Tw); Similar: **BAUMARE II** (NIS) ex-*Lake Biwa*

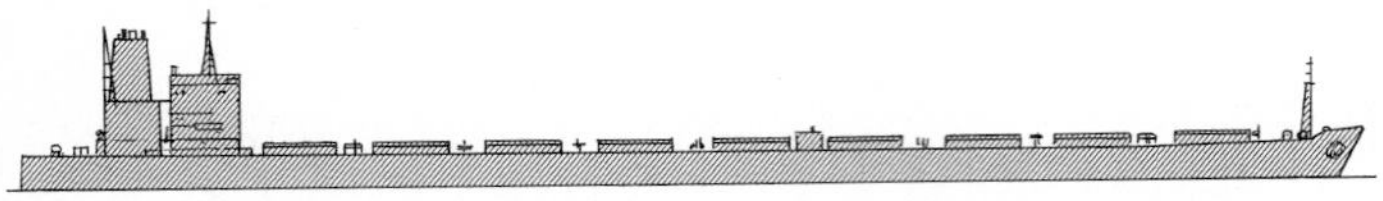

39 M^2CFM H
MERIDIAN SPICA My/Ja (Namura) 1986; B; 77,458 grt/146,939 dwt; 272.04 × 17.62 m *(892.52 × 57.81 ft)*; M (Sulzer); 13 kts; ex-*Shirasagi Maru*

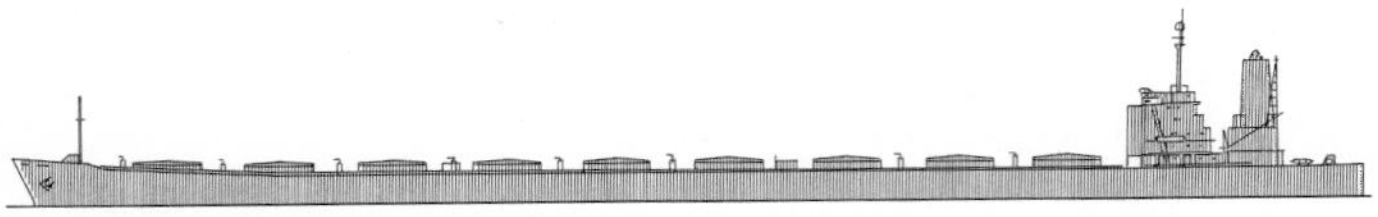

40 M^2CFM H
SETSUYO MARU Ja/Ja (IHI) 1985; B; 88,921 grt/170,808 dwt; 290 × 17.53 m *(951.44 × 57.51 ft)*; M (Sulzer); 13.5 kts
Similar (longer): **ONGA MARU** (Ja) (ore carrier)

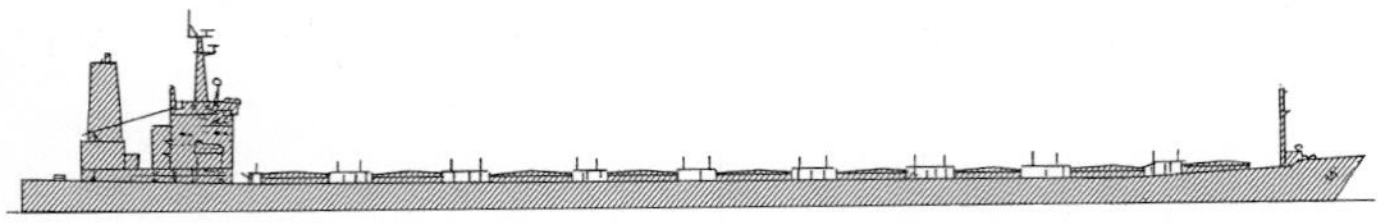

41 M^2DF H
IRON NEWCASTLE Au/Ja (IHI) 1985; B; 78,625 grt/148,140 dwt; 283.50 × 15.90 m *(929.88 × 52.15 ft)*; M (Sulzer); 14.25 kts
Sister: **IRON KEMBLA** (Au)

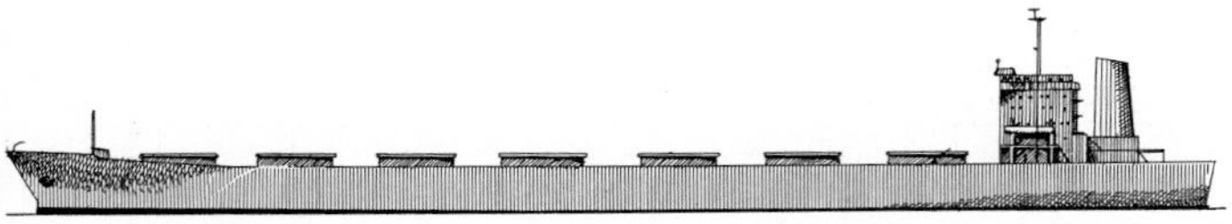

42 M^2F H
ATLANTICA Ma/De (B&W) 1975; B; 36,032 grt/63,990 dwt; 219.56 × 12.5 m *(720.34 × 41.01 ft)*; M (B&W); 15.75 kts; ex-*Caledonia*
Sisters: **CHANG YI HAI** (—) ex-*Calabria*; **PACIFICWAY** (Pa) ex-*Bonnieway*; **AGIA FOTIA** (Bs) ex-*Causeway*; **ATHINIOTISSA** (Ma); Launched as *Sheaf Crest*; **AIFANOURIOS** (Ma) ex-*Specialist*; **AGIOS MINAS** (Gr) ex-*Strategist*; **AEROSMITH** (Cy) ex-*Port Quebec*; **VANCOUVER** (Gr) ex-*Port Vancouver*; **ALISGLORIA** (Pa) ex-*Eredine*; **GUMBET** (Tu) ex-*Hamlet Beatrice*; **GULLUK** (Tu) ex-*Malacca*; **DA LUO SHAN** (RC) ex-*Morelia*; Sister (may have four deck cranes): **TOSCANA** (Gr) ex-*Eastern City*

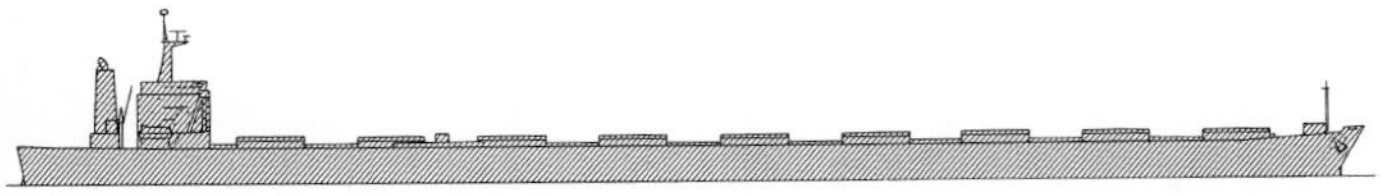

43 M^2F H
BARTOLOMEU DIAS Po/Ja (Sumitomo) 1990; B; 75,054 grt/151,227 dwt; 270.49 × 17.47 m *(887.43 × 57.32 ft)*; M (Sulzer); 14 kts
Similar: **FIRST SUN** (Pa)

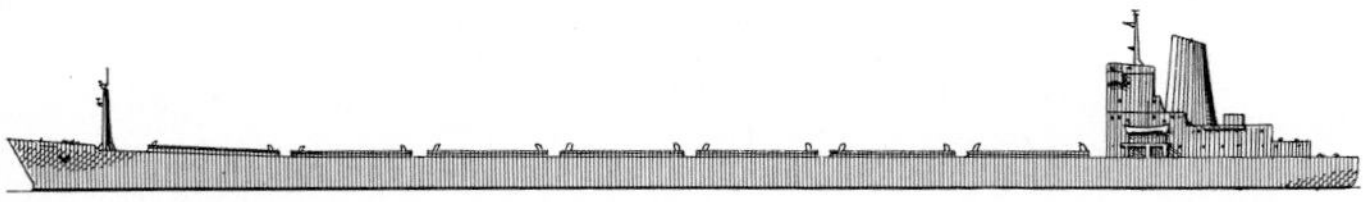

44 M^2F H
BONTRADER HK/Br (H&W) 1970; B; 35,460 grt/59,662 dwt; 224.04 × 12.52 m *(735.04 × 41.08 ft)*; M (B&W); 15.25 kts; ex-*Sydney Bridge*

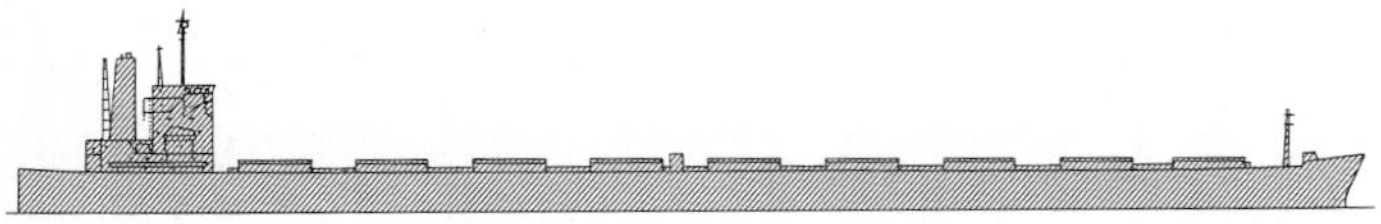

45 M^2F/MHF H
CHANNEL ENTERPRISE Pi/Ja (NKK) 1990; B; 77,304 grt/151,380 dwt; 273 × 17.42 m *(895.67 × 57.15 ft)*; M (B&W); 14 kts; ex-*Orient Enterprise*
Possible sisters: **CASTLE PEAK** (Pa); **KOHJU** (Sg); **LADY KADOORIE** (Pa)

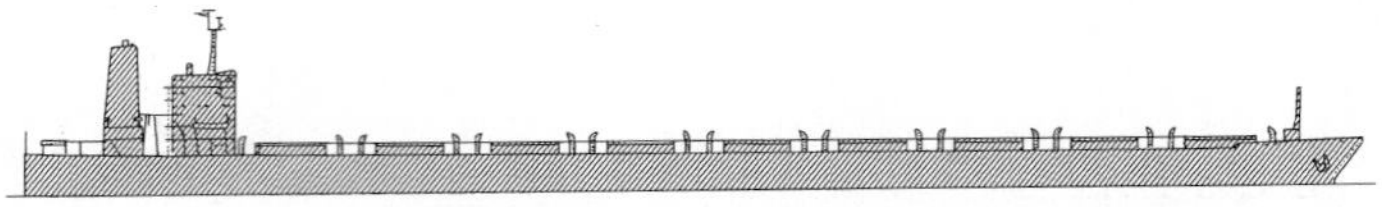

46 M^2F H
DOCECAPE Li/Bz (Verolme E R do Brasil) 1987; B; 79,184 grt/151,852 dwt; 276.99 × 17.61 m *(908.76 × 57.78 ft)*; M (B&W); 14 kts
Sisters: **DOCEBAY** (Li); **DOCERIVER** (Li)

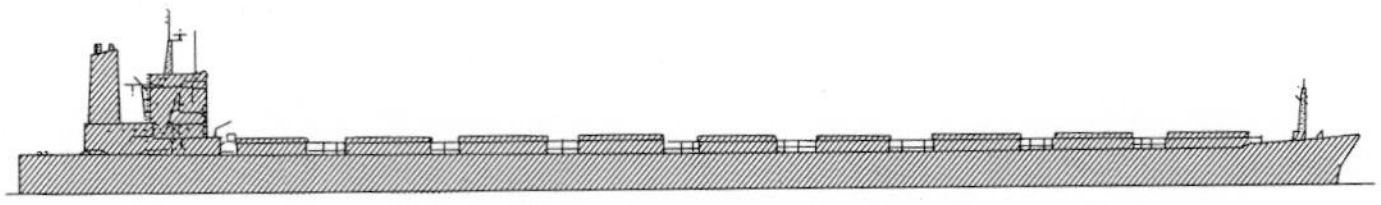

47 M^2F H
DOCERIO Bz/Bz (Verolme E R do Brasil) 1989; B; 90,633 grt/167,315 dwt; 290.03 × 17.61 m *(951.54 × 57.78 ft)*; M (B&W); 13.8 kts
Probable sister: **DOCESERRA** (Bz)

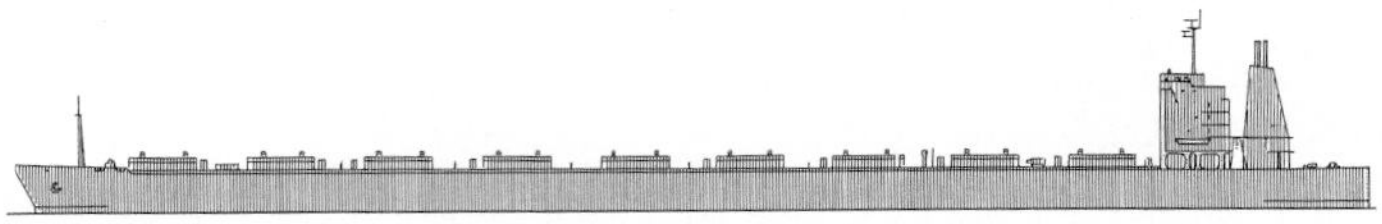

48 M^2F H
HUANG SHAN HK/Sp ('Astano') 1984; B; 92,568 grt/166,058 dwt; 290 × 17.05 m *(951.44 × 55.94 ft)*; M (B&W); 14.5 kts; Launched as *Patria*
Sister: **HADERA** (Li)

49 M^2F H
IDEAL PROGRESS Gr/FRG (LF-W) 1973; B; 43,980 grt/78,750 dwt; 255.91 × 14.2 m *(839.6 × 46.59 ft)*; M (MAN); 16 kts; ex-*Proserpina*
Sister: **DEPA GIULIA** (Bs) ex-*Propontis*; Similar (heavy masts aft): **ATLANTIC TRIDENT** (Cy) ex-*Johann Schulte*

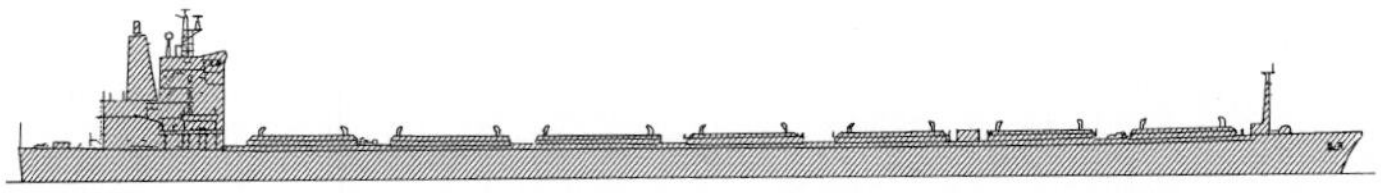

50 M^2F H
IGUAZU Bs/Bz (Verolme E R do Brasil) 1983; B; 41,010 grt/75,485 dwt; 241.89 × 13.60 m *(793.60 × 44.62 ft)*; M (MAN); 14 kts; ex-*Gulf Steel*
Sisters: **EL PAMPERO** (Bs) ex-*Gulf Grain*; **DIAVOLEZZA** (Sd) ex-*El Aalim*; **ST. CERGUE** (Sd) ex-*El Amaan*; Possible sisters: **DOCEMAR** (Br) ex-*Maria do Rosario*; **HILON OF SPARTA** (Cy) ex-*Doceangra*; **AFROS** (Cy) ex-*Carajas*

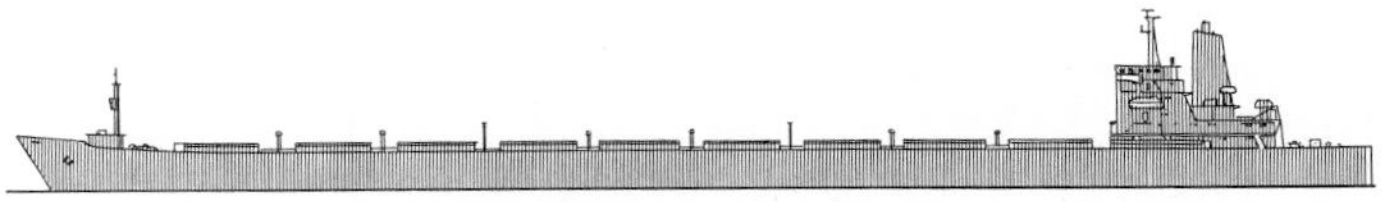

51 M^2F H
LIKA Gr/Ja (Mitsui) 1976; B; 64,627 grt/118,733 dwt; 259.82 × 16.45 m *(852.43 × 53.97 ft)*; M (B&W); 15.5 kts; ex-*Nortrans Elma*
Sister: **MEGA HILL** (Li) ex-*Moshill*; Similar: **PRINCESS CLIPPER** (HK) ex-*Polycrest*; **ROYAL CLIPPER** (HK) ex-*Polyclipper*; **SUNNY CLIPPER** (HK) ex-*Nanny Onstad*

See photo number 5/378

52 M^2F H
MAJA VESTIDA Pi/Ja (Sanoyas HM) 1994; B; 36,559 grt/70,213 dwt; 225.00 × 13.30 m *(738.19 × 43.64 ft)*; M (Sulzer); 14 kts; '70 BC' type.
SIMILAR TO DRAWING NUMBER 5/199

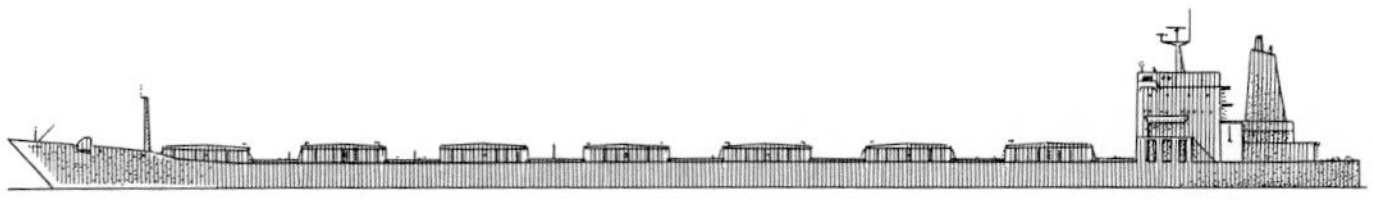

53 M^2F H
MATHEOS Cy/De (B&W) 1981; B; 35,223 grt/64,120 dwt; 225 × 13.1 m *(738.19 × 42.98 ft)*; M (B&W); 15 kts; ex-*Danelock*
Sisters: **LITROTIS** (Gr) ex-*Baumare*; **GOLDEN GLOW** (Gr) ex-*Susan B*; **MARINE RANGER** (Li); **NORTH DUCHESS** (Gr); **STAMOS** (Gr); **NORDSCOUT** (Cy) ex-*Karen T*; **BALTIC MERMAID** (Pa); **SUCCESS BULKER** (Li) ex-*Hydrolock*; **EDCO STAR** (Eg) ex-*Marilock*; **NAVARINO** (Bs) ex-*Fort Dufferin*; **CAPTAIN GEORGE L** ex-*Fort Frontenac*; **TAI ZHOU HAI** (RC); **LEI ZHOU HAI** (RC); **WEN ZHOU HAI** (RC); **QUAN ZHOU HAI** (RC); Possible sister: **MARE BALTICO** (It) ex-*Bridgeworth*

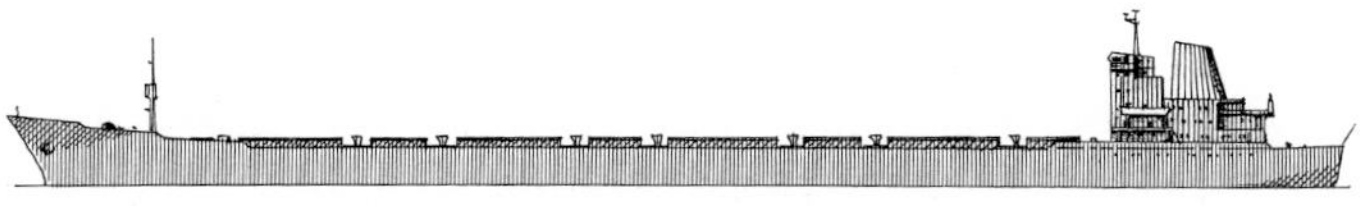

54 M^2F *H*

MERAKLIS Gr/FRG (Rhein Nordseew) 1975; B; 31,111 grt/53,836 dwt; 227.24 × 12.57 m *(745.54 × 41.24 ft)*; M (Sulzer); 16 kts
Sisters: **MARQUISE** (Gr); **MINOS** (Gr); **MISTER MICHAEL** (Gr)

55 M^2F *H*

OCEAN LADY Bs/Ja (NKK) 1974; B; 36,465 grt/67,688 dwt; 223.98 × 13.59 m *(734.84 × 44.59 ft)*; M (Sulzer); 14.75 kts; ex-*Scherpendrecht*
Sister: **MAVI** (Tu) ex-*Sliedrecht*; Possibly similar: **FLAG KARIN** (Gr) ex-*Zwijndrecht*; Similar: **SEAQUEEN III** (Ma) ex-*Hampton Bay*; **AVION** (Li) ex-*Ogden Amazon*; Probably similar: **STANDARD ENDEAVOUR** (Gr) ex-*Chalmette*

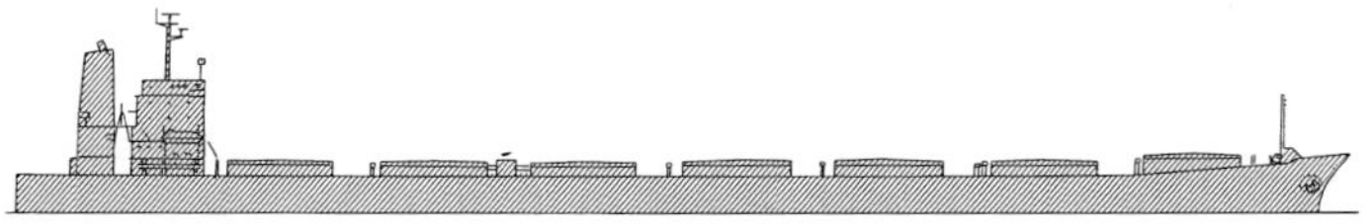

56 M^2F *H*

SAMJOHN LIGHT Gr/Ja (Hitachi) 1994; B; 38,077 grt/71,756 dwt; 223.70 × 13.46 m *(733.92 × 44.16 ft)*; M (B&W); 16.3 kts
Sister: **SAMJOHN SPIRIT** (Gr)

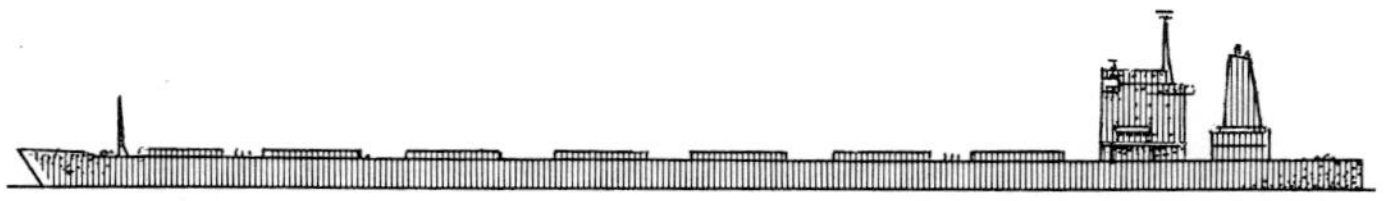

57 M^2F *H*

STANDARD VALOR Gr/Ih (Verolme Cork) 1977; B; 39,316 grt/72,311 dwt; 225.61 × 14.09 m *(740.19 × 46.23 ft)*; M (B&W); 16 kts; ex-*Irena Dan*
Sister: **NEPHELE** (Gr) ex-*Irish Spruce*

58 M^2F *H1*

AGHIA TRIAS Gr/Sw (Uddevalla) 1977; B; 64,264 grt/116,630 dwt; 253.65 × 15.91 m *(832.19 × 52.2 ft)*; M (B&W); 16 kts; ex-*Polycrusader*
Sister: **ABBEY** (Br) ex-*Andwi*

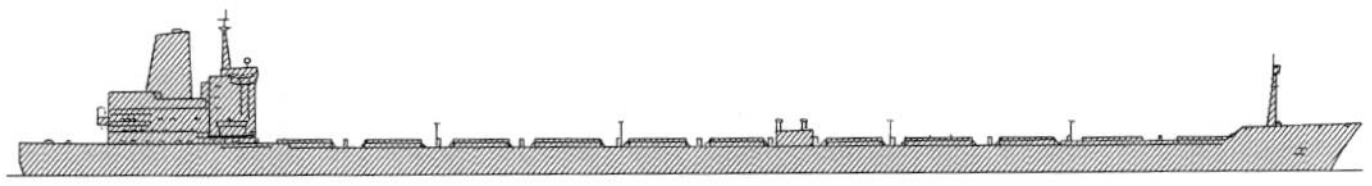

59 M^2F *H1*

AMICA NIS/FRG (B+V) 1971; B; 80,040 grt/147,522 dwt; 303.16 × 16.53 m *(994.62 × 54.23 ft)*; M (MAN); 16.25 kts; ex-*Widar*

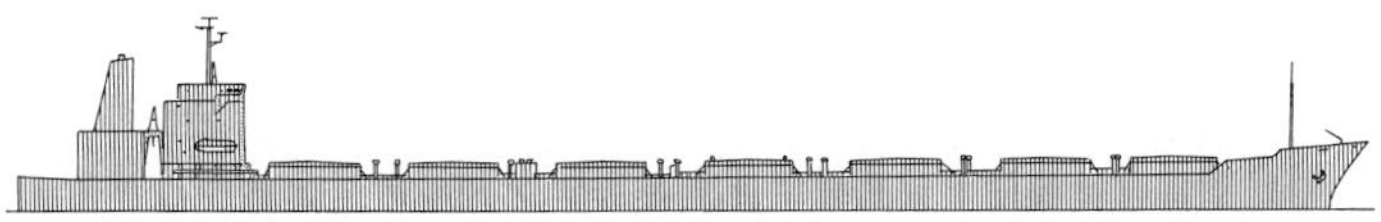

60 M^2F *H1*

CHINA PRIDE Li/RC (Jiangnan) 1990; B; 36,433 grt/65,656 dwt; 225.60 × 13.13 m *(740.16 × 43.08 ft)*; M (B&W); 14.4 kts
Sister: **CHINA GLORY** (Li); Possible sisters: **CHINA JOY** (Li); **CHINA SPIRIT** (Li); **CSK FORTUNE** (Pi); **CSK GLORY** (Pi); **HSING MAY** (Li); **YU MAY** (Li); **IRENE** (Gr) ex-*Pacific Ace*; **PACIFIC BRILLIANCE** (HK)

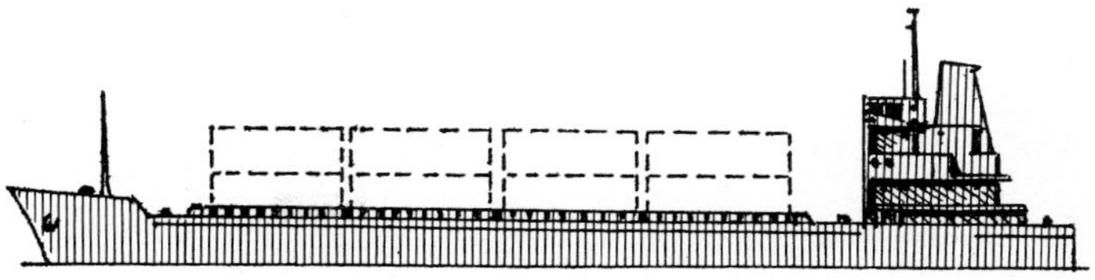

61 M^2F *H1*

DRACO DIS/FRG (Sietas) 1973; C/Con; 2,787 grt/2,661 dwt; 93.2 × 4.88 m *(305.77 × 16.01 ft)*; M (Atlas-MaK); 15 kts; ex-*Sagitta*; 195 TEU
Sisters: **SEVILLA** (At) ex-*Wiking*; **ELBE** (DIS); **WESER** (DIS); **THAMES STAR** (Tv) ex-*Janne Wehr*; Similar: **CASABLANCA** (At) ex-*Francop*

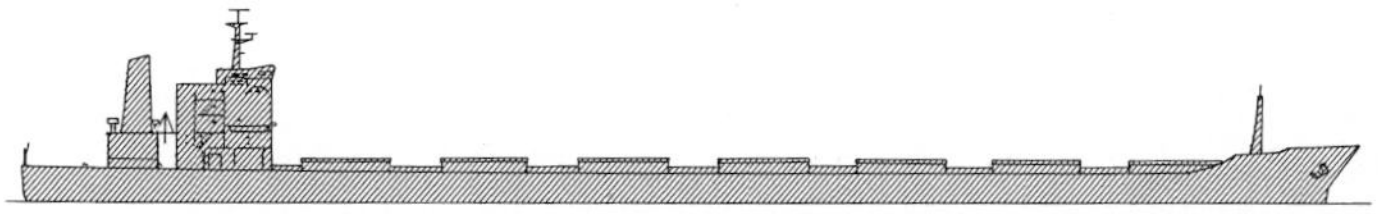

62 M^2F *H1*

DUBROVNIK Ma/Sp (AESA) 1983; B; 35,055 grt/61,318 dwt; 224.01 × 12.85 m *(734.94 × 42.16 ft)*; M (Sulzer); 14 kts; ex-*Ereaga*
Probable sister: **CASTILLO DE AREVALO** (Bs); Possible sisters: **CASTILLO DE ALMANSA** (Bs); **CASTILLO DE XATIVA** (Bs)

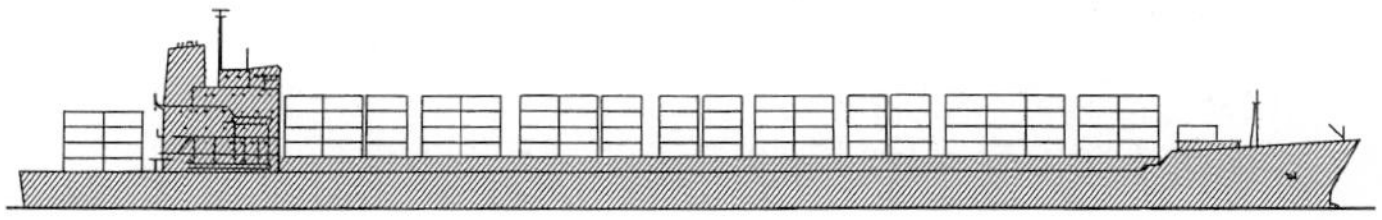

63 M^2F *H1*

ELLEN HUDIG Lu/Be (Boelwerf) 1983; B/Con; 27,758 grt/42,077 dwt; 209.10 × 11.58 m *(686.02 × 37.99 ft)*; M (Sulzer); — kts; 1,111 TEU
Sister: **CORNELIS VEROLME** (Lu)

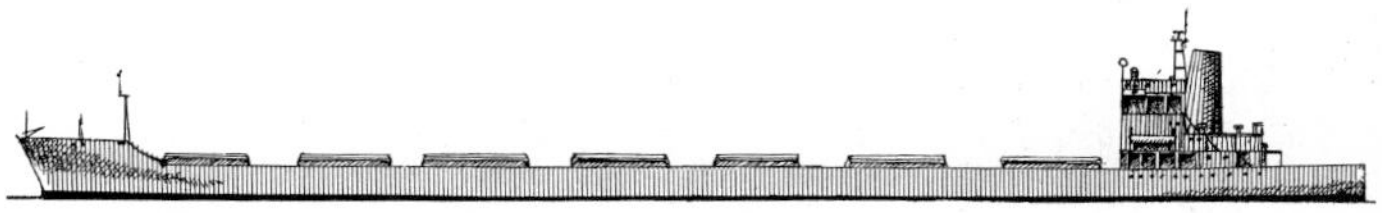

64 M^2F *H1*

HELEN Lu/Be (Cockerill) 1978; B/Con; 23,792 grt/42,566 dwt; 199.02 × 11.05 m *(652.95 × 36.25 ft)*; M (Sulzer); 16 kts; 1,097 TEU
Sister: **DELORIS** (Lu)

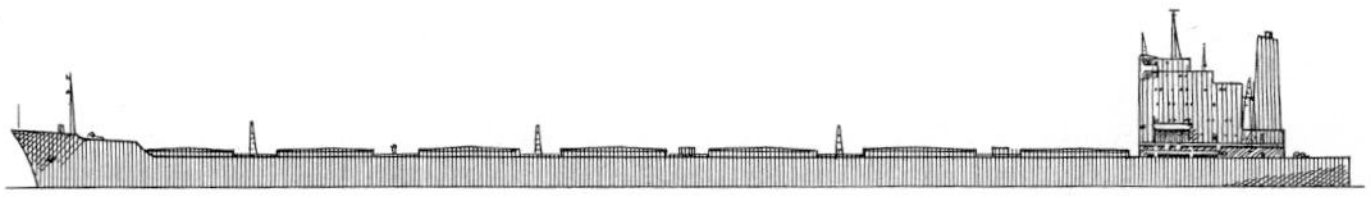

65 M^2F *H1*

JIN CHANG Va/Ja (Hitachi) 1977; B; 35,902 grt/60,767 dwt; 224.54 × 12.45 m *(736.68 × 40.85 ft)*; M (Sulzer); 15.25 kts; ex-*Adriatic Wasa*
Sisters: **MARIANN** (Bs) ex-*Pearl Castle*; **PAMPHILOS** (Cy) ex-*Pearl Crown*; **PETROPOLIS** (Cy) ex-*English Wasa*; **IOANNIS P** (Cy) ex-*Pearl Citadel*; **FLAG SUPPLIER** (Gr) Launched as *Sonette*; **NYON** (Sd) ex-*Pearl Corona*; Possible sister: **ANTHI P** (Cy) ex-*South Rainbow*; Similar: **ATHENA** (Gr) ex-*Argo Explorer*; **IOANNIS M** (Cy) ex-*Argo Enterprise*

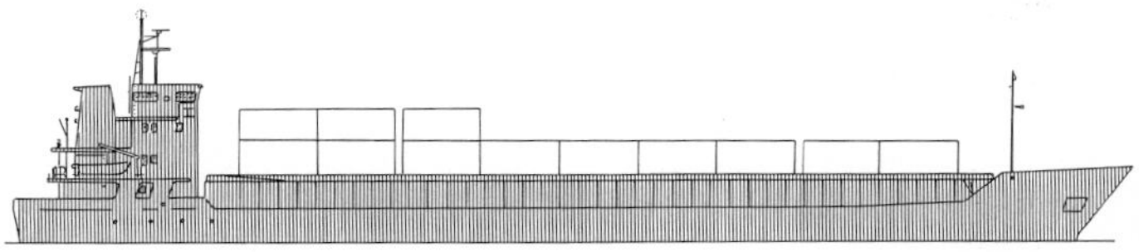

66 M^2F *H1*

JUPITER At/Ge (Peene-Werft) 1991; C; 2,450 grt/3,710 dwt; 87.85 × 5.47 m *(288.22 × 17.95 ft)*; M (Deutz); 10 kts; 180 TEU
Sister: **KATHARINA D** (Ge); Probable sisters: **BETTINA K** (At); **ELISABETH K** (At); **ELKE K** (At); **SCORPIUS** (At); **URANUS** (At); **SATURN** (At); **SUNRISE** (At); **ARIES** (At); **MARCEL** (At); **URSA** (At); **CORONA** (At)

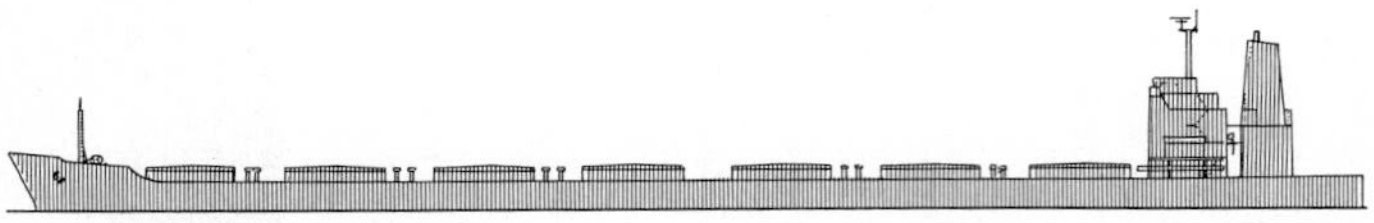

67 M^2F *H1*
KONKAR STAR Gr/Ja (Mitsui) 1985; B; 36,584 grt/69,582 dwt; 222.72 × 13.26 m *(730.71 × 43.5 ft)*; M (B&W); 15.2 kts; ex-*Bright Star*
Probable sisters: **ALLESANDRA D'AMATO** (It) ex-*Century Hope*; **RITA D'AMATO** (Ma) ex-*Century Progress*

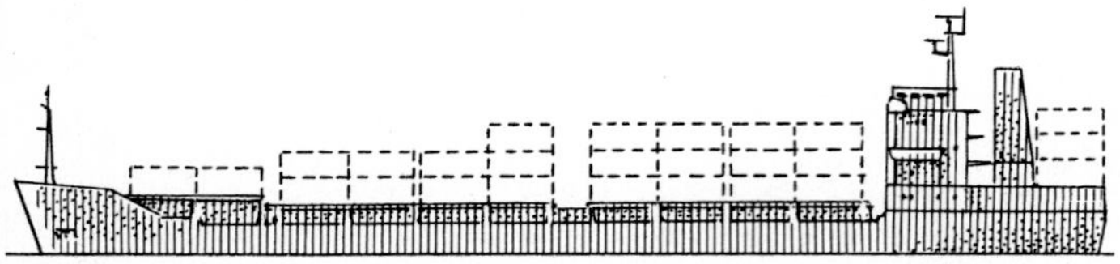

68 M^2F *H1*
LIAN MAO RC/FRG (Nobiskrug) 1980; C/Con; 1,599 grt/4,210 dwt; 99.95 × 5.09 m *(327.92 × 16.7 ft)*; M (KHD); 12.25 kts; ex-*Ymir*; 287 TEU
Sisters: **CAROLIN** (Cy) ex-*Njord*; **PRIME VIGOR** (Gr) ex-*Hermann Behrens*

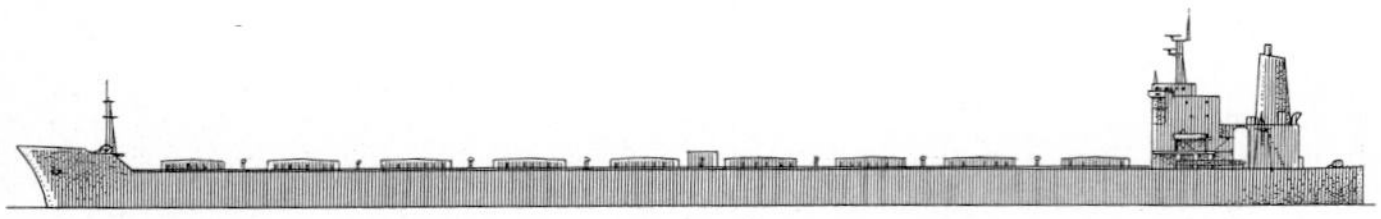

69 M^2F *H1*
NAVALIS HK/Ja (Hitachi) 1981; B; 74,672 grt/133,361 dwt; 270.9 × 16.35 m *(888.78 × 53.64 ft)*; M (B&W); 14.5 kts; ex-*World Dulce*

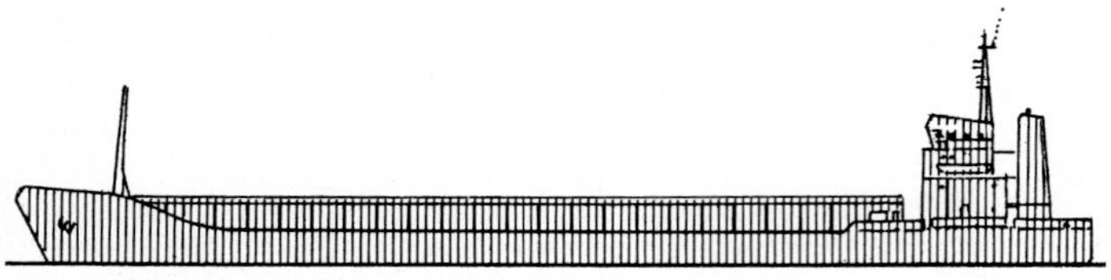

70 M^2F *H1*
ODIN Ge/FRG (M. Jansen) 1981; C/Con; 999 grt/2,860 dwt; 95.61 × 4.29 m *(314 × 14.07 ft)*; M (Krupp-MaK); 12.5 kts; ex-*Vela*; 157 TEU
Similar: **MAGNUS E** (At) ex-*Magnolia*

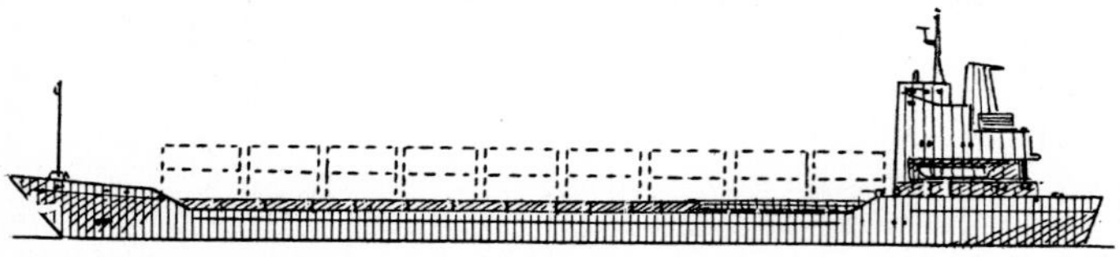

71 M^2F *H1*
OUEZZANE Mo/FRG (Sietas) 1976; C/Con; 1,536 grt/3,357 dwt; 93.38 × 5.56 m *(307.02 × 18.24 ft)*; M (Atlas-MaK); 14.5 kts; 195 TEU
Sisters: **OUARZAZATE** (Mo); **OUIRGANE** (Mo); **OUALIDIA** (Mo); **OULMES** (Mo)

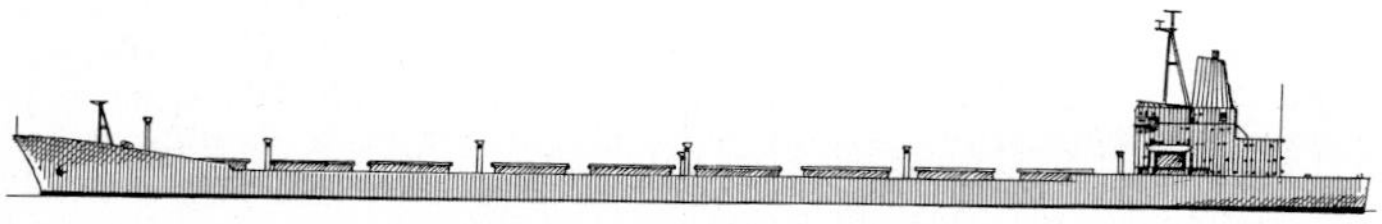

72 M^2F *H1*
PACIFIC ENVOY Pa/FRG (Flensburger) 1973; B/Con; 28,651 grt/50,550 dwt; 215.53 × 12.55 m *(707.12 × 41.17 ft)*; M (MAN); 15 kts; ex-*Meistersinger*; 1,242 TEU
Sisters: **BOREAS** (Ma) ex-*Adriano*; **YA MAWLAYA** (Cy) ex-*Hans Sachs*; **SVEA TRADER** (Cy) ex-*Tannhauser*; **SILVER DIGNITY** (Cy) ex-*Wien* (converted to bulk); **JOANNA V** (Cy) ex-*Wera Jacob* (bulk); **KATYA V** (Cy) ex-*Tom Jacob* (bulk)

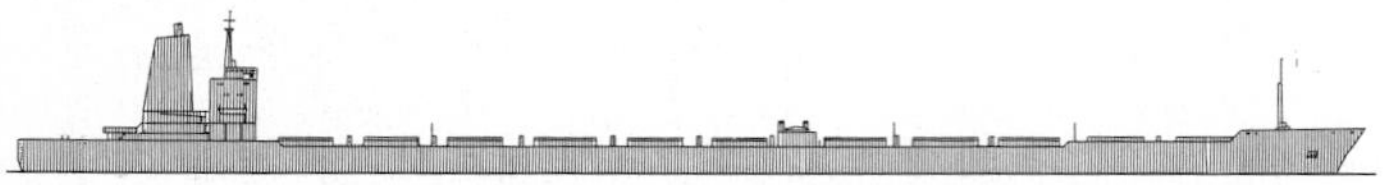

73 M^2F *H1*
PU AN HAI RC/FRG (B+V) 1973; B; 79,274 grt/148,200 dwt; 303.15 × 16.64 m *(994.59 × 54.59)*; M (MAN); 16 kts; ex-*Hermod*
Sister: **PANTANASSA** (Bs) ex-*Thor*

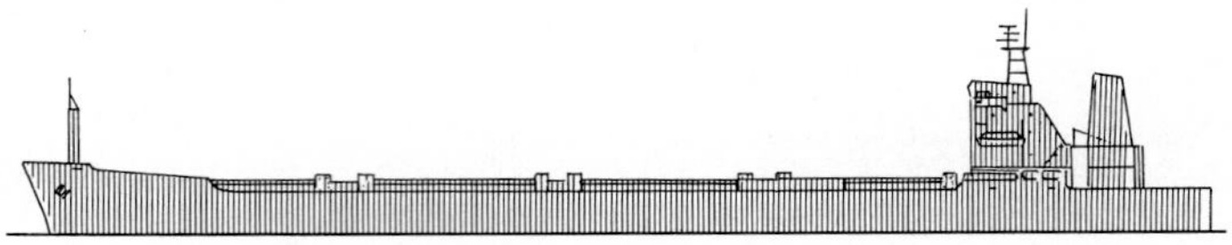

74 M^2F *H1*
SIR CHARLES PARSONS Br/Br (Govan) 1985; B; 14,201 grt/22,530 dwt; 154.87 × 9.02 m *(508.10 × 29.59 ft)*; M (Mirrlees Blackstone); 12.5 kts
Sisters: **LORD CITRINE** (Br); **LORD HINTON** (Br)

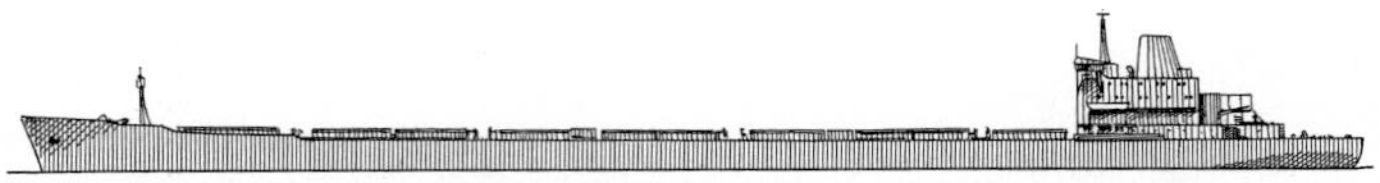

75 M^2F *H1*
SKY WIND Bs/Bz (Verolme E R do Brazil) 1974; B; 24,559 grt/51,121 dwt; 205.49 × 12.42 m *(674.18 × 40.75 ft)*; M (Sulzer); 15.5 kts; ex-*Docedelta*

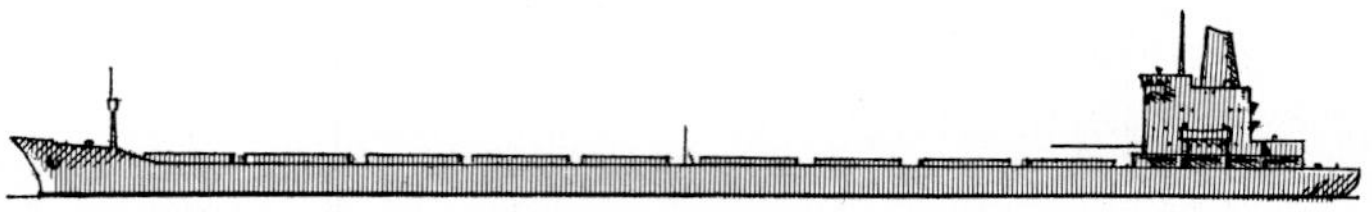

76 M^2F *H1*
TOXOTIS SV/Sp (AESA) 1975; B; 43,257 grt/79,493 dwt; 256.22 × 14.42 m *(840.62 × 47.31 ft)*; M (B&W); 15.75 kts; ex-*King George*
Sister: **FEDRA** (—) ex-*King William*

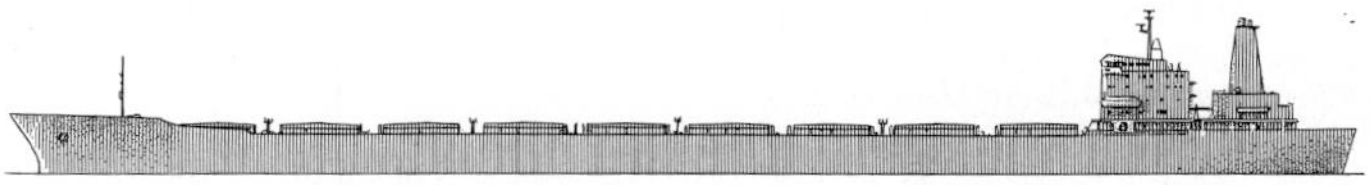

77 M^2F *H1*
TRADER Bs/Fi (Navire) 1976; B; 60,570 grt/110,444 dwt; 265.6 × 15.39 m *(871.39 × 50.49 ft)*; M (Sulzer); 14.5 kts; ex-*Horn Crusader*

78 M^2F *H123*
G. MOTHER Bl/Br (A. Hall) 1958; C; 1,280 grt/1,626 dwt; 76.21 × 4.25 m *(250.03 × 13.94 ft)*; M (British Polar); 11 kts; ex-*Ballylesson*; Lengthened 1964

79 M^2F *H123*
SOUHA Le/Br (Hall, Russell) 1963; C; 959 grt/1,961 dwt; 78.03 × 4.62 m *(256 × 15.16 ft)*; M (Polar); 11.5 kts; ex-*Ballyrory*
Sister: **KARIM** (SV) ex-*Ballyrush*

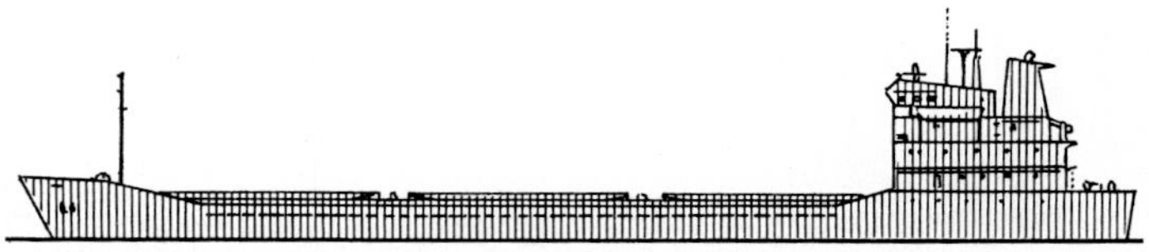

80 M^2F *H13*
ALDRINGTON Br/Br (Swan Hunter) 1978; B; 4,297 grt/6,570 dwt; 103.61 × 7.03 m *(340 × 23.06 ft)*; M (Mirrlees Blackstone); 14.75 kts
Sister (Builder Clelands): **ASHINGTON** (Br)

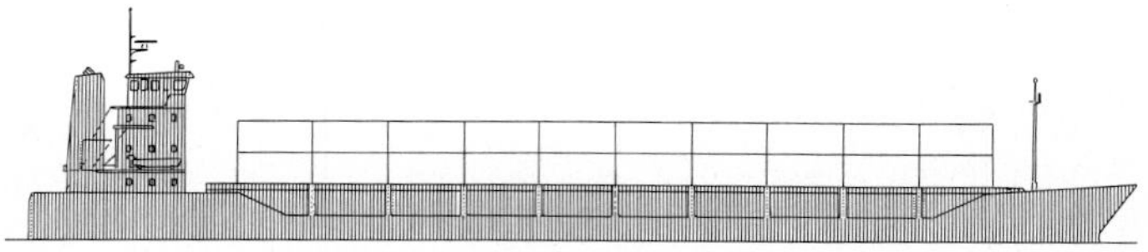

81 M^2F *H13*
ANJA II At/Ne (Slob) 1991; C; 2,705 grt/4,056 dwt; 89.48 × 5.34 m *(293.57 × 17.52 ft)*; M (Deutz); 12 kts; 220 TEU
Probable sister: **SARAH** (At)

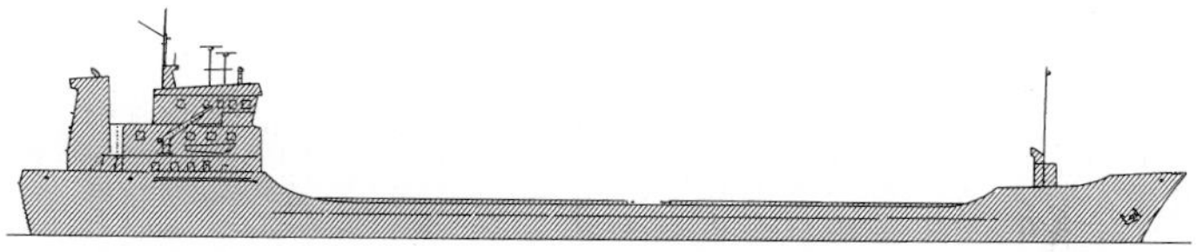

82 M^2F *H13*

ARROW Ne/Ne (Bodewes BV) 1988; C; 2,986 grt/5,150 dwt; 92.10 × 6.65 m *(302.17 × 21.82 ft)*; M (MaK); 11.5 kts
Probably similar: **ALERT** (Ne)

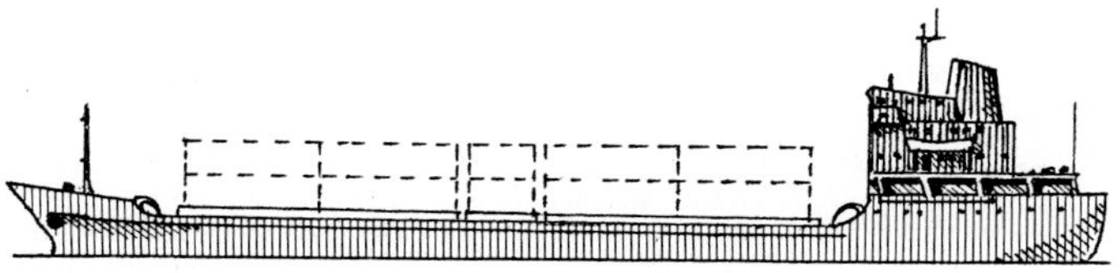

83 M^2F *H13*

ESLA Sp/Sp (Atlantico) 1977; C/Con; 3,311 grt/4,955 dwt; 99.73 × 6.9 m *(327.2 × 22.64 ft)*; M (MAN); 13 kts; Launched as *Gabriela de Perez*; 216 TEU
Sister: **TAJO** (Sp) ex-*Maria De Las Angustias*; Possibly similar (may have deck cranes): **FAREAST TRADER** (SV) ex-*Termancia*; **VASSILIS IX** (Cy) ex-*Galia*

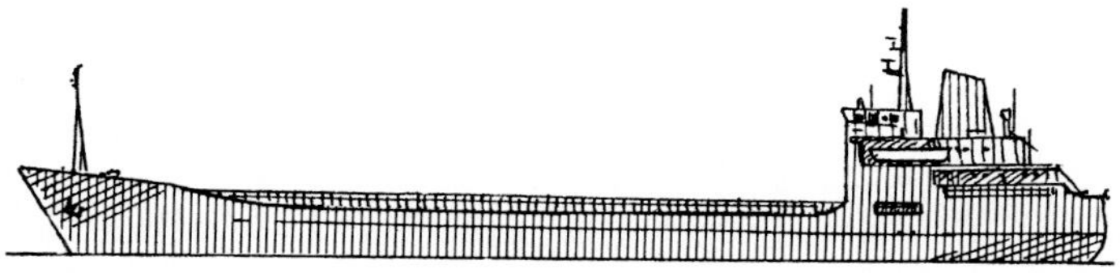

84 M^2F *H13*

ETZEL NIS/FRG (Sietas) 1971; C/Con; 2,397 grt/3,704 dwt; 88.5 × 5.28 m *(290.35 × 17.32 ft)*; M (Atlas-MaK); 14 kts; ex-*Heino*; 148 TEU
Similar (some may have deck cranes): **BREMER HANDEL** (NIS) ex-*Twiehausen*; **CORALLI** (NIS) ex-*Hannes Knuppel*; **KARAT II** (At) ex-*Bomberg*; **METS** (SV) ex-*Nautic*; **SEINEHAVEN** (At) ex-*Widukind*

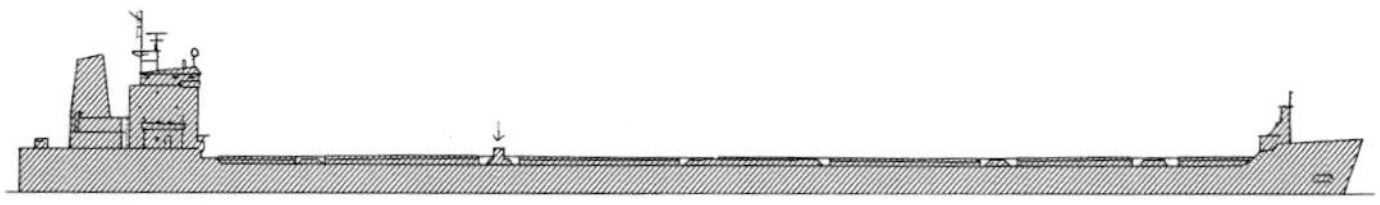

85 M^2F *H13*

FEDERAL FRASER HK/Br (Govan) 1983; B; 22,388 grt/35,315 dwt; 222.54 × 9.77 m *(730.12 × 32.05 ft)*; M (Sulzer); 12 kts; ex-*Selkirk Settler*
Sisters: **FEDERAL MACKENZIE** (HK) ex-*Canada Marquis*; **SASKATCHEWAN PIONEER** (Bs)

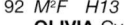

86 M^2F *H13*

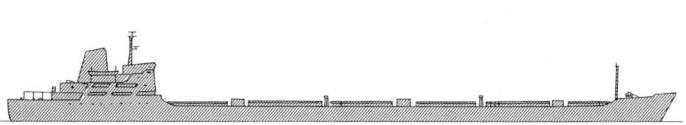

FROTAOESTE Bz/Bz (Ish do Brasil) 1973; B; 13,847 grt/25,231 dwt; 176.41 × 10.09 m *(578.77 × 33.10 ft)*; M (Sulzer); 14.5 kts
Probable sister: **OCEAN GR** (Ma) ex-*Omnium Pride*

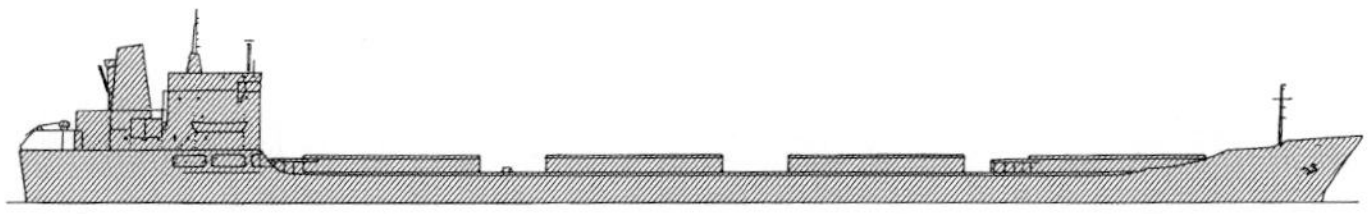

87 M^2F *H13*

GALASSIA It/It (FCNI) 1987; B; 17,599 grt/29,371 dwt; 186.01 × 10.40 m *(610.27 × 34.12 ft)*; M (Sulzer); 15.5 kts
Sister: **SAGITTARIUS** (It); Probable sister: **GEMINI** (It)

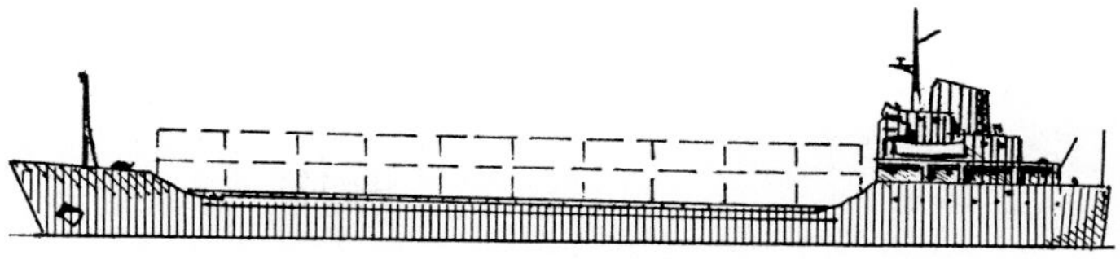

88 M^2F *H13*

JOHAN II My/FRG (Unterweser) 1969; C/Con; 1,963 grt/3,661 dwt; 95.20 × 5.72 m *(312.34 × 18.77 ft)*; M (KHD); 14.75 kts; ex-*Ida Blumenthal*; 150 TEU
Sister: **JOHAN III** (My) ex-*Johann Blumenthal*

89 M^2F *H13*

LESZEK G Pd/Br (Appledore) 1977; C; 1,991 grt/3,256 dwt; 91.52 × 5.16 m *(300.26 × 16.93 ft)*; M (Mirrlees Blackstone); 12.5 kts; ex-*Leslie Gault*; May have deck crames as indicated; 60 TEU
Sisters: **JERBA** (Tn) ex-*Cerinthus*; **GAUSS F** (Pd) ex-*Gallic Fjord*; **AO XIANG** (RC) ex-*Markinch*

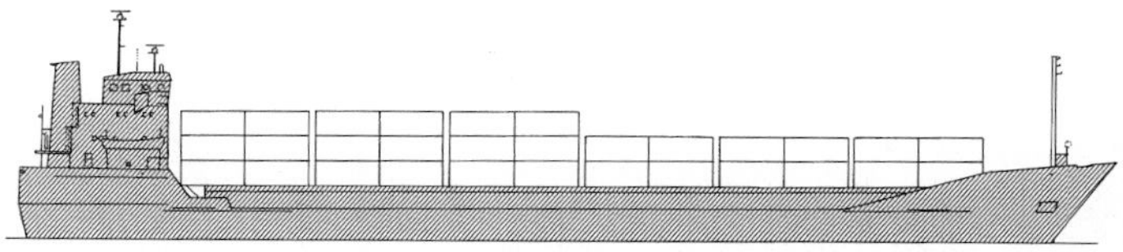

90 M^2F *H13*

MILD VICTORY Pa/FRG (Husumer) 1978; C/Con; 3,598 grt/5,849 dwt; 104.53 × 6.59 m *(342.95 × 21.62 ft)*; M (Deutz); 13 kts; ex-*Polaris*; 316 TEU

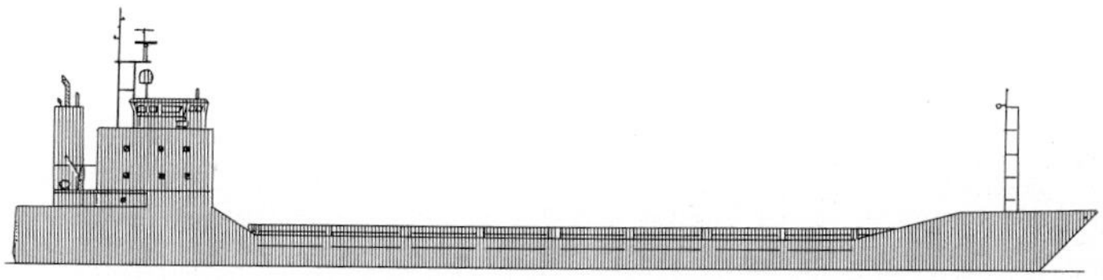

91 M^2F *H13*

NENUFAR UNO Sp/Tu (Madenci) 1992; C/Con; 3,779 grt/5,861 dwt; 92.80 × 6.56 m *(304.46 × 21.52 ft)*; M (MaK); 13.5 kts; ex-*Celtic Crusader*; 300 TEU
Probable sisters: **FAIRWIND** (Bs) ex-*Celtic Ambassador*; **FAIRWAY** (Bs) ex-*Celtic Commander*; **CELTIC WARRIOR** (Bs)

92 M^2F *H13*

OLIVIA Cy/Ne (Pattje) 1978; C; 1,990 grt/3,050 dwt; 80.68 × 5.12 m *(264.7 × 16.8 ft)*; M (MWM); 12 kts; ex-*Altappen*
Sisters: **GOLF STAR** (At) ex-*Silvia*; **SUSANNA** (Ma) ex-*Susanna*

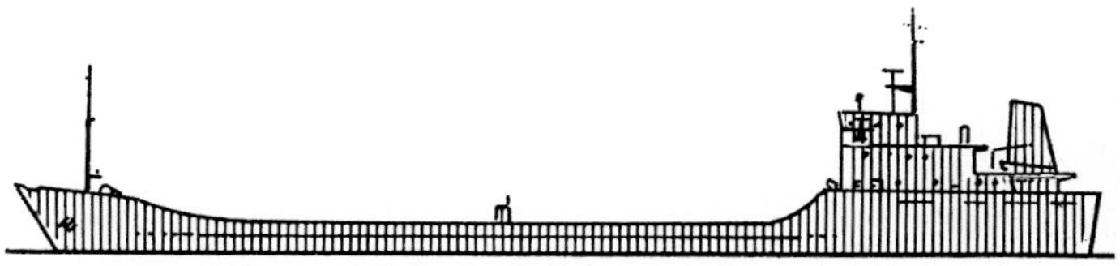

93 M^2F *H13*

REDTHORN Br/Br (Scott & Sons) 1978; C; 2,025 grt/3,070 dwt; 85.32 × 4.99 m *(279.92 × 16.37 ft)*; M (Mirrlees Blackstone); 12 kts; ex-*Pinewood*

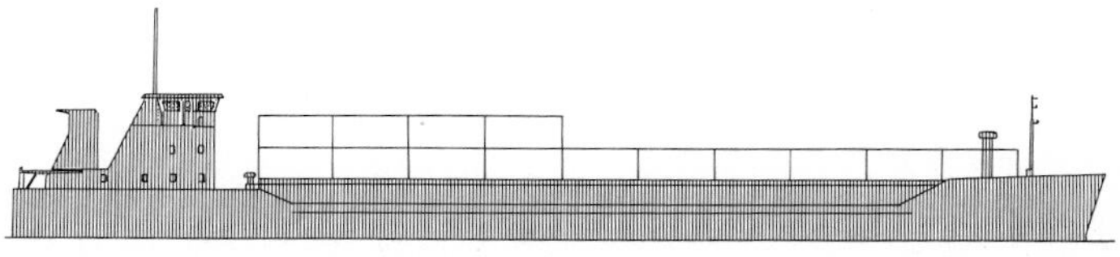

94 M^2F *H13*

RUTH At/Ge (Hitzler) 1991; C; 2,873 grt/4,557 dwt; 88.20 × 6.11 m *(289.37 × 20.05 ft)*; M (Deutz); 11 kts; 173 TEU
Sister: **TRANSPORTOR** (At)

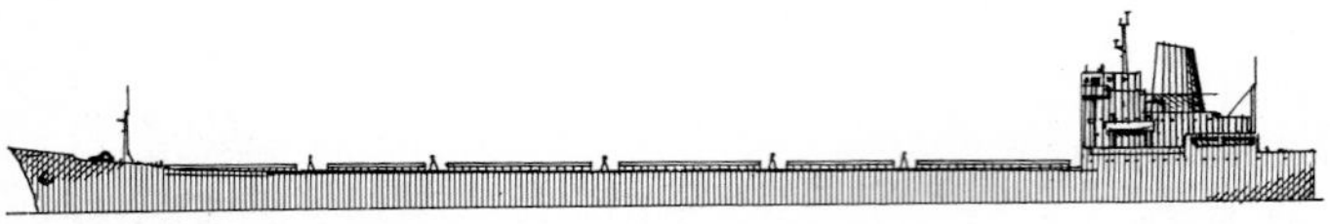

95 M^2F *H13*
SEAQUEEN Pa/No (Kaldnes) 1971; B; 14,750 grt/23,310 dwt; 165.21 × 10.22 m *(542.03 × 33.53 ft)*; M (Sulzer); 15 kts; ex-*Cape Race*

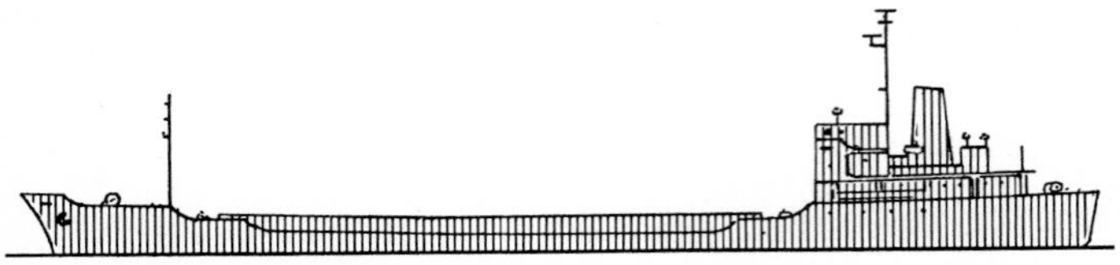

96 M^2F *H13*
SHOTOKU MARU RC/Ja (Usuki) 1978; C; 2,959 grt/4,916 dwt; 99.01 × 6.3 m *(324.84 × 20.67 ft)*; M (Hanshin); 13 kts

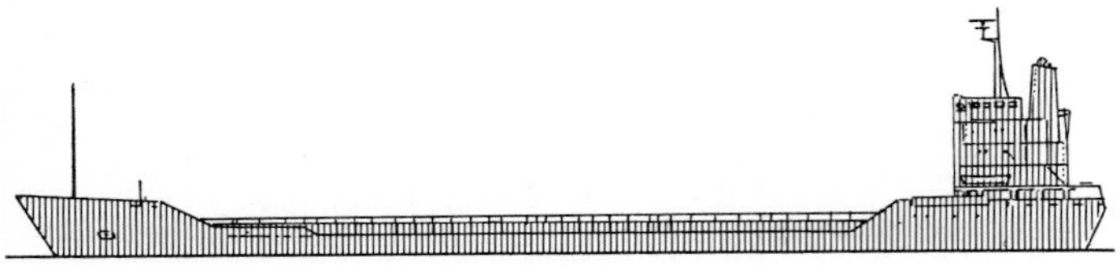

97 M^2F *H13*
SIGAL NIS/FRG (Sietas) 1980; C/Con; 5,378 grt/7,267 dwt; 126.27 × 6.51 m *(414.27 × 21.36 ft)*; M (MaK); 16.5 kts; ex-*Germanic*; 462 EU
Sisters: **PETER METZ** (VC) ex-*Peter Oltmann*; **KATHERINE BORCHARD** (At) ex-*Concordia*

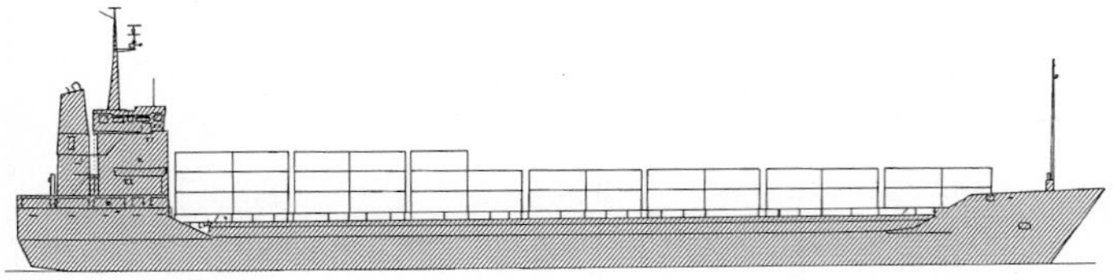

98 M^2F *H13*
ZIM NAPOLI At/FRG (Sietas) 1979; C/Con; 5,081 grt/6,907 dwt; 118.42 × 6.60 m *(388.52 × 21.65 ft)*; M (MaK); 14.5 kts; ex-*Caribic*; 542 TEU

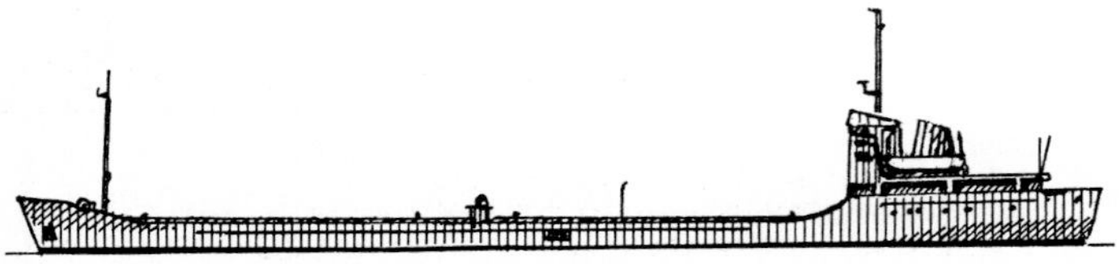

99 M^2F *P4*
MARK C Bb/Br (Dunston) 1971; C; 1,768 grt/2,823 dwt; 85.02 × 5.07 m *(278.94 × 16.63 ft)*; M (British Polar); 13 kts; ex-*Security*
Sister: **BARKET ALLAH** (Ho) ex-*Sincerity*

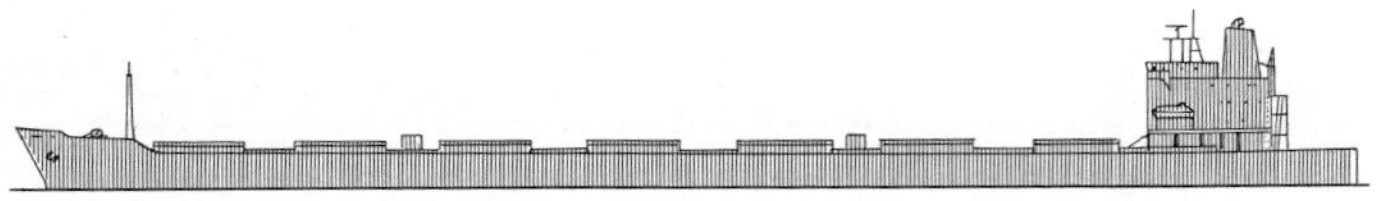

100 M^2FC *H1*
ANNA Gr/Ja (NKK) 1981; B; 35,160 grt/65,077 dwt; 224.54 × 12.84 m *(736.68 × 42.13 ft)*; M (Sulzer); 15.75 kts; ex-*Kapetan Yannis*
Possible sisters: **BANDAK** (NIS) ex-*Enard Hope*; **WESTERN TRADE** (Li) ex-*Kyriaki*; **HERAKLIA** (Gr) ex-*Ayiassos*; **LAMYRA** (Gr); **ANDROS** (Gr); **AMORGOS** (Gr); **SAMJOHN CAPTAIN** (Gr); **PERNAS ARANG** (My)

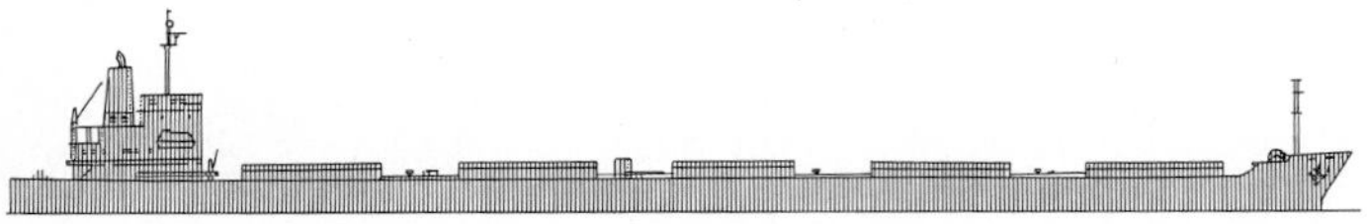

101 $M^2FC/MHFC$ *H1*
CORONA ACE Pi/Ja (Kawasaki) 1994; B; 42,869 grt/77,447 dwt; 230 × 12.79 m *(754.59 × 41.96 ft)*; M (B&W); 14 kts

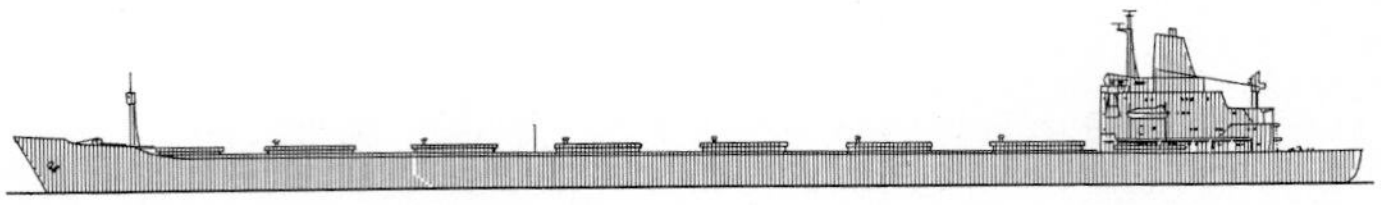

102 M^2FC *H1*
HUTA SENDZIMIRA Pd/Ja (Mitsubishi HI) 1976; B; 35,642 grt/64,334 dwt; 223.98 × 13.35 m *(735 × 43.8 ft)*; M (Sulzer); 14.5 kts; ex-*Varamis*
Sisters: **HUTA KATOWICE** (Pd) Launched as *Vigan*; **HUA TONG HAI** (RC) ex-*Vinstra*; **KAN SU HAI** (RC) ex-*Vesteroy*

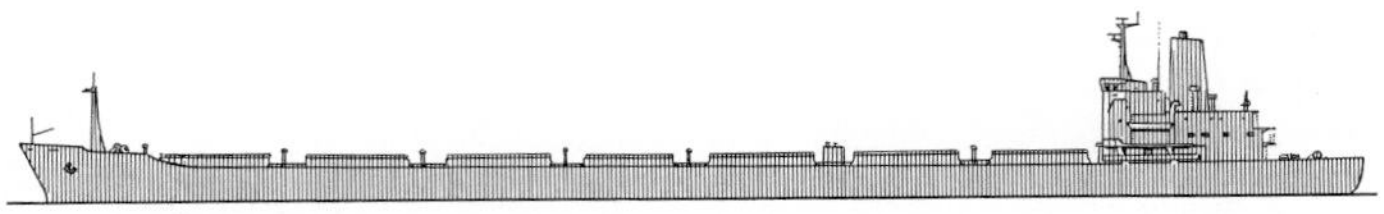

103 M^2FC *H1*
SEAEAGLE Ma/Ja (Koyo) 1981; B; 34,500 grt/58,412 dwt; 222.99 × 12.35 m *(732 × 40.52 ft)*; M (B&W); 16.75 kts; ex-*Brilliant Venture*
Sisters (some may have deck cranes): **CAPTAIN LEON CHR. LEMOS** (Gr) ex-*Eva Venture*; **STONE GEMINI** (Cy) ex-*Fa Fa Venture*; **CRUSADER VENTURE** (HK); **ORION II** (Cy) ex-*Slaney Venture*; **PRETTY LADY** (Ma) ex-*Anita Venture*; Probable sisters: **ALEXIA** (Gr) ex-*Sansan Venture*; **KIMISIS** (Gr) ex-*Pioneer Spirit*; **ELLI B** (Gr) ex-*Francois Venture*

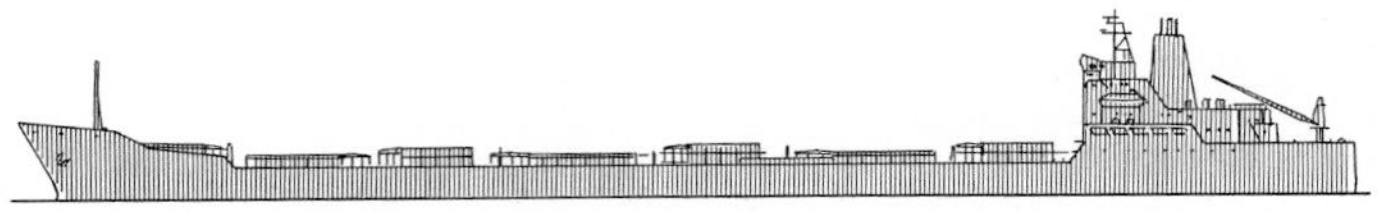

104 M^2FC *H13*
MAXHUTTE Ge/Bz (Emaq) 1985; B; 22,466 grt/37,613 dwt; 193.72 × 10.93 m *(635.56 × 35.86 ft)*; M (Sulzer); 14.5 kts; ex-*Bahia*
Sister: **STASSFURT** (Ge) ex-*Olinda*

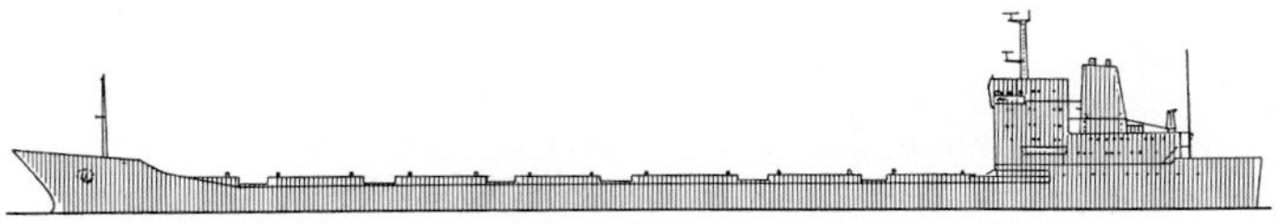

105 M^2FCM *H13*
GENERAL BERLING Pd/Bu (G Dimitrov) 1984; B; 23,306 grt/38,466 dwt; 198.56 × 11.20 m *(651.44 × 36.75 ft)*; M (Sulzer); 14.50 kts
Sisters: **GENERAL GROT-ROWECKI** (Pd); **LAKE MEAD** (Mi) ex-*General Dabrowski*; **YORDAN LUTIBRODSKI** (SV) (may have four cranes—see entry 7/140); **ALEXANDER DIMITROV** (Ma); **GEORGI GRIGOROV** (Ma); **DIMITROVSKY KOMSOMOL** (Ma)

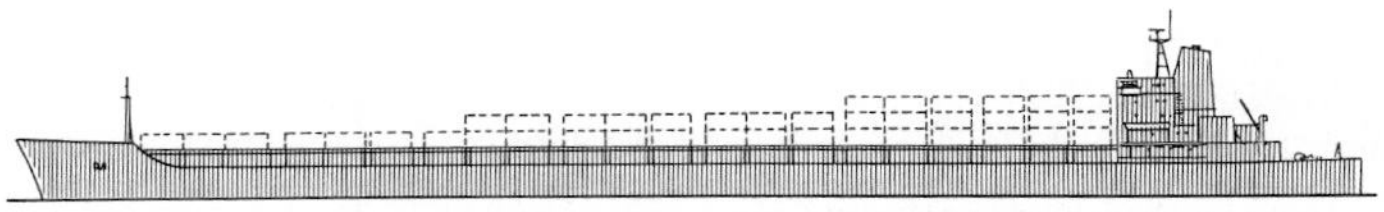

106 M^2FD *H1*
ANTWERPEN Lu/Be (Cockerill) 1979; B/Con; 25,599 grt/41,100 dwt; 199.02 × 10.52 m *(652.95 × 34.51 ft)*; M (Sulzer); 15.5 kts; 1,484 TEU
Sister: **BRUSSEL** (Lu)

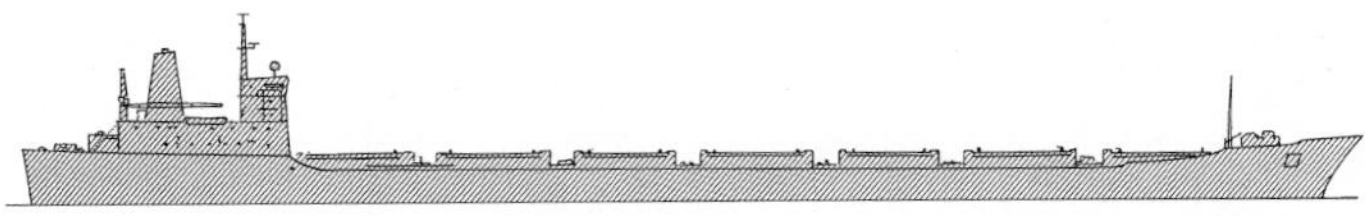

107 M^2FD *H13*
MARIASPERANZA F It/It (Tirreno) 1974; B; 32,427 grt/54,455 dwt; 223.12 × 12.34 m *(732.02 × 40.49 ft)*; M (B&W); 15 kts
Possible sisters: **CASPIAN TRIDENT** (Ma) ex-*Allegra F*; **PROVIDENTIA** (Bs) ex-*Ivanfrancesco F*; **PALVIA** (Pa) ex-*Massimiliano F*

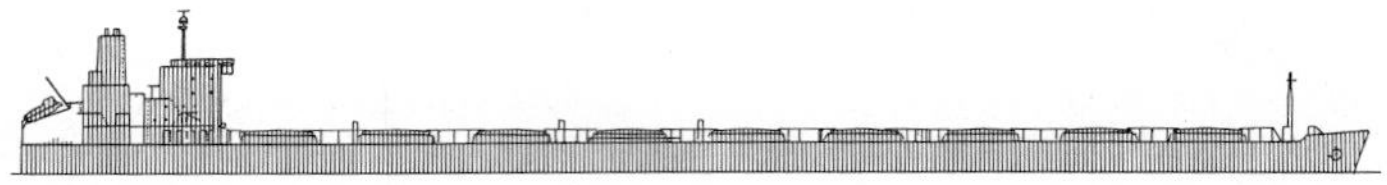

108 $M^2FL/MHFL$ *H*
ERRADALE Br/Br (H&W S&H) 1994; B; 82,701 grt/163,554 dwt; 283.73 × 17.78 m *(930.87 × 58.33 ft)*; M (B&W); 15.4 kts

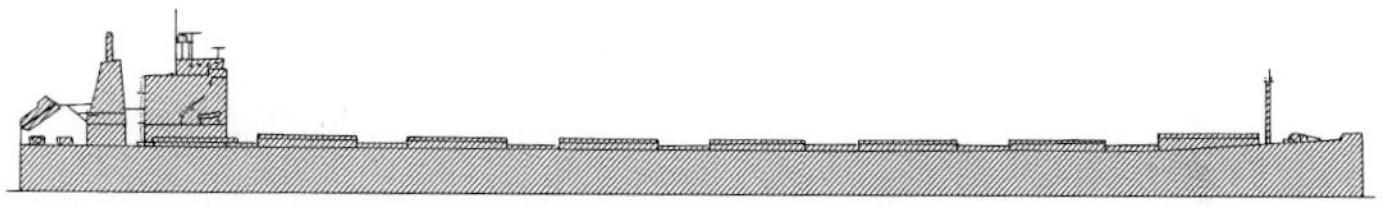

109 M^2FL *H*
ROMANDIE Sd/De (B&W) 1994; B; 39,422 grt/75,460 dwt; 225 × 14.34 m *(738.19 × 47.05 ft)*; M (Sulzer); 14.5 kts; 'BCT 70' (Mk V) type

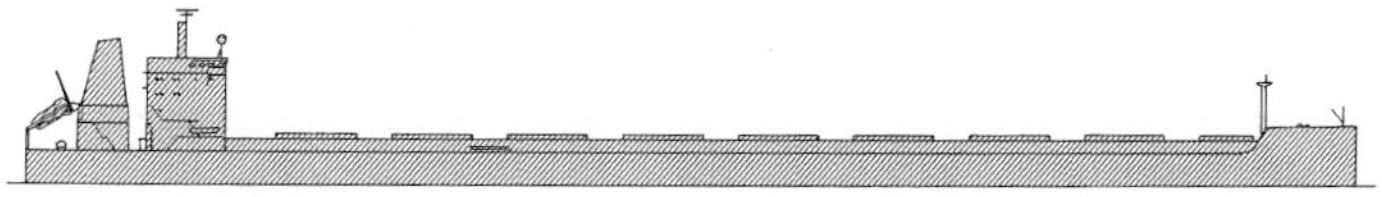

110 M^2FL *H1*
SOLIDARNOSC Pd/De (B&W) 1991; B; 41,252 grt/73,470 dwt; 228.60 × 14.12 m *(750.00 × 46.33 ft)*; M (B&W); 14.2 kts; 'BCT 70' type
Sisters: **ARMIA KRAJOWA** (Pd); **SZARE SZEREGI** (Pd); **POLSKA WALCZACA** (Pd); **ORLETA LWOWSKIE** (Pd)

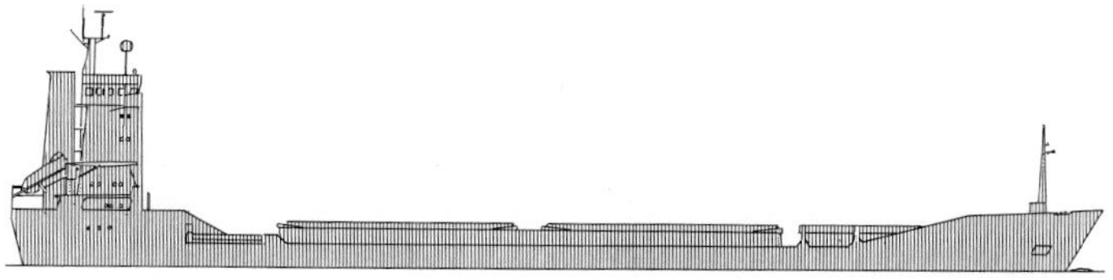

111 M^2FL *H13*
ZIM CONSTANTA NA/Ge (Husumer K) 1991; C; 7,398 grt/10,884 dwt; 122.60 × 8.29 m *(402.23 × 27.20 ft)*; M (MAN); 15 kts; ex-*Wodan*; 659 TEU

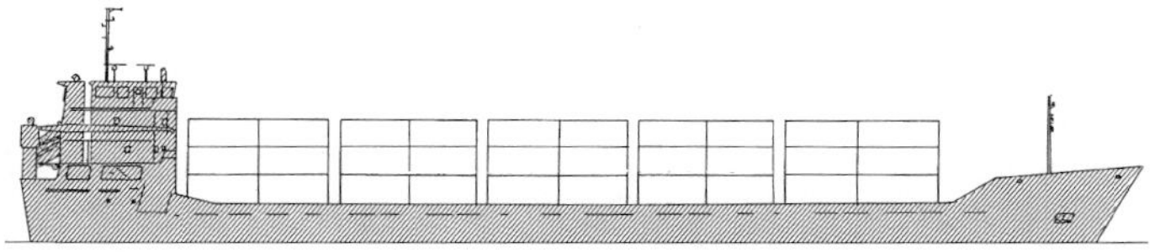

112 M^2FLR *H13*
ANGELA JURGENS Ge/FRG (Sietas) 1988; C/Con; 2,749 grt/3,376 dwt; 94.50 × 5.01 m *(310.04 × 16.44 ft)*; M (Wärtsilä); 14.30 kts; 'Type 122'; Crane aft on starboard, and lifeboat on port side; 262 TEU
Sisters: **AMAZONE** (Ge); **JAN BECKER** (Ge); **JAN KAHRS** (Ge); **OTTO BECKER** (Ge)

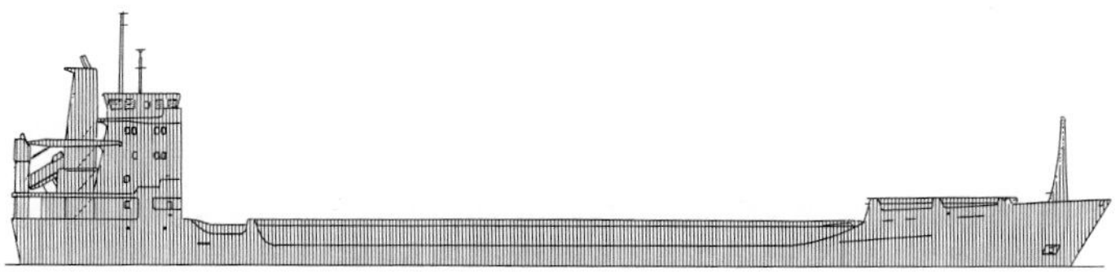

113 M^2FLR *H13*
CHURRUCA Ge/Ge (Sietas) 1991; C; 3,815 grt/4,654 dwt; 103.50 × 6.07 m *(339.57 × 19.91 ft)*; M (MaK); 14.5 kts; ex-*Cimbria*; 372 TEU; 'Type 129'
Sisters: **GRACECHURCH HARP** (At) ex-*Sven Dede*; **GRACECHURCH CROWN** (At) ex-*Zenit*; **CMBT CORVETTE** (Ge) ex-*Corvette*; **GRACECHURCH PLANET** (Ge) ex-*Schleswig Holstein*; **OPDR TEJO** (Ge) ex-*Nincop*; **EMMA** (At) ex-*Francop*; **RHEIN TRADER** (At); **MERKUR** (Ge); Similar ('Type 129a'—superstructure and other details differ): **CHRISTINA** (Fi); **KLENODEN** (Fi): **PASSADEN** (Fi); **SMARAGDEN** (Fi)

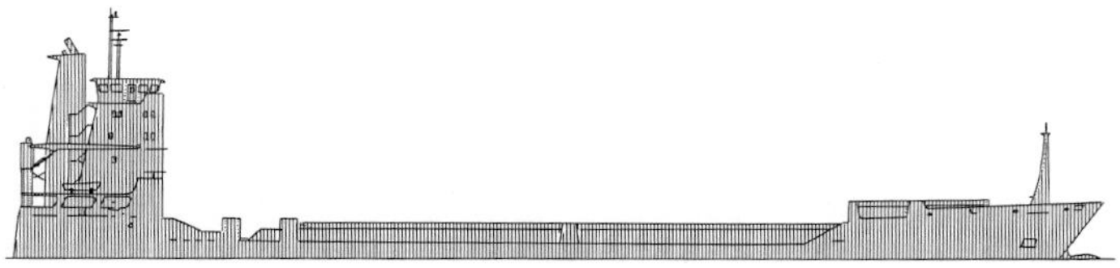

114 M^2FLR *H13*
SVEN OLTMANN At/Ge (Sietas) 1992; C; 5,006 grt/6,620 dwt; 116.82 × 6.87 m *(383.27 × 22.54 ft)*; M (MAN); 16.5 kts; 510 TEU; 'Type 148'
Sister: **ARMADA SPRINTER** (At) ex-*Inka Dede*; Probable sisters: **JUPITER** (Ge); **URANUS** (Ge)

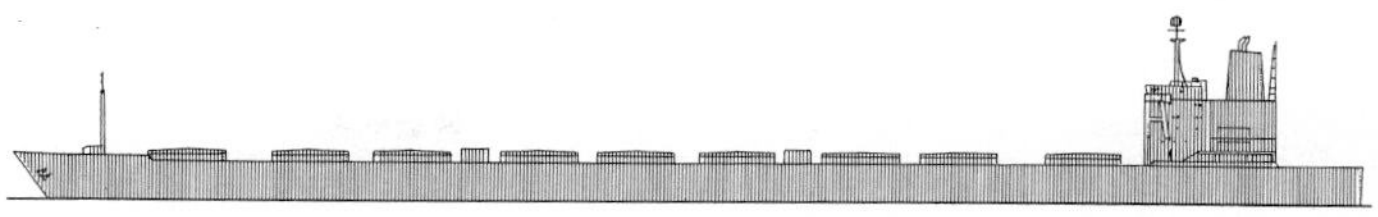

115 $M^2FM/MHFN$
OYASHIMA MARU Ja/Ja (Mitsubishi HI) 1981; O; 72,096 grt/131,987 dwt; 260.41 × 16.71 m *(854.36 × 54.82 ft)*; M (Sulzer); 14.25 kts; Probably has a goalpost radar mast
Similar: **CSK BRILLIANCE** (Sg) ex-*Shinei Maru*; **TREASURE SUNRISE** (Pa) ex-*Shinano Maru* (goalpost radar mast)

116 M^2FM *H*
ALINA SV/Ja (Mitsubishi HI) 1973; B; 68,169 grt/129,390 dwt; 261.02 × 17.58 m *(856.36 × 57.68 ft)*; M (Mitsubishi); 15.5 kts; ex-*Meynell*

117 M^2FM *H*
SOL Cy/Ja (Sumitomo) 1973; B; 65,064 grt/120,005 dwt; 257.03 × 16.93 m *(843.27 × 55.54 ft)*; M (Sulzer); 15.5 kts; ex-*Katori Maru*

118 M^2FM *H*
UNITY 1 Pa/Ja (Mitsubishi HI) 1973; B; 67,614 grt/129,542 dwt; 261.02 × 17.62 m *(856.36 × 57.81 ft)*; M (Sulzer); 14.75 kts; ex-*Elwood Mead*

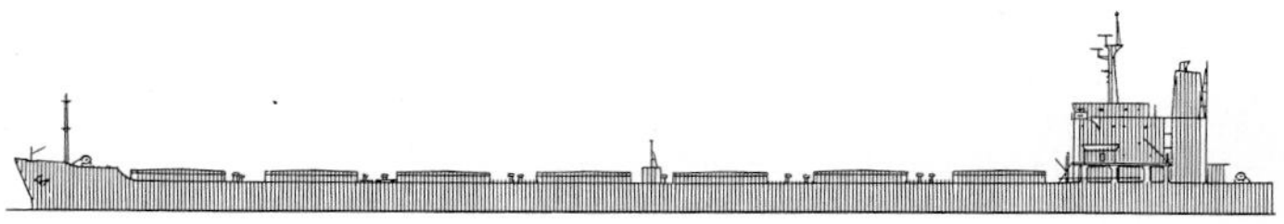

119 M^2FM *H1*
EVER CHAMPION Tw/Ja (Namura) 1982; B; 35,319 grt/62,343 dwt; 225.03 × 12.4 m *(738 × 40.68 ft)*; M (Sulzer); 14.75 kts; ex-*Ittersum*
Sister: **VITALI** (Gr) ex-*Hilversum* (24,510 grt)

120 M^2FM *H1*
PACIFIC JASMIN Li/Ja (Sumitomo) 1976; B; 73,141 grt/140,319 dwt; 266.99 × 16.54 m *(875.95 × 54.27 ft)*; M (Sulzer); 16 kts

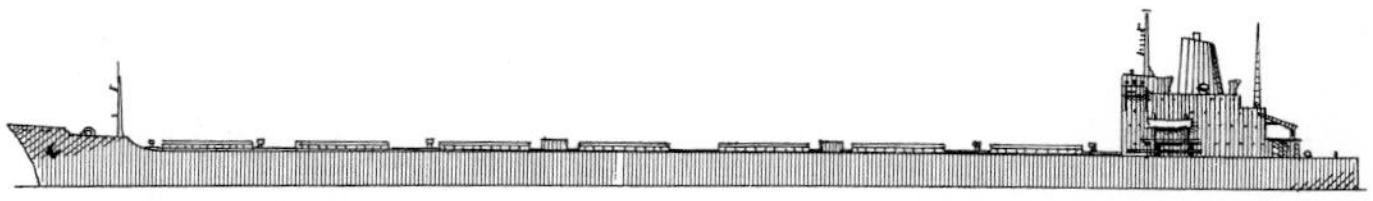

121 M^2FM *H1*
SHI HUI Pa/Ja (IHI) 1972; B; 36,250 grt/62,355 dwt; 223.02 × 12.82 m *(731.69 × 42.06 ft)*; M (Sulzer); 14.75 kts; ex-*Amelia Topic*
Probable sisters: **SV VICTORY** (Th) ex-*Kyriaki*; **LADY MOYNE** (Br) ex-*Olga Topic*; Possible sisters: **ANDROS MELTEMI** (Gr); **SV WINNER** (Th) ex-*Ocean Harmony*

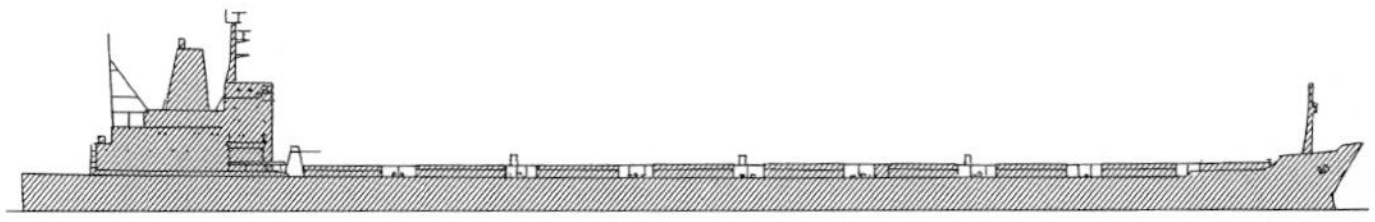

122 M^2FM *H1*
TAO JIANG HAI RC/Br (H&W) 1975; B; 63,509 grt/119,500 dwt; 261.53 × 16.2 m *(858.04 × 53.15 ft)*; M (B&W); 15.5 kts; ex-*Essi Camilla*
Sister: **APPLEBY** (Bs); Similar: **LACKENBY** (Bs) ex-*Otterpool*; **RAVENSCRAIG** (Bs)

123 M^2FM *H12*
KAILASH Ho/Br (A&P) 1958; C; 2,985 grt/4,430 dwt; 97.54 × 6.27 m *(320 × 20.57 ft)*; M (British Polar); 11 kts; ex-*Southwark*

124 M^2FM H13
DOCEORION Bz/Bz (Caneco) 1984; B; 28,330 grt/47,300 dwt; 218.45 × 10.70 m *(716.70 × 35.10 ft)*; M (MAN); 15 kts; **SIMILAR TO DRAWING NUMBER 5/196;** Appears identical to 5/196 but funnel is probably single; Others on this entry may be like Doceorion
Probable sister: **DOCETAURUS** (Bz)

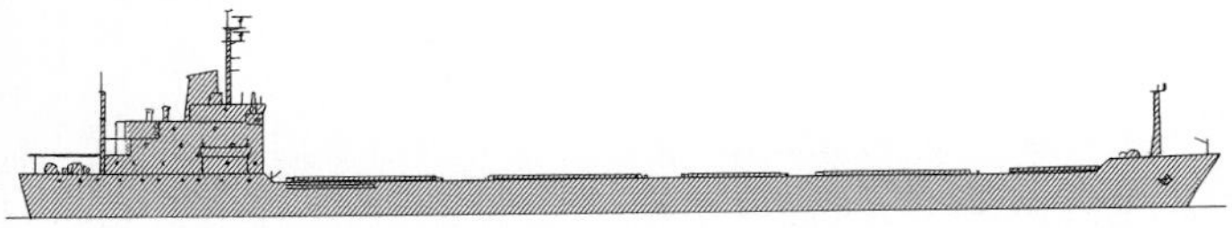

125 M^2FM H13
LEPETANE SV/Bz (Maua) 1984; B; 15,220 grt/26,700 dwt; 173.23 × 9.75 m *(568.34 × 31.99 ft)*; M (B&W); 13.75 kts; ex-*Libranave 1*
Sister: **ARMELLE** (SV) ex-*Libranave II*

126 M^2FM H13
S. M. SPIRIDON Li/Fr (Havre) 1967; C/Ch; 1,920 grt/2,730 dwt; 87 × 5.97 m *(285.43 × 19.59 ft)*; M (Werkspoor); 13.75 kts; ex-*Tyysterniemi*

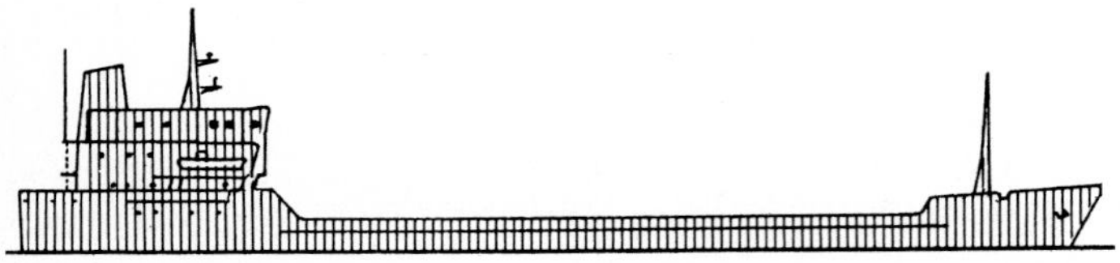

127 M^2FM H13
STELLA NORDIC Sw/Sw (Falkenbergs) 1978; C; 2,877 grt/4,958 dwt; 88.02 × 6.84 m *(288.78 × 22.44 ft)*; M (Polar); 12.50 kts; ex-*Nordanhav*

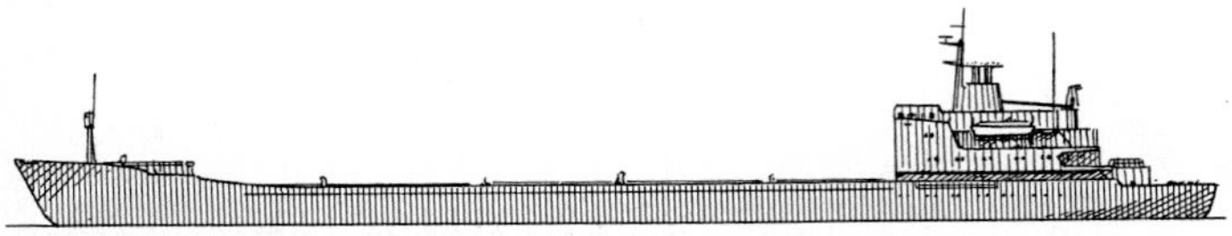

128 M^2FMC H1
KAPITONAS PANFILOV Lt/Ru (Kherson) 1975; B; 9,965 grt/14,631 dwt; 146.21 × 9.43 m *(479.69 × 30.94 ft)*; M (B&W); 14 kts; ex-*Kapitan Panfilov*; Crane is on starboard side
Sisters: **KAPITONAS CHROMCOV** (Lt) ex-*Kapitan Khromtsov*; **KAPITONAS DUBININ** (Lt) ex-*Kapitan Dubinin*; **KAPITONAS IZMIAKOV** (Lt) ex-*Kapitan Izhmyakov*; **KAPITONAS MESCERIAKOV** (Lt) ex-*Kapitan Meshchryakov*; **KAPITONAS REUTOV** (Lt) ex-*Kapitan Reutov*; **KAPITONAS GUDIN** (Lt) ex-*Kapitan Gudin*; **KAPITONAS STULIN** (Lt) ex-*Kapitan Stulov*; **KAPITONAS VAVILOV** (Lt) ex-*Kapitan Vavilov*; **KAPITONAS A. LUCKA** (Lt) ex-*Ivan Nesterov* **KAPITONAS STULPINAS** (Lt) ex-*Yustas Paleckis*

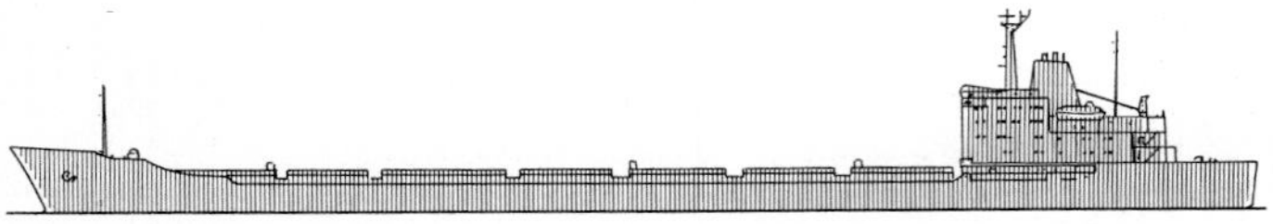

129 M^2FMC H13
BORIS LIVANOV Ru/Bu (G Dimitrov) 1986; B; 16,502 grt/23,940 dwt; 184.62 × 10.10 m *(605.71 × 33.14 ft)*; M (B&W); 15.50 kts; Mast aft is on port side
Sisters (some may have four deck cranes): **GUSTAV SULE** (Ea) ex-*Viktor Kingisepp*; **SEDOY** (Ma) ex-*Vasiliy Solovyev Sedoy*; **LEONID SOBOLYEV** (Ru); **SERGO ZAKARIADZE** (Ru); **ALEKSANDER KOLMPERE** (Ea) ex-*Skulptor Matveyev*; **KHUDOZHNIK KRAYNEV** (Ru); **GRIGORIY ALEKSANDROV** (Ru); **KOZNITSA** (Bu)

130 M^2FMC H13
COLDITZ Li/Ru (Baltic) 1980; B; 23,237 grt/38,250 dwt; 199.80 × 11.21 m *(655.51 × 36.78 ft)*; M (B&W); 16.20 kts; After crane is on starboard side
Sister: **PREMNITZ** (Ge)

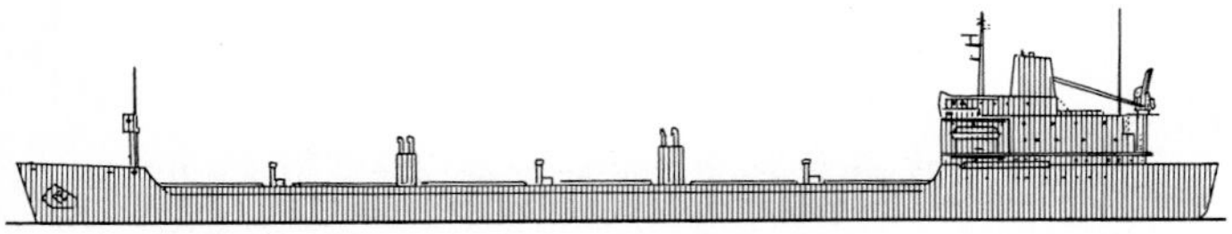

131 M^2FMC H13
DMITRIY DONSKOY Ru/DDR (Warnow) 1977; B/Con; 13,567 grt/ 19,885 dwt; 162.11 × 9.88 m *(532 × 32.41 ft)*; M (MAN); 15.25 kts; 'UL-ESC' type; 442 TEU
Sisters: **DMITRIY POZHARSKIY** (Ru); **ALEKSANDR NEVSKIY** (Ru); **ALEKSANDR SUVOROV** (Ru); **MIKHAIL KUTUZOV** (Ru); **ADMIRAL USHAKOV** (Ru); **KUZMA MININ** (Ru); **PETR VELIKIY** (Ru); **STEPAN RAZIN** (Ru); **YEMELYAN PUGACHEV** (Ru); **IVAN BOGUN** (Ru); **IVAN SUSANIN** (Ru)

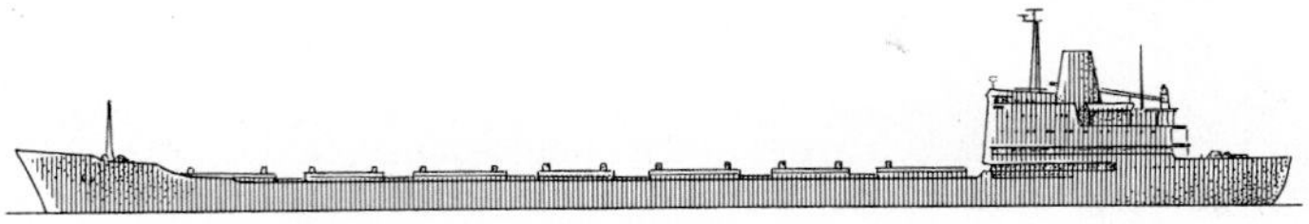

132 M^2FMC H13
KHUDOZHNIK FEDOROVSKIY Ru/Bu (G. Dimitrov) 1978; B; 15,643 grt/ 24,354 dwt; 185.22 × 10.1 m *(607.68 × 33.14 ft)*; M (Sulzer); 15.25 kts; This vessel may be fitted with four deck cranes—this could also apply to the sister ships
Sisters (some may have modified superstructure with six decks): **KHUDOZHNIK A GERASIMOV** (Gi); **KHUDOZHNIK GABASHVILI** (Gi); **KHUDOZHNIK KASIYAN** (Gi); **KHUDOZHNIK KUSTODIYEV** (Ru); **KHUDOZHNIK TOIDZE** (Gi); **KHUDOZHNIK VLADIMIR SEROV** (Gi); **GLENCORA** (Ho) ex-*Sovietskiy Khudozhnik*; **SHIPKA** (Bu); **RILA** (Bu); **RODOPI** (Bu); **VITOCHA** (or **VITOSHA**) (Bu); **MILIN KAMAK** (Bu); **SLAVIANKA** (Bu); **BALKAN** (Bu); **OKOLTCHITZA** (Bu); **KAPITAN GEORGI GEORGIEV** (Bu); **KAMENITZA** (Bu); **BUMBESTI** (Rm); **LIVEZINI** (Rm); **MOTRU** (Rm); **SALVA** (Rm); **VISEU** (Rm); **KAVO FLORA** (Cy) ex-*Lotru*; **KAVO MANGALIA** (Cy) ex-*Vidraru*

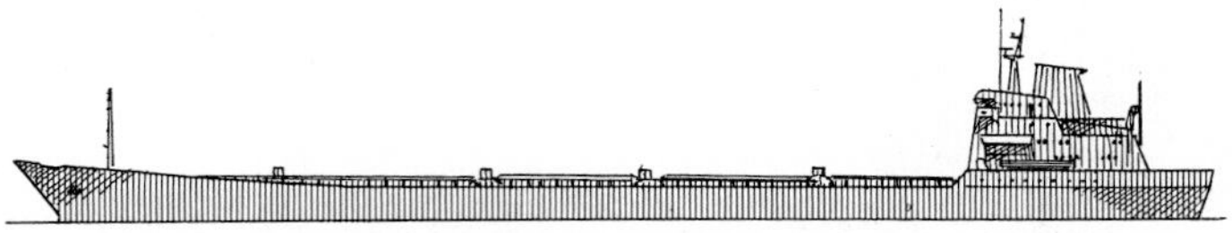

133 M^2FMD H13
HUTA ZGODA Pd/FRG (Schlichting) 1974; B; 9,268 grt/14,176 dwt; 145.65 × 8.35 m *(477.85 × 27.4 ft)*; M (B&W); 15 kts
Sisters: **HUTA ZYGMUNT** (Pd); **BUDOWLANY** (Pd); **ROLNIK** (Pd); **KOPALNIA SOSNOWIEC** (Pd); **KOPALNIA WALBRZYCH** (Pd); **KOPALNIA ZOFIOWKA** (Pd)

134 M^2FM^2 H1
AFRICA MI/Ja (Sumitomo) 1977; O; 73,328 grt/137,061 dwt; 267.01 × 16.6 m *(876.02 × 54.46 ft)*; M (Sulzer); 14.75 kts; ex-*Africa Maru*
Possible sister: **SGC SEAWIND** (Ma) ex-*Oceania Maru*

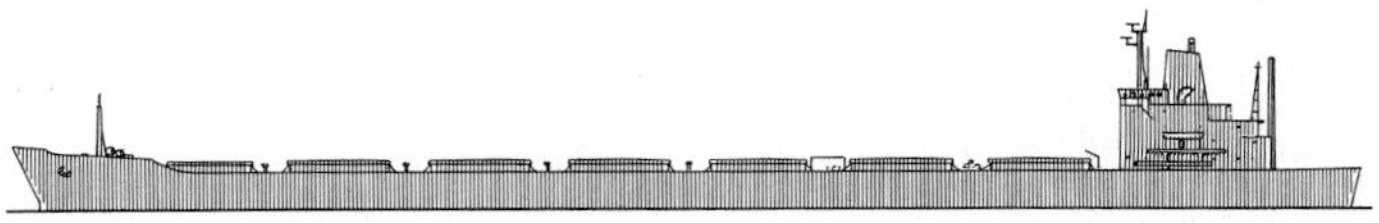

135 M^2FM^2 H1
AQUAMARINE Bs/Ja (Mitsui) 1979; B; 37,399 grt/64,911 dwt; 228.76 × 12.78 m *(750.52 × 41.93 ft)*; M (B&W); 15.25 kts; ex-*Kyokusho Maru*
Probably similar: **CAPETAN GIORGIS I** (Cy) ex-*Hoyo Maru*

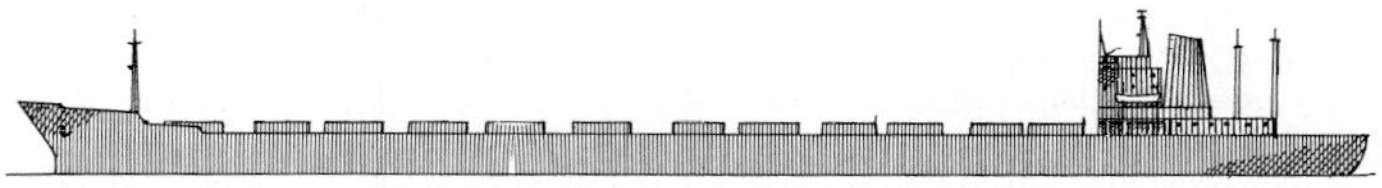

136 M^2FM^2 H1
HOPE SEA Pa/Ja (NKK) 1970; B; 32,752 grt/58,078 dwt; 226.88 × 12.3 m *(744.36 × 40.35 ft)*; M (B&W); 15.5 kts; ex-*W C van Horne*

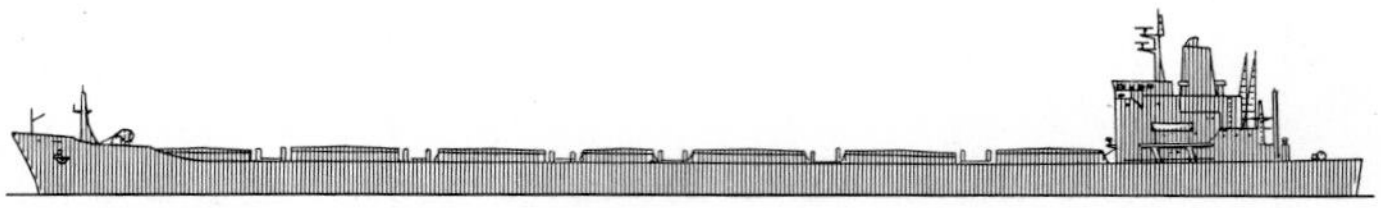

137 M^2FM^2CM H1
MONTAUK Gr/Ja (Tsuneishi) 1982; B; 37,318 grt/64,976 dwt; 228 × 12.78 m *(748.03 × 41.93 ft)*; M (B&W); 15 kts; ex-*Pacific Prosperity*
Sister: **ATLANTIC SPLENDOUR** (Gr) ex-*Pacific Pride*; Possible sisters: **DEERPOOL** (Br) ex-*Shannon Venture*; **CLIPPER STAR** (NIS) ex-*Hutland Venture*; Similar: **SUNNY GLORIOUS** (Pi) ex-*Ocean Prosper*

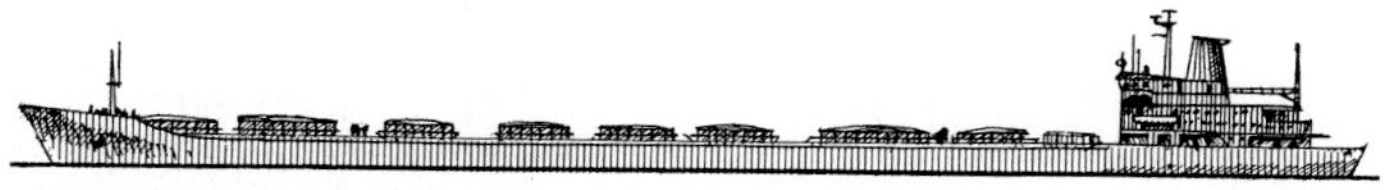

138 *MMFMR H1*
SEAGRACE II Cy/Pd ('Komuny Paryskiej') 1977; B; 34,609 grt/64,344 dwt; 251.16 × 12.35 m *(824.02 × 40.52 ft)*; M (Sulzer); 15.25 kts; ex-*Knut Mark*; 'B 526' type
Similar (Rm built—Constantza): **BAIA NOUA** (Rm) ex-*Stavroula*; Possibly similar (Rm built—Costanza): **BACESTI** (Li); **BAIA DE ARAMA** (Rm); **BAIA DE ARIES** (Rm); **BAIA DE CRIS** (Rm); **BAIA DE FIER** (Rm); **BANEASA** (Li); **BARAGANUL** (Rm); **TOMIS SPIRIT** (Ma) ex-*Baraolt*; **TOMIS GLORY** (Ma) ex-*Basarabi*; **BECHET** (Rm); **KAVO KALIAKRA** (Cy) ex-*Bistret*; **BOBILNA** (Cy); **TOMIS HOPE** (Ma) ex-*Borcea*; **BORZESTI** (Li); **KAVO MIDIA** (Cy) ex-*Branesti*; **BUJORENI** (Rm); **TOMIS FAITH** (Ma) ex-*Banisor*

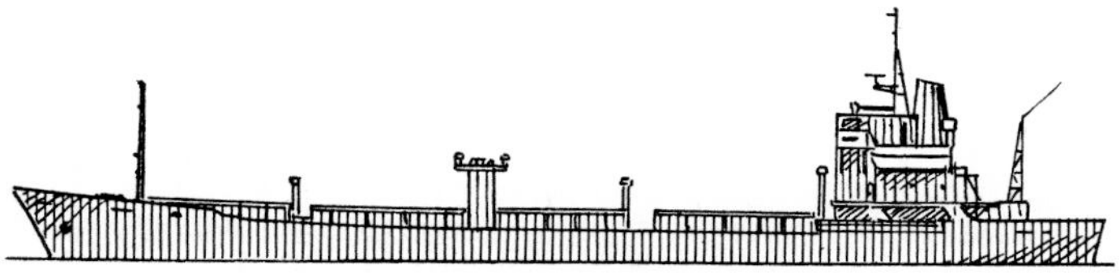

139 *M^2FN H*
ALAN Li/Ja (Tohoku) 1971; C/B; 2,900 grt/5,656 dwt; 85.83 × 7.45 m *(281.59 × 24.44 ft)*; M (Hanshin); 11 kts; ex-*Geneve*; 'Camit' type
Sisters: **LINA** (Ma) ex-*Hamburg*; **KIMOLOS II** (Gr) ex-*Ghent* (converted to cement carrier); **KAWAN** (Ma) ex-*Saint Nazaire*; **MEDI** (Ma) ex-*Tarragona*; **EARLY BIRD** (NIS) ex-*Sete* (lengthened to 105.971m (347.671ft))

140 *M^2FN H*
FLAG EMERALD Gr/Ja (Mitsui) 1972; B; 62,879 grt/111,064 dwt; 259.82 × 15.62 m *(852.43 × 51.25 ft)*; M (B&W); 15.25 kts; ex-*Ibaraki Maru*

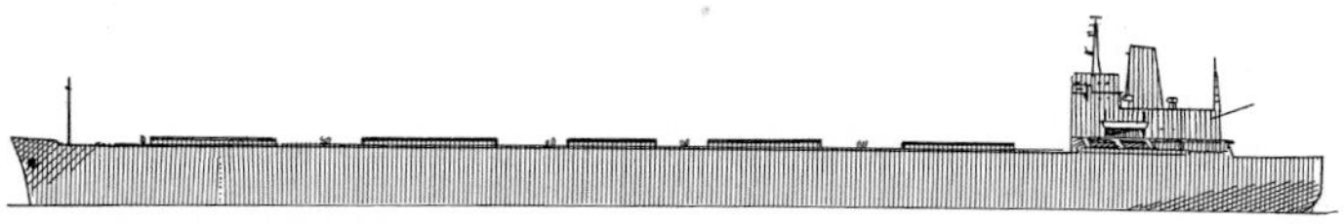

141 *M^2FN H*
FORTUNA DUCKLING Pa/Ja (Sumitomo) 1972; BWC; 31,107 grt/32,725 dwt; 196.02 × 9.7 m *(643.11 × 31.82 ft)*; M (Sulzer); 14.75 kts; ex-*Bunga Tembusu*
Sister: **FELIZ DUCKLING** (Pa) ex-*Bunga Melawis*; Probably similar: **VALENTINA** (Li)

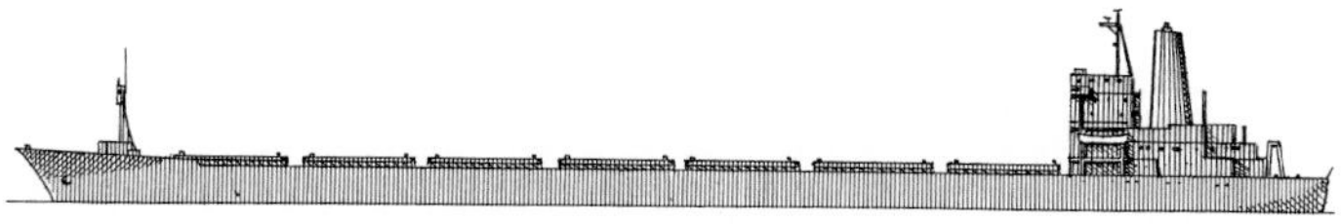

142 *M^2FN H*
GOLDEN LAND Pa/Ih (Verolme Cork) 1976; B; 28,422 grt/50,825 dwt; 205.49 × 12.33 m *(674.18 × 40.52 ft)*; M (MAN); 13.5 kts; ex-*Lutz Jacob*
Sisters: **ROVA** (Ma) ex-*Babette Jacob*; **SOYA QUEEN** (Bs) ex-*Margot Jacob*; **ZOUZOU** (Cy) ex-*Rolf Jacob*

143 *M^2FN H*
HANJIN CANBERRA Ko/Ja (Mitsui) 1973; B; 63,898 grt/118,435 dwt; 260.03 × 16.45 m *(853.12 × 53.97 ft)*; M (B&W); 16.5 kts; ex-*Polyviking*

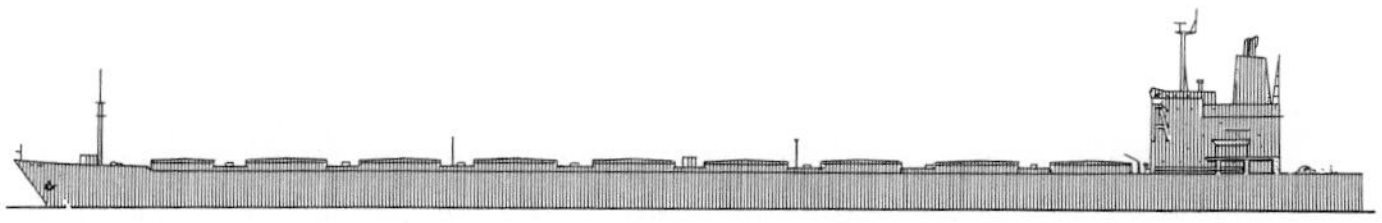

144 *M^2FN H*
IKAN TONGKOL Sg/Ja (Mitsubishi HI) 1982; B; 76,079 grt/138,490 dwt; 270.01 × 16.72 m *(886 × 54.86 ft)*; M (Sulzer); 14.5 kts

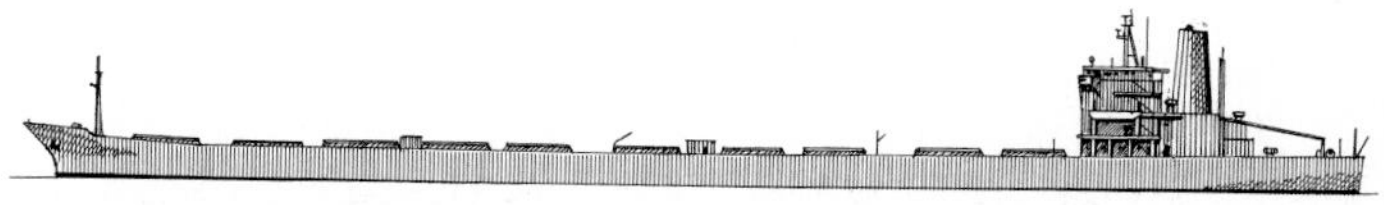

145 *M^2FN H*
PERICLES G C Cy/Be (Cockerill) 1974; B; 37,727 grt/65,085 dwt; 224.01 × 13.09 m *(734.94 × 42.95 ft)*; M (Sulzer); 15.5 kts; ex-*Zeebrugge*
Sisters: **AUK** (Cy) ex-*Martha*; **KVARNER** (Ma) ex-*Kyoto*; **REGAL TRADER** (NIS) ex-*Yaffa*; **NOBLE FORTUNE** (Pa) ex-*Ruth*; Similar: **MARINER C** (Pa) ex-*Maratha Mariner*; **POWER** (Gr) ex-*Maratha Melody*; Possibly similar (larger): **VICTORIA II** (Pa) ex-*Argosy Pacific*; **LIA M** (Cy) ex-*Leon & Pierre C*; Possibly similar: **SAMSARA** (Cy) ex-*Mineral Hoboken*; **CATHY** (Cy) ex-*Mineral Samitri*; **IPANEMA** (Cy) ex-*Mineral Luxembourg*

See photo number 5/338

146 *M^2FN H*
SAMRAT ASHOK In/Ja (Mitsubishi HI) 1974; B; 72,759 grt/129,513 dwt; 261.02 × 17.58 m *(856.36 × 57.68 ft)*; M (Sulzer); 15.5 kts; ex-*Gautama Buddha*

147 *M^2FN H*
TIGRIS Gr/Ja (Mitsubishi HI) 1973; B; 59,199 grt/122,647 dwt; 260.99 × 16.38 m *(856.27 × 53.74 ft)*; M (Mitsubishi); 15.25 kts; ex-*Shinrei Maru*
Similar: **CAPTAIN VENIAMIS** (Gr) ex-*Riko Maru*; **THEODORE A** (Li) ex-*Tweed Bridge*; **REGINA** (Pa) ex-*Orco Trader*; **DIMITRIOS** (Gr) ex-*Mermaid Jupiter*; Possibly similar: **BERLIN STAR** (SV) ex-*Chokai Maru*; **TIMAWRA** (Li) ex-*Amanda*; **ANGELIKI** (Gr) ex-*Taharoa Venturer*

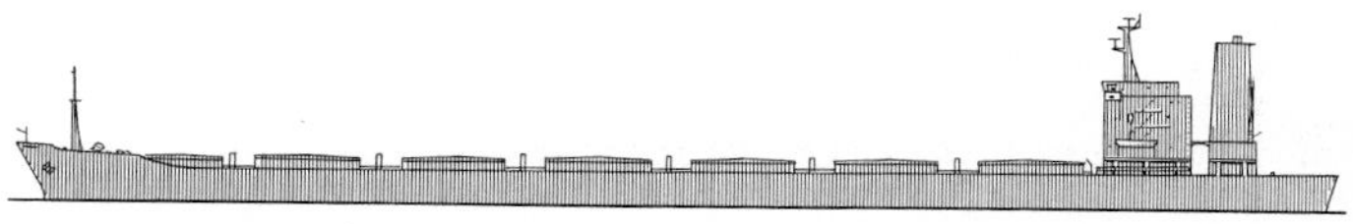

148 *M^2FN H1*
AGHIA MARKELLA Gr/Ja (Sumitomo) 1979; B; 36,237 grt/64,657 dwt; 230.21 × 13.02 m *(755 × 42.72 ft)*; M (Sulzer); 15 kts; ex-*Navios Monarch*
Similar: **HUA KAI** (RC) ex-*Navios Mariner* (shorter funnel); **TIMIOS STAVROS** (Cy) ex-*Navios Merchant*; **MARYLI** (Cy) ex-*Navios Miner*; **PANAMAX PRIDE** (Cy) ex-*Cerro Bolivar*

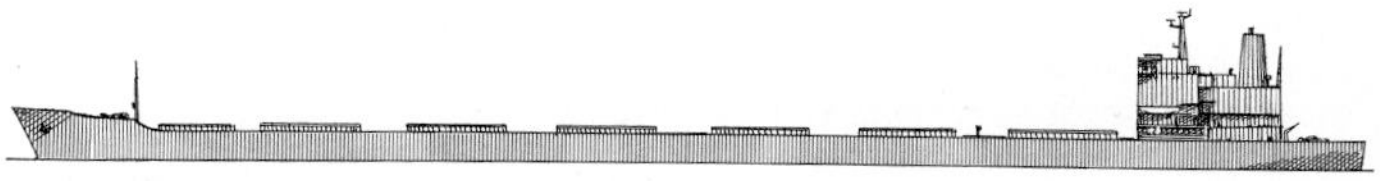

149 *M^2FN H1*
APOLLONIA LION Gr/Ja (Mitsubishi HI) 1977; B; 39,693 grt/72,044 dwt; 232.75 × 13.85 m *(736.62 × 45.44 ft)*; M (Sulzer); 15.5 kts; ex-*Aegean Lion*
Sister: **SEA UNION** (Gr) ex-*Anthony III*

150 *M^2FN H1*
GEORGIOS P Cy/FRG (Rhein Nordseew) 1968; B; 46,378 grt/82,445 dwt; 254.9 × 13.75 m *(836.29 × 45.11 ft)*; M (MAN); 16 kts; ex-*Aegir*
Sister: **ELISA P** (Cy) ex-*Brage*

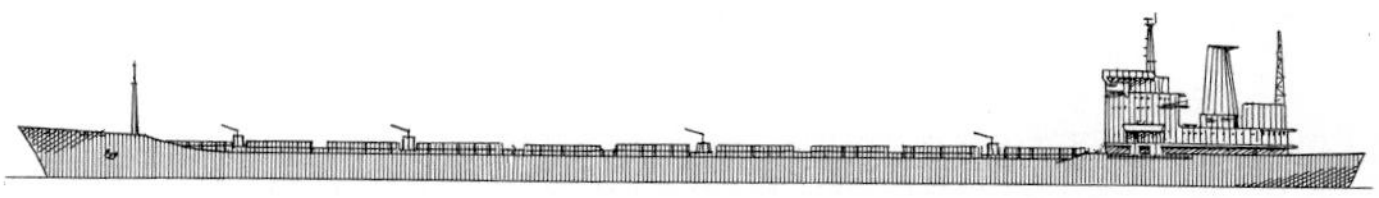

151 *M^2FN H1*
GOLDEN YANG Pa/Pd ('Komuny Paryskiej') 1976; B; 33,057 grt/54,443 dwt; 221.47 × 12.4 m *(726.61 × 40.68 ft)*; M (Sulzer); 15.75 kts; ex-*Amstelmolen*; 'B-521' type

152 *M^2FN H1*
INDOMITABLE Cy/Ja (Mitsui) 1972; B; 39,219 grt/77,996 dwt; 259.52 × 13.61 m *(851.44 × 44.65 ft)*; M (B&W); 16 kts; ex-*Konkar Indomitable*
Sisters: **KONKAR VICTORY** (Gr); **KONKAR INTREPID** (Gr)

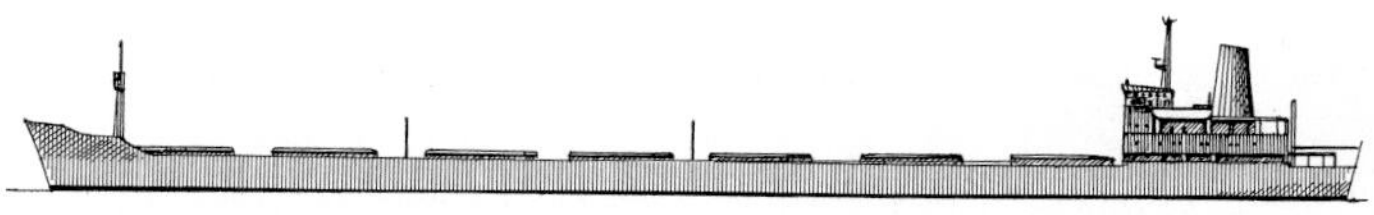

153 *M^2FN H1*
LUO FU SHAN RC/Sw (Eriksbergs) 1968; B; 29,418 grt/55,118 dwt; 217.58 × 12.82 m *(713.85 × 42.06 ft)*; M (B&W); 14.75 kts; ex-*King Alfred*

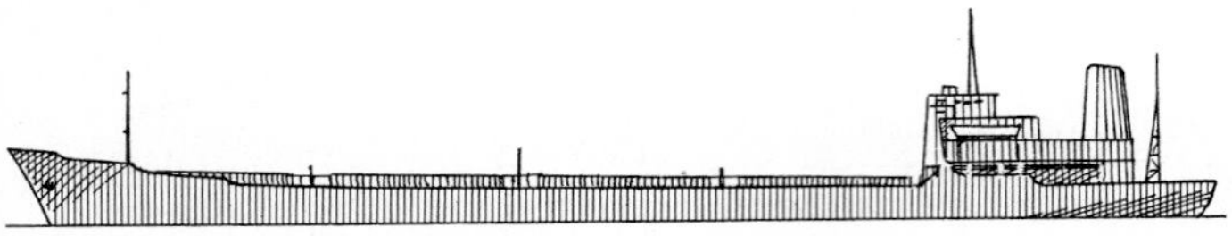

154 M^2FN *H1*
LYULIN Bu/Ja (Hakodate) 1965; B; 5,784 grt/9,308 dwt; 126.02 × 7.6 m *(413.45 × 24.93 ft)*; M (B&W); 13 kts
Sisters: **BELASITZA** (Bu); **HEMUS** (Bu); **OGRAJDEN** (Bu); **OSOGOVO** (Bu)

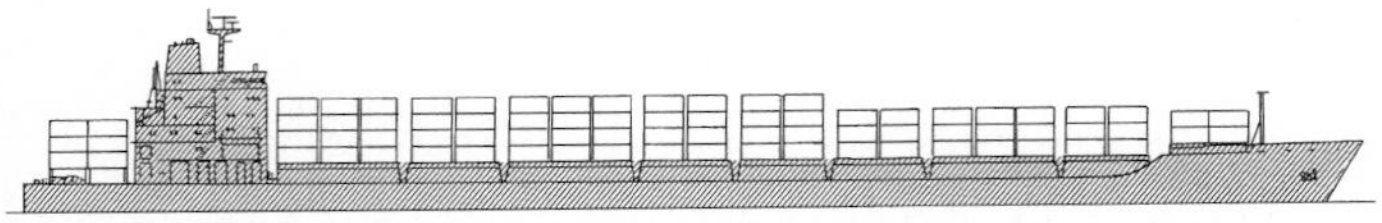

155 M^2FN *H1*
MARTHA II NIS/Ko (Samsung) 1984; B/Con; 29,223 grt/41,151 dwt; 209.40 × 11.60 m *(687.01 × 38.06 ft)*; M (Sulzer); 18.25 kts; ex-*TNT Express*; 1,922 TEU

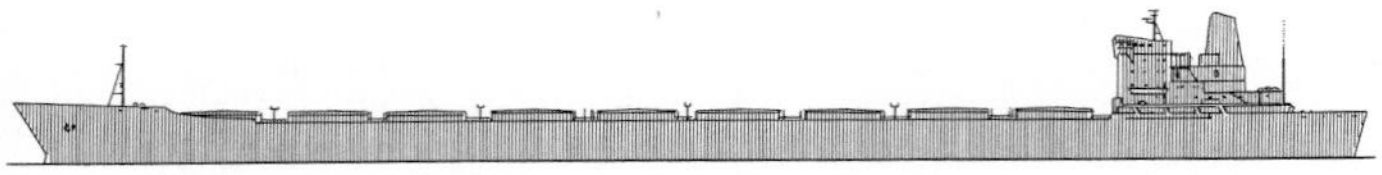

156 M^2FN *H1*
NESSIE Cy/No (Fredriksstad) 1972; B; 59,979 grt/110,342 dwt; 265.62 × 15.78 m *(871.46 × 51.77 ft)*; M (Sulzer); 15 kts; ex-*Jessie Stove*
Sisters: **EUROPA** (Li) ex-*Ariel*; **BELEM** (Cy) ex-*Olav Ringdal* (Kingpost on forecastle has a crow's nest); Similar: **VIVA** (NIS) ex-*Columbia*

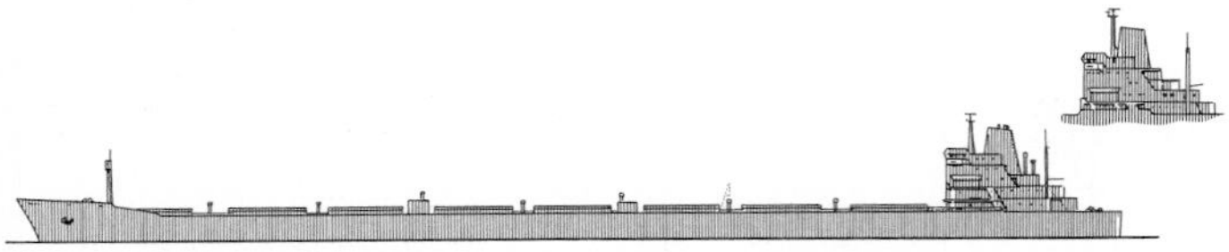

157 M^2FN *H1*
NEWAYS Pa/Ys ('3 Maj') 1972; B; 37,985 grt/69,886 dwt; 243.75 × 12.91 m *(799.7 × 42.36 ft)*; M (Sulzer); 15.5 kts; ex-*Ragna Gorthon*
Sisters: **FORUM GLORY** (Cy) ex-*Pacific Wasa*; **KOOKABURRA** (Gr) ex-*Cassiopeia*; Similar (see inset): **ANAFI** (Ma) ex-*Birte Oldendorff*; **DORA OLDENDORFF** (Sg); **UNITED V** (Cy) ex-*Helga Oldendorff*; **KYRENIA** (Cy) ex-*Ludolf Oldendorff*; Similar: **SHI TANG HAI** (RC) ex-*Dimitris A Lemos*; Possibly similar: **AKA** (Cy) ex-*Cetra Norma*

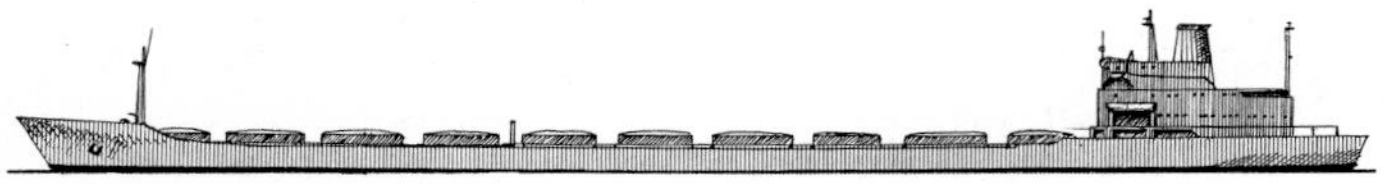

158 M^2FN *H1*
PENG HAI SV/Pd ('Komuny Paryskiej') 1972; B; 33,610 grt/54,976 dwt; 220 × 12.43 m *(721.78 × 40.78 ft)*; M (Sulzer); 15.75 kts; ex-*Hampton Bridge*; 'B-521' type
Possible sisters (some may be like drawing number 5/151 which see): **C NURFAN** (Tu) ex-*Jotunfjell*; **TRANSOCEAN** (Li) Launched as *Londrina*; **STAR OF MARIA** (Li) ex-*Gunnar Carlsson*; Sisters (Rm built—Constantza and Galatz): **MOUNT PENTELI** (Ma) ex-*Beius*; **JOHNNY C** (Pa) ex-*Bicaz*; **BIRLAD** (Rm); **BOCSA** (Rm); **BORSEC** (Rm); **BOTOSANI** (Rm); **HISTRIA SUN** (Rm) ex-*Breaza*; **GANZA** (Ma) Launched as *Stephanos D. Pateras*; **HISTRIA STAR** (Rm) ex-*Callatis*; **S K JUNIOR** (Gr) ex-*Tomis*; **MOUNT OLYMPUS** (Ma) ex-*Blaj*; **BUZIAS**; **FENG TAI** (Pa) ex-*Danube Sea*; **TRADE GREECE** (Cy) ex-*Ilona*; **HUDSON BAY** (Cy) ex-*Leandros*; **FENG HUA** (Pa) ex-*Tomis Sea*; **MOUNT YMITOS** (Ma) Launched as *Christine*; **MOUNT PARNITHA** (Ma) ex-*Bals*; **SPIGA** (Ma) ex-*Borsa*; **BRATULESTI** (Rm); **BALOTA** (Rm); Similar: **CENGIZ K** (Tu) ex-*Masovia*

159 M^2FN *H1*
RON Li/Sw (Uddevalla) 1972; B; 63,579 grt/117,949 dwt; 263.66 × 15.89 m *(865.03 × 52.13 ft)*; M (B&W); 15.5 kts; ex-*Norse Lion*
Sisters: **LEADER** (Cy) ex-*Constance*; **LOUSSIO** (Pa) ex-*Ronastar*; Similar: **ENTERPRISE** (HK) ex-*Varangfjell*

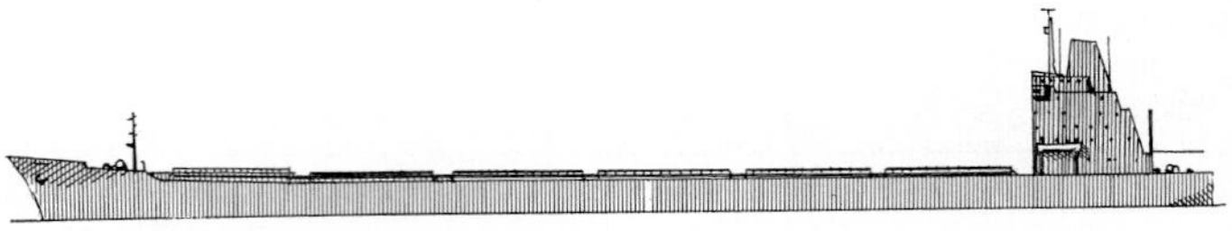

160 M^2FN *H1*
SUGAR ISLANDER US/US (Lockheed) 1972; B; 15,544 grt/29,984 dwt; 195.38 × 10.21 m *(641.01 × 33.5 ft)*; M (Fairbanks, Morse); 15 kts

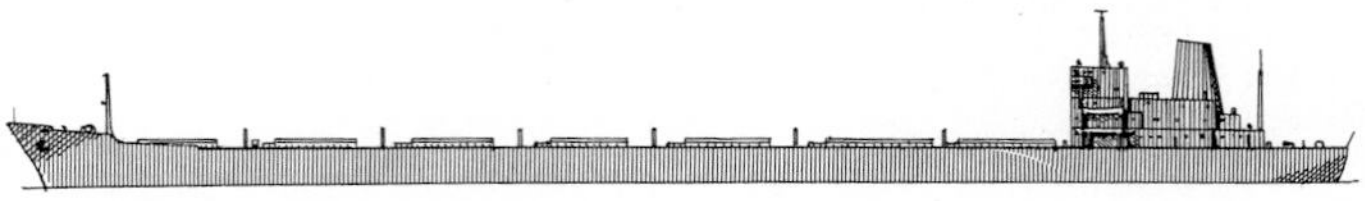

161 M^2FN *H1*
TRIANA Ma/Br (Doxford & S) 1968; B; 24,876 grt/51,046 dwt; 211.44 × 12.22 m *(693.7 × 40.09 ft)*; M (Doxford); 15.75 kts; ex-*Argonaut*

162 M^2FN *H1*
WEN DENG HAI RC/Br (H&W) 1968; B; 41,088 grt/77,871 dwt; 251.47 × 14.26 m *(825.03 × 46.78 ft)*; M (B&W); 16.5 kts; ex-*Essi Kristine*
Sister: **LUO SHAN HAI** (RC) ex-*Thara*

163 M^2FN *H13*
ADEN —/Pd (Szczecinska) 1971; B; 19,510 grt/32,208 dwt; 202.10 × 10.77 m; M (Sulzer); 13.5 kts; ex-*Cassinga*; 'B447' type. **SIMILAR TO DRAWING NUMBER 5/6**
Sister: **VERBIER** (Pa) ex-*Rio Zambeze*

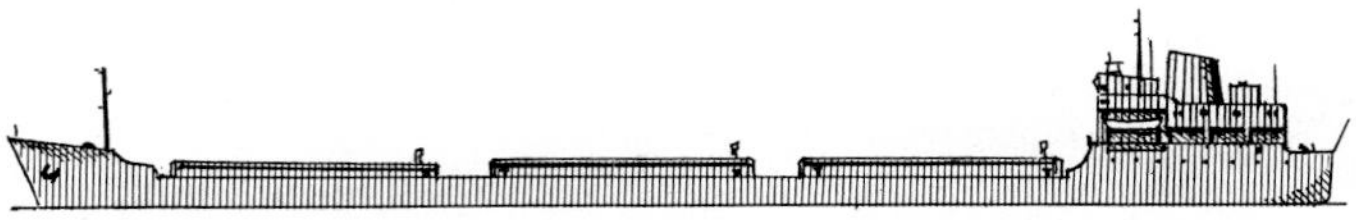

164 M^2FN *H13*
DALLINGTON Br/Ne (Verolme SH) 1975; B; 7,788 grt/12,140 dwt; 137.6 × 7.93 m *(451.44 × 26.02 ft)*; M (Stork-Werkspoor); 14 kts
Sisters: **DONNINGTON** (Br); **DURRINGTON** (Br); **STORRINGTON** (Br)

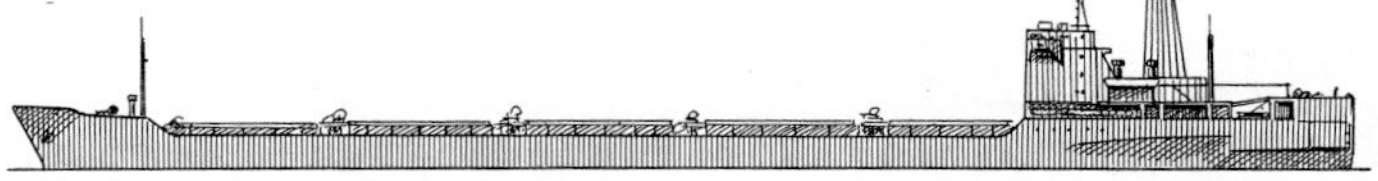

165 M^2FN *H13*
GOLD BOND TRAILBLAZER Li/Ja (Sasebo) 1974; O; 18,241 grt/26,608 dwt; 177.98 × 10.02 m *(583.92 × 32.87 ft)*; M (Sulzer); 15.25 kts; Main section ex-*Colon Brown*; Side doors; New mid body 1976

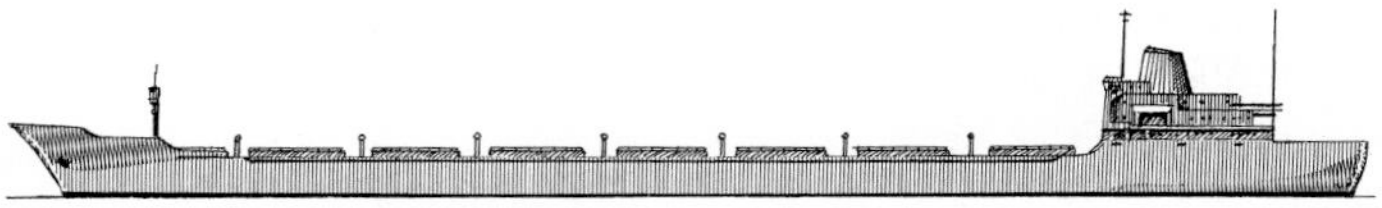

166 M^2FN *H13*
GULF TRIDENT Va/FRG (Rhein Nordseew) 1967; B; 29,911 grt/54,204 dwt; 222.51 × 12.92 m *(730.02 × 42.39 ft)*; M (B&W); 15 kts; ex-*Golden Master*

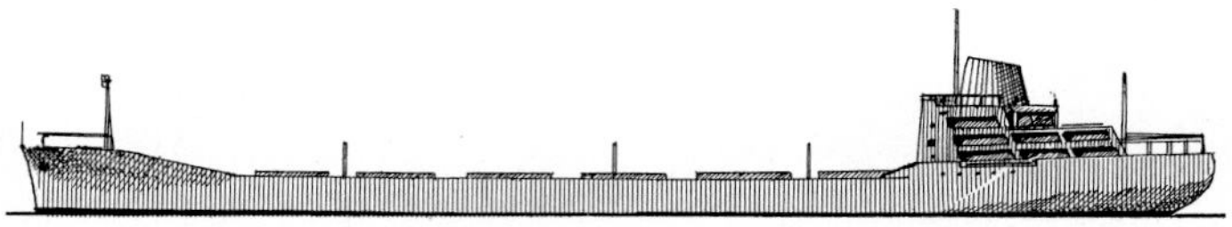

167 M^2FN *H13*
HONG QI 302 RC/Br (Lithgows) 1961; B; 13,548 grt/24,355 dwt; 173.54 × 10.26 m *(569.4 × 33.66 ft)*; M (Sulzer); 15 kts; ex-*Mylla*

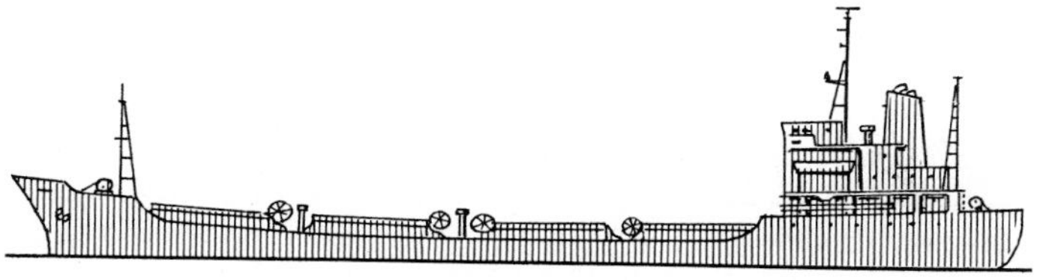

168 *M^2FN H13*
HUSNES Pa/Ja (Hashihama) 1977; B; 4,907 grt/7,174 dwt; 110.55 × 7.02 m *(363 × 23.03 ft)*; M (Mitsubishi); 15 kts; ex-*Sumburgh Head*
Sisters: **BARRA HEAD** (Ih); **HERNES** (Cy) ex-*Rora Head*

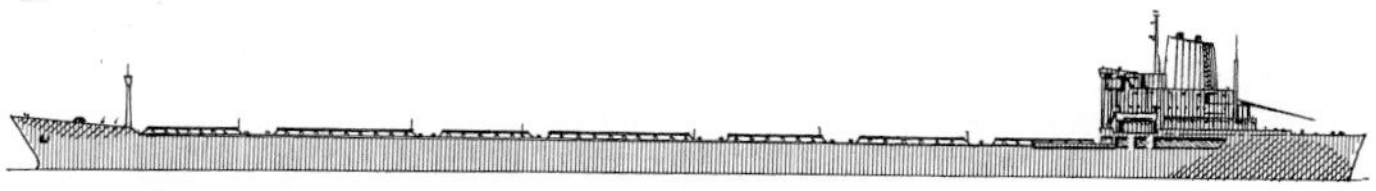

169 *M^2FN H13*
IOANNITSA Ma/De (B&W) 1973; B; 29,881 grt/51,913 dwt; 218.85 × 12.09 m *(718.01 × 39.66 ft)*; M (B&W); 15.5 kts; ex-*Thorunn*
Similar: **GIUSEPPE LEMBO** (It) ex-*Carlova*; **MARIJEANNIE** (Gr) ex-*Hector*; **UNIWERSYTET WARSZAWSKI** (Pd); **UNIWERSYTET WROCLAWSKI** (Pd); **SAMJOHN MARINER** (Pa); **SEABEE I** (Ma) ex-*Heering Christel*

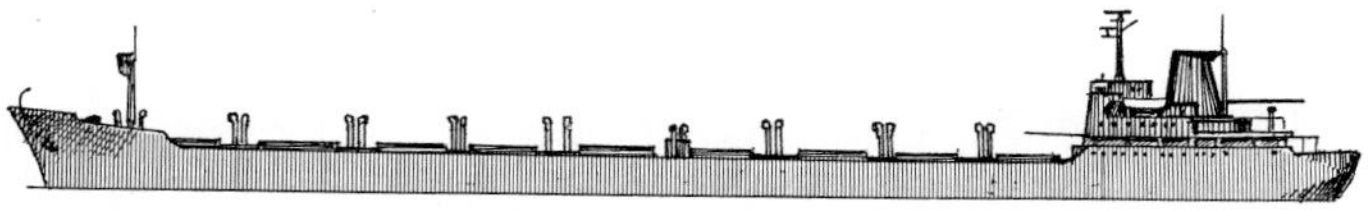

170 *M^2FN H13*
JU HAI RC/Sw (Uddevalla) 1966; B; 29,857 grt/47,602 dwt; 215.7 × 12.09 m *(707.68 × 39.67 ft)*; M (B&W); 16 kts; ex-*Vardaas*

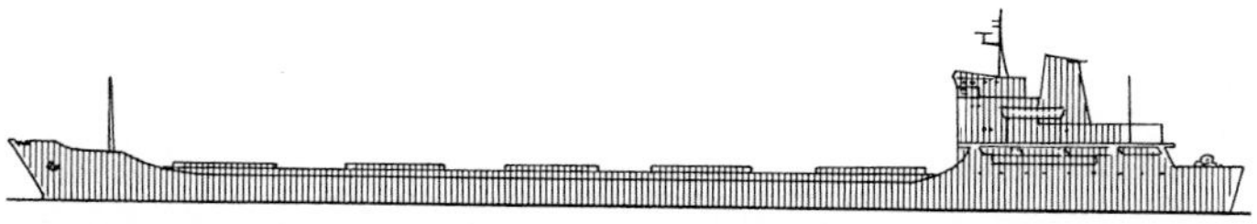

171 *M^2FN H13*
KOPALNIA JEZIORKO Pd/Sp (AESA) 1971; B; 8,721 grt/13,665 dwt; 146.77 × 8.27 m *(481.53 × 27.13 ft)*; M (Sulzer); 15.5 kts
Sister: **KOPALNIA PIASECZNO** (Pd)

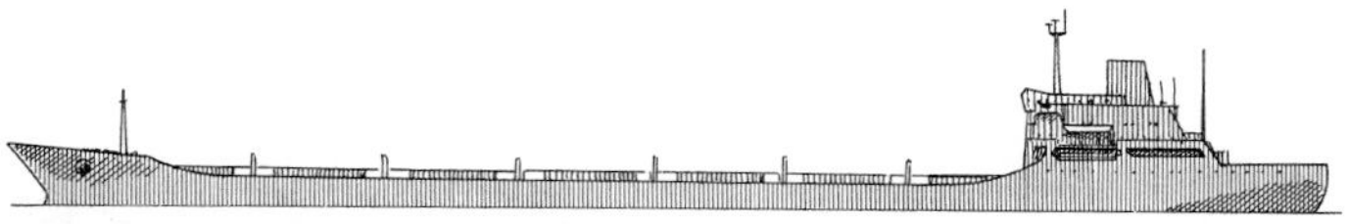

172 *M^2FN H13*
LAKE PLACID Ma/Bu (G. Dimitrov) 1973; B; 23,329 grt/37,844 dwt; 201.17 × 11.2 m *(660.01 × 36.75 ft)*; M (B&W); 17 kts; ex-*General Swierczewski*
Sisters: **GENERAL BEM** (Pd); **GENERAL JASINSKI** (Pd); **GENERAL MADALINSKI** (Pd); **GENERAL PRADZYNSKI** (Pd); **JORDANKA NIKOLOVA** (Bu); **PETIMATA OT RMS** (Bu); **ADALBERT ANTONOV** (Bu); Probable sister (may have four deck cranes): **MEKHANIK P KILIMENCHUK** (Uk) ex-*Kamar*

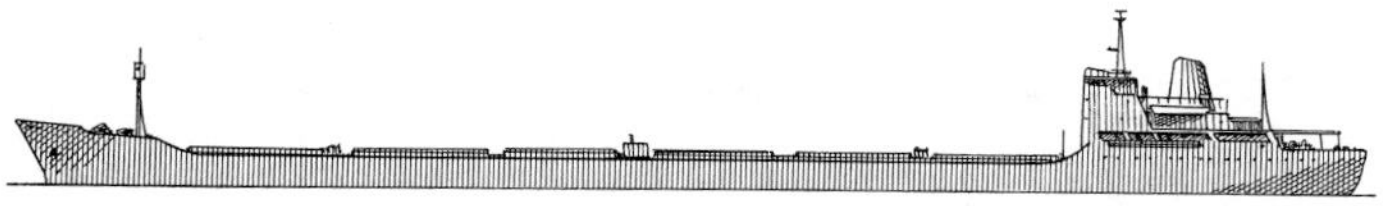

173 *M^2FN H13*
MARAMURES Rm/Ja (Hitachi) 1966; B; 15,426 grt/25,606 dwt; 181.13 × 9.5 m *(594.26 × 31.17 ft)*; M (B&W); 16 kts

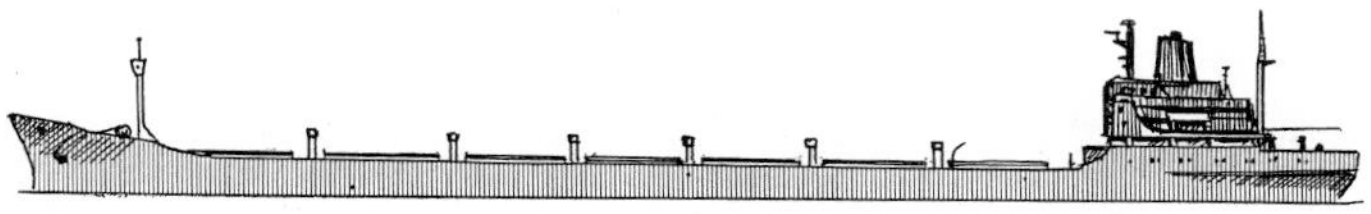

174 *M^2FN H13*
MARINAKI Ma/Ja (Mitsui) 1970; B; 25,481 grt/45,206 dwt; 203 × 12.49 m *(666 × 40.98 ft)*; M (B&W); 16 kts; ex-*Konkar Resolute*
Sister: **IOA** (Pa) ex-*Konkar Pioneer*

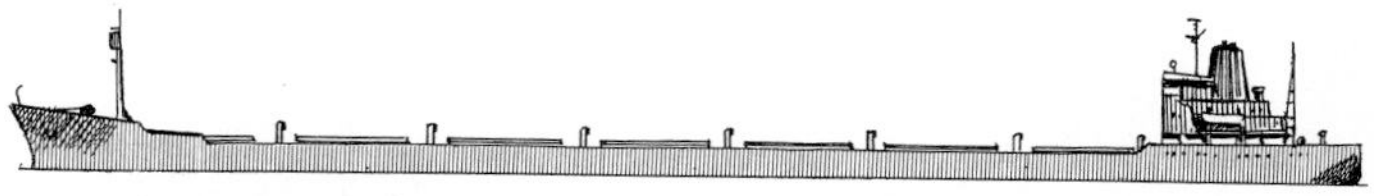

175 *M^2FN H13*
PAN UNION Ko/Ja (Hakodate) 1973; B; 35,967 grt/66,095 dwt; 219.01 × 13.62 m *(718.54 × 44.69 ft)*; M (Sulzer); 15 kts; ex-*Voywi*
Possible sisters: **EVANGELIA T** (Cy) ex-*Norse Duke*; **ESPEROS** (Bs) ex-*Ingwi*; **ERMIONI** (Cy) ex-*Gard*; **STANDARD VIRTUE** (Gr) ex-*Maro*; **YA ZHOU HAI** (RC) ex-*Balder Trader*; Similar: **SIRENA** (NIS) ex-*Moldanger*

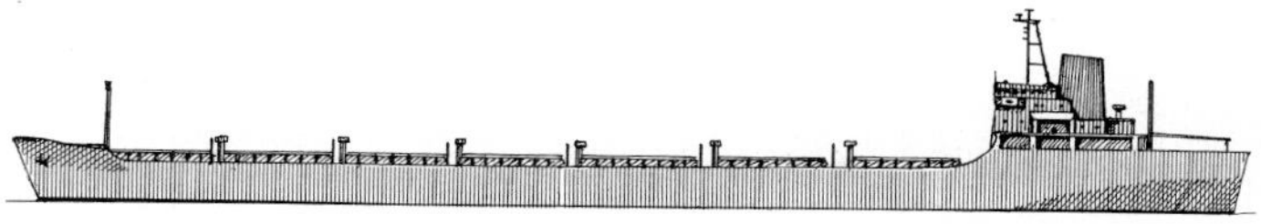

176 *M^2FN H13*
PENG YANG SV/Sp (AESA) 1973; B; 30,325 grt/53,439 dwt; 206.86 × 13.27 m *(678.67 × 43.54 ft)*; M (B&W); 16.5 kts; ex-*Seneca*
Sisters: **DYNAMIC** (Cy) ex-*Nicholas G. Papalios*; Similar (centre-line radar mast and taller funnel): **PIONEER STAR** (Cy) ex-*Ermua*

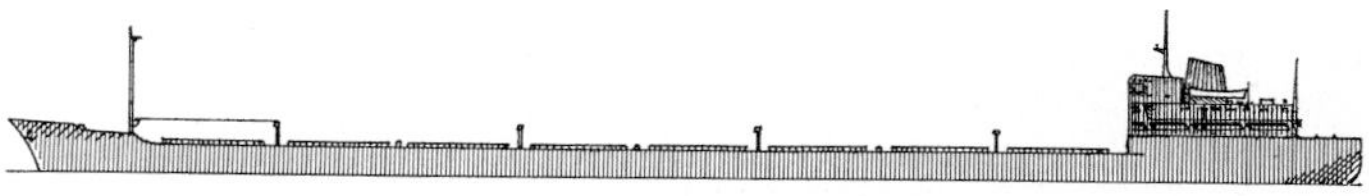

177 *M^2FN H13*
YANG MING SHAN RC/Ja (Hitachi) 1965; B; 25,395 grt/44,668 dwt; 206.03 × 12.32 m *(675.95 × 40.42 ft)*; M (B&W); 15 kts; ex-*Atherstone*

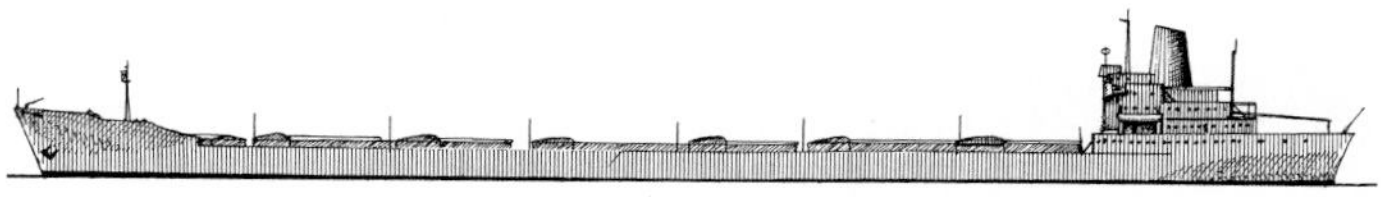

178 *M^2FN H13*
YELLOW ISLAND Pa/De (B&W) 1970; B; 30,038 grt/52,164 dwt; 218.85 × 12.1 m *(718 × 39.7 ft)*; M (B&W); 16 kts; ex-*Olga Maersk*
Sisters: **UNIWERSYTET JAGIELLONSKI** (Pd); **KARABI** (Bs) ex-*Uniwersytet Torunski*

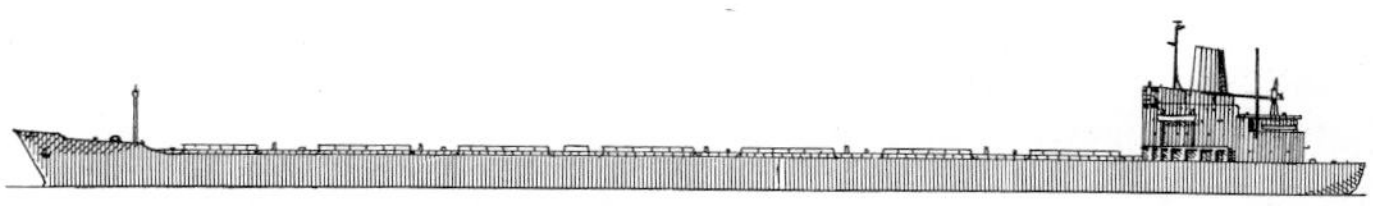

179 *M^2FNC H1*
PAN JOURNEY Ko/Ja (Mitsubishi HI) 1975; B; 35,787 grt/64,476 dwt; 224.01 × 13.32 m *(734.94 × 43.7 ft)*; M (Sulzer); 14.5 kts; ex-*Halla Grieg*; Crane is on port side

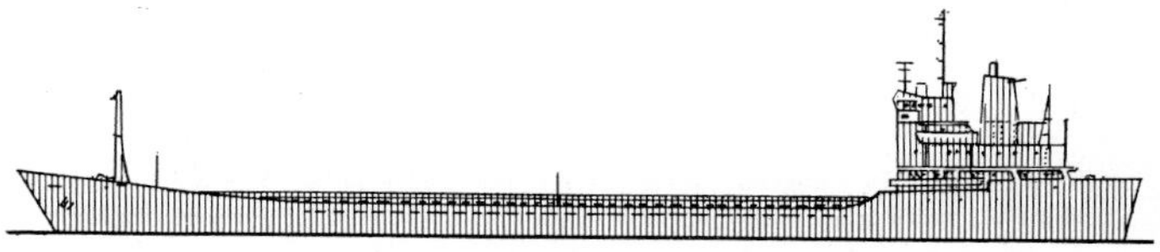

180 *M^2FN^2 H13*
WASHINGTON Cro/Ja (Kagoshima) 1977; B; 6,400 grt/9,008 dwt; 127.01 × 7.58 m *(417 × 24.87 ft)*; M (Pielstick); 14 kts

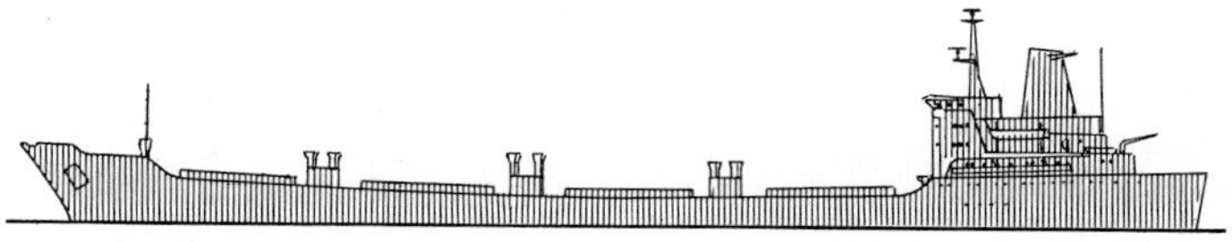

181 *M^2FNR H*
PIONIERUL Rm/Rm (Galatz) 1976; B; 10,394 grt/19,285 dwt; 145.12 × 10.14 m *(476 × 33.27 ft)*; M (Sulzer); 15 kts; Crane aft is on port side
Sisters: **TIRGU BUJOR** (Rm); **TIRGU LAPUS** (Rm); **TIRGU FRUMOS** (Rm); **TIRGU NEAMT** (Rm); **TIRGU OCNA** (Rm); **TIRGU SECUIESC** (Rm); **TIRGU TROTUS** (Rm)

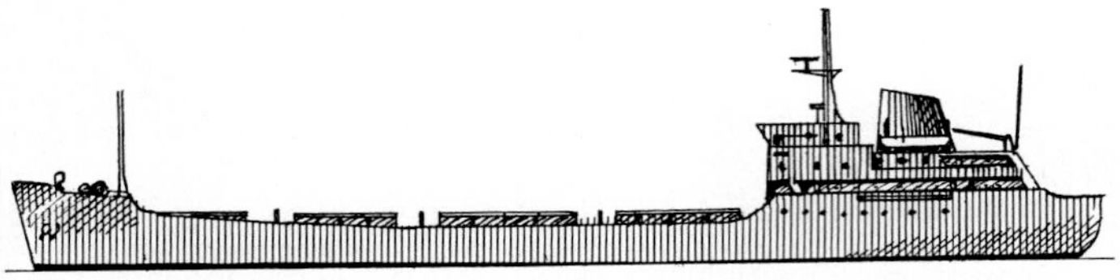

182 M^2FNS *H13*
SHANE Ma/Br (Readhead) 1965; C; 5,512 grt/8,422 dwt; 112.68 × 9.09 m *(369.69 × 29.82 ft)*; M (Doxford); 13.5 kts; ex-*Hudson Light*

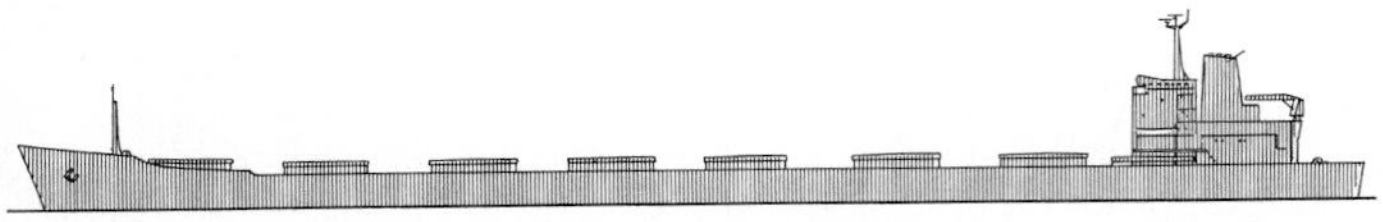

183 M^2FR *H1*
IOANNIS Gr/Br (Sunderland) 1982; B; 40,796 grt/77,300 dwt; 230 × 14.87 m *(755 × 48.79 ft)*; M (B&W); 14 kts; ex-*La Pampa*
Sister: **THEOMITOR** (Gr) ex-*La Chacra*

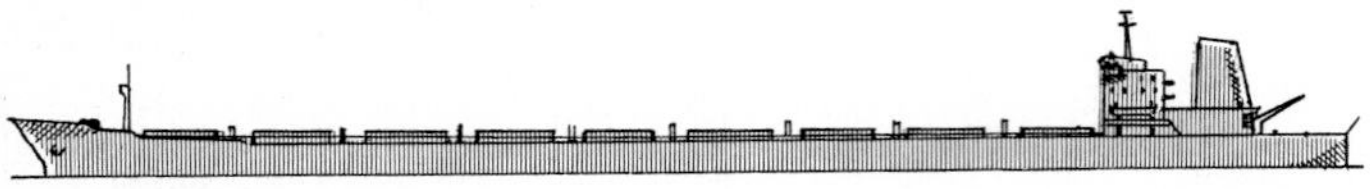

184 M^2FR *H1*
PROTECTOR 2 Cy/FRG (Rhein Nordseew) 1976; B; 64,670 grt/122,976 dwt; 272.32 × 16.08 m *(893.44 × 52.76 ft)*; M (Sulzer); 16 kts; ex-*Fernsea*
Sisters: **JOSTELLE** (HK) ex-*Fernhill*; **ENDEAVOR** (HK) ex-*Fernlane*; **PAN YARD** (Ko) ex-*Fernleaf*

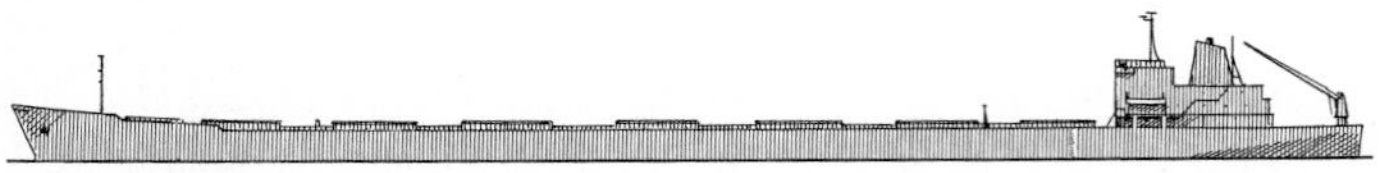

185 M^2FR *H1*
SEARADIANCE HK/Br (Sunderland) 1977; B; 38,412 grt/71,733 dwt; 228.12 × 14.05 m *(748.43 × 46.1 ft)*; M (Doxford); 15 kts; ex-*Orient City*
Sister: **ALBACORE** (Bs) ex-*Welsh City*

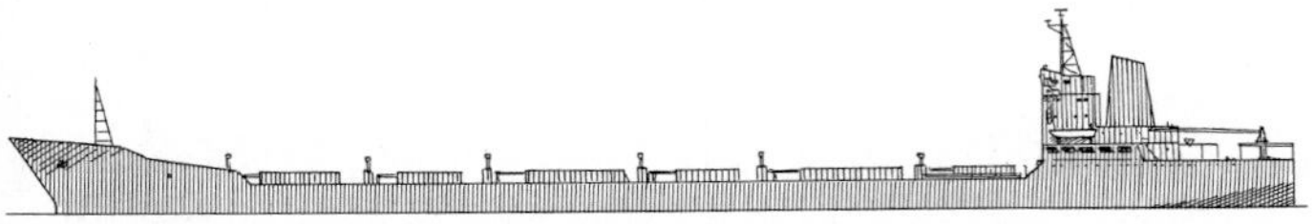

186 M^2FR *H13*
FEDRA Cy/Bz (Emaq) 1977; B; 22,094 grt/38,465 dwt; 193.86 × 10.9 m *(636.02 × 35.76 ft)*; M (Sulzer); 15 kts; ex-*Rio Verde*
Sister: **RIO NEGRO** (Bz); Sisters (superstructure extended aft): **RIO BRANCO** (Bz); **VORIOS IPIROS HELLAS** (Gr) ex-*Rio Grande*

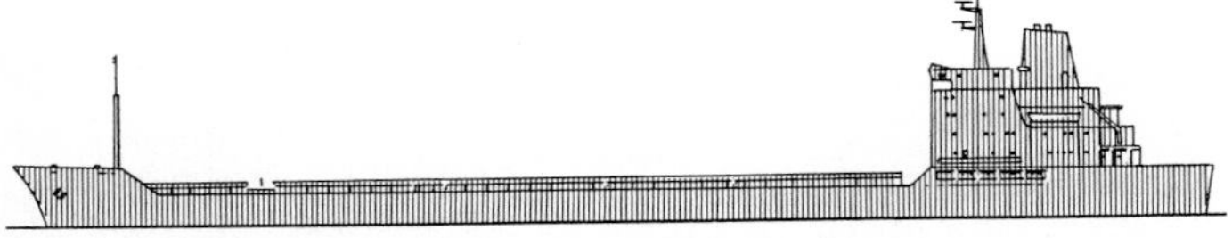

187 M^2FS *H13*
WADAG Ml/Br (Swan Hunter) 1980; B; 11,632 grt/16,753 dwt; 158.73 × 8.38 m *(521 × 27.49 ft)*; M (B&W); 14.75 kts; ex-*Kopalnia Siersza*; May be fitted with three cranes

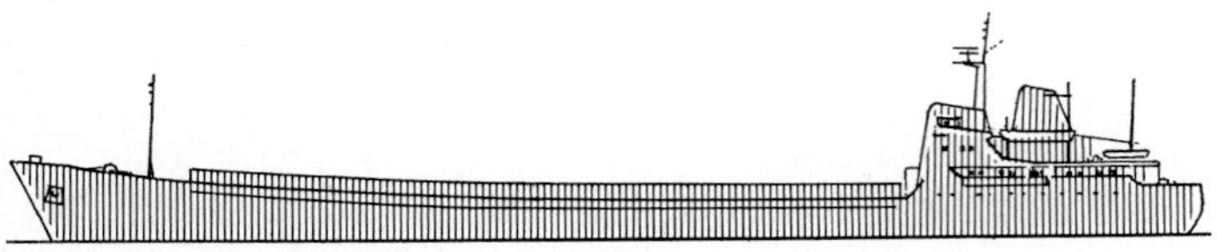

188 M^2F-M^2 *H13*
BASE WIND Ma/Ru (Navashinskiy) 1970; O; 3,688 grt/4,300 dwt; 123.53 × 4.80 m *(405 × 15.75 ft)*; TSM (Russkiy); 11.25 kts; ex-*Volnogorsk*; Hot ore carrier
Sisters: **GRIFO** (It) ex-*Arshintsevo*; **ARISTOPES** (SV) ex-*Azovstal*; **MAKAR MAZAY** (Uk); **CARENA** (It) ex-*Stepan Markyelov*; Sister (now converted to container ship): **YENAKIYEVO** (Uk)

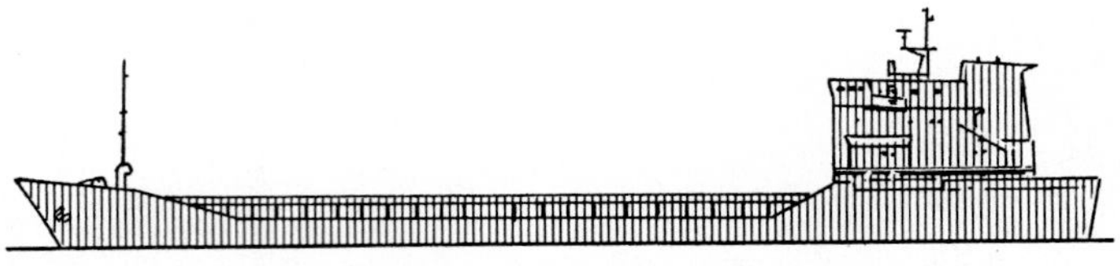

189 M^2F-S *H13*
MIELEC Ml/Br (Govan) 1980; B; 3,127 grt/4,456 dwt; 95 × 6.05 m *(312 × 19.85 ft)*; M (Sulzer); 13.5 kts
Sisters: **WARKA** (Ml) (builder—Scotstoun); **MALBORK II** (Ml); **GOLENIOW** (Ml) (builder—Ailsa); **BYTOM** (Ml) (builder—Robb Caledon)

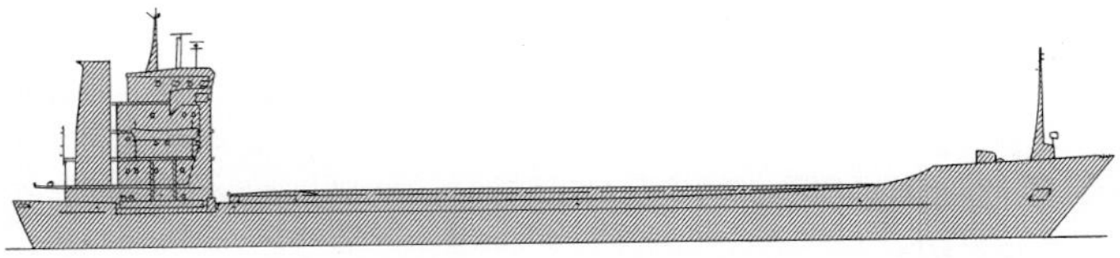

190 M^2G *H1*
ANGLIA Cy/FRG (Husumer) 1977; C/Con; 3,160 grt/3,732 dwt; 95.28 × 5.89 m *(312.60 × 19.32 ft)*; M (Deutz); 14.5 kts; ex-*Baldur*; 218 TEU

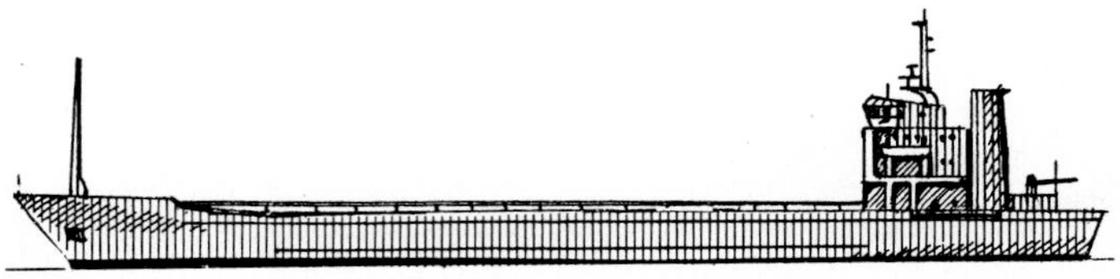

191 M^2G *H1*
CARI SKY Cy/FRG (Husumer) 1976; C/Con; 3,307 grt/3,900 dwt; 100.28 × 5.56 m *(329 × 18.24 ft)*; M (Atlas-MaK); 14 kts; ex-*Kaethe Johanna*; 218 TEU

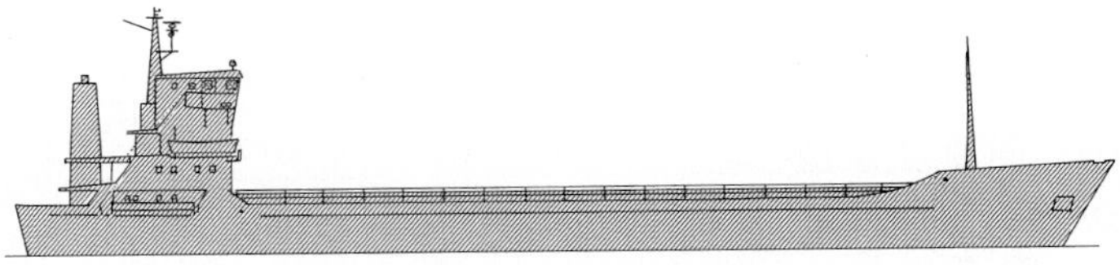

192 M^2G *H1*
LANDWIND At/Ne ('Hoogezand' JB) 1974; C; 2,592 grt/2,750 dwt; 87.89 × 4.85 m *(288.35 × 15.91 ft)*; M (KHD); 14 kts; ex-*Annika*; May be fitted with two deck-cranes; 184 TEU

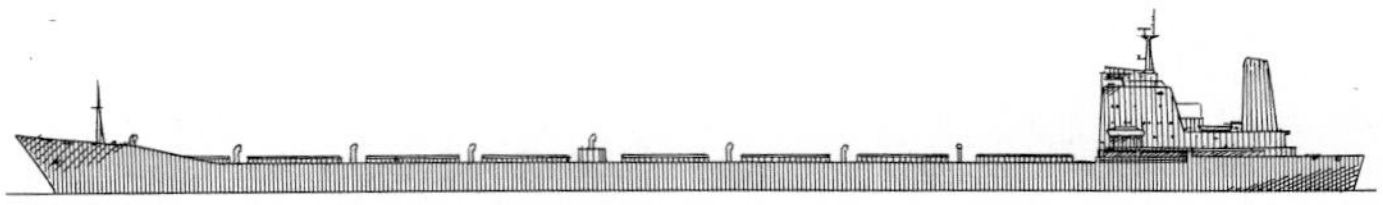

193 M^2G *H1*
ZOYA KOSMODEMYANSKAYA Uk/Ru (Okean) 1973; B; 30,070 grt/ 49,999 dwt; 215.37 × 11.73 m *(706.59 × 38.48 ft)*; M (B&W); 15.7 kts
Sisters: **ALEKSANDR MATROSOV** (Uk); **ION SOLTYS** (Uk) (small crane amidships; others may also have this); **IZGUTTY AYTYKOV** (Uk); **PARFENTIY GRECHANVYY** (Uk); **UNAN AVETISYAN** (Uk) (small crane amidships); Similar: **BULGARIA** (Bu); **RODINA** (Bu) (small crane amidships)

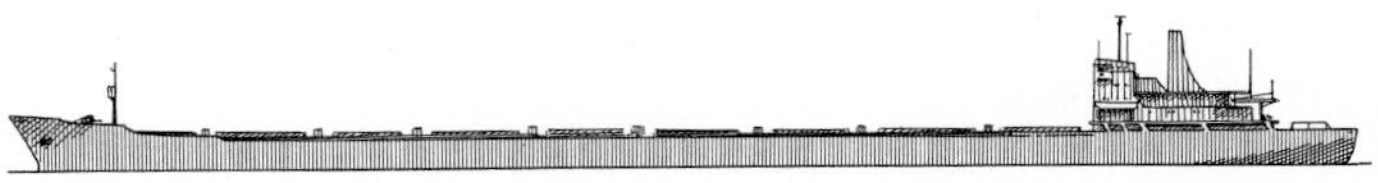

194 M^2GM *H1*
DAMODAR KAVERI In/FRG (Rhein Nordseew) 1974; B; 31,612 grt/ 65,343 dwt; 229.12 × 12.57 m *(751.71 × 41.24 ft)*; M (MAN); 15.25 kts; ex-*Damodar General T J Park*
Sister: **SEA SKY** (Ma) ex-*Jalvallabh*

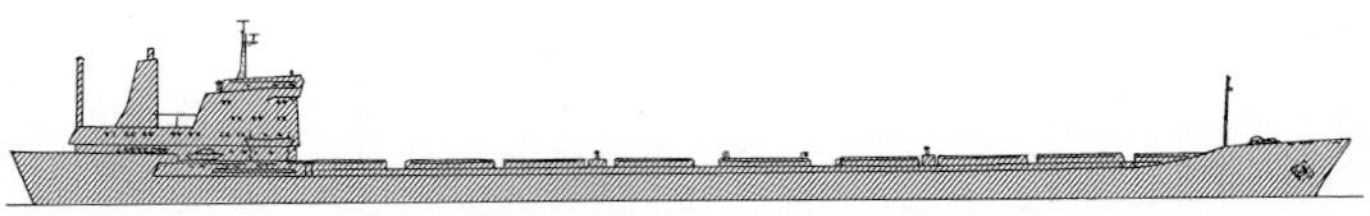

195 M^2GN *H13*
JIMILTA Ma/Pd (Szczecinska) 1974; B; 20,344 grt/31,881 dwt; 198.76 × 10.65 m *(652.10 × 34.94 ft)*; M (Sulzer); 15 kts; ex-*Bratislava*; 'B447' type
Sister: **TRINEC** (Cz)

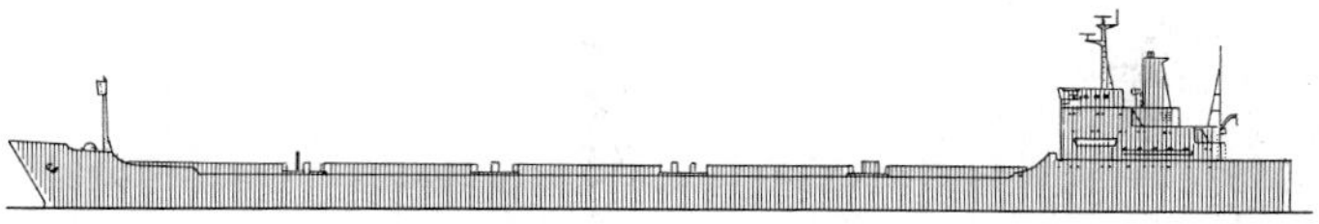

196 M^2GN *H13*
CHUSOVOY Cy/Bz (Caneco) 1981; B; 23,536 grt/37,483 dwt; 200.92 × 10.77 m *(659.19 × 35.33 ft)*; M (B&W); 15.25 kts; ex-*Doceorion*
Sisters: **CHKALOVSK** (Cy) ex-*Cyrena*; Sisters (some may be geared and some may have single funnel): **TUPI ANGRA** (Bz) ex-*Ana Torrealba*; **DA YU SHAN** (RC) ex-*Voluta*; **FORUM PRODUCT** (Cy) ex-*Rafaela*; **TUPI BUZIOS** (Bz) ex-*Arabela*; **MERCANTIL NITEROI** (Bz) ex-*Zuleika Borges*; **NORSUL IPU** (Bz) ex-*Docevega*; **FORUM CHEMIST** (Cy) ex-*Daniela*; **MACEDONIA HELLAS** (Gr) ex-*Docevirgo* (may have four cranes)

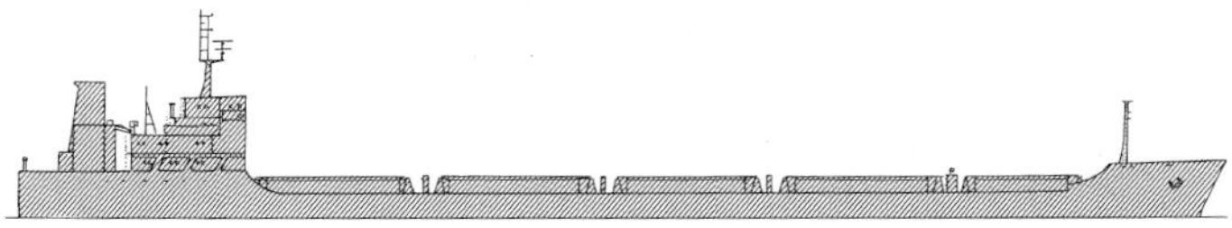

197 M^3CF *H13*
NORSUL TUBARAO Bz/Bz (Caneco) 1985; B/Con; 15,319 grt/27,911 dwt; 174.91 × 10.28 m *(573.85 × 33.73 ft)*; M (Sulzer); 14 kts; 522 TEU

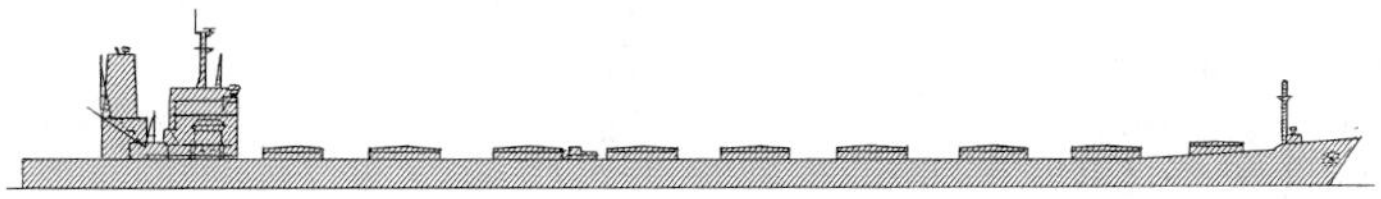

198 M^3CFM *H*
JAPAN PLATANUS Ja/Ja (IHI) 1987; B; 77,871 grt/149,986 dwt; 283.50 × 15.92 m *(930.12 × 52.23 ft)*; M (Sulzer); 13.30 kts

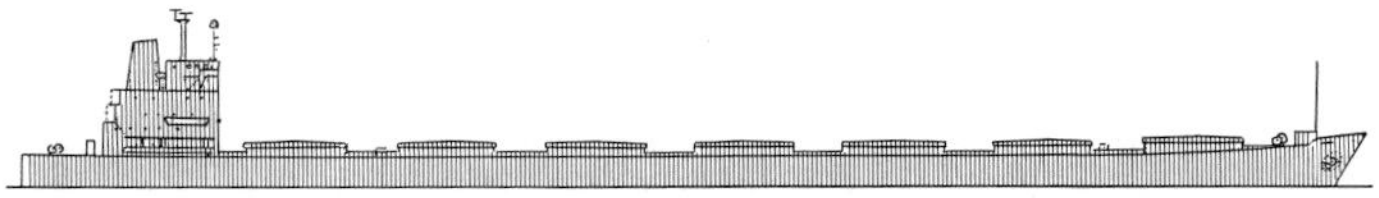

199 M^3F *H*
CIELO ESTA Pa/Ja (Sanoyas Corp) 1988; B; 36,520 grt/70,227 dwt; 225.00 × 13.30 m *(738.19 × 43.64 ft)*; M (Mitsubishi); 14 kts; ex-*West Point*; '70 BC' type
Sisters: **WESTERN TRADER** (Pi); **HAVBOR** (NIS) ex-*Malaya*; Probable sisters (some may be M^2F—see entry number 5/52. Some built by Sumitomo): **NORTH COUNTESS** (Gr) ex-*Louisiana Rainbow*; **ORIANA** (Pi); **ENERGY PIONEER** (HK); **ROYAL PILOT** (Pi); **DYNASTY** (Pa); **BESTORE** (Br) ex-*Bestor*; **GRAN TRADER** (Pi); **PACIFIC NOVA** (Pa)

200 M^3F *H*
HOKKAIDO STAR Pa/Ja (NKK) 1972; O; 85,899 grt/167,698 dwt; 295 × 17.01 m *(967.85 × 55.81 ft)*; M (Sulzer); 15.25 kts; ex-*Kohjusan Maru*

201 M^3F *H*
JASMINE Ko/Ko (Samsung) 1987; B; 95,748 grt/188,334 dwt; 291.40 × 18.03 m *(956.04 × 59.15 ft)*; M (B&W); 13 kts
Possible sister: **HANJIN SYDNEY** (Ko) ex-*Westin Nine*

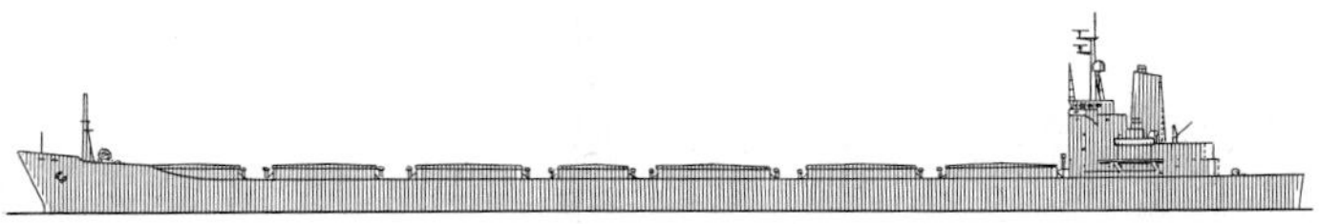

202 M^3FC *H1*
TITUS No/Ja (Tsuneishi) 1981; B; 37,323 grt/62,180 dwt; 228 × 12.33 m *(748.03 × 40.45 ft)*; M (MAN); 15.25 kts; ex-*Santa Vitoria Maru*
Probably similar: **EL HADJAR** (Ag) ex-*Orion Maru*; **MIHALIS P** (Gr) ex-*Oak Glory*; **SEORAX** (Pa) ex-*Miyagi Maru*; **TAI CHANG** (Pa) ex-*Panther*; **MADONNA LILY** (Pi) ex-*Santa Amelia Maru*; **ATLANTIC SAVIOR** (Gr) ex-*Tensho Maru*; **POLAR STAR** (Pi) ex-*Kinushima Maru*; **IRENE OLDENDORFF** (HK) ex-*Santa Teresa Maru*

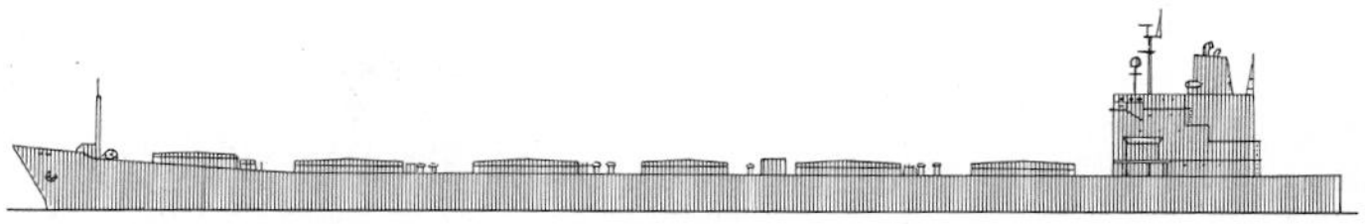

203 M^3FM *H*
ASIA UNION Pa/Ja (Mitsubishi HI) 1981; B; 43,651 grt/80,346 dwt; 227.60 × 13.63 m *(746.72 × 44.72 ft)*; M (MAN); 14.25 kts; ex-*Shoho Maru*
Sister: **SAIKAI MARU** (Ja)

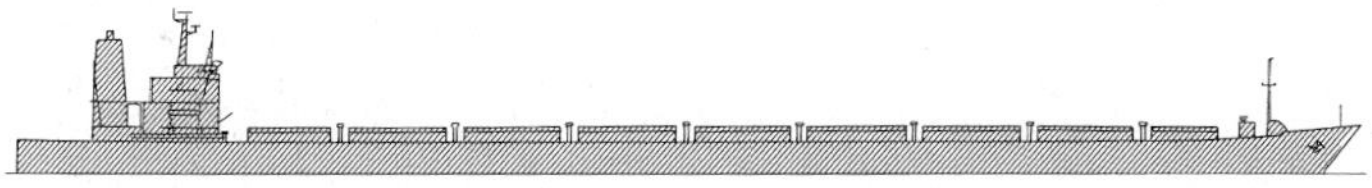

204 M^3FM *H*
CHINA STEEL TEAM Tw/Tw (China SB) 1984; B; 80,280 grt/131,333 dwt; 289.01 × 15.00 m *(948.20 × 49.21 ft)*; M (Sulzer); 14.75 kts
Sister: **CHINA STEEL ENTREPRENEUR** (Tw); Probably similar (fewer hatches): **CHINA STEEL INNOVATOR** (Tw); **CHINA STEEL REALIST** (Tw)

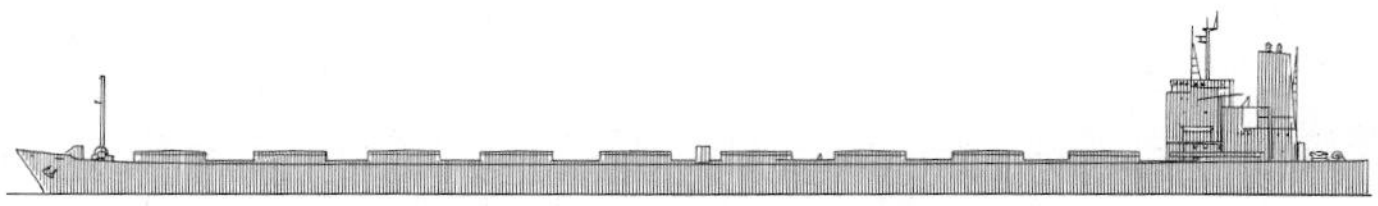

205 M^3FM *H*
JOYFUL SPIRIT Pa/Ja (Kawasaki) 1981; B; 74,449 grt/145,736 dwt; 280.02 × 16.98 m *(918.7 × 55.71 ft)*; M (MAN); 13 kts; ex-*Yashirokawa Maru*

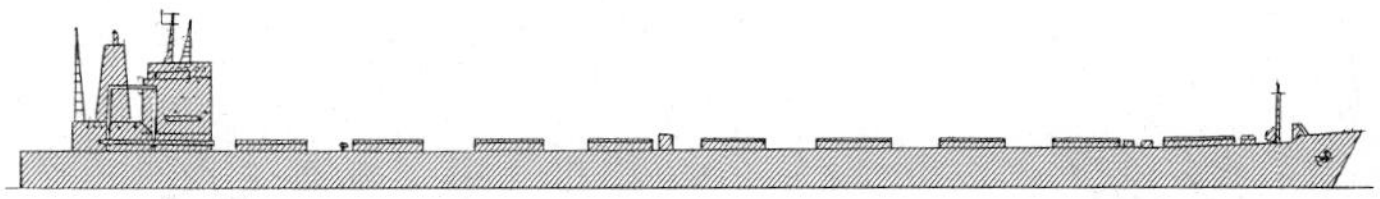

206 M^3FM *H*
KAMIKAWA MARU Ja/Ja (Kawasaki) 1986; B; 77,269 grt/149,532 dwt; 270.01 × 17.33 m *(885.86 × 56.86 ft)*; M (B&W); 13 kts

207 M^3FM *H*
KARTAL 4 Tu/Ja (NKK) 1974; B; 67,914 grt/131,260 dwt; 260 × 16.79 m *(853.02 × 55.09 ft)*; M (B&W); 15 kts; ex-*D C Coleman*
Sisters: **RIVER PLATE** (Pa) ex-*W M Neal*; **OCEANIC MINDORO** (Pi) ex-*Oceanic Crest*

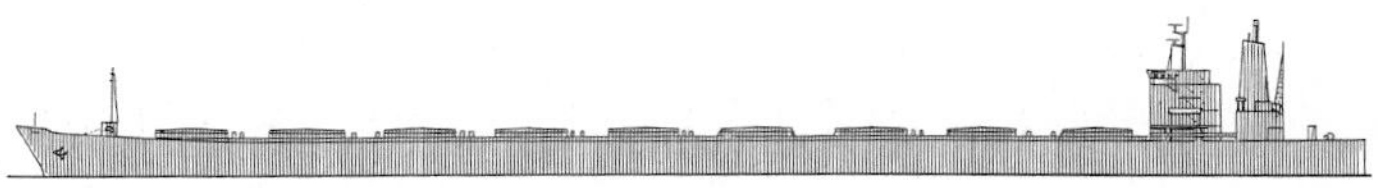

208 M^3FM *H*
LEOPARDI Li/Ja (Mitsui) 1982; B; 67,727 grt/129,088 dwt; 263.02 × 16.48 m *(863 × 54.07 ft)*; M (B&W); 14.5 kts; ex-*New Venture*
Sisters: **THALASSINI AVRA** (Gr) ex-*Kepwave*; **CATHERINE VENTURE** (Li); **PRIMO** (Li) ex-*Coal Venture*

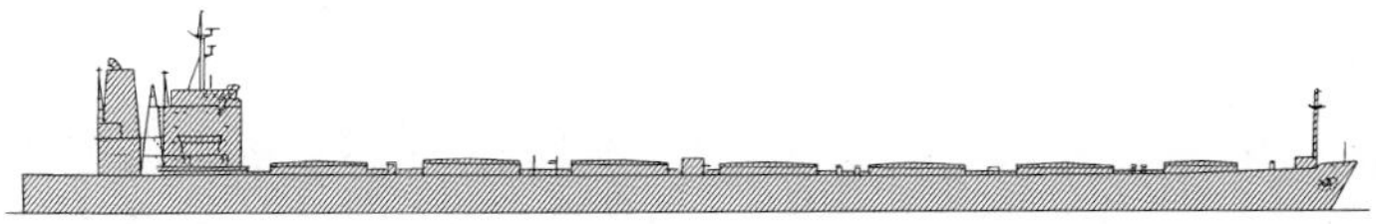

209 M^3FM *H*
PINA PRIMA Br/Ja (Sumitomo) 1984; B; 36,009 grt/68,405 dwt; 222.00 × 13.20 m *(728.35 × 43.31 ft)*; M (Sulzer); 15.5 kts; ex-*Pina*
Possibly similar: **THEONYMPHOS** (Gr) ex-*Pegasus Maru*

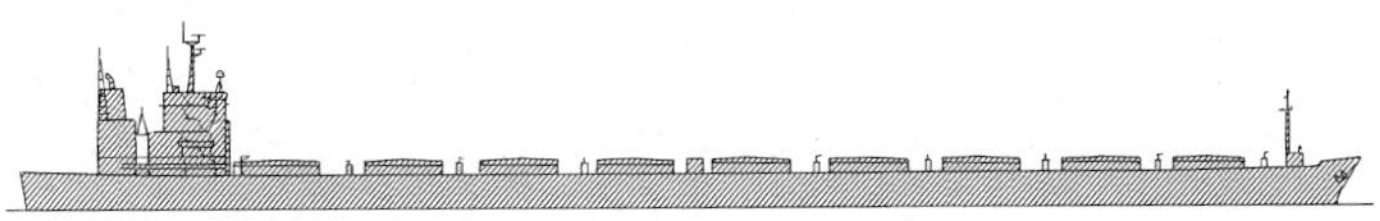

210 M^3FM *H*
SHINREI Pa/Ja (Mitsubishi HI) 1987; B; 76,324 grt/146,019 dwt; 268.00 × 17.30 m *(879.27 × 56.76 ft)*; M (Sulzer); 13.5 kts; ex-*Shinrei Maru*

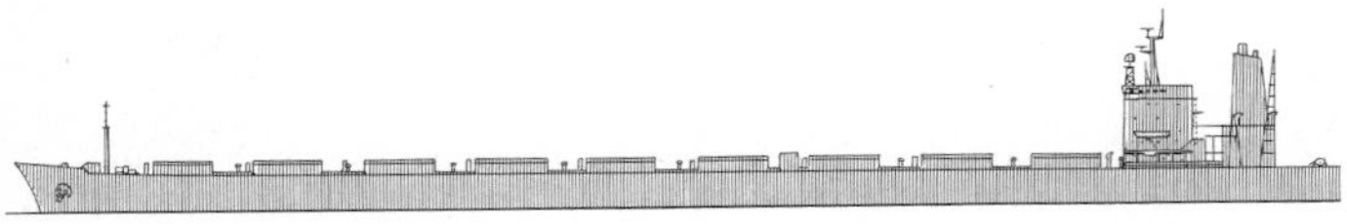

211 M^{3}FM *H*

SINGAPORE ACE Pa/Ja (Hitachi) 1982; B; 74,662 grt/133,082 dwt; 270 × 16.3 m *(886 × 53.48 ft)*; M (B&W); 13.3 kts; ex-*River Ace*

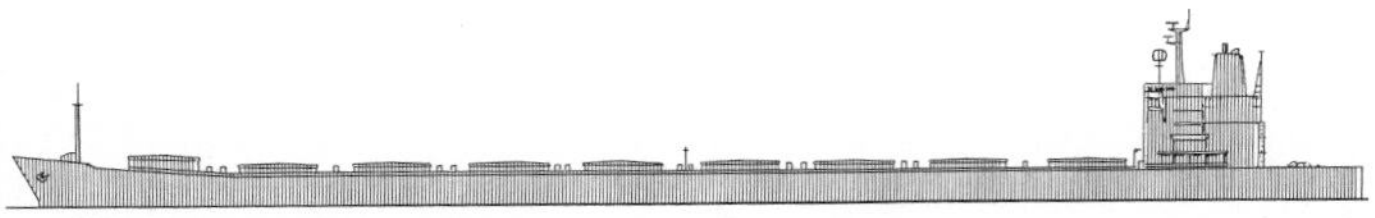

212 M^{3}FM *H*

VOYAGER Pa/Ja (Mitsubishi HI) 1982; B; 55,936 grt/94,994 dwt; 257.8 × 12.63 m *(846 × 41.44 ft)*; M (MAN); 13.3 kts; ex-*Sakaide Maru*

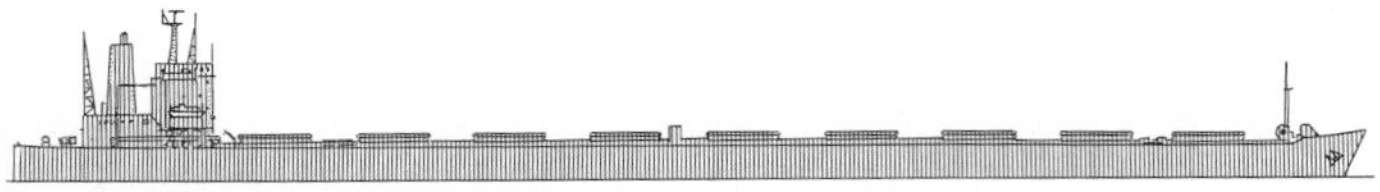

213 M^{3}FM *H*

YORK HK/Tw (China SB) 1990; B; 77,113 grt/149,503 dwt; 270 × 17.33 m *(885.83 × 56.86 ft)*; M (B&W); 13.5 kts
Possible sisters: **CAPE AFRICA** (Tw); **CAPE AMERICA** (Tw); **CAPE ASIA** (Tw); **CAPE AUSTRALIA** (Tw); **CAPE CATHAY** (Tw); **CAPE EUROPE** (Tw); **CAPE LILA** (Pi); **CAPE OCEANIA** (Tw); **CHINA ACT** (Tw); **CHINA FORTUNE** (Tw); **CHINA TRANSPORT** (Tw); **CHOU SHAN** (Tw); **DONAU ORE** (Tw) ex-*Wah Shan*; **TAI SHAN** (Tw); **WATERFORD** (HK)

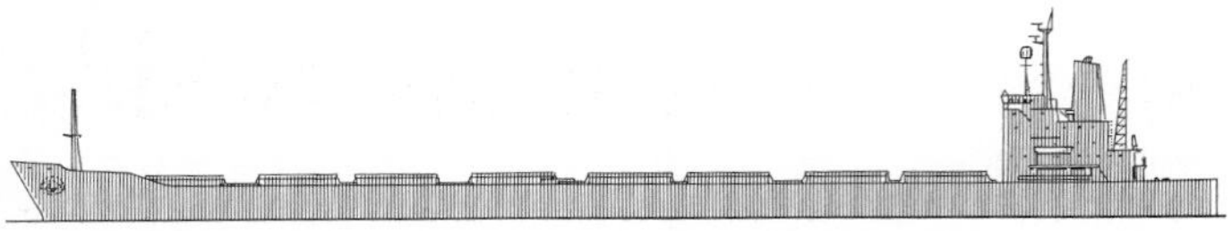

214 M^{3}FM *H1*

GLOBAL EPOCH HK/Ja (Tsuneishi) 1982; B; 42,627 grt/71,119 dwt; 228 × 12.53 m *(748 × 41.11 ft)*; M (MAN); 14.5 kts; ex-*Kurotakisan Maru*

215 M^{3}FM *H1*

PORT TALBOT Pa/Ja (Hitachi) 1970; O; 42,405 grt/81,612 dwt; 250.02 × 13.31 m *(820.28 × 43.67 ft)*; M (B&W); 15.25 kts; ex-*Kakogawa Maru*

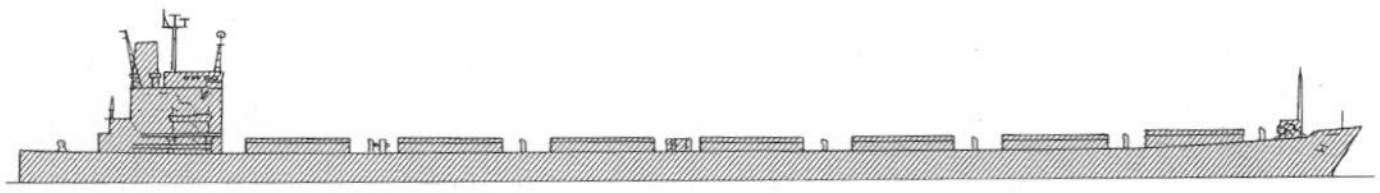

216 M^{3}FMC *H*

ORANGE PHOENIX Pa/Ja (Tsuneishi) 1986; B; 36,537 grt/69,561 dwt; 225.00 × 13.26 m *(738.19 × 43.50 ft)*; M (B&W); 14.5 kts
Probable sisters (some built by Hashihama): **MARIPOSA** (Pi) ex-*Mikasa*; **ANTONIS I ANGELICOUSSIS** (Gr); **KOSTRENA** (Ma); **EL FLAMENCO** (Gr); **MASS SUCCESS** (Pa) ex-*Channel Fortune*; **MASS WITS** (Pa) ex-*Allante*; **MILAMORES** (Pi); **PRESIDENT G** (Gr) ex-*Sindia*; **TORM MARINA** (DIS); **TORM TEKLA** (DIS); **YICK KAM** (Li) ex-*El Bravo*; Sisters (builder—Hashihama): **STELLAR VENUS** (Pa) ex-*Kumasachi Maru*; **HALLA ENDEAVOR** (Ko) ex-*Oriental Venus*; Possible sisters (builder—Hashihama): **DAITEN** (Va) ex-*Daiten Maru*; **TORM GERD** (DIS); **SCENERY SEA** (Pa) ex-*Channel Navigator*; **AEGEAN STAR** (Pi); **FULL SOURCES** (HK); **FULL SPRING** (HK); Possible sisters (builder—Tsuneishi): **NAVIOS MARINER** (Pi); **MASS ENTERPRISE** (Pa); **MASS GLORY** (Pa); **MASS MERIT** (Pa); **MASS PROSPERITY** (Pa); **OCEANIC STAR** (Pi); **RUBIN ENERGY** (Pi); **RIO VERDE** (Pi); **GLOBAL STAR** (Pa); **CHUNGJIN** (Pa)

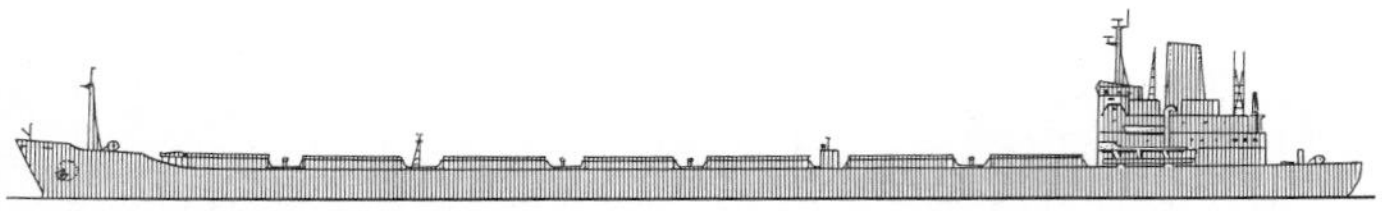

217 M^{3}FMC *H1*

TITIAN JAYA My/Ja (Koyo) 1982; B; 34,433 grt/61,769 dwt; 222.13 × 13.02 m *(729 × 42.72 ft)*; M (B&W); 14.75 kts; ex-*Miyajima Maru*
Possible sisters: **PILOT** (Bs) ex-*World Carmen Romano*; **MERCHANT PRELUDE** (Bs) ex-*Young Shinko*; **C MEHMET** (Tu) ex-*United Approach*; **NOSTOS T** (Gr) ex-*Bulk Venture*

218 M^{3}FN *H*

GERANIOS STYLIANOS —/Ja (Mitsui) 1974; O; 61,549 grt/115,976 dwt; 259.39 × 16.13 m *(851.02 × 52.92 ft)*; M (B&W); 15 kts; ex-*Sevenseas Conqueror*
Similar: **FORUM CAPE** (Cy) ex-*Chihirosan Maru*

219 M^{3}FN *H*

SLURRY EXPRESS Li/Ja (Hitachi) 1978; B (Slurry); 65,210 grt/125,180 dwt; 240.52 × 17.04 m *(821.92 × 55.91 ft)*; M (Sulzer); 13.5 kts

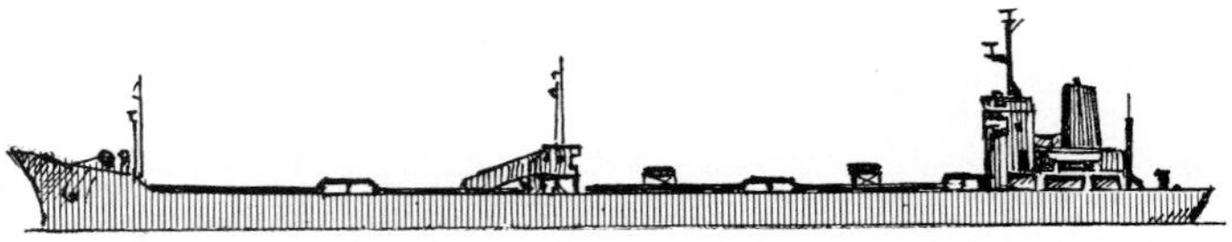

220 M^{3}FN *H1*

KIMITSU MARU Ja/Ja (Nipponkai) 1971; O; 10,741 grt/17,000 dwt; 136.18 × 8.28 m *(446.78 × 27.17 ft)*; M (IHI); 13 kts; Limestone carrier
Sister: **UCO XX** (Bn) ex-*Kimitetsu Maru*

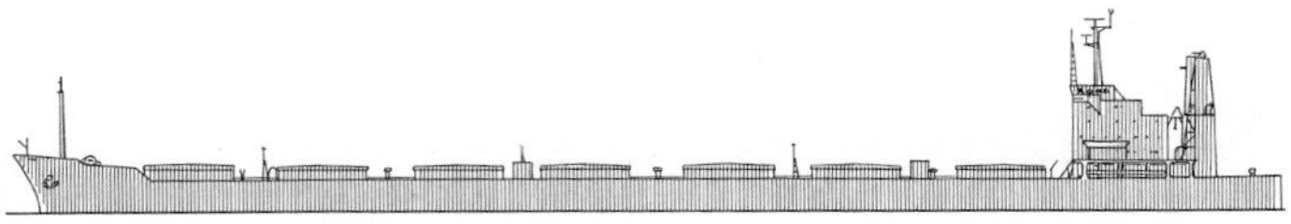

221 M^{3}F-M *H1*

THALIA Gr/Ja (Hitachi) 1982; B; 35,370 grt/64,135 dwt; 224.52 × 12.96 m *(737 × 42.52 ft)*; M (B&W); 15 kts; ex-*Maritime Baron*
Similar: **ASCONA** (Gr)

222 M^{3}G *H13*

RAFNES Cy/No (Kleven) 1976; B; 3,845 grt/6,258 dwt; 103.56 × 6.86 m *(339.68 × 22.50 ft)*; M (Normo); 13.5 kts; **SIMILAR TO DRAWING NUMBER 5/9**
Sisters: **RADNES** (Br); **RISNES** (Cy) ex-*Ronnes*; **EUROPEAN 1** (Pa) ex-*Ramnes*; **SAINT BREVIN** (Pa) ex-*Refsnes*; **SAINT BRICE** (Pa) ex-*Rossnes*; **NORNES** (Ma) ex-*Riknes*

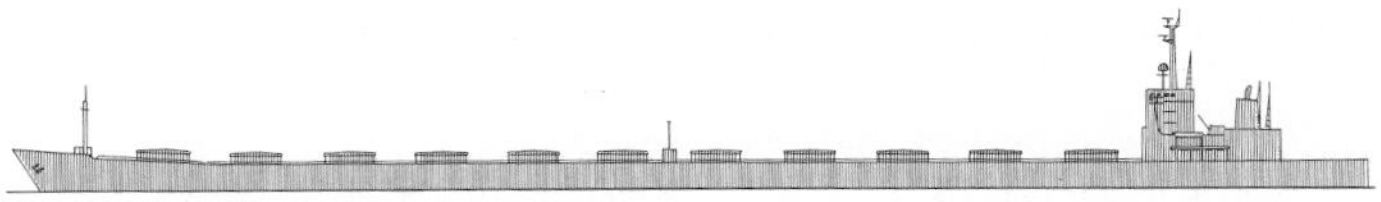

223 M^{4}DGM^2 *H*

SHIN-HOH Pa/Ja (Mitsubishi HI) 1982; B; 106,771 grt/208,952 dwt; 314.99 × 18.3 m *(1033.43 × 60.04 ft)*; M (Mitsubishi); 12.5 kts; ex-*Shinho Maru*

224 M^{4}F *H*

FINIX Gr/Sw (Gotav) 1976; B; 64,655 grt/123,125 dwt; 267.6 × 16.45 m *(877.95 × 53.97 ft)*; M (B&W); 16 kts; ex-*Montcalm*
Similar: **PU NING HAI** (RC) ex-*World Star*

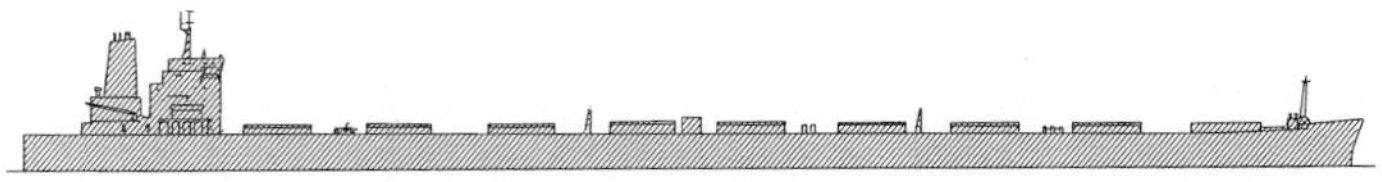

225 M^{4}F *H*

MINERAL ZULU HK/Ko (Hyundai) 1986; B; 87,709 grt/170,698 dwt; 290.00 × 17.55 m *(951.44 × 57.58 ft)*; M (B&W); 13 kts
Sister: **MINERAL EUROPE** (HK); Probable sister: **BELVAL** (Lu)

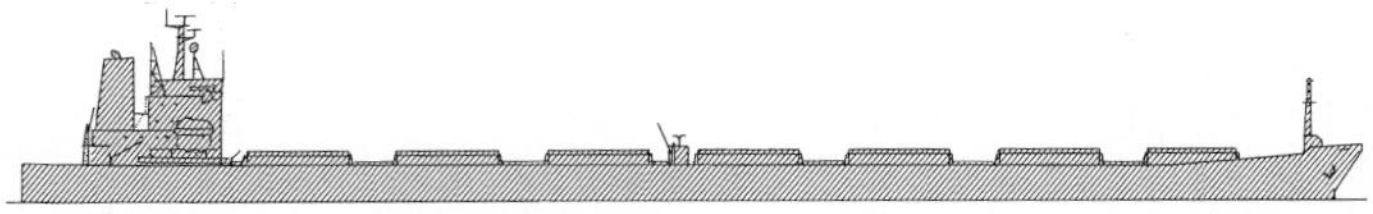

226 M^{4}FC *H*

ANANGEL VENTURE Gr/Ja (NKK) 1989; B; 36,781 grt/69,406 dwt; 225.00 × 13.27 m *(738.19 × 43.54 ft)*; M (Sulzer); 13.5 kts; ex-*Channel Enterprise*
Probable sister: **ANANGEL PROGRESS** (Gr) ex-*Channel Express*; Similar: **NORTHERN ENTERPRISE** (Br); **IOS** (Gr); **ALAM BARU** (My)

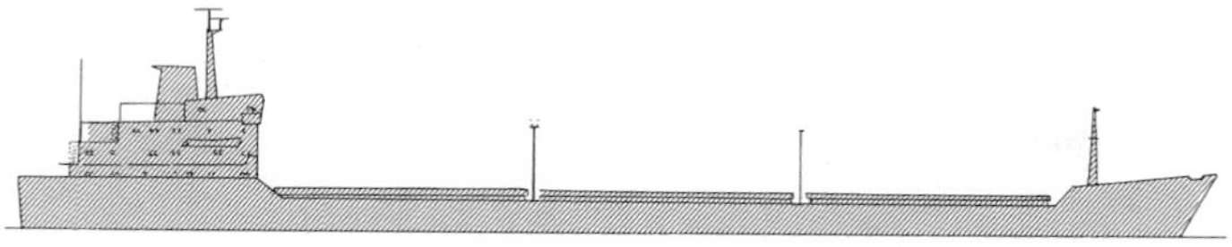

227 M^4FM *H13*
NORDEN Fi/FRG (Schuerenstedt) 1976; B; 7,764 grt/10,935 dwt; 143.31 × 7.57 m *(470.18 × 24.84 ft)*; M (MaK); 14.5 kts; ex-*Rautaruukki*
Probable sister: **MADZY** (Sw) ex-*Kuurtanes*

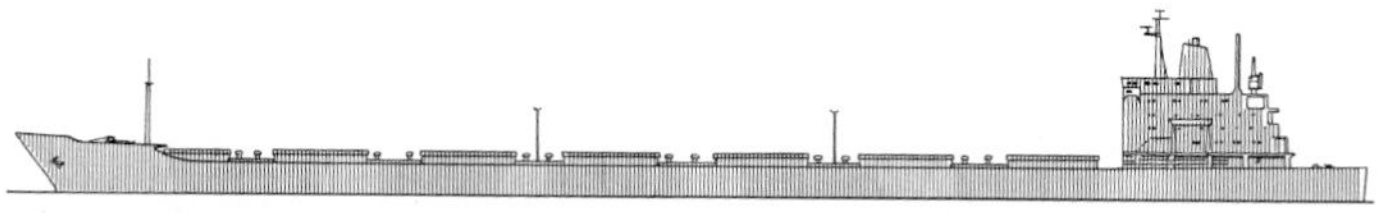

228 M^4FMC *H1*
BELCHATOW Pd/Ja (Mitsubishi HI) 1976; B; 40,030 grt/71,277 dwt; 232.37 × 13.85 m *(762 × 45.44 ft)*; M (Sulzer); 14.5 kts
Sister: **LAKE AVERY** (Ml) ex-*Turoszow*

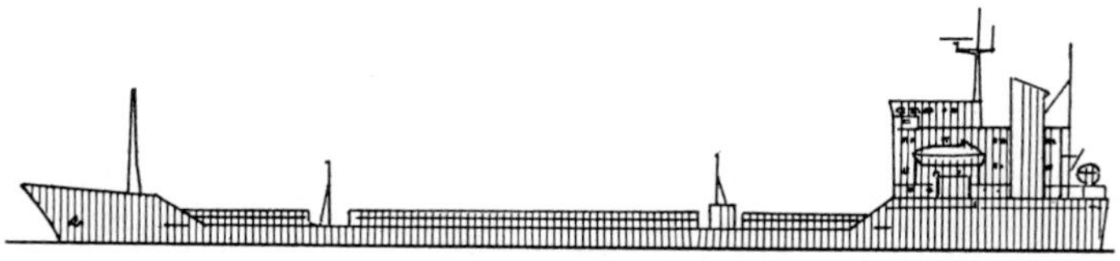

229 M^4G *H13*
GARNES Pa/No (Storviks) 1980/83; C; 3,967 grt/6,156 dwt; 107.02 × 6.49 m *(351.12 × 21.29 ft)*; M (Stork-Werkspoor); 13.5 kts; Lengthened 1983 (Fosen)
Sisters: **KORSNES** (Pa); **RAMNES** (Cy) ex-*Raknes*

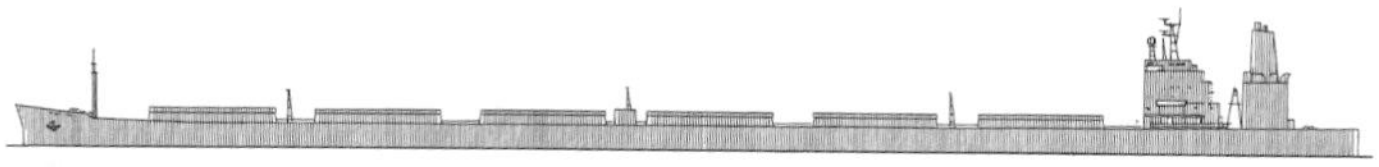

230 M^5F *H*
HITACHI VENTURE Li/Ja (Hitachi) 1982; O; 129,077 grt/267,889 dwt; 324.1 × 20.47 m *(1063 × 67.16 ft)*; M (B&W); 14.3 kts

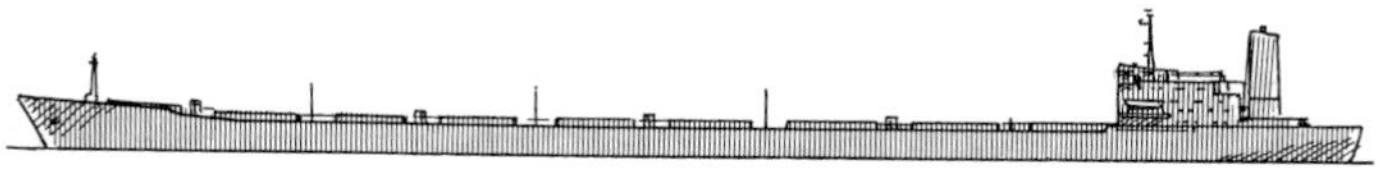

231 M^5F *H*
MACTRADER Cy/FRG (Flender) 1974; B; 44,084 grt/79,760 dwt; 260.79 × 14.2 m *(855.61 × 46.59 ft)*; M (B&W); 16.5 kts; ex-*Malmland*
Sister: **MIAN ZHU HAI** (RC) ex-*Ferroland*

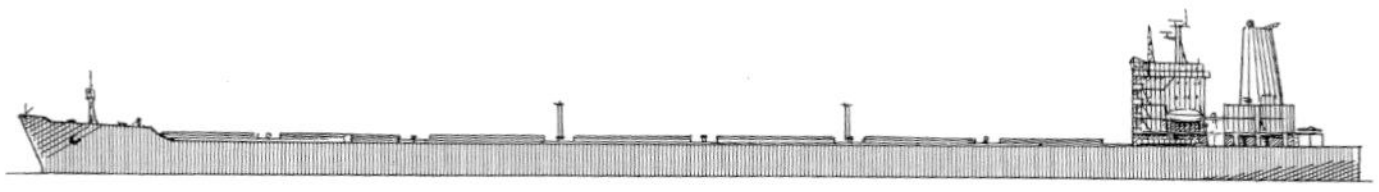

232 M^5F *H1*
DORIC CASTLE Gr/Ja (Mitsui) 1976; B; 43,393 grt/77,827 dwt; 239.05 × 14 m *(784.28 × 45.93 ft)*; M (B&W); 15.2 kts; ex-*Thorsdrake*

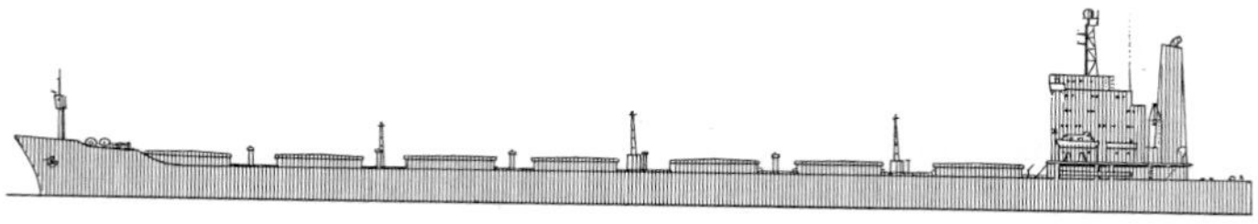

233 M^5F *H1*
PETRA Gr/Ja (Hitachi) 1981; B; 35,722 grt/64,848 dwt; 224.52 × 12.4 m *(737 × 40.68 ft)*; M (Sulzer); 15 kts; ex-*Jaraconda*
Sister: **MENITES** (Gr) ex-*Jasaka*

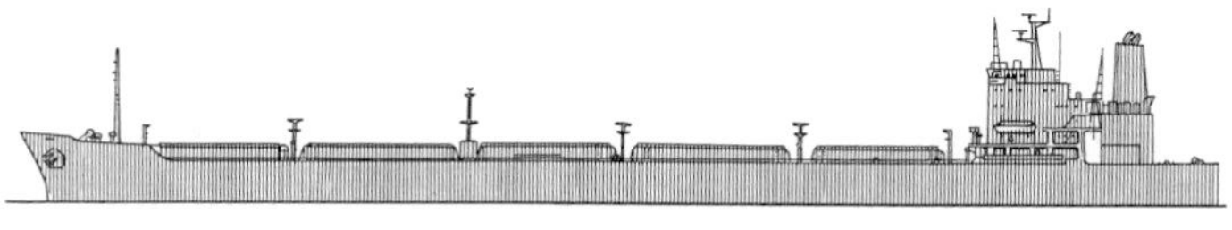

234 M^5F *H1*
SENTINEL II Li/Ja (Hitachi) 1982; B; 34,353 grt/47,503 dwt; 209 × 11 m *(686 × 36.09 ft)*; M (B&W); — kts; Caustic Soda carrier

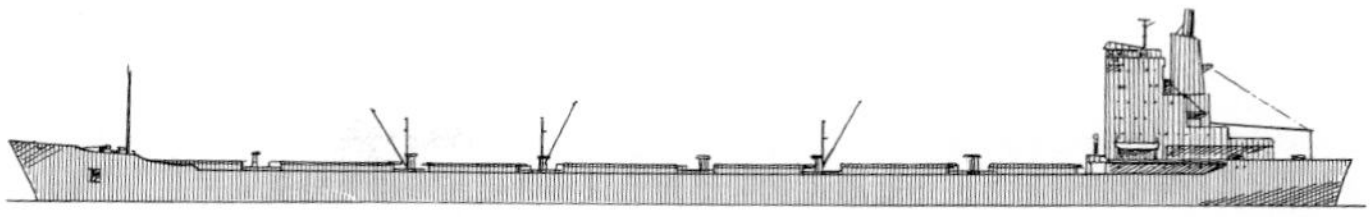

235 M^5F *H13*
STAR PETER Cy/De (B&W) 1974; B; 30,332 grt/52,327 dwt; 221.75 × 12.09 m *(727.53 × 39.67 ft)*; M (B&W); 16 kts; ex-*Milles*

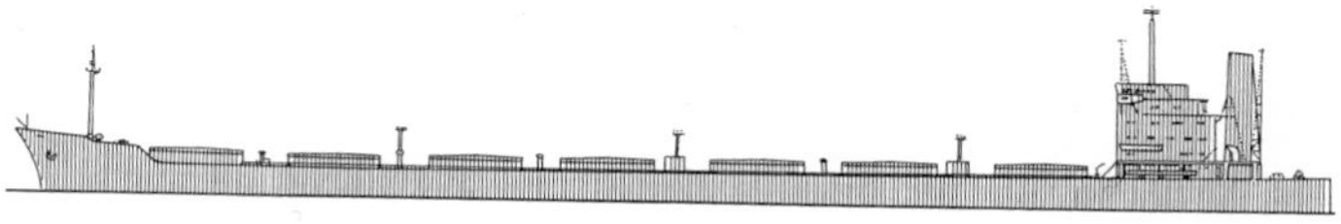

236 M^5HFN *H1*
EKTOR Cy/Ja (Hitachi) 1981; B; 35,911 grt/64,285 dwt; 224.52 × 12.96 m *(737 × 42.52 ft)*; M (B&W); 17.5 kts; ex-*Maersk Sentosa*
Sisters: **M G TSANGARIS** (Gr) ex-*Maersk Sebarok*; **BERNADETTE T** (Gr) ex-*Maersk Seletar*

237 M^6FM *H1*
ORFEAS Cy/Ja (Mitsubishi HI) 1973; B; 64,355 grt/120,143 dwt; 261.02 × 16.5 m *(856.36 × 54.13 ft)*; M (Sulzer); 15 kts; ex-*Erskine Bridge*

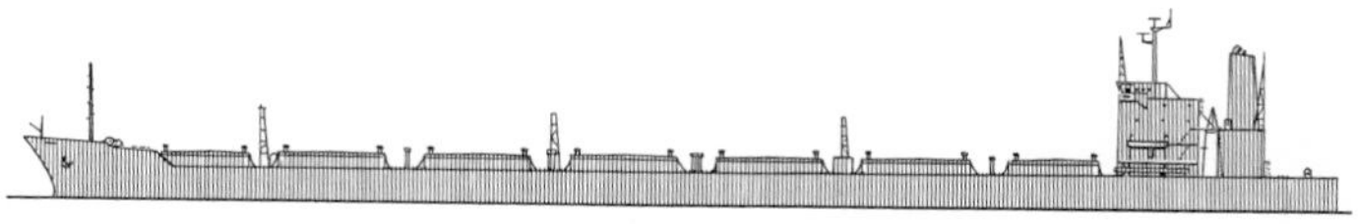

238 M^6FM *H1*
OTTERPOOL Bs/Ja (Hitachi) 1982; B; 35,750 grt/64,592 dwt; 225 × 12.4 m *(738 × 40.68 ft)*; M (B&W); 15 kts; ex-*Pacer*; 'Hitachi Panamax Mk II' type

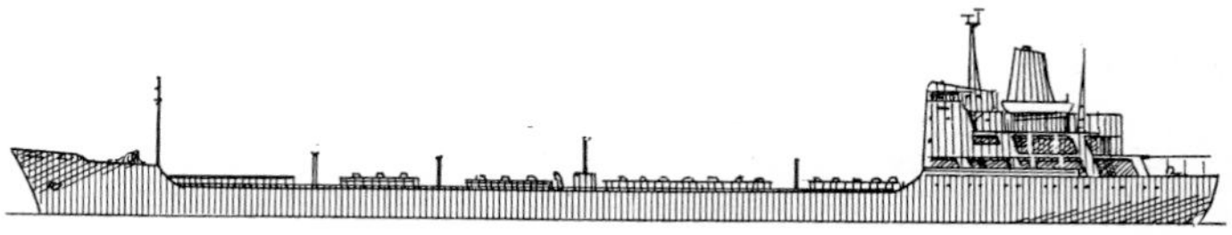

239 M^6FM *H13*
MUSALA Bu/Ja (Hitachi) 1967; B; 8,692 grt/14,030 dwt; 139.83 × 9.26 m *(458.76 × 30.38 ft)*; M (B&W); 14 kts
Sisters: **RUEN** (Bu); **VEJEN** (Bu)

240 M^6FN *H1*
DIAMOND SEA Ma/FRG (B+V) 1976; B; 74,966 grt/139,346 dwt; 282.07 × 16.43 m *(925.43 × 53.9 ft)*; M (B&W); 15 kts; ex-*Australian Prospector*
Sister: **TREASURE SEA** (Pa) ex-*Australian Progress*

241 M^6FN *H1*
THALIS OF MILITOS Cy/FRG (A G 'Weser') 1971; B; 73,652 grt/139,854 dwt; 282.23 × 16.42 m *(925.95 × 53.87 ft)*; M (B&W); 15.75 kts; ex-*Jacob Russ*

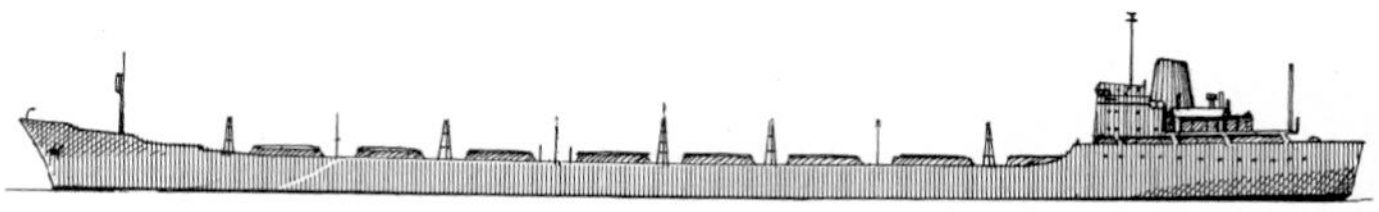

242 M^7FM *H13*
TIAN SHUI HAI RC/FRG (Bremer V) 1964; B; 23,073 grt/42,843 dwt; 214.18 × 11.63 m *(702.69 × 38.16 ft)*; M (MAN); 13 kts; ex-*Dorado*

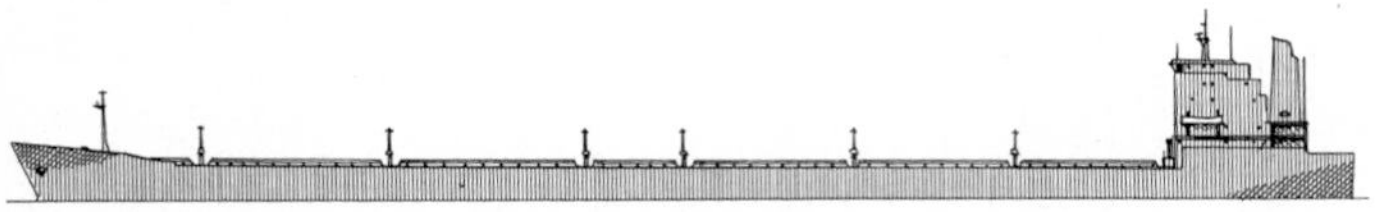

243 M^8F *H13*
HUI FU RC/Ko (Hyundai) 1978; B; 20,224 grt/38,568 dwt; 222.51 × 9.7 m *(730 × 31.82 ft)*; M (B&W); 14 kts; ex-*Federal Clyde*
Sisters: **TONG FU** (RC) ex-*Federal Calumet*; **STEEL FLOWER** (Pa) ex-*Federal Rhine*; **TRIAS** (Gr) ex-*Federal Schelde*; Similar (smaller funnel, lower superstructure and so on. Be built—(Cockerill): **LAKE ONTARIO** (MI) ex-*Federal Danube*; **LAKE MICHIGAN** (MI) ex-*Federal Maas*; **LAKE ERIE** (MI) ex-*Federal Ottawa*; **LAKE SUPERIOR** (MI) ex-*Federal Thames*

244 M^3FM *H1*
THEANO Ma/Br (Sunderland) 1974; B; 35,073 grt/72,063 dwt; 228.05 × 14.03 m *(748.20 × 46.03 ft)*; M (Doxford); 15 kts; ex-*Thetis*
Sister: **HUNTER** (Pa) ex-*Naiad*

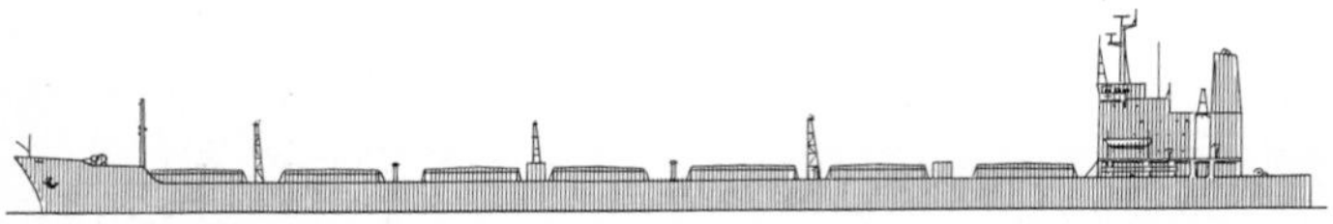

245 M^4NMF *H1*
OLYMPIC GALAXY Gr/Ja (Hitachi) 1982; B; 35,417 grt/64,931 dwt; 224.52 × 12.96 m *(737 × 42.52 ft)*; M (Sulzer); 14.75 kts; ex-*Ikan Bawal*

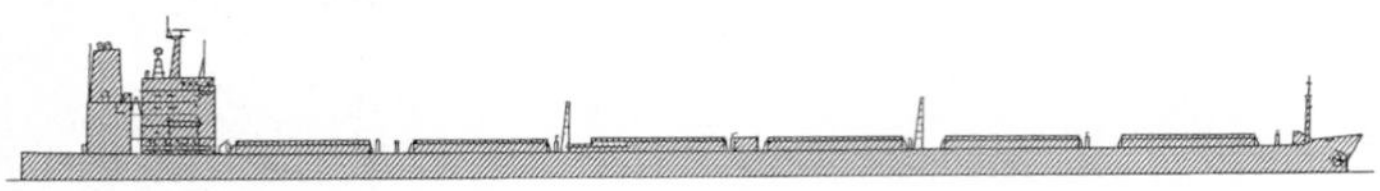

246 M^3NMFM *H*
OHTAKA MARU Ja/Ja (Hitachi) 1984; O; 97,183 grt/197,091 dwt; 300.01 × 17.83 m *(984.28 × 58.50 ft)*; M (B&W); 13.25 kts

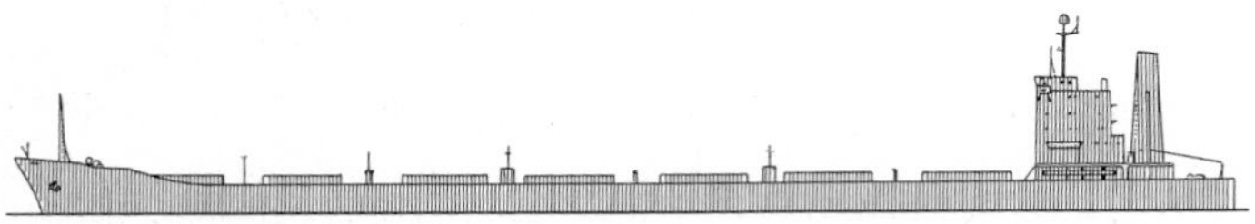

247 M^3N^2MF *H1*
OSSOLINEUM Pd/Ar (Alianza) 1986; B; 35,783 grt/61,013 dwt; 224.54 × 12.40 m *(736.68 × 40.68 ft)*; M (B&W); 14 kts
Sister: **MANIFEST PKWN** (Pd)

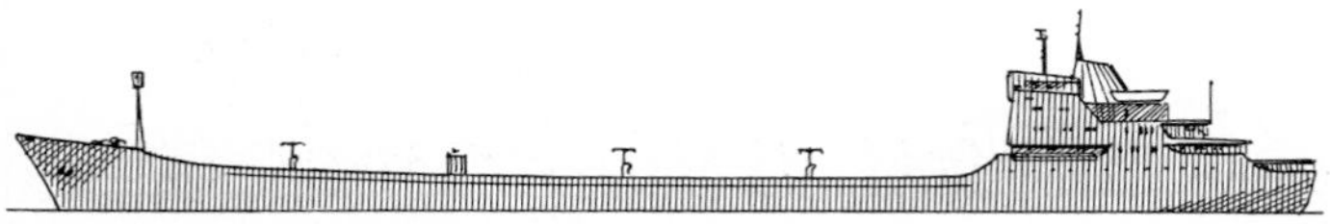

248 M^2M-FM *H12*
URICANI Rm/Rm (Galatz) 1971; B; 9,557 grt/12,540 dwt; 148.72 × 7.93 m *(487.93 × 26.02 ft)*; M (Sulzer); 12.5 kts
Sisters: **VEGA STAR ONE** (Rm) ex-*Anina*; **ROVINARI** (Rm); **VULCAN** (Rm); **MUSCEL** (Rm); **CIMPULUNG** (Rm); **AGNITA** (Rm)

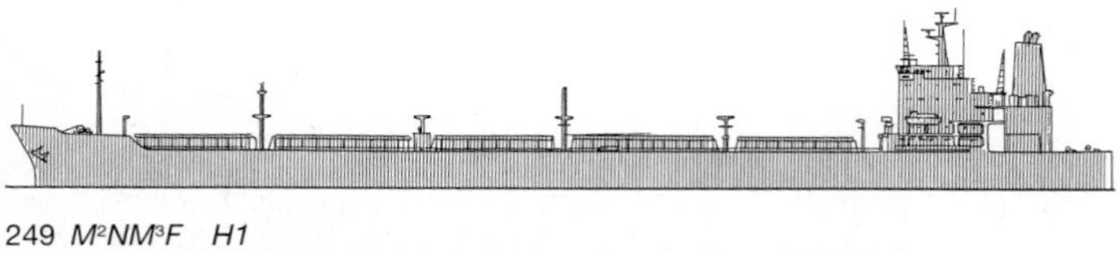

249 M^2NM^3F *H1*
PROSPECTOR II Li/Ja (Hitachi) 1982; B; 34,353 grt/47,535 dwt; 209.02 × 11 m *(686 × 36.09 ft)*; M (B&W); 14.75 kts; Launched as *Prospector*
Sister: **PATHFINDER II** (Li)

250 M^2RF *H*
BERGELAND NIS/Ko (Hyundai) 1992; O; 154,030 grt/322,941 dwt; 338.69 × 23 m *(1,111.19 × 75.46 ft)*; M (B&W); 14.5 kts

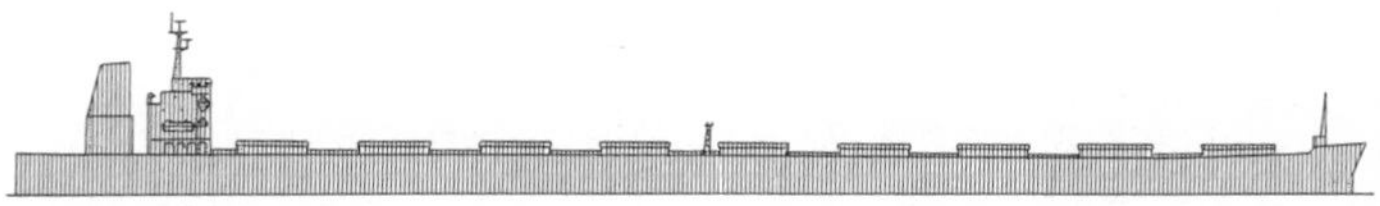

251 M^2RF *H*
HANJIN GLADSTONE Li/Ko (Hyundai) 1990; B; 110,541 grt/207,390 dwt; 309 × 18.02 m *(1,013.78 × 59.12 ft)*; M (B&W); 13 kts
Sister: **HANJIN DAMPIER** (Ko)

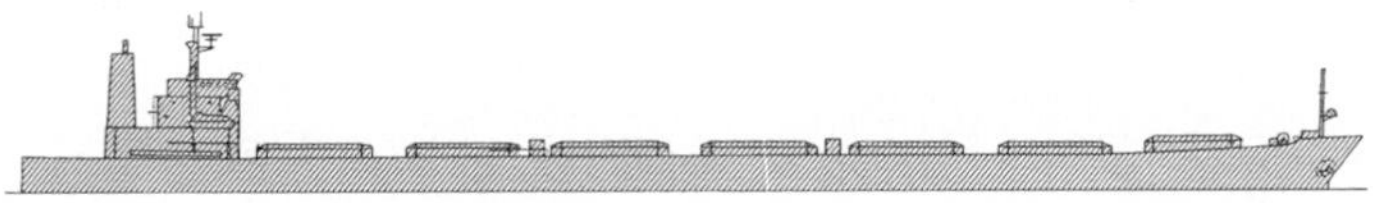

252 *MM-CF H*
BRAZILIAN VENTURE Li/Bz (IVI) 1995; B; 38,236 grt/70,728 dwt; 225.00 × 13.70 m *(738.19 × 44.95 ft)*; M (Sulzer); 14 kts; Crane is on starboard side

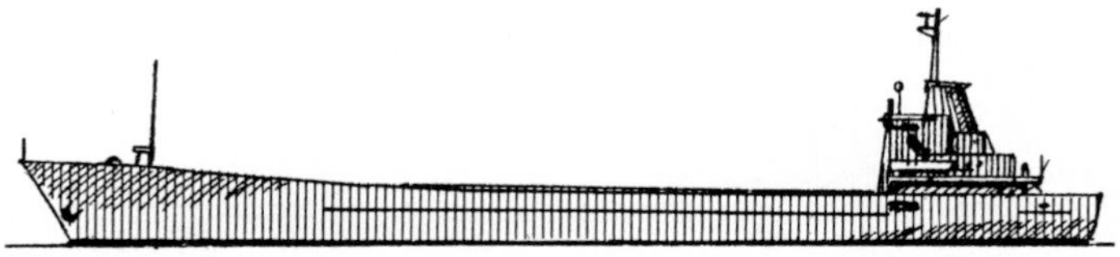

253 *MM-F H1*
KENMARE At/FRG (Schlichting) 1968; C/Con; 2,435 grt/2,290 dwt; 86.75 × 4.55 m *(284.61 × 14.93 ft)*; M (Atlas-MaK); 14.5 kts; ex-*Marietta Bolten*; 88 TEU

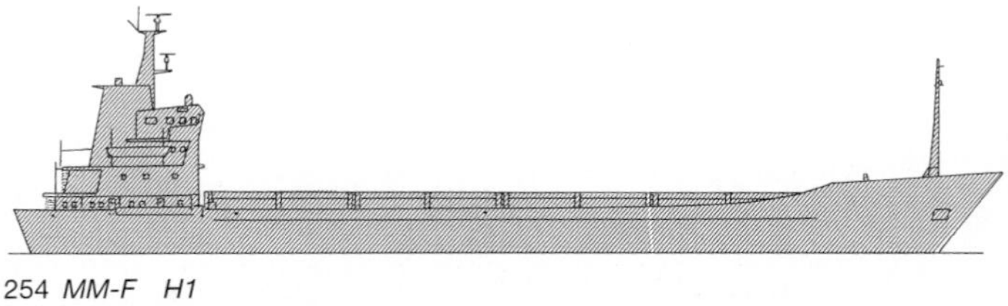

254 *MM-F H1*
LAGARD Fi/FRG (Husumer) 1976; C/Con; 998 grt/2,720 dwt; 84.26 × 4.96 m *(276.44 × 16.27 ft)*; M (Deutz); 14 kts; ex-*Hejo*; 174 TEU
Similar (longer enclosed superstructure. Lengthened to 991m (3,251ft). 198 TEU): **BOKELNBURG** (Cy)

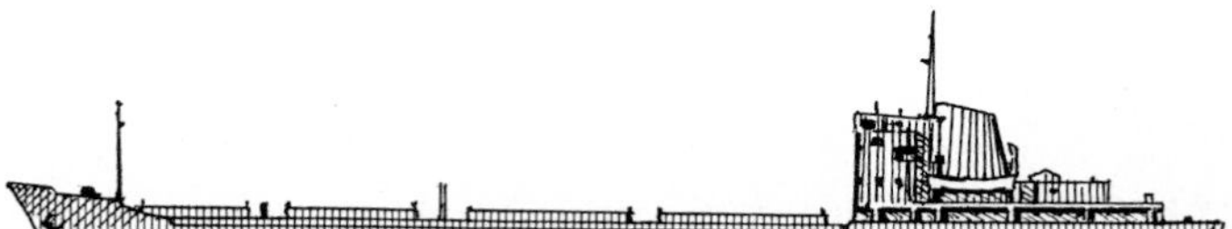

255 *MM-F H1*
MOON CYCLE SV/Br (Blyth) 1965; B; 4,886 grt/7,529 dwt; 112.76 × 7.32 m *(369.95 × 24.02 ft)*; M (British Polar); 12 kts; ex-*Corchester*

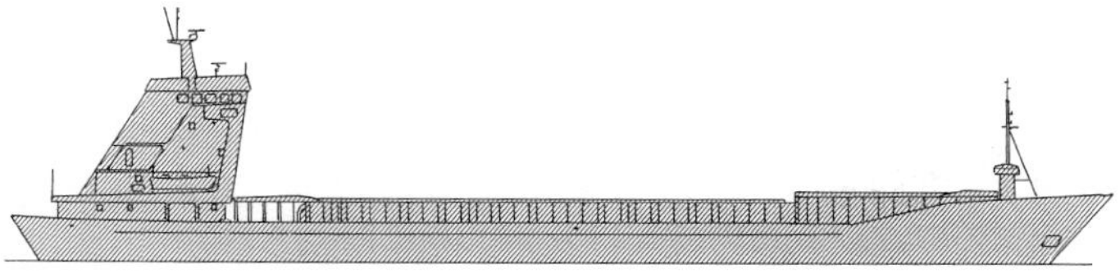

256 *MM-F H1*
NORDWIND Cy/FRG (H. Peters) 1976; C/Con; 2,161 grt/1,800 dwt; 87 × 4.73 m *(285.43 × 15.52 ft)*; M (Atlas-MaK); 13.25 kts; 115 TEU
Sisters: **THOR** (At) ex-*Brigitte Graebe*; **FAROS** (Ge) ex-*Lubeca*; Similar: **SPAROS** (Ge) ex-*Inka*; **DANFEEDER** (DIS) ex-*Barbara-Britt*; **SEEBRISE** (At) ex-*Lindaunis*; **CORONEL** (At) ex-*Christel*; **NAN YANG No 18** (RC) ex-*Isnis*; **BIRKENWALD** (At) ex-*Christopher Meeder*; **PINGUIN OCEAN DISTRICT** (At) ex-*Barbara-Chris*; **HAI DE WEI** (RC) ex-*Margret Catharina*; **CARINA I** (Ma) ex-*Frauke Catharina*; **MIAMI EXPRESS** (At) ex-*Thomas Mann*; **IRINA TRADER** (Ma) ex-*Boknis*; Similar (lengthened to 86.491m (283.761ft)): **CHRISTIAN** (Cy) ex-*Alita*

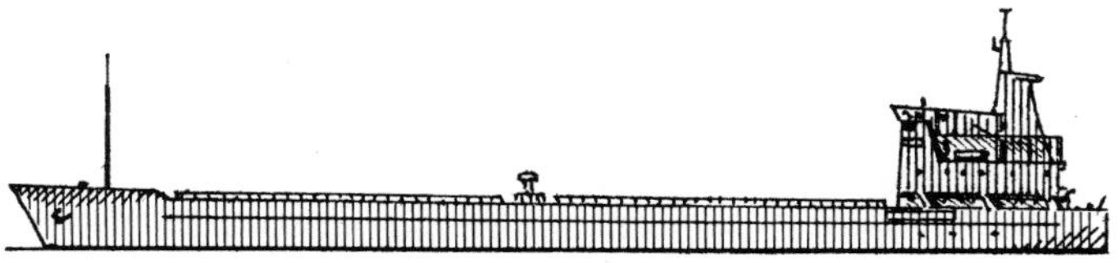

257 *MM-F H1*
SPECIALITY Bs/Br (Goole) 1977; C; 2,822 grt/4,245 dwt; 89.67 × 6.04 m *(294.19 × 19.82 ft)*; M (Alpha-Diesel); 12.5 kts
Possible sisters (may be geared): **STABILITY** (Bs); **RICCAM** (Pa) ex-*Jack Wharton*

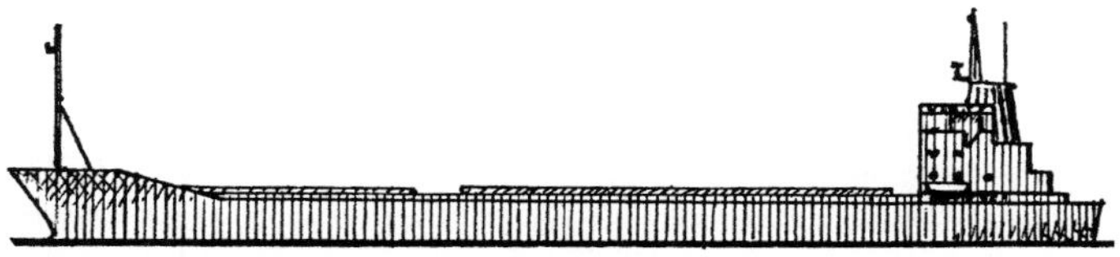

258 *MM-F H1*
VICTORIA NIS/Br (Appledore) 1977; C/Con; 2,764 grt/3,283 dwt; 95.18 × 4.87 m *(312.27 × 15.98 ft)*; M (Mirrlees Blackstone); 13 kts; ex-*Commodore Enterprise*; 194 TEU

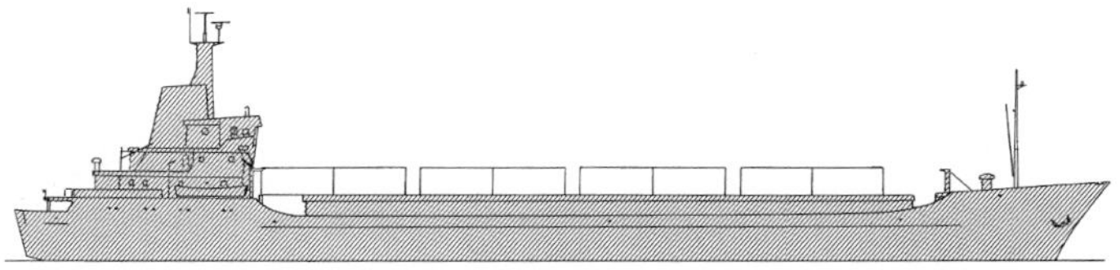

259 *MM-F H12*
GYLE Sw/FRG (Husumer) 1972; C/Con; 2,463 grt/2,400 dwt; 93.22 × 4.91 m *(305.84 × 16.11 ft)*; M (MAN); 14 kts; ex-*Duneck*; 146 TEU
Sister: **MATHILDE** (NIS) ex-*Anna Knuppel*

260 *MM-F H13*
AL NAJWA Sy/Ne (Van Diepen) 1972; C; 1,599 grt/2,920 dwt; 87.46 × 5.45 m *(286.94 × 17.88 ft)*; M (Atlas-MaK); 12 kts; ex-*Whitegate*
Sisters: **LEO** (Ma) ex-*Moidart*; **MINGARY** (It); **BONA FE** (Fi) ex-*Norrstal*; **BIRTA** (Ma) ex-*Regent's Park*; Possible sister: **MARIA I** (At) ex-*Highgate*

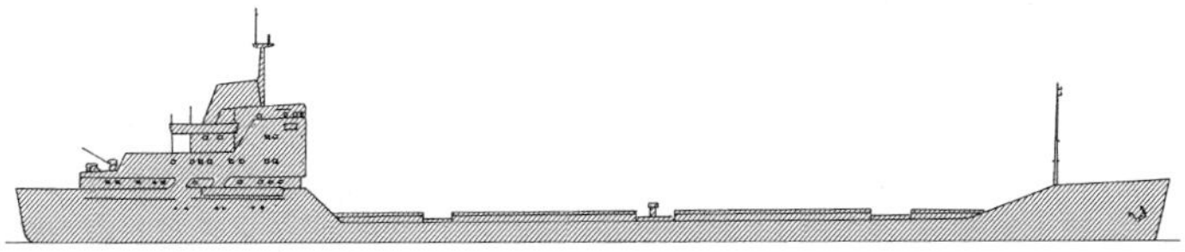

261 *MM-F H13*
LARVIKSTONE Bs/Pd (Gdanska) 1970; O; 3,923 grt/5,735 dwt; 108.77 × 6.86 m *(356.86 × 22.51 ft)*; M (Sulzer); 14 kts; ex-*Tarnow*; 'B-522' type
Sisters: **FINNSTONE** (SV) ex-*Kedzierzyn*; **NORSTONE** (SV) ex-*Nowy Sacz*; **WOODSTONE** (Bs) ex-*Eugenie Cotton*

262 *MM-F H13*
LUMINENCE Bs/Br (Clelands) 1977; C; 1,928 grt/3,210 dwt; 91.24 × 5.15 m *(299.34 × 16.9 ft)*; M (British Polar); 13 kts
Sister: **KINDRENCE** (Bs)

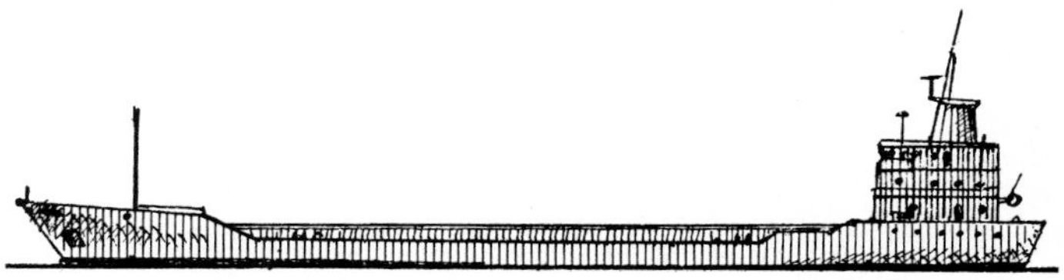

263 *MM-F H13*
NORMANNBAY NIS/Ne (Kramer & Booy) 1975; C; 2,630 grt/4,072 dwt; 93.6 × 5.64 m *(307.09 × 18.5 ft)*; M (Smit & Bolnes); 13 kts; ex-*Londonbrook*; 136 TEU
Sister: **ADRIATIC STAR** (Ma) ex-*Lancasterbrook*; Sisters (may be fitted with two travelling cranes): **EKOWAS TRADER II** (Ng) ex-*Leicesterbrook*; **GEVO VICTORY** (Li) ex-*Lincolnbrook*; Similar: **ANITA** (NIS) ex-*Junior Lotte*

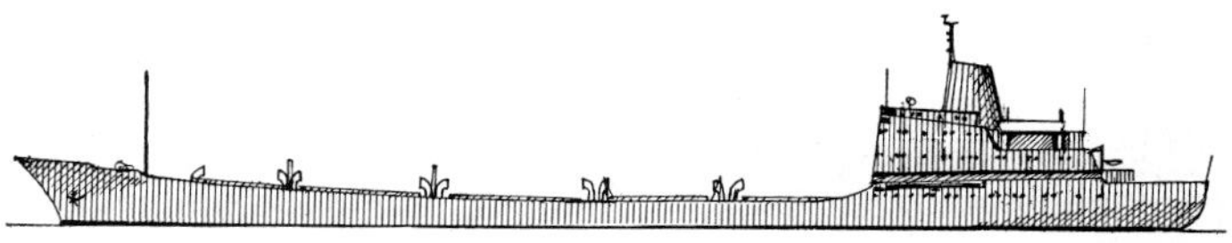

264 *MM-F H13*
VERILA Bu/Bu (G. Dimitrov) 1969; B; 7,361 grt/10,871 dwt; 134.02 × 7.48 m *(439.7 × 24.54 ft)*; M (B&W); 13 kts
Sisters: **VESLETS** (Bu); **VIDEN** (Bu); Probable sisters: **CHERNI VRAKH** (Bu); **CHUMERNA** (Bu)

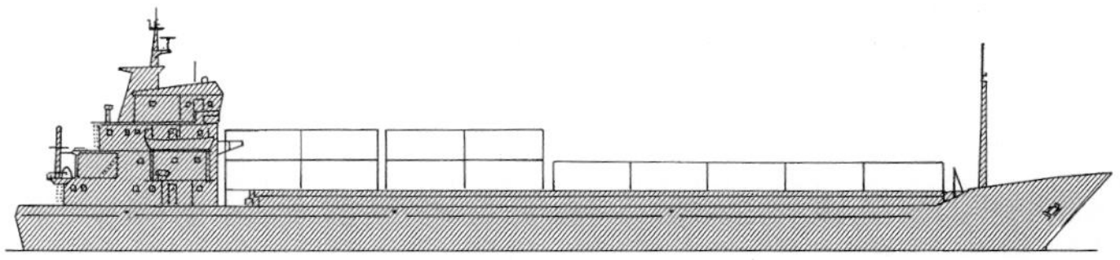

265 *MM-FD H1*
SOLAR At/Ja (Nichitsu) 1977; C/Con; 2,361 grt/2,680 dwt; 86.52 × 5.20 m *(283.86 × 17.06 ft)*; M (MaK); 12.5 kts; 140 TEU
Sisters: **REBENA** (At); **LYS-BRIS** (At) ex-*Virgo*; **SUNNANHAV** (At); **FLENSBURGER FLAGGE** (Ge) ex-*Schwinge*; **RANDI** (At) ex-*Argonaut*

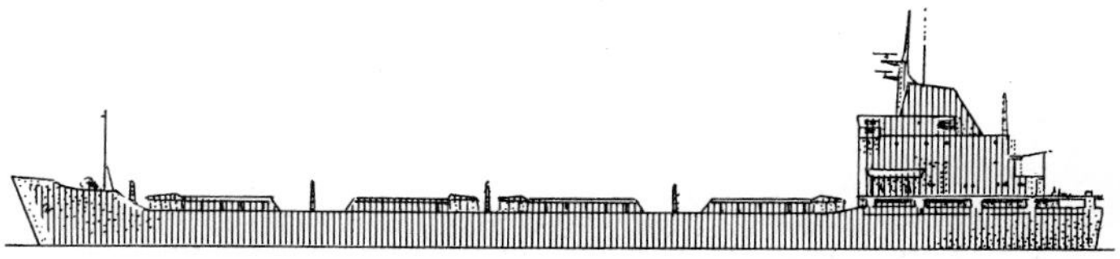

266 *MM-FM H1*
JEVINGTON Br/Br (Robb Caledon) 1977; B; 7,702 grt/12,330 dwt; 127.44 × 8.12 m *(418.11 × 26.64 ft)*; M (Pielstick); 13 kts; ex-*Garrison Point*

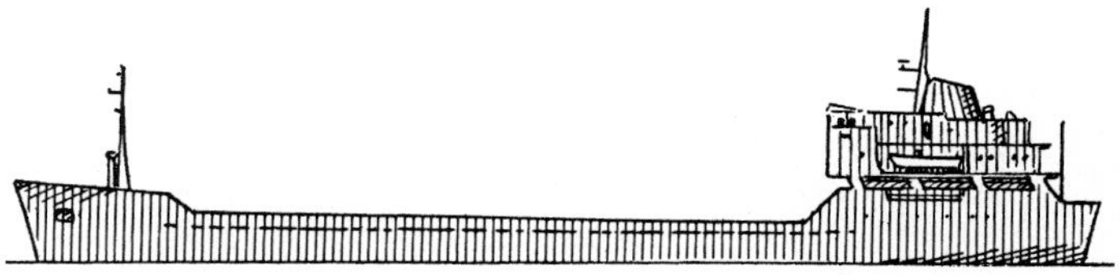

267 *MM-FM H13*
HARRIET SV/Sw (Falkenbergs) 1971; C; 2,092 grt/3,220 dwt; 87.03 × 4.96 m *(285.53 × 16.27 ft)*; M (Appingedammer Brons); 12 kts; ex-*Beeding*; 'M' aft is on starboard side

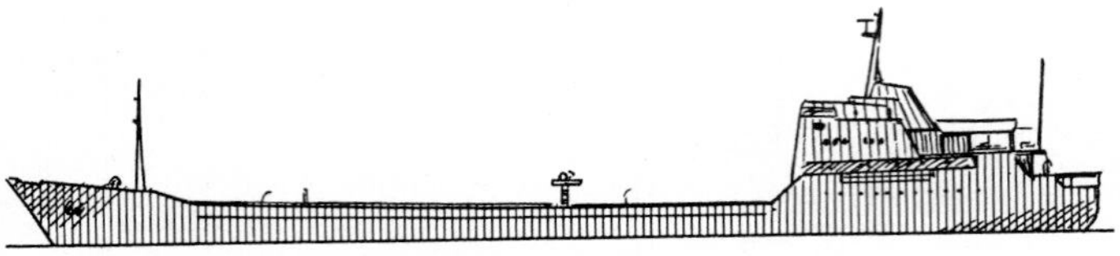

268 *MM-FM H13*
MARINA PEARL SV/Bu (G. Dimitrov) 1969; C; 2,516 grt/3,617 dwt; 95.89 × 5.66 m *(314.6 × 18.57 ft)*; M (Sulzer); 13 kts; ex-*Suwalki*
Sisters: **UNITY V** (SV) ex-*Kutno II*; **EMERALD PEARL** (SV) ex-*Piotrkow Trybunalski*; **ULLA PEARL** (SV) ex-*Wadowice*; **UNITY IV** (SV) ex-*Starachowice*; **ST. MALO PEARL** (SV) ex-*Przemysl*

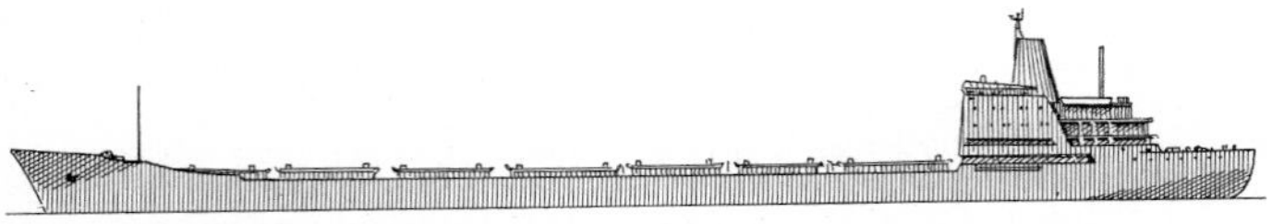

269 *MM-FN H13*
BELMEKEN Bu/Bu (G. Dimitrov) 1971; B; 16,151 grt/23,738 dwt; 185.2 × 9.86 m *(607.61 × 32.35 ft)*; M (Sulzer); 15 kts
Sisters: **GENERAL VLADIMIR ZAIMOV** (Bu); **ZIEMIA BIALOSTOCKA** (Pd); **ZIEMIA OLSZTYNSKA** (Pd); **LAKE TAHOE** (Ma) ex-*Ziemia Opolski*

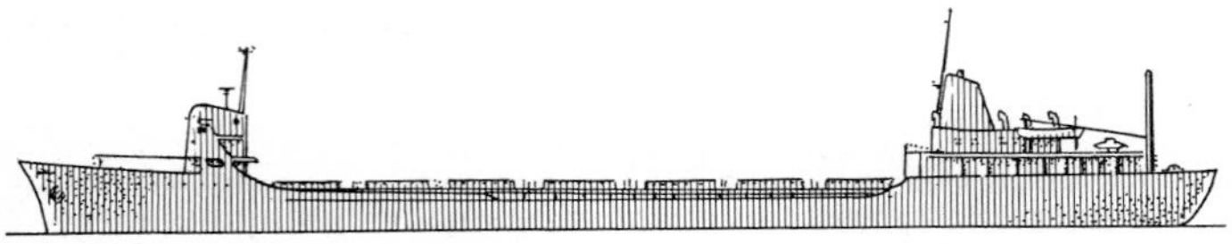

270 *MM-FN H13*
JOSIFF I Pa/Fr (La Seine) 1960; B; 7,319 grt/11,169 dwt; 135.9 × 7.72 m *(445.87 × 25.33 ft)*; T (GEC); 12 kts; ex-*Gypsum Countess*

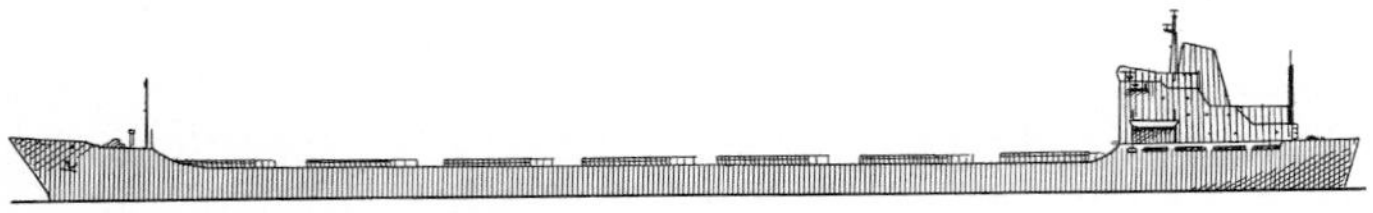

271 *MM-FN H13*
SAC MALAGA Pa/Sp (AESA) 1976; B; 17,169 grt/30,499 dwt; 190.66 × 10.69 m *(625.52 × 35.07 ft)*; M (Sulzer); 15 kts
Sister: **AROSA** (Cy) Launched as *Ponte Sampayo*; Similar: **GOLDEN SKY** (Cy) Launched as *Ponte Pasaje*; **VULCAN** (Cy) Launched as *Ponte Pedrido*

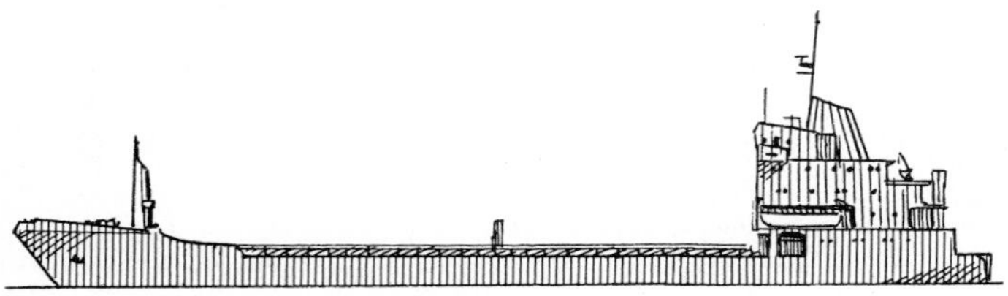

272 *MM-FND*
GIHO My/FRG (M. Jansen) 1971; C/Con; 2,812 grt/4,105 dwt; 94.01 × 5.6 m *(308.43 × 18.37 ft)*; M (KHD); 15 kts; Launched as *Ino J*; 174 TEU

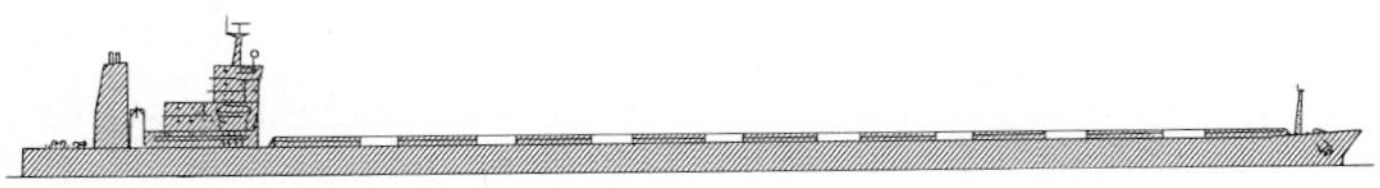

273 *MM-G H*
IRON PACIFIC Au/Ko (Samsung) 1986; B; 118,491 grt/231,851 dwt; 315.02 × 18.20 m *(1,033.53 × 59.71 ft)*; TSM (Sulzer); 13.5 kts

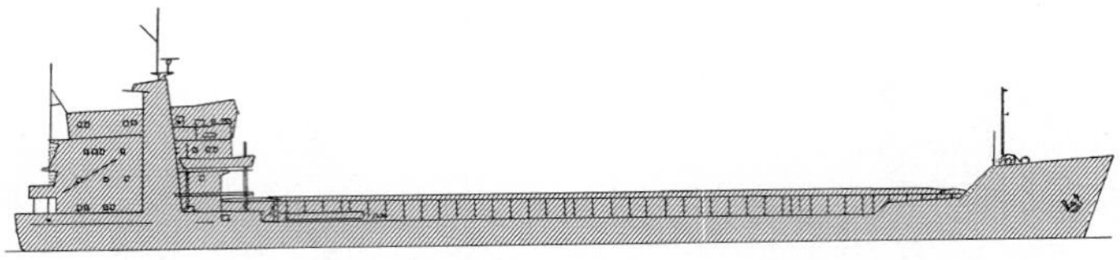

274 *MM-G H1*
ANIA B NIS/Ne (Giessen-De Noord) 1972; B/Con; 3,720 grt/6,200 dwt; 96.68 × 7.11 m *(317.19 × 23.33 ft)*; M (Atlas-MaK); 13 kts; ex-*Carlota Bolten*; 230 TEU
Similar (originally sisters. Now rebuilt and lengthened to 101.171m (331.921ft). 203 TEU): **ARTEMIS 1** (Cy) ex-*Susan Miller*; **CHRISTIANE SCHULTE** (Cy); **COSA** (Cy) ex-*Erika Fisser* (see photo number 5/334); **SERENADE** (Cy) ex-*Otto Porr*; **ESTHER** (Cy) ex-*Esther Bolten*

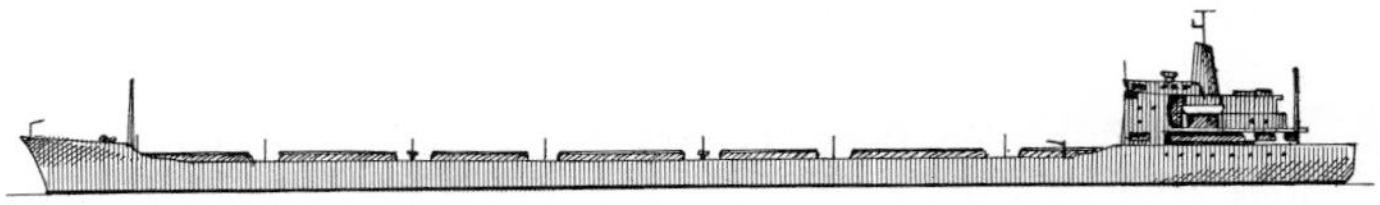

275 *MM-GN H13*
DYNAMIC SPIRIT Pa/Fr (France-Gironde) 1968; B; 18,210 grt/31,065 dwt; 196.58 × 10.79 m *(644.95 × 35.40 ft)*; M (B&W); 17 kts; ex-*Eglantine*

276 *MM-GY H1*
PISHRO Ir/FRG (Howaldts DW) 1978/81; DC/Con; 1,599 grt/4,514 dwt; 110.45 × 3.65 m *(362.37 × 11.98 ft)*; TSM (MaK); 10 kts; ex-*Sigrid Wehr*; Stern door/ramp; Lengthened 1981; Can operate without hatch covers; May be seen with hatch covers stowed foreward in 'piggy back' style; 336 TEU
Probable sister: **CONRO TRADER** (At) ex-*Areucon Caroline* (6,051 grt)

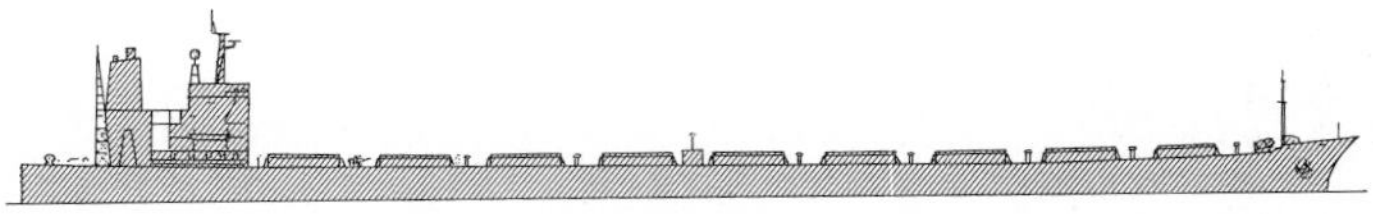

277 *MM-NFN H*
CHARIOT Pa/Ja (Hitachi) 1981; B; 70,595 grt/124,292 dwt; 259.52 × 16.13 m *(851.44 × 52.92 ft)*; M (B&W); 14.5 kts; ex-*Shin-Kakogawa Maru*

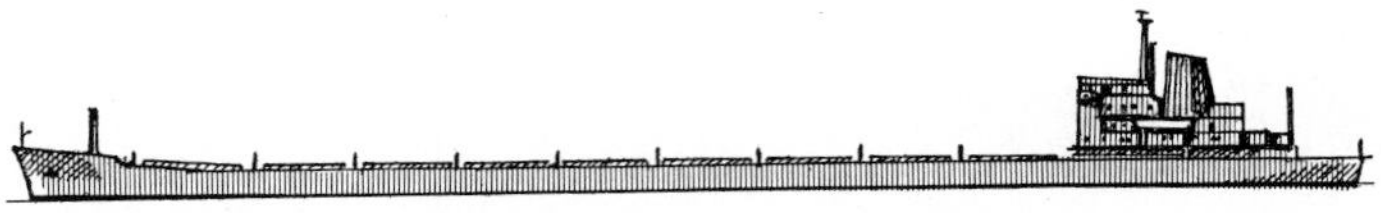

278 *MM-NFN H1*
AMBER Sg/Br (Lithgows) 1975; B; 41,906 grt/76,583 dwt; 245.37 × 13.83 m *(805.02 × 45.37 ft)*; M (B&W); 15.25 kts; ex-*Jalavihar*
Sister: **KASTURBA** (In)

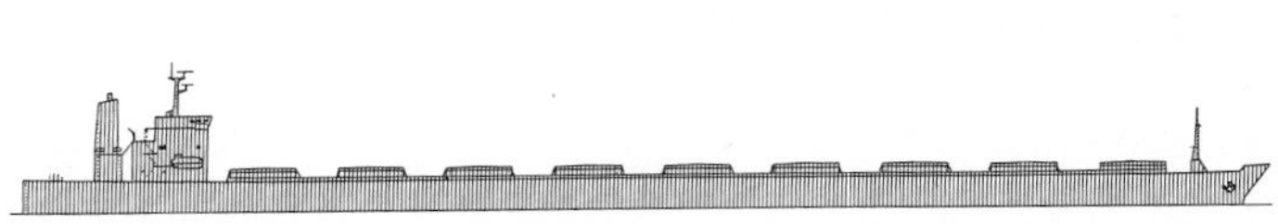

279 *MM-SF H*
ERIDGE HK/Ko (Daewoo) 1993; B; 65,153 grt/122,792 dwt; 266 × 15.42 m *(872.70 × 50.59 ft)*; M (B&W); 14 kts
Sister: **DUHALLOW** (HK)

280 *MNHF H*
KINOKAWA Pa/Ja (Sumitomo) 1982; B; 92,614 grt/179,618 dwt; 298.53 × 17.73 m *(979.43 × 58.17 ft)*; M (Sulzer); 13.80 kts; ex-*Kinokawa Maru*; **SIMILAR TO DRAWING NUMBER 5/286**
Similar: **BRAZIL STAR** (Pa) ex-*Tsukuba Maru*

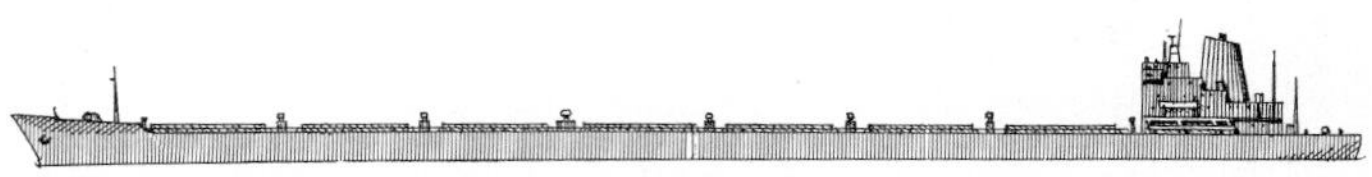

281 *MNHFM² H1*
GLOBAL DREAM Cy/Ja (Kawasaki) 1972; B; 31,935 grt/63,985 dwt; 228.61 × 12.93 m *(750.03 × 42.42 ft)*; M (MAN); 15 kts; ex-*Majesty*

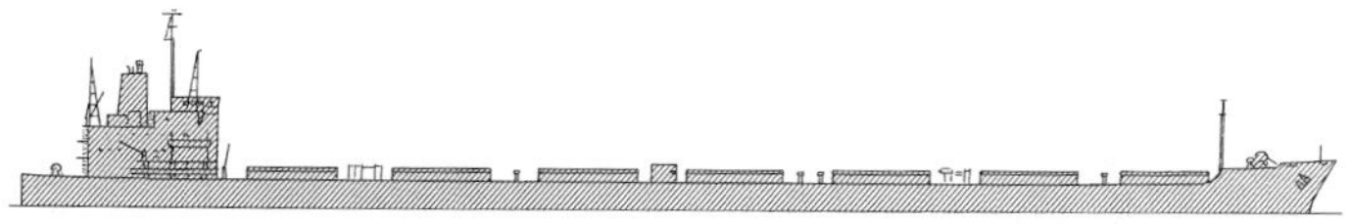

282 *MNHFN H1*
YICK JIA Pa/Ja (Kawasaki) 1986; B; 35,247 grt/67,395 dwt; 220.20 × 13.24 m *(722.44 × 43.44 ft)*; M (B&W); 13.75 kts; ex-*Sakura*
Sister: **GINA IULIANO** (It) ex-*Kris A*

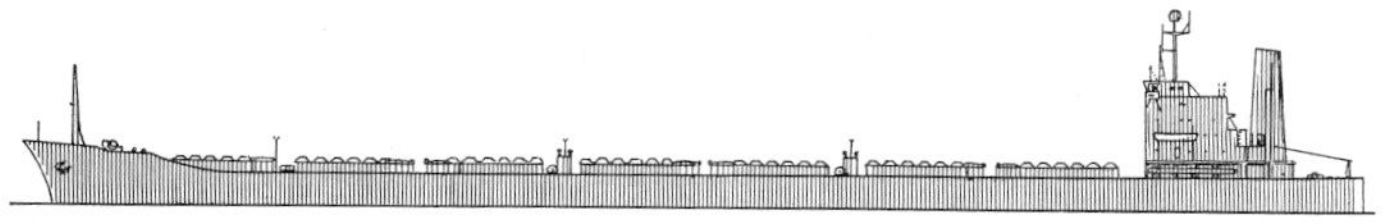

283 *MNHF-M H1*
MOUNT PENTELI Gr/Ja (Hitachi) 1980; B; 35,158 grt/63,569 dwt; 224.52 × 12.46 m *(737 × 40.88 ft)*; M (Sulzer); 14.5 kts; Kingpost alongside funnel
Sisters: **LUCKY SAILOR** (Ma) ex-*Mount Parnis*; **ASCENSION** (It) ex-*Mount Taygetos*

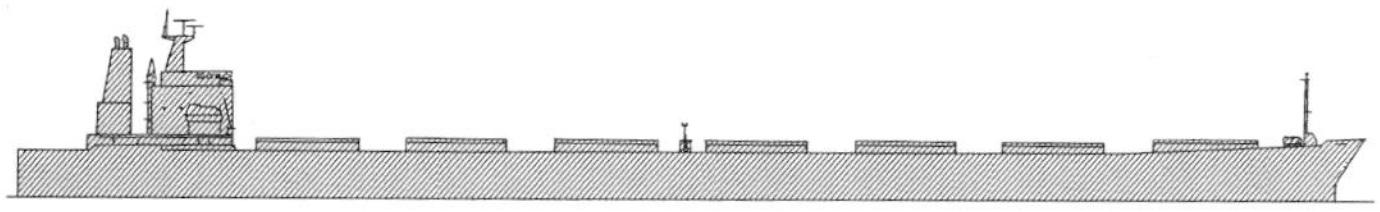

284 *MNMDF H*
THALASSINI TYHI Cy/Ko (Samsung S) 1994; B; 38,513 grt/73,205 dwt; 224.95 × 13.90 m *(738.02 × 45.60 ft)*; M (B&W); 14.5 kts
Sister: **THALASSINI NIKI** (Cy)

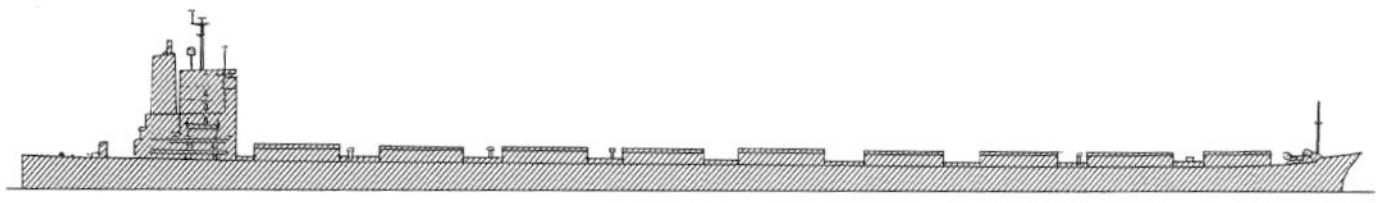

285 *MNMF H*
IJMUIDEN MARU Pa/Ja (Hashihama) 1986; B; 61,350 grt/111,695 dwt; 260.51 × 13.74 m *(854.69 × 45.08 ft)*; M (B&W); 13.5 kts

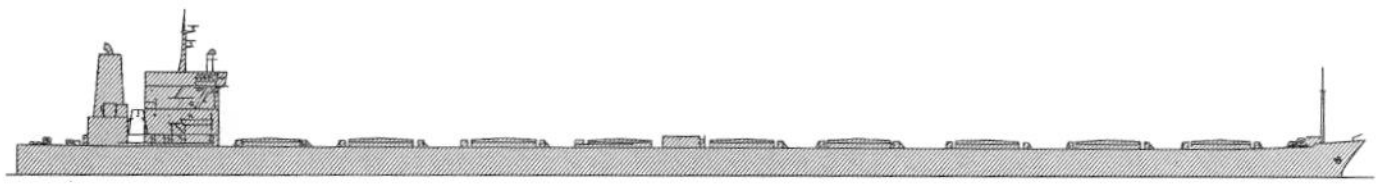

286 *MNMF H*
KII MARU Ja/Ja (Sumitomo) 1984; B; 93,049 grt/179,422 dwt; 298.53 × 17.73 m *(979.43 × 58.17 ft)*; M (Sulzer); 13 kts

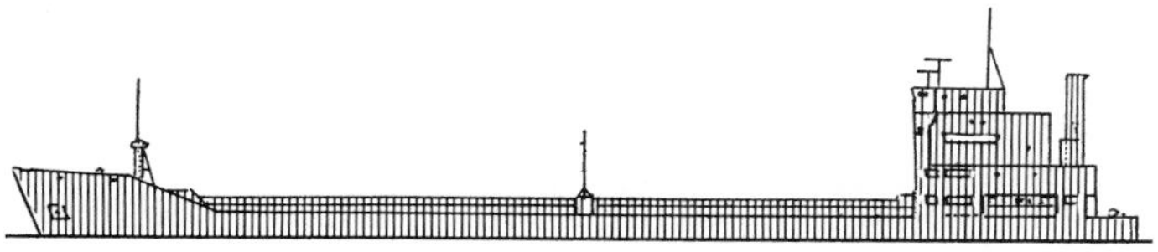

287 *MNMF H1*
BLANKENES Cy/Sw (Gotav Solvesborg) 1978; C; 4,061 grt/6,433 dwt; 105.64 × 6.84 m *(346.59 × 22.44 ft)*; M (Wärtsilä); kts; ex-*Black Sea*; 238 TEU
Sisters: **ALBONA** (As) (see photo number 5/383)

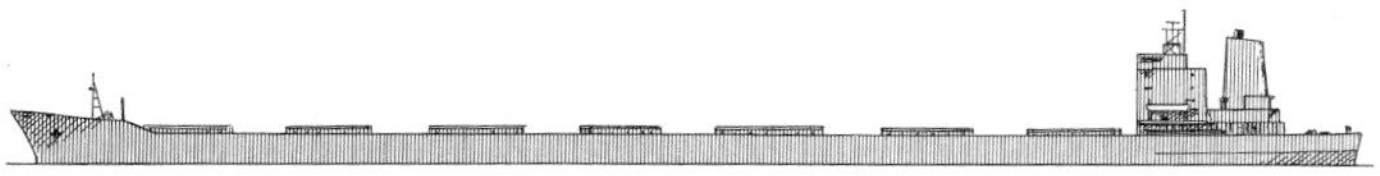

288 *MNMF H1*
RED ROSE Cy/Be (Boelwerf) 1978; B; 40,315 grt/75,724 dwt; 242.02 × 13.83 m *(794 × 45.37 ft)*; M (MAN); 16 kts; ex-*Eeklo*
Sister: **RED TULIP** (Ma) ex-*Temse*; Similar: **FERIDE** (Tu) ex-*Magritte*

289 *MNMFC H1*
SEA TRAMP Bs/Be (Cockerill) 1973; B; 32,624 grt/66,510 dwt; 234.8 × 13.27 m *(770.34 × 43.54 ft)*; M (MAN); 16 kts; ex-*Mineral Alegria*
Possible sister: **STRAHLHORN** (Li) ex-*Mineral Belgium*

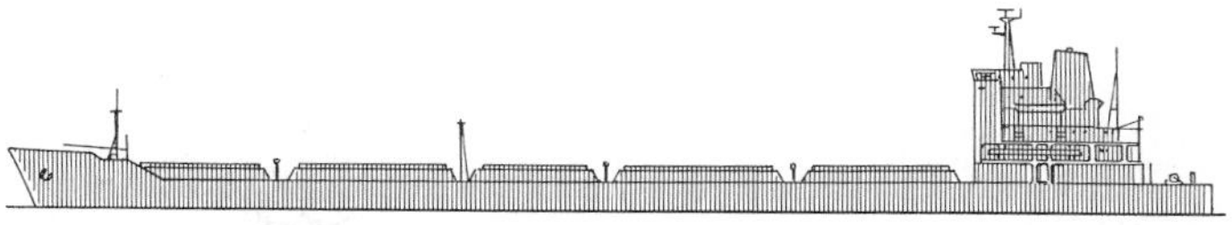

290 *MNMFM H12*
ZIEMIA SUWALSKA Pd/Ar (Alianza) 1984; B; 16,696 grt/26,706 dwt; 180.25 × 9.84 m *(591.37 × 32.28 ft)*; M (B&W); 14.50 kts
Sisters: **ZIEMIA CHELMINSKA** (Pd); **ZIEMIA GNIEZNIENSKA** (Pd); **ZIEMIA TARNOWSKA** (Pd); **ZIEMIA ZAMOJSKA** (Pd); **POMORZE ZACHODNIE** (Pd)

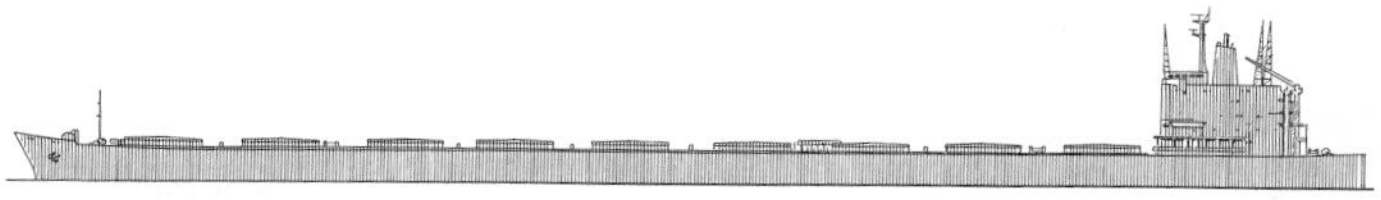

291 *MNMFM²S H*
HELLAS Li/Ja (Kawasaki) 1982; B; 72,934 grt/139,609 dwt; 280.02 × 16.15 m *(919 × 52.99 ft)*; M (MAN); 14 kts; ex-*Pengall*
Sisters: **CETRA CORONA** (Kn); **LA PAMPA** (Pa) ex-*Cetra Sagitta*; **LA SIERRA** (Pa) ex-*Gallant Lion*; Similar: **AMSTELWAL** (NA) ex-*Niels Onstad*; **GALLANT TIGER** (HK) ex-*Onstad Trader*

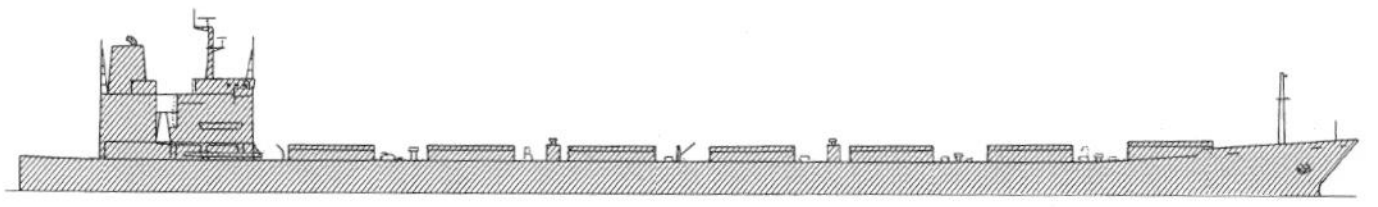

292 *MNMFN H*
MING WISDOM Tw/Tw (China SB) 1984; B; 36,303 grt/66,786 dwt; 229.75 × 13.27 m *(753.77 × 43.54 ft)*; M (Sulzer); 16.6 kts
Sisters: **MING COURAGE** (Tw); **MING MERCY** (Tw); **NEW HORIZON** (Cy) ex-*Panamax Cosmos*; **CHINA TRADER** (Tw); **MORNING CLOUD** (Pa) ex-*Panamax Neptune*; Probable sister: **CEMTEX YUAN** (Tw)

293 *MNMFN H*
NIIZURU Pa/Ja (Hitachi) 1971; O; 90,583 grt/165,188 dwt; 313.62 × 16.99 m *(1028.94 × 55.74 ft)*; M (B&W); 15.75 kts; ex-*Niizuru Maru*

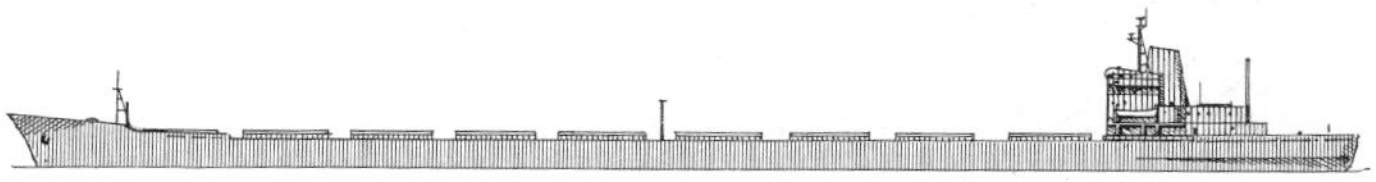

294 *MNMFN H1*
BELLINI Ma/Be (Boelwerf) 1971; B; 32,521 grt/65,455 dwt; 234.75 × 13.2 m *(770.18 × 43.31 ft)*; M (MAN); 15 kts; ex-*E R Brabantia*

295 *MNMFN H1*
JADRAN Ma/Br (Sunderland) 1976; B; 38,237 grt/72,149 dwt; 228.12 × 14.03 m *(748.43 × 46.03 ft)*; M (Doxford); 15 kts
Sisters: **KORDUN** (Ma); **KOSMAJ** (Ma); **ORJEN** (Ma); **SARAH** (Ma) ex-*Sutjeska*

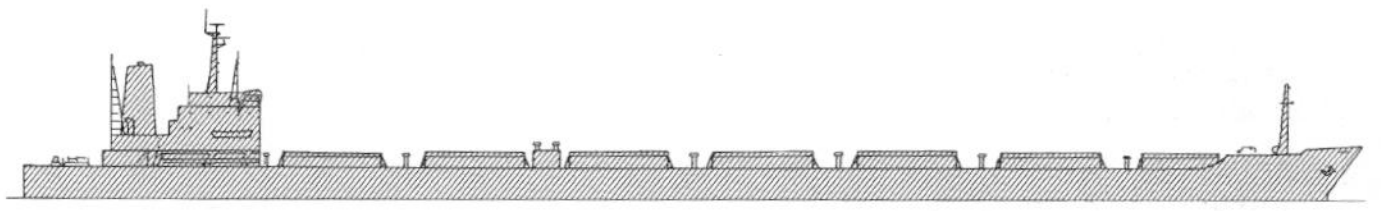

296 *MNMFN H1*
LONGEVITY Pi/Ja (Kasado) 1981; B; 37,939 grt/69,428 dwt; 238.16 × 13.25 m *(781.36 × 43.47 ft)*; M (B&W); 14.5 kts; ex-*Inverlock*
Sister: **NAVIOS BULKER** (HK) ex-*Fenlock*

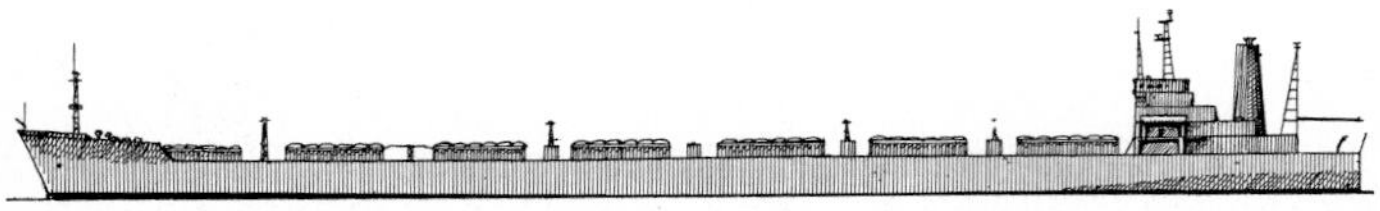

297 *MNMFN H1*
SIMEON CH Bs/Ja (Hitachi) 1977; B; 29,729 grt/61,709 dwt; 225.03 × 12.4 m *(738.29 × 40.68 ft)*; M (Sulzer); 14.75 kts; ex-*Golden Laurel*
Similar (may vary in details—particulary aft kingposts): **GLOBAL MAKATCHA** (Li) ex-*Ogden Danube*; **SAN FELICE** (Ma) ex-*Oslo Venture*; **ARCHANGELOS** (Gr); **FLAG ROLACO** (Gr) ex-*World Medal*; **MINERVA** (Li) ex-*Sapphire*; **MARIANT** (Gr) ex-*Showa Venture*; **REX FRIENDSHIP** (Gr) ex-*Continental Friendship*; **BULKAZORES** (Ma) ex-*Continental Trader*; **EVNIKI** (Li); **AMALTHEA** (Gr) ex-*Caryanda*; **BALTIC TRIDENT** (Ma) ex-*Mount Pindos*; **BIG ANGEL** (SV) ex-*Hoan Maru*; **MARYLOU II** (Cy) ex-*Zannis Michalos*

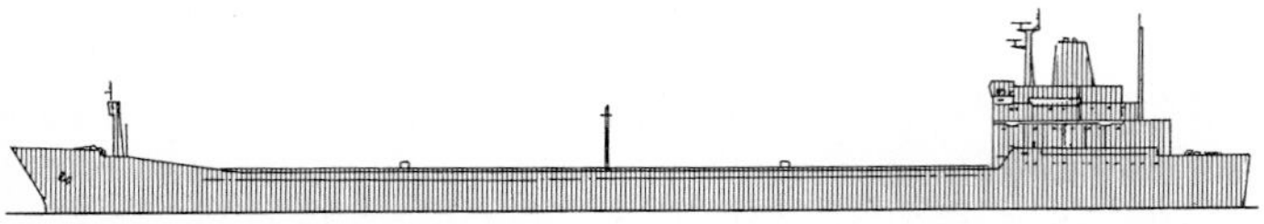

298 *MNMFN H13*
IONIAN SKY Pa/DDR (Mathias-Thesen) 1978; B/Con; 15,979 grt/23,308 dwt; 176.69 × 10.11 m *(580 × 33.17 ft)*; M (MAN); 16 kts; ex-*Jena*; 426 TEU
Sisters: **IONIAN STAR** (Pa) ex-*Meissen*; **IONIAN SUN** (Pa) ex-*Weimar*

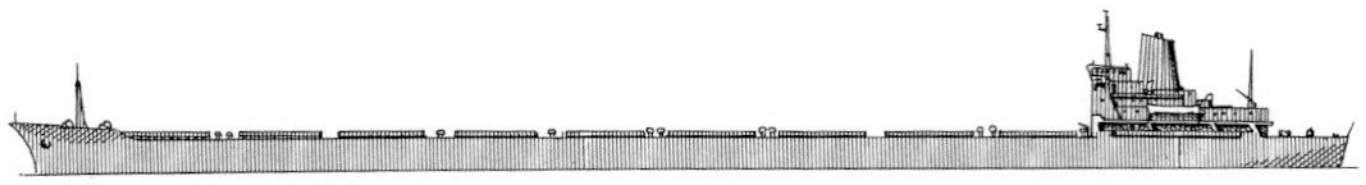

299 *MNMFNR H1*
OKTAY KALKAVAN Tu/Ja (Mitsui) 1970; B; 45,832 grt/82,617 dwt; 240.39 × 14.1 m *(788.68 × 46.26 ft)*; M (B&W); 15.25 kts; ex-*Rokkohsan Maru*
Similar (smaller-228.71 m (750.331 ft)): **FLAG MERSINIDI** (Gr) ex-*Mitsui Maru*; **DA YAO SHAN** (RC) ex-*Tetsuzui Maru*

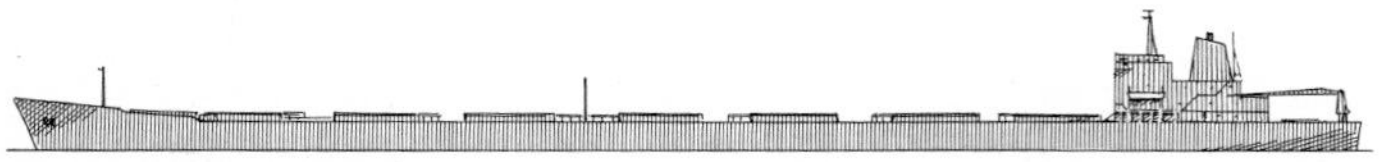

300 *MNMFNS H1*
ATLANTICWAY Pa/Br (Sunderland) 1978; B; 37,337 grt/72,100 dwt; 228.12 × 14.02 m *(748.42 × 45.99 ft)*; M (Doxford); 15 kts; ex-*Benhope*

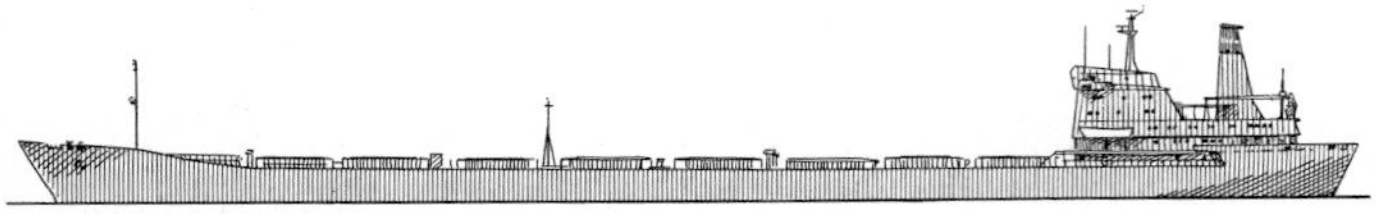

301 *MNMGMR H13*
REDUTA ORDONA Pd/Pd (Szczecinska) 1978; B; 20,357 grt/33,490 dwt; 198.18 × 11 m *(650.2 × 36.09 ft)*; M (Sulzer); 15.2 kts; ex-*Feliks Dzierzynski*; 'B-517' type
Sisters: **WALKA MLODYCH** (Pd); **UNIWERSYTET SLASKI** (Pd); **LAKE ONEIDA** (MI) ex-*Powstaniec Warszwaski*; **LAKE GEORGE** (MI) ex-*Janusz Kusocinski*; **SEADRIVE** (Cy) ex-*Sedge*

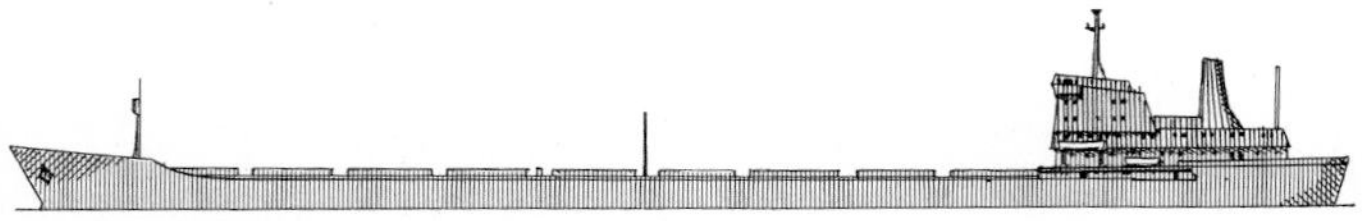

302 *MNMGN H13*
SYN PULKU Pd/Pd (Szczecinska) 1974; B; 20,593 grt/31,910 dwt; 199.17 × 10.63 m *(653.44 × 34.88 ft)*; M (Sulzer); 15.25 kts; 'B 447' type
Sisters: **CEDYNIA** (Pd); **MIROSLAWIEC** (Pd); **NARWICK II** (Pd); **POWSTANIEC WIELKOPOLSKI** (Pd); **STUDZIANKI** (Pd)

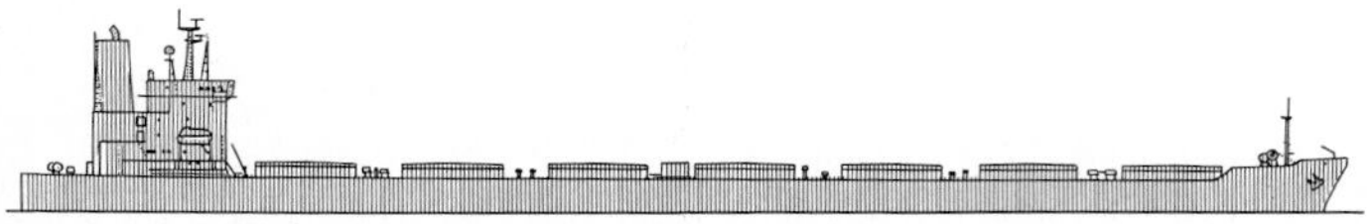

303 *MNM²FN H1*
CO-OP HARVEST Pi/Ja (Namura) 1988; B; 36,983 grt/68,377 dwt; 224.94 × 13.22 m *(737.99 × 43.37 ft)*; M (Sulzer); 14.70 kts
Sister: **CO-OP PARTNER** (Pi); Possible sisters: **CHARLES L D** (Pa) ex-*Lake River*; **GRACIOUS LADY** (Ma) ex-*Imari*; **NORTH EMPEROR** (Gr) ex-*Interbulk Valiant*; **C S ELEGANT** (Pa) ex-*Young Senator*

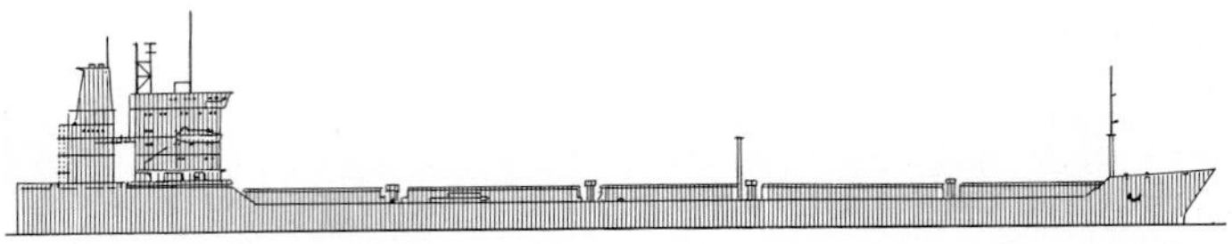

304 *MNM²M-F H13*
ARMIA LUDOWA Pd/Pd (Szczecinska) 1987; B; 21,458 grt/33,640 dwt; 195.33 × 10.65 m *(640.85 × 34.94 ft)*; M (Sulzer); 15.75 kts; 'B545' type
Sisters (some may be like drawing 5/306): **IGNACY DASZYNSKI** (Pd); **STANISLAW KULCZYNSKI** (Pd); **BATALIONY CHLOPSKIE** (Pd)

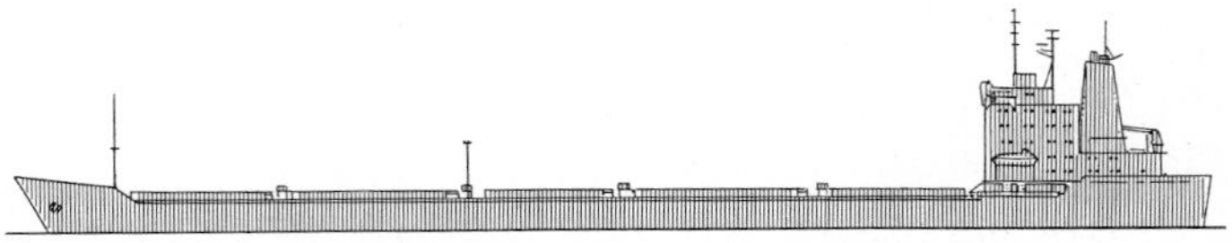

305 *MNM²M-FR H13*
MAJOR HUBAL Pd/Pd (Szczecinska) 1985; B; 21,531 grt/33,725 dwt; 195.21 × 10.68 m *(640.45 × 35.04 ft)*; M (Sulzer); 15 kts; 'B542' type
Sisters: **MACIEJ RATAJ** (Pd); **BATALION CZWARTAKOW** (Pd); **POWSTANIEC LISTOPADOWY** (Pd); **POWSTANIEC STYCZNIOWY** (Pd); **RODLO** (Pd); **BRAHMS** (Gr) ex-*Bronislaw Czech*

306 *MNMM-F H13*
OKSYWIE Pd/Pd (Szczecinska) 1987; B; 21,460 grt/33,580 dwt; 195.27 × 10.65 m *(640.65 × 34.94 ft)*; M (Sulzer); 15 kts; ex-*Wladyslaw Gomulka*; 'B545' type; Sister of drawing number 7/215 but without cranes and small uprights between hatches two and three—as on drawing 5/304; Some of the ships under the latter drawing may be sisters of OKSYWIE

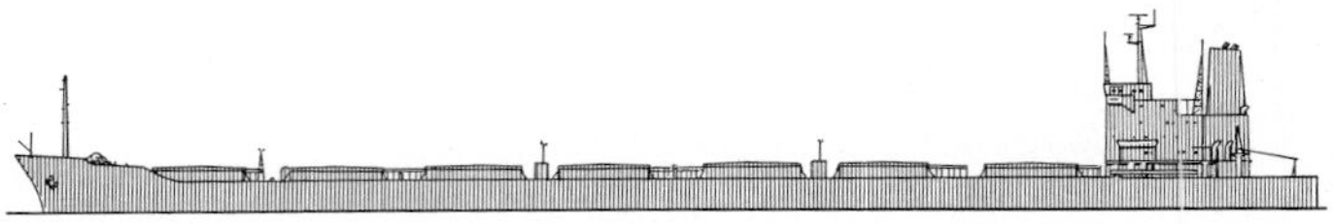

307 *MNMNF H1*
IOANNIS ZAFIRAKIS Gr/Ja (Hitachi) 1982; B; 35,304 grt/64,916 dwt; 224.52 × 12.95 m *(737 × 42.49 ft)*; M (B&W); 15 kts; ex-*Pacific Prominence*
Sister: **ATLANTIC STATESMAN** (Gr) ex-*Pacific Prestige*

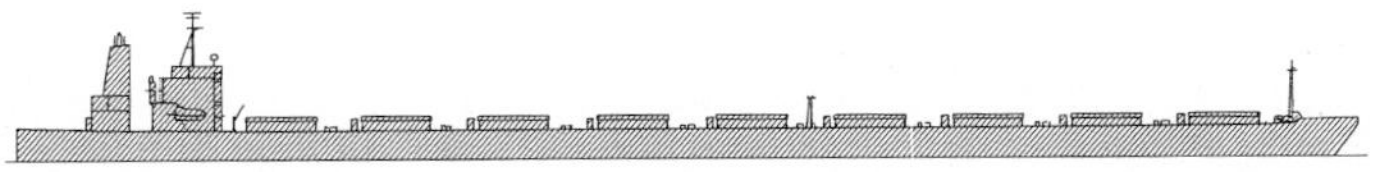

308 *MNMRF H*
MERCHANT PRESTIGE HK/Ko (Hyundai) 1995; B; 81,272 grt/161,010 dwt; 280.09 × 17.52 m *(918.93 × 57.48 ft)*; M (B&W); 14.52 kts
Sister: **MERCHANT PARAMOUNT** (HK)

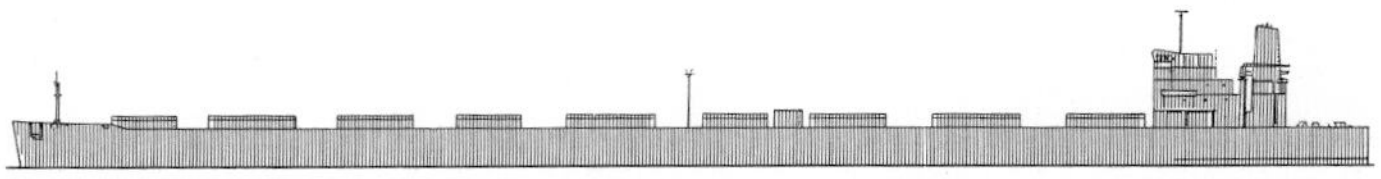

309 *MNMSF H*
MARINE HUNTER Pa/Be (Boelwerf) 1984; B; 83,784 grt/164,891 dwt; 265.01 × 17.42 m *(869.46 × 57.15 ft)*; M (B&W); 14 kts; ex-*Federal Hunter*
Sisters: **LA CORDILLERA** (Pa) ex-*Federal Skeena*; **PERIANDROS OF KORINTHOS** (Cy) ex-*Mineral Antwerpen*

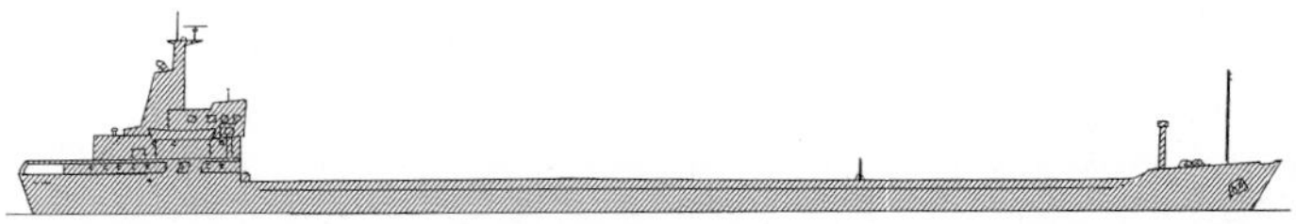

310 *MNM-F H1*
ST. ANTON As/Pd (Gdanska) 1976/83; C; 2,300 grt/4,028 dwt; 91.70 × 5.97 m *(300.85 × 19.59 ft)*; M (Fiat); 13.5 kts; ex-*Cairnash*; Lengthened and deepened 1983; 'B473' type
Sisters: **ST. CHRISTOPH** (As) ex-*Cairnelm*; **ST. JAKOB** (As) ex-*Cairnoak*

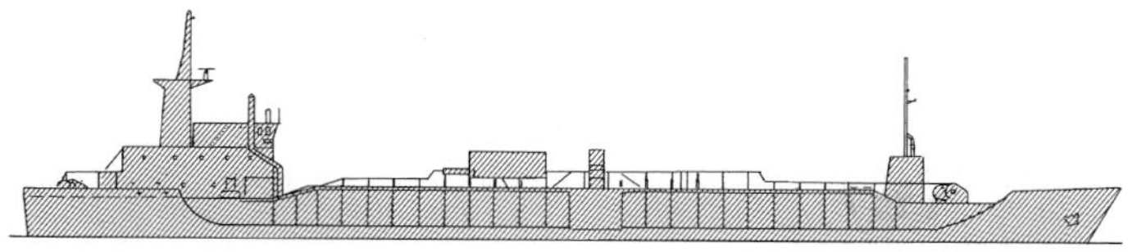

311 *MNM-F H13*
ACCOLADE II Au/Au (Carrington) 1982; B; 6,310 grt/8,140 dwt; 108.69 × 6.02 m *(356.59 × 19.75 ft)*; TSM (Fuji); 11.5 kts; Self-unloading limestone carrier

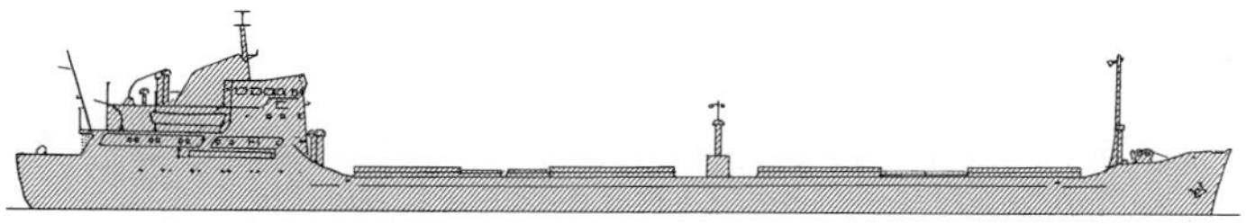

312 *MNM-FM H13*
VIDA Ma/Ne ('De Hoop') 1968; C; 4,154 grt/6,910 dwt; 110.42 × 6.85 m *(362.27 × 22.47 ft)*; M (MAN); 12.5 kts; ex-*Dunvegan Head*
Sister: **AMY** (Ma) ex-*Duncansby Head*

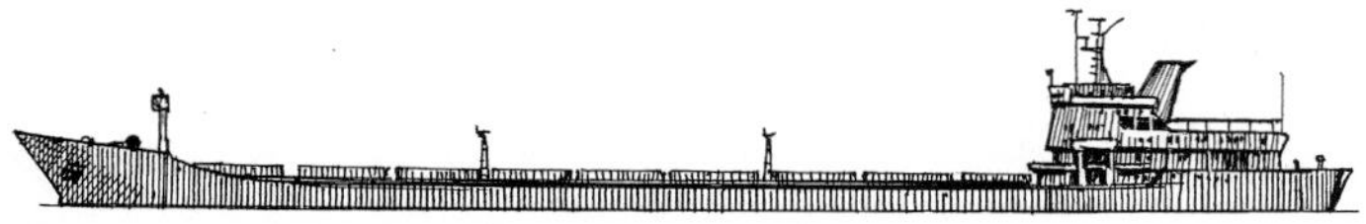

313 *MN^2MF H13*
FILIPP MAKHARADZE Gi/Pd (Szczecinska) 1972; B; 17,535 grt/32,404 dwt; 198.71 × 10.68 m *(651.93 × 35.03 ft)*; M (Sulzer); 15 kts; 'B447' type
Sisters: **NIKO K** (Ma) ex-*Niko Nikoladze*; **LEVAN** (Ma) ex-*Mikha Tskhakaya*; **OBRONCY POCZTY** (Pd); **POWSTANIEC SLASKI** (Pd); **LAKE WALES** (MI) ex-*Siekierki*; **TOBRUK** (Pd)

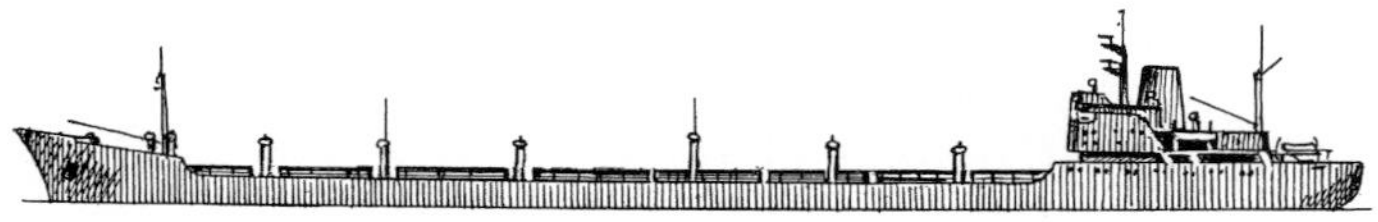

314 *MN^2MFH H13*
ZVENIGOROD Ru/Pd (Gdynska) 1967; B; 16,043 grt/22,895 dwt; 187.15 × 9.54 m *(614 × 31.29 ft)*; M (Sulzer); 15.5 kts; 'B 470' type
Sisters: **ZAPOROZHYE** (Uk); **ZAKARPATYE** (Uk); **ZADONSK** (Uk); **ZARECHENSK** (Ru); **ZLATOUST** (Uk); **ZORINSK** (Uk); **ZIEMIA KRAKOWSKA** (Pd); **ZIEMIA LUBELSKA** (Pd); **ZAGLEBIE MIEDZIOWE** (Pd)

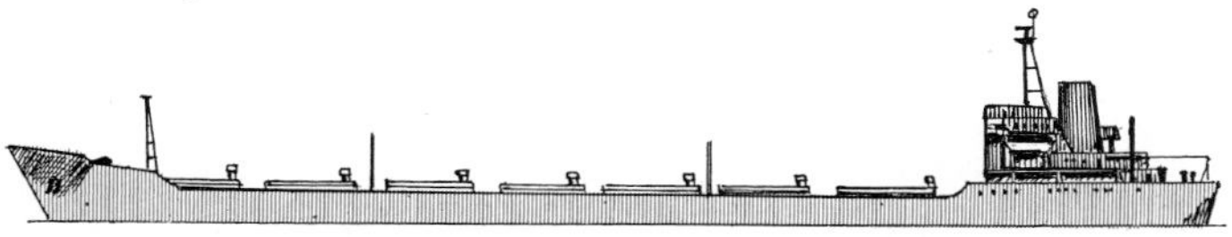

315 *MN^2MFN H13*
ALFA Cy/Sp (AESA) 1974; B; 29,824 grt/53,400 dwt; 206.76 × 13.28 m *(678.35 × 43.57 ft)*; M (Sulzer); 15.25 kts; ex-*King Charles*
Similar: **ALINDA** (Cy) ex-*Garthnewydd*; **JALAVIJAYA** (In) ex-*Graiglas*

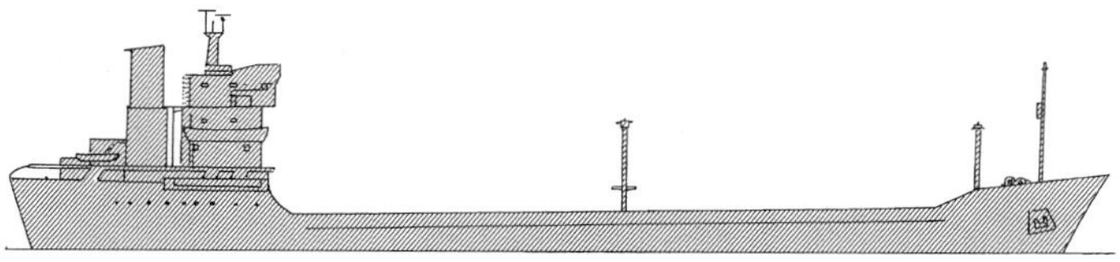

316 *MN^2MG H13*
KISH Bs/Pd (Gdanska) 1978; C; 1,961 grt/2,963 dwt; 84.18 × 5.73 m *(276.18 × 18.8 ft)*; M (Fiat); 14 kts; Launched as *Ran*; 'B-431' type
Sister: **CIBONEY** (SV) ex-*Lipsk N/Biebrza*

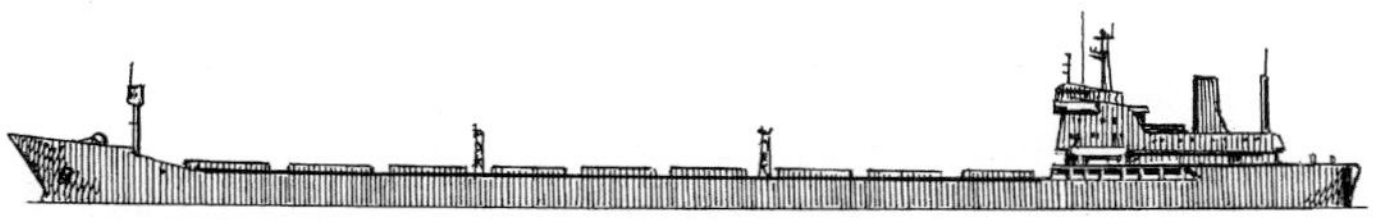

317 *MN^2MGN H13*
LEON Pa/Pd (Szczecinska) 1974; B; 20,513 grt/31,923 dwt; 202.34 × 10.64 m *(663.85 × 34.91 ft)*; M (Sulzer); 15 kts; ex-*Georgiy Leonidze*; 'B447' type
Sister: **ADJARIA** (Ma) ex-*General Leselidze*

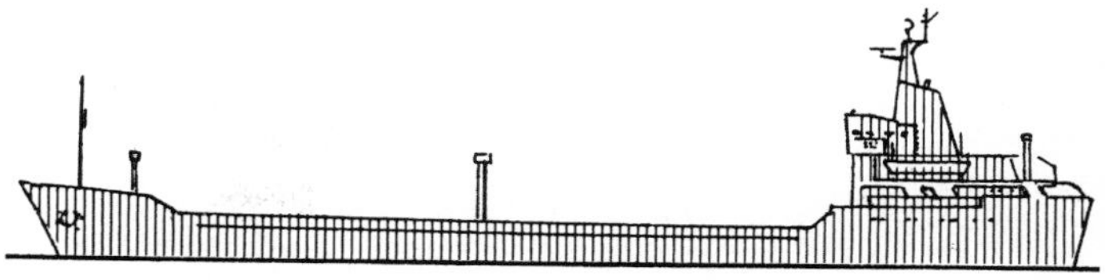

318 *MN^2M-F H13*
HASLO Ma/Pd (Gdanska) 1976; C; 1,895 grt/3,049 dwt; 84.13 × 5.32 m *(276 × 17.45 ft)*; M (GMT); — kts; ex-*Ask*; 'B-431' type
Sister: **GEILO** (Ma) ex-*Fro*

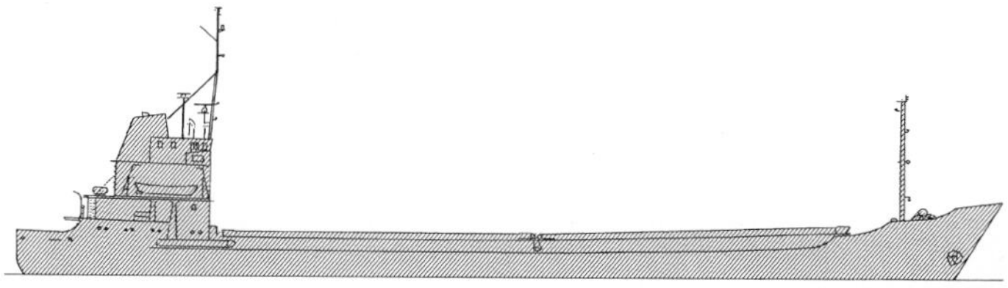

319 *MVF H12*
BLANKENESE At/FRG (Elsflether) 1984; C/Con; 2,882 grt/4,200 dwt; 89.2 × 5.23 m *(292.65 × 17.16 ft)*; M (Deutz); 11 kts; Lengthened to 99.801m (327.1ft) 1990—drawing shows vessel as built; 174 TEU

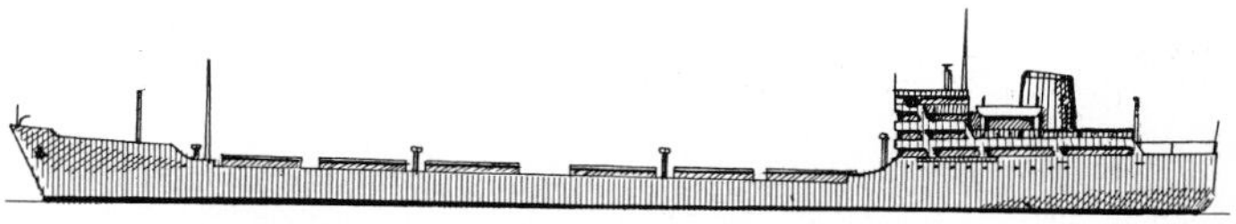

320 *NM^2FN H13*
BONG SAN RK/Br (J.L. Thompson) 1960; O; 12,733 grt/18,573 dwt; 160.03 × 9 m *(525.03 × 29.53 ft)*; M (Doxford); 12 kts; ex-*Lindisfarne*

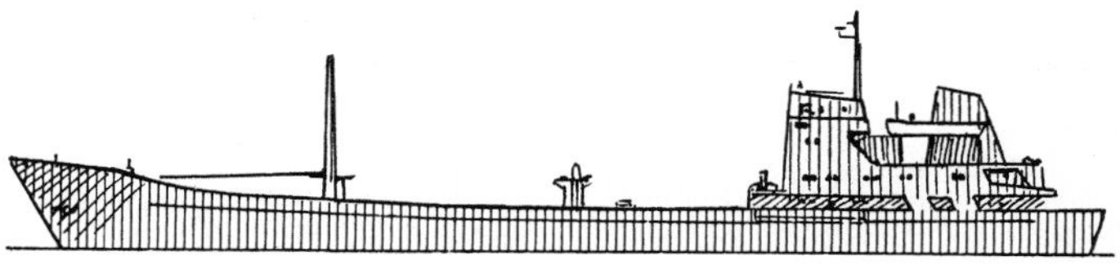

321 *VMF H1*
LEMBIT Ru/Rm (Turnu-Severin) 1970; C; 1,968 grt/2,063 dwt; 85.88 × 5.1 m *(281.76 × 16.73 ft)*; M (Sulzer); 14 kts; ex-*Naleczow*

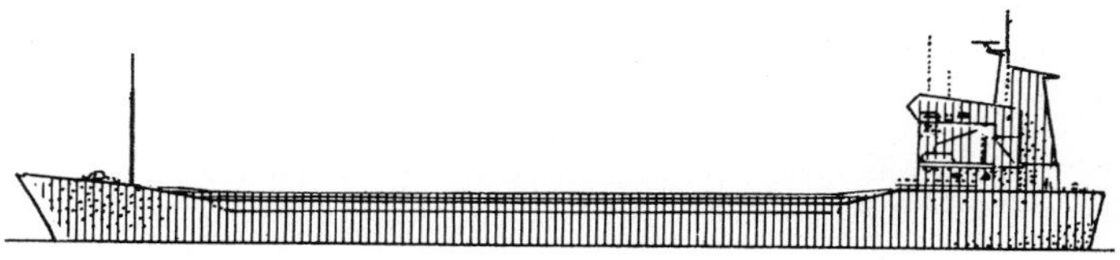

322 *VM-F H13*
BIRLING Br/Br (Clelands) 1977; C; 2,795 grt/4,300 dwt; 91.22 × 5.45 m *(299 × 17.88 ft)*; M (Mirrlees Blackstone); 14 kts
Sisters: **EMERALD** (Br); **HARTING** (Br); **STEYNING** (Br)

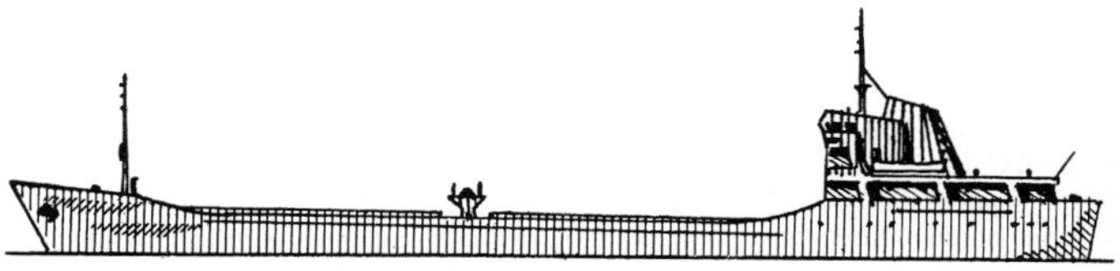

323 *V^2F H13*
SAGACITY Bs/Br (Goole) 1972; B; 1,926 grt/3,238 dwt; 91.14 × 5.14 m *(299.02 × 16.86 ft)*; M (British Polar); 12.75 kts
Sisters: **EMMA** (Ma) ex-*Serenity*; **LOBO** (NIS) ex-*Superiority*; **BARCO** (Ma) ex-*Suavity*; Similar: **RAUTZ** (As) ex-*Eildon*; **STUBEN** (As) ex-*Ettrick*; Similar (extended poop and forecastle): **RUTA** (Ma) ex-*Martindyke*; **GRETA C** (Bb) ex-*Mairi Everard*

324 Nessie *(Cy); 1972* *WSPL*

325 Angelic Grace *(Gr); 1971* *WSPL*

326 Lepanto Star *(Pa); 1973; (as Kanin)* *WSPL*

327 Kapitonas Mesceriakov *(Lt); 1978* *WSPL*

328 Samsara *(Cy); 1978; (as Mineral Hoboken)* *WSPL*

329 Ion Soltys *(Uk); 1976* *WSPL*

330 Lindesay Clark *(Au); 1985* *WSPL*

331 Ijmuiden Maru *(Pa); 1986* *WSPL*

332 Vedette *(Ne); 1990* *WSPL*

333 Gyle *(Sw); 1972; (as Rhein Merchant)* *WSPL*

334 Cosa *(Cy); 1972* *WSPL*

335 Rachel Borchard *(At); 1992* *Norman Thomson*

336 Petimata OT RMS *(Bu); 1978* *Norman Thomson*

337 Alexander *(Le); 1973; (as Global Makatcha)* *Norman Thomson*

338 Samrat Ashok *(In); 1974* *Norman Thomson*

339 Okolchitza *(Bu); 1982* *Norman Thomson*

340 Elizabeth C *(Bb); 1971; (as Mark C)* *Norman Thomson*

341 La Cordillera *(Pa); 1983; (as Federal Skeena)* *Norman Thomson*

342 Jalavijaya *(In); 1975* *Norman Thomson*

343 Levan *(Ma); 1972* *Norman Thomson*

344 Seniority *(Br); 1991* *FotoFlite*

345 Jevington *(Br); 1977* *FotoFlite*

346 Samson *(Li); 1978* *FotoFlite*

347 Saturn V *(Cy); 1980* *FotoFlite*

348 New Luck *(Gr); 1981* *FotoFlite*

349 Reliance Ocean *(HK); 1980; (as Senwa)* *FotoFlite*

350 Mineral Nippon *(HK); 1986* *FotoFlite*

351 Rena *(Gr); 1981; (as Ansgaritor)* *FotoFlite*

352 Elgin *(Li); 1981* *FotoFlite*

353 Yamato *(Pa); 1991* *FotoFlite*

354 Channel Enterprise *(Pi); 1990* *FotoFlite*

355 Ullswater *(HK); 1990* *FotoFlite*

356 Sea Clipper *(Pa); 1990* *FotoFlite*

357 Astrafederico *(Ar); 1981* *FotoFlite*

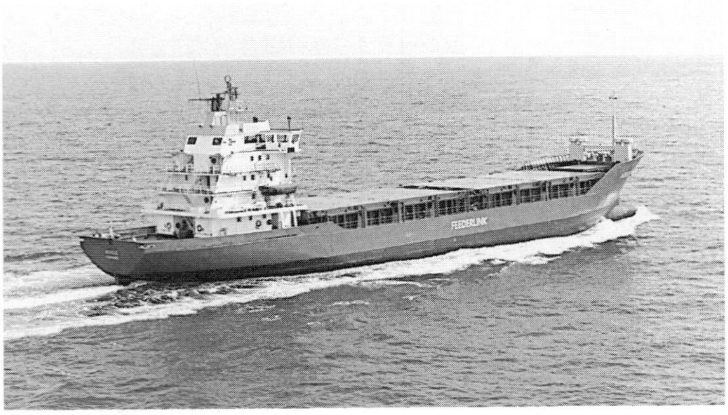

358 Nordia *(At); 1983* *FotoFlite*

359 Siderpollux *(It); 1982* *FotoFlite*

360 Portugal Bridge *(Ge); 1990; (as Gracechurch Comet)* *FotoFlite*

361 Bremon *(Sw); 1976* *FotoFlite*

362 Nunki *(Pa); 1979* *FotoFlite*

363 Laura Helena *(Cy); 1993* *FotoFlite*

364 Lowlands Sunrise *(Br); 1983* *FotoFlite*

365 Polycarp *(NIS); 1990* *FotoFlite*

366 Oceanic Enterprise *(Pa); 1995* *FotoFlite*

367 Stellar Cape *(Pa); 1990* *FotoFlite*

368 Mikasa *(Ja); 1991* *FotoFlite*

369 Maritime Nancy *(Pa); 1990* *FotoFlite*

370 Dyna Caroway *(HK); 1995* *FotoFlite*

371 Amagisan *(HK); 1993* *FotoFlite*

372 Cape Violet *(Pa); 1994* *FotoFlite*

373 Gran Trader *(Pi); 1994* *FotoFlite*

374 Chikuzen Maru *(Ja); 1993* *FotoFlite*

375 Merchant Pride *(HK); 1990* *FotoFlite*

376 Full Beauty *(Li); 1994* *FotoFlite*

377 Maritime Wisdom *(Sg); 1993* *FotoFlite*

378 Maja Vestida *(Pi); 1994* *FotoFlite*

379 Ispat Gaurav *(Li); 1994; (as Christitsa)* *FotoFlite*

380 Joy Sea *(Pa); 1990* *FotoFlite*

381 Alert *(Ne); 1984* *FotoFlite*

382 Anita *(NIS); 1975* *FotoFlite*

383 Albona *(As); 1980* *FotoFlite*

384 Olivier *(Ne); 1986* *FotoFlite*

385 Hyundai Oceania *(Ko); 1983* *FotoFlite*

386 Rosali *(Cy); 1972* *FotoFlite*

387 Emily Borchard *(At); 1978; (as Anglia)* *FotoFlite*

6 Gearless Dry Cargo Vessels (83.82 m (275 ft) and under)

6 Gearless Dry Cargo Vessels (83.82 m (275 ft) and under)

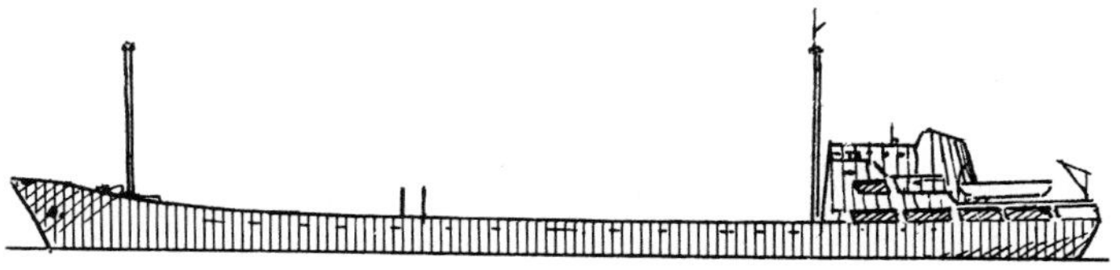

1 H^2F *H1*
UNITY III Ho/FRG (Hagelstein) 1957; C; 999 grt/2,227 dwt; 80.22 × 5 m *(263.19 × 16.4 ft)*; M (KHD); 11.5 kts; ex-*Dinklage*; Lengthened and deepened 1968
Similar: **ZAKARIA** (Ho) ex-*Berolina*

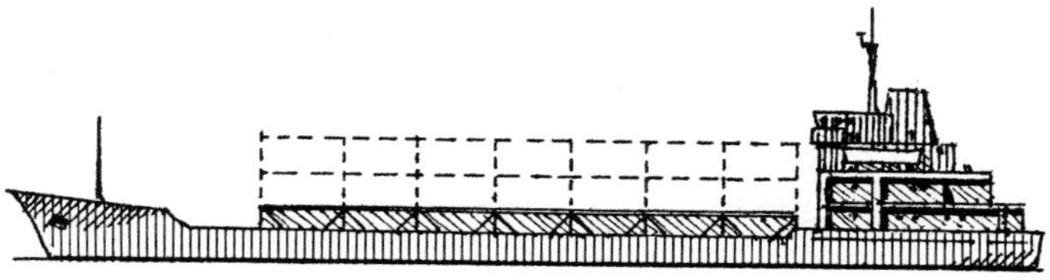

2 *MHF H1*
CORINNA At/FRG (Sietas) 1974; C/Con; 2,130 grt/2,450 dwt; 81.41 × 4.91 m *(267.09 × 16.11 ft)*; M (Atlas-MaK); 13.75 kts; ex-*Bell Vantage*; 144 TEU
Similar: **SVEALAND** (Ge) ex-*Osteclipper*; **STEFANIE** (At) ex-*Canopus*; **ANUND** (Cy) ex-*Odin*; **GERLINA** (NIS) ex-*Osteland*; **NAVIGIA** (Ge) ex-*Donar*; **TRAVEBERG** (Cy) ex-*American Comanche*; **COBURG** (At) launched as *Nautilus*; **HEINRICH BEHRMANN** (Ge) launched as *Komet*; **LAPPLAND** (Ge); **SYDGARD** (Fi) ex-*Ina Lehmann*; **SIEGFRIED LEHMANN** (Mr); **AROSIA** (At) launched as *Corvette*; **STENHOLM** (At) ex-*Suderelv*; **GERINA** (NIS) launched as Anna Becker; **NAUTILA** (At) launched as *Ute Wulff*; **HAJO** (At) ex-*Osterheide* (10 m (32 ft) shorter); **DUKE** (NIS) ex-*Jan Kahrs*; **NORRLAND** (Ge) ex-*Falkenstein* (shorter); **PASSAT** (Cy) (shorter); **VILLE DE MINA QABOOS** (At) ex-*Seevetal* (shorter); **GERLIN** (NIS) ex-*Orion*; **TONG AN** (RC) ex-*Niedermehnen* (shorter); **TALEA** (At) ex-*Parnass*; **ROSITA MARIA** (NIS); **LIBRA** (Ne) ex-*Melton Challenger*; **DOMAR** (Sw) ex-*Hove*; **SENTOSA JAYA** (Pa) ex-*Adeline* (shorter); **LU SHENG** (RC) ex-*Levern* (shorter); **BALTIC COURIER** (Cy) ex-*Jorn Dede* (shorter); **RONG DA** (RC) ex-*Hollwede* (shorter); **ANNIKA M** (Ge) ex-*Anja* (shorter); **HANNI** (Ge) ex-*G H Ehler*; **SCHULAU** (At) (shorter); **CUXHAVEN** (At); **TARAS** (Ne) ex-*Ikaria*; Similar (larger funnel): **MAJGARD** (Fi) ex-*Rie Bres*; **DORI BRES** (DIS); **NINA BRES** (DIS); **CLARA** (At) ex-*Heide-Catrin*; **RANAFJORD** (Ma) ex-*Ume*; **NORDFELD** (Cy); Probably similar (converted to cement carrier): **CAPO ROSSO** (Fr) ex-*Hornbaltic*

See photo number 6/78

3 *MH-F H1*
TARIK Mo/Ne ('Hoogezand' JB) 1969; C/Con; 1,270 grt/1,397 dwt; 75.70 × 3.58 m *(248.36 × 11.75 ft)*; M (MWM); 12.5 kts; ex-*Bell Vision*;
SIMILAR TO DRAWING NUMBER 6/42

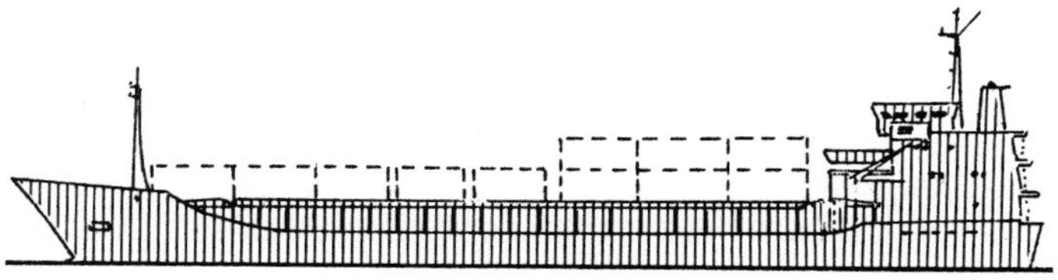

4 M^2F *H1*
ELIZA HEEREN At/FRG (Brand) 1981; C/Con; 2,023 grt/2,800 dwt; 79.71 × 5.07 m *(262 × 16.63 ft)*; M (Krupp-MaK); 12 kts; 144 TEU
Sister: **NORA HEEREN** (At)

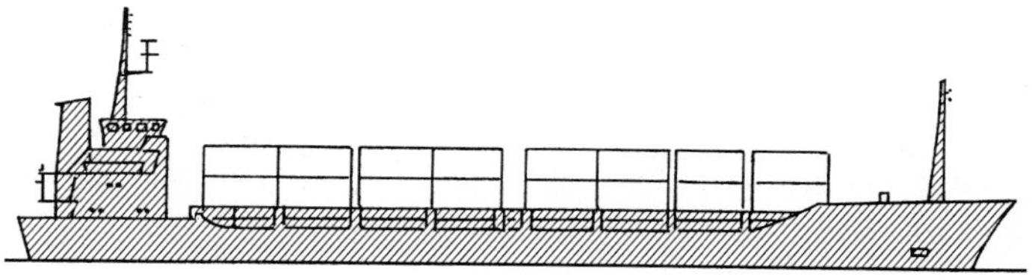

5 M^2F *H1*
FIGAROS At/FRG (Sietas) 1980; C/Con; 2,050 grt/3,254 dwt; 80.32 × 5.04 m *(263.52 × 16.54 ft)*; M (MaK); 13.50 kts; 132 TEU
Sister: **LADY BOS** (Sw); Similar: **KIRSTEN** (At) ex-*Craigavad*; **PELLWORM** (Ge) ex-*Craigantlet*

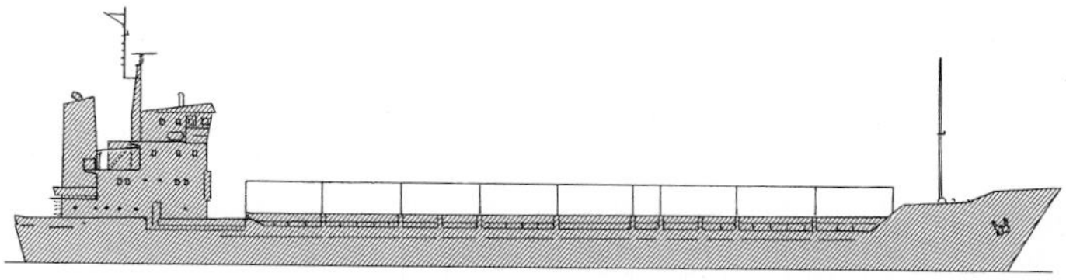

6 M^2F *H1*
PELTRADER Gr/Ne ('Friesland') 1978; Con/C; 2,315 grt/3,103 dwt; 81.84 × 5.65 m *(268.5 × 18.54 ft)*; M ('Bolnes'); 12.75 kts; ex-*Midsland*; 166 TEU
Sister (now lengthened to 95.81 m (314 ft)): **PELCHASER** (Gr) ex-*Sertan*

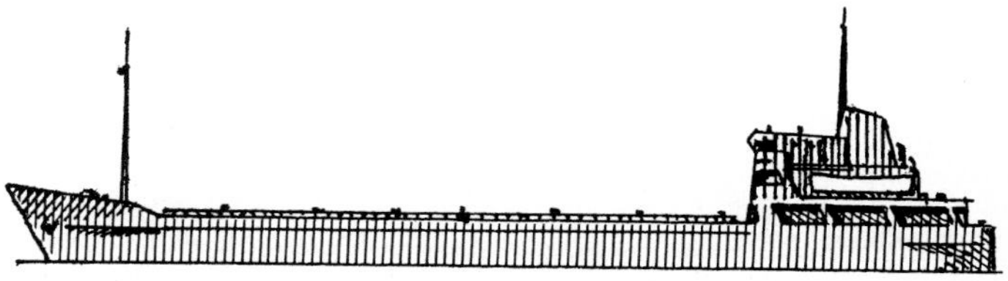

7 M^2F *H1*
SAFAD Pa/Ne ('Hoogezand' JB) 1970; C; 729 grt/1,521 dwt; 78.47 × 4.03 m *(257.45 × 13.22 ft)*; M (Atlas-MaK); 12.5 kts; ex-*Owenglas*
Sister: **CELINE M** (Ho) ex-*Hibernian Enterprise*

8 M^2F *H13*
AGROS Cy/Sp (Luzuriaga) 1981; C; 1,769 grt/2,839 dwt; 79.02 × 5.54 m *(259.25 × 18.18 ft)*; M (Alpha); 11.5 kts; ex-*Virgen de las Nieves*

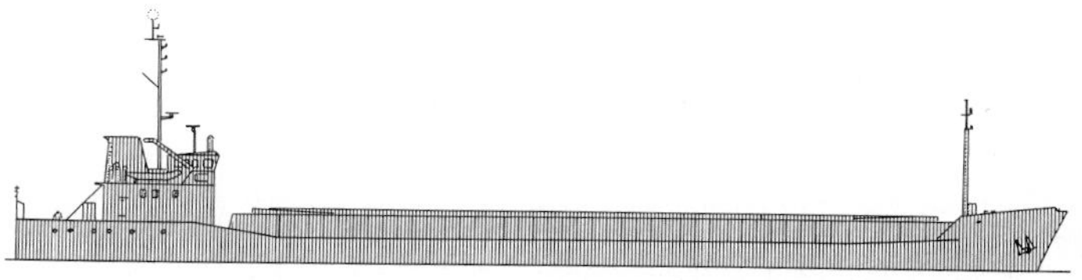

9 $\underline{M^2F}$ *H13*
ANDRINA F Ge/Ge (Arminius) 1990; C; 1,568 grt/1,890 dwt; 81.20 × 3.66 m *(266.40 × 11.98 ft)*; M (MaK); 9.5 kts; ex-*Simone*; 72 TEU
Possible sister: **TRINKET** (Cy)

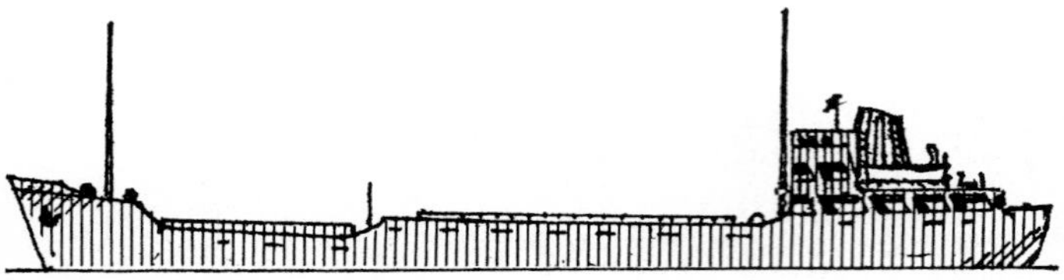

10 *M²F H13*
ARMENISTIS Gr/Ne ('Foxhol') 1965; C; 1,102 grt/1,623 dwt; 72.27 × 4.53 m *(237.11 × 14.86 ft)*; M (KHD); — kts; ex-*Eden Fisher*

11 *M²F H13*
ASTRAL 1 Pa/Ne (Coops) 1978; C; 1,248 grt/1,931 dwt; 71.38 × 4.53 m *(234.19 × 14.86 ft)*; M (Atlas-MaK); 12 kts; ex-*Star Venus*; May now have two cranes

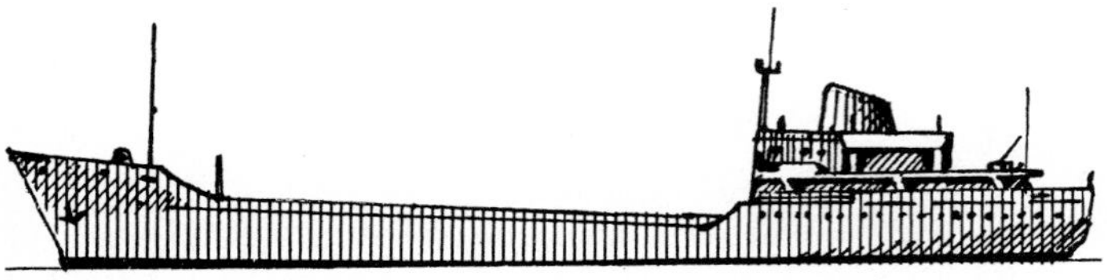

12 *M²F H13*
BULK CHALLENGE Ng/Hu (Angyalfold) 1968; C; 1,199 grt/1,950 dwt; 74.81 × 4.99 m *(245.44 × 16.37 ft)*; M (MWM); 11.75 kts; ex-*Petro Coco*
Sisters: **HAMAD ALLAH** (Eg) ex-*Petro Prince*; **HOSANNA** (It) ex-*Petro Duke*

13 *M²F H13*
CRAIGMORE Ho/Br (Dunston) 1966; C; 1,359 grt/1,710 dwt; 73.03 × 5.04 m *(239.6 × 16.54 ft)*; M (British Polar); 11 kts

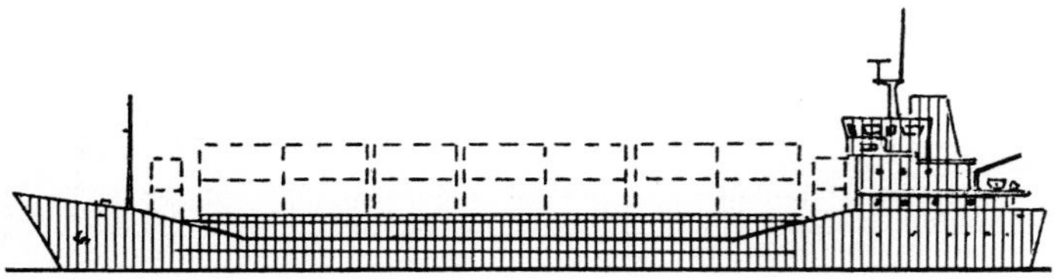

14 *M²F H13*
ENOL Po/Sp (Luzuriaga) 1982; C/Con; 2,016 grt/3,123 dwt; 77.07 × 5.8 m *(252.85 × 19.03 ft)*; M (Krupp-MaK); 11 kts; ex-*Punta Zabala*
Sister: **INISHOWEN** (Ih) ex-*Raimundo A*; Possible sisters: **XOVE** (Sp); **ERCINA** (Po) ex-*Salpa*

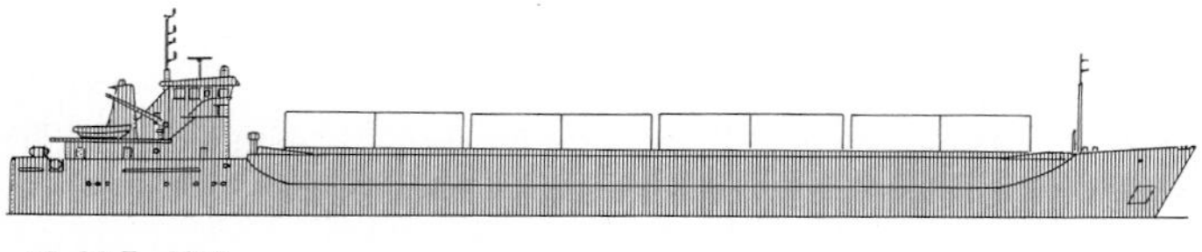

15 *M²F H13*
HANSE Ge/FRG (Diedrich) 1990; C; 1,508 grt/1,688 dwt; 79.70 × 3.53 m *(261.48 × 11.58 ft)*; M (Deutz); 10.5 kts; 80 TEU

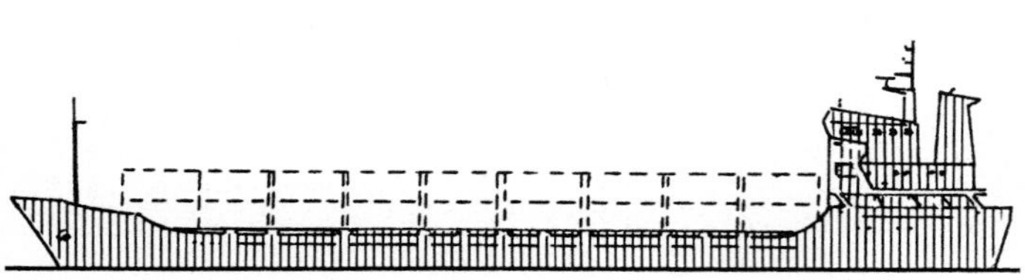

16 *M²F H13*
HUA JIAN SV/Ne (Sander) 1978; C/Con; 2,106 grt/2,222 dwt; 82 × 4.45 m *(269.03 × 14.6 ft)*; M (KHD); 12.5 kts; ex-*Yolanda*

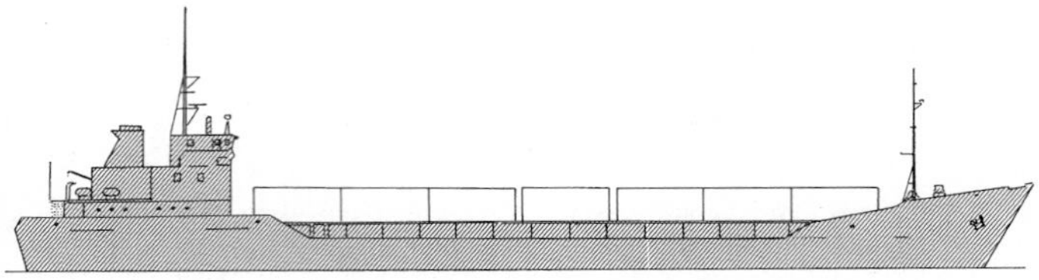

17 *M²F H13*
MAIRA Ea/DDR (Elbewerften) 1971; C/Con; 1,160 grt/1,120 dwt; 71.07 × 3.68 m *(233.17 × 12.07 ft)*; M (Liebknecht); 12 kts; ex-*Fritsis Rosin*
Sisters: **SOLAR BAY** (Ho) ex-*Gleb Sedin*; **HAI YU** (Ho) ex-*Warin*; **YUE XIU SHAN** (Ho) ex-*Bansin*; **YUE YANG** (Ho) ex-*Tessin*; **SHYAMLEE** (SV) ex-*Rechlin*

18 *M²F H13*
MERAK Cy/Ne (Gruno) 1976; C; 1,472 grt/2,340 dwt; 76.41 × 4.83 m *(250.69 × 15.85 ft)*; M (Appingedammer Brons); 10.75 kts

19 *M²F H13*
OCEAN FLEET Pa/Ne (E J Smit) 1975; C; 1,948 grt/3,016 dwt; 83.44 × 5.07 m *(273.75 × 16.63 ft)*; M (Atlas-MaK); 12.5 kts; ex-*Karen Danielsen*
Sisters: **CARIB TRADER** (Pa) ex-*Ulla Danielsen*; **WORTHING** (Br) ex-*Lis Danielsen* (builder—Suurmeyer); **MAGO** (It) ex-*Marie Helleskov*

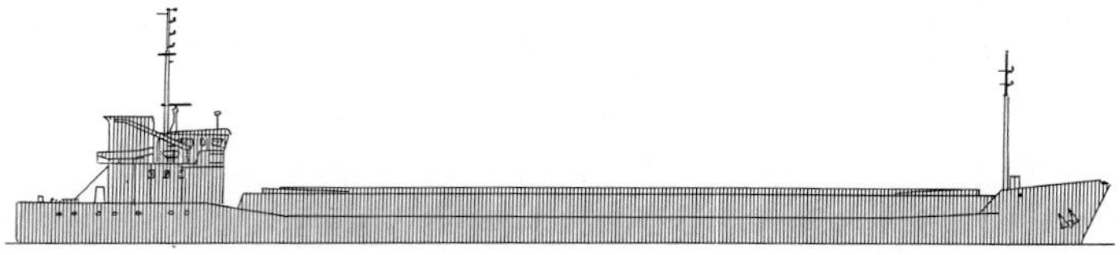

20 *M²F H13*
ONEGO Ru/Ge (Arminius) 1991; C; 1,574 grt/1,890 dwt; 81.20 × 3.65 m *(266.40 × 11.98 ft)*; M (MaK); 9.5 kts; 72 TEU
Possible sisters: **VYG** (Ru); **SEG** (Ru) (see photo number 6/110); **MEG** (Ru); **KENTO** (Ru); **KERET** (Ru)

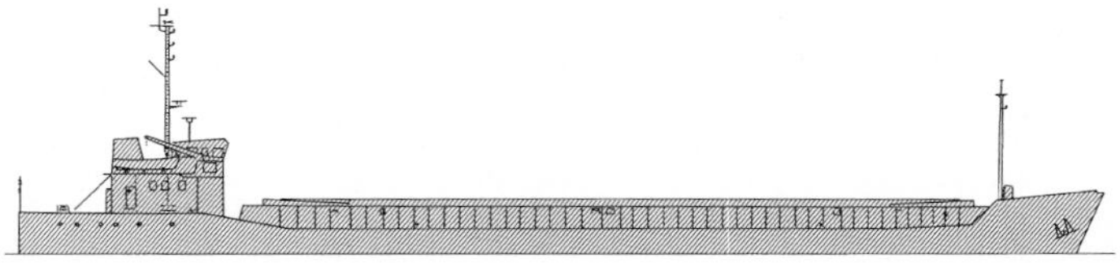

21 *M²F H13*
PETRA F Ge/FRG (Arminius) 1985; C/Con; 1,567 grt/1,748 dwt; 81.21 × 3.72 m *(266.44 × 12.20 ft)*; M (Wärtsilä); 9.75 kts; 72 TEU
Sister: **XANDRINA** (Ge)

See photo number 6/96

22 *M²F H13*
RMS MERCATOR Tv/FRG (Brand) 1986; C/Con; 2,006 grt/2,723 dwt; 81.87 × 4.52 m *(268.60 × 14.83 ft)*; M (Deutz); 11 kts; ex-*Atula*; 104 TEU
Sisters: **CLAUS** (Tv); **DIANA-MARIA** (Ge) ex-*Betula*

23 *M²F H13*
SCOTFIELD Cy/Ne (E J Smit) 1974; C; 1,952 grt/2,946 dwt; 83.5 × 5.13 m *(273.95 × 16.83 ft)*; M (Atlas-MaK); 12 kts; ex-*Syon Park*
Sisters: **MAXIM** (Ma) ex-*Mishnish*; **LANCING** (Br) ex-*Baxtergate*; Possibly similar: **COTINGA** (Bs); **MARATHON** (Cy) ex-*Flowergate*

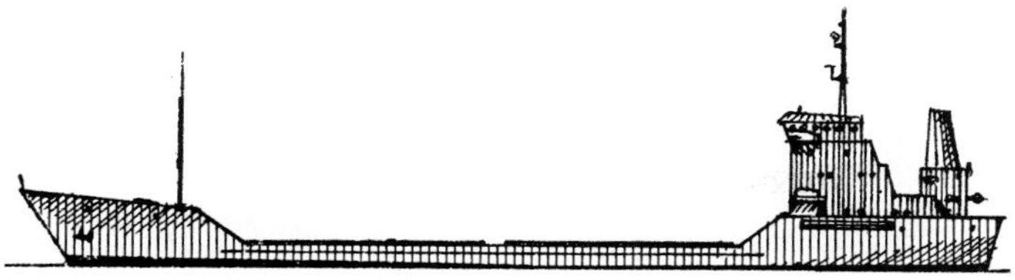

24 M^2F *H13*
SCOTIA NA/Ne (Tille) 1977; C; 1,599 grt/3,214 dwt; 81.72 × 5.5 m *(268.11 × 18.04 ft)*; M (Brons); 12.5 kts; ex-*Sylvia Alpha*
Sisters: **NORTH SEA** (NA) ex-*Sylvia Beta*; **LADY REA** (Cy) ex-*Sylvia Delta*; **SILKE** (NA) ex-*Sylvia Epsilon*; **CASPIC** (NA) ex-*Sylvia Gamma*; **BENGALEN** (NA) ex-*Sylvia Omega*

25 M^2F *H13*
SELECTIVITY Br/Br (Cochrane) 1984; C/Con; 1,892 grt/2,415 dwt; 79.02 × 4.55 m *(259.25 × 14.93 ft)*; M (Krupp-MaK); 10 kts; 94 TEU
Sisters: **PAMELA EVERARD** (Br) (builder—Richards); **SANGUITY** (Br) ex-*Willonia*; **SOCIALITY** (Br) ex-*Stevonia*

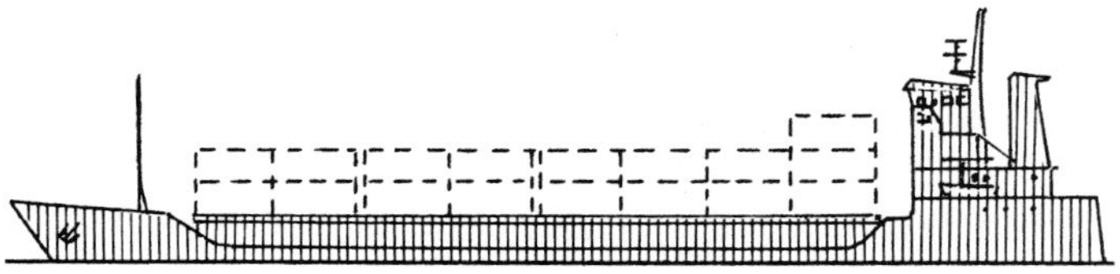

26 M^2F *H13*
SPRANTE Ge/FRG (Cassens) 1986; C/Con; 1,899 grt/2,295 dwt; 81,75 × 4.29 m *(268.21 × 14.07 ft)*; M (MWM); 11 kts; 147 TEU

27 M^2F *H13*
STATHIS G Pa/FRG (M Jansen) 1975; C; 1,770 grt/3,195 dwt; 79.51 × 5.55 m *(260.86 × 18.21 ft)*; M (Atlas-Mak); 12.5 kts; ex-*Breezand*; 72 TEU
Sisters: **ARMOUR** (Pa) ex-*Cairncarrier*; **BLUE LINE** (It) ex-*Cairnfreighter*; **FIVI** (Ma) ex-*Cairnleader*

See photo number 6/104

28 M^2F *H13*
SUDWIND Ge/FRG (Nobiskrug) 1978; C/Con; 1,624 grt/1,659 dwt; 79.23 × 3.5 m *(259.94 × 11.48 ft)*; M (Atlas-MaK); 12.5 kts; 142 TEU
Sister: **OSTWIND** (At) ex-*St Antonius*; Sisters (lengthened to 84.60 m (27 ft)): **MARIANNE** (Ge) ex-*Detlef Schmidt*; **EIDER** (Ge)

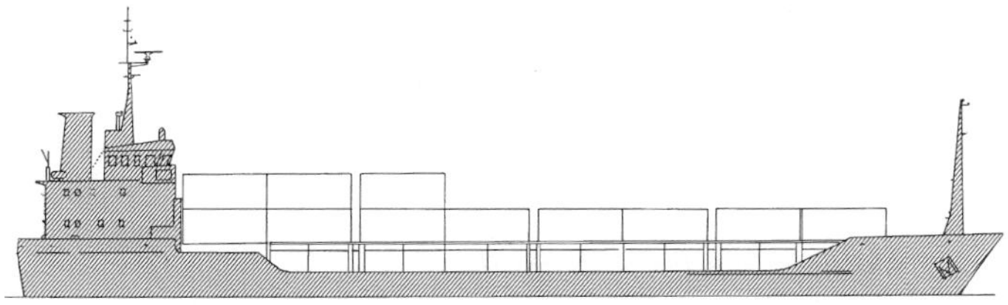

29 M^2F *H13*
URANIA Ge/FRG (Kroegerw) 1978; C/Con; 1,486 grt/1,626 dwt; 70.82 × 3.88 m *(232.35 × 12.73 ft)*; M (MaK); 11 kts; ex-*Ulsnis*; 140 TEU

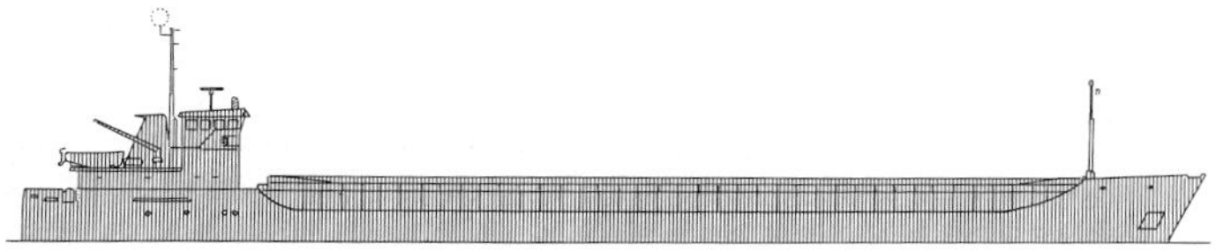

30 M^2F *H13*
VERA RAMBOW Ge/Ge (Diedrich) 1991; C; 1,559 grt/1,850 dwt; 79.70 × 3.68 m *(261.48 × 12.07 ft)*; M (Deutz); 10.1 kts; 80 TEU

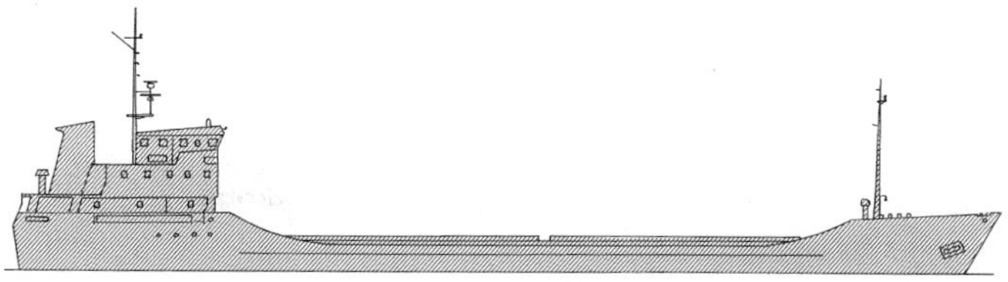

31 M^2F *H13*
VERENA Ne/Ne ('Voorwaarts') 1977; C; 1,769 grt/2,728 dwt; 75.11 × 5.37 m *(246.42 × 17.62 ft)*; M (Brons); 12 kts; ex-*Mathilde*
Probable sisters: **ERNA** (Ne) ex-*Menna*; **NORA** (Ne) (lengthened to 83.27 m (273 ft)): Similar: **MARY C** (Bb) ex-*Ligato*

32 M^2F *H13*
VERONA Ne/Ne (Bodewes NV) 1982; C; 1,923 grt/3,095 dwt; 80.02 × 5.55 m *(262.53 × 18.21 ft)*; M (Krupp-MaK); 12 kts
Sister: **ELECTRON** (Ne)

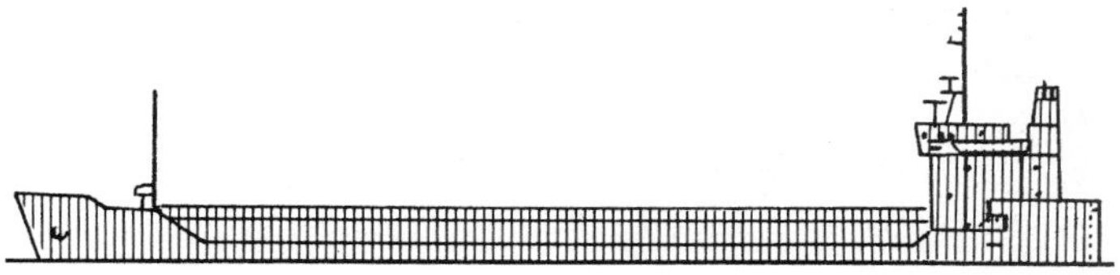

33 M^2F *H13*
WESTGARD Fi/Fi (Rauma-Repola) 1980; C/Con; 2,052 grt/2,730 dwt; 83.38 × 5.05 m *(273.56 × 16.57 ft)*; M (Wärtsilä); 12 kts; ex-*Lavola*; 128 TEU
Sisters: **STELLA ARCTIC** (Sw) ex-*Mustola*; **STELLA BALTIC** (Sw) ex-*Pohjola*; **BORRE AF SIMRISHAMN** (Sw) ex-*Repola*; **KAPTEN VOOLENS** (Ea) ex-*Kapitan Voolens*; **MEKHAANIK KRULL** (Ea) ex-*Mekhanik Krull*; **KAPTEN KONGA** (Ea) ex-*Yuriy Klementyev*

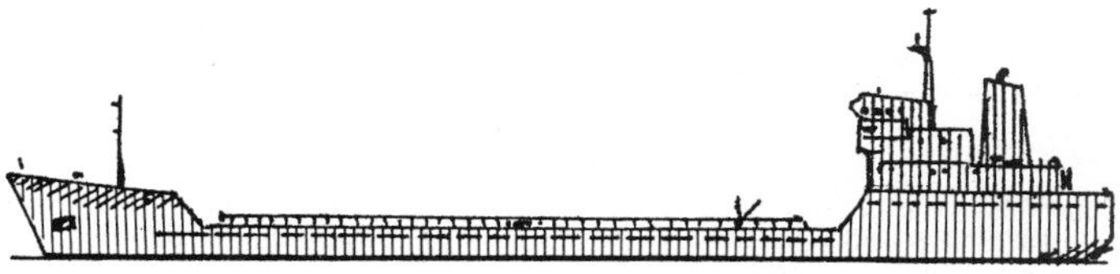

34 M^2F *H13*
ZWANET NA/Ne (Amels) 1977; C; 2,029 grt/3,100 dwt; 82.25 × 5.34 m *(269.85 × 17.52 ft)*; M (MWM); 12.5 kts; ex-*Deltasee*
Sister: **LIZRIX** (Br) ex-*Eriesee*

35 M^2FLM *H13*
RUSALKA II Pd/Pd ('Komuny Paryskiej') 1991; C; 1,948 grt/1,880 dwt; 75.96 × 4.50 m *(249.21 × 14.76 ft)*; M (Sulzer); 10.5 kts; 122 TEU; 'B564' type
Sisters: **NIMFA II** (Pd); **FORTUNA I** (SV) ex-*Goplana II*

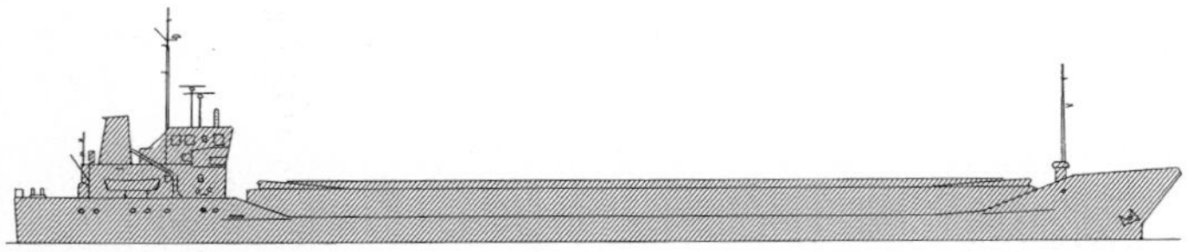

36 *M²FN H13*
SCOT TRADER Ge/FRG (Husumer K) 1986; C; 1,584 grt/1,900 dwt; 82.02 × 3.65 m *(269.09 × 11.98 ft)*; M (MAN); 10 kts; ex-*Wotan*
Sisters (differ in details such as position of mainmast, radar aerials and so on): **SILVIA** (Ge); **LEONA** (Ge); **MAIKE** (Ge); **LISA** (Ge) ex-*Edith*; **INGA** (Ge)

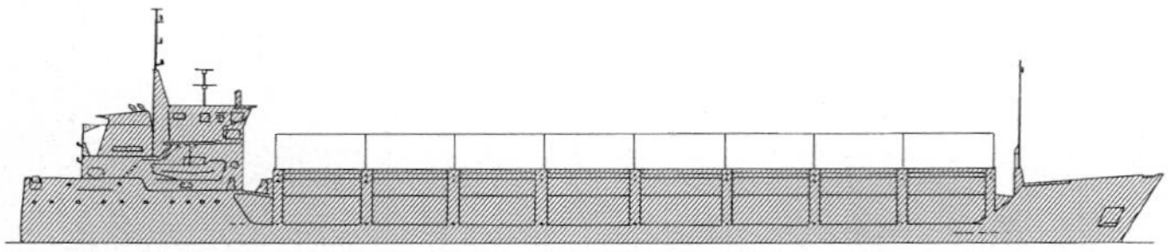

37 *M²FS H13*
BRANDARIS Ge/FRG (Hegemann) 1985; C/Con; 2,007 grt/2,460 dwt; 78.42 × 4.46 m *(257.28 × 14.63 ft)*; M (Deutz); 10 kts; 133 TEU

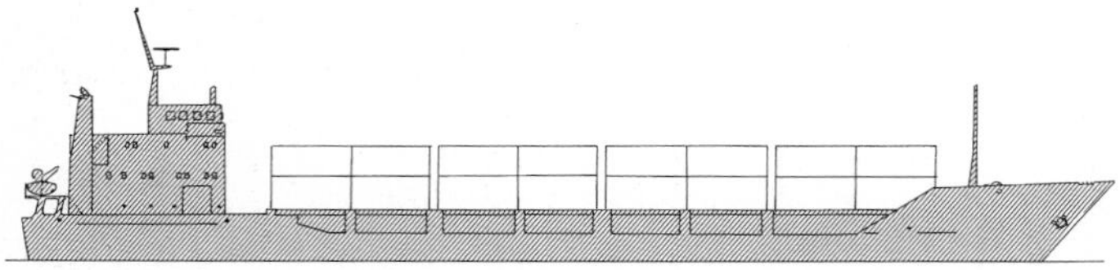

38 *M²G H1*
BRUCE It/Sp (Atlantico) 1981; C/Con; 2,337 grt/3,617 dwt; 80.90 × 6.01 m *(265.42 × 19.72 ft)*; M (Sulzer); 11.50 kts; ex-*Tresmares*; 162 TEU
Sister: **MIRA NOR** (No)

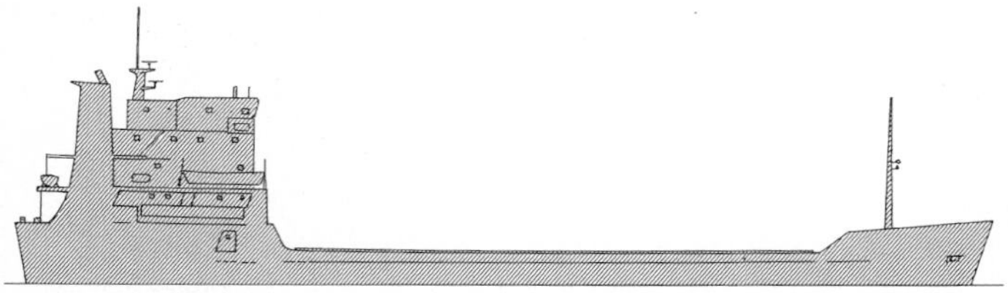

39 *MMG H13*
HAVANG Sw/No (Sterkoder) 1977; C; 2,021 grt/2,942 dwt; 80.12 × 5.32 m *(262.86 × 17.45 ft)*; M (Alpha); 13.5 kts; ex-*Fenix*
Sister (lengthened—98.58 m (323 ft)): **KAPALL** (As) (see photo number 6/112) ex-*Solklint*; Similar (converted to cement carrier; Structures and equipment in well; Lengthened): **NICCO** (Ma) ex-*Fenris*

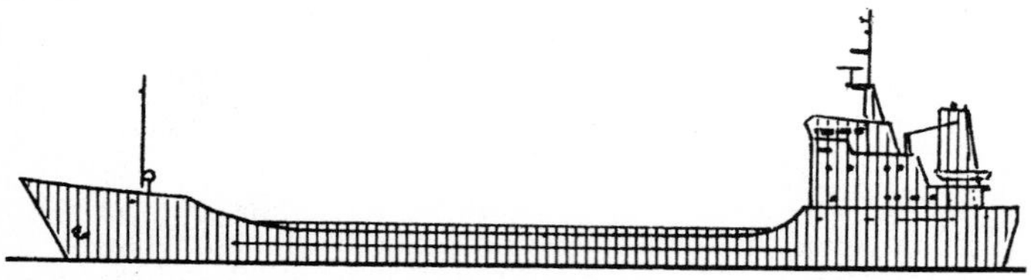

40 *M²RF H13*
ARKLOW ABBEY Ih/Ne (Ferus Smit) 1981; C; 1,171 grt/1,644 dwt; 70.59 × 4.24 m *(231 × 13.91 ft)*; M (Brons); 11 kts
Similar: **SHEVRELL** (Ih) (builder—Niestern-S); **ROSETHORN** (Br) ex-*Shamrock Endeavour* (builder—Coops); **SILVERTHORN** (Br) ex-*Shamrock Enterprise* (builder—Gruno); **NIQUEL** (Po) ex-*Angelique V* (builder—'Volharding'); Similar (lengthened to 83.75 m (275 ft)): **INISHARK** (Ih) ex-*Darell* (builder-Bijholt)

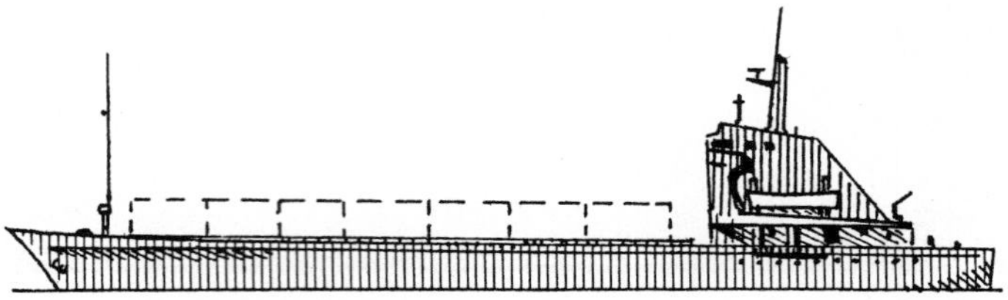

41 *MM-F H*
MINIFOREST Fi/FRG (H Peters) 1972; C/Con; 2,016 grt/2,545 dwt; 78.14 × 4.13 m *(256.36 × 13.55 ft)*; M (Atlas-MaK); 13 kts; ex-*Ilse Wulff*; 209 TEU
Similar: **ARA** (Ma) Launched as *Schwarzenberg*; **UNIKA** (At) ex-*Arnis*; **GARDSEA** (No) ex-*Gazelle*; **ROLF D** (At) Launched as *Heidberg*; **NORDFRAKT** (No) Launched as *Falkenberg*; **MIKA** (Cy) Launched as *Maria Graebe*; **HANNE CATHARINA** (DIS) ex-*Anne Catharina*; **NORDBULK** (NIS) Launched as *Seeberg*; **LILLGARD** (Fi) ex-*Gabriella*; **UNO** (De) Launched as *Jan Graebe*; **GARDWIND** (No) ex-*Kiefernberg*; **HANNA** (Sw) ex-*Johanna Catharina*

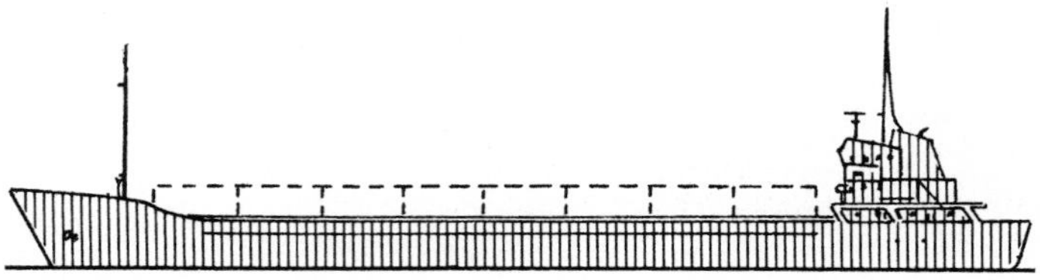

42 *MM-F H1*
AASLAND No/As (Korneuburg) 1971; C; 1,285 grt/1,298 dwt; 76.21 × 3.87 m *(250.03 × 12.7 ft)*; M (MWM); 12.5 kts; ex-*Geertien Bos*; Lifeboat on starboard side only; 74 TEU
Sisters: **ALLEGRO SEA** (SV) Launched as *Dorothee Bos*; **AHRENSHOOP** (Ge) ex-*Karen Oltmann*; **LEA** (Sw) Launched as *Liselotte Bos*; **STINA** (NIS) ex-*Lucia Bos*; **FEEDER B** (Ho) ex-*Gertrud Bos*

43 *MM-F H1*
CLARA At/FRG (Sietas) 1975; C/Con; 1,672 grt/2,130 dwt; 75.77 × 4.67 m *(248.59 × 15.32 ft)*; M (Deutz); 11 kts; ex-*Heide-Catrin*; 82 TEU; **SIMILAR TO DRAWING NUMBER 6/21**; 'Clara' appears under the latter drawing along with other similar ships

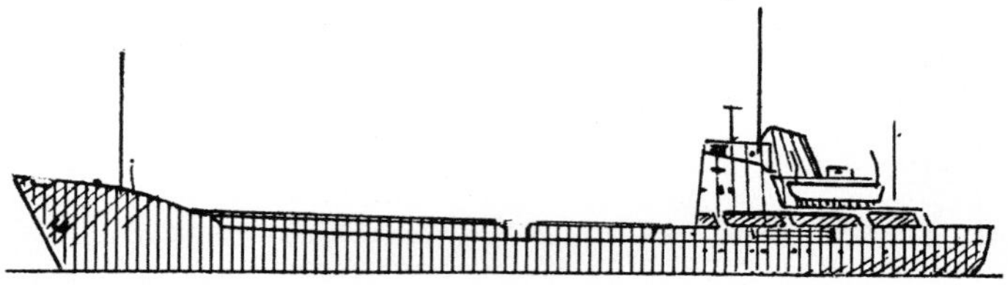

44 *MM-F H1*
IMAN M Sy/Pd ('Komuny Paryskiej') 1961; Con; 399 grt/1,356 dwt; 72.32 × 4.5 m *(237.27 × 14.76 ft)*; M (Alpha-Diesel); 11.5 kts; Lengthened 1978, 'B-57' type; 48 TEU
Sister: **ADRIATICO 1** (Ho) ex-*Wrozka*

See photo number 6/76

45 *MM-F H1*
ISABEL Ne/Ne ('Voorwarts') 1972; C; 1,472 grt/2,159 dwt; 71.28 × 4.97 m *(233.86 × 16.31 ft)*; M (Appingedammer Brons); 12 kts
Probable sister: **HELEEN C** (Bb) ex-*Irina*

46 *MM-F H1*
SOKNA NIS/FRG (Husumer) 1970; C/Con; 1,372 grt/1,370 dwt; 76.31 × 3.95 m *(250.36 × 12.96 ft)*; M (KHD); 13.25 kts; ex-*Arktis*; 72 TEU
Sisters: **FLENSIA** (Ma) ex-*Iris*; **ANTARES** (NIS) ex-*Bele*; **MERCATOR** (Ne) ex-*Heinrich Knuppel*; Sister (small housing against mainmast): **KORNI** (No) ex-*Ronan*; **TMP TAURUS** (Pa) ex-*Sea Maid*

47 *MM-F H13*
ATLANTIC COMET Cy/Ne ('Vooruitgang') 1971; C; 1,465 grt/1,971 dwt; 82.1 × 4.53 m *(269.36 × 14.86 ft)*; M (MWM); 13 kts; ex-*Cornelia Bosma*; Lengthened 1977

48 *MM-F H13*
BINISSALEM Sp/Sp (Balenciaga) 1978; C; 1,587 grt/2,730 dwt; 83.62 × 5.17 m *(274.34 × 16.96 ft)*; M (Deutz); 14.5 kts; ex-*Sota Aranzazu*
Sister: **AMIR KABIR** (Ir) ex-*Sota Sir Ramon*

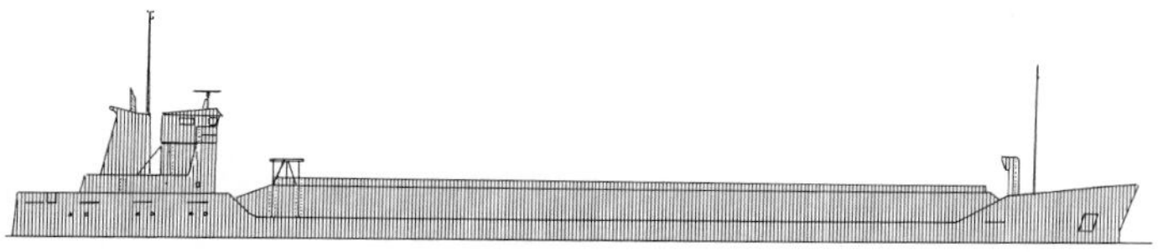

49 *MM-F H13*
CADY At/Ne (Ferus Smit) 1990; C; 2,374 grt/4,161 dwt; 88.29 × 5.74 m *(289.67 × 18.83 ft)*; M (Wärtsilä); 12 kts; ex-*Skagern*
Sisters: **EMJA** (At); **MB CLYDE** (Li); **MB HUMBER** (Li); **VENLO** (At);
Probable sisters: **MAGDALENA** (NA); **FLEVO** (Cy) ex-*Kirsten;* **CEMILE** (Ne)

50 *MM-F H13*
DUNKERQUE EXPRESS Ih/Ne (Tille) 1985; C/Con; 1,839 grt/2,230 dwt; 78.01 × 4.25 m *(255.94 × 13.94 ft)*; M (MaK); 12.3 kts; ex-*Elisa von Barssel*; 124 TEU; **SISTER OF DRAWING NUMBER 7/458** but crane removed

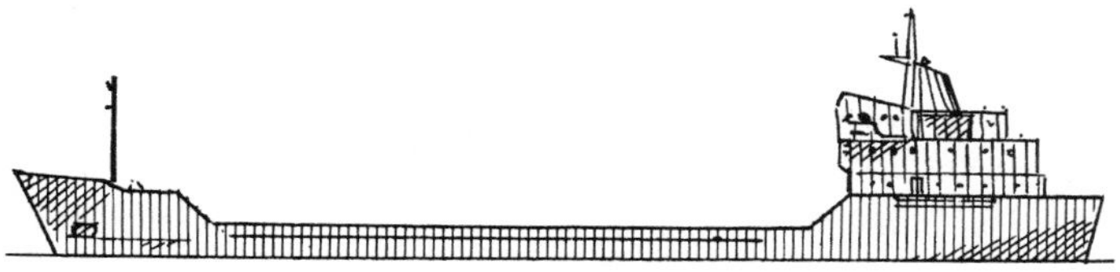

51 *MM-F H13*
ELSBORG Bb/Ne ('Friesland') 1977; C; 1,978 grt/3,150 dwt; 81.01 × 5.38 m *(265.78 × 17.65 ft)*; M (Polar); 12.5 kts; ex-*Carebeka IX*

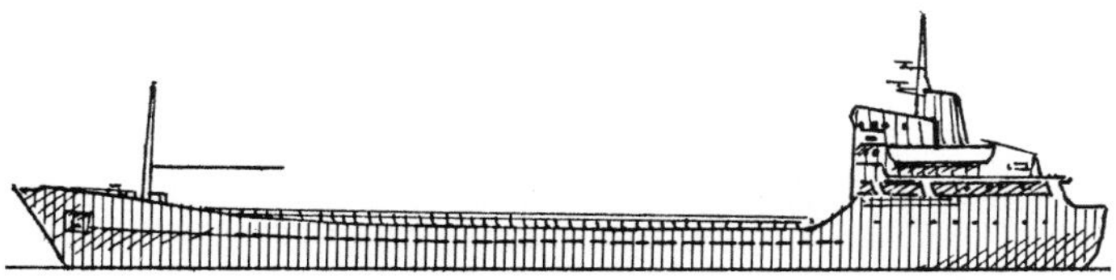

52 *MM-F H13*
EXTRAMAR NORTE Sp/Sp (Celaya) 1976; C; 1,338 grt/1,927 dwt; 77.02 × 4.52 m *(252.69 × 14.83 ft)*; M (Atlas-MaK); 11 kts; 76 TEU
Sister: **EIFFEL SUN** (Po) ex-*Extramar Este*; Similar: **EIFFEL STAR** (Po) ex-*Extramar Oeste*; **MUSTANSIR** (Pk) ex-*Extramar Sur*; Possible sisters: **HAI SHIOU SHAN** (Pa) ex-*Catalina Del Mar*; **JIA XIU SHAN** (RC) ex-*Mariona Del Mar*

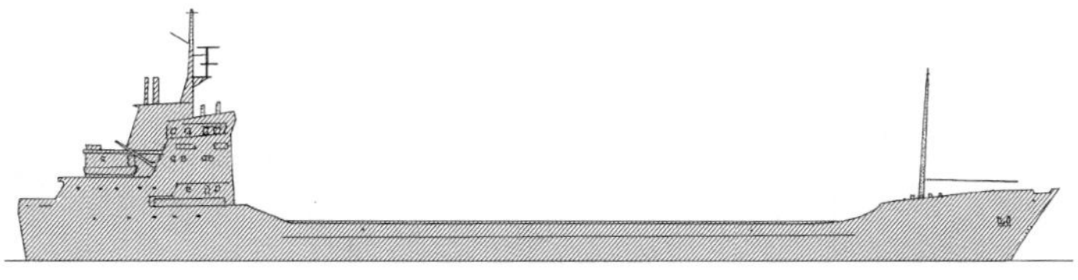

53 *MM-F H13*
FORTUNA At/Ne ('Harlingen') 1977; C; 1,793 grt/2,930 dwt; 80.22 × 5.56 m *(263.19 × 18.24 ft)*; M (MWM); 11.5 kts; ex-*Mallarsee*

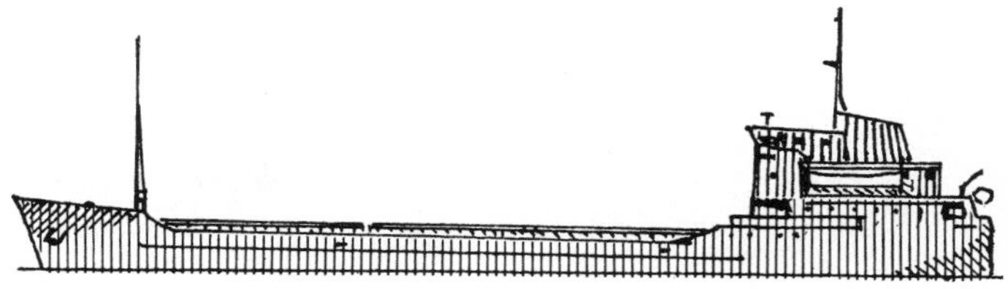

54 *MM-F H13*
LADY SANDRA Bb/Ne (Gruno) 1972; C; 1,507 grt/2,230 dwt; 76.43 × 4.64 m *(250.75 × 15.22 ft)*; M (Appingedammer Brons); 11.5 kts; ex-*Ventura*

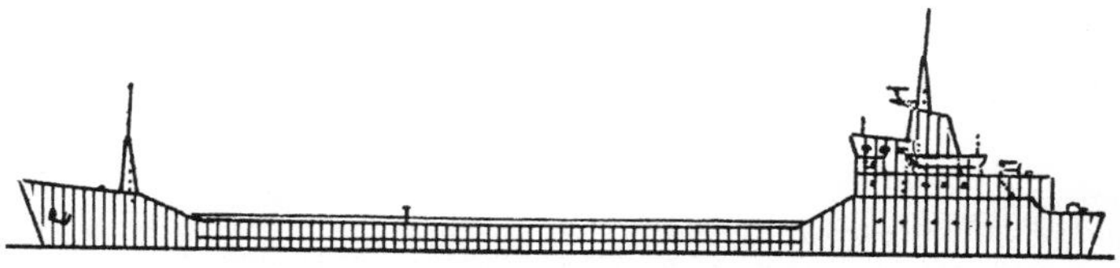

55 *MM-F H13*
MALTESE VENTURE Ma/Br (Cochrane) 1972/78; C; 1,007 grt/1,393 dwt; 72.73 × 3.76 m *(238.62 × 12.34 ft)*; M (MAN); 12 kts; ex-*Nellie M*; Lengthened 1978

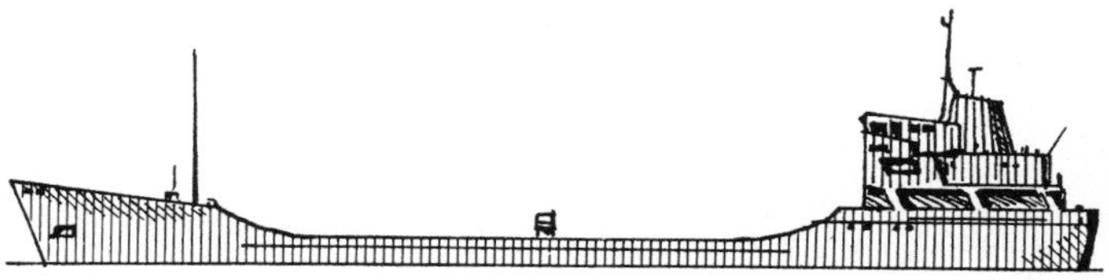

56 *MM-F H13*
MARC CHALLENGER Gr/Ne (Ferus Smit) 1975; C; 1,982 grt/3,050 dwt; 81.57 × 5.40 m *(267.95 × 17.65 ft)*; M (Smit-Bolnes); 12.5 kts; ex-*Veerhaven*
Similar (may have deck cranes): **DOLICHI** (Cy) ex-*Barendsz*

57 *MM-F H13*
MINEVA Ho/Pd (Gdanska) 1968; C; 1,672 grt/2,658 dwt; 82.17 × 4.89 m *(269.59 × 16.04 ft)*; M (Atlas-MaK); — kts; ex-*Hovin*; 'B-459' type; Lengthened 1973

58 *MM-F H13*
SEA WAVE NIS/FRG (Sietas) 1970; C; 1,223 grt/2,020 dwt; 73.84 × 5.04 m *(242.26 × 16.54 ft)*; M (KHD); 11.5 kts; ex-*Alicia*; 63 TEU
Sisters: **AROSETTE** (At); **JAN-RASMUS** (At) ex-*John Wulf*; **EURO CLIPPER** (At) ex-*Destel*; **WEISA** (At) ex-*Osterland*; **ARAWAK TRADER** (Bs) ex-*Ragna* (poop differs); **SYKRON** (Cy) ex-*Julia*; **RAMA** (Ho) ex-*Rhein*; Similar (smaller funnel etc): **JENLIL** (DIS) ex-*Osteriff*; **ARAWAK SUN** (Bs) ex-*Aros*; **EINSTEIN** (At) ex-*Eland*; **BRITTA** (At) launched as *Obotrita*; **BEATE** (At) launched as *Elke Kahrs*; **SEA VENTURE** (Ho) ex-*Zaanstroom*; **CASANDRA** (Fi) ex-*Owen Kersten*; **RAUK** (Sw) ex-*City of Dublin;* **BOREAS** (Cy) ex-*Heike Lehmann*; **IRLO** (Ge) ex-*Tina*

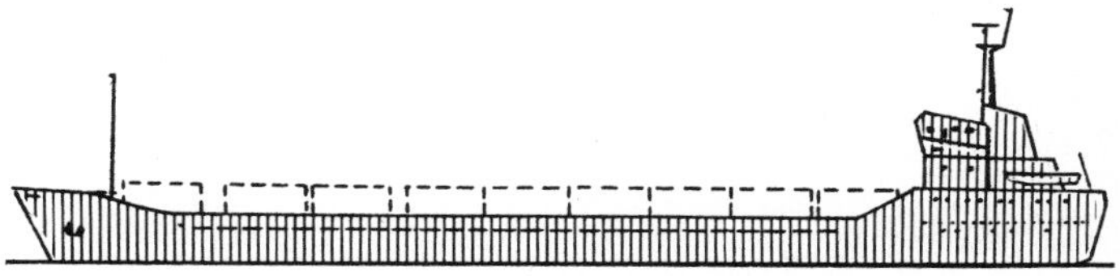

59 *MM-F H13*
SVETI JERE Ma/Ne (Duijvendijk's) 1971; B; 1,537 grt/2,515 dwt; 82.23 × 3.67 m *(269.78 × 12.04 ft)*; M (W H Allen); 12.5 kts; ex-*Guernsey Fisher*; Converted from general cargo 1984
Sister (builder—Ijsselwerf): **TMP AQUARIUS** (Po) ex-*Jersey Fisher*

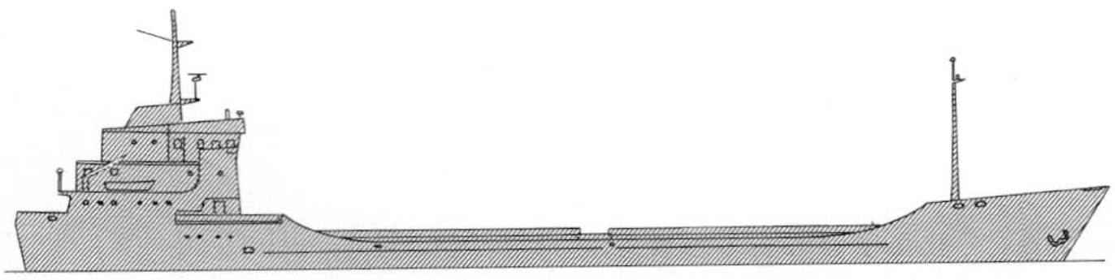

60 *MM-F H13*
TINA C Bb/Ne (Gruno) 1974; C; 1,458 grt/2,591 dwt; 78.77 × 5.02 m *(258.43 × 16.47 ft)*; M (Appingedammer Brons); 12 kts; ex-*Vanda*
Sister: **MINKA C** (Bb) ex-*Victory*; Similar: **VANESSA C** (Bb) ex-*Vanessa*

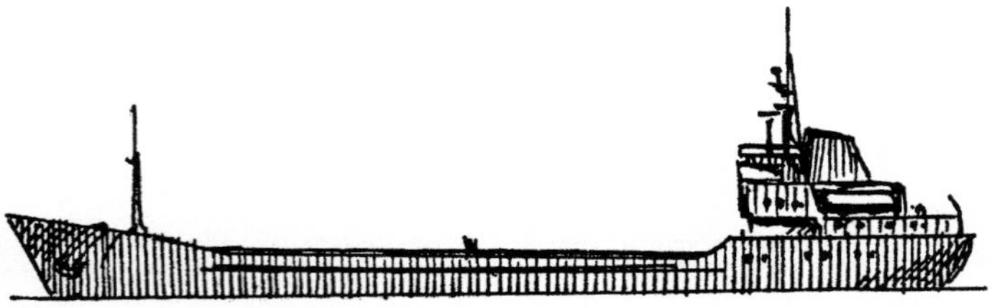

61 *MM-F H13*
VERONA Ma/Ne ('Hoogezand' JB) 1972; C; 1,508 grt/2,315 dwt; 78.01 × 4.92 m *(255.94 × 16.14 ft)*; M (Smit & Bolnes); 12 kts; ex-*Tuvana*

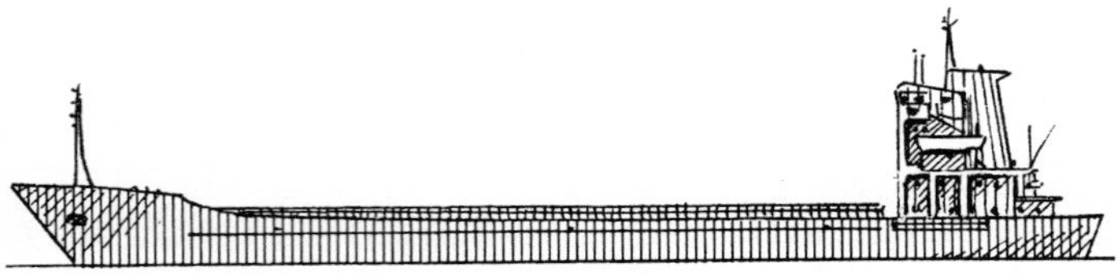

62 *MM-FM H1*
PETSAMO Fi/FRG (Husumer) 1976; C/Con; 2,356 grt/2,650 dwt; 83.52 × 4.96 m *(274.02 × 16.27 ft)*; M (Atlas-MaK); 14 kts; ex-*Voline*; 168 TEU
Sister: **SOMERS ISLES** (At) ex-*Theodor Storm*

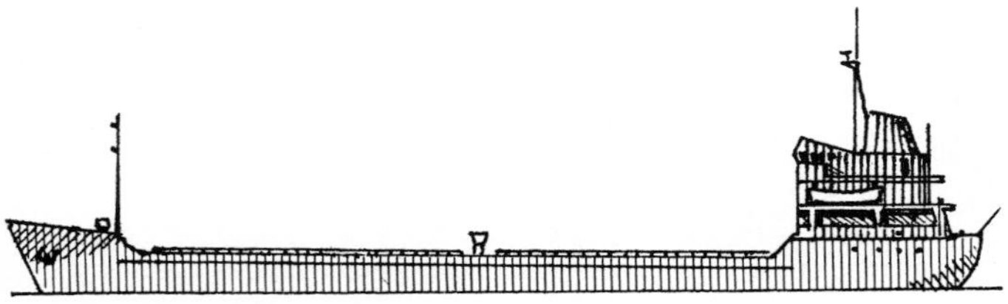

63 *MM-FM H13*
FLORIDA STAR Pa/Sp (Cadagua) 1976; C; 1,868 grt/3,000 dwt; 82.1 × 5.44 m *(269.36 × 17.85 ft)*; M (Deutz); 11.5 kts; ex-*Fer Baltico*
Sister: **EVITA** (Pa) ex-*Fer Balear*

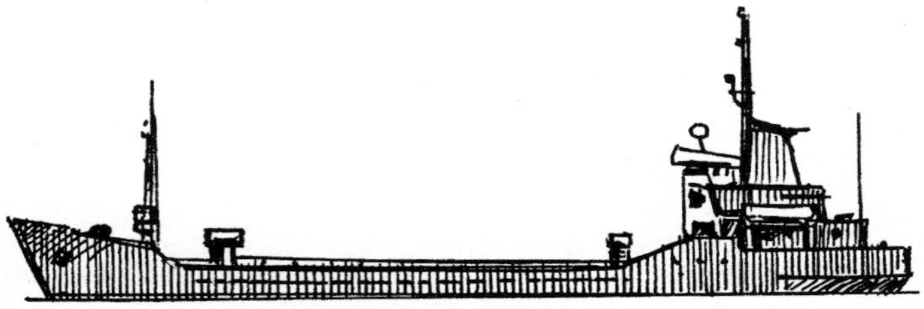

64 *MM-FM H13*
INHARRIME Mb/Sp (Duro Felguera) 1974; C; 1,569 grt/2,700 dwt; 81.82 × 5.6 m *(268.44 × 18.37 ft)*; M (Deutz); 14 kts; ex-*Allul*
Sister: **LUGELA** (Mb) ex-*Alfer*

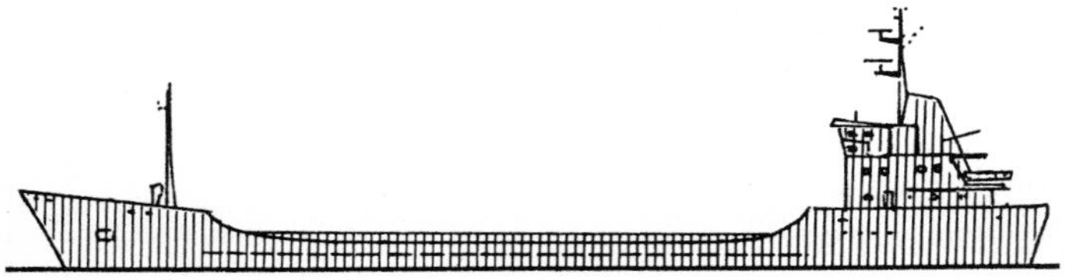

65 *MM-FM H13*
ROELOF Ne/Ne (Gruno) 1983; C; 1,599 grt/3,050 dwt; 81.62 × 5.38 m *(267.78 × 17.65 ft)*; M (MWM); 11.75 kts; ex-*Viking*
Probable sister: **ROMEO** (Cy) ex-*Andromeda*

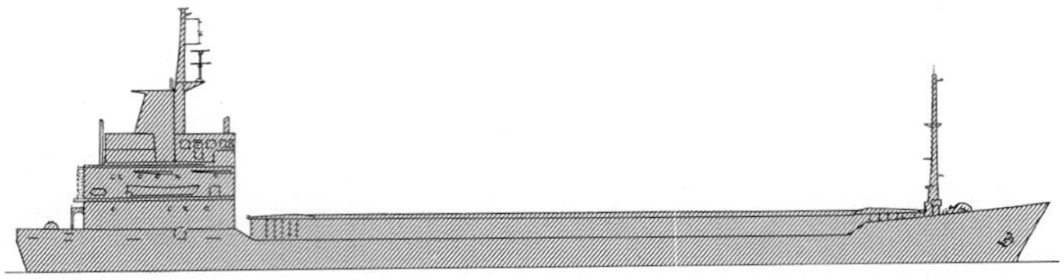

66 *MM-FN H*
SEA BOYNE Ih/Ja (Watanabe) 1977; C/Con; 999 grt/2,192 dwt; 79.10 × 4.77 m *(259.51 × 15.65 ft)*; M (Yanmar); 12 kts; ex-*Sybille*; 104 TEU
Sisters (some have four-deck superstructure): **SIGGEN II** (Tv) ex-*Siggen*; **STEFAN** (As) ex-*Sanderskoppel*; **GROUSE** (Cy) ex-*Oeland*; **JONRIX** (Bs) ex-*Langeland*; **LARK** (Cy) ex-*Aland*; **ANGUS** (Cy) ex-*Alsterberg*; **MATRISHA** (Bs) ex-*Boberg*; **MELISSA** (Cy) ex-*Messberg*; **BETTINA** (As) ex-*Nordholm*; **LIBRA II** (Tv) ex-*Libra*; Sisters (lengthened to 96.25 m (315.78 ft) (Hyundai): **KILLARNEY** (Ih) ex-*Neuwark*; **ULZBURG** (At) ex-*Neuwulmstorf*; **KYLEMORE** (Ih) ex-*Neukloster*

67 *MM-FN H1*
HELEN Fi/FRG (Norderwerft) 1979; C/Con; 1,826 grt/2,231 dwt; 79.79 × 4.43 m *(261.78 × 14.53 ft)*; M (MWM); 12 kts; ex-*Holger*; 145 TEU
Sister (builder—Sietas): **ANNE** (Fi) ex-*Trabant*

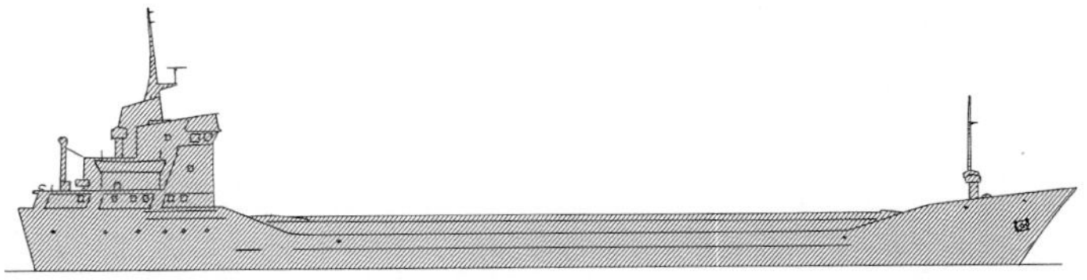

68 *MM-FN H13*
ELVINA Po/Sp (Murueta) 1976; C; 1,197 grt/1,924 dwt; 73.97 × 4.75 m *(242.68 × 15.58 ft)*; M (Cockerill); 12 kts; ex-*Danok*
Sister (may have superimposed wheelhouse): **KORTEZUBI** (Po)

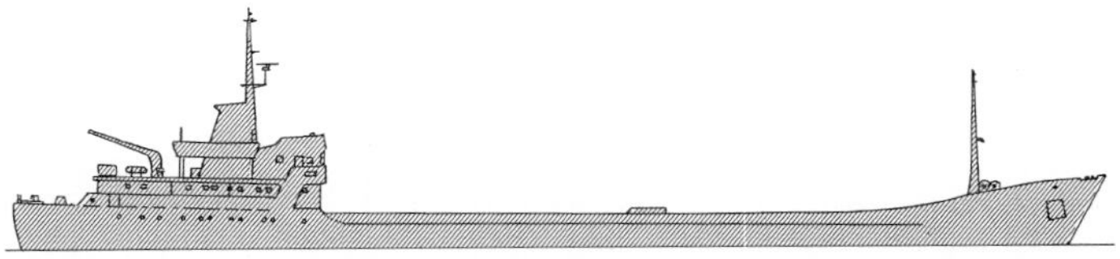

69 *MM-FS H1*
SEA ROVER Gr/Hu (Angyalfold) 1970; C; 1,510 grt/2,537 dwt; 76.41 × 5.31 m *(250.69 × 17.42 ft)*; M (MWM); 11 kts; ex-*Basalt*; Lengthened 1975
Sisters: **RANA M** (Sy) ex-*Diorit*; **SUNNY LADY** (Bs) ex-*Diabas*; **NAWAL** (Sy) ex-*Gabbro*; **WAHIB M** (Sy) ex-*Granit*; **DANA** (Ma) ex-*Dolomit*

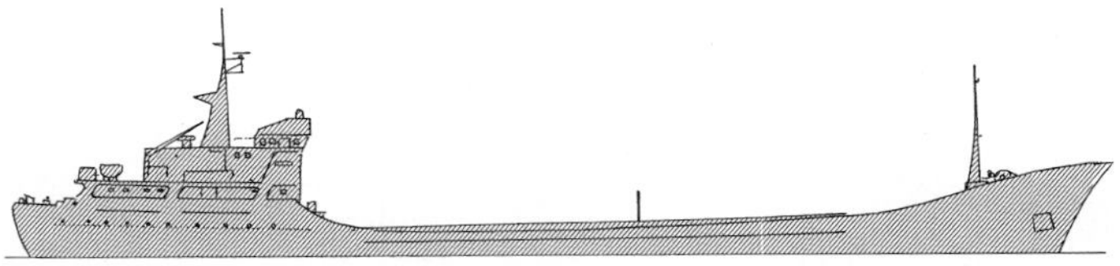

70 *MM-FS H13*
BLACKBIRD SV/FRG (Kremer) 1967; C; 935 grt/1,735 dwt; 75.24 × 4.42 m *(246.85 × 14.5 ft)*; M (KHD); 12.75 kts; ex-*Ortrud Muller*

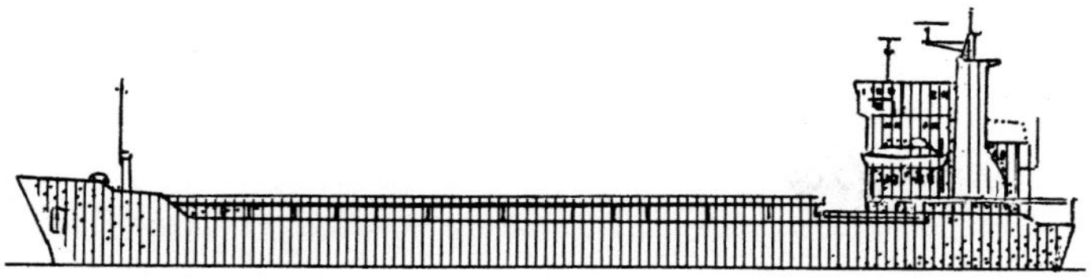

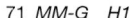

71 *MM-G H1*
WIND OCEAN SV/Sg (Far East-Levington) 1979; C/Con/NP; 3,416 grt/ 5,210 dwt; 80.78 × 7.21 m *(265.03 × 23.65 ft)*; M (MaK); 12 kts; ex-*Germa Team*; 145 TEU; May be fitted with a deck crane—see drawing number 7/ 460

72 *MVF H13*
HOPE Ih/Br (Goole) 1982; B; 1,785 grt/2,535 dwt; 77.09 × 4.96 m *(252.92 × 16.27 ft)*; M (Krupp-MaK); 12 kts; ex-*Ballygarvey*
Sister: **DUNANY** (Ih) ex-*Ballygrainey*

73 Sea Boyne *(Ih); 1977* *FotoFlite*

74 Miniforest *(Fi); 1972* *FotoFlite*

75 Sokna *(NIS); 1970* *FotoFlite*

76 Isabel *(Ne); 1972* *FotoFlite*

77 Ahrenshoop *(Ge); 1970* *FotoFlite*

78 Tarik *(Mo); 1969* *FotoFlite*

79 Somers Isles *(At); 1977* *FotoFlite*

80 Eliza Heeren *(At); 1981* *FotoFlite*

81 Peltrader *(Gr); 1978* *FotoFlite*

82 Enol *(Po); 1982* *FotoFlite*

83 Stella Arctic *(Sw); 1980* *FotoFlite*

84 Selectivity *(Br); 1984* *FotoFlite*

85 Fortuna *(At); 1977* *FotoFlite*

86 Inishark *(Ih); 1982* *FotoFlite*

87 Scotia *(NA); 1977* *FotoFlite*

88 Sprante *(Cy); 1986* *FotoFlite*

89 Verona *(Ne); 1982* *FotoFlite*

90 Olivia *(Cy); 1978* *FotoFlite*

91 Hope *(Ih); 1982* *FotoFlite*

92 Extramar Norte *(—); 1976* *FotoFlite*

93 Jan-Rasmus *(At); 1969* *FotoFlite*

94 Petra F *(Ge); 1985* *FotoFlite*

95 RMS Mercator *(Tv); 1986* *FotoFlite*

96 Brandaris *(Ge); 1985* *FotoFlite*

97 Havang *(Sw); 1977* *FotoFlite*

98 Freja *(At); 1975* *John Freestone*

99 Corinna *(At); 1974; (as Vantage)* *WSPL*

100 Nina Bres *(DIS); 1975* *WSPL*

101 East Med *(Bb); 1974; (as Betty C)* *WSPL*

102 Triumph *(Ne); 1986* *WSPL*

103 Marianne *(Ge); 1978; (as Detlef Schmidt)* *WSPL*

104 Eiffel Star *(Po); 1977; (as Extramar Oeste)* *WSPL*

105 Caspic *(NA); 1978; (as Vijverhof)* *WSPL*

106 Dana *(Ma); 1973; (as Lady Dorothy)* *WSPL*

107 Hoo Falcon *(Br); 1991* *WSPL*

108 Alliance *(Cy); 1979; (as Galliard)* *WSPL*

109 Seg *(Ru); 1993* *FotoFlite*

110 Rusalka II *(Pd); 1991* *FotoFlite*

111 Kapall *(As); 1978* *FotoFlite*

112 Barona *(Po); 1976; (as Kortezubi)* *FotoFlite*

113 Lisa *(Ge); 1986* *FotoFlite*

114 Agros *(Cy); 1981* *FotoFlite*

115 Roelof *(Ne); 1983* *FotoFlite*

116 Biscay *(Cy); 1982/89* *FotoFlite*

117 Klazina C *(Bb); 1983/88* *FotoFlite*

118 Gudrun II *(At); 1987* *FotoFlite*

119 Sian *(Ho); 1975* *FotoFlite*

120 Voyager *(Ne); 1975; (as Barok)* *FotoFlite*

121 Sea Wave *(NIS); 1970* *FotoFlite*

122 Nordica *(Sw); 1977* *FotoFlite*

123 Tina C *(Bb); 1974; (as Vanda)* *Norman Thomson*

124 Flevo *(Cy); 1991* *FotoFlite*

125 Phoenix II *(Cy); 1971* *FotoFlite*

126 Worthing *(Br); 1975* *FotoFlite*

127 Myrmo *(Bs); 1973/80* *FotoFlite*

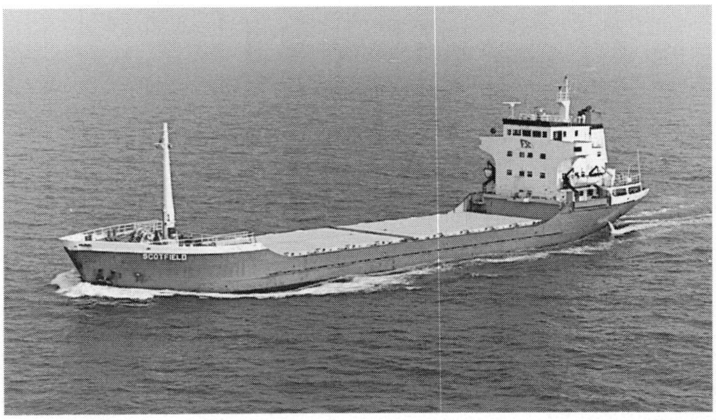

128 Scotfield *(Cy); 1974* *FotoFlite*

7 Dry Cargo Ships with Deck Cranes

7 Dry Cargo Ships with Deck Cranes

1 *$C^5M\text{-}FC^2$ H13*
HAI HUA Th/Fr (France-Gironde) 1971; C; 8,643 grt/13,814 dwt; 167 × 10.8 m *(548 × 35.75 ft)*; M (B&W); 23 kts; ex-*Zambeze*
Sister: **HAI SOONG** (Th) ex-*Zelande*

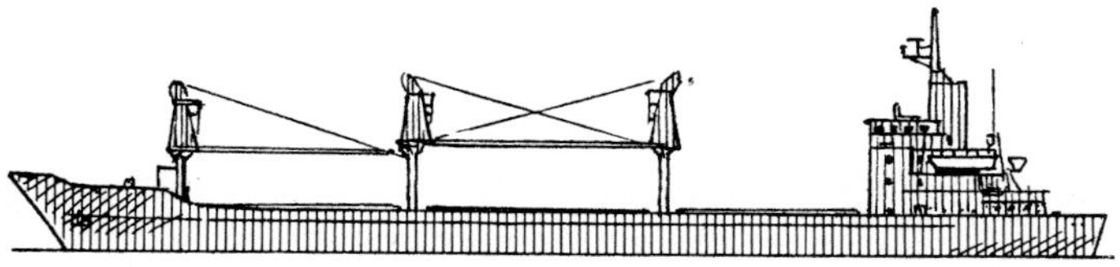

2 *$C^3M\text{-}F$ H1*
ESMERALDA At/Ne (Amels) 1970; C; 2,072 grt/2,532 dwt; 81.79 × 5.18 m *(268 × 16.99 ft)*; M (MWM); 13 kts; ex-*Rijnborg*
Sister: **JULIE** (NIS) ex-*Scheldeborg*

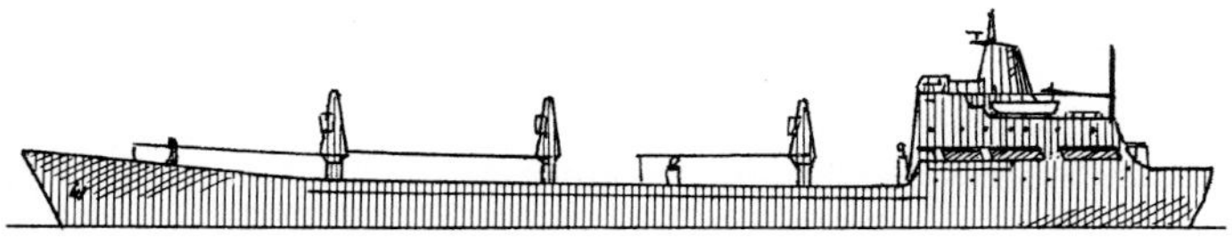

3 *$C^3M\text{-}FN$ H3*
SUNLUCK Cy/No (Sarpsborg) 1966; C; 3,314 grt/5,003 dwt; 105.36 × 6.42 m *(346 × 21.06 ft)*; M (B&W); 14 kts; ex-*Rudolf*

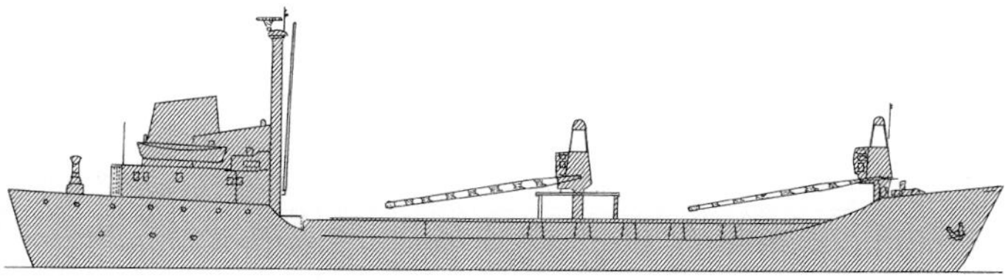

4 *C^2HF H13*
DOUA S Sy/FRG (LF-W) 1964; C; 1,589 grt/3,180 dwt; 81.23 × 5.87 m *(266.5 × 19.26 ft)*; M (MAN); 13 kts; ex-*Fredenhagen*

5 *HC^5MF H1*
PETRONIA —/FRG (Howaldts DW) 1981; B/Con; 18,691 grt/25,160 dwt; 169.04 × 9.96 m *(555 × 32.68 ft)*; M (Sulzer); 16.5 kts; ex-*Carmen*; 1,176 TEU
Sisters: **CAMPANIA** (Ge); **TRADE RICH** (HK) ex-*Conscience*; **TRADE WEALTH** (HK) ex-*Cranach*

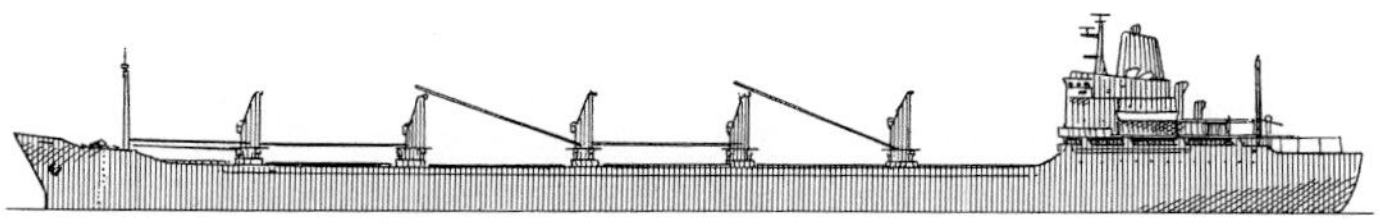

6 *HC^5MFN H13*
ANGELIKI D Cy/Ja (Mitsui) 1971; B; 16,598 grt/32,312 dwt; 182.61 × 10.69 m *(599.11 × 35.07 ft)*; M (Sulzer); 15 kts; ex-*Master Stefanos*

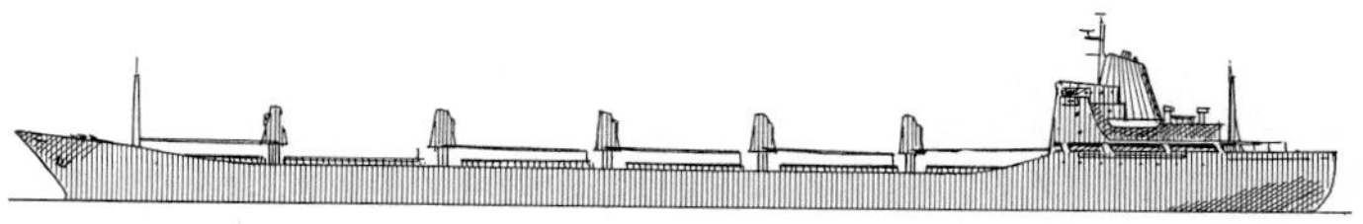

7 *$HC^5M\text{-}FN$ H13*
ONTARIO LAKER Gr/Ja (Hakodate) 1970; B; 14,687 grt/27,306 dwt; 182 × 10.64 m *(597.11 × 34.9 ft)*; M (Sulzer); 14.5 kts; ex-*Larry L*
Sisters: **OLYMPIA** (Ma) ex-*Catherine L*; **ATTICA** (Ma) ex-*Grace L*; **PELLA** (Ma) ex-*Patricia L*; Similar: **IONIAN EMPRESS** (Gr) ex-*Evy L*; **GEORGE L** (Gr); **MARKA L** (Gr); **PANTAZIS L** (Gr); **HAPPY DAY** (Cy) ex-*Tatiana L*

8 *HC^5NMFN H13*
DELTA STAR Pk/Sw (Oresunds) 1968; B; 16,638 grt/34,686 dwt; 175.27 × 10.24 m *(575.03 × 33.59 ft)*; M (Gotaverken); 15 kts; ex-*Valetta*

9 *HC^4HF H1*
NEDLLOYD SANTOS Cy/FRG (Howaldts DW) 1982; B/Con; 18,656 grt/25,085 dwt; 169.15 × 9.96 m *(555 × 32.68 ft)*; M (Sulzer); 16.5 kts; ex-*Rebecca Wesch*; 1,229 TEU
Sisters: **CALEDONIA** (Ge) ex-*Gabriele Wesch*; **PETRALIA** (Gr) ex-*Karsten Wesch*; **CALIFORNIA** (Li) ex-*Castor*; **BARRISTER** (Li) ex-*Carthago*; **CANDIA** (Li); **VICTORIA BAY** (Li) ex-*Caria*

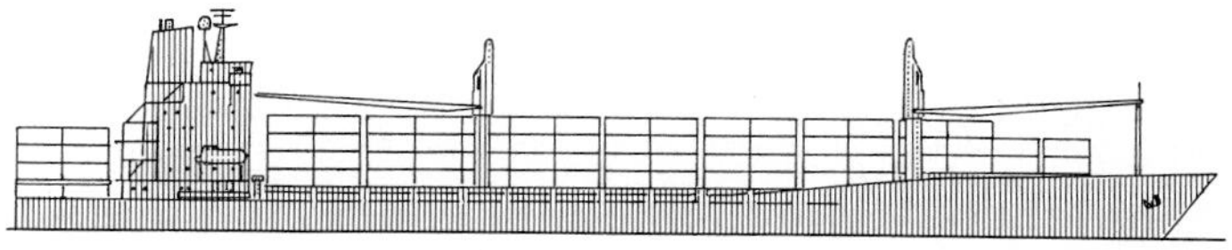

10 *HC^2M^2F H1*
CMB ENERGY Li/FRG (AG 'Weser') 1983; C/Con; 13,476 grt/19,440 dwt; 161.96 × 10.00 m *(531.36 × 32.81 ft)*; M (MaK); 17.75 kts; ex-*Helga Wehr*; 1,152 TEU; Currently in service as a container ship only
Sister: **MSC MAUREEN** (At) ex-*Holsten Bay*

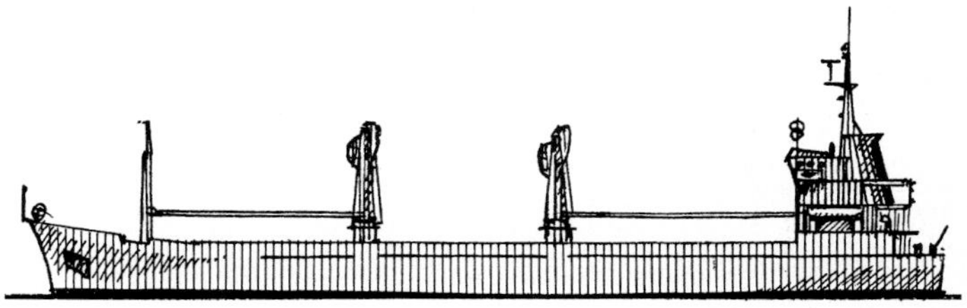

11 *$HC^2M\text{-}F$ H*
MUHU Ea/Ja (Miho) 1976; C; 3,466 grt/6,072 dwt; 80.22 × 5.98 m *(263.19 × 19.62 ft)*; M (Hanshin); 13.5 kts; ex-*Leliegracht*; Cranes on starboard side
Sisters: **FRISOHAVEN** (Ea) ex-*Leidsegracht*; **NAISSAAR** (Ea) ex-Lindengracht; **ABRUKA** (Ea) ex-*Lijnbaansgracht*; **VAINDLO** (Ea) ex-*Lauriergracht*; **VILSANDI** (Ea) ex-Looiersgracht; **SANDVIK** (Gr) ex-*Raamgracht*; **BLUE AQUAMARINE** (Cy) ex-*Realengracht*; **NIKKO MARU** (Ja) ex-*Reguliersgracht*; **ATLANTIC MERCADO** (At) ex-*Rijpgracht*; **HONG CHENG** (RC) ex-*Ringgracht*; **SUNNY** (Gr) ex-*Rozengracht*; **FOREST TRADER** (Pa) ex-*Schippersgracht*; **ROSAMAGDALENA** (Ve) ex-*Singelgracht*; **AL WAKRAH** (Qt) ex-*Spiegelgracht*; **FEROI** (Cy) ex-*Seliba*; **BAKENGRACHT** (Ne); **BARENTZGRACHT** (Ne); **BEURSGRACHT** (Ne); **BONTEGRACHT** (Ne); **BICKERSGRACHT** (Ne); **BATAAFGRACHT** (Ne); **BONAIRE** (Cy) ex-*Westafcarrier*; **FIDUCIA** (At) ex-*Westaftrader*

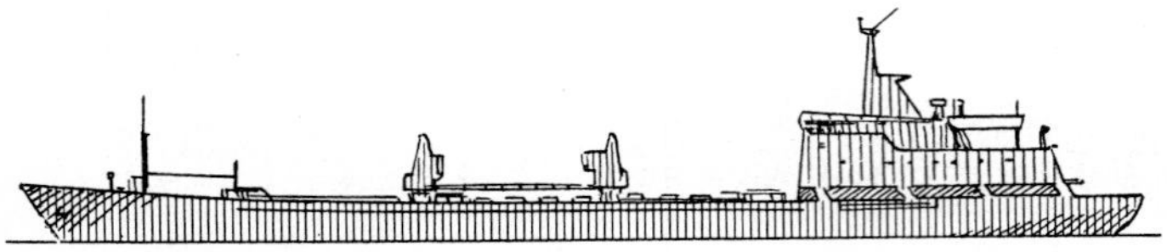

12 *HC^{2}M-F H*
PLANTA DE BETANIA Co/Sp (Ruiz) 1971; C; 2,426 grt/2,300 dwt; 96.93 × 3.86 m *(318.01 × 12.66 ft)*; TSM (MAN); 12 kts
Sister: **PLANTA DE MAMONAL** (Co)

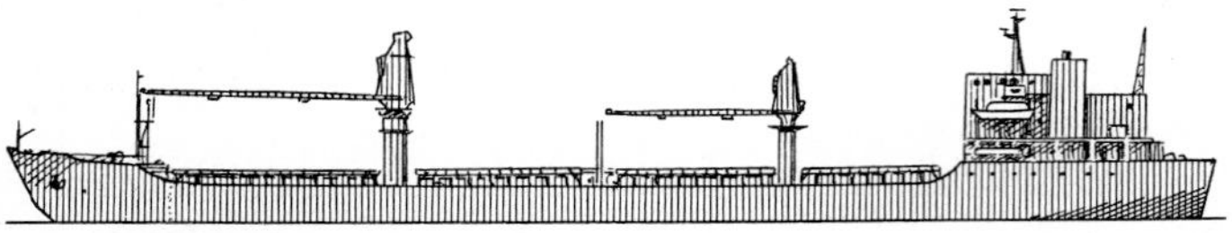

13 *HPCMGM H13*
FULLNES Pa/Ja (NKK) 1978; C; 8,960 grt/12,274 dwt; 134.52 × 8.67 m *(441.34 × 28.44 ft)*; M (Pielstick); 14.75 kts; ex-*Farnes*; After mast is on starboard side
Probable sister: **FURUNES** (Pa) ex-*Firmnes*

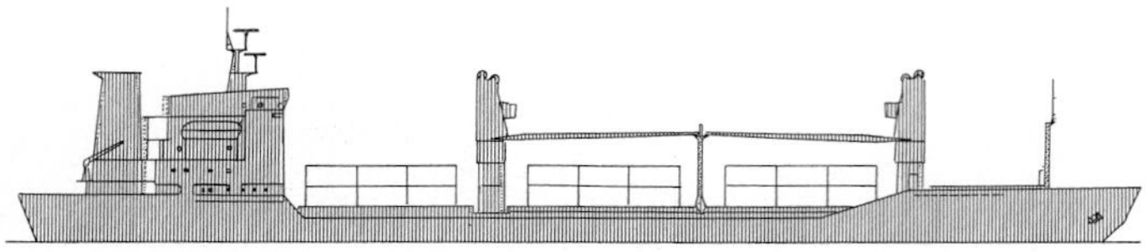

14 *HP^{2}MF H13*
IGOR ILYINSKIY Ru/Sp (Nervion) 1990; C/TC/Con; 6,775 grt/7,365 dwt; 132.71 × 6.88 m *(435.40 × 22.57 ft)*; M (B&W); 14.5 kts; 318 TEU
Sisters: **YELENA SHATROVA** (Ru); **VYSOKOGORSK** (Ru); **ABAKAN** (Ru); **SINEGORSK** (Ru); Possible sisters: **GOOD EASY** (Li); **GOOD MOST** (Li)

15 *HP^{2}M-FM H13*
CORRIENTES II Ar/Sp (AESA) 1977; C; 12,762 grt/20,717 dwt; 159.01 × 9.76 m *(521.69 × 32.02 ft)*; M (Sulzer); 16 kts; 'Santa Fe 77' type
Sisters: **FLINT** (Cy) ex-*Chaco*; **NICOLAS I K** (Cy) ex-*Entre Rios II*; **MAGNUS CHALLENGER** (Cy) ex-*Formosa*; **GEORGETTE K** (Cy) ex-*Rio Negro II*; **IOANNIS K** (Cy) ex-*Santa Cruz II*; **TIERRA DEL FUEGO II** (Ar); **MISIONES II** (Ar); **SEA SPIRIT** (Pa) ex-*Santa Fe II*; **MARIACHRIS K** (Cy) ex-*Chubut*

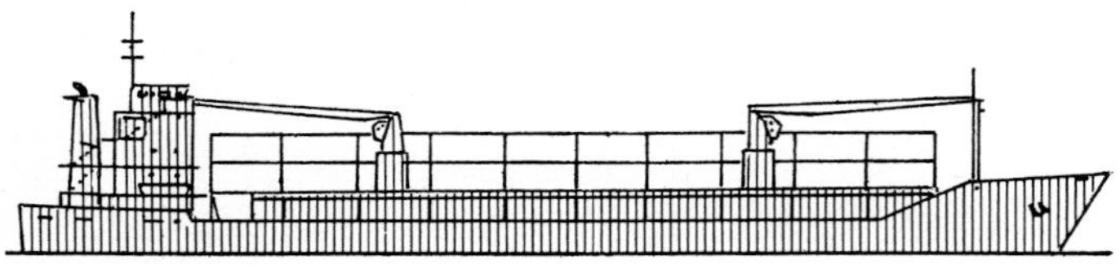

16 *HR^{2}MF H1*
HERM At/FRG (Buesumer) 1985; C/Con; 2,726 grt/2,957 dwt; 92.51 × 4.42 m *(303.51 × 14.50 ft)*; M (MaK); 12.25 kts; ex-*Herm Schepers*; 204 TEU; Cranes are on port side
Sister: **JETTY** (At) ex-Karola-S

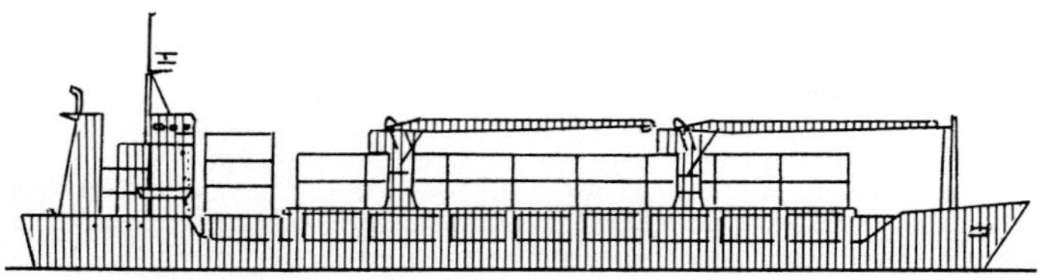

17 *HR^{2}M-FCL H13*
SANTA MARIA Ge/FRG (Cassens) 1985; C/Con; 3,062 grt/3,670 dwt; 99.42 × 5.10 m *(326.18 × 16.73 ft)*; M (MWM); 12 kts; 198 TEU
Sister: **SANTA HELENA** (Ge)

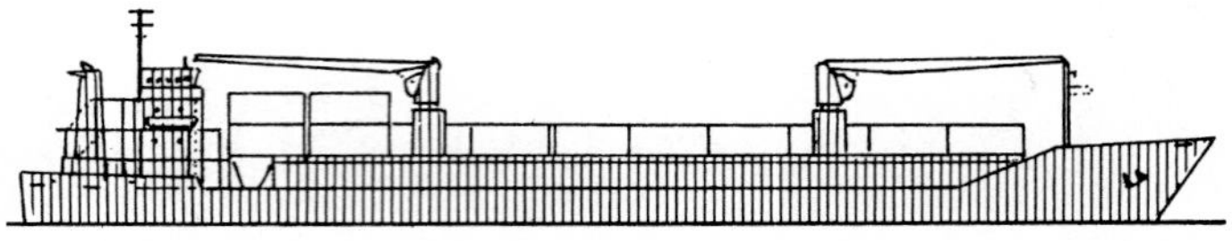

18 *HR^{2}NF H1*
KERSTIN Ge/Ge (Buesumer) 1984; C/Con; 2,683 grt/3,040 dwt; 92.51 × 4.45 m *(303.51 × 14.60 ft)*; M (MaK); 11.50 kts; 166 TEU; Cranes are on port side
Sisters : **MANDALA** (Ge); **BURGUNDIA** (At) ex-*Urte*; Probable sister: **MERLIN** (Ge)

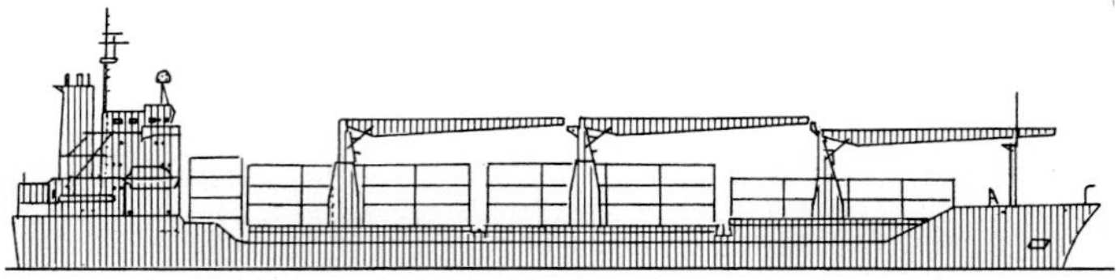

19 *HR^{3}MF H13*
ABITIBI CONCORD Li/FRG (Bremer V) 1985; C/NP/Con; 6,994 grt/9,650 dwt; 123.40 × 7.97 m *(404.86 × 26.15 ft)*; M (MAN); 16 kts; 504 TEU; Ice strengthened; Cranes are on port side
Sister: **ABITIBI MACADO** (Li)

20 *MC^{8}MFN H13*
MARIOS Ma/Rm (Galatz) 1974; B; 10,526 grt/18,003 dwt; 145.12 × 10.15 m *(476 × 33.30 ft)*; M (Sulzer); 16 kts; ex-*Lok Vihar*
Sister: **AGIA METHODIA** (Pa) ex-*Lok Palak*

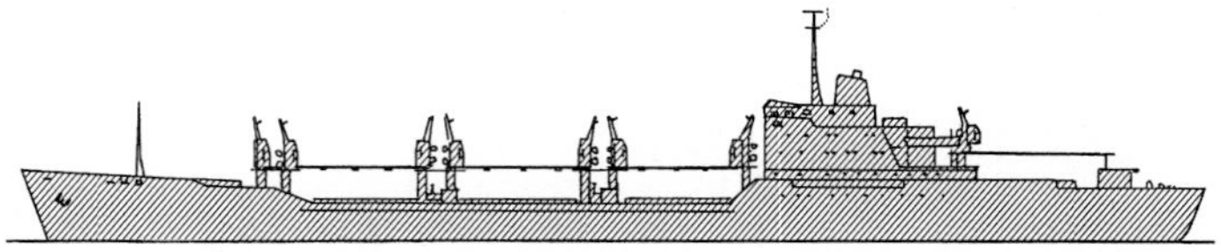

21 *MC^{7}MFC H13*
'IRKUTSK' class; 2483; Some of the vessels of this class may have this sequence now—see entry number 9/28

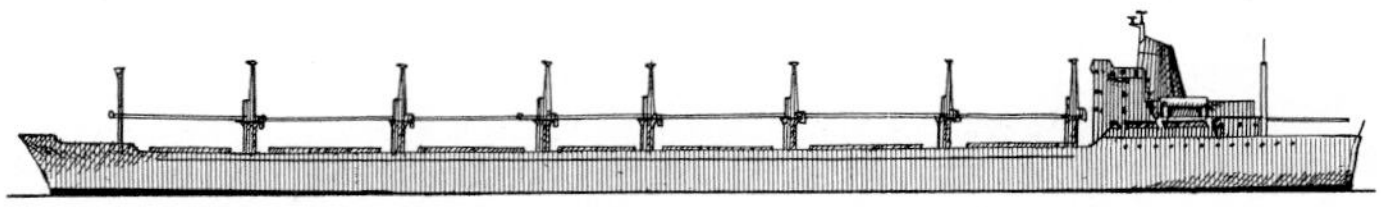

22 *MC^{7}M-FN H13*
IOANNA Ma/Br (Upper Clyde) 1969; B; 20,101 grt/38,457 dwt; 193.1 × 11.25 m *(633.53 × 36.91 ft)*; M (Sulzer); 15.5 kts; ex-*Volnay*

23 *MC^{6}MF H1*
ANANGEL EXPRESS Gr/Ja (Koyo) 1982; B; 34,407 grt/61,537 dwt; 223.15 × 13.02 m *(732 × 42.72 ft)*; M (B&W); 14.75 kts; ex-*Oak Sun*
Probable sisters: **WAIMEA** (Gr) ex-*Sabodine Venture*; **THEMIS PETRAKIS** (Cy) ex-*Krislock*; **SONIC YOUTH** (Cy) ex-*United Faith*; **MARIA** (Gr) ex-*World Acclaim*

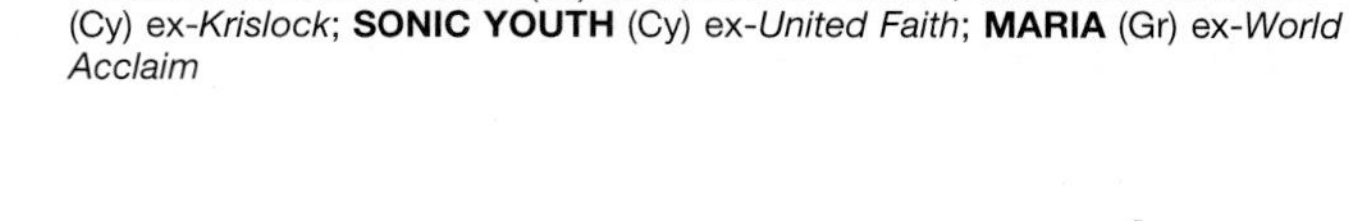

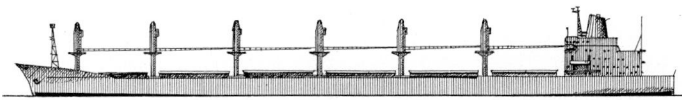

24 *MC^{6}MF H1*
SEAGUARDIAN Ma/FRG (Flensburger) 1976; B; 27,554 grt/50,250 dwt; 213.39 × 12.17 m *(700.09 × 39.93 ft)*; M (MAN); 16 kts; ex-*Warschau*
Sisters: **TOSCANA** (Bs) ex-*Emma Johanna*; **SEARIDER** (Ma) ex-*Dresden*; **GUANG YUAN** (RC) ex-*Thamesfield*

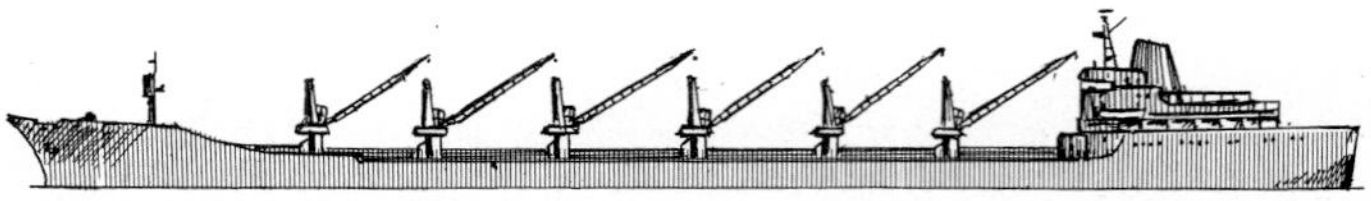

25 *MC^{6}MF H13*
KUANG HAI RC/No (Fredriksstad) 1965; B; 21,937 grt/35,560 dwt; 193.35 × 11.15 m *(634.35 × 36.58 ft)*; M (Gotaverken); 14.5 kts; ex-*Roald Jarl*

26 *MC^{6}MFM H1*
GU HAI RC/Sw (Uddevalla) 1968; B; 26,481 grt/54,996 dwt; 217.61 × 12.81 m *(714 × 42.03 ft)*; M (B&W); 15.5 kts; ex-*Spyros A Lemos*

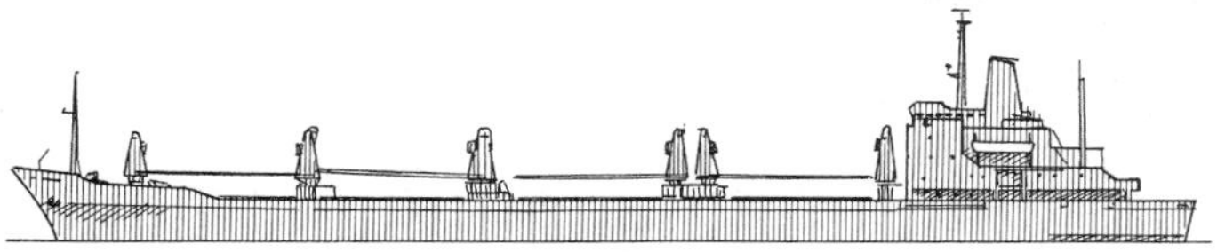

27 *MC^{6}MFN H1*
LUCIEN PAQUIN Ca/Sw (Eriksbergs) 1969; C; 10,034 grt/12,802 dwt; 140.04 × 9.52 m *(459.45 × 31.23 ft)*; M (Pielstick); 16.75 kts; ex-*Boreland*; 'Scandia' type
Sister: **MIN TAI 88** (RC) ex-*Birkaland*

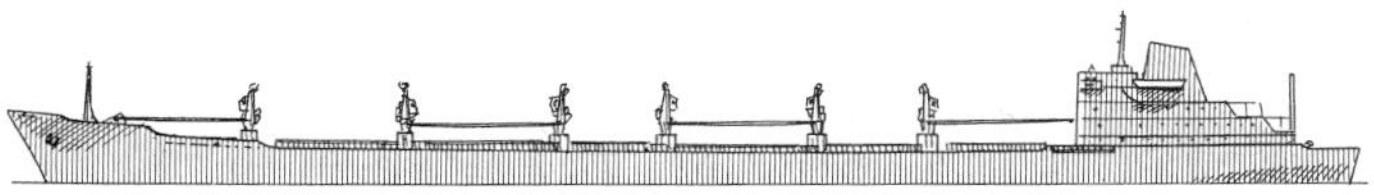

28 *MC^{6}MFN H1*
NICOLO ELISA SV/Br (A&P) 1975; B; 15,651 grt/26,702 dwt; 183.04 × 10.47 m *(600.52 × 34.35 ft)*; M (Sulzer); 15 kts; ex-*Anna M*; 'B-26' type
Sister: **ANNA** (Cy) ex-*Camilla M*

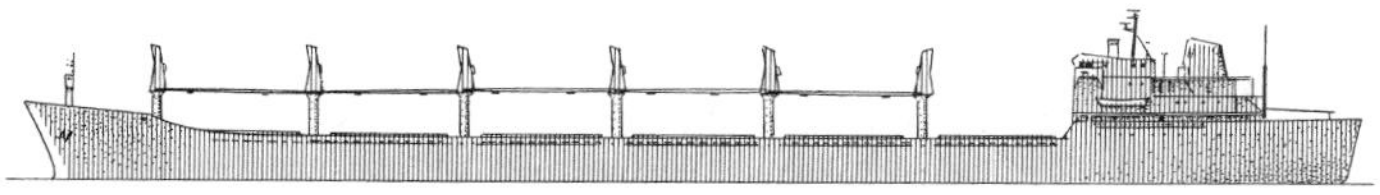

29 *MC^{6}MFN H13*
WESTERN GEORGIOS Gr/No (Fredriksstad) 1972; B; 22,614 grt/38,406 dwt; 193.45 × 11.76 m *(634.68 × 38.58 ft)*; M (Gotaverken); 15 kts; ex-*Belstar*
Similar: **NAND NAKUL** (In) ex-*Aleppo;* **MARGARO R** (Gr) ex-*Stove Campbell*; **FORTUNE BAY** (Cy) ex-*Stove Transport*; **AN HAI** (RC) ex-*Sandar*; **HU PO HAI** (RC) ex-*Bulk Promoter*; **JIN HAI** (RC) ex-*Ringstad*; **LIULINHAI** (RC) ex-*Belnor*; **MEI GUI HAI** (RC) ex-*Bulk Prospector*

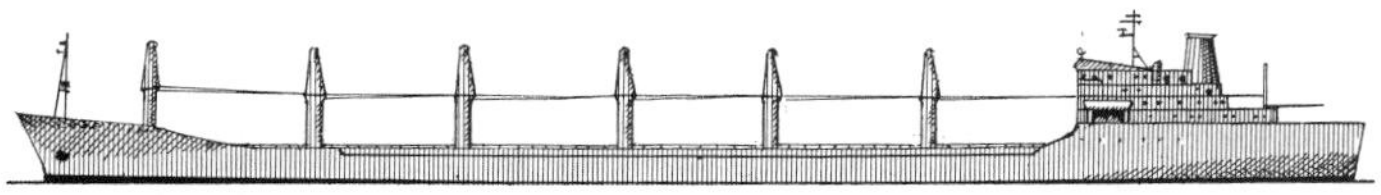

30 *MC^{6}MFN H13*
AL WAALIYU Pa/No (Fredriksstad) 1977; B; 22,614 grt/38,406 dwt; 193.45 × 11.77 m *(634.67 × 38.61 ft)*; M (Sulzer); — kts; ex-*Melsomvik*

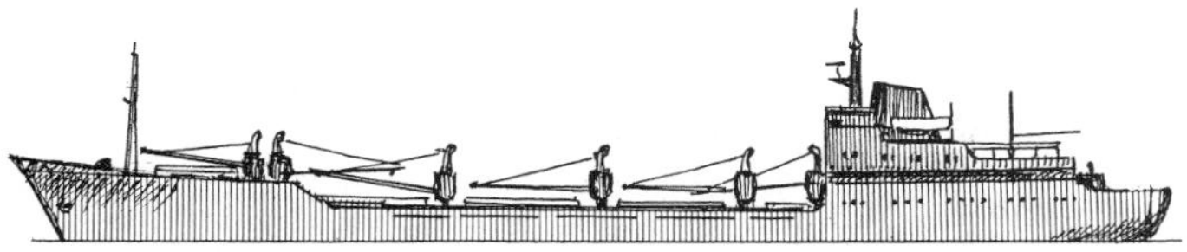

31 *MC^{6}MFN H13*
DONG NAI Vn/Sw (Lindholmens) 1965; C; 7,113 grt/9,734 dwt; 134.17 × 8.99 m *(440.19 × 29.49 ft)*; M (Pielstick); 17.5 kts; ex-*Lemnos*

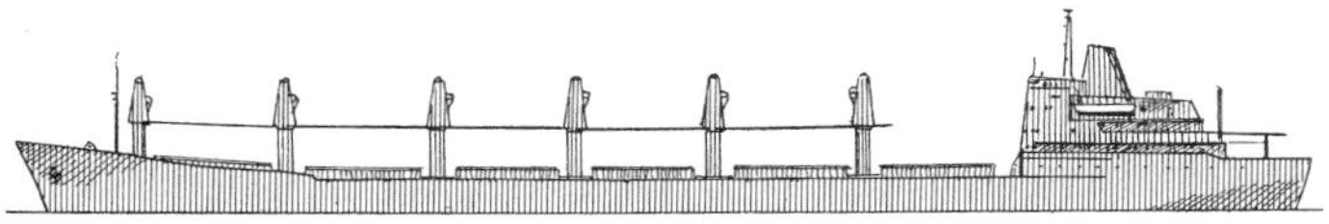

32 *MC^{6}MFN H13*
HACI SEFER KALKAVAN Tu/No (Haugesund) 1967; B; 12,433 grt/ 19,902 dwt; 161.55 × 9.7 m *(530.02 × 31.82 ft)*; M (Gotaverken); 15.5 kts; ex-*Cape Clear*

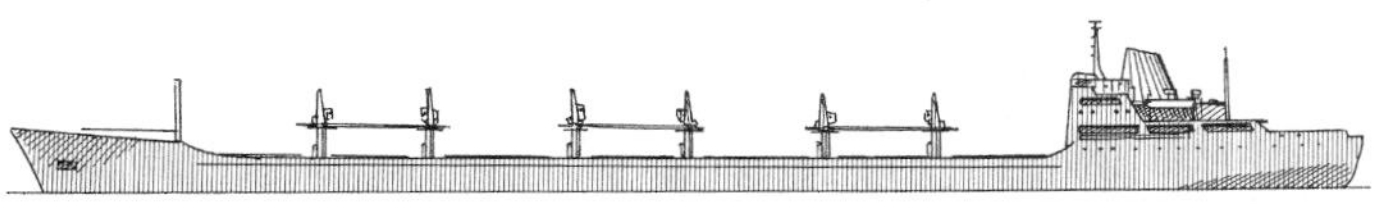

33 *MC^{6}MFN H13*
LARK Ma/Ys ('3 Maj') 1972; B; 18,401 grt/31,832 dwt; 196.6 × 10.86 m *(645.01 × 35.63 ft)*; M (Sulzer); 15.5 kts; ex-*Maritsa P Lemos*
Sister: **WU SHENG HAI** (RC) ex-*Nicolaos Pateras*; Similar: **ZHAO YANG HAI** (RC) ex-*Mericunda*; **HERCEGOVINA** (Ma)

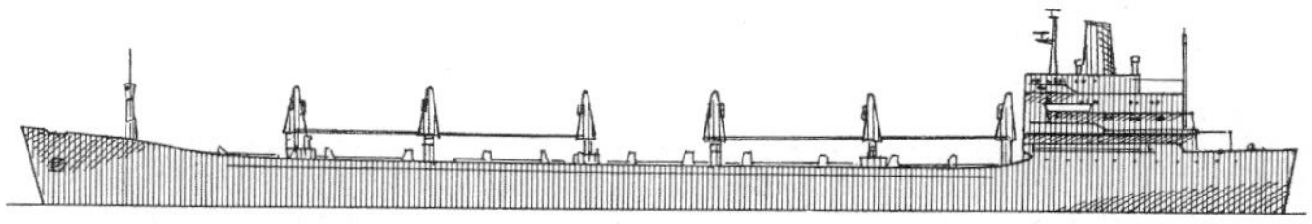

34 *MC^{6}MFN H13*
LYDI Gr/Sw (Uddevalla) 1970; B; 14,269 grt/22,394 dwt; 168.99 × 10.27 m *(554.43 × 33.69 ft)*; M (B&W); 16 kts; ex-*Norse Viking*
Sisters: **AVON** (Li) ex-*Norse Captain*; **HUA ZHU 2** (RC) ex-*Norse River*

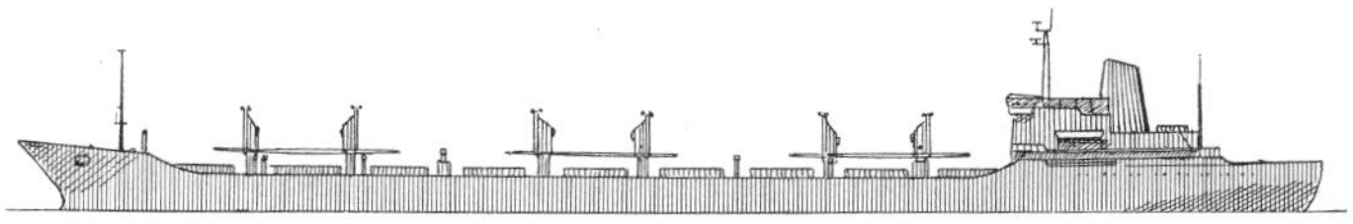

35 *MC^{6}MFN H13*
ON YEUNG Pa/Ru (Baltic) 1972; B; 20,818 grt/36,428 dwt; 199.9 × 11.23 m *(655.84 × 36.84 ft)*; M (B&W); 16 kts; ex-*Figaro*; 'Baltika' type
Similar: **ALKMINI A** (Ma) ex-*Madame Butterfly*; **AMAMI** (Cy), launched as *Renate* (may not have cranes)

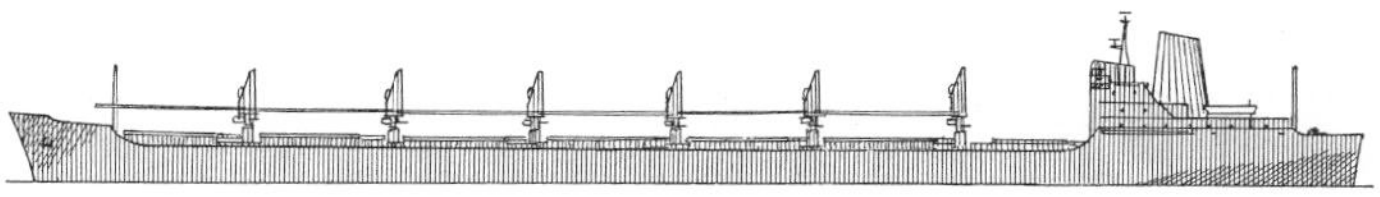

36 *MC^{6}MFN H13*
PRINARITIS Gr/Gr (Hellenic) 1973; B; 20,905 grt/37,580 dwt; 193.43 × 11.35 m *(634.61 × 37.23 ft)*; M (Sulzer); 15 kts; ex-*World Argus*
Similar: **LEPANTO GLORY** (Pa) ex-*World Apollo*; **WORLD ARES** (Gr); **WORLD AJAX** (Gr); **WORLD AGAMEMNON** (Gr); **WORLD ARETUS** (Gr); **ESPERANZA C** (Pa) ex-*World Marine*; **HAWK** (Cy) ex-*Daphne*; **CEMRE 2** (Tu) ex-*Aphrodite*; **TARPON SEALANE** (Cy); **WORLD AMPHION** (Gr); **KIKA** (Cy) ex-*Scapdale;* **WORLD ACHILLES II** (Gr); **NINA S** (Li) ex-*Fotini*; **SEDAT ERKOL** (Tu) ex-*Joanna*; **MATHILDAKI** (Cy) ex-*Scapwill*; Possible sister: **WORLD AEGEUS** (Gr)

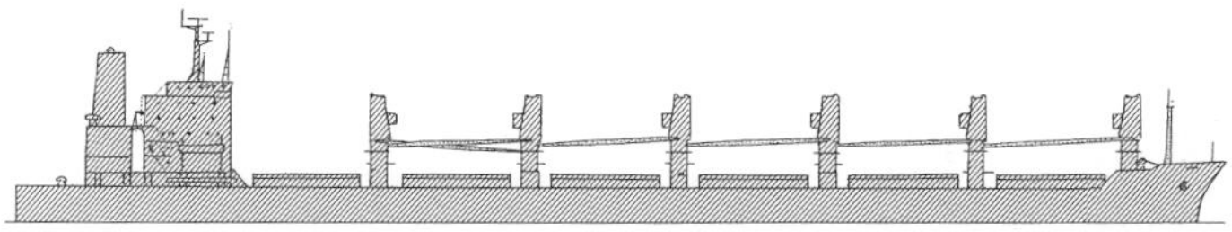

37 *MC^{6}M^{2}F H1*
APJ AKHIL In/Ja (Hitachi) 1989; B; 27,997 grt/39,989 dwt; 210.00 × 9.55 m *(688.98 × 31.33 ft)*; M (B&W); 14 kts
Probable sisters: **TAMIL ANNA** (In); **TAMIL KAMARAJ** (In); **TAMIL PERIYAR** (In)

38 *MC^{6}MNFNC H1*
CAPTAIN GEORGE TSANGARIS Gr/Ja (Koyo) 1982; B; 34,211 grt/ 61,349 dwt; 223.15 × 13.02 m *(732.12 × 42.72 ft)*; M (B&W); 14.5 kts; ex-*World Jade*

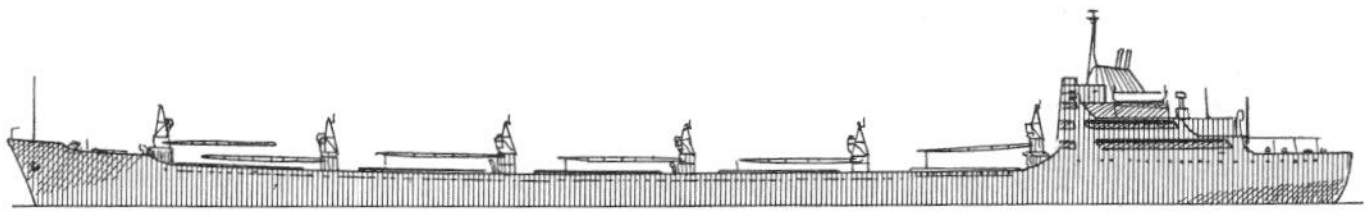

39 *MC^{6}M-F H13*
QING HAI RC/Br (Blyth) 1962; B; 16,177 grt/24,482 dwt; 188.63 × 9.78 m *(618.86 × 32.09 ft)*; M (Sulzer); 12.5 kts; ex-*Chapel River*

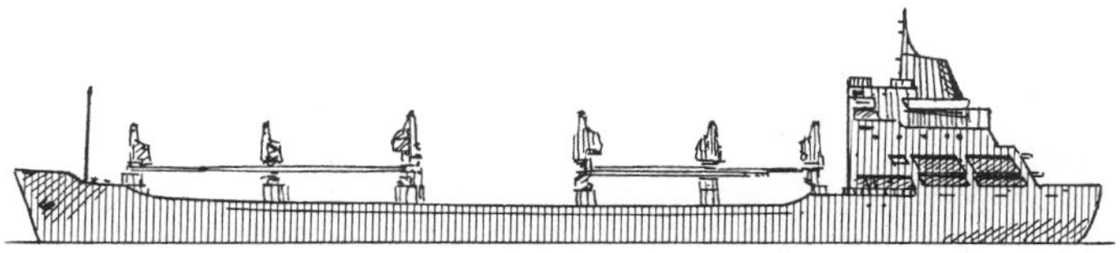

40 *MC^{6}M-F H13*
SEA HORSE Mv/Br (Caledon) 1966; C; 4,357 grt/6,177 dwt; 111.89 × 7.16 m *(367 × 23.49 ft)*; M (British Polar); 12.5 kts; ex-*Ngahere*
Sister: **FADEL G** (Le) ex-*Ngatoro*

41 *MC^{5}M-FN H13*
FLARE Cy/Ja (Hakodate) 1972; B; 16,947 grt/29,222 dwt; 180.8 × 10.68 m *(593.18 × 35.04 ft)*; M (Sulzer); 16.5 kts; ex-*Doric Flame*
Sister: **AGIOS NECTARIOS** (Ma) ex-*Apex*; Possible sisters: **DYNAMIC HORIZON** (Cy) ex-*Sapporo Olympics*; **SEAHOPE II** (Cy) ex-*Ellispontos*; **CHIOS GLORY** (Gr) ex-*Naftoporos*; **FIRST LADY** (Bs) ex-*Lokris*; Similar: **TEGEA** (Ma) ex-*Avlis*

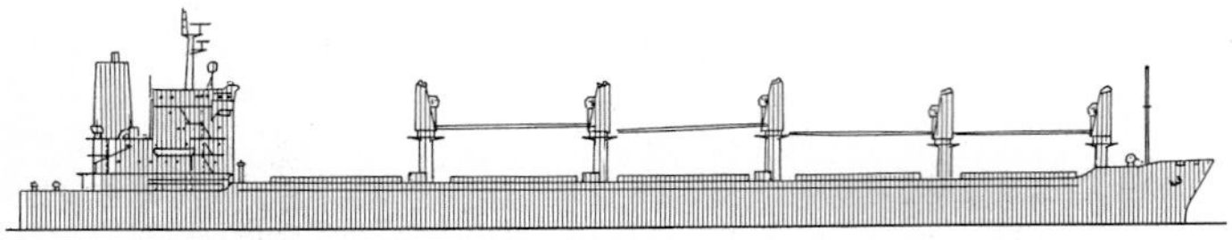

42 *MC^{5}MCF H1*
AYIA MARINA Gr/Ja (IHI) 1984; B; 22,511 grt/37,250 dwt; 187.03 × 10.74 m *(613.62 × 35.24 ft)*; M (Sulzer); 14.50 kts; ex-*Pacific Wave*; 'Future 32' type; Some vessels under drawing number 7/125 may have this appearance
Sisters: **PACIFIC OCEAN** (Li); **JAG RAHUL** (In) ex-*Fortunee*

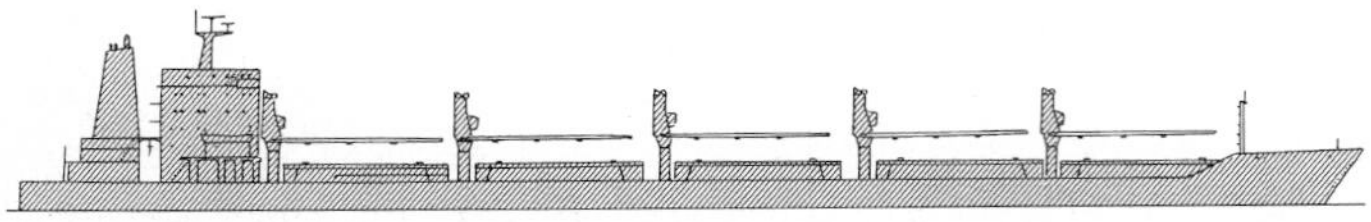

43 *MC^{5}MF H1*
DOMIAT Eg/Eg (Alexandria) 1985; B; 24,105 grt/38,391 dwt; 200.01 × 11.09 m *(656.20 × 36.38 ft)*; M (B&W); 15 kts; Launched as *Al Sedik*
Sister: **QENA** (Eg)

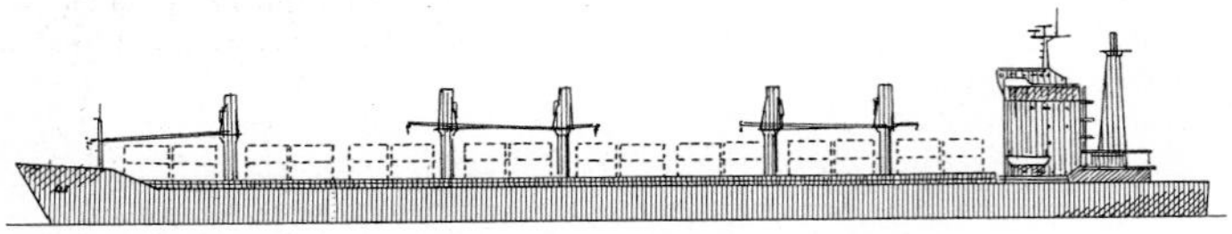

44 *MC^{5}MF H1*
LUAN HE RC/FRG (Howaldts DW) 1978; C/Con; 18,572 grt/25,550 dwt; 169.02 × 9.95 m *(554.53 × 32.64 ft)*; M (Pielstick); 15 kts; Launched as *Columbia*; 1,140 TEU
Sisters: **TUO HE** (RC) launched as *California*; **WEI HE** (RC) ex-*Caledonia*

45 *MC^{5}MF H13*
APJ ANJLI In/Ja (Kanasashi) 1982; B; 16,712 grt/27,192 dwt; 176.00 × 10.40 m *(577 × 34.12 ft)*; M (Sulzer); 14.8 kts
Sister: **APJ SUSHMA** (In)

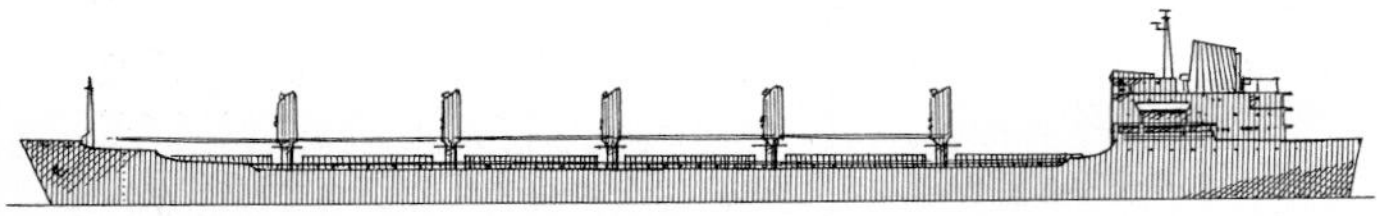

46 *MC^{5}MF H13*
GUANG SHUN RC/Br (Lithgows) 1972; B; 16,889 grt/32,738 dwt; 178.31 × 10.36 m *(585 × 33.99 ft)*; M (B&W); 15 kts; ex-*Bernes*

47 *MC^{5}MF H13*
TARTOUS Sy/Sp (Cadiz) 1964; C; 4,224 grt/5,829 dwt; 121.37 × 6.95 m *(398.19 × 22.8 ft)*; M (Gotaverken); 15 kts; ex-*Industria*; Lengthened 1968
Sisters: **NADEEN** (Bl) ex-*Scania*; **GADA** (Eg) ex-*Italia*; **XINDU** (RC) ex-*Dalmatia*

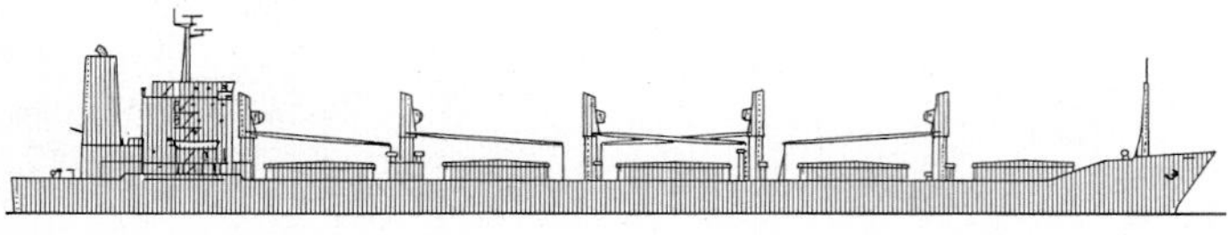

48 *MC^{5}MFC H1*
MAN HAI RC/Ja (Osaka) 1984; B; 26,959 grt/46,436 dwt; 189.68 × 11.44 m *(622.31 × 37.53 ft)*; M (B&W); 14.50 kts

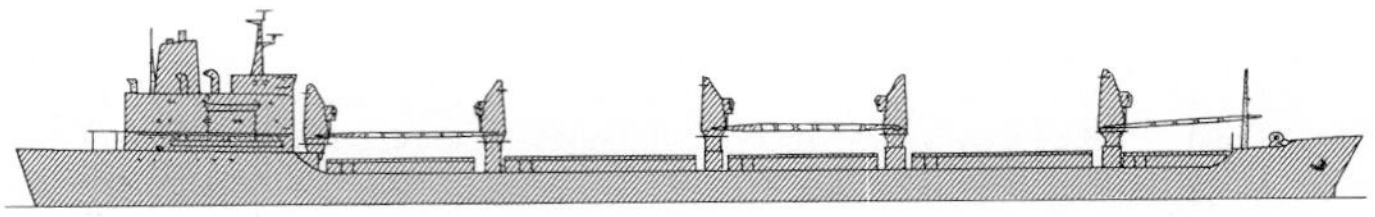

49 *MC^{5}MFM H13*
LUCKYMAN Cy/Ja (Hitachi) 1980; B; 16,223 grt/27,000 dwt; 178.21 × 10.57 m *(584.68 × 34.68 ft)*; M (B&W); 17.50 kts; ex-*O Sole Mio*

50 *MC^{5}MFM H13*
ZENO Gr/Ja (Sanoyasu) 1982; B; 23,381 grt/40,947 dwt; 182.68 × 12.12 m *(599 × 39.76 ft)*; M (Sulzer); 15.25 kts
Probable sisters: **ARTEMIS SB** (Cy) ex-*Artemis*; **MARLIN** (Ma) ex-*Alexander Venture*; **BELLE** (Cy) ex-*Belladona Venture*; **METIN KALKAVAN** (Tu) ex-*Petra*; **CRANE** (Cy) ex-*Antigone*; **MELOI** (Ma) ex-*Maritime Investor*; Similar: **DIMAN** (Cy) ex-*Bunga Sripagi*; **MARY L** (Gr) ex-*Holylight*

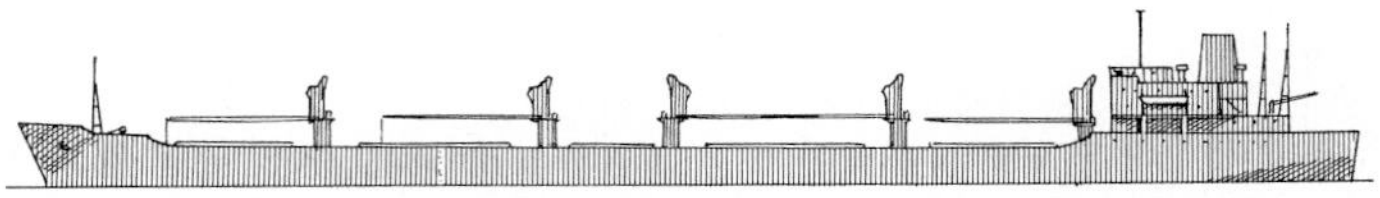

51 *MC^{5}MFM^2 H13*
ALEXANDER Gr/Ja (Osaka) 1975; B; 20,854 grt/35,244 dwt; 185.5 × 10.9 m *(608.59 × 35.76 ft)*; M (Sulzer); 15.25 kts; ex-*Cruzeiro Do Sol*
Sisters: **PARASKEVI M Y** (Gr) ex-*Diavolezza*; **NIRVANA** (Cy) ex-*Romandie*; Similar: **GEMINI EXPLORER** (Pa) ex-*Federal Katsura*; **RAFAEL** (Li) ex-*Federal Hudson*

52 *MC^{5}MFN*
XING HAI RC/FRG (Flensburger) 1961; B; 19,263 grt/30,746 dwt; 196.37 × 11 m *(644 × 36.09 ft)*; M (MAN); 15.5 kts; ex-*Naess Favorita*

53 *MC^{5}MFN H1*
ALAM AMAN My/Ja (Osaka) 1982; B; 16,927 grt/26,987 dwt; 169.60 × 9.62 m *(556 × 31.56 ft)*; M (Sulzer); 15 kts; ex-*Cavourella*
Probable sister: **JAG VIKRAM** (In) ex-*Mia*

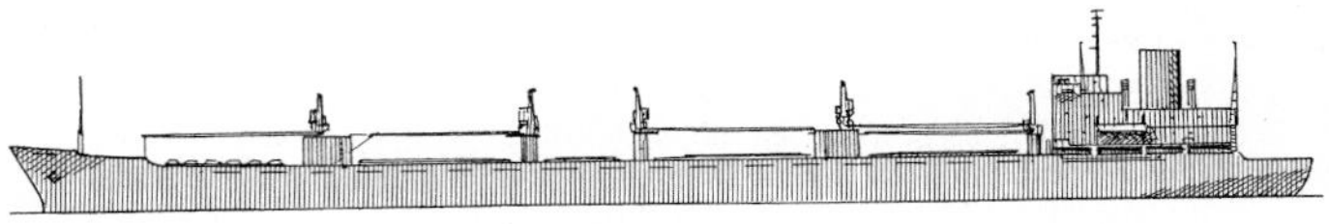

54 *MC^{5}MFN H1*
ALBATROSS Ma/Ja (Namura) 1971; B; 17,968 grt/30,228 dwt; 187 × 10.79 m *(613.52 × 35.4 ft)*; M (Sulzer); 14.5 kts; ex-*Toyota Maru No 14*
Sisters: **ALINDA** (Ma) ex-*Soyo Maru*; **GEORGIOS L** (Ma) ex-*Toyota Maru No 7*; **SEASONG** (Cy) ex-*Toyota Maru No 8*

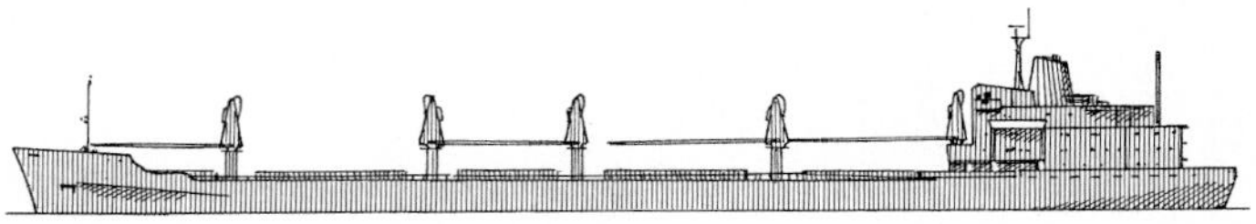

55 *MC^{5}MFN H1*
ARHON Pa/Br (Scotstoun) 1974; B; 14,802 grt/26,019 dwt; 175.11 × 9.98 m *(574.5 × 32.74); M (B&W); 15.5 kts; ex-Harfleur*

56 *MC^{5}MFN H1*
GREAT PRIZE Pa/Ja (Osaka) 1980; B; 16,021 grt/27,188 dwt; 170.52 × 10.06 m *(599 × 33.01 ft)*; M (B&W); 14.75 kts; ex-*World Prize*; N aft consists of tripod on port side and pole on starboard. They are slightly offset.
Sisters: **GREAT CHEER** (Pa) ex-*World Cheer*; **GREAT GLEN** (Pa) ex-*World Glen*; **KAPITAN TRUBKIN** (Uk) ex-Jaylock

57 *MC^{5}MFN H1*
IONIA Gr/Ja (Osaka) 1977; B; 20,567 grt/36,979 dwt; 186.01 × 11.07 m *(610.27 × 36.32 ft)*; M (Sulzer); 15 kts; ex-*Rimba Merbau*
Sister: **MARILY** (Pa) ex-*Rimba Sepetir*; Similar: **JAG RAVI** (In) ex-*Eastern Moon*

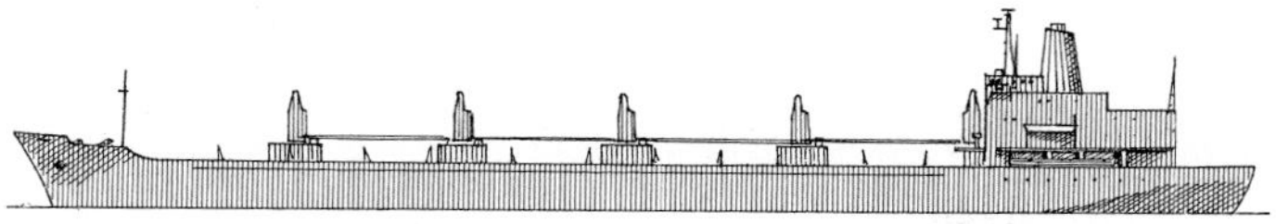

58 MC^5MFN *H1*
IRAN TORAB Ir/Ja (Sumitomo) 1971; B; 19,629 grt/29,569 dwt; 171.25 × 11.02 m *(561.84 × 36.15 ft)*; M (Sulzer); 16.7 kts; ex-*Asia Hunter*

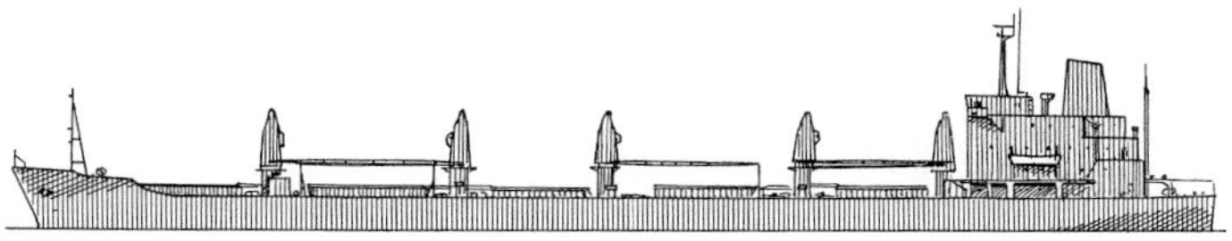

59 MC^5MFN *H1*
JAG VISHNU Br/Ja (Osaka) 1977; B; 16,931 grt/27,481 dwt; 169.63 × 9.62 m *(556.53 × 31.56 ft)*; M (Sulzer); 15 kts; ex-*Triton*

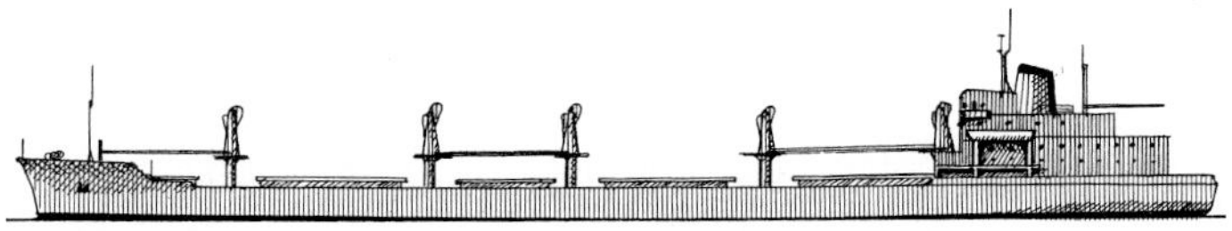

60 MC^5MFN *H1*
MALE II Pa/Br (Upper Clyde) 1970; B; 16,221 grt/26,289 dwt; 173.59 × 9.96 m *(569.52 × 32.67 ft)*; M (B&W); 15.25 kts; ex-*Vancouver City*; 'Cardiff' class
Sisters: **ABDUL RAHMAN S** (Sy) ex-*Port Alberni City;* **SINGA SKY** (RC) ex-*Prince Rupert City*; **MONOLIMA** (Ma) ex-*Victoria City*; **FORCE** (Cy) ex-*Tacoma City*; **MYOHYANG 2** (Rk) ex-*New Westminster City*; Similar: **SEAHORSE G** (Pa) ex-*Norse Pilot*; **AN DA HAI** (RC) ex-*Norse Trade*; **ONTARIO** (Cy) ex-*Cinchona*; **YUN FENG LING** (RC) ex-*Camara*; **TAHIR KIRAN** (Tu) ex-*Irish Oak*; **PARIS** (Ma) ex-*Norse Marshal*; **MARIA** (Li) ex-*Norse Herald*; **ARABELLA** (Ma) ex-*Irish Maple*; **NAZLI K** (Tu) ex-*Golden Oriole*; **ZEYNEP K** (Tu) ex-*Golden Anne*

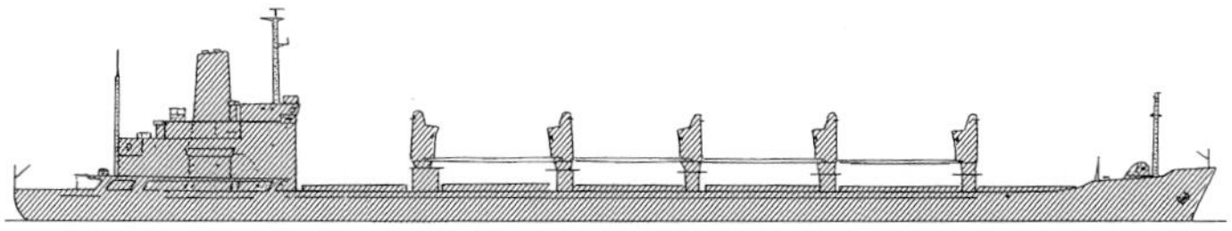

61 MC^5MFN *H1*
MORIAS Gr/Ja (Sumitomo) 1977; B; 13,409 grt/21,743 dwt; 163.51 × 9.60 m *(536.45 × 31.50 ft)*; M (Sulzer); 15.50 kts; ex-*Robin*

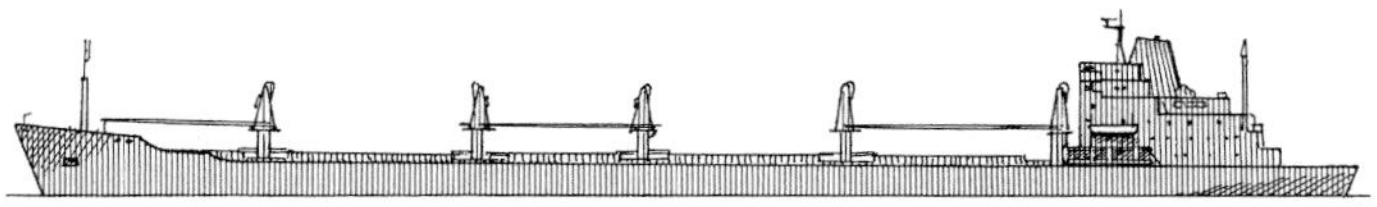

62 MC^5MFN *H1*
SINGA SAGA Li/Br (Govan) 1977; B; 16,103 grt/26,586 dwt; 175.14 × 9.96 m *(574.6 × 32.67 ft)*; M (B&W); 15 kts; ex-*Dona Paz*; 'Cardiff' class
Sisters: **GOLDEN EMPIRE** (Gr) ex-*Dona Hortencia II*; **SINGA SUN** (Li) ex-*Don Salvador III*

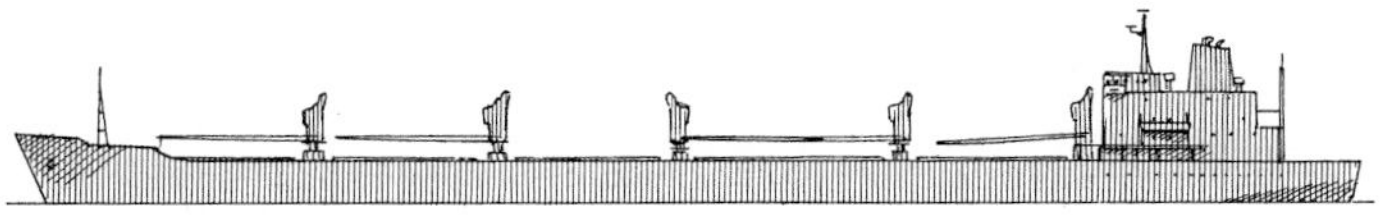

63 MC^5MFN *H1*
SUN II Pa/Ja (Osaka) 1975; B; 14,168 × 27,439 dwt; 169.63 × 9.57 m *(556.52 × 31.39 ft)*; M (Sulzer); 15.5 kts; ex-*Astros*
Sister: **MATHIOS** (Ma) ex-*Desert Wind*

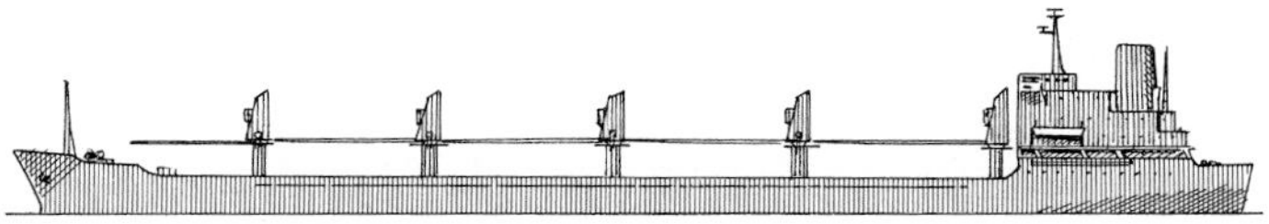

64 MC^5MFN *H13*
AMRO KALKAVAN Tu/Ja (Namura) 1976; B; 16,902 grt/27,849 dwt; 177.43 × 9.87 m *(582.12 × 32.38 ft)*; M (Sulzer); 15 kts; ex-*Rimba Meranti*
Possible sister: **RUBY** (Gr) ex-*Rimba Ramin*

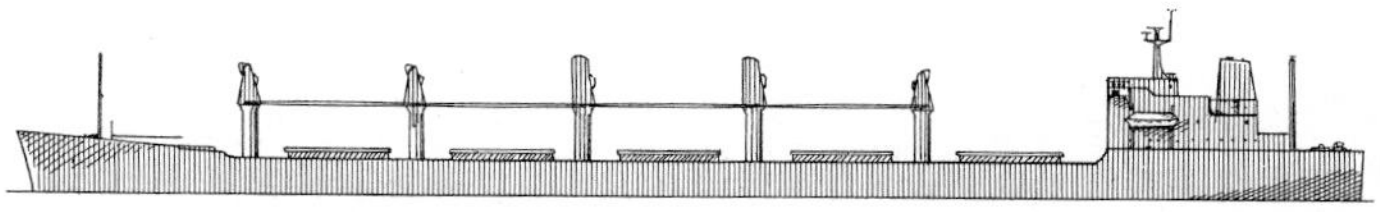

65 MC^5MFN *H13*
APTMARINER Li/Br (Sunderland) 1979; B; 17,677 grt/31,200 dwt; 188.75 × 10.66 m *(619.3 × 34.97 ft)*; M (Doxford); 15 kts; ex-*Devonbrook*
Sisters: **FEDERAL VIBEKE** (NIS) ex-*Nosira Lin*; **GUNAY A** (Tu) ex-*Nosira Sharon*; **HOPE 1** (Ma) ex-*Nosira Madeleine*; **DARYA KAMAL** (HK); **DARYA MA** (HK)

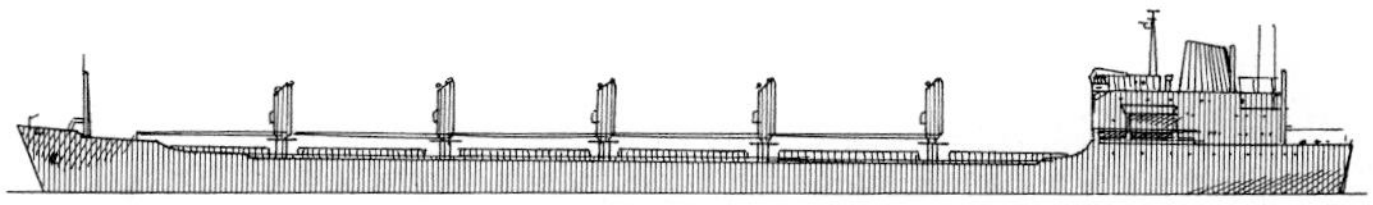

66 MC^5MFN *H13*
FEICUIHAI RC/Br (Lithgows) 1973; B; 18,972 grt/32,818 dwt; 178.31 × 10.38 m *(585.01 × 34.05 ft)*; M (B&W); 15 kts; ex-*Bravenes*

67 MC^5MFN *H13*
HUA JIN RC/Ja (NKK) 1980; B; 16,325 grt/30,869 dwt; 175.01 × 10.45 (m *(574 × 34.28 ft)*; M (Pielstick); 14.25 kts; ex-*Universal Beauty*
Sister: **HUA WAN** (RC) ex-*Universal Benefit*

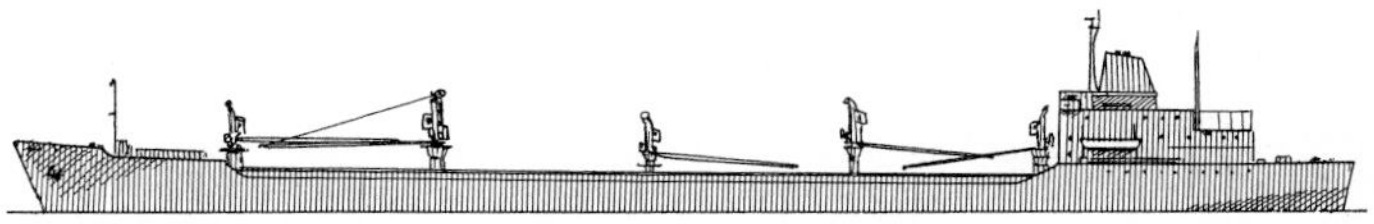

68 MC^5MFN *H13*
IBN ABDOUN Bn/Br (Scotstoun) 1976; C; 15,455 grt/23,890 dwt; 175.32 × 10.42 m *(575.19 × 34.18 ft)*; M (B&W); 16 kts; 'KUWAIT' Class
Sisters: **YI RONG** (RC) ex-*Ibn Bajjah*; **IBN HAZM** (Bn); **COSMAN II** (Cy) ex-*Ibn Sina*; **YI MING** (RC) ex-*Ibn Zuhr*; **COSMAN I** (Cy) ex-*Ibn Jubayr*; Similar (Ko built—Hyundai) (cranes are larger): **OCEAN BEAUTY** (Ko); **OCEAN CROWN** (Ko); **OCEAN DUKE** (Ko)

69 MC^5MFN *H13*
IRAN ADL Ir/RC (Hudong) 1983; B; 22,027 grt/37,537 dwt; 186 × 11.25 m *(610.23 × 36.91 ft)*; M (B&W); 15.25 kts; ex-*World Fraternity*
Possible sisters: **IRAN AFZAL** (Ir) launched as *Primelock*; **AKRA SOUNION** (Va) ex-*Star Orient*; Sisters (Ja built—Osaka & Imabari): **ORHAN EKINCI** (Tu) ex-*World Amity*; **HUA GUANG** (RC) ex-*World Aspiration* (builder—Imabari); **GREAT PEARL** (Pa) ex-*World Pearl* (builder—Imabari); **ASPILOS** (Ma) ex-*World Harvest*; **BLACK SEA** (Bs) ex-*World Oak*; **BALAJI VINTAGE** (In) launched as *World Teresa* (builder—Osaka)

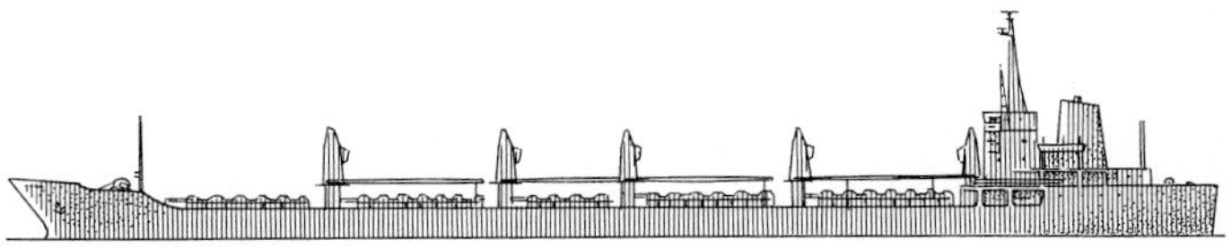

70 MC^5MFN *H13*
IRENE Ma/Ja (Kanasashi) 1976; B; 15,511 grt/27,947 dwt; 176.03 × 10.1 m *(577.53 × 33.14 ft)*; M (B&W); 15 kts; ex-*Splendid Albatross*
Sister: **MANYAS 1** (Tu) ex-*Sea Glory*; Probably similar: **ATHINOULA** (Cy) ex-*Truejoy*

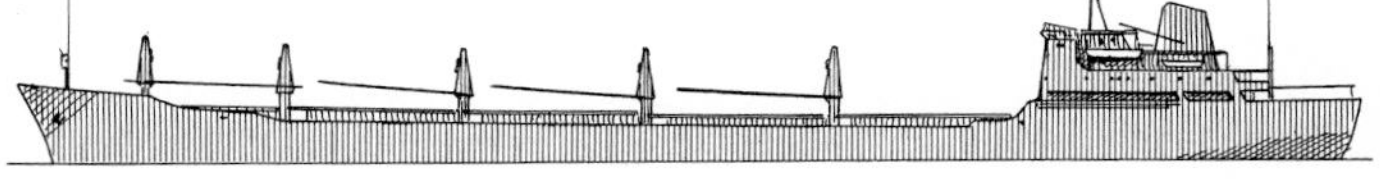

71 MC^5MFN *H13*
KEKOVA Tu/No (Fredriksstad) 1970; B; 11,832 grt/20,016 dwt; 165.67 × 9.31 m *(543.53 × 30.54 ft)*; M (Gotaverken); 15.5 kts; ex-*Melsomvik*
Similar: **SOPAL 1** (SV) ex-*Belocean*; **UNION AUCKLAND** (NZ) ex-*Columbia;* **AN JI HAI** (RC) ex-*Stove Friend*

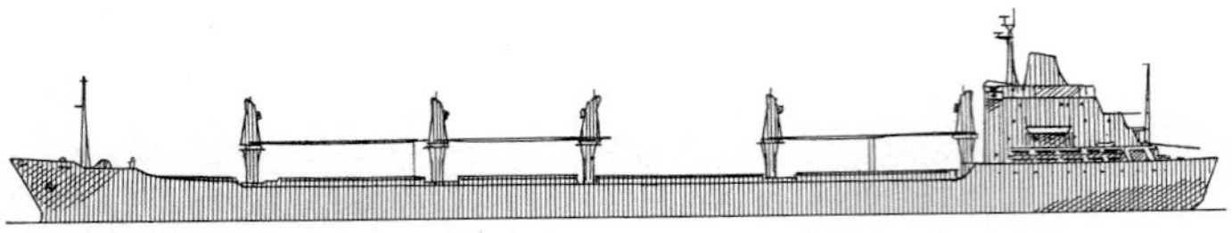

72 *MC^{5}MFN H13*
LAZAROS L Ma/Ja (Hayashikane) 1977; B; 15,592 grt/28,633 dwt; 176.82 × 10.35 m *(580.12 × 33.95 ft)*; M (B&W); 15 kts; ex-*Irish Cedar*
Sister: **AGIA PHILOTHEI** (Gr) ex-*Irish Rowan*

73 *MC^{5}MFN H13*
MARIA Ma/Ru (Baltic) 1971; B; 23,391 grt/38,201 dwt; 201.3 × 11.23 m *(660.43 × 36.84 ft)*; M (B&W); 15.5 kts; ex-*Nortrans Vision*; 'Baltika' type. Ice strengthened
Sister: **ARAYA** (Cy) ex-*Cresco*; Possible sister: **GUO FA** (SV) ex-*Nortrans Kathe*

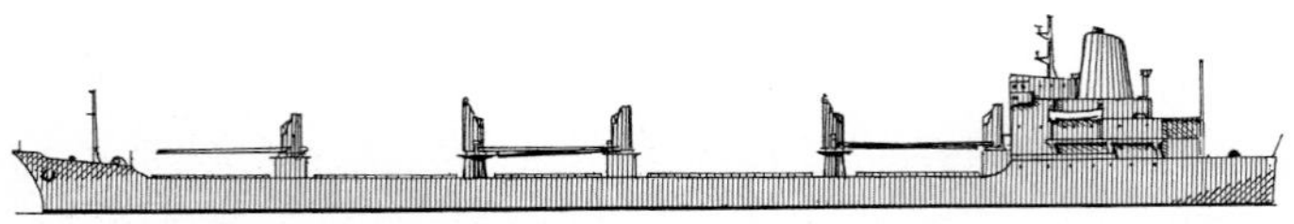

74 *MC^{5}MFN H13*
MARIA G L Gr/Ja (Namura) 1974; B; 14,961 grt/26,998 dwt; 178.49 × 10.42 m *(585.6 × 34.19 ft)*; M (Sulzer); 14.75 kts
Sister: **PONTOPOROS** (Gr) ex-*Odyssey 10*; Possible sister: **KALLIOPI L** (Gr); Similar: **XING LI** (SV) ex-*Ever Honor*; **ELIKI** (Cy) ex-*Pacbaron*; **HAO FA** (RC) ex-*Packing*; **FINIKI** (Cy) ex-*Pacduchess*; **MAURITIUS ENDEAVOUR** (Ms) ex-*Grand Enterprise*; **ISPARTA** (Tu); **URFA** (Tu); **SEAPEARL II** (Ma) ex-*Island Mariner*; **APIL** (Bs) ex-*Lucy*; Possibly similar: **PACDUKE** (Li)

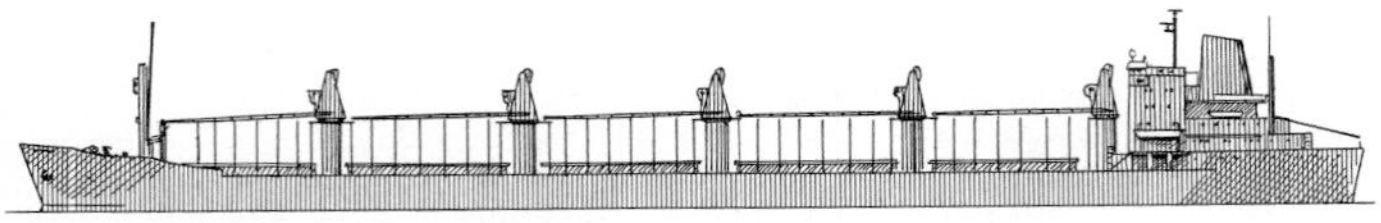

75 *MC^{5}MFN H13*
MED SALVADOR Ma/De (B&W) 1970; B; 23,081 grt/41,261 dwt; 192.06 × 10.12 m *(630.12 × 33.2 ft)*; M (B&W); 15.5 kts; ex-*Skogstad*
Sister: **MED CARRARA** (Ma) ex-*Roland Bremen*; Similar: **AGHIOS MINAS** (Ma) ex-*Janega*

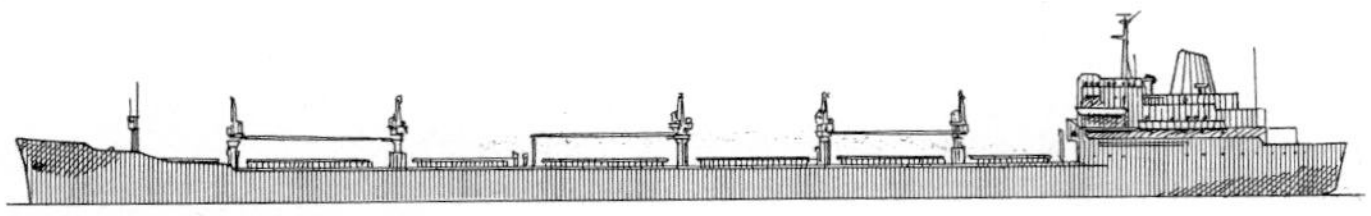

76 *MC^{5}MFN H13*
MING HAI RC/Sw (Gotav) 1967; B; 22,488 grt/39,055 dwt; 200.31 × 11.17 m *(657.19 × 36.42 ft)*; M (Gotaverken); 13 kts; ex-*Rudolf Olsen*
Similar: **JIA HAI** (RC) ex-*Pytheas*

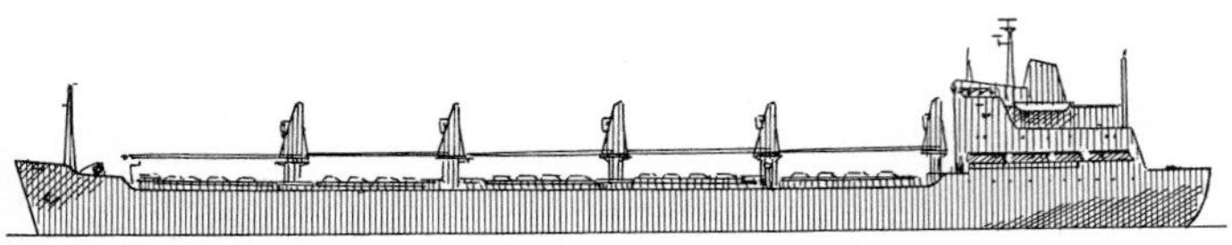

77 *MC^{5}MFN H13*
PATRICIA Ve/Ja (Namura) 1968; B; 10,713 grt/14,224 dwt; 147.02 × 8.49 m *(482.34 × 27.85 ft)*; M (B&W); 14 kts; ex-*William R Adams*

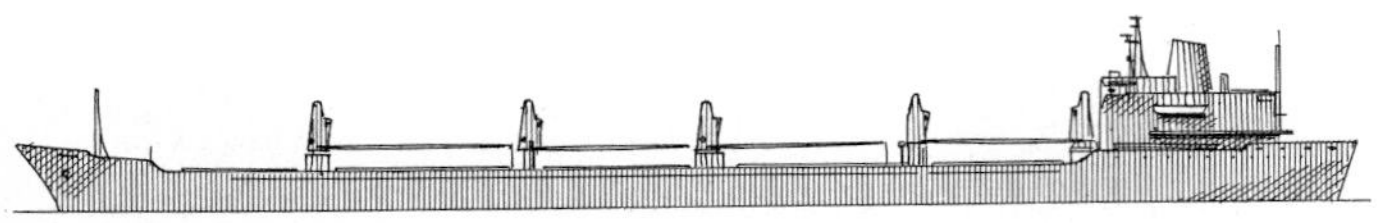

78 *MC^{5}MFN H13*
PHOENIX M Cy/Ja (Namura) 1976; B; 16,037 grt/26,874 dwt; 176.99 × 10.4 m *(580.67 × 34.12 ft)*; M (Sulzer); 15.5 kts; ex-*Georgis A Georgilis*
Sisters: **MACFRIENDSHIP** (Cy) ex-*Antonis P Lemos*; **ADITYA KIRAN** (In) ex-*Ilena*; Possibly similar: **JAG VIKAS** (In) ex-*Polychronis*

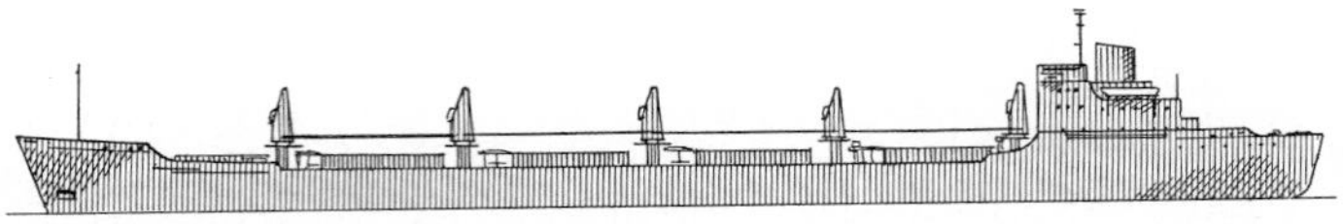

79 *MC^{5}MFN H13*
RED FOTINI Cy/Ne (Giessen-De Noord) 1970; B; 12,592 grt/20,015 dwt; 160.1 × 9.93 m *(526.26 × 32.58 ft)*; M (Sulzer); 14.5 kts; ex-*Putten*
Sister: **EUROBULKER I** (Ma) ex-*Voorne*

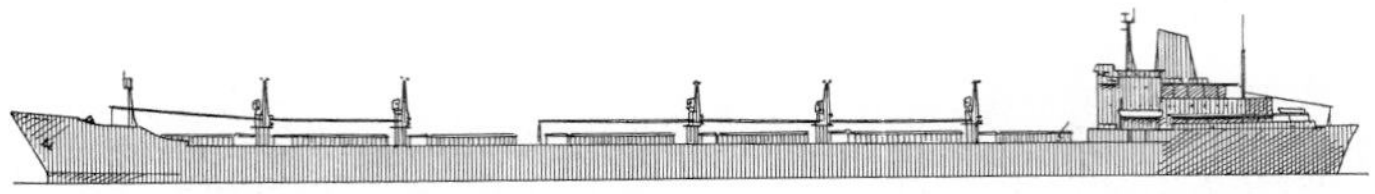

80 *MC^{5}MFN H13*
TRAMCO AMITY HK/De (B&W) 1969; B/Con; 29,967 grt/51,652 dwt; 218.85 × 12.1 m *(718.01 × 39.69 ft)*; M (B&W); 15.5 kts; ex-*Bianca*
Sister: **VITORANDIS** (Li) ex-*Berit*

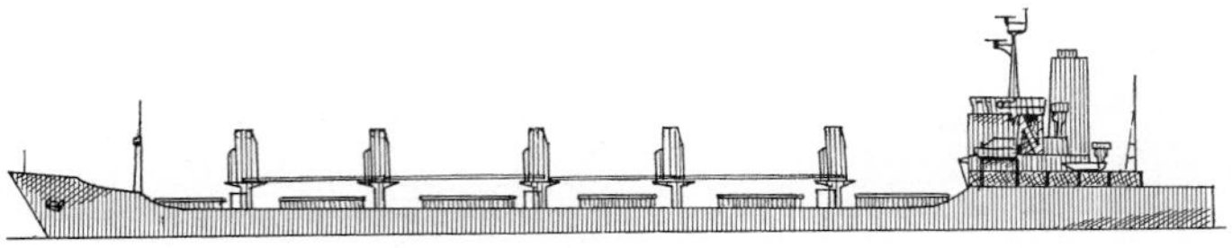

81 *MC^{5}MFN H13*
TRANS COMFORT Pa/Ja (NKK) 1976; B; 20,350 grt/35,208 dwt; 177.02 × 11.16 m *(580.77 × 36.61 ft)*; M (Sulzer); 15.5 kts; ex-*Bolnes*
Sisters: **VLADIMIR GAVRILOV** (Uk) ex-*Borgnes*; **DENIZATI** (Tu) ex-*Bravenes*; **PYOTR SMORODIN** (Uk) ex-*Becknes*; **NOMADIC DIXIE** (Bs) ex-*Bellnes*; **CALLIAN S** (Li) ex-*Birknes); **PEARL LUCK** (In) ex-*Brooknes*; **MIKHAIL STELMAKH** (Uk) ex-*Briskneś*; **ALEXANDER** (Gr) Launched as *Bergnes*

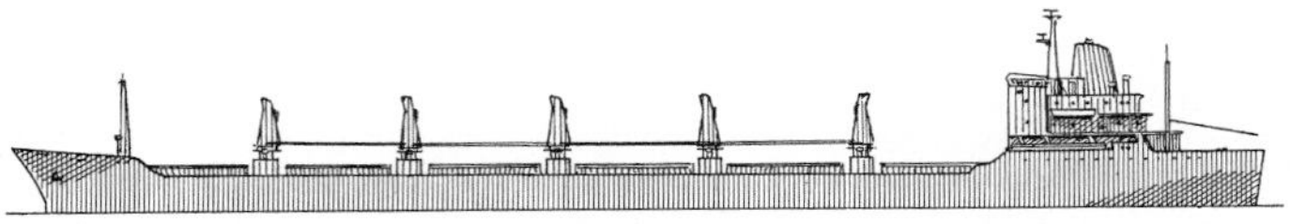

82 *MC^{5}MFN H13*
WINNER Gr/Ja (Mitsui) 1972; B; 15,653 grt/27,152 dwt; 176.77 × 10.66 m *(579.95 × 34.97 ft)*; M (B&W); 15.25 kts; ex-*Achilles*
Sisters: **CANNES** (Pa) ex-*Ajax*; **AITODOR** (Ma) ex-*Anchises*; **FREEDOM K** (Pa) ex-*Agamemnon*; **SOLBULK** (NIS) ex-*Antenor*; Similar (Foreward end of superstructure not extended outboard in some ships): **WINNER** (Cy) Launched as *Ocean Retla*; **A ALAMDAR** (Li) ex-*Shenandoah*; **AL ALIYU** (Li) ex-*Kentucky Home*; **LYRA** (Cy) ex-*S A Sabie*; **PROSPATHIA** (Cy) ex-*Presidente Allende*; **ALMA** (Cy) ex-*Endeavor*; Possibly similar: **PERIANDROS** (Ma) ex-*Skukuza*

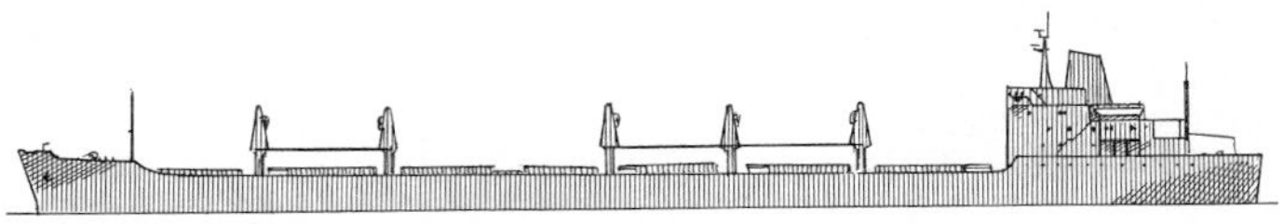

83 *MC^{5}MFN H13*
YIN SHAN HAI Pa/Br (Upper Clyde) 1972; B; 15,904 grt/27,498 dwt; 176.99 × 10.62 m *(580.68 × 34.84 ft)*; M (B&W); 11 kts; ex-*Vancouver Island*

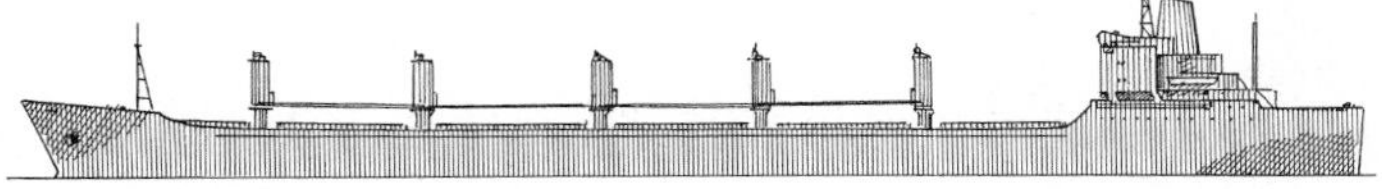

84 *MC^{5}MFN H13*
ZIYA K Tu/Be (Boelwerf) 1976; B; 17,900 grt/30,165 dwt; 190.02 × 10.79 m *(623.42 × 35.4 ft)*; M (MAN); 15.75 kts; ex-*Rubens*

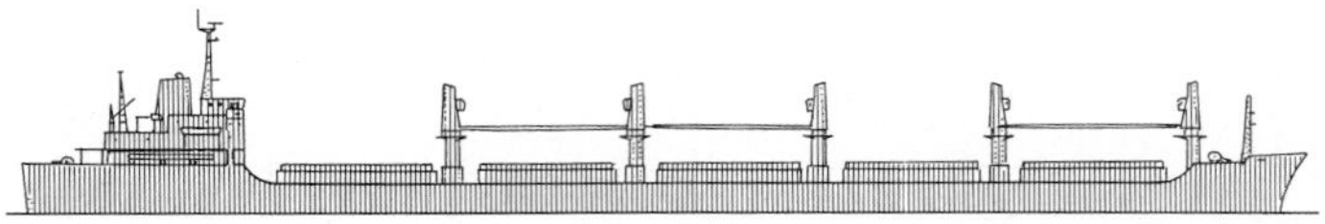

85 *MC^{5}MFNC H13*
MONTGOMERY Bs/Ja (Nipponkai) 1984; B/Con; 24,791 grt/41,373 dwt; 188.40 × 10.78 m *(618.11 × 35.37 ft)*; M (B&W); — kts; ex-*Orly*; 844 TEU

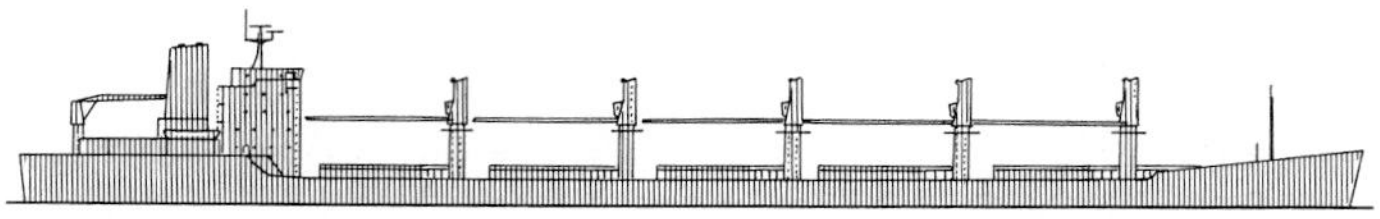

86 MC^5MFR *H13*
RADNIK Pa/Br (Sunderland) 1984; B/Con; 17,882 grt/30,960 dwt; 188.17 × 10.63 m *(617.36 × 34.88 ft)*; M (B&W); — kts; 542 TEU
Sister (cranes of different sizes): **NEA DOXA** (Gr) ex-*Alberta*

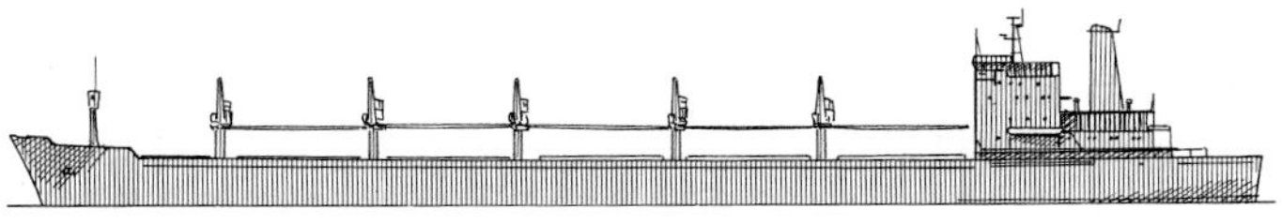

87 MC^5MG *H1*
KARRINGTON SV/Ys ('Uljanik') 1969; B; 18,693 grt/27,248 dwt; 163.02 × 11.09 m *(534.84 × 36.38 ft)*; M (B&W); 15.5 kts; ex-*Borgestad*
Sister: **EUROBULKER II** (Ho) ex-*Silvermain*

88 $\underline{MC^5M^2FM}$ *H1*
MOSDEEP Bs/Ja (Kasado) 1981; B; 29,709 grt/49,000 dwt; 190.03 × 12.12 m *(623 × 39.76 ft)*; M (Mitsubishi); 14 kts; ex-*Yamaoki Maru*

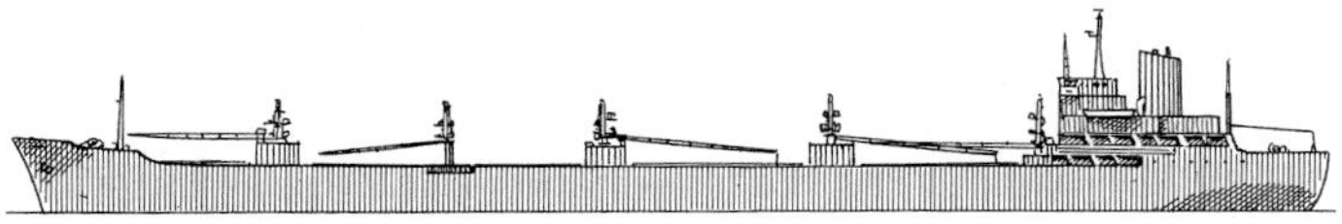

89 $\underline{MC^5M^2FM}$ *H13*
ELENA A Cy/Ja (Maizuru) 1970; B; 16,127 grt/27,110 dwt; 175.52 × 10.91 m *(575.85 × 35.79 ft)*; M (B&W); 14.5 kts; ex-*Hiratsuka Maru*
Possible sister: **ALTAIR** (Cy) ex-*Tochigi Maru*

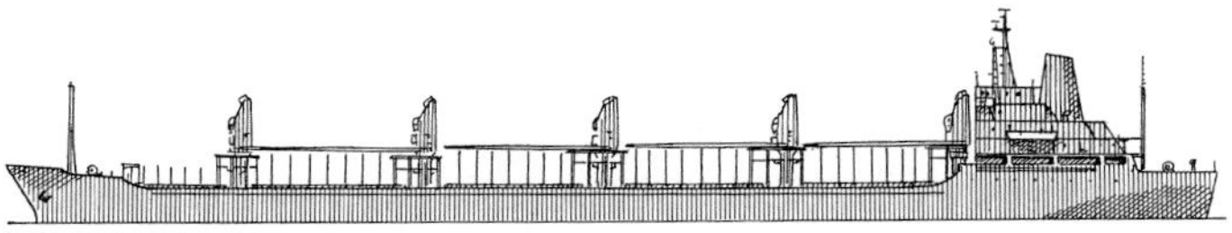

90 $\underline{MC^5M^2FM}$ *H13*
INCE-B Tu/Ja (Hayashikane) 1977; B; 15,990 grt/27,832 dwt; 176.89 × 10.34 m *(580.34 × 33.92 ft)*; M (B&W); 15 kts; ex-*Eastern Bride*

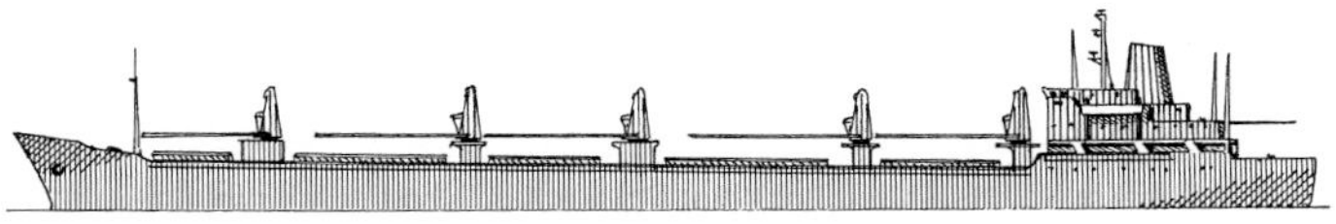

91 $\underline{MC^5M^2FM^2}$ *H13*
AHMET UZUNDEMIR Tu/Ja (Namura) 1978; B; 16,234 grt/26,867 dwt; 177.04 × 10.41 m *(580.84 × 34.16 ft)*; M (Sulzer); 15.5 kts; ex-*Toxon*

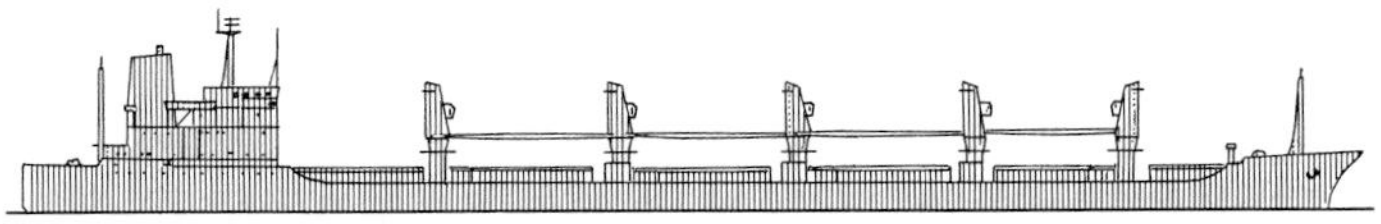

92 MC^5M^2FN *H13*
FEDERAL NORD NIS/Ja (Hakodate) 1981; B; 16,890 grt/29,002 dwt; 179.81 × 10.65 m *(589.93 × 34.94 ft)*; M (Sulzer); 16.50 kts; ex-*Violetta*
Similar (small differences—Focsle plating, superstructure and so on): **PONTOKRATIS** (Cy); **FEDERAL BERGEN** (NIS) ex-*High Peak*; Probably similar: **CAPETAN MICHALIS** (Gr) ex-*Vasiliki*; **IKAN SELAYANG** (Sg) ex-*Yannis C*; **ASIA TRADER** (Pa) ex-*High Light*

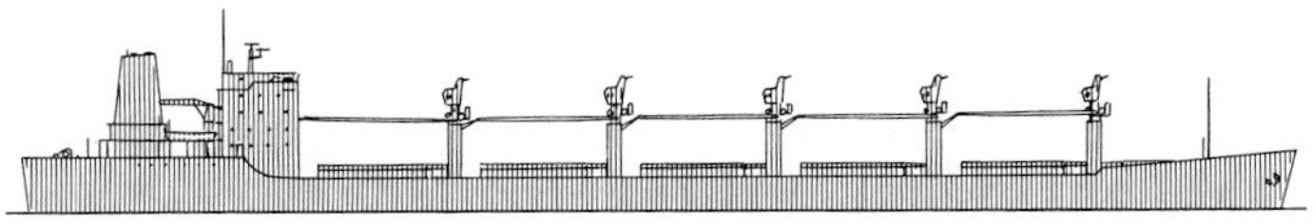

93 MC^5M^2RF *H13*
BROOMPARK Br/Br (Sunderland) 1982; B; 17,842 grt/30,670 dwt; 188.17 × 10.66 m *(617.36 × 34.97 ft)*; M (Sulzer); 15 kts

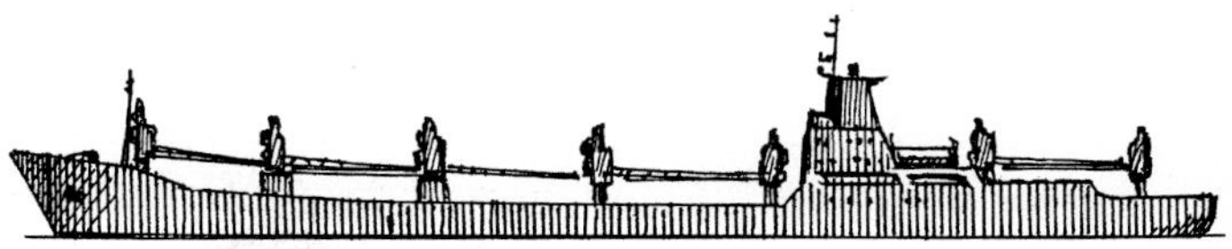

94 $MC^5M\text{-}FC^2$ *H13*
AHORA NA/Fi (Rauma-Repola) 1963; C; 5,014 grt/6,838 dwt; 130.7 × 7.3 m *(430 × 24.1 ft)*; M (Sulzer); 16 kts; ex-*Argo*; Lengthened 1970

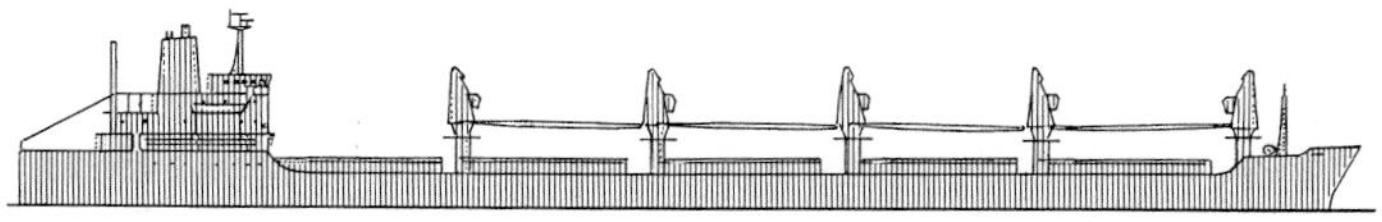

95 MC^5NFN *H13*
ENGIN KAPTANOGLU Tu/Ja (Mitsui) 1981; B; 23,077 grt/40,750 dwt; 182.08 × 11.16 m *(597.38 × 36.61 ft)*; M (B&W); 16.75 kts; ex-*Zannis*
Possible sister: **JAG RASHMI** (In) ex-*Hunan*

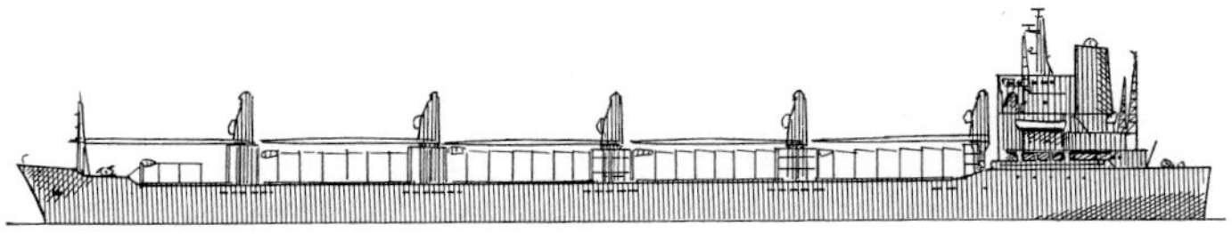

96 MC^5NMFM^2 *H13*
NIKAIA Ma/Ja (Sanoyasu) 1977; B; 16,317 grt/27,606 dwt; 169.58 × 10.3 m *(556.36 × 33.99 ft)*; M (Sulzer); 14.75 kts; ex-*Kako Maru*

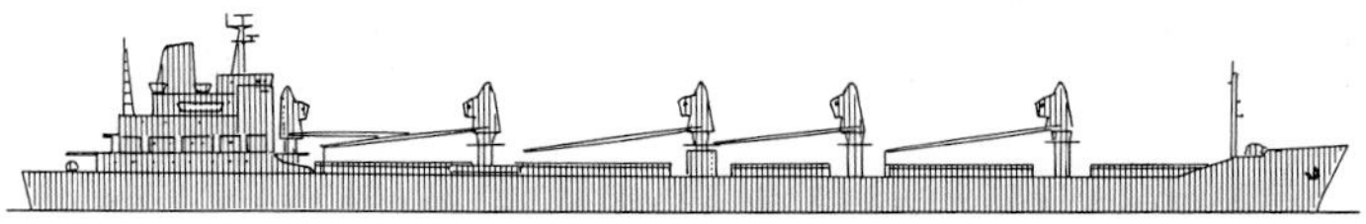

97 MC^5NMFN *H12*
IRA Li/Ja (Hitachi) 1979; B; 16,466 grt/26,697 dwt; 180.19 × 9.87 m *(591.17 × 32.38 ft)*; M (B&W); 17.75 kts
Sister: **IVI** (Li)

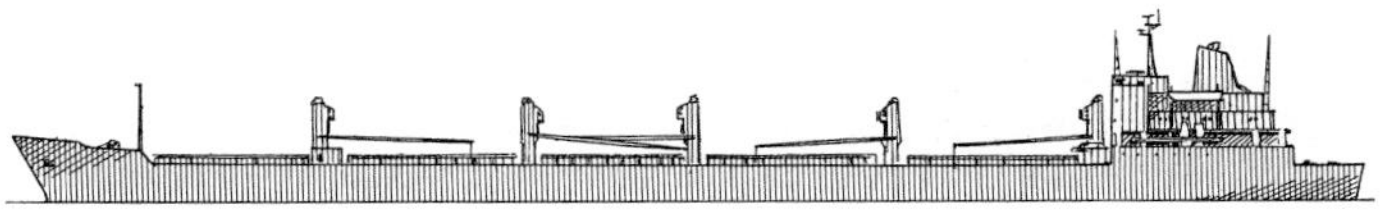

98 MC^5NMFN *H12*
NEDROMA Ag/Ja (Hitachi) 1978; B; 15,909 grt/26,593 dwt; 172.27 × 10.25 m *(565.19 × 33.63 ft)*; M (B&W); 16.25 kts
Sister: **NEMEMCHA** (Ag)

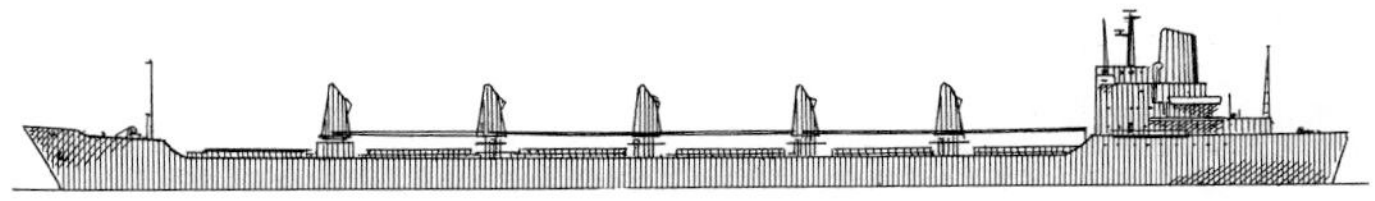

99 MC^5NMFN *H13*
CHEROKEE BELLE Pa/Ja (NKK) 1973; B; 15,819 grt/27,571 dwt; 174.1 × 10.97 m *(571.19 × 35.99 ft)*; M (Sulzer); 15.5 kts; ex-*Wayfarer*
Sisters: **OCEAN SPIRIT** (Pa) ex-*Wanderer*; **OURIOS** (Cy) ex-*Warrior*; Similar: **SALVADOR 1** (Pa) ex-*Roseline*

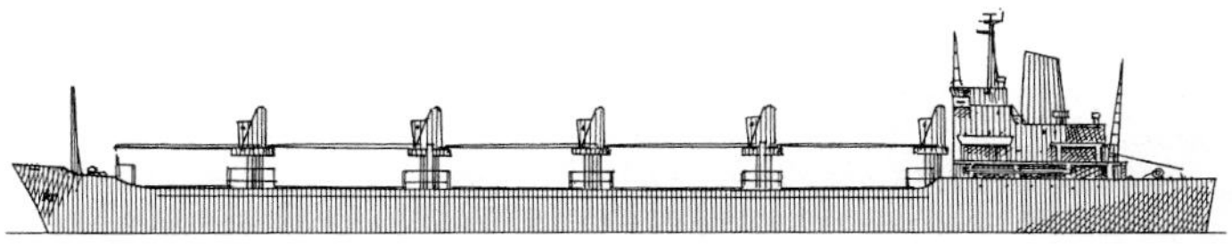

100 MC^5NMFN *H13*
FERNANDO PESSOA Po/Ja (Usuki) 1976; B; 17,085 grt/26,463 dwt; 172.5 × 10.35 m *(565.94 × 33.95 ft)*; M (Sulzer); 13 kts; ex-*Michel Delmas*

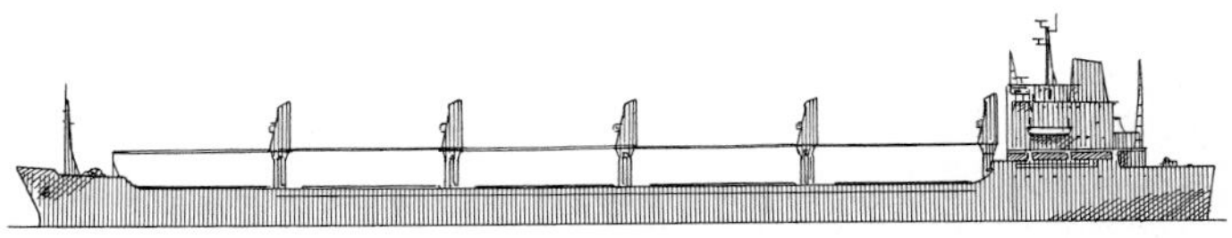

101 MC^5NMFN *H13*
ISMINI Cy/Ja (Sanoyasu) 1975; B; 22,030 grt/25,974 dwt; 184 × 11.06 m *(603.67 × 36.28 ft)*; M (B&W); 15 kts; ex-*Fort Nelson*
Sisters: **GALEA** (Ma) ex-*Fort Calgary*; **LEO** (Li) ex-*Leda*

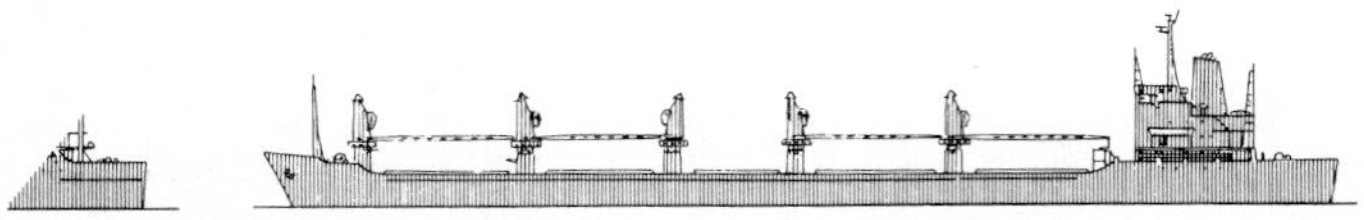

102 *MC^{5}NMFN H13*
KAPITAN PENKOV Li/Ja (Minami) 1981; B; 18,605 grt/33,041 dwt; 183.50 × 10.76 m *(602.03 × 35.30 ft)*; M (Sulzer); 17 kts; ex-*Carrianna Rose*
Sister: **PODOLSK** (Li) ex-*Carrianna Orchid*; Possible sisters: **DARYA SHUBH** (Li) ex-*Celtic Princess*; **DONA V** (Li) ex-*Menina Christina*; **VAN WARRIOR** (Li); **CALYPSO N** (Cy) ex-*Celtic Venture*; **SETIF II** (Ag) ex-*Kildonan Venture*

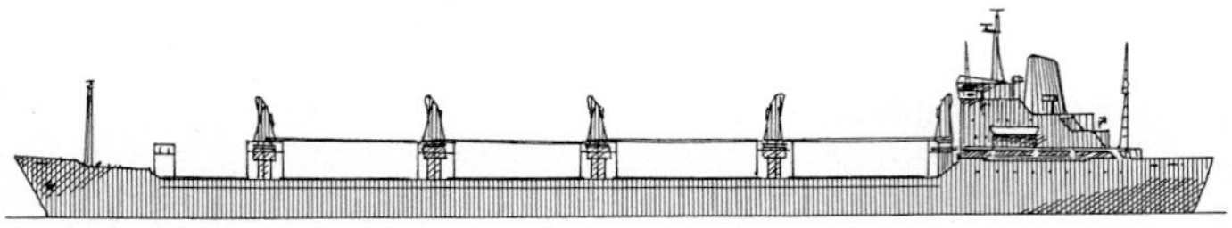

103 *MC^{5}NMFN H13*
LASSIA Cy/Ja (Hayashikane) 1975; B; 15,833 grt/28,042 dwt; 176.94 × 10.31 m *(580.51 × 33.82 ft)*; M (Sulzer); 14.75 kts; ex-*Jade City*
Sisters: **NOMADIC LADY** (NIS), launched as *Pearl City*; **KARINA** (Li) ex-*Opal City*; **ADAMASTOS** (Cy) ex-*Emerald City*; Probable sister; **PACIFIC CHUNGSAM** (Tw) ex-*Euroasia Concorde*

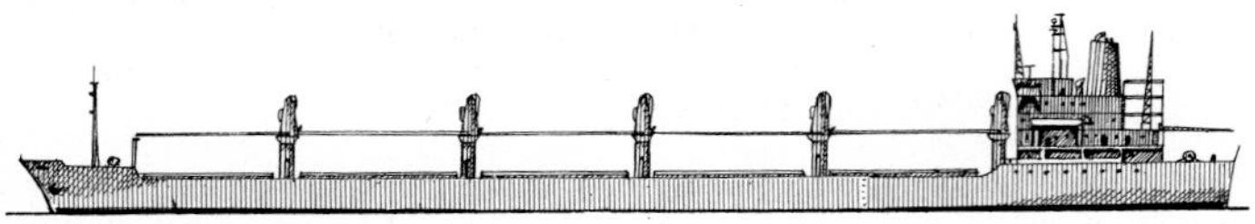

104 *MC^{5}NMFN H13*
MASTER PANOS Cy/Ja (Sanoyasu) 1977; B; 16,255 grt/28,317 dwt; 172.85 × 10.40 m *(567.09 × 34.12 ft)*; M (B&W); 15.75 kts; ex-*Fort Yale*
Sisters: **HULDRA** (Li) ex-*Fort Kamloops*; **IONIS** (Gr) ex-*Fort Victoria*

105 *MC^{5}NMFN H13*
PAHOM MAKARENKO Uk/Ja (Mitsui) 1977; B; 18,707 grt/34,811 dwt; 179.00 × 10.95 m *(587.27 × 35.93 ft)*; M (B&W); 15 kts; ex-*Kamahi*
Probable sisters: **GOOD FRIDAY** (Bs) ex-*Nan Feng*; **XING SU HAI** (RC) ex-*Keyaki*

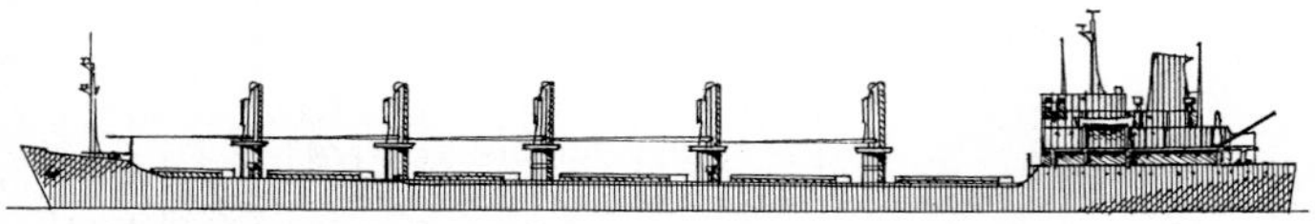

106 *MC^{5}NMFNC H13*
NOMADIC PRINCESS NIS/Ja (Kasado) 1978; B; 15,856 grt/26,991 dwt; 172.02 × 10.63 m *(564.37 × 34.88 ft)*; M (Sulzer); 17 kts; ex-*Dona Sophia*
Similar: **NAND SRISHTI** (In) ex-*Georgis Gerontas*

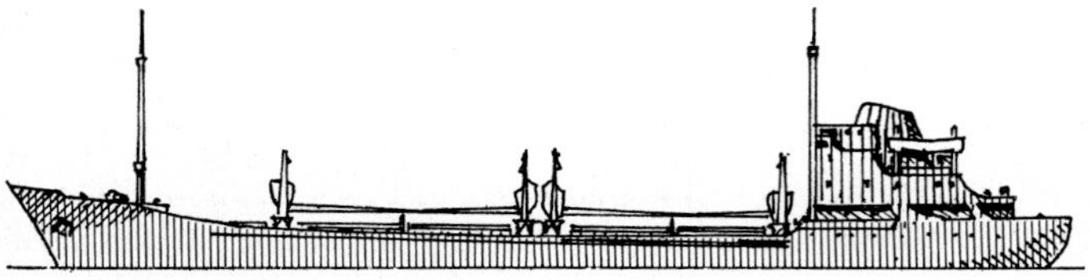

107 *MC^{4}HF H1*
AVENTURE Ho/Fi (Crichton-Vulcan) 1960; C; 2,569 grt/3,597 dwt; 101.12 × 6.13 m *(331.76 × 20.11 ft)*; M (Sulzer); 13 kts; ex-*Arcturus*; Lengthened 1968
Sister: **EASTERN GLORY** (My) ex-*Hektos*

108 *MC^{4}HF H1*
WESTWOOD FUJI Sg/Sw (Oresunds) 1982; B/Con; 26,964 grt/41,800 dwt; 186.54 × 11.90 m *(612 × 39.04 ft)*; M (B&W); 16 kts; Launched as *Waardrecht*; 1,502 TEU
Sisters: **WESTWOOD HALLA** (Sg) ex-*Wieldrecht*; **NEDLLOYD ABIDJAN** (Sg) ex-*Woensdrecht*

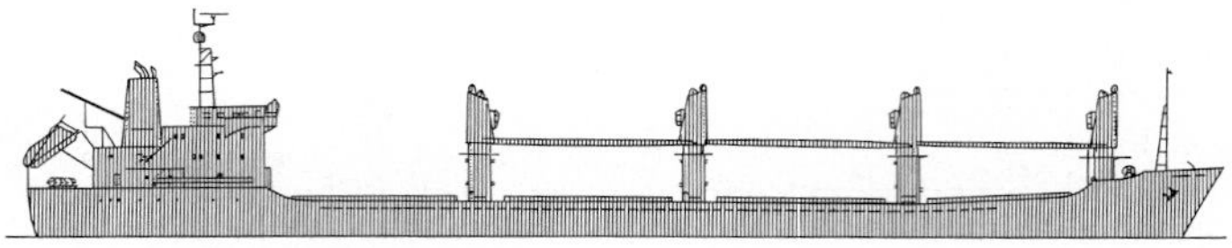

109 *MC^{4}HFL H13*
ERNA OLDENDORFF Li/Ja (Shikoku) 1994; B; 11,267 grt/18,355 dwt; 148.30 × 9.17 m *(486.55 × 30.09 ft)*; M (B&W); 14 kts
Sister: **ANNA OLDENDORFF** (Li)

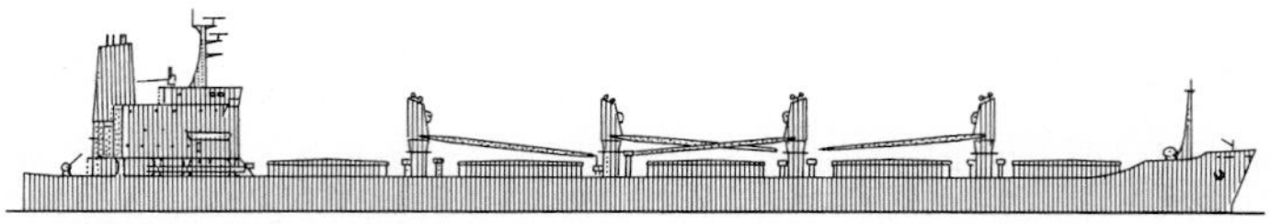

110 *MC^{4}MCF H1*
SHOU GUANG HAI RC/Ja (Namura) 1985; B; 27,766 grt/45,149 dwt; 189.00 × 11.24 m *(620.08 × 36.88 ft)*; M (B&W); 14.50 kts
Sisters: **SHOU CHANG HAI** (RC); **SHOU NING HAI** (RC)

111 *MC^{4}MF H*
ANGEL WING Pa/Ja (Hakodate) 1994; B; 25,457 grt/44,950 dwt; 184.53 × 11.32 m *(605.41 × 37.14 ft)*; M (B&W); 14.30 kts

112 *MC^{4}MF H*
IKAN BILIS Sg/De (B&W) 1982; B/Con; 35,455 grt/63,800 dwt; 225.03 × 13.08 m *(738 × 42.91 ft)*; M (B&W); 15 kts; ex-*Rangelock*
Sister: **SOUILLAC** (Ms) ex-*Sealock*; Probable sister (may have three cranes only): **MARE VIKINGO** (It) ex-*Annalock*

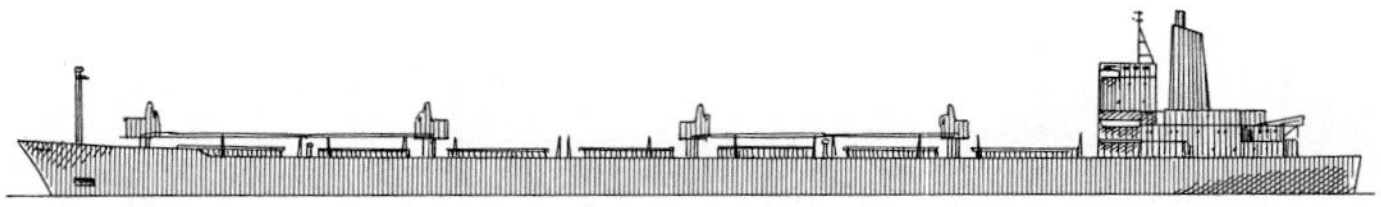

113 *MC^{4}MF H*
MI YUN HAI RC/Ih (Verolme Cork) 1968; B; 19,672 grt/38,378 dwt; 192.67 × 11.38 m *(632.12 × 37.33 ft)*; M (MAN); 15.5 kts; ex-*Irish Elm*

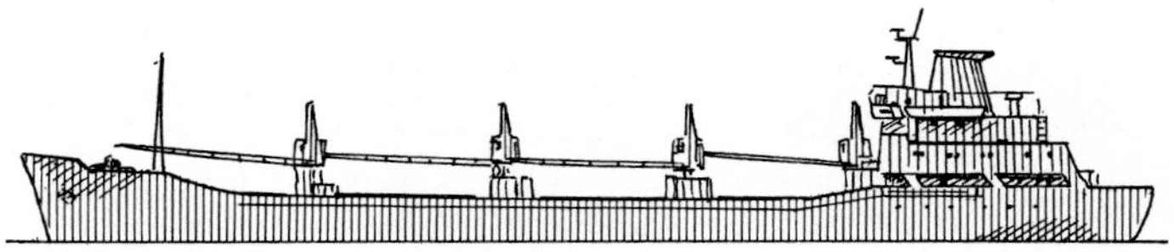

114 *MC^{4}MF H1*
AYYOUB Sy/Fi (Wärtsilä) 1966; C; 4,073 grt/5,709 dwt; 102.11 × 7.58 m *(335 × 24.86 ft)*; M (Sulzer); 15 kts; ex-*Nils Gorthon*
Sisters: **KADDOUR I** (Sy) ex-*Margit Gorthon*; **ALMAHDY** (Ho) ex-*Gregerso*

115 *MC^{4}MF H1*
CARLO M Li/Ja (IHI) 1977; B; 22,263 grt/37,657 dwt; 187.74 × 10.76 m *(615.94 × 35.3 ft)*; M (Sulzer); 15.5 kts; 'Future 32' type
Sister: **LLAIMA** (Ch) ex-*Costanza M*; Similar: **MARIA TOPIC** (Li)

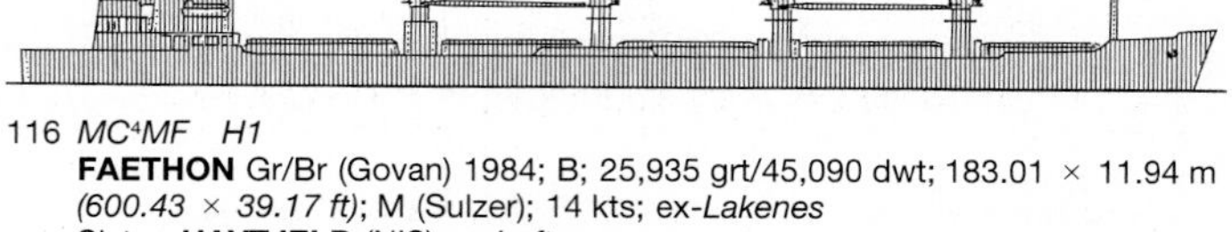

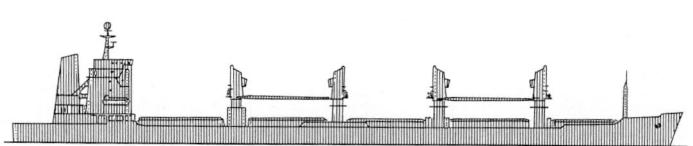

116 *MC^{4}MF H1*
FAETHON Gr/Br (Govan) 1984; B; 25,935 grt/45,090 dwt; 183.01 × 11.94 m *(600.43 × 39.17 ft)*; M (Sulzer); 14 kts; ex-*Lakenes*
Sister: **HAVTJELD** (NIS) ex-*Loftnes*

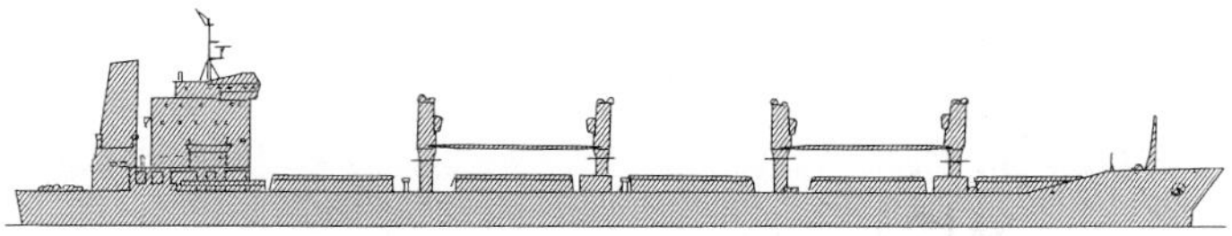

117 MC^{4}MF H1

IRAN ESHRAGI Ir/Ko (Daewoo) 1985; B; 25,768 grt/43,369 dwt; 190.00 × 11.62 m *(623.36 × 38.12 ft)*; M (B&W); — kts
Probable sisters: **IRAN ABOZAR** (Ir); **IRAN ASHRAFI** (Ir); **IRAN CHAMRAN** (Ir); **IRAN DASTGHAYB** (Ir); **IRAN EGHBAL** (Ir); **IRAN GHAFARI** (Ir); **IRAN GHAZI** (Ir); **IRAN GHODOUSI** (Ir); **IRAN HAMZEH** (Ir); **IRAN JAMAL** (Ir); **IRAN KASHANI** (Ir); **IRAN MADANI** (Ir); **IRAN MUFATEH** (Ir); **IRAN NAVAB** (Ir); **IRAN SADOUGHI** (Ir); **IRAN SADR** (Ir); **IRAN SAEIDI** (Ir); **IRAN SHARIATI** (Ir); **IRAN TALEGHANI** (Ir)

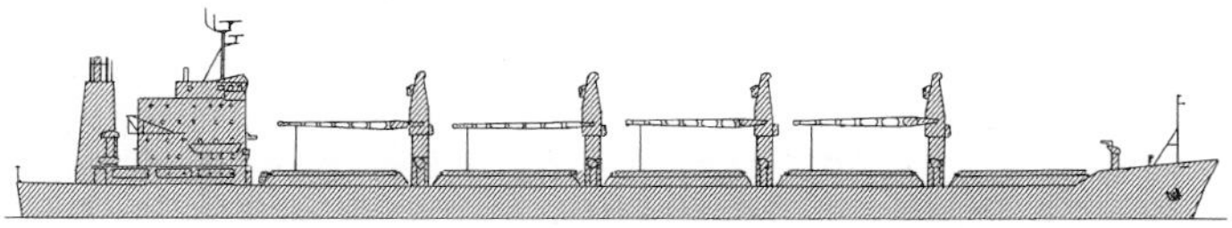

118 MC^{4}MF H1

KONTULA Fi/Fi (Wärtsilä) 1980; B/IB; 19,854 grt/31,850 dwt; 179.46 × 11.05 m *(588.78 × 36.25 ft)*; M (Sulzer); 15 kts

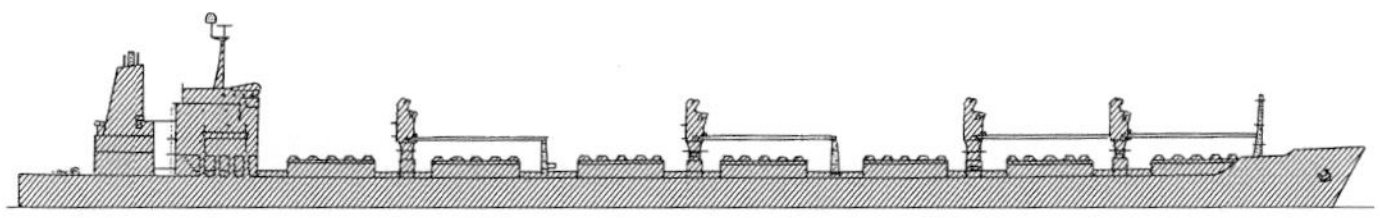

119 MC^{4}MF H1

LIBERTY WAVE US/Ko (Hyundai) 1984; B; 33,784 grt/63,463 dwt; 225.00 × 13.12 m *(738.19 × 43.04 ft)*; M (B&W); 15 kts; ex-*Archon*; 400 TEU
Sisters: **LIBERTY SPIRIT** (US) ex-*Altair*; **LIBERTY STAR** (US) ex-*Arion*; **LIBERTY SUN** (US) ex-*Aspen*; **LIBERTY SEA** (US) ex-*Aurora* (may be gearless)

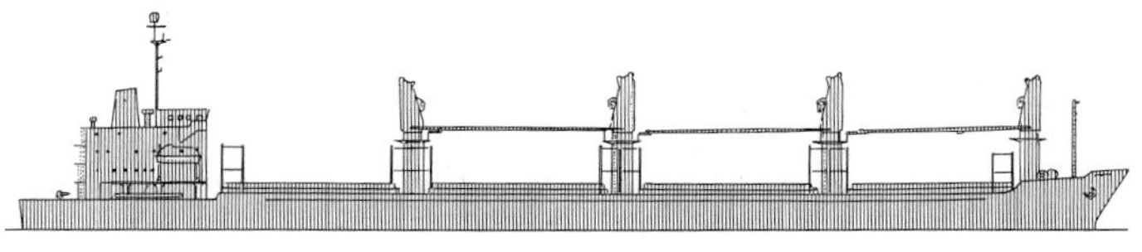

120 MC^{4}MF H1

LUCY OLDENDORFF Li/Ja (Saiki) 1992; B; 13,696 grt/22,160 dwt; 157.00 × 9.12 m *(515.09 × 29.92 ft)*; M (Mitsubishi); 14 kts
Probable sisters (some parts built by Onomichi); **DORTHE OLDENDORFF** (Li); **ELISABETH OLDENDORFF** (Li); **GRETKE OLDENDORFF** (Li); **CAROLINE OLDENDORFF** (Li); **DOROTHEA OLDENDORFF** (Li); Possible sisters: **KEN EI** (Pa); **RUBIN IRIS** (Pa); **BLUE OCEAN** (Pa); **LONG BEACH** (Pa); **EDELWEISS** (HK); **ORIENTE GRACE** (Pa); **OCEAN SERENE** (Pa)

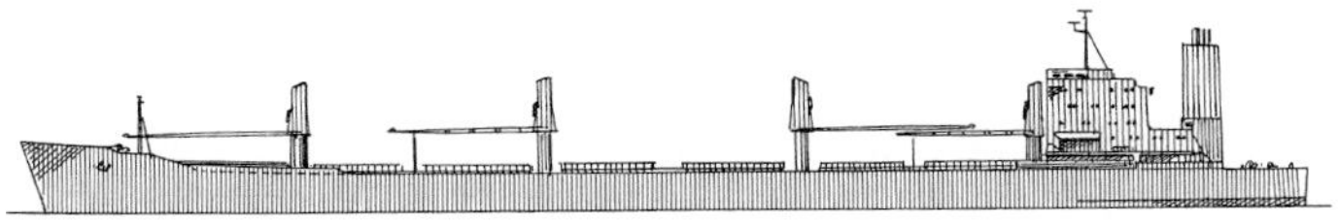

121 MC^{4}MF H1

MELGAR Sg/Sw (Gotav) 1978; B/Con; 26,718 grt/44,600 dwt; 191.4 × 11.33 m *(627.95 × 37.17 ft)*; M (B&W); 15 kts; ex-*Meerdrecht*; 'Columbus 44' type. 1,402 TEU
Sisters: **MAINIT** (Sg) ex-*Mijdrecht*; **CARGO ENTERPRISE** (Gr) ex-*Arlberg*; **DEVOTION** (Pa); **FRUITION** (Ml); **UNISON** (Pa); **GRAZ** (Sg) ex-*Moordrecht*

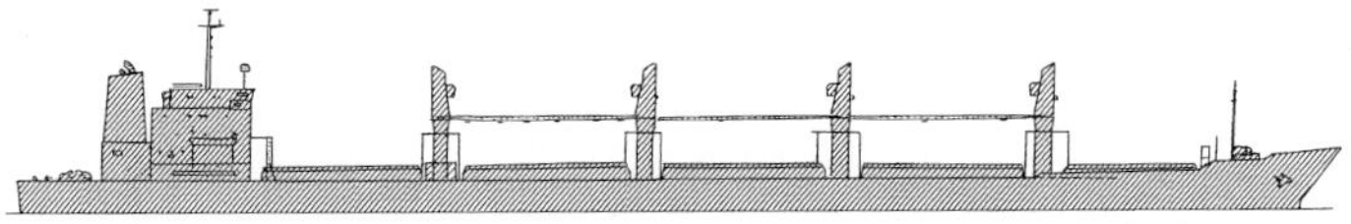

122 MC^{4}MF H1

NEO PELARGONIUM Li/Ja (Osaka) 1984; B; 23,279 grt/40,501 dwt; 184.82 × 11.02 m *(606.36 × 36.15 ft)*; M (Sulzer); 14 kts; ex-*Sanko Pelargonium*
Probable sisters: **SEA PHOENIX** (Li) ex-*Sanko Platanus*; **MANILA PROGRESS** (Pi) ex-*Sanko Poinsettia*

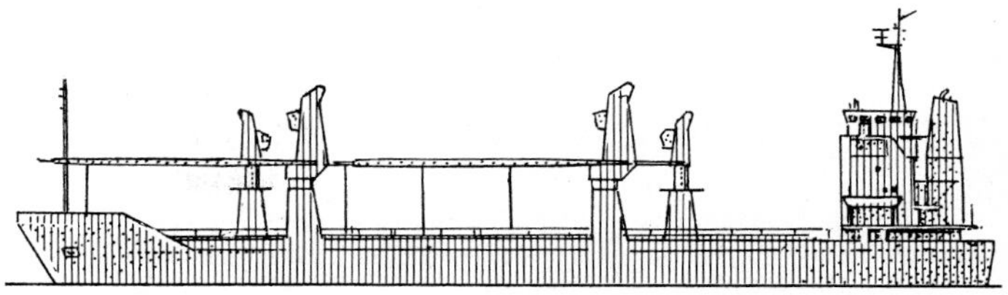

123 MC^{4}MF H1

SALIF BAY At/FRG (Sietas) 1979; C/Con; 4,351 grt/6,142 dwt; 100.13 × 6.94 m *(328.51 × 22.77 ft)*; M (Atlas-MaK); 15 kts; ex-*Conti Britania*; Smaller cranes are on starboard side and larger ones on port; 324 TEU

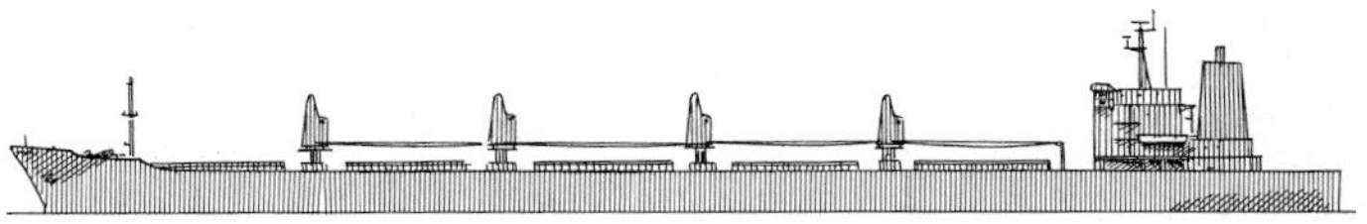

124 MC^{4}MF H1

THEOTOKO Gr/Ja (IHI) 1983; B; 22,076 grt/37,612 dwt; 187.74 × 9.75 m *(615.94 × 31.99 ft)*; M (Sulzer); 15 kts; 'Future 32' type
Sister: **PLATITERA** (Gr) ex-*Boucraa*; Similar (some may have five cranes): **ROSINA TOPIC** (Li); **AGIA EIRINI** (Cy) ex-*Sovereign Venture*; **PAN EXPRESS** (Ko) ex-*Primula*; **PAN QUEEN** (Ko) ex-*Primavera*; **ANDROS OCEANIA** (Gr); **CHC No. 2** (Pa) ex-*Fairness*; **IKAN SELANGAT** (Sg) ex-*Magic Sky*; **JAG RAHUL** (In) ex-*Fortunee*; **NEPTUNE SCHEDAR** (Sg); **AL QAWYYU** (Pa) ex-*Neptune Seginus*; **DONG FANG HAI** (RC) ex-*Neptune Sheratan*; **LEADER** (Pa); **SERAFIN TOPIC** (Li); Possibly similar (may be gearless); **CRUSADER** (Pa); **LEIRA** (Bs) ex-*Hellespont Vanguard*

125 MC^{4}MF H1

VERNER Pa/Ja (Kanasashi) 1984; B; 22,009 grt/37,660 dwt; 188.02 × 10.86 m *(616.86 × 35.63 ft)*; M (Sulzer); 14 kts; ex-*Sanko Cedar*
Sisters: **SPRINGWOOD** (Pa) ex-*Sanko Hawk*; **AYIA MARKELLA** (Gr) ex-*Sanko Cypress*; Possible sisters: **PRABHU JIVESH** (In) ex-*Sanko Eagle*; **SANKO MOON** (Pa); **SANKO SOUTH** (Pa); **HANEI STAR** (Pa) ex-*Sanko Star*; **CANELA** (Bs) ex-*Sanko Chestnut*; **HANEI PEARL** (Pa) ex-*Sanko Pearl*; **CEDRELA** (Bs) ex-*Sanko Poplar*; **PEARL SEA** (Pa) ex-*Sanko Diamond*; **CHC No 1** (Pa) ex-*Sanko Lily*; **RELIANCE TRADER** (Li) ex-Sanko Reliance; **GOLDEN VENTURE**; (Pa) ex-*Sanko Lilac*; **SEAL CORAL** (Li) ex-*Sanko Ruby*; Probably similar: **STAR NITSA** (Cy) ex-*Asian Beauty*; **GOKCAN** (Tu) ex-*Asian Brilliance*

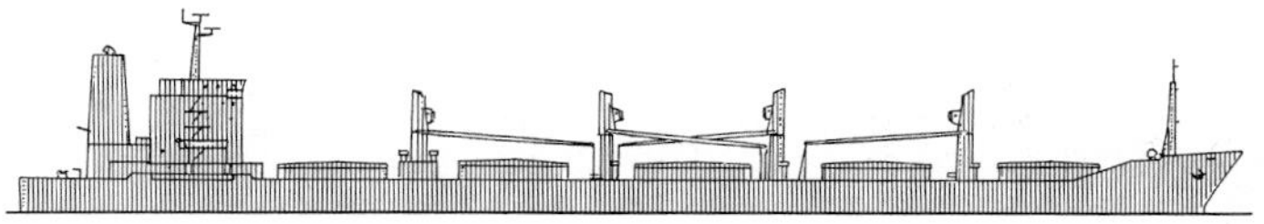

126 MC^{4}MF H1

YI HAI RC/Ja (Osaka) 1984; B; 26,959 grt/46,482 dwt; 189.68 × 11.44 m *(622.31 × 37.53 ft)*; M(B&W); 14.50 kts
Similar (RC built—Hudong): **TAI AN HAI** (RC); **TAI GU HAI** (RC); **TAI KANG HAI** (RC); **TAI HE HAI** (RC); **TAI PING HAI** (RC); **TAI SHAN HAI** (RC)

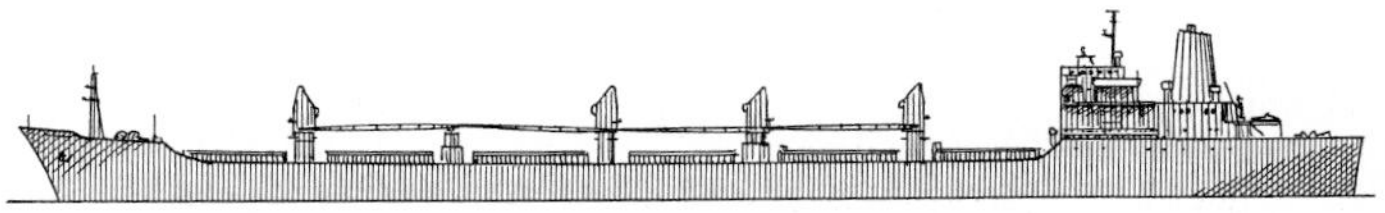

127 MC^{4}MF H13

AYANE Tu/Ja (NKK) 1977; B; 15,573 grt/28,406 dwt; 178.11 × 10.9 m *(584.35 × 35.76 ft)*; M (Sulzer); 15.5 kts; ex-*Kieldrecht*
Sister: **PYLOS** (Gr) ex-*Katendrecht*

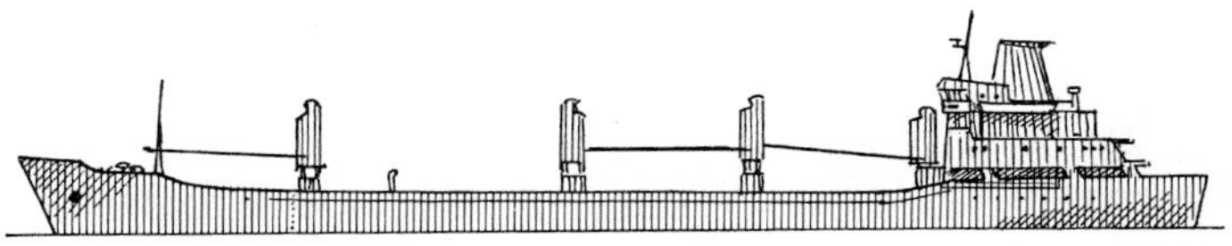

128 MC^{4}MF H13

CELIKSAN Tu/Fi (Wärtsilä) 1969; C; 4,543 grt/6,476 dwt; 116.01 × 7.41 m *(380.61 × 24.31 ft)*; M (Sulzer); 15 kts; ex-*Germundo*

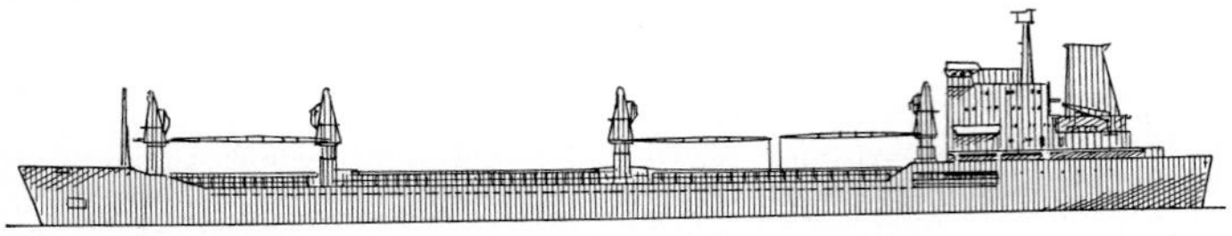

129 MC^4MF *H13*
CLIPPER FAME Pa/Sp (Juliana) 1977; B; 12,409 grt/14,829 dwt; 159.21 × 9.15 m *(522.34 × 30.02 ft)*; M (Sulzer); 16 kts; ex-*Lotila*
Sisters: **FINNFIGHTER** (Bs) ex-*Kaipola*; **CLIPPER FOREST** (Cy) ex-*Walki*; **BRAVADEN** (Fi) ex-*Walki Paper*; **ALOUETTE ARROW** (NIS) ex-*Finnarctis*; **VARJAKKA** (Fi); **POKKINEN** (Fi)

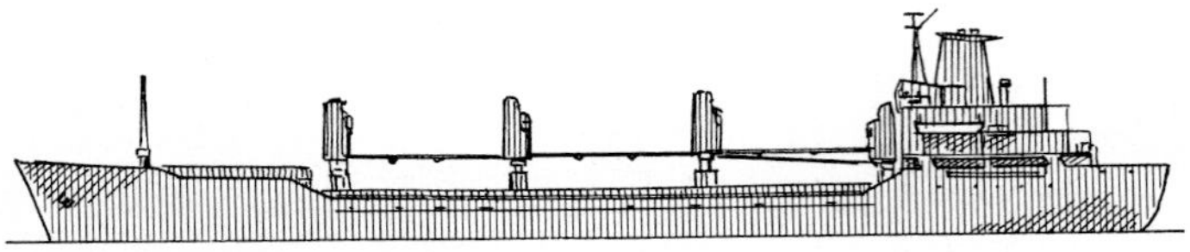

130 MC^4MF *H13*
KIMOLOS Pa/Fi (Wärtsilä) 1971; C; 5,523 grt/5,511 dwt; 118.32 × 6.41 m *(388.2 × 21.03 ft)*; M (Sulzer); 14.75 kts; ex-*Kaipola*
Sisters: **YUE LU SHAN** (RC) ex-*Valkeokoski*; **SALAMA** (Eg) ex-*Koiteli*; **BALTIC STONE** (Bs) ex-*Tuira*

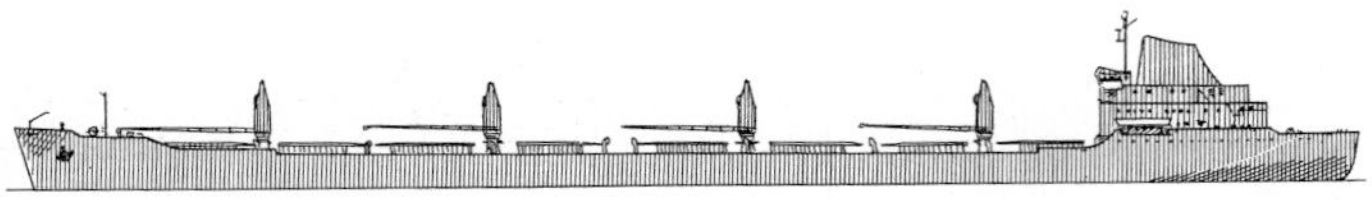

131 MC^4MF *H13*
TRADE WILL Cy/Gr (Eleusis) 1973; B; 23,785 grt/43,841 dwt; 205.01 × 11.74 m *(672.6 × 38.51 ft)*; M (Sulzer); 15.5 kts; ex-*Althea*
Sister: **AKTEA** (Cy)

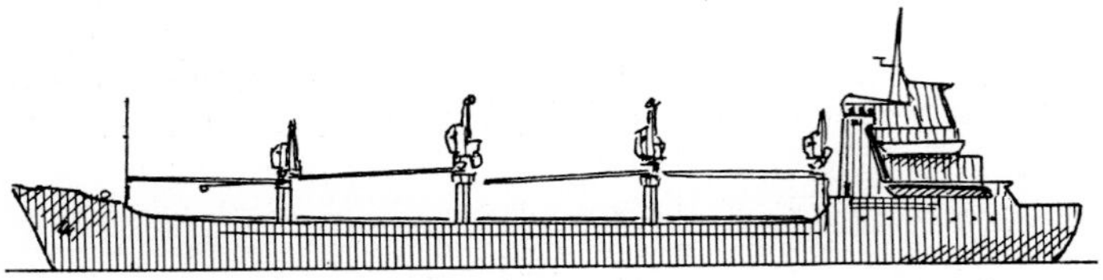

132 MC^4MF *H13*
YEMAYA Bl/Sw (Finnboda) 1967; C; 2,710 grt/4,135 dwt; 93.81 × 6.6 m *(307.77 × 21.65 ft)*; M (Atlas-MaK); 14 kts; ex-*Alca*
Sisters: **MONA S** (Sy) ex-*Doris*; **LIMANI** (Le) ex-*Hamno*

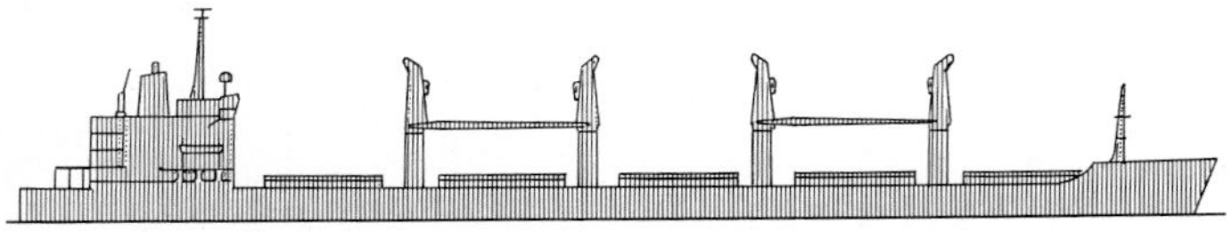

133 MC^4MFC *H1*
HALIS KALKAVAN Tu/Ko (Hyundai) 1984; B/Con; 22,629 grt/36,800 dwt; 186.70 × 11.05 m *(612.53 × 36.25 ft)*; M (Sulzer); 13 kts; ex-*Esmeralda*; 898 TEU; Drawing is approximate
Sisters: **ANGARA** (Ru) ex-*Esperanza*; Similar: **YENISEI** (Ru) ex-C A Margaronis; Probably similar: **CHENNAI NERMAI** (In); **CHENNAI POLIVU** (In); **CHENNAI VALARCHI** (In); **CHENNAI VEERAM** (In); **ESER KAPTANOGLU** (Tu) ex-*Asia No 16*; **HYUNDAI NO 17** (Pa) ex-*Asia No 17*; **ALMAR** (Gr) ex-*Hyundai No 18* (builder—Inchon); **DORY** (Gr) ex-*Hai Mong*; **KOREAN PIONEER** (Ko)

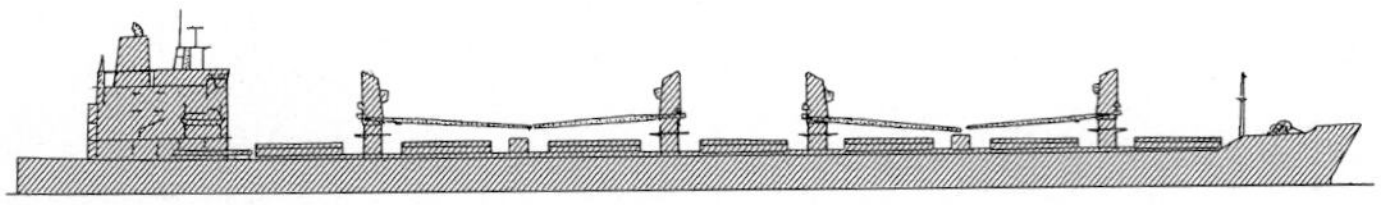

134 MC^4MFC *H1*
SALLY STOVE NIS/Ja (NKK) 1981; B; 35,586 grt/64,535 dwt; 224.52 × 12.86 m *(736.61 × 42.19 ft)*; M (Sulzer); — kts; ex-*Sagay Stove*

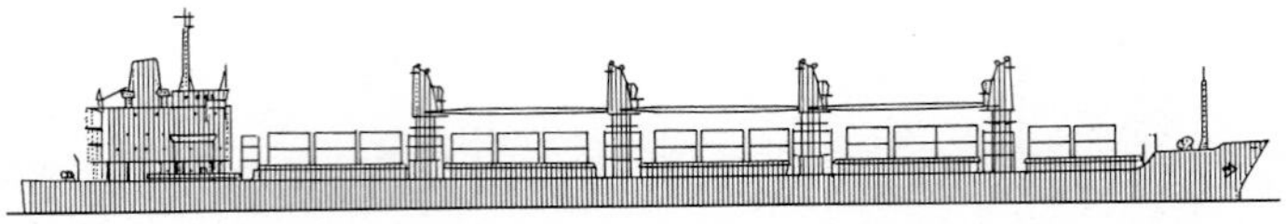

135 MC^4MFC *H1*
SANMAR PIONEER In/Ja (Sanoyas Corp) 1986; B/Con; 23,531 grt/ 40,836 dwt; 182.76 × 11.19 m *(599.61 × 36.71 ft)*; M (Sulzer); 14 kts; ex-*Amor Amor*; 824 TEU
Possible sisters: **FEDERAL PESCADORES** (Pa); ex-*Louisiana Mama* (May have five cranes); **PINE BEAUTY** (Pa) ex-*Sanko Beauty*; **BENARITA** (Pa) ex-*Sanko Elegance*

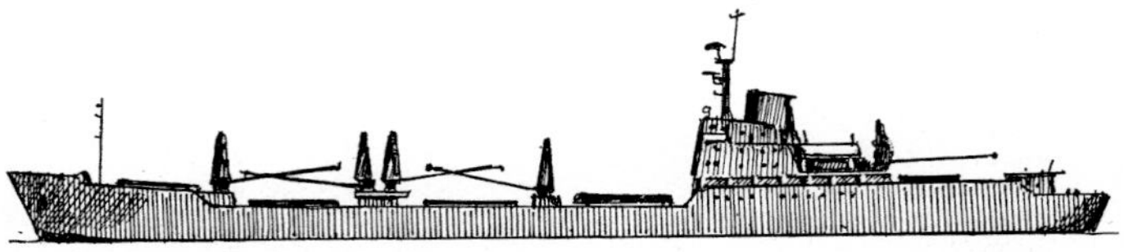

136 MC^4MFC *H12*
SVETLOGORSK Uk/USSR (Kherson) 1970; C; 8,874 grt/13,738 dwt; 152.7 × 9.3 m *(501 × 30.85 ft)*; M (B&W); 17 kts
Sisters: **AKADEMIK EVGENIY PATON** (Uk); **ILYA KULIK** (Uk); **SEREBRYANSK** (Uk); **SEVAN** (Uk); **SYZRAN** (Uk); Similar (smaller cranes arranged in pairs): **SARNY** (Uk); **SEROV** (Uk); **SEVERODONETSK** (Uk); **SLAVYANSK** (Uk); **SVANETIYA** (Uk); **VEGA** (Uk) ex-*Komsomolskaya Slava*; **SOCHI** (Uk)

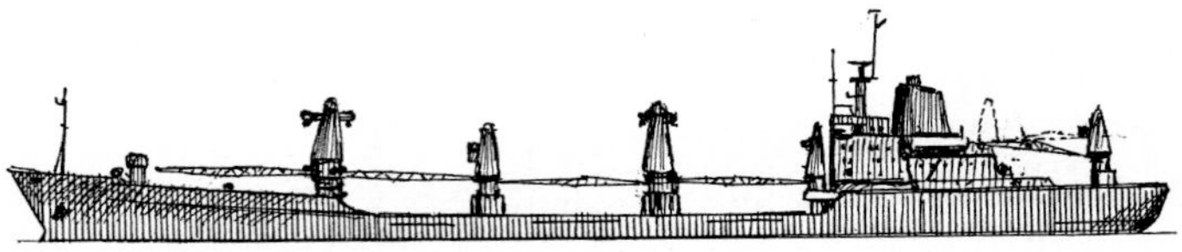

137 MC^4MFC *H13*
EQUATOR RUBY Sg/Ne ('De Schelde') 1972; C; 14,135 grt/12,147 dwt; 165 × 9.7 m *(543 × 32 ft)*; M (Sulzer); 21 kts; ex-*Straat Nagasaki*
Sisters: **SIN LOONG** (Sg) ex-*Straat Napier*; **EQUATOR STAR** (Sg) ex-*Straat Nassau*

138 MC^4MFC *H13*
TRADEWIND Gr/Ja (Oshima) 1981; B; 13.711 grt/27,471 dwt; 169.81 × 9.8 m *(557.12 × 32.15 ft)*; M (Sulzer); 17.5 kts
Probable sister: **EASTWIND** (Gr)

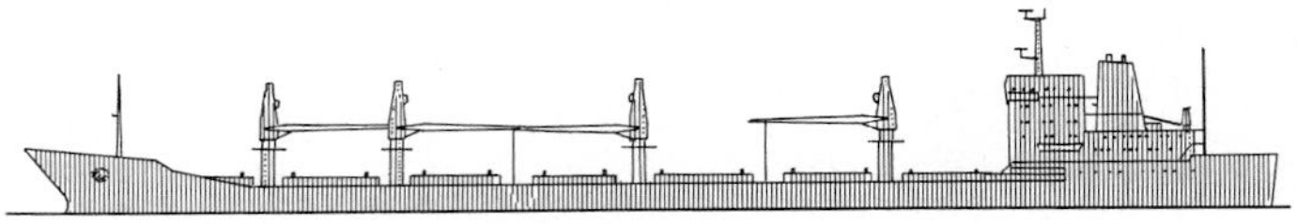

139 MC^4MFCM *H13*
CAPE CORNWALL Li/Bu (G Dimitrov) 1984; B; 23,609 grt/38,377 dwt; 198.61 × 11.20 m *(651.61 × 36.75 ft)*; M (Sulzer); — kts; ex-*Jonathan J*; After crane is on starboard side
Sister: **YORKGATE** (Li); Probable sisters: **TRIBUNO** (Li); **YORDAN LUTIBRODSKI** (SV) (may be gearless—see entry 5/105); **ARETE** (Gr) ex-*Garth*

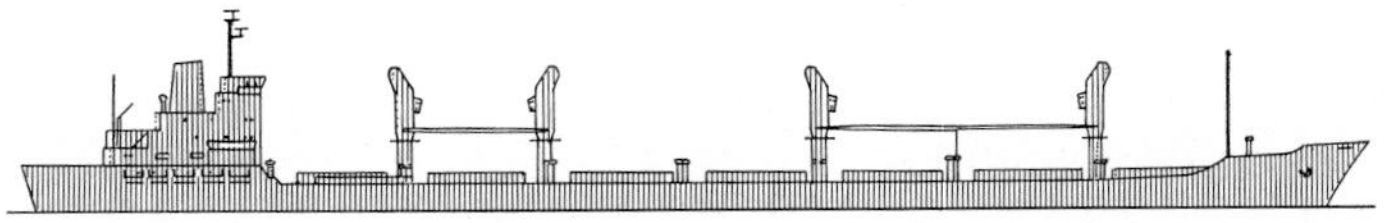

140 MC^4MFCN *H13*
BAR Ma/Sp (AESA) 1986; B; 17,460 grt/30,070 dwt; 189.41 × 10.65 m *(621.42 × 34.94 ft)*; M (B&W); 15.50 kts
Sister: **UTVIKEN** (Bs) ex-*Bijelo Polje*

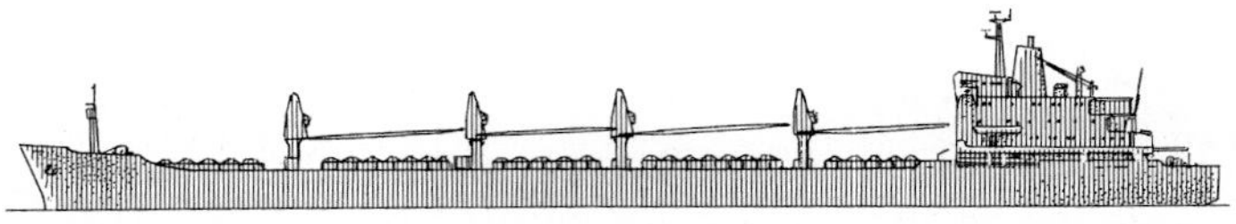

141 MC^4MFCR *H1*
JIAN HUA LING RC/Ja (Sumitomo) 1976; B; 17,710 grt/29,168 dwt; 169.89 × 10.26 m *(557.68 × 33.66 ft)*; M (Sulzer); 15 kts; ex-*Mosriver*
Sister: **SILVER YU** (SV) ex-*Moslake*

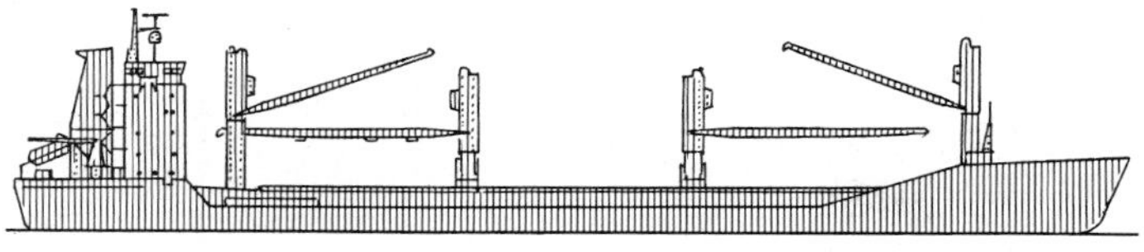

142 *MC^{4}MFL H13*
NORDLAND Ge/FRG (M Jansen) 1986; C/Con; 7,562 grt/9,050 dwt; 127.01 × 8.08 m *(416.70 × 26.51 ft)*; M (MaK); 16 kts; 560 TEU

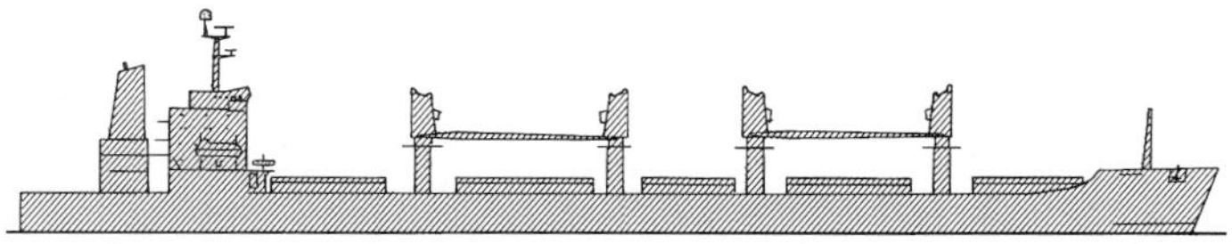

143 *MC^{4}MFM H1*
JORITA NIS/Ko (Daewoo) 1985; B; 23,981 grt/36,726 dwt; 179.03 × 10.60 m *(587.37 × 34.78 ft)*; M (B&W); 14.5 kts
Sisters: **GEORGIY BERNACHUK** (Li) ex-*Anita*; **KAPITAN BETKHER** (Cy) ex-*Tinita*; **OB** (Ru) ex-*Rosita*

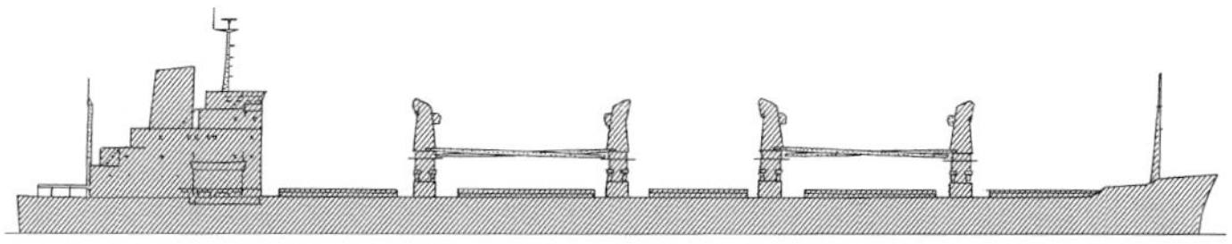

144 *MC^{4}MFM H1*
KOREAN PIGEON Ko/Ko (Korea SB) 1979; B; 16,898 grt/26,811 dwt; 170.01 × 9.63 m *(557.78 × 31.59 ft)*; M (Sulzer); 16.50 kts
Sister: **KOREAN PEACE** (Ko)

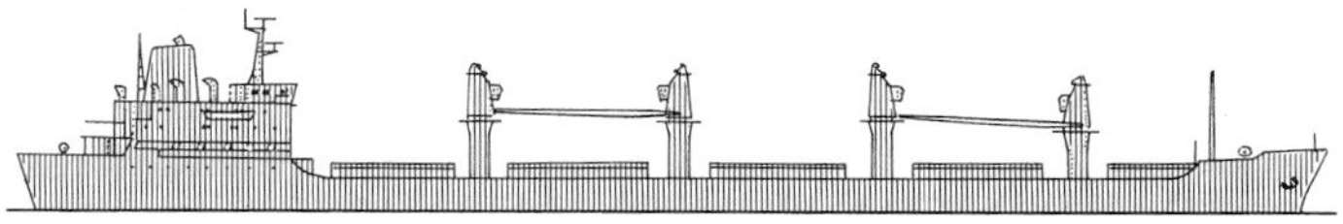

145 *MC^{4}MFM H13*
ALAM UNITED My/Ja (Hitachi) 1984; B; 17,065 grt/27,223 dwt; 178.21 × 10.59 m *(584.68 × 34.74 ft)*; M (Sulzer); 14.50 kts; ex-*Silver Leader*
Sisters (some differ slightly): **ANTALINA** (Cy) ex-*Union Pioneer*; **MARILIS T** (Cy) ex-*Union Peace*; **UNION** (HK) ex-*Socrates*; **ISLAND GEM** (Gr); **ALAM SEMPURNA** (My) ex-*Saint Laurent*; Possible sisters: **ALAM SENANG** (My) ex-*Goldean Alliance*; **FEDERAL MANITOU** (NIS) ex-*Kalliopi II*; **ALAM UNIVERSITY** (My) ex-*Rich Alliance*; **HANDY LAKER** (Pi) ex-*Cathariness*; **ISLAND SKIPPER** (Gr); **YICK HUA** (Pa) ex-*Pacific Defender*

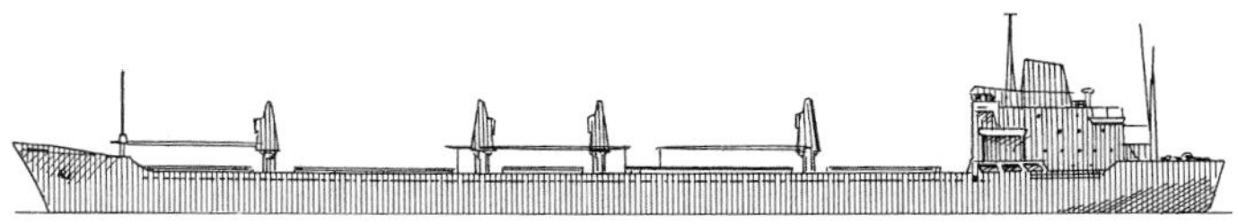

146 *MC^{4}MFM H13*
ANGELIKI R Cy/Sp (AESA) 1974; C; 12,143 grt/20,949 dwt; 159.01 × 9.77 m *(521.68 × 32.05 ft)*; M (Sulzer); — kts; ex-*Aegis Majestic*; 'SANTA FE 77' type
Sisters: **BOTIC** (Li) ex-*Aegis Athenic*; **TEMPO** (Ma) ex-*Aegis Atomic*; **HELIOS II** (Th) ex-*Aegis Baltic*; **MED AFRICA LINK** (Ma) ex-*Aegis Britannic*; **GEOHART** (Ma) ex-*Aegis Doric*; **ANASTASIA** (Pa) ex-*Aegis Dynamic*; **OCEAN GRACE** (Cy) ex-*Aegis Harmonic*; **PAULINE OLIVIERI** (Pa) ex-*Aegis Hellenic*; **MARULIC** (Li) ex-*Aegis Ionic*; **STORMY ANNIE** (Pa) ex-*Aegis Logic*; **SEA BARON** (Cy) ex-*Aegis Lyric*; **MITERA VASSILIKI** (Cy) ex-*Aegis Magic*; **ALYCIA** (Ma) ex-*Aegis Mystic*; **OCEAN LAKE** (Cy) ex-*Aegis Practic*; **AMBASSADOR I** (Cy) ex-*Aegis Sonic*; **ACTIVE** (Cy) ex-*Aegis Topic*;
Possible sister: **PRAGATI** (Cy) ex-*Lok Vikas*

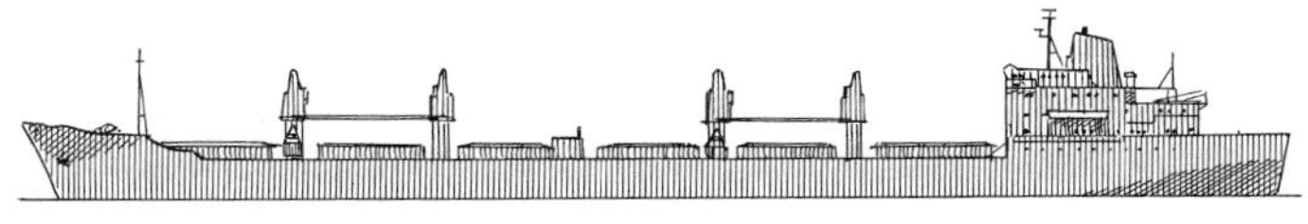

147 *MC^{4}MFM H13*
BAI YU LAN RC/No (Horten) 1971; B; 12,098 grt/21,950 dwt; 159.21 × 9.76 m *(522.34 × 32.02 ft)*; M (Sulzer); 15 kts; ex-*Baron Maclay*
Sister: **CHIOS FORTUNE** (Gr) ex-*Cape Leeuwin*

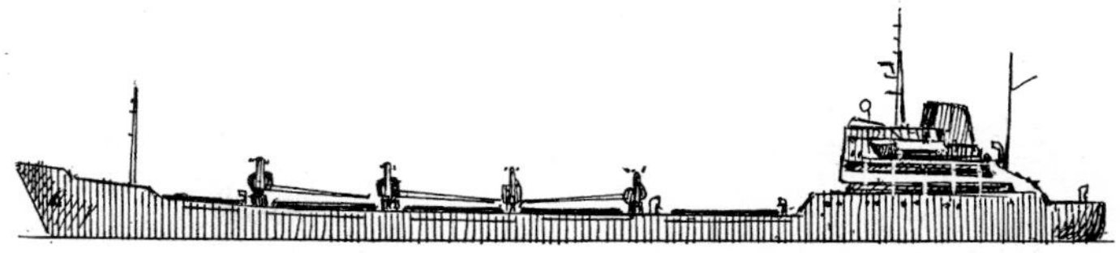

148 *MC^{4}MFM H13*
DNEPRODZERZHINSK Ru/DDR (Warnow) 1960; O; 6,753 grt/10,033 dwt; 139.5 × 8.12 m *(457.68 × 26.64 ft)*; M (MAN); 14.25 kts; Cranes may be removed
Sister (may have three cranes): **DEDOVSK** (Ru)

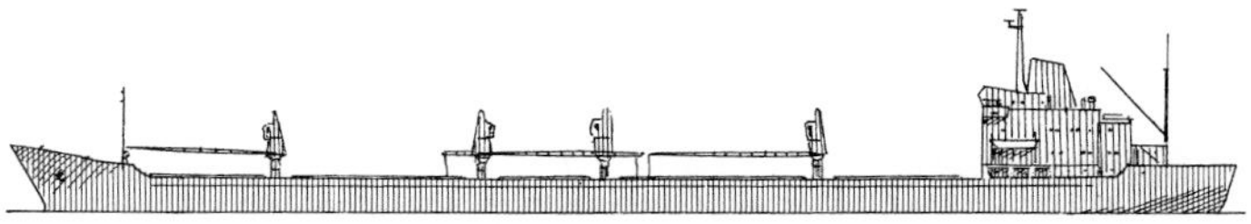

149 *MC^{4}MFM H13*
HERO II Th/Sp (U N de Levante) 1977; C; 12,771 grt/21,069 dwt; 159.01 × 9.77 m *(521.68 × 32.05 ft)*; M (Sulzer); 15.5 kts; ex-*Mishref*; 'SANTA FE 77' type
Sister: **HERAKLES** (Th) ex-*Jumairah*

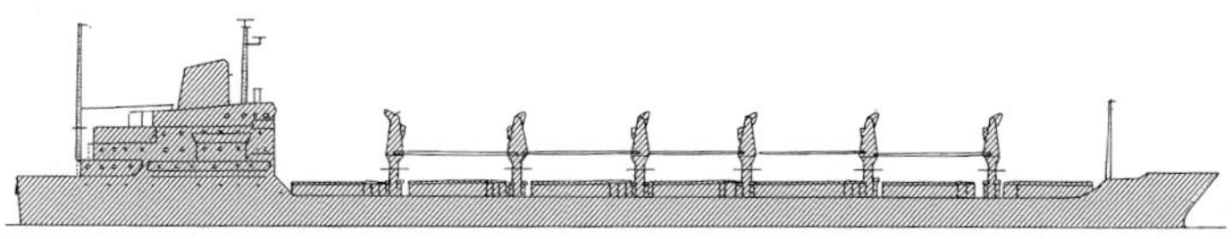

150 *MC^{4}MFM H13*
LOK PRATIMA In/In (Garden Reach) 1989; B; 15,952 grt/26,872 dwt; 172.20 × 10.90 m *(564.96 × 35.76 ft)*; M (MAN); 15 kts; 'GR 26' type
Probable sister: **LOK PRAGATI** (In)

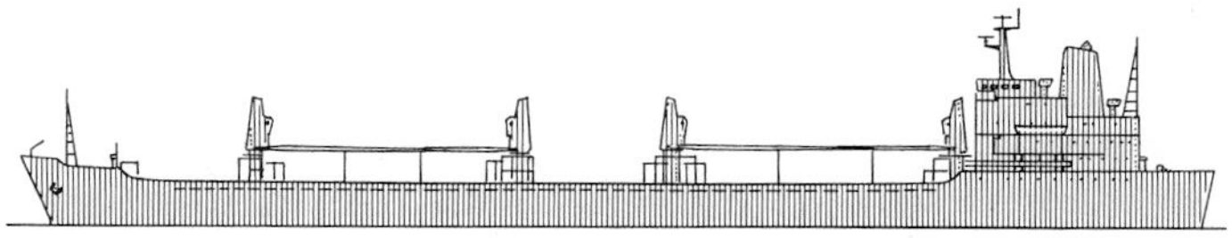

151 *MC^{4}MFM H13*
SUMY Uk/Ja (Osaka) 1978; B; 14,136 grt/22,904 dwt; 164.60 × 9.94 m *(540.03 × 32.61 ft)*; M (B&W); 13 kts; ex-*Ikan Belanak*
Possible sister: **DONG SHAN LING** (RC) ex-*Maritime Noble*

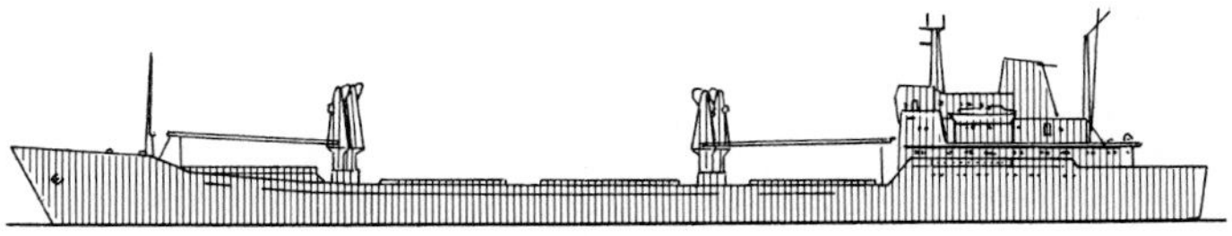

152 *MC^{4}MFM H13*
VASILIY SHUKSHIN Uk/Ru (Navashinskiy) 1978; C (Sea/River); 4,417 grt/5,550 dwt; 124.39 × 5.5 m *(408 × 18.04 ft)*; TSM (Russkiy); 13 kts; Has four deck cranes
Sisters: **MAKSIM RYLSKIY** (Uk); **MIKHAIL LUKONIN** (Ru); **SADRIDDIN AYNI** (Ru); **SERGEY SMIRNOV** (Uk); **VIKTOR KHARA** (Uk); **YURIY KRIMOV** (Uk); **MIKHAIL ISAKOVSKIY** (Uk); **TIKHON SYOMUSHKIN** (Ru); **VITALIY DYAKONOV** (SV); **KHAMZA** (Uk); **MUKHTAR AUEZOV** (SV); **BORIS LAVROV** (Ru); **AKADEMIK POZDYUNIN** (Ru); **PROFESSOR BUBNOV** (Ru); **PROFESSOR PAPKOVICH** (Ru); **PAVEL SHCHEPELEV** (Ru); **PROFESSOR VIKTOR VOLOGDIN** (Ru); **PROFESSOR VLADIMIR POPOV** (Ru); **PROFESSOR VOSKRESENSKIY** (Ru); **VALERIY KUZMIN** (Ru); **AKADEMIK RASPLETIN** (Ru); **NIKOLAY DOLINSKIY** (Ru)

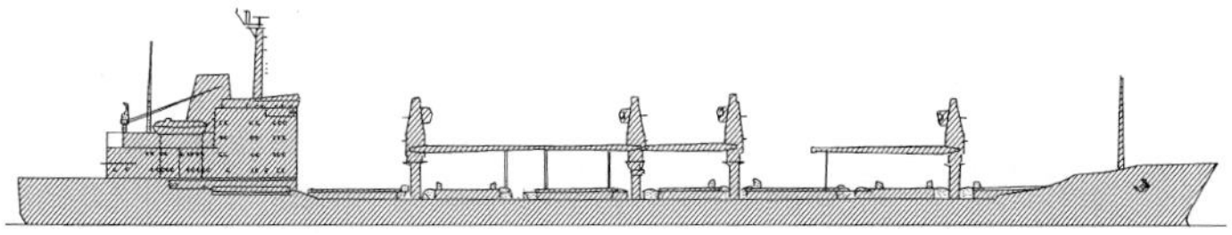

153 *MC^{4}MFMC H13*
BORIS LIVANOV type Ru/Bu (G Dimitrov) 1986; B; 16,502 grt/23,940 dwt; 184.62 × 10.10 m *(605.71 × 33.14 ft)*; M (B&W); 15.50 kts; Presence of deck cranes unconfirmed; see gearless appearance—drawing number 5/129; Any of the vessels under the latter drawing may have cranes; Aftermast is on the port side

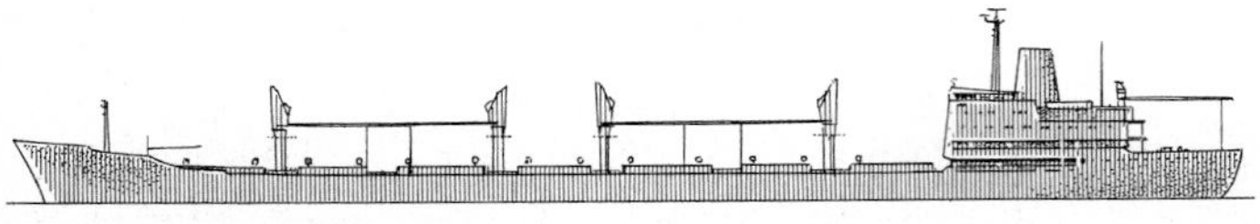

154 MC^4MFMC *H13*
EPOS Cy/Bu (G Dimitrov) 1975; B; 14,732 grt/24,750 dwt; 185.43 × 10.25 m *(608.37 × 33.63 ft)*; M (Sulzer); 15 kts
Sister: **POLLUX I** (Pa) ex-*Boujniba*; Similar (some may have a modified superstructure with six decks, and some may be gearless—see drawing number 5/132): **CORATO** (Br); **ROJEN** (Bu); **AYSE ANA** (Tu) ex-*El Carrier*; **JANICE AUNG** (Bs) ex-*El Commodore*; **MYSON** (Ma) ex-*El Crusader*; **AGHIA MARKELLA** (Cy) ex-*Kithaironas*; **MARIANIC K** (Cy) ex-*Tarpon Star*; **MINA-S** (Tu) ex-*Tarpon Sun*; **CHRISTIANE** (Bs) ex-*Juventia*; **MALYOVITZA** (Bu); **CORAL** (Ma) ex-*Yeral*; Probably similar: **GULF VENTURE** (Cy) ex-*26 De Julio*; **GULF WAVE** (Cy) ex-*Antonio Maceo*

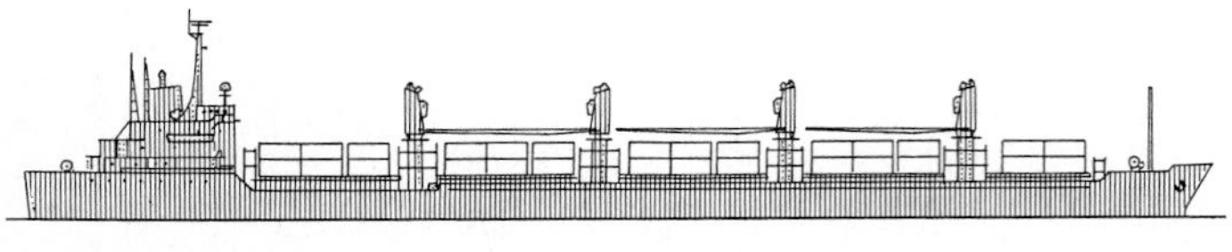

155 $MC^4MFM^2C^2$ *H13*
SANKO HUMANITY Pa/Ja (Mitsubishi HI) 1984; B; 19,340 grt/33,022 dwt; 174.71 × 10.63 m *(573.20 × 34.88 ft)*; M (Mitsubishi); 14 kts
Sisters: **AURORA OPAL** (Pa) ex-*Sanko Heart*; **NEGO WES** (HK) ex-*Sanko Heritage*; Possible sister: **HANDY BONITA** (Pi) ex-*Sanko Symphony*; **SAMSUN EARNEST** (Ko) ex-*Sanko Honesty*

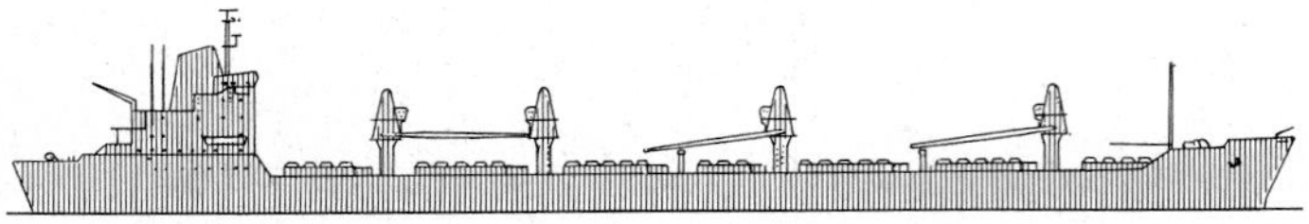

156 MC^4MFM^2R *H13*
SEVILLA WAVE Cy/Sp (AESA) 1986; B; 15,933 grt/26,858 dwt; 183.09 × 10.51 m *(600.69 × 34.48 ft)*; M (Sulzer); 17.75 kts
Probable sister: **ERIKOUSA WAVE** (Cy); Possible sister: **ALEXIS** (Ma) ex-*Ocean Crony*

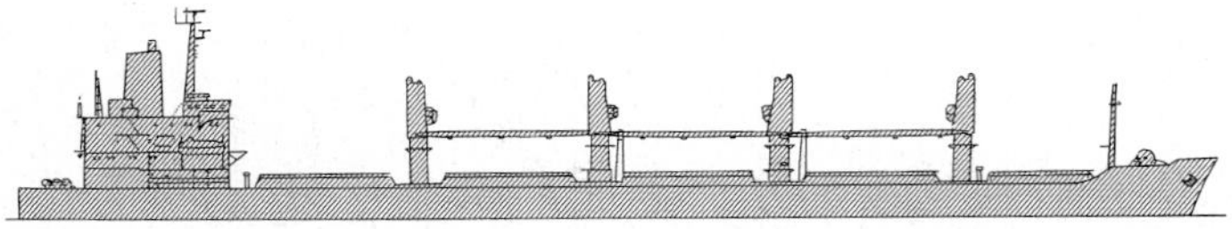

157 MC^4MFMN *H1*
ARKADIA Fi/Ja (NKK) 1983; B; 28,330 grt/47,442 dwt; 189.01 × 11.68 m *(620.11 × 38.32 ft)*; M (Sulzer); 15 kts

158 MC^4MFN *H1*
C FILYOS Tu/Br (A&P) 1982; B; 15,384 grt/26,450 dwt; 181.29 × 10.38 m *(594.78 × 34.06 ft)*; M (Sulzer); 14.5 kts; ex-*Ingenious*; 'B-26' type
Sisters: **HARDMAN H** (Cy) ex-*Carrianna Peony*; **TAMMANY H** (Cy) ex-*Carrianna Primrose*

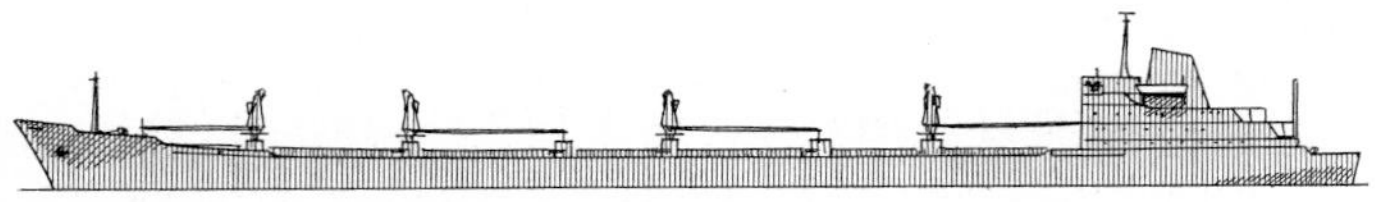

159 MC^4MFN *H1*
JEANNIE Gr/Br (A&P) 1977; B; 15,627 grt/27,541 dwt; 183.04 × 10.71 m *(600.5 × 35.14 ft)*; M (Sulzer); 15 kts; ex-*London Baron*; 'B-26' type
Sisters: **ITHAKI** (Cy) ex-*London Earl*; **KALISTI** (Gr) ex-*London Viscount*; **AUDACIOUS** (Bs) ex-*Welsh Voyager*

160 MC^4MFN *H1*
ROMAN KARMEN Uk/Ja (Osaka) 1981; B; 21,463 grt/38,625 dwt; 188.58 × 11 m *(619 × 36.09 ft)*; M (Sulzer); 17.75 kts; ex-*Maritime Victor*
Sisters: **KAPITAN POLIN** (Uk) ex-*Maritime Leader*; **VASILIY MATUZENKO** (Uk) ex-*Maritime Pride*; **PYOTR TOMASEVICH** (Uk) ex-*Maritime Queen*

161 MC^4MFN *H1*
TIGER VIEW HK/Br (A&P) 1984; B; 18,964 grt/30,650 dwt; 179 × 9.94 m *(587.27 × 32.61 ft)*; M (Sulzer); 14.5 kts; ex-*Fayrouz II*; 'B30' type
Sisters: **TIGER ISLAND** (HK) ex-*Fayrouz I*; **EDO** (Cy) ex-*Fayrouz III*; **TIGER BAY** (HK) ex-*Fayrouz IV*

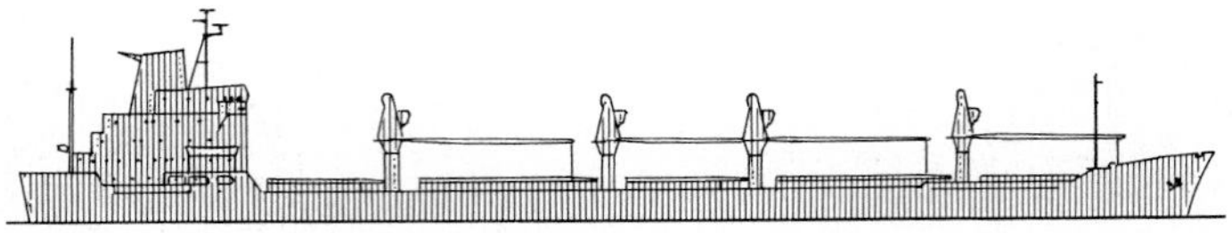

162 MC^4MFN *H13*
AGIOS NIKOLAOS Cy/Sp ('Bazan') 1977; C; 9,222 grt/14,854 dwt; 148.06 × 8.96 m *(485.76 × 29.4 ft)*; M (MAN); 15.5 kts; ex-*Angel Perez*; 'CARTAGO' class; 336 TEU
Probable sisters: **JURINA** (Bs) ex-*Elena Perez*; **MANLEY HAVANT** (SV) ex-*Alvaro Perez*; **AL SHAMS** (Ma) ex-*Ramon Perez*; **AGIOS ANDREAS** (Cy) ex-*Gabriel Perez*; Possible sister: **FRANINA** (Bs) ex-*Antonio Maura*

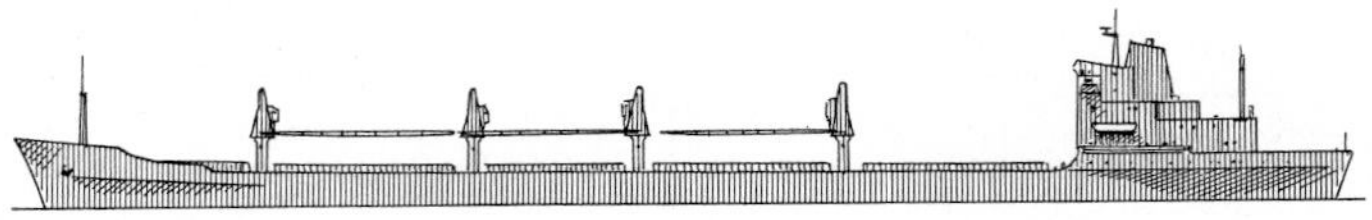

163 MC^4MFN *H13*
ANDAXIOS Cy/Br (Govan) 1976; B; 16,368 grt/26,931 dwt; 175.11 × 10.14 m *(574.51 × 33.27 ft)*; M (B&W); 15 kts; ex-*Cape Ortegal*; 'CARDIFF' class
Sister: **CHL INNOVATOR** (Sg) ex-*Cape Rodney*; (Now converted to BIBO (Bulk in/Bag out) type—probably altered in appearance); Similar: **KALE I** (Tu) ex-*Baron Napier*; **HUA ZHEN** (RC) ex-*Baron Pentland*

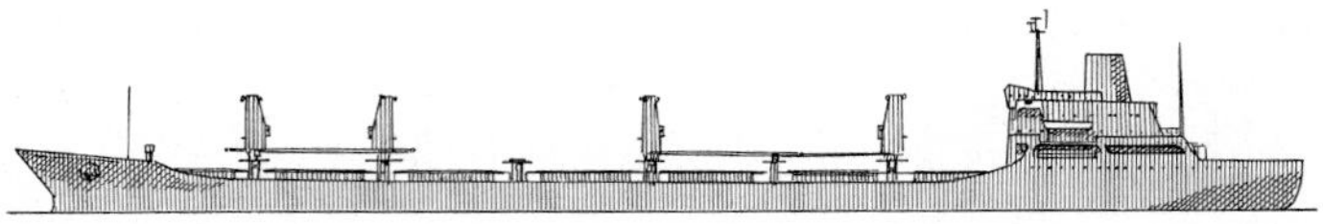

164 MC^4MFN *H13*
ARIETTA Cy/Bu (G Dimitrov) 1973; B; 23,060 grt/37,765 dwt; 201.3 × 11.23 m *(660.43 × 36.84 ft)*; M (B&W); 15 kts; ex-*Tropwind*
Similar (different types of cranes): **MARE** (Va) ex-*Amstelvliet*; **CAPE HATTERAS** (Li) ex-*Amstelvaart*; **OSLAND** (Va) ex-*Amstelvoorn*; **FALCON SEA** (Pa); **PROSPERITY SEA** (Va) **LAKE MARION** (Ml) ex-*Roc Sea*; **SVILEN RUSSEV** (Bu); **LILIANA DIMITROVA** (Bu); Similar (may not have deck cranes): **MEKHANIK P KILIMENCHUK** (Uk) ex-*Kamar*

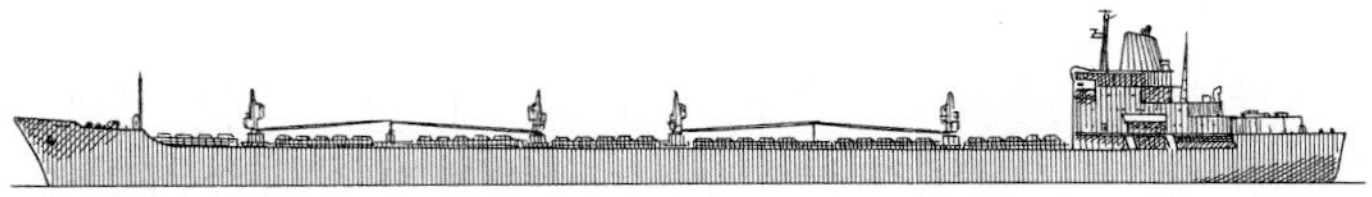

165 MC^4MFN *H13*
CAPETAN LEFTERIS Gr/Ja (IHI) 1968; B; 28,708 grt/47,392 dwt; 202.72 × 12.27 m *(665.09 × 49.26 ft)*; M (Sulzer); 15.5 kts
Similar: **ALEXANDROS** (Gr) ex-*Aquaglory*; **GIORGOS** (Cy) ex-*M G Tsangaris*

166 MC^4MFN *H13*
DINARA Ma/Sp (AESA) 1974; B; 15,734 grt/27,020 dwt; 182.71 × 10.53 m *(599 × 34.55 ft)*; M (Sulzer); 16 kts
Sisters: **CVIJETA ZUZORIC** (Cro); **RUDER BOSKOVIC** (Ma); Similar: **MARIEL** (Ma) ex-*Beograd*; **FAVORE** (NA) ex-*Danilovgrad*

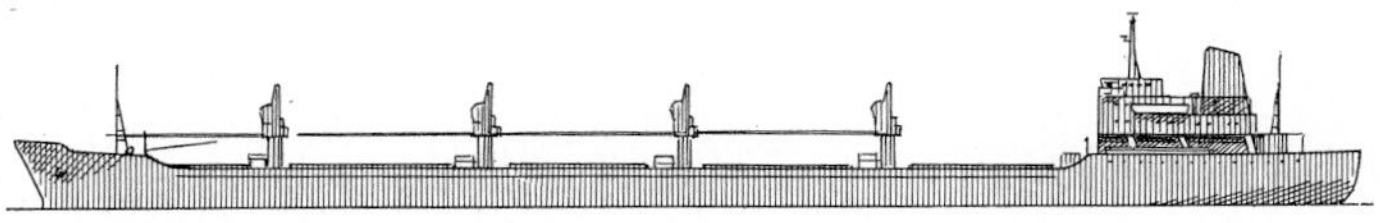

167 MC^4MFN *H13*
EVANDROS K Pa/Ja (Osaka) 1971; B; 14,555 grt/24,561 dwt; 174.5 × 9.92 m *(572.5 × 32.54 ft)*; M (Sulzer); 14.5 kts; ex-*Asia Hawk*
Sister: **BRITANNIA** (Cy) ex-*Asia Swallow*

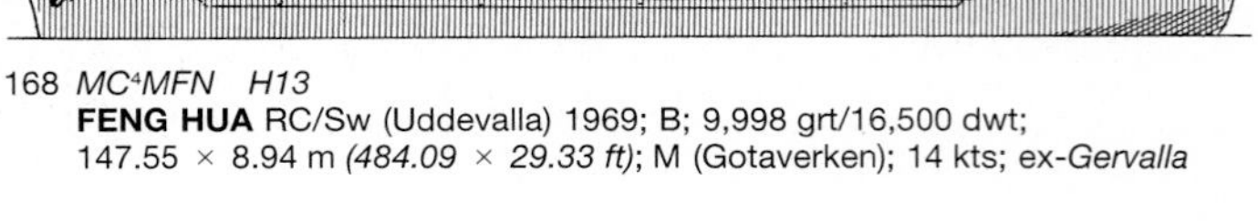

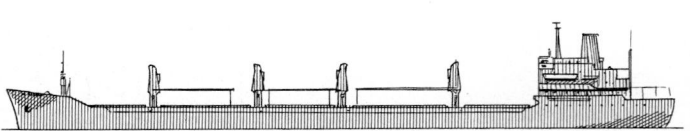

168 MC^4MFN *H13*
FENG HUA RC/Sw (Uddevalla) 1969; B; 9,998 grt/16,500 dwt; 147.55 × 8.94 m *(484.09 × 29.33 ft)*; M (Gotaverken); 14 kts; ex-*Gervalla*

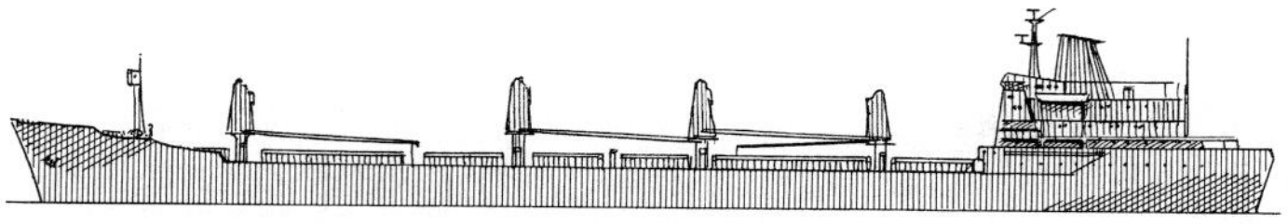

169 *MC^{4}MFN H13*
FLAG ADRIENNE Gr/Fi (Wärtsilä) 1968; B; 11,855 grt/18,289 dwt; 158.32 × 9.59 m *(519.42 × 31.46 ft)*; M (Sulzer); 14.5 kts; ex-*Kotkaniemi*

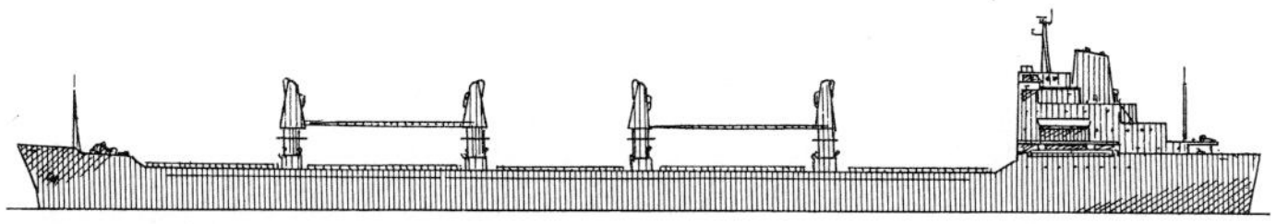

170 *MC^{4}MFN H13*
FLORA C Gr/Ja (Koyo) 1978; B; 17,537 grt/27,384 dwt; 169 × 9.72 m *(556.43 × 31.89 ft)*; M (Sulzer); 16 kts
Sisters: **NANI** (Cy) ex-*John C*; **SOPHIE C** (Gr); Similar: **CHRISTINA C** (Gr); **EUGENIE C** (Gr); **BUENA FORTUNA** (Gr); **DESERT FALCON** (Gr)

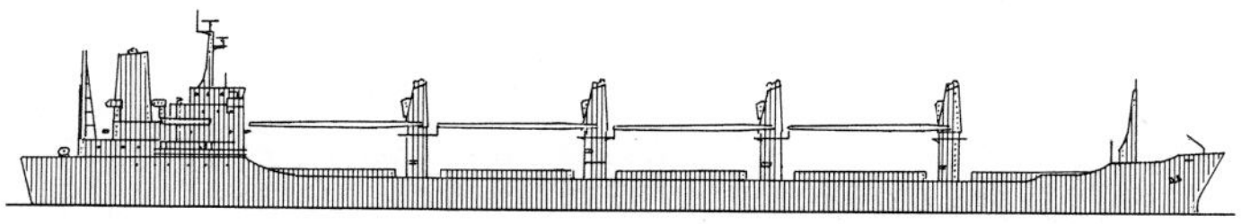

171 *MC^{4}MFN H13*
HILAL II Tu/Ja (Osaka) 1981; B; 15,357 grt/25,845 dwt; 178.31 × 9.58 m *(585.01 × 31.43 ft)*; M (B&W); — kts; ex-*Yin Kim*; Of the masts aft, starboard side is a pole and port side a tripod
Probable sister: **KAVO YERAKAS** (Gr) ex-*Gema Phosphate*

172 *MC^{4}MFN H13*
HOLCK-LARSEN In/Ja (Rinkai/Nipponkai) 1980/81; B; 16,798 grt/ 27,036 dwt; 191.29 × 9.5 m *(628 × 31.17 ft)*; M (B&W); — kts; ex-*Eggarlock*; Foreward section built Rinkai 1980; After section built Nipponkai 1981
Sisters: **SOREN TOUBRO** (In) ex-*Oak Star;* **MINA CEBI** (Tu) ex-*El General*; **OCEAN LEADER** (Ma) ex-*Regent Palm*

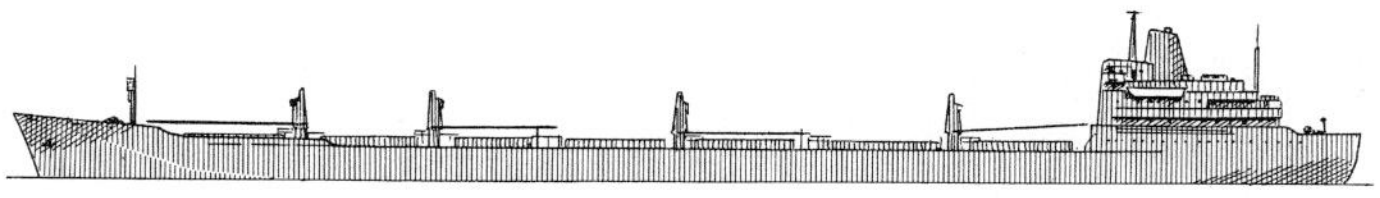

173 *MC^{4}MFN H13*
HUA SHUN RC/No (Haugesund) 1966; B; 17,777 grt/34,260 dwt; 187.03 × 11.26 m *(613.62 × 36.9 ft)*; M (Sulzer); 16.5 kts; ex-*Skausund*
Sister (may have seven cranes): **WEI HAI** (RC) ex-*Lysland*

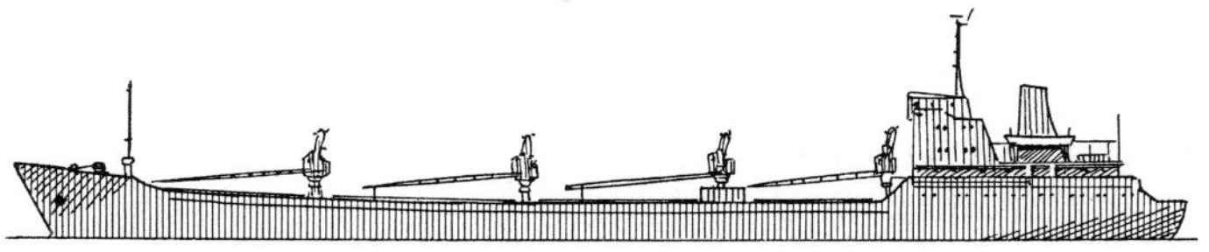

174 *MC^{4}MFN H13*
INTERNATIONAL 2 Rm/Rm (Galatz) 1974; C; 5,987 grt/8,750 dwt; 130.77 × 8.1 m *(429.04 × 26.57 ft)*; M (Sulzer); 15.75 kts; ex-*Radauti*
Sisters (some built by Tulcea): **OSCAR JUPITER** (Rm) ex-*Faget*; **FIERBINTI** (Rm); **SAMMARINA 2** (Rm) ex-*Filioara*; **CALIMANESTI** (Rm); **FAUREI** (Rm); **FAGARAS** (Rm); **BUSTENI** (Rm); **TELEORMAN** (Rm); **INTERNATIONAL 1** (Rm) ex-*Firiza*; **BIHOR** (Rm); **FILIASI** (Rm); **SATU MARE** (Rm); **INTERNATIONAL 5** (Rm) ex-*Odorhei*; **SAMMARINA 4** (Rm) ex-*Simeria*; **GORJ** (Rm); **FRUNZANESTI** (Rm); **FRASINET** (Rm); **PONOR** (Rm) ex-*Dolj*; **CACIULATA** (Rm); **FIENI** (Rm); **RUPEA** (Rm); **HATEG** (Rm); **ORAVITA** (Rm); **GOVORA** (Rm); **ATILLA K** (Rm) ex-*Fundulea*; **GIURGIU** (Rm); **HIRSOVA** (Rm); **HUSI** (Rm); **CRISTIAN B** (Rm) ex-*Grivita*; **GIURGENI** (Rm); **DANUBE TRADER** (Rm) ex-*Gradistea*; **HOREZU** (Rm); **STEFAN KARADJA** (Bu); **ZAHARI STOIANOV** (Bu); **CALUGARENI** (Rm); **COSTINESTI** (Rm); **INTERNATIONAL 4** (Rm) ex-*Falciu*; **FELDIOARA** (Rm); **FELEAC** (Rm); **FAIR SKY** (Rm) ex-*Filaret*; **FINTINELE** (Rm); **CRISTIAN C** (Rm) ex-*Moldovita*; **CRISTIAN A** (Rm) ex-*Filipesti*; **FLORESTI** (Rm); **SAMMARINA 1** (Rm) ex-*Foisor*; **SAMMARINA 5** (Rm) ex-*Frasin*; **FUNDENI** (Rm); **GORGOVA** (Rm); **GORUN** (Rm); **GRUIA** (Rm); **HAGIENI** (Rm); **HUMULESTI** (Rm); **ILFOV** (Rm); **LUGOJ** (Rm); **MOINESTI** (Rm); **NICORESTI** (Rm); **SAMMARINA 3** (Rm) ex-*Plataresti*; **MEHEDINTI** (Rm); **MIZIL** (Rm); **VILCEA** (Rm); **MIRCESTI** (Rm)

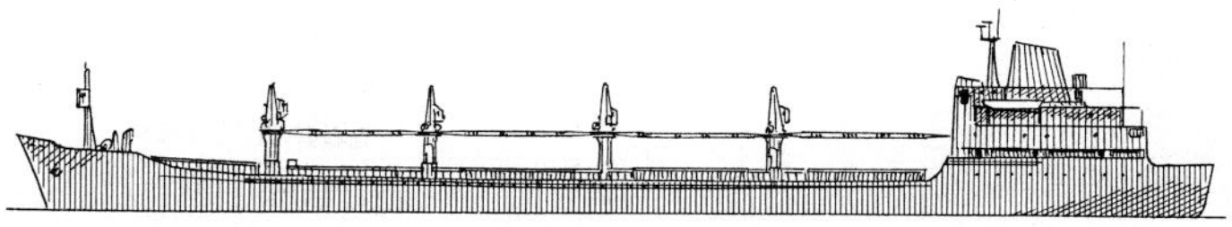

175 *MC^{4}MFN H13*
JIN HUI RC/Br (Scotts' SB) 1970; B; 12,077 grt/20,395 dwt; 158.53 × 9.51 m *(520.11 × 31.2 ft)*; M (Sulzer); 15 kts; ex-*Norita*, ex-*Ingeren*

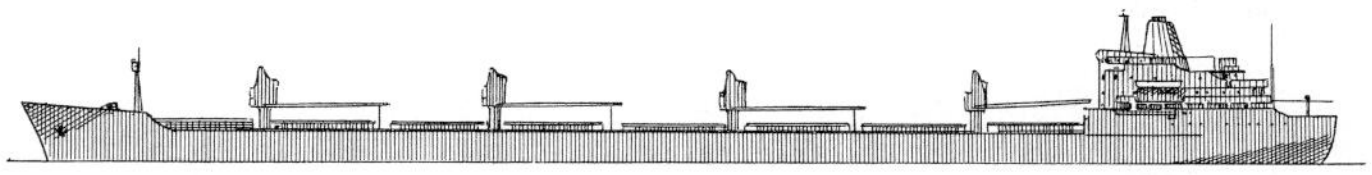

176 *MC^{4}MFN H13*
JULPHA A UAE/No (Haugesund) 1969; B; 19,257 grt/36,080 dwt; 216.14 × 10.99 m *(709.12 × 36.06 ft)*; M (Sulzer); 16 kts; ex-*Andwi*

177 *MC^{4}MFN H13*
KUPA Ma/Ys ('3 Maj') 1973; B; 18,669 grt/30,832 dwt; 196.6 × 10.82 m *(645 × 35.5 ft)*; M (Sulzer); 15.75 kts; ex-*Adriatik*
Sister: **SAVA** (Ma)

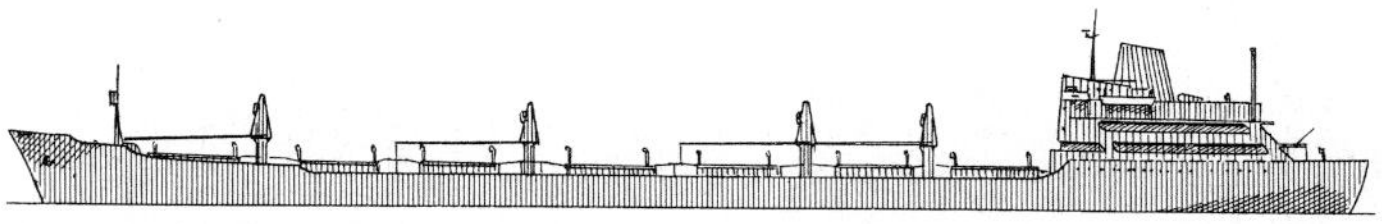

178 *MC^{4}MFN H13*
LING LONG HAI RC/No (Bergens) 1963; B; 17,373 grt/30,700 dwt; 185.66 × 11.2 m *(609.12 × 36.75 ft)*; M (Gotaverken); 11.5 kts; ex-*Norbu*

179 *MC^{4}MFN H13*
MATUMBA Ma/Sp (AESA) 1974; B; 19,473 grt/35,264 dwt; 196.02 × 11.15 m *(643.1 × 36.58)*; M (Sulzer); 15 kts; ex-*Galea*
Sisters: **DELFINI** (Gr) ex-*Matai*; **MILAGRO** (Ma) ex-*Forano*; **LENINSK** (Ru) ex-*Lita*; **NAN FUNG** (SV); **GORLOVKA** (Ru) ex-*Pampero*; **ADIB** (Ir) ex-*Patricia*; **AMIN** (Ir) ex-*Caldereta*; **VITALITY** (Ml) ex-*Levante*

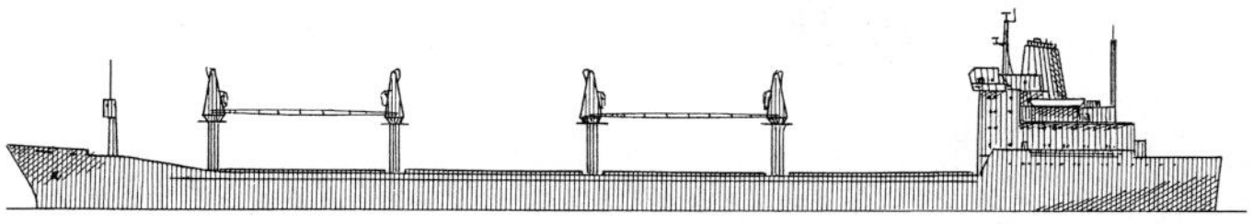

180 *MC^{4}MFN H13*
MED LERICI Pa/DDR (Mathias-Thesen) 1972; B/Con; 15,986 grt/23,222 dwt; 176.16 × 10.11 m *(579.59 × 33.17 ft)*; M (MAN); 15.5 kts; ex-*Arctic Wasa*
Sisters: **MED GENOA** (Ma) ex-*Celtic Wasa*; **ANAMELI** (Gr) ex-*Gothic Wasa*; **GAGICH** (Ma) ex-*Finntimber*; **RIO CHAMA** (Ve) ex-*Sylvo*; Similar (four-deck superstructure with funnel on topmost deck—others may be like this): **PIONEER SUN** (Cy) ex-*Baltic Wasa*; **MED VENICE** (Ma) ex-*Delphic Wasa*; **PAL MARINOS** (Cy) ex-*Maya IV*

181 *MC^{4}MFN H13*
SEA MONARCH Ma/RC (Dalian) 1984; B; 18,025 grt/28,251 dwt; 195 × 10 m *(639.76 × 32.81 ft)*; M (B&W); 14.5 kts; ex-*Sea Monarch*
Sisters: **AURORA TOPAZ** (Li) ex-*Sea Fortune*; **SEASTAR II** (Cy) ex-*Sea Glory*; **DANIA PORTLAND** (DIS) ex-*Sea Prosperity*

182 *MC^{4}MFN H13*
SERSOU Ag/Ja (Mitsubishi HI) 1982; B; 19,672 grt/34,100 dwt; 178 × 10.74 m *(584 × 35.24 ft)*; M (Mitsubishi); 14.7 kts; ex-*Pepe Le Moko*
Sisters: **ADITYA PRAKASH** (In) ex-*Sky Hawk*; **ANANGEL EAGLE** (Gr) ex-*Libexport*; Probable sisters: **HANDY SUCCESS** (Pi) ex-*Crest 1*; **HANDY EXPLORER** (Pi) ex-*Lappland*; **JIN BI** (Pa) ex-*Libextrade*; **ANANGEL POWER** (Gr) ex-*Libexpress*

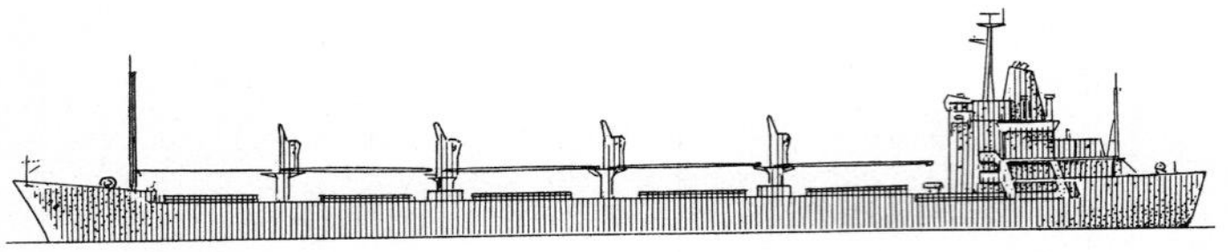

183 *MC^{4}MFN H13*
TOGO CHARM Cy/Ja (NKK) 1977; B; 12,510 grt/21,400 dwt; 155.71 × 9.9 m *(510.86 × 32.48 ft)*; M (Sulzer); 17.5 kts; ex-*Sachsenhausen*
Probable sister: **LEROS STRENGTH** (Cy) ex-*Benetnasch*; Sisters (longer—172.001 m (564.1ft)): **GOLDEN TRADER** (Gr); **GOLDEN CHALLENGER** (Pa); **GOLDEN POLYDINAMOS** (Gr); **JAG VIJAY** (In) ex-*Golden Polykleitos*

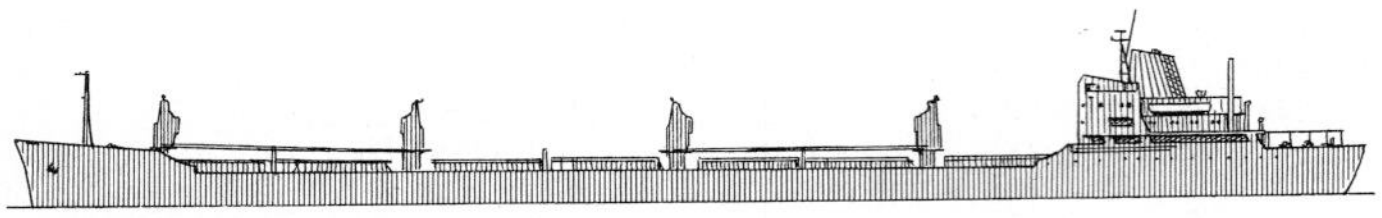

184 *MC^{4}MFN H13*
TROPICANA Ho/Ne (Verolme Scheeps) 1967; B; 19,541 grt/34,114 dwt; 183.93 × 11.16 m *(603.44 × 36.61 ft)*; M (Sulzer); 12.8 kts; ex-*Amstelpark*; Tripod radar mast
Sister: **SEAVENUS** (Ma) ex-*Amstellaan*

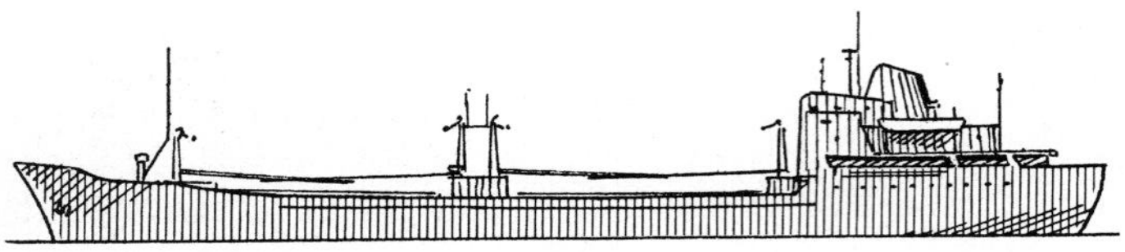

185 *MC^{4}MFN H13*
UNITED I Eg/De (Langesunds) 1963; C; 2,635 grt/3,840 dwt; 93.88 × 6.37 m *(307.68 × 20.9 ft)*; M (Sulzer); 13.5 kts; ex-*Nina*

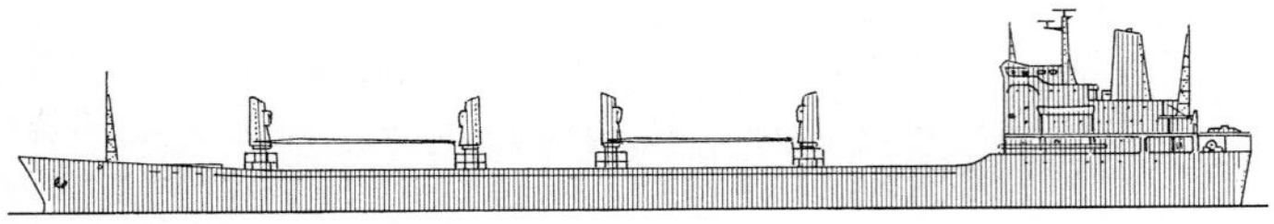

186 *MC^{4}MFNC H3*
AVDEEVKA Uk/Ja (Hayashikane) 1977; B; 16,576 grt/26,398 dwt; 174.02 × 10.45 m *(570.93 × 34.28 ft)*; M (Sulzer); 14.50 kts; ex-*Goldensari 1*
Sister: **ADITYA KANTI** (In) ex-*Bogasari Satu*; Similar: **RECAI B** (Tu) ex-*Rimba Keruing*; **BETA LUCK** (Gr) ex-*Rimba Balau*

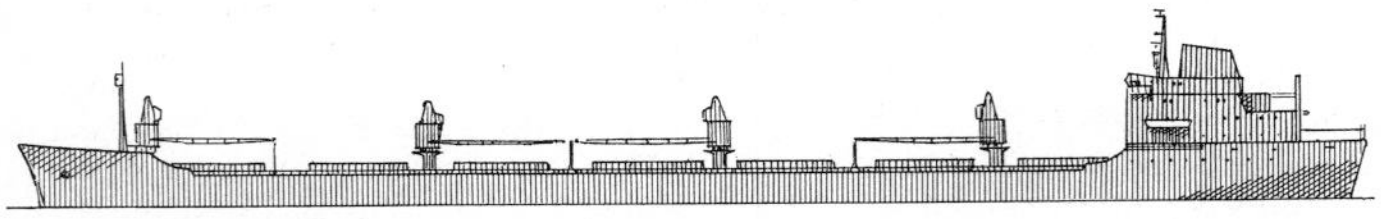

187 *MC^{4}MFNM H13*
EXPEDITIONER Pa/Br (Cammell Laird) 1972; B; 19,572 grt/34,424 dwt; 180.96 × 11.23 m *(593.7 × 36.84 ft)*; M (Doxford); 15 kts; ex-*Letchworth*
Sisters: **HUA CHANG** (Li) ex-*Naworth*; **AU YIN LENG** (—) ex-*Oakworth*

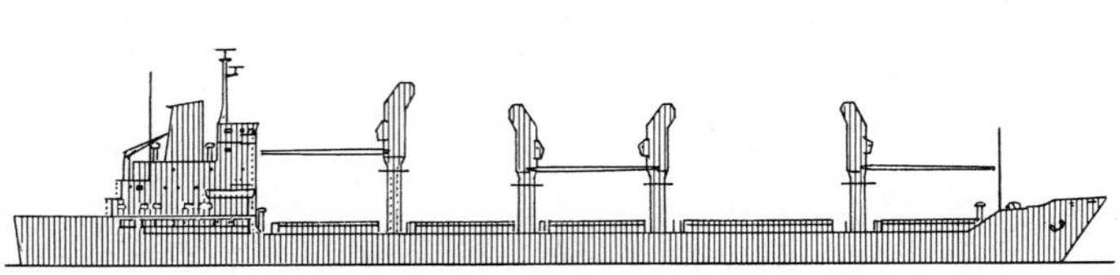

188 *MC^{4}MFNS H13*
CARVIK Cy/Sp (AESA) 1986; C/Con; 10,572 grt/16,223 dwt; 149.05 × 9.41 m *(488.85 × 30.87 ft)*; M (B&W); 14 kts; ex-*Bahia de Cardenas*; 519 TEU
Sisters: **CIENVIK** (Cy) ex-*Bahia de Cienfuegos*; **HAVIK** (Cy) ex-*Bahia de Habana*; **MANZAVIK** (Cy) ex-*Bahia de Manzanillo*; **NUEVIK** (Cy) ex-*Bahia de Nuevitas*; **HONVIK** (Cy) ex-*Bahia Honda*; **TOPAVIK** (Cy) ex-*Bahia de Puerto Padre*

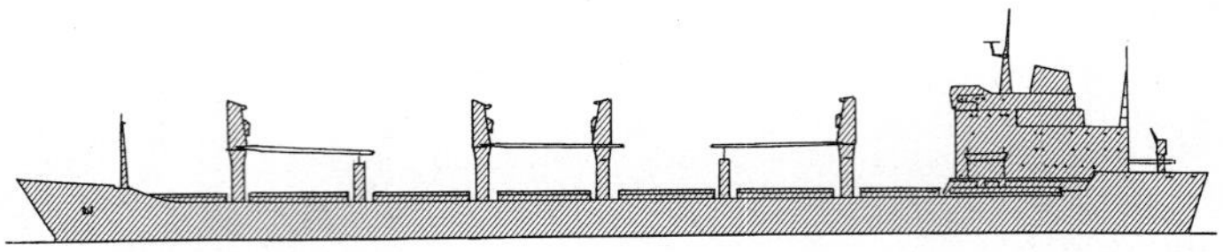

189 *MC^{4}MFNS H13*
KAPITAN SOROKA Uk/Pd ('Komuny Paryskiej') 1981; B/Con; 20,755 grt/34,170 dwt; 186.39 × 11.02 m *(611.52 × 36.15 ft)*; M (Sulzer); 15 kts; ex-*Sah Kim*; 700 TEU; 'B533' type
Sister: **KAPITAN FOMENKO** (Uk) ex-*Bah Kim*

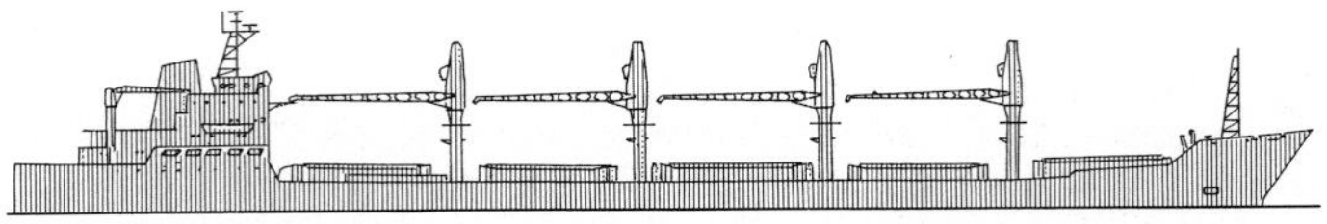

190 *MC^{4}MFR H13*
CHENNAI SADHANAI In/Bz (Emaq) 1984; B/Con; 23,525 grt/37,635 dwt; 193.84 × 11.07 m *(635.96 × 36.32 ft)*; M (B&W); 15.50 kts; ex-*Ajax*; 913 TEU
Sister: **CHENNAI JAYAM** (In) ex-*Atlas*

191 *MC^{4}MFR H13*
FROTAMERICA Bz/Bz (Emaq) 1979; B; 21,733 grt/37,930 dwt; 193.81 × 10.91 m *(636 × 35.79 ft)*; M (Sulzer); 15 kts
Sisters (some may be gearless): **THORNHILL** (Va) ex-*Frotabrasil*; **FROTACHILE** (Bz); **FROTARGENTINA** (Bz); **FROTAURUGUAY** (Bz); **M AKSU** (Tu) ex-*Almirante Aniceto*; **CORCOVADO** (Ch) ex-*Frotacanada*; Similar (after crane in different position): **CARGO TRADER** (Gr) ex-*Mulheim*; **CARGO EXPLORER** (Gr) ex-*Bentheim*; Similar (centre-line mast on focsle and different design of crane aft): **KRAS** (SV) ex-*Docevenus*; **DOCEMARTE** (Bz) (may not have deck cranes)

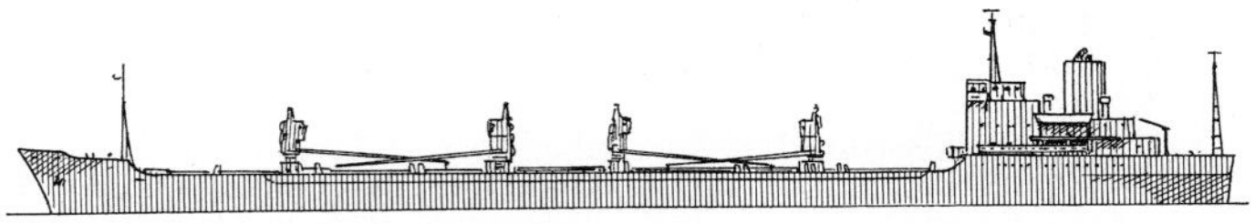

192 *MC^{4}MFR H13*
IRAN NASR Ir/Ja (NKK) 1971; B; 12,257 grt/19,874 dwt; 155.48 × 9.9 m *(510.1 × 32.48 ft)*; M (Sulzer); 14 kts; ex-*Asia Flamingo*
Sisters: **SAADI** (Ir) ex-*Asia Gold*; **IRAN SABR** (Ir) ex-*Asia Loyalty*

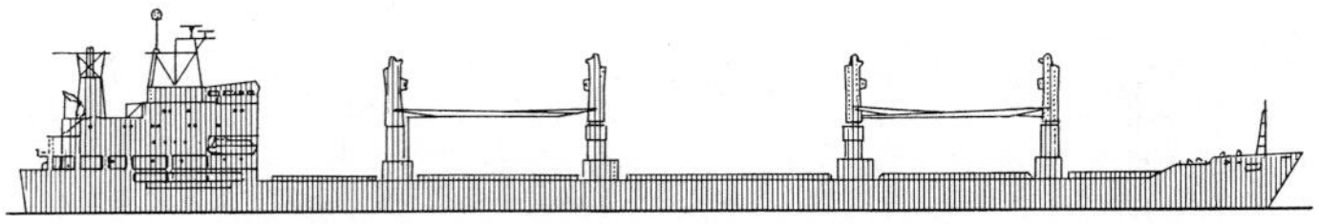

193 *MC^{4}MFS H13*
T A EXPLORER Li/Br (North East) 1987; C/Con; 17,101 grt/22,500 dwt; 187.41 × 9.50 m *(614.86 × 31.17 ft)*; M (B&W); 16.50 kts; ex-*Dietrich Oldendorff*; 1,000 TEU; 'ECOFLEX' type
Sister: **T A VOYAGER** (Li) ex-*Johanna Oldendorff*

194 *MC^{4}MF-MD*
NATHALIE DELMAS Fr/Fr (L'Atlantique) 1982; C/Con; 20,424 grt/26,287 dwt; 177 × 11.42 m *(581 × 37.47 ft)*; M (Pielstick); 18 kts; 988 TEU; Funnel on port side opposite tripod mast on starboard side
Sisters: **PATRICIA DELMAS** (Fr); **CGM MASCAREIGNES** (Fr) ex-*Renee Delmas*; **SUZANNE DELMAS** (Fr)

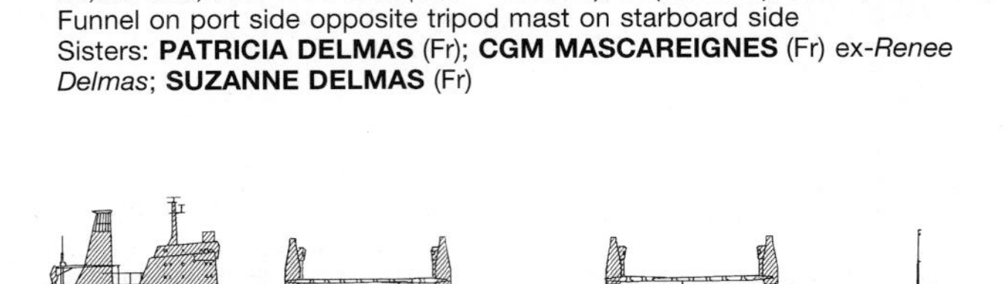

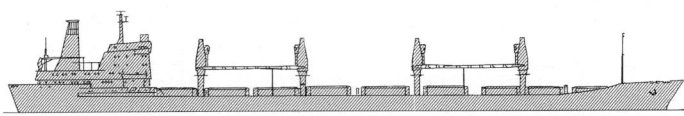

195 *MC^{4}MGMR H13*
SEADRIVE Cy/Pd (Szczecinska) 1982; B; 17,419 grt/33,500 dwt; 198.18 × 11.00 m *(650.20 × 36.10 ft)*; M (Sulzer); 16 kts; ex-*Sedge*; 'B517' type; Aftermast is on port side and crane aft is centreline

196 *MC^{4}MGN H13*
ADRIANA At/Bz (Caneco) 1983; B; 23,519 grt/38,913 dwt; 200.90 × 10.75 m *(659.12 × 35.27 ft)*; M (B&W); 17.10 kts; ex-*Natica*

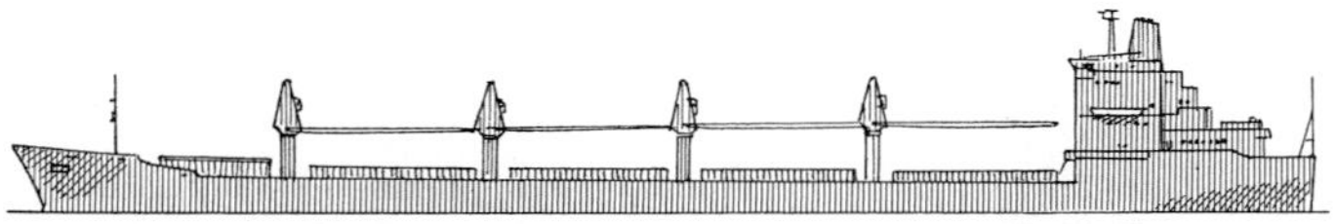

197 MC^4MGN H13
PEARL OF DUBAI Cy/No (Haugesund) 1972; B; 15,329 grt/24,090 dwt; 162.87 × 10.42 m *(534.35 × 34.18 ft)*; M (Stork-Werkspoor); 15.5 kts; ex-*Temple Inn*
Sisters: **YOUMING** (Pa) ex-*Sneland*; **PLATINUM KRIS** (Pa) ex-*Vestland*

198 MC^4MHFN H1
MAERSK SERANGOON Sg/Ja (Hitachi) 1983; B; 36,196 grt/63,686 dwt; 224.5 × 12.96 m *(737 × 42.52 ft)*; M (B&W); 16 kts
Sister: **MAERSK SEMBAWANG** (Sg)

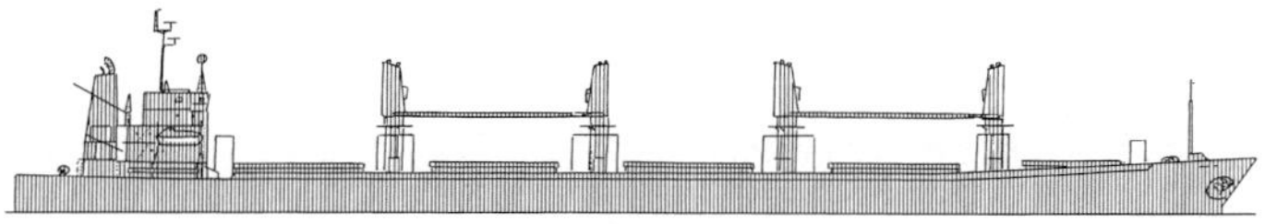

199 MC^4M^2CF H
PACIFIC ENDEAVOR Li/Ja (Oshima Z) 1992; B; 24,139 grt/43,366 dwt; 184.80 × 11.22 m *(606.30 × 36.81 ft)*; M (Sulzer); 14.3 kts
Probable sisters: **PACIFIC EMBOLDEN** (Li); **PACIFIC CAREER** (Li); **PACIFIC VIGOROUS** (Li); **MARITIME JADE** (Sg); **MARITIME LAPIS** (—); **MARITIME PEARL** (Sg); **MARITIME DIAMOND** (Pa); **BATIS** (Pi); **WESTERN BELL** (NIS); Possible sisters: **MARITIME SKILL** (Pa); **AMBER HALO** (Pa); **NIKKEI EAGLE** (Pa); **GOLDEN WING** (Pa); **ANGEL FEATHER** (Pa); **YOU SHENG** (Pa); **YOU LIANG** (Pa); **YOU MEI** (Pa); **KIRILLIS BARBARA** (Pa); **K-CHRISTINA** (Pi); **VELEBIT** (Li); **GOLDEN LADY** (Ma); **OCEANIC SUCCESS** (Pi); **SUNNY SUCCESS** (Pa); **SUN MASTER** (Pa); **KAYAX** (Pa)

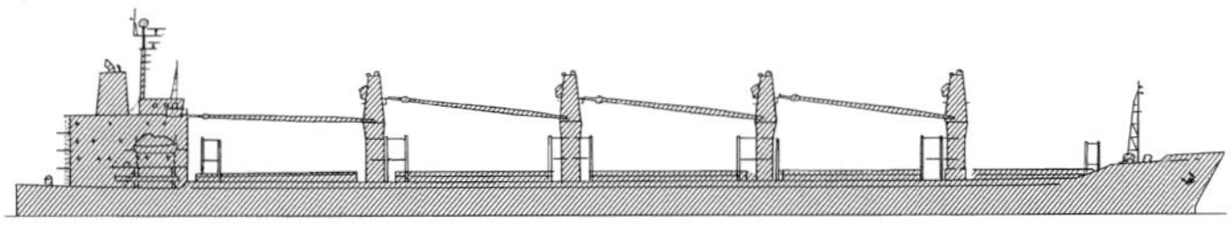

200 MC^4M^2F H1
ATLANTIC BULKER Pa/Ja (Kanasashi) 1995; B; 17,075 grt/27,860 dwt; 176.62 × 9.50 m *(579.46 × 31.17 ft)*; M (Mitsubishi); 14 kts

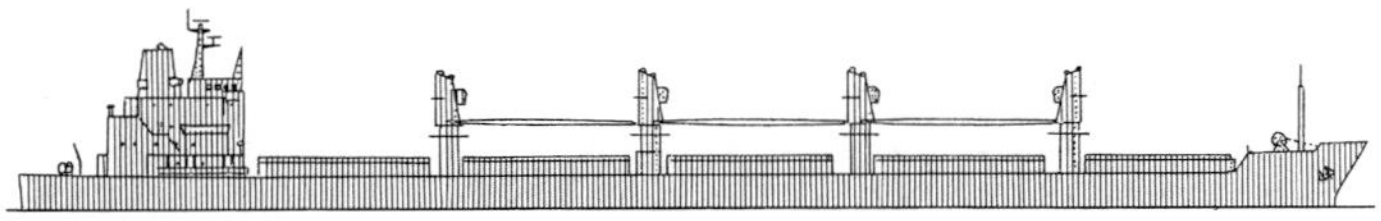

201 MC^4M^2F H1
NIKOS N Cy/Ja (Sanoyas Corp) 1984; B; 23,186 grt/41,093 dwt; 182.76 × 11.19 m *(599.61 × 36.71 ft)*; M (Sulzer); 16.25 kts; ex-*Alfi*
Possible sisters: **WESTERN VILLAGE** (Pi) ex-*Sea Elfi*; **TOP GLORY** (Li) ex-*Star Delfi*

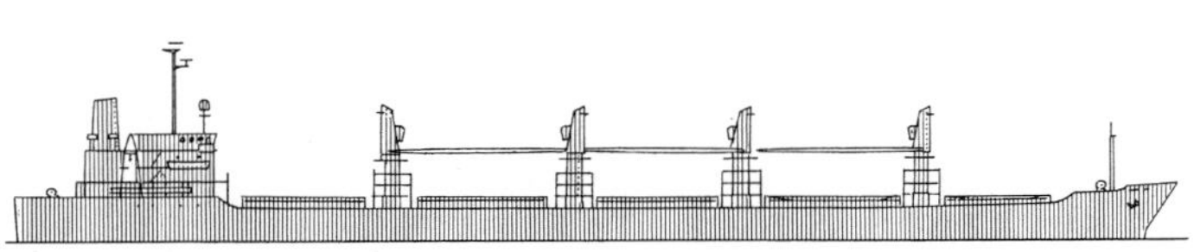

202 MC^4M^2F H13
SEA SPARKLE Li/Ja (Koyo) 1984; B; 23,207 grt/38,380 dwt; 189.97 × 11.02 m *(623.26 × 36.15 ft)*; M (B&W); 14 kts; ex-*Sanko Lapis*
Probable sisters (some may have five-deck superstructure): **SEA RIPPLE** (Li) ex-*Sanko Topaz*; **COSTIS** (Gr): ex-*Sanko Amethyst*; **LIBERTY VICTORY** (Pi) ex-*Bluebell*; **JIN SHENG** (Pa) ex-*Star Vanri*; **JIN YI** (Pa) ex-*Junri*; **VIVITA** (NIS) ex-*Sunny Wisteria*; The following have five-deck superstructures; **SEA SWIFT** (Pa) ex-*Oriental Ruby*; **NAND NEETI** (In) ex-*Stove Tradition*

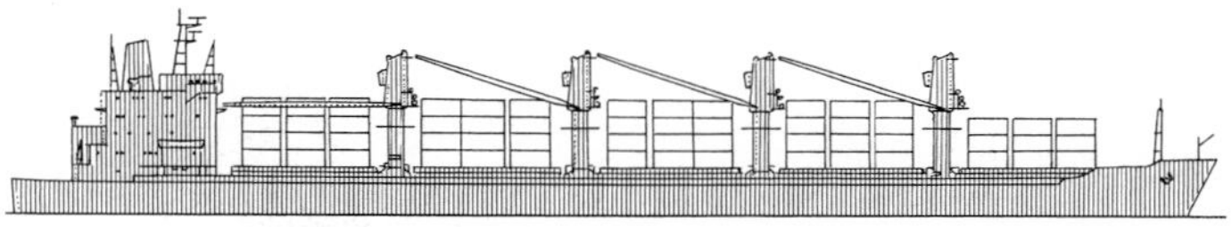

203 MC^4M^2FM H1
WESTERN SHORE NIS/Ja (Tsuneishi) 1984; B/Con; 26,257 grt/43,681 dwt; 185.83 × 11.32 m *(609.68 × 37.14 ft)*; M (B&W); 14 kts; ex-*Eastern Jay*; 1,076 TEU; 'TESS 40' type
Probable sister (some may be like drawing number 7/242): **SEA CROWN** (Pa) ex-*Southern Jay*; Possible sisters: **GLENITA** (Pa) ex-*Gleneagles*; **GOLDEN VICTORY** (Pa); **OCEAN PRIZE** (Pi) ex-*Western Jay*; **DARYA CHAND** (Li) ex-*Soarer Cupid* (builder—Hashihama); **CHETTINAND TRADITION** (In) ex-*Soarer Diana* (builder—Hashihama); **SOARER BELLONA** (Pi); **MARINE WORLD** (Pa) ex-*Big Glory* (builder-Hashihama)

204 $MC^4M^2FM^2$ H1
ROSITA NIS/Ja (Hashihama) 1984; B; 25,777 grt/42,972 dwt; 185.83 × 11.33 m *(609.68 × 37.17 ft)*; M (B&W); 13.50 kts; ex-*Nisshu Maru*

205 $MC^4M^2FM^2$ H13
WESTERN WINNER Pa/Ja (NKK) 1982; B; 17,858 grt/30,396 dwt; 175 × 10.45 m *(574 × 34.28 ft)*; M (Sulzer); 15.2 kts; ex-*Flores*
Sister: **YPAPADI** (Pa) ex-*Farisi*

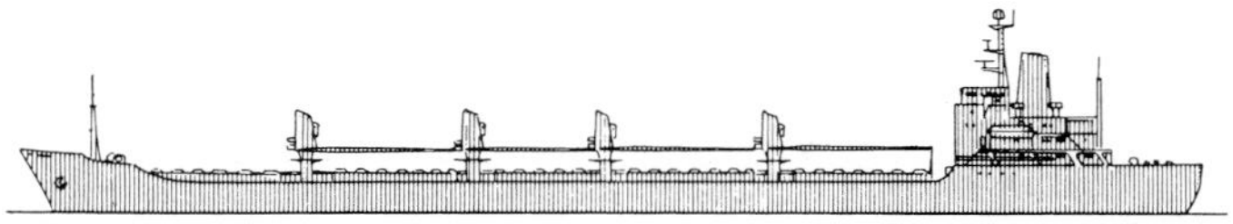

206 MC^4M^2FN H13
VASILIY AZHAYEV Uk/Ja (Sumitomo) 1977; B; 20,222 grt/34,545 dwt; 180.02 × 10.89 m *(590.62 × 35.73 ft)*; M (Sulzer); 15.50 kts; ex-*Binsnes*
Sisters: **DNEPROGES** (Uk) ex-*Brunes*; **PEARL PROSPERITY** (In) ex-*Barknes*; **JADE ORIENT** (Li) ex-*Bergnes*; **JADE PACIFIC** (Li) ex-*Bessnes*; **MERKUR** (Tu) ex-*Baynes*

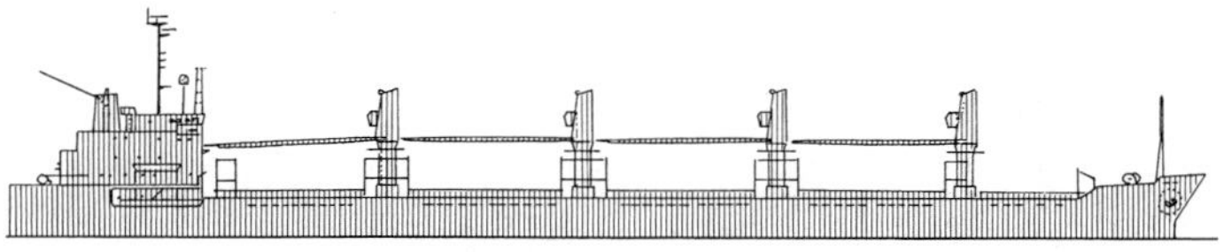

207 MC^4M^2F-C H13
HANDY ISLANDER Pi/Ja (Kanasashi) 1985; B; 15,833 grt/26,587 dwt; 167.21 × 9.54 m *(548.59 × 31.30 ft)*; M (B&W); 14 kts; ex-*Citrus Island*
Possible sisters: **EAST TRADER** (Pa) ex-*Sanko Diligence*; **SANKO POPPY** (Pa); **SANKO LAUREL** (Pa); **SANKO SPRUCE** (Pa); **VIRGINIA** (Pa) ex-*Sanko Walnut*; **MARIF** (Pa); **HAKUFU** (Pa) ex-*Blue Mary*; Sisters (builder—Hakodate): **NEGO NOMIS** (HK) ex-*Matsumae*; **ALTAMONTE** (Pi); **GOLDEN ALPHA** (Pa) ex-*Marimo*; **NEGO KIM** (HK) ex-*Mashu*; Probable sisters (builder Hakodate): **GLORIOUS SUCCESS** (Pi); **SEVEN OCEAN** (Pi); **OCEAN ORCHID** (Pa); **YUO XIU** (HK); **YOU YUE** (HK); **TRICHORD SUCCESS** (Pi); **GREEN SYLVAN** (Pa); **OCEAN LYDIA** (Pa); **COLUMBIA BAY** (Pa); **FOREST CHAMPION** (Pa)

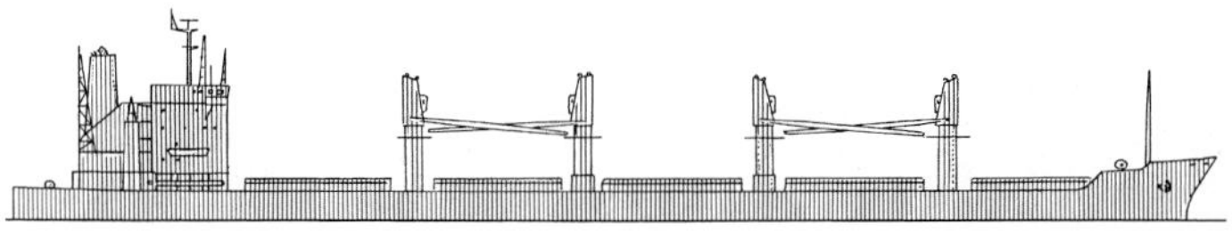

208 MC^4M^3FM H1
GEM OF MADRAS In/Ja (NKK) 1986; B; 25,131 grt/41,938 dwt; 191.01 × 10.72 m *(626.67 × 35.17 ft)*; M (B&W); 14 kts; ex-*Expeditor*

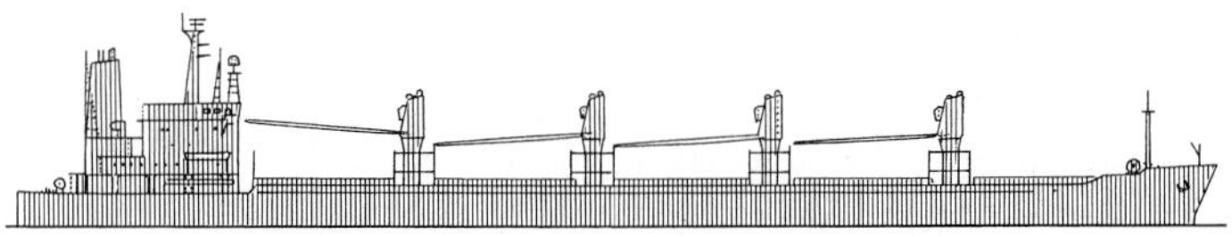

209 MC^4M^3FM H1
NEW CRYSTAL Li/Ja (Namura) 1984; B; 23,536 grt/39,333 dwt; 181.03 × 11.01 m *(593.93 × 36.12 ft)*; M (Sulzer); 14 kts; ex-*Sanko Crystal*
Sisters: **NEW JADE** (Li) ex-*Sanko Jade*; **SEA MARINER** (SV) ex-*Sanko Coral*; **SEA ANGEL** (Li) ex-*Sanko Turquoise*

210 *MC^{4}M^{3}FM H1*
SEA BRILLIANCE Li/Ja (Kawasaki) 1984; B/Con; 22,361 grt/38,307 dwt; 179.41 × 10.82 m *(588.62 × 35.50 ft)*; M (B&W); 14 kts; ex-*Sanko Dignity*; 140 TEU
Probable sisters: **SANKO EMERALD** (Li); **SEA RAINBOW** (Li) ex-*Sanko Eternity*; **NEW NOBLE** (Pi) ex-*Sanko Noble*; **NIMET PISAK** (Tu) ex-*Sanko Sapphire*; **MIDAS** (Pa) ex-*Sanko Sovereign*

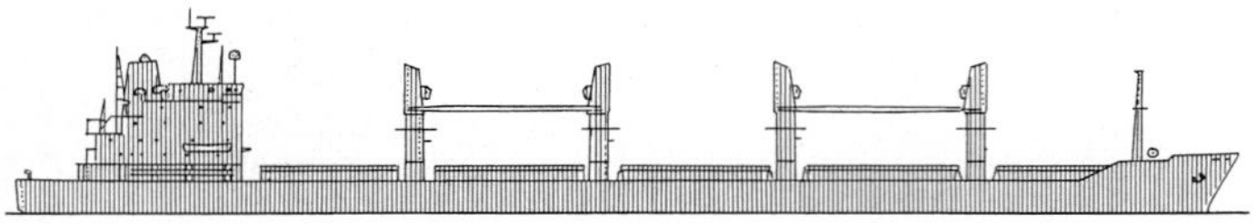

211 *MC^{4}M^{3}FMC* H1
TETIEN Gr/Ja (Hayashikane) 1984; B/Con; 24,705 grt/40,045 dwt; 190.00 × 11.26 m *(623.36 × 37.27 ft)*; M (Sulzer); 14 kts; 948 TEU
Possible sister: **MARO L** (Gr)

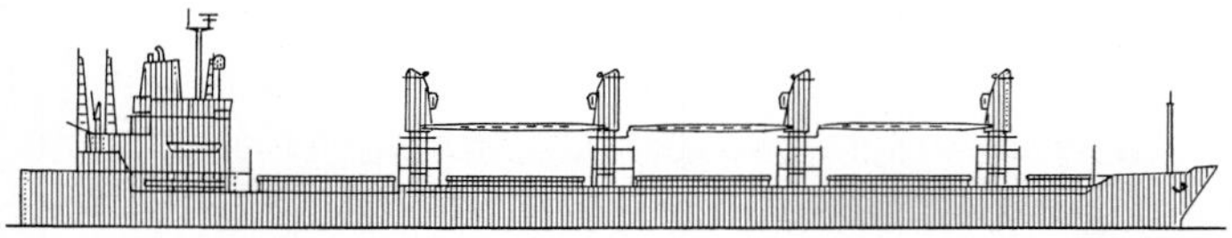

212 *MC^{4}M^{3}FMCM H13*
ALASKA Mr/Ja (Mitsui) 1986; B; 16,608 grt/27,174 dwt; 168.30 × 9.77 m *(552.17 × 32.05 ft)*; M (B&W); 14.50 kts; ex-*Sanko Prosperity*; Of the after masts, the foreward one is on the port side and the after on the starboard
Sisters: **SEA ROSE** (Mr) ex-*Sanko Daring*; **SANKO PEACE** (Pa); **BROTHERS** (Cy) ex-*Sanko Pinnacle*; **NORDIC BULKER** (Pa) ex-*Sanko Defiant*; **BALTIC BULKER** (Pa) ex-*Sanko Probity*

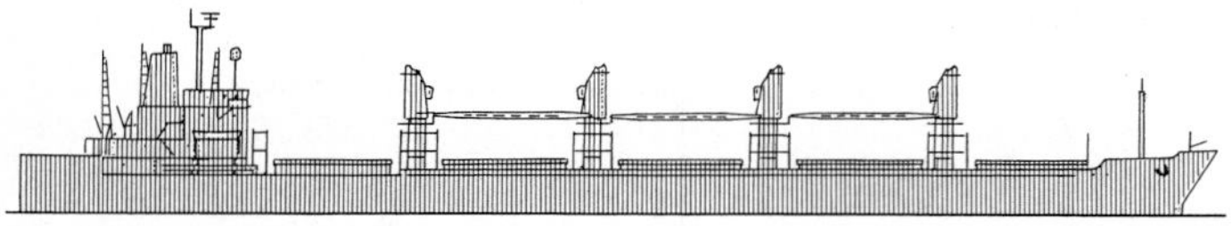

213 *MC^{4}M^{3}FMCM H13*
HANSA MERCHANT Li/Ja (Mitsui) 1987; B; 24,646 grt/41,574 dwt; 182.81 × 11.02 m *(599.77 × 36.15 ft)*; M (B&W); 14 kts; ex-*Sanko Jupiter*
Sisters: **NAND SWASTI** (In) ex-*Sanko Altair*; **SERIFE** (Tu) ex-*Sanko Falcon*; **SPRING STORK** (Li) ex-*Sanko Stork*; **SPRING SWIFT** (Li) ex-*Sanko Swift*; **SPRING DRAKE** (Li) ex-*Sanko Drake*; **ANANGEL DIGNITY** (Gr) ex-*Sanko Antares*; **ANANGEL SUCCESS** (Gr) ex-*Sanko Deneb*; **MASSY PHOENIX** (Pi) ex-*Sanko Phoenix*; Possible sisters: **FUJI ANGEL** (Va); **ALAM SAYANG** (My) ex-*Yuko Maru*; **BULK GALAXY** (Pa); **SURYA KRIPA** (In) ex-*Bulk Garland*; **ATALANTI** (Gr) ex-*Bulk Garnet*; **TINITA** (Pa) ex-*Bulk Genie*; Similar (some have full length focsle): **STAR CENTAURUS** (Gr) ex-*Jovian Laurel* (may have five cranes); **MATRU KRIPA** (In) ex-*Pacific Hawk*; **NAND SHWETA** (In) ex-*Kepbreeze*; **PANDIAS** (Li) ex-*Kepbay*; **MARIA** (NIS) ex-*Kepbrave*; **STAR ANTARES** (Gr) ex-*Cape Breton*; **WESTERN MARINER** (Pi) ex-*Cape Wrath*; **BERGEN MALAYA** (Pi) ex-*Baron Dunmore*; **AGHIA SOPHIA** (Gr)

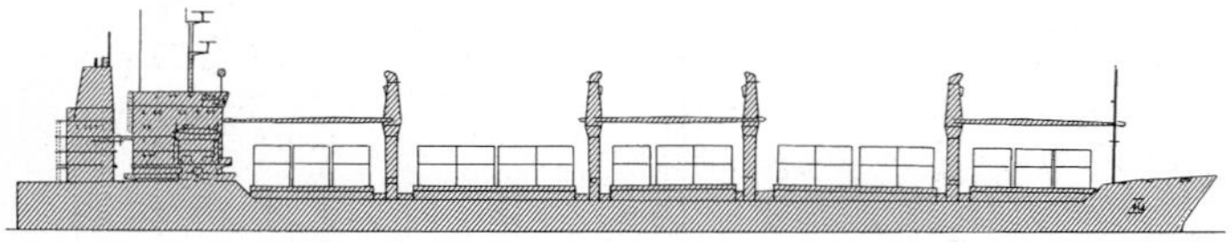

214 *MC^{4}MM-F H13*
DUNAJ Cz/Pd (Szczecinska) 1989; B/Con; 21,399 grt/33,230 dwt; 195.11 × 10.69 m *(640.12 × 35.07 ft)*; M (Sulzer); 14.52 kts; 575 TEU; 'B545' type
Sister: **LABE** (Cz)

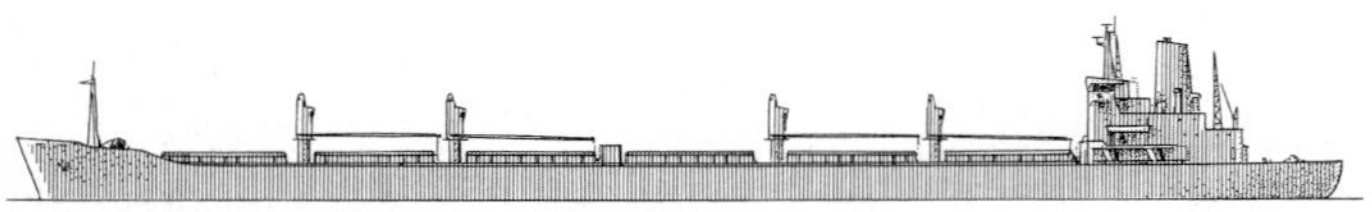

215 *MC^{4}MNFMC H1*
ALKYONIS Pa/Ja (Koyo) 1976; B; 30,962 grt/61,869 dwt; 222.29 × 12.32 m *(731.59 × 40.42 ft)*; M (B&W); 14.5 kts; ex-*Pacific Master*
Possible sister: **PANAMAX PEARL** (—) ex-*New Apollo*

216 *MC^{4}MNFN H1*
PANDESIA Gr/Ja (Koyo) 1982; B; 34,395 grt/61,806 dwt; 223.15 × 12.45 m *(732 × 40.85 ft)*; M (B&W); 14.5 kts; ex-*Limelock*
Possible sister: **JIAO ZHOU HAI** (RC) ex-*Koyo Venture*

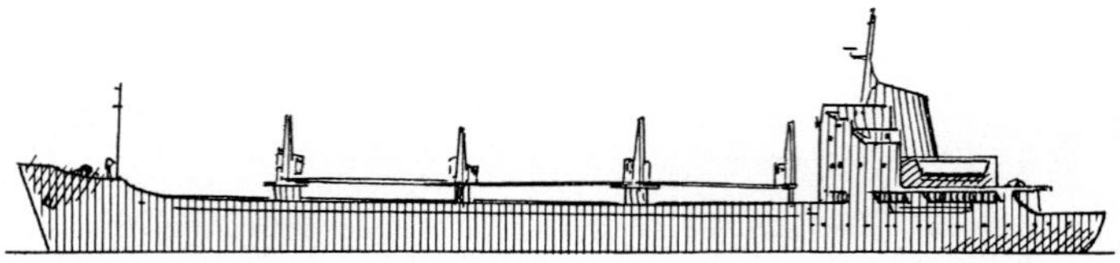

217 *MC^{4}M-F H1*
LING JIANG RC/Fi (Rauma-Repola) 1960; C; 1,994 grt/3,627 dwt; 96.91 × 5.81 m *(317.94 × 19.06 ft)*; M (MAN); 13 kts; ex-*Simpele*
Sister: **KAO JIANG** (RC) (may be spelt **AO JIANG**) ex-*Kaipola*

218 *MC^{4}M-F H1*
MARINER 1 SV/FRG (Norderwerft) 1966; C; 2,751 grt/4,216 dwt; 95.97 × 5.16 m *(314.86 × 16.93 ft)*; M (KHD); 13.75 kts; ex-*Martha Russ*

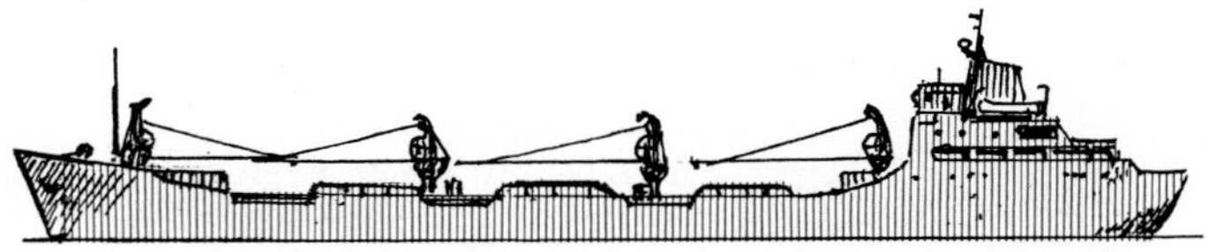

219 *MC^{4}M-F H13*
MABROUK Ho/Sw (Solvesborgs) 1966; C; 3,470 grt/5,697 dwt; 110.06 × 5.41 m *(361.09 × 17.75 ft)*; M (Gotaverken); 14.5 kts; ex-*Michael Salman*; Side door; Lengthened 1971

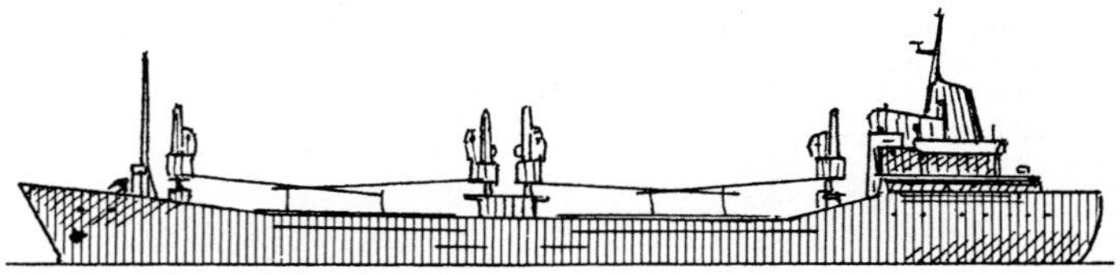

220 *MC^{4}M-F H13*
MARINE STAR Eg/Sp (Juliana) 1971; C; 2,116 grt/2,540 dwt; 87 × 4.87 m *(285.43 × 15.97 ft)*; M (Stork-Werkspoor); 13.5 kts; ex-*Benimusa*
Sisters: **ANNA S** (SV) ex-*Benimamet*; **FAISAL NIAGA** (Ia) ex-*Benisalem*; **ABDELRAHMAN** (Eg) ex-*Beniajan*; **DANAU LIMBOTO** (Ia) ex-*Benifaraig*; Similar (shorter—80.75 m (265 ft)): **UGARIT** (Sy) ex-*Benimar*; **SOFALA** (Pa) ex-*Benisa*; **SANG THAI NEPTUNE** (Th) ex-*Beniali*

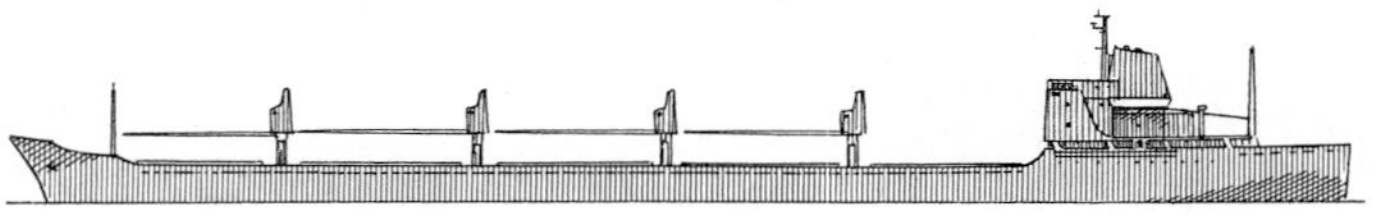

221 *MC^{4}M-FN H13*
BLUEBELL SUSANNAH Li/Ja (Hakodate) 1973; B; 16,378 grt/27,329 dwt; 177.96 × 10.69 m *(583.86 × 35.07 ft)*; M (Sulzer); 15 kts; ex-*Star Capella*
Sisters: **AYNUR KALKAVAN** (Tu) ex-*Star Kerry*; **ODYSSEAS I** (Cy) ex-*Star Nestor*; Possible sisters: **LEROS SPIRIT** (Cy) ex-*Star Castor*; **RATNA VANDANA** (In) ex-*Star Lily*; **VIENNA SKY** (SV) ex-*Star Kestrel*

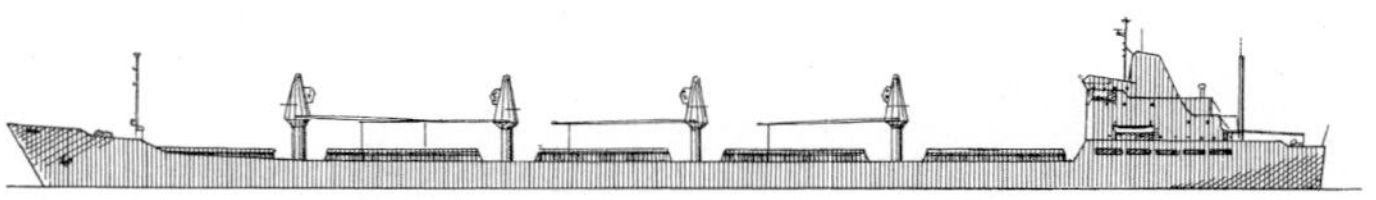

222 *MC^{4}M-FN H13*
CORDIALITY Pa/Sp (AESA 1979; B; 20,284 grt/35,110 dwt; 197.6 × 11.11 m *(648.3 × 36.45 ft)*; M (Sulzer); 15 kts; ex-*Angela Pando*
Sisters: **IRAN MOTAHARAI** (Ir) ex-*Marcoplata*; **VAN K** (Tu) ex-*Sokorri*; **MARIANNA** (Li) ex-*Sokorri*; Probable sisters: **BLED** (SV); **BOHINJ** (At); **HUA PENG** (RC) ex-*Free Spirit*; **TAMASOS** (Cy) ex-*Ocean King*; **STEFANIA** (SV) ex-*Wayfarer*; **EPTALOFOS** (Ma) ex-*Kin Ip*; **CYCLADES** (Ma) ex-*Kin Shing*; **AGIA SOFIA** (Ma) ex-*King Wang*; **KALMA** (Gr) ex-*Macaye*; **NEDI** (Gr) ex-*Marcoalbelay*; Similar: **IRAN AKHAVAN** (Ir) ex-*Philippine Success*; **IRAN AMANAT** (Ir) ex-*Manila Pride*; **IRAN SARBAZ** (Ir); **ADITYA PRABHA** (In) ex-*Kin Wai*; **AKER** (Tu) ex-*Therean Skipper*; Similar (differently shaped funnel, five-deck superstructure, small cranes aft and so on): **LEADER** (Gr) ex-*Ocean Wind*

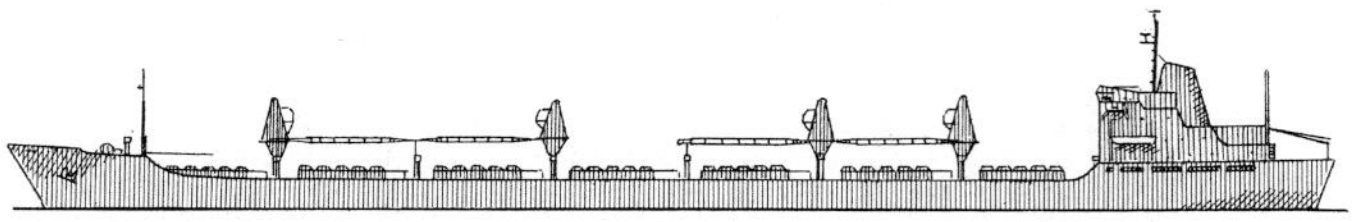

223 *MC^{4}M-FN H13*
GEORGIOS D Gr/Sp (AESA) 1977; B; 16,765 grt/30,242 dwt; 181.11 × 10.65 m *(594.19 × 34.94 ft)*; M (Sulzer); 15 kts; ex-*Kara*
Sisters: **BARBARA H** (Cy) ex-*Kelo*; **PRAXITELIS** (Gr) ex-*Pamela*; **POLYDEFKIS** (Gr) ex-*Peter*; **KAMARI I** (Cy) ex-*Puhos*; Probable sister: **AROSA** (Cy) ex-*Castellblanch*

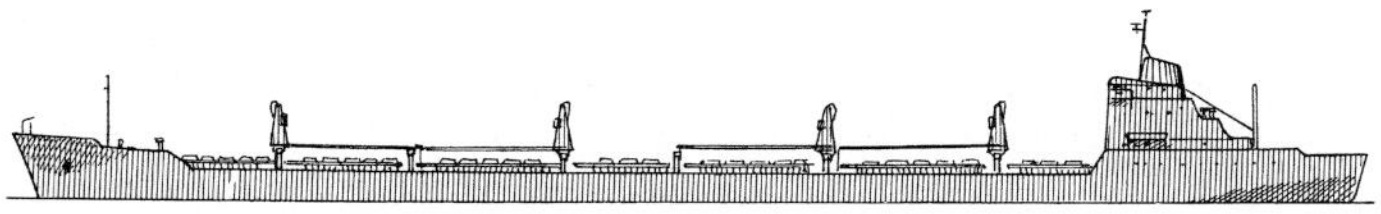

224 *MC^{4}M-FN H13*
JAG SHAKTI In/Sp (AESA) 1972; B; 15,678 grt/27,071 dwt; 182.84 × 10.55 m *(599.88 × 34.61 ft)*; M (Sulzer); 15.5 kts; ex-*Cunard Caravel*; 'Euskalduna 27' type
Sisters: **NORBEL BULK** (Li) ex-*Cunard Carrier*; **FANNIE ANNE** (Gr) ex-*Cunard Chieftain*; **MASTROGIORGIS B** (Cy) ex-*Cunard Calamanda*; **MERYEM ANA** (Tu) ex-*Cunard Carronade*; **LEADER A** (Ma) ex-*Swedish Wasa*; **HASAN B** (Tu) ex-*Spanish Wasa*; Similar; **CORINTHIAN TRADER** (Gr) ex-*Cobetas*; **CRETAN TRADER** (Gr) ex-*Deusto*; **LASERBEAM** (Ma) ex-*Laurentine*; **CAPRICORN I** (Cy) ex-*Penmen*

225 *MC^{4}M-FN H13*
TUPI PONTA NEGRA Bz/Bz (CCN) 1980; B; 16,490 grt/26,223 dwt; 173.18 × 9.72 m *(568 × 31.89 ft)*; M (Man); 15 kts; ex-*Regina Ferraz*
Sisters: **TUPI ILHA BELA** (Bz) ex-*Graziella Ferraz*; **ALCYON** (Bz); **ALMARIS** (Bz); **MERCANTIL ARARUAMA** (Bz) ex-*Taquy*; **NORSUL SOBRAL** (Bz) ex-*Felicidade Ferraz*; **MANSURNAVE II** (Bz) ex-*Antonio Ferraz*; Probable sisters: **ALNAVE** (Bz); **SERAM** (Pa) ex-*Alison*; Similar (smaller funnel separated from radar mast): **ATLANTIS TWO** (Cy) ex-*Cape Arnhem;* **ATLAS** (Cy) ex-*Cape Finisterre*; **EPTA** (Cy) ex-*Cape Trafalgar*; **MARITIME BANGKOK** (Pa) ex-*Baron Kinnaird*; Probably similar: **SEA BREAKER** (Pa) ex-*Criciuma*

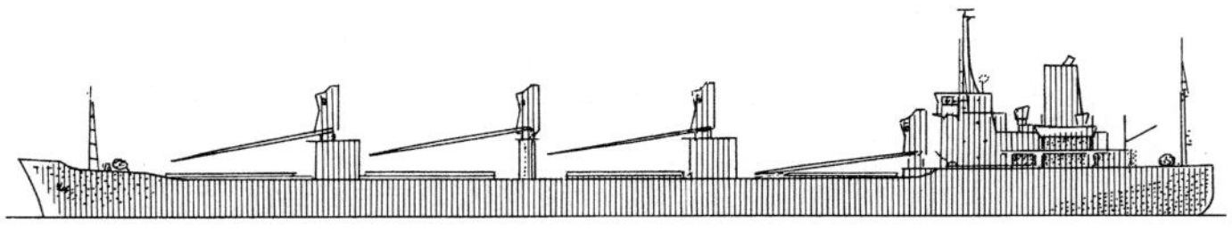

226 *MC^{4}M-NFM H13*
WU LIN RC/Ja (Kanasashi) 1970; B; 10,900 grt/18,534 dwt; 155.1 × 9.19 m *(508.86 × 30.15 ft)*; M (B&W); 14.75 kts; ex-*Kinko Maru*
Probable sisters: **EUROFREEDOM** (Cy) ex-*Kaneshizu Maru*; **SEABREEZE ONE** (Ma) ex-*Kanekiyo Maru*

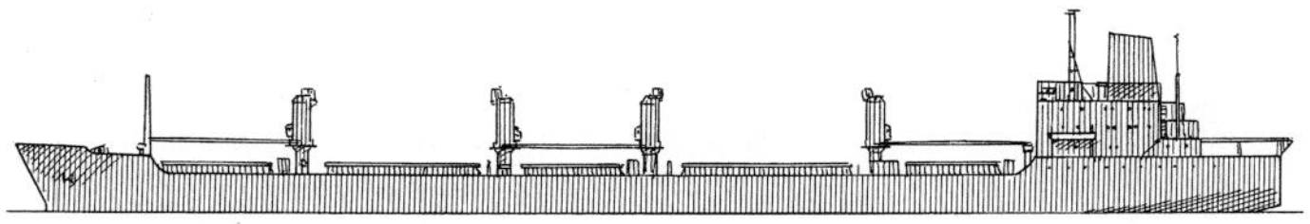

227 *MC^{4}NFN H13*
KOTA INTAN Sg/FRG (A G 'Weser') 1976; C/Con; 16,332 grt/24,580 dwt; 171.41 × 10.45 m *(562.37 × 34.28 ft)*; M (Sulzer); 13.5 kts; ex-*Pagnol*; 'Key 26' type
Sister: **KOTA INDAH** (Sg) ex-*Raimu*

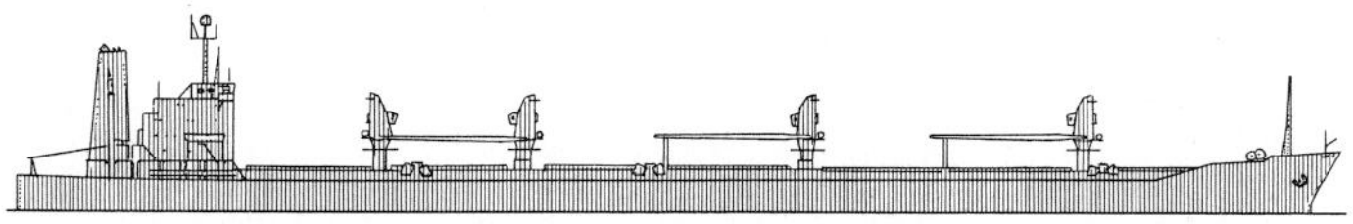

228 *MC^{4}NHF-N H1*
ALPHEOS Li/Ja (Hitachi) 1984; B; 35,119 grt/62,635 dwt; 224.52 × 12.46 m *(736.61 × 40.88 ft)*; M (Sulzer); 16.75 kts; ex-*Jackie*
Sister: **TRIDENT FORTUNE** (Gr) ex-*Captain Stamatis*; Probable sisters: **ARGOLIS** (Li) ex-*Maroula*; **JAG MANEK** (In) ex-*Rayna*

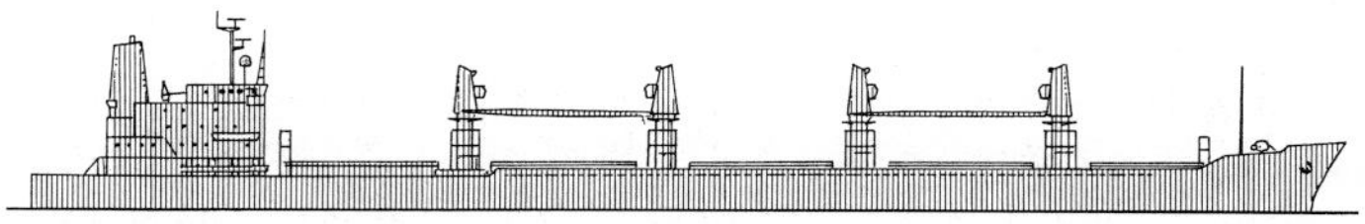

229 *MC^{4}NMCF H1*
CHINA MOUNTAIN HK/Ja (Hitachi) 1984; B; 22,564 grt/37,740 dwt; 185.00 × 10.91 m *(606.96 × 35.79 ft)*; M (B&W); 14 kts; ex-*Sanko Iris*
Probable sisters: **PARITA** (Ma) ex-*Sanko Helianthus*; **DARYA LAKSHMI** (Li) ex-*Sanko Helenium*; **TELINA** (Pa) ex-*Sanko Amaryllis*; **NEO HIBISCUS** (Pa) ex-*Sanko Hibiscus*; **VINCA** (Li) ex-*Sanko Honeysuckle*

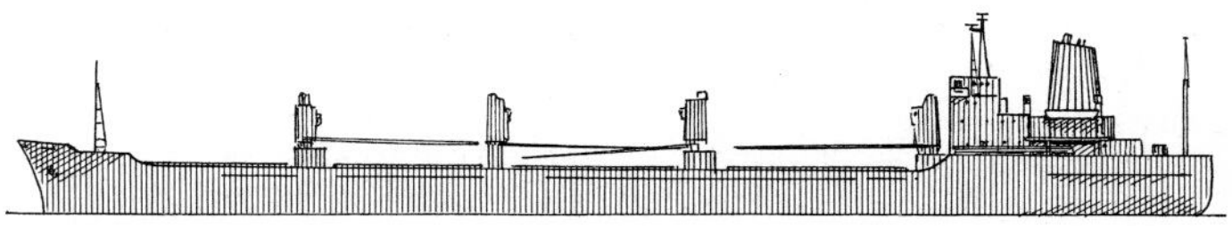

230 *MC^{4}NMFM H13*
LINDEN Cy/Ja (Namura) 1972; B; 12,102 grt/19,717 dwt; 150.12 × 9.73 m *(492.52 × 31.92 ft)*; M (Sulzer); 14.5 kts; ex-*Amazon Maru*

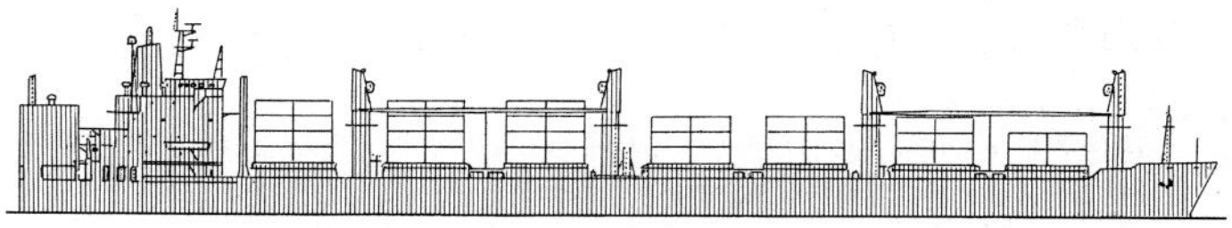

231 *MC^{4}NMFM^2 H1*
WESTERN GALLANTRY Ge/Ja (Tsuneishi) 1985; OBO; 25,865 grt/ 43,467 dwt; 185.83 × 11.30 m *(609.68 × 37.07 ft)*; M (B&W); — kts; ex-*Pacific Gallantry*; Converted from 'TESS 40' type bulk carrier 1987 (Bremer V)
Sisters: **WESTERN GREETING** (Ge) ex-*Pacific Greeting*; **WESTERN GUARDIAN** (Ge) ex-*Pacific Guardian*

232 *MC^{4}NMFM^2 H13*
AIN TEMOUCHENT Ag/Ja (Tsuneishi) 1982; B; 19,084 grt/32,131 dwt; 179 × 11.53 m *(587 × 37.83 ft)*; M (B&W); 14.5 kts; ex-*Baron Minto*
Sister: **MARINE GRACE** (Pa) ex-*Felicia*

233 *MC^{4}NMFN H1*
SOTIRAS Gr/Ja (Hitachi) 1982; B/V; 36,704 grt/58,055 dwt; 210.01 × 12.42 m *(689 × 40.75 ft)*; M (B&W); 14 kts; Side doors (port and starboard)
Sister: **KARDAMYLA** (Gr) ex-*Co-Op Express II*

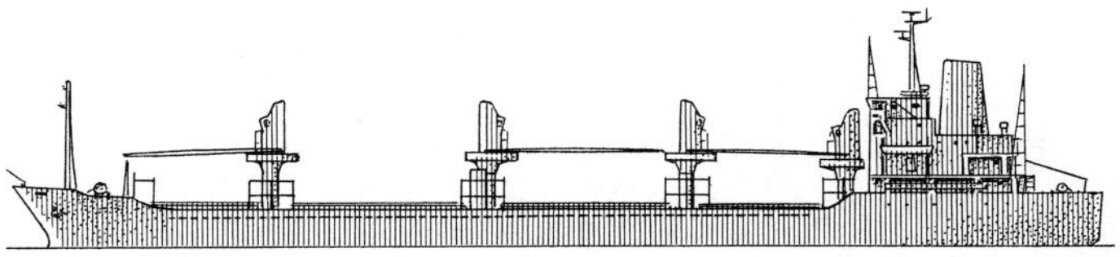

234 *MC^{4}NMFN H13*
ANDRE DELMAS Bs/Ja (Usuki) 1976; B; 14,555 grt/21,839 dwt; 156.01 × 10.35 m *(511.84 × 33.96 ft)*; M (Sulzer); 15.5 kts
Probable sister (may have kingposts): **LUCIEN DELMAS** (Bs)

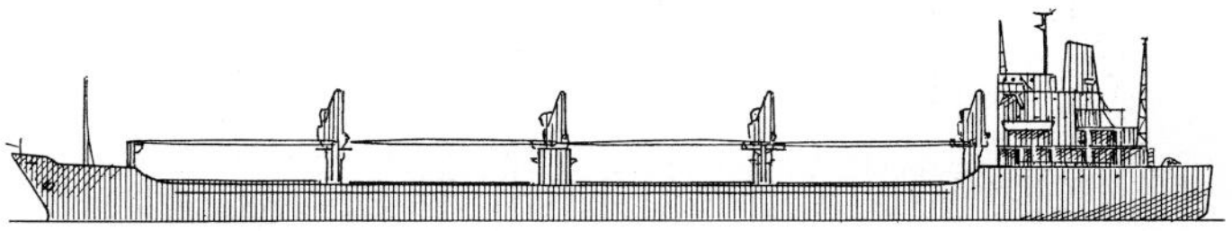

235 *MC^{4}NMFN H13*
CAPTAINYANNIS L Ma/Ja (Usuki) 1977; B; 14,500 grt/24,350 dwt; 160.03 × 9.92 m *(525.03 × 32.55 ft)*; M (Pielstick); 14.5 kts; ex-*Seiyei Maru*

236 *MC^{4}NMFN H13*
DUDEN Tu/Ja (Naikai) 1981; B; 16,211 grt/26,975 dwt; 173.01 × 10.63 m *(567.62 × 34.88 ft)*; M (B&W); 15 kts; ex-*Armenistis*
Probable sister: **ALIKRATOR** (Gr)

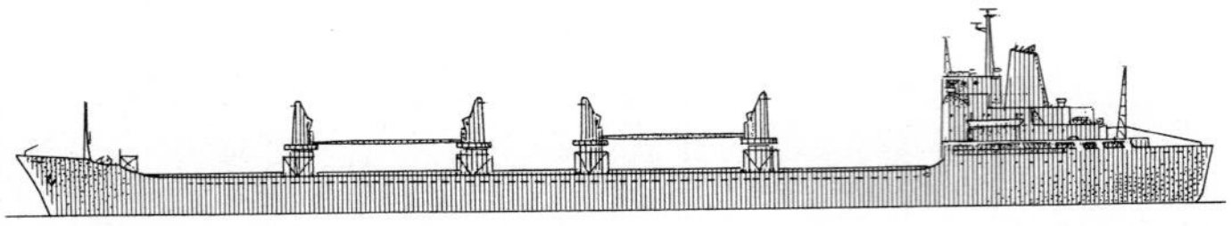

237 *MC^{4}NMFN H13*
FLECHA Cy/Ja (Usuki) 1974; B; 18,960 grt/30,910 dwt; 178.39 × 10.65 m *(585.27 × 34.94 ft)*; M (Sulzer); 15.5 kts; ex-*Cedrela*

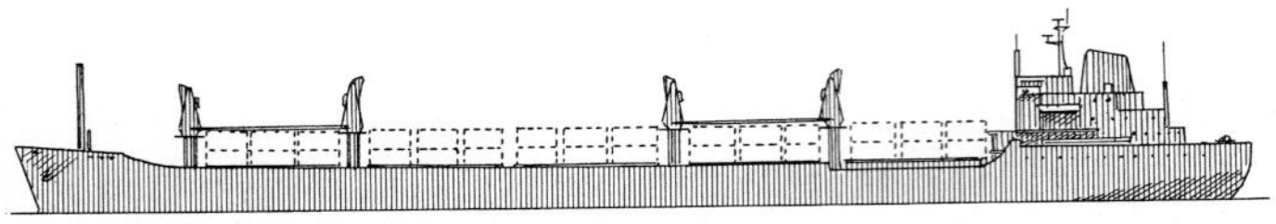

238 *MC^{4}NMFN H13*
NIAXO V Ar/Br (Upper Clyde) 1970; C/Con; 17,626 grt/26,368 dwt; 175.27 × 9.88 m *(575.03 × 32.41 ft)*; M (Sulzer); 15.25 kts; ex-*Kyoto Forest*; Converted from bulk carrier and shortened 1975

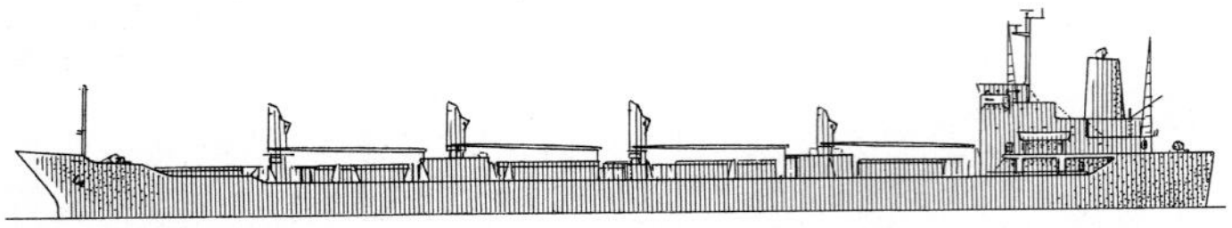

239 *MC^{4}NMFN H13*
SEA CONCERT Cy/Ja (Kurushima) 1976; B; 18,114 grt/35,571 dwt; 178.87 × 11.12 m *(586.84 × 36.48 ft)*; M (MAN); 15.4 kts; ex-*Toshu Maru*

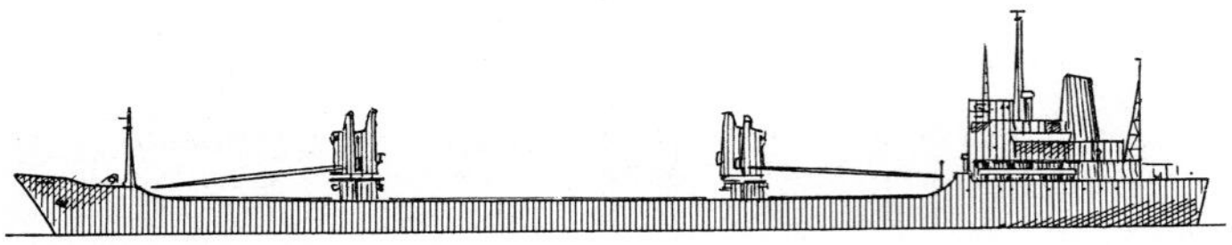

240 *MC^{4}NMFN H13*
SEA KING Ho/Ja (Shikoku) 1972; B; 7,248 grt/12,126 dwt; 130 × 8.3 m *(426.51 × 27.23 ft)*; M (Sulzer); 14 kts; ex-*Siam Venture*

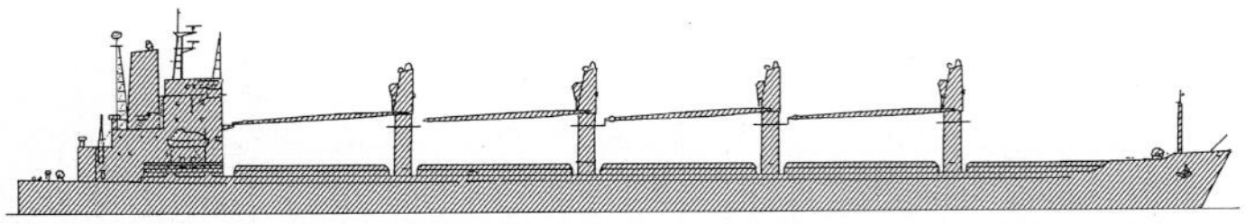

241 *MC^{4}NMFNC H1*
AVENTICUM Sd/Ja (Tsuneishi) 1989; B/Con; 25,891 grt/43,665 dwt; 185.84 × 11.32 m *(609.71 × 37.14 ft)*; M (B&W); 14 kts; ex-*World River*; 'TESS 40' type; 1,082 TEU
Sisters (some may be like drawing number 7/204): **LUCKY FORTUNE** (Li) ex-*Universal River*; **SCHWYZ** (Sd) ex-*Orient River*; Possible sisters (some may be like drawing number 7/204): **EDIP KARAHSAN** (Tu) ex-*Soarer Yoga*; **LIBRE** (Pa) ex-*Casuarina*; **YOU XUAN** (Va); **GREAT LAKE** (HK); **BIG GLORY** (Pa) ex-*Antsumo*; **ORIENT RIVER II** (Pa); **LEPTA VENUS** (Pa); **GRAND FESTIVAL** (Pa); **SOARER ZEN** (Pa); **SOARER ADONIS** (Pi); Possible sisters (builder—Hashihama): **SINCERE OCEANUS** (Pa) ex-*Ocean Bloom*; **SINCERE APOLLO** (Pa) ex-*Ocean Commander*; **KASTILYO** (Pi): ex-*Gresik*

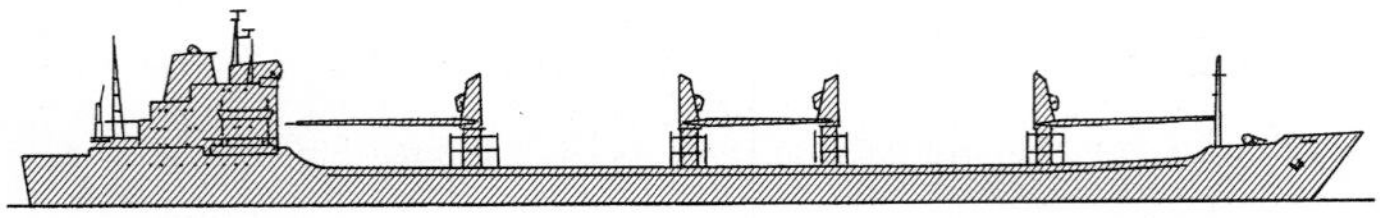

242 *MC^{4}NMFND H13*
MAKEEVKA Uk/RC (Jiangnan) 1982; B; 17,989 grt/28,136 dwt; 196.45 × 10.24 m *(644.52 × 33.60)*; M (B&W); 14.50 kts; ex-*World Shanghai*; May be spelt **MAKEYEVKA**
Sisters: **DOBRUSH** (Uk) ex-*World Goodwill*; **SAMRAT RUCAKA** (In) ex-*Baronia*

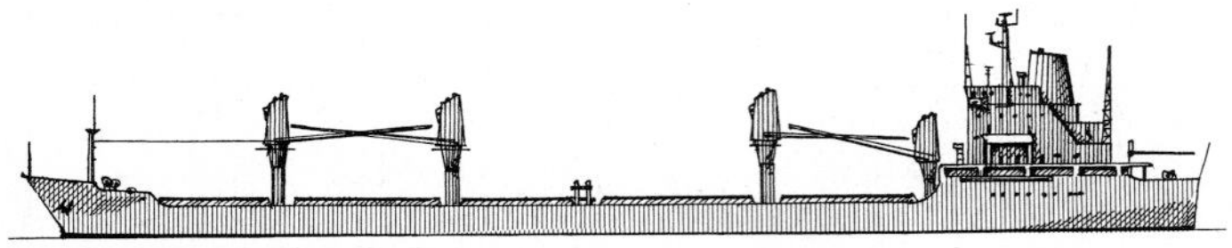

243 *MC^{4}NMFND H13*
NAVA AVRA Cy/Ja (Mitsubishi HI) 1977; B; 18,328 grt/29,554 dwt; 170.01 × 10.21 m *(557.77 × 33.5 ft)*; M (Sulzer); 15.5 kts; ex-*Wellpark*
Sisters: **XUE FENG LING** (RC) ex-*Clarkspey*; **NAVA MARIA** (Cy) ex-*Trongate*

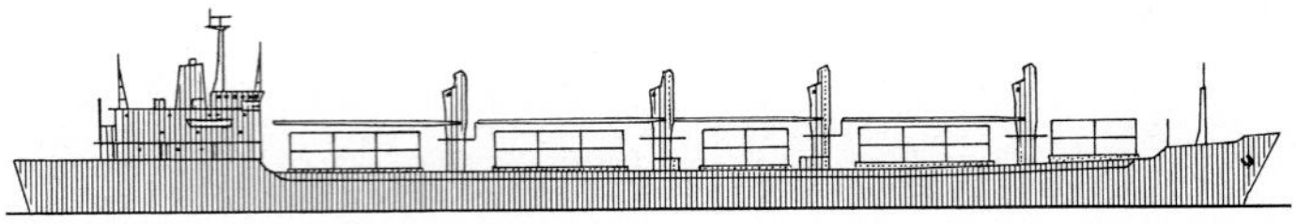

244 *MC^{4}NMFN^2 H13*
TRIDENT MARINER Gr/Ja (Mitsubishi HI) 1984; B/Con; 17,210 grt/ 29,617 dwt; 179.91 × 10.50 m *(590.26 × 34.45 ft)*; M (Sulzer); 16.50 kts; 432 TEU
Probable sister: **IKAN SEPAT** (Sg) ex-*Trident Venture*

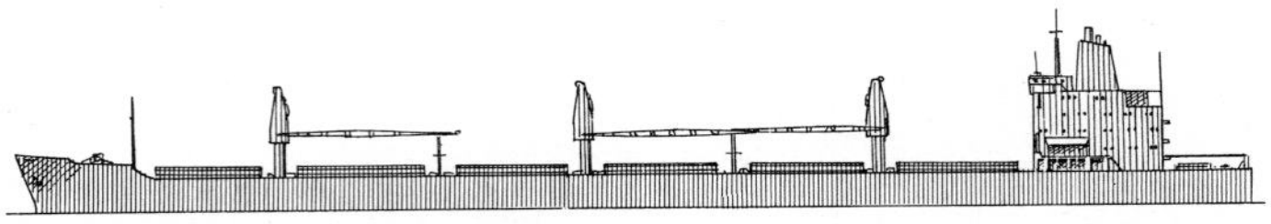

245 *MC^{3}HF H1*
VASILIY KOVAL Uk/De (Odense) 1977; B; 26,712 grt/44,750 dwt; 182.99 × 11 m *(600.4 × 36.1 ft)*; M (Sulzer); 15 kts; ex-*Torm Herdis*
Sisters: **PROFESSOR KOSTIUKOV** (Uk) ex-*Torm Helvig*; **ALEKSANDR SAVELYEV** (Uk) ex-*Torm Hilde*; **INZHENER PARKHONYUK** (Uk) ex-*Torm Helene*

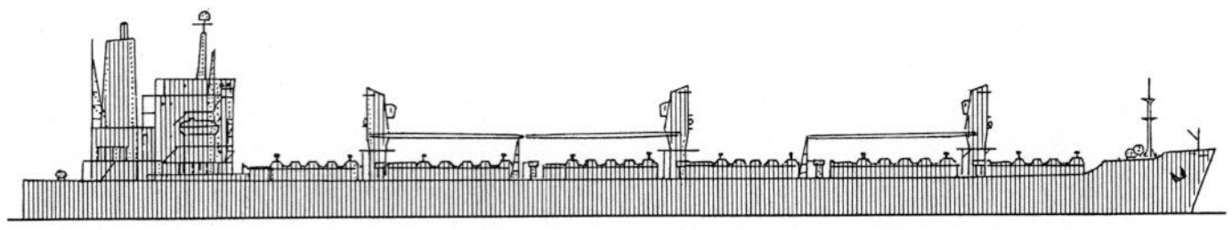

246 *MC^{3}HFN* H1
FEYZA Tu/Ja (Namura) 1984; B; 27,798 grt/47,882 dwt; 189.08 × 12.00 m *(620.34 × 39.37 ft)*; M (Sulzer); 14.75 kts; ex-*Lindnes*
Sisters: **BIBI M** (Tu) ex-*Lockness*; **PILION** (Ma) ex-*Langnes*

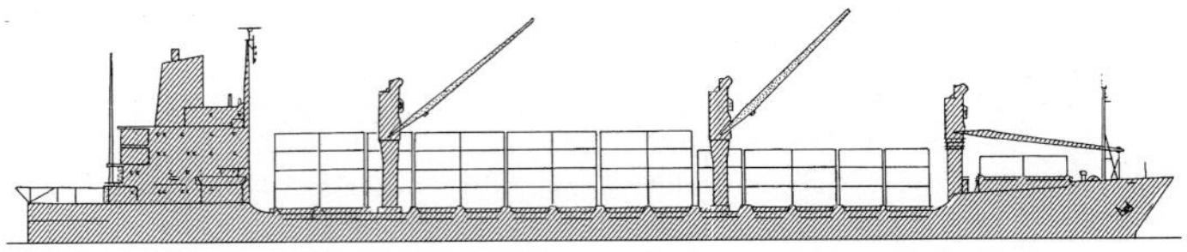

247 *MC^{3}HFN H13*
SAN DIEGO Cy/FRG (A G 'Weser') 1980; C Con; 10,871 grt/14,198 dwt; 159.40 × 8.21 m *(522.97 × 26.94 ft)*; M (MaK); 17.75 kts; ex-*Holstencruiser*; 'Key 12' type; 934 TEU; Lengthened 1989
Similar: **SAVANNAH** (Ge)

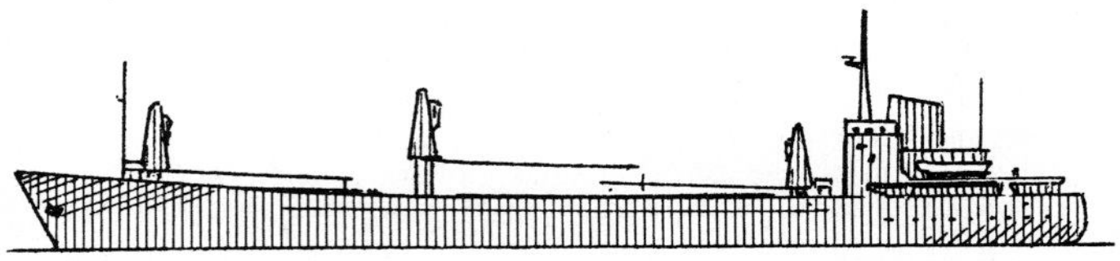

248 *MC^{3}MF H*
PERIDOT Pa/Sw (Falkenbergs) 1964; C; 1,325 grt/2,033 dwt; 83.55 × 3.67 m *(274.11 × 12.04 ft)*; M (MWM); 12 kts; ex-*Aspen*

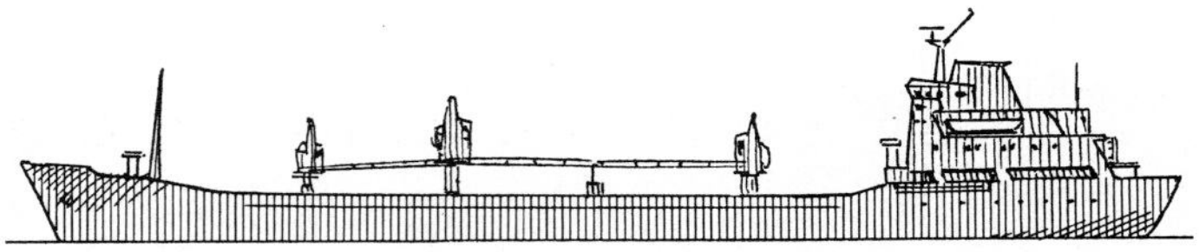

249 *MC^{3}MF H1*
ARVAGH SV/Fi (Crichton-Vulcan); C; 3,175 grt/4,490 dwt; 105.29 × 6.54 m *(345.44 × 21.46 ft)*; M (Sulzer); 14.5 kts; ex-*Fennia*; Lengthened 1970; Side doors

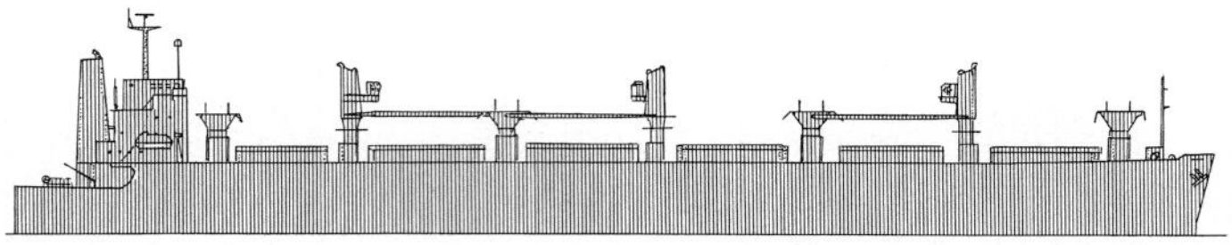

250 *MC^{3}MF H1*
DIXIE MONARCH Pa/Ja (Sanoyas Corp) 1991; BWC; 39,023 grt/44,679 dwt; 199.99 × 10.72 m *(656.14 × 35.17)*; M (Sulzer); 14.3 kts
Probable sister: **GRANDIS** (Pa)

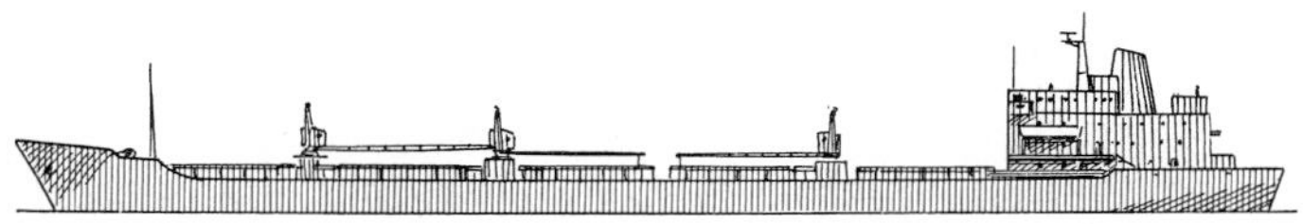

251 *MC^3MF H1*
EUROBULKER Cy/Sp (AESA) 1972; B; 7,934 grt/14,036 dwt; 145.01 × 8.36 m *(475.75 × 27.43 ft)*; M Sulzer; 16 kts; ex-*Kopalnia Grzybow*
Sister: **KOPALNIA MACHOW** (Pd)

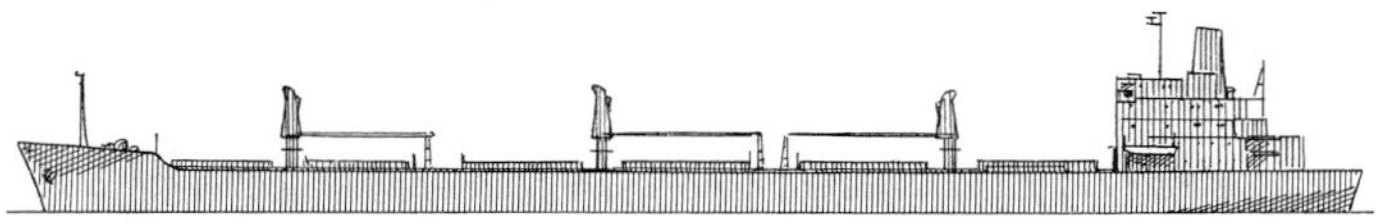

252 *MC^3MF H1*
EUROPEGASUS Cy/Ne (Verolme SH) 1972; B; 14,072 grt/26,615 dwt; 170.36 × 10.27 m *(558.92 × 33.69 ft)*; M (MAN); 15.5 kts; ex-*Pegasus*

253 *MC^3MF H1*
GOSPIC SV/Ja (IHI) 1977; B; 22,372 grt/37,836 dwt; 187.74 × 10.76 m *(616 × 35.30 ft)*; M (Sulzer); 14.5 kts; 'Future 32' type
Sisters: **MOLAT** (SV); **PAKRAC** (SV) ex-*Rudo*

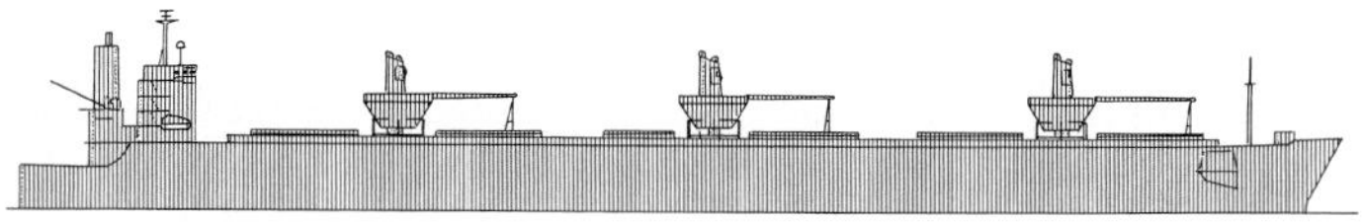

254 *MC^3MF H1*
PEARL VENUS Li/Ja (Mitsubishi HI) 1991; BWC; 44,802 grt/53,679 dwt; 227.00 × 10.83 m *(744.75 × 35.53)*; M (Mitsubishi); 13 kts

255 *MC^3MF H1*
PHA SHWE GYAW YWA Mr/De (Aarhus) 1964; C; 1,262 grt/1,575 dwt; 77.35 × 5.00 m *(253.77 × 16.40 ft)*; M (B&W); 13.5 kts; ex-*Bergenhus*

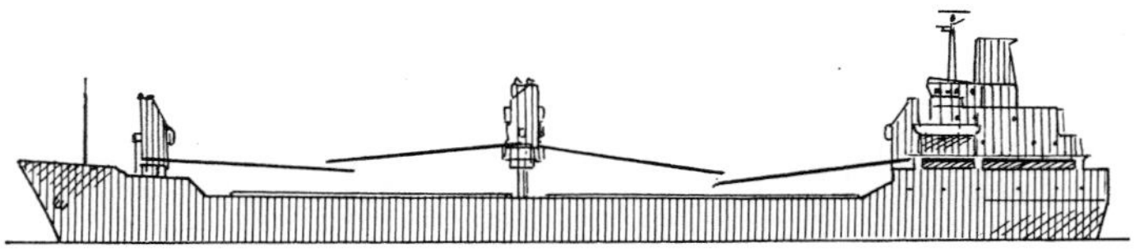

256 *MC^3MF H13*
JIA FA RC/No (Kleven) 1972; C; 4,036 grt/5,919 dwt; 106.61 × 7.08 m *(349.77 × 23.23 ft)*; M (Stork-Werkspoor); 14 kts; ex-*Finnmaster*

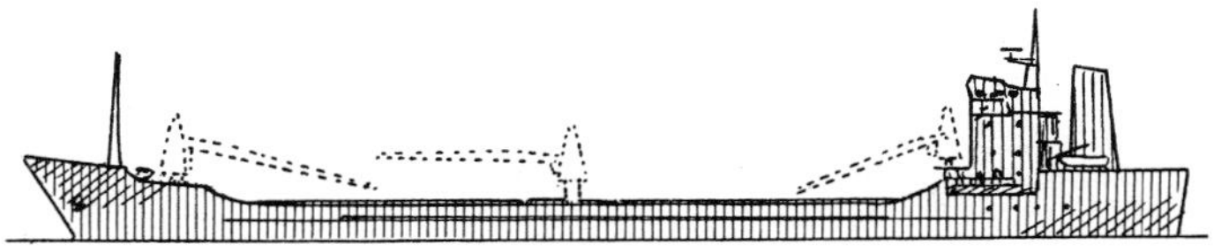

257 *MC^3MF H13*
LESZEK K Pd/Br (Appledore) 1977; C; 1,991 grt/3,256 dwt; 91.52 × 5.16 m *(300.26 × 16.93 ft)*; M (Mirrlees Blackstone); 12.5 kts; ex-*Leslie Gault*; Deck cranes may be removed
Sisters: **JERBA** (Tn) ex-*Cerinthus;* **GAUSS F** (Pd) ex-*Gallic Fjord*; **AO XIANG** (RC) ex-*Markinch*

258 *MC^3MF H13*
NORDON Sw/No (Lothe) 1977; C; 5,420 grt/7,884 dwt; 113.01 × 7.14 m *(370.77 × 23.43 ft)*; M (MaK); 14 kts; ex-*Pasila*

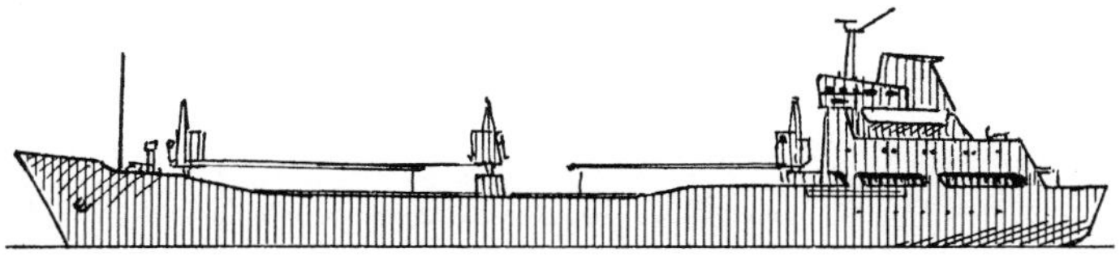

259 *MC^3MF H13*
ROSE III Pa/Fi (Wärtsilä) 1967; C; 2,747 grt/3,697 dwt; 91.55 × 6.52 m *(300.36 × 21.39 ft)*; M (Sulzer); 13.5 kts; ex-*Auriga*

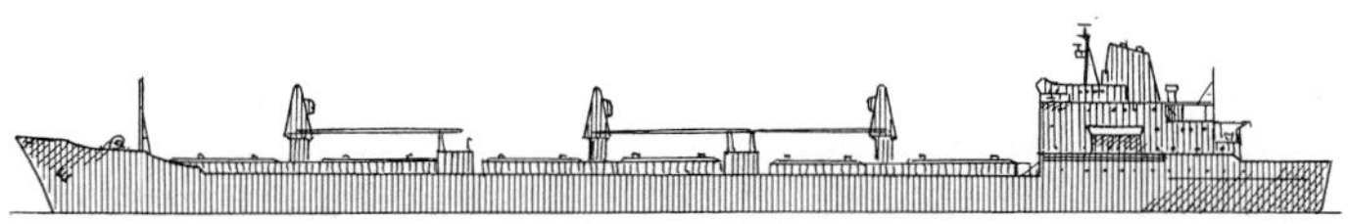

260 *MC^3MF H13*
SAABA SV/No (Horten) 1969; B; 12,087 grt/22,373 dwt; 159.82 × 9.78 m *(524.34 × 32.09 ft)*; M (Sulzer); 15 kts; ex-*Cape York*

261 *MC^3MF H13*
SOLTA Ma/Ys ('Split') 1984; B/Con; 18,259 grt/29,785 dwt; 189.59 × 10.82 m *(622.01 × 35.50 ft)*; M (MAN); 15.75 kts
Probable sisters: **MARIA SJ** (Li) ex-*Bihac*; **MLJET** (Ma)

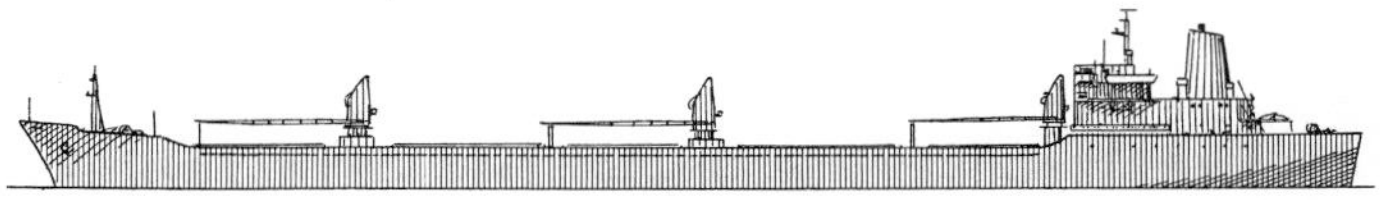

262 *MC^3MF H13*
STEPAN ARTEMENKO Uk/Ja (NKK) 1977; B; 15,949 grt/27,536 dwt; 178.21 × 10.92 m *(584.68 × 35.83 ft)*; M (Sulzer); 15.5 kts; ex-*Lavinia V*
Sisters: **KAPITAN MEDVEDEV** (Uk) ex-*Felicia V*; **MEKHANIK DREN** (Uk) ex-*Patricia V*

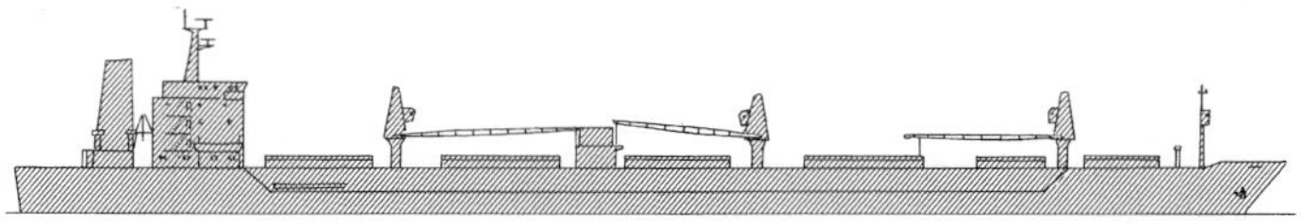

263 *MC^3MF H13*
TIGER CAPE Cy/Sp (AESA) 1981; B/Cem; 27,638 grt/43,576 dwt; 189.26 × 11.91 m *(620.93 × 39.07 ft)*; M (B&W); — kts; ex-*Castillo de Javier*
Sister: **HAI HUANG** (RC) ex-*Castillo de Monterrey*

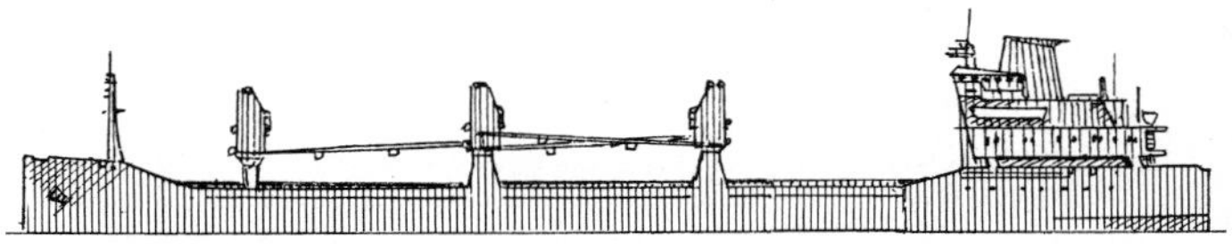

264 *MC^3MF H13*
WHITE STONE Bs/Fi (Hollming) 1970; C; 5,438 grt/7,869 dwt; 144.31 × 8.08 m *(473.4 × 28.47 ft)*; M (B&W); 15 kts; ex-*Maria Gorthon*; Lengthened 1975
Sisters: **VERA** (SV) ex-*Ada Gorthon*; **CECILIA DESGAGNES** (Ca) ex-*Carl Gorthon*; **BLUE STONE** (Bs) ex-*Ivan Gorthon*

265 *MC^3MF H13*
WIGRY MI/Br (Govan) 1979; B; 11,676 grt/16,653 dwt; 158.53 × 8.38 m *(520 × 27.49 ft)*; M (B&W); 15 kts; ex-*Kopalnia Jastrzebie*
Sisters: **ROS** (MI) ex-*Kopalnia Myslowice*; **MAMRY** (MI) ex-*Kopalnia Siemianowice*; **TALTY** (MI) ex-*Kopalnia Szombierki*

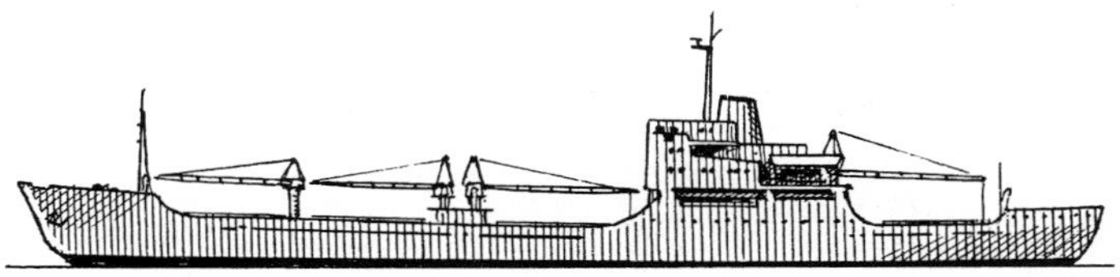

266 *MC^3MFC H123*
PERM Ru/USSR (Vyborg) 1969; C; 4,562 grt/6,540 dwt; 122 × 7.2 m *(400 × 23.5 ft)*; M (B&W); 14.5 kts
Sisters: **PALANGA** (Ru); **PARAMUSHIR** (Ru); **PAROMAY** (Ru); **PARGOLOVO** (Ru); **PAVLOVO** (Ru); **PECHENGA** (Ru); **PERTOMINSK** (Ru); **PETROKREPOST** (Ru); **PETROVSKIY** (Ru); **PETROZAVODSK** (Ru); **PLESETSK** (Ru); **POMORYE** (Ru); **PONOY** (Ru); **MARGARET** (—) ex-*Prokopyevsk*; **PRZHEVALSK** (Ru); **PULKOVO** (Ru); **PUSHLAKHTA** (Ru); **PUSTOZERSK** (Ru); **UNIARCH** (Ma) ex-*Pamir*

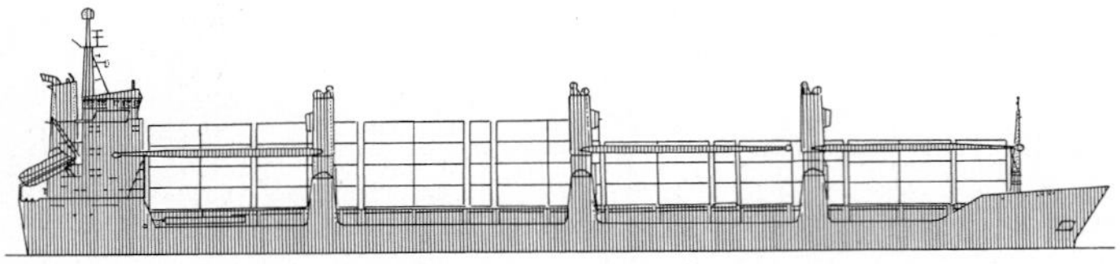

267 MC^3MFL *H13*
ADMIRALENGRACHT Ne/Ne (Frisian) 1990; C/Con; 7,949 grt/12,000 dwt; 129.80 × 8.60 m *(425.85 × 28.22 ft)*; M (Wärtsilä); — kts; 679 TEU; Cranes are on starboard side
Sisters: **ARTISGRACHT** (Ne); **ALEXANDERGRACHT** (Ne); **ANKERGRACHT** (Ne); **APOLLOGRACHT** (Ne); **ARCHANGELGRACHT** (Ne); **ATLASGRACHT** (Ne); Sisters (builder—Giessen-De Noord): **ANJELIERSGRACHT** (Ne); **AMSTELGRACHT** (Ne); **ACHTERGRACHT** (Ne)

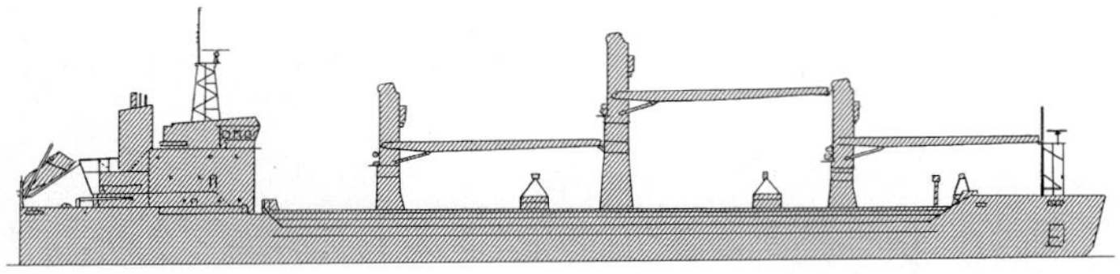

268 MC^3MFL *H13*
HESPERIA Fi/Fi (Rauma OS) 1991; B; 10,374 grt/13,565 dwt; 135.29 × 8.19 m *(443.86 × 26.87)*; M (B&W); 14 kts; Cranes and lifeboat on port side

269 MC^3MFM
ALEKSANDR POKALCHUK UK/Ru (Navashinskiy) 1968; C (sea/river); 3,629 grt/4,150 dwt; 123.53 × 4.5 m *(405.28 × 14.76 ft)*; TSM (Russkiy); 11.75 kts
Sisters (Some may have cranes removed or reduced to one): **VEGA II** (Pa) ex-*Gorkovskaya Komsomoliya*; **NIKOLAY SHCHETININ** (Ru) ex-*Buor-Khaya*; **PETR GUTCHENKO** (Uk); **CIRCEO** (It) ex-*Shura Burlachenko*; **GORNYAK** (Ru); **KELME** (Uk); **MUOSTAKH** (—); **SERGEY BURYACHEK** (Uk)

270 MC^3MFM *H13*
MARIGOULA K Cy/De (B&W) 1974; B; 30,616 grt/41,602 dwt; 221.75 × 12.09 m *(727.53 × 39.67 ft)*; M (B&W); 17.5 kts; ex-*Rodin*; Cranes on starboard side but may now be removed

See photo number 7/507

271 MC^3MFM *H13*
NEGO BREEZE Pi/Ja (Shin Yamamoto) 1983; B; 12,905 grt/21,340 dwt; 152.66 × 9.71 m *(500.85 × 31.86 ft)*; M (B&W); 13.5 kts; ex-*Ocean Breeze*
Sister: **GOLDEN LEAF** (Pa) ex-*Green Wood*; Possible sisters: **EVELYN** (Cy) ex-*Oriental Angel*; **PLOVER** (Pa) ex-*Cosmos*; **SAMSUN ATRAXIA** (Ko) ex-*Arishima Maru*; **ASEAN VICTORY** (Pa) ex-*Seitaku Maru*; **SHINSHIMA** (Li) ex-*Shinshima Maru*; **NEPTUNE JACINTH** (Sg) ex-*Green Master*; **KAKUSHIMA** (Li) ex-*Kakushima Maru*; **RUBY C** (RC) ex-*Olympic Sun*; **PRINCESS CASTLE** (Pa); **ROYAL VENTURE** (Pa) ex-*White Coral*; Similar (builder Imabari—taller funnel one deck lower): **ARCTIC TRADER** (Pa); **MUKDA NAREE** (Th) ex-*Ocean Trader;* **ORIENTAL HONEY** (Pa) ex-*Oriental Hope*; **SINCERE SPLENDOR** (Pi) ex-*Prosperidad*; **SOUTHGATE** (Li) ex-*Oriental Swan*; **BLUE COSMO** (Mr); **NOBLE EMPRESS** (Pa) ex-*World Crystal*; **TSAKALOFF** (Ma) ex-*Stella Filipinas*; **MARITIME CHIANGMAI** (Sg) ex-*Sun Glorious*; **ROJAREK NAREE** (Th) ex-*Hemlock Queen*; **FLORA** (Pa); **IST** (Ma) ex-*Nissho Maru*; **ASTURIAS** (Pi) ex-*Atlantic Trader*; **DOOYANG VICTOR** (Ko) ex-*Aishima Maru*; **BALDER QUEEN** (Pa); **HILDA** (Pa) ex-*Hosho Maru*; **MARITIME VALOUR** (Pa) ex-*Kasina*; **HANDY DIAMOND** (Pi) ex-*World Diamond*; **WHITE OPAL** (Gr) ex-*Sunrise Ocean*; Probably similar (builder—Imabari); **ACACIA** (Ch) ex-*Young Sky*; **MAY STAR** (Ko) ex-*Diligence*; **AROMO** (Ch) ex-*Ocean Crown*; **NIRA NAREE** (Th) ex-*Garza Star*; **MARITIME CARE** (Pa) ex-*Sun Grace*; **PRIAMOS** (Ma) ex-*Sanwa Maru*

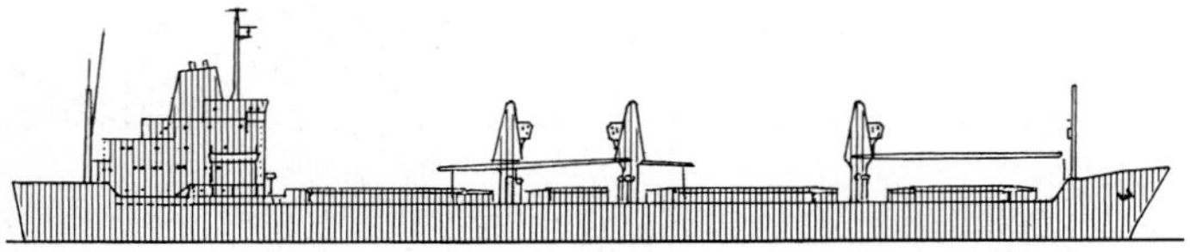

272 MC^3MFM *H13*
QI XIA SHAN RC/Sp (AESA) 1978; C; 9,513 grt/15,985 dwt; 144.00 × 8.90 m *(472.44 × 29.20 ft)*; M (B&W); 14 kts; ex-*Aegis Seaman*; 'TD 15' type
Sisters: **TIAN MU SHAN** (RC) ex-*Aegis Agent*; **NAN PING SHAN** (RC) ex-*Aegis Sailor*; **TAI BAI SHAN** (RC) ex-*Aegis Captain*

273 MC^3MFMC *H13*
VIKTOR TKACHYOV Ru/DDR (Warnow) 1981; B/Con; 13,520 grt/19,240 dwt; 162.11 × 9.88 m *(532 × 32.41 ft)*; M (MAN); 14.75 kts; Ice strengthened; 'UL-ESC' type; 442 TEU; After mast on port side
Sisters: **KAPITAN BOCHEK** (Cy); **KAPITAN CHUKHCHIN** (Ru); **KAPITAN SVIRIDOV** (Ru); **KAPITAN TSIRUL** (Ru); **KAPITAN VODENKO** (Cy); **IVAN BOGUN** (Ru); **KAPITAN KUDLAY** (Cy); **KAPITAN VAKULA** (Cy); **ANATOLIY LYAPIDEVSKIY** (Ru); **KAPITAN NAZAREV** (Cy); **TIM BUCK** (Cy); **PAVEL VAVILOV** (Ru); **MIKHAIL STREKALOVSKIY** (Ru)

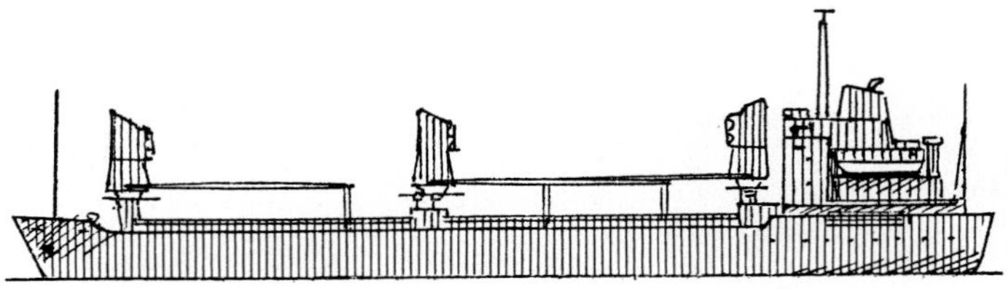

274 MC^3MFN *H*
TANTO MULTI Ia/Ja (Miho) 1976; C; 3,044 grt/4,382 dwt; 86.01 × 6.39 m *(282.18 × 20.96 ft)*; M (Hanshin); 12.5 kts; ex-*Bunga Setawar*; 81 TEU
Sisters: **TANTO MITRA** (Ia) ex-*Bunga Mas*; **THAI YANG No. 2** (My) ex-*Bunga Bindang*; Probable sister: **TANTO MANDIRI** (Ia) ex-*Bunga Gelang*

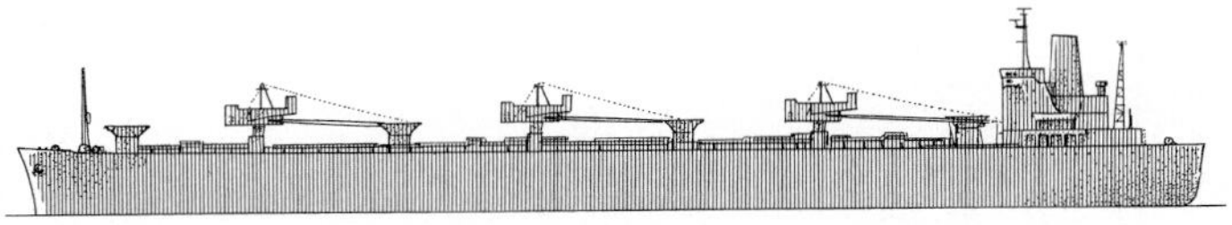

275 MC^3MFN *H*
WORLD WOOD Li/Ja (Hayashikane) 1974; BWC; 36,785 grt/46,599 dwt; 205.44 × 11.3 m *(674.02 × 37.07 ft)*; M (Sulzer); 13.5 kts
Possibly similar: **RICO DUCKLING** (Pa) ex-*Oriental Taio*; **CORTESIA DUCKLING** (Pa) ex-*Universal Taio*

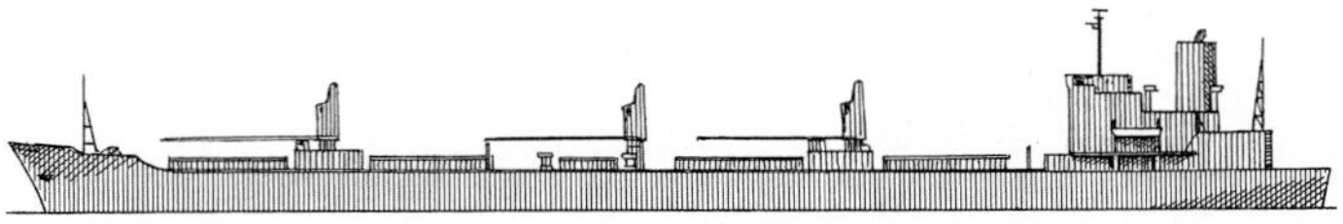

276 MC^3MFN *H1*
KARTERIA Cy/Ja (Osaka) 1974; B; 21,266 grt/34,899 dwt; 184.97 × 11.34 m *(606.85 × 37.2 ft)*; M (Sulzer); 14.75 kts; ex-*World Finance*
Sisters: **SOLDROTT** (NIS) ex-*Stream Bollard*; **VERA** (Ma) ex-*Stream Dolphin*; **SUPERITAS** (Ma) ex-*Stream Hawser*; Similar: **FLAG TOM** (Gr) ex-*Asia Heron*; **MARATHA DEEP** (In) ex-*Asia Industry*

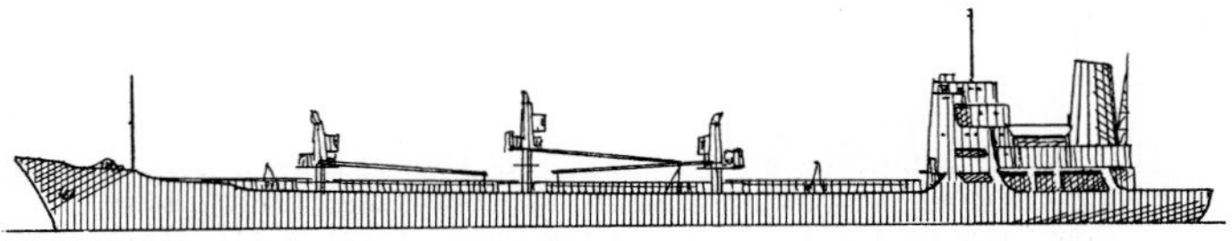

277 MC^3MFN *H1*
PIRIN Bu/Ja (Hakodate) 1965; B; 5,786 grt/9,383 dwt; 126.02 × 7.6 m *(413.45 × 24.93 ft)*; M (B&W); 13 kts
Sisters: **SREDNA GORA** (Bu); **STARA PLANINA** (Bu)

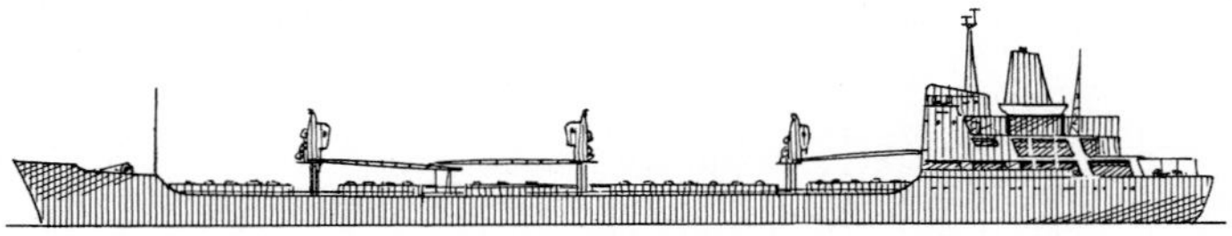

278 MC^3MFN *H13*
BUZLUDJA Bu/Ja (Setoda) 1968; B; 8,692 grt/13,904 dwt; 139.83 × 9.26 m *(458.75 × 30.38 ft)*; M (B&W); 15 kts
Sisters: **MURGASH** (Bu); **LUDOGORETZ** (Bu); **OBORISHTE** (Bu)

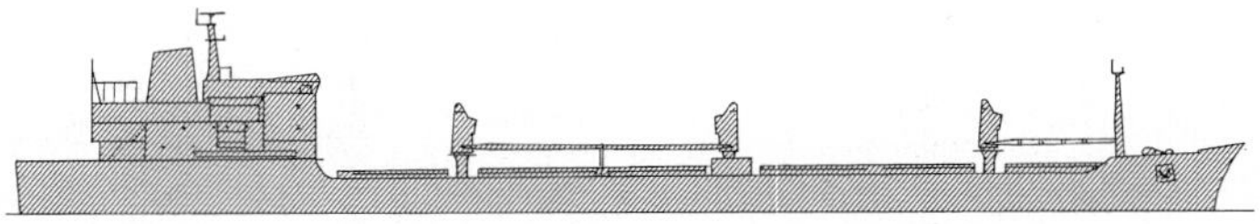

279 MC^3MFN *H13*
HUA DE RC/Au (NSW Govt) 1977; B; 17,705 grt/27,500 dwt; 171.30 × 10.10 m *(562.01 × 33.14 ft)*; M (B&W); 14.5 kts; ex-*Flinders Range*

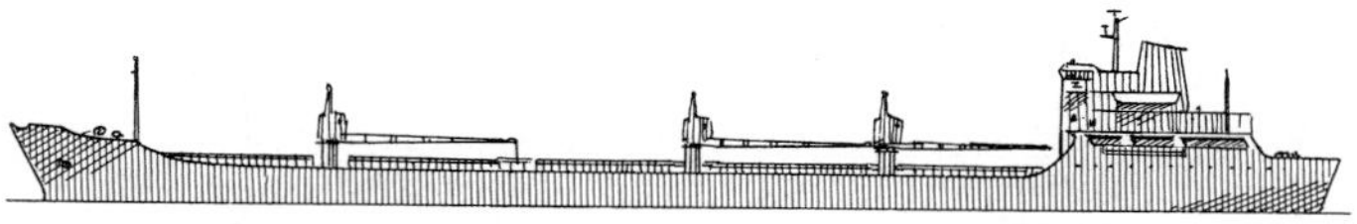

280 *MC^{3}MFN H13*
KOPALNIA PIASECZNO Pd/Sp (AESA) 1971; B; 8,721 grt/13,665 dwt; 146.72 × 8.27 m *(481.36 × 27.13 ft)*; M (Sulzer); 15.5 kts
Sister: **KOPALNIA JEZIORKO** (Pd)

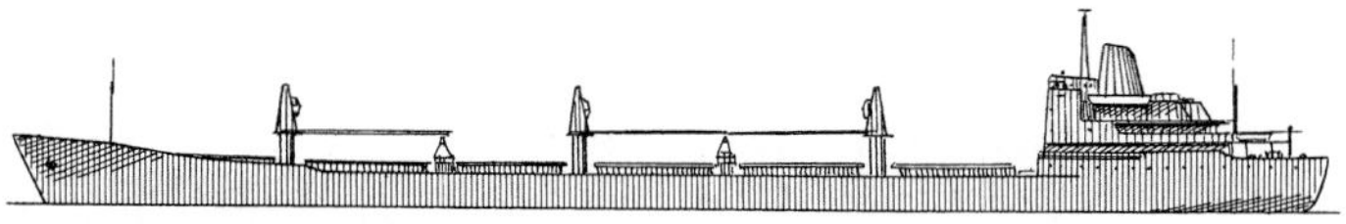

281 *MC^{3}MFN H13*
THALASSOPOROS Gr/No (Haugesund) 1968; B; 12,678 grt/20,278 dwt; 161.55 × 9.7 m *(530 × 31.82 ft)*; M (Sulzer); 16 kts; ex-*Baron Dunmore*

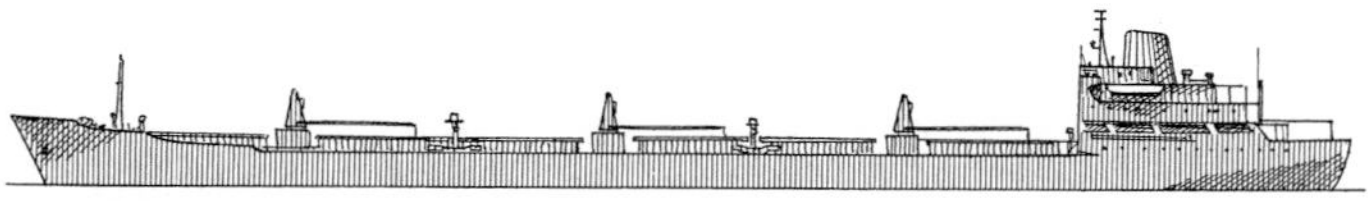

282 *MC^{3}MFN H13*
YASENA Ho/No (Kaldnes) 1967; B; 15,810 grt/25,929 dwt; 180.3 × 10.21 m *(591.54 × 33.5 ft)*; M (Gotaverken); 15.5 kts; ex-*Ragnhild*

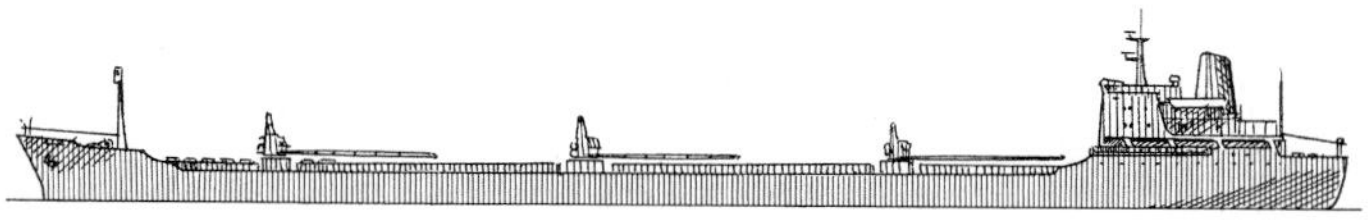

283 *MC^{3}MFN H13*
YING GE HAI RC/Ja (Fujinagata) 1967; B; 15,576 grt/25,046 dwt; 178.01 × 10.17 m *(584.02 × 33.37 ft)*; M (B&W); 15 kts; ex-*Normandiet*

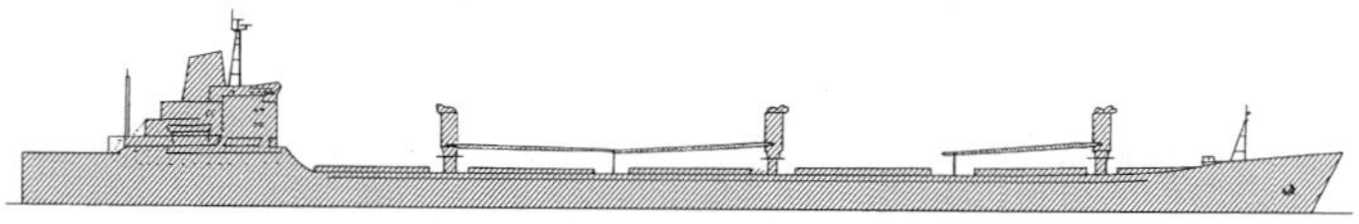

284 *MC^{3}MFN H13*
YIUFA Pa/Be (Boelwerf) 1974; B; 17,544 grt/29,750 dwt; 190.00 × 10.81 m *(623.36 × 35.47 ft)*; M (MAN); 15 kts; ex-*Hasselt*

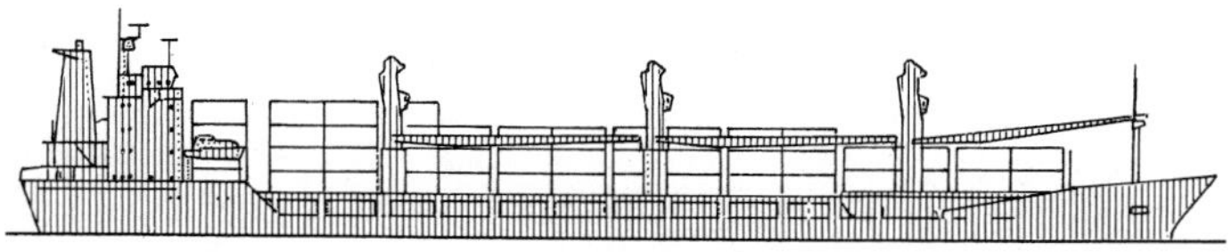

285 *MC^{3}MFR H13*
CAPE RAY Cy/FRG (Schichting) 1984; C/Con/Pap; 8,183 grt/10,700 dwt; 135.06 × 8.25 m *(443.11 × 27.07 ft)*; M (MAN); 15 kts; ex-*Bridgewater*; 601 TEU; Cranes are on port side

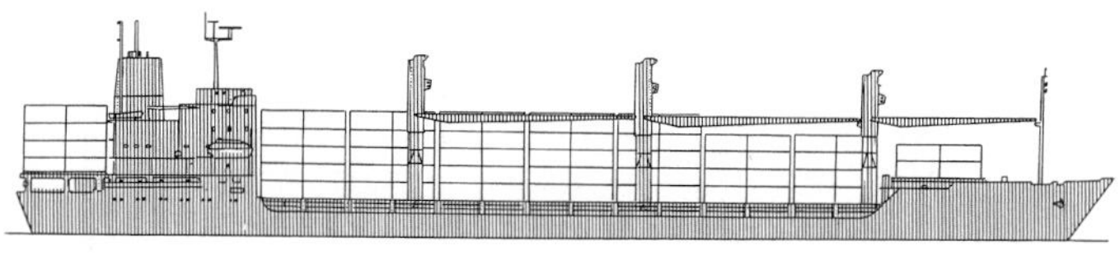

286 *MC^{3}MF-M H13*
SERENITY Li/Ge ('Neptun' GmbH) 1990; C/Con; 13,315 grt/17,175 dwt; 158.91 × 10.09 m *(521.36 × 33.10 ft)*; M (Sulzer); 16.2 kts; 1,033 TEU; 'MPC NEPTUN 900' type
Sisters: **ZIM RIO** (Li) ex-*Mikhail Tsarev*; **ZIM SANTOS** (Bs) ex-*Kapitan N Kladko*; **NEDLLOYD CRISTOBAL** (Bs) ex-*Kapitan Moshchinskiy*; Sisters (some may be gearless): **PROSPERITY** (Li); **KAPITAN L GOLUBEV** (Bs); **ZIM ITAJAI** (Bs) ex-*Kapitan V Kiris*; **ZIM NEW YORK** (Bs) ex-*Kapitan A Krivobokov*; **SEAL MAURITIUS** (Bs) ex-*Kapitan E Freyman*; **SEAL MADAGASCAR** (Bs) ex-*Kapitan A Dotsenko*; **SEAL REUNION** (Bs) ex-*Kapitan N Petrosyan*; **NEDLLOYD EVEREST** (Li) ex-*Aleksandr Marinesko*

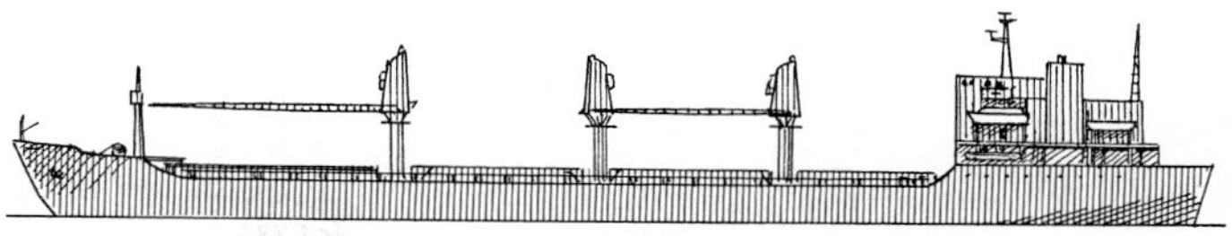

287 *MC^{3}MGM H13*
FRINES Pa/Ja (NKK) 1978; C; 8,967 grt/12,358 dwt; 134.52 × 8.67 m *(441.34 × 28.44 ft)*; M (Pielstick); 14.75 kts
Sister: **FINNSNES** (Pa)

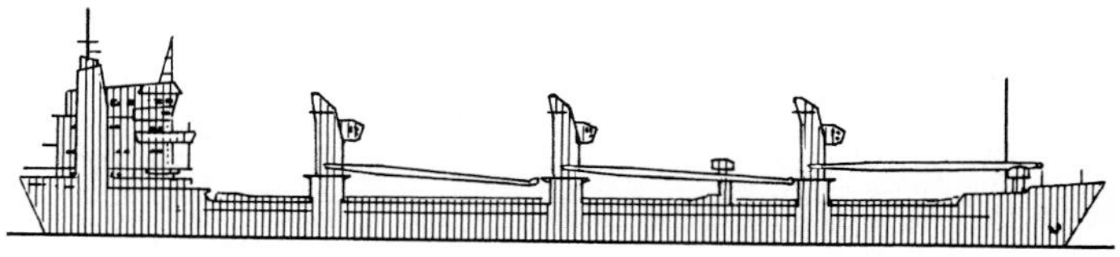

288 *MC^{3}MH-G H13*
CAROLA I Cy/Ne (Groot & VV) 1983; C; 5,943 grt/9,620 dwt; 113.49 × 8.60 m *(372.34 × 28.22 ft)*; M (Werkspoor); 12.50 kts; ex-*Carola Smits*; Cranes are on starboard side
Sister: **CARIANA I** (Cy) ex-*Carina Smits*

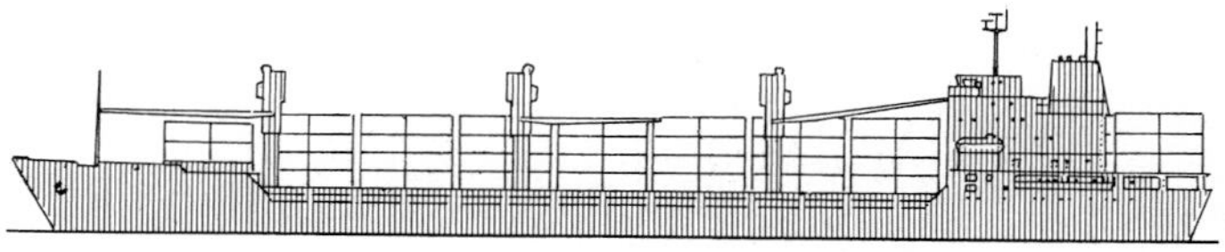

289 *MC^{3}MM-FM* H13
IRON FLINDERS Au/DDR ('Neptun') 1986; C/Con; 13,315 grt/17,370 dwt; 158.07 × 10.10 m *(518.60 × 33.14 ft)*; M (MAN); 16 kts; ex-*Atinuke Abiola*; 928 TEU 'Aequator' type
Sister: **AQUITANIA** (It) ex-*Binta Yar'adua*

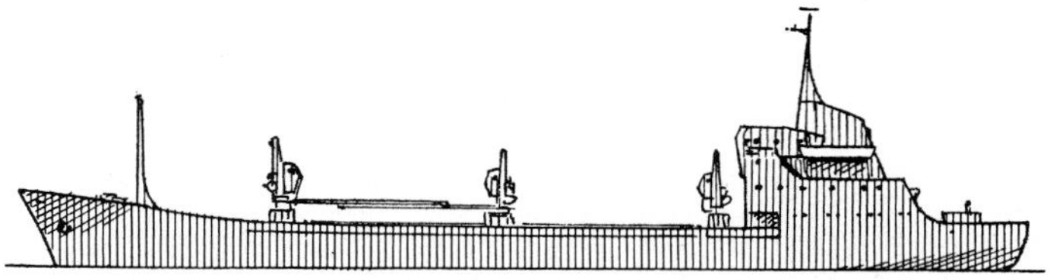

290 *MC^{3}M-F H1*
PROGRESS LIBERTY Mv/Br (Doxford) 1965; C/V; 1,766 grt/3,391 dwt; 97.9 × 5.5 m *(321.2 × 18.05 ft)*; M (MAN); 14 kts; ex-*Baltic Venture*; Side doors; Can carry vehicles and pallets

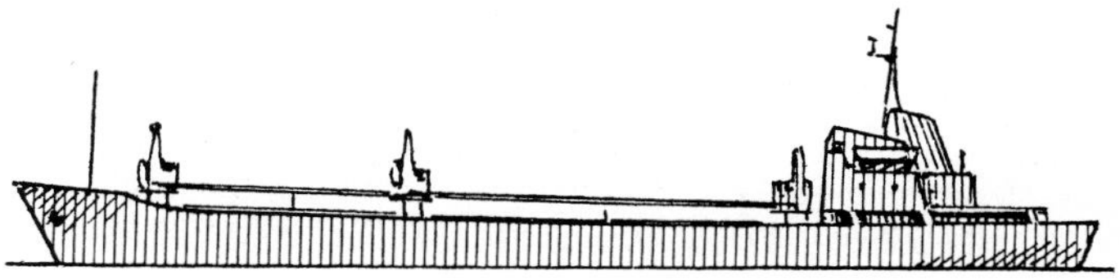

291 *MC^{3}M-F H1*
TWEIT IV Le/FRG (Unterweser) 1966; C; 399 grt/1,443 dwt; 73.36 × 5.39 m *(240.68 × 17.68 ft)*; M (KHD); 12.5 kts; ex-*Fortuna*
Similar (builder—Lürssen): **AMINA MOON** (Le) ex-*Astarte*

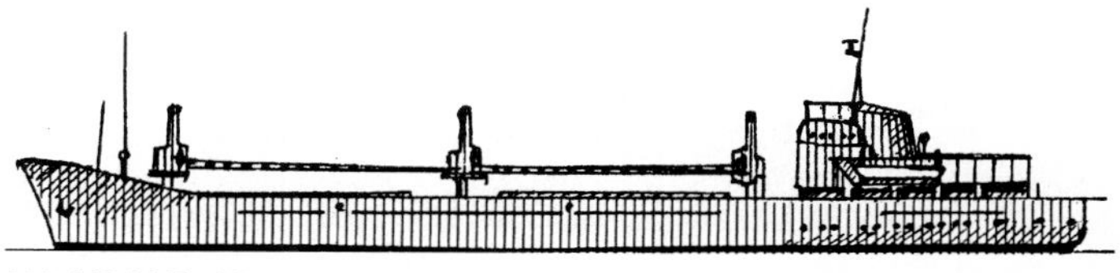

292 *MC^{3}M-F H1*
USTRINE SV/FRG (Kroegerw) 1960; C; 1,542 grt/2,627 dwt; 80.17 × 5.64 m *(263.02 × 18.5 ft)*; M (MAN); 13 kts; ex-*Baltic Sprite*

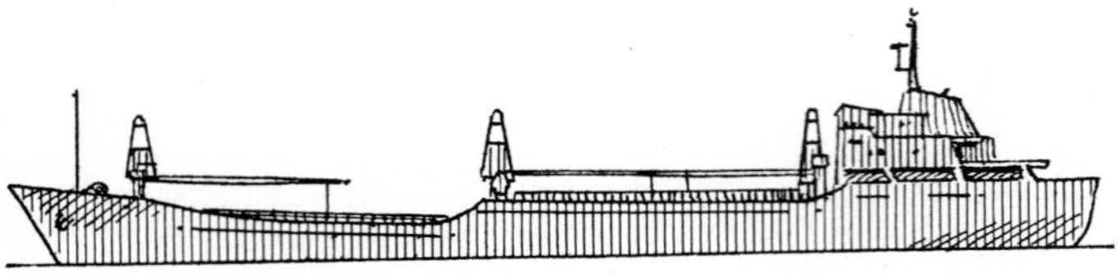

293 MC^3M-F *H123*
AHMAD S Sy/FRG (Elsflether) 1966; C; 1,599 grt/2,780 dwt; 85.81 × 5.12 m *(281.53 × 16.79 ft)*; M (MaK); 12.5 kts; ex-*Erich Retzlaff*

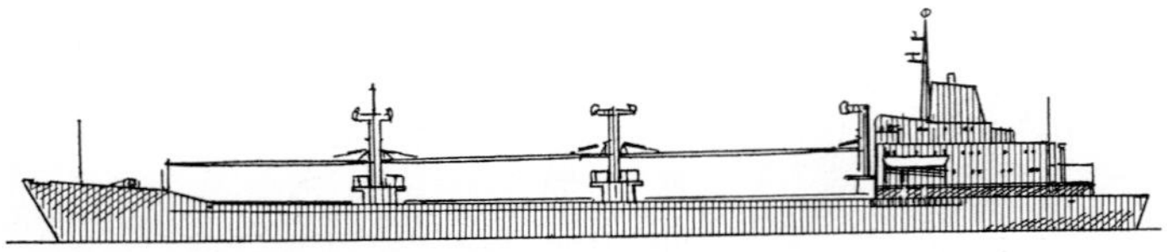

294 MC^3M-FN *H1*
GOZDE B Tu/FRG (Nobiskrug) 1971; C; 4,956 grt/7,499 dwt; 125.02 × 6.56/7.65 m *(410.17 × 21.52/25.1 ft)*; M (B+V); 17 kts; ex-*Cap Matapan*
Sister: **OFFSHORE MASTER** (—) ex-*Cap Anamur*

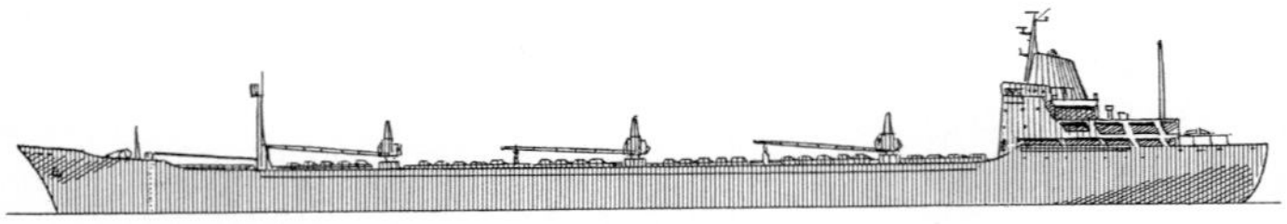

295 MC^3NMFM *H13*
HUA DONG RC/Ja (Uraga HI) 1965; B; 19,411 grt/35,906 dwt; 193.02 × 11.17 m *(633.26 × 36.64 ft)*; M (Sulzer); — kts; ex-*Marina*

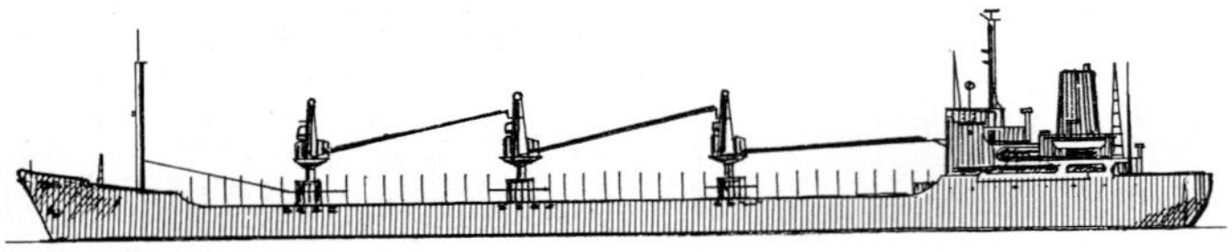

296 MC^3NMFN *H13*
OSMAN BEY Tu/Ja (Mitsui) 1965; C; 9,624 × 15,757 dwt; 147.02 × 8.61 m *(482.34 × 28.25 ft)*; M (B&W); 15 kts; ex-*Wakasugisan Maru*

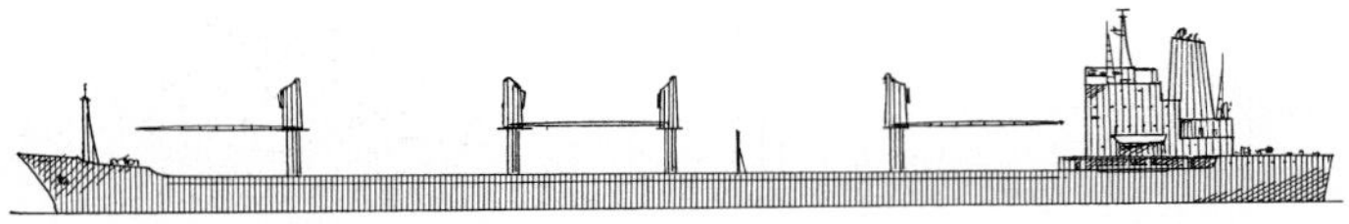

297 MC^3NMFN *H13*
SPRING Pa/Tw (China SB) 1978; C; 18,352 grt/29,129 dwt; 172.02 × 10.6 m *(564.37 × 34.78 ft)*; M (Sulzer); 17 kts; ex-*Ming Spring*
Sisters: **SUMMER** (Ma) ex-*Ming Summer*; **AUTUMN** (Ma) ex-*Ming Autumn*; **WINTER** (Ma) ex-*Ming Winter*; Probable sisters: **TAO YUAN** (Tw) ex-*Tai Hsiung*; **YE LAN** (Tw) ex-*Tai Lung*

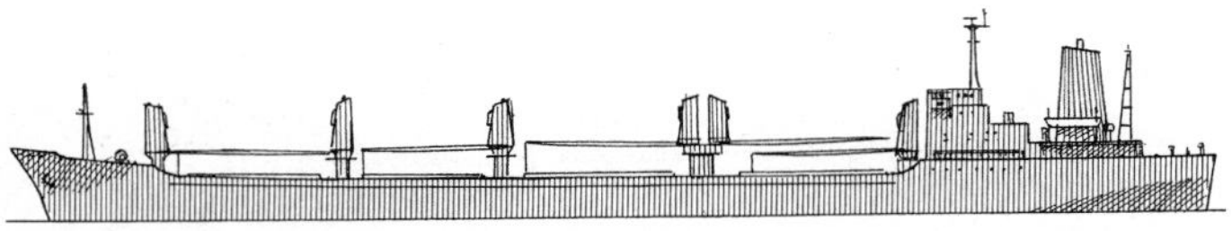

298 MC^3PCMFN *H13*
ASTRA PEAK Li/Ja (NKK) 1976; C; 13,412 grt/20,425 dwt; 161.02 × 10.37 m *(528.28 × 34.02 ft)*; M (Sulzer); 17 kts
Sisters: **GLORIA PEAK** (Pa); **PRIMERA PEAK** (Pa); **APOLLO PEAK** (Pa); Similar (taller superstructure and solid kingpost aft): **CONTINENTAL PARTNER** (Pa) ex-*Solar Peak*

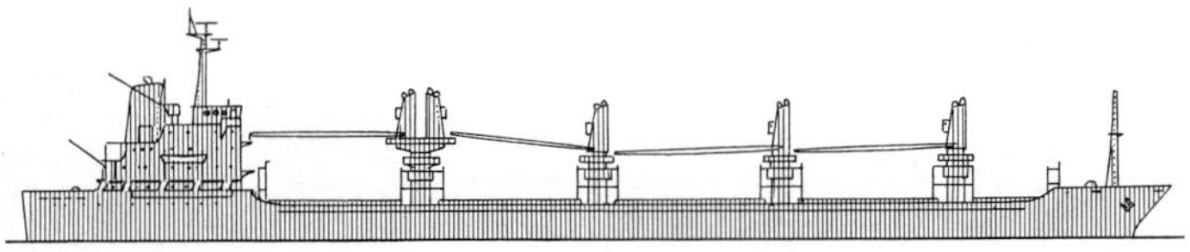

299 MC^3PMCFC *H13*
VAN TRADER Li/Ja (IHI) 1986; B/Con; 18,003 grt/28,468 dwt; 174.99 × 10.23 m *(574.11 × 33.56 ft)*; M (Sulzer); 14 kts; 501 TEU

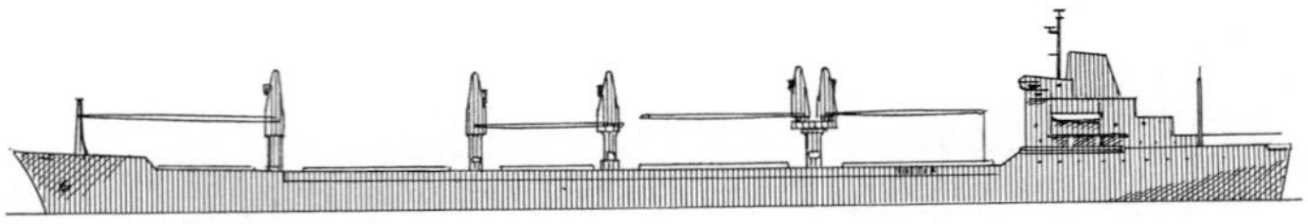

300 MC^3PMFN *H13*
BLUE SKY Li/Bz (CCN) 1977; B; 16,622 grt/26,107 dwt; 173.18 × 9.72 m *(568.17 × 31.89 ft)*; M (MAN); 15.5 kts; 'Prinasa 26/15' type; 676 TEU
Possible sisters: **MULTIBULK EXPRESS** (Cy) ex-*Atacama*; **MINOAN FAME** (Ma) ex-*Arauco*

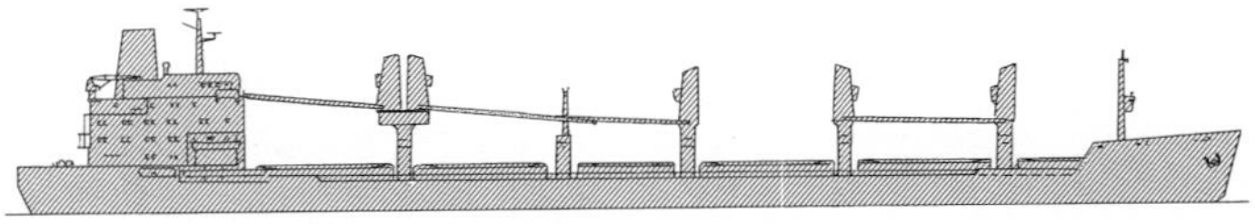

301 MC^3PMFS *H13*
THULELAND Sg/Sw (Eriksbergs) 1977; B; 22,157 grt/31,900 dwt; 185.86 × 11.28 m *(609.77 × 37 ft)*; M (B&W); 16 kts
Sister: **COLUMBIALAND** (Sg)

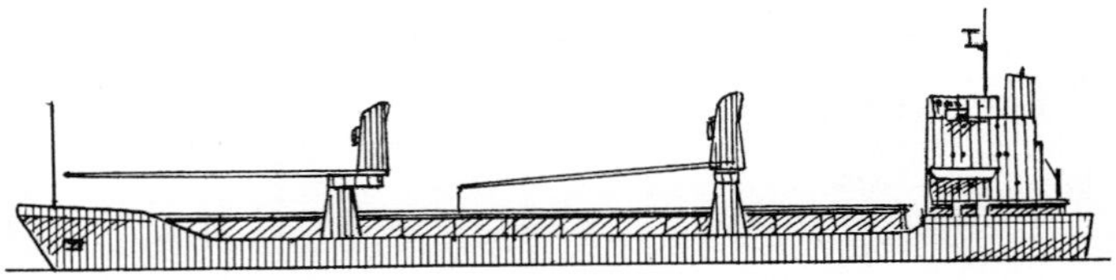

302 MC^2HF *H1*
ZIM ESPANA Br/FRG (Sietas) 1977; C/Con; 3,807 grt/4,150 dwt; 97.54 × 5.39 m *(320.01 × 17.68 ft)*; M (Atlas-Mak); 14 kts; ex-*Westermoor*; 284 TEU; Cranes on port side

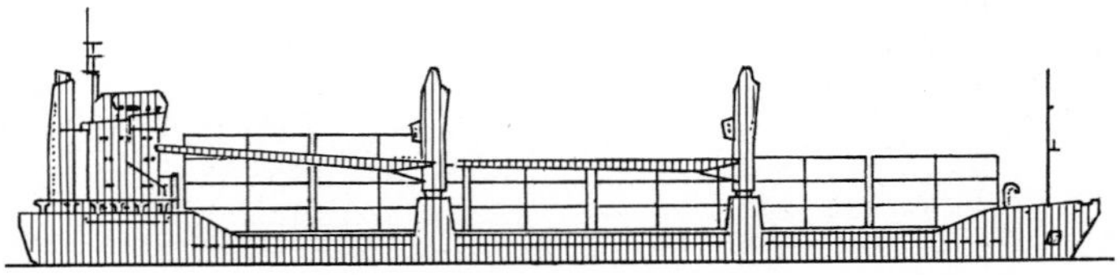

303 MC^2HF *H13*
EXPLORER Sg/Ne (Groot & VV) 1984; C/Con; 3,949 grt/6,120 dwt; 106.63 × 6.60 m *(349.84 × 21.65 ft)*; M (Werkspoor); 14.50 kts; ex-*Samsun Express*; 419 TEU; Cranes are on starboard side
Sisters: **ELSA** (Ne) ex-*Samsun Glory*; **FAITH** (Sg) ex-*Samsun Faith*; **CORCOVADO** (Ch) ex-*Frisian Hope*

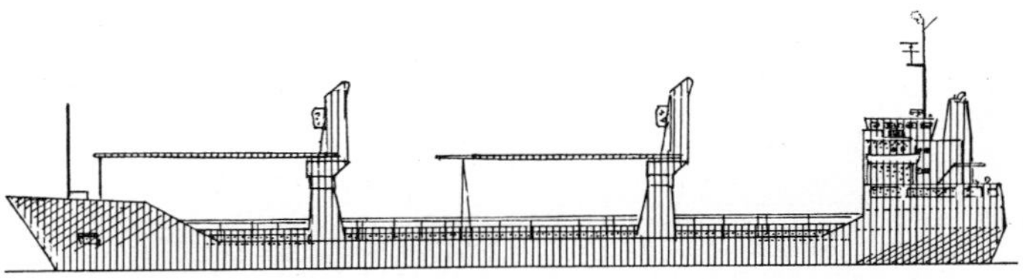

304 MC^2HF *H13*
HANSETOR At/FRG (Sietas) 1978; C/Con; 4,126 grt/5,650 dwt; 104.84 × 6.61 m *(343.96 × 21.69 ft)*; M (Atlas-MaK); 15 kts; 302 TEU; Cranes are on port side
Sisters: **SKOGAFOSS** (At) ex-*Ostebay*; **NEDLLOYD ANTILLES** (At) ex-*Hansedam*; **REYKJAFOSS** (At) ex-*Regulus*

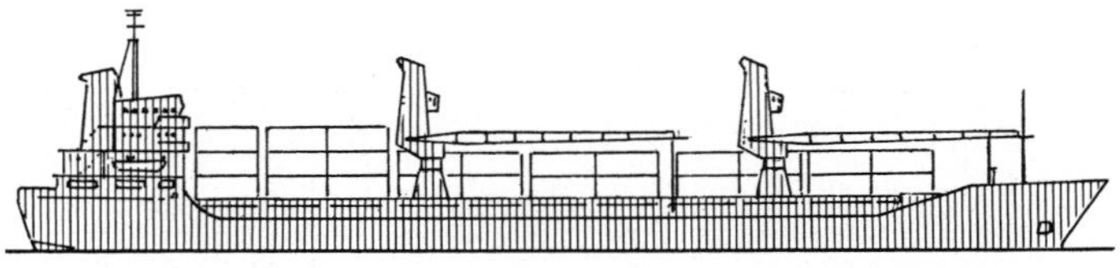

305 MC^2HF *H13*
SKAGERN Sw/RC (Zhong Hua) 1983; C/Con; 4,426 grt/6,150 dwt; 105.95 × 6.99 m *(347.60 × 22.93 ft)*; M (Mitsubishi); 13.50 kts; 310 TEU; Cranes are on port side
Sisters (some may be gearless): **ALKAID** (Cy) ex-*Schwabenland*; **ATLANTIS** (Po) ex-*Emsland*; **ALSTERN** (Sw) ex-*Friesland*; **AHLERS BELGICA** (At) ex-*Shetland*; **NOREN** (Sw) ex-*Nordland*; **CANTERBURY EXPRESS** (Br) ex-*Katania*; **AUCKLAND EXPRESS** (Br) ex-*Karthago*; **SOMMEN** (Sw)

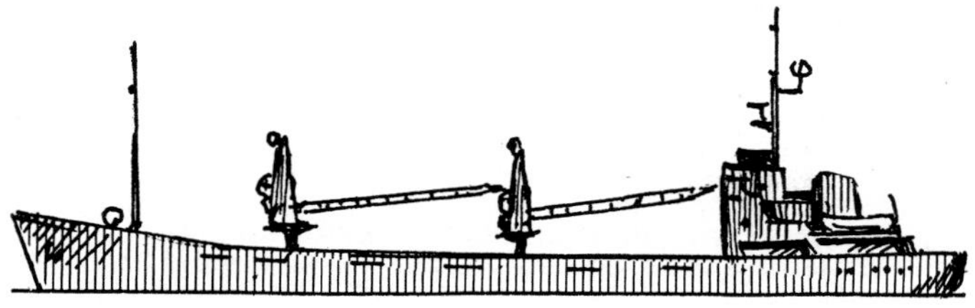

306 MC^{2}MF H
FLORIDA Ho/Ne (Arnhemsche) 1962; C; 1,404 grt/1,250 dwt; 79.18 × 4.1 m *(259 × 13.45 ft)*; M (Werkspoor); 12.5 kts; ex-*Texelstroom*

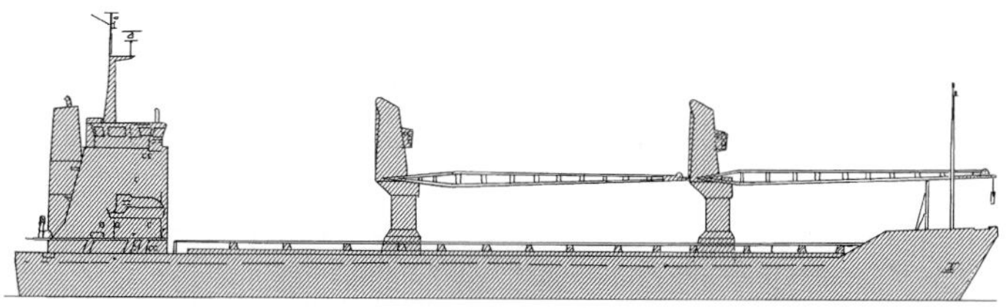

307 MC^{2}MF H1
CPC HELVETIA At/FRG (Sietas) 1984; C/Con; 4,366 grt/5,902 dwt; 99.90 × 6.95 m *(327.76 × 22.80 ft)*; M MaK; 13.75 kts; ex-*Conti Helvetia*; 323 TEU; Cranes are on port side
Sisters: **CPC HOLANDIA** (At) ex-*Conti Holandia*; **ALMANIA** (At) ex-*Conti Almania*

308 MC^{2}MF H1
DETTIFOSS Cy/FRG (Sietas) 1982; C/Con; 5,424 grt/7,752 dwt; 106.48 × 7.71 m *(349 × 25.3 ft)*; M (Krupp-MaK); 15 kts; ex-*Isle Wulff*; 'Sietas Type 111a'
Sisters: **BAKKAFOSS** (At) ex-*Helios*; **GODAFOSS** (At) ex-*Oriolus*; **DRAGON** (Ge) launched as *Marjon*; Similar (with free-fall lifeboat system aft—some previous vessels may also have this): **MANDEB BAY** (At) ex-*Inka Dede*; **MULAFOSS** (At) ex-*Calypso*; **MONIKA** (—) ex-*Albatros*; **CAYENNE** (At) ex-*Tequila Sunshine*; **RANGITANE** (At) ex-*Antje*; **RANGITOTO** (At) ex-*Sleipner*; **LIBRA** (Ge) ex-*Dorado*; **TINTO** (Ge) ex-*Tinto*; **RANGINUI** (At) ex-*Anke*; **ESPERANZA** (Ge); **BLUE BIRD** (At) ex-*Gretl*

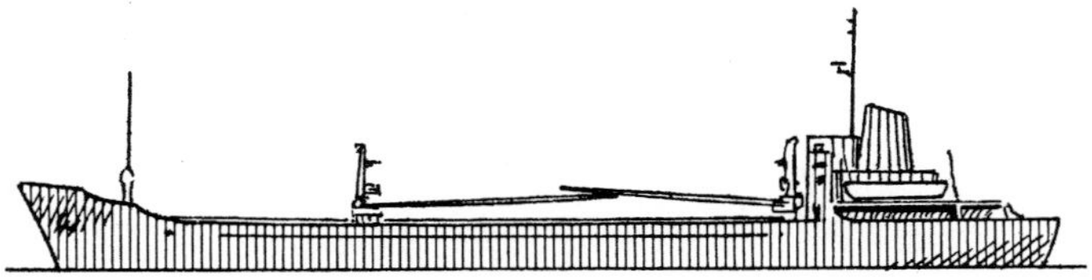

309 MC^{2}MF H1
PALATIAL II Pa/Ne (Arnhemsche) 1963; C; 1,514 grt/2,098 dwt; 81.03 × 5.10 m *(265.85 × 16.73 ft)*; M (Deutz); 12 kts; ex-*Vega*; Lengthened 1969
Sister (now converted to livestock carrier): **BERGER B** (Le) ex-*Edda*; Similar (unlengthened): **ALAATI ALAAH** (Ho) ex-*Ask*

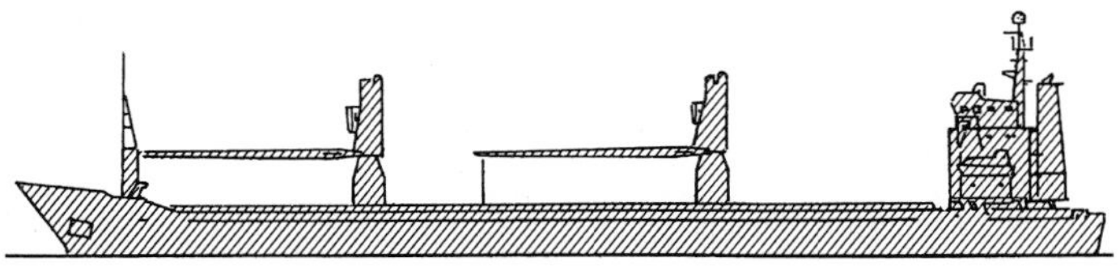

310 MC^{2}MF H1
PIJLGRACHT Ne/Ja (Miho) 1985; C/Con; 5,974 grt/9,515 dwt; 113.01 × 6.40 m *(370.77 × 20.99 ft)*; M (Hanshin); 14 kts; 474 TEU; Cranes are on starboard side
Sisters: **PIETERSGRACHT** (Ne); **PAUWGRACHT** (Ne); **PALEISGRACHT** (Ne); **POOLGRACHT** (Ne); **PARKGRACHT** (Ne); **PALMGRACHT** (Ne); **PRINSENGRACHT** (Ne); Sisters (some built by Mitsubishi HI): **CMBT TANA** (Cy) ex-*Timca*; **MEKHANIK KURAKO** (Cy) ex-*Printca*; **NICOLE GREEN** (Cy) ex-*Carpulp*; **NATALIE GREEN** (possibly **NATHALIE GREEN)** (Cy) ex-*Kraftca*; **LEMMERGRACHT** (Ne) ex-*Woodca*; **LINDENGRACHT** (Ne) ex-*Newca*; **LEVANTGRACHT** (Ne) ex-*Pulpca*; **LOOTSGRACHT**; (Ne) ex-*Poleca*; **LAURIERGRACHT** (Ne); **LIJNBAANSGRACHT** (Ne); **KOCHNEV** (Cy) ex-*Conca*; **ALEKSANDROV** (Cy) ex-*Steelca*

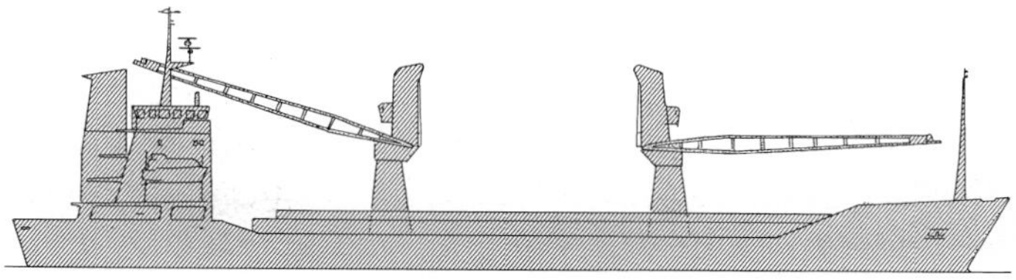

311 MC^{2}MF H1
TIMBUS Ge/FRG (Sietas) 1983; C/Con; 4.043 grt/6,231 dwt; 94.98 × 7.42 m *(311.61 × 24.34 ft)*; M (MaK); 14 kts; ex-*Hans-Gunther Bulow*; 290 TEU; Crane is on port side; 'Type 120'

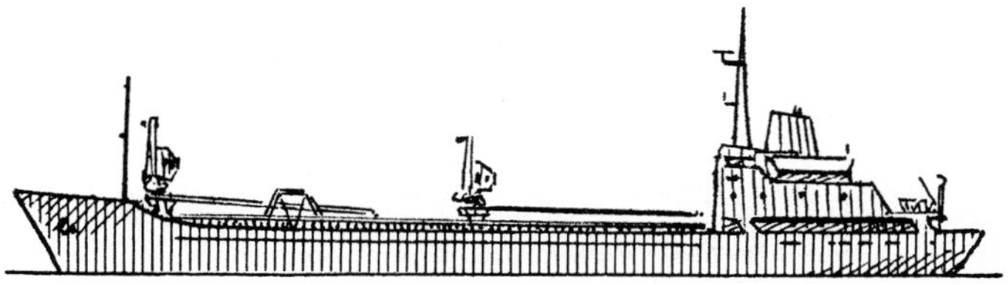

312 MC^{2}MF H1
ZHAN QIONG No 1 RC/Sw (Oskarshamns) 1965; C; 1,296 grt/2,155 dwt; 71.64 × 5.46 m *(235.04 × 17.91 ft)*; M (Deutz); 12.5 kts; ex-*Bore XI*
Sisters: **MELAKA JAYA III** (My) ex-*Bore VIII*

313 MC^{2}MF H13
ALTONA At/FRG (Sietas) 1980; C/Con; 5,307 grt/6,660 dwt; 113.16 × 6.49 m *(371 × 21.29 ft)*; M (MaK); 15 kts; ex-*Karyatein*; 436 TEU; Cranes are on port side
Similar (some may have a free-fall lifeboat, and handling crane, aft): **WESTERHAMM** (Li); **MAERSK CANARIAS** (Sp), launched as *Alcyone*; **LEVANT WESER** (At), launched as *Birte Ritscher*; **SEA TRADER** (At) ex-*Estetrader*; **LEVANT NEVA** (Ge) ex-*Hansewall*; Similar: (Be built—St Pieter): **BREEZE** (Cy) ex-*Ahlers Breeze*; **LMOTSE** (Cy) ex-*Ahlers Bridge*; Similar (may not have extended poop): **INSULANO** ex-*Esteclipper*; Probably similar: **JOANNA BORCHARD** (At) ex-*Caravelle*; Similar (lengthened 1991 to 146.901m (481.961ft; 760 TEU)); **HISPANIOLA** (Ge) ex-*Germania*

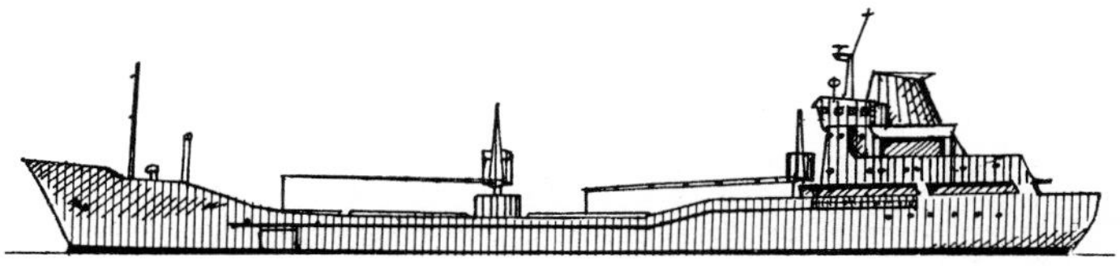

314 MC^{2}MF H13
DELTA EXPRESS UAE/Fi (Wärtsilä) 1966; C; 2,666 grt/3,697 dwt; 91.55 × 6.52 m *(300.36 × 21.4 ft)*; M (Sulzer); 13.4 kts; ex-*Algenib*

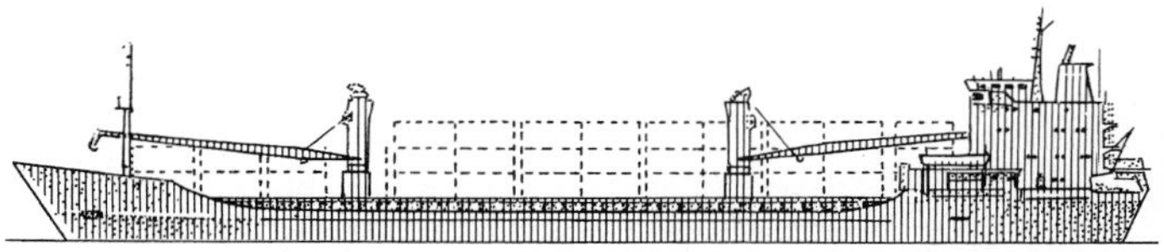

315 MC^{2}MF H13
HELGAFELL Ic/FRG (Brand) 1978; C/Con; 5,215 grt/7,209 dwt; 117.20 × 6.08 m *(384.51 × 19.95 ft)*; M (MaK); 16 kts; ex-*Bernhard S*; 644 TEU; Cranes are on starboard side

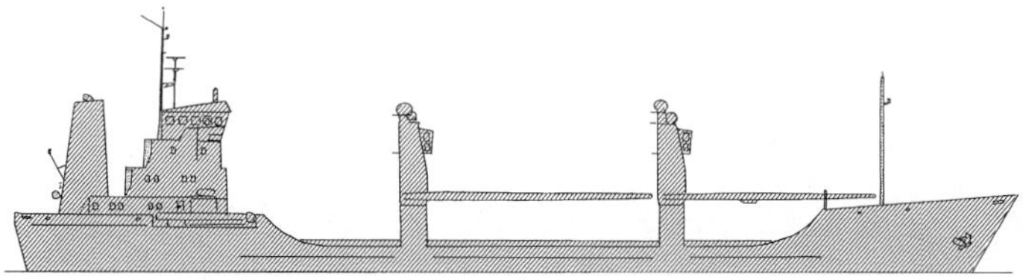

316 MC^{2}MF H13
JOHANNA TRADER At/Ne (Bijlholt) 1983; C/Con; 1,600 grt/3,009 dwt; 81.72 × 5.38 m *(268.11 × 17.65 ft)*; M (MAN); 11.5 kts; ex-*Vrouwe Johanna*; 95 TEU; Cranes are on starboard side

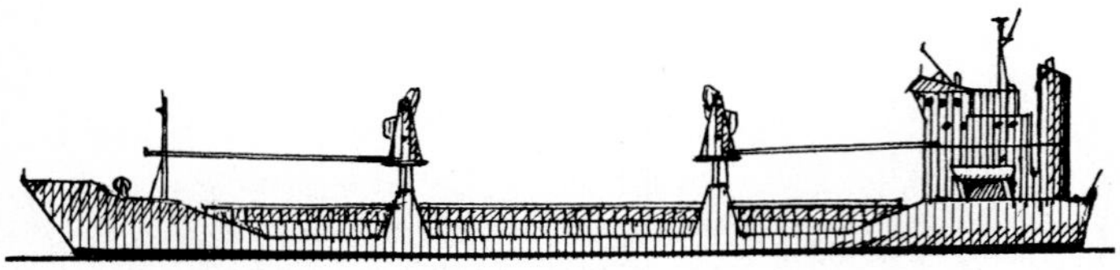

317 *MC²MF H13*
LAMONE It/Ne (Amels) 1977; C; 3,331 grt/5,623 dwt; 83.88 × 7.62 m *(275.2 × 34.99 ft)*; M (Atlas-MaK); 13 kts; ex-*Visten*

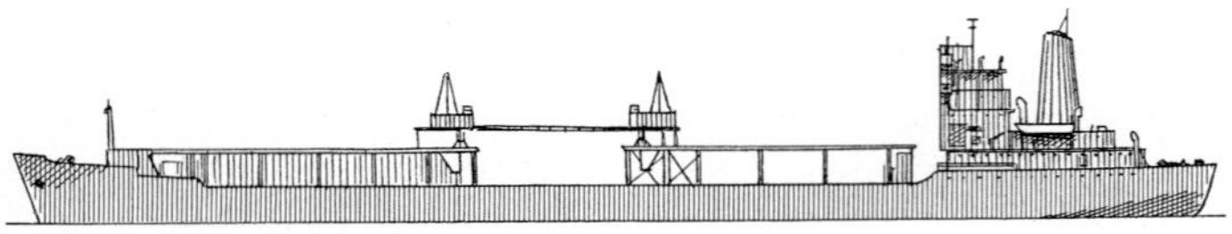

318 *MC²MF H13*
MAINE US/US (Marinship) 1944/67; TF/V; 8,025 grt/12,446 dwt; 170.67 × 8.25 m *(559.94 × 27.07 ft)*; T-E (GEC); 16 kts; ex-*Seatrain Maine*; Constructed from parts of three, 'T-2' type, tankers
Sister: **WASHINGTON** (US) ex-*Seatrain Washington*

319 *MC²MF H13*
MEKHANIK YARTSEV Ru/As (Osterreichische) 1990; C; 2,489 grt/2,657 dwt; 85.20 × 5.05 m *(279.53 × 16.57 ft)*; M (B&W); 12.60 kts; Cranes and lifeboat on starboard side; Funnel offset to starboard
Sisters: **MEKHANIK PYATLIN** (Ru); **MEKHANIK BRILIN** (Ru); **MEKHANIK FOMIN** (Ru); **MEKHANIK KOTTSOV** (Ru); **MEKHANIK KRASKOVSKIY** (Ru); **MEKHANIK MAKARIN** (Ru); **MEKHANIK SEMAKOV** (Ru); **MEKHANIK TYULENEV** (Ru); **MEKHANIK PUSTOSHNYY** (Ru)

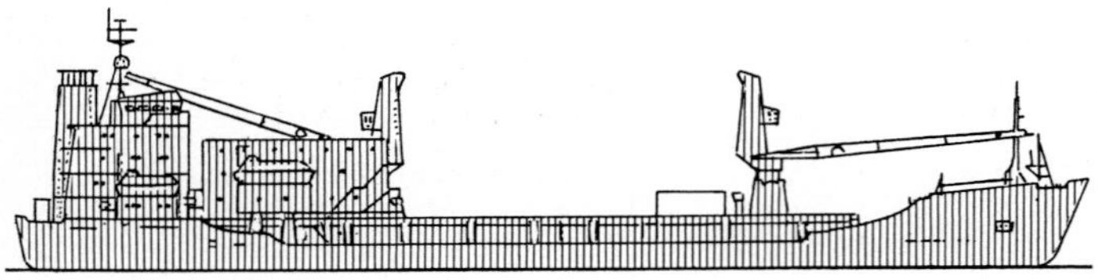

320 *MC²MF H13*
POLAR BIRD NIS/FRG (Brand) 1984; C/Con/Sply; 5,156 grt/6,433 dwt; 109.71 × 7.65 m *(359.94 × 25.10 ft)*; M (MaK); 14.75 kts; ex-*Icebird*; 389 TEU; Cranes are on port side; Housing forward of bridge is detachable and is used to house scientists and so on, when vessel is used for polar research

321 *MC²MF H13*
RANGIOARA At/FRG (Brand) 1984; C/Con; 3,784 grt/5,189 dwt; 99.5 × 6.5 m *(326.44 × 21.33 ft)*; M (Krupp MaK); 14 kts; ex-*Weser Guide*; 350 TEU; Cranes are on port side

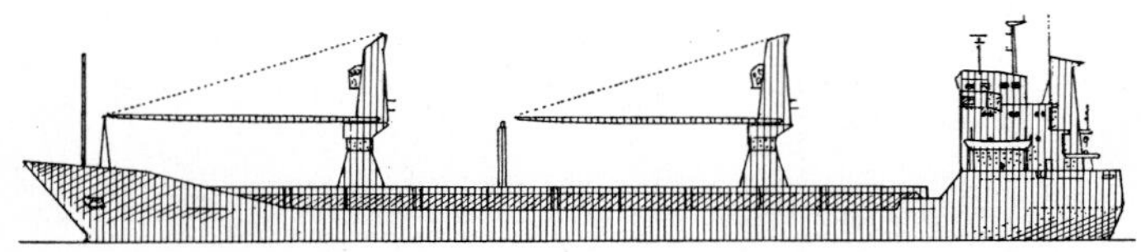

322 *MC²MF H13*
RIJMOND NA/FRG (Husumer) 1979; C; 3,998 grt/5,628 dwt; 104.5 × 6.65 m *(343.85 × 21.82 ft)*; M (Deutz); 13 kts; ex-*Matthias Claudius*; 300 TEU; Cranes are on port side
Sister: **SHUN PING** (Pa) ex-*Kalkara*

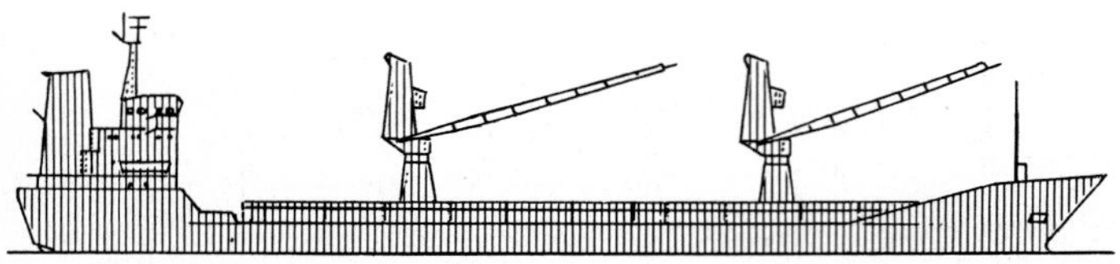

323 *MC²MF H13*
SILVER YING SV/FRG (Husumer) 1981; C/Con; 4,532 grt/6,500 dwt; 110.27 × 6.54 m *(361.78 × 21.46 ft)*; M (MaK); 13.50 kts; ex-*Theodor Fontaine*; 343 TEU

324 *MC²MF H13*
SOVIETSKIY VOIN Ru/Ru (Vyborg) 1968; C; 1,684 grt/2,360 dwt; 82 × 5.43 m *(269.03 × 17.82 ft)*; M (Skoda); 12.75 kts; May be spelt **SOVETSKIY VOIN**
Sisters: **KONSTANTIN SHESTAKOV** (Ru); **ALEKSANDR PANKRATOV** (Ru); **ARSENIY MOSKVIN** (Ru); **EVGENIY NIKONOV** (or **YEVGENIY NIKONOV**) (Ru); **KONSTANTIN SAVELYEV** (Ru); **ANDREY IVANOV** (Ru); **EVGENIY ONUFRIEV** (or **YEVGENIY ONUFRIEV**) (Ru); **YAKOB KUNDER** (Ru); **KONSTANTIN KORSHUNOV** (Ru); **NEREUS** (Ho) ex-*Narvskaya Zastava*; **VYBORGSKAYA STORONA** (Ru); **LENINGRADSKIY OPOLCHENETS** (Ru); **LENINGRADSKIY PARTIZAN** (Ru); **SOVIETSKIY POGRANICHNIK** (or **SOVETSKIY POGRANICHNIK**) (Ru); **ALEKSANDR MIROSHNIKOV** (Ru); **NIKOLAY EMELYANOV** (Ru); **SOVIETSKIY MORYAK** (or **SOVETSKIY MORYAK**) (Ru); **VYACHESLAV DENISOV** (Ru); **YAKOV REZNICHENKO** (Ru)

325 *MC²MF H13*
THEA S At/FRG (Brand) 1982; C/Con; 6,377 grt/8,350 dwt; 124.01 × 7.72 m *(406.86 × 25.33 ft)*; M (Krupp-Mak); 15 kts; ex-*Thea S*; 504 TEU; Cranes are on starboard side

326 *MC²MF H13*
WESTERLAND At/FRG (Sietas) 1981; C/Con; 8,389 grt/11,708 dwt; 133.31 × 8.67 m *(437 × 28.44 ft)*; M (B&W); 16 kts; 'Type 114'; 605 TEU; Cranes are on port side
Sisters: **ARGONAUT** (At) ex-*Amaranta*; **JOHANNA** (Cy) ex-*Tumilco*; **UMFOLOZI** (Cy) ex-*Pacific*; **FMG CARTAGENA** (At) ex-*Ursus*; **EAGLE PROSPERITY** (Cy) launched as *David Bluhm*

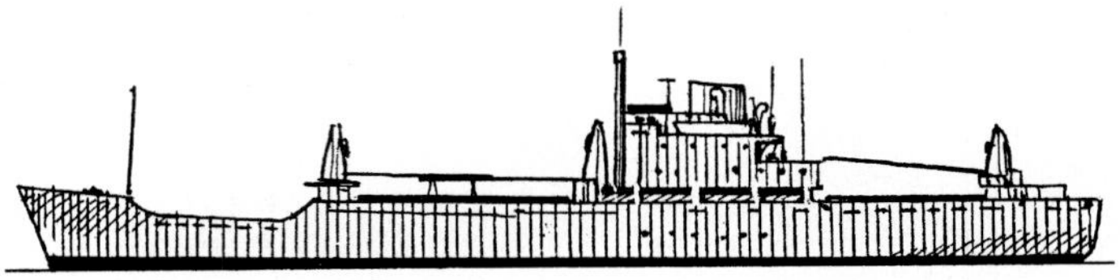

327 *MC²MFC H13*
BLUE PEARL SV/Br (H Robb) 1959; C; 2,880 grt/3,120 dwt; 100 × 4.9 m *(329 × 16.4 ft)*; M (Sulzer); 11 kts; ex-*Poolta*; Lengthened 1968

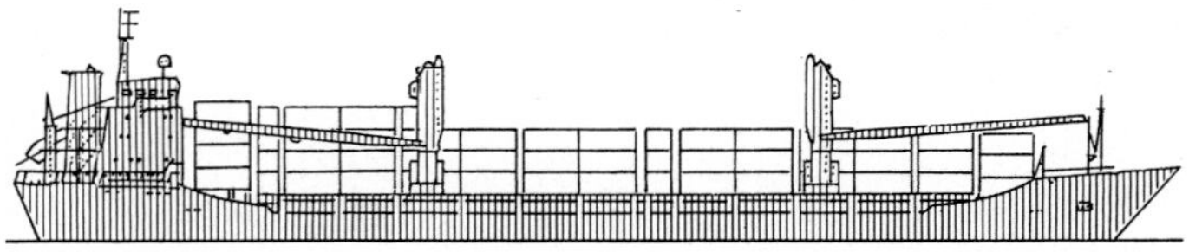

328 *MC²MFCL H13*
FAS ISTANBUL At/FRG (Brand); C/Con; 6,638 grt/9,729 dwt; 126.09 × 8.25 m *(413.68 × 27.07 ft)*; M (MaK); 15.70 kts; ex-*Helgis*; 618 TEU; Cranes are on port side

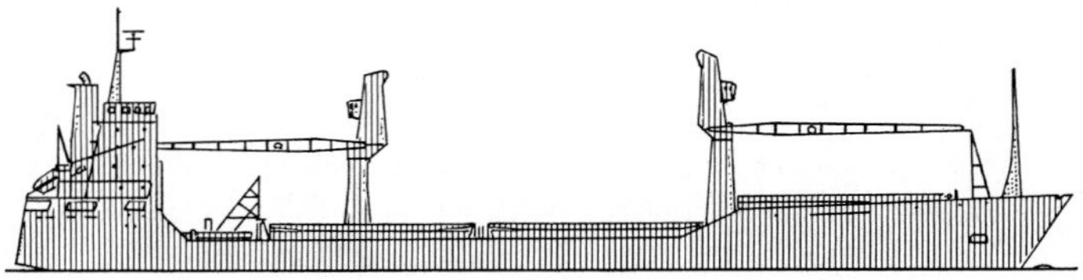

329 *MC²MFCL H13*
JAN RITSCHER Ge/FRG (Sietas) 1986; C/Con; 8,641 grt/9,373 dwt; 133.38 × 7.58 m *(437.60 × 24.87 ft)*; M (MAN); 16 kts; ex ACT II; 754 TEU; Cranes on port side; Probably used as container ship only; May have a free-fall lifeboat
Similar: **GUATEMALA** (Ge) ex-*John Wulff*; **MAERSK CARACAS** (At) ex-*Wiking*

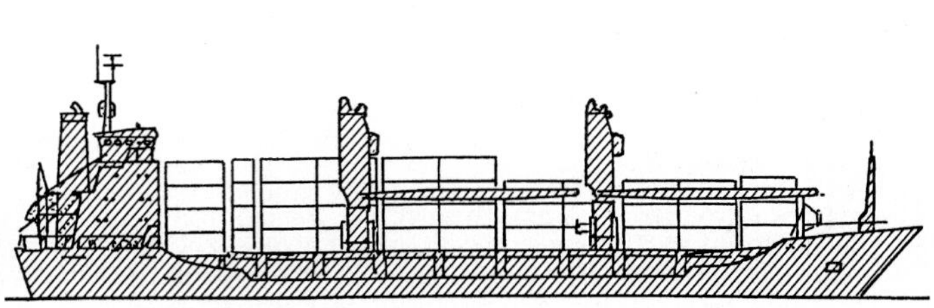

330 *MC²MFCL H13*
RANGITATA At/FRG (Brand) 1985; C/Con; 3,412 grt/4,104 dwt; 95.97 × 6.35 m *(314.86 × 20.83 ft)*; M (MaK); 14 kts; ex-*Christa Thielemann*; 323 TEU; Cranes are on port side

331 *MC²MFL H3*
INDEPENDENT VOYAGER Ge/FRG (Bremer V) 1985; C/Con; 10,282 grt/13,346 dwt; 146.67 × 8 m *(481.2 × 26.25 ft)*; M (B&W); 18 kts; ex-*Noble Eagle*; 'BV 1000' type; 1,022 TEU
Sisters: **INDEPENDENT ENDEAVOR** (Ge) ex-*Brave Eagle*; **HANSA CORAL** (Ge) ex-*Fine Eagle*; **BUXMAID** (Ge) ex-*Proud Eagle*; **INDEPENDENT MERCHANT** (Ge) ex-*Wild Eagle*; **INDEPENDENT PIONEER** (Ge) ex-*Bold Eagle*; **DORIA** (Ge)

332 *MC²MFLC H1*
MANDEB BAY At/FRG (Sietas) 1984; C/Con; 3,113 grt/4,286 dwt; 88.63 × 6.45 m *(290.78 × 21.16 ft)*; M (Wärtsilä); 12 kts; ex-*Inka Dede*; 256 TEU; Cranes on port side; **SIMILAR TO NUMBER 7/309,** but has free-fall lifeboat (port) and crane aft (starboard); List of sisters are under the latter entry

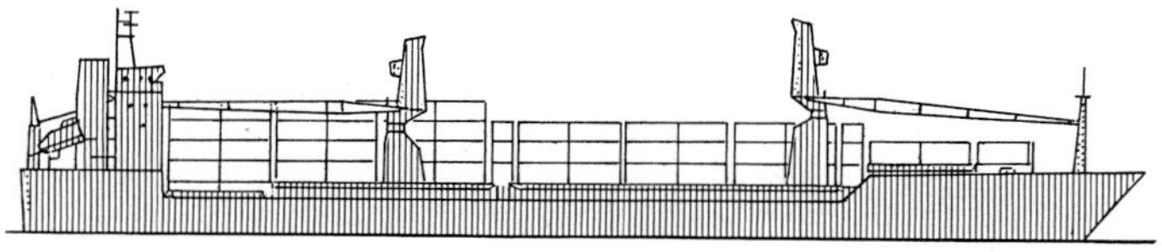

333 *MC²MFLC* H13
SEA REGINA Cy/FRG (Schichau-U) 1984; C/Con; 8,902 grt/8,968 dwt; 136.30 × 7.02 m *(447.18 × 23.03 ft)*; M (MaK); 16 kts; ex-*Capricornus*; 755 TEU; Cranes are on port side; Crane aft is on port side and lifeboat on starboard; Superstructure block abreast funnel on port side

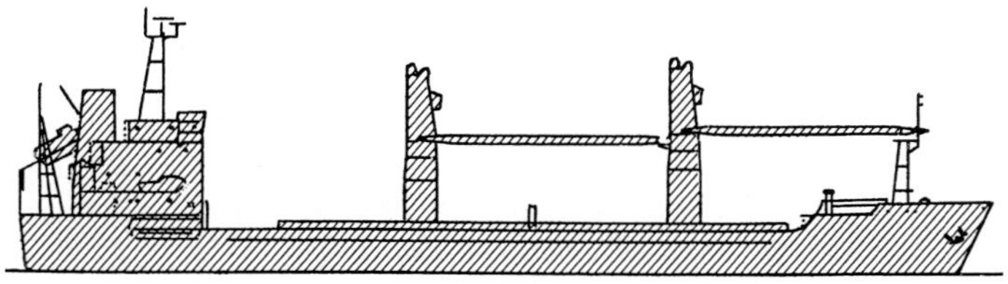

334 *MC²MFLM H13*
SUSAK Cy/Ys ('3 Maj') 1987; C/Con; 4,839 grt/5,896 dwt; 99.22 × 6.16 m *(325.52 × 20.21 ft)*; M (Sulzer); 13.25 kts; 336 TEU; Cranes are on port side
Sisters: **SRAKANE** (Cy); **GOOD RIDER** (Pa) ex-*Orlec*; **GOOD SUCCESS** (Pa) ex-*Orjula*; **LIAN FENG** (Pa) ex-*Ilovik*

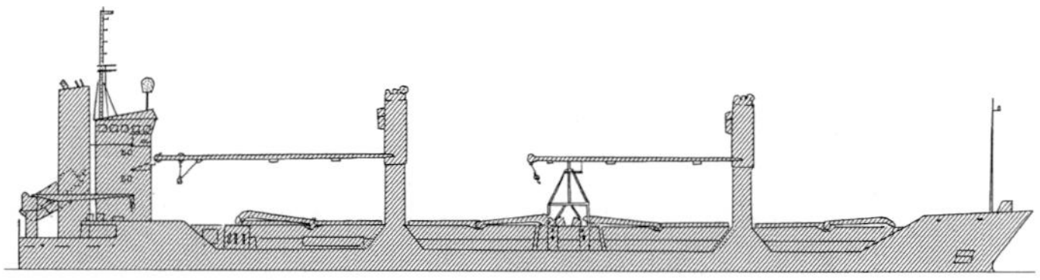

335 *MC²MFLR H12*
COLDSTREAM SHIPPER NA/Ne (Giessen-De Noord) 1989; C/Tk/Con; 4,059 grt/6,275 dwt; 99.55 × 6.52 m *(326.61 × 21.39 ft)*; M (Normo); 12 kts; ex-*Norrsundet*; 253 TEU; Cranes are on starboard side; lifeboat on port and after crane on starboard; 'COB' Type (Container/Oil/Bulk)
Sisters: **COLDSTREAM TRADER** (NA) ex-*Aldabi*; **COLDSTREAM MERCHANT** (NA) ex-*Skutskar*

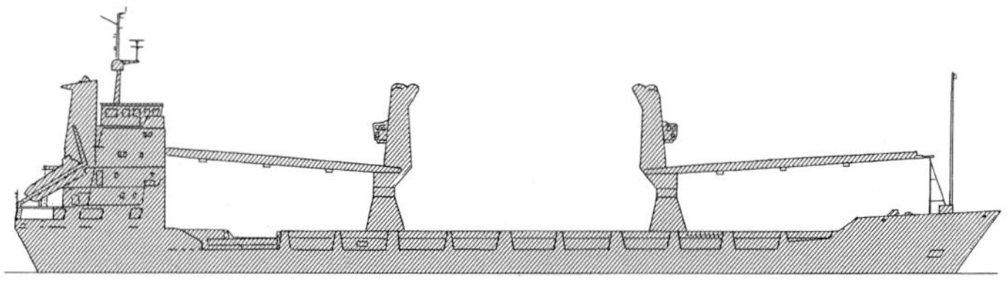

336 *MC²MFLR H13*
CPC GALLIA Ge/FRG (Sietas) 1987; C/Con; 6,500 grt/8,914 dwt; 114.92 × 8.10 m *(377.03 × 26.57 ft)*; M (Wärtsilä); 15 kts; ex-*Conti Gallia*; 539 TEU; Cranes are on port side
Probable sister: **CPC NIPPON** (Ge) ex Conti Nippon

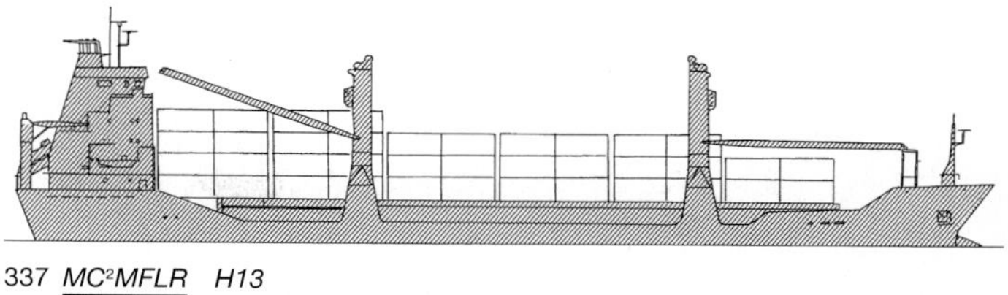

337 *MC²MFLR H13*
GASTRIKLAND Ge/Ge (H Peters) 1992; C/Con; 4,090 grt/4,450 dwt; 111.10 × 5.98 m *(364.50 × 19.62 ft)*; M (Mak); 15.3 kts; 357 TEU
Possible sister (may be gearless): **BIRGIT JURGENS** (Ge)

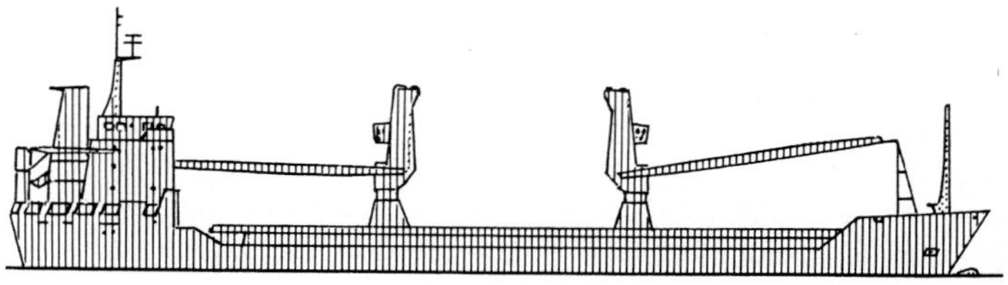

338 *MC²MFLR H13*
SVENJA At/FRG (Sietas) 1987; C/Con; 5,755 grt/7,751 dwt; 107.45 × 7.88 m *(352.53 × 25.85 ft)*; M (Wärtsilä); 13.50 kts; ex-*Elbstrom*; 461 TEU; Cranes are on port side; 'Type 132'
Sisters: **REGINE** (At); **ANTJE** (At); **LENA** (At) ex-*Annegret*; **GRIETJE** (At); **ANNEGRET** (At); Probable sister: **PAULA** (At)

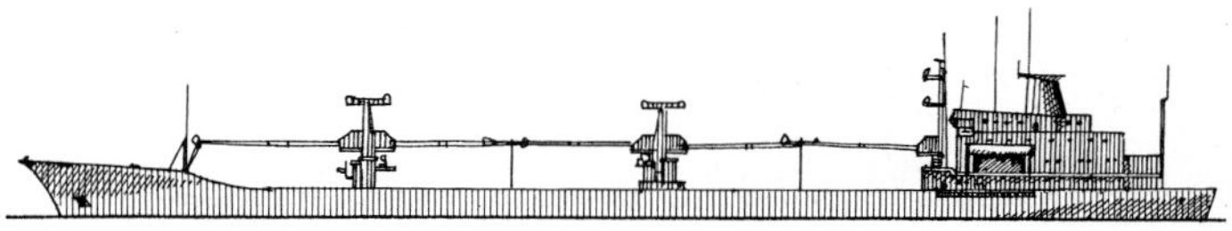

339 *MC²MFM H1*
YING KOU RC/FRG (Lindenau) 1970; C; 5,784 grt/8,140 dwt; 129.94 × 7.51 m *(426.31 × 24.64 ft)*; M (Atlas-MaK); 15.5 kts; ex-*Barbarella*
Possible sister: **FUNDA C** (Tu) launched as *Stintfang*

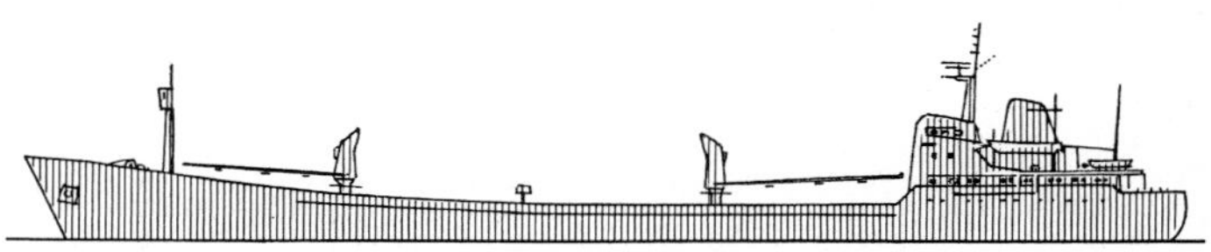

340 *MC²MFM² H13*
SOVIETSKAYA YAKUTIYA Ru/Ru (Navashinskiy) 1972; C (Sea/River); 3,590 grt/3,984 dwt; 123.53 × 4.5 m *(405.28 × 14.76 ft)*; TSM (Russkiy); 11.75 kts; May be spelt **SOVETSKAYA YAKUTIYA**
Sisters: **AFANASIY BOGATYREV** (Ru); **FYODOR POPOV** (Ru); **YAKUB KOLAS** (Ru); **IVAN STROD** (Ru); **KONSTANTIN ZASLONOV** (Uk); **KOZELSK** (Uk); **KHUDOZHNIK KUINDZHA** (Uk); **YANKA KUPALA** (Uk); **FIZULI** (Az); **VAGIF** (Az); **VASILIY YAN**; **BAKY** (Az) ex-*Avetik Isaakyan*; **MUGAN** (Az) ex-*Berdy Kerbabayev*; **BULUNKHAN** (Ru); **KIGILYAKH** (Ru); **DANUBE VOYAGER** (Ma) ex-*Andrey Kizhevatov*; **KHUDOZHNIK PLASTOV** (Uk); **SERGEY GRITSEVETS** (Uk); **FYODOR OKHLOPOV** (Ru); **RESHID BEHBUDOV** (Az) ex-*Komandarm Gay*; **ISIDOR BARAKHOV** (Ru); **ILYA SELVINSKIY** (Uk); **MAKSIM AMMOSOV** (Ru); **NIKOLAY ZABOLOTSKIY** (Uk); **NIZAMI** (Az); **PLATON OYUNSKIY** (Ru); **OGNYAN NAYDOV** (Uk); **ASHUG ALEKSER** (Az); **DZHAFER DZHABARLY** (Az); **SHIRVAN** (Az) ex-*Kosta Khetagurov*

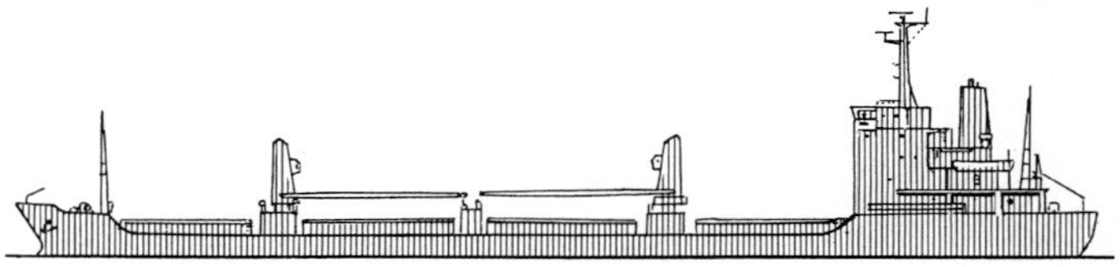

341 *MC²MFN H13*
AFRICAN GARDENIA Li/Ja (Shimoda) 1981; B; 6,498 grt/9,101 dwt; 135.52 × 6.32 m *(447 × 20.73 ft)*; M (Mitsubishi); 15 kts
Probable sisters: **AFRICAN CAMELLIA** (Li); **AFRICAN DAHLIA** (Li); **AFRICAN EVERGREEN** (Li); **AFRICAN FERN** (Li); Possible sisters: **AFRICAN AZALEA** (Li); **AFRICAN BEGONIA** (Li)

342 *MC²MFN H13*
ZHE YAN RC/FRG (Nobiskrug) 1972; C; 6,266 grt/9,450 dwt; 147.70 × 7.68 m *(484.58 × 25.20 ft)*; M (MaK); 16 kts; ex-*Sandhorn*; 264 TEU

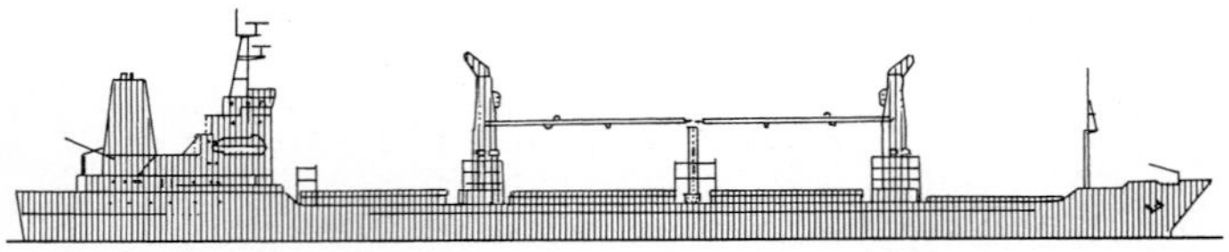

343 MC^2MFR *H13*
PIRAN SV/Ys ('Uljanik') 1987; B/Con; 12,533 grt/18,242 dwt; 151.01 × 9.02 m *(495.44 × 29.59 ft)*; M (B&W); 14.25 kts; 621 TEU
Possible sister: **CLIPPER DREAM** (Ma) ex-*Portoroz*

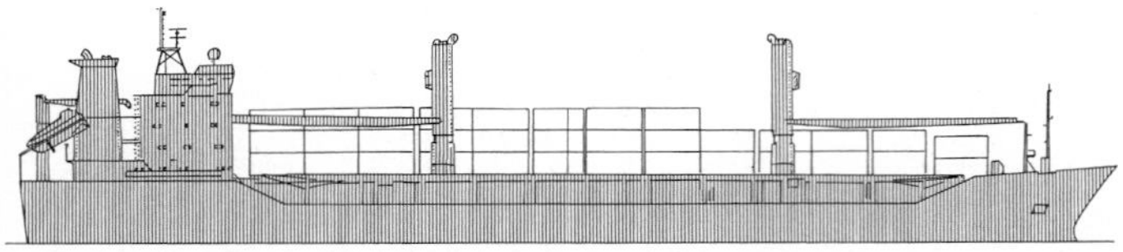

344 MC^2MFRL *H13*
GERMANIA Ge/Ge (Brand) 1993; C/Con/RoC; 8,721 grt/8,814 dwt; 125.20 × 8.02 m *(410.76 × 26.31 ft)*; M (MaK); 16.40 kts; 645 TEU; Cranes on starboard side

345 MC^2MFS *H13*
VARNA Bu/Sp (Juliana) 1987; C/Con; 7,455 grt/8,075 dwt; 123.63 × 8.00 m *(405.61 × 26.25 ft)*; M (B&W); 14 kts; 446 TEU; Cranes are on port side
Sister: **BURGAS** (Bu)

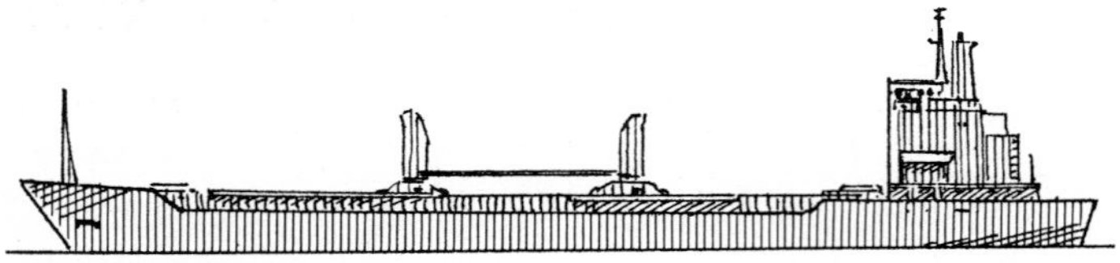

346 MC^2MG *H1*
LAGARFOSS At/FRG (Sietas) 1977; C; 3,083 grt/3,806 dwt; 93.53 × 6.06 m *(306.86 × 19.88 ft)*; M (Atlas-MaK); 14.5 kts; ex-*John Wulff*; Travelling cranes; 128 TEU
Sister: **CELLUS** (Ge) ex-*Hildegard Wulff*

347 MC^2MGM *H13*
ALTNES NIS/No (Kleven) 1978; C; 3,961 grt/6,105 dwt; 107 × 6.4 m *(351 × 21 ft)*; M (Stork-Werkspoor); 13.5 kts; Lengthened 1980
Sister: **VIGSNES** (Pa)

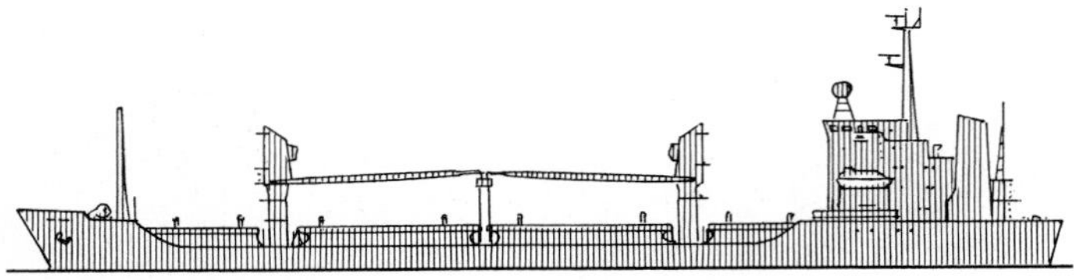

348 MC^2MGN *H13*
SARINE 2 Sd/Ja (Miho) 1982; B; 8,351 grt/12,334 dwt; 129.04 × 8.42 m *(423 × 27.62 ft)*; M (Pielstick); 14.5 kts; ex-*Fjellnes*
Sister: **FANLING** (HK) ex-*Fossnes*; Probable sisters: **URI** (Sd) ex-*Falknes*; **KAMTIN** (HK) ex-*Fjordnes*

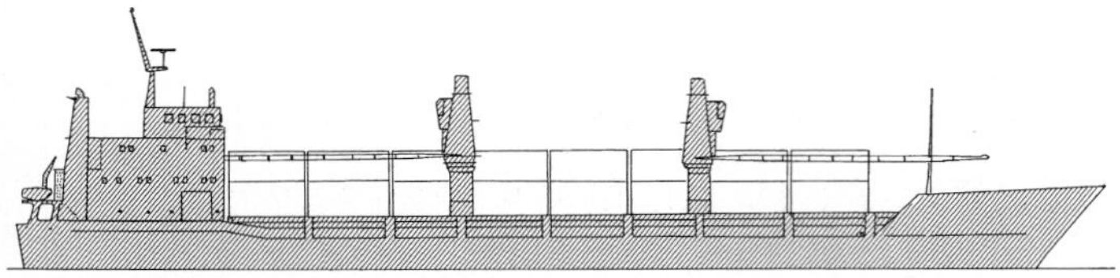

349 MC^2MGS *H1*
IREGUA Cy/Sp (Atlantico) 1983; C/Con; 2,287 grt/3,116 dwt; 80.90 × 5.70 m *(265.42 × 18.70 ft)*; M (Sulzer); 10 kts; ex-*Pena Sagra*; 162 TEU; Cranes on port side
Probable sister (may not have cranes): **TORMES** (Cy) ex-*Pena Labra*

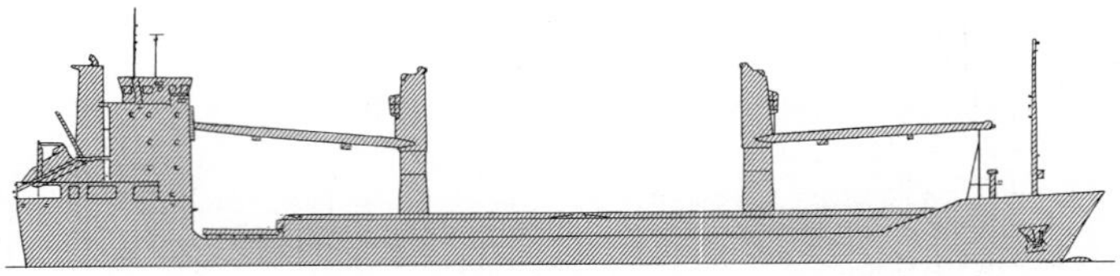

350 MC^2M^2FL *H13*
JENOLIN Fi/Pd (Marynarki) 1992; C/Con; 4,303 grt/5,314 dwt; 105.25 × 6.20 m *(345.31 × 20.34 ft)*; M (Wärtsilä); 13.5 kts; 283 TEU; Cranes are on port side; Lifeboat is on starboard side; 'NS 101' type
Sister: **JULIA** (Fi)

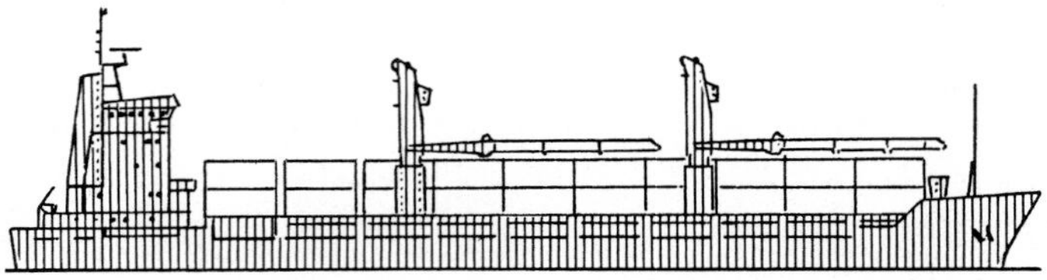

351 MC^2M-F *H1*
BRABO Cy/Be (Belgian SB) 1984; C/Con; 2,859 grt/4,800 dwt; 89.92 × 6.65 m *(295.01 × 21.82 ft)*; M (ABC); 13 kts; 245 TEU; Cranes are on port side
Sisters: **BOUGUENAIS** (Kn) ex-*Bayard*; **BEAULIEU** (Cy) ex-*Uilenspiegel*

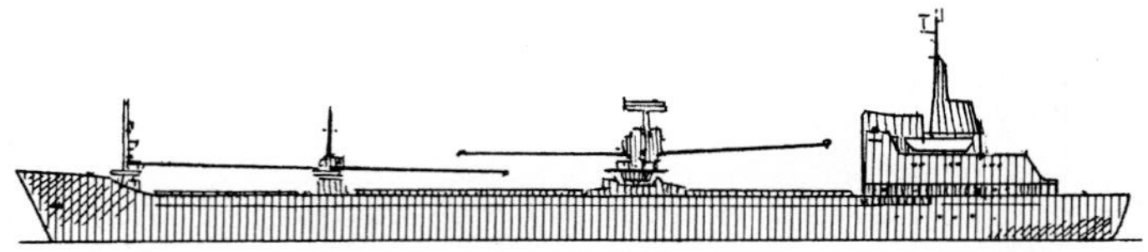

352 MC^2M-F *H1*
HELLA At/FRG (Norderwerft) 1970; C; 2,875 grt/4,100 dwt; 97.24 × 5.2 m *(319.02 × 17.06 ft)*; M (KHD); 14.5 kts; ex-*Ilse Russ*

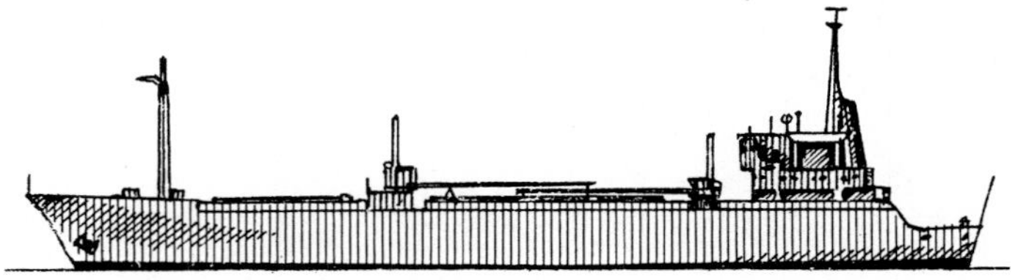

353 MC^2M-F *H1*
HVITANES Pa/No (Kaldnes) 1966; C; 2,517 grt/2,345 dwt; 83.47 × 5.30 m *(273.85 × 17.39 ft)*; M (Deutz); 14.5 kts; ex-*Baltique*
Similar: **CYRUS** (Le) ex-*Bretagne* (converted to livestock carrier)

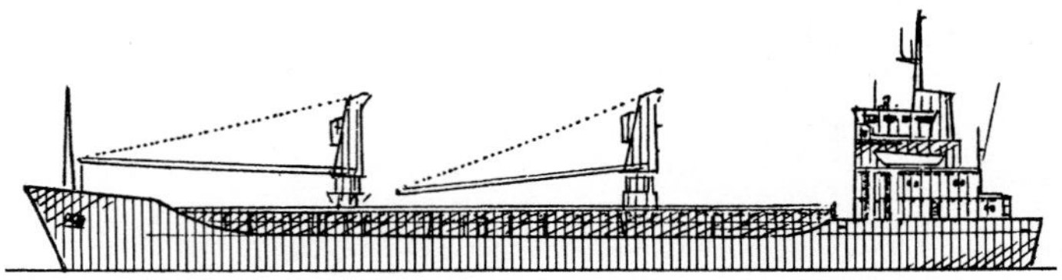

354 MC^2M-F *H1*
ROSEN DIS/FRG (Sietas) 1976; C/Con; 2,250 grt/2,560 dwt; 81.41 × 5.04 m *(267.09 × 16.54 ft)*; M (Atlas-MaK); 13.25 kts; ex-*Elbstrom*; Travelling cranes; 110 TEU
Sister: **DOMAR** (Sw) ex-*Hove* (deck cranes may be removed); Similar: **PICO GRANDE** (Po) ex-*Jacob Becker*

355 MC^2M-F *H1*
ROSY RIVER Pa/FRG (H Peters) 1978; C/Con; 1,599 grt/4,089 dwt; 104.22 × 5.75 m *(341.93 × 18.86 ft)*; M (MaK); 15.75 kts; ex-*Maria Catharina*; Cranes are on travelling gantries; 330 TEU

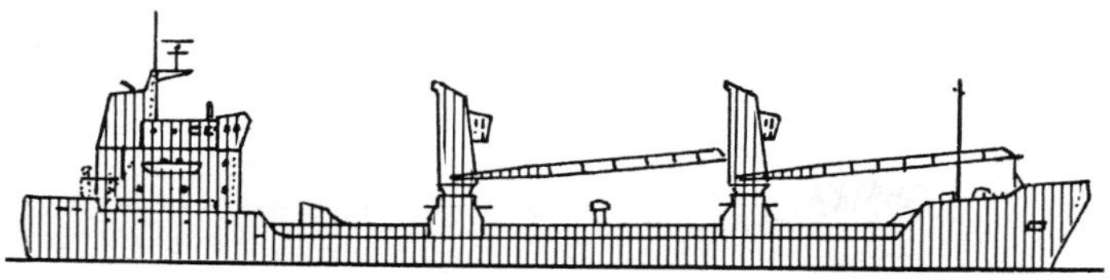

356 *MC²M-F H13*
AL GHARRAFAH Qt/Ne ('Friesland') 1981; C/Con; 2,723 grt/4,878 dwt; 81.56 × 7.24 m *(267.59 × 23.75 ft)*; M (Deutz); 12 kts; ex-*Javazee*; 131 TEU; Cranes are on starboard side

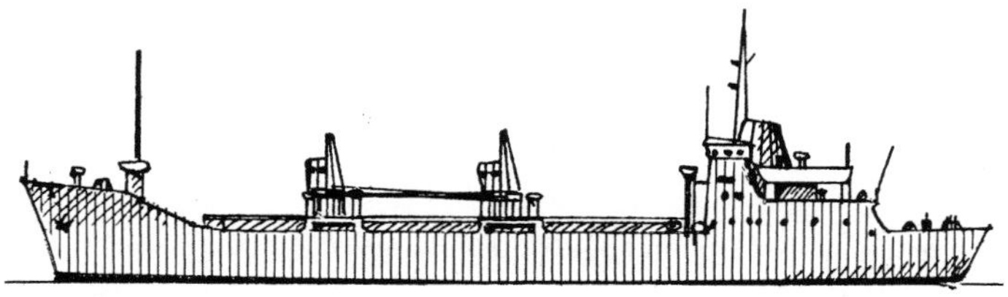

357 *MC²M-F H13*
ALKARAMA Eg/Fi (Laiva) 1965; C; 1,685 grt/2,108 dwt; 75.42 × 5.41 m *(247.44 × 17.75 ft)*; M (Wärtsilä); 13.75 kts; ex-*Capella*; Side doors
Sister: **VIVIETTE** (Co) ex-*Canopus*

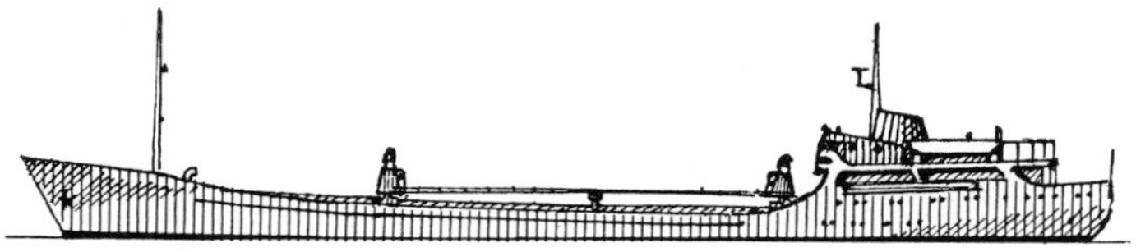

358 *MC²M-F H13*
BATAK Bu/Bu (Ivan Dimitrov) 1966; C; 1,599 grt/2,255 dwt; 80.65 × 5.29 m *(264.6 × 17.36 ft)*; M (Sulzer); 12 kts
Sisters (some are reported to have a third crane on focsle. Some may be converted to container ships): **KALOFER** (Bu); **BAY STAR** (Ho) ex-*Perustica*; **KOTEL** (Bu); **TROJAN** (Bu); **KOPRIVSTICA** (Bu) (may be converted to LGC); **ZERAVNA** (Bu); **KLISURA** (Bu); **ZLATOGRAD** (Bu); **HONG QI 191** (RC) ex-*Melnik*; **HONG QI 192** (RC) ex-*Razlog*

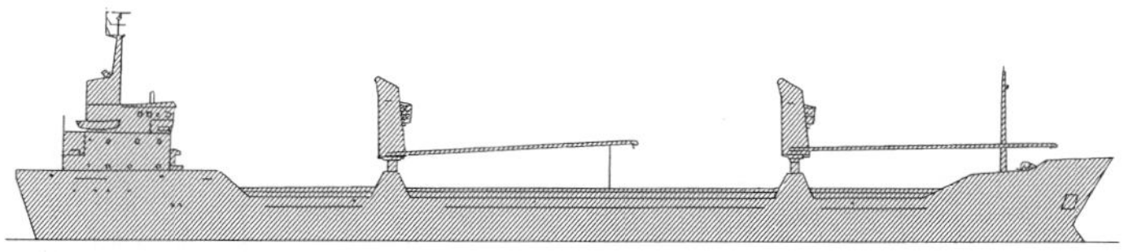

359 *MC²M-F H13*
BUMI RAYA Pa/Ne (Amels) 1977; C; 3,971 grt/4,640 dwt; 98.91 × 5.99 m *(324.51 × 19.65 ft)*; M (Atlas-MaK); 13 kts; ex-*Jan Tavenier*; 130 TEU; Lengthened 1984

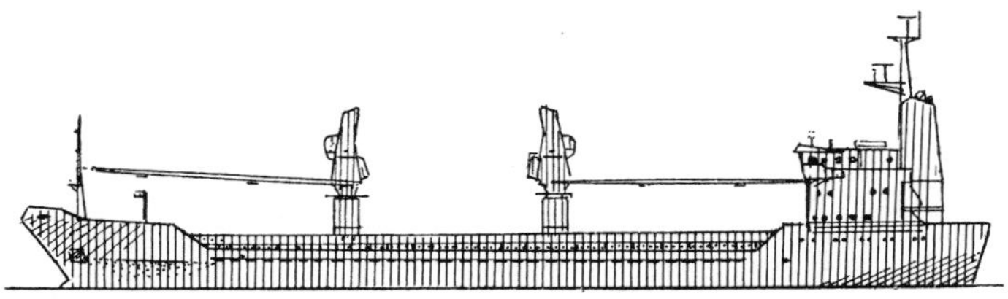

360 *MC²M-F H13*
DELFBORG Ne/Ne (Amels) 1978; C; 3,699 grt/5,575 dwt; 83.06 × 7.8 m *(272.5 × 25.59 ft)*; M (Polar); 11.75 kts; 181 TEU; Cranes are on starboard side

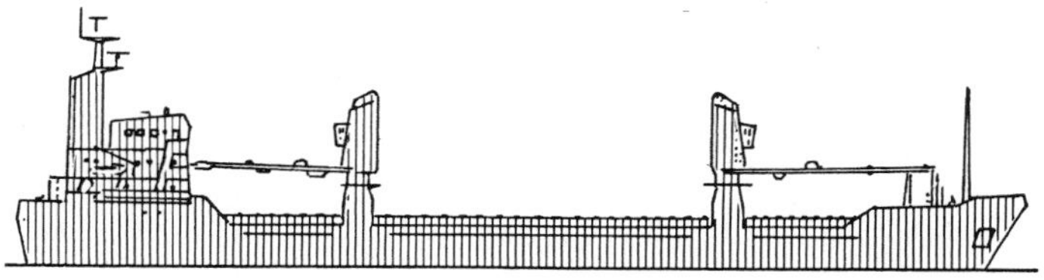

361 *MC²M-F H13*
IJSSELLAND Ne/Ne (Nieuwe Noord) 1985; C/Con; 3,757 grt/6,446 dwt; 96.78 × 7.14 m *(317.52 × 23.43 ft)*; M (Wärtsilä); 12 kts; 215 TEU; Cranes are on starboard side
Similar (shorter—82.38 m (270.28 ft)): **LENNEBORG** (Ne); **LINDEBORG** (Ne); **HENDRIK B** (Ne) ex-*Polarborg*

362 *MC²M-FRL H13*
SIAM BAY At/FRG (Rickmers) 1986; C/Con; 6,072 grt/8,049 dwt; 129.55 × 6.60 m *(425.03 × 21.65 ft)*; M (Deutz); 16 kts; ex-*Britta Thien*; 582 TEU; 'RW39' type; **SIMILAR TO ENTRY NUMBER 7/364** but for free-fall lifeboat aft; Others under latter entry may also have this feature; Cranes are on port side

363 *MC²M-FS H13*
HARI BHUM Sg/FRG (Rickmers) 1981; C/Con; 5,938 grt/7,754 dwt; 126.29 × 6.56 m *(414.34 × 21.52 ft)*; M (Mitsubishi); 15.5 kts; ex-*Champion*; 'RW39' type; 584 TEU
Sisters (Superstructure differs on some): **CAM IROKO EXPRESS** (At) ex-*Esteturm*; **LUSO** (At) ex-*Tauria*; **DHAULAGIRI** (RC) ex-*Wejadia*; **EWL VENEZUELA** (At) ex-*Premier*; **EWL ROTTERDAM** (Li) ex-*Gothia*; **UWA BHUM** (Ge) ex-*Vanellus*; **SEA LAUREL** (Ge) ex-*Marivia*; **LEERORT** (At); **EWL SURINAME** (At) ex-*Lilienthal*; **ELIZA** (Ma) ex-*Estebrugge*; **HUSUM** (Cy); Probable sisters: **EWL COLOMBIA** (At) ex-*Heide*; **INTRA BHUM** (Sg) ex-*Dorte*

364 *MC²M-G H13*
CLAUDIA I Cy/Ne (Groot & VV) 1981; C; 3,692 grt/5,900 dwt; 84.21 × 8.38 m *(276 × 27.49 ft)*; M (Stork-Werkspoor); 11 kts; ex-*Claudia Smits*; Cranes are on starboard side
Sisters: **CECILIA I** (Cy) ex-*Cecilia Smits*; **CHRISTINA I** (Cy) ex-*Christina Smits*

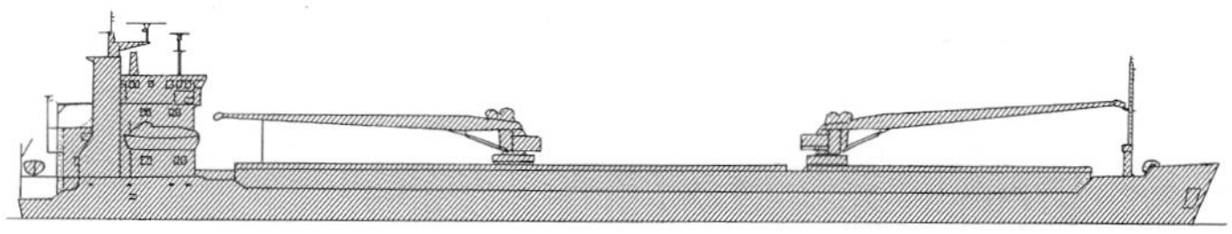

365 *MC²M-G H13*
UNITED WAY Pa/Sg (Singapore Slip) 1979/88; C/Con; 5,060 grt/7,906 dwt; 106.80 × 7.22 m *(350.39 × 23.69 ft)*; M (MaK); 13 kts; ex-*Katawa*; Lengthened 1988; 303 TEU
Sisters: **ZHU FENG SHAN** (RC); ex-*Germa Tara;* **HELLE STEVNS** (DIS) ex-*Lina*

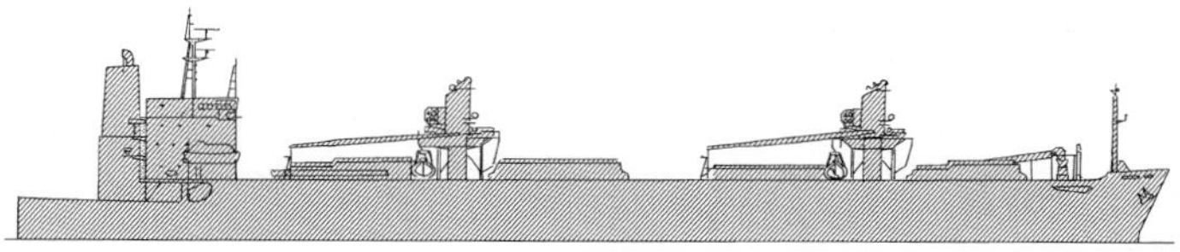

366 *MC²NMF H1*
TROPICAL VENTURE Pa/Ja (Tsuneishi) 1988; BWC; 18,203 grt/21,989 dwt; 153.00 × 8.82 m *(501.97 × 28.94 ft)*; M (Mitsubishi); 12.60 kts

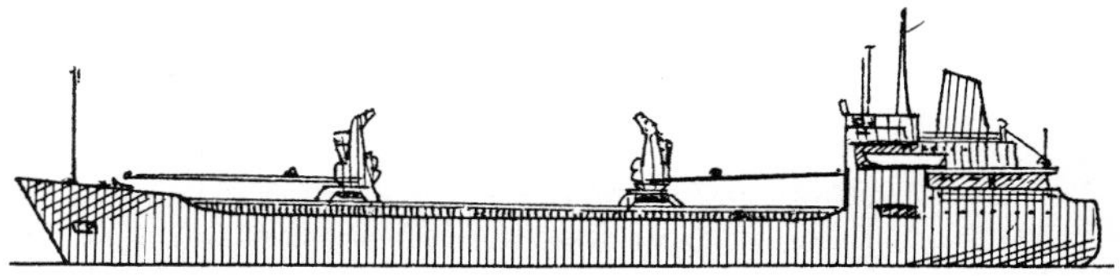

367 *MC²NMFC H1*
STEVNS SEA At/FRG (Sietas) 1972; C/Con; 2,333 grt/3,610 dwt; 88.50 × 5.27 m *(290.34 × 17.32 ft)*; M (Atlas-MaK); 14 kts; ex-*Estebogen*; 423 TEU
Sisters: **AROSSEL** (Cy) ex-*Scol Progress*; **BALTICA** (Ho); **KIEFERNWALD** (At) ex-*Ursa*; **STEVNS TRADER** (DIS) ex-*Patricia*

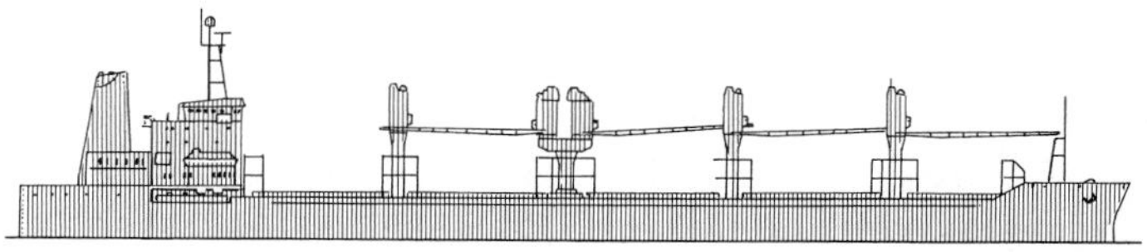

368 *MC²PCMF H13*
BLANDINE DELMAS Fr/Fr (L'Atlantique) 1986; C/Con; 23,275 grt/33,660 dwt; 176.36 × 10.50 m *(578.61 × 34.45 ft)*; M (B&W); 14 kts; 918 TEU
Sister: **CAROLINE DELMAS** (Fr); Sisters (builder—'3 Maj'): **ADELINE DELMAS** (Fr); **DELPHINE DELMAS** (Fr)

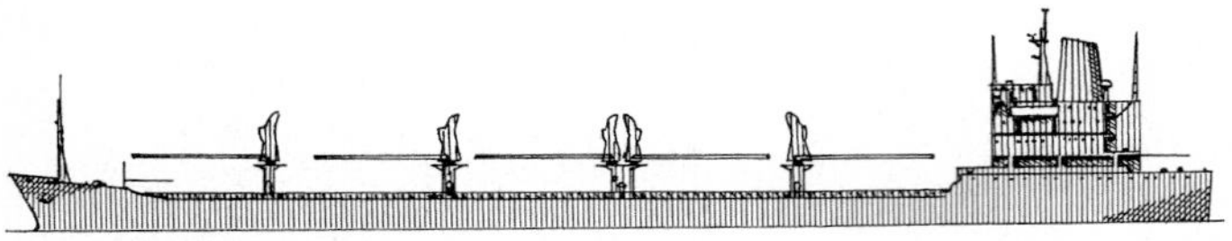

369 *$MC^2PCNMFN$ H13*
GREVENO Gr/Ja (Sanoyasu) 1978; B; 13,823 grt/22,170 dwt; 169.9 × 9.79 m *(527.95 × 32.12 ft)*; M (B&W); 14 kts; ex-*Fort Hamilton*
Sisters: **DANIS KOPER** (Tu) ex-*Fort Carleton*; **PANY R** (Ma) ex-*Fort Walsh*

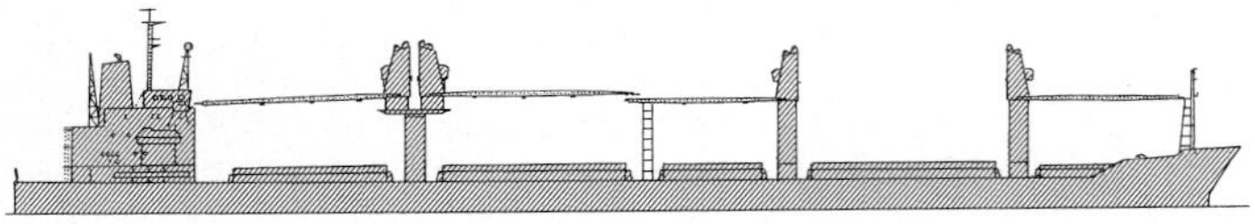

370 *MC^2PNMFM H1*
SAPAI Mr/Ja (Shin Kurushima) 1989; C; 17,590 grt/28,860 dwt; 170.02 × 10.10 m *(557.81 × 33.14 ft)*; M (Mitsubishi); 14 kts

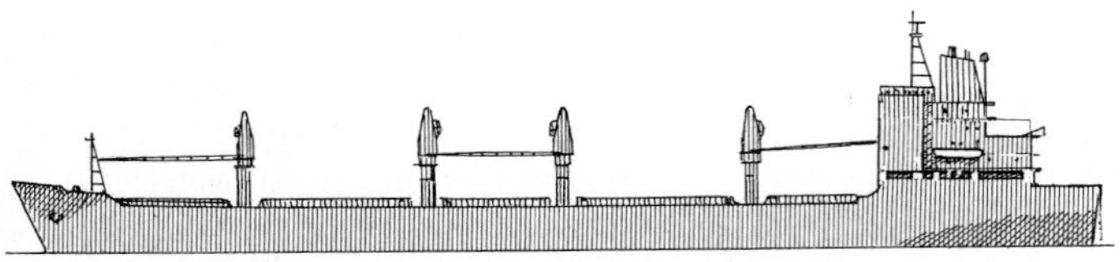

371 *MC^2P^2MFM H13*
MASHALLAH Cy/De (Nakskov) 1978; C/Con; 16,199 grt/23,720 dwt; 159.42 × 10.2 m *(523.03 × 33.46 ft)*; M (B&W); 16 kts; ex-*Samoa*
Sisters: **IRAN TAKHTI** (Ir) ex-*Sargodha*; **LIKA 1** (Ma) ex-*Siena*; **KRASICA 1** (Ma) ex-*Sinaloa*; **MAKRAN** (Pk); **IRAN TEYFOURI** (Ir) ex-*Simba*

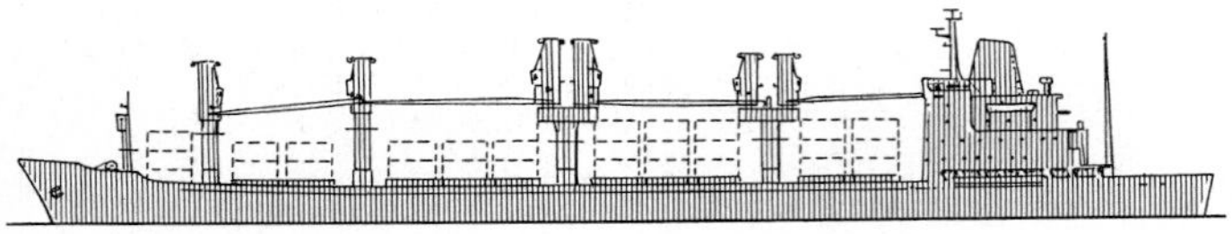

372 *MC^2P^2MFN H1*
MSC TARGA Bs/Ja (Mitsubishi HI) 1977; C/Con; 13,610 grt/18,628 dwt; 162.03 × 9.85 m *(531.59 × 32.32 ft)*; M (Sulzer); 18 kts; ex-*Thana Varee*
Sister: **GREGOR** (Cy) ex-*Chai Varee*

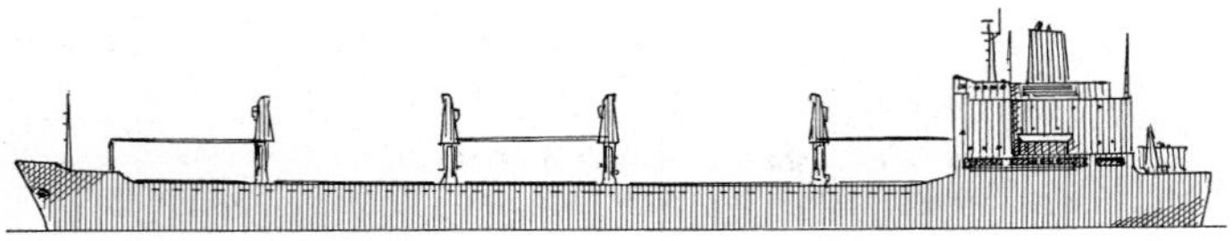

373 *$MC^2P^2M^2FM^2$ H13*
SONIA Bs/Ja (Mitsui) 1977; B/Con; 16,699 grt/23,314 dwt; 158.02 × 10.59 m *(518.44 × 34.74 ft)*; M (B&W); 16.25 kts; ex-*Songkhla*; 792 TEU
Sister: **KORNAT** (SV) ex-*Sumbawa*

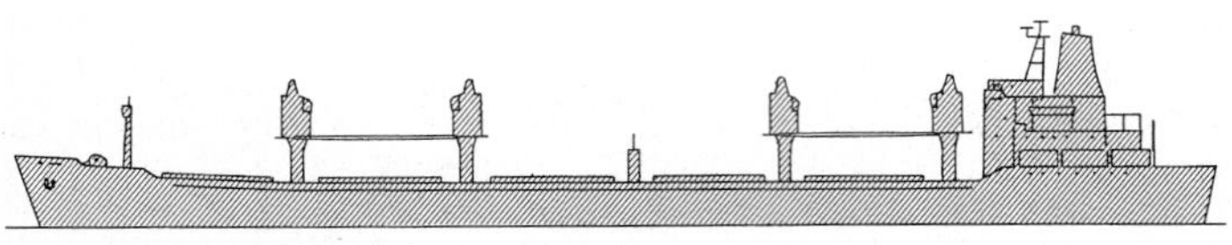

374 *MC^2XC^2MFN H13*
CANAN ARICAN Tu/Br (Swan Hunter) 1972; B; 16,285 grt/26,324 dwt; 182.89 × 10.36 m *(600.03 × 33.99 ft)*; M (Sulzer); 15 kts; ex-*Capulet*

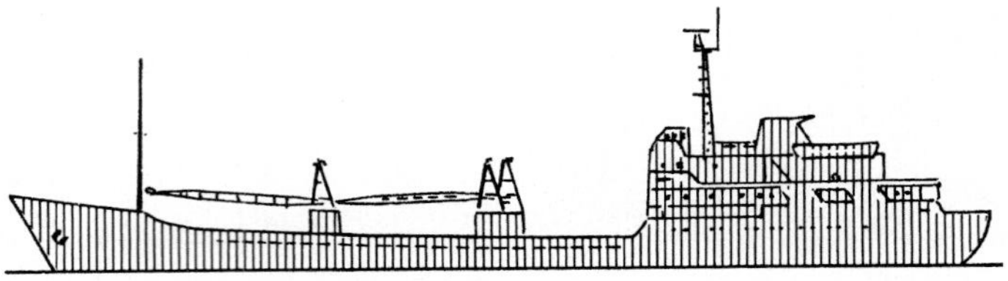

375 *MCDMF H13*
CHEREPOVETS Ru/Rm (Constantza) 1970; C; 1,531 grt/1,851 dwt; 80.27 × 4.9 m *(263.35 × 16.08 ft)*; M (Sulzer); 12 kts
Sisters: **SOSNOVETS** (Ru); **SARATA** (Uk); **SOSNOVKA** (Uk); **SUVOROVO** (Uk); **SERNOVODSK** (Ru); **SNEZHNOGORSK** (Ru); **SUDAK** (Uk); **SLAUTNOYE** (Ru); **SOFIYSK** (Ru); **SURGUT** (Ru); **FREEDOM STAR 1** (Rm) ex-*Nazarcea*; **PALAS** (Rm); **POIANA** (Rm); **FREEDOM STAR 3** (Rm) ex-Novaci

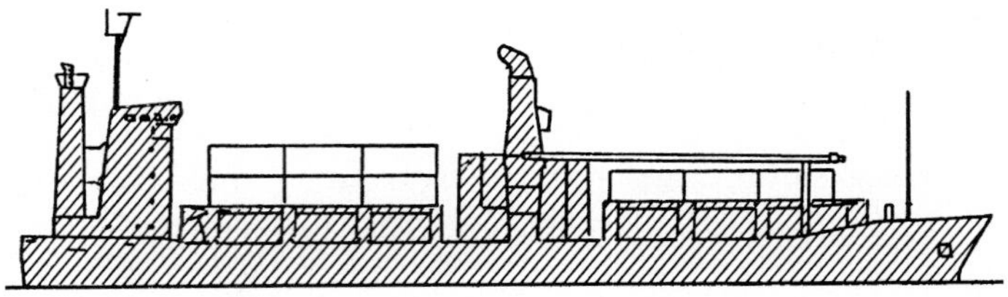

376 *MCMF H*
BREMER REEDER NIS/FRG (Luersson) 1984; C/Con/Pal; 2,191 grt/1,492 dwt; 77.70 × 3.51 m *(254.92 × 11.52 ft)*; M (Deutz); 11 kts; 120 TEU; Side door on port side

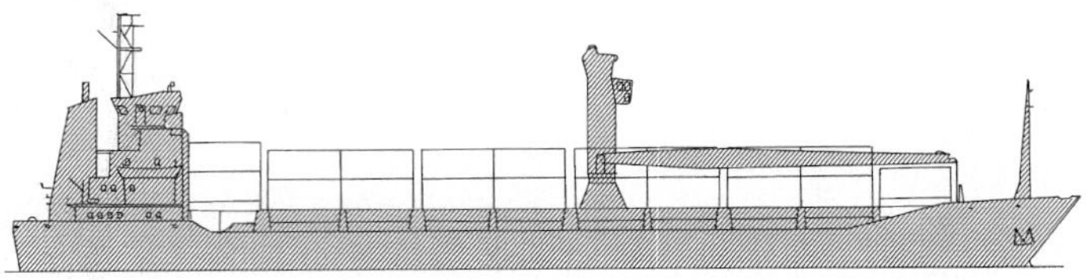

377 *MCMF H1*
CARIBBEAN BREEZE At/FRG (Kroegerw) 1984; C/Con; 2,969 grt/2,880 dwt; 89.79 × 4.85 m *(294.59 × 15.91 ft)*; M (MWM); 13 kts; ex-*Grimsnis*; 221 TEU

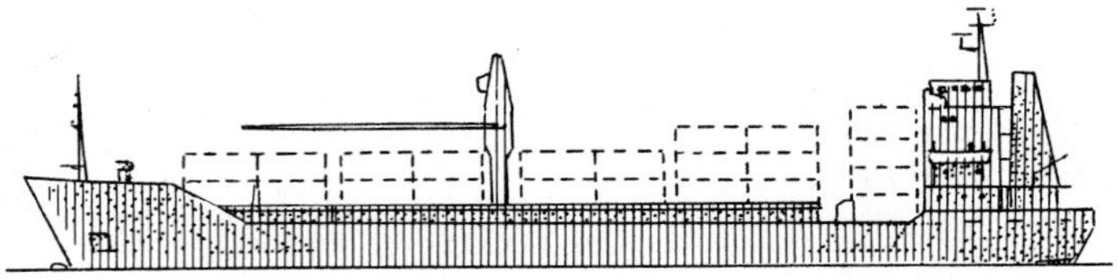

378 *MCMF H1*
MIN MAO RC/FRG (Nobiskrug) 1980; C/Con; 999 grt/3,220 dwt; 89.38 × 4.95 m *(293.24 × 16.24 ft)*; M (KHD); 13.2 kts; ex-*Heidkamp*; 218 TEU
Sister: **FAREAST BONNIE** (SV) ex-*Algeria*

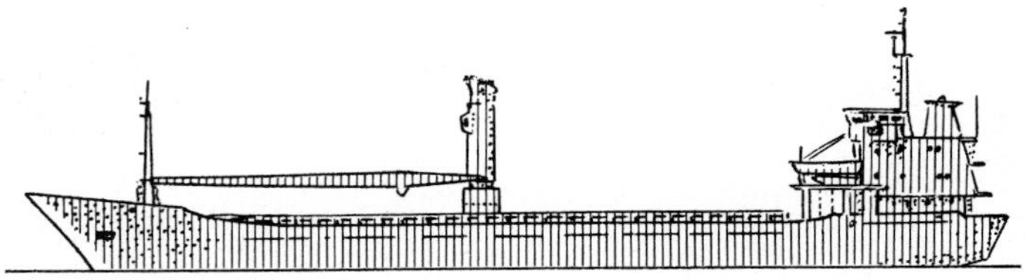

379 *MCMF H1*
RANGIKURA At/FRG (Brand) 1979; C/Con; 2,481 grt/3,932 dwt; 86.2 × 4.87 m *(283 × 15.98 ft)*; M (Atlas-MaK); 13.5 kts; ex-*Christa Thielemann*; 153 TEU; Crane is on starboard side
Sisters: **VITORIO NEMESIO** (Po) ex-*Nicole*; **MAELIFELL** (At) ex-*Stenholm*; Similar (Taller crane, satcom aerial on after end of superstructure, and so on): **ANDRA** (At) ex-*Sandra*

380 *MCMFL H1*
RANGITIKEL At/FRG (Brand) 1985; C/Con; 2,732 grt/4,000 dwt; 90.40 × 6.27 m *(296.59 × 20.57 ft)*; M (MaK); 13.5 kts; ex-*Lisa Heeren*; 177 TEU; Crane on starboard side; **SIMILAR TO DRAWING NUMBER 7/379** but has free-fall lifeboat
Probable sister: **MARINA HEEREN** (At)

381 *MCMFM H1*
ANDRA At/FRG (Brand) 1983; C/Con; 2,605 grt/3,235 dwt; 90.02 × 5.58 m *(295.34 × 18.31 ft)*; M (MaK); 13 kts; ex-*Sandra*; 177 TEU; **SIMILAR TO DRAWING NUMBER 7/379** but for satcom mast aft

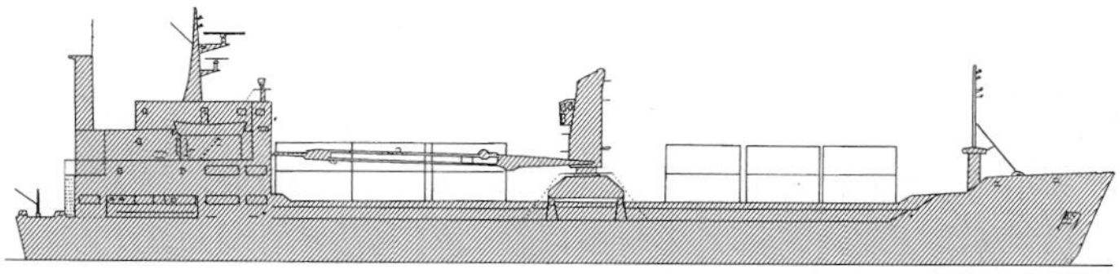

382 *MCMM-F H1*
VELA It/Sw (Gotav Solvesborg) 1979; C/Con; 3,155 grt/5,166 dwt; 89.62 × 7.09 m *(294.03 × 23.26 ft)*; M (Alpha); 12.50 kts; ex-*White Sea*; 192 TEU

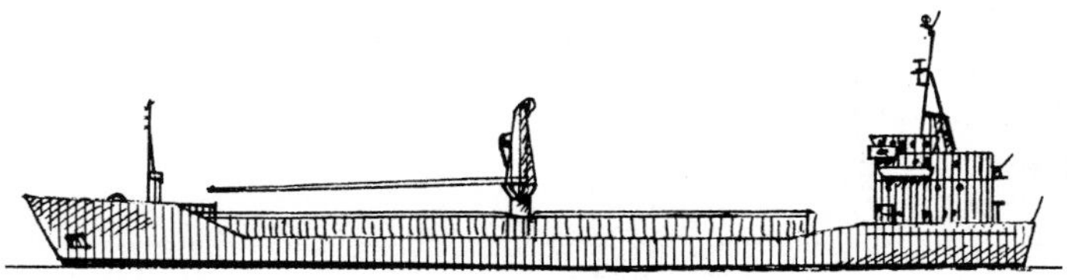

383 *MCM-F H1*
AROS FORCE Sw/FRG (Werftunion) 1977; C; 2,068 grt/2,189 dwt; 81.06 × 4.83 m *(265.94 × 15.85 ft)*; M (Atlas-MaK); 13.5 kts; ex-*Norrland*

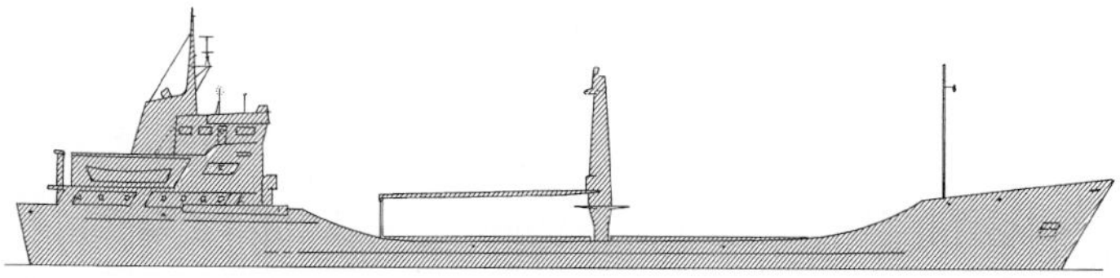

384 *MCM-F H13*
ATLANTIC COAST Bs/Ne ('Hoogezand' JB) 1977; C; 1,943 grt/3,124 dwt; 81.72 × 5.40 m *(268.11 × 17.72 ft)*; M (Polar); 13 kts; ex-*Fivel*; May be sail-assisted

385 *MCM-F H13*
MANASLU Li/Gr (Salamis) 1977; C/Con; 4,387 grt/6,107 dwt; 102.09 × 6.32 m *(334.94 × 20.73 ft)*; TSM (Deutz); 16 kts; ex-*Meteor 1*; 389 TEU; May now be gearless

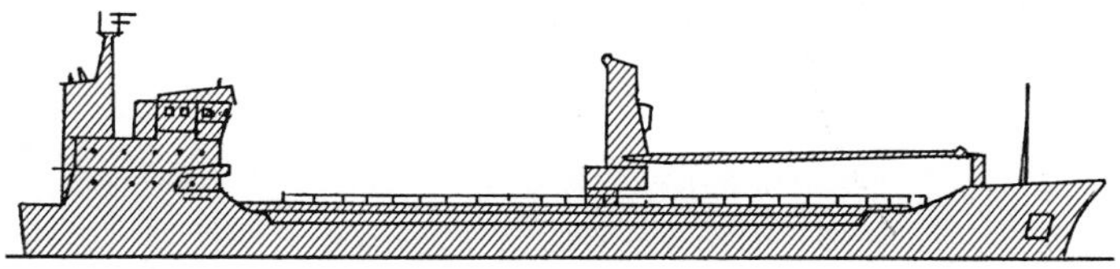

386 *MCM-F H13*
UNDEN Sw/Ne (Nieuwe Noord) 1984; C/Con; 2,610 grt/3,175 dwt; 87.03 × 5.98 m *(285.53 × 19.62 ft)*; M (Wärtsilä); 14.25 kts; 135 TEU; Crane is on port side
Sister: **MANGEN** (Sw)

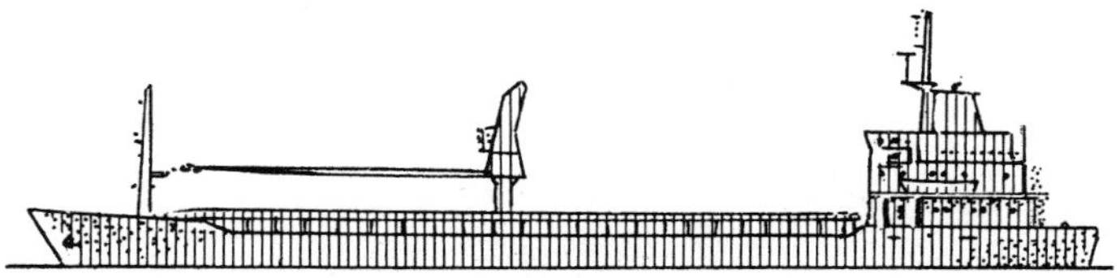

387 *MCM-FN H*
DELLACH As/Ja (Nishi Z) 1977; C; 1,980 grt/2,770 dwt; 79.10 × 5.42 m *(259.51 × 17.78 ft)*; M (Yanmar); 10.5 kts; ex-*Dalsland*; 100 TEU
Sisters: **KELS** (Cy) ex-*Gotaland*; **SWALLOW** (Cy) ex-*Vaermland*

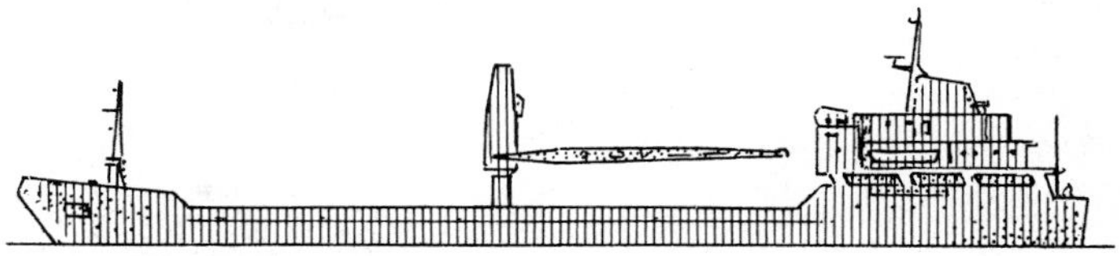

388 *MCM-FN H13*
SALAMA Ma/Sw (Falkenbergs) 1970; C/Con; 2,092 grt/3,251 dwt; 87.03 × 4.96 m *(285.53 × 16.27 ft)*; M (Wichmann); — kts; ex-*Alice*
Similar: **ARACHOVITIKA** (Gr), launched as *Isotat*

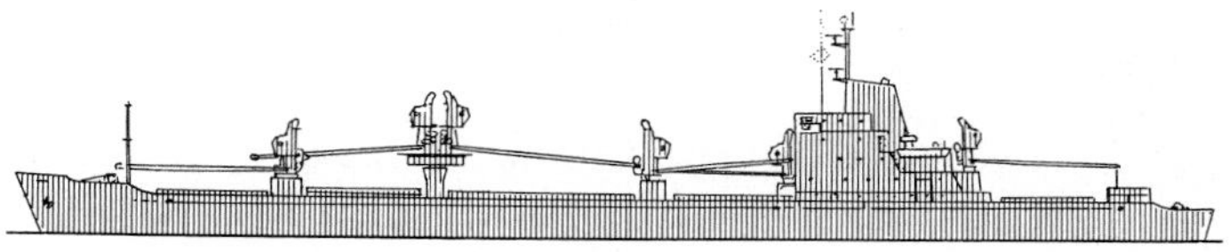

389 *MCPC²M-FC H1*
CHALLENGER IV Pa/Bz (CCN) 1981; C; 10,295 grt/14,650 dwt; 160.03 × 9.21 m *(525 × 30.22 ft)*; M (MAN); 17.5 kts; ex-*Lloyd Alegrete*
Sister: **LLOYD BAHIA** (Bz)

390 *MCPCMFN H13*
VISHVA PANKAJ In/Br (Sunderland) 1980; C/Con; 12,648 grt/16,169 dwt; 152.03 × 9.52 m *(499 × 31.23 ft)*; M (Sulzer); 15.75 kts; 396 TEU
Sisters: **VISHVA PALLAV** (In); **VISHVA PARIMAL** (In); **VISHVA PARIJAT** (In); **VISHVA PARAG** (In); **VISHVA PRAFULLA** (In)

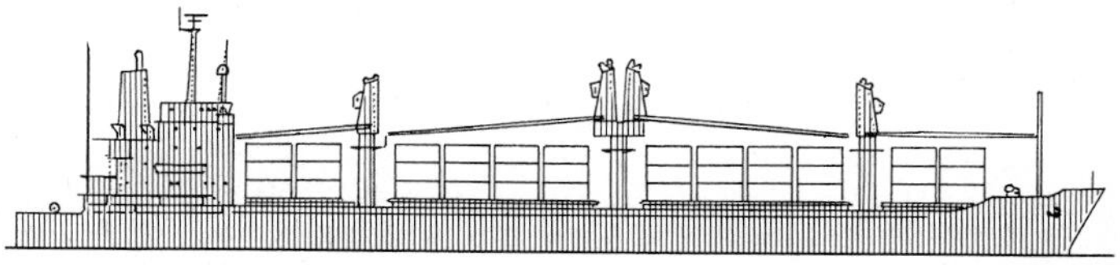

391 *MCPCM²FN H1*
ALS EXPRESS Li/Ja (Mitsubishi HI) 1986; C/Con; 12,963 grt/20,482 dwt; 146.51 × 9.82 m *(480.68 × 32.22 ft)*; M (Sulzer); 14.75 kts; ex-*Kriti Gold*; 734 TEU
Sisters: **T A PATHFINDER** (Pa) ex-*Kriti Silver*; **T A PIONEER** (Pa) ex-*Kriti Platinum*; **ALS STRENGTH** (Pa) ex-*Kriti Amber*

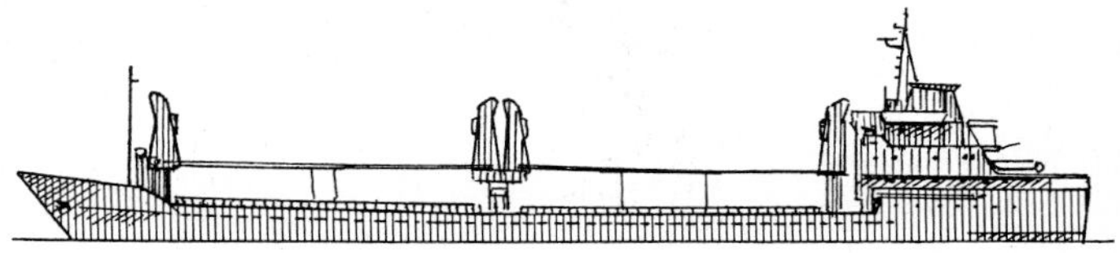

392 *MCPCM-F H13*
DIMARCO Ho/DDR ('Neptun') 1971; C; 2,992 grt/4,344 dwt; 104.12 × 5.79 m *(341.6 × 19 ft)*; M (DMR); 13.5 kts; ex-*Hanseatic*
Sister: **MOONLIGHT** (Cy) ex-*Brunvard*; Probably similar: **GOOD FIGHTER** (—) ex-*Brunhild)*

393 *MCPCNMFN H13*
ASHLEY Li/Ja (Kanda) 1980; B; 21,098 grt/32,770 dwt; 183 × 10.88 m *(600 × 35.7 ft)*; M (Sulzer); — kts; ex-*Aracruz Venture*
Sister: **CIELO DI FIRENZE** (At) ex-*Brazil Venture*

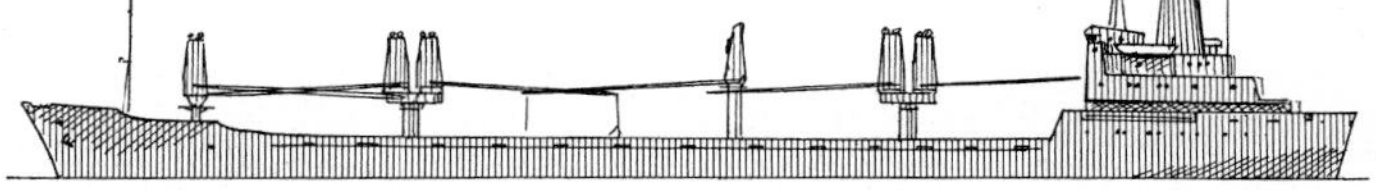

394 *MCPCPMF H13*
ARIEL Bs/De (Helsingor) 1970; C; 7,661 grt/9,529 dwt; 147.02 × 6.79/7.7 m *(482.34 × 22.28/25.26 ft)*; M (B&W); 17.5 kts; Lengthened 1974
Sister: **PALLAS** (Bs)

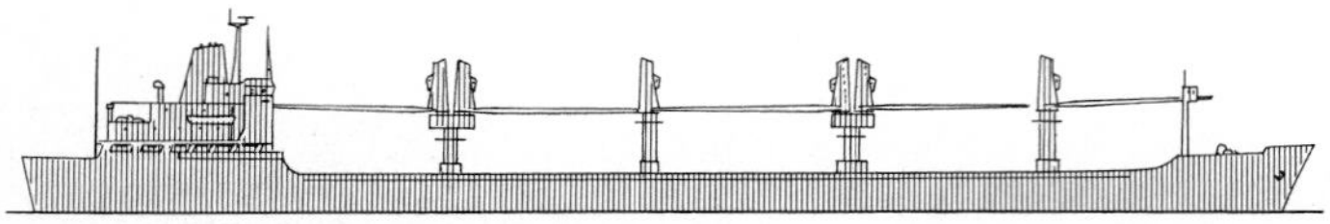

395 *MCPCPNMFN H13*
TOPAZ Gr/Ja (Mitsubishi HI) 1977; C/Con; 14,989 grt/24,424 dwt; 179.03 × 10.37 m *(587.37 × 34.02 ft)*; M (Sulzer); 15.25 kts; ex-*Muncaster Castle*; 628 TEU
Sister: **DSR-SENATOR IVORY** (HK) ex-*Merry Viking*

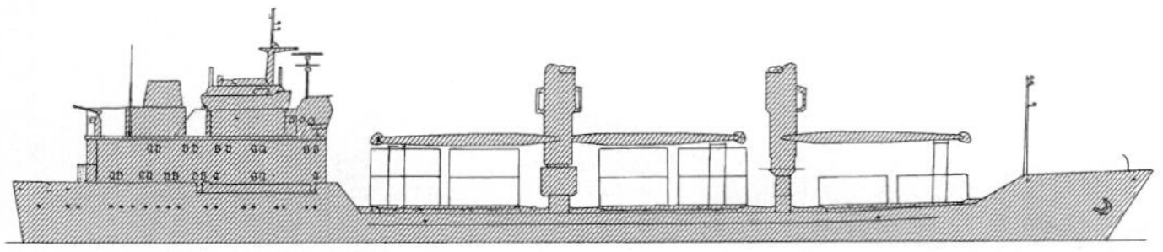

396 *MCPMFM H13*
YOU YI 16 RC/Bu (G Dimitrov) 1988; C/Con; 3,728 grt/5,259 dwt; 100.09 × 7.03 m *(328.38 × 23.06 ft)*; M (B&W); — kts; ex-*You Yi 6*; 98 TEU
Probable sister: **YOU YI 28** (RC)

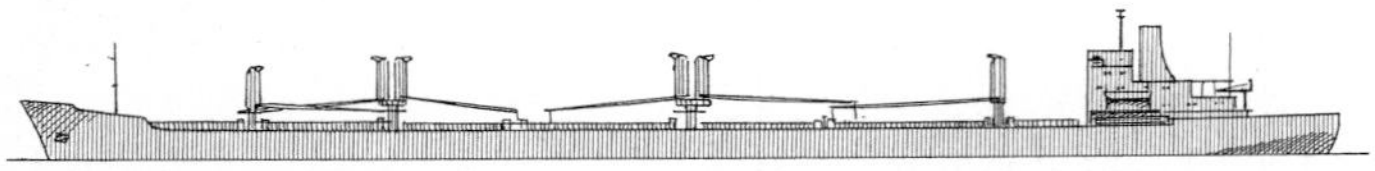

397 *MCP^{2}CMF H1*
KAPETAN ELIAS Cy/FRG (Bremer V) 1971; B; 24,594 grt/43,442 dwt; 203.18 × 11.6 m *(666.6 × 38.06 ft)*; M (MAN); 16 kts; ex-*Budapest*
Sister: **SANTORINI I** (Cy) ex-*Prag*

398 *MCP^{2}CMF H13*
TORM FREYA DIS/De (Aalborg) 1982; C/Con; 16,507 grt/23,700 dwt; 159.57 × 10.35 m *(524 × 33.96 ft)*; M (B&W); 16.5 kts; ex-*Ove Skou*; 760 TEU

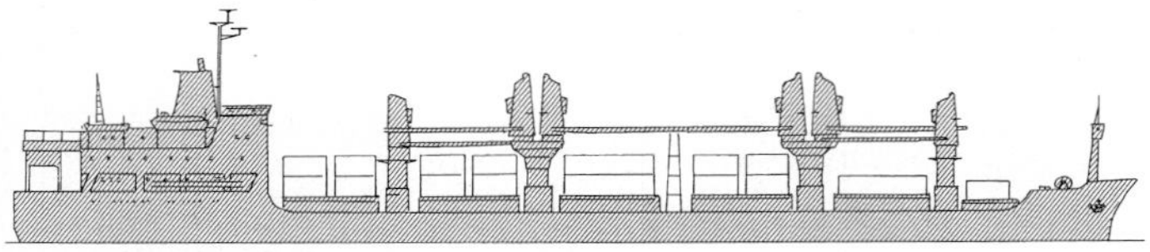

399 *MCP^{2}CMFN H13*
MAULLIN Ch/Ja (Nipponkai) 1978; C/Con; 11,492 grt/15,011 dwt; 152.28 × 9.23 m *(499.61 × 30.28 ft)*; M (B&W); 16 kts; ex-*Salvador*; 449 TEU
Sister: **SANTA FE** (Cy)

400 *MCP^{2}CM^{2}F H13*
ADMAS Et/Pd ('Komuny Paryskiej') 1986; C/Con; 11,573 grt/13,593 dwt; 149.51 × 9.14 m *(490.52 × 29.99 ft)*; M (Sulzer); 16.80 kts; ex-*Warszawa II*; 302 TEU; 'B354' type
Sisters: **LUBLIN II** (Pd); **SZCZECIN** (Pd); **KRAKOW II** (Pd); **LODZ II** (Pd); **UNISELVA** (NA) ex-*Polonia*; **UNISIERRA** (NA) ex-*Radom*; **MIRA** (Li) ex-*Bydgoszcz*

401 *MCP^{2}HFN H13*
NEDLLOYD CALIFORNIA Ge/FRG (A G 'Weser') 1980; C/Con; 10,835 grt/13,992 dwt; 145.01 × 8.21 m *(476 × 26.94 ft)*; M (MaK); 17.75 kts; ex-*Holstencarrier*; 'Key 12' type; 950 TEU
Sister: **ST NICOLAS X** (Cy) ex-*Holstenracer*

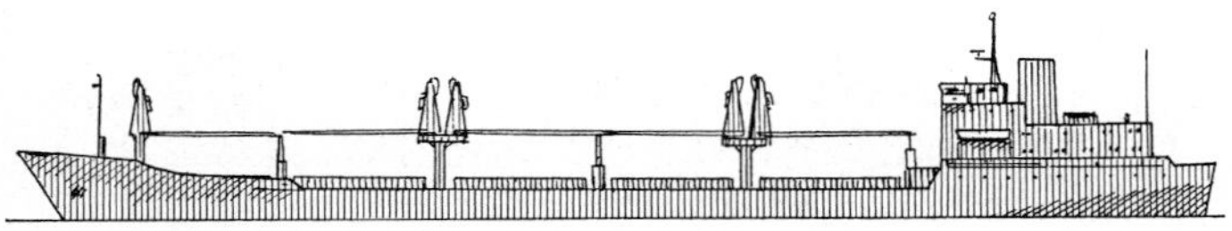

402 *MCP^{2}MF H13*
HUA SHENG RC/Fi (Valmet) 1971; C; 6,179 grt/8,627 dwt; 129.09 × 7.97 m *(423.52 × 26.15 ft)*; M (B&W); 17 kts; ex-*Herakles*; 285 TEU

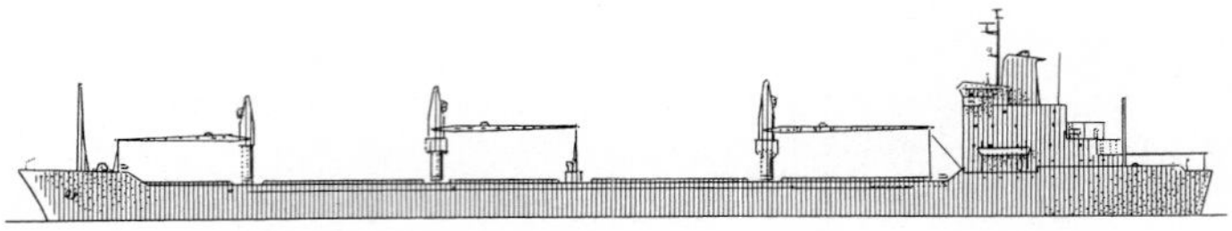

403 *MCP^{2}MFN H13*
FINDIKLI Tu/Bz (Maua) 1978; B; 16,704 grt/26,272 dwt; 173.19 × 9.72 m *(568.17 × 31.89 ft)*; M (MAN); 15.5 kts; ex-*Alexandros G Tsavliris*; 'Prinasa 26/16' type; 592 TEU
Sister: **SEA SONNET** (Cy) ex-*Claire A Tsavliris*

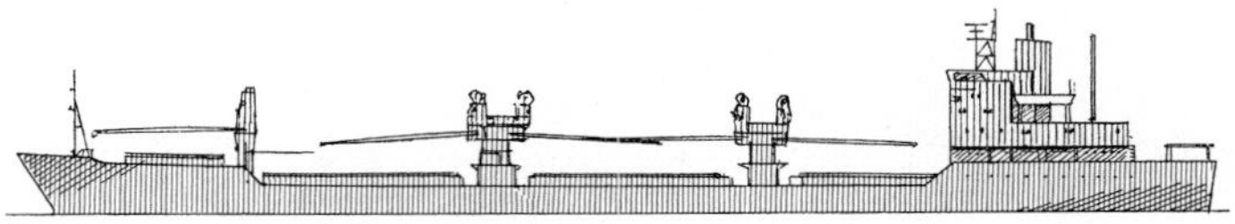

404 *MCP^{2}MFN H13*
MOANA PACIFIC DIS/Be (Boelwerf) 1978; C/Con; 14,023 grt/19,775 dwt; 163.5 × 10.25 m *(536.5 × 33.6 ft)*; M (MAN); 17 kts; ex-*E R Brugge*; 697 TEU
Sister: **MSC CARLA** (Cy) ex-*E R Brussel*

405 *MCP^{2}MFN H13*
OCEANGLORY Pa/RC (Chung Hua) 1981; C/Con; 12,245 grt/18,950 dwt; 164.32 × 9.74 m *(539 × 31.96 ft)*; M (B&W); 16 kts; ex-*Sea Architect*

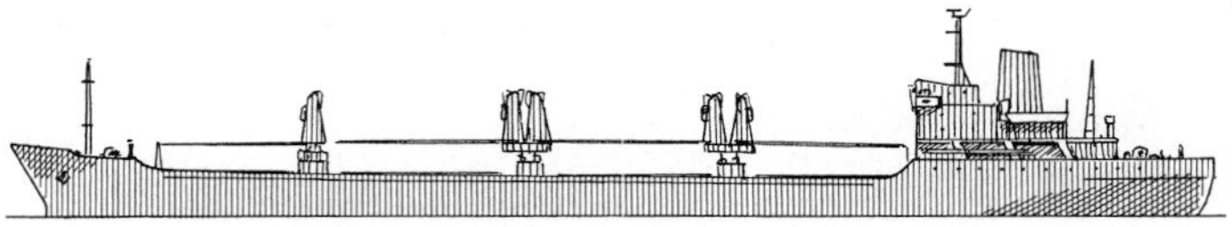

406 *MCP^{2}MFN H13*
XIANG CHENG RC/Ja (Mitsui) 1976; C; 11,418 grt/18,755 dwt; 147.71 × 9.63 m *(484.61 × 31.59 ft)*; M (B&W); 15 kts; ex-*Aristeidis*; 'Mitsui-Concord 18' type
Sisters: **RONG CHENG** (RC) ex-*Aristoxenos*; **PRAPTI** (Cy) ex-*Aristonofos*; Possible sisters: **YUN CHENG** (RC) ex-*Aristodikos*; **TONG CHENG** (RC) ex-*Aristonidas*; **ARUNACHAL PRADESH** (In), launched as *Aristolaos*; **JIN CHENG** (RC) ex-*Aristomachos*

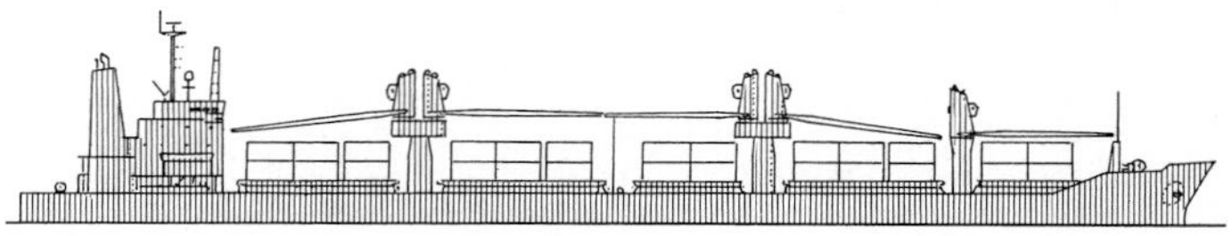

407 *MCP^{2}M^{2}F H1*
OHFU Pa/Ja (Kurushima) 1987; C/Con; 14,499 grt/23,325 dwt; 160.51 × 10.12 m *(526.61 × 33.20 ft)*; M (Mitsubishi); 14 kts; 581 TEU
Sister (builder—Hayashikane): **CHOFU** (Pa)

408 *MCP^{3}HFN H13*
PACIFIC MARU Ja/Ja (Mitsubishi HI) 1981; C/Con; 17,137 grt/22,597 dwt; 169.5 × 10.04 m *(556.1 × 32.94 ft)*; M (Sulzer); 17.75 kts
Sister: **PANAMA MARU** (Ja)

See photo number 7/505

409 *MCP^{3}MFN H1*
OCEAN ELITE Pa/Ja (Mitsubish HI) 1977; C/Con; 13,436 grt/18,284 dwt; 162.24 × 9.87 m *(532.28 × 32.38 ft)*; M (Sulzer); 16 kts
Sisters: **OCEAN BRILLIANCY** (Pa) ex-*Ocean Esperance*; **OCEAN CONFIDENCE** (Sg) ex-*Ocean Espoir*; **OCEAN COMPETENCE** (Sg) ex-*Ocean Eminence*; Similar (lower superstructure): **SALVADOR EXPRESS** (Bs) ex-*Ocean Harvest*; **KOTA PUSAKA** (Sg) ex-*Ocean Harmonia*; **LA PAIX** (Pa) ex-*Ocean Hope*

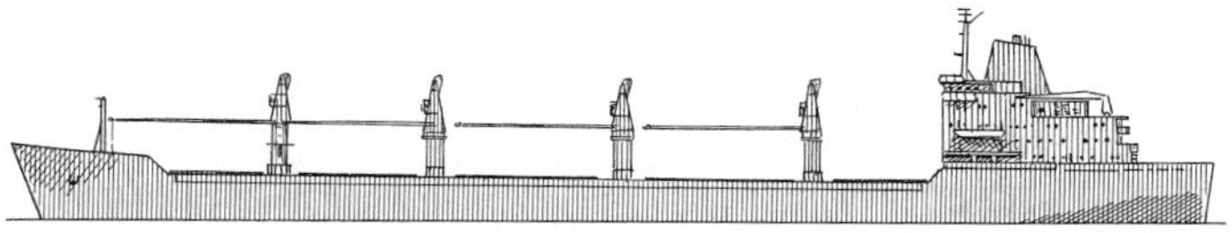

410 *MCP^{3}MFR H13*
CLIPPER SALVADOR Ma/De (Nakskov) 1974; C/Con; 16,119 grt/17,249 dwt; 170.69 × 10.27 m *(560.01 × 33.69 ft)*; M (B&W); 20.5 kts; ex-*Marchen Maersk*; 628 TEU
Sisters: **CLIPPER SAO LUIZ** (Ma) ex-*Margrethe Maersk*; **CLIPPER SAO PAULO** (Ma) ex-*McKinney Maersk*; **CLIPPER SANTOS** (Ma) ex-*Mathilde Maersk*

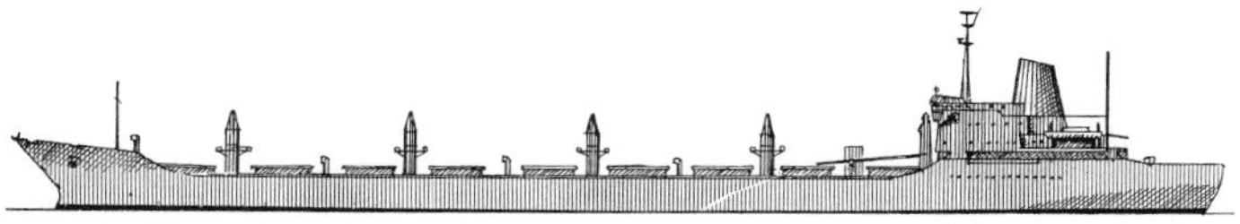

411 *MD^{5}MFN H13*
POROS Gr/Ru (Baltic) 1971; B; 23,192 grt/38,203 dwt; 201.33 × 11.23 m *(660.53 × 36.84 ft)*; M (B&W); 15.5 kts; ex-*Gerlena*; 'Baltika' type
Possible sisters: **HUA MING** (RC) ex-*Tento*; **CAPTADIMITRIS** (Cy) ex-*Gerlin*

412 *MDMM-F H13*
DOLICHI Cy/Ne (Bijlholt) 1975; C; 1,927 grt/3,020 dwt; 81.67 × 3.38 m *(267.95 × 11.09 ft)*; M (Smit-Bolnes); 12.50 kts; ex-*Barendsz*; Cranes may now be removed; **SIMILAR TO DRAWING NUMBER 6/56**

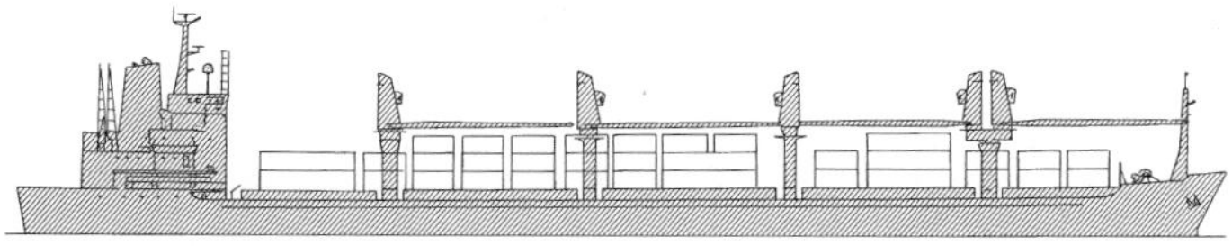

413 *MPC^{2}PNMFN H13*
DSR-TIANJIN Pa/Ja (Sanoyasu) 1983; C/Con; 17,126 grt/26,320 dwt; 166.40 × 9.68 m *(545.93 × 31.76 ft)*; M (Mitsubishi); 15 kts; ex-*C C Long Beach*; 1,022 TEU
Sisters: **HEIYO** (Pa) ex-*C C Oakland*; **HEIAN** (Pa) ex-*C C Portland*; **GLADIATOR** (Li) ex-*C C Los Angeles*; **RICKMERS SHANGHAI** (HK) ex-*C C Seattle*; **SAWAT** (Li) ex-*C C San Francisco*

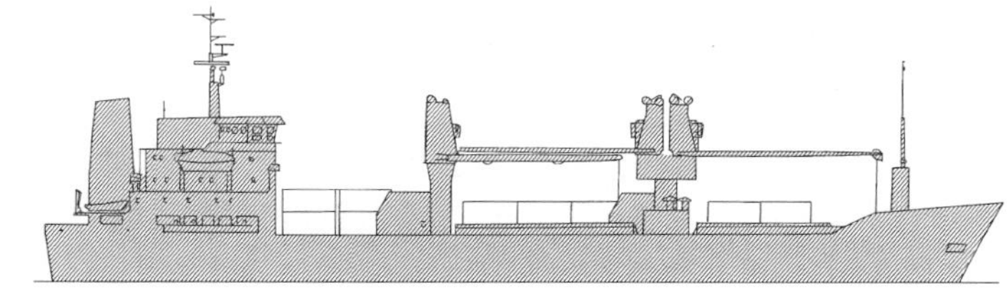

414 *MPCHF H1*
ARINA ARCTICA DIS/De (Orskov C) 1984/94; Con; 6,759 grt/4,330 dwt; 110.01 × 6.24 m *(360.93 × 20.47 ft)*; M (B&W); 16 kts; ex-*Nuka Ittuk*; 274 TEU; Converted from cargo/pallets carrier 1994; Drawing shows vessel's original appearance so there are probably some alterations now

415 *MPCMF H13*
NAN XI JIANG RC/De (Aalborg) 1970; C; 3,003 grt/4,450 dwt; 95.56 × 7.17 m *(313.52 × 23.52 ft)*; M (B&W); 14 kts; ex-*Dettifoss*
Sister: **MYOHYANG 5** (Rk) ex-*Manafoss*

416 *MPCPMFN H1*
VERDON Cy/Br (A&P) 1981; B; 14,582 grt/26,350 dwt; 181.29 × 10.4 m *(594.78 × 34.12 ft)*; M (Sulzer); 15 kts; ex-*El Challenger*; 'B-26' type

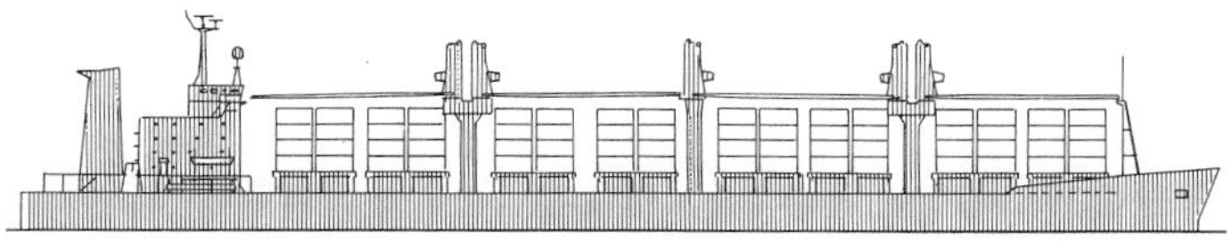

417 *MPCPM^{2}F H1*
COLIMA Pi/Br (Sunderland) 1985; C/Con; 29,660 grt/45,913 dwt; 196.04 × 12.22 m *(643.18 × 40.09 ft)*; M (B&W); 17.50 kts; 1,590 TEU
Sister: **MITLA** (Pa)

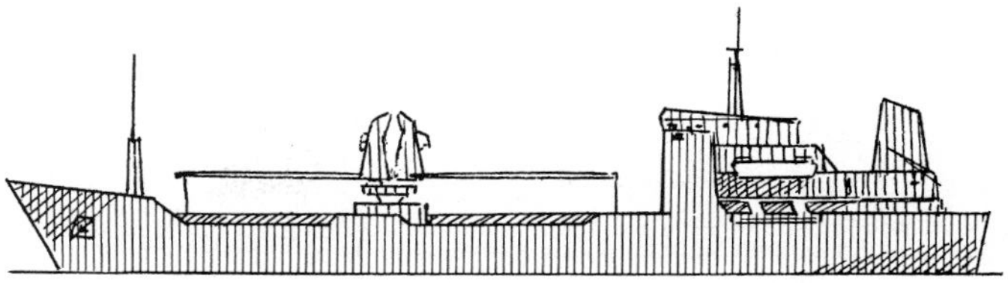

418 *MPHF H1*
SNOW BIRD Cy/De (Dannebrog) 1979; C; 4,961 grt/3,704 dwt; 95.51 × 5.3 m *(313.35 × 17.39 ft)*; M (Alpha-Diesel); 14.5 kts; ex-*Magnus Jensen*; side door
Sister: **JANET I** (Sg) ex-*Johan Petersen*

419 *MPM–F H13*
EVAN SV/Ne ('Friesland') 1976; C; 2,892 grt/3,821 dwt; 81.92 × 6.05 m *(268.77 × 19.85 ft)*; M (KHD); 12 kts; ex-*Annette*

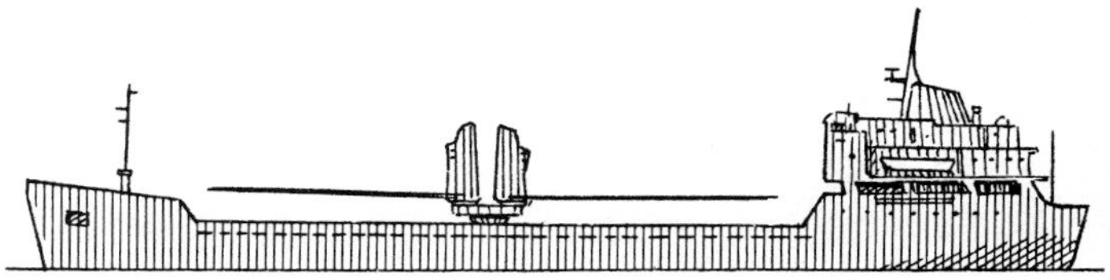

420 *MPM-F H13*
MEONIA Cy/Sw (Falkenbergs) 1972; C; 2,756 grt/4,954 dwt; 87.03 × 6.83 m *(285.53 × 22.4 ft)*; M (Nydqvist & Holm); 11.5 kts; ex-*Eos*
Similar: **SALAMA** (Ma) ex-*Alice*

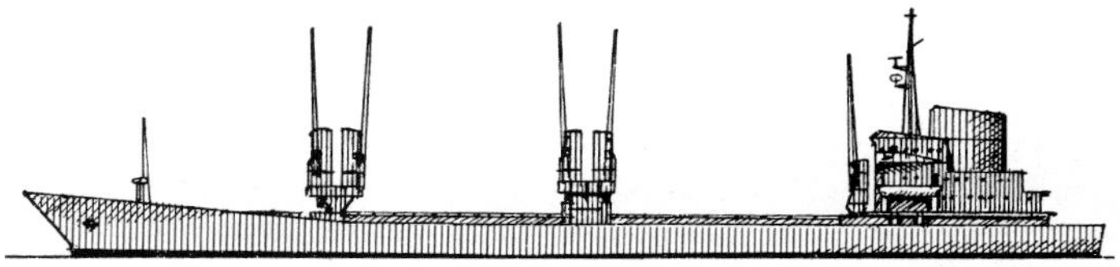

421 *MP^{2}CMF H*
WAN XIANG RC/FRG (O&K) 1971; C; 5,084 × 7,550 dwt; 117.2 × 7.53 m *(384.51 × 24.7 ft)*; M (Atlas-MaK); 16.5 kts; ex-*Bellatrix*
Sister: **DIMITRIS P** (Bl) ex-*Beteigueze*

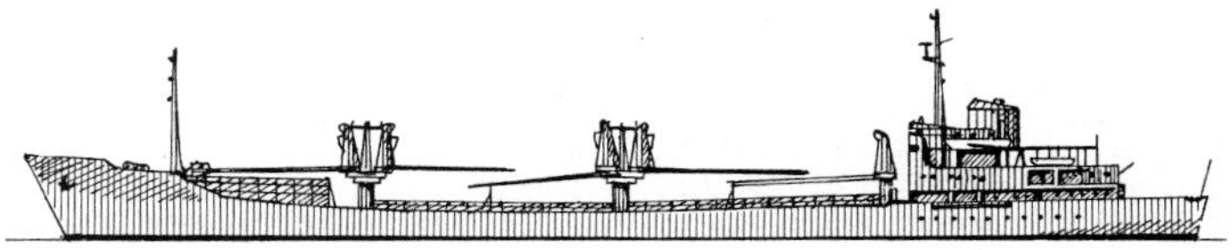

422 *MP^{2}CMF H1*
HUA YING RC/FRG (Unterweser) 1969; C; 5,512 grt/7,244 dwt; 124.49 × 7.55 m *(408.43 × 24.77 ft)*; M (KHD); 17 kts; ex-*Ede Sottorf*; 258 TEU
Sisters: **JIN QIAO** (RC) ex-*Willi Reith*; **MSC SANDRA 5** (Pa) ex-*Meta Reith*;
Similar: **XIN HAI HUA** (RC) ex-*Matthias Reith*; **SI QI** (RC) ex-*Grethe Reith*

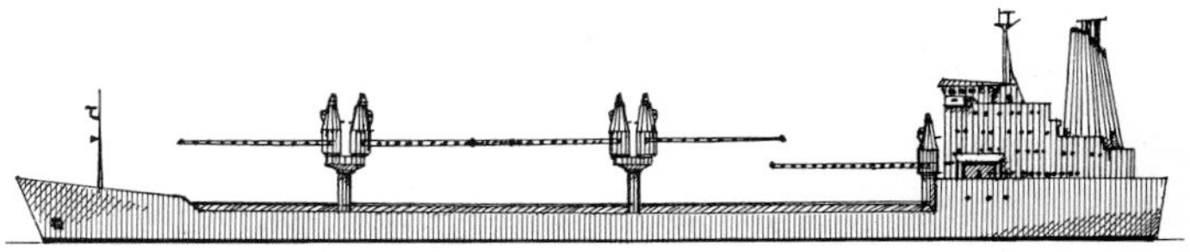

423 *MP^{2}CMF H13*
NOMADIC POLLUX NIS/No (Haugesund) 1977; C; 14,013 grt/17,161 dwt; 154.97 × 9.2 m *(508.43 × 30.18 ft)*; M (Sulzer); 17 kts; ex-*Pollux*
Sister: **NOMADIC PATRIA** (NIS) ex-*Patria*

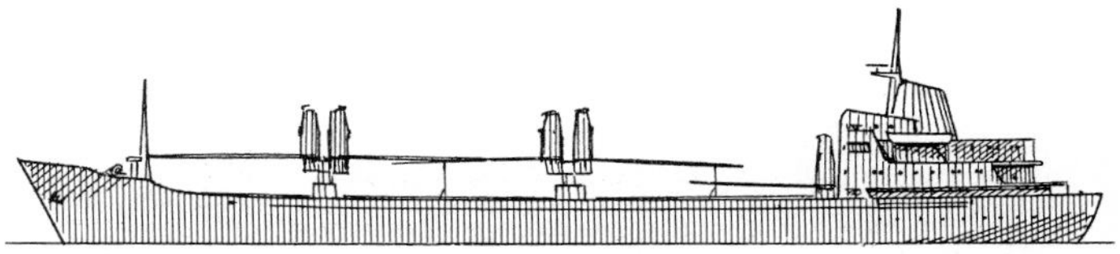

424 *MP^{2}CM-F H1*
LAS PERLAS Cy/FRG (O&K) 1967; C; 4,925 grt/7,027 dwt; 123.4 × 7.59 m *(405 × 24.9 ft)*; M (MAN); — kts; ex-*Galila*

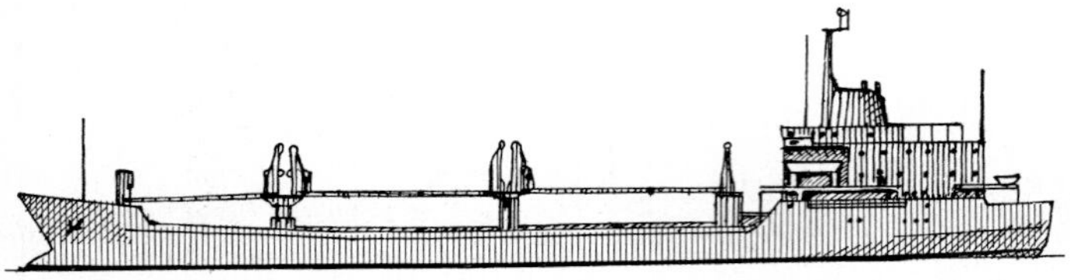

425 *MP^2CM-FN H13*
LITSA K Cy/DDR ('Neptun') 1977; C; 4,338 grt/7,084 dwt; 120.61 × 7.83 m *(395.7 × 25.69 ft)*; M (MAN); 16.75 kts; ex-*Liebenwalde*
Sisters: **FORTUNE OCEAN** (SV) ex-*Cunewalde*; **ST THOMAS** (Cy) ex-*Luckenwalde*; **MICO** (Bs) ex-*Schonwalde*; **GREEN ISLAND** (Eg) ex-*Geringswalde*; **OTS URANUS** (Cy) ex-*Mittenwalde*; **LUCKY OCEAN** (SV) ex-*Furstenwalde*; **DAN DONG** (Ma) ex-*Eichwalde*; **ARABIA** (Ma) ex-*Rudolf Diesel*; **JIN JI SHAN** (RC) ex-*Blankensee*; **SAMSUN** (Pa) ex-*Muggelsee*; **ST GEORGE** (At) ex-*Werbellinsee*; **CORTO** (Ma) ex-*Kolpinsee*; **CARTHAGE** (Tn) ex-*Inselsee*; **HANNIBAL** (Tn) ex-*Rhinsee*; **CHANG WANG** (RC) ex-*Schwielosee*; **ST MARTIN** (At) ex-*Trenntsee*

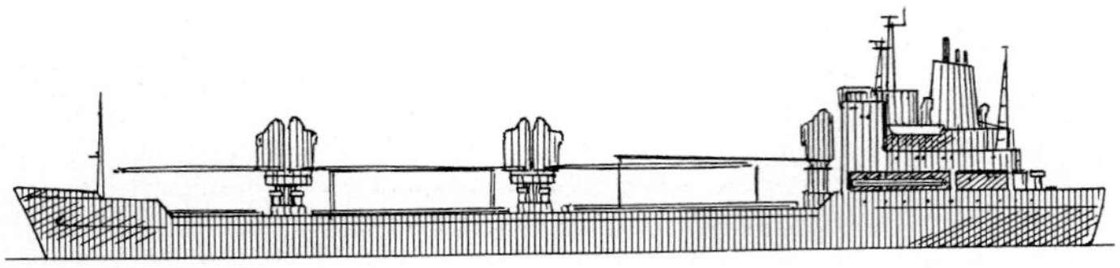

426 *MP^2CNMFN H13*
TOZEUR Tn/Ja (Naikai) 1977; C; 6,977 grt/8,628 dwt; 127.29 × 7.9 m *(417.62 × 25.92 ft)*; M (B&W); 18 kts
Possible sister: **EL JEM** (Tn); Possibly similar: **TOYOFUJI No 2** (Ja)

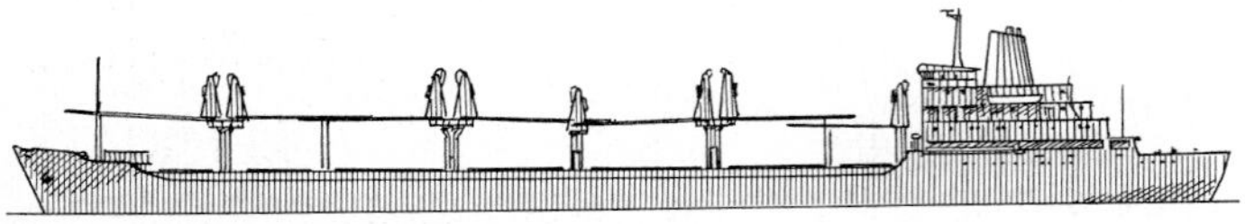

427 *MP^2CPCMF H13*
JUTHA PARIYANAT Th/Br (Smith's D) 1972; C; 11,863 grt/13,537 dwt; 159.77 × 9.17 m *(522.21 × 30.09 ft)*; M (Sulzer); 19 kts; ex-*Atlanta*; 118 TEU
Sister: **JUTHA NATTAKA** (Th) ex-*Aurora*

428 *MP^2CPM-FC H13*
SKOPELOS Gr/Ca (Marine Indust) 1978/80; C/Con; 15,011 grt/16,927 dwt; 187.15 × 8.37 m *(614.01 × 27.46 ft)*; M (MAN); 17.25 kts; ex-*Marindus Rimouski*; Lengthened 1980 (NKK); 594 TEU
Sisters: **SKYROS** (Gr) ex-*Marindus Quebec*; **SAMOS** (Gr) ex-*Marindus Trois Rivieres*

429 *MP^2MF H1*
HUA QIONG RC/FRG (Unterweser) 1972; C/Con; 5,829 grt/8,150 dwt; 124.52 × 8.1 m *(408.53 × 26.57 ft)*; M (KHD); 17.5 kts; ex-*Lotte Reith*

430 *MP^2MF H1*
KOTA MESRA My/FRG (O&K) 1971; C; 5,705 grt/8,220 dwt; 126.83 × 7.36 m *(416.1 × 24.14 ft)*; M (Atlas-MaK); 16.5 kts; ex-*Katjana*
Sister: **LU FENG** (RC) ex-*Steindamm*

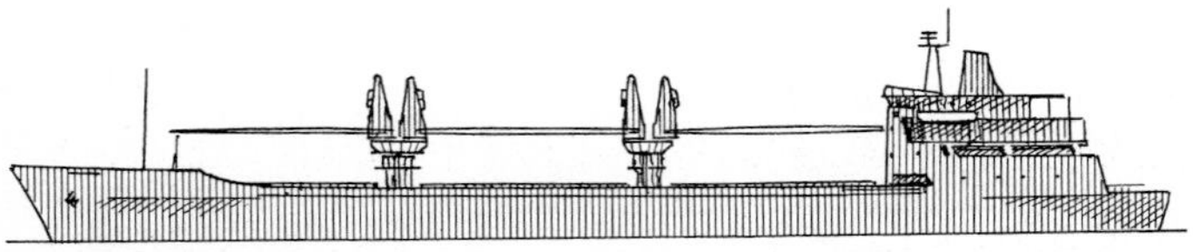

431 *MP^2MF H12*
KOTA MACHAN Sg/Au (Adelaide) 1973; C; 6,285 grt/8,543 dwt; 119.7 × 7.71 m *(392.72 × 25.30 ft)*; M (MAN); 16.75 kts; ex-*Cape York*; One side door
Sister: **HAI FENG** (SV) ex-*Cape Arnhem*

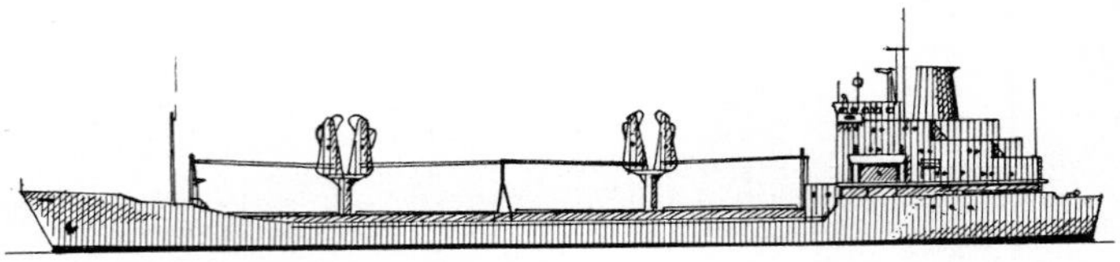

432 *MP^2MF H13*
AN GUO RC/Fi (Valmet) 1971; C; 6,616 grt/8,123 dwt; 129.39 × 8.07 m *(424.51 × 24.48 ft)*; M (B&W); 17.25 kts; ex-*Finnpine*
Sisters: **SU LIN** (RC) ex-*Finntrader*; **J SISTER** (SV) ex-*Finnwood*

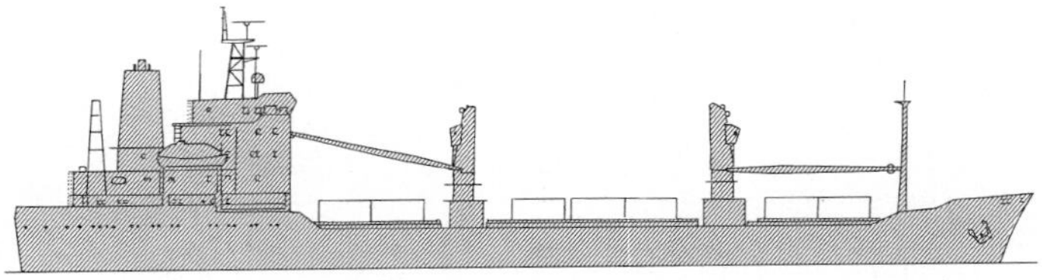

433 *MP^2MFK H13*
SUPERFLEX BOND Cy/RC (Xingang) 1989; C/Con; 6,425 grt/7,920 dwt; 119.01 × 7.40 m *(390.45 × 24.28 ft)*; M (Sulzer); 13.50 kts; ex-*Berounka*; 126 TEU
Sisters: **SUPERFLEX BEAUTY** (Cy) ex-*Sazava*; **ZILINA** (Sk) ex-*Vltava*; **OTAVA** (Sk)

434 *MP^2MFR H13*
ZIM TEXAS Li/FRG (Flender) 1981; C/Con; 9,582 grt/11,640 dwt; 147.4 × 8.16 m *(484 × 26.77 ft)*; M (Krupp-Mak); 16 kts; ex-*Sirius*; 737 TEU
Similar (funnel differs): **EAGLE SEA** (At) ex-*Katjana*; Possible sister (may not have cranes): **APOLLONIA** (At) launched as *Apollonia*

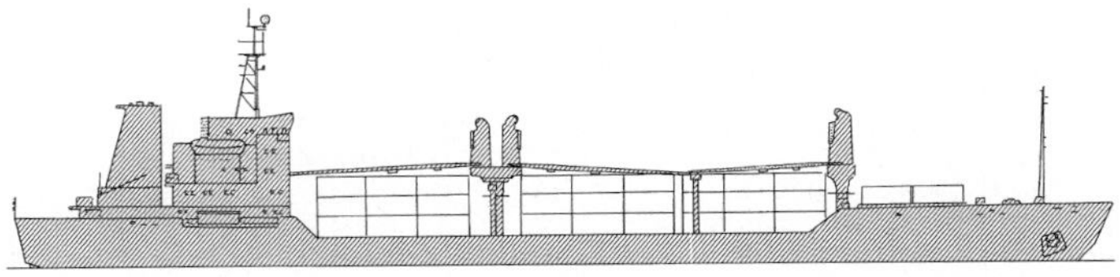

435 *MP^2MFS H13*
PAVLIN VINOGRADOV Ru/Pd (Gdanska) 1987; C/Con; 6,395 grt/7,850 dwt; 131.60 × 7.00 m *(431.76 × 22.97 ft)*; M (B&W); 14.90 kts; 274 TEU; 'B352' type
Sisters: **INZHENER PLAVINSKIY** (Ru); **KAPITAN GLOTOV** (Ru); **KAPITAN PONOMARYOV** (Ru) (possibly **KAPITAN PONOMAREV**); **A SIBIRYAKOV** (Ru); **AKADEMIK GLUSHKO** (Ru); **TEODOR NETTE** (Ru); **JOHANN MAHMASTAL** (Ru); Sisters (Maltese built—Malta SB; 'B479' type; Funnel has a framework extension): **KAPITAN GONCHAROV** (Cy); **KAPITAN KHABALOV** (Ru); **KAPITAN CHMUTOV** (Ru); **KAPITAN ZUZENKO** (Ru); **KAPITAN PRIMAK** (Cy); **MIKHAIL PANFILOV** (Ru); **RADIST NESMENOVA** (Ru)

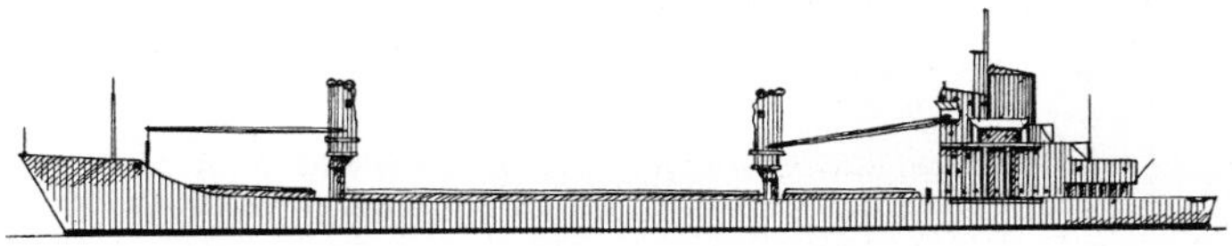

436 *MP^2MM-F H1*
GOOD EXPLORER Pa/FRG (Schichau-U) 1973; C; 6,261 grt/8,985 dwt; 132.52 × 8 m *(434.77 × 26.24 ft)*; M (KHD); 17 kts; ex-*Ede Sinstorf*; 358 TEU
Similar: **LU YU** (RC) ex-*Macaela Drescher*

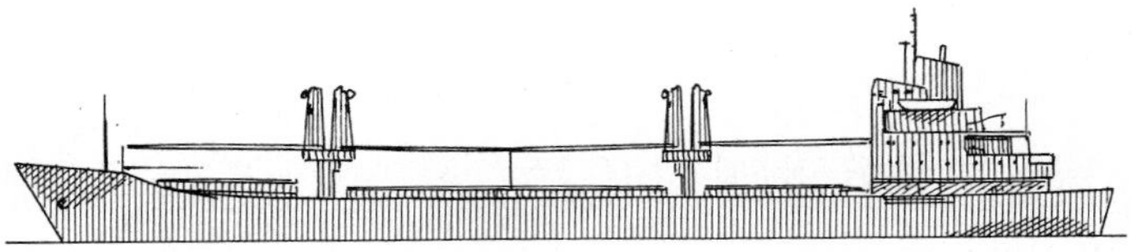

437 *MP^2M-F H1*
GOLDEN SHINE SV/FRG (Unterweser) 1972; C; 5,939 grt/8,100 dwt; 124.52 × 8.12 m *(408.53 × 26.64 ft)*; M (KHD); 17 kts; ex-*Ede Wittorf*

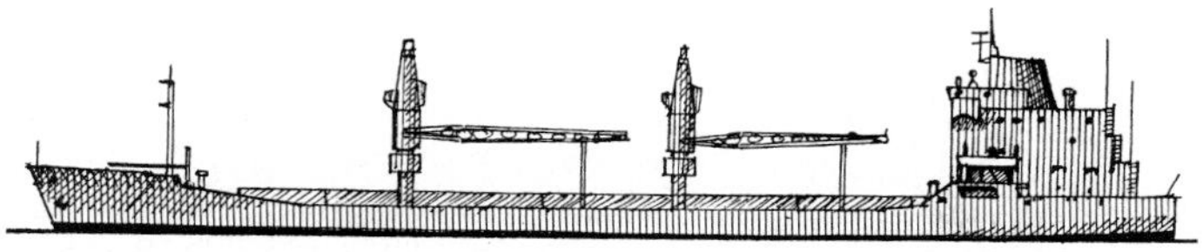

438 *MP²M-FN H13*
RED STONE Bs/Br (Robb Caledon) 1972; C/Pap; 6,704 grt/9,985 dwt; 122.81 × 8.1 m *(402.92 × 26.57 ft)*; M (Pielstick); 15 kts; ex-*Ida Lundrigan*
Sister: **GIDO** (Pa) ex-*Ria Jean McMurtry*

439 *MP²NMFN H1*
RASELTIN Eg/Ja (Setouchi) 1976; C; 5,769 grt/8,232 dwt; 119.06 × 7.45 m *(390.61 × 24.44 ft)*; M (B&W); 14.5 kts
Sisters: **ALANFUSHI** (Eg); **ALCHATBY** (Eg); **ALIBRAHIMIYA** (Eg)

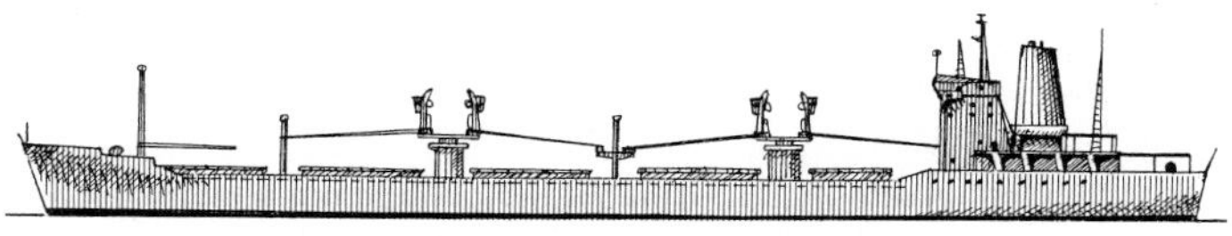

440 *MP²NMFN H13*
ANGELINA L Gr/Ja (Hitachi) 1975; C; 13,731 grt/21,196 dwt; 161.6 × 9.93 m *(530.18 × 32.58 ft)*; M (B&W); 15.5 kts; ex-*Jamaica Farewell*; 'Hitachi UT-20' type
Sister: **SEA HARVEST** (Li) ex-*Mari Boeing*

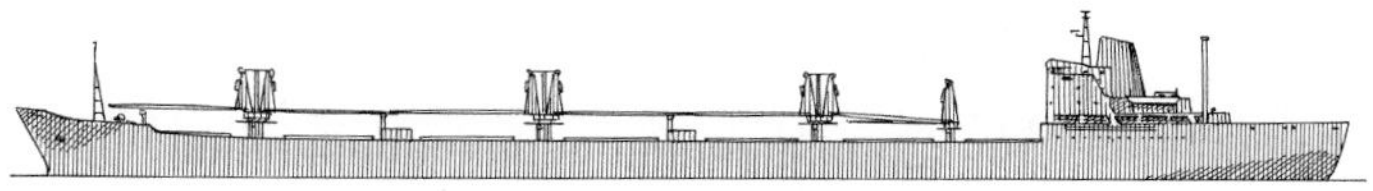

441 *MP³CMFN H13*
CONQUISTADOR Ma/Be (Boelwerf) 1969; B; 24,025 grt/40,095 dwt; 203.77 × 11.37 m *(668.53 × 37.3 ft)*; M (MAN); 15.5 kts; ex-*E R Scaldia*

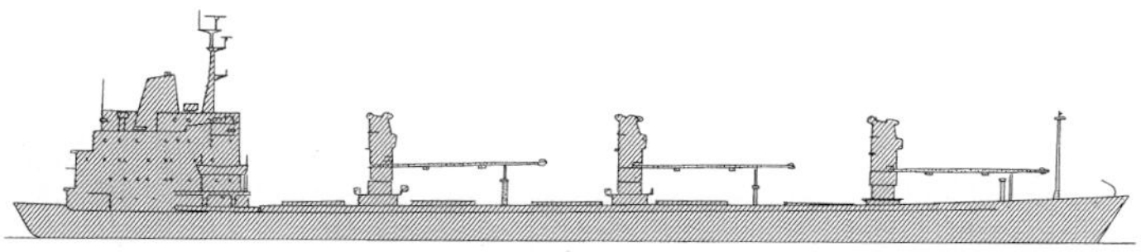

442 *MP³MF* H
PANORMOS WIND Cy/Ar (Alianza) 1977; C/Con; 9,590 grt/15,895 dwt; 144.79 × 9.35 m *(475.03 × 30.68 ft)*; M (Sulzer); 15 kts; ex-*Cordoba*; Modified 'Freedom-Hispania' type; 162 TEU
Sister: **PANORMOS BAY** (Cy); ex-*La Pampa*; **ADONIS** (Pa) ex-*Buenos Aires*

See photo number 7/515

443 *MP³MF H13*
HUMBOLDT CURRENT SV/Ys ('Uljanik') 1981; C/Con; 16,992 grt/24,432 dwt; 193.17 × 10.2 m *(634 × 33.46 ft)*; M (B&W); 16.75 kts; ex-*Konkar Thetis*
Sister: **CALIFORNIA CURRENT** (Li) ex-*Konka Triaina*; Probable sisters: **ROSSEL CURRENT** (SV) ex-*Konkar Doris*; **KARLOBAG** (Ma) ex-*Konkar Nereus*; **SLAVONIJA** (Ma) ex-*Konkar Poseidon*; **GULF CURRENT** (Li) ex-*Konkar Triton*

444 *MP³MF H13*
MANDALAY Mr/FRG (A G 'Weser') 1983; C/Con; 10,024 grt/13,105 dwt; 148.82 × 8.05 m *(488.25 × 26.41 ft)*; M (MAN); 17 kts; ex-*Mahndalay*; 383 TEU
Sisters: **BAGO** (Mr) ex-*Pago*; **SAGAING** (Mr) (builder—Seebeck); **MAGWAY** (Mr) ex-*Magwe* (builder—Seebeck)

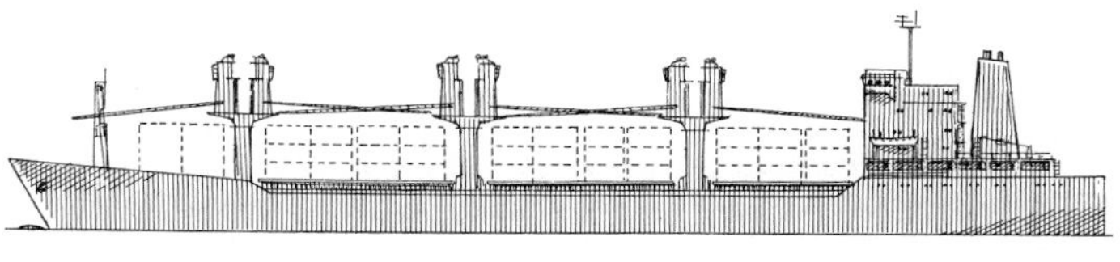

445 *MP³MF H13*
XOUR INA Pa/Ko (Korea SB) 1979; C/Con; 13,603 grt/17,056 dwt; 155.02 × 10.04 m *(508.6 × 32.94 ft)*; M (Sulzer); 17 kts; ex-*Unido*
Sister: **XOUR GEMINI** (Sg) ex-*Amado*

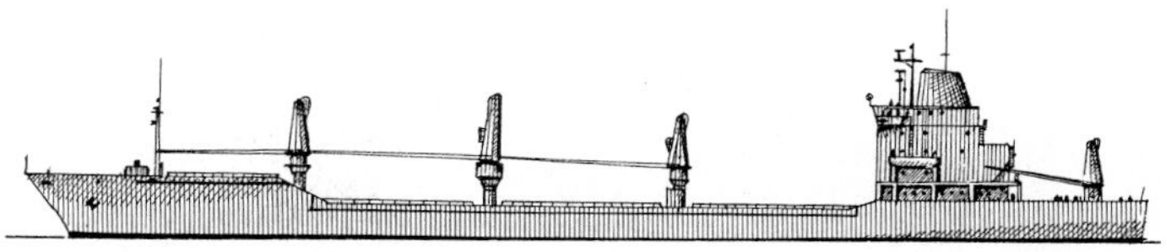

446 *MP³MFC H13*
ANGELIQUE Ma/Ca (Marine Indust) 1975; C; 11,461 grt/17,636 dwt; 160.15 × 10.05 m *(525.43 × 32.97 ft)*; M (MAN); 18 kts; ex-*La Pallice*; 'MARINDUS' class
Sisters: **NICOLE** (Bs) ex-*La Rochelle*; **JUBILEE I** (Bs) ex-*Poitiers*; **SILVER GLORY** (Cy) ex-*Rochefort;* **SILVER CHARIOT** (Cy) ex-*Royan*; **MC PEARL** (Bs) ex-*Tours*; **BABOR** (Ag); **BIBAN** (Ag); **GLOBAL EXPRESS 6** (Cy) ex-*Aristandros*; **NZOL CONTENDER** (Bs) ex-*Aristeides*; **LADY MURIEL** (Cy) ex-*Aristarchos*

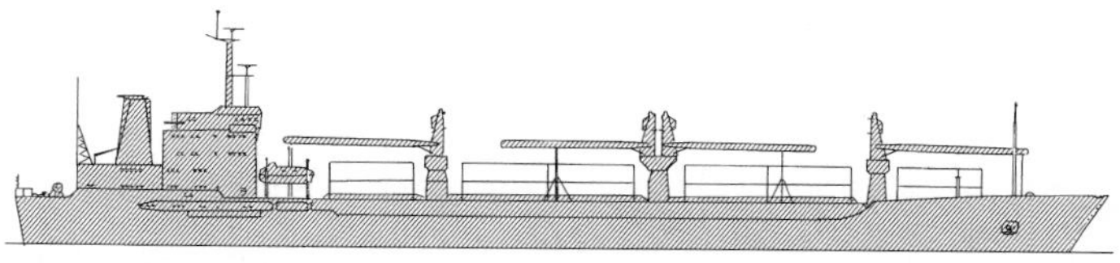

447 *MP³MFM H13*
SEANAV I Rm/Rm (Galatz) 1988; C/Con; 11,561 grt/16,166 dwt; 158.71 × 10.09 m *(520.70 × 33.10 ft)*; M (MAN); 15.50 kts; ex-*Vulcana Bai*; 420 TEU
Sisters: **AVRIG** (Rm); **MARAKI** (Rm) ex-*Amara*

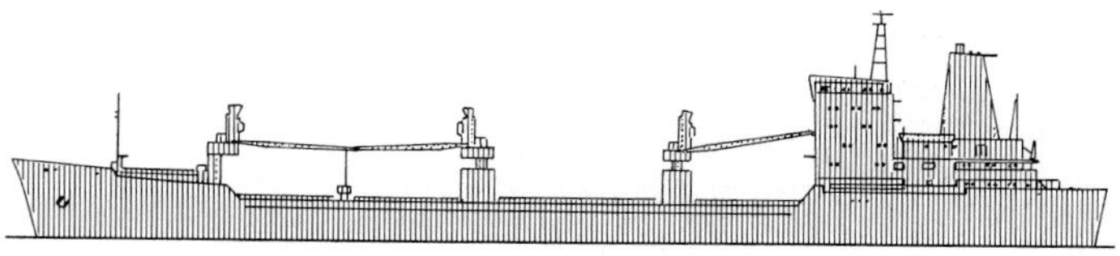

448 *MP³MFMC H13*
CEYNOWA Pd/Pd (Gdanska) 1982; C/Con; 15,235 grt/15,623 dwt; 156.75 × 9.30 m *(514.27 × 30.51 ft)*; M (Sulzer); 16 kts; 412 TEU; 'B348' type
Sisters: **JAN DLUGOSZ** (Pd); **KARLOWICZ** (Pd); **PARANDOWSKI** (Pd)

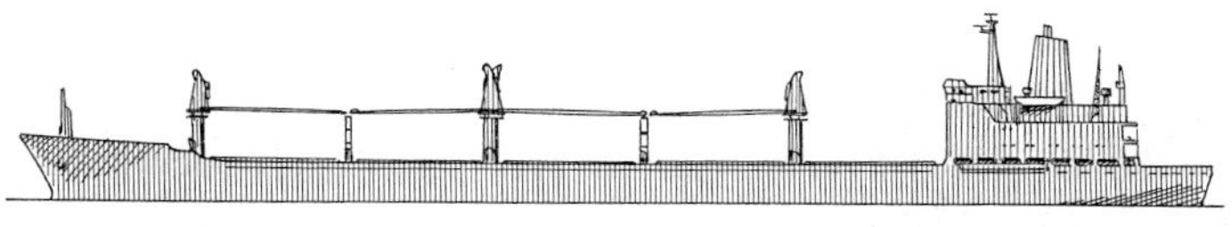

449 *MP³MFMD H1*
LONGAVI Li/Ja (Sasebo) 1977; C/Con; 16,088 grt/20,632 dwt; 164.12 × 10.01 m *(538.45 × 32.84 ft)*; M (Sulzer); 16.5 kts; ex-*Van Dyck*; 656 TEU
Sister: **LOA** (Li) ex-*Quellin*

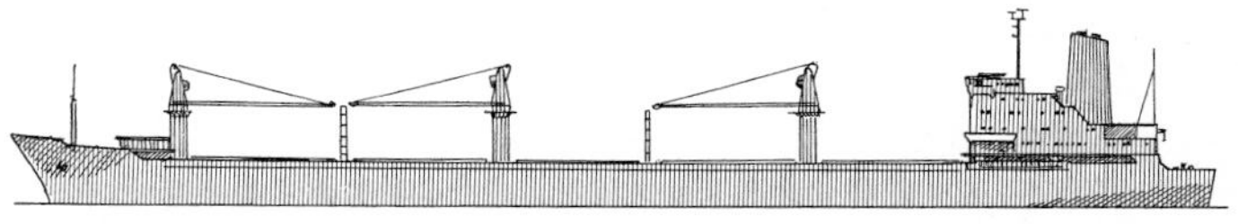

450 *MP³MFN H1*
AKTI Cy/Ys ('3 Maj') 1971; C/Con; 21,738 grt/33,791 dwt; 183.32 × 11.37 m *(601.44 × 37.3 ft)*; M (Sulzer); 15 kts; ex-*Arctic Troll*; 450 TEU
Sisters: **BARBICAN SPIRIT** (Pi) ex-*Troll Lake*; **MSC LAURA** (Pa) ex-*Troll Park*; **BARBICAN STAR** (It) ex-*Troll River* (converted to container ship 1977)

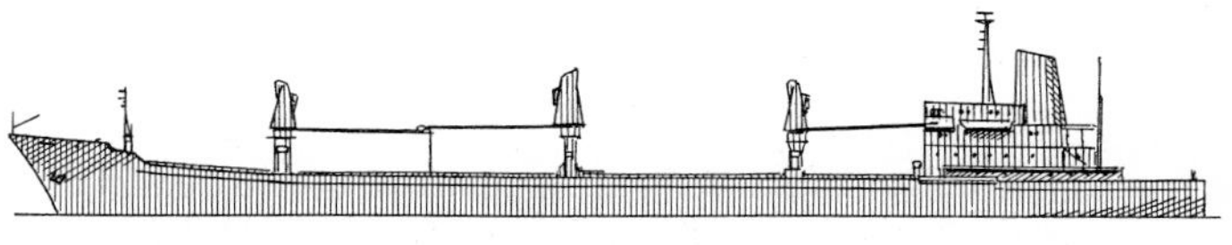

451 *MP³MFN H1*
IRAN MEEZAN Ir/FRG (A G 'Weser') 1975; C; 9,888 grt/16,265 dwt; 149.79 × 9.26 m *(488.85 × 30.38 ft)*; M (MAN); 16.5 kts; ex-*Arya Soroosh*; '36-L' type
Sisters: **IRAN SOKAN** (Ir) ex-*Arya Navid*; **IRAN BORHAN** (Ir) ex-*Arya Gohar*; **IRAN EHSAN** (Ir) ex-*Aristaios*; **IRAN VOJDAN** (Ir), launched as *Aristonidas*; **IRAN BAYAN** (Ir) ex-*Aristonimos*

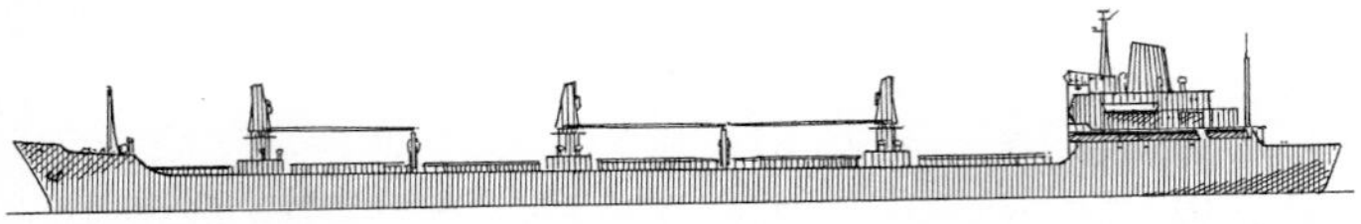

452 *MP^{3}MFN H13*
ALAM ACAPULCO My/Ja (Mitsui) 1975; B; 19,728 grt/34,260 dwt; 179.03 × 10.97 m *(587.37 × 35.99 ft)*; M (B&W); 15 kts; ex-*Nordkap*
Sisters: **ALAM MEXICO** (My) ex-*Nordpol*; **KENT EXCELLENT** (Pa) ex-*Nordtramp*; **CHIOS BEAUTY** (Gr) ex-*Nordkyn*; **AGAPI** (Gr) ex-*Nordhval*; **KAPITAN FOMIN** (Uk) ex-*Gunvor Cord*

453 *MP^{3}MFN H13*
CYCLADES Pa/DDR (Mathias-Thesen) 1980; C/Con; 16,600 grt/22,042 dwt; 178.52 × 10.11 m *(586 × 33.17 ft)*; M (MAN); 15 kts; ex-*Papagena*; 'MBC' type
Sisters: **THORSWAVE** (Li) ex-*Stephan Reeckmann* (Now given a new 80 ft forward section which adds 20 ft to the overall length); **IRON DAMPIER** (Au) ex-*Palapur*; **SPLIT** (SV) ex-*Paloma*; **VEGA** (Sg) ex-*Pamina*; **PENELOPE II** (Pa) ex-*Dagmar Reeckmann*

454 *MP^{3}M^{2}F-MC H13*
BERDYANSK Uk/Ja (NKK) 1977; B/Con; 16,585 grt/27,554 dwt; 178.11 × 10.90 m *(584.35 × 35.76 ft)*; M (Sulzer); 15.7 kts; ex-*Baltic Skou*; 550 TEU; Mast by funnel is on port side
Sister: **MARIUPOL** (Uk) ex-*Arctic Skou*

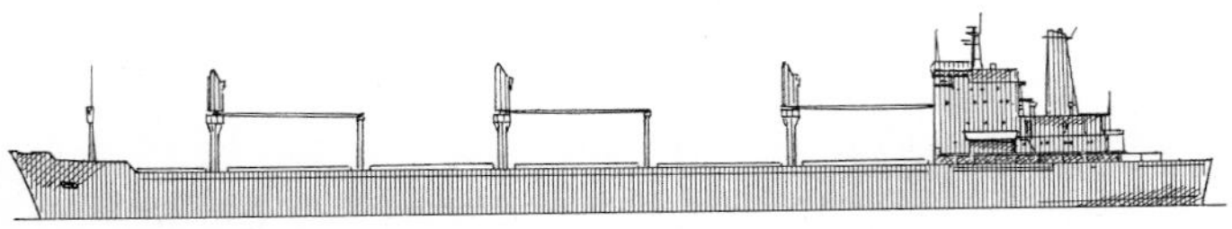

455 *MP^{3}NMG H1*
SILVERFJORD Li/Ys ('Uljanik') 1972; B; 20,584 grt/34,509 dwt; 179 × 11.09 m *(587.27 × 36.38 ft)*; M (B&W); 16 kts
Sisters: **BLUE MASTER** (Sg); **GOLDEN ISLE** (Li) ex-*Norbeth*

456 *MRC^{2}RMF H13*
PRIME VIVID At/FRG (Brand) 1981; C/Con; 5,934 grt/7,805 dwt; 112.86 × 5.1/7.59 m *(370 × 16.73/24.9 ft)*; M (MaK); 16 kts; ex-*Karin*; Lengthened 1986; Length is now 127.21 m (417.36 ft); 472 TEU; larger (C) cranes are on starboard and smaller (R) cranes on port
Sister: **CARL METZ** (SV) ex-*Doris*

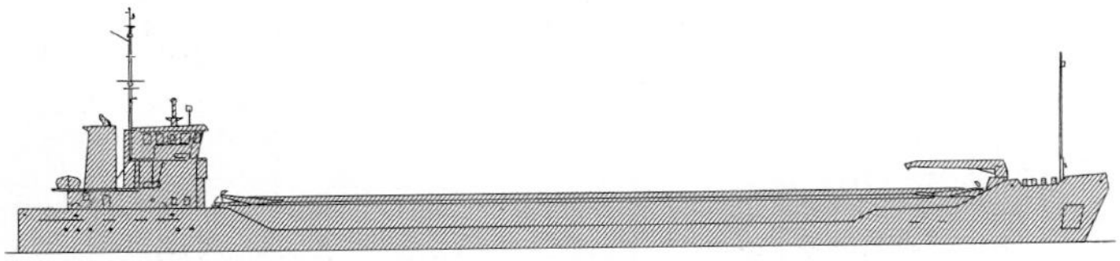

457 *MRMF H13*
BOTHNIABORG Ne/Ne; C/Con; 1,999 grt/3,015 dwt; 82.00 × 4.94 m *(269.03 × 16.21 ft)*; M (Caterpillar); 11.50 kts
Sisters: **FLINTERBORG** (Ne); **RIJNBORG** (Ne); Possible sisters: **BALTICBORG** (Ne); **EEMSBORG** (Ne); **SCHELDEBORG** (Ne)

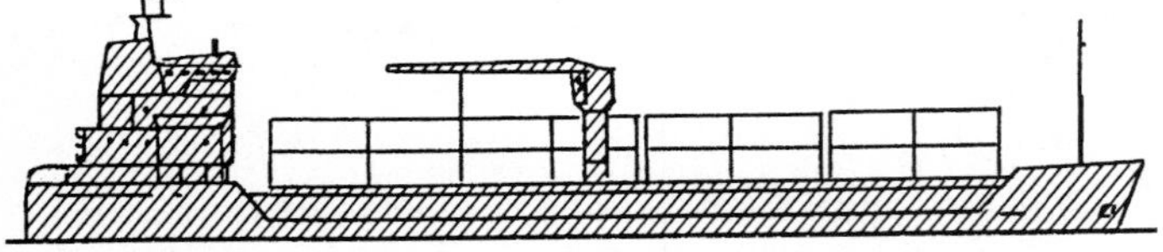

458 *MRMF H13*
JUPITER Ne/Ne (Gruno) 1985; C/Con; 1,839 grt/2,167 dwt; 78.59 × 4.25 m *(257.84 × 13.94 ft)*; M (Bolnes); 12 kts; ex-*Dirk*; 124 TEU

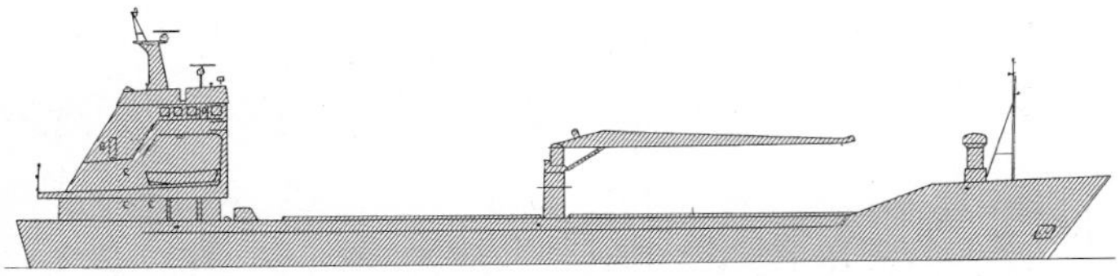

459 *MRM-F H1*
RUGARD At/FRG (H Peters) 1977; C/Con; 1,889 grt/2,159 dwt; 80.40 × 4.87 m *(263.78 × 15.98 ft)*; M (MaK); 13.25 kts; 128 TEU

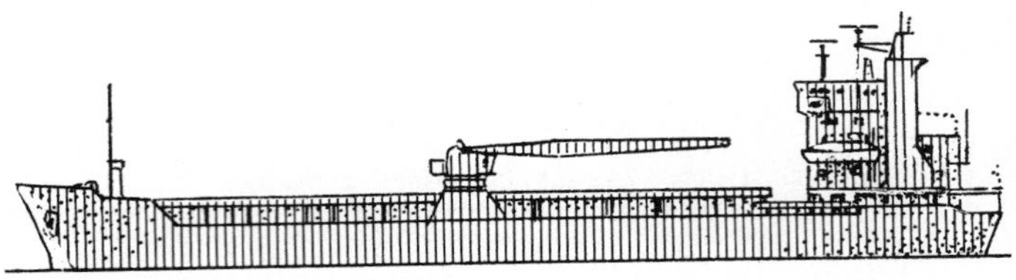

460 *MRM-G H1*
AVANT No/Sg (Singapore Slip) 1979; C/NP/Con; 3,340 grt/5,210 dwt; 80.78 × 7.22 m *(265.03 × 23.69 ft)*; M (MaK); 13 kts; ex-*Germa Fondal*; The crane may not be fitted; This could also apply to any, or all, of the sisters; The deck crane may be obscured when containers are carried; 145 TEU; Crane is on port side
Sisters: **SIO** (Hu) ex-*Germa Karma*; **ATLAS** (NIS) ex-*Germa Forest*; **BALATON** (Hu) ex-*Germa Fram*; **HELLE STEVNS** (DIS) ex-*Lina*; **KAPOS** (Hu) ex-*Lionel*; **MARMORBULK** (No) ex-*Germa Pride*; **SIRT** (Tu) ex-*Germa Lady*

461 *MR^{2}MF H1*
KATHE SIF DIS/De (Orskovs) 1981; C/Con; 4,238 grt/4,380 dwt; 101.3 × 5.54 m *(332 × 18.18 ft)*; M (Mak); 13.5 kts; ex-*Frellsen Annette*; 326 TEU; Cranes on port side
Sisters: **JOAN SIF** (DIS) ex-*Frellsen Birgitte*; **CHARLOTTE SIF** (DIS) ex-*Lotte Scheel*; **TIGER FORCE** (DIS) ex-*Mette Sif*; **PENHIR** (Kn) ex-*Frellsen Eva*; **VILLE DE DAMIETE** (Bs) ex-*Peter Sif*; **BRAVO SIF** (DIS); **EDEL SIF** (DIS) ex-*Edel Scheel*; **MAJ SIF** (DIS) ex-*Maj Sandved*; **SAAD** (SV) ex-*Sigga Sif*; **MEKONG VITESSE** (DIS) ex-*Ocean Sif*; **BARBARA E** (Br) ex-*Finn Sif*; **CYGNE** (Kn) ex-*Faroe Trader*

462 *MR^{2}MF H13*
BREMER EXPORT NIS/Ne ('Volharding') 1991; C/Con; 2,641 grt/3,628 dwt; 88.00 × 5.42 m *(288.71 × 17.78 ft)*; M (Alpha); 13 kts; 200 TEU

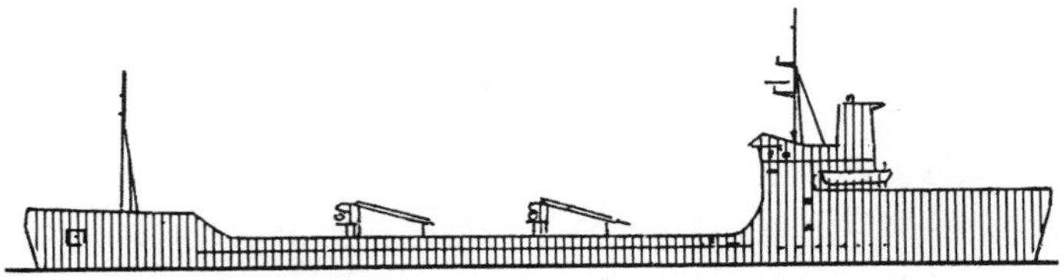

463 *MR^{2}MF H13*
CARIB ALBA Va/De (Sonderborg) 1976; C; 1,399 grt/2,997 dwt; 78.8 × 5 m *(258.53 × 16.4 ft)*; M (Alpha-Diesel); 12.5 kts; ex-*Susan Silvana*; Now sail-assisted—sail not shown on drawing; Cranes are on starboard side
Sister (probably not sail-assisted): **HONG YAN 3** (RC) ex-*Vibeke Silvana*

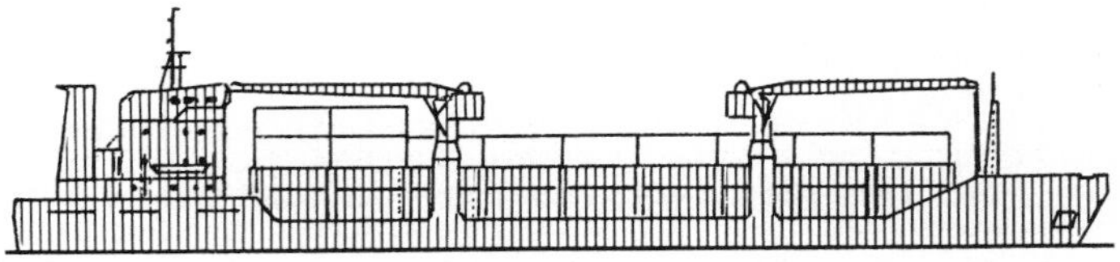

464 *MR^{2}MF H13*
MEKONG FORTUNE AT/FRG (Hegemann) 1987; C/Con; 2,610 grt/2,873 dwt; 87.03 × 4.60 m *(285.53 × 15.09 ft)*; M (Alpha); 11.80 kts; ex-*Magdlena R*; 153 TEU; Cranes are on starboard side
Sister: **TRICOLOR STAR II** (At) ex-*Carola R*

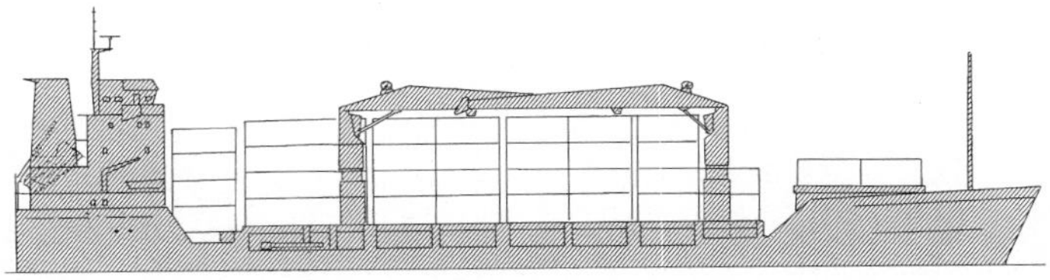

465 *MR^{2}MF H13*
SLOMAN CHALLENGER At/Eg (Alexandria) 1995; C/Con; 4,489 grt/5,665 dwt; 100.70 × 6.65 m *(330.38 × 21.82 ft)*; M (MaK); 14.50 kts; 380 TEU; Cranes are on port side
Sisters: **SLOMAN CHAMPION** (At); **SLOMAN COMMANDER** (At)

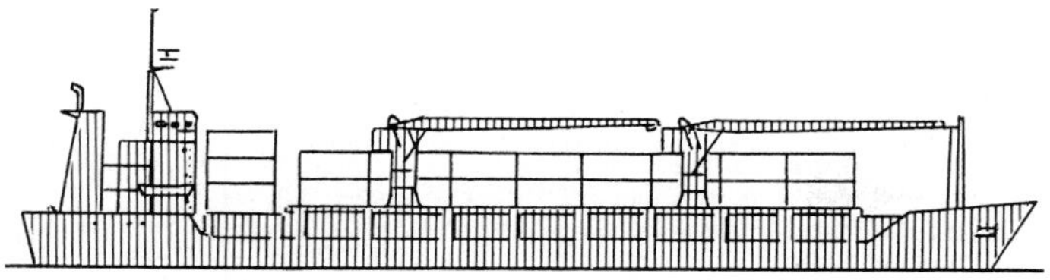

466 *MR^2MF H13*
VALIANT At/FRG (Seebeck) 1985; C/Con; 2,800 grt/2,980 dwt; 85.55 × 4.40 m *(280.68 × 14.44 ft)*; M (Deutz); 11.50 kts; ex-*Stadt Leer*; 246 TEU; Cranes are on port side
Sister: **STADT NORDEN** (At)

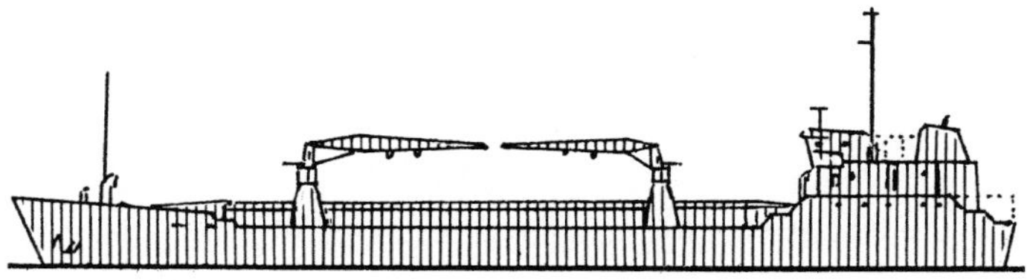

467 *MR^2MF H3*
LOMUR NIS/De (Nordso) 1983; C/Con; 1,516 grt/2,600 dwt; 72.45 × 3.56 m *(237.7 × 11.68 ft)*; M (Krupp-MaK); 10 kts; ex-*Karen Dania*; 67 TEU; Cranes are on port side
Sister: **SVANUR II** (Ic) ex-*Jette Dania*

468 *MR^2MFC H1*
IRAN BASHEER Ir/FRG (H Peters) 1982; C/Con; 2,563 grt/2,885 dwt; 93.63 × 4.41 m *(307 × 14.47 ft)*; M (Deutz); 10.5 kts; ex-*Uranos*; 141 TEU; Cranes are on port side
Sister: **RA EES ALI** (Ir) ex-*Hammonia*

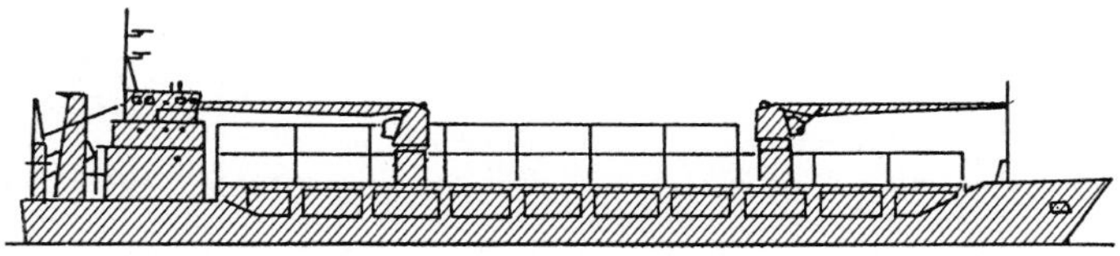

469 *MR^2MFCL H13*
NIOBA Ge/FRG (Mutzelfeldt) 1985; C/Con; 2,816 grt/2,923 dwt; 91.17 × 4.36 m *(299.11 × 14.30 ft)*; M (Wärtsilä); 12.50 kts; ex-*Rudolf Karstens*; 187 TEU; Cranes are on port side

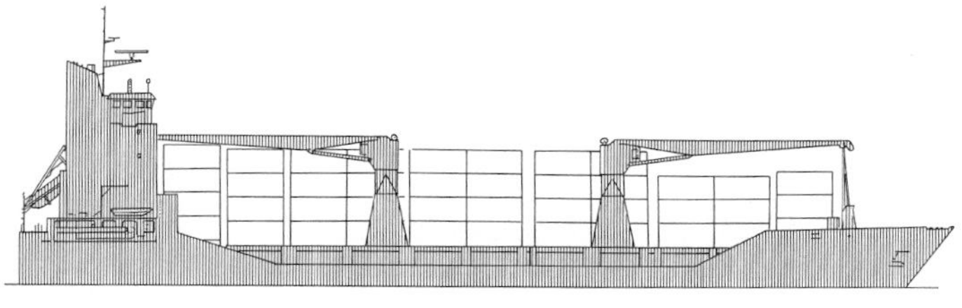

470 *MR^2MFL* H13
ARKTIS FIGHTER DIS/De (Aarhus) 1994; C/Con; 4,980 grt/7,120 dwt; 101.10 × 7.30 m *(331.70 × 23.95 ft)*; M (MaK); 15.70 kts; 444 TEU; Cranes are on port side; Lifeboat is on port side
Sisters: **ARKTIS FANTASY** (DIS); **ARKTIS FAITH** (DIS)

471 *MR^2MFL* H13
FLS COLOMBIA Cy/Ge★ (Mutzelfeldt) 1994; C/Con; 3,978 grt/5,273 dwt; 104.75 × 6.55 m *(343.67 × 21.49 ft)*; M (MAN); 15 kts; ex-*Arcadian Faith*; 373 TEU; Cranes are on port side. Lifeboat is on starboard side. ★Hull constructed in Mexico by 'Auver'
Sister: **FRONTIER AMERICA** (Cy) ex-*Arcadian Sky*

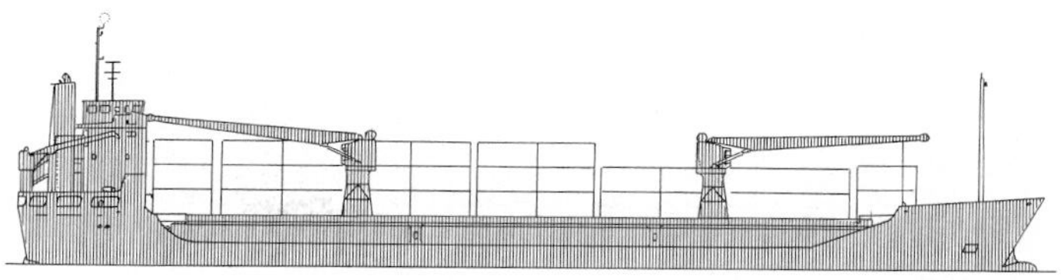

472 *MR^2MFLR H13*
HALSINGLAND Ge/Ge (Sietas) 1990; C/Con; 3,845 grt/4,334 dwt; 104.85 × 5.86 m *(344.00 × 19.23 ft)*; M (MaK); 14.60 kts; 'Type '145A'; 326 TEU; Cranes are on port side
Sister: **ANGERMANLAND** (Ge)

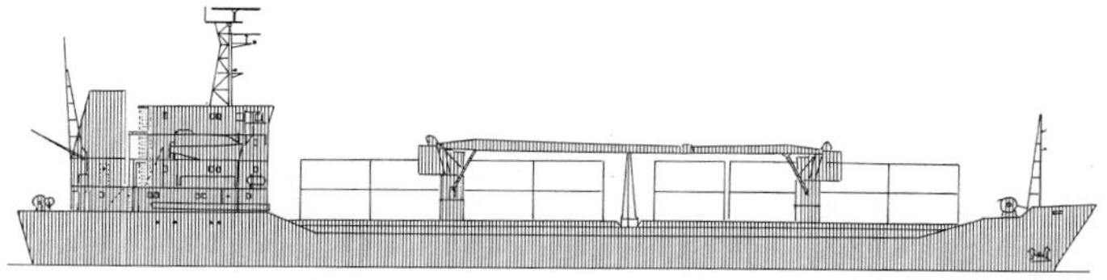

473 *MR^2MFM H13*
FAS COLOMBO Cy/RC (Wenchong) 1990; C/Con; 3,186 grt/4,200 dwt; 93.00 × 6.26 m *(305.12 × 20.54 ft)*; M (B&W); 12.5 kts; ex-*Wila Buck*; 180 TEU
Sisters: **SOUTHERN CROSS** (Cy) ex-*Bartok*; **NILS R** (Bs) ex-*Kodaly*

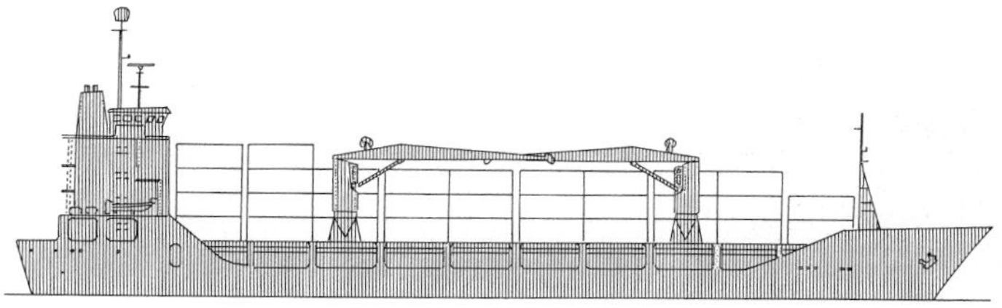

474 *MR^2M^2F H13*
BREMER MERKUR SV/Au (Australian SBI) 1990; C/Con; 3,113 grt/3,487 dwt; 92.70 × 5.31 m *(304.13 × 17.42 ft)*; M (B&W); 12 kts; ex-*Roberta Jull*; 270 TEU; Funnel is on starboard side and cranes on port
Sisters: **BREMER WESTEN** (SV) ex-*Frank Konecny*; **BREMER MAKLER** (SV) ex-*Gordon Reid*

475 *MR^2M-F H1*
RUTHENSAND At/FRG (Luehring) 1981; C/Con; 1,834 grt/2,623 dwt; 78.59 × 4.6 m *(258 × 15.09 ft)*; M (Krupp-MaK); 10.25 kts; 88 TEU

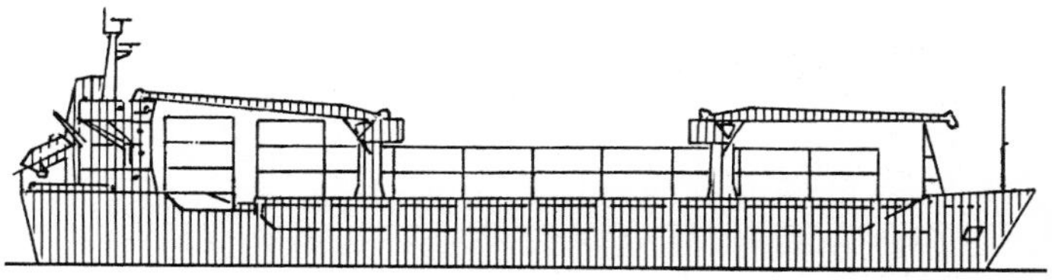

476 *MR^2M-F H13*
ANNE CATHARINA Ge/FRG (Nobiskrug) 1986; C/Con; 3,147 grt/3,324 dwt; 90.02 × 4.70 m *(295.34 × 15.42 ft)*; M (MaK); 12.50 kts; 276 TEU; Cranes are on port side; Funnel is on port side and lifeboat on starboard
Similar: **SEA BIRD** (DIS); **OCEAN BIRD** (DIS); **MARTIN** (At)

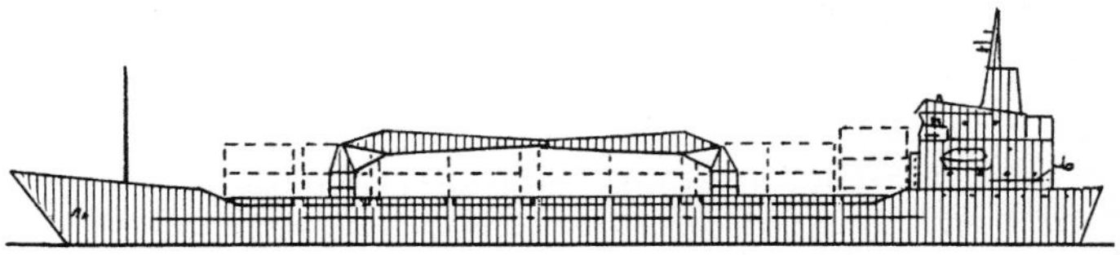

477 *MR^2M-F H13*
DONG FENG SHAN RC/Ne (Stroobos) 1977; C/Con; 1,600 grt/3,645 dwt; 93.07 × 5.57 m *(305.35 × 18.27 ft)*; M (Alpha-Diesel); 13.2 kts; ex-*Helge Folmer*; 159 TEU; Cranes are on starboard side

478 *MR^2M-F H13*
OCEAN TRAMP DIS/De (Orskovs) 1976; C/Con; 1,523 grt/1,424 dwt; 71.89 × 3.56 m *(235.86 × 11.68 ft)*; M (Alpha-Diesel); 12.5 kts; ex-*Pep Sea*; 54 TEU; Cranes are on starboard side
Sister: **OCEAN TRADER I** (Bs) ex-*Pep Sky*

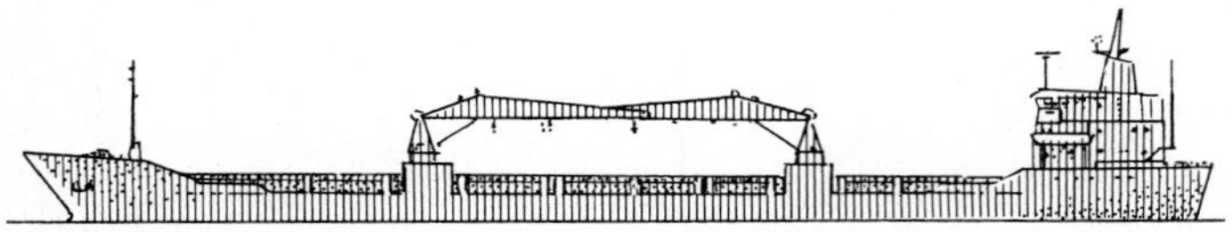

479 *MR²M-F H13*
YONG AN RC/Ne (Kramer & Booy) 1974/79; C/HL; 1,999 grt/4,695 dwt; 106.43 × 5.58 m *(349.18 × 18.31 ft)*; M (Alpha); 12 kts; ex-*Junior Lilo*; Converted from cargo and lengthened 1979 (Helsingor); New engines 1984; Cranes are on port side

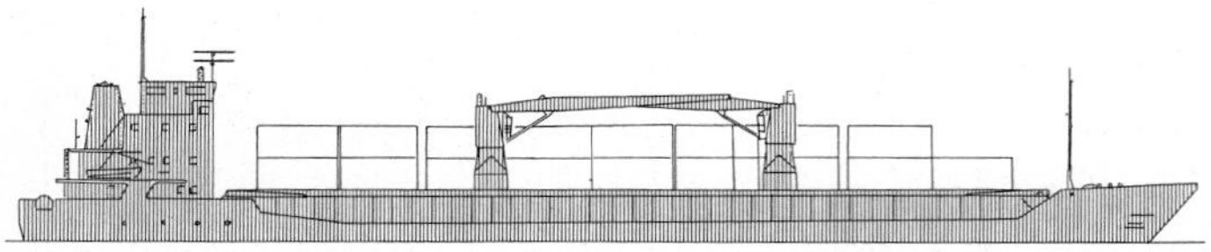

480 *MR²VF H13*
FISCHLAND Ge/Cz (Slovenske) 1994; C/Con; 2,514 grt/3,560 dwt; 87.68 × 5.52 m *(287.66 × 18.11 ft)*; M (Alpha); 11.5 kts; 168 TEU; Cranes are on port side; 'NL ROSTOCK' type
Sisters: **HIDDENSEE** (Ge); **POEL** (Ge); **RUGEN** (Ge); **USEDOM** (Ge); **VILM** (Ge)

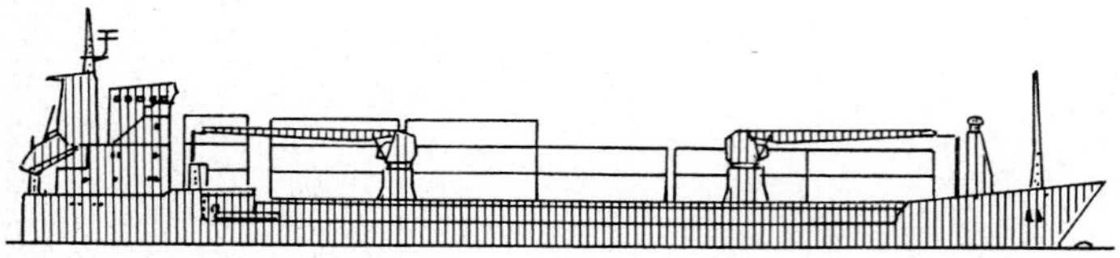

481 *MXR²M-FCL H13*
AMKE Ge/FRG (Cassens) 1986; C/Con; 3,219 grt/4,260 dwt; 100.62 × 5.25 m *(330.12 × 17.22 ft)*; M (MWM); 12 kts; ex-*Norbrit Weser*; 240 TEU; Cranes are on port side
Sisters: **SUN BAY** (Ge) ex-*Karin B*; **ANNY AUSTRAL** (SV) ex-*Julia*; **SUN BIRD** (Ge) ex-*Thule*; **JAN LUIKEN** (Ge); **TRICOLOR STAR II** (At); **CORINGLE BAY** (At) ex-*Ditzum*; **SINA** (At) ex-*Emma Helene* (SA built—Dorbyl)

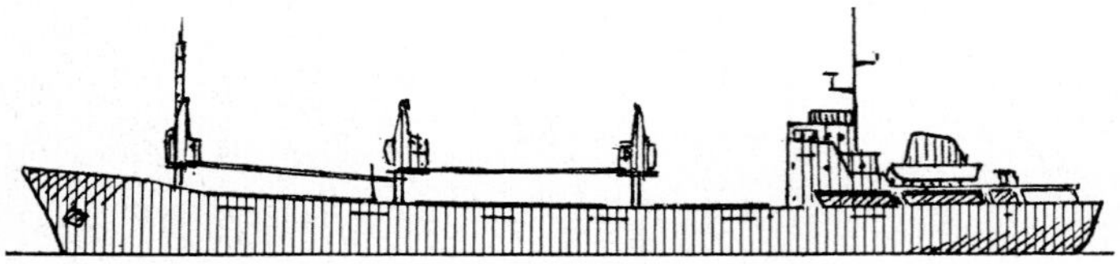

482 *M-CC²MF H*
HYE PROSPERITY 1388 Ho/No (Sarpsborg) 1964; C; 793 grt/1,303 dwt; 79.18 × 4.11 m *(259.78 × 13.48 ft)*; M (Werkspoor); 12.5 kts; ex-Spaarnestroom

483 *M-NC⁴MFN H13*
HENNIGSDORF Ge/DDR (Mathias-Thesen) 1986; C/Con; 16,794 grt/23,929 dwt; 176.55 × 10.46 m *(579.23 × 34.32 ft)*; M (MAN); 15 kts; 802 TEU; 'OBC' type
Sisters: **ORANIENBURG** (Ge) ex-*Brandenburg*; **RESA** (Ge); **CHERKASSY** (Ru) ex-*Thalassini Hara*; **CHEREMKHOVO** (Ru) ex-*Thalassini Axia*; **CHELYABINSK** (Ru) ex-*Pantelis A Lemos*; **ADAMANTIA** (Sg) ex-*Fremo Scorpius*; **SOLIN** (Ma) ex-*Spyros A Lemos*; **COSMIC** (SV) ex-*Wismar*; **CARIBBEAN PRINCESS** (Cy) ex-*Santa Rosa*; **CARIBBEAN QUEEN** (Cy) ex-*Santa Rita*; **MED PISA** (Ma) ex-*Fengtien*; Sisters (lengthened to 199.8 m (655.5 ft) between third and fourth cranes; 828 TEU): **LAS BOLINAS** (Pa) ex-*Fontenoy*; **NECAT A** (Tu) ex-*Federal Elbe*; **WINTER STAR** (Cy) ex-*Federal Hudson*

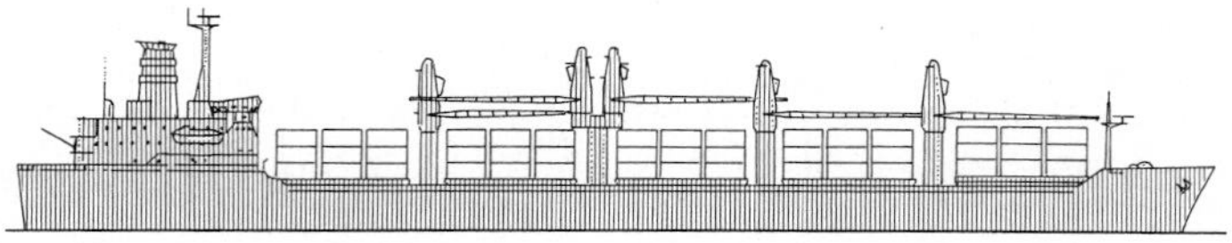

484 *M-NC²PCMF H13*
GREAT TRANS Pa/Ja (NKK) 1983; C/Con; 24,869 grt/37,425 dwt; 182.51 × 11.53 m *(598.79 × 37.83 ft)*; M (Sulzer); 15 kts; ex-*Taurus*; 1,104 TEU
Sister: **RECIFE** (Pa) ex-*Tellus*

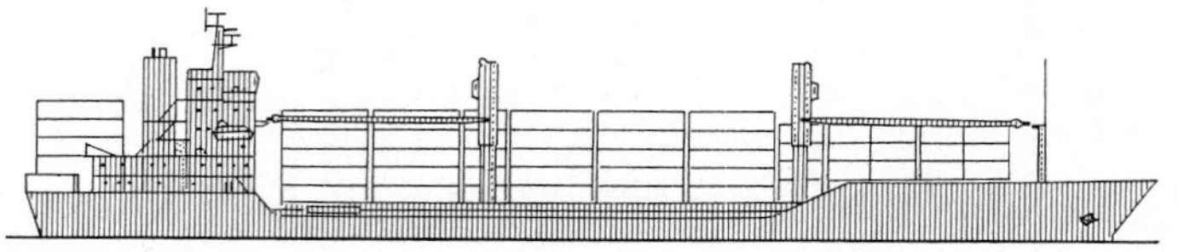

485 *M-NCPMFS H13*
ZIM BRASIL II Bs/DDR (Mathias-Thesen) 1987; C/Con; 11,977 grt/14,101 dwt; 156.88 × 8.58 m *(514.70 × 28.15 ft)*; M (Sulzer); 16 kts; ex-*Waterschout*; 1,034 TEU. 'UCC 14' type
Sisters: **NEDLLOYD MAAS** (Ne) ex-*Waterkoning*; **NEDLLOYD MERWE** (Ne) ex-*Waterstoker*; **KEDAH** (Sg) ex-*Watergraaf*; **NEDLLOYD MAIN** (Ne) ex-*Waterklerk*; **TRANZTAS TRADER** (Au) ex-*Watergeus*

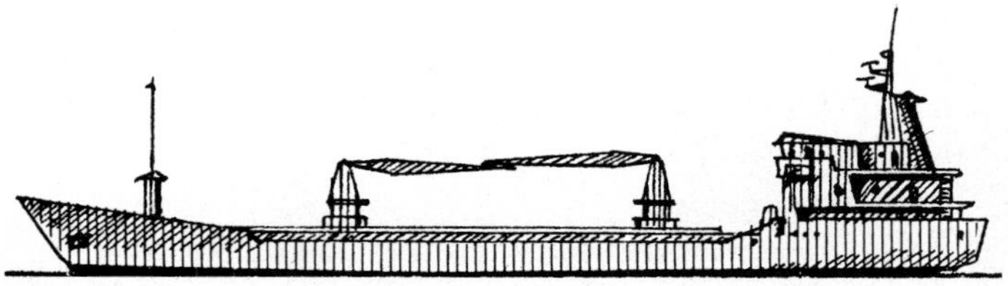

486 *VR²M-F H13*
MARINA Ia/De (Orskovs) 1977; C; 499 grt/1,440 dwt; 73.65 × 3.55 m *(241.63 × 11.65 ft)*; M (Atlas-MaK); 13 kts; ex-*Pep Star*; 54 TEU; Cranes are on port side
Sisters: **BISON** (Bs) ex-*Pep Sun*; **FAST LIFT** (Bs) ex-*Pep Spica*; **DILZA** (CV) ex-*Pep Sirius*

487 Saad *(Mo); 1982; (as Maersk Forto)* *WSPL*

488 Marina Star *(Bs); 1990* *Norman Thomson*

489 Zenovia *(Li); 1976; (as Hakuko Maru)* *WSPL*

490 Kwangtung *(HK); 1986* *WSPL*

491 Capo Mele Secondo *(It); 1978; (as Lake Barrine)* *WSPL*

492 Golden Evagelistra *(Gr); 1973* *WSPL*

493 Evangelia IV *(Cy); 1986; (as Baltic Sun)* *FotoFlite*

494 Chopin *(Pd); 1988* *WSPL*

495 Talana *(Li); 1977; (as Louisa)* *WSPL*

496 Pacduke *(Li); 1975* *WSPL*

497 Vola *(Bu); 1992* *WSPL*

498 Kirzhach *(Ru); 1991* *WSPL*

499 European *(Pa); 1979; (as Char Ching)* *WSPL*

500 Costis *(Gr); 1985; (as New Amethyst)* *WSPL*

501 Hans *(Pa); 1977; (as Georgia Rainbow)* *WSPL*

502 Bao Chang *(Pa); 1977; (as Parnassos)* *WSPL*

503 Pantazis L *(Gr); 1974* *WSPL*

504 La Paix *(Pa); 1973* *WSPL*

505 Silver Yu *(SV); 1976; (as Moslake)* *WSPL*

506 Ist *(Ma); 1981; (as Nissho Maru)* *WSPL*

507 Gregor *(Cy); 1977; (as Chai Varee)* *WSPL*

508 Flecha *(Cy); 1974; (as Cedrela)* *WSPL*

509 Alouette Arrow *(NIS); 1980; (as Finnarctis)* *WSPL*

510 Bickersgracht *(Ne); 1981* *WSPL*

511 Blue Master *(Sg); 1971* *WSPL*

512 Galet *(Ma); 1981; (as Merchant Pilot)* *WSPL*

513 Liliana Dimitrova *(Bu); 1982* *WSPL*

514 Karlobag *(Ma); 1980; (as Konkar Nereus)* *WSPL*

515 Yevgeniy Onufriyev *(Ru); 1970* *WSPL*

516 Ibn Al Haitham *(Bn); 1976* *WSPL*

517 Oak *(Pa); 1971; (as Noble Duckling) (wood chip)* *FotoFlite*

518 Maersk La Plata *(Ge); 1984; (as Hannoverland)* *FotoFlite*

519 Bob L *(Pa); 1980* *FotoFlite*

520 Steinkirchen *(Ge); 1987* *FotoFlite*

521 Spica *(DIS); 1988; (as Fortuna Coast)* *FotoFlite*

522 Lee Frances *(Cy); 1985* *FotoFlite*

523 Fonnes *(Pa); 1978* *FotoFlite*

524 Heerengracht *(Ne); 1981* *FotoFlite*

525 Marmil *(Pa); 1980; (as Sprante Rubin)* *FotoFlite*

526 Turnu Severin *(Rm); 1990* *FotoFlite*

527 Gutterman *(Cy); 1989; (as Albonica)* *FotoFlite*

528 Century Star *(Li); 1990* *FotoFlite*

529 Maersk Timonel *(Pi); 1994* *FotoFlite*

530 Victoria Bay *(Pi); 1994* *FotoFlite*

531 Scarlet Success *(Pi); 1994* *FotoFlite*

532 Iman *(Tu); 1982* *FotoFlite*

533 Antigoni B *(Cy); 1977* *FotoFlite*

534 Pacprince *(Li); 1986* *FotoFlite*

535 Balsa *(NIS); 1981; (as Wani Bird)* *FotoFlite*

536 Nand Rati *(In); 1984* *FotoFlite*

537 Jag Rahul *(In); 1984* *Norman Thomson*

538 Manaslu *(Li); 1976; (as Euro Challenger)* *Norman Thomson*

539 Marbonita *(Li); 1982* *Norman Thomson*

540 Lark *(Ma); 1972; (as Eleftherotria)* *Norman Thomson*

541 Golden Condor *(Gr); 1983* *FotoFlite*

542 Full City *(Pa); 1995* *FotoFlite*

543 Griffin *(Pa); 1994* *FotoFlite*

544 Kula *(Tu); 1984* *FotoFlite*

545 Clary *(Sg); 1979* *FotoFlite*

546 Wind Ocean *(SV); 1979* *FotoFlite*

547 Kamilla *(At); 1985* *FotoFlite*

548 Banglar Urmi *(Bh); 1984* *FotoFlite*

8 Dry Cargo Ships with Derrick Posts

8 Dry Cargo Ships with Derrick Posts

1 *H^2F H1*
BEGA Rm/Rm (Turnu-Severin) 1972; C; 1,907 grt/1,979 dwt; 85.88 × 5.1 m *(281.76 × 16.73 ft)*; M (Sulzer); 13.25 kts
Sisters: **MEDIAS** (Rm); **TIMIS** (Rm); **DROBETA 1850** (Rm)

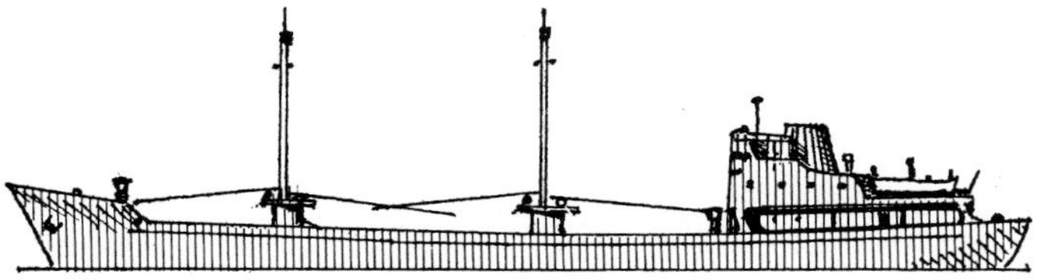

2 *H^2F H1*
HARIS —/Sp (Construcciones SA) 1964; C; 1,148 grt/1,942 dwt; 86.57 × 4.81 m *(284.02 × 15.78 ft)*; M (B&W); 12 kts; ex-*La Laja*
Sister: **RISING SUN I** (—) ex-*La Rabida*

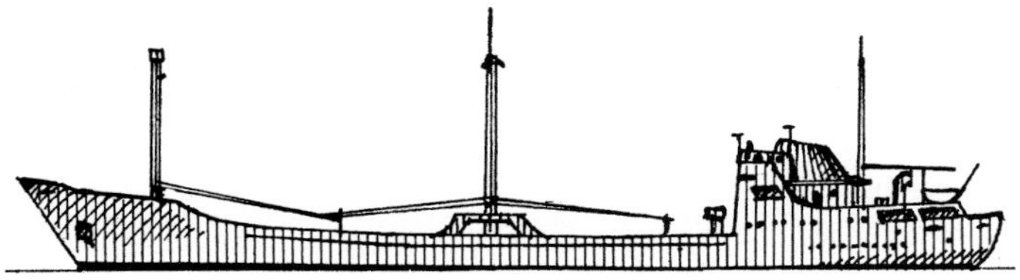

3 *H^2FM H1*
ANNE M SV/Ne (Boot) 1963; C; 498 grt/1,219 dwt; 72.67 × 3.82 m *(238.42 × 12.53 ft)*; M ('De Industrie'); 12 kts; Launched as *Breewijd*

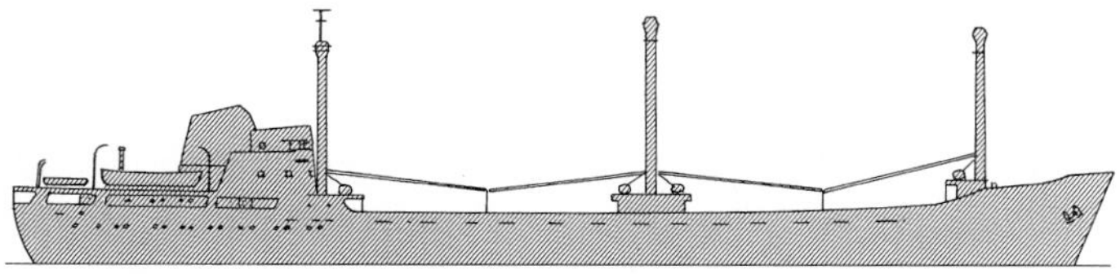

4 *H^3F H1*
KURILA Cro/FRG (Lindenau) 1958; C; 1,987 grt/3,090 dwt; 79.13 × 5.9 m *(259.61 × 19.36 ft)*; M (MAN); 12 kts; ex-*Ragni*
Sisters: **CARA TIMUR TIGA** (My) ex-*Sunny Girl*; **LOUCY** (Sy) ex-*Angelica Schulte*

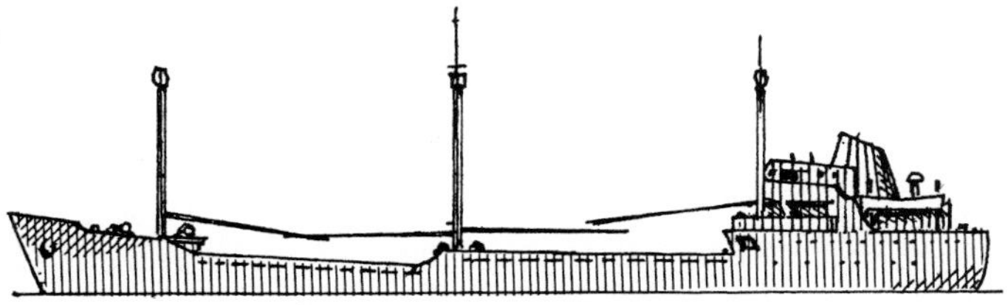

5 *H^3F H123*
OZGE S Tu/FRG (Meyer) 1958; C; 1,860 grt/2,763 dwt; 80.7 × 5.96 m *(264.76 × 19.55 ft)*; M (KHD); 12.5 kts; ex-*Akko*
Sister: **DELTA STAR** (Pa) ex-*Ashdod*; Possibly similar: DADO (Is) ex-*Kesarya*

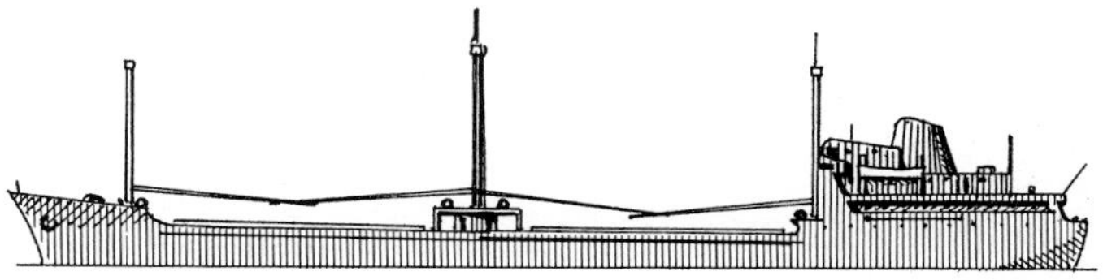

6 *H^3F H13*
AJMER Bl/Sp (Euskalduna) 1964; C; 2,570 grt/4,083 dwt; 93.68 × 6.13 m *(307.35 × 20.11 ft)*; M (MAN); 11.5 kts; Launched as *Malkenes*

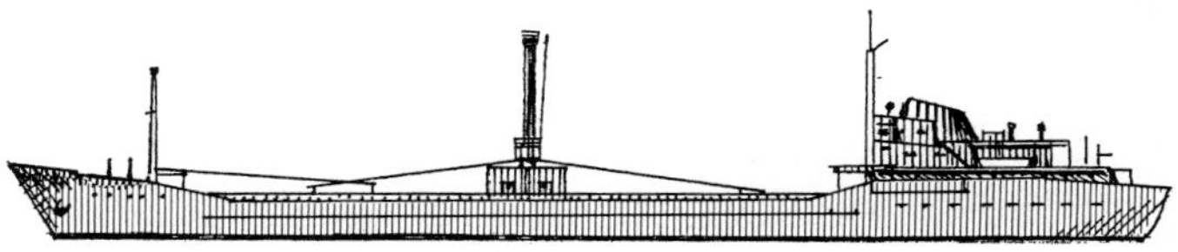

7 *H^3F H13*
FERAS Sy/Sp (UN de Levante) 1967; C; 3,319 grt/6,500 dwt; 124.21 × 7.10 m *(407.51 × 23.29 ft)*; M (B&W); 13 kts; ex-*Sorolla*

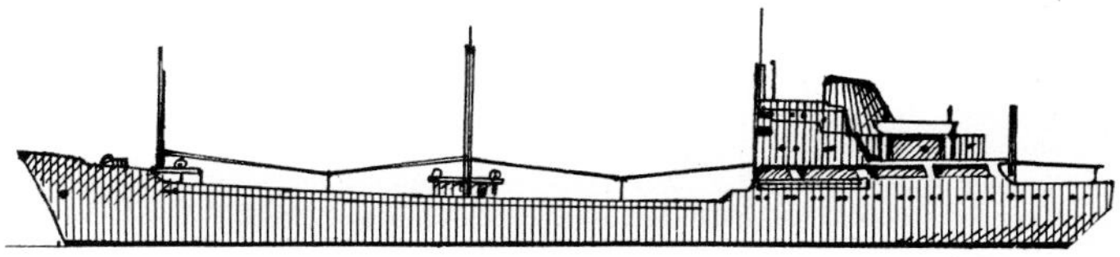

8 *H^3FM H13*
REEF STAR SV/Ys ('Jozo Lozovina-Mosor') 1968; C; 3,194 grt/3,230 dwt; 102.14 × 5.67 m *(335.1 × 18.6 ft)*; M (B&W); 14.5 kts; ex-*Korcula*

9 *H^4F H*
FAYSAL Ho/Rm (Galatz) 1965; C; 3,090 grt/4,400 dwt; 98.30 × 6.58 m *(322.51 × 21.59 ft)*; M (Sulzer); 12.5 kts; ex-*Baia Mare*

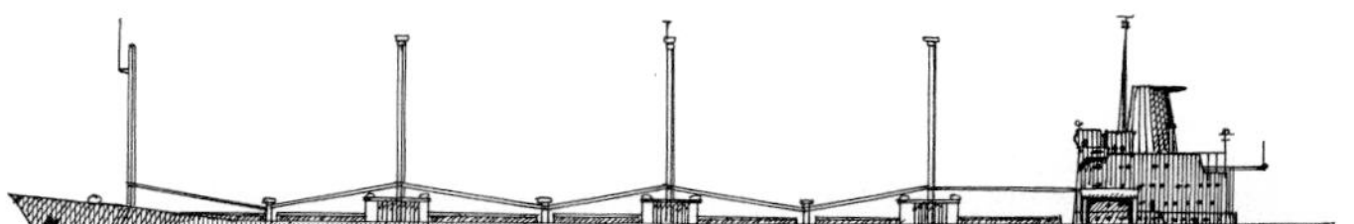

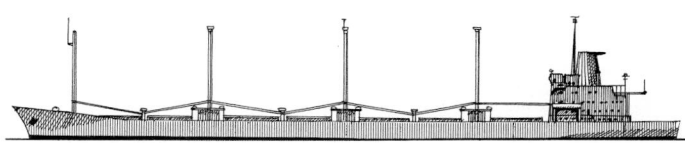

10 *H^4MF H*
HUA DA RC/FRG (LF-W) 1970; B; 18,643 grt/33,373 dwt; 196.32 × 10.95 m *(644 × 35.76 ft)*; M (Borsig); 16.5 kts; ex-*Evelyn Bolten*
Sister: **HUA FANG** (RC) ex-*Hermann Schulte*

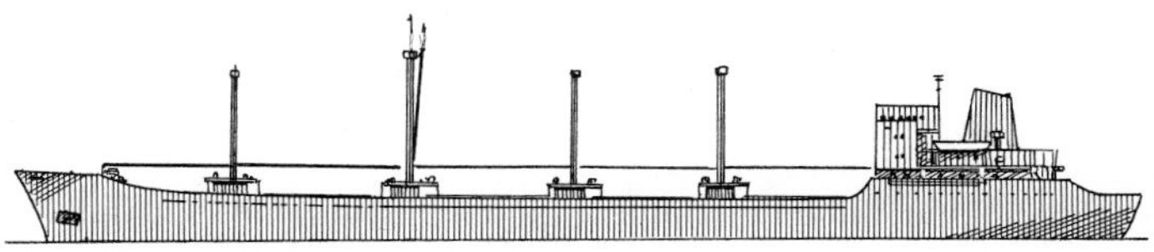

11 *H^4MF H13*
PETKO R SLAVEJNOV Bu/Ys ('Uljanik') 1968; C; 10,569 grt/13,270 dwt; 143.64 × 8.87 m *(471.26 × 29.1 ft)*; M (B&W); 15 kts; Launched as *Atria*
Sister: **IVAN VAZOV** (Bu) Launched as *Almak*; Similar (Heavier radar mast): **HELIOPOLIS WIND** (Eg) ex-*Omdurman*

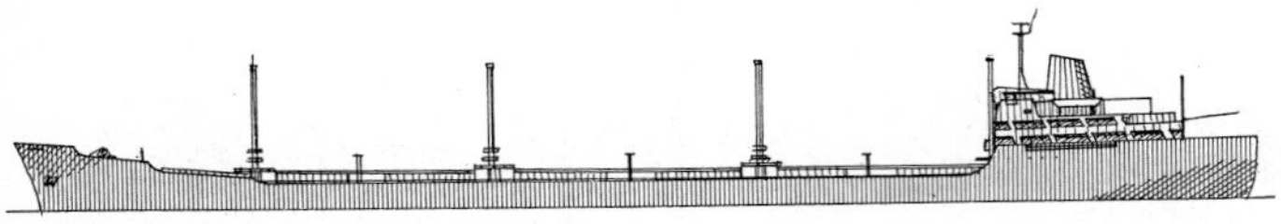

12 H^4MFN *H13*
DONG HAI RC/Br (Smith's D) 1965; B; 17,402 grt/30,839 dwt; 184.63 × 10.80 m *(605.74 × 35.43 ft)*; M (Sulzer); 13.5 kts; ex-*Riley*

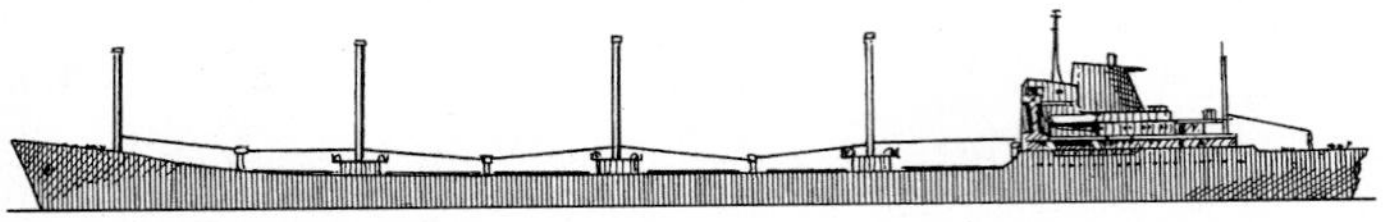

13 H^4MFN *H13*
FU JIN HAI RC/FRG (LF-W) 1965; B; 15,395 grt/22,690 dwt; 189.92 × 9.8 m *(623.1 × 32.15 ft)*; M (Fiat); 15 kts; ex-*Marie Luise Bolten*
Sister: **HUA BEI** (RC) ex-*Margrethe Bolten*

14 H^4MFN *H13*
LONG HAI RC/Be (Boelwerf) 1968; B; 20,527 grt/40,484 dwt; 203.77 × 11.48 m *(668.54 × 37.66 ft)*; M (MAN); 12 kts; ex-*Agioi Victores*
Sister: **PING HAI** (RC) ex-*Ioannis N Pateras*

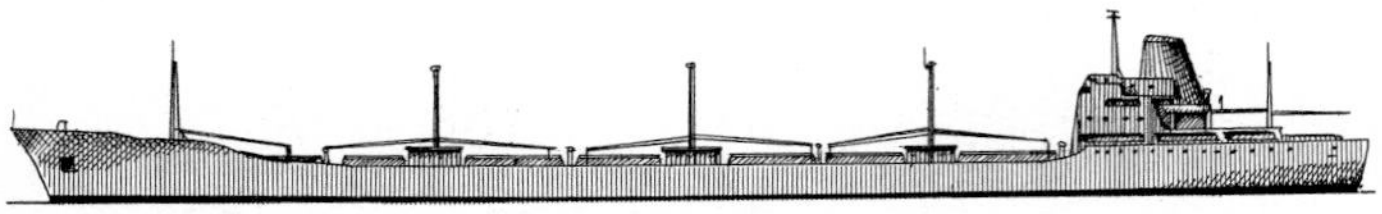

15 H^4MFN *H13*
PROSPERITY X Ma/Ys ('3 Maj') 1968; B; 18,958 grt/30,593 dwt; 199.63 × 10.85 m *(655 × 35.6 ft)*; M (Sulzer); 15.5 kts; ex-*Welsh Minstrel*
Sisters: **JIN ZHOU HAI** (RC) ex-*Doric Arrow*; **OMIROS** (Ma) ex-*Hellas in Eternity*; **LAS ROSAS** (Pa) ex-*Apollon*; Probable sister: **HUA PU** (RC) ex-*Iatis*

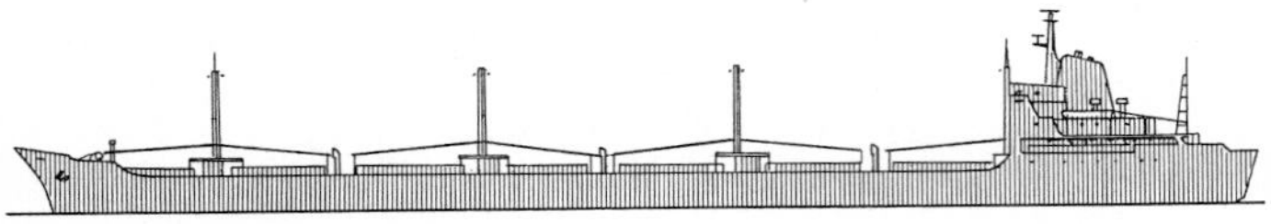

16 $H^4M–FN$ *H13*
DALAKI Ma/Ja (Hakodate) 1969; B; 16,852 grt/29,156 dwt; 180.8 × 10.69 m *(593.18 × 35.07 ft)*; M (Sulzer); 15 kts; ex-*Atlantic Hero*
Sisters: **EVRIALI** (Ma) ex-*Atlantic Hawk*; **RODANTHI** (Gr) ex-*Atlantic Heritage*; **CONSTANTINOS M** (Cy) ex-*Chrysanthi G L*; **MARIA D** (Ma) ex-*Glafkos*; **MAYFLOWER** (Li) ex-*Maria Voyazides*; **IONIAN KING** (Ma) ex-*Antaios*; **EUROSTAR** (Gr) ex-*Ioannis Zafirakis*; **IKTINOS** (Cy) ex-*Dias*; **AILSA** (Li) ex-*Cornilios*; **CLEANTHES** (Pa); **MALINI** (SV) ex-*Strymon*; **HENG CHUN HAI** (RC) ex-*Venthisikimi*; **JIANG LING HAI** (RC) ex-*Triton*; **GAO LAN DAO** (RC) ex-*Dimitros Criticos*; **ATTICOS** (Pa); **ZARA** (Li) ex-*Zephyros*

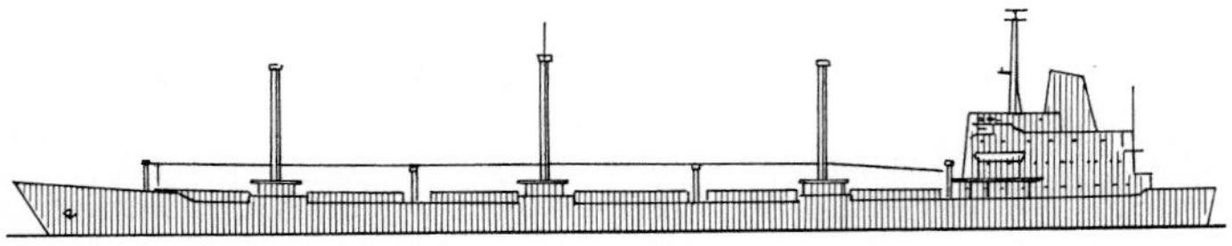

17 H^3MF *H*
'FREEDOM-HISPANIA' type —/Sp (AESA/Cadiz/UN de Levante) and Ar (Alianza) 1968–76; approx 9,200–9,800 grt/approx 16,000-16,500 dwt; 143.69 × 9.29 m *(471.42 × 30.48 ft)*; M (Sulzer); 15.5 kts
Sisters: **SPRING BREEZE** (Ma) ex-*Marbonita*; **OCEAN TRADER** (Pa) ex-*Lago Maihue*; **TRIDENT** (Pa) ex-*Marlinda*; **AGHIOS RAFAEL** (Ma) ex-*Cigoitia*; **RIZE K** (Tu) ex-*Aiboa*; **SHAHPUR** (Bh) ex-*Lago Rinihue*; **ALLISSA** (Sg) ex-*Nonna Raffaella*; **SEA ENERGY** (Pa) ex-*Aysen*; **SONG RIM** (RK) ex-*Tivano*; **OURANIA** (Pa) ex-*Getaldic*; **PAVLINA ONE** (Pa) ex-*Gundulic*; **HAI LEE** (Th) ex-*Ivo Vojnovic*; **GUAMA** (Ma) ex-*Kolasin*; **HALLVARD** (Th) ex-*Mavro Vetranic*; **JUPITER** (Cy) ex-*Virpazar*; **VERONA** (Cy) ex-*Ancud*

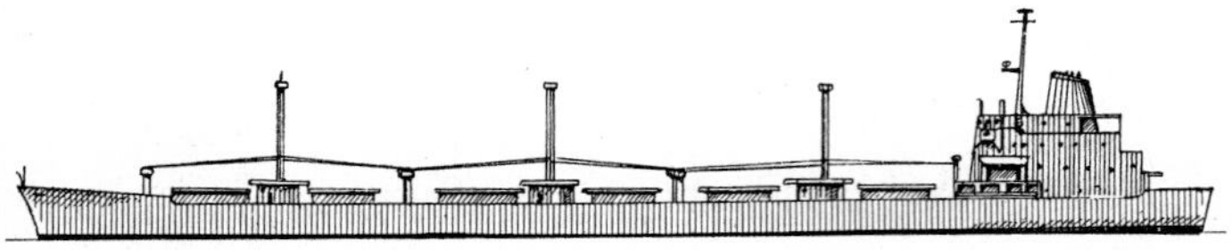

18 H^3MF *H*
PANIKOS Pa/Ja (IHI) 1969; C; 8,982 grt/14,924 dwt; 142.27 × 9.06 m *(466.77 × 29.72 ft)*; M (Pielstick); 13.5 kts; ex-*Khian Sun*; Early version of 'FREEDOM' type
Similar: **TORY HILL** (Pa) ex-*Khian Hill*

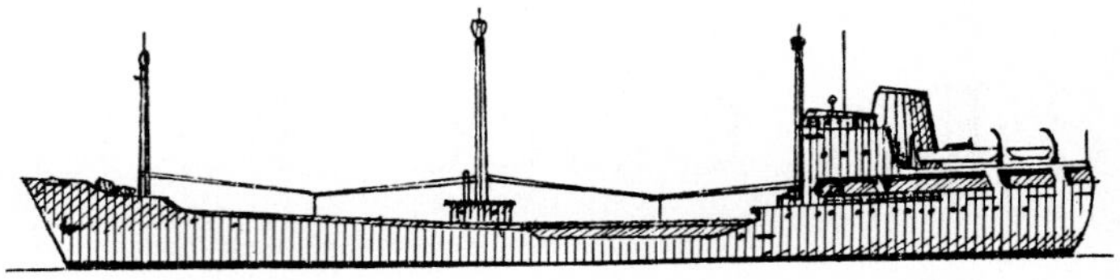

19 H^3MF *H13*
BUILDER III My/FRG (Lindenau) 1960; C; 1,956 grt/3,165 dwt; 84.69 × 5.6 m *(277.85 × 18.37 ft)*; M (MAN); 12 kts; ex-*Fossheim*

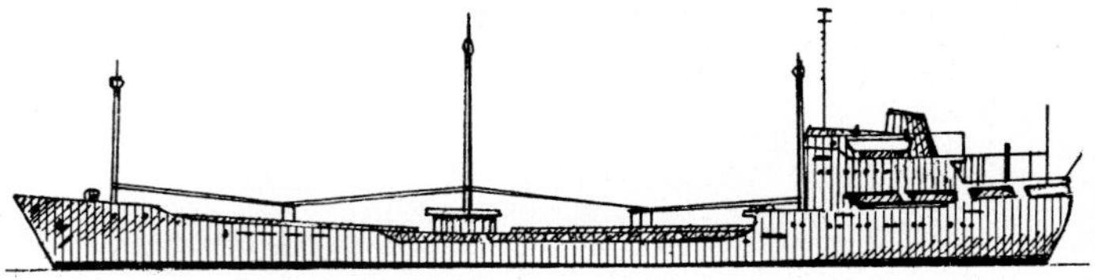

20 H^3MF *H13*
DIMACHK Sy/No (Sarpsborg) 1963; C; 2,706 grt/4,064 dwt; 91.52 × 6.03 m *(300.26 × 19.78 ft)*; M (MAN); 12.25 kts; ex-*Anneliese Porr*

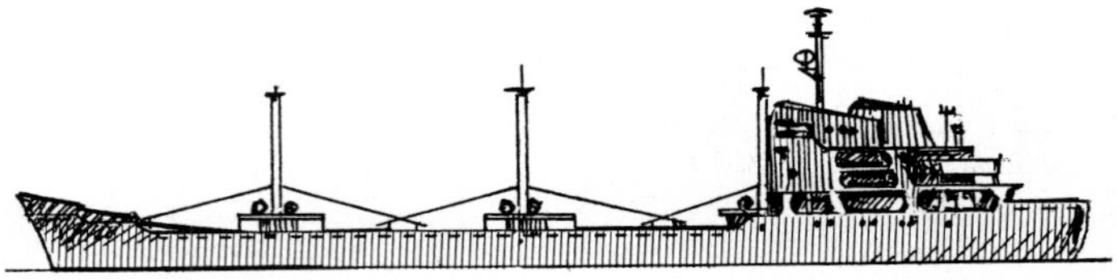

21 H^3MF *H13*
SEATRA EXPRESS Pa/Ja (Hakodate) 1961; C; 4,213 grt/5,751 dwt; 108.82 × 6.52 m *(357.02 × 21.39 ft)*; M (MAN); — kts; ex-*Gunung Kerintji*

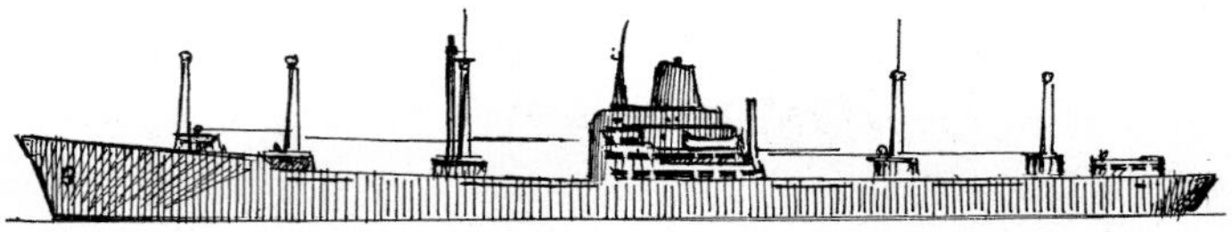

22 H^3MFH^3 *H1*
CAPE JOHNSON US/US (National Steel) 1961; C; 12,724 grt/14,699 dwt; 172 × 9.7 m *(565 × 31.7 ft)*; T (GEC); 20 kts; ex-*M M Dant*; US Government owned
Sisters: **CAPE JOHN** (US) ex-*C E Dant*; **CAPE JUBY** (US) ex-*Hawaii*; **MORMACWAVE** (US) ex-*Washington*; **CAPE JACOB** (US) ex-*California*

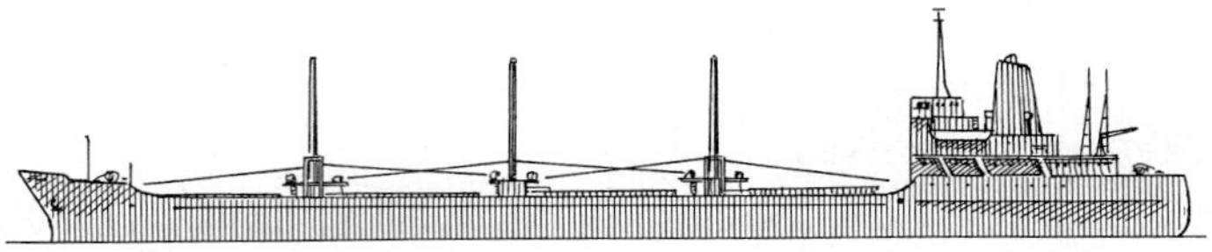

23 H^3MFM^2R *H13*
FU PING RC/Ja (Osaka) 1968; C; 9,858 grt/15,824 dwt; 145.7 × 9.27 m *(478.02 × 30.41 ft)*; M (B&W); 15.5 kts; ex-*Margaret Cord*; 'Mitsui Concord' type

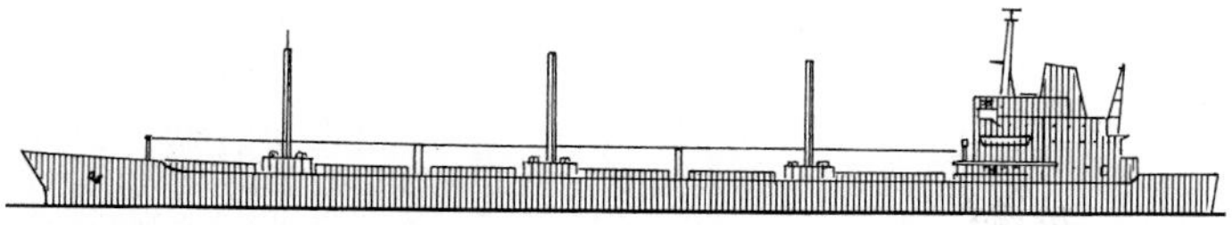

24 *H^{3}MFN H*

'FREEDOM' type —/Ja (IHI) & Sg (Jurong Spyd) 1968–1978; C; approx 9,000 grt/approx 15,000 dwt; 142.3 × 9.06 m *(466.86 × 29.72 ft)*; M (Pielstick); 14.5 kts; Some later ships have heavy-lift derrick
Sisters: **ELENI** (Ma) ex-*Acritas*; **PURNIMA** (Bs) ex-*Aeolos*; **AR RAQIB** (Pa) ex-*Agenor*; **FIDELITY** (—) ex-*Amyntas*; **ANNOULA** (Gr); **PROGRESS EXCELLENCE** (Mv) ex-*Anthemios*; **JHELUM** (Ma) ex-*Aquamarine*; **MUN SU BONG** (RK) ex-*Argos*; **TANARAY STAR** (Pa) ex-*Prosperity*; **OLMA** (Cy) ex-*Comet*; **CAPE KENNEDY** (Cy); **CAPE MONTEREY** (Cy) ex-*Kastraki*; **SAN SEBASTIAN** (Cy) ex-*Estina*; **AS SALAAM** (Pa) ex-*Dimos Halcoussis*; **CATRIONA** (Bs) ex-*Efthitis*; **DELTA FREEDOM** (Pk) ex-*Elpis*; **SYMPLEA** (Cy) ex-*Epos*; **ZULFIKAR** (Cy) ex-*Evnia*; **SEA STAR** (—) ex-*Frinton*; **FILIO** (Gr) ex-*Fronisis*; **VIVA TREASURE** (SV) ex-*Sharpeville*; **MARIGO** (Gr); **NAXOS** (Gr) ex-*Athens*; **SEA CHAMP** (Ho) ex-*Prospathia*; **RIZCUN ENTERPRISE** (Br) ex-*Santo Pioneer*; **NOBLE STAR** (Cy) ex-*Sea Tide*; **MULTISTAR** (SV) ex-*Silver Athens*; **JUPITER I** (Th) ex-*Teti N*; HAI HING (Th) ex-*Titika Halcoussi*; **FLYING DRAGON** (Vn) ex-*Sea Bird*; **ZHI KONG** (RC) ex-*Unity*; **HAI MENG** (Th) ex-*Yannis Halcoussis*; **CAPE SYROS** (Cy) ex-*Pola*; **HALLDIS** (Th) ex-*Ponza*; **HELMOS** (Cy) ex-*Akrata*; **ALEXANDRAKI** (Cy) ex-*Sea Star*; **ALAM TANGKAS** (My) ex-*Al Rakeeb*; **hATLANTA** (Cy) ex-*Neptune Sakura*; **PANANDROS** (Cy) ex-*Arkandros*; **DALIA** (SV) ex-*Endurance Express*; **GIOS** (SV) ex-*Georgios Matsas*; **FERARA** (Cy) ex-*Michalis*; **LADY OF LORNE** (Sg) ex-*Volta Friendship*; **GALAXY III** (Pa) ex-*Aramis*; **SAINT SPIRIDON** (Cy) ex-*Bounteous*; **RADNOR** (Cy) ex-*Hermina*; **NORBULK NAMIR** (Ma) ex-*Al Rahim*; **OURANIA 1** (Ma) ex-*Al Redha*; **GALLANTRY** (Pa) ex-*Santo Fortune*; **NAVARINO** (Gr) ex-*Long Beach*; **MAKRON** (Gr) ex-*Oakland*; **KALLANG** (Ma) ex-*Lydia*; **SAVANNAH I** (Pa) ex-*Pacprince*; **ADVENTURE** (Cy) ex-*Pacprincess*; **RIZCUN TRADER** (Br) ex-*Regina S*; **ZALCO SHARIFF** (Pa) ex-*Adamas*; **TRUST 38** (Pa) ex-*Wistaria Marble;* **PLATON** (Cy) ex-*Marabou*; **PORTAITISSA** (Ma) ex-*Duteous*; **APOSTOLIS II** (Ma) ex-*Spacious*; **ANNA JOHN** (Ma) ex-*Neptune Cyprine*; **SAI KUNG** (HK) ex-*Neptune Iolite*; **NEPTUNE IRIS** (Sg); **AL BAKY** (Pa) ex-*Neptune Kiku*; **BRIGHT STAR** (Sg) ex-*Neptune Peridot*; **ZULJENAH** (Pa) ex-*Neptune Ruby*; **FONTANA** (Cy) ex-*Neptune Sardonyx*; **LAEMTHONG PRIDE (Th) ex-***Neptune Spinel*; **WINDSTAR** (Li) ex-*Neptune Tourmaline*; **LAEMTHONG GLORY** (Th) ex-*Neptune Turquoise*; **SHANNON** (Cy) ex-*Wistaria Coral*: **TAI PAN** (HK) ex-*Wistaria Pearl*; **RUVU** (Ta) ex-*Sea Horse*; **LINCOLN K** (Ma) ex-*Pozega*; **KAVERI** (Ma) ex-*Pericles Halcoussis*; **TEESTA** (Ma) ex-*Indian Fraternity*; **GUI JIANG** (RC) ex-*Sea Falcon*; **LAN CANG JIANG** (RC) ex-*Zografnia Y*; **QU JIANG** (RC) ex-*Sea Swan*; **XUAN CHENG** (RC) ex-*Theodoros A S*; **WU JIANG** (RC) ex-*Sea Eagle*; Similar (Tw built (China SB): **LAI KING** (Gr) ex-*Glorious Trader*; **EVANTHIA** (Ma) ex-*Sincere Trader*; Similar (shorter third mast and superstructure differs. Some vessels in the above list may also have this appearance): **ANEMI** (Gr) ex-*Lucky Wave*; **PERICLES** (Cy) ex-*Leonis Halcoussis*; **LUCKY O** (Cy) ex-*Free Wave*; **ALAM TABAH** (My) ex-*Al Raziq*; **MAIROULI** (Cy) ex-*Telfair Pioneer*; **FORTUNE CELIA** (Pa) ex-*Kyriacos AS;* **YA SAMADU** (Pa) ex-*Nata*; **RELIANT** (Gr); **NEARCHOS** (Cy) ex-*Al Rashed*; **ZARA** (Bh) ex-*Al Rahman*; **CLIPPER FIDELITY** (Bs) ex-*Carnival Venture*; **ALAM TENAGA** (My) ex-*Al Raouf*; **GEMSTAR I** (Li) ex-*Al Razak*

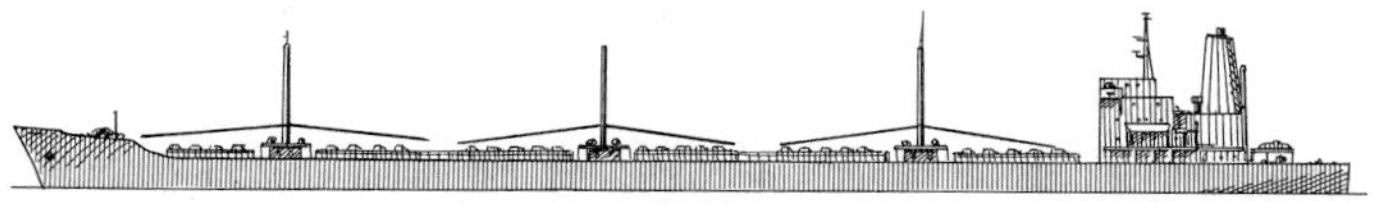

25 *H^{3}MFN H1*

ALMOND Pa/Ja (Sumitomo) 1972; B; 24,519 grt/41,872 dwt; 194.01 × 11.44 m *(636.52 × 37.53 ft)*; M (Sulzer); 14.75 kts; ex-*Inveralmond*; N aft consists of pole on port side and lattice-tripod on starboard

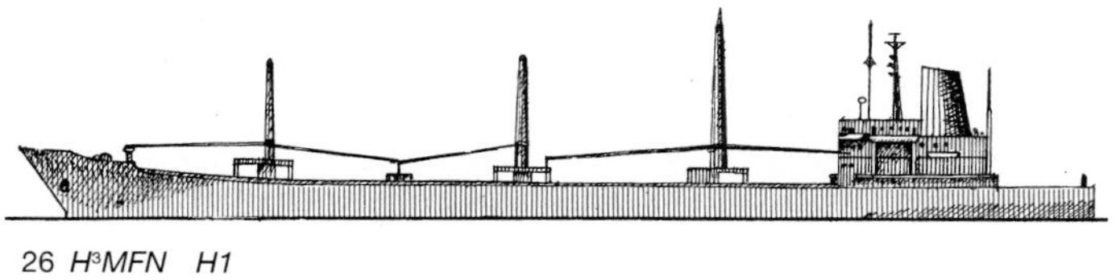

26 *H^{3}MFN H1*

GUR MAIDEN Bs/FRG (A G 'Weser') 1976; C; 9,886 grt/16,251 dwt; 149.82 × 9.28 m *(491.54 × 30.45 ft)*; M (MAN); 16.5 kts; ex-*Luise Bornhofen*; '36-L' type; 228 TEU
Similar (Some have five-deck super structure): **SAN EVANS** (Cy) ex-*Hugo Oldendorff*; **SOLAR GLORY** (SV) ex-*Gretke Oldendorff* (Pa); **ZANET II** (Ma) ex-*Almut Bornhofen*; **LYDIA II** (Gr) ex-*Karin Bornhofen*; **QIAN SHAN** (RC) ex-*Charlotte Kogel*; **SPINOZA** (Cy) ex-*Elise Schulte*; **DA SHA PING** (RC) ex-*Tarpon Seaway*; **DA SHI ZHAI** (RC) ex-*Tarpon Sands*; **JIN JIANG** (RC) ex-*Ilse Schulte*; **NEI JIANG** (RC) ex-*Elisabeth Schulte*; **WAN RU** (RC) ex-*Boleslaw Prus*

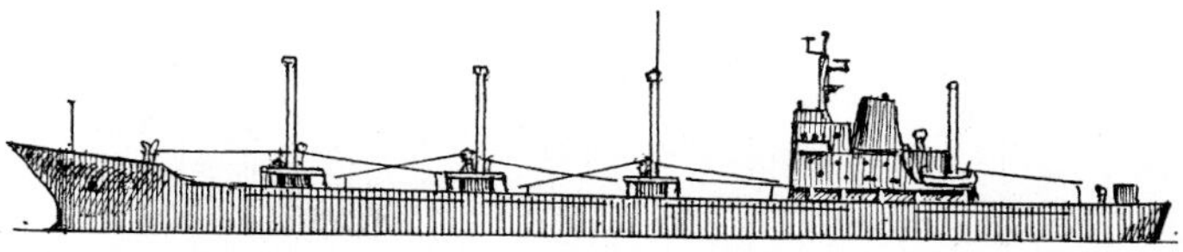

27 *H^{3}MFN H1*

RUCHI Pa/Ys ('3 Maj') 1969; C; 9,419 grt/15,124 dwt; 145 × 9.1 m *(476 × 29.10 ft)*; M (Sulzer); 15.5 kts; ex-*Betelgeuse*; 'Zagreb' type
Sisters: **JIN CHENG JIANG** (SV) ex-*Arcturus*; **GOLDEN HANSOME** (SV) ex-*Bellatrix*; **TAE CHON** (RK) ex-*Denebola*; Similar (five deck superstructure and centre-line kingposts): **ELKE** (SV) ex-*Crikvenica*; **LOSINJ** (SV); **OPATIJA** (SV); **RAB** (SV)

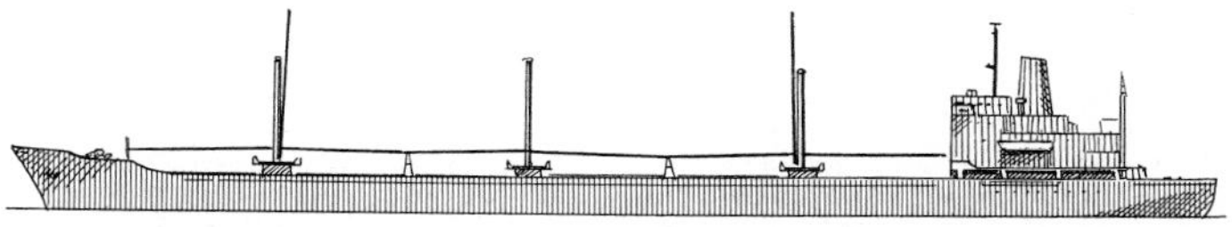

28 *H^{3}MFN H1*

TRIAS Gr/Ja (Sumitomo) 1970; B; 13,589 grt/21,939 dwt; 163.51 × 9.63 m *(536.45 × 31.59 ft)*; M (Sulzer); 16.5 kts; ex-*Seafox*

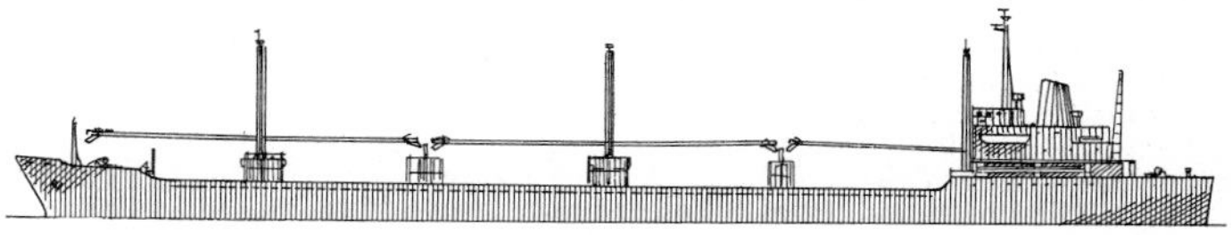

29 *H^{3}MFN H13*

GALAXY Pa/Ja (Onomichi) 1975; B; 16,511 grt/27,213 dwt; 172.35 × 10.25 m *(565.45 × 33.63 ft)*; M (Sulzer); 17.4 kts; ex-*Frank Delmas*
Possible sister: **GRECIAN STAR** (Cy) ex-*Fidelity*

30 *H^{3}MFN H13*

GLAFKOS Cy/Tw (Taiwan SB) 1977; B; 17,344 grt/27,800 dwt; 181.31 × 10.28 m *(594.85 × 33.73 ft)*; M (Sulzer); 15 kts; ex-*Polly*
Sister: **SPYRIDON CH** (Cy) ex-*Juliana*; Similar: **PROGRESO I** (Pa) ex-*Camerona*; **FORTUNE** (Cy) ex-*Union Harvest*; **ELINA** (SV) launched as *Pacific Endeavour*
Possibly similar: **PROGRESS** (Cy) ex-*Anita*; **EVANGELOS CH** (Cy) ex-*Christina*; **LEROS COURAGE** (Cy) ex-*Harriet*; **TAI SHING** (Tw); **STELLA TINGAS** (Cy) ex-*Lucina*; **HUA LIAN** (RC) ex-*Silver Clipper*; **IASON** (Cy) ex-*Tauros*; **HARMONY SEA** (Va) ex-*Justina*

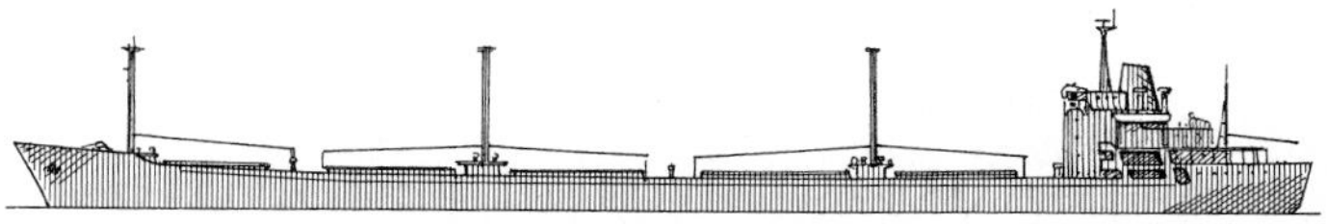

31 *H^{3}MFN H13*

GOLDEN TENNYO Pa/Ja (NKK) 1977; B; 14,382 grt/24,738 dwt; 172.27 × 9.78 m *(565.19 × 32.09 ft)*; M (Sulzer); 15 kts
Sisters (length 155m (508ft)): **GOLDEN CHASE** (Gr); **GOLDEN HORIZON** (Gr); **GOLDEN PANAGIA** (Pa); **GOLDEN SHIMIZU** (Pa); **TOCOPILLA** (Ch) ex-*Polytropos*; Similar (length 155m (508ft)): **GOLDEN SPEAR** (Gr); **ALRAHIM** (Ma) ex-*Golden Sword*; **STELLA** (Gr) ex-*Papyros*

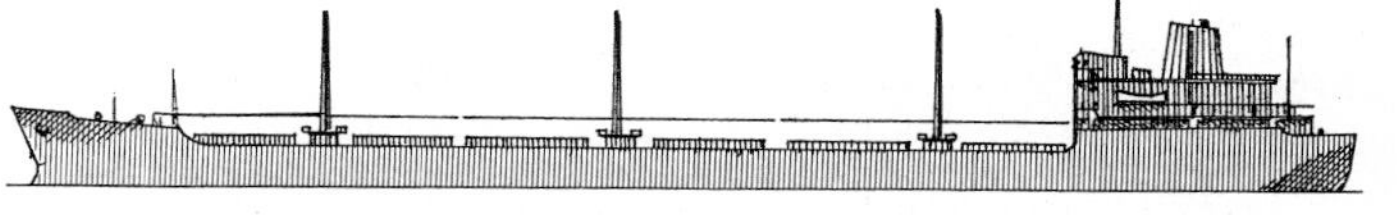

32 *H^{3}MFN H13*

JIANG HE RC/Ja (Kawasaki D) 1967; B; 14,444 grt/25,379 dwt; 178.52 × 10.39 m *(585.7 × 34.09 ft)*; M (MAN); 12.75 kts; ex-*Hoegh Mallard*

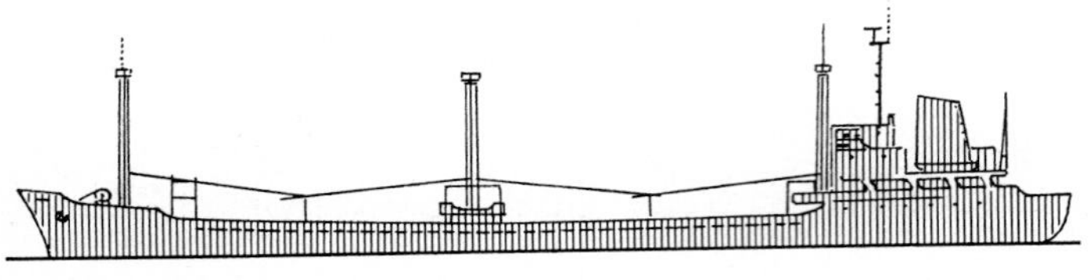

33 *H³MFN H13*
KOBE Pa/Ko (Dae Dong) 1984; C; 4,045 grt/6,500 dwt; 109.51 × 6.76 m *(359.28 × 22.18 ft)*; M (B&W); 12.5 kts
Possible sisters: **GAYA DUA** (My) ex-*Napili*; **NEW LEADING** (Pa); **JUBITER** (Pa) ex-*Sun Pheonix*; GAYA SATU (My) ex-*Lucky Pine*; **HARPOON** (Pi) ex-*Osa Vigoroso*; **HYUN AM** (Ko) ex-*Kee Expander*; Similar (smaller funnel and so on): **HANIFAH** (Pa) ex-*Ocean Rainbow*

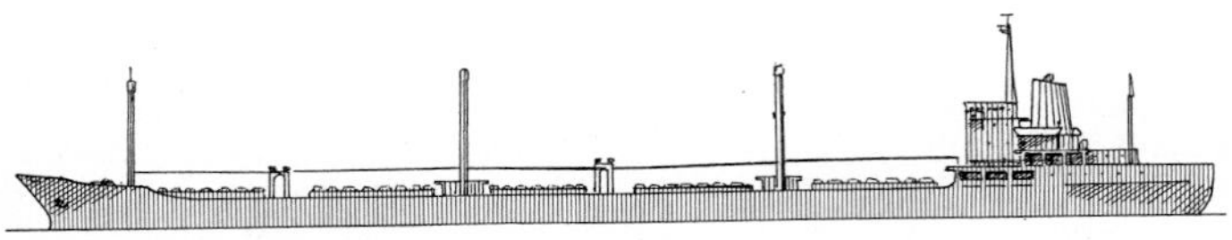

34 *H³MFN H13*
PROTAGORAS Cy/Ja (Kanasashi) 1974; B; 19,867 grt/33,652 dwt; 182.2 × 10.92 m *(597.77 × 35.83 ft)*; M (B&W); 16 kts; ex-*Toxotis*
Sisters: **PTOLEMEOS** (Cy) ex-*Didymi;* **FIVI** (Cy) ex-*Hydrohos*; **TILEMAHOS** (Cy) ex-*Zygos*; **SUN VIL** (Gr) ex-*Aegokeros*; **ANTIGONOS** (Cy) ex-*Ihthis*; **DIOMIDES** (Cy) ex-*Scorpius*; Similar: **TRIGLAV** (SV) ex-*Nova Gorica*; **BUFFALO** (Ko) ex-*Cascade Maru*
Possibly similar: **PANAYIOTA** (Li) ex-*Mammoth Fir*; **SEAGULL FORTUNE** (Li) ex-*Mammoth Pine*; **LEROS STAR** (Cy) ex-*Zinnia*; **GULSUM ANA** (Tu) ex-*Stadion*; **TOMAHAWK** (Cy) ex-*Trophy*

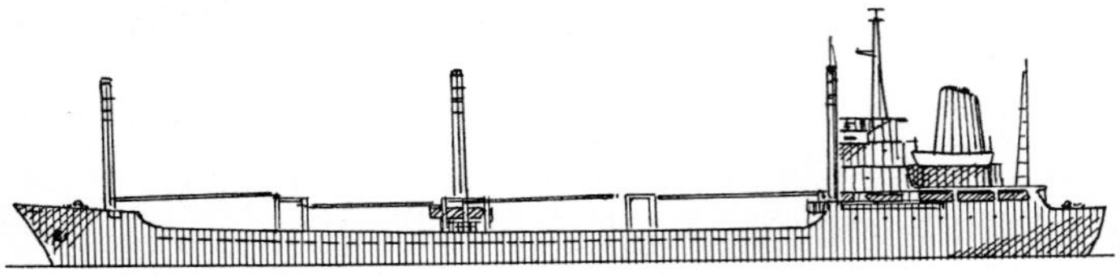

35 *H³MFN H13*
RAINBOW SV/Ja (Setoda) 1970; C; 4,099 grt/6,174 dwt; 111 × 6.7 m *(364.17 × 21.98 ft)*; M (B&W); 13 kts; ex-*Dona Amalia*
Sister: **TONALA** (Pa) ex-*Don Ambrosia*

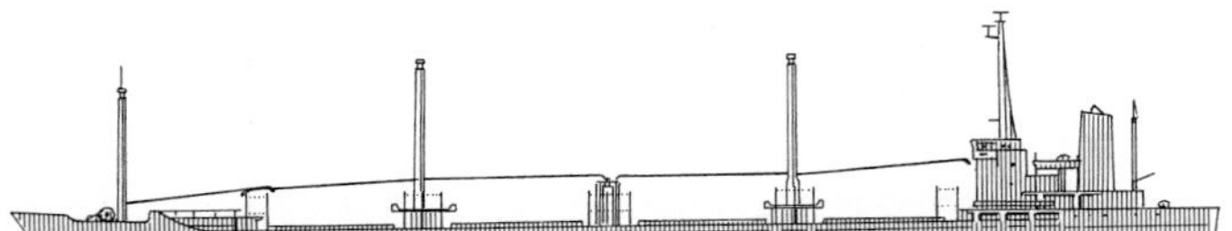

36 *H³MFN H13*
SEA JADE Li/Ja (Kanda) 1974; B; 16,047 grt/25,314 dwt; 175.85 × 9.62 m *(577 × 31.56 ft)*; M (Sulzer); 14.5 kts; ex-*Asia Beauty*
Sisters: **SEA DIAMOND** (Li) ex-*Asia Bravery*; **SEA FORTUNE** (Li) ex-*Asia Honesty*; Similar (shorter funnel): **LORI E** (Li) ex-*Genista*; Probable Sisters: **SEA BELLS** (Li); **SEA FAN** (Li)

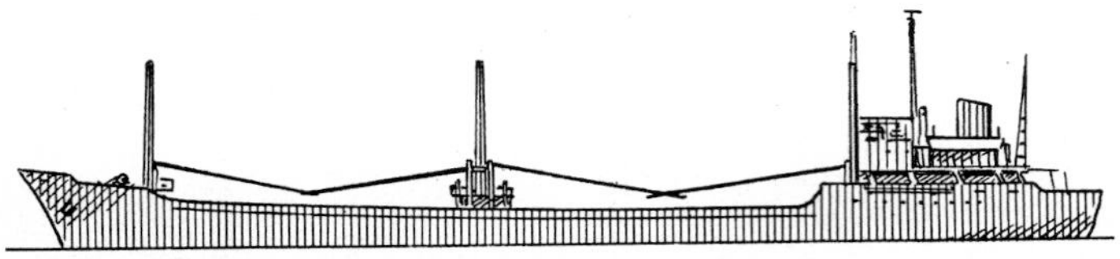

37 *H³MFN H13*
TAVEECHO MARINE Th/Ja (Kurushima) 1969; C; 3,054 grt/5,125 dwt; 97.21 × 6.38 m *(318.93 × 20.93 ft)*; M (Akasaka); 13 kts; ex-*Chang Chun*
Possibly similar: **CHUN JIN** (Ko) ex-*Shinnan Maru*; **TARAKAN** (Pa) ex-*Hashihama Maru*

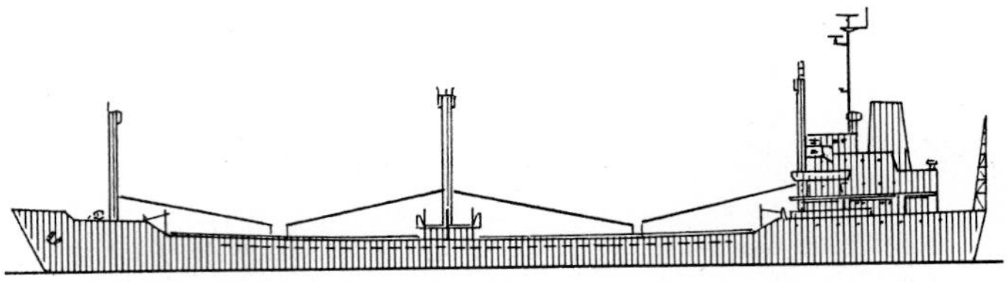

38 *H³MFN H13*
YAYASAN LAPAN My/My (Sabah) 1984; C/Log; 5,106 grt/8,027 dwt; 113.01 × 7.23 m *(370.77 × 23.72 ft)*; M (B&W); 12 kts
Sisters: **YAYASAN ENAM** (My); **YAYASAN LIMA** (My); **YAYASAN TUJUH** (My)
Possible sisters (Ja built—Taihei): **YAYASAN DUA** (My); **YAYASAN SATU** (My); **YAYASAN TIGA** (My)

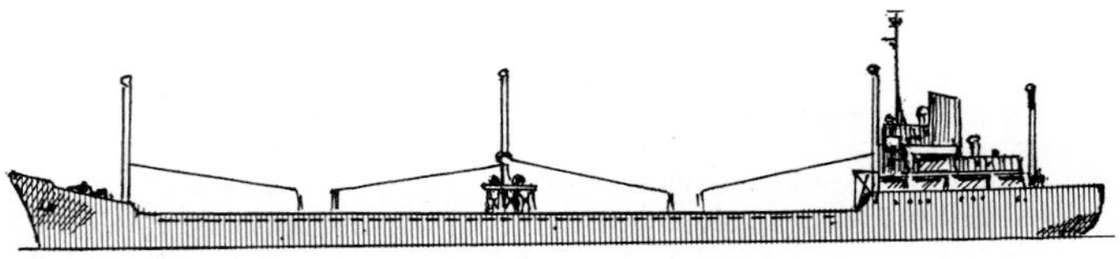

39 *H³MFN H13*
YUAN DA RC/Ja (Usuki) 1971; B; 9,827 grt/15,964 dwt; 147.2 × 9.09 m *(482.94 × 29.82 ft)*; M (Sulzer); 14.5 kts; ex-*Skyline*

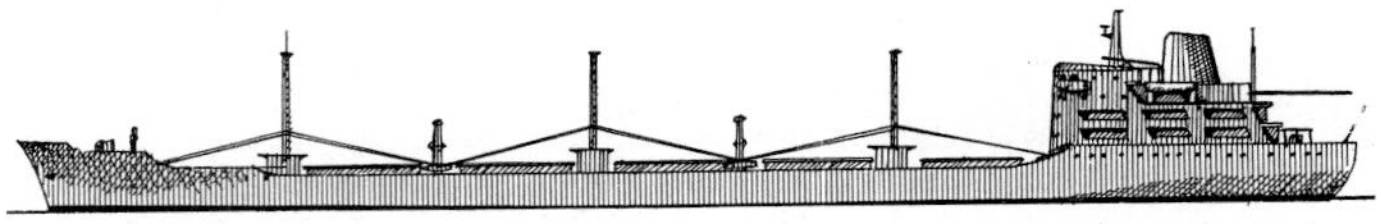

40 *H³MFN H13*
ZHEN HAI RC/Fr (L'Atlantique) 1963; B; 15,468 grt/23,426 dwt; 178.24 × 10.02 m *(584.78 × 32.87 ft)*; M (B&W); 13 kts; ex-*Destrehan*

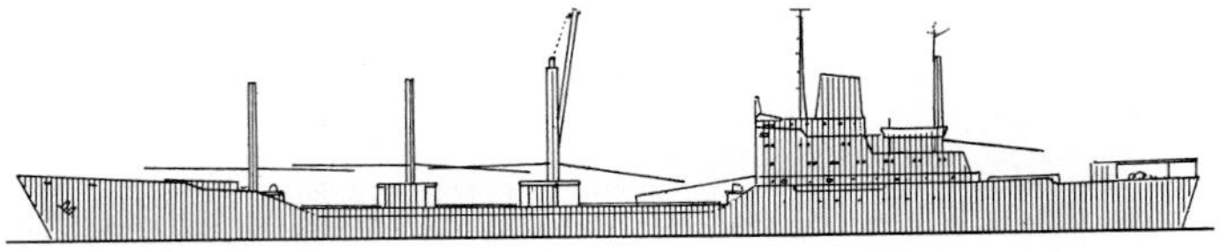

41 *H³MFT H13*
QIMEN RC/DDR (Warnow) 1973; C; 10,058 grt/13,884 dwt; 151.72 × 9.3 m *(498 × 30.35 ft)*; M (MAN); 17 kts; 'Ozean' type
Sisters: **DOUMEN** (RC); **HONGMEN** (RC); **LONGMEN** (RC); **YU QIANG** (RC) ex-*Tianmen*; **WUMEN** (RC); **XIAMEN** (RC); **YANMEN** (RC); **YIMEN** (RC); **YONGMEN** (RC); **MARO** (Ma) ex-*Mir*; **COTNARI** (Rm); **DRAGASANI** (Rm); **FOCSANI** (Rm)

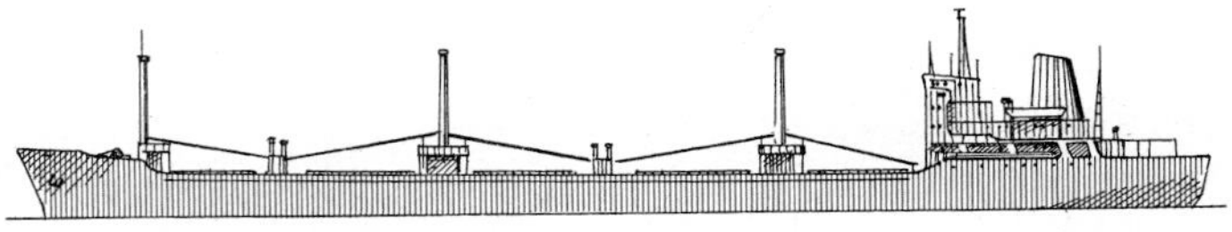

42 *H³M²FN H13*
SPYROS B Cy/Ja (Hitachi) 1966; B; 11,961 grt/19,470 dwt; 156.01 × 9.48 m *(511.8 × 31.1 ft)*; M (B&W); 14 kts; ex-*Coronia*; 'Hitachi Standard 19' type
Sisters: **ALEXIS** (Li) ex-*Wilshire Boulevard*; **OREO** (Pa) ex-*Orestia*; **GOLD RING** (Ma) ex-*Sea Pioneer*; **THETIS K** (Pa) ex-*Antiocha*; **NASOS S** (Pa) ex-*Olynthia*

43 *H³M–F H*
"FREEDOM-HISPANIA" type dwt; Sequence variation on drawing number 8/17

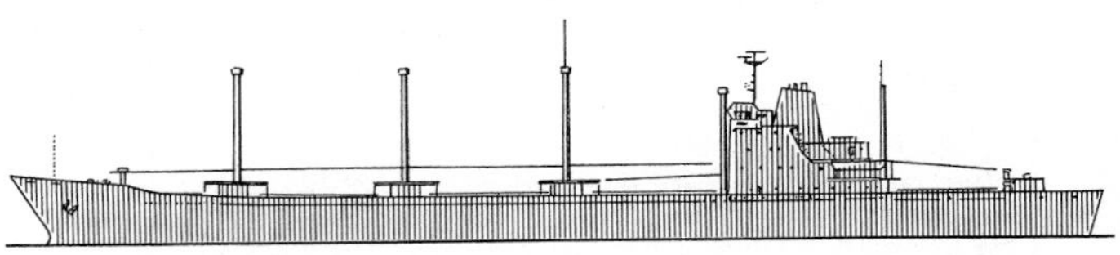

44 *H³NMFN H1*
AREITO Cu/Ys ('3 Maj') 1977; C; 10,057 grt/15,193 dwt; 148.01 × 8.99 m *(486 × 29.49 ft)*; M (Sulzer); 16 kts; ex-*Aracelio Iglesias*; 198 TEU
Sisters: **MAISI** (Cu) ex-*Jesus Menendez*; **VARADERO** (Cu) ex-*Lazaro Pena*

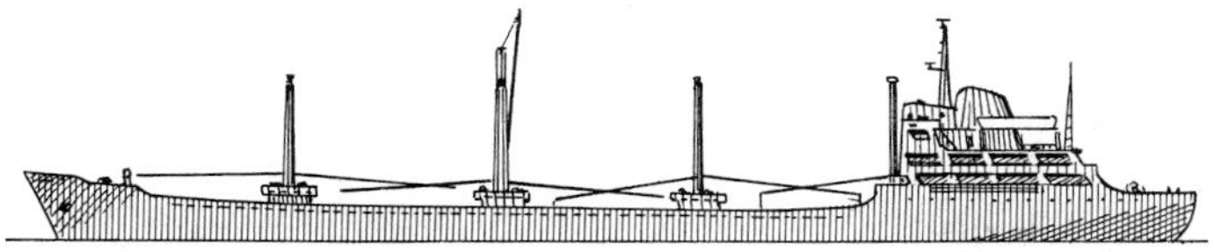

45 *H³NMFN H13*
IRENE Pi/Ja (Hayashikane) 1966; C; 7,074 grt/9,511 dwt; 131.93 × 7.6 m *(432.8 × 24.9 ft)*; M (B&W); 15 kts

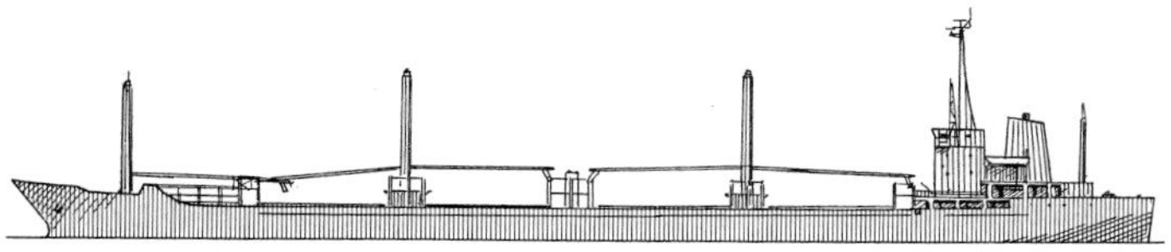

46 *H³NMFN H13*
WAN LING RC/Ja (Kanasashi) 1977; B; 15,863 grt/25,882 dwt; 175.8 × 9.6 m *(576.77 × 31.5 ft)*; M (MAN); 14.5 kts; ex-*Lucent Star*
Sisters: **SEA LANTERN** (Li) ex-*Brilliant Star*; **YUN LING** (RC) ex-*Radiant Star*; **LEVENT K** (Tu) ex-*Shining Star*; **EVPO AGNIC** (Pa) ex-*World Candour*; **DA PENG** (RC) ex-*World Probity*
Probable sisters—may have cranes: **EVPO AGSA** (Ma) ex-*Morning Glory*; **ANATOLI** (Ma) ex-*Red Arrow*

47 *H³NMFNH H13*
BAI YIN SHAN RC/Ja (Hitachi) 1966; C; 10,100 grt/12,653 dwt; 157.03 × 9.45 m *(517 × 31 ft)*; M (B&W); 18.5 kts; ex-*Izumo Maru*

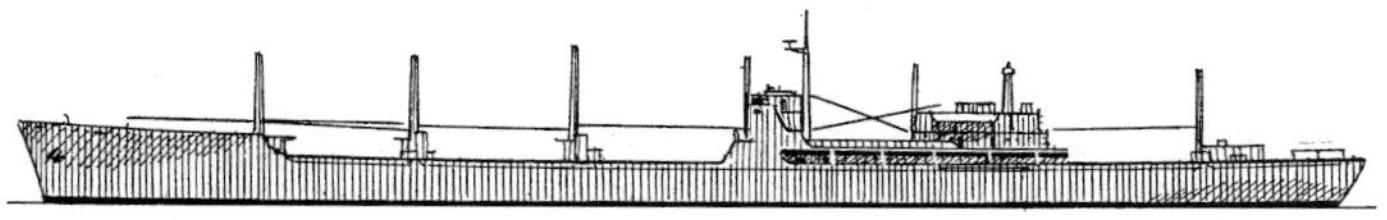

48 *H³NMNGK H1*
BRINTON LYKES US/US (Bethlehem Steel) 1962; C/Con; 11,891 grt/ 14,515 dwt; 180.6 × 9.79 m *(593 × 32.12 ft)*; T (GEC); 18 kts; lengthened 1972 (Todd). Lengthened 'Pacer' or 'Gulf Pride' class; US Government owned
Sisters: **VELMA LYKES** (US) ex-*Jean Lykes*; **SHIRLEY LYKES** (US); **SOLON TURMAN** (US)

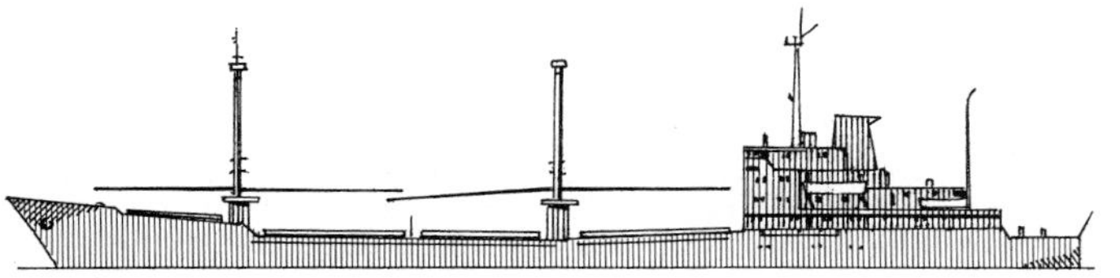

49 *H²MFM H1*
ARMADA GLORY Ia/Ru (Vyborg) 1977; C; 6,479 grt/8,520 dwt; 136.81 × 7.49 m *(448.85 × 24.57 ft)*; M (B&W); 16.25 kts; ex-*Nopal Yona*; 274 TEU 'Universal' type
Sisters: **JI MA** (RC) ex-*Nopal Camille*; **NIKOLAY ZHUKHOV** (Ru); **NIKOLAY MOROZOV** (Uk); **GRIGORIY KOVALCHUK** (Ru); **VASILIY BYELOKONYENKO** (Uk); **VITALIY KRUCHINA** (Ru); **IVAN KOROTEYEV** (Uk); **MIKHAIL STENKO** (Uk); **NIKOLAY SHCHUKIN** (Uk); **PYOTR STAROSTIN** (Uk); **ANDRIAN GONCHAROV** (Uk); **INZHENER YAMBURENKO** (Uk)

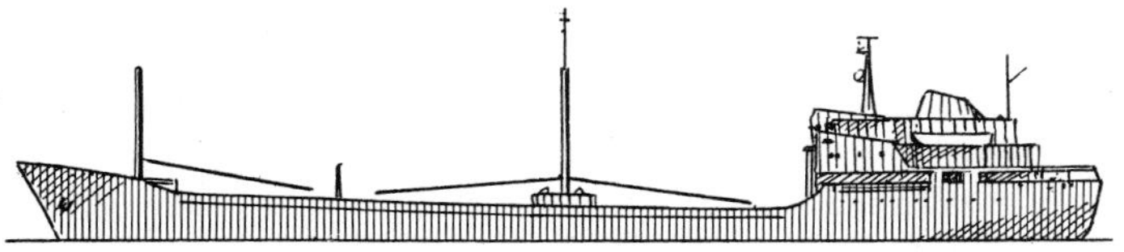

50 *H²MFM H13*
BRAD Rm/Rm (Galatz) 1971; C; 3,532 grt/4,795 dwt; 106.2 × 7.06 m *(348.43 × 23.16 ft)*; M (Sulzer); 14 kts
Sisters (Some built by Braila): **AZUGA** (Rm); **TIRGU JIU** (Rm); **CODLEA** (Rm); **SULINA** (Rm); **TIRNAVENI** (Rm); **RIMNICU VILCEA** (Rm); **PLOPENI** (Rm); **SACELE** (Rm); **DUMBRAVENI** (Rm); **CALARASI** (Rm); **GHEORGHIENI** (Rm); **SADOVA** (Rm); **SNAGOV** (Rm); **SOVEJA** (Rm); **OSCAR SATURN** (Rm) ex-*Sovata*; **ROMANATI** (Rm) ex-*Segarcea*; **SAVINESTI** (Rm); **SAVENI** (Rm); **SUCEVITA** (Rm); **SOUSA** (Rm); **SALISTE** (Rm); **SABARENI** (Rm); **SLANIC** (Rm); **SEBES** (Rm); **LOVECH** (Bu); **GEVO EXPRESS** (Le) ex-*Arya Marmar*; **IRAN TOWHEED** (Ir) ex-*Arya Noosh*; **HE XIN** (SV) ex-*Sarmisegetuza*; **SEIMENI** (Rm); **SOLCA** (Rm); **SUCIDAVA** (Rm); **SMIRDAN** (Rm)
Probable sisters (builder—Braila): **COVASNA** (Rm); **DRAGANESTI** (Rm); **SALONTA** (Rm); **STEFANESTI** (Rm); **TELEGA** (Rm); **ZARNESTI** (Rm); **ZIMNICEA** (Rm) (builder—Galatz); **VICTORIA** (SV) ex-*Sascut*

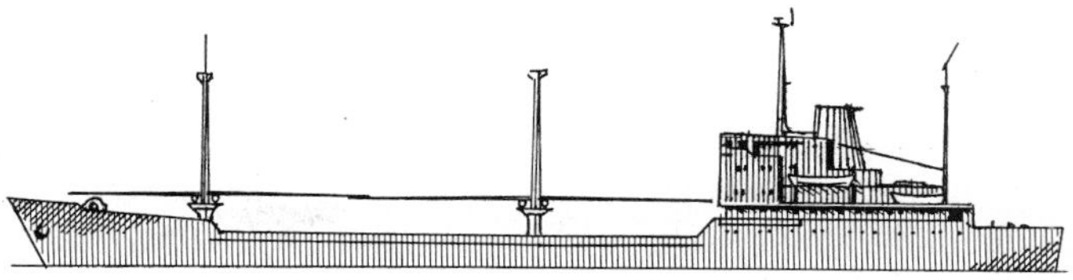

51 *H²MFM H13*
PIONER MOSKVY Ru/Ru (Vyborg) 1973; C; 4,814 grt/6,780 dwt; 130.31 × 7.36 m *(428 × 24.15 ft)*; M (B&W); 15.5 kts
Sisters: **PIONER ARKHANGELSKA** (Ru); **PIONER SAKHALINA** (Ru); **PIONER YUZHNO SAKHALINSKA** (Ru); **PIONER CHUKOTKI** (Ru); **PIONER KHOLMSKA** (SV); **PIONER ONEGI** (Ru); **PIONER ESTONII** (Ru); **PIONER KAMCHATKI** (SV); **PIONER ROSSII** (Ru); **PIONER BURYATII** (SV); **PIONER LITVY** (Ru); **PIONER SEVERODVINSKA** (Ru); **PIONER SLAVYANKI** (Ru); **PIONER BELORUSSII** (Ru); **PIONER KARELII** (Ru); **PIONER KAZAKHSTANA** (Ru); **PIONER KERGIZII** (Ru); **PIONER KOLY** (Ru); **PIONER MOLDAVII** (Ru); **PIONER UZBEKISTANA** (Ru); **IVAN RYABOV** (Ru) ex-*Heidenau*; **TEKHNOLOG KONYUKHOV** (Ru) ex-*Rabenau*

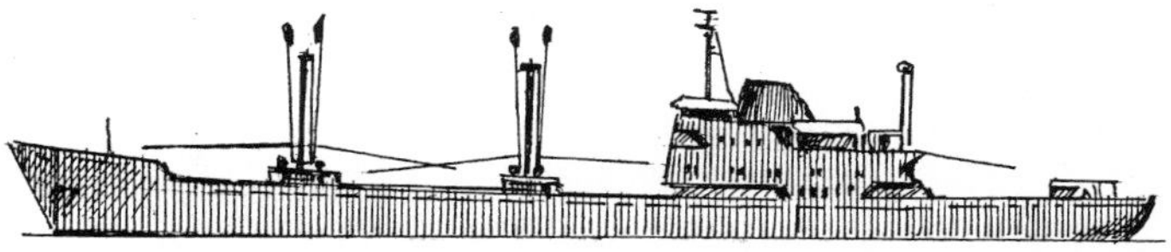

52 *H²MFN H1*
FARAMITA SV/Pd (Szczecinska) 1970; CP; 5,296 grt/5,923 dwt; 124 × 6.9 m *(407 × 23 ft)*; M (Sulzer); 16 kts; ex-*Krivan*; 'B455' type
Sisters: **ROSHNI** (SV) ex-*Blanik*

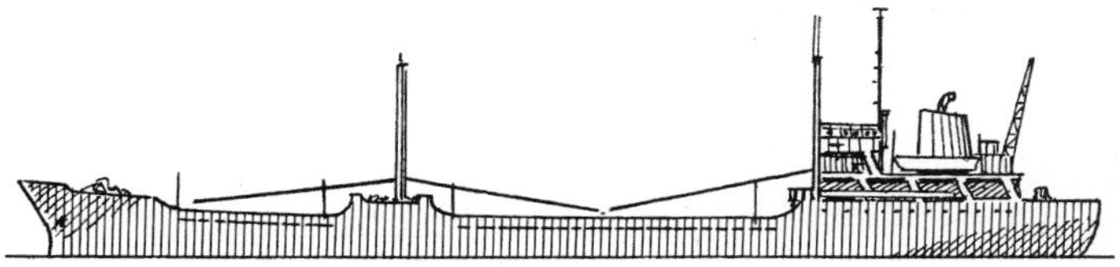

53 *H²MFN H123*
TA TUNG No 2 Tw/Ja (Nishi Z) 1969; C; 1,998 grt/3,861 dwt; 91.9 × 6.42 m *(301.51 × 21.06 ft)*; M (Ito Tekkosho); 13 kts; ex-*Marukichi Maru No 3*
Possible sisters: **SHUN ZHI** (RC) ex-*Kyoho Maru*; **SENTOSA** (Ia) ex-*Shorei Maru*

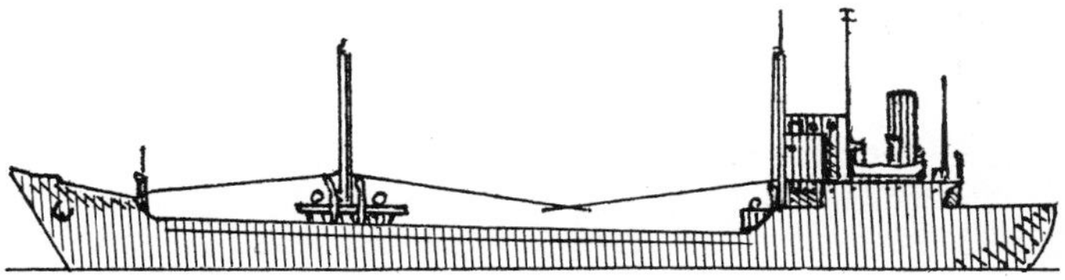

54 *H²MFN H13*
NAM SAN Ko/Ko (Dae Sun) 1972; C; 1,534 grt/2,551 dwt; 82.66 × 5.26 m *(271.19 × 17.26 ft)*; M (Akasaka); 10.5 kts

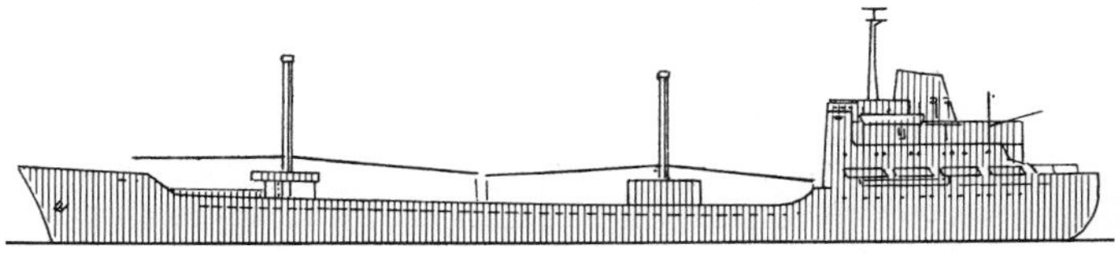

55 *H²MFN H13*
PARADISE SV/Ja (Setoda) 1967; C; 5,756 grt/8,406 dwt; 120.3 × 7.88 m *(395 × 25.85 ft)*; M (B&W); 13 kts; ex-*Tropical Plywood*

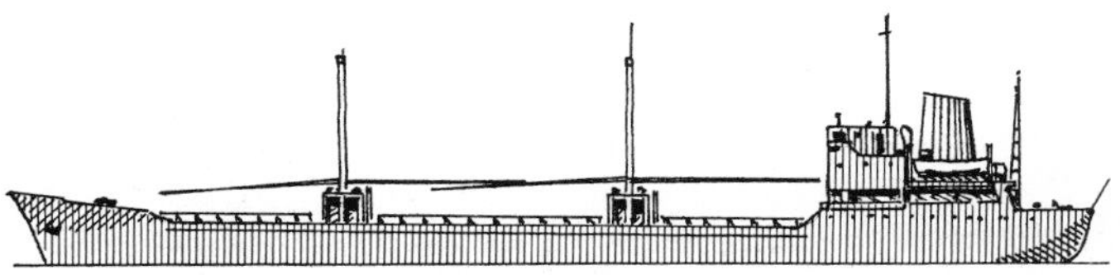

56 *H²MFN H13*
STEVE GLORY Pa/Ja (Osaka) 1962; C; 3,883 grt/5,681 dwt; 108.92 × 6.83 m *(357.35 × 22.41 ft)*; M (Mitsubishi); 12 kts; ex-*Toyo Maru No 2*

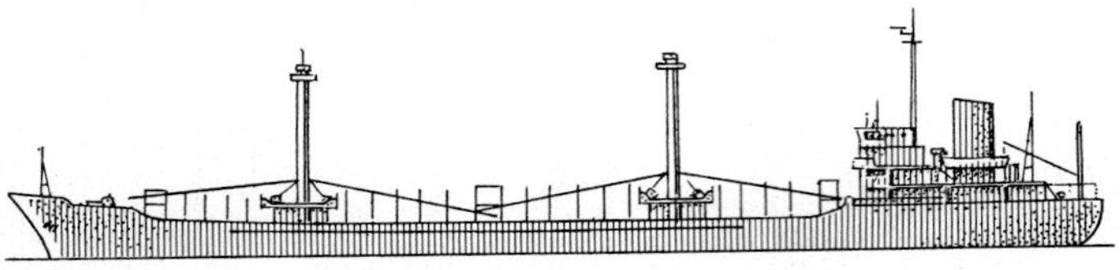

57 H^2M^2FNM *H13*
BLACK SEA T SV/Ja (Tohoku) 1969; C; 6,390 grt/10,157 dwt; 127.41 × 7.25 m *(418 × 23.79 ft)*; M (B&W); 12.75 kts; ex-*Rinsei Maru*
Similar (Superstructure differs): **LOYAL BIRD** (Bh) ex-*Allied Enterprise*
Possibly similar: **YING YOU SHAN** (RC) ex-*Kosei Maru*; **CHIOS FAITH** (Pa) ex-*Crystal Camellia*

58 H^2M–FNH *H1*
ZHENJIANG RC/FR (France-Gironde) 1966; C; 10,596 grt/15,688 dwt; 158 × 9.4 m *(520 × 31 ft)*; M (B&W); — kts
Sister: **JIU JIANG** (RC)

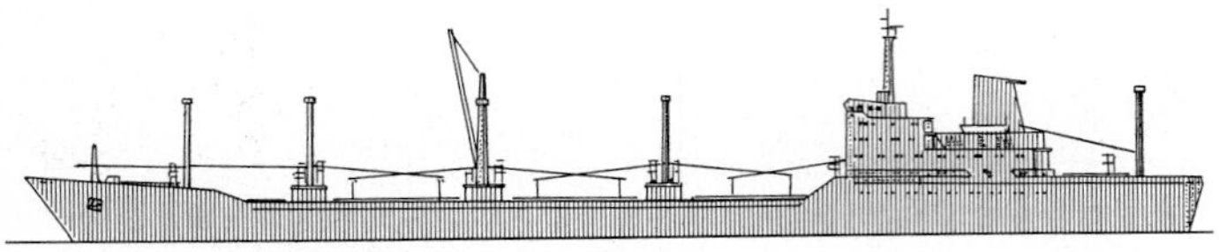

59 H^2NHMFH *H13*
KORINTHOS Pd/Ys ('Uljanik') 1978; C/Con; 18,022 grt/15,613 dwt; 180.42 × 9.65 m *(592 × 31.66 ft)*; M (Sulzer); 22 kts; ex-*Profesor Szafer*; 366 TEU. May be spelt **KHORINTHOS**
Sisters: **KASSOS** (Pd) ex-*Profesor Mierzejewski*; **KALYMNOS** (Pd) ex-*Profesor Rylke*

60 H^2NHNGN *H1*
CAPE CHALMERS US/US (Bethlehem Steel) 1963; C/Con; 9,296 grt/11,473 dwt; 150.8 × 10.3 m *(495 × 34.5 ft)*; T (GEC); 18 kts; ex-*Adabelle Lykes*; US Government owned
Sisters: **CAPE CANSO** (US) ex-*Aimee Lykes*; **CAPE CANAVERAL** (US) ex-*Allison Lykes*; **CAPE CHARLES** (US) ex-*Charlotte Lykes*; **CAPE CATOCHE** (US) ex-*Christopher Lykes*; **CAPE COD** (US) ex-*Sheldon Lykes*; **CAPE CLEAR** (US) ex-*Mayo Lykes*

61 H^2NMFMH^2 *H1*
AMBASSADOR US/US (New York SB) 1960; C; 7,848 grt/11,197 dwt; 150.1 × 8.5 m *(493 × 28.1 ft)*; T (GEC); 18.5 kts; ex-*Export Ambassador*; US Government owned
Sisters: **ADVENTURER** (US) ex-*Export Adventurer*; **AIDE** (US) ex-*Export Aide*; **AGENT** (US) ex-*Export Agent*

62 H^2NMFNH *H1*
QING FENG ER HAO RC/Sw (Oskarshamns) 1960; CP; 8,970 grt/12,675 dwt; 147.9 × 9.1 m *(485 × 29.11 ft)*; M (Gotaverken); 15 kts; ex-*Gyda*

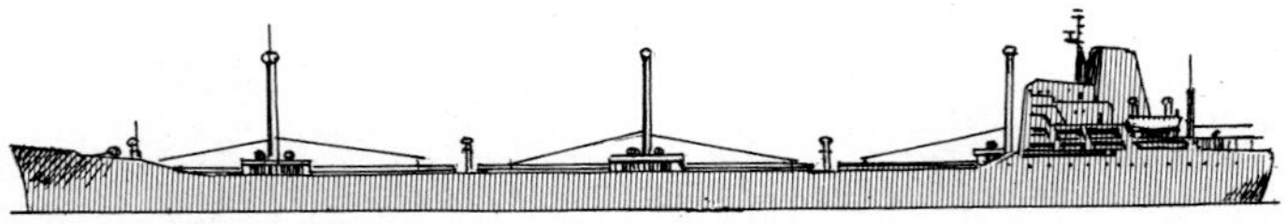

63 H^2N^2MFN *H13*
OCEAN K Pa/Ja (Fujinagata) 1964; B; 15,260 grt/25,701 dwt; 178.19 × 9.83 m *(584.61 × 32.25 ft)*; M (Sulzer); 12 kts; ex-*Tokyo Olympics*

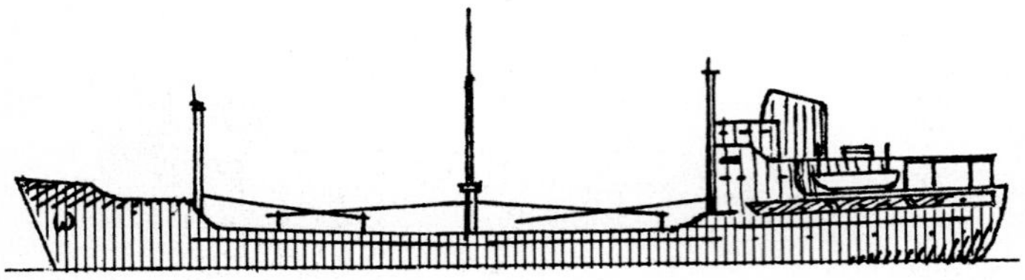

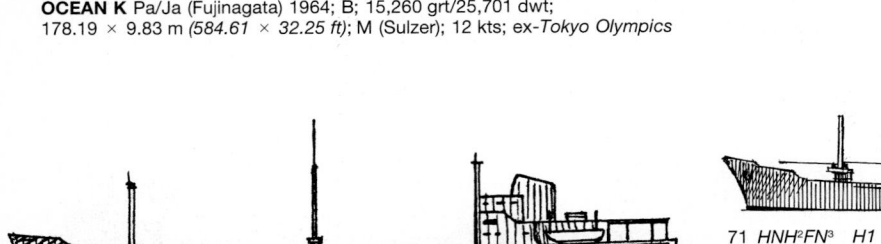

64 *HMHF H13*
VATSY Mg/No (Drammen) 1957; C; 1,437 grt/1,715 dwt; 72.55 × 4.74 m *(238.02 × 15.55 ft)*; M (Polar); 12 kts; ex-*Le Scandinave*

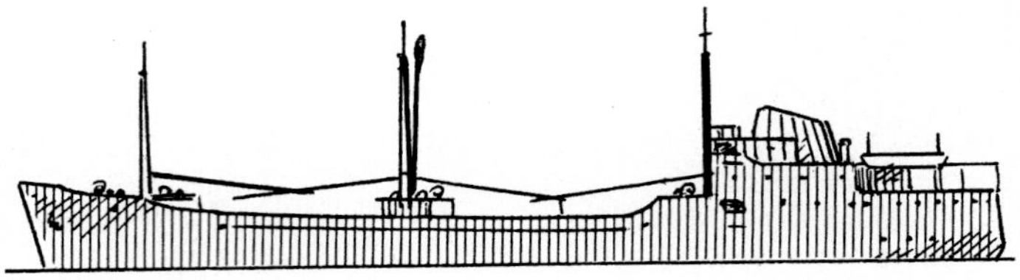

65 *HMHMF H12*
ANAS Sy/Br (Grangemouth) 1963; C; 1,672 grt/2,512 dwt; 74.73 × 5.77 m *(245.18 × 18.93 ft)*; M (Mirrlees); 13.5 kts; ex-*Palomares*
Sisters: **PISANG PERAK** (Ia) ex-*Pelayo*

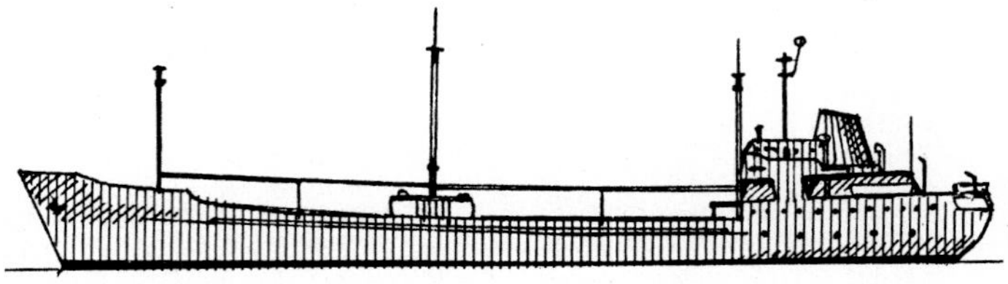

66 *HMHMF H13*
MARY TH Sr/FRG (Hagelstein) 1961; C; 1,252 grt/2,042 dwt; 76.1 × 5.03 m *(249.67 × 16.5 ft)*; M (KHD); 12 kts; ex-*Karl-Heinz Parchmann*

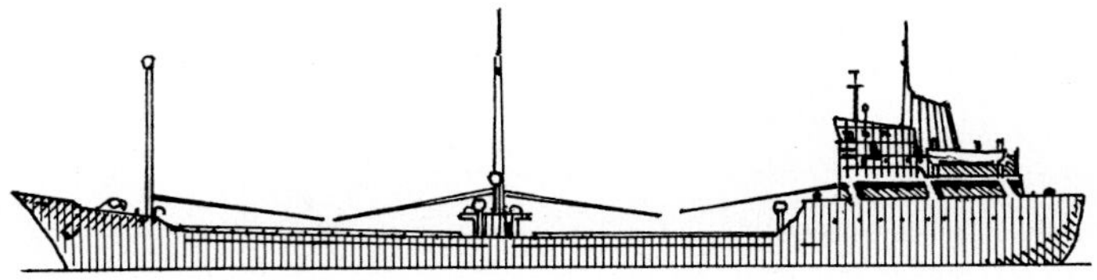

67 *HMM–F H13*
CAPTAIN NIKOLAS Ma/Sp (Espanola) 1967; C; 2,046 grt/3,658 dwt; 93.02 × 5.37 m *(305.18 × 17.62 ft)*; M (Sulzer); 11 kts; ex-*Liana*

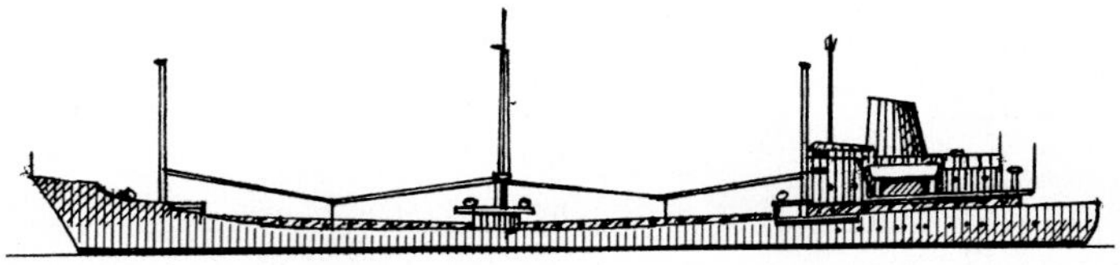

68 *HMNMF H1*
ADNAN Sy/FRG (Nobiskrug) 1966; C; 2,705 grt/3,220 dwt; 90.05 × 5.67 m *(295.44 × 18.6 ft)*; M (MAN); 13.75 kts; ex-*Botany Bay*
Sister: **ABDUL LATIF-S** (Sy) ex-*Saturn*

69 *HNFH H13*
NAZ K Tu/Br (Caledon) 1961; C; 3,726 grt/5,410 dwt; 99.17 × 7.46 m *(325.36 × 24.48 ft)*; M (Sulzer); 12 kts; ex-*Phyllis Bowater*

70 *HNFNH H1*
TONG AN RC/Sp (UN de Levante) 1964; PC; 7,225 grt/7,080 dwt; 133.1 × 7.6 m *(437 × 25 ft)*; M (B&W); 17 kts; ex-*Villa de Bilbao*

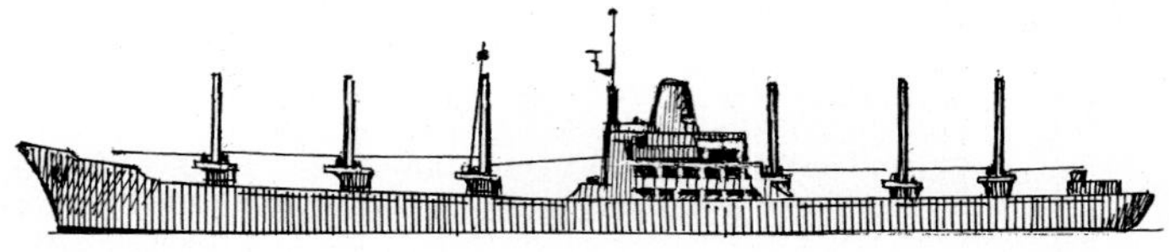

71 HNH^2FN^3 *H1*
CAPE ALAVA US/US (Ingalls SB) 1962; C; 11,309 grt/12,932 dwt; 174.3 × 9.4 m *(572 × 30.1 ft)*; T (GEC); 20 kts; ex-*African Comet*; US Government owned
Sisters: **DAWN** ex-*African Dawn* (US); **CAPE ALEXANDER** (US) ex-*African Mercury*; **CAPE ANN** (US) ex-*African Meteor*; **CAPE ARCHWAY** (US) ex-*African Neptune*; **CAPE AVINOF** (US) ex-*African Sun*

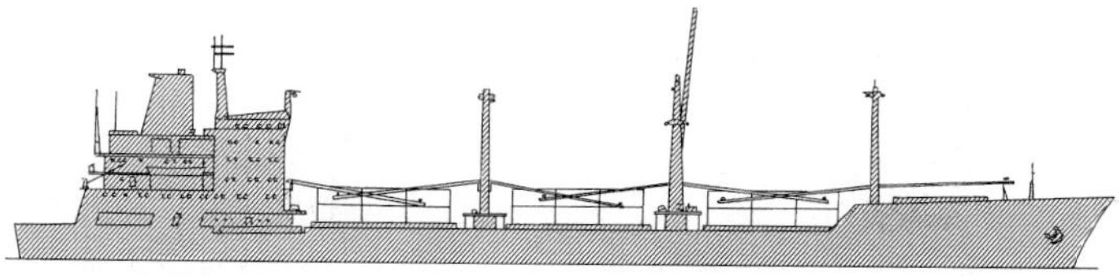

72 *HNH^{2}MFM H1*
INDIAN EXPRESS Va/Pd (Gdanska) 1982; C/Con; 13,251 grt/17,279 dwt; 155.23 × 9.70 m *(509.28 × 31.82 ft)*; M (Sulzer); 16 kts; ex-*Kriti Jade*; 381 TEU; 'B346' type
Sisters: **IBERIAN EXPRESS** (Va) ex-*Kriti Coral*; **ISTRIAN EXPRSS** (Va) ex-*Kriti Garnet*; **ITALIAN EXPRESS** (Va) ex-*Kriti Peridot*; **IONIAN EXPRESS** (Va) ex-*Kriti Amethyst*

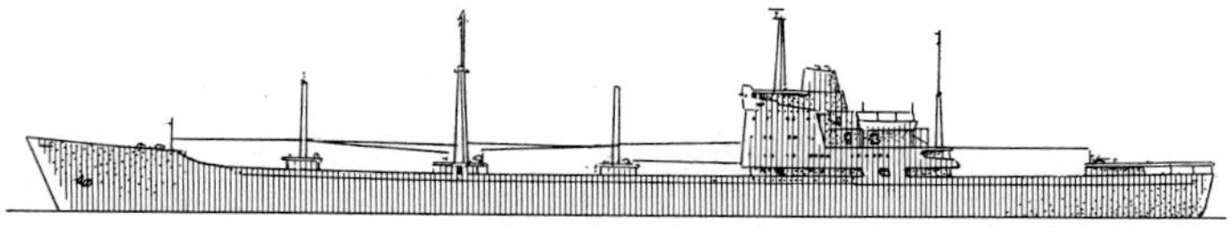

73 *HNHMFH H1*
URSUS Li/Pd (Gdanska) 1972; C; 9,847 grt/12,313 dwt; 154.67 × 8.97 m *(507.4 × 29.43 ft)*; M (Sulzer); 17.75 kts; 'B442' type
Sister: **SWIECIE** (Li)

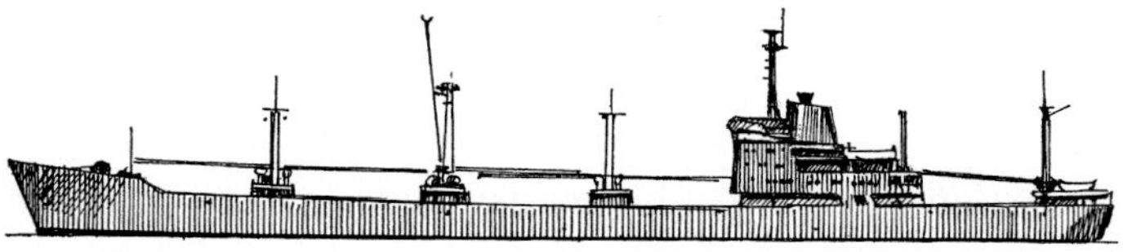

74 *HNHMFNH H1*
IGNATIY SERGEYEV Uk/Pd (Gdanska) 1968; C; 10,028 grt/12,640 dwt; 154.5 × 9.5 m *(507 × 29.6 ft)*; M (Sulzer); 16.5 kts; 'B40/B401' type 'Kommunist' class
Sisters: **GEORGIY CHICHERIN** (Uk); **GEORGIY DIMITROV** (Uk); **ERNST THALMANN** (Uk); **GIUSEPPE DI VITTORIO** (Uk); **DENEB** (Uk); **HO CHI MIN** (Ru); **INESSA ARMAND** (Uk); **IONA YAKIR** (Uk); **JEANNE LABOURBE** (Uk); **KARL LIEBKNECHT** (Ru); **KOMMUNIST** (Uk); **SIRIUS** (Uk) ex-*Kommunisticheskoye Znamya*; **BELA KUN** (Uk); **DMITRY POLUYAN** (Uk); **NIKOLAY KREMLYANSKIY** (Uk); **FRIEDRICH ENGELS** (Uk); **ROZA LUKSEMBURG** (Uk); **FRANZ BOGUSH** (Uk); **TOYVO ANTIKAYNEN** (Uk); B442 type: **GENERAL A F CEBESOY** (Ru); **GENERAL K ORBAY** (Ru); **GENERAL R GUMUSPALA** (Ru); **GENERAL Z DOGAN** (Ru); **KONIN** (Li)

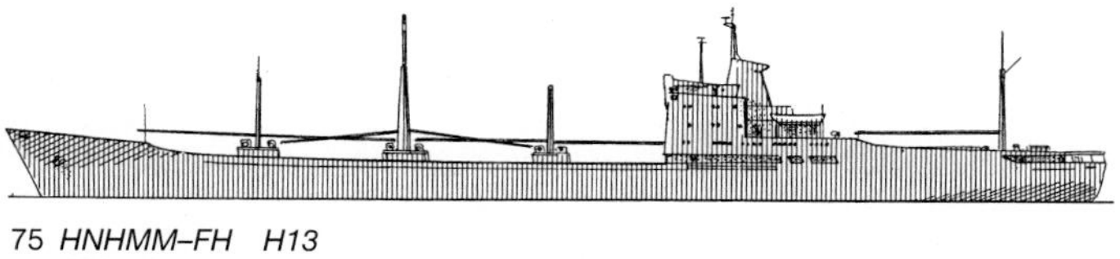

75 *HNHMM–FH H13*
YAN AN WU HAO RC/Pd (Gdanska) 1971; C; 10,119 grt/12,181 dwt; 153.74 × 8.97 m *(504.4 × 29.43 ft)*; M (Sulzer); 18 kts; ex-*Wlaydyslaw Orkan*; Modified 'B442' type
Sister: **SU XIA** (RC) ex-*Lucjan Szenwald*

76 *HNHNF H*
AL BAHR AL SABAH UAE/Rm (Galatz) 1963; C; 3,090 grt/4,400 dwt; 98.30 × 6.58 m *(322.51 × 21.59 ft)*; M (Sulzer); 12.5 kts; ex-*Brasov*
Sisters: **SUNRISE K** (Ho) ex-*Deva*; **OSCAR 10** (Rm) ex-*Iasi* **SIBIU** (Rm); **HALIMA K** (Ho) ex-*Tirgoviste*; **TIRGU MURES** (Rm); **CHANG AN** (RC); **HONG QI 150** (RC); **HONG QI 151** (RC); **HONG QI 152** (RC); **HONG QI 153** (RC); **HUAI AN** (RC); **HONG QI 160** (RC) ex-*Ilia*; **XIN AN** (RC)

77 *HNHNF H1*
TAI WU SHAN RC/Fi (Rauma-Repola) 1960/70; C; 2,440 grt/3,430 dwt; 100.44 × 4.92 m *(329.53 × 16.15 ft)*; M (Sulzer); 13 kts; ex-*Tellus*; Lengthened 1970
Sisters: **TAI YANG SHAN** (RC) ex-*Titania*; **JORDAN** (Eg) ex-*Triton*

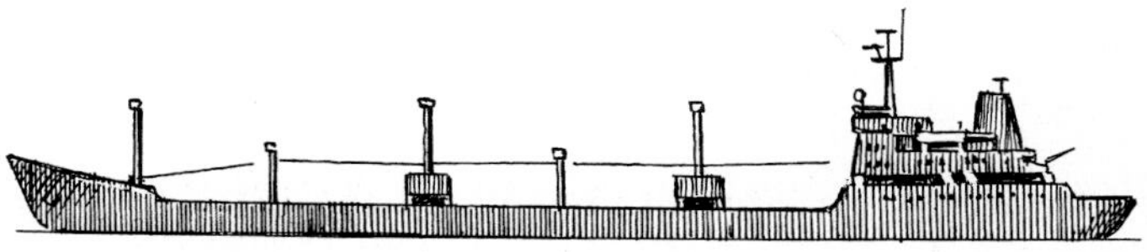

78 *HNHNHMF H13*
NIKOLAY NOVIKOV Ru/Pd (Gdanska) 1973; B/TC; 10,150 grt/13,950 dwt; 150.27 × 8.69 m *(493.01 × 28.51 ft)*; M (Sulzer); 15.75 kts; 'B-436' type
Sisters: **IVAN SYRYKH** (Ru); **VLADIMIR MORDVINOV** (Ru); **VLADIMIR TIMFEYEV**. The following sisters are 'B-540' type: **KAPITAN MOCHALOV** (Ru); **KAPITAN BAKANOV** (Ru); **KAPITAN KIRIY** (Ru); **KONSTANTIN PETROVSKIY** (Ru); **MEKHANIK GORDIYENKO** (Ru); **VLAS NICHKOV** (Ru); **KAPITAN DUBLITSKIY** (Ru); **KAPITAN MILOVZOROV** (Ru); **KAPITAN SAMOYLENKO** (Ru); **PETR SMIDOVICH** (Ru); **VASILIY MUSINSKIY** (Ru); **KAPITAN BURMAKIN** (Ru); **KAPITAN GLAZACHYEV** (Ru): **CHALKA (or CHAIKA)** (Ma) ex-*Kapitan Vasilyevskiy*; **KAPITAN ZAMYATIN** (Ru); **YURIY SAVINOV** (Ru); **BOTSMAN MOSHKOV** (Ru); **FEDOR VARAKSIN** (Ru); **KAPITAN SHEVCHENKO** (Ru); **KAPITAN LYUBCHENKO** (Ru); **PETR STRELKOV**

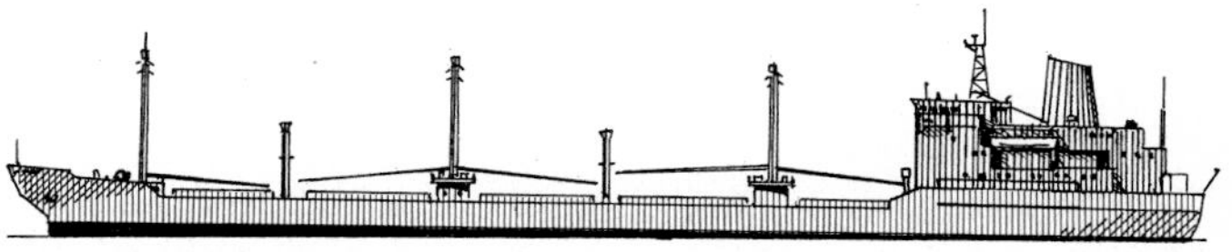

79 *HNHNHMFN H13*
PUFFIN —/Ys ('Uljanik') 1968; B; 8,648 grt/14,475 dwt; 138.46 × 9 m *(454.27 × 29.53 ft)*; M (B&W); 12 kts; ex-*Kras*

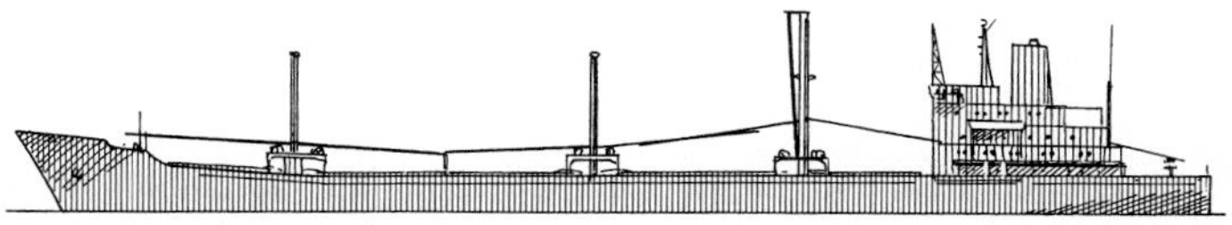

80 *HNHNMFN H1*
PING GU RC/FRG (A G 'Weser') 1977; C; 9,862 grt/15,820 dwt; 149.82 × 9.25 m *(491.54 × 30.35 ft)*; M (MAN); 16.5 kts; ex-*Hildesheim*; '36-L' type; 228 TEU
Sisters: **AQUA SIERRA** (Cy) ex-*Rudesheim*; **M MELODY** (Bs) ex-*Ingelheim*; **ZETA** (Ma) ex-*Russelsheim*; **STEFANOS** (Gr) ex-*Heidenheim*; **GUR MASTER** (Bs) ex-*Unterturkheim*

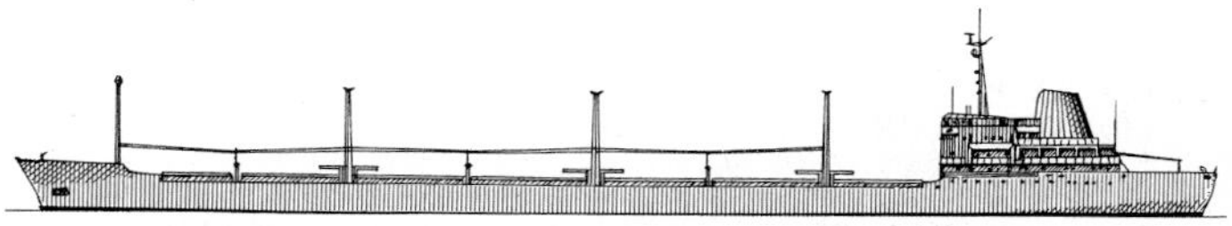

81 *HNHNMFN H13*
PU XING RC/FRG (Howaldts DW) 1968; B; 13,858 grt/25,721 dwt; 186.93 × 10.59 m *(613.3 × 34.7 ft)*; M (MAN); 17 kts; ex-*Pacific Skou*
Sister: **CHERRY** (Sg) ex-*Atlantic Skou*

82 *HNMH^{2}FN H13*
HUA TAI RC/Ys ("Uljanik") 1963; B; 15,810 grt/26,513 dwt; 191.47 × 10.86 m *(628.18 × 35.63 ft)*; M (Fiat); 16 kts; ex-*Atlantic Champion*
Similar: **HUA YANG** (RC) ex-*Atlantic Eagle*; **HUA HONG** (RC) ex-*Atlantic Star*

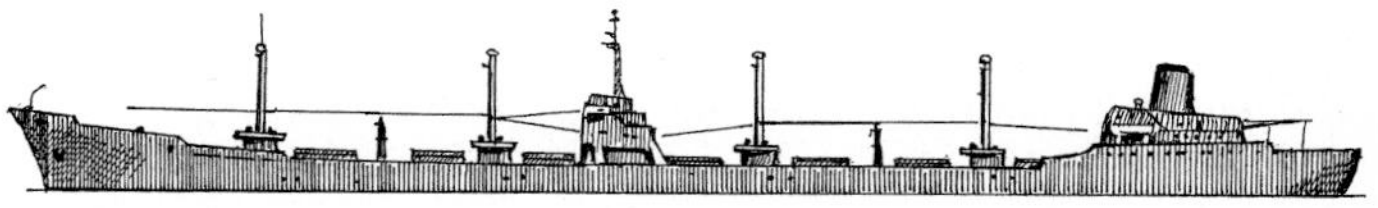

83 *HNMN^{2}F H13*
MISS MARIETTA Gr/FRG (Rhein Nordseew) 1966; C; 24,538 grt/41,150 dwt; 204.96 × 11.37 m *(672.44 × 37.3 ft)*; M (Sulzer); 14 kts
Sisters: **MICHALAKIS** (Gr); **MARY** (Gr); **MASTER PETROS** (Gr)

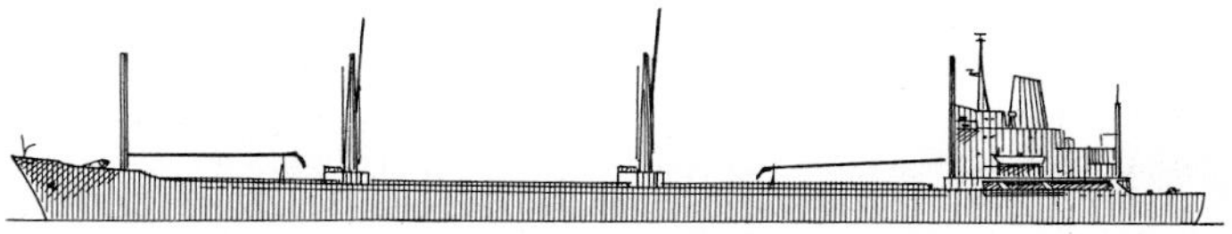

84 *HN^{2}HMFN H1*
HUMBER Bs/Ja (Sumitomo) 1972; B; 16,474 grt/25,920 dwt; 162.01 × 10.64 m *(531.53 × 34.91 ft)*; M (Sulzer); 14.5 kts; ex-*Eastern Wiseman*

85 *HN^{2}HMFN   H13*
NOA Li/Ja (Hakodate) 1971; B; 16,225 grt/26,093 dwt; 160.99 × 10.79 m *(528.2 × 35.4 ft)*; M (Sulzer); 14.5 kts; ex-*Pacific Saga*

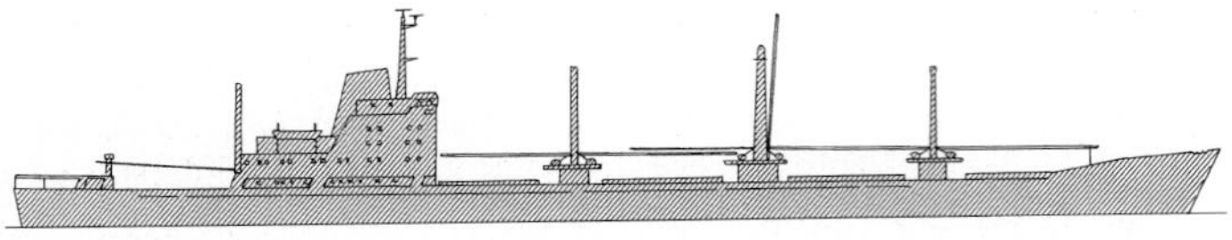

86 *HN^{2}MFN   H1*
QING YANG RC/RC (Jiangnan) 1973; C; 10,267 grt/14,145 dwt; 161.50 × 9.23 m *(529.86 × 30.28 ft)*; M (Hudong); 17.5 kts
Sisters: **LI YANG** (RC); **YI YANG** (RC)

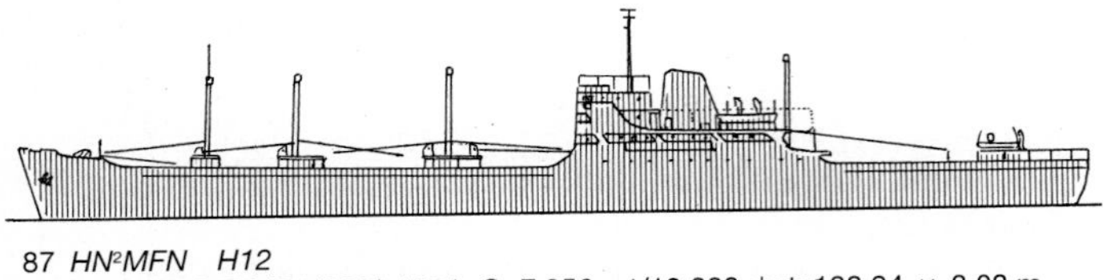

87 *HN^{2}MFN   H12*
YU HONG RC/Br (A&P) 1961; C; 7,956 grt/10,229 dwt; 138.94 × 8.08 m *(456 × 26.52 ft)*; M (Sulzer); 15.5 kts; ex-*Torr Head*

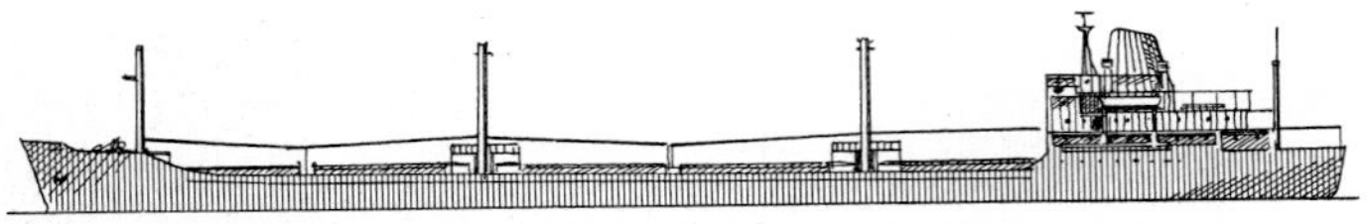

88 *HN^{2}MFN   H13*
CUMBERLAND SKY SV/Br (Scotts' SB) 1969; B; 12,308 grt/19,356 dwt; 158.5 × 9.26 m *(520.01 × 30.38 ft)*; M (Sulzer); 14.75 kts; ex-*Eriskay*

89 *HN^{2}MFN^{2} H1*
PIONEER COMMANDER US/US (Bethlehem) 1963; C; 11,105 grt/ 13,752 dwt; 170.85 × 9.63 m *(561 × 31.7 ft)*; T (Bethlehem); 22 kts; ex-*American Commander*; US Government owned
Sisters: **PIONEER CONTRACTOR** (US) ex-*American Contractor*; **PIONEER CRUSADER** (US) ex-*American Crusader*

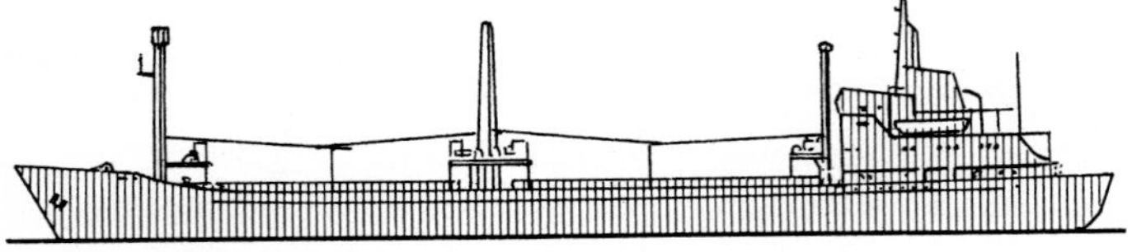

90 *HN^{2}MM–F   H1*
MARIGOLD Ho/FRG (Norderwerft) 1971; C; 2,899 grt/4,100 dwt; 97.24 × 6.44 m *(319 × 21.13 ft)*; M (Atlas-MaK); 15 kts; ex-*Arete*; 64 TEU

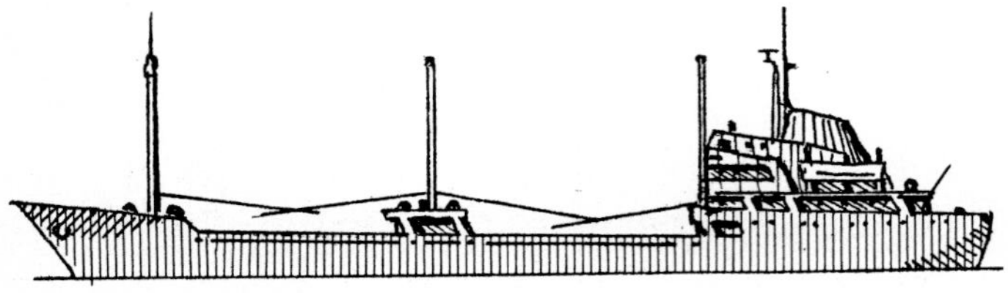

91 *HN^{2}M–F   H13*
EL NIEL Ho/DDR ('Neptun') 1962; C; 1,744 grt/2,733 dwt; 82.33 × 5.75 m *(270.11 × 18.86 ft)*; M (Halberstadt); 11.5 kts; ex-*Pinguin*

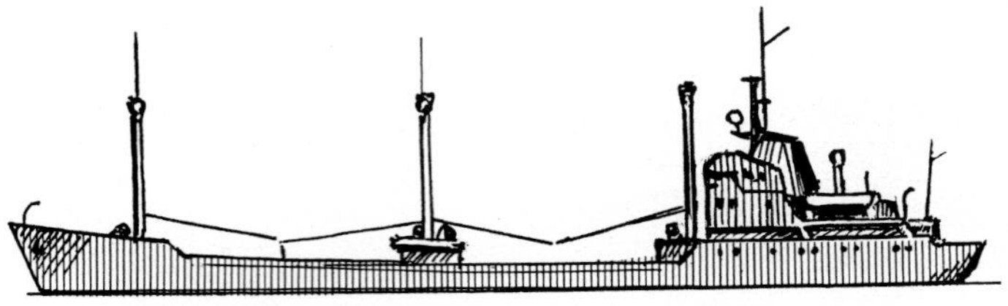

92 *HN^{2}M–F   H13*
MOHAMED S Sy/DDR ('Neptun') 1967; C; 2,546 grt/3,639 dwt; 92.82 × 5.92 m *(304.53 × 19.42 ft)*; M (SKL); 12.75 kts; ex-*Oelsa*
Sisters: **KARIM M** (Ho) ex-*Eisenberg*; **SADOUN** (Sy) ex-*Hellerau*; **LUBNA S** (Sy) ex-*Themar*; **HASAN S** (Sy) ex-*Zeulenroda*

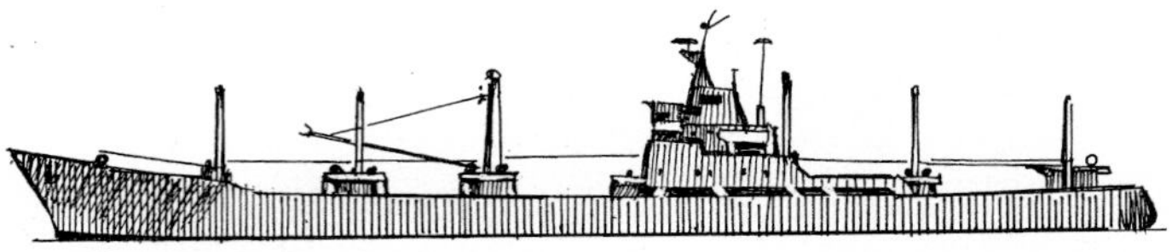

93 *HN^{2}M–FN^{3} H1*
AMERICAN RACER US/US (Sun SB) 1964; C/Con; 11,202 grt/13,477 dwt; 166 × 9.74 m *(542 × 31.96 ft)*; T (GEC); 21 kts; US Government owned
Sisters: **AMERICAN RANGER** (US); **AMERICAN RELIANCE** (US); **MORMACDAWN** (US) ex-*American Resolute*; **MORMACMOON** (US) ex-*American Rover*

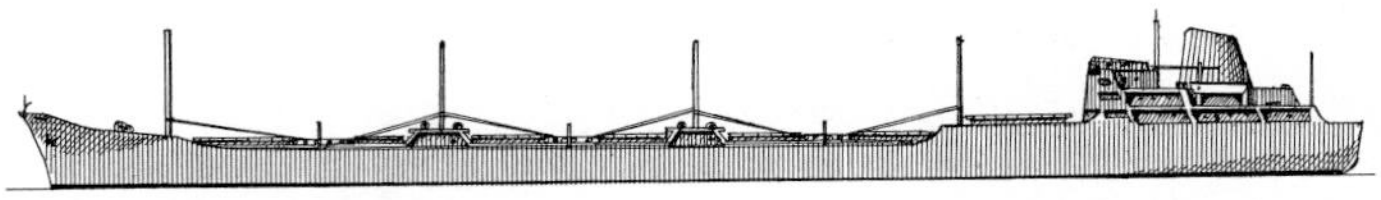

94 *HN^{3}HFN   H13*
WU TONG SHAN RC/Br (Furness) 1965; B; 20,056 grt/34,000 dwt; 192.03 × 10.75 m *(630 × 35.3 ft)*; M (Sulzer); 15.5 kts; ex-*Simonburn*

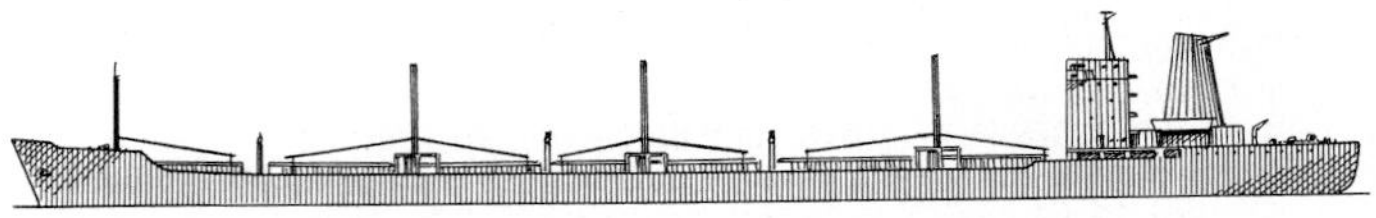

95 *HN^{3}MF   H13*
FUTURO Ch/It (Muggiano) 1974; B; 14,521 grt/27,169 dwt; 178.44 × 10.12 m *(585.43 × 33.2 ft)*; M (GMT); 14.75 kts; ex-*Drava*
Sisters: **MELODIA** (Cy) ex-*Kidric B*; **DESTINO** (Pa) ex-*Kraigher B*

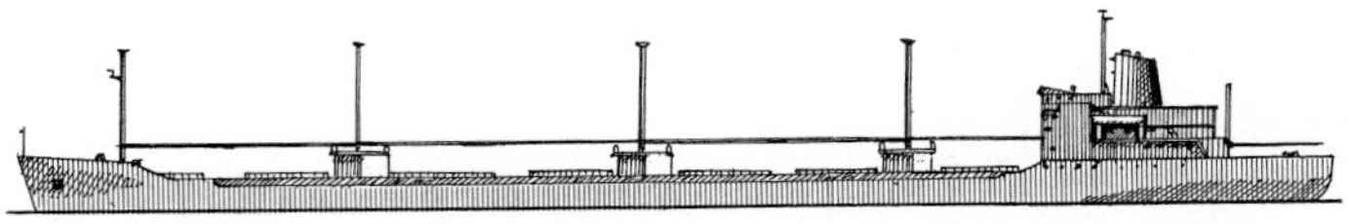

96 *HN^{3}MFN   H13*
GOLD BRIDGE I Pa/Br (Doxford & S) 1970; B; 18,738 grt/32,280 dwt; 182.58 × 10.67 m *(599.01 × 35.01 ft)*; M (Doxford); 16 kts; ex-*Berkshire*
Sisters: **SUNLIGHT** (—) ex-*Cheshire*; **MIKE K** (Cy) ex-*Oxfordshire*

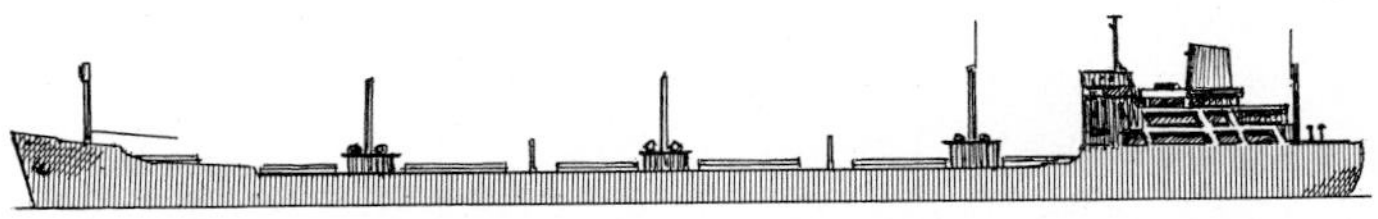

97 *HN^{3}MFN   H13*
HONG QI 303 RC/Br (J L Thompson) 1963; B; 16,527 grt/27,243 dwt; 182.43 × 10.52 m *(598.52 × 34.51)*; M (Gotaverken); 12 kts; ex-*Kollfinn*

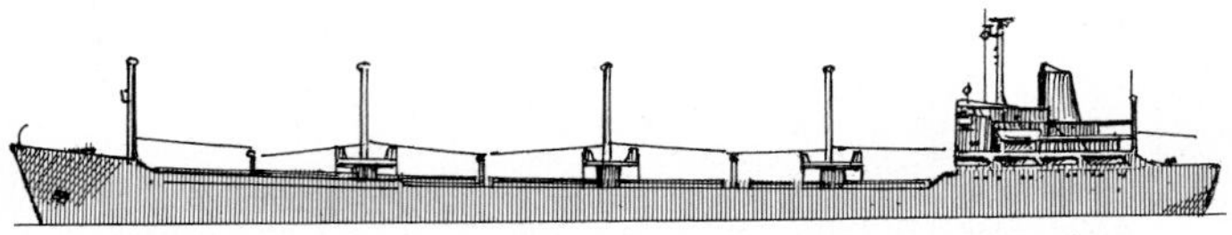

98 *HN^{3}MFN   H13*
RYONG GANG RK/FRG (Kieler H) 1967; B; 13,799 grt/25,585 dwt; 186.9 × 10.55 m *(613.2 × 34.6 ft)*; M (MAN); 17 kts; ex-*Stadt Wolfsburg*

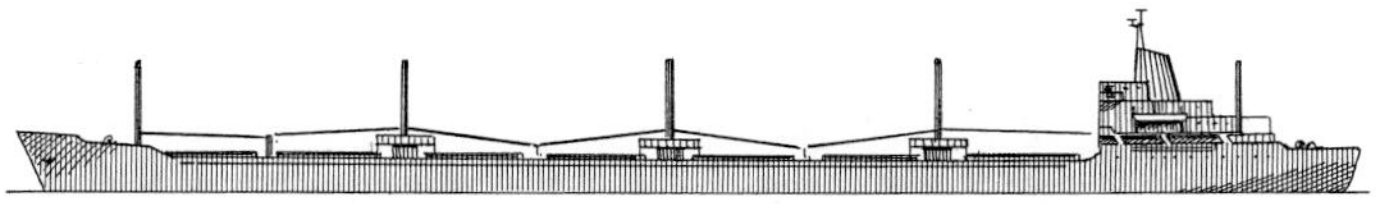

99 *HN^{3}M–FN H13*
FLAG PAOLA Gr/Br (Scotts' SB) 1971; B; 18,619 grt/32,010 dwt; 186.11 × 10.83 m *(610.6 × 35.53 ft)*; M (Sulzer); 14 kts; ex-*Cumbria*

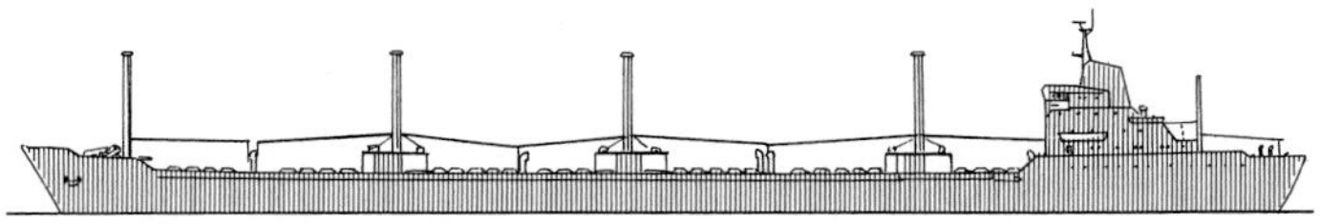

100 *HN^{3}M–FN H13*
VITAGRAIN Gr/Sp (AESA) 1970; B; 15,780 grt/26,958 dwt; 183.12 × 10.58 m *(600.79 × 34.71 ft)*; M (MAN); 16 kts; ex-*Arenal*
Sisters (some have taller radar masts and other, smaller, differences): **SERIFOS** (SV) ex-*Triana*; **ECEM** (Tu) ex-*Erzurum*; **ATANUR** (Tu) ex-*Erdemir*; **ADONIS** (Cy) ex-*Torre Del Oro*; **IONIAN CORAL** (Cy) ex-*Giralda*

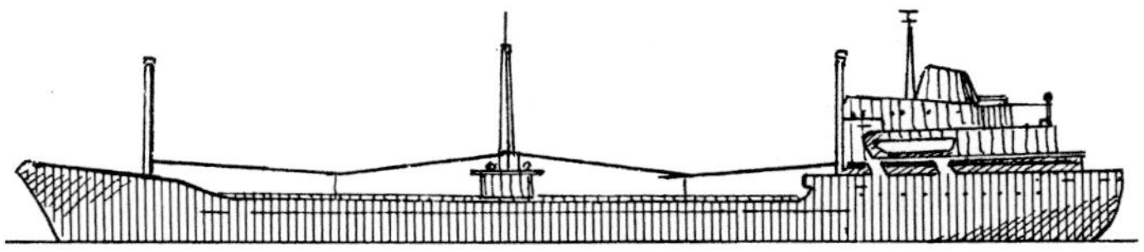

101 *HTNMF H13*
SOANKA Le/FRG (Lindenau) 1965; C; 2,335 grt/3,220 dwt; 92.06 × 5.6 m *(302.03 × 18.37 ft)*; M (Sulzer); 13 kts; ex-*Matthias Rehder*

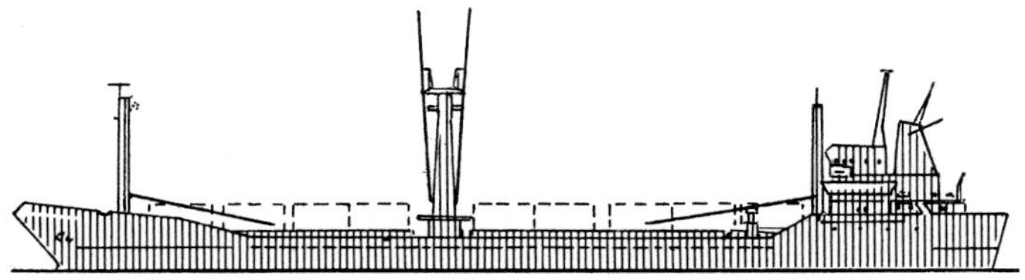

102 *HTNMM–F H13*
LUBA Pa/Sp (Barreras) 1979; C/Con; 2,717 grt/4,029 dwt; 97.36 × 6.24 m *(319 × 20.47 ft)*; M (Deutz); 15 kts; ex-*Algarmi*; 125 TEU
Sisters: **TANGA** (SV) ex-*Alalma*; **NOVA** (Pa) ex-*Alyolex*

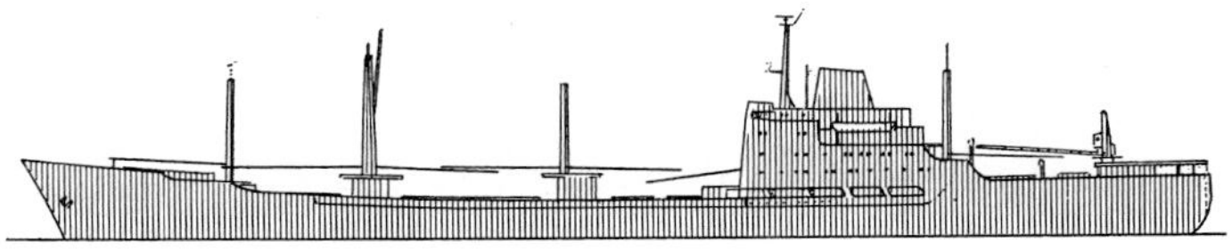

103 *HUHMFHC H13*
LUFENG RC/DDR (Warnow) 1970; C; 5,745 grt/8,220 dwt; 150.68 × 8.92 m *(494 × 29.27 ft)*; M (MAN); — kts
Sister: **XINFENG** (RC)

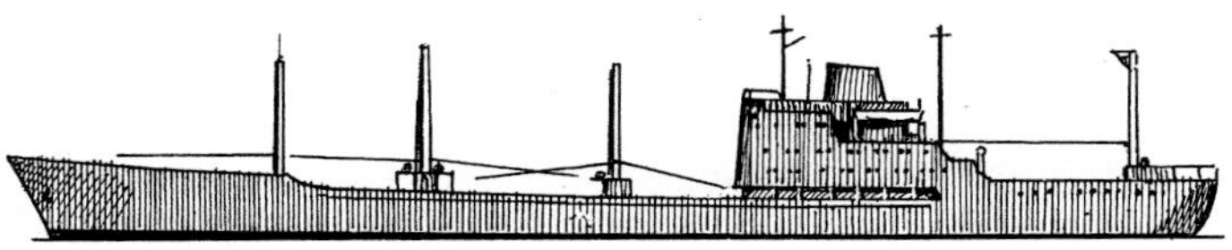

104 *HUHMFMT H13*
HE FU RC/DDR (Warnow) 1969; C; 8,822 grt/12,540 dwt; 150.5 × 8.8 m *(494 × 29.3 ft)*; M (MAN); 17 kts; ex-*Haifeng*; 'Ozean' type

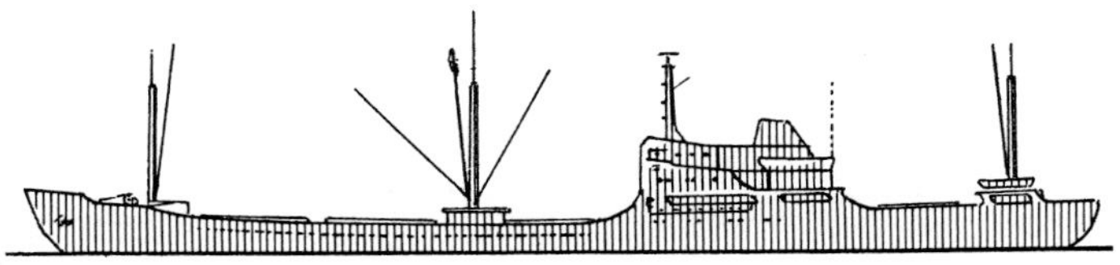

105 *HVMFH H13*
DOVE Ma/Rm (Galatz) 1965; C/TC; 2,856 grt/3,265 dwt; 100.67 × 6 m *(330 × 19.69 ft)*; M (Fiat); 13.75 kts; ex-*Aleksandr Dovzhenko*
Sisters: **GEORGIY VASILYEV** (Uk); **SERGEY EYZENSHTEIN** (Uk); **SERGEY VASILYEV** (Uk); **SARA JUNIOR** (Le) ex-*Vsevolod Pudovkin*

106 *HVMFH H13*
"SIBIRLES" class dwt; Variation on this class, with goalposts. **See drawing number 8/612**

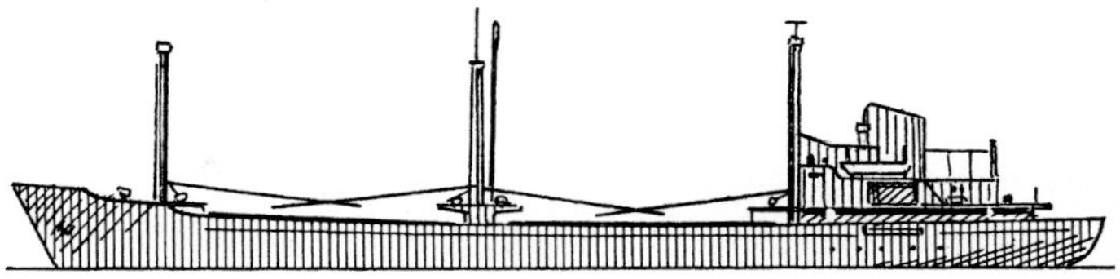

107 *HVNF H1*
DAVUT 1 Tu/FRG (Unterweser) 1967; C; 1,788 grt/2,858 dwt; 88.45 × 5.22 m *(290.19 × 17.13 ft)*; M (Deutz); 14 kts; ex-*Marie Reith*
Sisters: **ILZE** (La) ex-*Susanne Reith*; **MERCS UHANA** (Sr) ex-*Emil Reith*
Possible sister: **GENCA TERZO** (It) ex-*Elisabeth Reith*

108 *MFM H12*
ELCANO Pi/Ja (Hitachi) 1955; PC; 2,047 dwt; 87.3 × 5 *(288 × 16.7)*; M (Hitachi); 13.5
Sister: **SULU** (Pi) ex-*Legazpi*

109 *MFNH H1*
LAI CHANG Vn/Fi (Crichton-Vulcan) 1958; C; 1,700 dwt; 94.2 × 5.7 *(309 × 18.7)*; M (Sulzer); 13.5; ex-*Fastov*
Sister: **THACH HAN** (Vn) ex-*Floreshty*

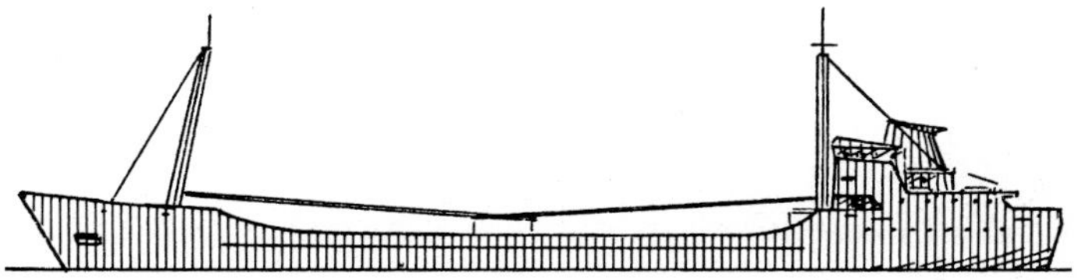

110 *MHF H13*
BUMI JAYA Pa/Ne (Stroobos) 1978; C; 1,886 grt/3,001 dwt; 81.01 × 5.21 m *(265.78 × 17.09 ft)*; M (Alpha-Diesel); 13.5 kts; ex-*Gera Holwerda*

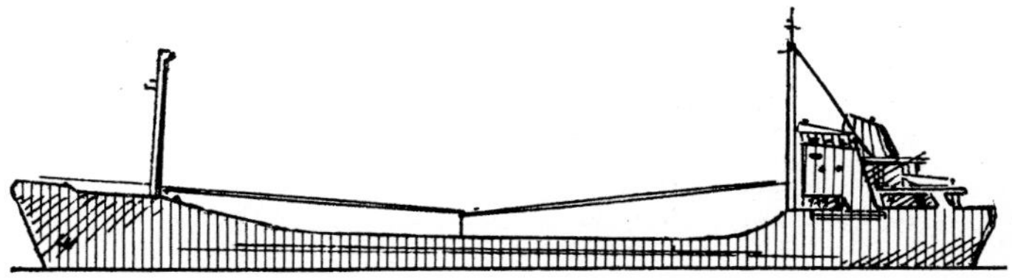

111 *MHF H13*
FLINTERDIJK Ne/Ne (Peter's Schpsbw) 1978; C; 1,863 grt/2,955 dwt; 80.22 × 5.45 m *(263.19 × 17.88 ft)*; M (Brons); 12.5 kts; ex-*Maritta Johanna*

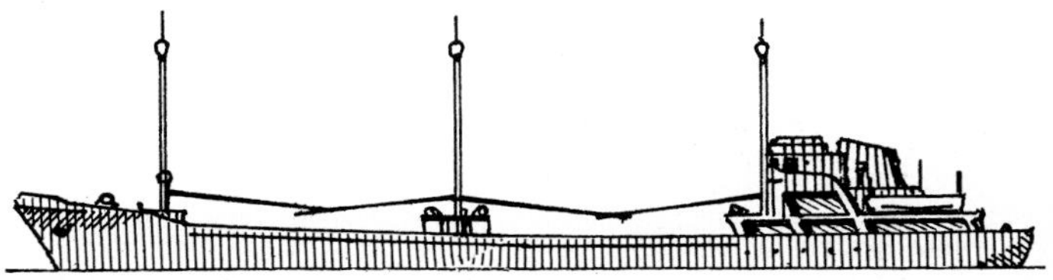

112 *MH^{2}F H1*
ENDIBE Pa/Sp ('Corbasa') 1963; C; 1,541 grt/2,797 dwt; 82.53 × 5.98 m *(270.77 × 19.62 ft)*; M (Werkspoor); 13 kts; ex-*Sierra Andia*

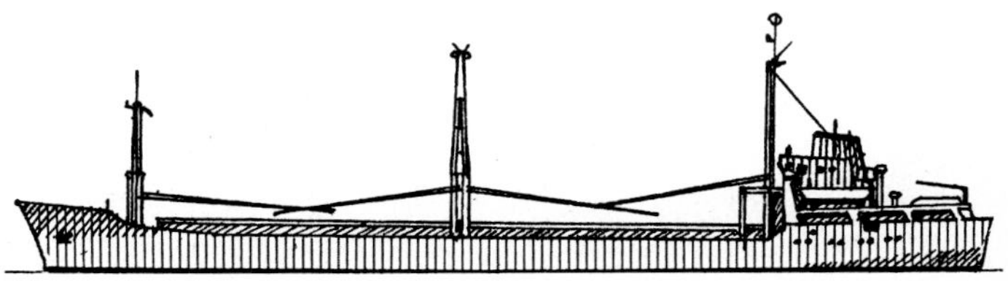

113 *MH^{2}F H1*
NELIE It/No (Aukra) 1972; C/Con; 1,968 grt/2,640 dwt; 77.09 × 5.1 m *(252.92 × 16.73 ft)*; M (Atlas-MaK); 14 kts; ex-*Anneliese Oltmann*; 93 TEU

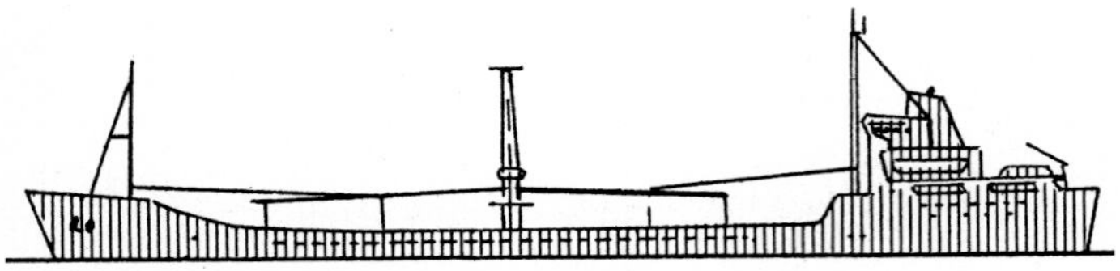

114 MH^2F *H13*
ATHINOULA Pa/No (Aukra) 1972; C; 1,454 grt/2,489 dwt; 77.17 × 4.76 m *(253 × 15.61 ft)*; M (Atlas-MaK); 13 kts; ex-*Nortrio*
Sisters: **KAMANDALU** (Ia) ex-*Norcato*; **ATLANTIC RIVER** (Cy) ex-*Norimo*

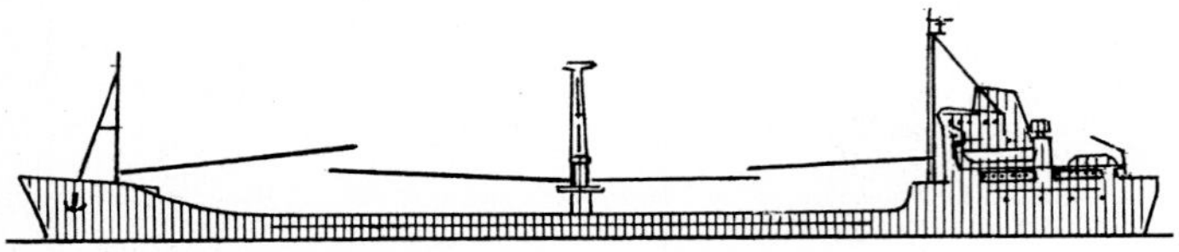

115 MH^2F *H13*
PRAMS PRAKASH At/No (Aukra) 1970/78; C; 1,705 grt/2,922 dwt; 89.11 × 4.73 m *(292 × 15.52 ft)*; M (Atlas-MaK); 13.5 kts; ex-*Nordfjord*; Lengthened 1978
Sisters: **PAT** (SV) ex-*Sudfjord*; **SALAM** (Ho) ex-*Westfjord* (may have centre-line mast foreward)

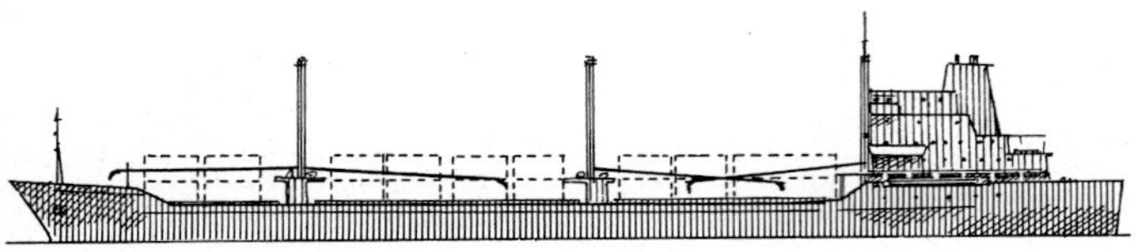

116 MH^3F *H13*
KOTA MAWAR Sg/Ja (Yamanishi) 1978; C/Con; 6,789 grt/8,676 dwt; 129.32 × 7.83 m *(424.3 × 25.7 ft)*; M (B&W); 16 kts; ex-*Esteblick*; 314 TEU
Sisters: **PHAROS** (SV) ex-*Nordwelle*; Similar: **SEA HORSE** (SV) ex-*Atalanta*; **KAIROS** (SV) ex-*Germanic*; **KOTA MEGAH** (Sg) ex-*Impala*; Probably similar: **EVER CHEER** (Pa) ex-*Hilda Wesch*

117 MH^4FN *H12*
DR JUAN B ALBERDI Pa/Pd (Szczecinska) 1985; C/Con; 17,700 grt/20,169 dwt; 184.28 × 9.95 m *(604.59 × 32.64 ft)*; M (Sulzer); 18 kts; ex-*Euro Sun*; 1095 TEU. 'B 181' type. **SIMILAR TO DRAWING NUMBER 8/125** but has seven-deck superstructure and goalpost radar mast

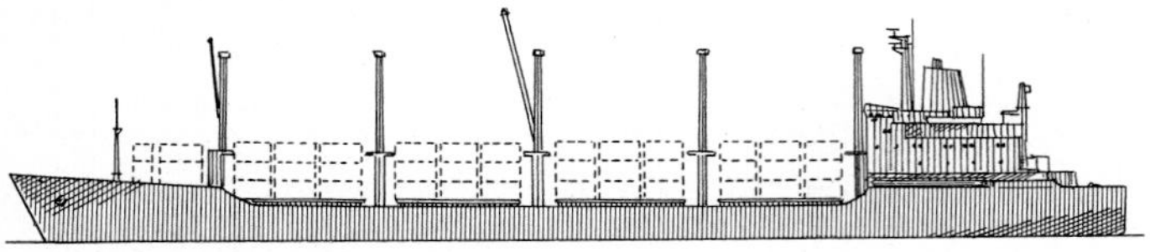

118 MH^5MFMC *H13*
MSC NICOLE SV/Ja (Mitsubishi HI) 1977; C/Con; 17,180 grt/21,881 dwt; 164.52 × 10.62 m *(540 × 34.84 ft)*; M (Sulzer); 18 kts; ex-*Menelaus*; 'MP-20' type; 773 TEU; Mast abaft funnel is on starboard side
Sisters: **HAI XIONG** (Pa) ex-*Memnon*; **WOERMANN EXPERT** (HK) ex-*Menestheus*; **CMB EBONY** (HK) ex-*Melampus* Sisters (Br-built: Scotts' SB): **MERCHANT PATRIOT** (HK) ex-*Maron*; **TAMATIKI** (Br) ex-*Mentor*; **TAMAMONTA** (HK) ex-*Myrmidon*

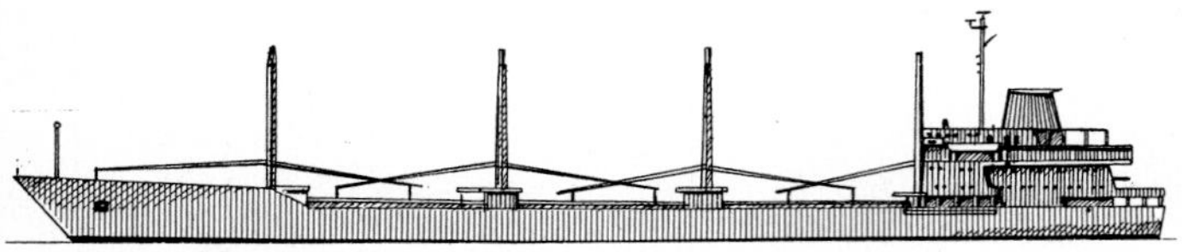

119 MH^4MF *H1*
EXCELSIOR LUCK Pa/Pd (Szczecinska) 1973; C/Con; 9,590 grt/11,618 dwt; 145.73 × 8.4 m *(478.12 × 27.56 ft)*; M (Sulzer); 16.5 kts; ex-*Shonga*; 'B-430' type; 322 TEU
Sisters: **MENG YANG** (Sg) ex-*Sherbro*; **TRADE VIGOUR** (Pa) ex-*Hasselburg*; **DAE JIN** (Sg) ex-*Monsun*; **ORIENT GANGES** (Cy) ex-*River Hadejia*; Sister (radar mast has tripod legs extending to funnel top): **ORIENT CHALLENGE** (Cy) ex-*Schauenberg*

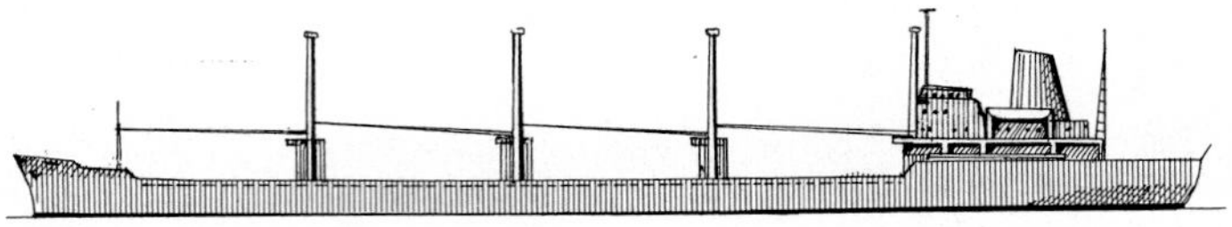

120 MH^4MFN *H13*
QUEEN Cy/Ja (Hitachi) 1968; B; 11,413 grt/19,297 dwt; 156.17 × 9.53 m *(512.37 × 31.27 ft)*; M (B&W); 15 kts; ex-*Maritine Queen*; 'Hitachi Standard 18' type
Sister: **HARVEST** (Pa) ex-*Maritime Pioneer*

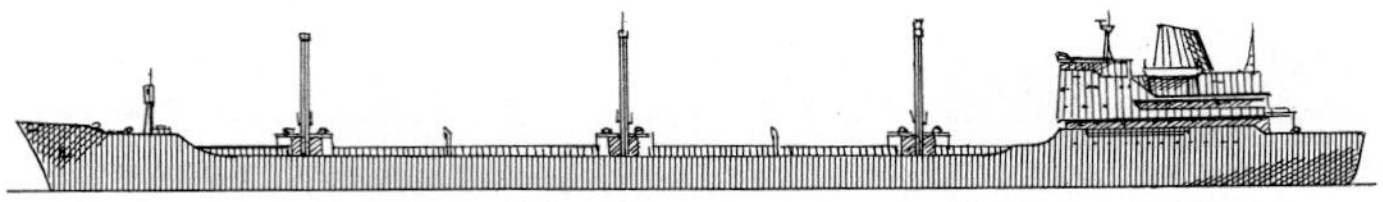

121 MH^3MF *H13*
BAI YUN HAI RC/Ys ('Uljanik') 1967; B; 13,481 grt/20,030 dwt; 174.05 × 9.02 m *(571.03 × 29.59 ft)*; M (B&W); — kts; ex-*Sunima*

122 MH^3MF *H13*
KOTA MELATI Sg/Ja (Yamanishi) 1978; C/Con; 6,709 grt/8,812 dwt; 129.32 × 7.82 m *(424.28 × 25.66 ft)*; M (B&W); 15 kts; ex-*Lotte Scheel*; 308 TEU; **SIMILAR TO DRAWING NUMBER 8/116**; Principally differs from latter by having radar mast from bridge top

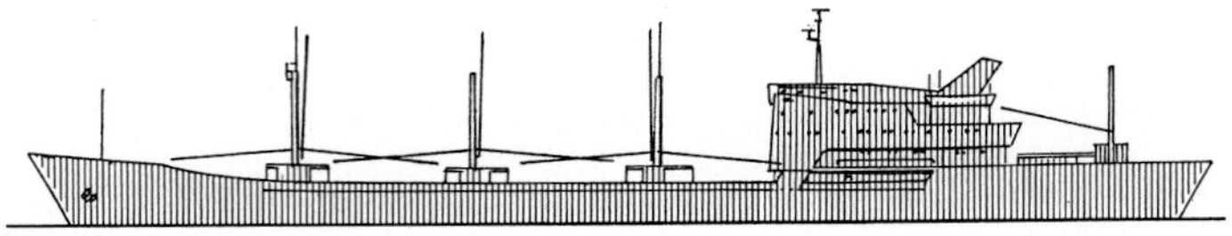

123 MH^3MFH *H13*
PEARL 1 SV/Pd (Szczecinska) 1968; C; 6,576 grt/7,081 dwt; 135.41 × 7.67 m *(444.26 × 25.16 ft)*; M (Sulzer); 17 kts; ex-*Zakopane*; 'B-446' type
Sisters: **ZAMBROW** (Pd); **ZAWICHOST** (Pd); Similar: **FENG CHENG** (RC); **YAN CHENG** (RC)

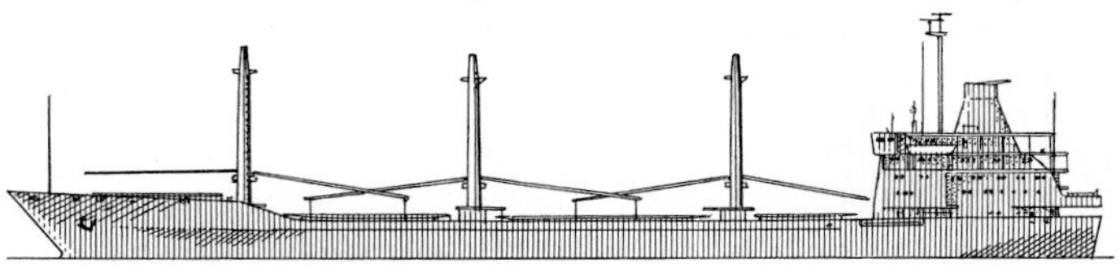

124 MH^3MFN *H1*
MENG KIAT Sg/Pd (Szczecinska) 1979; C/Con; 9,605 grt/11,455 dwt; 146.16 × 8.44 m *(479.53 × 27.69 ft)*; M (Sulzer); 16.8 kts; ex-*Sokoto*; 'B-430' type; 454 TEU
Sisters: **WING SON** (Pa) ex-*Sekondi*; **SAINT PIERRE** (Cy) ex-*Sapele*; **CMBT EFFORT** (Li) ex-*Guatemala*; **ANDREA BROVIG** (NIS) ex-*Honduras*; **ECHO PIONEER** (NIS) ex-*Costa Rica*

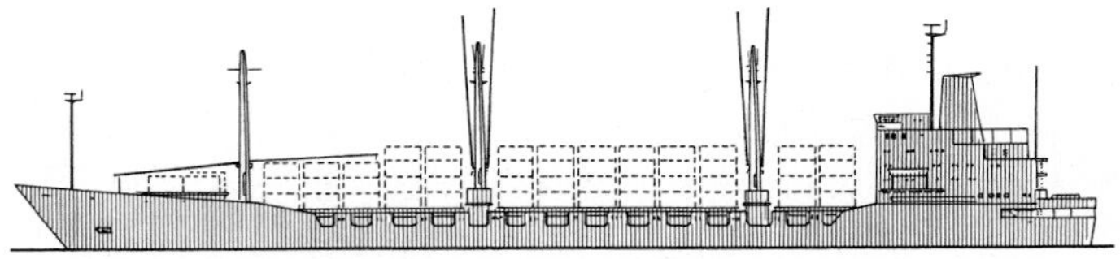

125 MH^3MFN *H12*
CMBT EMERALD Bs/Pd (Szczecinska) 1981; C/Con; 14,136 grt/19,035 dwt; 175.57 × 10.01 m *(576 × 32.84 ft)*; M (Sulzer); 17.5 kts; ex-*Medi Star*; 'B 181' type; 970 TEU
Sisters: **VIDAL** (Bs) ex-*Medi Sea*; **BORIS ANDREYEV** (Uk) ex-*Lagos Palm*; **MEKHANIK BARDETSKIY** (Uk) ex-*Lokoja Palm*; **PRESIDENTE SARMIENTO** (Pa) ex-*Euro Star*; **OCEAN CENTAURUS** (Pa) ex-*Toledo*; **HONOUR** (Pa) ex-*Laredo*; **ST BLAIZE** (Bs) ex-*Euro Sea*

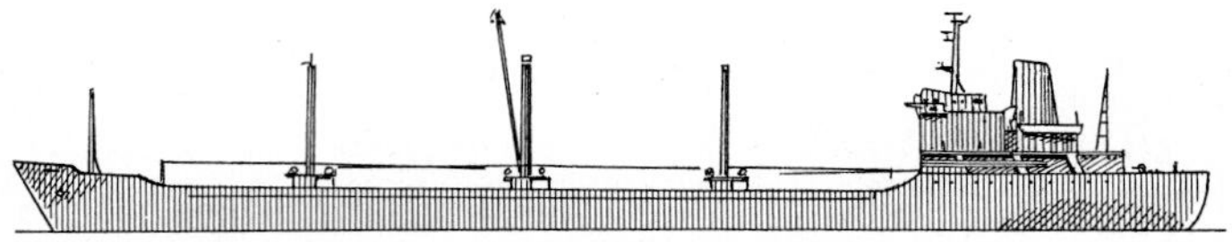

126 MH^3MFN *H13*
INDIAN PRESTIGE In/Ja (Mitsui) 1971; C; 11,802 grt/18,854 dwt; 147.71 × 9.63 m *(484.61 × 31.59 ft)*; M (B&W); 15 kts; ex-*Aristagoras*; 'Mitsui-Concord 18' type
Sisters: **INDIAN PROGRESS** (In) ex-*Aristodimos*; **INDIAN PROSPERITY** (In) ex-*Ioanna*

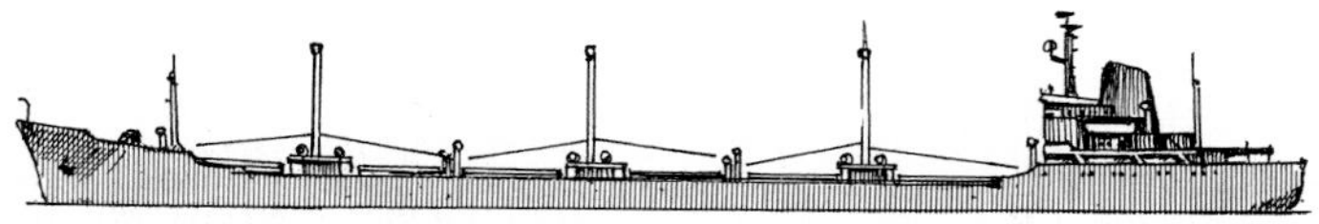

127 *MH^{3}MFN H13*
JIA YU HAI RC/Ja (Mitsui) 1969; B; 15,918 grt/27,475 dwt; 178.01 × 10.57 m *(584 × 34.7 ft)*; M (B&W); 15 kts; ex-*Lorina*

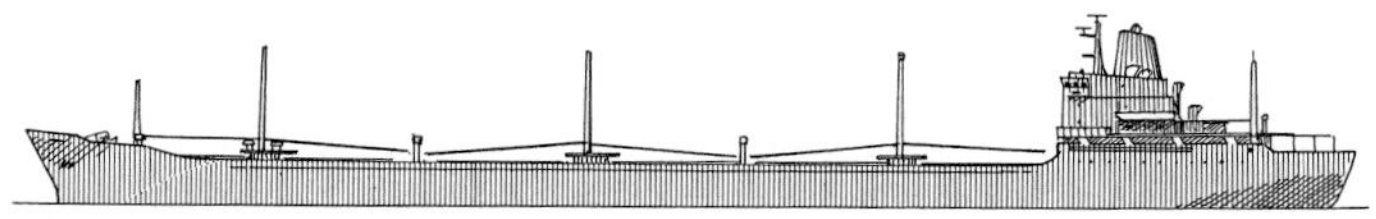

128 *MH^{3}MFN H13*
MARINA Ma/Ja (Mitsui) 1970; B; 19,428 grt/32,427 dwt; 182.61 × 10.63 m *(599.11 × 34.88 ft)*; M (Sulzer); 16 kts; ex-*Agia Erini II*
Sisters: **AFROS** (Pa) ex-*Froso*; **SAMSUN BOOSTER** (Ko) ex-*Cindy*; **PENELOPE A** (SV) ex-*Silvaplana*; Similar: **VASOS** (Ma) ex-*Karen*; **JAY DURGA** (In) ex-*Ruby*

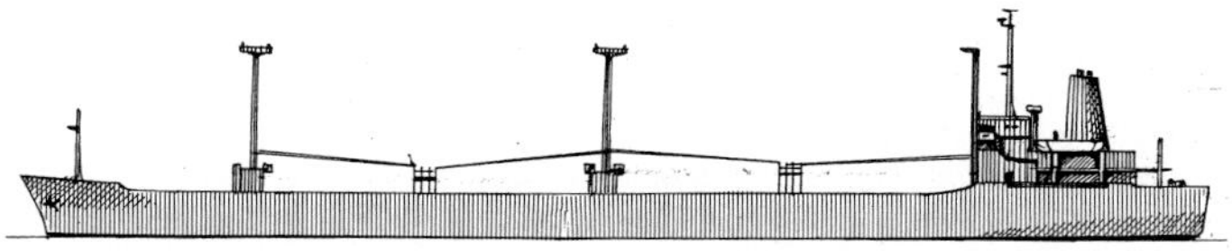

129 *MH^{3}MFN H13*
SPARKLE SUN Pa/Ja (Shin Yamamoto) 1974; B; 16,999 grt/27,575 dwt; 181.52 × 10.06 m *(592.26 × 34.74 ft)*; M (Sulzer); 15 kts; ex-*Seiho Maru*

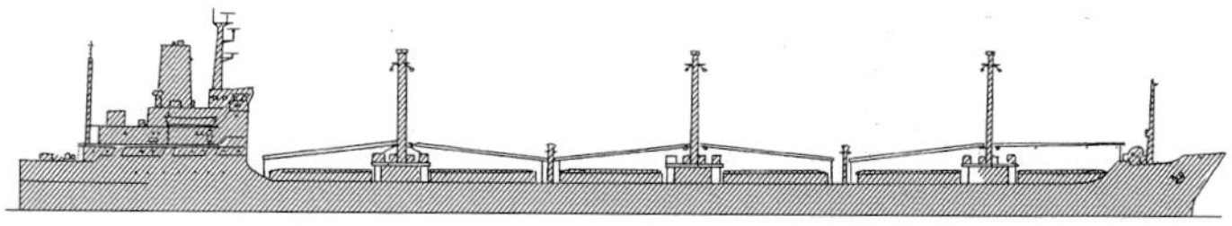

130 *MH^{3}MFN H13*
ZARA Li/Ja (Hakodate) 1977; B; 16,573 grt/29,171 dwt; 180.83 × 10.96 m *(593.27 × 35.96 ft)*; M (Sulzer); 15 kts; ex-*Zephyros II*

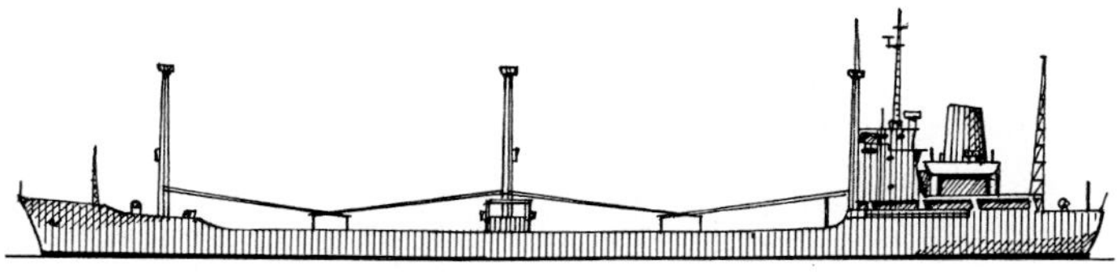

131 *MH^{3}MFN H13*
ZHE HAI 717 RC/Ja (Shikoku) 1970; C; 4,065 grt/6,830 dwt; 110.5 × 6.86 m *(362.53 × 22.51 ft)*; M (Mitsubishi); 12.75 kts; ex-*Ryusei Maru*

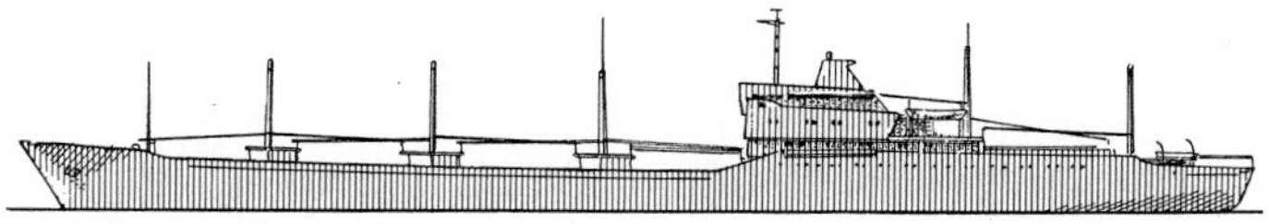

132 *MH^{3}MFNH H*
OSCAR CASTOR Rm/Pd (Szczecinska) 1976; C; 8,097 grt/11,741 dwt; 145.07 × 9.08 m *(476 × 29.79 ft)*; M (Sulzer); 18.5 kts; ex-*Alba Iulia*; 'B478' type
Sister: **CURTEA DE ARGES** (Rm)

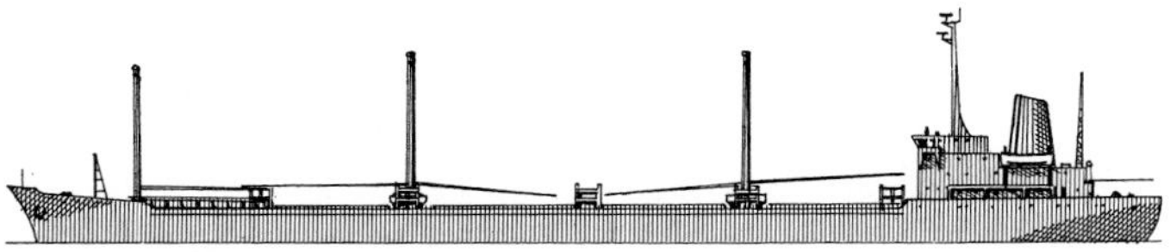

133 *MH^{3}M^{2}FN H13*
IRAN AZADI Ir/Ja (Onomichi) 1979; B; 20,672 grt/35,839 dwt; 179.91 × 11.26 m *(590.26 × 36.94 ft)*; M (B&W); 15 kts; ex-*Oinoussian Friendship*
Sisters: **IRAN JOMHOURI** (Ir) ex-*Oinoussian Leadership*; **IRAN ENTEKHAB** (Ir) ex-*Oinoussian Prestige*; **IRAN ESTEGHLAL** (Ir) ex-*Oinoussian Virtue*; **IRAN ESLAMI** (Ir) ex-*Shuko Maru*
Probable sisters: **GUNS AND ROSES** (Ma) ex-*Thames Maru*; **LEOPARD** (Ko) ex-*Seine Maru*; **DELFI** (Cy) ex-*Kenryu Maru*; **JIAN GE HAI** (RC) ex-*Rhein Maru*; **KENT ADVENTURE** (Pa) ex-*Maria Rubicon*

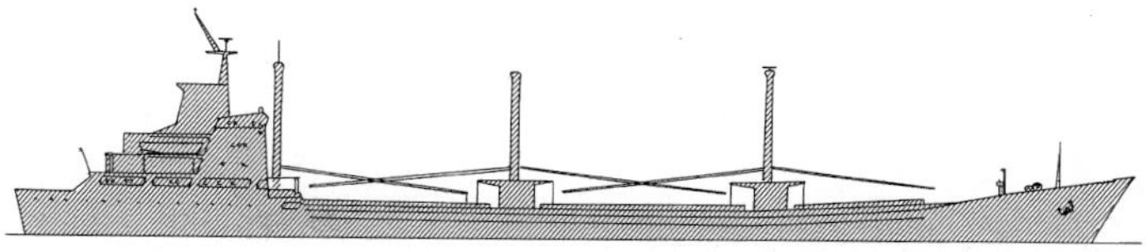

134 *MH^{3}M–F H13*
HAI HANG RC/Sp (Ruiz) 1975; B; 6,633 grt/9,152 dwt; 133.87 × 7.58 m *(439.21 × 24.87 ft)*; M (B&W); 14 kts; ex-*Ibn Zaidoun*
Sisters: **UN HA** (RK) ex-*Valle de Carranza*; **ACHILEAS P** (Cy) ex-*Valle de Lujua*; **HAE NAM** (RK) ex-*Valle de Orduna*; **LAUREL STAR** (Pa) ex-*Valle de Ayala*; **SU FA** (RC) ex-*Ibn Majid*; Probably similar (larger—138m (453 ft)): **SAMSUN TRUST** (Cy) ex-*Valle de Ibaizabal*; **OCEAN TRAMP** (At) ex-*Golfo de Uraba*; **ALEXANDROS P** (Cy) ex-*Valle de Unza*; **LONG TENG** (SV) ex-*Valle de Cadagua*

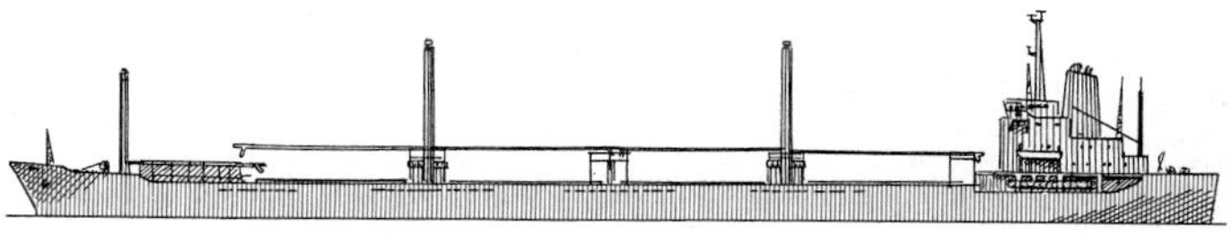

135 *MH^{3}NMFM^2 H13*
BETA Bs/Ja (Sanoyasu) 1977; B; 23,705 grt/40,110 dwt; 183.67 × 12 m *(602.59 × 39.37 ft)*; M (Sulzer); 15.5 kts; ex-*Federal Fraser*
Sisters: **GAMMA** (Li) ex-*Federal Sumida*; Similar: **HUA NAN** (RC) ex-*Seine Maru;* **HEREKE 4** (Tu) ex-*Thames Maru*; **AGAMEMNON SB** (Cy) ex-*Rhein Maru*; **LUCIJA** (At) ex-*Suiko Maru*

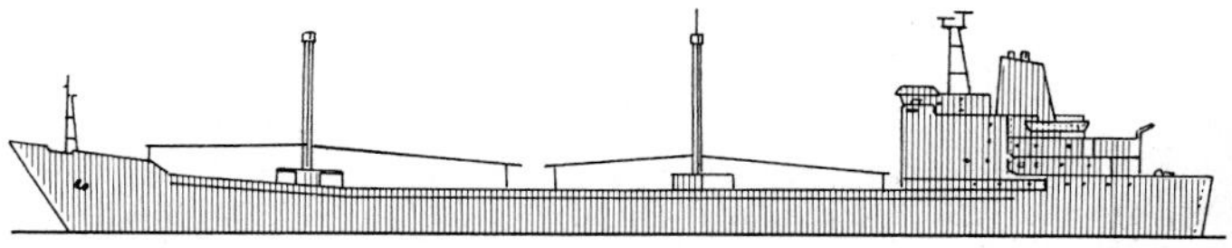

136 *MH^{2}MF H13*
SLAPY Cz/Ys ("3 Maj") 1981; C; 10,512 grt/15,236 dwt; 145.55 × 9.12 m *(477.53 × 29.92 ft)*; M (Sulzer); 14.75 kts
Sisters: **LIPNO** (Cz) (Stülcken derrick); **ORAVA** (Cz)

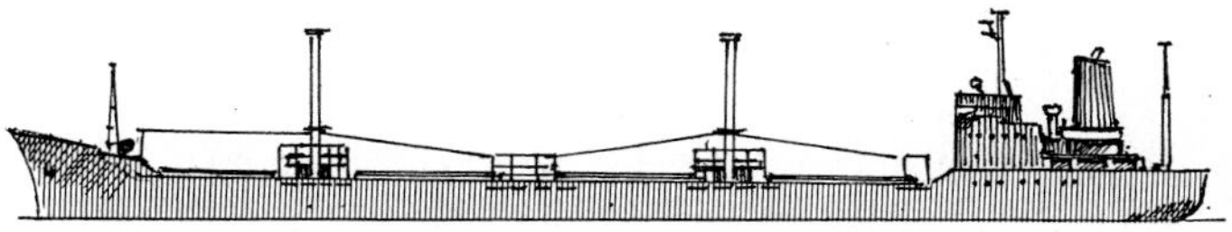

137 *MH^{2}MFM H13*
ASEAN ENTERPRISE Ma/Ja (Mitsui) 1969; B; 11,585 grt/18,875 dwt; 154.05 × 9.19 m *(505.41 × 30.15 ft)*; M (B&W); 14.75 kts; ex-*Hiko Maru*
Similar: **EASTERN TRUST** (Li) ex-*Montrose*
Similar (Korean built-Korea SB): **PAN KOREA** (Bl); **KOREAN TRADER** (Li) ex-*Glory River*; **SAPANCA** (Tu) ex-*Alkaios*; **ARGUS** (Li) ex-*Great River*; **SKRADIN** (Ma) ex-*Korean Fir*; **BILICE** (Ma) ex-*Korean Pride*; **ELITE B** (Cy) ex-*Boo Yang*

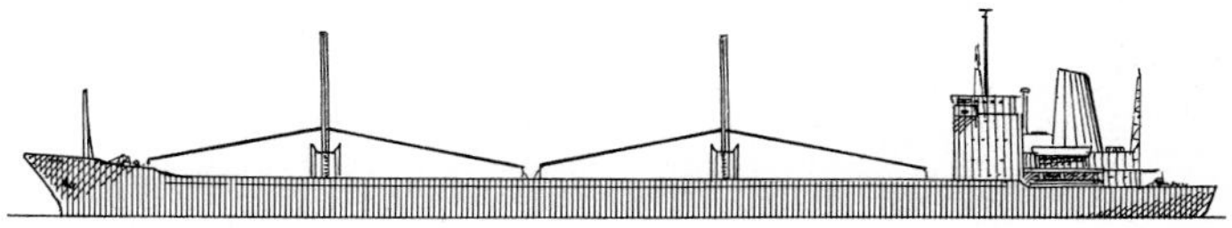

138 *MH^{2}MFN H1*
A VERMEZ Tu/Ja (Shin Yamamoto) 1973; B; 14,030 grt/22,869 dwt; 154.11 × 10.52 m *(505.61 × 34.51 ft)*; M (Sulzer); 15.5 kts; ex-*Trans Ruby*

139 *MH^{2}MFN H13*
RENESSI Gr/Ja (Osaka) 1970; B; 11,503 grt/18,985 dwt; 154.34 × 9.18 m *(506.36 × 30.12 ft)*; M (Sulzer); 15 kts; ex-*Edelweiss*; **SIMILAR TO DRAWING NUMBER 8/277**

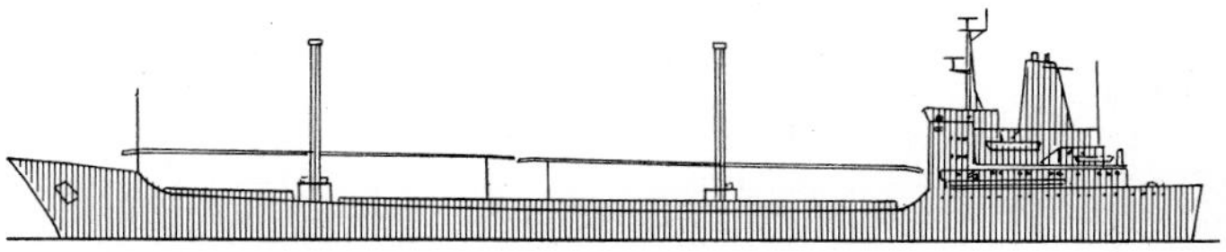

140 *MH^{2}MFN H13*
RIURENI Rm/Rm (Galatz) 1981; C/Con; 11,025 grt/15,082 dwt; 145.11 × 9.20 m *(476.08 × 30.18 ft)*; M (MAN); 15 kts; ex-*Posada*; 278 TEU
Sisters: **OITUZ** (Rm); **ELENI** (Rm) ex-*Marasti*; **DRAGOMIRESTI** (Rm) ex-*Med Fidelity*; **IRENES DIAMOND** (Cy) ex-*Calugareni*

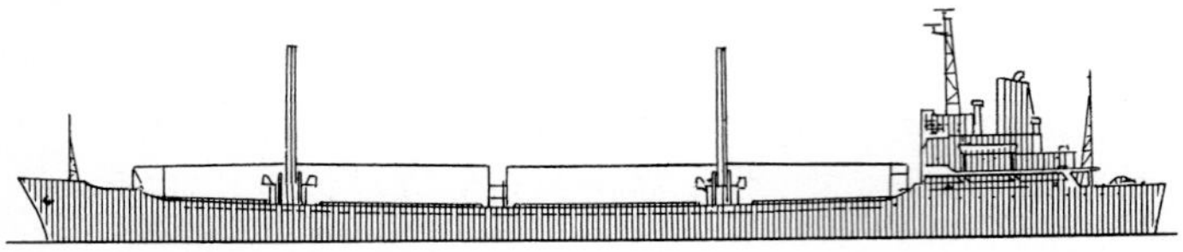

141 *MH²MFN H13*
VINTA Bs/Ja (Imai Z) 1976; B; 9.833 grt/16,583 dwt; 143.39 × 9.39 m *(470 × 30.81 ft)*; M (Mitsubishi); 15.5 kts; ex-*Blue Neptune*
Sisters: **MARIA DIAMANTO** (Cy) ex-*Royal Sapphire*; **TULIP** (Pa) ex-*Nichigaku Maru*; Possible sisters: **APJ PRITI** (In); **QI LIAN SHAN** (RC) Launched as *Duck Yang Rose*; **SV VENTURE** (Th) ex-*Easter Lily*; **WOODPECKER** (Cy) ex-*Scarlet Mare*

142 *MH²MM–F H3*
RUNGHOLTSAND At/FRG (Buesumer) 1979; R; 2,462 grt/3,416 dwt; 95.03 × 5.81 m *(311.78 × 19.06 ft)*; M (MaK); 14 kts

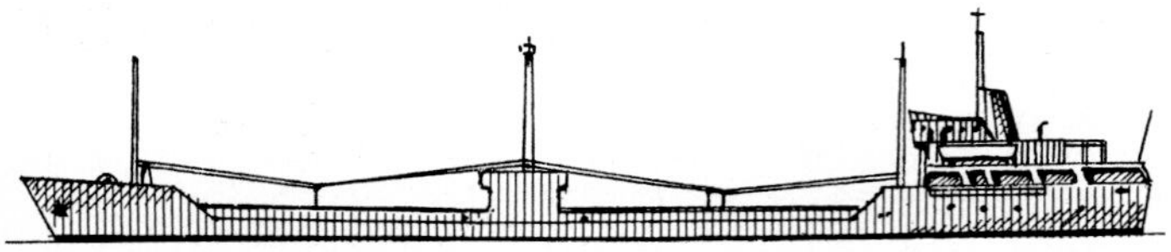

143 *MH²M–F H13*
ANGLO No/Pd (Gdanska) 1972; C; 2,326 grt/3,665 dwt; 93.73 × 5.57 m *(307.51 × 18.27 ft)*; M (KHD); 13 kts; ex-*Enid*; 'B-431' type
Sisters: **JOSEPHINA I** (SV) ex-*Cupid*; **COSTAS S** (Pa) ex-*Eldrid*; **OLGA M** (Pa) ex-*Gudrid*; **NICOLAS S** (Ma) ex-*Sigrid*

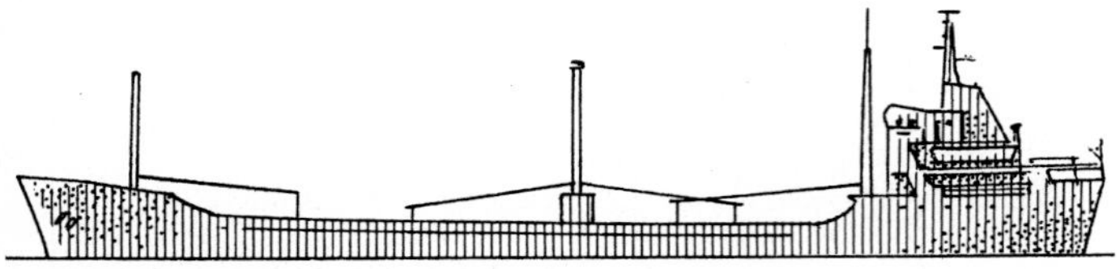

144 *MH²M–F H13*
DINA M Sy/Pd (Gdanska) 1967; C; 1,597 grt/2,780 dwt; 87.58 × 4.81 m *(287.34 × 15.78 ft)*; M (Atlas-MaK); 12 kts; ex-*Gdynia*; Lengthened 1970 (Gdanska); 'B-459' type
Sisters: **NADINE** (Sy) ex-*Germa Lord*; **JAD** (Sy) ex-*Geisha*; **DANY M** (Ho) ex-*Gdansk*; Similar (not lengthened): **EUROLADY** (Ma) ex-*Lionel*

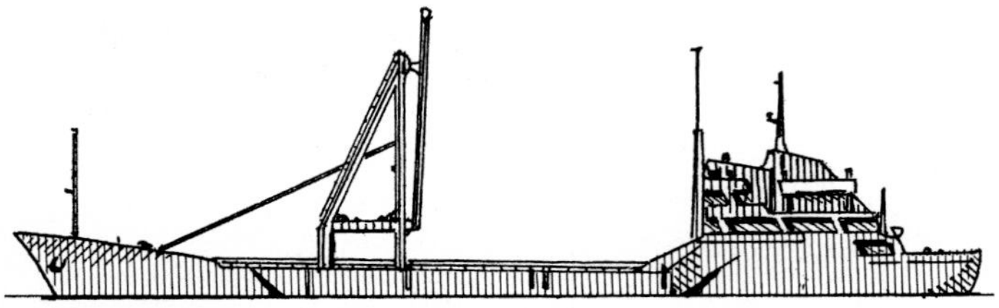

145 *MH²M–F H13*
GIANT Ve/Fr (Havre) 1969; C/HL; 1,443 grt/1,585 dwt; 90.23 × 5.9 m *(296.03 × 19.36 ft)*; M (Werkspoor); 15.5 kts; ex-*La Gavotte*; Converted from general cargo

146 *MH²NMFN H13*
PATCHAREE NAREE Th/Ja (Yamanishi) 1977; C/TC; 11,030 grt/18,845 dwt; 146.08 × 9.31 m *(479.27 × 30.54 ft)*; M (Akasaka); 14 kts; ex-*Glory Ocean*
Sisters: **KYDONIA** (Cy) ex-*Sweet Sultan*; **LUCKY PIONEER** (Pa) ex-*Seaward Ace*; **ROUBINI** (Cy) ex-*Scan Trader*; **EVER WISE** (Pa) ex-*Clipper Hope*; **CHADA NAREE** (Th) ex-*Grand Wood*; Similar: **MANDARIN SEA** (Sg) ex-*Pacific Charger*; **HANDY VIKING** (Pi) ex-*Balder Hope*

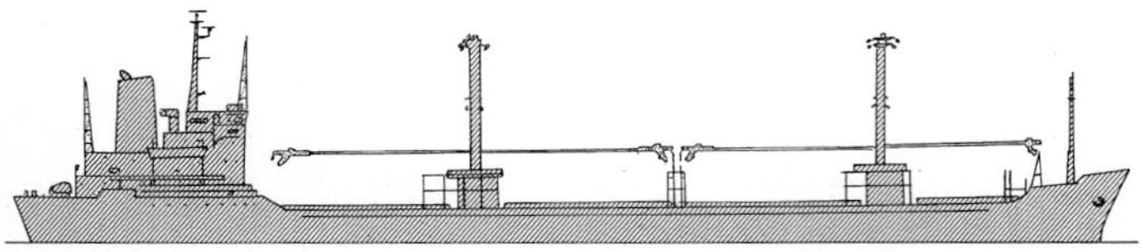

147 *MH²NMFN H13*
PERSEAS I Pa/Ja (Kochi Jukogyo) 1976; B; 10,013 grt/16,613 dwt; 141.96 × 9.10 m *(465.75 × 29.86 ft)*; M (Mitsubishi); 12.80 kts; ex-*Diamond Star*
Possible sister: **HUA HAI** (Pa) ex-*Cattleya*

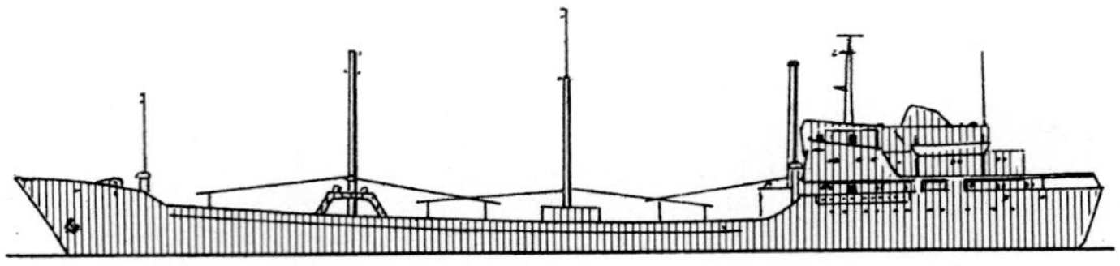

148 *MH²NMFN H13*
SLOBOZIA Rm/Rm (Galatz) 1973; C; 3,532 grt/4,600 dwt; 106.2 × 7.06 m *(348 × 23.16 ft)*; M (Sulzer); 14 kts
Sisters: **SELESA MAJU** (My) ex-*Pitria Galaxy*; **MENADO** (Ia) ex-*Evros 1*; **PIONEER ELEGANT** (Mv) ex-*Ardas*

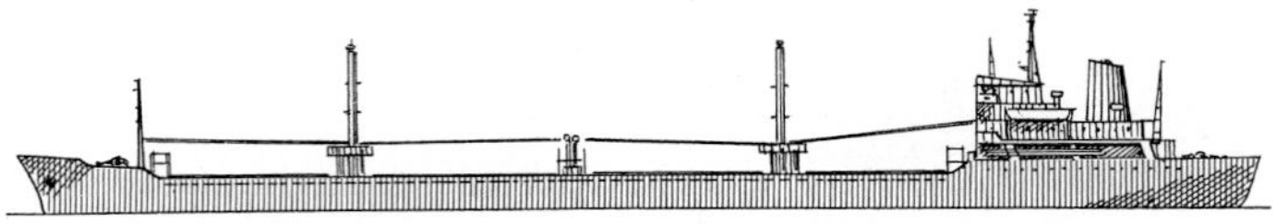

149 *MH²NMFN H13*
YA RAB Pa/Ja (Hitachi) 1971; B; 11,061 grt/19,469 dwt; 156.17 × 9.29 m *(512.37 × 30.48 ft)*; M (B&W); 15 kts; ex-*Woermann Sanaga*
Sisters: **HOPE GLORY** (Pa) ex-*Woermann Sassandra*; **HEI HU QUAN** (RC) ex-*Woermann Sankuru*; **ALMENDRO** (Ch) ex-*Swakop*; **ARIA** (Ma) ex-*Woermann Sambesi*; **CACHIMBA** (Ga) Launched as *Woermann San Pedro*; **NGOWE** (Ga) ex-*Woermann Senegal*; Similar (some may have centre-line posts): **SAN JOHN I** (Cy) ex-*Maritime Victor*; **HAI JING** (RC) ex-*Van Warrior*; **SEA DESTINY** (SV) ex-*Van Hawk*; **GUANG FU QUAN** (RC) ex-*World Hercules*; **ZINI** (Gr); **GEORTINA** (Gr); Possibly similar (some may have centre-line posts): **ISLAND SKY** (GR); **NEW GROWTH** (Pa) ex-*World Pride*; **DOOYANG BRAVE** (Ko) ex-*Golden Explorer*

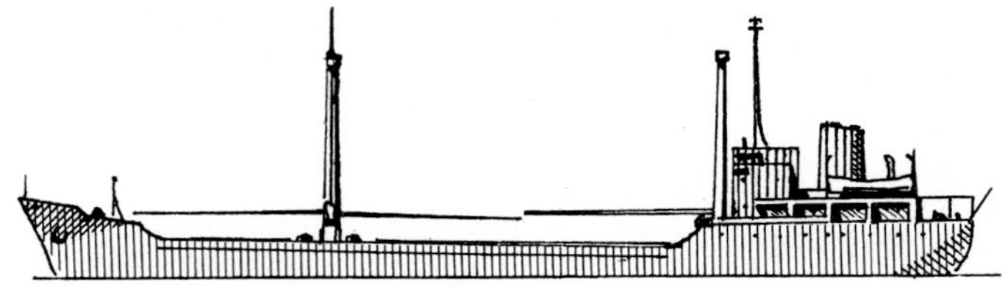

150 *MHMF H13*
CHANG DUCK No 5 Ko/Ja (Hitachi) 1962; C; 1,847 grt/2,930 dwt; 86.98 × 5.46 m *(285.37 × 17.91 ft)*; M (Hanshin); 11 kts; ex-*Futuba Maru No 3*

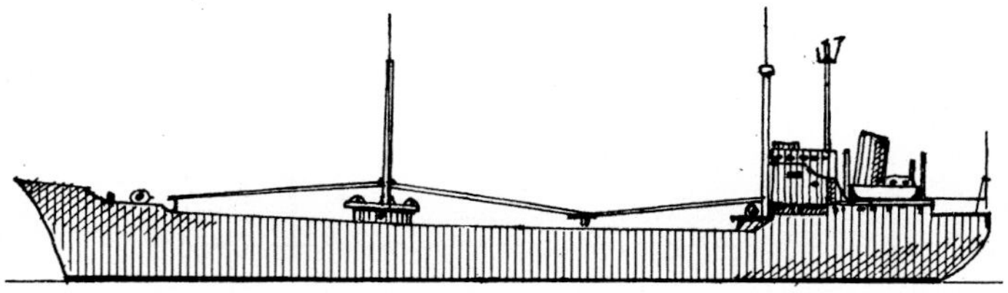

151 *MHMF H13*
WEASEL Pi/Ja (Shikoku) 1964; C; 1,738 grt/2,996 dwt; 85.58 × 5.44 m *(280.77 × 17.85 ft)*; M (Ito Tekkosho); 12 kts; ex-*Ichiyo Maru*
Possible sisters: **HAE SUNG No 7** (Ko) ex-*Houzan Maru*; **DONG SEONG** (Ko) ex-*Kensho Maru*; **BANGPO** (Th) ex-*Kinyo Maru*

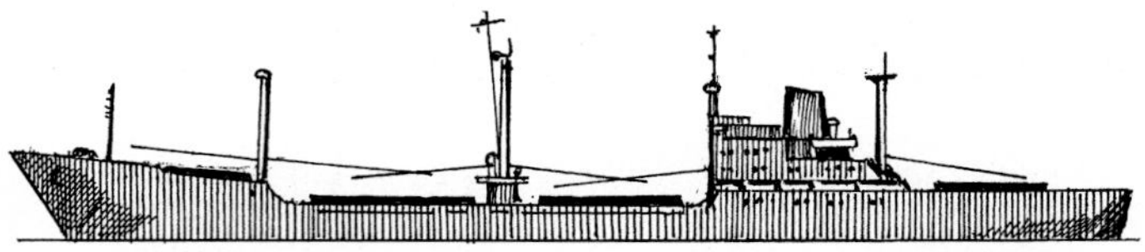

152 *MHNHFM H13*
TONG ZHOU RC/DDR (Warnow) 1972; C; 7,755 grt/13,845 dwt; 152.86 × 9.40 m *(501 × 31.0 ft)*; M (MAN); 18.5 kts; ex-*Joruna*; 'Ozean' type
Sisters: **HAI MAO** (SV) ex-*Anne Reed*; **SENICOLI SIERRA** (Gr) ex-*Karen Reed*; **JANBAZ III** (Cy) ex-*Salland* Probable sisters: **JI LIN** (RC) ex-*Aludra*; **HERMION** (Th) ex-*Torasund*; **HALLBORG** (Th) ex-*Torafjord*

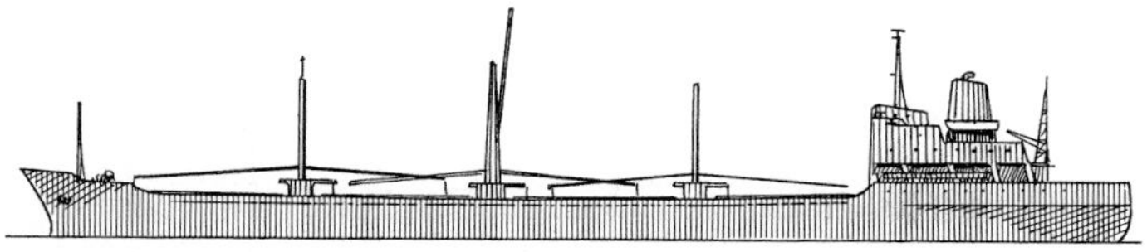

153 *MHNHMFN H13*
LONG CHUAN JIANG RC/Ja (Mitsui) 1971; C/Con; 10,199 grt/14,880 dwt; 147.7 × 9.1 m *(478 × 29.8 ft)*; M (B&W); 17 kts; ex-*Heelsum*; 'Mitsui-Concord 15' type; 202 TEU
Sister: **JIN CHENG JIANG** (RC) ex-*Leersum*

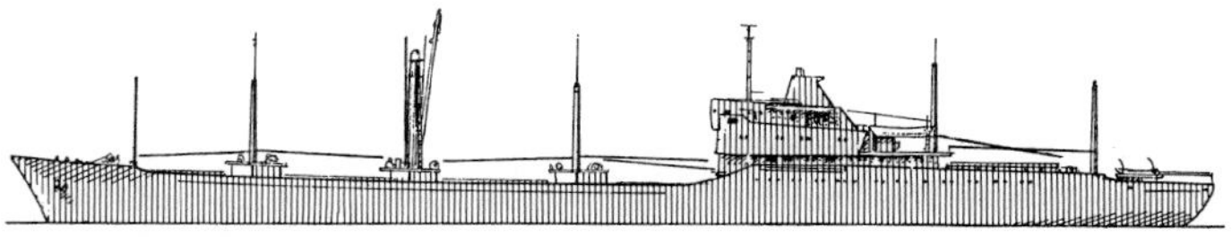

154 *MHNHMFNH H13*
WLADYSLAW JAGIELLO Pd/Pd (Szczecinska) 1971; C; 8,309 grt/ 11,570 dwt; 145.37 × 7.36/9.09 m *(476.94 × 24.15/29.82 ft)*; M (Sulzer); 17.5 kts; 'B445' type
Sisters: **WLADYSLAW LOKIETEK** (Pd); **ZYGMUNT AUGUST** (Pd); **ZYGMUNT STARY** (Pd); **ZYGMUNT III WAZA** (Pd): **IRAN EKRAM** (Ir) ex-*Arya Rokh*; **IRAN ELHAM** (Ir) ex-*Arya Kish* **JIANG CHENG** (Pd) ex-*Wladyslaw IV* Sisters ('B474' type): **CSOKONAI** (Hu); **RADNOTI** (Hu)

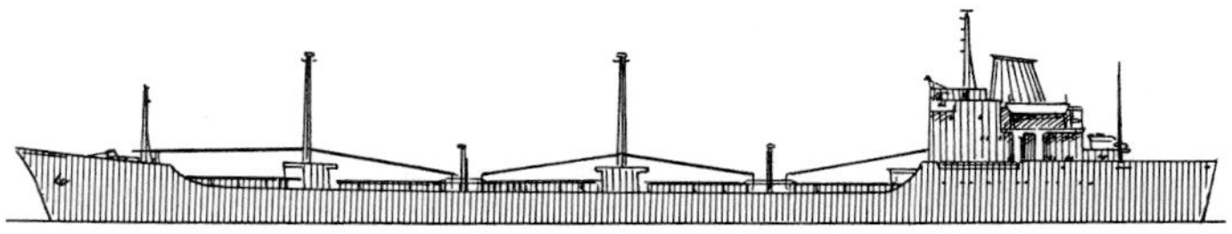

155 *MHNHNMFN H13*
FLORIANA Ma/De (Nakskov) 1968; B; 8,355 grt/11,780 dwt; 141.71 × 8.2 m *(464.93 × 26.9 ft)*; M (B&W); 15.25 kts; ex-*Kopalnia Moszczenica*
Sisters: **KLEOFAS** (Ma) ex-*Kopalnia Kleofas*; **SUBHAN ALLAH** (Ho) ex-*Kopalnia Marcel*; **CHOPOL** (Pd) ex-*Kopalnia Sosnica*; **KOPALNIA SZCZYGLOWICE** (Pd); **WIREK** (Ml) ex-*Kopalnia Wirek*; **REDA ALLAH** (Sy) ex-*Gliwice II*

156 *MHNMFNM H1*
YE XING RC/Sw (Oskarshamns) 1961; C; 8,872 grt/13,198 dwt; 147.8 × 9.3 m *(485 × 29.11 ft)*; M (Gotaverken); 13.5 kts; ex-*Salvada*

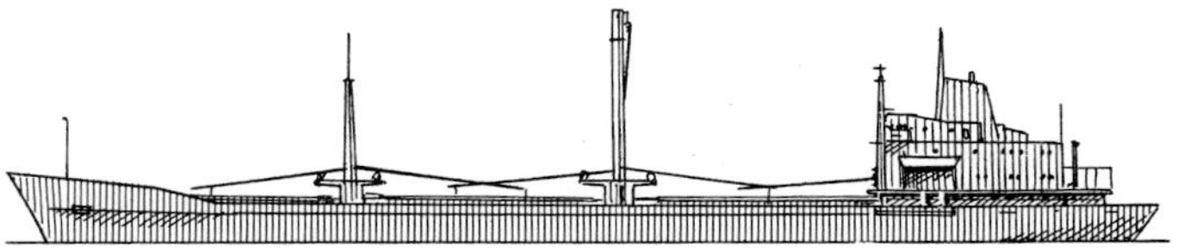

157 *MHNM–FN H1*
CHENG DA RC/FRG (Nobiskrug) 1969; C; 5,163 grt/7,500 dwt; 124.97 × 7.67 m *(410 × 25.16 ft)*; M (Atlas-MaK); 16.5 kts; ex-*Juno*
Sisters: **HUA YUE** (RC) ex-*Jupiter*
Probable sister: **HAPAG LLOYD AMAZONAS** (Pa) ex-*Neptun*

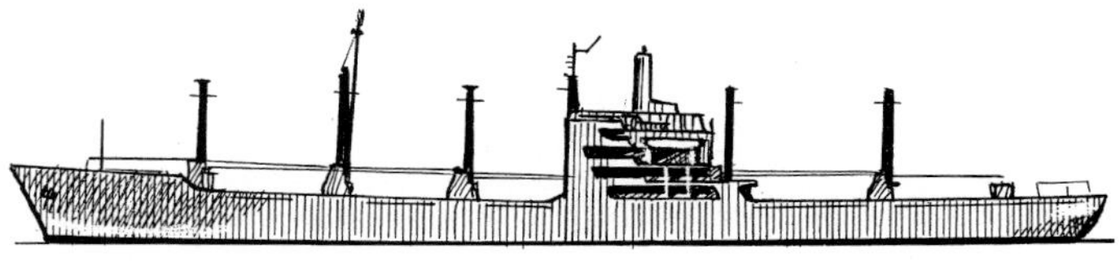

158 *MHN²HGN² H1*
CAPE BOVER US/US (Avondale) 1967; C; 10,723 grt/14,897 dwt; 165 × 9.9 m *(540 × 31.8 ft)*; T (De Laval); 19 kts; ex-*Frederick Lykes*; US Government owned
Sisters (some US Government owned): **CAPE BORDA** (US) ex-*Howell Lykes*; **GALVESTON BAY** (US) ex-*Mallory Lykes*; **CAPE BLANCO** (US) ex-*Mason Lykes*; **TAMPA BAY** (US) ex-*Stella Lykes*; **CAPE BON** (US) ex-*Velma Lykes*; **CAPE BRETON** (US) ex-*Dolly Turman*

159 *MHN²MFH² H13*
UNITED FUNG Pa/Pd (Gdanska) 1974; C/Con; 11,511 grt/11,632 dwt; 161 × 9.7 m *(529 × 32 ft)*; M (Sulzer); 15 kts; ex-*Bronislaw Lachowicz*; 'B438' type; 218 TEU
Sisters: **EUGENIUSZ KWIATKOWSKI** (Pd); **OCEAN TRADER** (Pd) ex-*Mieczyslaw Kalinowski*; **ANNY L** (Ma) ex-*Roman Pazinski*; **TADEUSZ OCIOSZYNSKI** (Pd); **ANDRONIKOS P** (Ma) Launched as *Aleksandr Rylke*; **CONSTANTINOS D** (Ma) ex-*Isla Baltra*; **CLEO D** (Ma) ex-*Cantuaria*

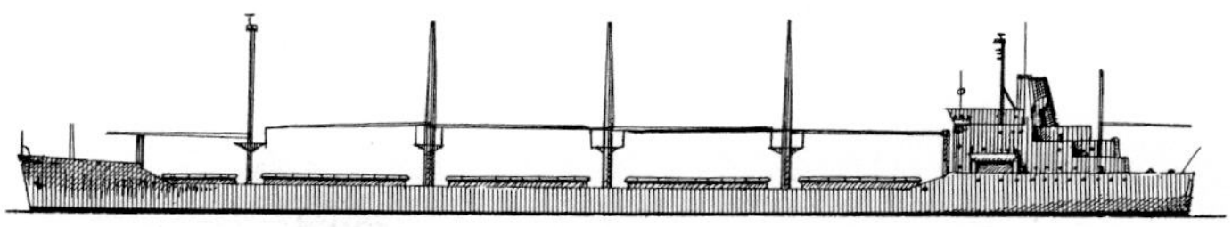

160 *MHN³M²FN H13*
NEDLLOYD INCA Li/Ne (Verolme Scheeps) 1973; B/Con; 20,375 grt/ 32,629 dwt; 181.67 × 11.24 m *(596.03 × 36.88 ft)*; M (MAN); 16 kts; ex-*Hamburger Wappen*; Converted from bulk carrier 1978 (B+V); 980 TEU; Small wheelhouse superimposed on bridge top (not on drawing)
Sisters: **MSC LUCY** (Cy) ex-*Hamburger Flagge* (1,204 TEU)

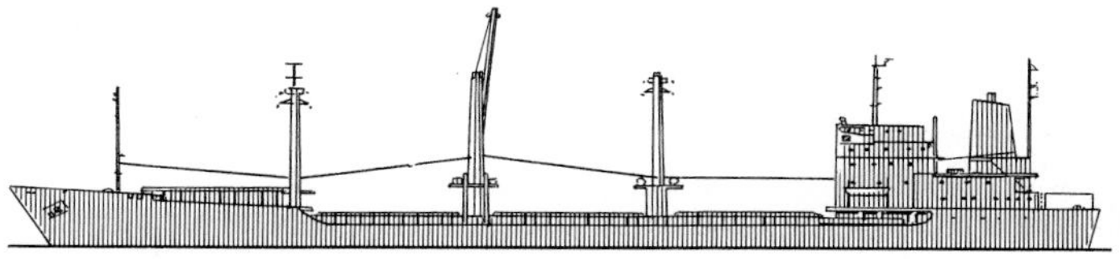

161 *MHUHMFM H13*
TAGAMA At/DDR (Warnow) 1982; C/Con; 12,811 grt/17,400 dwt; 158.05 × 10.18 m *(519 × 33.4 ft)*; M (MAN); 13 kts; ex-*Wahehe*; 'MONSUN' type 642 TEU
Sisters: **THEOFANO** (Cy) ex-*Wangoni*; **PAL WIND** (Li) ex-*Wadai*; **DURMITOR** (Ma); **LOVCEN** (Ma); Similar (bulwark plating in well and poop, taller funnel and so on): **GRIGORIY KOZINTSEV** (Uk) ex-*Faneos*: **PYOTR ALEYNIKOV** (or **PETR ALEYNIKOV**) (Uk) ex-*Filon*
Probably similar: **VALENTIN ZOLOTARYEV** (Uk) ex-*Athenian Spirit*; **SEVASTAKI** (Li) ex-*Eastern Moon*; **CANOPUS** (Sg); **CMBT EQUATOR** (Li) ex-*Woermann Wameru*; **PEARL MERCHANT** (Cy) ex-*Family Irini*; Similar: **INDUSTRIAL ADVANTAGE** (Ml) ex-*Radebeul*

162 *MHUHNMFM H13*
WADAI At/DDR (Warnow) 1983; C/Con; 12,811 grt/17,330 dwt; 158.05 × 10.18 m *(518.54 × 33.40 ft)*; M (MAN); 16.8 kts; 642 TEU; 'MONSUN' type; **SIMILAR TO DRAWING NUMBER 8/161**; Principally differs from latter by additional uprights from bridge front
Possible sisters: **PEARL MERCHANT** (Cy) ex-*Family Irini*; **CMBT EQUATOR** (Li) ex-*Woermann Wameru*

163 *M²F H1*
ST CHRISTOPHER SV/Sw (Solvesborgs) 1959; C; 999 grt/1,272 dwt; 74.07 × 4.12 m *(243 × 13.52 ft)*; M (Alpha-Diesel); 12 kts; ex-*Vinia*; Lengthened 1963

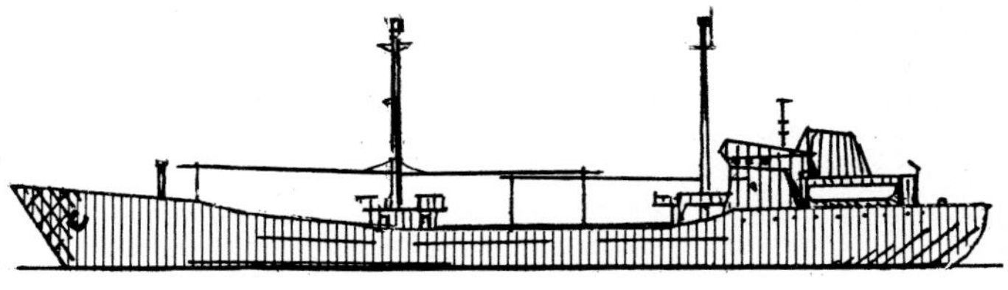

164 *M²F H13*
ALMIRANTE ERASO Co/FRG (Kremer) 1965; C; 1,337 grt/2,233 dwt; 74.73 × 4.2/5.4 m *(245.18 × 13.78/17.72 ft)*; M (General Motors); — kts; ex-*Langa*; New engines 1993

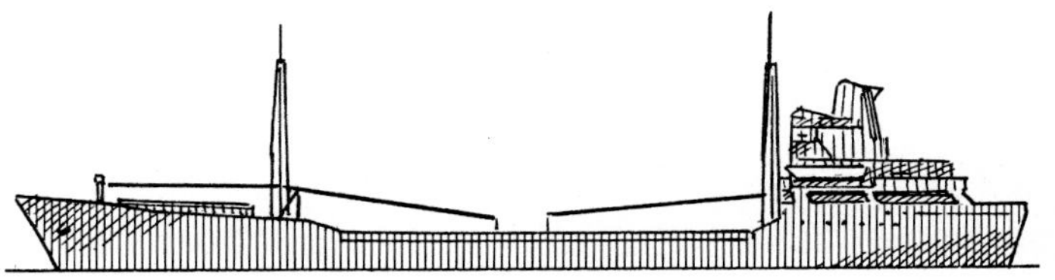

165 *M²F H13*
EQUATOR JOY Sg/Sw (Oresunds) 1972; C; 2,225 grt/3,090 dwt; 93.22 × 5.13 m *(305.84 × 16.83 ft)*; M (Atlas-MaK); 15 kts; ex-*Jota*

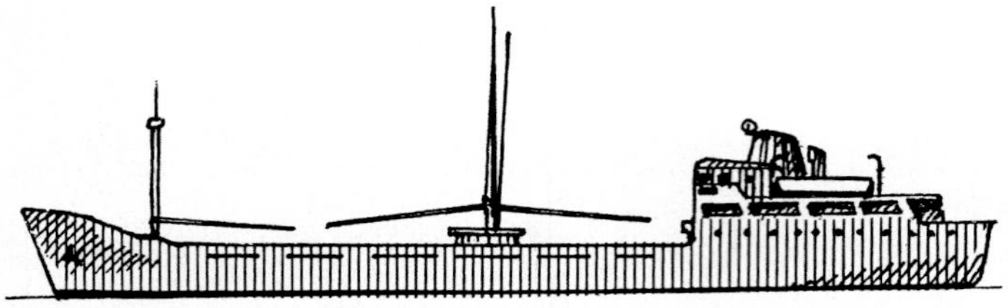

166 M^2F *H13*
TEUTA Al/It (Apuania) 1960; C; 1,094 grt/1,711 dwt; 72.42 × 4.77 m *(237.6 × 15.65 ft)*; M (Fiat); 11.75 kts

167 $\underline{M^2FM}$ *H*
TACLOBAN CITY Pi/Ja (Sanoyasu) 1962; C; 1,965 dwt; 91 × 4.5 *(299 × 14.6)*; M (Mitsubishi); 18.5; ex-*Naminoue Maru*

168 M^2FM *H1*
NAVARIN Ru/Ru (Leninskogo) 1967; C; 7,461 grt/9,190 dwt; 133 × 8.9 m *(436 × 30 ft)*; D–E (Fairbanks, Morse); 15 kts; Ice strengthened
Similar (some have helicopter deck): **PAVEL PONOMARYEV** (Ru); **VASILIY FEDOSEYEV** (Ru); **MIKHAIL SOMOV** (Ru) (operated as a research ship. Superstructure extended to mainmast. Fitted with Helo pad.)

169 M^2FM *H123*
DUBAI TRADER SV/Ru ('Zhdanov') 1963; C; 4,482 grt/6,459 dwt; 122 × 6.78 m *(400 × 22.24 ft)*; M (B&W); 14.5 kts; ex-*Chulymles*
Sisters: **ISAKOGORKA** (Ru); **IVAN CHERNYKH** (Ru); **SABIN** (Sy) ex-*Kildin*; **NADOR** (Ho) ex-*Krasnaya Gorka*; **COOT** (Ma) ex-*Nizhniy Tagil*;**NOVAYA LADOGA** (Ru); **YANNIS** (Pa) ex-*Novaya Zemlya*; **ALLAH KABEER** (Bl) ex-*Porkhov*; **MARWAN** (Sy) ex-*Taymyr*; **AL BUSHRA** (—) ex-*Vasya Alekseyev*; **LINA M** (Ma) ex-*Voskhod*; **UNIPOWER** (Ma) ex-*Vostok 2*; **AL WAFIC** (Ma) ex-*Vostok 5*; **SAMRA** (Sy) ex-*Yamal*; **KATERINA ONE** (Ma) ex-*Zolotitza*; **OCEAN HUNTER** (Ma) ex-*Oka*

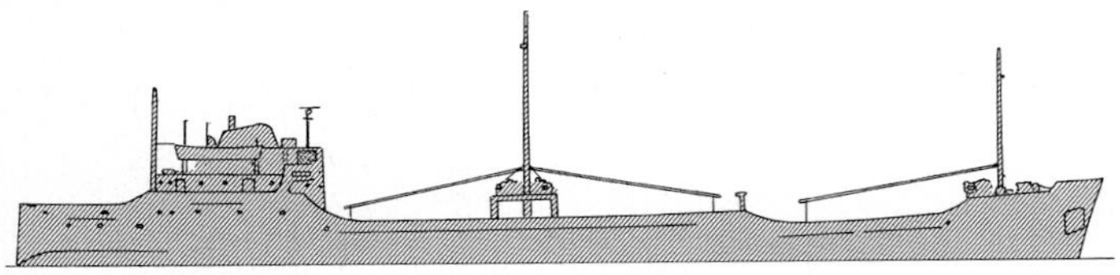

170 M^2FM *H123*
GEORGIOS Ho/Br (Clelands) 1963; C; 1,588 grt/2,597 dwt; 81.23 × 5.16 m *(266.5 × 16.93 ft)*; M (British Polar); — kts; ex-*Gillian Everard*; Mast aft is on starboard side
Sisters: **ELPIDA** (Gr) ex-*Penelope Everard*; **BERLICE** (Ho) ex-*Rosemary Everard*; **YGIA** (Ho) ex-*Corkbrook*; **CHIOS I** (Gr) ex-*Caernarvonbrook*; **ECOWAS TRADER I** (Ng) ex-*William J Everard*

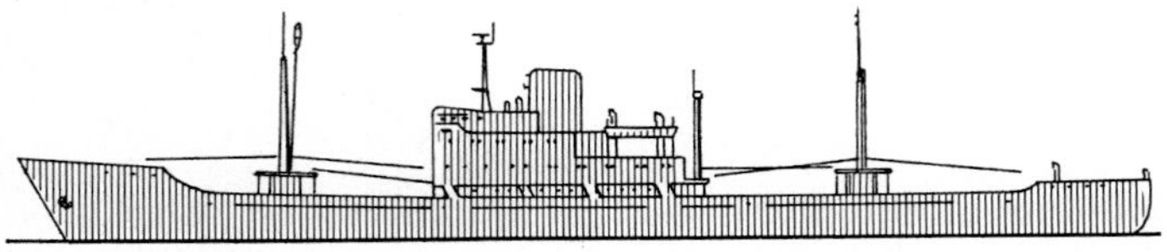

171 $\underline{M^2FM^2}$ *H13*
TUAN JIE RC/RC (Dalian) 1964; C; 4,939 grt/6,096 dwt; 121.01 × — m *(397 × — ft)*; M (—); — kts; May be spelt **TUAN CHIEH**

172 M^2FNM *H1*
DA PING SHAN RC/Ys ('Uljanik') 1958; C; 9,189 grt/12,762 dwt; 149.3 × 8.9 m *(490 × 29.2 ft)*; M (B&W); 15 kts; ex-*Polet*

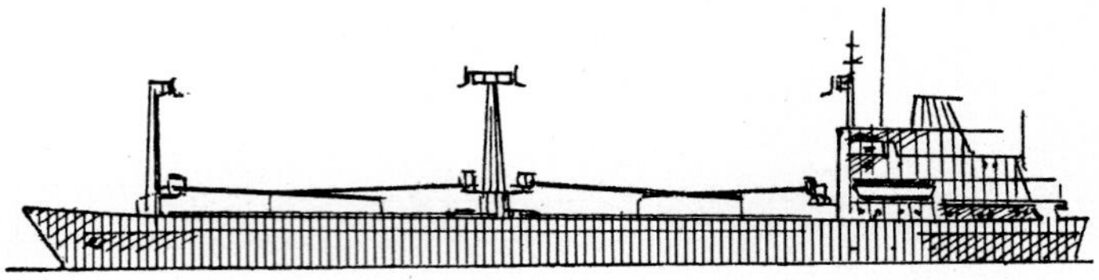

173 M^2HF *H*
ALEDREESI Iq/FRG (Buesumer) 1976; C/Con; 1,599 grt/3,549 dwt; 81.62 × 6.1 m *267.78 × 20.1 ft)*; M (Atlas-MaK); 12.5 kts; 108 TEU
Sisters: **ALZAWRAA** (Iq); **ALKHANSAA** (Iq); **ZANOOBIA** (Iq); Similar: **UB PROSPER** (Bs) ex-*Rosa Dania*; **UB PREMIER** (Bs) ex-*Agnes Dania*; **LIAN JIANG** (RC) ex-*Anett Bentsen*; **HUAN JIANG** (RC) ex-*Susann Bentsen*: **PERNILLE** (NIS) ex-*Mercandian Sea*; **PROGRESS LILY** (Mv) ex-*Mercandian Sky*

174 M^2HF *H*
SHARAF ALDDIN Ho/Sw (Falkenbergs) 1961; C; 399 grt/1,850 dwt; 74.5 × 3.67 m *(244.42 × 12.04 ft)*; M (MWM); 10.5 kts; ex-*Nordpol*
Sister: **MAGO** (Sao) ex-*Vaasa*

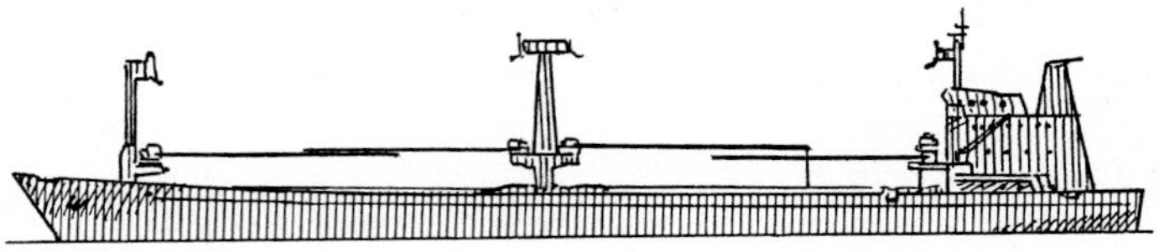

175 M^2HF *H*
UB PRESTIGE Bs/FRG (Buesumer) 1977; C; 2,853 grt/4,135 dwt; 93.3 × 5.93 m *(306.1 × 19.46 ft)*; M (Alpha-Diesel); 12.5 kts; ex-*Mercandian Moon*; 122 TEU
Sister: **UB PIONEER** (Bs) ex-*Mercandian Star*

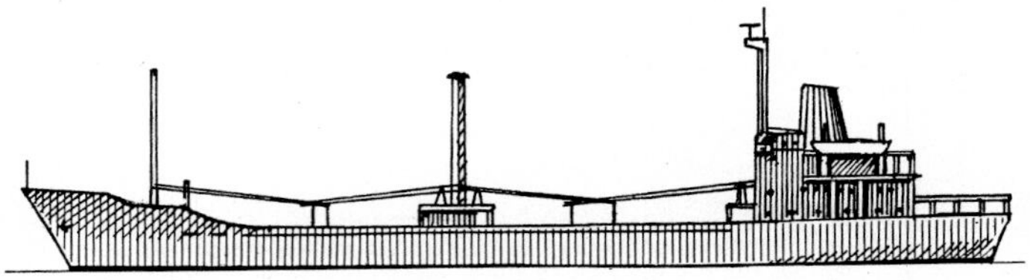

176 M^2HF *H1*
A M SPIRIDON Le/Br (H Robb) 1968; C; 1,460 grt/2,476 dwt; 94.24 × 5.01 m *(309.19 × 16.44 ft)*; M (Mirrlees); 13 kts; ex-*Mediterranian*

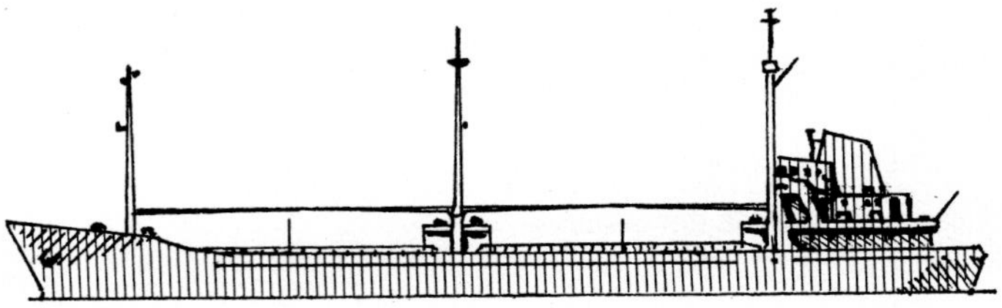

177 M^2HF *H1*
ARUNA SV/De (Svendborg) 1972; C; 1,422 grt/1,340 dwt; 75.42 × 3.47 m *(247.44 × 11.38 ft)*; M (Atlas-MaK); 11 kts; ex-*Oceania*; 71 TEU
Sisters: **VASILIS** (SV) ex-*Anne Mette*; **SUNMAR STAR** (US) ex-*Elin S*; **ANDREAS M** (SV) ex-*Sigrid S*

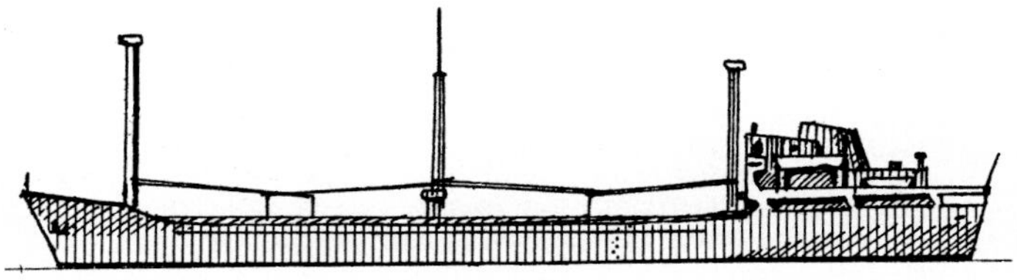

178 M^2HF *H1*
EBENEZER C Ho/Sp (Euskalduna) 1963; C; 998 grt/1,847 dwt; 74.78 × 4.89 m *(245.34 × 16.04 ft)*; M (MaK); 13 kts; ex-*Linglea*

179 M^2HF *H1*
MARSHALL Bl/FRG (Sietas) 1964; C; 1,572 grt/2,561 dwt; 83.72 × 5.89 m *(274.67 × 19.32 ft)*; M (MAN); 14 kts; ex-*Thesee*

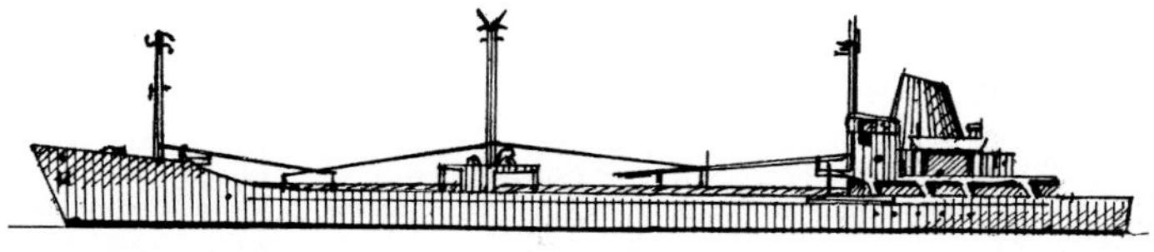

180 *M^2HF H1*
RASHIDAH SV/Br (Clelands) 1970; C; 2,373 grt/2,635 dwt; 86.87 × 5.07 m *(285 × 16.63 ft)*; M (Ruston); 13.5 kts; ex-*Mendip Prince*
Sisters: **THANG LOI 2** (Vn) ex-*Chiltern Prince*; **THANG LOI 1** (Vn) ex-*Malvern Prince*; **COTSWOLD PRINCE** (NZ)

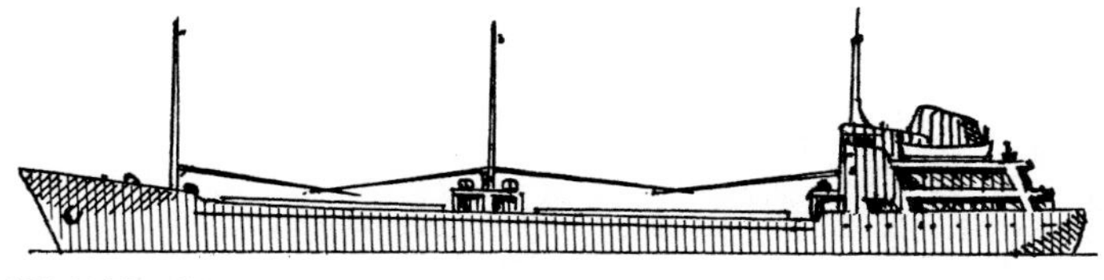

181 *M^2HF H1*
ROMIOS Cy/FRG (Brand) 1968; C; 1,598 grt/2,880 dwt; 80.09 × 6.05 m *(262.76 × 19.85 ft)*; M (KHD); 13 kts; ex-*Eckwardersand*
Sisters: **NEREUS** (Cy) ex-*Boitwardersand*; **NAFIS** (Ir) ex-*Lemwardersand*

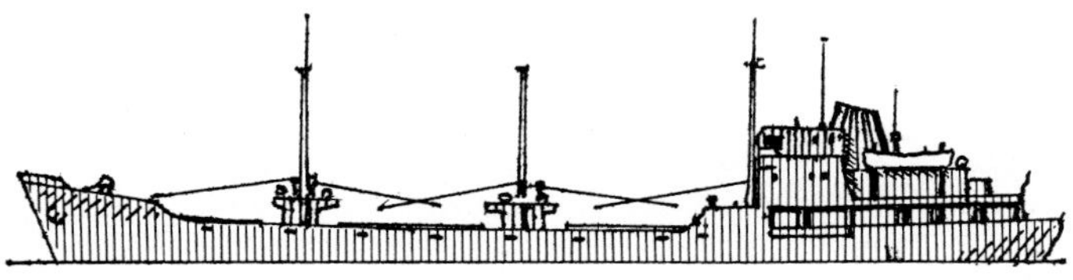

182 *M^2HF H1*
SONITA Ma/Ne (Duijvendijk's) 1959; C; 2,123 grt/2,543 dwt; 88.09 × 5.26 m *(289 × 17.26 ft)*; M (Werkspoor); 13 kts; ex-*Stalheim*

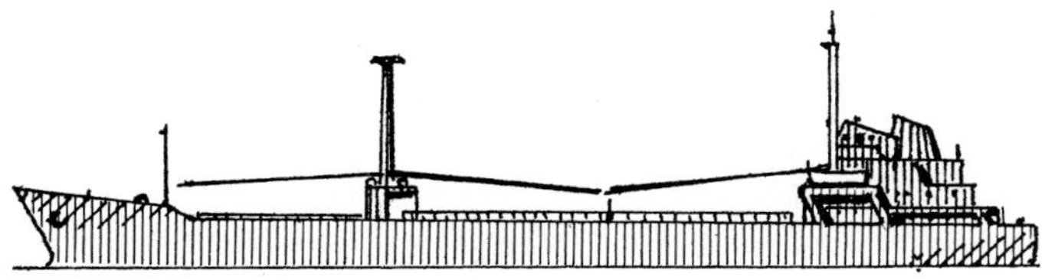

183 *M^2HF H1*
VASSILIS VII Ho/Ne ('De Biesbosch') 1969; C; 2,426 grt/3,750 dwt; 84.26 × 6.68 m *(276.44 × 21.92 ft)*; M (MWM); — kts; ex-*Iris*

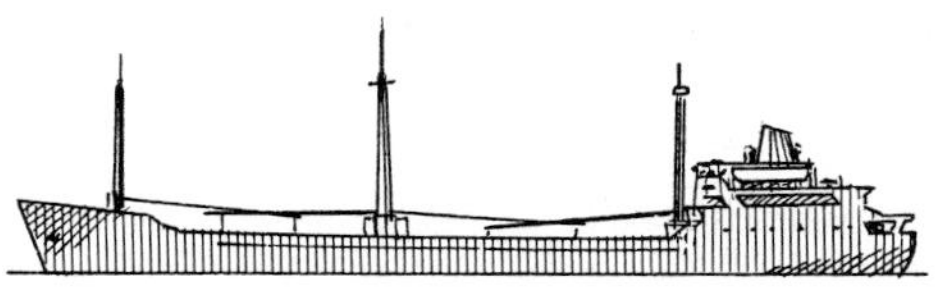

184 *M^2HF H12*
DOMNA MARIA Ho/No (Kristiansands) 1965; C; 1,210 grt/2,330 dwt; 71.73 × 5.31 m *(235.33 × 17.42 ft)*; M (MaK); 12.5 kts; ex-*Marmorfjell*

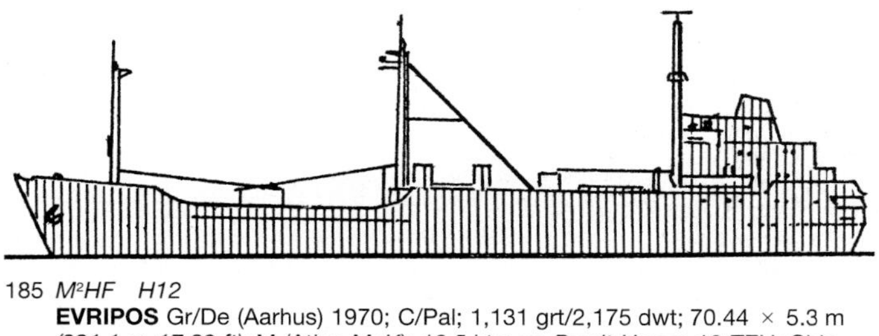

185 *M^2HF H12*
EVRIPOS Gr/De (Aarhus) 1970; C/Pal; 1,131 grt/2,175 dwt; 70.44 × 5.3 m *(231.1 × 17.39 ft)*; M (Atlas-MaK); 12.5 kts; ex-*Dorrit Hoyer*; 12 TEU; Side door (port)

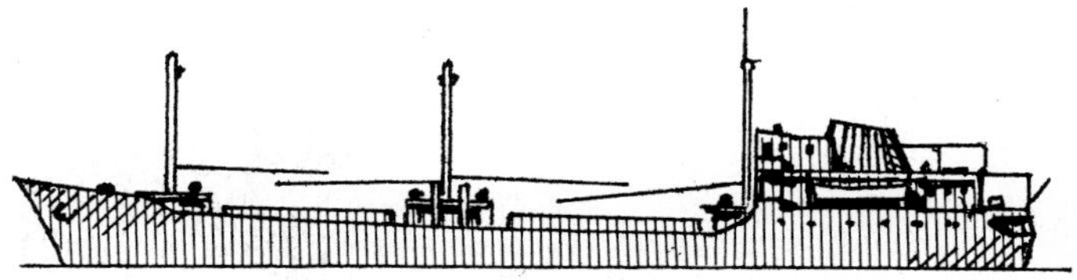

186 *M^2HF H13*
AL HAJ OSSMAN Sy/FRG (Schuerenstedt) 1966; C; 1,299 grt/2,329 dwt; 73.61 × 5.28 m *(241.5 × 17.32 ft)*; M (MaK); 12.5 kts; ex-*Tantzen*; may be spelt **AL HAJ OTHMAN**

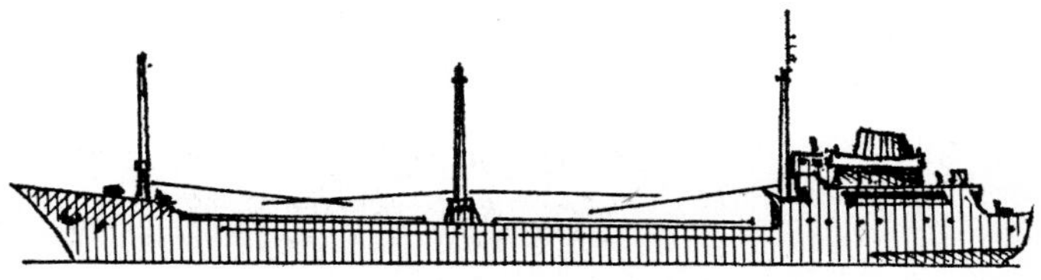

187 *M^2HF H13*
DONA PETRA M R Pa/Ne ('Hoogezand' JB) 1966; C; 1,051 grt/1,270 dwt; 73.06 × 4.27 m *(239.7 × 14 ft)*; M (Appingedammer Brons); 12.5 kts; ex-*Jan*
Sister (Hu built—Angyalfold): **BLUE JADE** (Mv) ex-*Jodonna*

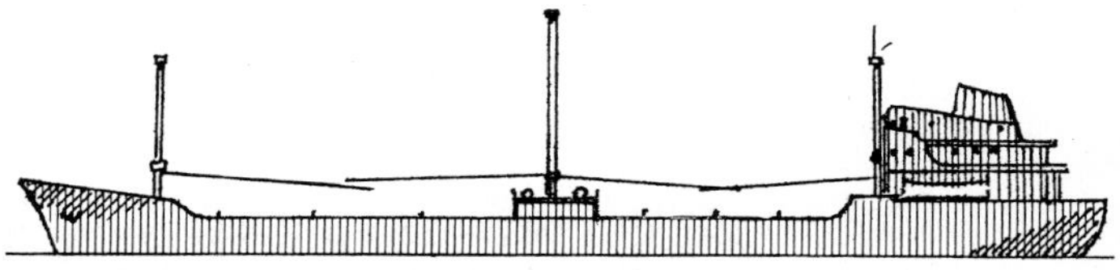

188 *M^2HF H13*
EQUATOR GRAND Sg/FRG (M Jansen) 1970; C/Con; 2,896 grt/4,480 dwt; 100.51 × 6.33 m *(329.76 × 20.77 ft)*; M (MWM); 13 kts; ex-*Kathe Bos*
Similar: **TINHINAN** (Ag) ex-*Johannes Bos*; **HODNA** (Ag) ex-*Annette Bos*

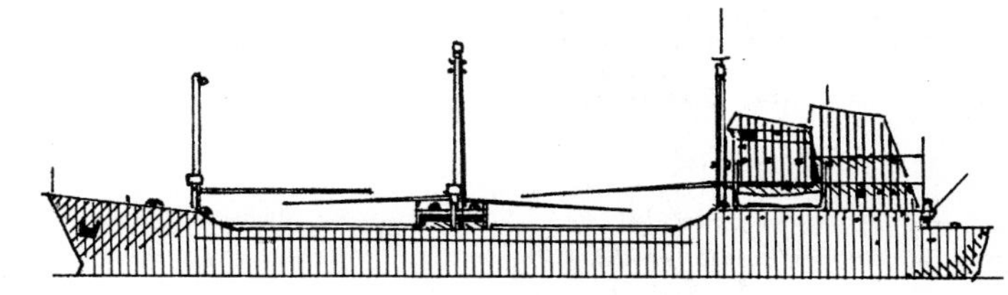

189 *M^2HF H13*
HOTAMA Pa/Ne (Pattje) 1970; C; 1,599 grt/2,976 dwt; 79.69 × 5.89 m *(261.45 × 19.32 ft)*; M (MWM); 13 kts; ex-*Hendrik Bros*
Sister: **ORIANA** (It) ex-*Gerd Bos*
Probable sister: **KABANJAHE** (Ia) ex-*Irmgard Bos*

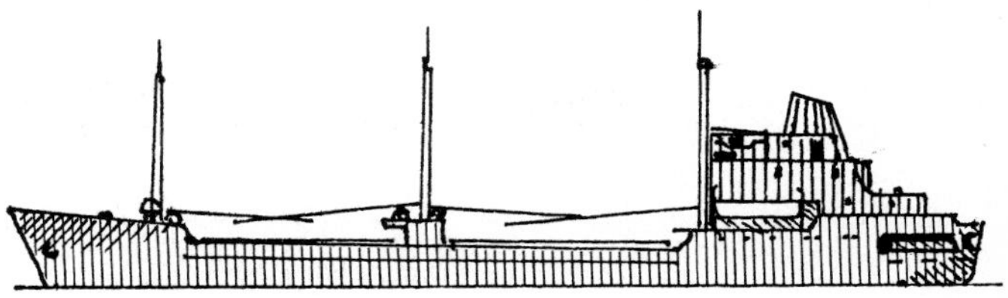

190 *M^2HF H13*
KAHURIPAN Ia/De (Aarhus) 1969; C; 1,181 grt/2,220 dwt; 70.44 × 5.54 m *(231.1 × 18.18 ft)*; M (Atlas-MaK); 12.5 kts; ex-*Lotte Nielsen*

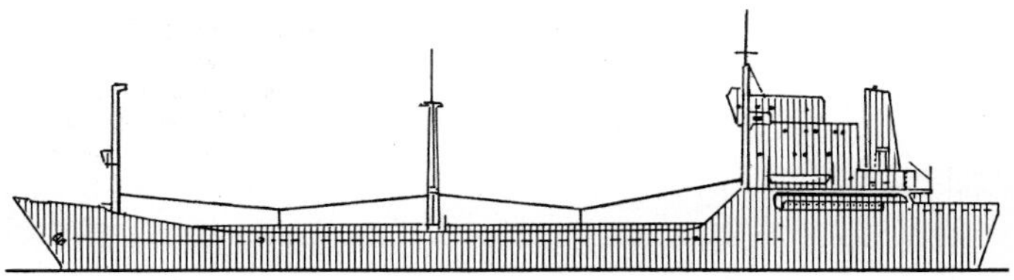

191 *M^2HF H13*
LA BRIANTAIS Kn/No (Sterkoder) 1977; C; 4,576 grt/7,020 dwt; 110.75 × 7.19 m *(363.35 × 23.59 ft)*; M (KHD); 13.5 kts; ex-*Kings River*

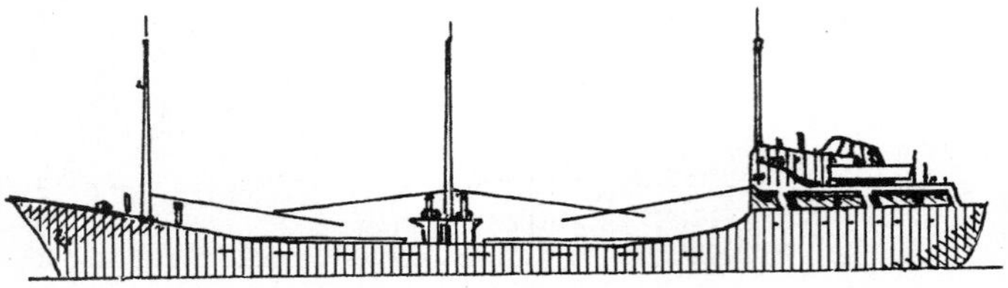

192 *M^2HF H13*
LEILA Sy/FRG (Brand) 1959; C; 499 grt/1,585 dwt; 72.47 × 4.32 m *(237.76 × 14.17 ft)*; M (MaK); 11 kts; ex-*Rotesand*

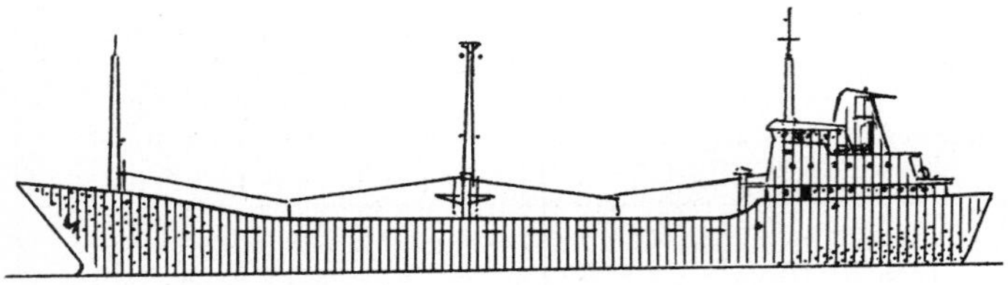

193 *M^2HF H13*
LUCILLE Ho/De (Frederikshavn) 1972; C; 1,507 grt/1,327 dwt; 76.61 × 3.47 m *(251.35 × 11.38 ft)*; M (Alpha-Diesel); 12 kts; ex-*Merc Continental*; Starboard side superstructure differs
Sisters: **RACHMANUEL 1** (Ia) ex-*Merc Polaris*; **RACHMANUEL 2** (Ia) ex-*Merc Aequator*; **NORIENT** (Pa) ex-*Merc Orientalis*; **AL ANDALUS** (Ho) ex-*Merc Africa*; **ULSUND** (No) ex-*Merc America*; Similar: **IARKO** (Sg) ex-*AES*; **OCEAN HERO** (At) ex-*Peder Most*; **ANGEL** (Pa) ex-*Britannia*; **JUAN DIEGO** (Cy) ex-*Charlotte S*; **JOANNE I** (Pa) ex-*Mogens S*; **PATRICIA STAR** (SV) ex-*Patricia S*

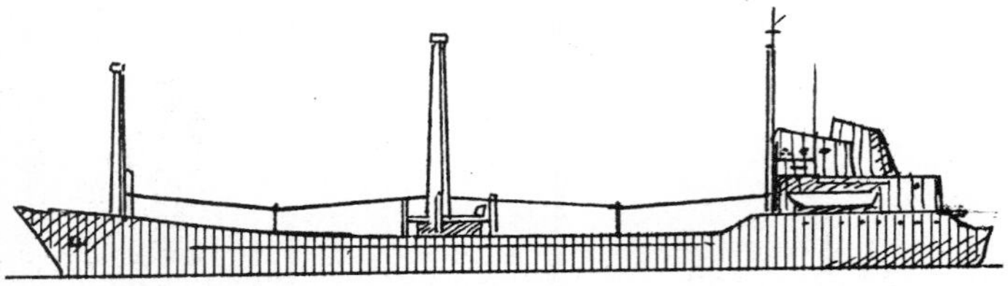

194 *M^2HF H13*
NIAGA XXIV Ia/FRG (M Jansen) 1969; C; 1,492 grt/2,780 dwt; 75.49 × 6.00 m *(247.6 × 19.68 ft)*; M (KHD); 13 kts; Launched as *Bele*
Sister: **ALBERT J** (Bl) ex-*Tasso*

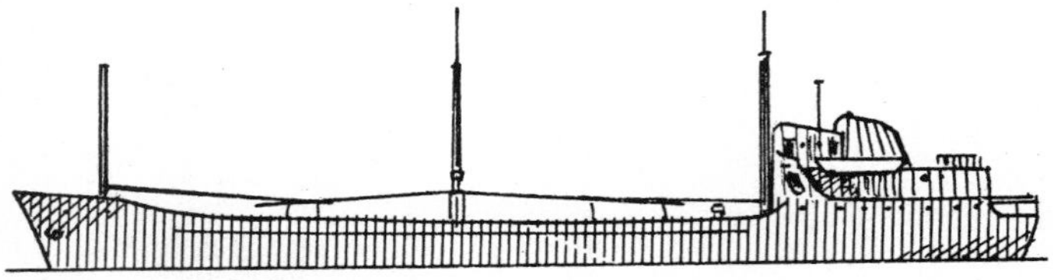

195 *M^2HF H13*
NICOLAOS H Ho/Sp (Juliana) 1963; C; 1,133 grt/1,930 dwt; 74.71 × 5.04 m *(245.11 × 16.54 ft)*; M (MAN); 14 kts; ex-*Monte Cinco*
Similar: **VIOLA** (Pa) ex-*Eco Gabriela*; **AGAETE** (Pa) Launched as *Monte Uno*

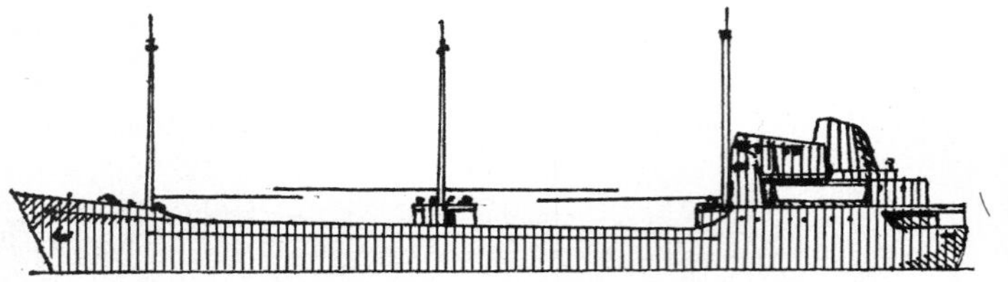

196 *M^2HF H13*
SALINA Ma/FRG (Sietas) 1967; C; 1,437 grt/2,400 dwt; 75.34 × 5.55 m *(247.18 × 18.21 ft)*; M (Deutz); 13 kts; ex-*Kehdingen*
Similar: **IOANNA** (Gr) ex-*Wilken*

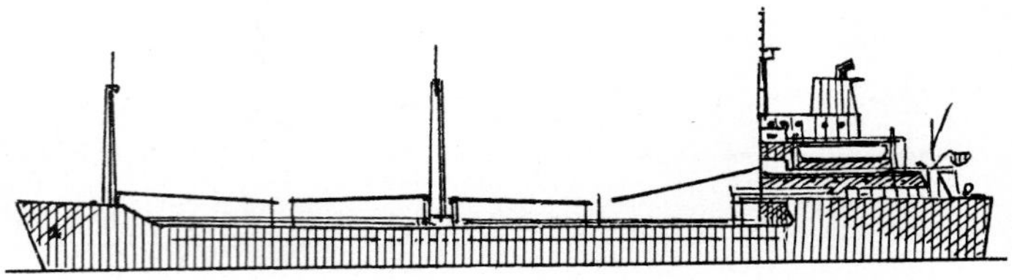

197 *M^2HF H13*
SAVA It/No (Sterkoder) 1972; C; 1,903 grt/3,068 dwt; 79.91 × 5.28 m *(262.17 × 17.32 ft)*; M (Polar); 14 kts; ex-*Mini Sun*
Sisters: **UNI YAMANI** (Eg) ex-*Mini Cloud*; **MINI MOON** (Ho); **IPPOCRATIS** (SV) ex-*Mini Sky*; **PINDOS** (SV) ex-*Mini Star*

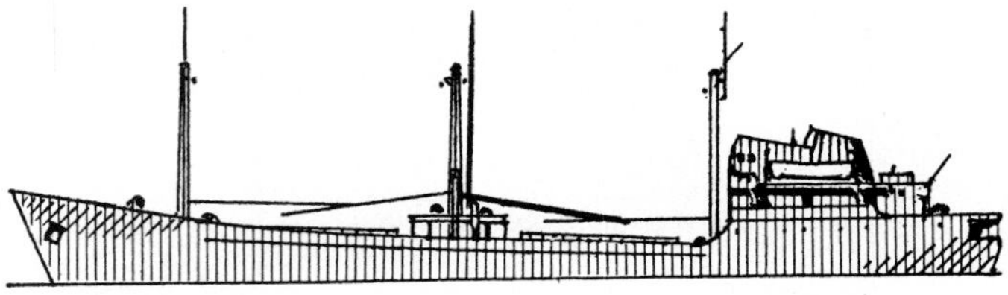

198 *M^2HF H13*
SOLARA Le/FRG (Meyer) 1966; C; 1,477 grt/2,564 dwt; 74.81 × 5.75 m *(245.44 × 18.86 ft)*; M (KHD); 13.5 kts; ex-*Seeadler*

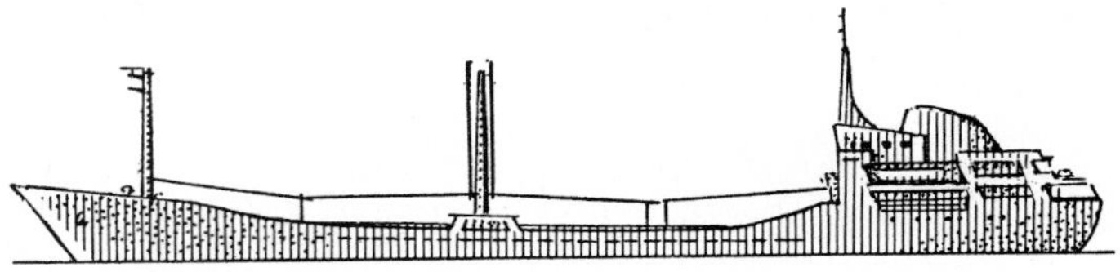

199 *M^2HF H13*
SPEEDY FORTUNE Ia/FRG (Brand) 1970; C; 2,170 grt/3,326 dwt; 92.31 × 6.10 m *(303 × 20.01 ft)*; M (Deutz); 15.5 kts; ex-*Stollhammersand*; 121 TEU
Sisters: **RAINBOW GLORY** (Ho) ex-*Marocsand*; **AHMAD J** (Sy) ex-*Seefeldersand*

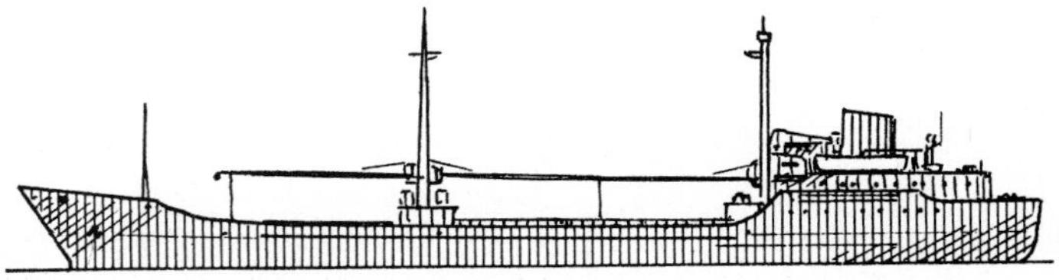

200 *M^2HF H13*
VAEANU Fr/FRG (Sietas) 1967; C; 1,540 grt/2,420 dwt; 76.66 × 5.81 m *(261.35 × 19.06 ft)*; M (MAN); 13.5 kts; ex-*Cadiz 1981*; Now has passenger accommodation and may be altered in appearance
Sister: **MAMIRI** (Ia) ex-*Sevilla*

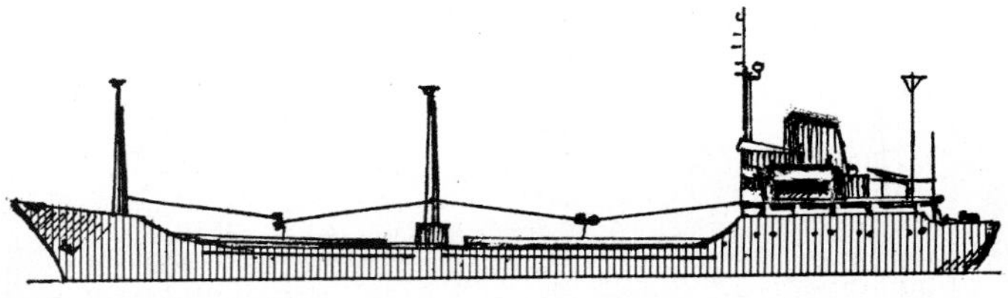

201 *M^2HFM H13*
BOSUT Cro/FRG (Luerssen) 1967; C; 2,707 grt/4,476 dwt; 95.81 × 6.36 m *(314.34 × 20.87 ft)*; M (Bergens); 12.25 kts; ex-*Raknes*
Sisters: **CIKOLO** (Cro) ex-*Tinnes*; **AMALIJA** (Cro) ex-*Vigsnes*; **MAR GRANDE** (It) ex-*Telnes*; **MINA** (Le) ex-*Altnes*; **JOHN HOPE** (Ho) ex-*Korsnes*; **DAKIS I** (Bl) ex-*Garnes*; **MARINA I** (Le) ex-*Fritre*

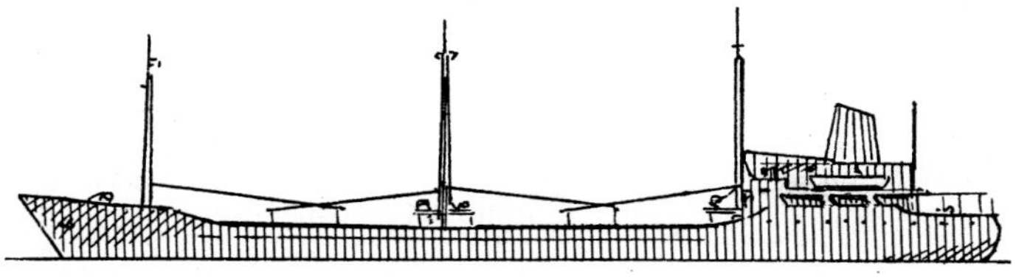

202 *M²HFM H13*
MUHIEDDINE I Sy/Ne (E J Smit) 1968; C; 1,529 grt/2,580 dwt; 77.55 × 5.74 m *(254.43 × 18.83 ft)*; M (Atlas-MaK); 12 kts; ex-*Holland Park*
Sisters: **SHEREEN A** (Le) ex-*Cairnventure*; **ANTALAHA** (Mg) ex-*Corato*; **MARIOS K** (SV) ex-*Voreda*; **QIONG XI** (RC) ex-*Calandria*; **BERGER A** (Le) ex-*Hyde Park*; **LADY NINA** (Le) ex-*Saltersgate*; Similar: **KAMASAN** (Ia) ex-*Gudrun Danielsen*; **OSMAN J** (Ho) ex-*White Crest*; **ARANA** (SV) Launched as *Cairntrader*; **JIU LONG** (RC) ex-*Jytte Danielsen*; (larger): **VEGA** (SV) ex-*Cairnrover*; **SAMER** (SV) ex-*Cairnranger*; **VENUSIA** (It) ex-*Thea Danielsen*
Similar (Sp built—Construcciones SA): **ARISTEA** (SV) ex-*Narya*

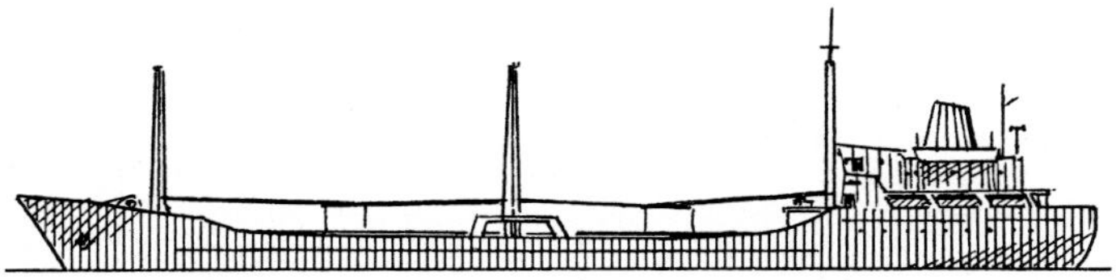

203 *M²HFM H13*
SAIDA STAR Le/Sp (Construcciones SA) 1971; C; 1,594 grt/2,840 dwt; 84.82 × 5.67 m *(278.28 × 18.6 ft)*; M (Deutz); 11 kts; ex-*Nenya*
Sister: **LYDIA FLAG** (SV) ex-*Waynegate*

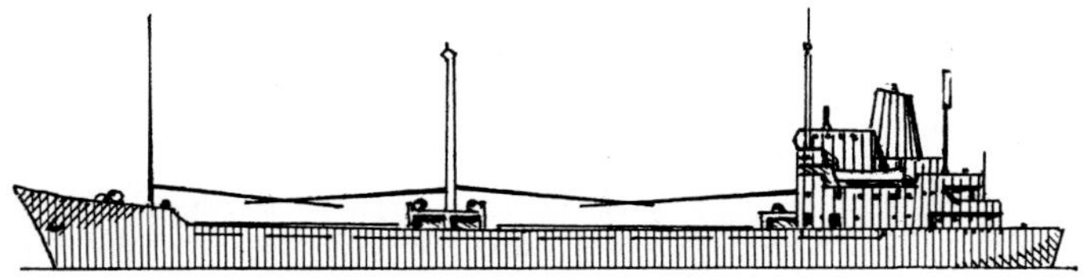

204 *M²HFN H1*
FRANKY Ia/Ne ('Freisland') 1971; C; 1,496 grt/3,125 dwt; 94.52 × 5.4 m *(310.1 × 17.72 ft)*; M (MWM); 14 kts; ex-*Karlsburg*
Similar: **SARI** (Sy) ex-*Trias*

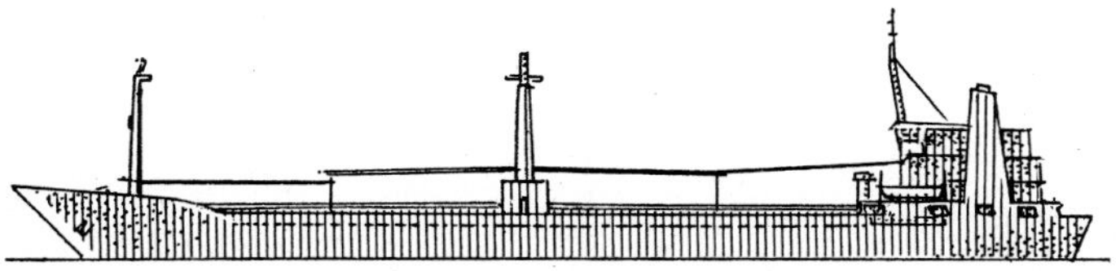

205 *M²HG H1*
KAREN WINTHER De/De (Frederikshavn) 1977; C/Con; 3,437 grt/4,100 dwt; 96.53 × 5.64 m *(316.69 × 18.5 ft)*; M (Atlas-MaK); 12.5 kts; 154 TEU

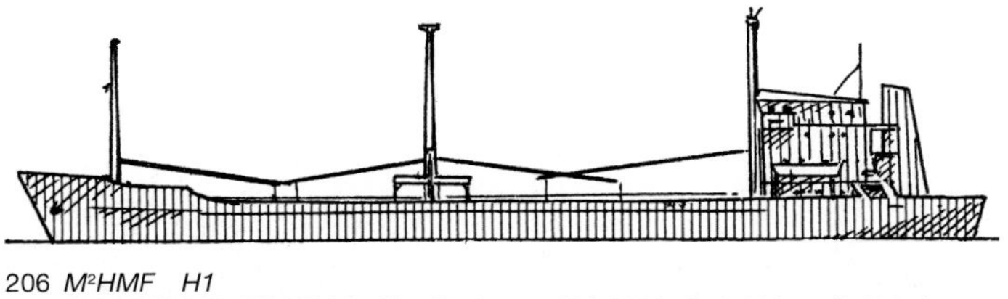

206 *M²HMF H1*
BIANCO DANIELSEN Cy/Ne (Bodewes BV) 1976; C; 1,836 grt/2,350 dwt; 79.48 × 4.83 m *(260.76 × 15.85 ft)*; M (MaK); 12.5 kts; ex-*Pia Danielsen*
Similar: **GUDRUN DANIELSEN** (Bs) ex-*Gudrun Danielsen*; **JYTTE DANIELSEN** (Bs); **BONGO DANIELSEN** (Bs) ex-*Grete Danielsen*; **HERMAN BODEWES** (Cy); **EVDOKIA STAR** (Pa) ex-*Geert Bodewes*; **REGENT PARK** (Bs) ex-*Madeline Danielsen*; **HYDE PARK** (Bs) ex-*Margriet Danielsen* (sloping uprights to goalpost): **PULAU SAMUTERA** (Ia) ex-*Hille Frellsen*

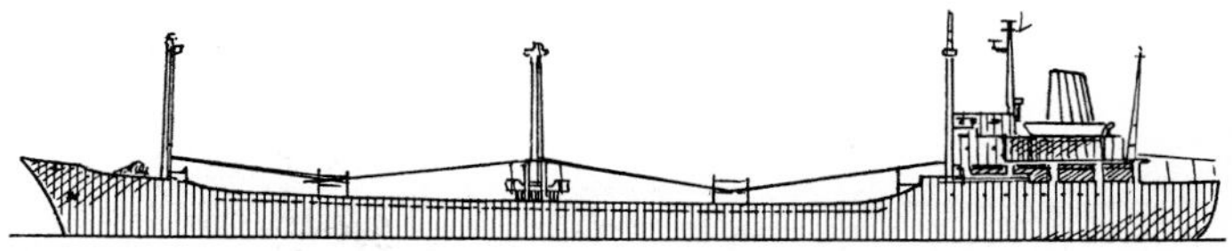

207 *M²HMFN H13*
CHANG LONG RC/Ja (Shinhama) 1975; C; 3,632 grt/6,099 dwt; 106.46 × 6.6 m *(349.28 × 21.65 ft)*; M (Mitsubishi); 12.5 kts; ex-*Musashi*

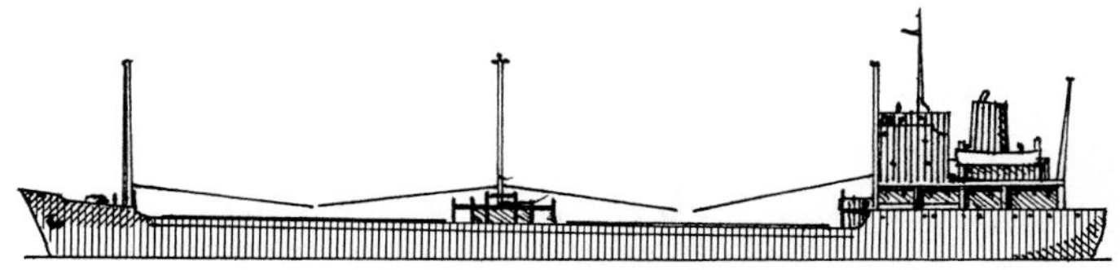

208 *M²HMFN H13*
FU DA RC/Ja (Geibi) 1975; C; 4,359 grt/7,164 dwt; 107.85 × 6.75 m *(353.84 × 22.15 ft)*; M (Hanshin); 13 kts; ex-*Bela Kosmo*
Possible sisters: **GREAT CHINA NO 1** (Pa) ex-*Andhika Adiraja*; **MARTASATU** (Ia) ex-*Adhiguna Dharma*

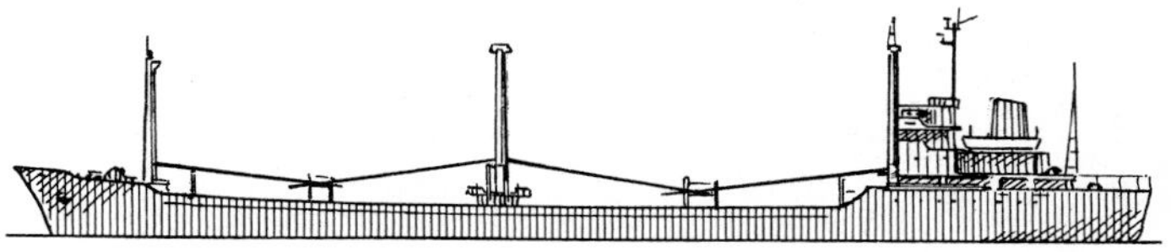

209 *M²HMFN H13*
HAI LIH Pa/Ja (Shinhama) 1974; C; 3,526 grt/6,074 dwt; 106.28 × 6.58 m *(348.69 × 21.59 ft)*; M (Hanshin); 13 kts; ex-*Wooster King*

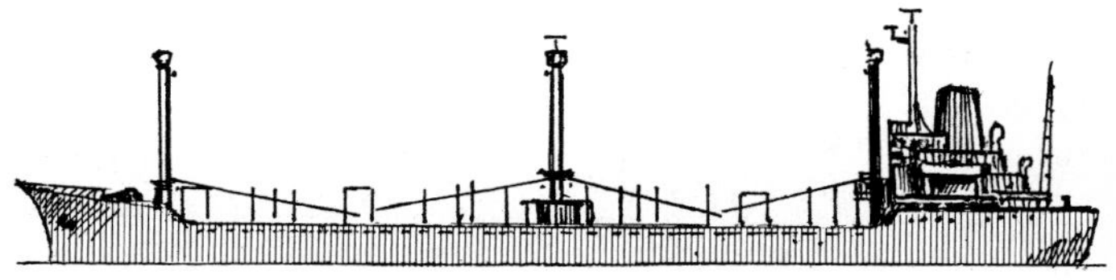

210 *M²HMFN H13*
HONG CHANG Pa/Ja (Imabari) 1971; C; 5,905 grt/9,948 dwt; 124.31 × 7.52 m *(407.84 × 24.67 ft)*; M (Mitsubishi); 11.5 kts; ex-*Hosho Maru*
Similar: **INCE 1** (Tu) ex-*Seiwa Maru*
Probably similar: **FAKREDINE** (Le) ex-*Higashikawa Maru*; **SOUTHERN TRADER** (Pa) ex-*Kyowa Maru No 8*

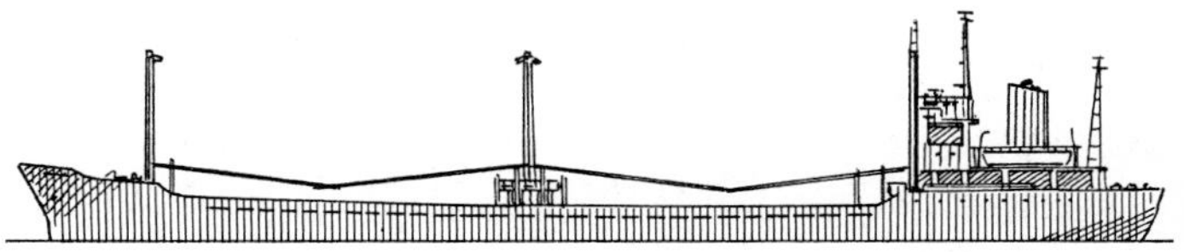

211 *M²HMFN H13*
JIN GANG LIN RC/Ja (Kurinoura) 1974; C; 4,214 grt/7,346 dwt; 109.05 × 7.01 m *(357.78 × 23 ft)*; M (Makita); 14.5 kts; ex-*Gulf President*
Probable sisters: **NAN GUAN LING** (RC) ex-*Gulf King*; **DRACO NO 1** (Pa) ex-*Tres Mar*; **SOUTHERN PEARL** (Pa) ex-*Garza Ocean*; **RIMBA EMPAT** (Ia) ex-*May Breeze*; **BANGBUA** (Th) ex-*Sun Salvia*; **GEMINI BURI** (SV) ex-*Ocean Star No 1*; **KIAN ANN** (Sg) ex-*Sanyo Maru*

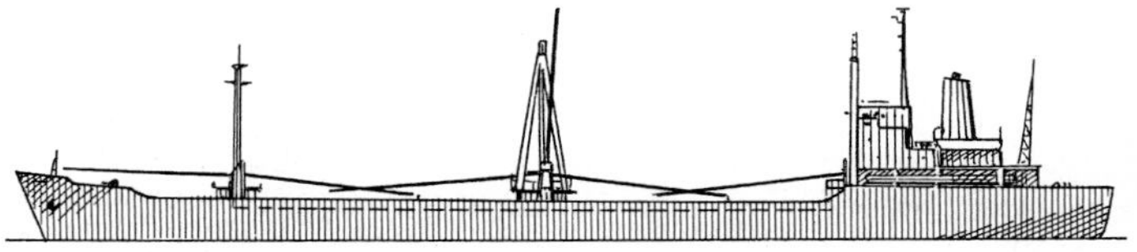

212 *M²HMFN H13*
KEE ANN Sg/Ja (Kanasashi) 1970; C/HL; 5,680 grt/9,201 dwt; 122.05 × 7.7 m *(400.43 × 25.26 ft)*; M (Pielstick); 13.5 kts; ex-*Kamo Maru*
Possible sister: **HOE ANN** (Sg) ex-*Kitano Maru*

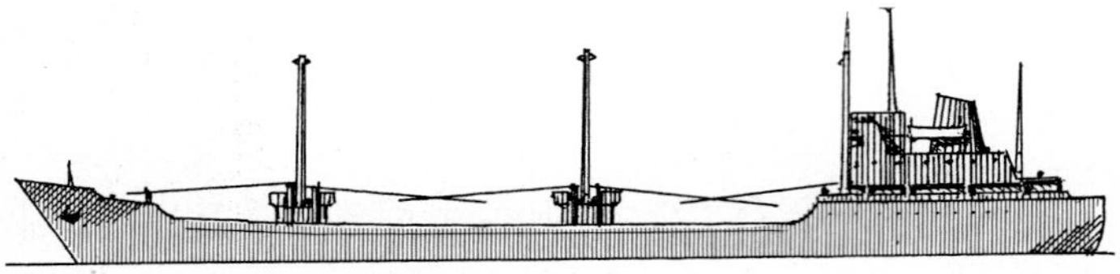

213 *M^2HMFN H13*
MERIDIAN —/Ja (Hayashikane) 1969; C; 4,864 grt/7,469 dwt; 117.53 × 6.99 m *(385.60 × 22.93 ft)*; M (Mitsubishi); 15 kts; ex-*Lung Yung*
Possible sister: **NAZLICAN** (Tu) ex-*Mui Kim*

214 *M^2HMFN H13*
SAMSUN PARTNER Ko/Ja (Hashihama) 1970; C; 3,049 grt/5,928 dwt; 101.05 × 6.61 m *(331.53 × 21.69 ft)*; M (Mitsubishi); 12.75 kts; ex-*Kobe Maru No 7*
Possible sisters: **TRIPAL** (SV) ex-*Kaisei Maru*; **MAHARDI** (Ia) Launched as *Kenyo Maru*; **SANG THAI POWER** (Th) ex-*Shinwa Maru*; **MAHALIM** (Ia) ex-*Shinyo Maru*; **TANTO RAYA** (Ia) ex-*Shunyo Maru*; **HOAM** (Ko) ex-*Horyu Maru*; **SEATRAN SILVIA** (My) ex-*Hoei Maru*; **IMA TELLINA** (Pa) ex-*Kowa Maru*; **MAHALENE** (Bl) ex-*Rokko Maru*; **SOUTHERN OPAL** (Pa) ex-*Reiyo Maru*; **TSANG JIA** (Pa) ex-*Shuho Maru*; Possibly similar: **SEA BROS** (—) ex-*Taiyo Maru*; **JAMBO** (Pa) ex-*Shuyo Maru*

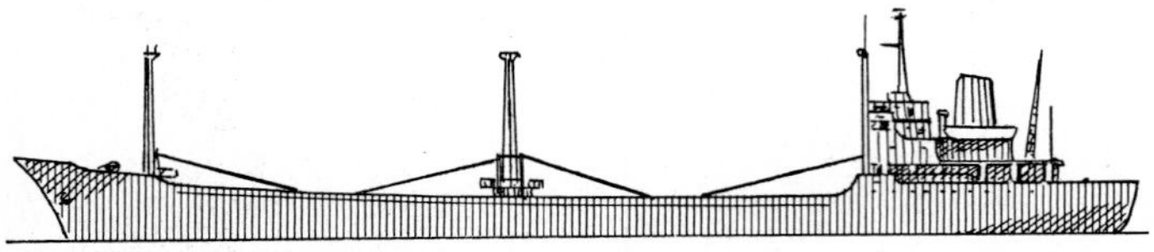

215 *M^2HMFN H13*
SANEM Tu/Ja (Hayashikane) 1970; C; 3,989 grt/6,382 dwt; 110.98 × 6.66 m *(364.11 × 21.85 ft)*; M (Mitsubishi); 15.5 kts; ex-*Sincere No 2*
Similar: **JACKSON OCEAN** (Tw) ex-*Sincere No 1*; **IRUVAI HUDHU** (Mv) ex-*Dawn Ray*

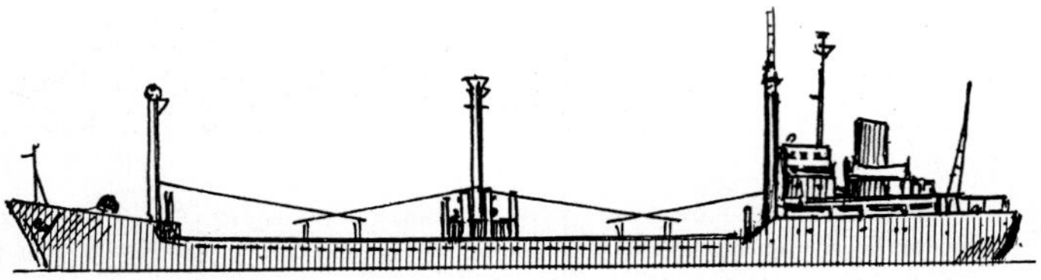

216 *M^2HMFN H13*
SIGMA RC/Ja (Hashihama) 1970; C; 3,992 grt/6,225 dwt; 110.7 × 6.66 m *(363.19 × 21.85 ft)*; M (Mitsubishi); 12 kts; ex-*Laguna*
Possibly similar: **SARUNTA 1** (Pa) ex-*Yushin Maru*; **YU NAM No 6** (Ko) ex-*Yufuku Maru*

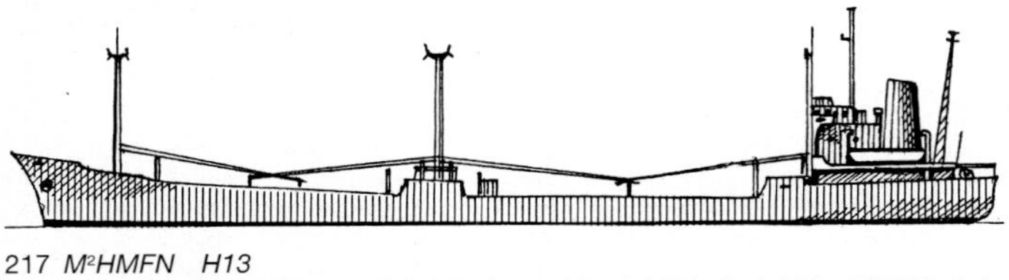

217 *M^2HMFN H13*
TAKASAGO MARU NO 12 RC/Ja (Kurushima) 1971; C; 2,988 grt/5,978 dwt; 101.12 × 6.81 m *(331.76 × 22.34 ft)*; M (Kobe); 12.5 kts
Sister: **AN LI** (RC) ex-*Eimei Maru*
Possible sisters: **MANTA RAY** (Pi) ex-*Tokei Maru No 2*; **MOGES AGATHIS** (Ia) ex-*Umiyama Maru*; **WOO YANG PRINCE** (Ko) ex-*Maya Maru*; **JIN SHAN** (RC) ex-*Masaharu Maru*; **SINGA GOLD** (—) ex-*Kuching*; **GOLDEN STAR** (Th) ex-*Geppo Maru*; **MASAGANA** (Pi) ex-*Kodai Maru*; **RUAMCHAI LOTUS** (Th) ex-*Kinriki Maru No 21*; **CAFER AHMET** (Tu) ex-*Kairyu Maru*; **SUN PRIDE** (Bl) ex-*Hoso Maru*; **PACIFIC SAKTI** (Ia) ex-*Amagi Maru*; **EAST SHING** (SV) ex-*Shinko Maru*

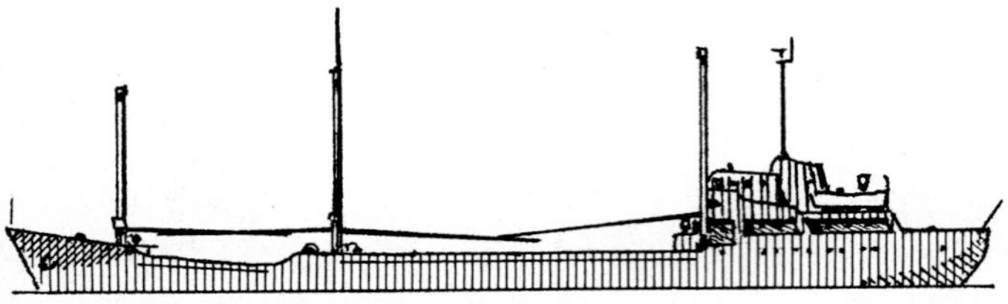

218 *M^2HM–F H123*
EOLOS SV/FRG (Abeking) 1958; C; 1,542 grt/2,450 dwt; 79.2 × 5.24 m *(259.84 × 17.19 ft)*; M (MaK); 12 kts; ex-*Inga Bastian*; Lengthened 1959

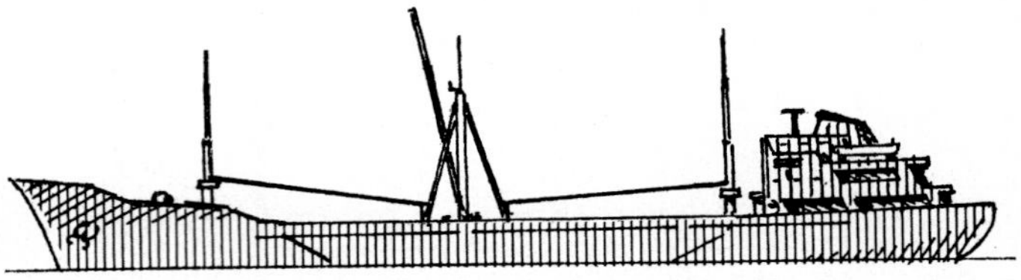

219 *M^3F H1*
CABO BOJADOR Ho/Ne ('Friesland') 1966; C/HL; 1,273 grt/1,840 dwt; 75.42 × 5.0 m *(247.44 × 16.44 ft)*; M (Werkspoor); 10 kts; ex-*Valkenburg*; Widened 1969

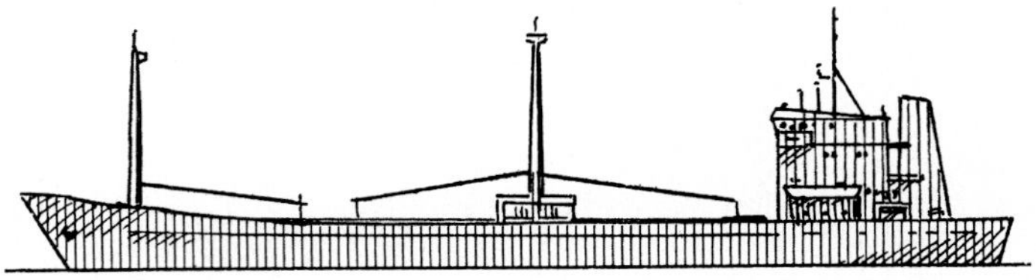

220 *M^3F H1*
DARPO SEPULUH Ia/Ne (Van Diepen) 1974; C; 890 grt/2,204 dwt; 76 × 4.45 m *(249.34 × 14.6 ft)*; M (Atlas-MaK); 11 kts; ex-*Amigo Express*
Similar (Some have radar mast at after end of superstructure): **NEW GROVE** (Cy) ex-*Kaspar Sif*; **TARUNA ABADI** (Ia) ex-*Jette Sif*; **SAND SWAN** (Cy) ex-*Ann Sandved*; **LEONIE** (Pa) ex-*Balton*; **LIBERTY STAR** (Pa) ex-*Gerda Lonborg*; **HERMANN** (Cu) ex-*Gerda Lonborg*; **SWIFT TRADER** (Br) ex-*Swift*; **PULAU KALIMANTAN** (Ia) ex-*Erik Sif*; **PINECONE** (Cy) ex-*Grete Sif*; **MERATUS PRIMA** (Ia) ex-*Pia Sandved*; **FREEDOM STAR** (Pa) ex-*Lotte Scheel*
Possible sisters (may have lower superstructure): **PIA DANIELSEN** (Cy) ex-*Anny Danielsen*; **ULLA DANIELSEN** (Cy) ex-*Dien Danielsen*

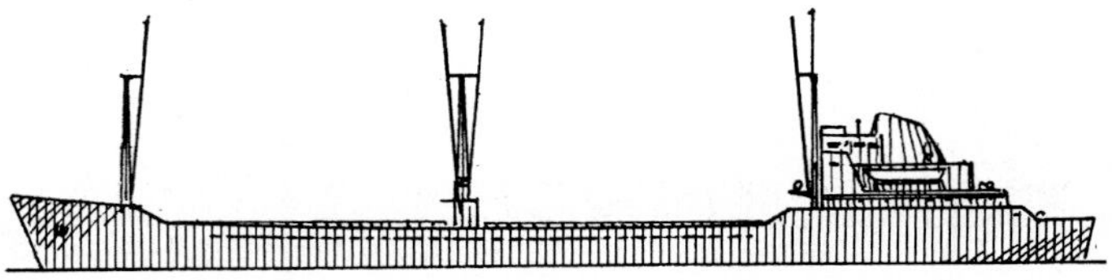

221 *M^3F H1*
ELPIDA SV/Br (Cochrane) 1970; C; 1,769 grt/2,982 dwt; 86.34 × 5.03 m *(283.27 × 16.5 ft)*; M (Ruston); 12 kts; ex-*Solentbrook*
Sisters: **MANDARIN** (—) ex-*Somersetbrook*; **SERENADE** (SV) ex-*Surreybrook*; **GOLD STAR I** (SV) ex-*Sussexbrook*

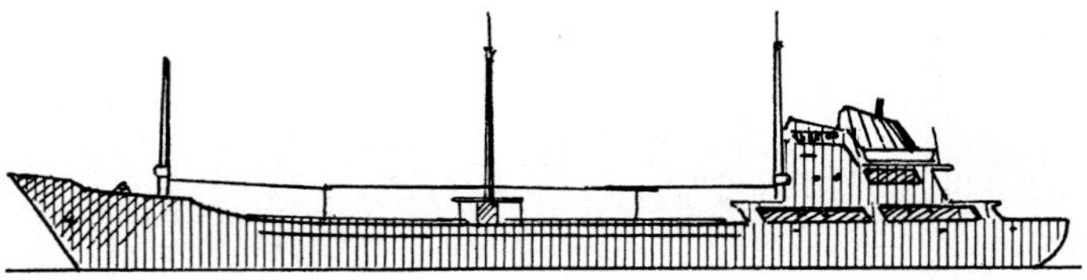

222 *M^3F H1*
JARASH Eg/Ne (Kramer & Booy) 1966; C; 1,450 grt/1,968 dwt; 75.14 × 4.50 m *(246.52 × 14.76 ft)*; M (Deutz); 13 kts; ex-*Andromeda*
Similar: **NOVA 1** (SV) ex-*Brandaris*

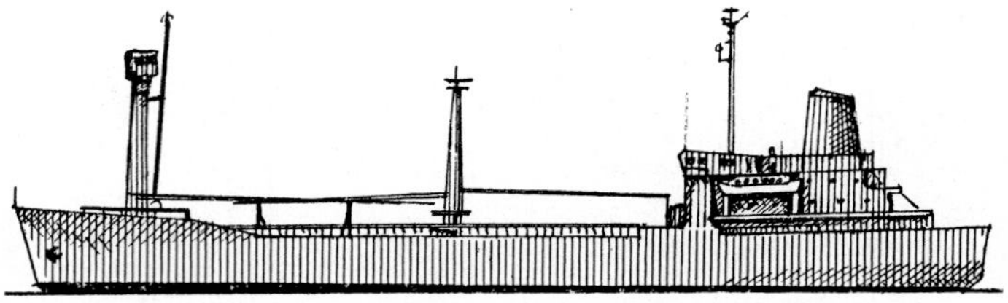

223 *M^3F H1*
KISTA ARCTICA DIS/Fi (Nystads) 1973; C; 4,209 grt/4,990 dwt; 93.93 × 7.36 m *(308.16 × 24.14 ft)*; M (Pielstick); 14.5 kts; ex-*Gronland*; Side doors

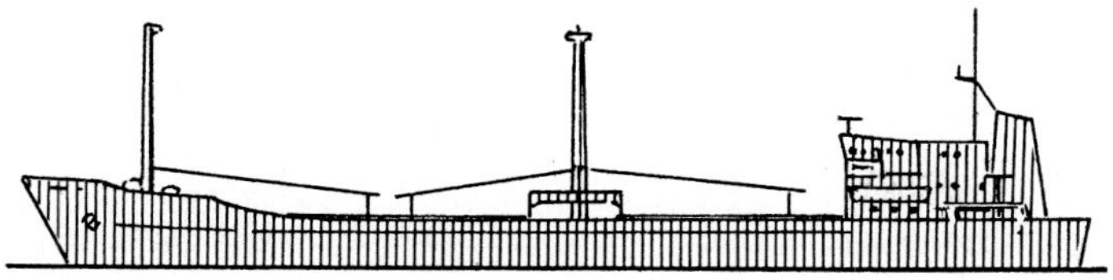

224 M^3F *H1*
MAYLIN Cy/Ne (E J Smit) 1977; C; 1,140 grt/2,585 dwt; 79.18 × 5.17 m *(259.78 × 16.96 ft)*; M (MaK); 12.25 kts; ex-*Mariane Danielsen*
Sisters: **GOLDEN BANNER** (Pa) launched as *Inge Danielsen*; **RIKA** (Pa) ex-*Ketty Danielsen*; **LOKA** (Pa) launched as *Otto Danielsen*; **MARCO DANIELSEN** (Cy) ex-*Winni Helleskov*
Possible sisters (may have taller superstructure): **PIA DANIELSEN** (Cy) ex-*Anny Danielsen*; **ULLA DANIELSEN** (Cy) ex-*Dien Danielsen*

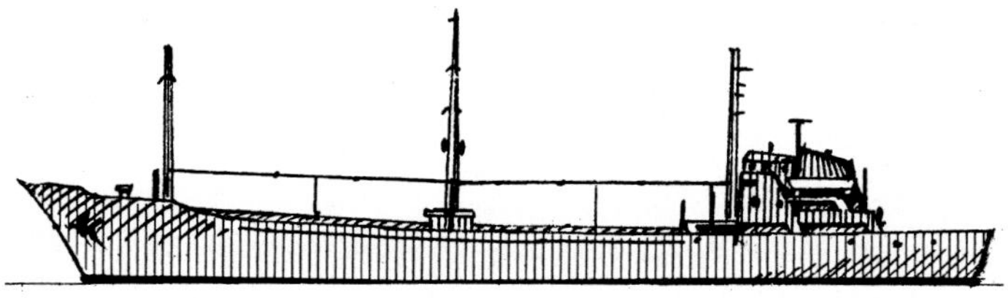

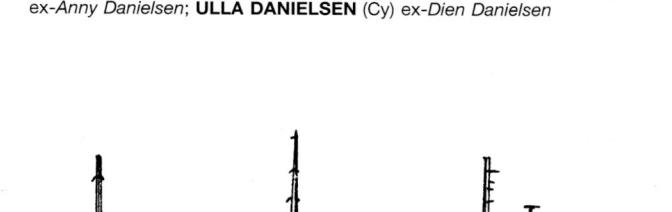

225 M^3F *H1*
PREVEZE Tu/Tu (Denizcilik) 1973; C; 1,431 grt/2,658 dwt; 80.02 × 5.51 m *(262.53 × 18.08 ft)*; M (Atlas-MaK); 10.5 kts
Sister: **FIGEN AKAT** (Tu) ex-*Nigbolu*
Probable sisters: **AGRI** (Tu); **ANTAKYA** (Tu); **ARTVIN** (Tu); **CALDIRAN** (Tu); **MOHAC** (Tu)

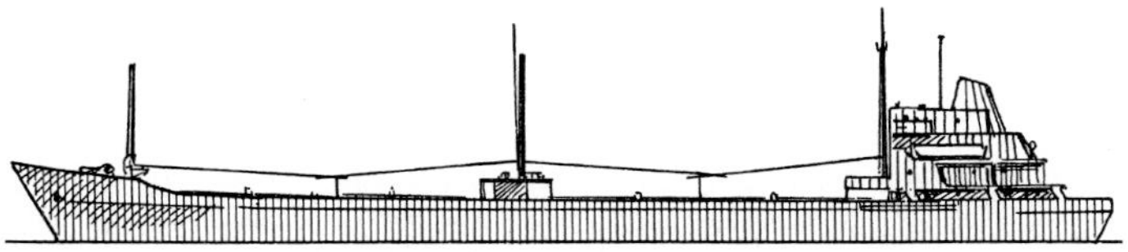

226 M^3F *H1*
QU JIANG RC/FRG (Meyer) 1970; C; 3,258 grt/5,085 dwt; 103.38 × 6.37 m *(339.17 × 20.89 ft)*; M (KHD); 15.5 kts; Launched as *Peter Wehr*

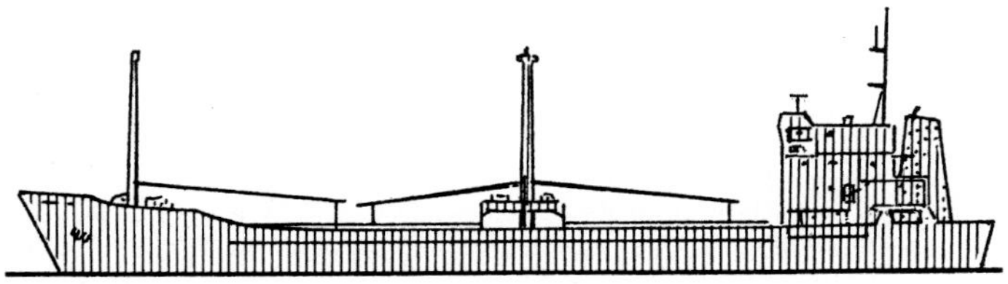

227 M^3F *H1*
REIFENS Cy/Ne (Van Diepen) 1979; C; 1,282 grt/2,578 dwt; 79.81 × 5.3 m *(261.84 × 17.39 ft)*; M (MaK); 12.25 kts; ex-*Amigo Defender*
Sisters: **HERO A** (Cy) ex-*Amigo Express*; **OTTO DANIELSEN** (Cy) ex-*Amigo Fortuna*; Probably similar (original sister probably converted to livestock carrier): **DUNA** (Cy) ex-*Marie Helleskov*

228 M^3F *H12*
ALDEBARAN Ho/Br (Grangemouth) 1957; C; 1,542 grt/1,893 dwt; 73.44 × 4.79 m *(290.94 × 19.72 ft)*; M (Newbury); — kts; ex-*Alfred Everard*
Similar: **EMMA** (Ma) ex-*Serenity*; **KALKAVANLAR** (Tu) ex-*Singularity*

229 M^3F *H123*
FANAM Mv/Ne (Amels) 1961; C; 1,354 grt/2,240 dwt; 81.79 × 4.31 m *(268.34 × 14.14 ft)*; M ('De Industrie'); 13 kts; ex-*Nassauborg*; Lengthened 1969
Sisters: **LAURA** (Cy) ex-*Prinsenborg*

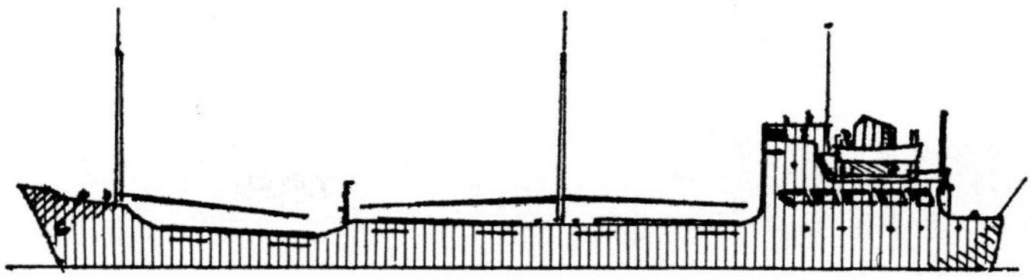

230 M^3F *H123*
NOURA 1 Le/Br (Lamont) 1960; C; 1,323 grt/1,580 dwt; 70.03 × 4.59 m *(229.76 × 15.06 ft)*; M (Mirrlees); 11 kts; ex-*Laksa*

231 M^3F *H13*
ARION Ho/FRG (H Peters) 1964; C; 992 grt/1,875 dwt; 71.63 × 4.93 m *(235 × 16.17 ft)*; M (Deutz); 10 kts; ex-*Christian Matthiesen*

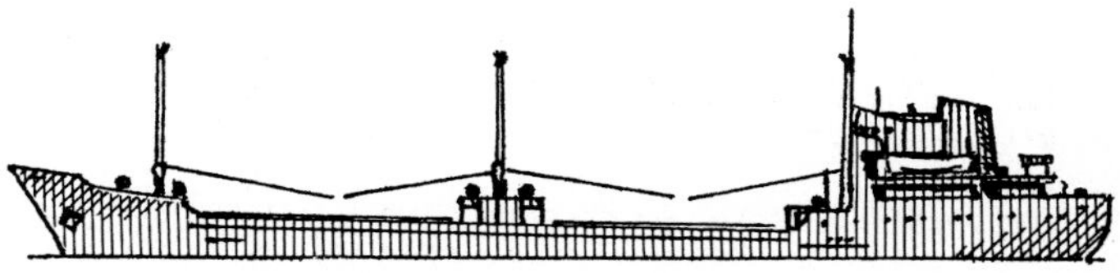

232 M^3F *H13*
ARUNTO Fa/DDR ('Neptun') 1966; C; 1,316 grt/2,439 dwt; 78.59 × 5.06 m *(257.84 × 16.6 ft)*; M (MaK); 11.5 kts; ex-*Brunto*
Similar: **NEDAL** (Sy) ex-*Brunette*; **RAFIK J** (Sy) ex-*Recto*; **SALEM** (Sy) ex-*Hanseatic*; **WARBURG II** (At) ex-*Brunita*; **ALEX** (Ho) ex-*Jobella*; **NABIL M** (Sy) ex-*Jocefa*; **PALMAVERA** (It) ex-*Stokktind* (longer, 84m (276ft), and may have a deck crane); **MAYA** (It) ex-*Hanseat*; **SAPPHIRE** (Ma) ex-*Fro*; **RAMITA** (Sy) ex-*Hansa*; **K GEORGIOS** (Ho) ex-*Gol*

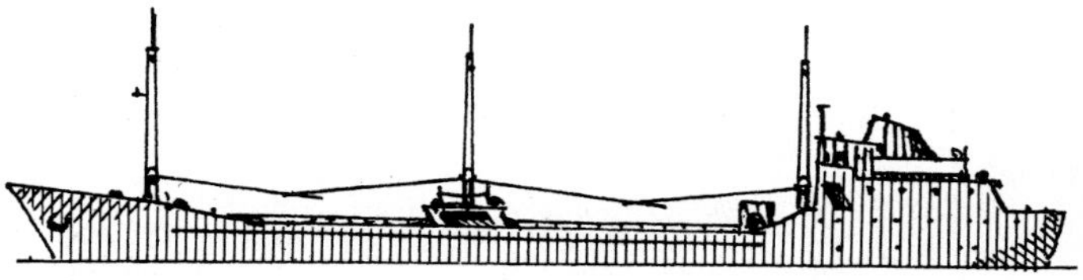

233 M^3F *H13*
ASSEM Ho/DDR ('Neptun') 1964; C; 1,130 grt/1,943 dwt; 75.24 × 5.19 m *(246.85 × 17.03 ft)*; M (KHD); 11.5 kts; ex-*Bari IV*
Sister: **TALAAT** (Eg) ex-*Bari II*

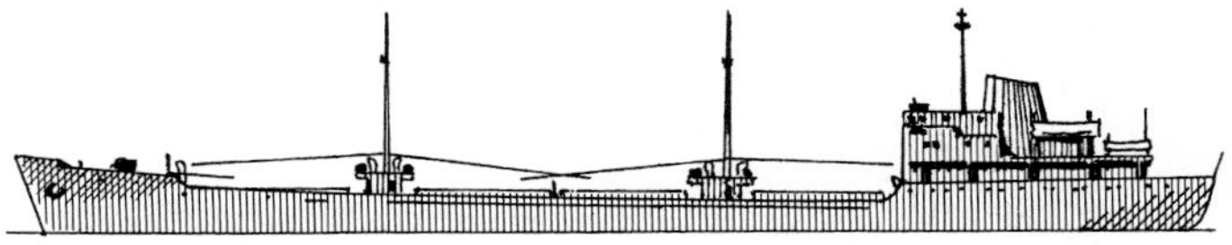

234 M^3F *H13*
CATHERINE DESGAGNES Ca/Br (Hall, Russell) 1962; C; 5,675 grt/8,395 dwt; 125.05 × 7.58 m *(410.27 × 24.87 ft)*; M (Sulzer); 13.5 kts; ex-*Gosforth*

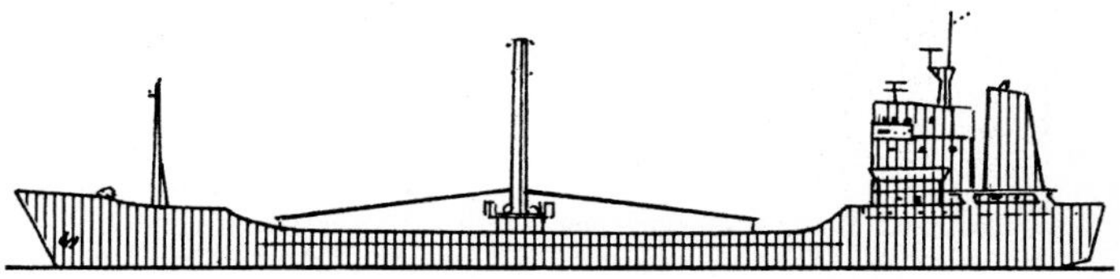

235 M^3F *H13*
CHAHAYA SEJATI Pa/Ne (Sander) 1976; C; 1,532 grt/3,067 dwt; 83.52 × 5.19 m *(274 × 17.03 ft)*; M (MaK); 12.5 kts; ex-*Gallic Wave*

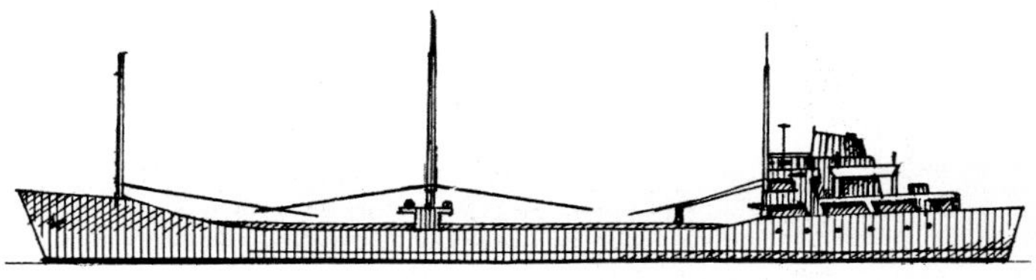

236 M^3F *H13*
DANAH I Pa/Br (Goole) 1967; C; 1,597 grt/3,130 dwt; 92 × 5.2 m *(301.84 × 17.06 ft)*; M (Mirrlees); 11.5 kts; ex-*Somersbydyke*

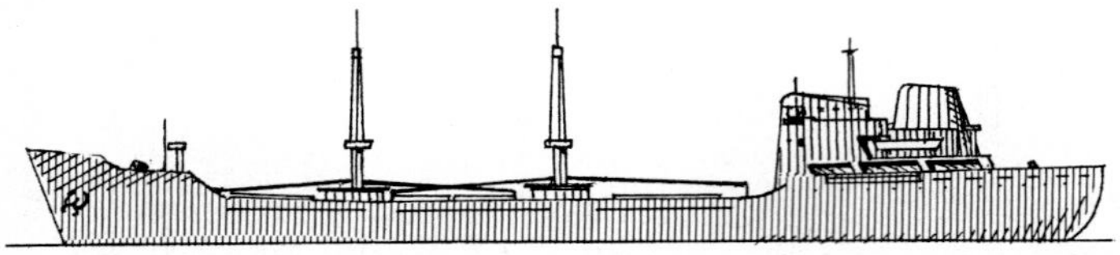

237 M^3F *H13*
FAIR RAINBOW Pa/Ne ('De Hoop') 1962; C; 3,963 grt/5,410 dwt; 109.43 × 4.71 m *(359.02 × 15.45 ft)*; M (MAN); 15 kts; ex-*Sifnos*

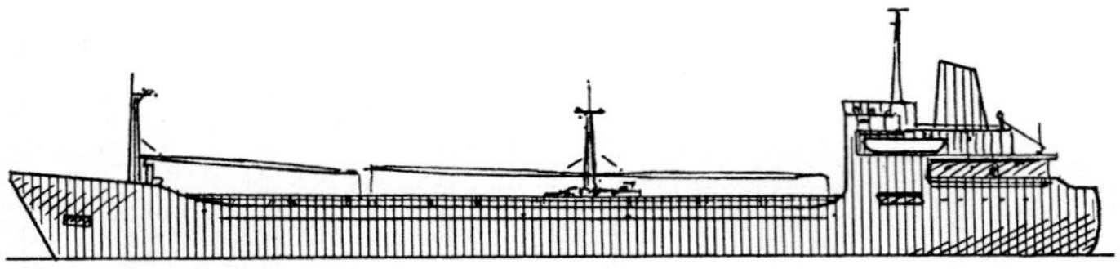

238 M^3F *H13*
LUO JIANG RC/FRG (Sietas) 1970; C; 999 grt/2,393 dwt; 87.61 × 5.29 m *(287.43 × 17.35 ft)*; M (KHD); 14 kts; Launched as *Svealand*; 123 TEU

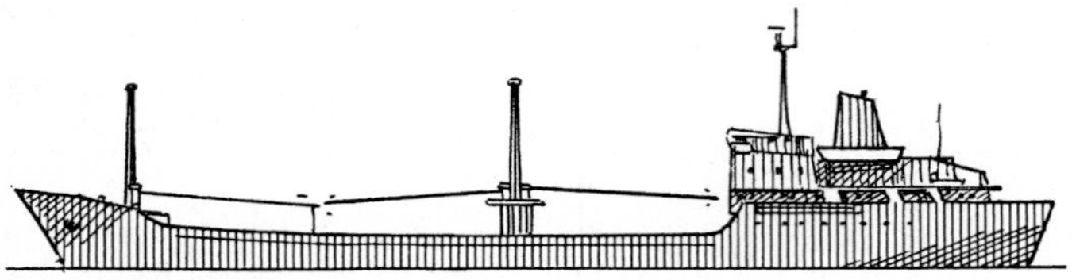

239 M^3F *H13*
SUNSEA SV/Rm (Turnu-Severin) 1974; C; 2,136 grt/2,180 dwt; 88.75 × 5.2 m *(291.17 × 17.06 ft)*; M (Sulzer); 13 kts; ex-*Anton Gubaryev*
Sisters: **SUNWAVE** (SV) ex-*Dzhems Bankovich*; **GRISHA PODOBEDOV** (Ru); **SVENTOJI** (Lt) ex-*Khendrik Kuyvas*; **LIDA DEMESH** (Ru); **SUNSTAR** (SV) ex-*Maldis Skreya*; **NIDA** (Lt) ex-*Marat Kozlov*; **NADE RIBAKOVAYTE** (Ru); **NYURA KIZHEVATOVA** (Uk); **PETYA KOVALYENKO** (Uk); **PETYA SHITIKOV** (Uk); **SUNCITY** (SV) ex-*Richardas Bukauskas*; **TANYA KARPINSKAYA** (Uk); **SUNMAR** (SV) ex-*Valya Kurakina*; **RUSNE** (Lt) ex-*Vanya Kovalyev*; **YASHA GORDIYENKO** (Uk); **SUNSET** (SV) ex-*Vasya Stabrovskiy*; **VASYA KURKA** (Ru); **VITYA NOVITSKIY** (Uk); **KIBU** (Ma) ex-*Yunyy Partizan*

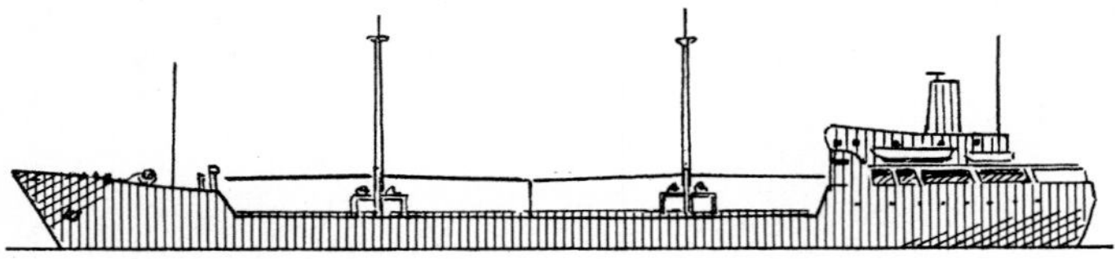

240 M^3FM *H13*
MAYSSAA I Sy/Ne (Van Diepen) 1971; C; 1,585 grt/2,870 dwt; 87.61 × 5.37 m *(287.43 × 17.62 ft)*; M (Atlas-MaK); 12 kts; ex-*Troup Head*
Sister: **PEGY** (Cy) ex-*Tod Head*

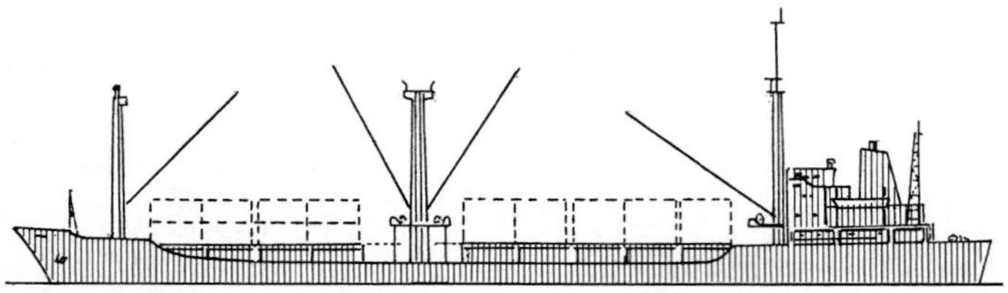

241 M^3FM *H13*
MITRANS EXPRESS Pa/Ja (Kagoshima) 1978; C/Con; 5,548 grt/8,056 dwt; 116.97 × 7.29 m *(384 × 23.92 ft)*; M (Mitsubishi); 15 kts; ex-*Leo Tornado*; 325 TEU

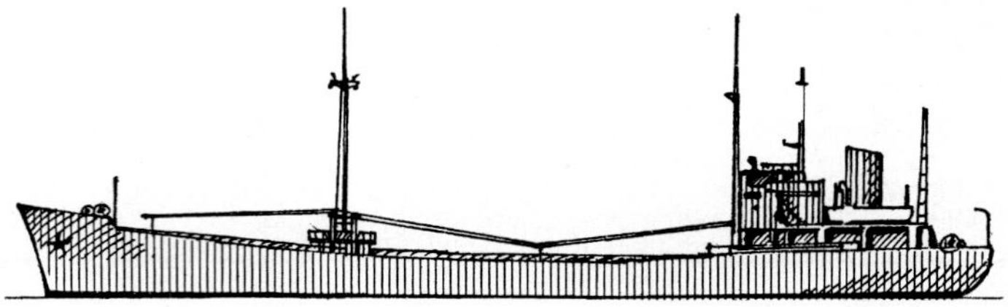

242 M^3FM *H13*
SEVEN LOG MASTER Pi/Ja (Ujina) 1969; C; 2,067 grt/3,444 dwt; 89.62 × 5.72 m *(294 × 18.77 ft)*; M (Nippon Hatsudoki); 12.25 kts; ex-*Shinkyo Maru*
Probable sister: **WILCON II** (Pi) ex-*Kyoluku Maru*

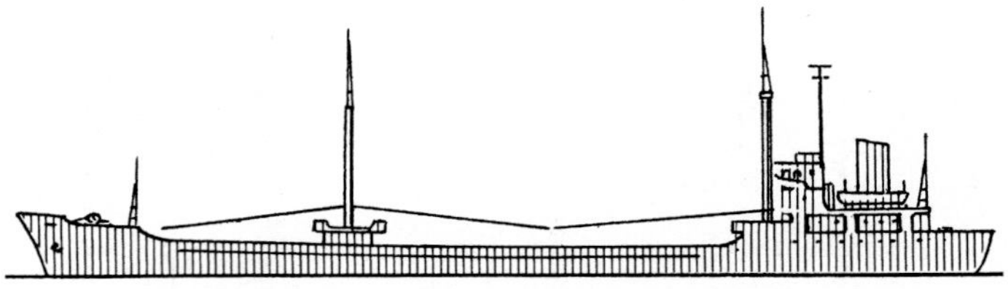

243 M^3FM *H13*
SOO GEUN HO RK/Ja (Shin Naniwa) 1970; C; 1,990 grt/3,407 dwt; 88.02 × 5.59 m *(289 × 18.34 ft)*; M (Akasaka); 13 kts; ex-*Yamafuji Maru*

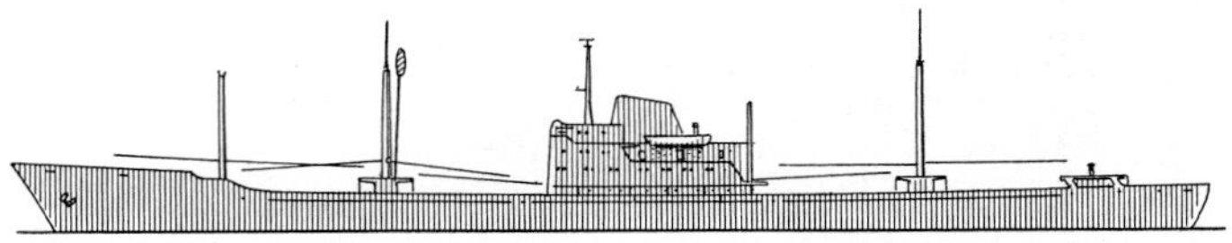

244 M^3FM^2 *H1*
CHAO YANG RC/RC (Jiangnan) 1968; C; 10,142 grt/14,325 dwt; 161.5 × 9.5 m *(530 × 31.17 ft)*; M (Sulzer); 15.5 kts
Sister: **XIANG YANG** (RC) ex-*Gao Yang*

245 M^3FM^2 *H13*
HUANG JIN SHAN RC/FRG (Bremer V) 1961; C; 7,957 grt/11,132 dwt; 144 × 8.5 m *(473 × 28 ft)*; M (MAN); 14 kts; ex-*Beer Sheva*

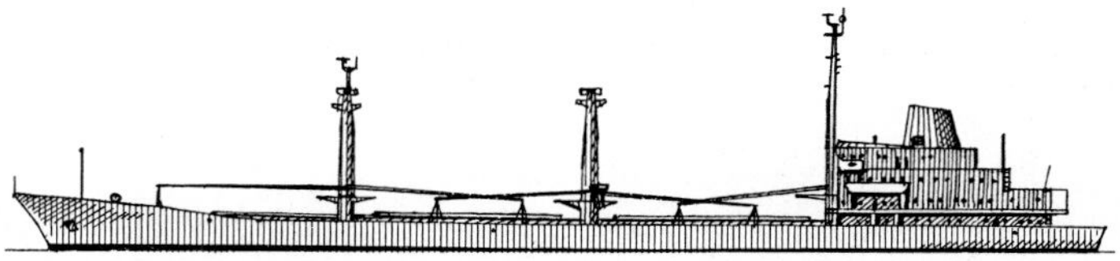

246 M^3FN *H1*
SU XIN SV/FRG (Nobiskrug) 1972; C; 5,213 grt/7,450 dwt; 125 × 7.64 m *(410.1 × 25.07 ft)*; M (MAN); 17 kts; ex-*Emma Jebsen*
Sister: **TANTO PERMAI II** (Ia) ex-*Heinrich Jessen*

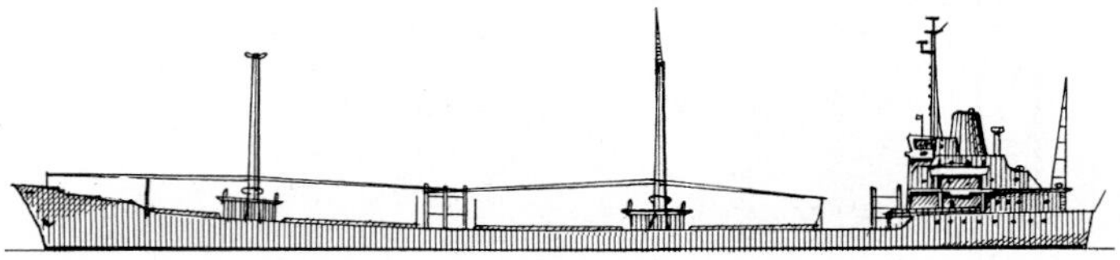

247 M^3FN *H13*
PANAGIA TINOU Ma/Ja (Mitsubishi HI) 1971; C; 8,208 grt/13,769 dwt; 141.28 × 8.81 m *(464 × 29 ft)*; M (Kobe); 14.5 kts; ex-*Kyosei Maru*

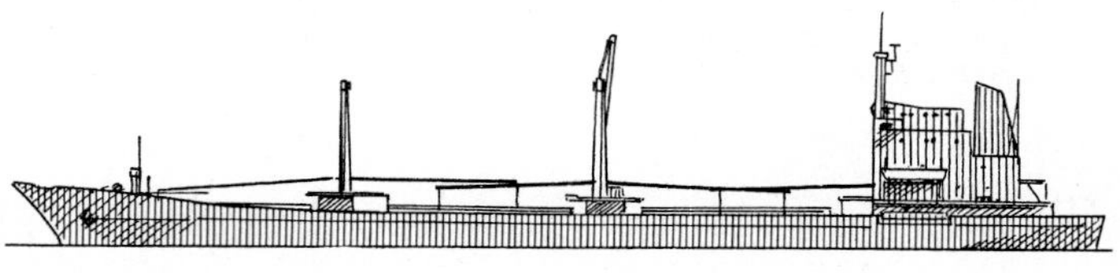

248 M^3HFM *H1*
EZZ-ELDIN REFAAT Eg/FRG (O&K) 1978; C; 5,091 grt/7,402 dwt; 116.64 × 7.52 m *(382.68 × 24.67 ft)*; M (Atlas-MaK); 15.25 kts; ex-*Flensau*; 249 TEU
Sister: **IBN SINA** (Eg) ex-*Krusau*

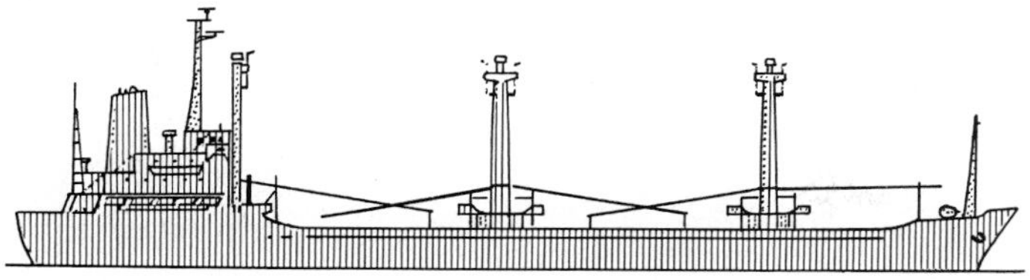

249 *M^3HMFN H13*
ANGLO-ALLIANCE Pa/Ja (Honda) 1982; C; 5,801 grt/9,588 dwt; 118.57 × 7.52 m *(389.01 × 24.67 ft)*; M (Mitsubishi); 13 kts; ex-*Boe Sound*
Possible sister: **LONG AN** (Pa) ex-*Golden Mermaid*

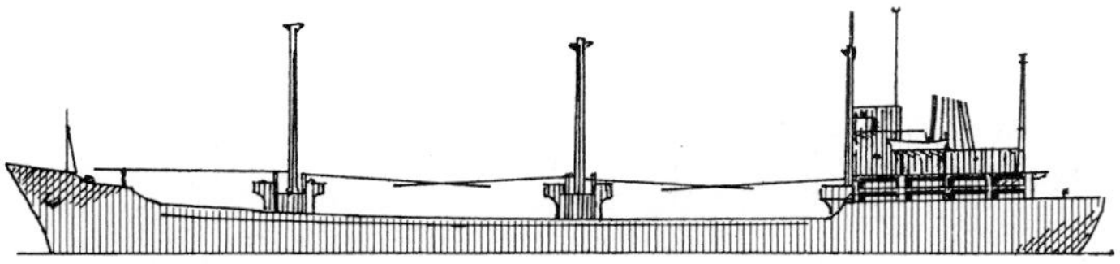

250 *M^3HMFN H13*
RAINBOW SPLENDOUR Pa/Ja (Shimoda) 1976; C; 5,815 grt/8,940 dwt; 116.06 × 7.62 m *(380.77 × 24.99 ft)*; M (Ito Tekkosho); 12.5 kts; ex-*Happusan Maru*

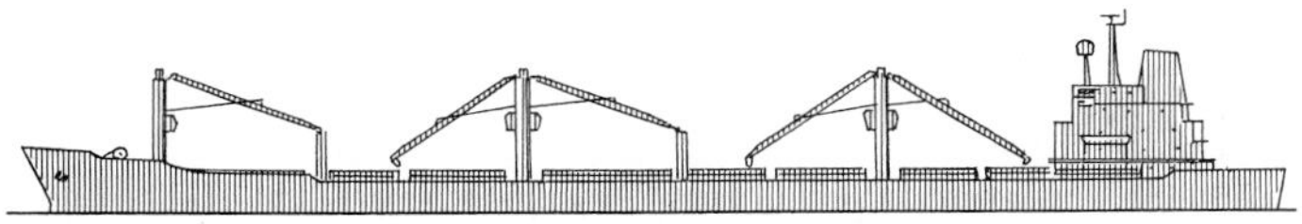

251 *M^4F H1*
ARABELLA Gr/Ja (IHI) 1983; C/Con; 14,160 grt/23,440 dwt; 164.34 × 10.10 m *(539.17 × 33.14 ft)*; M (Pielstick); 14.5 kts; 'Friendship' type; 707 TEU
Sisters: **CLIPPER AMARYLLIS** (Gr) ex-*Amaryllis*; **AGAMEMNON** (Gr); **DEVON** (Gr) ex-*Pilos*; **DOVER** (Gr) ex-*Poros*; Similar (no satcom aerial): **SAKURA** (Bs) ex-*Dimitris E*; **ALPHA BRAVERY** (Gr) ex-*Anangel Leader*; **ALPHA JUPITER** (Gr); **ARISTOTELIS** (Gr)

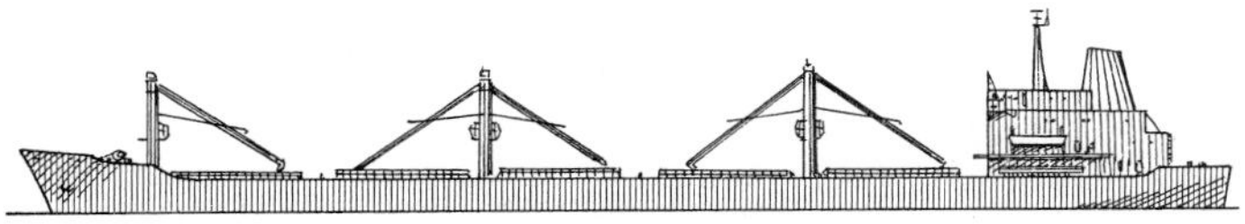

252 *M^4F H1*
'FREEDOM' MARK II type —/Ja (IHI) 1977 onwards; C; approx 10,300 grt/approx 17,000 dwt; 145.5 × 9.45 m *(478 × 31 ft)*; M (Pielstick); 13.5 kts; Also licensed to be built in Brazil; 367 TEU
Sisters: **ANANGEL ARES** (Gr) launched as *Al Ahad*; **ROTHNIE** (Br) ex-*Antiopi*; **ALAM TENTERAM** (My) ex-*Altis*; **ANTHOS** (Bs); **ALAM TELADAN** (My) ex-*Athlon*; **AVLIS** (Gr); **ALKMINI** (Gr); **IKAN TANDA** (Sg) ex-*Amazon*; **ALAM TEGUH** (My) ex-*Aran*; **EFDIM HOPE** (Gr); **EFDIM JUNIOR** (Gr) ex-*Al Awal*; **GHIKAS** (Gr); **CLIPPER MAJESTIC** (Bs) ex-*Milos Island*; **ALAM TEGAS** (My) ex-*Nemea*; **PELLA** (Gr); **ANANGEL SKY** (Gr) ex-*Anangel Sky*; **ANANGEL VICTORY** (Gr) ex-*Anangel Victory*; **PACIFIC TRADER** (Gr) ex-*Anangel Apollo*; **IKAN TAMBAN** (Sg) ex-*Amarantos*; **NARRATOR** (Cy) ex-*Naxos Island*; **PROMOTER** (Cy) ex-*Poros Island*; **ANANGEL PRUDENCE** (Gr) ex-*Alpha Challenge*; **ANANGEL ATLAS** (Gr); **CLIPPER ALPHA** (Bs) ex-*Yorktown*; Similar (improved version with satellite aerial from radar mast, small upright at after end of superstructure, and so on): **CLIPPER ARITA** (Bs) ex-*Arita*; **CLIPPER MANDARIN** (Bs) ex-*Sifnos Island*; **ANANGEL PRUDENCE** (Gr) ex-*Alpha Challenge*; **MAGIC** (Cy) ex-*Andros Island*; **ALAM TALANG** (My) ex-*Alkimos* (may not have satcom aerial); **ALAM TENGGIRI** (My) ex-*Aramis* (may not have satcom aerial); **AN BAO JIANG** (RC) ex-*Ruby Ocean*; **AN HUA JIANG** (RC) ex-*Ruby Sea*

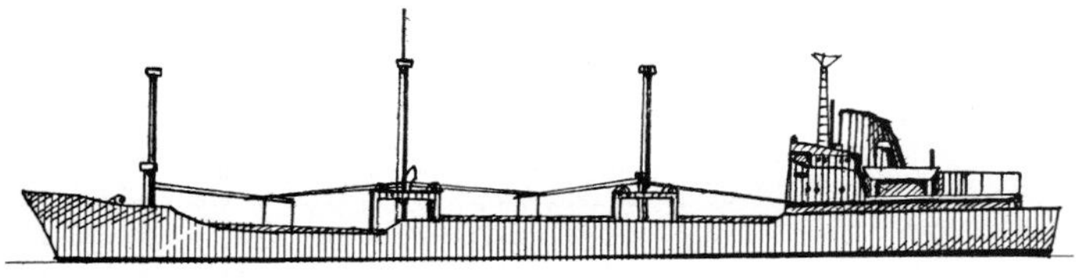

253 *M^4F H123*
MONTONE It/FRG (Nobiskrug) 1963; C; 3,021 grt/4,380 dwt; 105.92 × 6 m *(347.51 × 19.69 ft)*; M (MAN); 14.5 kts; ex-*Jobst Oldendorff*
Sister: **RIMA G** (Le) ex-*Erna Oldendorff*

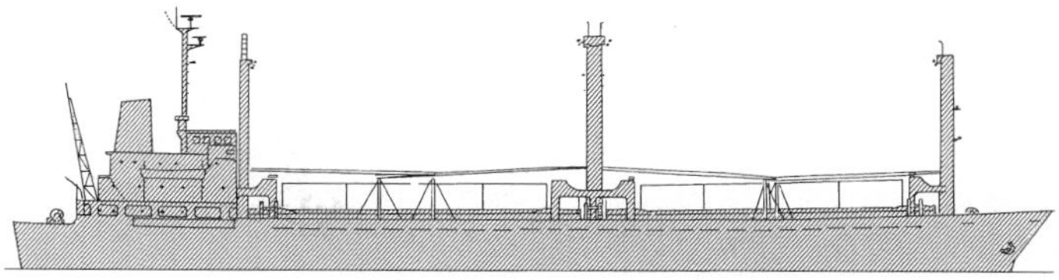

254 *M^4FM H*
KUEI WEI Pa/Ja (Kegoya) 1984; C/Con; 4,619 grt/5,968 dwt; 98.25 × 6.57 m *(322.34 × 21.56 ft)*; M (Akasaka); 11.25 kts; ex-*Ocean Fairy*; 148 TEU

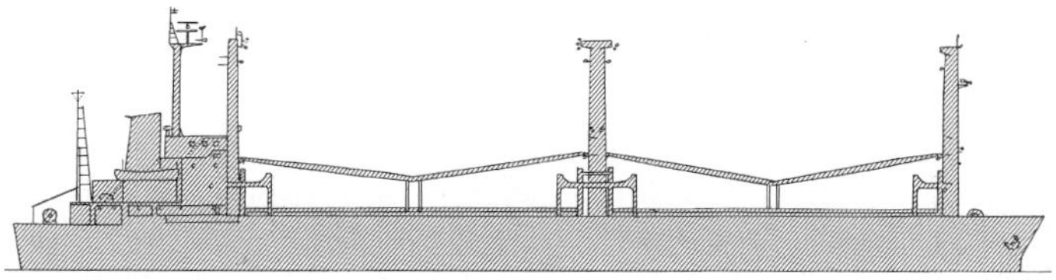

255 *M^4FM H*
SIRIUS Bs/Ko (Dong Hae) 1986; C; 5,561 grt/6,700 dwt; 107.70 × 7.00 m *(353.35 × 22.97 ft)*; M (B&W); 12.50 kts
Possible sister: **RIGEL** (Pa)

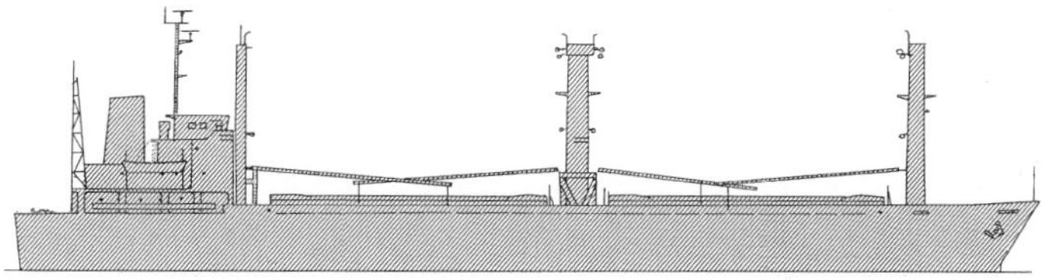

256 *M^4FM H*
TERANG Pa/Ja (Fukuoka) 1984; C/Con; 5,479 grt/6,522 dwt; 96.81 × 7.31 m *(317.62 × 23.98 ft)*; M (Mitsubishi); 12.25 kts; ex-*Ofelia*; 132 TEU
Possible sister: **JULIE PACIFIC** (Pa) ex-*Cristina C*

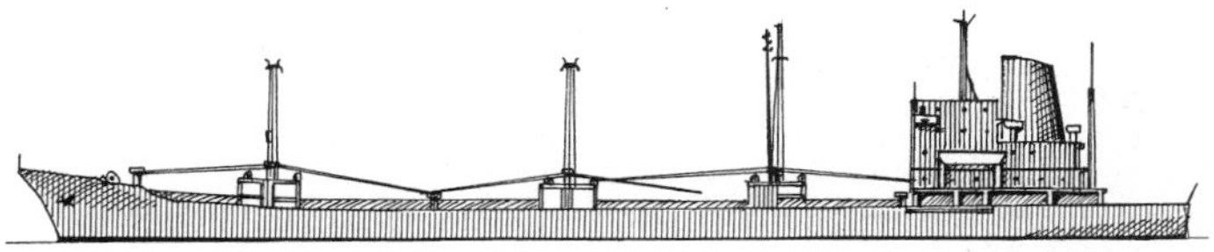

257 *M^4FM H1*
JUN LIANG CHENG RC/FRG (A G 'Weser') 1970; C; 9,966 grt/16,350 dwt; 150.15 × 9.27 m *(492.62 × 30.41 ft)*; M (MAN); 16 kts; ex-*Arabonne*; '36-L' type; 245 TEU
Sister: **ARBERIA** (Al) ex-*Arapride*
Sisters (second mast is heavier and has a heavy-lift derrick): **MANLEY FALMOUTH** (Ma) ex-*Araluck*; **MANLEY GOSPORT** (Li) ex-*Gordian*

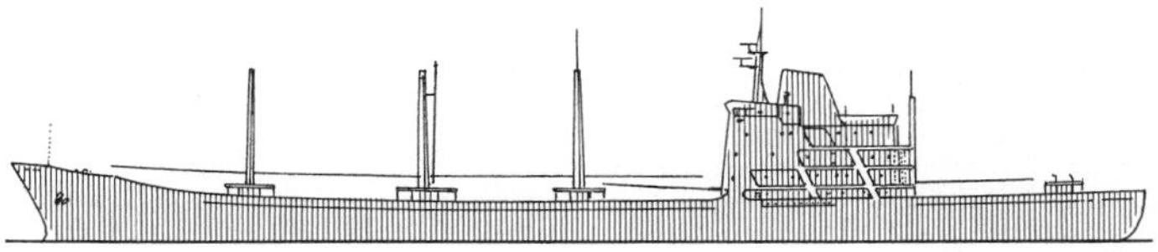

258 *M^4FM H1*
STN 1 Bl/Sp ('Bazan') 1969; C/Con; 8,484 grt/10,493 dwt; 148.57 × 8.42 m *(487 × 27.62 ft)*; M (Sulzer); 18 kts; ex-*Litija*

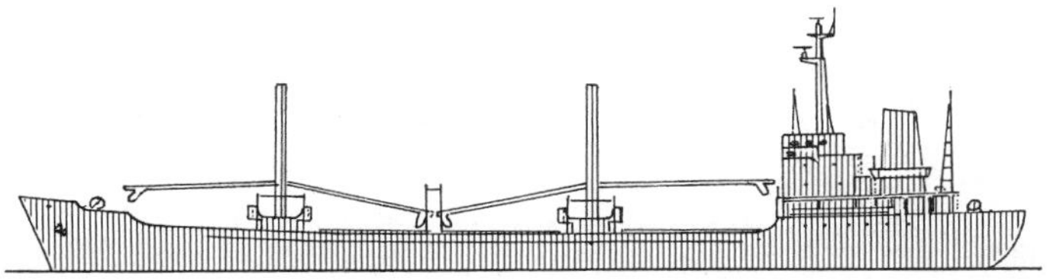

259 *M^4FM H13*
CANOPUS Ma/Ja (Mitsubishi HI) 1978; C; 5,630 grt/8,815 dwt; 119.51 × 7.3 m *(392.09 × 23.95 ft)*; M (Mitsubishi); 9.5 kts; ex-*Paradise Moon*
Sister: **NEW FORTUNE** (Pa) ex-*Eternal Moon*

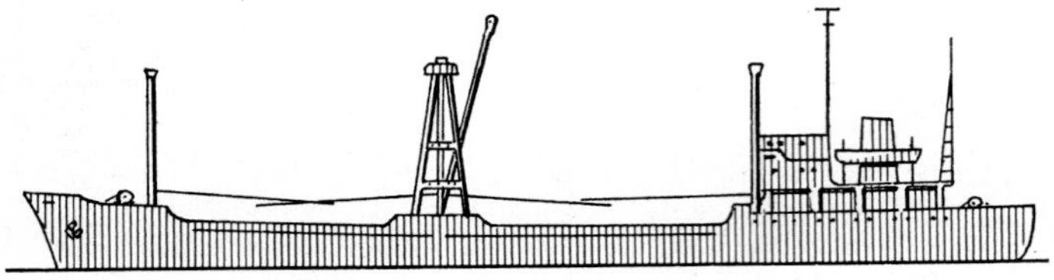

260 M^4FM *H13*
LIN HAI 16 RC/Ja (Shikoku) 1970; C/HL; 3,128 grt/5,500 dwt; 99.47 × 6.35 m *(326 × 20.83 ft)*; M (Hanshin); 12.5 kts; ex-*Don Rufino*
Sister: **LIN HAI 20** (RC) ex-*Dona Marcelina*

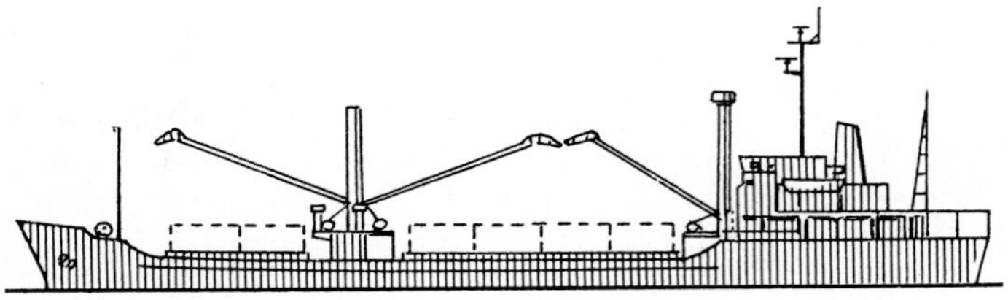

261 M^4FM *H13*
MARISCAL JOSE FELIX ESTIGARRIBIA Py/Ja (Kanrei) 1984; C/Con; 2,281 grt/2,999 dwt; 89.52 × 5.01 m *(293.7 × 16.44 ft)*; M (Daihatsu); 12.5 kts; 48 TEU
Sister: **BLAS GARAY** (Py)

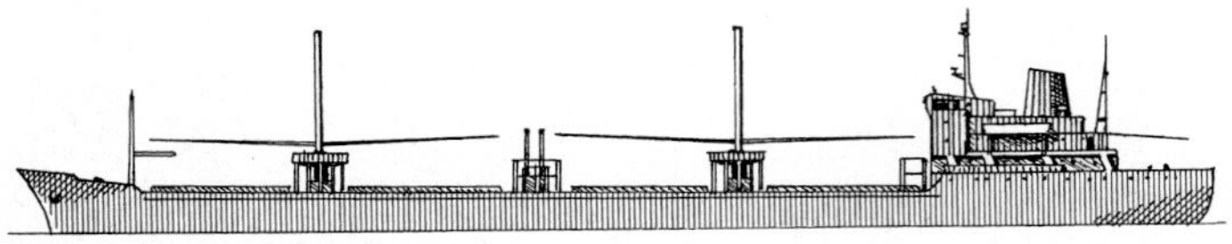

262 M^4FM *H13*
ROSANA Gr/Ja (Hitachi) 1978; B; 11,998 grt/19,509 dwt; 156.24 × 9.5 m *(512.6 × 31.17 ft)*; M (B&W); 15.5 kts
Possibly similar: **MANA** (Pa) ex-*Young Statesman*; **RUBIES** (Sg) ex-*Providence*

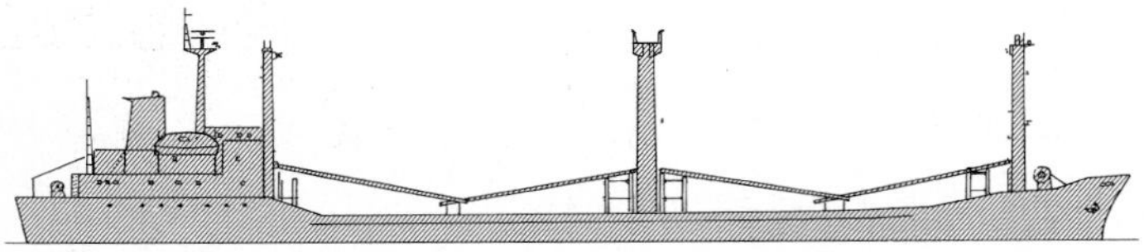

263 M^4FM *H13*
SKY MOON Pa/Ko (Dong Hae) 1988; C; 4,189 grt/6,835 dwt; 110.15 × 6.75 m *(361.38 × 22.15 ft)*; M (B&W); 14.65 kts; ex-*Dooyang Ruby*

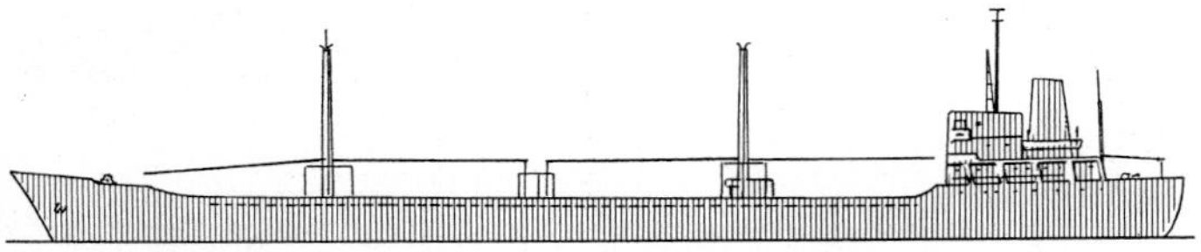

264 M^4FM *H13*
WAN DA 1 RC/Ja (Kanasashi) 1968; C; 9,815 grt/16,011 dwt; 148.04 × 8.68 m *(486 × 28.48 ft)*; M (B&W); 14 kts; ex-*Kanetoshi Maru*
Possible sister: **OLIVE** (Pa) ex-*Daikei Maru*

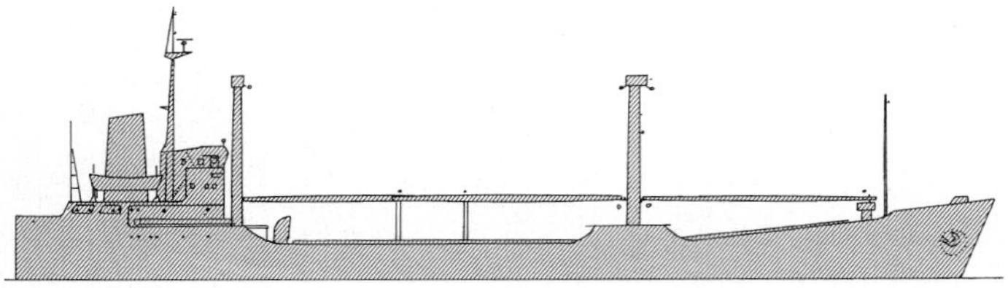

265 M^4FM *H23*
ADHIGUNA MULIAMARGA Ia/Ko (Dae Dong) 1984; C; 3,509 grt/3,675 dwt; 93.00 × 4.96 m *(305.12 × 16.27 ft)*; TSM (Niigata); 10.75 kts; Asphalt carrier
Sisters: **ADHIGUNA PURNAMAGA** (Ia); **ADHIGUNA RAYAMARGA** (Ia)

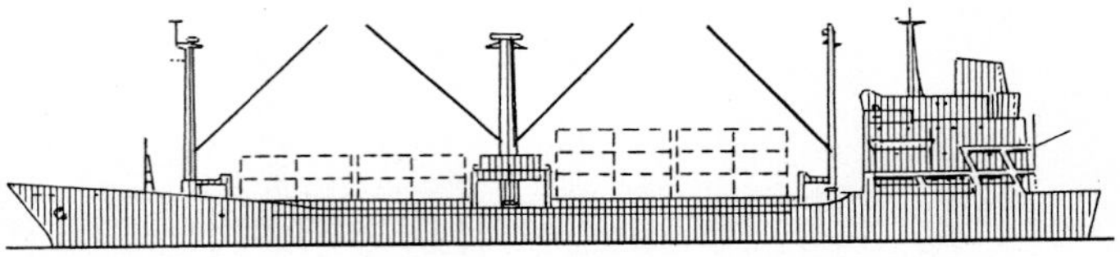

266 M^4FM *H3*
SU HE RC/Ja (Kagoshima) 1976; C/Con; 5,721 grt/7,679 dwt; 120.50 × 8.19 m *(395.34 × 26.87 ft)*; M (B&W); 14.5 kts; ex-*Seevetal*; 292 TEU

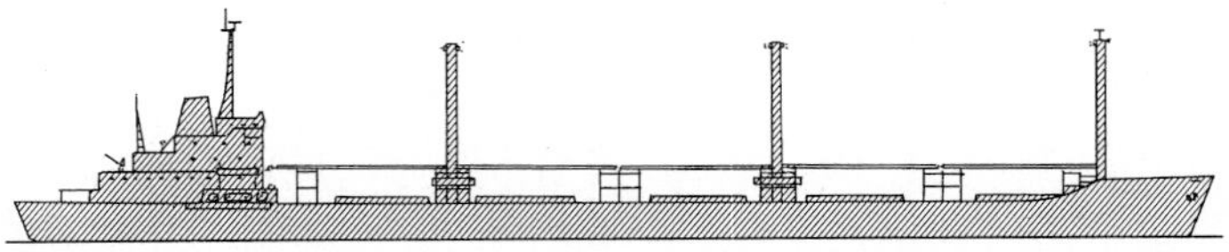

267 M^4FMC *H1*
IOLCOS LEGEND Cy/Ko (Hyundai) 1980; B; 19,103 grt/35,295 dwt; 177.03 × 10.91 m *(580.81 × 35.79 ft)*; M (Sulzer); 14 kts; ex-*Jasmine*

268 M^4FM^2 *H1*
TONG JIANG RC/Ne (Sulzer) 1960; C; 10,442 grt/14,935 dwt; 158 × 9.3 m *(517 × 30.5 ft)*; M (Sulzer); 16 kts; ex-*Argo Altis*

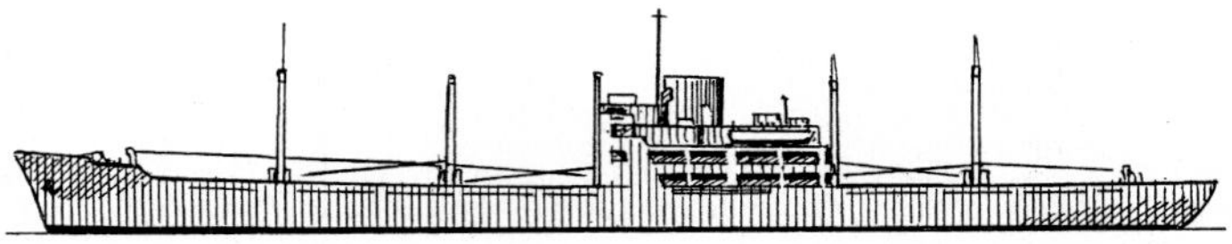

269 M^4FM^2 *H1*
YONG JIN RK/Ja (Nipponkai) 1958; C; 7,358 grt/11,353 dwt; 137.27 × 8.57 m *(433.9 × 28.12 ft)*; M (Sulzer); 13.75 kts; ex-*Chuoh Maru*

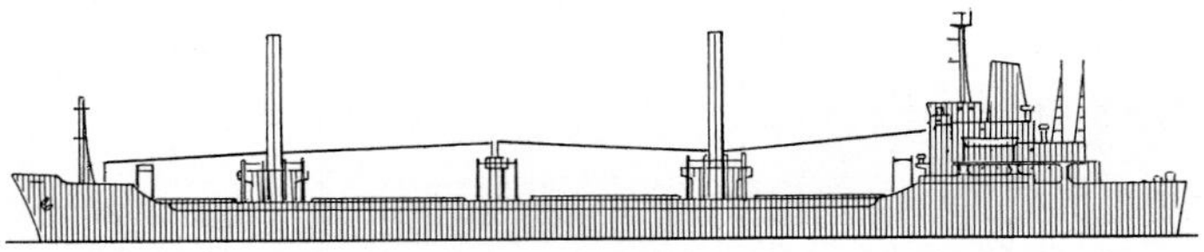

270 M^4FM^2 *H13*
ASIAN CONFIDENCE Cy/Ko (Hyundai) 1978; B; 11,686 grt/19,395 dwt; 151.21 × 9.61 m *(496.1 × 31.53 ft)*; M (B&W); 15.25 kts; ex-*Korean Zircon*
Sisters: **EPIC** (Cy) ex-*Korean Jade*; **PETREL** (Cy) ex-*Korean Ruby*; **MARABU** (Cy) ex-*Korean Sapphire*; **KYZIKOS** (Ma) ex-*Korean Topaz*;
Similar: **EAGLE II** (Cy) ex-*Asia Samho*; **DONGNAMA POHANG** (Ko) ex-*Asia Yukho*; **IMPERIAL CONFIDENCE** (Cy) ex-*Asia Oho*; **SAMSUN HONOUR** (Ko) ex-*Asia Chilho*; **DONGNAMA INCHON** (Ko) ex-*New Song Do*

271 M^4FM^2 *H13*
REX SV/FRG (Rhein Nordseew) 1972; C/Con; 10,779 grt/16,424 dwt; 158.4 × 9.6 m *(520 × 31.7 ft)*; M (MAN); 16.25 kts; ex-*Jalayamini*

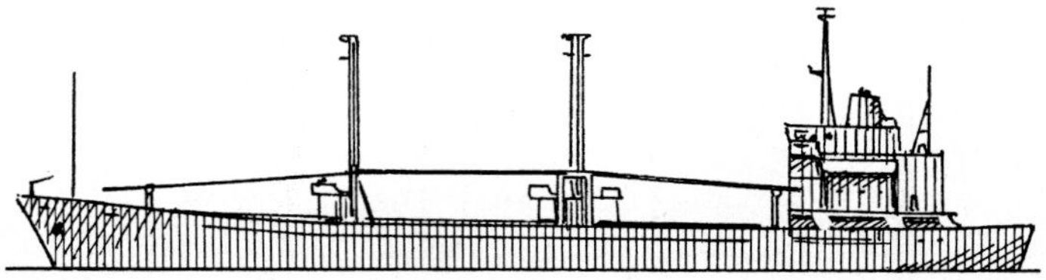

272 M^4FN *H*
GOPHER Pi/Ja (Tohoku) 1972; C; 3,166 grt/5,391 dwt; 85.83 × 7.44 m *(281.6 × 24.41 ft)*; M (Hanshin); 12 kts; ex-*Union Australia*; 'Camit' type; 76 TEU
Sisters: **CHIPMUNK** (Pi) ex-*Union New Zealand*; **PROTOPOROS** (Gr) ex-*Union Trans Tasman*

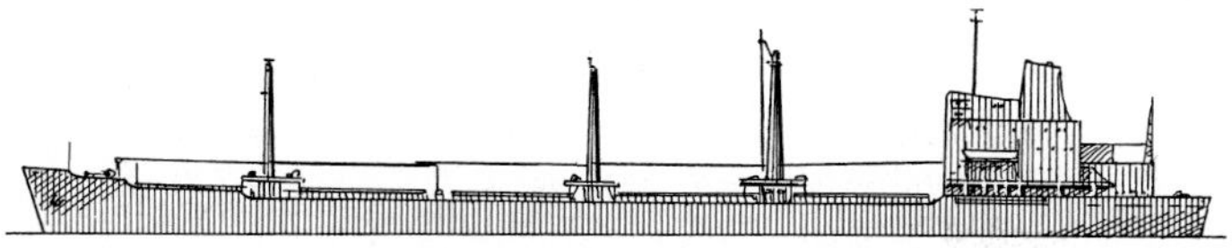

273 M^4FN *H1*
HA R BIN RC/FRG (Bremer V) 1970; C; 9,166 grt/15,406 dwt; 139.58 × 9.19 m *(457.94 × 30.15 ft)*; M (MAN); 16 kts; ex-*Atlantis*; 'German Liberty' type
Sisters: **HAN YIN** (RC) ex-*Okeanis*; **XIN AN JIANG** (RC) ex-*Octavia*; **FAR EAST** (SV) ex-*Niriis*; **MATTZ VEGA** (Bs) ex-*Altavia*; **VIVA VICTORIA** (Pa) ex-*Megalopolis*

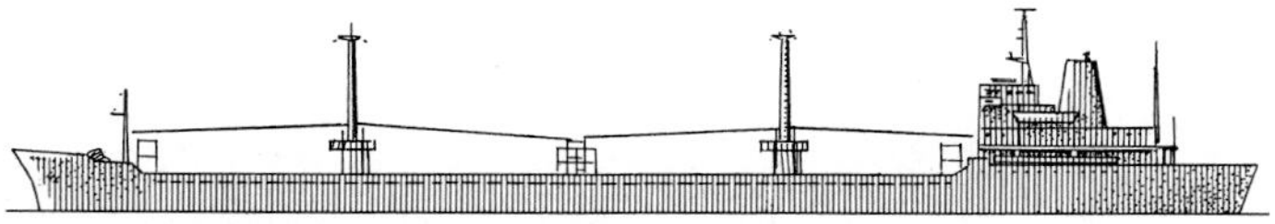

274 M^4FN *H13*
ASEAN PIONEER Ma/Ja (Maizuru) 1969; B; 10,708 grt/19,440 dwt; 156.17 × 9.54 m *(512.37 × 31.3 ft)*; M (B&W); 15 kts; ex-*Asia Brightness*
Sisters: **BALTIC TRANSPORTER** (Tu) ex-*Asia Grace*; **TRINITY** (Cy) ex-*Eastern Mary*

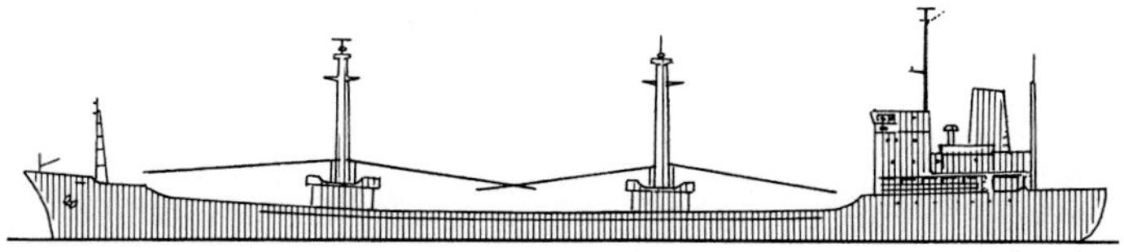

275 M^4FN *H13*
HANS LEONHARDT Cy/Ja (Ujina) 1976; C/Con; 7,244 grt/11,680 dwt; 129.27 × 8.24 m *(424.11 × 27.03 ft)*; M (B&W); 14 kts; 260 TEU
Sister: **INGRID LEONHARDT** (Cy)

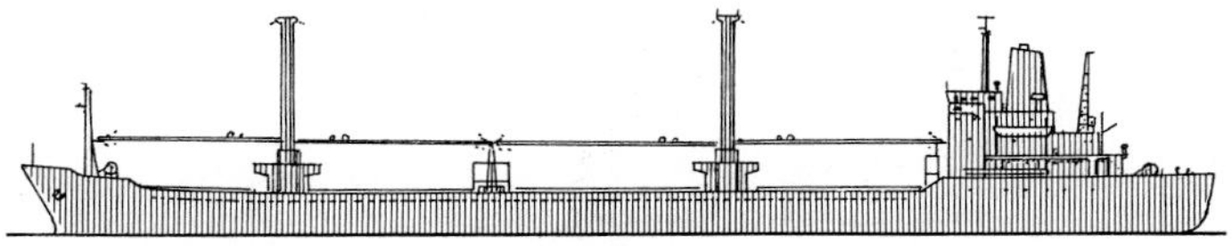

276 M^4FN *H13*
JOINT SUCCESS Ma/Ja (Tsuneishi) 1977; B; 11,069 grt/17,583 dwt; 145.98 × 9.28 m *(478.94 × 30.45 ft)*; M (B&W); 15 kts; ex-*Scan Fuji*
Sister: **PACIFIC SWAN** (Pa) ex-*Tensha Maru No 1*; Probable sister: **FERENIKI** (Gr) ex-*Scan Eastern*; Possible sisters: **HAKKI UZUNOGLU** (Tu) ex-*Young Seagull*; **HELLENIC CONFIDENCE** (Cy) ex-*Wakayoshi Maru*; **ST NICOLAS** (Pa) ex-*Court Lady*; **HAFNIA** (Cy) ex-*Elbhoff*; **MERIDIAN VENUS** (My) ex-*Marigold*; **S ARAZ** (Tu) ex-*Oceanic Confidence*; **VENTO** (Cy) ex-*Tensha Maru No 3*; **PLATON** (Gr) ex-*Tetsuzan Maru*; **UNITED CONFIDENCE** (Cy) ex-*Daisy*; **OPAL NAREE** (Th) ex-*Tenkei Maru*; **SAINT JOHN** (Cy) ex-*Young Scope*; **LACONIAN CONFIDENCE** (Cy) ex-*C S Valiant*

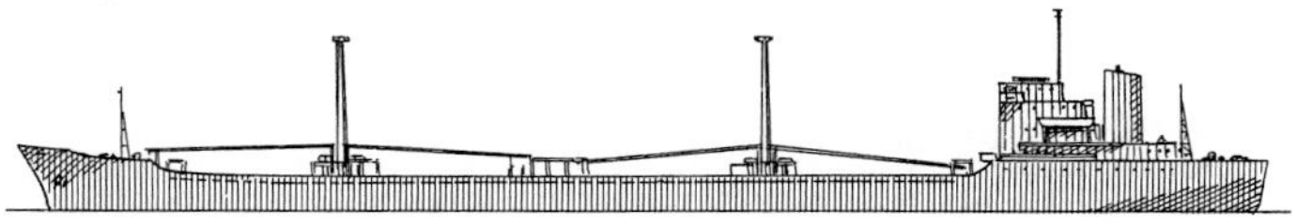

277 M^4FN *H13*
MYOHYANG 3 RK/Ja (Osaka) 1970; B; 10,913 grt/16,800 dwt; 154.34 × 9.18 m *(506.36 × 30.12 ft)*; M (B&W); 15 kts; ex-*Federal Yodo*
Sister: **AIS NIKOLAS** (Cy) ex-*Federal Mackenzie*

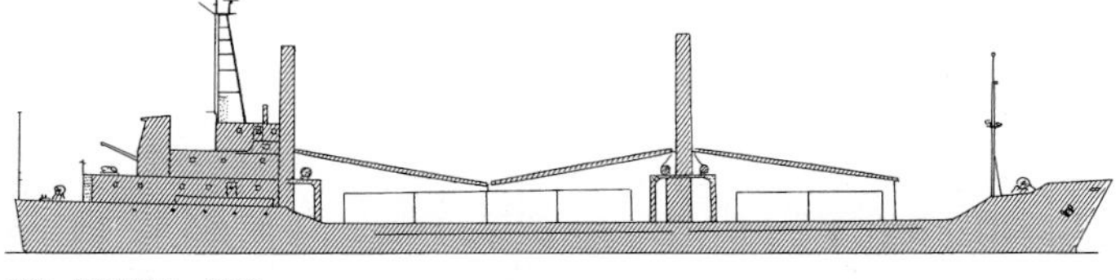

278 M^4FRM *H13*
HWANG YOUNG Ko/Ko (Shin-A) 1988; C/Con; 2,831 grt/3,459 dwt; 90.00 × 5.55 m *(295.28 × 18.21 ft)*; M (Hanshin); 12.5 kts; ex-*Sam Kyung*; 75 TEU
Possible sister: **DONG YOUNG** (Ko)

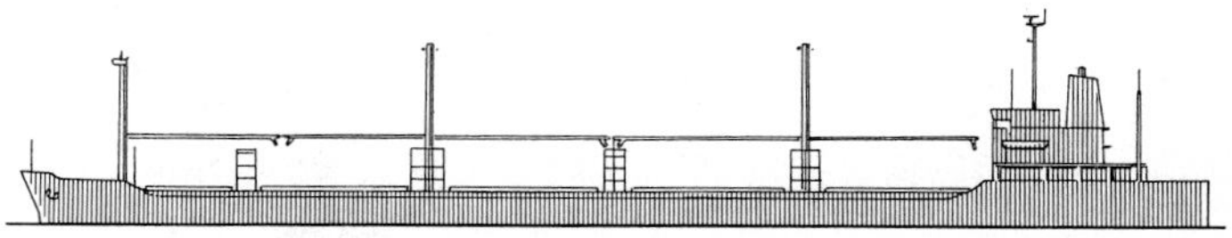

279 M^5FM *H13*
KOTOR SV/Ja (NKK) 1982; B; 17,436 grt/30,435 dwt; 175.01 × 10.45 m *(574 × 34.28 ft)*; M (Pielstick); 14.5 kts; ex-*Ocean Steelhead*

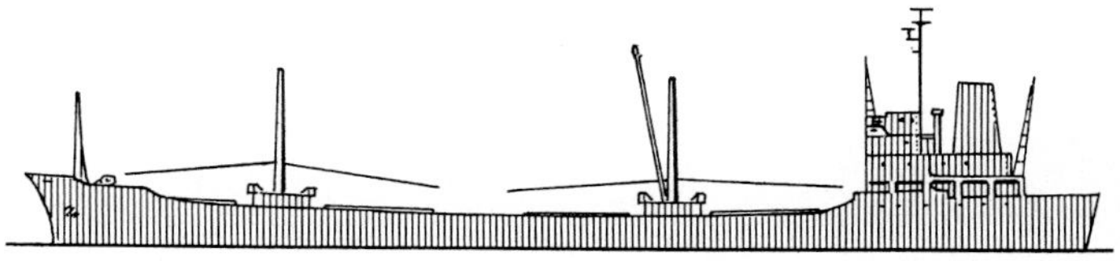

280 M^5FM *H13*
TONG GON AE HUK HO RK/Ja (Imai Z) 1976; C; 5,378 grt/11,525 dwt; 117.48 × 7.64 m *(385 × 25.07 ft)*; M (Hanshin); 13.5 kts; ex-*Ae Guk*

281 M^5FM *H13*
XING YE 1 RC/Tw (China SB) 1979; C; 3,814 grt/6,543 dwt; 108.51 × 6.66 m *(356 × 21.85 ft)*; M (Mitsubishi); 14.25 kts; ex-*Ocean Constructor*
Probable sisters: **SUTLA** (Cro) ex-*Chiang Wei*; **CONDOR** (SV) ex-*Jackson Pioneer*; **CHARLENE** (Pa) ex-*Hailung No 1*; **BLANCHE** (Pa) ex-*Hailung No 2*

282 M^5FM^2 *H1*
SONG SAI GON Vn/Ja (Kawasaki D) 1965; C; 8,774 grt/10,784 dwt; 151 × 8.8 m *(496 × 29.2 ft)*; M (MAN); 17.5 kts; ex-*Denmark Maru*

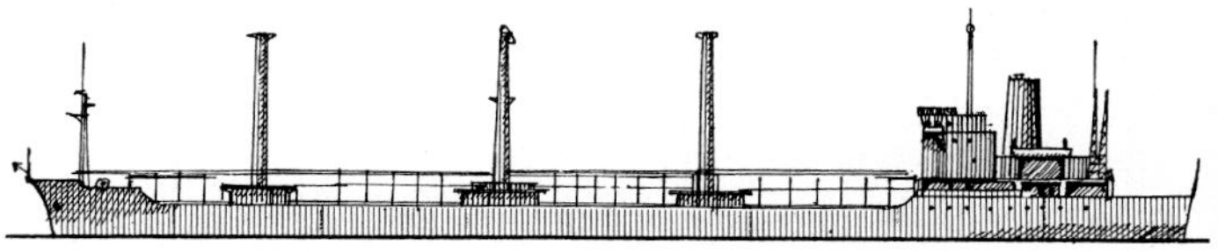

283 M^5FM^2 *H13*
KOSTANDIS F Gr/Ja (Tsuneishi) 1977; B; 10,396 grt/15,202 dwt; 144 × 8.87 m *(472.4 × 29.1 ft)*; M (B&W); 14.25 kts; ex-*Montmartre*
Sister: **VICTORIUS** (Gr) ex-*Montparnasse*

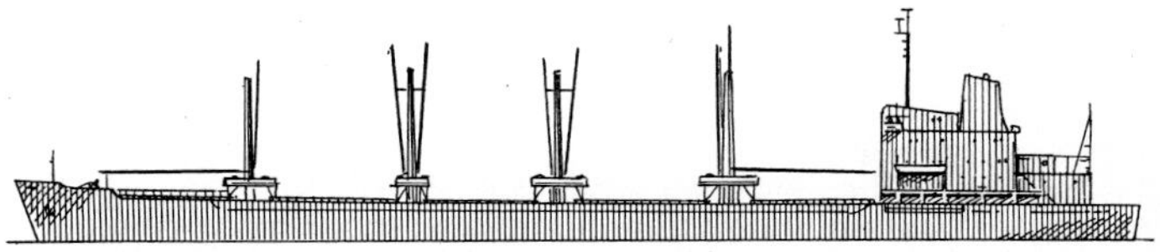

284 M^5FN *H1*
GOLDEN STAR Sg/FRG (Bremer V) 1974; C; 9,497 grt/15,082 dwt; 139.55 × 9.17 m *(457.84 × 30.09 ft)*; M (MAN); 16 kts; ex-*Lumumba*; 'German Liberty' type
Sisters: **TOLIS** (Cy) ex-*Bandundu*; **CITY OF BEIRUT** (Ma) ex-*Bukavu*; **EMIL S II** (Cy) ex-*Mbandaka*; **EMIL S** (Cy) ex-*Mbuji-Mayi*

285 M^3M^2FN *H13*
JING HAI RC/Br (Lithgows) 1968; B; 12,404 grt/20,025 dwt; 159.06 × 9.47 m *(521.85 × 31.07 ft)*; M (B&W); 14.75 kts; ex-*Baynes*

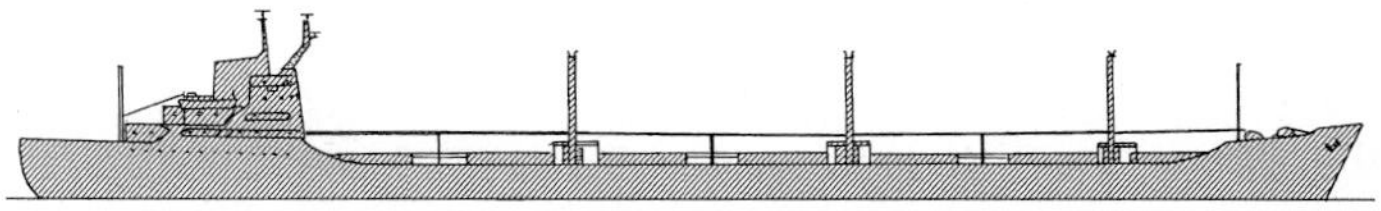

286 $M^5M\text{–}FM$ *H13*
LU HAI RC/Br (J Brown) 1965; B; 16,942 grt/31,013 dwt; 186.08 × 11.63 m *(610.50 × 38.16 ft)*; M (Sulzer); 13.5 kts; ex-*Vennacher*
Sister: **XI QIAO SHAN** (RC) ex-*British Monarch*

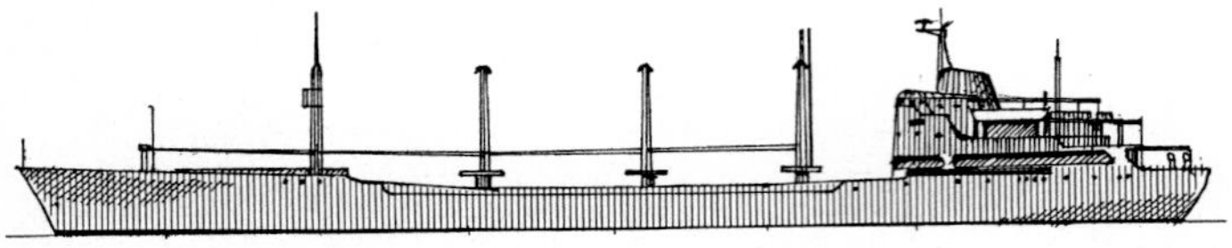

287 *M^4M–FN H13*
HAI JIAO RC/Sw (Uddevalla) 1962; C; 7,051 grt/7,934 dwt; 129.29 × 7.94 m *(424.18 × 26.05 ft)*; M (Gotaverken); 16 kts; ex-*David Salman*

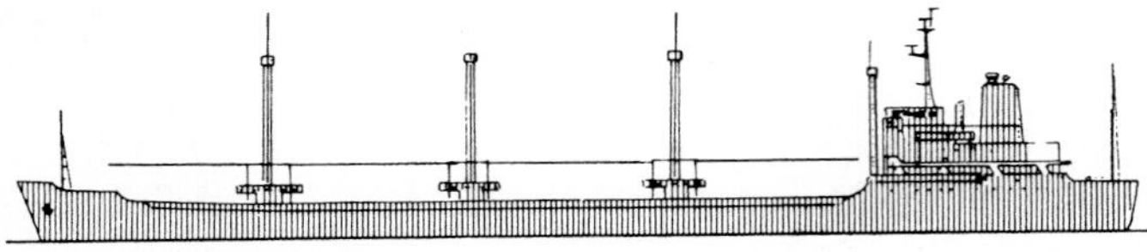

288 *M^4NMFM H13*
UELEN Uk/Ja (Sanoyasu) 1968; B; 9,745 grt/16,557 dwt; 143.72 × 9.04 m *(471.52 × 29.66 ft)*; M (MAN); 14.50 kts; ex-*Windford*

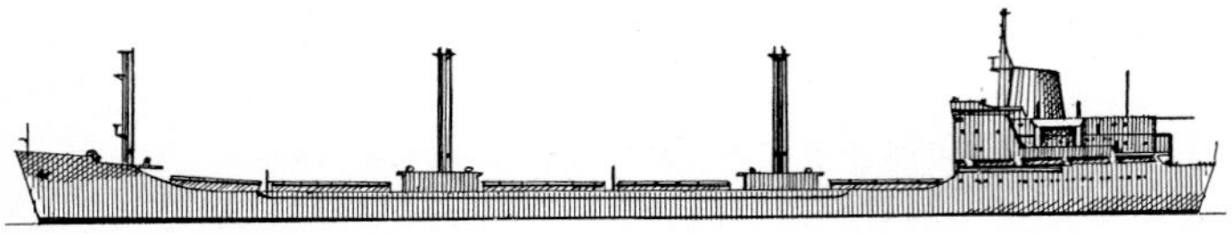

289 *M^3M–F H13*
SOUNION Gr/Br (Lithgows) 1968; B; 13,575 grt/20,930 dwt; 167.65 × 9.58 m *(550.03 × 31.43 ft)*; M (B&W); 15.5 kts; ex-*Sugar Refiner*

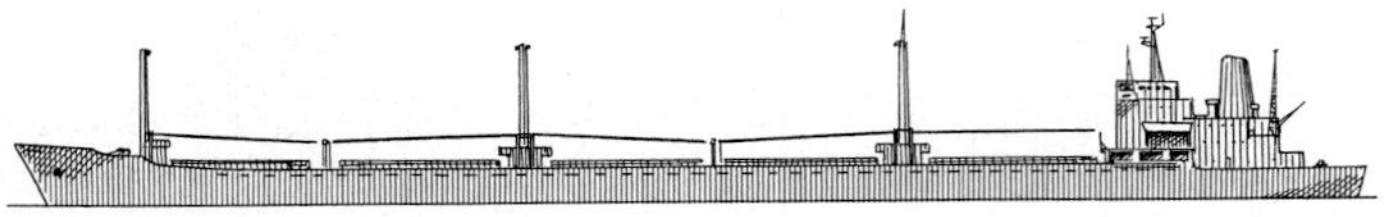

290 *M^3NMFN H1*
MARKELLA Cy/Ja (Hitachi) 1977; B; 21,107 grt/37,534 dwt; 182.23 × 11.28 m *(597.87 × 37.01 ft)*; M (B&W); 14.75 kts; ex-*Chieftain Bulker*
Sisters: **HUA KUN** (RC) ex-*Cavalier Bulker*; **MARIA K** (Ma) ex-*Centurion Bulker*; **GUANG NAN** (RC) ex-*Conqueror Bulker*

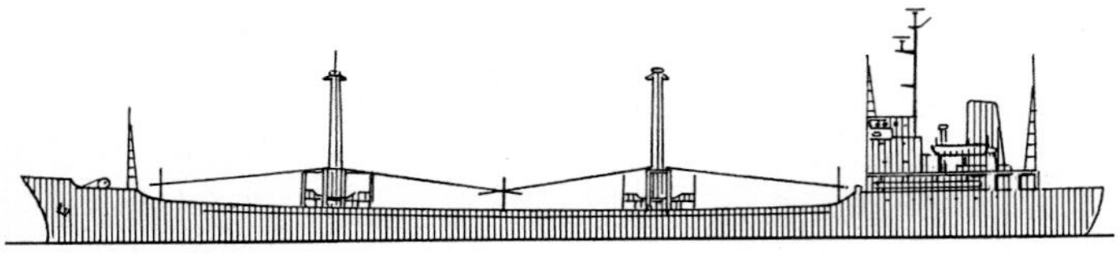

291 *M^3NMFN H13*
DIMITRIS N Cy/Ja (Ujina) 1974; B; 6,177 grt/12,020 dwt; 127.77 × 8.25 m *(419.19 × 27.07 ft)*; M (Ito Tekosho); 13.25 kts; ex-*Oriental Victory*
Sisters: **QIN LING** (RC) ex-*Myoken Maru*; **UNA** (Cro) ex-*Hand Loong*; **ISIS I** (Ma) ex-*Hand Fortune*; **DIAMOND DRAGON** (Pa) ex-*Golden Valley*; Possible sisters: **OMER** (Tu) ex-*Cherryfield*; **KNIGHT** (Ko) ex-*Sun Deneb*; **JELAU** (Pa) ex-*Akitaka Maru*; **KYRAKOULA** (Ma) ex-*Golden Dragon*; **SUN RITCHIE TWO** (SV) ex-*Shuwa Maru*; **THAPAR KALINADI** (In) ex-*Yancey*; **ASLINUR** (Tu) ex-*Blue Jupiter*; **OSMAN GAZI** (or **OSMANGAZI**) (Tu) ex-*Yu-Lin*; **SOYA** (Th) ex-*Lusty*; **CETI** (Pa) ex-*Golden Breeze*; **REGENT** (Ko)

292 *M^3NMFN H13*
GRAND OCEAN 1 Pa/Tw (China SB) 1978; C; 7,246 grt/11,688 dwt; 127.82 × 8.05 m *(419.36 × 26.41 ft)*; M (Mitsubishi); 13.25 kts; ex-*Union River*; **SIMILAR TO DRAWING NUMBER 8/304**; Only difference to latter is mast on focsle; Some sisters on number 8/304 may also have this

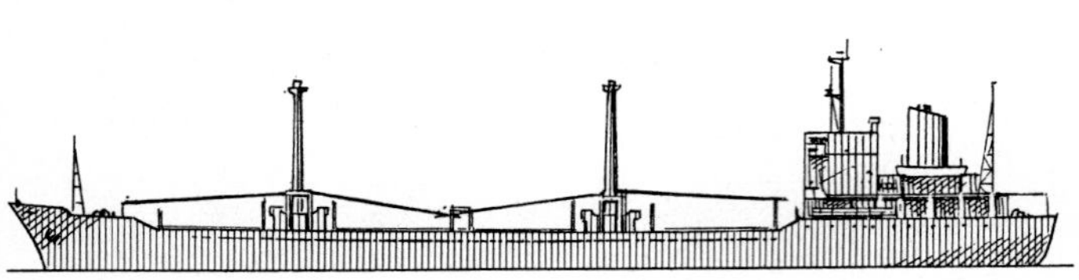

293 *M^3NMFN H13*
LADY NADA Ma/Ja (Onomichi) 1971; C; 4,724 grt/7,460 dwt; 114.2 × 7.04 m *(374.67 × 23.1 ft)*; M (Kobe); 13 kts; ex-*Kisshu Maru*

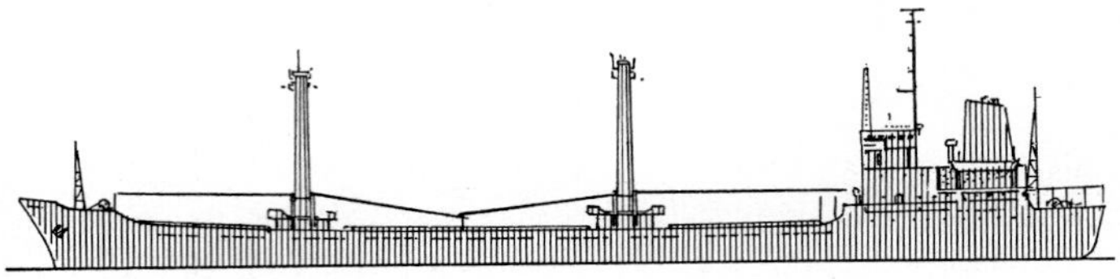

294 *M^3NMFN H13*
PANSY Ia/Ja (Hashihama) 1969; C; 5,973 grt/9,664 dwt; 127.62 × 7.53 m *(419 × 24.7 ft)*; M (Kobe); 13.5 kts; ex-*Shotai Maru*
Sisters: **KAREMA** (Ma) ex-*Shintai Maru*

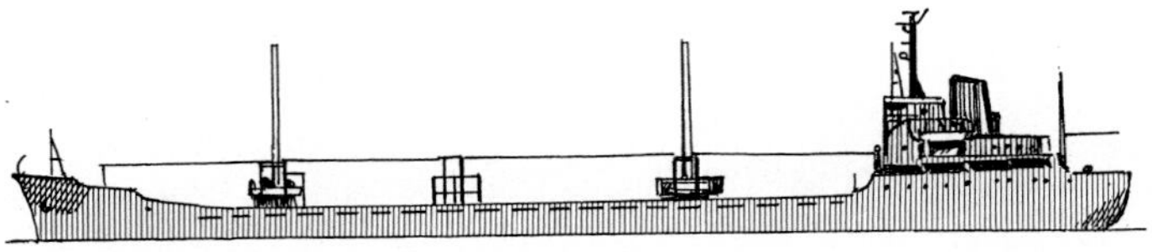

295 *M^3NMFN H13*
SEA TRADITION SV/Ja (IHI) 1969; B; 10,168 grt/16,734 dwt; 145.65 × 9.11 m *(477.85 × 29.89 ft)*; M (Sulzer); 16.5 kts; ex-*Eastern Ace*

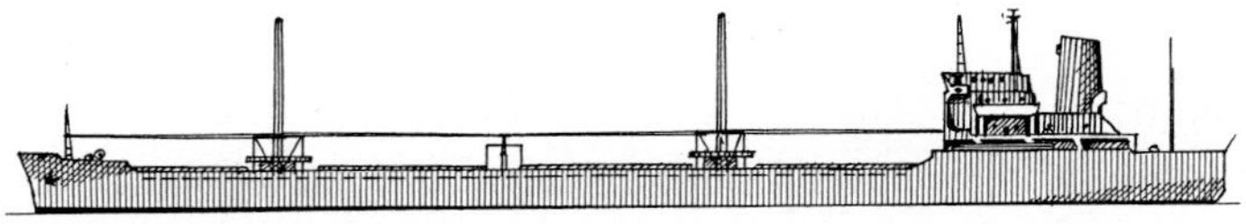

296 *M^3NMFN H13*
VICTOR III Pa/Ja (Namura) 1969; B; 10,165 grt/16,992 dwt; 143.71 × 9.16 m *(477.36 × 30.45 ft)*; M (Sulzer); 14.75 kts; ex-*Cosmos Eltanin*

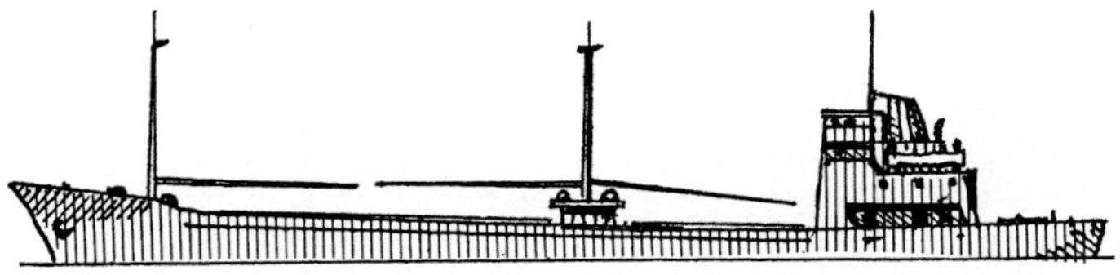

297 *M^2M–F H1*
MERCS HENDALA Sr/Ne (Zaanlandsche) 1967; C; 1,403 grt/2,210 dwt; 76.94 × 5.28 m *(252 × 17.32 ft)*; M (Werkspoor); 13.5 kts; ex-*Leonard Bohmer*

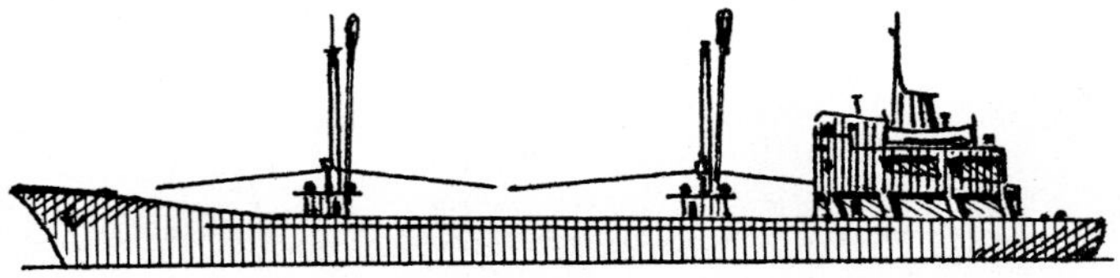

298 *M^2M–F H1*
SUEZ FLOWER Eg/Sp (Duro Felguera) 1970; C; 1,179 grt/1,727 dwt; 72.7 × 5.19 m *(238.5 × 16.96 ft)*; M (Deutz); 15 kts; ex-*Atlan Esmeralda*
Sister: **NEW IRIS** (Eg) ex-*Atlan Rubi*; Possibly similar (reefers): **HAI YI** (RC) ex-*Lian*; **MONTEBLANCO** (Ve) ex-*Lian Dos*

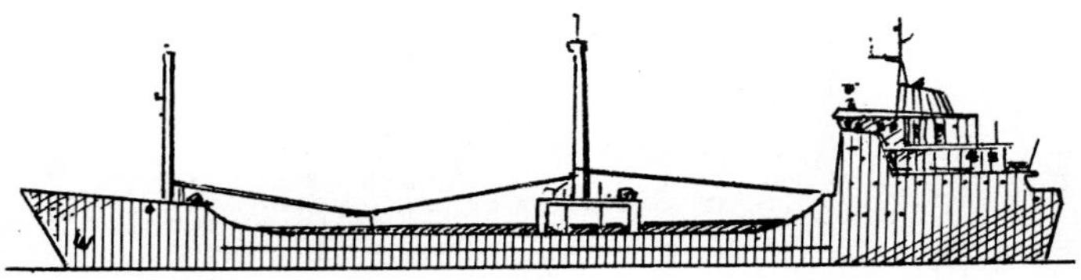

299 *M^2M–F H13*
HOOP Cy/Ne (Bodewes Bergum) 1978; C; 1,691 grt/2,555 dwt; 78.67 × 5.04 m *(258.1 × 16.54 ft)*; M (Caterpillar); 11 kts

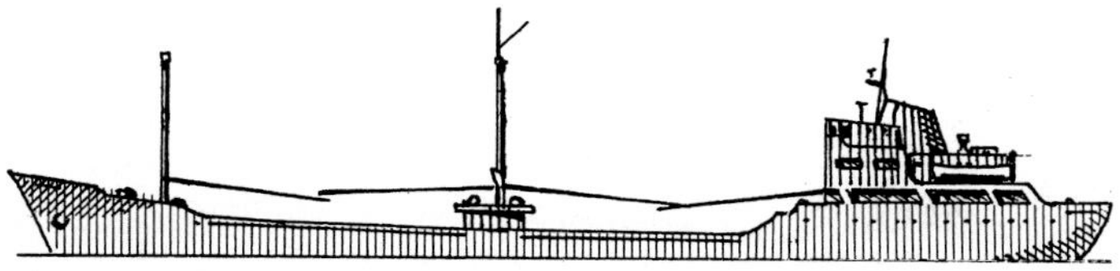

300 *M^2M–F H13*
SEA MELODY —/Sp (AESA) 1968; C; 2,185 grt/3,577 dwt; 93.02 × 5.37 m *(305.18 × 17.62 ft)*; M (B&W); 12.5 kts; ex-*Anamilena*
Sister: **VILA DHOADHI** (Ho) ex-*Adriana*

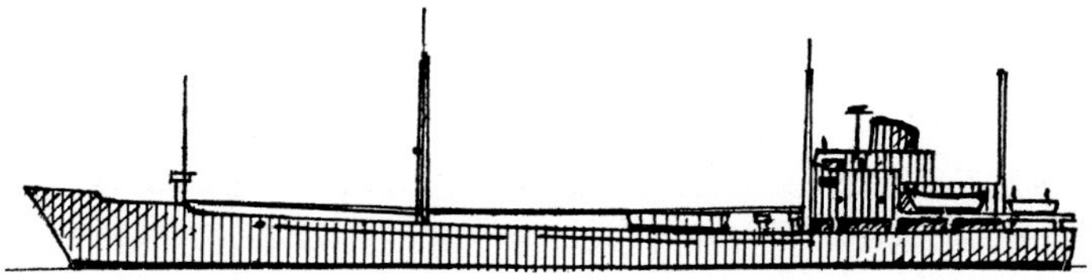

301 *M^2NFM H1*
NERA II Pa/Ne (Boele's Sch) 1961; C; 799 grt/1,160 dwt; 77.17 × 4.02 m *(253.18 × 13.19 ft)*; M (Werkspoor); 11.25 kts; ex-*Adara*
Sisters: **ISLA BOLIVAR** (Co) ex-*Situla*; **SONIA G** (Ho) ex-*Talita*; **ZAHER II** (Ho) ex-*Nashira*

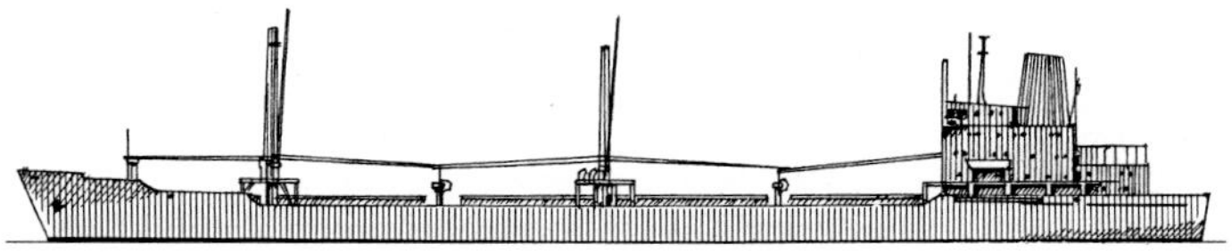

302 *M^2NMF H1*
MANA ELENI Ma/FRG (Flensburger) 1968; C; 9,278 grt/15,550 dwt; 139.73 × 9.02 m *(458.4 × 29.6 ft)*; M (MAN); 15 kts; ex-*Pitria*; 'German Liberty' type
Possible sister (may have poop — see drawing number 8/549): **AMNA S** (Sy) ex-*Marita Leonhardt*; Similar: **BRIHOPE** (My) ex-*Attika Hope*

303 *M^2NMFN H1*
MATTZ DENEB Bs/FRG (Bremer V) 1970; C/Con; 9,166 grt/15,406 dwt; 139.55 × 9.17 m *(457.84 × 30.09 ft)*; M (MAN); 15.5 kts; ex-*Novia*; 315 TEU; Modified 'German Liberty' type; **SIMILAR TO DRAWING NUMBER 8/273**

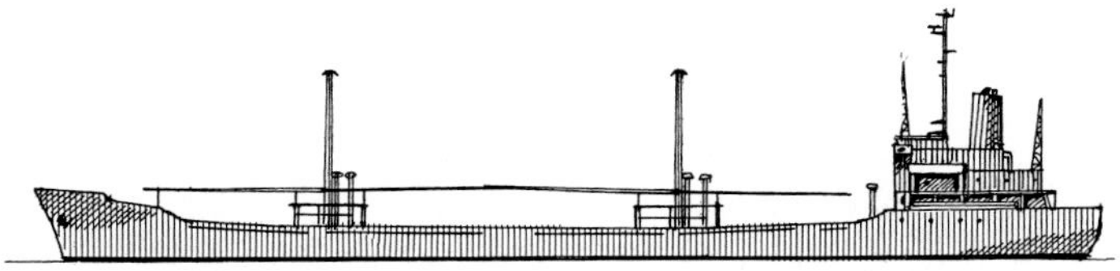

304 *M^2NMFN H13*
NEW HAITENG Pa/Ja (Fukuoka) 1976; C/Con; 7,593 grt/11,488 dwt; 127.79 × 8.05 m *(419.26 × 26.41 ft)*; M (Mitsubishi); 16.75 kts; ex-*Zepsea*; 400 TEU
Sisters: **ABDUL M** (SV) ex-*Lily Venture* (may now have a light tripod on focsle); **BUGA** (Cro) ex-*Ocean Ace*; **DRAGON TEKONG** (Pa) ex-*Zephawk*; **DAIZU MARU** (Th) ex-*Bright Star*;
Possible sister: **DIGNITY** (Cy) ex-*Kitty Porr*; Similar: **MARYGOLD** (Pa) ex-*Yue Hope* (builder: Minami) Probable sister: **KANG DA** (SV) ex-*Kreon*
Probably similar: **GEMINY** (Pa) ex-*Marguerite Venture*

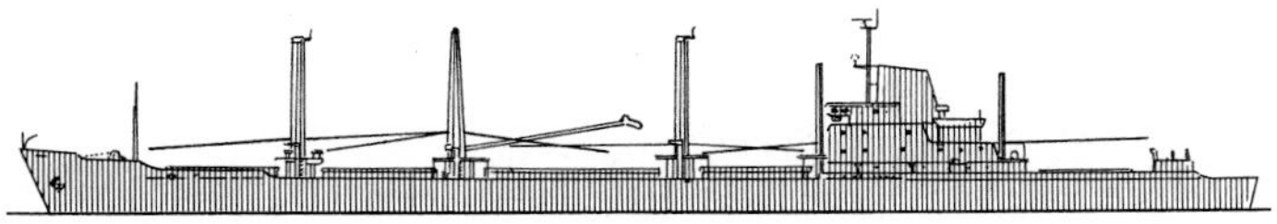

305 *M^2NMNMFN H1*
GOLDEN FUTURE Pa/Bz (Maua) 1975; C; 10,266 grt/14,321 dwt; 160.05 × 9.22 m *(525 × 30.25 ft)*; M (MAN); 17 kts; ex-*Caicara*; 'Prinasa 121' type
Probable sisters: **YONG TONG** (RC); ex-*Amalia*; **PANGLIMA** (Sg) ex-*Joana*

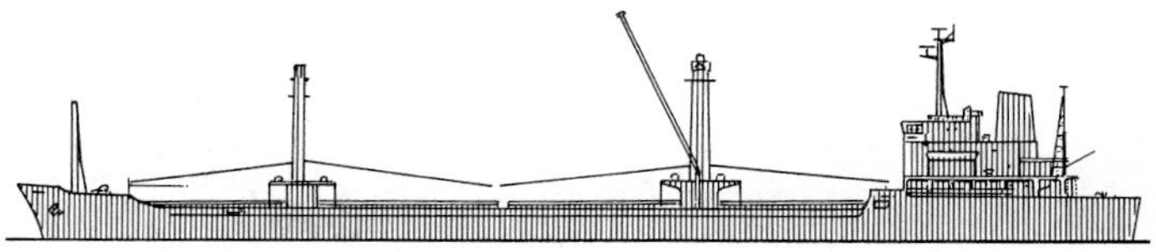

306 *M^2TMFN H13*
MATTHEOS L SV/Ja (Hashihama) 1977; C; 11,006 grt/16,363 dwt; 148.39 × 9.12 m *(487 × 29.92 ft)*; M (Sulzer); 14.5 kts; ex-*Nicolaos Angelakis*; 288 TEU
Possible sister: **SYNESSIOS L** (Pa) ex-*Duke Star*

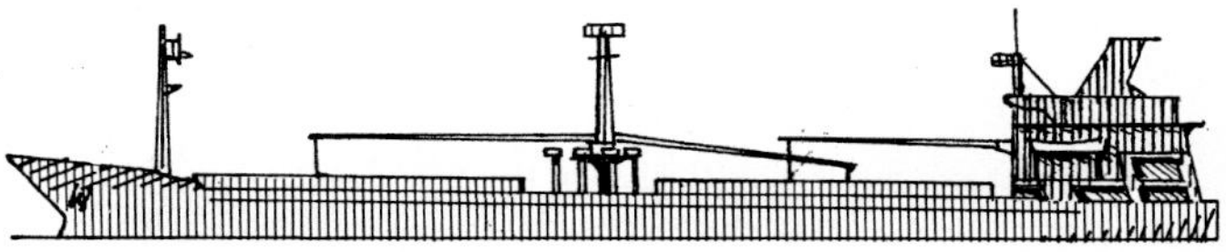

307 *M^2VF H1*
LIAN HUA FENG RC/De (Aalborg) 1977; C; 3,260 grt/5,524 dwt; 96.53 × 6.8 m *(316.69 × 22.3 ft)*; M (Alpha-Diesel); 12 kts; ex-*Mercandian Atlantic*
Sister: **SANTIAGO** (It) ex-*Mercandian Pacific*

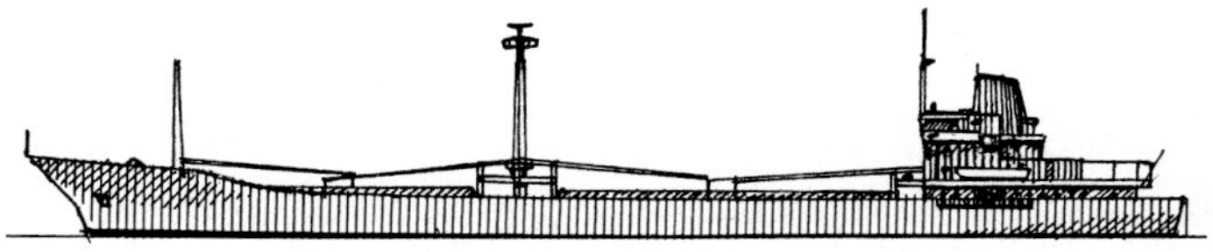

308 *M^2VF H1*
MAN CHENG RC/FRG (Husumer) 1975; C; 1,599 grt/4,114 dwt; 91.47 × 6.12 m *(300 × 20 ft)*; M (KHD); 15 kts; ex-*Lindinger Light*
Sisters: **XIONG ER SHAN** (RC) ex-*Lindinger Karat*; **KUAN CHENG** (RC) ex-*Lindinger Ivory*; **TIAN LI SHAN** (RC) ex-*Lindinger Jade*; **A CHENG** (RC) ex-*Lindinger Nimbus*; **HAI CHENG** (RC) ex-*Lindinger Moonstone*; **LI CHENG** (RC) ex-*Lindinger Silver*; **FILAOS** (Bs) ex-*Lindinger Topaz*; **ANGELA** (Ma) ex-*Gert Staerke*; **SOLID SUN** (Pi) ex-*Lindinger Unique*
Possible sisters: **ROOK TRADER** (Pa) ex-*Lindinger Opal*; **SHI ZUI SHAN** (RC) ex-*Lindinger Quetzal*; **ROOK MARINER** (Pa) ex-*Lindinger Ruby*

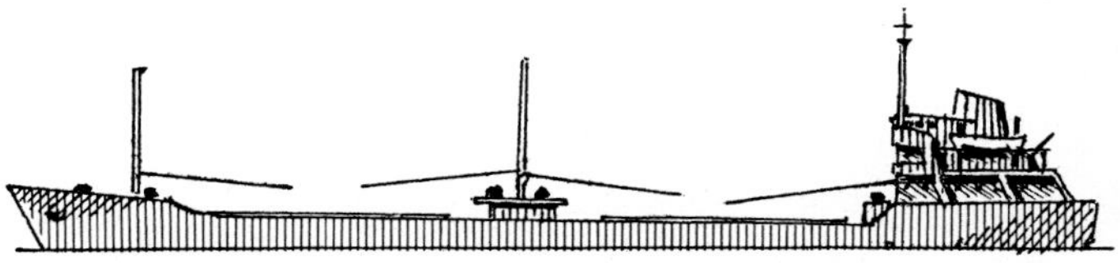

309 *M^2VF H13*
MARIANN Pa/Ma (Malta DD) 1972; C; 1,953 grt/3,015 dwt; 91.37 × 5.12 m *(299.77 × 16.8 ft)*; M (Atlas-MaK); 14 kts
Sister: **THERESE** (Cy)

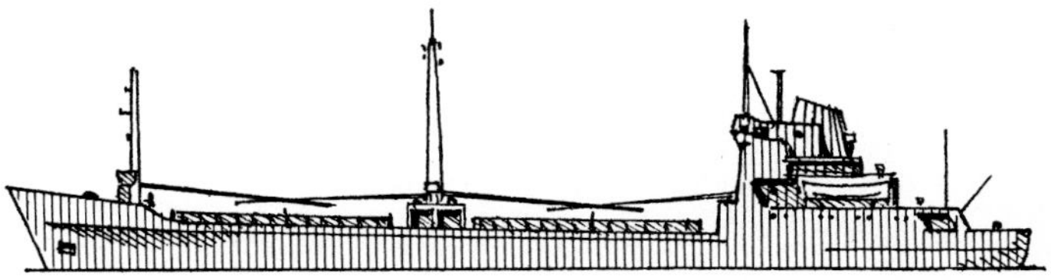

310 *M^2VFM H12*
OCEAN VICTOR At/FRG (Husumer) 1970; C; 1,850 grt/3,377 dwt; 83.8 × 5.05/6.33 m *(274.93 × 16.57/20.77 ft)*; M (Werkspoor); 13.5 kts; ex-*Anna von Bargen*
Sisters: **MARIALENA** (Pa) ex-*Gitta von Bargen*; **CARIBE** (Pa) ex-*Susann von Bargen*; **SURYA PACIFIC** (Ia) ex-*Moevensteert*; **GIGI** (My) ex-*Dukegat*;
Similar (Lengthened. Now 90.89m (298ft)): **SENIOR M** (Eg) ex-*Vela*

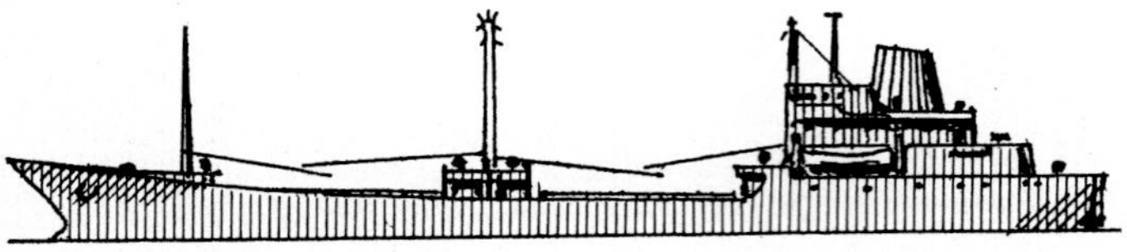

311 M^2VMF *H3*
MAHASEN Sr/FRG (Husumer) 1972; C; 1,598 grt/2,906 dwt; 81.01 × 5.49 m *(265.78 × 18.01 ft)*; M (Alpha-Diesel); 13 kts; ex-*Lindinger Brilliant*; 52 TEU
Sisters: **TAPAC III** (Ia) ex-*Lindinger Emerald*; **MINDELO** (CV) ex-*Lindinger Facet*; **ZARKA** (Qt) ex-*Lindinger Coral*; **SAMI III** (To) ex-*Lindinger Amber*; **NURIA (SV) ex-***Lindinger Diamond*
Possible sisters: **ILHA DE KOMO** (CV) ex-*Lindinger Hyacinth*; **SELAT MAS** (Ia) ex-*Lindinger Gold*

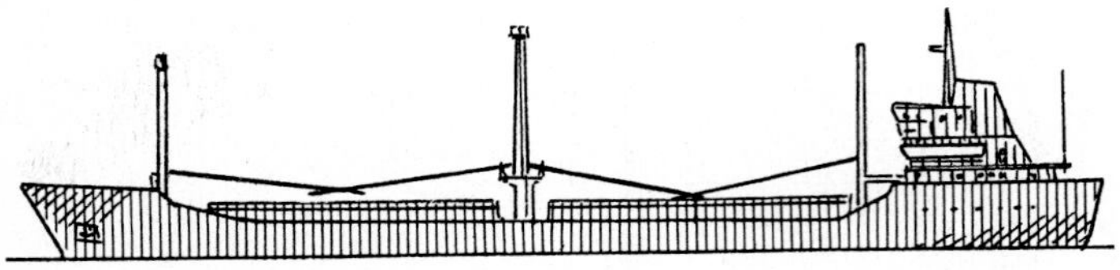

312 $M^2VM{-}F$ *H13*
CHRISSI P Ma/No (Batservice) 1971; C; 1,834 grt/3,017 dwt; 80.02 × 5.32 m *(262.53 × 17.45 ft)*; M (Polar); 13 kts; ex-*Lyshav*
Sister: **THALASSA** (Sw) ex-*Rondane*; Similar: **AGIOS VISSARION** (Pa) ex-*Mornes*; **GALTEAM** (Ma) ex-*Blankenburg*; **BIBA** (It) ex-*Delta*; **RACHMANUEL** (Ia) ex-*Kalmarvind*; **CAPRICORN SEA** (Pa) ex-*Karin Lehmann*; **MAIK PRIMO** (It) ex-*Rudolf Kurz*; **MARIKA** (Fi) ex-*Pingvin*; Similar (Gr built-Argo) (taller radar masts): **TIFFANY** (Ma) ex-*Argo Challenge*; **CURRENT** (Ma) ex-*Argo Glory*; **AGIOS FANOURIOS** (Ma) ex-*Argo Hope*; **ARGO PIONEER** (Gr); **TRADER BULK** (No) ex-*Argo Valour*; **LAZANI** (SV) ex-*Argo Faith*

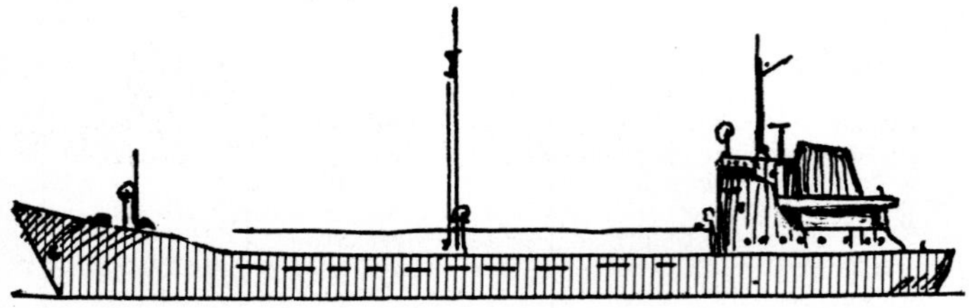

313 *MM–F H1*
MARINER Na/Ne (Van Diepen) 1966; C; 1,148 grt/1,821 dwt; 73 × 5.02 m *(239.5 × 16.47 ft)*; M (Werkspoor); 11 kts; ex-*Kraftca*
Similar (Some have mast from funnel): **DIAMOND I** (Ho) ex-*Schoonebeek*; **MOEZ 2** (Eg) ex-*Lijnbaansgracht*; **NIKOLIS PALLIS** (Gr) ex-*Comtesse*; **MITCHELL EXPRESS** (Pa) ex-*Arrow*

314 *MNFM H1*
VIANGTHALAE Th/FRG (Ottensener) 1958; C; 5,770 grt/8,669 dwt; 129.1 × 8.1 m *(424 × 26.5 ft)*; M (Ottensener); 14.5 kts; ex-*Danholm*

315 *MNFM H13*
LEONID LEONIDOV Ru/Be (Boel) 1957; C; 3,106 grt/5,664 dwt; 120.5 × 6.71 m *(395.34 × 22.01 ft)*; M (Sulzer); 13.5 kts

316 *MNFM H13*
NIREUS Gr/FRG (Kieler H) 1956; C; 7,289 grt/13,956 dwt; 155.2 × 9.3 m *(509 × 30.6 ft)*; M (Sulzer); 15.75 kts; ex-*Orpheus*

317 *MNFMN H1*
SKENDERBEG Al/Bu (G Dimitrov) 1959; C; 1,925 grt/3,206 dwt; 92.5 × 4.7 m *(304 × 15.8 ft)*; M (Liebknecht); 13 kts; Also known as **GJERGJ KASTRIOTI**
Sisters: **PKHEN HOA** (RK); **PYENG HOA** (Rk) ex-*Mir*

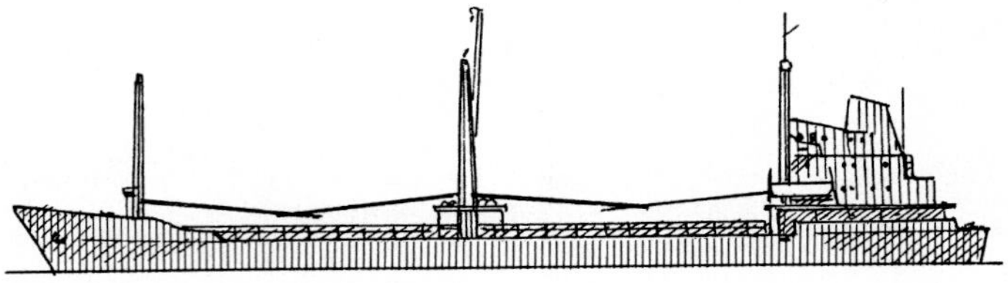

318 *MNHF H13*
SULTENG I Ia/FRG (M Jansen) 1973; C; 1,463 grt/3,440 dwt; 96.45 × 5.19 m *(316.44 × 17.03 ft)*; M (KHD); 14.5 kts; ex-*Cairngorm*

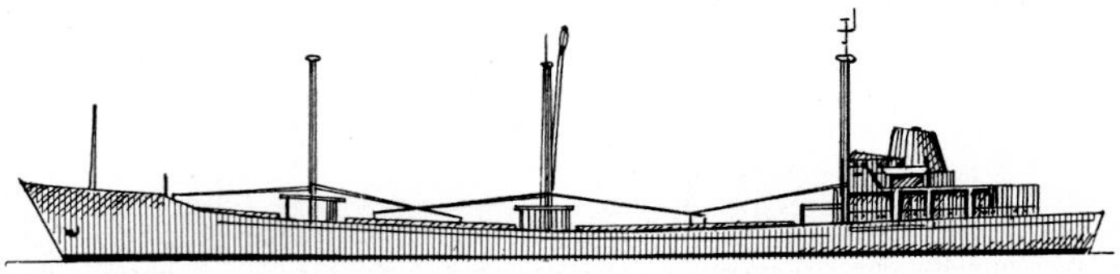

319 MNH^2F *H1*
HAGAAR Ia/FRG (Unterweser) 1969; C/Con; 5,499 grt/8,130 dwt; 124.49 × 8 m *(404.4 × 26.2 ft)*; M (KHD); 17 kts; ex-*Helene Roth*; 189 TEU
Sisters: **OCEAN CREST** (Pa) ex-*Erika Schulte*; **CHIANGRAI** (Th) ex-*Gunther Schulte*; **XIN FENG** (Pa) ex-*Auguste Schulte*

320 *MNHMF H13*
LIPNO Cz/Ys ("3 Maj") 1981; C; 10,512 grt/15,173 dwt; 145.55 × 9.10 m *(477.53 × 29.86 ft)*; M (Sulzer); 14.75 kts; **SIMILAR TO DRAWING NUMBER 8/136**; Lipno differs by having a Stülcken derrick between hatches one and two

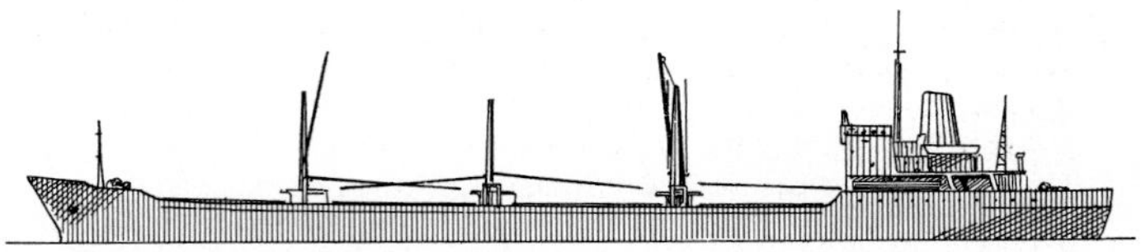

321 *MNHNHFN H13*
VELENJE Ys/Ja (Mitsui) 1976; C/Con/HL; 12,117 grt/18,485 dwt; 147.71 × 9.63 m *(484.61 × 31.59 ft)*; M (B&W); 15 kts; 'Mitsui-Concord 18' type; 232 TEU
Sisters: **MARIBOR** (SV); **KRANJ** (SV); **CELJE** (SV); **KAMNIK** (Sg)

322 $MNHN^2M{-}FN^2$ *H13*
"SAPPHIRE STAR" class dwt; Sequence variation for some sisters listed under drawing number 8/358

323 *MNMF H13*
POROS Gr/Ne ('De Merwede') 1955; Cem; 1,524 grt/2,266 dwt; 85.37 × 4.92 m *(280.09 × 16.14 ft)*; M (Werkspoor); 11 kts; ex-*Pargasport*

324 *MNMFM H1*
HONG QI 138 RC/FRG (A G 'Weser') 1957; C; 9,207 grt/14,022 dwt; 153.7 × 9 m *(504 × 29.7 ft)*; M (MAN); 14 kts; ex-*Captantonis*

325 *MNMFM H13*
HONG QI 116 RC/It (Taranto) 1957; C; 8,661 grt/12,900 dwt; 151 × 8.9 m *(495 × 29.2 ft)*; M (Fiat); 12 kts; ex-*Calliope*

326 *MNMFNM H1*
CALANDA Ho/FRG (Rickmers) 1963; C; 4,794 grt/7,050 dwt; 126.8 × 7.6 m *(415 × 25 ft)*; M (Sulzer); 15 kts; ex-*Calanda*

327 *MNMFNM H1*
SONG NHUE Vn/Ja (Harima) 1960; C; 7,125 grt/10,395 dwt; 136.6 × 8.4 m *(448 × 26.9 ft)*; M (Sulzer); 15.75 kts; ex-*Soei Maru*

328 *MNMFNM H13*
MING LONG RC/FRG (B+V) 1962; C; 5,196 grt/7,375 dwt; 126.32 × 7.88 m *(414.44 × 25.85 ft)*; M (MAN); 14 kts; ex-*Tunis*

329 *MNM²F H123*
BHA EXPRESS Ho/Ne (Amels) 1960; C; 1,519 grt/2,488 dwt; 78.80 × 5.00 m *(258.53 × 16.40 ft)*; M (Werkspoor); 11 kts; ex-*Bothniaborg*

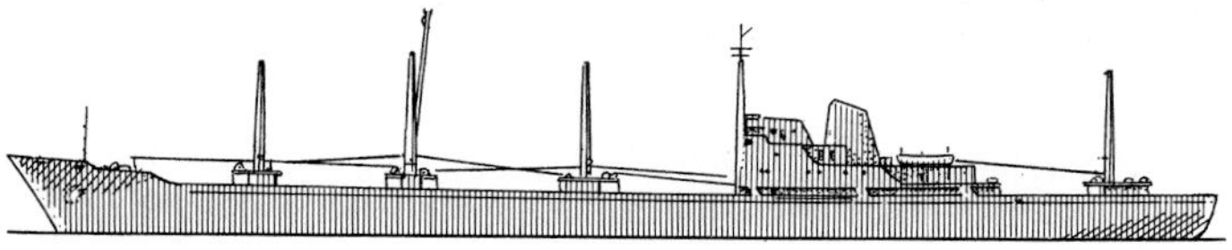

330 *MNM²FM H1*
DALIA Ho/Ar (Astarsa) 1976; C; 8,183 grt/9,754 dwt; 147.63 × 8.26 m *(484.35 × 27.1 ft)*; M (GMT); 18 kts; ex-*Rio Esquel*
Sisters: **SIBA** (SV) ex-*Rio Deseado*; **SAFINA-E-ISMAIL 2** (Pk) ex-*Rio Olivia*

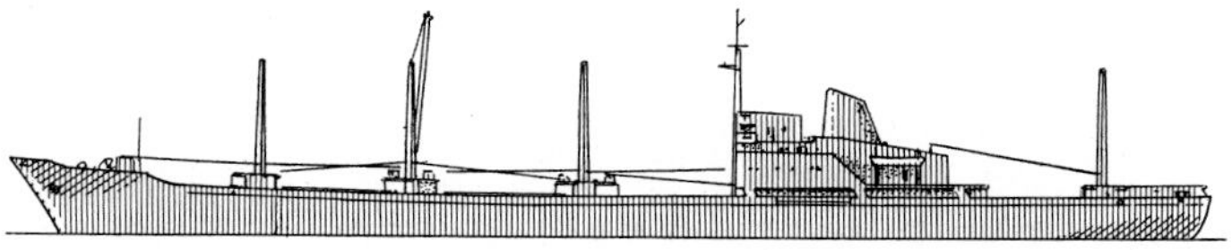

331 *MNM²FM H1*
HELIOPOLIS SPRING Eg/Ar (AFNE) 1970; C; 8,202 grt/10,070 dwt; 152.71 × 8.68 m *(501.02 × 28.48 ft)*; M (GMT); 17.5 kts; ex-*Rio Calchaqui*

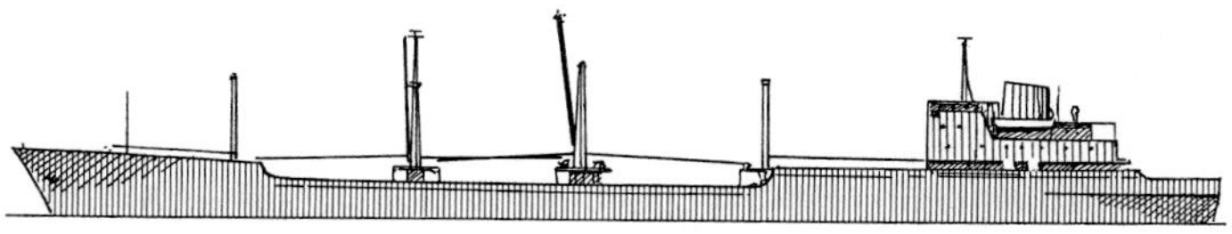

332 *MNMN²MF H13*
SHENG YUAN RC/FRG (A G 'Weser') 1974; C; 9,632 grt/15,100 dwt; 145.04 × 9.43 m *(475.85 × 30.94 ft)*; M (MAN); 16 kts; ex-*Adam Asnyk*; '36-L' type
Sisters: **DONG FA** (RC) ex-*Changxing*; **SU YANG** (RC) ex-*Dexing*

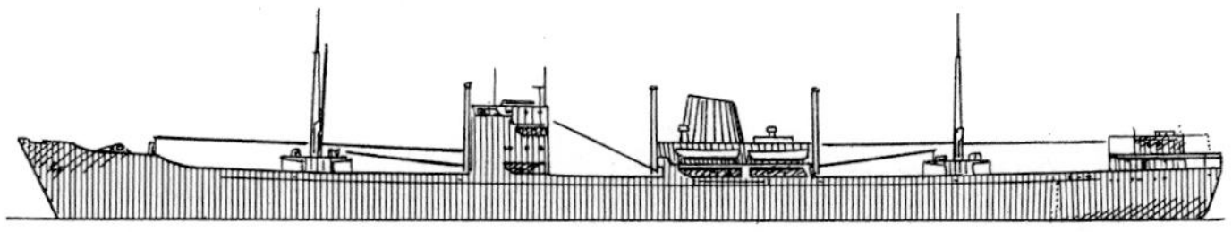

333 *MN²FNM H1*
YU LIANG SHAN RC/No (Framnaes) 1960; C; 5,754 grt/8,382 dwt; 146.06 × 8.09 m *(479.2 × 26.54 ft)*; M (Sulzer); 16.5 kts; ex-*Thorstream*

334 *MN²FNMN H13*
HONG QI 134 RC/FRG (Deutsche Werft) 1956; C; 8,976 grt/10,300 dwt; 151.14 × 8.1 m *(496 × 26.57 ft)*; M (B&W); 15.5 kts; ex-*Hoegh Cliff*

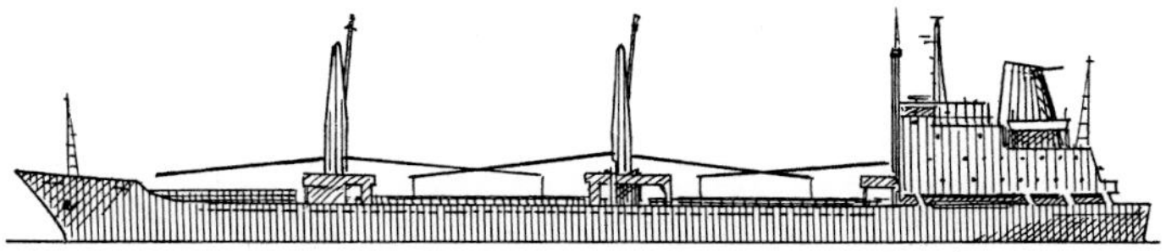

335 *MN²HMFN H1*
TIAN XING RC/Ja (Setouchi) 1977; C; 6,249 grt/7,956 dwt; 119.41 × 7.41 m *(391.77 × 24.31 ft)*; M (B&W); 14 kts; ex-*Laurie U*
Sister: **TIAN CHANG** (RC) ex-*Maria U*

336 *MN²HN²M–F H13*
HANG CHEONG Pa/FRG (B+V) 1970; C/Con; 10,119 grt/14,738 dwt; 162.75 × 8.94 m *(533.96 × 29.33 ft)*; M (Pielstick); 15.5 kts; ex-*Iberia*; 'PIONEER' Type; 348 TEU

337 *MN²MF H13*
PHILIPPOS Ho/FRG (Sterkrade) 1954; C; 1,598 grt/2,885 dwt; 86.77 × 5.7 m *(284.68 × 18.7 ft)*; M (MAN); 11.5 kts; ex-*Mercator*

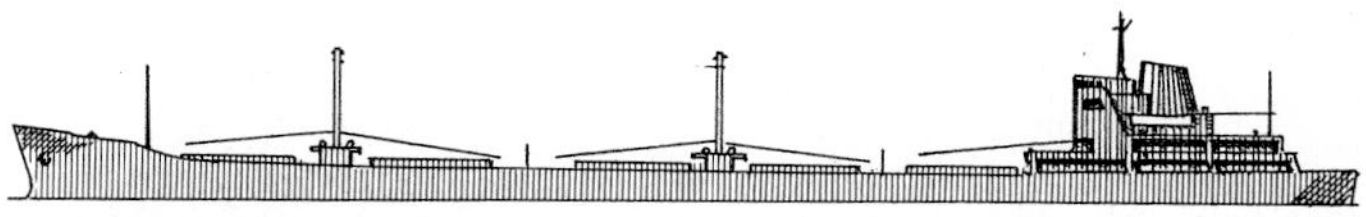

338 *MN²MFN H1*
NAN DU JIANG RC/Br (Doxford & S) 1969; B; 11,539 grt/20,747 dwt; 160.03 × 9.15 m *(525.03 × 30.02 ft)*; M (Sulzer); 15.5 kts; ex-*Federal Lakes*

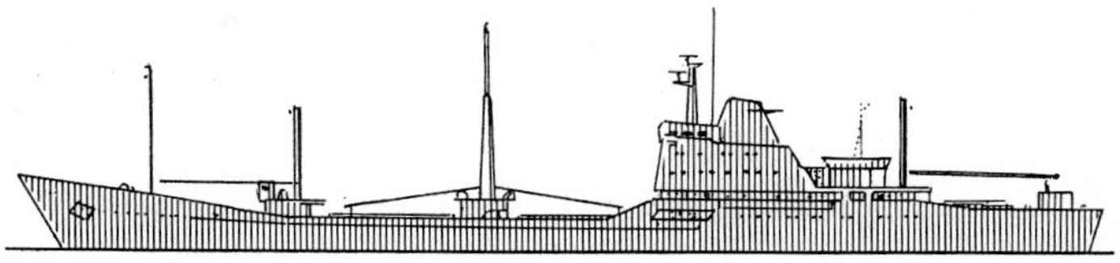

339 *MN²MFN H13*
TARKHANSK Ru/Pd (Szczecinska) 1978; C/FC; 5,467 grt/5,816 dwt; 123.93 × 7.32 m *(406 × 24.02 ft)*; M (Sulzer); 15.75 kts; 'B432' type
Sisters: **ALEXANDERE** (Li) ex-*Kashirskoye*; **KULIKOVO** (Ru); **SARATOVSK** (Ru); **TALNIKI** (Ru); **TARASOVSK** (Ru); **TEREKHOVSK** (Ru); **TERNOVSK** (Ru); **TIMOFEYEVSK** (Ru); **TITOVSK** (Ru); **TOKARYEVSK** (Ru); **TRUNOVSK** (Ru); **TULSK** (Ru)

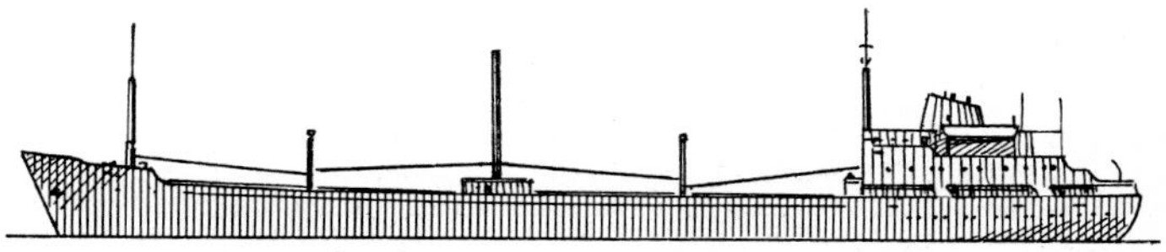

340 *MN³HF H1*
BOTEVGRAD Bu/No (Kristiansands) 1962; C; 2,334 grt/4,013 dwt; 102.77 × 6.01 m *(337.17 × 19.72 ft)*; M (B&W); 14 kts; ex-*Germa*

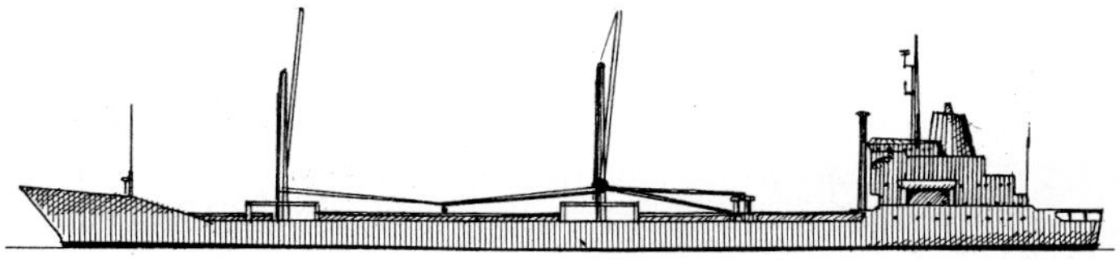

341 *MN³MF H13*
REI FENG SV/FRG (O&K) 1972; C/Con; 8,598 grt/12,478 dwt; 143.8 × 8.33 m *(471.78 × 27.33 ft)*; M (Pielstick); 18 kts; Launched as *Edith Howaldt*; 1053 TEU
Sisters: **LORCON MINDANAO** (Pa); ex-*Rheingold*; **LORCON LUZON** (Pa) Launched as *Walkure*

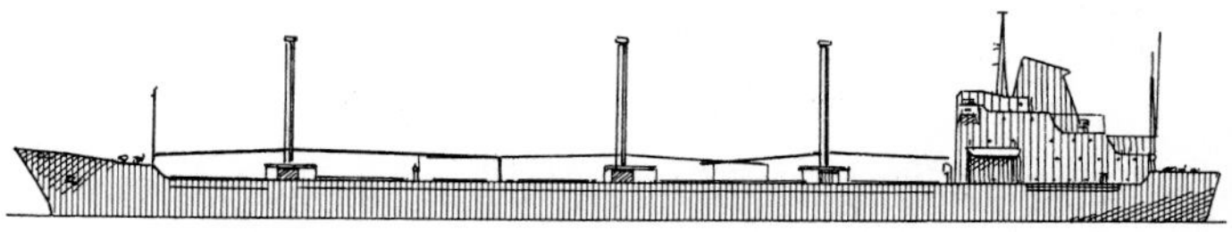

342 *MN³MFM H13*
GOLDEN IMMENSITY Pa/Sp (AESA) 1970; C; 11,599 grt/19,524 dwt; 147.02 × 10.06 m *(482.34 × 32.40 ft)*; M (MAN); 16 kts; ex-*Jocelyne*; 'SANTA FE' type

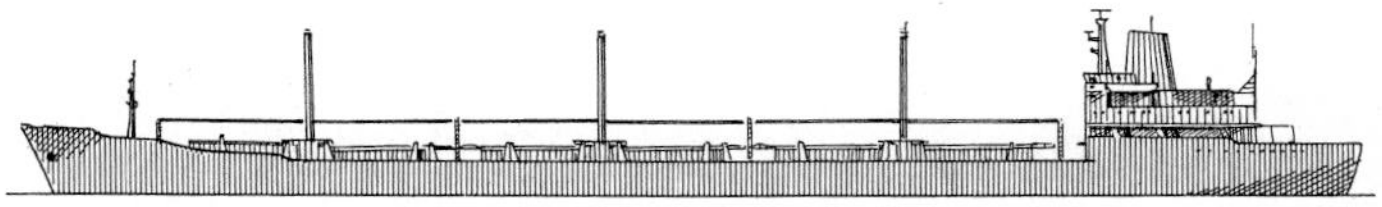

343 *MN³MFN H13*
BAJDA Ma/No (Kaldnes) 1969; B; 15,655 grt/25,782 dwt; 180.32 × 10.21 m *(591.6 × 33.5 ft)*; M (B&W); 15 kts; ex-*Maersk Commander*
Sisters: **MAS PROSPERITY** (SV) ex-*Maersk Cadet*; **SEAWAYS** (Ma) ex-*Hoegh Minerva*; **GEORGE** (Ma) ex-*Hoegh Miranda*

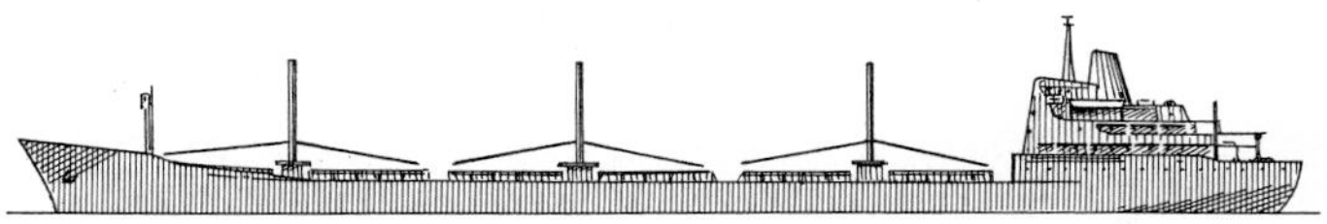

344 *MN³MFN H13*
CHANG HAI RC/No (Haugesund) 1964; B; 12,750 grt/20,080 dwt; 162.16 × 9.7 m *(532 × 31.8); M (B&W); 14.5 kts; ex-Bris*
Sister: **FOUR M** (Ho) ex-*Valhall*

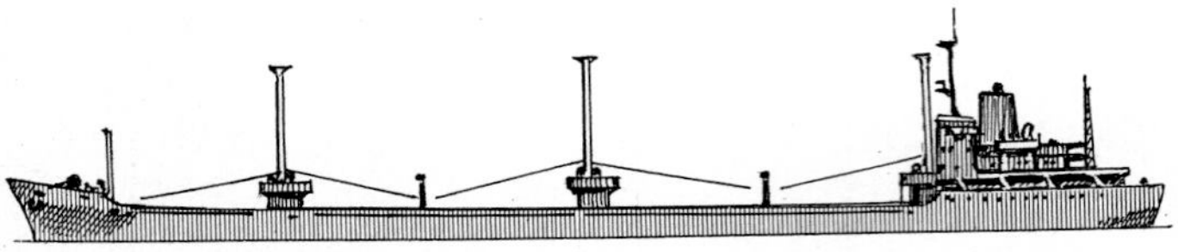

345 *MN^{3}MFN H13*
COPERNICO Ch/Ja (Hitachi) 1971; B; 15,665 grt/25,714 dwt; 174.71 × 10.31 m *(573.2 × 33.8 ft)*; M (B&W); 15.5 kts; ex-*Island Archon*
Sister: **CHINA BRIGHT** (Pa) ex-*Island Sun*

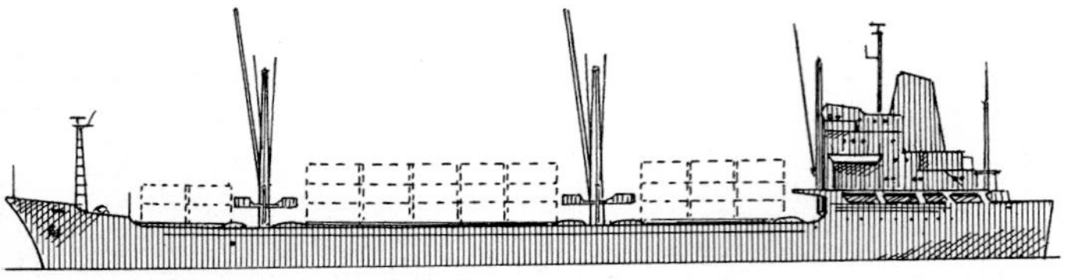

346 *MN^{3}MFN H13*
KARIPANDE An/Ja (Ujina) 1977; C/Con; 8,521 grt/12,977 dwt; 133.2 × 8.83 m *(437.01 × 28.97 ft)*; M (B&W); 15 kts; ex-*Bianka Leonhardt*; 378 TEU

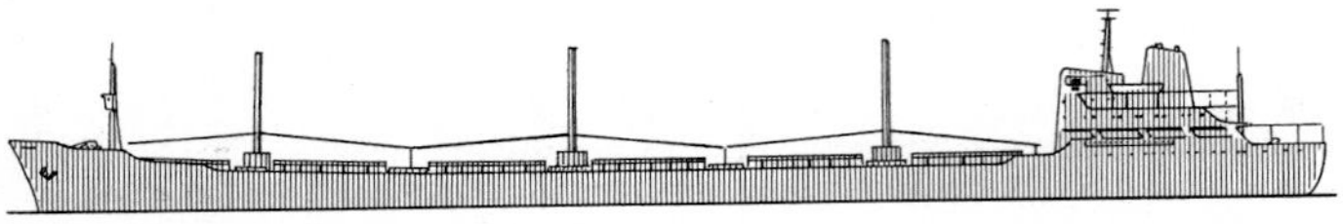

347 *MN^{3}MFN H13*
LIAO HAI RC/Ja (Mitsubishi Z) 1961; B; 15,718 grt/26,739 dwt; 176.79 × 10.66 m *(580 × 34.97 ft)*; M (MAN); 15.25 kts; ex-*Mosdale*

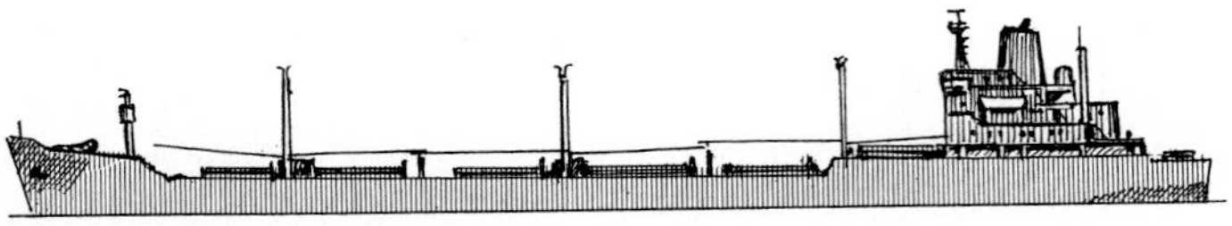

348 *MN^{3}MFN H13*
WAN LI RC/FRG (Rhein Nordseew) 1969; B; 14,357 grt/21,240 dwt; 169.02 × 10.12 m *(554.5 × 33.2 ft)*; M (Fiat); 16 kts; ex-*Long Charity*
Sister: **ASENA 1** (Tu) ex-*Fernside*

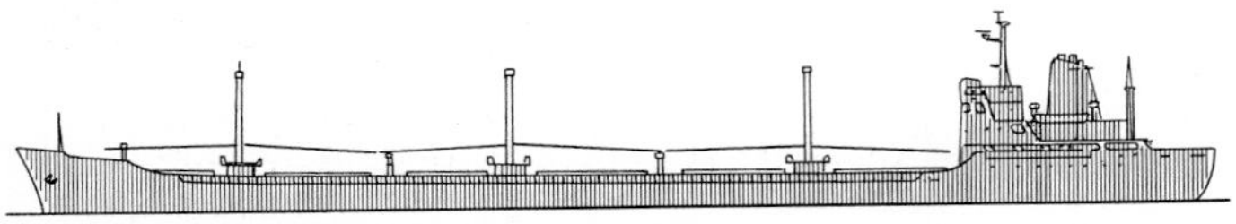

349 *MN^{3}MFN^2 H13*
ALEXIA Cy/Tw (Taiwan SB) 1973; B; 17,355 grt/28,843 dwt; 181.21 × 10.28 m *(594.52 × 33.73 ft)*; M (Sulzer); 15 kts; ex-*Eleranta*

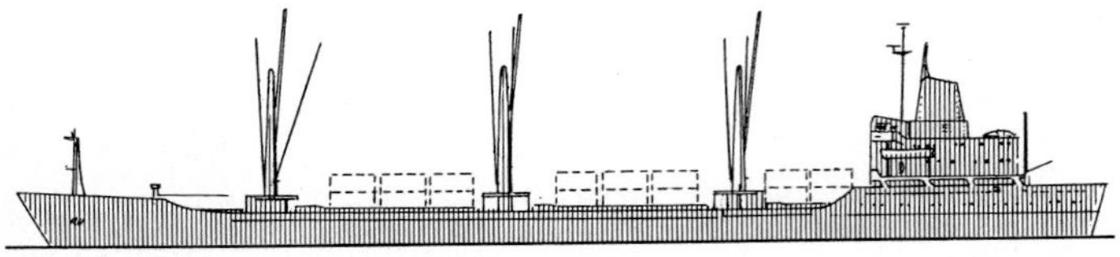

350 *MN^{3}MM–FN H13*
JIN HAI YANG RC/FRG (Flensburger) 1972; C/Con; 11,082 grt/16,780 dwt; 154.87 × 9.8 m *(508 × 32.15 ft)*; M (MAN); 17 kts; ex-*Lutz Jacob*; May be fitted with a travelling crane; 501 TEU
Sister: **ARMIN STAR** (Ma) ex-*Renate Jacob*

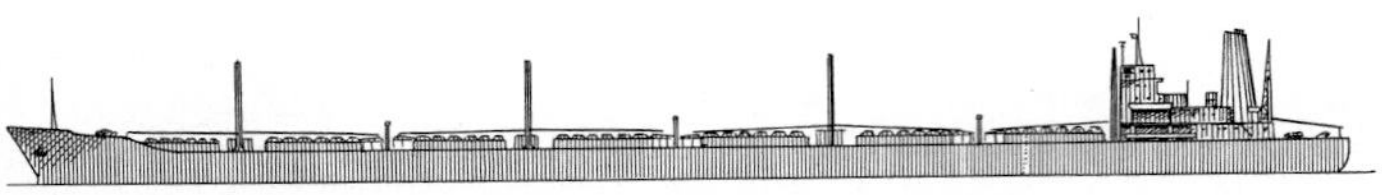

351 *MN^{4}MFN H1*
HORIZON A Ma/Ja (Hitachi) 1971; B; 34,932 grt/60,503 dwt; 225 × 12.46 m *(738.19 × 40.88 ft)*; M (Sulzer); 14.75 kts; ex-*Evelyn*
Sisters: **AURELIA** (Va) ex-*Ivory*; **DELTA PRIDE** (Pk) ex-*Peace Venture*; **VELOS** (Cy) ex-*Vela*

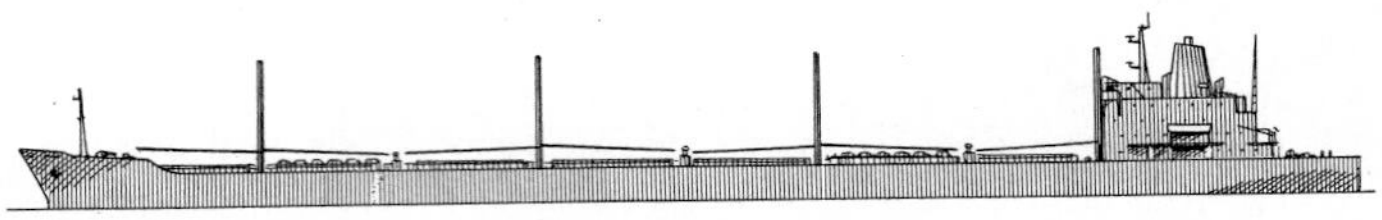

352 *MN^{4}MFN H1*
WEST STAR Li/Ja (IHI) 1970; B; 31,424 grt/51,091 dwt; 208.01 × 11.73 m *(682.45 × 38.48 ft)*; M (Sulzer); 14.75 kts; ex-*Choko Maru*
Similar: **MEXICANA** (Cy) ex-*Mexican Gulf*; **FENG CHANG** (Pa) ex-*Spray Derrick*; **MERCURY** (Li) ex-*Tonin*

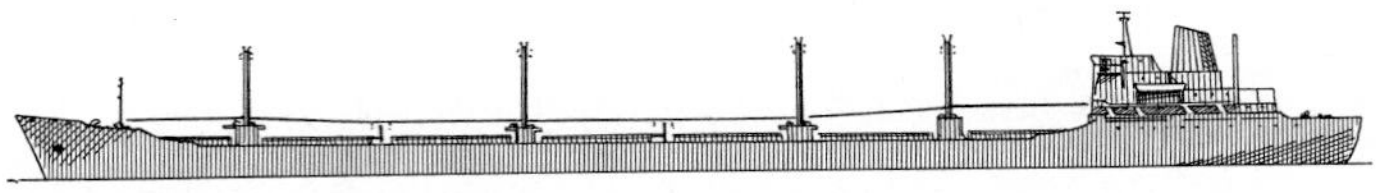

353 *MN^{4}MFN H13*
BELLE Ma/Br (Scotts' SB) 1969; B; 23,919 grt/41,869 dwt; 201.78 × 11.61 m *(662 × 38.09 ft)*; M (Sulzer); 15 kts; ex-*Grecian Legend*
Sister: **HOMER** (Cy) ex-*Grecian Spirit*

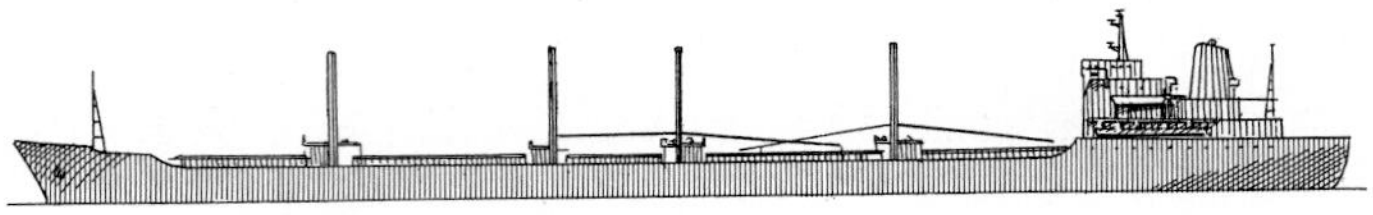

354 *MN^{4}MFN H13*
DARIA I Pa/Ja (Osaka) 1971; B; 20,464 grt/34,241 dwt; 185.5 × 11.15 m *608.6 × 36.58 ft)*; M (Sulzer); 14.75 kts; ex-*Maritime Ace*
Sisters: **XIN LONG JIANG** (RC) ex-*Eastern Hornet*; **IRAN FALLAHI** (Ir) ex-*Eastern Lilac*; **SUPPORT** (Pa) ex-*Golden Daisy*; **ASTORIA** (Cy) ex-*Bunga Chempaka*; Similar: **MARIKA** (Gr) ex-*Erradale*; **MAGDA P** (Gr) ex-*Maritime Unity*; **MARIA M** (Cy) ex-*Golden Dolphin*; **HOI CHEUNG** (Va) ex-*Maritime Justice*; **HERON** (Cy) ex-*Maritime Harmony*; **ANURADHA** (Bs) ex-*Maritime Fortune*; **MAYSTAR** (Ma) ex-*Maritime Trader*

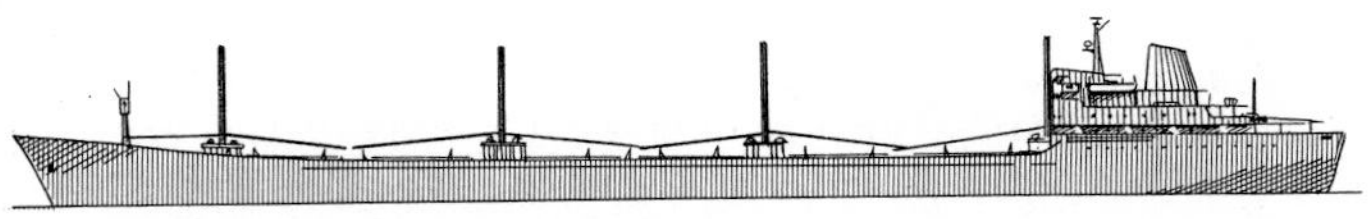

355 *MN^{4}MFN H13*
TRANCISCO —/No (Fredriksstad) 1966; B; 15,784 grt/24,879 dwt; 190.79 × 10.12 m *(625.95 × 33.2 ft)*; M (Gotaverken); 17.5 kts; ex-*Norse Transporter*

356 *MN^{4}M–FN^2 H13*
"SAPPHIRE STAR" class dwt; Sequence variation for some sisters listed under drawing number 8/358

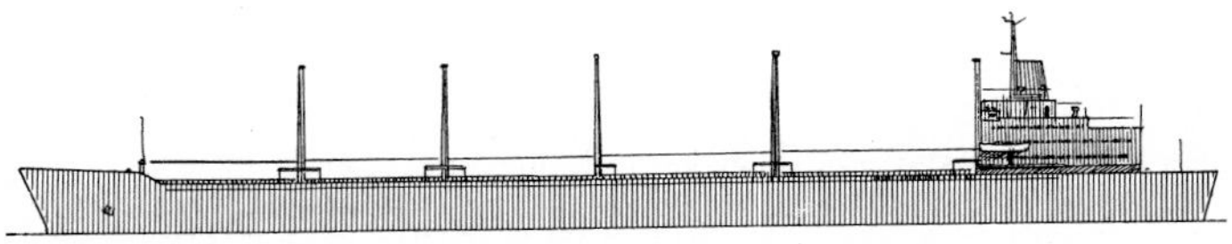

357 *MN^{5}M-F HI*
GRONERS JADE Pa/FRG (B+V) 1969; C; 13,392 grt/21,404 dwt; 162.21 × 10.38 m *(532.19 × 34.06 ft)*; M (Pielstick); 15 kts; ex-*Jag Deesh*; 'Pioneer' type
Sisters: **SAGAR** (Ma) ex-*Jag Dhir*; **HAINAN 3** (RC) ex-*Indian Glory*

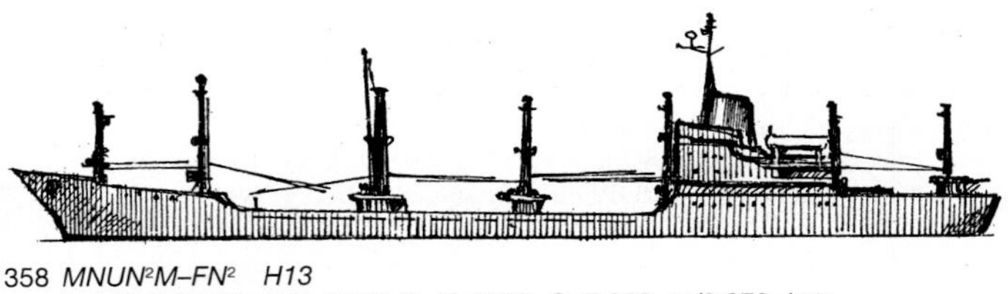

358 *MNUN^{2}M–FN^2 H13*
SAPPHIRE STAR Pa/FRG (B+V) 1967; C; 7,066 grt/8,873 dwt; 135.8 × 7.42/8.6 m *(446 × 24/28 ft)*; M (B+V); 18.75 kts; ex-*Trier*
Sisters (third mast is a goalpost or a Stulcken in some vessels): **HUANG LONG SHAN** (RC) ex-*Hagen*; **TAI HANG SHAN** (RC) ex-*Hamburg*; **EMERALD STAR** (—) ex-*Speyer*; **MIAO FENG SHAN** (RC) ex-*Hattingen*; **SU FENG** (RC) ex-*Heidelberg*; **CORAIN 1** (Co) ex-*Hanau*; **CORAIN II** (Co) ex-*Heilbronn*

359 *MTFNM H*
ANDINO Pe/Ne (Duijvendijk's) 1956; C; 1,816 grt/3,256 dwt; 109 × 5.3 m *(358 × 17.6 ft)*; M (Sulzer); 14.5 kts; ex-*Crispin*; Lengthened 1964

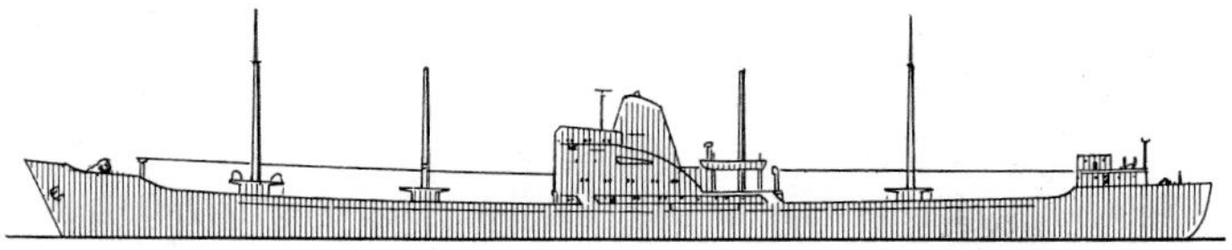

360 *MTFTM H13*
BANGLAR SAMPAD Bh/In (Hindustan) 1971; C; 8,933 grt/12,880 dwt; 154.13 × 9.22 m *(506 × 30.25 ft)*; M (Sulzer); 14 kts; ex-*Vishva Darshan*

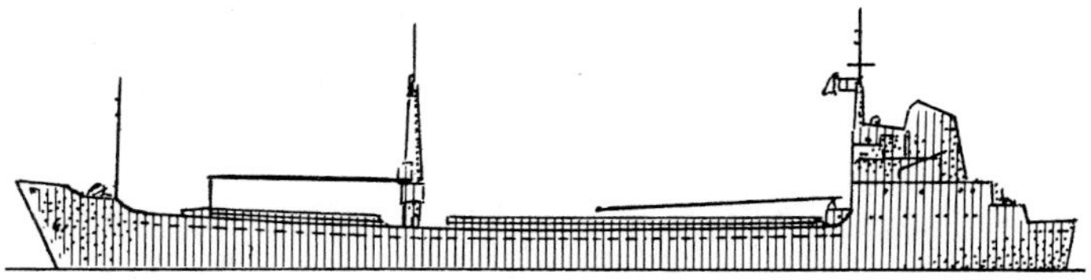

361 *MTHF H12*
AVRA Cy/In (Mazagon) 1978; C/Con; 2,916 grt/3,716 dwt; 91.19 × 5.58 m *(299.18 × 18.31 ft)*; M (Alpha-Diesel); 14.5 kts; ex-*Oued Sebou*; 128 TEU

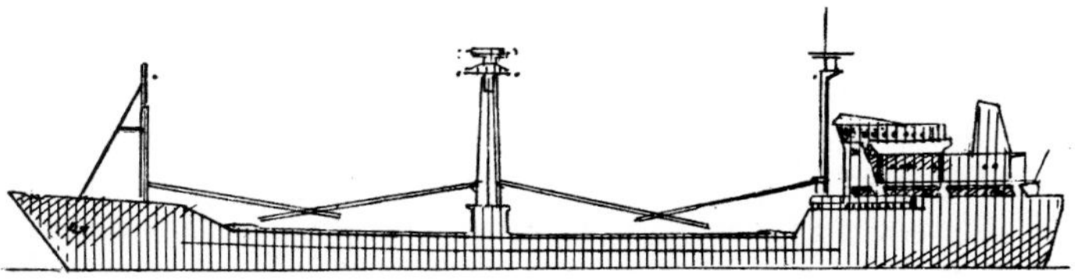

362 *MTHF H13*
ACORIANO Po/No (Aukra) 1978; C; 1,529 grt/2,864 dwt; 79.46 × 5.35 m *(260.7 × 17.55 ft)*; M (Alco); 14 kts; ex-*Hirma*; 94 TEU

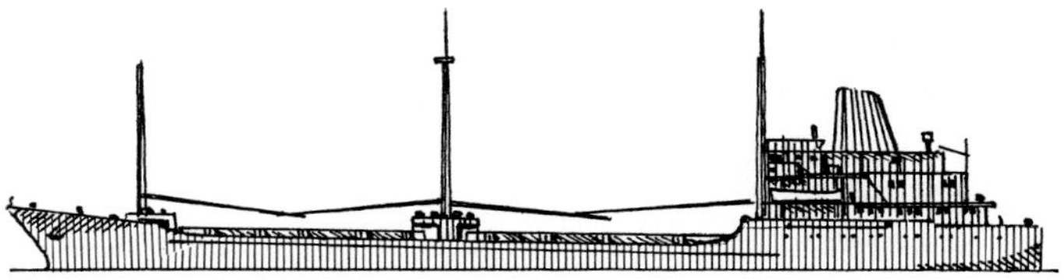

363 *MTHF H13*
HUA JIA RC/FRG (Sietas) 1970; C; 3,254 grt/4,478 dwt; 100.56 × 6.77 m *(329.92 × 22.21 ft)*; M (Deutz); 15.5 kts; ex-*Weser Broker*

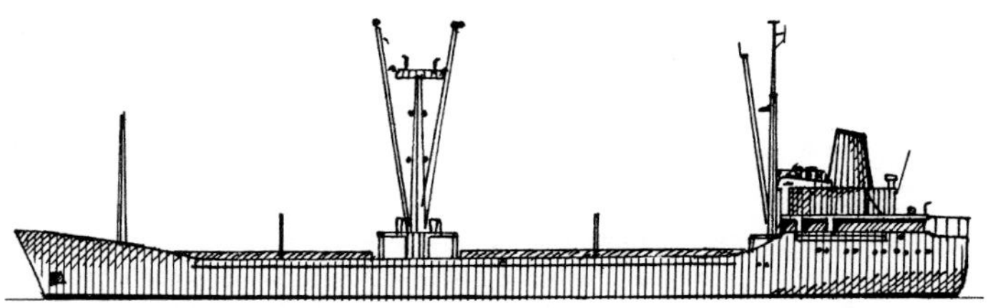

364 *MTHF H13*
STRAITS VENTURE Sg/FRG (Sietas) 1970; C; 2,477 grt/4,000 dwt; 90.81 × 6.50 m *(297.93 × 21.33 ft)*; M (Atlas-MaK); 14 kts; Launched as *Taurus*

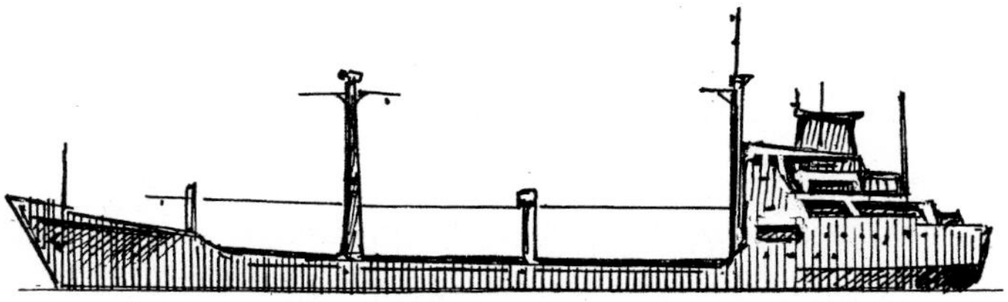

365 *MTHFM H13*
APUOLE Lt/Fi (Nystads) 1973; C/TC; 3,184 grt/4,471 dwt; 97.31 × 6.7 m *(319.26 × 21.98 ft)*; M (B&W); 14 kts; ex-*Abram Arkhipov*
Sisters (Some built by Hollming or Valmet): **VELIUONA** (Lt) ex-*Vladimir Favorskiy*; **KREVA** (Lt) ex-*Mitrofan Grekov*; **MEDININKAI** (Lt) ex-*Vasiliy Polenov*; **MERKINE** (Lt) ex-*Nikolay Yaroshenko*; **KERNAVE** (Lt) ex-*Nikolay Kasatkin*; **KONSTANTIN YUON** (Ru); **IGOR GRABAR** (Ru); **IVAN SHADR** (Ru); **MIKHAIL CHEREMNYKH** (Ru); **VERA MUKHINA** (Ru); **EKATERINA BELASHOVA** (Ru)

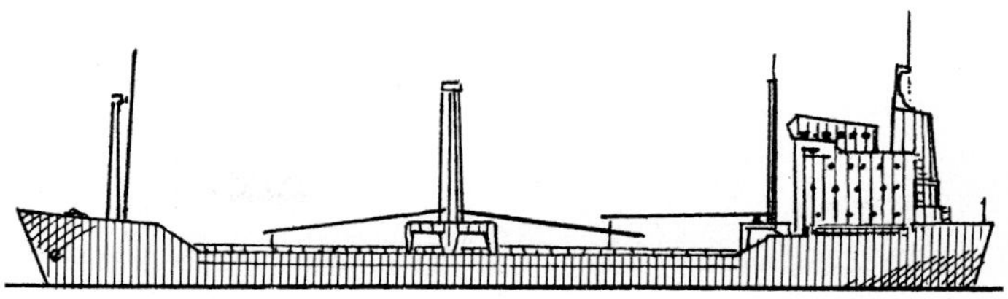

366 *MTHH–F H13*
MOON BIRD NA/Ne (Jonker) 1978; C; 3,457 grt/3,787 dwt; 82.12 × 6.41 m *(269.42 × 21.03 ft)*; M (MWM); 12.5 kts; ex-*Alamak*; 30 TEU

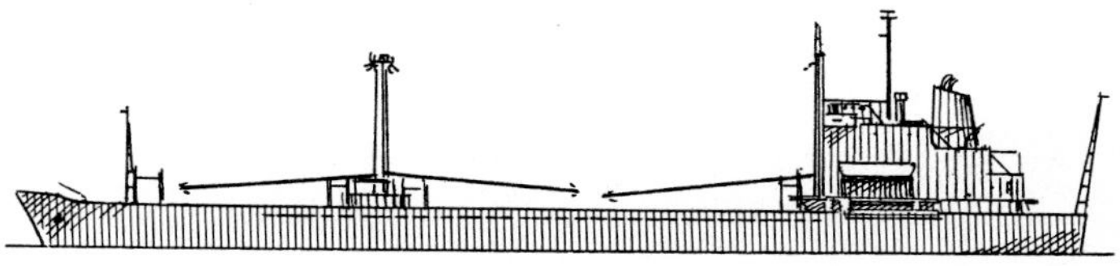

367 *MTHMFN H*
INDOBARUNA 1 Ia/Ja (Asakawa) 1975; C; 4,756 grt/6,150 dwt; 102.16 × 6.02 m *(335.17 × 19.75 ft)*; TSM (Akasaka); 12 kts; ex-*Masbon*
Sisters: **RASA** (Cro) ex-*Minarosa*; **VIJERA** (Cro) ex-*Minador*

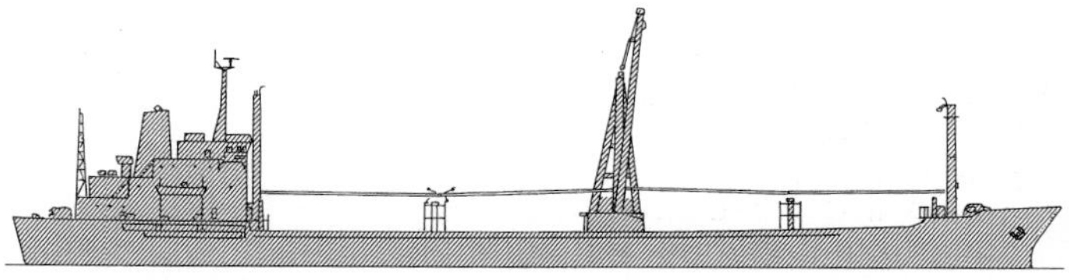

368 *MTHMFN H123*
KEDMA Is/Ja (Namura) 1978; C/HL; 9,231 grt/16,436 dwt; 145.04 × 8.90 m *(475.85 × 29.20 ft)*; M (B&W); 16 kts; ex-*Moncey*
Probable sisters: **LU LONG No 1** (RC) ex-*L'Acropole*; **KELTIC CONFIDENCE** (Pi) ex-*Kilbride*

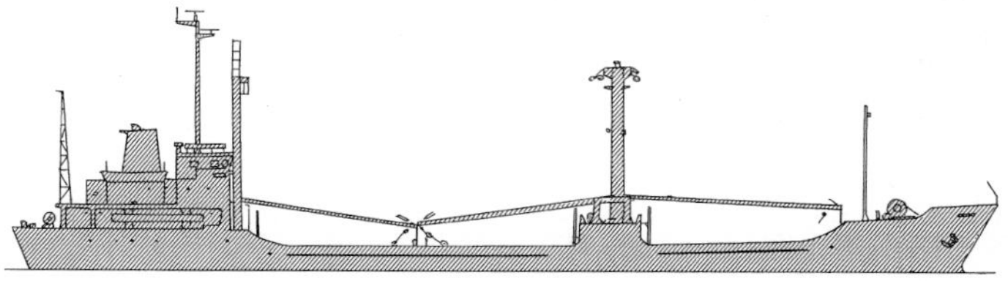

369 *MTHMFN H13*
FU WEI RC/Ja (Imai S) 1983; C; 2,866 grt/4,824 dwt; 90.51 × 6.41 m *(296.95 × 21.03 ft)*; M (Akasaka); 11 kts; ex-*Tasman Friendship*
Sister: **JASMIN PRINCE** (Pa) ex-*Blue Columbia*
Probable sisters: **YAN FU** (RC) ex-*Hop Arrow*; **WEINING 3** (Pa) ex-*New Arrow*; **SANG THAI QUARTZ** (Th) ex-*Sea Arrow*; **LA BONITA** (Bs) ex-*Lotus King*; **HUNG VUONG 1** (Vn) ex-*Prince*; **LINDA K** (Pa); **EASTERN LUCKY** (Pa); **WESTERN LUCKY** (Pa)
Sister (larger crosstree on mast amidships): **SECIL DINAMARCA** (Pa)

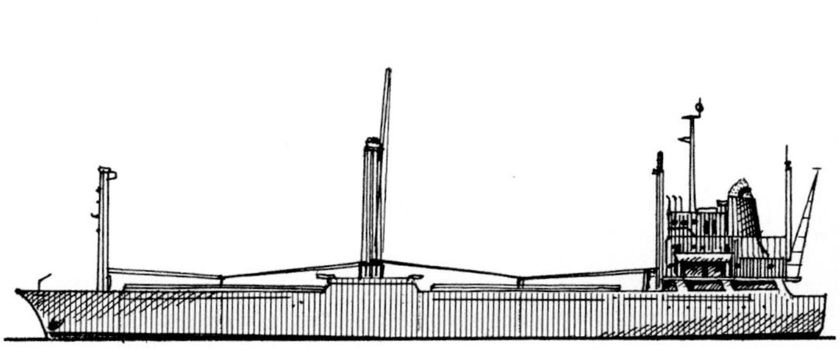

370 *MTHMFN[2] H2*
EBN JUBAIR Ly/Ja (Asakawa) 1976; C; 6,229 grt/7,769 dwt; 105.7 × 7.62 m *(346.78 × 25 ft)*; M (B&W); 13 kts
Sister: **EBN BATUTA** (Ly)

371 *MTHNMFN H13*
QING ANN Sg/Ja (Hashihama) 1976; C; 6,375 grt/9,930 dwt; 128.99 × 7.95 m *(423.20 × 26.08 ft)*; M (Mitsubishi); 13.50 kts; ex-*Regent Scorpio*; **SIMILAR TO DRAWING NUMBER 8/420**. Some ships on latter entry may also have a goalpost mast

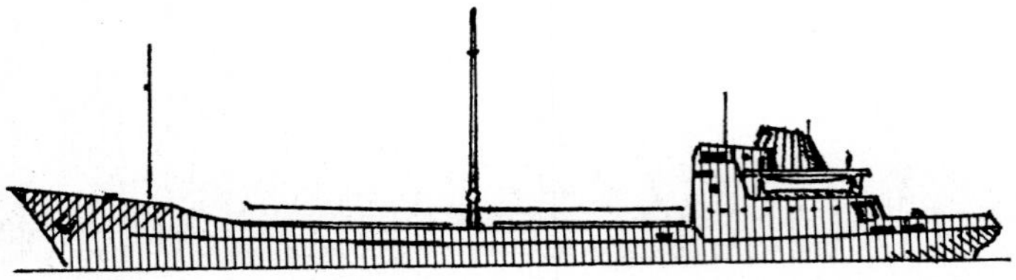

372 *MTMF H1*
SHOVELLER Ho/Ne (Boot) 1967; C; 1,377 grt/2,546 dwt; 79.61 × 5.77 m *(261.19 × 18.93 ft)*; M ('De Industrie'); 12.5 kts; ex-*Schippersgracht*

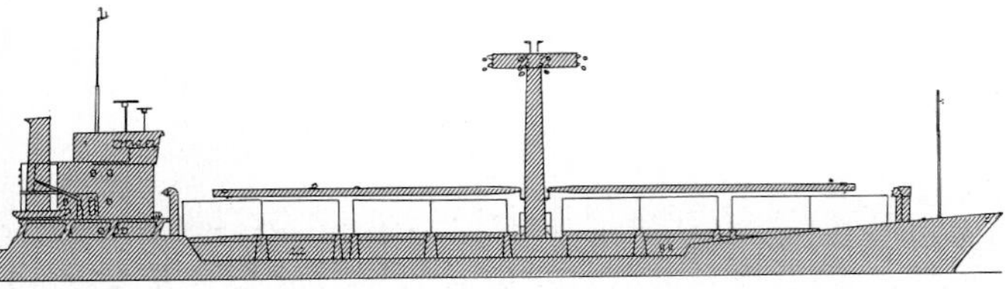

373 *MTMF H13*
CLEARWATER BAY DIS/De (Nordso) 1989; C/Con; 1,829 grt/2,676 dwt; 79.57 × 5.18 m *(261.06 × 16.99 ft)*; M (MaK); 11.7 kts; ex-*Arktis Queen*; 118 TEU
Sisters: **ARKTIS TRADER** (DIS); **ARKTIS BREEZE** (DIS); **ARKTIS OCEAN** (DIS); **ARKTIS RIVER** (DIS); **ARKTIS SKY** (DIS); **ARKTIS SIRIUS** (DIS); **ARKTIS PRINCESS** (DIS); **ARKTIS CARRIER** (DIS); **ARKTIS GRACE** (DIS)

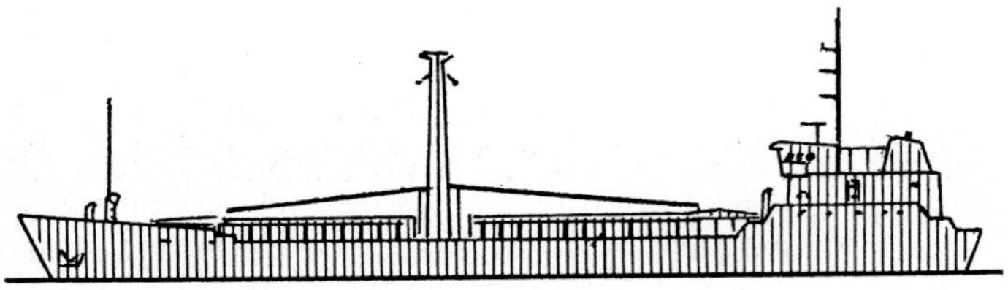

374 *MTMF H3*
TCI SHAKTI In/De (Nordso) 1982; C; 1,510 grt/2,156 dwt; 72.47 × 3.8 m *(237.76 × 12.47 ft)*; M (B&W Alpha); 11 kts; ex-*Kraka*; May be sail-assisted (not shown on drawing); 54 TEU
Sisters (Some may be sail-assisted): **JEANIE BROWN** (Cy) ex-*Karolina*; **BHORUKA VIKRAM** (In) ex-*Arktis Moon*; **ARKTIS SEA** (DIS); **EMILIE K** (DIS) ex-*Arktis Star*; **ARKTIS SUN** (DIS); **ARKTIS BAY** (DIS); **GUADALUPE** (Cy) ex-*Edith M*; **SEA FLOWER** (DIS) ex-*Kirsten Frank*

375 *MTMFNMN H13*
TANG YIN RC/FRG (LF-W) 1960; C; 9,224 grt/12,995 dwt; 151.4 × 9.3 m *(497 × 30.4 ft)*; M (MAN); 14 kts; ex-*Hanse*

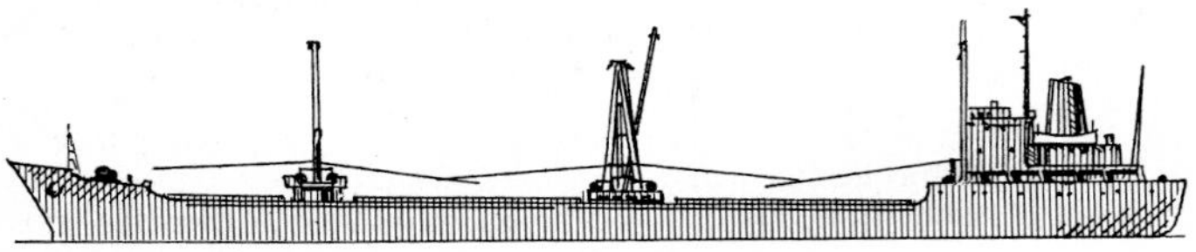

376 *MTMHMFN H123*
RUN ZHOU SV/Ja (Kurushima) 1973; C; 6,066 grt/9,585 dwt; 126.04 × 7.85 m *(413.52 × 25.75 ft)*; M (Mitsubishi); 14 kts; ex-*Katsura Maru*

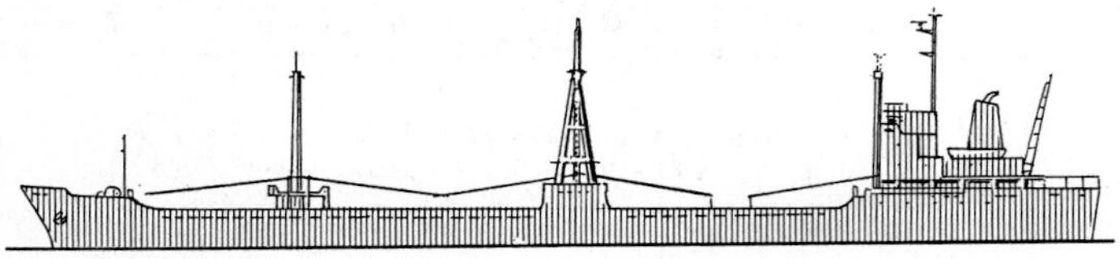

377 *MTMHMFN H13*
HUANG JIN SHAN SV/Ja (Kurushima) 1976; C/HL; 7,359 grt/11,132 dwt; 131.81 × 8.3 m *(432 × 27.23 ft)*; M (MAN); 14 kts; ex-*Azalea*
Similar (goalpost mast from bridge): **HUA BAO** (Pa) ex-*Yucaly*; Similar: **SAFINA-E-NAJJAM** (Pk) ex-*Asunaro*; **MARINA LAURI** (Sg) ex-*Hamanasu*; **MARINA CATHYA** (Sg) ex-*Acacia*

378 *MTMTMFCN H13*
FENG NING RC/Fi (Crichton-Vulcan) 1964; CP; 9,237 grt/10,936 dwt; 152 × 8.6 m *(500 × 28.7 ft)*; M (Sulzer); 16 kts; ex-*Finnenso*; Lengthened 1969

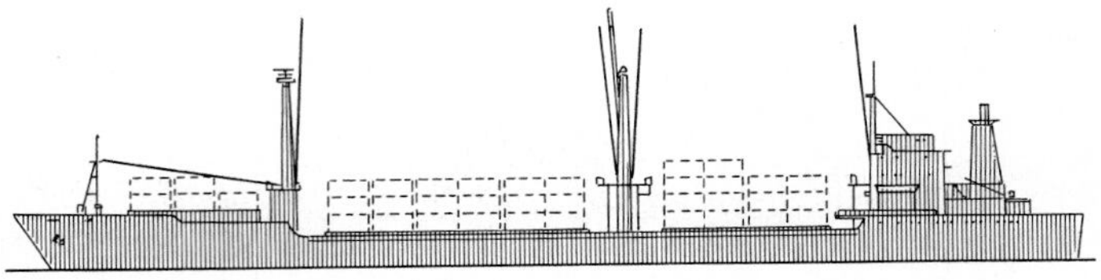

379 *MTNHFC H13*
OSTFRIESLAND Sg/FRG (Howaldts DW) 1978; C/Con/HL; 12,754 grt/ 17,750 dwt; 159.95 × 9.65 m *(524.77 × 31.66 ft)*; M (Sulzer); 17.25 kts; ex-*Ostfriesland*; 733 TEU
Sister: **MARIA S** (Gr) ex-*Elbeland*

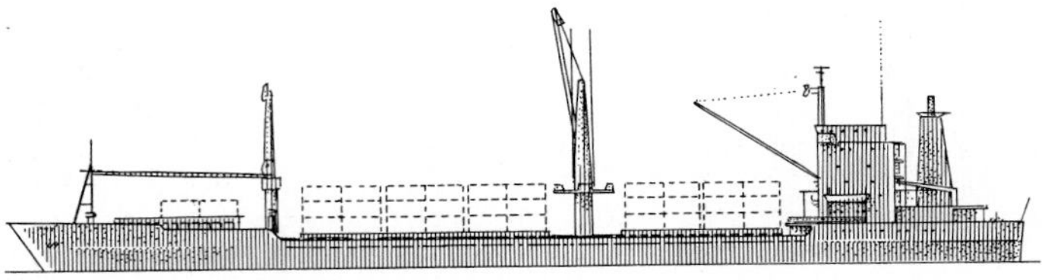

380 *MTNHFR*
KOTA BERJAYA Sg/FRG (Howaldts DW) 1978; C/Con/HL; 13,501 grt/ 18,283 dwt; 163.02 × 9.62 m *(535 × 31.56 ft)*; M (MAN); 16.5 kts; ex-*Mosel*; 800 TEU; Crane aft is on port side
Sister: **CMBT ENSIGN** (Cy) ex-*Elbe*

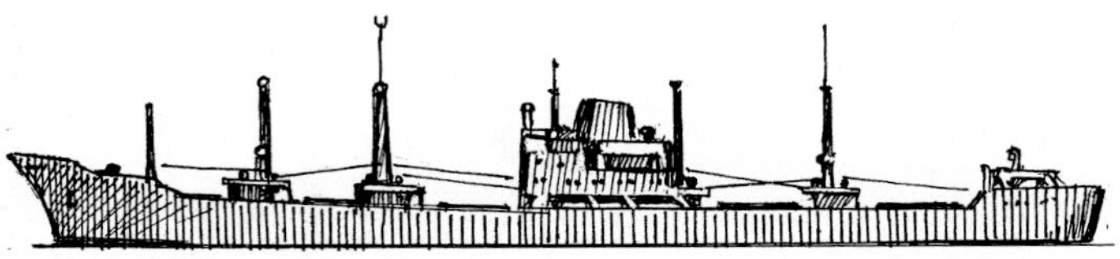

381 *MTNMFNM H13*
PINYA Mr/Ja (Hitachi) 1963; C; 7,234 grt/10,011 dwt; 137.9 × 8.4 m *(452 × 27.5 ft)*; M (B&W); 15 kts
Sister: **MERGUI** (Mr)

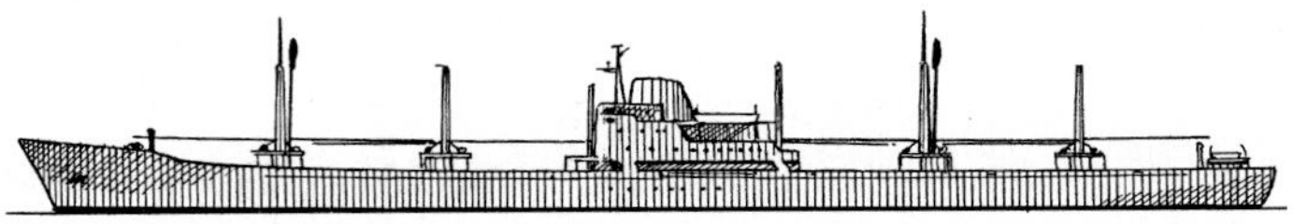

382 *MTNMFNMT H1*
VICTORIA DE GIRON Cu/Sw (Uddevalla) 1969; C; 10,972 grt/15,363 dwt; 161.9 × 9.8 m *(531 × 32.6 ft)*; M (B&W); — kts
Sister: **BAHIA DE COCHINOS** (Cu)

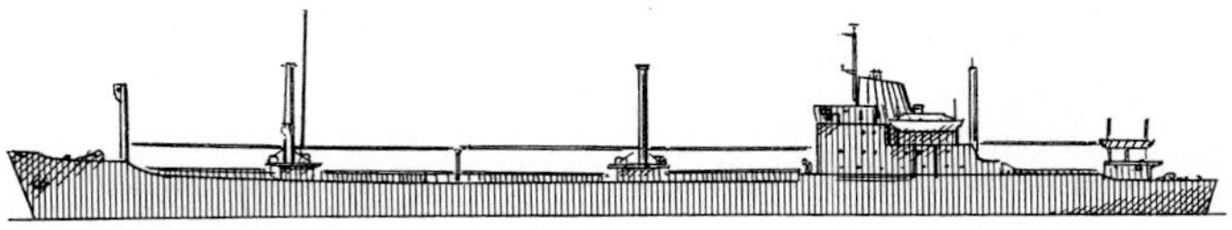

383 *MTNM–FN H1*
RONG JIANG RC/Br (A&P) 1978; C; 9,117 grt/15,189 dwt; 141 × 8.86 m *(462 × 29.07 ft)*; M (Sulzer); 14.75 kts; ex-*Morviken*; 'SD 14' type
Sisters: **MAXIMO GOMEZ** (Cu) ex-*Australind*; **KIFANGONDO** (An) ex-*Sea Hawk*; **LUNDOGE** (An) ex-*Aegira*; **THAI-BINH** (Vn); **LUCNAM** (Vn); **TO-LICH** (Vn); **SONG DUONG** (Vn) ex-*Dalworth*; **YUANJIANG** (RC); **HUNJIANG** (RC); **PING JIANG** (RC) ex-*Funing*; **HANBONN CONCORD** (SV) ex-*Derwent*; **RIO B** (Ma) ex-*Belloc*; **SHUN YI** (RC) ex-*Boswell*; **SAFE STAR** (Ma) ex-*Bronte*; **FORTUNATE STAR** (Ma) ex-*Browning*; **AN SAI JIANG** (RC) ex-*African Express*; **AN LU JIANG** (RC) ex-*European Express*; **EMPROS** (Gr); **AN YANG JIANG** (RC) ex-*Grand Faith*; **SAIGON 3** (Ml) ex-*Jade 11*; **SCANDINAVIAN EXPRESS** (Pi) ex-*Jade 111*; **PETRA WAVE** (Cy) ex-*United Drive*; **FAR EAST** (Bs) ex-*United Enterprise*; **NAVAL LADY** (Ma) ex-*United Spirit*; **LILAC ISLANDS** (Pa) ex-*Carrianna Lilac*; **LOTUS ISLANDS** (Pa) ex-*Carrianna Lotus*; **ROSE ISLANDS** (Pa) ex-*Sunderland Venture*; **HANBONN BROTHER** (SV) ex-*Darya Lok*; Similar ('SD15' type—almost identical, slightly larger): **EAST ISLANDS** (Cy); **NORTH ISLANDS** (Cy); **SOUTH ISLANDS** (Cy); **WEST ISLANDS** (Cy)

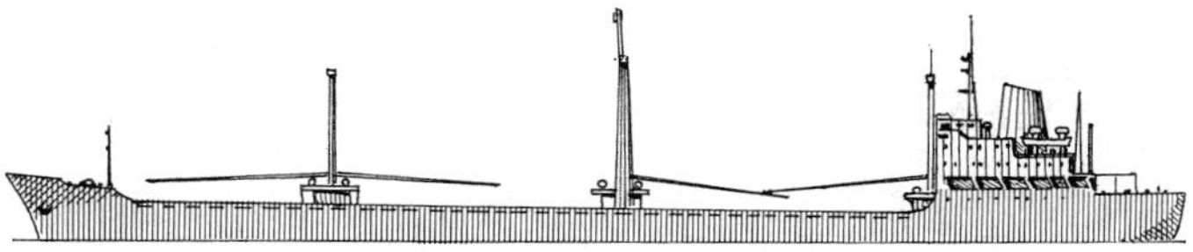

384 MTN^2MFN^2 *H13*
DA CHENG RC/Ja (Hitachi) 1973; C/HL; 11,288 grt/14,522 dwt; 154.95 × 9.08 m *(508.37 × 29.79 ft)*; M (B&W); 15.5 kts
Sister: **DA TIAN** (RC)

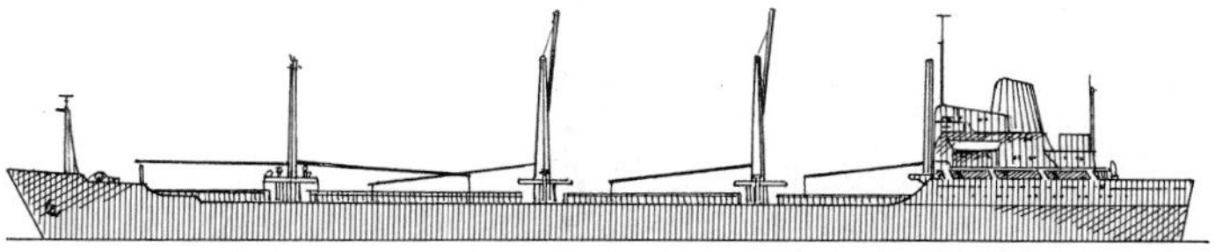

385 MTN^3MFN *H13*
LUISE LEONHARDT Cy/FRG (Flensburger) 1971; C/Con; 11,103 grt/16,950 dwt; 154.87 × 9.79 m *(508.1 × 32.12 ft)*; M (MAN); 18.5 kts; 371 TEU

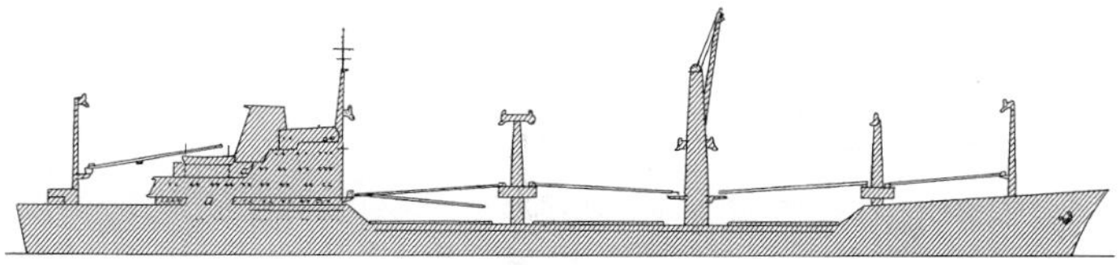

386 *MTNTHFT H13*
IRAN KOLAHDOOZ Ir/Pd (Gdanska) 1977; C/Con/HL; 13,914 grt/16,641 dwt; 169.83 × 9.76 m *(557.18 × 32.02 ft)*; M (Sulzer); 18 kts; ex-*Stratheden*; 'B-466' type; 368 TEU
Sisters: **IRAN BROOJERDI** (Ir) ex-*Strathelgin*; **IRAN BAGHAEI** (Ir) ex-*Stratherrol*; **IRAN BAGHERI** (Ir) ex-*Strathesk*; **TRIATIC POWER** (Cy) ex-*Strathettrick*; **IRAN MAHALLATI** (Ir) ex-*Strathewe*

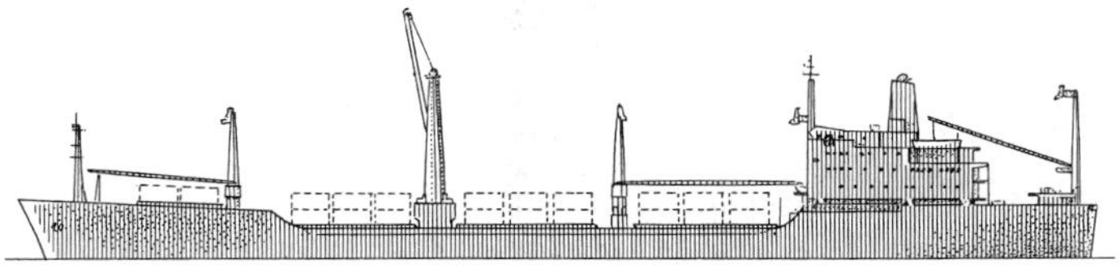

387 *MTNTHFT H13*
RIO ATRATO Co/Ja (Mitsui) 1978; C/Con/HL; 14,660 grt/17,350 dwt; 169 × 9.75 m *(554.46 × 31.99 ft)*; M (B&W); 18 kts; ex-*Strathfife*; 302 TEU
Sister: **RIO TRUANDO** (Co) ex-*Strathfyne*

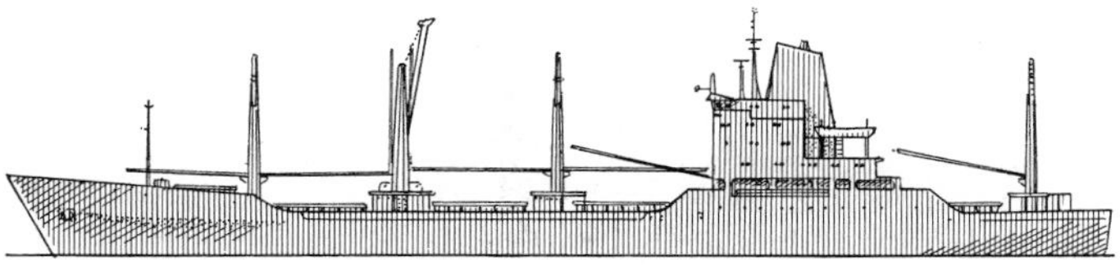

388 *MTNTMFT H12*
ENARXIS Gr/Ko (Hyundai) 1979; C/Con; 11,536 grt/11,664 dwt; 147.26 × 8.56 m *(483.14 × 28.08 ft)*; M (B&W); 16.1 kts; ex-*River Jimini*; 500 TEU
Sisters: **NDONI RIVER** (Ng) ex-*River Aboine*; **RIVER ASAB** (Ng); **KRIOS** (Li) ex-*River Osse*; **JUTHA KASAMPHAN** (Th) ex-*River Rima*; **RIVER MADA** (Ng); **RIVER ANDONI** (Ng); **JUTHA MALEE** (Th) ex-*River Guma*; **KINZAN MARU** (Th) ex-*River Kerawa*; **SIMEON TH** (Gr) ex-*River Ngada*; **RIVER IKPAN** (Ng)

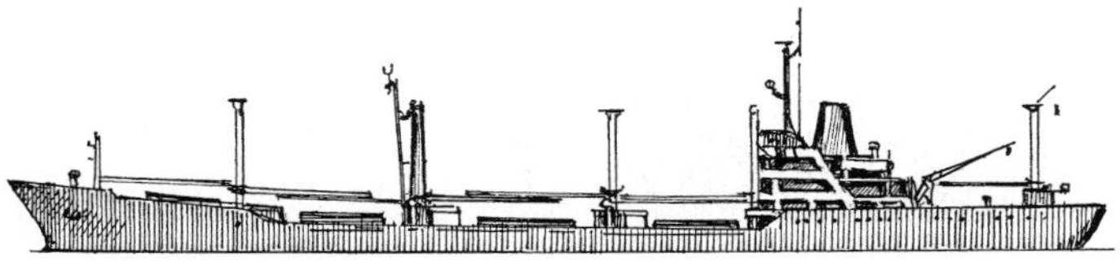

389 *MTNTNMFRT H13*
AHMED ARAB Si/Fi (Wärtsilä) 1971; C; 10,255 grt/10,596 dwt; 159 × 9.8 m *(523 × 32 ft)*; M (Sulzer); 18 kts; ex-*Hellenic Pride*
Sister: **LIAN HUA SHAN** (RC) ex-*Hellenic Star*

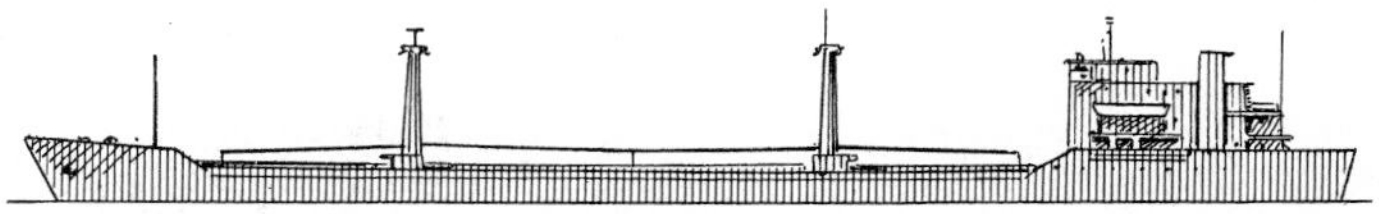

390 MT^2G *H13*
POLICOS Gr/FRG (Luerssen) 1972; Cem; 5,036 grt/7,174 dwt; 123.27 × 6.85 m *(404.43 × 22.47 ft)*; M (Normo); 13.5 kts; ex-*Falknes*; Converted from general cargo 1988—drawing shows vessel before conversion

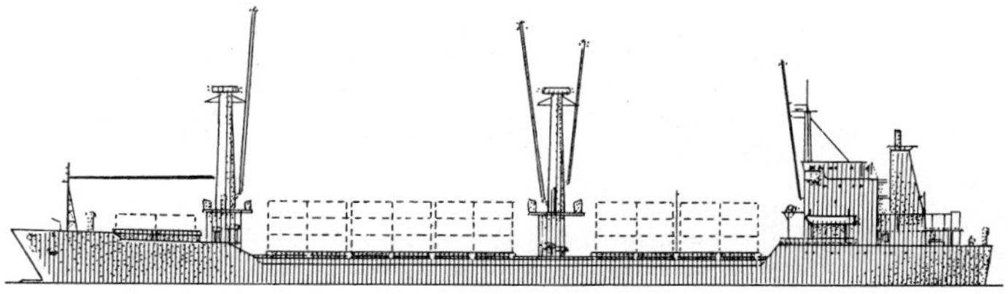

391 MT^2HF *H13*
EQUATOR EMERALD Sg/FRG (Howaldts DW) 1978; C/Con; 9,310 grt/12,692 dwt; 151.03 × 8.13 m *(495.51 × 26.67 ft)*; M (Atlas-MaK); 17 kts; ex-*Carolina*; Modified 'CL 10' type; 517 TEU
Sister: **SRIMANEE** (Th) ex-*Charlotta*

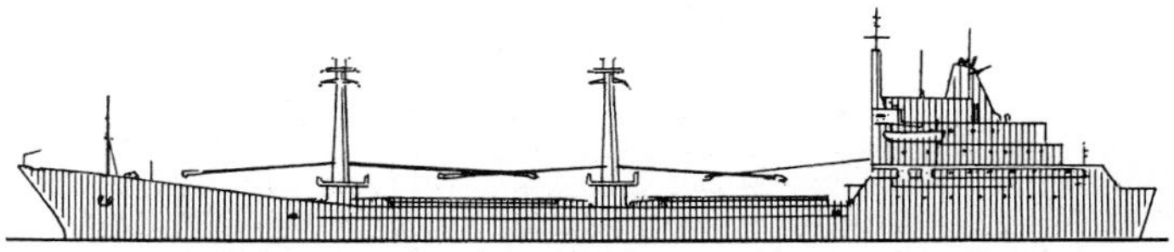

392 MT^2HF *H13*
MANDARIN STAR Bl/Bz (Ebin/So) 1977; C; 5,868 grt/8,135 dwt; 127.39 × 8.06 m *(418 × 26.44 ft)*; M (Pielstick); 15 kts; ex-*Alvorada*
Sisters: **STAR-ACE** (Ho) launched as *Lis Bewa*; **HAI RONG** (RC) launched as *Kirsten Bewa*; **JOY** (Ho) ex-*Aurora* Probable sisters: **ELINDA** (SV) ex-*Marianna*; **IBN KHALDOUN** (Eg) ex-*Saronic*; **VALBRENTA** (It) launched as *Syros Island*; **TROPICANA I** (Pa) launched as *Limnos Island*; **AL ZAHRAA** (Eg) launched as *Naxos Island*; **AL SHAYMAA** (Eg) launched as *Nicolas Condaras*

393 MT^2HFN *H13*
GHADAMES Ag/Ja (Fukuoka) 1977; C/Con; 8,627 grt/11,200 dwt; 136.38 × 8.33 m *(447.44 × 27.33 ft)*; M (Mitsubishi); 17.5 kts; ex-*Jenny Porr*; 437 TEU
Sisters: **KASSANTINA** (Ly); **SHENG CAI** (Li) ex-*Henriette Schulte*; **ASIAN JUMBO** (Pi) ex-*Wilhelm Schulte*; **WELCOME** (SV) ex-*Renate Schulte*; Similar: **TRADE LINK** (Pa) ex-*Regina*

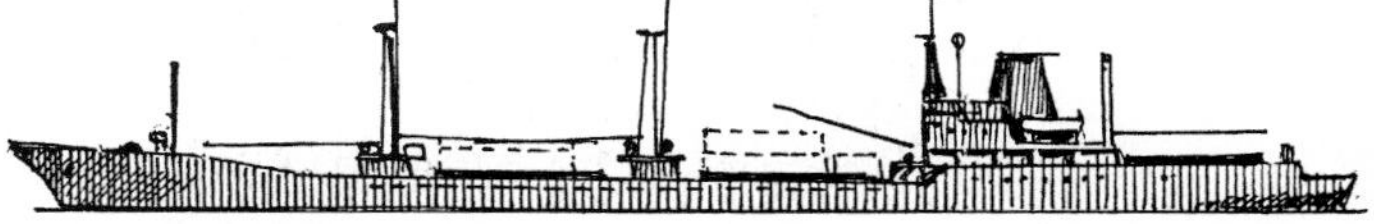

394 MT^2HFN *H13*
GOLDPATH SV/FRG (Schlichting) 1972; C; 6,472 grt/9,304 dwt; 131 × 8.2 m *(431 × 27 ft)*; M (MAN); 18 kts; ex-*Wilhelm Bornhofen*
Sisters: **SUN SPEED** (Pa) ex-*Hans Bornhofen*; **XIONG YUE CHENG** (RC) ex-*Elisabeth Bornhofen*

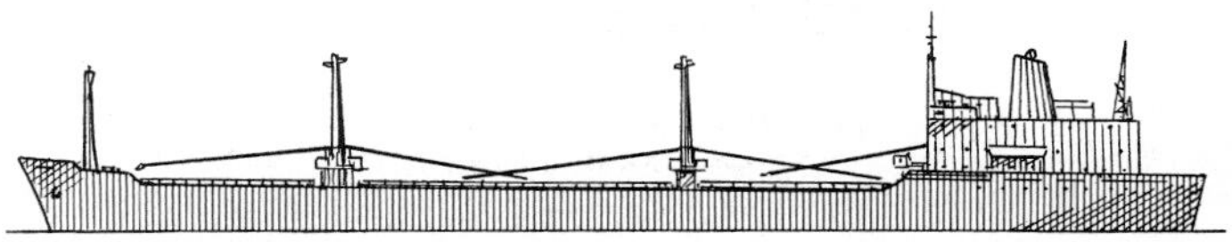

395 MT^2HFND *H13*
SOUTH COUNTY Cy/Ko (Dae Sun) 1976; C/Con; 6,769 grt/9,119 dwt; 125 × 7.56 m *(410.1 × 24.8 ft)*; M (Mitsubishi); 12.50 kts; ex-*Roebuck*; 234 TEU
Sister: **AFRICAN GLORY** (Gr) ex-*Ravenswood*

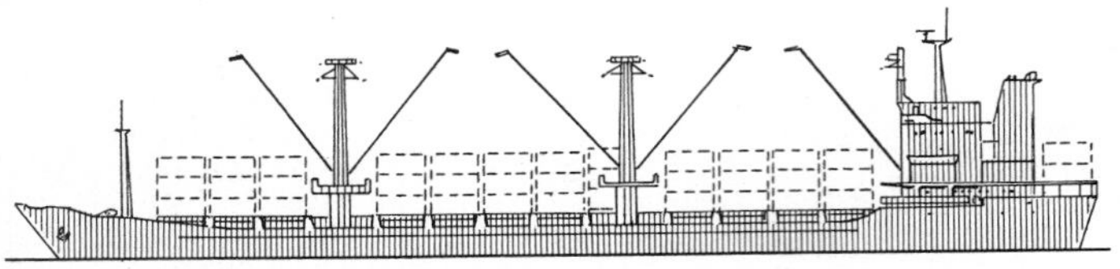

396 *MT^2HMF H13*
ANDROMEDA STAR Sg/Ko (Dong Hae) 1982; B/Con; 8,431 grt/11,243 dwt; 135.3 × 7.7 m *(444 × 25.26 ft)*; M (Mitsubishi); 15.46 kts; 594 TEU
Sisters: **ANDROMACHE** (Sg); **ZIM MEXICO** (Cy) ex-*Esther Schulte*; **MARIANNE SCHULTE** (Cy) (square funnel): **MANORA BAY** (Cy) ex-*Elisabeth Schulte*

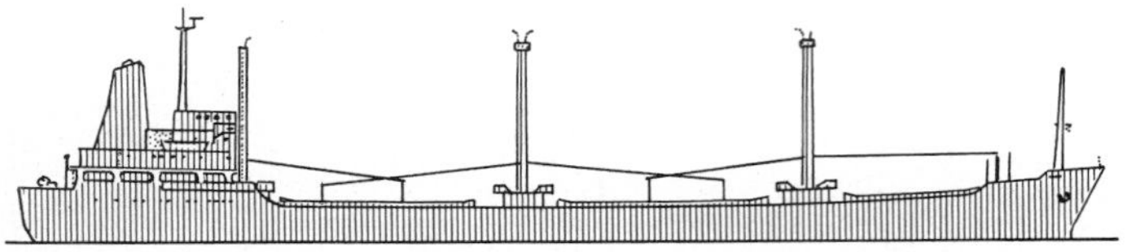

397 *MT^2HMF H13*
NICOLA D Cy/Ja (Watanabe) 1977; B; 6,376 grt/9,267 dwt; 133.84 × 6.95 m *(439.11 × 22.80 ft)*; M (Mitsubishi); 14.50 kts; ex-*Clivia*

398 *MT^2HMFM^2R H13*
B ONAL Tu/Ja (Sasebo) 1971; B; 15,662 grt/25,110 dwt; 174.53 × 10.19 m *(572.6 × 33.43 ft)*; M (Sulzer); 15 kts; ex-*Asia Fidelity*

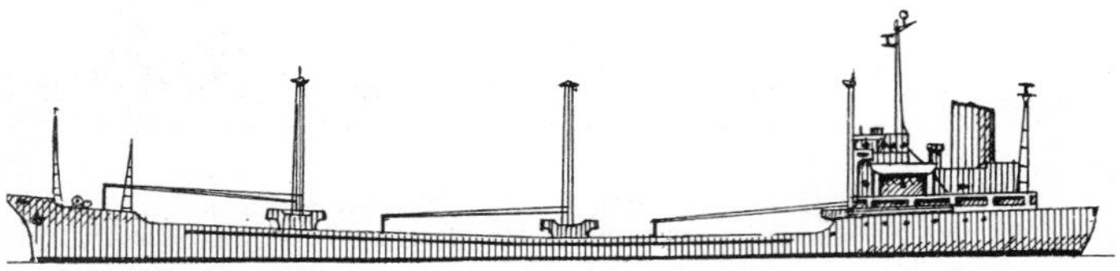

399 *MT^2HMFN H13*
TROPIVENTURE Cy/Ja (Watanabe) 1976; C; 5,201 grt/8,197 dwt; 117.61 × 7.3 m *(385.8 × 23.9 ft)*; M (Mitsubishi); 14 kts; ex-*Anita*
Sisters: **NORDHEIM** (Cy); **ORION PROGRESS** (Pa); ex-*Nordfels*; **NORDHOLM** (Cy); **NORDMARK** (Cy); **KINSALE** (Cy) ex-*Rhombus*; **LIAN HUA LING** (RC) ex-*Kirsten Wesch*; **KAREN D** (Cy) ex-*Helen Schulte*; **KIRBY D** (Cy) ex-*Johanna Schulte*; **KENMARE** (Cy) ex-*Raute*; **KAREN** (Cy); **PERGAMOS** (Pa) ex-*Coral Volans*; **TAXIARCHIS** (Cy) ex-*Neptune Volans*; **LONG HAI** (Vn) ex-*Rainbow Volans*; **TURKAY B** (Tu) ex-*Rio Explorer*

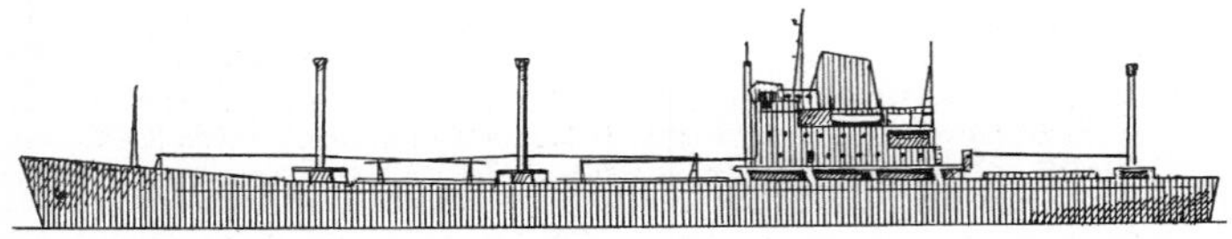

400 *MT^2HMFNT H1*
JENNIFER R Pa/Br (Cammell Laird) 1973; Pt. Con; 12,309 grt/18,080 dwt; 162 × 9.8 m *(530 × 32.4 ft)*; M (B&W); 18 kts; ex-*Orduna*
Sisters: **GEORGE B** (Pa) ex-*Ortega*; **ANTWERP EXPRESS** (SV) ex-*Orbeta*

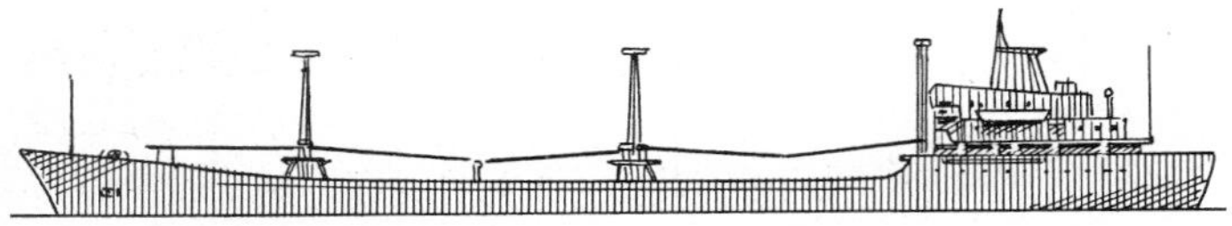

401 *$MT^2HM–F$ H13*
ADELAIDE Cy/FRG (Lindenau) 1972; C; 5,202 grt/7,450 dwt; 124.49 × 7.07 m *(408.43 × 23.2 ft)*; M (Atlas-MaK); 15 kts; ex-*Leo Schroder*
Sister: **SENYA** (Cy) ex-*Lutz Schroder*

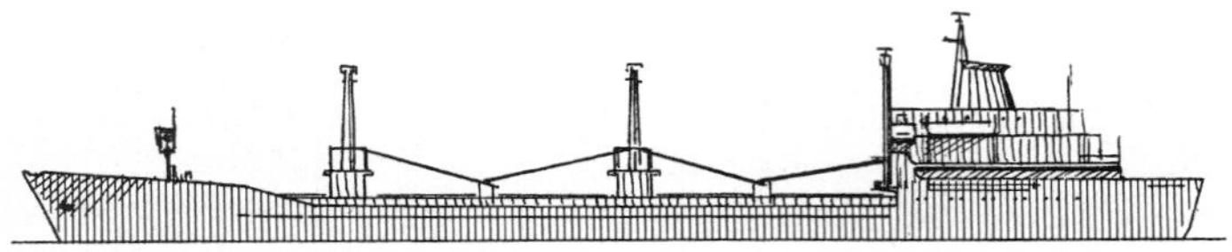

402 *$MT^2HM–F$ H13*
ISMAIL M Sy/FRG (Lindenau) 1969; C; 4,217 grt/6,450 dwt; 112.83 × 6.9 m *(370.18 × 22.64 ft)*; M (Sulzer); 13.75 kts; ex-*Fossheim*

403 *$MT^2HM–FM^2$ H13*
CAPE NELSON SV/DDR ("Neptun") 1984; C/Con; 10,018 grt/12,768 dwt; 150.20 × 9.05 m *(492.78 × 29.69 ft)*; M (MAN); 17 kts; ex-*Rydal*; 428 TEU; Typical of later units of 'Neptun 421' type; Principally distinguished by staggered masts aft see drawing number 8/446

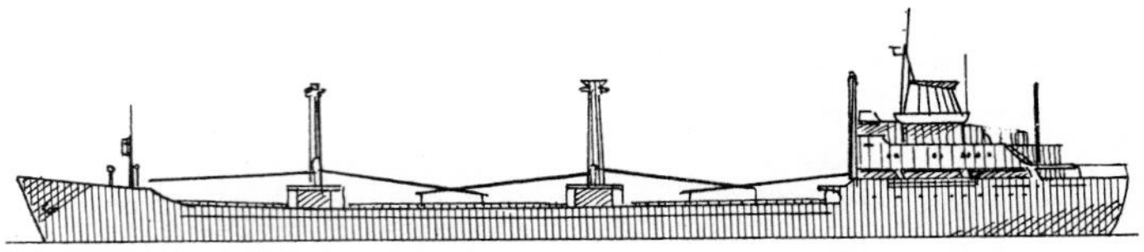

404 *$MT^2HM–FN$ H13*
BABTAI Lt/DDR ('Neptun') 1968; C; 4,070 grt/6,010 dwt; 114.71 × 6.48 m *(376.35 × 21.26 ft)*; M (MAN); 14 kts; ex-*Sigyn*; Mast amidships may be removed (also on *Wadeiaa*)
Sisters: **WADEIAA** (Sy) ex-*Joselin*; **A BEDEVI** (Tu) ex-*Joulla*

405 *$MT^2HM–FN$ H13*
"NEPTUN 421" type dwt; **SIMILAR TO DRAWING NUMBER 8/446**. Several ships under latter drawing will have this sequence

406 *MT^2MF H1*
PICO CASTELO Po/De (Aalborg) 1973; C/R; 6,842 grt/7,620 dwt; 135.11 × 7.62 m *(443.3 × 25 ft)*; M (B&W); 17 kts; ex-*Bamsa Dan*

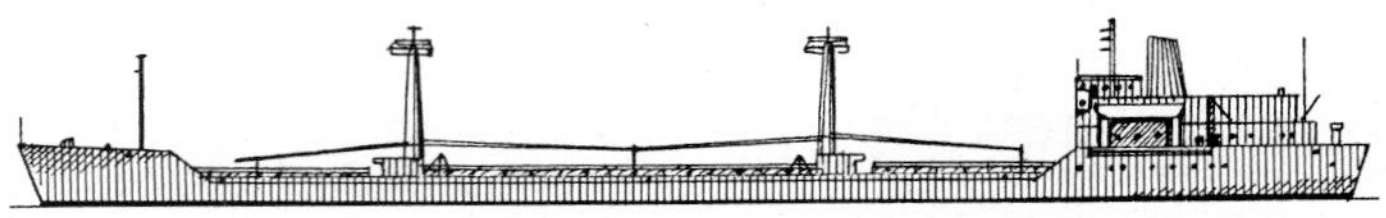

407 *MT^2MF H13*
DRNIS Ma/FRG (Luerssen) 1972; C; 4,821 grt/7,702 dwt; 123.32 × 6.85 m *(404.59 × 22.47 ft)*; M (Normo); 13.25 kts; ex-*Furunes*
Sister: **PRIMOSTEN** (SV) ex-*Fjordnes*

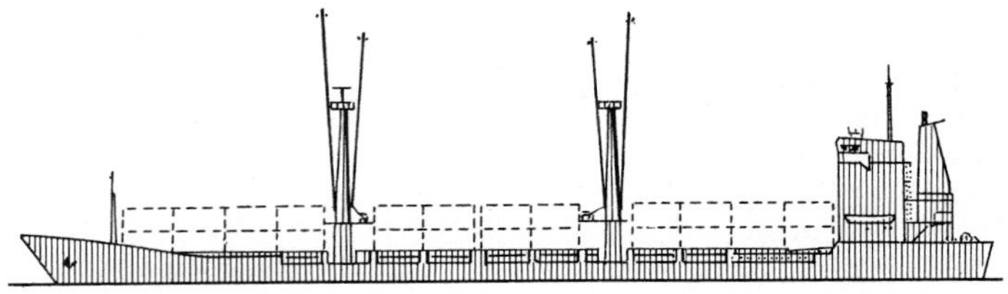

408 *MT^2MF H13*
SINGANG Sg/FRG (Flensburger) 1979; C/Con; 4,858 grt/7,550 dwt; 117.71 × 5.97 m *(386.19 × 19.59 ft)*; M (MaK); 14 kts; Launched as *Flensburg*; 371 TEU
Sister: **ARUBA** (Na) Launched as *Breslau*

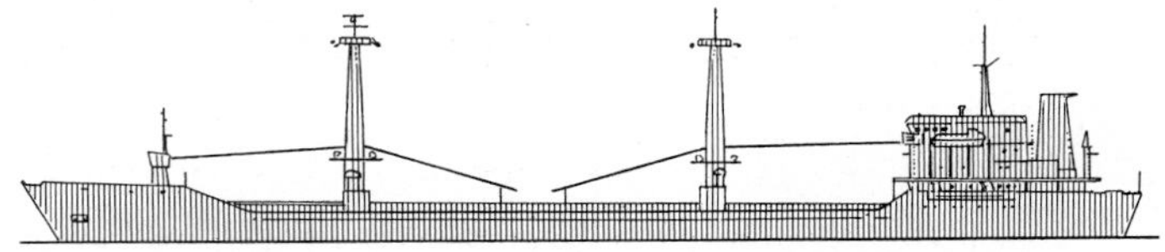

409 *MT^2MFD H13*
ARIES NIS/FRG (Lindenau) 1979; C/Con; 8,547 grt/11,121 dwt; 146.44 × 7.92 m *(480.45 × 25.98 ft)*; M (MaK); 16 kts; ex-*Fossum*; 515 TEU

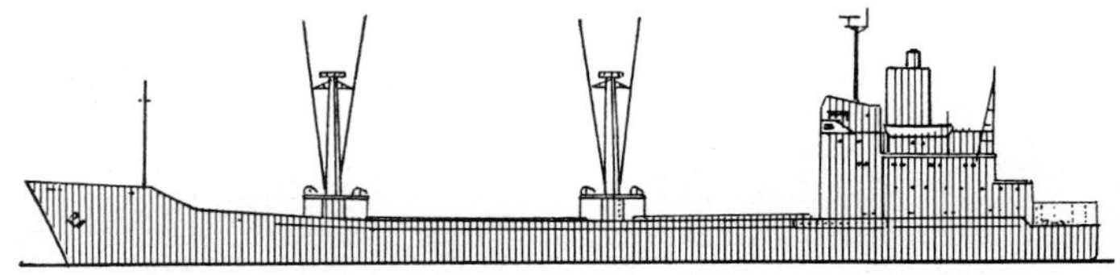

410 *MT^2MFN H1*
ZAMET Cro/Bz (Emaq) 1979; C/Con; 5,120 grt/5,344 dwt; 115.65 × 6.5 m *(379 × 21.33 ft)*; M (MAN); 15 kts; ex-*Benedict*; 105 TEU
Sister: **PECINE** (Cro) ex-*Boniface*

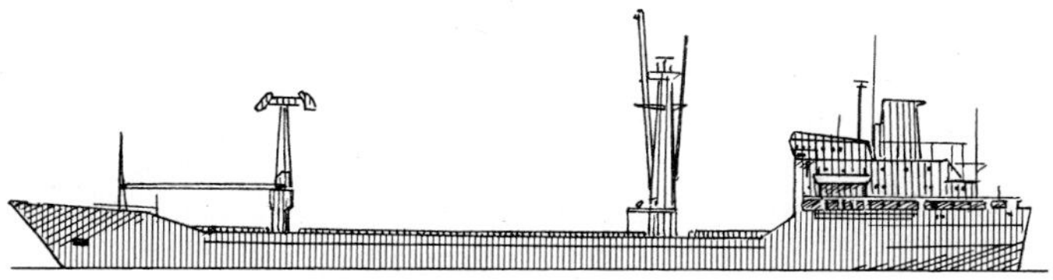

411 *MT*^{2}*MFN H13*
EQUATOR CRYSTAL Sg/FRG (Schuerenstedt) 1977; C/Con; 7,045 grt/9,805 dwt; 131.6 × 8.03 m *(431.76 × 26.35 ft)*; M (Atlas-MaK); 15 kts; ex-*Scilla*; 336 TEU

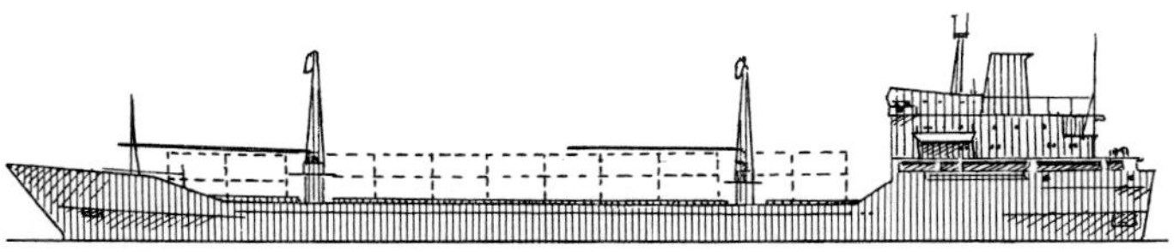

412 *MT*^{2}*MFN H13*
RICKMERS BRASIL Pa/FRG (Schuerenstedt) 1977; C/Con; 7,012 grt/9,945 dwt; 131.71 × 8.03 m *(432.12 × 26.35 ft)*; M (Atlas-MaK); 15.25 kts; ex-*Uranus*; 330 TEU

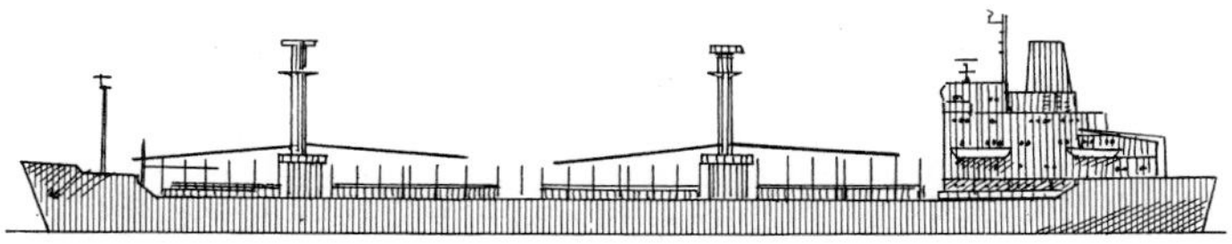

413 *MT*^{2}*MFS H13*
FLORENZ Pa/FRG (Bremer V) 1977; C; 9,996 grt/15,327 dwt; 142.07 × 9.06 m *(466.11 × 29.72 ft)*; M (MAN); 14.5 kts; 'Modified German Liberty' type; 358 TEU
Sister: **WILLIAM SHAKESPEARE** (Pa)

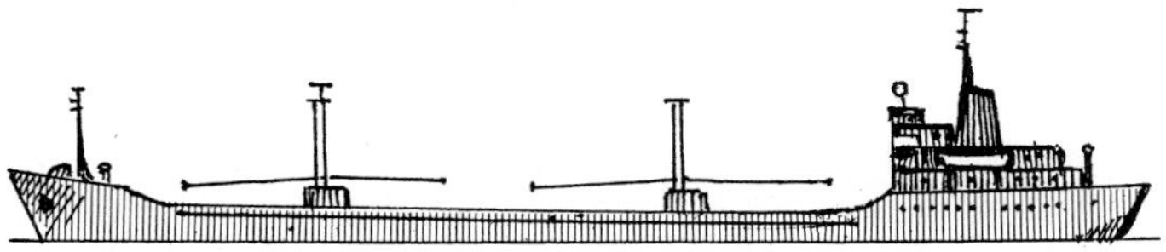

414 *MT*^{2}*M–F H13*
VILLACH Cy/FRG (Luerssen) 1970; C; 4,769 grt/7,611 dwt; 123.25 × 6.99 m *(404.36 × 22.93 ft)*; M (Normo); 13.25 kts; ex-*Brinknes*; Lengthened 1974 (Swan Hunter)

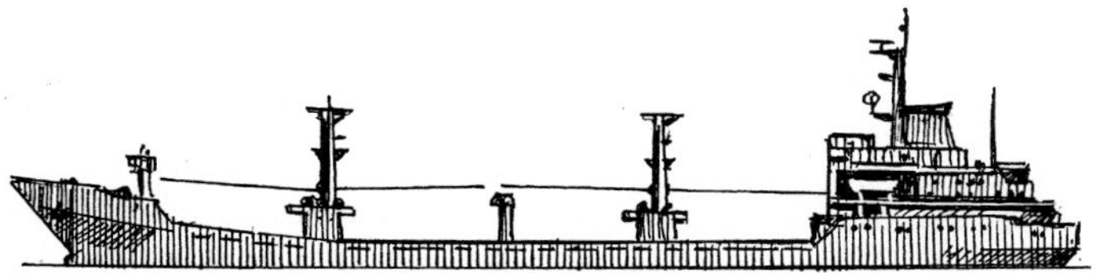

415 *MT*^{2}*M–FN H13*
CHITA Ru/DDR ('Neptun') 1973; C; 4,497 grt/5,657 dwt; 117.79 × 6.92 m *(386.45 × 22.7 ft)*; M (MAN); 16.5 kts; 'POSEIDON' class
Sisters: **KHASAN** (Ru); **NOVOCHERKASSK** (Uk); **RYSHKANY** (Uk); **RUSHANY** (Uk); **RUDNYY** (Ru); **ROMNY** (Uk); **RUBEZHNOYE** (Uk); **RZHEV** (Ru); **RAKHOV** (Uk); **REUTOV** (Uk); **RATNO** (Uk); **RADOMYSHL** (Uk); **RYAZAN** (Ru); **ROSLAVL** (Ru); **RYBINSK** (Uk); **MAGO** (Ru)

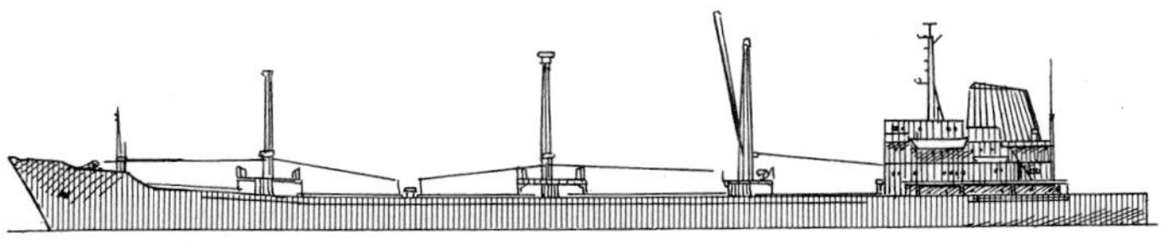

416 *MT*^{2}*NMFN H1*
GREAT POWER Cy/FRG (A G 'Weser') 1977; C/Con; 9,892 grt/16,120 dwt; 149.82 × 9.26 m *(491.53 × 30.38 ft)*; M (MAN); 16.5 kts; ex-*Argolikos*; '36-L' type; 305 TEU
Sister: **SANDY PRIDE** (Cy) ex-*Laconikos*; Possible sister: **ASPASIA L** (Cy) ex-*Saronikos*

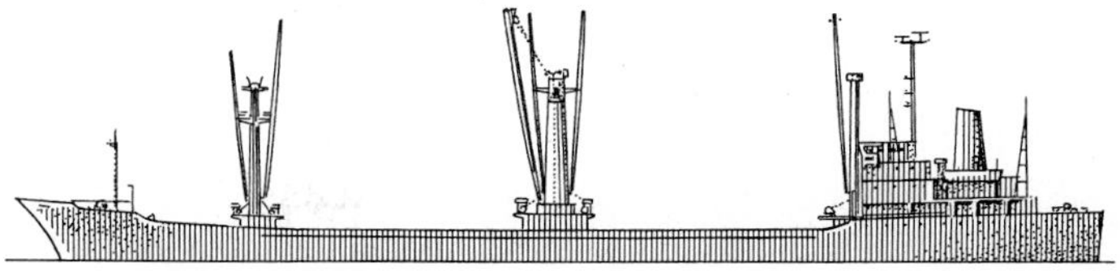

417 *MT*^{2}*NMFN H13*
AL SWAMRUZ Bh/Ja (Tohoku) 1974; C/HL; 8,522 grt/12,350 dwt; 143.52 × 8.36 m *(470.87 × 27.43 ft)*; M (Mitsubishi); 15 kts; ex-*Amazon Maru*

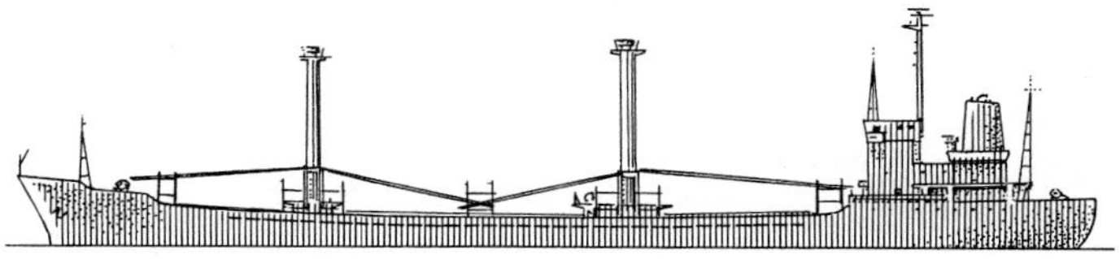

418 *MT*^{2}*NMFN H13*
EGASCO MARINA Eg/Ja (Kochiken) 1975; C/TC; 6,242 grt/10,178 dwt; 129.98 × 7.75 m *(426.4 × 25.43 ft)*; M (Mitsubishi); 13.25 kts; ex-*Kong Hoi*
Sisters: **LINK STAR** (Ma) ex-*Yue Man*; **PERNAS SUASA** (My) ex-*Bright Melbourne*; **KIM LIEN** (Vn) ex-*Grace Adelaide*; Possible sisters: **JUPITER 2** (Th) ex-*Pearl Lotus*; **SARINDERJIT** (Sg) ex-*Ocean Explotar*; **HONG FAN** (RC) ex-*Great Success*; **TELSTA** (Pa) ex-*Ruby Lotus*; **EGASCO STAR** (Eg) ex-*Ho Chung*; **RANGER 1** (Cy) ex-*Sunny Sydney;* **UNIJE** (Pa) ex-*Matsufukujin Maru*; **BUDHI PERKASA** (Ia) ex-*Timber Leader*; **NAZLI DENIZ** (Tu) ex-*Sun Antares*

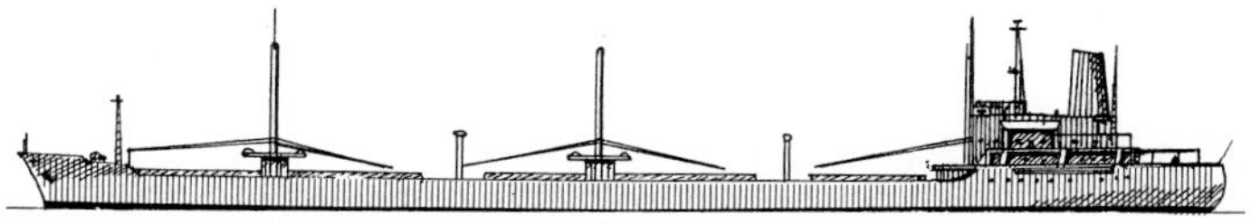

419 *MT*^{2}*NMFN H13*
GOLDEN UNION Ma/Ja (Hitachi) 1972; C; 9,715 grt/15,160 dwt; 145.01 × 9.08 m *(475.75 × 29.79 ft)*; M (B&W); 14.5 kts; ex-*Leidenschaft*; 'UT-15' type
Sister: **HYOK SIN** (RK) ex-*Liechtenstein*

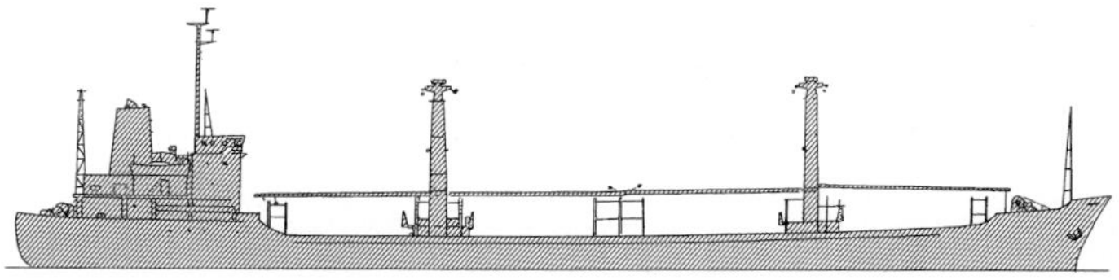

420 *MT*^{2}*NMFN H13*
SONG THUONG Vn/Ja (Kochiken) 1976; C; 6,051 grt/10,028 dwt; 127.07 × 7.77 m *(416.90 × 25.49 ft)*; M (Mitsubishi); 14.40 kts; ex-*Shing Ta*
Sisters (some built by Hashihama): **POLAR** (Pa) ex-*Eva Sun*; **SALINDO PERDANA I** (Ia) ex-*Nancy Moon*; **AMARYNTHOS** (Cy) ex-*Asia Luna*; **BARBAROS OKTAY** (Tu) ex-*Berth Star*; **UNISON GREAT** (Pa) ex-*Nusantara IV*; **HUNG YUN** (Pa) ex-*Regent Leo*; **SOUTHERN HOPE** (Pa) ex-*Regent Radiance*; **SUN KUNG No 3** (Pa) ex-*Regent Ranger*; **LAPTOP PIONEER** (My) ex-*Regent Ruth*; **SONG DAY** (Vn) ex-*Houng Ta*; **AURORA GOLD** (Li) ex-*Yeong Ta*; **PAN JIN HAI** (RC) ex-*Kwong Ta*

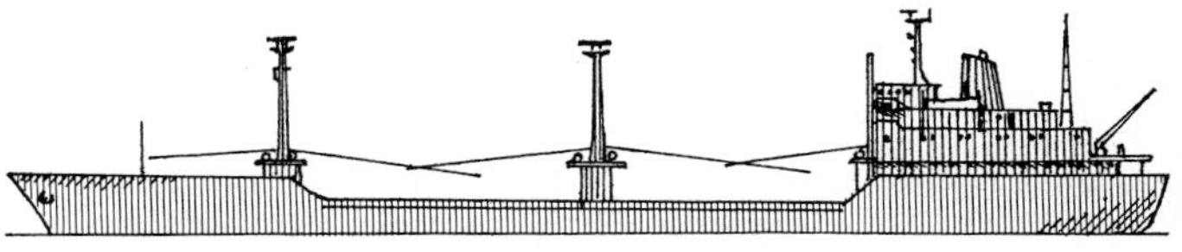

421 *MT*^{2}*NMFNS H13*
TIGER SPRING Pa/Ja (Fukuoka) 1977; C; 8,598 grt/10,272 dwt; 144 × 8.22 m *(472.44 × 26.97 ft)*; M (IHI); 16.5 kts; ex-*Oslofjord*; 330 TEU
Sister: **DRAGON WELL** (Pa) ex-*Bergensfjord*; Possibly similar: **AMBALIKA** (Ia) ex-*Tanafjord*

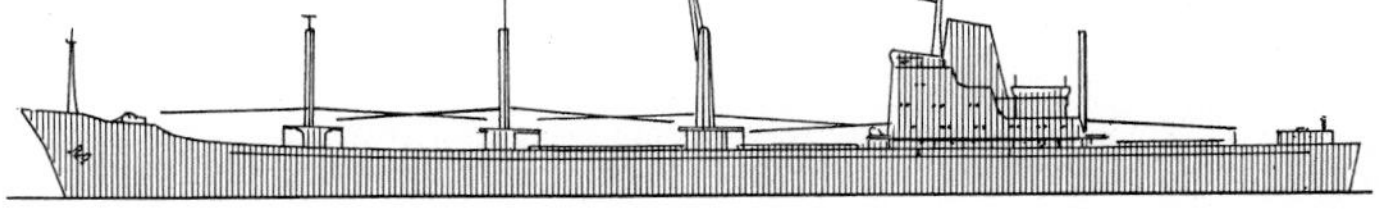

422 *MT*^{2}*NMFT H1*
AMER ASHA Pa/Br (Doxford & S) 1972; C; 11,391 grt/16,975 dwt; 161.45 × 9.76 m *(530 × 32.02 ft)*; M (Doxford); 16.5 kts; ex-*Lancashire*

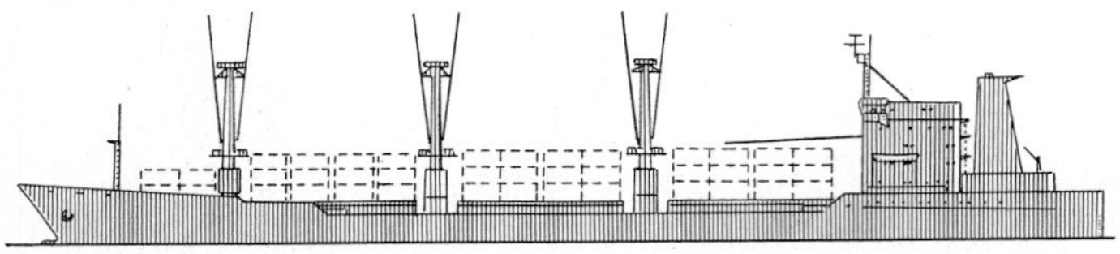

423 MT^3HF *H13*
CMBT ECHO Cy/Ko (Korea SB) 1979; C/Con; 14,085 grt/18,229 dwt; 169.48 × 9.95 m *(556.04 × 32.64 ft)*; M (MAN); 17 kts; ex-*Christina Isabel*; 796 TEU
Sister: **WOURI** (Pa) ex-*Mount Sabana*

424 MT^3HF *H13*
GREEN RIDGE US/FRG (Howaldts DW) 1979; C/Con; 9,515 grt/12,487 dwt; 154.57 × 8.17/7.16 m *(507.12 × 26.80 ft)*; M (Atlas-MaK); 17.5 kts; ex-*Sloman Mercur*; Cranes can rotate; 543 TEU
Sister: **GREEN WAVE** (US) ex-*Sloman Mira*

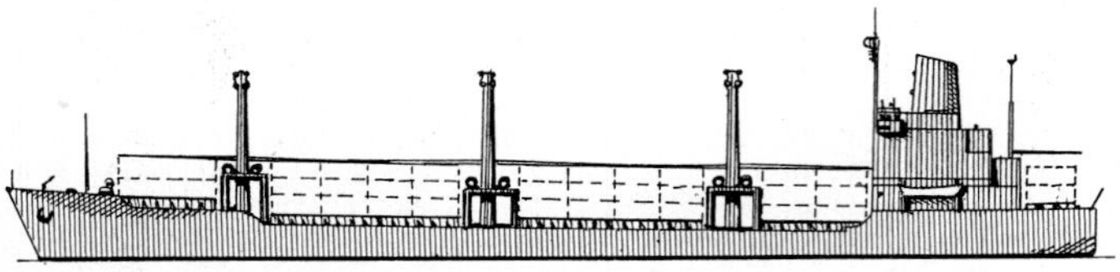

425 MT^3HFN *H13*
CARRYMAR SV/FRG (A. G. 'Weser') 1978; C/Con; 9,688 grt/12,430 dwt; 146.01 × 8.16 m *(479.04 × 26.77 ft)*; M (Atlas-MaK); 18.25 kts; ex-*Holstensailor*; 'Key 12' type; 576 TEU
Sisters: **BUZET** (Ma) ex-*Holstenclipper*; **ORIENT SHREYAS** (Cy) ex-*Holstentrader*

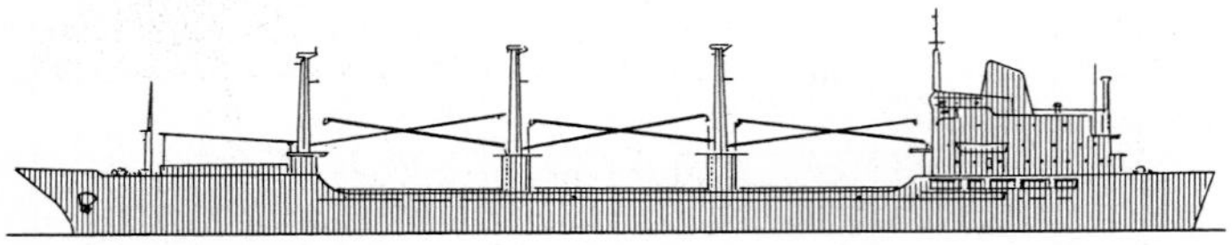

426 MT^3HFN *H13*
MOSLAVINA Ma/Sp (AESA) 1978; C/Con; 11,771 grt/16,000 dwt; 157.66 × 9.95 m *(517.26 × 32.64 ft)*; M (Sulzer); 18 kts; ex-*Bondoukou*; 450 TEU
Sisters: **ELEIN K** (Cy) ex-*Bonoua*; **CITY OF LOME** (Cy) ex-*Bouake*

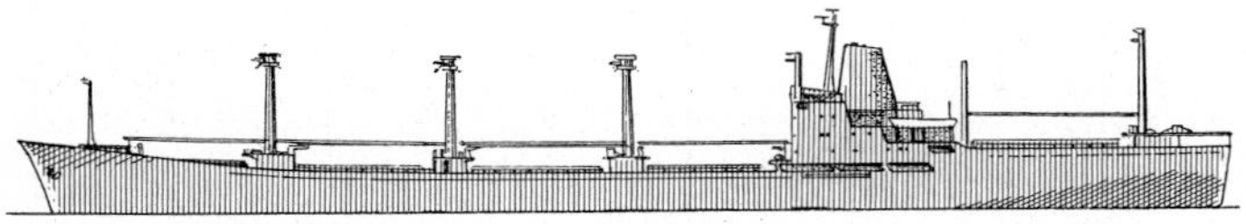

427 MT^3HMFNT *H13*
ANNA L Gr/Br (Sunderland) 1979; C/Con; 12,917 grt/18,501 dwt; 161.82 × 9.95 m *(530.9 × 32.64 ft)*; M (Doxford); 16.6 kts; ex-*Dacebank*
Sisters: **WESTMAN** (Cy) ex-*PIKEBANK*; **DEVO** (Bs) ex-*Roachbank*; **LADY REBECCA** (HK) ex-*Ruddbank*; **CLINTON K** (HK) ex-*Tenchbank*; **BRIJ** (Bs) ex-*Troutbank*

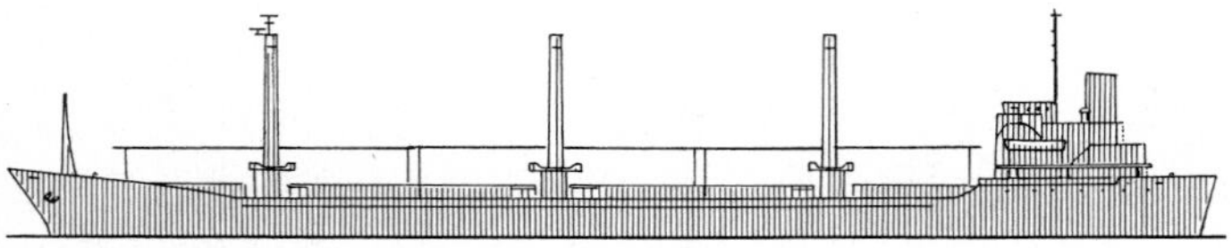

428 MT^3MF *H13*
MC EMERALD Bs/Ja (Minami) 1977; C/Con; 11,030 grt/16,590 dwt; 156.88 × 9.35 m *(514.7 × 30.68 ft)*; M (MAN); 15 kts; Launched as *Maretania*; 650 TEU
Sister: **ENIF** (Sg) ex-*Maretrader*

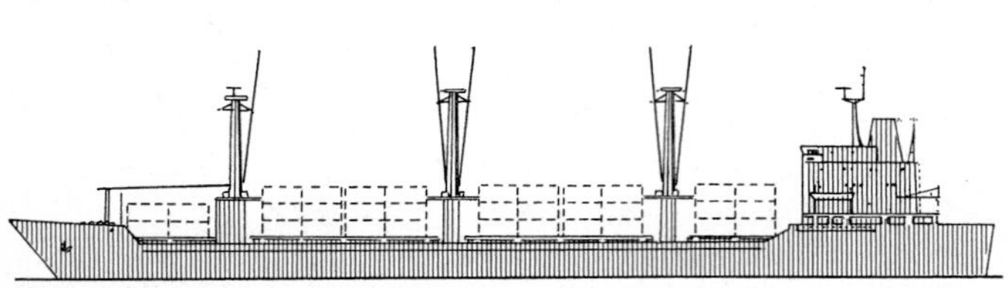

429 MT^3MFM *H13*
CMBT EAGLE Bs/Ko (Hyundai) 1979; C/Con; 11,200 grt/14,822 dwt; 149.82 × 9.64 m *(492 × 31.63 ft)*; M (MAN); 17 kts; ex-*Bamenda Palm*; 597 TEU

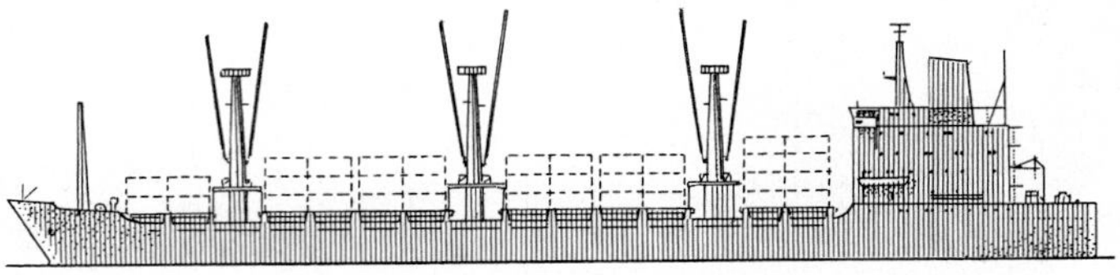

430 MT^3MFM *H13*
MYKINAI Gr/FRG (A G 'Weser') 1979; C/Con; 12,349 grt/16,600 dwt; 152.20 × 9.71 m *(499.34 × 31.86 ft)*; M (MAN); 15.5 kts; ex-*Cam Ilomba*; 686 TEU. Mast aft is on port side
Sisters: **CMBT EXPRESS** (Bs) ex-*Cam Iroko*; Sisters (Fr built-L'Atlantique): **CAM BILINGA** (Cn); **CAM EBENE** (Cn)

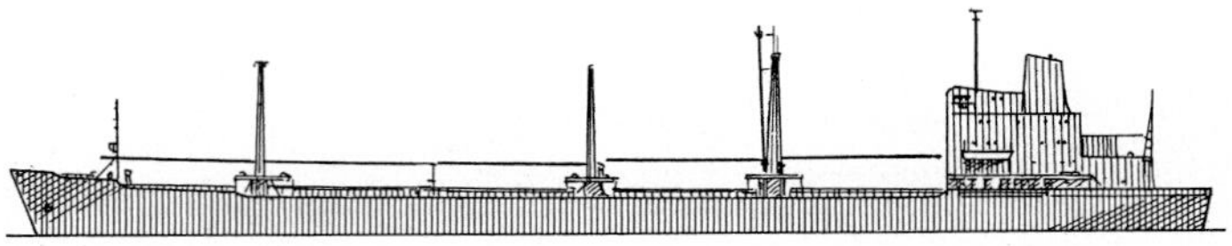

431 MT^3MFN *H1*
BISMIHITA'LA Li/FRG (Rickmers) 1976; C; 9,326 grt/15,342 dwt; 139.58 × 9.17 m *(457.94 × 30.09 ft)*; M (MAN); 16 kts; ex-*Susanne*; 'German Liberty' type

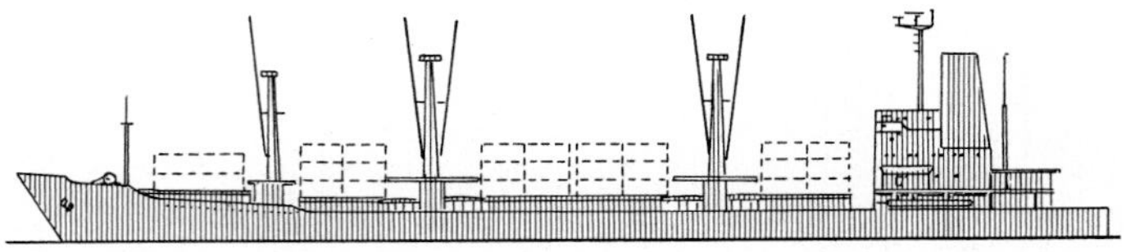

432 MT^3MFN *H1*
MARINE CONFIDENCE Pa/FRG (A.G. 'Weser') 1982; C/Con; 10,929 grt/17,240 dwt; 147.4 × 9.78 m *(484 × 32.09 ft)*; M (MaK); 16.6 kts; ex-*Highsea Success*; 'Key 17' type; 434 TEU

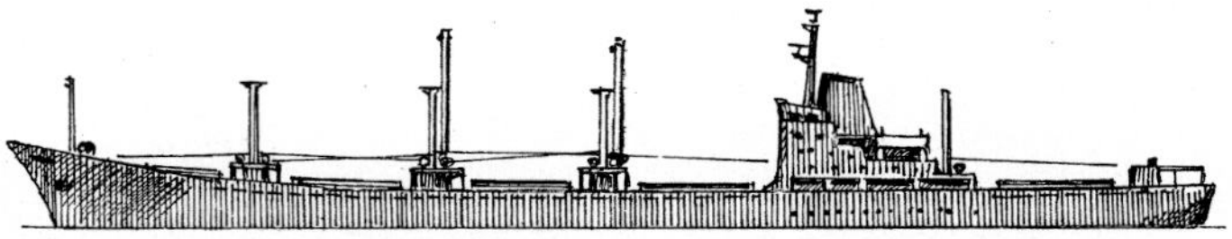

433 MT^3MFN *H1*
TAMAMIMA HK/Br (Sunderland) 1978; C; 12,021 grt/18,400 dwt; 161.5 × 9.7 m *(529.86 × 31.82 ft)*; M (Doxford); 16 kts; ex-*Crestbank*
Sister: **DIMITRAKIS** (Gr) ex-*Fenbank*

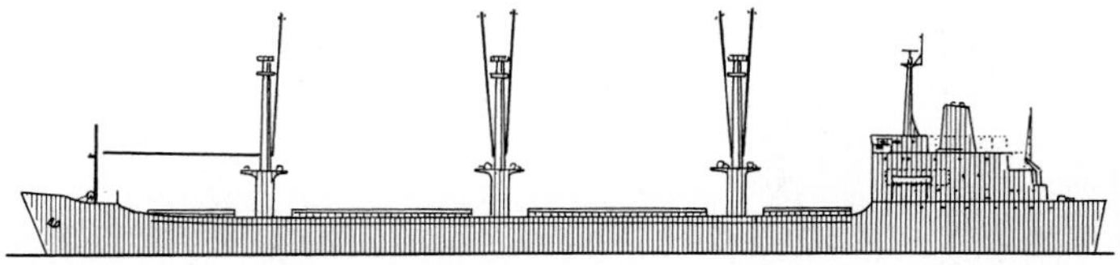

434 MT^3MFN *H13*
CORDIGLIERA Pa/Br (Sunderland) 1979; C/Con; 12,025 grt/16,525 dwt; 154.67 × 9.55 m *(507.45 × 31.33 ft)*; M (Doxford); 16.75 kts; ex-*Badagry Balm*; Five side doors (port). Five side doors (starboard); 600 TEU

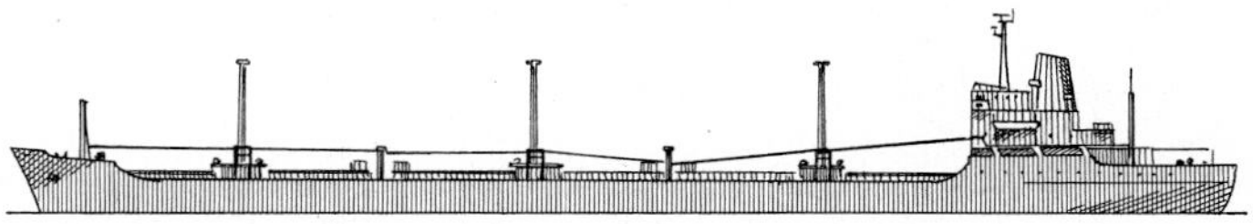

435 MT^3MFN *H13*
EFESSOS Ma/Ja (Mitsui) 1973; B; 20,610 grt/34,273 dwt; 179.03 × 10.96 m *(587.4 × 36 ft)*; M (B&W); 15.25 kts; ex-*Jill Cord*

436 MT^3MFNTM *H13*
YANG CHENG RC/Br (Fairfield SB) 1962; C; 11,537 grt/11,455 dwt; 166 × 9.1/9.5 m *(544 × 30.1/31.5 ft)*; M (Sulzer); 20 kts; ex-*Glenogle*
Sister: **QING HE CHENG** (RC) ex-*Glenfalloch*

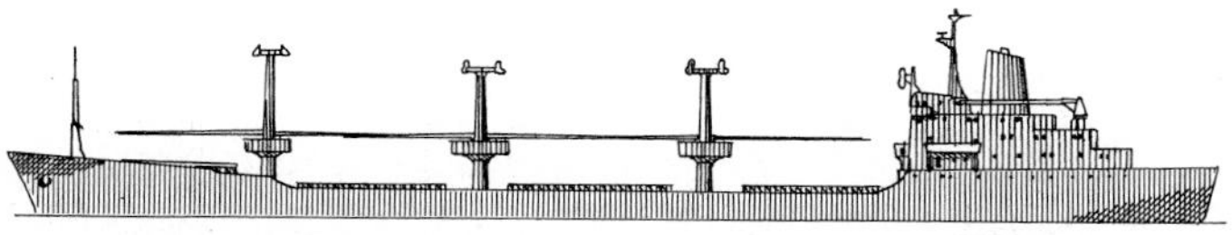

437 *MT^{3}MFR H13*
IRAN GHEYAMAT Ir/Ja (Sumitomo) 1978; C/Con; 14,856 grt/19,212 dwt; 166.61 × 10.52 m *(546.62 × 34.51 ft)*; M (B&W); 18 kts; ex-*Arya Shams*; 366 TEU
Sisters: **IRAN VAHDAT** (Ir) ex-*Arya Keyhan*; **IRAN ADALAT** (Ir) ex-*Arya Sepehr*; **IRAN NABUVAT** (Ir) ex-*Arya Shahab*

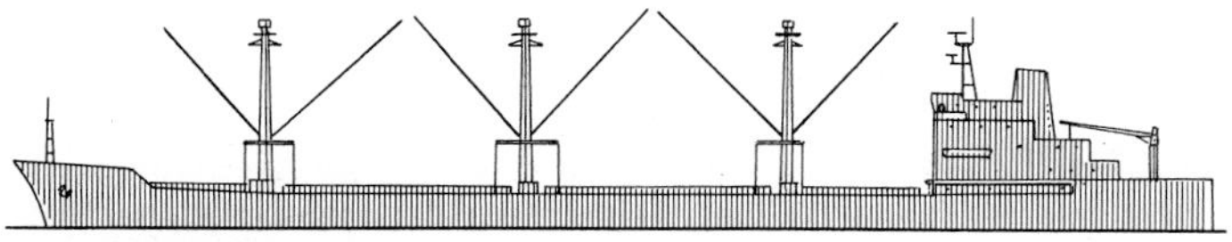

438 *MT^{3}MFR H13*
LIANG SHAN RC/Ys ('3 Maj') 1984; C/Con; 12,448 grt/16,670 dwt; 157.54 × 9.30 m *(516.86 × 30.51 ft)*; M (Sulzer); 15.25 kts; 512 TEU
Sister: **SONG SHAN** (RC)

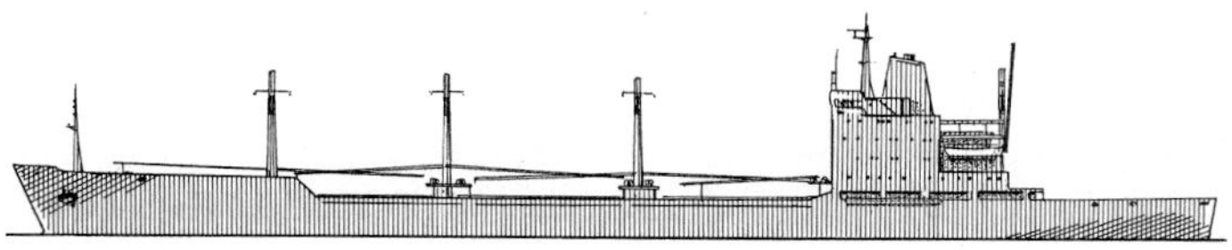

439 *MT^{3}MFT H1*
RIVER ADADA Ng/Ys ('Split') 1979; C/Con; 13,164 grt/16,487 dwt; 173 × 9.15 m *(567.59 × 30.02 ft)*; M (Sulzer); 19 kts
Sisters: **RIVER OJI** (Ng); **RIVER MAJIDUN** (Ng); **RIVER OLI** (Ng); **RIVER OGBESE** (Ng); **RIVER MAJE** (Ng); **WINDFALL** (Na) ex-*River Oshun*

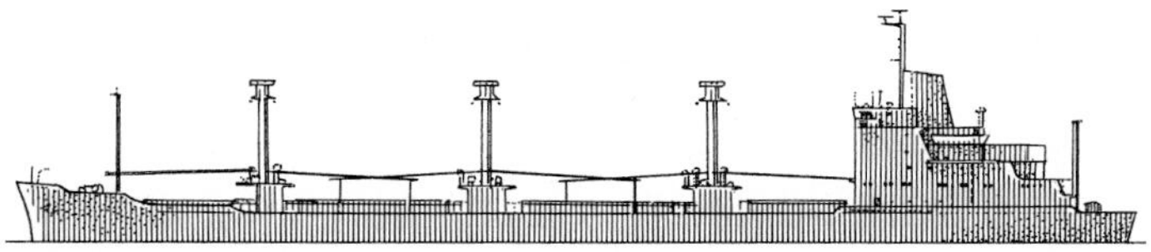

440 *MT^{3}M–FN H1*
AYUBIA Pk/Br (A&P) 1981; C; 12,030 grt/18,050 dwt; 152.03 × 9.49 m *(498.79 × 31.14 ft)*; M (Sulzer); 15.75 kts; ex-*Murree*; 'SD 18' type; 494 TEU
Sister: **KAGHAN** (Pk)

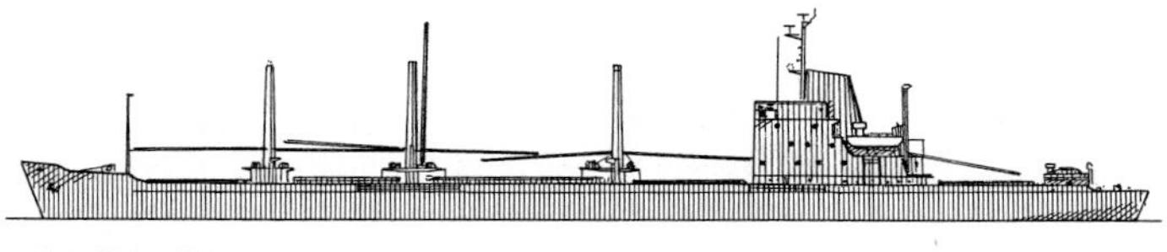

441 *MT^{3}M–FN H1*
PROMETHEUS Cy/Bz (CCN) 1979; C; 10,304 grt/14,236 dwt; 160.02 × 9.21 m *(525 × 30.22 ft)*; M (MAN); 17 kts; ex-*Lloyd Mandu*; 'Prinasa 121' type
Sister: **ANTEOS** (Cy) ex-*Lloyd Tupiara*

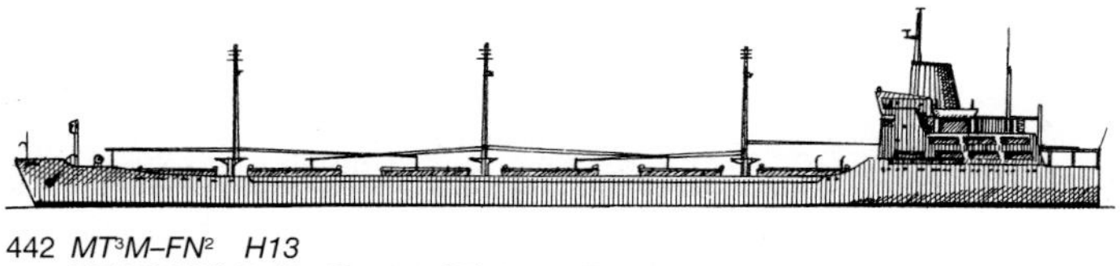

442 *MT^{3}M–FN^2 H13*
EXCELLUS Pa/Br (Scotts' SB) 1970; B; 11,716 grt/21,546 dwt; 158.6 × 9.54 m *(520 × 31.3 ft)*; M (B&W); 12.5 kts; ex-*Bulknes*

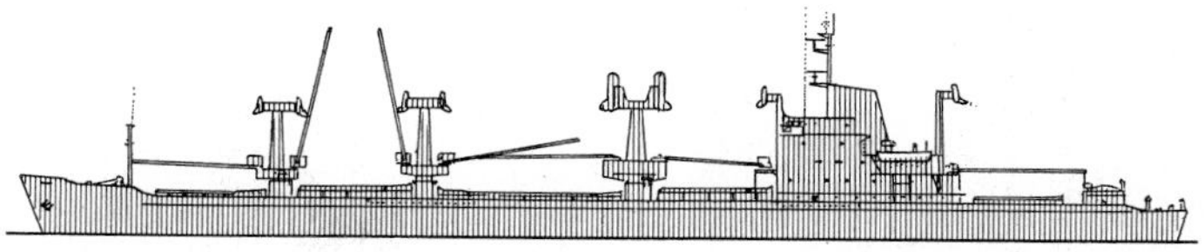

443 *MT^{3}M–FT H1*
FROTADURBAN Ms/Bz (CCN) 1980; C; 6,267 grt/14,319 dwt; 160.03 × 9.21 m *(525 × 30.22 ft)*; M (MAN); 17 kts; 'Prinasa 121' type; 80 TEU
Sister: **FROTASINGAPORE** (Ms); Probable sisters: **BEL AZUR** (Ms) ex-*Frotamanila*; **SEA LADY I** (Ma) ex-*Celina Torrealba*; Possible sister: **UNILAGO** (NA) ex-*Nicia*

444 *MT^{3}NMFT H12*
VERANO Cy/Ko (Hyundai) 1980; C/Con; 13,387 grt/16,633 dwt; 167.32 × 10.18 m *(548.95 × 33.40 ft)*; M (Sulzer); — kts; ex-*Tano River*; 500 TEU; **SIMILAR TO DRAWING NUMBER 8/388** (which has a Stülcken derrick between hatches three and four).
Sisters: **KETA LAGOON** (Gh); **VOLTA RIVER** (Gh); **LIBRA CHILE** (Cy) ex-*Sissili River*

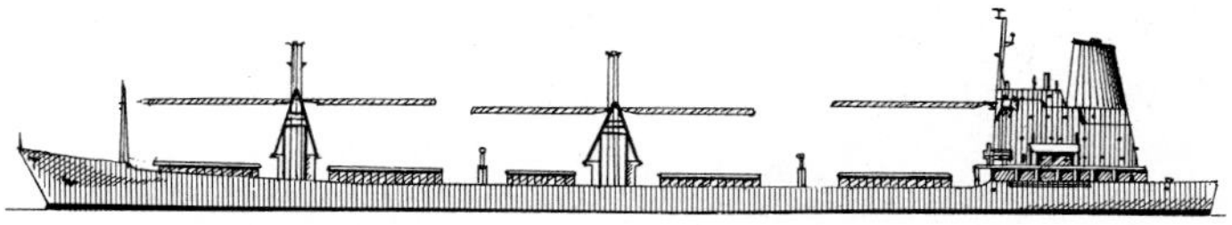

445 *MT^{2}VF H*
'FORTUNE' type —/Ja (IHI) 1971 onwards; B; approx 13,800 grt/approx 22,600 dwt; 164.34 × 9.87 m *(539.2 × 32.4 ft)*; M (Pielstick); 14.5 kts
Sisters: **POLIS** (Gr) ex-*Acropolis*; **AKRAGAS** (Gr) ex-*Akritas*; **EVA MARIA** (Ma) ex-*Alkyonis*; **AMILLA** (Gr); **SPYROS** (Gr) ex-*Anangel Glory*; **ANANGEL HONOUR** (Gr); **ANANGEL HOPE** (Gr); **ANANGEL LIBERTY** (Gr); **ANANGEL PROSPERITY** (Gr); **ANANGEL TRIUMPH** (Gr); **ANANGEL WISDOM** (Gr); **MENTOR** (Cy) ex-*Andros Mentor*; **ARETI** (Gr); LUCK (Pa) ex-*Asterion*; **ELLINIS P** (Gr) ex-*Astir*; **CHERRY FLOWER** (Gr); **EVIMERIA** (Gr); **PISTIS** (Gr); **IKAN SELAR** (Sg) ex-*Santorini*; **ANDRIOTISSA** (Ma) ex-*Sea Tiger*; **TREASURE ISLAND** (Gr) ex-*Theano*; **SAMOS** (Gr); ex-*Atreus*; **MARIA K** (Gr) ex-*Anangel Fortune*; **LIBERTA** (Ma) ex-*Anangel Happiness*; **NEREIS P** (Gr) ex-*Anangel Peace*; **ATHINAIS P** (Gr) ex-*Arion*; **CHERRY** (Gr); **WAN LING** (Sg) ex-*Fortune Leader*; **CAPTA SPYROS** (Pa) ex-*Apollon*; **IOANNIS L** (Gr) ex-*Akademos*; **GOLDEN SUN** (Va) ex-*Zuiho*; **EURASIAN GLOW** (Pi) ex-*Al Salaam*; **MEGHNA** (Ma) ex-*Al Samad*; **ANGELIA P** (Gr) ex-*Al Samie*; **MARIKA STRAVELAKIS** (Li) ex-*Andros Transport*; **NELSON** (Gr) ex-*Australian Grain*; **ARCADIA** (Bs) ex-*Vera Venture*; **ZEPHYROS** (Gr) ex-*Pacglory*; **PHILIA** (Gr) ex-*Loucas N*; **LADY FORTUNE** (Pa) ex-*Unique Fortune*; **PAN HOPE** (Ko) ex-*Ryuho*; **AMBAR** (Pi) ex-*Jasper*; **XIFIAS** (Cy) ex-*Benignity*; **GTS HORIZON** (Sg) ex-*Honesty*; **FOTINI** (Pa) ex-*Attica*; **KARLOVY VARY** (Cz) ex-*Everray*; **ARETHUSA** (Cy) ex-*Maria N*; **JOLLITY** (Pa) ex-*Everjust*; **COMMENCEMENT** (Cy) ex-*Tradewind West*; **NESTOR** (Li) ex-*Stella Prima*; **ESPERANZA** (Pa) ex-*Tradewind East*; **KOCAELI 1** (Tu); **ATHOL** (Sg); **LEDI** (Cy) ex-*XIII Congreso*; **DUGI OTOK** (SV); **NIN** (SV); **NOVIGRAD** (SV); **RAVNI KOTARI** (SV); **CHINA POWER** (HK) ex-*Chimo*

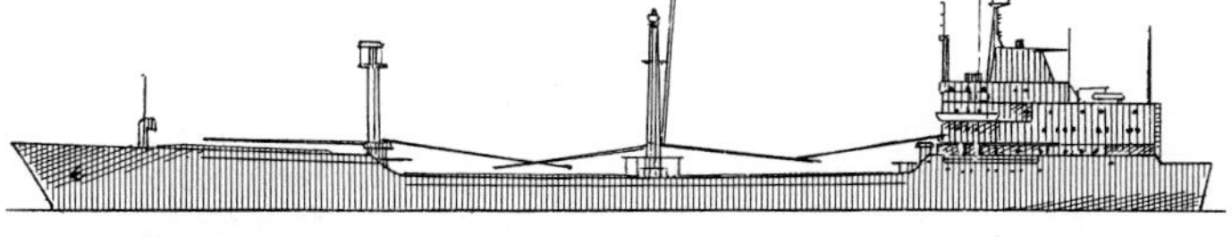

446 *MTUHM–FN H13*
LAURISSA Sg/DDR ('Neptun') 1977; C/Con; 9,799 grt/13,150 dwt; 150.17 × 9.07 m *(492.68 × 29.76 ft)*; M (MAN); 15 kts; ex-*Claudia Maria*; 442 TEU. *"Neptun 421" type*
Similar (Some have the sequences MT^{2}HM–FN or MT^{2}HM–FM^2): **YIN FENG** (RC) Launched as *Ivory Uranus*; **KOTA RAKYAT** (Sg) ex-*Ivory Tellus*; **HAU GIANG 2** (Vn) ex-*Vestland*; **PATRICK DELMAS** (Cy) ex-*Thesee*; **LOUIS** (Bs) ex-*Soldrott*; **JUTHA SARUNPAK** (Th) ex-*Sagaland*; **DELMAS KOUROU** (It) ex-*Merkur Sea*; **GEORGES DELMAS** (Cy) ex-*Merkur River*; **PAL VASSILIS** (Cy) ex-*Merkur Bay*; **BANGLAR ROBI** (Bh) ex-*Merkur Island*; **ST GERASIMOS I** (Cy) ex-*Merkur Lake*; **KOTA MUTIARA** (Sg) ex-*Pacific Dragon*; **FLORA V** (Pa) ex-*Sainte Alexandrine*; **SIGMUND JAHN** (Li) ex-*Fliegerskosmonaut der DDR Sigmund Jahn*; **PRITZWALK** (Li); **PASEWALK** (Li); **GLACHAU** (Li); **CRIMMITSCHAU** (Li); **SHUN AN** (Li) ex-*Neptun*; **JUTHA RACHAVADEE** (Th) ex-*Merkur Delta*; **JUTHA SUPHANNIKA** (Th) ex-*Merkur Beach*; **BANGLAR MONI** (Bh) ex-*Antje*; **ELISE D** (Ma) ex-*L'Abanga*; **ALEXIS II** (Ma) ex-*La Mpassa*; **DECO OLDENBURG** (Cy) ex-*Merkur Beach*; **CAPITAINE KERMADEC** (Th) ex-*Merkur Delta*; **GOTLANDIA** (Li) ex-*Saxonia*; **CGM MANA II** (Cy) ex-*Nuestra Senora del Rosario*; **CASTOR** (Sg) ex-*Dirk*; **CMBT EQUINOX** (Li) ex-*Laplandia*; **CAPE YORK** (SV) ex-*Nordwoge*; **CAPE NELSON** (SV) ex-*Nordstrand*; **MEGAH JAYA** (My) ex-*Annemarie Kruger*; **JOHAN CRYSTAL** (My) ex-*Hans Kruger*

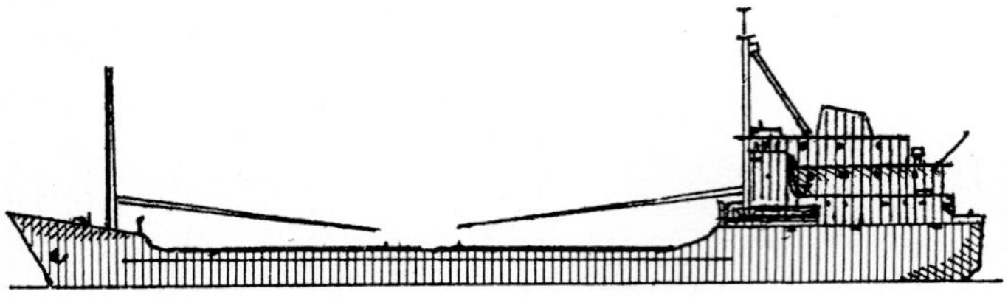

447 *MVF H13*
MARATHON Ne/Ne (Bijlholt); 1976; C dwt; 1,655/2,575; 78.67 × 5.03 *(258.1 × 16.5)*; M (Appingedammer Brons); 11.5; ex-*Vrouwe Alida*

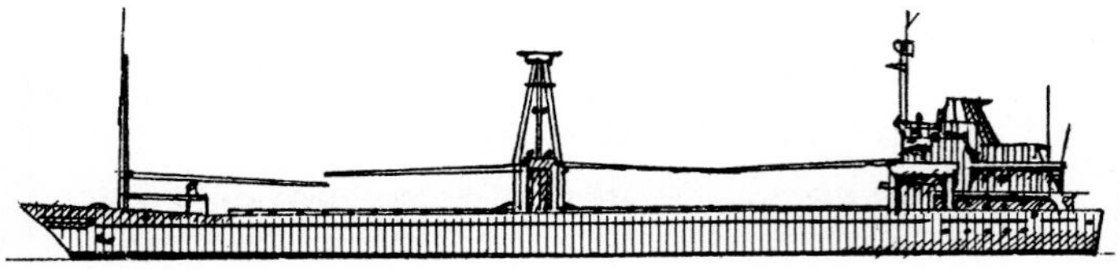

448 *MVHF H*
SEA PEARL FRG (Buesumer) 1973; C/Con; 2,593 grt/3,615 dwt; 89.34 × 5.86 m *(293 × 19.23 ft)*; M (Alpha-Diesel); 13 kts; ex-*Wivi Bewa*; 146 TEU; Lengthened 1977
Similar: **HAI BAO** (RC) ex-*Conny Bewa*; **ARWAD** (Sy) ex-*Viggo Scan*; **REUNION** (SV) ex-*Heavy Scan*; **CONTI BLUE** (SV) ex-*Super Scan*; **CHI WAN 301** (RC) ex-*Sally Bewa*

449 *MVMFN H13*
TAINO Cu/De (Helsingor) 1977; C/TS; 12,170 grt/13,021 dwt; 149.1 × 9 m *(489 × 30 ft)*; M (B&W); 16.5 kts; ex-*Jose Marti*
Sister: **IBN KHALDOON** (Iq)

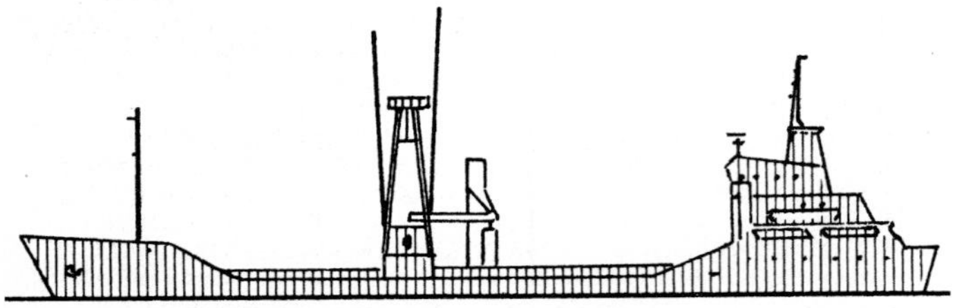

450 *MVM–F H13*
AKOLI Ng/No (Eides) 1972; C; 1,229 grt/2,337 dwt; 70.01 × 5.27 m *(229.69 × 17.29 ft)*; M (Atlas-MaK); 12.5 kts; ex-*Brunette*

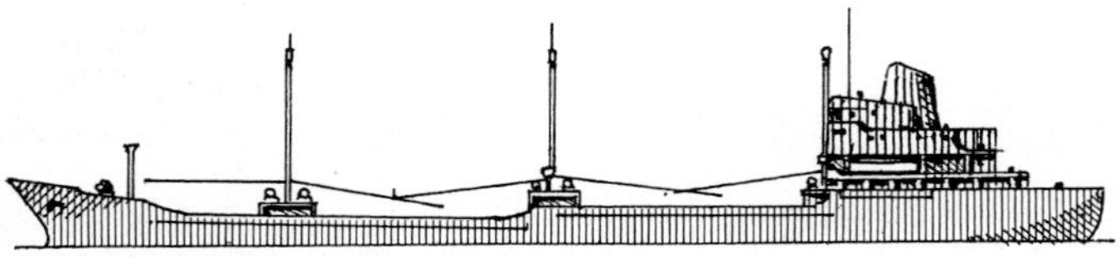

451 *MV²HF H123*
PAN SHAN RC/FRG (Meyer) 1967; C; 4,173 grt/6,070 dwt; 110.5 × 7.57 m *(362.53 × 24.84 ft)*; M (Fiat); 14 kts; ex-*Inge Kruger*

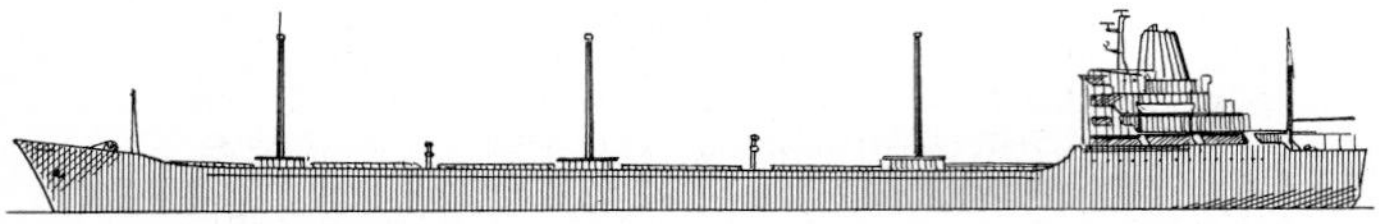

452 *MV³MFN H13*
ZHI HAI RC/Ja (Mitsui) 1968; B; 15,353 grt/25,934 dwt; 176.60 × 9.03 m *(579.40 × 29.63 ft)*; M (Sulzer); 13.50 kts; ex-*Aurora II*
Similar: **MILENAKI** (Gr) ex-*Agios Nikolaos III*; **SHAO SHAN** (SV) ex-*George S Embiricos*; **KEA** (Gr) ex-*Maistros*; **DORYFOROS** (Bs); **LEON** (Bs) ex-*Nicolaos S Embiricos*; **YONG FENG HAI** (RC) ex-*Costas Frangos*

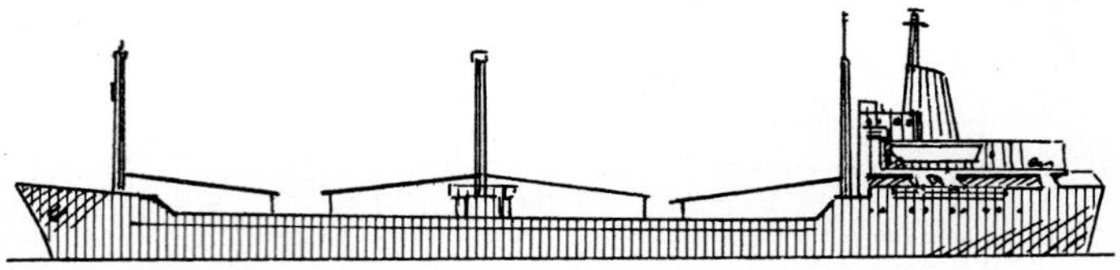

453 *NH²M–F H13*
EVANGELIA 1 Cy/Pd (Gdanska) 1973; C; 1,908 grt/2,943 dwt; 84.18 × 5.3 m *(276.18 × 17.39 ft)*; M (Deutz); 14.75 kts; ex-*Sig*; 'B-431' type
Sisters: **VENIA** (It) ex-*Eir*; **BULK MASTER** (Ma) ex-*Soknatun*; **NAUSICA** (It) ex-*Hop*; **POSITANO** (It) ex-*Germa*; **MARE NOSTRUM** (Ma) ex-*Eva*; **CLEOPATRA** (SV) Launched as *Lionel*; **NEW FLORA** (Eg) ex-*Germa Gracia*; **THEOFILOS S** (Pa) ex-*Germa Girl*; **YVETTE** (SV) ex-*Lyspol*; **HAJJI-KHADIJA** (Sy) ex-*Garli*

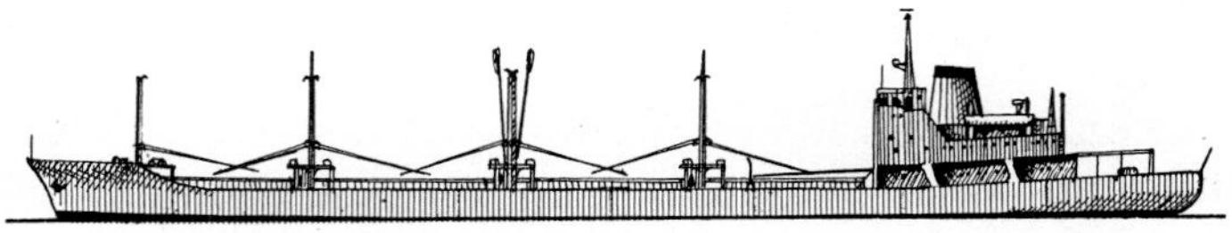

454 *NH²N²MFN H1*
PRESIDENTE KENNEDY Bz/Bz (Ish do Brazil) 1965; C; 9,091 grt/13,330 dwt; 145.5 × 8.75 m *(477.36 × 28.7 ft)*; M (Sulzer); 15.5 kts

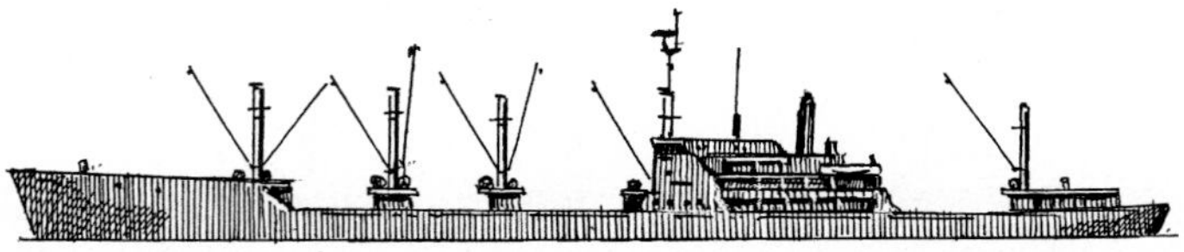

455 *NHNHGN H1*
GULF BANKER US/US (Avondale) 1964; C; 8,970 grt/11,549 dwt; 151 × 9.8 m *(495 × 32 ft)*; T (GEC); 18 kts; GULF ANDES class; US Govenment owned
Sisters: **GULF FARMER** (US); **GULF MERCHANT** (US); **GULF SHIPPER** (US); **GULF TRADER** (US)

456 *NHN²F H1*
ABOITIZ CONCARRIER XII Pi/Sw (Norrkopings) 1957; CP; 1,341 grt/2,174 dwt; 89.09 × 6.09 m *(292.29 × 19.98 ft)*; M (MAN); 13 kts; ex-*Vega*; Converted from cargo ship

457 *NM³NF H12*
UNITED TRUST Ma/De (Aalborg) 1964; C; 3,447 grt/4,887 dwt; 110.5 × 6.27 m *(362.53 × 20.57 ft)*; M (B&W); 14.5 kts; ex-*Concordia*

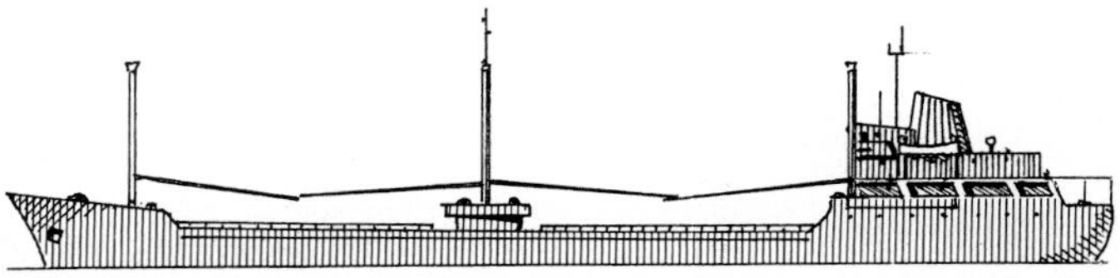

458 *NMNMF H13*
SARA II Ho/FRG (Rickmers) 1968; C; 4,570 grt/7,274 dwt; 110.75 × 7.29 m *(363.35 × 23.92 ft)*; M (Deutz); — kts; ex-*Alexandra Botelho*

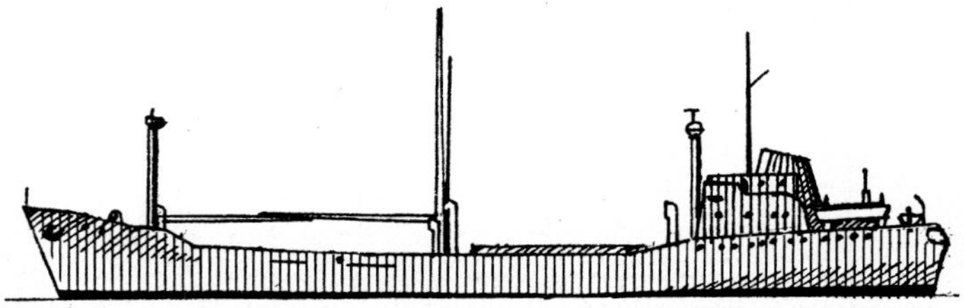

459 *NMNMF H13*
STORM Pa/FRG (Renck) 1953; C; 1,943 grt/3,484 dwt; 73.43 × 6.48 m *(240.91 × 21.26 ft)*; M (MaK); 12 kts; ex-*Johanna*

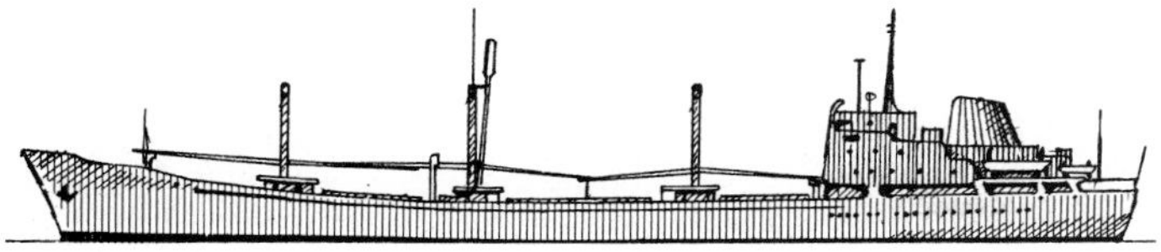

460 *NMNMFN H1*
SOUAD M Le/Sw (Ekensbergs) 1960; C; 3,922 grt/6,071 dwt; 114.33 × 7.19 m *(375 × 23.59 ft)*; M (B&W); 14.5 kts; ex-*Bindal*

461 *NMNMFNH H13*
QIN HUAI RC/FRG (Kieler H) 1960; C; 4,998 grt/7,280 dwt; 143.2 × 8.5 m *(470 × 27.1 ft)*; M (MAN); 17 kts; ex-*Nopal Express*

462 *NMNM–FN^3 H1*
MORMACGLEN US/US (Todd) 1961; C; 9,258 grt/12,590 dwt; 147.3 × 9.58 m *(483 × 31.4 ft)*; T (GEC); 19 kts; US Government owned
Similar (Operated by US Navy (Military Sealift Command) as Cargo Ships): **NORTHERN LIGHT** ex-*Mormaccove*; **SOUTHERN CROSS** ex-*Mormactrade*

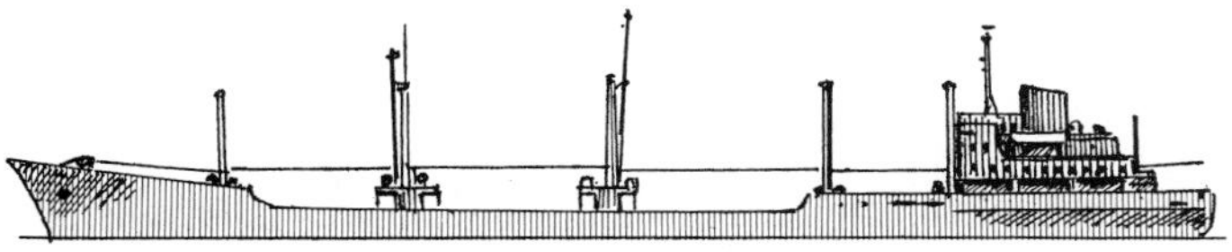

463 *NMN^{3}MFN H13*
INDIAN VALOUR In/FRG (A G 'Weser') 1971; C; 9,629 grt/15,550 dwt; 144.91 × 9.42 m *(475.43 × 30.91 ft)*; M (MAN); 16 kts; '36-L' type

464 *N^{2}HNF H1*
NATALI —/Sw (Norrkoping) 1956; C; 1,307 grt/2,174 dwt; 89.01 × 6.06 m *(292.03 × 19.88 ft)*; M (MAN); 13 kts; ex-*Mira*

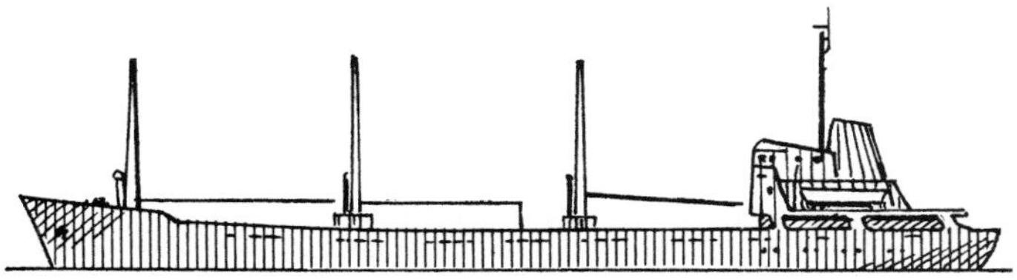

465 *N^{3}MF H1*
EMMANUEL SV/FRG (Hitzler) 1966; C; 961 grt/2,422 dwt; 77.60 × 5.39 m *(254.59 × 17.68 ft)*; M (Atlas-MaK); 11.5 kts; ex-*Uthorn*

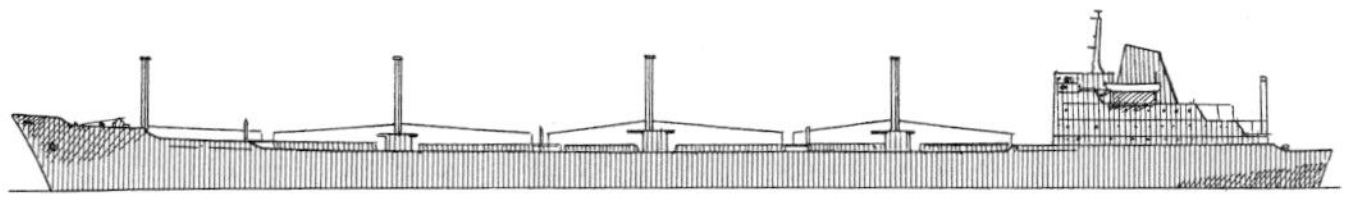

466 *N^{4}MFN H1*
SEAKITTIE Li/Br (A&P) 1975; B; 15,584 grt/26,620 dwt; 183.04 × 10.47 m *(600.53 × 34.35 ft)*; M (Sulzer); 15.5 kts; ex-*Cairnsmore*; 'B-26' type
Sisters: **CHIOS CHARM** (Pa) ex-*Lynton Grange*; **ORGULLO** (Pa) ex-*Upwey Grange*; **SENTOSA** (Cy) ex-*Leon*; Possible sister: **MARIA A** (Cy) ex-*Righteous*

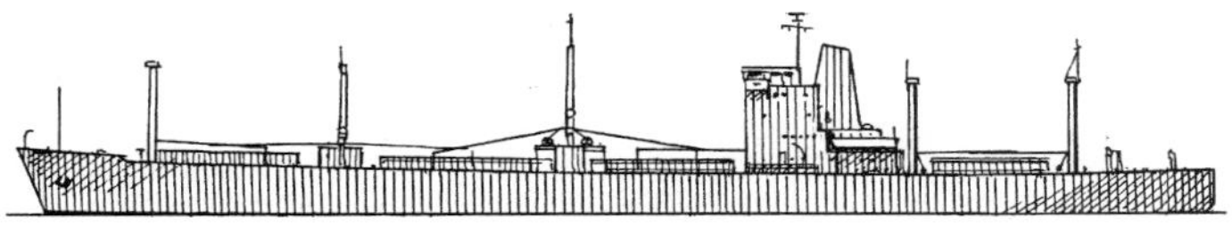

467 *NT^{2}MFN^2 H*
KELLYS MARK Bl/Be (Cockerill) 1969; C; 9,001 grt/16,030 dwt; 141 × 9.27 m *(461 × 30.41 ft)*; M (Stork); 14 kts; ex-*Matija Gubec*; 'Unity' type

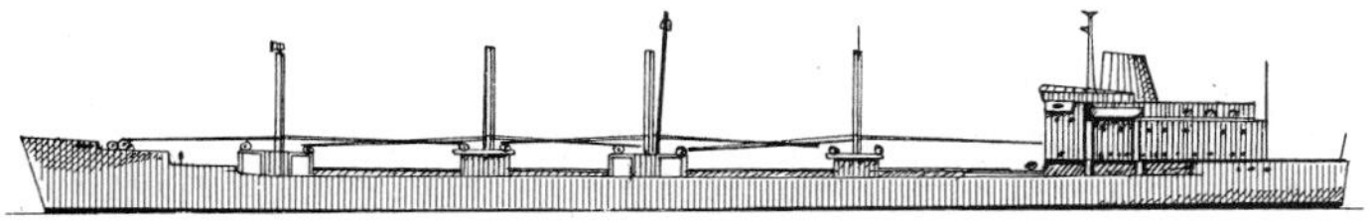

468 *NT^{3}MFN H13*
LONG KHANH Vn/Br (Upper Clyde) 1968; C; 9,373 grt/16,240 dwt; 152.25 × 9.11 m *(499.5 × 29.9 ft)*; M (Pielstick); 16 kts; ex-*Cornish City*

469 *NVFVN H123*
LIRIJA Al/Pd (Szczecinska) 1959; C; 2,561 grt/3,251 dwt; 94.7 × 5.5 m *(308 × 18 ft)*; R ('Zgoda'); 11.5 kts; 'B32' type
Similar: **PARTIZANI** (Al)

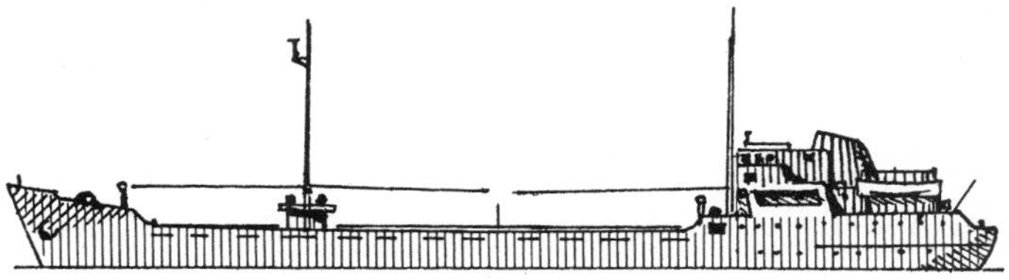

470 *THF H13*
TWEIT VI Le/Ne (Arnhemsche) 1960; C; 1,200 grt/1,928 dwt; 81.29 × 4.73 m *(266.7 × 15.52 ft)*; M (MAN); 12 kts; ex-*City of Cork*

471 *THFHN H13*
SAONA Pa/Fr (Bretagne) 1961; C; 3,096 grt/— dwt; 99.2 × 5.7 m *(325 × 19 ft)*; M (Pielstick); 19 kts; ex-*Boree*

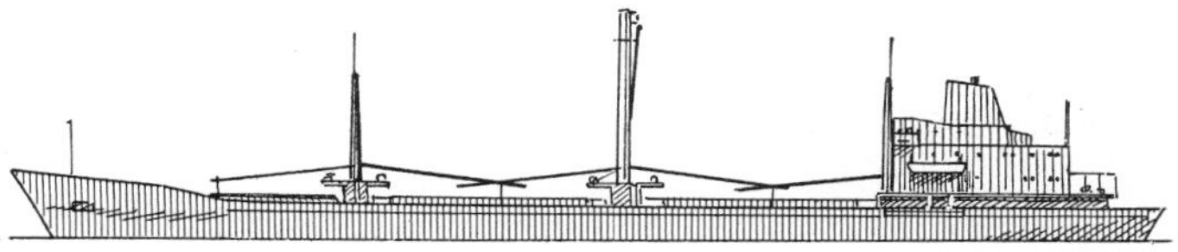

472 *TH^{2}FN H1*
SU CHANG Pa/FRG (Nobiskrug) 1971; C/Con; 4,960 grt/7,500 dwt; 125.02 × 7.62 m *(410.17 × 25 ft)*; M (Atlas-MaK); 16.5 kts; ex-*Pallas*; 210 TEU
Sister: **HAPAG LLOYD AMAZONAS** (Pa) ex-*Neptun*

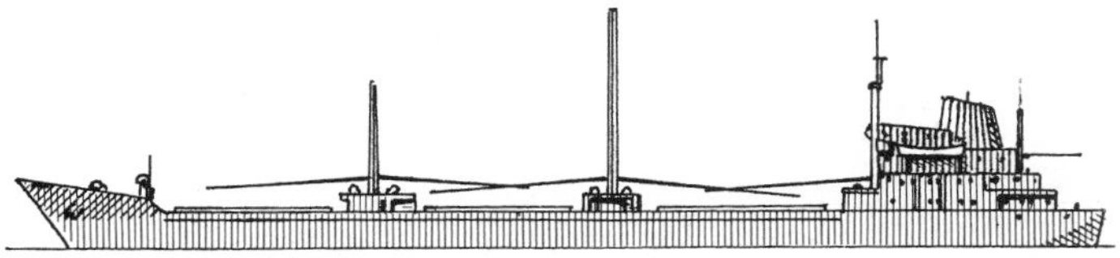

473 *TH^{2}FN H1*
YUN LONG RC/FRG (O&K) 1971; C/Con; 4,810 grt/7,405 dwt; 116.72 × 7.53 m *(382.94 × 24.7 ft)*; M (Atlas-MaK); 15.25 kts; ex-*Gebe Oldendorff*; 226 TEU

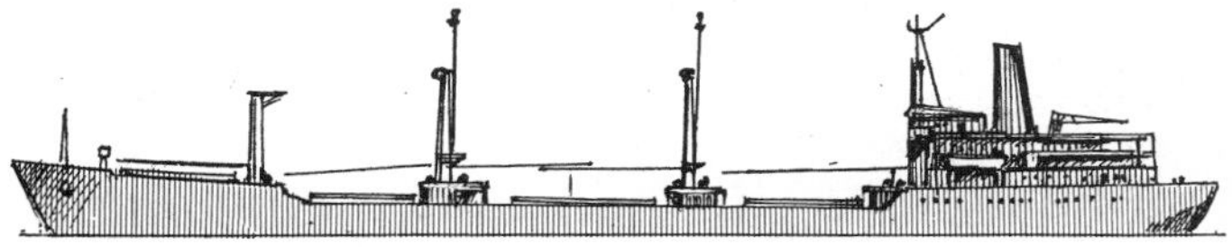

474 *TH^{3}G*
OCEAN LINER Pa/Sp (AESA) 1972; C/Con; 10,966 grt/15,893 dwt; 154.64 × 10.36 m *(507.35 × 33.99 ft)*; M (B&W); 18 kts; ex-*Gioacchino Lauro*; 335 TEU
Sister: **MSC ANIELLO** (Pa) ex-*Turmalin*

475 *TH^{2}MFN H13*
WONFU SV/Ja (Hashihama) 1973; C/Con; 7,060 grt/11,526 dwt; 129.06 × 7.98 m *(423.43 × 26.18 ft)*; M (Mitsubishi); 13.5 kts; ex-*Luxuriant*; 210 TEU

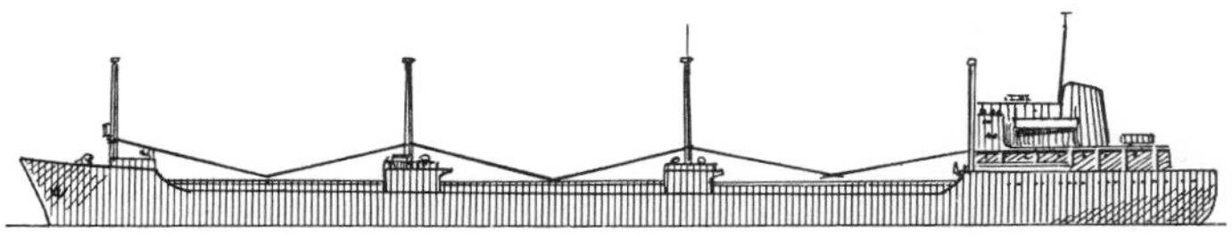

476 *TH^{2}NM–F H13*
ANNA SIERRA Cy/No (Porsgrunds) 1971; C; 7,537 grt/12,934 dwt; 140.14 × 8.71 m *(459.78 × 28.58 ft)*; M (MAN); 13 kts; ex-*Diagara*

477 *THM–FN H1*
"SD14" type dwt; Sequence variation on drawing number 8/500

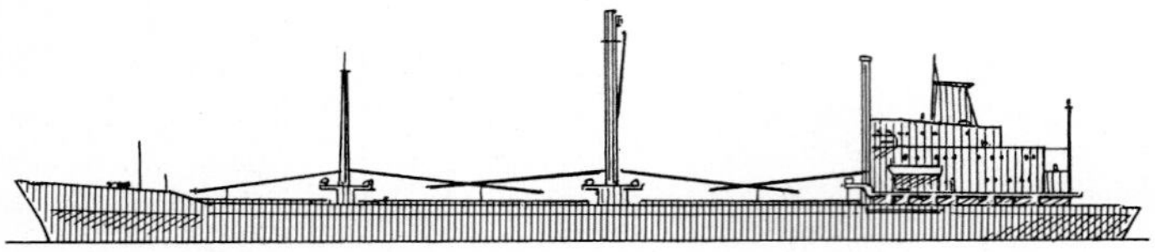

478 *THNM–FN H1*
MUHIEDDINE VI Sy/FRG (Lindenau) 1969; C; 5,079 grt/7,490 dwt; 125.18 × 7.64 m *(410.7 × 25.07 ft)*; M (MAN); 12 kts; ex-*Kathe Wiards*

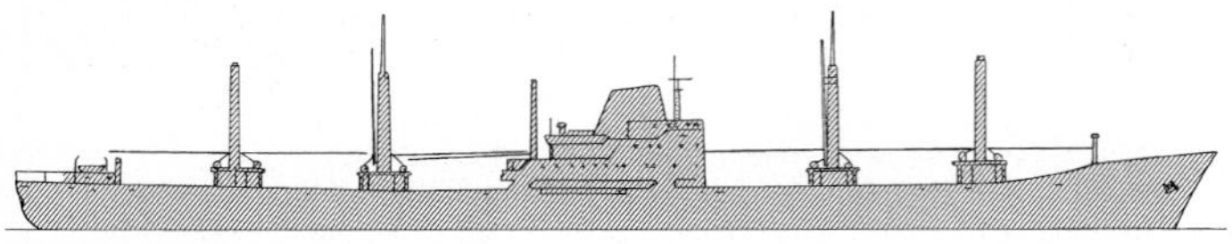

479 *TMFNMT H1*
LI MING RC/Sw(Uddevalla) 1963; C; 10,678 grt/15,372 dwt; 161.92 × 9.53 m *(531.23 × 31.27 ft)*; M (Gotaverken); 16.5 kts; ex- *London Tradesman*

480 *TMHMFN H123*
RUN ZHOU SV/Ja (Kurushima) 1972; C/HL; 6,066 grt/9,585 dwt; 126.02 × 7.88 m *(413.45 × 25.85 ft)*; M (Mitsubishi); 14 kts; ex-*Katsura Maru*; **ALTERNATIVE SEQUENCE FOR NUMBER 8/376**

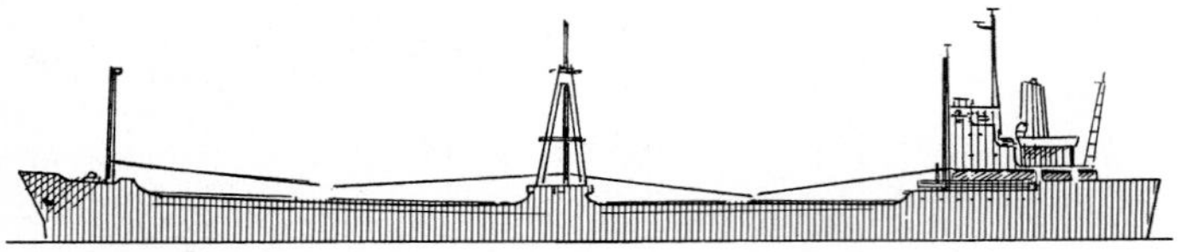

481 *TMHMFN H13*
RICO My/Ja (Kurushima) 1971; C/HL; 7,094 grt/11,603 dwt; 131.81 × 8.23 m *(432.5 × 26 ft)*; M (Kobe); 14 kts; ex-*Seiyo Maru*
Sisters: **CANDO** (Pa) ex-*Sakura Maru*; **YANG YANG** (My) ex-*Tachibana Maru*

482 *TM^{2}FMN H1*
HONG QI 131 RC/Br (Gray) 1958; C; 8,414 grt/12,350 dwt; 145.7 × 9.1 m *(478 × 30 ft)*; M (B&W); 14.5 kts; ex-*Cleveland*

483 *TM^{2}FN H13*
YU QING RC/Ja (Mitsui) 1966; C; 6,264 grt/7,723 dwt; 130.99 × 7.89 m *(429.7 × 25.88 ft)*; M (B&W); 17 kts; ex-*Transmichigan*
Sister: **YU YING** (RC) ex-*Transontario*

484 *TM^{3}FN H13*
VISHVA KARUNA In/In (Hindustan) 1973; C; 9,795 grt/13,967 dwt; 154 × 9.2 m *(506 × 30.6 ft)*; M (Sulzer); 17.5 kts
Sisters: **VISHVA MADHURI** (In); **VISHVA BANDHAN**; (In) **VISHVA YASH** (In)

485 *TM^{3}FN H13*
WAN LONG RC/FRG (Deutsche Werft) 1965; C; 9,659 grt/13,550 dwt; 156 × 9 m *(511 × 30 ft)*; M (MAN); 17 kts; ex-*Taveta*

486 *TMNFNM H13*
AVA Mr/FRG (A G 'Weser') 1963; C; 7,140 grt/10,120 dwt; 135 × 8.4 m *(455 × 27.56 ft)*; M (B&W); 15.5 kts
Sister: **PATHEIN** (Mr) ex-*Bassein*

487 *TMNFT H1*
WAN PING RC/FRG (Bremer V) 1957; C; 4,874 grt/6,725 dwt; 126 × 7.5 m *(414 × 26.8 ft)*; M (Bremer V); 14 kts; ex-*Spreestein*

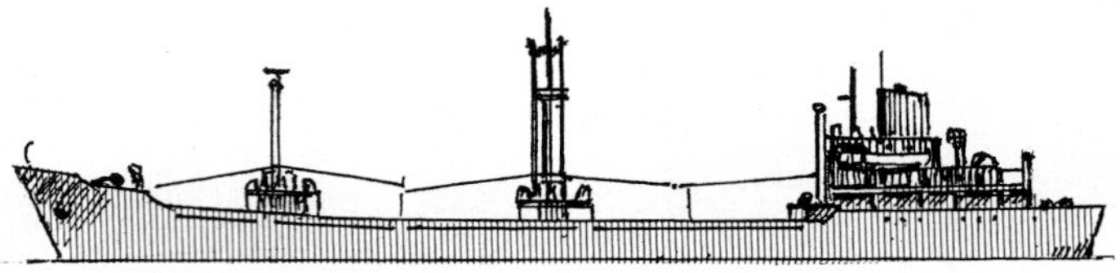

488 *TMNMF H13*
NAN JING RC/Br (Burntisland) 1968; C; 5,008 grt/7,670 dwt; 121.62 × 7.89 m *(399 × 25.89 ft)*; M (B&W); 16 kts; ex-*Paul Schroder*
Sister: **FANG CHENG** (RC) ex-*Peter Schroder*

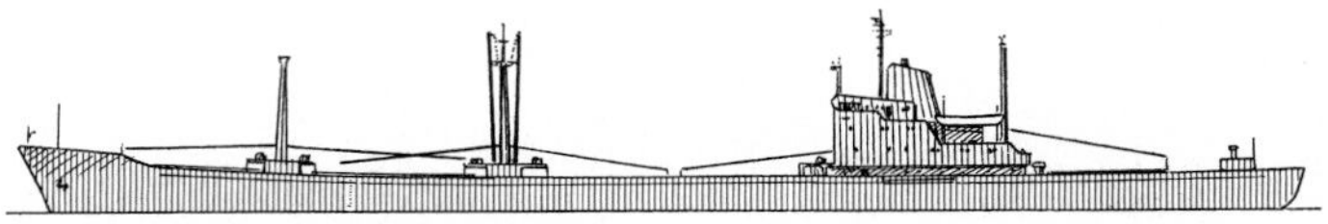

489 *TMNMFN H1*
TILLY Pa/FRG (Deutsche Werft) 1967/74; C; 8,084 grt/7,650 dwt; 151.47 × 8.03 m *(496.95 × 26.35 ft)*; M (MAN); 17.75 kts; ex-*Tilly Russ*; Lengthened 1974
Sister **PAUL** (Pa) ex-*Paul Lorenz Russ*

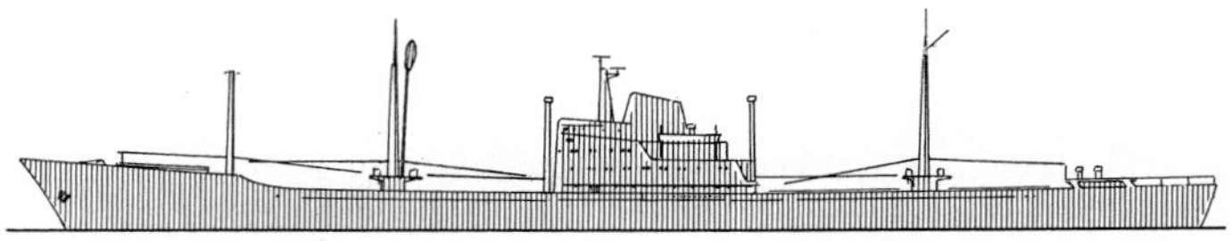

490 *TMNMFNM H1*
LIAO YANG RC/RC (Guangzhou) 1974; C; 9,910 grt/14,683 dwt; 161.25 × 9.53 m *(529 × 31.27 ft)*; M (Sulzer); 17 kts; Differs from **FENG QING** (see number 8/492) only by radar mast being separated from funnel. Other vessels of this class may also have this feature

491 *TMNMFN^2 H13*
QING FENG SAN HAO RC/Br (Lithgows) 1962; C; 9,733 grt/13,774 dwt; 159 × 9.4 m *(502 × 31 ft)*; M (B&W); 15 kts; ex-*Clarkforth*; May be reported as **QING FENG 3**

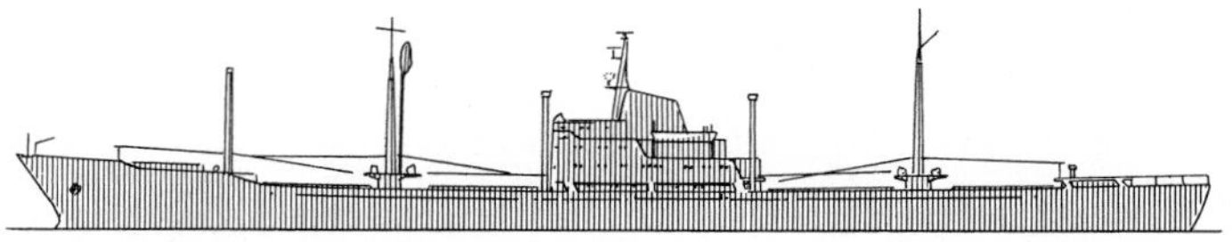

492 *TMNM–FNM H1*
FENG QING RC/RC (Kiangran) 1974; C; 9,921 grt/14,802 dwt; 161.6 × 9.1 m *(530 × 30 ft)*; M (Hudong); 16 kts
Sister: **FENG SHENG** (RC) (builder–Zhong Hua); Probable sisters (some may have radar mast from bridge—see number 8/490) **FENG CAI** (RC); **FENG GE** (RC); **FENGTAI** (RC); **FENGTAO** (RC); **FENGXIANG** (RC); **FENGYAN** (RC); **FENGYANG** (RC); **FENGYI** (RC); **FENGYING** (RC); **HUI YANG** (RC); **YANG CHENG** (RC); ex-*Jieyang*; **XINYANG** (RC); **YUEYANG** (RC); **TRANSPACE** (Pa) ex-*Feng Lei*

493 *TMN^{2}MFNMN H13*
GOLDEN SPLENDOUR SV/FRG (Rhein Nordseew) 1970; C; 11,384 grt/13,161 dwt; 163 × 9 m *(534 × 30 ft)*; M (Sulzer); 18 kts; ex-*Weserland*

494 *TMN^{2}M–FN H1*
SEA HAWK 1 Pa/De (Odense) 1963; CP; 10,362 grt/14,429 dwt; 153.3 × 9.1 m *(503 × 30 ft)*; M (B&W); 16 kts; ex-*Dlugosz*

495 *TMTMFN^2 H13*
DONG RU RC/FRG (Deutsche Werft) 1966; C; 10,527 grt/13,500 dwt; 156 × 9.2 m *(509 × 30.6 ft)*; M (MAN); 19 kts; ex-*Tugelaland*

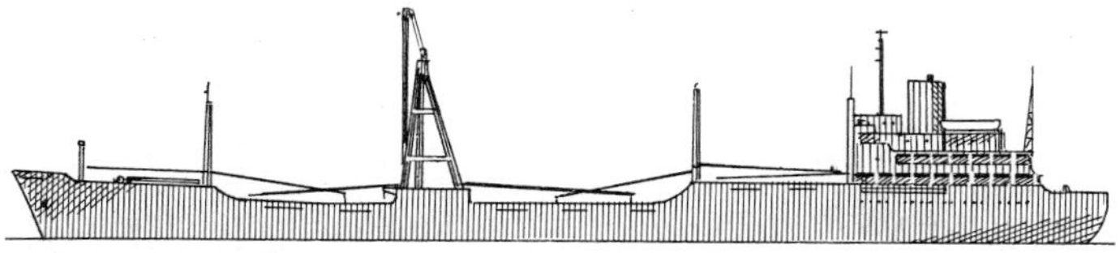

496 *TMTNHFN H123*
RONG HUA SHAN RC/Ja (Namura) 1969; C/HL; 7,673 grt/11,896 dwt; 138.51 × 8.81 m *(454.43 × 28.90 ft)*; M (B&W); 14.75 kts; ex-*Wakaura Maru*

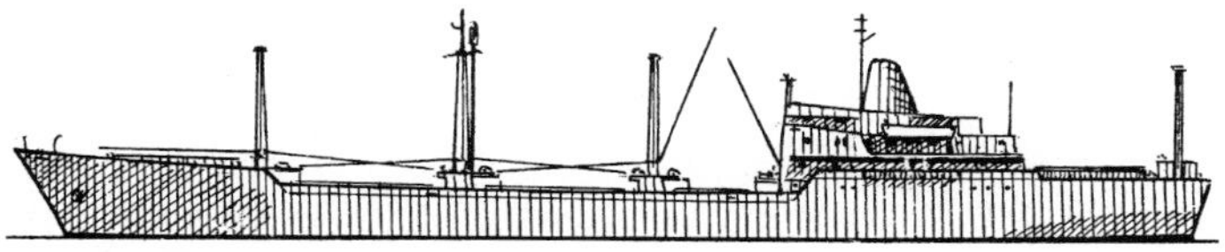

497 *TMTNMFN H13*
GUANG YUN RC/FRG (Howaldts DW) 1969; C; 4,303 grt/7,382 dwt; 133.4 × 7.4 m *(438 × 24.4 ft)*; M (MAN); 17.5 kts; ex-*Hornmeer*
Sisters: **YU CAI** (RC) ex-*Horngolf*; **YACU WAYO** (Pe) ex-*Hornwind*

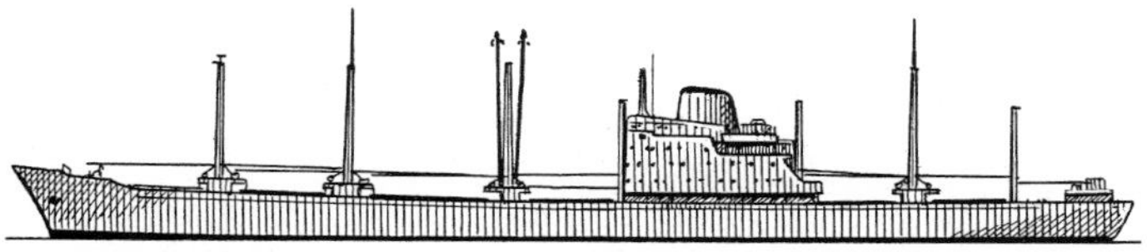

498 *TMTNMFNMN H1*
HONG YIN RC/FRG (Howaldts) 1960; CP; 9,788 grt/12,310 dwt; 162 × 9 m *(533 × 30 ft)*; M (Fiat); 18.5 kts; ex-*Ostriesland*

499 *TNHF H1*
IBN KHALDOUN II Ag/FRG (Schlichting) 1977; C/Con; 5,400 grt/8,190 dwt; 126.47 × 7.35 m *(414.93 × 24.11 ft)*; M (MaK); 15.5 kts; **SIMILAR TO DRAWING NUMBER 8/505** but has 80-tonne Stülcken derrick
Sisters: **IBN SINA II** (Ag)

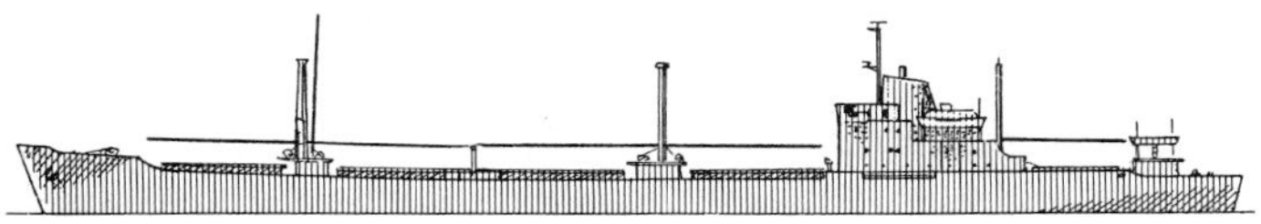

500 *TNM–FN H1*
'SD 14' type —/Br etc 1968 onwards; C; approx 8,700–9,800 grt/approx 14,600–15,300 dwt; 141 × 8 m *(463 × 29 ft)*; M (Sulzer; MAN; Doxford); 14 kts; Standard British 'Liberty' replacement design. Built in Br (A&P; Bartram; Smith's Dock) and under licence in Bz (CCN; Maua) and Gr (Hellenic). Ships vary slightly in appearance (mast houses; taller superstructure; heavy derricks and so on. Some have a goalpost mast between hatches and some have a radar mast offset to starboard on bridge top.)
Sisters: **AGIOS GERASSIMOS** (SV) ex-*Sea Moon*; **ALAN** (Ma) ex-*Santa Ines*; **FLOATING MOUNTAIN** (Pa) ex-*Anna Dracopoulos*; **VRISSI** (Cy) ex-*Athanassia*; **AMANECIDA** (Ho) ex-*Serra Verde*; **ELINKA** (Ma) ex-*Serra Azul*; **VALI P** (Cy); **AL HAFIZU** (Pa) ex-*Collin*; **KYONG SONG** (RK) ex-*Despina*; **SAM HAE** (RK) ex-*John Michalos*; **TRINITY SIERRA** (Cy) ex-*Nefos II*; **HONG XIANG** (Ma) ex-*Panaghis Vergottis*; **MARE** (Pa) ex-*Rea*; **MARINER** (Cy) ex-*Scapwind*; **ANDY** (Ma) ex-*Silver Cloud*; **MIN JIANG** (RC) ex-*Stephanos Vergottis*; **LIA P** (Cy) ex-*Tanganyika*; **TOPAZ** (Bl) ex-*Toxotis*; **IOANNIS I** (Cy) ex-*London Bombardier*; **PANDA FAGET** (Cy) ex-*Babitonga*; **ASTRON** (Cy); ex-*Ceresio*; **HAE GUM GANG** (RK) ex-*Miguel de Larrinaga*; **FAWAZ** (Pa) ex-*L L Antuerpia*; **PETRA STAR** (Cy) ex-*Katerina Dracopoulos*; **FULVIA** (Pa) ex-*L L Peru*; **ALEXANDRA** (Li) ex-*L L Chile*; **ZALCO PIONEER** (Pa) ex-*L L Equador*; **PROCYON** (Cy) ex-*L L Colombia*; **ICARUS** (Cy) ex-*Lloyd Hamburgo*; **DANCING SISTER** (Ma) ex-*Lloyd Liverpool*; **KAVO GERANOS** (Ma) ex-*Lloyd Bras*; **PHAETHON** (Cy) ex-*Lloyd Genova*; **NONG GOONG SHANG NO 8** (RC) ex-*Lloyd Marselha*; **ELINA** (Li) ex-*Semiramis*; **DELIGHT GLORY** (Pa) ex-*Catharina Oldendorff*; **SINFA** (Sg) ex-*Dorthe Oldendorff*; **FAIR SPIRIT** (Li) ex-*Eibe Oldendorff*; **FEAX** (Cy) ex-*Hille Oldendorff*; **NIKA** (Ma) ex-*Hinrich Oldendorff*;

(continued in next column)

TECHMAT PIONEER (Pa) ex-*Imme Oldendorff*; **ACHILLES** (Cy) ex-*Santa Ursula*; **GOOD FAITH** (Li); **GLOBE TRADER** (Li); **1 CONGRESO DEL PARTIDO** (Cu) ex-*Maisi*; **SEVERN** (Ma) ex-*Belic*; **AVON** (Ma) ex-*Carlos Manuel de Cespedes*; **IGNACIO AGRAMONTE** (Cu); **CALIXTO CARCIA** (Cu) ex-*Ajanna*; **OLEBRATT** (Cy) ex-*Strathdirk*; **MAGISTER** (Cy) ex-*Strathdevon*; **AMORE** (Pa) ex-*Cosmonaut*; **OCEAN CROWN** (SV) ex-*Cluden*; **MANTIS** (SV) ex-*Erawan*; **AL JOHFFA** (Pa) ex-*Santa Maja*; **LIAN FENG** (RC) ex-*Santa Vassiliki*; **CORMORANT** (Ma) ex-*Cosmostar*; **MERRYTRANS** (SV) ex-*Santa Katerina*; **SAIGON 2** (Vn) ex-*Welsh Trident*; **HARMONY BREEZE** (Ma) ex-*Natal*; **AVANTI** (Pa) ex-*Cosmokrat*; **EXPEDIENT** (Pa) ex-*Togo*; **GHULAM** (SV) ex-*Venturer*; **SAIGON I** (Vn) ex-*Welsh Endeavour*; **SOCRATES** (Cy) ex-*London Cavalier*; **HALLDOR** (Th) ex-*Dunelmia*; **HERMES** (Th) ex-*Capetan Markos*; **LIA P** (Cy) or *Tanganyika*; **EMERALD ISLANDS** (Ma) ex-*Strathdoon*; **SILVER KRIS** (Ma) ex-*Santa Amalia*; **SAE BYOL** (Cb) ex-*Santa Isabella*; **PYONG CHON** (RK) ex-*Niki*; **XIN HAI TENG** (RC) ex-*Virtus*; **ALAMINOS** (Cy) ex-*Strathduns*; **NAVIRA EXPRESS** (Va) ex-*Welsh Troubador*; **MAR COURRIER** (Pa) ex-*Maria*; **GELI P** (Cy) ex-*Aracaju*; **VARUNA KACHHAPI** (In) ex-*Capetan Manolis*; **BANGLAR BAANI** (Bh) ex-*Industria*; **HOJI YA HENDA** (An) ex-*Anax*; **EBO** (An) ex-*Rio Conquista*; **YUE YANG** (SV) ex-*Cosmopolit*; **TIAN YUAN XING** (SV) ex-*London Grenadier*; **SOUTH ISLANDS** (Cy); **PHEASANT** (Cy) ex-*Ariadne*; **NIKA II** (Cy) ex-*Patricia M*; **SUNLIGHT** (SV) ex-*Rinoula*; **OCEAN ENVOY** (Pk); **ZENITH** (Cy) ex-*Strathdare*; **GUARDIAN ANGEL** (SV) ex-*Arrino*; **MEI JIANG** (RC) ex-*Ormos*; **NAN JIANG** (RC) ex-*Sea Lion*; **RIVER BREEZE** (Cy) ex-*Marsha*; **ANIXIS** (Ma) ex-*Serra Branca*; **SULU EXPRESS** (Pi) ex-*Lindenhall*; **SAINT SPIRIDONAS** (Cy) ex-*Leonor*; **JORDAN II** (Pa) ex-*Tucurui*

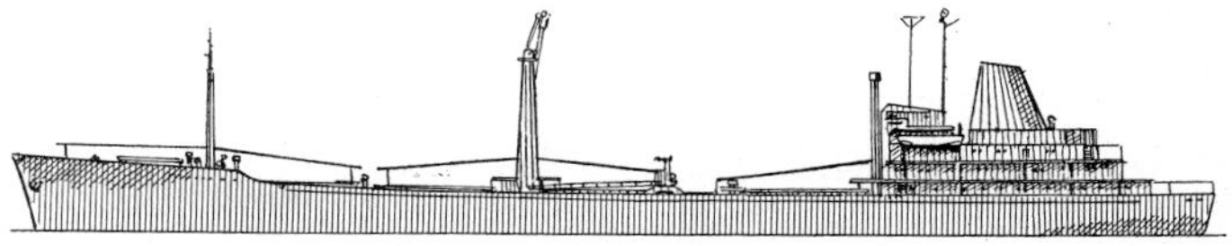

501 *TN^2MF H1*
DA LONG TIAN RC/Ja (A G 'Weser') 1966; C/HL; 9,441 grt/12,991 dwt; 152.25 × 9.48 m *(499.5 × 31.1 ft)*; M (MAN); 19 kts; ex-*Crostafels*
Sisters: **DA HONG QIAO** (RC) ex-*Kybfels*; **WU YI SHAN** (RC) ex-*Birkenfels*; **DA QING SHAN** (RC) ex-*Schonfels*

502 *TN^2MFN H1*
REDESTOS Cy/Br (A&P) 1974; C; 8,953 grt/15,180 dwt; 141 × 8.9 m *(463 × 29 ft)*; M (Sulzer); 15 kts; ex-*Waterland*; 'SD 14' type

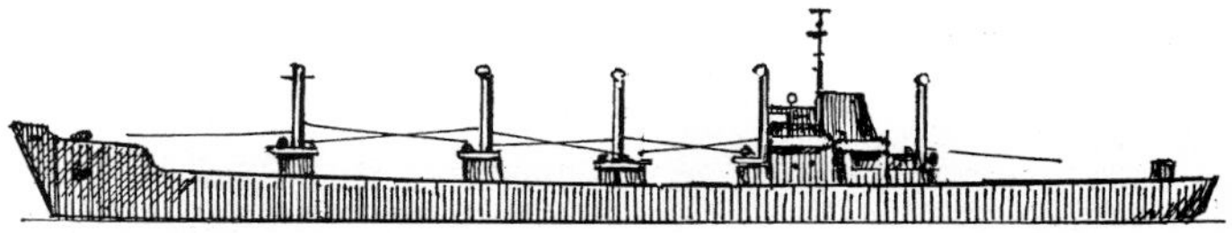

503 *$TN^3M–FN$ H1*
PRUDENT VOYAGER SV/Gr (Hellenic) 1971; CP; 8,892 grt/15,153 dwt; 143 × 7.82 m *(470 × 25.66 ft)*; M (MAN); 16.5 kts; ex-*Hellenic Ideal*; 'SD 14' Liner type
Sisters: **KUM GANG** (RK) ex-*Hellenic Navigator*; **SAFAR** (Pa) ex-*Grigorios C IV*; Similar ('SD 14' type): **OCEAN HO** (Ho) ex-*Belle Rose*; **TEPHYS** (Cy) ex-*Westland*

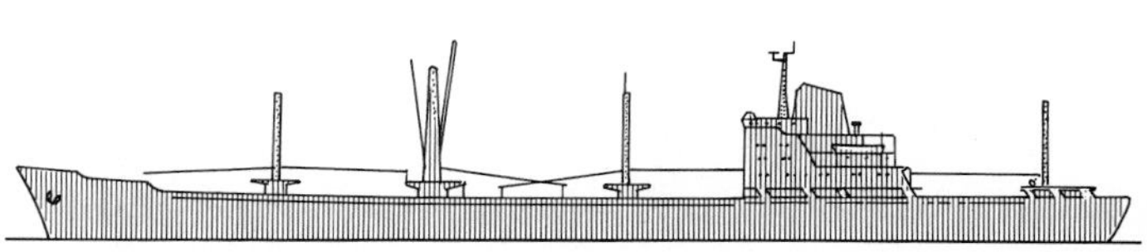

504 *TNTMFN H1*
DA LI RC/RC (Dalian) 1974; C; 10,129 grt/13,000 dwt; 163.00 × 9.10 m *(534.78 × 29.86 ft)*; M (Sulzer); 17 kts
Sisters: **DA FENG** (RC); **DA XING** (RC); **DA YE** (RC)

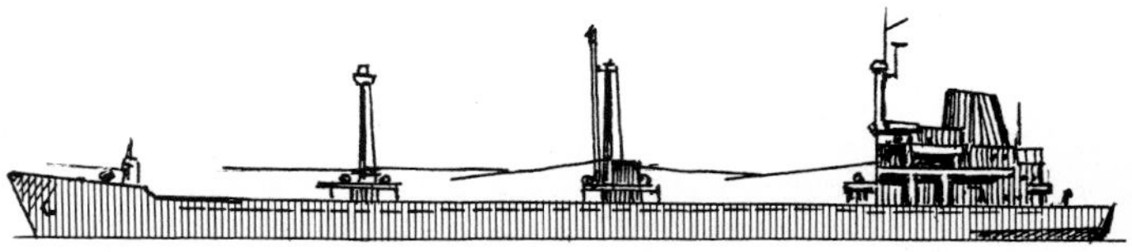

505 *T^2HF H1*
IBN ROCHD Ag/FRG (Schlichting) 1973; C/Con; 4,932 grt/7,435 dwt; 116.69 × 7.52 m *(328.84 × 24.67 ft)*; M (Atlas-MaK); 15.75 kts; 'Trampco' type; 226 TEU
Sisters (Some are 10m (33ft) longer): **IBN BADIS** (Ag); **IBN BATOUTA** (Ag); **IBN SIRAJ** (Ag); **AURES** (Ag); **DJORF** (Ag); **DJURDJURA** (Ag); **EDOUGH** (Ag); **QUARSENIS** (Ag)
Sisters (with Stülcken derrick): **IBN KHALDOUN II** (Ag); **IBN SINA II** (Ag)

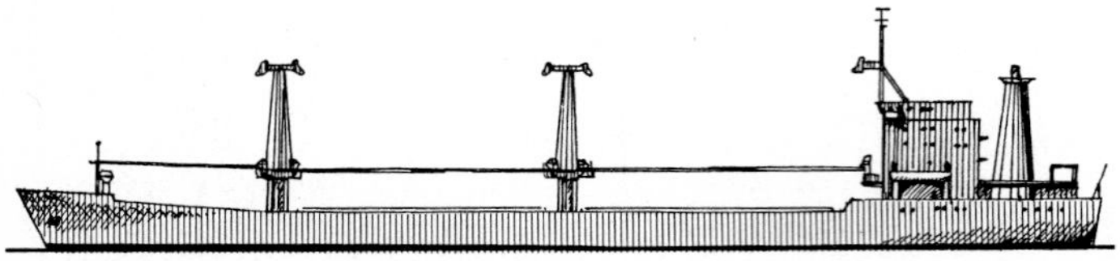

506 *T^2HF H13*
CORDILLERA Ch/FRG (Howaldts DW) 1977; C; 7,759 grt/10,480 dwt; 129.52 × 6.87/8.06 m *(424.93 × 22.53/26.44 ft)*; M (Atlas-MaK); 17 kts; ex-*Sloman Nereus*; 'CL-10' type
Sisters: **CONDOR** (Ch) ex-*Sloman Najade*; **BELGRANO** (Cy) ex-*Stubbenhuk*; **COPIHUE** (Ch) ex-*Steinhoft*

507 *T^2HF H13*
FU SHUN CHENG RC/FRG (Elsflether) 1969; C/Con; 5,382 grt/7,047 dwt; 117.35 × 7.06 m *(385.01 × 23.16 ft)*; M (Pielstick); 17 kts; ex-*Jorg Kruger*; 202 TEU
Sister: **PING XIANG CHENG** (RC) ex-*Britta Kruger*

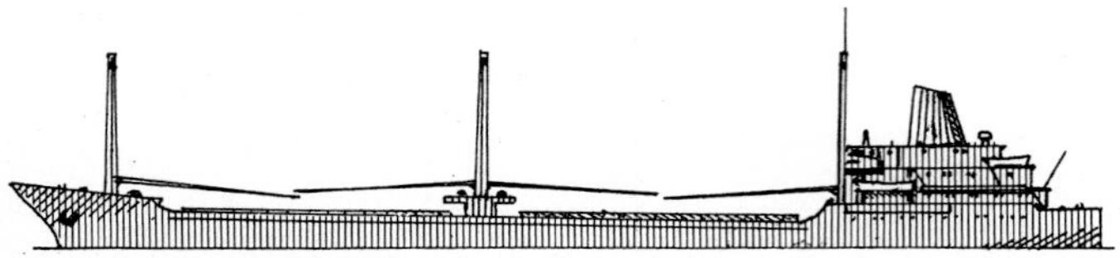

508 *T^2HF H13*
LIAN HONG My/FRG (Sietas) 1970; C/Con; 3,897 grt/4,250 dwt; 116.62 × 6.48 m *(382.61 × 21.26 ft)*; M (Atlas-MaK); 15 kts; ex-*Victrix* 1983; ex-*Al Hodeidah* 1982, ex-*Carolina* 1978; Lengthened 1973; 226 TEU
Similar (lengthened): **SWEE LONG SATU** (My) ex-*Arosia*
Similar (unlengthened): **EQUATOR RISE** (Sg) ex-*Isabella*; **WAH YEE** (RC) Launched as *Suderfehn*; **AL BATTANI** (Eg) ex-*Birte Andrea*; **EQUATOR PRIDE** (Sg) Launched as *Anita-Adele*

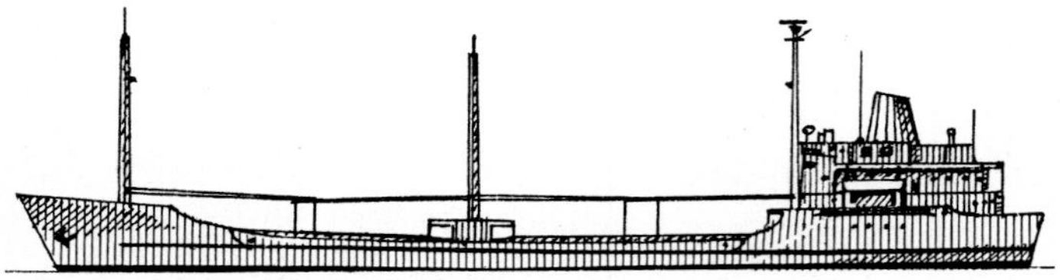

509 *T^2HF H13*
LUJIANG Sg/FRG (Sietas) 1970; C; 3,267 grt/4,572 dwt; 100.56 × 6.76 m *(329.92 × 22.17 ft)*; M (KHD); 12 kts; ex-*Apus*

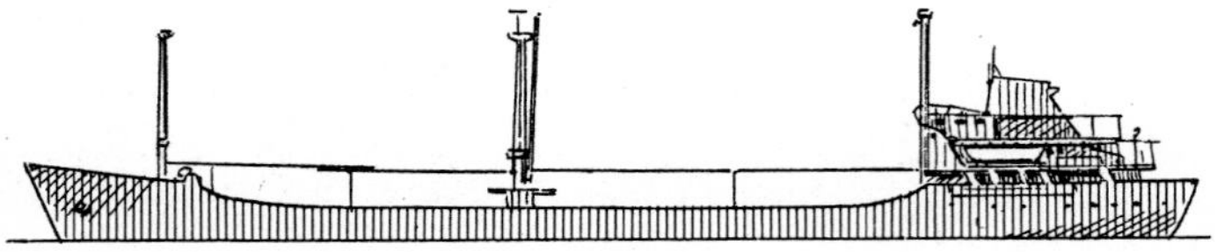

510 *T^2HF H13*
MAREM Ma/FRG (Elsflether) 1970; C/Con; 1,999 grt/3,358 dwt; 95.28 × 5.53 m *(312.6 × 18.14 ft)*; M (Atlas-MaK); 14.5 kts; ex-*Baltrumersand*; 80 TEU
Similar: **LIVA** (Ma) ex-*Mellumersand*

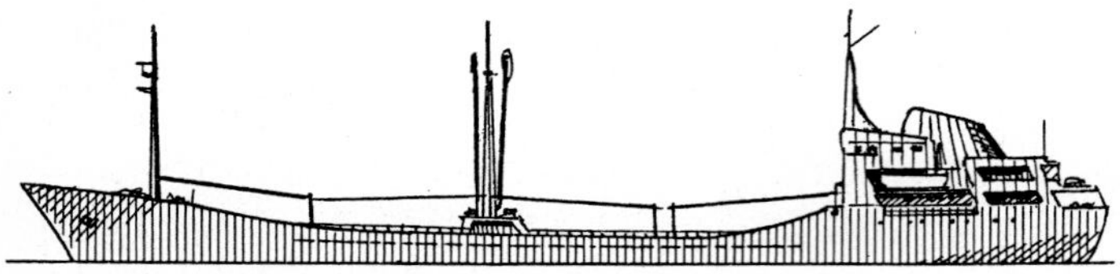

511 *T^2HF H13*
MUHIEDDINE V Sy/FRG (Brand) 1969; C; 1,999 grt/3,321 dwt; 92.33 × 6.1 m *(302.92 × 20.01 ft)*; M (Deutz); 15 kts; ex-*Tegelersand*

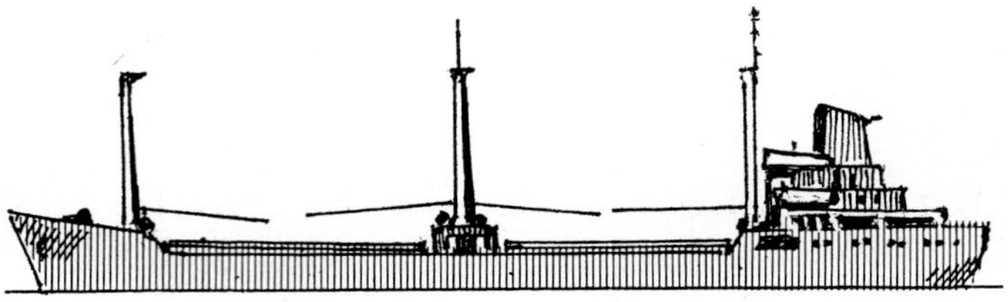

512 *T^2HF H13*
PERDANA PUTERA Pa/Ne (Sander) 1971; C; 2,999 grt/4,399 dwt; 103.51 × 6.52 m *(339.51 × 21.39 ft)*; M (Atlas-MaK); 15 kts; ex-*Westerfehn*; 170 TEU

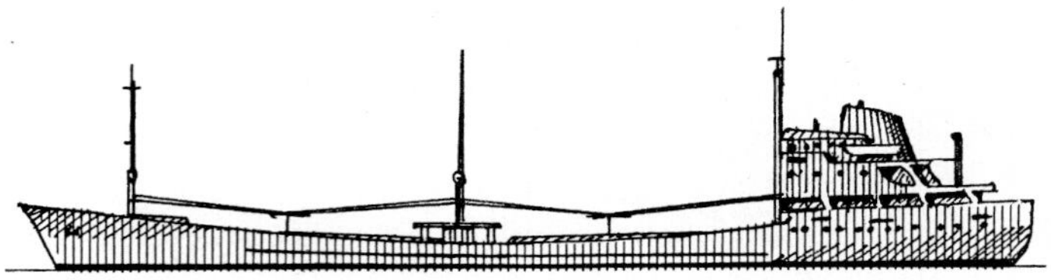

513 *T^2HF H13*
SAMER I SV/FRG (Elsflether) 1967; C; 1,848 grt/2,824 dwt; 86.01 × 5.14 m *(282.19 × 16.86 ft)*; M (Deutz); 12.75 kts; ex-*Bremersand*
Sisters: **GERASIMOS** (SV) ex-*Wesersand*; **ARTEMIS** (SV) ex-*Nordseesand*

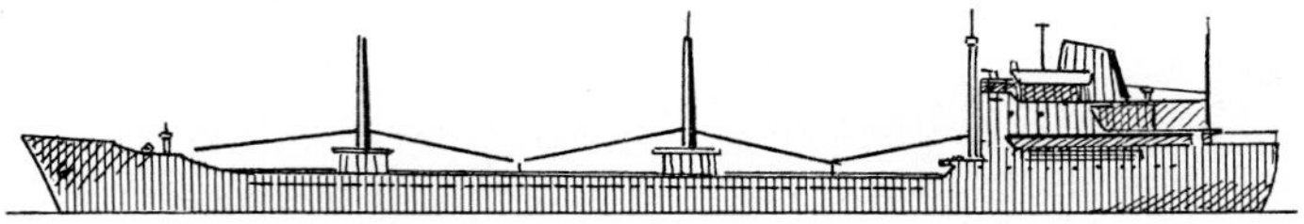

514 *T^2HFM H13*
AL BASHIR SV/No (Framnaes) 1966; C; 3,838 grt/5,842 dwt; 111.36 × 6.33 m *(365 × 20.77 ft)*; M (Sulzer); 13 kts; ex-*Fossum*

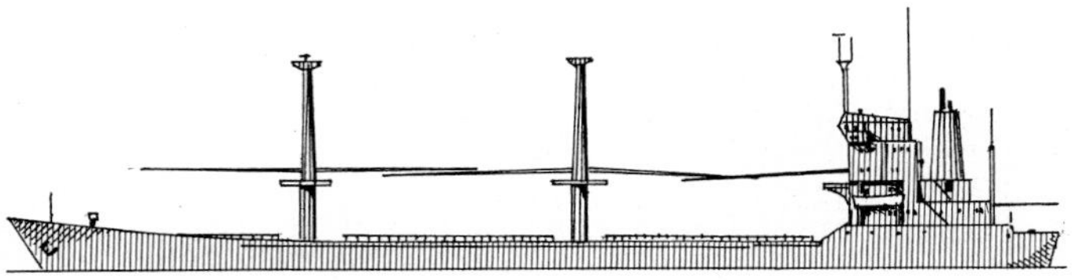

515 *T^2HFN H13*
MENG LEE Sg/FRG (Flensburger) 1978; C; 7,560 grt/11,690 dwt; 133.81 × 8.25 m *(439.01 × 27.07 ft)*; M (Atlas-MaK); 15 kts; ex-*Hodo*; 454 TEU
Sisters: **MAWLAMYINE** (Mr) ex-*Maw-La-Myaing*; **SITTWE** (Mr) ex-*Sit-Tway*

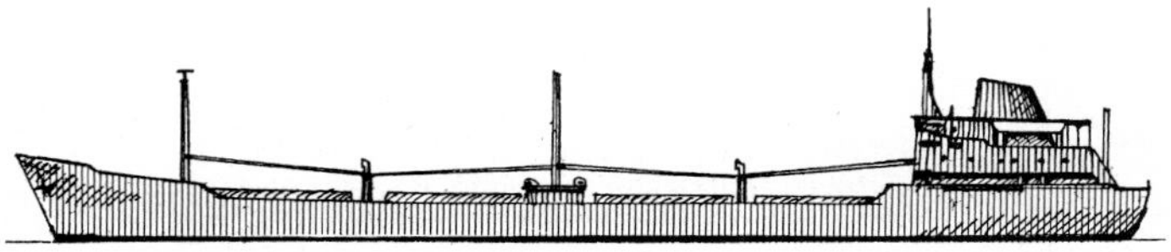

516 *T^2HFN H13*
PAN Ma/Br (Caledon) 1967; C; 4,816 grt/7,290 dwt; 123.81 × 7.1 m *(406.2 × 23.29 ft)*; M (British Polar); 14 kts; ex-*Lyminge*

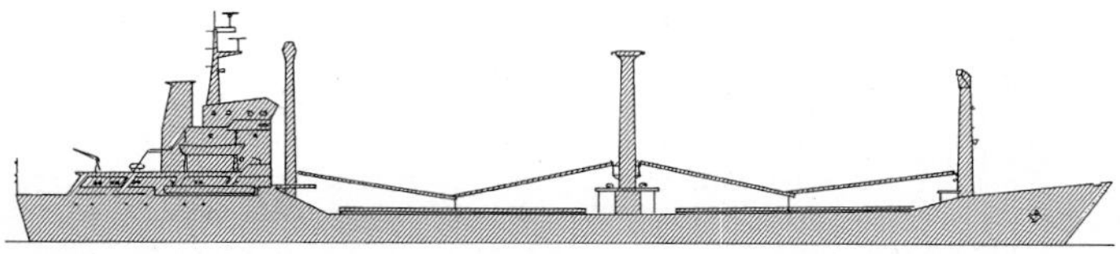

517 *T^2HMF H13*
ROMANCE Li/Sp (Juliana) 1984; C/Con; 5,868 grt/8,522 dwt; 119.51 × 7.43 m *(392.09 × 24.38 ft)*; M (Werkspoor); 13.25 kts; ex-*Abedul*; 160 TEU
Sisters: **LEX NARANJO** (Va) ex-*Ebano*; **ZLARIN** (Ma) ex-*Asturies*

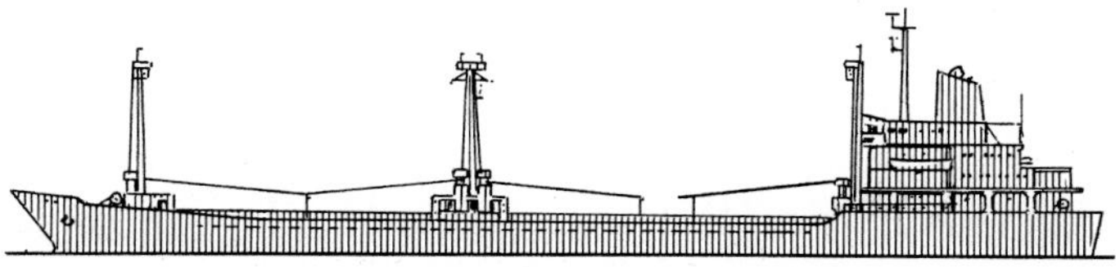

518 *T^2HMF H13*
YU MEN Pa/Ja (Watanabe) 1977; C; 5,408 grt/6,600 dwt; 118.70 × 7.10 m *(389 × 23.29 ft)*; M (Mitsubishi); 14 kts; ex-*Cap Anamur*; 174 TEU
Similar: **STARTRAMP** (At) launched as *Cap Andreas*

519 *T^2HMFN H1*
YONG NIAN SV/FRG (Bremer V) 1969; C/Con; 9,369 grt/15,315 dwt; 139.48 × 9.19 m *(457.61 × 30.15 ft)*; M (MAN); 15.75 kts; ex-*Caroline Oldendorff*; 238 TEU; **SIMILAR TO DRAWING NUMBER 8/273** but has tall goalpost between fourth and fifth hatches
Sisters: **TAI PING YANG** (RC) ex-*Elisabeth Oldendorff*; **BI JIA SHAN** (Pa) ex-*Maria Oldendorff*

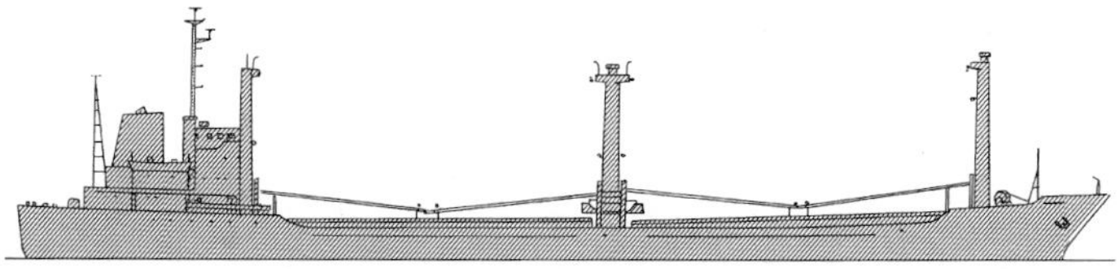

520 *T^2HMFN H13*
IKARIADA Cy/Ja (Kagoshima) 1976; C; 5,915 grt/9,780 dwt; 119.00 × 8.20 m *(390.42 × 26.90 ft)*; M (Mitsubishi); 12.25 kts; ex-*Lagada*
Similar: **ALL ROUND** (Sg) ex-*Leo Tempest*

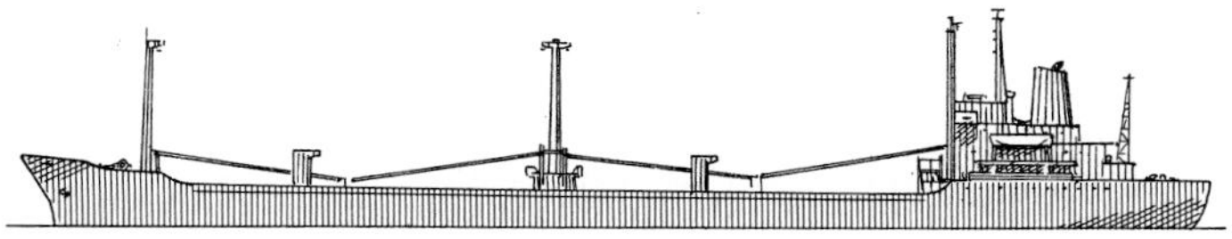

521 *T^2HMFN H13*
PAULINA Pa/Ja (Kochi) 1977; B; 7,881 grt/20,752 dwt; 141.97 × 9.1 m *(465.78 × 29.86 ft)*; M (Mitsubishi); 14 kts; ex-*Camphor*
Sisters: **ALVIC** (Cy) ex-*Scan Crusaders*; **NAVIGATOR D** (Cy) ex-*Eastern Hope*; **LAMDA** (Ma) ex-*Scan Commander*; **YA FENG** (RC) ex-*Pacific Arrow*; **WOOD PIONEERS** (Pa) ex-*New Pioneer*; **EVPO AGNAR** (Pa) ex-*Pine Tree*
Possible sisters: **SMYRNI** (Cy) ex-*Ace Hero*; **AURORA RUBY** (Pa) ex-*Scan Challenger*; **ASEAN PREMIER** (Ma) ex-*Eastern Fuji*; **FAITH** (Cy) ex-*Shinzan Maru*; **BOWEN KING** (—) ex-*Kalmia*; **ATLANTIS A** (Cy) ex-*Toshin Maru*; **ROMINA** (Ma) ex-*Toho Maru*

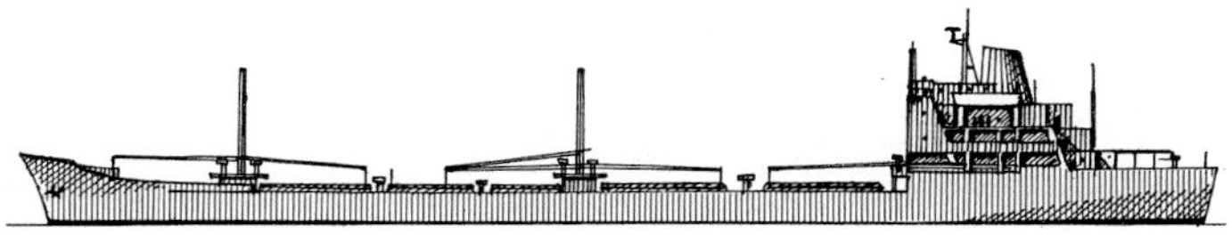

522 *T^2HMFN H13*
RIHA TRANSPORTER SV/Be (Boel) 1967; B; 9,081 grt/14,270 dwt; 149.41 × 8.59 m *(490.19 × 28.18 ft)*; M (B&W); 11 kts; ex-*Koper*
Sister: **RIHA TRADER** (SV) ex-*Krpan*

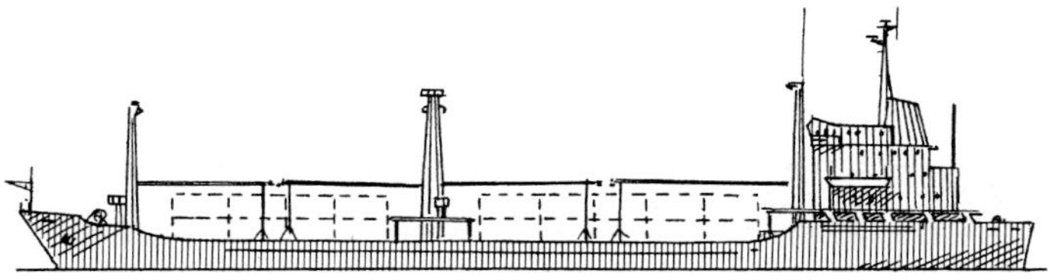

523 *T^2HMFN H13*
ULA Tu/Ja (Ujina) 1977; C/Con; 4,817 grt/6,516 dwt; 116.01 × 6.94 m *(380.61 × 22.77 ft)*; M (MAN); 16.75 kts; ex-*Max Bastian*; 177 TEU

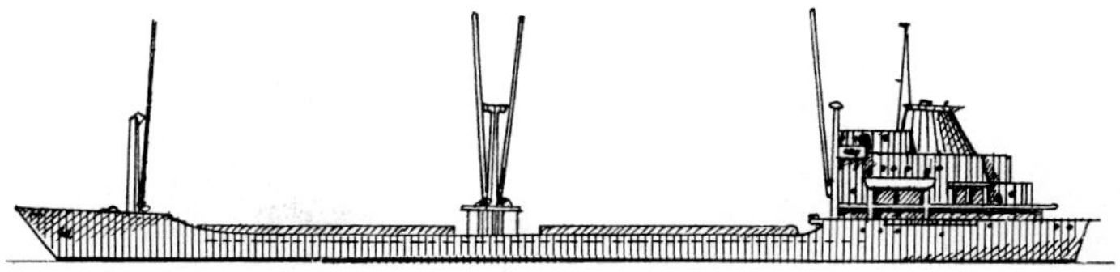

524 *T^2HM–F H13*
BLUE OCEAN Bh/Gr (Eleusis) 1973; C/Con; 3,979 grt/5,932 dwt; 107.52 × 6.69 m *(352.76 × 21.95 ft)*; M (MAN); 14.5 kts; ex-*Okeanis*; 155 TEU
Sister: **CONSTANTIA V** (Ma) ex-*Tithis*

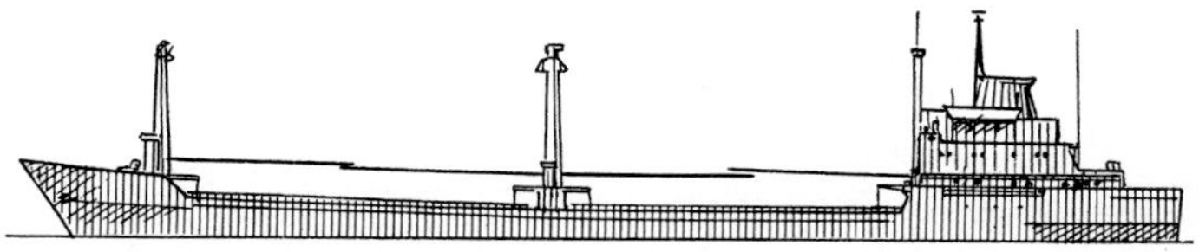

525 *T^2HM–F H13*
MAHER Ho/DDR ('Neptun') 1972; C/Con; 3,200 grt/4,631 dwt; 104.91 × 6.39 m *(344.19 × 20.97 ft)*; M (DMR); 14.5 kts; ex-*Klosterfelde*; 154 TEU
Sisters: **IBRAHIM** (Ho) ex-*Neuhausen*; **AYATT** (Ho) ex-*Radeberg*

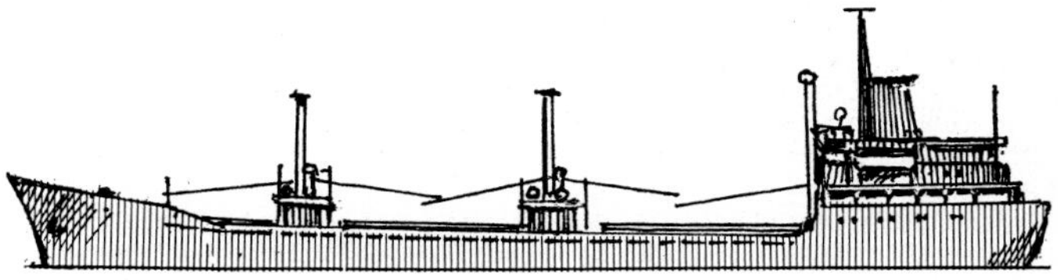

526 *T^2HM–F H13*
PRVIC Ma/No (Lothe) 1972; C; 4,165 grt/6,450 dwt; 112.83 × 6.89 m *(370.18 × 22.6 ft)*; M (Stork-Werkspoor); 13.50 kts; ex-*Lindo*

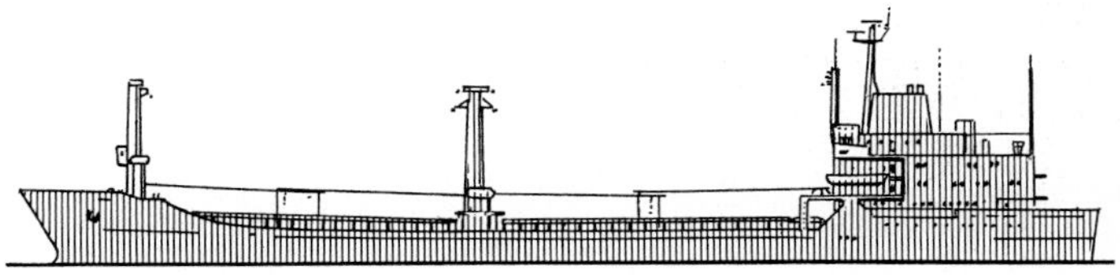

527 *T^2HM–FN H13*
CLIPPER UNITY Bs/DDR ('Neptun') 1973; C; 5,919 grt/8,001 dwt; 121.75 × 7.73 m *(399.44 × 25.36 ft)*; M (MAN); 15.5 kts; ex-*Jobella*; 215 TEU; 'Neptun 477' type
Sisters: **YUAN MING** (RC) ex-*Brunla*; **BULK TRADER** (Ma) ex-*Brunhorn*; **ACCORD** (SV) ex-*Jocare*; **CLIPPER PACIFIC** (Cy) Launched as *Jodew*; **CLIPPER ATLANTIC** (Cy) ex-*Joada*; **GIWI II** (My) ex-*Hansa*; **MING ZHOU 8** (RC) ex-*Moutsaina*; **HETTSTEDT** (Li) ex-*Jobebe*; **ABEER S** (Ma) ex-*Joboy*; **BREMEN STAR** (Br) ex-*Aken*; **FREITAL** (Li); **KOTHEN** (Ge); **KONSTANTINOVKA** (Ru) ex-*Baunton*; **GENERAL BLAZHEVICH** (Uk) ex-*Traun*; **KRAMATORSK** (Uk) ex-*Wellwood*; **FASTOV** (Ru) ex-*Gaviota II*; **SUPERTRAMP** (At) ex-*Yiannis L*; **FATEZH** (Uk) ex-*Alexander Schulte*; **BERGEN** (Li)

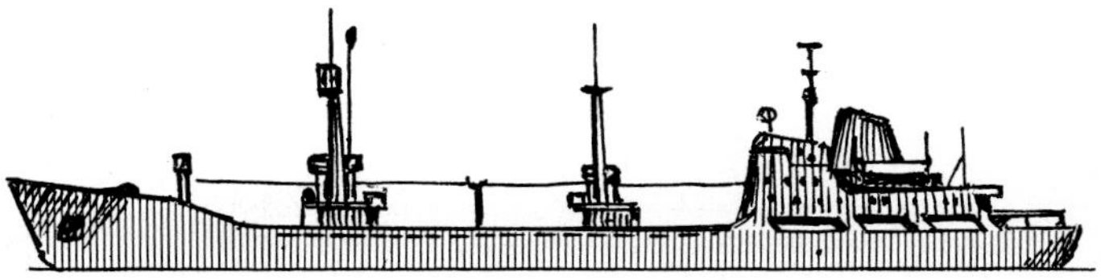

528 *T^2MF H1*
KUWAIT Eg/Ne ('De Noord') 1961; C; 3,113 grt/3,759 dwt; 96.96 × 6.64 m *(318.11 × 21.78 ft)*; M (B&W); 13.5 kts; ex-*Ritva Dan*

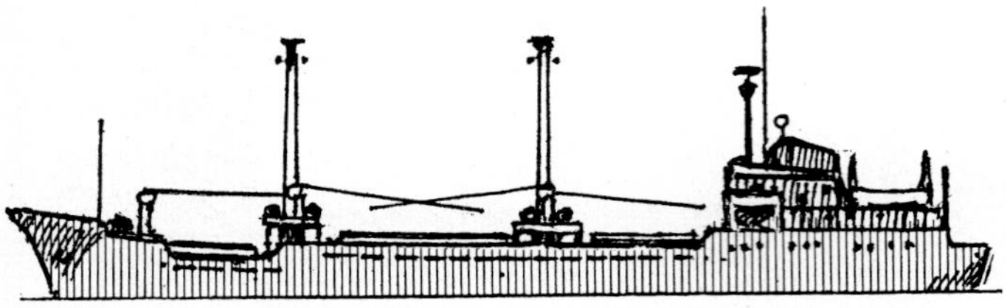

529 *T^2MF H13*
CAMURI Ve/Ne (Amsterdamsche D) 1964; C; 2,303 grt/3,390 dwt; 87.89 × 6.31 m *(288.35 × 20.7 ft)*; M (Werkspoor); 13 kts; ex-*Rahel*
Sister: **REINA DEL MAR** (Ho) ex-*Devora*

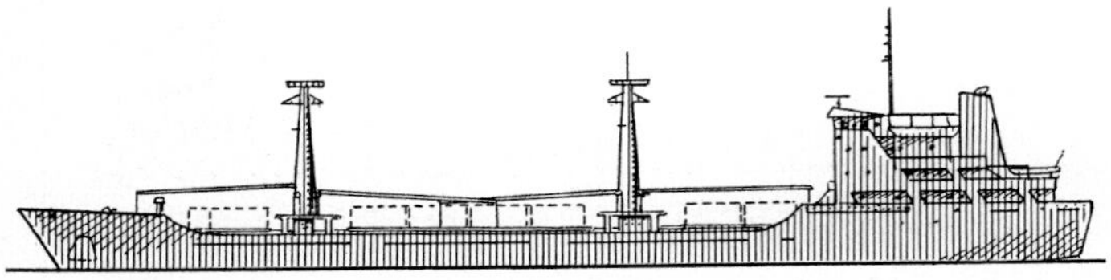

530 *T^2MF H13*
NOUR ALLAH Cy/Ne (Amels/'Friesland') 1980; C/Con; 4,051 grt/6,019 dwt; 114.05 × 6.65 m *(374 × 21.82 ft)*; M (Stork-Werkspoor); 15 kts; ex-*Saramacca*; 120 TEU

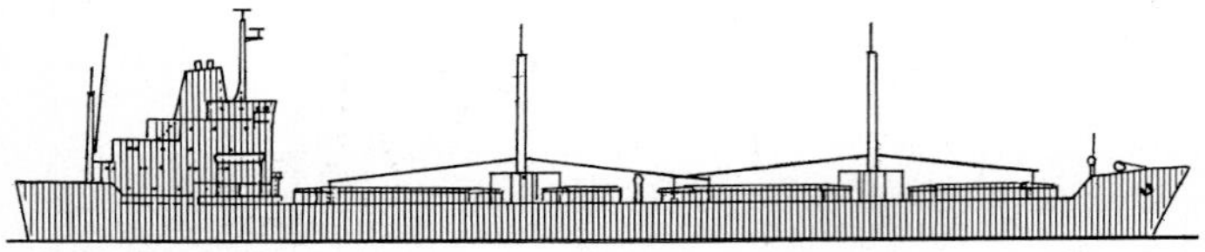

531 *T^2MFM H13*
RAFFIU Cy/Sp (AESA) 1978; C; 9,721 grt/15,883 dwt; 144.00 × 8.97 m *(472.44 × 29.43 ft)*; M (B&W); 14 kts; ex-*Ponte Sampayo*; 'TD15' type
Possible sisters (may have cranes aft): **ZI JIN SHAN** (RC) ex-*Aegis Pilot*; **WIND** (Cy) ex-*Patricia Adriana S*; **LARAK** (Cy) ex-*Karen S*; **NEREUS** (Ma) ex-*Mirta S*; **PERSEUS** (Ma) ex-*Richard S*

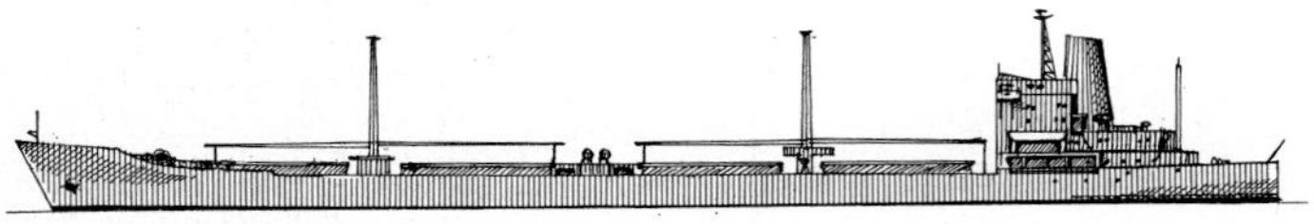

532 *T^2MFN H1*
ZHONG SHAN RC/Be (Boelwerf) 1969; C/Con; 12,979 grt/20,349 dwt; 160.03 × 9.88 m *(525.03 × 32.41 ft)*; M (MAN); 15.5 kts; ex-*Zelzate*; 406 TEU
Sisters: **HUALIEN EXPRESS** (SV) ex-*Charleroi*; **BARAKA** (Bs) ex-*Chertal*; **VIGO EXPRESS** (Bs) ex-*Belval*

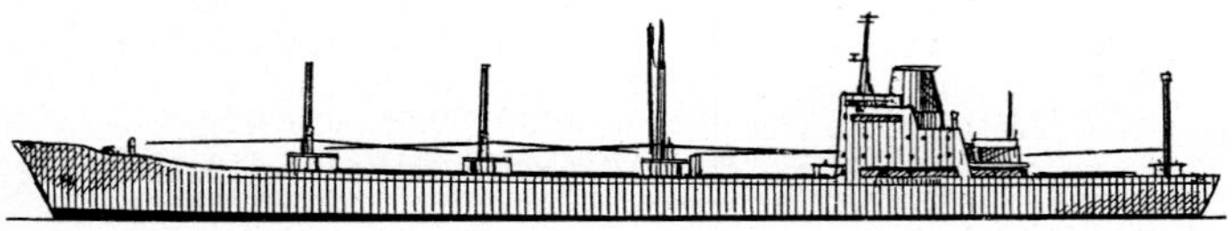

533 *T^2M^2FMN H1*
GARCILASO Pe/Fi (Wärtsilä) 1969; C; 7,902 grt/13,920 dwt; 150.5 × 9.4 m *(494 × 30.8 ft)*; M; 17 kts
Sisters: **CHOCANO** (Pe); **TELLO** (Pe)

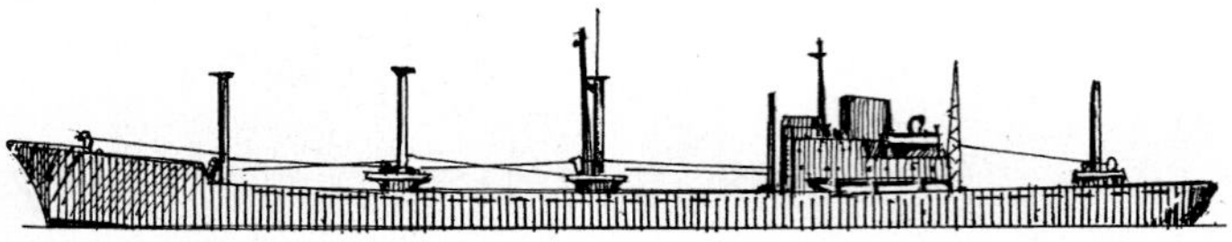

534 *T^2MNMFN^2 H1*
KIM AN Li/Ja (Hitachi) 1966; C; 8,838 grt/12,197 dwt; 141 × 9.18 m *(462.60 × 30.12 ft)*; M (B&W); 16 kts; ex-*Columbia Maru*

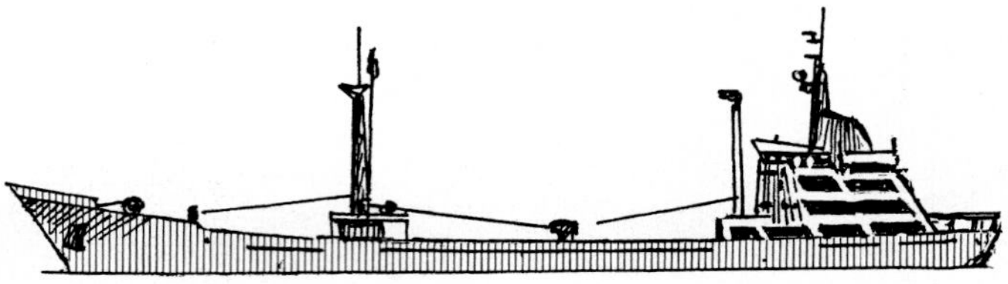

535 *T^2M–F H1*
VILA CARRIER Mv/Ne (Amels) 1968; C; 2,725 grt/4,147 dwt; 101.99 × 6.17 m *(334.61 × 20.24 ft)*; M (Deutz); 15 kts; ex-*Corantijn*

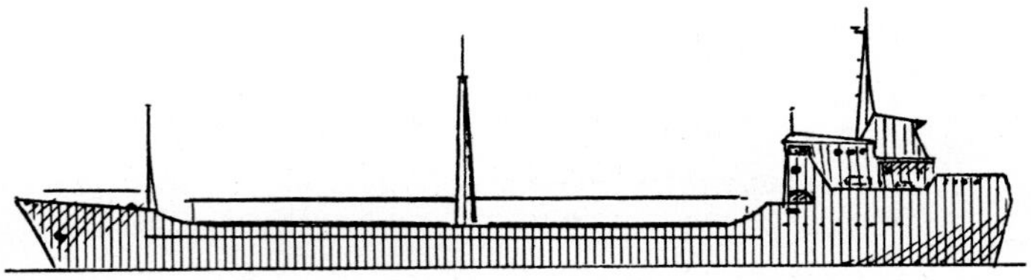

536 *T^2M–F H13*
SEA GRAPES Ma/Ne ('Harlingen') 1976; C; 1,598 grt/2,893 dwt; 79.81 × 5.44 m *(261.84 × 17.85 ft)*; M (Alpha-Diesel); 11 kts; ex-*Frisian Trader*

537 *T^2M–FN H1*
SALTA Ar/Br (Robb Caledon) 1976; C/Con; 9,236 grt/14,980 dwt; 141 × 8.9 m *(463 × 29 ft)*; M (Doxford); 15.5 kts; Modified 'SD 14' type; 138 TEU
Sisters: **QAMAR** (Pa) ex-*Jujuy II*; **MUZAFFAR AZIZ** (Pa) ex-*Tucuman*; **JANBAZI I** (Cy) ex-*Almirante Storni*; Possible sisters (Ar built-AFNE): **PRUDENT CHALLENGER** (SV) ex-*Libertador General Jose de San Martin*; **PRESIDENTE RAMON S CASTILLO** (Ar); **PANORMITIS** (Cy) ex-*Neuquen II*; **ASTIVI** (Ma) ex-*Dr Atilio Malvagni*; **GENERAL MANUEL BELGRANO** (Ar)

538 *T^2M–FN H1*
"SD14" type dwt; Sequence variation on drawing number 8/500

539 *T^2NF H12*
SROUR Le/FRG (Elsflether) 1961; C; 1,574 grt/2,366 dwt; 77.81 × 5.4 m *(255.28 × 17.72 ft)*; M (MaK); 12 kts; ex-*Else Retzlaff*

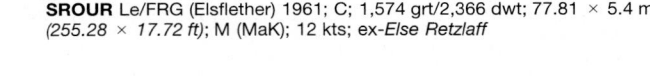

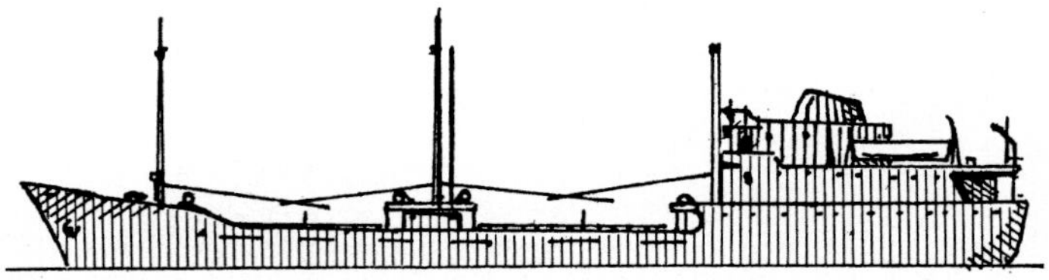

540 *T^2NF H13*
DIEU SI BON Pa/Ne (Arnhemsche) 1962; C; 738 grt/1,199 dwt; 73.54 × 3.96 m *(241.27 × 12.99 ft)*; M (Werkspoor); 12.5 kts; ex-*Nico P W*

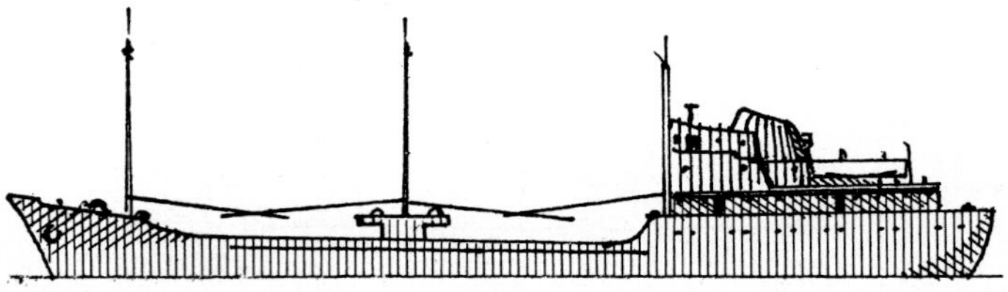

541 *T^2NF H13*
IOANNIS H Ho/Ne (Zaanlandsche) 1962; C; 1,510 grt/2,200 dwt; 79.15 × 4.9 m *(259.68 × 16.08 ft)*; M (Werkspoor); 12 kts; ex-*Lis Frellsen*
Sister: **ALBERTO** (It) ex-*Thea Danielsen*

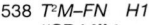

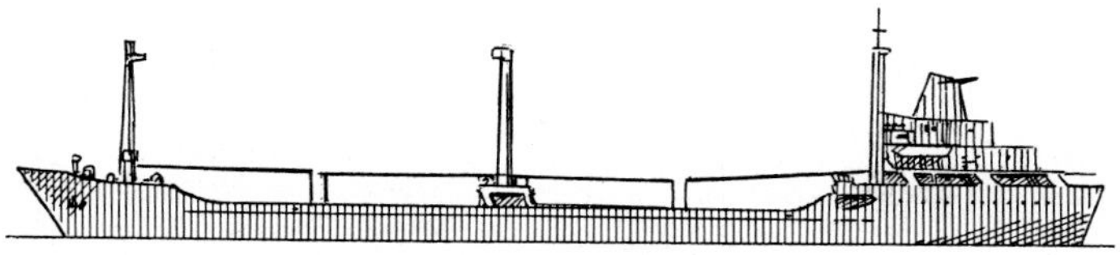

542 *T^2NF H13*
MAZINA Mv/Sp (Cadagua) 1971; C/Con; 3,082 grt/4,399 dwt; 104.25 × 6.53 m *(342 × 21.42 ft)*; M (Deutz); 12 kts; ex-*Dollart*; 235 TEU
Probable sister: **PATTU** (Bl) ex-*Amasis*

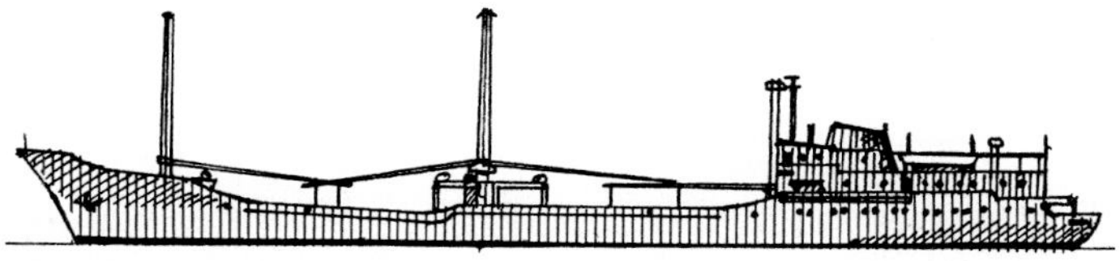

543 *T^2NF H13*
NEPTUNE WIND Ho/Is (Israel Spyds) 1965; C; 1,993 grt/3,027 dwt; 84.31 × 6.27 m *(276.61 × 20.57 ft)*; M (Werkspoor); 12.5 kts; ex-*Hanna*
Sisters: **SAWAMINEE** (Pa) ex-*Lea*; **PANNARAI** (Th) ex-*Miryam*

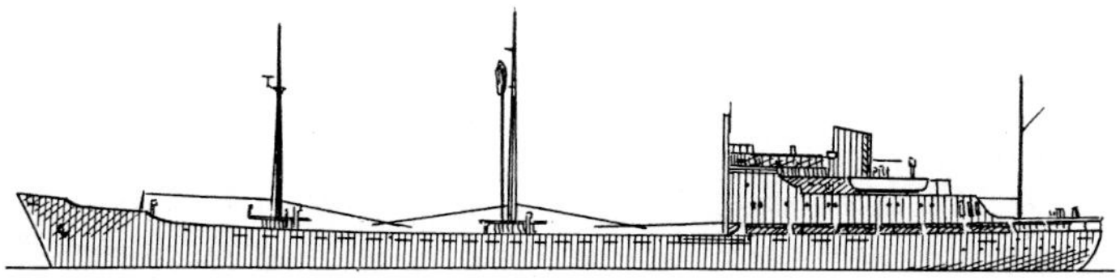

544 *T^2NFM H1*
ARTURO MICHELINA Ve/Ne (Vuyk) 1959; C; 3,840 grt/4,890 dwt; 119.49 × 6.41 m *(392 × 21.03 ft)*; M (Stork); 16 kts; ex-*Ammon*; Lengthened 1966
Sister: **NELA ALTOMARE** (Ve) ex-*Chiron*

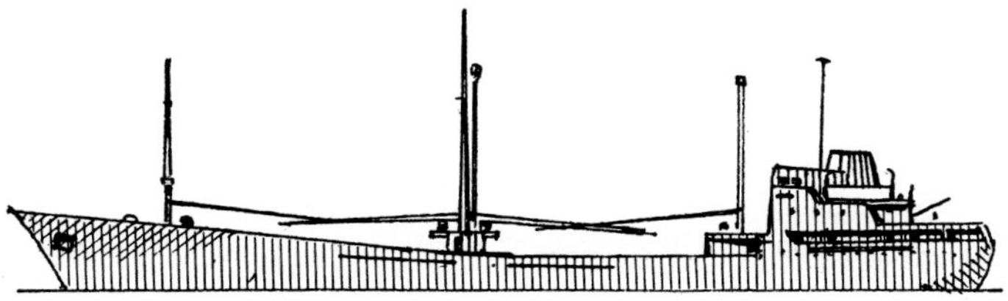

545 *T^2NMF H*
CRISANTA Pi/FRG (Schlichting) 1961; C; 1,481 grt/2,036 dwt; 81.82 × 5.27 m *(268.44 × 17.29); M (KHD); 14.5 kts; ex-Vinland Saga*

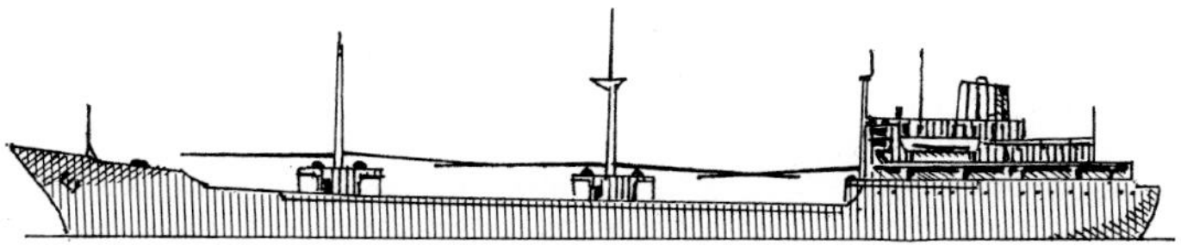

546 *T^2NMF H13*
MIN FU Pa/FRG (Rickmers) 1965; C; 4,289 grt/6,424 dwt; 116.74 × 7.54 m *(383.01 × 24.74 ft)*; M (Fiat); 15 kts; ex-*Martin Schroder*
Sister: **SHOU SHAN** (Pa) ex-*Monique Schroder*

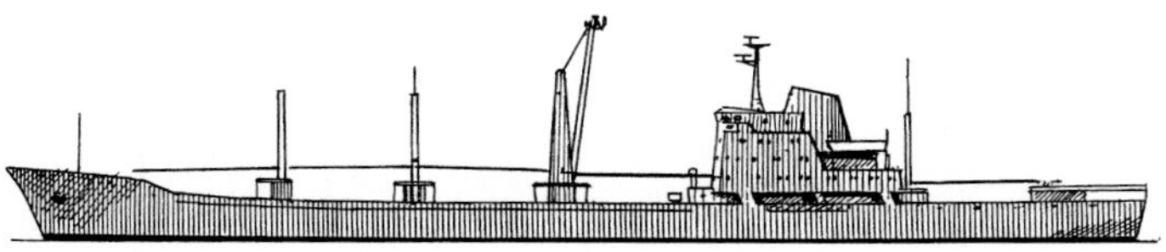

547 *T^2NMFN H1*
HULIN RC/Ys ('Split') 1974; C; 9,705 grt/13,427 dwt; 160 × 9.4 m *(525 × 30.1 ft)*; M (MAN); 19.25 kts
Sisters: **CHUNLIN** (RC); **SONGLIN** (RC); **TIANLIN** (RC); **YANGLIN** (RC); **YULIN**(RC); **TAOLIN** (RC)

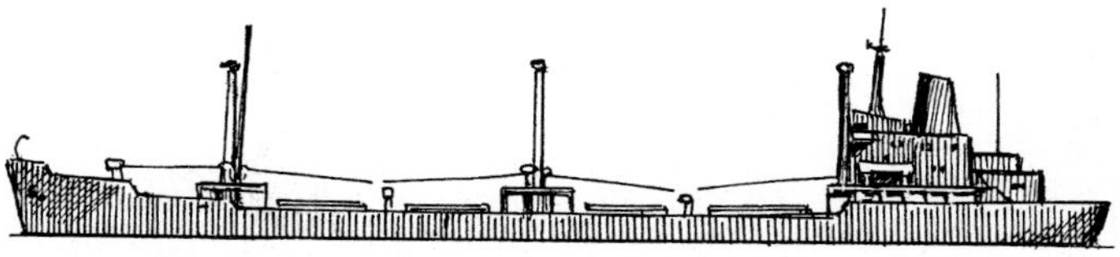

548 *T^2NMFN H13*
HUA YU RC/FRG (Bremer V) 1969; C; 9,373 grt/15,202 dwt; 139.45 × 9.2 m *(457.51 × 30.18 ft)*; M (MAN); 15.5 kts; ex-*Jens Jost*; 'German Liberty' type
Similar: **DAIANA P** (Ma) Launched as *Franciska Fisser*; **LI LONG** (RC) ex-*Olga Jacob*; **MATTZ ALTAIR** (Bs) ex-*Elisabeth Roth*; **PING DING SHAN** (RC) ex *Verena Wiards*; **HARVEST** (UAE) ex-*Irmgard Jacob*; **MANNAN** (Ma) ex-*Pitria Star*; **MSC SHAULA S** (Pa) ex-*Paula Howaldt*

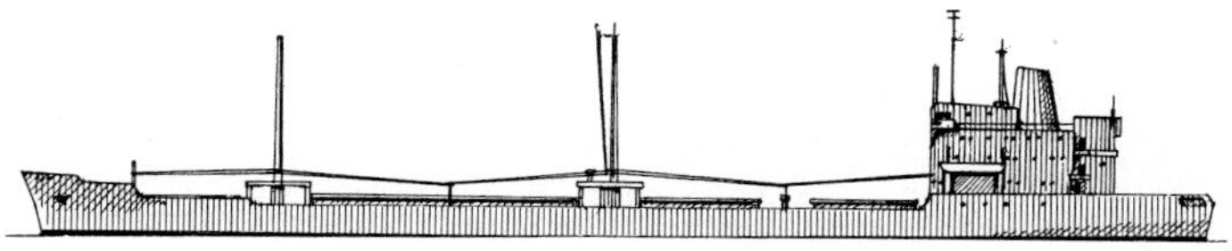

549 *T^2NMFN H13*
HUI FENG SV/FRG (Flensburger) 1971; C; 9,391 grt/15,088 dwt; 139.76 × 9.18 m *(458.53 × 30.12 ft)*; M (MAN); 16 kts; ex-*Lina Fisser*; 'Germany Liberty' type; 236 TEU
Probable sister (may not have poop–see drawing number 8/302): **AMNA S** (Sy) ex-*Marita Leonhardt*; Similar: **AZIMUTH** (Ma) Launched as *Carl Fisser*; **ALI S** (Sy) ex-*Finn Heide*; **MSC ILARIA M** (Pa) ex-*Klaus Leonhardt*; **GOLDEN BEAR** (Sg) ex-*Sunbaden*

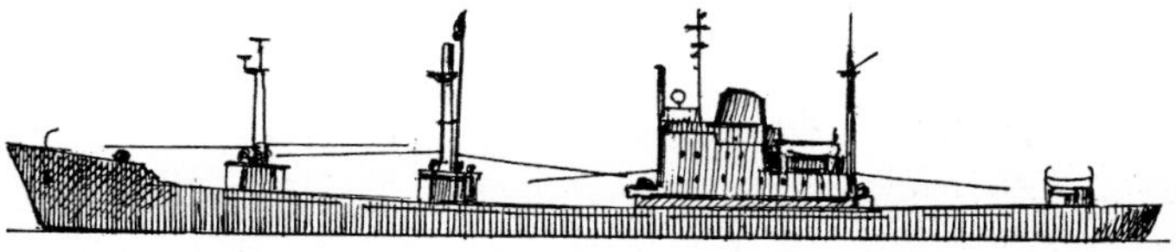

550 *T^2NMFT H1*
SHEN DA RC/DDR (Mathias-Thesen) 1968; C; 5,715 grt/6,950 dwt; 129.4 × 7.6 m *(424 × 25 ft)*; M (MAN); 16 kts; ex-*Wismar*; 'AFRIKA' type
Sisters: **SU XIANG** (SV) ex-*Stollberg*; **SU RUN** (SV) ex-*Wittenberg*; **FALCON EYE** (SV) ex-*Sonneberg*

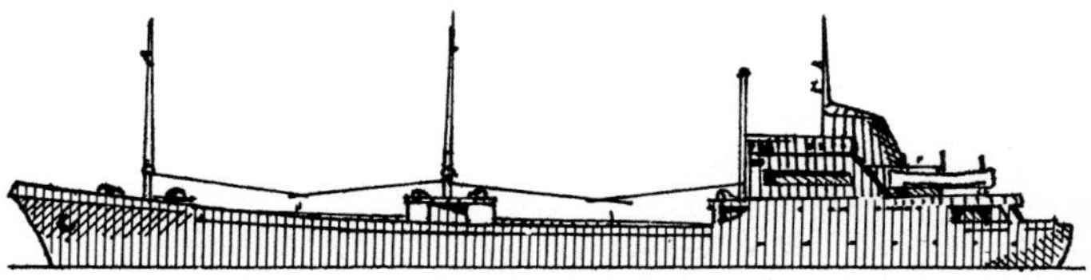

551 *T^2NM-F H12*
POLLUX Ma/Sp (Ruiz) 1966; C; 1,596 grt/2,896 dwt; 82.5 × 6 m *(270.67 × 19.69 ft)*; M (Stork-Werkspoor); 11 kts; ex-*Marichu*
Sister: **KAPTAN DURSUN AKBAS** (Tu) ex-*Maria Dolores Tartiere*

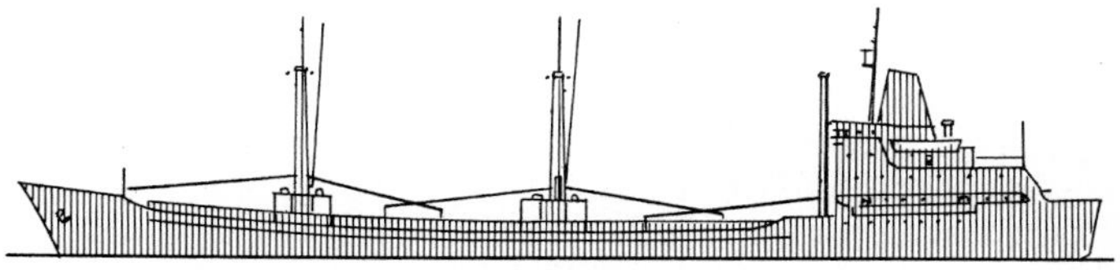

552 *T^2NM–F H13*
MAX VICTORY RC/Sp (Juliana) 1972; C; 4,975 grt/7,596 dwt; 118.12 × 7.35 m *(388 × 24.11 ft)*; M (B&W); 14 kts; ex-*Miraflores*
Sisters: **WEI GUANG** (RC) ex-*Jupiter*; **VIGOROUS LUCK** (Pa) Launched as *Monte Albertia*; **SKY ONE** (RC) ex-*Monte Abril*; **JUNIOR M** (Eg) ex-*Monte Ayala*; **DONG SHENG** (Pa) ex-*Monte Almnanzor*

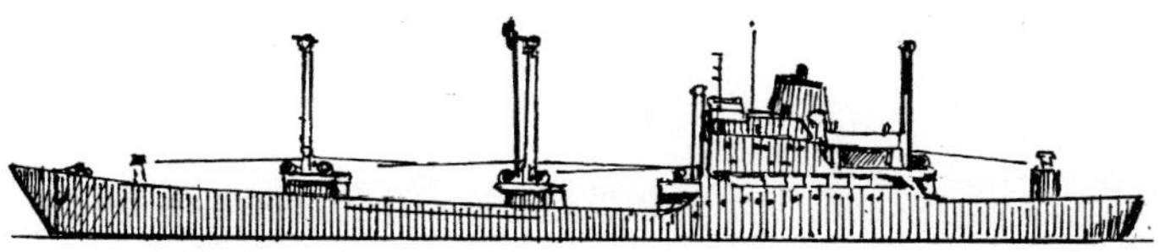

553 *T^2NM–FN H13*
CAPELLA–1 Pa/Ne (Verolme Dok) 1966; C; 5,182 grt/6,655 dwt; 121 × 8 m *(397 × 26 ft)*; M (MAN); — kts; ex-*Lion of Judah*
Sister: **QUEEN OF SHEEBA** (Et)

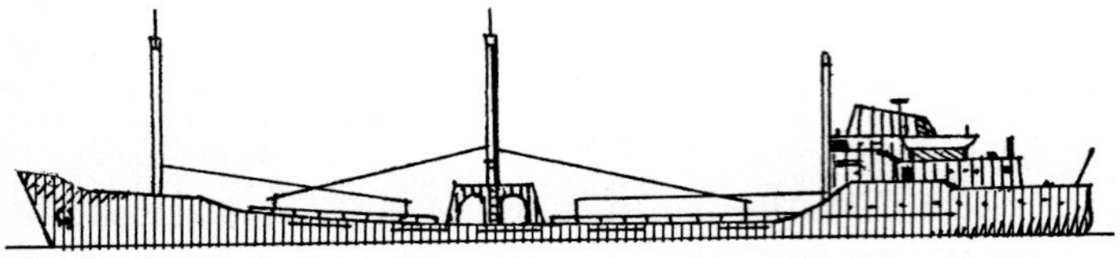

554 T^3F *H13*
AMAFHH TWO —/Br (Ailsa) 1962; C; 1,596 grt/2,469 dwt; 81.62 × 5.21 m *(267.78 × 17.09 ft)*; M (KHD); 13 kts; ex-*Topaz*
Sister: **AKRAM V** (Ho) ex-*Tourmaline*

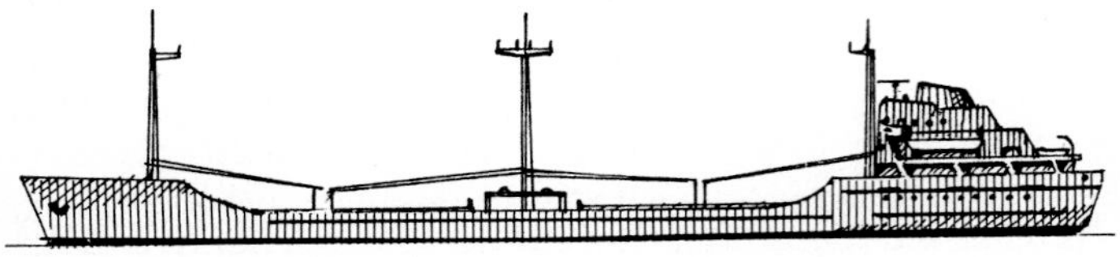

555 T^3F *H13*
ANIS ROSE Sy/Ne (Nieuwe Noord) 1969; C; 1,928 grt/2,967 dwt; 90.76 × 5.19 m *(297.77 × 17.03 ft)*; M (KHD); 12 kts; ex-*Gem*

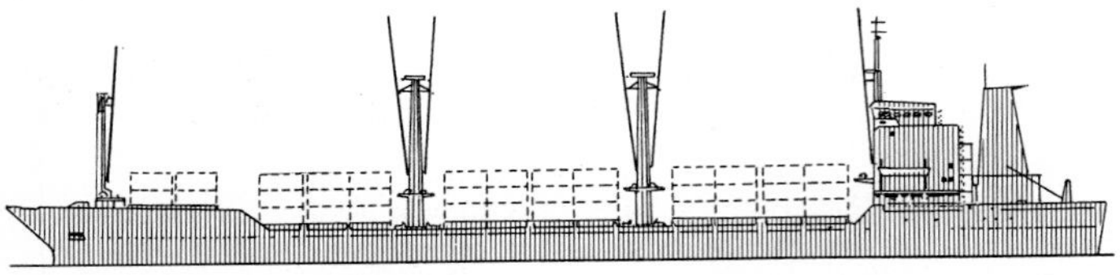

556 T^3HFD *H13*
SRIWIJAYA la/FRG (Schlichting) 1981; C/Con; 13,084 grt/17,618 dwt; 158.38 × 9.50 m *(520 × 31.17 ft)*; M (MAN); 17 kts; 686 TEU
Sister: **MATARAM** (la)

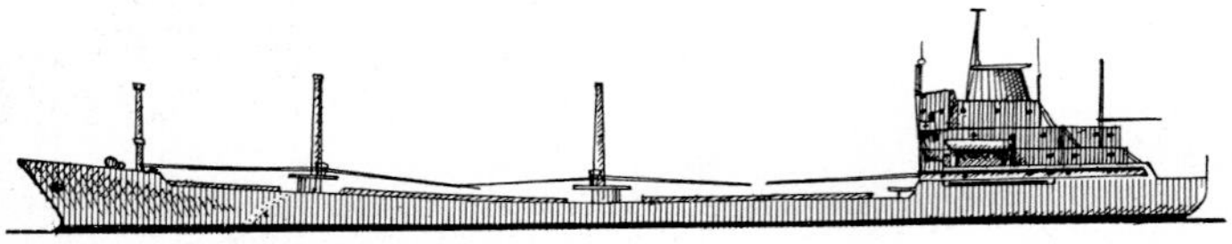

557 $T^3HM\text{–}FN$ *H13*
MSC MARINA Pa/DDR ('Neptun') 1970; C/Con; 8,245 grt/11,029 dwt; 146.23 × 8.89 m *(479.76 × 29.17 ft)*; M (MAN); 14.50 kts; Launched as *Hamburger Damm*; 300 TEU
Similar: **ELIZA** (Bs) ex-*Sol Michel*; **JUTHA PHANSIRI** (Th) ex-*Sol Neptun*; **EVER FORTUNE** (Pa) ex-*Anna Presthus*; **SU YU** (RC) ex-*Brageland*; **ROSE STONE** (SV) ex-*Balticland*; **LU HAI 65** (RC) ex-*Bardaland*

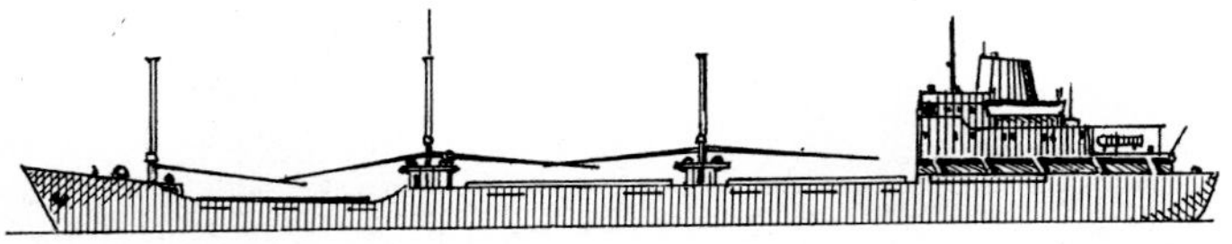

558 T^3MF *H123*
LA TATA Pa/FRG (Rhein Nordseew) 1962/70; C; 3,244 grt/4,622 dwt; 110 × 6.14 m *(360.89 × 20.14 ft)*; M (MaK); 13 kts; ex-*Mak Hugo Stinnes*; Lengthened 1970

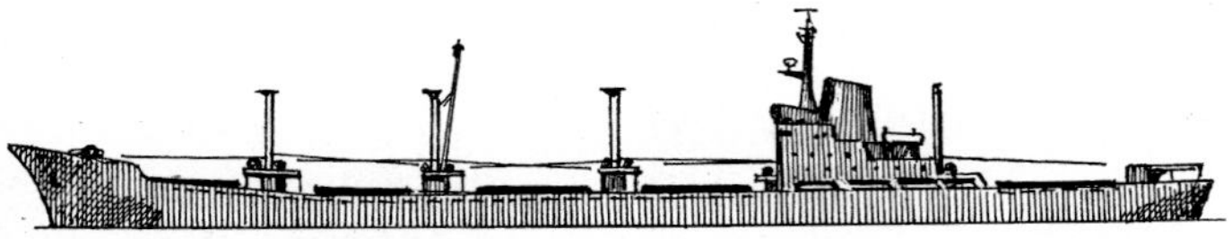

559 T^3MFN *H1*
VIGOROUS SWAN Pa/Br (Doxford & S) 1972; C; 11,045 grt/16,901 dwt; 161.45 × 9.75 m *(530 × 32 ft)*; M (Doxford); 17 kts; ex-*Beaverbank*
Sisters: **LIBANUS** (Ma) ex-*Birchbank*; **IRENE** (Gr) ex-*Cedarbank*; **FRATZIS M** (Cy) ex-*Riverbank*; **AMER PRABHA** (Cy) ex-*Streambank*; **MARIE H** (Cy) ex-*Cloverbank*; **AGIOS SPYRIDON** (Ma) ex-*Firbank*; **GEORGE** (Bs) ex-*Nessbank*

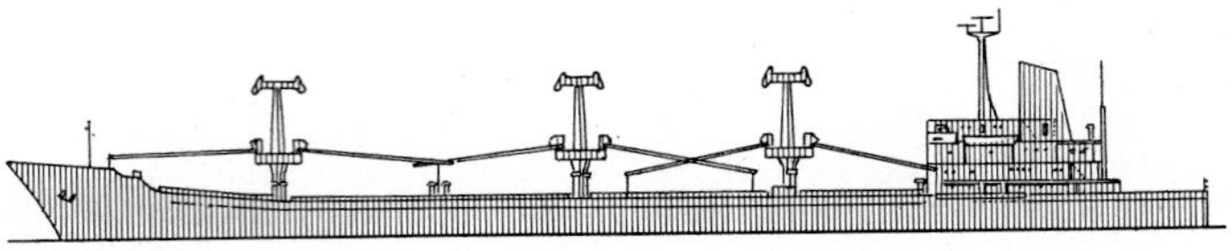

560 T^3MFN *H1*
XIANG JIANG RC/FRG (A G 'Weser') 1978; C/Con; 9,792 grt/16,270 dwt; 149.79 × 9.26 m *(491 × 30.38 ft)*; M (MAN); 16.5 kts; '36-L' type; 247 TEU
Sisters: **MIN JIANG** (RC); **YONG JIANG** (RC); **PU CHENG** (RC) ex-*Yong Xing*; **FLOURISH ORIENTAL** (SV) ex-*Leopold Staff*; **RUA HA** (Ta) ex-*Aristanax*; **AL MUBARAQ** (Cy) ex-*Aristagelos*; **YONGSHUN** (SV) ex-*Aristogenis*

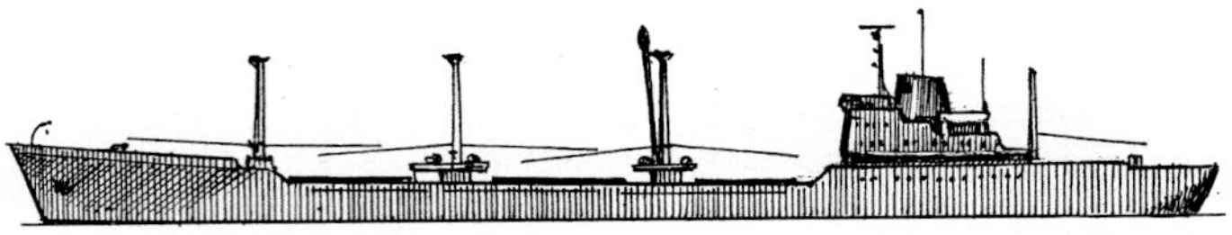

561 T^3MFN *H13*
ANTING RC/Fi (Rauma-Repola) 1970; C; 9,796 grt/14,517 dwt; 151.8 × 8.7/9.8 m *(498 × 28.5/32 ft)*; M (Gotaverken); 18 kts; ex-*Kunlungshan*
Sisters: **CHANGTING** (RC) ex-*Wutaishan*; **HUATING** (RC) ex-*Liupanshan*; **JIANGTING** (RC) ex-*Dahsueshan*; **WANGTING** (RC) ex-*Taihanshan*; Possible sisters: **YANTING** (RC); **YUTING**

562 T^3MFN *H13*
BLUEWEST Ma/Be (Boelwerf) 1970; B; 17,698 grt/30,184 dwt; 190.02 × 10.81 m *(623.43 × 35.47 ft)*; M (MAN); 15 kts; ex-*Ektor*
Sisters: **NIRJA** (Pa) ex-*Ermis*; **SNOWBIRD** (SV) ex-*Rossetti*; **GUANG SHEN** (RC) ex-*Reynolds*

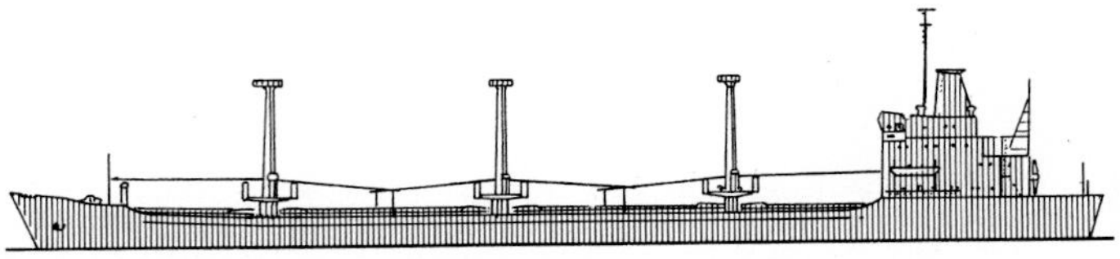

563 T^3MFN *H13*
HONG YUAN Pa/FRG (Rickmers) 1976; C/Con; 7,095 grt/10,151 dwt; 139.33 × 7.82 m *(457 × 25.66 ft)*; M (MaK); 12 kts; ex-*Florence Schroder*; 266 TEU
Sister: **YONG QING** (SV) ex-*Frank Schroder*

564 T^3NMFN *H12*
SONG SAN Ho/FRG (Flensburger) 1970; C; 9,366 grt/14,745 dwt; 139.75 × 9.19 m *(458.53 × 30.15 ft)*; M (Bremer V); 15 kts; ex-*Alpina*; 'German Liberty' type
Possible sister: **GU YUE** (Pa) ex-*Ascona*

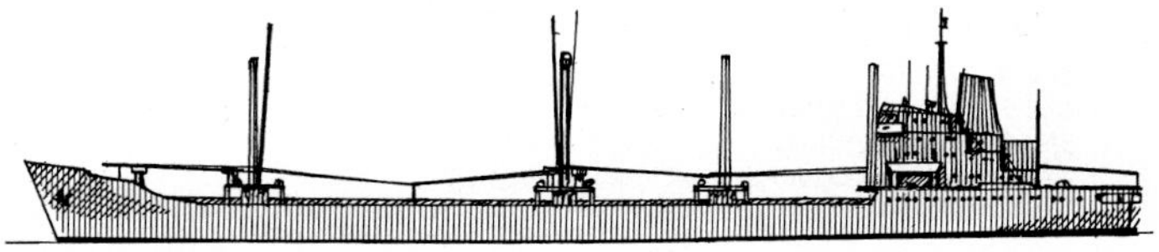

565 T^3NMFN *H13*
KANGSON Cb/FRG (Flensburger) 1970; C/Con; 9,366 grt/14,745 dwt; 139.76 × 9.19 m *(458.53 × 30.15 ft)*; M (Sulzer); 15 kts; ex-*Alpina*; 'German Liberty' type; 512 TEU;
Possible sister: **GU YUE** (Pa) ex-*Ascona*

566 T^3NMFN *H13*
MIKOLAJ REJ Pd/Fi (Rauma-Repola) 1965; C; 9,936 grt/14,605 dwt; 151 × 9.7 m *(496 × 32 ft)*; M (Gotaverken); 18 kts; ex-*Wirta*
Sister: **FRYCZ MODRZEWSKI** (Pd) ex-*Wilma*

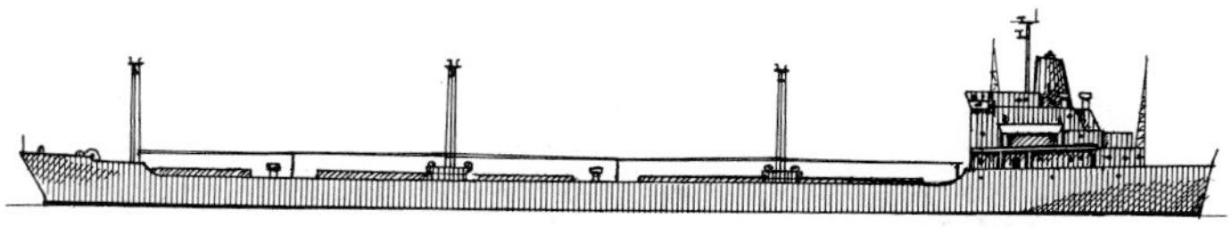

567 *T^3NMFN H13*
PROTEUS Cy/Ja (NKK) 1972; B; 12,668 grt/21,916 dwt; 155.53 × 9.84 m *(510.27 × 32.28 ft)*; M (Pielstick); 15.5 kts; ex-*Swiftnes*
Sisters: **VARNAKOVA** (Pa) ex-*Saltnes*; **KINGFISHER** (Cy) ex-*Sealnes*; **GEORGIOS** (Gr) ex-*Spraynes*; **ISIDORA** (Ma) ex-*Sharpnes*; **MED TRANSPORTER** (Tu) ex-*Surenes*

568 *T^3NM–FH H12*
JIN HU QUAN RC/Sp (AESA) 1967; C; 8,229 grt/9,699 dwt; 142.5 × 9.4 m *(468 × 30.6 ft)*; M (Sulzer); 16 kts; ex-*Mar Cantabrico*

569 *T^3NM-FH H13*
JIN HU QUAN RC/Sp (AESA) 1967; C; 8,229 grt/9,699 dwt; 143 × 9.3 m *(468 × 30.6 ft)*; M (Sulzer); 15 kts; ex-*Mar Cantabrico*

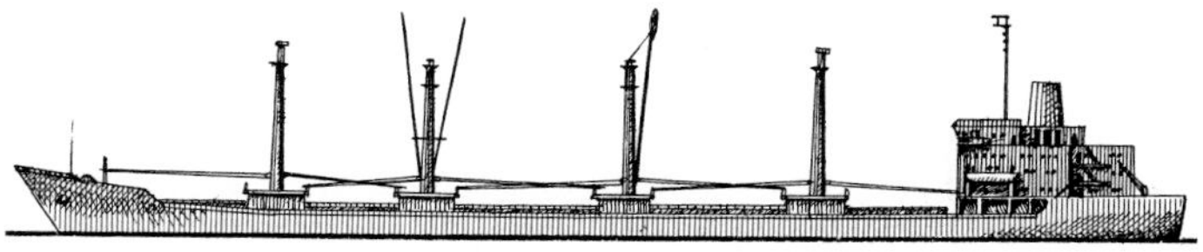

570 *T^4MF H13*
HER AN Sg/FRG (Bremer V) 1977; C/Con; 10,786 grt/17,057 dwt; 157.38 × 8.07/9.28 m *(516.34 × 26.48/30.45 ft)*; M (MAN); 16 kts; ex-*Flavia*; Bremen Progress 'B' type; 460 TEU

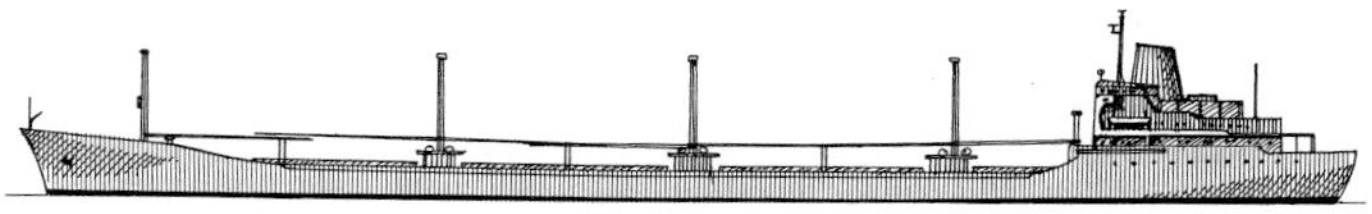

571 *T^4MFN H13*
YUN HAI RC/Sw (Uddevalla) 1963; B; 20,121 grt/34,239 dwt; 196.32 × 10.88 m *(644.09 × 35.7 ft)*; M (Gotaverken); 11 kts; ex-*Robert Stove*

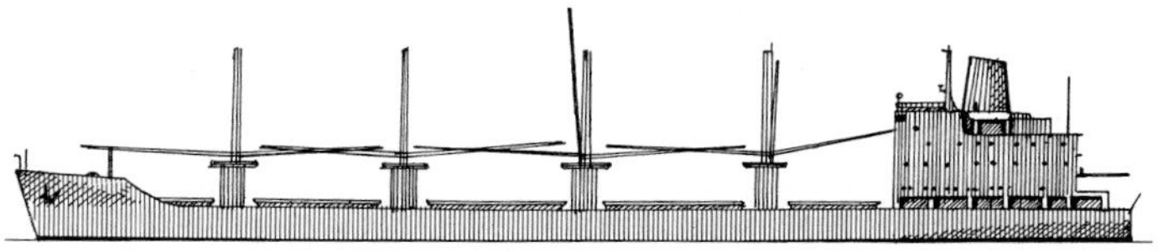

572 *T^4MFS H1*
MERCHANT PREMIER HK/Br (Lithgows) 1978; C; 14,275 grt/17,944 dwt; 163.15 × 9.68 m *(535.27 × 31.76 ft)*; M (Sulzer); 16.25 kts; ex-*Oroya*; 476 TEU
Sister: **MERCHANT PRINCIPAL** (HK) ex-*Oropesa*

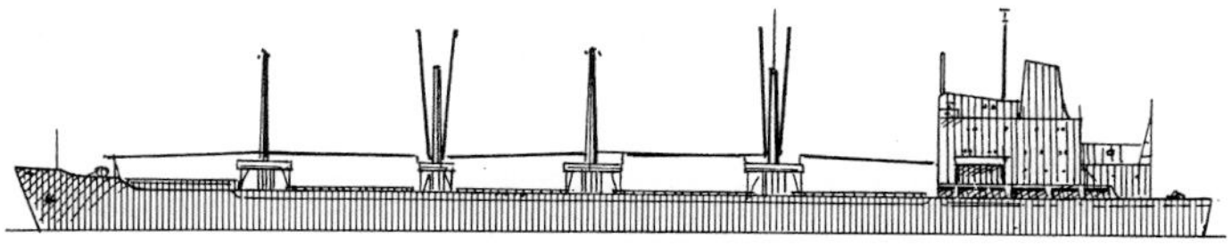

573 *T^4NMFN H1*
MANLEY EXETER Ma/FRG (Rickmers) 1971; C/Con; 9,282 grt/14,556 dwt; 139.55 × 9.19 m *(457.84 × 30.15 ft)*; M (MAN); 15.5 kts; ex-*Nedlloyd Niger*; 'German Liberty' type
Sister: **MANLEY DEVON** (Ma) ex-*Nedlloyd Nile*

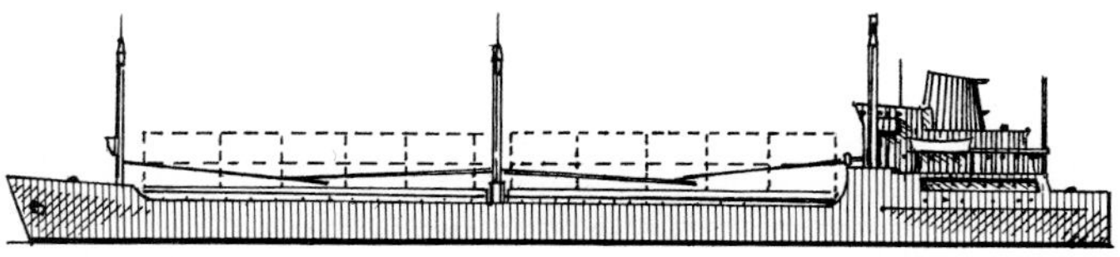

574 *T^2VFN H13*
EQUATOR PEARL Sg/Rm (Galatz) 1975; C/Con; 5,078 grt/8,447 dwt; 105.97 × 8.24 m *(347.67 × 27.03 ft)*; M (MWM); 15.5 kts; ex-*Bow Ek*; 236 TEU
Sisters: **JI HAO** (RC) Launched as *Frendo-Fellowship*; **ALLAH KAREEM** (Ho) ex-*Frendo-Membership*

575 *TVM–FV H13*
BIRYUSA Uk/DDR ('Neptun') 1963; C; 3,212 grt/4,302 dwt; 106 × 6.6 m *(347 × 21.3 ft)*; M (MAN); 12.5 kts; 'Povonets' type
Sisters: **GRUMANT** (—); **GULBENE** (Ea); **HARVEST 2** (SV) ex-*Heltermaa*; **YIANNIS P** (Pa) ex-*Kokhtla*; **KOVDOR** (Ru); **LINDA** (—) ex-*Kypu*; **MURMAN** (Ru); **OLENEGORSK** (Ru); **TRI-AN** (Vn) ex-*Pereslavl–Zalessik*; **OCEAN PEARL** (SV) ex-*Segezha*; **WORLDTREND 2** (—) ex-*Selemdzha*; **BAIKAL 1** (Vn) ex-*Shilka*; **HENG TONG** (RC) ex-*Spassk–Dalniy*; **STEPANS HALTURINS** (La) ex-*Stepan Khalturin*; **BAIKAL 2** (Vn) ex-*Svirsk*; **SYKTYVKAR** (Uk); **HAI YEN 1** (Vn) ex-*Tunguska*; **TAN TRAO** (Vn) ex-*Ussuri*; **LADA** (Ru) ex-*Vilyany*; **VICTORY** (—) ex-*Vyru*; **DIMA** (Sy) ex-*Zapolyarnyy*

576 *VFNV H123*
DURRESI Al/Pd (Gdanska) 1961; C; 3,804 dwt; 108.3 × 6.6 *(355 × 21.8)*; R (Zgoda); 12; 'B-31' type

577 *VFV H123*
SONG DA 2 Vn/DDR ('Neptun') 1958; C; 3,174 grt/4,296 dwt; 104.2 × 6.6 m *(341 × 22 ft)*; M (Goerlitzer); 10 kts; ex-*Andizhan*; 'LEVANT' type or 'KOVEL' type
Sisters: **DALNERECHENSK** (—) ex-*Iman*; **LOVELY LADY** (SV) ex-*Holmogory*; **HONG HA 2** (Vn) ex-*Namangan*; **RAKVERE** (Ru); **PHA LAI** (Vn) ex-*Reni*; **SEA EXPRESS** (SV) ex-*Sobolevo*; **SIGULDA** (Ma)

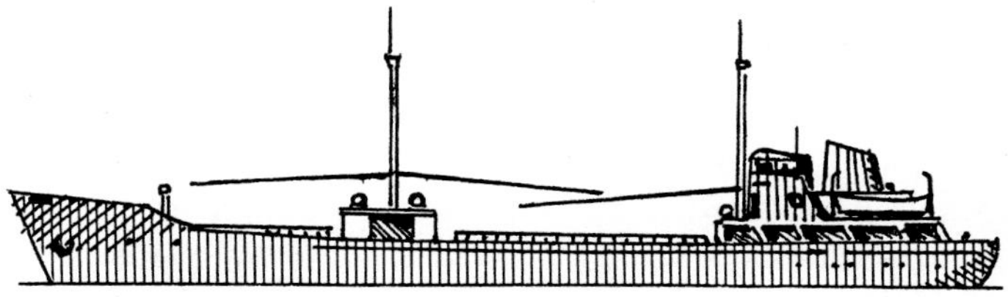

578 *VHF H1*
AGROTAI Sp/Sp ('Elcano') 1960; C; 686 grt/1,200 dwt; 72.6 × 3.91 m *(238.19 × 12.83 ft)*; M (Smit & Bolnes); 12.5 kts
Sisters: **BRIGANTIUM** (Sp) ex-*Formentor*; **BARBARA** (Bl) ex-*Marimar*

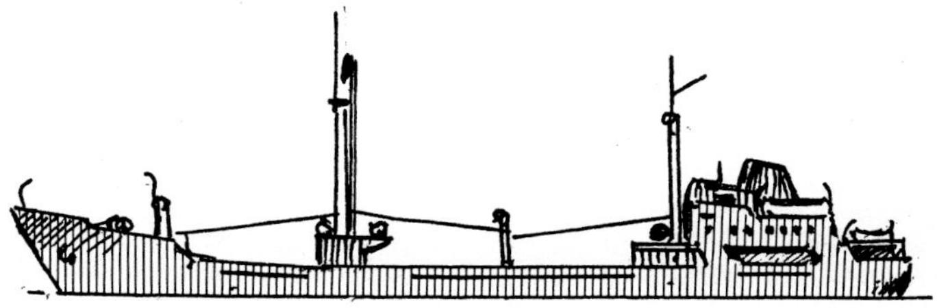

579 *VHF H1*
ALEJANDRA SV/No (Liaaen) 1964; C; 1,575 grt/1,595 dwt; 80.04 × 4.41 m *(262.6 × 14.47 ft)*; M (MaK); 13 kts; ex-*Skanderborg*

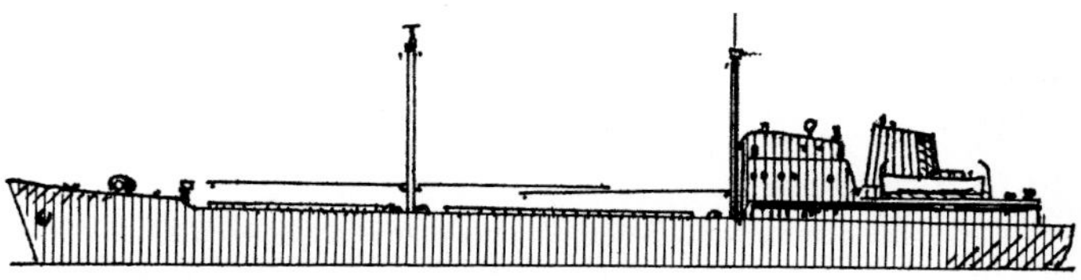

580 *VHF H1*
OCEAN FREEZE Pa/FRG (F Schichau) 1962; C; 1,539 grt/1,587 dwt; 83.29 × 6.23 m *(273.26 × 20.44 ft)*; M (Deutz); 13 kts; ex-*Holstenau*

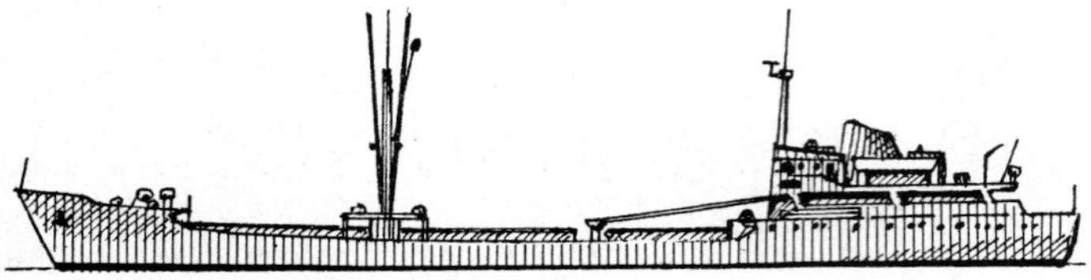

581 *VHF H13*
ARTSIZ Uk/Hu (Angyalford) 1966; C; 1,161 grt/1,609 dwt; 74.55 × 4.67 m *(244.59 × 15.32 ft)*; M (Lang Gepgyar); 11.5 kts
Sisters: **PIA II** (Pa) ex-*Kunda*; **OTEPYA** (Ru); **LIVADIYA** (Uk); **KUYVASTU** (Ru); **LUCINGO** (Mb) ex-*Massandra*; **TIRASPOL** (Uk); **VEZIRA** (Ho) ex-*Vyandra*; **KALMIUS** (Uk); **SOLOMBALA** (Ru); **HELJE** (Ea) ex-*Virtsu*; **PINE KING** (Ho) ex-*Karl Krushteyn*; **ISOLA** (Ho) ex-*Osmussaar*; **PINE QUEEN** (Ho) ex-*Takhkuna*; **LADY NOHA** (Bl) ex-*Heviz*; **HATZVI** (Pa) ex-*Hajduszoboszlo*; **HASAN ATASOY** (Tu) ex-*Herend*; **OMOGY** (Pa) ex-*Somogy*; **CYNTHIA** (Ho) ex-*Tata*: **DACCA** (Bh) ex-*Ambla*; **KHULNA** (Bh) ex-*Imatra*; **NADA** (Sy) ex-*Sagastrand*; **ARMADA PERMAI** (Ia) ex-*Sawu*; **PUTRA JAYA** (Ia) ex-*Selayar*; **KOTA SILAT IV** (Ia) ex-*Lovatj*; **HERO QUEEN** (Ho) ex-*Palana*

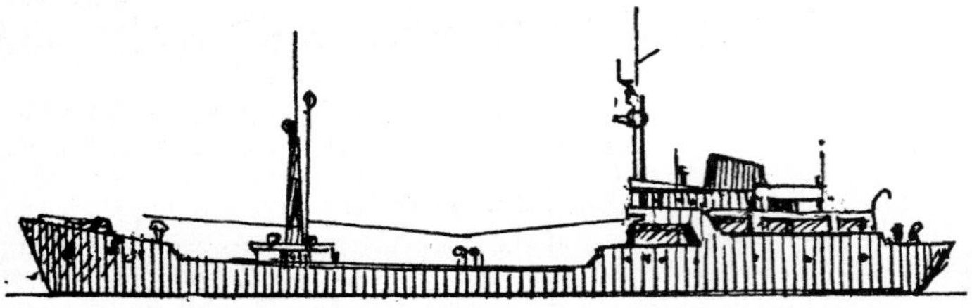

582 *VHF H13*
IVAN BOLOTNIKOV Ru/Hu (Angyalfold) 1969; C; 1,350 grt/1,722 dwt; 77.81 × 4.73 m *(255.28 × 15.52 ft)*; M (Sulzer); 12.5 kts; ex-*Spartak*
Sisters (Some, perhaps all, of these ships have an upswept deflector on funnel): **KONDRATIY BULAVIN** (Ru); **NIKOLAY BAUMAN** (Ru); **PYOTR KAKHOVSKIY** (Ru); **SALAVAT YULAYEV** (Ru); **AEGNA** (Ea); **ANGYALFOLD** (Ea); **PAKRI** (Ea) ex-*August Kulberg*; **MOHNI** (Ea); **KABALA** (Ea) ex-*Kabona*; **PAUGI** (Sv) ex-*Semyon Roshal*; **ORTOS** (Sv) ex-*Teriberka*; **GOLDOBIN** (Ru) ex-*Ambla*; **RAPLA** (Ea); **ADEN** (Ye) ex-*Mate Zalka*

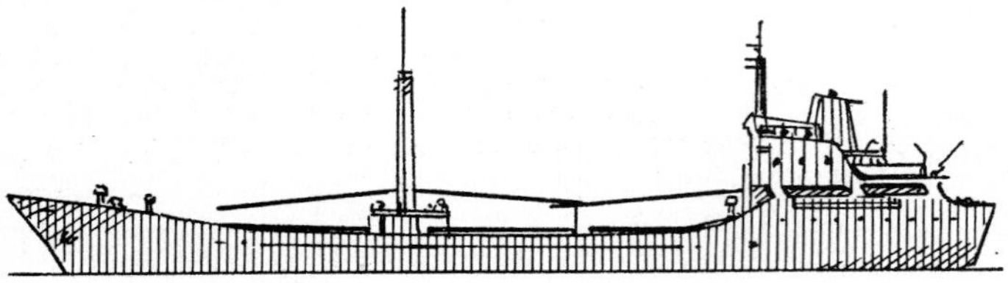

583 *VHFN H13*
CAN DEVAL Tu/Tu (Gaye) 1978; C; 1,590 grt/2,750 dwt; 87.18 × 5.40 m *(286.02 × 17.72 ft)*; M (Atlas-MaK); 12 kts; ex-*Kemal Kolotoglu*
Probable sister: **HACI ARIF KAPTAN** (Tu)

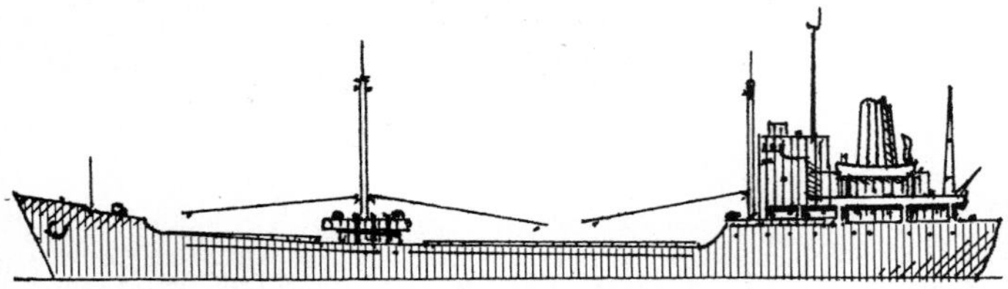

584 *VHMFN H13*
OCEAN LEGEND —/Ja (Kanasashi) 1966; C; 1,988 grt/3,354 dwt; 90.48 × 5.59 m *(296.85 × 18.34 ft)*; M (Ito Tekkosho); 12 kts; ex-*Eitoku Maru*

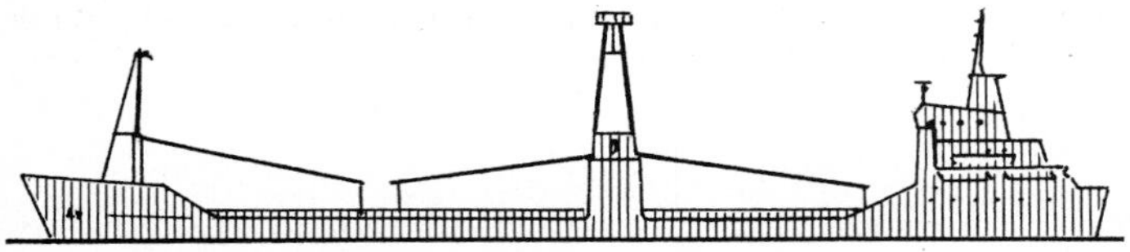

585 *VHM–F H123*
DURA BULK DIS/No (Eides) 1973; C; 2,950 grt/3,500 dwt; 87.79 × 5.04 m *(288.02 × 16.54 ft)*; M (Atlas-MaK); 15 kts; ex-*Brunborg*

586 *VMFV H1*
SALEM SIX Eg/De (Aalborg) 1966; C; 3,021 grt/3,645 dwt; 99.6 × 6.3 m *(327 × 22.3 ft)*; M (B&W); 14.25 kts; ex-*Sandomierz*
Sisters: **SALEM SEVEN** (Eg) ex-*Sanok*; **INDOBARUNA III** (Ia) ex-*Slupsk*

587 *VMNV^{2}FN H13*
CHENG SHAN RC/Ys ('Split') 1959; C; 9,231 grt/13,044 dwt; 153.09 × 8.95 m *(502.26 × 29.36 ft)*; M (Fiat); 13.5 kts; ex-*Chopin*

588 *VMV^{2}FN H13*
HUA XING RC/Ys ("Split") 1960; C; 9,246 grt/12,666 dwt; 153.08 × 8.98 m *(502.23 × 29.46 ft)*; M (Fiat); 15 kts; ex-*Moniuszko*
Sisters: **FANG XING** (RC) ex-*Szymanowski*; **HUA XI** (RC) ex-*Wieniawski*

589 *VM–FV^2 H123*
ALDANLES Ru/Pd (Gdanska) 1960; C/TC; 4,499 grt/6,525 dwt; 123.9 × 7.23 m *(406 × 23.72 ft)*; M (Sulzer); 14.75 kts; 'B-514' type
Similar: **ALATYRLES** (Ru); **KOMILES** (Ru); The following are of the later 'B-45' type: **ALTAYLES** (Ru); **ARGUN** (Ru); **VIEN HAI I** (Vn) ex-*Barnaul*; **BAYKONUR** (Ru); **Y LAN** (Vn) ex-*Bodaybo*; **DZHURMA** (Ru); **ELEKTROSTAL** (Ru); **XI SHAN** (RC); ex-*Kungur*; **KHATANGA** (Ru); **KHOLMSK** (Ru); **MEKHANIK RYBACHUK** (Ru); **OREKHOVO—ZUYEVO** (Ru); **PORONIN** (Ru); **CHAU LONG** (Vn) ex-*Putyatin*; **POBYEDINO** (Ru); **HAI YEN 2** (Vn) ex-*Rubtsovsk*; **ORIENTE OCEANO (Pa) ex-***Sakhalinles* (Ru); **SHADRINSK** (Ru); **SHATURA** (Ru); **RAYCHIKHINSK** (Ru); **VISION** (Ma) ex-*Selengales*; **PYONG WON** (RK) ex-*Taygonos*; **TAYGA** (Ru); **ULAN-UDE** (Ru); **GAFOOR** (Ma) ex-*Vetlugales*; **ZABAYKALSK** (Ru)

590 *VNMF H13*
KOTOVSK Ru/Hu ('Gheorghiu Dej') 1960; C; 1,156 grt/1,310 dwt; 74.00 × 4.00 m *(242.78 × 13.12 ft)*; M (Russkiy); 11 kts
Sisters: **PINAR** (Tu) ex-*Tartu*; **KOVO** (SV) ex-*Vilkovo*; **VICTORY II** (Ho) ex-*Sergey Kirov*; **PALDISKI** (Ru); **EKA** (La) ex-*Engure*; **SONG THAO** (Vn) ex-*Tymlat*; **WIJAYA INDAH** (Ia) ex-*Vychegda*; **NEW ROAD** (Eg) ex-*Adnan El Malki*

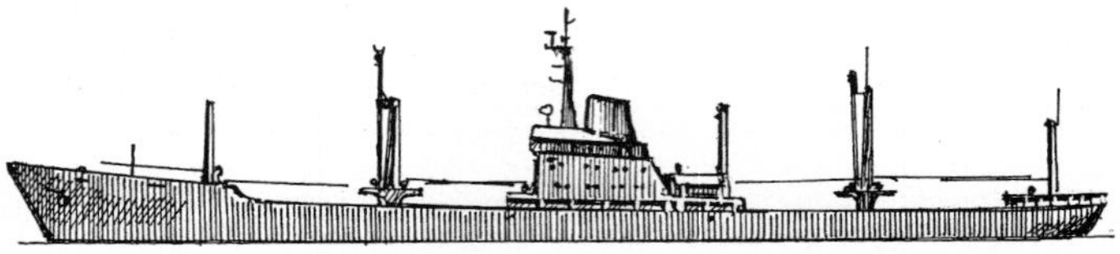

591 *VNMFNVN H1*
IRAN SEEYAM Ir/Po (Viana) 1974; C; 9,206 grt/12,140 dwt; 153 × 9.1 m *(501 × 30 ft)*; M (Sulzer); 18 kts; ex-*Arya Sun*
Sisters: **MAJOR SUCHARSKI** (Li); **MARIAN BUCZEK** (Li); **IRAN SALAM** (Ir) ex-*Arya Zar*

592 *VNM–FNVN H1*
TIRANA Al/Pd (Gdynska) 1970; CP; 8,701 grt/12,038 dwt; 153 × 9 m *(502 × 29.9 ft)*; M (Sulzer); 16.25 kts; 'B41' type

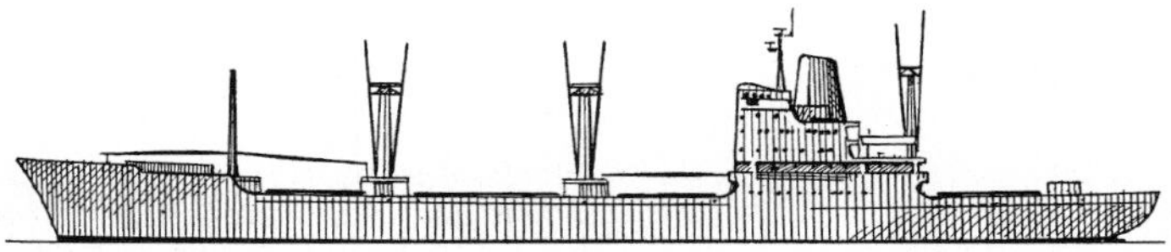

593 *VT^{2}MFT H12*
LONG XU RC/Be (Cockerill) 1968; C; 11,478 grt/16,562 dwt; 161 × 9.9 m *(528 × 32.6 ft)*; M (B&W); 19 kts; ex-*Montaigle*
Sister: **GREAT BEST 1** (Pa) ex-*Montsalva*

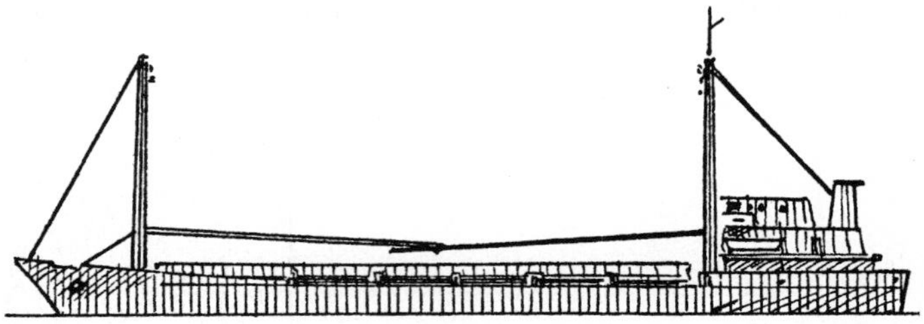

594 *V^{2}F H1*
TEGE No/FRG (Buesumer) 1971; C/Con/HL; 1,344 grt/1,278 dwt; 71.4 × 3.98 m *(234.25 × 13.06 ft)*; M (B&W); 14 kts; ex-*Atlas Scan*; 77 TEU
Sisters: **MIN DA** (RC) ex-*Unit Scan*; **BEI FENG SHAN** (RC) ex-*Hercules Scan*

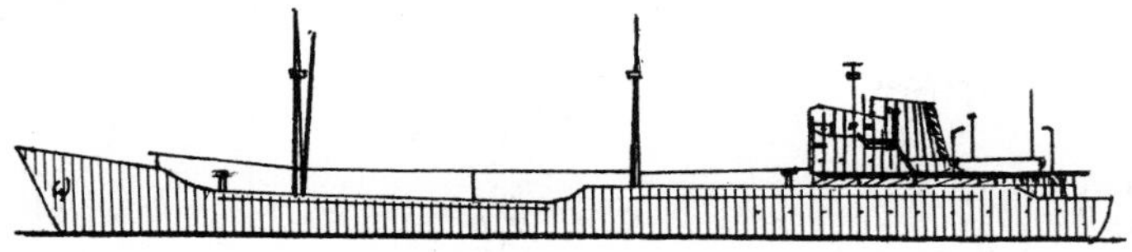

595 V^2F *H13*
MOUNT Ho/FRG (S&B) 1958; C; 1,827 grt/3,018 dwt; 80.17 × 6.55 m *(263.02 × 21.49 ft)*; M (Werkspoor); — kts; ex-*Geertje Buisman*

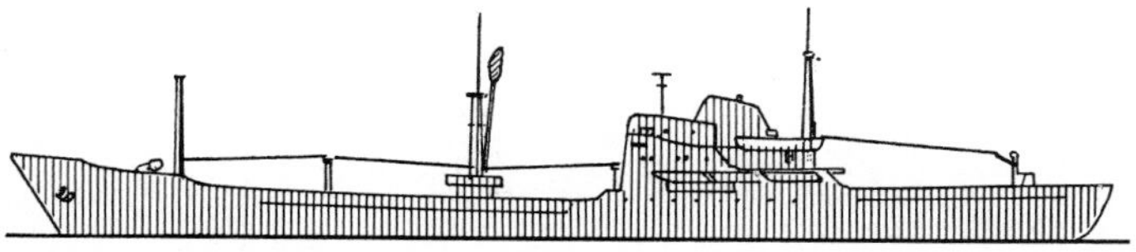

596 V^2FV *H13*
AL-BILAL —/Fi (Valmet) 1965; C/TC; 2,609 grt/3,446 dwt; 102 × 6 m *(334 × 19.6 ft)*; M (B&W); 13.75 kts; ex-*Indiga*; some (possibly all) of this class have a deflector fitted to the funnel
Sisters: **ALEXANDRE** (Cb) ex-*Janales*; **KHATANGALES** (Ru); **KOSTROMALES** (Ru); **KODINO** (Ru); **KABERNEEME** (Ea) ex-*Nevales*; **OLYUTORKA** (Ru); **DIKSON** (Ru); **KOLGUYEV** (Ru); **PERVOURALSK** (Ru); **SALDUS** (Ru); **SHEKSNALES** (Ru); **ZEYALES** (Ru); **DIBSON 1** (Bl) ex-*Kamales*

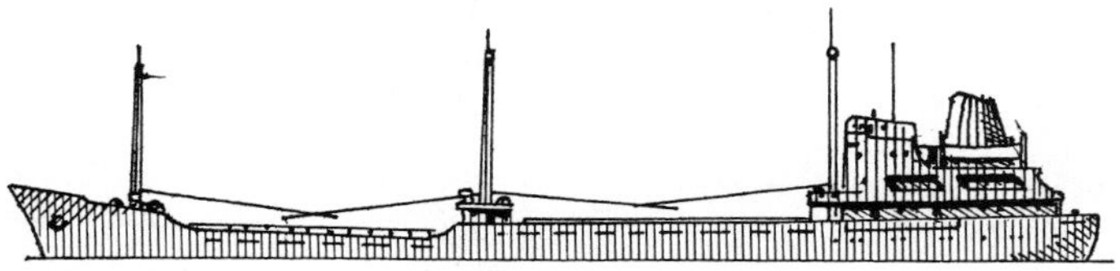

597 V^2HF *H1*
AL HABIB–II Sy/FRG (Meyer) 1961; C; 2,939 grt/4,348 dwt; 94.01 × 6.77 m *(308.43 × 22.21)*; M (MAN); 12.5 kts; ex-*Jan Ten Doornkaat*

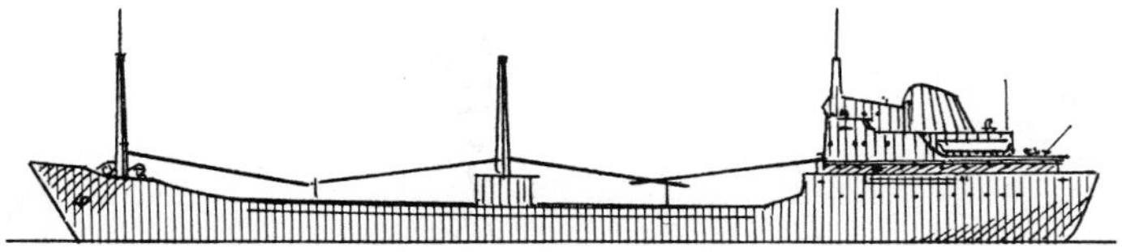

598 V^2HF *H13*
BREEHELLE Sy/Fi (Valmet) 1961; C; 1,630 grt/2,300 dwt; 85.81 × 5.39 m *(281.53 × 17.68 ft)*; M (Deutz); 13 kts; ex-*Pulptrader*

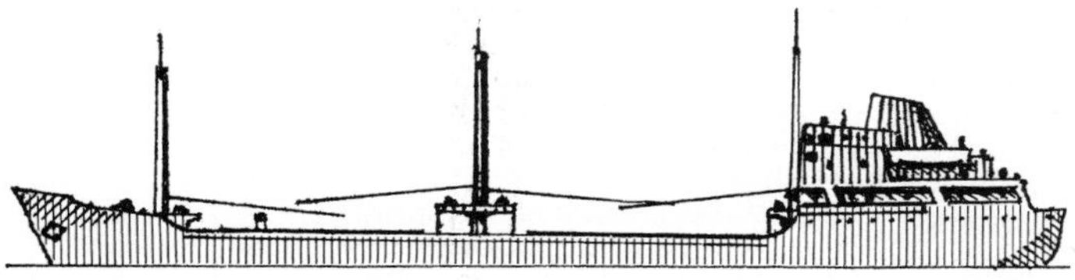

599 V^2HF *H13*
EDITH NIELSEN SV/De (Aalborg) 1967; C; 2,745 grt/4,044 dwt; 94.11 × 6.62 m *(308.76 × 21.72 ft)*; M (B&W); 14.5 kts

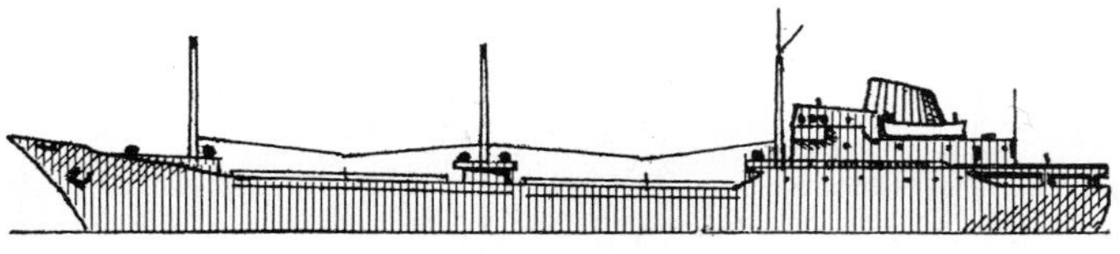

600 V^2HF *H13*
MERCS KOMARI Sr/De (Aalborg) 1965; C; 2,453 grt/3,942 dwt; 95.61 × 6.58 m *(313.68 × 21.59 ft)*; M (B&W); 14 kts; ex-*Reykafoss*
Sister: **MERCS KUMANA** (Sr) ex-*Skogafoss*

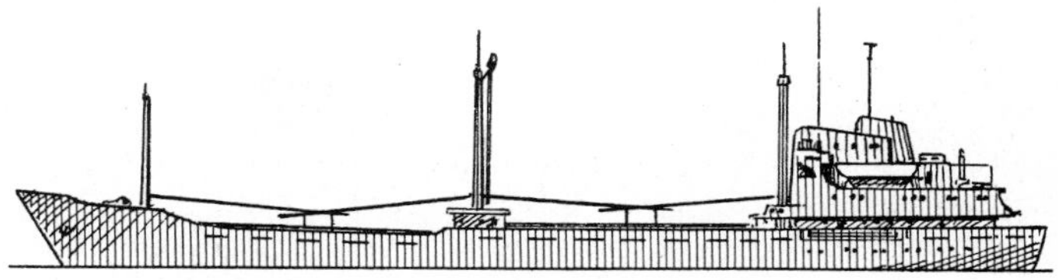

601 $V^2HM–F$ *H1*
OMIROS Ho/FRG (Lindenau) 1964; C; 2,796 grt/4,310 dwt; 94.29 × 8.61 m *(309.35 × 28.25 ft)*; M (MAN); 14.5 kts; ex-*Friederike Ten Doornkat*

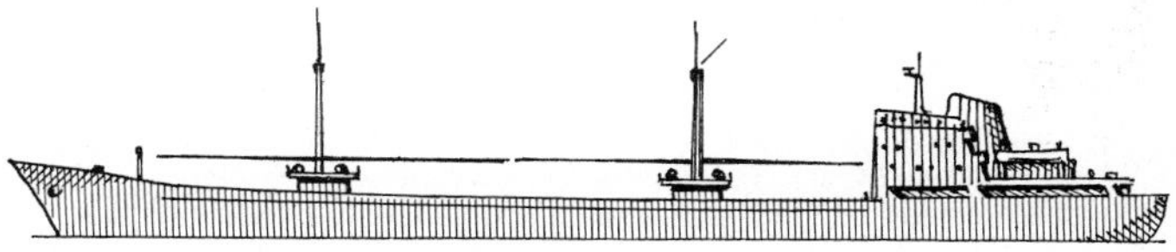

602 V^2MF *H*
GESAN Tu/De (Helsingor) 1962; C; 4,307 grt/6,597 dwt; 119.54 × 7.01 m *(392.19 × 23 ft)*; M (B&W); 15 kts; ex-*Heering Rose*; May now be fitted with deck cranes

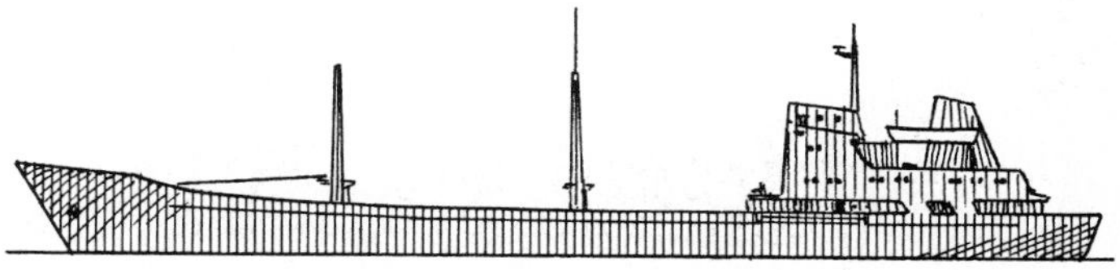

603 V^2MF *H1*
GULF SPLENDOUR —/Rm (Turnu-Severin) 1970; C; 1,585 grt/1,911 dwt; 85.91 × 5.1 m *(281.86 × 16.73 ft)*; M (Sulzer); 13 kts; ex-*Iwonicz Zdroj*
Sisters (Superstructure varies): **FENES** (Pa) ex-*Ciechocinek*; **MARIA X** (Ma) ex-*Duszniki Zdroj*; **GULF SEAGULL** (Pa) ex-*Cieplice Zdroj*; **MANSOURA 1** (Eg) ex-*Rabka Zdroj*; **PHOENICIA** (Sy) ex-*Polczyn Zdroj*

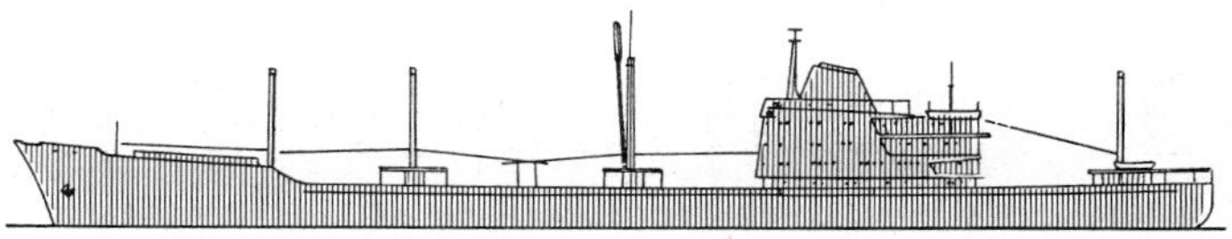

604 V^2MFMV *H1*
ROMASHKA Ho/Pd (Gdanska) 1965; C; 9,695 grt/12,432 dwt; 155 × 9 m *(508 × 29.10 ft)*; M (Sulzer); 17.25 kts; ex-*Medyn*
Sisters (some have modified superstructure. Some are 'B441' type): **MEZHDURECHENSK** (Uk); **MEZHGORYE** (Uk); **MUKACHEVO** (Uk); **MOLODOGVARDEYSK** (Uk); **MYTISHCHI** (Uk); **ALEKSEY TOLSTOY** (Uk); **BORIS GORBATOV** (Uk); **LILY** (Uk) ex-*Ivan Goncharov*; **NIKOLAY NEKRASOV** (Uk); **DUBAI SUCCESS** (Ma) ex-*Samuil Marshak*; **ANTON MAKARENKO** (Uk); **BORIS LAVRENEV** (Uk); **ROMEN ROLLAN** (Uk)

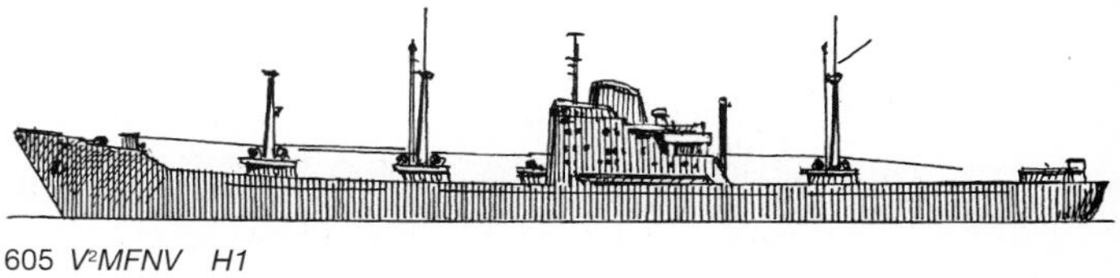

605 V^2MFNV *H1*
GRUNWALD Pd/De (Nakskov) 1967; CP; 10,188 grt/12,027 dwt; 154 × 7.9/8.5 m *(504 × 26/28 ft)*; M (Sulzer); 16 kts

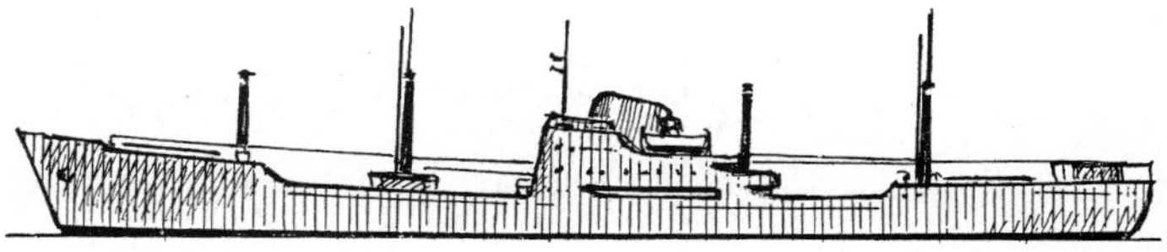

606 V^2MFNV *H13*
SHU YU QUAN RC/FRG (Kieler H) 1961; CP; 7,075 grt/9,250 dwt; 138 × 8.6 m *(453 × 28.1 ft)*; M (MAN); 16.5 kts; ex-*Maren Skou*

607 *V^{2}MFNVN H1*
NEZABUDKA Ho/Pd (Gdanska) 1962; C; 9,151 grt/12,460 dwt; 155 × 7.8/8.9 m *(508 × 26/29.3 ft)*; M (Sulzer); 15 kts; ex-*Salavat*; 'B43' type

608 *V^{2}MFNVT H1*
YU HUA RC/Pd (Szczecinska) 1965; C; 6,563 grt/10,400 dwt; 154 × 8.3 m *(505 × 27.4 ft)*; M (Sulzer); 15 kts; ex-*Henryk Jendza*; 'B454' type

609 *V^{2}MFV H1*
ARAB MAZIN Si/Br (Hall, Russell) 1967; C; 4,385 grt/6,183 dwt; 114 × 6.5/7.4 m *(374 × 21.4/24.3 ft)*; M (MAN); 15.25 kts; ex-*Duburg*

610 *V^{2}MFV H1*
LEWANT SV/De (Aalborg) 1967; C; 4,289 grt/4,600 dwt; 114.5 × 6.3 m *(375 × 20.6 ft)*; M (B&W); 16 kts; ex-*Lewant II*
Sister: **DOLPHINS 1** (SV) ex-*Lechistan II*

611 *V^{2}MFV H1*
TAISHAN RC/Sw (Oresunds) 1957; CP; 4,530 grt/6,565 dwt; 112.5 × 6.4/7.5 m *(369 × 20.9/24.7 ft)*; M (Gotaverken); 13 kts; ex-*Nordica*

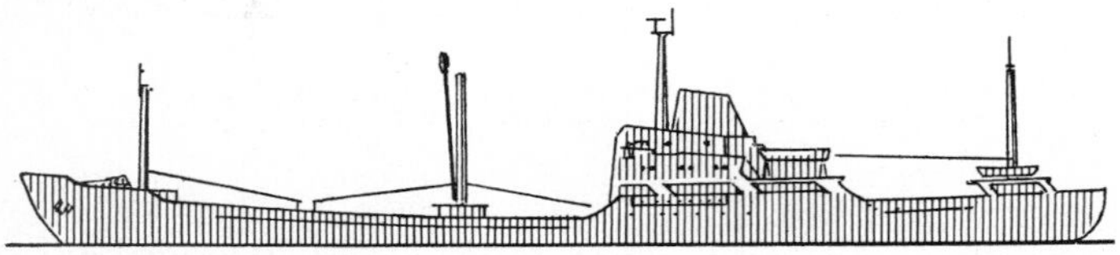

612 *V^{2}MFV H13*
ALDAN Ru/Ru (Navashinsky) 1967; C/TC; 3,179 grt/4,140 dwt; 104.5 × 6.05 m *(343 × 19.85 ft)*; M (B&W); 13.5 kts; Some sisters have goalpost on forecastle and poop; "Sibirles" class; See entry number 8/106
Sisters (Ru built): **EGVEKINOT** (Ru); **YANA** (Ru); **KEM** (Ru); **SON CA** (Vn) ex-*Kondopoga*; **SOFIA** (Ru) ex-*Korsakov*; **LAKHTA** (Ru); **OMOLON** (Ru); **SELENGA** (Ru); **SIBIRLES** (Ru); **SIBIRTSYEVO** (Ru) ex-*Manzovka*; **TERNEY** (Ru); **VYATKALES** (Ru); **VZMORYE** (Ru) Sisters (Rm built (Galatz)): **ANTON BUYUKLY** (Ru); **BORIS NIKOLAICHUK** (Ru); **CHERNIGOV** (Uk); **KARAGA** (Ru); **KATANGLI** (Ru); **KAVALEROVO** (Ru); **KAZATIN** (Uk); **KILIYA** (Uk); **BARBARA** (Ru) ex-*Kirensk*; **KOREIZ** (Uk); **KRASNOARMEYSK** (Uk); **KRASNOPOLYE** (Ru); **KRASNOTURINSK** (Ru); **KRYMSK** (Uk); **KULUNDA** (Ru); **KUSTANAY** (Uk); **KUZNETSK** (Ru); **LEONID SMIRNYKH** (Ru); **STEPAN SAVUSHKIN** (Ru); **TUSHINO** (Uk); **TYMOVSK** (Ru); **YEVGENIY CHAPLANOV** (Ru)

613 *V^{2}MFV H13*
LENALES Ru/Fi (Nystads) 1964; C/TC; 2,921 grt/4,009 dwt; 102 × 6.2 m *(334 × 20.4 ft)*; M (B&W); 13.75 kts; **SIMILAR TO ENTRY NUMBER 8/619**

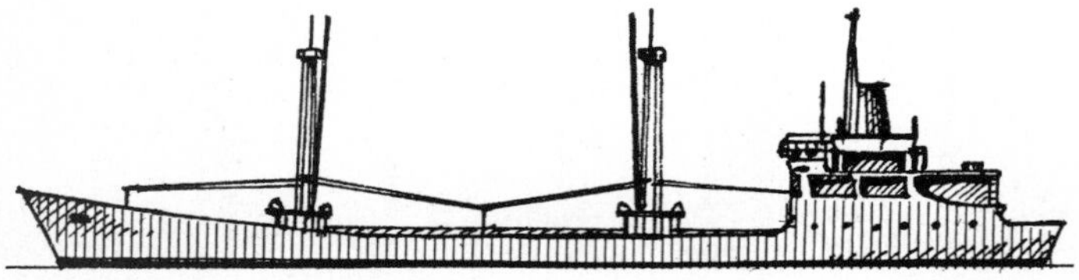

614 *V^{2}M–F H*
AL BIRUNI Eg/Sp (Duro Felguera) 1971; C/R; 1,414 grt/2,096 dwt; 77.4 × 5.32 m *(253.94 × 17.45 ft)*; M (Deutz); 15 kts; ex-*Atlan Turquesa*
Sister: **AL IDRISI** (Eg) ex-*Atlan Diamante*

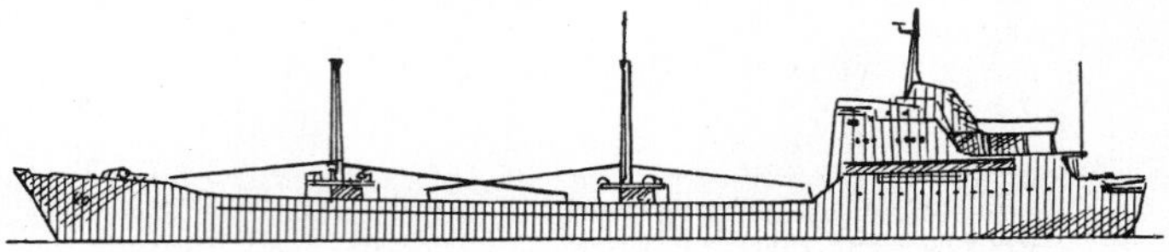

615 *V^{2}M–F H12*
MARINA SV/Bu (G Dimitrov) 1968; C; 2,416 grt/3,496 dwt; 95.89 × 5.64 m *(314.6 × 18.5 ft)*; M (Sulzer); 13 kts; ex-*Warna*
Sisters (Some have heavier radar mast and some have cowl around funnel top): **TOOT** (Eg) ex-*Plock*; **HAPPY FORTUNE** (Ho) ex-*Oswiecim*; **UNITY VIII** (Ho) ex-*Chrzanow*; **LILLI PEARL** (SV) ex-*Jelcz II*; **OMADHOO FORTUNE** (Ho) ex-*Jelenia Gora*

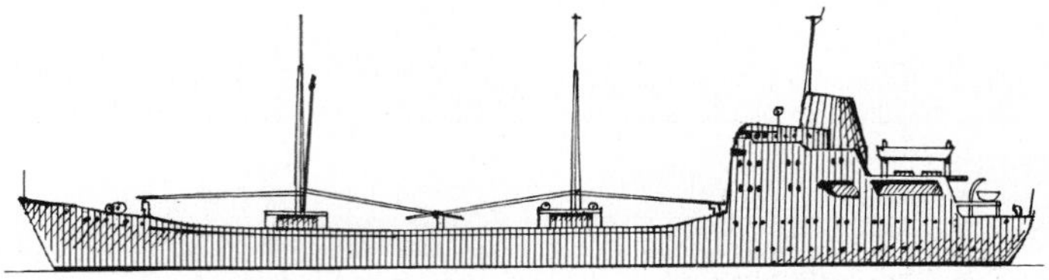

616 *V^{2}M–F H13*
MARINER II SV/Bu (G Dimitrov) 1963; C; 3,353 grt/6,310 dwt; 114.18 × 7.54 m *(374.61 × 24.74 ft)*; M (MAN); 14 kts; ex-*Sofia*
Sister: **DIMITRAKIS** (—) ex-*Veliko Tirnovo*

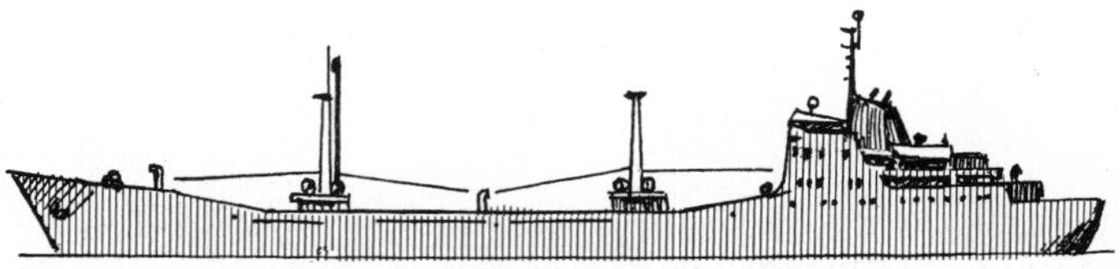

617 *V^{2}M–F H13*
SUN JOY Pa/Bu (G Dimitrov) 1971; C; 2,857 grt/4,870 dwt; 114.26 × 6.55 m *(374.87 × 21.49 ft)*; M (MAN); 13.5 kts; ex-*Safia*
Sisters: **YANG ZI JIANG 4** (RC) ex-*Woolgar*; **TAI SHAN** (RC) ex-*Tai An*; **TAI NING** (RC); **TAI SHUN** (RC)

618 *V^{2}M–FNV H1*
ZHEN XING RC/Pd (Gdanska) 1963; C; 9,107 grt/11,895 dwt; 153.88 × 9.02 m *(505 × 29.59 ft)*; M (Sulzer); 16 kts; ex-*Konopnicka*; 'B54' type
Sister: **CHI CHENG** (RC) ex-*Guo Ji*

619 *V^{2}M–FV H13*
BIRZAI Lt/Fi (Valmet) 1968; C/TC; 2,873 grt/3,930 dwt; 102 × 6.2 m *(335 × 20.2 ft)*; M (B&W); 13.5 kts; ex-*Bereznik*
Sisters: **MARIJAMPOLE** (Lt) ex-*Kapsukas*; **KELME** (Lt) ex-*Kashino*; **ROKISKIS** (Lt) ex-*Kara*; **KALININGRAD** (Ru); **KEDAINIAI** (Lt); **KINGISEPP** (Ru); **KOPORYE** (Ru); **LEJA** (Bl) ex-*Krasnoborsk*; **NERINGA** (Lt) ex-*Kostino*; **HELENA** (Cb) ex-*Kuzminki*; **KUPISKIS** (Lt); **KURSENAI** (Lt) ex-*Kuntsevo*; **LAZDIJAI** (Lt) ex-*Lyuban*; **JOSE DIAS** (Ru); **LYDIA** (Bl) ex-*Turku*; **VENTA** (Lt) ex-*Voronezh*; **SOFIYA PEROVSKAYA** (Ru); **EL BILLY 1** (Ma) ex-*Tsiglomen*; **ANNA** (Ma); **KIKHCHIK** (Ru); **KAMCHADAL** (Ru); **TAMPERE** (Ru); **SHUSHENSKOYE** (Ru); **KIMRY** (Ru); **NINA** (Ma) ex-*Kapitan Gastello*; **LIGOVO** (Ru); **KRASNOYARSK** (Ru); **HELENA 1** (Cb) ex-*Gus-Khrustalnyy*; **VAGA** (Ru); **PALANA** (Ru); **MIRNYY** (Ru); **PAKRUOJIS** (Lt) ex-*Pravda*; **KOZYREVSK** (Ru); **KRETINGA** (Lt); **DOCTOR RAMI** (Bl) ex-*Yantarnyy*; **TOBOL** (Ru); **IGNALINA** (Lt) ex-*Ilyichyovo*; **ILYINSK** (Ru); **BLAGOVESHCHENSK** (Ru); **CHAZHMA** (Ru); **YASSMIN M** (Sy) ex-*Lomonosova*; **BARBA** (Ma) ex-*Kharlov*

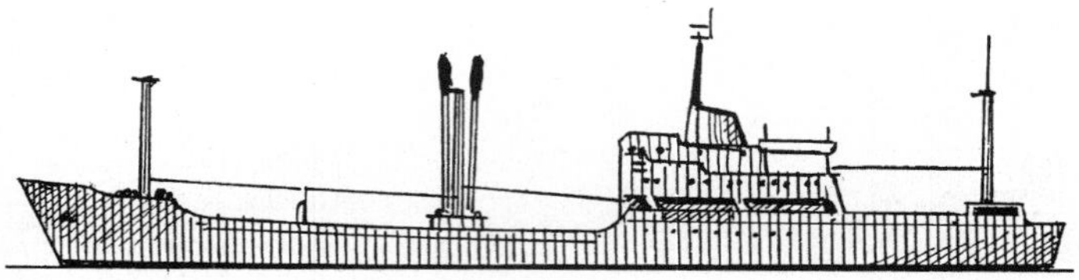

620 *V^{2}M–FV H13*
LYONYA GOLIKOV Ru/DDR ('Neptun') 1968; C; 3,601 grt/4,638 dwt; 105.7 × 6.8 m *(347 × 22.4 ft)*; M (MAN); 13.75 kts; May be other ships of this class with this sequence.

621 V^2M–FV *H13*
SHURA KOBER Ru/DDR ('Neptun') 1971; C; 3,685 grt/4,687 dwt; 105.7 × 6.7 m *(347 × 21.6 ft)*; M (MAN); 13.75 kts; 'Pioner' type. Some of this class may have a smoke deflector on the funnel
Sisters: **ARKADIY KAMANIN** (Ru); **BORYA TSARIKOV** (Ru); **NAJIB** (SV) ex-*Galya Komleva*; **KOLYA MYAGOTIN** (Ru); **LARA MIKHEYENKO** (Ru); **LYONYA GOLYKOV** (Ru); **MARAT KAZEY** (Ru); **NINA KUKOVEROVA** (Ru); **PAVLIK LARISHKIN** (Ru); **PIONER** (Ru); **PIONERSKAYA PRAVDA** (Ru); **PIONERSKAYA ZORKA** (Ru); **SASHA BORODULIN** (Ru); **SASHA KONDRATYEV** (Ru); **SASHA KOTOV** (Ru); **VIRGO III** (Pa) ex-*Sasha Kovalyov*; **TOLYA KOMAR** (Ru); **TOLYA SHUMOV** (Ru); **TONYA BONDARCHUK** (Ru); **VALYA KOTIK** (Ru); **VALERIY VOLKOV** (Ru); **VASYA KOROBKO** (Ru); **URGA** (Ru) ex-*Vasya Shishkovskiy*; **VITYA CHALENKO** (Ru); **VITYA KHONENKO** (Ru); **VITYA SITNITSA** (Ru); **VOLODYA SHCHERBATSEVICH** (Ru); **YUTA BONDAROVSKAYA** (Ru); **ZINA PORTNOVA** (Ru)

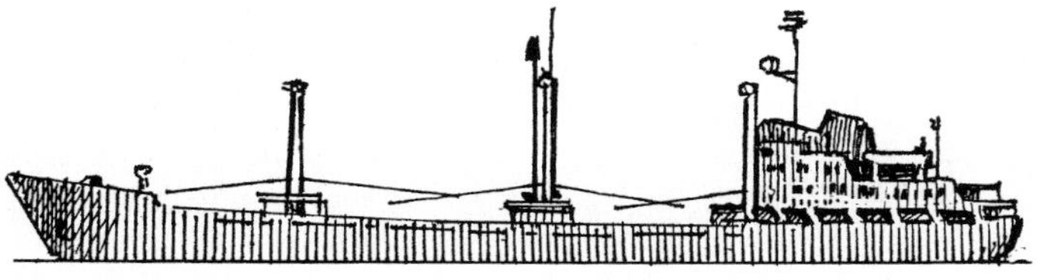

622 V^2NMF *H*
DANUBE STREAM Pa/Rm (Galatz) 1963; C; 3,327 grt/4,220 dwt; 100.59 × 6.55 m *(330.02 × 21.49 ft)*; M (Sulzer); 12.5 kts; ex-*Novy Bug*
Sisters: **NOVY DONBASS** (Uk); **NOVORZHEV** (Uk); **NOVOSHAKHTINSK** (Uk)

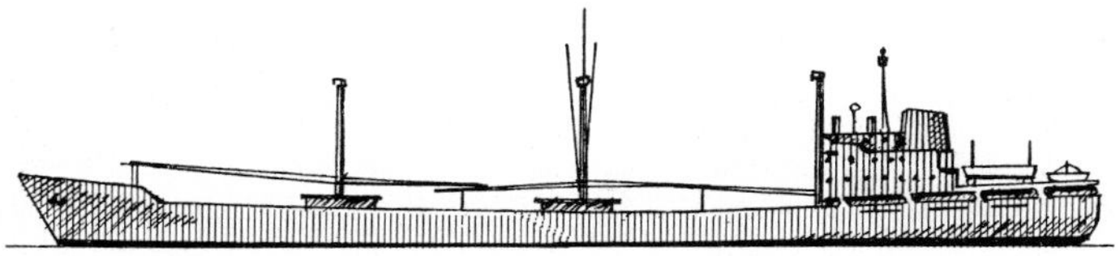

623 V^2NMF *H1*
BODRUM Tu/FRG (A G 'Weser') 1961; C; 4,164 grt/6,270 dwt; 115.73 × 7.16 m *(379.69 × 23.49 ft)*; M (MAN); 14 kts
Sisters: **MARMARIS 1** (Tu); **MUGLA** (Tu)

624 V^2NMFNM *H1*
HONG QI 103 RC/FRG (Flensburger) 1958; CP; 8,432 grt/12,000 dwt; 147.9 × 8.5 m *(485 × 27.9 ft)*; M (MAN); 12.5 kts; ex-*Indus*

625 V^2NMFNV^2 *H13*
HONG QI RC/RC (Dalian) 1964; C; 11,090 grt/15,925 dwt; 169.91 × 9.73 m *(557.4 × 31.92 ft)*; T (Kirov); 17 kts

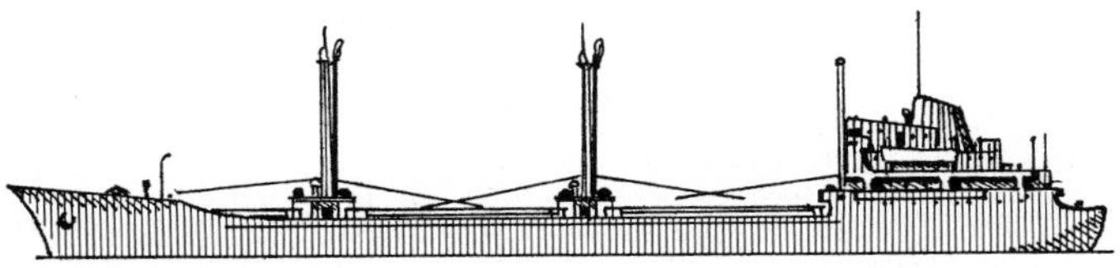

626 V^2NM–F *H13*
MERCS WADDUWA Sr/FRG (Lindenau) 1967; C; 3,506 grt/5,710 dwt; 107.85 × 7.42 m *(353.84 × 24.34 ft)*; M (MAN); 15.5 kts
Sister: **YING ZHOU** (RC) ex-*Moritz Schulte*

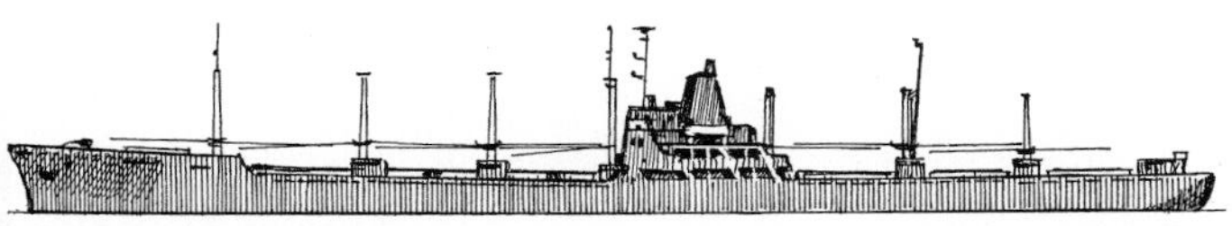

627 V^3HMFH^2V *H1*
CAPE GIRARDEAU US/US (Newport News) 1968; C/Con; 15,949 grt/22,564 dwt; 184.4 × 10.7 m *(605 × 35 ft)*; T (GEC); 21 kts; ex-*Alaskan Mail*; US Government owned
Sisters: **CLEVELAND** (US) ex-*American Mail*; **CAPE GIBSON** (US) ex-*Indian Mail*; **SUE LYKES** (US) ex-*Hong Kong Mail*

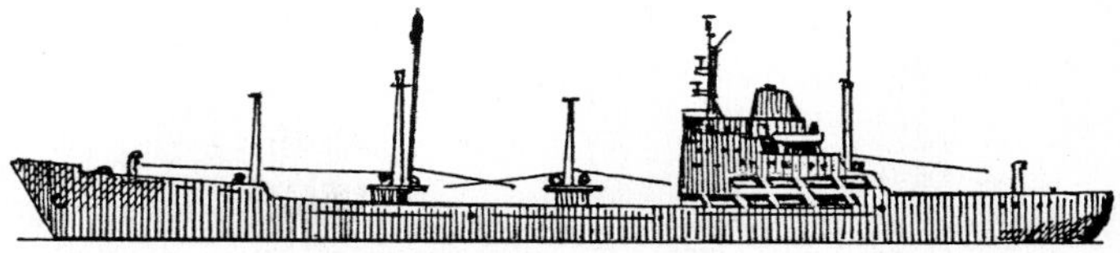

628 V^3MFH *H13*
IFIGENIA Ma/DDR (Warnow) 1964; C; 8,461 grt/12,295 dwt; 150.6 × 8.8 m *(494 × 29.3 ft)*; M (MAN); 16.5 kts; ex-*Vereya*
Similar: **JIANGMEN** (RC); **VOLZHSK** (Ru)

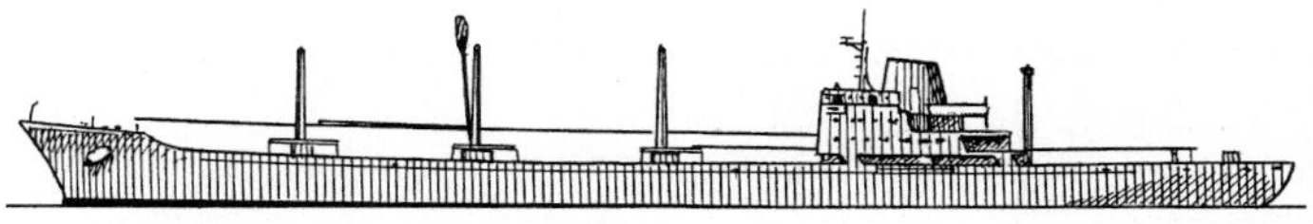

629 V^3MFN *H1*
GOKHAN KALKAVAN Tu/Ys ('Jozo Lozovina-Mosor') 1971; C; 8,570 grt/13,085 dwt; 154.3 × 9.3 m *(506 × 30.6 ft)*; M (MAN); — kts; ex-*Keban*
Sisters: **ARAS** (Tu); **DICLE** (Tu); **FIRAT** (Tu); **GEDIZ** (Tu); **MERIC** (Tu)

630 V^3MFN *H13*
ASTRA Ho/Ys ('Uljanik') 1964; C; 10,109 grt/14,868 dwt; 160 × 9.7 m *(525 × 32 ft)*; M (B&W); 18 kts; ex-*Pula*
Sisters: **THALLIA** (Ma) ex-*Aleksandr Blok*; **ALEKSANDR GRIN** (Uk); **EFSTRATIOS G** (Ma) ex-*Aleksandr Serafimovich*; **ALEKSANDR VERMISHEV** (Ru); **EASTERN STAR** (Ma) ex-*Alisher Navoi*; **ARKADIY GAYDAR** (Uk); **DEMYAN BEDNYY** (Uk); **UNITED GLORY** (Ma) ex-*Makhtum-Kuli*; **MUSA DZHALIL** (Uk); **NIKOLAY DOBROLYUBOV** (Uk); **NIKOLAY GOGOL** (Uk); **NIKOLAY KARAMZIM** (Ru); **NIKOLAY OGAREV** (Uk); **SAINT NEKTARIOS** (Ma) ex-*Ovanes Tumanyan*; **VISSARION BELINSKIY** (Uk); **UNITED PIONEER** (Ma); ex-*Vladimir Korolenko*

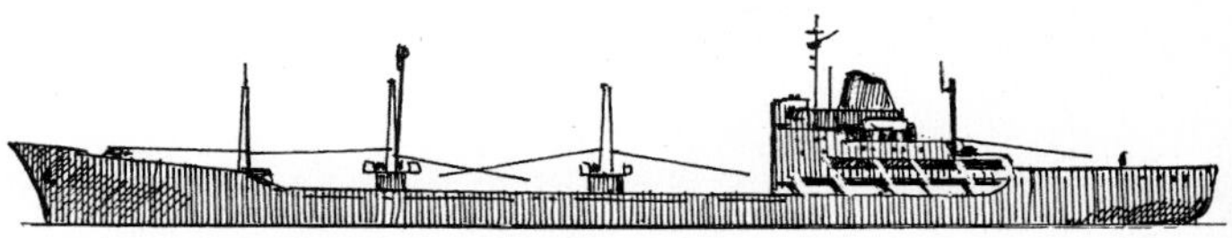

631 V^3MFN *H13*
DONG GUANG RC/DDR (Warnow) 1969; C; 9,736 grt/12,680 dwt; 151.2 × 9 m *(496 × 29.8 ft)*; M (MAN); 20 kts; ex-*Neptune Amethyst*; 'Ozean' type

632 V^3MFN *H13*
TONGSHUN Pa/Br (Doxford & S) 1971; C; 11,630 grt/17,029 dwt; 163 × 9.7 m *(540 × 31.9 ft)*; M (Sulzer); 18 kts; ex-*Ion*
Sisters: **XIN JI** (RC) ex-*Iason*; **FEI TENG** (RC) ex-*Iktinos*; **GANG CHENG** (RC) ex-*Ion*; **CADMUS** (Le) ex-*Atalanti*; Similar: **PARNASSUS** (Le) ex-*Feax*; **MYO HANG 3** (RK) ex-*Faethon*

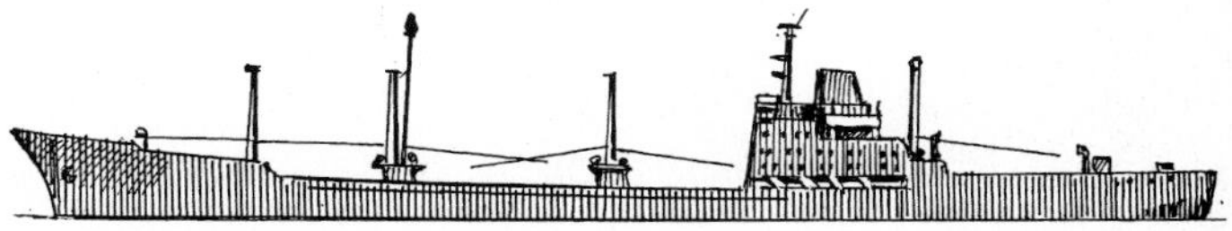

633 V^3MFN *H13*
XING LONG RC/DDR (Warnow) 1968; C; 9,630 grt/12,430 dwt; 151 × 8.8 m *(494 × 29.3 ft)*; M (MAN); 15 kts; ex-*Haimen*

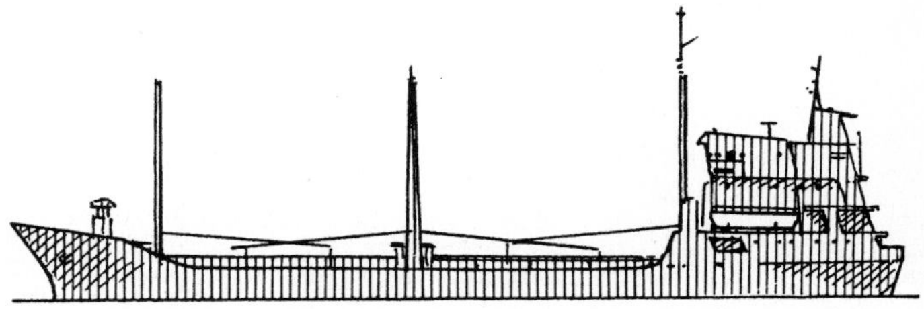

634 V^2M–F *H13*
DARPO SEMBILAN Ia/De (Orskovs) 1972; C; 1,435 grt/2,620 dwt; 71.48 × 5.67 m *(235 × 18.6 ft)*; M (Alpha-Diesel); 12 kts; ex-*Chris Lion*
Similar (Lengthened): **WAKENITZ** (Cy) ex-*Mette Christensen*

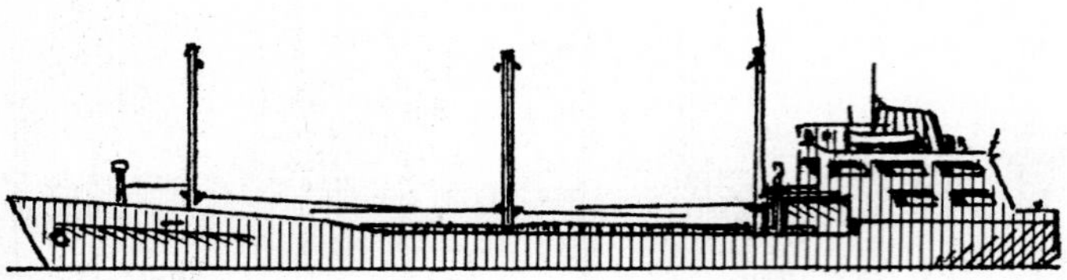

635 *V³M–F H13*
MINAMAR Ho/De (Sonderborg) 1971; C; 499 grt/1,800 dwt; 70.82 × 4.3 m *(232.35 × 14.11 ft)*; M (Alpha-Diesel); 12 kts; ex-*Kirsten Bech*

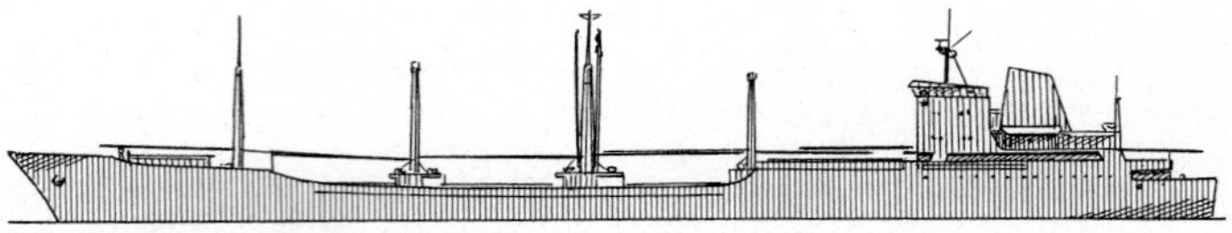

637 *V³NMFN H13*
AKROGIALI Cy/De (Helsingor) 1976; C; 9,244 grt/14,763 dwt; 154.11 × 9.51 m *(506 × 31.2 ft)*; M (B&W); 18 kts; ex-*Juarez*; 152 TEU
Sisters: **DAIQUIRI** (Cu) ex-*O'Higgins*; **SANTANITA** (Cy) ex-*San Martin*; **SOUL** (Bl) ex-*Sandino*

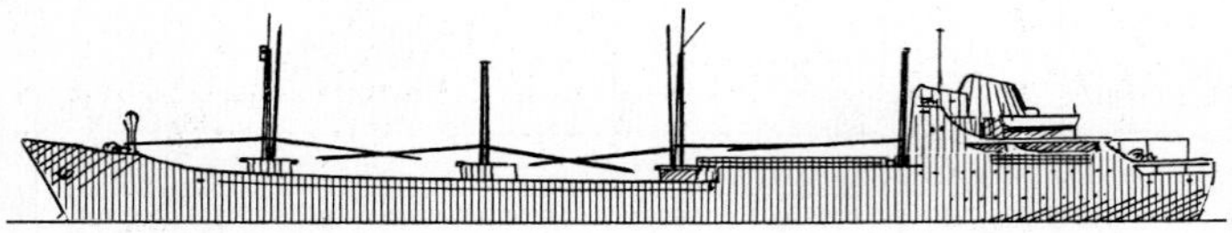

636 *V³NMF H13*
LU DING RC/Fi (Valmet) 1959; C; 4,784 grt/7,625 dwt; 121.54 × 7.67 m *(398.75 × 25.16 ft)*; M (B&W); 15 kts; ex-*Amazonas*

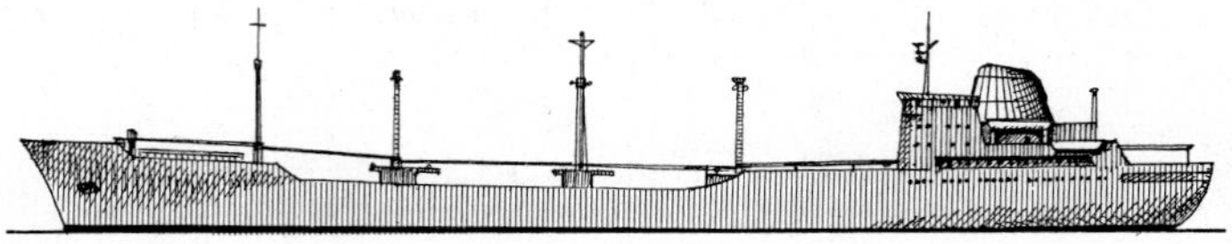

638 *V³NMFN H13*
SHENG MAO SV/De (Helsingor) 1969; C; 9,854 grt/10,780 dwt; 156.37 × 8.07 m *(513.02 × 26.48 ft)*; M (B&W); 18 kts; ex-*Dinna Skou*
Similar: **SHENG KAI** (RC) ex-*Diana Skou*; **KOTA RATNA** (Sg) ex-*Dolly Skou*; **KOTA RATU** (Sg) ex-*Dorit Skou*; **LONG PING** (RC) ex-*Dagny Skou*

639 Shun-Ei *(Pa); 1983; (as Shun-Ei Maru)* *FotoFlite*

640 Lutro *(NIS); 1975* *FotoFlite*

641 Enko *(Tu); 1983* *FotoFlite*

642 Necati Atasoy *(Tu); 1983; (as Yuksel Guler)* *FotoFlite*

643 Baltic Horizon *(Ma); 1977; (as Atlantic Horizon)* *FotoFlite*

644 Erdal *(Tu); 1976* *FotoFlite*

645 Fortune Bell *(Pa); 1976* *FotoFlite*

646 Euroliberty *(Cy); 1974* *FotoFlite*

647 Iro *(Gr); 1976* *FotoFlite*

648 Hawk One *(Cy); 1982; (as Lux Hawk)* *FotoFlite*

649 Rattana Naree *(Th); 1977; (as Sangkulirang No 7)* *FotoFlite*

650 Rea *(Cy); 1973* *FotoFlite*

651 Indian Endurance *(In); 1975* *FotoFlite*

652 Danica Rainbow *(DIS); 1987* *FotoFlite*

653 Texas *(It); 1982* *FotoFlite*

654 Southway *(Cy); 1979; (as Midway)* *FotoFlite*

655 Super Vision *(Pi); 1986* *FotoFlite*

656 Arctic Confidence *(Pi); 1977* *FotoFlite*

657 Kouilou *(Pa); 1979; (as Algenib)* *FotoFlite*

658 Tango *(SV); 1979; (as Ralu)* *FotoFlite*

659 Sirt *(Ly); 1981* *FotoFlite*

660 Overseas Harriette *(US); 1978* *FotoFlite*

661 Marine Express *(Tu); 1981* *FotoFlite*

662 Lydra *(Bs); 1979; (as MC Diamond)* *FotoFlite*

663 Riomar *(Cy); 1983* *FotoFlite*

664 Jingshun *(Sg); 1979; (as Novmenchu)* *FotoFlite*

665 Rafah *(Eg); 1977* *FotoFlite*

666 Qing Long 88 *(RC); 1979; (as Fredro)* *FotoFlite*

667 Shui Cheng *(RC); 1978* *FotoFlite*

668 Regina *(NIS); 1971; (as Coast Pride)* *FotoFlite*

669 Norbulk Seraya *(Ma); (as Kriti Pearl)* *WSPL*

670 Adventure *(Cy); 1971* *Norman Thomson*

671 Grunwald *(Pd); 1968* *Norman Thomson*

672 Long Hai *(RC); 1968* *WSPL*

673 Woermann Expert *(HK); 1977; (as Lloyd Parana)* *WSPL*

674 Mini Moon *(Ho); 1972* *WSPL*

675 Abdul M *(SV); 1974; (as Lily Venture)* *WSPL*

676 Hermes *(Th); 1977; (as Caly)* *WSPL*

677 Rainbow Splendour *(Pa); 1976* *WSPL*

678 Ibn Sina II *(Ag); 1978* *WSPL*

679 Mawlamyine *(Mr); 1979; (as Mawlamyaing)* *WSPL*

680 Unipampa *(NA); 1979; (as Frankfurt/Oder)* *WSPL*

681 Ibn Khaldoon *(Iq); 1978* *WSPL*

682 Dien Bien 3 *(Vn); 1975; (as Grenada)* *WSPL*

683 Bintang Harapan *(Ko); 1974* *WSPL*

684 Khatulistiwa *(Ia); 1980; (as Maju Terus)* *WSPL*

685 Spyros B *(Cy); 1970* *Norman Thomson*

686 Silver Feng *(Li); 1976* *Norman Thomson*

687 Aros *(Bs); 1985; (as Secil Congo)* *Norman Thomson*

688 Toro *(Cy); 1975; (as Sensei)* *John Freestone*

689 Pat *(SV); 1971; (as Patricia)* *Norman Thomson*

690 Cape Nelson *(SV); 1984; (as Nordstrand)* *Norman Thomson*

691 Novigrad *(SV); 1978* *Norman Thomson*

692 Futuro *(Pa); 1974; (as Drava)* *Norman Thomson*

693 Queen of Sheeba *(Et); 1966* *John Freestone*

694 Deneb *(DIS); 1981* *FotoFlite*

j003

695 Brigantium *(Po); 1976; (as Noruega)* *FotoFlite*

696 Salem Ten *(Eg); 1969; (as Alba)* *FotoFlite*

9 Dry Cargo Ships with Mixed Cargo Gear

9 Dry Cargo Ships with Mixed Cargo Gear

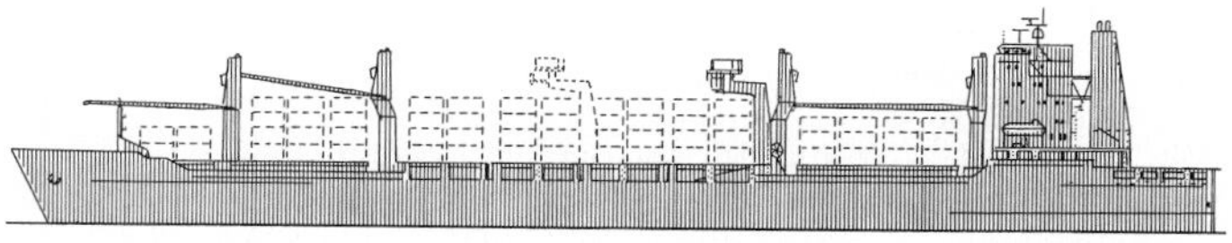

1 C^2KC^2MF *H12*
HOEGH DYKE Br/Fi (Wärtsilä) 1984; C/Con/V; 30,150 grt/41,600 dwt; 197.7 × 12 m *(648.62 × 39.37 ft)*; M (Sulzer); 16.5 kts; Gantry normally stowed by number 3 crane; 1656 TEU
Sister: **HOEGH DRAKE** (Br); Similar: **HOEGH DENE** (Br); **HOEGH DUKE** (Br) (Br built—Swan Hunter; machinery—B&W)

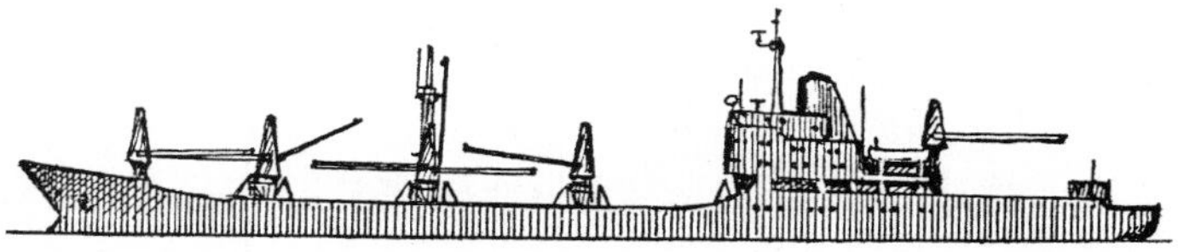

2 C^2TCMFC *H13*
ALEXANDER PEREDERIY Uk/Ru ('Zhdanov') 1968; C; 6,212 grt/8,260 dwt; 129.9 × 7.8 m *(426 × 25.7 ft)*; M (B&W); 16.5 kts; ex-*Pyatidyesyatiletiye Komsomola*; 'Kaliningrad' type

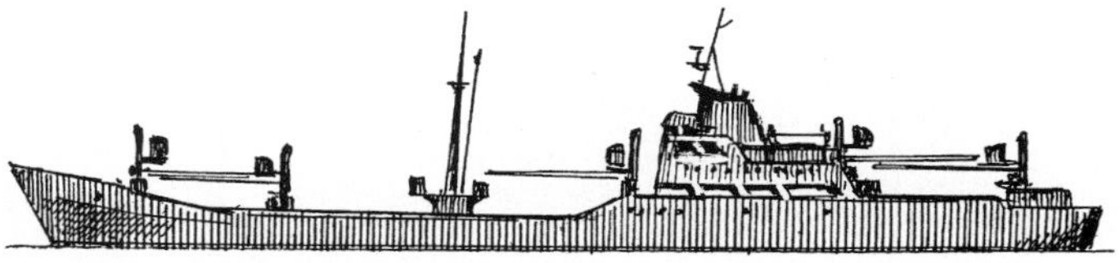

3 $C^2TCM\text{–}FC^2$ *H13*
SU CHENG RC/Br (H&W) 1961; C; 6,176 grt/7,601 dwt; 129.88 × 7.79 m *(426 × 25.56 ft)*; M (B&W); 16 kts; ex-*Bombala*
Sister: **YANG ZI JIANG 3** (RC) ex-*Bamora*

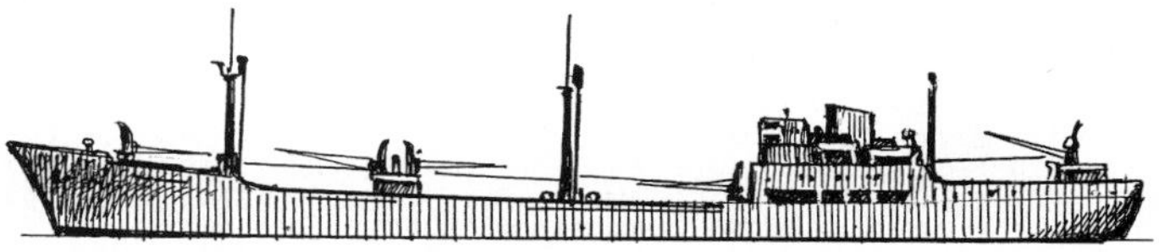

4 CTC^2TCFNC *H13*
LI SHUI RC/Ne ('De Noord') 1960; C; 6,115 grt/9,760 dwt; 151.13 × 7.99 m *(496 × 26.2 ft)*; M (Stork); 15.5 kts; ex-*Aludra*
Sister: **GUANGSHUI** (RC) ex-*Alchiba*

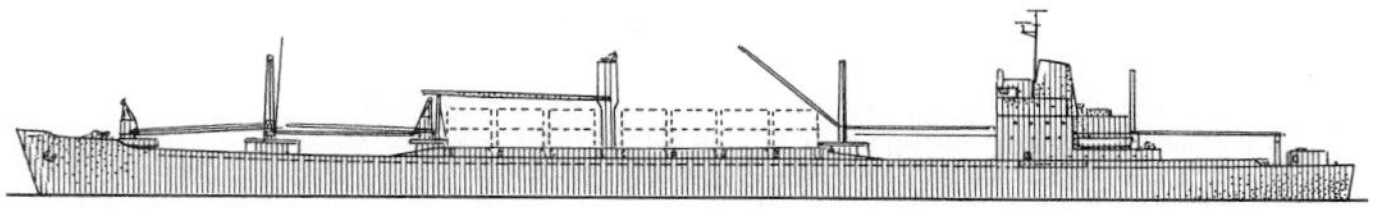

5 $CTC^2TM\text{–}FN$ *H1*
HAI HING Th/Br (Bartram) 1970/78; C/Con; 8,303 grt/14,572 dwt; 172.19 × 7.55 m *(564.93 × 24.77 ft)*; M (Sulzer); 16 kts; ex-*Saint Francois*; Modified 'SD 14' type converted from general cargo 1978 (Lisnave). 410 TEU

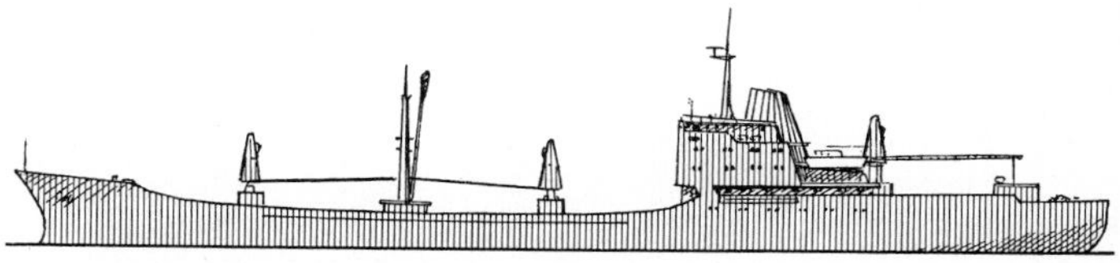

6 *CTCMFC H13*
'KALININGRAD' type —/Ru ('Zhdanov') 1969; C; 5,950 grt/8,290 dwt; 129 × 7.83 m *(426 × 25.69 ft)*; M (B&W); 16 kts; There are two types—the earlier ones having cranes by the foremast; some may have a mast on the Focsle
Sisters: **TAHSIN** (Le) ex-*Donetskiy Komsomolets*; **ASHA MANAN** (SV) ex-Donetskiy Khimik; **ASHA GLOBAL** (SV) ex-*Donetskiy Metallurg*; **DONETSKIY SHAKHTYOR** (Uk); **ASHAKRUPA** (SV) ex-*Komsomolets*; **BRYANSKIY MASHINOSTROITEL** (Uk); **KAPITAN PAAPKOV** (Uk) ex-*Leninskiy Iskry*; **KOMSOMOLETS ARMENII** (Uk); **KOMSOMOLETS AZERBAYDZHANA** (Uk); **KOMSOMOLETS MOLDAVII** (Uk); **KOMSOMOLETS ROSSII** (Uk); **KOMSOMOLETS ADZHARII** (Uk); **KAPITAN KISSA** (Uk) ex-*Komsomolets Byelorussii*; **MOSKOVSKIY KOMSOMOLETS** (Uk); **KAPITAN KLUNNIKOV** (Uk) ex-*Zhdanovskiy Komsomolets*; **GANG NAM** (RK) ex-*Krasnoyarskiy Komsomolets*; **KOMSOMOLETS SPASSKA** (Ru); **KOMSOMOLETS USSURIYSKA** (Ru); **KOMSOMOLETS VLADIVOSTOKA** (Ru); **KOMSOMOLETS KAZAKHSTANA** (Ru); **KOMSOMOLETS TURKMENII** (Ru); **RABOCHAYA SMENA** (Ru); **STARYY BOLSHEVIK** (Ru); **SALAJ** (Rm); **NASAUD** (Rm); Sisters (Eg built–Alexandria): **SALEM FIVE** (Eg) ex-*Ramses II*; **NEFERTITI** (Eg); **ISIS** (Eg); **AMOUN** (Eg); **THUTMOSE** (eg); **AHMOS** (eg); **IKHNATON** (Eg); **MEMPHIS** (eg); **15 MAY** (Eg)

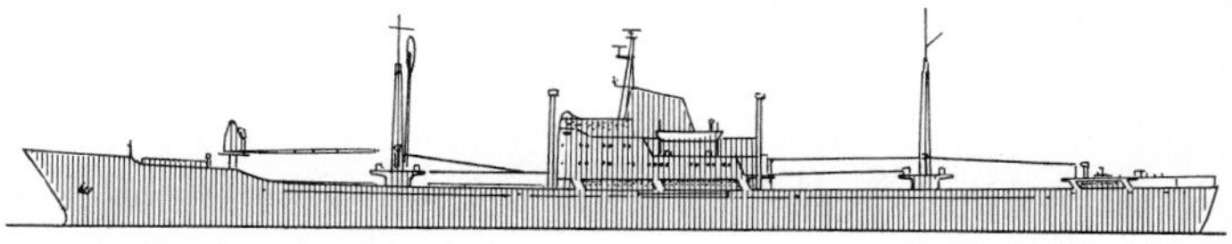

7 *CTNM–FNT H1*
FENG HANG RC/RC (Shanghai SY) 1975; C; 9,998 grt/14,770 dwt; 161.5 × 9 m *(530 × 30 ft)*; M (—); — kts; ex-*Feng Bao*; Cranes abreast mainmast
Sisters: **FENG JIN** (RC) ex-*Feng Lang*; **FENG GUANG** (RC); **FENG YUN** (RC) ex-*Feng Jin*; **FENG MAO** (RC); **FENG MING** (RC); **FENG ZHAN** (RC)
Note: some of these may have a crane aft

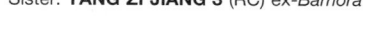

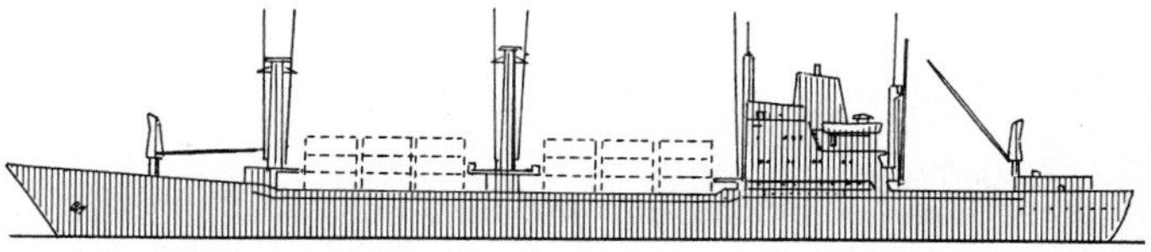

8 CT^2HFTC *H*
MARFRIO Li/De (Helsingor) 1970; C/Con/R; 8,080 grt/10,750 dwt; 136.61 × 9.32 m *(448 × 30.58 ft)*; M (B&W); 19.25 kts; ex-*Cap Melville*

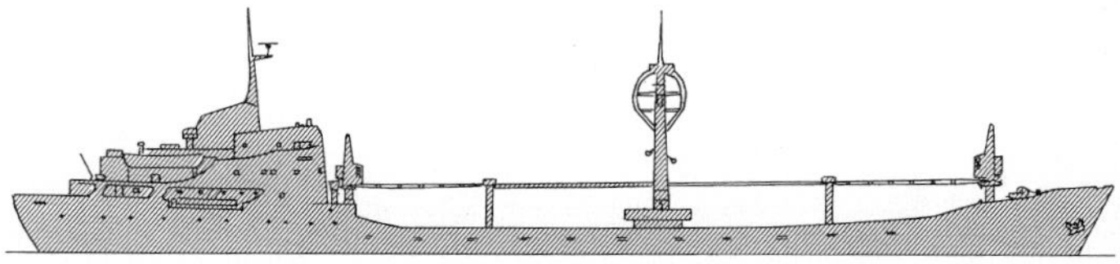

9 *CXCM–F H13*
SHAHER M Ma/Fi (Valmet) 1963; C; 2,714 grt/3,584 dwt; 102.32 × 5.91 m *(335.7 × 19.39 ft)*; M (B&W); 13 kts; ex-*Izhevskles*
Sisters: **MOUSTAFA S** (Sy) ex-*Inkurles*; **SEDA** (La) ex-*Irbitles*; **ALI M** (Sy) ex-*Ilmenles*; **AL-BASHAR** (Sy) ex-*Irtyshles*; **CLAIRE** (Bl) ex-*Izhorales*; **MAKKIA** (Sy) ex-*Istra*

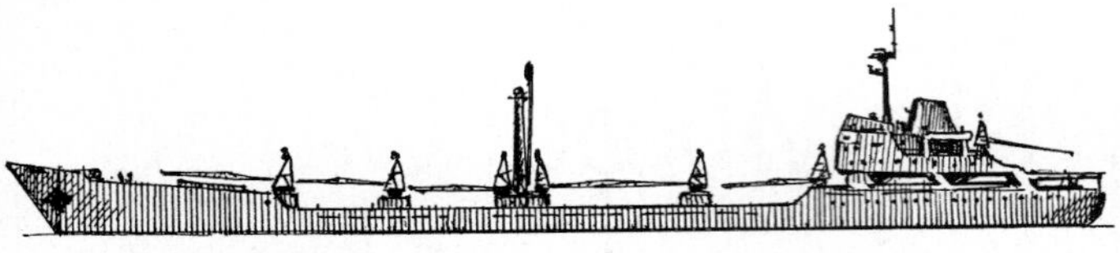

10 *D^{2}M–DD^{2}MFC H13*
DUBAI PIONEER Ma/Ru (Nosenko) 1962; C; 8,992 grt/13,940 dwt; 155.68 × 9.09 m *(510.76 × 29.82 ft)*; M (B&W); 15 kts; ex-*Podolsk*
Sisters: **HOA MAI** (Ho) ex-*Pavlovsk*; **PRIDNEPROVSK** (—); **HOA LU 2** (Vn) ex-*Berislav*; **BALASHIKHA** (Uk); Similar: **XIN TONG** (SV) ex-*Ady*; **HAI SHENG** (SV) ex-*Petofi*; **BAGHDAD** (Iq); **BABYLON** (Iq); **STEVE II** (Pa) ex-*Basrah*; **ALTAAWIN ALARABI** (Iq) ex-*Sindbad*; **XIANG HE** (SV) ex-*Al Salehiah*; **UMANG** (SV) ex-*Vishva Umang*

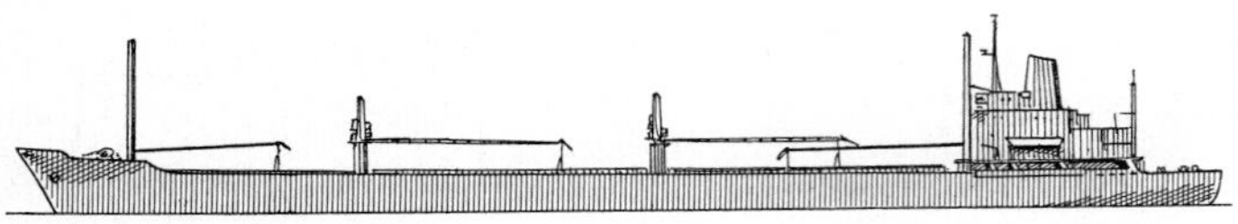

11 *HC^{2}HMFN H1*
DONA Li/Ja (Uruga HI) 1968; B; 15,674 grt/26,074 dwt; 162.01 × 10.61 m *(531.53 × 34.81 ft)*; M (Sulzer); 15 kts; ex-*Princess Aurora*
Sister: **RIO EXPRESS** (Li) ex-*Snow White*

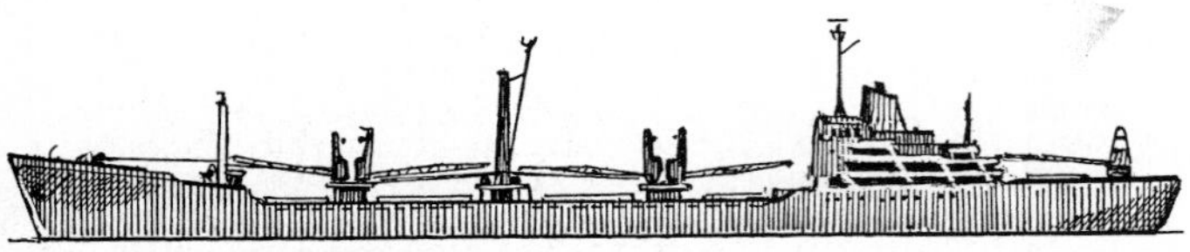

12 *HC^{2}NC^{2}MFMC H13*
HONG SHOU SHAN RC/Fr (La Ciotat) 1966; C; 10,427 grt/13,800 dwt; 158 × 9.5 m *(516 × 32 ft)*; M (Sulzer); 19 kts; ex-*Ango*
Sisters: **LIAN YUN SHAN** (RC) ex-*Dupleix*; **WU TAI SHAN** (RC) ex-*Forbin*

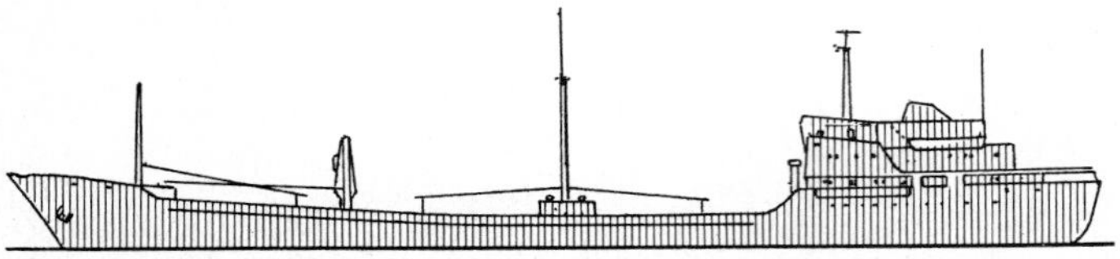

13 *HCHMFM H13*
BAO AN RC/Rm (Galatz) 1975; C; 3,578 grt/4,665 dwt; 106.13 × 7.1 m *(348 × 23.29 ft)*; M (Sulzer); 14.5 kts
Sisters: **DONG AN** (RC); **JIANG AN** (RC)

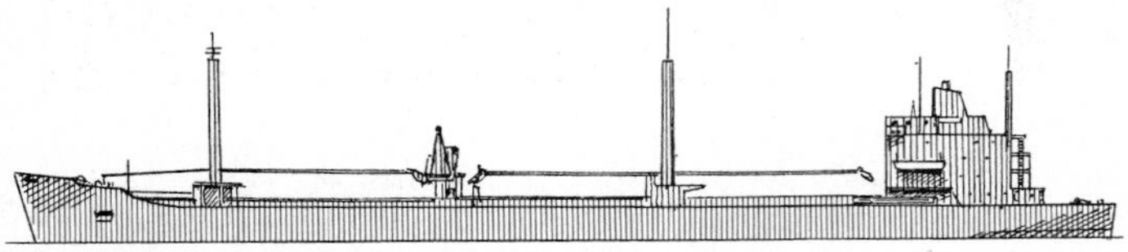

14 *HCHMFN H1*
LADY ANAIS Bs/Br (Upper Clyde) 1971; C/Con; 11,656 grt/18,623 dwt; 147.2 × 10 m *(482.93 × 32.81 ft)*; M (Sulzer); 18.75 kts; ex-*Sig Ragne*; 'CLYDE' class; 461 TEU
Sisters: **LADY BELLA** (Bs) ex-*Samjohn Governor*; **LADY CHARMAIN** (Bs) ex-*Samjohn Pioneer*

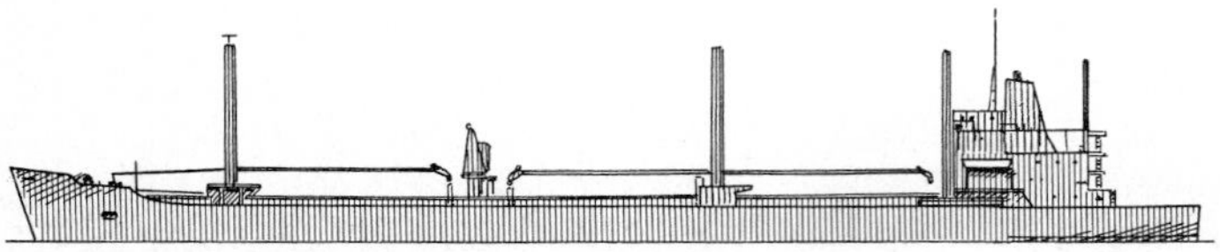

15 *HCHNMFN H1*
AFRICA STAR HK/Br (Upper Clyde) 1973; C; 11,484 grt/18,863 dwt; 147.2 × 10.02 m *(482.93 × 32.87 ft)*; M (Sulzer); 16 kts; ex-*Alisa*; 'CLYDE' class; 507 TEU
Sisters: **AFRO ASIA STAR** (HK) ex-*Hilla*; **OYSTER BAY** (HK) ex-*Orli*; **ASIA STAR** (HK) ex-*Varda*

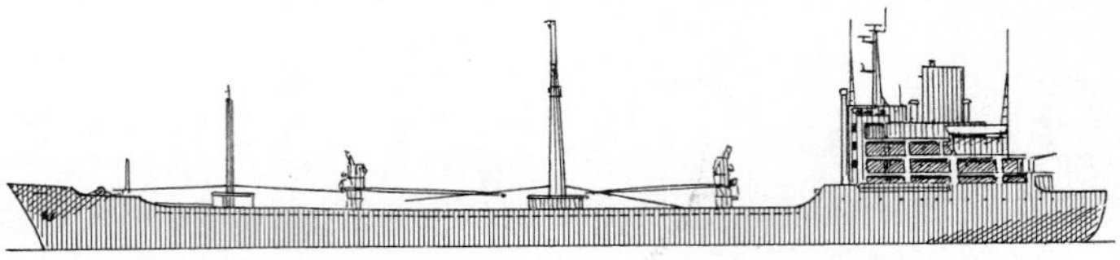

16 *HCNCNMFN H13*
CYCLOPUS K Ma/Ja (Hayashikane) 1973; C; 9,445 grt/13,602 dwt; 155.56 × 9.3 m *(510.36 × 30.51 ft)*; M (MAN); 16.75 kts; ex-*Shinkawa Maru*

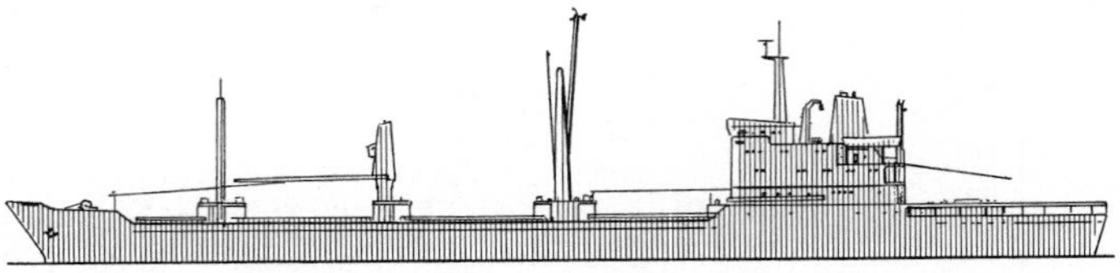

17 *HCNMFN H13*
EL OBEID Su/Ys ('3 Maj') 1979; C/Con; 9,691 grt/12,111 dwt; 149.41 × 8.77 m *(490 × 28.77 ft)*; M (B&W); 17 kts; 178 TEU
Sisters: **GEDAREF** (Su); **DONGOLA** (Cy); **MERAWI** (Cy); **DARFUR** (Cy)

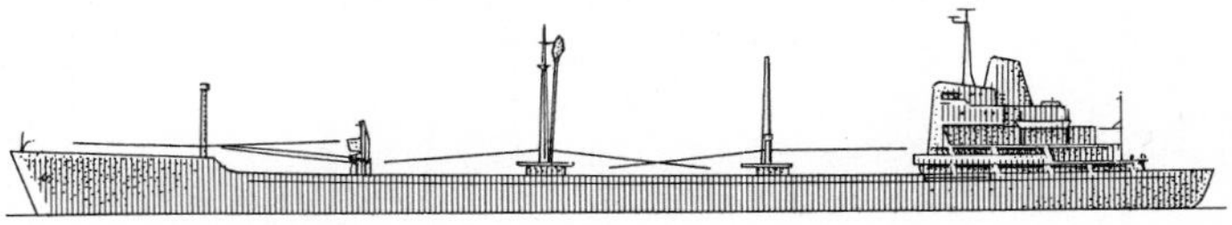

18 *HCT^{2}MFN H1*
KAPTAI Pk/FRG (A G 'Weser') 1967; C; 9,605 grt/13,120 dwt; 153.88 × 9.27 m *(504.86 × 30.41 ft)*; M (MAN); 14 kts

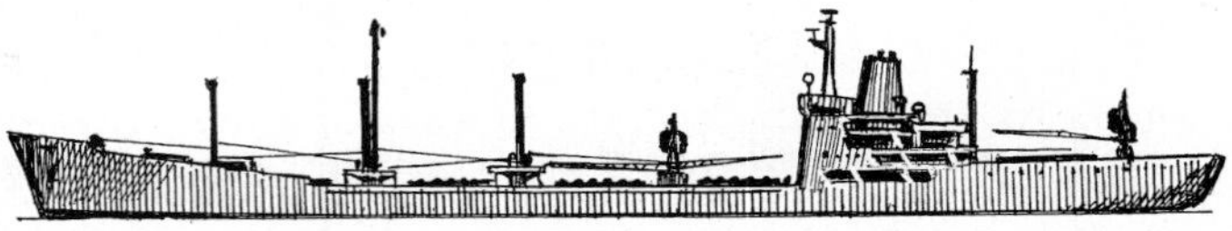

19 *H^{3}DMFNC H13*
MOWLAVI Ir/Ja (Mitsubishi) 1967; C; 10,463 grt/12,554 dwt; 166.02 × 9.00 m *(544.6 × 29.53 ft)*; M (Sulzer); 20.75 kts; ex-*Barcelona Maru*

20 *H^{4}FC H13*
SANTA ROSA DE LIMA Pe/Fr (La Ciotat) 1970; C; 10,742 grt/17,257 dwt; 171 × 7.7/9.7 m *(561 × 25.6/32 ft)*; M (Sulzer); 19 kts; ex-*Leonce Vieljeux*
Sisters: **SANTA RITA I** (Pe) ex-*Christian Vieljeux*; **CSAV TENO** (Pa) ex-*Patrick Vieljeux*; **UNITED** (Cy) ex-*Stephane Vieljeux*

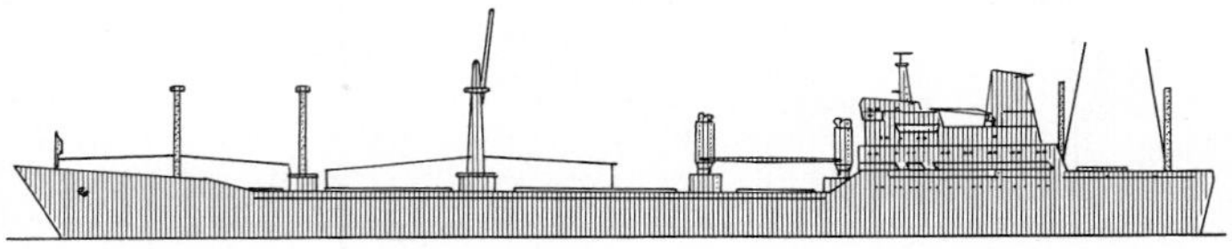

21 *H^{2}NC^{2}MFH^2 H13*
MAERSK NARA Ma/Pd (Gdanska) 1978; C/Con; 20,408 grt/21,648 dwt; 180.7 × 11.02 m *(592.85 × 36.15 ft)*; M (Sulzer); 17.25 kts; ex-*Ciudad de Armenia*; 356 TEU; 'B469' type; Stülcken derrick
Sisters: **DIANA** (Ma) ex-*Ciudad de Pasto*; **EASTERN TRADER** (Pa) ex-*Ciudad de Quito*

See photo number 9/200

22 *HJHM–G H1*
MICHELLE Ma/De (Svendborg) 1975; C/Con; 3,123 grt/4,240 dwt; 94.21 × 6.01 m *(309.09 × 19.72 ft)*; M (Alpha-Diesel); 13 kts; ex-*Amulet*; Travelling cranes; 150 TEU
Sisters: **AASTUN** (NIS) ex-*Talisman*; **IRAFOSS** (At) ex-*Charm*; **FETISH** (DIS); **MEDALLION** (DIS); **MAGIC** (DIS); **SCARAB** (DIS)

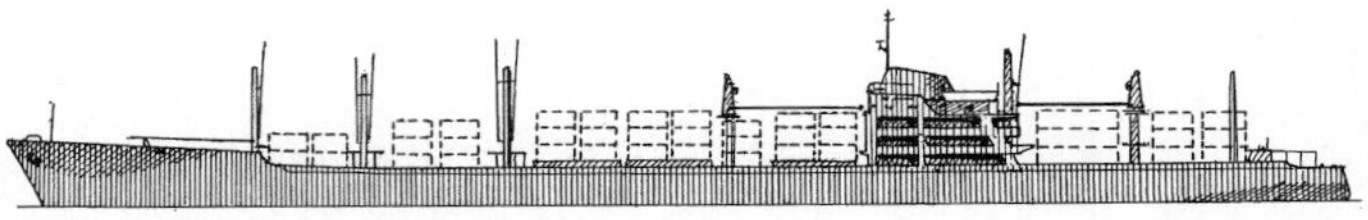

23 *HN^{2}CM–FNCN H1*
MAGALLANES US/US (Ingalls SB) 1965/76; C/Con; 14,081 grt/15,244 dwt; 203 × 9.5 m *(666 × 31.17 ft)*; T (GEC); 21 kts; ex-*Mormacargo*; Converted from cargo ship and lengthened 1976 (Todd); owned by US Government
Probable sisters: **CORPUS CHRISTI** (US) ex-*Mormaclynx*; **MALLORY LYKES** (US) ex-*Mormacrigel*; **ALLISON LYKES** (US) ex-*Mormacvega*

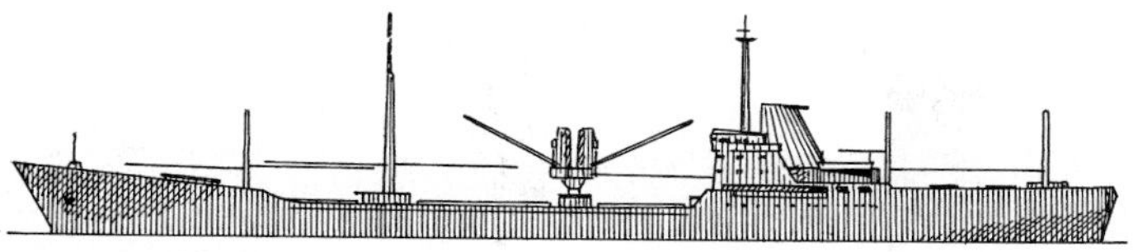

24 *HNPMFH^2 H13*
IONIAN SEA Bs/Pd (Gdanska) 1972; C/Con; 11,301 grt/12,193 dwt; 161 × 9.7 m *(528 × 30 ft)*; M (Sulzer); 20.5 kts; ex Ciudad de Manta; 'B434' type

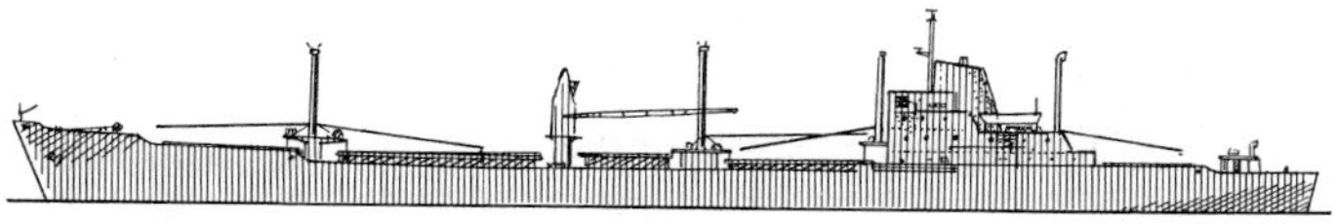

25 *HPN^{2}M–FN H1*
LITSA Cy/Bz (Maua) 1976; C; 9,079 grt/14,500 dwt; 140.98 × 8.82 m *(462.53 × 28.94 ft)*; M (MAN); 15 kts; ex-*Santa Teresa*; 'SD14' type (Modified)

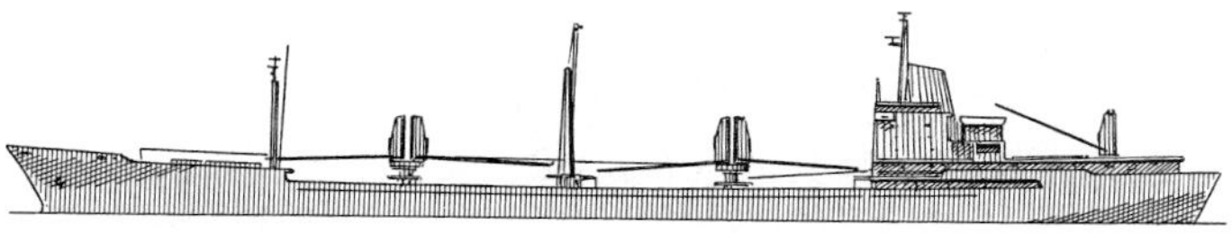

26 *HPNPM–FC H13*
FRATZESCOS M Ma/Fr (La Ciotat) 1972; C/Con; 13,657 grt/16,265 dwt; 171.2 × 9.71 m *(561.68 × 31.86 ft)*; M (Sulzer); 20 kts; ex-*Ville de Valence*; 208 TEU
Sister: **TAMARIN I** (Ma) ex-*Ville de Genes*

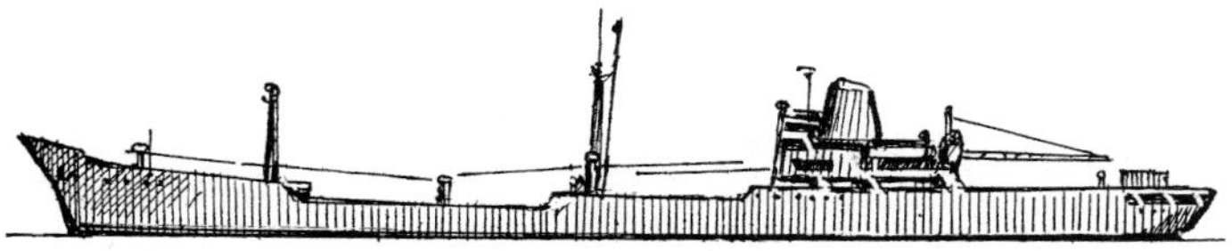

27 *HTFC H12*
MONTE ASHA Bh/Sp (Euskalduna) 1965; C; 8,275 grt/14,931 dwt; 145.93 × 9.58 m *(478.77 × 31.43 ft)*; M (MAN); 16 kts; ex-*Garciani*

28 *MC^{7}MFCM H13*
IRKUTSK Uk/DDR (Warnow) 1968; C; 8,521 grt/12,882 dwt; 151 × 8.8 m *(497 × 29.9 ft)*; M (MAN); 17 kts; Some may have aftermast removed—see drawing number 7/22
Sisters: **IZMAIL** (Uk); **IOKASTI** (Ma) ex-*Tula*; **SANTIAGO DE CUBA** (Ru) ex-*Ilovaysk*; **AKADEMIK IOSIF ORBELI** (Ru); **AKADEMIK SHUKHOV** (Ru); **ISMINI** (Ma) ex-*Akademik Yuryev*

29 *MC^{4}HMFN H13*
STORK Cy/Ja (Hakodate) 1970; B; 14,760 grt/26,765 dwt; 171.71 × 10.09 m *(563.00 × 33.10 ft)*; M (B&W); 15; ex-*Spray Cap*
Sisters: **SPYRIDOULA** (Ma) ex-*Spray Stan*

See photo number 9/194

30 *MC^{4}HMFN H13*
TAESCHORN Li/Ja (Sumitomo) 1971; B; 20,270 grt/34,867 dwt; 180.02 × 10.87 m *(591 × 35.66 ft)*; M (Sulzer); 15.25 kts; ex-*Bluesky*
Probable sisters: **TRADE AMBASSADOR** (Li) ex-*Grace Boeing*; **TRADE BANNER** (Li) ex-*Mozart Festival*; Similar: **HUA XI** (RC) ex-*Asia Falcon*

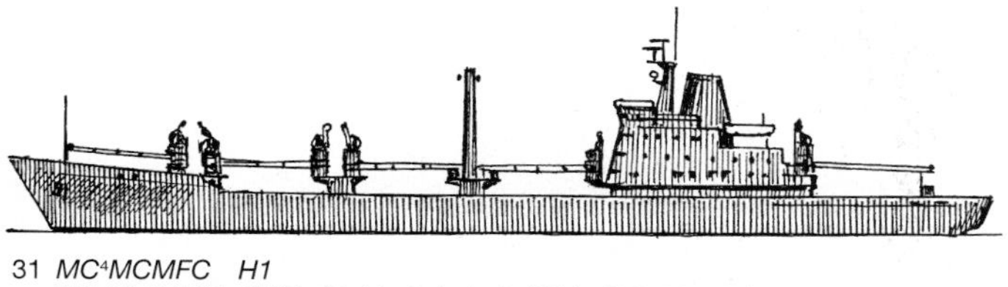

31 *MC^{4}MCMFC H1*
MAGDALENA SV/Br (Robb Caledon) 1971; C; 9,767 grt/13,488 dwt; 153 × 9.1 m *(502 × 30.9 ft)*; M (Doxford); 18 kts; ex-*City of Hull*

32 *MC^{4}M^{2}FM^2 H1*
KAPITAN A POLKOVSKIY Li/Ja (Hitachi) 1978; B; 15,563 grt/26,016 dwt; 172.88 × 9.73 m *(567 × 31.92 ft)*; M (Sulzer); 15 kts; ex-*Kopelia*

See photo number 9/193

33 *MC^{4}NMFN H1*
ALKMINI Ma/Ja (Osaka) 1970; B; 15,912 grt/26,739 dwt; 170.52 × 10.06 m *(559.45 × 33 ft)*; M (B&W); 15 kts; ex-*Maritime Brilliance*
Sisters: **ASTRA SKY** (Ma) ex-*Golden Lotus*; **MASTER NIKOS** (Ma) ex-*Golden Orchid*; **BLUENORTH** (Ma) ex-*Zenko Maru*; **APOLLON** (Cy) ex-*Bunko Maru*

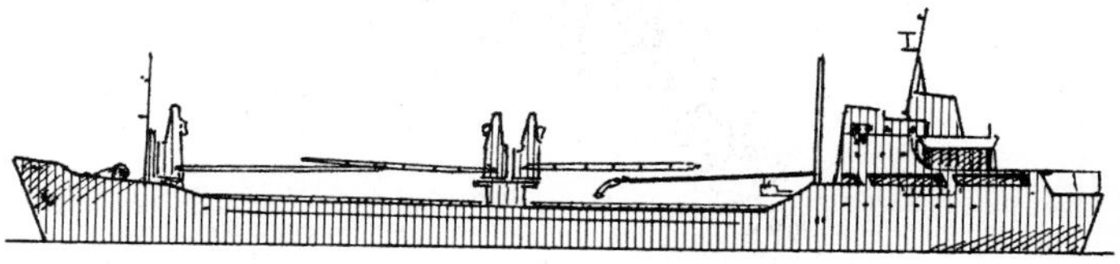

34 *MC^{3}HM–F H13*
SEA PRINCESS SV/Br (H Robb) 1967; C; 2,644 grt/2,391 dwt; 93.88 × 5.08 m *(308 × 16.66 ft)*; M (Mirrlees); 13 kts; ex-*Sorrento*
Sister: **GENIKI** (My) ex-*Salerno*

35 *MC^{3}MC^{5}MFNC H1*
OLGA I Ho/Ja (Hitachi) 1964; C; 10,842 grt/15,015 dwt; 154.77 × 9.59 m *(507.78 × 31.46 ft)*; M (B&W); 17.25 kts; ex-*Ola*

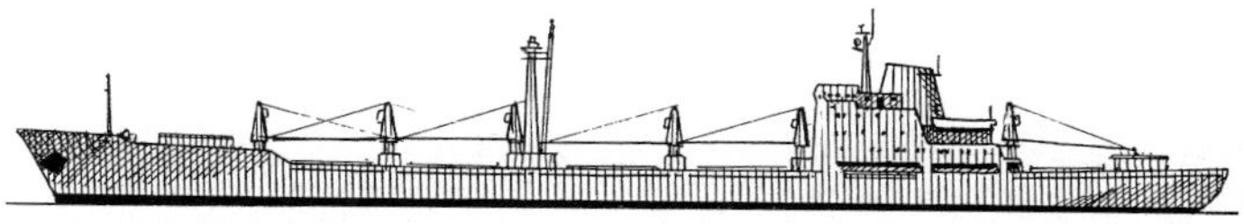

36 *MC^{3}MC^{2}MFC H1*
WON SAN RK/USSR ('Chernomorskiy') 1971; C; 11,347 grt/16,700 dwt; 169.86 × 10.06 m *(557.28 × 33.01 ft)*; M (B&W); kts; 18 ex-*Tropico*; 'FEODOSIYA' type
Similar: **NEGOTIATOR** (Cy) ex-*Monsoon*; **KAPITAN ALEKSEYEV** (Uk); **KAPITAN DZHURASHEVICH** (Uk); **KAPITAN KADETSKIY** (Uk); **KAPITAN KAMINSKIY**; **KAPITAN KUSHNARENKO** (Uk); **KAPITAN ANISTRATENKO** (Uk); **KAPITAN GEORGIY BAGLAY** (Uk); **KAPITAN LEONTIY BORISENKO** (Uk); **KAPITAN LEV SOLOVYEV** (Uk); **KAPITAN MODEST IVANOV** (Uk); **KAPITAN SLIPKO** (Uk)

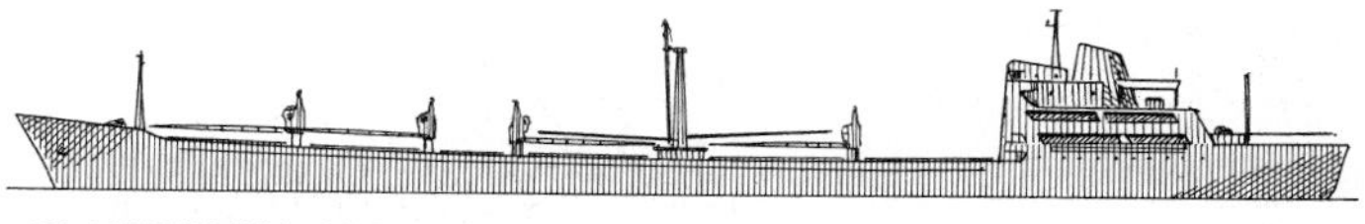

37 *MC^{3}TCMFN H13*
PREDEAL Rm/Br (Doxford & S) 1966; C; 10,838 grt/15,095 dwt; 162.46 × 9.38 m *(533 × 30.77 ft)*; M (B&W); 18.25 kts

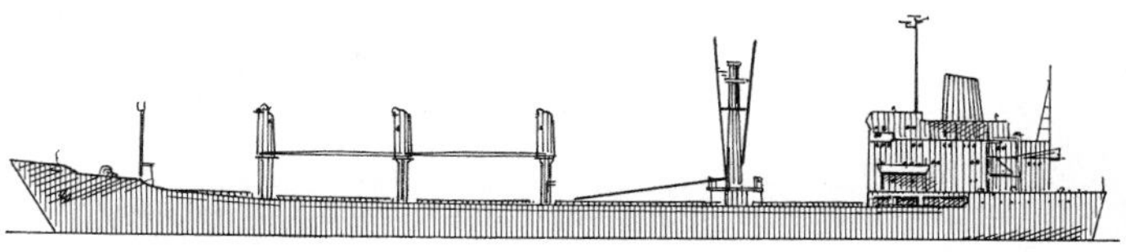

38 *MC^{3}TMFN H13*
LADY SHARON HK/FRG (Bremer V) 1976; C/Con; 10,415 grt/16,330 dwt; 150.66 × 9.35 m *(494.26 × 30.68 ft)*; M (MAN); 15 kts; ex-*City of Winchester*; 'Bremen Progess' type (Series A); 322 TEU
Sisters: **LADY JULIET** (HK) ex-*City of Canterbury*; **FELICITA** (Ma) ex-*City of York*

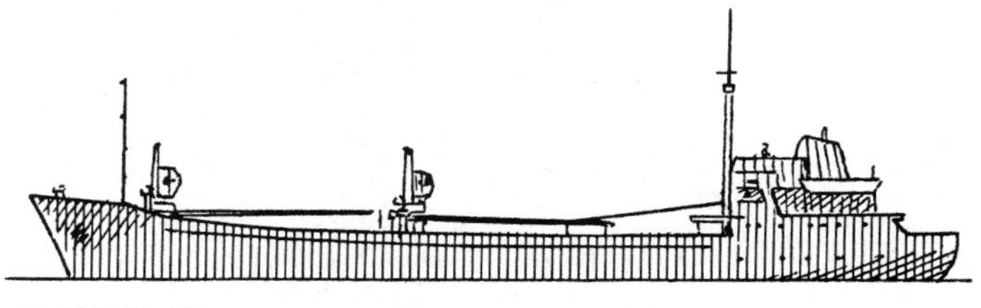

39 *MC^{2}HF H1*
SENTOSA My/Fi (Laiva) 1961; C; 997 grt/1,790 dwt; 73.21 × 5 m *(240.19 × 16.4 ft)*; M (Crossley); 11.5 kts; ex-*Vikla*

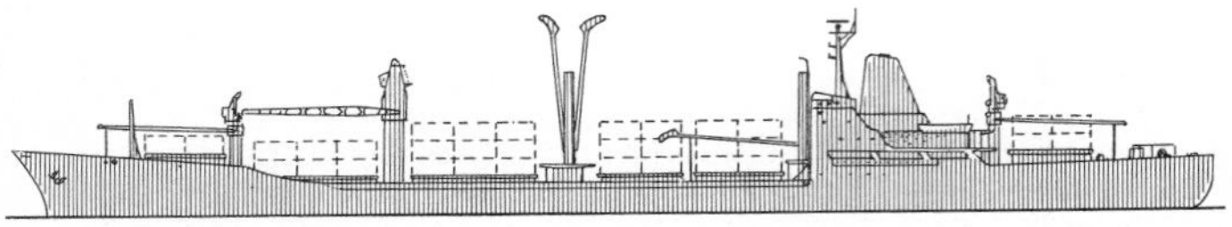

40 MC^2H^2MFC *H13*
ITAITE Bz/Bz (Ish. do Brazil) 1971/81; C/Con; 11,985 grt/14,042 dwt; 176.94 × 9.6 m *(581 × 31.5 ft)*; M (Sulzer); 20 kts; Converted from cargo and lengthened 1981 (Thyssen)
Sisters: **ITANAGE** (Bz); **ITAPE** (Bz); **ITAPAGE** (Bz); **ITAQUATIA** (Bz)

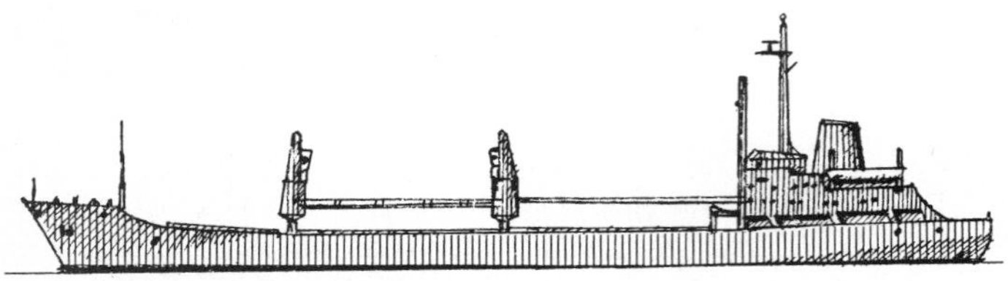

41 MC^2HMF *H1*
STRAITS STAR Ia/SA (Barens) 1969; C; 3,077 grt/4,572 dwt; 95.71 × 6.55 m *(314.01 × 21.49 ft)*; M (Sulzer); 11 kts; ex-*Tugela*
Sister: **ASIAN VENTURE** (Sg) ex-*Pongola*; Probable sister: **MERUBI** (Ho) ex-*Sezela*

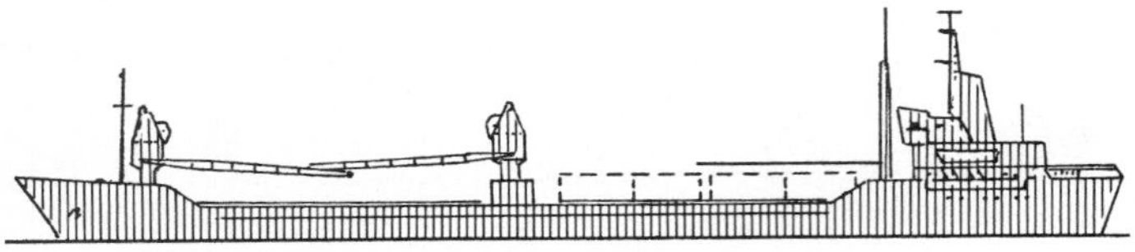

42 $MC^2HM\text{–}F$ *H13*
BODROG Hu/Pd (Gdanska) 1977; C; 2,191 grt/3,605 dwt; 93.53 × 5.58 m *(306.86 × 18.31 ft)*; M (GMT); 13 kts; 'B479' type
Sisters: **KOROS** (Hu); **SAJO** (Hu); **BANSKA BYSTRICA** (Sk)

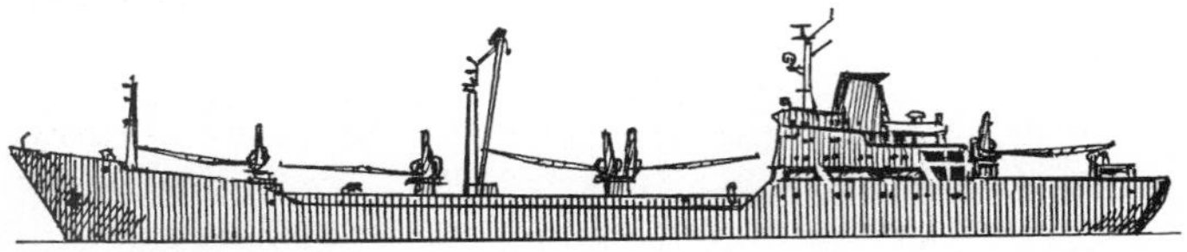

43 MC^2MC^2MFC *H13*
NOVGOROD Ru/Fi (Wärtsilä) 1967; C; 8,802 grt/13,650 dwt; 150.9 × 9 m *(495 × 29.5 ft)*; M (Sulzer); 18 kts; Heavy lift derrick is not normally fitted
Sisters: **NOVOSIBIRSK** (Ru); **NOVOKUZNETSK** (Ru); **NOVOKUYBYSHEVSK** (Ru); **NOVOMOSKOVSK** (Ru); **MITRO** (Ma) ex-*Novovyatsk*; **NOVOALTAYSK** (Ru); **NOVOMIRGOROD** (Ru); **NOVOPOLOTSK** (Ru); **NOVODRUZHESK** (Ru); **NOVOLVOVSK** (Ru); **NOVOZYBKOV** (Ru); **NOVOGRUDOK** (Ru); **NOVOVOLYNSK** (Ru)

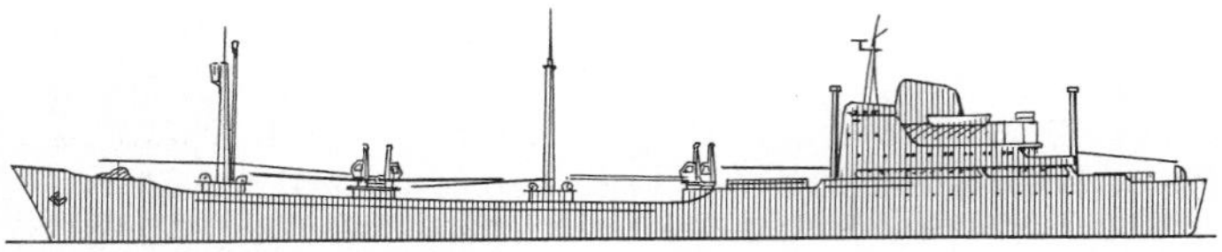

44 MC^2MC^2NMFN *H13*
TRUONG SON Vn/No (Kaldnes) 1960; C; 9,663 grt/12,000 dwt; 155.58 × 8.45 m *(510.43 × 27.72 ft)*; M (B&W); 19.5 kts; ex-*Tonsberg*

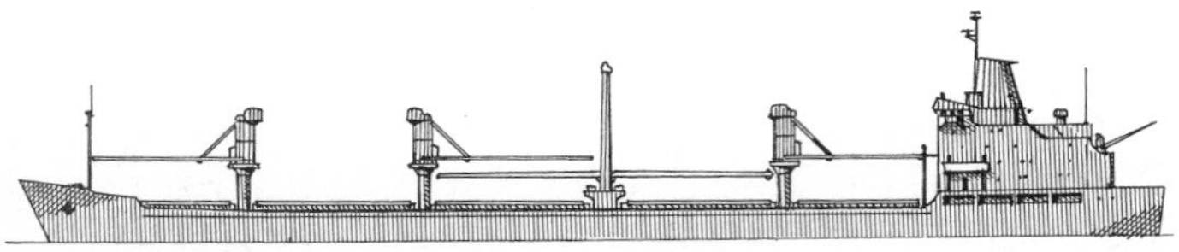

45 $MC^2MCM\text{–}FMC$ *H13*
COMET Gr/Sp (AESA) 1978; C/Con; 16,547 grt/24,300 dwt; 173.01 × 10.5 m *(567.62 × 34.45 ft)*; M (Pielstick); 17.5 kts; ex-*Ville de Brest*; Stülcken derrick amidships; 670 TEU
Sisters: **VAST JOLLITY** (HK) ex-*Ville de Reims*; **ACRITAS** (Bs) ex-*Ville de Rouen*

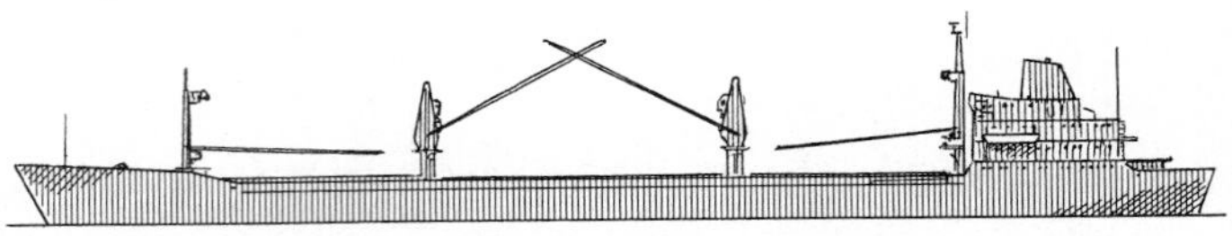

46 MC^2MFN *H12*
MAR CORAL Ve/FRG (Nobiskrug) 1972; C/Con; 6,266 grt/9,450 dwt; 142.73 × 7.68 m *(468.27 × 25.2 ft)*; M (Atlas-MaK); 16 kts; ex-*Fleethorn*; 264 TEU
Sister: **ZHE YAN** (RC) ex-*Sandhorn*

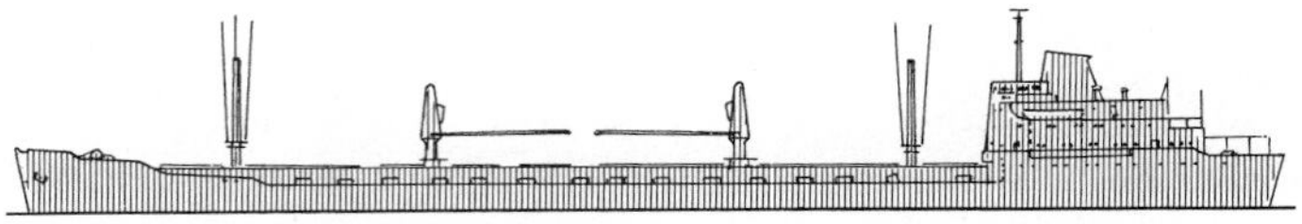

47 MC^2M^2F *H13*
XING LONG RC/Sw (Lindholmens) 1963; B; 11,470 grt/16,735 dwt; 152.53 × 9.1 m *(500 × 29.86 ft)*; M (Gotaverken); 13.5 kts; ex-*Matumba*

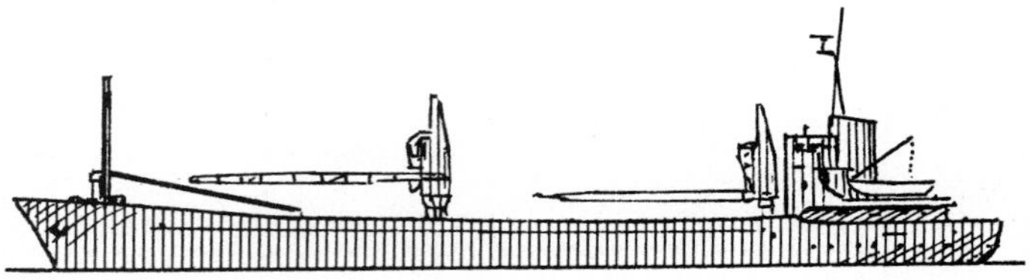

48 $MC^2M\text{–}F$ *H*
ALBARKA-3 Sy/FRG (Kroegerw) 1965; C; 499 grt/1,245 dwt; 72.07 × 3.71 m *(236.45 × 12.17 ft)*; M (Deutz); 12 kts; ex-*Fryken*

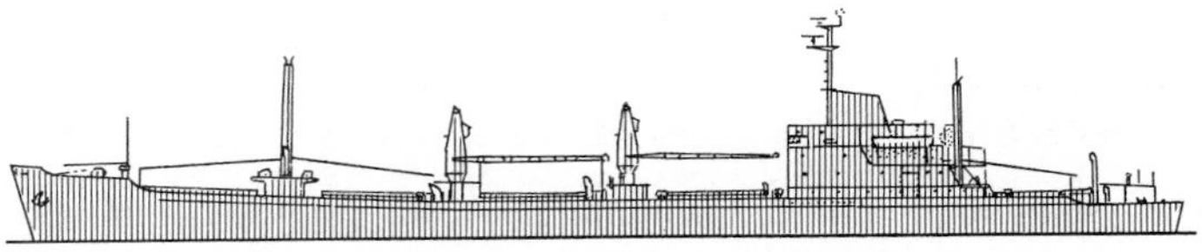

49 $MC^2M\text{–}FM$ *H1*
STELLA F Pa/Bz (CCN) 1981; C; 8,976 grt/14,854 dwt; 141 × 8.82 m *(463 × 28.94 ft)*; M (MAN); 15 kts; ex-*Lloyd Argentina*; 'SD14' (modified) type
Sisters: **ESPERANZA III** (Pa) ex-*Lloyd Mexico*; **ROSE** (Cy) ex-*Lux Rose* 1989; ex-*Lloyd Venezuela*; **ARISTOTELES** (Cy) ex-*Lloyd Houston*; **FU SHAN** (Pa) ex-*Renata*

50 MC^2NCMF *H13*
ALBA Rm/Rm (Galatz) 1977; C; 6,115 grt/8,400 dwt; 130.77 × 8.10 m *(429.04 × 26.57 ft)*; M (Deutz); 16 kts; ex-*Ludmila C*; Stülcken derrick; **SAME AS DRAWING NUMBER 7/175** but a Stücken derrick replaces third crane

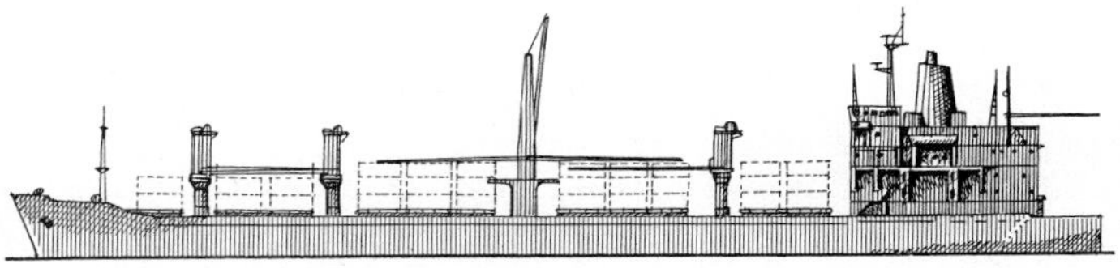

51 $MC^2NCNMFND$ *H1*
CSAV RAPEL Pa/Ja (Mitsubishi HI) 1977; C/Con; 17,379 grt/20,754 dwt; 163.02 × 10 m *(534.84 × 32.81 ft)*; M (Sulzer); 18 kts; ex-*Eiffel*; 620 TEU
Sisters: **CSAV RALUN** (NIS) ex-*Haussmann*; **CSAV RENAICO** (Bs) ex-*Mansart*; **LONDON BRIDGE** (Bs) ex-*Soufflot*

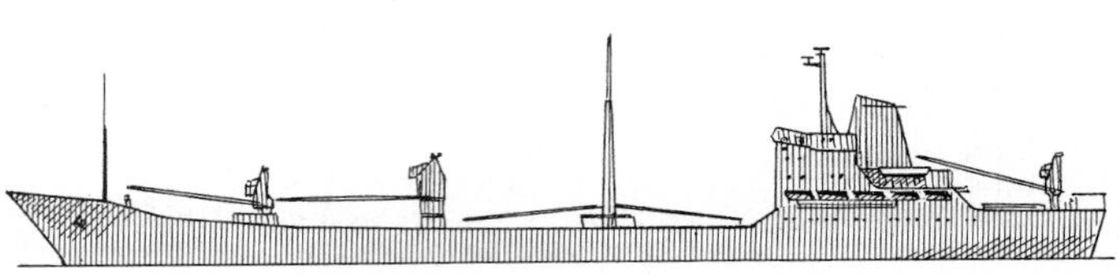

52 MC^2NMFC *H13*
FROTA MARABA Bz/Bz (Emaq) 1976; C; 7,777 grt/8,437 dwt; 142.02 × 7.67 m *(465.95 × 25.16 ft)*; M (Sulzer); 18 kts; ex-*Lloyd Maraba*; 94 TEU
Sister: **GUO CAI** (SV) ex-*Lloyd Cuiaba*

See photo number 9/188

53 *MC²NMFC H13*
RADZIONKOW Pd/Pd (Szczecinska) 1973; C; 5,916 grt/6,380 dwt; 124 × 7.3 m *(407 × 24.1 ft)*; M (Sulzer); 15.5 kts; 'B432' type
Sisters: **BOCHNIA** (Ma); **CHELM** (Ma); **GARWOLIN** (Pd); **OSTROLEKA** (Pd); **SIEMIATYCZE** (Ma); **WIELICZKA** (Ma); **TRANS CARGO III** (Eg); **AL HAMRAA** (Eg); **ASMAA** (Eg)
AL YARMOUK (Sy); **BARADA** (Sy)

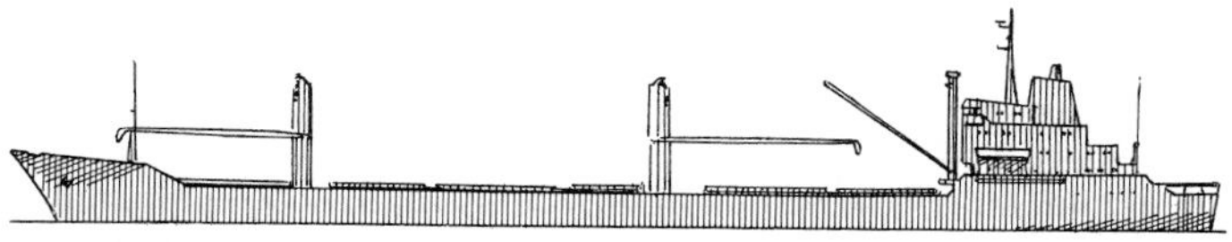

54 *MC²NMFN H12*
VIRA BHUM Sg/FRG (O&K) 1974; C/Con; 8,412 grt/12,470 dwt; 143.85 × 8.31 m *(471.99 × 27.26 ft)*; M (Pielstick); 16 kts; ex-*Tristan*; 422 TEU
Sister: **OOCL ARROW** (Li) ex-*Rienzi*; **TIGER SPEED** (Sg) Launched as *Senta*

55 *MC²TCMFCT H13*
SU YUAN RC/Sw (Lindholmens) 1964; C; 5,584 grt/7,609 dwt; 124 × 8.2 m *(407 × 26.9 ft)*; M (Gotaverken); 17 kts; ex-*Discoverer*
Sister: **WU CHANG** (RC) ex-*Novelist*

See photo number 9/179

56 *MC²UC³MFNC H13*
NATALIE Ru/DDR (Warnow) 1971; C; 9,323 grt/13,150 dwt; 151.5 × 9 m *(497 × 29.5 ft)*; M (MAN); 17 kts; ex Harry Pollitt; Some sisters vary in details. Some have small kingpost abaft funnel as indicated in drawing
Sisters: **VALERIAN KUIBYSHEV** (Ru); **WILLIAM FOSTER** (Ru); **ANATOLIY LUNACHARSKIY** (Ru); **BLUE OCEAN** (SV) ex-*Anna Ulyanova*; **CLIO** (Ma) ex-*Aleksandr Ulyanov*; **ILYA ULYANOV** (Ru); **NIKOLAY KRYLENKO** (Ru); **NIKOLAY POGODIN** (Ru); **NIKOLAY TULPIN** (Ru); **OLGA ULYANOVA** (Ru); **VLADIMIR ILICH** (Ru); **BORIS ZHEMCHUZIN** (Ru)

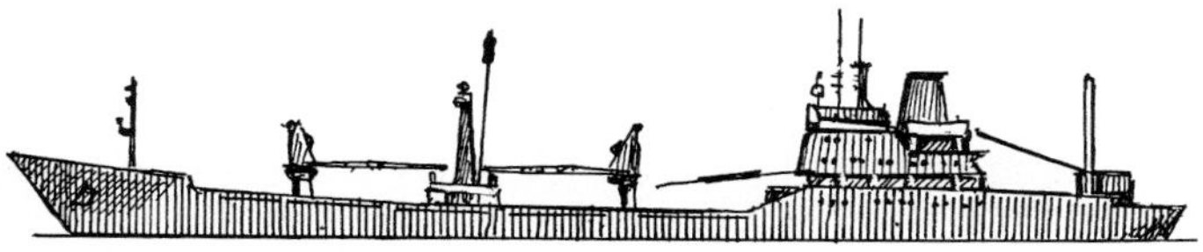

57 *MCHCMFH H12*
EMEL I Ea/Pd (Szczecinska) 1972; C; 6,876 grt/7,400 dwt; 135 × 7.5 m *(443 × 24.5 ft)*; M (Sulzer); 15.5 kts; ex-*Aleksandr Vinokurov*; 'B46' type
Sisters: **MAGIC K** (Ma) ex-*Aleksandra Artyukhina*; **AMBER II** (Ma) ex-*Andrey Andreyev*; **FEDOR PETROV** (Ru); **GLEB KRZHIZHANOVSKIY** (Uk); **VESLEO** (Bb) ex-*Iosif Dubrovinskiy*; **VALKLA** (Ea) ex-*Ivan Byelostotskiy*; **ORIS** (SV) ex-*Ivan Pokrovskiy*; **LEON POPOV** (Uk); **LYUDMILA STAL** (Ru); **MATVEY MURANOV** (Uk); **APOSTLE ANDREY** (Ma) ex-*Maksim Litvinov*; **MIKHAIL VLADIMIRSKY** (Ru); **MIKHAIL OLMINSKIY** (Ru); **NIKOLAY SEMASHKO** (Ru); **SOMPA** (Ea) ex-*Nikolay Shvernik*; **KUIVASTU** (Ea) ex-*Olga Varentsova*; **OSIP PYATNITSKIY** (Ru); **PANTELEYMON LEPESHINSKIY** (Ru); **SERGEY GUSEV** (Uk); **SUREN SPANDARYAN** (Uk); **PIHTLA** (Ea) ex-*Vera Lebedyeva*; **VIKTOR KURNATOVSKIY** (Uk); **VASILY SHELGUNOV** (Ru); **PARILA** (Ea) ex-*Pavel Dauge*; **YEMELYAN YAROSLAVSKIY** (Ru)

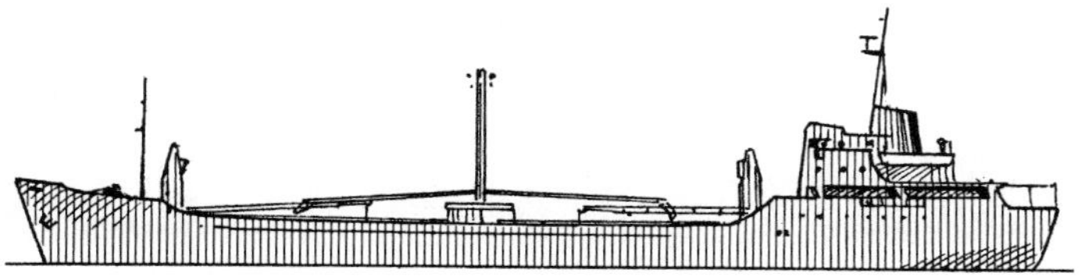

58 *MCHCM–F H13*
CAPTEN KHALED Sy/Br (H Robb) 1968; C; 2,583 grt/3,825 dwt; 93.88 × 5.08 m *(308 × 16.67 ft)*; M (Mirrlees); 13 kts; ex-*Silvio*
Sister: **MELINA II** (Ia) ex-*Sangro*

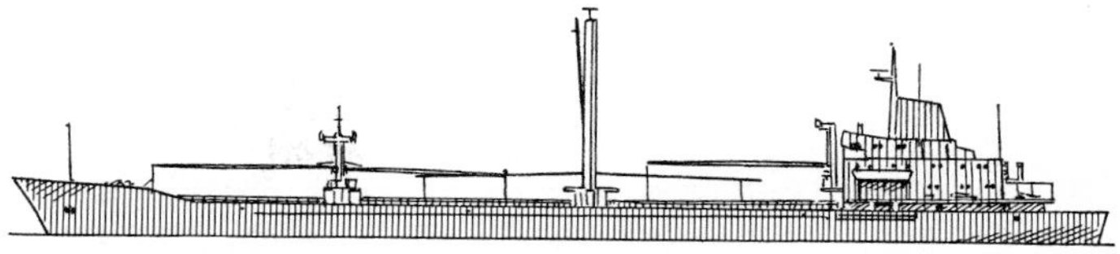

59 *MCHCM–FN H1*
JIN RUN RC/FRG (Nobiskrug) 1970; C; 5,034 grt/7,470 dwt; 125.02 × 7.64 m *(410.17 × 25.06 ft)*; M (Atlas-MaK); 17 kts; ex-*Cap Serrat*
Sisters: **JAK KONG** (SV) ex-*Cap Sunion*; **SHENG RONG** (RC) ex-*Cap Sidero*; **FEI YUE** (RC) ex-*Cap Saray*

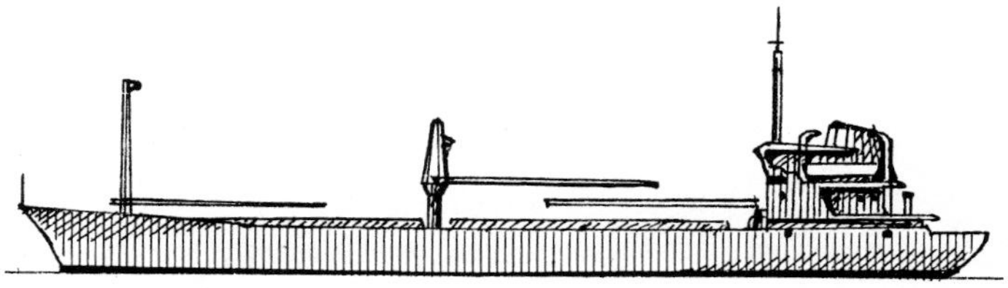

60 *MCHF H*
ADRA NIS/FRG (Luehring 1968; C; 1,956 grt/2,264 dwt; 83.9 × 4.61 m *(275.26 × 15.12 ft)*; M (Atlas-MaK); 12.5 kts; ex-*Sommen*; Lengthened 1973

61 *MCHF H*
FIRAS 1 Ho/No (Kristiansands) 1965; C; 397 grt/1,925 dwt; 72.73 × 4.61 m *(238.62 × 15.12 ft)*; M (Caterpillar); 12.75 kts; ex-*Bastant*

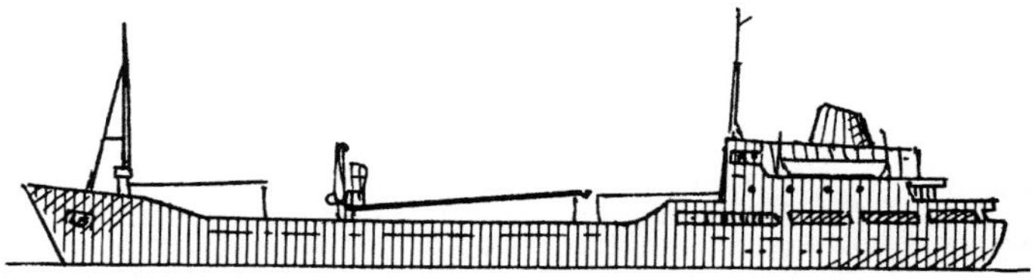

62 *MCHF H1*
ADMIRAL ONE Ca/No (Soviknes) 1965; C; 1,110 grt/1,311 dwt; 70.8 × 3.62 m *(232.28 × 11.8 ft)*; M (Deutz); 12.5 kts; ex-*Blikur*; Lengthened 1971

63 *MCHF H1*
CAPITAL BAY SV/Ko (Dong Hae) 1980; C/Con; 3,263 grt/4,950 dwt; 96.37 × 6.6 m *(316 × 21.65 ft)*; M (MWM); 15.75 kts; ex-*Sunny Christina*; 218 TEU
Sister: **PONTA DE SAGRES** (Po) ex-*Sunny Bettina*

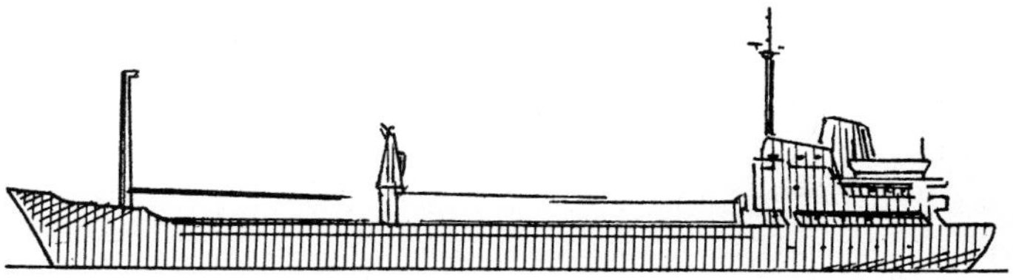

64 *MCHF H1*
ROSA PRIMA It/Ne ('Friesland') 1969; C; 1,564 grt/2,854 dwt; 77.65 × 5.83 m *(254.75 × 19.12 ft)*; M (Atlas-MaK); 12 kts; ex-*Mangen*
Sister: **LUNDENO** (SV) ex-*Unden*

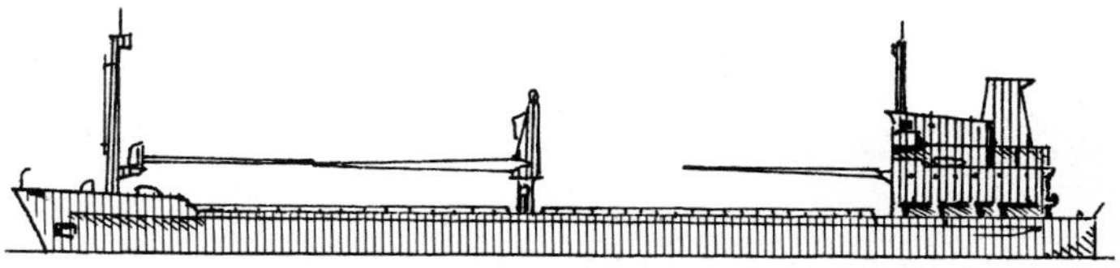

65 *MCHF H1*
SINGOLARITA It/Br (Swan Hunter) 1977; C/Con; 2,803 grt/4,156 dwt; 89.72 × 6.04 m *(294.36 × 19.82 ft)*; M (Alpha-Diesel); 12.5 kts; ex-*Singularity*; 122 TEU

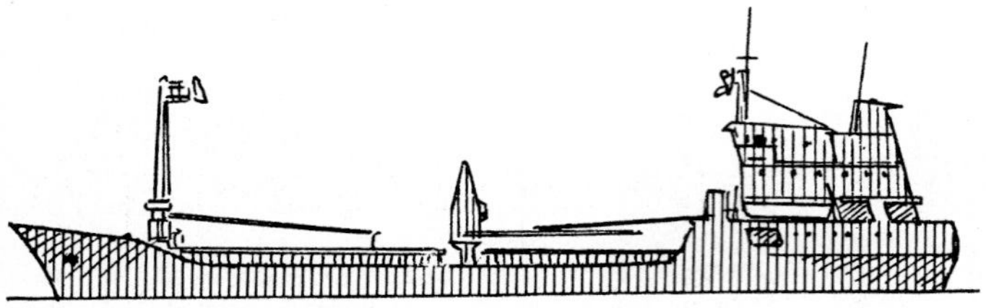

66 *MCHF H13*
COMBI TRADER Ne/De (Orskovs) 1975; C; 1,399 grt/2,807 dwt; 71.48 × 5.74 m *(234.51 × 18.83 ft)*; M (Atlas-MaK); 12 kts; ex-*Ocean Coast*; 64 TEU
Sisters: **CAPRICORN** (SV) ex-*Pacific Coast*; **YUSR** (UAE) ex-*Atlantic Coast*; Similar: **SAMIR** (SV) Launched as *Janne*; **INDIAN** (NIS) ex-*Indian Coast* (Lengthened 1979–Solvesborgs)

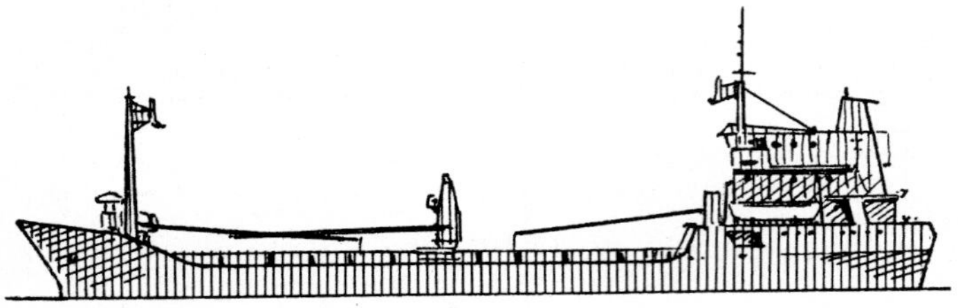

67 *MCHF H13*
UNIVERSE ADMIRAL —/De (Orskovs) 1973; C; 1,399 grt/2,666 dwt; 71.48 × 5.68 m *(234.51 × 18.63 ft)*; M (Alpha-Diesel); 12 kts; ex-*Lita Bewa*
Sister: **BEWA** (NIS) ex-*Karin Bewa*; Possible sister: **NIAGA XX** (Ia) ex-*Nina Bewa*

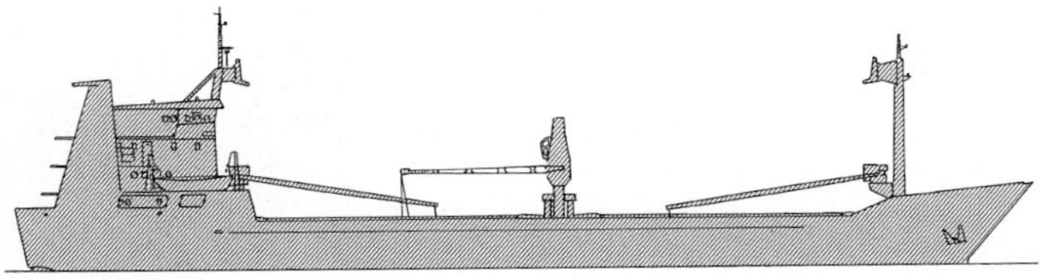

68 *MCHG H1*
APACHE Cy/De (Frederikshavn) 1974; C; 1,547 grt/3,099 dwt; 78.52 × 5.67 m *(257.61 × 18.6 ft)*; M (Alpha-Diesel); 13 kts; ex-*Mercandian Exporter*
Sisters: **BEHCET CANBAZ** (Tu) ex-*Mercandian Supplier*; **CHELIA** (Ag) ex-*Mercandian Agent*; **QIN HAI 108** (Pa) ex-*Mercandian Carrier*; **SANG THAI HONOR** (Th) ex-*Mercandian Transporter*; **EMELIE** (Pa) ex-*Mercandian Supplier*; **EUROPE 92** (It) ex-*Mercandian Shipper*

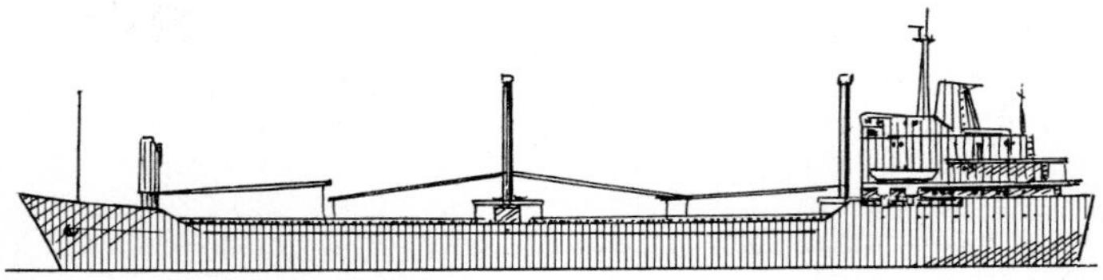

69 *MCH^{2}MF H13*
KWIDZYN Pd/Pd (Gdanska) 1974; C; 4,120 grt/3,891 dwt; 106.38 × 5.68 m *(349.02 × 18.64 ft)*; M (Sulzer); 14 kts; 'B472' type; 119 TEU
Sisters: **LEBORK** (Pd); **WEJHEROWO** (Pd)

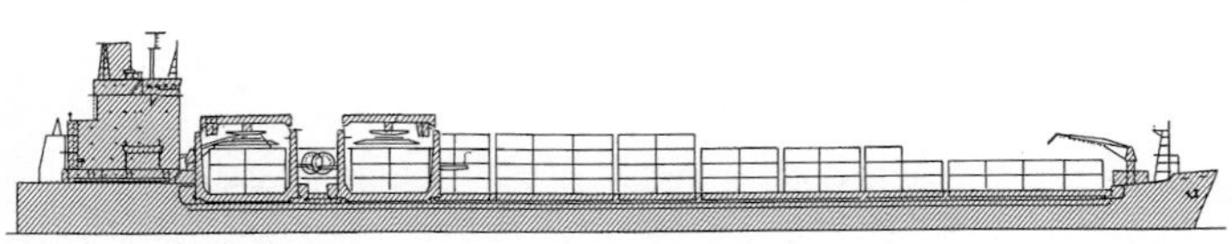

70 *MCK^{2}M^{2}F H13*
CITY OF ALBERNI Bb/Ja (Tsuneishi) 1985; C/Con/TC; 27,470 grt/39,260 dwt; 199.4 × 10.79 m *(654.2 × 35.4 ft)*; M (B&W); 15 kts; ex-*Belwood*; 1,692 TEU
Sister: **CITY OF NANAIMO** (Bb) ex-*Beltimber*
Probable sister: **CITY OF NEW WESTMINSTER** (Bb) ex-*Belforest*

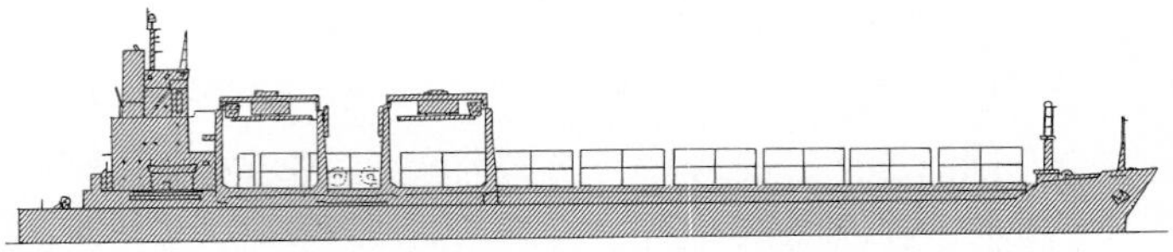

71 *MCK^{2}NHFS H1*
HOEGH MISTRAL Pa/Ja (Kurushima) 1986; C/Con/TC; 20,125 grt/30,402 dwt; 168.5 × 10.97 m *(552.82 × 35.99 ft)*; M (Sulzer); 15 kts; ex-*Texas Rainbow*; 1204 TEU
Probable sister: **NORTHERN DAWN** (Bs) ex-*New York Rainbow*

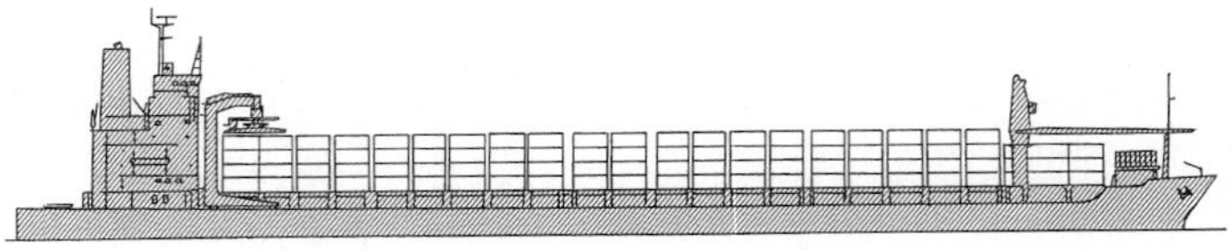

72 *MCKNMF H1*
STAR EVANGER NIS/Ja (Kawasaki) 1984; C/Con/TC; 30,163 grt/44,959 dwt; 211.21 × 11.52 m *(692.95 × 37.80 ft)*; M (B&W); 15.75 kts; ex-*Lily Star*; 2303 TEU

73 *MCMCHM–FC H13*
ELPIS Ma/Ca (Marine Indust) 1973; C/Con; 12,287 grt/17,110 dwt; 159.01 × 8.18 m *(521.68 × 26.83 ft)*; M (Pielstick); 18.5 kts; ex-*Cantal*; 'Marindus' type; 376 TEU
Sister: **MSC ANGELA** (Pa) ex-*Calvados*

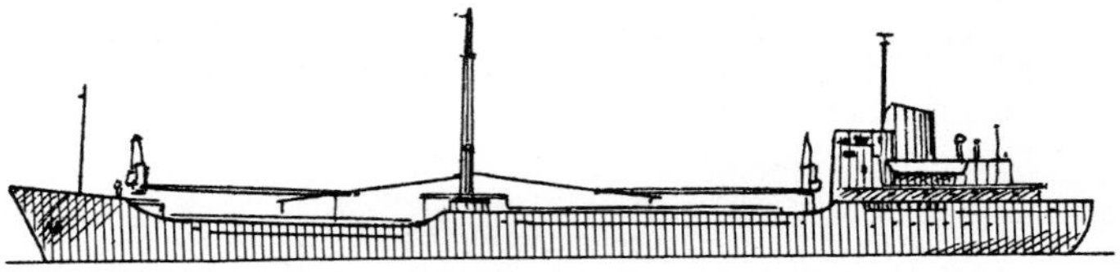

74 *MCMCM–F H123*
BIG STAR Sy/FRG (Kroegerw) 1960; C; 1,576 grt/2,489 dwt; 87.08 × 4.98 m *(285.7 × 16.34 ft)*; M (MaK); 12.5 kts; ex-*Indal*

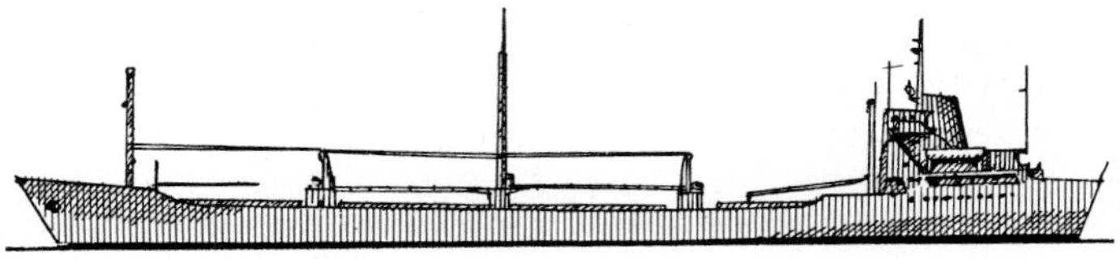

75 *MCMCNM–FN H13*
SALEM TWO Eg/Pd (Gdanska) 1968; C; 4,143 grt/6,705 dwt; 116.52 × 7.24 m *(382.28 × 23.75 ft)*; M (Mirrlees); 13.5 kts; ex-*Seahawk*; 'B448' type

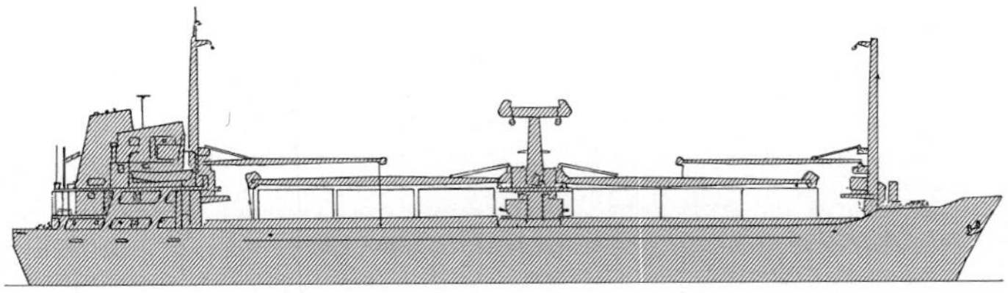

76 *MCMF H1*
KORIMU Pa/Ne (Nieuwe Noord) 1970; C; 1,918 grt/1,768 dwt; 80.73 × 4.14 m *(264.48 × 13.58 ft)*; M (British Polar); 13.5 kts; ex-*Supremity*; 68 TEU

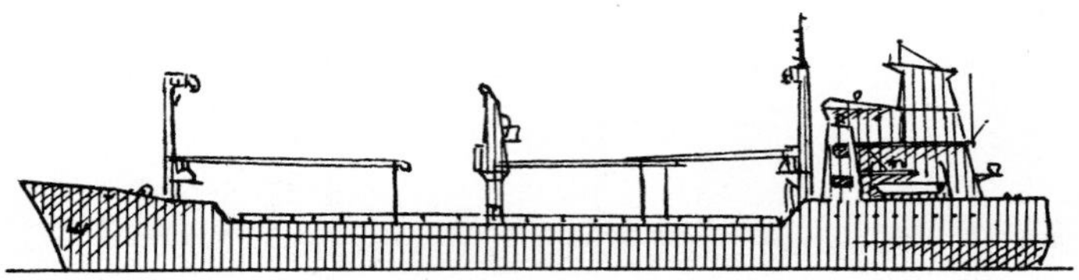

77 *MCMF H13*
MIRAH Ia/Ne ('Vooruitgang') 1973; C; 1,526 grt/2,968 dwt; 77.09 × 5.81 m *(252.92 × 19.06 ft)*; M (Atlas-MaK); 12.5 kts; ex-*Aerdenhout*
Sisters: **ARACHOVITIKA BAY** (Ma) ex-*Groesbeek*; **DIANA K** (Le) ex-*Wedlooper*

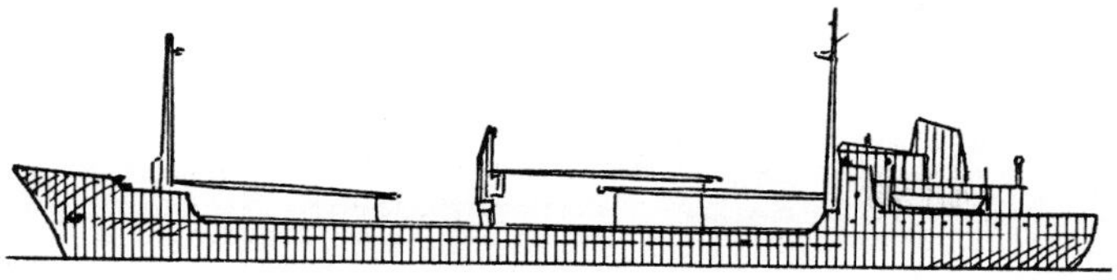

78 *MCMF H13*
PANTAI MAS Ia/Ne ('Vooruitgang') 1970; C; 1,548 grt/2,860 dwt; 78.75 × 5.84 m *(258.37 × 19.16 ft)*; M (Werkspoor); 12 kts; ex-*Hilvarenbeek*
Sister: **NIAGA XXXII** (Ia) ex-*Noordwal*

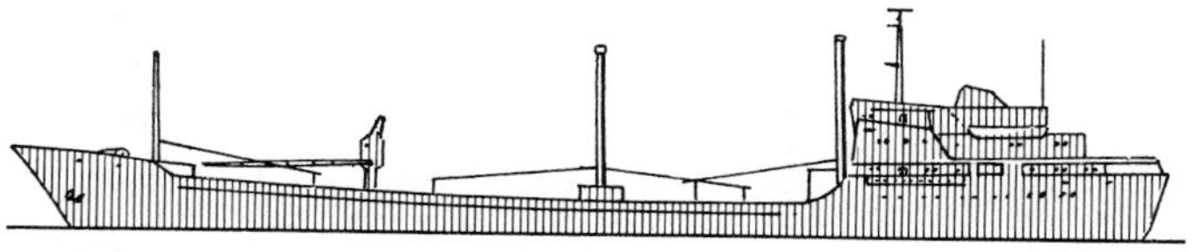

79 *MCM^{3}FM H13*
BEI AN RC/Rm (Galatz) 1974; C; 4,980 grt/7,771 dwt; 106.13 × 7.04 m *(348 × 23.1 ft)*; M (Sulzer); 14 kts

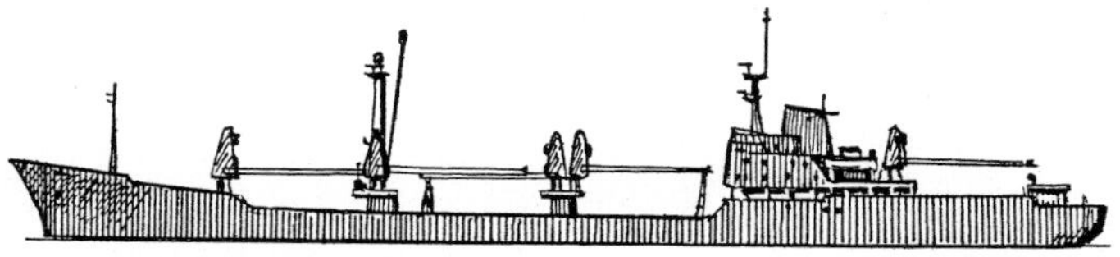

80 *MCM–DC^{2}MFC H13*
SOSNOGORSK Uk/USSR (Kherson) 1969; C; 8,874 grt/13,738 dwt; 153 × 9.1 m *(501 × 29.8 ft)*; M (B&W); 17 kts; Cranes abreast mast
Sisters: **SIDOR KOVPAK** (Ru); **SOKOL** (Uk); **KAPITAN PLAUSHEVSKIY** (Uk); **STOLETIYE PARIZHSKOY KOMMUNY** (Ru); **IVAN KOROBTSOV** (Ru); **GENERAL VLADIMIR ZAIMOV** (Bu); **VALERIY MEZHLAUK** (Uk); **VALENTIN KHUTORSKOY** (Ru); **KAPITAN LUKHMANOV** (Uk); **ALEKSANDR TSYURUPA** (Uk); **ANDREY LAVROV** (Ru); **KAPITAN SHANTSBERG** (Ru); **KLIM VOROSHILOV** (Uk); **KOMANDARM MATVEYEV** (Uk); **PROFESSOR BUZNIK** (Uk); **AKADEMIK YANGEL** (Uk)
Sisters (Cranes ahead of bridge may be abreast) (Eg built— Alexandria): **ISMAILIYA** (Uk); **PORT SAID** (Uk); **SUEZ** (Uk)

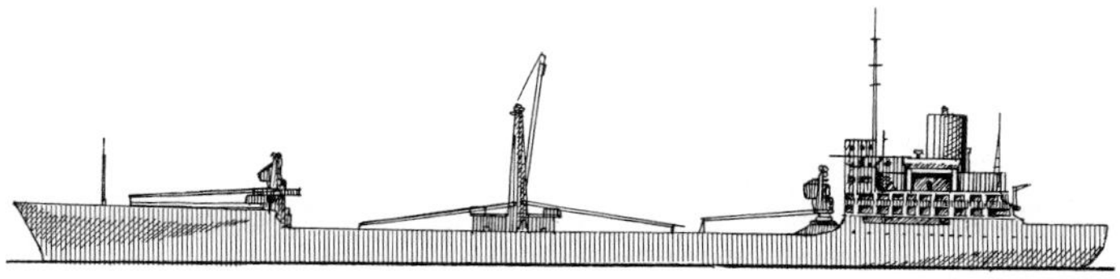

81 *MCNCHFN H13*
PIPOB SAMUT Th/Ja (Namura) 1970; C/HL; 9,916 grt/13,859 dwt; 156.55 × 9.02 m *(513.61 × 29.59 ft)*; M (B&W); 16.75 kts; ex-*Wakaume Maru*

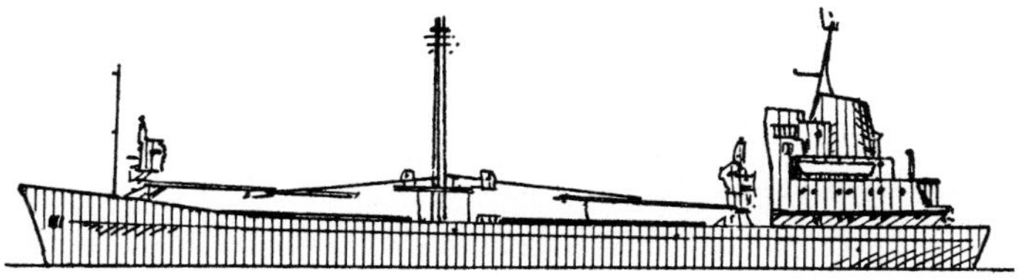

82 *MCNCM–F H1*
ARCTIC VIKING Ca/FRG (Kroegerw) 1967; C; 1,599 grt/2,073 dwt; 74.53 × 5.17 m *(244.52 × 16.96 ft)*; M (MWM); 14 kts; ex-*Baltic Viking*

83 *MCNJNCMF H1*
PRESIDENTE FREI Cu/FRG (LF-W) 1970; C/Con/HL; 10,932 grt/14,436 dwt; 153.27 × 10.12 m *(502.85 × 33.2 ft)*; M (MAN); 17 kts; ex-*Steinfels*; 528 TEU
Sisters (ships with 'MSC' prefix may have had some, or all, cargo gear removed): **MSC EMILIA 5** (Pa) ex-*Sternenfels*; **MSC FRANCESCA** (Pa) ex-*Stockenfels*; **FADEL ARAB** (Si) ex-*Strahlenfels*; **MSC ARIANE** (Pa) ex-*Goldenfels*; **MSC VALERIA** (Pa) ex-*Gutenfels*

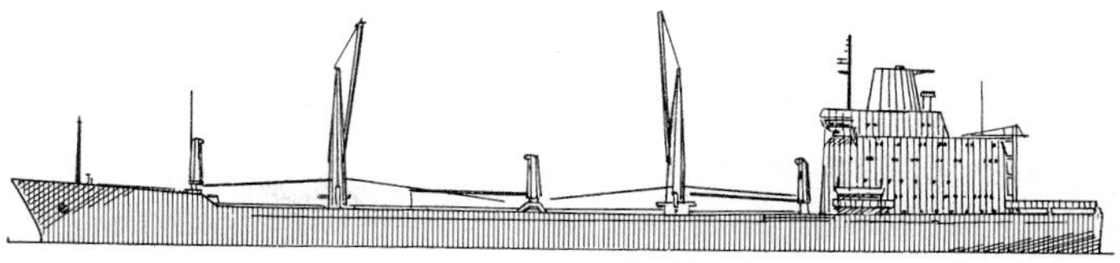

84 *MCNJNJMF H1*
ORANTUS Ma/FRG (LF-W) 1972; C/Con/HL; 11,506 grt/14,036 dwt; 153.24 × 10.07 m *(502.75 × 33.2 ft)*; M (MAN); 20 kts; ex-*Sturmfels*; 122 TEU

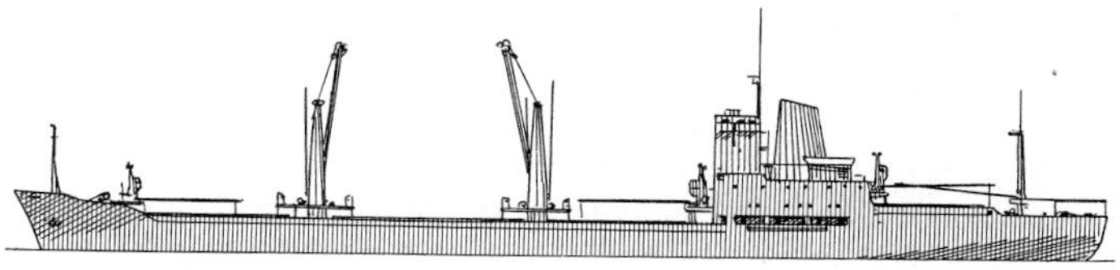

85 *MCN^{2}CMFCT H13*
CHRISTINA J Cy/Br (Doxford & S) 1972; C/HL; 10,219 grt/12,550 dwt; 162.01 × 9.36 m *(531.52 × 30.7 ft)*; M (Sulzer); 17 kts; ex-*Craftsman*

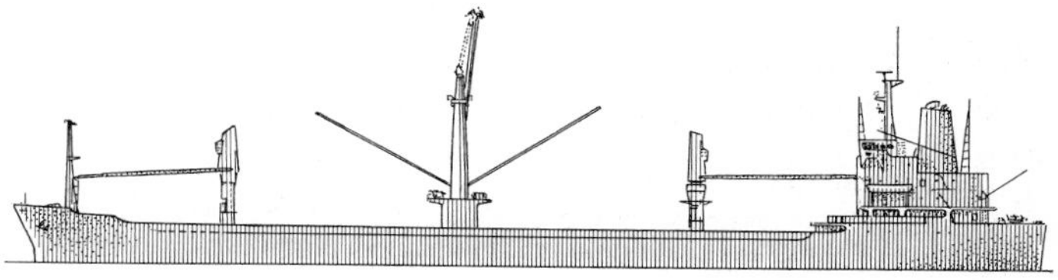

86 *MCNPNMFN H13*
ALTAI Li/Ja (Sanoyasu) 1979; C/Con/HL; 16,325 grt/23,284 dwt; 166.12 × 10.39 m *(545 × 34.09 ft)*; M (Sulzer); 16 kts; ex-*Altai Maru*; 664 TEU
Sister: **KILIMANJIRO** (Pa) ex-*Himalaya Maru*

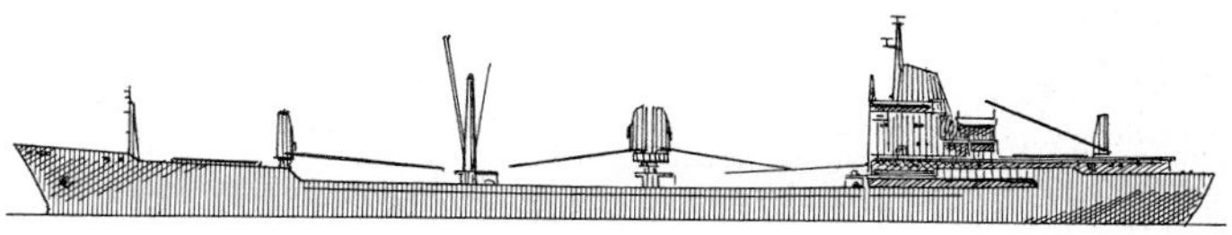

87 *MCNPNM–FC H13*
AMER SHANTI Cy/Fr (La Ciotat) 1974; C; 12,750 grt/16,570 dwt; 171.02 × 9.7 m *(561.08 × 31.82 ft)*; M (Sulzer); 16 kts; ex-*Ville de Marseille*; 236 TEU
Sister: **AMER SHAKTI** (Cy) ex-*Ville de Nantes*

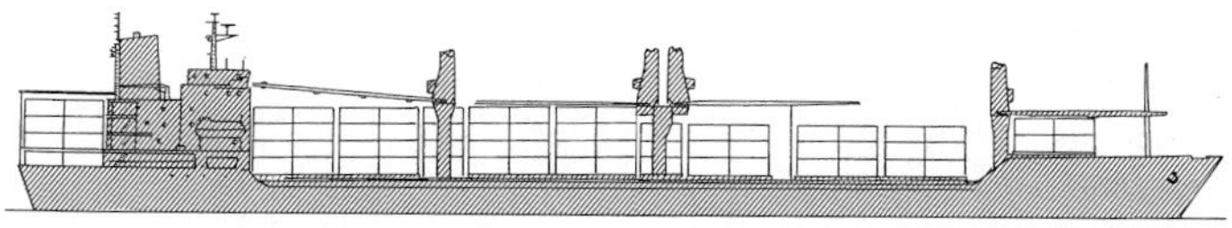

88 *MCPCMFM H13*
T A MARINER Li/DDR (Warnow) 1989; C/Con; 15,520 grt/20,377 dwt; 181.15 × 9.84 m *(594.32 × 32.28 ft)*; M (Sulzer); 16 kts; ex-*Octavia*; Lengthened 1989; 1,128 TEU; 'PASSAT' type; Mast aft is on starboard side
Sister: **T A ADVENTURER** (Li) ex-*Maria Oldendorff*
Sisters (unlengthened—165m (541ft)): **BRISA** (Ma) ex-*Ivangrad*; **AIRE F** (Ma) ex-*Obod*

89 *MCPNPMF H13*
BIBI Br/Ja (Hitachi) 1979; C/Con/HL; 17,128 grt/22,378 dwt; 178.26 × 10.41 m *(584.84 × 34.15 ft)*; M (B&W); 19 kts; 816 TEU
Sisters: **JALISCO** (Pa) ex-*Barbara Mariana*; **NACIONAL VITORIA** (Cy) ex-*Gina Luisa*; **MERIDA** (Cy) ex-*Silvia Sofia*

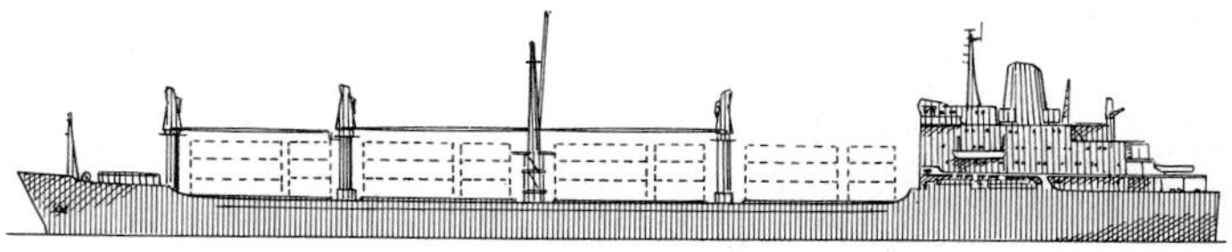

90 *MCPNPMFNC^2 H13*
KASSIAKOS Cy/Ja (Mitsui) 1977; C/Con; 16,872 grt/21,793 dwt; 165 × 10.48 m *(451.34 × 34.38 ft)*; M (B&W); 18.5 kts; ex-*Amerika*; 728 TEU
Sister: **JOHNNY TWO** (Cy) ex-*Nigeria*

91 *MCPNPNMFNR H1*
OLIVEBANK Pa/No (Kaldnes) 1977; C/Con/HL; 17,006 grt/24,270 dwt; 171.41 × 10.55 m *(562.4 × 34.61 ft)*; M (B&W); 18.25 kts; ex-*Nara*; 536 TEU
Sisters: **RICKMERS DALIAN** (Cy) ex-*Nausicaa*; **NOBLE STAR** (US) ex-*Concordia Star*; **B. PRUS** (Pd) ex-*Concordia Sun*

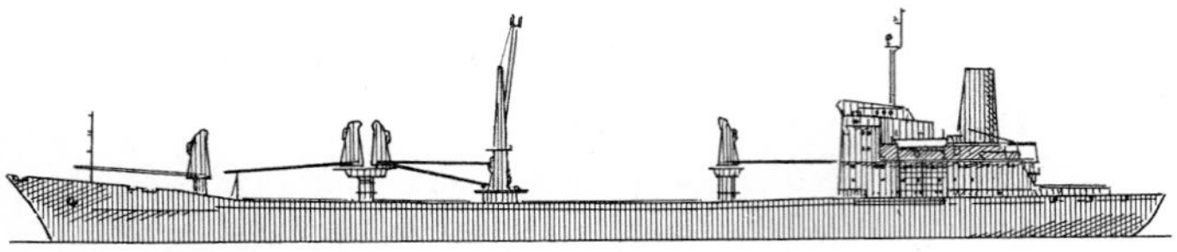

92 *MCPN–DPMF H1*
IVAN ZAGUBANSKI Bu/Ru (Kherson) 1975; C; 10,569 grt/13,480 dwt; 162.31 × 9.17 m *(532.51 × 30.09 ft)*; M (B&W); 18 kts; 'Dnepr' type; 388 TEU
Sisters: **CHRISTO BOTEV** (Bu); **GOTZE DELCHEV** (Bu); **LUBEN KARAVELOV** (Bu); **KAPITAN PETKO VOIVODA** (Bu); **VASIL LEVSKY** (Bu); **VALERIYA BARSOVA** (Uk) ex-*Athenian Anna*; **ALEKSANDR OGNIVTSEV** (Uk) ex-*Athina K*; **GRIGORIY PETRENKO** (Uk); **NIKITA MITCHENKO** (Uk); **PETR DUTOV** (Uk); **IVAN SHEPETKOV** (Uk); **IVAN MOSKALENKO** (Uk); **GEROI PANFILOVTSY** (Uk); **VASILIY KLOCHKOV** (Uk); **NIKOLAY ANANYEV** (Uk); **NIKOLAY MAKSIMOV** (Uk); **PETR YEMTSOV** (Uk): **YAKOV BONDARENKO** (Uk); **ALBEBARAN (Uk) (or ALDEBARAN)** ex-*Sovietskiye Profsoyuzy*; **ARAM KHACHATURYAN** (Uk); **BORIS BABOCHKIN** (Uk); **IVAN PEREVERZEV** (Uk); **ALKA** (SV) ex-*Admiral Purisic*; **JELSA** (SV) ex-*Heroj Paic*; **MARJAN I** (SV) ex-*Heroj Kosta Stamenkovic*; **OMIS** (SV) ex-*Heroj Senjanovic*; **RUNNER B** (Cy) ex-*Kapetan Pavlovic*; **BOL** (SV) ex-*Pristina*; **RIDER B** (Cy) ex-*Jugoagent*; **KALO** (Rm) ex-*Zalau*; **RILOS** (Ma) ex-*Jose A Echeverria*; **LURIC** (Ma) ex-*Julio Antonio Mella*; **KAPPARA** (Ma) ex-*30 De Noviembre*; **SIRENS** (Ma) ex-*XI Festival*; **SANDY PRIDE** (Cy) ex-*Antonio Guiteras*; **MULTIDIAMOND** (Cy) ex-*Ruben Martinez Villena*; **VOROSMARTY** (Hu); **ANTHONY** (Cy) ex-*Family Anthony*; **AGIOS IOANNIS** (Cy) ex-*Santa Elena*; **JOY D** (Cy) ex-*Laertes*; **BAO SHAN** (RC) ex-*Family Fotini*; **ELEFTHERIA K** (Pa) ex-*Lycaon*

93 *MCPN–DPMF–M H13*
KAPITAN TEMKIN Uk/Bu (G Dimitrov) 1985; C/Con; 12,174 grt/16,954 dwt; 158.88 × 9.96 m *(521.26 × 32.68 ft)*; M (B&W); 17.10 kts; ex-*Bacho Kiro*; 330 TEU
Sisters: **KAPITAN V OVODOVSKIY** (Uk); **LADY EMILY** (HK) ex-*Turid*; **CLELIA HF** (Gr); **WEALTHY STAR** (Pa) ex-*Varnita Tween*
The following were originally sisters but have been converted to container ships. Some, or all, cargo gear may have been removed: **PEYO YAVOROV** (Bu); **GEO MILEV** (Bu); **ALEKO KONSTANTINOV** (Bu)

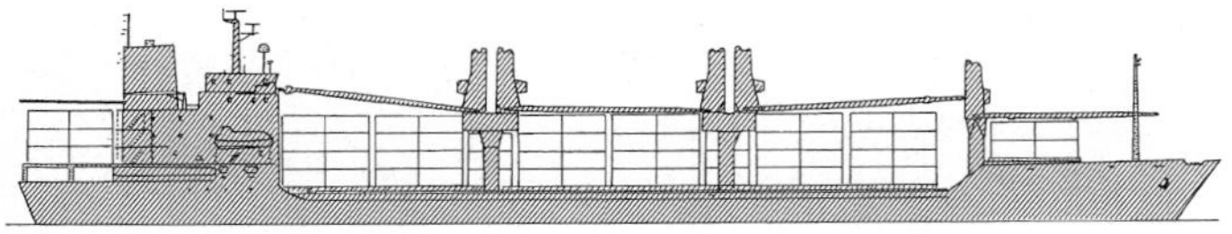

94 *MCP^{2}MF–M H13*
NORVIKEN Bs/DDR (Warnow) 1990; C/Con; 13,651 grt/18,145 dwt; 165.5 × 10.07 m *(542.98 × 33.04 ft)*; M (Sulzer); 15.9 kts; ex-*Moraca*; 670 TEU; 'PASSAT' type
Sister: **TORM AMERICA** (SV) ex-*Vardar*
Probable sisters: **MAYOR** (Gr) ex-*Vodice*; **THRAKI HELLAS** (Gr) ex-*Boka*; **TORM BIRGITTE** (Bs) ex-*Jezera*; **RAMA** (Cy) ex-*Kupres*

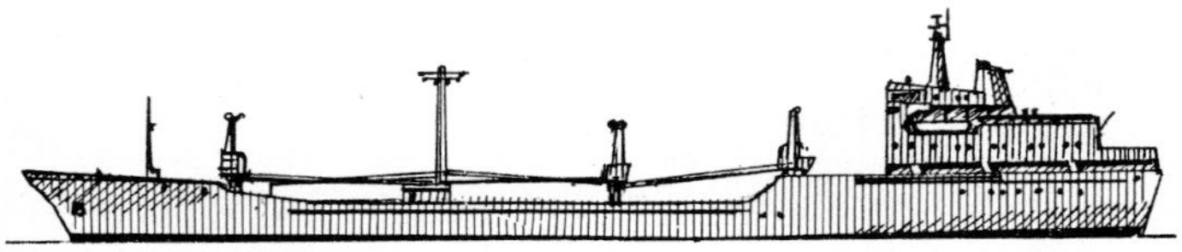

95 *MCTC^{2}MF H13*
HENG LONG RC/FRG (Meyer) 1968; C/Con; 4,797 grt/6,775 dwt; 119.97 × 7.6 m *(393.6 × 24.93 ft)*; M (Deutz); 15 kts; ex-*Madeleine*; 148 TEU
Sister: **QIAN TANG JIANG** (RC) ex-*Madeleine*

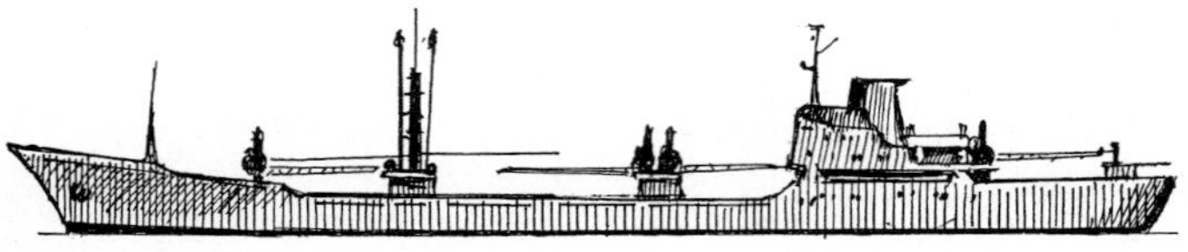

96 *MCTC^{2}MFC H13*
KRASNOKAMSK Ru/Fi (Wärtsilä) 1964; C; 8,540 grt/12,844 dwt; 147 × 9.1 m *(482 × 30 ft)*; M (Sulzer); 17.5 kts
Sister: **KOMSOMOLETS LITVY** (Ru)

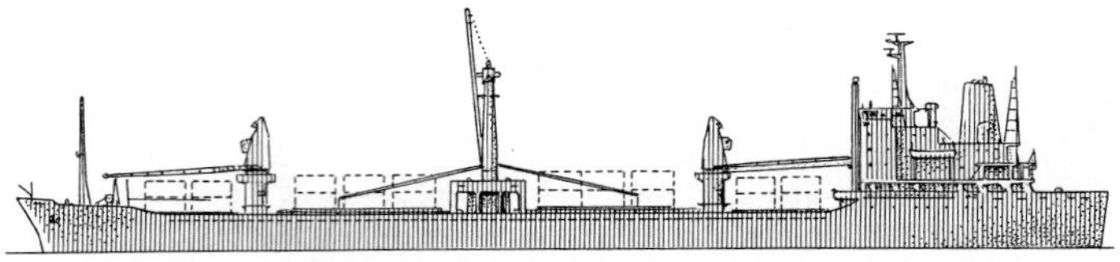

97 *MCTCN^{2}MFN H13*
YOUNG SPORTSMAN Pa/Ja (Onomichi) 1979; C; 12,666 grt/17,884 dwt; 156.53 × 9.1 m *(513.55 × 29.86 ft)*; M (Sulzer); 17.8 kts; ex-*Van Ocean*
Possible sister: **KAPTAN CEBI** (Tu) ex-*Van Enterprise*

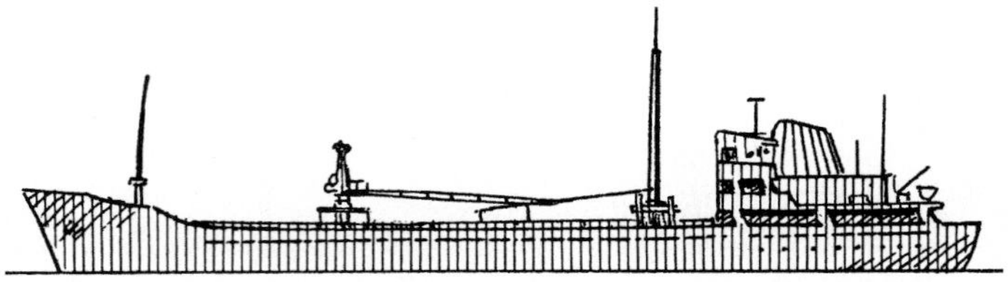

98 *MCTFM H1*
TROPICAL SEA Pa/Ne (E J Smit) 1965; C; 981 grt/1,043 dwt; 71.99 × 3.82 m *(236.18 × 12.53 ft)*; M (MAN); 12.75 kts; ex-*Zeeburgh*

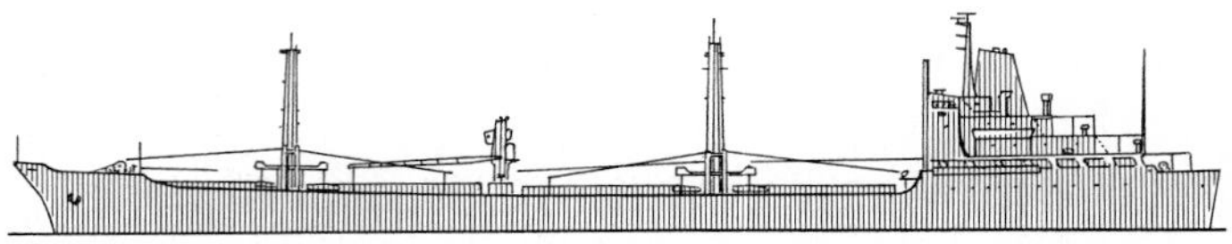

99 *MCTHMFN H13*
FALCON CARRIER Li/Ja (Mitsubishi HI) 1975; C; 13,915 grt/21,367 dwt; 162.1 × 10.6 m *(532 × 34.78 ft)*; M (Sulzer); 15 kts; ex-*Maritime Carrier*
Similar: **MARNI** (Ma) ex-*Atlantic Albatross*

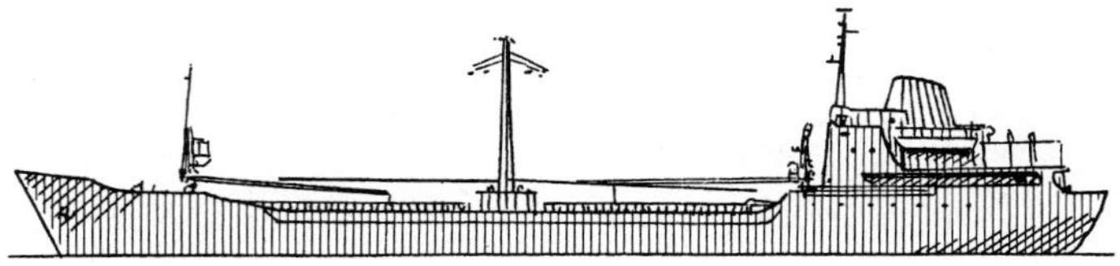

100 *MCVCMF H13*
ALDABRA SV/Sw (Finnboda) 1964; C; 2,763 grt/3,134 dwt; 93.81 × 5.76 m *(307.77 × 18.9 ft)*; M (Fiat); 13.5 kts; ex-*Gondul*
Similar: **REEF ISLAND** (SV) ex-*Asta*; **GINA II** (My) ex-*Berit*

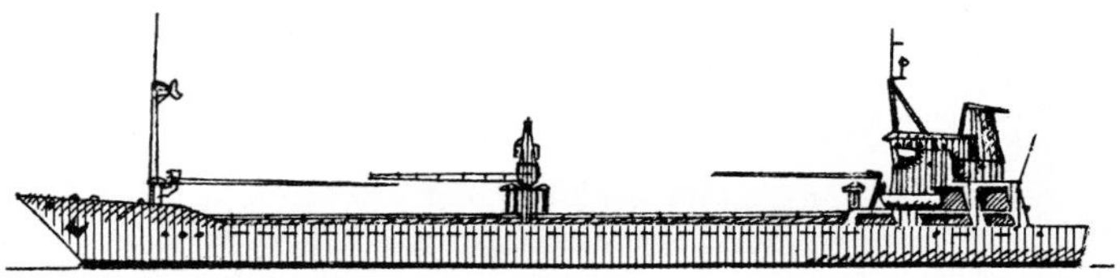

101 *MCVF H1*
LOIRE Ma/De (Frederikshavn) 1977; C/Con; 2,919 grt/4,150 dwt; 96.53 × 5.64 m *(316.69 × 18.51 ft)*; M (Atlas-MaK); 12.25 kts; ex-*Mercandian Prince*; 'COMMANDER' class; 90 TEU
Sisters: **ATLANTIC MOON** (Bs) ex-*Mercandian Admiral*; **CASABLANCA S** (It) ex-*Mercandian Ambassador*; **EVANGELINE** (SV) ex-*Mercandian Commander*; **GARONNE** (Ma) ex-*Mercandian Queen*

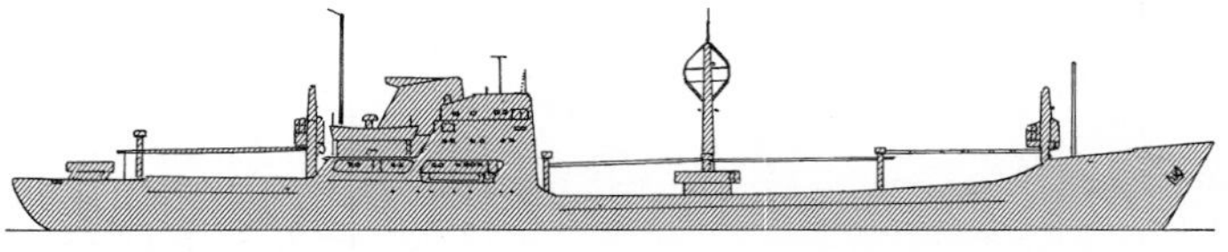

102 *MCXMFMC H13*
KIROVSKLES Ru/Fi (Nystads) 1962; TC/C; 2,925 grt/3,779 dwt; 102 × 5.7 m *(335 × 18.9 ft)*; M (B&W); 12.25 kts
Sisters: **KASUGA II** (Pa) ex-*Baykalles*; **KIM LONG** (Vn) ex-*Kareliyales*; **SONDRA** (Ho) ex-*Kolymales*; **KRASNOGORSKLES** (Ru); **UNIPROGRESS** (Ma) ex-*Kungurles*; **HONG LONG** (Vn) ex-*Kovdales*; **AMIR A** (Sy) ex-*Vologdales*

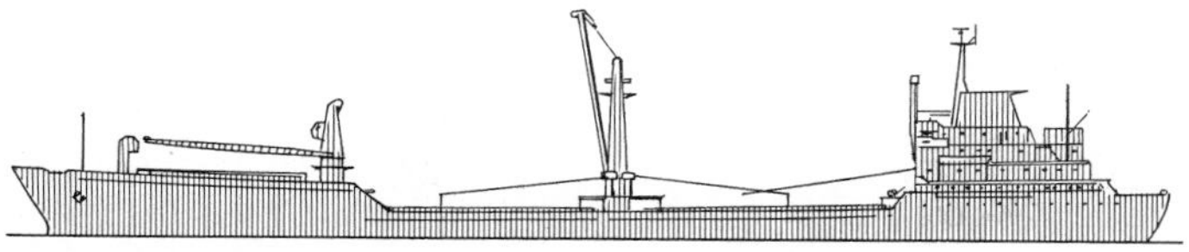

103 *MDNHM–FN H13*
J TRUSTER SV/DDR ('Neptun') 1974; C/Con/HL; 10,211 grt/12,764 dwt; 150.37 × 9.05 m *(493 × 29.69 ft)*; M (MAN); 17 kts; Launched as *Bari*; 420 TEU
Sister: **J FASTER** (SV) ex-*Neuenburg*

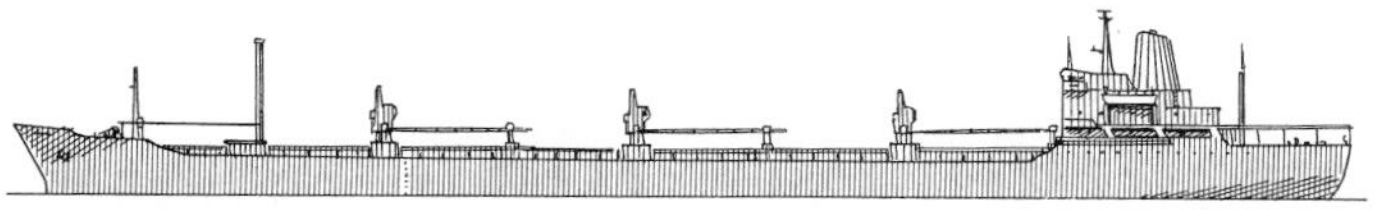

104 *MHC^{3}M^{2}FN H13*
IOS Pa/Ja (Mitsui) 1968; B; 15,473 grt/26,397 dwt; 178.14 × 10.27 m *(584.45 × 33.69 ft)*; M (Sulzer); 13.5 kts; ex-*Continental Shipper*

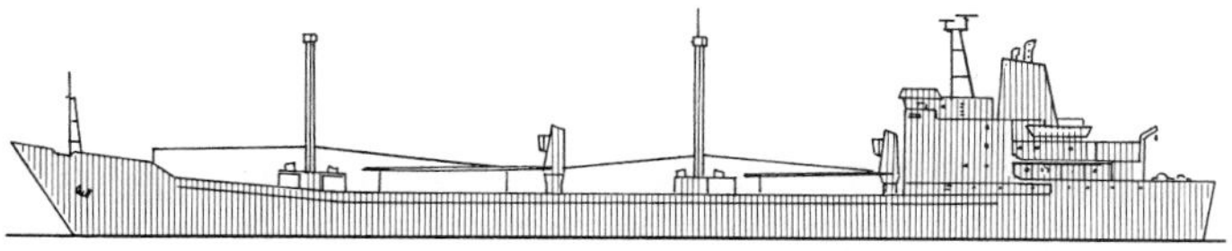

105 *MHCHCMF H13*
ORLIK Cz/Ys ("3 maj") 1980; C; 10,512 grt/15,236 dwt; 145.55 × 9.12 m *(477.53 × 29.92 ft)*; M (Sulzer); 14.75 kts; May be others of this type with this sequence—see LIPNO and so on (see drawing number 8/136)

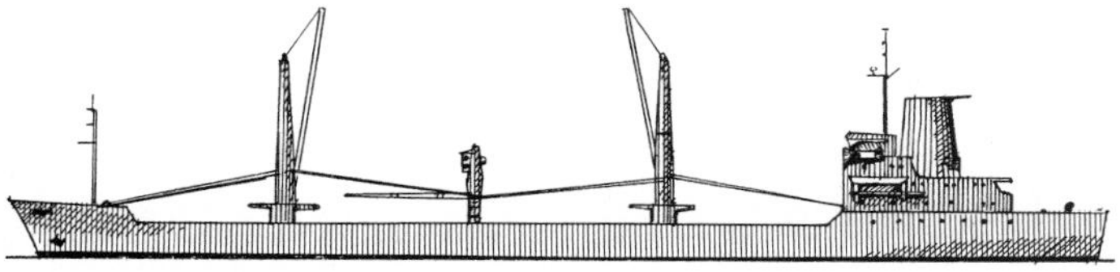

106 *MHCHMF H13*
BARENBELS Gr/FRG (Flender) 1976; C/HL; 12,158 grt/18,500 dwt; 149.16 × 9.6 m *(489.37 × 31.5 ft)*; M (MAN); 15.5 kts; ex-*Barenfels*
Sister: **ATLAS** (Ma) ex-*Brauenfels*

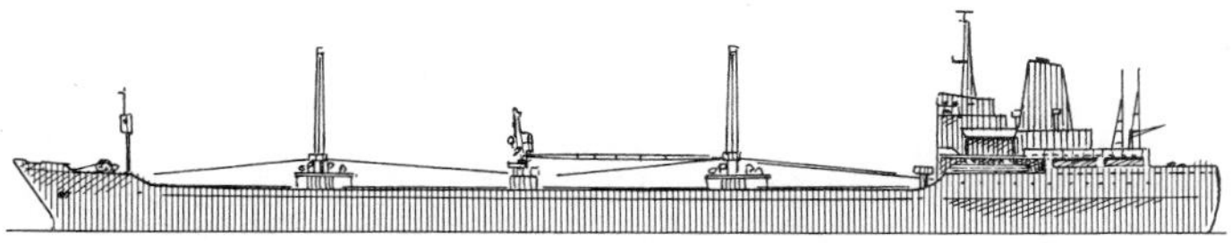

107 *MHCHMFM^2 H13*
HAE WOO No 3 Bl/Ja (Mitsui) 1971; C; 10,130 grt/15,167 dwt; 145.7 × 9.27 m *(478.02 × 30.41 ft)*; M (B&W); 16 kts; ex-*Ranenfjord*; 'Concord' type
Sister: **HAE WOO No 2** (Bl) ex-*Lyngenfjord*

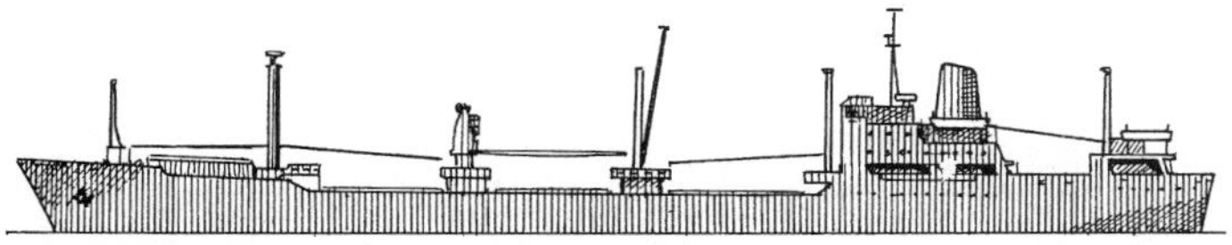

108 *MHCHNMFN H13*
JUTHA JESSICA Th/De (Nakskov) 1972; C; 11,082 grt/13,579 dwt; 153.6 × 9.4 m *(504 × 30.9 ft)*; M (B&W); 18 kts; ex-*Afrika*
Sister: **JUTHA CHANATHIP** (Th) ex-*Bretagne*

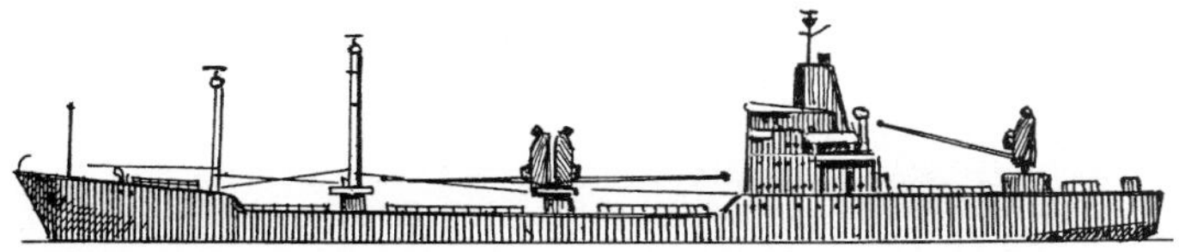

109 *MH^{2}PM–FC H13*
UNIPUNA NA/FRG (Luebecker F-W) 1972; C; 10,281 grt/14,120 dwt; 149 × 9.4 m *(488 × 30.7 ft)*; M (B+V); 19 kts; ex-*Santa Cruz*

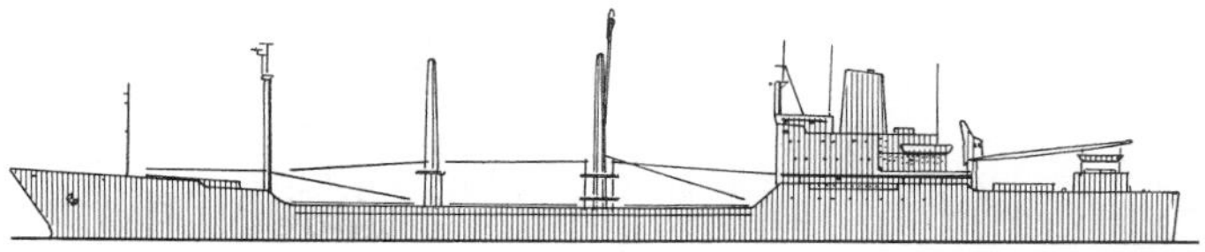

110 *MH^{2}UHFNC H13*
XING CHENG RC/DDR (Warnow) 1973; C; 9,348 grt/12,824 dwt; 144.99 × 7.3 m *(492 × 23.95 ft)*; M (MAN); 17 kts; ex-*Union Aotearoa*; 'Meridian' type
Sisters: **RINOS** (Cy) ex-*Hawk*; **PANDA** (SV) ex-*Merlin 1*; **COLMY** (Cy) ex-*Phenix 1*; **RITA** (Cy) ex-*Condor*; **ETHNOS** (Pa) ex-*Krasica*; **KRK** (Cro); **MOSCENICE** (Cro); **MOTOVUN** (Cro); **SU YUN** (RC) ex-*Falcon*; Similar (superstructure differs): **AFRIS WAVE** (Cy) ex-*Cottbus*; **UNIPAMPA** (NA) ex-*Frankfurt/Oder*; **UNICOSTA** (NA) ex-*Erfurt*; **UNISOL** (NA) ex-*Berlin-Haupstadt DER DDR*; **UNIVALLE** (NA) ex-*Leipzig*; **KATERINA L** (Gr) ex-*Potsdam*; **HERCEG NOVI** (Ma); **SLOVENIJA** (Ma); **GROBNIK** (Ma) ex-*Vojvodina*; **TIVAT** (Ma); **EUROTWIN** (Cy) ex-*Risan*; **VISHVA NANDINI** (In); **DUBAI VISION** (Ma); **DUBAI VALOUR** (Ma); **VISHVA KAUMUDI** (In); **UNIMAR** (NA) ex-*Schwerin*

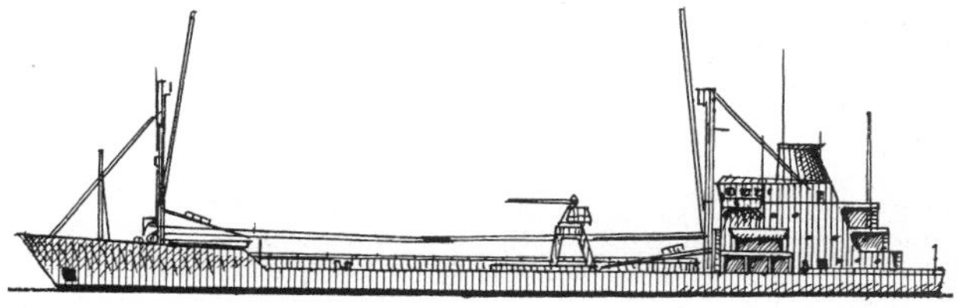

111 *MHJHF H1*
BARDE TEAM NIS/FRG (M Jansen) 1976; C/Con/HL; 4,093 grt/7,113 dwt; 94.49 × 7.9 m *(310 × 25.92 ft)*; M (Alpha-Diesel); — kts; ex-*Samson Scan*; Travelling cranes; 192 TEU

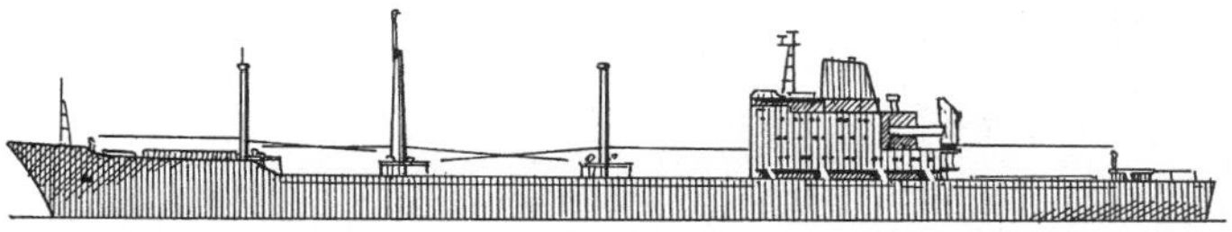

112 *MHNNMFC H1*
JIANG CHUAN RC/Ys ('3 Maj') 1973; C; 10,740 grt/15,475 dwt; 157 × 9.2 m *(519 × 30.5 ft)*; M (Sulzer); 18 kts
Sisters: **HAN CHUAN** (RC); **YIN CHUAN** (RC); **TONG CHUAN** (RC)

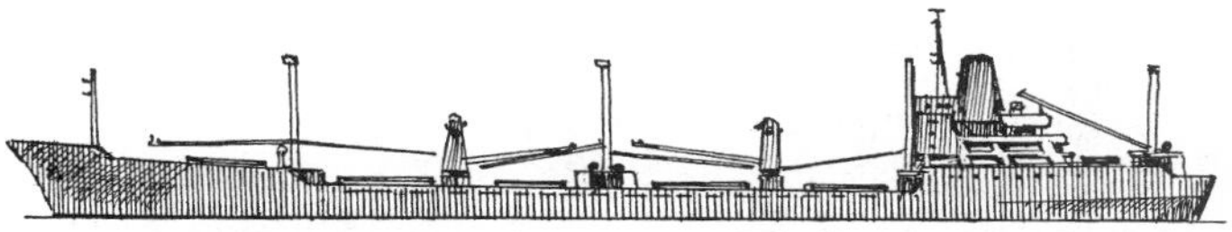

113 *MHPHPNMFN^{2}H H13*
SIN TONG Sg/Ja (Mitsubishi HI) 1971; C; 12,403 grt/16,920 dwt; 162 × 10.4 m *(533 × 34 ft)*; M (Sulzer); 17 kts; ex-*Nedlloyd Kingston*
Sisters: **MANLEY APPLEDORE** (Pa) ex-*Nedlloyd Kimberley*; **JUTHA TRITHIP** (Th) ex-*Nedlloyd Kyoto*; Similar (plated superstructure): **ZHONG FA** (Pa) ex-*Nedlloyd Katwijk*

114 *MHPNM–FC H1*
SEA DIAMOND H Cy/Sp ('Bazan') 1972/81; C/Con; 4,910 grt/9,513 dwt; 155.78 × 7.5 m *(511 × 24.6 ft)*; M (Sulzer); 18 kts; ex-*Roncesvalles*; Lengthened 1981 ('Astano')
Sisters: **AL MOHAMMED** (Ma) ex-*Belen*; **JIN XIANG** (RC) ex-*Galeona*; **DIAMOND H** (Cy) ex-*Valvanuz*

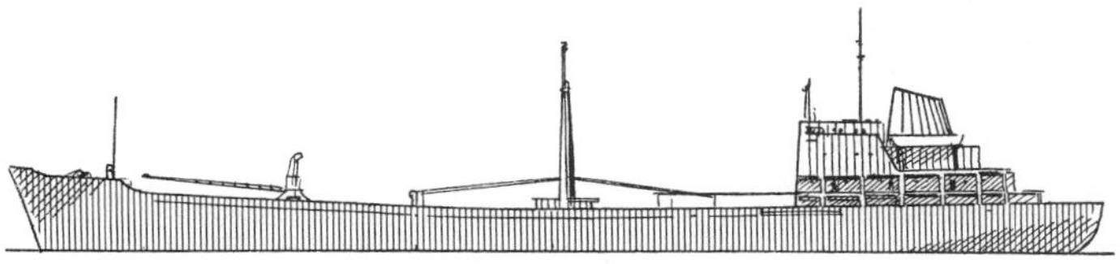

115 *MJN^{2}MF H13*
MYOMA YWA Mr/FRG (A G 'Weser') 1962; C/HL; 5,184 grt/7,189 dwt; 127.11 × 7.78 m *(417.03 × 25.52 ft)*; M (B&W); 15.75 kts; ex-*Altenfels*; Travelling crane

116 *M^{2}FMC H*
JIN XIAN QUAN RC/Sw (Lindholmens) 1959; C; 5,893 grt/7,956 dwt; 129.11 × 8.14 m *(423.59 × 26.71 ft)*; M (Gotaverken); 15 kts; ex-*Topdalsford*

117 *M^{5}FCM H13*
XIN CHANG RC/Fi (Crichton-Vulcan) 1963; C; 6,327 grt/7,850 dwt; 134.7 × 8.2 m *(445 × 26.1 ft)*; M (Gotaverken); 16 kts; ex-*Sagaholm*

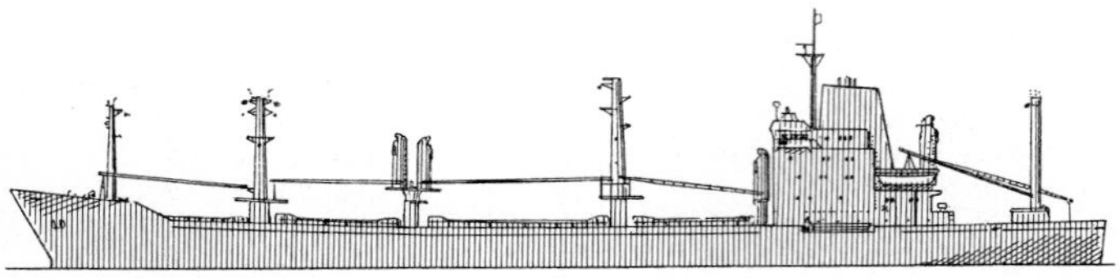

118 *M^{2}PMCMFCN H1*
SECIL NAMIBIA Bs/Ne (Giessen-De Noord) 1977; C/Con; 10,573 grt/14,746 dwt; 142 × 9.5 m *(466 × 31 ft)*; M (Stork-Werkspoor); approx 16.25 kts; ex-*Aldabi*
Sisters: **GOLD ASIA** (Pa) ex-*Alhena*; **MOONLIGHT 1** (SV) ex-*Alnati*; **SUNFLOWER 1** (SV) ex-*Alphacca*

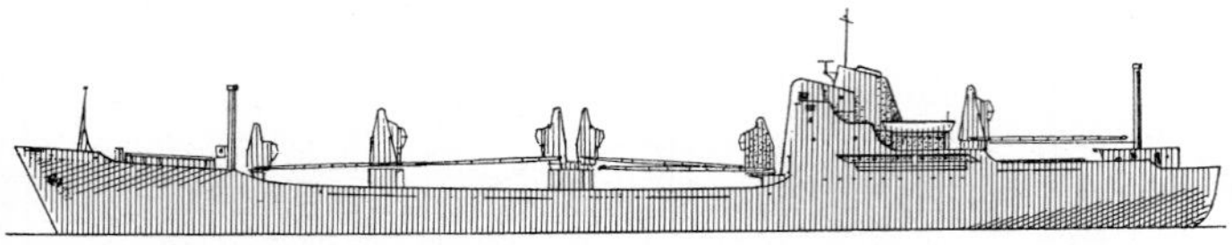

119 *MNC^{5}M–FCN H13*
ARAB HIND Si/Br (Burntisland) 1965; C; 6,589 grt/7,620 dwt; 130.77 × 7.77 m *(429 × 25.6 ft)*; M (B&W); 14.5 kts; ex-*Nova Scotia*

120 *MNCNCMFC H13*
KUZNICA Pd/De (Nakskov) 1970; C; 12,167 grt/14,078 dwt; 166.7 × 9.7 m *(547 × 31.9 ft)*; M (B&W); 20.75 kts
Sisters: **JASTARNIA-BOR** (Pd); **JURATA** (Pd); **WLADYSLAWOWO** (Pd)

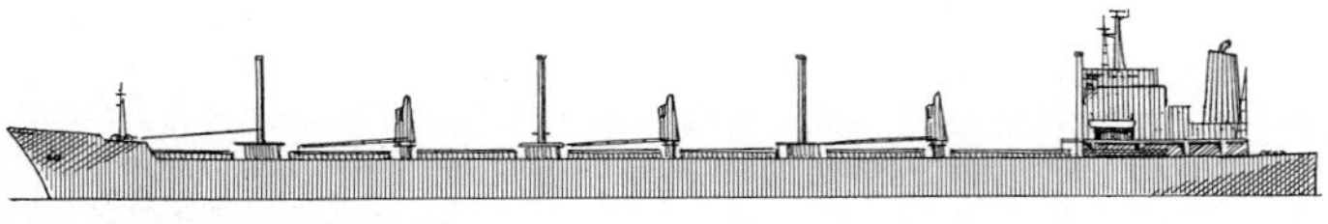

121 *MNCNCNCNMFN H1*
TRADE CARRIER Li/Ja (Hitachi) 1976; C; 30,617 grt/51,672 dwt; 199.98 × 12.42 m *656.1 × 40.75 ft)*; M (Sulzer); 15.5 kts; 'Hi-bulk 50' type
Sister: **TANGLAW** (Pa) ex-*Kyuko Maru*
Sisters (builder—Mitsubishi HI): **ICL RAJA RAJAN** (In) ex-*Yuko Maru*; **MANA** (Gr) ex-*Zenko Maru*
Sisters (builder-IHI): **VENUS** (Li) ex-*Venus Venture*; **HAPPYMAN** (Cy) ex-*Queendom Venture*
Probable sisters (builder—Sanoyasu): **ICL PARTHIBAN** (In) ex-*Sanko Maple*; **ICL VIKRAMAN** (In) ex-*Sanko Daisy* (see photo number 9/213)

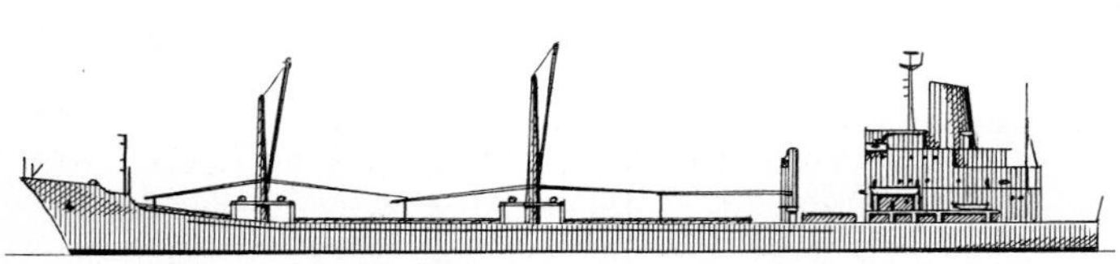

122 *MN^{2}CMFN H1*
MAGNUS SINCERITY Cy/FRG (A G 'Weser') 1977; C/Con; 9,673 grt/15,513 dwt; 149.82 × 9.25 m *(491.54 × 30.35 ft)*; M (Sulzer); 16.5 kts; ex-*Mendoza*; '36-L' type; 253 TEU
Sisters: **AURORA** (Cy) ex-*Catamarca II*; **LA RIOJA** (Ar); **SAN JUAN** (Ar); **TAI TAI** (Cy) ex-*San Luis*

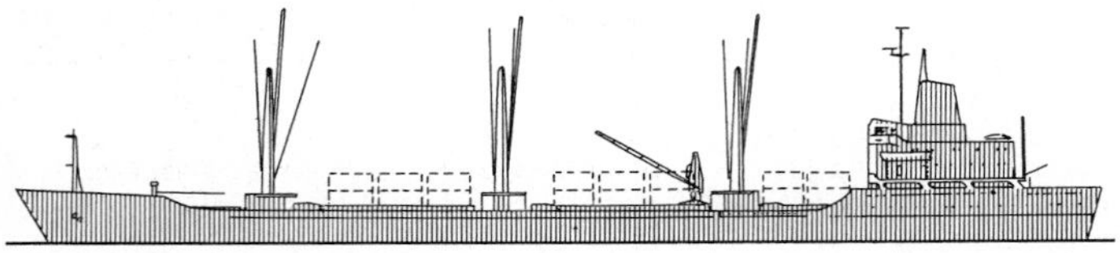

123 *MN^{2}JNMM–FN H13*
JIN HAI YANG RC/FRG (Flensburger) 1972; C/Con; 11,082 grt/16,780 dwt; 154.87 × 9.8 m *(508 × 32.15 ft)*; M (MAN); 18.5 kts; ex-*Lutz Jacob*; Travelling crane may be removed; 501 TEU
Sister: **ARMIN STAR** (Ma) ex-*Renate Jacob*

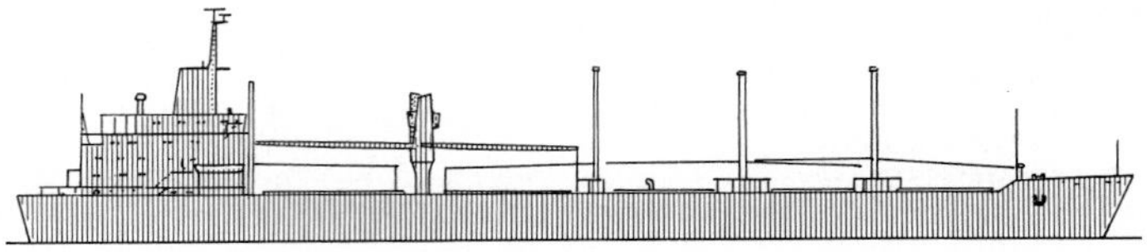

124 *MN^{3}PNMFN H1*
HALIM TOPAZ Ko/In (Hindustan) 1979; C/Con; 13,455 grt/20,914 dwt; 162.21 × 10.38 m *(532.19 × 34.06 ft)*; M (Pielstick); 16 kts; ex-*Jalagodavari*; 348 TEU; 'PIONEER' type
Sisters: **TRIMBAKESHWAR** (In) ex-*Jalagovind*; **SEA LION I** (Pa) ex-*Jalagopal*; **VEER SAVARKAR** (In) ex-*Jalagouri*

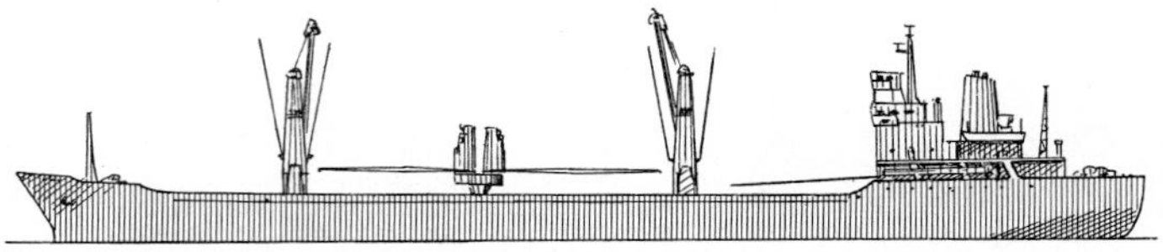

125 *MNPNMFN H13*
TRIBELS Gr/Ja (Nipponkai) 1974; C/HL; 11,980 grt/18,029 dwt; 147.71 × 9.63 m *(484.61 × 31.59 ft)*; M (B&W); 18.5 kts; ex-*Aristogenis*; Converted from 'Mitsui-Concord' type cargo vessel
Sister: **TRAUTENBELS** (Cy) ex-*Aristokleidis*

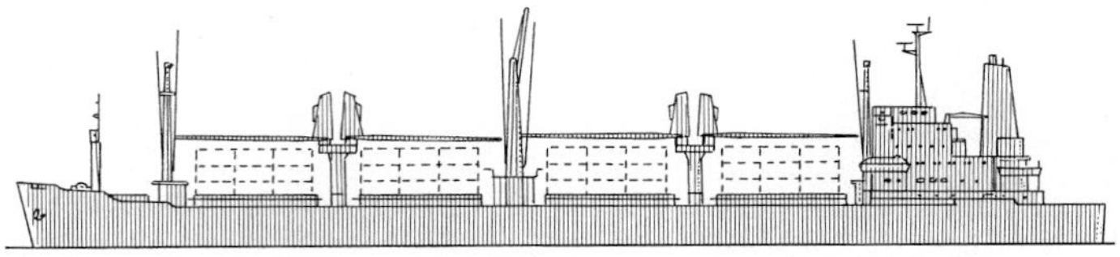

126 *MNPNPNMFM H1*
EVER HAPPY Cy/Ja (NKK) 1977; C/Con/HL; 18,846 grt/22,060 dwt; 171 × 9.97 m *(561.02 × 32.71 ft)*; M (Sulzer); 17.5 kts; ex-*Tsu*; 726 TEU
Sisters: **ADVANTAGE** (US) ex-*Thermopylae*; **POKOJ** (Pd) ex-*Terrier*; **PRACA** (Pd) ex-*Tennessee*; **CARNIVAL** (Cy) ex-*Tysla*

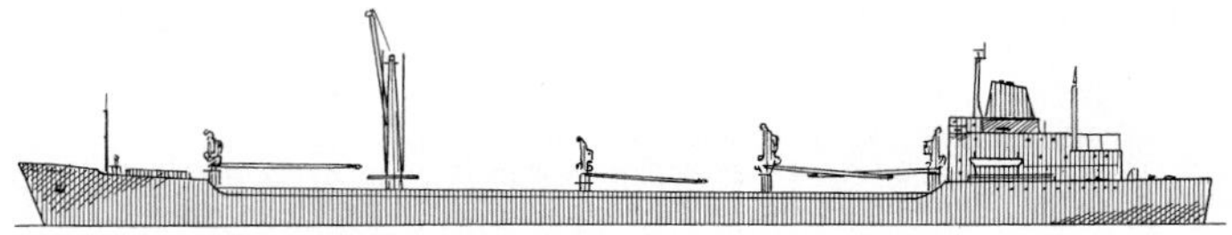

127 *MPNCPCMFN H13*
IBN SHUHAID UAE/Ko (Hyundai) 1977; C; 15,455 grt/23,618 dwt; 175.32 × 10.4 m *(575.2 × 34.12 ft)*; M (B&W); 16 kts; 'KUWAIT' class; 386 TEU
Sisters (some Br built (Govan)): **IBN AL-ATHEER** (Si); **IBN AL-MOATAZ** (Si); **IBN ASAKIR** (Qt); **IBN BASSAM** (Qt); **IBN BATTOTAH** (Ku); **HARWICH STAR** (SV) ex-*Ibn Duraid*; **IBN HAYYAN** (UAE); **KRISTIN STAR** (SV) ex-*Ibn Khaldoon*; **IBN KHALLIKAN** (Ku); **IBN MALIK** (UAE); **IBN QUTAIBAH** (Si); **IBN RUSHD** (Ku); **IBN TUFAIL** (Ku); **IBN YOUNUS** (Qt); **AL SALIMIAH** (Ku); **AL MUBARAKIAH** (UAE); **AL YAMAMAH** (Si); **AL FUJAIRAH** (UAE); **TOGO BEAUTY** (Cy) ex-*Al Muharraq*; **AL RAYYAN** (Qt); **AHMAD AL-FATEH** (Bn); **ARAFAT** (Si); **DANAH** (Ku); **FATHULKHAIR** (Qt); **HIJAZ** (Qt); **JILFAR** (UAE); **KUBBAR** (Ku); **SALAH ALDEEN** (UAE); **KORAT NAVEE** (Th) ex-*Theekar*; **TABUK** (Si); **IBN AL-NAFEES** (Qt); **IBN AL-ABBAR** (Qt)

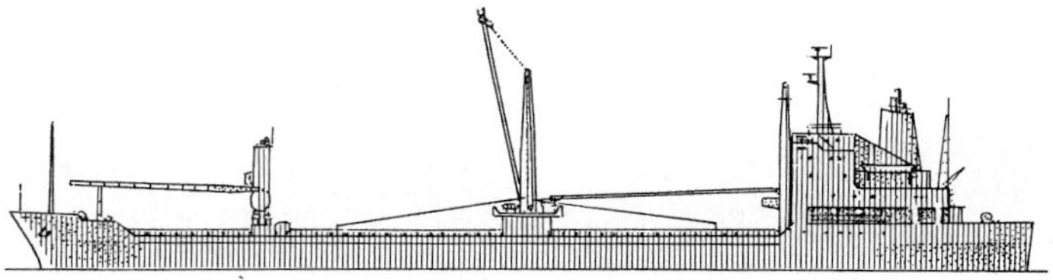

128 *MPNHMFN H13*
BIZERTE Tn/Ja (Naikai) 1979; C/B; 8,205 grt/8,312 dwt; 137.31 × 7 m *(450.49 × 22.97 ft)*; M (B&W); 17.25 kts; Designed for the transportation of phosphate rock
Sister: **KAIROUAN** (Tn)

See photo number 9/199

129 *MPNPHFN H13*
PIONEER WAVE Pa/Ja (Mitsubishi HI) 1978; C/Con/HL; 14,478 grt/22,107 dwt; 162.52 × 10.45 m *(533.2 × 34.28 ft)*; M (MAN); 18 kts; ex-*Wakanami Maru*; 458 TEU
Sister: **PHAYAO NAVEE** (Th) ex-*Wakamizu Maru*; Similar (second pair of cranes on travelling gantry, heavier KP foreward): **UTHAI NAVEE** (Th) ex-*Wakagiku Maru*; **SEA FAYE** (Cy) ex-*Wakatake Maru*

See photo number 9/196

130 *MPNPMF H13*
ADRIAN NA/FRG (Howaldts DW) 1979; C/Con; 8,193 grt/10,800 dwt; 141.69 × 7.85 m *(465 × 25.75 ft)*; M (MAN); 15.75 kts; ex-*Sandra Wesch*; 590 TEU
Sisters: **BALKAN** (NA) ex-*Christian Wesch*; **AN WU JIANG** (RC) ex-*Jonny Wesch*; **AN TAO JIANG** (RC) ex-*Magdalene Wesch*

131 *MPNPMFN H13*
CAPE MORETON Gr/Ja (Kanawa) 1977; C/Con; 11,309 grt/16,250 dwt; 148.01 × 9.45 m *(485.6 × 31 ft)*; M (MAN); 16 kts; ex-*Neckar*; 505 TEU

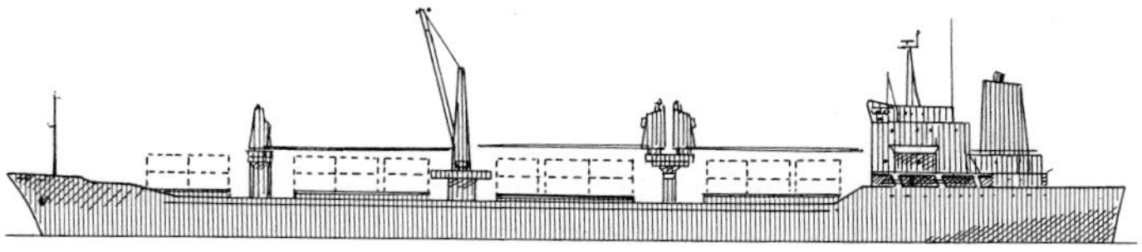

132 *MPNPNMF H13*
WAKAMBA Pa/Ja (Hitachi) 1977; C/Con; 13,381 grt/20,435 dwt; 161.53 × 9.97 m *(529.95 × 32.71 ft)*; M (B&W); 16.25 kts; ex-*Tabora*; 'UC20' type; 454 TEU
Sister: **MARINGA** (Pa) Launched as *Transkei*

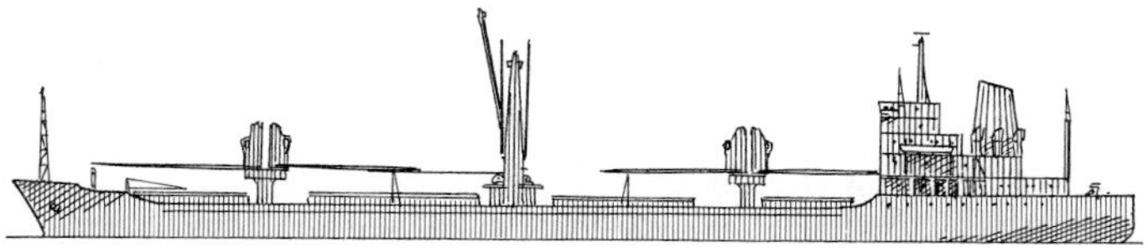

133 *MPNPNMFN H13*
KSAR ETTIR Ag/Ja (Kanasashi) 1977; C/HL; 13,135 grt/19,782 dwt; 156.11 × 9.9 m *(512.77 × 32.48 ft)*; M (B&W); 15 kts
Sisters: **KSAR CHELLALA** (Ag); **KSAR EL BOUKHARI** (Ag)

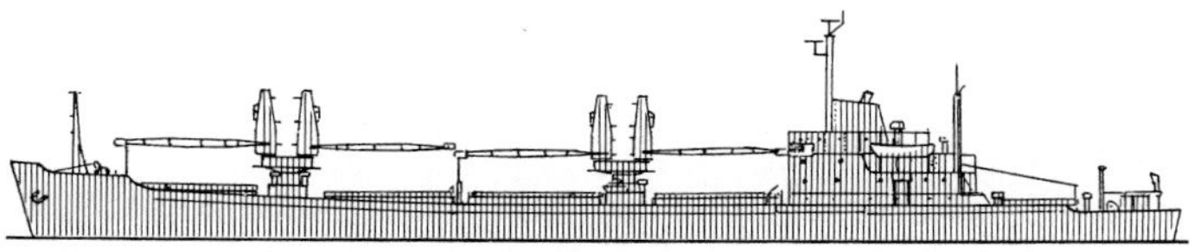

134 *MP*^{2}*M–FN H1*
REGENT Bs/Bz (CCN) 1979; C; 9,328 grt/14,328 dwt; 140.95 × 8.92 m *(462 × 29.27 ft)*; M (MAN); 15 kts; ex-*Monte Alto*; 'SD14' type
Sister: **EDWARD R** (Pa) ex-*Monte Cristo*; **MONTE PASCOAL** (Bz); Similar (radar mast just forward of funnel): **ANA LUISA** (Bz) Probably similar: **JOBST OLDENDORFF** (Li) ex-*Alessandra* (Bz); **NACIONAL SANTOS** (Bz) ex-*Anisio Borges*; **NACIONAL RIO** (Bz) ex-*Rodrigo*

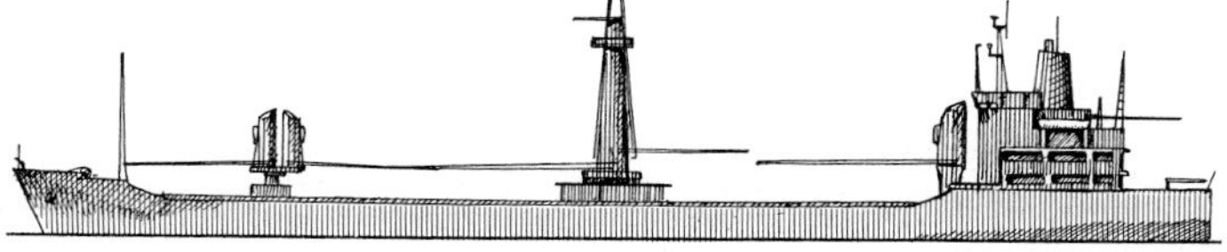

135 *MPTCNMFRN H13*
ENLIVENER HK/Ja (Mitsubishi HI) 1978; C/HL; 15,628 grt/20,763 dwt; 161.02 × 9.5 m *(528.28 × 31.16 ft)*; M (Sulzer); 15.25 kts; ex-*Atlas Maru*
Sister: **ENCOURAGER** (HK) ex-*Andes Maru*

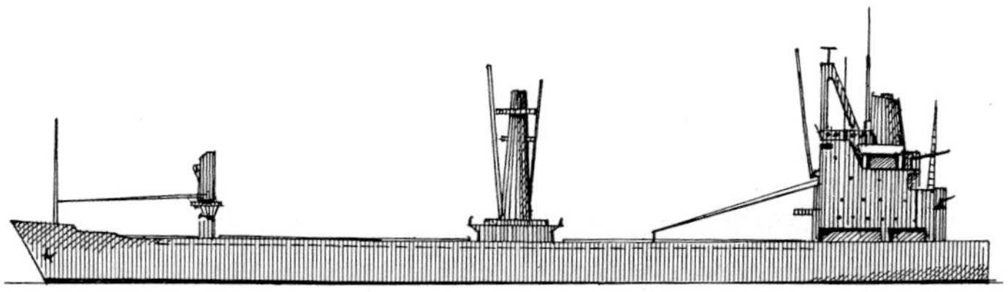

136 *MPTHFMM–R H1*
CHAINAT NAVEE Th/Ja (Kawasaki) 1978; C/HL; 15,938 grt/20,258 dwt; 157.03 × 9.5 m *(515.19 × 31.17 ft)*; M (MAN); 15.5 kts; ex-*Malacca Maru*

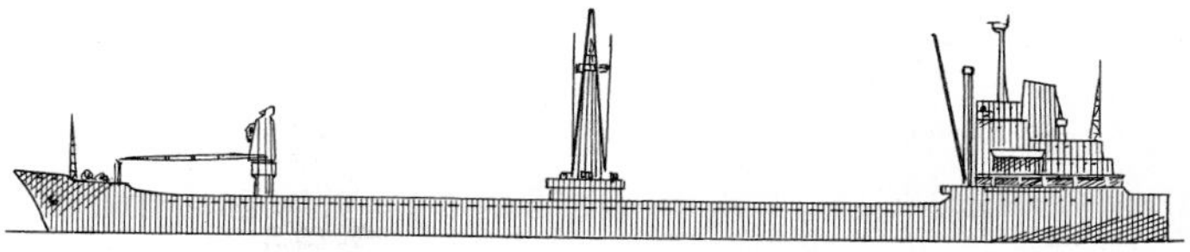

137 *MPTNMFN H13*
ASEAN JUMBO Sg/Ja (Onomichi) 1976; C/HL; 12,313 grt/18,435 dwt; 154.41 × 9.58 m *(506.59 × 31.43 ft)*; M (Pielstick); 15 kts; ex-*Kasuga Maru*
Probable sister: **KASHIMA** (Pa) ex-*Kashima Maru*; Similar (larger): **ASEAN WINNER** ex-*Katori Maru* (Pa)

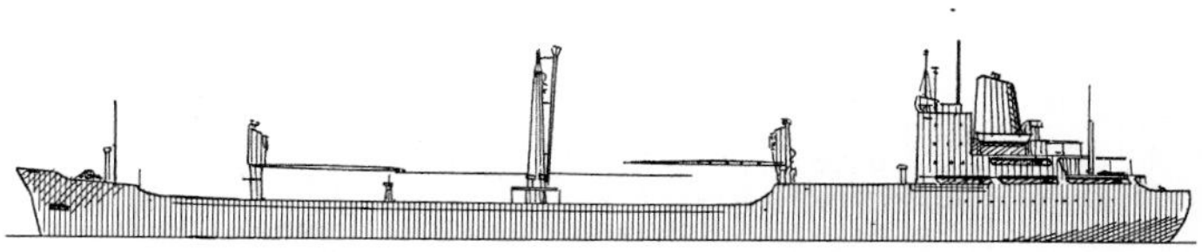

138 *MPTPMFN H13*
GAN JIANG RC/No (Framnaes) 1970; C; 12,611 grt/16,277 dwt; 155.53 × 9.4 m *(510.26 × 30.84 ft)*; M (B&W); 16.5 kts; ex-*Norbella*

139 *MPUPMFMC H1*
WARNEMUNDE Ru/DDR (Warnow) 1972; C; 7,192 grt/12,347 dwt; 150.2 × 8.9 m *(493 × 29 ft)*; M (MAN); 19.25 kts; 'MERCATOR' type. Ships may vary slightly
Sisters: **MARINA** (SV) ex-*Palekh* (Ru); **PAVLODAR** (Ru); **PAVLOGRAD** (Ru); **PESTOVO** (Ru); **PETRODVORETS** (Ru); **PRAVDINSK** (Ru); **PRIMORSK** (Ru); **PUTIVL**; **PERVOMAYSKI**; **PRIOZERSK** (Ru) ex-*Walter Ulbright*; **DEKABRIST** (Ru); **NADEZHDA KRUPSKAYA** (Ru); Similar: **UMGENI** (SV) ex-*Muhlhausen*; **PONGOLA** (SV) ex-*Nordhausen*; **SEZELA** (SV) ex-*Sangerhausen*; **AFRIS PIONEER** (Cy) ex-*Sonderhausen*

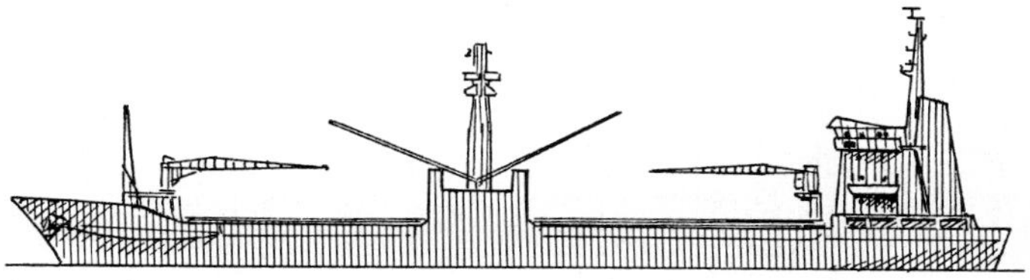

140 *MRTRM–F H1*
WOLWOL Et/De (Orskovs) 1977; C/Con; 3,720 grt/4,135 dwt; 98.96 × 5.73 m *(324.67 × 18.79 ft)*; M (Alpha-Diesel); 14 kts; ex-*Pep Coral*; 180 TEU
Sister: **KEIY KOKEB** (Et) ex-*Pep Comet*

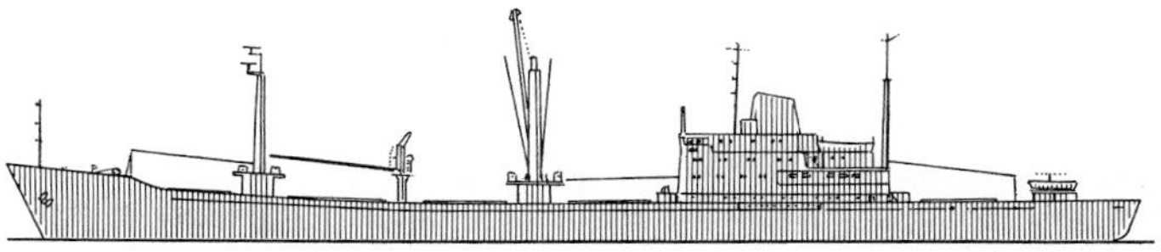

141 *MTCUNMFT H1*
MILOS L Pa/DDR (Warnow) 1967; C; 6,799 grt/10,080 dwt; 150.2 × 8.2 m *(493 × 26.11 ft)*; M (MAN); 17 kts; ex-*Bernburg*; 'XD' type
Sisters: **CARL METZ** (SV) ex-*Boizenburg*; **LADY BANA** (Ho) ex-*Eilenburg*; **MAJESTIC** (Ho) ex-*Naumburg*; **PABLO METZ** (SV) ex-*Oranienburg*; **METZ BELGICA** (SV) ex-*Quedlinburg*; **METZ BEIRUT** (SV) ex-*Rostock*; **BRANDENBURG** (Ms) ex-*Neubrandenburg*

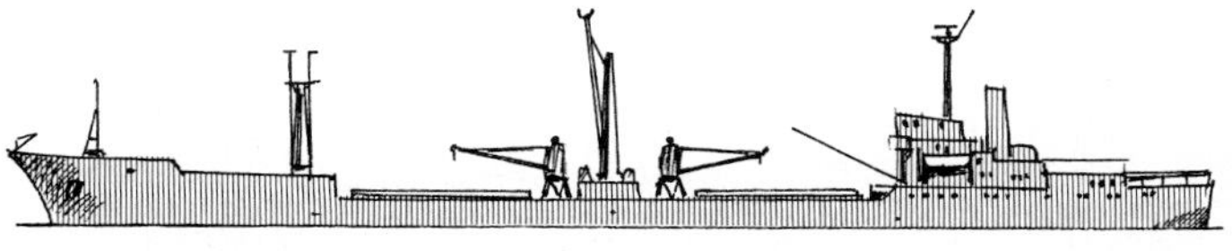

142 *MTJNJMG H13*
IRAN MEEAD Ir/Be (Cockerill) 1970; C; 11,700 grt/16,580 dwt; 160.51 × 9.79 m *(526.6 × 32.12 ft)*; M (B&W); 19 kts; ex-*Arya Gam*; Travelling cranes
Sisters: **IRAN MEELAD** (Ir) ex-*Arya Nur*; **IRAN ABAD** (Ir) ex-*Arya Taj*; **IRAN ERSHAD** (Ir) ex-*Arya Tab*; **IRAN JAHAD** (Ir) ex-*Arya Pas*

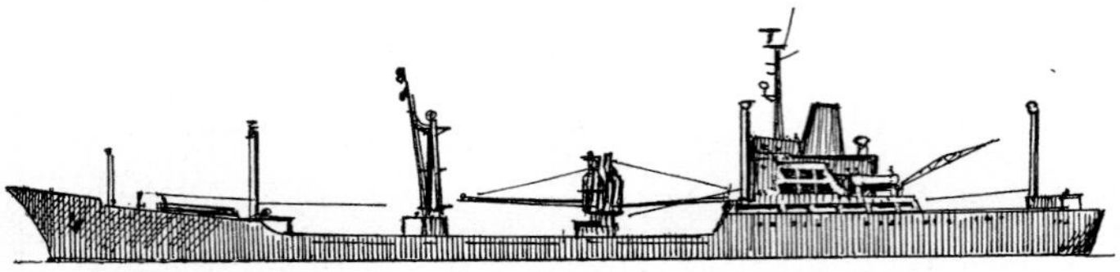

143 *MTNPNMFRT H13*
TIA ANGELICA Pa/Fi (Navire) 1976; C; 11,084 grt/14,814 dwt; 159 × 9.8 m *(522 × 32 ft)*; M (Sulzer); 18.25 kts; ex-*Tachira*
Sisters: **CATHERINE HELEN** (Pa) ex-*Trujillo*; **MICHAEL R** (Pa) ex-*Aragua*; **MAYPRINCE** (Ma)

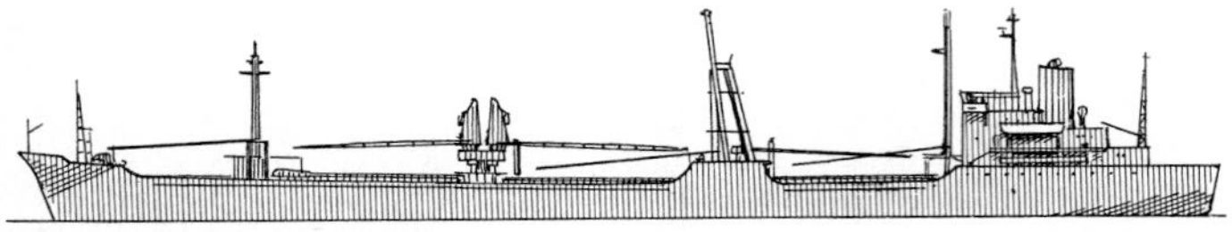

144 *MTPMHMFN H13*
YAN SHAN RC/Ja (Kanawa) 1976; C; 11,275 grt/16,213 dwt; 148.01 × 9.5 m *(485.6 × 31.17 ft)*; M (B&W); 15 kts; ex-*Aloha*; 425 TEU

145 *M–C³MM–F H1*
DEBORA Sw/FRG (Nobiskrug) 1965; C; 2,331 grt/3,228 dwt; 94.01 × 4.67 m *(308.43 × 15.32 ft)*; M (MaK); 13.5 kts; ex-*Cremon*

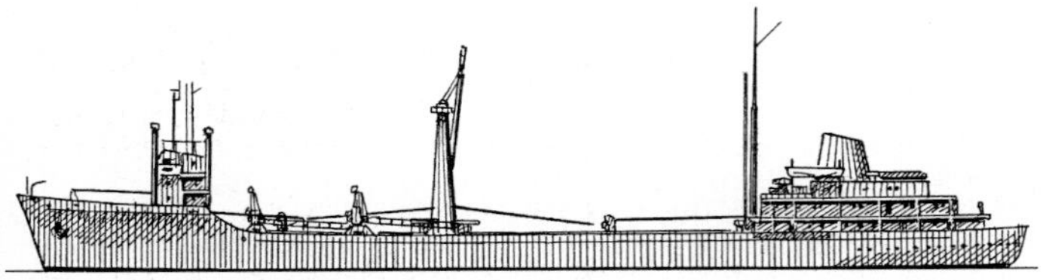

146 *NMNC²NTF H1*
DA DE RC/FRG (A G 'Weser') 1962; C/HL; 9,555 grt/12,623 dwt; 152.25 × 9.35 m *(499.51 × 30.68 ft)*; M (MAN); 17 kts; ex-*Werdenfels*; Cranes move along main deck

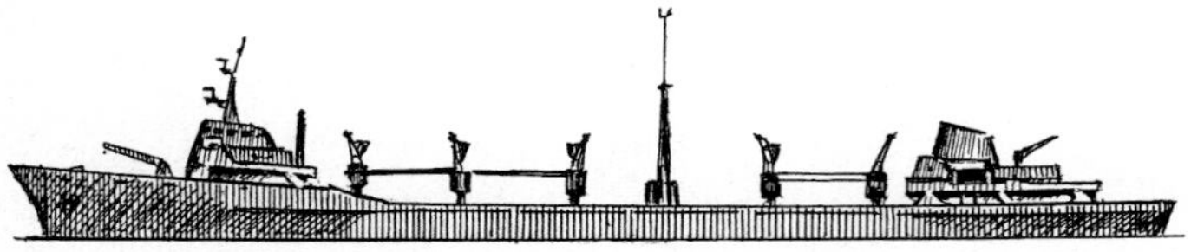

147 *SMNC³NC²FS H1*
DEL MONTE US/US (Ingalls) 1968; C/HL; 10,396 grt/13,248 dwt; 159.11 × 9.47 m *(522.01 × 31.07 ft)*; T (GEC); 18.5 kts; ex-*Delta Brasil*; Owned by US Government
Sisters: **DEL VIENTO** (US) ex-*Delta Mexico*; **DEL VALLE** (US) ex-*Delta Uruguay*

148 *TC²NM–F H*
RAINBOW HOPE US/US (Equitable) 1980; Con/C/R; 983 grt/2,000 dwt; 90.07 × 4.5 m *(295.5 × 14.76 ft)*; M (Fairbanks, Morse); 13.75 kts; ex-*Amazonia*; 99 TEU

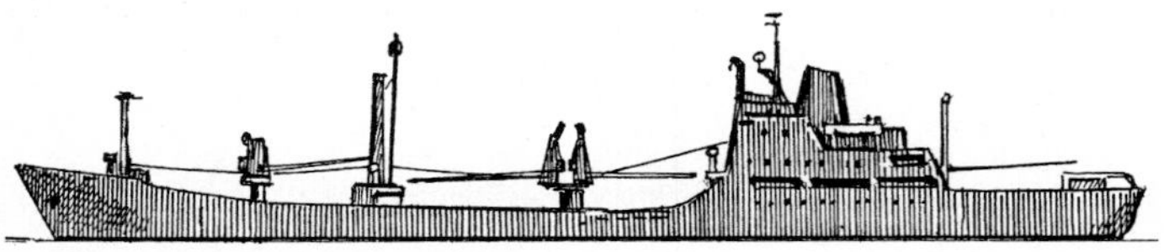

149 *TC²TC²NMFN H13*
CLYDEBANK Br/Br (Swan Hunter) 1974; C; 11,956 grt/15,460 dwt; 148.5 × 9.6 m *(520 × 31.7 ft)*; M (Doxford); 18.75 kts
Sisters: **FORTHBANK** (Br); **IVYBANK** (Br); **PRO ATLANTICA** (Cy) ex-*Meadowbank*; **MORAYBANK** (Br) ex-*Toana Papua*

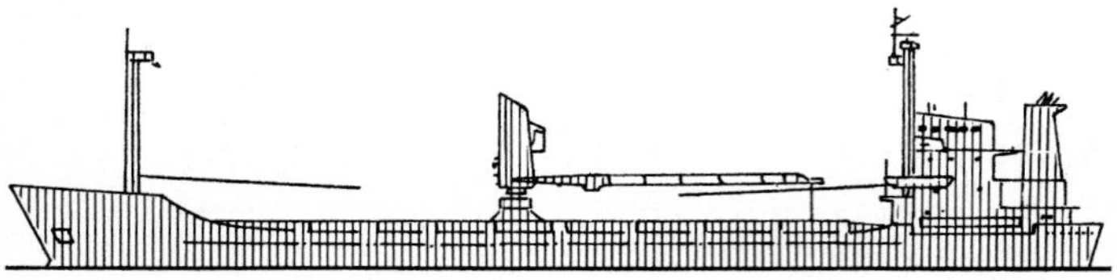

150 *TCHF H1*
HASKERLAND Ne/Ne (Stroobos) 1982; C/Con; 4,047 grt/6,081 dwt; 92.44 × 8.11 m *(303 × 26.61 ft)*; M (Stork-Werkspoor; 12 kts; ex-*Samsun Carrier*; 249 TEU; Crane is on starboard side

151 *TCHF H1*
SEA ATALANTI I Cy/Ne (Stroobos) 1982; C/Con; 3,982 grt/6,705 dwt; 82.7 × 8.35 m *(271 × 27.4 ft)*; M (Stork-Werkspoor); 12 kts; ex-*Roelof Holwerda*; Crane on starboard side; Now lengthened to 91.80m (301ft)

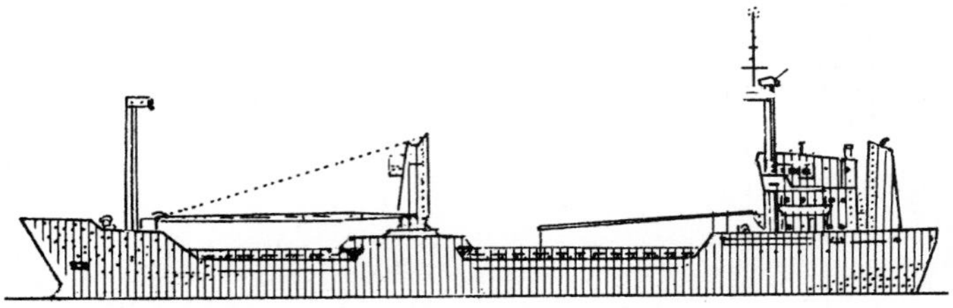

152 *TCHF H13*
CAPITAINE FEARN Va/Ne (Amels) 1979; C/Con; 3,119 grt/3,478 dwt; 82.78 × 5.93 m *(271.59 × 19.46 ft)*; M (Stork-Werkspoor); 13 kts; ex-*Nestor*; Crane is on port side
Sisters: **TADORNE II** (Fr) ex-*Mentor*; **LA PAIMPOLAISE** (Fr) ex-*Stentor*

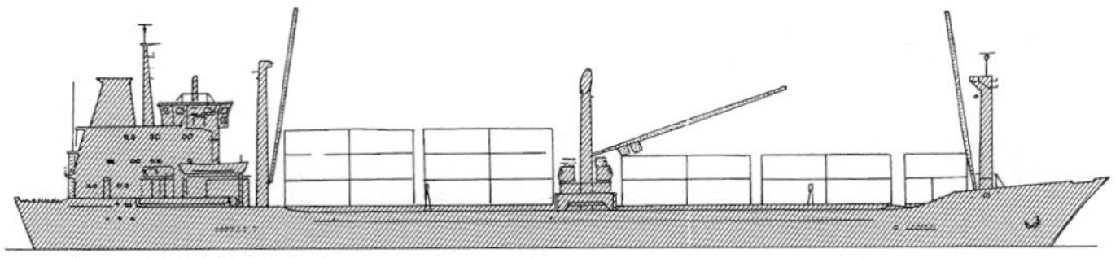

153 *TCHMF H13*
UMAG SAINT MALO NA/FRG (Brand) 1977; C/Con; 3,747 grt/6,200 dwt; 102.88 × 7.29 m *(337.53 × 23.92 ft)*; M (Atlas-MaK); 15 kts; ex-*Marlene S*; 268 TEU

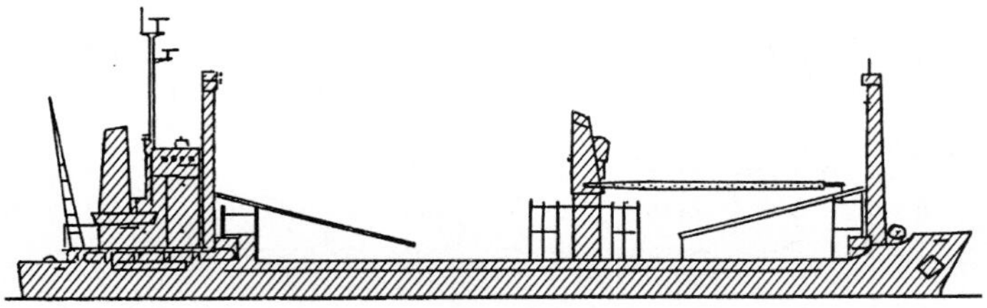

154 *TCHMFN H1*
DERYOUNG STAR Pa/Ja (Kegoya) 1984; C; 3,952 grt/5,547 dwt; 96.02 × 5.09 m *(315.03 × 16.7 ft)*; M (Hanshin); 13 kts; ex-*Amur No 1*
Sister: **AMUR No 3** (Cy)
Probable sisters: **AMUR No 2** (Pa) (builder—Shinhama); **DIAN LAUT** (Cy) ex-*Amur No 5* (builder—Kambara)

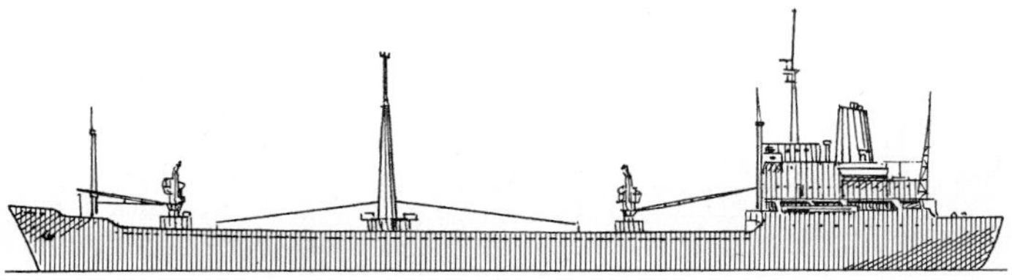

155 *TCNCNMFN H13*
SAMSUN DOLPHIN Ko/Ja (Hitachi) 1970; C; 8,442 grt/12,139 dwt; 140.06 × 8.99 m *(459.51 × 29.49 ft)*; M (B&W); 15.5 kts; ex-*Yamashige Maru*
Sister: **TUO JIANG** (RC) ex-*Niishige Maru*

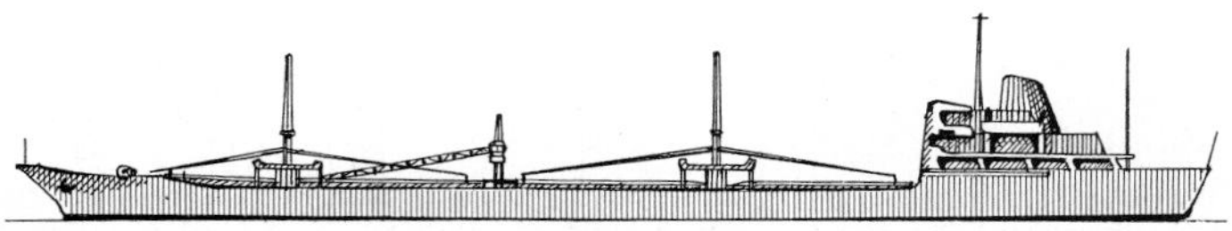

156 *TCTMFN H13*
HONG GU CHENG RC/Ja (Mitsubishi HI) 1970; C; 10,707 grt/15,895 dwt; 151.16 × 9.17 m *(496 × 30.09 ft)*; M (Sulzer); 15 kts; ex-*Nils Amelon*; 'MM–14' type

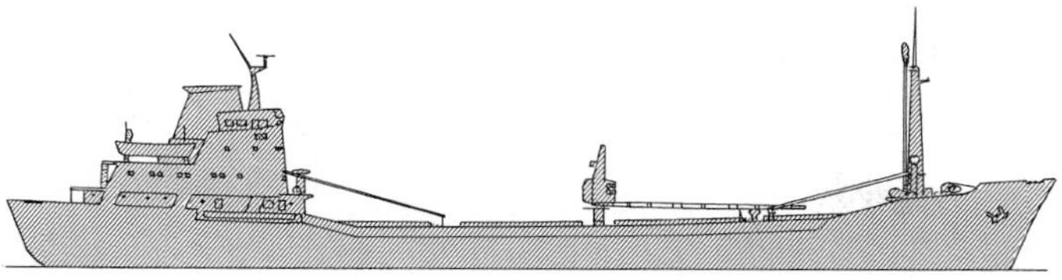

157 *TDMF H13*
WAN FU SV/Fi (Crichton-Vulcan) 1964; C; 2,563 grt/3,810 dwt; 91.57 × 6.67 m *(300.43 × 21.88 ft)*; M (Sulzer); 14.5 kts; ex-*Finnfighter*
Sisters: **AN DA** (RC) ex-*Finnseal*; **LILY** (SV) ex-*Lotila*

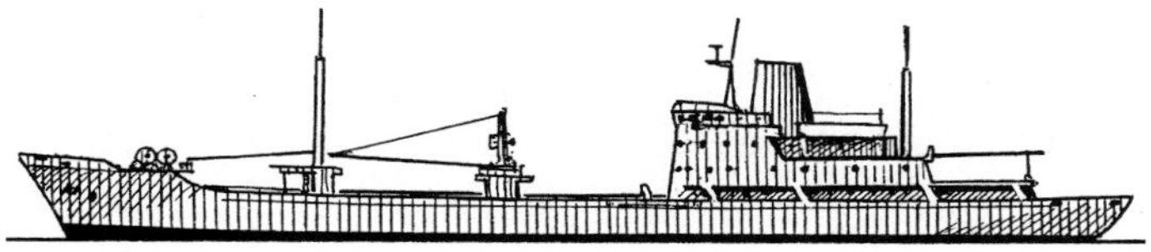

158 *TDMFT H1*
WINDSOR III Ho/Br (Robb Caledon) 1969; CP; 4,418 grt/5,791 dwt; 112 × 7.6 m *(367 × 25 ft)*; M (Mirrlees); 15 kts; ex-*Eigamoiya*

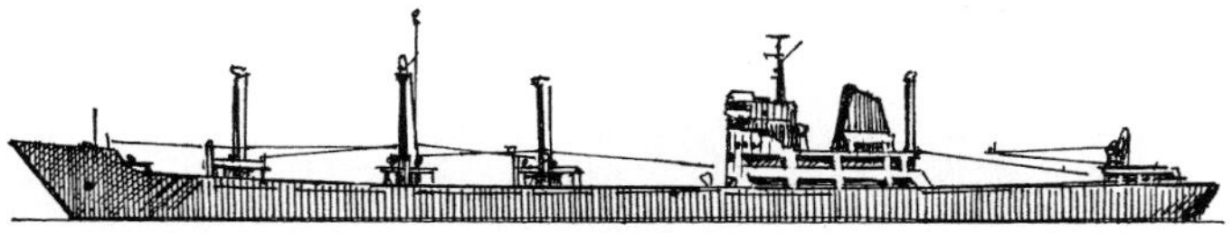

159 *TNTMFTC H1*
SAMUDRA SAMRAT Bh/Sp ('Bazan') 1973; C; 8,591 grt/10,232 dwt; 150.9 × 7.6/8.2 m *(495 × 25/27.1 ft)*; M (Sulzer); 18 kts; ex-*Rio los Sauces*
Sisters: **SAMUDRA RANI** (Bh) ex-*Rio Calingasta*; **A.J.1** (Cy) ex-*Rio Marapa*; **HARMONY II** (Cy) ex-*Rio Neuquen*; **YUAN DONG I** (RC) ex-*Rio Pilcomayo*

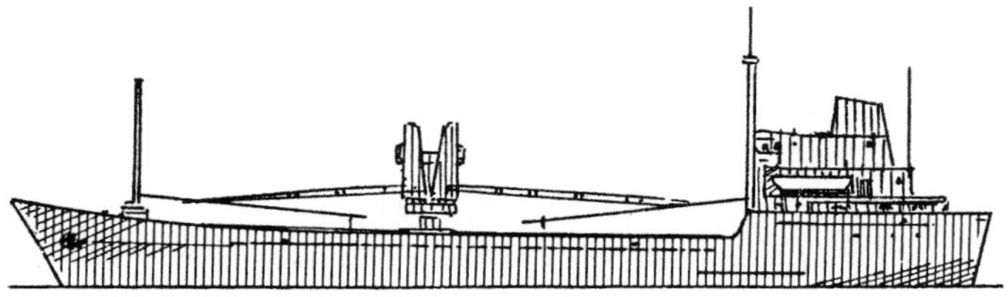

160 *TPHFN H13*
TMP LIBRA Pa/FRG (Buesumer) 1971; C; 1,759 grt/2,613 dwt; 80.17 × 4.07/5.87 m *(263.02 × 13.36/19.25 ft)*; M (KHD); 14 kts; ex-*Hvassafell*

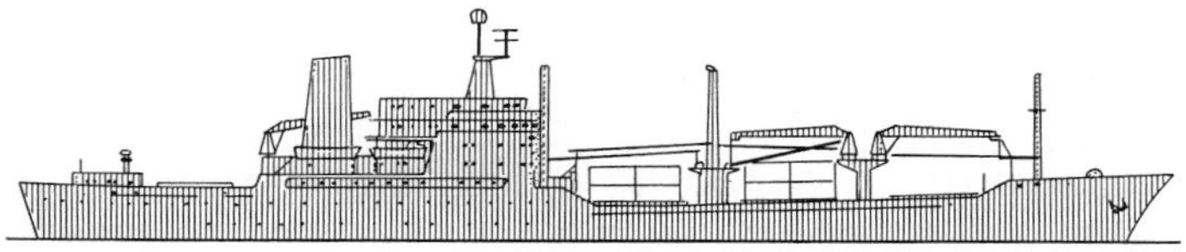

161 *TPHNMFR H13*
NAUTICAS MEXICO Me/Ne ("De Merwede") 1981; C/Con/TSi; 12,095 grt/12,796 dwt; 150.53 × 9.22 m *(493.86 × 30.25 ft)*; M (Sulzer); 18 kts; 48 TEU

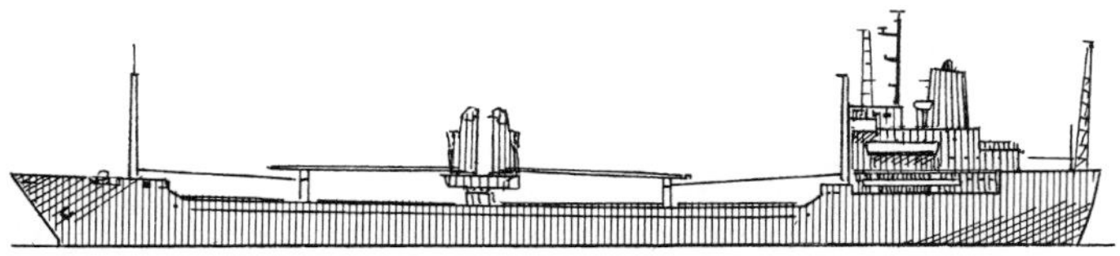

162 *TPN²MFN H13*
ABUQIR Eg/Ja (Kurushima) 1976; C; 4,715 grt/7,525 dwt; 114.33 × 7.25 m *(375.1 × 23.79 ft)*; M (Mitsubishi); 16.75 kts
Sisters: **AGIOS SPYRIDON** (Cy) ex-*Almountazah 1*; **MARYUT** (Eg)

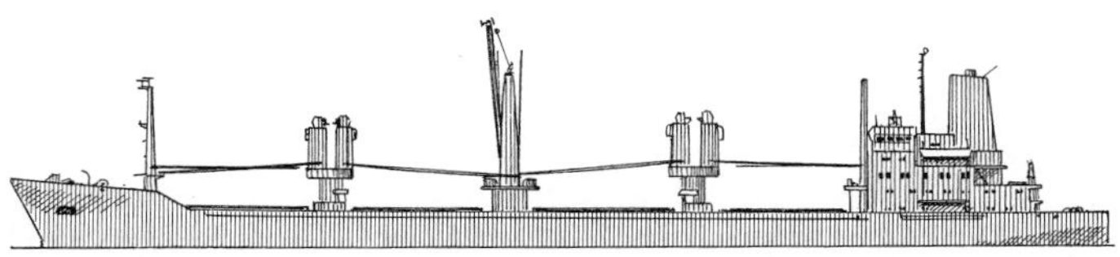

163 *TPNPNMFS H1*
CHARLES LYKES Pa/Ne (Giessen-De Noord) 1978; C; 18,792 grt/22,500 dwt; 173.03 × 10 m *(567.68 × 32.81 ft)*; M (Sulzer); 17 kts; ex-*Nedlloyd Bahrain*; 676 TEU
Sisters: **AGULHAS** (Pa) ex-*Nedlloyd Baltimore*; **COLUMBINE** (Pa) ex-*Nedlloyd Bangkok*; **DOCTOR LYKES** (Pa) ex-*Nedlloyd Barcelona*

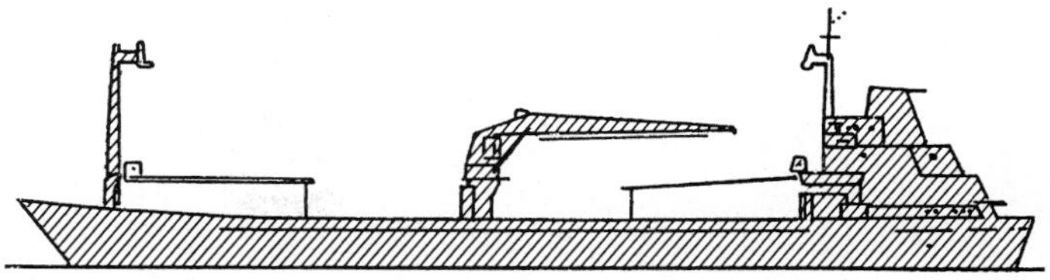

164 *TRHF H*
UFUK Tu/FRG (Buesumer) 1976; C/Con; 2,667 grt/4,040 dwt; 89.77 × 6.04 m *(294.52 × 19.82 ft)*; M (Alpha); 13 kts; ex-*Mercandian Sun*; 122 TEU
Sister: **KONG TONG DAO** (Pa) ex-*Alice Steen*

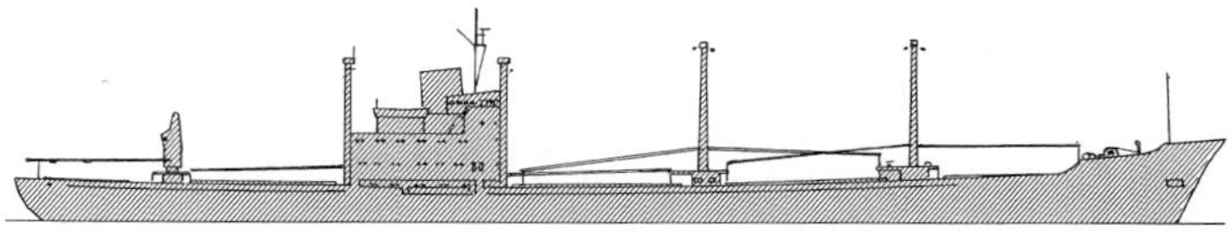

165 *T²NMFNC H13*
HELIOPOLIS SKY Eg/Ne (P. Smit) 1969; C; 4,846 grt/10,645 dwt; 148 × 7 m *(484 × 23.4 ft)*; M (Sulzer); 15.5 kts; ex-*Gooiland*

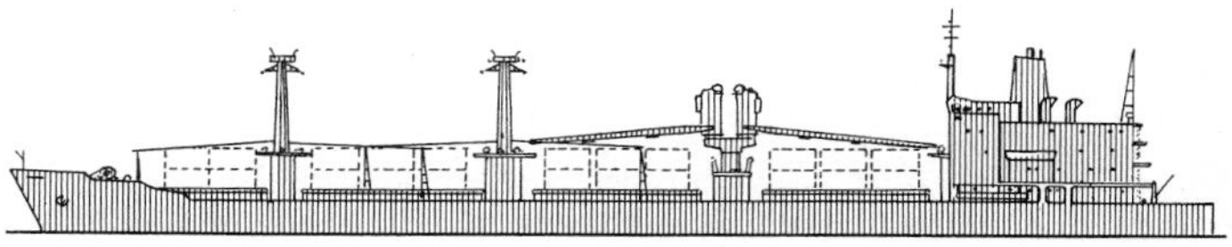

166 *T²PHFN H1*
BOLAN Pk/Ja (Kawasaki) 1980; C/Con; 12,395 grt/18,145 dwt; 153.02 × 9.75 m *(502 × 31.99 ft)*; M (MAN); — kts; 386 TEU
Sisters: **CHITRAL** (Pk); **IRAN TAKHTI** (Ir) ex-*Sargodha*; **HYDERABAD** (Pk); **MULTAN** (Pk); **MALAKAND** (Pk)

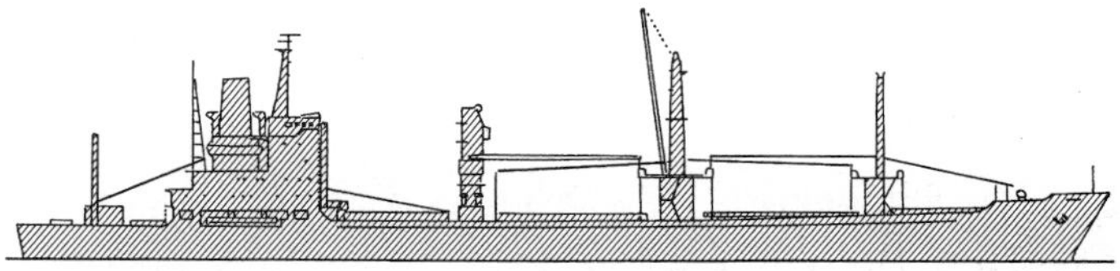

167 *T²PNMFN² H1*
BANGLAR MAMATA Bh/Ja (Mitsubishi HI) 1980; C/Con; 11,764 grt/15,877 dwt; 154.16 × 9.0 m *(505.77 × 29.53 ft)*; M (Sulzer); 16 kts; 256 TEU
Sister: **BANGLAR MAYA** (Bh)

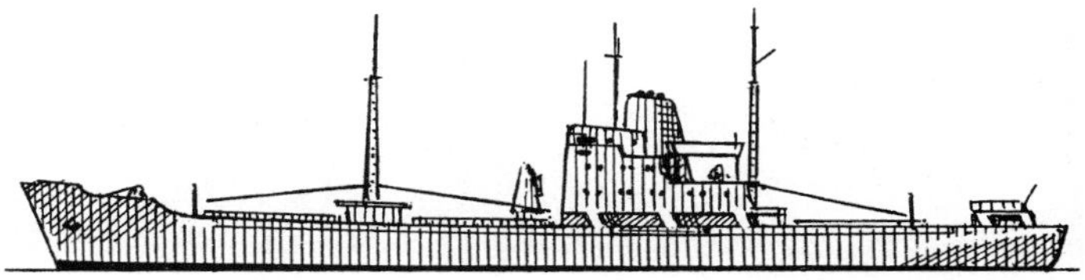

168 *VCMFV H1*
NOOR UAE/De (Aalborg) 1967; C; 2,309 grt/3,350 dwt; 101.5 × 6 m *(335 × 19.8 ft)*; M (Sulzer); 15 kts; ex-*Jaslo*

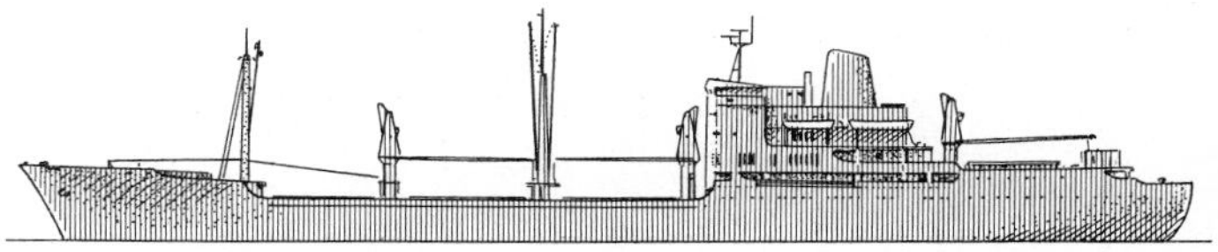

169 *VCTCMFC H13*
HAI HUA Pa/Be (Cockerill) 1972; PC; 13,303 grt/15,350 dwt; 161.14 × 9.89 m *(528.67 × 32.48 ft)*; M (B&W); 20 kts; ex-*Fabiolaville*
Sister: **NORBEL OMAN** (Li) ex-*Kananga*

170 *V²MFSV H13*
DAI YUN SHAN RC/De (Nakskov) 1965; CP; 7,486 grt/9,750 dwt; 137.5 × 7.1/8.7 m *(451 × 23/28.6 ft)*; M (B&W); 17.5 kts; ex-*Jytte Skou*
Sister: **BAI YUN SHAN** (RC) ex-*Susanne Skou*

171 Rio Express *(Li); 1968* *Norman Thomson*

172 Gallant II *(Pa); 1976; (as Gallant Pioneer)* *WSPL*

173 Nyanza *(Bs); 1978; (as Harmony)* *WSPL*

174 Great Universe *(Pa); 1976* *WSPL*

175 Faarabi *(Ir); 1977; (as Kimishige Maru)* *WSPL*

176 Biskra *(Ag); 1979* *WSPL*

177 Niaga XXXII *(Ia); 1970* *WSPL*

178 Umgeni *(SV); 1976; (as Muhlhausen Thomas-Muntzer-Stadt)* *WSPL*

179 Clio *(Ma); 1970; (as Aleksandr Ulyanov)* *WSPL*

180 Ibn Al-Moataz *(Si); 1977* *WSPL*

181 Noble Star *(US); 1977; (as Hoegh Star)* *WSPL*

182 Kitsa *(Cy); 1976; (as Hellespont Courage)* *WSPL*

183 Africa Star *(HK); 1973; (as Gold Alisa)* *WSPL*

184 Komsomolets Moldavii *(Uk); 1971* *FotoFlite*

185 Jobst Oldendorff *(Li); 1983; (as Nobility)* *FotoFlite*

186 Itaite *(Bz); 1971/81* *FotoFlite*

187 Stella F *(Pa); 1981* *FotoFlite*

188 Radzionkow *(Pd); 1973* *FotoFlite*

189 Emel 1 *(Ea); 1975* *FotoFlite*

190 Secil Namibia *(Bs); 1977* *FotoFlite*

191 Tai Angelica *(Pa); 1976* *FotoFlite*

192 Herceg Novi *(Ma); 1981* *FotoFlite*

193 Alkmini *(Ma); 1970* *FotoFlite*

194 Trade Ambassador *(Li); 1976* *FotoFlite*

195 Valeriya Barsova *(Uk); 1982* *FotoFlite*

196 Adrian *(NA); 1979* *FotoFlite*

197 Comet *(Gr); 1978* *FotoFlite*

198 Ksar Chellala *(Ag); 1977* *FotoFlite*

199 Phayao Navee *(Th); 1978* *FotoFlite*

200 Aastun *(NIS); 1975; (as Talisman)* *FotoFlite*

201 Veer Savarka *(In); 1981; (as Jalagouri)* *FotoFlite*

202 Maersk Nara *(Ma); 1978; (as Ciudad de Armenia)* *FotoFlite*

203 Nauticas Mexico *(Me); 1981* *FotoFlite*

204 Banglar Maya *(Bh); 1980* *FotoFlite*

205 City of New Westminster *(Bb); 1985; (as Belforest)* *FotoFlite*

206 Star Evanger *(NIS); 1984* *FotoFlite*

207 Kong Tong Dao *(RC); 1976; (as South Winner)* *FotoFlite*

208 Brisa *(Ma); 1988; (as Ivangrad)* *FotoFlite*

209 Pitak Samut *(Th); 1978; (as Vanil)* *FotoFlite*

210 Chang Ping *(RC); 1970* *FotoFlite*

211 General Delgado *(Pi); 1985* *FotoFlite*

212 Joy Venture *(Li); 1976* *FotoFlite*

213 ICL Vikraman *(In); 1979; (as Sanko Daisy)* *FotoFlite*

214 Pascale Delmas *(Bs); 1979; (as Mahajanga)* *FotoFlite*

215 Cosmos *(Cy); 1979; (as Perla One)* *FotoFlite*

216 Thomas Delmas *(Bs); 1977; (as Yamoussoukro)* *FotoFlite*

217 Laser Santiago *(Cy); 1978; (as Tarpon Santiago)* *FotoFlite*

218 Gao Ling *(RC); 1975* *FotoFlite*

219 Wing Lee No 2 *(Pa); 1978; (as Pembroke)* *FotoFlite*

220 Gulf Champion *(SV); 1978; (as Agboville)* *FotoFlite*

221 Yacu Puma *(Bs); 1977; (as Popi P)* *FotoFlite*

222 Banglar Kallol *(Bh); 1988* *FotoFlite*

223 Pattaya Navee *(Pa); 1978; (as MC Jade)* *FotoFlite*

224 Pal Falcon *(Gr); 1980* *FotoFlite*

225 City of Akaki *(Cy); 1978/86; (as Angol)* *FotoFlite*

226 Maria P I *(Cy); 1978; (as Apure)* *FotoFlite*

227 Mayqueen *(Ma); 1977; (as Guarico)* *FotoFlite*

228 Ken Sun *(Li); 1980; (as Lancelot Sun)* *FotoFlite*

229 Kutai *(Ia); 1983* *FotoFlite*

230 Feng Chi *(RC); 1975* *FotoFlite*

231 Baab Ullah *(Ia); 1983* *FotoFlite*

232 Apman II *(Pa); 1977* *FotoFlite*

233 Yon Pung Ho *(HK); 1978* *FotoFlite*

234 Christina K *(Pa); 1972; (as Evita)* *FotoFlite*

10 Dry Cargo Ships with Travelling Cranes and Self-Unloading Gear

10 Dry Cargo Ships with Travelling Cranes and Self-Unloading Gear

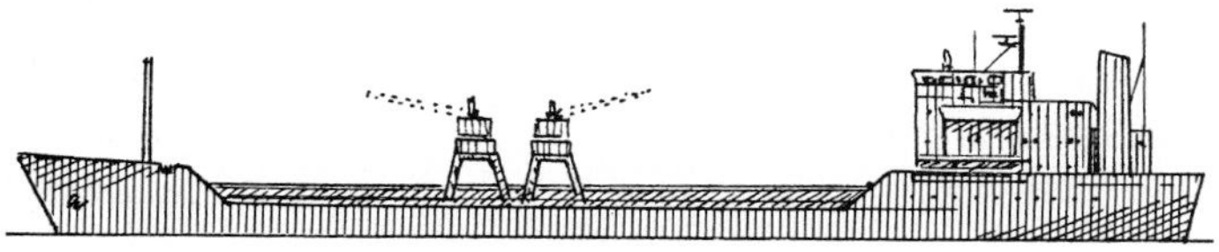

1 *HJ²MG H13*
SUNRANA NIS/Br (Appledore) 1976; C; 3,663 grt/5,482 dwt; 102.04 × 6.93 m *(334.78 × 22.74 ft)*; M (Mirrlees Blackstone); 13.75 kts; ex-*Sandgate*; Travelling cranes
Sisters: **AGIOS SPYRIDON I** (Cy) ex-*Southgate*; **ANJANA D** (Bs) ex-*Green Park* (crane may be removed)

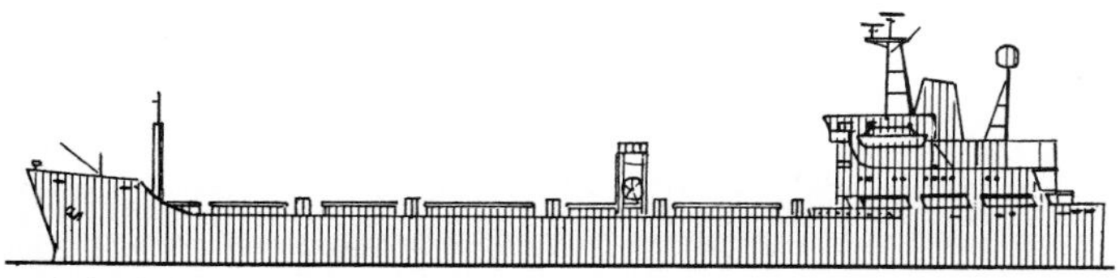

2 *HKMFM H1*
PACIFIC TEAL Br/Br (Swan Hunter) 1982; C; 4,648 grt/3,702 dwt; 103.92 × 6.02 m *(341 × 19.75 ft)*; TSM (A P E Allen); 13 kts; Spent nuclear fuel carrier
Probable sister (builder—Appledore): **PACIFIC SANDPIPER** (Br)

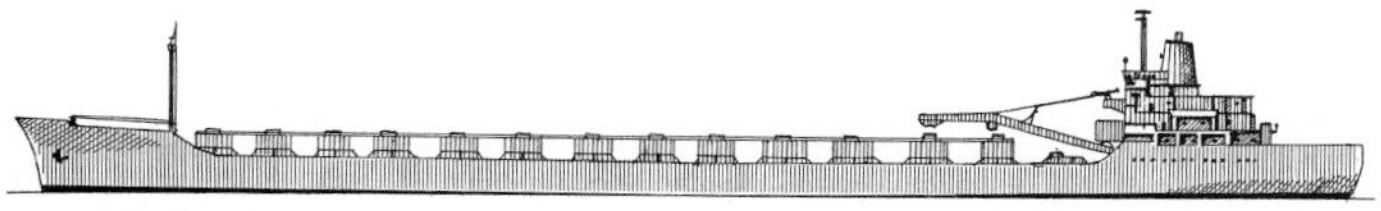

3 *HOMF H13*
DON JORGE Pa/FRG (Howaldts DW) 1970; B; 28,565 grt/52,415 dwt; 226.7 × 12.79 m *(743.76 × 41.96 ft)*; T (Allgemeine); 17.5 kts; ex-*David P Reynolds*

4 *MCHFN H13*
LIBEXCEL Pa/Ja (Sumitomo) 1969; O; 17,261 grt/30,176 dwt; 175.04 × 11 m *(574.28 × 36.09 ft)*; M (Sulzer); 14.25 kts; ex-*Nikkei Maru No 3*; N aft consists of a pole on port side and a tripod on starboard side

5 *MGMFN H1*
XOUR SINGAPORE Sg/Ja (Miho) 1977/81; C/Con; 7,187 grt/8,710 dwt; 132.11 × 7.02 m *(433.43 × 23.03 ft)*; M (B&W); 15 kts; ex-*Papuan Chief*; Lengthened 1981 (Miho); 392 TEU
Sister: **SRI SAMUT** (Th) ex-*Nimos*; Sister (unlengthened): **SEA GALLANT** (Sg) ex-*Coral Chief*

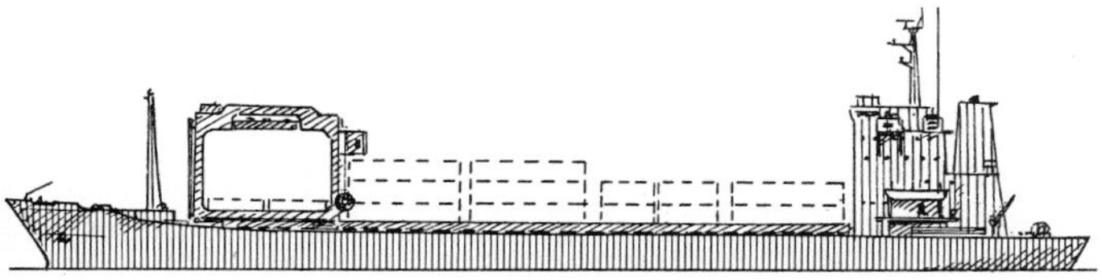

6 *MGMFS H1*
SEA GLORY Sg/Ja (Miho) 1977; C/Con; 6,145 grt/7,747 dwt; 118.12 × 7.42 m *(387.53 × 24.34 ft)*; M (B&W); 15 kts; ex-*Strathkeith*; 372 TEU
Sister: **KOTA PANJANG** (My) ex-*Strathkirn*

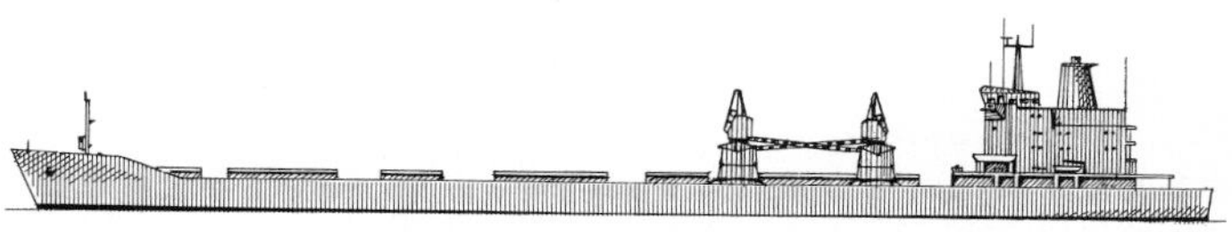

7 *MJ²MF H1*
ARISTOTELIS Li/FRG (Howaldts DW) 1977; B; 23,584 grt/40,300 dwt; 182.91 × 11.89 m *(600.1 × 39.01 ft)*; M (MAN); 14.75 kts; ex-*Havorn*; Travelling cranes
Sisters: **ARISTOGEITON** (Li) ex-*Havfalk*; **ARISTOGENIS** (Li) ex-*Havjo*

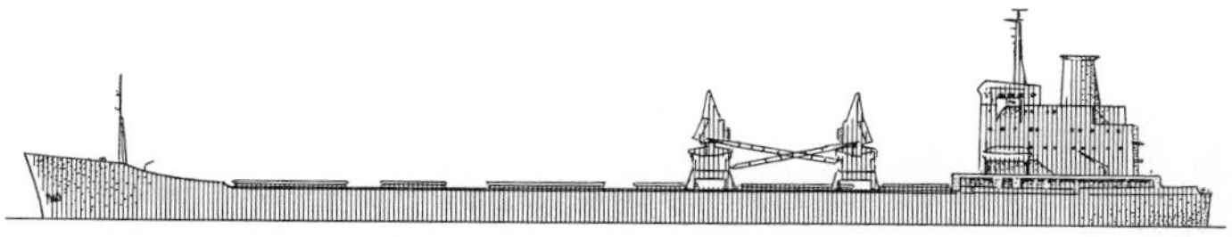

8 *MJ²MF H1*
DYVI PACIFIC NIS/Pd (Gdynska) 1978; B; 21,630 grt/34,232 dwt; 176.59 × 11.51 m *(579.36 × 37.76 ft)*; M (Sulzer); 16 kts; ex-*Beth*; 'B515' type; Travelling cranes
Sisters: **SWAN CLIFF** (Li) ex-*Bardu*; **BARRY** (NIS); **BAUCHI** (NIS); **LUCKY TRADER** (Li) ex-*Bavang*; **DYVI ATLANTIC** (NIS) ex-*Bergo*

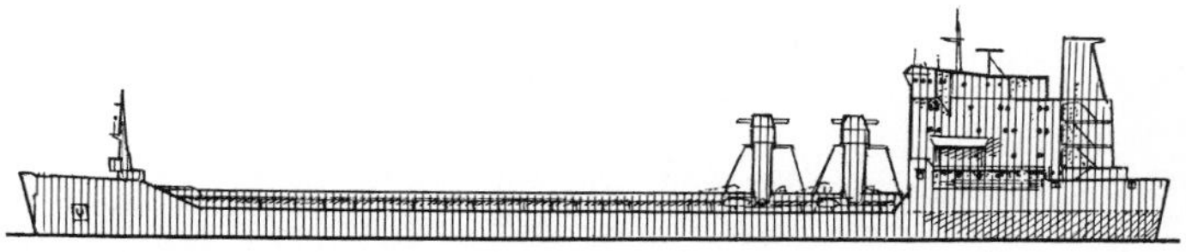

9 *MJ²MF H13*
AQUARIUS It/Sw (Kalmar) 1978; B/TC; 6,355 grt/8,139 dwt; 121 × 7.62 m *(396.98 × 25 ft)*; M (B&W); 14.6 kts; ex-*Boxy*; Travelling cranes; The jibs are normally stowed athwartships as shown; 289 TEU
Sister (has been lengthened to 135 m (443 ft) and probably has one crane): **HOLMON** (Sw) ex-*Dania*

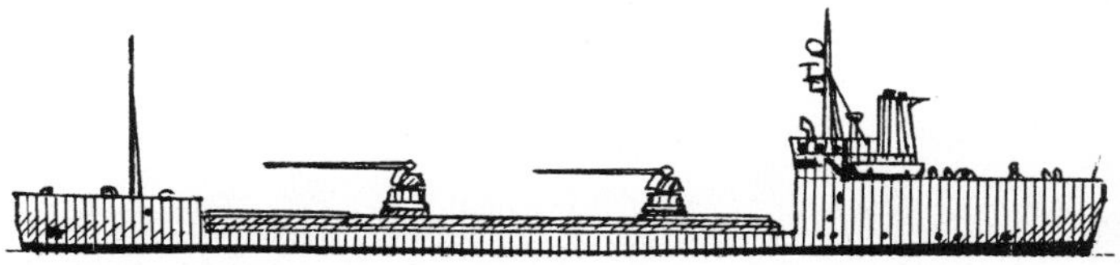

10 *MJ²MF H13*
CARIB DAWN Va/De (Sonderborg) 1975; C; 1,399 grt/2,997 dwt; 78.77 × 5.06 m *(258.43 × 16.6 ft)*; M (Alpha-Diesel); 12.5 kts; ex-*Esther Bech*; Travelling cranes
Sister (can operate as a research ship): **CARIB EVE** (Va) ex-*Louise Bravo*

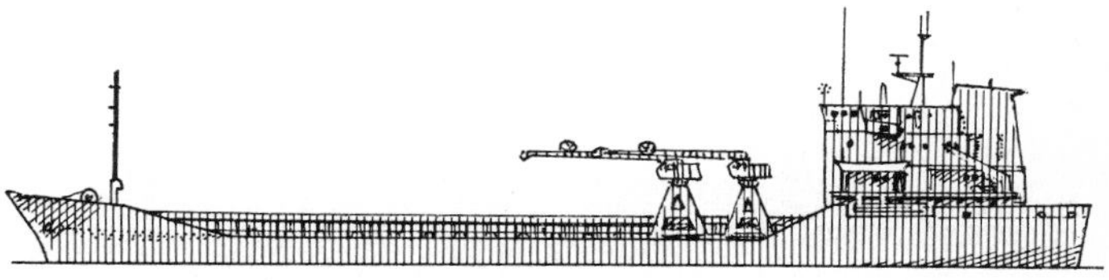

11 *MJ²MF H13*
CHORZOW Ml/Br (Scotstoun) 1980; B; 3,127 grt/4,361 dwt; 95 × 6.08 m *(311.68 × 19.95 ft)*; M (Sulzer); 12.25 kts; Travelling cranes
Sisters (some may not have cranes): **WYSZKOW** (Ml); **MLAWA** (Ml); **GNIEZNO II** (Ml); **SIERADZ** (Ml); **BYTOM** (Ml); **ZGORZELEC** (Ml); **KOSCIERZYNA** (Ml); **LOMZA** (Ml); **WIELUN** (Ml)

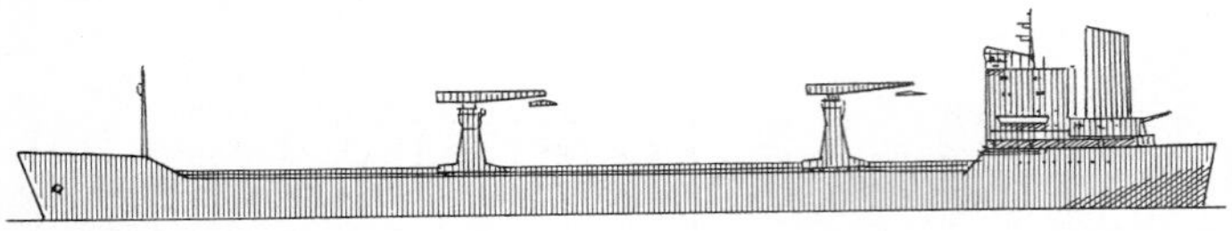

12 *MJ²MF H13*
CLIPPER GOLDEN HIND Li/Ko (Hyundai) 1978; B/Con/NP; 12,804 grt/ 16,560 dwt; 163.96 × 8.65 m *(537.93 × 28.38 ft)*; M (MAN); 15.75 kts; ex-*Antares*; Travelling cranes; 540 TEU; 'HD16F' type
Sisters: **STAR SKOGANGER** (NIS) Launched as *Aldebaran*; **STAR SKARVEN** (NIS) ex-*Atalaya*; **STRILBERG** (NIS) ex-*Astrea*; **STAR STRONEN** (NIS) ex-*Anderso*; **C MARTIN** (Ma) ex-*Baldero*

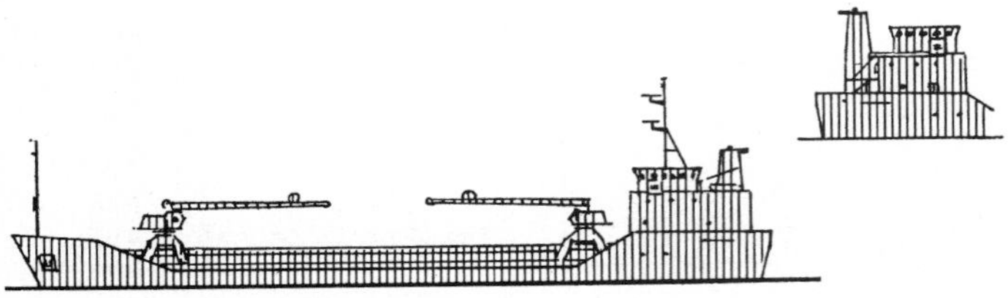

13 *MJ²MF H13*
NATACHA C Bb/Br (Cochrane) 1982; C/Con; 1,636 grt/2,467 dwt; 70.13 × 4.96 m *(230 × 16.27 ft)*; M (APE Allen); 10 kts; ex-*Norbrit Faith*; Travelling cranes; 70 TEU
Sister: **CHERYL C** (Bb) ex-*Norbrit Hope*

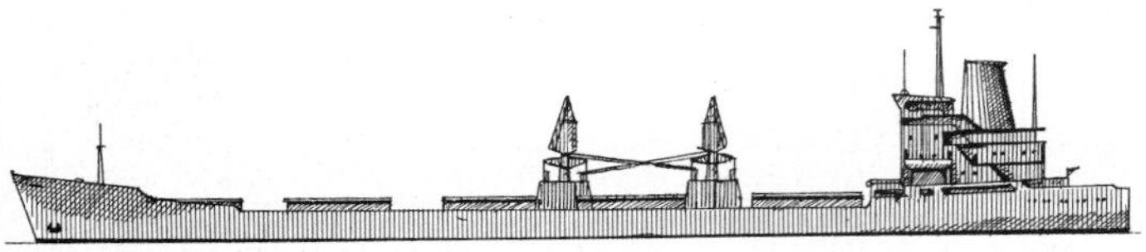

14 *MJ²MFN H1*
BJORN Pa/Pd (Gdynska) 1971; B; 17,564 grt/27,279 dwt; 163.2 × 10.99 m *(535.43 × 36.05 ft)*; M (Sulzer); 15 kts; ex-*Havbjorn*; Travelling cranes; 'B523' type
Sisters: **R PETER M ELRICK** (Li) ex-*Havkatt*; **TROLL** (Li) ex-*Havtroll*; **NORCAPE** (Bs) ex-*Bajka*; **VERNAL STAR** (Pa) ex-*Bakar*; **HANG SHUN** (Pa) ex-*Banta*; **SWAN HILL** (Bs) ex-*Barwa*; **ADRIATIC** (NIS) ex-*Bergljot*; **BALTIC** (NIS) ex-*Blix*; **NORQUEST** (Bs) ex-*Stavern*; **IONIAN MASTER** (Pa) ex-*Trym*; **PU DONG** (Pa) ex-*Baro*

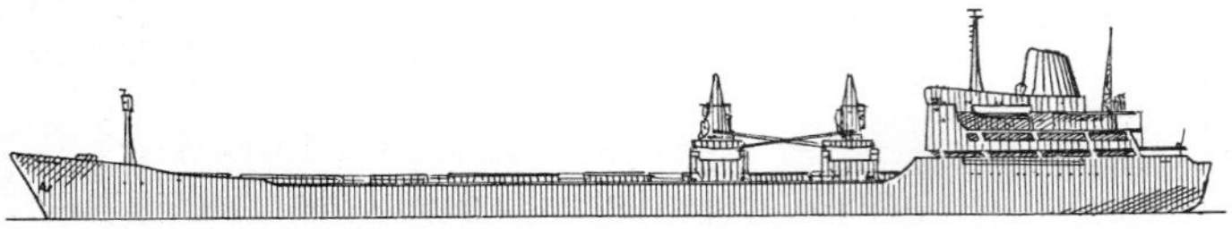

15 *MJ²MFN H13*
JI HAI 10 RC/Ja (IHI); B; 11,686 grt/20,331 1967 dwt; 153.93 × 10.24 m *(505.02 × 33.6 ft)*; M (Sulzer); 16.5 kts; ex-*Havfru*; Travelling cranes

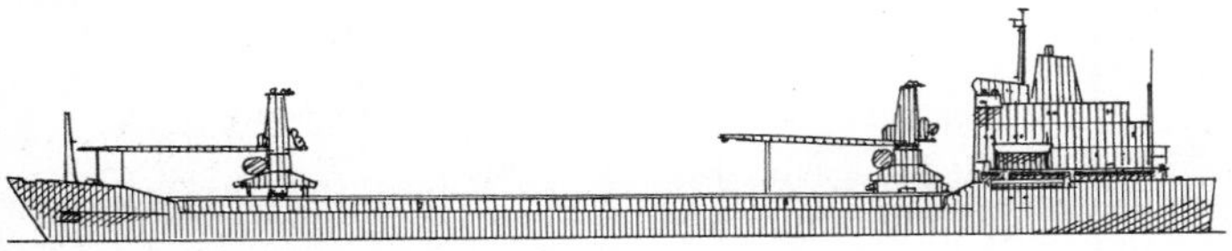

16 *MJ²MFN H13*
SINO CREDIT SV/FRG (Schuerenstedt) 1975; C/Con; 8,142 grt/10,220 dwt; 143.82 × 7.54 m *(471.85 × 24.74 ft)*; M (MAN); 15.5 kts; ex-*Vinland*; Travelling cranes; 456 TEU
Sister: **TRADE BLISS** (Pa) ex-*Skotland*

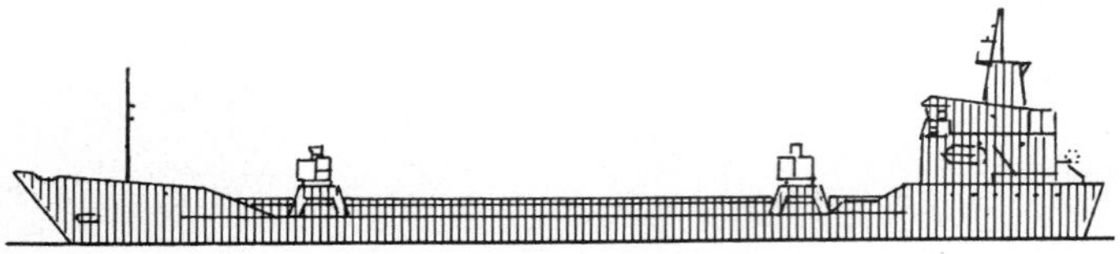

17 *MJ²M–F H13*
ECOWAS TRADER II Ng/Ne (Tille) 1977; C/Con; 1,599 grt/3,700 dwt; 93.6 × 5.6 m *(307.09 × 18.37 ft)*; M (Alpha-Diesel); 12.5 kts; ex-*Leicesterbrook*; Has travelling cranes which may now be removed; 172 TEU
Sister: **GEVO VICTORY** (Le) ex-*Lincolnbrook*

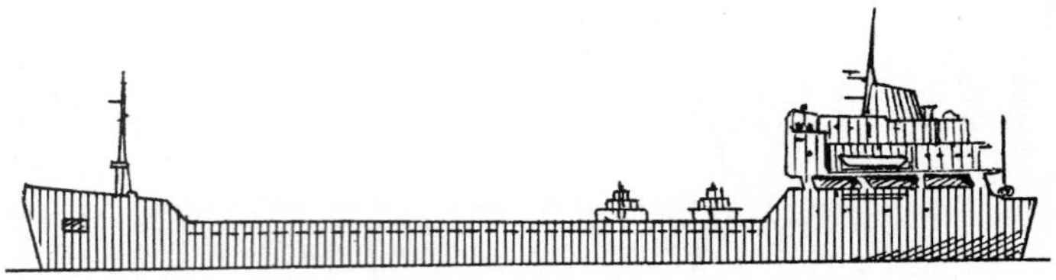

18 *MJ²M–F H13*
HUBRO Ma/Sw (Falkenbergs) 1971; C; 2,092 grt/3,203 dwt; 87.03 × 4.96 m *(285.53 × 16.27 ft)*; M (Appingedammer Brons); 12 kts; ex-*Anders*; Cranes may have been removed

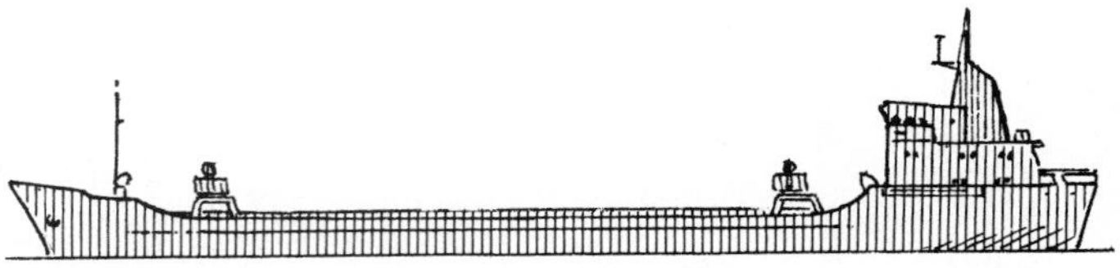

19 *MJ²M–F H13*
MARGARETHA It/Ne (Groot & VV) 1976; C; 2,643 grt/3,854 dwt; 84.21 × 6.32 m *(276.8 × 20.73 ft)*; M (Smit & Bolnes); 13 kts; ex-*Margaretha Smits*; Travelling cranes
Sister (may have cranes removed): **MALIN SEA** (Va) ex-*Marijke Smits*
Probable sisters: **TRI FRAKT** (No) ex-*Makiri Smits*; **MARIVAN** (Ho) ex-*Marinus Smits*

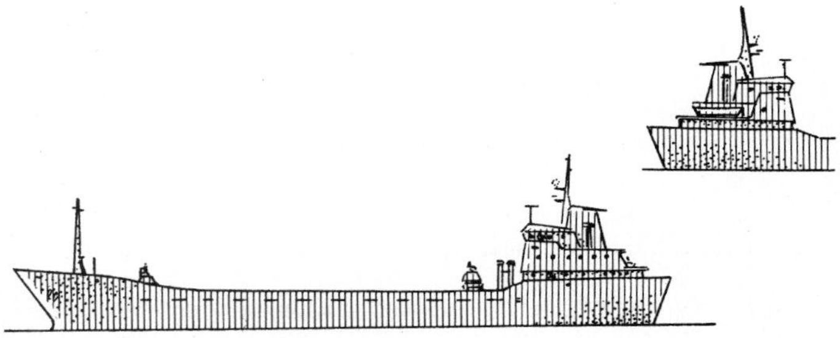

20 *MJ²M–F H13*
TYSEER Sy/De (Frederikshavn) 1971; C; 1,366 grt/2,126 dwt; 76.46 × 4.75 m *(250.85 × 15.58 ft)*; M (Alpha-Diesel); 12 kts; ex-*Merc Europa*; Travelling cranes; Starboard side of superstructure differs (see inset); 54 TEU
Sisters: **CARIMA** (Pa) ex-*Merc Phoenecia*; **KAI YUAN** (RC) ex-*Merc Continental*; **NORPOL PRIDE** (—) ex-*Merc Australia*; **ROSAYELENA** (Ve) ex-*Merc Groenlandia*

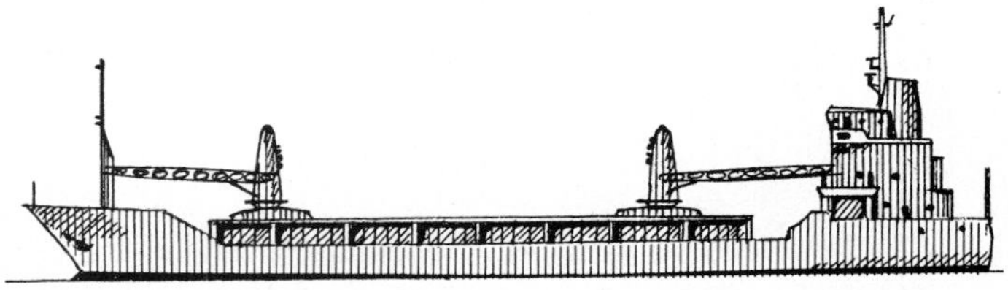

21 *MJ²M–FM H13*
GARDSKY NIS/FRG (S&B) 1976; C; 2,978 grt/4,450 dwt; 91.09 × 6.79 m *(298.85 × 22.28 ft)*; M (KHD); 14.5 kts; ex-*Dollart*; Travelling cranes; 155 TEU; See photo number 10/67
Sisters: **SKY BIRD** (NA) ex-*Jan Wilhelm*; **GARDSUN** (No) ex-*Osterems*; **GARDWAY** (No) ex-*Luhe*; See photo number 10/112

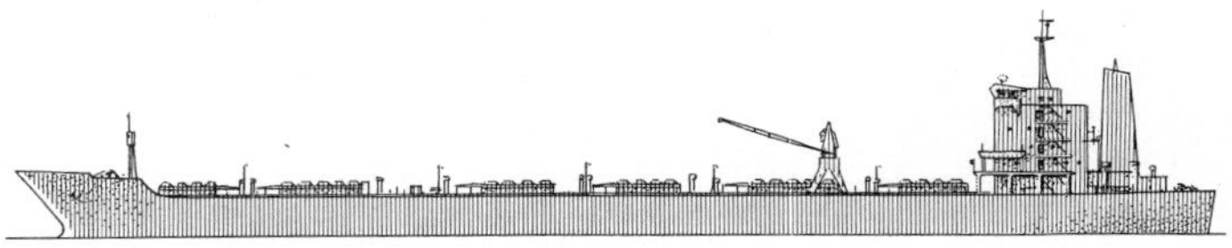

22 *MJMF H1*
MARIA DOLORES Po/Sp (AESA) 1979; B/Cem; 22,352 grt/38,401 dwt; 186.65 × 9.75 m *(612.37 × 31.99 ft)*; M (Sulzer); 14 kts; ex-*Baroja*; Travelling crane
Sisters: **FAIR LADY** (Ma) ex-*Unamuno*; **ADVENTURE I** (Ma) ex-*Guridi*

23 *MJMF H13*
GRINNA SV/De (Frederikshavn) 1972; C; 1,545 grt/2,647 dwt; 76.6 × 3.47 m *(251.31 × 11.38 ft)*; M (Alpha); 12 kts; ex-*Merc Asia*; **SIMILAR TO DRAWING NUMBER 10/20**; Grinna was originally a sister of latter but cranes have been replaced by an excavator

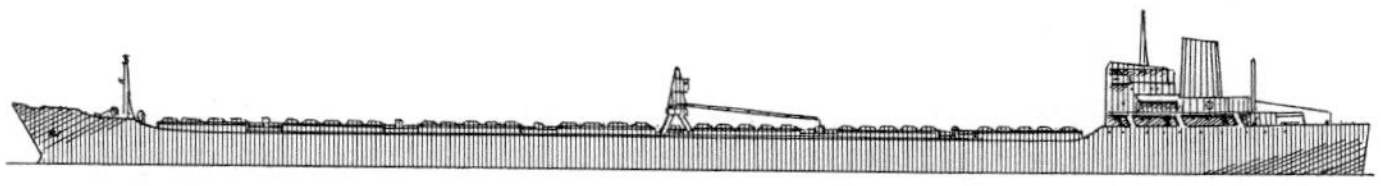

24 *MJMFN H13*
MAR CASPIO Ar/Sp (AESA) 1971; B; 28,021 grt/53,489 dwt; 206.86 × 13.35 m *(678.67 × 43.79 ft)*; M (Sulzer); 16 kts; ex-*Aralar*; Travelling crane may now be removed
Similar (tripod radar mast): **BONSAI** (Ma) ex-*Pilar Maria*

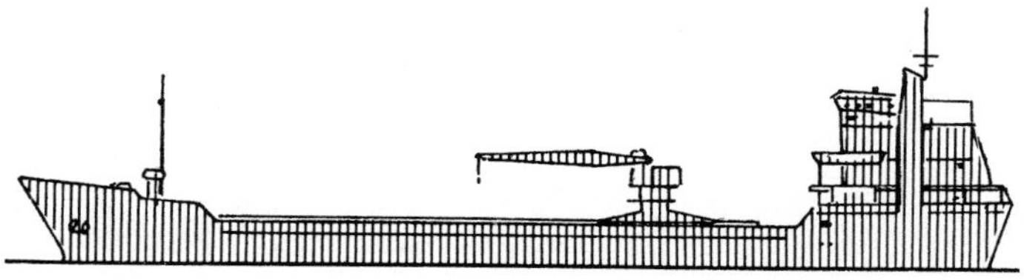

25 *MJMG H13*
ALIDON Cy/Ne (Groot & VV) 1978; C; 3,702 grt/6,110 dwt; 83.7 × 8.38 m *(275 × 27.49 ft)*; M (Atlas-MaK); 11 kts; ex-*Alida Smits*; Cranes are tandem and ram-luffing type
Sisters: **ALSYDON** (Cy) ex-*Alsyta Smits*; **ANDREALON** (Cy) ex-*Andrea Smits*; Similar (longer sisters—98.1m (322ft)): **AMANDA 1** (Cy) ex-*Amanda Smits*; **ANITA 1** (Cy) ex-*Anita Smits*

See photo number 10/105

26 *MJMG H13*
NOR VIKING No/No (Sterkoder) 1977; C; 1,992 grt/3,048 dwt; 80.12 × 5.58 m *(262.86 × 18.31 ft)*; M (Alpha); 10.5 kts; ex-*Norrviken*; **SIMILAR TO DRAWING NUMBER 6/39** but *Nor Viking* has an excavator crane added

See photo number 10/104

27 *MJMG H13*
REKSNES Pa/No (Lothe) 1977; B; 3,885 grt/6,258 dwt; 103.56 × 6.85 m *(339.76 × 22.47 ft)*; M (Normo); 13.5 kts; **SIMILAR TO DRAWING NUMBER 5/9**; *Reksnes* has been fitted with an excavator crane
Sister: **ROGNES** (Pa)

28 *MJM–F H1*
PIONER No/As (Korneuberg) 1970; C; 1,357 grt/1,397 dwt; 76.21 × 3.7 m *(250.03 × 12.14 ft)*; M (MWM); 12 kts; ex-*Windle Surf*; **SIMILAR TO DRAWING NUMBER 6/42**. *Pioner* has been fitted with an excavator crane

29 *MJM–F H13*
MINERVA No/No (Eides) 1973; C; 1,480 grt/2,378 dwt; 70.01 × 5.27 m *(229.69 × 17.29 ft)*; M (Atlas-MaK); 12.5 kts; ex-*Brunita*; fitted with excavator crane

30 *MJM–F H13*
SARA 3 Sy/Ne (Groot & VV) 1976; C; 1,599 grt/3,640 dwt; 84.31 × 6.32 m *(276.6 × 20.73 ft)*; M (Smit & Bolnes); 13 kts; ex-*Kirsten Smits*; Travelling crane; 122 TEU
Probable sisters: **MARIVAN** (Ho) ex-*Marinus Smits*; **GIAVA** (It) ex-*Pauline Lonborg*

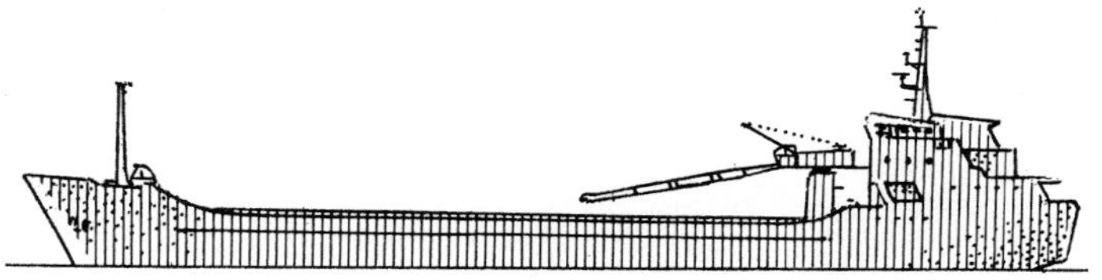

31 *MJM–F H13*
STEPENITZ Cy/Ne (Bijlsma) 1977; C; 1,595 grt/2,820 dwt; 81.44 × 4.78 m *(267.2 × 15.68 ft)*; M (Atlas-MaK); 11.5 kts; ex-*Noordland*

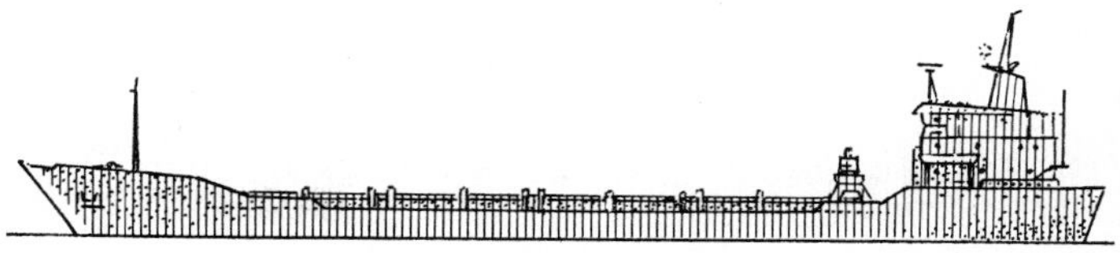

32 *MJM–FN H13*
ANITA NIS/Ne (Kramer & Booy) 1975; C; 2,627 grt/3,739 dwt; 93 × 5.58 m *(305.12 × 18.31 ft)*; M (Alpha-Diesel); 13 kts; ex-*Junior Lotte*; Travelling crane; 186 TEU
Sister: **MARIE** (Sw) ex-*Junior Lone*

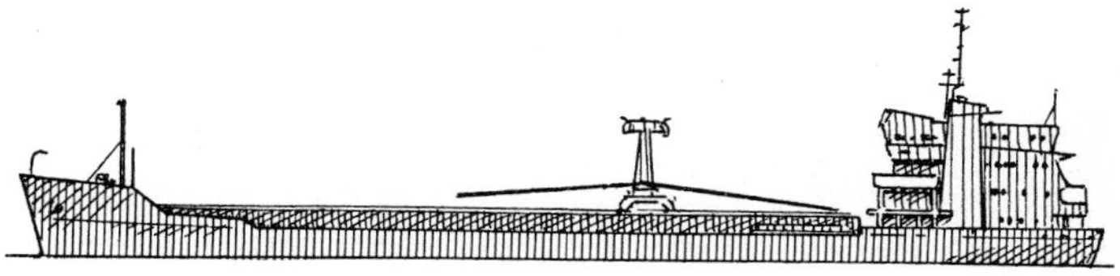

33 *MJM–G H1*
ROSALI Cy/Po (Viana) 1972; B/Con; 4,255 grt/6,126 dwt; 96.6 × 7.19 m *(316.93 × 23.6 ft)*; M (Atlas-MaK); 13 kts; ex-*Alice Bolten*; Travelling cranes; 180 TEU
Probably similar (original sisters, now lengthened and rebuilt): **PYRGOS** (Cy) ex-*Elisabeth Fisser*; **OKAPI** (Cy) ex-*Imela Fisser*

34 *MJOMF H1*
KURE Li/Ja (IHI) 1971; B; 89,623 grt/159,162 dwt; 303.82 × 17.45 m *(996.78 × 57.25 ft)*; T (IHI); 15.5 kts; Launched as *Cedros Pacific*; Travelling cranes

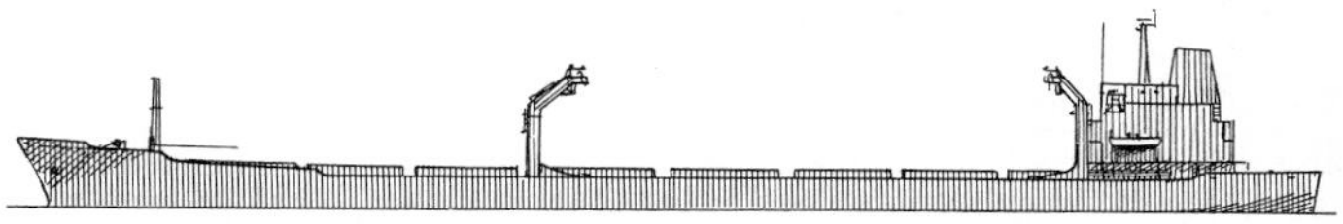

35 *MK^{2}MF H1*
ADAMAS Bs/Ja (IHI) 1978; B; 14,153 grt/22,823 dwt; 164.34 × 9.4 m *(539.11 × 30.84); M (Pielstick); 15 kts; ex-Falcon*; 'Friendship' type
Sisters: **ANANGEL MIGHT** (Gr); **ANANGEL SPIRIT** (Gr); **CLIPPER AQUAMARINE** (Bs) Launched as *Efdim Junior*; **KAWA** (Bs) ex-*George*; **ANANGEL ENDEAVOUR** (Gr); **ANANGEL FIDELITY** (Gr); **CLIPPER YAMA** (Bs) ex-*Therean Mariner*; **CLIPPER AMETHYST** (Bs) ex-*Amethyst*

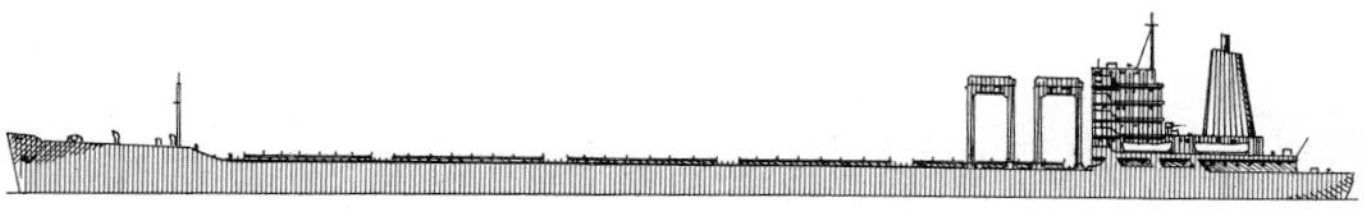

36 *MK^{2}MF H1*
INGER US/US (Sun SB) 1945/62; B; 14,192 grt/23,997 dwt; 190.81 × 9.26 m *(626.02 × 30.38 ft)*; T–E (Westinghouse); 14 kts; ex-*Fort Caspar*; Converted from 'T–2' type tanker 1962 (Schlieker); gantries have now been removed

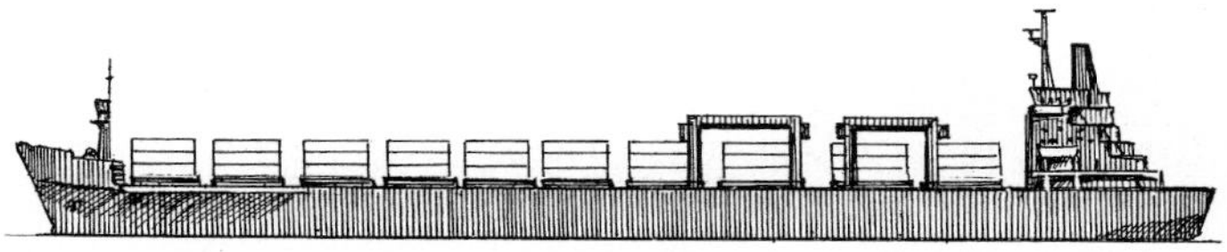

37 *MK^{2}MF H1*
SEA PEARL Cy/Fi (Wärtsilä) 1971; C/TC; 23,569 grt/31,889 dwt; 184.21 × 10.78 m *(604.36 × 35.37 ft)*; M (Pielstick); 16.5 kts; ex-*Pacific*
Sister: **ICEPEARL** (Cy) ex-*Suecia*

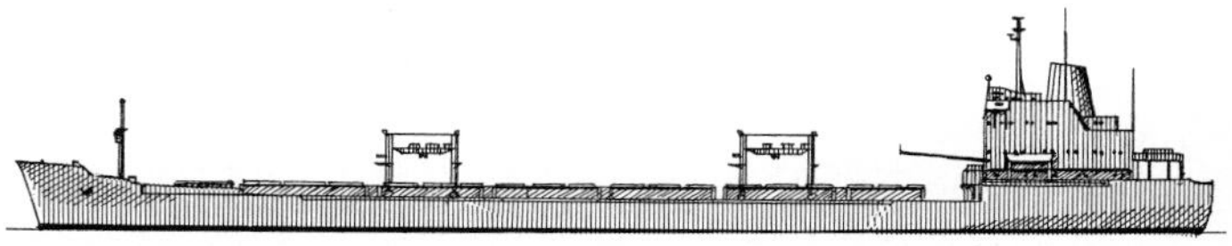

38 *MK^{2}MF H13*
MED CARRARA SV/No (Bergens) 1969; B/Con; 19,033 grt/29,709 dwt; 171.91 × 10.41 m *(564 × 34.15 ft)*; M (MAN); 15.75 kts; ex-*Taranger*; 694 TEU
Similar (some have gantries of different design): **IONIAN SAILOR** (Pa) ex-*Star Atlantic*; **IONIAN BREEZE** (Pa) ex-*Star Assyria*; **STAR CEBU** (Pi) ex-*Star Boxford*

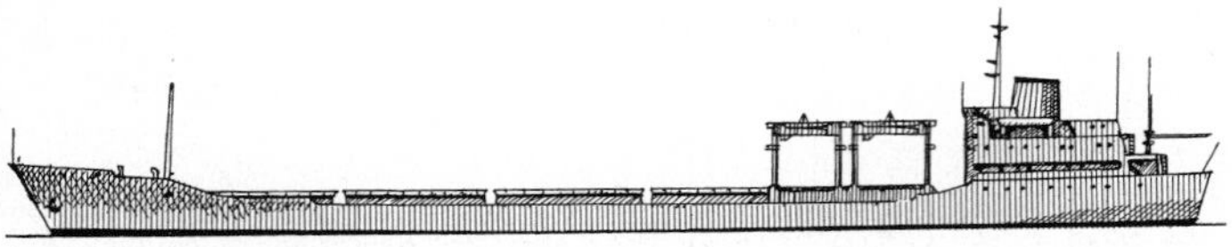

39 *MK²MFM H13*
MUNKSUND Sw/Sw (Lindholmens) 1968; C/TC; 9,261 grt/12,497 dwt; 153.4 × 8.4 m *(503.28 × 27.56 ft)*; M (Pielstick); 16.5 kts
Sisters: **HOLMSUND** (Sw); **TUNADAL** (Sw)

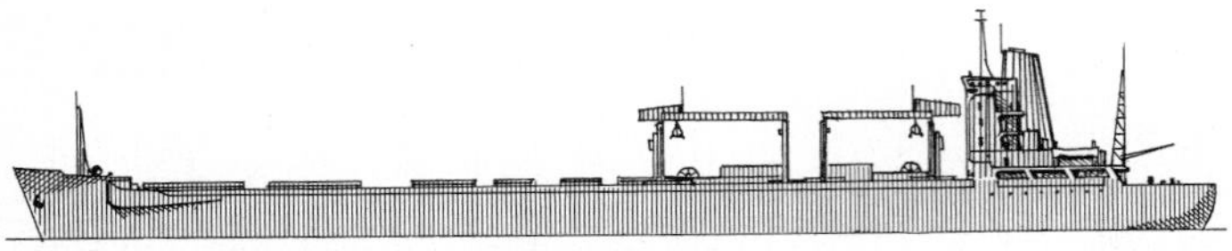

40 *MK²MFN H1*
JIANG YANG RC/Ja (Mitsui) 1967; B; 19,922 grt/28,210 dwt; 176 × 10.7 m *(577.43 × 35.1 ft)*; M (B&W); 14 kts; ex-*Chuetsusan Maru*

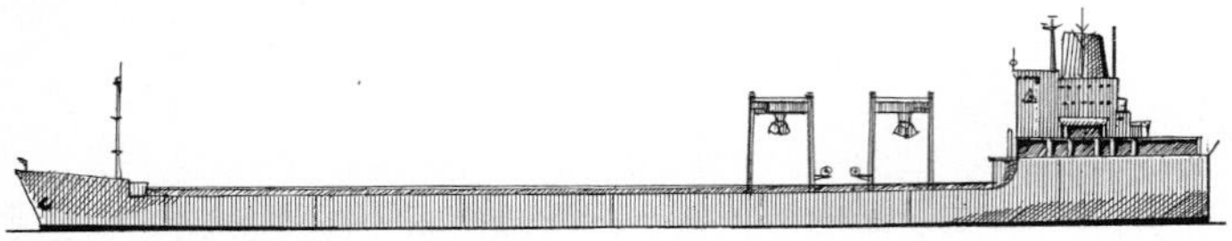

41 *MK²MFN H13*
STAR EUROPA Li/Ja (Kawasaki) 1977; B/TC/Con; 30,719 grt/45,063 dwt; 200.51 × 11.51 m *(657.84 × 37.62 ft)*; M (MAN); 15.25 kts; ex-*Hoegh Mallard*; 1,800 TEU
Sisters: **MASCOT** (Bs) ex-*Hoegh Mascot*; **HOEGH MARLIN** (Bs); Similar: **HOEGH MERCHANT** (Bs); **HOEGH MERIT** (Bs); **HOEGH MINERVA** (Bs); **HOEGH MUSKETEER** (Bs); **HOEGH MIRANDA** (Bs)

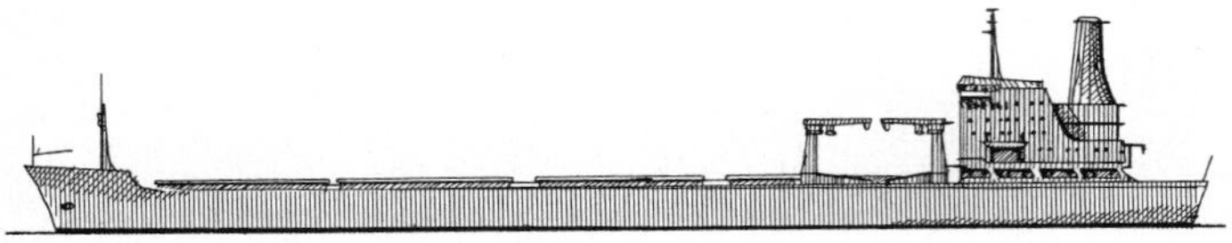

42 *MK²MG H1*
BORC NIS/Be (Cockerill) 1972; B; 20,139 grt/28,106 dwt; 172.52 × 10.52 m *(566 × 34.51 ft)*; M (B&W); 15.25 kts; ex-*Borg*

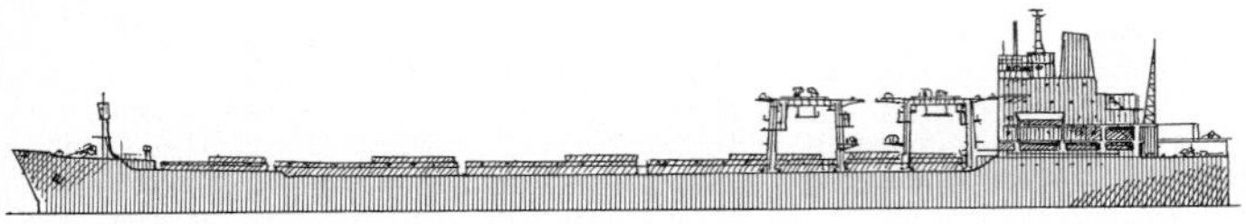

43 *MK²M²FN H13*
FALCON ARROW Bs/Ja (Mitsui) 1977; B/TC/Con; 25,929 grt/38,747 dwt; 182 × 11.55 m *(597 × 37.89 ft)*; M (B&W); 14.5 kts; 1,100 TEU
Sister: **SWAN ARROW** (Bs); Similar: **BORRENMILL** (Bs) ex-*La Ensenada*; **BIO BIO** (Li) ex-*La Primavera*; **LARKFIELD** (Bs) ex-*Alain L-D*; **NANDU ARROW** (Bs); **RAVEN ARROW** (Bs); **RICHFIELD** (Bs) ex-*Louis L-D*; **SUN SUMA** (Bs) ex-*La Costa*; **DOVE ARROW** (Bs) ex-*Egda*; **PELICAN ARROW** (Bs) ex-*Folga*; **HATO ARROW** (Bs) ex-*Grena*; **GULL ARROW** (Bs) ex-*Horda*; **CONDOR ARROW** (NIS) ex-*Molda*; **DIPPER ARROW** (NIS) ex-*Kiwi Arrow*; **TOKI ARROW** (Bs); **TSURU ARROW** (Bs); **EAGLE ARROW** (Bs) ex-*Gerard L-D*; **PRINCEFIELD** (Bs) ex-*Jean L-D*; **RHONE** (Bs) ex-*La Cordillera*; **HERON ARROW** (Bs) ex-*Strinda*; **BERGEN ARROW** (Bs) ex-*Bergen Thistle*

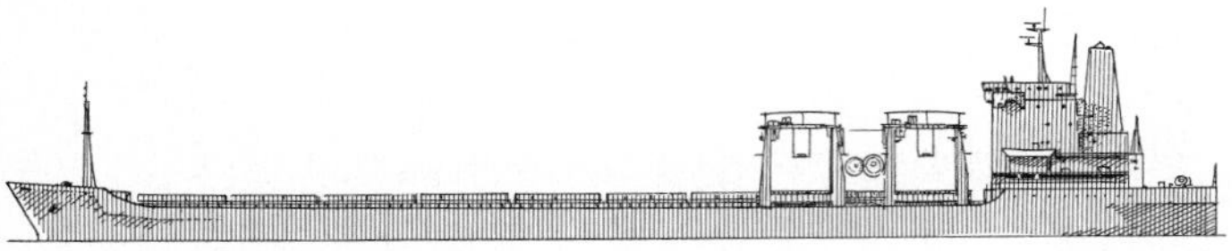

44 *MK²MNF H13*
STAR DROTTANGER NIS/Ja (Mitsui) 1978; B/Con; 27,735 grt/43,051 dwt; 182.91 × 12.03 m *(600.1 × 39.47 ft)*; M (B&W); 15 kts; ex-*Star Magnate*; 1,344 TEU
Sisters: **STAR DRIVANGER** (NIS) ex-*Star Hong Kong*; **STAR DJERVANGER** (NIS) ex-*Star World*; Similar: **STAR DIEPPE** (NIS); **STAR DOVER** (NIS

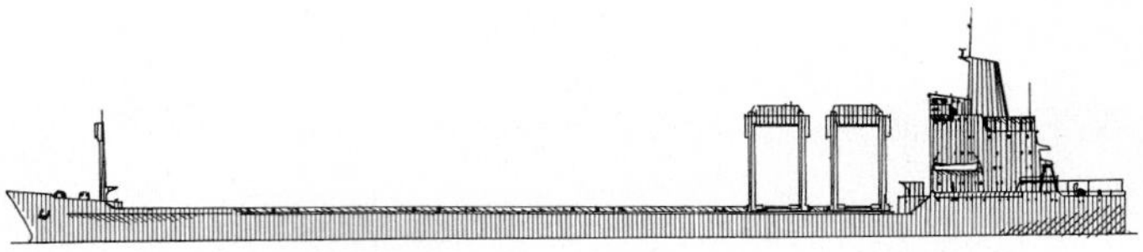

45 *MK²M-F H13*
EVER ACCESS Pa/Br (H&W) 1970; B; 17,372 grt/25,299 dwt; 167.57 × 10.37 m *(549.77 × 34.02 ft)*; M (B&W); 14.5 kts; ex-*Bulk Eagle*
Sisters: **YOUTH STRONG** (Pa) ex-*La Pampa*; Similar: **FILIPOS** (Ma) ex-*Heina*; **LI NING** (Pa) ex-*Lista* (built in Norway—Bergens): **VISAYAS VICTORY** (Pi) ex-*Ogna*

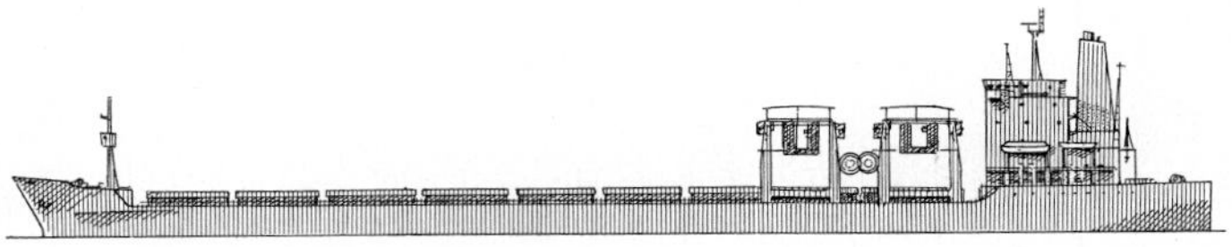

46 *MK²NMFM H13*
STAR DAVANGER NIS/Ja (Kawasaki) 1978; B/Con; 27,125 grt/43,793 dwt; 183 × 12.05 m *(600.39 × 39.53 ft)*; M (MAN); 15.5 kts; ex-*Star Enterprise*; 1,464 TEU
Sister: **STAR DERBY** (NIS) ex-*Star Carrier*

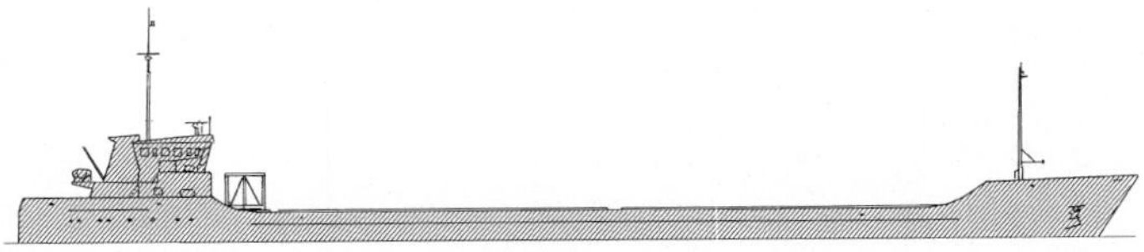

47 *MKMF H13*
PLUTO Ne/Ne (E J Smit) 1986; C; 1,998 grt/3,697 dwt; 88.14 × 5 m *(289.17 × 16.4 ft)*; M (MaK); 10.5 kts
Sisters: **JAMBO** (Cy); **JUMBO** (Ne); **PLATO** (Cy)

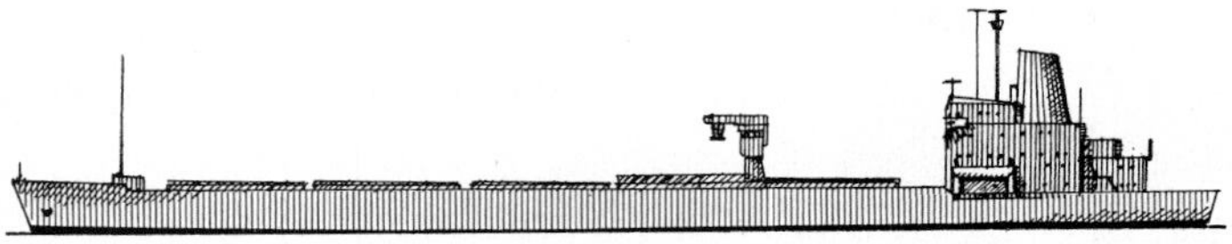

48 *MKMFN H*
EAGLE Va/FRG (Rickmers) 1972; B/V; 9,514 grt/10,079 dwt; 141.61 × 7.27 m *(464.6 × 23.85 ft)*; M (MAN); 16 kts; ex-*Weyroc*; Four side doors and two ramps (port)

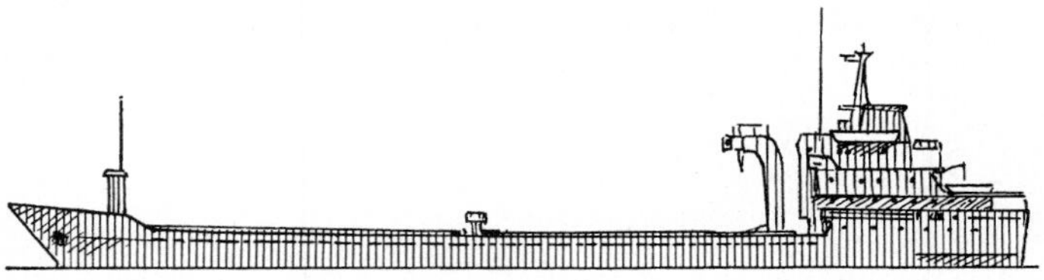

49 *MKM-F H13*
SEA EMPRESS SV/DDR ('Neptun') 1970; C; 3,011 grt/4,410 dwt; 102.98 × 5.85 m *(338 × 19.19 ft)*; M (Atlas-MaK); 13.5 kts; ex-*Hansa Trade*; Gantry crane may have been removed and replaced by conventional cranes. This could also apply to some, or all, of the similar ships
Similar: **ORION STAR** (Pa) ex-*Hanseat*; **LINZ** (Cy) ex-*Samba*; **MIMINA DORMIO** (It) ex-*Ringfalck*

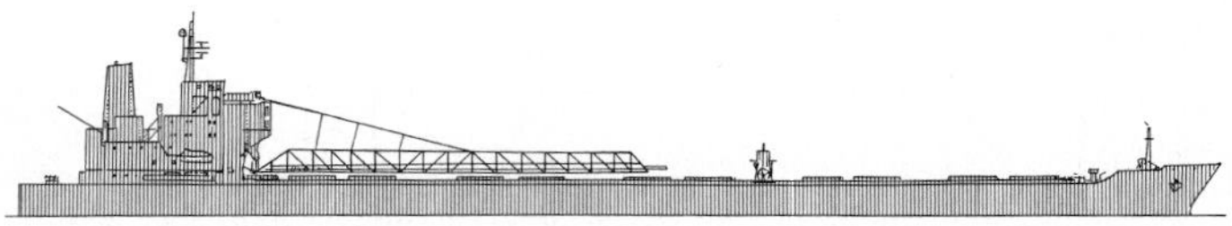

50 *MKOMFC H1*
WESTERN BRIDGE Bs/Ja (Hashihama) 1991; B; 55,695 grt/96,772 dwt; 249.9 × 15.02 m *(819.88 × 49.28 ft)*; M (B&W); 15 kts
Sister: **EASTERN BRIDGE** (Bs)

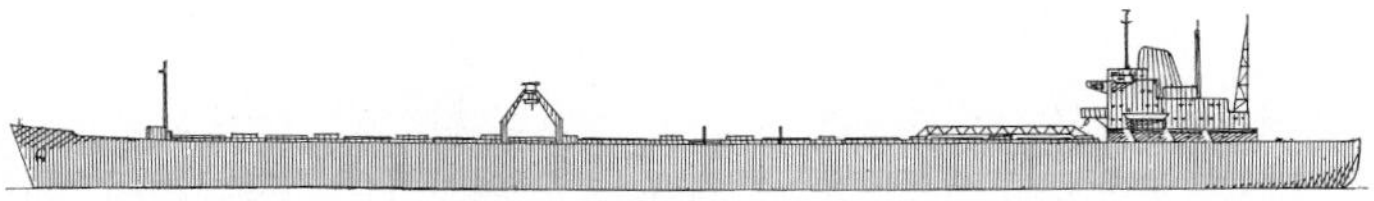

51 *MKOMFM^2 H*
CONVEYOR Li/Ja (Kure) 1968; B; 44,099 grt/75,608 dwt; 243.5/9 × 14.55 m *(799.18 × 47.74 ft)*; T (GEC); 15.5 kts; ex-*Universe Conveyor*

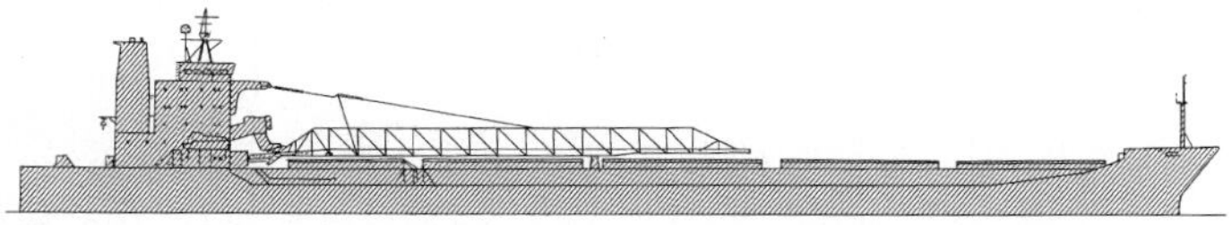

52 *MOMF H13*
HAI WANG XING RC/Ge (Bremer VW) 1995; B; 24,964 grt/37,944 dwt; 186.58 × 9.8 m *(612.14 × 32.15 ft)*; M (B&W); 14.5 kts
Sister: **TIAN LONG XING** (RC)

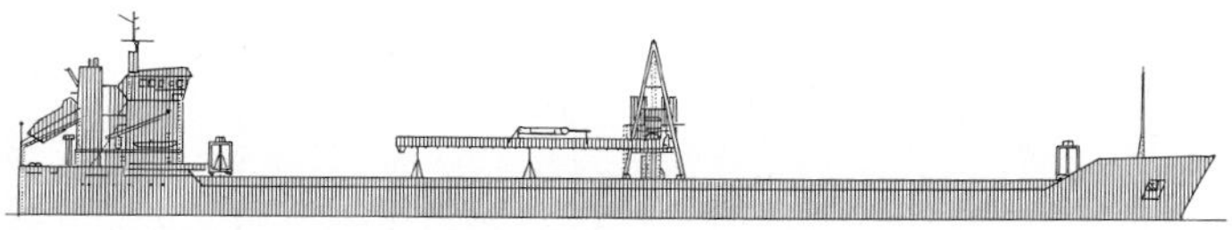

53 *MOMFL H13*
MALMNES NIS/Ne (Ferus Smit) 1993; B; 5,883 grt/9,891 dwt; 126.7 × 7.69 m *(415.68 × 25.23 ft)*; M (Wärtsilä); 13.5 kts
Sisters: **MORNES** (NIS); **MOXNES** (NIS)

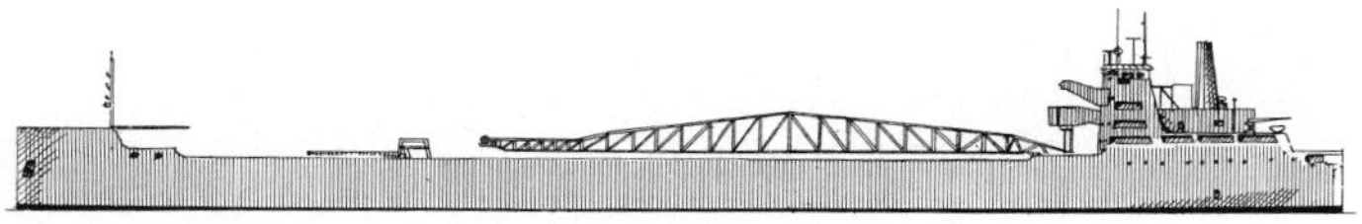

54 *MOMG H12*
CANADIAN PROGRESS Ca/Ca (Port Weller) 1968; B; 21,436 grt/ 31,751 dwt; 222.51 × 8.73 m *(730 × 28.56 ft)*; M (Caterpillar); 13.5 kts

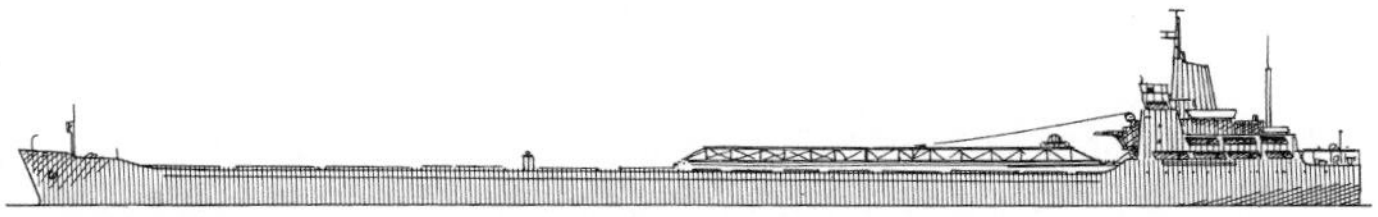

55 *MOM–FN H13*
SAUNIERE Ca/Br (Lithgows) 1970; B; 16,522 grt/24,481 dwt; 195.94 × 9.54 m *(642.85 × 31.29 ft)*; M (MaK); 13 kts; ex-*Brooknes*; Lengthened 1976 (Swan Hunter)

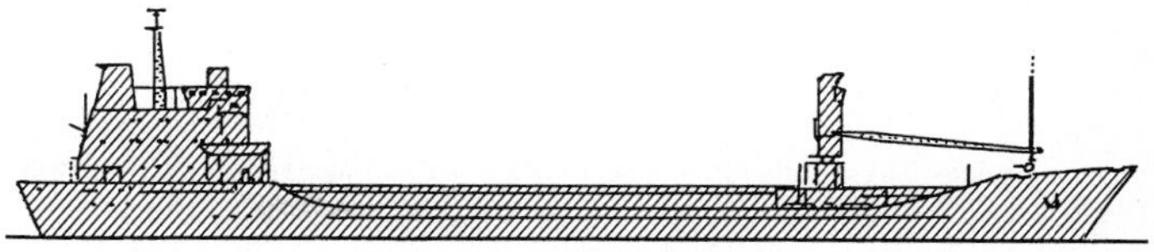

56 *MPMF H13*
ADRIATIC QUEEN Ma/FRG (Brand) 1976; C/Con; 4,399 grt/7,852 dwt; 106.61 × 7.85 m *(349.77 × 25.75 ft)*; M (MaK); 13.50 kts; ex-*Bernhard Schulte*; 246 TEU

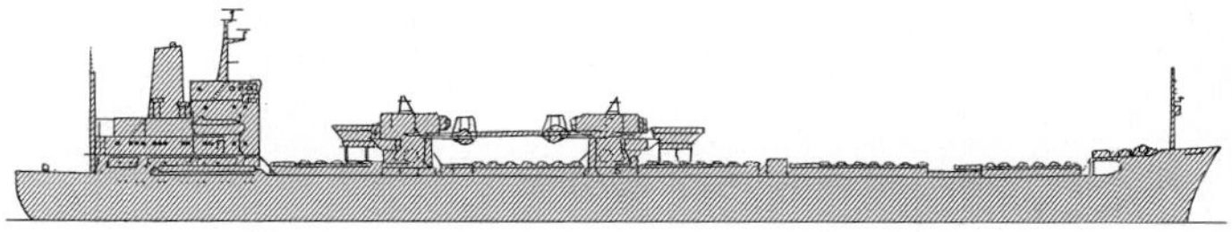

57 *MX^{2}MFN H1*
GRIGORIY ALEKSEYEV Ru/Ja (Hitachi) 1974; BWC; 18,398 grt/23,606 dwt; 169.45 × 9.88 m *(555.94 × 32.41 ft)*; M (B&W); 14.5 kts; Travelling cranes
Sister: **PAVEL RYBIN** (Ru)

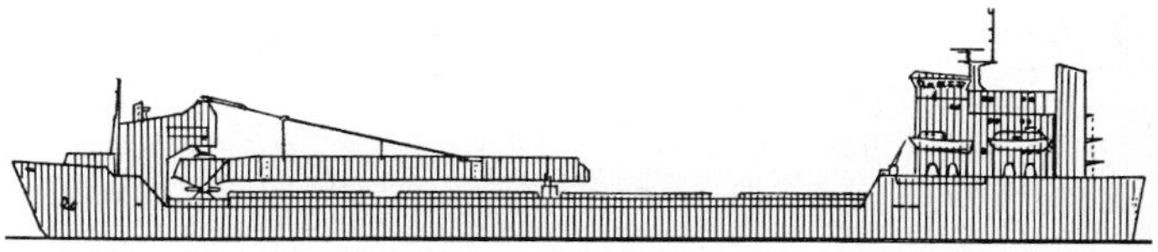

58 *M–OMG H13*
TELNES Pa/No (Kleven) 1982; B; 6,944 grt/10,110 dwt; 117.71 × 8.47 m *(386.19 × 27.79 ft)*; M (Stork-Werkspoor); 14 kts; Fitted with self-discharging elevator
Sister: **TINNES** (NIS)

59 *X^{2}KMFX^3*
LINCOLN US/US (Bethlehem PC) 1962; C/Con; 13,367 grt/14,473 dwt; 172 × 9.6 m *(564 × 31.8 ft)*; T (Bethlehem Steel); 20 kts; ex-*President Lincoln*; US Government owned; Both vessels transferred to US Reserve Fleet
Sister: **PRESIDENT** (US) ex-*President Tyler*

60 Aristogeiton *(Li); 1977* *FotoFlite*

61 Carima *(SV); 1972* *FotoFlite*

62 Chorzow *(MI); 1980* *FotoFlite*

63 Aquarius *(It); 1978* *FotoFlite*

64 Natacha C *(Bb); 1982* *FotoFlite*

65 Star Skoganger *(NIS); 1977* *FotoFlite*

66 Troll *(Li); 1973* *FotoFlite*

67 Gardsky *(NIS); 1976* *FotoFlite*

68 Fair Lady *(Ma); 1979* *FotoFlite*

69 Stepenitz *(Cy); 1977* *FotoFlite*

70 Telnes *(Pa); 1982* *FotoFlite*

71 Eagle *(Va); 1972* *FotoFlite*

72 Sea Pearl *(Cy); 1971; (as Malahat)* *FotoFlite*

73 Borc *(NIS); 1972; (as Borg)* *FotoFlite*

74 Kota Jade *(Sg); 1976; (as Gulf Pioneer)* *WSPL*

75 Belo Oriente *(HK); 1987* *WSPL*

76 Yeoman Bank *(Li); 1982* *WSPL*

77 Windfield *(Bs); 1980* *WSPL*

78 Toki Arrow *(Bs); 1974* *FotoFlite*

79 Sea Glory *(Sg); 1977; (as Kota Sahabat)* *WSPL*

80 Star Hidra *(NIS); 1994* *FotoFlite*

81 Star Trondanger *(NIS); 1975* *FotoFlite*

82 Star Grip *(NIS); 1986* *FotoFlite*

83 Alanya *(Pa); 1986; (as Rio Purus)* *FotoFlite*

84 Star Eagle *(NIS); 1981* *FotoFlite*

85 Teal Arrow *(Bs); 1984* *FotoFlite*

86 Harefield *(Bs); 1985* *FotoFlite*

87 Westwood Cleo *(NIS); 1987* *FotoFlite*

88 Star Geiranger *(Li); 1986* *FotoFlite*

89 Star Florida *(NIS); 1985* *FotoFlite*

90 Harmac Dawn *(NIS); 1980* *FotoFlite*

91 Pacific Pintail *(Br); 1987* *FotoFlite*

92 Tornes *(Pa); 1984* *FotoFlite*

93 Trollnes *(NIS); 1985* *FotoFlite*

94 Nan Ji Zhou *(RC); 1986* *FotoFlite*

95 Nelvana *(Va); 1983* *FotoFlite*

96 Adriatic Queen *(Ma); 1976; (as Bernhard Schulte)* *FotoFlite*

97 Mina *(NIS); 1972; (as Mira Bulk)* *FotoFlite*

98 Eos *(NIS); 1976/84* *FotoFlite*

99 Yeoman Brook *(Li); 1991* *FotoFlite*

100 Western Bridge *(Bs); 1991* *FotoFlite*

101 Nordanhav *(Sw); 1992* *FotoFlite*

102 Saga Breeze *(NIS); 1992* *FotoFlite*

103 Alberni Dawn *(Li); 1980* *FotoFlite*

104 Reksnes *(Pa); 1977; (before addition of excavator)* *FotoFlite*

105 Nor Viking *(No); 1977; (as Norro); (before addition of excavator)* *FotoFlite*

106 Bauchi *(NIS); 1980* *Norman Thomson*

107 West Sky *(Sw); 19868* *FotoFlite*

108 Grethe *(No); 1972; (as Grunnvaag)* *FotoFlite*

111 Anangel Might *(Gr); 1978* *David Key*

109 Pluto *(Ne); 1986* *FotoFlite*

112 Gardway *(NIS); 1978* *WSPL*

110 Konstantina K *(Cy); 1976* *FotoFlite*

113 Arklow Brook *(Ih); 1995* *FotoFlite*

11 Refrigerated Cargo Ships (Reefers)

11 Refrigerated Cargo Ships (Reefers)

See photo number 11/218

1 $CRC^{2}MG$ *H1*
KYKNOS 1 Pa/Ne (Ysselwerf) 1977/83; R; 2,965 grt/3,459 dwt; 96.45 × 5.11 m *(316.44 × 16.77 ft)*; M (MaK); 15 kts; ex-*Klipper*; Lengthened 1983 (Giessen-De Noord)
Sister (sequence is $C^{2}RCMG$): **KHERSONES 1** (Cy) ex-*Klipper II*; **OMEGA BAY** (Pa) ex-*Pacific Queen*

2 $HC^{3}M\text{–}F$ *H1*
DAE SUNG No 11 Pa/Sp (AESA) 1967; R; 1,598 grt/2,333 dwt; 91.01 × 5.56 m *(298.59 × 18.24 ft)*; M (B&W); 16 kts; ex-*Playa del Medano*

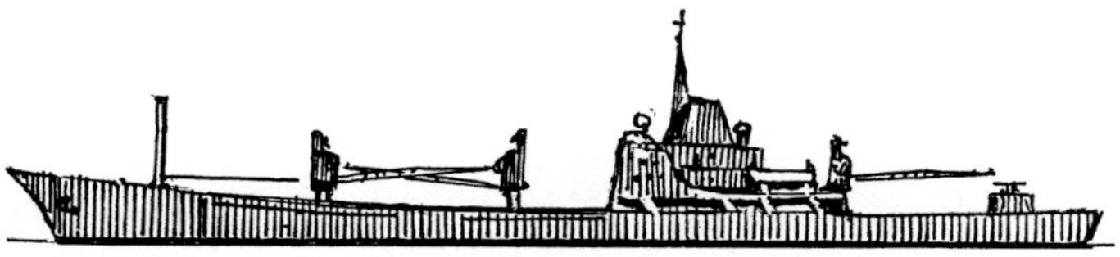

3 $HC^{2}M\text{–}FC$ *H*
USHUAIA Ar/Sp ('Astano') 1969; R; 4,334 grt/3,761 dwt; 110 × 6.5 m *(361 × 21.2 ft)*; M (B&W); 17.5 kts; ex-*Playa de Naos*

4 $HC^{2}N^{2}MFC^{2}$ *H1*
SERIFOS Pa/Br (Stephen) 1967; R; 8,932 grt/12,435 dwt; 166 × 9.8 m *(546 × 32.4 ft)*; M (Sulzer); 19 kts; ex-*Britannic*

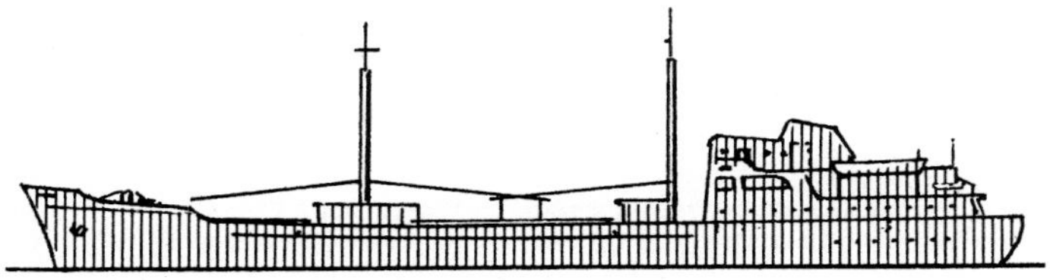

5 $H^{2}F$ *H1*
LAS MERCEDES Cu/Sp (Palma) 1966; R; 1,237 grt/1,199 dwt; 72.75 × 4.47 m *(239 × 14.67 ft)*; M (Werkspoor); 14 kts

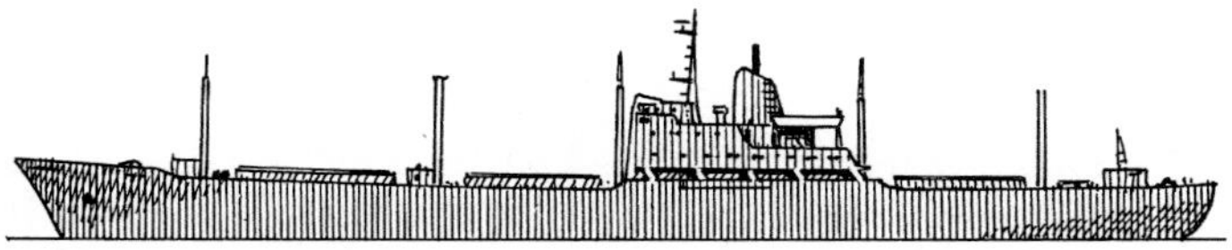

6 $H^{3}MFH^{2}$ *H*
OVERSEA FRUIT Pa/Ja (Hayashikane) 1971; R; 6,275 grt/6,564 dwt; 134 × 7.5 m *(440 × 24.8 ft)*; M (Sulzer); 21.75 kts
Sister: **PARAISO** (Tw) ex-*Comfort*

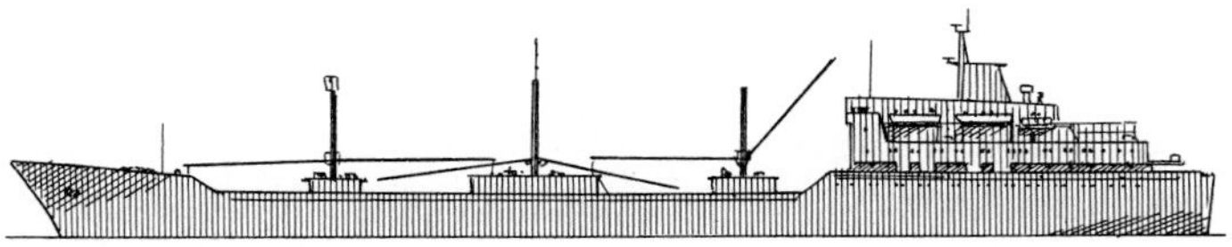

7 $H^{3}M\text{–}F$ *H13*
ZULAWY Pd/Pd (Gdanska) 1974; R/FC; 8,120 grt/8,439 dwt; 151.31 × 7.4 m *(496.42 × 24.28 ft)*; M (Sulzer); 19 kts; 'B68' type
Sisters: **KASZUBY II** (Pd); **WINETA** (Pd); **MAZURY** (Pd)

8 $H^{3}NMFN$ *H1*
MORILLO Pi/No (Bergens) 1971; R; 9,983 grt/10,800 dwt; 155.8 × 9.2 (511 × 33) m; M (B&W); 22
Sisters: **IRISH SEA** (Bs) ex-*Tangelo*; **RIO GUAYAS** (Ec) ex-*Maranga*; **PELAGOS** (Bs) ex-*Cantaloup*; **PERSEUS** (Bs) ex-*Orange*; **R P CAYMAN** (Pi) ex-*Cherry*

9 $H^{2}MF$ *H12*
FRIMARO Cu/Sp (UN de Levante) 1966; R; 1,661 grt/2,378 dwt; 87 × 5.77 m *(285.43 × 18.93 ft)*; M (B&W); — kts; ex-*Frimar*

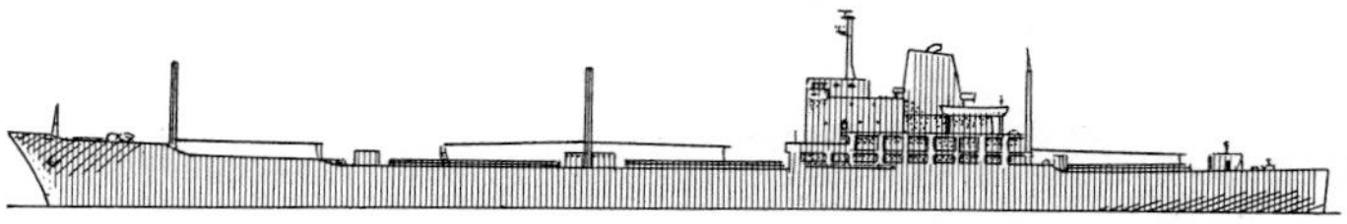

10 $H^{2}MFH$ *H1*
ACAPULCO Li/Ja (Kanda) 1973; R; 10,219 grt/10,851 dwt; 163.02 × 8.99 m *(534.84 × 29.49 ft)*; M (B&W); 20 kts; ex-*Ryutu Reefer*
Sisters: **KINAROS V** (Pa) ex-*Pacific Reefer*; **RIO PARANA** (Pa) ex-*Sonoda Reefer*; **GOLFO DE BATABANO** (Cu); **ORION REEFER** (Cu) ex-*Golfo de Guacanaybo*; **GOLFO DE GUANAHACABIBES** (Cu); **OCEANO ATLANTICO** (Cu); **OCEANO ARTICO** (Cu)

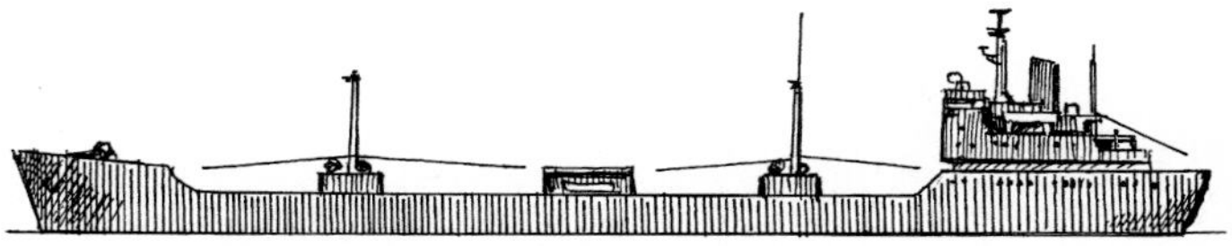

11 $H^{2}MFM$ *H13*
RUSU SALA Lt/Sw (Lindholmens) 1969; FC; 6,693 grt/10,200 dwt; 150.55 × 7.47 m *(494 × 24.51 ft)*; M (Pielstick); 18.25 kts; ex-*Ostrov Russkiy*
Sisters: **ATLASOVO SALA** (Lt) ex-*Ostrov Atlasova*; **RONU SALA** (La) ex-*Ostrov Kotlin*; **LITKES SALA** (Lt) ex-*Ostrov Litke*; **OSTROV SHOKALSKOGO** (Ru); **DOLES SALA** (La) ex-*Ostrov Sibiryakova*; **OSTROV USHAKOVA** (Ru); **BERINGA SALA** (La) ex-*Ostrov Beringa*

12 $H^{2}MFN$ *H*
VICTORIA Tw/Tw (Taiwan SB) 1968; R; 3,629 grt/5,669 dwt; 106.99 × 7.12 m *(351.02 × 23.36 ft)*; M (MAN); 14.5 kts; ex-*Union Evergreen*

13 $H^{2}MFN$ *H1*
AMAZON REEFER Li/No (Bergens) 1971; R; 9,548 grt/10,963 dwt; 156 × 9.1 m *(511 × 30.1 ft)*; M (B&W); 21 kts; ex-*Wild Auk*
Sister: **ALPINA I** (Pa) ex-*Wild Avocet*

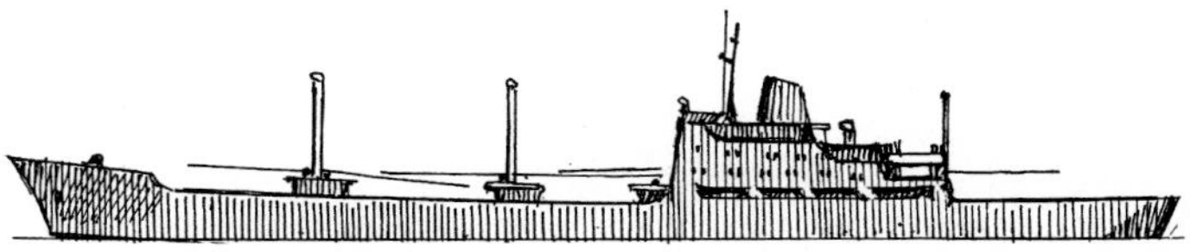

14 $H^{2}MFN$ *H1*
CLEMENTINA Mr/No (Bergens) 1971; R; 8,360 grt/9,750 dwt; 148 × 9.1 m *(485 × 30 ft)*; M (B&W); 20 kts

15 $H^{2}MFN$ *H13*
SAJO DOLPHIN Ko/Ja (Shikoku) 1968; R; 2,654 grt/3,519 dwt; 104.5 × 5.84 m *(342.85 × 19.16 ft)*; M (Pielstick); 15 kts; ex-*Tonichi Maru*
Sister: **KIN PING HAI** (Tw) ex-*Mishima Maru*

16 *H²M–F H13*
SAN HSIEH 303 Pa/Sp (Cadagua) 1969; R; 1,787 grt/1,938 dwt; 84 × 5 m *(275.59 × 16.4 ft)*; M (Cadiz); 13 kts; ex-*Horus*

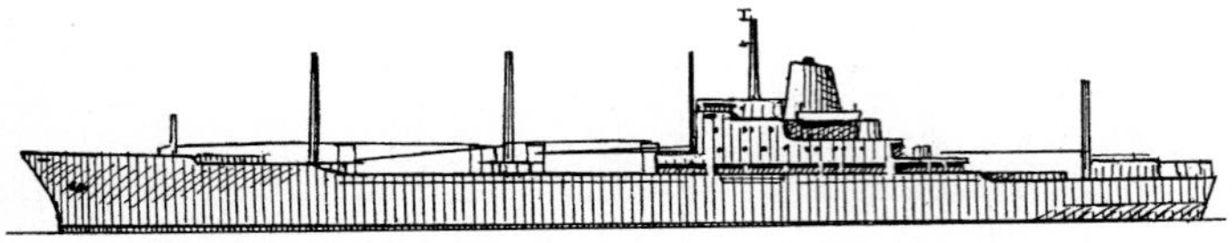

17 *H²NMFN H1*
AL ZOHAL Si/Ja (Kawasaki) 1969; R; 8,769 grt/6,072 dwt; 145 × 7.4 m *(474 × 24.4 ft)*; M (MAN); 20.5 kts; ex-*Morant*
Sister: **AL ZAHRAH** (Si) ex-*Musa*

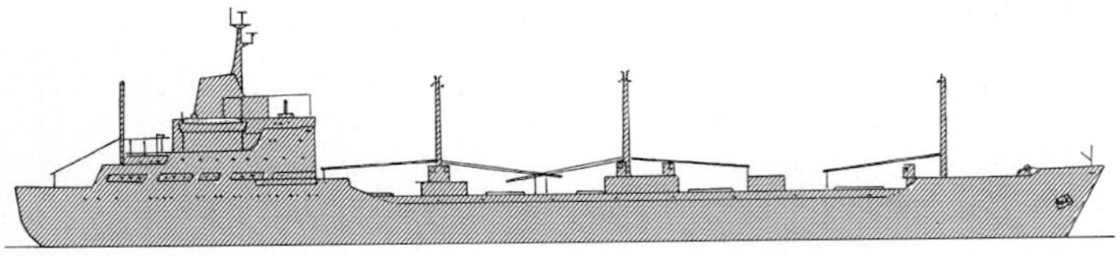

18 *HN²M–FN H13*
RIZHSKIY ZALIV Uk/Fr (Dubigeon-Normandie) 1969; FC; 12,454 grt/11,816 dwt; 164.62 × 7.01 m *(540.09 × 23 ft)*; M (Pielstick); 17.25 kts
Sisters: **AMURSKIY ZALIV** (Uk); **DVINSKIY ZALIV** (Uk); **SUOMIJOS ILANKA** (Lt) ex-*Finskiy Zaliv*; **KANDALAKSHSKIY ZALIV** (Uk); **NARVOS ILANKA** (Lt) ex-*Narvskiy Zaliv*; **ONEZHSKIY ZALIV** (Uk); **TAGANROGSKIY ZALIV** (Uk); **USSURIYSKIY ZALIV** (Uk)

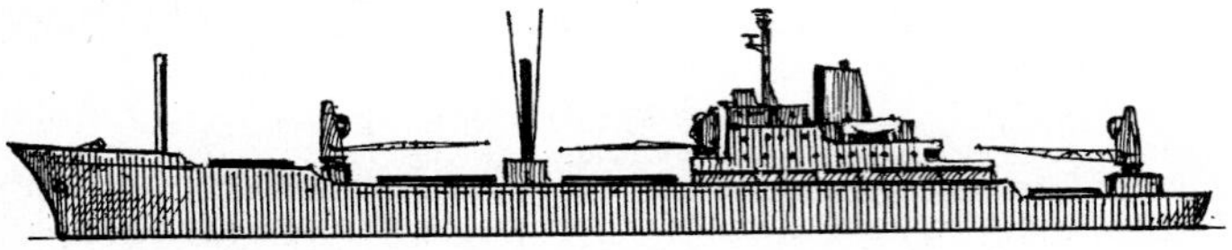

19 *HPHM²FC H1*
ALLIANORA Cy/Ja (Kawasaki) 1972; R; 6,513 grt/6,127 dwt; 144.5 × 7.4 m *(474 × 24.5 ft)*; M (MAN); 20.5 kts; ex-*Manistee*
Sisters: **MYRTIA** (Bs) ex-*Magdalena*; **MARGARITA** (Bs) ex-*Manzanares*; **MAGNOLIA** (Bs) ex-*Mazatec*

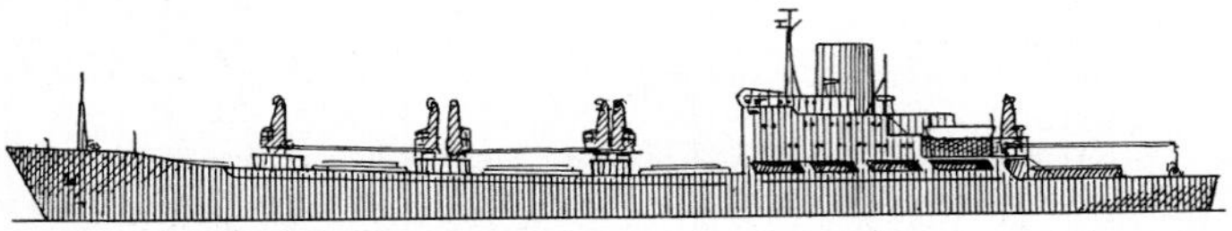

20 *MC⁵MFNC H1*
AFRIC STAR Bs/Br (Smith's D) 1975; R; 10,012 grt/11,092 dwt; 155.81 × 9.17 m *(511 × 30.05 ft)*; M (B&W); 22 kts
Sisters: **ALMEDA STAR** (Bs); **AVELONA STAR** (Bs); **AVILA STAR** (Bs) ex-*Almeria Star*; **SWAN LAKE** (As) ex-*Avila Star*

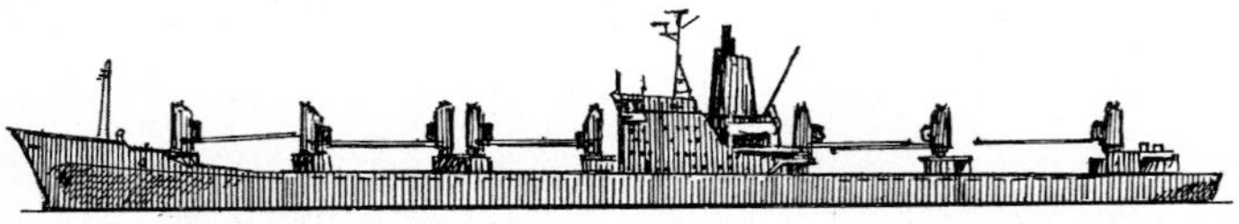

21 *MC⁵MFNC³ H1*
SNOW DELTA Bs/Fr (La Ciotat) 1972; R; 14,512 grt/12,782 dwt; 173 × 9.3 m *(569 × 30.5 ft)*; M (Sulzer); 22 kts; ex-*Snow Flake*; Side doors
Sisters: **SNOW CAPE** (Bs) ex-*Snow Ball*; **SNOW CRYSTAL** (Br); **SNOW DRIFT** (Bs) **SNOW FLOWER** (Bs); **KYMA** (Pa) ex-*Snow Land*; **HOOD** (Ir) ex-*Snow Storm*; **NOOR** (Ir) ex-*Snow Hill* (See photo number 11/191)

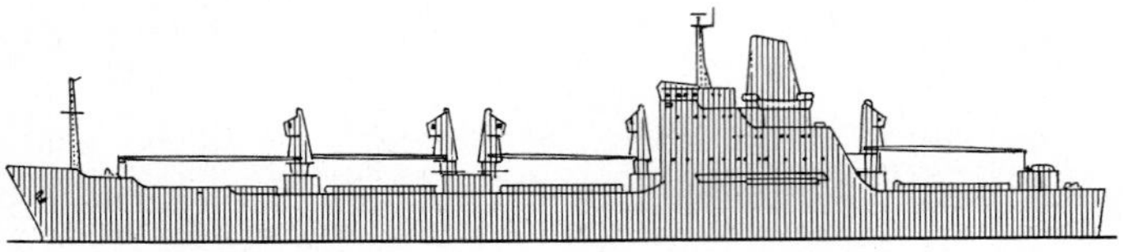

22 *MC⁴MFC H1*
ATLANTIC UNIVERSAL Sr/Ja (Mitsubishi HI) 1984; R/Con; 13,299 grt/12,271 dwt; 150 × 9.83 m *(492.13 × 32.25 ft)*; M (Sulzer); 20.5 kts; 141 TEU; Eight side doors (four port/four starboard)
Sister: **PACIFIC UNIVERSAL** (Sr)

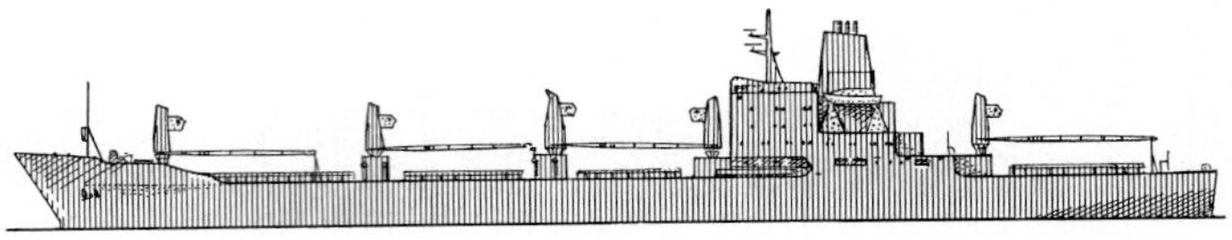

23 *MC⁴MFC H1*
SPRINTER Bs/No (Framnaes) 1979; R; 12,061 grt/12,475 dwt; 155.7 × 9.8 m *(510.9 × 32.1 ft)*; M (Sulzer); 22 kts; ex-*Hilco Sprinter* 1988
Sisters: **SCAMPER** (Bs) ex-*Hilco Scamper*; **IRAN MOFID** (Ir) ex-*Hilco Speedster*

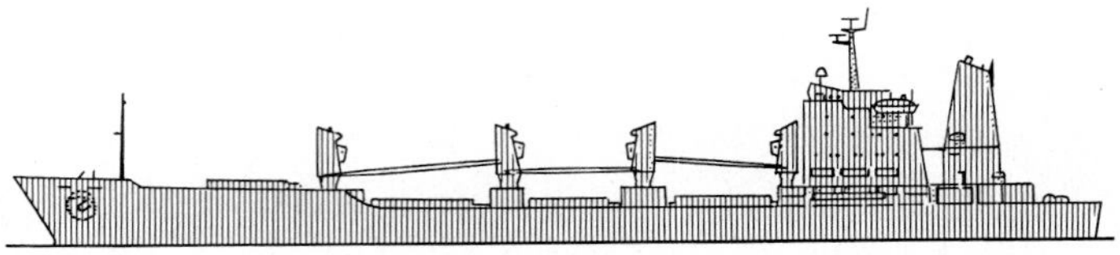

24 *MC⁴MF–M H1*
ARCTIC UNIVERSAL Sr/Ja (Hayashikane) 1987; R; 10,298 grt/11,022 dwt; 145.5 × 9.22 m *(477.36 × 30.25 ft)*; M (B&W); 18.5 kts; 66 TEU; Eight side doors (four port/four starboard); Mast aft is on starboard side
Sisters: **BALTIC UNIVERSAL** (Sr); **LINCOLN UNIVERSAL** (Sr); **TASMAN UNIVERSAL** (Sr)

25 *MC³MF H13*
SANTISTA Bz/Bz (Ish do Brazil) 1973; B; 13,847 grt/24,858 dwt; 176.41 × 10.08 m *(578.77 × 33.07 ft)*; M (Sulzer); 14.5 kts

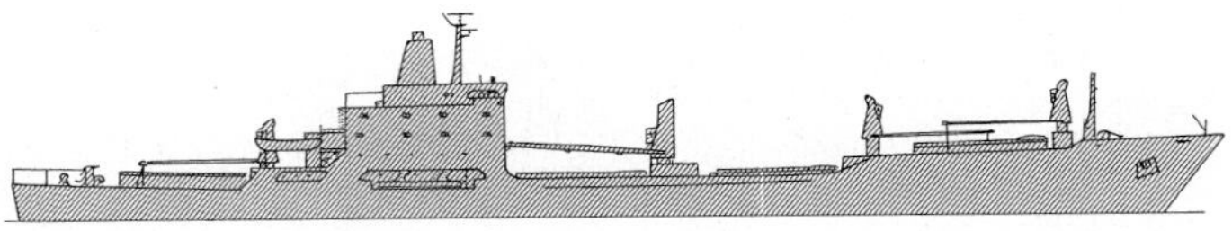

26 *MC³MFC H1*
CAHOKIA SV/It (Muggiano) 1976; R; 10,404 grt/9,750 dwt; 152.8 × 9.2 m *(503 × 30 ft)*; M (GMT); 23 kts; ex-*Punta Stella*; now broken up
Sisters: **CORAL SEA** (Bs) ex-*Punta Verde* (Sulzer engines); **CAP SOUNION** (Pa) ex-*Punta Sole*; **BERING SEA** (Bs) ex-*Punta Bianca* 1994 (Sulzer engines)

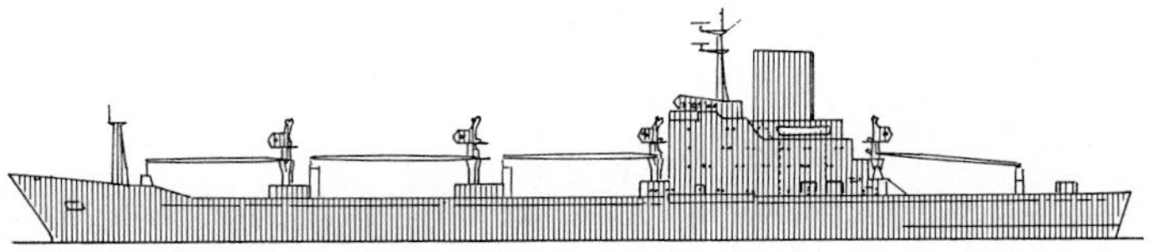

27 *MC³MFC H1*
SCOTTISH STAR Bs/Br (H&W) 1985; R; 10,291 grt/13,058 dwt; 150.76 × 9.38 m *(494.62 × 30.77 ft)*; M (B&W); — kts; Side doors
Sisters: **CANTERBURY STAR** (Bs); **AUCKLAND STAR** (Bs); **ENGLISH STAR** (Bs)

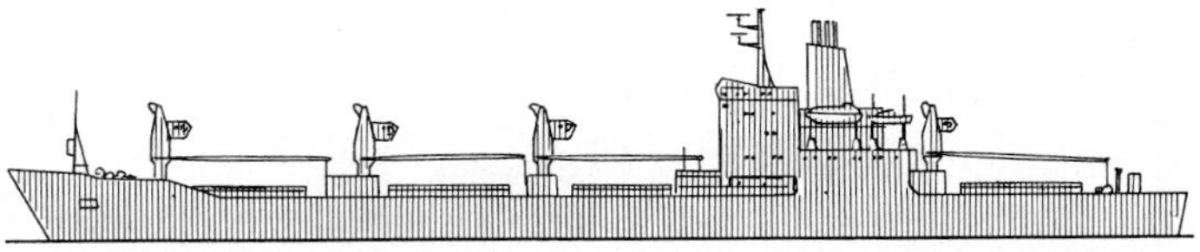

28 *MC³MFC H1*
SKIER Bs/No (Framnaes) 1981; R; 8,835 grt/12,475 dwt; 156.17 × 9.82 m *(512.37 × 32.22 ft)*; M (Sulzer); 22 kts; ex-*Hilco Skier*; Side doors
Sister: **SKATER** (Bs) ex-*Hilco Skater*

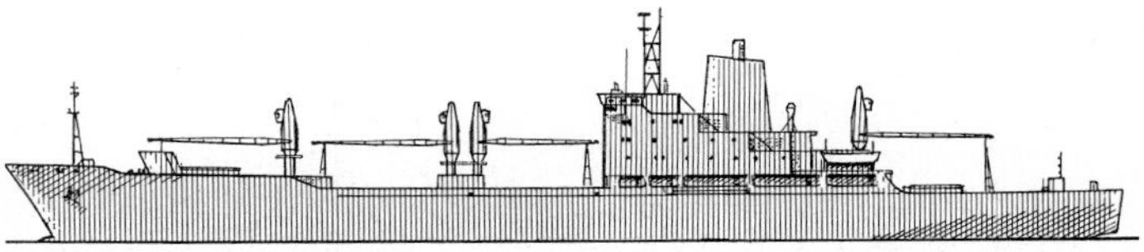

29 *MC³MFC H1*
SWAN STREAM NIS/Be (Boelwerf) 1979; R; 10,424 grt/9,852 dwt; 151.26 × 8.7 m *(496.26 × 28.54 ft)*; M (MAN); 21 kts; ex-*Pocantico*
Sisters: **SWAN LAGOON** (NIS) ex-*Pocahontas*; **SWAN LAKE** (NIS) ex-*Potomac*; **RACISCE** (Cro) (Ys built—'Split')

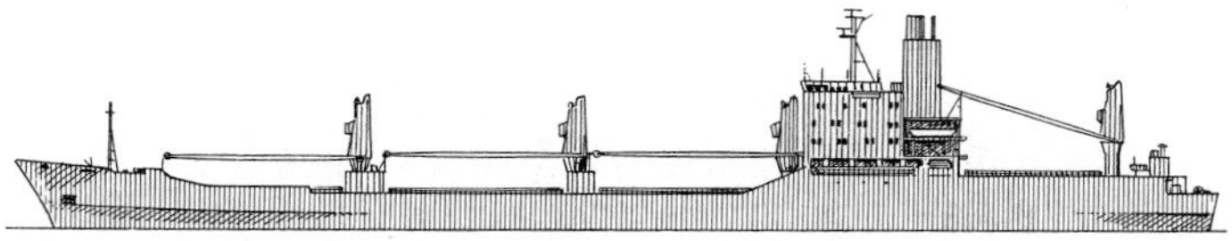

30 MC^3MFC *H12*
WINTER WATER Bs/Sw (Gotav) 1979; R; 15,833 grt/15,100 dwt; 169 × 10.1 m *(554.46 × 33.14 ft)*; M (B&W); 21.9 kts; ex-*Winter Water*
Sisters: **WINTER MOON** (Bs); **WINTER SEA** (Bs); **WINTER STAR** (Bs); **WINTER SUN** (Bs); **WINTER WAVE** (Sw)

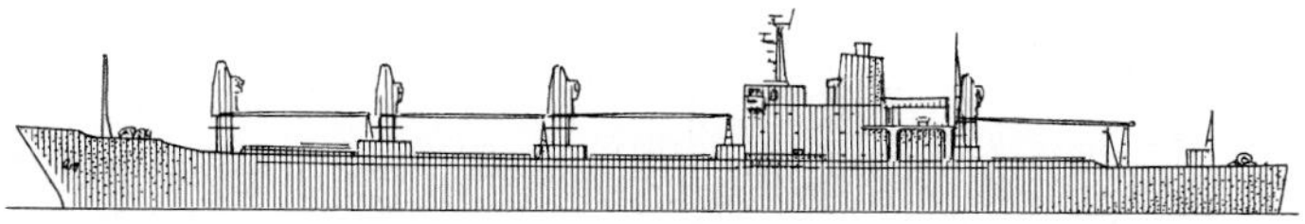

31 MC^3MFC–*N H1*
AFRICAN PRINCESS Li/Ja (Kochi Jukogyo); R; 9,018 grt/9,125 dwt; 151.11 × 8.62 m *(495.77 × 28.28 ft)*; M (Pielstick); 20 kts; ex-*Hawaii*
Sisters: **ROYAL REEFER** (Pi) ex-*Barrios*; **AFRICAN QUEEN** (Pa) ex-*Turbo*

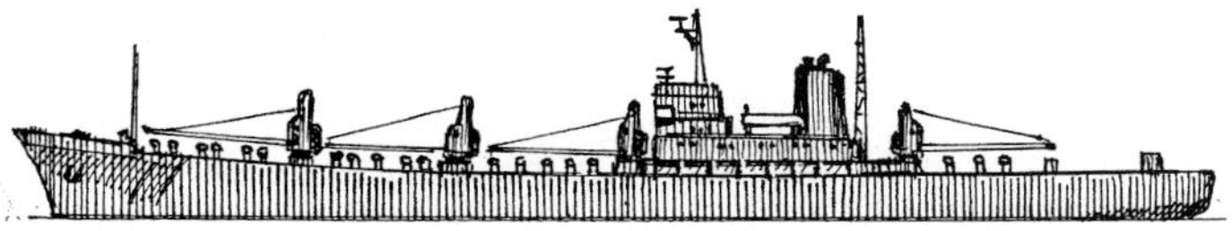

32 MC^3MFMC *H*
RAINFROST Pa/Ja (Kochi Jukogyo) 1973; R; 7,246 grt/6,827 dwt; 141.1 × 8.1 m *(463 × 26 ft)*; M (MAN); 21 kts; ex-*Toei Maru*
Sister: **EAST LIGHT** (Bs) ex-*Toyu Maru*

33 MC^3MFN *H1*
FRIO JAPAN Cy/Sp (AESA) 1980; R; 3,835 grt/4,392 dwt; 103.74 × 6.3 m *(340.35 × 20.67 ft)*; M (B&W); 15.25 kts; ex-*Frigo America*
Sisters: **FRIO KOREA** (Cy) ex-*Frigo Africa*; **DIAMOND REEFER** (Bs) ex-*Frigo Asia*; **FRIO ARGENTINA** (Cy) ex-*Frigo Espana*; **FRIO CANADA** (Pa) ex-*Frigo Europa*; **FRIO AMERICA** (Cy) ex-*Frigo Oceania*; **FRIO BRASIL** (Cy) ex-*Frigo Las Palmas*; **FRIO ESPANA** (Cy) ex-*Frigo Tenerife*

34 MC^3MFN *H13*
MINAS DEL FRIO Cu/Sp (Juliana) 1982; R; 3,456 grt/4,133 dwt; 103.73 × 6.67 m *(340 × 21.88 ft)*; M (B&W); 15.7 kts; ex-*Barrueta*
Sister: **GRAN PIEDRA** (Cu) ex-*Guiard*

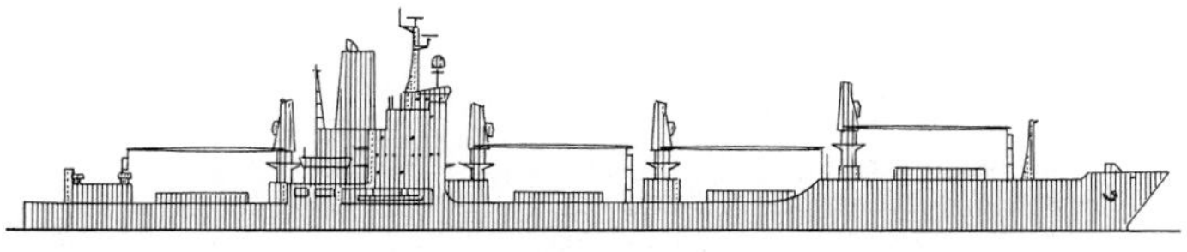

35 MC^3MFNC *H1*
CHIQUITA BARU Br/Ja (Sasebo) 1984; R/V; 12,659 grt/13,556 dwt; 169.09 × 9.5 m *(554.76 × 31.17 ft)*; M (B&W); 22.5 kts; ex-*Vivian M*; Eight side doors (four port/four starboard)
Sisters: **CHIQUITA BARACOA** (Br) ex-*Ellen D*; **SUMMER MEADOW** (Br) ex-*Irma M*; **SUMMER WIND** (Br) ex-*Edyth L*

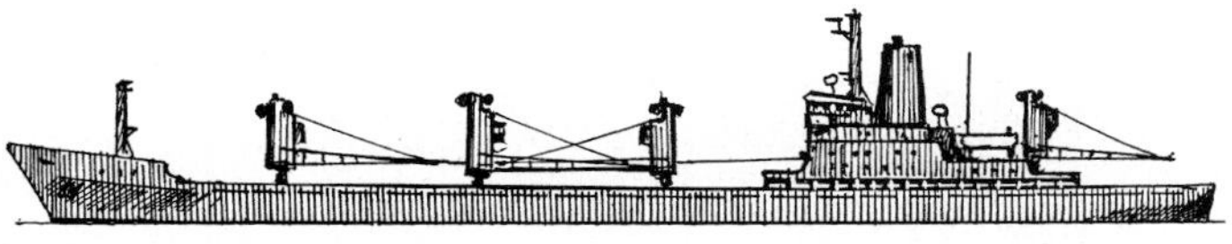

36 MC^3MFNC *H1*
EASTCAPE Bs/Br (Scotstoun) 1975; R; 10,808 grt/10,746 dwt; 157.3 × 9.3 m *(516 × 30 ft)*; M (B&W); 20.5 kts; ex-*Loch Maree*
Sister: **STAR HAVEN** (Bs) ex-*Loch Lomond*

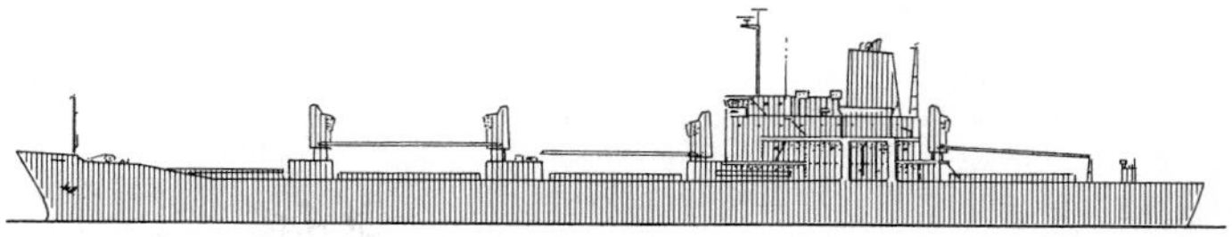

37 MC^3MFNC *H1*
SWAN BAY NIS/Ja (Kurushima) 1979; R; 10,853 grt/10,976 dwt; 160.51 × 8.67 m *(526.61 × 28.44 ft)*; M (MAN); 19.5 kts; ex-*Caribbean Maru*; side doors; Can carry vehicles
Sister: **SWAN RIVER** (NIS) ex-*California Maru*

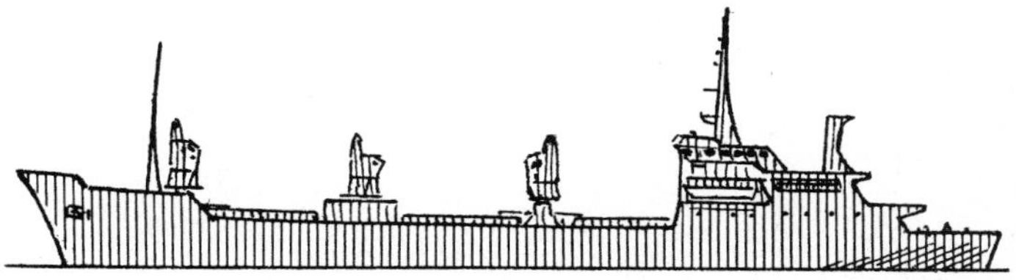

38 MC^3MG *H1*
AFKO 106 Gh/No (Ulstein) 1967; C; 1,419 grt/2,540 dwt; 75.85 × 6.05 m *(248.85 × 19.85 ft)*; M (Caterpillar); 12 kts; ex-*Lorena Horn*

39 MC^3M^2FL–*R H1*
WINDFROST Bs/FRG (Flender) 1984; R; 9,268 grt/11,150 dwt; 145.6 × 9.45 m *(478 × 31 ft)*; M (MAN); 21.7 kts; ex-*Helene Jacob*; Free-fall lifeboat system aft, on port side, can obscure a crane on the starboard side; Eight side doors (four port/four starboard)
Sister: **WALTER JACOB** (Tv)

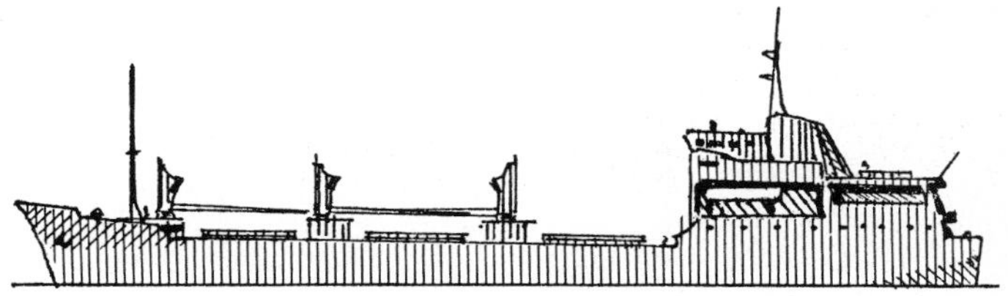

40 MC^3M–*F H12*
CARIBIC Cy/No (Ulstein) 1967; R; 1,468 grt/2,469 dwt; 75.77 × 6.02 m *(248.59 × 19.75 ft)*; M (Atlas-MaK); 15 kts; ex-*Caribia*

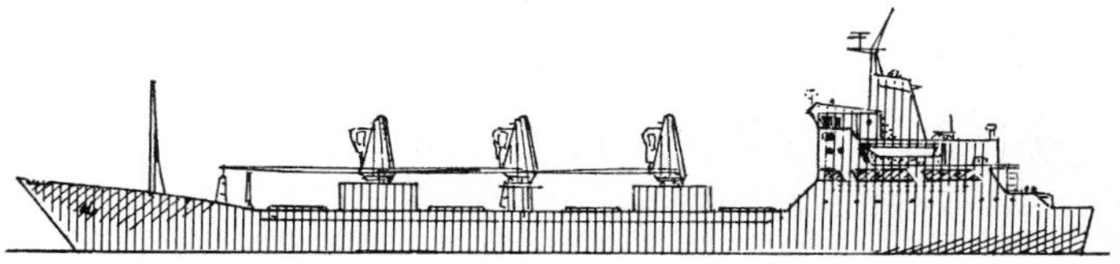

41 MC^3M–*F H12*
SIERRA ARACENA Pa/Sp (Cadagua) 1979; R; 2,502 grt/2,694 dwt; 90.4 × 5.11 m *(296.6 × 16.77 ft)*; M (Deutz); 14 kts; ex-*Puerto Cadiz*
Sisters: **SIERRA ARALAR** (Pa) ex-*Fero Cadiz*; **ALBACORA FRIGO DOS** (Sp) ex-*Mar Cadiz*

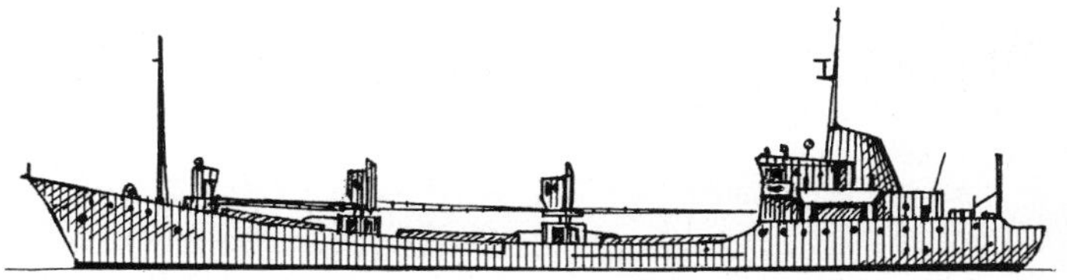

42 MC^3M–*FN H2*
FREESIA Pi/Sp (Juliana) 1970; R; 1,725 grt/2,026 dwt; 88.8 × 5.25 m *(291.34 × 17.22 ft)*; M (MAN); 14 kts; ex-*Pinguino*

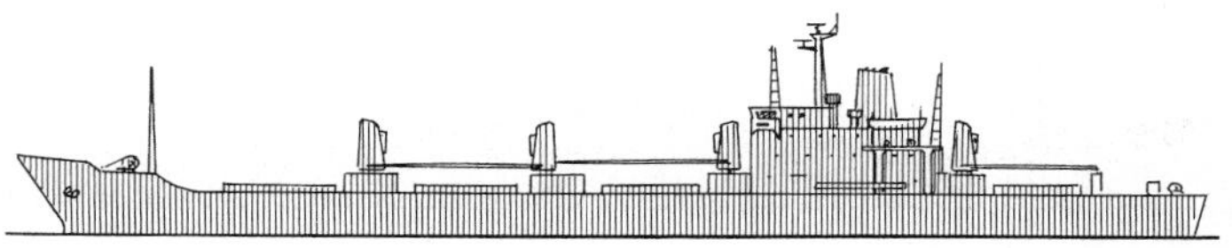

43 MC^3NMFNC *H1*
FRIO IPANEMA Bs/Ja (Kurushima) 1978; R; 7,194 grt/7,764 dwt; 143.52 × 8.52 m *(471 × 27.95 ft)*; M (Pielstick); 20 kts; ex-*Puma*
Sister: **OSAKA BAY** (SV) ex-*Panther*

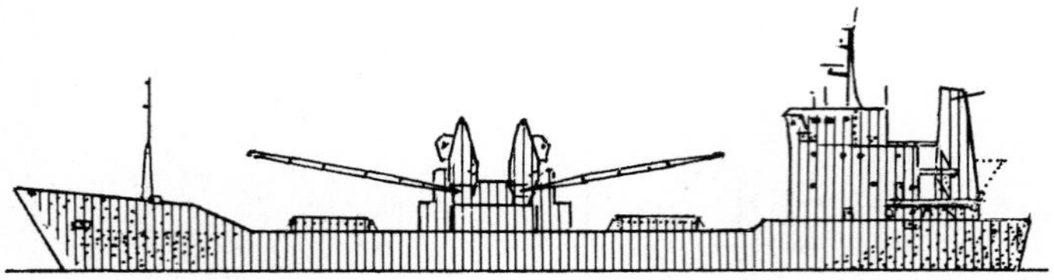

44 *MC^{2}MF H1*
QUN YING RC/De (Orskovs) 1979; R; 1,021 grt/1,778 dwt; 80.2 × 4.71 m *(263.12 × 15.45 ft)*; M (Atlas-MaK); 14 kts; ex-*Ice Star*; Side door

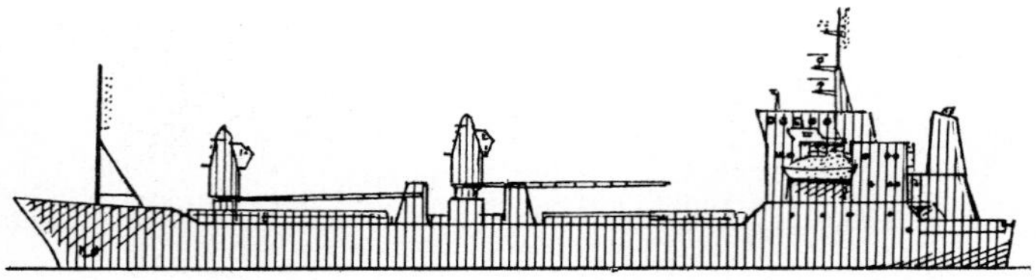

45 *MC^{2}MF H12*
GREEN FRIO NIS/No (Ulstein H) 1979; FC; 2,249 grt/2,432 dwt; 79.44 × 5.12 m *(260.63 × 16.8 ft)*; M (Atlas-MaK); 14 kts; ex-*Norcan*

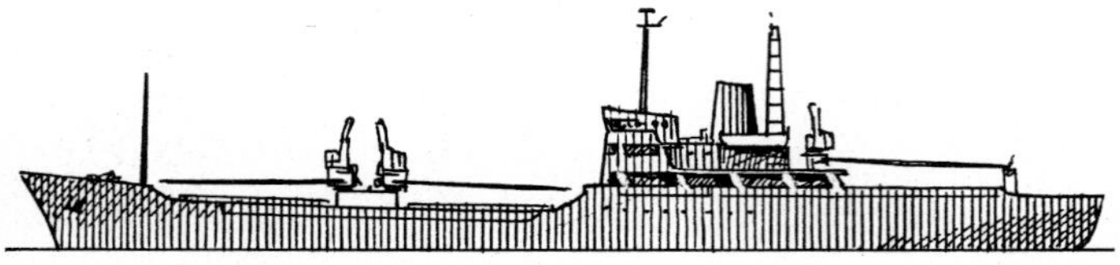

46 *MC^{2}MFMC H13*
JIA YOW Pa/Ja (Hayashikane) 1967; R; 3,686 grt/4,590 dwt; 111 × 6.8 m *(364 × 22.6 ft)*; M (Kobe); 16 kts; ex-*Hayashikane Maru No 1*
Sister: **SEA PLENTY No 1** (Pa) ex-*Hayashikane Maru No 2*

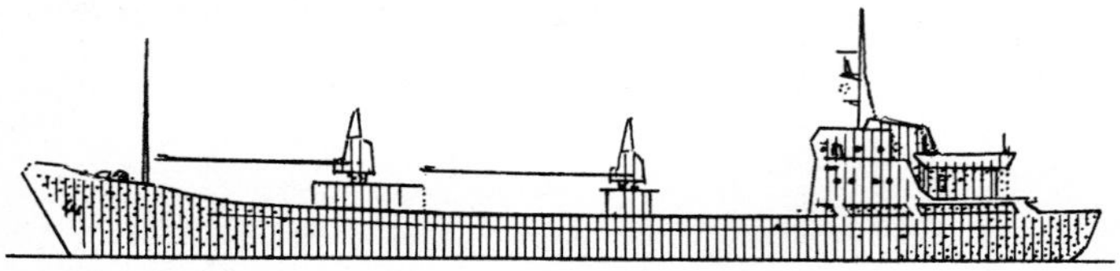

47 *MC^{2}M–F H1*
FRENASO Pa/Sp ('Corbasa') 1967; R; 1,517 grt/1,869 dwt; 83.47 × 5.01 m *(273.85 × 16.44 ft)*; M (Stork-Werkspoor); 16 kts; ex-*Sierra Lucena*
Sister: **CARMEN CASTELLANO** (Sp) ex-*Sierra Luna*

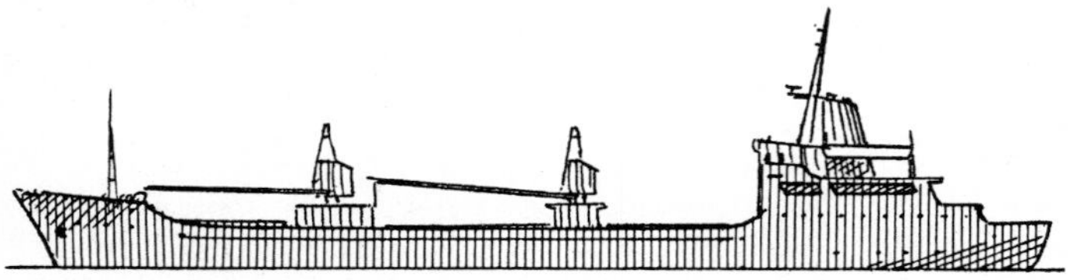

48 *MC^{2}M–F H13*
ITFA 2 Th/Sp ('Astano') 1967; R; 1,770 grt/1,996 dwt; 86.24 × 5.02 m *(282.94 × 16.47 ft)*; M (B&W); 13.5 kts; ex-*Rio Nansa*
Probably similar: **SAMOS REEFER** (Ma) ex-*Trevinca*

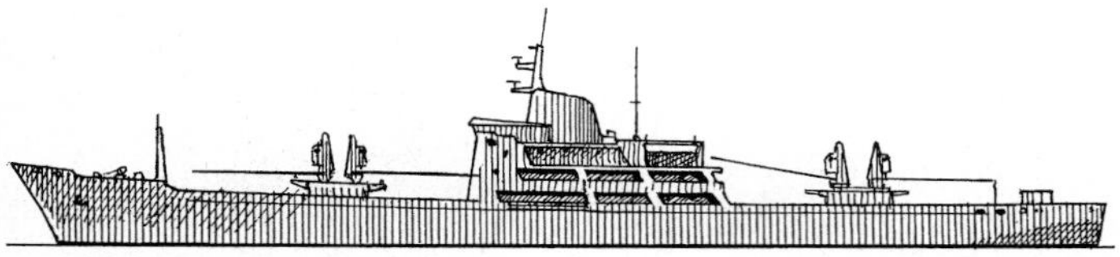

49 *MC^{2}M–FC^2 H1*
UB PARADE Bs/Fr (France–Gironde) 1968; R; 8,697 grt/6,625 dwt; 144.1 × 7.5 m *(473 × 24.8 ft)*; M (B&W); 21.5 kts; ex-*Aquilon*
Sisters: **CHATEAULIN** (Bs) ex-*Fort Sainte Marie*; **UB PRIDE** (Bs) ex-*Ivondro*; **UB PRELUDE** (Bs) ex-*Narval*; **BLUMENAU REEFER** (Ma) ex-*Marsouin*

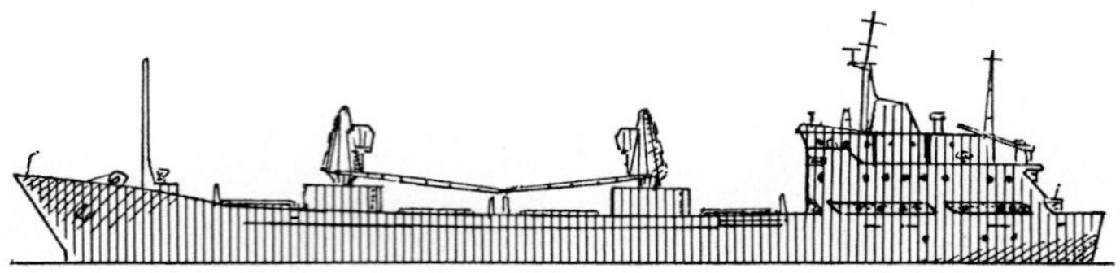

50 *MC^{2}M–FMC H*
SIERRA GUADARRAMA Pa/Sp (Musel) 1979; R; 2,477 grt/2,480 dwt; 85.9 × 4.9 m *(281.82 × 16.08 ft)*; M (Deutz); 13 kts
Probable sisters (lengthened to 97.62 m (320 ft), may have three cranes): **SIERRA GRANA** (Pa); **SIERRA GRANERA** (Pa); **SIERRA GUADELUPE** (Pa); **SIERRA GREDOS** (Pa)

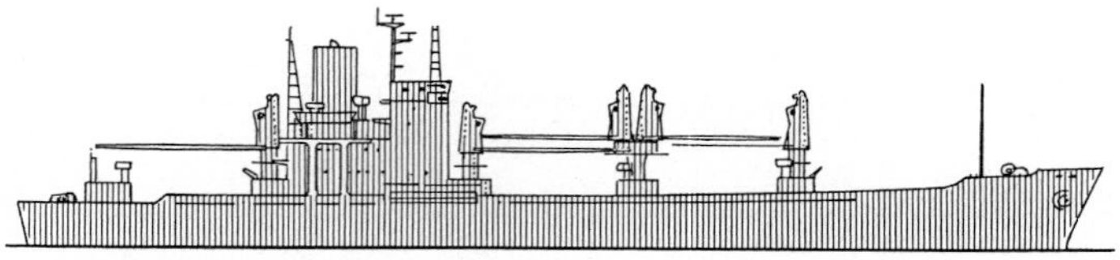

51 *MCPCNMFNC H1*
BALTIC STAR Li/Ja (Sasebo) 1983; R/V; 9,628 grt/9,464 dwt; 140.49 × 8.82 m *(460.93 × 28.94 ft)*; M (Mitsubishi); 19.5 kts; 54 TEU; Eight side doors (four port/four starboard)
Sister: **TASMAN STAR** (Pa); Similar (longer—151.52 m (497 ft)): **ATLANTIC STAR** (Pa); **PACIFIC STAR** (Li)

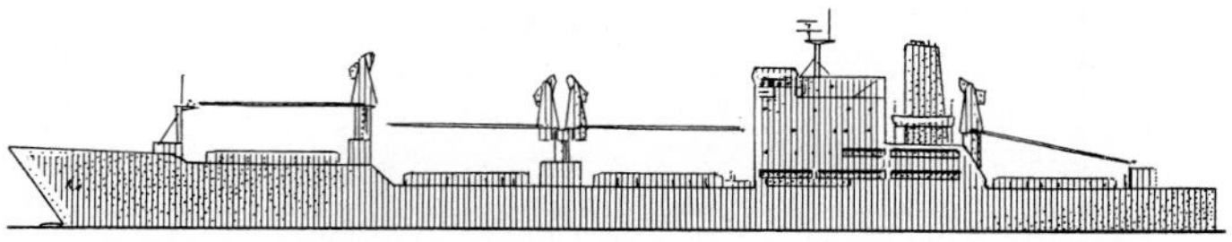

52 *MCPMFC H1*
GLACIAR AMEGHINO Ar/Ar (Alianza) 1981; R; 9,013 grt/10,452 dwt; 146.51 × 9.23 m *(480.7 × 30.28 ft)*; M (Sulzer); 20 kts; Side doors
Sisters: **GLACIAR PERITO MORENO** (Ar); **KEA** (Gr) ex-*Glaciar Viedma*

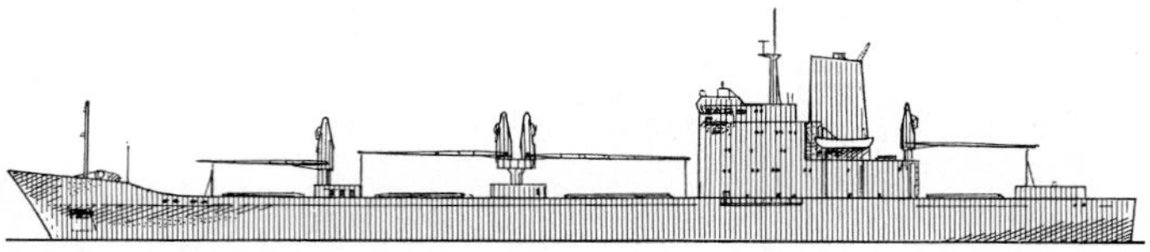

53 *MCPMFC H1*
HONOLULU NA/Ne (Giessen-de Noord) 1979; R; 11,312 grt/10,598 dwt; 155 × 8.8 m *(508.53 × 28.87 ft)*; M (Sulzer); 21.6 kts
Sisters: **KING** (Bs) ex-*Christina*; **QUEEN** (Bs) ex-*Lanai*; **RIO FRIO** (NA); **TINEKE** (NA); **PEGGY DOW** (NA)

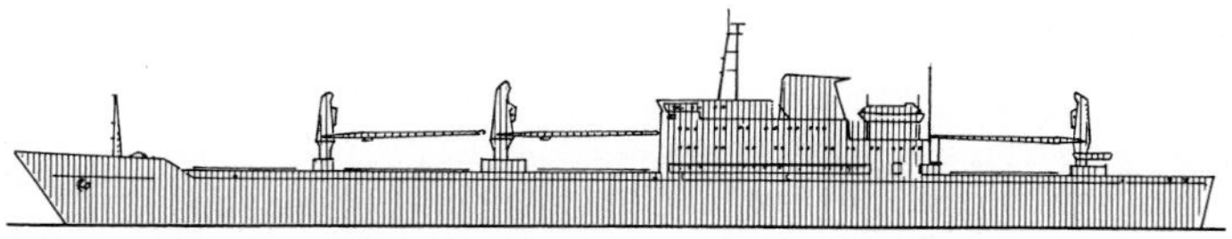

54 *MCPMFMC H1*
KURSKA La/Pd (Gdanska) 1983; R; 8,960 grt/7,496 dwt; 146.62 × 8.1 m *(481.04 × 26.57 ft)*; M (B&W); 21.75 kts; ex-*Kursk*; Side doors; 'B365' type
Sisters: **PURE** (La) ex-*Arvid Pelshe*; **AKADEMIS BOCVARS** (La) ex-*Akademik Bochvar*; **KAMILO SJENFUEGOS** (La) ex-*Camilo Cienfuegos*; **AKADEMIS CELOMEJS** (La) ex-*Akademik Chelomey*; **BELGORODA** (La) ex-*Byelgorod*; **PERLE** (La) ex-*Yan Kalnberzin*

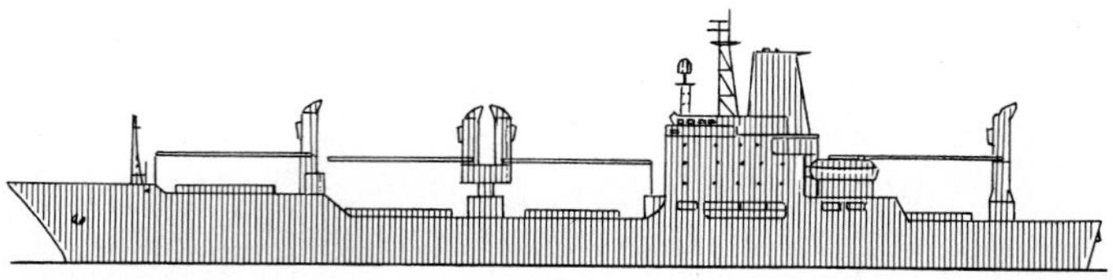

55 *MCPM^{2}FC H1*
AKADEMIKIS VAVILOVS La/De (Aalborg) 1985; R; 9,552 grt/7,673 dwt; 138.21 × 8.2 m *(453.44 × 26.9 ft)*; M (B&W); 20.25 kts; ex-*Akademik N Vavilov*; Side doors (four port—four starboard)
Sisters: **AKADEMIKIS ZAVARICKIS** (La) ex-*Akademik Zavaritskiy*; **SKULPTORS TOMSKIS** (La) ex-*Skulptor Tomskiy*

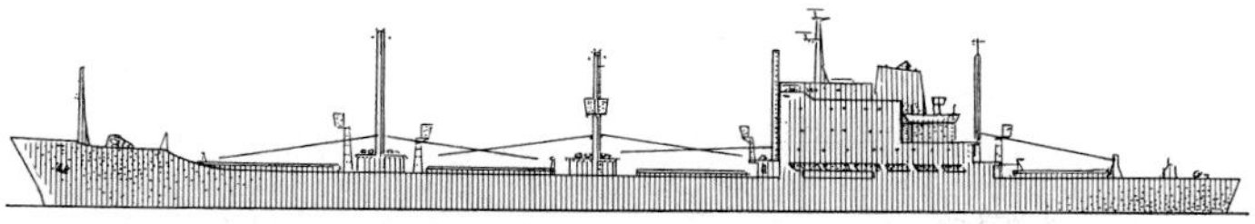

56 *MH³MFH H1*
SAXON STAR SV/Ja (Koyo) 1979; R; 10,153 grt/9,996 dwt; 168.05 × 8.65 m *(551.35 × 28.38 ft)*; M (Sulzer); 21 kts; ex-*Tasman Rex*
Probable sister: **NORMAN STAR** (SV) ex-*Humboldt Rex*

57 *MH³NMFN H1*
CARINA Bs/De (Aalborg) 1972; R; 12,530 grt/12,182 dwt; 175 × 9.1 m *(575 × 30.1 ft)*; M (B&W); 23.5 kts; ex-*Gladiola*
Sister: **CAPRICORN** (Bs) ex-*Chrysantema*

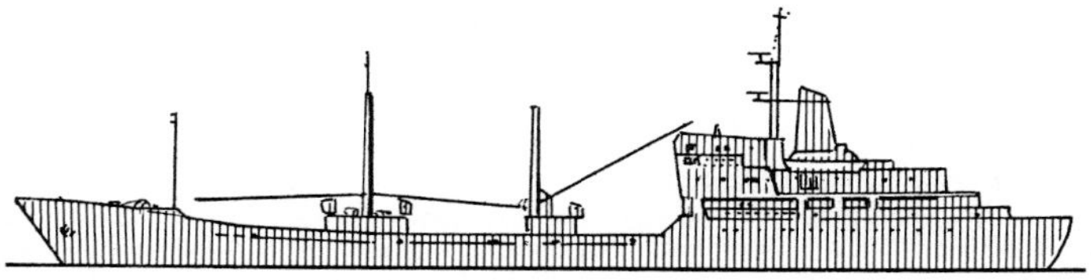

58 *MH²MF H13*
TATARSTAN Ru/Ru (Zelenodolskiy) 1977; FC; 2,381 grt/1,880 dwt; 95.28 × 5.48 m *(313 × 17.98 ft)*; M (Skoda); 13.5 kts
Sisters: **TURKMENISTAN** (Ru); **UZBEKISTAN** (Ru); **KOMSOMOLIYA KALININGRADA** (Ru); **KOMSOMOLSKAYA SMENA** (Ru)

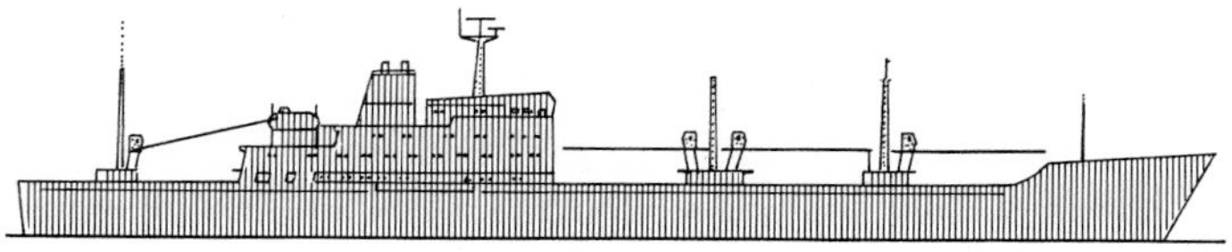

59 *MH²MFH H1*
KOCIEWIE Cy/Pd (Gdanska) 1986; FC; 8,864 grt/6,333 dwt; 139.69 × 7.4 m *(458.3 × 24.28 ft)*; M (B&W); 18 kts; 'B364' type
Sisters: **POWISLE** (Cy); **KURPIE** (Cy); **PODLASIE** (Li); **WARMIA** (Li); **ROZTOCZE** (Cy)
Possible sister ('B364/2' type): **AMATA** (Cy) ex-*Mazowsze*

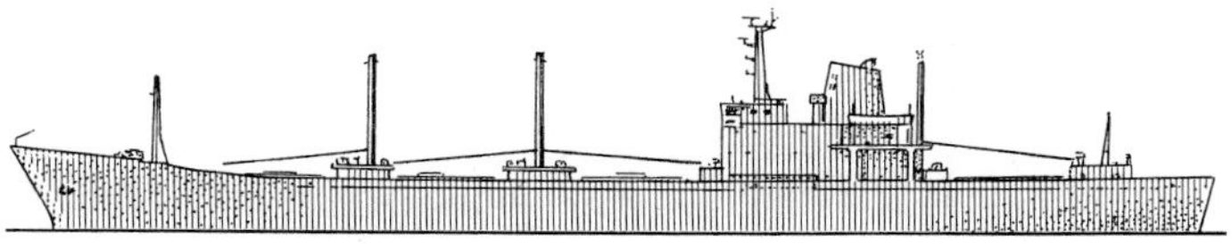

60 *MH²MFHM H1*
ALONTRA Ma/Ja (Kochi Jukogyo) 1978; R; 7,608 grt/7,649 dwt; 140.67 × 8.32 m *(461.52 × 27.3 ft)*; M (IHI); 20 kts; ex-*Freezer King*
Sisters: **ARIZONIA** (Bs) ex-*Freezer Prince*; **NISSOS KRITI** (Gr) ex-*Freezer Queen*; **AKAROA** (Sv) ex-*Khalij Reefer*
Possible sisters: **ARAWAK E** (SV) ex-*Khalij Freezer*; **AITAPE** (Sv) ex-*Khalij Frost*; **ANAKAN** (SV) ex-*Khalij Cooler*; **COLORADO** (Bs) ex-*Freezer Ace*

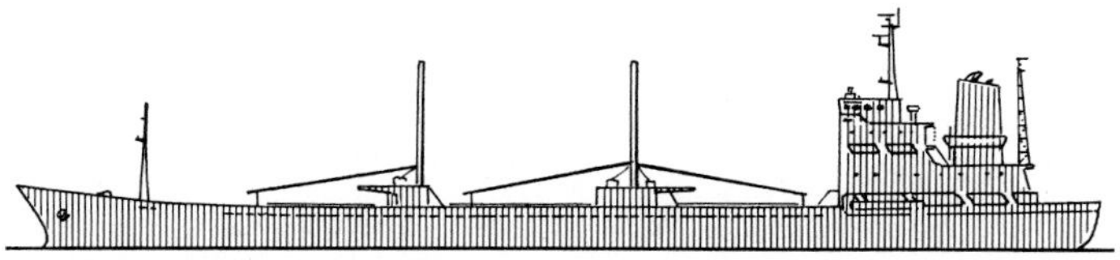

61 *MH²MFN H*
ABDALLAH BNOU YASSINE Mo/Ja (Honda) 1978; R; 3,086 grt/5,179 dwt; 120.58 × 6.4 m *(395.6 × 21 ft)*; M (Pielstick); 18 kts; ex-*Hirotsuki Maru*

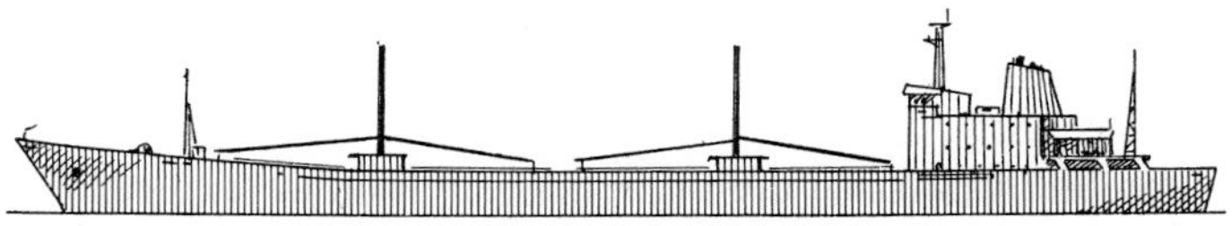

62 *MH²MFN H*
FRIO ITALIA Cy/Ja (Nishii) 1977; R; 5,432 grt/5,787 dwt; 127.41 × 7.07 m *(418.01 × 23.2 ft)*; M (Mitsubishi); 18 kts; ex-*Eitoku Maru*
Similar: **FRIO GALICIA** (Pa) ex-*Nittoku Maru*

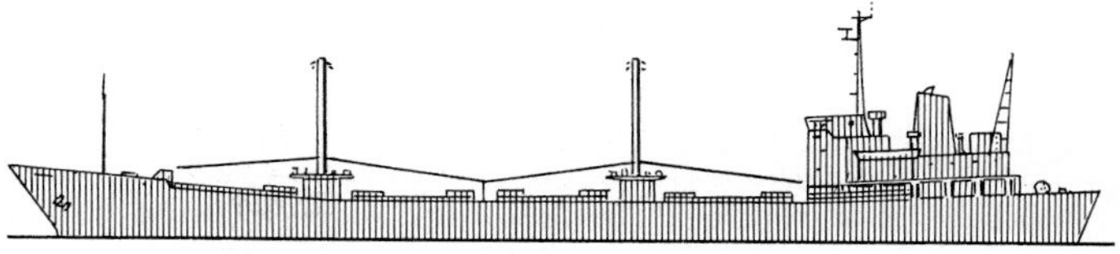

63 *MH²MFN H*
RASHA ONE Ma/Ja (Miyoshi) 1978; R; 6,221 grt/7,926 dwt; 126.29 × 8.67 m *(414.34 × 28.44 ft)*; M (Pielstick); 18 kts; ex-*Takatsuki Maru*
Probable sister: **FANGHAI** (Pa) ex-*Takeshima Maru*

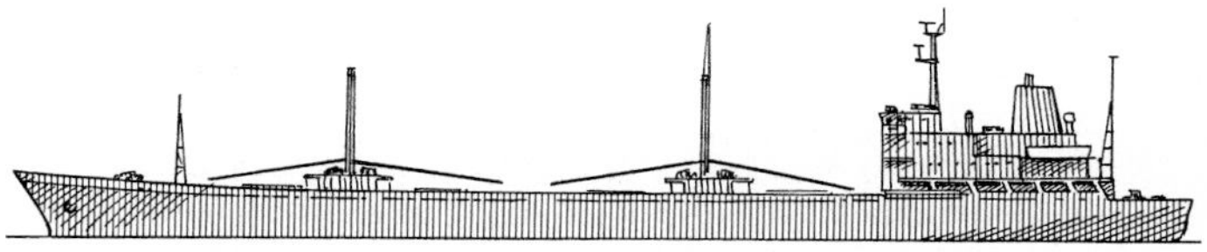

64 *MH²MFN H*
REEFER No 1 Ko/Ja (Shikoku) 1975; R; 3,858 grt/6,049 dwt; 131.48 × 6.99 m *(431.36 × 22.93 ft)*; M (Mitsubishi); 17.5 kts; ex-*Rose Daphne*
Sisters: **FRIO CARIBIC** (Pa) ex-*Rose Mallow*; **IONIAN SPRINTER** (Pa) ex-*Rose Acacia*; **FRIO OCEANIC** (Pa) ex-*Aden Maru*

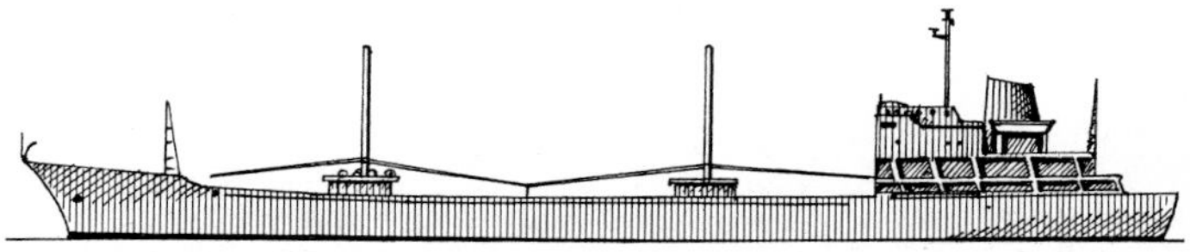

65 *MH²MFN H1*
REEFER No 2 Ko/Ja (Kishimoto) 1975; R; 3,566 grt/5,688 dwt; 124.08 × 6.92 m *(407.08 × 22.7 ft)*; M (B&W); 17.5 kts; ex-*Ocean Dynamic*
Sister: **REEFER No 3** (Ko) ex-*Ocean Fresh*

66 *MH²MFN H13*
FORTUNA VOYAGER Bs/Ja (Shikoku) 1972; R; 2,919 grt/4,320 dwt; 109.02 × 6.73 m *(357.68 × 22.08 ft)*; M (Kobe); 16.5 kts; ex-*Nipponham Maru No 1*
Probably similar: **WIN SHUN SHING** (Tw) ex-*Dairyo Maru*

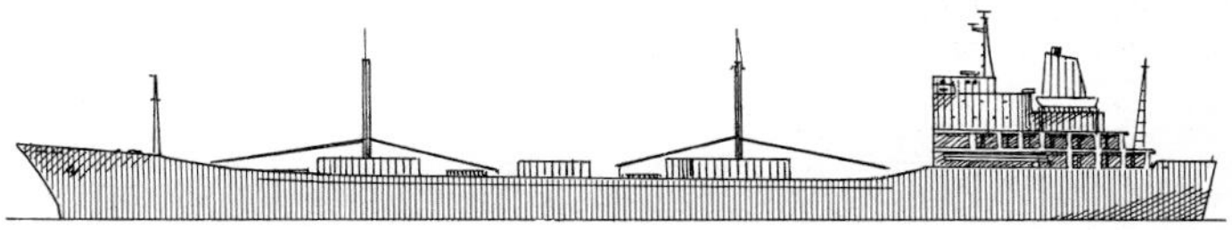

67 *MH²MFN H13*
TAISEI No 98 Pa/Ja (Shin Yamamoto) 1977; R/FC; 10,670 grt/10,325 dwt; 155 × 8.22 m *(508.53 × 26.97); M (Mitsubishi); 19.75 kts; ex-Taisei Maru No 98*

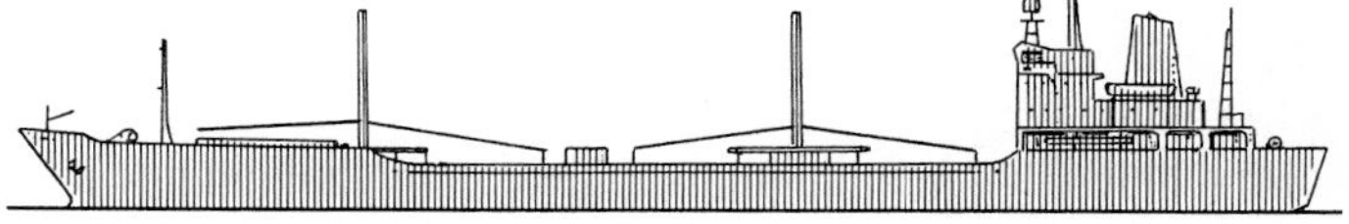

68 *MH²M²FN H13*
FRIO BERGEN Ma/Ja (Kyokuyo) 1983; R; 6,150 grt/7,118 dwt; 137.83 × 7.7 m *(452.2 × 25.26 ft)*; M (Mitsubishi); 17 kts; ex-*Yoshino Reefer*

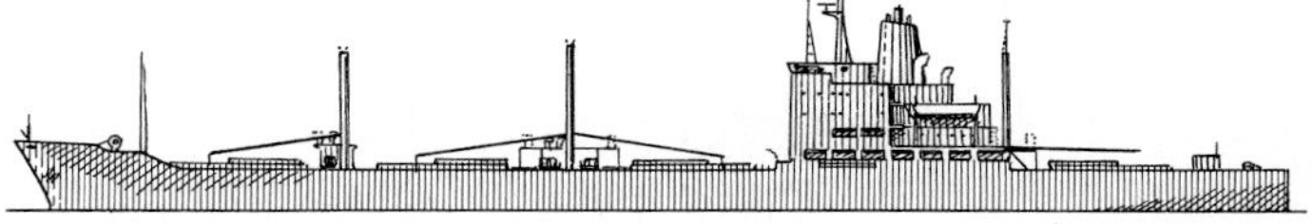

69 *MH²NMFH H1*
FUJI STAR SV/Ja (Hitachi) 1979; R; 7,095 grt/8,084 dwt; 144.95 × 8.07 m *(475.56 × 26.48 ft)*; M (B&W); 20 kts; ex-*Fuji Reefer*
Sisters: **SAKURA REEFER** (Gr); **ARIAKE STAR** (SV) ex-*Ariake Reefer*; **AKEBONO STAR** (SV) ex-*Akebono Reefer*; **TOKYO BAY** (SV) ex-*Tokyo Reefer*

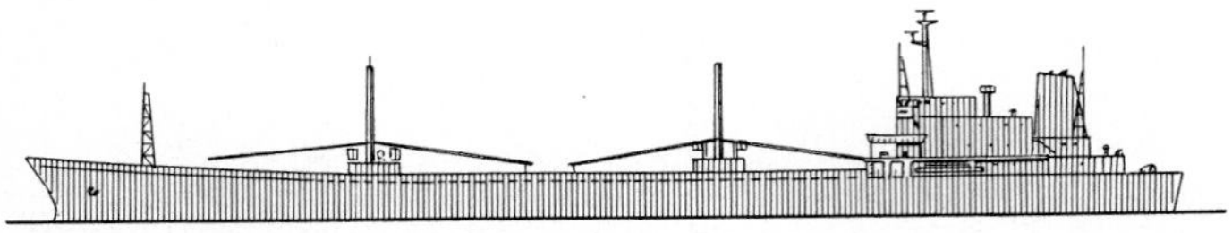

70 *MH^2NMFN H*
ALBA STAR Pa/Ja (Shikoku) 1982; R; 6,183 grt/6,404 dwt; 145.5 × 6.82 m *(477.36 × 22.38 ft)*; M (B&W); 17.4 kts; ex-*Daikoh Maru*

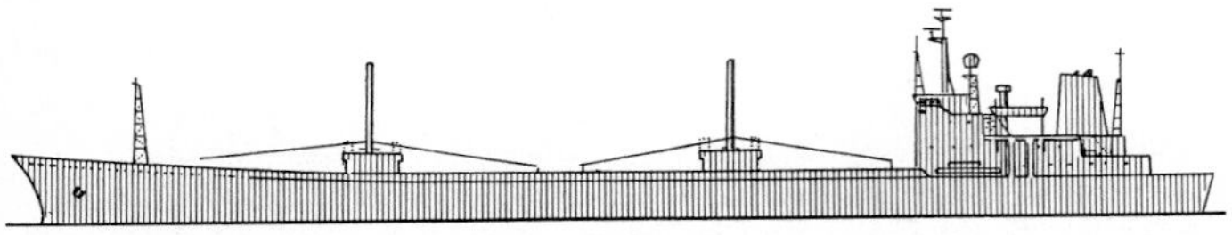

71 *MH^2NMFN H*
CALAMO Pa/Ja (Shikoku) 1982; R; 6,089 grt/6,370 dwt; 145.52 × 6.77 m *(477 × 22.21 ft)*; M (B&W); 17.25 kts; ex-*Hamanasu*
Sisters: **ASUKA REEFER** (Pa); **IONIAN** (Bs) ex-*Trans Reefer*; **REEFER PENGUIN** (Ja)
Possible sister: **WHITE SUN** (As) ex-*Hideshima Maru*; Similar (tripod radar mast surmounted by satcom aerial): **SUZURAN** (Pa)

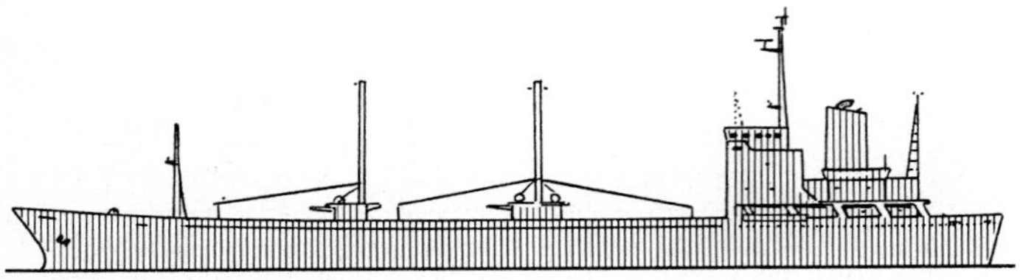

72 *MH^2NMFN H*
KONAH Pa/Ja (Honda) 1979; R; 2,687 grt/4,517 dwt; 107.42 × 6.51 m *(352.43 × 21.36 ft)*; M (Pielstick); 17 kts; ex-*Fumizuki Maru*
Similar (slightly taller funnel. Small housing abaft funnel): **OCEAN EXPRESS** (Ko) ex-*Wakatsuki Maru*

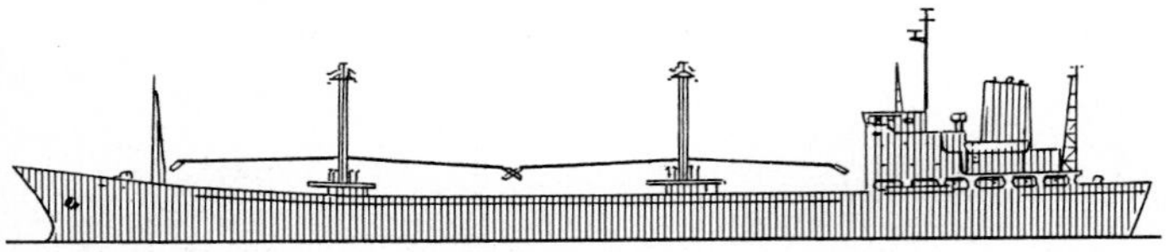

73 *MH^2NMFN H*
MIDELT Mo/Ja (Miyoshi) 1980; R; 2,825 grt/5,030 dwt; 122.48 × 6.65 m *(401.84 × 21.82 ft)*; M (Mitsubishi); 14 kts; ex-*Miyashima Maru*

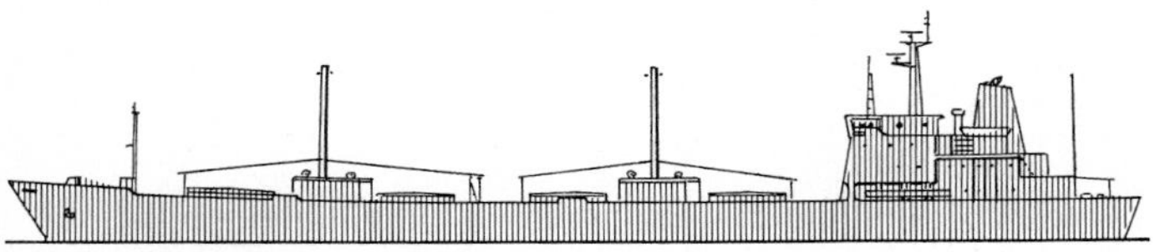

74 *MH^2NMFN H*
NIPPON REEFER Bs/Ja (Kyokuyo) 1982; R; 7,858 grt/8,657 dwt; 142.40 × 8.62 m *(467 × 28.28 ft)*; M (Pielstick); 17.25 kts
Sister: **NEW ZEALAND REEFER** (Bs)

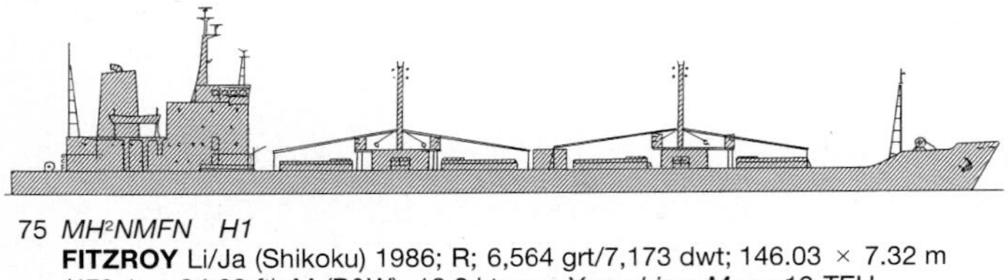

75 *MH^2NMFN H1*
FITZROY Li/Ja (Shikoku) 1986; R; 6,564 grt/7,173 dwt; 146.03 × 7.32 m *(479.1 × 24.02 ft)*; M (B&W); 18.2 kts; ex-*Yasushima Maru*; 12 TEU
Sister: **COPIHUE** (Pa)
Possible sisters: **SARAMATI** (Sg) ex-*Ohgishima Maru*; **VINSON** (Li) ex-*Kaneshima*; **WHITE CASTLE** (Pa); **KOWHAI** (Pa); **ELBRUS** (Li) ex-*Tomishima Maru*; Similar: **SANTORINI REX** (Va) ex-*Cap Domingo*; **GLACIER BAY** (Pa) ex-*Cap Delgado*

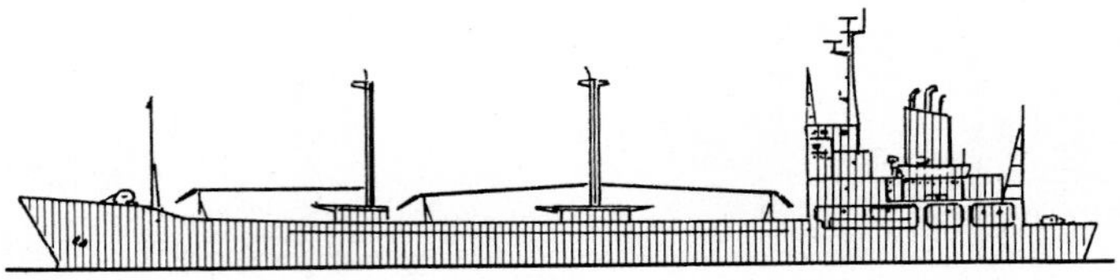

76 *MH^2NMFN H1*
GLOBAL MARINER Pa/Ja (Kitanihon) 1981; R; 3,363 grt/5,009 dwt; 99.01 × 6.71 m *(324.84 × 22.01 ft)*; M (Mitsubishi); 15.5 kts; ex-*Mizuho Reefer*

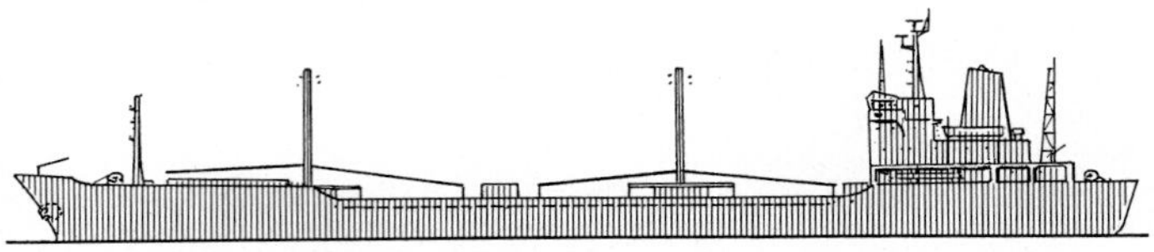

77 *MH^2NMFN H13*
EW ASPEN Li/Ja (Towa) 1983; R; dwt; 137.83 × 7.51 *(452.2 × 24.64)*; TSM (B&W); 17; ex-*Sun Beauty*
Possible sister: **SUN PRINCESS** (Pa) ex-*Sun Field*

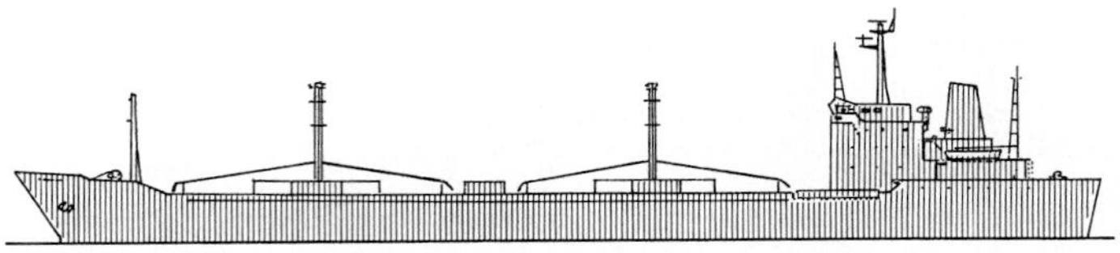

78 *MH^2NMFN H13*
WINFAST REEFER Pa/Ja (Towa) 1982; R; 8,041 grt/8,778 dwt; 139.93 × 8.78 m *(459.09 × 28.81 ft)*; M (Mitsubishi); 18 kts; ex-*Kijima*
Similar: **KIWI** (Ma) ex-*Southern Universal*

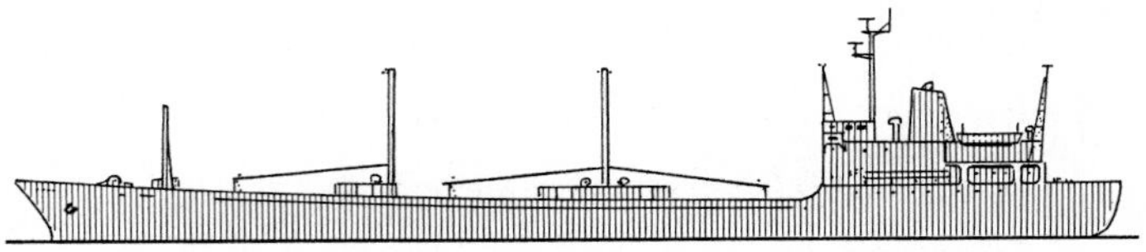

79 *MH^2NMFN H3*
KLAIPEDA Pa/Ja (Imabari) 1978; R; 5,707 grt/5,603 dwt; 130.31 × 6.9 m *(427.53 × 22.64 ft)*; M (Sulzer); 17.5 kts; ex-*Kendrick*; Three side doors

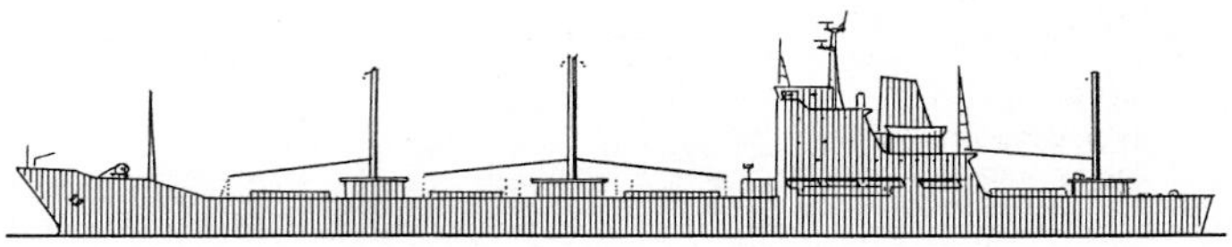

80 *MH^2NMFNH H1*
ATHENIAN REX Cy/Ja (Hayashikane) 1979; R; 7,246 grt/8,872 dwt; 140.52 × 8.82 m *(461 × 28.94 ft)*; M (Sulzer); 20 kts; ex-*Royal Lily*; Four side doors
Possibly similar: **NISSOS HYDRA** (Va) ex-*Seki Rex*

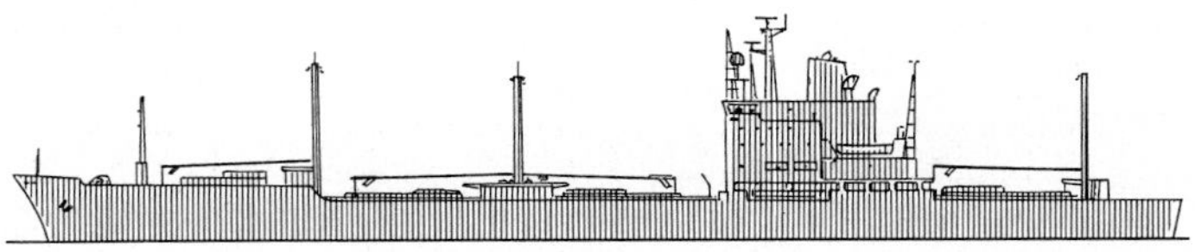

81 *MH^2NM^2FNH H1*
ARIMAO UNIVERSAL Cy/Ja (Hitachi) 1984; R; 9,274 grt/10,641 dwt; 149.89 × 9.02 m *(491.77 × 29.59 ft)*; M (B&W); 19 kts; ex-*Kasuya Reefer*; Side doors
Sisters: **GEMINI** (Cy); **LIBRA** (Cy); **PASADENA UNIVERSAL** (Pa)

82 *MHMFH H*
YANIS RAYNIS Ru/Pd (Gdanska) 1971; R; 5,215 grt/4,428 dwt; 119.4 × 7.3 m *(393 × 23.11 ft)*; M (B&W); 19 kts; 'B443' type
Sisters: **ALEKSANDRA KOLLONTAY** (Ru); **HENRI BARBUSSE** (Ru); **LARISA REYSNER** (Ru); **PAOLA** (Pa) ex-*Karlis Ziedins*; **KLARA ZETKIN** (Ru); **MARINA RASKOVA** (Ru); **OTOMAR OSHKALN** (Ru); **POLINA OSIPENKO** (Ru); **YANIS LENTSMANIS** (Ru); **ROBIN** (Pa) ex-*Yakov Alksnis*

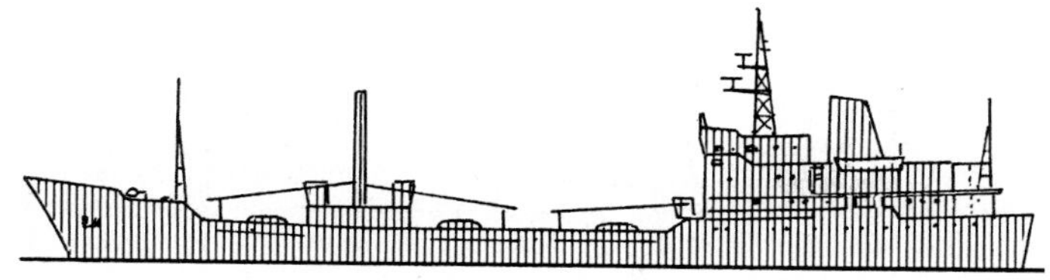

83 *MHMFM H13*
VEGA Lt/Pd (Gdynia) 1980; FC; 2,778 grt/1,928 dwt; 90.99 × 5.35 m *(298.52 × 17.55 ft)*; M (Sulzer); 15.5 kts; ex-*Terral*; 'B361' type
Sister: **NEPTUNAS** (Lt) ex-*Zonda*

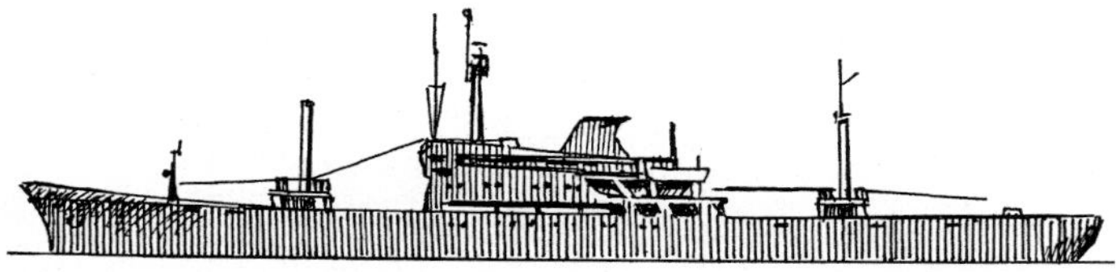

84 *MHMFMH H*
APRIL Ma/Pd (Gdanska) 1972; FC; 5,216 grt/4,555 dwt; 120 × 7.3 m *(394 × 24 ft)*; M (B&W); 18 kts; ex-*Lewanter*; 'B433' type

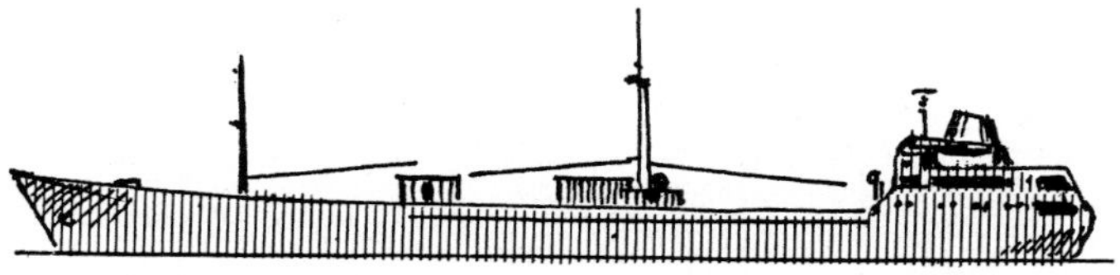

85 *M^3F H*
ORIENT REEFER Ho/No (Kleven) 1968; R; 1,369 grt/2,047 dwt; 81.44 × 5.02 m *(267.19 × 16.47 ft)*; M (Bergens); 16 kts; ex-*Frio Trader*

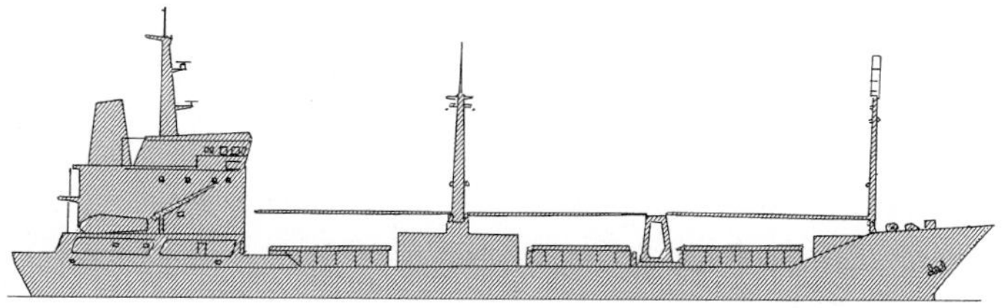

86 *M^3F H1*
REEFER COUNTESS At/De (Frederikshavn) 1978; R; 1,753 grt/2,225 dwt; 74.5 × 5.01 m *(244.42 × 16.44 ft)*; M (Alpha-Diesel); 11.5 kts; ex-*Gomba Reefer 1*; '613-B' type
Sister: **REEFER EMPRESS** (Cy) ex-*Gomba Reefer II*

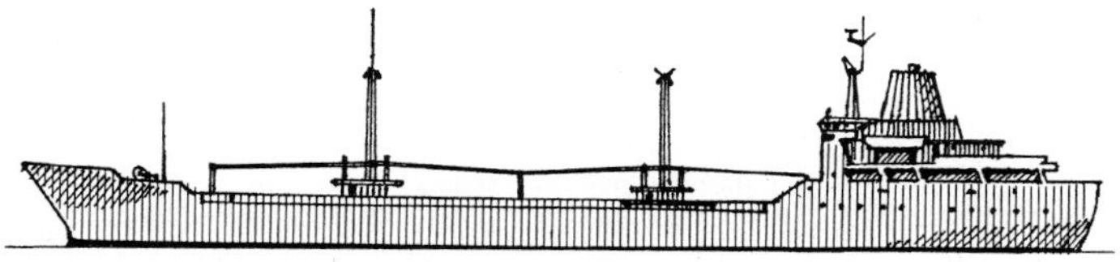

87 *M^3F H13*
BLISSFUL REEFER 2 Pa/Sw (Solvesborgs) 1970; R; 2,965 grt/2,965 dwt; 98.81 × 5.92 m *(324.18 × 19.42 ft)*; M (Pielstick); 16.5 kts; ex-*Polar Kristall*
Sisters: **BLUE ICE** (Pa) ex-*Tizi N'Test*; **NEAMMA** (SV) ex-*Polar Diamant*

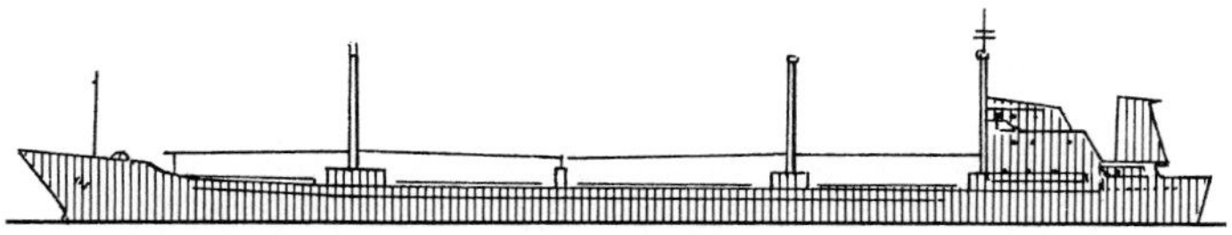

88 *M^3HG H1*
DAKOTA Cy/Ne (Nieuwe Noord) 1977/83; R; 2,989 grt/3,507 dwt; 101.94 × 5.3 m *(334 × 17.39 ft)*; M (KHD); 14 kts; ex-*Jan-Willem*; Lengthened 1983 (Nederlandse)
Sisters: **CALAFIA** (Bs); **CASABLANCA** (NA); **INCA** (Cy); **SWALAN** (NA) ex-*Laura Christina*; **MAGDALENA** (NA); **LIMA** (NA) ex-*Mathilda*; **MAYA** (NA)

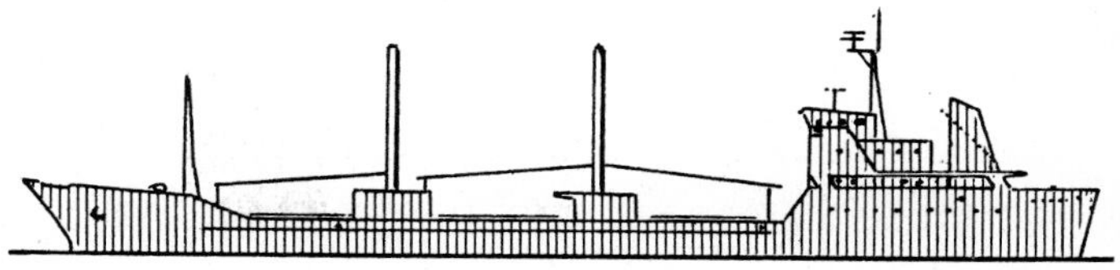

89 *M^4F H13*
ARGOSEA SV/Sp (Cadagua) 1981; R; 1,774 grt/2,557 dwt; 83.70 × 5.20 m *(274.61 × 17.06 ft)*; M (Deutz); 12 kts; ex-*Extrelago*
Probable sister: **ARGOMAR** (SV) ex-*Extremar*

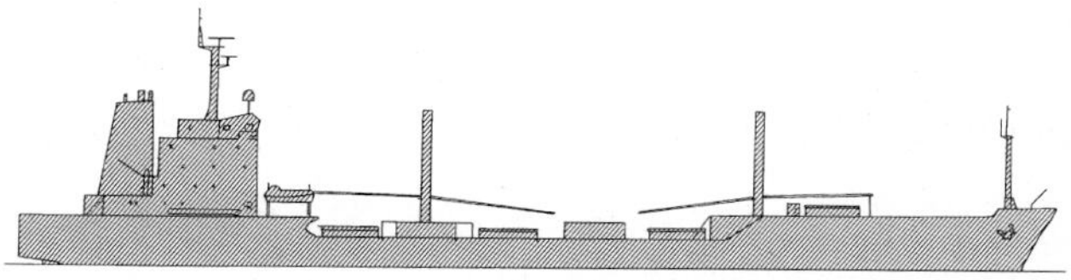

90 *M^4F H13*
URANUS Si/Ko (Dong Hae) 1989; R; 7,212 grt/6,518 dwt; 137 × 7.4 m *(449.48 × 24.28 ft)*; M (B&W); 18.5 kts
Probable sister: **PLUTO** (Si)

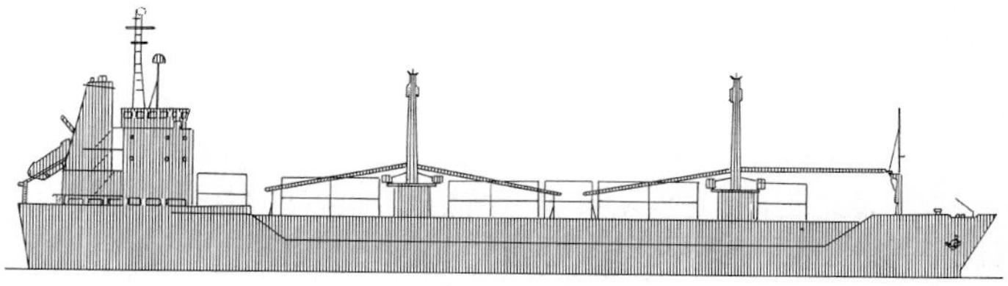

91 *M^4FL H13*
BLUE FROST Cy/RC (Shanghai SY) 1991; R/Con; 6,419 grt/6,050 dwt; 120.50 × 7.88 m *(395.34 × 25.85 ft)*; M (Sulzer); 18.4 kts; ex-*Blue Ice*; 228 TEU
Sisters: **BLUE CREST** (Li); **BLUE CRYSTAL** (Cy) ex-*Blue Cloud*; **BLUE REEFER** (Cy) ex-*Blue Sky*; **CAPE FINISTERRE** (Cy); **CAPE COD** (Li); **CAPE CAVO** (Li); **CAPE VINCENTE** (At)

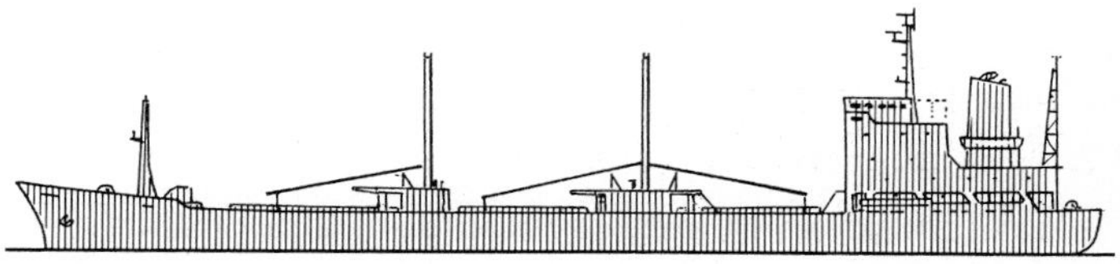

92 *M^4FN H1*
OKBA BNOU NAFIA Mo/Ja (Honda) 1978; R; 3,085 grt/5,179 dwt; 120.55 × 6.49 m *(395.5 × 21.29 ft)*; M (Pielstick); 18 kts; ex-*Akizuki Maru*

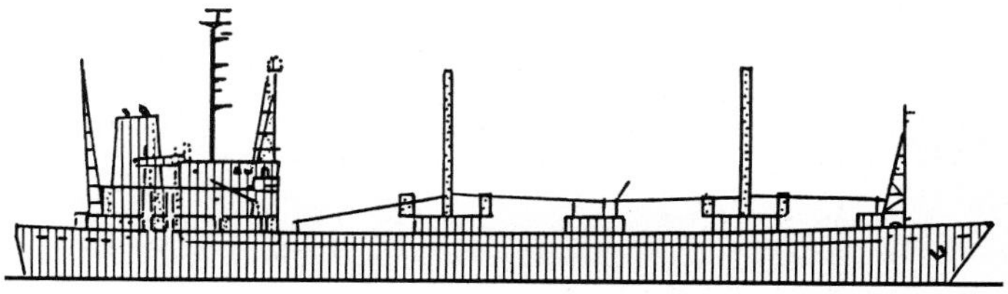

93 *M^5FM H*
SEKINO V Pa/Ja (Kanasashi) 1988; R/FC; 2,426 grt/2,267 dwt; 86.33 × 4.97 m *(283.23 × 16.31 ft)*; M (Hanshin); 12.75 kts; ex-*Sekino Maru*

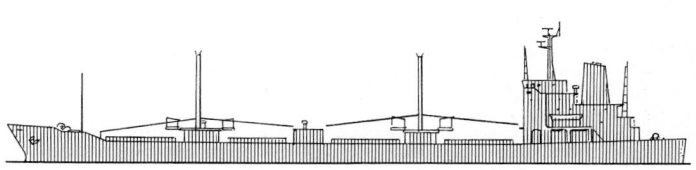

94 *M^5FM H1*
PUNENTE Pa/Ja (Towa) 1984; R/V/Con; 7,736 grt/8,556 dwt; 139.05 × 7.58 m *(456.2 × 24.87 ft)*; M (Mitsubishi); 17 kts; 53 TEU
Possible sisters: **LEVANTE** (Pa); **CHIRICANA** (Pa) ex-*Juvante*

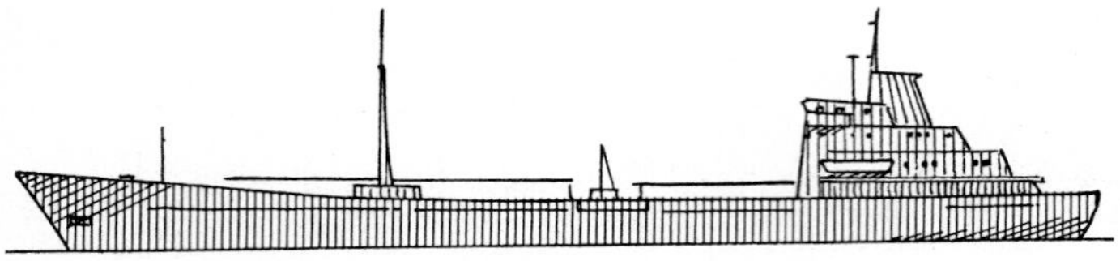

95 *M^2M–F H*
TROPICAL REEFER Pa/FRG (Schlichting) 1969; R; 1,942 grt/2,462 dwt; 93.71 × 5.51 m *(307.45 × 18.08 ft)*; M (Deutz); 17.5 kts; ex-*Cooler Scan*

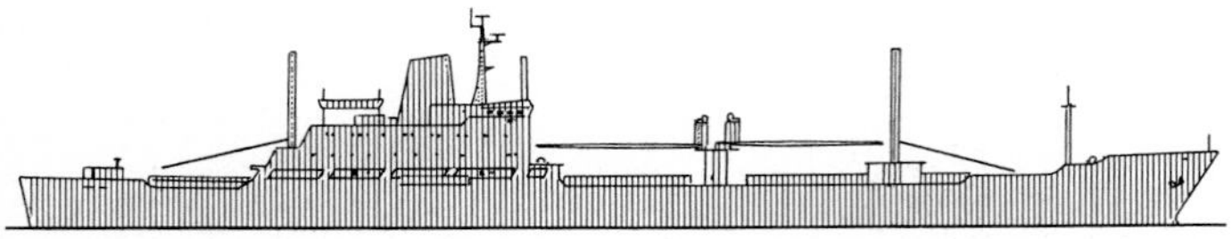

96 *M^2PM^2FM H1*
BORA UNIVERSAL Br/Ja (Mitsubishi HI) 1979; R; 11,032 grt/9,175 dwt; 154.01 × 8.5 m *(505.28 × 27.89 ft)*; M (Sulzer); 21 kts
Sister: **SCIROCCO UNIVERSAL** (Br)

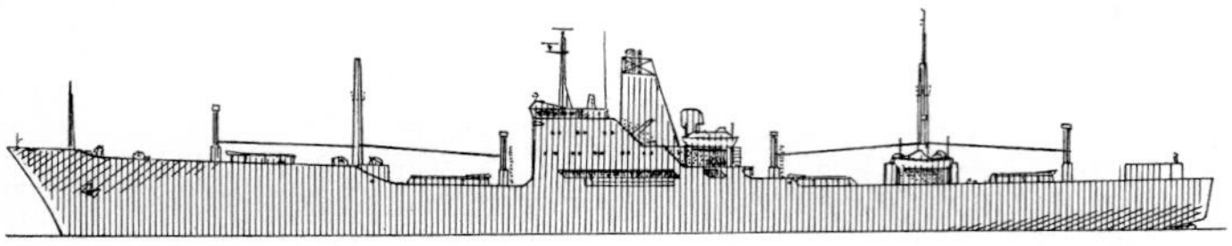

97 *M^2TM^2FMTM H1*
UB POLARIS NIS/No (Drammen) 1978; R; 7,179 grt/9,269 dwt; 144.45 × 9.01 m *(473.92 × 29.56 ft)*; M (Sulzer); 21.9 kts; ex-*Ragni Berg*; 'Drammen' type
Sisters: **ORENOCO REEFER** (Cy) ex-*Rio Palora*; **ZAIN AL-QAWS** (Iq) ex-*Elisabeth Berg*; Similar: **MALIBU REEFER** (cy) ex-*Rio Chone*; **BALBAO REEFER** Ec) ex-*Rio Esmeraldas*; **CURACAO REEFER** (Cy) ex-*Rio Babahoya*

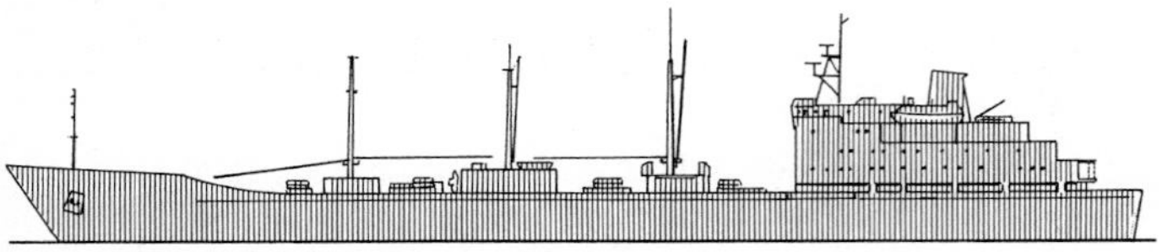

98 *MNMNMF H1*
FROST 1 Li/DDR (Mathias-Thesen) 1978; FC; 12,383 grt/9,360 dwt; 152.69 × 8 m *(500.95 × 26.25 ft)*; M (MAN); 17 kts; ex-*Almaznyy Bereg*; 'KRISTAL' type
Sisters: **AMURSKIY BEREG** (Ru); **BALTIYSKIY BEREG** (Ru); **BEREG MECHTY** (Ru); **BEREG NADEZHDY** (Ru); **CHUKOTSKIY BEREG** (Ru); **KAMCHATSKIY BEREG** (Ru); **KAPTEINIS KULINICS** (La) ex-*Kapitan Kulinich*; **KHRUSTALNY BEREG** (Ru); **FROST 2** (Li) ex-*Primorskiy Bereg*; **TAMBOV** (Ru); **VOSTOCHNIY BEREG** (Ru); **ZVYOZDNYY BEREG** (Ru); Similar ('KRISTAL II' type): **KOMSOMOLETS PRIMORYA** (Ru); **FROST 3** (Li) ex-*Zolotye Dyuny*; **TAYOZHNYY BEREG** (Ru); **REF VEGA** (Pa) ex-*Bereg Yunosti*; **REF STAR** (Pa) ex-*Kaliningradskiy Bereg*; **MOTOVSKIY ZALIV** (Cy); **OLYUTORSKIY ZALIV** (Ru); **ULBANSKIY ZALIV** (Ru); **USSURIYSKAYA TAYGA** (Ru); **FROST 4** (Li) ex-*Bereg Vetrov*; **PENZHINSKIY ZALIV** (Ru); **HERMANN MATERN** (Cy); **HAMBURG TRADER** (Bs) ex-*Reutershagen*; **REF LIRA** (Pa) ex-*Burya*; **KLAJPEDSKIJ BEREG** (Cy); **PAMYAT KIROVA** (Cy); **FROST 5** (Li) ex-*Baltiyskiye Zory*; **KOLSKIY ZALIV** (Cy); **ATMODA** (La) ex-*Rizhskiy Bereg*; **VASILIY POLESHCHUK** (Cy); **BALTIJAS CELS** (Pa) ex-*Bereg Baltiki*; **DUBRAVA** (Cy); **PAMYAT ILYICHA** (Cy); **KILDINSKIY PROLIV** (Cy)

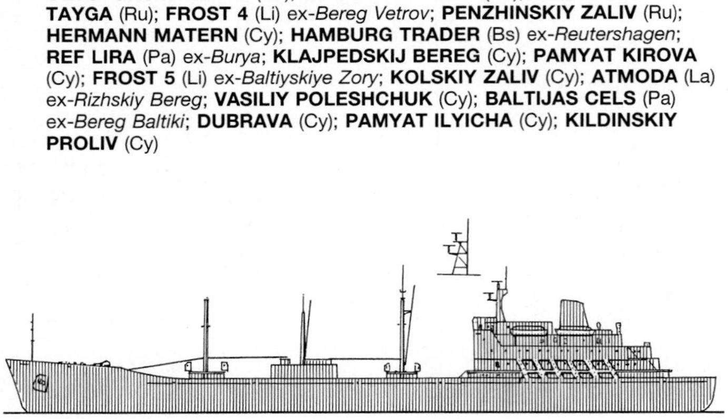

99 *MNMNMF H1*
HAMMOND Lt/DDR (Mathias-Thesen) 1974; FC; 8,323 grt/9,600 dwt; 152.25 × 8.17 m *(499.51 × 25.8 ft)*; M (MAN); 17.25 kts; Launched as *Ignalina*; 'Polar' type
Sisters (some have tripod radar mast—see inset): **DIMANTS** (La) ex-*Dimant*; **ERNST THALMANN** (Ru); **FRITZ HECKERT** (Ru); **GRANITNYY BEREG** (Ru); **IZUMRUDNYY BEREG** (Ru); **MATHIAS THESEN** (Ru); **OTTO GROTEWOHL** (Ru); **ROZA LUXEMBURG** (Ru); **SKALISTYY BEREG** (Ru); **WILHELM PIECK** (Ru); **ZHEMCHUZNYY BEREG** (Ru); **ROMAN ARCTIC** (Pa) ex-*Polar III*; **ROMAN BLIZZARD** (Cy) ex-*Polar V*; **ROMAN COOLER** (Cy) ex-*Polar VI*; **INVINCIBLE** (Pa) ex-*Lichtenhagen*

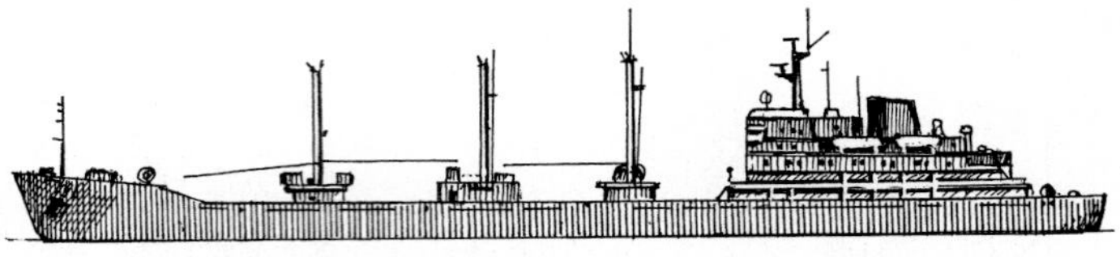

100 *MNMNMF H1*
KARL LIBKNEKHT Ru/DDR (Mathias-Thesen) 1970; FC; 8,410 grt/9,288 dwt; 155 × 7.79 m *(508.53 × 25.58 ft)*; M (MAN); 17.25 kts; 'Polar' type
Sisters: **LAZURNYY BEREG** (Ru); **SOLNECHNYY BEREG** (Ru); **YANTARNYY BEREG** (Ru)

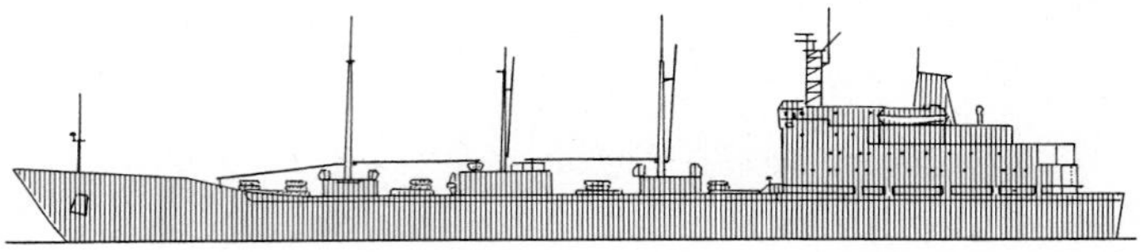

101 *MNMNMF H1*
KOMSOMOLETS PRIMORYA Ru/DDR (Mathias-Thesen) 1983; FC; 7,701 grt/9,360 dwt; 152.79 × 7.45 m *(501.28 × 24.44 ft)*; M (MAN); 17.5 kts; 'Kristal II' type
Sisters: **FROST 3** (Li) ex-*Zolotye Dyuny*; **TAYOZHNYY BEREG** (Ru); **REF STAR** (Pa) ex-*Kaliningradskiy Bereg*; **MOTOVSKIY ZALIV** (Cy); **OLYUTORSKIY ZALIV** (Ru); **ULBANSKIY ZALIV** (Ru); **USSURIYSKAYA TAYGA** (Ru); **FROST 4** (Li) ex-*Bereg Vetrov*; **PENZHINSKIY ZALIV** (Ru); **HERMANN MATERN** (Cy); **REF VEGA** (Pa) ex-*Bereg Yunosti*; **HAMBURG TRADER** (Bs) ex-*Reutershagen*; **REF LIRA** (Pa) ex-*Burya*; **KLAJPEDSKIJ BEREG** (Cy); **PAMYAT KIROVA** (Cy); **FROST 5** (Li) ex-*Baltiyskiye Zory*; **KOLSKIY ZALIV** (Cy); **ATMODA** (La) ex-*Rizhskiy Bereg*; **VASILIY POLESHCHUK** (Cy); **BALTIJAS CELS** (Pa) ex-*Bereg Baltiki*; **DUBRAVA** (Cy); **PAMYAT ILYICHA** (Cy); **KILDINSKIY PROLIV** (Cy)

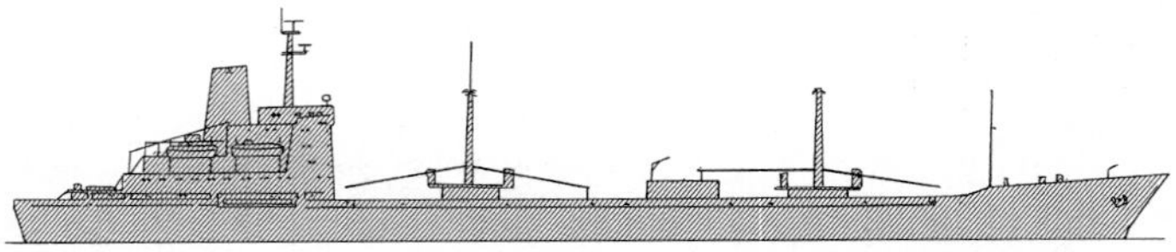

102 *MN^2MF H1*
PYATIDYESYATILYETIYE SSSR Ru/Ru ('61 Kommunar') 1973; FC; 10,104 grt/11,420 dwt; 172.12 × 8.1 m *(564.7 × 26.57 ft)*; M (B&W); 19 kts; Also known as **50 LET SSSR**
Sisters: **STRAUME** (La) ex-*Beringov Proliv*; **IRBENSKIY PROLIV** (Ru); **PROLIV LAPERUZA** (Ru); **PROLIV SANNIKOVA** (Uk); **CHYORNOE MORE** (Uk); **KERCHENSKIY PROLIV** (Uk); **SKRIVERI** (La) ex-*Proliv Kruzenshterna*; **PROLIV NADEZHDY** (Ru); **60 LET OKTYABRYA** (Uk); **UKRAINSKIY KOMSOMOLETS** (Ru); **PROLIV DIANY** (Ru); **PROLIV LONGA** (Uk); **PROLIV VIKTORIYA** (Uk); **KAMCHATSKIY PROLIV** (Uk); **PROLIV VILKITSKOGO** (Ru); **SELDERI** (La) ex-*Sangarskiy Proliv*

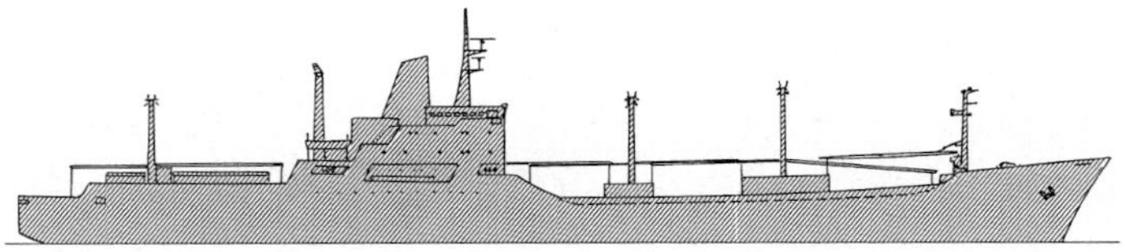

103 *MN^2MFTN H12*
RAINBOW REEFER Li/Fr (CNIM) 1969; R; 9,716 grt/8,712 dwt; 148.4 × 8.5 m *(487 × 28 ft)*; M (Pielstick); 20.5 kts

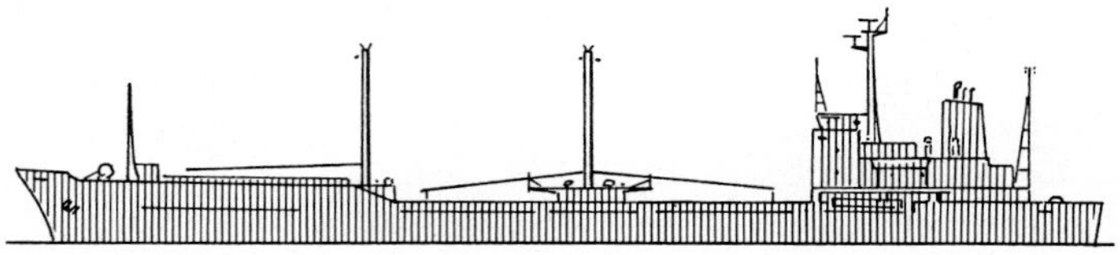

104 *MN^3MFN H1*
FRESA Ma/Ja (Kitanihon) 1984; R; 4,364 grt/5,522 dwt; 109 × 7.67 m *(357.61 × 25.16 ft)*; M (Mitsubishi); 16 kts; Launched as *Subaru*
Possible sister: **ISLA BONITA** (Pa) ex-*East Breeze*

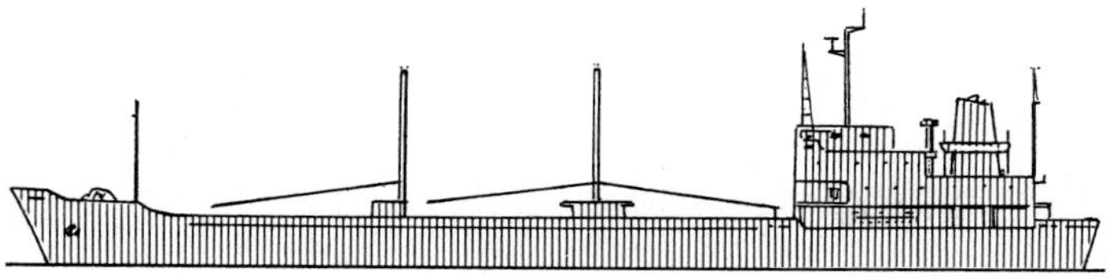

105 *MN^{3}MFN H1*
HAI FENG 301 RC/Ja (Kanasashi) 1978; R/FC; 2,968 grt/4,258 dwt; 107.02 × 6.25 m *(351.12 × 20.51 ft)*; M (Mitsubishi); 17 kts; ex-*Daigen Maru*

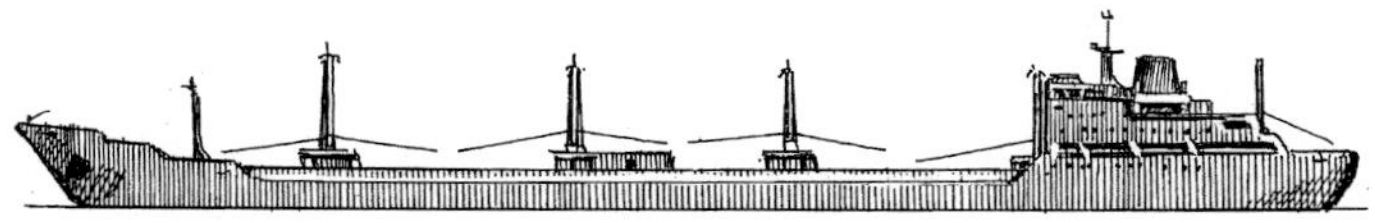

106 *MN^{4}MFN H13*
LAFAYETTE Ma/Fr (CNIM) 1972; FC; 18,871 grt/14,947 dwt; 186.8 × 7.75 m *(612.86 × 25.43 ft)*; M (Pielstick); 19 kts; ex-*Karskoye More*

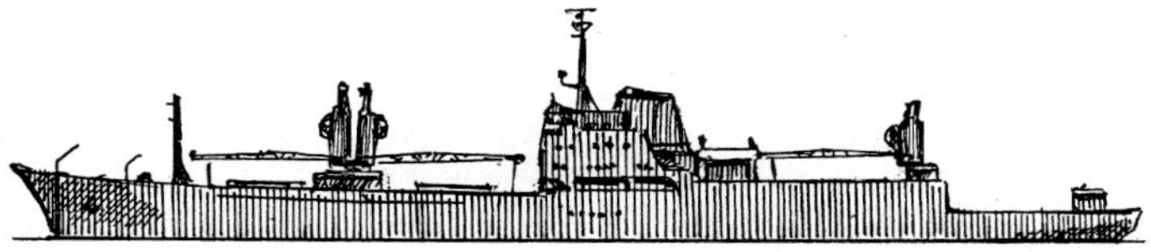

107 *MPMFP H12*
LLOYD BAGE Bz/Bz (Caneco) 1973; R; 5,379 grt/7,459 dwt; 140 × 8.3 m *(459 × 27.3 ft)*; M (Sulzer); 21 kts

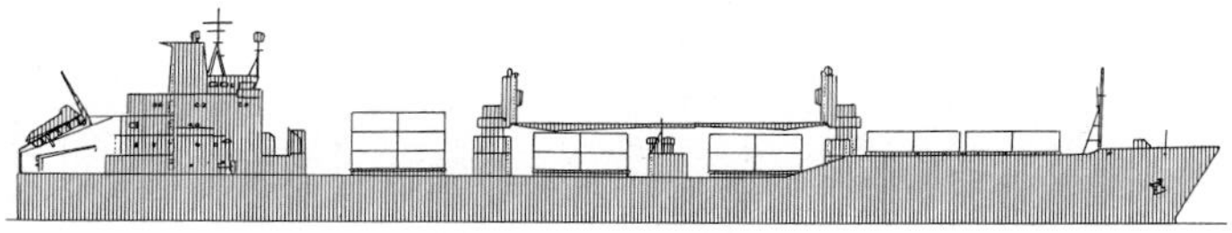

108 *MP^{2}HFL H1*
HANSA LUBECK Ge/Ge (Bremer V) 1990; R/Con; 10,842 grt/12,350 dwt; 156.53 × 9.51 m *(513.55 × 31.20 ft)*; M (B&W); 21 kts; 290 TEU; Side doors (port)
Sisters: **HANSA BREMEN** (Ge); **HANSA VISBY** (Ge); **HANSA STOCKHOLM** (Ge)

See photo number 11/243

109 *MP^{2}MFC H1*
SPRING BEE Li/Ja (Koyo) 1984; R/Con; 12,113 grt/10,113 dwt; 150.7 × 8.63 m *(494.4 × 28.3 ft)*; M (B&W); 19 kts; ex-*Spring Bird*; Eight side doors (four port, four starboard)
Sisters: **SPRING BOB** (NA) ex-*Spring Blossom*; **SPRING PANDA** (NA) Launched as *Spring Blossom*

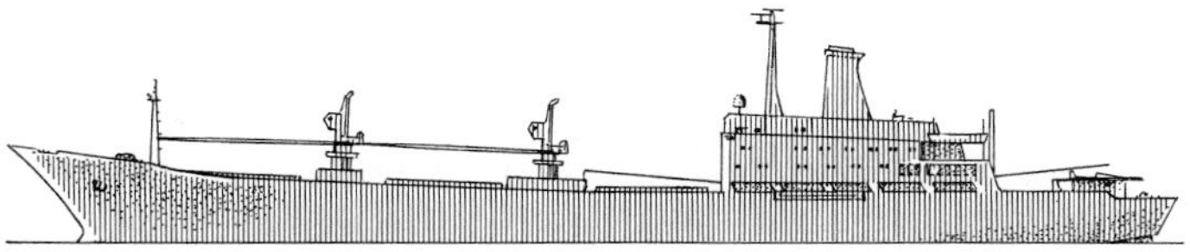

110 *MP^{2}MGN H1*
MAGELLAN REEFER Pa/Br (Smith's D) 1981; R/CP; 10,364 grt/9,970 dwt; 159.07 × 8.82 m *(521.8 × 28.94 ft)*; M (B&W); 19.5 kts; ex-*Geestbay*
Sister: **BAHIANA REEFER** (Pa) ex-*Geestport*

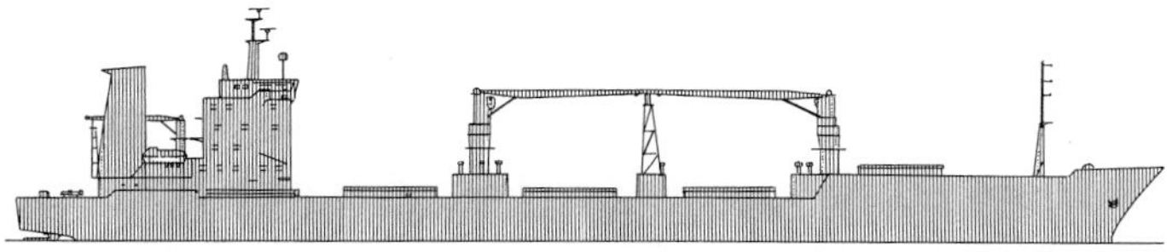

111 *MP^{2}MRF H1*
TUNDRA KING Li/Sp (AESA) 1990; R/Con; 11,658 grt/12,714 dwt; 158.53 × 9.12 m *(520.11 × 29.92 ft)*; M (B&W); 20 kts; ex-*Del Monte Pride*; 362 TEU
Sisters: **TUNDRA PRINCESS** (Li) ex-*Del Monte Spirit*; **TUNDRA QUEEN** (Li) ex-*Del Monte Quality*; **DEL MONTE CONSUMER** (Li); **DEL MONTE TRADER** (Li)

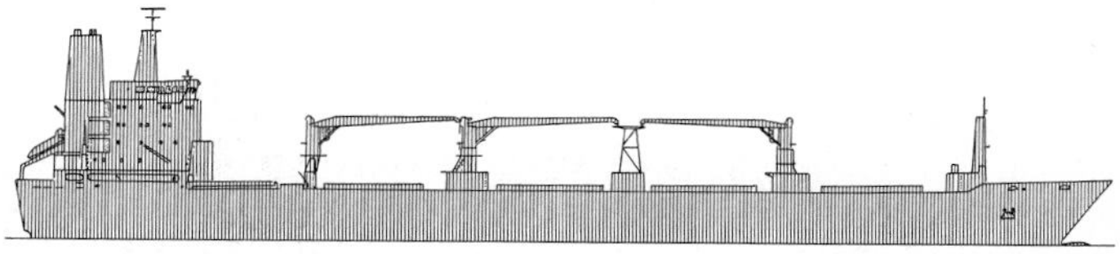

112 *MPR^{2}MFL H*
CHIQUITA NEDERLAND Bs/De (Danyard) 1991; R/Con; 13,049 grt/ 13,958 dwt; 158.13 × 10.02 m *(518.8 × 32.87 ft)*; M (B&W); 22 kts; 439 TEU
Sisters: **CHIQUITA DEUTSCHLAND** (Bs); **CHIQUITA SCHWEIZ** (Bs); **CHIQUITA SCANDINAVIA** (Bs); **CHIQUITA ITALIA** (Bs); **CHIQUITA BELGIE** (Bs)

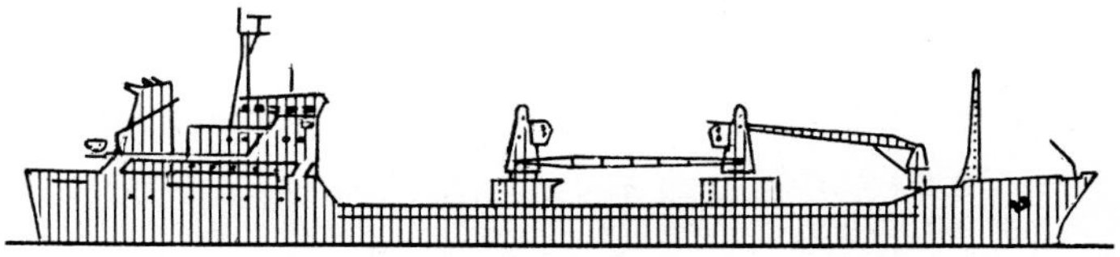

113 *MRM^{2}FS H13*
PETREL SV/Sp (Cadagua) 1981; R; 1,835 grt/2,255 dwt; 83.7 × 5.31 m *(275 × 17.42 ft)*; M (Deutz); 13.4 kts; ex-*F J Garaygordobil*
Similar (kingpost on forecastle and first crane aft of forecastle): **QUEEN OF HEAVEN** (Bl) ex-*Luis Calvo*

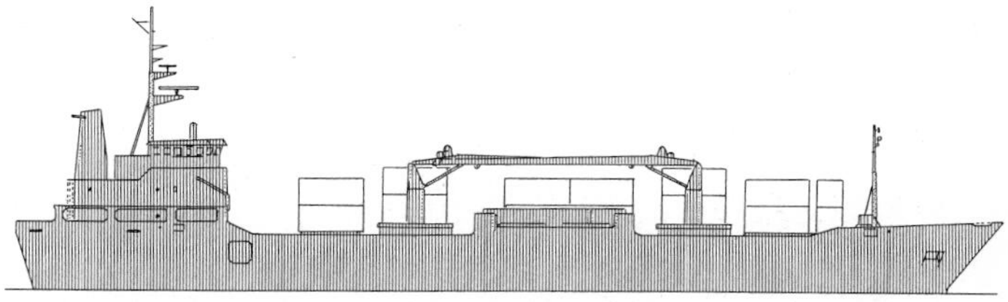

114 *MR^{2}MF H*
ICE STAR DIS/De (Aarhus) 1990; R/Pal; 3,625 grt/3,039 dwt; 92.90 × 5.17 m *(304.79 × 16.96 ft)*; M (B&W); 13 kts; 42 TEU; Two side doors (starboard)
Sisters: **ICE CRYSTAL** (DIS); **ICE BIRD** (DIS) ex-*Ice Clipper*

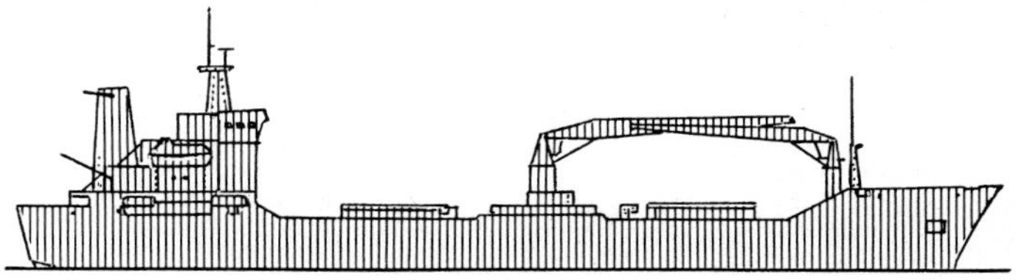

115 *MR^{2}MF H1*
NORDJARL No/De (Orskov C) 1985; R/Con; 3,968 grt/2,607 dwt; 95.51 × 5.18 m *(313.35 × 16.99 ft)*; M (MaK); 15 kts; ex-*Ice Pearl*; 54 TEU; Two side doors; Cranes are on starboard side

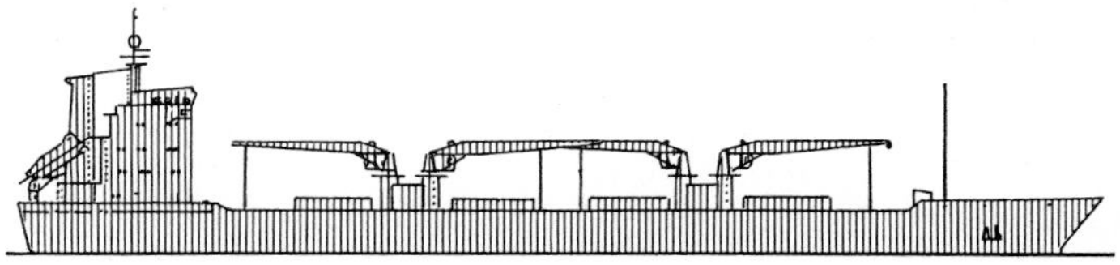

116 *MR^{4}HFLR H*
ICE FLAKE Br/Ne (Ysselwerf) 1987; R; 5,966 grt/6,985 dwt; 118.40 × 8.09 m *(388.45 × 26.54 ft)*; M (MAN); 18 kts; ex-*Prins Willem van Oranje*; 48 TEU; Four side doors (port)
Sister: **PRINS CASIMIR** (Ne)

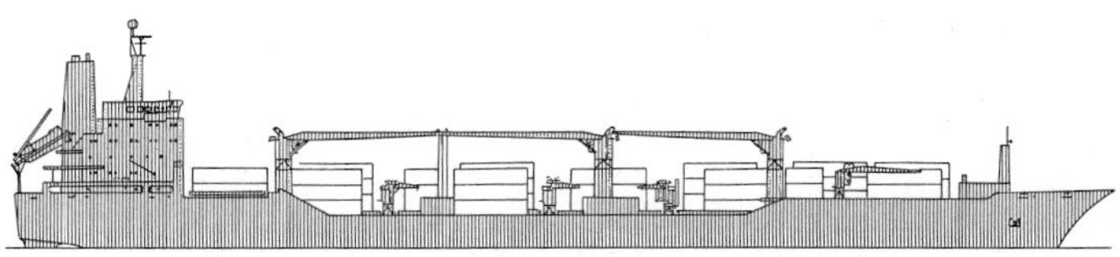

117 *MR^{4}MFL H13*
ALBEMARLE ISLAND Bs/De (Danyard) 1993; R/Con; 14,061 grt/14,160 dwt; 178.5 × 9.22 m *(585.63 × 30.25 ft)*; M (B&W); 21.5 kts; 434 TEU
Sisters: **BARRINGTON ISLAND** (Bs); **CHARLES ISLAND** (Bs); **DUNCAN ISLAND** (Bs); **HOOD ISLAND** (Bs)

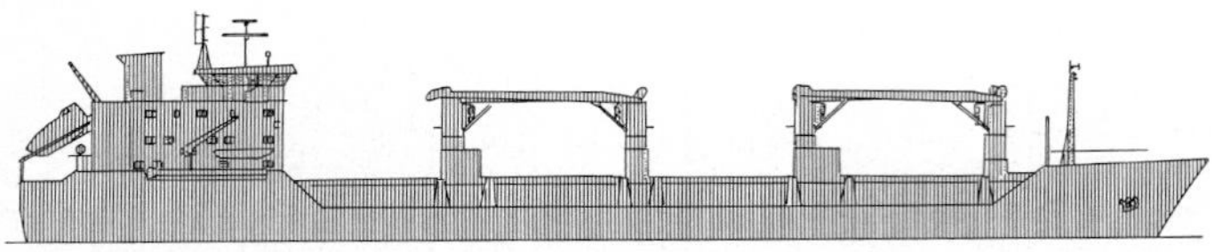

118 *MR⁴MFL H13*
ERIKSON FREEZER Bs/No (K Kleven L) 1991; R/Con; 5,084 grt/6,120 dwt; 109 × 7.41 m *(357.61 × 24.31 ft)*; M (Wärtsilä); 16 kts; 90 TEU
Sisters (various builders): **ERIKSON COOLER** (Bs); **ERIKSON CRYSTAL** (Bs); **ERIKSON FROST** (Bs); **ERIKSON NORDIC** (Bs); **ERIKSON SNOW** (Bs); **ERIKSON WINTER** (Bs); **BELINDA** (Bs) ex-*Erikson Arctic*; **IBERIAN REEFER** (DIS) ex-*Erikson Polar*; **INDIAN REEFER** (DIS) ex-*Erikson Reefer*
Possible sisters: **ITALIAN REEFER** (DIS); **CARMENCITA** (NIS)

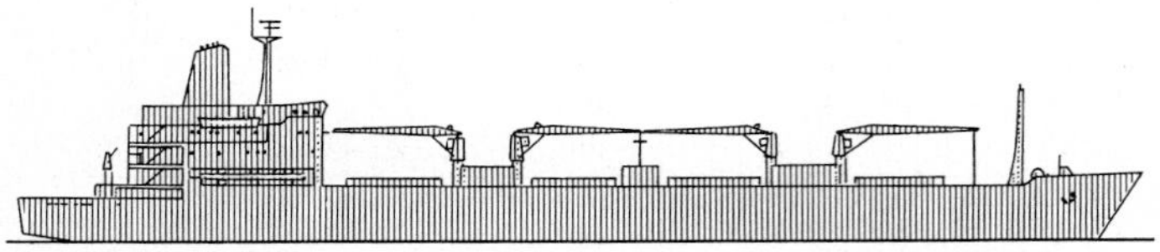

119 *MR⁴MFR H1*
AUSTRALIAN REEFER DIS/Ko (Hyundai) 1984; R/Con; 12,411 grt/14,499 dwt; 144.76 × 10 m *(474.93 × 32.8 ft)*; M (B&W); 18 kts; 148 TEU; Four side doors (starboard)
Sisters: **AMERICAN REEFER** (Bs); **AFRICAN REEFER** (DIS); **REEFER JAMBU** (Bs)

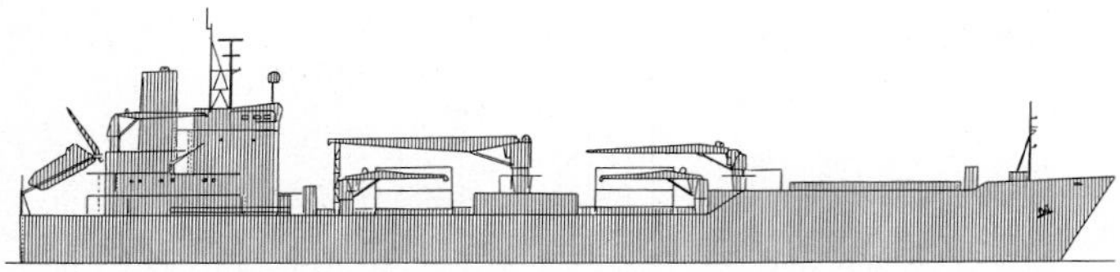

120 *MR⁴MFRL H1*
CRYSTAL PRIDE Lu/Be (Boelwerf) 1992; R/V/Pal; 7,743 grt/7,726 dwt; 131.25 × 8.85 m *(430.61 × 29.04 ft)*; M (B&W); 19.6 kts; 54 TEU; Two side doors (port)
Sisters: **CRYSTAL PIONEER** (Lu); **CRYSTAL PILGRIM** (Lu); **CRYSTAL PRIMADONNA** (Lu) (see photo number 11/184); **CRYSTAL PRINCE** (Lu); **CRYSTAL PRIVILEGE** (Lu)

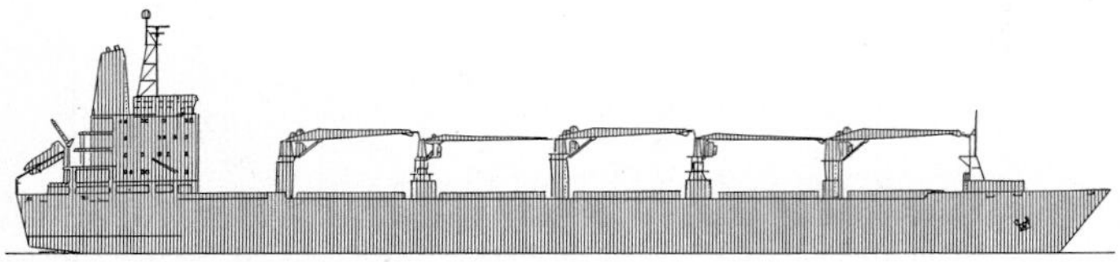

121 *MR⁵MFRL H*
DITLEV LAURITZEN DIS/De (Danyard) 1990; R/Con; 14,406 grt/16,950 dwt; 164.33 × 10 m *(539.14 × 32.81 ft)*; M (B&W); 20.2 kts; 480 TEU
Similar: **IVAR LAURITZEN** (DIS) (solid mast foreward); **JORGEN LAURITZEN** (DIS); **KNUD LAURITZEN** (DIS)

122 *MR⁸MFL H13*
ALBEMARLE ISLAND dwt; **Sequence variation on drawing number 11/117**. There are four small cranes on starboard side which could be obscured by containers

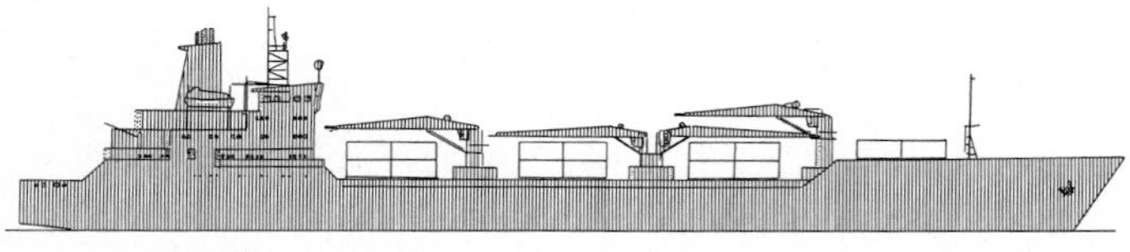

123 *MRR–R²MF H12*
JUSTINIAN Bs/Pd (Gdanska) 1992; R/V/Con; 10,629 grt/10.620 dwt; 150.35 × 9.27 m *(493.27 × 30.41 ft)*; M (Sulzer); 21 kts; 178 TEU; 'B369' type
Sisters: **POLAR ARGENTINA** (Li) ex-*Gordian*; **POLAR BRASIL** (Li) ex-*Numerian*; **POLAR COLOMBIA** (Li) ex-*Appian*; **HADRIAN** (Bs); **TRAJAN** (Bs)
Possible sisters ('B369/1' type): **HORNBREEZE** (Sr); **HORNCLOUD** (Sr)

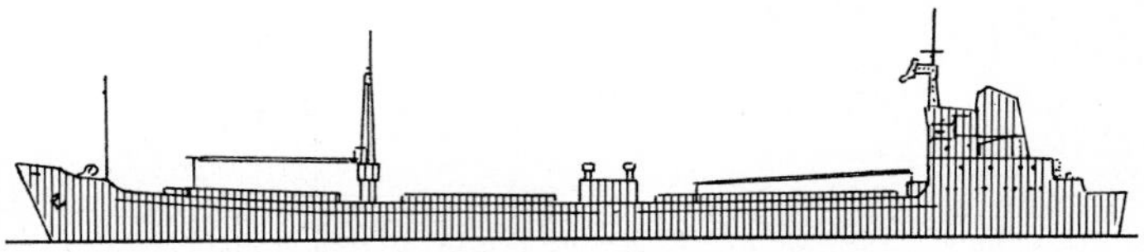

124 *MTHF H12*
GREEN TULIP Bs/In (Mazagon) 1977/83/84; R; 3,624 grt/4,352 dwt; 107.68 × 5.46 m *(353.28 × 17.91 ft)*; M (Alpha-Diesel); 14.5 kts; Launched as *Gomba Venture*; Converted from general cargo 1983; Lengthened 1984 (Nederlandsche)
Sisters: **GREEN FREESIA** (Bs) Launched as *Gomba Challenge*; **GREEN LILY** (Bs) Launched as *Gomba Endeavour*; **GREEN ROSE** (Bs) ex-*Gomba Endeavour*; **GREEN VIOLET** (Bs) ex-*Gomba Venture*

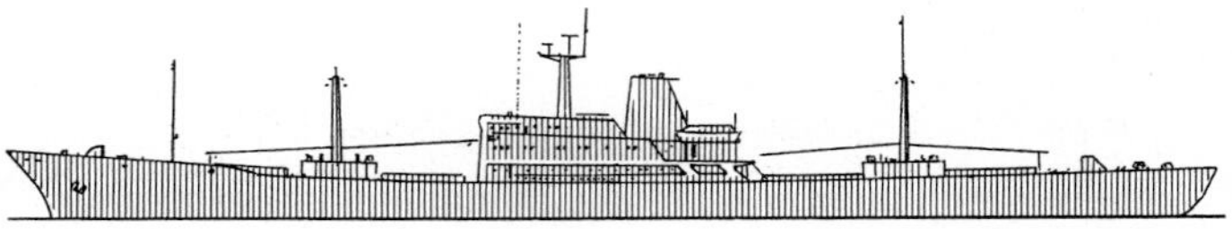

125 *MTMFT H*
BALTIC TRADER Bs/Po (Alfeite) 1978; R; 6,414 grt/5,657 dwt; 139.63 × 7.78 m *(458 × 25.52 ft)*; M (Sulzer); 22.5 kts; ex-*Dzieci Polskie*; Eight side doors; 'B437' type; Completed in Poland (Gdanska).
Sisters (Po built): **ARCTIC TRADER** (Bs) ex-*Gydnski Kosynier* (Builder—Lisnave); **AQUILA II** (Bs) ex-*Zyrardow*
Sisters (Pd built—Gdanska): **RIO CUYAMEL** (Bs); **RIO ULUA** (Bs) ex-*Rio Sixaola*; **SPARTIAN** (Bs)

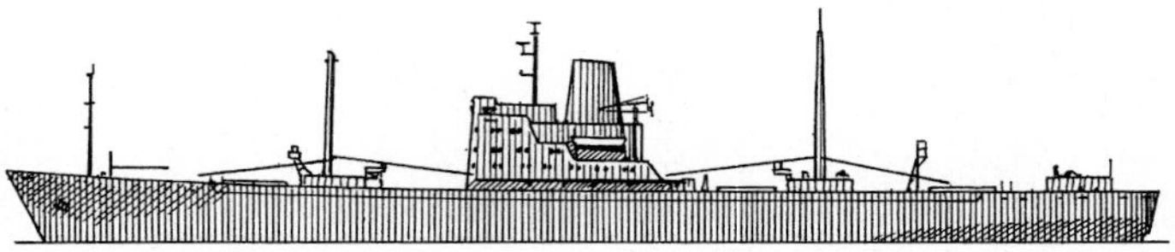

126 *MTMFT H*
FLAMINGO REEFER Pa/FRG (LF-W) 1973; R; 9,609 grt/9,315 dwt; 155 × 8.8 m *(507 × 28.7 ft)*; M (MAN); 22.5 kts; ex-*Wild Cormorant*
Sisters: **POLAR COSTA RICA** (Bs); **POLAR HONDURAS** (Bs)

127 *MTMFT H*
NIKOLAJS KOPERNIKS La/Pd (Gdanska) 1974; R; 6,391 grt/5,887 dwt; 140 × 7.7 m *(460 × 25.6 ft)*; M (Sulzer); 21.75 kts; ex-*Nikolay Kopernik*; 'B437' type
Sisters (some have a light pole foreward): **ARISTARHS BELOPOLSKIS** (LA) ex-*Aristarkh Byelopolskiy*; **FJODORS BREDIHINS** (LA) ex-*Fedor Bredikhin*; **MIHAILS LOMONOSOVS** (LA) ex-*Mikhail Lomonosov*; **PAVELS PARENAGO** (LA) ex-*Pavel Parenago*; **PAVELS STERNBERGS** (LA) ex-*Pavel Shternberg*; **VASILIJS FESENKOVS** (LA) ex-*Vasiliy Fesenkov*; **VASILIJS STRUVE** (LA) ex-*Vasiliy Struve*; **IVANS POLZUNOVS** (LA) ex-*Ivan Polzunov*; **IVANS KULIBINS** (LA) ex-*Ivan Kulibin*; **AKADEMIKIS ARTOBOLEVSKIS** (LA) ex-*Akademik Artobolevskiy*; **AKADEMIKIS HOHLOVS** (LA) ex-*Akademik Khokhlov*
Sisters: **RIO ULUA (Bs); RIO CUYAMEL** (Bs); **SPARTIAN** (Bs); **ARCTIC TRADER** (Bs) ex-*Gdynski Kosynier*; **BALTIC TRADER** (Bs) ex-*Dzieci Polskie*; **AQUILA II** (Bs) ex-*Zyrardow*
PROFESSOR POPOV (Ru); **ILYA METCHNIKOV** (Ru)

128 *MTMFT H1*
IONIC REEFER Gr/No (Drammen) 1977; R; 7,216 grt/9,592 dwt; 144.5 × 9 m *(474 × 29.8 ft)*; M (Sulzer); 22.75 kts; ex-*Wild Gannet*; 'DRAMMEN' type
Sister: **AEOLIC REEFER** (Gr) ex-*Wild Grebe*

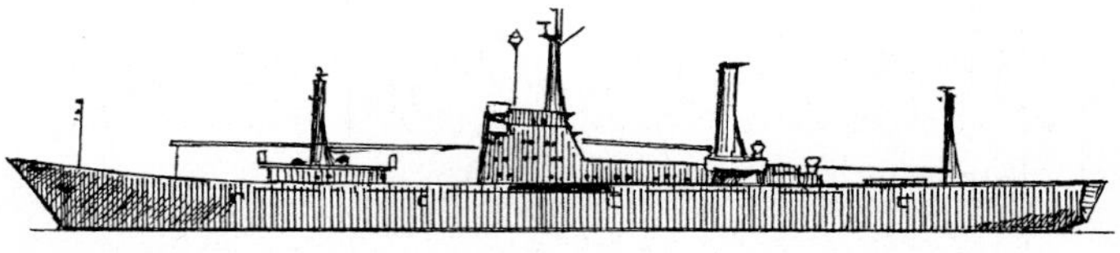

129 *MTMGT H*
MIRAMAR Cy/FRG (B+V) 1968; R; 7,807 grt/7,949 dwt; 148 × 8.2 m *(485 × 27 ft)*; M (Ottensener); 23 kts; ex-*Polar Colombia*
Sister: **LOLA** (Cy) ex-*Polar Uruguay*

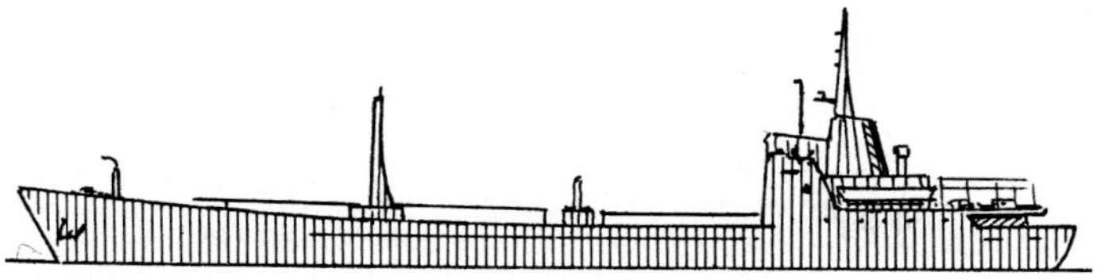

130 *MTMM–F H2*
CRYSTAL REEFER Pa/FRG (Schlichting) 1966; R; 1,223 grt/1,697 dwt; 75.57 × 5.02 m *(247.93 × 16.47 ft)*; M (MaK); 13 kts; ex-*Keppo*

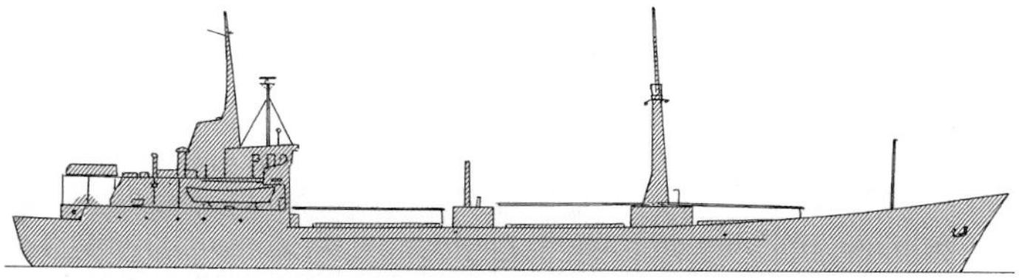

131 *MTMM–F H2*
GOLDEN PACIFIC Pa/FRG (Buesumer) 1968; R; 1,232 grt/1,705 dwt; 75.6 × 5 m *(248.03 × 16.4 ft)*; M (Atlas-MaK); 14.75 kts; ex-*Freezer Scan*
Sisters: **CHOKE REEFER 1** (Pa) ex-*Frigo Scan*; **JACMAR** (Pa) ex-*Bymos*
Probable sister: **REEM** (Ho) ex-*Ahmos*

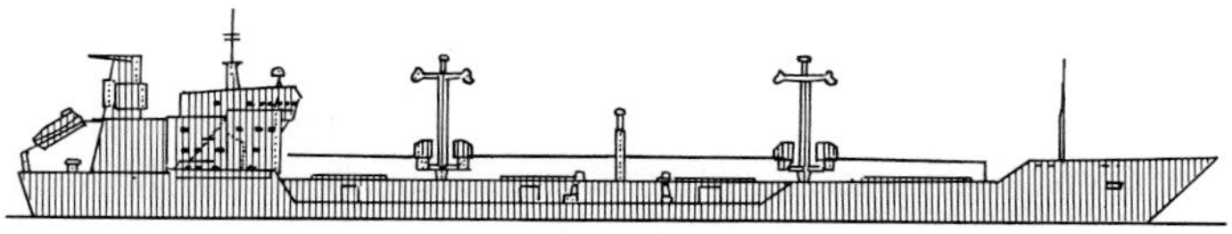

132 *MTNTMFL H13*
MYSTIC Ne/Ne (Van Diepen) 1988; R; 5,089 grt/6,105 dwt; 135.69 × 7.6 m *(445.18 × 24.93 ft)*; M (MaK); 20 kts; Side doors
Sister: **MAJESTIC** (Ne)

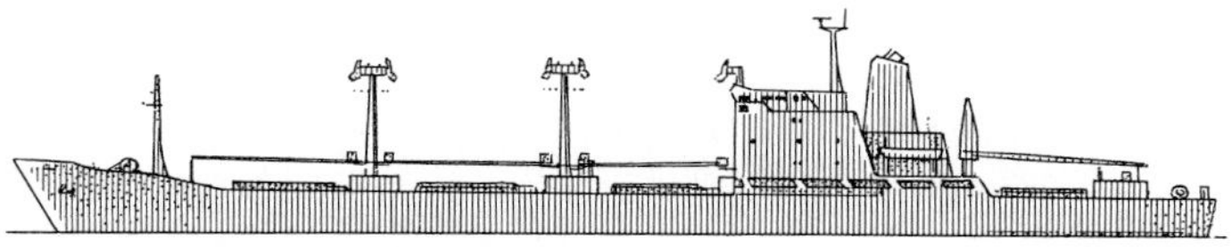

133 *MT²MFC H1*
CANADIAN REEFER NIS/De (Aalborg) 1979; R; 11,243 grt/12,570 dwt; 144.35 × 10.14 m *(473.59 × 33.27 ft)*; M (B&W); 22 kts
Sister: **ECUADORIAN REEFER** (NIS)
Sisters (Japanese built—Hayashikane): **ASIAN REEFER** (Gr); **BALKAN REEFER** (Gr)

134 *MT²MFT H1*
ARABIAN SEA Bs/De (Aalborg) 1968; R; 7,238 grt/11,902 dwt; 145.3 × 8.8 m *(477 × 28.11 ft)*; M (B&W); 22.5 kts; ex-*Italian Reefer*
Sisters: **CELTIC SEA** (Bs) ex-*Nippon Reefer*; **ORANGE REEFER** (Bs) ex-*Persian Reefer*; **MANGO REEFER** (Bs) ex-*Roman Reefer*

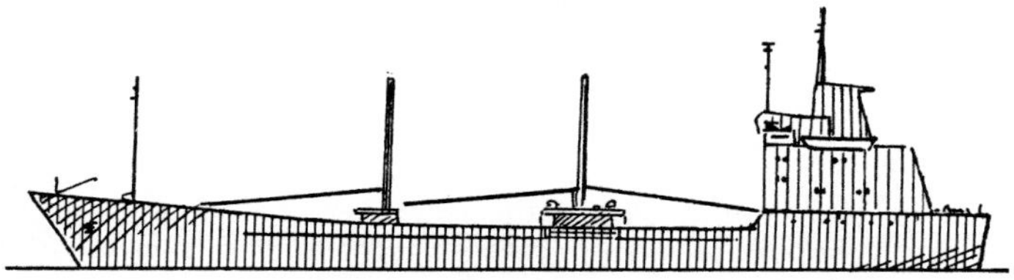

135 *MT²MM–F H13*
GROOTSAND Cy/FRG (Buesumer) 1978; R; 1,727 grt/2,175 dwt; 78.11 × 5.75 m *(256.27 × 18.86 ft)*; M (MaK); 13.5 kts
Sisters: **WITTSAND** (Cy) (may be sail assisted); **BASILEA** (Cy); **TURICIA** (Cy)
Sisters (lengthened to 95.60m (314ft). Larger gap between second and third masts): **YORKSAND** (Cy) ex-*Reefer Knight*; **KNIEPSAND** (Cy)

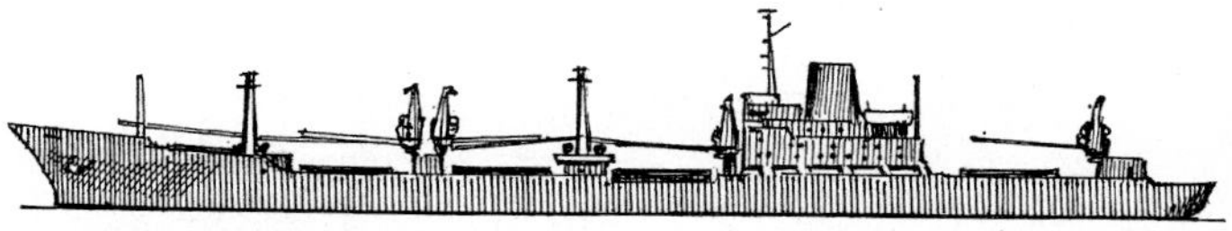

136 *MVC²VCMFNC H1*
LIMON TRADER Gr/Ja (Mitsui) 1968; R; 12,778 grt/11,893 dwt; 164 × 9.2 m *(540 × 30.2 ft)*; M (Mitsui); 21 kts; ex-*Manapouri*
Sister: **BOLERO REEFER** (Pa) ex-*Mataura*

137 *MVMFV H13*
TA CHUN Tw/Ja (Hayashikane) 1967; R; 3,582 grt/4,512 dwt; 111 × 6.9 m *(365 × 23 ft)*; M (Kobe); 16 kts; ex-*Reiyo Maru*

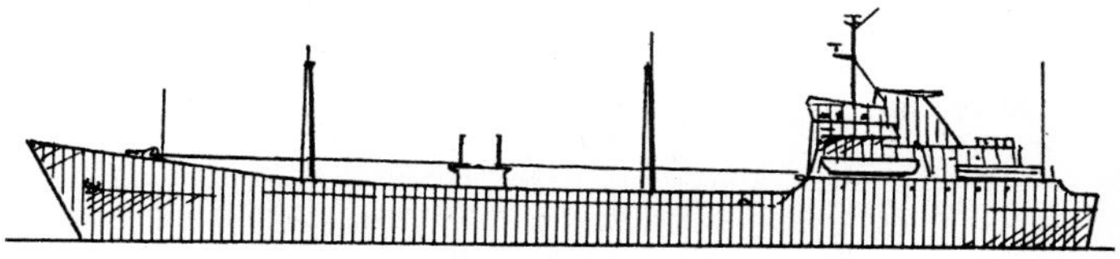

138 *MV²MFN H12*
ANACAONA Cu/Fi (Nystads) 1975; R; 1,327 grt/1,582 dwt; 74.12 × 4.71 m *(243.18 × 15.45 ft)*; M (Bofors); 14 kts; ex-*Batalla de Santa Clara*
Sister: **GUARIONEX** (Cu) ex-*Batalla de Yaguajay*

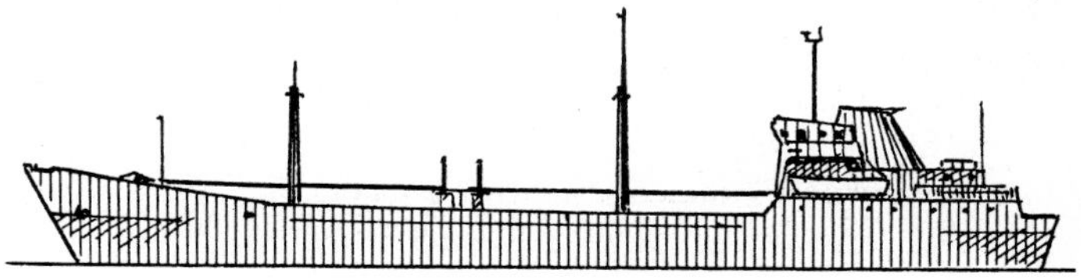

139 *MV²MFN H12*
FISKO Fi/Fi (Nystads) 1974; R; 1,327 grt/1,666 dwt; 74.12 × 4.8 m *(243.18 × 15.75 ft)*; M (Polar); 13.5 kts
Sister: **IGLOO LION** (Bs) ex-*Lindo*

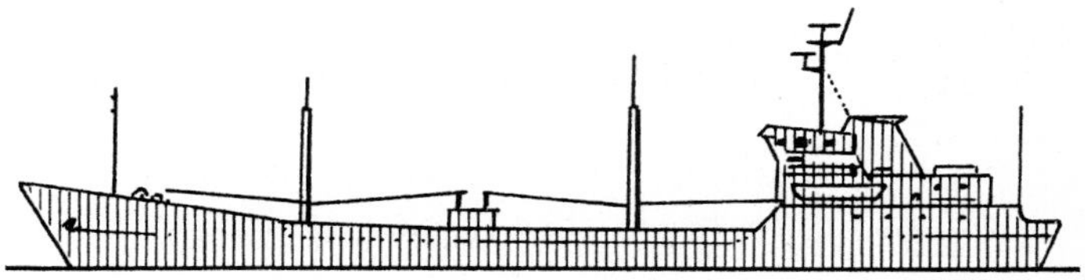

140 *MV²MFN H12*
SUNNY TINA Bs/Fi (Rauma-Repola) 1979; R; 1,328 grt/1,660 dwt; 74.61 × 4.7 m *(245 × 15.42 ft)*; M (Polar); 14 kts; ex-*Asko*
Sisters: **IGLOO FINN** (Bs) ex-*Finno*; **FRIO LIBRA** (Ma) ex-*Terso*

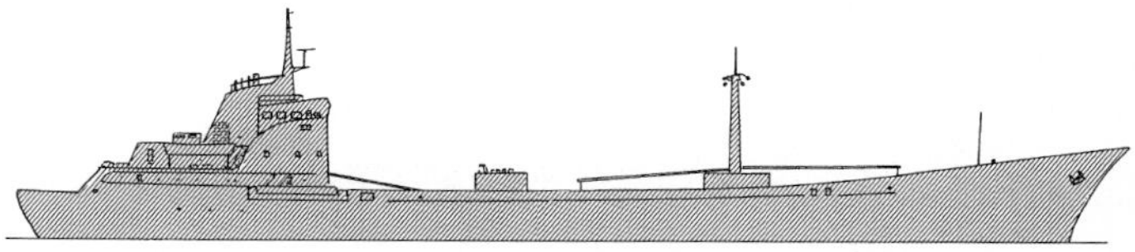

141 *NTM–F H*
PRASLIN REEFER Pa/Fr (La Rochelle) 1970; R; 2,943 grt/3,651 dwt; 100.44 × 6.2 m *(329.53 × 20.34 ft)*; M (KHD); — kts; ex-*Sirara*
Sister: **FRIO ARCTIC** (Pa) ex-*Ea*

142 *TCTCHF H1*
JOSE MARIA RAMON Sp/Sp (Cadagua) 1973; R; 3,382 grt/1,611 dwt; 108.39 × 4.16 m *(355.61 × 13.65 ft)*; M (MAN); 18 kts
Sister: **MAERE** (Ma) ex-*Pedro Ramirez*

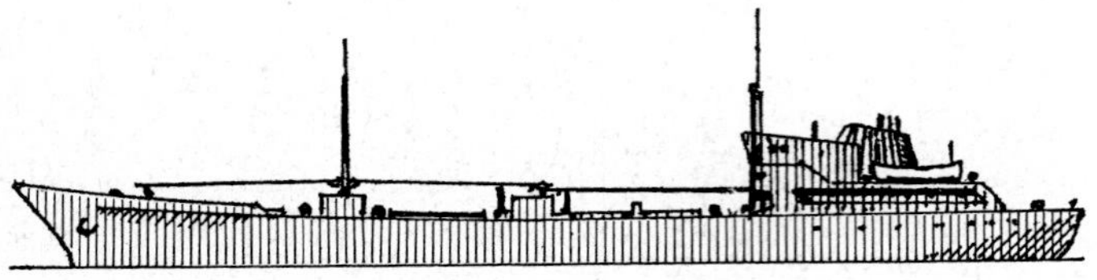

143 *THF H*
AFRICAN STAR Pa/Fr (La Rochelle) 1968; R; 2,195 grt/2,743 dwt; 86.67 × 6.21 m *(284.35 × 20.37 ft)*; M (Deutz); 14.5 kts; ex-*Barrad Wave*

144 *THF H1*
FRIGO AROSA Sp/Sp ('Astano') 1965; C; 1,189 grt/1,021 dwt; 75.14 × 3.75 m *(246.52 × 12.30 ft)*; M (Werkspoor); 13.5 kts; ex-*San Cyr*

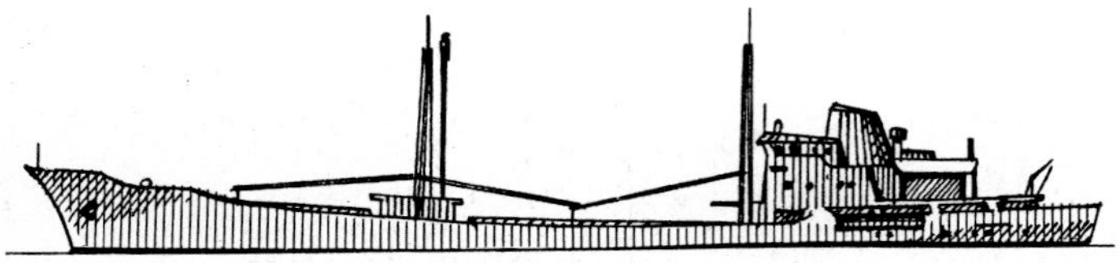

145 *THF H1*
M A ULUSOY Tu/Sp ('Astano') 1965; R; 1,600 grt/1,877 dwt; 81.69 × 5 m *(267.88 × 16.4 ft)*; M (MWM); 15 kts; ex-*Glaciar Rojo*
Sister: **ORHAN AYANOGLU** (Tu) ex-*Glaciar Negro*

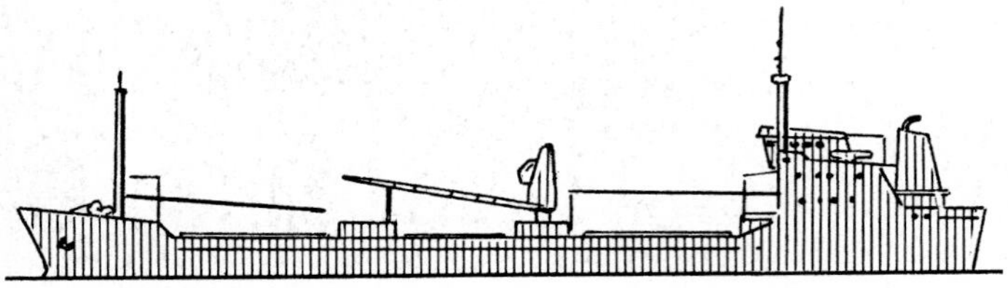

146 *TMCHG H13*
CELTIC ICE NA/Ne ('Friesland') 1979/82; R; 1,198 grt/2,468 dwt; 81.74 × 5.05 m *(268.18 × 16.57 ft)*; M (KHD); — kts; ex-*Celtic*; Lengthened 1982
Sisters: **ATLANTIC ICE** (NA) ex-*Atlantic*; **BALTIC ICE** (NA) ex-*Baltic*

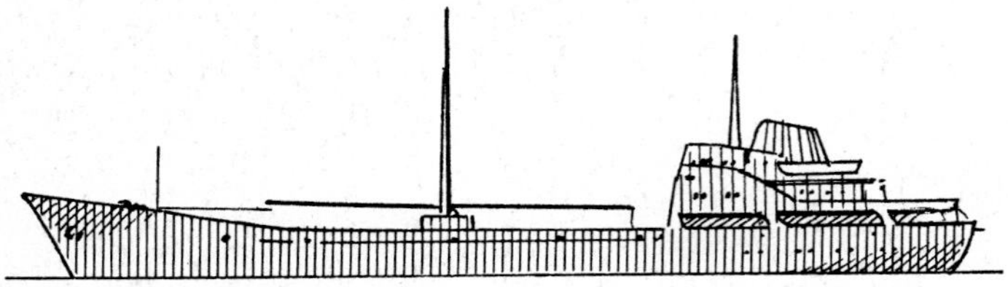

147 *TMF H1*
NOVI T Le/FRG (Sietas) 1959; R; 1,312 grt/1,363 dwt; 75.09 × 4.5 m *(246.36 × 14.76 ft)*; M (Deutz); 12.5 kts; ex-*Fjell Reefer*
Sister: **MUDI** (Le) ex-*Heinz Horn*

148 *TMF H1*
PAULEMOSE R–1 Ho/FRG (Mutzelfeldt) 1959; R; 1,237 grt/934 dwt; 75.19 × 4.13 m *(246.69 × 13.55 ft)*; M (KHD); 13 kts; ex-*Tsefat*

149 *TMFMT H1*
YEYSKIY LIMAN Uk/FRG (Howaldts DW) 1968; R; 4,903 grt/6,560 dwt; 139 × 7.6 m *(456 × 25.2 ft)*; M (MAN); 22.75 kts; ex-*Sloman Alsterpark*

150 *TMFT H1*
AZALEA Bs/Be (Boelwerf) 1969; R; 7,576 grt/7,340 dwt; 149.2 × 7.8 m *(489 × 25.8 ft)*; M (MAN); 22 kts; ex-*Pontos*

151 *TMFT H1*
KULOY Ru/FRG (O&K) 1955; FC; 3,782 grt/3,640 dwt; 111.2 × 6.2 m *(365 × 21 ft)*; M (MAN); 14 kts
Sisters: **TULOMA** (Ru); **UMAN** (Ru)

152 *TMFT H1*
PACIFIC TRADER Bs/No (Drammen) 1970; R; 6,682 grt/8,984 dwt; 140.7 × 9 m *(462 × 30); M (Sulzer); 22.5 kts; ex-Greenland*; 'DRAMMEN' type
Sisters: **TROPICAL ESTORIL** (Li) ex-*Frigoantartico*; **TROPICAL SINTRA** (Li) ex-*Frigoartico*; **RIO DAULE** (Li) ex-*Golar Frost*; **BALTIC SEA** (Bs) ex-*Golar Girl*; **GOLDEN B** (Pa) ex-*Cardiff Clipper*; **BRASILIA REEFER** (Ma) ex-*Ifni*; **IMILCHIL** (Mo); **TROPICANA REEFER** (Pa) ex-*Imouzzer*; **MAGELLANIC** (Pa) ex-*Theodor Korner*; **BANANOR** (Pa) ex-*Teeside Clipper*; **FARID F** (SV) ex-*Lapland*; **METONIC** (Pa) ex-*Heinrich Heine*

153 *TMFT H1*
SHKVAL Uk/Sw (Oresunds) 1963; R; 4,104 grt/4,680 dwt; 126.4 × 7.3 m *(415 × 24 ft)*; M (Gotaverken); 17 kts; ex-*Bakke Reefer*

154 *TMFT H1*
TROPICAL SUN Li/FRG (Howaldts) 1968; R; 6,171 grt/5,354 dwt; 130.66 × 7.20 m *(428.67 × 23.62 ft)*; M (MAN); 20 kts; ex-*Brunshausen*; Side doors
Sisters: **URAGAN** (Uk) ex-*Brunsbuttel*; **DNEPROVSKIY LIMAN** (Uk) ex-*Brunstor*

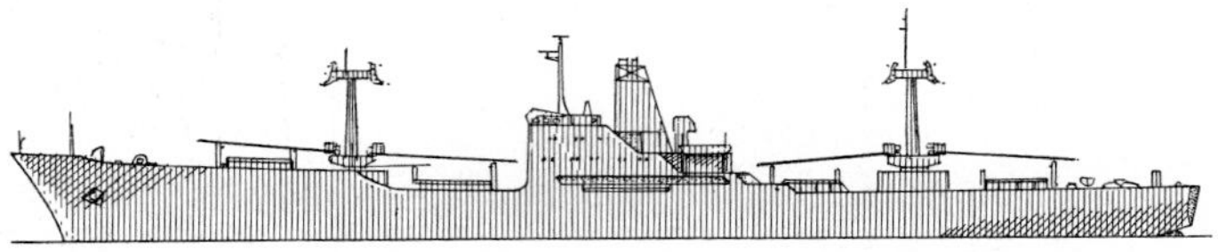

155 *TMFT H1*
UB PRINCE NIS/No (Drammen) 1976; R; 7,213 grt/9,612 dwt; 144.2 × 8.99 m *(473.1 × 29.49 ft)*; M (Sulzer); 22.75 kts; ex-*Emanuel*; 'DRAMMEN' type

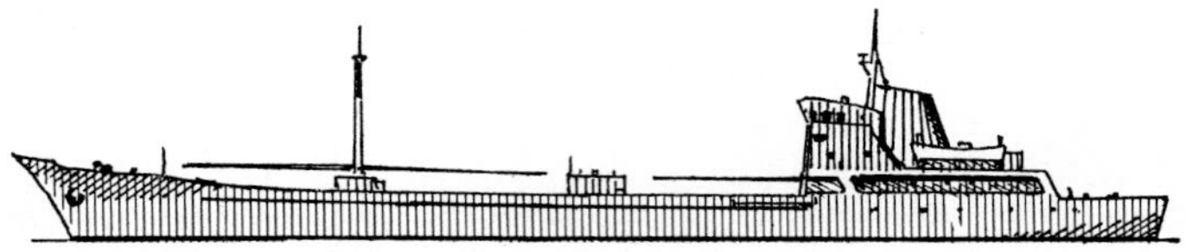

156 *TM–F H*
GREEN LEAF Pa/Fr (La Rochelle) 1968; R; 1,590 grt/3,439 dwt; 97.01 × 6.22 m *(318.27 × 20.41 ft)*; M (KHD); — kts; ex-*Barrad Foam*

157 *TM–FN H*
MAHE REEFER Pa/Fr (La Ciotat) 1966; R; 4,426 grt/3,259 dwt; 111.8 × 6.5 m *(367 × 21.4 ft)*; M (Sulzer); 19.75 kts; ex-*Oyonnax*

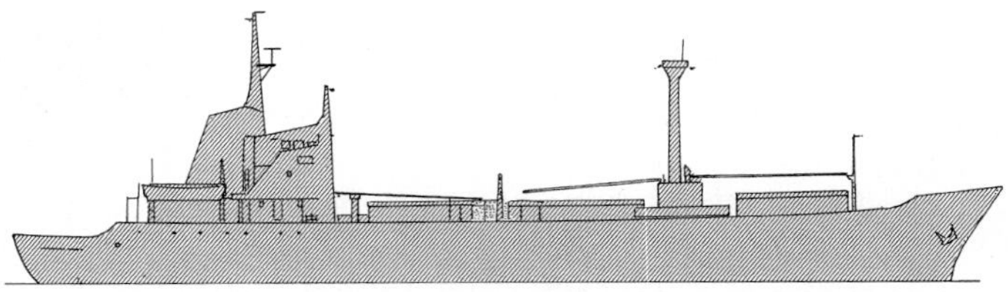

158 *TNM–F H1*
CHOKE REEFER 2 Pa/Fr (Havre) 1968; R; 1,864 grt/1,771 dwt; 75.55 × 5.11 m *(247.86 × 16.76 ft)*; M (Atlas-MaK); 15 kts; ex-*Jofrigo*
Sisters: **NATIONAL REEFER** (Eg); ex-*Joquita*; **REEFER ACE** (Ho) ex-*Jo-Rivka*; **TEMEHANI II** (Fr) ex-*Jogela*

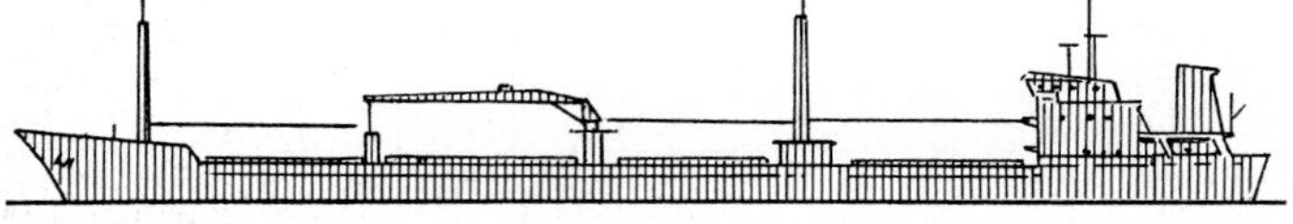

159 *TRTHG H1*
SCORFF Cy/Ne (Van Diepen) 1979/83; R; 2,966 grt/3,514 dwt; 101.26 × 5.28 m *(332 × 17.32 ft)*; M (KHD); 13.5 kts; ex-*Icelandic*; Lengthened 1983 (Boele's Sch)
Sisters: **STEIR** (Kn) ex-*Arctic*; **STER LAER** (Kn) ex-*Indianic*; **STYVAL** (Kn) ex-*Tempo*

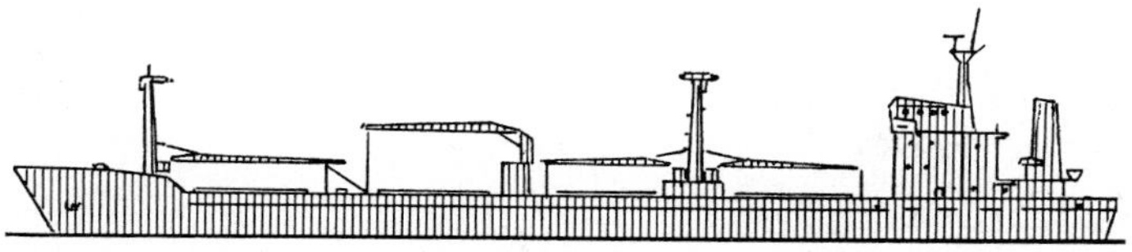

160 *TRTMF H1*
ICE EXPRESS Va/Ne (Ysselwerf) 1979/83; R; 2,768 grt/3,387 dwt; 94.49 × 5.12 m *(310 × 16.8 ft)*; M (KHD); 14.5 kts; Lengthened 1983 (Ysselwerf)
Sister: **COLD EXPRESS** (Va)

161 *T^2F H1*
ATLANTIC REEFER II Ho/Ne (Nieuwe Noord) 1963; R; 487 grt/935 dwt; 78.36 × 3.71 m *(257.09 × 12.17 ft)*; TSM (MAN); 16 kts; ex-*Sonja*

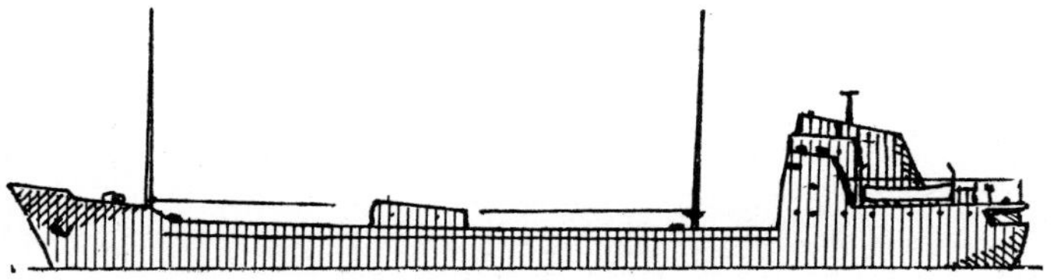

162 *T^2F H13*
HYBUR STAR At/Ne (Noord) 1962; R; 1,126 grt/1,577 dwt; 74.12 × 4.73 m *(243.18 × 15.52 ft)*; M (Deutz); 13 kts; ex-*Arctic*

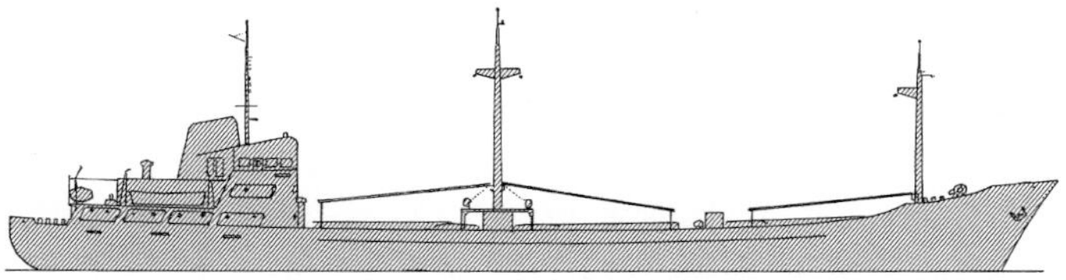

163 *T^2HF H1*
AL-SHEBLI REEFER SV/Ne (Nieuwe Noord) 1967; R; 1,444 grt/1,795 dwt; 80.96 × 4.92 m *(265.62 × 16.14 ft)*; M (Deutz); 15 kts; ex-*Antarctic*
Similar: **HUA LUNG REEFER** (Pa) ex-*Spitsbergen*

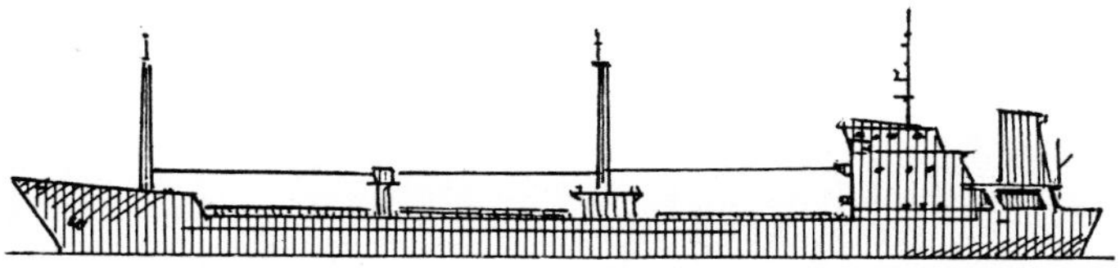

164 *T^2HG H1*
OCEANIC ICE NA/Ne (Nieuwe Noord) 1977; R; 2,244 grt/2,404 dwt; 82.73 × 5.01 m *(271.42 × 16.44 ft)*; M (Deutz); 13 kts; ex-*Oceanic*

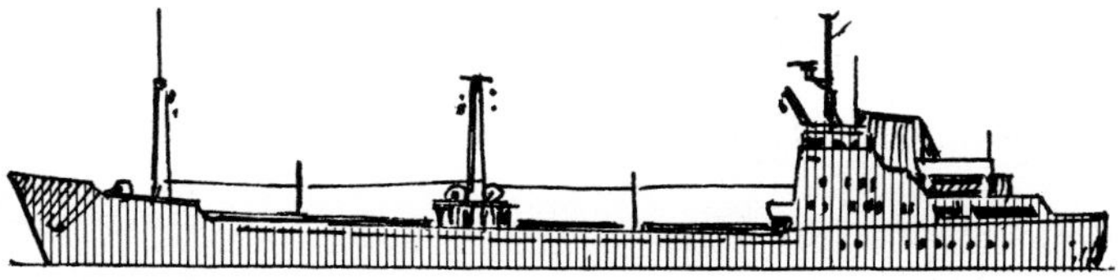

165 *T^2HMF H1*
MAYA REEFER Ho/Br (Grangemouth) 1964; R; 2,189 grt/2,860 dwt; 89.46 × 5.35 m *(293.5 × 17.55 ft)*; M (Deutz); — kts; ex-*Hofsjokull*

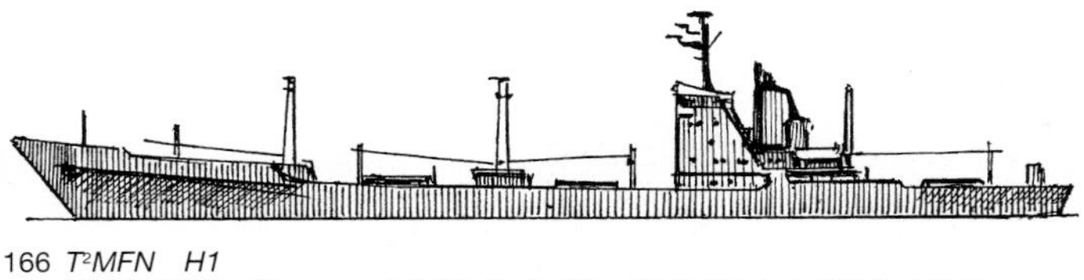

166 *T^2MFN H1*
TAJIN SV/No (Drammen) 1975; R; 8,479 grt/11,300 dwt; 143.4 × 9.4 m *(470 × 31 ft)*; M (Pielstick); 23.5 kts; ex-*Bremerhaven*
Sister (with tripod mast): **WINDFROST** (Bs) ex-*Blumenthal*

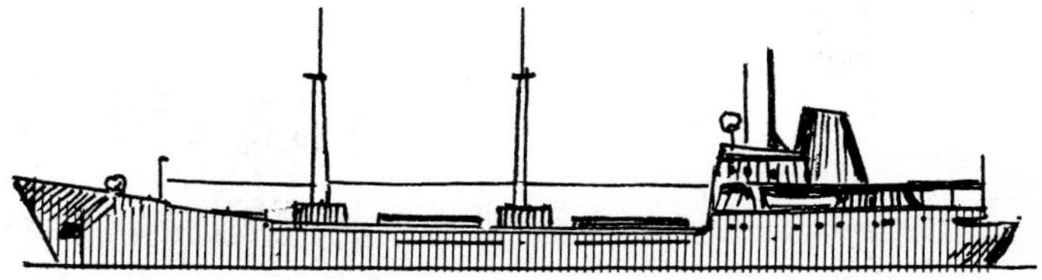

167 *T^2M^2F H2*
MACEDONIA Ma/FRG (Schlichting) 1967; R; 1,558 grt/1,947 dwt; 88.7 × 5.21 m *(291.01 × 17.09 ft)*; M (Atlas-MaK); 16 kts; ex-*Fahrmannsand*
Sisters: **SWEET ORANGE** (SV) ex-*Luhesand*; **ART REEFER** (Pa) ex-*Pagensand*

168 *T^2M–F H1*
PEARL REEFER Pa/It (Esercizio) 1969; R; 1,580 grt/1,647 dwt; 82.81 × 4.81 m *(271.69 × 15.78 ft)*; M (MAN); — kts; ex-*Geleszae*
Sister: **TRINACRIA** (Ho) ex-*Doroty*

169 *VCM–FV H*
NORTH SEA Bs/It (Apuania) 1968; R; 6,787 grt/5,598 dwt; 140.49 × 7.62 m *(461 × 25 ft)*; M (Fiat); — kts
Sister: **OCEANO PACIFICO** (Cu)

170 *VMFV H1*
KOTOVSKIY Uk/It (Breda) 1968; R; 4,079 grt/4,772 dwt; 121.7 × 7.5 m *(401 × 24 ft)*; M (Fiat); 18 kts
Sisters: **NIKOLAY SHCHORS** (Uk); **PARKHOMENKO** (Uk); **SERGEY LAZO** (Uk); **CHAPAEV** (Uk)

171 *VMFV H13*
SUN LONG No 8 Tw/Ja (Hayashikane) 1968; R; 3,411 grt/4,512 dwt; 111.1 × 6.9 m *(365 × 22.6 ft)*; M (Kobe); 16 kts; ex-*Juyo Maru*

172 *VMVF H123*
NIKOLAJS ZICARS La/Ru (Baltic) 1964; FC; 5,794 grt/4,670 dwt; 130.92 × 6.72 m *(429.53 × 22.05 ft)*; D-E (Fairbanks, Morse); 16.25 kts
Sisters: **VOLCHANSK** (Ru); **KOMISSAR POLUKHIN** (Ru) ex-*Karel*; **ZABAYKALYE** (Ru)

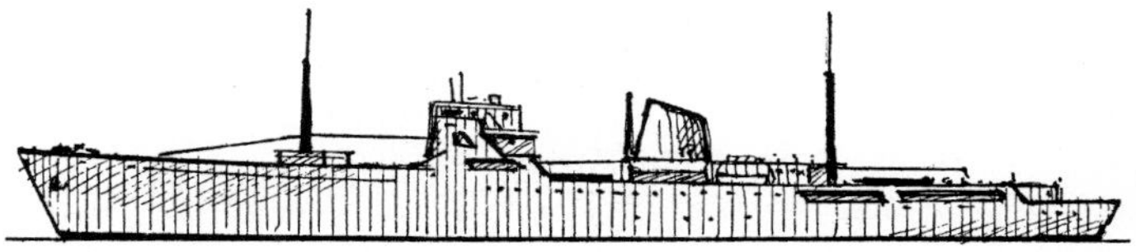

173 *VNFV H1*
VICTORIA REEFER Pa/Fr (Nantes) 1962; R; 4,731 grt/3,707 dwt; 115.27 × 6.1 m *(378.18 × 20.01 ft)*; M (Pielstick); 17 kts; ex-*Espadon*

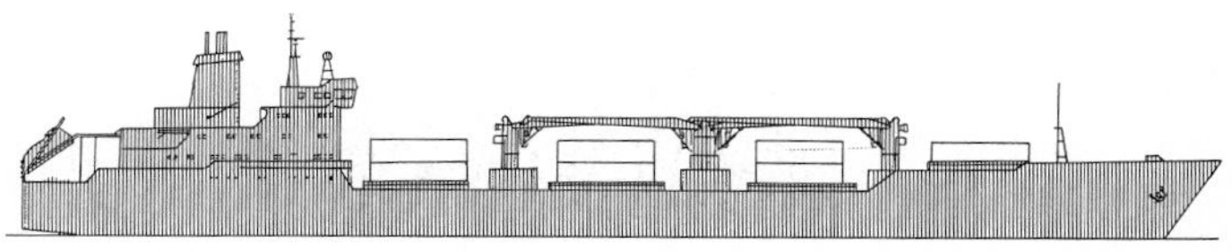

174 *VR^4MFL H12*
DOLE AMERICA Li/Pd (Gdanska) 1994; R; 10,584 grt/10,600 dwt; 150.3 × 9.1 m *(493.11 × 29.86 ft)*; M (B&W); 21.8 kts; 'B369/2' type; 264 TEU
Sisters: **DOLE AFRICA** (Li); **DOLE ASIA** (Li); **DOLE EUROPA** (Li)

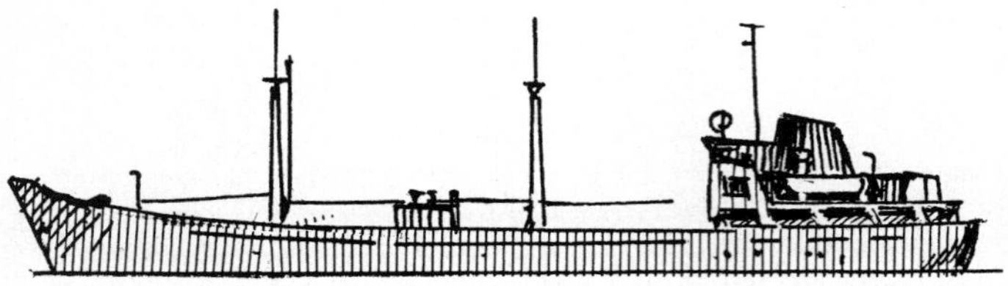

175 V^2MF *H1*
FAHD Sy/Fi (Nystads) 1961; R; 489 grt/844 dwt; 71.81 × 3.62 m *(235.6 × 11.88 ft)*; M (KHD); 14 kts; ex-*Jarso*
Similar: **VANILLA** (Pi) ex-*Tingo*; **SUNNY SARAH** (Bs) ex-*Herro*

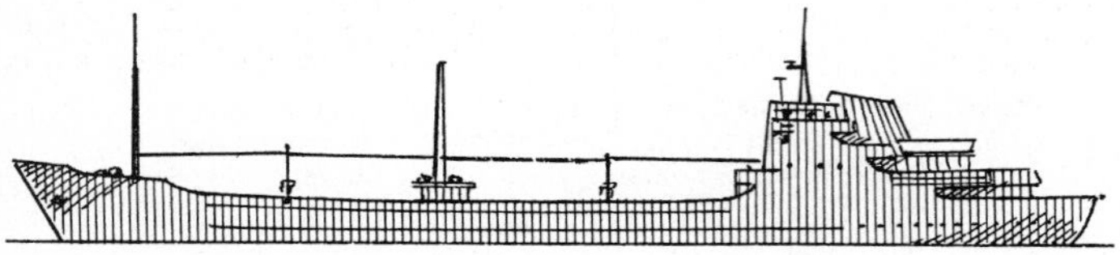

176 V^2MF *H12*
BONG DAE SAN RK/Ne (van der Werf) 1961; R; 1,209 grt/1,882 dwt; 86.01 × 5.02 m *(282.19 × 16.47 ft)*; M (KHD); 13 kts; ex-*Drangajokull*; Probably used as a fish carrier
Sister: **LA PAL SAN** (RK) ex-*Langjokul*

177 V^2MF *H13*
SAN BENEDETTO Ho/Sw (Solvesborgs) 1964; R; 1,221 grt/1,676 dwt; 72.8 × 5 m *(238.85 × 16.47 ft)*; M (Polar); 14.5 kts; ex-*Polar Viking*

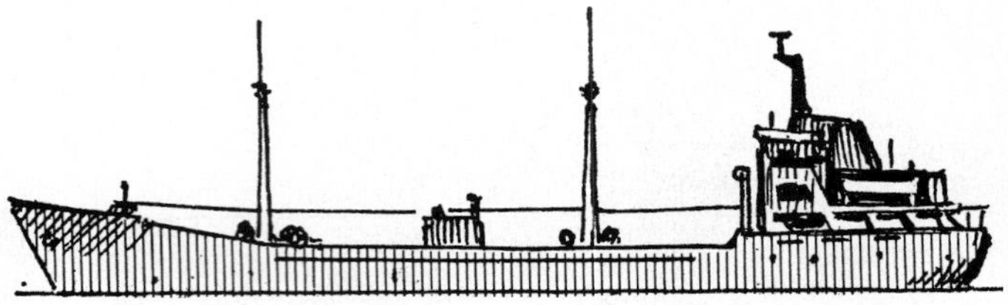

178 $V^2M\text{–}F$ *H1*
IMG 1 Th/Fi (Nystads) 1966; R; 1,116 grt/1,545 dwt; 73.82 × 4.71 m *(242.19 × 15.45 ft)*; M (Deutz); 13.5 kts; ex-*Ranno*
Sister: **HAI FENG 832** (Pa) ex-*Saggo*

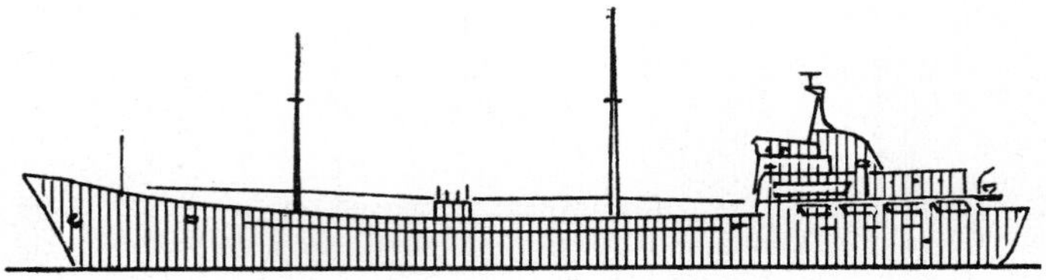

179 $V^2M\text{–}F$ *H1*
IMG 2 Th/Fi (Nystads) 1969; R; 1,138 grt/1,581 dwt; 73.82 × 4.71 m *(242.19 × 15.45 ft)*; M (Atlas-MaK); 13.5 kts; Launched as *Arctic Scan*
Sisters: **POLAR** (Th) ex-*Polar Scan*; **ITFA 1** (Th) ex-*Reefer Scan*

180 Prince of Waves *(Bs); 1993* *WSPL*

181 Chiquita Italia *(Bs); 1992* *WSPL*

182 Breiz Klipper *(Kn); 1991* *WSPL*

183 Pioneer Express *(Pi); 1982; (as Pioneer Reefer)* *WSPL*

184 Crystal Primadonna *(Lu); 1992* *WSPL*

185 Horncliff *(Li); 1992* *WSPL*

186 Maveric *(Ne); 1993* *WSPL*

187 Kea *(Pa); 1982; (as Kos V)* *WSPL*

188 Reefer No 5 *(Ko); 1973; (as Ocean Violet)* *WSPL*

192 Ivory Eagle *(Ja); 1992* *WSPL*

189 Bothnian Reefer *(Li); 1992* *Norman Thomson*

193 Mediteran Frigo *(Ma); 1979* *WSPL*

190 Royal Klipper *(Ml); 1987* *WSPL*

194 Athenian Rex *(Cy); 1979; (as Royal Lily)* *WSPL*

191 Noor *(Ir); 1974* *WSPL*

195 Scamper *(Bs); 1980* *WSPL*

196 Akademikis Zavarickis *(Cy); 1986* *WSPL*

197 Chacabuco *(Li); 1990* *FotoFlite*

198 Chiquita Bremen *(Br); 1992* *WSPL*

199 Nauru *(Pa); 1993; (as Chiquita Maru)* *WSPL*

200 April *(Ma); 1972* *WSPL*

201 Reefer Fresh *(Pa); 1987* *FotoFlite*

202 Frio Dolphin *(Pa); 1979* *FotoFlite*

203 Stevens *(Va); 1982* *FotoFlite*

204 Iglo Express *(Pi); 1979/85* *FotoFlite*

205 Avocado Carmel *(Is); 1972/79* *FotoFlite*

206 Seavic Reefer *(Pa); 1979; (as Azur Trader)* *FotoFlite*

207 Spring Delight *(HK); 1984* *FotoFlite*

208 Saronic Pride *(Pa); 1979/83; (as Pacific Princess)* *FotoFlite*

209 Reefer Jambu *(Bs); 1985* *FotoFlite*

210 Brest *(Bs); 1985* *FotoFlite*

211 Orange Klipper *(Ne); 1991* *FotoFlite*

212 Geest Dominica *(Bs); 1993* *FotoFlite*

213 Pacifik Frigo *(SV); 1990* *FotoFlite*

214 Cap Changuinola *(Li); 1988* *FotoFlite*

215 Shinano Reefer *(Pa); 1993* *FotoFlite*

216 Diamond Reefer *(Pa); 1992; (as Hudson Rex)* *FotoFlite*

217 Uruguayan Reefer *(Pa); 1993* *FotoFlite*

218 Khersones *(Pa); 1978/83; (as Pacific Marchioness)* *FotoFlite*

219 Cottica *(HK); 1991* *FotoFlite*

220 Rambynas *(Lt); 1985; (as Tornado)* *FotoFlite*

221 White Dolphin *(Pa); 1988* *FotoFlite*

222 Ural Mountains *(Pa); 1984; (as Mistrau)* *FotoFlite*

223 Nyantic *(NA); 1984* *FotoFlite*

224 Fenland *(Bs); 1979* *FotoFlite*

225 Reefer Cape *(At); 1979* *FotoFlite*

226 Atlantic Dawn *(Bs); 1983; (as Nienburg)* *FotoFlite*

227 Reefer Dolphin *(Pa); 1983* *FotoFlite*

228 White Arrow *(Pa); 1983* *FotoFlite*

229 Green Arctic *(NIS); 1980; (as San Carlos)* *FotoFlite*

230 Longva Stream *(Bs); 1982; (as Frio Baltic)* *FotoFlite*

231 Spring Tiger *(NA); 1984* *FotoFlite*

232 Slavyanka *(Ru); 1989* *FotoFlite*

233 Ping Quan *(RC); 1984* *FotoFlite*

234 Tropical Mist *(Li); 1986* *FotoFlite*

235 Chaiten *(Li); 1988* *FotoFlite*

236 Goose Bay *(Bs); 1979; (as Ikoma)* *FotoFlite*

237 Arctic Goose *(Bs); 1974/88; (as Tunisian Reefer)* *FotoFlite*

238 Cuenca *(Bs); 1981* *FotoFlite*

239 Chilean Reefer *(NIS); 1984* *FotoFlite*

240 Tasman Universal *(Sr); 1988* *Norman Thomson*

241 Indian Reefer *(DIS); 1991* *WSPL*

242 Tauu *(Pa); 1993; (as Hornstrait)* *FotoFlite*

243 Spring Bee *(Mr); 1984* *FotoFlite*

12 Gearless Container Ships

12 Gearless Container Ships

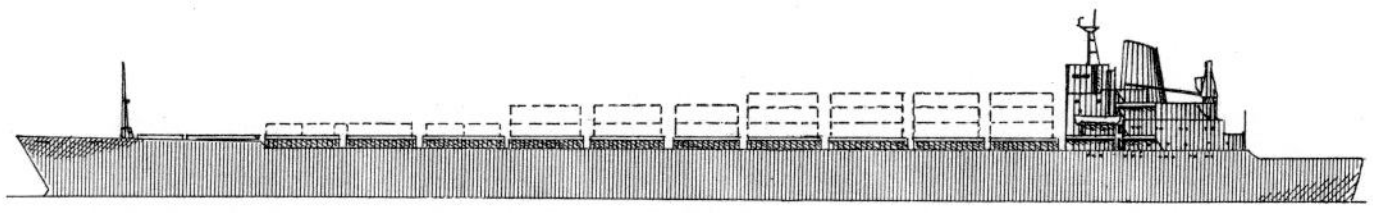

1 *HMFC H1*
CANMAR EUROPE Br/Be (Cockerill) 1970; Con; 30,491 grt/29,283 dwt; 231.55 × 10.08 m *(759.68 × 33.07 ft)*; M (Sulzer); 21 kts; ex-*Dart Europe*; 1,556 TEU
Sister: **OOCL CHALLENGE** (HK) ex-*Dart America*

2 *HM–FH H1*
SEA-LAND EXPEDITION US/US (Ingalls SB) 1973; Con; 21,687 grt/ 19,845 dwt; 203.7 × 9.6 m *(669 × 31.5 ft)*; T (Westinghouse); 23 kts; ex-*Austral Ensign*
Sister: **SEA-LAND HAWAII** (US) ex-*Austral Endurance*; Similar: **PRESIDENT JEFFERSON**; (US) **JEAN LYKES** (US) ex-*President Pierce*; **THOMPSON LYKES** (US) ex-*President Johnson*; **HOWELL LYKES** (US) ex-*President Madison*

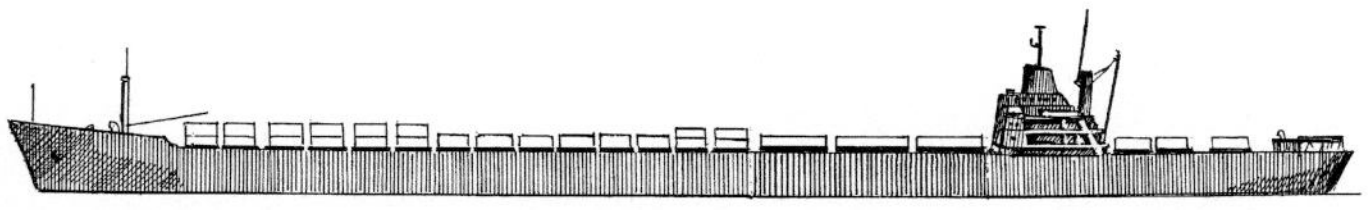

3 *HM–FH H1*
SEA-LAND NAVIGATOR MI/US (Ingalls SB) 1972/77; Con; 28,807 grt/ 28,200 dwt; 247.81 × 10.08 m *(813.02 × 33.07 ft)*; T (Westinghouse); 23 kts; ex-*Austral Envoy*; Lengthened 1977; This vessel was lengthened again in 1983; The drawing shows it before this; Sisters also lengthened
Sisters: **SEA-LAND TRADER** (US) ex-*Austral Entente*; **SEA-LAND PACIFIC** (US) ex-*Austral Pioneer*; **SEA-LAND ENTERPRISE** (US) ex-*Austral Puritan*

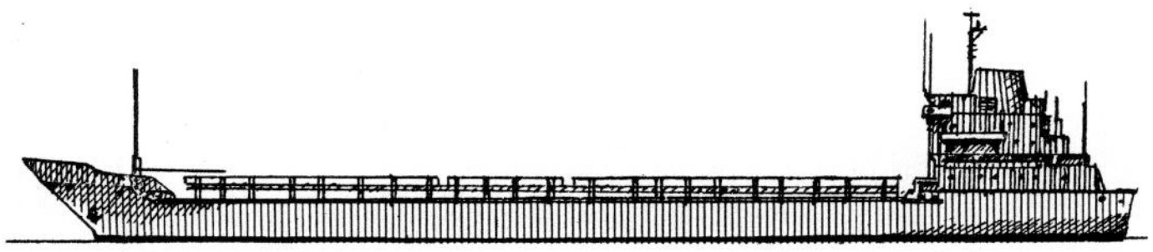

4 *HM–FRM H1*
PACIFIC LADY Bl/Br (Appledore) 1973; Con; 4,993 grt/6,235 dwt; 112.1 × 6.38 m *(367.78 × 20.93 ft)*; M (Pielstick); 15 kts; ex-*Manchester Zeal*; 296 TEU

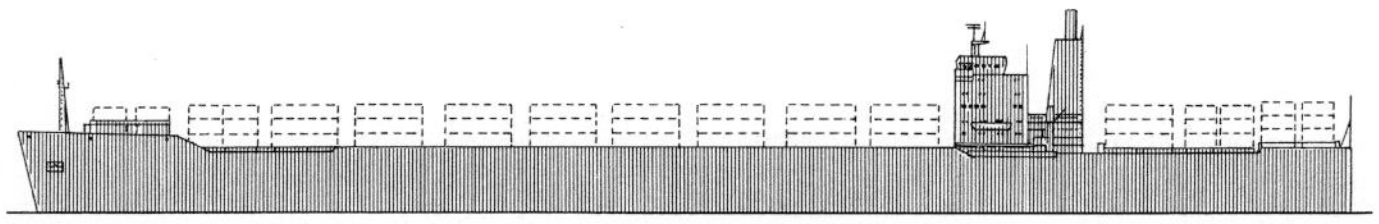

5 *MHF H1*
DUESSELDORF EXPRESS Sg/FRG (Flender) 1977/85; Con; 38,991 grt/ 40,624 dwt; 240.52 × 11.02 m *(789.11 × 36.15 ft)*; M (MAN); 21.5 kts; Lengthened 1985 (B+V)
Sisters: **KOLN EXPRESS** (Ge); **NURNBERG EXPRESS** (Ge); **STUTTGART EXPRESS** (Ge)

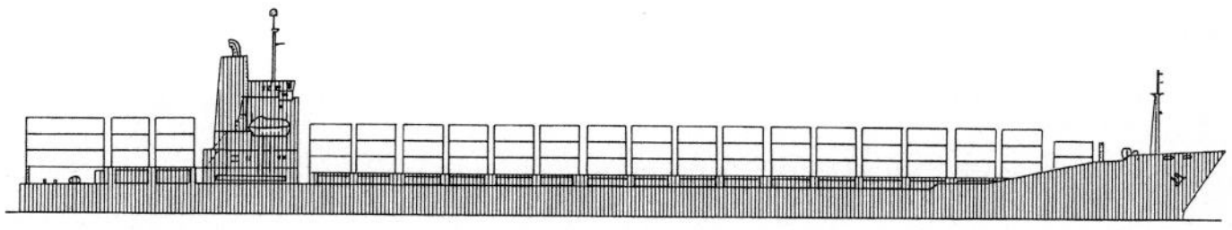

6 *MHF H1*
KOTA WIJAYA Sg/Ja (Kanasashi) 1991; Con; 16,731 grt/22,695 dwt; 184.50 × 9.53 m *(605.31 × 31.27 ft)*; M (Mitsubishi); 19 kts; 1,182 TEU
Sister: **KOTA WIRAWAN** (Sg)

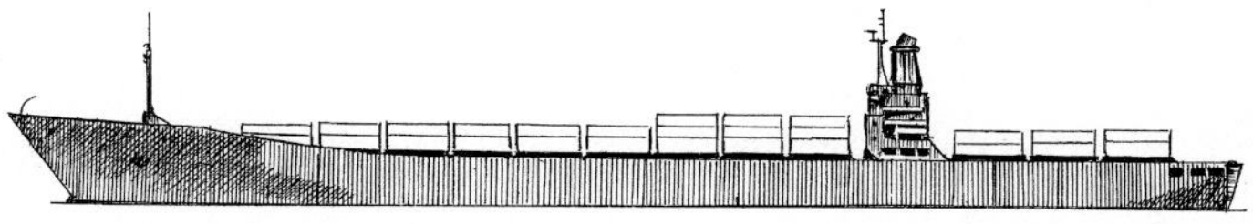

7 *MHF H1*
NERD 1 Li/FRG (Rhein Nordseew) 1971; Con; 30,490 grt/31,814 dwt; 243 × 10.7 m *(799 × 35.2 ft)*; TSM (Stork-Werkspoor); 20 kts; ex-*Eurofreighter*, now broken up
Sisters: **VILLE DE TITANA** (Bs) ex-*Asialiner*; **CANMAR ENTERPRISE** (Bs) ex-*Asiafreighter*

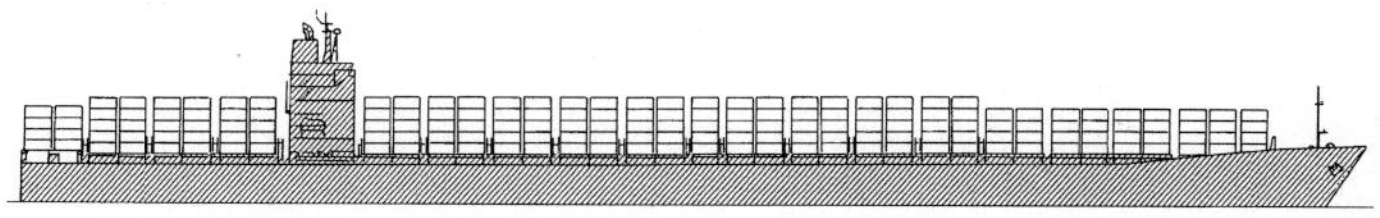

8 *MHF H1*
NYK ALTAIR Pa/Ja (IHI) 1994; Con; 60,117 grt/63,163 dwt; 299.95 × 13.03 m *(984.09 × 42.75 ft)*; M (MaK); 23.5 kts; 4,730 TEU
Probable sister: **NYK PROCYON** (Pa); Similar (builder—Mitsubishi HI): **NYK VEGA** (Pa)

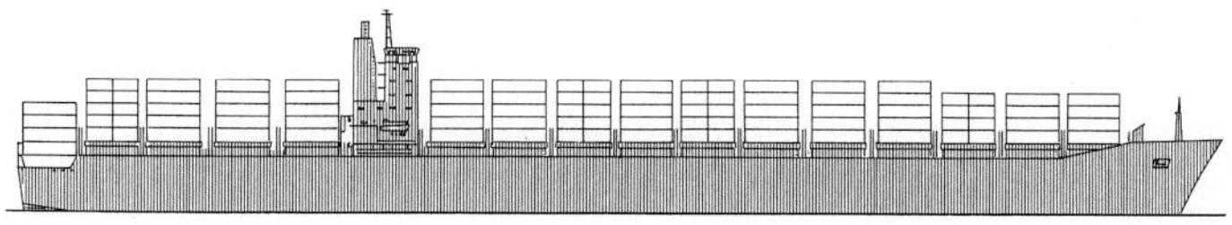

9 *MHF H1*
PRESIDENT TRUMAN US/FRG (Howaldts DW) 1988; Con; 61,926 grt/ 54,700 dwt; 275.22 × 12.73 m *(902.95 × 41.77 ft)*; M (Sulzer); 24.3 kts; 4,340 TEU
Sisters: **PRESIDENT ADAMS** (US); **PRESIDENT JACKSON** (US); **PRESIDENT KENNEDY** (US); **PRESIDENT POLK** (US)

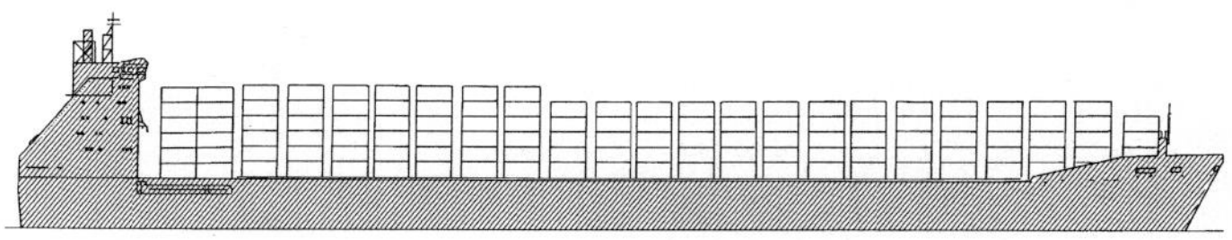

10 *MHF H1*
TRADE APOLLO HK/Ge (Flensburger) 1994; Con; 28,892 grt/38,270 dwt; 202.80 × 11.93 m *(665.35 × 39.14 ft)*; M (B&W); 20 kts; ex-*Trade Sol*; 2,480 TEU; 'ECOBOX CC42' type
Probable sisters: **TRADE ETERNITY** (HK); **TRADE SELENE** (HK); **JAMES LYKES** (Li); **JOSEPH LYKES** (Li)

11 *MHF H1*
ZHONG HE RC/Ge (Bremer VW) 1994; Con; 48,311 grt/51,280 dwt; 275.10 × 12.50 m *(902.56 × 41.01 ft)*; M (Sulzer); 24 kts; 3,764 TEU
Sisters: **TENG HE** (RC); **YUAN HE** (RC); **FEI HE** (RC) (builder—Howaldts DW)

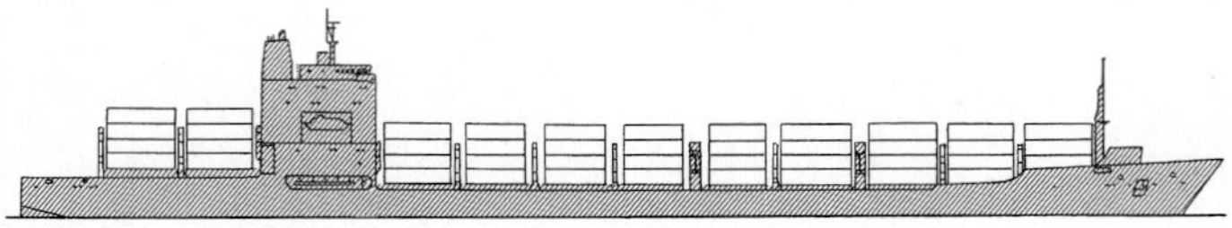

12 *MHF H13*
SEA-LAND ANCHORAGE US/US (Bay) 1987; Con; 20,965 grt/20,668 dwt; 216.42 × 10.35 m *(710.04 × 33.96 ft)*; M (B&W); 20 kts; 1,402 TEU
Sisters: **SEA-LAND KODIAK** (US); **SEA-LAND TACOMA** (US)

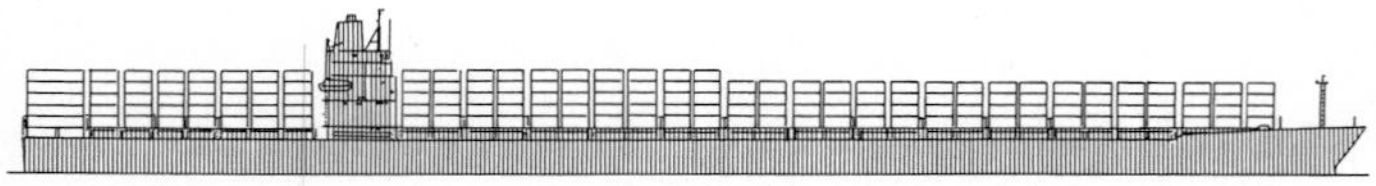

13 *MHFC H*
MARSTAL MAERSK DIS/Ja (Mitsui) 1990; Con; 49,779 grt/55,971 dwt; 294.06 × 13.02 m *(964.76 × 42.72 ft)*; M (B&W); 24.5 kts; ex-*Arosia*; 4,000 TEU
Sister: **MUNKEBO MAERSK** (DIS) ex-*Alsia*

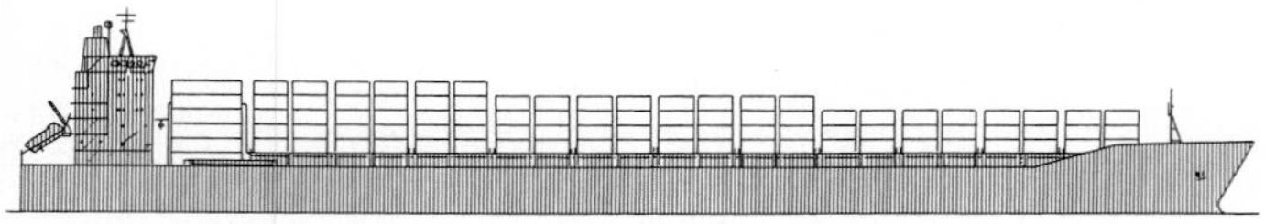

14 *MHFL H1*
DSR-BALTIC Ge/Ge (Bremer VW) 1992; Con; 34,231 grt/45,696 dwt; 216.19 × 12.52 m *(709.28 × 40.03 ft)*; M (Sulzer); 19.7 kts; 2,680 TEU; 'BV2700' type
Sisters: **DSR EUROPE** (Ge); **LONDON SENATOR** (Ge)
Sisters ('BV 3000' type—but identical appearance): **SEA PROGRESS** (Ge) ex-*Tokyo Senator*; **WASHINGTON SENATOR** (Ge); **SEA INITIATIVE** (Ge) ex-*California Senator*

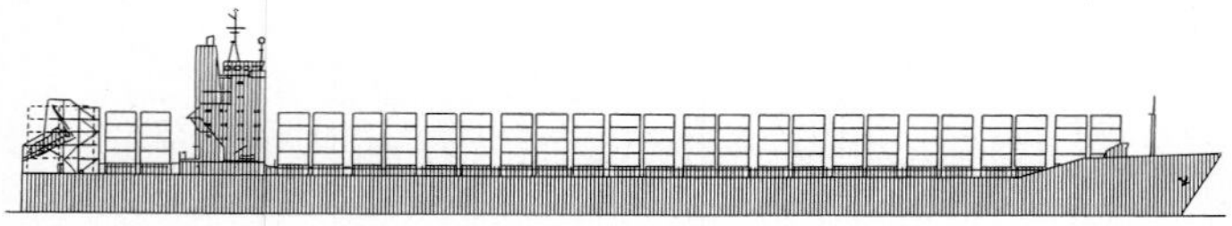

15 *MHFLR/MHFL H1*
DSR SENATOR Li/Ge (Bremer VW) 1991; Con; 37,071 grt/46,600 dwt; 237.00 × 11.98 m *(777.56 × 39.30 ft)*; M (B&W); 21 kts; 2,668 TEU; 'CS2700' type
Sisters: **DSR-ROSTOCK** (Li); **BREMEN SENATOR** (Li); **VLADIVOSTOK SENATOR** (Li); **CHOYANG MOSCOW** (Li); **BERLIN SENATOR** (Li); **ST PETERSBURG SENATOR** (Li); **SOVCOMFLOT SENATOR** (Li); **HAMBURG SENATOR** (Li); **CHOYANG VOLGA** (Li)

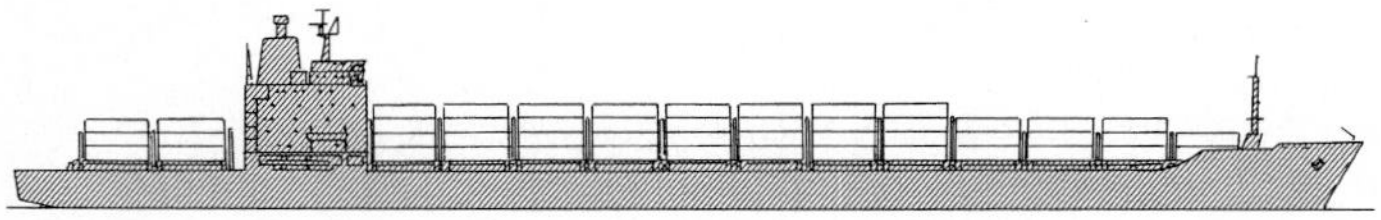

16 *MHFM H1*
SEA-LAND PATRIOT US/Ja (Mitsubishi HI) 1980; Con; 32,629 grt/ 30,225 dwt; 257.51 × 10 m *(844.62 × 32.81 ft)*; M (Sulzer); 22 kts; 2,472 TEU
Sisters (also lengthened. Some have extra bridge level): **SEA-LAND DEFENDER** (US); **SEA-LAND DEVELOPER** (US); **SEA-LAND EXPLORER** (US); **SEA-LAND INDEPENDENCE** (US); **SEA-LAND LIBERATOR** (US); **SEA-LAND EXPRESS** (US); **SEA-LAND VOYAGER** (US); **SEA-LAND FREEDOM** (US); **SEA-LAND MARINER** (US)
Sisters (also lengthened. Ko built—Hyundai): **SEA-LAND ENDURANCE** (US); **SEA-LAND INNOVATOR** (US)

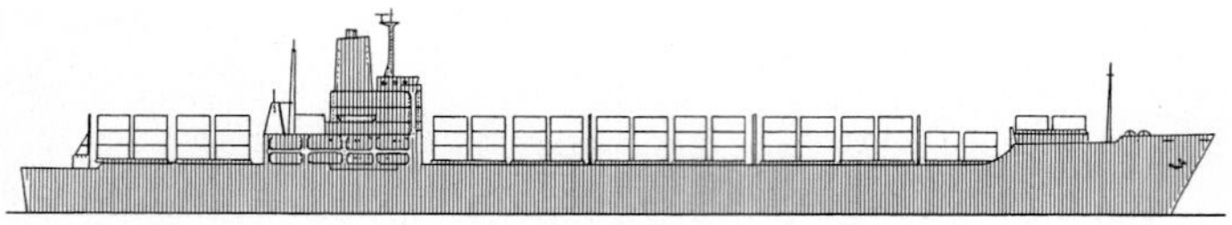

17 *MHFN H1*
ACX APRICOT Sg/Ja (Mitsubishi HI) 1974; Con; 31,608 grt/27,203 dwt; 218.50 × 11.23 m *(716.86 × 36.84 ft)*; M (Mitsubishi); 22 kts; ex-*Hakata Maru*; 1,409 TEU

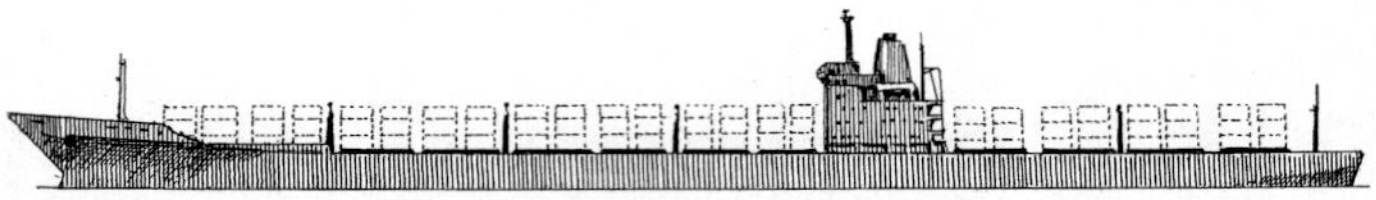

18 *MHFN H1*
BRIGIT MAERSK DIS/Ja (IHI) 1974; Con; 40,390 grt/32,153 dwt; 260 × 11.8 m *(851 × 38.6 ft)*; M (Sulzer); 26.5 kts; ex-*Svendborg Maersk*

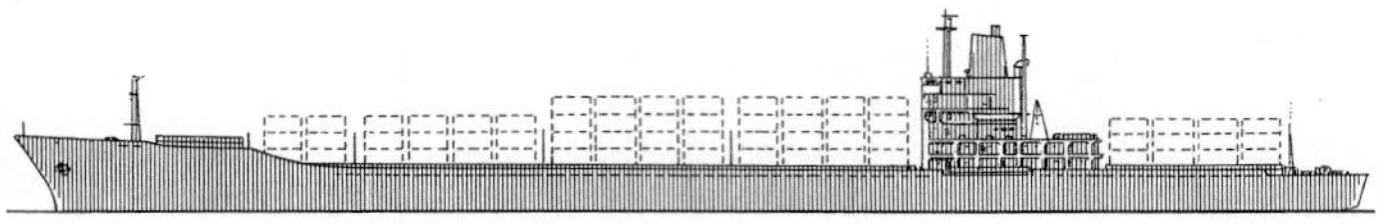

19 *MHFN H1*
HIKAWA II Li/Ja (NKK) 1974; Con; 25,848 grt/23,513 dwt; 213 × 10.52 m *(700 × 34.51 ft)*; M (Sulzer); 23 kts; ex-*Hikawa Maru*

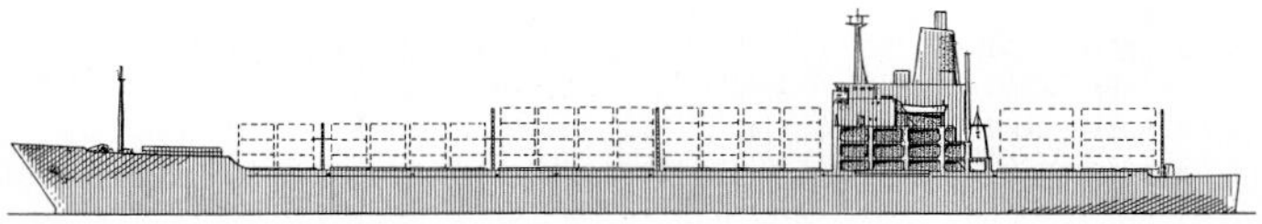

20 *MHFN H1*
NEPTUNE RHODONITE Li/Ja (Mitsubishi HI) 1978; Con; 30,575 grt/ 31,227 dwt; 214.61 × 10.5 m *(704 × 34.45 ft)*; M (Sulzer); 23 kts; ex-*Hira Maru*

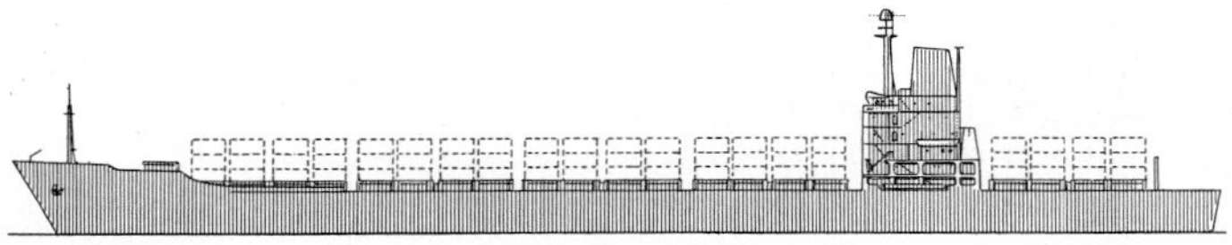

21 *MHFN H1*
OSAKA Pa/Ja (Mitsubishi HI) 1981; Con; 31,942 grt/33,185 dwt; 211 × 11.62 m *(692 × 38.12 ft)*; M (Sulzer); 18 kts
Possible sister: **PACIFIC LINK** (Pa) ex-*Hayakawa Maru*

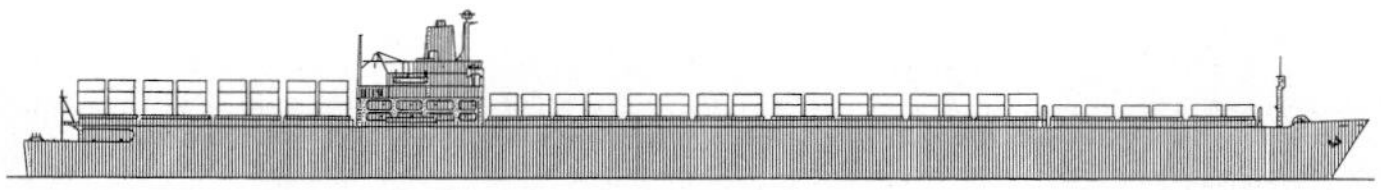

22 *MHFNM H1*
KASUGA I Pa/Ja (Mitsubishi HI) 1976; Con; 57,587 grt/44,538 dwt; 289.50 × 12.23 m *(949.80 × 40.12 ft)*; TSM (Sulzer); 23.25 kts; ex-*Kasuga Maru*; 2,326 TEU

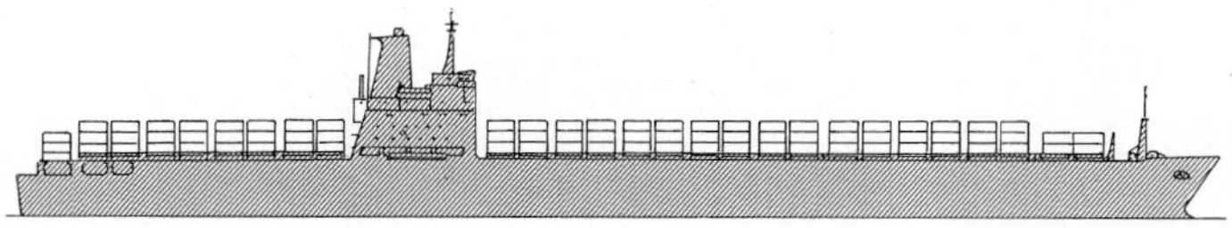

23 *MHGN H1*
BUNGA PERMAI My/Ja (Sumitomo) 1979; Con; 43,470 grt/49,228 dwt; 267 × 13 (875.98 × 42.65) m; M (Sulzer); 26
Sister: **BUNGA SURIA** (My)

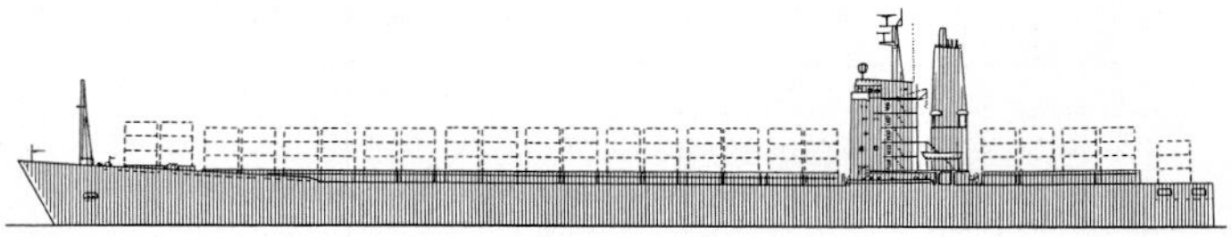

24 *M²F H*
MAPLE RIVER Pa/FRG (Thyssen) 1982; Con; 33,267 grt/34,589 dwt; 216.08 × 11.02 m *(709 × 36.15 ft)*; M (B&W); 17.5 kts; ex-*Tor Bay*
Sister: **RIVER CRYSTAL** (Pa) ex-*Providence Bay*

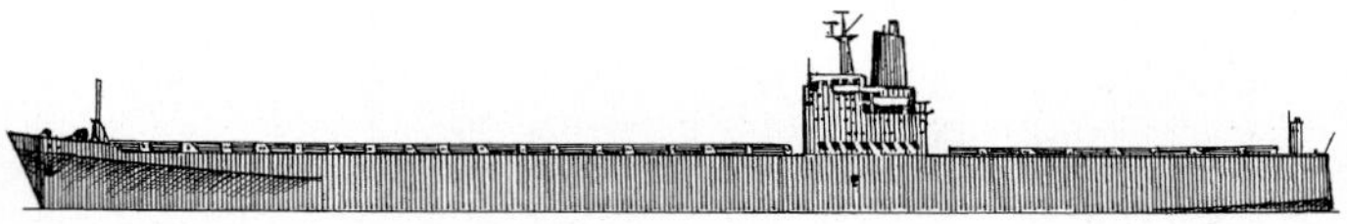

25 *M²F H*
S A SEDERBERG SA/Fr (France-Gironde) 1978; Con; 52,615 grt/48,878 dwt; 258.53 × 13 m *(841.48 × 42.65 ft)*; TSM (Sulzer); 21 kts
Sisters: **S A HELDERBERG** (SA); **S A WATERBERG** (SA); **S A WINTERBERG** (SA)

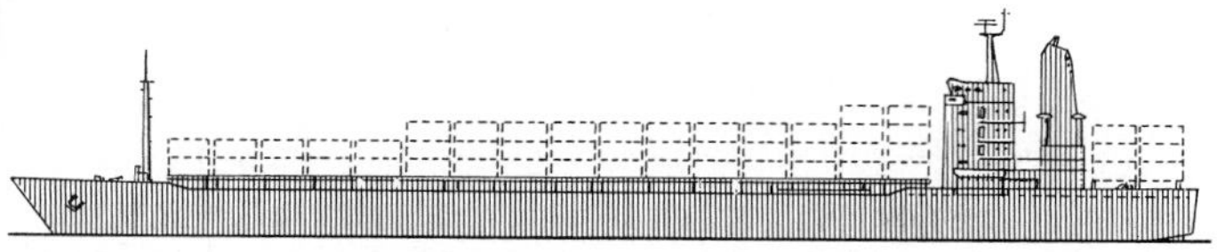

26 M^2F *H*
SEVEN SEAS BEACON Pa/FRG (Thyssen) 1980; Con; 16,868 grt/21,569 dwt; 164.01 × 10.32 m *(538 × 33.86 ft)*; M (MAN); 18 kts; ex-*Balandra*; 1,253 TEU
Sister: **ZURA BHUM** (At) ex-*Barbarossa*

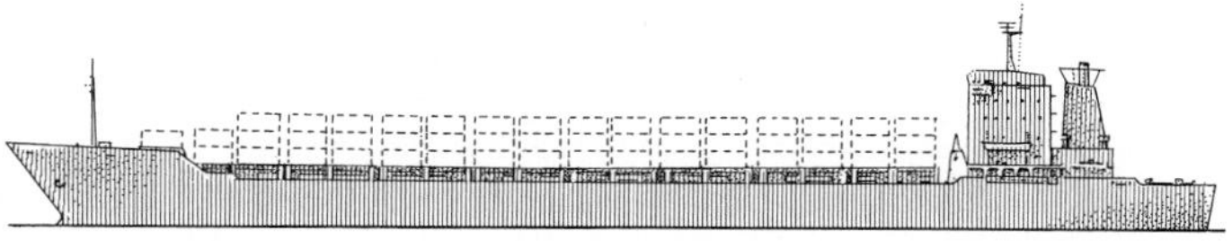

27 M^2F *H1*
ADDIRIYAH Si/Ko (Hyundai) 1979; Con; 20,526 grt/20,275 dwt; 183.24 × 10.02 m *(601 × 32.87 ft)*; M (B&W); 17.75 kts; 1,612 TEU
Sisters: **AL WATTYAH** (Ku); **BAR'ZAN** (Qt); **JEBEL ALI** (UAE)

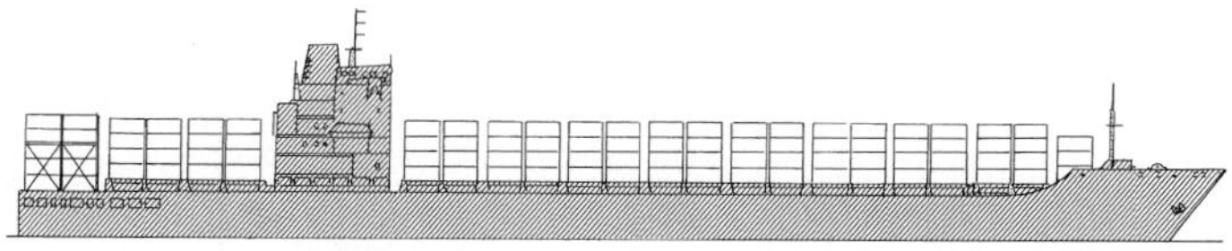

28 M^2F *H1*
CRISTOFORO COLOMBO It/It (FCNI) 1989; Con; 32,630 grt/28,800 dwt; 206.45 × 11.50 m *(677.33 × 37.73 ft)*; M (Sulzer); 19.5 kts; 2,232 TEU
Sister: **AMERIGO VESPUCCI** (It)

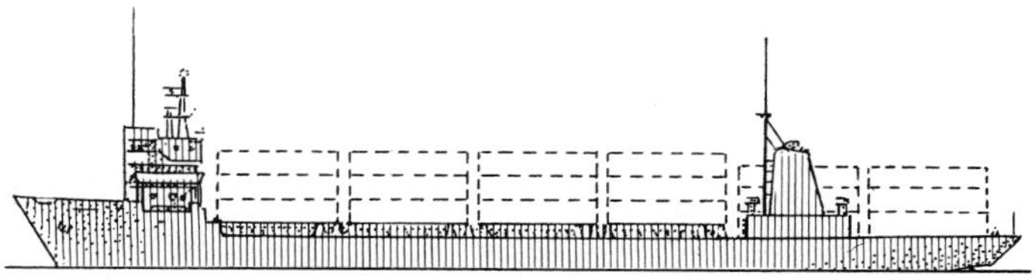

29 M^2F *H1*
DESAFIO Sp/Sp (Lorenzo) 1979; Con; 4,062 grt/6,648 dwt; 103.45 × 6.43 m *(339.4 × 21.1 ft)*; M (Deutz); 14 kts; 193 TEU

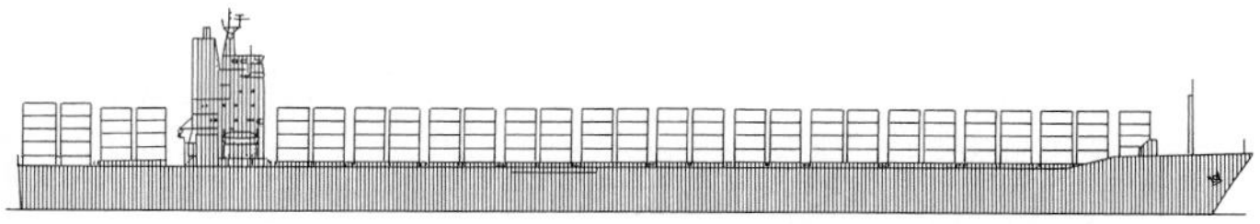

30 M^2F *H1*
GAO HE RC/Ge (Howaldts DW) 1990; Con; 37,143 grt/47,625 dwt; 236.00 × 12.00 m *(774.28 × 39.37 ft)*; M (B&W); 19 kts; 2,761 TEU
Sisters: **DONG HE** (RC); **MIN HE** (RC)

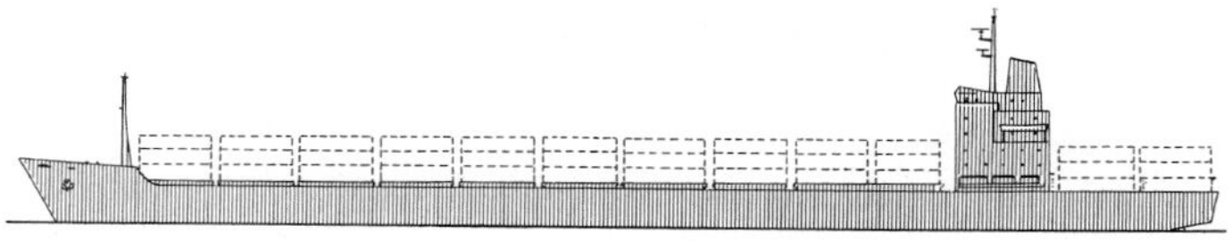

31 M^2F *H1*
HANJIN BUSAN Ko/Ko (Hyundai) 1979; Con; 17,682 grt/18,700 dwt; 200.62 × 8.34 m *(658 × 27.36 ft)*; M (Sulzer); 18.75 kts; 1,150 TEU
Sister: **HANJIN POHANG** (Ko); **HANJIN SEOUL** (Ko)

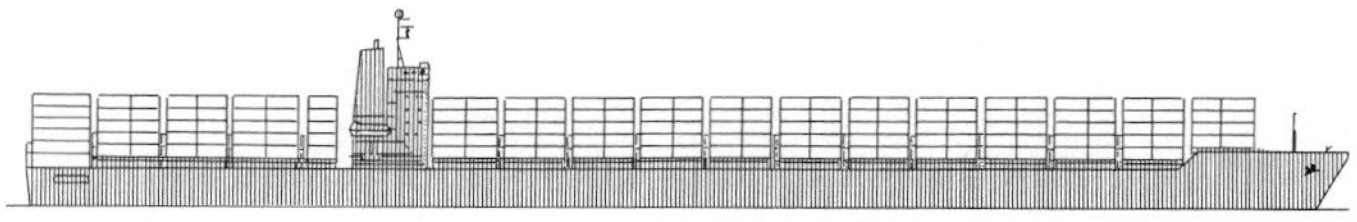

32 M^2F *H1*
HANJIN TONGHAE Ko/Ko (Hyundai) 1979; Con; 26,796 grt/25,444 dwt; 207.5 × 10.86 m *(681 × 35.63 ft)*; T (Kawasaki); 23.75 kts; ex-*Korean Jacewon*; 1,528 TEU
Sister: **HANJIN MASAN** (Ko) ex-*Korean Jacejin*; Similar (superstructure differs—pipe from funnel is different shape, and so on. Motor ship): **HANJIN CHUNGMU** (Ko) ex-*Korean Wonis Seven*

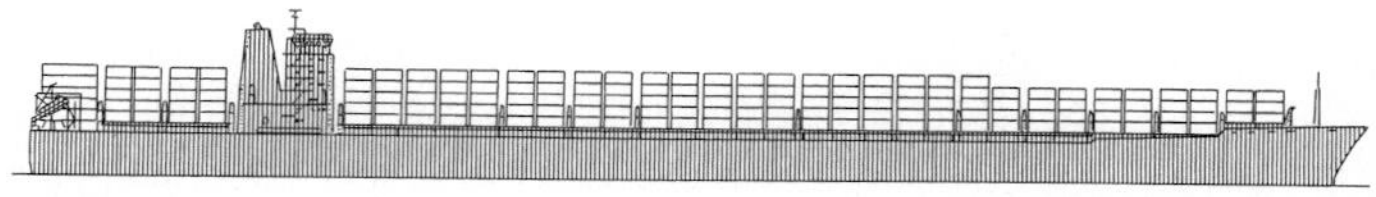

33 M^2F *H1*
HOECHST EXPRESS Ge/Ko (Samsung) 1991; Con; 53,833 grt/67,684 dwt; 294.00 × 13.50 m *(964.57 × 44.29 ft)*; M (B&W); 23 kts; 4,422 TEU; There is a free-fall lifeboat aft which is not included in the sequence because it is obscured by container stacks
Sisters: **HANNOVER EXPRESS** (Ge); **LEVERKUSEN EXPRESS** (Ge); **DRESDEN EXPRESS** (Ge); **LUDWIGSHAFEN EXPRESS** (Ge)

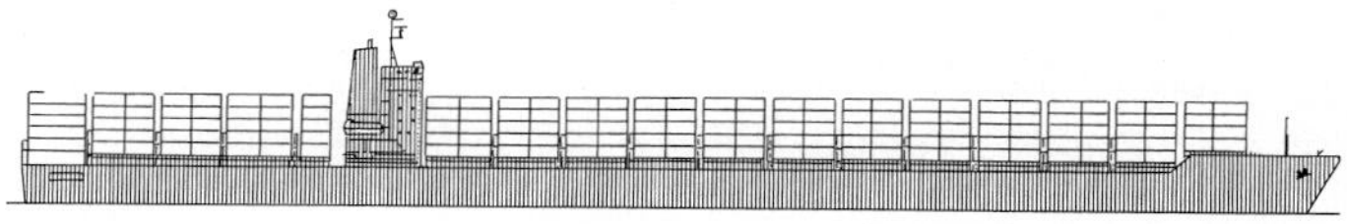

34 M^2F *H1*
HYUNDAI ADMIRAL Ko/Ko (Hyundai) 1992; Con; 51,836 grt/61,152 dwt; 275.10 × 13.62 m *(902.56 × 44.69 ft)*; M (B&W); 24.5 kts; 4,469 TEU
Sisters: **HYUNDAI BARON** (Ko); **HYUNDAI COMMODORE** (Pa); **HYUNDAI DUKE** (Pa); **HYUNDAI EMPEROR** (Pa)

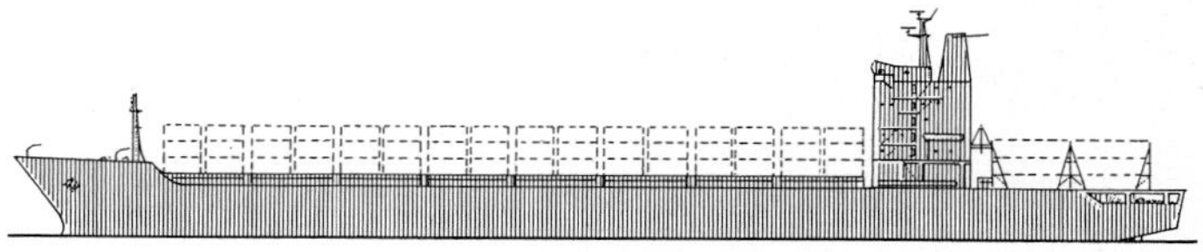

35 M^2F *H1*
IRENES HORIZON Cy/Sp (AESA) 1982; Con; 19,872 grt/19,185 dwt; 184 × 9.52 m *(604 × 31.23 ft)*; M (B&W); 20 kts; ex-*Almudena*; 1,202 TEU
Sister: **ACX CLOVER** (Cy) ex-*Pilar*

36 M^2F *H1*
MSC AURORA Cy/FRG (LF-W) 1971; Con; 13,276 grt/11,911 dwt; 174.86 × 9.9 m *(573.69 × 32.48 ft)*; M (MAN); 19.5 kts; ex-*Gruenfels;* Lengthened 1974 (A G 'Weser'); 886 TEU
Sister: **MSC ALEXA** (Pa) ex-*Geyerfels*

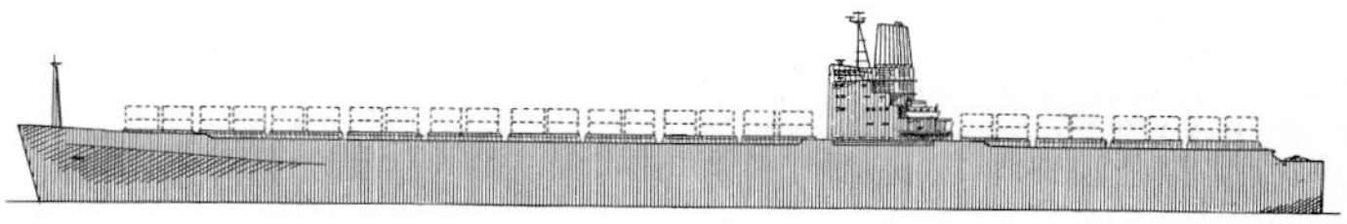

37 M^2F *H1*
NEDLLOYD HOUTMAN Ne/Ne (Verolme Dok (aft section); Nederlandsche (fwd section)) 1977; Con; 52,007 grt/49,262 dwt; 258.5 × 13.03 m *(848.1 × 42.75 ft)*; TSM (Sulzer); 21.5 kts
Sister: **NEDLLOYD HOORN** (Ne)

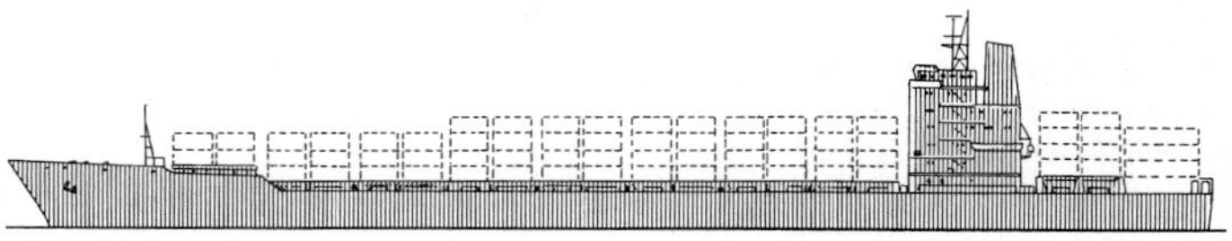

38 M^2F *H1*
NOLIZWE Br/Be (Boelwerf) 1981; Con; 20,799 grt/25,070 dwt; 186.01 × 10.82 m *(610 × 35.5 ft)*; M (B&W); 20 kts; ex-*Plantin*; 1,270 TEU

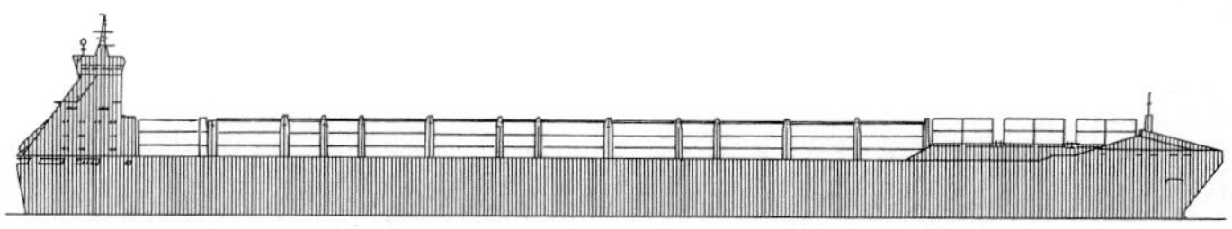

39 M^2F *H1*
NORASIA HONG KONG Li/Ge (Howaldts DW) 1994; Con; 42,323 grt/41,570 dwt; 242.00 × 11.00 m *(793.96 × 36.09 ft)*; M (Mitsubishi); 22.5 kts; 2,780 TEU
Sisters: **NORASIA FRIBOURG** (Ma); **NORASIA KIEL** (Ma); **NORASIA SHARJAH** (Li)

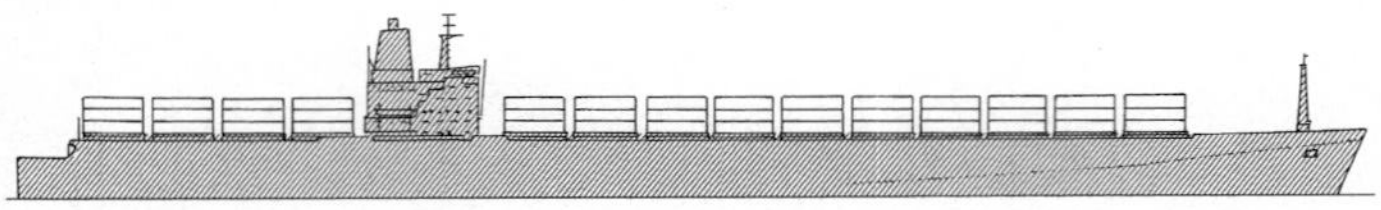

40 *M²F H1*
OOCL FAME Li/FRG (Bremer V) 1972; Con; 55,576 grt/47,838 dwt; 187 × 12 m *(942 × 39.6 ft)*; T (Stal-Laval); 23 kts; ex-*Bremen Express*
Sisters: **OOCL FRONTIER** (Hk) ex-*Hongkong Express*; **NEDLLOYD DEJIMA** (Ne) (Motor ship—Sulzer); **NEDLLOYD DELFT** (Ne) (Motor ship—Sulzer)

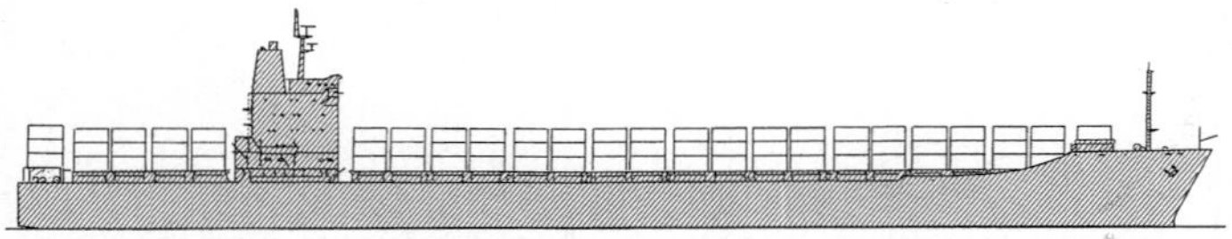

41 *M²F H1*
SKY RIVER Li/Ja (IHI) 1984; Con; 31,714 grt/36,021 dwt; 212.50 × 11.63 m *(697.18 × 38.16 ft)*; M (Sulzer); 19.25 kts; ex-*Asian Venture*; 1,960 TEU

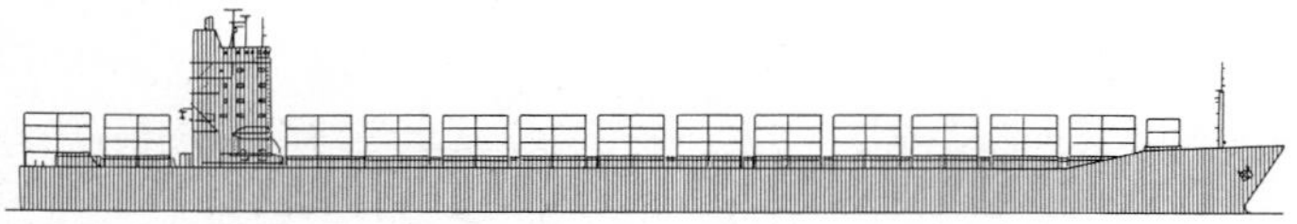

42 *M²F H1*
ZIM CANADA Is/Ge (Howaldts DW) 1990; Con; 37,209 grt/47,230 dwt; 236.00 × 10.50 m *(774.28 × 34.45 ft)*; M (Sulzer); 21 kts; 2,402 TEU
Sisters: **ZIM ITALIA** (Is); **ZIM KOREA** (Is); **ZIM JAPAN** (Is); **ZIM HONG KONG** (Is); **ZIM ISRAEL** (Is); **ZIM AMERICA** (Is)

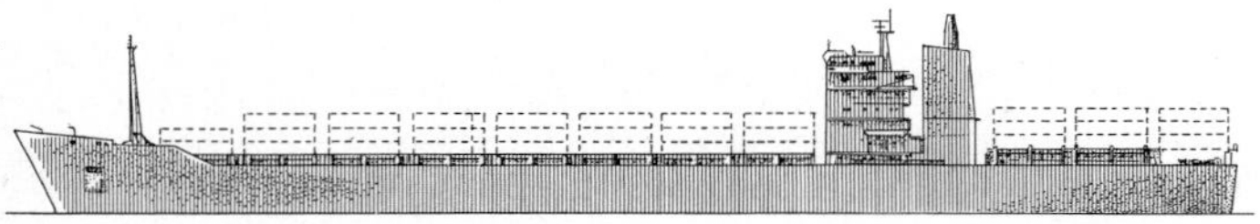

43 *M²F H1*
ZIM KEELUNG Is/Ne (Giessen-De Noord) 1981; Con; 36,263 grt/39,967 dwt; 210.22 × 11.5 m *(689.7 × 37.73 ft)*; M (Sulzer); 22.5 kts; lengthened 1991; Drawing shows vessel as built; Length is now 238.77 m (783.3 ft)
Sisters (lengthened): **ZIM SAVANNAH** (Is); **ZIM IBERIA** (Is)

44 *M²F H13*
CARMEN DOLORES H Sp/Ne ('De Hoop' L) 1994; Con; 7,424 grt/ 11,007 dwt; 133.00 × 8.25 m *(436.35 × 27.07 ft)*; M (Wärtsilä); 17.5 kts; 758 TEU

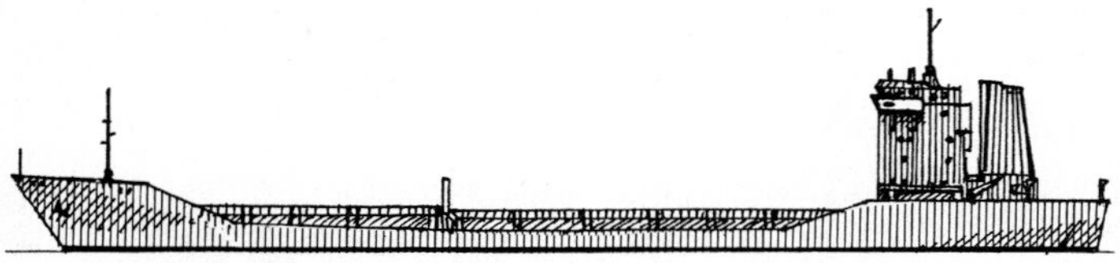

45 *M²F H13*
CERVANTES Br/Br (Appledore) 1978; Con; 3,992 grt/4,352 dwt; 104.17 × 5.56 m *(341.77 × 18.24 ft)*; M (Doxford); 14.5 kts; ex-*City of Plymouth*; 'AS-300' type; 300 TEU
Sisters: **ERKA SUN** (Cy) ex-*City of Perth*; **CITY OF MANCHESTER** (Br) ex-*City of Hartlepool*; **PELMARINER** (Gr) ex-*City of Ipswich*; **HYUNDAI MALACCA** (Bs) ex-*City of Oxford*

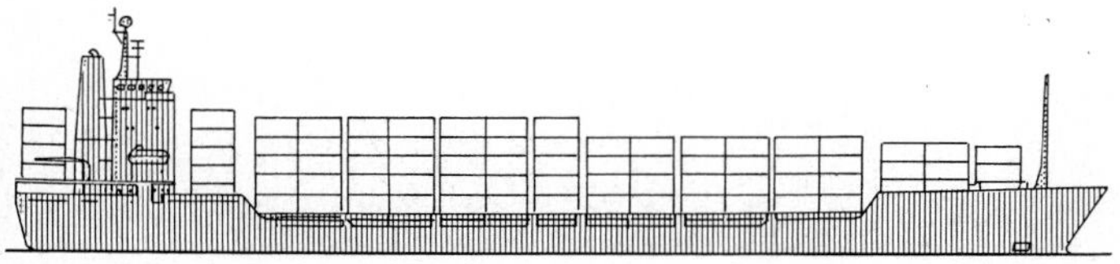

46 *M²F H13*
CTE MAGALLANES Li/FRG (Nobiskrug) 1983; Con; 10,544 grt/14,271 dwt; 151.01 × 8.33 m *(495.44 × 27.33 ft)*; M (MaK); 16.3 kts; ex-*Westermarsch*; 932 TEU
Sister: **ORA BHUM** (Li) ex-*Westertal*

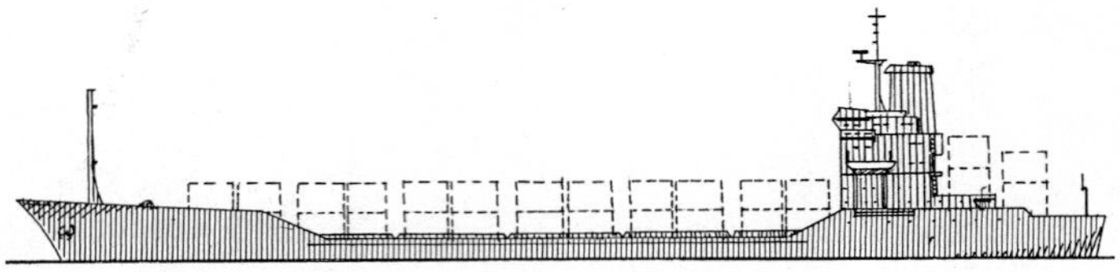

47 *M²F H13*
FAIRBRIDGE —/Ne (Giessen-De Noord) 1971; Con; 7,850 grt/8,723 dwt; 144.94 × 7.62 m *(475.52 × 25 ft)*; M (MAN); 13.5 kts; ex-*Fiery Cross Isle*; 436 TEU; now broken up
Sister: **ALACRITY** (—) ex-*Lord of the Isle*

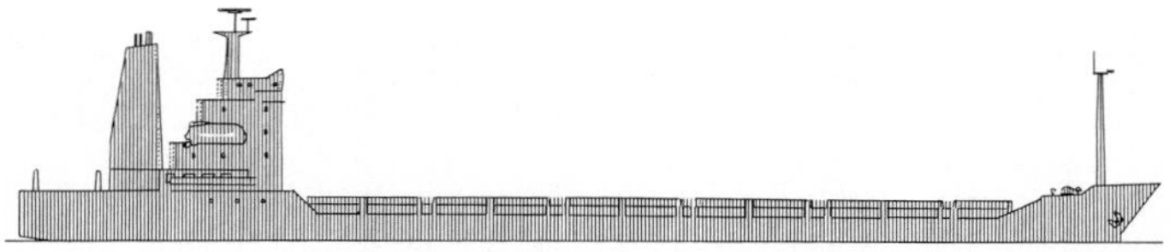

48 *M²F H13*
HANJIN BANGKOK Ko/Ko (Hanjin SB) 1991; Con; 5,833 grt/8,075 dwt; 121.00 × 6.61 m *(396.98 × 21.69 ft)*; M (B&W); 14 kts; 414 TEU

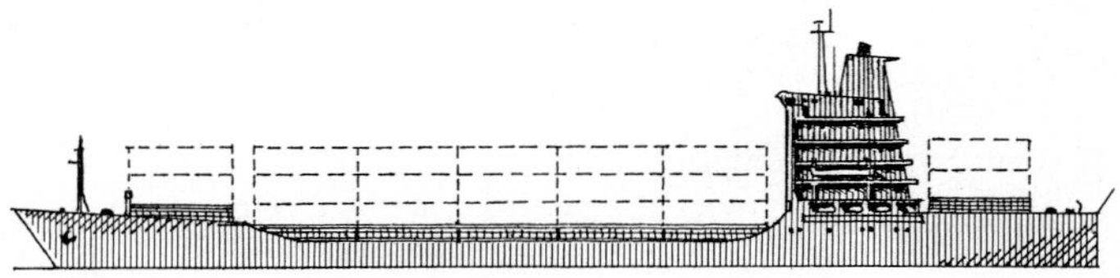

49 *M²F H13*
HUA NING HE RC/FRG (Elsflether) 1971; Con; 5,997 grt/9,050 dwt; 128.43 × 8.07 m *(421.36 × 26.48 ft)*; M (Atlas-MaK); 18 kts; ex-*Visurgis*; 424 TEU

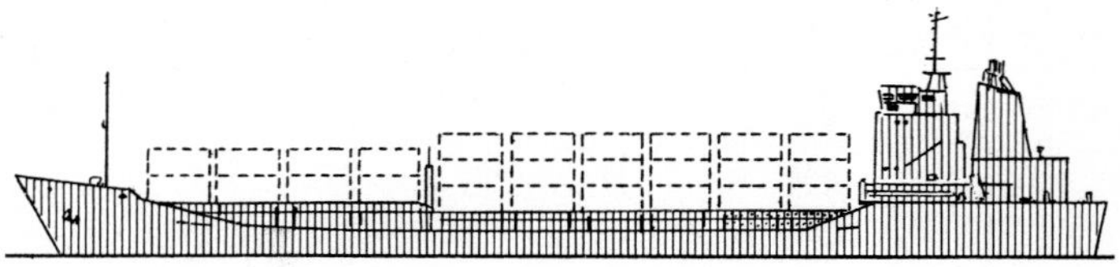

50 *M²F H13*
JIN FA Pa/Br (Swan Hunter) 1979; Con; 4,036 grt/4,280 dwt; 104.2 × 5.69 m *(342 × 18.67 ft)*; M (Doxford); 15 kts; ex-*Crown Prince*; 288 TEU
Sister: **HOST COUNTRY** (Pa) ex-*Royal Prince*

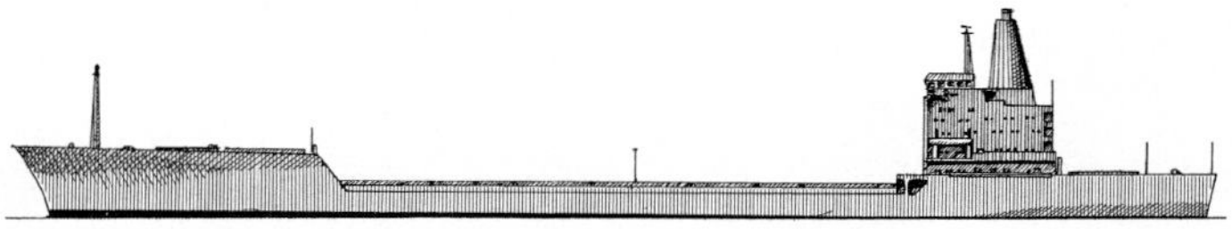

51 *M²F H13*
MSC BRIANNA Gr/FRG (B+V) 1970; Con; 28,896 grt/34,734 dwt; 226.47 × 11.56 m *(743 × 37.93 ft)*; T (Stal-Laval); 21 kts; ex-*Sydney Express*; 1,685 TEU
Similar (It built—Muggiano): **MSC GIOVANNA** (Pa) ex-*Lloydiana*

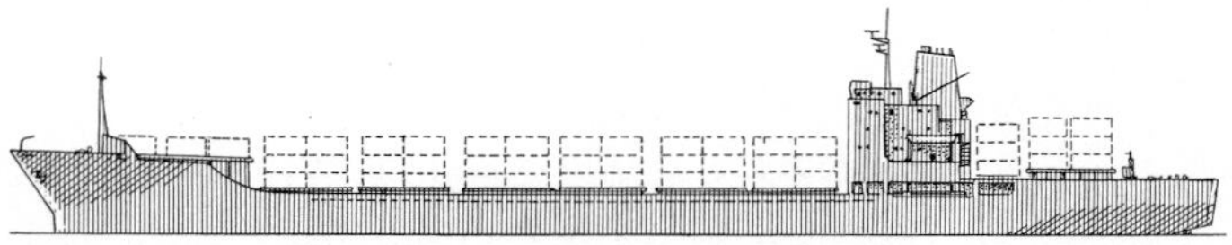

52 *M²F H13*
OOCL ASSURANCE HK/Ja (Namura) 1979; Con; 15,145 grt/18,643 dwt; 177.03 × 10.13 m *(583.96 × 33.12 ft)*; M (Sulzer); 19 kts; ex-*Seatrain Oriskany*; 1,061 TEU
Sisters: **OOCL ALLIANCE** (Tw) ex-*Seatrain Bennington*; **CANMAR VICTORY** (Br) ex-*Seatrain Chesapeake*; **CANMAR CONQUEST** (Br) ex-*Seatrain Yorktown*; **CANMAR TRIUMPH** (Br) ex-*Seatrain Independence*; **CANMAR GLORY** (Br) ex-*Seatrain Saratoga*

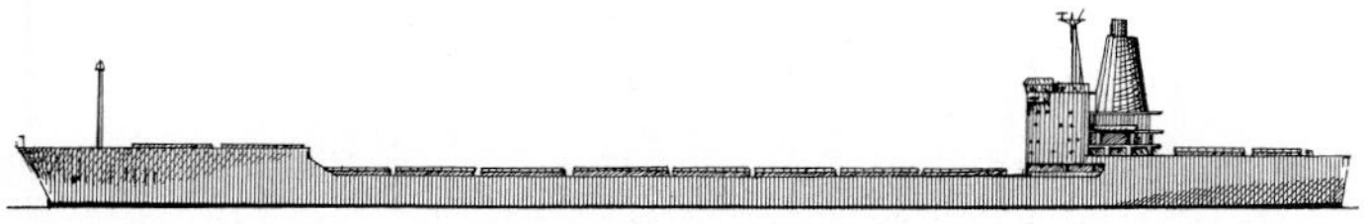

53 *M^2F H13*
OOCL BRAVERY HK/FRG (Bremer V) 1978; Con; 26,383 grt/33,869 dwt; 218.6 × 11.77 m *(717.19 × 38.62 ft)*; M (MAN); 23 kts; ex-*Dart Canada*; 1,737 TEU

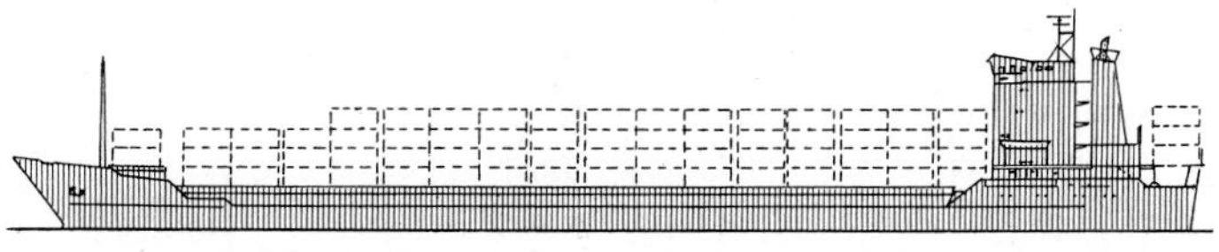

54 *M^2F H13*
PRECIOUS RIVER Pa/FRG (O&K) 1982; Con; 9,948 grt/14,003 dwt; 153.63 × 8.25 m *(504 × 27.07 ft)*; M (Krupp-MaK); 16.5 kts; ex-*Arktic*; 827 TEU
Sister: **NOBLE RIVER** (Pa) Launched as *Nautic*

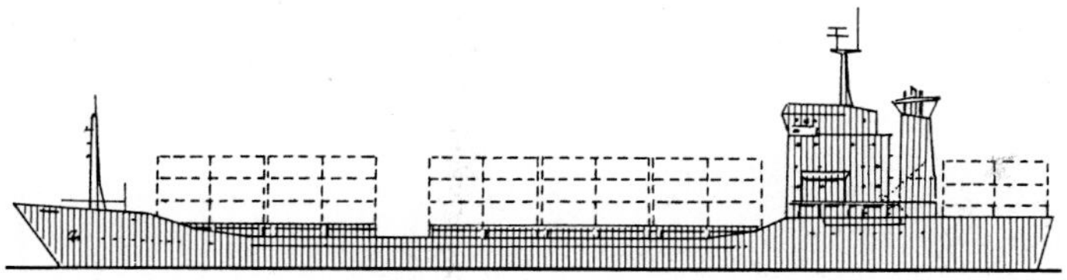

55 *M^2F H13*
TONG YUN RC/Tw (China SB) 1980; Con; 6,256 grt/6,539 dwt; 118.01 × 8 m *(387 × 26.25 ft)*; M (MAN); 15.75 kts; ex-*Atlantic*; 443 TEU
Sisters: **ROOK CARRIER** (Pa) Launched as *Altonic*; **MILD UNION** (Pa) ex-*Hanseatic*; **YAN TONG** (Pa) ex-*Holsatic*; **BEI DAI HE** (RC) Launched as *Arctic*; **MILD SUN** (Pa) ex-*Nan Hwa*

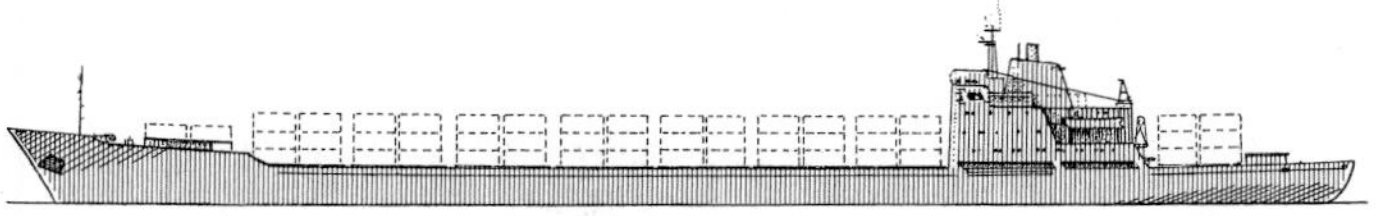

56 *M^2FC H1*
AL AHMADIAH Si/Ru (Nosenko) 1969/80; Con; 14,539 grt/15,763 dwt; 194.33 × 9.5 m *(637.57 × 31.17 ft)*; M (B&W); 17 kts; Converted from cargoship of 'Feodosiya' type 1980 (AESA); 800 TEU
Sister: **AL SHAMIAH** (UAE)

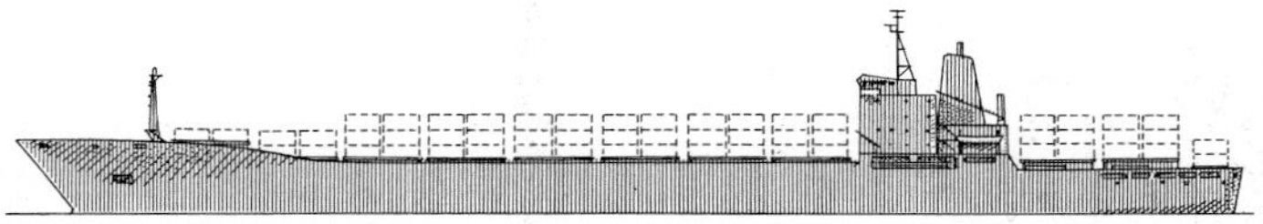

57 *M^2FC H1*
SEXTUM Pa/It (Italcantieri) 1980; Con; 27,073 grt/25,868 dwt; 208.12 × 10.66 m *(682.81 × 34.97 ft)*; M (GMT); 22 kts; ex-*Ercole Lauro*

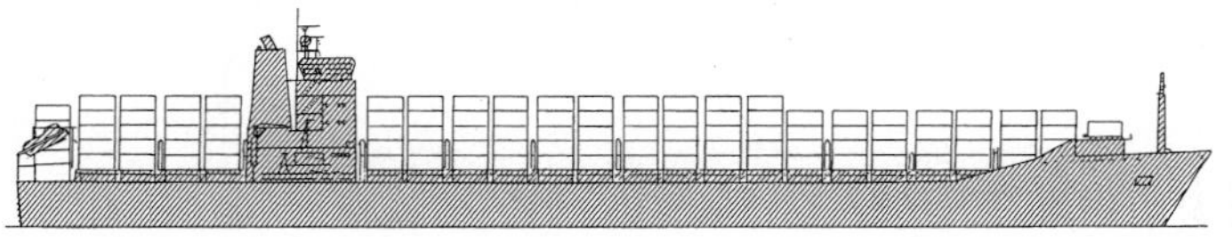

58 *M^2FL H1*
BONN EXPRESS Ge/FRG (Howaldts DW) 1989; Con; 35,919 grt/45,977 dwt; 235.65 × 12.50 m *(773.13 × 41.01 ft)*; M (B&W); 20.5 kts; 2,803 TEU; Lengthened 1992—drawing shows original appearance (206 m (676 ft))
Sister: **HEIDELBERG EXPRESS** (Ge)

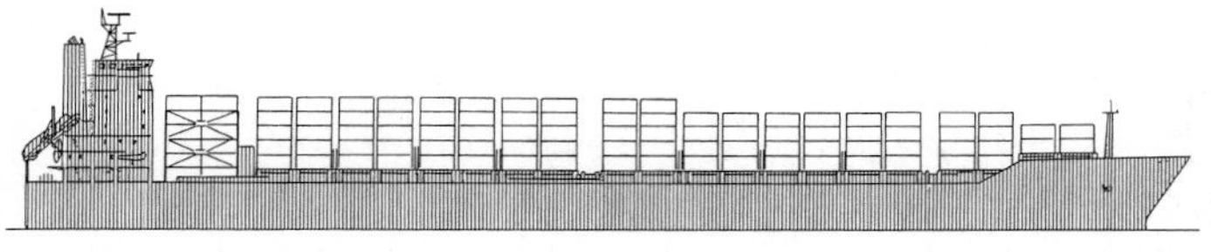

59 *M^2FL H1*
NUEVO LEON Me/Sp (AESA) 1994; Con; 30,971 grt/36,887 dwt; 202.00 × 12.52 m *(662.73 × 41.08 ft)*; M (B&W); 20 kts; 2,394 TEU
Sisters: **SONORA** (Me); **YUCATAN** (Me)

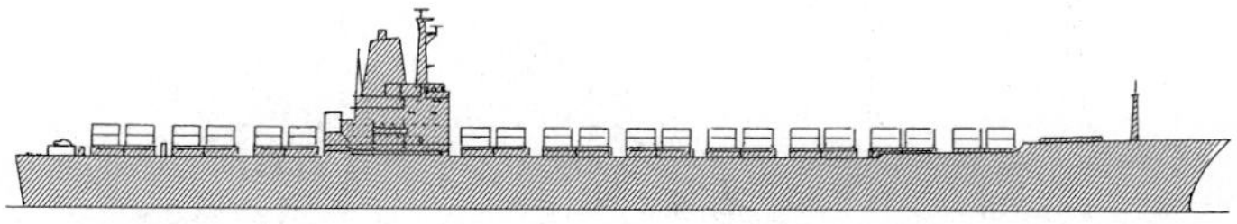

60 *M^2FM H*
BERLIN EXPRESS Br/Br(Swan Hunter) 1973; Con; 35,303 grt/42,224 dwt; 252 × 11 m *(827 × 32.6 ft)*; M (Sulzer); 21 kts; ex-*Remuera*; Mast aft is on port side

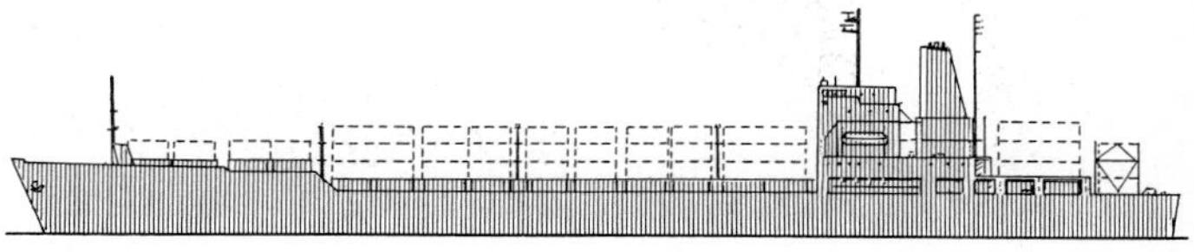

61 *M^2FM H1*
TAVIRA Cy/DDR (Warnow) 1982; Con; 21,584 grt/21,370 dwt; 173.92 × 9.82 m *(570.60 × 32.22 ft)*; M (B&W); 20 kts; ex-*Kapitan Kanevskiy*; Now lengthened to 203.06 m (666 ft); Drawing shows vessel to original appearance; Container capacity is now 1,254 TEU; 'MERKUR II' type
Sisters (also lengthened): **LISBOA** (Cy) ex-*Kapitan Gavrilov*; **MIDEN AGAN** (Ru) ex-*Kapitan Kozlovskiy*; **AVEIRO** (Cy) ex-*Nikolay Tikhonov*; **LEIXOES** (Cy) ex-*Tikhon Kiselyev*; **SPEVDE VRADEOS** (Cy) ex-*Professor Tovstykh*; **BOLSHEVIK M TOMAS** (Uk)
Sisters (unlengthened): **ORIENT CORD** (Uk) ex-*Kapitan V Ushakov*; **KAPITAN V TRUSH** (Uk); **TRANSKORD** (Uk) ex-*Geroi Monkadiy* (widened)

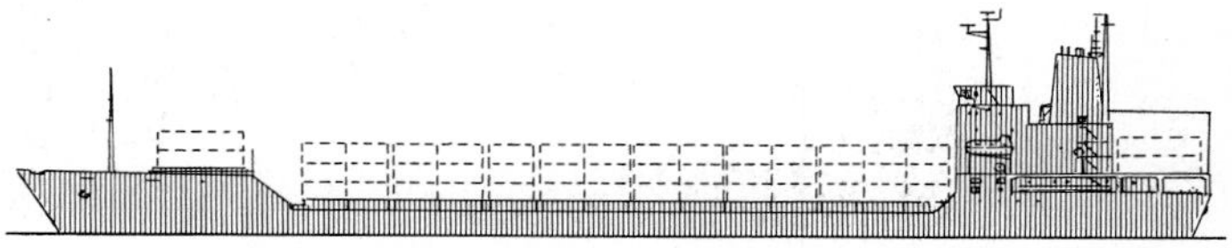

62 *M^2FM^2 H13*
TIGER CAPE Sg/DDR (Warnow) 1985; Con; 13,769 grt/18,155 dwt; 165.51 × 10.05 m *(543.01 × 32.97 ft)*; M (MAN); 16 kts; ex-*Ruhland*; 946 TEU
Sisters: **MERKUR BAY** (Li) ex-*Rubeland*; **WIDAR** (At) ex-*Fahrland*; **ARNOLD SCHULTE** (Cy) ex-*Sohland*

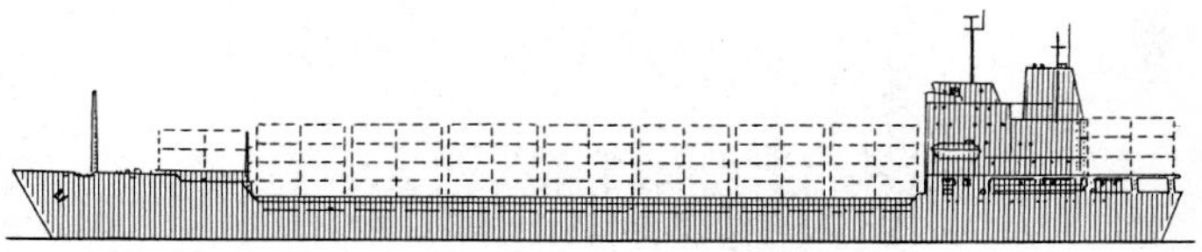

63 *M^2FM^2 H13*
VOGTLAND Ge/DDR ("Neptun") 1986; Con; 13,335 grt/17,088 dwt; 158.07 × 10.11 m *(518.60 × 33.17 ft)*; M (MAN); 16 kts; 896 TEU
Sisters: **HAVELLAND** (Ge)

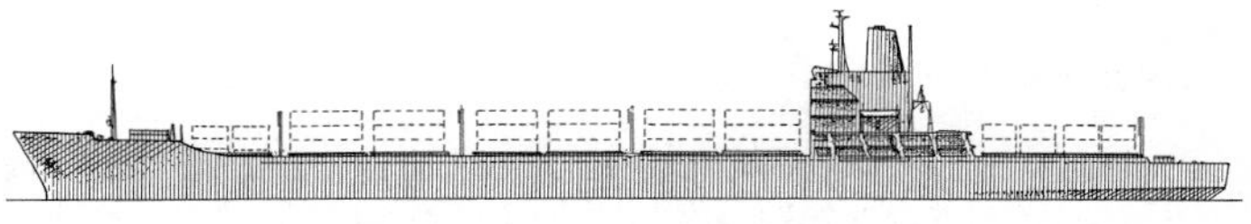

64 *M^2FN H1*
ALIGATOR MIRACLE Sg/Ja (Mitsubishi HI) 1973; Con; 29,342 grt/ 29,581 dwt; 209 × 10.6 m *(686 × 35 ft)*; M (Sulzer); 22.5 kts; ex-*Alaska Maru*; Now lengthened to 238 m (781 ft); Drawings show original appearance
Possible sister (unlengthened): **ACX LOTUS** (Pa) ex-*Hakusan Maru*

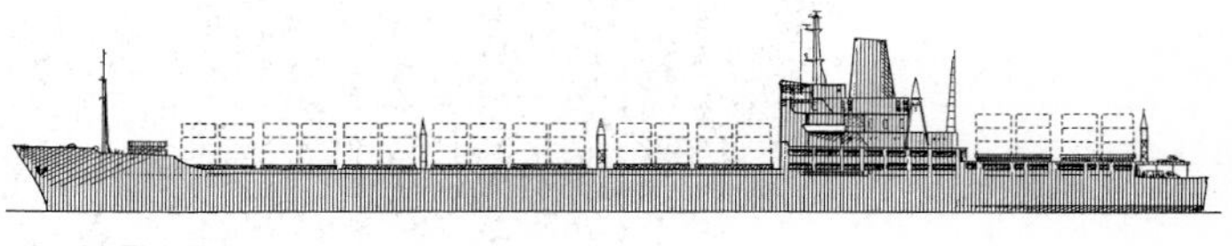

65 *M^2FN H1*
CHITRAL Br/Ja (Mitsubishi HI) 1970; Con; 25,093 grt/23,009 dwt; 211.49 × 10.53 m *(693.86 × 34.55 ft)*; M (B&W); 23 kts; ex-*Arafura*

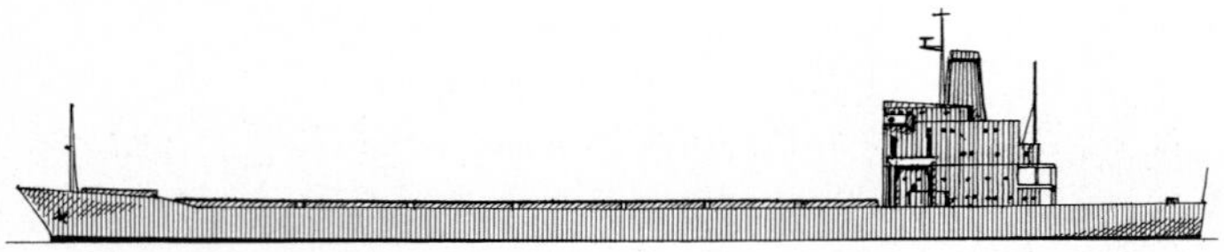

66 *M^2FN H1*
CHOYANG LAND Ko/Ne ('De Hoop') 1972; Con; 12,810 grt/13,440 dwt; 172.52 × 8.17 m *(566.01 × 26.80 ft)*; M (MAN); 21 kts; ex-*Plutos*; 732 TEU

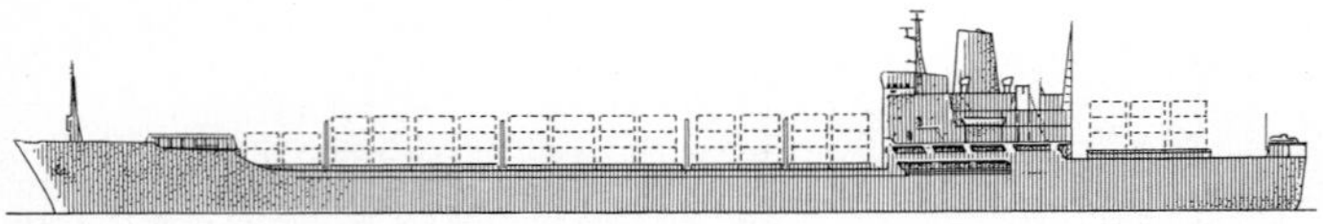

67 *M^2FN H1*
FISHGUARD BAY HK/Ja (Mitsui) 1970; Con; 25,407 grt/23,415 dwt; 213 × 10.5 m *(700 × 34.5 ft)*; M (B&W); 23 kts; ex-*Ariake*

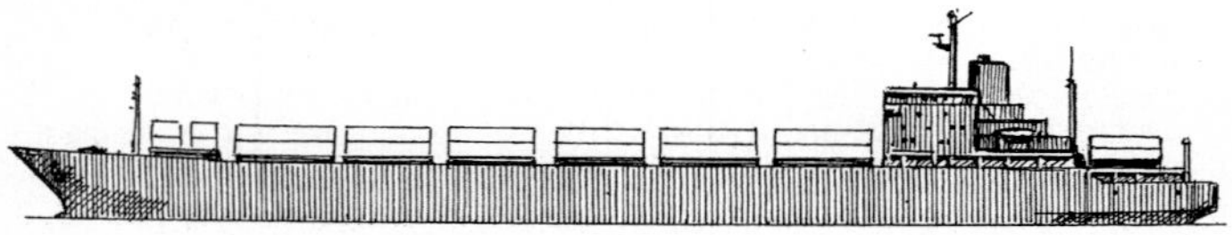

68 *M^2FN H1*
IRENES SONG Cy/DDR (Warnow) 1975; Con; 15,305 grt/14,490 dwt; 169.63 × 9.2 m *(556.52 × 30.18 ft)*; M (Sulzer); 20 kts; ex-*Khudozhnik Saryan*; 'Mercur' type; 712 TEU
Sisters: **ZIM ODESSA** (Ma) ex-*Khudozhnik Pakhomov*; **TIGER ISLAND** (HK) ex-*Khudozhnik Prorokov*; **TIGER BAY** (Cy) ex-*Khudozhnik Repin*; **MOR EUROPE** (Cy) ex-*Khudozhnik Romas*; **MOR UK** (Cy) ex-*Nadezhda Obukhova*; **MOR CANADA** (Cy) ex-*Nikolay Golovanov*
Sisters (lengthened to 198.90 m (652 ft). 1,254 TEU): **KHUDOZHNIK IOGANSON** (Ru); **KHUDOZHNIK ZHUKOV** (Ru); **MAKSIM MIKHAYLOV** (Ru)

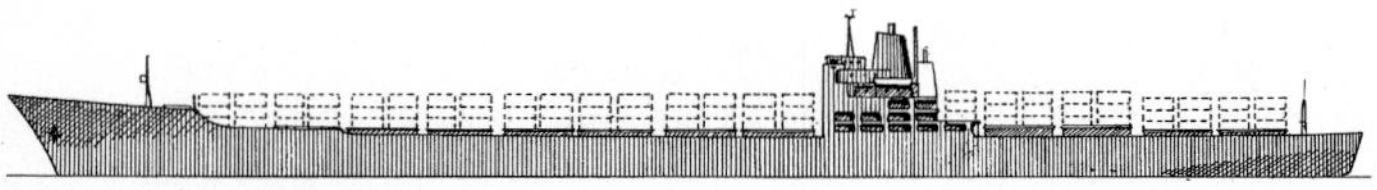

69 *M^2FN H1*
MED NAGOYA Li/Ja (IHI) 1973; Con; 38,997 grt/33,106 dwt; 261 × 11.8 m *(857 × 38.6 ft)*; M (Sulzer); 21.3 kts; ex-*Kiso Maru*

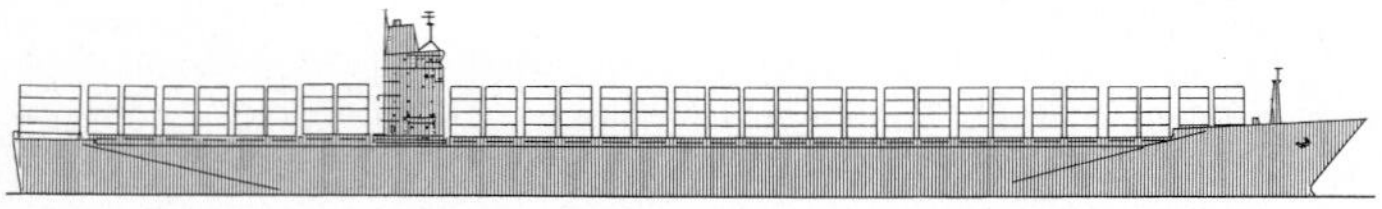

70 *M^2FN H1*
MING PEACE Tw/Tw (China SB) 1986; Con; 40,464 grt/40,744 dwt; 269.68 × 11.53 m *(884.78 × 37.83 ft)*; M (Sulzer); 20.5 kts; 3,266 TEU
Sisters: **MING PLEASURE** (Tw); **MING PLENTY** (Tw); **MING PROGRESS** (Tw); **MING PROMINENCE** (Tw); **MING PROMOTION** (Tw); **MING PROPITIOUS** (Tw); **MED TAIPEI** (Tw) ex-*Ming Prosperity*

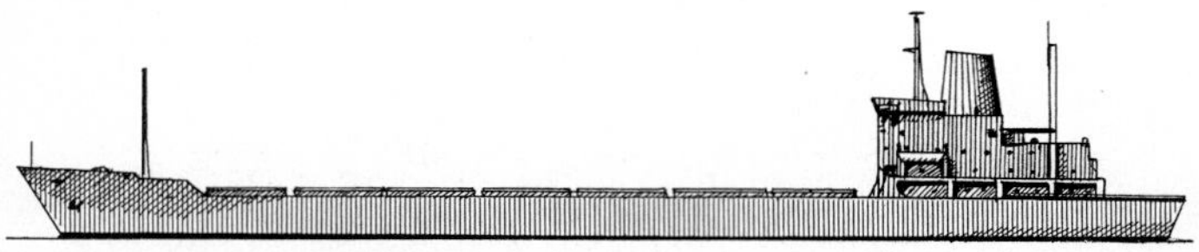

71 *M^2FN H1*
MSC REBECCA SV/Br (Cammell Laird) 1970; Con; 15,576 grt/16,963 dwt; 167.09 × 9.17 m *(548.2 × 30.9 ft)*; M (B&W); 19 kts; ex-*CP Voyageur*; 779 TEU
Sisters: **CANMAR VENTURE** (HK) ex-*CP Discoverer*; **CANMAR SPIRIT** (HK) ex-*CP Trader*

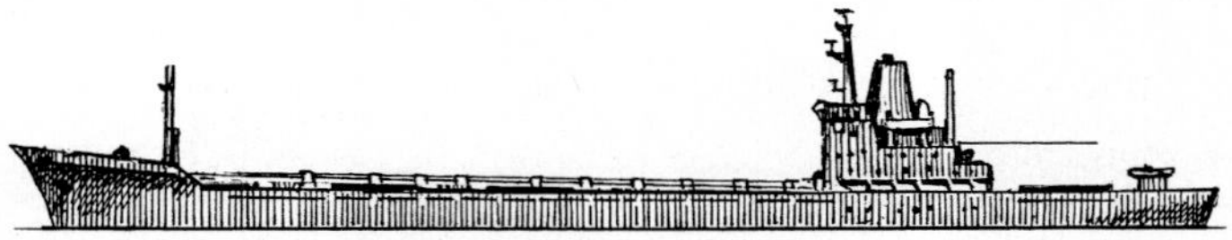

72 *M^2FN H1*
ORIENT STRENGTH Pa/Ja (Mitsubishi HI) 1972/77; Con; 11,490 grt/12,580 dwt; 155.96 × 8.68 m *(511.35 × 28.48 ft)*; M (Sulzer); 17 kts; Converted from general cargo 1977 (Malaysian Spyd)
Sisters: **BUNGA TERATAI** (My); **BUNGA SEROJA** (My); **ORIENT SPIRIT** (Pa) ex-*Bunga Melati*

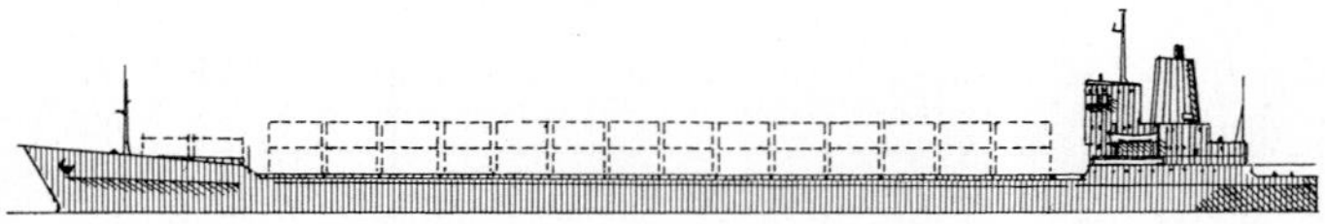

73 *M^2FN H12*
ACX CANARY Pi/FRG (O&K) 1976; Con; 10,233 grt/14,833 dwt; 159.01 × 8.26 m *(521.69 × 27.1 ft)*; M (Pielstick); 16.5 kts; ex-*Sovereign Express*; 662 TEU
Sister: **ACX ROBIN** (Pi) ex-*Sovereign Accord*

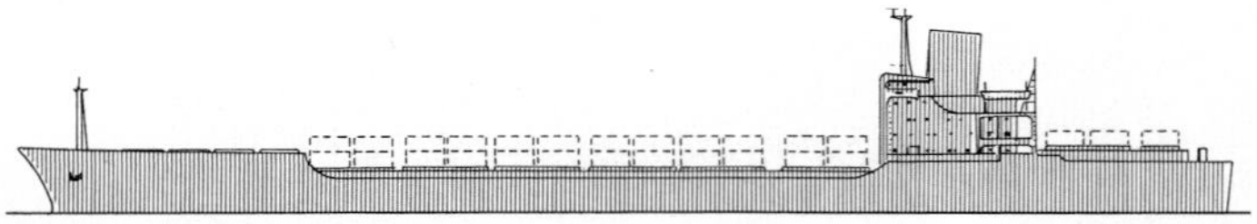

74 *M^2FN H13*
FREMANTLE STAR Sg/FRG (Bremer V) 1971; Con; 18,882 grt/19,114 dwt; 189 × 10 m *(616 × 33 ft)*; M (MAN); 21.5 kts; ex-*California Star*
Sister: **NEW ZEALAND STAR** (Sg) ex-*Columbia Star*

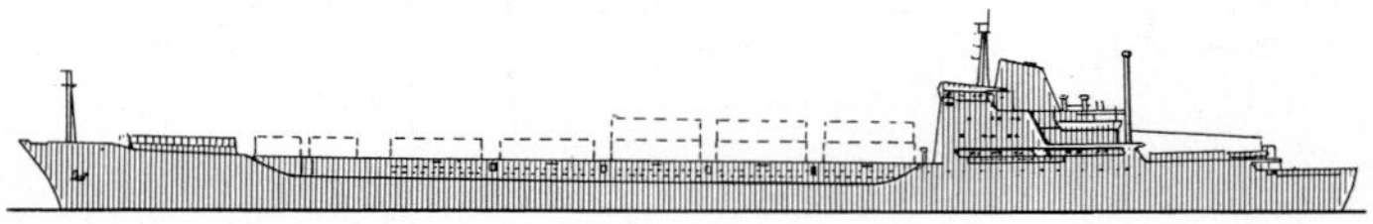

75 *M^2FN H13*
GAMZAT TSADASA Ru/Ys ('Uljanik') 1971/80; Con; 12,280 grt/14,141 dwt; 176.23 × 9.80 m *(578 × 32.15 ft)*; M (B&W); 17.75 kts; Converted to container and lengthened 1980 (Jurong Spyd)
Sisters: **IVAN KOTLYAREVSKIY** (Ru); **KONSTANTIN PAUSTOVSKIY** (Ru); **NOVIKOV PRIBOY** (Ru)

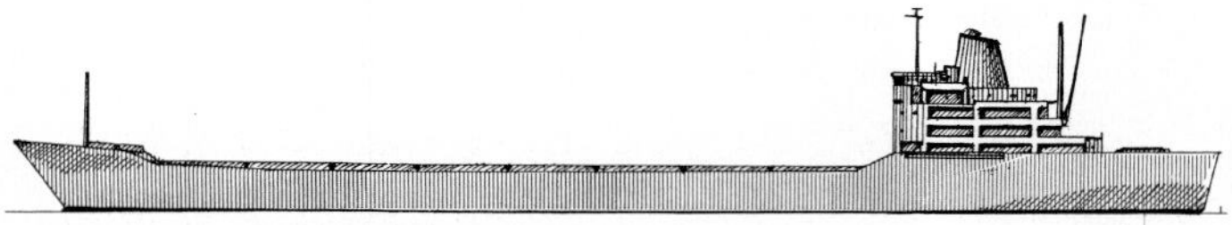

76 *M^2FN H13*
MAERSK AUSTRALIA Gr/De (Nakskov) 1971; Con; 20,325 grt/20,215 dwt; 201.86 × 9.48 m *(662.27 × 31.1 ft)*; M (B&W); 21.5 kts; ex-*Falstria*; 918 TEU
Sister: **MAERSK OCEANIA** (Gr) ex-*Meonia*

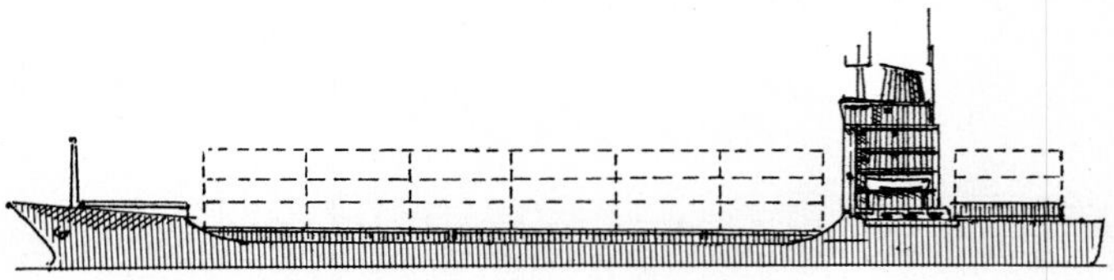

77 *M^2FN H13*
VERED Is/Is (Israel Spyds) 1978/85; Con; 7,723 grt/9,404 dwt; 129.85 × 8.07 m *(426.02 × 26.48 ft)*; M (Sulzer); 17 kts; Now lengthened to 144.81 m (475 ft); Drawing shows vessel to original appearance; Container capacity is now 578 TEU
Sisters (also lengthened): **ZIM VALENCIA** (Is) (foreward section—ex-*Sigal*; aft section—ex-*Palmah II*); **RAQEFET** (Is)

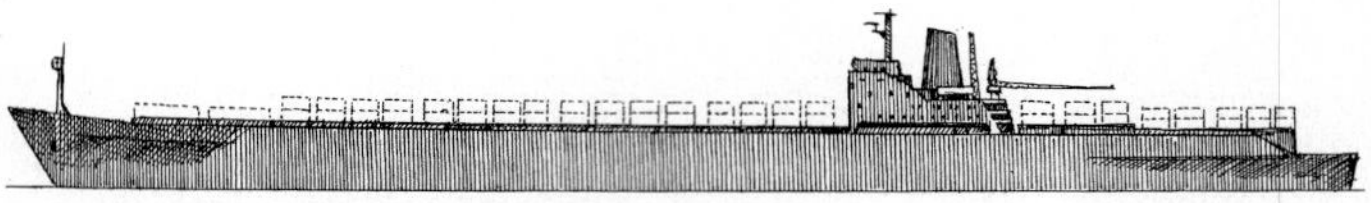

78 *M^2FNC H1*
MAERSK NANHAI Bs/Ja (Mitsui) 1972/84; Con; 57,079 grt/39,948 dwt; 289.49 × 11.61 m *(949.77 × 38.09 ft)*; TrS M (B&W); 26.25 kts; ex-*Toyama*; Lengthened by 15 m (49.21 ft) 1984 (Hyundai). Drawing shows vessel prior to this conversion

79 *M^{2}FNC H13*
WINDWARD Gr/Ja (Mitsui) 1974/78; Con; 14,400 grt/21,885 dwt; 169.46 × 9.38 m *(555.97 × 30.77 ft)*; M (B&W); 18 kts; ex-*Aristotelis*; Converted from 'Mitsui-Concord' type cargo ship 1978 (Jurong Spyd); May now be fitted with three deck cranes; Same applies to sisters—see entry number 13/9; 924 TEU; Crane aft is on starboard side
Sisters: **LEEWARD** (Gr) ex-*Aristarchos*; **HEUNG-A GRACE** (Gr) ex-*Aristandros*

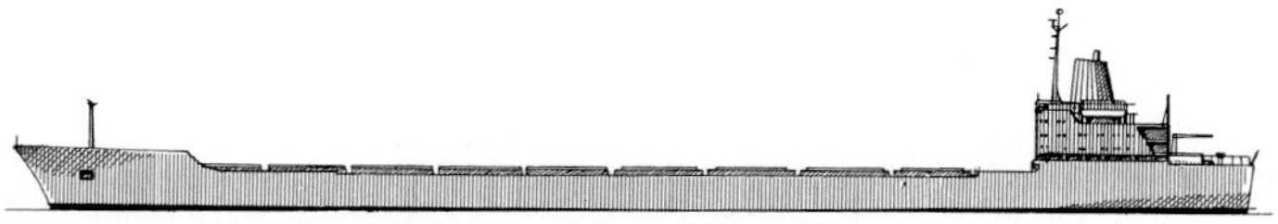

80 *M^{2}FNS H13*
DISCOVERY BAY Br/FRG (Bremer V) 1969; Con; 24,699 grt/28,225 dwt; 217.25 × 10.83 m *(712.76 × 35.53 ft)*; T (Stal-Laval); 19.5 kts; ex-*ACT 1*; 1,414 TEU
Sister: **MORETON BAY** (Br) ex-*ACT 2*; Similar: **QUEENSLAND STAR** (Bs) ex-*ACT 6* (Motor ship—Sulzer, 15 knots)

81 *M^{2}FR H1*
VILLE DE VELA Ge/Ko (Hyundai) 1994; Con; 35,595 grt/42,085 dwt; 240.39 × 11.72 m *(788.68 × 38.45 ft)*; M (B&W); 22 kts; 3,538 TEU
Sisters: **VILLE DE LIBRA** (Ge); **VILLE DE SAGITTA** (Ge)

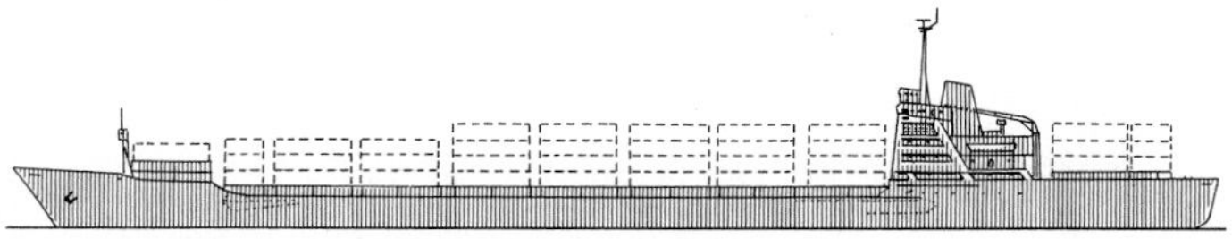

82 *M^{2}FR H13*
HUA QING HE RC/Fi (Wärtsilä) 1972/82; Con; 14,040 grt/21,465 dwt; 190.43 × 9.42 m *(624.77 × 30.91 ft)*; M (Sulzer); — kts; ex-*Hellenic Faith*; Converted from general cargo; Lengthened and widened 1982 (Riuniti); 1,200 TEU
Sisters: **HUA SHUN HE** (RC) ex-*Hellenic Wave*; **HUA LI HE** (RC) ex-*Hellenic Sun*; **ZIM MELBOURNE** (Gr) ex-*Hellenic Sea*

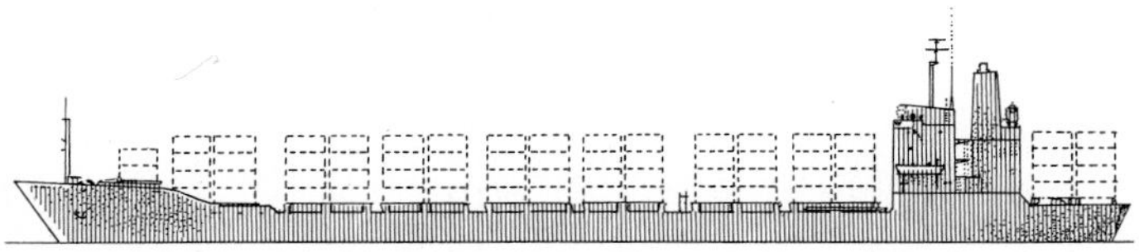

83 *M^{2}FR H13*
MERIT HK/FRG (Flensburger) 1980; Con; 15,689 grt/21,232 dwt; 170.21 × 9.65 m *(558.43 × 31.66 ft)*; M (MAN); 18.5 kts; ex-*Ambrosia*; 1,152 TEU
Sister: **KOTA MAJU** (Sg) ex-*TFL Adams*

84 *M^{2}FR–L H13*
MARE ADRIATICUM Ge/Pd (Szczecinska) 1993; Con; 9,581 grt/12,721 dwt; 149.50 × 8.26 m *(490.49 × 27.10 ft)*; M (B&W); 17.5 kts; 1,012 TEU; 'B183' type; **SIMILAR TO DRAWING NUMBER 13/38**. The latter is a sister of *Mare Adriaticum* but has deck cranes, which *Mare Adriaticum* probably does not have
Sister: **KAPITAN KONEV** (Ru)

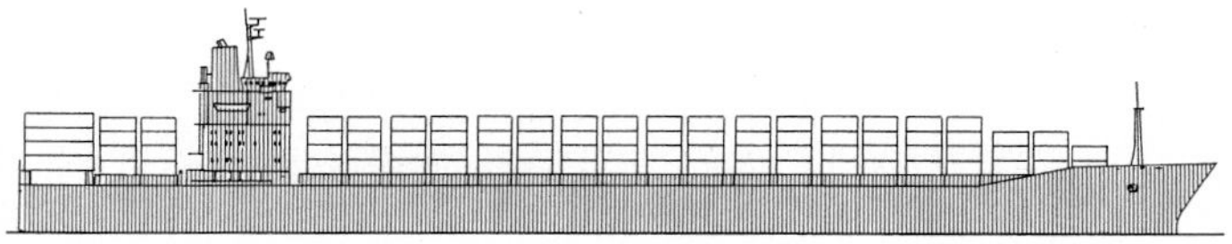

85 *M^{2}FS*
MED BARCELONA Lu/Be (Boelwerf) 1984; Con; 32,696 grt/38,981 dwt; 207.02 × 12.00 m *(679.20 × 39.37 ft)*; M (B&W); 19.5 kts; ex-*Maeterlinck*; 1,997 TEU
Sister: **MED SINGAPORE** (Lu) ex-*Verhaeren*

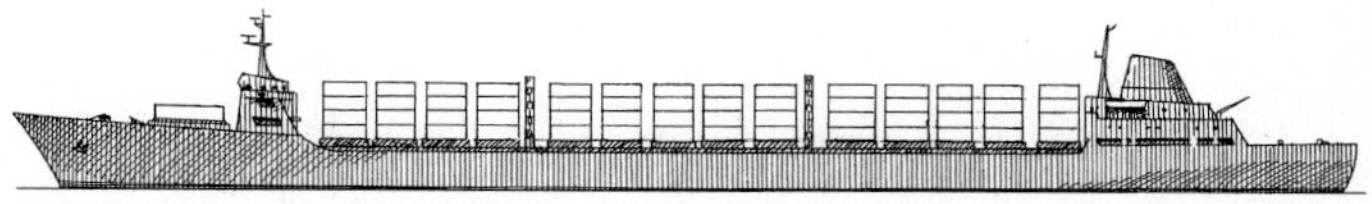

86 *M^{2}FS H1*
MANUKAI US/US (Bethlehem Steel) 1970; Con; 23,785 grt/27,107 dwt; 219.62 × 10.4 m *(720.53 × 34.12 ft)*; T (Stal-Laval); 19.75 kts; ex-*Hawaiian Enterprise*; 1,120 TEU
Sister: **MANULANI** (US) ex-*Hawaiian Progress*; Similar (bridge superstructure one deck lower): **SEA-LAND CONSUMER** (US) ex-*Australia Bear*; **SEA-LAND PRODUCER** (US) ex-*New Zealand*
Similar (bridge further foreward and one deck higher): **MAUI** (US); **KAUAI** (US)

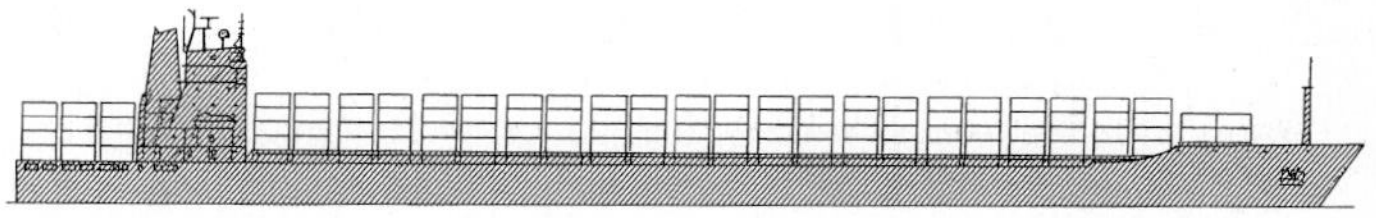

87 *M^{2}FS H1*
TAI HE RC/Br (K Govan) 1989; Con; 35,963 grt/45,987 dwt; 236.12 × 12.00 m *(774.67 × 39.37 ft)*; M (B&W); 19 kts; 2,716 TEU
Sister: **PU HE** (RC)

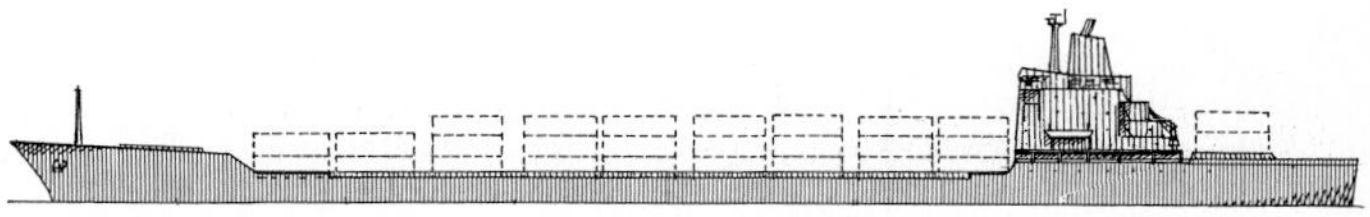

88 *M^{2}FS H13*
ZIM ELAT Is/FRG (Bremer V) 1973; Con; 25,120 grt/31,846 dwt; 218.6 × 11.51 m *(717.19 × 37.76 ft)*; T (Stal-Laval); 23.5 kts; ex-*Zim Montreal*; 1,504 TEU
Sister: **ZIM VENEZIA** (Is) ex-*Zim Hong Kong*

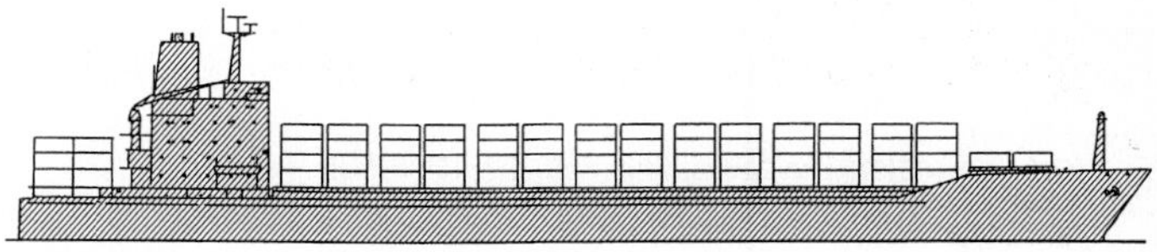

89 *M^{2}F–MR H1*
CHUN HE RC/FRG (Seebeck) 1984; Con; 19,835 grt/25,955 dwt; 170.02 × 10.72 m *(560.43 × 35.17 ft)*; M (B&W); 17 kts; 1,322 TEU
Sister: **CHAO HE** (RC)
Sisters (lengthened version—199.20 m (653 ft)): **SONG HE** (RC); **ZHUANG HE** (RC)

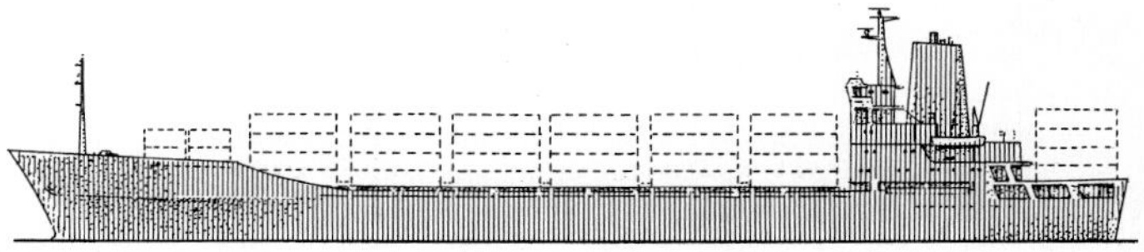

90 *M^{2}F–ND H1*
HEUNG-A STRAIT Gr/Ja (Hitachi) 1979; Con; 16,471 grt/19,621 dwt; 157.05 × 9.19 m *(515 × 30.15 ft)*; M (Sulzer); 18 kts; ex-*Alltrans Enterprise*; Lengthened to 178.60 m (585.96 ft) in 1990; Drawing shows vessel to original appearance; Container capacity is now 1,181 TEU
Sisters (also lengthened): **ZIM YOKOHAMA** (Gr) ex-*TFL Independence*; **ZIM OSAKA** (Gr) ex-*TFL Liberty*
Sisters (unlengthened): **RATANA PAILIN** (Gr) ex-*TFL Democracy*; **CHOYANG EXPRESS** (Gr) ex-*Alltrans Express*; **EAGLE NOVA** (Gr) ex-*TFL Freedom*

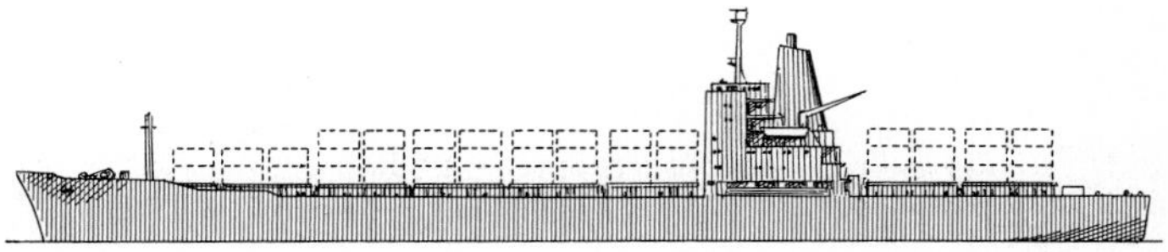

91 *MMF–S H1*
OOCL ALLIANCE Hk/Br (Smith's D) 1980; Con; 16,544 grt/17,607 dwt; 168.89 × 9.15 m *(554.1 × 30.03 ft)*; M (Sulzer); 19 kts; ex-*Manchester Venture*; 946 TEU
Sister: **EAGLE RESPECT** (Li) ex-*Manchester Vanguard*

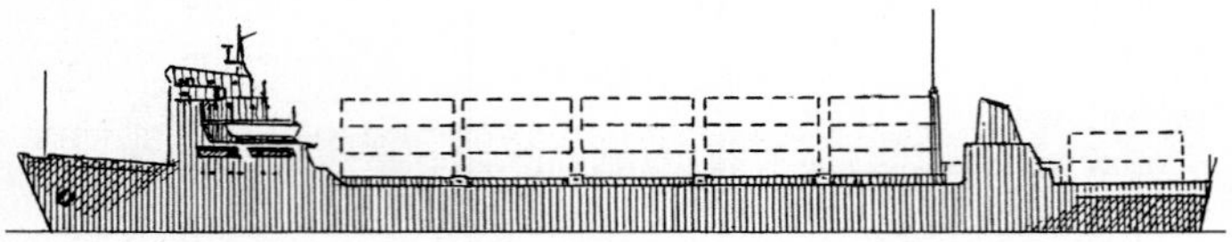

92 *M^2G H*
MERSIN SV/Ne (van der Werf) 1970; Con; 4,944 grt/4,250 dwt; 114.51 × 4.15 m *(375.69 × 13.62 ft)*; TSM (MWM); 14.5 kts; ex-*Greyhound*; 383 TEU

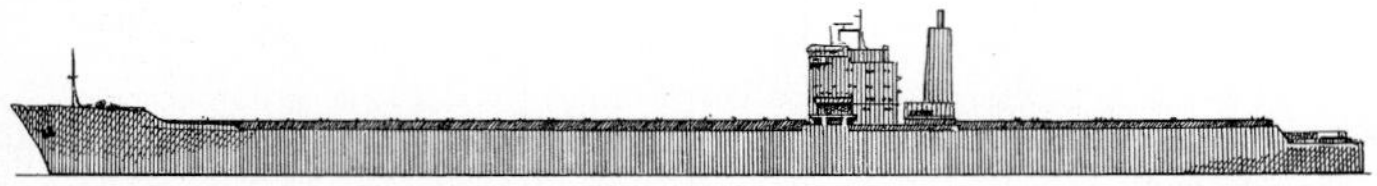

93 *M^2G H1*
ARIAKE Br/FRG (Flender) 1976; Con; 37,287 grt/34,346 dwt; 238 × 11.6 m *(781 × 38 ft)*; TSM (MAN); 26 kts

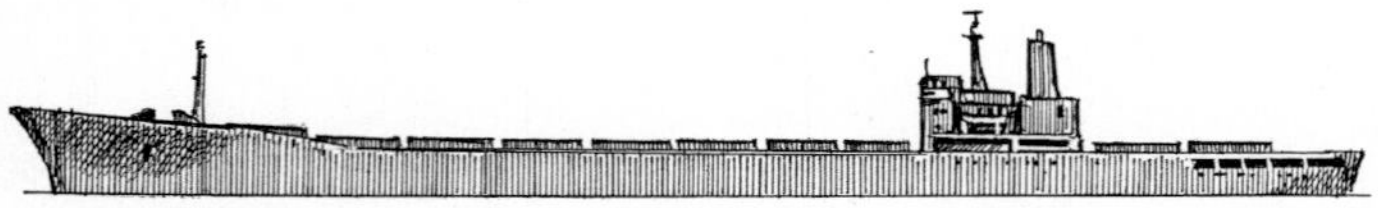

94 *M^2G H1*
MSC VIVIANA Pa/It (Italcantieri) 1971; Con; 25,827 grt/25,045 dwt; 208 × 10.4 m *(683 × 34.1 ft)*; T (Westinghouse); 23.5 kts; ex-*Taeping*
Sisters: **ZIM ALEXANDRIA** (Is) ex-*Zim Genova*; **ZIM HAIFA** (Ma); **ZIM TOKYO** (Ma); Similar: **MSC LUISA** (Pa) ex-*Mediterranea*; **MSC MARIA LAURA** (Pa) ex-*Nipponica*; **MSC DANIELA** (Pa) ex-*Africa*; **MSC FEDERICA** (Pa) ex-*Europa*; **MSC JADE** (Cy) ex-*S A Langeberg*; **MSC SABRINA** (Pa) ex-*Americana*; **MSC CHIARA** (Pa) ex-*Italica*

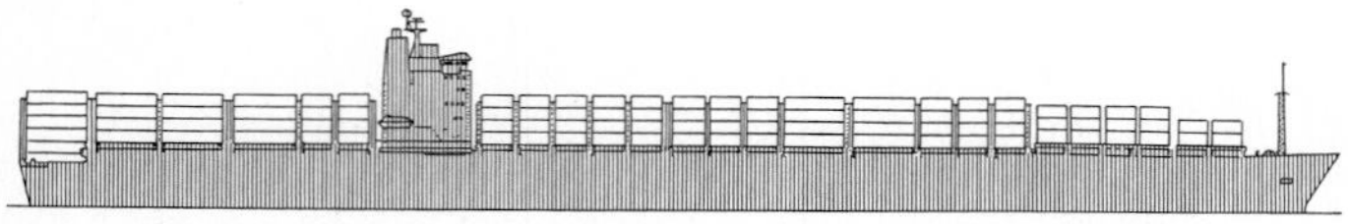

95 *M^2G H1*
NEDLLOYD EUROPA Ne/Ja (Mitsubishi HI) 1991; Con; 48,508 grt/47,157 dwt; 266.00 × 12.50 m *(872.70 × 41.01 ft)*; M (Sulzer); 21.5 kts; 3,568 TEU
Sisters: **NEDLLOYD AFRICA** (Ne); **NEDLLOYD AMERICA** (Ne); **NEDLLOYD ASIA** (Ne); **NEDLLOYD OCEANIA** (Ne); Similar (larger): **NEDLLOYD HONGKONG** (Ne); **NEDLLOYD HONSHU** (Ne)

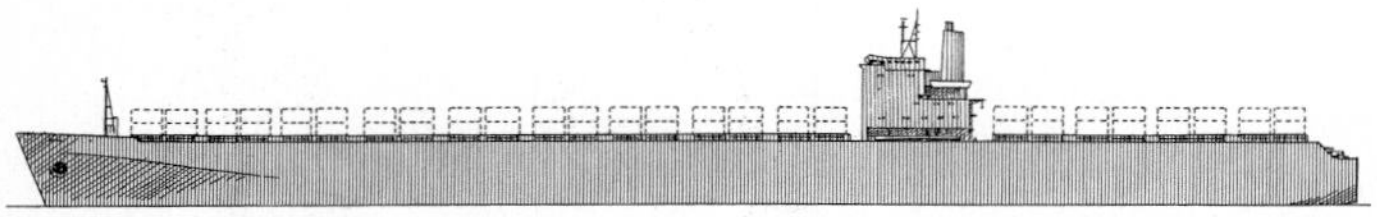

96 *M^2G H1*
TRANSVAAL Li/Be (Boelwerf) 1978; Con; 52,682 grt/50,313 dwt; 258.53 × 13 m *(848.2 × 42.65 ft)*; TSM (Sulzer); 22.75 kts; ex-*Ortelius*

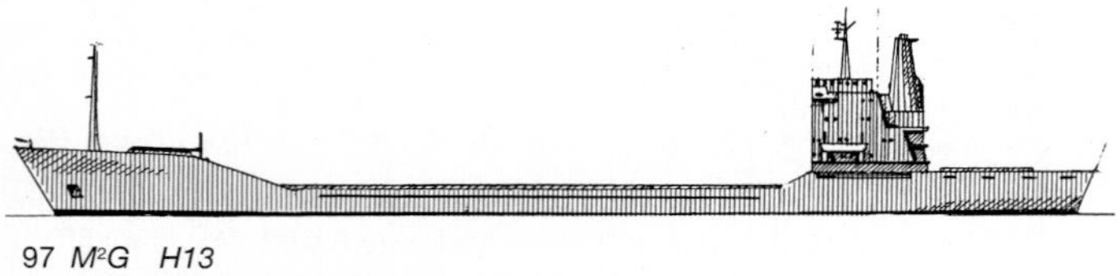

97 *M^2G H13*
HRELJIN Cro/FRG (Sietas) 1977; Con; 8,819 grt/11,031 dwt; 153.88 × 8.59 m *(504.86 × 28.18)*; M (Pielstick); 16.5 kts; 574 TEU
Sister: **SUSAK** (Cro)

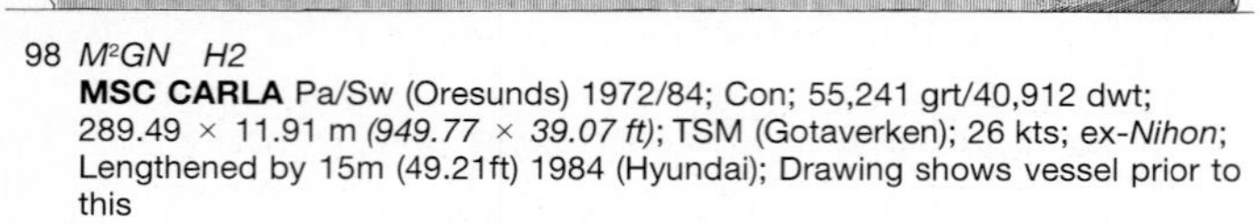

98 *M^2GN H2*
MSC CARLA Pa/Sw (Oresunds) 1972/84; Con; 55,241 grt/40,912 dwt; 289.49 × 11.91 m *(949.77 × 39.07 ft)*; TSM (Gotaverken); 26 kts; ex-*Nihon*; Lengthened by 15m (49.21ft) 1984 (Hyundai); Drawing shows vessel prior to this

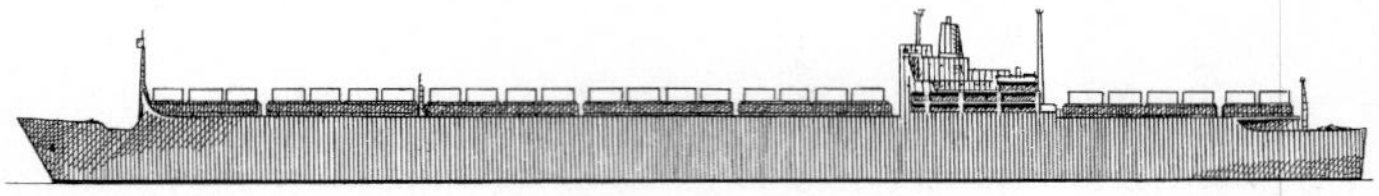

99 *M^2GN H2*
MSC CLAUDIA Pa/Ja (Mitsubishi HI) 1971; Con; 50,303 grt/35,737 dwt; 261 × 12 m *(856 × 39.1 ft)*; TSM (B&W); 24 kts; ex-*Kamakura Maru*
Sisters: **ZIM JAMAICA** (Gr) ex-*Kitano Maru*; **KURAMA** (Pa) ex-*Kurama Maru*; **SEA DOMINANCE** (Pa) ex-*Rhine Maru*

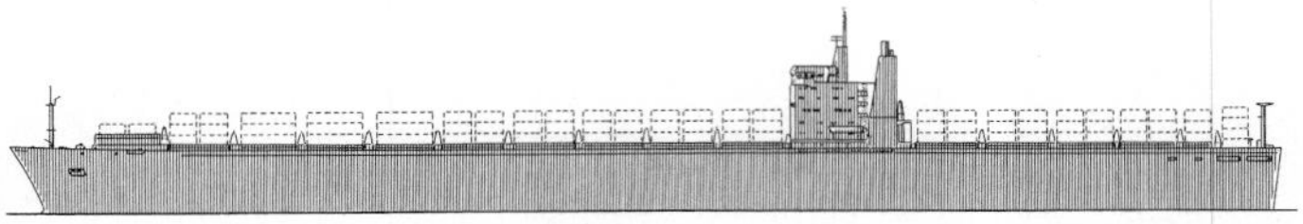

100 *M^2GS H*
FRANKFURT EXPRESS Sg/FRG (Howaldts DW) 1981; Con; 57,540 grt/51,540 dwt; 287.71 × 13.03 m *(944 × 42.75 ft)*; TSM (MAN); 23 kts

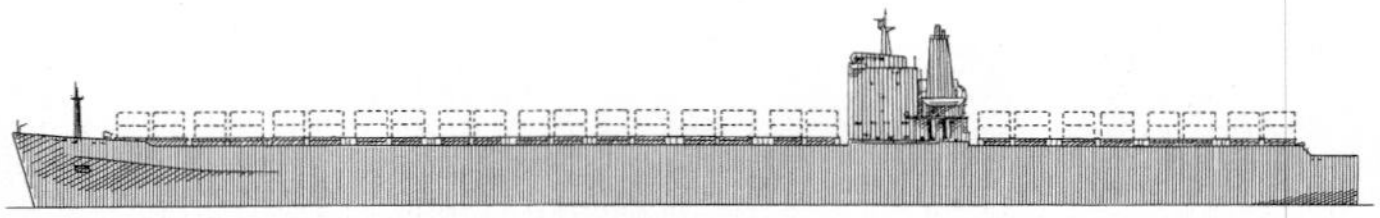

101 *MMGS H1*
HEEMSKERCK Ne/FRG (Howaldts DW) 1978; Con; 51,982 grt/49,730 dwt; 258.53 × 13.02 m *(848.2 × 42.72 ft)*; TSM (MAN); 23 kts; ex-*Transvaal*

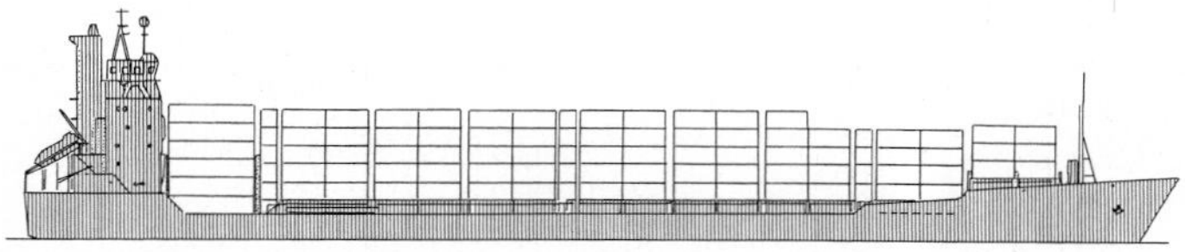

102 *M^2HFL H13*
CONTSHIP JORK Ge/Ge (Schichau See); Con; 16,236 grt/23,596 dwt; 163.33 × 10.66 m *(535.86 × 34.97 ft)*; M (B&W); 17.7 kts; 1,599 TEU; May be fitted with three cranes; 'BV 1600' type
Sister: **BUXLADY** (Ge) ex-*Contship La Spezia*; Similar (larger sisters. 'BV 1800' type. Some may be geared—see drawing number 13/3): **NEDLLOYD ZAANDAM** (Ge) ex-*Hongkong Senator*; **BUXCROWN** (Ge) ex-*Singapore Senator*; **PANAMA SENATOR** (Ge); **HANSA CARRIER** (Ge); **HANSA CLIPPER** (Ge) ex-*CGM Provence*; **CHOYANG PRIDE** (Ge) ex-*Paris Senator*; **ARABIAN SENATOR** (Ge); **JAPAN SENATOR** (Ge)

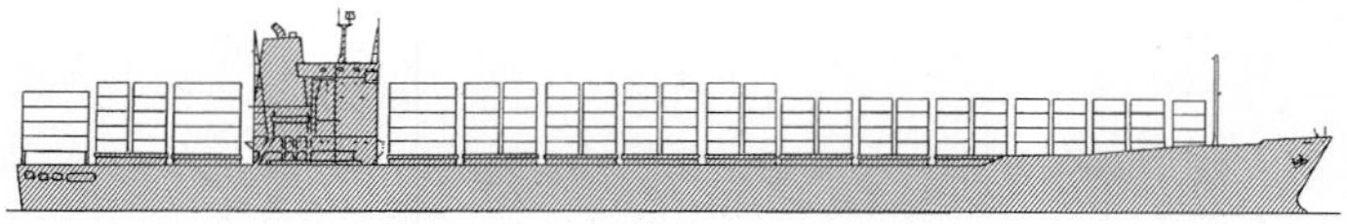

103 *M^2HFM*
GEORGE WASHINGTON BRIDGE Ja/Ja (Kawasaki) 1986; Con; 42,000 grt/40,928 dwt; 240.95 × 12.52 m *(790.52 × 41.08 ft)*; M (B&W); 22.5 kts; 2,878 TEU; Mast aft is on starboard side
Sisters: **HENRY HUDSON BRIDGE** (Ja); **MACKINAC BRIDGE** (Ja)
Possible sister: **MANHATTAN BRIDGE** (Ja); Similar (smaller—226.80 m (744 ft)): **GOLDEN GATE BRIDGE** (Ja); **TOWER BRIDGE** (Li); **BAY BRIDGE** (Li)
Similar (larger—276.52 m (907 ft). Superstructure differs): **HUMBER BRIDGE** (Ja)

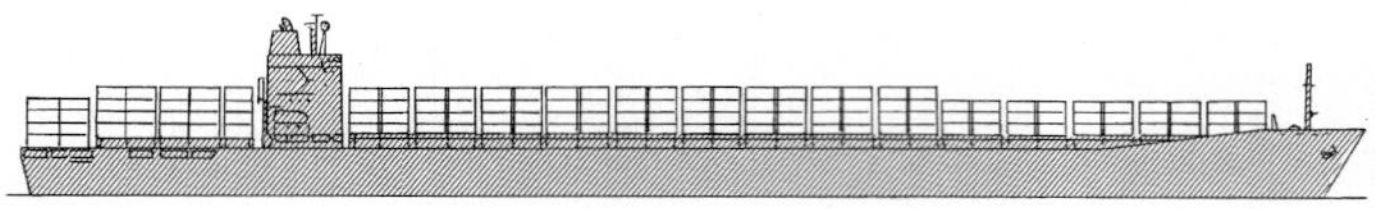

104 *M^3F H1*
LA SEINE Pa/Ja (IHI) 1988; Con; 50,030 grt/59,488 dwt; 289.52 × 13.03 m *(949.87 × 42.75 ft)*; M (Sulzer); 23.5 kts; 3,613 TEU
Sister: **KAMAKURA** (Pa)

105 *M^3F H1*
MSC INSA Pa/Ja (Mitsui) 1972; Con; 51,608 grt/35,229 dwt; 269 × 11.9 m *(883 × 39.4 ft)*; TrS M (B&W); 27.5 kts; ex-*Elbe Maru*

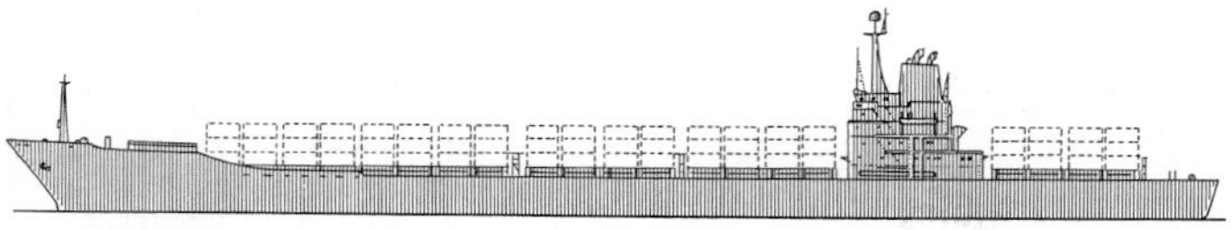

106 M^3FM *H1*
CANMAR SUCCESS Pa/Ja (Mitsui) 1982; Con; 31,570 grt/32,207 dwt; 222.51 × 11.62 m *(730 × 38.12 ft)*; M (B&W); 22.25 kts; ex-*America Maru*

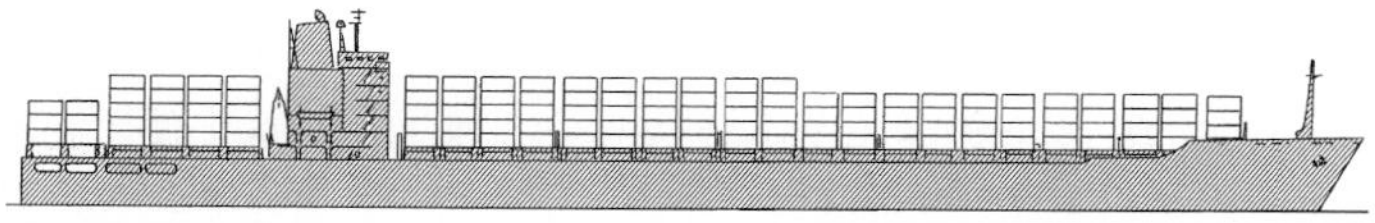

107 M^3FM *H1*
RAINBOW BRIDGE Pa/Ja (Tsuneishi) 1986; Con; 42,260 grt/45,743 dwt; 241.00 × 12.54 m *(790.68 × 41.14 ft)*; M (Sulzer); 22.5 kts; 2,875 TEU
Probable sister: **AMBASSADOR BRIDGE** (Pa)
Sister (heavier radar mast): **OOCL FRIENDSHIP** (Li) ex-*Oriental Friendship*; Similar (builder—Mitsubishi. Shorter focsles and other differences): **OOCL FAIR** (Li) ex-*Oriental Fair*; **OOCL FAITH** (Li) ex-*Oriental Faith*; **OOCL FORTUNE** (Li) ex-*Oriental Fortune*; **OOCL FREEDOM** (HK) ex-*Oriental Freedom*; **BROOKLYN BRIDGE** (Pa)

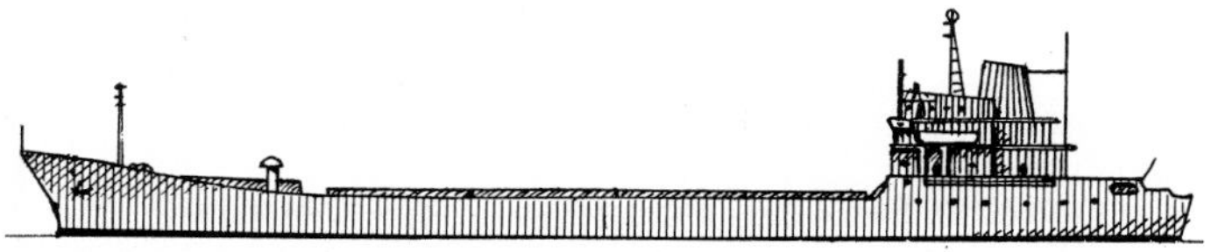

108 M^3FM *H12*
PIONIR Cro/FRG (Schuerenstedt) 1973; Con; 4,247 grt/5,580 dwt; 118.88 × 6.4 m *(390.03 × 21 ft)*; M (MAN); 15.5 kts; ex-*Maritime Champ*; 304 TEU; May be fitted with a deck crane
Similar (smaller): **MILD OCEAN** (Pa) ex-*Maritime Ace*

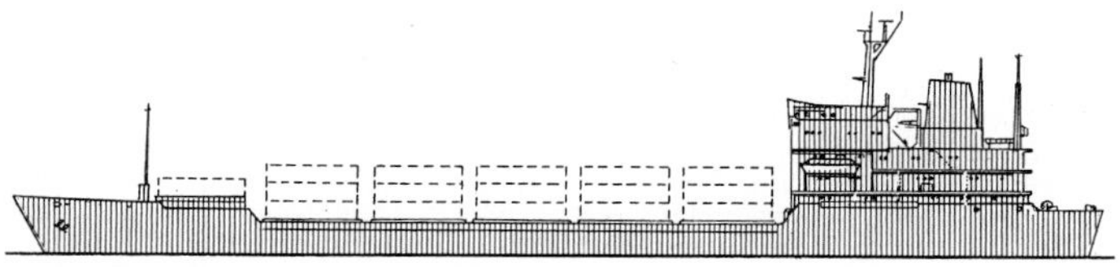

109 M^3FM^2 *H13*
AUSMA LEADER Cy/Bu (G Dimitrov) 1981; Con; 9,548 grt/9,141 dwt; 148.67 × 7.65 m *(488 × 25.1 ft)*; M (B&W); 18 kts; ex-*Simon Bolivar*; 490 TEU
Sisters: **AUSMA TRADER** (Cy) ex-*Pyer Puyyad*; **GENERAL GORBATOV** (Uk); **KAPITAN ARTYUKH** (Ru); **KAPITAN LYASHENKO** (Ru); **KAPITAN KUD** (Uk); **KRASNOGVARDEYETS** (Ru); **KHUDOZHNIK N RERIKH** (Ru); **PAVEL MIZIKEVICH** (Uk); **YURIY LEVITAN** (Uk); **MEDSKY** (Uk) ex-*Leninskiy Pioner*; **STOYKO PEEV** (Bu); **ROSTOV NA DONU** (Ru); **STANKO STAIKOV** (Bu)

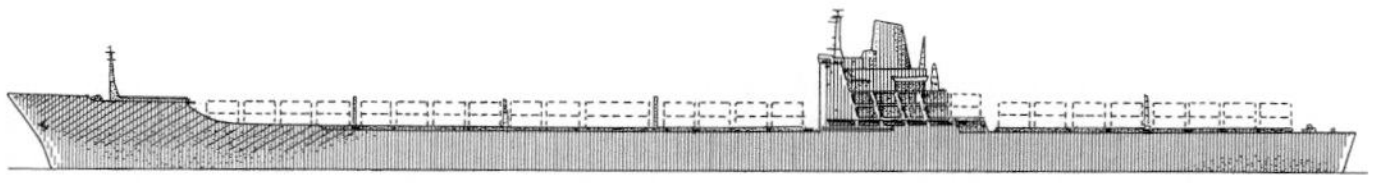

110 M^3FN *H1*
AN HE RC/Ja (Mitsui) 1973; Con; 39,240 grt/33,034 dwt; 263.28 × 11.5 m *(863.78 × 37.73 ft)*; TSM (B&W); 26 kts; ex-*New Jersey Maru*

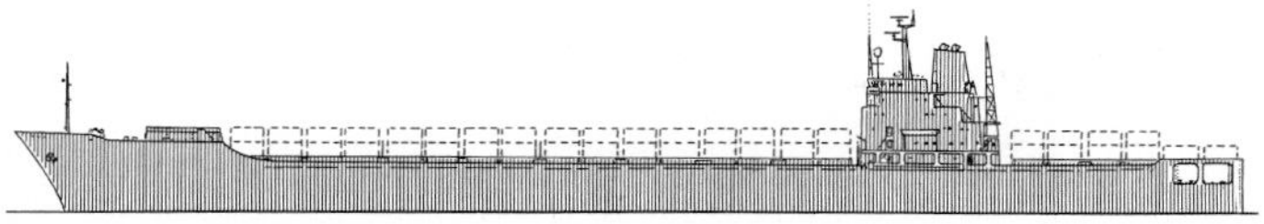

111 M^3FN *H1*
CALIFORNIA CERES Pa/Ja (Hitachi) 1981; Con; 31,694 grt/28,615 dwt; 221.5 × 11.03 m *(727 × 36.19 ft)*; M (B&W); 22.75 kts; ex-*Shin-Kashu Maru*
Similar: **MAERSK YOKOHAMA** (Sg) ex-*Shin-Beishu Maru*

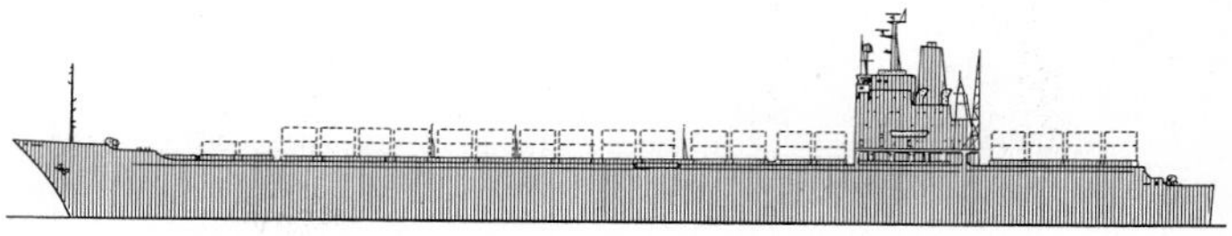

112 M^3FN *H1*
NICHIGOH MARU Ja/Ja (Hitachi) 1980; Con; 36,912 grt/32,023 dwt; 217.18 × 11.53 m *(712 × 37.83 ft)*; M (B&W); 21 kts

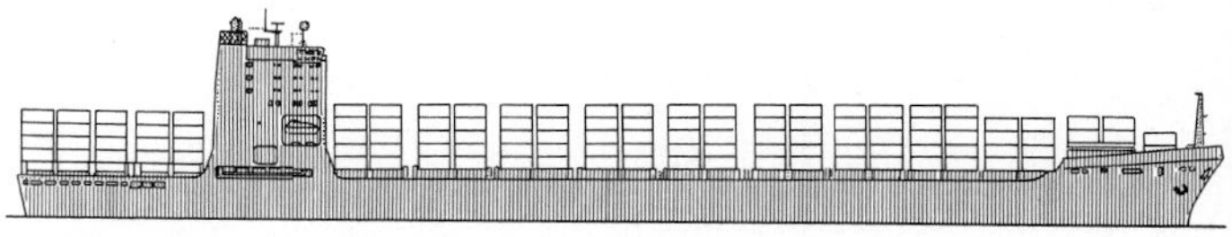

113 M^3G *H1*
CGM LA PEROUSE Kn/Ko (Samsung) 1988; Con; 36,389 grt/42,513 dwt; 228.85 × 12.40 m *(750.82 × 40.68 ft)*; M (Sulzer); 20.5 kts; 2,505 TEU

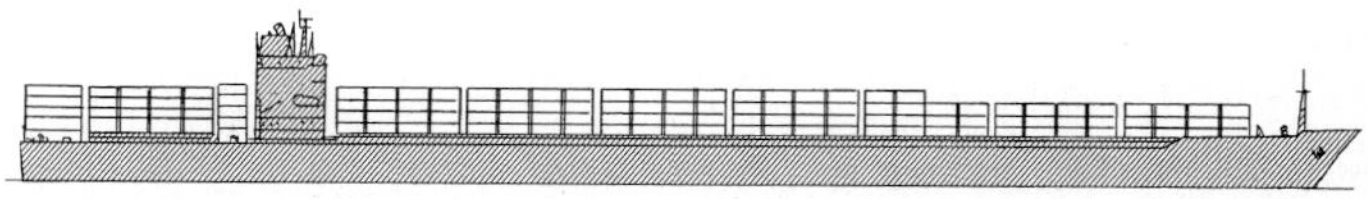

114 M^4FM *H1*
KAGA Ja/Ja (Koyo) 1988; Con; 51,047 grt/59,533 dwt; 288.31 × 13.03 m *(945.90 × 42.75 ft)*; M (B&W); 23 kts; 3,618 TEU
Possible sister: **KITANO** (Ja)

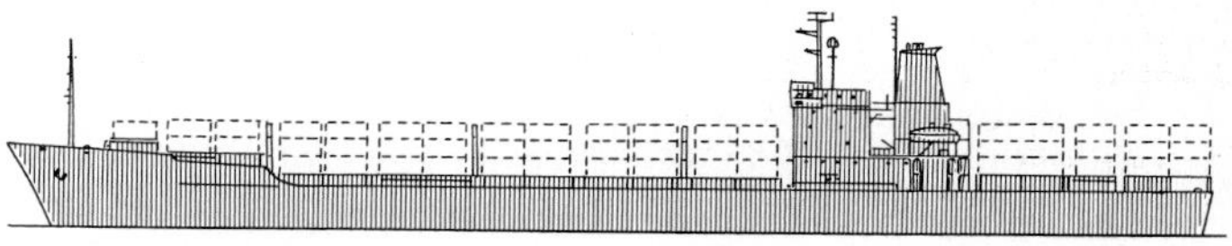

115 $M^3M–F$ *H1*
MECKLENBURG Ge/DDR (Warnow) 1987; Con; 18,353 grt/19,710 dwt; 172.42 × 10.40 m *(565.68 × 34.12 ft)*; M (MAN); 17 kts; ex-*Ernst Thalmann*; 1,164 TEU; 'SATURN' type
Sisters: **BRANDENBURG** (Ge) ex-*Wilhelm Pieck*; **SACHSEN** (Ge) ex-*Otto Grotewohl*; **SHANGHAI EXPRESS** (Ge) ex-*Walter Ulbricht*

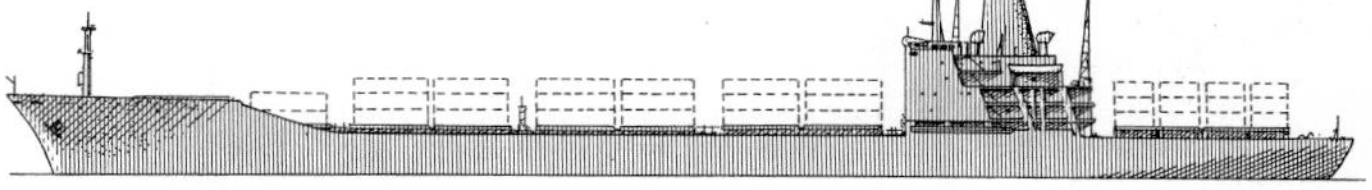

116 M^2NFN *H1*
MONT BLANC MARU Ja/Ja (Mitsui) 1974; Con; 29,955 grt/28,849 dwt; 217 × 11.71 m *(711.94 × 38.42 ft)*; M (B&W); 23 kts

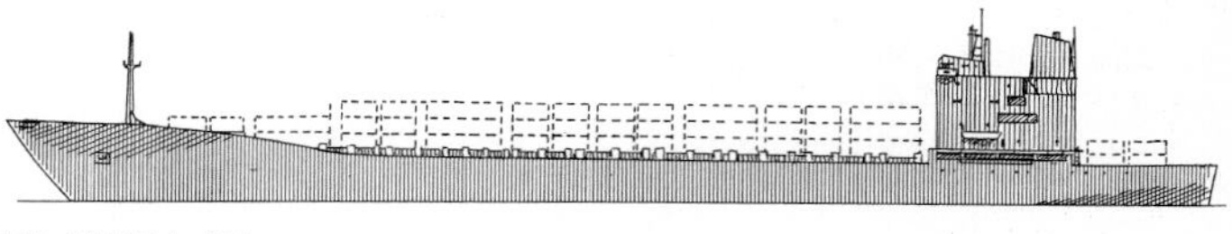

117 M^2NFN *H1*
MSC DOMINIQUE Pa/Fr (CNIM) 1977; Con; 27,721 grt/27,653 dwt; 208.13 × 10.39 m *(682.84 × 34.09 ft)*; T (GEC); 24 kts; ex-*Chevalier Valbelle*; 1,482 TEU
Sisters (lengthened to 252 m (827 ft) by Hyundai Mipo in 1981): **ZIM PUSAN** (Gr) ex-*Chevalier Roze*; **ZIM LIVORNO** (Gr) ex-*Chevalier Paul*; **MSC MAEVA** (Pa) ex-*Mercator* (motor ship—Sulzer); Similar (superstructure different. Lengthened as previous group): **OOCL EXECUTIVE** (Li) ex-*Oriental Executive* (lengthened 1981; Motor ship); **OOCL EDUCATOR** (Li) Launched as *Oriental Chevalier* (lengthened 1982; Motor ship); **OOCL EXPLORER** (Li) ex-*Oriental Statesman* (lengthened 1982; Motor ship)

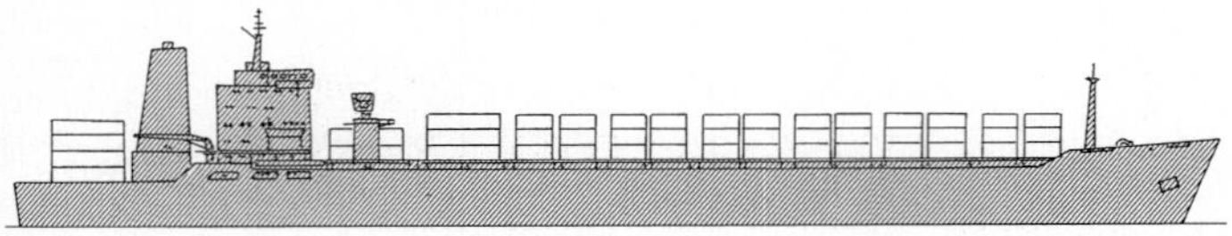

118 *M²SF H1*
CARIBIA EXPRESS Gr/Pd (Gdanska) 1976; Con; 27,971 grt/27,828 dwt; 203.99 × 10 m *(669.26 × 32.81 ft)*; M (Sulzer); 21 kts; 'B-463' type; 1,202 TEU; Gantry crane may be removed (also appears in Section 13)
Sisters: **SIERRA EXPRESS** (Gr) ex-*Cordillera Express*; **URUGUAY EXPRESS** (Ur) ex-*Allemania Express*; **OOCL BEACON** (Cy) ex-*America Express*; **LASER STREAM** (Gr) ex-*Adviser*; **CARAIBE** (Gr); **NEDLLOYD NEERLANDIA** (Ne) ex-*Hollandia*; **AUTHOR** (Br); **WEALTHY RIVER** (Pa) ex-*Astronomer*

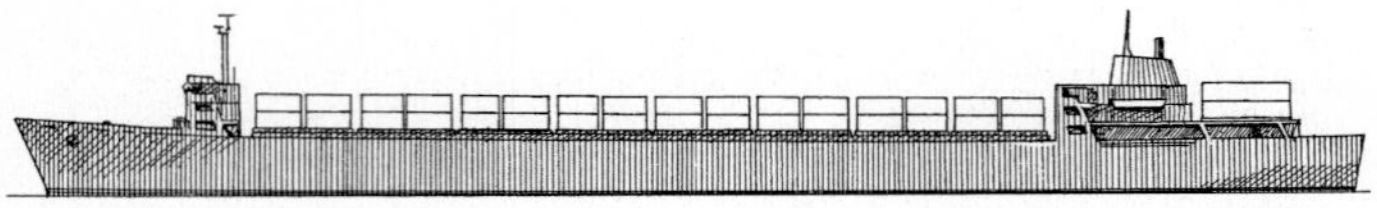

119 *MM–F H*
EXPORT FREEDOM US/US (Bath) 1973; Con; 17,904 grt/16,605 dwt; 185.93 × 9.63 m *(610.01 × 31.59 ft)*; T (GEC); 21 kts; 1,070 TEU
Sisters: **EXPORT PATRIOT** (US); **ARGONAUT** (US); **RESOLUTE** (US) (Government owned)

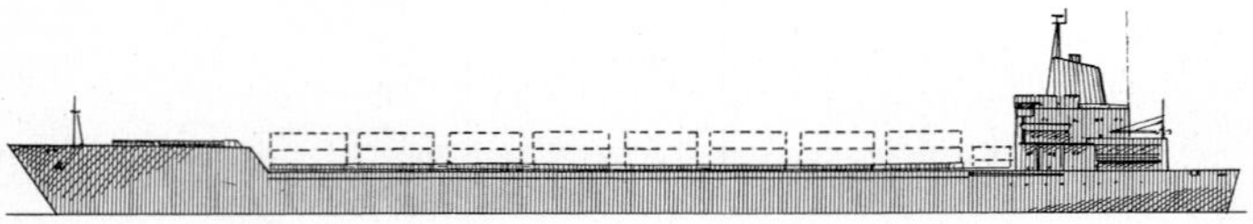

120 *MM–F H1*
ADABELLE LYKES US/FRG (Bremer V) 1968; Con; 16,757 grt/15,400 dwt; 201.00 × 7.89 m *(659.45 × 25.89 ft)*; M (MAN); 19.5 kts; ex-*Mosel Express*; Lengthened 1973; 1,104 TEU
Similar (taller funnel): **SHELDON LYKES** (US) ex-*Alster Express*
Similar (unlengthened—170.87 m (560 ft): **LONG HAI HE** (RC) ex-*Main Express*; **XING HAI HE** (RC) ex-*Rhein Express*

121 *MM–F H1*
COLUMBUS AUSTRALIA Ge/FRG (Howaldts DW) 1971; Con; 21,278 grt/ 22,435 dwt; 193.94 × 10.85 m *(636.29 × 35.6 ft)*; M (B&W); 18.5 kts; 1,380 TEU; Gantry crane probably removed
Sisters: **COLUMBUS AMERICA** (Ge); **COLUMBUS NEW ZEALAND** (Ge)

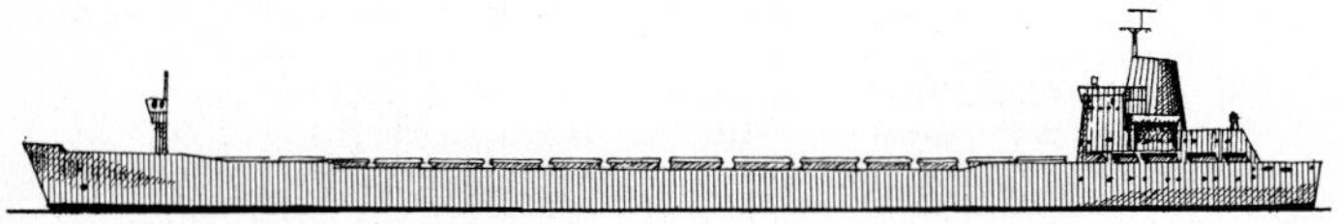

122 *MM–F H1*
OOCL AWARD Li/Br (Smith's D) 1974; Con; 12,102 grt/13,867 dwt; 161.47 × 8.26 m *(529.76 × 27.1 ft)*; M (Pielstick); 19.5 kts; ex-*Manchester Reward*; 584 TEU

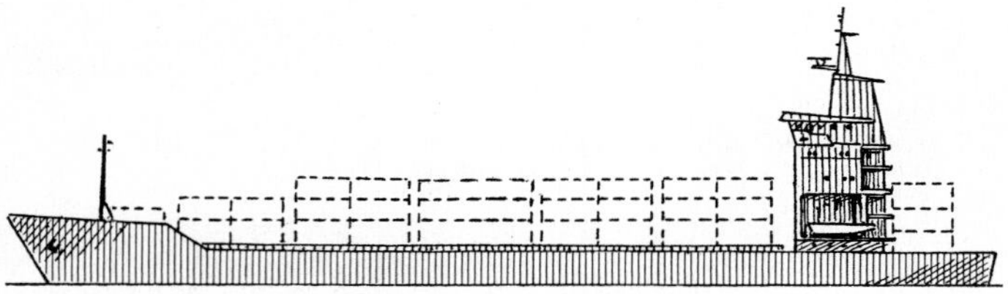

123 *MM–F H1*
PELFISHER Gr/Gr (Salamis) 1977; Con; 4,345 grt/6,107 dwt; 102.16 × 5.01 m *(394 × 16.44 ft)*; M (KHD); 16 kts; ex-*Meteor II*; 384 TEU; May be fitted with a deck crane—see entry in Section 7
Sister: **MANASLU** (Li) ex-*Meteor 1*

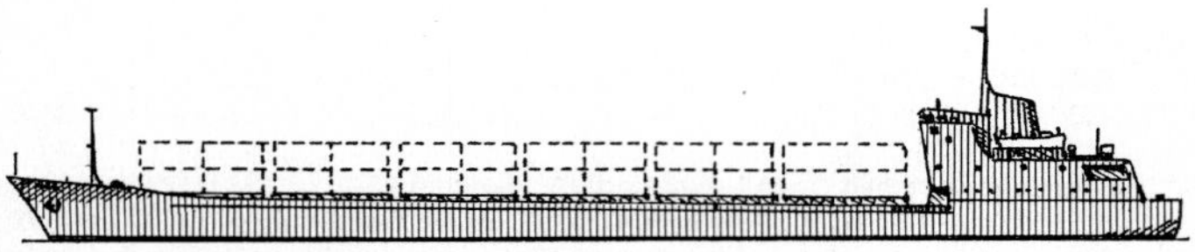

124 *MM–F H1*
SHERYN M SV/Br (Doxford & S) 1966/77; Con; 3,964 grt/4,826 dwt; 118.73 × 6.5 m *(389.53 × 21.33 ft)*; M (MAN); 14.75 kts; ex-*Baltic Vanguard*; Converted from cargo and lengthened 1977 (Middle Docks); 213 TEU

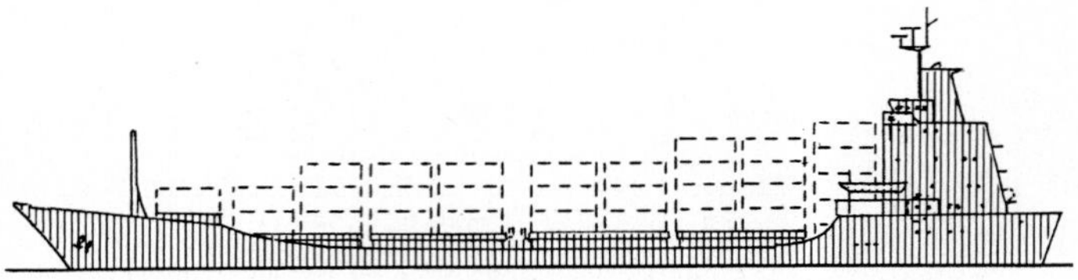

125 *MM–F H13*
FAIR COSMOS Pa/FRG (Elsflether) 1980; Con; 4,146 grt/5,983 dwt; 102.9 × 6.98 m *(337.6 × 22.9 ft)*; M (MAN); 14 kts; ex-*Carald*; 293 TEU

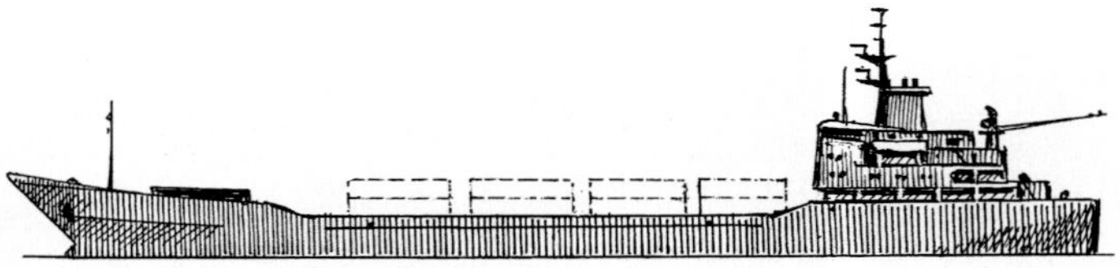

126 *MM–FC H13*
ALEKSANDR FADEYEV Ru/Ru (Kherson) 1973; Con; 6,478 grt/6,458 dwt; 130.21 × 7.5 m *(427 × 24.61 ft)*; M (B&W); 16.25 kts; 304 TEU
Sisters: **ALEKSANDR PROKOFYEV** (Ru); **ALEKSANDR TVARDOVSKIY** (Ru); **MIKHAIL PRISHVIN** (Ru); **MIKHAIL SVETLOV** (Ru)

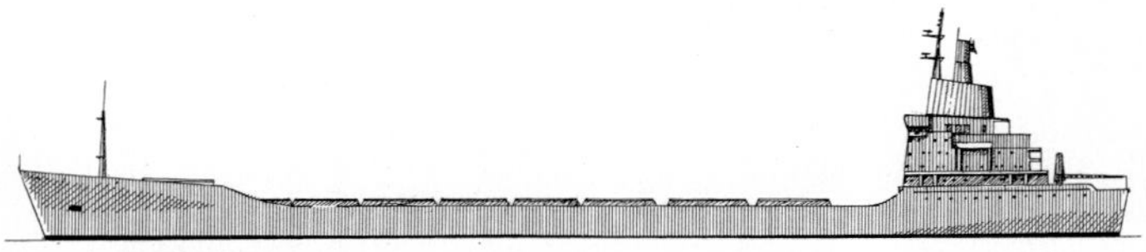

127 *MM–FD H13*
ENCOUNTER BAY Br/FRG (Howaldts DW) 1969; Con; 27,835 grt/ 28,794 dwt; 227.31 × 10.69 m *(745.77 × 35.07 ft)*; M (B&W); 19.5 kts; 1,578 TEU
Sisters: **BOTANY BAY** (Br); **DIRECT KEA** (Bs) ex-*Discovery Bay*; **FLINDERS BAY** (Br); **DIRECT KOOKABURRA** (Bs) ex-*Moreton Bay*

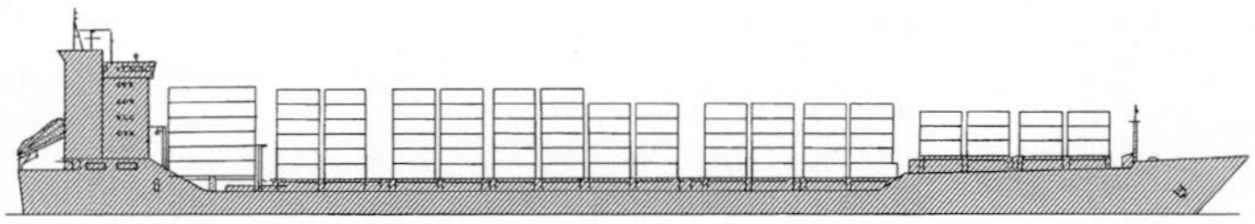

128 *MM–FL H13*
CAPE NATAL Li/Pd (Gdanska) 1995; Con; 15,800 grt/22,800 dwt; 175.00 × 9.00 m *(574.15 × 29.53 ft)*; M (B&W); 20.4 kts; 1,500 TEU; 'B191' type; Funnel is on starboard side. There is also a structure on the port side, giving the impression of twin funnels
Sisters: **CAPE NEGRO** (—); **CAPE NELSON** (Cy); **CAPE NORMAN** (Cy); **MASOVIA** (Li)

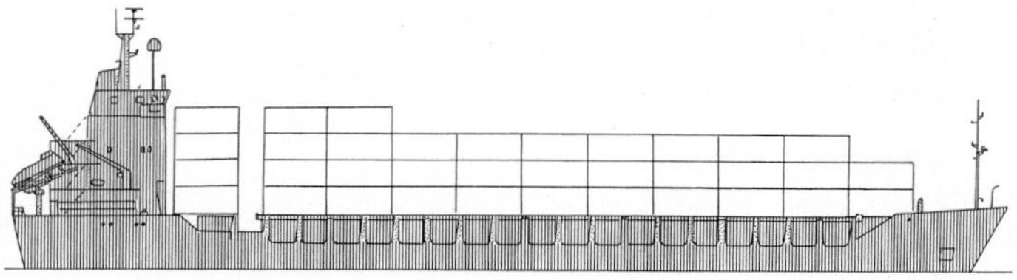

129 *MM–FL H13*
RUTH BORCHARD Ge/Tu (Marmara) 1991; C/Con; 3,469 grt/4,706 dwt; 96.65 × 6.01 m *(317.09 × 19.72 ft)*; M (MaK); 14 kts; 343 TEU
Sister: **JUDITH BORCHARD** (Ge)

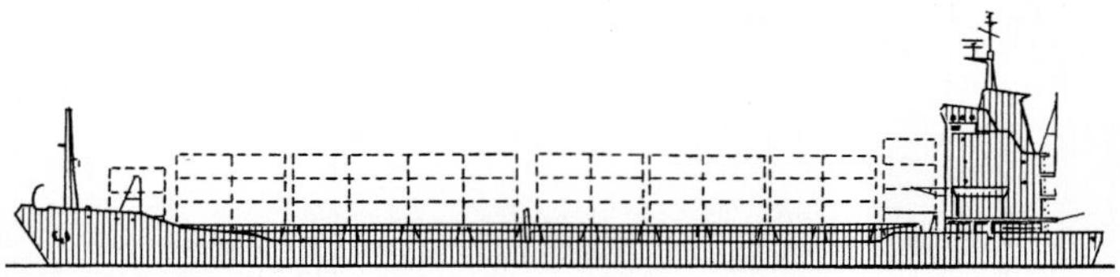

130 *MM–FN H1*
GRAND RIVER Pa/Sg (Singapore SB) 1979; Con; 5,262 grt/7,635 dwt; 120.53 × 6.5 m *(395 × 21.33 ft)*; M (Mitsubishi); 13.5 kts; ex-*Tauria*; 431 TEU
Sisters: **JIN PENG** (RC) ex-*Nordwelle*; **TRADE RANK** (Cy) ex-*Nordwind*; **TRADE LUCK** (Cy) ex-*Nordheide*; **NORDBAY** (Cy); **NORDSTAR** (Cy)
Probable sister: **NORDSUND** (Cy) ex-*Nordsund*; Possibly similar: **JIN FAN** (RC) ex-*Pegasia*; **ORIENT PROSPERITY** (In) ex-*Este*

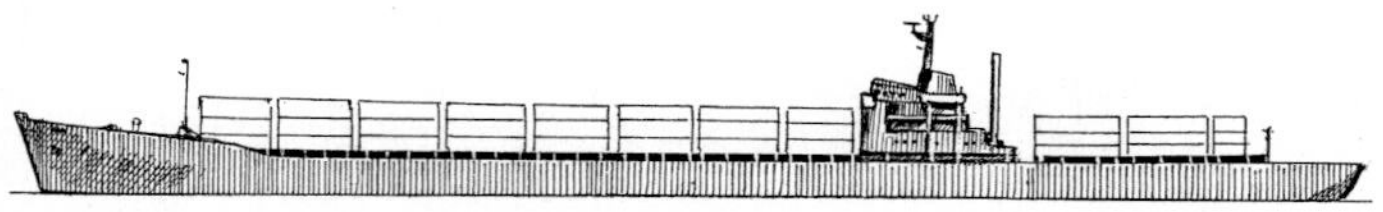

131 *M^2–FN H1*
HUMACAO US/US (Sun SB) 1969; Con; 19,046 grt/22,582 dwt; 214 × 9.8 m *(701 × 32.2 ft)*; T (GEC); 22 kts; ex-*American Lancer*
Sisters: **SEA-LAND CHALLENGER** (US) ex-*American Legion*; **SEA-LAND DISCOVERY** (US) ex-*American Liberty*; **SEA-LAND CRUSADER** (US) ex-*American Lark*; **MAYAGUEZ** (US) ex-*American Lynx*; **GUAYAMA** ex-*American Astronaut*; **NUEVO SAN JUAN** (US) ex-*American Apollo*; **CAROLINA** (US) ex-*American Aquarius*

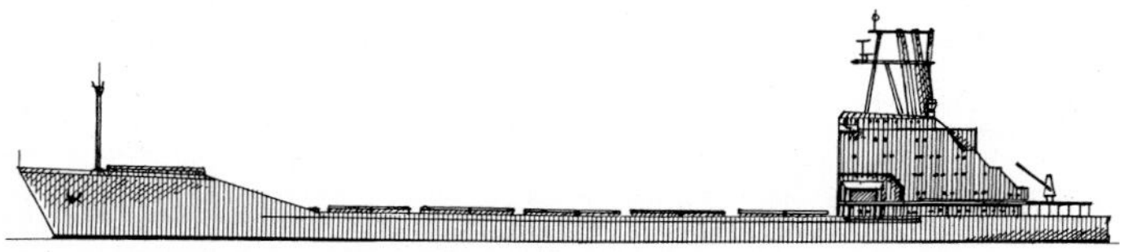

132 *MM–FR H1*
KOTA BERLIAN Sg/FRG (A G 'Weser') 1976; Con; 15,011 grt/15,790 dwt; 161.02 × 9.42 m *(528.28 × 30.91 ft)*; M (MAN); 18.5 kts; ex-*Columbus Victoria*; 750 TEU
Sisters: **KOTA BERKAT** (Sg) ex-*Columbus Virginia*; **KOTA BERANI** (Sg) ex-*Columbus Wellington*

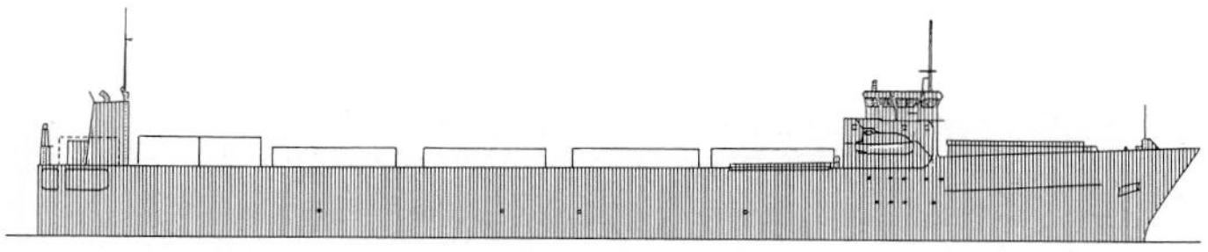

133 *MM–FS H1*
BELL PIONEER Ih/Ja (Teraoka) 1990; Con; 6,111 grt/4,833 dwt; 114.50 × 5.92 m *(375.66 × 19.42 ft)*; M (Wärtsilä); 14.5 kts; 303 TEU; No hatch covers on holds 2, 3 and 4
Probably similar: **EURO POWER** (Ih)

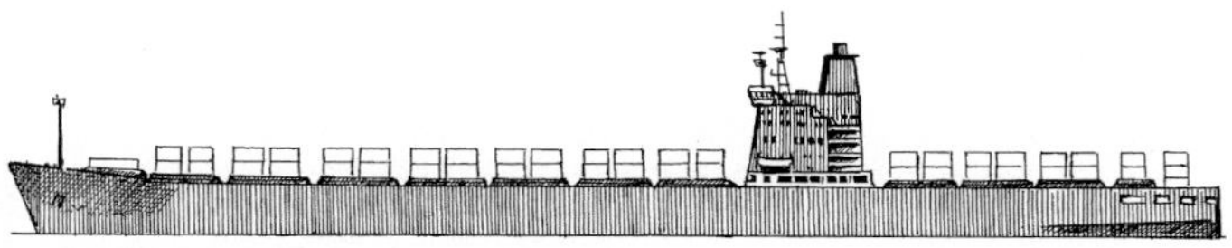

134 *MNMF H*
AUSTRALIAN VENTURE Au/FRG (Bremer V) 1977; Con; 44,154 grt/ 39,454 dwt; 249 × 11 m *(820 × 37 ft)*; TSM (MAN); 24 kts
Sisters: **PALLISER BAY** (Br) ex-*Act 7*; **RESOLUTION BAY** (Br); **MAIRANGI BAY** (Br); **NEW ZEALAND PACIFIC** (HK)

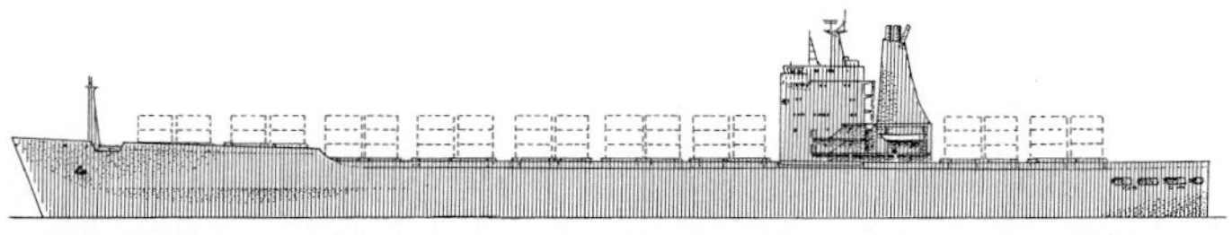

135 *MNMF H1*
FORT ROYAL Fr/Fr (Dunkerque-Normandie) 1979; Con; 32,671 grt/ 30,998 dwt; 210 × 11.02 m *(688.98 × 36.15 ft)*; TSM (Pielstick); 22 kts; carries refrigerated containers
Sister: **FORT FLEUR d'EPEE** (Fr)

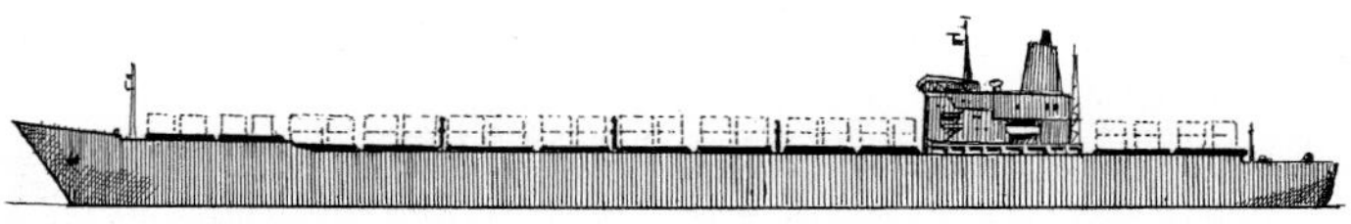

136 *MNMFN H1*
IBN MAJID Pa/Ja (Hitachi) 1972; Con; 36,585 grt/30,576 dwt; 246 × 10.5 m *(807 × 34.7 ft)*; M (B&W); 19.5 kts; ex-*Tohbei Maru*

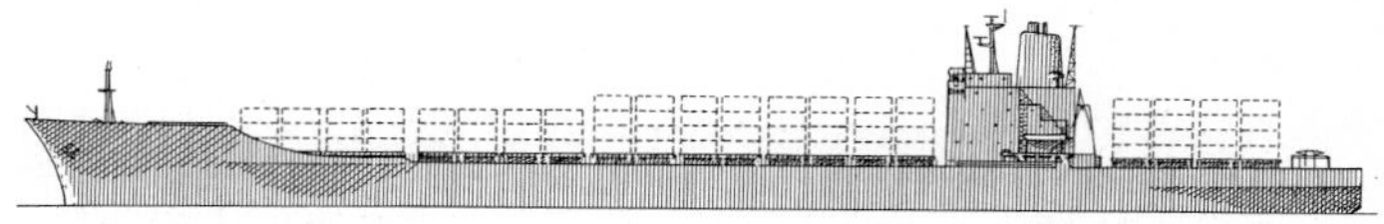

137 *MNMFN H1*
OOCL ENVOY Li/Tw (China SB) 1979; Con; 37,238 grt/39,766 dwt; 221.7 × 11.5 m *(727.36 × 37.73 ft)*; M (Sulzer); 23 kts; ex-*China Container*; lengthened 1982; Length is now 250.55 m (822 ft); Drawing shows original appearance
Similar (unlengthened): **MSC CLORINDA** (Pa) ex-*Ace Concord;* **MSC LAUREN** (Pa) ex-*Oriental Patriot*; **NEPTUNE PEARL** (Sg); **NEPTUNE CORAL** (Sg)
Similar—shorter: **MING GALAXY** (Tw); **MING GLORY** (Tw); **MING MOON** (Tw); **MING OCEAN** (Tw); **MING STAR** (Tw); **MING SUN** (Tw); **MED GENOVA** (Tw) ex-*Ming Universe*; **MING COMFORT** (Tw); **MED KEELUNG** (Tw) ex-*Ming Energy*; **MING FORTUNE** (Tw); **MED HONG KONG** (Tw) ex-*Ming Longevity*
Similar (shorter. Builder IHI): **VAAL** (SV) ex-*S A Vaal*
Similar (231 m): **NEPTUNE AMBER** (Sg); **NEPTUNE CRYSTAL** (Sg); **NEPTUNE DIAMOND** (Sg)
Similar (260 m): **PRESIDENT EISENHOWER** (US) ex-*Neptune Garnet*; **PRESIDENT F D ROOSEVELT** (US) ex-*Neptune Jade*

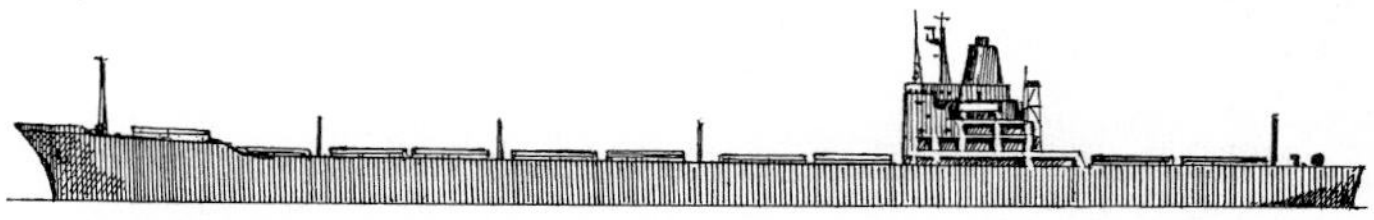

138 *MNMFN H1*
PACIFIC ARROW Ja/Ja (IHI) 1973; Con; 30,576 grt/26,836 dwt; 219 × 11 m *(719 × 36.1 ft)*; M (Sulzer); 22 kts

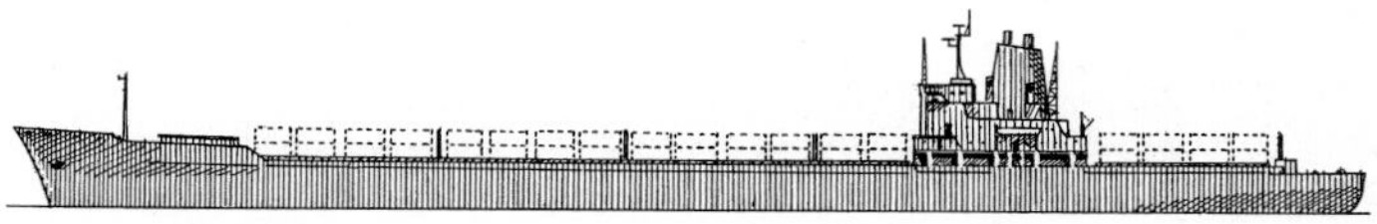

139 *MNMFN H1*
SEA RANGER Mr/Ja (Hitachi) 1974; Con; 24,415 grt/25,297 dwt; 212.99 × 10.82 m *(698.79 × 35.5 ft)*; M (B&W); 22.5 kts; ex-*Yamashin Maru*

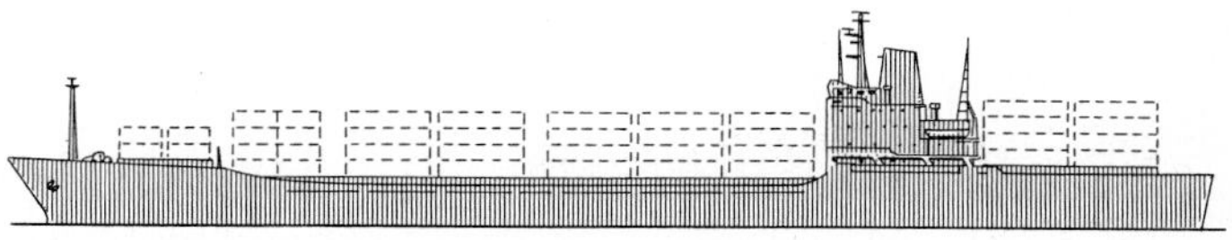

140 *MNMFN H13*
UNI-SHINE Tw/Ja (Hayashikane) 1976/77; Con; 14,153 grt/15,764 dwt; 174.33 × 9.4 m *(572 × 31 ft)*; M (B&W); 20 kts; ex-*Ever Shine*; Lengthened 1977
Sisters: **UNI-SPRING** (Tw) ex-*Ever Spring*; **UNI-SUMMIT** (Tw) ex-*Ever Summit*; **UNI-SUPERB** (Tw) ex-*Ever Superb*

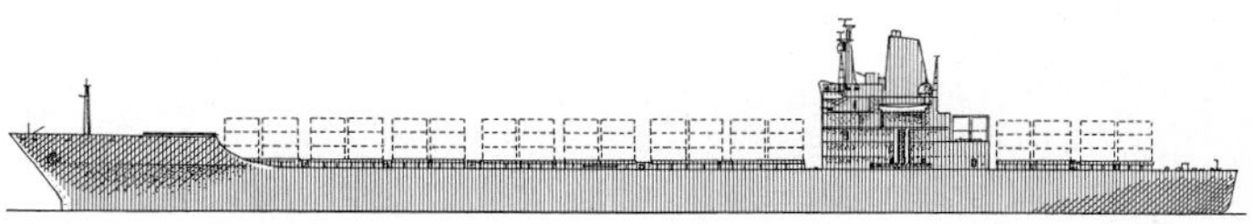

141 *MNMF–CN H1*
WELLINGTON MARU Ja/Ja (Mitsui) 1979; Con; 32,163 grt/29,888 dwt; 216.3 × 11.52 m *(709.64 × 37.8 ft)*; M (B&W); 22.3 kts; ex-*Canberra Maru*

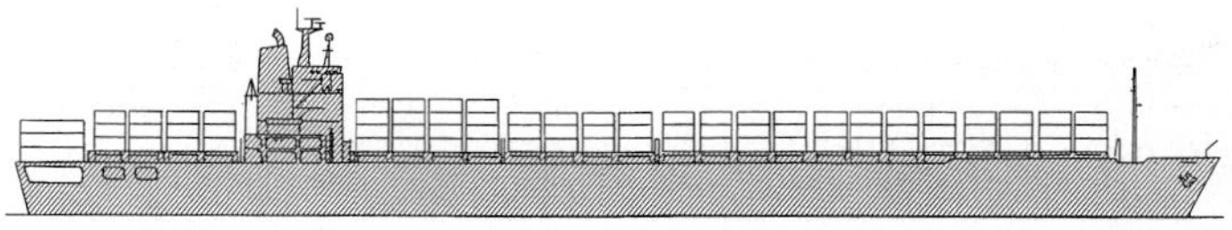

142 *MNMF–N H1*
ALLIGATOR FORTUNE Li/Ja (Tsuneishi) 1986; Con; 40,354 grt/41,539 dwt; 226.42 × 11.62 m *(742.85 × 38.12 ft)*; M (Sulzer); 19.5 kts; 2,512 TEU

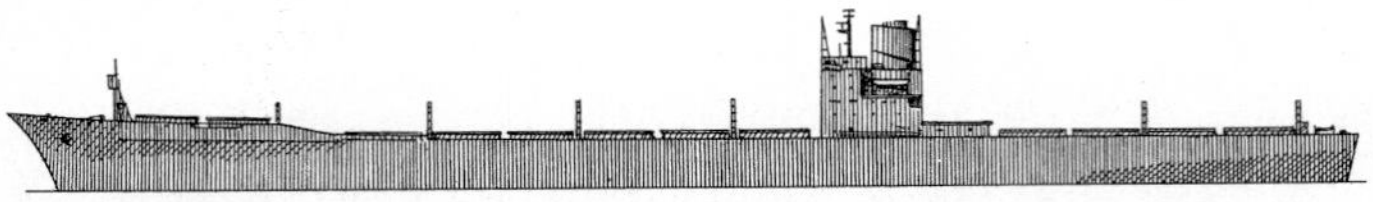

143 *MNMF–SN H1*
MSC SAMIA Pa/Ja (Kawasaki) 1973; Con; 40,944 grt/35,480 dwt; 265 × 11.9 m *(868 × 39 ft)*; TSM (MAN); 26.5 kts; ex-*Verrazano Bridge*
Similar: **POL AMERICA** (Pa) ex-*Seven Seas Bridge*; **MSC RITA** (Pa) ex-*Hong Kong Container*

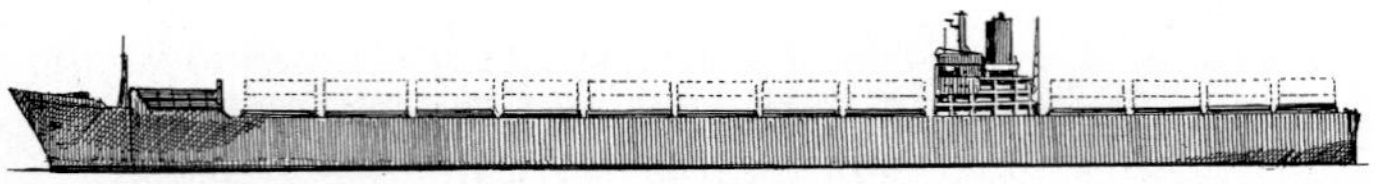

144 *MNMGN H1*
KANG HE RC/Ja (Mitsubishi HI) 1972; Con; 38,826 grt/33,281 dwt; 263 × 11.5 m *(863 × 37.9 ft)*; TSM (Sulzer); 24.75 kts; ex-*New York Maru*

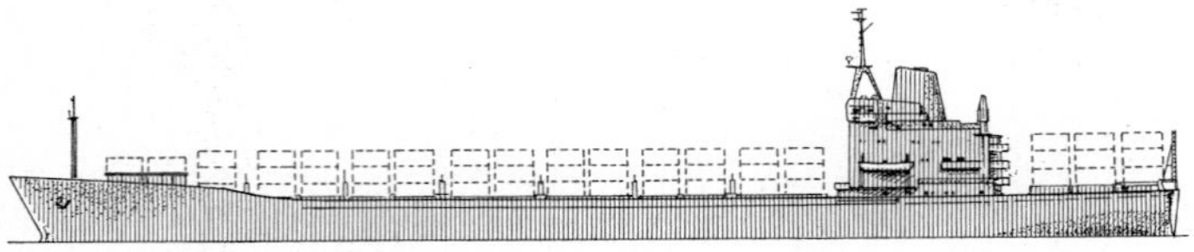

145 *MVFD H1*
MSC ANASTASIA Pa/FRG (Howaldts DW) 1970/78; Con; 16,670 grt/21,307 dwt; 176.49 × 10.59 m *(579 × 34.74 ft)*; M (MAN); 20.5 kts; ex-*Leverkusen*; Converted from general cargo, lengthened and widened 1978 (Bremer V)
Sisters: **MSC MEE MAY** (Cy) ex-*Erlangen*; **MSC GIULIA** (Gr) ex-*Ludwigshafen*

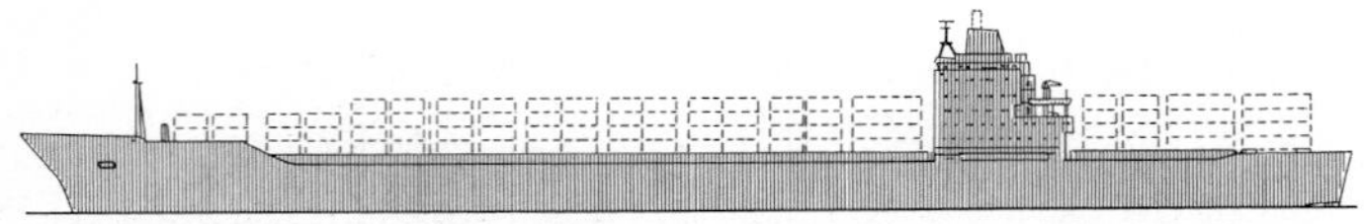

146 *MVFMR H1*
ANDERS MAERSK DIS/FRG-FRG (B+V) 1976/78/83; Con; 33,401 grt/37,129 dwt; 239.28 × 11.52 m *(785.04 × 37.8 ft)*; M (B&W); — kts; After section ex-*Arthur Maersk*; Lengthened 1978; Lengthened 1983 (B+V)
Sisters: **AXEL MAERSK** (DIS) After section ex-*Anna Maersk*; **MAERSK VANCOUVER** (Gr) ex-*Alva Maersk* (Builder—Flender); **ANNA MAERSK** (DIS) After section ex-*Anders Maersk*; **MAERSK HOUSTON** (Gr) ex-*Arild Maersk* (Builder—Flender); **ARTHUR MAERSK** (DIS) (Builder B+V; rebuilt by Hitachi 1983)

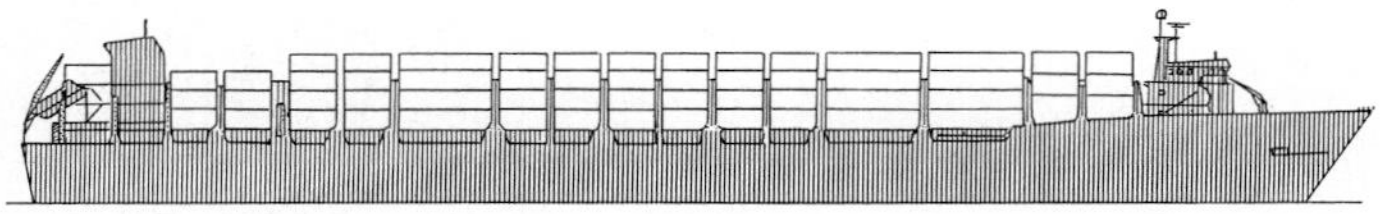

147 *RMFL H1*
ATLANTIC LADY Bs/Ne (Verolme SH) 1992; Con; 19,562 grt/19,984 dwt; 173.62 × 9.00 m *(569.62 × 29.53 ft)*; M (Stork-Werkspoor); 18 kts; 1,646 TEU; Hatchless on holds 1 to 5
Probable sister: **FRESHWATER BAY** (Ne) ex-*European Express*

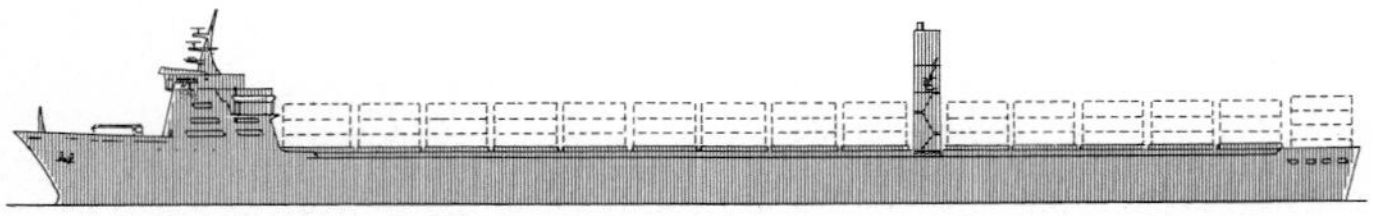

148 *SMF–S H1*
MANOA US/US (Avondale) 1982; Con; 40,627 grt/30,825 dwt; 262.14 × 10.68 m *(860 × 35.04 ft)*; M (Sulzer); 23.25 kts
Sisters: **PRESIDENT MONROE** (US); **PRESIDENT WASHINGTON** (US)

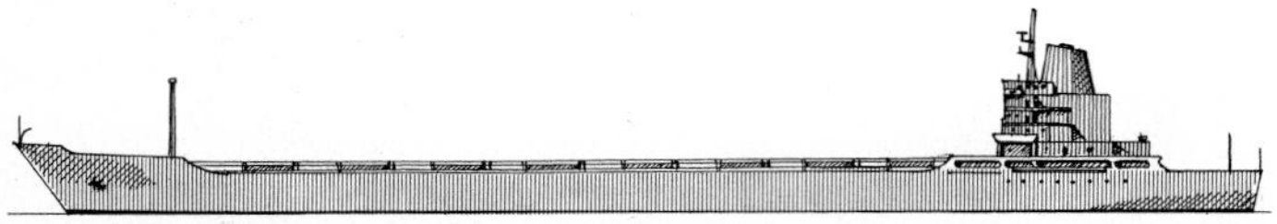

149 *TMFN H1*
MSC ROSEMARY Pa/Fr (CNIM) 1971; Con; 24,602 grt/27,667 dwt; 234.5 × 9.68 m *(769.36 × 31.76 ft)*; M (Sulzer); 22.25 kts; ex-*Oriental Educator*; Lengthened 1976; 1,466 TEU
Similar: **OOCL CONCORD** (HK) ex-*Oriental Commander*; **MSC ALEXANDRA** (Pa) ex-*Oriental Chevalier*

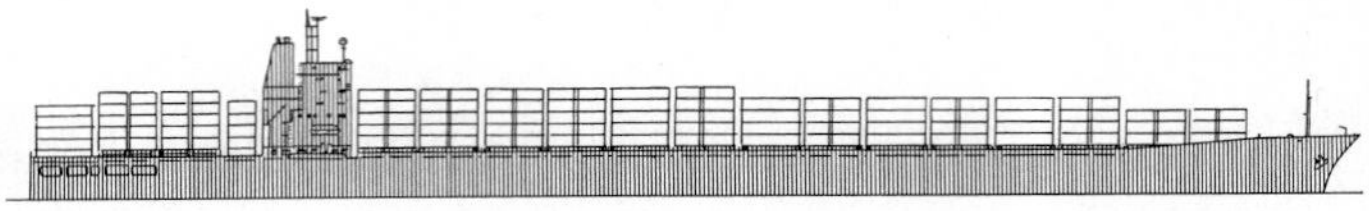

150 *VHF H*
HANJIN OSAKA Pa/Ko (Hanjin HI) 1992; Con; 50,792 grt/62,681 dwt; 289.50 × 13.00 m *(949.80 × 42.65 ft)*; M (Sulzer); 24 kts; 4,024 TEU
Sisters: **HANJIN BARCELONA** (Pa); **HANJIN MALTA** (Ko); **HANJIN MARSEILLES** (Pa); **HANJIN PORTLAND** (Pa); **HANJIN TOKYO** (Pa); **HANJIN COLOMBO** (Pa); **HANJIN SHANGHAI** (Pa)

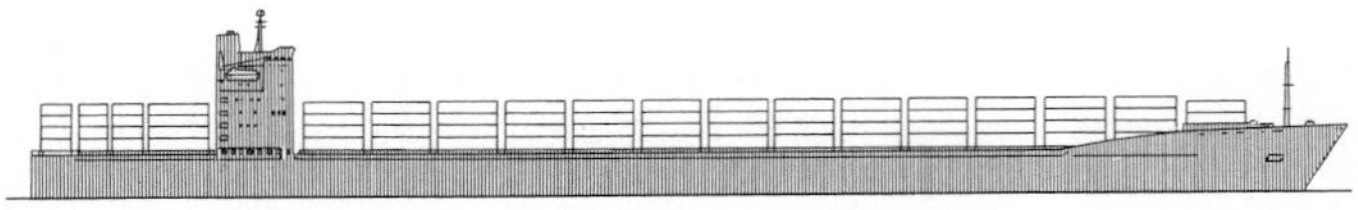

151 *VHF–D H1*
EVER GIVEN Tw/Ja (Onomichi) 1986/87; Con; 46,410 grt/53,240 dwt; 269.68 × 11.63 m *(884.78 × 38.16 ft)*; M (Sulzer); 21 kts; 3,428 TEU; 'GX' type; Lengthened 1987 (China SB)
Sisters: **EVER GAINING** (Tw); **EVER GALLANT** (Tw); **EVER GARLAND** (Pa); **EVER GENERAL** (Tw); **EVER GLAMOUR** (Pa); **EVER GLEEFUL** (Tw); **EVER GLOWING** (Tw); **EVER GOODS** (Tw); **EVER GROUP** (Tw); **EVER GUEST** (Tw)

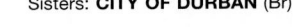

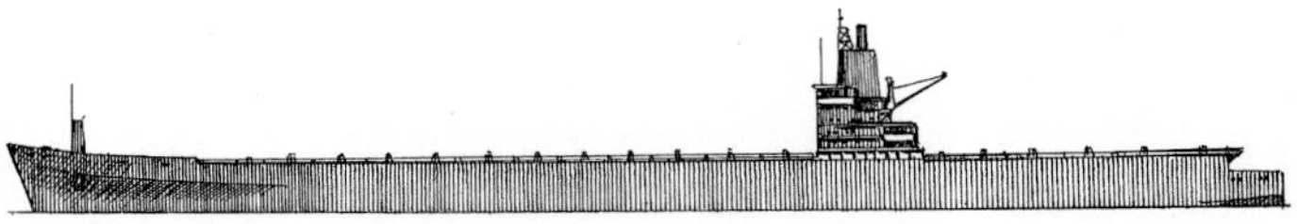

152 *VH–FD H1*
TABLE BAY Br/FRG (AG 'Weser') 1977; Con; 52,055 grt/47,197 dwt; 258.55 × 13.02 m *(848.26 × 42.72)*; TSM (MAN); 21.5 kts
Sisters: **CITY OF DURBAN** (Br)

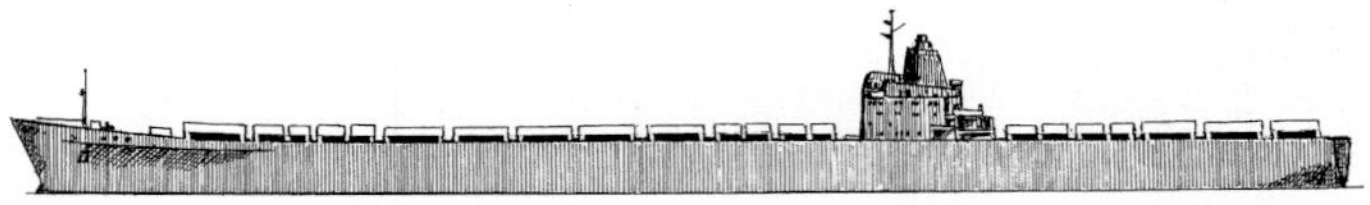

153 *VMF H*
LIVERPOOL BAY Br/FRG (Howaldts DW) 1972; Con; 56,822 grt/47,442 dwt; 290 × 13 m *(950 × 42.9 ft)*; TSM (Sulzer); — kts
Sisters: **CARDIGAN BAY** (Br); **KOWLOON BAY** (Br); **OSAKA BAY** (Br); **TOKYO BAY** (Br)

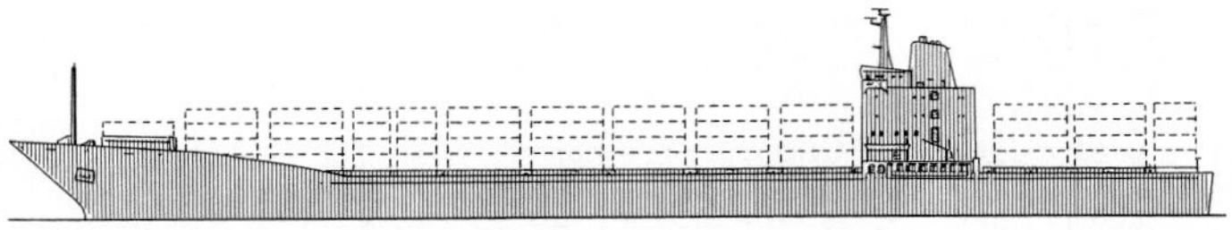

154 *VMF H1*
EVER LEVEL Tw/Ja (Onomichi) 1980; Con; 24,804 grt/28,898 dwt; 202.6 × 11.23 m *(665 × 36.84 ft)*; M (Sulzer); 21 kts; ex-*Ever Light*
Sisters: **EVER LAUREL** (Tw) ex-*Ever Large*; **EVER LIVING** (Tw) ex-*Ever Lucky*; **EVER LYRIC** (Tw) ex-*Ever Loyal*; **EVER LINKING** (Pa); **EVER LOADING** (Pa)

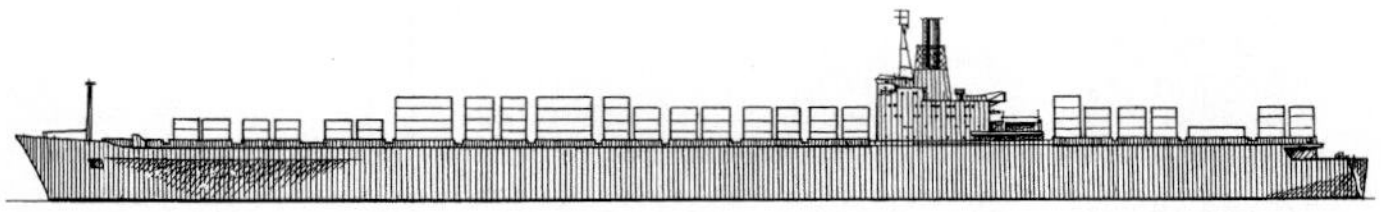

155 *VMF H1*
LONDON MAERSK DIS/FRG (Howaldts DW) 1972; Con; 55,889 grt/49,593 dwt; 290 × 13 m *(950 × 42.7 ft)*; TSM (MAN); — kts; ex-*Benalder*
Sisters: **PARIS MAERSK** (DIS) ex-*Benavon*; **EDINBURGH MAERSK** (DIS) ex-*City of Edinburgh*

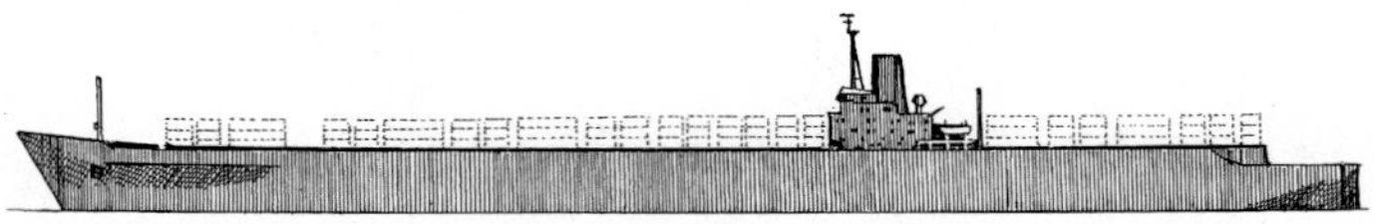

156 *VMFN H1*
NEDLLOYD KORRIGAN Fr/FRG (Howaldts DW) 1973; Con; 57,304 grt/48,850 dwt; 289 × 13 m *(947 × 42.7 ft)*; TSM (Sulzer); 22.5 kts; ex-*Korrigan*

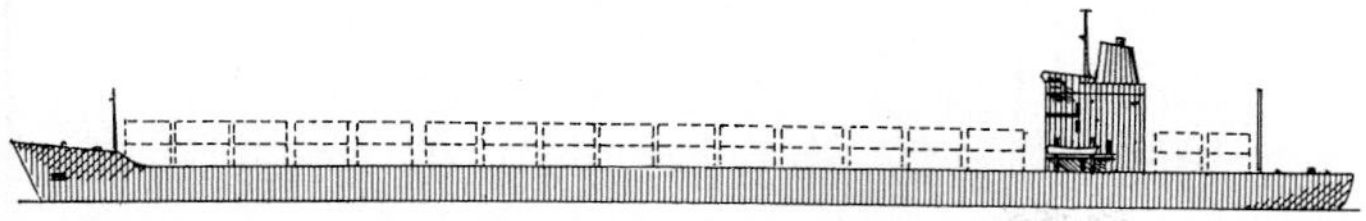

157 *VMFN H1*
XOUR TINGGI Sg/Fr (Dubigeon-Normandie) 1973; Con; 15,656 grt/22,311 dwt; 163.91 × 7.8 m *(537.76 × 25.59 ft)*; M (Pielstick); 19 kts; ex-*Medorfea*; Now lengthened to 191.31 m (627.66 ft); Drawing shows vessel to original appearance; Container capacity is now 1,208 TEU
Sisters (also lengthened): **NICOSIA** (Cy) ex-*Medariana*; **PIRAEUS** (Ma) ex-*Medelena*; **ZIM KAOHSIUNG** (Gr) ex-*Atlantic Marseille*

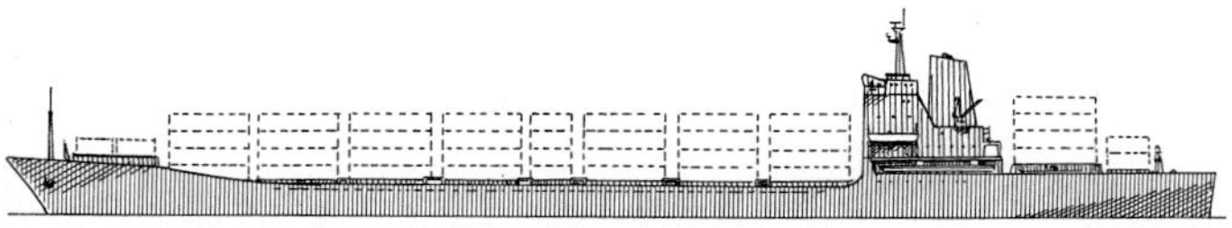

158 *VMF–S H13*
HANJIN KUNSAN Pa/Ja (Hayashikane) 1977; Con; 15,560 grt/18,834 dwt; 186.75 × 10.02 m *(612.7 × 32.87 ft)*; M (Sulzer); 22 kts; ex-*Ever Valiant*
Similar: **HANJIN KWANGYANG** (Ko) ex-*Ever Victory*; **HANJIN CHEJU** (Ko) ex-*Ever Voyager*; **UNI-VIGOR** (Pa) ex-*Ever Vigor*; **UNI-VITAL** (Pa) ex-*Ever Vital*
Probably similar: **UNI-VALOR** (Pa) ex-*Ever Valor*; **UNI-VALUE** (Pa) ex-*Ever Value*

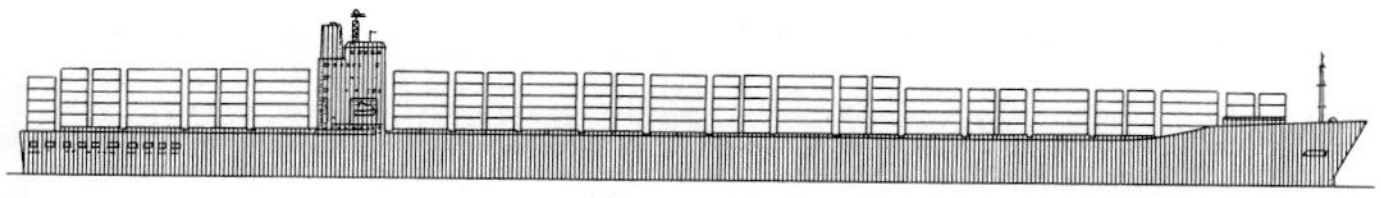

159 *VMG H*
EVER RACER Pa/Ja (Onomichi) 1994; Con; 53,359 grt/57,904 dwt; 294.13 × 12.63 m *(964.99 × 41.44 ft)*; M (Sulzer); 23.2 kts; 4,229 TEU
Sisters: **EVER REACH** (Pa); **EVER REFINE** (Pa); **EVER RENOWN** (Pa); **EVER REPUTE** (Pa); **EVER RESULT** (Pa); **EVER REWARD** (Pa); **EVER RIGHT** (Pa); **EVER ROUND** (Pa); **EVER ROYAL** (Pa)

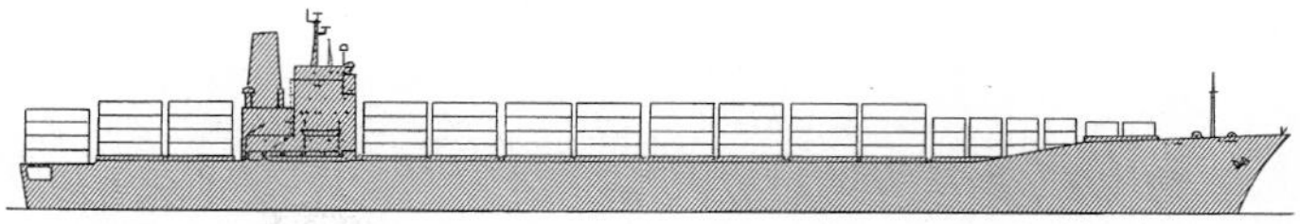

160 *VM²F H1*
HANJIN NEWYORK Pa/Ja (Hitachi) 1986; Con; 35,610 grt/43,270 dwt; 241.10 × 11.73 m *(791.01 × 38.48 ft)*; M (Sulzer); 24 kts; 2,668 TEU
Sisters: **HANJIN LONGBEACH** (Pa); **HANJIN YOKOHAMA** (Pa)
Sisters (Ko built—Daewoo): **HANJIN HONGKONG** (Li); **HANJIN KOBE** (Li); **HANJIN KEELUNG** (Pa): **HANJIN SAVANNAH** (Ko); **HANJIN SEATTLE** (Ko); **HANJIN OAKLAND** (Ko); **HANJIN VANCOUVER** (Ko); **HANJIN ROTTERDAM** (Ko) (builder—Samsung); **HANJIN LE HAVRE** (Ko) (builder—Samsung); Similar (Ko built—Hanjin): **HANJIN KAOHSIUNG** (Ko); **HANJIN SINGAPORE** (Ko); **HANJIN ELIZABETH** (Ko); **HANJIN BREMEN** (Ko); **HANJIN FELIXSTOWE** (Ko) (builder—Samsung); **HANJIN HAMBURG** (Ko) (builder—Samsung)

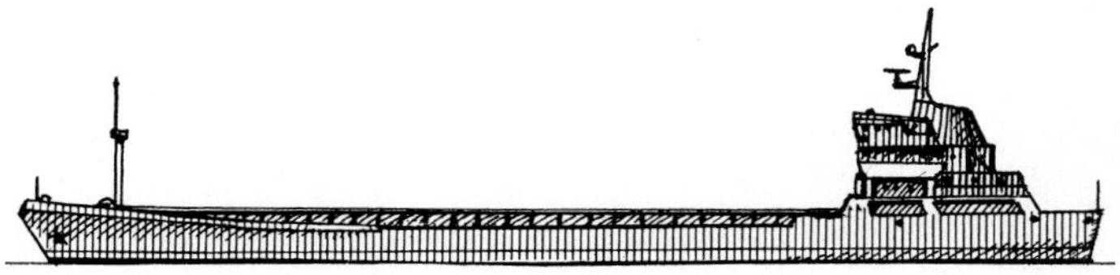

161 *VM–F H*
VINCE Bl/Ih (Verolme Cork) 1973; Con; 3,440 grt/3,664 dwt; 99.60 × 5.22 m *(326.77 × 17.13 ft)*; M (MAN); 15 kts; ex-*Wicklow*; 177 TEU

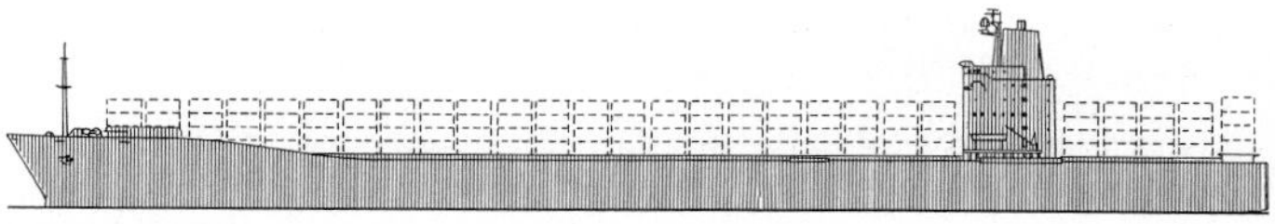

162 *VM–F H1*
EVER GUARD Pa/Ja (IHI) 1983/84; Con; 37,042 grt/43,198 dwt; 230.82 × 11.63 m *(757.28 × 38.16 ft)*; M (Sulzer); 20.5 kts; Lengthened 1984
Sisters: **EVER GUIDE** (Pa); **EVER GOING** (Pa); **EVER GRADE** (Pa); **EVER GIANT** (Pa); **EVER GRACE** (Pa)
Sisters (Builder Onomichi): **EVER GLORY** (Pa); **EVER GLOBE** (Pa); **EVER GREET** (Pa); **EVER GRAND** (Pa)
Sisters (Builder China SB.): **EVER GATHER** (Pa); **EVER GARDEN** (Tw); **EVER GENIUS** (Tw); **EVER GENTRY** (Tw); **EVER GENTLE** (Tw); **EVER GIFTED** (Tw); **EVER GROWTH** (Tw); **EVER GOLDEN** (Tw); **EVER GLEAMY** (Tw); **EVER GOVERN** (Tw)

163 Leverkusen Express *(Ge); 1991* *WSPL*

167 Nedlloyd Korrigan *(Kn); 1973; (as Korrigan)* *WSPL*

164 Kitano *(Ja); 1990* *WSPL*

168 Hanjin Masan *(Ko); 1979; (as Korean Jacejin)* *WSPL*

165 Kasuga 1 *(Pa); 1976* *WSPL*

169 MSC Maria Laura *(Pa); 1973; (as Nipponica)* *WSPL*

166 Kowloon Bay *(Br); 1972* *WSPL*

170 Jebel Ali *(USE); 1979* *WSPL*

171 Malacca Bridge *(Tw); 1982; (as Ming Comfort)* *WSPL*

172 Nedlloyd Asia *(Ne); 1991* *WSPL*

173 Ever Giant *(Pa); 1984* *WSPL*

174 Hanjin Bremen *(Ko); 1991* *WSPL*

175 Zim Pusan *(Gr); 1976/81; (as Chevalier Roze)* *WSPL*

176 Kurama *(Pa); 1972; (as Kurama Maru)* *WSPL*

177 Table Bay *(Br); 1977; (as Tolaga Bay)* *WSPL*

178 Elbe *(Ja); 1990* *WSPL*

179 Zagreb Express *(Ma); 1989* *WSPL*

180 New Haihung *(Pa); 1981; (as Johore Bridge)* *WSPL*

181 Bhatra Bhum *(Sg); 1979; (as Glory Ace)* *WSPL*

182 Luna Maersk *(DIS); 1982; (as Newport Bay)* *WSPL*

183 MSC Rita *(Pa); 1974; (as Hongkong Container)* *WSPL*

184 Mont Blanc Maru *(Ja); 1974* *WSPL*

185 Neptune Garnet *(Sg); 1986* *FotoFlite*

186 Transworld Bridge *(Li); 1980* *WSPL*

187 Newark Bay *(US); 1985* *WSPL*

188 Choyang Victory *(Ko); 1990* *WSPL*

189 APL Japan *(MI); 1995* *FotoFlite*

190 Louis Maersk *(DIS); 1984* *FotoFlite*

191 Tyson Lykes *(US); 1985* *FotoFlite*

192 Genova *(It); 1988* *FotoFlite*

193 Zim Manila III *(Cy); 1973; (as Carrybox 4)* *FotoFlite*

194 Choyang Chance *(Ko); 1978/88* *FotoFlite*

195 MSC Gina *(Cy); 1974/84* *FotoFlite*

196 City of Salerno *(Is); 1983; (as Zim Antwerpen)* *FotoFlite*

197 Axel Maersk *(DIS); 1975/84* *FotoFlite*

198 Marchen Maersk *(DIS); 1988* *FotoFlite*

199 Medspirit *(Ma); 1978; (as Casilda del Mar)* *FotoFlite*

200 Canopus *(Rm); 1988; (as Piatra Olt)* *FotoFlite*

201 Oahu *(Pa); 1980* *FotoFlite*

202 Navicon *(Sp); 1981* *FotoFlite*

203 Fort Desaix *(Kn); 1980* *FotoFlite*

204 Dubai *(UAE); 1982* *FotoFlite*

205 Ming America *(Tw); 1992* *FotoFlite*

206 River Elegance *(Pa); 1994* *FotoFlite*

207 Choyang Giant *(Ko); 1991* *FotoFlite*

208 Shan He *(RC); 1994* *FotoFlite*

209 Kirishima *(Pa); 1993* *FotoFlite*

210 Baltic Tern *(Br); 1989* *FotoFlite*

211 Aquitaine Challenge *(Ge); 1992; (as German)* *FotoFlite*

212 Nedlloyd Normandie *(Kn); 1991* *FotoFlite*

213 Largs Bay *(Li); 1994* *FotoFlite*

214 Tokio Express *(Sg); 1973* *FotoFlite*

215 Jervis Bay *(Br); 1992* *FotoFlite*

216 Thames *(Pa); 1990* *FotoFlite*

217 NOL Amazonite *(Sg); 1993; (as Neptune Amazonite)* *FotoFlite*

218 Cape Natal *(Li); 1995* *Stocznia Gdanska*

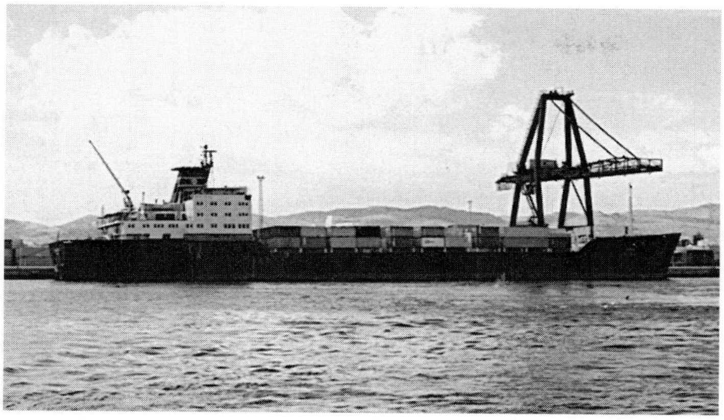

219 Universal *(Pa); 1979; (as Kalidas)* *Norman Thomson*

220 Palliser Bay *(Br); 1977; (as ACT 7)* *Norman Thomson*

221 Shenzhen Bay *(Br); 1994* *FotoFlite*

222 Rich Star *(SV); 1978/83; (as Wotan)* *FotoFlite*

223 Repulse Bay *(Br); 1992* *FotoFlite*

224 Navipor *(Sp); 1982; (as Maersk Mango)* *FotoFlite*

225 NYK Lisboa *(Cy); 1977; (as Carrybox Sun)* *FotoFlite*

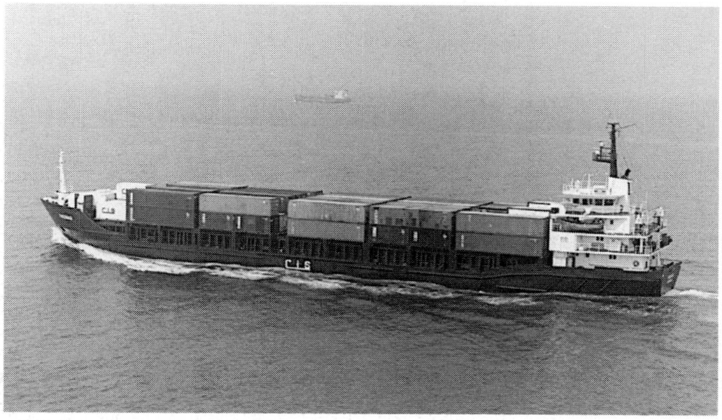

226 Prime View *(Gr); 1979/82; (as Thunar)* *FotoFlite*

13 Geared Container Ships

13 Geared Container Ships

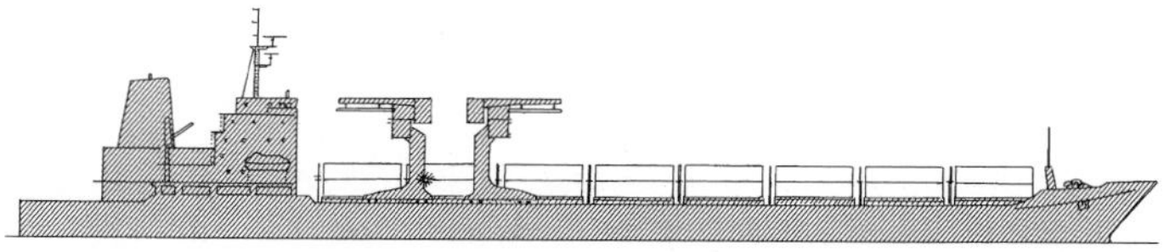

1 HJ^2MCF *H1*
DOLE CALIFORNIA It/It (FCNI) 1989; R/Con; 16,488 grt/11,800 dwt; 179.00 × 8.67 m *(587.27 × 28.44 ft)*; M (Sulzer); 20 kts; 890 TEU; Travelling cranes
Sisters: **DOLE COSTARICA** (It); **DOLE ECUADOR** (It)

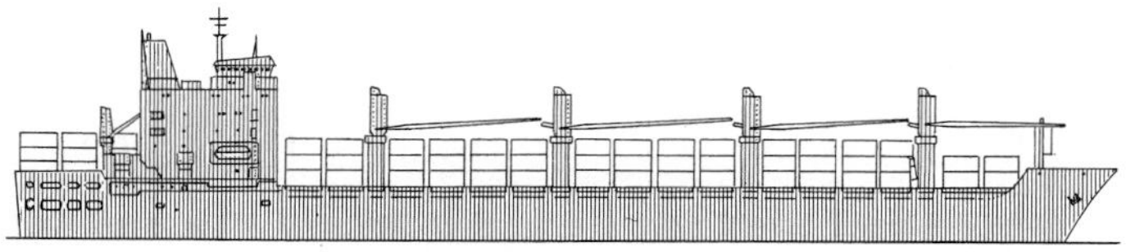

2 $MC^4MF\text{–}MD$ *H1*
VERONIQUE DELMAS Fr/Fr (L'Atlantique) 1984; Con; 30,750 grt/ 31,983 dwt; 189.01 × 11.42 m *(620.11 × 37.47 ft)*; M (Sulzer); 18 kts; 1,417 TEU; Funnel is on port side with mast adjacent on starboard side
Sisters: **THERESE DELMAS** (Fr); **URSULA DELMAS** (Fr); **NEDLLOYD PERNAMBUCO** (Cy) ex-*Yolande Delmas*

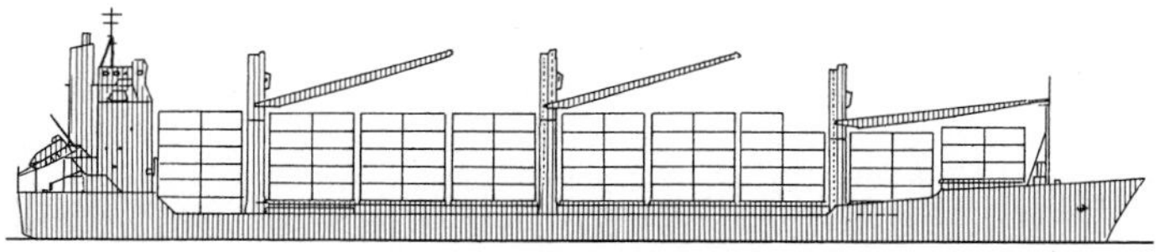

3 MC^3HFC *H13*
CSAV RUPANCO At/FRG (Bremer V) 1986; Con; 16,250 grt/23,465 dwt; 163.30 × 10.55 m *(535.76 × 34.61 ft)*; M (B&W); 18.7 kts; ex-*Ville de Jupiter*; 1,597 TEU; 'ECONPROGRESS BV 1600' type
Sisters (some may not have cranes—see drawing no 12/102): **CMB MEDAL** (Ge) ex-*Ville de Mercure*; **CMB MELODY** (Ge) ex-*Ville de Pluton*; **CMB ANTWERP** (Ge) ex-*Ville de Saturne*
Sisters ('BV 1600' type but may be gearless): **CONTSHIP BARCELONA** (Ge); **CONTSHIP GERMANY** (Ge); **CONTSHIP ITALY** (Ge); **CONTSHIP LAVAGNA** (Ge); **MILDBURG** (Ge) ex-*Contship Australia*; **CONTSHIP FRANCE** (Ge); **CONTSHIP ASIA** (Ge); **CONTSHIP PACIFIC** (Ge); **CONTSHIP ATLANTIC** (Ge); **CONTSHIP NEW ZEALAND** (Ge); **CONTSHIP SINGAPORE** (Ge); **CONTSHIP EUROPE** (Ge); Similar ('BV 1800' type. Longer—176.71m (580ft). Extra hatch between second and third cranes): **CGM IGUACU II** (Ge) ex-*Ville de Neptune*; **DEPPE FLORIDA** (Ge) ex-*Ville de Venus*; **CMBT CONCORD** (Br) ex-*Ville de Mars*; **HANSA CARRIER** (Ge); **HANSA CLIPPER** (Ge) ex-*CGM Provence*

4 MC^3MFC *H1*
SEA EXPRESS Sg/Br (Smith's D) 1978; Con; 16,498 grt/16,114 dwt; 168.87 × 9.37 m *(554.04 × 39.74 ft)*; M (Sulzer); 18 kts; ex-*Australia Star*

See photo number 13/78

5 MC^3MFCL *H13*
CMBT ASIA Li/FRG (Howaldts DW) 1985; C/Con; 21,887 grt/31,290 dwt; 173.39 × 11.20 m *(568.86 × 36.75)*; M (B&W); 17 kts; ex-*Norasia Samantha*; 1,893 TEU; Now lengthened to 189.38m (621ft). Drawing shows vessel as built; There is probably an extra hatch between first and second cranes
Sisters: **CMBT EUROPE** (Ge) ex-*Norasia Susan*; **MSC AUGUSTA** (Ma) ex-*Norasia Pearl*; **MSC FLORIANA** (Ma) ex-*Norasia Princess*; **MSC ADELE** (Ms) ex-*Norasia Sharjah*

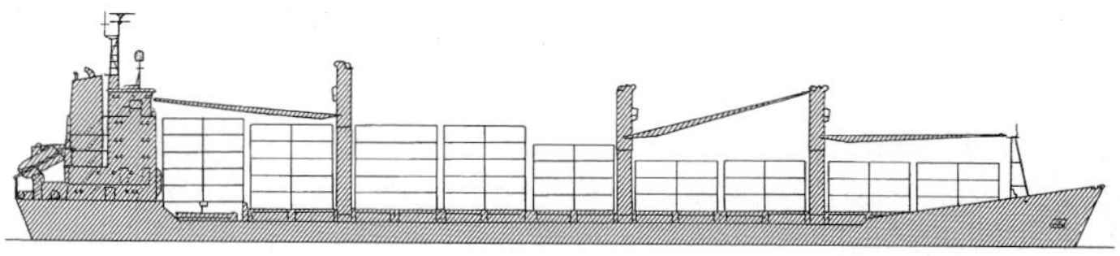

6 MC^3MFLR *H13*
KARAWA At/Pd (Szczecinska) 1993; Con; 10,778 grt/14,103 dwt; 162.87 × 8.30 m *(534.35 × 27.23 ft)*; M (B&W); 17.77 kts; ex-*Maria Rickmers*; 1,156 TEU; 'B183/2' type (lengthened)
Sisters: **KAIAMA** (At) ex-*Peter Rickmers*; **LUKAS** (At); **ZIM ARGENTINA** (At) ex-*Paul Rickmers*; **HASSELWERDER** (At)
Possible sister: **CAECILIA SCHULTE** (Li)

See photo number 13/115

7 MC^3MFLR *H13*
TSL GALLANT Li/Ge (MTW) 1994; Con; 15,908 grt/22,343 dwt; 168.37 × 10.81 m *(552.39 × 35.47 ft)*; M (Sulzer); 19.5 kts; ex-*Westerdeich*; 1,572 TEU; 'CC1600' type
Sister: **CCNI ATACAMA** (Ge) ex-*Westerhever*
Probable sisters: **CSAV RAULI** (At) ex-*Elbe Trader*; **TRAVE TRADER** (Ge)
Possible sister: **MARLENE S** (At)

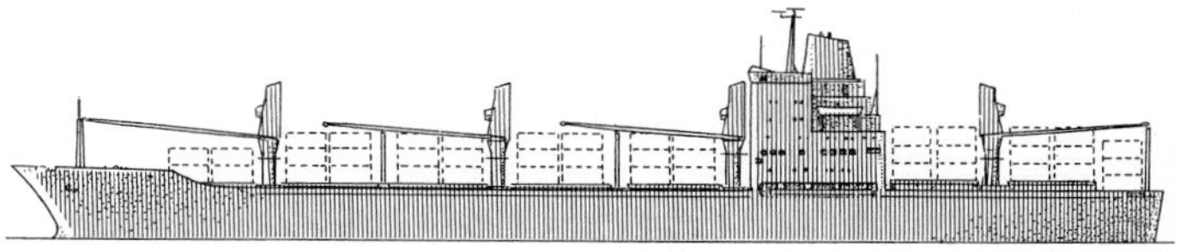

8 MC^3MFMC *H1*
CALIFORNIA STAR Bs/Br (Smith's D) 1980; Con; 18,236 grt/16,511 dwt; 171.3 × 9.35 m *(561.45 × 30.68 ft)*; M (B&W); 19 kts; ex-*Willowbank*

9 MC^3MFN *H13*
BARBICAN SUCCESS Pi/Ja (Nipponkai) 1973/79; Con; 14,466 grt/ 21,357 dwt; 170.77 × 9.36 m *(560 × 30.71 ft)*; M (B&W); 16 kts; ex-*Aristipos*; 904 TEU; Cranes are on port side; Converted from 'Mitsui-Concord' type cargo vessel and lengthened 1979; Others of this class may also have deck cranes now—see entry number 12/79

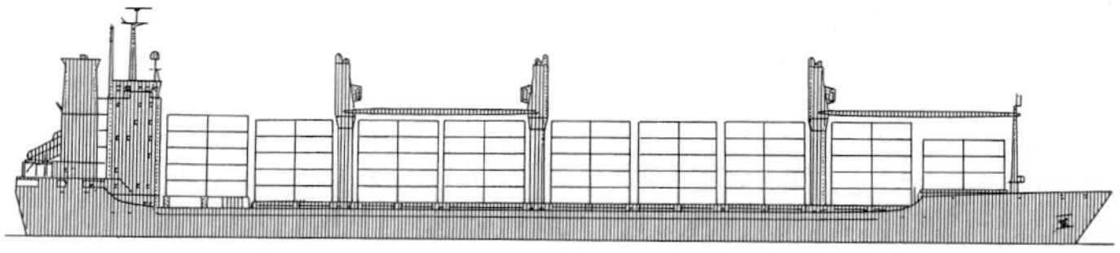

10 MC^3M^2FL *H13*
CABO BLANCO Cy/Ge (Kvaerner Warnow) 1994; Con; 14,869 grt/ 18,950 dwt; 167.24 × 9.80 m *(548.69 × 32.15 ft)*; M (Sulzer); 19 kts; ex-*Marwan*; 1,338 TEU
Sisters: **CHARLOTTE SCHULTE** (Cy); **NORDWELLE** (Cy); **NORDWOGE** (Cy); **NEDLLOYD SINGAPORE** (Li) ex-*Westermuhlen*; **NAUTIQUE** (Cy); **EXPORTER** (Ge) ex-*Wieland*; **EMERALD** (Cy) ex-*Teval*; **ELITE** (At) ex-*Merian*; **CONCORD** (At); **CSAV RAHUE** (At) ex-*Courier*; **CCNI ANAKENA** (Ge) ex-*Birte Ritscher*; **SEA NOVIA** (Li) ex-*Novia*; **SEA OLIVIA** (Li) ex-*Olivia*; **ENERGY** (Cy) ex-*Norplius*

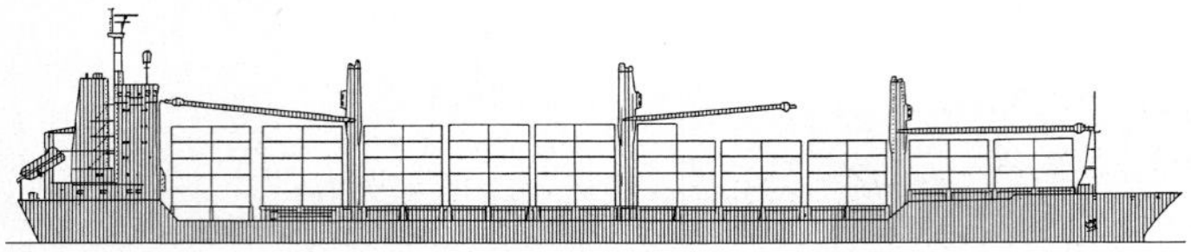

11 $MC^{3}M^{2}FRL$ *H13*
NORDLAKE Cy/Pd (Szczecinska) 1994; Con; 16,202 grt/22,450 dwt; 179.18 × 9.94 m *(587.86 × 32.61 ft)*; M (Sulzer); 19 kts; 1,496 TEU, 'B186' type
Sisters: **TSL BOLD** (Li) ex-*Dorian*; **CSAV RANCO** (Cy) ex-*Mare Ibericum*; **NORDCLOUD** (Cy); **SAN MARINO** (Cy) ex-*Nordpol*; **SAN MIGUEL** (Cy); **CALAPEDRA** (Cy) ex-*Bernhard Schulte*; **RENATE SCHULTE** (Li)

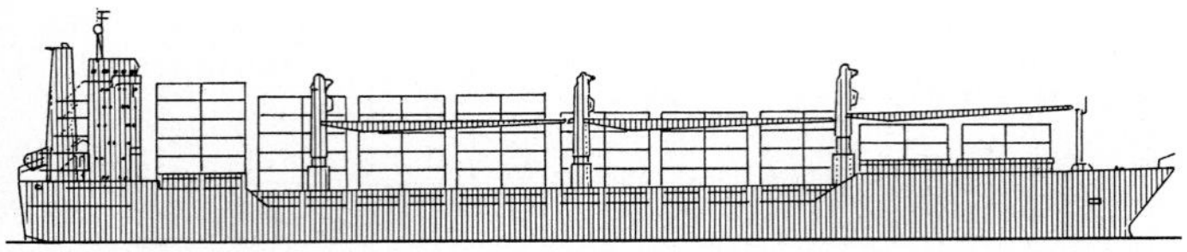

12 $MC^{3}NFL$ *H13*
KAPITAN KUROV Ru/FRG (Schlichting) 1986; Con; 14,068 grt/19,560 dwt; 161.53 × 9.80 m *(529.95 × 32.15 ft)*; M (MaK); 18 kts; ex-*Sandra K*; 1,317 TEU; Cranes are on port side
Sister: **KAPITAN SERYKH** (Ru) ex-*Contado*

See photo number 13/75

13 $MC^{3}NMFR$ *H1*
LONTUE Li/No (Kaldnes) 1978/82; Con; 21,669 grt/28,800 dwt; 200.57 × 10.34 m *(658.04 × 33.92 ft)*; M (B&W); 16.5 kts; ex-*Ville de Bordeaux*; Converted from general cargo and lengthened 1982 (L'Ouest); 1,201 TEU; **LIMARI** may be like this now (see entry number 13/43)

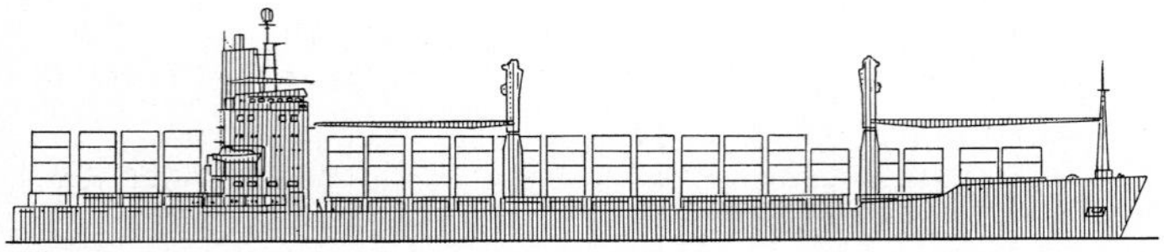

14 $MC^{2}HFS$ *H1*
NEDLLOYD VAN DIEMEN Ne/Ne (Giessen-De Noord) 1984; Con; 23,790 grt/29,730 dwt; 182.76 × 11.60 m *(599.61 × 38.06 ft)*; M (Sulzer); 17.5 kts; 1,444 TEU
Sister: **NEDLLOYD VAN NOORT** (Ne)

15 $MC^{2}MF$ *H1*
AZAPA At/Ne (E J Smit) 1986; Con; 3,790 grt/4,250 dwt; 106.61 × 5.50 m *(349.77 × 18.04 ft)*; M (Wärtsilä); 14.75 kts; ex-*Pacheco*; 354 TEU; Cranes are on port side
Sister: **ALINA I** (Cy) ex-*Palacio*

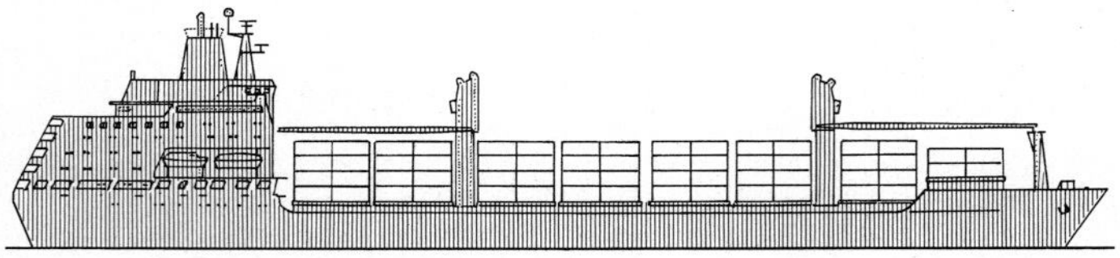

16 $MC^{2}MF$ *H13*
AMERICANA NIS/Ko (Hyundai) 1988; P/Con; 19,203 grt/19,830 dwt; 176.71 × 9.52 m *(579.76 × 31.23 ft)*; M (B&W); 18.25 kts; 1,120 TEU

See photo number 13/109

17 $MC^{2}MF$ *H13*
GU CHENG RC/RC (Dalian) 1985; Con; 9,683 grt/13,058 dwt; 147.5 × 7.9 m *(483.92 × 25.92 ft)*; M (B&W); 15.5 kts; 724 TEU
Sisters: **BIN CHENG** (RC); **SHANG CHENG** (RC); **MING CHENG** (RC); **GAO CHENG** (RC); **SONG CHENG** (RC)
Sisters (builder—Shanghai SY): **KENT MERCHANT** (Sg) ex-*Actuaria*; **NORDKAP** (Cy); **NORDSINO** (Cy); **ZIM SAN JUAN** (Sg) ex-*Arabella*; Probably similar (may have a free-fall lifeboat): **KOTA CAHAYA** (Sg); **TRADE FAST** (Cy)

18 $MC^{2}MF$ *H13*
HYUNDAI TIANJIN Cy/Sp (Juliana) 1985; Con; 6,819 grt/7,960 dwt; 122.13 × 8.02 m *(400.69 × 26.31 ft)*; M (SKL); 14.5 kts; ex-*Rudolstadt*; 440 TEU; Cranes are on port side
Sisters: **STAR LIGHT** (At) ex-*Halberstadt*; **KRIS TERASEK** (My) ex-*Arnstadt*; **IMKE WEHR** (At) ex-*Johangeorgenstadt*; **WAN NING HE** (RC) ex-*Neustadt*; **FMG AMERICA** (At) ex-*Johstadt*

See photo number 13/107

19 $MC^{2}MF$ *H13*
NEPTUNE BERYL Sg/RC (Jiangnan) 1984; Con; 13,488 grt/18,436 dwt; 161.02 × 8 m *(528.28 × 26.25 ft)*; M (Pielstick); 17.5 kts; 859 TEU
Sister: **NEPTUNE JASPER** (Sg)

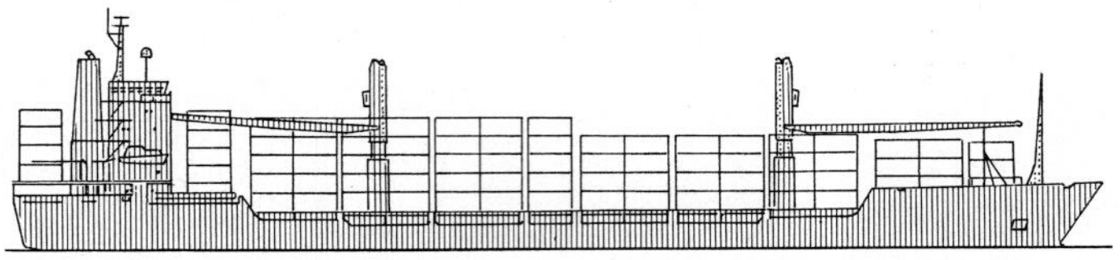

20 $MC^{2}MF$ *H13*
ZIM PARAGUAY Li/FRG (Nobiskrug) 1985; Con; 10,524 grt/14,180 dwt; 151.01 × 8.35 m *(495.44 × 27.40 ft)*; M (MaK); 18 kts; ex-*Westerbrook*; 962 TEU; Cranes are on port side
Sisters (different design of crane): **ANIKA** (At) ex-*Anika Oltmann*; **FRANCOLI** (Sp) ex-*Karen S*

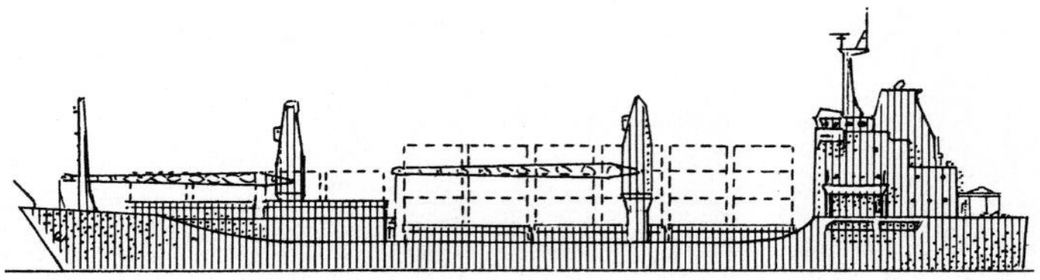

21 $MC^{2}MFC$ *H13*
BUNGA PENAGA My/Ja (Osaka) 1979; Con; 3,927 grt/5,362 dwt; 102.4 × 6.2 m *(335.96 × 20.34 ft)*; M (Pielstick); 13.5 kts; 196 TEU; First crane on starboard side and second on port
Sister: **BUNGA DAHLIA** (My)

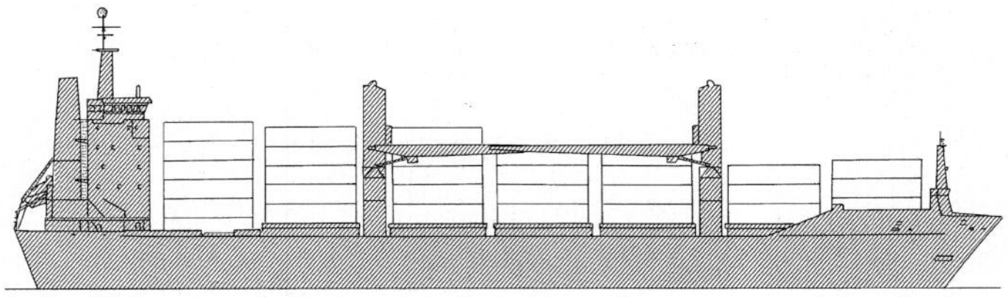

22 $MC^{2}MFL$ *H1*
SEA ARCTICA DIS/De (Danyard) 1994; Con; 11,612 grt/9,566 dwt; 132.50 × 8.01 m *(434.71 × 26.28 ft)*; M (MAN); 13.75 kts; ex-*Naja Arctica*; 782 TEU

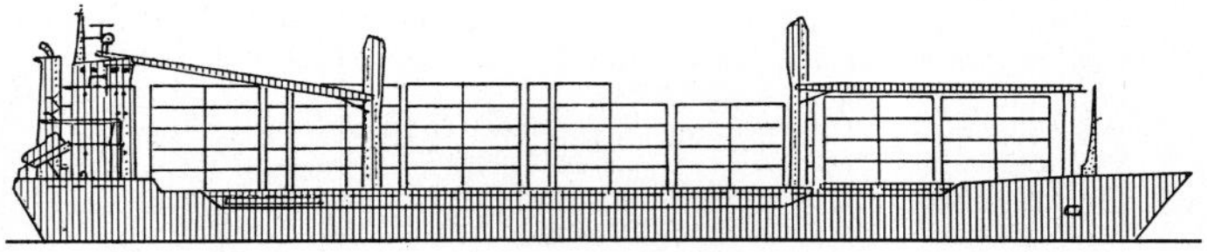

23 $MC^{2}MFL$ *H13*
KENT TRADER Ge/FRG (M Jansen) 1986; Con; 8,106 grt/9,393 dwt; 132.70 × 7.53 m *(435.37 × 24.70 ft)*; M (MAN); 17 kts; ex-*Maria Sibum*; 885 TEU; Cranes are on port side

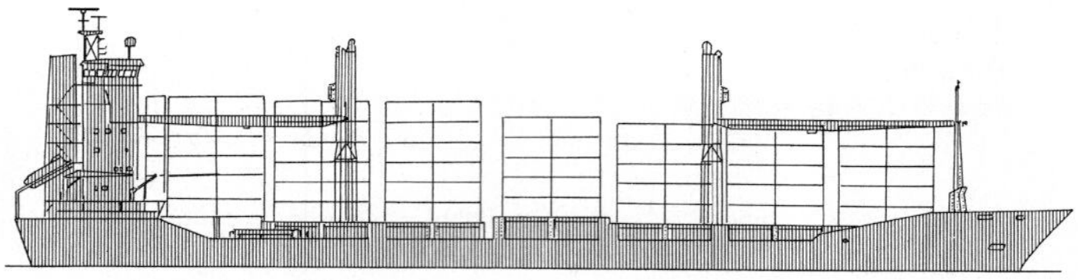

24 $MC^{2}MFL$ *H13*
SEA-LAND HONDURAS DIS/De (Orskov C) 1990; Con; 8,908 grt/9,766 dwt; 133.70 × 7.60 m *(438.65 × 24.93 ft)*; M (MaK); 17.2 kts; ex-*Flemming Sif*; 976 TEU
Sisters: **SEA-LAND GUATEMALA** (DIS) ex-*Kathrine Sif*; **SEA-LAND COSTA RICA** (DIS) ex-*Colleen Sif*; Similar (lower superstructure, different focsle shape): **MAERSK EURO PRIMO** (DIS) ex-*Lotte Sif*; **MAERSK EURO QUARTO** (DIS) ex-*Maersk Forto*; **MAERSK EURO QUINTO** (DIS) ex-*Heidi B*

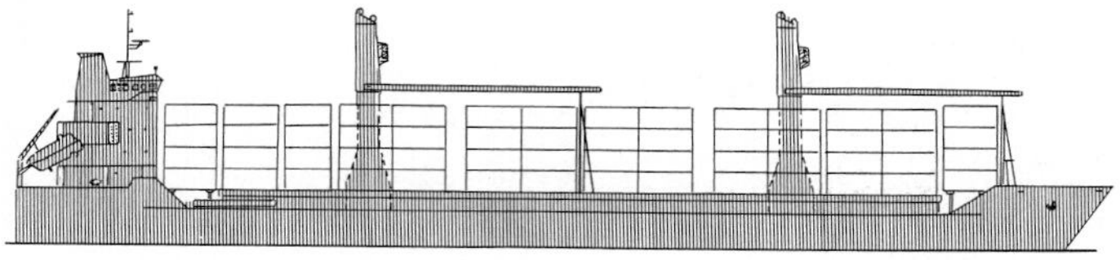

25 *MC^{2}MFL H13*
SECIL ANGOLA Bs/Sg (Atlantis) 1992; Con; 7,197 grt/10,000 dwt; 123.50 × 6.50 m *(405.18 × 21.33 ft)*; M (B&W); 15 kts; 604 TEU

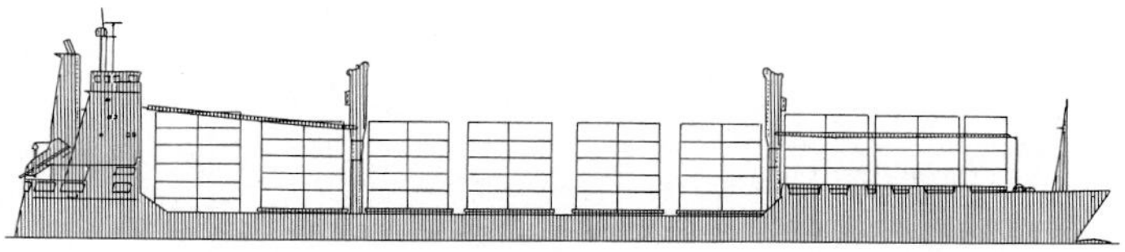

26 *MC^{2}MFL H13*
ULF RITSCHER Ge/Ge (Sietas) 1990; Con; 10,868 grt/15,174 dwt; 157.69 × 8.97 m *(517.36 × 29.43 ft)*; M (MaK); 18.4 kts; 1,048 TEU
Sisters: **WIDUKIND** (Ge); **ATLANTA** (Ge) ex-*Kollmar*
Probable sisters: **LANKA RUWAN** (At) ex-*Elbstrom*; **LANKA AMILA** (At) ex-*Antje*; **CAROLA** (Ge)

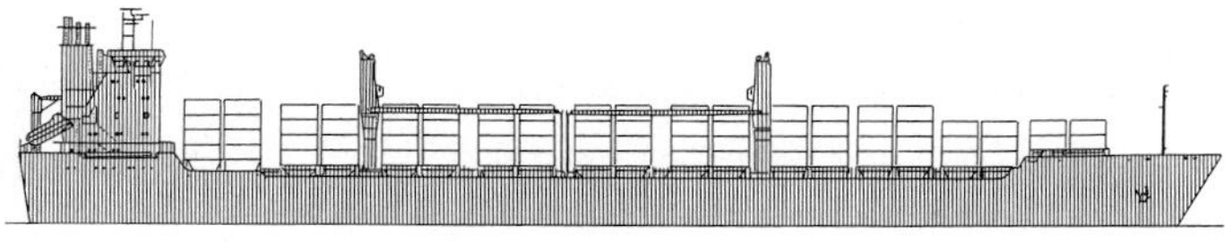

27 *MC^{2}MFLR H13*
CAP POLONIO Ge/FRG (Flender) 1990; Con; 29,739 grt/33,221 dwt; 200.23 × 12.00 m *(656.92 × 39.37 ft)*; M (Sulzer); 18.5 kts; 1,960 TEU
Sisters: **CAP FINISTERRE** (Ge); **CAP TRAFALGAR** (Ge)

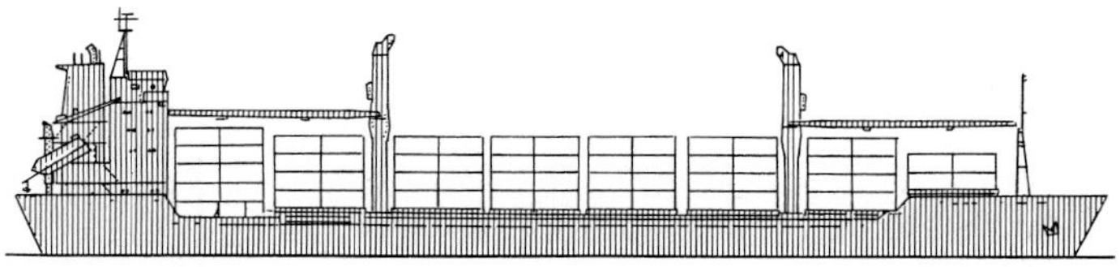

28 *MC^{2}MFLR H13*
SANTOS NIS/FRG (Flender) 1985; Con; 12,569 grt/17,261 dwt; 151.31 × 9.77 m *(496.42 × 32.05 ft)*; M (Sulzer); 17 kts; ex-*Torenia*; 1,042 TEU; 'Flender 1100' type
Sisters (smaller crane, pole radar mast): **ARGONIA** (Cy) ex-*Altonia*

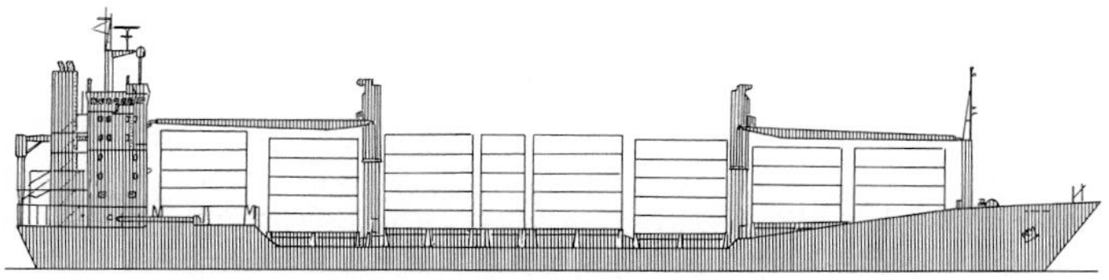

29 *MC^{2}MFL–R H13*
CAPE HATTERAS Cy/Ge (MTW) 1992; Con; 10,396 grt/12,854 dwt; 146.72 × 8.65 m *(481.36 × 28.38 ft)*; M (MaK); 17.4 kts; ex-*Cape Hatteras*; 923 TEU; 'MMC 900' type
Sisters: **TIGER OCEAN** (Sg) ex-*Cape Henry*; **MAERSK LA PAZ** (Li) ex-*Cape Horn*; **KIMANIS** (Sg) ex-*Cape Hermes*

30 *MC^{2}MFN H12*
SEA WIND Gr/FRG (O&K) 1976; Con; 8,647 grt/12,798 dwt; 143.82 × 8.32 m *(471.85 × 27.3 ft)*; M (Pielstick); 18 kts; ex-*Anemos*; 626 TEU
Sister: **SEA WAVE** (Gr) ex-*Pelagos*

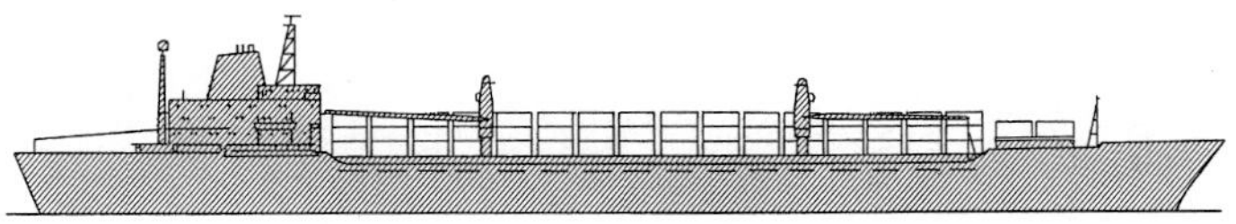

31 *MC^{2}MFN H13*
CMBT AMERICA HK/De (Nakskov) 1977; Con; 20,295 grt/19,974 dwt; 201.76 × 9.90 m *(661.94 × 32.48 ft)*; M (B&W); 22 kts; ex-*Fionia*; 974 TEU
Sister: **NOMZI** (Br) ex-*Boringia*

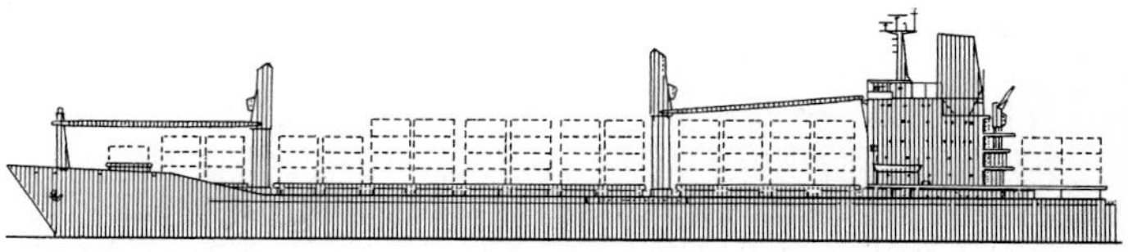

32 *MC^{2}MFR H1*
LUO HE RC/FRG (A G 'Weser') 1983; Con; 19,915 grt/26,025 dwt; 170.21 × 10.73 m *(558 × 35.2 ft)*; M (MAN); 17.75 kts; 1,234 TEU
Sisters: **SHA HE** (RC); **LIAO HE** (RC)

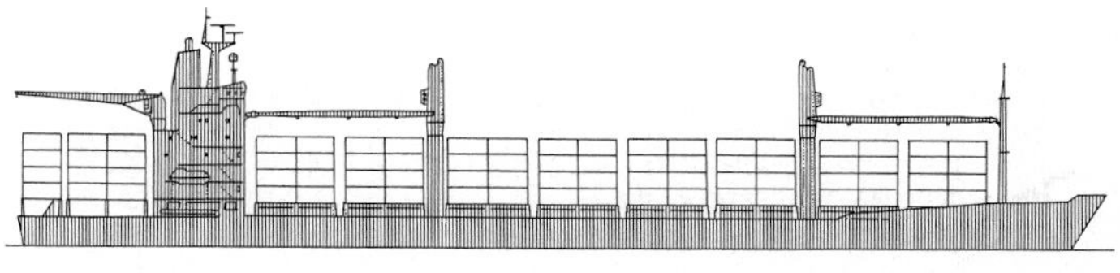

33 *MC^{2}MFR H1*
NEDLLOYD RIVER PLATE Li/Ko (Hanjin HI) 1994; Con; 16,927 grt/27,780 dwt; 167.98 × 9.20 m *(551.12 × 30.18 ft)*; M (B&W); 19 kts; ex-*Hansa Riga*; 1,641 TEU
Probable sisters: **BEIRUT** (At) ex-*Harmony*; **NEDLLOYD RECIFE** (Li); **NEDLLOYD RIO** (At) ex-*Triumph*

See photo number 13/108

34 *MC^{2}MFR H12*
FENHE RC/FRG (Schlichting) 1982; Con; 16,108 grt/20,828 dwt; 170.21 × 9.66 m *(558 × 31.69 ft)*; M (MAN); 18.75 kts; 1,152 TEU
Sisters: **QING HE** (RC); **TANG HE** (RC); Similar (builder—Flensburger): **COPACABANA** (Bz); **FLAMENGO** (Bz)

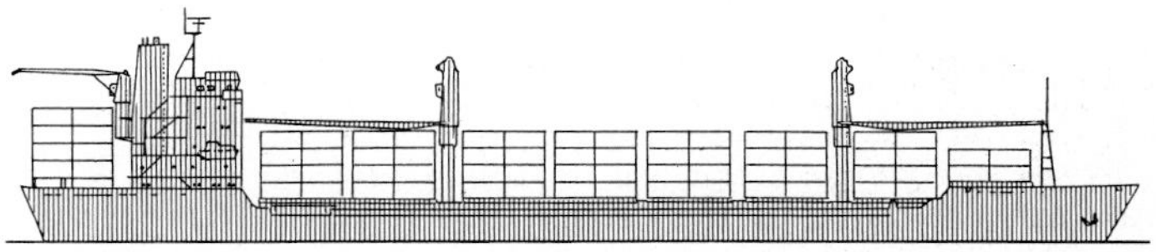

35 *MC^{2}MFR H13*
EAGLE WIND Ko/FRG (Flender) 1985; Con; 14,455 grt/19,187 dwt; 165.72 × 9.60 m *(543.70 × 31.50 ft)*; M (B&W); 17 kts; ex-*San Martin*; 1,012 TEU; 'FW 1200' type
Similar: **SAN LORENZO** (Ge); **SAN VICENTE** (Ge); **SAN ISIDRO** (Ge); **SAN ANTONIO** (NIS); **SAN CLEMENTE** (Ge)

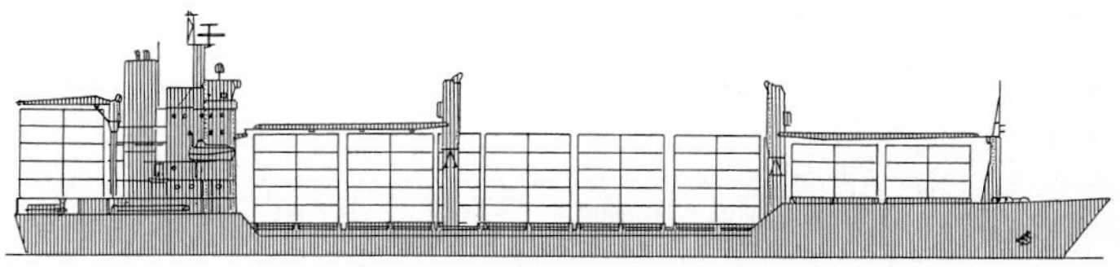

36 *MC^{2}MFR H13*
NORDLIGHT Cy/DDR (Mathias-Thesen) 1990; Con; 11,998 grt/14,140 dwt; 156.70 × 8.62 m *(514.11 × 28.28 ft)*; M (Sulzer); 17.8 kts; 1,034 TEU; 'UCC-14M' type
Sisters: **ALASKA** (Cy) ex-*Nordsky*; **LANKA ABHAYA** (Cy) ex-*Nordsun*; **LANKA ARUNA** (Cy) ex-*Nordbeach*; **LANKA ASITHA** (Cy) ex-*Nordcliff*; **MAERSK ASIA OCTAVO** (Cy) ex-*Nordisle*; **ZIM URUGUAY** (At) ex-*Tallahassee*; **NEDLLOYD CATARINA** (At) ex-*Kalamazoo*

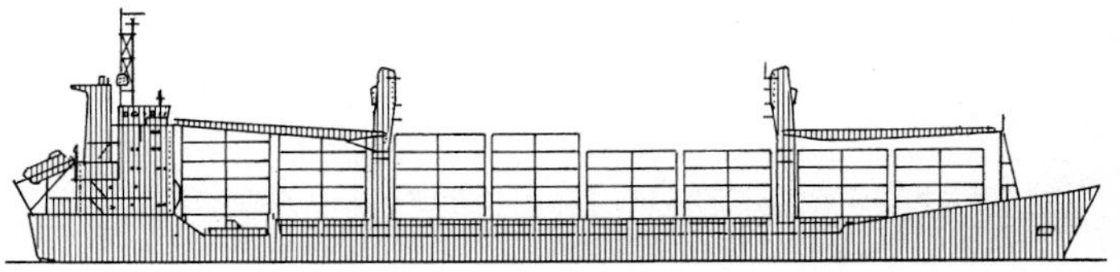

37 *MC^{2}MFRL H13*
LILA BHUM Ge/FRG (Rickmers) 1985; Con; 9,392 grt/12,622 dwt; 146.01 × 8.29 m *(479.04 × 27.20 ft)*; M (Sulzer); 17.5 kts; ex-*Heike*; 1,002 TEU; 'RW 49' type
Sisters: **OLANDIA** (Ge); **FAS GULF** (At) ex-*Jens Knuppel*

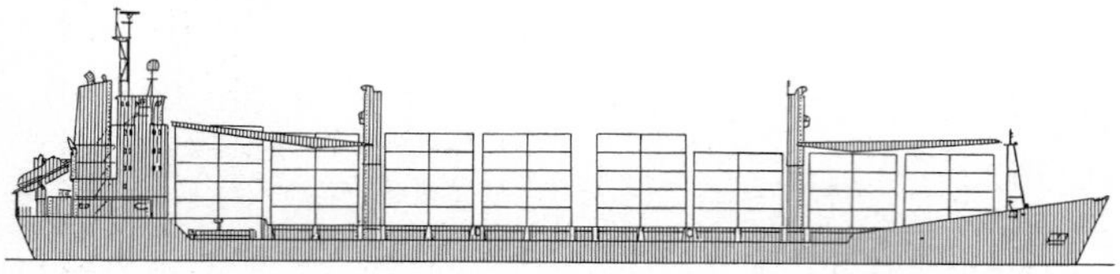

38 *MC²MFR–L H13*
NOBLE At/Pd (Szczecin) 1992; Con; 9,601 grt/12,583 dwt; 149.70 × 8.25 m *(491.14 × 27.07 ft)*; M (B&W); 17.5 kts; ex-*Kairo*; 1,012 TEU; 'B183' type
Sisters (differ in details, such as superstructure arrangement. Some may not have cranes. See drawing number 12/84): **NEDLLOYD CALDERA** (At) ex-*R C Rickmers*; **NEDLLOYD RECIFE** (At) ex-*Ankara*; **ST IRENE** (Cy) ex-*Mai Rickmers*; **MAERSK SANTIAGO** (Li) ex-*Hansa London*; **SEA-LAND COLOMBIA** (At) ex-*Major*; **TSL BRAVO** (Li) ex-*Merkur Bridge*; **MARE BALTICUM** (Cy); **NEDLLOYD CURACAO** (Li) ex-*Hansa Wismar*; **EAGLE WAVE** (Li) ex-*Hansa Stralsund*; **FAS LATTAQUIE** (Li) ex-*Judith Schulte*; **MARE ADRIATICUM** (At) (probably gearless); **HANSA BERLIN** (Ge); **BASTION** (HK); **LIBRA GENOVA** (Ge) ex-*Merkur Lake*; **KAPITAN BYANKIN** (Ru); **YURIY OSTROVSKIY** (Ru); **MAERSK MIAMI** (Sg) ex-*Fiona I*; **HANSA ROSTOCK** (Li); **MAERSK SANTOS** (HK) ex-*Bulwark*; **MARE HIBERNUM** (Li); **SEA NORDIC** (At) ex-*Mare Doricum*

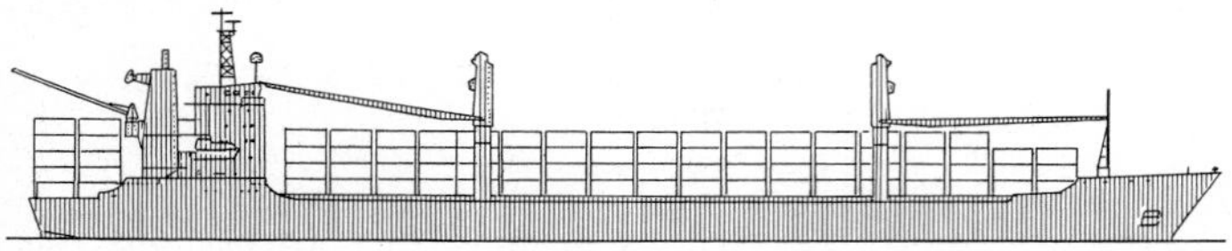

39 *MC²MF–R H12*
ARKONA Cy/FRG (Bremer V) 1985; Con; 18,145 grt/25,088 dwt; 179.84 × 10.30 m *(590.03 × 33.79 ft)*; M (B&W); 17.3 kts; 1,382 TEU; 'CMPC 1300' type
Similar (basically a sister. Differences include different design of radar mast. Funnel may be taller): **MERKUR ISLAND** (Ge)

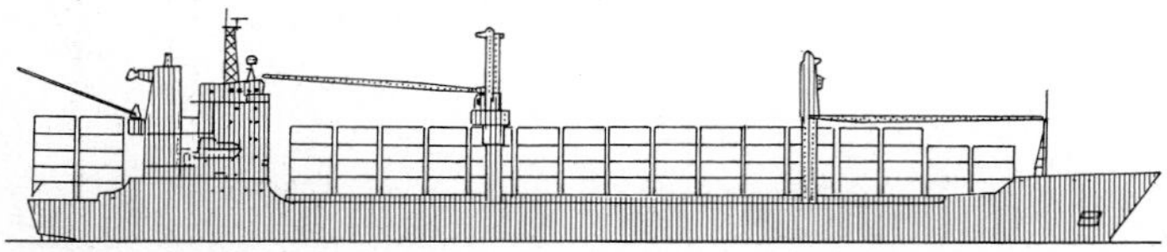

40 *MC²MF–R H12*
CSAV RAUTEN Cy/FRG (Bremer V) 1984; Con; 16,517 grt/22,233 dwt; 166.45 × 10.30 m *(546.10 × 33.79 ft)*; M (B&W); 18 kts; 1,160 TEU
Sisters: **MARCON** (Cy); **CITY OF GLASGOW** (Cy) ex-*Merkur Sea*

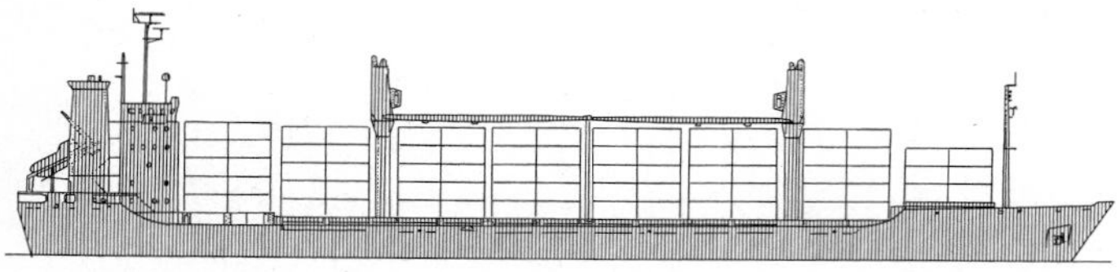

41 *MC²M²FL H13*
AMERICA Cy/Ge (Neptun-Warnow) 1991; Con; 12,997 grt/17,610 dwt; 150.22 × 10.03 m *(492.85 × 32.91 ft)*; M (Sulzer); 17.2 kts; ex-*Carolina*; 1,208 TEU; 'Warnow 1200' type
Sisters: **CSAV ROBLE** (Cy) ex-*Auguste Schulte*; **ELISE SCHULTE** (Cy); **ALABAMA** (Cy) ex-*Donata Schulte*

See photo number 13/79

42 *MC²M–G H1*
TANGER At/Sg (Singapore SB) 1982; Con; 5,371 grt/7,826 dwt; 120.61 × 6.49 m *(396 × 21.29 ft)*; M (Pielstick); 15 kts; ex-*Hellenic Island*; 431 TEU; Cranes are on port side
Sisters: **CADIZ** (At) ex-*Hellenic Cape*; **LISBOA** (At) ex-*Hellenic Dawn*

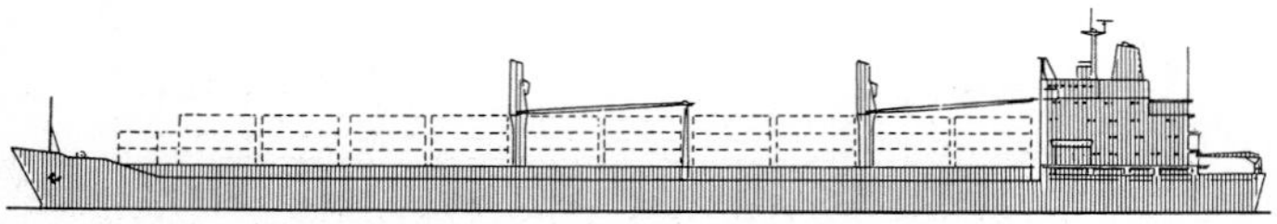

43 *MC²NMFR H1*
LIMARI Li/No (Tangen) 1977/80; Con; 21,449 grt/29,240 dwt; 198.05 × 10.36 m *(649.77 × 33.99 ft)*; M (B&W); 20 kts; ex-*Ville D'Anvers*; Lengthened and converted from general cargo 1980 (Riuniti); Probably has a crane foreward; May be like drawing no 13/13; see photo number 13/106; 1,225 TEU

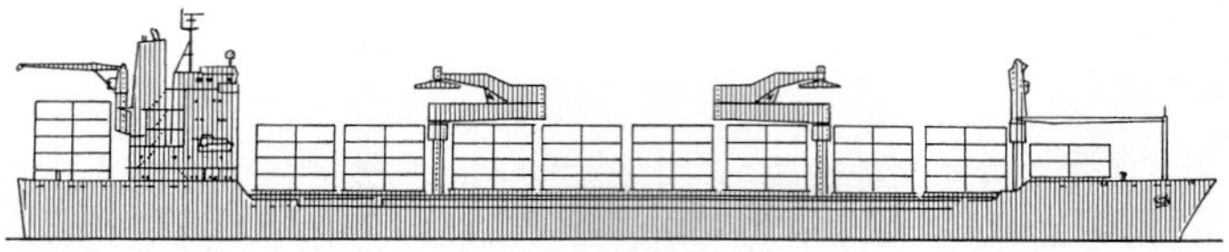

44 *MCJ²MF–R H13*
ZIM AUSTRALIA Br/FRG (Flender) 1986; Con; 21,054 grt/29,995 dwt; 182.10 × 11.54 m *(597.44 × 37.86 ft)*; M (B&W); 18 kts; ex-*Santa Catarina*; 1,631 TEU; 'FW 1600' type

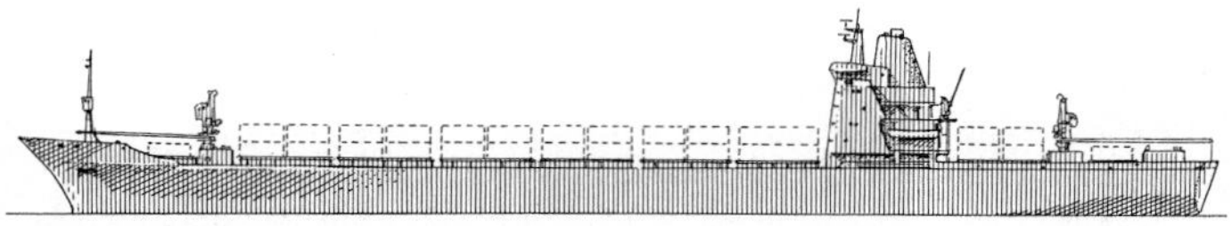

45 *MCMFC H1*
MSC DIEGO Pa/Fi (Wärtsilä) 1970; Con; 15,769 grt/16,070 dwt; 174.25 × 10.08 m *(571 × 33.07 ft)*; TSM (Pielstick); 23 kts; ex-*San Francisco*
Sister: **MSC REGINA** (Pa) ex-*Antonia Johnson*

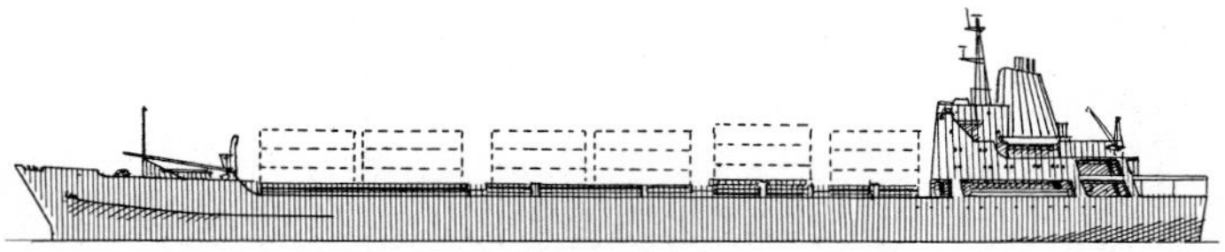

46 *MCMFD H1*
FARO Gr/Au (Whyalla) 1969; Con; 12,373 grt/14,279 dwt; 156.67 × 9.17 m *(514 × 30.08 ft)*; M (Sulzer); 17.5 kts; ex-*Kanimbla*; 620 TEU

See photo number 13/85

47 *MCMFMCM H1*
MSC MICHELE Pa/FRG (Howaldts DW) 1971/79; Con; 16,670 grt/21,185 dwt; 181.44 × 10.59 m *(595.28 × 34.74 ft)*; M (MAN); 20.5 kts; ex-*Hoechst*; 951 TEU; Converted from general cargo, lengthened and widened, 1978 (Bremer V); **SIMILAR TO DRAWING No 12/145** but with crane added foreward

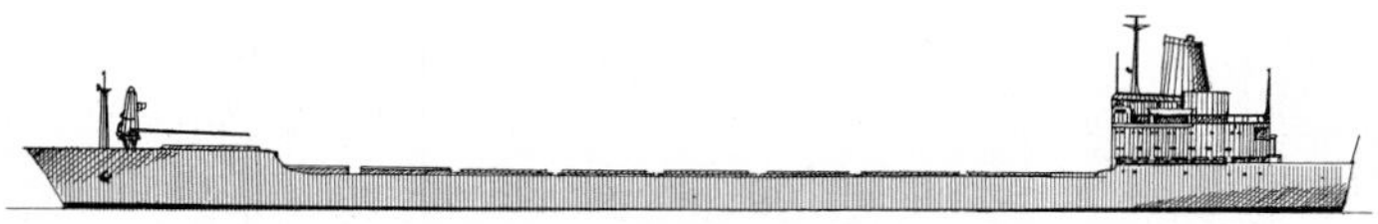

48 *MCMFN H13*
AMERICA STAR Bs/FRG (Bremer V) 1971; Con; 24,907 grt/27,953 dwt; 217.25 × 10.52 m *(712.76 × 34.51 ft)*; M (Sulzer); — kts; ex-*Act 3*; 1,472 TEU
Sisters: **MELBOURNE STAR** (Bs) ex-*Act 4*; **SYDNEY STAR** (Bs) ex-*Act 5*; **MSC MIRELLA** (Pa) ex-*Australian Exporter* (Turbine Machinery—19.5k)

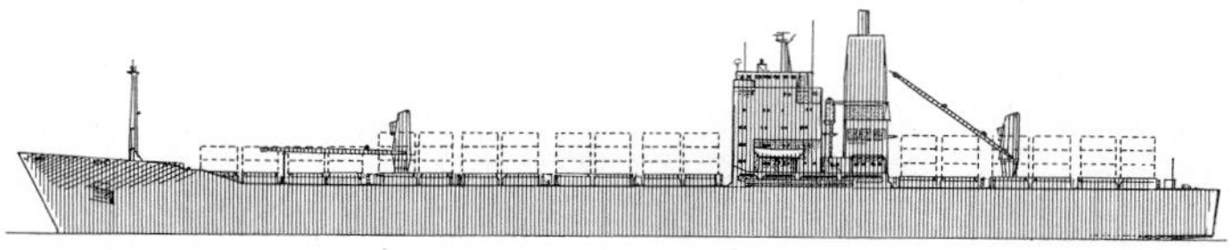

49 *MCMRFRC H1*
GULF SPIRIT Li/Ne (Nederlandsche) 1979; Con; 30,249 grt/27,738 dwt; 202 × 10.5 m *(662.73 × 34.45 ft)*; M (Sulzer); 21 kts; ex-*Incotrans Spirit*
Sister: **HYUNDAI VANCOUVER** (Li) ex-*Incotrans Speed*

50 *MCPCNMF H13*
POLYNESIA Li/Ja (IHI) 1979; Con; 10,774 grt/14,646 dwt; 137.5 × 8 m *(451.11 × 26.25 ft)*; M (Sulzer); 16 kts; 1,091 TEU; Now lengthened to 162.08 m (532 ft)

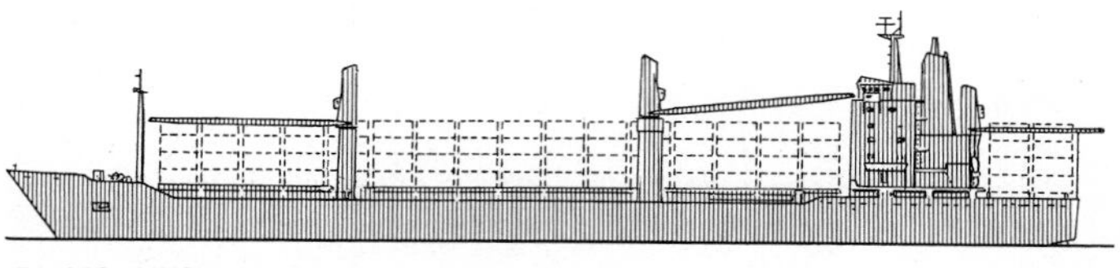

51 *MCPMFC H1*
CONCORDIA Cy/FRG (Thyssen) 1983; Con; 17,468 grt/25,412 dwt; 166.07 × 11.61 m *(545 × 38.09 ft)*; M (B&W); 18.75 kts; ex-*Concordia*; 1,282 TEU
Sister: **CITY OF LONDON** (Cy) ex-*Corona*

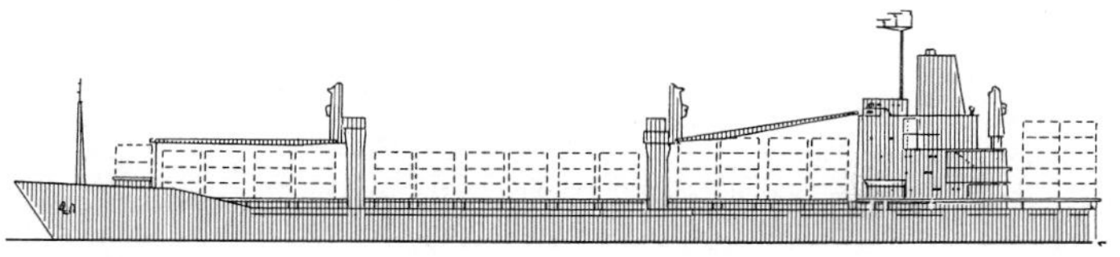

52 *MCPMFC H1*
SEA TRADE Li/FRG (A G 'Weser') 1982; Con; 20,345 grt/28,422 dwt; 173.98 × 11.22 m *(571 × 36.81 ft)*; M (B&W); 18.7 kts; ex-*Usaramo*; 1,346 TEU
Sisters: **SEA MERCHANT** (Li) ex-*Ubena*; **SEA COMMERCE** (Li) ex-*Usambara*

53 $MCP^{2}MF$ *H1*
KOTA SURIA Sg/Ru (Kherson) 1976/79; Con; 12,549 grt/15,128 dwt; 162.52 × 10.12 m *(533 × 33.2 ft)*; M (B&W); 16.5 kts; ex-*Santa Rosa*; Converted from 'DNEPR' class cargo vessel 1979 (Flender); 531 TEU
Sister: **KOTA SABAS** (Sg) ex-*Santa Rita*

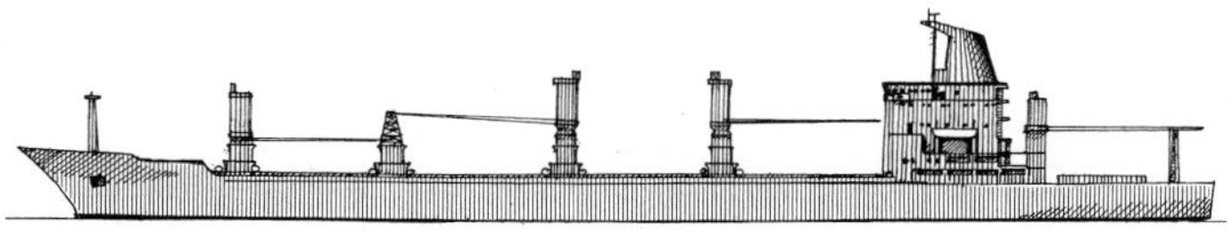

54 $MCP^{2}MFC$ *H1*
DIRECT FALCON Bs/Fr (L'Atlantique) 1978; Con; 20,537 grt/24,946 dwt; 188.63 × 11.42 m *(618.86 × 37.47 ft)*; M (Pielstick); 20.8 kts; ex-*Helene Delmas*; 921 TEU
Sisters: **DIRECT KIWI** (Bs) ex-*Irma Delmas*; **DIRECT EAGLE** (Bs) ex-*Lucie Delmas*; **PADRONE** (Bs) ex-*Marie Delmas*

55 $MCP^{3}NMFS$ *H1*
LAJA Li/Ja (Kawasaki) 1978; C/Con; 22,149 grt/23,709 dwt; 174.02 × 10.15 m *(570.93 × 33.3 ft)*; M (MAN); 17.5 kts; ex-*John Bakke*; Now converted to a container ship (1,017 TEU)
Sister: **LIRCAY** (Li) ex-*Marie Bakke*

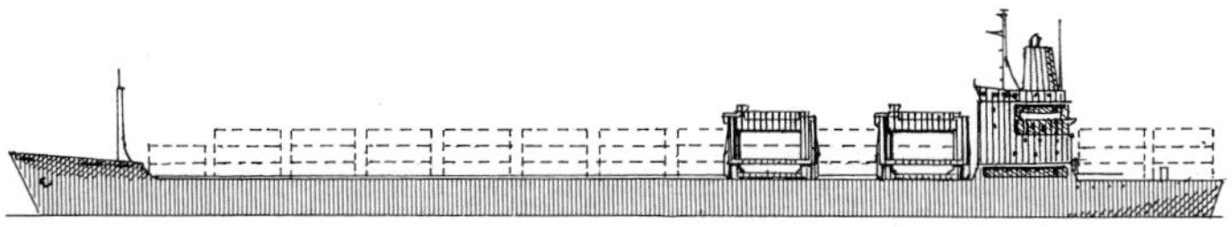

56 $MG^{2}MFM$ *H1*
SEA LEADER Bs/FRG (Schlieker) 1962/78; Con; 17,618 grt/15,417 dwt; 201.84 × 8.28 m *(662.2 × 27.17 ft)*; M (Sulzer); 18 kts; ex-*Elizabethport*; 1978; Foreward and aft sections built 1978 (Mitsubishi HI)
Sisters: **SEA ADVENTURE** (Bs) ex-*San Francisco*; **SEA-LAND PACER** (US) ex-*San Juan*; **SEA PIONEER** (Bs) ex-*Los Angeles*

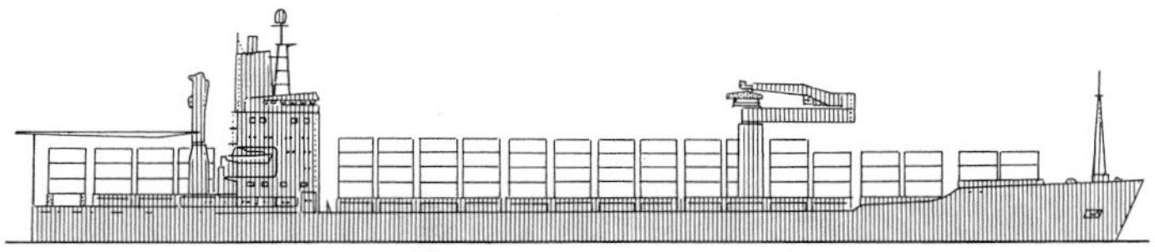

57 *MJHFC H1*
NEDLLOYD VAN NECK Ne/Ne (Giessen-De Noord) 1983; Con; 23,930 grt/ 29,730 dwt; 182.76 × 11.25 m *(599.61 × 36.91 ft)*; M (Sulzer); 17.5 kts; 1,444 TEU

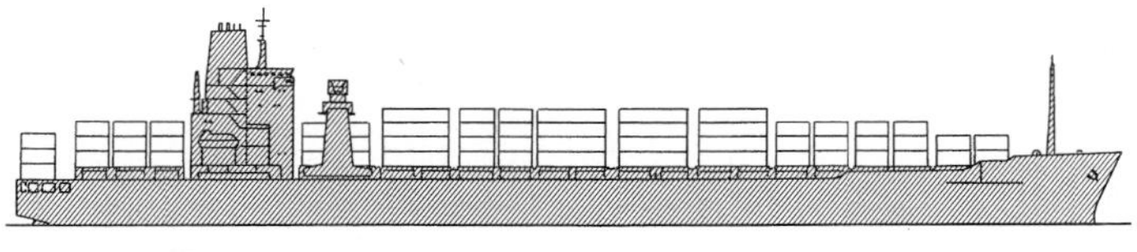

58 *MJHFMD H1*
LASER PACIFIC Li/Ja (NKK) 1984; Con; 31,446 grt/34,680 dwt; 201.02 × 11.52 m *(659.51 × 37.80 ft)*; M (Pielstick); — kts; ex-*Bo Johnson*; 1,905 TEU

59 $MJ^{2}MFR$ *H12*
MAJAPAHIT Ia/FRG (Flensburger) 1982; Con; 16,135 grt/20,815 dwt; 170.21 × 9.68 m *(558 × 31.76 ft)*; M (MAN); 19 kts; 1,152 TEU
Sisters: **ANRO GOWA** (Ia) ex-*Gowa*; **ANRO JAYAKARTA** (Ia) ex-*Jayakarta*

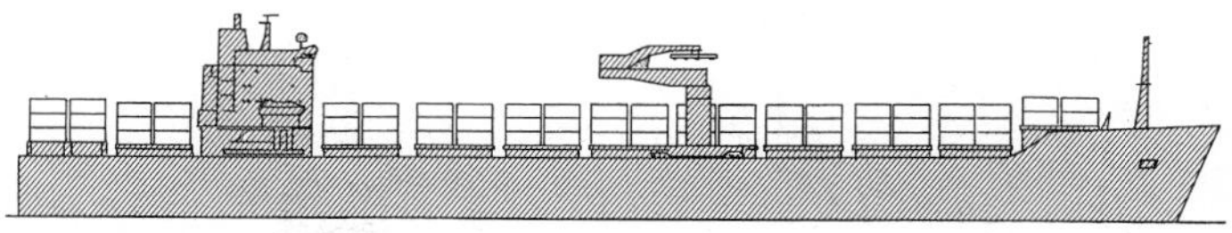

60 *MJMF H1*
CGM MAGELLAN HK/Ko (Hyundai) 1984; Con; 32,150 grt/37,042 dwt; 202.55 × 12.02 m *(664.53 × 39.44 ft)*; M (B&W); — kts; ex-*Andes*; 2,145 TEU

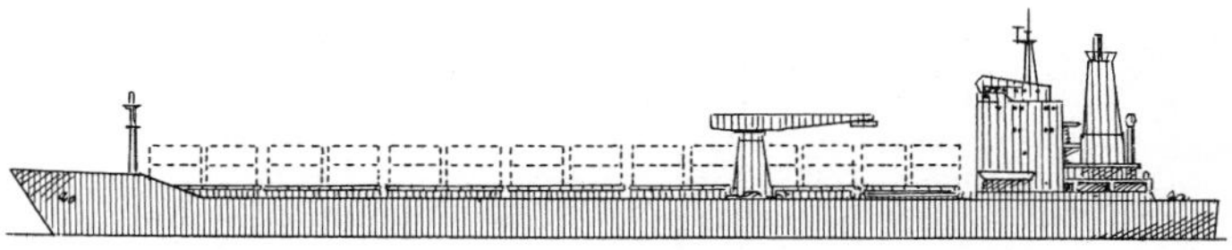

61 *MJMF H1*
KHYBER HK/FRG (Howaldts DW) 1977; Con; 11,217 grt/13,880 dwt; 145.01 × 9.02 m *(475.75 × 29.59 ft)*; M (MAN); 17 kts; Launched as *Brabant*; 550 TEU
Sisters: **MARIN** (Bs) Launched as *Ulanga*; **HANNE BAKKE** (NIS) Launched as *Eschenbach*

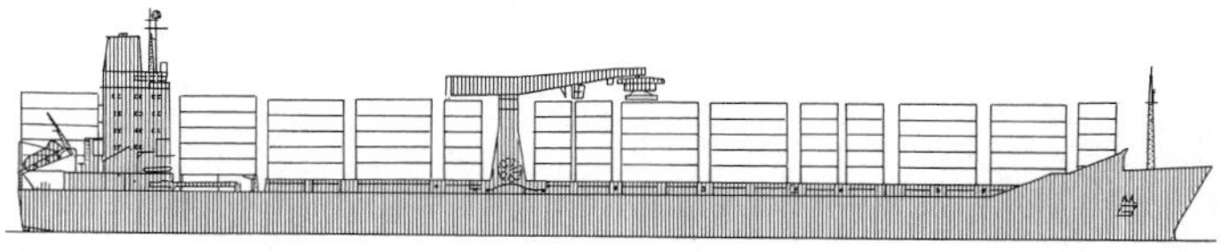

62 *MJMFL H1*
CECILIE MAERSK DIS/De (Odense) 1994; Con; 20,842 grt/28,550 dwt; 190.48 × 10.30 m *(624.93 × 33.79 ft)*; M (Mitsubishi); 18.7 kts; 1,400 TEU
Sisters: **CAROLINE MAERSK** (DIS); **CLAES MAERSK** (DIS); Similar (smaller—176m (577ft)): **CLARA MAERSK** (DIS); **CHRISTIAN MAERSK** (DIS) Similar (smaller—162m (531ft)): **CLIFFORD MAERSK** (DIS); **CORNELIA MAERSK** (DIS); **CHARLOTTE MAERSK** (DIS); **CHASTINE MAERSK** (DIS)

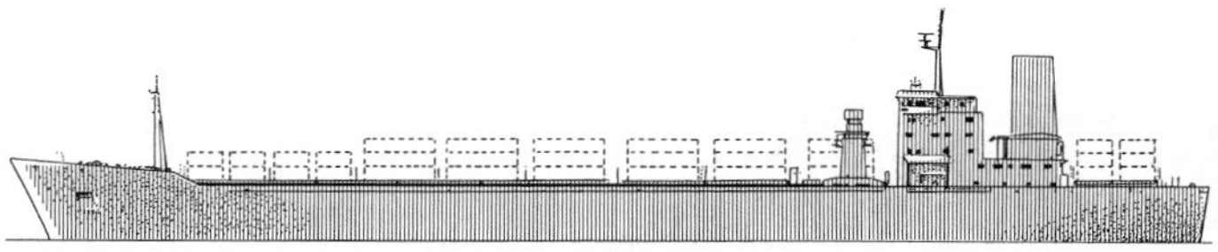

63 *MJMFS H1*
NEDLLOYD ZEELANDIA Ne/Ne (Giessen-De Noord) 1980; Con; 30,175 grt/ 23,678 dwt; 204.02 × 10.21 m *(669.36 × 33.5 ft)*; M (Sulzer); 21.25 kts; ex-*Benattow*; 1,460 TEU

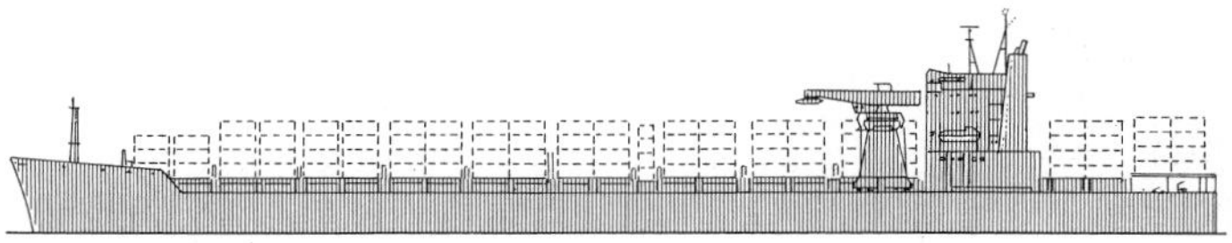

64 $MJM^{2}G$ *H1*
HUMBOLDT EXPRESS Ge/Ko (Samsung) 1984; Con; 32,444 grt/ 34,037 dwt; 206 × 11.72 m *(675.85 × 38.45 ft)*; M (B&W); 18.5 kts; Crane is normally stowed athwartships; 2,181 TEU
Sister: **ISLA DE LA PLATA** (Pa) ex-*Cordillera Express*

See photo number 13/113

65 *MJM–FR H1*
MONTE ROSA Ge/FRG (A G 'Weser') 1981; Con; 24,270 grt/23,520 dwt; 184.89 × 10.02 m *(607 × 32.87 ft)*; M (Sulzer); 18 kts; 1,185 TEU
Sisters: **COLUMBUS CALIFORNIA** (Ge) ex-*Monte Cervantes*; **COLUMBUS QUEENSLAND** (Ge); Similar (originally shorter but lengthened 1985 (Seebeck) to 183.7m (603ft)): **COLUMBUS CANADA** (Li) ex-*Columbus Canterbury*; **COLUMBUS VICTORIA** (Ge) ex-*Columbus Louisiana*

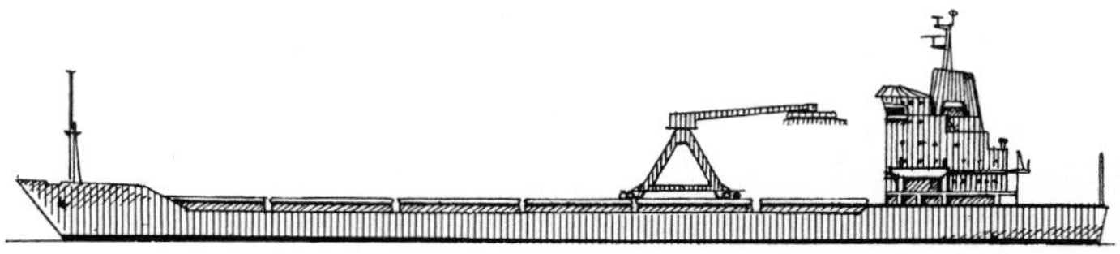

66 *MJM–GN H1*
KOTA JADE Sg/Ja (Yamanishi) 1976; C/Con; 3,741 grt/6,340 dwt; 117.46 × 6.49 m *(385.36 × 21.29 ft)*; M (MAN); 16.25 kts; ex-*Zepatlantic*; Travelling cranes; 358 TEU
Sister: **WEN HE** (RC) ex-*GULF Sailor*

See photo number 13/112

67 M^2SF *H1*
CARIBIA EXPRESS Alternative sequence for entry no 12/118; Crane may be removed

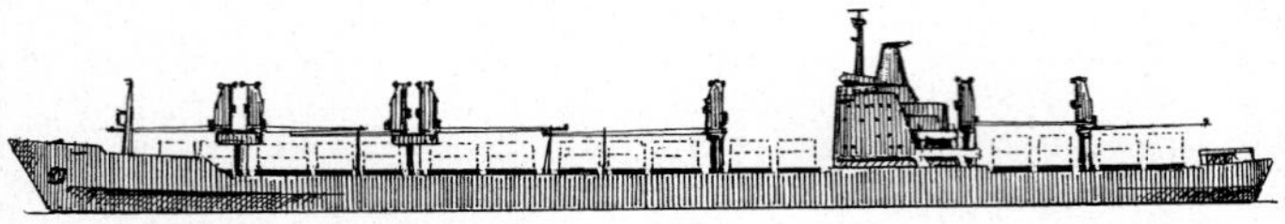

68 MP^2CMGC^2 *H1*
MSC RAFAELA Pa/Fi (Wärtsilä) 1974; Con; 22,042 grt/20,770 dwt; 209.23 × 9.88 m *(686 × 32.41 ft)*; TSM (Sulzer); 22.5 kts; ex-*Tamara*; Cranes may be removed
Sisters: **MSC GINA** (Cy) ex-*Malmros Monsoon*; **TA HE** (Pa) ex-*Nagara*

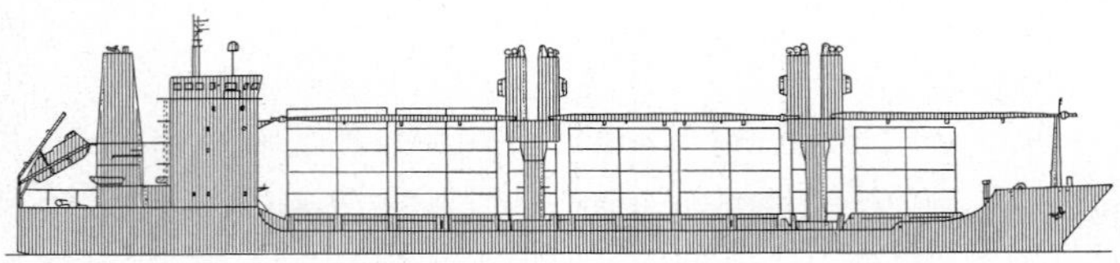

69 MP^2MFL *H13*
FROTABELEM Bz/Bz (EMAQ-Verolme) 1994; Con; 9,182 grt/11,256 dwt; 133.40 × 8.06 m *(437.66 × 26.44 ft)*; M (B&W); 16 kts; 666 TEU
Sister: **FROTAMANAUS** (Bz)

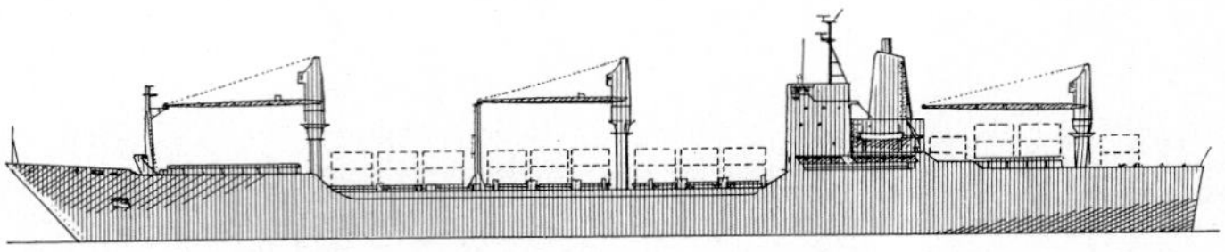

70 MP^2MFP *H13*
MSC ROSA M Cy/It (Italcantieri) 1978; C/Con; 20,418 grt/20,185 dwt; 186.44 × 10.02 m *(611.68 × 32.87 ft)*; M (GMT); 23 kts; ex-*D'Albertis*
Sisters: **MSC DEILA** (Pa) ex-*Da Mosto*; **MSC CARMEN** (Pa) ex-*Pancaldo*

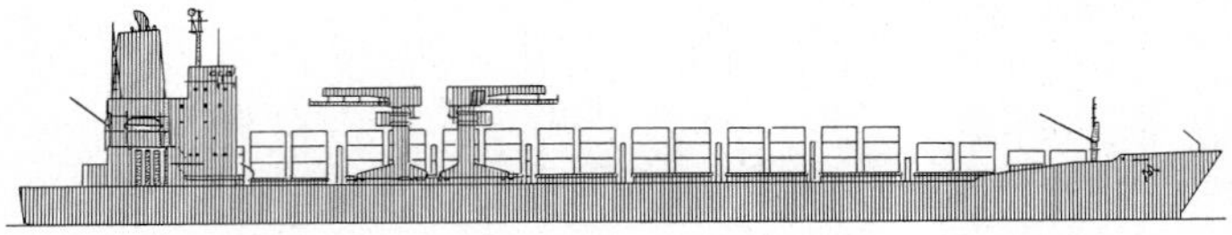

71 $M\text{–}CJ^2HF\text{–}M$ *H1*
COURTNEY L Br/Ja (Tsuneishi) 1992; Con/R; 19,595 grt/15,593 dwt; 203.00 × 8.33 m *(666.01 × 27.33 ft)*; M (B&W); 21.5 kts; 868 TEU
Sisters: **EDYTH L** (Bs); **FRANCES L** (Bs)

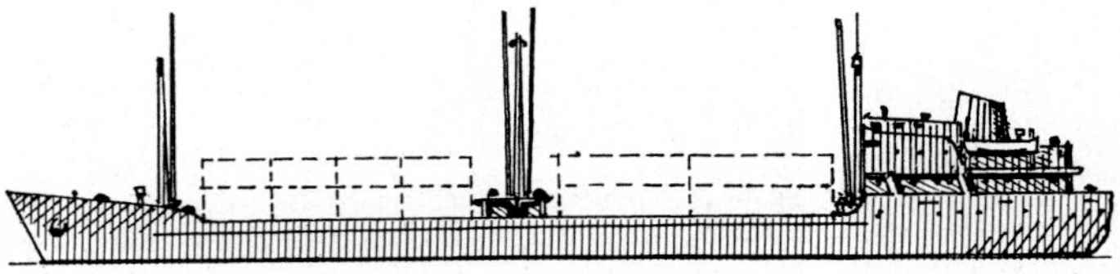

72 *TNHF* *H13*
ACOR SV/FRG (Rolandwerft) 1970; Con; 2,961 grt/4,780 dwt; 102.42 × 6.24 m *(336.02 × 20.47 ft)*; M (Atlas-MaK); 11 kts; Launched as *Norderfehn*; 170 TEU

73 Liao Cheng *(RC); 1975/79* *WSPL*

74 Sha He *(RC); 1983* *WSPL*

75 Lontue *(Li); 1978/82; (as Ville de Bordeaux)* *WSPL*

76 Cap Trafalgar *(Ge); 1990* *WSPL*

77 Bunga Penaga *(My); 1979* *WSPL*

78 CMBT Asia *(Ge); 1985; (as Norasia Samantha)* *WSPL*

79 Lisboa *(At); 1981; (as Hellenic Dawn)* *WSPL*

80 Paraguay Express *(Pa); 1967/81; (as CMB Tabora)* *WSPL*

81 Nedlloyd Inca *(Li); 1973; (as MSC Laurence)* *FotoFlite*

82 Brisbane Star *(Bs); 1978* *FotoFlite*

83 Columbus Olivos *(Bs); 1980/86; (as Monte Pascoal)* *FotoFlite*

84 Ouro Do Brasil *(Li); 1993; (fruit juice carrier)* *FotoFlite*

85 MSC Michele *(Pa); 1971/79* *FotoFlite*

86 Beirut *(At); 1994* *FotoFlite*

87 Lloyd Atlantico *(Bz); 1986* *FotoFlite*

88 Maersk San Antonio *(Sg); 1993; (as ACX Fresia)* *FotoFlite*

89 Maersk Euro Primo *(DIS); 1991* *FotoFlite*

90 Melfi Canada *(Bs); 1992; (as Secil Angola)* *FotoFlite*

91 Castor *(Ne); 1990* *FotoFlite*

92 Alabama *(Cy); 1991; (as Atlantic Express)* *FotoFlite*

93 Eagle Prestige *(Ge); 1983; (as Puritan)* *FotoFlite*

94 Maipo *(Li); 1984* *FotoFlite*

95 Isla Gran Malvina *(Ar); 1987* *FotoFlite*

96 Argentina Star *(Bs); 1979/86* *FotoFlite*

97 World Lynx *(Li); 1979* *FotoFlite*

98 E Cheng *(RC); 1978* *Norman Thomson*

99 Karawa *(At); 1993* *John Freestone*

100 Uruguay Express *(Ur); 1978* *WSPL*

101 Nedlloyd Zeelandia *(Ne); 1980* *WSPL*

102 Greenland Saga *(DIS); 1989* *FotoFlite*

103 MSC Rosa M *(Cy); 1978* *FotoFlite*

104 MSC Regina *(Pa); 1971* *FotoFlite*

105 Direct Eagle *(Bs); 1978* *FotoFlite*

106 Limari *(Li); 1977; (as Ville d'Anvers)* *FotoFlite*

107 Neptune Jasper *(Sg); 1984* *FotoFlite*

108 Copacabana *(Bz); 1984* *FotoFlite*

109 Nordsino *(Cy); 1982* *FotoFlite*

110 City of London *(Cy); 1983* *FotoFlite*

111 Humboldt Express *(Sg); 1984* *FotoFlite*

112 Caribia Express *(Gr); 1976* *FotoFlite*

113 Monte Rosa *(Ge); 1981* *FotoFlite*

117 San Miguel *(Cy); 1994* *FotoFlite*

114 Caecilia Schulte *(Li); 1995* *FotoFlite*

118 Ulf Ritscher *(Ge); 1990* *FotoFlite*

115 Trave Trader *(At); 1994* *FotoFlite*

119 Sea-Land Costa Rica *(DIS); 1991; (as Colleen Sif)* *FotoFlite*

116 CSAV Rosario *(At); 1995* *FotoFlite*

120 Eagle Dawn *(Cy); 1992; (as Cape Hatteras)* *FotoFlite*

121 Clifford Maersk *(DIS); 1992* *FotoFlite*

122 CMBT Concord *(Br); 1988* *FotoFlite*

123 Laser Pacific *(Li); 1984* *FotoFlite*

124 Levant Weser *(At); 1983* *WSPL*

125 Columbus Olinda *(Li); 1987* *FotoFlite*

126 Arkona *(Cy); 1985*

14 Small Gearless Container Ships (Ten 20 ft Stacks or less)

14 Small Container Ships (Ten 20 ft Stacks or Less)

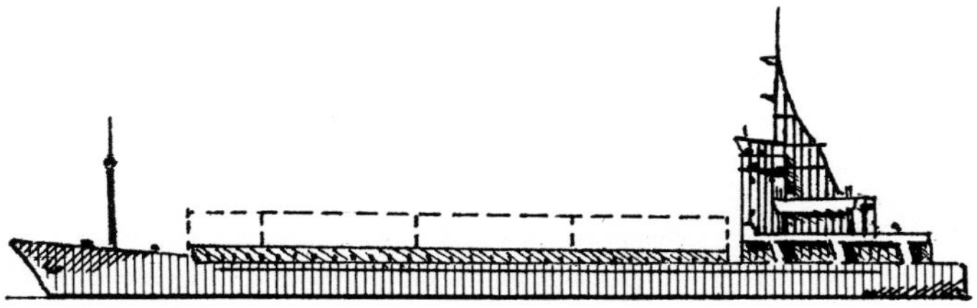

1 *HM–F H*
SAMANTHA Cy/Sp (Luzuriaga) 1972; Con; 1,919 grt/1,829 dwt; 74.71 × 4.24 m *(245.11 × 13.91 ft)*; M (Stork-Werkspoor); 12.5 kts; ex-*Astiluzu 201*; 102 TEU; May be fitted with a deck crane

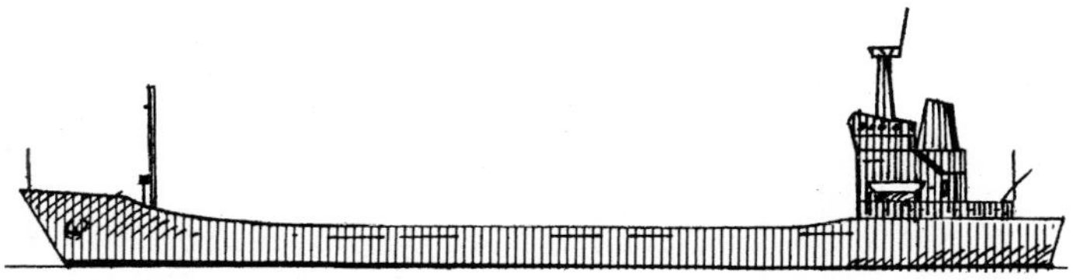

2 M^2F *H1*
ANA RAQUEL —/Ne (Vuyk) 1969; Con; 1,457 grt/2,210 dwt; 85.32 × 4.71 m *(279.92 × 15.45 ft)*; M (Werkspoor); 16 kts; ex-*Minho*; 'Hustler' class; 124 TEU
Sisters: **DINA** (Pa) ex-*Tormes*; **HALCON DEL MAR** (Pa) ex-*Tua*; **FILIPPOS** (SV) ex-*Tamega*; **HYBUR CLIPPER** (At) ex-*Tiber*; **PANAMA FLYER** (Br) ex-*Mondego*; **APPLE** (Pa) ex-*England*; **HYBUR INTREPID** (At) ex-*Tronto*

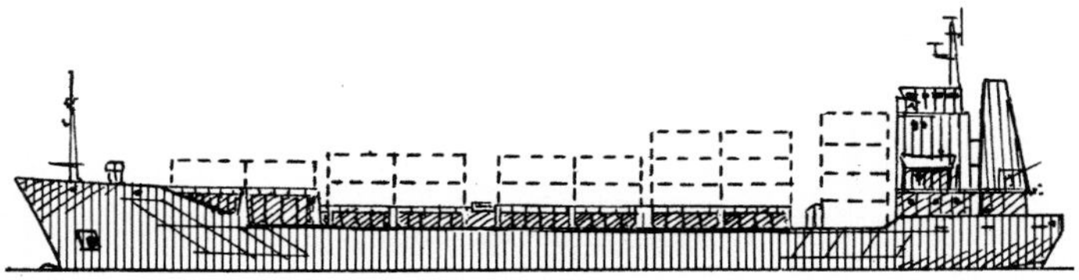

3 M^2F *H1*
CORVO Po/FRG (Nobiskrug) 1980; C/Con; 2,937 grt/3,224 dwt; 89 × 4.95 m *(292 × 16.24 ft)*; M (KHD); 13 kts; ex-*Stemwede*; May now have a deck crane; 218 TEU
Sisters (lengthened to 103.41m (339ft): **YAN XING** (Pa) ex-*Donar*; **LE YU QUAN** (RC) ex-*Thiassi*; Similar (May have a deck crane): **PRIME VELVET** (Gr) ex-*Lusitania*

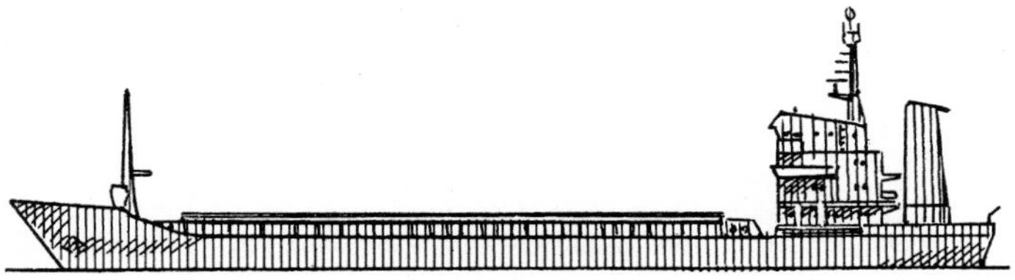

4 M^2F *H1*
DELTA FRG/FRG (M Jansen) 1978; C/Con; 2,108 grt/2,280 dwt; 82.02 × 4.9 m *(269.09 × 16.08 ft)*; M (MaK); 13 kts; 122 TEU

5 M^2F *H1*
FLAMINGO Sn/Br (Hill) 1962/72; Con; 1,343 grt/1,771 dwt; 78.64 × 5.04 m *(258.01 × 16.54 ft)*; M (British Polar); 13 kts; ex-*Buffalo*; Converted from cargo 1972; 84 TEU

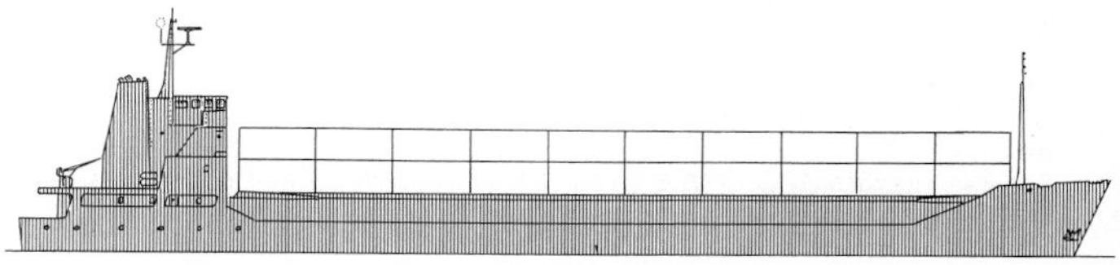

6 M^2F *H1*
RHEIN FEEDER At/Po (Viana) 1991; C/Con; 2,463 grt/3,269 dwt; 87.42 × 5.08 m *(286.81 × 16.67 ft)*; M (Alpha); 12.5 kts; ex-*Liesel*; 202 TEU
Sisters (some built by Mondego): **INTERMODAL MALTA** (At) ex-*Wannsee*; **HERM J** (At); **HIGHLAND** (At) ex-*Sirrah*; **INTERMODAL LEVANT** (At) ex-*Queensee*; **INTERMODAL EGYPT** (At) ex-*Anna J*; **INTERMODAL MARE** (At) ex-*Adele J*; **INTERMODAL CARRIER** (At) ex-*Heide J*

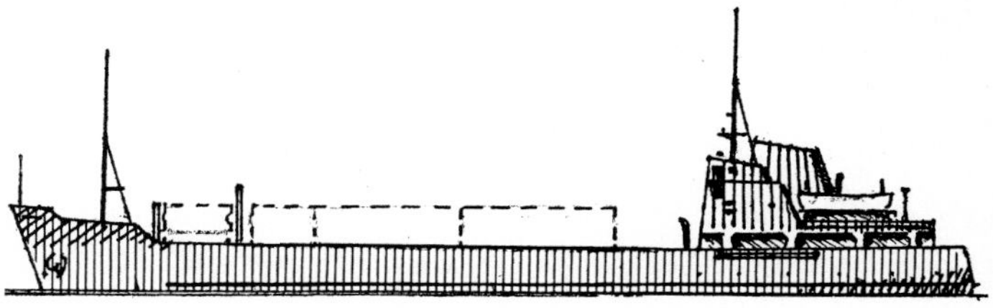

7 M^2F *H1*
SEA CONTAINER Ho/Br (Ailsa) 1958; C; 999 grt/1,219 dwt; 80.09 × 4.08 m *(262.76 × 13.39 ft)*; M (British Polar); 10 kts; ex-*Container Enterprise*; 47 TEU
Sister: **SEA MIST** (Pa) ex-*Container Venturer*

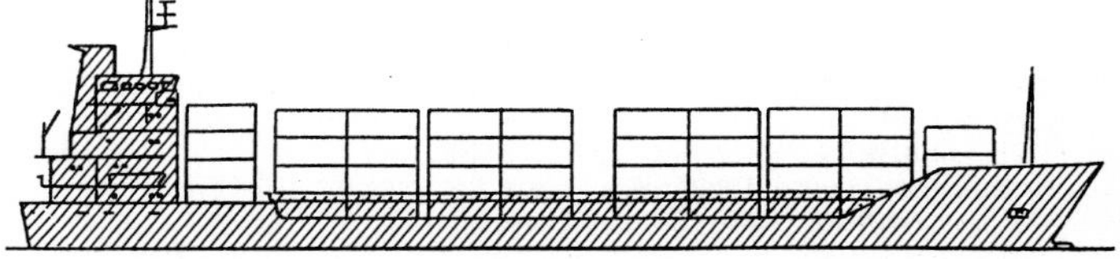

8 M^2FD *H1*
BORSTEL At/FRG (Sietas) 1980; C/Con; 3,228 grt/3,996 dwt; 93.30 × 5.78 m *(306.10 × 18.96 ft)*; M (Deutz); 14 kts; ex-*Clipper*; 263 TEU
Sister: **PRIME VENTURE II** (Gr) ex-*Concord*

9 M^2FN *H1*
EAGLE MOON Sg/Ja (Mitsubishi HI) 1979; Con; 7,179 grt/8,050 dwt; 120.3 × 6.91 m *(394.69 × 22.67 ft)*; M (Mitsubishi); 14 kts; ex-*Benvalla*; 426 TEU

10 M^2FT *H13*
PIONER NAKHODKI Ru/Ru (Vyborg) 1972; Con; 4,787 grt/6,270 dwt; 130.31 × 6.93 m *(427.53 × 22.74 ft)*; M (Sulzer); 15 kts; 218 TEU
Sisters: **SESTRORETSK** (Ru); **PIONER ODESSY** (Uk); **PIONER VLADIVOSTOKA** (Ru); **PIONER PRIMORYA** (Ru); **PIONER VYBORGA** (Ru)

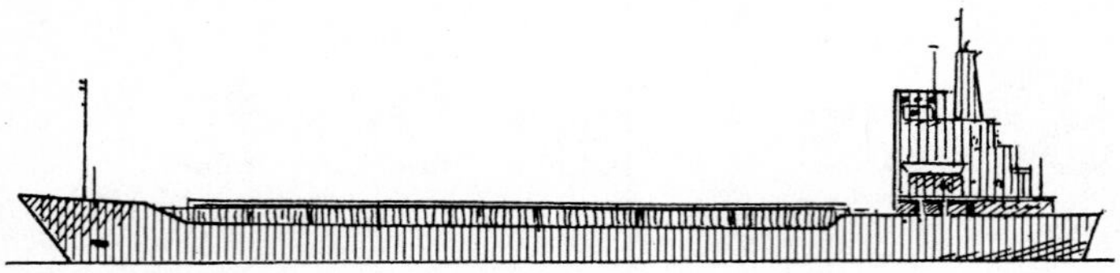

11 *M²M–GD H1*
KOMET At/FRG (Sietas) 1976; C/Con; 1,599 grt/3,882 dwt; 93.53 × 6.08 m *(306.86 × 19.88 ft)*; M (KHD); 14.5 kts; ex-*Regine*; 210 TEU
Sisters: **BELL SWIFT** (At) ex-*Jan*; **EASTWIND** (Cy) ex-*Nordic*; **ARAWAK CHIEF** (At) ex-*Triton*; Similar (mast from bridge): **RABAT** (At) ex-*Diana*; **SAFI** (At) ex-*Liberta*

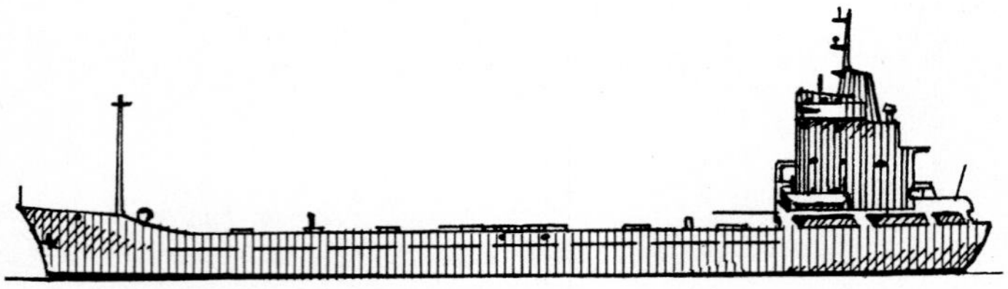

12 *MM–F H1*
BISANZIO SV/Ne (Zaanlandsche) 1970; Con; 2,166 grt/2,520 dwt; 81.64 × 5.03 m *(267.85 × 16.5 ft)*; M (Werkspoor); — kts; ex-*Rane*; 167 TEU
Sisters: **ALEXANDRIA STAR** (Pa) ex-*Ring* (Spanish built—Cadagua); **KARIN** (NIS) ex-*Brage*

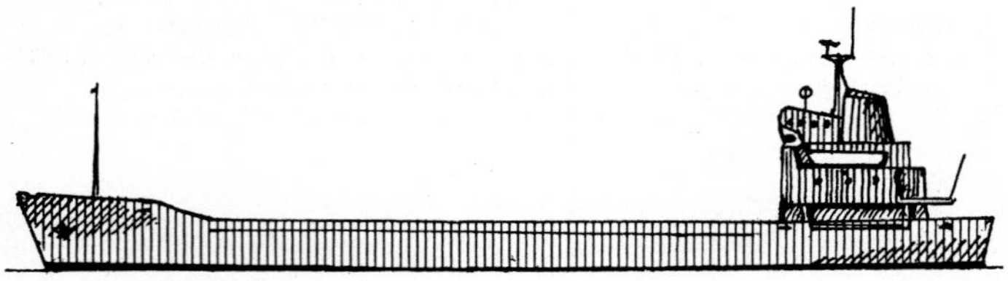

13 *MM–F H1*
GINA My/FRG (Schuerenstedt) 1969; Con; 630 grt/1,450 dwt; 82.1 × 3.82 m *(269.36 × 12.53 ft)*; M (Atlas-MaK); 15 kts; ex-*Kormoran Isle*; 126 TEU

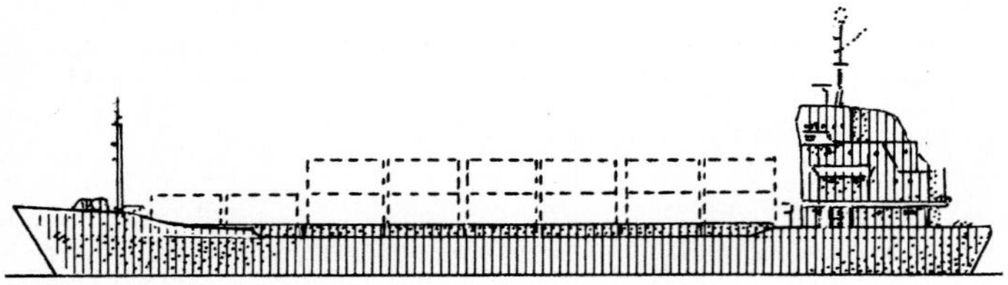

14 *MM–F H1*
LING FENG RC/Ja (Kagoshima) 1976; Con/C; 1,839 grt/2,213 dwt; 79.58 × 4.61 m *(261.09 × 15.12 ft)*; M (Atlas-MaK); 13.75 kts; ex-*Bell Rover*; 122 TEU
Sisters: **LAURA I** (Pa) ex-*Bell Raider*; **ESTRELLA I** (Pa) ex-*Bell Rebel*; **OLA** (Pa) ex-*Bell Renown*; **ERIZO** (Pa) ex-*Bell Reliant*; **HUA JIE** (RC) ex-*Bell Resolve*; **FAREAST FAIR** (SV) ex-*Bell Rival*
Sisters (lengthened by 13m (42.65ft)): **BELL RACER** (Ih); **BELL RULER** (Ih); **BELL RANGER** (Ih)

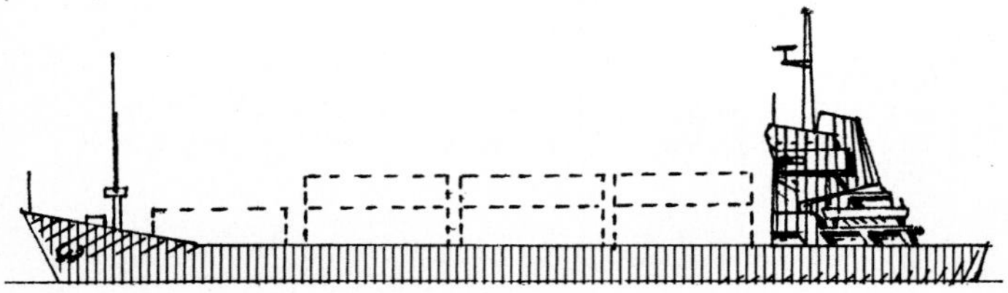

15 *MM–F H1*
MONA Gr/Ne (van der Werf) 1968; C/Con; 499 grt/1,221 dwt; 73.84 × 4.48 m *(242.26 × 14.70 ft)*; M (MWM); 13.5 kts; ex-*Stadt Aschendorf*
Similar: **LAS AVES** (Ve) ex-*Nieuwland*; **EQUATOR JEWEL** (Sg) ex-*Plainsman*

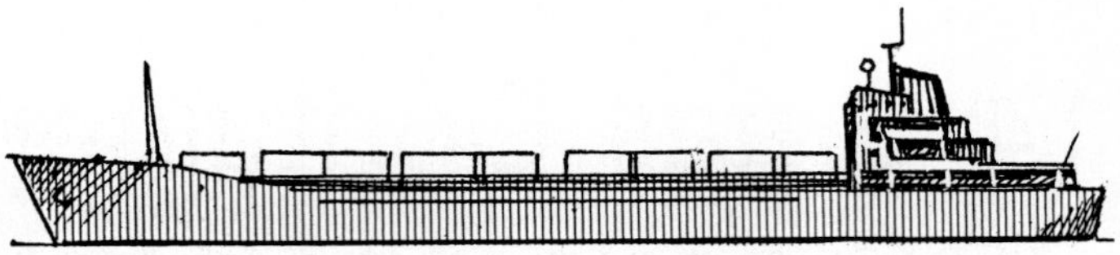

16 *MM–F H1*
RODRIGUES CABRILHO Po/FRG (Schuerenstedt) 1969; Con; 2,978 grt/2,923 dwt; 95.59 × 5.07 m *(313.62 × 16.63 ft)*; M (MaK); 12 kts; ex-*Ellen Isle*; 152 TEU

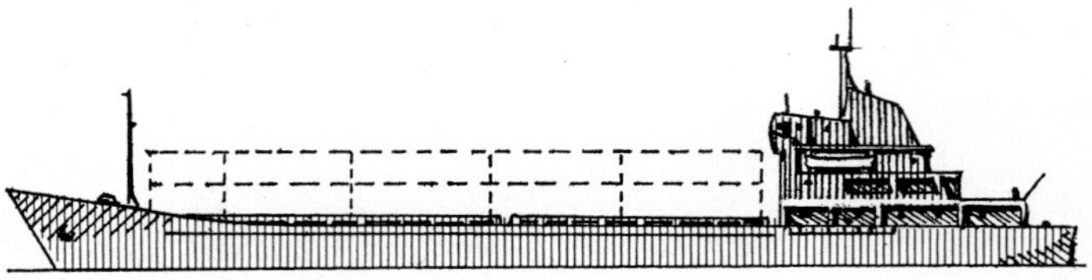

17 *MM–F H1*
XIU SHAN RC/Ne (Giessen-De Noord) 1969; Con; 2,910 grt/3,780 dwt; 95.61 × 4.85 m *(313.68 × 15.91 ft)*; M (Atlas-MaK); 15 kts; ex-*Sally Isle*; 152 TEU

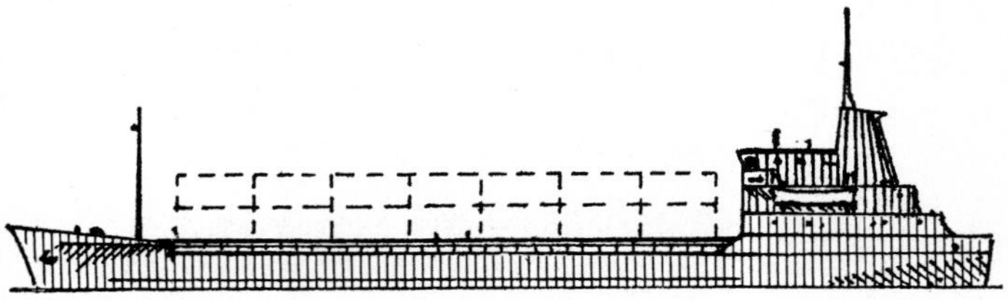

18 *MM–F H12*
C EXPRESS Th/FRG (Schlichting) 1968; C/Con; 1,597 grt/1,330 dwt; 78.06 × 3.62 m *(256.1 × 11.88 ft)*; M (Atlas-MaK); 13 kts; ex-*Kildare*; 74 TEU

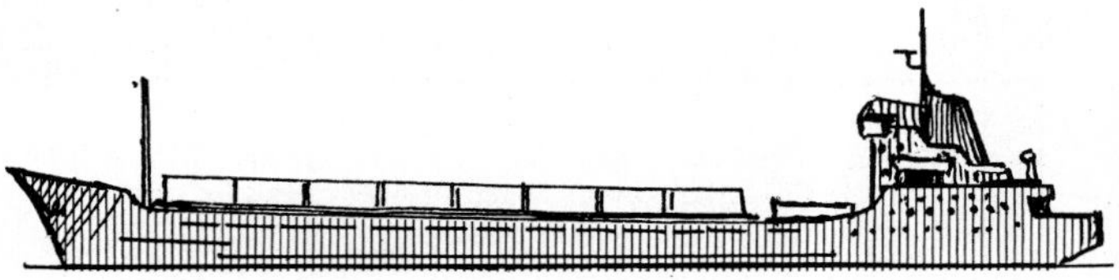

19 *MM–F H12*
WEST SKY Sw/Ne (van der Werf) 1968; C/Con; 2,544 grt/2,523 dwt; 90.12 × 4.64 m *(295.67 × 15.22 ft)*; M (KHD); 14.5 kts; ex-*Solway Fisher*; 89 TEU

20 *MM–F H13*
ELENA Bu/Bu (Ivan Dimitrov) 1970; Con; 1,599 grt/2,239 dwt; 80.73 × 5.31 m *(264.86 × 17.42 ft)*; M (Sulzer); — kts; Converted from general cargo; Others of this class may be similarly converted; May have two deck cranes

See photo number 14/57

21 *MM–F H13*
PELBOXER Gr/Sp (Construcciones SA) 1970; Con; 2,663 grt/3,260 dwt; 88.22 × 5 m *(289.44 × 16.4 ft)*; M (Stork-Werkspoor); 12 kts; ex-*Isla del Mediterraneo*; 182 TEU
Sister: **JOHAN PEARL** (My) Launched as *Ardan*

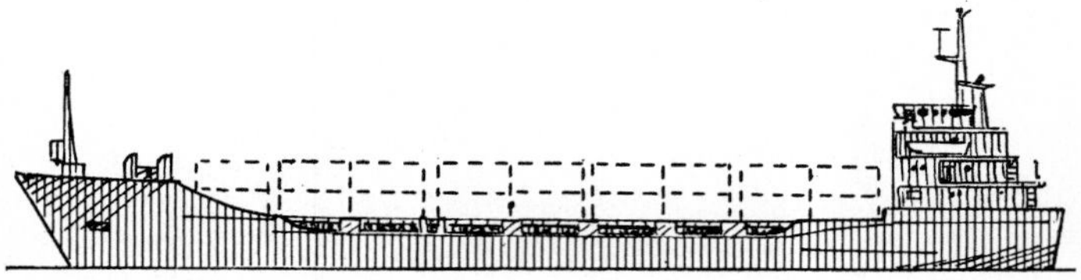

22 *MM–F H13*
PRIME VIEW Gr/FRG (Norderwerft/Sietas) 1979; Con; 3,296 grt/4,133 dwt; 88.65 × 4.88 m *(290.85 × 16.01 ft)*; M (KHD); 14.5 kts; ex-*Thunar*; 267 TEU; 'Sietas type 81'; aft section built by Norderwerft, foreward section built by Sietas. Lengthened 1982 to 103.18m (339ft). Drawing shows vessel before lengthening
Sister: **RICH STAR** (SV) ex-*Wotan*
Sisters (not lengthened): **NORDSEE** (At); **ATLANTIS** (At); **GOTALAND** (Ge) ex-*Helene Waller*; **PHILIPP** (At) ex-Karat

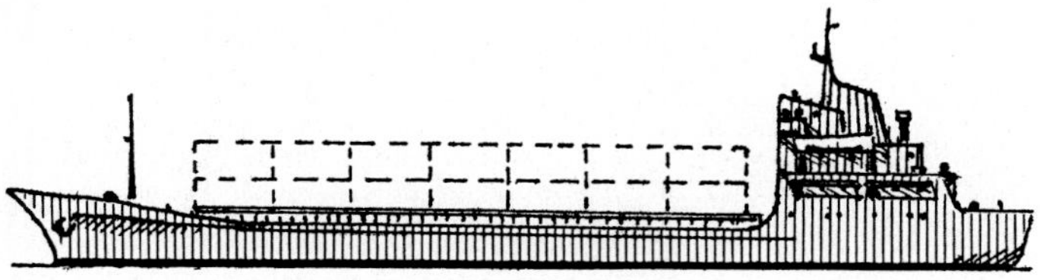

23 *MM–F H13*
VENTO Ma/Sp (Musel) 1971; Con; 1,940 grt/2,837 dwt; 79.94 × 5.65 m *(262.27 × 18.54 ft)*; M (Deutz); 13 kts; Launched as *Esther del Mar*; 143 TEU
Sister: **PHOENIX II** (Cy) ex-*Manchester Mercurio*

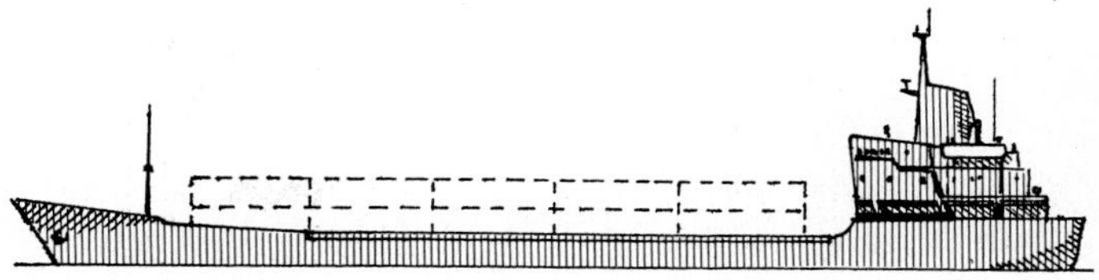

26 *MM–FMD H13*
WING SING Pa/Sp (Construcciones SA) 1972; Con; 3,452 grt/2,905 dwt; 104.53 × 4.89 m *(342.95 × 16.04 ft)*; M (MAN); 16 kts; ex-*American Main*; 176 TEU

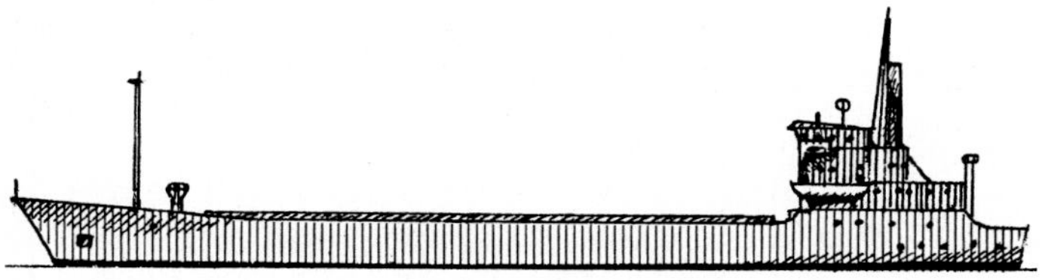

24 *MM–F H2*
LING TONG RC/FRG (Jadewerft) 1972; Con; 980 grt/2,161 dwt; 88.3 × 4.35 m *(289.7 × 14.27 ft)*; M (MWM); 14 kts; ex-*Kalkgrund*; 148 TEU

See photo number 14/59

27 *MM–FN H13*
PANCON 3 Bl/Ne (van der Werf) 1971; C/Con; 3,671 grt/5,463 dwt; 105.92 × 6.36 m *(347.51 × 20.87 ft)*; M (KHD); 14.5 kts; ex-*Brathay Fisher*; 185 TEU

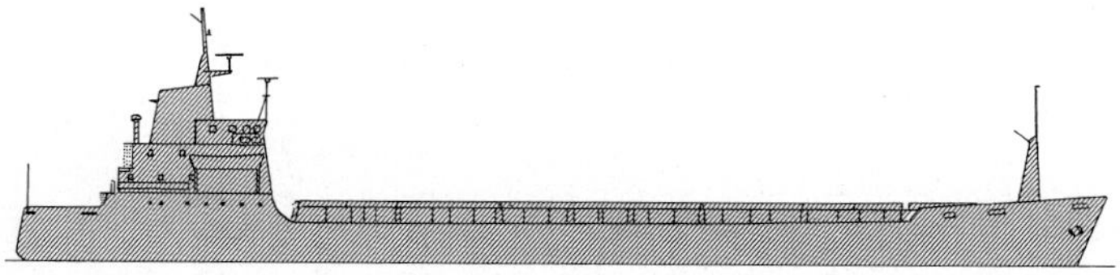

25 *MM–F H2*
PELTAINER Cy/Ih (Verolme Cork) 1970; Con; 4,079 grt/4,914 dwt; 107.14 × 4.44 m *(351.51 × 14.57 ft)*; TSM (Mirrlees Blackstone); 14 kts; ex-*Brian Boroime*; 182 TEU
Sister: **PELINER** (Cy) ex-*Rhodri Mawr*

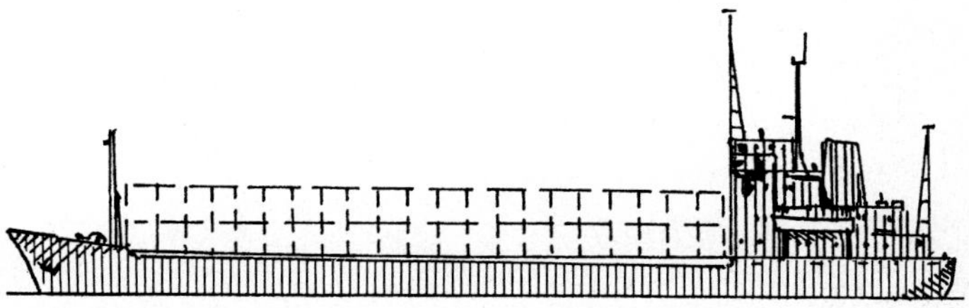

28 *MNMFN H1*
NIKKO No 53 —/Ja (Imai S); 1976; C grt/Con dwt; 1,982/3,908 m; 76.76 × 5.18 *(251.84 × 17)*; TSM (Akasaka); 9.5; ex-*Tungho No. 1*
Probable sisters: **WILCON V** (Pi) ex-*Tungho No.2*; **SENEI MARU** (Ja) ex-*Tungho No.3*

29 Coburg *(At); 1975* *WSPL*

30 Casablanca *(At); 1974* *Norman Thomson*

31 St Georg *(At); 1993* *FotoFlite*

32 St Pauli *(At); 1992* *FotoFlite*

33 Bell Ady *(At); 1995* *FotoFlite*

34 Danfeeder *(DIS); 1975* *FotoFlite*

35 Westgard *(Fi); 1980; (as Laura)* *FotoFlite*

36 Prime Velvet *(Gr); 1980* *WSPL*

37 UB Jaguar *(Ge); 1994; (as Iberian Bridge)* *FotoFlite*

38 Bermuda Islander *(Ne); 1995* *FotoFlite*

39 Gerassimos *(Pa); 1978; (as Melly)* *FotoFlite*

40 Rhein Merchant *(Ge); 1991; (as Sybille)* *FotoFlite*

41 Long Tong *(RC); 1972; (as Baltic Osprey)* *FotoFlite*

42 Komet *(At); 1976; (as Steinkirchen)* *FotoFlite*

43 Bell Swift *(At); 1976; (as Jan)* *FotoFlite*

44 Arawak Chief *(At); 1976* *FotoFlite*

45 Rabat *(At); 1975* *FotoFlite*

46 Safi *(At); 1975* *FotoFlite*

47 Bisanzio *(SV); 1970; (as Trade Sky)* *FotoFlite*

48 Karin *(NIS); 1970; (as Samo)* *FotoFlite*

49 Erizo *(Pa); 1978* *FotoFlite*

50 Bell Racer *(Ih); 1978* *FotoFlite*

51 Panama Flyer *(Br); 1972; (as Hustler Indus)* *FotoFlite*

52 Nordsee *(At); 1978* *FotoFlite*

53 Atlantis *(At); 1979* *FotoFlite*

54 Philipp *(At); 1978* *FotoFlite*

55 Alfama *(Po); 1978* *FotoFlite*

56 Corvo *(Po); 1980; (as Espana) (crane probably removed)* *FotoFlite*

57 Johan Pearl *(My); 1971; (as Ratana Bhum)* *FotoFlite*

58 Vento *(Ma); 1971; (as Esther del Mar)* *FotoFlite*

59 Pancon 3 *(Bl); 1971* *FotoFlite*

60 Sea Container *(Ho); 1958; (as Container Enterprise)* *FotoFlite*

61 Rhein Feeder *(At); 1991* *FotoFlite*

62 Intermodal Carrier *(At); (as Heide J)* *FotoFlite*

63 Lady Linda *(Cy); 1989; (as Mellum)* *FotoFlite*

64 Borstel *(At); 1980; (as Iberian Bridge)* *FotoFlite*

65 Prime Venture II *(Gr); 1981; (as Concord)* *FotoFlite*

66 Schulau *(At); 1978* *FotoFlite*

67 City of Manchester *(Br); 1979; (as Laxfoss)* *FotoFlite*

68 Werfen *(As); 1991* *FotoFlite*

69 Vince *(Bl); 1971; (as Wilke)* *FotoFlite*

70 Dunkerque Express *(Ih); 1985* *FotoFlite*

71 Lu Sheng *(RC); 1977; (as Diana D)* *FotoFlite*

72 Churruca *(Ge); 1991; (as Cimbria)* *FotoFlite*

73 Teutonia *(NIS); 1972/76* *Ian Pakeman*

74 Jorund *(Cy); 1976* *WSPL*

75 Ursula C *(Cy); 1996* *WSPL*

76 Nautilus *(NA); 1991* *WSPL*

77 Heereplein *(Ne); 1991* *WSPL*

78 Jan Kahrs *(Ge); 1988* *WSPL*

79 Northsea Trader *(At); 1995* *WSPL*

80 Baltic Amber *(Cy); 1979; (as Nora Heeren)* *WSPL*

81 Highland *(At); 1990; (as Sirrah)* *WSPL*

82 Kate *(Ge); 1986* *WSPL*

83 Durnstein *(As); 1986; (as Visurgis)* *WSPL*

84 Gisela Bartels *(Ge); 1985/86* *WSPL*

15 Low-airdraught Ships (Sea/River)

15 Low-airdraught Ships (Sea/River)

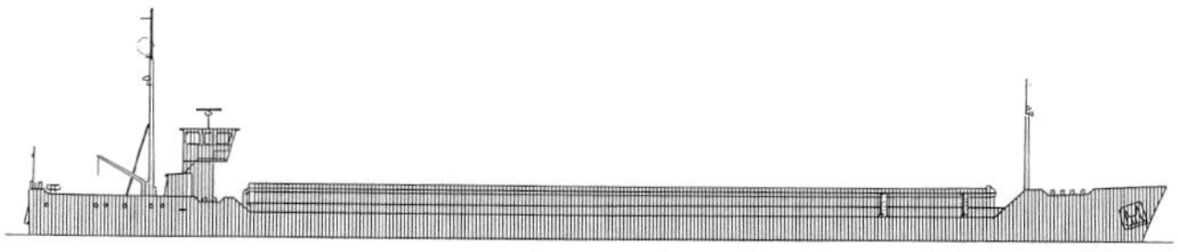

1 *HFH H1*
SEA ORADE Ge/Ge (Bayerische) 1990; C/Con; 1,354 grt/1,609 dwt; 77.00 × 3.17 m *(252.62 × 10.40 ft)*; TSM (Penta); 10.5 kts; ex-*Orade*; 94 TEU; Funnel on starboard side

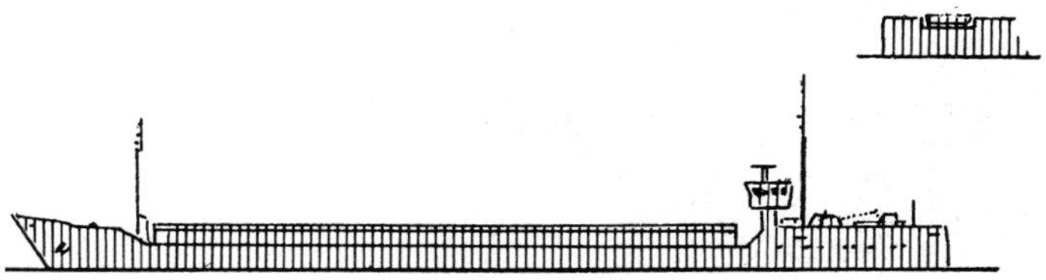

2 *H²F H13*
RMS SCOTIA Ge/FRG (Koetter) 1981; C; 1,022 grt/1,092 dwt; 75.01 × 2.91 m *(246 × 9.55 ft)*; M (KHD); 10 kts; ex-*Lucky Star*; Sea/river type; Lifeboat on starboard side (see inset)
Sisters: **RMS BAVARIA** (Ge) ex-*Gerhard Prahm*; **WARFLETH** (Ge) (builder—Hegemann); **RMS ANGLIA** (Ge) ex-*Sheila Hammann*

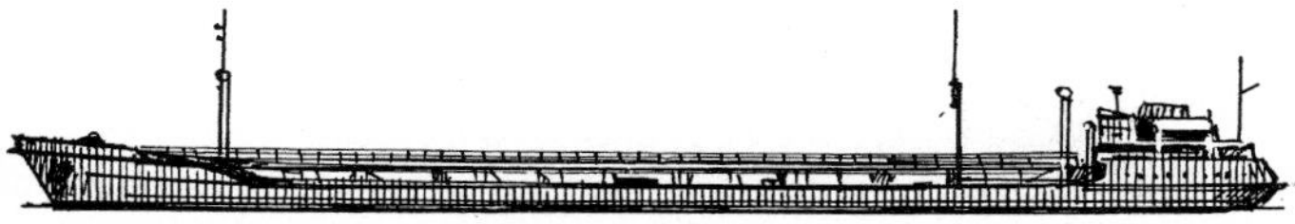

3 *HMNMFM H13*
VOLGONEFT type Ru/Ru and Bu (Volgograd/G Dimitrov) 1969/72; Tk; 3,400 grt/4,200 dwt; 135.01 × 3.5 m *(442.95 × 11.48 ft)*; TSM (Liebknecht); 10.5 kts; This drawing represents the later vessels of this type; Names have the prefix 'VOLGONEFT' and a number; There are approximately 27 in the whole group; See photo number 15/96

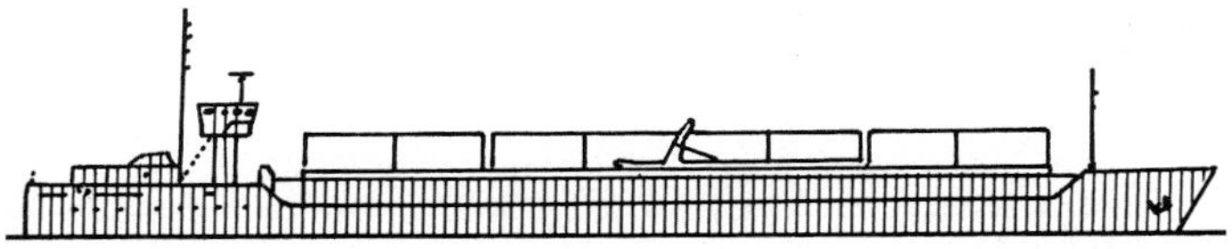

4 *MCMF H13*
MARI CLAIRE SV/FRG (Koetter) 1984; C/Con; 1,409 grt/1,545 dwt; 79.00 × 3.30 m *(259.19 × 10.83 ft)*; M (Deutz); 10 kts; ex-*Kirsten*; 80 TEU; Deck crane could be obscured by deck cargo—see drawing number 15/13
Similar: **MARI FRANCE** (Ge) ex-*Simone*

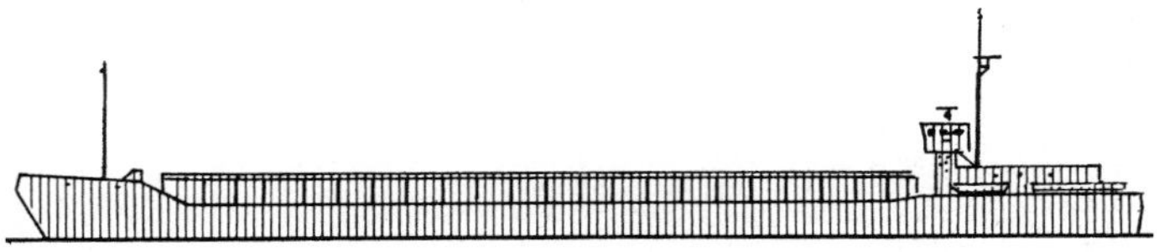

5 *MH H1*
GOLF Ge/FRG (Cassens) 1981; Pal/Pap; 3,060 grt/3,154 dwt; 95.71 × 4.4 m *(314 × 14.44 ft)*; M (Krupp-MaK); 11 kts; Sea/river type; Side door (port); 118 TEU

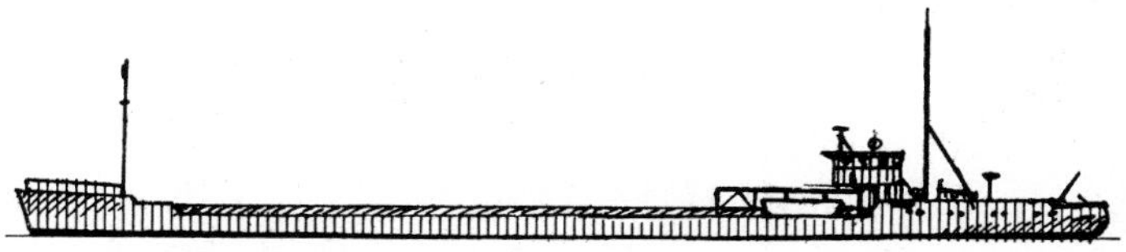

6 *MH H13*
NOORDERLING Ne/Ne (Kramer & Booy) 1973; C (sea/river); 967 grt/1,400 dwt; 80.02 × 3.18 m *(262.53 × 10.43 ft)*; M (Liebknecht); 10 kts; ex-*Bielefeld* 1984; ex-*Cargo-Liner 1* 1981; Masts and bridge can be lowered
Sisters: **DEO GRATIAS** (Ne) ex-*Cargo-Liner II*; **MANJA** (Cy) ex-*Cargo-Liner IV*; **COMPAEN** (Ne) ex-*Cargo-Liner V*; **JOY** (Pa) ex-*Cargo-Liner VI*
Sister (converted to cement carrier—probably altered in appearance): **GORGULHO** (Po) ex-*Cargo-Liner III*

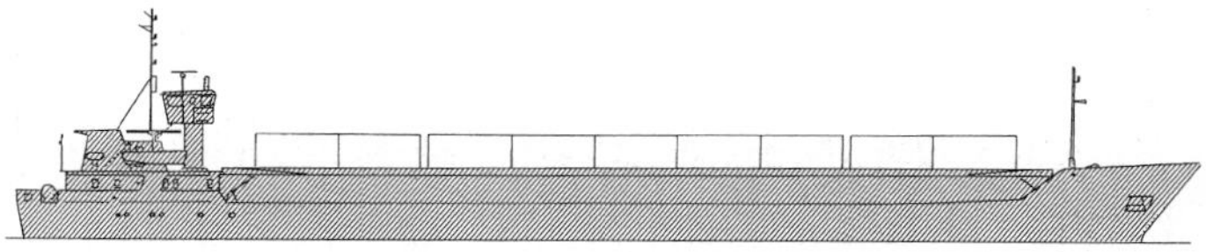

7 *MHF H1*
MARIA D Ge/FRG (Suerken) 1986; C/Con; 2,370 grt/2,760 dwt; 87.84 × 4.45 m *(288.19 × 14.60 ft)*; M (Deutz); 11.5 kts; 144 TEU
Sisters: **ISARTAL** (Ge); **WACHAU** (As) ex-*Ruhrtal*; **DURNSTEIN** (As) ex-*Visurgis*

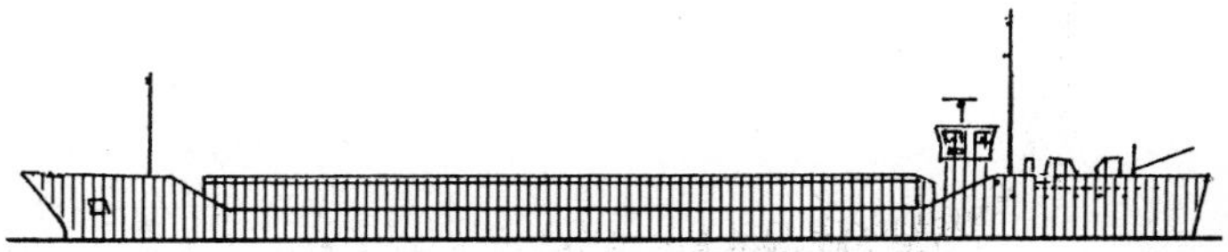

8 *MHF H13*
ALADIN Cy/FRG (H Peters) 1982; C; 1,499 grt/1,768 dwt; 82.48 × 3.54 m *(270.6 × 11.61 ft)*; M (KHD); 10.5 kts; Sea/river; 48 TEU
Sisters (some have bridge on taller tower): **FALKO** (At) Launched as *Christa Schutt*; **ANKE BETTINA** (At) ex-*Hammaburg*; **PIROL** (Cy) ex-*Meridian II*: **PAX** (DIS); **MIKE** (At) ex-*Patria*; **AQUA PIONEER** (Ma) ex-*Poseldorf*; **ANGA** (NA) ex-*Vineta*; **ALI ZEE** (At) ex-*Bungsberg*; **PERNILLE W** (DIS) ex-*Pionier*; **PHONIX I** (Cy) ex-*Osterberg*; **DEO VOLENTE** (Ne) ex-*Elbstrand*; **SINDBAD** (Cy); **SESAM** (Cy); **UNION ARBO** (Bs) ex-*Birka*; **ROGER** (At) ex-*Gudrun*; **PIRAT** (Cy) ex-*Haithabu*; **GEORG LUHRS** (Ge); **DANIA CARINA** (Ge); **PERO** (Ge); **PALOMA** (Ge) ex-*Landkirchen*; **SABINE L** (Ge); **TRUSO** (Ge); **JAN MEEDER** (Ge)
Probable sisters: **ALI BABA** (Cy); **DIOLI** (NA) ex-*Baltica*; **UNION VENUS** (Bb) ex-*Hansa*; **CLIFF** (At) ex-*Kiebitzberg*; **POSEIDON** (Ge)

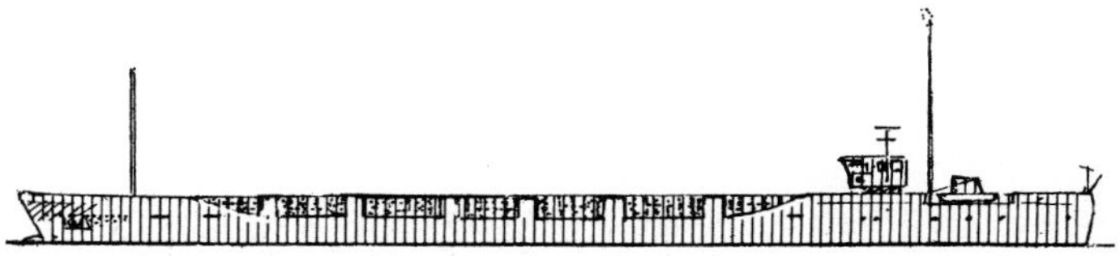

9 *MHF H13*
CONDOR Ge/FRG (Sietas) 1978; C (sea/river); 1,252 grt/1,623 dwt; 73.11 × 3.4 m *(239.86 × 11.15 ft)*; M (KHD); 11 kts; 70 TEU
Sister: **MEDWIND** (Po) ex-*Angela Jurgens*

10 *MHF H13*
ELIANE TRADER Ma/FRG (M Jansen) 1978; C (sea/river); 1,384 grt/1,623 dwt; 81.62 × 3.28 m *(267.78 × 10.76 ft)*; M (MWM); 10 kts; ex-*Konigsee*; Hinged masts

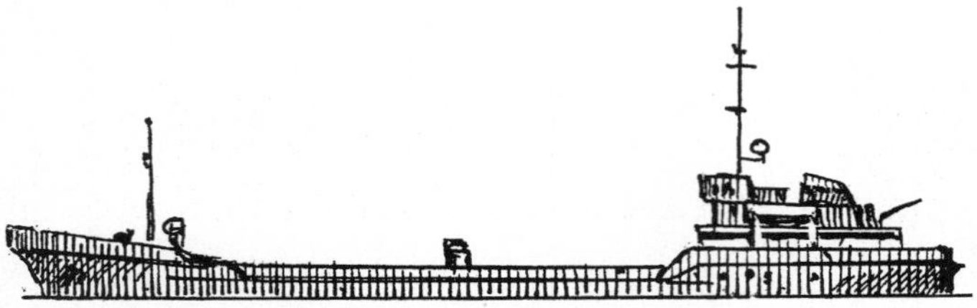

11 *MHF H13*
'LADOGA' type Ru/Fi (Laiva) 1972–74; C (sea/river); 1,568 grt/1,968 dwt; 81.01 × 4.01 m *(265.78 × 13.16 ft)*; TSM (Liebknecht); 12 kts
Sisters (funnels vary in shape and height): **LADOGA 1** (Ru); **LADOGA 2** (Ru); **LADOGA 3** (Ru); **LADOGA 4** (Ru); **LADOGA 5** (Ru); **LADOGA 6** (Ru); **LADOGA 7** (Ru); **LADOGA 8** (Ru); **LADOGA 9** (Ru)

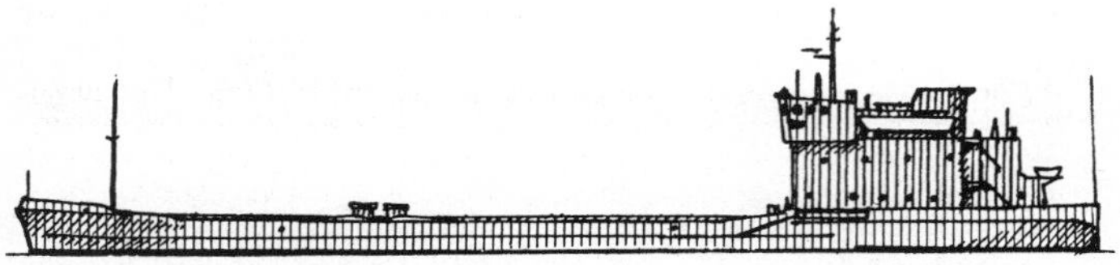

12 *MHF H13*
SAYMENSKIY KANAL Ru/Fi (Rauma-Repola) 1978; C (sea/river); 1,578 grt/1,855 dwt; 81.01 × 4 m *(265.78 × 13.12 ft)*; TSM (SKL); 12.25 kts; ex-*Ladoga 10*
Sisters: **LADOGA 11** (Ru); **LADOGA 12** (Ru); **LADOGA 13** (Ru); **LADOGA 14** (Ru); **LADOGA 15** (Ru); **LADOGA 16** (Ru); **LADOGA 17** (Ru); **LADOGA 18** (Ru); **LADOGA 19** (Ru)

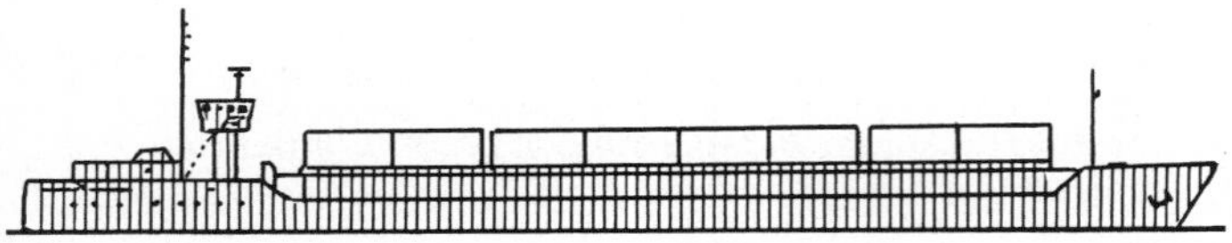

13 *MHF H13*
SEA EMS SV/FRG (Diedrich) 1984; C/Con; 1,410 grt/1,562 dwt; 79.00 × 3.31 m *(259.19 × 10.86 ft)*; M (Deutz); 10.5 kts; 80 TEU
Similar (has a small crane which could be obscured by deck cargo—see drawing number 15/3): **MARI CLAIRE** (SV) ex-*Kirsten*; **MARI FRANCE** (Ge) ex-*Simone*

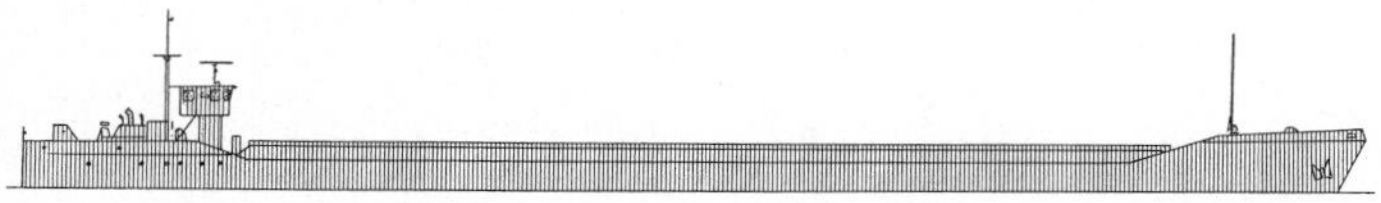

14 *MHF H13*
UNION JUPITER Bb/Br (Cochrane) 1990; C/Con; 2,230 grt/3,274 dwt; 99.73 × 4.26 m *(327.20 × 13.98 ft)*; M (Alpha); 11.2 kts; 114 TEU
Sisters: **VECTIS ISLE** (Bb) ex-*Union Mercury*; **SUPERIORITY** (Br); **SHORT SEA TRADER** (Br); **NORTH SEA TRADER** (Br); **UNION PEARL** (Bb) ex-*Bromley Pearl* (builder—Dunston); **ANJA C** (SV) ex-*Union Saturn* (builder—Dunston)

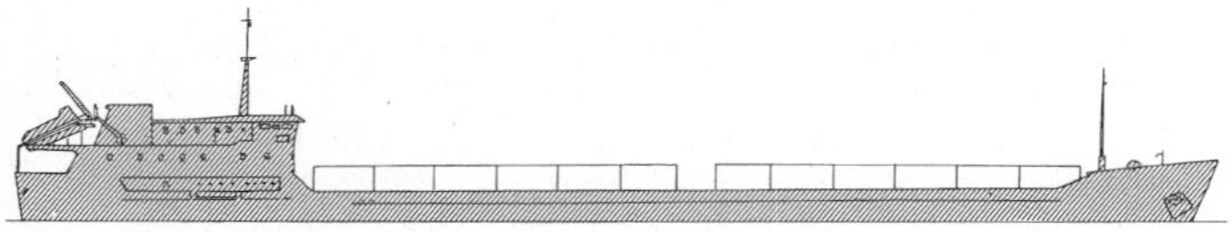

15 *MHFL H13*
SORMOVSKIY-3063 Ru/Po (Viana) 1989; C/Con; 3,048 grt/3,134 dwt; 119.20 × 3.75 m *(391.08 × 12.30 ft)*; TSM (SKL); 10.5 kts; 90 TEU
Sisters (some ships under number 15/18 may have this appearance): **SORMOVSKIY-3064** (Ru); **PYOTR ANOKHIN** (Ru) ex-*Sormovskiy-3065*; **SORMOVSKIY-3066** (Ru); **SORMOVSKIY-3067** (Ru); **SORMOVSKIY-3068** (Ru); **GAZANFAR MUSABEKOV** (Az) ex-*Sormovskiy-3062*; **TEYMUR EHMEDOV** (Az) ex-*Sormovskiy-3061*

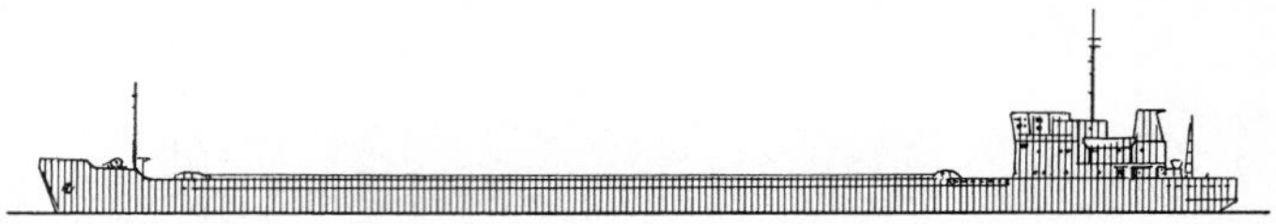

16 *MHFM H1*
SIBIRSKIY 2113 Ru/Fi (Hollming) 1980; C/Con (sea/river); 3,743 grt/3,505 dwt; 129 × 2.5 m *(423 × 8.2 ft)*; TSM (Russkiy); 10.2 kts; 144 TEU
Sisters: **SIBIRSKIY 2110** (Ru); **SIBIRSKIY 2111** (Ru); **SIBIRSKIY 2112** (Ru); **SIBIRSKIY 2114** (Ru); **SIBIRSKIY-2115** (Ru); **SIBIRSKIY 2116** (Ru); **SIBIRSKIY 2117** (Ru); **SIBIRSKIY 2118** (Ru); **SIBIRSKIY 2119** (Ru); **SIBIRSKIY 2130** (Ru); **SIBIRSKIY 2131** (Ru); **SIBIRSKIY 2132** (Ru); **SIBIRSKIY 2133** (Ru)

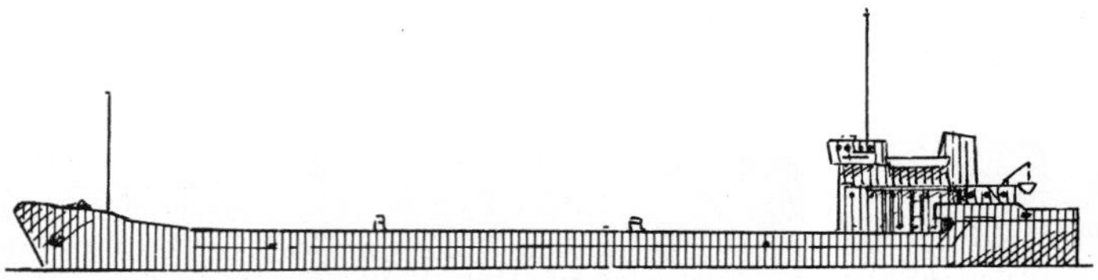

17 *MHFM H13*
BALTIYSKIY 101 Ru/Fi (Laiva) 1978; C/Con (sea/river); 1,987 grt/2,554 dwt; 95 × 4 m *(311.68 × 13.12 ft)*; TSM (SKL); 12.5 kts; Hinged masts; 83 TEU
Sisters: **BALTIYSKIY 102** (Ru); **BALTIYSKIY 103** (Ru); **VASILIY MALOV** (Ru) ex-*Baltiyskiy 104*; **BALTIYSKIY 105** (Ru); **BALTIYSKIY 106** (Ru); **BALTIYSKIY 107** (Ru); **BALTIYSKIY 108** (Ru); **BALTIYSKIY 109** (Ru); **BALTIYSKIY 110** (Ru); **BALTIYSKIY 111** (Ru)

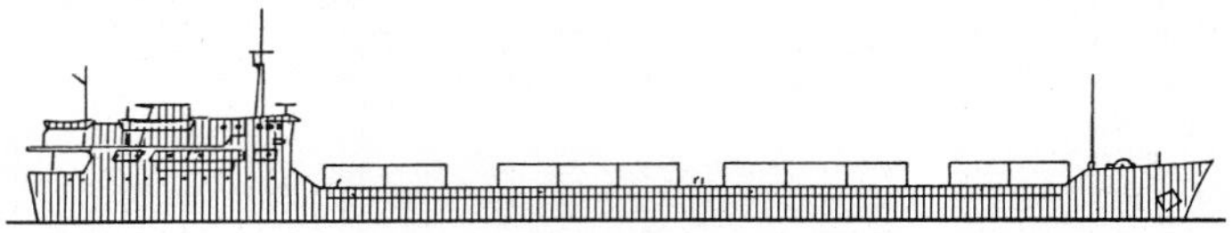

18 *MHFM H13*
SORMOVSKIY 3058 Ru/Po (Viana) 1987; C/Con; 3,041 grt/3,134 dwt; 119.21 × 3.73 m *(391.11 × 12.24 ft)*; TSM (SKL); 10.5 kts; 90 TEU
Sisters (some may have a pole radar mast—see entry number 15/36): **SORMOVSKIY-3048** (Ru) ex-*XVII Syezd Profsoyuzov*; **SORMOVSKIY-3049** (Ru) ex-*XI Pyatiletka*; **SORMOVSKIY-3050** (Ru) ex-*0065 Let Sovetskoy Vlasti*; **SORMOVSKIY-3051** (Ru); **SORMOVSKIY-3052** (Ru); **SORMOVSKIY-3053** (Ru); **SORMOVSKIY-3054** (Ru); **SORMOVSKIY-3055** (Ru); **SORMOVSKIY-3056** (Ru); **SORMOVSKIY-3057** (Ru); **SORMOVSKIY-3058** (Ru); **SORMOVSKIY-3060** (Ru); **ALEKSANDR SHOTMAN** (Ru) ex-*Sormovskiy-3059*

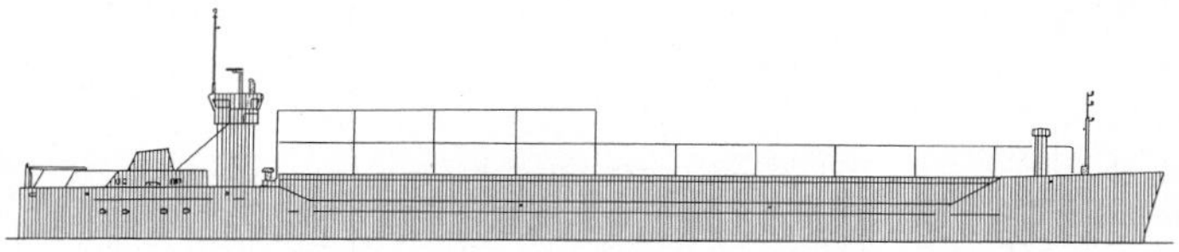

19 *MHFR H13*
ARKLOW VALOUR Ih/Ge (H Peters) 1990; C/Con; 2,827 grt/4,258 dwt; 88.20 × 5.81 m *(289.37 × 19.06 ft)*; M (MaK); 11 kts; 173 TEU
Sisters: **ARKLOW VILLA** (Ih); **ARKLOW VIEW** (Ih); **ARKLOW VALLEY** (Ih); **ARKLOW VENTURE** (Ih); **ARKLOW VIKING** (Ih); **ARKLOW VALE** (Ih)
Sisters (smaller—73.85m (242ft)): **ARKLOW MANOR** (Ih); **ARKLOW MARSH** (Ih); **ARKLOW MILL** (Ih); **ARKLOW BAY** (Ih); **ARKLOW MOOR** (Ih) (builder—Hitzler); **ARKLOW MEADOW** (Ih) (builder—Hitzler)

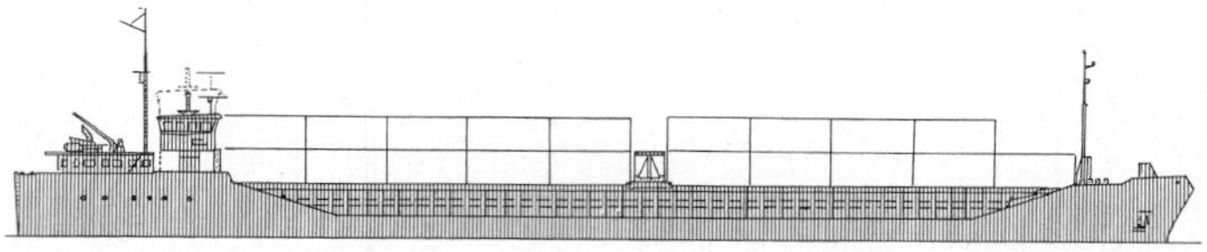

20 *MHRF H13*
MORGENSTOND I Ne/Ne (Ferus Smit H) 1993; C/Con; 2,650 grt/4,000 dwt; 89.00 × 5.65 m *(291.99 × 18.54 ft)*; M (Stork-Werkspoor); 11.8 kts; 190 TEU; telescopic wheelhouse (as indicated on drawing)
Possible sister: **GERARDA** (Ne)

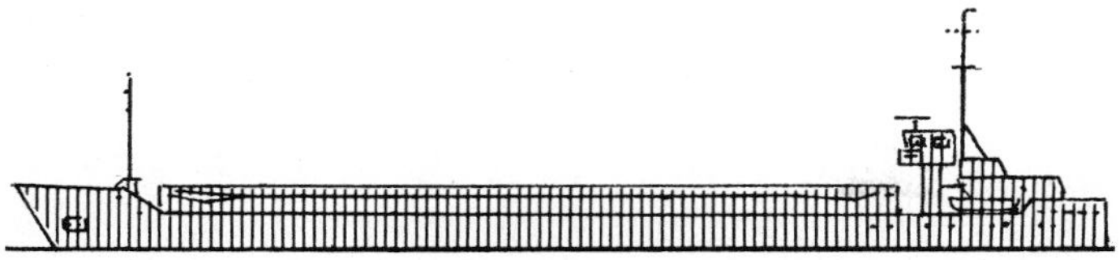

21 *MH–F H1*
CLAUDIA L Ge/FRG (Suerken) 1983; C; 1,300 grt/1,506 dwt; 74.81 × 3.3 m *(254.44 × 10.83 ft)*; M (KHD); 10.25 kts; Sea/river
Sisters: **KAY L** (At); **MARC L** (At); **RICHARD C** (At); **RMS FRANCIA** (Cy) ex-*Sea Tamar*; **KATHARINA CHARLOTTE** (Cy); **JOHANNA** (Ne) ex-*Sea Trent*; **SEA TYNE** (Ge); **WERDER BREMEN** (At)
Probable sisters: **NEIL B** (At); **AMISIA** (Ge); **RHENUS** (Ge); **JEROME H** (At); **MARIA H** (At); **OSTERHUSEN** (At) ex-*Jessica S*; **MOSA** (Ge); **ELKE** (At) ex-*Mareike B*

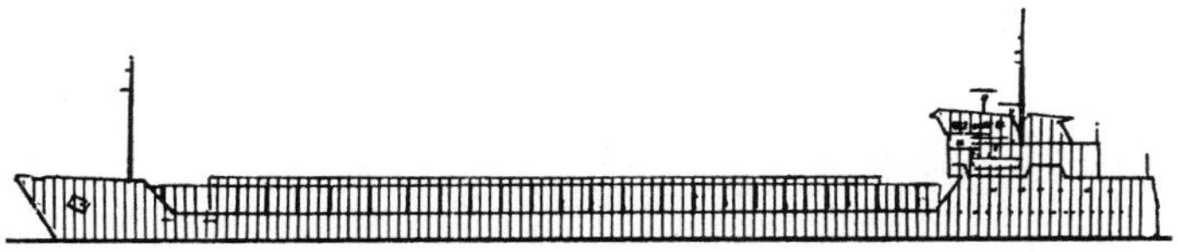

22 *MH–F H13*
LOUISE TRADER Ma/FRG (Hegemann) 1982; C (sea/river); 1,716 grt/2,319 dwt; 80.29 × 4.25 m *(263 × 13.94 ft)*; M (KHD); 11 kts; ex-*Selena*
Sisters: **LENA-S** (Ge); **SIMONE** (Ge); Similar (funnel top slopes upward from front): **DANUBIA** (Ge); **MARGARETA** (Ge)
Similar (Larger—84.9m (278.54ft)): **ANTINA** (Ge); **ASSIDUUS** (Ge); **CHRISTOPHER** (Ge)

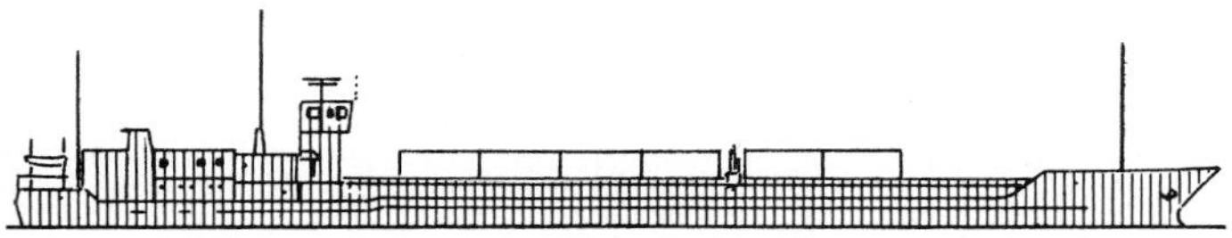

23 *MJMGM H1*
GEORGIY AGAFONOV Uk/As (Osterreichische) 1987; R/Con; 2,060 grt/2,099 dwt; 91.90 × 3.37 m *(301.51 × 11.06 ft)*; TSM (Wärtsilä); 12 kts; 96 TEU
Sisters: **VALERIAN ZORIN** (Uk); **IVAN PROKHOROV** (Uk); **ARKADIY SVERDLOV** (Uk); **ALEKSANDR ARZHAVKIN** (Uk); **VADIM GLAZUNOV** (Uk); **NIKOLAY SAVITSKIY** (Uk); **KAPITAN PETRUSHEVSKIY** (Uk); **VENEDIKT ANDREYEV** (Uk); **LEONID LUGOVOY** (Uk)

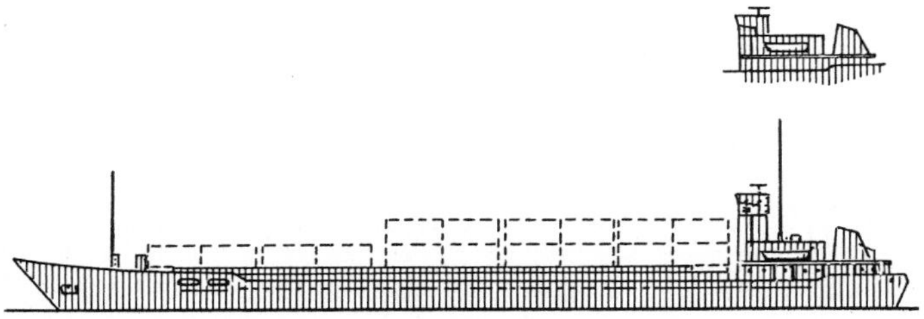

24 *MMF H1*
CANOPUS I Cy/FRG (Elsflether) 1979; C/Con; 2,862 grt/2,507 dwt; 98.71 × 3.76 m *(323.85 × 12.34 ft)*; M (MaK); 12.5 kts; ex-*Canopus*; Sea/river; 204 TEU; telescopic wheelhouse—see inset

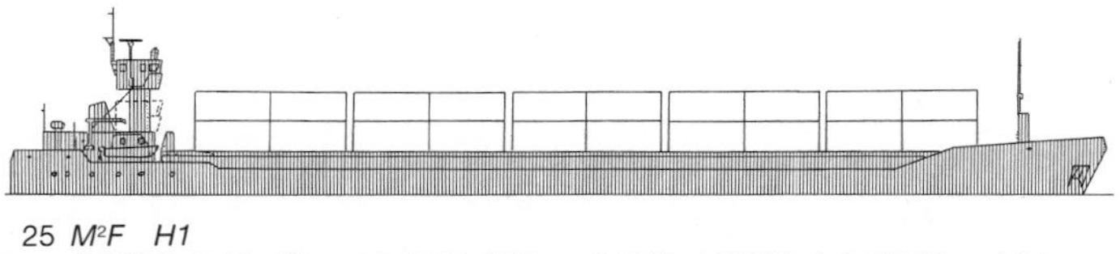

25 *M^2F H1*
JENS R At/Ne (Damen) 1990; C/Con; 1,960 grt/2,980 dwt; 88.32 × 4.61 m *(289.76 × 15.12 ft)*; M (Caterpillar); 11.5 kts; 158 TEU; Hydraulic bridge
Sisters: **MINDFUL** (At) ex-*Christian R*; **KARIN** (Ge) (may not have hydraulic bridge); Similar (shorter focsle): **JADE** (At) ex-*Sea Jade*; **METE** (Li) ex-*Six Madun*; **ERIKA H** (Cy) ex-*Wilma*; **ELISABETH WE** (Cy) ex-*Elisabeth W*; **JACQUELINE** (Bs); **NADINE** (Cy) ex-*Niels*

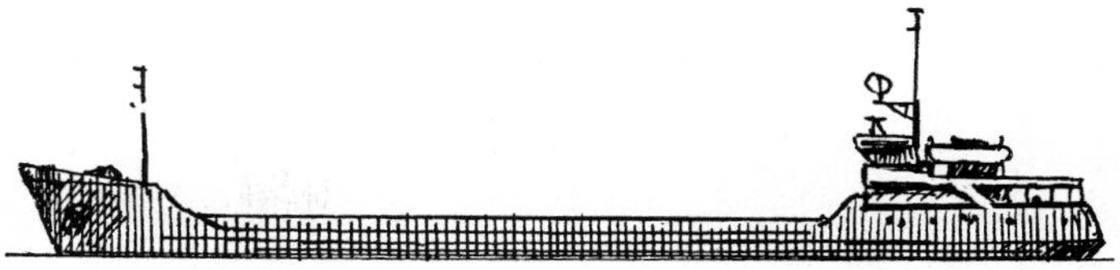

26 *MMF H13*
'BALTIYSKIY' type Ru/Ru ('Krasnoye S') 1962–68; C (sea/river); 1,865 grt/2,128 dwt; 95.61 × 3.26 m *(313.68 × 10.7 ft)*; TSM (Liebknecht); 10 kts;
Most of this class have the sequence M^2FM—see entry number 15/35;
Funnel heights vary
Among vessels known to be M^2F: **VLAS CHUBAR** (Uk)

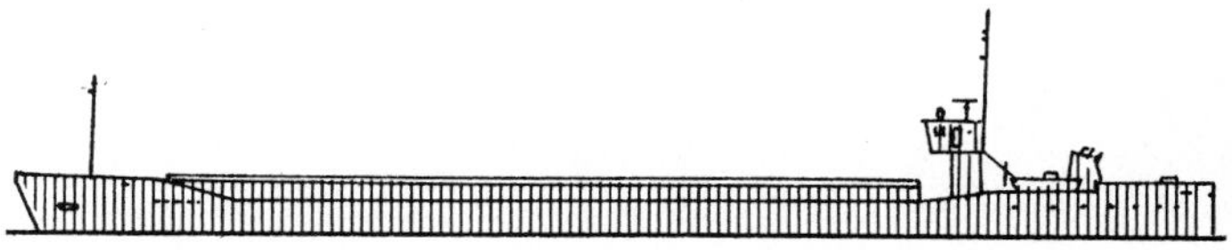

27 *M^2F H13*
DEIKE At/FRG (Sietas) 1981; C (sea/river); 1,939 grt/2,890 dwt; 87.97 × 4.67 m *(289 × 15.32 ft)*; M (KHD); 11.5 kts; 90 TEU
Sisters: **LANIA** (Cy) ex-*Carola*; **TAFELBERG** (Ge) ex-*Helga*; **MARGARETHA** (Ge); **BREITENBURG** (Cy) ex-*Jule*; **CATHARINA** (Ge); **NIEDERELBE** (Ge); **KAAKSBURG** (Ge) ex-*Tini*; **COMET** (At); **ILKA** (At); **HUMBER STAR** (Tv) ex-*Katja*; **SEA WESER** (At); **CHRISTA KERSTIN** (At) ex-*Esteburg*; **WASEBERG** (Ge); **MUHLENBERG** (Ge); **COIMBRA** (Cy) ex-*Gerda Rambow*; **KATHARINA S** (Ge) ex-*Katharina Siemer*; **POLTERBERG** (Ge); Similar (larger funnel): **HEIDBERG** (Ge); **BAURSBERG** (Ge)

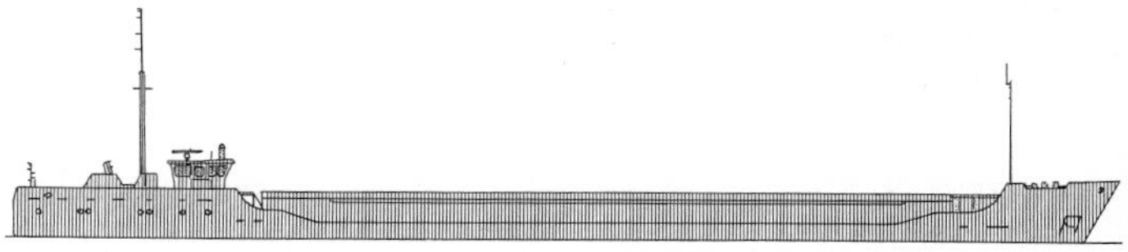

28 *M^2F H13*
FREYA Ge/Ne (Vervako) 1991; C/Con; 1,548 grt/2,412 dwt; 79.63 × 4.39 m *(261.25 × 14.40 ft)*; M (Deutz); 10 kts; 78 TEU
Possible sister: **REMMER** (Cy); Similar: **RUBY** (NA); **DIAMOND** (NA)

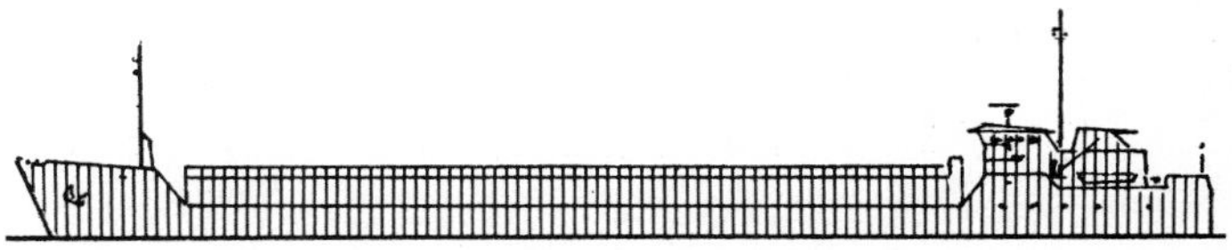

29 *M^2F H13*
HEIMATLAND Ge/FRG (Diedrich) 1984; C; 1,372 grt/1,573 dwt; 75.01 × 3.71 m *(246.1 × 12.17 ft)*; M (Krupp-MaK); 11 kts
Sisters: **BETA** (Ge) (builder—Koetter); **MARSCHENLAND**

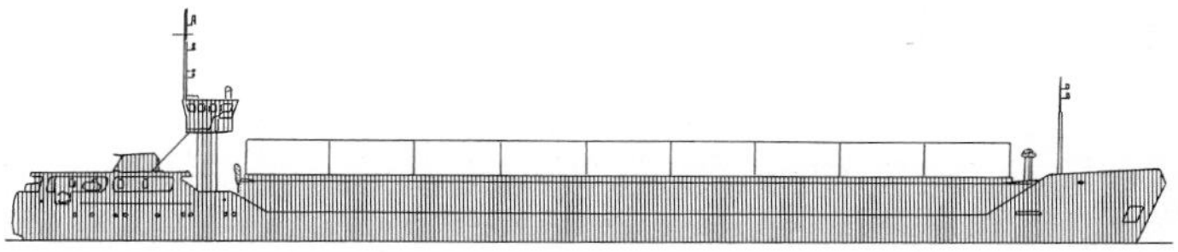

30 *M^2F H13*
HEINKE Cy/FRG (Koetter) 1990; C/Con; 1,690 grt/1,857 dwt; 82.50 × 4.50 m *(270.67 × 14.76 ft)*; M (Deutz); 10.5 kts; 84 TEU
Similar (Mast abaft bridge. Builder—Rosslauer): **SAAR EMDEN** (At) ex-*Rysum*; **SAAR LISBOA** (At) ex-*Eilsum*; **SAAR MADRID** (At); **SAAR ANTWERP** (At); **SAAR ROTTERDAM** (Ge) ex-*Pilsum*

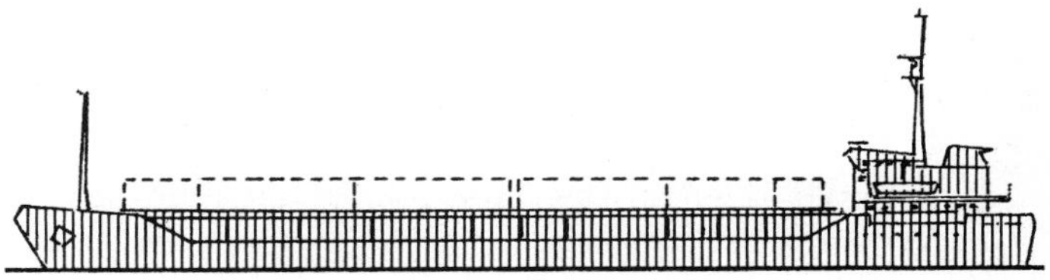

31 *MMF H13*
ROMA Ru/FRG (Werftunion) 1981; C/Con; 2,363 grt/2,700 dwt; 80.8 × 4.66 m *(265 × 15.29 ft)*; M (Krupp); 11.9 kts; 120 TEU

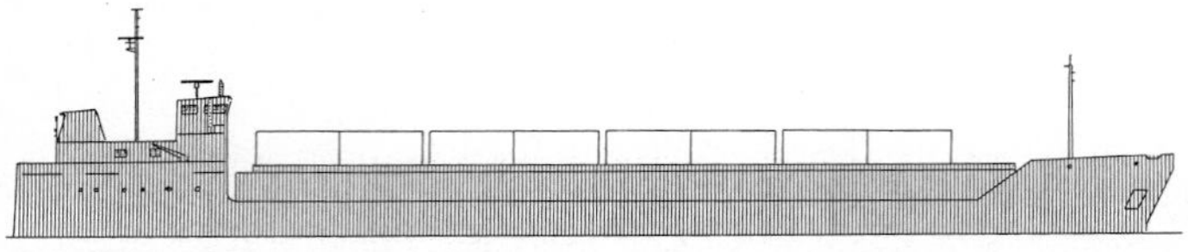

32 M^2F *H13*
STAR Ge/Ge (Cassens GmbH) 1991; C/Con; 2,237 grt/2,700 dwt; 82.50 × 4.69 m *(270.67 × 15.39 ft)*; M (Deutz); 11.5 kts; 138 TEU

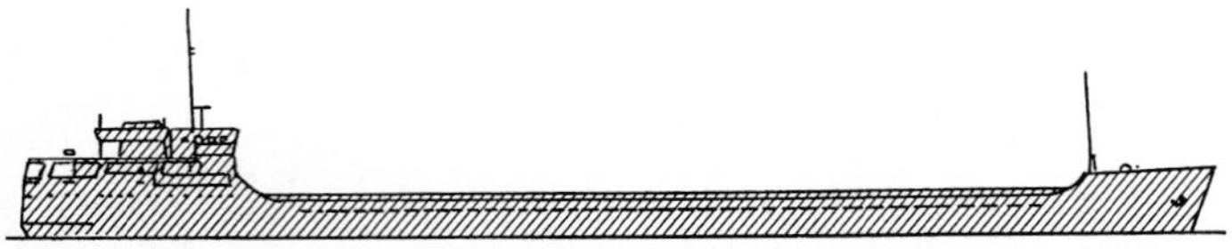

33 M^2F *H13*
VOLGO-BALT type Ru/Ru and Cz ('Krasnoye Sormovo' and Zavody) 1964–86; C; 2,400 grt/2,907 dwt; 114.00 × 3.64 m *(374.02 × 11.94 ft)*; TSM (SKL); 10.5 kts; Class of over 100 ships; Most have names with the prefix 'VOLGO-BALT' followed by a number between 8 and 248

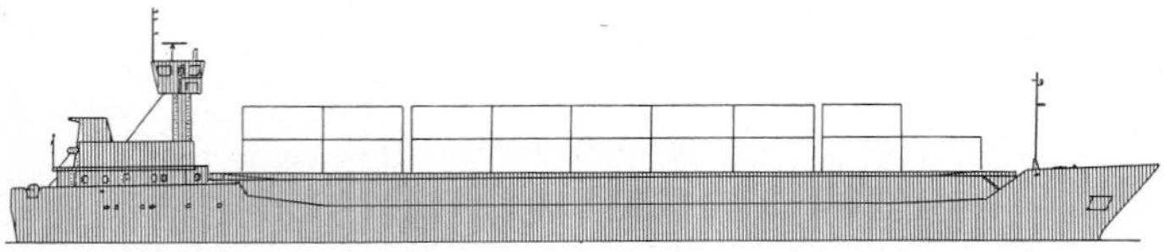

34 M^2F *H13*
WITTENBERGEN Cy/Cz (Slovenske) 1992; C/Con; 2,381 grt/3,700 dwt; 87.90 × 5.45 m *(288.39 × 17.88 ft)*; M (Deutz); 10.6 kts; 176 TEU
Sisters: **RHEINFELS** (Cy): **CLAVIGO** (At)
Possible sisters: **SAAR BERLIN** (Cy) ex-*Julia Isabel*; **PADUA** (Cy); **PANDORA** (Cy); **PRIWALL** (Cy); **SAAR BREDA** (At) ex-*Preussen*

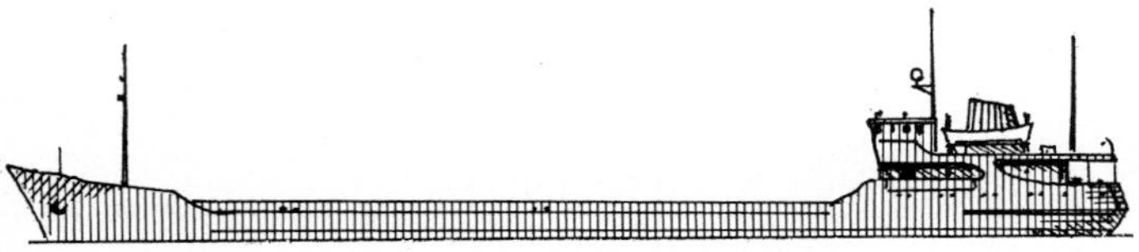

35 M^2FM *H13*
BALTIYSKIY type Ru and Uk/Ru ('Krasnoye S') 1962–68; C (sea/river); 1,865 grt/2,121 dwt; 96.02 × 3.26 m *(315.03 × 10.7 ft)*; TSM (Liebknecht); 10 kts; Some have lower funnels; Aftermast omitted on some vessels; Large class of approximately 50 ships but are being sold or scrapped; Most have names with the prefix 'BALTIYSKIY' followed by a number between 1 and 73; Many will have flags other than Ru or Uk, having been sold

36 M^2FM *H13*
LENINSKIY KOMSOMOL Ru/Po (Viana) 1978; Con; 2,780 grt/3,146 dwt; 118.5 × 3.73 m *(388.78 × 12.24 ft)*; TSM (SKL); 11.25 kts; **SIMILAR TO DRAWING NUMBER 15/18** but latter has goalpost radar mast
Sisters (some may have goalpost radar mast—see note above): **DRUZHBA NARODOV** (Ru); **ZNAMYA OKTYABRYA** (Ru); **SOVIETSKAYA RODINA** (Ru)

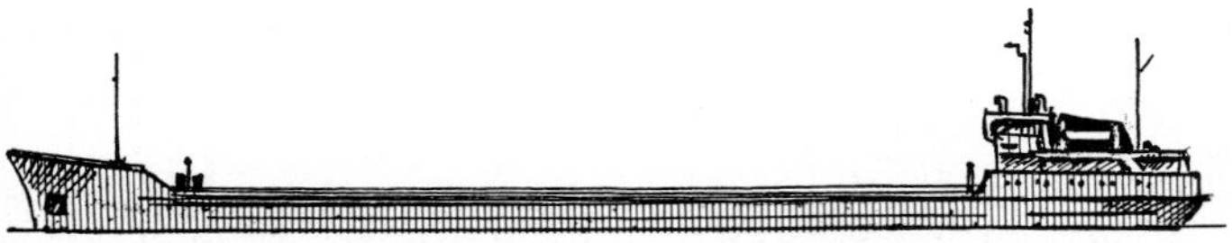

37 M^2FM *H13*
NEFTERUDOVOZ type Ru/Ru (Kama) 1972/77; OO (sea/river); 2,699 grt/2,848 dwt; 118.93 × 3.42 m *(390.19 × 11.22 ft)*; TSM (Liebknecht); 11 kts
Sisters (Ru flag): from **NEFTERUDOVOZ 8M** to **NEFTERUDOVOZ 58M** (excluding 35M)

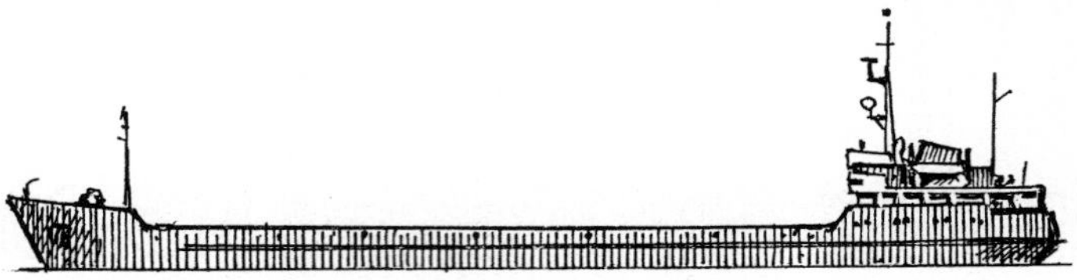

38 M^2FM *H13*
SORMOVSKIY Ru/Ru ('Krasnoye S'/Volodarskiy and so on) 1967–85; C (sea/river); 2,484 grt/3,000 dwt; 114.2 × 3.42 m *(374.67 × 11.22 ft)*; TSM (Liebknecht); 10.5 kts; a class of around 120 ships; Most have names with the prefix 'SORMOVSKIY' followed by a number; At least three under Bulgarian flag

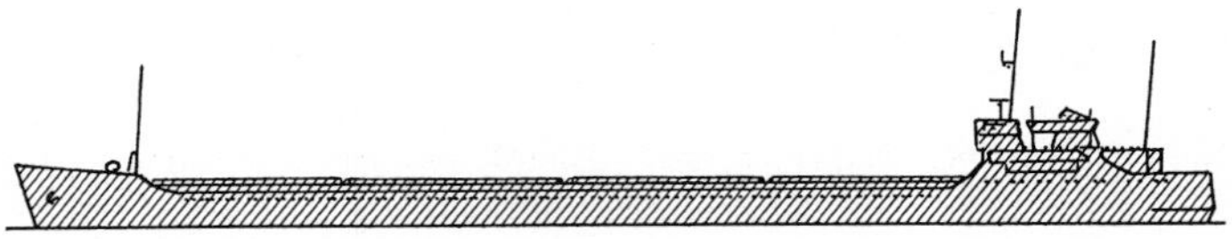

39 M^2FM *H13*
VOLGO-BALT type; dwt; Variation on this type—see text under drawing number 15/33

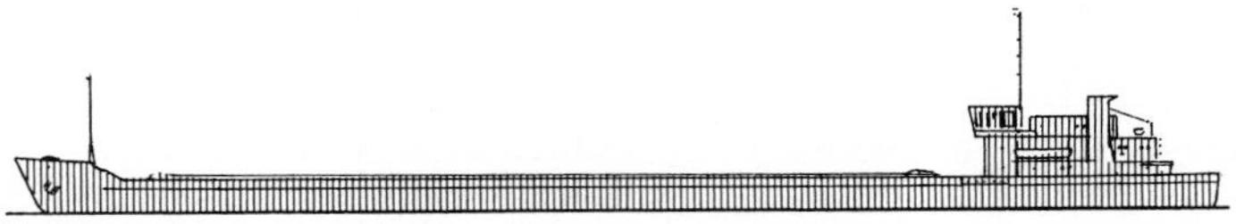

40 M^2GCH *H1*
SIBIRSKIY 2101 Ru/Fi (Valmet) 1979; C (Riv); 3,409 grt/3,050 dwt; 127.5 × 3 m *(418 × 9.84 ft)*; M (Russkiy); 10.5 kts; 48 TEU
Sisters: **SIBIRSKIY 2102** (Ru); **SIBIRSKIY 2103** (Ru); **SIBIRSKIY 2104** (Ru); **SIBIRSKIY 2106** (Ru); **SIBIRSKIY 2108** (Ru); **SIBIRSKIY 2109** (Ru); **SIBIRSKIY 2123** (Ru); **SIBIRSKIY 2124** (Ru); **SIBIRSKIY 2125** (Ru); **SIBIRSKIY 2128** (Ru); **SIBIRSKIY 2129** (Ru)

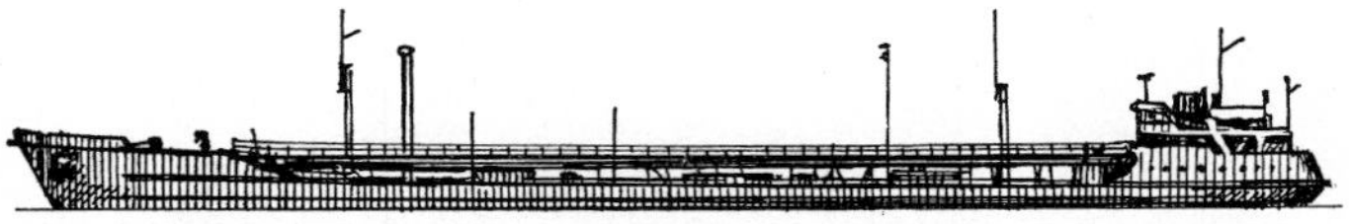

41 M^4FM *H13*
'VOLGONEFT' type Ru/Ru and Bu (G Dimitrov/Volgograd) 1966–69; Tk; 3,400 grt/4,200 dwt; 132.59 × 3.58 m *(435 × 11.75 ft)*; TSM (Liebknecht); 10.5 kts; This drawing represents the earlier vessels of this type; Names have the prefix **'VOLGONEFT'** and a number; Approximately 27 in the whole group

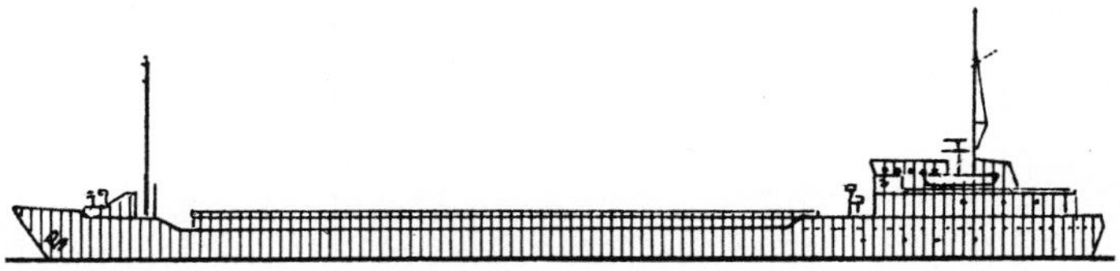

42 *MM–F* *H1*
NAVIGATOR Ge/FRG (Luehring); C/Con; 1,811 grt/2,668 dwt; 78.59 × 4.6 m *(258 × 15.09 ft)*; M (Krupp-MaK); 10.25 kts; Sea/river type; 88 TEU

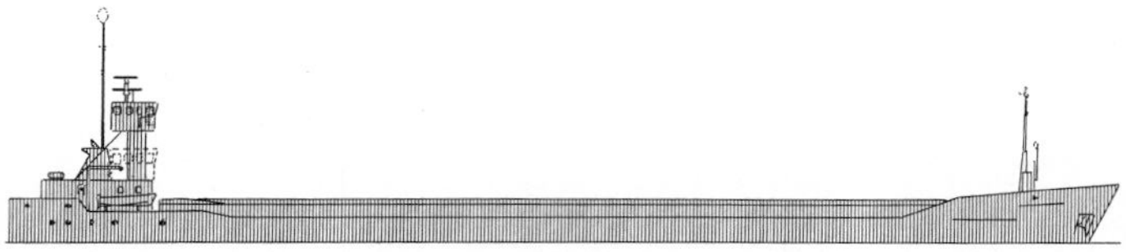

43 *MM–F* *H1*
NORDSTRAND At/Ne (Damen) 1991; C/Con; 1,960 grt/2,800 dwt; 88.30 × 4.60 m *(289.70 × 15.09 ft)*; M (Caterpillar); 11.5 kts; ex-*Nicole*; 158 TEU; Hydraulic wheelhouse
Sisters: **FRANZ KELLER** (At) ex-*Tima Jupiter*; **KARIBU** (At) ex-*Petra*; **INGRID** (Cy); **COSMEA** (Ge); **SAAR LONDON** (At) ex-*Rex*
Possible sisters: **SAGITTA** (Ge) ex-*Rosemarie*; **KOPERSAND** (At); **LEYSAND** (At); **SAAR GENOVA** (At) ex-*Freepsum*; **ALPHA** (At) ex-*Barbel*; Similar (mast from front of funnel): **BORSTELER BERG** (At); **SONJA B** (At); **WALDTRAUT B** (At)

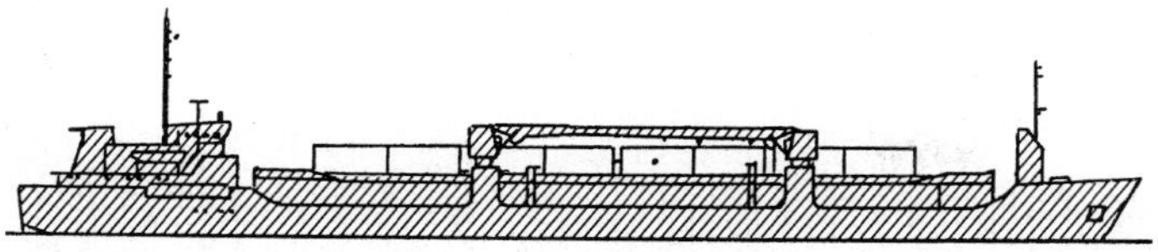

44 *MR²HF H13*
UPPLAND Ge/FRG (Hegemann) 1984; C/Con; 3,093 grt/3,185 dwt; 95.51 × 4.40 m *(313.35 × 14.44 ft)*; M (Deutz); 12 kts; 207 TEU; Cranes are on starboard side
Sister: **ARTEMIS** (Ge) ex-*Marlen-L*

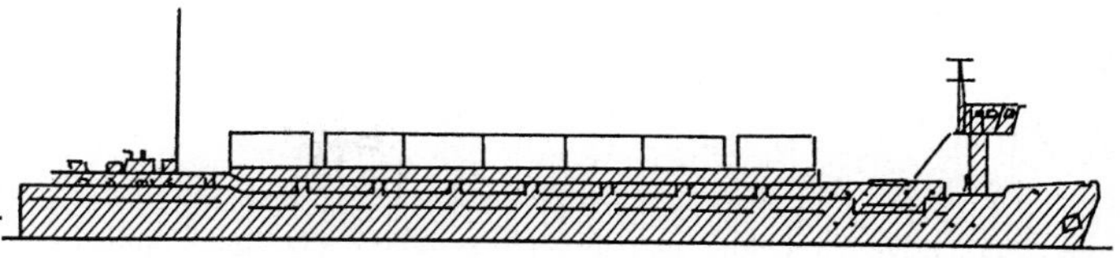

46 *MVF H*
LADOGA-101 Ru/Fi (Rauma-Repola) 1988; C/Con; 1,853 grt/2,075 dwt; 82.50 × 4.00 m *(270.67 × 13.12 ft)*; TSM (SKL); 10.3 kts; 84 TEU
Sisters: **LADOGA-102** (Ru); **LADOGA-103** (Ru); **LADOGA-104** (Ru); **LADOGA-105** (Ru); **LADOGA-106** (Ru); **LADOGA-107** (Ru); **LADOGA-108** (Ru); **LADOGA-109** (Ru)

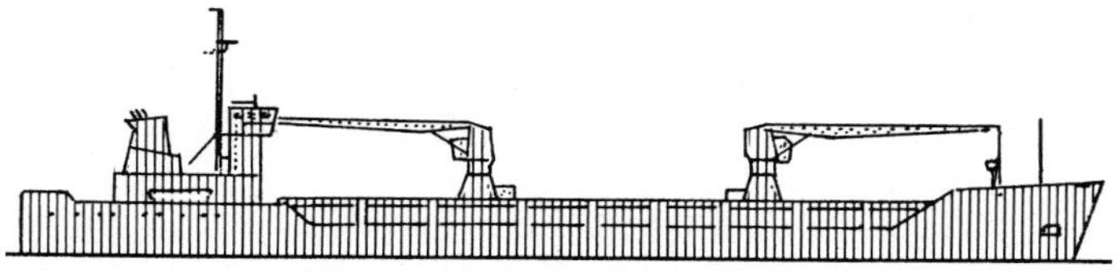

45 *MR²HF H13*
ZIM COLOMBIA At/FRG (Seebeck) 1984; C/Con; 2,472 grt/3,065 dwt; 90.02 × 4.46 m *(295.34 × 14.63 ft)*; M (Deutz); 11.5 kts; ex-*Dithmarsia*; 134 TEU; Cranes are on port side
Sisters: **JUSTINE** (At) ex-*Heino*; **ORIENTAL DRAGON** (Pa) ex-*Paul*; **SYLT** (At); **POINT LISAS** (Ge) ex-*Holsatia*; **INA LEHMANN** (At) ex-*Werner*

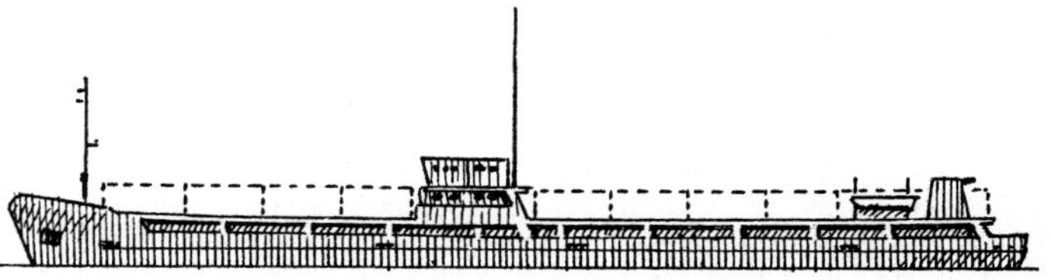

47 *MVG H*
ISHIM Ru/DDR (Elbe B/R) 1977; C/Con; 1,521 grt/1,755 dwt; 81.85 × 3.40 m *(268.54 × 11.15 ft)*; TSM (SKL); 11.5 kts; 70 TEU. Sea/river design
Probable sisters: **BAKHTEMIR** (Uk); **YENOTAYEVSK** (Ru); **ZELENGA** (Ru); **KONDA** (Ru); **LOZVA** (Ru); **STAROVOLZHK** (Uk): **SOSVA** (Bu); **PUR** (Ru); **YEKATERINBURG** (Ru) ex-*Kazim*; **ZARYA** (Ru) ex-*STK-1010*; **LIBERTY** (—) ex-*Tavda*; **OM** (Ru); **VAGAY** (Ru); **BERSUT** (Ru); **TARKHANY** (Ru); **KRASNOVIDOVO** (Ru); **VOLGORECHENSK** (Ru); **NIKOLSKOYE** (Ru); **LONG XIANG** (RC) ex-*Impuls*; **STK-1001** (Ru); **STK-1002** (Ru); **STK-1003** (Ru); **STK-1004** (Ru); **STK-1005** (Ru); **GULF ROSE** (Cy) ex-*STK-1006*; **STK-1007** (Ru); **STK-1008** (Ru); **STK-1009** (Ru); **STK-1011** (Ru); **STK-1012** (Ru); **STK-1016** (Ru); **STK-1017** (Ru); **STK-1018** (Ru); **STK-1019** (Ru); **STK-1020** (Ru); **STK-1021** (Ru); **STK-1022** (Ru); **STK-1023** (Ru); **STK-1024** (Ru); **STK-1025** (Ru); **STK-1026** (Ru); **STK-1028** (Ru); **STK-1029** (Ru); **STK-1031** (Ru); **NEVA** (Ru); **YENISEY** (Ru) ex-*STK-1032*; **TAVRIYA-2** (Uk) ex-*TK-2*; **TAVRIYA-3** (Uk) ex-*TK-3*; **TAVRIYA-4** (Uk) ex-*TK-4*; **TAVRIYA-5** (Uk) ex-*TK-5*; **TAVRIYA-6** (Uk); **TK-6** (—); **TK-7** (—); **STK-1036** (Ru); **YUNDA** (SV) ex-*Sun-Beam*; **SHENGDA** (SV) ex-*Sun-Shine*; **HAIDA** (SV) ex-*Sun-Ward*; **ZARNISTA** (Ru) ex-*STK-1015*; **SVEZDA** (Ru) ex-*STK-1024*; **STK-1037** (Ru)

48 Tomfield *(Bs); 1978; (as Nascence)* *FotoFlite*

49 Brigitta *(Ge); 1979* *FotoFlite*

50 Inter Mare *(Cy); 1983; (as Vanernsee)* *FotoFlite*

51 Montania *(Cy); 1981* *FotoFlite*

52 Fast Filip *(Pd); 1980; (as Smaragd)* *FotoFlite*

53 Suntis *(Ge); 1985* *FotoFlite*

54 Eldor *(Ge); 1981* *FotoFlite*

55 Batavier *(Cy); 1986; (as Bromley Sapphire)* *FotoFlite*

56 Anne *(At); 1980* *FotoFlite*

57 Guimaraes *(Po); 1979* *FotoFlite*

58 Sarah Rousing *(DIS); 1979; (as Alexander)* *FotoFlite*

59 Katrin *(Ge); 1986* *FotoFlite*

60 Sea Magula *(Ge); 1980* *FotoFlite*

61 Shearwater *(Sc); 1976; (as Matador)* *FotoFlite*

62 RMS Westfalia *(At); 1980; (as Atoll)* *FotoFlite*

63 Helena 1 *(Pa); 1985; (as Almaris)* *FotoFlite*

64 Silvia *(It); 1980; (as Union Arrow)* *FotoFlite*

65 Marinier *(Ne); 1986* *FotoFlite*

66 Amstelborg *(Ne); 1978* *FotoFlite*

67 Anders Rousing *(DIS); 1979; (as Norbox)* *FotoFlite*

68 Eberstein *(At); 1979* *FotoFlite*

69 Heike Lehmann *(At); 1985* *FotoFlite*

70 Galatea *(Ne); 1985; (as Galaxa)* *FotoFlite*

71 Pia *(Ge); 1987* *FotoFlite*

72 Sea Rhone *(SV); 1995* *FotoFlite*

73 Saar Madrid *(At); 1993* *FotoFlite*

74 Piano *(At); 1987* *FotoFlite*

75 Vectis Isle *(Bb); 1990* *FotoFlite*

76 Lass Mars *(Ge); 1992* *FotoFlite*

77 Rhine Trader *(Cy); 1982; (as River Trader)* *FotoFlite*

78 Lys Coast *(Ge); 1984* *FotoFlite*

79 Claudia *(Ge); 1986* *FotoFlite*

80 Jan V *(At); 1985* *FotoFlite*

81 Fast Wal *(At); 1985; (as Sabine)* *FotoFlite*

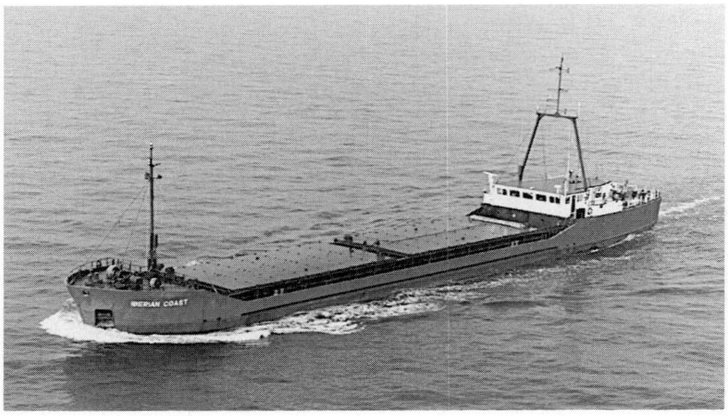

82 Iberian Coast *(Bs); 1979* *FotoFlite*

83 Stridence *(Bs); 1983* *FotoFlite*

84 Euklid *(At); 1984; (as Maelo)* *FotoFlite*

85 Scorpio *(Ne); 1984; (as Morgenstond)* *FotoFlite*

86 Nescio *(Ne); 1993* *WSPL*

87 Catharina *(Ge); 1982* *WSPL*

88 Union Arbo *(Bs); 1984* *WSPL*

89 Ruth W *(Ge); 1984* *WSPL*

90 Laola *(DIS); 1980; (as Emsdiech)* *WSPL*

91 Neermoor *(At); 1993* *WSPL*

92 Sabine L *(Ge); 1983* *WSPL*

93 Volga 4006 *(Ru); 1989* *WSPL*

94 Ladoga 102 *(Ru); 1988* *WSPL*

95 Aleksandr Pashkov *(Ru); 1968* *WSPL*

96 Volgoneft 251 *(Ru); 1975* *WSPL*

97 Lena S *(Ge); 1982* *Norman Thomson*

98 Lady Anna *(Cy); 1989; WSPL*

99 Jehan *(Ne); 1985* *WSPL*

100 Osiris *(Ne); 1985* *WSPL*

101 Marschenland *(Ge); 1985* *Norman Thomson*

102 Regina *(Lu); 1987; (tanker)* *FotoFlite*

103 Stephanie S *(Ge); 1980; (as RMS Lettia)* *FotoFlite*

16 RO-RO/Container (Gearless)

16 RO-RO/Container (Gearless)

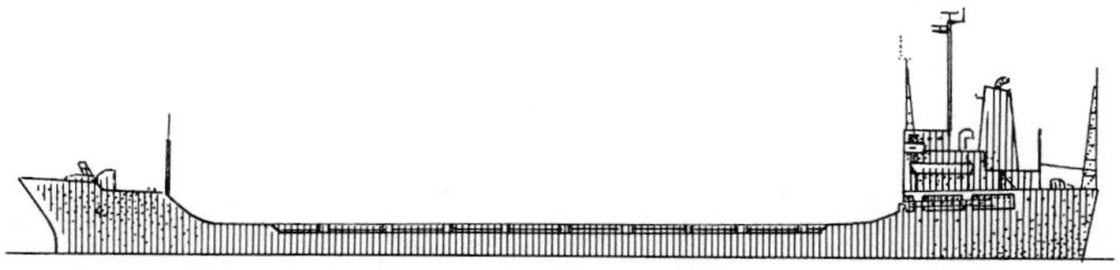

1 *HNMFNM H13*
SEICREDIT Pa/Ja (Kurushima) 1977; RoC/Con; 5,011 grt/7,218 dwt; 113.49 × 6.87 m *(372.34 × 22.54 ft)*; M (Mitsubishi); — kts; ex-*R S Ixion*; 326 TEU; Bow door/ramp
Sister: **LATMOS** (Cy) ex-*R S Jason*

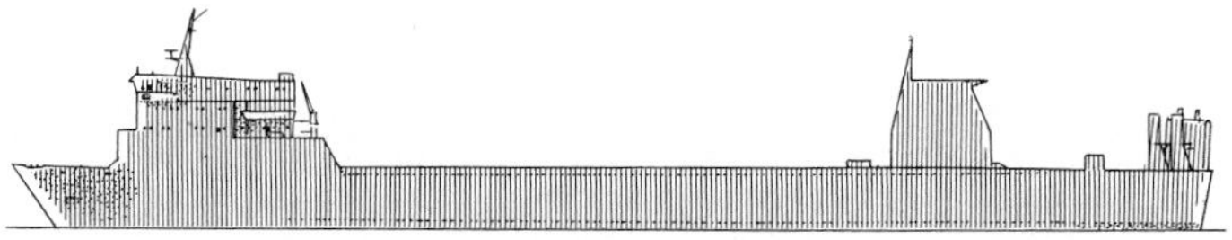

2 *MDM–FY H2*
STENA SHIPPER Bs/FRG (Meyer) 1980; RoC/Con; 12,337 grt/9,259 dwt; 168.8 × 6.45 m *(553.8 × 21.16 ft)*; M (Stork-Werkspoor); 17 kts; ex-*Nestor*; Slewing stern door/ramp; 600 TEU

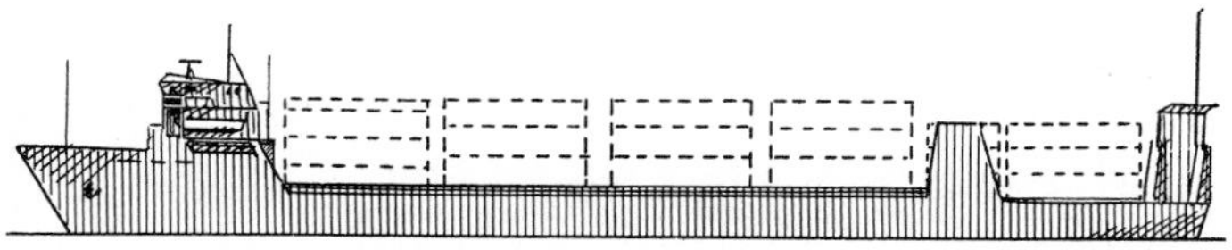

3 *MGM–A H1*
FAIR HOPE Pa/No (Mandal) 1979; RoC/Con; 3,377 grt/4,161 dwt; 103.8 × 5.15 m *(340.55 × 16.9 ft)*; M (Wichmann); 16 kts; ex-*Seatrain Leonor*; quarter ramp (starboard); 300 TEU

4 *M²F H12*
GREAT LAND US/US (Sun SB) 1975; RoC; 17,527 grt/16,397 dwt; 241 × 9.02 m *(791 × 29.59 ft)*; T (GEC); 25 kts

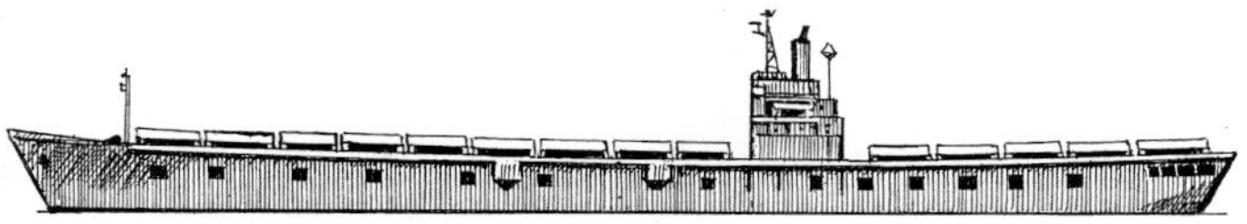

5 *M²F H2*
PONCE US/US (Sun SB) 1968/81; RoC/Con; 17,594 grt/18,725 dwt; 241.03 × 9.02 m *(790.78 × 29.59 ft)*; T (GEC); 25.5 kts; ex-*Ponce de Leon*; Lengthened 1981; (note—vessel is drawn to original length and there is now an extra deck level foreward of bridge)
Similar: **BAYAMON** (US) ex-*Eric K Holzer*; **KAINALU** (US) ex-*El Taino*; (Lengthened to 241m (1976) and now has extra deck level foreward of bridge); **NORTHERN LIGHTS** (US) ex-*Puerto Rico*; **KAIMOKU** (US) ex-*Westward Bridge* (extra deck foreward of bridge)

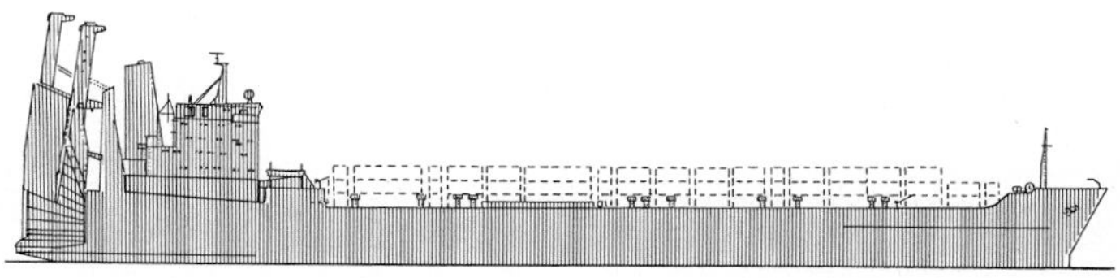

6 *M²FA H1*
JOLLY BIANCO It/Sp (AESA) 1982; RoC/Con; 30,969 grt/21,334 dwt; 199.50 × 9.52 m *(654.53 × 31.23 ft)*; M (Sulzer); 18.5 kts; ex-*Poznan*; 1,200 TEU; Angled stern door/ramp
Sisters: **KAGORO** (NIS) ex-*Katowice*; **JOLLY ROSSO** (It) ex-*Gdansk II*; **JOLLY VERDE** (It) ex-*Wroclaw*

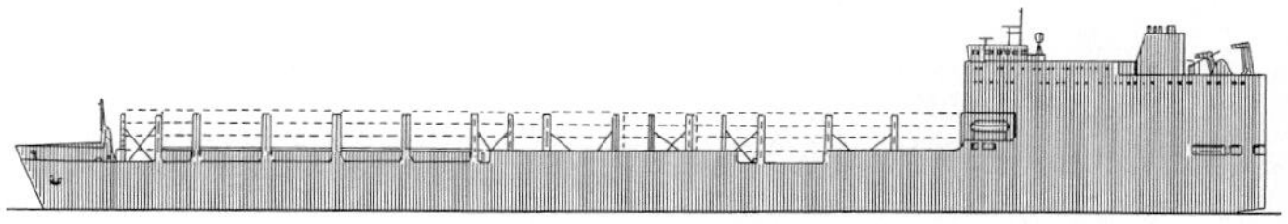

7 *M²FA H13*
ATLANTIC CONVEYOR Bs/Br (Swan Hunter) 1985; RoC/Con; 58,438 grt/ 44,988 dwt; 249.99 × 10.89 m *(820.18 × 35.73 ft)*; M (B&W); 18 kts; Angled stern door/ramp (starboard); Now lengthened to 291.92m (958ft) (Scott Lithgow). Drawing shows original appearance; Container capacity is now 2,908 TEU; Funnel is on starboard side; 'G3' type (see photo number 16/87)
Similar (differences in accommodation superstructure): **ATLANTIC CARTIER** (Bs) (Builder—Nord Med) (see photo number 16/64)

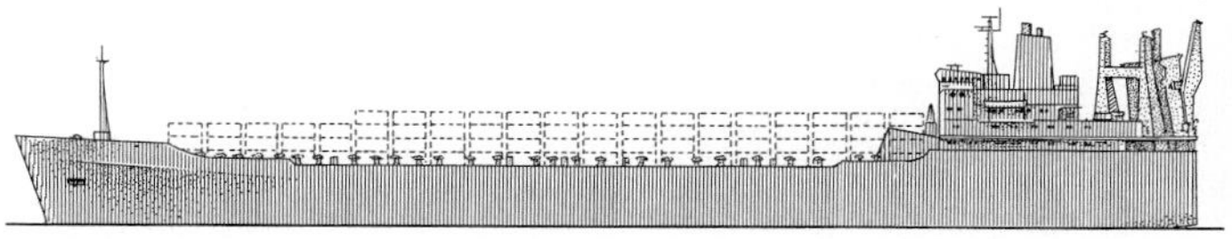

8 *M²FA H13*
CAPE KNOX US/Ja (NKK) 1978; RoC/Con; 36,450 grt/29,218 dwt; 212.1 × 10.72 (696 × 35.17) m; M (Sulzer); 19; ex-*Nedlloyd Rouen*; Quarter ramp (starboard); 1,550 TEU; owned by US Government
Sister (owned by US Government): **CAPE KENNEDY** (US) ex-*Nedlloyd Rosario*

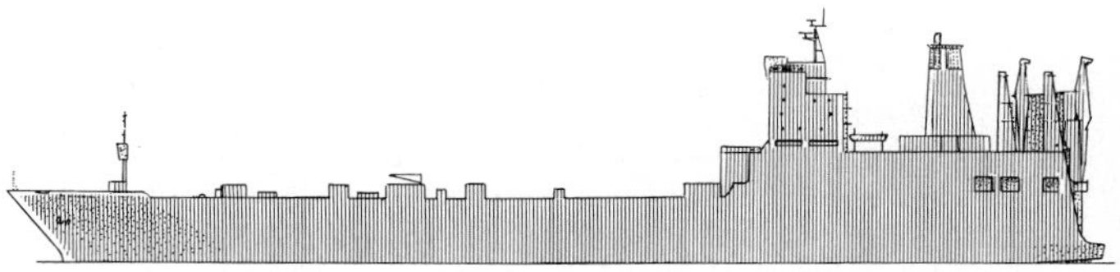

9 *M²FA H3*
SAUDI QASSIM Si/It (Italcantieri) 1980; RoC/Con; 43,841 grt/38,000 dwt; 194.37 × 10.8 m *(637.7 × 35.43 ft)*; M (GMT); 19 kts; ex-*Andrea Merzario*; Quarter ramp on starboard side; Lengthened 1983 by 31m (102ft) (Riuniti); Drawing shows vessel prior to this; 1,455 TEU; see photo number 16/70
Sister (also lengthened): **SAUDI HAIL** (Si) ex-*Comandante Revello*

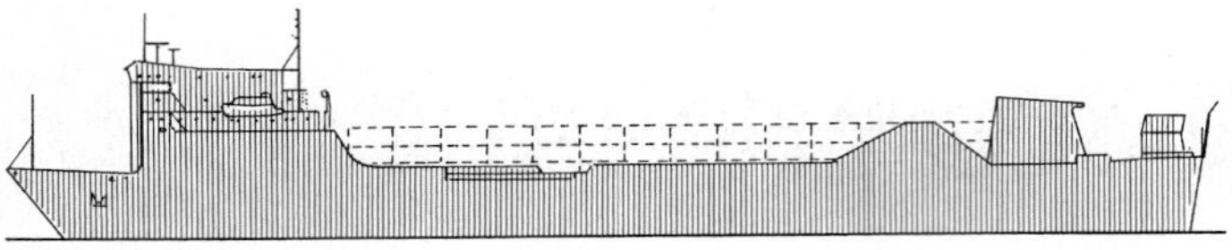

10 *M^{2}FAY H2*
SEABOARD VOYAGER Pa/FRG (Schichau-U) 1985; RoC/Con; 14,351 grt/11,294 dwt; 157.71 × 7.2 m *(517.42 × 23.62 ft)*; M (Krupp-MaK); 15.5 kts; ex-*Kintampo*; Side door/ramp (starboard side aft); quarter stern door/ramp; 865 TEU; Funnel is on starboard side

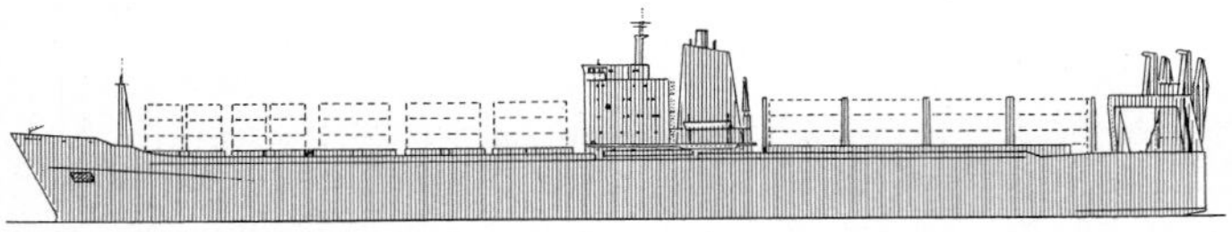

11 *M^{2}FCA H1*
SINGAPORE EXPRESS Li/Fr (La Ciotat) 1981; RoC/Con; 31,207 grt/27,970 dwt; 200.26 × 9.52 m *(657 × 31.23 ft)*; M (Sulzer); 20.75 kts; ex-*Tadeusz Kosciusko*; Starboard quarter ramp
Sisters: **PYRMONT BRIDGE** (Li) ex-*Kazimierz Pulaski*; **SAUDI RIYADH** (Li) ex-*Stefan Starzynski*; **SAUDI MAKKAH** (Si) ex-*Wladyslaw Sikorski*

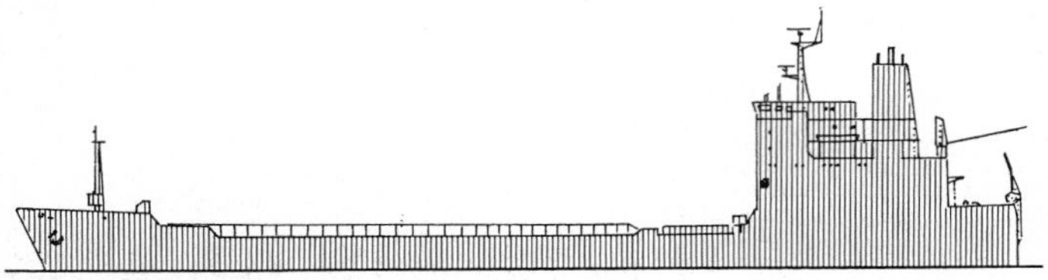

12 *M^{2}FC–RY H13*
THELISIS Gr/Sw (Kalmar) 1979; RoC/Con; 8,904 grt/9,450 dwt; 132.8 × 6.3 m *(435.7 × 20.67 ft)*; M (Pielstick); 14 kts; ex-*Merzario Arcadia*; Two stern doors/ramps; 521 TEU
Sister: **GALINI** (Gr) ex-*Merzario Fenicia*

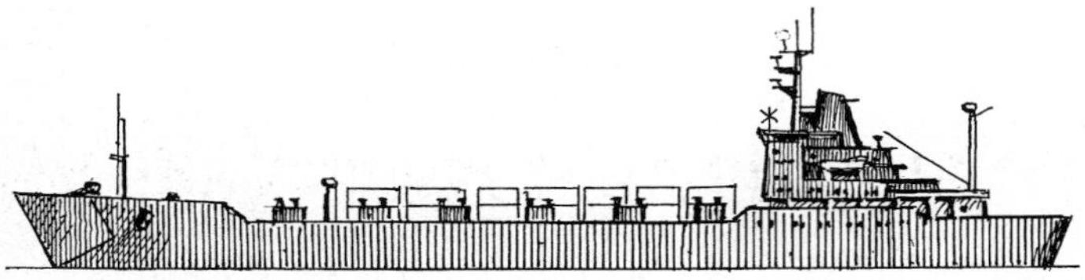

13 *M^{2}FM H1*
IVAN SKURIDIN Ru/Ru ('Zhdanov') 1975; RoC/Con; 3,954 grt/4,600 dwt; 139.6 × 6.62 m *(458 × 21.72 ft)*; M (B&W); 17 kts; Bow door/ramp; 242 TEU; 'Neva' type
Sisters (some have bow and stern doors): **GAVRILL KIRDISHCHEV** (Ru); **YURIY SMIRNOV** (Ru); **RAKVERE** (Ea) ex-*Nikolay Vilkov*; **IVAN DERBENYEV** (Ru); **ZNAMYA OKTYABRYA** (Uk); **KATYA ZELENKO** (Uk); **VALGA** (Ea) ex-*Aleksandr Osipov*; **NARVA** (Ea) ex-*Timur Frunze*; **VILJANDI** (Ea) ex-*Boris Buvin*; **VIKTOR TALALIKHIN** (Uk); **VERA KHORUZHAYA** (Uk); **LIVORNO BRIDGE** (Bs) ex-*Aleksa Dundic* **VALENCIA BRIDGE** (Bs) ex-*Marjan*; Similar (sisters but 12m (40ft) longer): **JURIS AVOTS** (La) ex-*Yuriy Avot*; **NIKOLAY PRZHEVALSKIY** (Ru); **SHANTAR** (Ru) ex-*Devyatnadtsatyy Syezd Vlksm*; **DONETSK** (Uk); **KUZMA GNIDASH** (Ru); **HAAPSALU** (Ea) ex-*Nikolay Yanson*; **ALEKSANDR STAROSTENKO** (Ru)

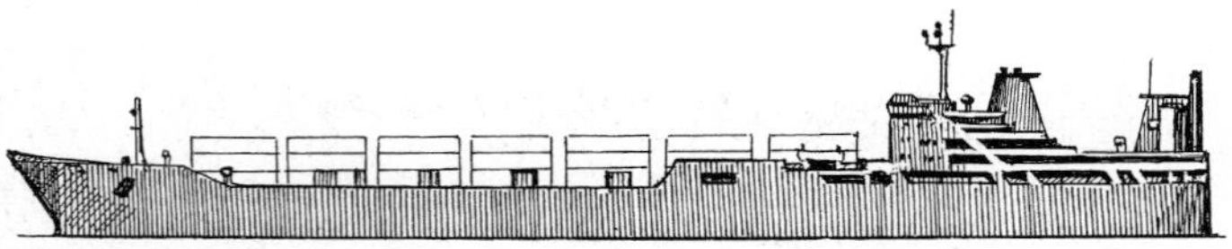

14 *M^{2}FN–A H1*
KIDIRA Bs/Pd (Gdanska) 1975; RoC/Con; 12,718 grt/18,462 dwt; 181.41 × 9.64 m *(595.18 × 31.63 ft)*; M (Sulzer); 20.5 kts; ex-*Skulptor Konenkov*; Stern door/quarter ramp; 'B-481' type; 634 TEU
Sisters: **UTARI** (Pa) ex-*Skulptor Vuchetich*; **SKULPTOR GOLUBKINA** (Uk); **ATLANTIC HOPE** (Li) ex-*Skulptor Zalkalns*; **NIKOLAY CHERKASOV** (Uk); **AGOSTINHO NETO** (Uk) ex-*Boris Limanov*; **EUROSHIPPING ONE** (Ru) ex-*Pyotr Masherov*; **ATLANTIC HERALD** (Li) ex-*Georgiy Pyasetskiy*; **YURIY MAKSARYOV** (Uk); **AKADEMIK GORBUNOV** (Ru)

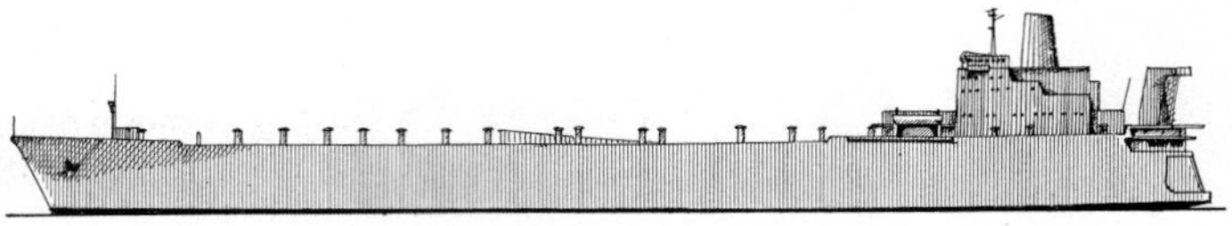

15 *M^{2}FRA H*
CAPE DOUGLAS US/Sw (Eriksbergs) 1974; RoC/Con; 23,972 grt/24,204 dwt; 207.4 × 9.58 m *(680.45 × 31.43 ft)*; M (Pielstick); 22.75 kts; ex-*Lalandia*; 1,495 TEU; Quarter stern door/ramp; Owned by US Government
Similar (Superstructure varies): **CAPE DUCATO** (US) ex-*Barranduna*; **CAPE DOMINGO** (US) ex-*Tarago*; **CAPE DECISION** (US) ex-*Tombarra*; **CAPE DIAMOND** (US) ex-*Tricolor*

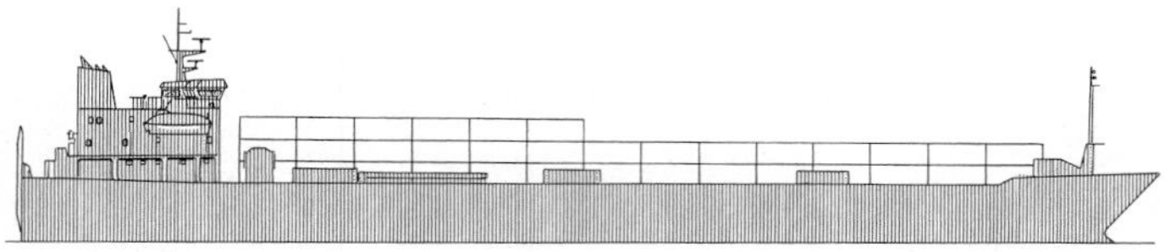

16 *M^{2}FY H*
HAMNO Fi/Ys ('Sava') 1991; RoC/Con; 6,620 grt/5,387 dwt; 122.00 × 6.17 m *(400.26 × 20.24 ft)*; M (Wärtsilä); 16.5 kts; 296 TEU; Stern door/ramp; Paper carrier
Sisters: **GRANO** (Fi); **AHTELA** (Fi); **STYRSO** (Fi); **AMBER** (No); **AKNOUL** (Pa)

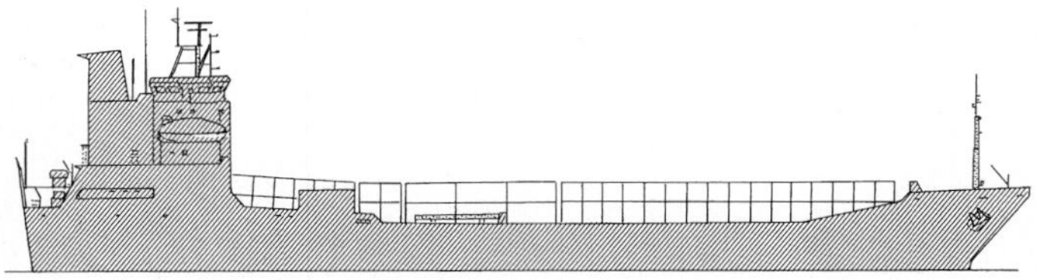

17 *M^{2}FY H13*
FENICIA It/It (Apuania) 1989; RoC/Con; 7,363 grt/5,000 dwt; 121.56 × 5.61 m *(398.82 × 18.41 ft)*; M (GMT); 15 kts; 305 TEU; Stern door/ramp
Sister: **EGIZIA** (It)

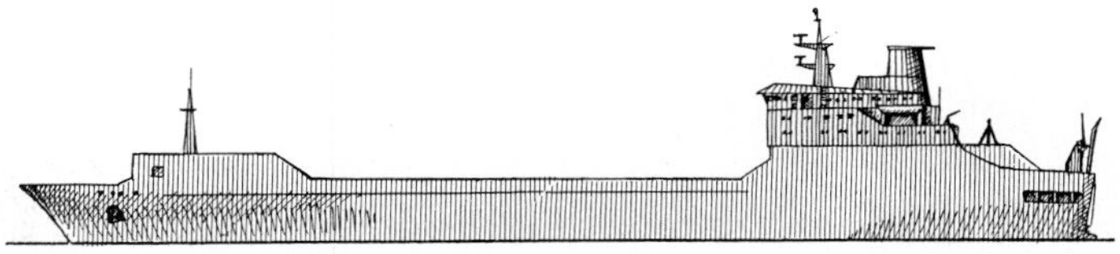

18 *M^{2}FY H2*
STENA CARRIER Br/Ko (Hyundai) 1977; RoC/Con; 13,117 grt/8,661 dwt; 151.01 × 7.32 m *(495.44 × 24.02 ft)*; M (Pielstick); 16 kts; ex-*Imparca Express 1*; Stern door/ramp; 562 TEU
Sisters: **ATLANTIC FREIGHTER** (Bs) ex-*Tor Felicia*; **STENA FREIGHTER** (Sw) ex-*Merzario Ausonia*; Similar (lengthened sister—163.61m (537ft)): **ELK** (Br)

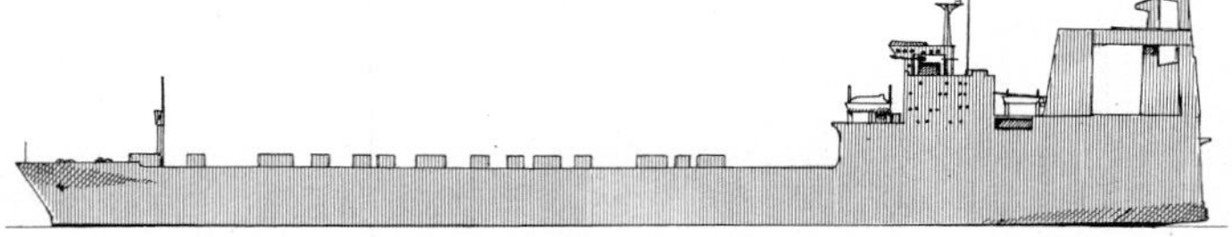

19 *M^{2}F–A H3*
TAPIOLA NIS/Ja (Mitsubishi HI) 1978; RoC/Con; 39,535 grt/31,456 dwt; 228.51 × 9.05 m *(749.7 × 29.69 ft)*; M (Sulzer); 22 kts; ex-*Boogabilla*; Angled stern door/ramp; 1,772 TEU; Funnel is on starboard side
Sisters: **CGM RIMBAUD** (Kn) ex-*Elgaren*; **TOURCOING** (NIS); **CGM RACINE** (Kn) ex-*Kolsnaren*

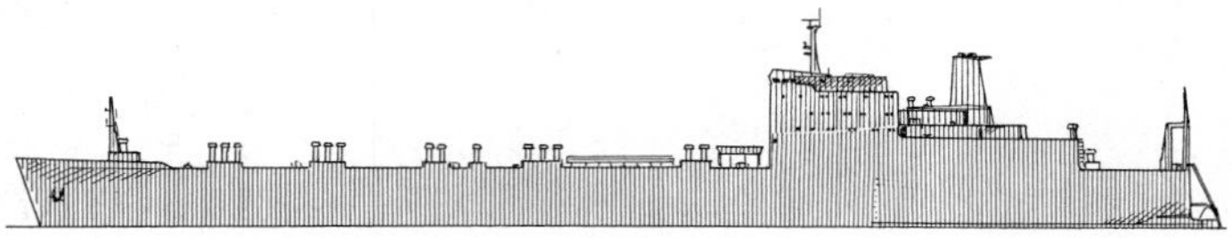

20 *M^{2}F–RZ H2*
BORAC NIS/Sw (Oskarshamns) 1978; RoC/Con; 20,165 grt/14,763 dwt; 183.5 × 8.44 m *(602.03 × 27.69 ft)*; M (Sulzer); 18.5 kts; ex-*Emirates Express*; Two stern doors/ramps; 840 TEU

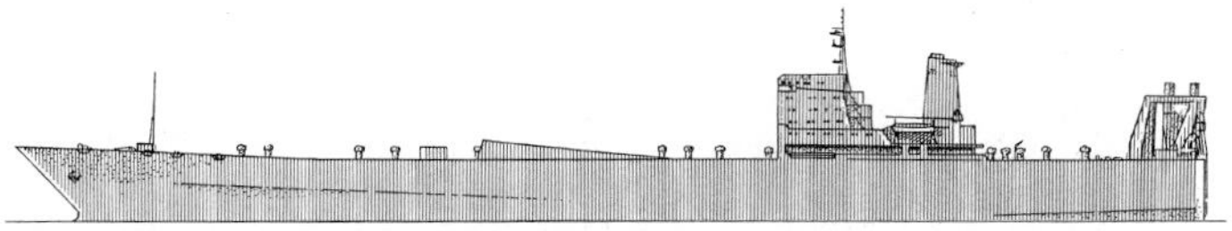

21 *M^{2}GA H*
KAPITAN SMIRNOV Uk/Ru ('Chernomorskiy') 1979; RoC/Con; 14,345 grt/20,075 dwt; 227.3 × 9.87 m *(745.74 × 32.38 ft)*; TS GT/M; — kts; Quarter ramp
Sisters: **KAPITAN MEZENTSEV** (Uk); **INZHENER YERMOSHKIN** (Uk); **VLADIMIR VASLYAYEV** (Uk)

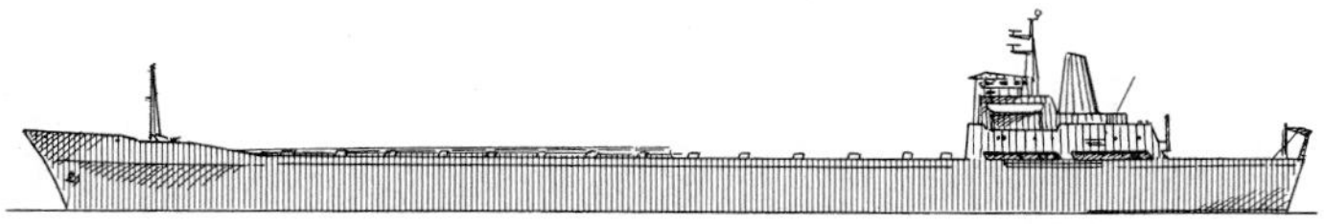

22 *M^{2}GMY H1*
MARMARA PRINCESS Tu/Fi (Wärtsilä) 1972/78; RoC/Con; 10,600 grt/9,511 dwt; 162.36 × 7.22 m *(532.68 × 23.69 ft)*; TSM (Pielstick); 17 kts; ex-*Mont Royal*; Stern door/ramp. Lengthened and converted 1978 (Nobiskrug); 133 TEU
Sister: **ARION** (—) ex-*Montmorency*

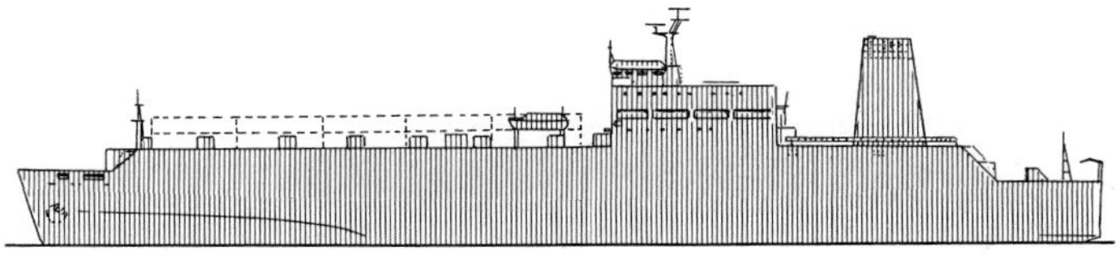

23 *M^{2}GMY H2*
AURORA NIS/Fi (Rauma-Repola) 1982; RoC/Con; 20,381 grt/13,090 dwt; 155.02 × 8.46 m *(509 × 27.76 ft)*; M (Pielstick); 18.5 kts; ex-*Arcturus*; Stern door/ramp; 608 TEU
Similar: **FINNMERCHANT** (Fi); **OIHONNA** (Fi); **BALTIC EIDER** (Br) (Ko built—Hyundai)

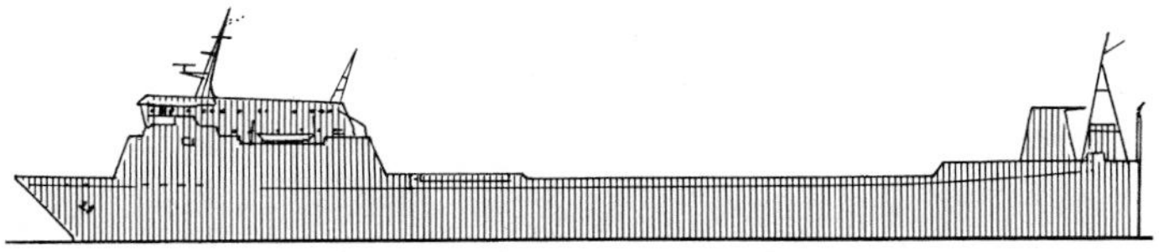

24 *M^{2}GMY H23*
AZILAL Mo/De (Frederikshavn) 1983; RoC/Con; 7,955 grt/7,225 dwt; 131.7 × 6.16 m *(432 × 20.21 ft)*; M (Krupp-MaK); 15.5 kts; ex-*Mercandian Ambassador*; Side ramp/door (starboard) and stern ramp/door; 414 TEU
Sisters: **AZROU** (Mo) ex-*Mercandian Diplomat*; **NEPTUNE OLYMPIC** (Gr) ex-*Mercandian Prince II*; **SEALIFT** (NZ) ex-*Mercandian Queen II*; **MERCANDIAN SENATOR** (DIS); **CANARIAS EXPRESS** (Sp) ex-*Mercandian Duke*; Similar (original sisters, extra accommodation block added to upper deck and other differences): **KRAKA** (De) ex-*Mercandian Governor*; **LODBROG** (De) ex-*Mercandian President*; **HEIMDAL** (De) ex-*Mercandian Admiral II*

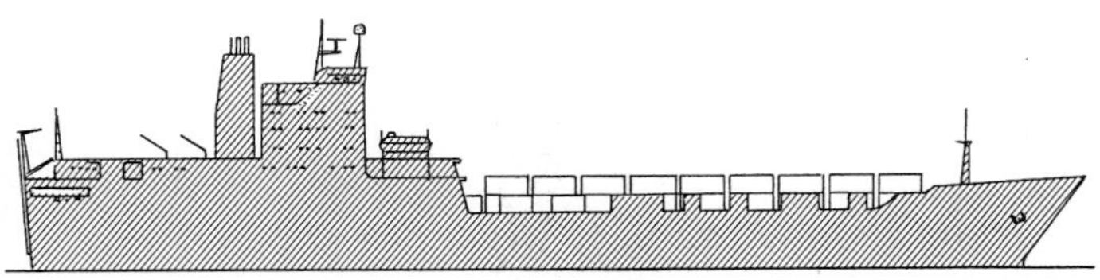

25 *M^{2}GS^{2}MY H12*
ZERAN Pd/Pd ('Komuny Paryskiej') 1986; RoC/Con; 15,414 grt/7,328 dwt; 147.45 × 6.80 m *(483.76 × 22.31 ft)*; TSM (Sulzer); 14.5 kts; Stern door/ramp; 400 TEU; 'B481' type
Sisters: **TYCHY** (Pd); **JOLLY BLU** (It) ex-*Debica*; **CHODZIEZ** (Pd); **WLOCLAWEK** (Pd)

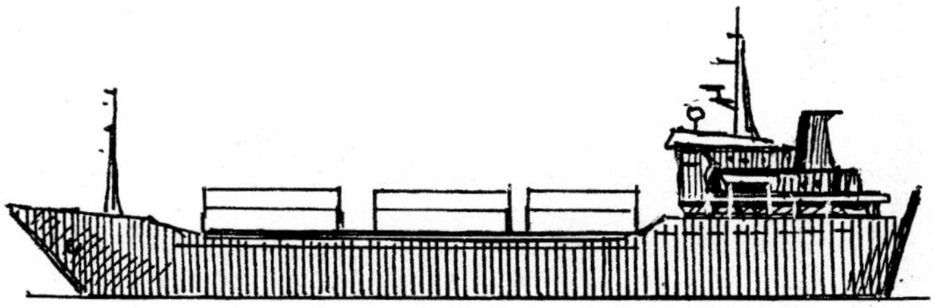

26 *M^{2}GY H13*
KESSULAID Ea/Tu (Beykoz) 1972; RoC/Con; 2,317 grt/2,120 dwt; 80.22 × 4.15 m *(263.19 × 13.62 ft)*; M (Alpha-Diesel); 13 kts; ex-*Wotan*; Stern door/ramp; 115 TEU
Similar: **MANILAID** (Ea) ex-*Thunar*; **SUURLAID** (Ea) ex-*Donar*
Similar (FRG built (Suerken)): **HEINLAID** (Ea) Launched as *Ymir* (see photo number 16/48); **VIIRELAID** (Ea) ex-*Thiassi*; **NIKOLAS** (—) ex-*Bibiana*

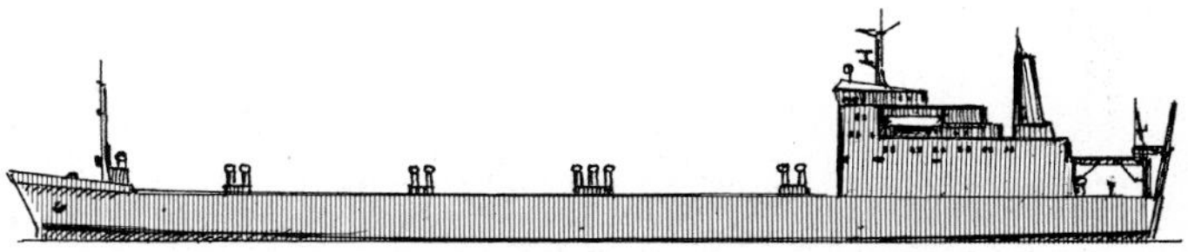

27 *M^{2}GY H2*
LOVERVAL Pa/Sw (Lodose) 1977; RoC/Con; 10,931 grt/9,019 dwt; 162.11 × 6.6 m *(531.86 × 21.65 ft)*; TSM (Sulzer); 17.25 kts; ex-*Vullmo*; Stern door/ramp; 308 TEU
Sister: **DANA HAFNIA** (DIS) ex-*Linne* 1985. (Funnel variation); Similar: **EUROMAGIQUE** (Bs) ex-*Kaprifol* (extra superstructure) (see photo number 16/62

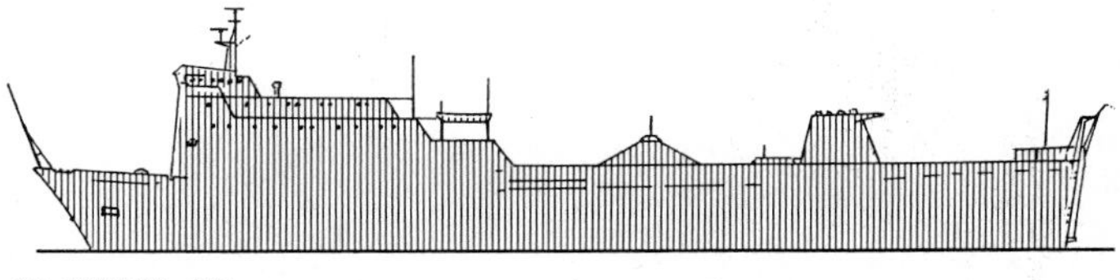

28 *M^{3}FMY H2*
TABA Eg/FRG (Schlichting) 1985; RoC/Con; 2,039 grt/3,133 dwt; 117.2 × 5.25 m *(384.51 × 17.22 ft)*; TSM (Krupp-MaK); 17 kts; Stern door/ramp; 257 TEU; Funnel is on port side
Sisters: **AL HUSSEIN** (Eg) ex-*Nuweiba*; **RAS MOHAMED** (Eg); Similar (converted to passenger/RoRo—extra superstructure): **DAHAB** (Eg) ex-*Sharm El Sheikh*
Similar (RoRo cargo): **GHARDAIA** (Ly); **TAJURA** (Ag)

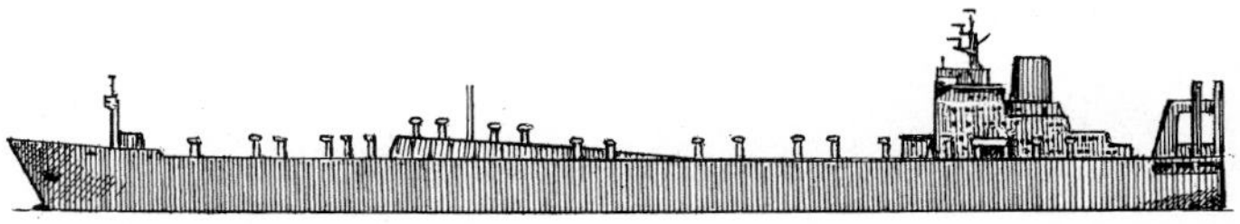

29 *M^{3}FM–RA H*
MAGNITOGORSK Ru/Fi (Valmet) 1975; RoC/Con; 15,709 grt/21,002 dwt; 205.8 × 9.7 m *(675.2 × 31.82 ft)*; M (B&W); 21.75 kts; Stern door/quarter ramp; 1,346 TEU
Sister: **KOTLINI** (Cy); Similar (lifeboats ahead of bridge): **ANATOLIY VASILYEV** (Ru); **SMOLENSK** (Ru)

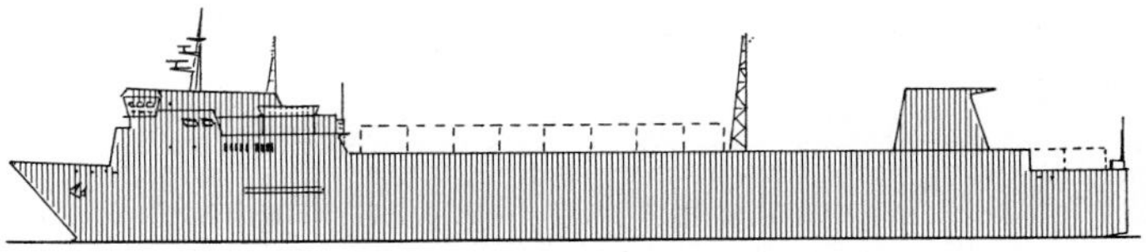

30 *M^{3}FZ H2*
DANA CIMBRIA DIS/De (Frederikshavn) 1986; RoC/Con; 12,189 grt/7,057 dwt; 145 × 6.55 m *(475.72 × 21.49 ft)*; M (MaK); 17.5 kts; ex-*Mercandian Express II*; 458 TEU; three stern ramps; FV 2070 type

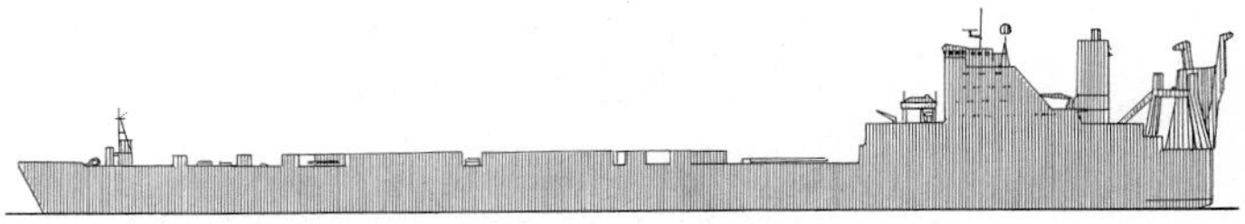

31 *M^{3}RFA H3*
SAUDI ABHA Si/Sw (Kockums) 1982; RoC/Con; 44,171 grt/42,600 dwt; 248.72 × 10.8 m *(816 × 35.43 ft)*; M (B&W); 18.5 kts; 2,025 TEU; Quarter ramp/door; Side door/ramp; Funnel is on starboard side
Sisters: **SAUDI DIRIYAH** (Si); **SAUDI HOFUF** (Si); **SAUDI TABUK** (Si)

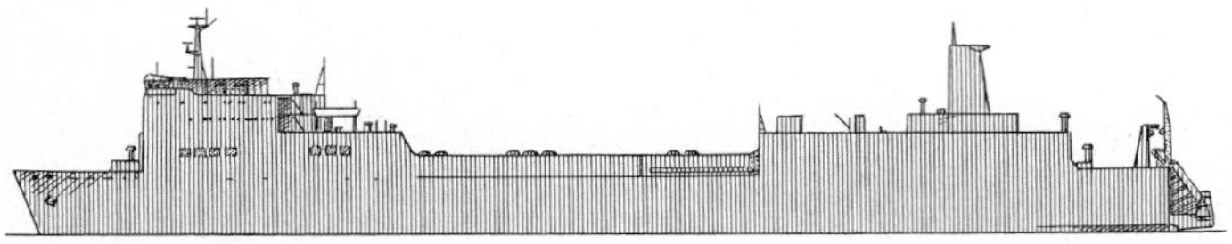

32 *M^2NM–FZ H2*
UND HAYRI EKINCI Tu/Sw (Oskarshamns) 1979; RoC/Con; 21,213 grt/14,522 dwt; 183.14 × 8.47 m *(600.85 × 27.79 ft)*; M (Sulzer); 18.5 kts; ex-*Finneagle*; Two stern ramps (slewing); 840 TEU
Sister: **UND DENIZCILIK** (Tu) ex-*Gulf Express*; Similar: **BORACAY** (NIS) ex-*Bandar Abbas Express*

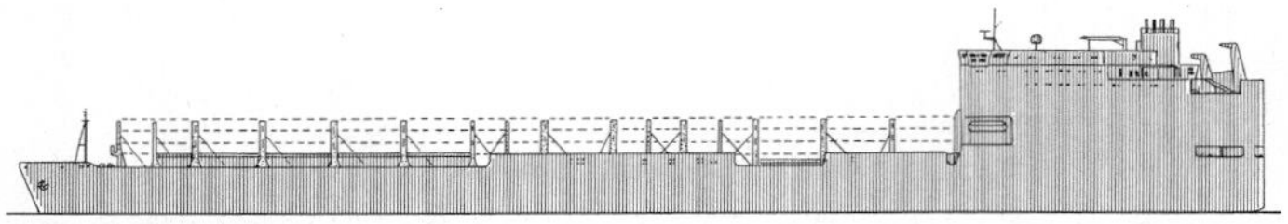

33 *M^2RFA H3*
ATLANTIC COMPANION Sw/Sw (Kockums) 1984; RoC/Con; 57,255 grt/51,648 dwt; 249.44 × 10.89 m *(818.37 × 35.73 ft)*; M (B&W); 18 kts; Angled stern door/ramp (starboard); Now lengthened to 291.92m (958ft) (Hyundai Mipo); Drawing shows original appearance; Container capacity is now 2,908 TEU; Funnel is on starboard side; G3 type (see photo number 16/86)
Sisters (also lengthened): **ATLANTIC COMPASS** (Sw); **ATLANTIC CONCERT** (Sw)

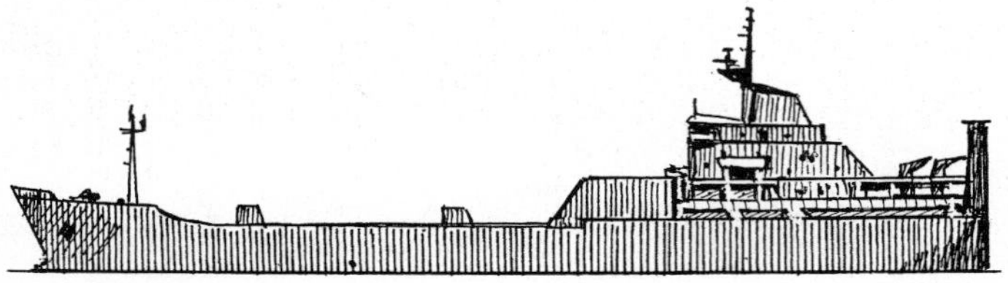

34 *MM–FA H1*
AKADEMIK ARTSIMOVICH Uk/Fr (CNIM) 1975; RoC/Con; 7,662 grt/4,460 dwt; 119.03 × 5.77 m *(390.52 × 18.93 ft)*; M (Pielstick); 16.75 kts; Angled stern door and ramp; 235 TEU
Sisters: **AKADEMIK GUBER** (Uk); **AKADEMIK KUPREVICH** (Uk); **AKADEMIK MILLIONSCHIKOV** (Uk); **AKADEMIK STECHKIN** (Uk); **AKADEMIK TUPOLEV** (Uk)

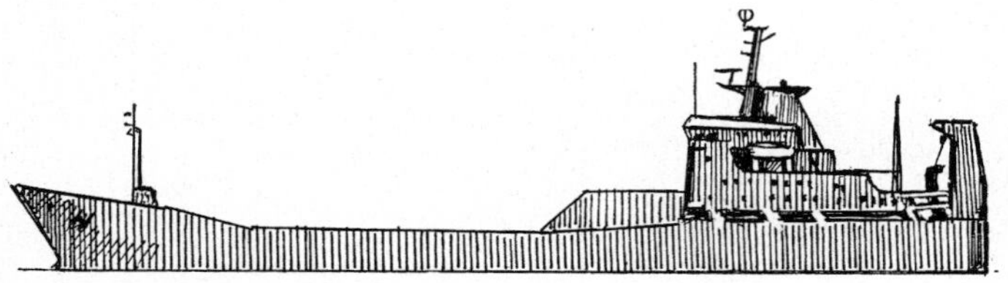

35 *MM–FNA H1*
INZHENIER MACHULSKIY Ru/Fi (Hollming) 1975; RoC/Con; 4,009 grt/6,128 dwt; 124.21 × 6.6 m *(407.51 × 21.65 ft)*; M (Pielstick); 16.2 kts; Quarter ramp; Stern door; 239 TEU
Sisters: **INZHENIER BASHKIROV** (Ru); **INZENIERIS SUHORUKOVS** (La) ex-*Inzhenier Sukhorukov*; **INZENIERIS KREILIS** (La) ex-*Inzhenier Kreylis*; **MEKHANIK KONOVALOV** (Ru); Similar (stern ramp and no extension before bridge-front): **INZENIERIS NECIPORENKO** (La) ex-*Inzhenier Nechiporenko*; **MEHANIKIS FJODOROVS** (La) ex-*Mekhanik Fedorov*; **MEKHANIK YEVGRAFOV** (Ru); **MEHANIKIS GERASIMOVS** (La) ex-*Mekhanik Gerasimov*

36 *MM–FNY H1*
INZENIERIS NECIPORENKO type; dwt; **SEE DRAWING NUMBER 16/35.** The vessels with in-line stern ramps under this drawing will have the above sequence

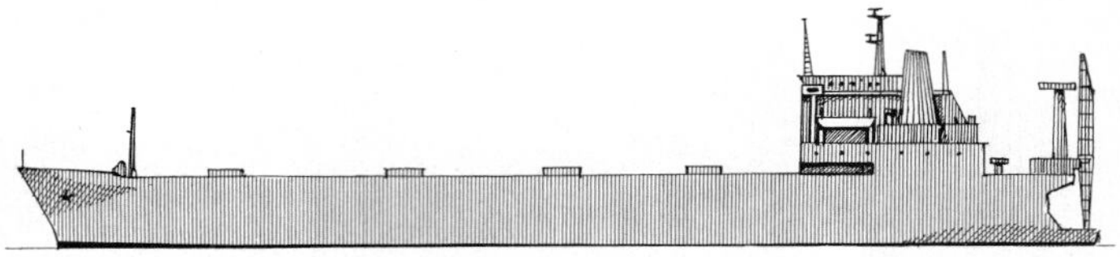

37 *MNGNY H*
JOLLY SMERALDO It/Ja (Sasebo) 1978; RoC/Con; 29,119 grt/31,262 dwt; 190.53 × 11.9 m *(625.1 × 39.04 ft)*; TSM (MAN); 17 kts; ex-*Hellenic Valor*; 1,107 TEU; Slewing stern ramp/door
Sisters: **JOLLY RUBINO** (It) ex-*Hellenic Explorer*; **JOLLY TURCHESE** (It) ex-*Hellenic Innovator*

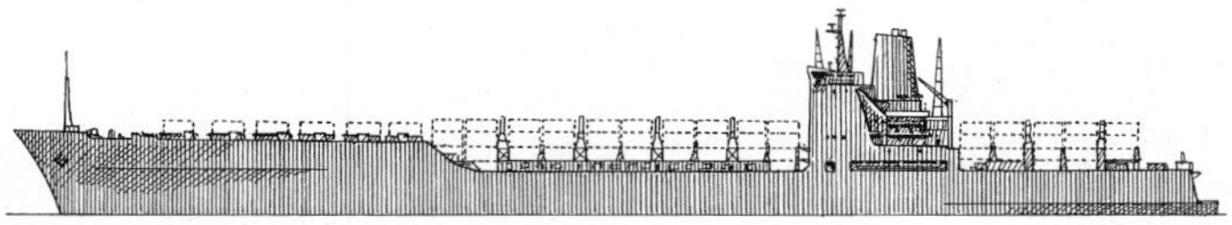

38 *MN^2FNS H1*
MARILIA A Ma/Ja (Kawasaki) 1975; RoC/Con; 19,928 grt/23,476 dwt; 222.3 × 10.5 m *(731 × 35 ft)*; M (MAN); 22.75 kts; ex-*Australian Emblem*; Stern door
Sister: **MAKEDON** (Cy) ex-*James Cook*

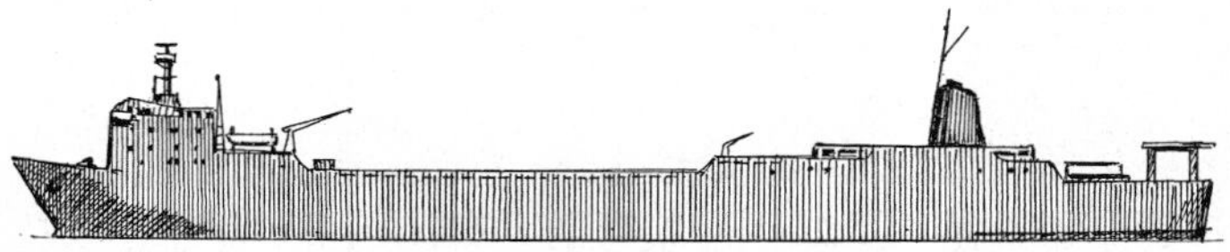

39 *MNS^2M–FY H2*
CAPE RAY US/Ja (Kawasaki) 1977; RoC; 14,825 grt/22,735 dwt; 197.52 × 10.03 m *(648.03 × 32.91 ft)*; M (MAN); 14 kts; ex-*Seaspeed Asia*; Stern door and side door; 1,315 TEU; Owned by US Government
Sisters: **CAPE RACE** (US) ex-*Seaspeed America*; **CAPE RISE** (US) ex-*Seaspeed Arabia*

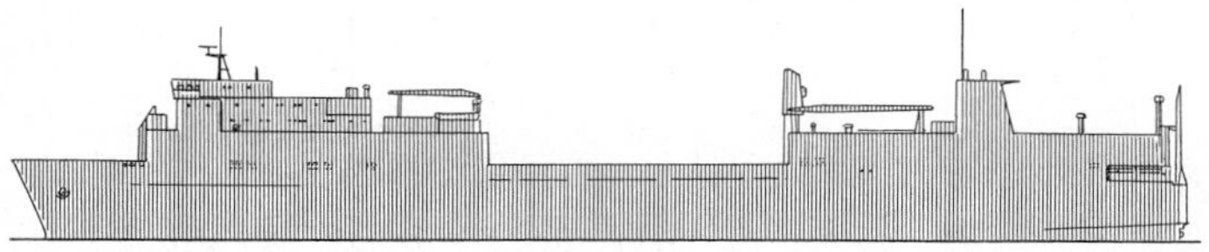

40 *MRCM–FZ H23*
CAPE ORLANDO US/Sw (Kockums) 1981; RoC/Con; 15,632 grt/20,731 dwt; 194.01 × 9.22 m *(637 × 30.25 ft)*; TSM (Sulzer); 19.75 kts; ex-*Finneagle*; Two slewing stern door/ramps; 1,050 TEU; US Government owned
Sisters: **AMERICAN FALCON** (US) ex-*Finnclipper*; **AMERICAN CONDOR** (US) ex-*Kuwait Express*

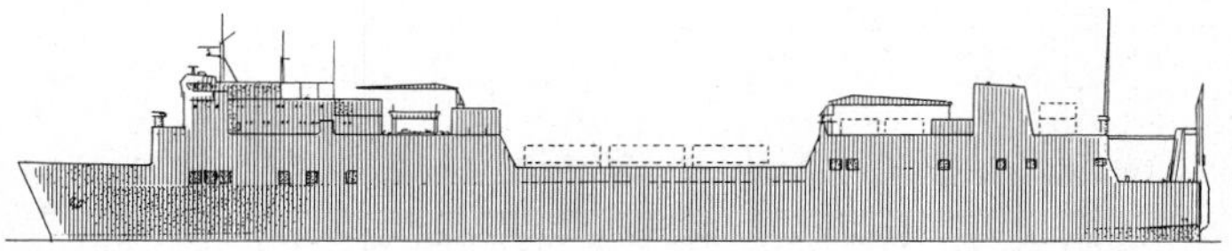

41 *MR^2FMZ H2*
LUBECK LINK Fi/Sw (Oskarshamns) 1980; RoC/Con; 33,163 grt/18,541 dwt; 194.11 × 8.4 m *(636.84 × 27.56 ft)*; TSM (Sulzer); 19.2 kts; ex-*Finnrose*; 1,132 TEU; Now converted to RoRo passenger ferry—may have extra superstructure; Bow door/ramp
Sister: **MALMO LINK** (Sw) ex-*Finnhawk*

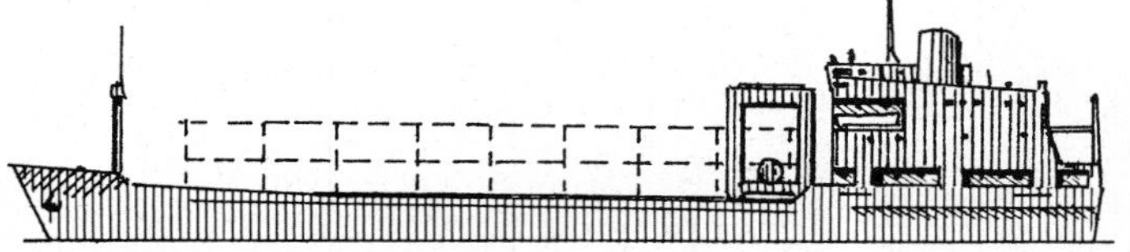

42 *M–NKMGY*
VIENTO DEL SIROCO Sp/Ne (Zaanlandsche) 1971; RoC/Con; 1,523 grt/1,893 dwt; 85.32 × 4.71 m *(279.92 × 15.45 ft)*; M (Werkspoor); 15 kts; ex-*Vento di Scirocco*; Stern ramp; 113 TEU; 'Tarros' type
Sisters: **WALTER F** (Pa) ex-*Bergen Juno*; **PISHGAM** (Ir) ex-*Vento di Maestrale*; **SERAYA JAYA** (Pa) ex-*Cheshire Venture*

43 Marilia A *(Ma); 1975* *FotoFlite*

44 Inzhener Yermoshkin *(Uk); 1980* *FotoFlite*

45 Singapore Express *(Li); 1981; (as Tadeusz Kosciusko)* *FotoFlite*

46 Marmara Princess *(Tu); 1972/78; (as Canada Maritime)* *FotoFlite*

47 Kessulaid *(Ea); 1972* *FotoFlite*

48 Heinlaid *(Ea); 1971* *FotoFlite*

49 Aurora *(NIS); 1982; (as Arcturus)* *FotoFlite*

50 Baltic Eider *(Br); 1989* *FotoFlite*

51 Thelisis *(Gr); 1979* *FotoFlite*

52 Ivan Derbenyev *(Ru); 1978* *FotoFlite*

53 Juris Avots *(La); 1983* *FotoFlite*

54 Latmos *(Cy); 1977; (as Kapitan Yakovlev)* *FotoFlite*

55 Jolly Rubino *(It); 1978* *FotoFlite*

56 Mehanikis Gerasimovs *(La); 1977* *FotoFlite*

57 Borac *(NIS); 1978; (as Foss Eagle)* *FotoFlite*

58 Kotlini *(Cy); 1976; (as Komsomolsk)* *FotoFlite*

59 Anatoliy Vasilyev *(Ru); 1981* *FotoFlite*

60 Jolly Verde *(It); 1983* *FotoFlite*

61 Loverval *(Pa); 1977* *FotoFlite*

62 Euromagique *(Bs); 1977* *FotoFlite*

63 Cape Knox *(US); 1978; (as Rouen)* *FotoFlite*

64 Atlantic Cartier *(Bs); 1985/87* *FotoFlite*

65 Atlantic Freighter *(Bs); 1978; (as Stena Grecia)* *FotoFlite*

66 Saudi Diriyah *(Si); 1983* *FotoFlite*

67 Tapiola *(NIS); 1978* *FotoFlite*

68 CGM Racine *(Kn); 1978* *FotoFlite*

69 Saudi Qassim *(Si); 1980* *FotoFlite*

70 Seaboard Voyager *(Pa); 1985; (as Kintampo)* *FotoFlite*

71 Ghardaia *(Ly); 1980* *FotoFlite*

72 American Falcon *(US); 1981* *FotoFlite*

73 Azilal *(Mo); 1983* *FotoFlite*

74 Dana Cimbria *(DIS); 1986* *FotoFlite*

75 Stena Shipper *(Bs); 1980* *FotoFlite*

76 Boracay *(NIS); 1978* *FotoFlite*

77 Inzenieris Neciporenko *(La); 1976* *FotoFlite*

78 ASL Sanderling *(Ca); 1977; (as Onno)* *FotoFlite*

79 Tarago *(Bs); 1979* *FotoFlite*

80 Ahtela *(Fi); 1991* *FotoFlite*

81 Astrea *(Fi); 1990* *FotoFlite*

82 Bore Nordia *(Fi); 1991* *FotoFlite*

83 Anke S *(At); 1985* *Norman Thomson*

84 Britannia *(Ge); 1985; (as Linda Buck)* *FotoFlite*

85 Laila *(At); 1983* *FotoFlite*

86 Atlantic Companion *(Sw); 1984/87* *FotoFlite*

87 Atlantic Conveyor *(Bs); 1985/87* *FotoFlite*

88 Nedlloyd Rotterdam *(Ne); 1978* *FotoFlite*

89 Zeran *(Pd); 1987* *FotoFlite*

90 Anro Australia *(Au); 1977/81* *FotoFlite*

91 American Condor *(US); 1981; (note slewing ramps)* *Norman Thomson*

92 Taba *(Eg); 1985* *WSPL*

93 Akademik Stechkin *(Uk); 1975* *WSPL*

94 Inzhener Machulskiy *(Ru); 1974* *WSPL*

95 Livorno Bridge *(Ma); 1982* *WSPL*

96 Cidade de Funchal *(Po); 1981* *FotoFlite*

97 Und Prenses *(Tu); 1987; (as Mount Cameroon)* *FotoFlite*

98 Inzhener Bashkirov *(Ru); 1975* *WSPL*

17 RO-RO/LO-LO

17 RO-RO/LO-LO

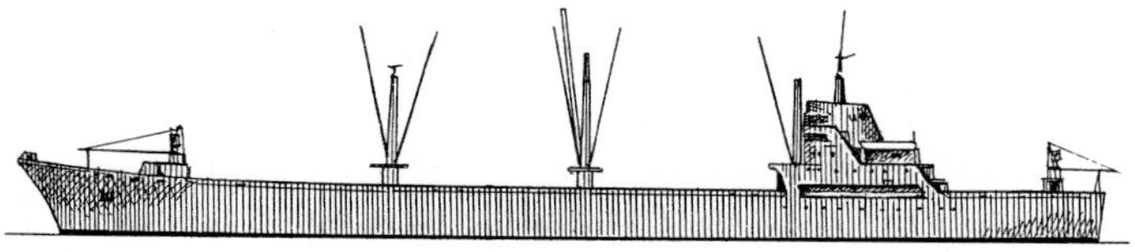

1 *CH^3M–FCY H*
CAPE NOME US/US (Ingalls SB) 1969; RoC/C; 11,757 grt/15,946 dwt; 183.2 × 10.4 m *(603 × 34.1 ft)*; T (GEC); 23.5 kts; ex-*Mormacstar*; US Government owned
Sisters (converted to RoC/Logistics): **CURTISS** (US) ex-*Mormacsky*

See photo number 17/77

2 *HC^2MGY H13*
UNION GLORY Pa/FRG (Cassens) 1982; RoC/Con; 4,729 grt/6,181 dwt; 99.95 × 6.08 m *(328 × 19.95 ft)*; M (MaK); 13 kts; ex-*Maris*; Stern door/ramp; 402 TEU; Cranes are on port side
Sisters: **LIAN SHAN** (RC) ex-*Stephan-J*; **MARIA J** (At); **UNION LUCKY** (Pa) ex-*Rewi*

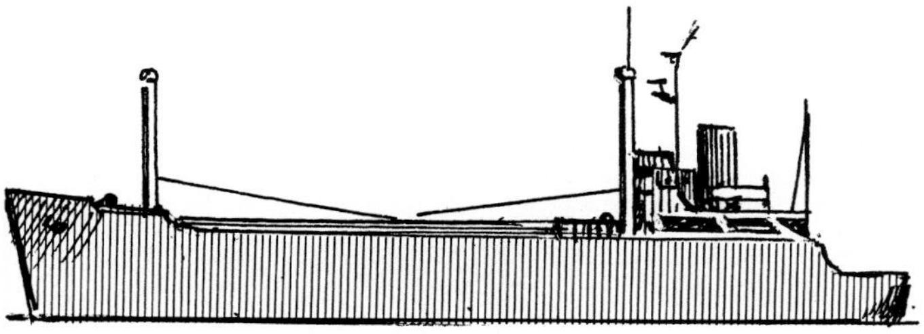

3 *H^2MFN H1*
JUNIOR SV/Ja (Miho) 1970; RoC; 4,776 grt/2,946 dwt; 87.30 × 4.98 m *(286.42 × 16.34 ft)*; TSM (Daihatsu); 11.5 kts; ex-*Cosmos No 2*; Bow door/ramp

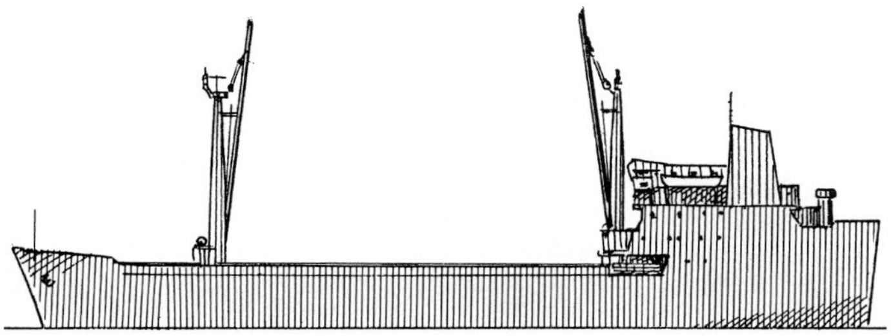

4 *H^2M–GY H3*
ATLAS Si/Fr (La Rochelle) 1972; C/HL/RoC; 5,426 grt/4,106 dwt; 97.90 × 6.39 m *(321.19 × 20.96 ft)*; M (Werkspoor); 15 kts; Stern door
Sisters: **GARA DJEBILET** (Ag); **TINDOUF** (Ag)

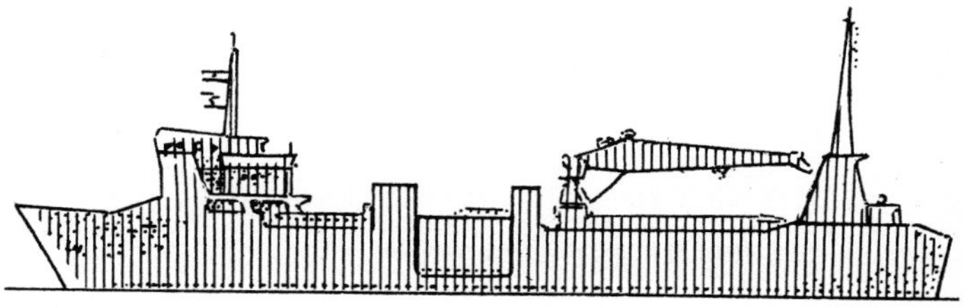

5 *MARM–F H*
ROYKSUND No/No (Lothe) 1979; Pal/Con; 2,028 grt/1,250 dwt; 70.8 × 4.57 m *(232.28 × 14.99 ft)*; M (Wichmann); 14 kts; Side door (port); 48 TEU
Sister (lengthened to 89.41m (293ft). Has two cranes): **KARMSUND** (No)

6 *MA–CM–F H*
NORDKYN No/No (Fosen) 1979; Pal/Con; 2,503 grt/1,385 dwt; 77.63 × 5.13 m *(254.69 × 16.83 ft)*; M (Wärtsilä); 14 kts; Side door (port); 26 TEU
Sisters (lengthened to 88.80 (291.34ft)): **BLIKUR** (Fa); **LOMUR** (Fa)

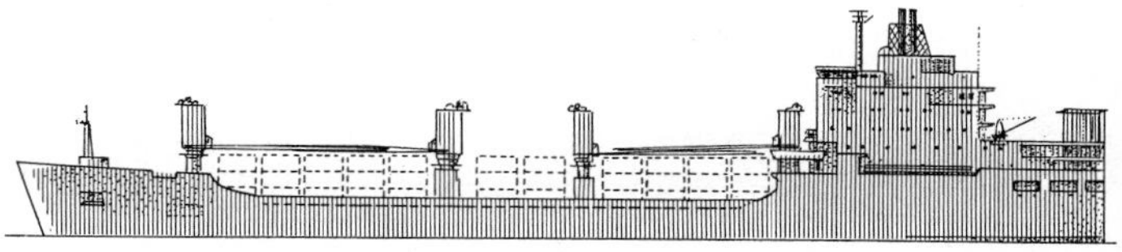

7 *MC^4MFMCA H13*
ILE DE LA REUNION Bs/Fr (L'Atlantique) 1977; RoC/Con; 13,928 grt/19,669 dwt; 163.79 × 10.74 m *(537.36 × 35.23 ft)*; M (Pielstick); 18.5 kts; ex-*Degas*; Quarter stern door/ramp; 637 TEU
Sisters: **ILE MAURICE** (Bs) ex-*Cezanne*; Similar (lengthened sisters—204.12m (670ft)): **PROSO** (Bs) ex-*Renoir*; **BUFFALO SOLDIER** (US) ex-*Monet*; **VERGINA** (Pa) ex-*Gauguin*; **AMERICAN MERLIN** (US) ex-*Utrillo*

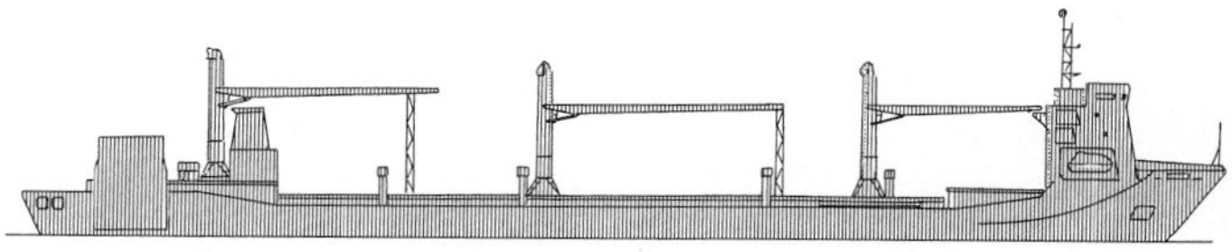

8 *MC^3FA H13*
INTREPIDO Bz/Bz (Caneco) 1991; RoC/Con; 15,768 grt/17,512 dwt; 173.42 × 8.20 m *(568.96 × 26.90 ft)*; M (Sulzer); 15.2 kts; two side doors/ramps (starboard); 1,341 TEU
Sister: **INDEPENDENTE** (Bz)

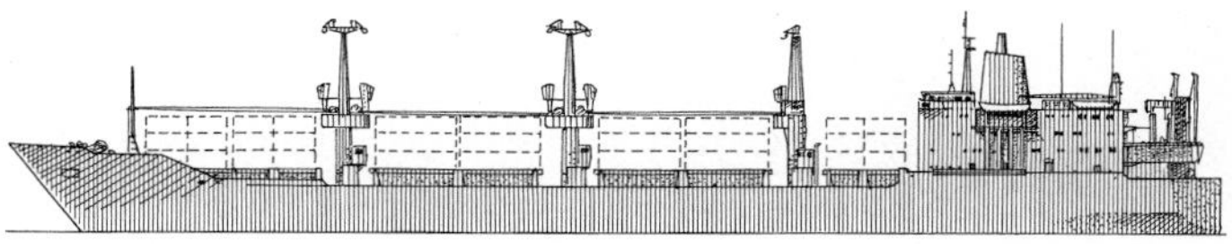

9 *MC^3HFCA H13*
MAERSK CONSTELLATION US/De (Odense) 1980; RoC/Con/C; 20,529 grt/21,213 dwt; 182.28 × 11.85 m *(598 × 38.88 ft)*; M (Sulzer); 18.5 kts; ex-*Elisabeth Maersk*; Quarter ramp (starboard); 566 TEU; 'Carolina' type

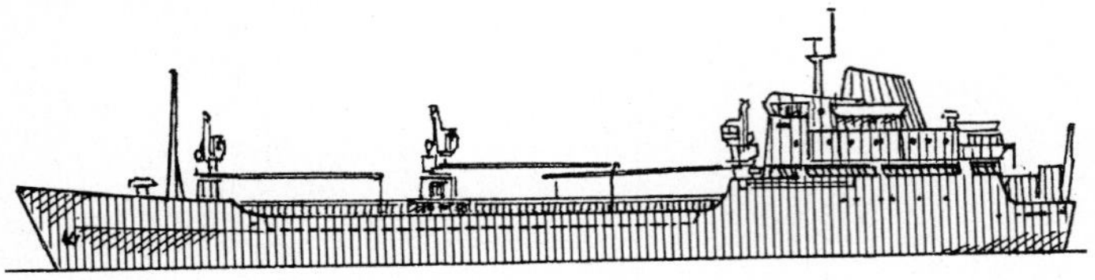

10 *MC^{3}MFY H12*
SPLENDID FORTUNE Ia/Fi (Rauma-Repola) 1967; RoC; 3,206 grt/3,825 dwt; 100.01 × 6.22 m *(328.11 × 20.41 ft)*; M (MWM); 15 kts; ex-*Bore VI*; Stern door
Sister: **IRISMED** (SV) ex-*Bore V*

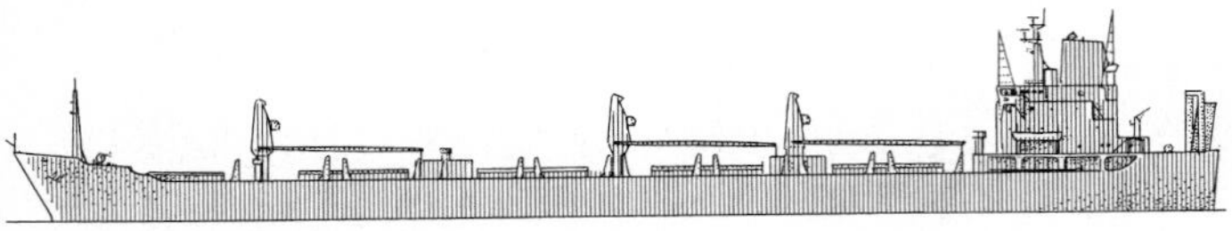

11 *MC^{3}M^{2}F–MRA H13*
FILOKTITIS Cy/Ja (Sanoyasu) 1978; B/RoVC; 25,465 grt/37,484 dwt; 184.72 × 12 m *(606.04 × 39.37 ft)*; M (MAN); 16 kts; ex-*Meiho Maru*; Stern quarter ramp
Sister: **EVRIMEDON** (Cy) ex-*Nippou Maru*

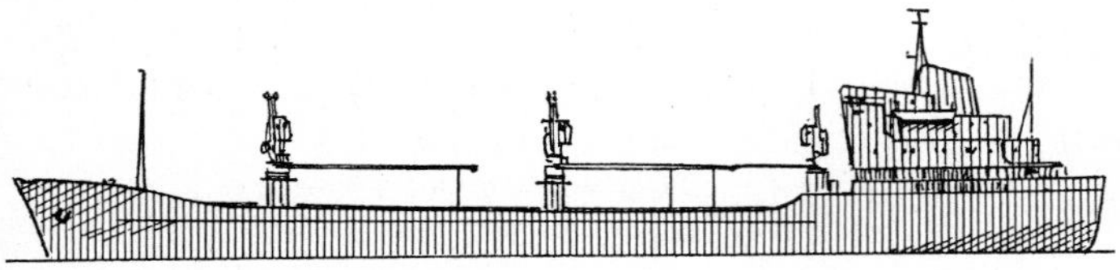

12 *MC^{3}M–FNY H13*
LADY FRANKLIN Ca/FRG (Kroegerw) 1970; C/RoC; 3,702 grt/3,627 dwt; 103.43 × 5.94 m *(339.33 × 19.49 ft)*; M (MAN); — kts; ex-*Baltic Valiant*; Stern door/ramp

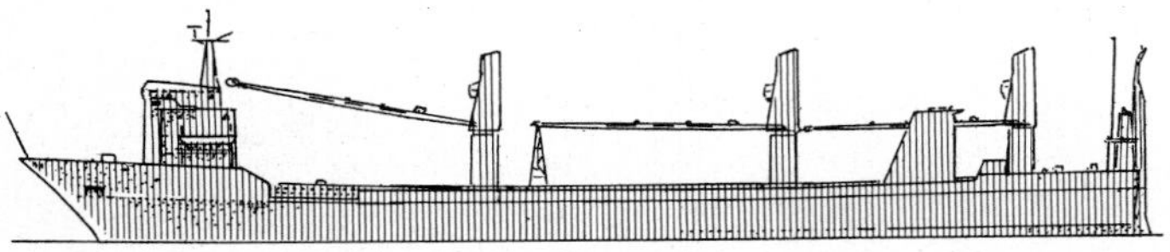

13 *MC^{2}FCMY H1*
PELRIDER Gr/FRG (Schlichting) 1978; C/Con/RoC; 7,235 grt/9,302 dwt; 124 × 8.2 m *(406.8 × 26.9 ft)*; TSM (Atlas-MaK); 15 kts; ex-*Neugraben*; 555 TEU; Funnel is on port side and cranes on starboard
Sister: **IRVING TIMBER** (Br) ex-*Uta-Sabine* (now fitted with a side-loading device between the first and second cranes)

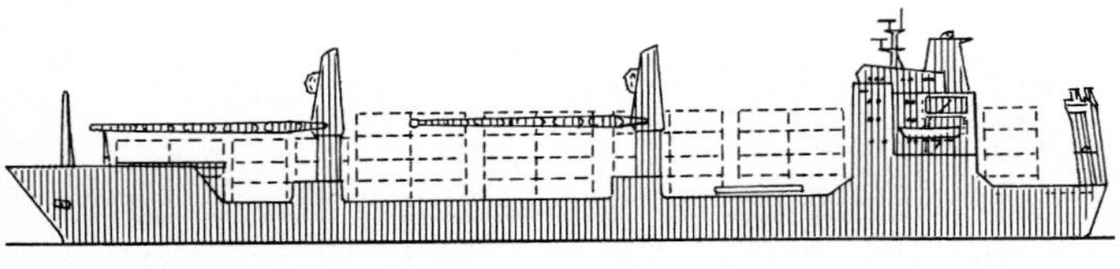

14 *MC^{2}MFA H12*
JULIA DEL MAR Sp/Sp (Barreras) 1981; RoC/Con/C; 3,860 grt/8,492 dwt; 122.71 × 8.17 m *(402.59 × 26.8 ft)*; M (Deutz); 14.5 kts; Quarter door/ramp; 533 TEU; Cranes are on port side
Sisters: **GLORIA DEL MAR** (Sp); **GALA DEL MAR** (Sp); **GRACIA DEL MAR** (Sp)

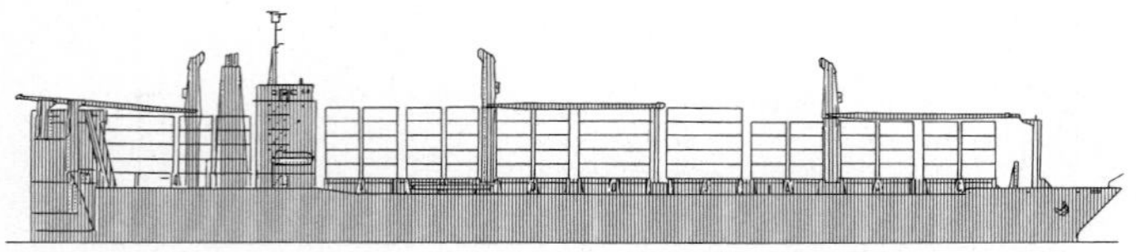

15 *MC^{2}MFCA H*
BETELGEUSE Bz/Bz (Emaq) 1992; RoC/Con; 30,225 grt/33,621 dwt; 192.20 × 11.90 m *(630.58 × 39.04 ft)*; M (Sulzer); 19 kts; Quarter ramp/door (starboard); 2,233 TEU
Sister: **BELATRIX** (Bz)

See photo number 17/79 and 17/80

16 *MC^{2}M–FLR H13*
HELENE Ge/FRG (Nobiskrug) 1985; RoC/C/Con; 5,608 grt/7,120 dwt; 116.52 × 6.16 m *(382.28 × 20.21 ft)*; M (Krupp-MaK); 13 kts; Launched as *Heinrich J*; Stern door/ramp; Free-fall lifeboat system on port side at stern; 574 TEU; Cranes are on port side and funnel on starboard
Sisters: **CARIB FAITH** (Ge) ex-*Helene*; **CAM IROKO EXPRESS** (At) ex-*Navigare*; **CAM AYOUS EXPRESS** (At) Launched as *Kathe Husmann*
Sisters (Be built—Boelwerf): **VENTO DI TRAMONTANA** (Lu) ex-*L Craeybeckx*; **TRANPORT SCHELDE** (Lu) ex-*L Delwaide*; Similar (poop is longer, giving more space abaft superstructure): **CAM AZOBE EXPRESS** (At) ex-*Thies*

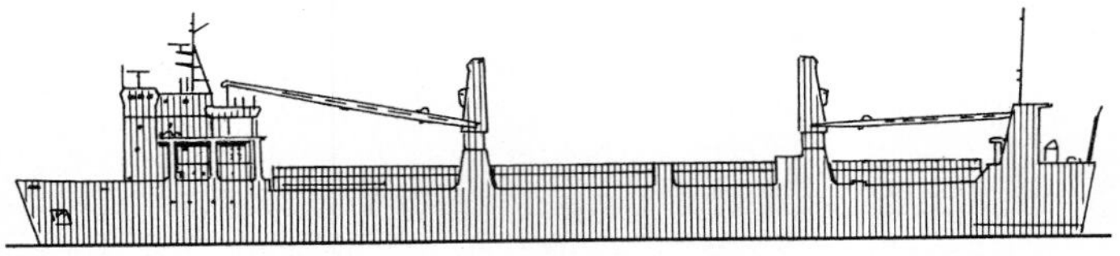

17 *MC^{2}M–GY H3*
RAGNA GORTHON Sw/Sw (Finnboda/Marstrands) 1979; RoC/C; 10,165 grt/7,583 dwt; 119.89 × 5.97 m *(393 × 19.59 ft)*; M (MaK); 14.5 kts; Stern door/ramp; Side door (starboard); 465 TEU; Now lengthened and converted to carry pallets (134.90m (443ft)); Drawing shows vessel as built; Cranes are on port side; Fwd section built by Marstrands, aft section built by Finnboda
Sisters (also lengthened): **LOVISA GORTHON** (Sw); **STIG GORTHON** (Sw)

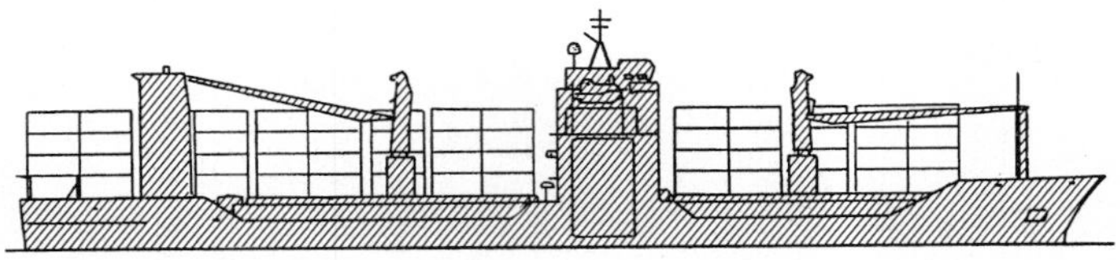

18 *MCMCF H123*
ABITIBI CLAIBORNE Ge/FRG (Bremer V) 1986; C/Pap/Pal; 7,580 grt/7,879 dwt; 123.02 × 7.39 m *(403.61 × 24.25 ft)*; M (MAN); 14.5 kts; ex-*Weser-Importer*; 604 TEU; Side door (starboard); Cranes and funnel on port side
Sister: **ABITIBI ORINOCO** (Ge) ex-*Weser-Harbour*

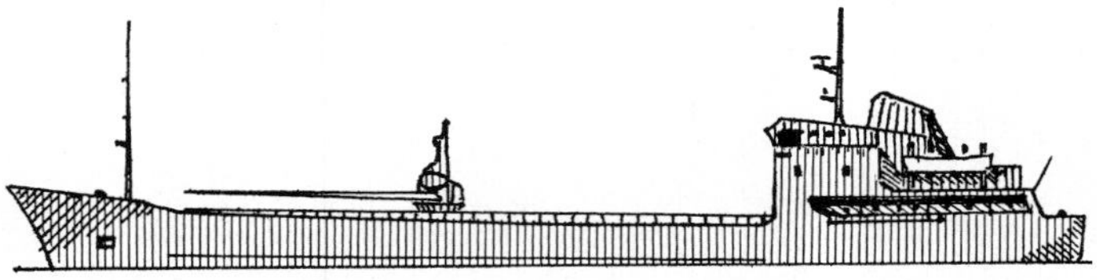

19 *MCMF H1*
NAWAF Si/It (Felszegi) 1966; RoC; 1,211 grt/1,472 dwt; 94.19 × 3.73 m *(390.02 × 12.24 ft)*; M (Atlas-MaK); 14 kts; Launched as *Forenede*; Stern door; Lengthened 1969 (Boele's Sch)
Sister: **SATTAM** (Si) Launched as *United*

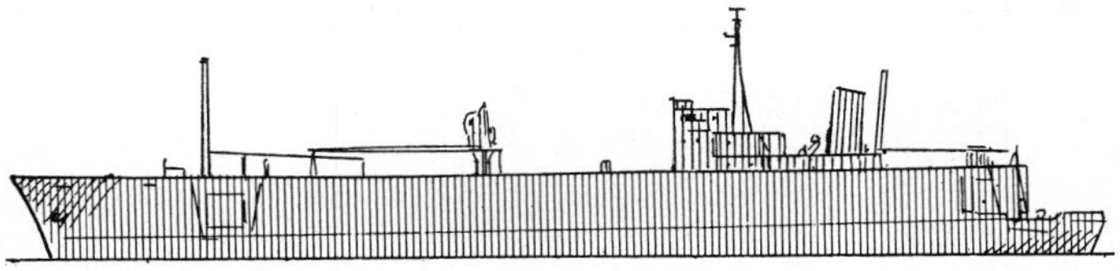

20 *MCMFM H1*
MALIGAYA Pi/Ja (Hayashikane) 1969; RoC; 2,406 grt/2,286 dwt; 107.7 × 4.49 m *(353.34 × 14.73 ft)*; TSM (Niigata); 13 kts; ex-*Hokuo Maru*; Stern door/ramp

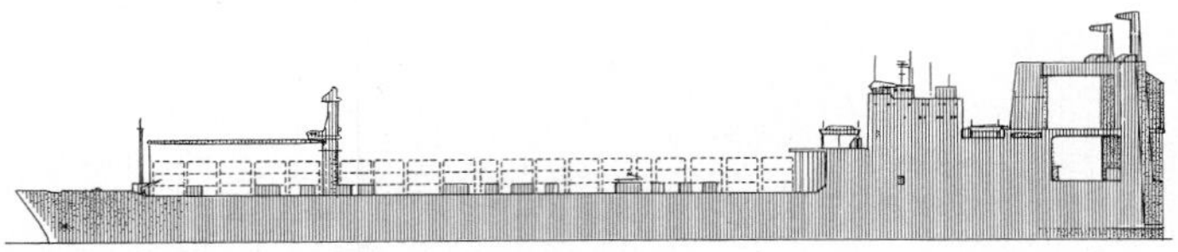

21 *MCMF–A H2*
CAPE HORN US (Navy)/No (Kaldnes) 1979; RoC/Con; 37,812 grt/31,800 dwt; 228.5 × 10.8 m *(749.67 × 35.43 ft)*; M (B&W); 22 kts; ex-*Barber Tonsberg*; Starboard quarter ramp; 1,772 TEU; Owned by US Government
Sister: **CAPE HUDSON** (US) ex-*Barber Taif*; Similar (Ja built—Mitsubishi HI; Differences include funnel shape, design of crane and so on): **CAPE HENRY** (US) ex-*Barber Priam*; **TALABOT** (NIS) ex-*Barber Perseus*; **TOBA** (NIS) ex-*Barber Toba*; **TAMPERE** (NIS) ex-*Barber Nara*

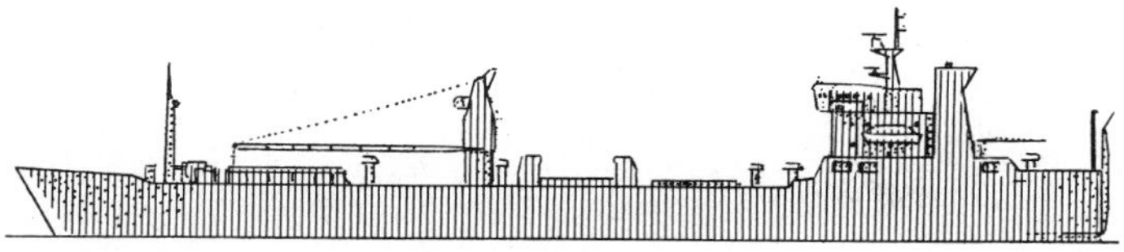

22 *MCMGMY H3*
TUNGENES NIS/No (Fosen) 1979; RoC/Con; 4,234 grt/3,041 dwt; 109 × 4.79 m *(357.61 × 15.72 ft)*; M (MaK); 15.5 kts; ex-*Astrea*; Stern ramp; Side door on starboard side; 75 TEU

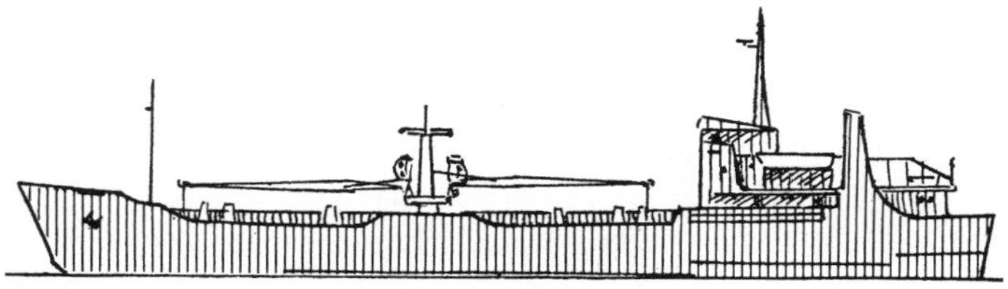

23 *MCMGY H1*
CENK II Tu/FRG (Sietas) 1967; RoC; 999 grt/1,377 dwt; 78.03 × 4.29 m *(256 × 14.07 ft)*; M (Atlas-MaK); — kts; ex-*Wasa*; Bow and stern doors; 50 TEU
Sister: **CENK K** (Tu) ex-*Hansa*

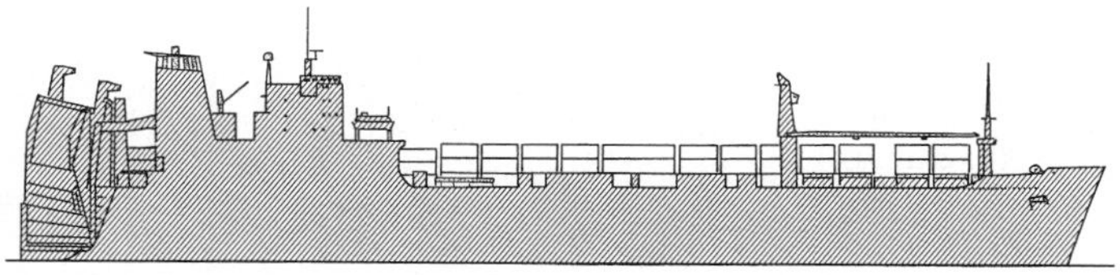

24 *MCM²CFA H13*
ROSA BLANCA Li/Ja (NKK) 1985; RoC/Con; 32,924 grt/27,601 dwt; 185.02 × 11.25 m *(607.02 × 36.91 ft)*; M (Pielstick); 16 kts; Quarter door/ramp (starboard); 1,446 TEU
Sister: **ROSA TUCANO** (Li)

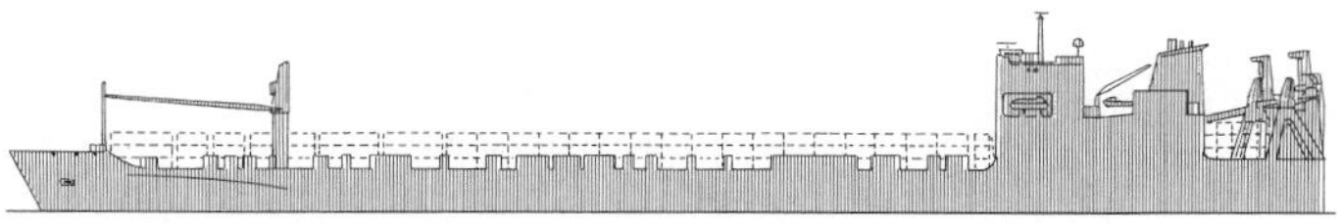

25 *MCMSFA H12*
TAMPA NIS/Ko (Hyundai) 1984; RoC/Con; 49,326 grt/44,013 dwt; 262.01 × 11.7 m *(859.61 × 38.39 ft)*; M (B&W); 21 kts; ex-*Barber Tampa*; Side door/ramp (starboard); Angled stern door/ramp (starboard); 2,455 TEU; No inset lifeboat on starboard side of superstructure; Funnel is on starboard side
Sisters: **TAIKO** (NIS) ex-*Barber Hector*; **TEXAS** (NIS) ex-*Barber Texas*

26 *MCM–F H1*
GULF STAR Cy/Br (Cochrane) 1969; Pal; 1,427 grt/1,824 dwt; 75.32 × 3.4 m *(247.11 × 11.15 ft)*; TSM (Mirrlees Blackstone); 13.75 kts; ex-*Dangeld*; Two side doors (starboard)

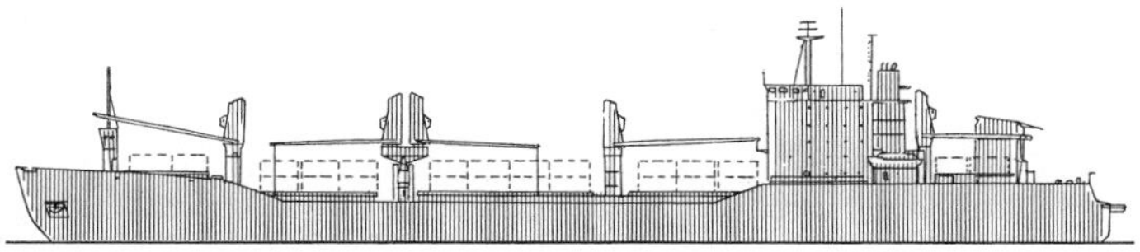

27 *MCPCHNFCA H12*
NORILSK Cy/Fi (Wärtsilä) 1982; C/Con/RoC; 18,627 grt/19,943 dwt; 174.02 × 10.52 m *(570.9 × 34.51 ft)*; M (Sulzer); 17 kts; Side ramp; 'SA 15' type. Some sisters built by Valmet; 576 TEU
Sisters: **MONCHEGORSK** (Cy); **ARKHANGELSK** (Cy); **NIZHNEYANSK** (Ru); **SPEYBANK** (Br); **TIKSI** (Ru); **IGARKA** (Ru); **ARUNBANK** (Br); **KOLA** (Ru); **AMDERMA** (Ru): **KANDALAKSHA** (Ru); **KEMEROVO** (Ru); **ANADYR** (Ru); **NIKEL** (Ru); **ANATOLIY KOLESNICHENKO** (Ru); **KAPITAN MAN** (Ru); **YURIY ARSHENENSKIY** (Ru); **VASILIY BURKHANOV** (Ru); **KAPITAN DANILKIN** (Ru)

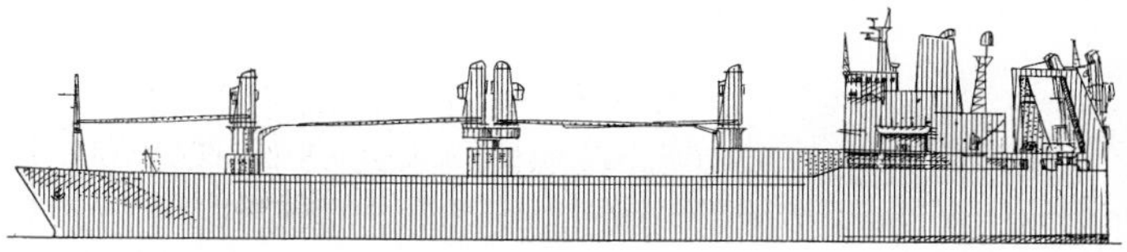

28 *MCPCNMFMA H3*
SEABOARD STAR Pa/Ja (Tsuneishi) 1979; Con/RoC; 15,108 grt/12,161 dwt; 152 × 9.08 m *(498.7 × 29.79 ft)*; M (Pielstick); 17 kts; ex-*Seki Rokako*; Quarter stern door/ramp; 650 TEU
Sister: **SEABOARD FLORIDA** (Pa) ex-*Seki Rokel*

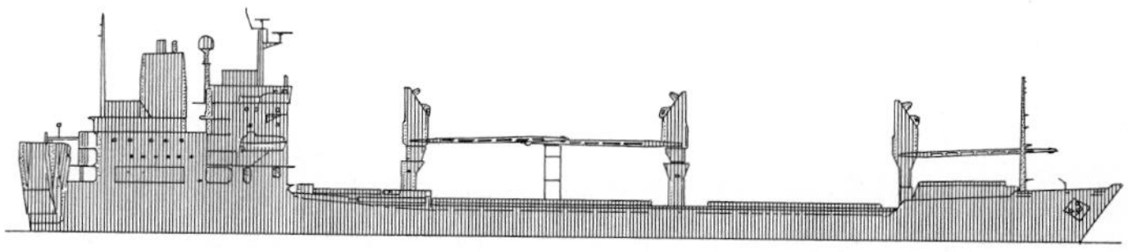

29 *MCP²MFMA H13*
BELOOSTROV Ru/Ge (Kvaerner Warnow) 1992; C/RoC/Con; 16,075 grt/17,420 dwt; 173.50 × 10.02 m *(569.23 × 32.87 ft)*; M (Sulzer); 18 kts; ex-*Krasnograd*; Quarter door/ramp (starboard); 518 TEU

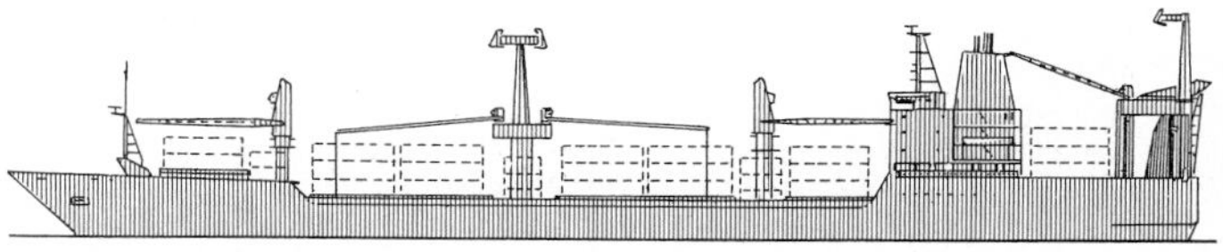

30 *MCTCMFT–A H13*
GREEN CAPE Li/It (Italcantieri) 1981; C/RoC/Con; 21,826 grt/28,052 dwt; 177.37 × 11.55 m *(582 × 37.89 ft)*; M (GMT); 18 kts; ex-*Costa Arabica*; Starboard quarter ramp; 918 TEU
Sister: **DIAMOND LAND** (Li) ex-*Costa Ligure*

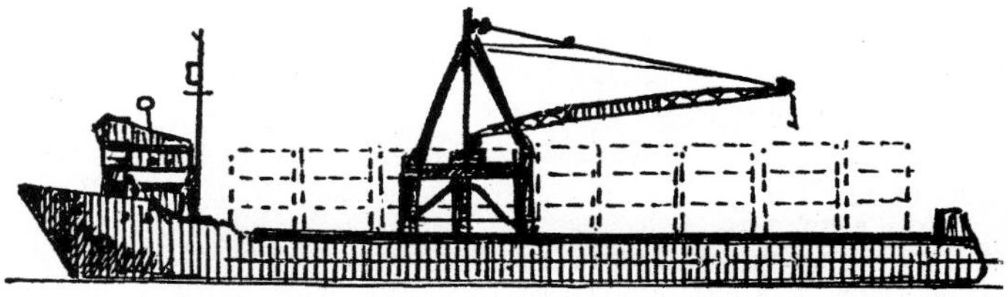

31 *MJG H1*
TRANS-PORT I Sg/HK (Highfield) 1975; RoC/DC/Con; 2,161 grt/2,686 dwt; 76.23 × 3.83 m *(250.09 × 12.56 ft)*; TSM (KHD); 11 kts; ex-*Deckship Arabella*; 190 TEU; Stern ramp; 'Deckship' type
Sisters: **MACAU VENTURE** (Li) ex-*Deckship Brigida*; **CHIANG MAI** (Th) ex-*Pegasus Peace*; Similar (ramp and crane differ and so on): **TRANS-PORT II** (Sg) ex-*Eleanora*; **HARTA I** (My) ex-*Gisela*

32 *MJMGC–Y H1*
LEDENICE Ma/Ys ('3 Maj') 1979; RoC/Con/C; 5,575 grt/7,478 dwt; 144.4 × 6.5 m *(473.75 × 21.33 ft)*; M (Pielstick); 17.9 kts; Travelling gantry (with slewing deck crane); Stern slewing ramp; 416 TEU; Crane aft is on starboard side of ramp gantry
Probable sister: **BRIBIR** (Ma)

See photo number 17/102

33 *MK²GH H1*
BROCKEN Pa/Ne ('Holland') 1976; RoC/HL; 2,371 grt/1,375 dwt; 81.01 × 3.95 m *(265.78 × 12.96 ft)*; TSM (Liebknecht); 10 kts; Bow door/ramp; two stern ramps; 80 TEU

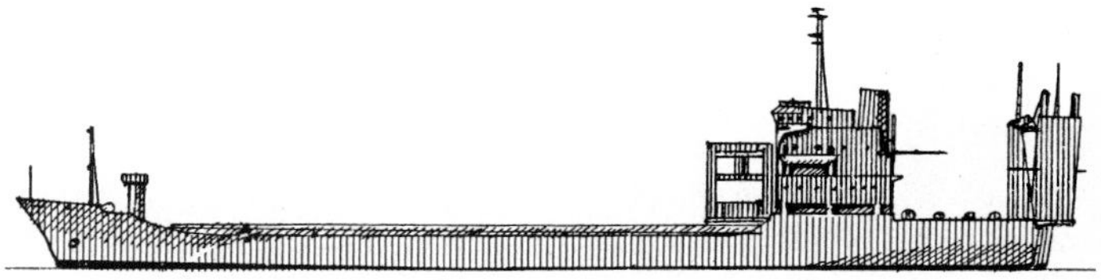

34 *MKMFMN–A H13*
KOTA RIA Sg/Ja (Shinhama) 1975; RoC/Con; 5,664 grt/6,430 dwt; 119.61 × 7.47 m *(392.42 × 24.51 ft)*; M (MAN); 16.75 kts; ex-*Aqaba Crown*; Quarter ramp; 'Strider' type; 329 TEU; Funnel is on port side
Sisters: **SEA DRAGON** (Sg) ex-*Strider Broadsword*; **ORIENT COURIER** (In) ex-*Saudi Crown*; Similar (some have larger funnels): **CARTAGENA** (Li) ex-*Strider Gallant*; **KLANG REEFER** (Bs) ex-*Opal Bounty*; **SANTA MARTA** (Li) Launched as *Strider Hero*; **SWAN REEFER** (Bs) ex-*Turquoise Bounty*

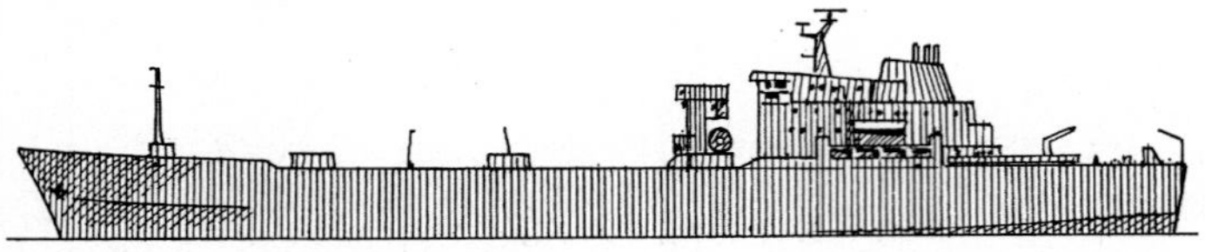

35 *MKMFRY H*
DANA CORONA NIS/Fi (Rauma-Repola) 1972; RoC/Con; 12,110 grt/5,710 dwt; 138 × 6.7 m *(451 × 21.1 ft)*; TSM (Stork-Werkspoor); 18 kts; ex-*Antares*; Stern door
Sisters: **RIJNHAVEN** (Ma) ex-*Orion*; **FINNMASTER** (Fi) ex-*Sirius*; **LIPA** (Li) ex-*Baltic Enterprise*; **PARKHAVEN** (Ma) ex-*Baltic Progress*

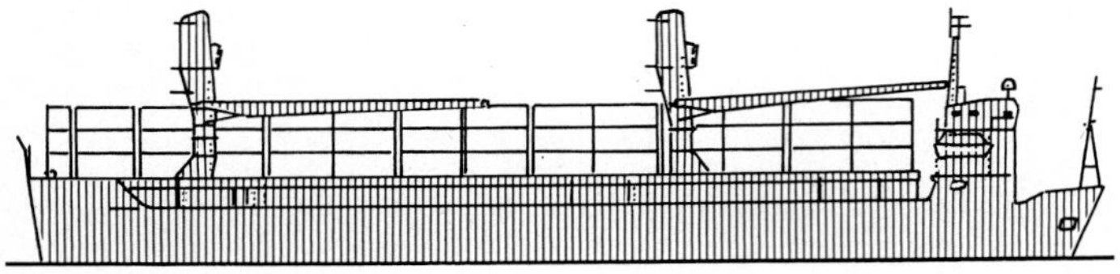

36 *M^2C^2 H3*
CONDOCK IV Ge/FRG (Rickmers) 1984; Dk/RoC/Con; 6,786 grt/4,490 dwt; 106.03 × 3.70 m *(347.87 × 12.14 ft)*; TSM (MaK); 13.25 kts; ex-*Este Submerger II*; 467 TEU; Stern door/ramp; There is a very low funnel on port side just foreward of the second crane; Cranes are on port side
Sister (cranes of different design): **OSTARA** (NA) ex-*Callisto*

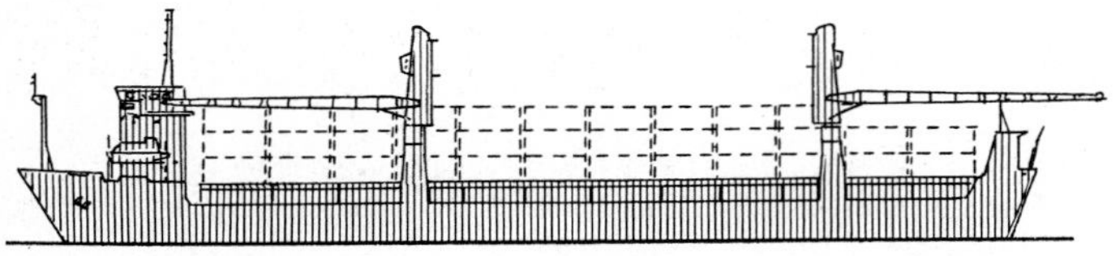

37 *M^2C^2GY H13*
NORLANDIA NA/FRG (Rickmers) 1983; RoC/Con; 4,998 grt/4,250 dwt; 105.5 × 4.56 m *(346 × 14.96 ft)*; M (Wichmann); 12.5 kts; 'RW 29' type; 334 TEU; Stern door/ramp; Cranes are on port side
Sisters: **NORDICA** (At) ex-*Hans Behrens*; **FLAMARES** (Bs) ex-*Johanna*

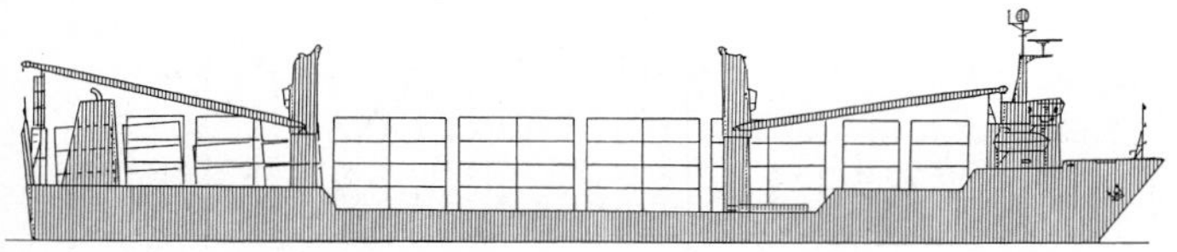

38 *M^2C^2GY H13*
TROPIC TIDE Pa/Sg (Singapore T) 1993; RoC/Con; 6,536 grt/7,430 dwt; 121.20 × 6.30 m *(397.64 × 20.67 ft)*; TSM (MaK); 15 kts; Stern door/ramp; 392 TEU
Sister: **TROPIC SUN** (Pa)

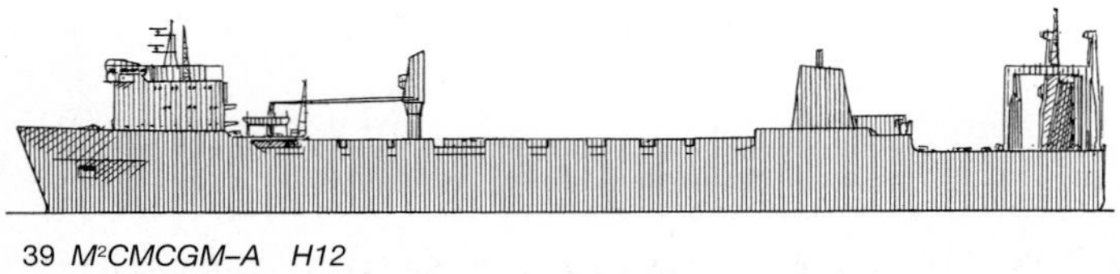

39 *M^2CMCGM–A H12*
THEBELAND Sw/Ja (Mitsui) 1978; RoC/Con; 16,477 grt/12,200 dwt; 165 × 8 m *(541.34 × 26.25 ft)*; TSM (B&W); 16.5 kts; quarter ramp/door; 800 TEU; Large crane is on starboard side
Sisters: **TYRUSLAND** (Sw); **VEGALAND** (Sw)
Sister (larger crane—further aft): **VIKINGLAND** (Sw)
Sisters (covered area over entire upper deck): **CORTIA** (Sw) ex-*Timmerland*; **CELIA** (Sw) ex-*Vasaland*

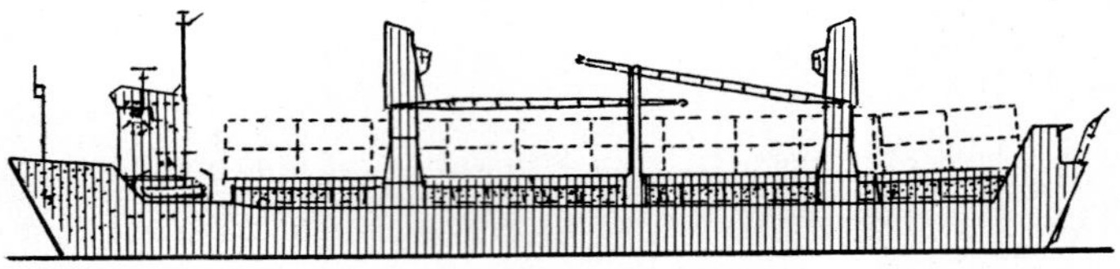

40 *M^2CMCGY H1*
SLOMAN RANGER At/FRG (Howaldts DW) 1979; RoC/Con; 3,922 grt/2,570 dwt; 92.07 × 3.65 m *(302 × 11.98 ft)*; TSM (KHD); 12.5 kts; Stern ramp/door; 319 TEU; Cranes are on port side
Sisters: **SLOMAN RECORD** (At); **SLOMAN RIDER** (At); **RAWAN I** (Cy) ex-*Sloman Rover*; **NORTHERN PHOENIX** (Cy) Launched as *Tilia*; **SLOMAN RUNNER** (At); **SLOMAN REGENT** (At); Similar: **AGDAL** (Mo) ex-*Adele J*; **ROSELLEN** (Cy) ex-*Bangui*; **SLOMAN ROVER** (At) ex-*Paoua*; **PUNTLAND II** (So) ex-*Heinrich Husmann*; **MICAELA** (It) ex-*Petra Scheu*; **BALTIC SPRINTER** (Cy) ex-*Obotrita*; **SPIRIT OF PROGRESS** (At) ex-*Sloman Royal* (lower superstructure—Bz built (CCN): **ATLANTICA** (NA) ex-*Amaragy*; **APODY** (At); **JESSICA** (NA) ex-*Amambahy*; **CINDYA** (NA) ex-*Araguary*

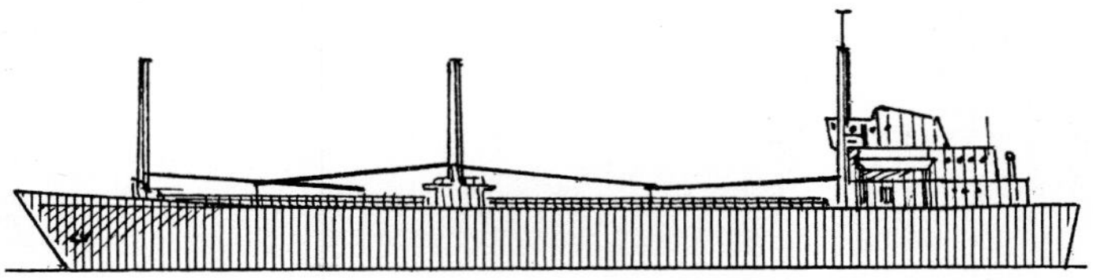

41 *M^2HF H*
OSOR Cro/No (Ulstein) 1970; RoC/C; 1,516 grt/2,822 dwt; 87.03 × 6.15 m *(285.53 × 20.18 ft)*; M (Stork-Werkspoor); 14.75 kts; ex-*Braga*; Side doors (starboard); Stern door/ramp
Sister: **ZAHER III** (Le) ex-*Bismillah*

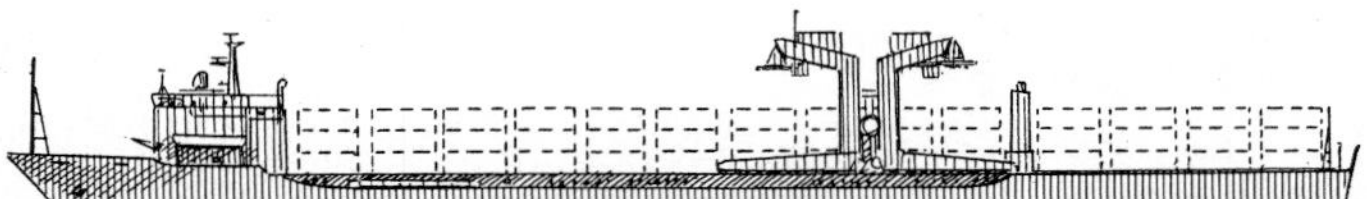

42 *M^2K^2FMY H1*
CGM ST LAURENT Gr/Ja (Kanda) 1978; RoC/Con; 11,138 grt/8,979 dwt; 137.15 × 6.51 m *(449.97 × 21.36 ft)*; M (MAN); 17.75 kts; ex-*Levante Express*; Stern door/ramp; Side door/ramp (starboard); 550 TEU; 'Boxer' type
Sisters: **PELAMBER** (Gr) ex-*Fenicia Express*; **EAGLE CLOUD** (Br) ex-*Boxer Captain Cook*

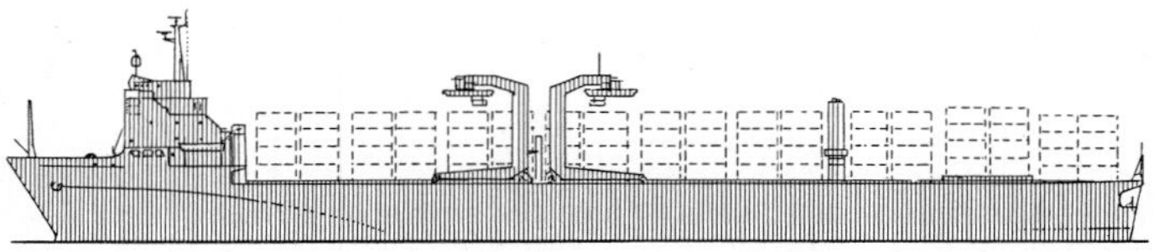

43 *M^2K^2GY H1*
PUERTO CORTES Bs/It (Breda) 1981; RoC/Con; 11,445 grt/17,993 dwt; 173.01 × 8.19 m *(568 × 26.87 ft)*; TSM (Pielstick); 19 kts; ex-*Contender Argent*; Quarter bow door/ramp; three side door/ramps; 1,108 TEU

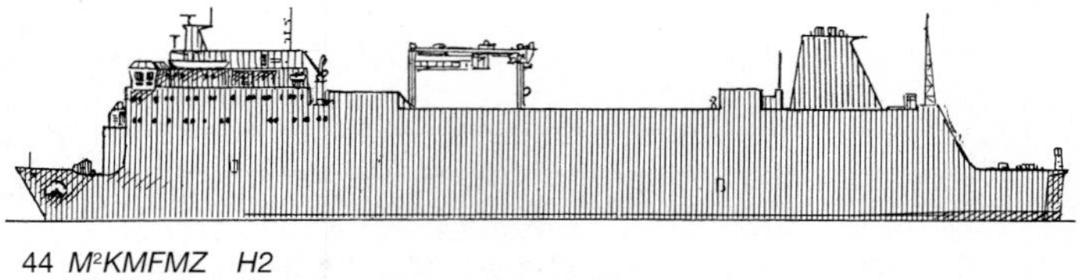

44 *M^2KMFMZ H2*
DANA MAXIMA DIS/Ja (Hitachi) 1978; RoC; 13,303 grt/3,980 dwt; 141.51 × 6.56 m *(464.27 × 21.52 ft)*; TSM (Pielstick); 18.2 kts; Two stern doors/ramps; Now lengthened to 173.00m (567.59 ft). Drawing shows vessel as built; Funnel is on port side. See photo number 17/101

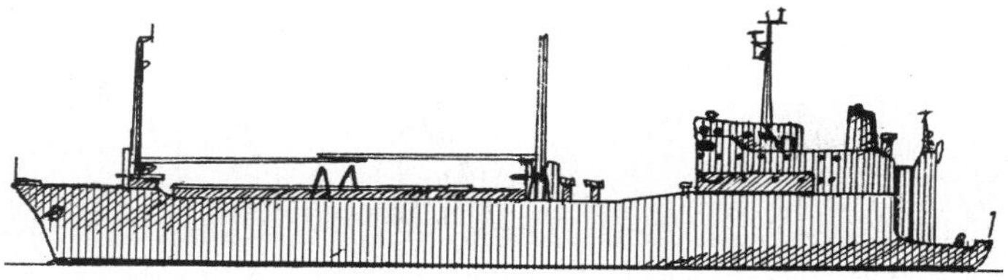

45 *M^{3}GM–B H1*
NIKI AGUSTINA Ia/Ja (Miho) 1969; RoC; 2,175 grt/3,600 dwt; 95.41 × 6 m *(313.02 × 19.69 ft)*; M (Pielstick); 14 kts; ex-*Shinju Maru*; Quarter stern door/ramps (port and starboard)

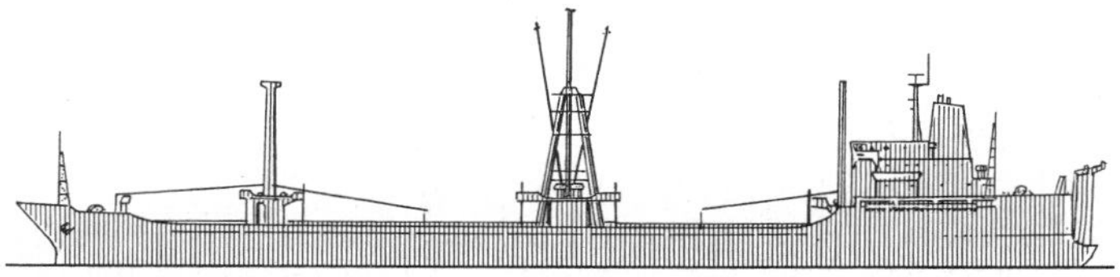

46 *M^{3}HMFNB H13*
SUPHAN NAVEE Th/Ja (Narasaki) 1977; C/RoC/HL; 13,094 grt/18,258 dwt; 156.22 × 10.17 m *(513 × 33.37 ft)*; M (MAN); 14.75 kts; ex-*Nigeria Venture*; Quarter ramps (port and starboard); 191 TEU; Funnel is on starboard side
Sister: **UBON NAVEE** (Th) ex-*Lagos Venture*

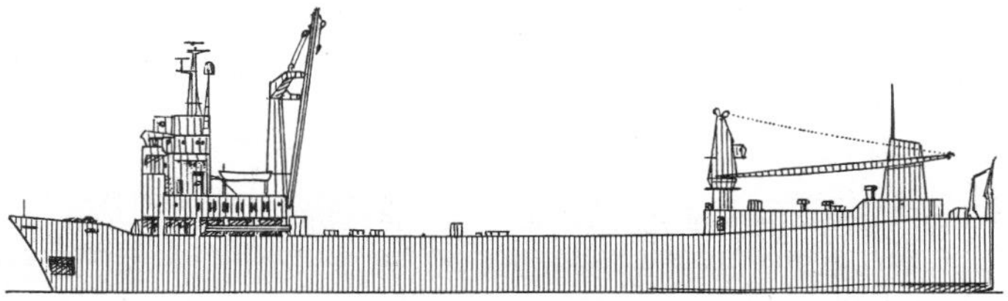

47 *M^{2}TCM–FY H*
STJERNEBORG DIS/Ja (NKK) 1979; RoC/Con/HL; 12,076 grt/8,002 dwt; 145.3 × 6.68 m *(442.91 × 21.92 ft)*; M (B&W); 15.3 kts; ex-*Dana America*; Side door (starboard); stern door/ramp; 120 ton derrick; 476 TEU
Sisters: **SKODSBORG** (DIS) ex-*Dana Africa*; **SKANDERBORG** (DIS) ex-*Dana Arabia*; **SCHACKENBORG** (DIS) ex-*Dana Caribia*

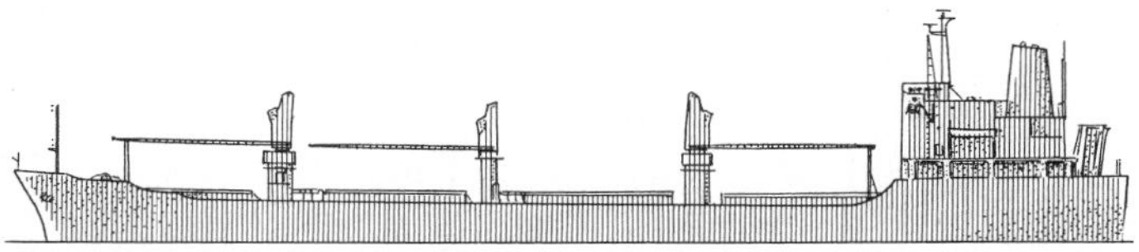

48 *MPCPNMFNA H13*
CORAL ISLANDER Pa/Ja (Namura) 1977; C/RoC/Con; 14,294 grt/15,567 dwt; 155.53 × 8.92 m *(510.27 × 29.27 ft)*; M (MAN); 16 kts; ex-*Fiji Maru*; Two quarter stern door/ramps; 432 TEU

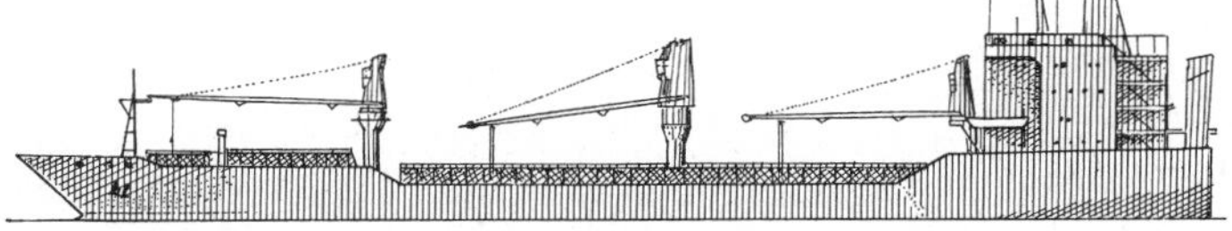

49 *MP^{2}CMFA H13*
WHITE NILE Su/De (B&W) 1979; RoC/Con/C/HL; 9,874 grt/12,905 dwt; 132.9 × 9.4 m *(436 × 30.84 ft)*; M (B&W); 15 kts; Quarter stern ramp; 372 TEU; 'Hamlet-Multiflex' type
Sister: **BLUE NILE** (Su); Similar: **ABU EGILA** (Eg); **ABURDEES** (Eg); **ABU ZENIMA** (Eg)

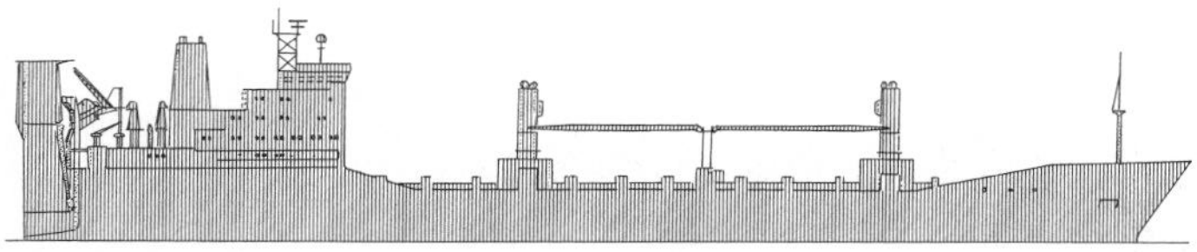

50 *MP^{2}MFR^{2}A H13*
HORNBAY Li/Ys ("Uljanik") 1990; R/RoC/Con; 12,887 grt/9,096 dwt; 153.50 × 8.72 m *(503.61 × 28.61 ft)*; M (B&W); 20 kts; Quarter ramp/door (starboard); 322 TEU
Sisters: **HORNCAP** (Li); **HORNCLIFF** (Li)

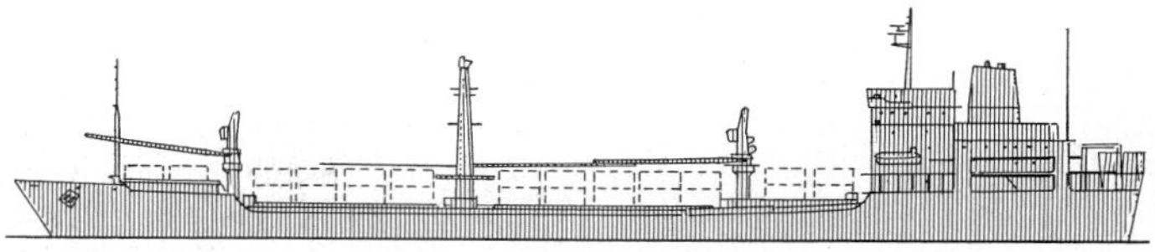

51 *MPUPMFMA H13*
ASTRAKHAN Ru/DDR (Warnow) 1983; RoC/C/Con; 15,893 grt/17,850 dwt; 172.32 × 10.02 m *(565.35 × 32.87 ft)*; M (MAN); 17 kts; Quarter door/ramp; 533 TEU
Sisters: **ROSTOV** (Ru); **VINNITSA** (Uk); **KREMENCHUG** (Uk); **BUDAPESHT** (Ru); **BREST** (Uk); **ROVNO** (Uk); **KOSTROMA** (Ru); **SVERDLOVSK** (Ru); **ULAN-BATOR** (Ru); **KORSUN-SHEVCHENKOVSKIY** (Uk); **SAMARKAND** (Ru); **TRUSKAVETS** (Ru); **ZHITOMIR** (Uk); **BALTIYSK** (Cy); **VYBORG** (Cy); **KOLPINO** (Cy); **VLADIMIR** (Cy)

See photo number 17/84

52 *MRMF H1*
GREEN ICE Bs/No-Sw (Fosen/Marstrands) 1985; R/Pal/Con; 3,399 grt/2,900 dwt; 84.61 × 4.47 m *(277.59 × 14.67 ft)*; M (Wärtsilä); 15 kts; ex-*Svanur*; Foreward section built by Marstrands; Aft section built by Fosen; Side door; 78 TEU

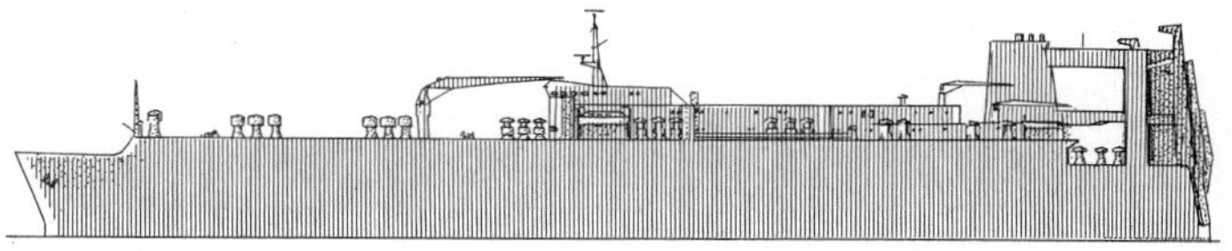

53 *MRMRF–R–A H2*
G AND C PARANA NIS/No (Frederiksstad) 1979; RoC/Con; 41,905 grt/42,424 dwt; 182.51 × 12.02 m *(598.79 × 39.44 ft)*; M (B&W); 14.8 kts; ex-*Skaubord*; Stern quarter ramp/door; 895 TEU

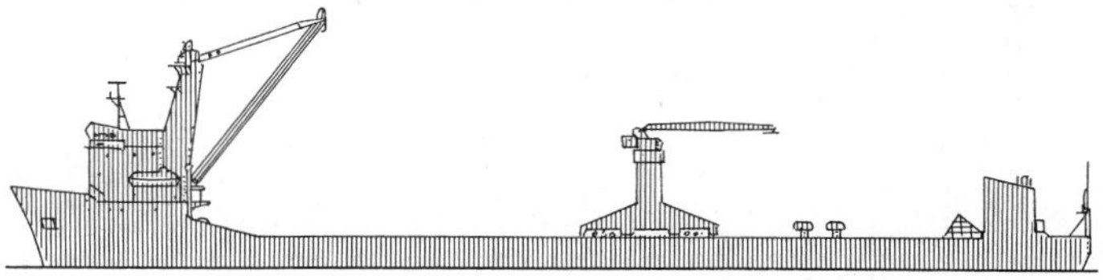

54 *MTJGMY H1*
STRONG VIRGINIAN US/FRG (Bremer V) 1984; RoC/C/HL; 16,169 grt/21,541 dwt; 156.06 × 8.63 m *(512.01 × 28.31 ft)*; TSM (Krupp-MaK); 16.5 kts; ex-*St Magnus*; Stern ramp; 1413 TEU; 'J' crane is tandem

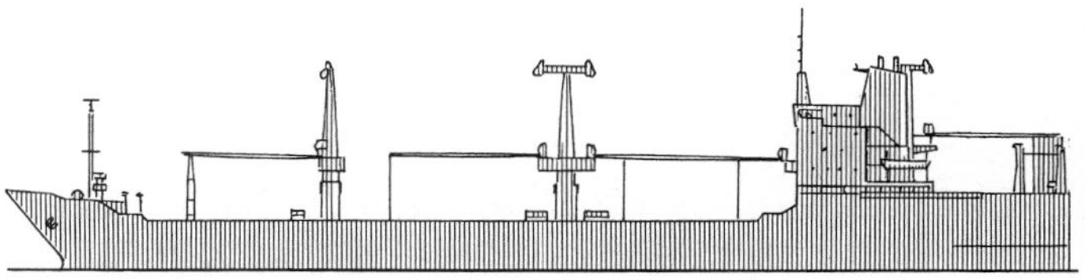

55 *MT^{2}HF–TA H13*
PACHITEA Pa/It (Italcantieri) 1982; RoC/C/Con; 8,281 grt/15,984 dwt; 154.24 × 9.05 m *(506.04 × 29.69 ft)*; M (GMT); 16 kts; Launched as *Transatlantico*; 600 TEU; Quarter door/ramp; Funnel is on starboard side; launched 1979—completed 1982
Sisters: **MANTARO** (Pa) Launched as *Transmediterraneo*; **BANDAMA EXPRESS** (SV) Launched as *Transbaltico*; **GUYANE** (SV) Launched as *Transpacifico*

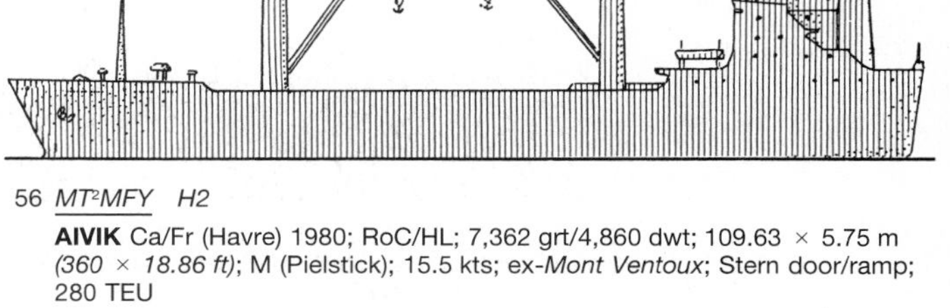

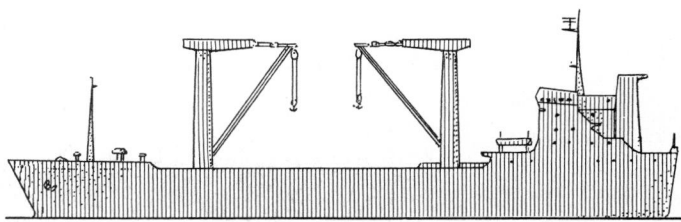

56 *MT^{2}MFY H2*
AIVIK Ca/Fr (Havre) 1980; RoC/HL; 7,362 grt/4,860 dwt; 109.63 × 5.75 m *(360 × 18.86 ft)*; M (Pielstick); 15.5 kts; ex-*Mont Ventoux*; Stern door/ramp; 280 TEU

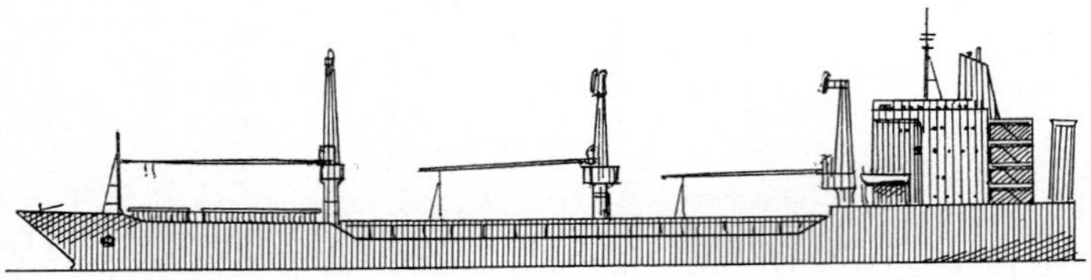

57 *MT^{3}MFA H13*
HAU GIANG Vn/De (B&W) 1977; RoC/C/Con; 9,415 grt/12,800 dwt; 132.92 × 9.4 m *(436.09 × 30.84 ft)*; M (Alpha-Diesel); 15 kts; Launched as *Hamlet Alice*; 'Hamlet-Multiflex' type; Quarter ramp/door; 380 TEU
Sisters: **ASIA EXPRESS** (Li) ex-*Hamlet Arabia*; **HAMLET SAUDIA** (Pa); **HAN ZHONG MEN** (RC) ex-*Nopal Audrey*; **IZVESTIYA** (Uk); **CIUDAD DE OVIEDO** (Cy) ex-*Kimberley*; **KNUD JESPERSON** (Uk) ex-*Aleksey Stakhanov*

See photo number 17/93

58 *TCHFY H*
FB PIONEER Ma/No (Trondhjems) 1970; RoC/C; 3,130 grt/2,873 dwt; 87 × 6.13 m *(285.43 × 20.11 ft)*; M (Werkspoor); 15 kts; ex-*Bomma*; Stern door/ramp; Side doors (starboard)
Sisters: **HASSNAA** (Ho) ex-*Barok*; **NEPTUNE SUN** (Ma) ex-*Berby*; **UB PROGRESS** (Bs) ex-*Borre*; **IONIAN KORTI** (Ma) ex-*Bard*; **IKIZTEPE** (Tu) ex-*Bolt*

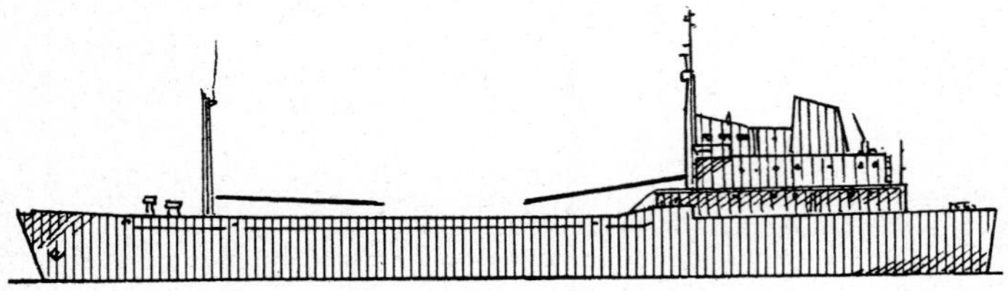

59 *THFY H*
CONTENDER Br/Fr (Havre) 1973; RoC; 2,292 grt/1,357 dwt; 78.87 × 4.22 m *(258.76 × 13.85 ft)*; M (Deutz); 15 kts; ex-*Antinea*; Stern door/ramp; Two side doors (one port, one starboard); 28 TEU
Similar (larger): **MOANA III** (Fr) ex-*Anahita*

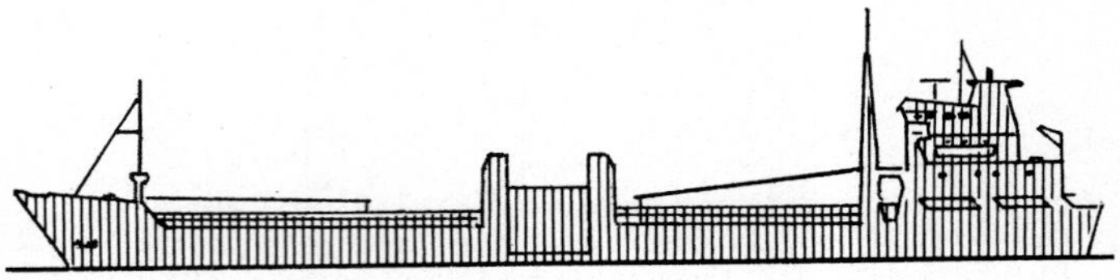

60 *VAHM–FC H1*
BREMER IMPORT La/No (Orens) 1974/80; C; 685 grt/1,755 dwt; 82.48 × 3.68 m *(270.6 × 12.07 ft)*; M (Wichmann); 12.5 kts; ex-*Lysvik*; Side door (port); Lengthened 1980; New engines 1979

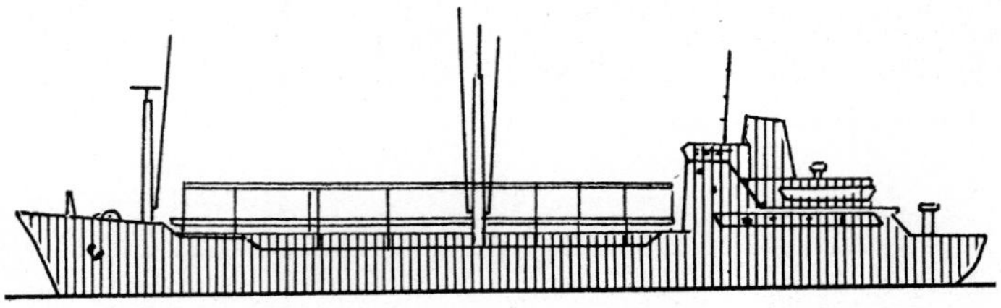

61 *V^{2}MF H*
KALBA III Ho/Sw (Ekensbergs) 1964; RoC/C; 1,590 grt/2,235 dwt; 75.57 × 5.1 m *(248 × 16.77 ft)*; M (MWM); 12 kts; ex-*Elektra*; Bow door and ramp

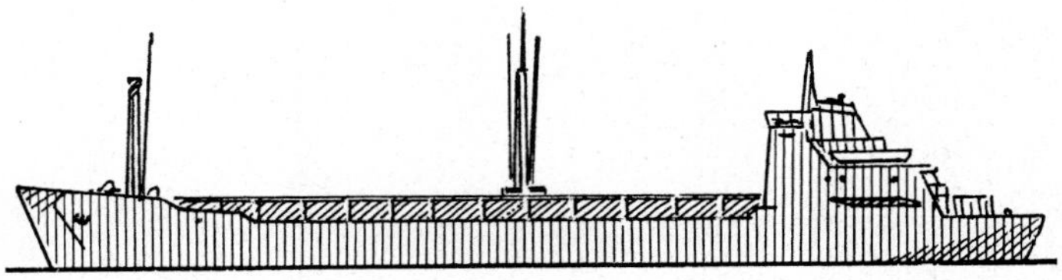

62 *V^{2}M–F H1*
SIM FORNY SV/Sw (Ekensbergs) 1965; RoC; 2,200 grt/3,740 dwt; 80.85 × 6.53 m *(256.26 × 21.42 ft)*; M (MWM); 11 kts; ex-*Don Juan*; Bow door and ramp
Sister: **SEA MIST II** (Bl) ex-*Don Carlos*

63 Condock IV *(Ge); 1984* *FotoFlite*

64 Ostara *(NA); 1983* *FotoFlite*

65 Monchegorsk *(Cy); 1983* *FotoFlite*

66 Lipa *(Li); 1973* *FotoFlite*

67 Puerto Cortes *(Bs); 1981; (as Contender Argent)* *FotoFlite*

68 G and C Parana *(NIS); 1979; (as G and C Forest)* *FotoFlite*

69 Seaboard Star *(Pa); 1979; (as Seki Rokako)* *FotoFlite*

70 Ile de la Reunion *(Bs); 1977* *FotoFlite*

71 Vergina *(Pa); 1977/86; (as Ville du Havre)* *FotoFlite*

72 Lady Franklin *(Ca); 1970* *FotoFlite*

73 Maersk Constellation *(US); 1980* *FotoFlite*

74 Evrimedon *(Cy); 1978* *FotoFlite*

75 White Nile *(Su); 1979* *FotoFlite*

76 Abu Zenima *(Eg); 1983* *FotoFlite*

77 Union Glory *(Pa); 1982* *FotoFlite*

78 Fas Var *(Ge); 1985; (as Heinrich J)* *FotoFlite*

79 Helene *(Ge); 1985; (as Carib Faith)* *FotoFlite*

80 Vento Di Tramontana *(Lu); 1987; (as Transport Maas)* *FotoFlite*

81 Julia Del Mar *(Sp); 1981* *FotoFlite*

82 Astrakhan *(Ru); 1983* *FotoFlite*

83 Green Cape *(Li); 1981* *FotoFlite*

84 Green Ice *(Bs); 1985* *FotoFlite*

85 Tampa *(NIS); 1984* *FotoFlite*

86 Toba *(NIS); 1979* *FotoFlite*

87 Hau Giang *(Vn); 1977* *FotoFlite*

88 Aivik *(Ca); 1980; (as Mont Ventoux)* *FotoFlite*

89 Mantaro *(Pa); 1982* *FotoFlite*

90 Bremer Import *(La); 1974/80* *FotoFlite*

91 Cartagena *(Li); 1977* *FotoFlite*

92 Hassnaa *(Ho); 1971; (as Venus)* *FotoFlite*

93 UB Progress *(Bs); 1970* *FotoFlite*

94 Atlas *(Si); 1972* *FotoFlite*

95 Sloman Ranger *(At); 1979* *FotoFlite*

96 Baltic Sprinter *(Cy); 1980; (as Oparis)* *FotoFlite*

97 Cindya *(NA); 1984* *FotoFlite*

98 Ragna Gorthon *(Sw); 1979* *FotoFlite*

99 Cortia *(Sw); 1978; (as Hektos)* *FotoFlite*

100 Skodsborg *(DIS); 1979* *FotoFlite*

101 Dana Maxima *(DIS); 1978* *FotoFlite*

102 Brocken *(Pa); 1976* *FotoFlite*

103 Beloostrov *(Ru); 1992* *FotoFlite*

104 Abitibi Claiborne *(Ge); 1986* *FotoFlite*

105 Rosa Tucano *(Li); 1985* *FotoFlite*

106 Pioneer Spirit *(Pa); 1977; (as Unique)* *FotoFlite*

107 Kolomna *(Ru); 1989* *FotoFlite*

108 Horncap *(Li); 1991* *FotoFlite*

109 Belatrix *(Bz); 1992* *FotoFlite*

110 Intrepido *(Bz); 1991* *FotoFlite*

111 Sea Wolf *(US); 1984* *FotoFlite*

112 Arneb *(Ge); 1986; (as Alster Rapid)* *FotoFlite*

113 Ariana *(Ge); 1988* *FotoFlite*

114 Roxane Delmas *(Bs); 1979; (as Saint Roland)* *FotoFlite*

115 Saint Roch *(Fr); 1980* *FotoFlite*

116 Ingrid Gorthon *(Sw); 1977/91* *FotoFlite*

117 Repubblica Di Amalfi *(It); 1989/90* *FotoFlite*

118 Forte *(Ne); 1989* *Norman Thomson*

119 Al-Zahraa *(Iq); 1983* *FotoFlite*

120 Kumasi *(Br); 1976* *FotoFlite*

121 MN Toucan *(Kn); 1995* *FotoFlite*

122 Guyane *(SV); 1981; (as Ganda Gama)* *WSPL*

18 RO-RO Cargo

18 RO-RO Cargo

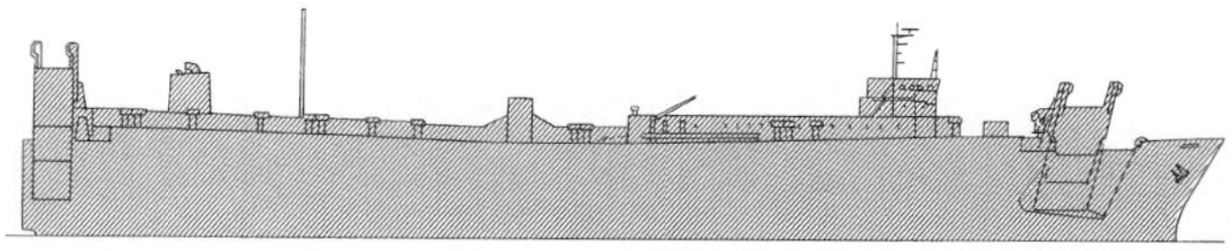

1 *AM^{3}FA H2*
SHUTTLE ACE Ja/Ja (Kurushima) 1993; RoC/V; 8,280 grt/5,271 dwt; 161.52 × 6.72 m *(529.92 × 22.05 ft)*; M (Pielstick); 20.2 kts; Angled door/ramp (starboard foreward); Quarter door/ramp (starboard)

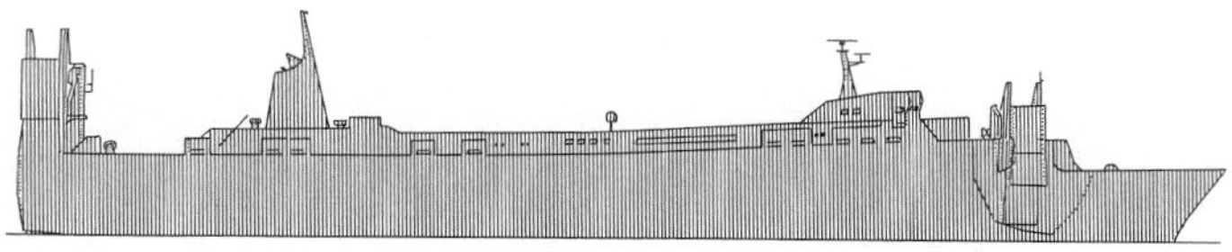

2 *AMM–FA H2*
HOKUREN MARU Ja/Ja (Imabari) 1993; RoC; 7,096 grt/5,517 dwt; 153.62 × 6.99 m *(504.00 × 22.93 ft)*; M (Pielstick); 23.5 kts; Angled door/ramp (starboard foreward); Quarter door/ramp (starboard)

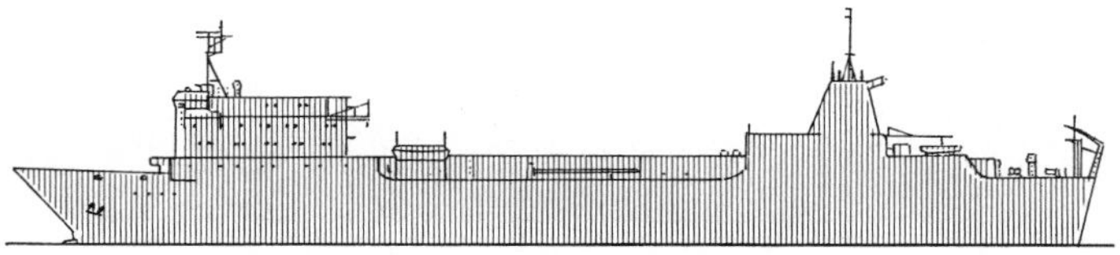

3 *HM–GY H2*
GLEICHBERG Ge/DDR (Mathias-Thesen) 1982; RoC; 10,243 grt/6,704 dwt; 138.53 × 7.23 m *(454.5 × 23.72 ft)*; TSM (SKL); 14.5 kts; Stern door/ramp; 344 TEU
Sisters: **AUERSBERG** (Ge); **KAHLEBERG** (Ge) (extra passenger accommodation); **TUTOVA** (Cy) ex-*Ritzberg*; **TUZLA** (Cy) ex-*Spiegelberg*

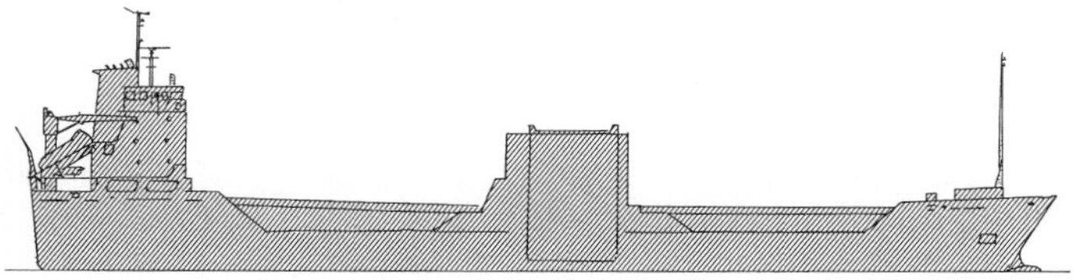

4 *MAM^{2}FLRY H13*
LINK STAR Fi/FRG (Sietas) 1989; RoC/Pal; 5,627 grt/4,453 dwt; 106.50 × 6.10 m *(349.41 × 20.01 ft)*; M (Wärtsilä); 15.3 kts; Side door (starboard); Stern door/ramp; 290 TEU; Funnel is on port side
Sisters: **MINI STAR** (Fi); **MARTHA RUSS** (At)

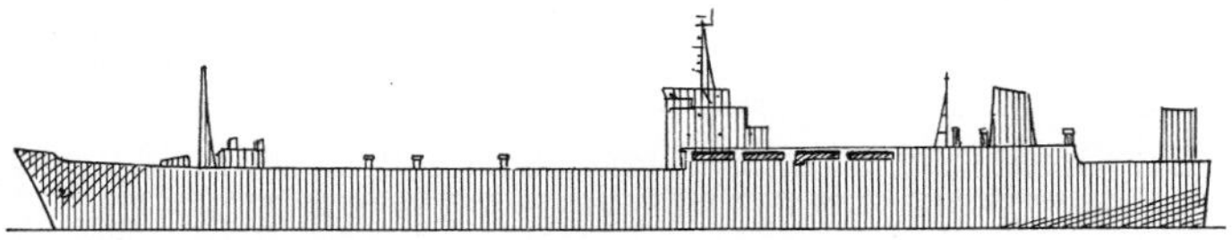

5 *MAM^{2}GA H*
RO-RO RUNNER Pa/Ja (Shimoda) 1974; RoC; 3,945 grt/4,838 dwt; 130 × 6.02 m *(426.51 × 19.75 ft)*; M (Pielstick); 17 kts; ex-*Kushiro Maru*

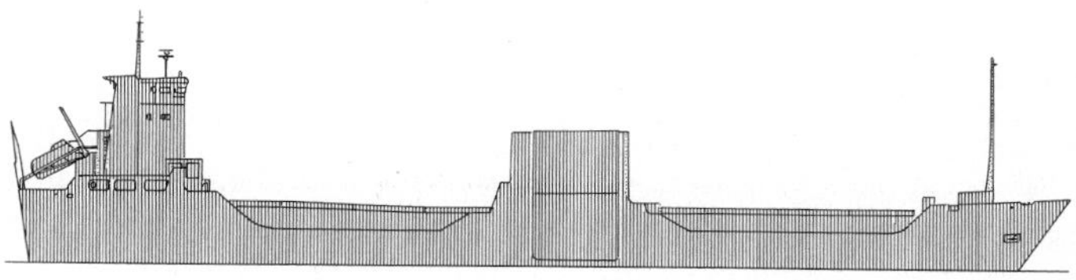

6 *MAM–FLY H*
ORTVIKEN Ge/SA (Dorbyl) 1990; RoC/Pal; 5,599 grt/4,300 dwt; 114.00 × 5.90 m *(374.02 × 19.36 ft)*; M (Deutz); 15.3 kts; ex-*Alteland*; Side door (starboard); Stern door/ramp; 180 TEU

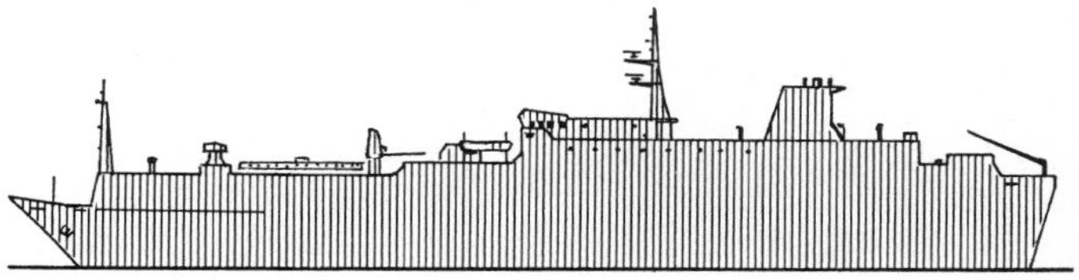

7 *MCMGR H2*
MONTLHERY Kn/Fr (La Rochelle) 1982; RoC; 1,597 grt/2,439 dwt; 116.52 × 5.25 m *(382 × 17.22 ft)*; TSM (Pielstick); 15.5 kts; Stern door/ramp
Sister: **LE CASTELLET** (Kn)

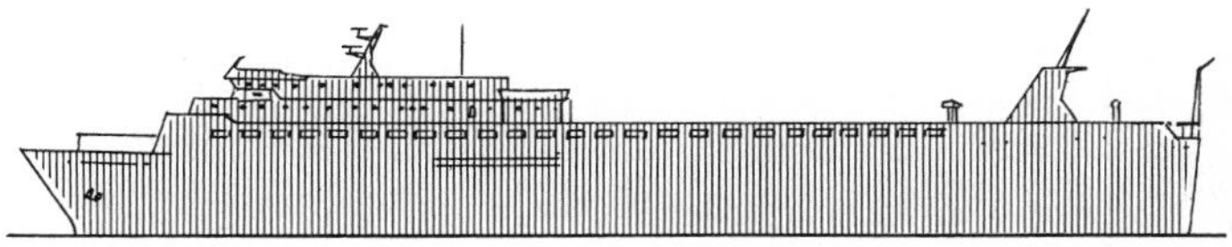

8 *MCM–GY H2*
FLEUR-DE-LYS Cy/Sp (Lorenzo) 1982; RoC; 8,553 grt/5,273 dwt; 122.8 × 6.38 m *(403 × 20.93 ft)*; TSM (MAN); 17.5 kts; ex-*Roll Galicia*; Stern door/ramp; 284 TEU
Sisters: **CIUDAD DE BURGOS** (Sp) ex-*Roll Vigo*; Similar (slightly smaller): **CIUDAD DE ALICANTE** (Sp) ex-*Rollman*; **CIUDAD DE CADIZ** (Sp) ex-*Roll-Al*

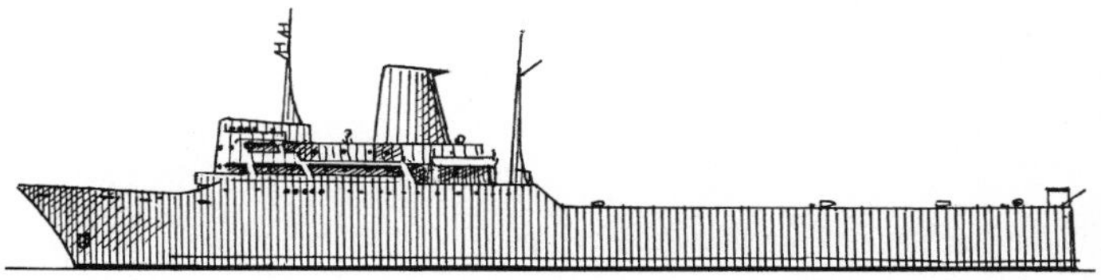

9 *MFM H2*
AFRODITE II Cy/Br (Swan Hunter) 1968; RoC; 3,778 grt/1,608 dwt; 137.6 × 4.6 m *(451 × 15.2 ft)*; TSM (Pielstick); 19.25 kts; ex-*Europic Ferry*; Stern door

10 *MFM H2*
IGOUMENITSA EXPRESS Gr/Br (Ailsa) 1961; RoC; 3,333 grt/1,007 dwt; 110.2 × 3.9 m *(361 × 12.1 ft)*; TSM (Davey, Paxman); 18 kts; ex-*Cerdic Ferry*; Stern door/ramp

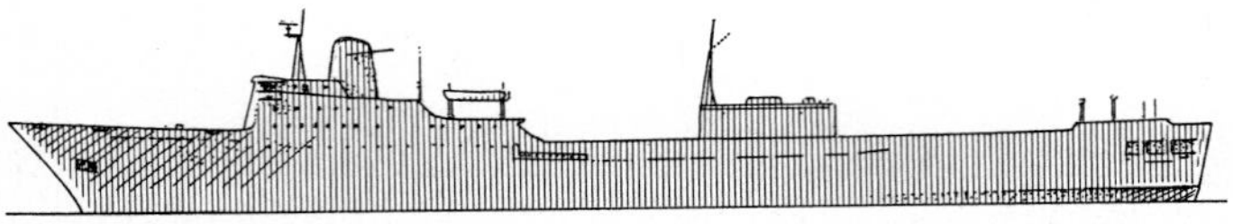

11 *MFMY H12*
CONCORD Pa/It (Apuania) 1969; RoC/P; 4,736 grt/3,373 dwt; 141.03 × 5.88 m *(462.7 × 19.29 ft)*; TS D-E (Fiat); 17.5 kts; ex-*Canguro Giallo*; Stern door
Sisters: **CANGURO GRIGIO** (It); **AL SALAM 91** (Pa) ex-*Canguro Biondo;* **CANGURO FULVO** (It)

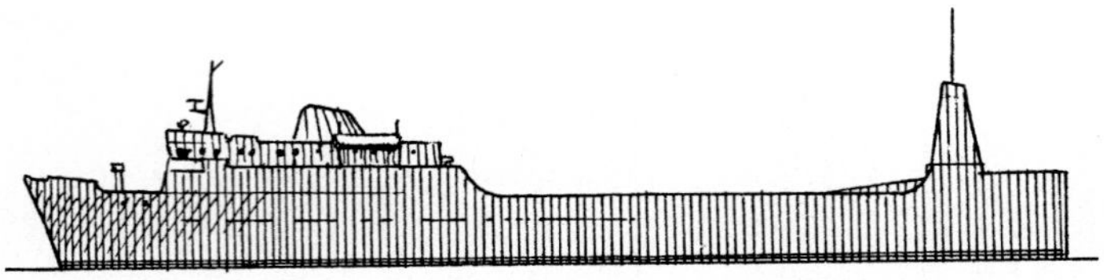

12 *MFM–G H2*
MONARCH QUEEN Ho/Sp (Mallorca) 1971; RoC; 1,123 grt/2,076 dwt; 88.91 × 4.18 m *(291.69 × 13.71 ft)*; M (B&W); 17 kts; ex-*Cala Marsal*
Sister: **CALA LLONGA** (Sp)

13 *MG H2*
PRINCESS SUPERIOR Ca/Ca (Burrard DD) 1974; RoC/F; 3,838 grt/ 4,941 dwt; 116.44 × 5.37 m *(382.02 × 17.62 ft)*; TSM (General Motors); 15 kts; ex-*Incan Superior*
Similar: **GEORGES ALEXANDRE LEBEL** (Ca) ex-*Incan St Laurent*

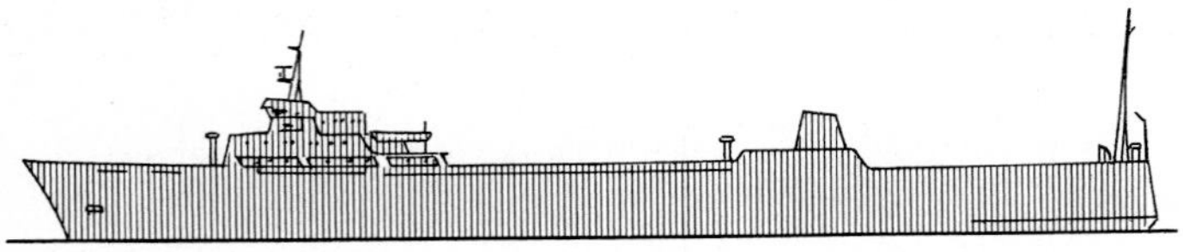

14 *MGMY H*
SEA ROAD It/FRG (Meyer) 1969/71; RoC; 6,151 grt/4,145 dwt; 123.34 × 5.38 m *(404.66 × 17.65 ft)*; TSM (KHD); 17 kts; ex-*Servus*; Stern door/ramp; Lengthened 1971 (Amsterdamsche D)

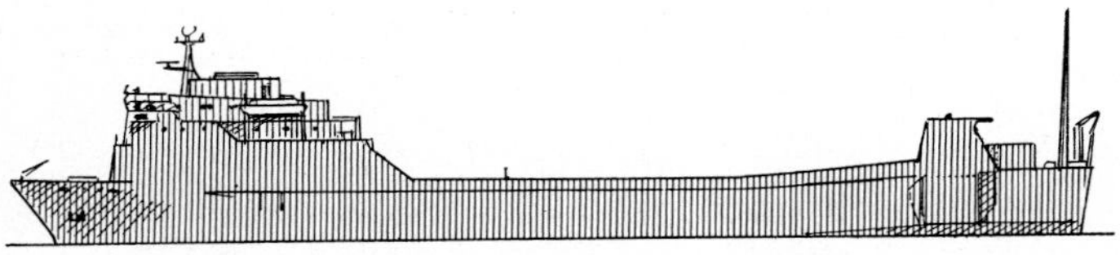

15 *MGMY H2*
MAERSK ANGLIA Br/Ja (Ishikawajima S & C) 1977; RoC; 6,862 grt/ 3,526 dwt; 122.94 × 4.77 m *(403.35 × 15.65 ft)*; TSM (Pielstick); 15 kts; ex-*Admiral Caribe*; Stern door/ramp; 283 TEU
Sister: **MAERSK FLANDERS** (Ne) ex-*Admiral Atlantic*
Sister (now converted to RoRo passenger ferry. Will have extra accommodation block): **AL SALAM 89** (Eg) ex-*Admiral Pacific*

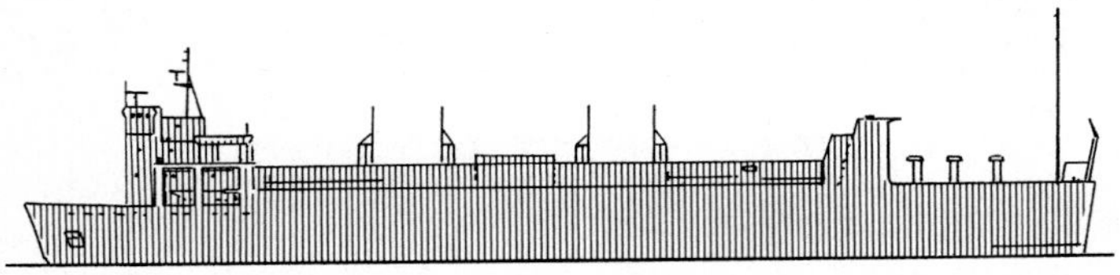

16 *MGMY H2*
NORDIC LINK Ne/Sw (Finnboda) 1981; RoC; 5,006 grt/6,704 dwt; 120.2 × 6.22 m *(394 × 20.41 ft)*; M (Pielstick); 14.5 kts; Two side doors (starboard); Stern door/ramp; 65 TEU
Sister (Finnish built—Rauma-Repola): **BALTIC LINK** (Ne); Similar (raised housing foreward of funnels): **FINNPINE** (Fi) ex-*Solano*
Similar (larger—134.6m (441.60ft). Extra housing foreward of funnels): **DEGERO** (Fi)

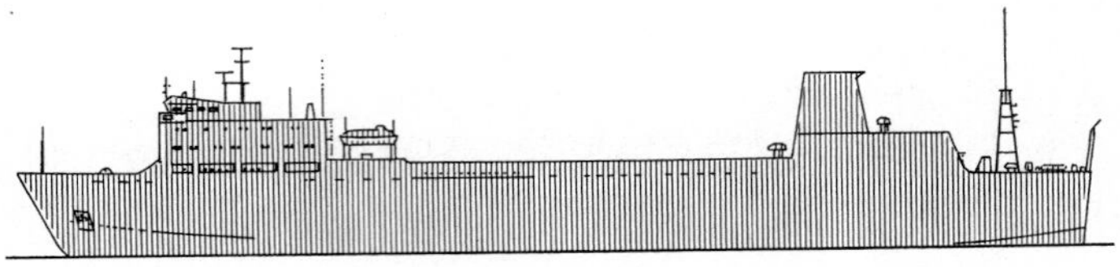

17 *MGMY H2*
NORQUEEN Fi/Fi (Rauma-Repola) 1980; RoC; 14,398 grt/7,984 dwt; 142.09 × 7.62 m *(466 × 25 ft)*; TSM (MaK); 17.5 kts; ex-*Bore Queen*; Stern door/ramp; 514 TEU
Sister: **NORKING** (Fi) ex-*Bore King*

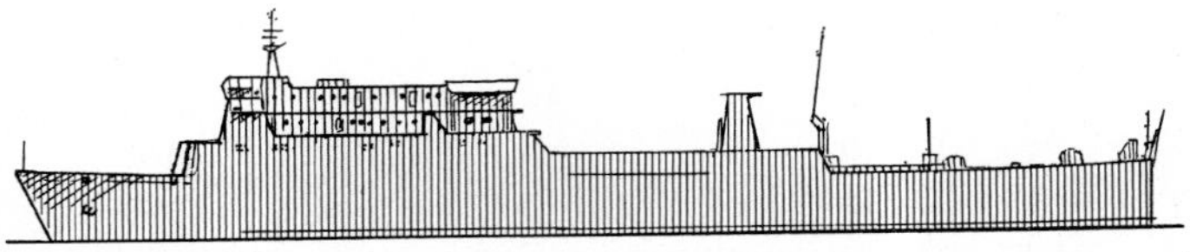

18 *MGMY H2*
PICASSO Bb/FRG (Rickmers) 1977; RoC; 1,599 grt/2,670 dwt; 115.12 × 5.30 m *(377.7 × 17.39 ft)*; TSM (Atlas-MaK); 17 kts; ex-*Wuppertal*; Stern door/ramp

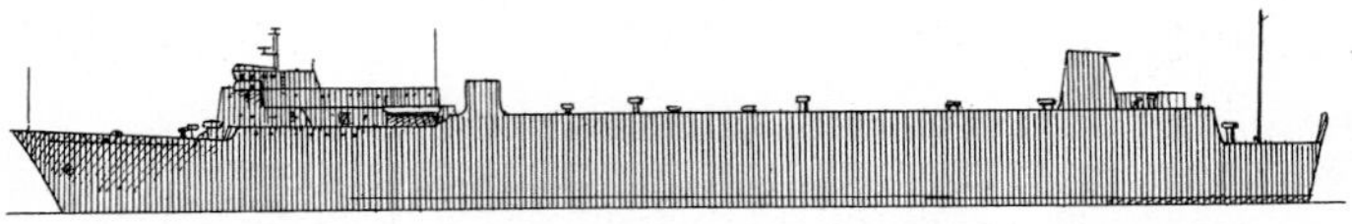

19 *MGMY H2*
TOR CALEDONIA DIS/No (Frederiksstad) 1977; RoC; 14,424 grt/12,200 dwt; 162.77 × 6.2 m *(534.02 × 20.34 ft)*; TSM (Pielstick); 18.5 kts; ex-*Tor Caledonia*; Stern ramp; 453 TEU; Now lengthened to 188.67m (619ft); Drawing shows vessel as built
Similar (lengthened to 163.48m (536ft)): **ASSI SKAN LINK** (Ne) ex-*Tor Finlandia*; **TOR HOLLANDIA** (Sw) ex-*Tor Dania* (see photo number 18/213)

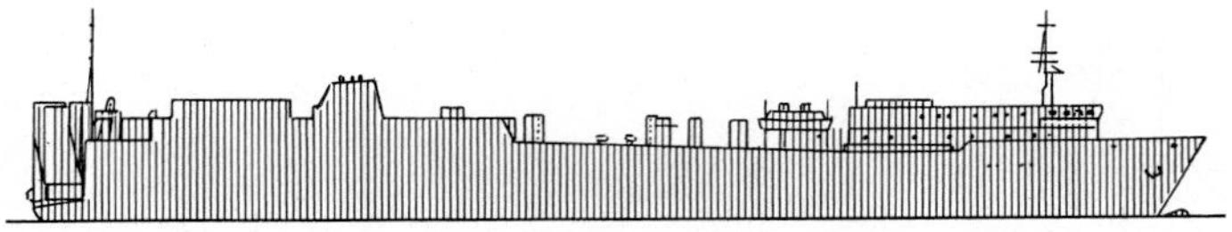

20 *MGV–A H2*
NIKOLAY CHERNYSHEVSKIY Uk/DDR ('Neptun') 1987; RoC/Pal; 6,894 grt/ 4,673 dwt; 125.90 × 5.66 m *(413.06 × 18.57 ft)*; TSM (SKL); 15.75 kts; Quarter ramp (starboard); 66 TEU
Sisters: **KOMPONISTS CAIKOVSKIS** (La) ex-*Kompozitor Chaykovskiy*; **KOMPOZITOR DARGOMYZHSKIY** (Uk); **KOMPOZITOR MUSORGSKIY** (Ru); **KOMPOZITOR NOVIKOV** (Uk); **KOMPOZITOR RAKHMANINOV** (Uk); **KOMPOZITOR RIMSKIY-KORSAKOV** (Uk); **BESTEKAR FIKRET AMIROV** (Az) ex-*Kompozitor Glinka*; **BESTEKAR GARA GARAEV** (Az) ex-*Kompozitor Kara Karayev*; **SIAULIAI** (Lt) ex-*Kompozitor Borodin*

21 *MGY H*
FJARDVAGEN Fi/No (Ankerlokken) 1972; RoC; 6,040 grt/2,677 dwt; 109.51 × 4.93 m *(359.28 × 16.17 ft)*; TSM (Pielstick); 18 kts; ex-*Anu*; Bow door/ramp; Stern door/ramp
Sister: **MIE MOLS** (De) ex-*Lalli* (may have extra superstructure)

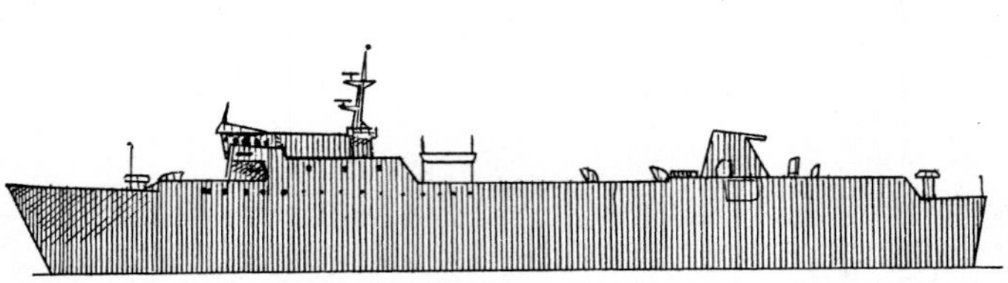

22 *MGY H2*
COUTANCES Fr/Fr (Havre) 1978; RoC; 6,507 grt/1,779 dwt; 110 × 4.5 m *(360.89 × 14.7 ft)*; M (Atlas-MaK); 17.5 kts; Bow and stern door; lengthened 1986 (Havre) now 125.17m (411ft). Drawing shows vessel before this modification (see photo number 18/182)
Sister: **PURBECK** (Fr)

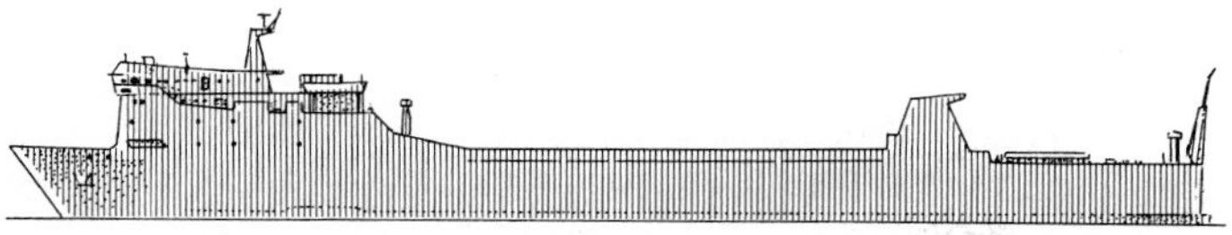

23 *MGY H2*
KIRK MARINA Bs/Ne (Vuyk) 1973/75; RoC; 7,955 grt/5,375 dwt; 142.22 × 5.94 m *(467 × 19.49 ft)*; TSM (Werkspoor); 18 kts; ex-*Stena Sailer*; Lengthened 1975; Bow and stern doors
Sister: **STENA SCANRAIL** (Sw) Launched as *Stena Seatrader*

24 *MHG H*
BRAHMAN EXPRESS Pi/Ne (Arnhemsche) 1966; RoVC/C/LS; 554 grt/931 dwt; 80.80 × 3.36 m *(265.09 × 11.02 ft)*; M (MAN); 14 kts; ex-*Rijnstroom*; Now converted to livestock carrier—appearance may be altered

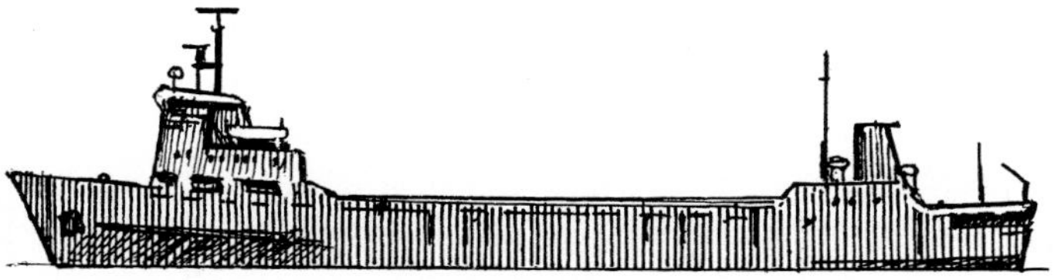

25 *MHGMRY H1*
PUERTO EDEN Ch/Fi (Rauma-Repola) 1972; RoC; 6,709 grt/4,700 dwt; 113.52 × 6.25 m *(372.44 × 20.51 ft)*; M (Atlas-MaK); 16 kts; ex-*Bore VII*; Stern door/ramp; 247 TEU; Now fitted with large, four-deck, housing abaft superstructure — not on drawing
Similar: **ASCHBERG** (Ge) ex-*Bore IX*; **BEERBERG** (Ge) ex-*Bore X*; **FEEDERTEAM** (Pa) ex-*Bore XI*

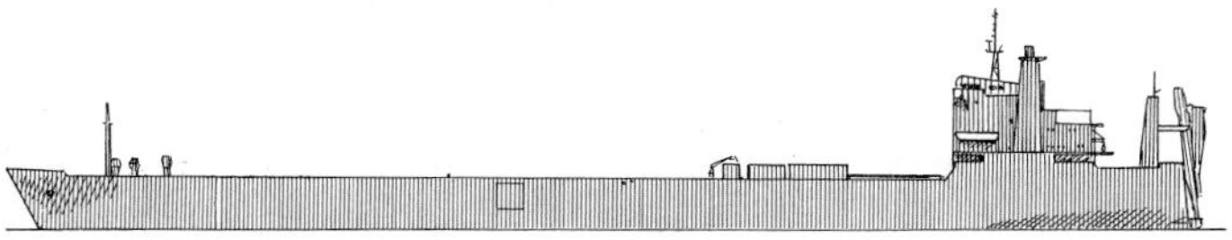

26 *MHGY H3*
CAPE TEXAS US/FRG (Howaldts DW) 1977; RoC; 12,159 grt/15,074 dwt; 193.33 × 8.61 m *(634.28 × 28.25 ft)*; M (MAN); 19 kts; ex-*Reichenfels*; Slewing stern ramp; Side door/ramps (one port, one starboard); 340 TEU; Owned by US Government
Sister: **CAPE TRINITY** (US) ex-*Rheinfels*

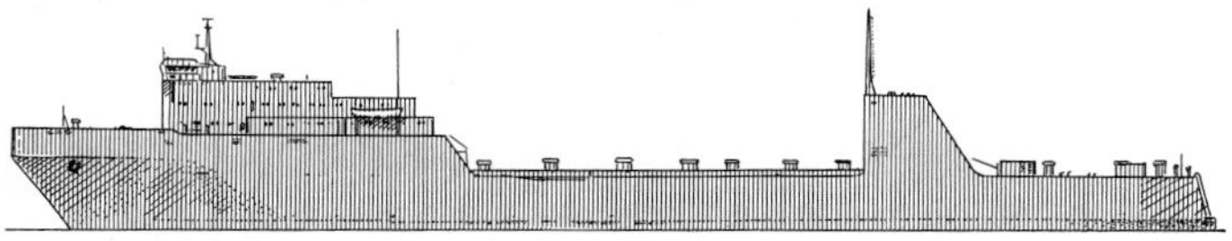

27 *MHM–G H1*
GEROITE NA SEVASTOPOL Bu/No (Framnaes) 1978; RoC/TF; 19,518 grt/12,900 dwt; 185.45 × 7.42 m *(608.43 × 24.34 ft)*; TSM (B&W); 19 kts; Stern door
Sister (builder—Frederiksstad): **GEROITE NA ODESSA** (Bu); Similar (Ys built—'Uljanik'): **GEROI PLEVNY** (Uk); **GEROI SHIPKI** (Uk)

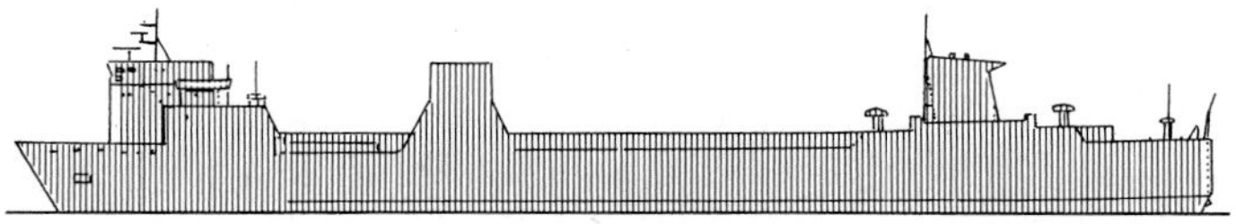

28 *MH–FY H*
TOR SCANDIA Sw/Sw (Gotav) 1978; RoC; 16,947 grt/8,412 dwt; 143.26 × 5.2 m *(470 × 17.06 ft)*; TSM (Alpha-Diesel); 16 kts; ex-*Britta Oden*; Stern door/ramp; 431 TEU; Now lengthened to 170.26m (558ft); Extra deckhouse added. Drawing shows vessel as built; Funnel is on starboard side
Sisters: **TOR FLANDRIA** (Sw) ex-*Anna Oden*; **TOR BELGIA** (Sw) ex-*Eva Oden* (see photo number 18/186)

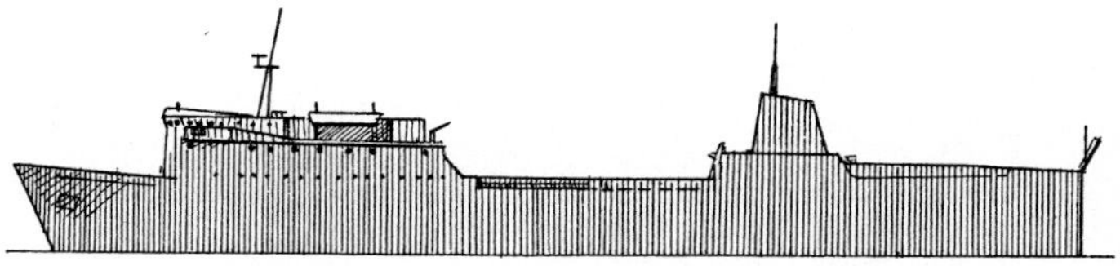

29 *MH–FY H2*
FAST ALEXANDRIA Eg/Sp (Cadagua) 1977; RoC; 6,860 grt/3,501 dwt; 110.6 × 5.61 m *(362.86 × 18.41 ft)*; M (Werkspoor); 15.5 kts; ex-*Cala d'Or*; Lengthened 1977; Stern door/ramp; 162 TEU

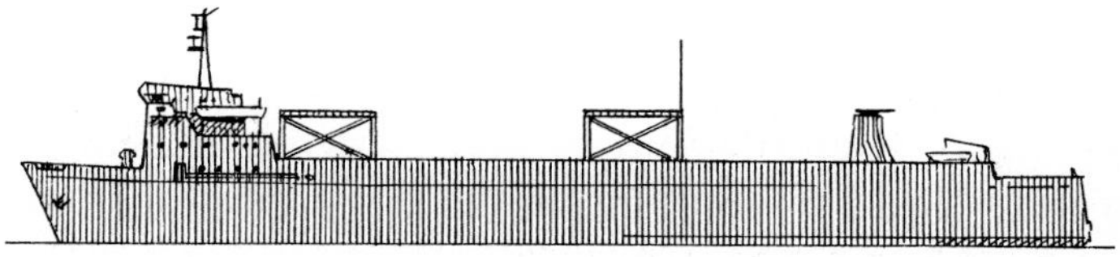

30 *MKM–KG H*
MISTRAL SV/Sp (Juliana) 1978; RoC; 4,878 grt/3,040 dwt; 101.66 × 5.66 m *(333.53 × 18.57 ft)*; TSM (Pielstick); 18 kts; ex-*Monte Buitre*; Stern door
Sister (may be fitted with two deck cranes): **DALIAN** (RC) Launched as *Monte Bustelo*

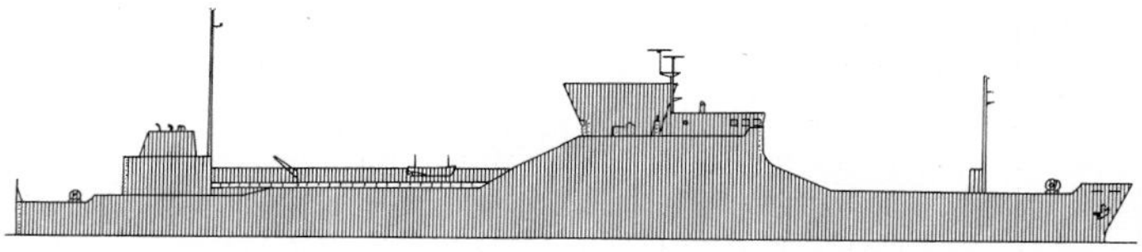

31 *M^{2}AMF H2*
HAKURYU MARU Ja/Ja (NKK) 1991; Pal; 5,195 grt/2,510 dwt; 115.00 × 5.01 m *(377.30 × 16.44 ft)*; M (B&W); 15 kts; Side door/ramp (port)
Sister: **ORYU MARU** (Ja); Similar: **SHIRYU MARU** (Ja)

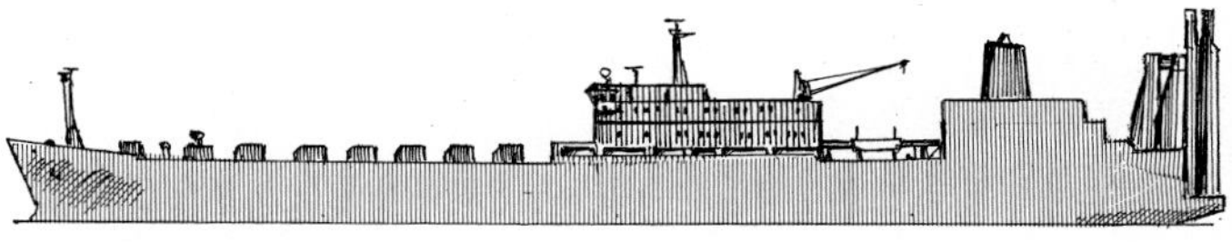

32 *M^{2}CGA H3*
IRON MONARCH Au/Au (Whyalla) 1973; RoC; 10,577 grt/14,885 dwt; 179.33 × 8.87 m *(588.35 × 29.1 ft)*; GT (GEC); 20.5 kts; Angled stern door and ramp (starboard); 227 TEU

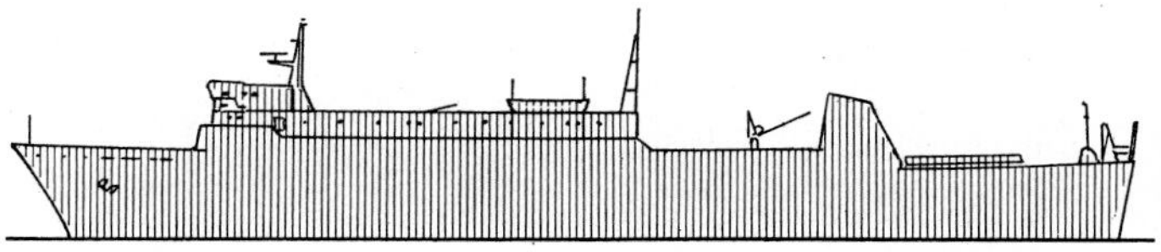

33 *M^{2}CGMY H2*
CAP AFRIQUE Fr/Ja (Tokushima ZS) 1978; RoC; 1,583 grt/2,401 dwt; 108.64 × 4.98 m *(356 × 16.34 ft)*; M (Pielstick); 17.1 kts; ex-*Catherine Schiaffino*; Stern door/ramp; 150 TEU

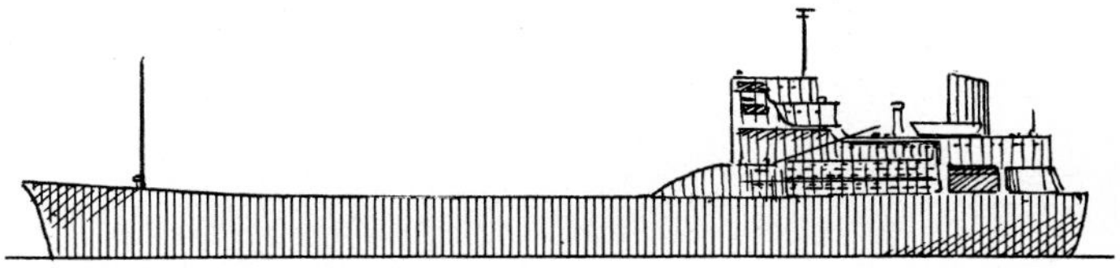

34 *M^{2}F H*
ANTARA My/Ja (Setoda) 1964; RoC; 2,787 grt/1,354 dwt; 88.55 × 4.5 m *(290.52 × 14.76 ft)*; M (Ito Tekkosho); 13 kts; ex-*Prince Maru No 2*

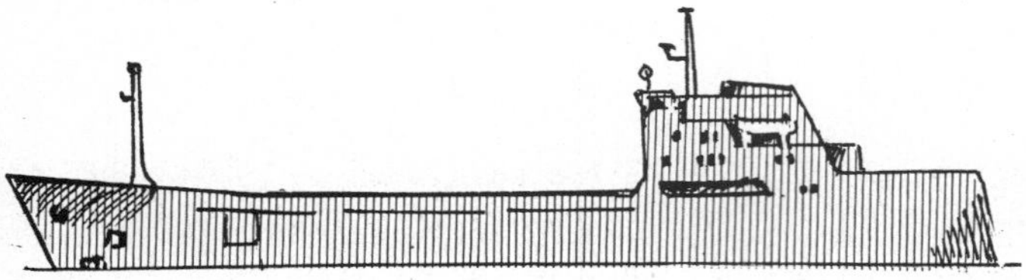

35 M^2F H
BADER Ho/Fr (Havre) 1969; RoC; 2,085 grt/3,300 dwt; 99.68 × 4.5 m *(327.03 × 14.76 ft)*; TSM (Ruston & Hornsby); 15.5 kts; ex-*Monte Cinto*; Stern door

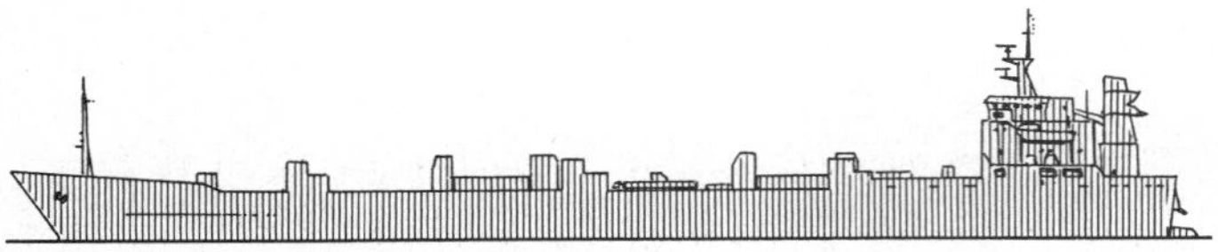

36 M^2F H
BENCOMO Pa/Sw (Marstrands) 1982; RoC/R; 6,182 grt/4,200 dwt; 128.1 × 5.57 m *(420.28 × 18.27 ft)*; M (Krupp-MaK); 20 kts; Two side door/ramps (starboard); 164 TEU; Pallets carrier; Crane on starboard side of funnel
Sister: **BENTAGO** (Pa)

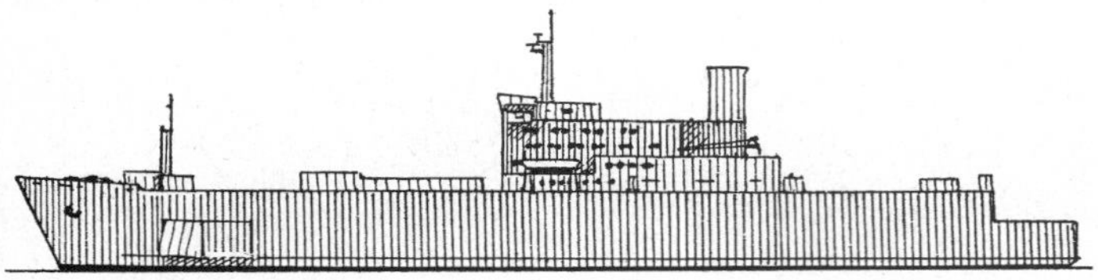

37 M^2F H1
FINNMAID Fi/Fi (Wärtsilä) 1969; RoC; 13,070 grt/5,300 dwt; 137.4 × 5.7 m *(451 × 18.9 ft)*; TSM (Pielstick); 18 kts; ex-*Hans Gutzeit*; Stern doors
Similar (original sister now converted to passenger/car and train ferry—lengthened by 40m (131ft)): **STENA SEARIDER** (Sw) ex-*Finncarrier*
Similar (converted to passenger/RoRo cargo): **FINNFELLOW** (Fi)

38 M^2F H1
SIRIO Ma/Br (Hawthorn, L) 1963; RoC/TF; 2,516 grt/1,854 dwt; 122.8 × 3.7 m *(440 × 12.2 ft)*; TSM (Mirrlees); 13.5; ex-*Cambridge Ferry*; The upper deck is now extended to the stern

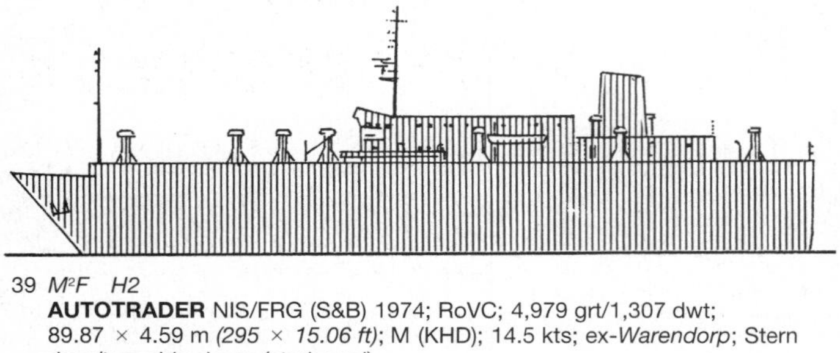

39 M^2F H2
AUTOTRADER NIS/FRG (S&B) 1974; RoVC; 4,979 grt/1,307 dwt; 89.87 × 4.59 m *(295 × 15.06 ft)*; M (KHD); 14.5 kts; ex-*Warendorp*; Stern door/two side doors (starboard)

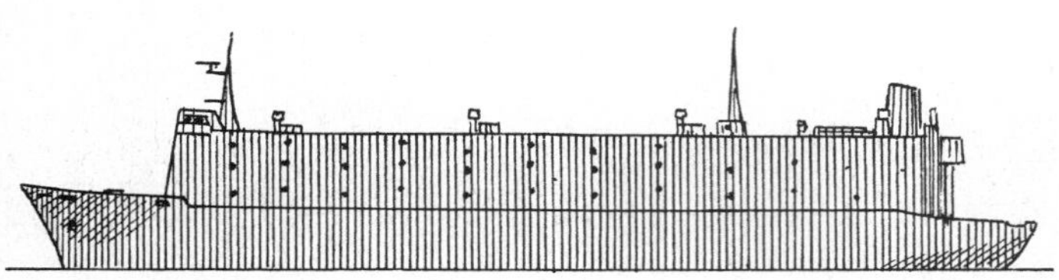

40 M^2F H2
DANAU MAS Ia/Ja (Onomichi) 1967; RoC; 5,097 grt/1,315 dwt; 96.7 × 4.8 m *(317.26 × 15.75 ft)*; M (B&W); 13.5 kts; ex-*Aichi Maru*

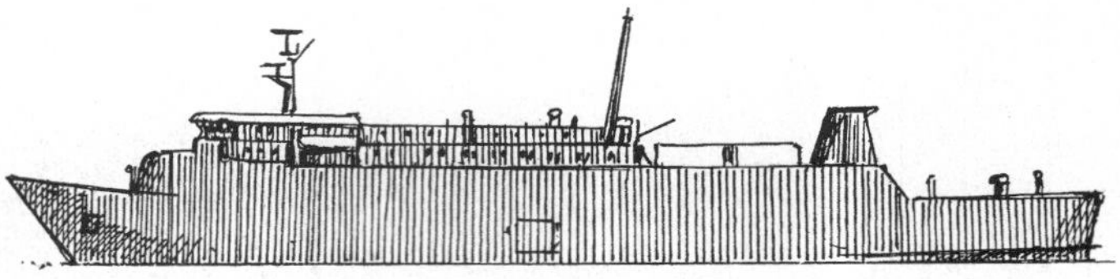

41 M^2F H2
EXCALIBUR Bs/No (Trosvik) 1976; RoC; 9,737 grt/5,675 dwt; 132.52 × 6.58 m *(434.78 × 21.59 ft)*; M (Sulzer); 18.5 kts; ex-*Seaspeed Dana*; Funnel is on port side only; two side doors (one port, one starboard); Stern door/ramp; 300 TEU
Sister: **ENDEAVOUR** (Bs) ex-*Seaspeed Dora*

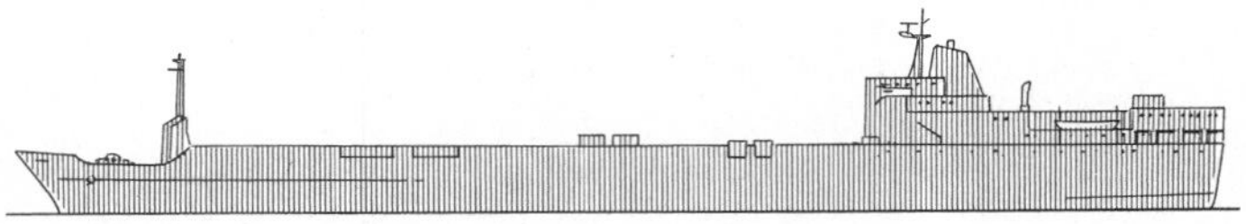

42 M^2F H2
FRECCIA BLU It/It (Breda) 1970; RoC/P; 13,265 grt/3,940 dwt; 163.96 × 5.98 m *(537.93 × 19.62 ft)*; TSM (Fiat); 20 kts; Three stern doors/ramps; Lengthened 1977; Now has extra superstructure on foredeck and aft
Similar (extra superstructure on foredeck): **FRECCIA ROSSA** (It)

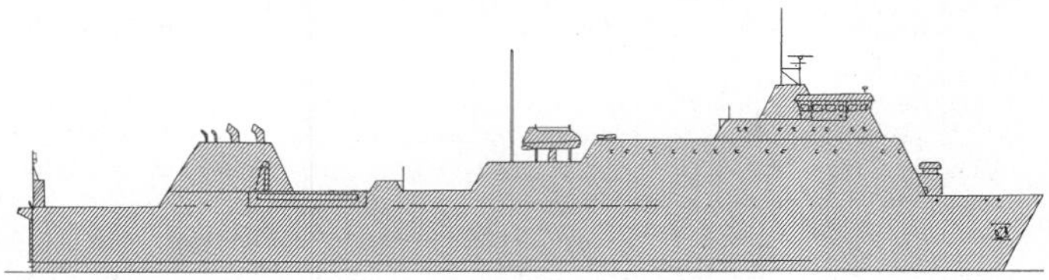

43 M^2F H2
ISLAND COMMODORE Bs/Ne (Scheldegroep) 1995; RoC; 11,166 grt/5,215 dwt; 126.40 × 5.80 m *(414.70 × 19.03 ft)*; TSM (MaK); 25 kts; Stern door/ramp; 40 TEU
Sister: **COMMODORE GOODWILL** (Bs)

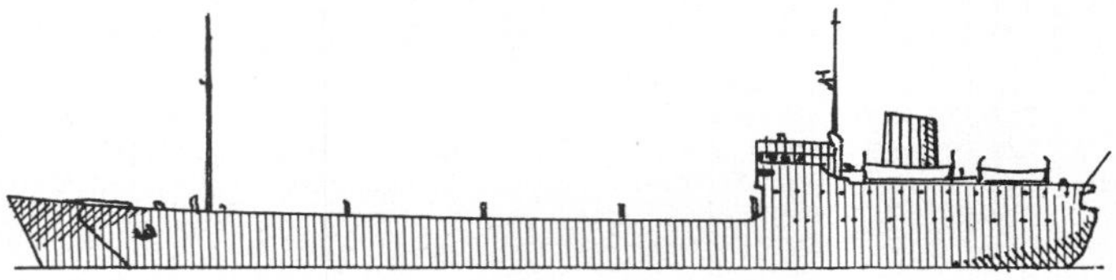

44 M^2F H3
MARITZA ARLETTE Pa/FRG (Norderwerft) 1952/66; RoC/LS; 1,121 grt/1,247 dwt; 90.91 × 4.06 m *(298.26 × 13.32 ft)*; M (MaK); 11.5 kts; ex-*Anna Catharina*; Converted from tanker 1966 (Giessen-De Noord)

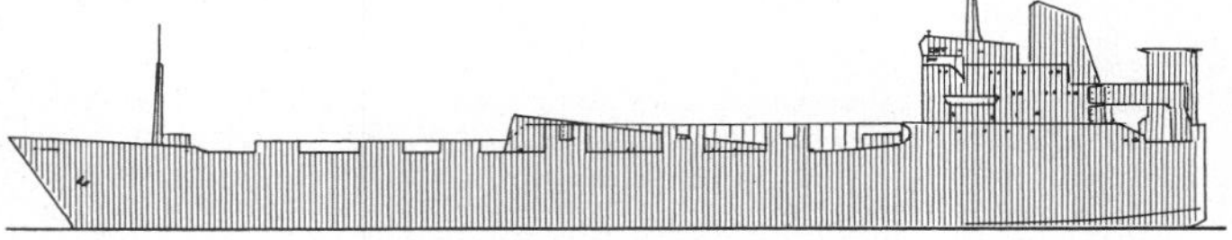

45 M^2FA H2
ROLLCARGO Bz/Br (Smith's D) 1984; RoC; 13,683 grt/7,450 dwt; 149.84 × 6.9 m *(491.6 × 22.64 ft)*; M (Pielstick); 15.5 kts; ex-*Karisma*; Quarter stern door/ramp; 375 TEU; Funnel is on starboard side

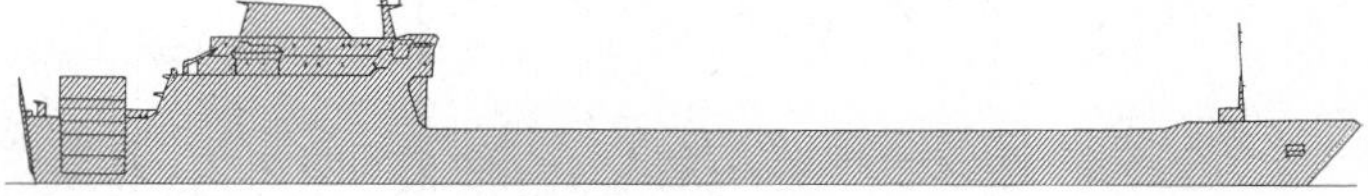

46 M^2FAY H2
NORSE MERSEY It/It ('Visentini') 1995; RoC/F; 13,500 grt/11,000 dwt; 174.50 × 6.50 m *(572.51 × 21.33 ft)*; M (Wärtsilä); 19.5 kts; Side ramp (port aft); Stern ramp
Sister: **LINDA** (It)

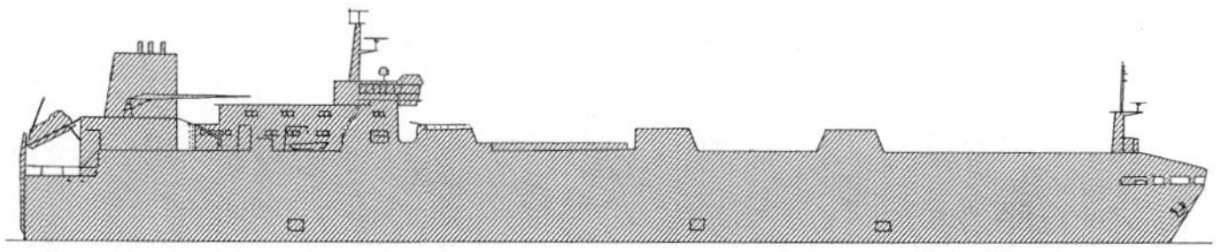

47 *M^2FLY H*
OBBOLA Sw/Sp (AESA) 1995; RoC/Pap; — grt/9,200 dwt; — × — m *(— × — ft)*; M (—); — kts; Funnel and Free-Fall lifeboat are both on port side (see photo number 18/232
Sisters: **OSTRAND** (Sw); **ORTVIKEN** (Sw)

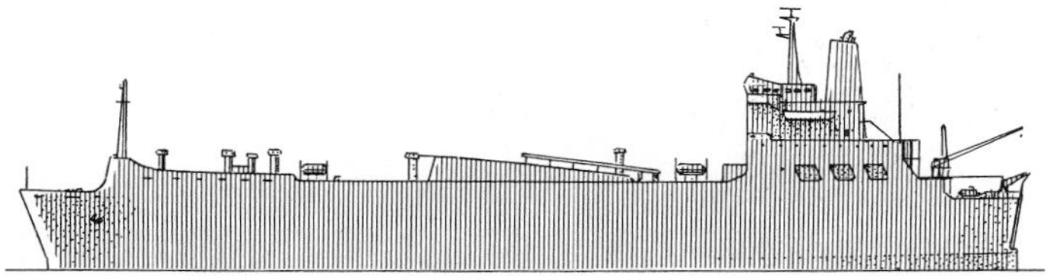

48 *M^2FMC–RZ H2*
JOLLY GRIGIO It/Ja (Kawasaki) 1977; RoC/Con; 22,945 grt/10,665 dwt; 142.91 × 9.02 m *(468.86 × 29.59 ft)*; M (MAN); 14 kts; ex-*Bellman*; converted from RoRo/Tanker/Bulk carrier 1985; Stern door
Sister: **JOLLY AMARANTO** (It) ex-*Taube*

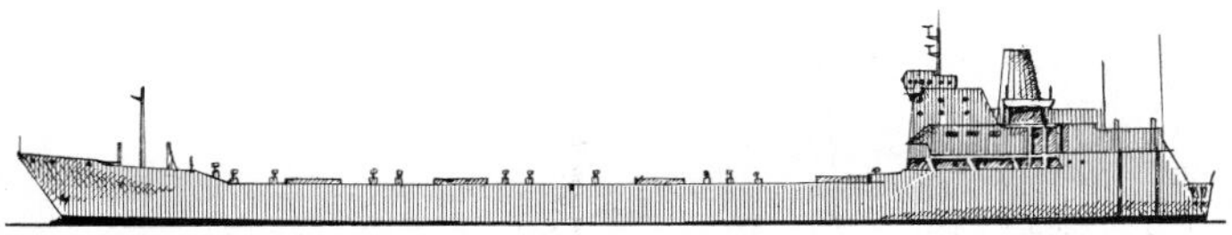

49 *M^2FM^2 H12*
CAPE LOBOS US/Ca (Port Weller) 1972; RoC; 22,286 grt/20,545 dwt; 208.19 × 9.3 m *(683.04 × 30.51 ft)*; TSM (Pielstick); 19 kts; ex-*Laurentian Forest*; Two side doors/ramps (starboard); Owned by US Government
Sister: **CAPE LAMBERT** (US) ex-*Avon Forest*

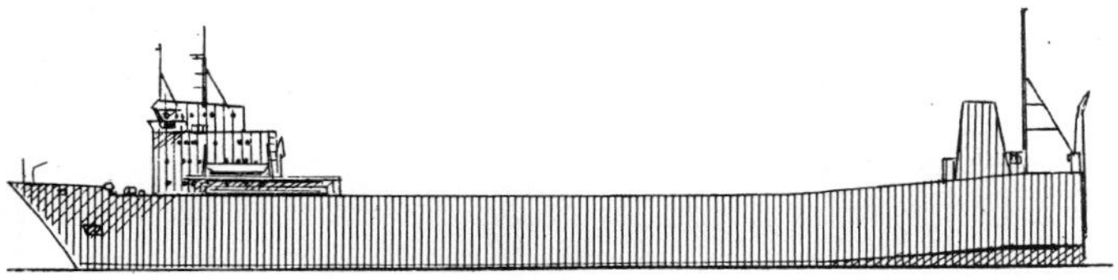

50 *M^2FMY H*
KIRK CHALLENGER Bs/De (Helsingor) 1979; RoC; 5,945 grt/3,390 dwt; 105.62 × 4.95 m *(347 × 16.24 ft)*; M (MaK); 15.3 kts; ex-*Dana Minerva*; Stern door/ramp; Side door/ramp (starboard); 274 TEU; Funnel is on starboard side

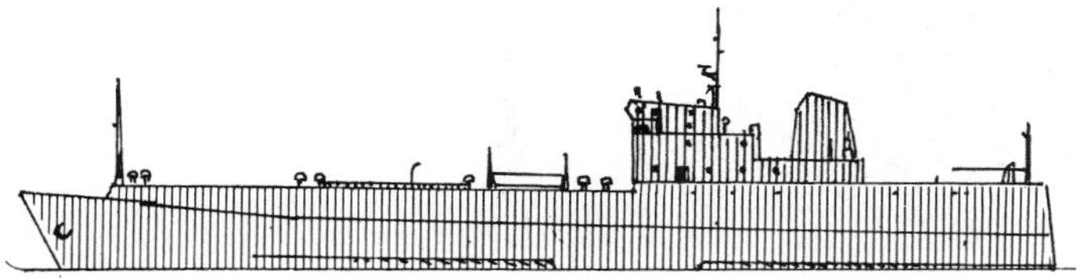

51 *M^2FN H2*
AUTOSTRADA NIS/No (Langvik) 1971; RoVC; 3,548 grt/857 dwt; 92.36 × 3.89 m *(303 × 12.76 ft)*; M (Bergens); 14.25 kts; Stern door/ramp
Sister: **KHALED IV** (Le) ex-*Autoroute*

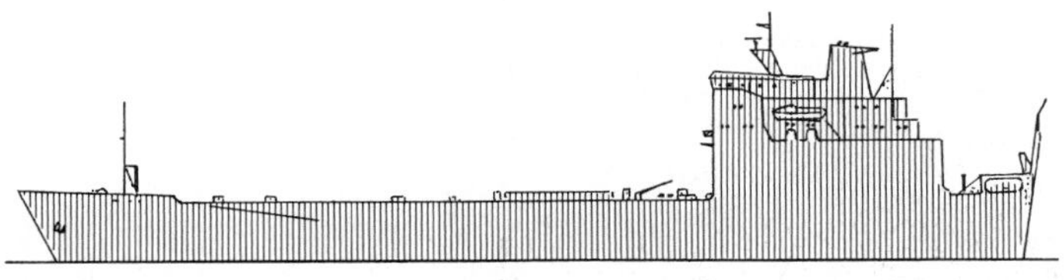

52 *M^2FNSZ H2*
RIVER LUNE Bs/Rm (Galatz) 1983; RoC; 7,765 grt/5,000 dwt; 121.49 × 5.33 m *(398.59 × 17.49 ft)*; TSM (MaK); 15.5 kts; ex-*Balder Vik*; Stern door/ramp; 450 TEU
Sisters: **CITY OF BURNIE** (Br) ex-*Balder Strand*; **BAZIAS 1** (Rm) ex-*Balder Fjord*; **DART 2** (Rm) ex-*Balder Hav*; **PERSEUS** (Rm) ex-*Balder Ra*; **SALLY EUROROUTE** (Bs) ex-*Balder Sten*; **SALLY EUROLINK** (Bs) ex-*Balder Bre*; **CITY OF PORT MELBOURNE** (Br) ex-*Balder Sund*

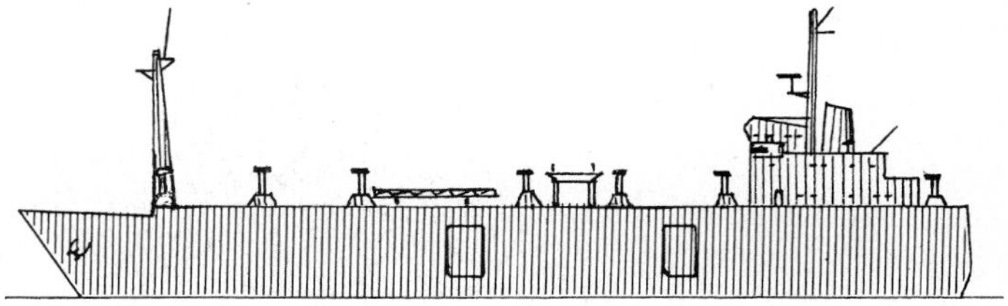

53 *M^2FR H*
FEEDERMATE Be/FRG (S&B) 1973; RoC; 3,495 grt/1,194 dwt; 92.56 × 4.30 m *(303.67 × 14.11 ft)*; M (KHD); 14 kts; ex-*Ramsgate*; Stern and side doors

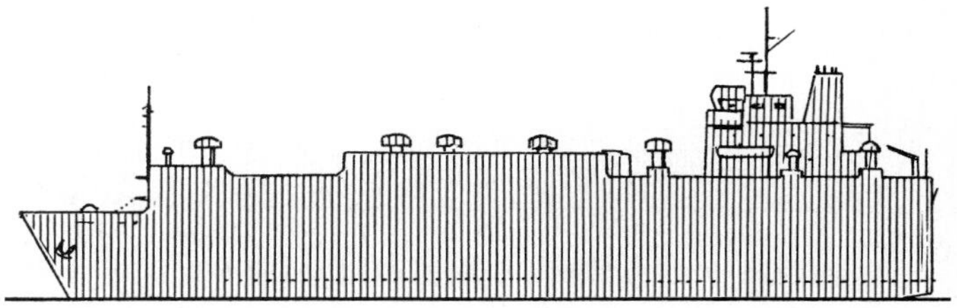

54 *M^2FR H2*
AUTOCARRIER NIS/FRG (Flender) 1982; RoVC; 6,421 grt/1,472 dwt; 89.52 × 4.26 m *(294 × 13.98 ft)*; M (MaK); 13.5 kts; ex-*Castorp*; Side door/ramp; Stern door/ramp

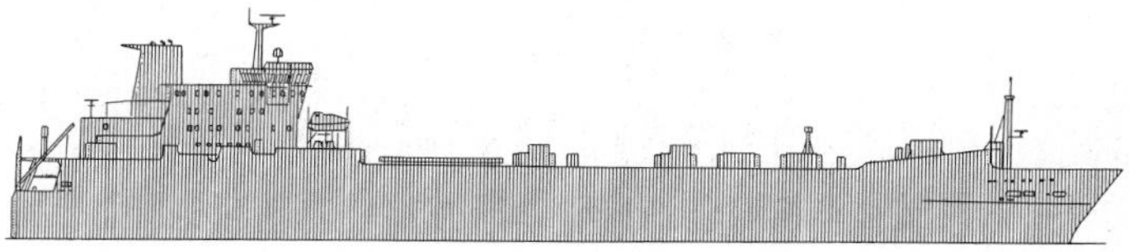

55 *M^2FRY H*
HELENA Sw/Ko (Daewoo) 1991; RoC/Pal; 22,193 grt/12,968 dwt; 169.80 × 6.70 m *(557.09 × 21.98 ft)*; M (Wärtsilä); 14.6 kts; Stern door/ramp; 24 TEU

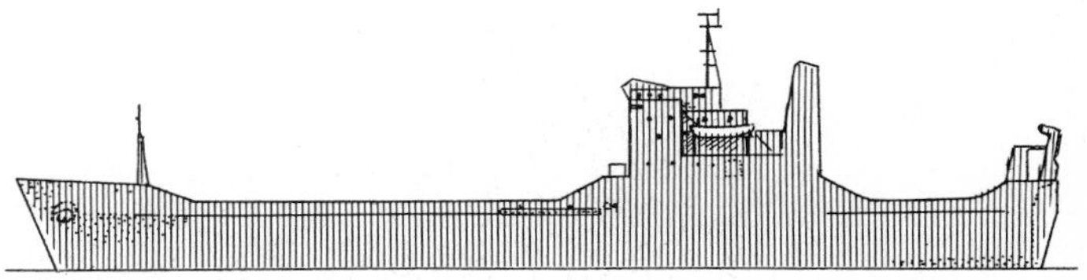

56 *M^2FY H123*
BELVAUX Pa/Be (Cockerill) 1979; RoC; 6,832 grt/5,064 dwt; 16.7 × 6.2 m *(382.87 × 20.34 ft)*; M (Mirrlees Blackstone); 15 kts; Stern slewing ramp; Funnel is on port side
Sister: **CHANG HANG** (RC) ex-*Clervaux*

57 *M^2FY H13*
JAMAICA PROVIDER Bl/FRG (Sietas) 1968; RoC; 2,676 dwt; 91.5 × 4.5 m *(300 × 14.1 ft)*; TSM (KHD); 16; ex-*Jamaican Provider*; Funnel is on port side

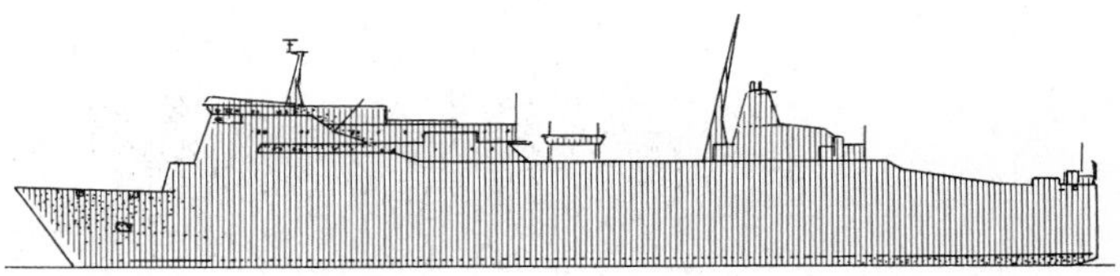

58 *M^2FY H2*
ROSEBAY Cy/FRG (Sietas) 1976; RoC; 13,700 grt/5,233 dwt; 135.45 × 6.05 m *(444.39 × 19.85 ft)*; TSM (MAN); 19 kts; ex-*Transgermania*; Stern ramp

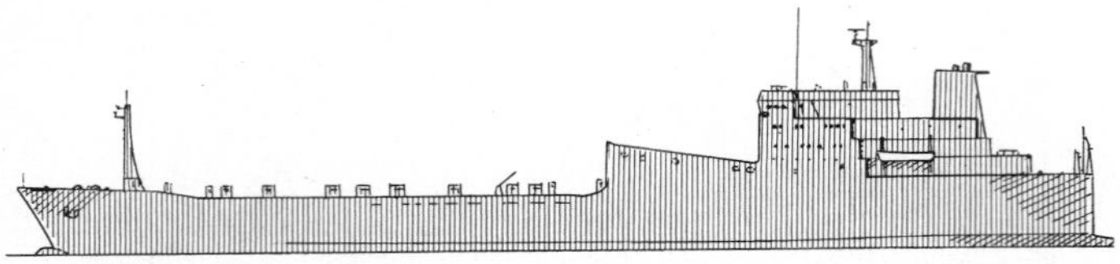

59 *M^2FY H3*
TOR ANGLIA Sw/FRG (Lindenau) 1977; RoC; 17,492 grt/8,700 dwt; 144.48 × 6.7 m *(474.02 × 21.98 ft)*; TSM (Atlas-MaK); 18 kts; ex-*Merzario Gallia*; Stern door; 723 TEU; Now lengthened to 171.94m (564ft); Drawing shows vessel as built; Funnel is on starboard side

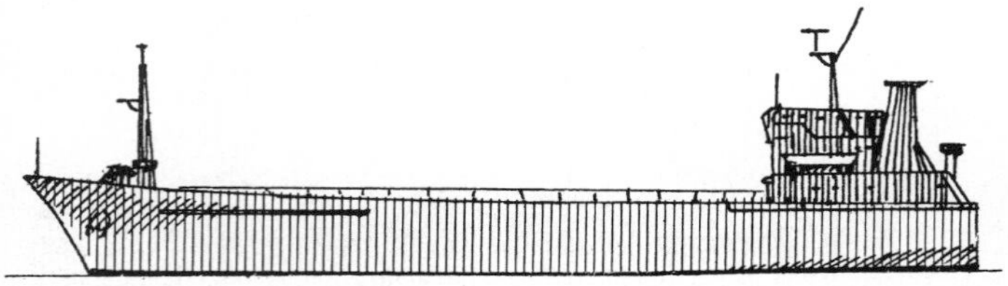

60 *M^2G H*
MAKEDONIA 1 Gr/FRG (Schlichting) 1967; RoC; 495 grt/1,084 dwt; 76.43 × 4.22 m *(250.75 × 13.85 ft)*; M (MAN); 14.5 kts; ex-*Arneb*; Stern door

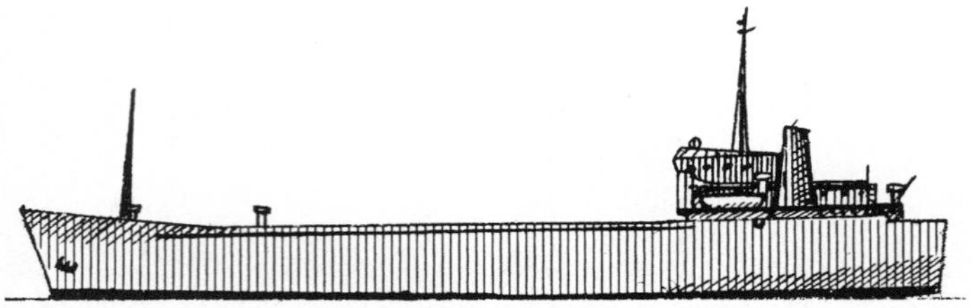

61 *M^2G H*
MAKEDONIA 2 Gr/FRG (S&B) 1970; RoC; 491 grt/1,186 dwt; 77.98 × 3.86 m *(255.84 × 12.66 ft)*; M (MAN); 12.5 kts; ex-*Monte d'Oro*; 70 TEU; Stern door/ramp

62 *MMG H*
NIOBE 1 Pa/Fr (CNIM) 1968; RoC/P/Con; 5,684 grt/1,829 dwt; 104.02 × 4.7 m *(341.27 × 15.42 ft)*; TSM (MWM); 16 kts; ex-*Transcontainer 1*; Stern door/ramp; 192 TEU

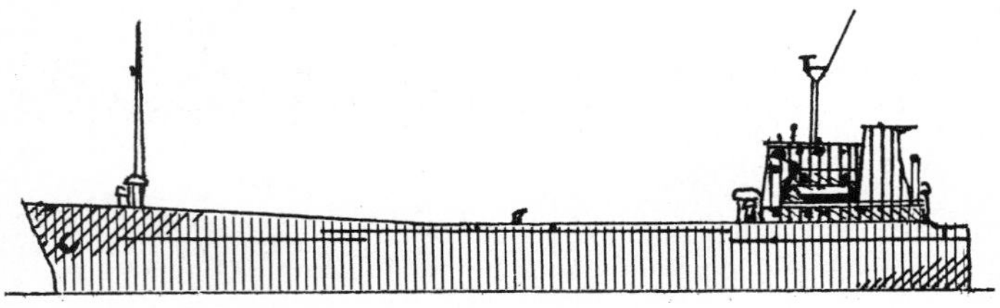

63 *M^2G H1*
EL MALEK KHALED Eg/FRG (Buesumer) 1969; RoC/C; 499 grt/1,046 dwt; 76.41 × 4.18 m *(251 × 13.71 ft)*; M (MAN); 14.5 kts; ex-*Cogolin*; Stern door/ ramp; two side doors/ramps (starboard)
Sister: **RAS EL KHAIMA** (Eg) ex-*Cotignac*

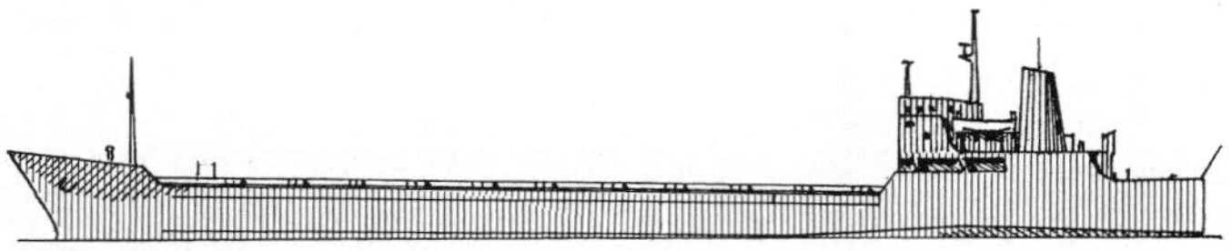

64 *M^2G H13*
DELLYS Ag/Sp (Construcciones SA) 1974; RoC; 1,598 grt/2,337 dwt; 107 × 4.85 m *(351.05 × 15.91 ft)*; TSM (Deutz); 18 kts; Side door; stern door/ramp
Sister: **TENES** (Ag)

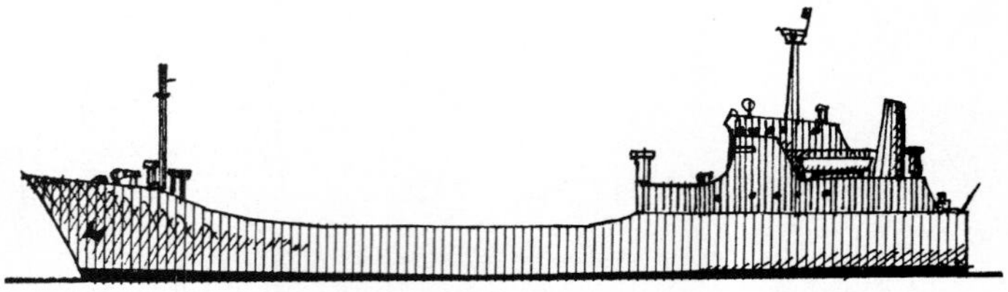

65 *M^2G H13*
PANTELLERIA It/Ne (Vuyk) 1969; RoC; 885 grt/1,080 dwt; 74.99 × 4.19 m *(246.03 × 13.75 ft)*; M (MWM); 15 kts; ex-*Duke of Holland*; Stern door
Sister: **DUKE OF TOPSAIL** (Br) ex-*Duke of Norfolk*

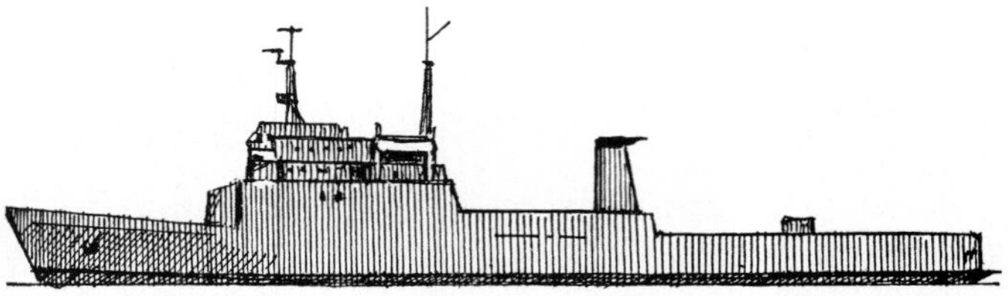

66 *M^2G H2*
NUSA MULIA Ia/FRG (Rickmers) 1971; RoC; 1,873 grt/2,920 dwt; 114.9 × 5.7 m *(377 × 18.1 ft)*; TSM (Atlas-MaK); 17 kts; ex-*Fuldatal*
Sisters: **CHARME** (It) ex-*Travetal*; **DANA BALTICA** (NIS) ex-*Wesertal*; Similar: **PICASSO** (Bb) ex-*Canaima*

67 *M^2G H2*
SPIRIT OF FREE ENTERPRISE Fj/Fr (Havre) 1968; RoC; 997 grt/1,555 dwt; 92.03 × 4.76 m *(301.94 × 15.63 ft)*; TSM (Atlas-MaK); 15 kts; ex-*Sealord Contender*; Stern ramp

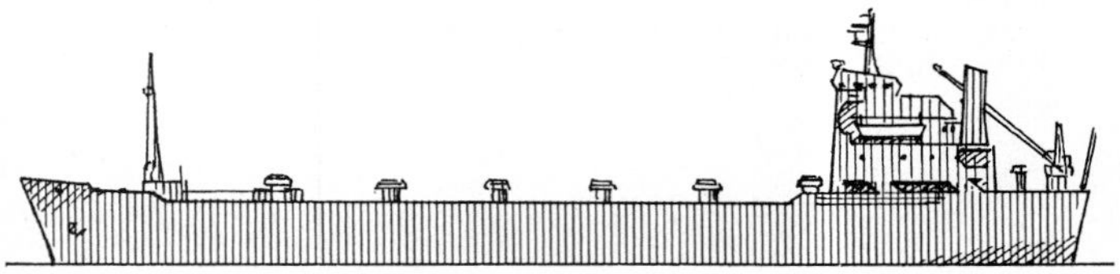

68 *M^2GCY H*
PHOENIX SPIRIT Ho/FRG (Meyer) 1966; RoC; 1,599 grt/4,457 dwt; 99.22 × 5.83 m *(325.52 × 19.13 ft)*; M (KHD); 13 kts; ex-*Salome*; Lengthened 1969; Side doors; Stern door/ramp
Sisters: **LUCKY RAIDER** (Ho) ex-*Aida*; **FAGR** (Ho) ex-*Otello* (deck house forward of bridge)

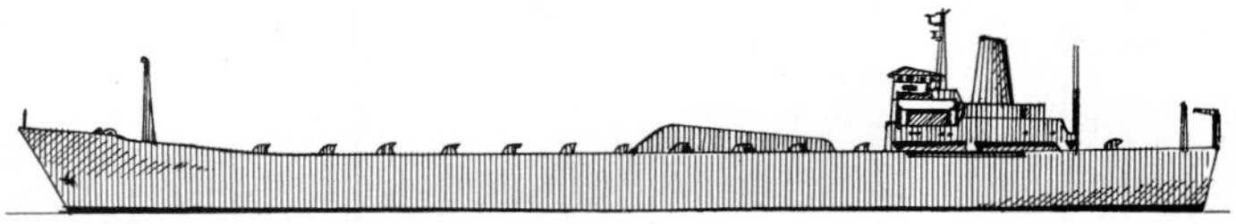

69 *M^2GM^2Y H*
SEABOARD TRADER Pa/Fi (Wärtsilä) 1972; RoC; 3,977 grt/6,604 dwt; 162.36 × 7.72 m *(532.68 × 23.69 ft)*; TSM (Pielstick); 17.5 kts; ex-*Mont Laurier*; Lengthened 1978 (Wärtsilä); Stern door/ramp; 482 TEU

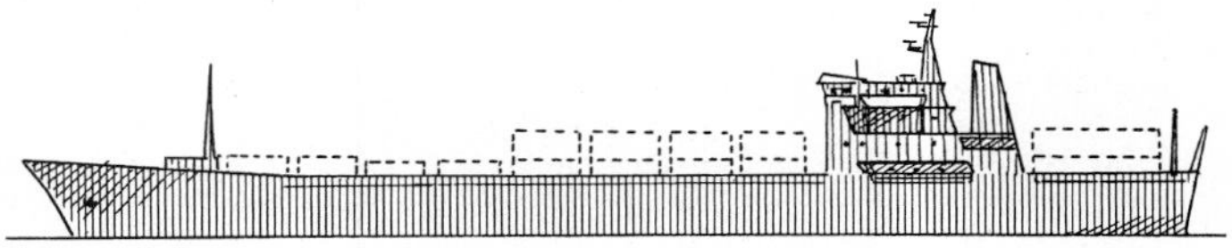

70 *M^2GMY H*
LUCKY RUNNER Ho/Sw (Finnboda) 1970; RoC; 2,885 grt/5,182 dwt; 112.71 × 6.82 m *(369.78 × 22.38 ft)*; M (Atlas-MaK); 16 kts; ex-*Mignon*; Stern door/ramp; 180 TEU

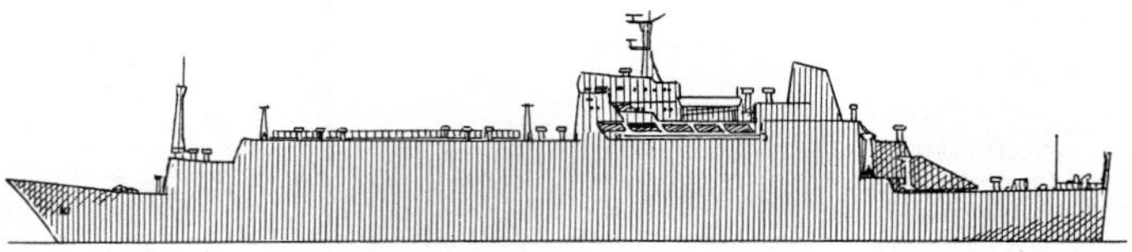

71 *M^2GMY H2*
BOUNDARY SV/Sw (Finnboda) 1972; RoC; 11,400 grt/5,618 dwt; 138.26 × 7.01 m *(453.61 × 23 ft)*; M (Stork-Werkspoor); 18 kts; ex-*Sibelius*

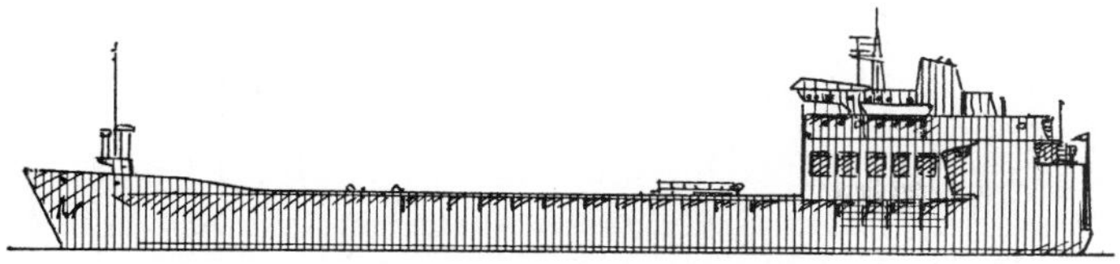

72 *M^2GMY H3*
SUNSHINE PEARL Cy/Ne (Pattje) 1979; RoC; 3,353 grt/1,770 dwt; 93.9 × 3.53 m *(308.07 × 11.58 ft)*; TSM (Polar); 15 kts; ex-*Balder Haren*; Two stern door/ramps; 52 TEU
Sister: **CASALICCHIO** (It) ex-*Balder Eems*

See photos numbers 18/180 and 18/222
73 *M^2GR H2*
DONINGTON NIS/Fr (Graville) 1976; RoC; 5,351 grt/1,400 dwt; 100.52 × 4.15 m *(330 × 13.62 ft)*; M (MaK); 15 kts; ex-*Tertre Rouge*; Stern door/ramp
Similar: **HOCKENHEIM** (Kn) ex-*Hunaudieres*

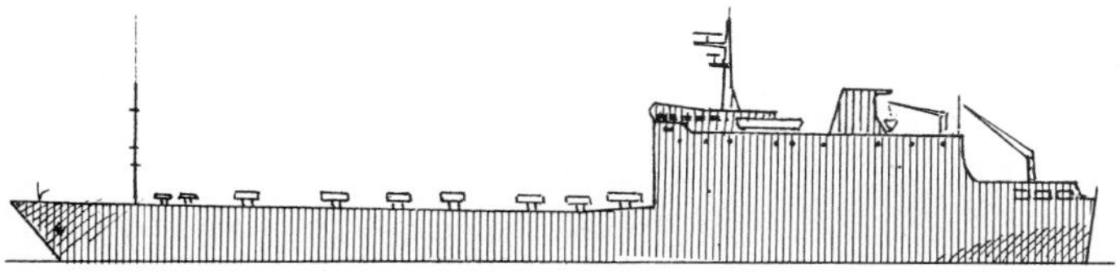

74 *M^2GR^2Y H2*
JUNIPER Cy/Fr (Havre) 1977; RoC; 1,575 grt/2,700 dwt; 109.71 × 5.21 m *(359.94 × 17.09 ft)*; TSM (Atlas-MaK); 16 kts; ex-*Cap Benat*; Stern door/ramp; 130 TEU
Sisters: **CAP CANAILLE** (Kn) ex-*Cap Lardier*; **ANWAL** (Mo) ex-*Cap Taillat*

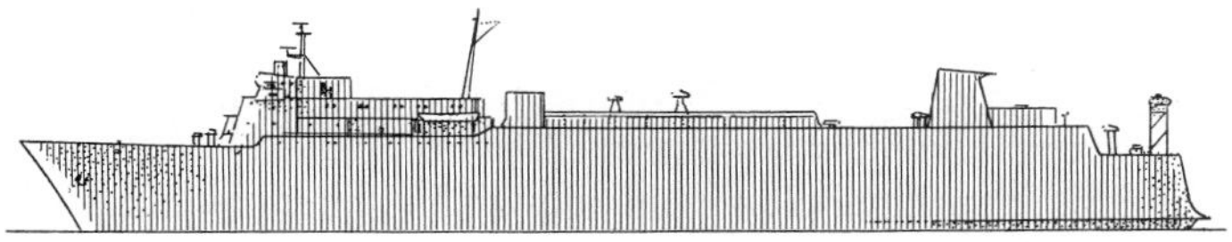

75 *M^2GV H2*
FAST TRADER Eg/No (Framnaes) 1977; RoC; 9,771 grt/7,299 dwt; 135.79 × 7.17 m *(445.5 × 23.52 ft)*; TSM (Pielstick); 18.5 kts; ex-*Union Lyttelton*; Stern door; 283 TEU

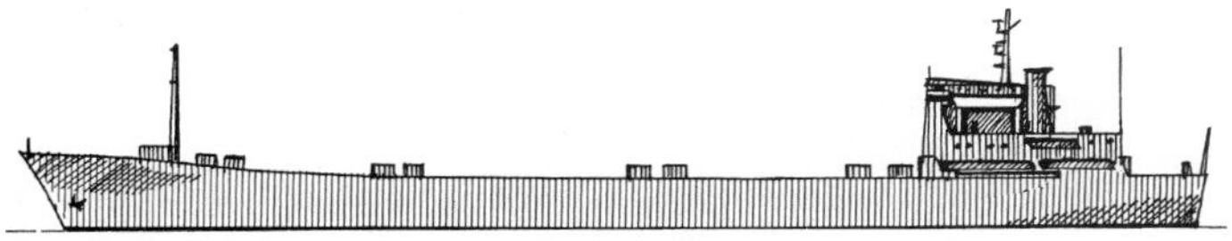

76 *M^2GY H*
ALMA LLANERA Pa/Sw (Lodose) 1972; RoC; 4,055 grt/6,879 dwt; 130.71 × 6.74 m *(428.84 × 22.11 ft)*; M (Ruston Paxman); 14.75 kts; ex-*Valerie*; Now has a large breakwater foreward (not on drawing); Stern door/ramp; 200 TEU (see photo number 18/179)
Sister: **ABLE ADMIRAL** (My) ex-*Vallann*

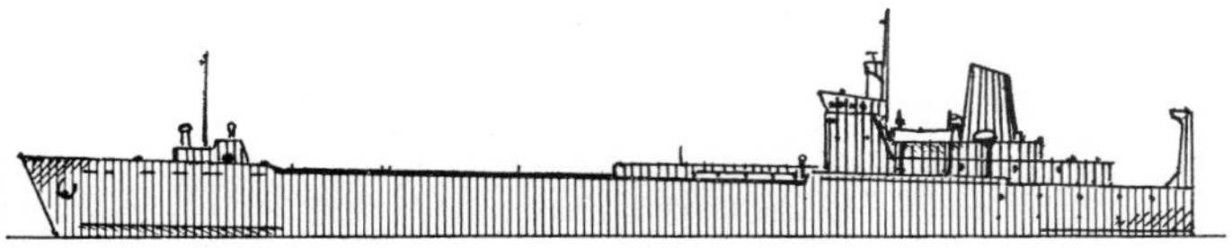

77 *M^2GY H*
CENK III Tu/Ne (Boele's Sch) 1971; RoC; 4,977 grt/3,337 dwt; 101.2 × 5.18 m *(332.02 × 16.99 ft)*; M (B&W); 15 kts; ex-*Mary Holyman*; Stern door/ramp; 150 TEU

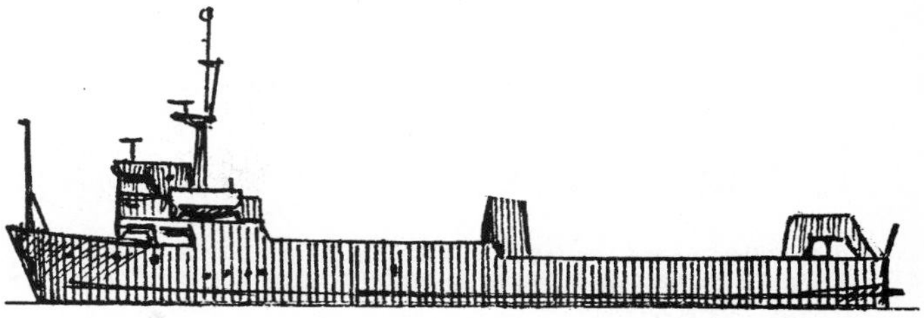

78 *M^2GY H*
PRESIDENT YEIWENE Fr/Fr (Dubigeon-Normandie) 1973; P/RoC; 3,523 grt/724 dwt; 74.99 × 3.2 m *(262.43 × 10.5 ft)*; TSM (Alpha-Diesel); 13 kts; ex-*Poole Antelope*

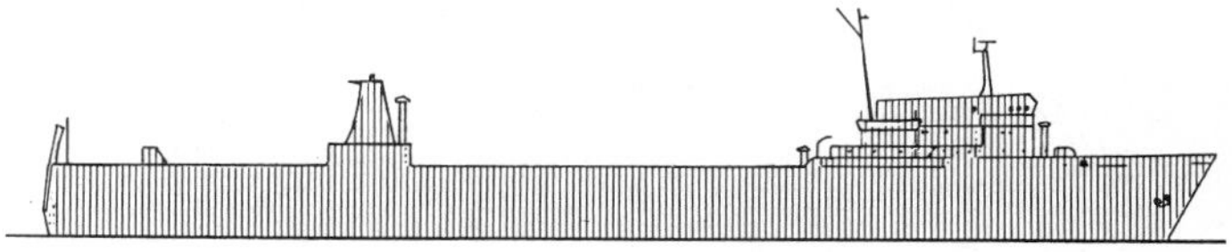

79 *M^2GY H*
SERDIKA Ma/No (Langvik) 1972/78; RoC; 2,693 grt/5,864 dwt; 130.21 × 6.18 m *(427.20 × 20.28 ft)*; TSM (Pielstick); 14 kts; ex-*Domino*; Stern door; Lengthened 1978
Sister: **PRESLAV** (Bu) ex-*Destro*; Similar (superstructure differs. Tripod radar mast): **PLISKA** (Bu) ex-*Tor Scandia*; **CHRISTIAN I** (Pa) ex-*Tor Mercia*

80 *M^2GY H*
SPHEROID Br/No (Langvik) 1971; RoC; 7,171 grt/2,838 dwt; 109.81 × 4.95 m *(360 × 16.24 ft)*; TSM (MAN); 17.5 kts; ex-*Starmark*; Stern door; lengthened to 124m (407ft) in 1990

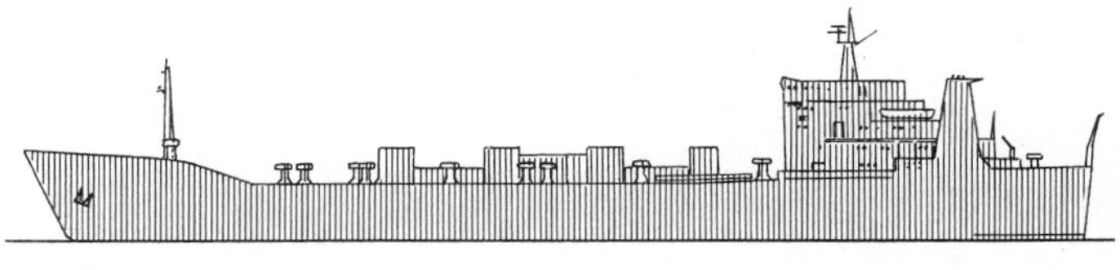

81 *M^2GY H1*
CAMILLA Fi/FRG (Kroegerw) 1982; RoC/Pap; 10,085 grt/7,000 dwt; 133.41 × 6.87 m *(437.7 × 22.54 ft)*; M (Stork-Werkspoor); 14.5 kts; Two side doors (starboard); Stern door/ramp; 399 TEU

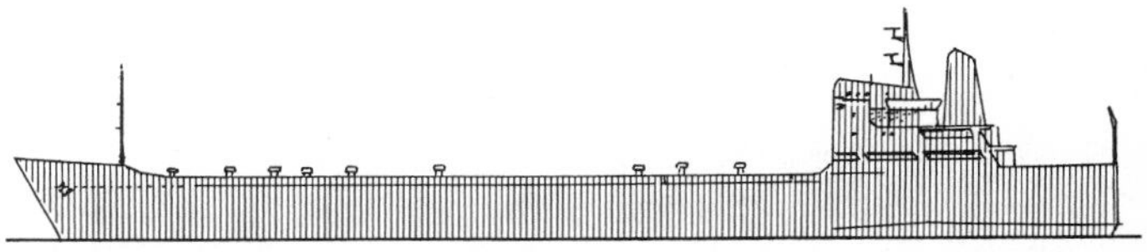

82 *M^2GY H1*
FOREST LINK NIS/Sp (Construcciones SA) 1973; RoC/Con; 7,107 grt/5,924 dwt; 127.26 × 6.4 m *(418 × 21 ft)*; TSM (Deutz); 17.5 kts; ex-*Stellaria*; Side door (starboard); Stern door/ramp; Lengthened 1977; 200 TEU
Sister: **WHITE SEA** (NIS) ex-*Fragaria*

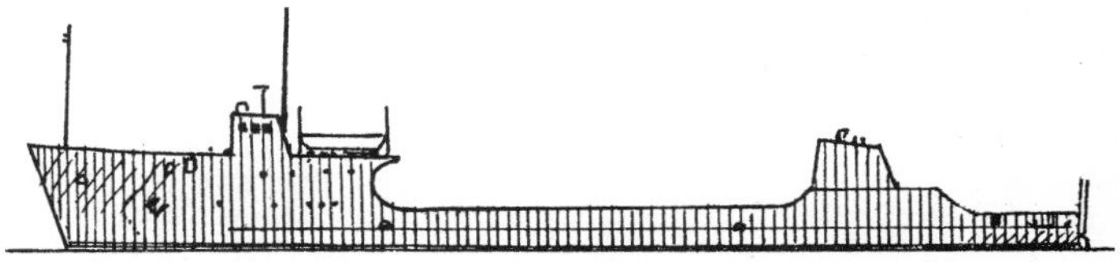

83 *M^2GY H1*
NEW LIGHT Bs/US (Levingston) 1970; RoC/LC; 788 grt/2,208 dwt; 81.51 × 3.49 m *(267.4 × 11.45 ft)*; TrS M (Caterpillar); 12 kts; ex-*Inagua Light*; Landing craft; Bow door/ramp; Stern ramp
Sisters: **SEA BEACH** (Pa) ex-*Inagua Beach*; **HYBUR TRADER** (At) ex-*Inagua Sound*
Possible sisters: **PARU MERU** (Pa) ex-*Inagua Bay*; **RORA MERU** (Ve) ex-*Inagua Surf*; **CMS ISLAND EXPRESS** (SV) ex-*Inagua Island*; **TROPIC OPAL** (SV) ex-*Inagua Shore*; **RIO PACUARE** (Pa) ex-*Inagua Espana* (Sp built—Freire)

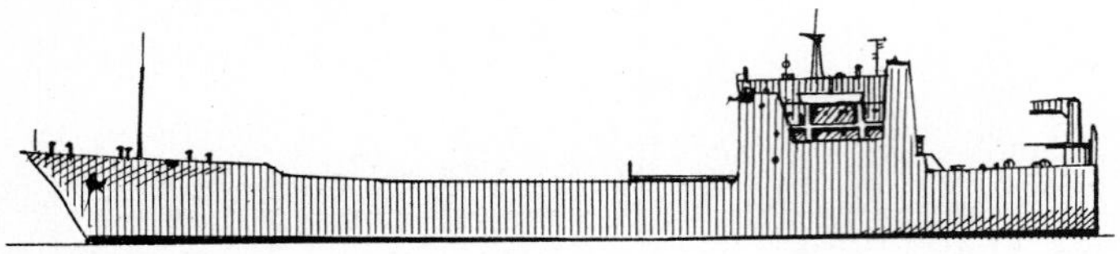

84 *M^{2}GY H12*
VALENTINO Cy/Br (Robb Caledon) 1971; RoC/P; 4,469 grt/4,084 dwt; 117.48 × 6.32 m *(385.43 × 20.73 ft)*; TSM (Pielstick); 17.5 kts; ex-*Caribbean Progress*; Stern door/ramp
Similar (FRG built—Sietas): **CARIBE TRADER** (Pa) ex-*Caribbean Endeavour*

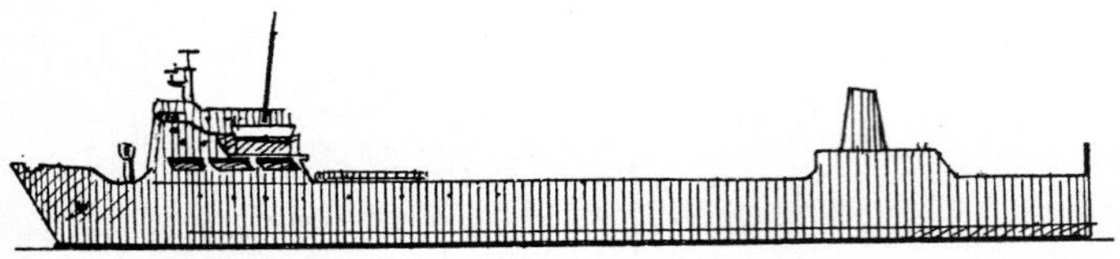

85 *M^{2}GY H2*
AGIOS DIONISSOS S Gr/Sp (Construcciones SA) 1972; RoC; 3,395 grt/3,207 dwt; 99.17 × 5.81 m *(325.36 × 19.06 ft)*; TSM (Deutz); 16 kts; ex-*Lilac*; Stern door/ramp
Similar: **GUAYCURA** (Me) ex-*Jasmine*

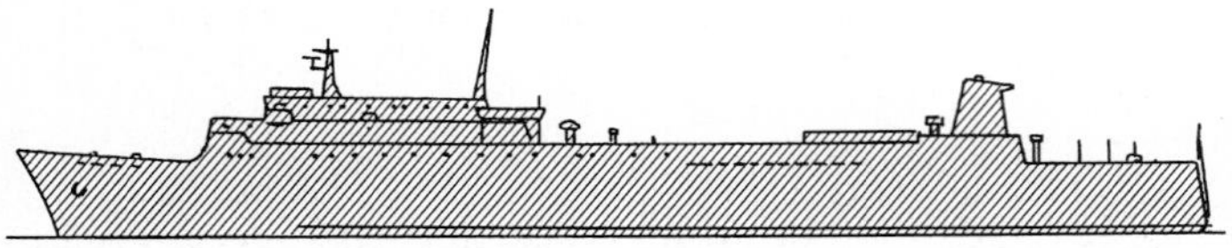

86 *M^{2}GY H2*
ELBLAG SV/No (Kristiansands) 1972; RoC; 6,057 grt/3,979 dwt; 118.42 × 5.98 m *(388.52 × 19.62 ft)*; TSM (Sulzer); 17 kts; ex-*Leo*; Stern door/ramp; 125 TEU
Sister: **COMMODORE CLIPPER** (NIS) ex-*Juno*

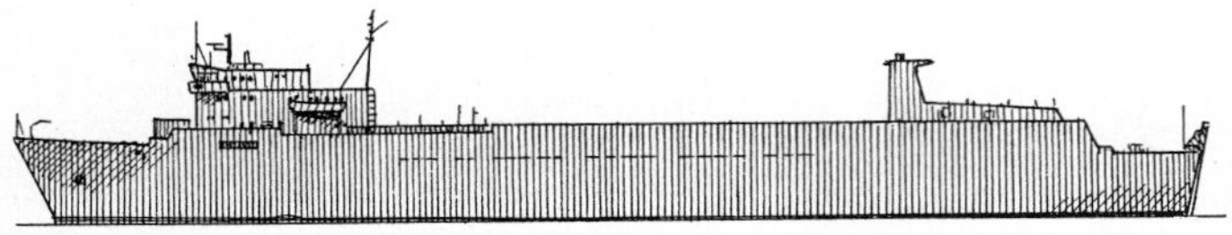

87 *M^{2}GY H2*
ISOLA DELLE STELLE It/No (Ankerlokken) 1975; RoC; 6,113 grt/10,320 dwt; 167.52 × 6.21 m *(549.61 × 20.37 ft)*; TSM (Pielstick); 18.5 kts; ex-*Bayard*; Stern door and ramps; Lengthened 1981 (Frederikshavn)—drawing shows vessel before lengthening
Sisters: **ISOLA DELLE PERLE** (It) ex-*Bohemund*; **BALDUIN** (NIS)

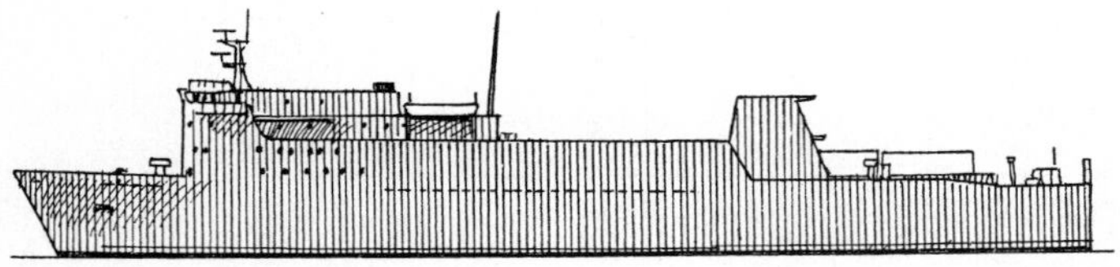

88 *M^{2}GY H2*
MARINE EVANGELINE Bs/No (Kristiansands) 1974; RoC; 2,793 grt/1,856 dwt; 110.14 × 5.75 m *(361.35 × 18.86 ft)*; TSM (Normo); 18.5 kts; ex-*Duke of Yorkshire*; Bow, side and stern doors

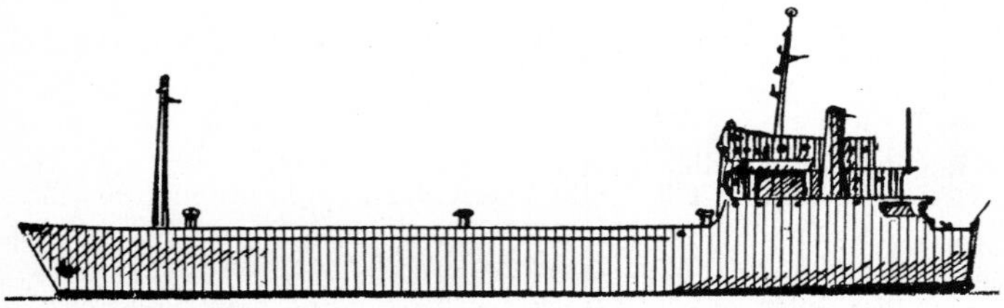

89 *M^{2}GY H2*
MARTIN POSADILLO Sp/Sp (Duro Felguera) 1974; RoC; 1,923 grt/1,283 dwt; 75.01 × 4.27 m *(246.1 × 14.01 ft)*; M (MWM); 15 kts; ex-*Rivanervion*
Sister: **CALA GALDANA** (Sp) ex-*Rivamahon*
Possible sisters: **NARAVAL** (It) ex-*Rivanalon*; **BALTIC METEOR** (Pa) ex-*Rivagijon*

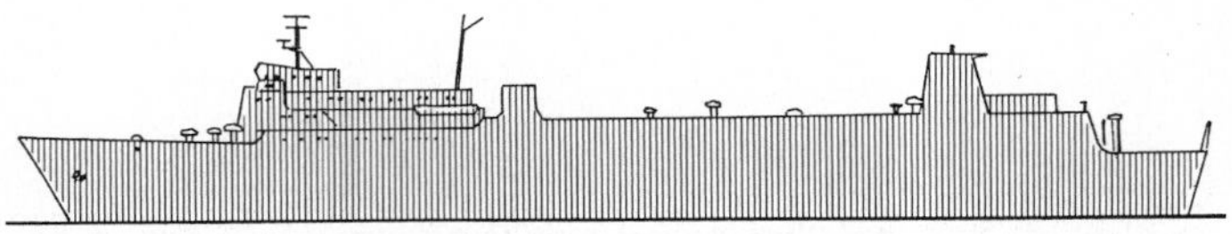

90 *M^{2}GY H2*
MELBOURNE TRADER Au/No (Framnaes) 1975; RoC; 14,406 grt/11,925 dwt; 139.91 × 7.16 m *(459.02 × 23.49 ft)*; M (Pielstick); 16 kts; Stern door/ramp; 198 TEU; Now lengthened to 188.67m (619ft). Drawing shows vessel as built
Similar (unlengthened): **DANA MINERVA** (Ge) ex-*Tor Caledonia*

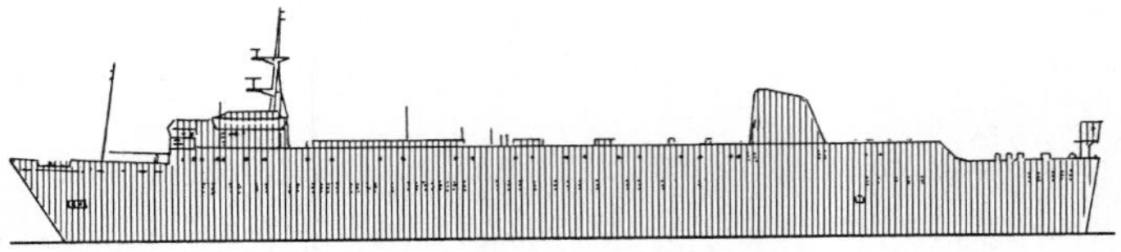

91 *M^{2}GY H2*
PAULIS Rm/Rm (Galatz) 1983; RoC; 8,110 grt/4,100 dwt; 128.39 × 6.56 m *(421.23 × 21.52 ft)*; TSM (MAN); 20 kts; 200 TEU; Stern door
Sisters: **PALTINIS** (Rm); **PASCANI** (Rm); **PERIS** (Rm)

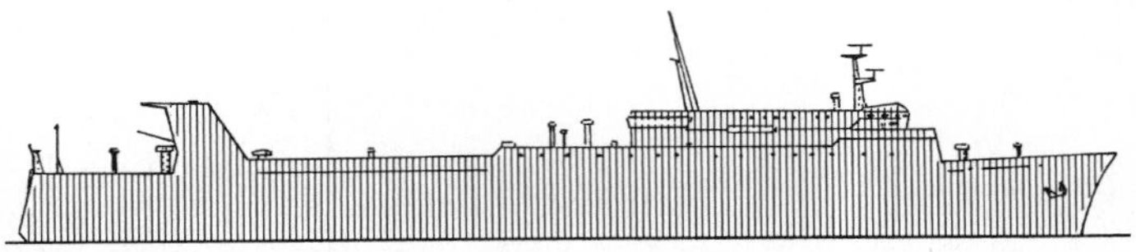

92 *M^{2}GY H2*
PEVERIL Br/No (Kristiansands) 1971; RoC; 5,254 grt/1,685 dwt; 106.28 × 4.97 m *(348.69 × 16.31 ft)*; TSM (Pielstick); 14 kts; ex-*Holmia*; Bow door/ramp; Stern door/ramp
Similar (larger): **GUNILLA** (Fi); **TRANSESTONIA** (Ea) ex-*Arona*; **PUCK** (SV) ex-*Grano*; **DONATA** (Pa) ex-*Silvia*; **DERNA** (Ly); **GHAT** (Ly)

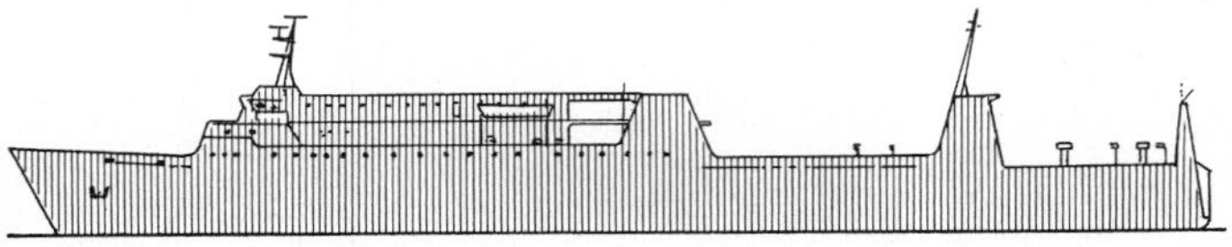

93 *M^{2}GY H2*
SUBIC ADVENTURE Pa/No (Trosvik) 1971; RoC/TF; 6,665 grt/3,120 dwt; 124.67 × 4.95 m *(409 × 16.24 ft)*; TSM (Wichmann); 13 kts; ex-*Stubbenkammer*; Bow door and ramp; Stern door/ramp; lengthened 1984 (Fosen). Drawing shows vessel before this; Superstructure now longer. Mast between funnels now moved to after-end of superstructure

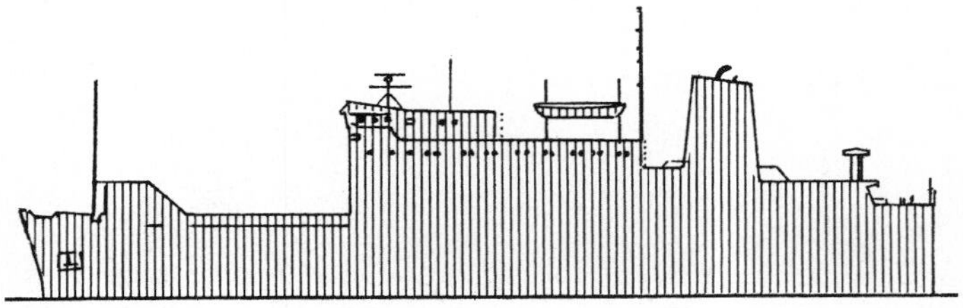

94 *M^{2}GY H2*
SV DUJE SV/Ne (Amels) 1981; RoC; 4,476 grt/2,022 dwt; 79.43 × 4.4 m *(261 × 14.44 ft)*; TSM (KHD); 14.5 kts; ex-*Duke of Holland II*; Stern door/ramp

95 *M^{2}GY H2*
TOR DANIA DIS/Fr (Dunkerque-Normandie) 1978; RoC; 19,412 grt/— dwt; 169.25 × 7.74 m *(555.2 × 25.3 ft)*; M (CCM); 16.5 kts; ex-*Ville De Dunkerque*; Stern door/ramp; Side doors; lengthened 1995
Sisters: **TOR BRITANNIA** (Sw) ex-*Ville du Havre* (probably lengthened); **SEABOARD EXPRESS** (Pa) ex-*Ro-Ro Manhattan*; **SEABOARD INTREPID** (Pa) ex-*Ro-Ro Genova*

96 *M^{2}GY H2*
TOR GOTHIA Sw/No (Framnaes) 1971/77; RoC; 12,259 grt/9,928 dwt; 163.48 × 7.10 m *(536.35 × 23.29 ft)*; TSM (Pielstick); 18.5 kts; Stern door/ramp; 458 TEU; Lengthened 1977

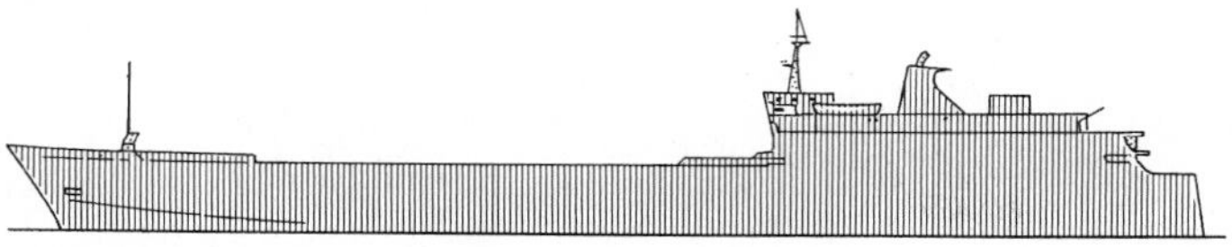

97 *M^{2}GZ H2*
SREDETZ Bu/It (Cassaro) 1975; RoC/P; 3,263 grt/4,937 dwt; 141.71 × 5.82 m *(464.93 × 19.09 ft)*; TSM (Werkspoor); 14.5 kts; ex-*Laura Russotti*; two stern door/ramps (one port, one starboard)

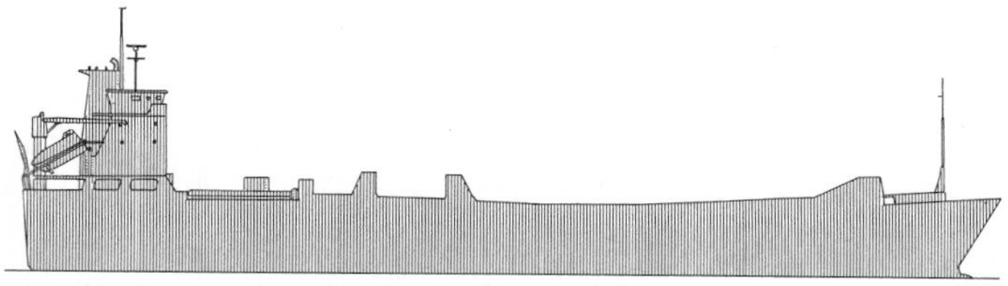

98 *M^{3}FLRY H*
BORE SEA Fi/FRG (Sietas) 1990; RoC/Pap; 5,873 grt/4,234 dwt; 108.35 × 5.80 m *(355.48 × 19.03 ft)*; M (Wärtsilä); 15.3 kts; Stern door/ramp; 120 TEU; Funnel is on port side; Side door on starboard side
Sister: **MIMER** (Fi) ex-*Bore Star*

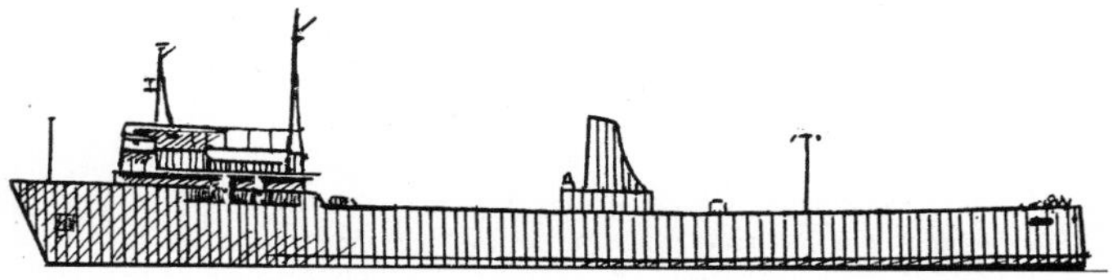

99 *M^{3}FMY H*
AGIOS RAFAEL Gr/FRG (Sietas) 1968; RoC/F; 1,804 grt/2,267 dwt; 95 × — m *(312 × — ft)*; TSM (KHD); 16 kts; ex-*Golfo Paradiso*; Stern door; Now has extended superstructure and raised deck abaft funnel—not on drawing

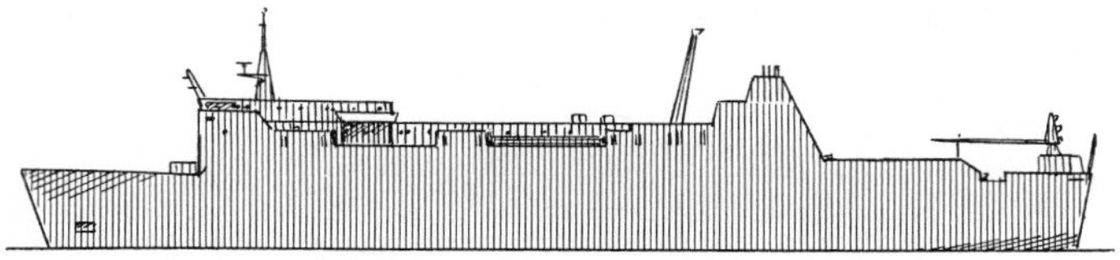

100 *M^{3}GDY H2*
LAN QIAO RC/Fr (Dubigeon-Normandie) 1978; RoC; 4,156 grt/3,884 dwt; 120.33 × 5.9 m *(394.78 × 19.36 ft)*; TSM (Atlas-MaK); 16 kts; ex-*Le Mans*; Stern door/ramp; Side doors

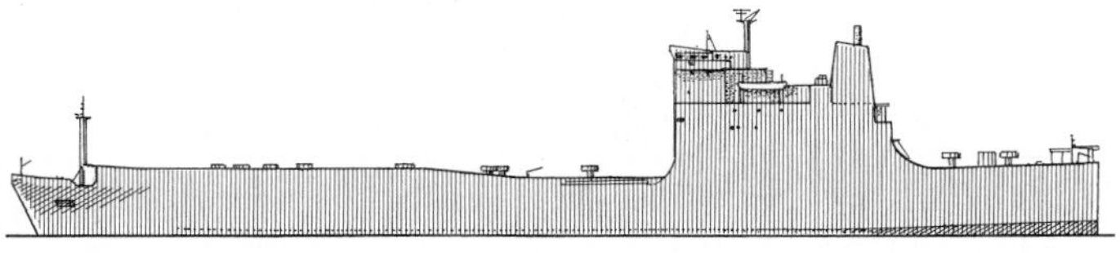

101 *M^{3}GY H2*
TOR DANIA DIS/Fr (Dunkerque-Normandie) 1978; RoC; 19,412 grt/10,800 dwt; 169.25 × 7.74 m *(555.2 × 25.3 ft)*; TSM (Sulzer); 16.5 kts; ex-*Ville De Dunkerque*; Stern door/ramp; Side door ramp (starboard); 693 TEU
Sister: **TOR BRITANNIA** (Sw) ex-*Ville Du Havre*; Similar: **SEABOARD EXPRESS** (Pa) ex-*Ro-Ro Manhattan*; **SEABOARD INTREPID** (Pa) ex-*Ro-Ro Genova*

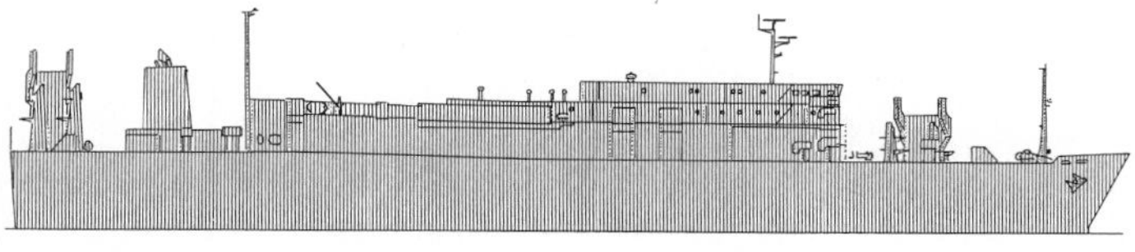

102 *MMM^{2}FA H2*
SHINKA MARU Ja/Ja (Hakodate) 1990; RoC/Pap; 6,163 grt/5,720 dwt; 139.72 × 6.92 m *(458.40 × 22.70 ft)*; M (Pielstick); 17.75 kts; Angled door/ramp (port foreward); Quarter door/ramp (port)

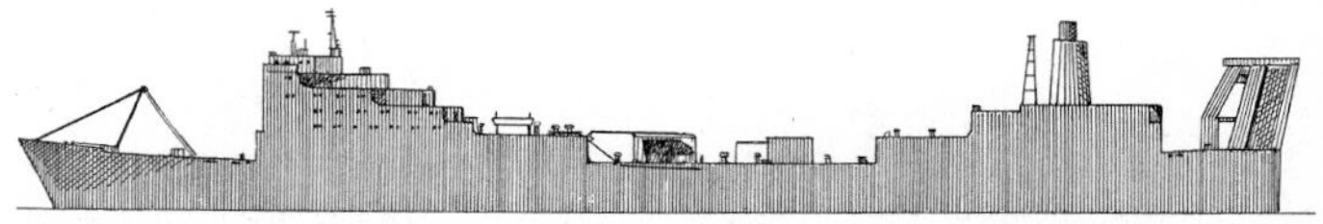

103 *M^{4}FA H2*
UNION ROTORUA NZ/Au (Whyalla) 1976; RoC; 22,228 grt/20,270 dwt; 203.21 × 9.53 m *(666.6 × 31.2 ft)*; TS D-E (Wärtsilä); — kts; Bow door/ramp; Angled stern door and ramp; 646 TEU
Sister: **UNION ROTOITI** (NZ)

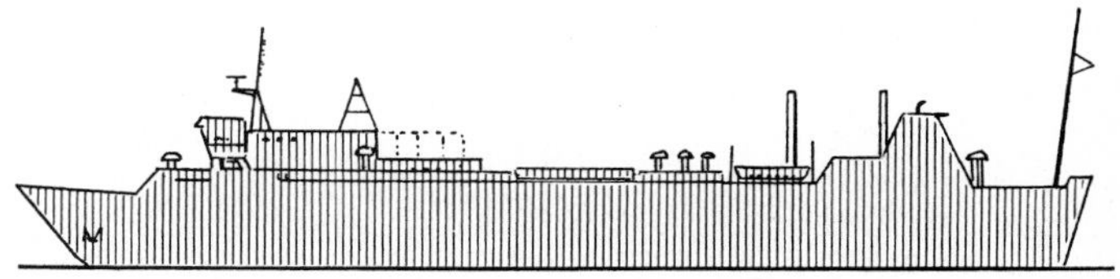

104 *M^{4}GMY H2*
LOULAN Pa/No (Trosvik) 1978; RoC; 1,321 grt/2,435 dwt; 96.22 × 5.51 m *(315.68 × 18.08 ft)*; TSM (Hedemora); 14.5 kts; ex-*Ramses Carrier*; Stern door/ramp; 150 TEU
Sisters: **SV JOSIP** (SV) ex-*Ramses Trailer* (builder—Porsgrunn); **FENG TIAN** (Pa) ex-*Ramses Freighter*

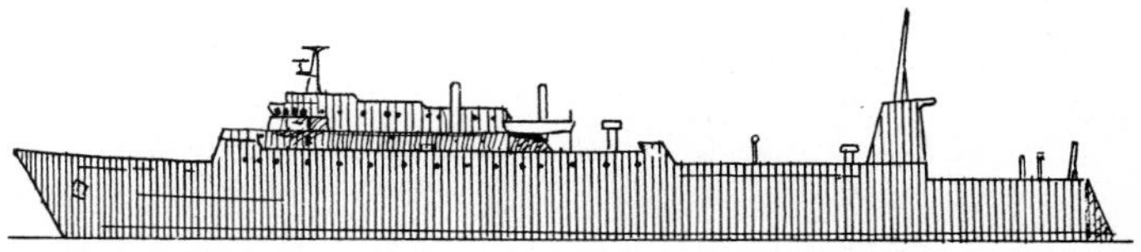

105 *M^{3}M–GY H2*
FJARDVAGEN Fi/No (Kristiansands) 1970; RoC/P; 4,979 grt/1,157 dwt; 105.9 × 4.95 m *(347.44 × 16.24 ft)*; TSM (Normo); 16 kts; ex-*Stena Carrier*; Bow, stern and side doors
Sister: **LAMPUNG** (Ia) ex-*Stena Trailer*; Similar: **CTMA VOYAGEUR** (Ca) ex-*Anderida*

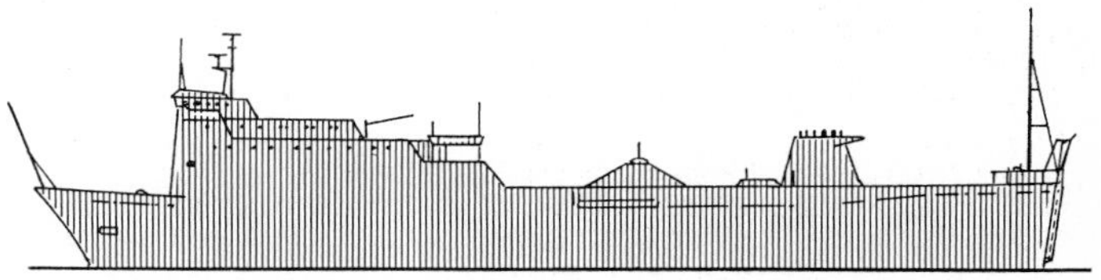

106 *M^{3}RNFMY H2*
SAGA MOON Li/FRG (Schlichting) 1984; RoC/P; 7,746 grt/2,900 dwt; 116.62 × 5.22 m *(382.61 × 17.13 ft)*; M (Krupp-MaK); 17.5 kts; ex-*Lidartindur*; Side door/ramp (starboard); Stern door/ramp; Now lengthened to 134.50m (441.27m); Drawing shows vessel as built

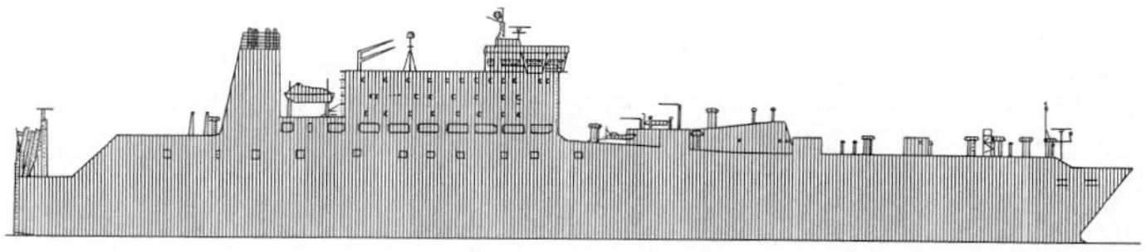

107 *M^{3}SGY H2*
FINNHANSA Fi/Pd (Gdanska) 1994; RoC/P; 32,531 grt/11,600 dwt; 183.00 × 7.40 m *(600.39 × 24.28 ft)*; M (Sulzer); 18 kts; Stern door/ramp; 423 TEU; 'B501' type
Sisters: **FINNPARTNER** (Fi); **FINNTRADER** (Fi); **TRANSEUROPA** (Ge)

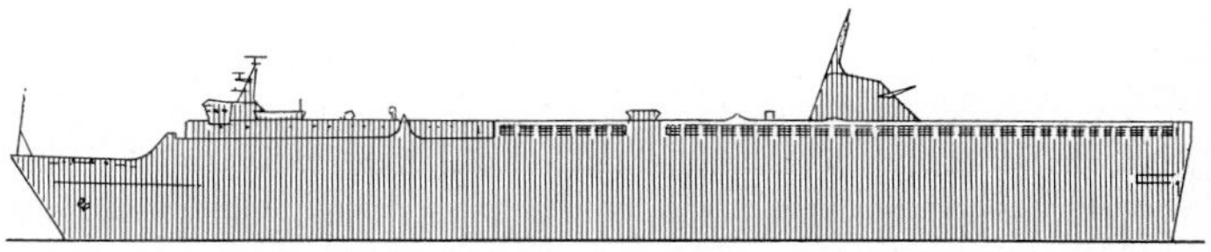

108 *M^{2}M–F H2*
PO Ma/It (Apuania) 1974/83; RoC; 15,095 grt/4,960 dwt; 159.85 × 6.2 m *(524.44 × 20.34 ft)*; TSM (Fiat); 18.5 kts; Stern door/ramp; Five side doors/ramps; Lengthened 1983 by 24.5m (80.40ft)
Similar (also lengthened): **DORA BALTEA** (Ma)
Similar (unlengthened): **DORA RIPARIA** (Ma)

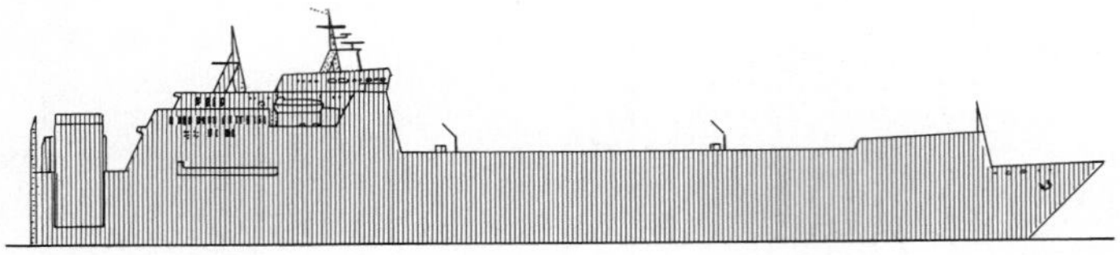

109 M^2M–*FSAZ H2*
UND SAFFET BAY Tu/De (Danyard) 1987; RoC; 19,689 grt/14,107 dwt; 163.81 × 8.82 m *(537.46 × 28.94 ft)*; M (MaK); 17.5 kts; ex-*Mercandian Pacific*; Side door/ramp (port aft); Two stern door ramps (one port/one starboard); 'FV2800' type
Sisters: **UND PRENSES** (Tu) ex-*Mercandian Nautic*; **TJOET NYA DHIEN** (Sg) ex-*Rosa Dan*

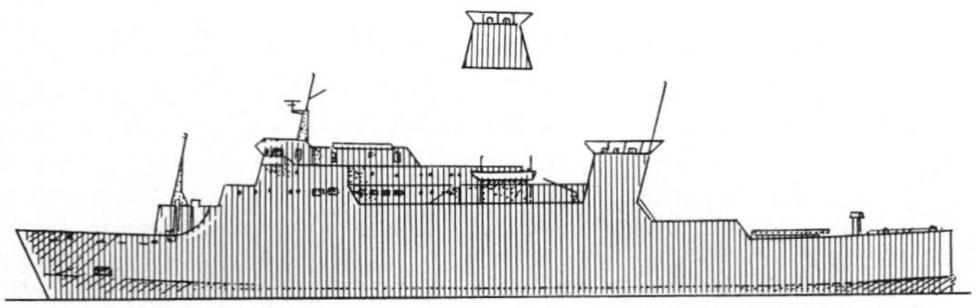

110 M^2M–*G H2*
EUROPEAN CLEARWAY Br/FRG (Schichau-U) 1976; RoC; 8,023 grt/3,927 dwt; 118.32 × 5.82 m *(388.2 × 19.09 ft)*; TSM (Stork-Werkspoor); 18.5 kts; Bow door/ramp and stern door/ramp
Sister: **EUROPEAN TRADER** (Br); Similar (funnel shape differs—see inset): **EUROPEAN ENDEAVOUR** (Br)

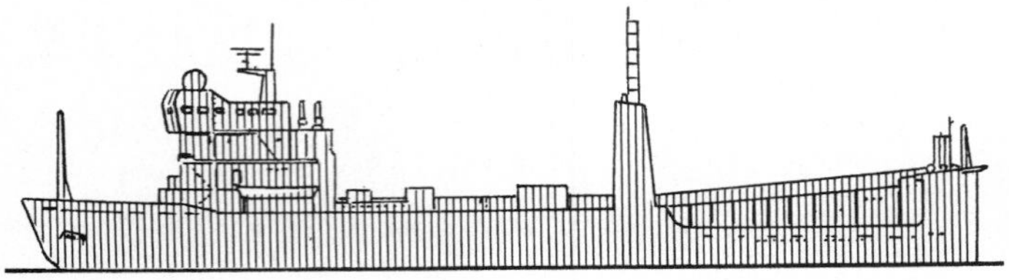

111 M^2M–*GY H13*
SIGYN Sw/Fr (Havre) 1982; RoC; 4,166 grt/2,044 dwt; 90.02 × 3.99 m *(295 × 13.09 ft)*; TSM (B&W); 11 kts; Stern door; Bow thrusters; Irradiated nuclear fuel carrier

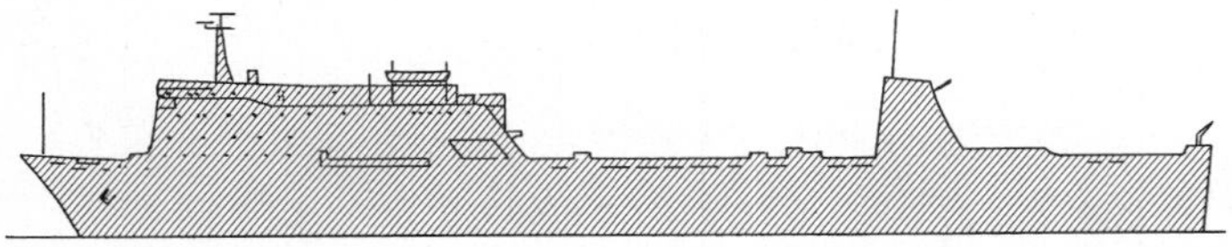

112 M^2M–*GY H2*
ASK De/It (Apuania) 1981/82; RoC/F; 11,160 grt/6,235 dwt; 150.81 × 5.67 m *(388.52 × 18.60 ft)*; TSM (Wärtsilä); 18.5 kts; ex-*Lucky Rider*; Stern door/ramp
Sister: **URD** (De) ex-*Easy Rider*

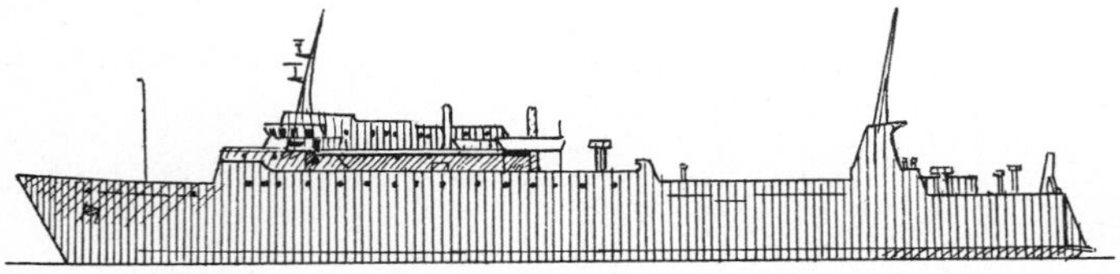

113 M^2M–*GY H2*
CTMA VOYAGEUR Ca/No (Trosvik) 1971; RoC; 1,578 grt/2,500 dwt; 106 × 4.94 m *(347.76 × 16.2 ft)*; TSM (Normo); 16 kts; ex-*Anderida*; Bow door and ramp; Stern door/ramp; Side doors; 30 TEU

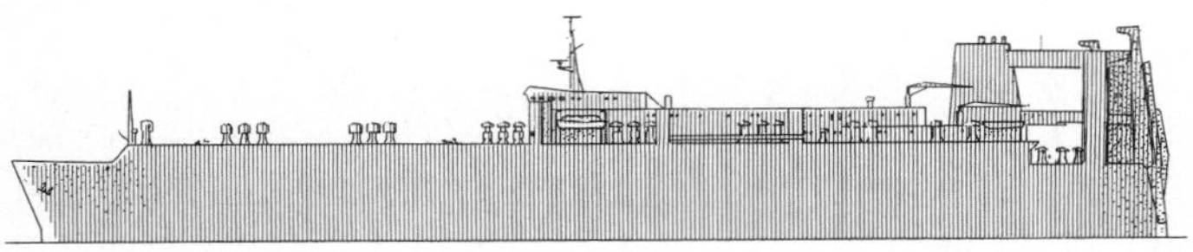

114 M^2RF–*A H2*
SKAUGRAN NIS/No (Fredriksstad) 1979; RoC; 41,905 grt/42,424 dwt; 182.5 × 11.99 m *(598.75 × 39.34 ft)*; M (B&W); 14.8 kts; Stern quarter ramp/door (starboard); 895 TEU; Funnel is on starboard side
Sister: **SKAUBRYN** (NIS) ex-*Skeena*

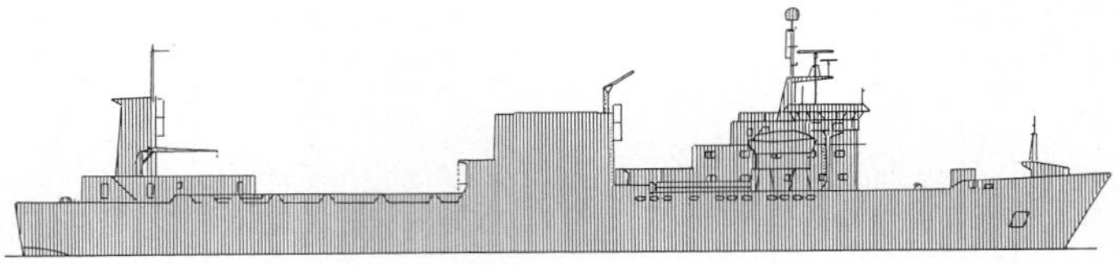

115 M^2RM–*F*–*R H*
NORNEWS SUPPLIER No/FRG (Suerken) 1990; Pal; 5,603 grt/4,944 dwt; 115.86 × 4.28 m *(380.12 × 14.04 ft)*; M (Normo); 15 kts; ex-*Gold River*; Side door (starboard)
Similar: **NORNEWS LEADER** (No); **TRANS DANIA** (NIS); **NORNEWS EXPRESS** (No)

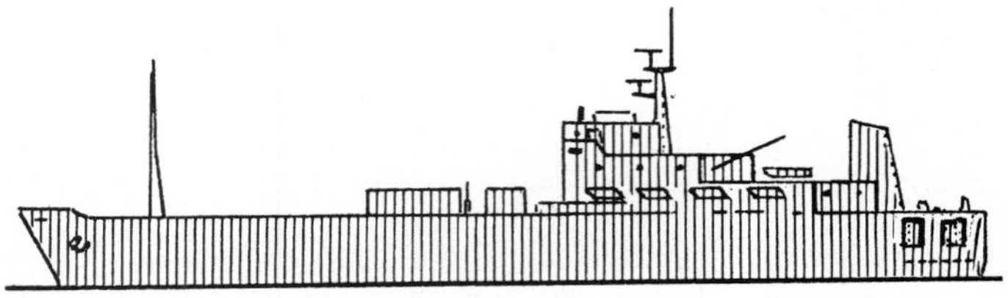

116 M^2SGY *H*
ISIS Ma/Sp (Construcciones SA) 1981; RoC/R; 1,570 grt/1,928 dwt; 74.71 × 4.57 m *(245.11 × 14.99 ft)*; M (Alpha); 12 kts; ex-*El Sexto*; Side door; Stern door/ramp
Sister: **HURACAN** (Ma) ex-*El Quinto*
Possible sisters (builder—Huelva): **OLYMPIAN DUCHESS** (Bs) ex-*El Primero*; **RIVEIRA** (Sp) ex-*El Tercero*

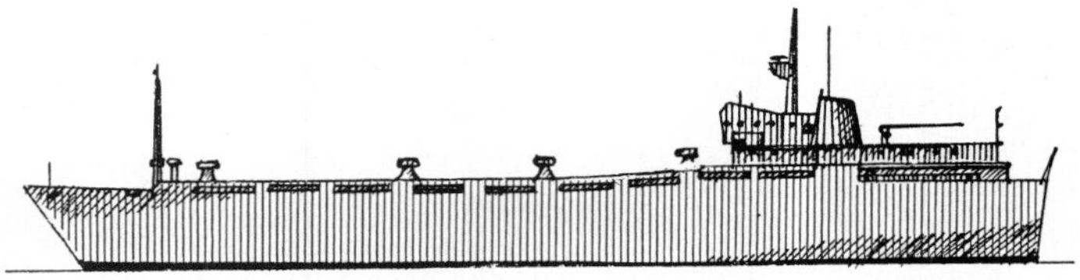

117 M^2SY *H2*
DIMITRIOS MIRAS Gr/Fr (Havre) 1972; RoC; 499 grt/861 dwt; 100.51 × 3.99 m *(329.76 × 13.09 ft)*; TSM (MAN); 14.55 kts; ex-*Monaco*; Stern door/ramp
Sister: **FEEDERMASTER** (Cy) ex-*Monza*

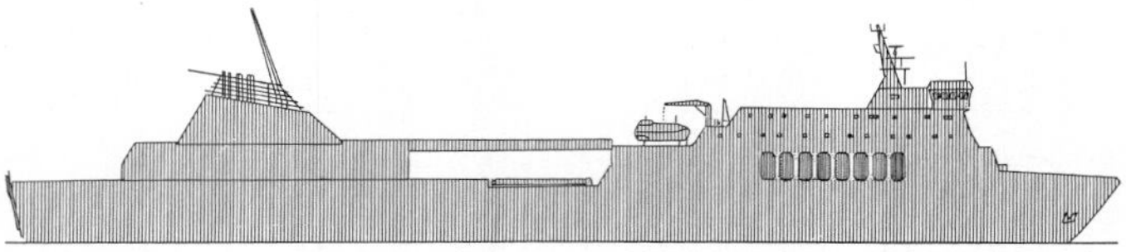

118 M^2–*F H*
VIA ADRIATICO It/Ne (Frisian) 1992; RoC/P; 14,398 grt/6,200 dwt; 150.43 × 5.60 m *(493.54 × 18.37 ft)*; TSM (Sulzer); 19 kts; Stern door/ramp
Sisters: **VIA TIRRENO** (It); **ESPRESSO RAVENNA** (It)
Probable sister (It built—FCNI): **ESPRESSO CATANIA** (It) ex-*Via Mediterraneo*

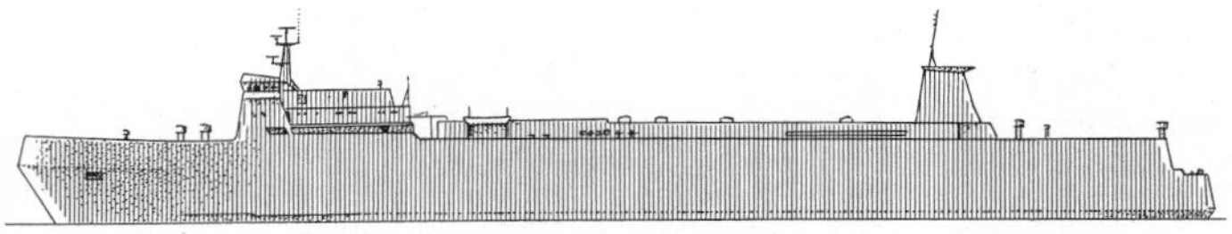

119 *MM*–*F H1*
RAILSHIP 1 Fi/FRG (Rickmers) 1975/80; RoC/TF; 17,864 grt/8,970 dwt; 177.22 × 6.32 m *(581.43 × 20.73 ft)*; TSM (Atlas-MaK); 20.5 kts; Stern door; Lengthened 1979 (A G 'Weser')

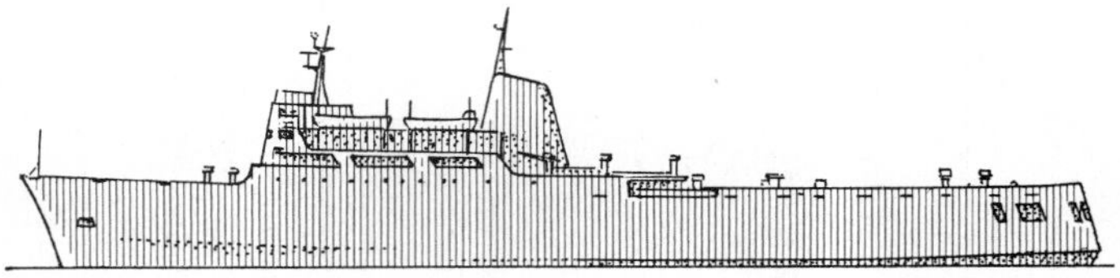

120 *MM*–*F H2*
DUCHESS M Cy/HK (Taikoo) 1970; RoC; 2,786 grt/2,601 dwt; 112.5 × 4.44 m *(369.1 × 14.57 ft)*; TSM (Pielstick); 17.5 kts; ex-*Wanaka*; Stern door/ramp

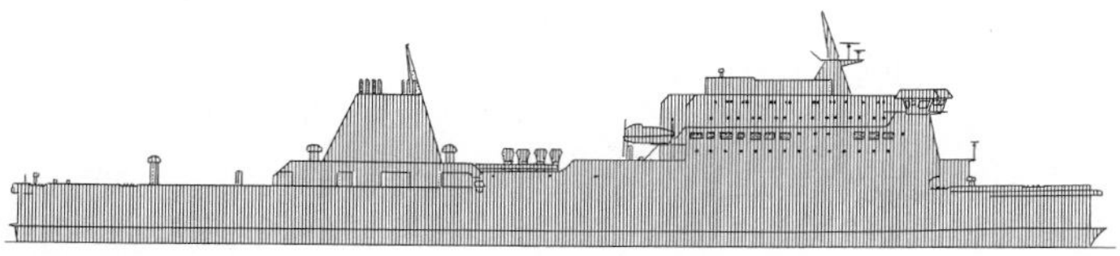

121 *MM–F H2*
EUROPEAN SEAWAY Br/Ge (Schichau See) 1991; RoC/P; 22,986 grt/6,584 dwt; 179.70 × 6.25 m *(589.57 × 20.51 ft)*; TSM (Sulzer); 21 kts; Bow door; Stern door
Sisters: **EUROPEAN HIGHWAY** (Br); **EUROPEAN PATHWAY** (Br)

122 *MM–F H2*
O'SHEA EXPRESS Le/Br (Robb Caledon) 1970; RoVC; 398 grt/1,054 dwt; 91.5 × 3.93 m *(300.2 × 12.89 ft)*; M (MaK); — kts; ex-*Speedway*; Side loading

123 *MM–FAY H23*
SPIRIT OF FREEDOM NZ/De (Frederikshavn) 1979; RoC; 4,925 grt/3,297 dwt; 105.62 × 4.97 m *(346.52 × 16.31 ft)*; M (MaK); 15 kts; ex-*Mercandian Exporter II*; Side door/ramp (starboard-aft); Stern door/ramp; 200 TEU. **SIMILAR TO DRAWING NUMBER 18/136**
Sisters: **MARC SPYROS** (Gr) ex-*Mercandian Trader II*; **OMO WONZ** (Et) ex-*Mercandian Merchant II*; **CIDADE DE FUNCHAL** (Po) ex-*Mercandian Supplier II*

124 *MM–FMY H2*
BORDEN Fi/No (Frederiksstad) 1977; RoC; 10,100 grt/6,615 dwt; 142.22 × 7 m *(466.6 × 22.97 ft)*; TSM (MWM); 17 kts; ex-*Bore Sky*; Stern door/ramp; 420 TEU
Sisters: **GARDEN** (Fi) ex-*Bore Sun*; **NORCOVE** (Sw) ex-*Rolita*

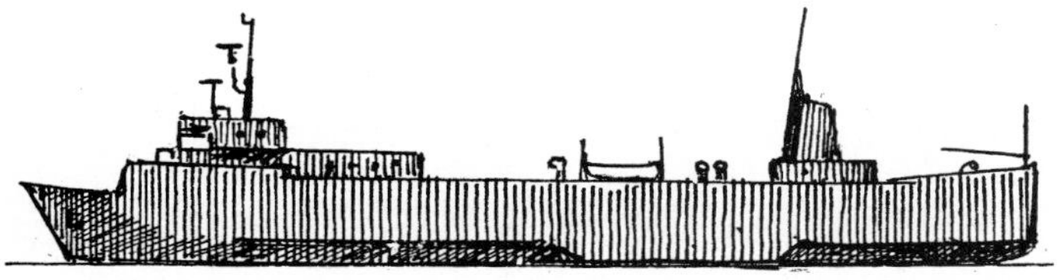

125 *MM–FN H2*
AUTOBAHN NIS/No (Batservice) 1972; RoVC; 3,559 grt/864 dwt; 92.46 × 3.88 m *(303.35 × 12.73 ft)*; TSM (Normo); 14 kts; Stern door/ramp

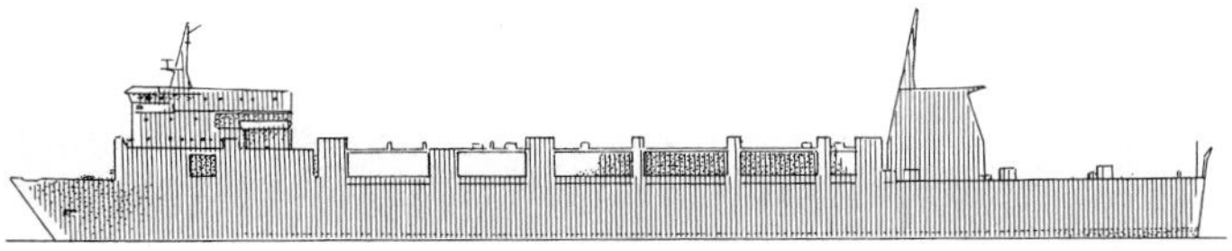

126 *MM–FY H*
AMBASSADOR US/FRG (Meyer) 1980; RoC; 13,412 grt/8,995 dwt; 168.8 × 6.45 m *(553.8 × 21.16 ft)*; M (Stork-Werkspoor); 17 kts; Stern door/ramp; 400 TEU
Sister (extra housing above the bridge, adjoining foremast): **SENATOR** (US) ex-*Diplomat*

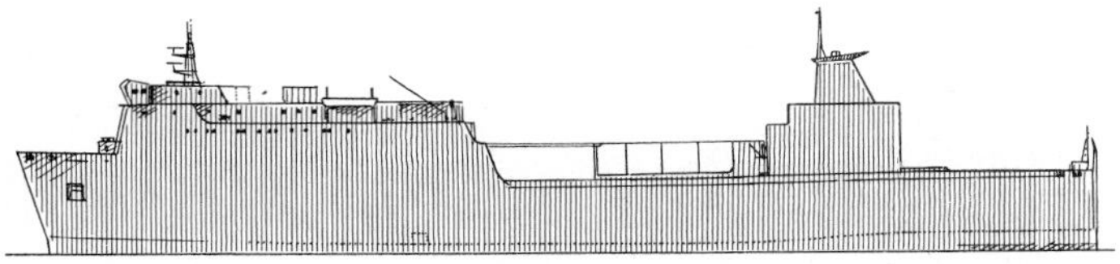

127 *MM–FY H1*
NORSKY Br/Ja (Mitsui) 1979; RoC; 14,077 grt/5,024 dwt; 150 × 5.12 m *(492 × 16.8 ft)*; TSM (Mitsui); 19 kts; ex-*Ibex*; Stern door/ramp; 240 TEU
Sister: **NORCAPE** (Ne) ex-*Puma*

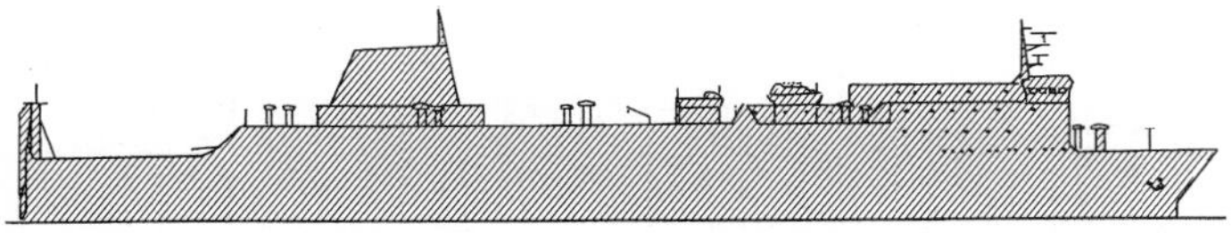

128 *MM–FY H2*
JAN SNIADECKI Cy/Sw (Gotav) 1988; RoC/P/TF; 14,417 grt/5,583 dwt; 155.19 × 5.10 m *(509.15 × 16.73 ft)*; TSM (Sulzer); 16 kts; Side door (starboard); Stern door

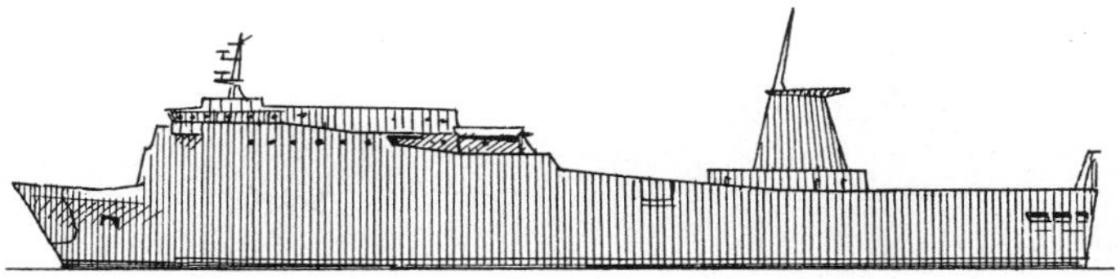

129 *MM–FY H2*
LORETO Me/As (Osterreichische) 1977; RoC; 6,461 grt/3,537 dwt; 114.38 × 5.7 m *(375.26 × 18.7 ft)*; TSM (KHD); 18 kts; ex-*Stena Timer*; Stern door/ramp; 110 TEU

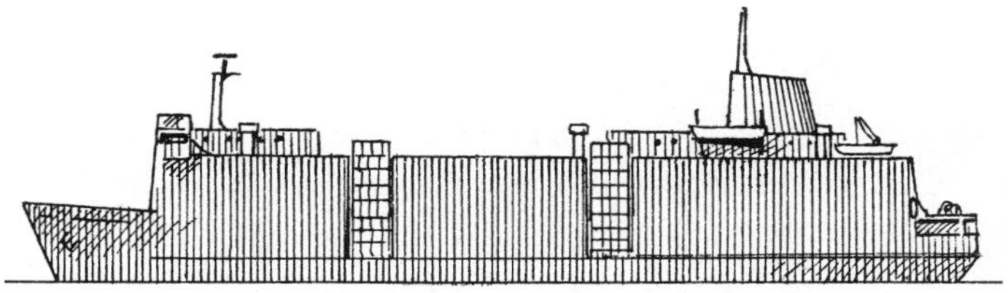

130 *MM–FY H2*
NEPTUNE SKY Gr/Br (Grangemouth) 1967; RoC; 3,462 grt/926 dwt; 88.55 × 4.34 m *(290.52 × 14.24 ft)*; M (Mirrlees); 14 kts; ex-*Carway*

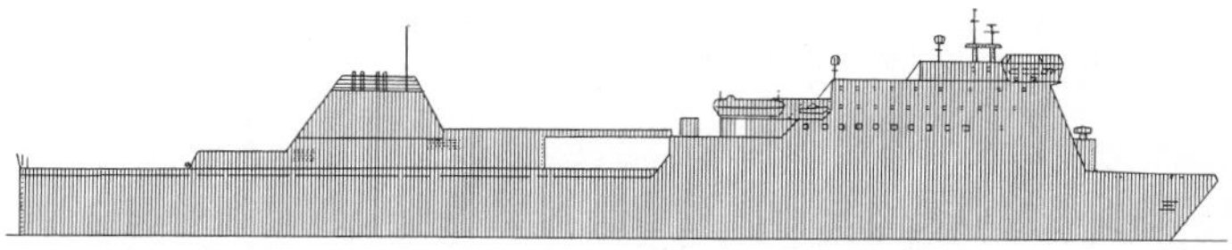

131 *MM–FY H2*
NORBANK Ne/Ne (Giessen-De Noord) 1993; RoC/P; 17,464 grt/6,791 dwt; 166.77 × 6.02 m *(547.15 × 19.75 ft)*; TSM (Sulzer); 23 kts; Stern door/ramp
Sister: **NORBAY** (Br)

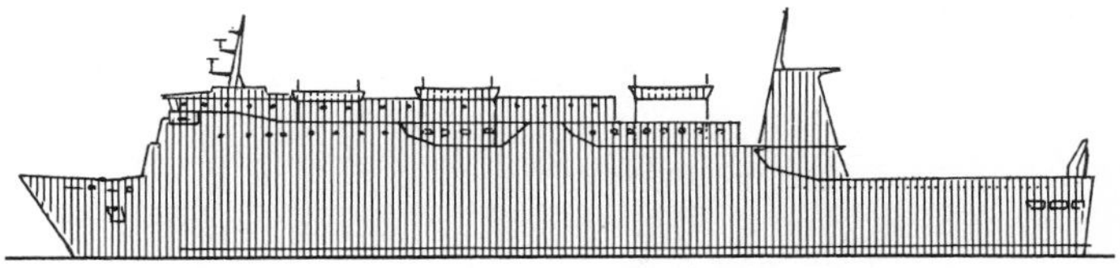

132 *MM–FY H2*
NORD NEPTUNUS Sw/As (Osterreichische) 1977/82; RoC/P; 8,457 grt/1,791 dwt; 114.02 × 5.76 m *(374.08 × 18.90 ft)*; TSM (KHD); 18 kts; ex-*Darnia*; Launched as *Stena Topper*; Bow door/ramp; Stern door/ramp; Rebuilt 1982

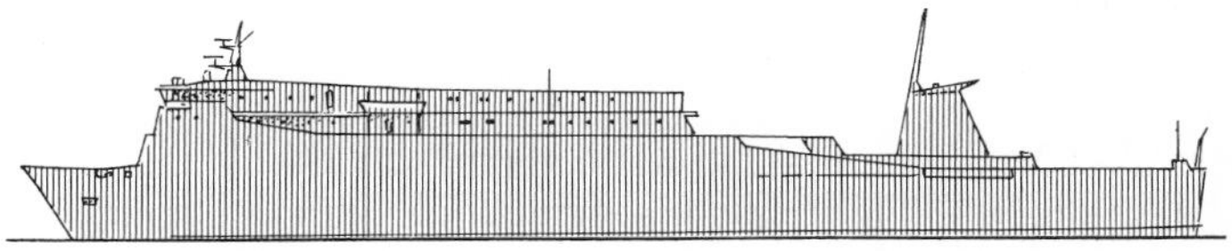

133 *MM–FY H2*
PUMA Br/FRG (Sietas) 1975; P/RoC; 10,957 grt/4,035 dwt; 141.81 × 5.81 m *(465.26 × 19.06 ft)*; TSM (KHD); 18 kts; ex-*Union Melbourne*; Lengthened 1975; Stern door/ramp; 200 TEU
Similar: **BUFFALO** (Br)
Similar (extra cargo deck added over weather deck. It extends from existing superstructure to stern): **BISON** (Br)

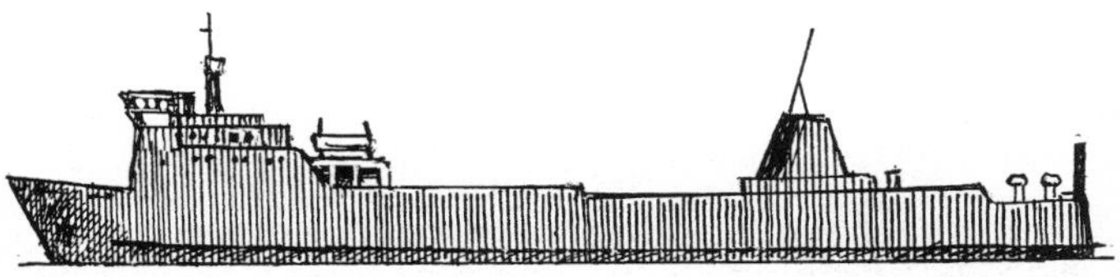

134 *MM–FY H2*
SALLY EUROBRIDGE Bs/FRG (Rickmers) 1977; RoC; 6,041 grt/3,046 dwt; 116.01 × 5.38 m *(380.61 × 17.65 ft)*; TSM (MaK); 15 kts; ex-*Mashala*; Side doors (one port, one starboard); Stern door/ramp; 140 TEU
Sisters: **MERCHANT VALIANT** (Bs) ex-*Salahala*; **MERCHANT VICTOR** (Bs) ex-*Emadala*

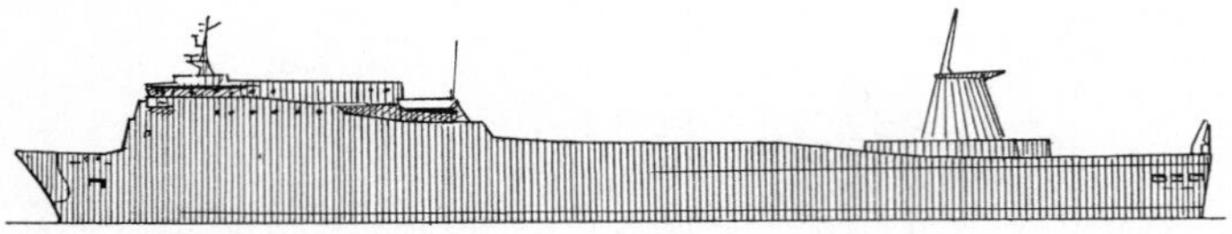

135 *MM–FY H2*
VIKING TRADER Br/As (Osterreichische) 1977; P/RoC; 9,085 grt/3,775 dwt; 144.07 × 5.7 m *(472.67 × 18.7 ft)*; TSM (KHD); 18 kts; ex-*Stena Tender*; Bow door and stern ramp; Completed in Romania and lengthened in West Germany 1977 (Nobiskrug); Now has some passenger accommodation. May have extension to superstructure

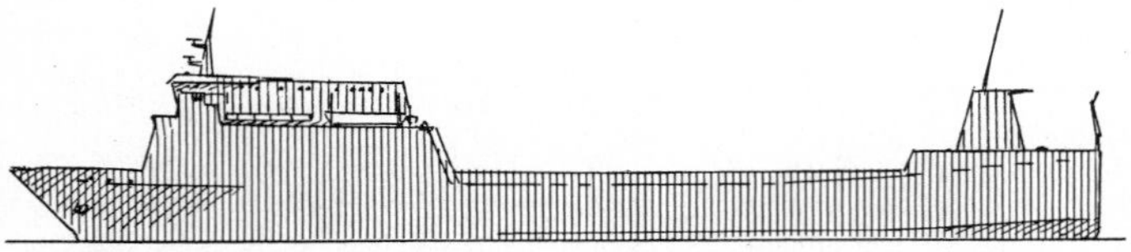

136 *MM–FY H23*
PINTO Ma/De (Frederikshavn) 1978; RoC; 1,599 grt/3,708 dwt; 105.62 × 4.97 m *(346.52 × 16.31 ft)*; M (MaK); 15 kts; ex-*Mercandian Transporter II*; Stern door; Side door (starboard); 'Merc Multiflex' type
Sister: **BELARD** (Br) ex-*Mercandian Carrier II*
Sisters (lengthened by 13.1m (43ft) by Howaldts DW): **CALA SALADA** (Sp) ex-*Dana Atlas*; **CALA FUSTAM** (Sp) ex-*Mercandian Importer II*

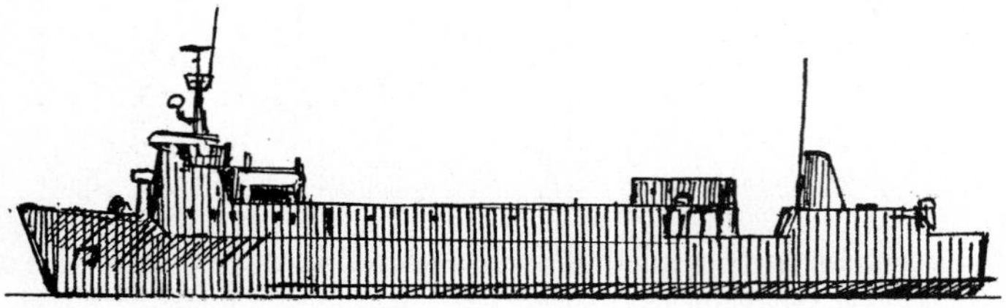

137 *MM–G H*
AL ZAHER II Ma/No (Hatlo) 1972; RoC; 3,194 grt/998 dwt; 91.04 × 4.42 m *(298.69 × 14.5 ft)*; TSM (Alpha-Diesel); 15.75 kts; ex-*Admiral Carrier 1*; Stern door
Sister: **LA GOLETA** (Ve) ex-*Admiral Carrier*

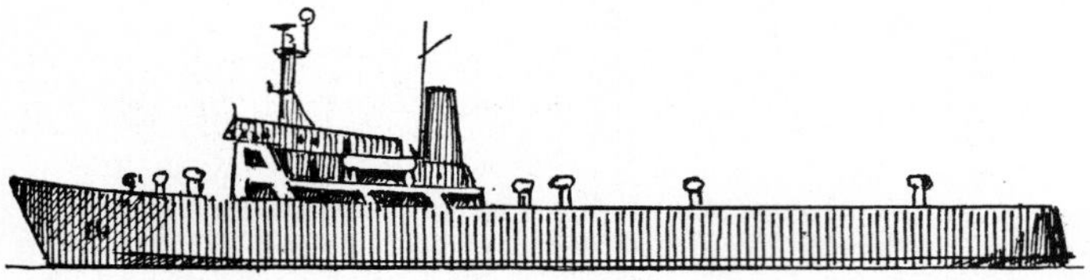

138 *MM–G H*
ALBA SV/FRG; (Kroegerw) 1970; RoC dwt; 915/1,225; 97 × 4.1 *(319 × 13.6)*; TSM (Atlas-MaK); 16; ex-*Neckartal*; Stern door
Similar: **CARIBE MERCHANT** (Br) ex-*Thule*; **PARSETA** (Pd) ex-*Donautal*; **ZEBBUG** (Ma) ex-*Antwerpen*

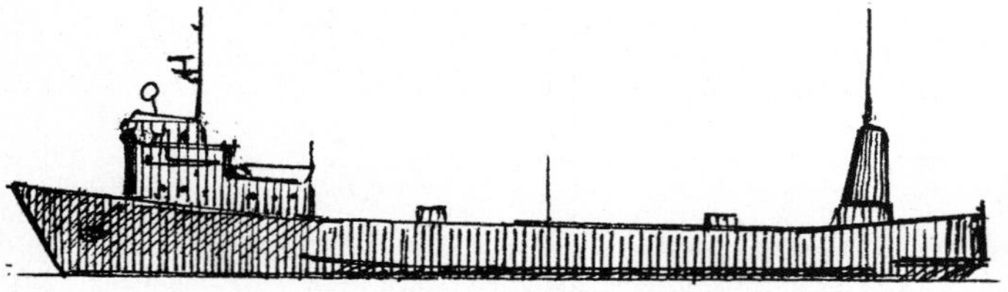

139 *MM–G H*
FAWZIAH Ho/No (Trondhjems) 1972; RoC; 369 grt/967 dwt; 91.9 × 3.16 m *(301.51 × 10.37 ft)*; TSM (Normo); 15 kts; ex-*Ostend Express*; Two stern door/ramps

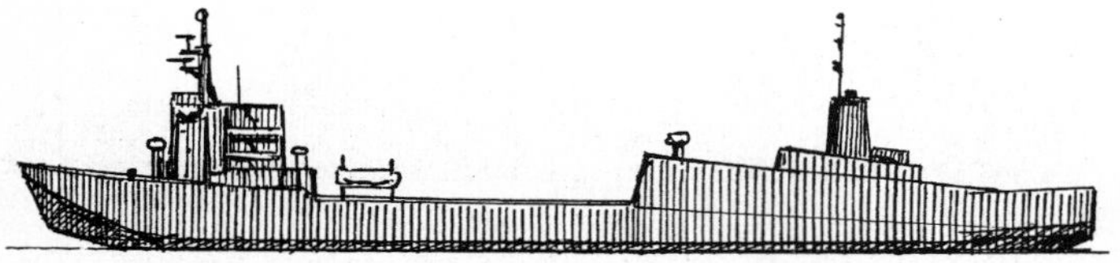

140 *MM–G H*
TUI CAKAU III Fj/Fi (Navire) 1975; RoC; 6,563 grt/4,580 dwt; 129.85 × 6.4 m *(458.83 × 21 ft)*; TSM (Normo); 12 kts; ex-*Bia*; Stern door/ramp; 303 TEU; 'KATATRAN' type; Semi-catamaran hull

141 *MM–G H1*
ATHENS EXPRESS Gr/Au (Evans Deakin) 1969; RoC; 11,003 grt/4,510 dwt; 136.68 × 6.42 m *(454.99 × 21.06 ft)*; TSM (MAN); 16 kts; ex-*Brisbane Trader*; Stern door/ramp

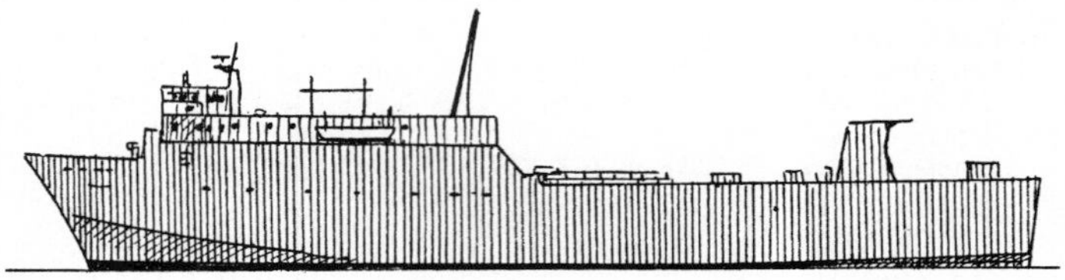

142 *MM–G H1*
ISLA DE LAS VOLCANES Sp/Fr (La Rochelle) 1977; RoC; 1,141 grt/1,600 dwt; 90.71 × 4.45 m *(297.60 × 14.60 ft)*; M (Pielstick); 13.5 kts; ex-*Luberon*; Stern door
Sisters: **L'AUDE** (Bs); **FES** (Mo) ex-*L'Ardeche*; **CAP BON** (Tn) ex-*Aurelia*; **ANTHENOR EXPRESS** (Ma) ex-*Anthenor*

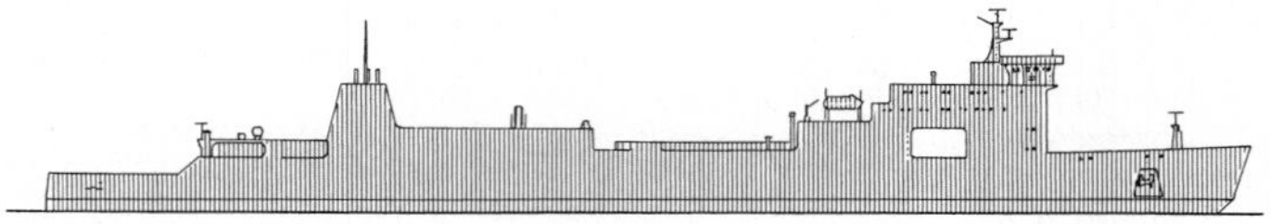

143 *MM–G H12*
ORESUND Sw/No (Moss R) 1986; RoC/TF; 16,925 grt/6,772 dwt; 186.02 × 5.64 m *(610.30 × 18.50 ft)*; TSM (MAN); 15 kts; Bow door

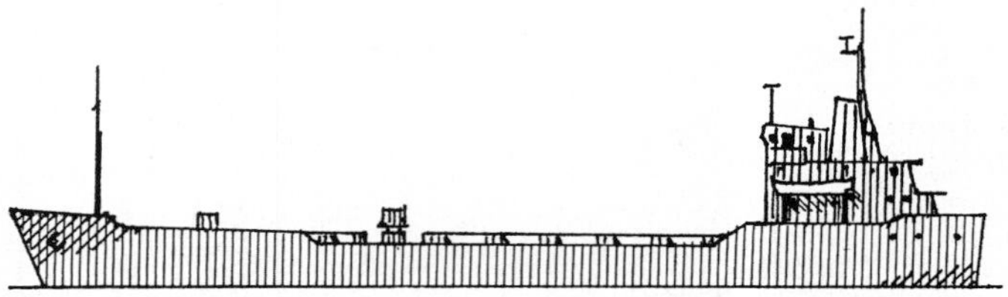

144 *MM–G H13*
IONIAN FAME Ma/Sp (Construcciones SA) 1971; RoC; 895 grt/1,881 dwt; 79.33 × 4.7 m *(260.27 × 15.42 ft)*; M (Stork-Werkspoor); 14 kts; ex-*Cometa*; Stern door/ramp; 95 TEU; 'Porter' type
Sister: **BENI SAF** (Ag) ex-*Arcade*

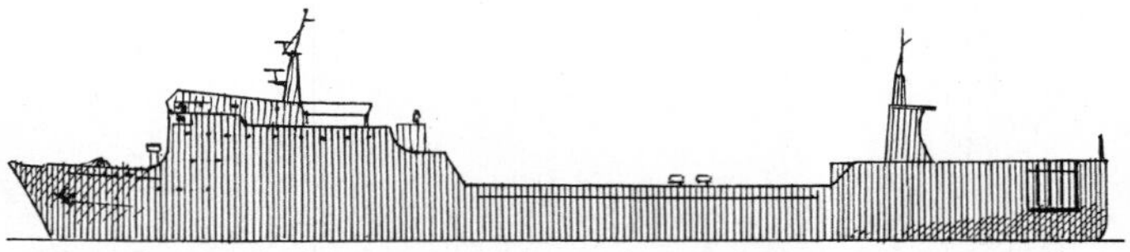

145 *MM–G H13*
ROLON NORTE Sp/Sp (Cadagua) 1977; RoC; 3,863 grt/3,264 dwt; 111.03 × 4.6 m *(364.27 × 15.09 ft)*; M (Sulzer); 14 kts; Two side doors (one port, one starboard); Stern door/ramp
Sister: **ROLON SUR** (Sp)

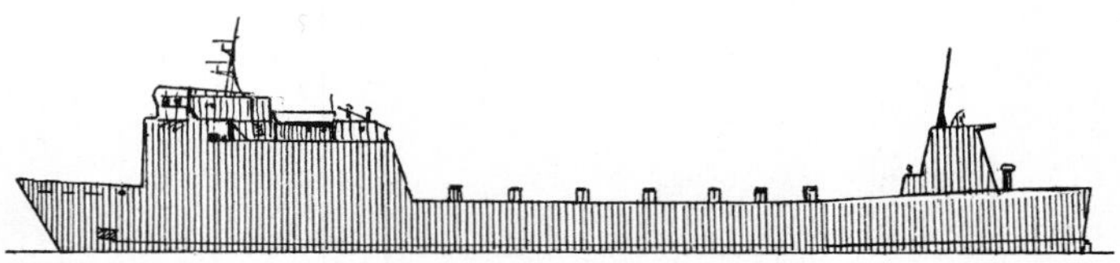

146 *MM–G H2*
AMADEO Ch/FRG (Schichau-U) 1977; RoC; 4,787 grt/2,358 dwt; 109.20 × 4.07 m *(358.27 × 13.35 ft)*; TSM (Polar); 15 kts; ex-*Miriam*; Stern door/ramp

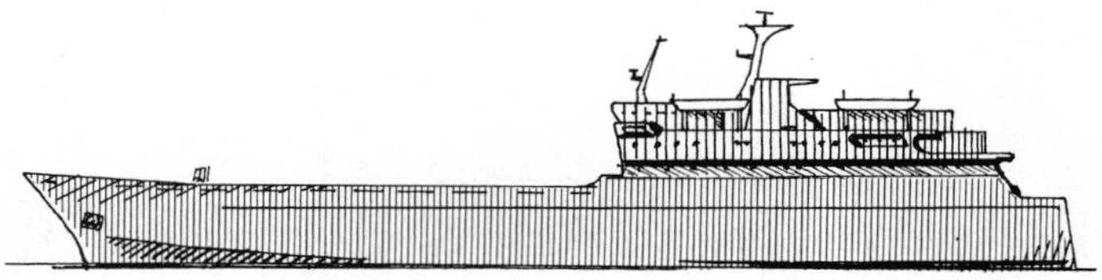

147 *MM–G H2*
MERNGUE EXPRESS Br/It (Cassaro) 1973; RoC/P; 7,818 grt/1,634 dwt; 115.12 × 5.97 m *(377.69 × 19.59 ft)*; TSM (Stork-Werkspoor); 14.5 kts; ex-*Monica Russoti*; two stern door/ramps; 124 TEU

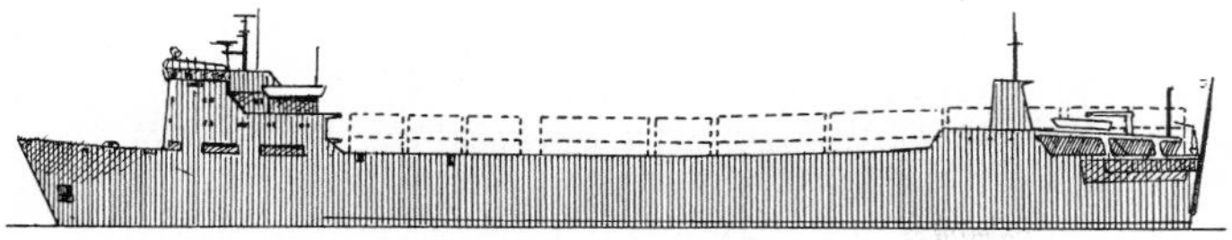

148 *MM–GRR–Y H*
BORE SONG Fi/Fi (Rauma-Repola) 1977; RoC; 8,188 grt/6,100 dwt; 128.91 × 6.3 m *(422.93 × 20.67 ft)*; M (Atlas-MaK); 17 kts; ex-*Abha*; Stern door/ramp; 367 TEU
Sister: **VILLARS** (Sd) ex-*Buraidah*

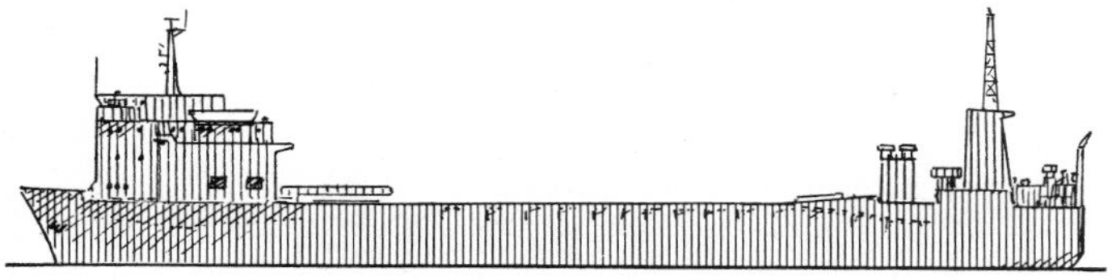

149 *MM–GY H*
IVA Cro/Ja (Teraoka) 1978; RoC; 3,287 grt/3,406 dwt; 93.81 × 3.52 m *(307.78 × 11.55 ft)*; TSM (Niigata); 14 kts; two stern door/ramps (port and starboard); 130 TEU
Sister: **ANI** (Cro)

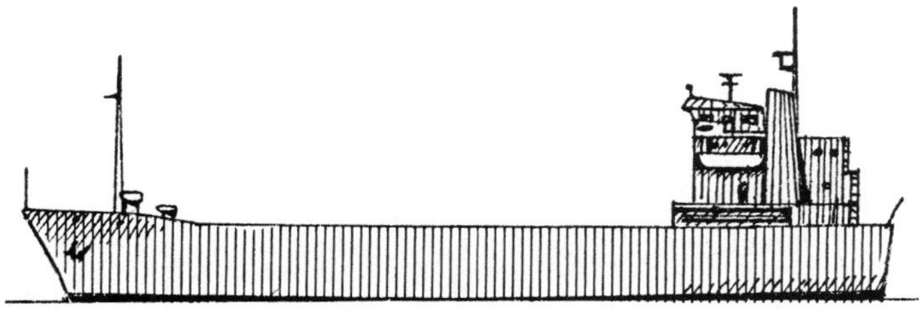

150 *MM–GY H*
YTONG 1 Bb/FRG (S&B) 1973; RoC/C/Con; 2,332 grt/1,580 dwt; 79.41 × 4.24 m *(260.53 × 13.91 ft)*; M (KHD); 12.5 kts; ex-*Henry Stahl*; Lengthened 1975; Stern door/ramp; 144 TEU

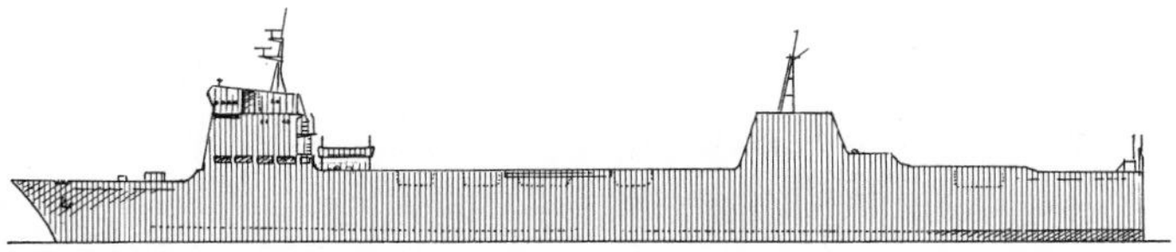

151 *MM–GY H2*
CICERO Ca/Br (Smith's D) 1978; RoC; 11,819 grt/6,985 dwt; 147.12 × 6.88 m *(482.68 × 22.57 ft)*; TSM (Pielstick); 18 kts; Stern door/ramp
Sister: **CABOT** (Ca) ex-*Cavallo*; Similar: **JACQUELINE** (Bz)

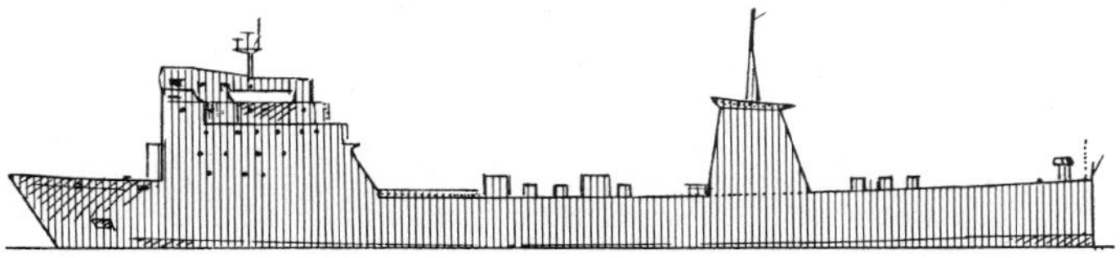

152 *MM–GY H2*
KAPTAN NECDET OR Tu/FRG (Schichau-U) 1977; RoC; 2,212 grt/2,742 dwt; 110.52 × 4.98 m *(362.6 × 16.34 ft)*; TSM (MAN-Sulzer); 17 kts; Bow door and ramp; stern door/ramp

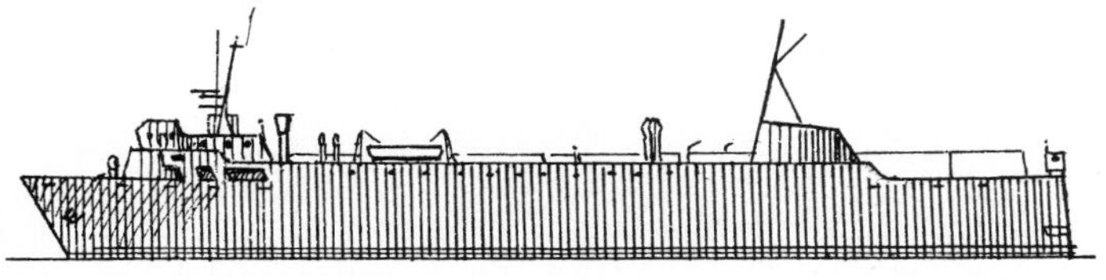

153 *MM–GY H2*
MAR CARIBE Br/FRG (O&K) 1967; RoC; 2,658 grt/3,165 dwt; 104 × 5.4 m *(342 × 18)*; M (Atlas-MaK); 18 kts; Stern door
Similar: **ST ROGNVALD** (Br) ex-*Rhonetal*

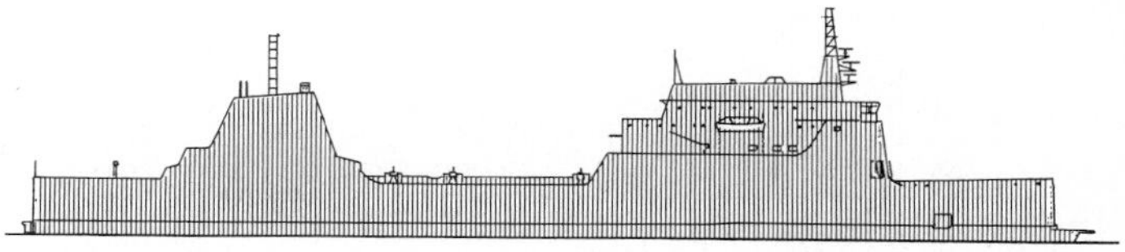

154 *MM–GY H2*
NORD PAS-DE-CALAIS Fr/Fr (NORMED) 1987; RoC/P/TF; 13,727 grt/4,284 dwt; 160.08 × 5.94 m *(525.20 × 19.49 ft)*; TSM (Sulzer); 21.5 kts; Bow door and ramp; Stern door/ramp

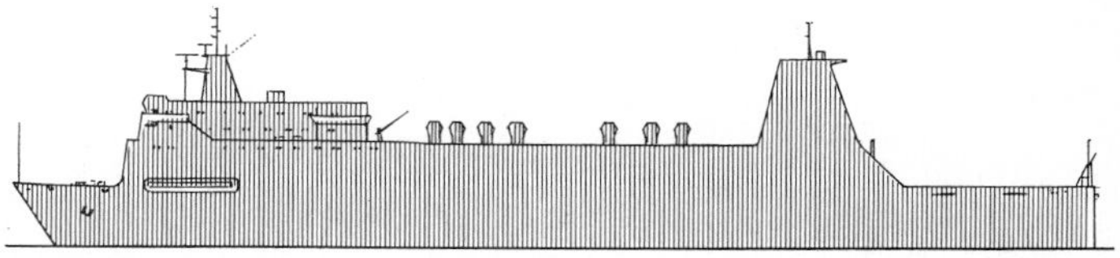

155 *MM–GY H2*
TRANSFINLANDIA Ge/FRG (Flender) 1981; RoC; 19,524 grt/11,645 dwt; 157.82 × 8.24 m *(518 × 27.03 ft)*; TSM (B&W); 19 kts; Stern door/ramp; 552 TEU

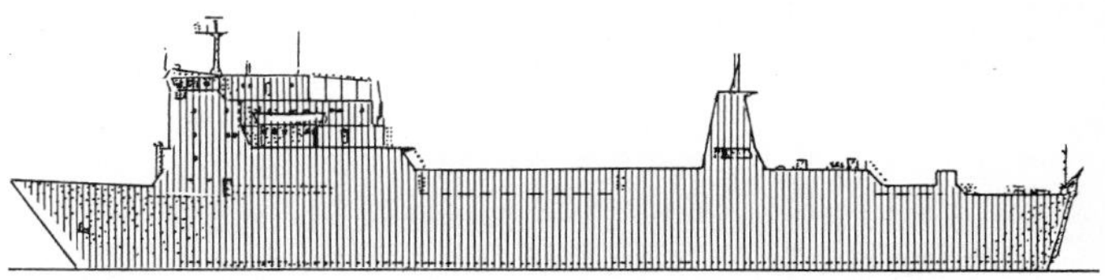

156 *MM–GY H2*
YUSUF ZIYA ONIS Tu/No (Ankerlokken) 1979; RoC; 2,399 grt/3,295 dwt; 113.4 × 5.51 m *(372 × 18.08 ft)*; M (Normo); 15.1 kts; ex-*Dr Adnan Biren*; Stern door/ramp
Sister: **ROLON ALCUDIA** (Sp) ex-*Transdeniz*

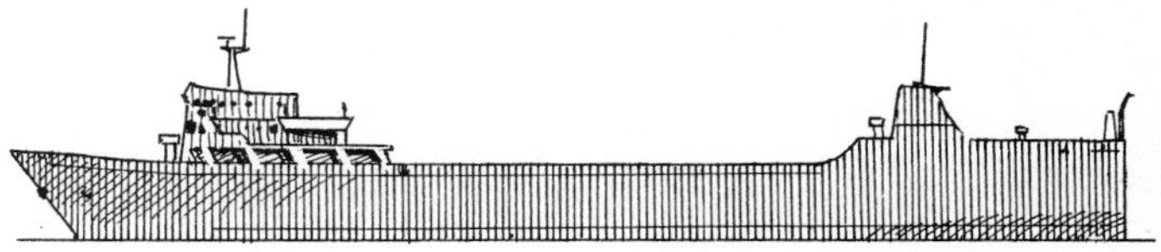

157 *MM–GY H3*
RAPOCA Li/Sp (Lorenzo) 1976; RoC; 4,605 grt/4,243 dwt; 106.36 × 6.2 m *(348.95 × 20.34 ft)*; M (Werkspoor); 17.25 kts; ex-*Antonio Suardiaz*; Stern door/ramp
Sister: **SOFIA** (Li) ex-*Rivainfanzon*

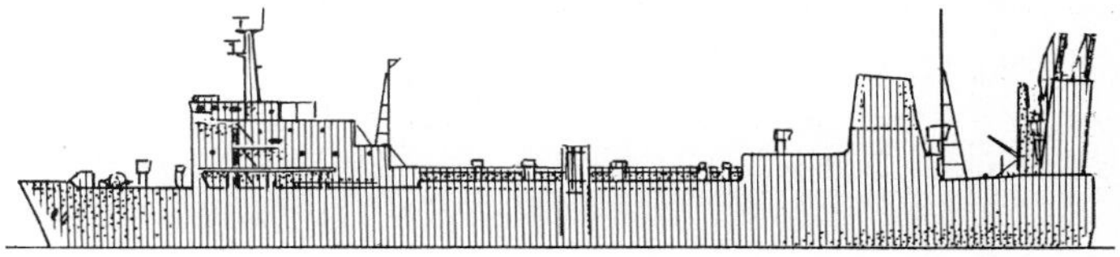

158 *MNFMA H2*
OUR LADY OF THE SACRED HEART Pi/Ja (Mitsui) 1978; RoC; 4,388 grt/3,834 dwt; 112.53 × 6.01 m *(369.2 × 19.72 ft)*; M (Mitsui); 16.75 kts; ex-*Shinsei Maru*; Stern door/ramp

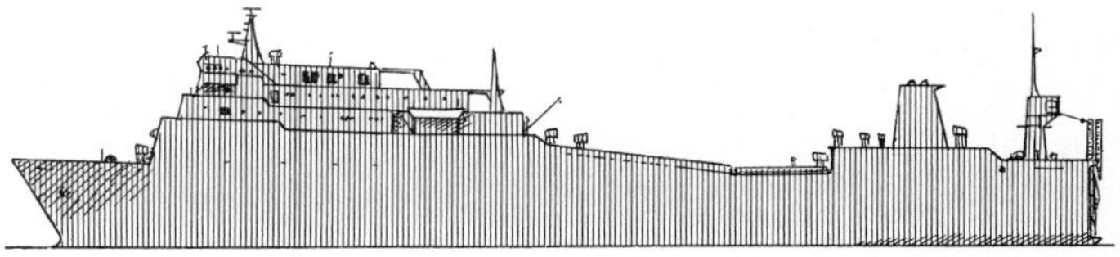

159 *MNGTY H2*
C R TANGER Bs/Ja (Minami) 1978; RoC/Con; 14,444 grt/9,332 dwt; 140.85 × 7.65 m *(462.1 × 25 ft)*; TSM (Sulzer); 14 kts; ex-*TFL Progress*; Foreward ramp (starboard) and stern slewing ramp; 510 TEU; Hance at after end of midcastle is steeper on the starboard side
Sister: **PACIFIC PROSPERITY** (Gr) ex-*TFL Prosperity*

160 *MNMGNTY H3*
CAPE TAYLOR US/Ja (Sasebo) 1977; RoC; 13,098 grt/15,175 dwt; 193.20 × 9.12 m *(633.86 × 29.92 ft)*; M (MAN); 16.5 kts; ex-*Rabenfels*; Slewing stern door/ramp; 1,127 TEU; Owned by US Government. **SIMILAR TO DRAWING NUMBER 18/26**
Sister: **ASL SANDERLING** (Ca) ex-*Rauenfels*

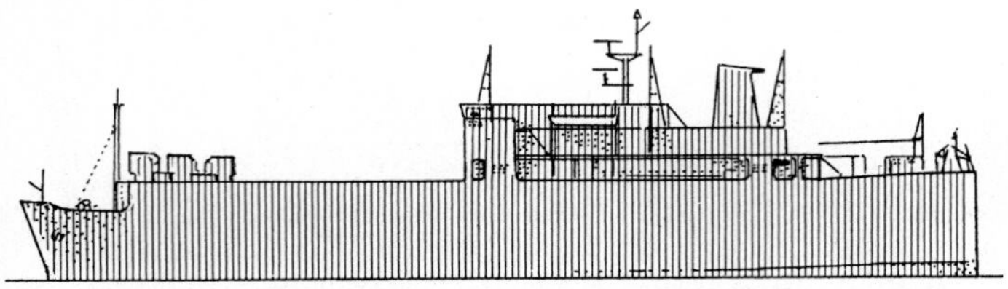

161 *MNM^{2}FMCY H2*
AUTOROUTE NIS/Ja (Mitsui) 1979; RoVC; 7,114 grt/1,849 dwt; 100.01 × 4.21 m *(328.12 × 13.81 ft)*; M (B&W); 15.25 kts; Stern door/ramp

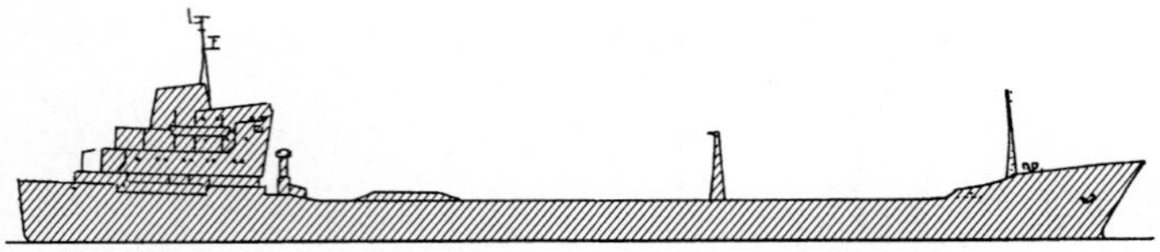

162 *MNM–F H13*
CEDAR CAR Le/FRG (Kroegerw) 1972/81; RoC; 6,623 grt/5,599 dwt; 126.60 × 6.05 m *(415.35 × 19.85 ft)*; M (MAN); 15 kts; ex-*Algol*; Stern door/ramp; Lengthened 1981

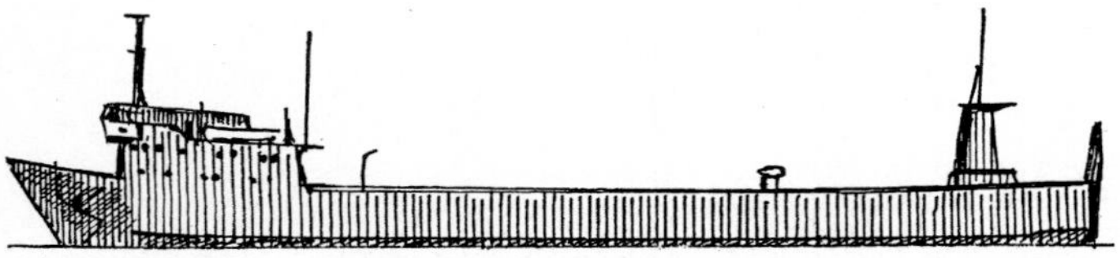

163 *MNM–GY H*
NUSA DHARMA Ia/No (Trondhjems) 1973; RoC; 1,436 grt/1,714 dwt; 105.39 × 3.52 m *(345.77 × 11.55 ft)*; TSM (Normo); 15 kts; ex-*Jarl Transporter*; Bow and stern doors
Sister: **CARIBBEAN TRAILER** (Pa) ex-*Stena Trailer*

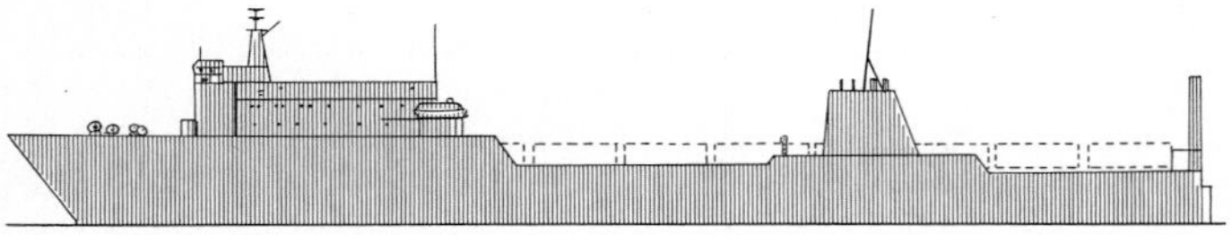

164 *MNM–GY H12*
KLAIPEDA Lt/DDR (Mathias-Thesen) 1987; RoC/TF; 21,890 grt/11,910 dwt; 190.38 × 7.18 m *(624.61 × 23.56 ft)*; TSM (SKL); 15.5 kts; Stern door
Sisters (extra passenger accommodation—superstructure may be increased): **KAUNAS** (Lt); **VILNIUS** (Lt)

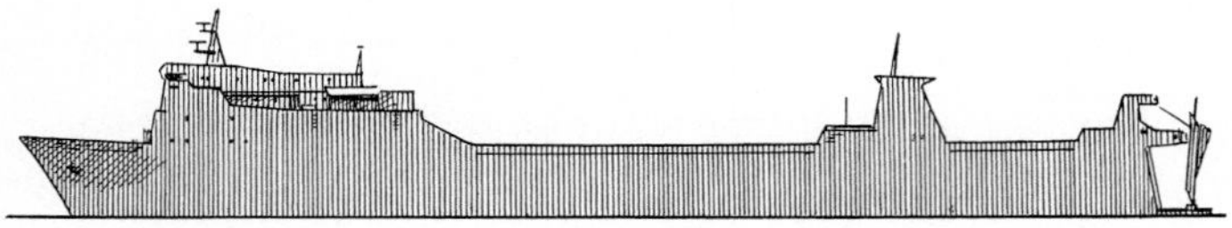

165 *MNM–GY H2*
TIDERO STAR NIS/Ne (Vuyk) 1978; RoC; 3,894 grt/5,482 dwt; 151 × 6.2 m *(495.41 × 20.34 ft)*; M (Sulzer); 17 kts; ex-*Anzere*; Slewing stern door/ramp; 356 TEU

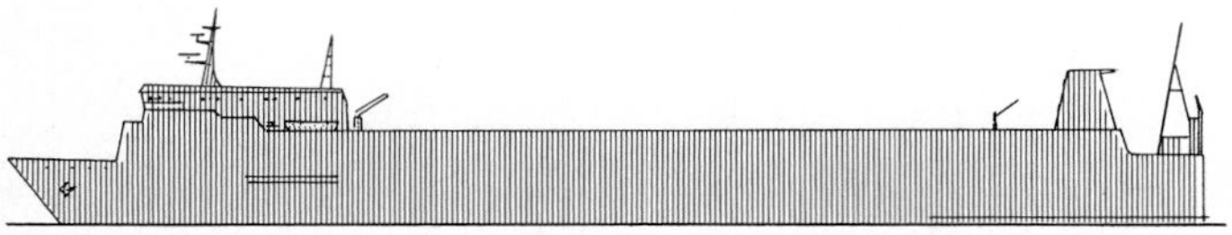

166 *MNR^{2}GMY H2*
ROCON I Pi/De (Frederikshavn) 1984; RoC; 15,375 grt/9,250 dwt; 160.51 × 6.73 m *(526.61 × 22.08 ft)*; M (MaK); 16 kts; ex-*Mercandian Gigant*; Side door/ramp (starboard side aft); Stern door/ramp; 558 TEU; 'FV2100' type
Sisters: **RO-RO SENTOSA** (Sg) ex-*Mercandian Continent*; **SEABOARD UNIVERSE** (Li) ex-*Mercandian Universe*; **SEABOARD OCEAN** (Li) ex-*Mercandian Ocean*; **SEABOARD SUN** (Li) ex-*Mercandian Sun II*; **MERCANDIAN GLOBE** (DIS); **MERCANDIAN ARROW** (DIS); **SEABOARD CARIBE** (Li) ex-*Mercandian Sea II*

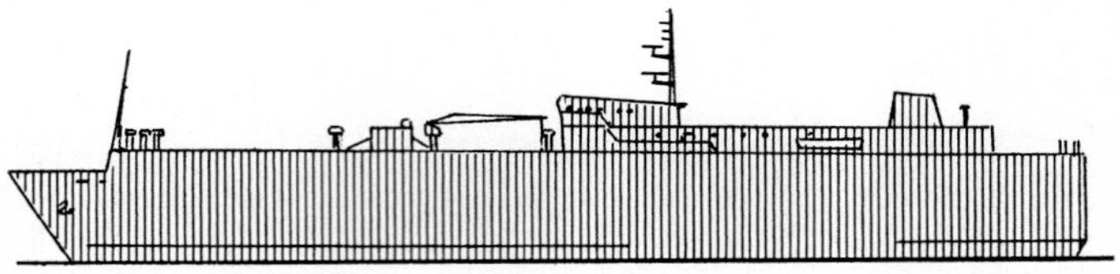

167 *MRMF H2*
AUTOWEG NIS/No (Batservice) 1973; V; 3,946 grt/1,042 dwt; 91.8 × 3.86 m *(301.18 × 12.66 ft)*; M (Normo); 14 kts; Side doors

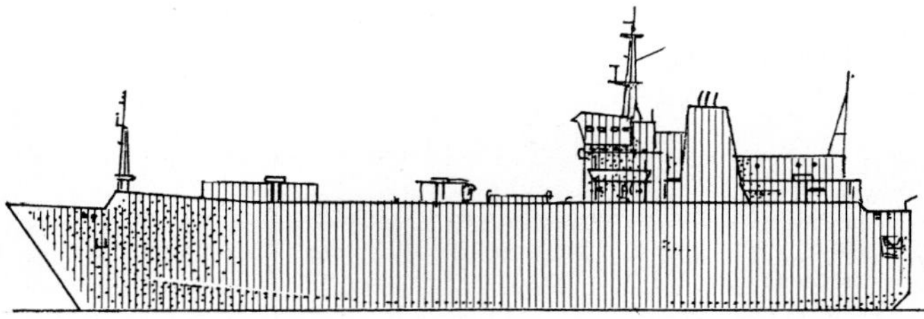

168 *MRMGNY H*
AUTOFREIGHTER NIS/Ne (Vuyk) 1977; RoC; 5,927 grt/1,313 dwt; 89.34 × 4.23 m *(293.11 × 13.88 ft)*; M (Atlas-MaK); 13.5 kts; ex-*Fredenhagen*; Bow door/ramp; Stern door/ramp; Side door/ramp (starboard)

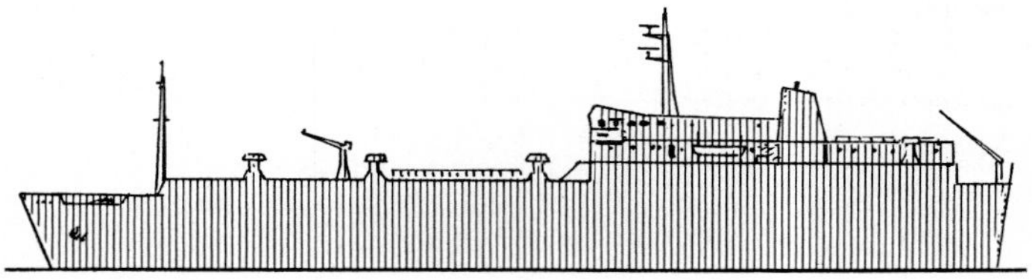

169 *MRMGRY H2*
GOODWOOD Kn/Fr (Havre) 1974; RoC; 5,180 grt/1,400 dwt; 100.46 × 4.38 m *(330 × 14.37 ft)*; TSM (Atlas-MaK); 15 kts; ex-*Mulsanne*; Stern door/ramp
Sister: **ESTORIL** (Kn) ex-*Arnage*; Similar (no crane foreward): **DONINGTON** (NIS) ex-*Tertre Rouge*
Probably similar: **HOCKENHEIM** (Kn) ex-*Hunaudieres*

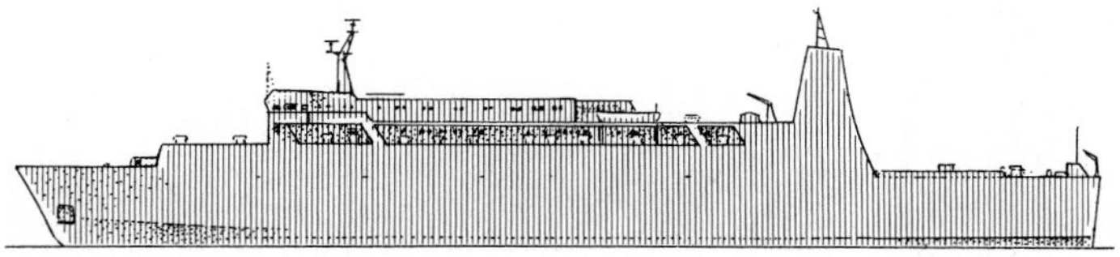

170 *MRM–GZ H2*
BALTIC EAGLE Br/Fi (Rauma-Repola) 1979; RoC; 14,738 grt/9,450 dwt; 137.12 × 8.21 m *(449.87 × 26.94 ft)*; TSM (Stork-Werkspoor); 18 kts; Two stern doors/ramps
Sister: **INOWROCLAW** (Pd)

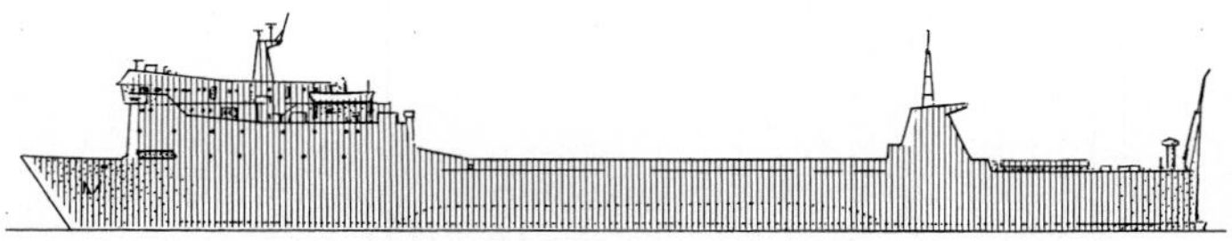

171 *MV–GY H2*
NORMANDIE SHIPPER Fr/Ne (Vuyk) 1973/77; RoC/P/F; 4,078 grt/5,555 dwt; 142.27 × 5.92 m *(466.77 × 19.42 ft)*; TSM (Werkspoor); 18 kts; ex-*Union Wellington*; Launched as *Stena Shipper*; Bow door and ramp; Stern door/ramp; Lengthened 1977; Now has superstructure extended and extra housing just aft of funnel —not shown on drawing (see photo number 18/185)

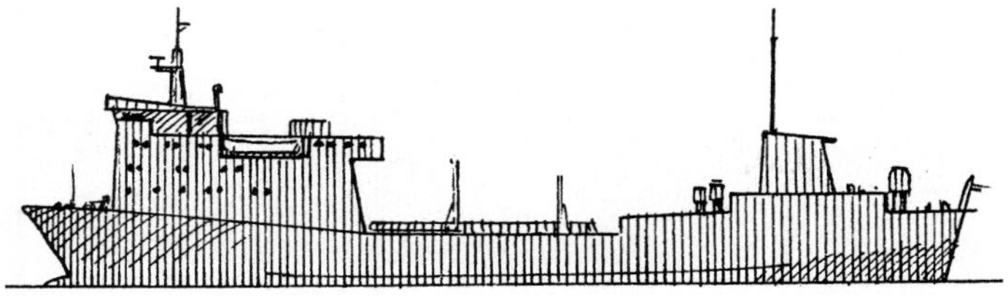

172 *MV–GY H2*
NUSA BAHAGIA Ia/Ne ('De Biesbosch-Dordrecht') 1972; RoC; 3,555 grt/1,810 dwt; 98 × 3.85 m *(321.52 × 12.63 ft)*; TSM (MWM); 15 kts; ex-*Ador*; Bow and stern doors
Sister: **EVANGELISTAS** (Ch) ex-*Condor*

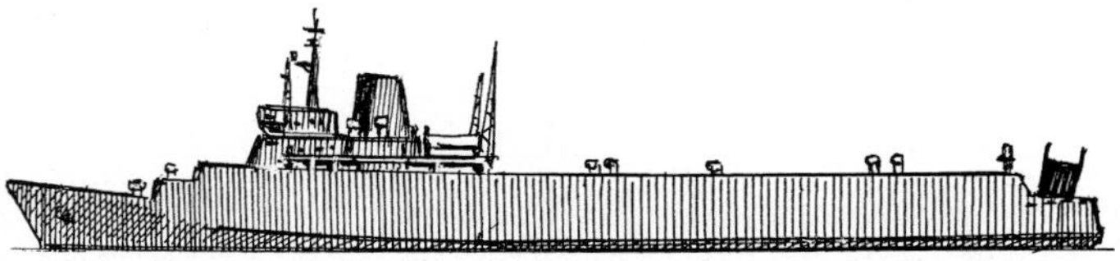

173 *NMFM–NA H2*
TOKYO MARU Ja/Ja (Hayashikane) 1976; RoC; 6,737 grt/4,407 dwt; 147.5 × 6.6 m *(484 × 21.7 ft)*; M (MAN); 19.5 kts

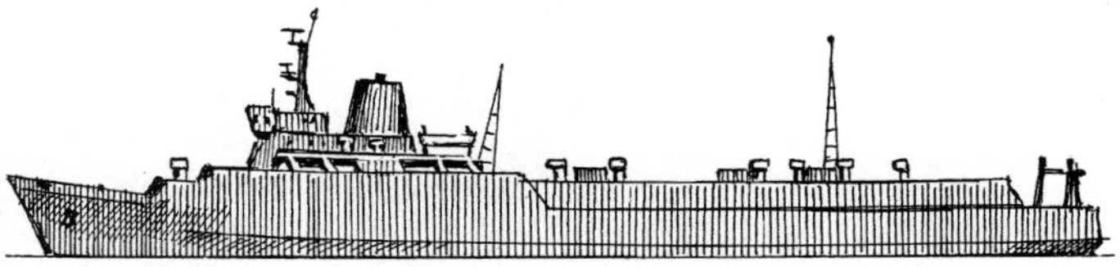

174 *NMFNMA H2*
CALABRIA It/Ja (Hayashikane) 1976; RoC; 3,651 grt/4,412 dwt; 147.6 × 6.6 m *(484 × 21.8 ft)*; M (MAN); 19.5 kts; ex-*Serenissima Express*; Stern and quarter doors
Sisters: **SICILIA** (It) ex-*Anglia Express*; **SARDEGNA** (It) ex-*Allemagna Express*

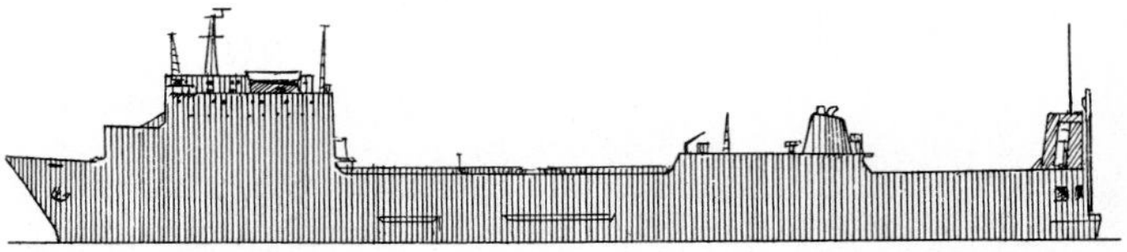

175 *NMN²FMY H2*
NAN KOU RC/Ja (Kawasaki) 1978; RoC; 3,748 grt/5,692 dwt; 136.19 × 6.81 m *(446.84 × 22.34 ft)*; M (MAN); 17.7 kts; ex-*Ocean Transporter*; Slewing stern door/ramp; 404 TEU; Funnel is on port side
Similar (longer—146.55m (480ft)): **BAI HE KOU** (RC); **HUA YUAN KOU** (RC); **ZHI JIANG KOU** (RC); **TAI PING KOU** (RC); **XIAO SHI KOU** (RC)

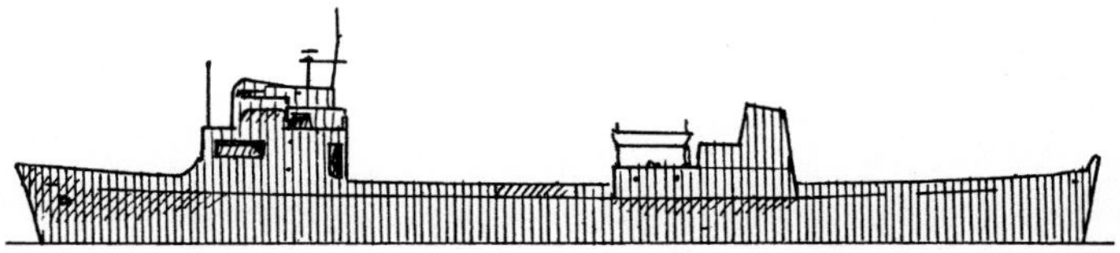

176 *VMGY H*
ULUSOY-1 Tu/It ('L Orlando') 1969; RoC; 3,739 grt/3,014 dwt; 105.5 × 5 m *(346 × 16.9 ft)*; TSM (Fiat); — kts; ex-*Espresso Campania*

See photo number 18/217

177 *VMGY H2*
RAVENNA BRIDGE Bs/It ('L Orlando') 1975; RoC; 7,110 grt/4,462 dwt; 117.51 × 5.07 m *(385.5 × 16.62 ft)*; TSM (GMT); 20 kts; ex-*Corriere Dell'Ouest*; Lengthened 1980; Drawing shows vessel as built; Length is now 140m (459ft)
Sister (also lengthened): **FILIPPOS** (Gr) ex-*Corriere Del Nord*
Sisters (unlengthened—119m (390ft)): **ELEFSIS** (Gr) ex-*Buona Speranza*; **ATLANTIS** (Gr) ex-*Nuova Ventura*

178 Baltic Meteor *(Pa); 1971* *FotoFlite*

179 Alma Llanera *(Pa); 1972* *FotoFlite*

180 Hockenheim *(Kn); 1976* *FotoFlite*

181 Olympian Duchess *(Bs); 1981* *FotoFlite*

182 Coutances *(Fr); 1978; (after lengthening)* *FotoFlite*

183 Fjardvargen *(Fi); 1972; (as Norman Commodore)* *FotoFlite*

184 ASSI Euro Link *(Ne); 1972/77* *FotoFlite*

185 Normandie Shipper *(Fr); 1973* *FotoFlite*

186 Tor Belgia *(Sw); 1979/88; (after rebuilding)* *FotoFlite*

187 Gabriele Wehr *(Ge); 1978/82* *FotoFlite*

188 Roline *(Sp); 1980* *FotoFlite*

189 Asian Century *(NIS); 1978; (as Bassro Polar)* *FotoFlite*

190 Car Express *(Bs); 1977* *FotoFlite*

191 Rodona *(Sw); 1980/82* *FotoFlite*

192 Und Transfer *(Tu); 1978/89; (as Stena Transfer)* *FotoFlite*

193 Feedersailor *(Ma); 1972/91* *FotoFlite*

194 Stena Clipper *(Bs); 1978* *FotoFlite*

195 Roseanne *(Cy); 1982* *FotoFlite*

196 Don Pedro *(Sp); 1984* *FotoFlite*

197 Arcade Eagle *(NIS); 1981* *FotoFlite*

198 Cape Victory *(US); 1984; (as Merzario Britannia)* *FotoFlite*

199 Bul Pride *(SV); 1980; (as Nordic Pride)* *FotoFlite*

200 Imola *(Po); 1981* *FotoFlite*

201 Olivia *(Bs); 1982* *FotoFlite*

202 Maria Gorthon *(Sw); 1984* *FotoFlite*

203 Joh Gorthon *(Sw); 1977/82* *FotoFlite*

204 Nornews Express *(No); 1987* *FotoFlite*

205 Seaboard Venture *(NIS); 1978; (as Railro)* *FotoFlite*

206 Transbaltica *(Cy); 1990; (as Ahlers Baltic)* *FotoFlite*

207 Autoracer *(NIS); 1994* *FotoFlite*

208 City of Barcelona *(Br); 1993* *FotoFlite*

209 Autotransporter *(NIS); 1983* *FotoFlite*

210 Espresso Ravenna *(It); 1993* *WSPL*

211 European Freeway *(Br); 1978/81; (as Cerdic Ferry)* *WSPL*

212 Trekroner *(De); 1979/86* *WSPL*

213 Tor Hollandia *(Sw); 1973/77* *WSPL*

214 Donata *(Pa); 1972/83; (as Feederteam)* *WSPL*

215 Cap Canaille *(Kn); 1977; (as Seafowl)* *WSPL*

216 Filippos *(Gr); 1975/80; (as Ro-Ro Primula)* *WSPL*

217 Dana Cimbria *(DIS); 1986* *WSPL*

218 Dana Hafnia *(DIS); 1979* *WSPL*

219 Rosebay *(Cy); 1976* *WSPL*

220 Finnmerchant *(Fi); 1983* *WSPL*

221 Maersk Flanders *(Ne); 1978* *WSPL*

222 Donington *(NIS); 1976* *WSPL*

223 Marine Evangeline *(Bs); 1974; (as Spirit of Boulogne)* *WSPL*

224 Symphorine *(Pa); 1988* *WSPL*

225 Sea Wind II *(Sw); 1979; (as Sally Sun)* *WSPL*

226 Arroyofrio Dos *(Sp); 1985* *WSPL*

227 Transeuropa *(Ge); 1995* *Stocznia Gdanska*

228 Polaris *(Cy); 1975/85* *FotoFlite*

229 Al Ahamad *(Si); 1970; (as Feederman)* *FotoFlite*

230 Mundial Car *(Le); 1965* *FotoFlite*

231 Thebeland *(Sw); 1978/95* *FotoFlite*

232 Obbola *(Sw); 1996* *FotoFlite*

233 Viola Gorthon *(Sw); 1987* *FotoFlite*

19 Vehicle Carriers

19 Vehicle Carriers

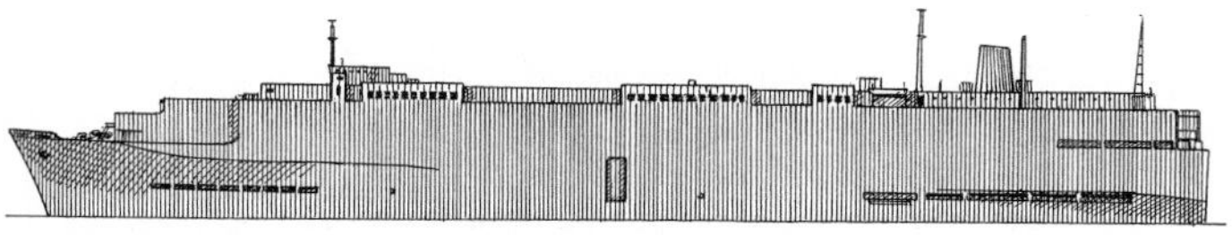

1 *HMFMNA H2*
OLIVE ACE Li/Ja (Mitsui) 1977; RoVC; 38,772 grt/13,873 dwt; 176.26 × 9.03 m *(578.28 × 29.63 ft)*; M (B&W); 19 kts; Two quarter door/ramps (one port, one starboard); Side door/ramp (port)
Sister: **NOBLE ACE** (Pi) ex-*Suzukasan Maru*

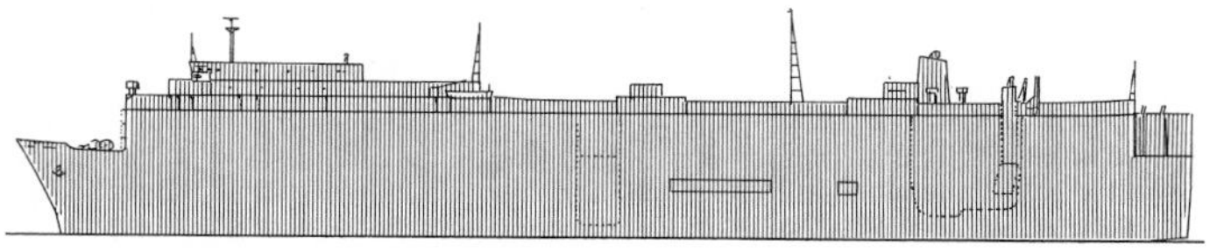

2 *HNMFAM H2*
ASTRO COACH Li/Ja (Tsuneishi) 1980; RoVC; 41,969 grt/13,950 dwt; 186.01 × 9 m *(610 × 29.53 ft)*; M (B&W); 18.5 kts; two side doors (one port, one starboard); one stern door/ramp
Similar: **VIKING STAR** (Li) ex-*Paramount Ace*

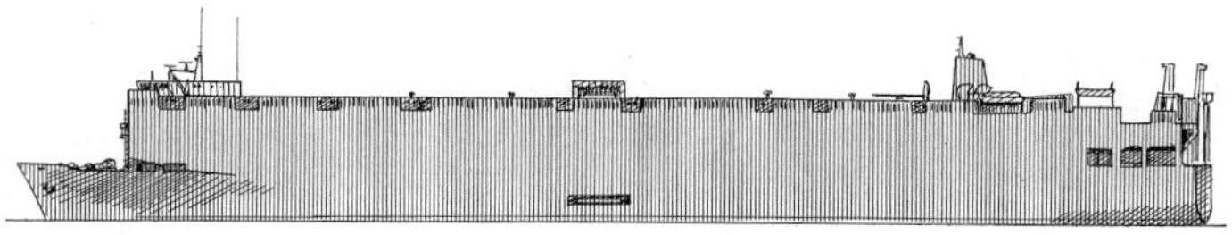

3 *MCM–FA H2*
NOSAC RANGER US/Ja (Mitsui) 1978; RoVC; 47,089 grt/17,406 dwt; 194.52 × 8.2 m *(638.19 × 26.9 ft)*; M (B&W); 19.75 kts; ex-*Nopal Mascot*; Side door/ramp (starboard); Quarter door/ramp (starboard)

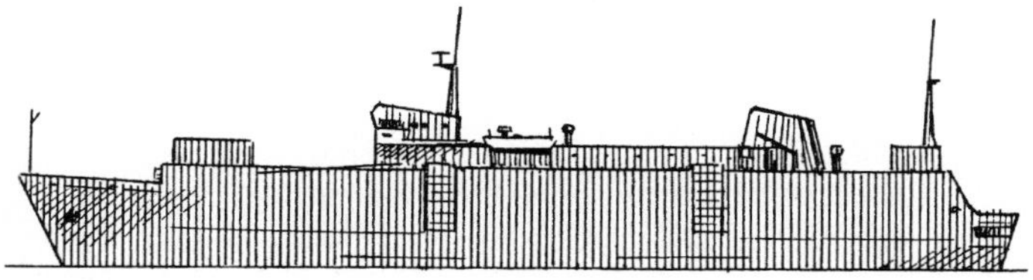

4 *MFM H2*
TAMARA I Pa/Sp (Construcciones SA) 1976; RoVC; 4,343 grt/2,175 dwt; 88.02 × 5.18 m *(288.78 × 16.99 ft)*; M (Deutz); 14 kts; ex-*Canabal*; Side doors; two side door/ramps (starboard); Stern door
Sister: **ELENORE** (Pa) ex-*Cobres*

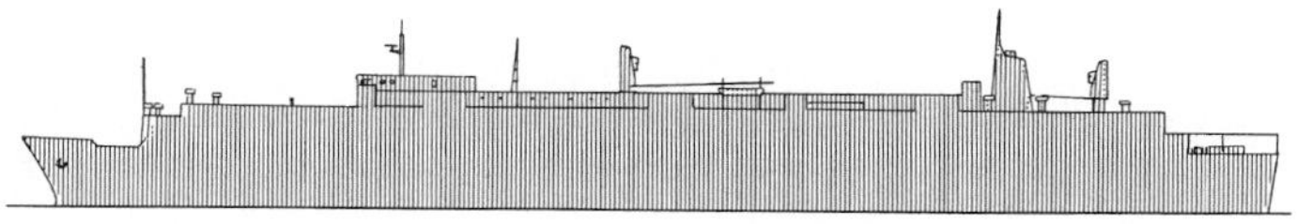

5 *MHNCM–FC H2*
SILVER RAY Pa/Ja (Imabari) 1978; V; 39,147 grt/18,748 dwt; 199.42 × 9.33 m *(654.27 × 30.61 ft)*; M (Sulzer); 18 kts; ex-*Canadian Highway*
Probable sisters: **PACIFIC EXPLORER** (Li) ex-*Asian Highway*; **MORNING QUEEN** (Pa) ex-*Golden Ace*

6 *MHNDM–FC H2*
PACIFIC RUNNER Li/Ja (Imabari) 1977; RoVC; 38,754 grt/17,830 dwt; 199.40 × 9.33 m *(654.20 × 30.61 ft)*; M (Sulzer); 20 kts; Side doors; **SIMILAR TO DRAWING NUMBER 19/5**; Principal difference is pair of cranes amidships

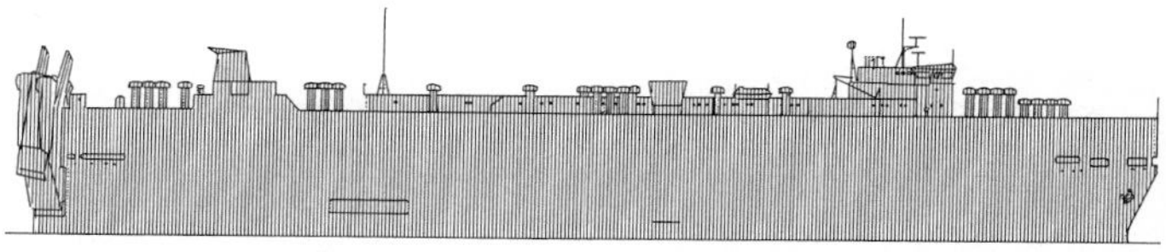

7 *M^2FA H*
AIDA Sw/Ja (Hitachi) 1991; RoVC; 52,288 grt/29,213 dwt; 199.00 × 9.50 m *(652.89 × 31.17 ft)*; M (B&W); 19.2 kts; Side door/ramp (starboard); Quarter door/ramp (starboard)
Sister: **OTELLO** (Sw)

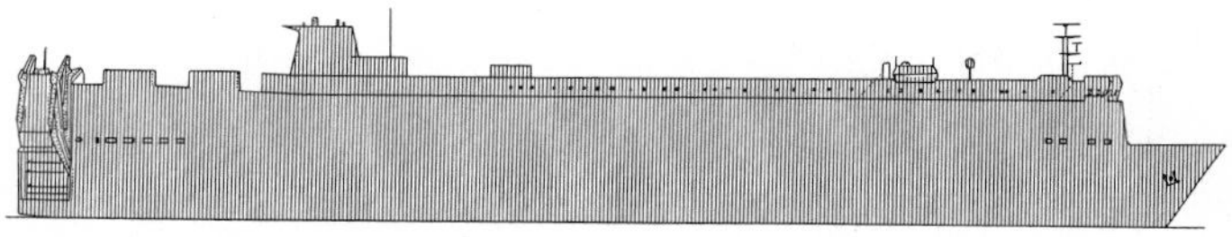

8 *M^2FA H2*
FIDES It/Ge (Flender) 1993; RoVC/P/Con; 33,411 grt/16,806 dwt; 178.09 × 7.60 m *(584.28 × 24.93 ft)*; M (Sulzer); 19 kts; Quarter door/ramp (starboard); 504 TEU
Sister: **SPES** (It)

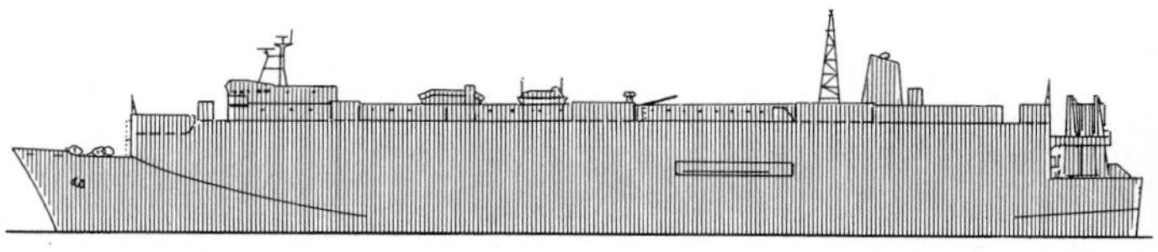

9 *M^2FA H2*
HUAL TRACER Bs/Ja (Kanasashi)1981; RoVC; 33,236 grt/12,961 dwt; 180.02 × 8.82 m *(591 × 28.94 ft)*; M (B&W); 17.6 kts; Side door/ramp (starboard); quarter door/ramp (starboard)
Sister: **HUAL TRAPPER** (Bs)

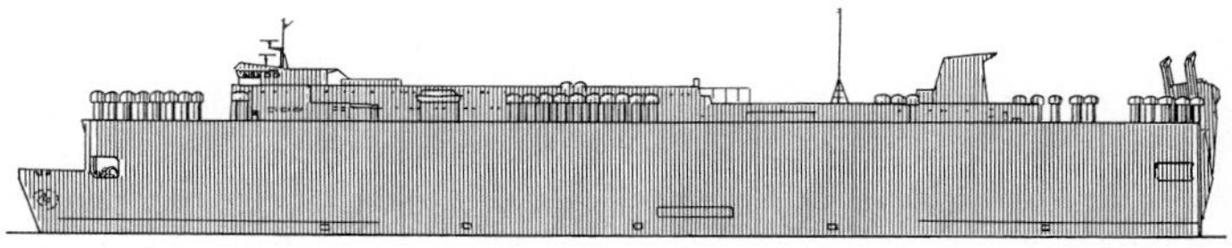

10 *M^2FA H2*
MADAME BUTTERFLY Sg/Sw (Kockums) 1981; RoVC; 50,681 grt/28,223 dwt; 199.7 × 11.61 m *(655 × 38.22 ft)*; M (Gotaverken); 19.5 kts; Side door/ramp (starboard); Quarter ramp (starboard)
Sisters: **CARMEN** (Sw); **FIGARO** (Sw); **MEDEA** (Sg); **TRISTAN** (Sw); **ISOLDE** (Sw)

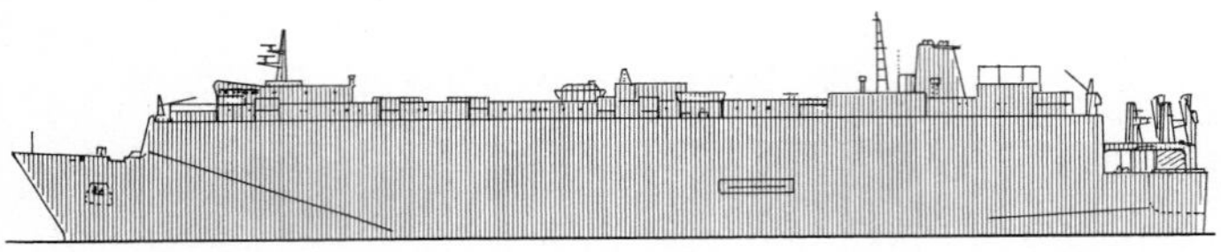

11 M^2FCA *H2*
HUAL ANGELITA NIS/Ja (Tsuneishi) 1981; RoVC; 33,374 grt/11,977 dwt; 180.02 × 8.52 m *(591 × 27.95 ft)*; M (B&W); 17.75 kts; ex-*Angelita*; Side door/ramp (starboard); quarter door/ramp (starboard)
Sisters: **HUAL INGRITA** (NIS) ex-*Ingrita*; **HUAL LISITA** (NIS) ex-*Lisita*; **HUAL ROLITA** (NIS) ex-*Rolita*

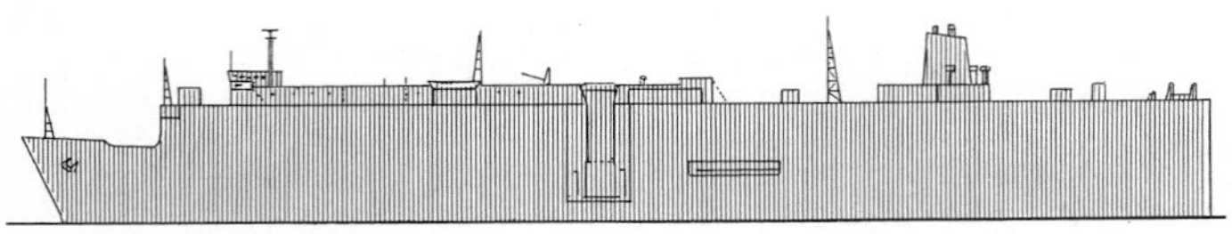

12 M^2HNMFA *H2*
CHIJIN Pi/Ja (Tsuneishi) 1982; RoVC; 29,889 grt/12,582 dwt; 176 × 8.22 m *(577 × 26.97 ft)*; M (B&W); 17.5 kts; ex-*Chijin Maru*; Two side door/ramps (one port, one starboard); quarter ramp (starboard)
Sister: **ASTRO VENUS** (Pi) ex-*Shojin Maru*
Possible sister: **SEA VENUS** (Pa) ex-*Orchid Ace*

13 $M^2HNM–FC$ *H2*
MORNING LIGHT Pi/Ja (Hitachi) 1978; RoVC; 30,070 grt/10,601 dwt; 180.02 × 7.50 m *(590.62 × 24.61 ft)*; M (B&W); 18.2 kts; Side door/ramps; **SIMILAR TO DRAWING NUMBER 19/22**; Main difference is goalpost mast on *Morning Light*

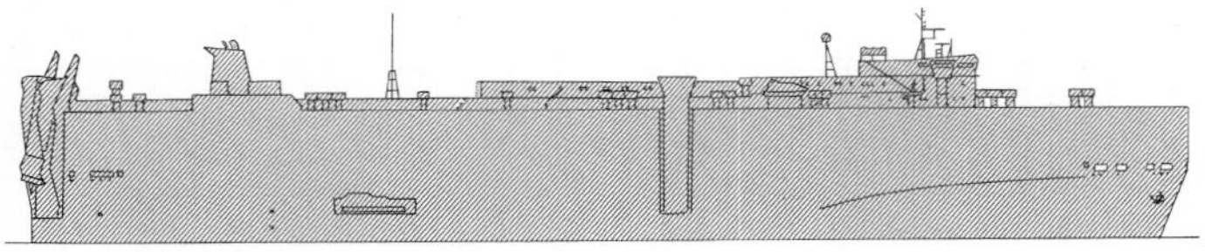

14 M^3FA *H*
TITUS Sw/Ko (Daewoo) 1994; RoVC; 55,598 grt/15,199 dwt; 199.11 × 9.52 m *(653.25 × 31.23 ft)*; M (B&W); 20.25 kts; side ramp (starboard); Quarter door/ramp (starboard)
Sister: **TURANDOT** (Sw)

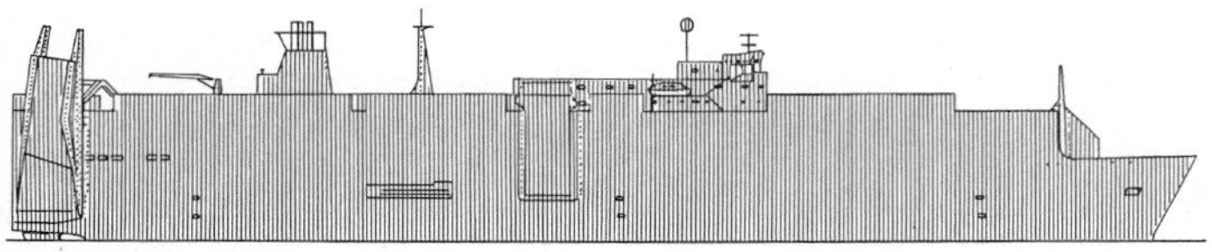

15 M^3FRA *H2*
NOSAC EXPRESS NIS/Ko (Daewoo) 1985; RoVC; 48,357 grt/21,900 dwt; 195.03 × 11.06 m *(639.86 × 36.29 ft)*; M (B&W); 19 kts; Side door/ramp (starboard); Quarter door/ramp (starboard); Funnel is on starboard side
Sister: **NOSAC EXPLORER** (NIS) ex-*Nosac Tasco*

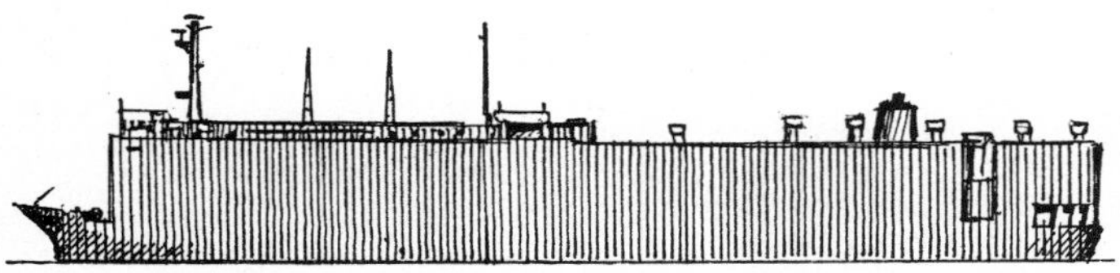

16 M^3G *H2*
SILVER HOPE 1 Pa/Ja (Ube Dock) 1976; RoVC; 4,668 grt/4,733 dwt; 120.1 × 8.93 m *(394.02 × 29.29 ft)*; M (Pielstick); 17.75 kts; ex-*Blue Andromeda*; Side doors

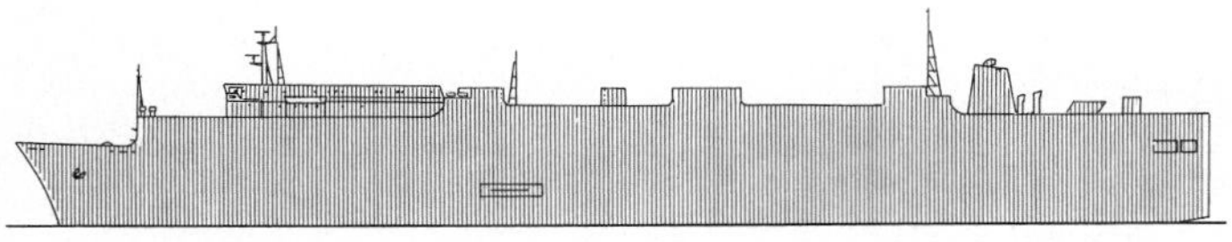

17 M^5F *H2*
TRANS PACIFIC 3 Pa/Ja (Naikai) 1981; RoVC; 33,935 grt/10,848 dwt; 190.08 × 8.02 m *(624 × 26.31 ft)*; M (B&W); 18 kts; ex-*Toyofuji No 7*; Two side door/ramps (starboard)

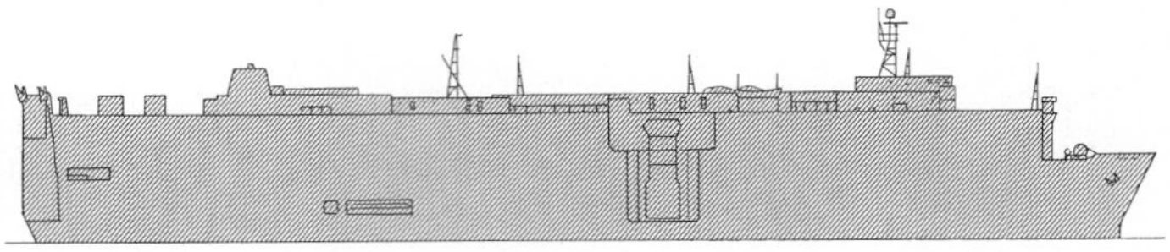

18 M^6FA *H2*
MARINE RELIANCE MI/Ja (Sumitomo) 1987; RoVC; 35,750 grt/11,676 dwt; 175.17 × 8.42 m *(574.70 × 27.62 ft)*; M (Sulzer); 17.9 kts; Two side door/ramps (one port/one starboard); Quarter door/ramp
Possibly similar: **EURASIAN CHARIOT** (Pi) ex-*Ocean Cheer*

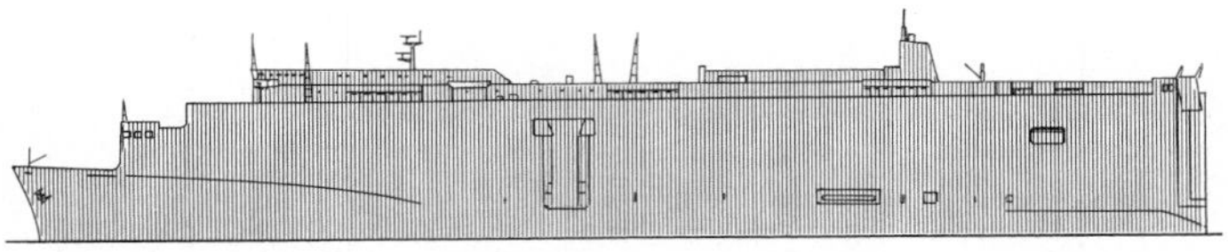

19 $M^5NM–FB$ *H2*
PRINCESS ARROW Pa/Ja (Sumitomo) 1981; RoVC; 47,847 grt/17,637 dwt; 190 × 8.92 m *(623 × 29.27 ft)*; M (Sulzer); 19.5 kts; ex-*European Venture*; two side door/ramps (one port, one starboard)

20 $M^3M–FCA$ *H2*
OPAL RAY Ma/Ja (Hitachi) 1972; RoVC; 22,454 grt/8,678 dwt; 174.5 × 7.21 m *(572.5 × 23.67 ft)*; M (B&W); 18 kts; ex-*Sagami Maru*; Slewing stern ramp

21 M^3NMFCA *H2*
CANADIAN ACE II Pa/Ja (Naikai) 1976; RoVC; 23,679 grt/8,773 dwt; 174.5 × 7.2 m *(572.5 × 23.63 ft)*; M (B&W); 18 kts; ex-*Laurel*; Stern door

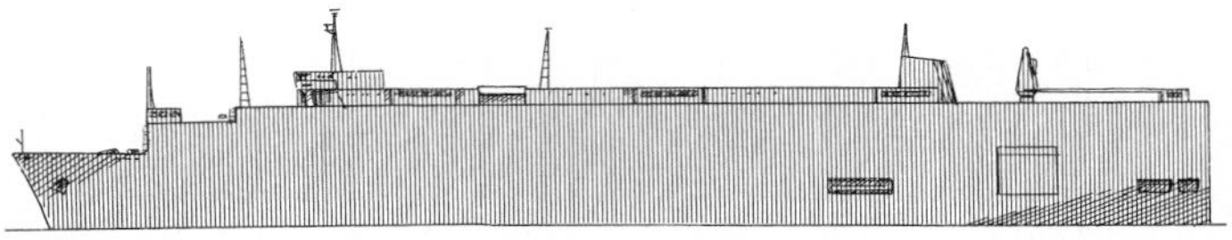

22 $M^3NM–FC$ *H2*
GUANAJUATO Li/Ja (Hitachi) 1977; V; 30,256 grt/10,535 dwt; 180.02 × 7.5 m *(590.62 × 24.61 ft)*; M (B&W); 18 kts; ex-*President*; Side doors; crane aft is on starboard side
Sister: **LERMA** (Li) ex-*Nissan Silvia*

23 M^2NDFC *H2*
EASTERN HIGHWAY Ja/Ja (Tsuneishi) 1977; RoVC; 16,588 grt/7,305 dwt; 152.3 × 7.62 m *(499.67 × 25 ft)*; M (B&W); 18.5 kts; Side doors (two on starboard side)

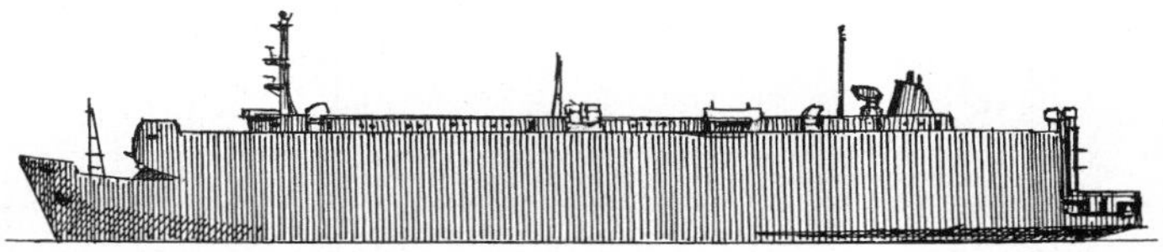

24 M^2NMFB *H2*
GOLDEN RAY Pa/Ja (Mitsubishi HI) 1973; RoVC; 22,293 grt/8,870 dwt; 169.12 × 7.21 m *(554.8 × 23.6 ft)*; M (MAN); 17 kts; ex-*Prince Maru No 7*; stern ramps

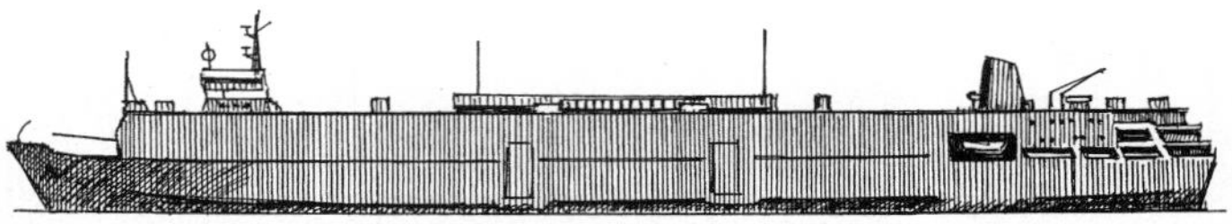

25 M^2NMFS *H2*
ARNO It/Ne (P Smit) 1973; RoVC; 25,312 grt/9,652 dwt; 187.51 × 8.01 m *(615.19 × 26.27 ft)*; M (Sulzer); 18 kts; ex-*Dyvi Skagerak*; Side doors (see photo number 19/80)
Sisters: **DYVI KATTEGAT** (NIS); **ARMACUP PATRICIA** (NIS) ex-*Dyvi Adriatic*; **TRIGGER** (Li) ex-*Hoegh Trigger*; Similar (tall pipes from funnel): **SEA TRANSIT** (Li) ex-*Nopal Sel*

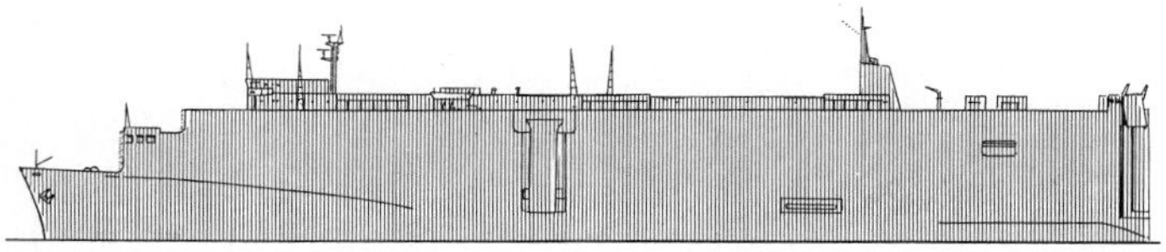

26 *M²NM²NM–FSB H2*
HUAL TRINITA Li/Ja (Sumitomo) 1981; RoVC; 45,365 grt/17,938 dwt; 190 × 8.92 m *(623 × 29.27 ft)*; M (Sulzer); 19.2 kts; ex-*Yokohama Maru*; side doors/ramps (one port, one starboard); two quarter doors/ramps (one port, one starboard)
Sister: **SAN MARCOS** (Li) ex-*Oppama Maru*

27 *M²NMNM–FB H2*
KYUSHU Li/Ja (Hitachi) 1981; 45,573 grt/17,650 dwt; 190.00 × 92 m *(623.36 × 29.27 ft)*; M (B&W); 19.25 kts; ex-*Kyushu Maru*; two quarter door/ramps; two side door/ramps; **SIMILAR TO DRAWING NUMBER 19/28**; Latter does not have quarter ramps
Sister: **HONSHU 1** (Cy) ex-*Zama Maru*

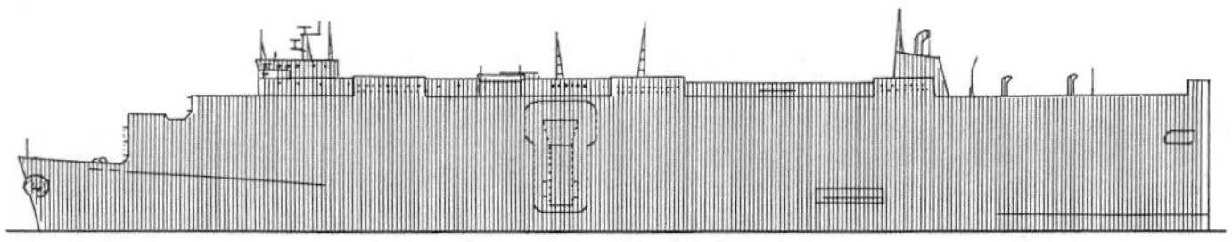

28 *M²N²MNM–FS H2*
GLORIOUS ACE Ja/Ja (Hitachi) 1981; RoVC; 16,880 grt/17,743 dwt; 190 × 8.92 m *(623 × 29.27 ft)*; M (B&W); 19 kts; two side ramps (one port, one starboard); one stern door/ramp
Similar (two side ramps and two quarter ramps): **KYUSHU** (Li) ex-*Kyushu Maru*; **HONSHU 1** (Cy) ex-*Zama Maru*

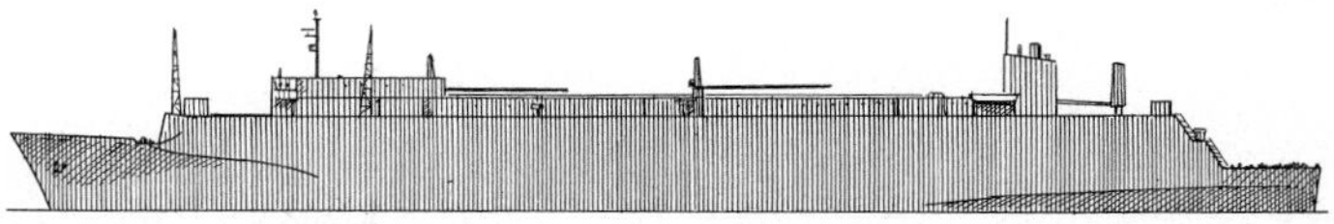

29 *NMNCDM–FC H2*
GABRIELA R Br/Ja (Kawasaki) 1977; RoVC; 24,361 grt/11,290 dwt; 192.08 × 8.03 m *(630.18 × 26.34 ft)*; M (MAN); 20.5 kts; ex-*Atlantic Highway*; Two side doors (one port, one starboard). Stern door

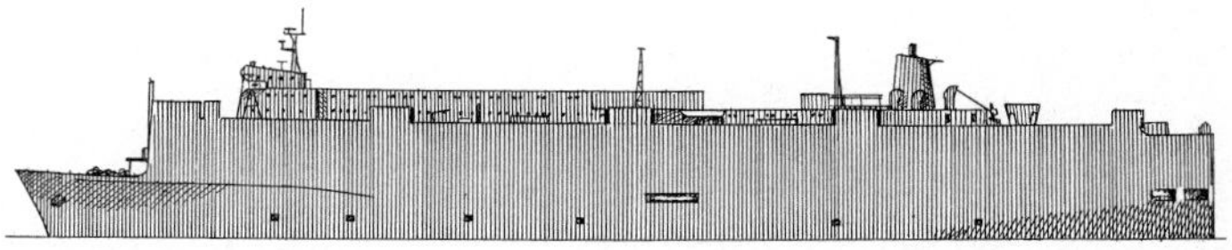

30 *NMNMF H2*
RIGOLETTO Sw/Ja (Hitachi) 1977; RoVC; 43,487 grt/13,438 dwt; 190.02 × 8.5 m *(623.4 × 27.8 ft)*; M (Sulzer); 19.25 kts; Side door/ramp (starboard); Angled side door/ramp (port and starboard)
Sister: **TRAVIATA** (Sw)

31 Kentucky Highway *(Ja); 1987* *FotoFlite*

32 Harmony Ace *(HK); 1992* *FotoFlite*

33 Sea Pride *(NIS); 1980; (as Ferngolf)* *FotoFlite*

34 Hume Highway *(Pa); 1985* *FotoFlite*

35 Automobil Ace *(Pa); 1980* *FotoFlite*

36 Nosac Rover *(NIS); 1982* *FotoFlite*

37 Hual Karinita *(NIS); 1980* *FotoFlite*

38 Auto Atlas *(Ko); 1988* *FotoFlite*

39 Parsifal *(Sg); 1978* *FotoFlite*

40 Green Bay *(US); 1987* *FotoFlite*

41 Sapphire Highway *(Pa); 1986; (as London Highway)* *FotoFlite*

42 Maersk Wind *(Sg); 1981* *FotoFlite*

43 Meiyo Maru *(Ja); 1981* *FotoFlite*

44 Nosac Takara *(Li); 1986* *FotoFlite*

45 Orion Diamond *(Va); 1982* *FotoFlite*

46 Koh Jin *(Va); 1981* *FotoFlite*

47 Eurasian Dream *(Pi); 1984; (as Japan Carryall)* *FotoFlite*

48 Hyundai No 107 *(Pa); 1987* *FotoFlite*

49 Hual Traveller *(Bs); 1983* *FotoFlite*

50 Falstaff *(Sw); 1985* *FotoFlite*

51 Tepozteco II *(Br); 1985; (as Nissan Bluebird)* *FotoFlite*

52 Wolfsburg *(Mr); 1988* *FotoFlite*

53 European Emerald *(Pa); 1984; (as Nissan Maru)* *FotoFlite*

54 Mercury Ace *(Ja); 1985/87* *FotoFlite*

55 Freccia *(Pa); 1987; (as Kassel)* *FotoFlite*

56 Ingolstadt *(Pa); 1987* *FotoFlite*

57 Franconia *(Li); 1985* *FotoFlite*

58 Maersk Crest *(Sg); 1983; (as Rich Queen)* *FotoFlite*

59 Maersk Sky *(Sg); 1982* *FotoFlite*

60 African Highway *(Pa); 1982* *FotoFlite*

61 Eternal Ace *(Pa); 1988* *FotoFlite*

62 Marico *(Pa); 1978; (as Northern Highway)* *FotoFlite*

63 Triton Highway *(Ja); 1987* *FotoFlite*

64 Maersk Sea *(Sg); 1987* *FotoFlite*

65 Aegean Breeze *(Sg); 1983* *FotoFlite*

66 Eternal Glory *(Li); 1982* *FotoFlite*

67 Nada II *(Li); 1981* *FotoFlite*

68 Sun Ace *(Pa); 1981* *FotoFlite*

69 Nosac Takayama *(Li); 1983* *FotoFlite*

70 Solar Wing *(Li); 1988* *FotoFlite*

71 Aniara *(Sg); 1978* *FotoFlite*

72 Ocean Kmir *(Li); 1977; (as Nada)* *FotoFlite*

73 Indianapolis *(NIS); 1980* *FotoFlite*

74 Nosac Sun *(NIS); 1987* *FotoFlite*

75 Hojin *(Va); 1990* *FotoFlite*

76 Century Highway No 5 *(Pa); 1986* *FotoFlite*

77 Feederchief *(Ma); 1993* *WSPL*

78 Southern Ace *(Pi); 1980; (as Arcadia Ace)* *WSPL*

79 Pelander *(Pa); 1979* *WSPL*

80 Atlantic Breeze *(Li); 1986* *WSPL*

81 Arno *(It); 1973; (as Dyvi Skagerak)* *WSPL*

82 Nosac Ranger *(US); 1978* *WSPL*

83 Hual Trinita *(Li); 1981; (as Yokohama)* *WSPL*

84 Tosca *(Sg); 1978* *WSPL*

85 Margherita *(Va); 1981* *WSPL*

86 Adige *(Ma); 1976* *WSPL*

87 Sanwa *(Li); 1985; (as Sanwa Maru)* *WSPL*

88 Morning Prince *(Pa); 1979; (as Prince No 10)* *WSPL*

89 Suijin *(Pa); 1984* *WSPL*

90 Astro Mercury *(Pa); 1978* *FotoFlite*

91 Baltic Breeze *(Sg); 1983* *Ian Pakeman*

92 Melbourne Highway *(Pa); 1983* *David Key*

93 Morning Light *(Pa); 1978* *David Key*

94 Kaijin *(Pa); 1994* *David Key*

20 Passenger Ships (including Ferries)

20 Passenger Ships (including Ferries)

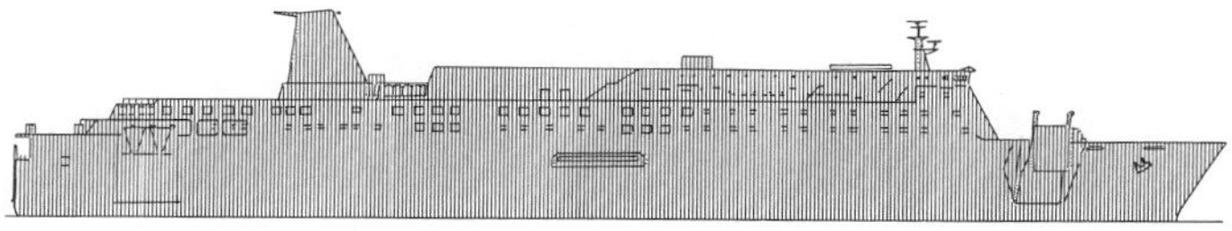

1 *AMF H*
ISHIKARI Ja/Ja (Mitsubishi HI) 1991; RoPCF; 14,257 grt/6,938 dwt; 192.5 × 6.92 m *(631.56 × 22.7 ft)*; TSM (MAN); 21.5 kts; Bow door/ramp; Quarter bow door/ramp; Two side door/ramps (one port/one starboard); Stern door/ramp

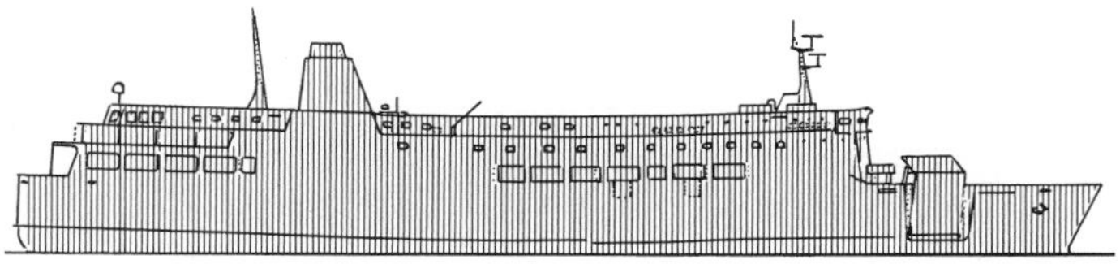

2 *AMGM H*
DA-IN Pa/Ja (Mitsubishi HI) 1988; RoC/F; 12,365 grt/3,363 dwt; 134.6 × 5.72 m *(441.6 × 18.77 ft)*; TSM (Pielstick); 20 kts; ex-*Venilia*; Bow door and ramp; Side door/ramp (starboard); Stern door/ramp

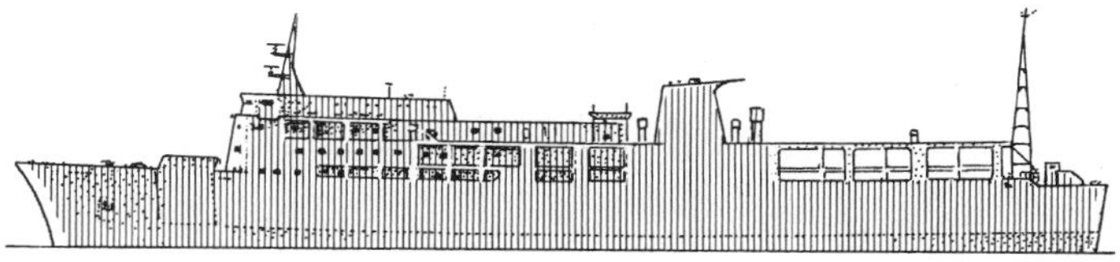

3 *AMGM H*
VELA Ja/Ja (Naikai) 1979; RoPF; 3,664 grt; 120.58 × 5.3 m *(395.6 × 17.39 ft)*; TSM (NKK); 21 kts; Bow door/ramp; Stern door/ramp; Side doors/ramps
Sister: **VESTA** (Ja)

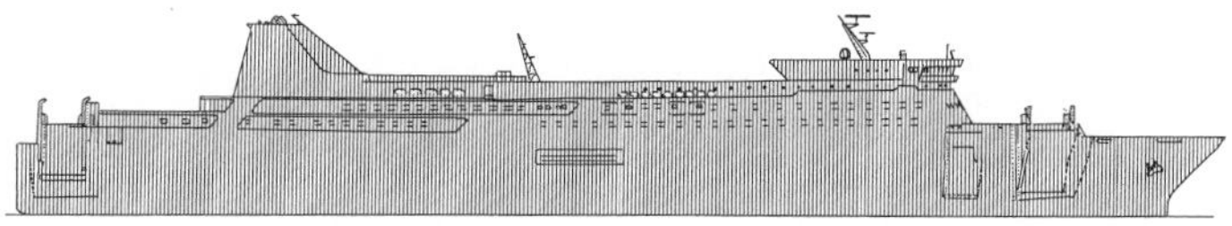

4 *AMNFA H*
SABRINA Ja/Ja (Kanda) 1990; RoPCF; 12,524 grt/6,281 dwt; 186.5 × 6.85 m *(611.88 × 22.47 ft)*; M (Pielstick); 23.2 kts; Quarter bow door/ramp; Side door/ramp (starboard aft); Stern door/ramp
Sister: **BLUE ZEPHYR**

5 *AMNM-F H*
MARIMO Ja/Ja (Setoda) 1972; RoPCF; 9,627 grt; 166 × 6.3 m *(545 × 20.6 ft)*; TSM (MAN); 22 kts; Stern door/ramp; Two side doors/ramps; Superstructure may now be extended aft

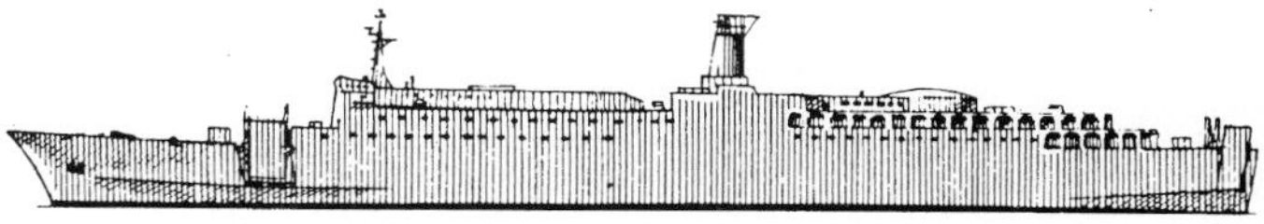

6 *BMFB H*
SUN FLOWER Ja/Ja (Kawasaki) 1972; RoPF; 12,130 grt; 185 × 6.4 m *(607 × 21 ft)*; TSM (MAN); 24.75 kts
Sisters: **SUN FLOWER 2** (Ja); **SUN FLOWER OSAKA** (—) ex-*Sun Flower 5*; **SUN FLOWER TOSA** (Ja) ex-*Sun Flower 8*

7 *CDMFM H*
NORDSTJERNEN No/Ge (B+V) 1956; P; 2,191 grt; 80.78 × 4.5 m *(268 × 14.9 ft)*; M (B&W); 15.5 kts
Sister: **CARIBBEAN MERCY** (Pa) ex-*Polarlys*

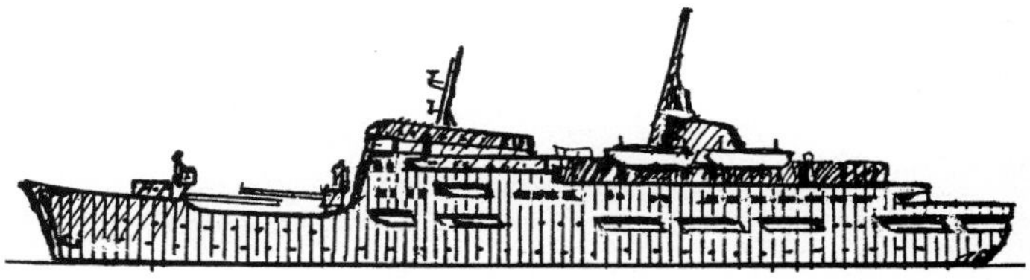

8 *CDMM-F H*
HARALD JARL No/No (Trondhjems) 1960; P; 2,600 grt; 87.4 × 4.6 m *(287 × 15.09 ft)*; M (B&W); 16 kts

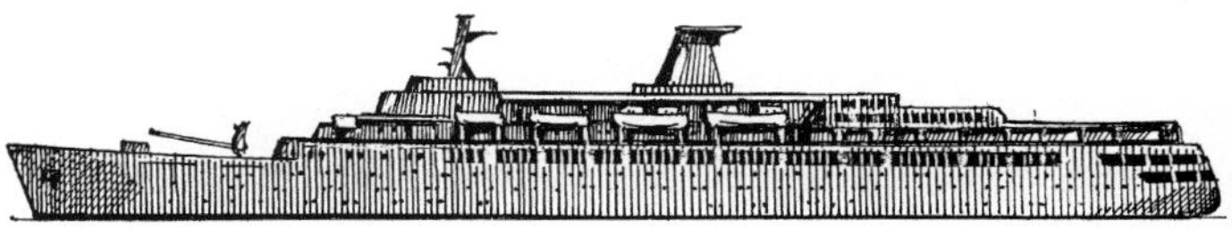

9 *CMF H*
DAPHNE Bs/Br (Swan Hunter) 1955/75; P; 9,436 grt; 162 × 10 m *(533 × 32.8 ft)*; TSM (Doxford); 17 kts; ex-*Port Sydney*; Rebuilt from a cargo ship 1975 (Khalkis)
Sister: **PRINCESS DANAE** (Pa) ex-*Port Melbourne*

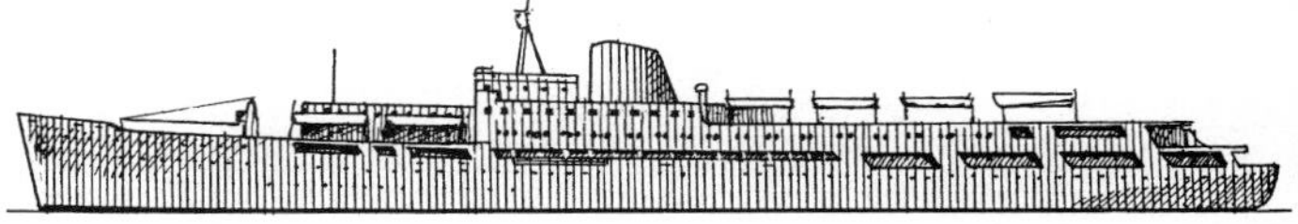

10 *CMF H*
ROMANTICA Cy/Ge (B+V) 1939; P; 9,511 grt; 148 × 6.7 m *(488 × 21.98 ft)*; D-E (MAN); 16 kts; ex-*Huascaran*

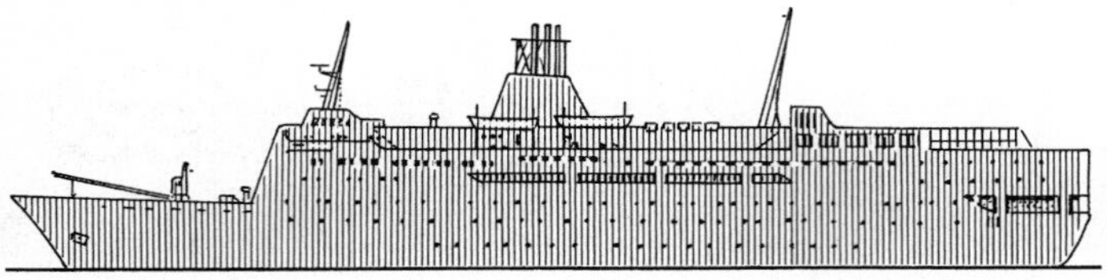

11 *CMFM H*
PRINCESA CYPRIA Cy/It (Tirreno) 1968; RoPF; 9,984 grt; 124.95 × 5.62 m *(411 × 18.44 ft)*; TSM (B&W); 18 kts; ex-*Prinsesse Margrethe*; Rebuilt 1975

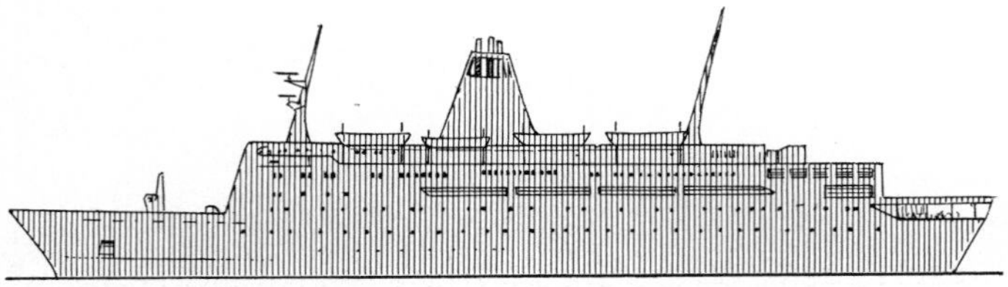

12 *CMFM H*
TIAN E RC/It (Tirreno) 1969/80; RoPF; 8,000 grt; 124.85 × 5.21 m *(410 × 17.09 ft)*; TSM (B&W); 21 kts; ex-*Aalborghus*; Bow, stern and side doors; Rebuilt 1980 (Aalborg)

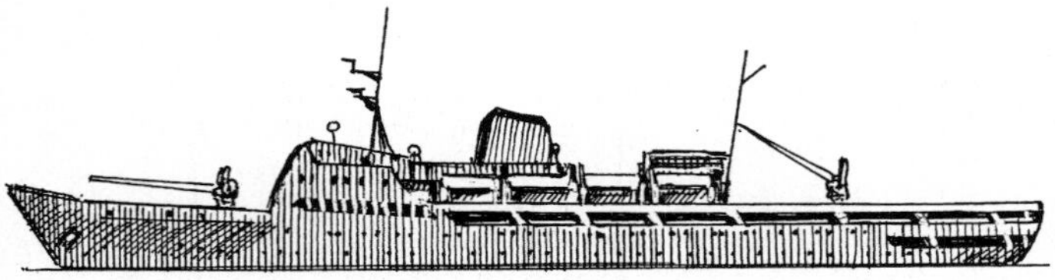

13 *CMFMC H*
ADZHARIYA Uk/DDR (Mathias-Thesen) 1964; P; 4,804 grt; 122 × 5.2 m *(401 × 17 ft)*; TSM (MAN); 17 kts

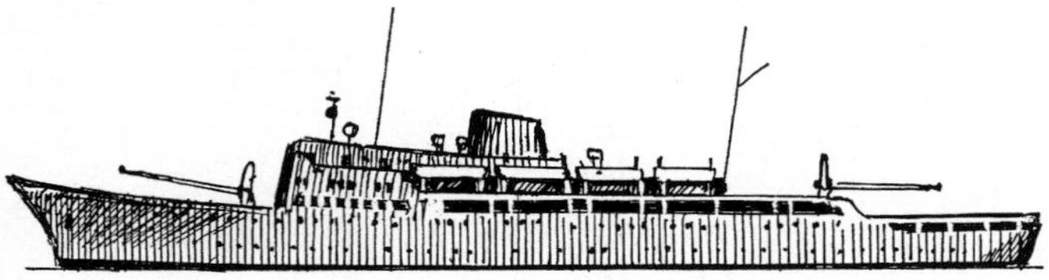

14 *CMFMC H*
BAYKAL Ru/DDR (Mathias-Thesen) 1962; P; 5,200 grt; 122.1 × 5.2 m *(401 × 17 ft)*; TSM (MAN); 17 kts
Similar (vary in details): **G ORDZHONIKIDZE** (Ma) ex-*Grigoriy Ordzhonkidze*; **EXCELSIOR MERCURY** (Ho) ex-*Mariya Ulyanova*; **NIKOLAYEVSK** (Ru); **BOSPHOR** (—)

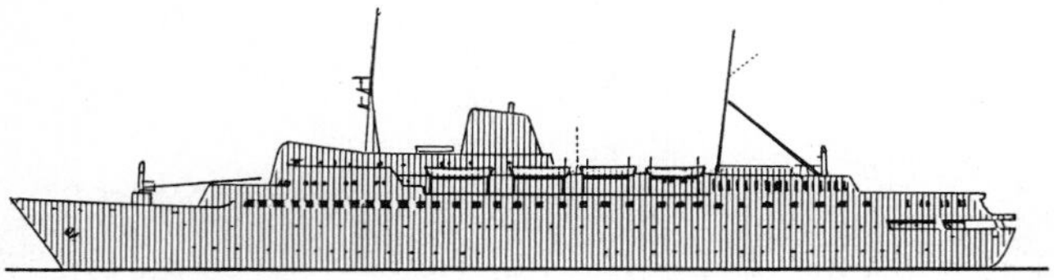

15 *CMFMC H*
ESTONIYA Ru/DDR (Mathias-Thesen) 1960; P; 5,035 grt; 122 × 5.2 m *(401 × 17 ft)*; TSM (MAN); 17 kts
Sister: **FU JIAN** (RC) ex-*Litva*

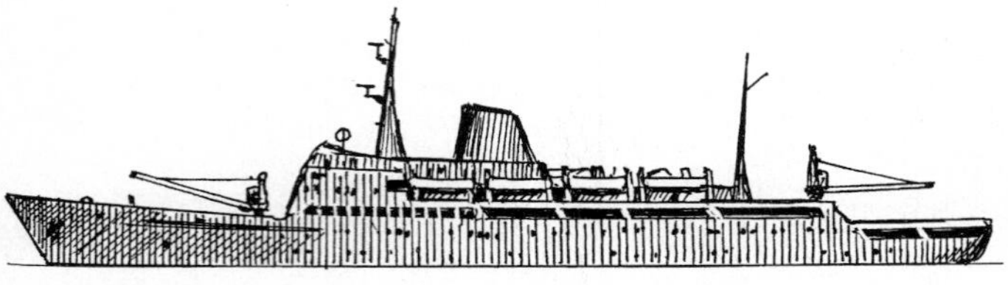

16 *CMFMC H*
ODESSA SONG Ma/DDR (Mathias-Thesen) 1964; P; 5,261 grt; 122.15 × 5.27 m *(400.75 × 17.29 ft)*; TSM (MAN); 17 kts; ex-*Bashkiriya*

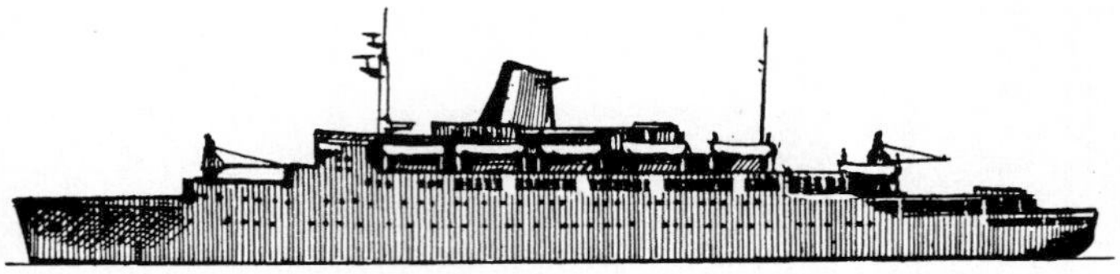

17 *CMFMC H*
STEFAN Ma/Ne (Wilton-Fije) 1952; P; 11,693 grt; 153.3 × 8.7 m *(503 × 28.54 ft)*; T (GEC); 16.5 kts; ex-*Maasdam*

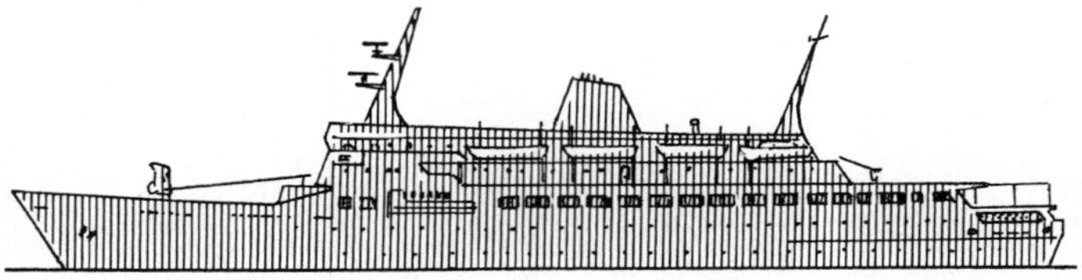

18 *CMFMS H*
ANTONINA NEZHDANOVA Ru/Ys (Titovo) 1978; P; 3,900 grt; 100.01 × 4.65 m *(328 × 15.26 ft)*; TSM (B&W); 17.25 kts
Sisters: **OLGA SADOVSKAYA** (Ru); **KLAVDIYA YELANSKAYA** (Ru).
Possible sister: **OLGA ANDROVSKAYA** (Ru)

19 *CM²F H*
KOLKHIDA Ru/Ru ('Zhdanov') 1961; P; 3,200 grt; 101.5 × 4 m *(333 × 13 ft)*; TSM (CKD Praha); 14.5 kts; Some ships have taller funnel; Some ships may not have crane
Sisters: **ALESSIA** (It) ex-*Moldavia*; **WANG FU** (RC) ex-*Tadzhakistan*; **TALLINN** (Ea) ex-*Svanetiya*; **TATARIYA** (Ru); **ODESSA SUN** (Ma) ex-*Uzbekistan*

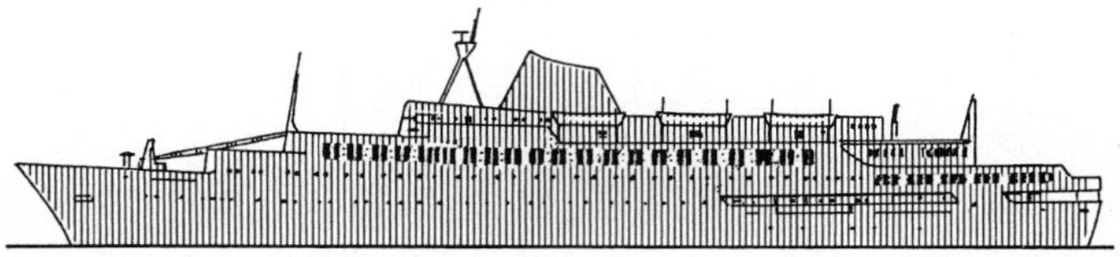

20 *CM²FN H*
DALMACIJA Cro/Ys ('Uljanik') 1965; P; 5,619 grt; 116.87 × 5.28 m *(383.43 × 17.32 ft)*; TSM (Sulzer); 17 kts
Sister: **ASTRA** (Uk) ex-*Istra*

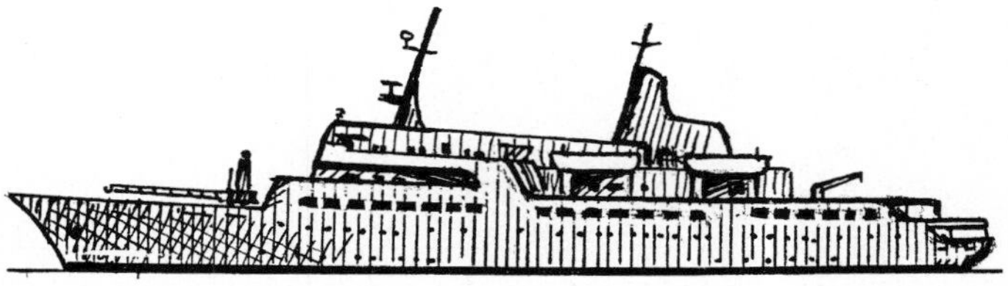

21 *CMM-F H*
BALTIC STAR Ge/FRG (Howaldts) 1963; P; 2,800 grt; 91.4 × 3.8 m *(300 × 12.46 ft)*; TSM (KHD); 18 kts; ex-*Helgoland*

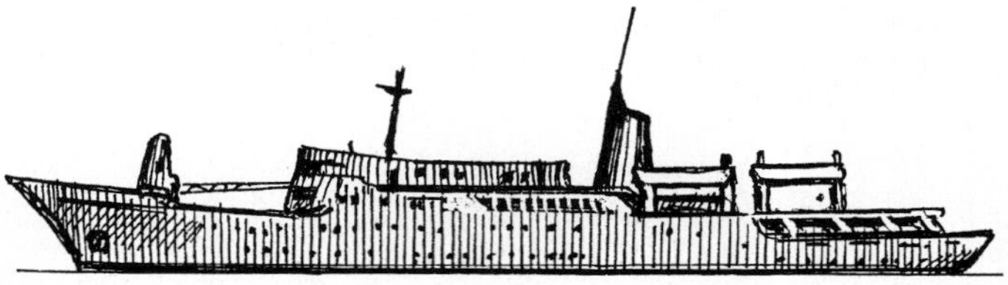

22 *CMM-F H*
GALAPAGOS EXPLORER Ec/It (Apuania) 1962; P; 2,200 grt; 95 × 3.7 m *(312 × 12.13 ft)*; TSM (Fiat); 19.5 kts; ex-*Gentile Da Fabriano*
Sister: **MARAM** (Si) ex-*Andrea Mantegna*

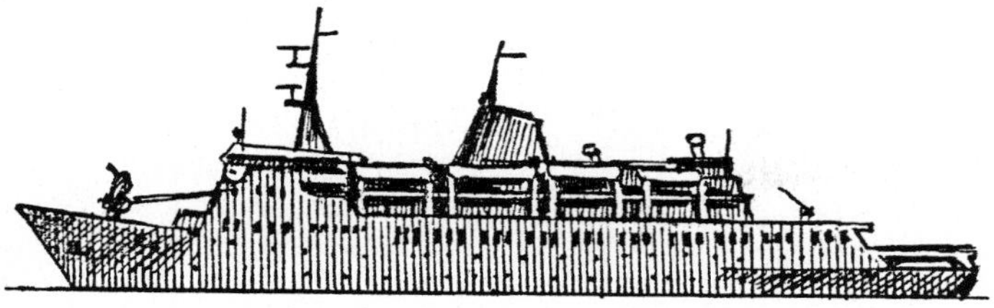

23 *CMM-FD H*
MARIYA YERMOLOVA Ru/Ys ('Titovo') 1974; P; 4,364 grt; 100 × 4.5 m *(328 × 14.1 ft)*; TSM (B&W); 17 kts
Sisters: **ALLA TARASOVA** (Ru); **LYUBOV ORLOVA** (Ru); **MARIYA SAVINA** (Ru); **OLGA ANDROVSKAYA** (Ru)

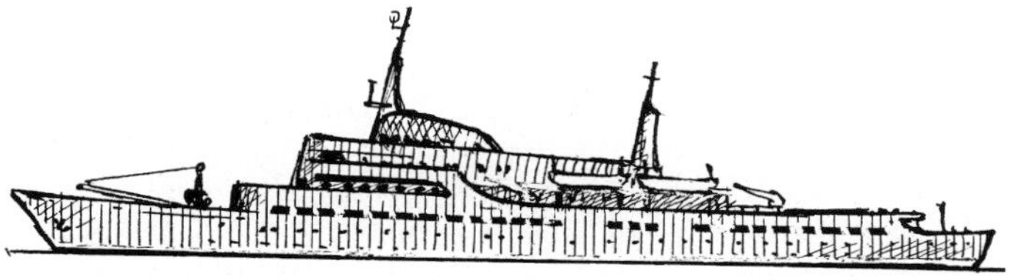

24 *CM-FM-G H*
HELGOLAND Ge/FRG (B+V) 1962; P; 3,800 grt; 104 × 4 m *(341 × 13.2 ft)*; TSM (Ottensener); 21 kts; ex-*Wappen Von Hamburg*

25 *CM-FM-G H*
WAPPEN VON HAMBURG Ge/FRG (Howaldts) 1965; P; 4,192 grt; 109.7 × 4.2 m *(360 × 13.7 ft)*; TSM (MAN); 21.5 kts

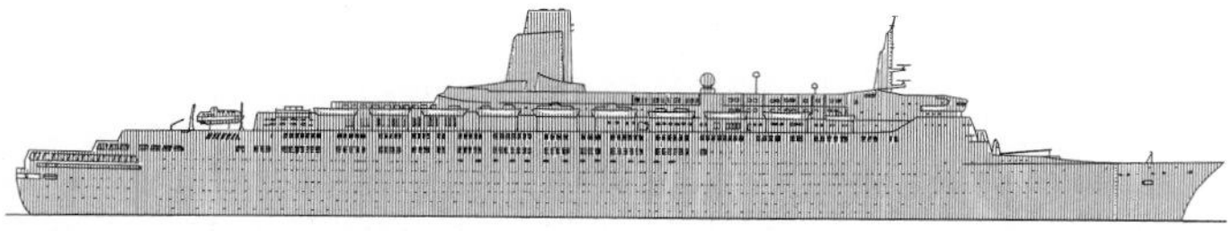

26 *C-RMF H*
QUEEN ELIZABETH 2 Br/Br (Upper Clyde) 1969; P; 70,327 grt; 293 × 10 m *(963 × 32.8 ft)*; TS D-E (MAN/GEC); 28.5 kts

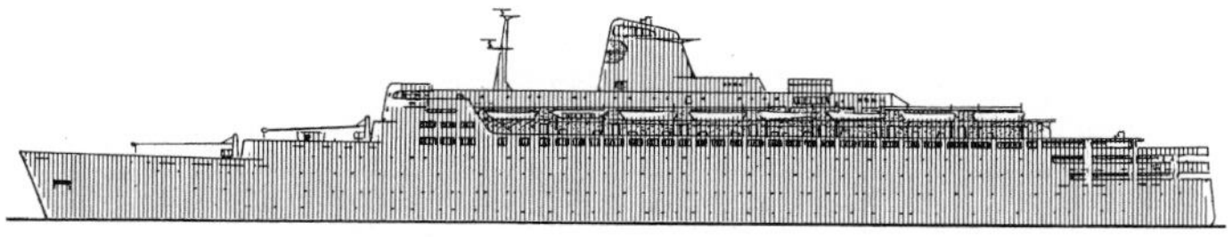

27 *D^2MF H*
ALBATROS Bs/Br (J Brown) 1957; P; 24,803 grt; 185.3 × 8.9 m *(608 × 29.19 ft)*; TST (J Brown); 20 kts; ex-*Sylvania* (see photo number 20/403
Sister: **REGENT ISLE** (—) ex-*Carinthia*

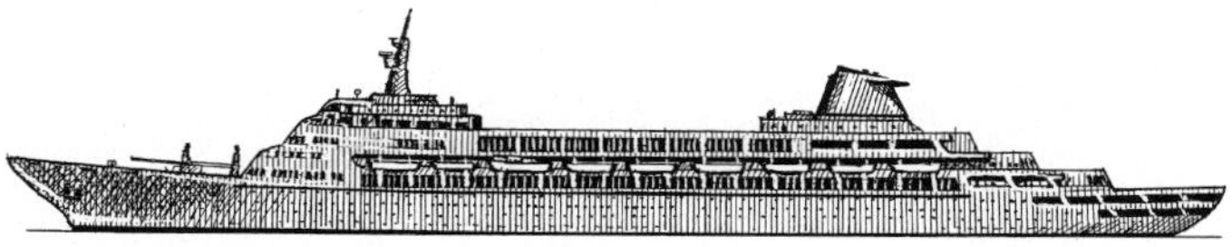

28 *D^2MF H*
STARSHIP OCEANIC Bs/It (Adriatico) 1965; P; 19,500 grt; 238 × 8.6 m *(782 × 28.4 ft)*; TST (Adriatico); 26.5 kts; ex-*Oceanic*

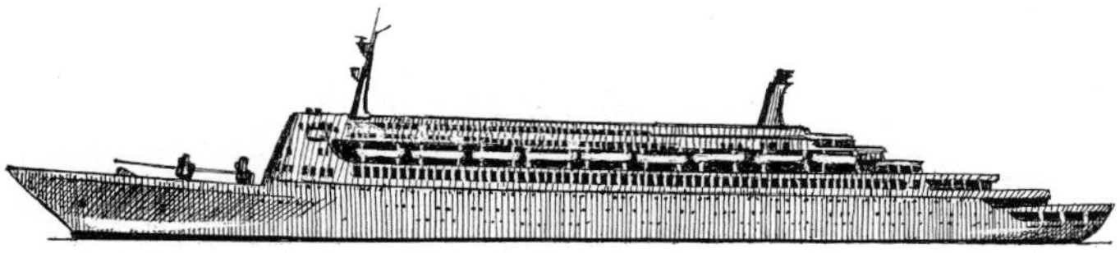

29 *D^2MG H*
EUGENIO COSTA It/It (Adriatico) 1966; P; 30,600 grt; 217 × 8.6 m *(773 × 28.4 ft)*; TST (De Laval); 27 kts; ex-*Eugenio C*

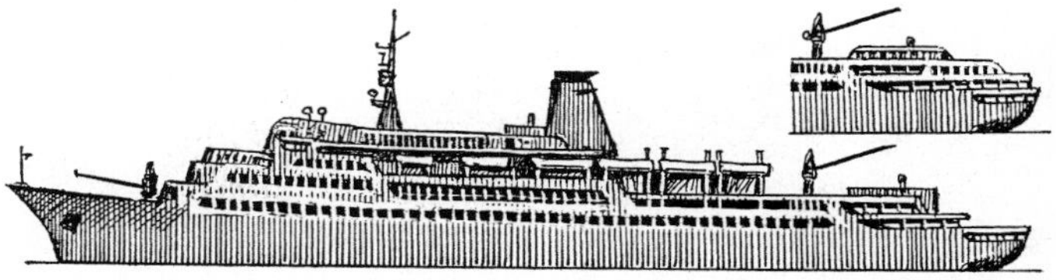

30 *DMFD H*
TARAS SHEVCHENKO Li/DDR (Mathias-Thesen) 1965; P; 21,100 grt; 176 × 8 m *(577 × 26.24 ft)*; TSM (Sulzer); 20.5 kts
Similar: **IVAN FRANKO** (Uk)

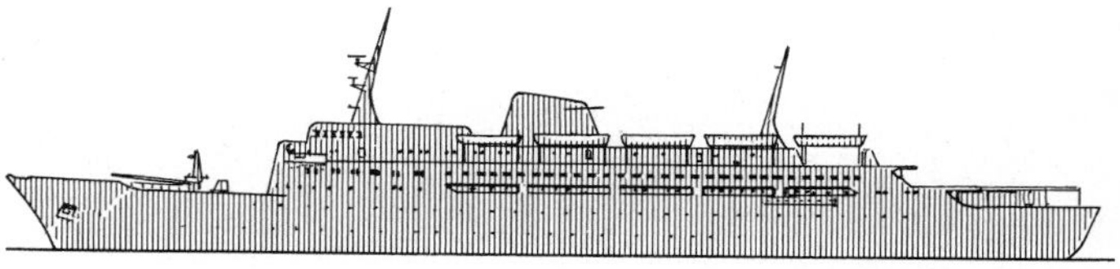

31 *DMFM H*
EUROPA Gr/De (Helsingor) 1964; RoPF; 4,986 grt; 140 × 5.5 m *(459 × 18.0 ft)*; TSM (B&W); 21 kts; ex-*England*

32 *DMFM H*
SAPPHO Gr/Br (Cammell Laird) 1966; RoPF; 6,500 grt; 140 × 5.4 m *(460 × 17.7 ft)*; TSM (Mirrlees); 18 kts; ex-*Spero*; Lengthened 1971

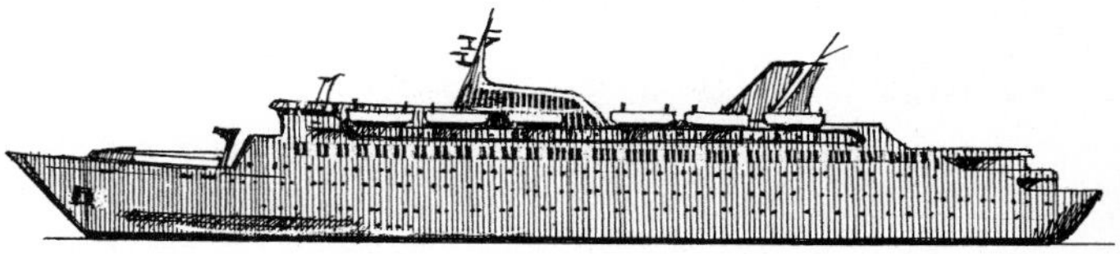

33 *DMGM H*
BOLERO Pa/FRG (AG 'Weser') 1968; P; 12,900 grt; 160 × 6.3 m *(525 × 20.66 ft)*; TSM (MAN); 21 kts; ex-*Starward*; Side doors
Similar: **LEISURE WORLD** (Bs) ex-*Skyward*

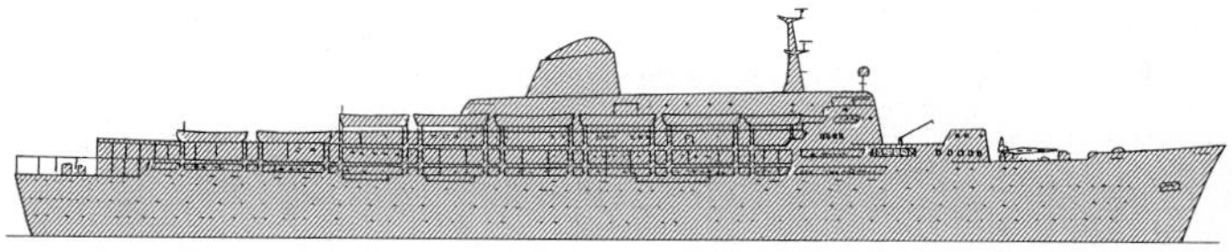

34 *DMSMF H*
FAIRSTAR Li/Br (Fairfields) 1957; P; 23,180 grt; 185.6 × 8.4 m *(609 × 27.7 ft)*; TST (Fairfield); 20 kts; ex-*Oxfordshire*

35 *HDMFN H*
ANASTASIS Ma/It (Adriatico) 1953; P; 11,701 grt; 159.09 × 7.19 m *(522 × 23.59 ft)*; TSM (Fiat); 19.75 kts; ex-*Victoria*

36 *H^2FH H1*
MISAMIS OCCIDENTAL Pi/Ja (Hayashikane) 1970; PC; 1,900 grt; 88.9 × 4.9 m *(292 × 16.1 ft)*; M (B&W); 18 kts

37 *HMF H1*
AMBASADOR I Ec/Ys ('Split') 1958; P; 2,210 grt; 90 × 4.7 m *(296 × 15.4 ft)*; TSM (Sulzer); 16.5 kts; ex-*Jedinstvo*
Similar: **HERMES** (Gr) ex-*Jugoslavija*

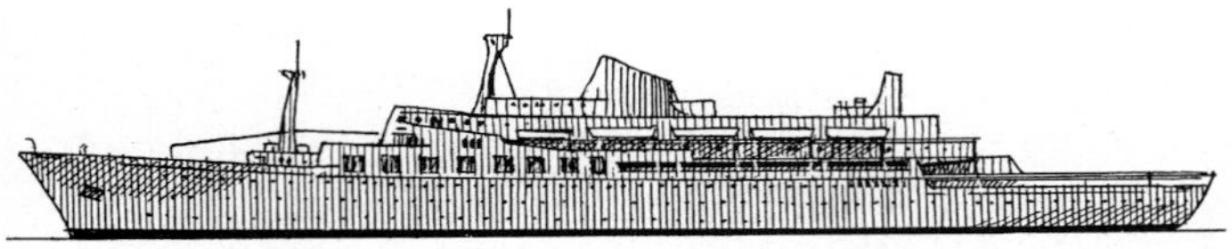

38 *HMFG H*
REGENT SPIRIT Bs/Ys ('Uljanik') 1962; P; 7,952 grt; 150 × 5.5 m *(492 × 18.0 ft)*; TSM (B&W); 18.5 kts; ex-*Anna Nery*
Sister: **ATHIRAH** (Ia) ex-*Rosa Da Fonseca*

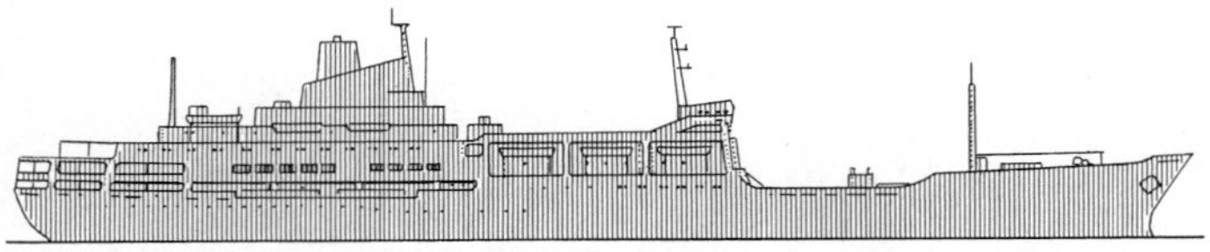

39 *HMM-FN H12*
SHIN SAKURA MARU Ja/Ja (Mitsubishi HI) 1972/81; PC; 19,811 grt/4,700 dwt; 175.83 × 7.93 m *(576.87 × 26.02 ft)*; M (Mitsubishi); 21.25 kts; Converted from passenger cargo/exhibition ship 1981

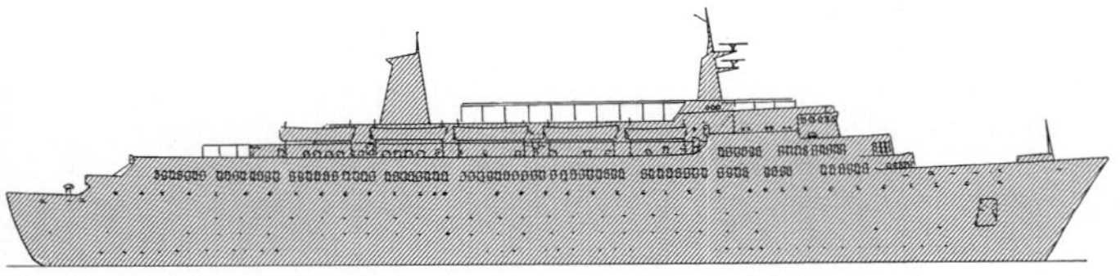

40 *KMM-G H*
FREEWINDS Pa/Fi (Wärtsilä) 1968; P; 9,780 grt; 134 × 5.5 m *(441 × 18.1 ft)*; TSM (Sulzer); 20 kts; ex-*Boheme*

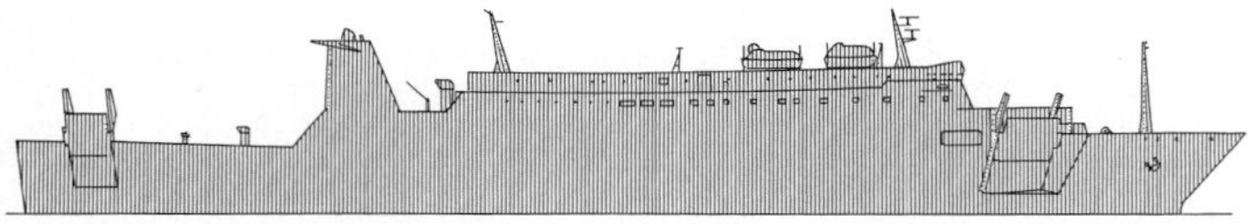

41 *MAM^{2}GA H2*
WAKANATSU OKINAWA Ja/Ja (Saiki) 1991; RoPCF; 8,052 grt/3,900 dwt; 151.13 × 6.4 m *(495.83 × 21 ft)*; M (Pielstick); 21 kts; Quarter bow door/ramp (starboard); Quarter stern door/ramp; 179 TEU

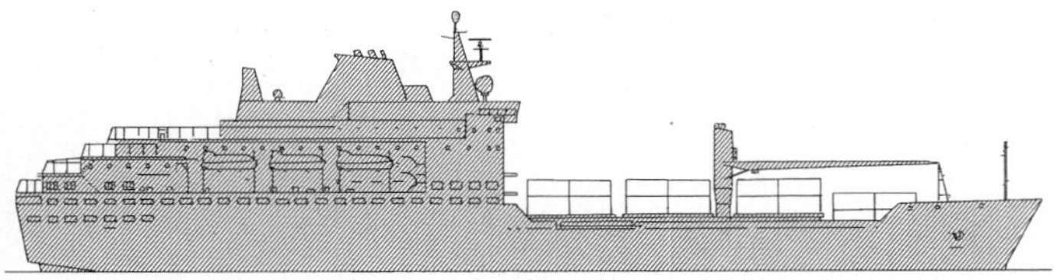

42 *MCMF^2 H12*
ZI YU LAN RC/Ge (MTW) 1995; P/Con; 16,071 grt/6,526 dwt; 150.45 × 6.85 m *(493.6 × 22.47 ft)*; M (MaK); 20 kts; 286 TEU

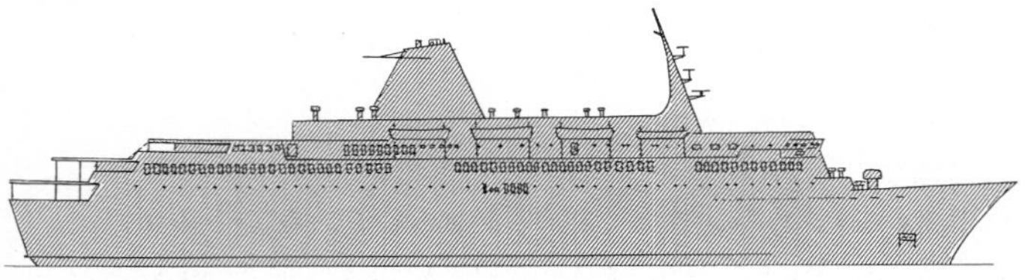

43 *MF H*
AMBASSADOR II Cy/FRG (Nobiskrug) 1970; RoPF; 11,403 grt; 134 × 4.9 m *(440 × 16.07 ft)*; TSM (Pielstick); 22 kts; ex-*Prins Oberon*; Bow door/ramp; Stern door/ramp; Has alterations to after end of superstructure—not shown on drawing
Similar: **NIEBOROW** (Pd) ex-*Prinz Hamlet*; **NORRONA** (Fa) ex-*Gustav Vasa* (small mast from funnel—superstructure extended from foremast to bridge top)

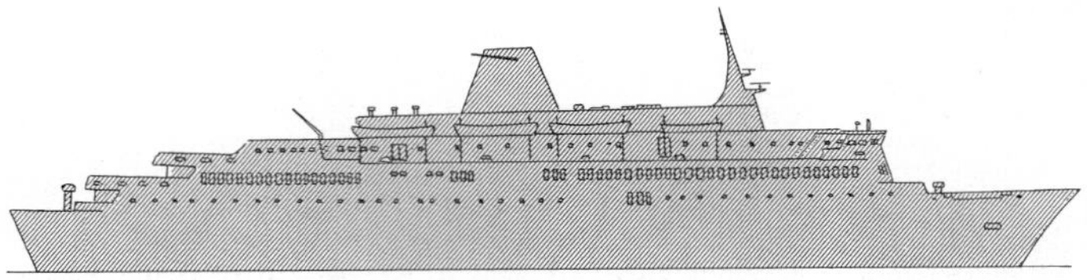

44 *MF H*
BEAUPORT Bs/FRG (Unterweser) 1970; RoPF; 7,747 grt; 118.5 × 4.75 m *(389 × 15.58 ft)*; TSM (Pielstick); — kts; ex-*Prince of Fundy*; Bow, stern and side doors
Sister: **DIMITRIOS EXPRESS** (Gr) ex-*Saint Patrick*. Similar: **MARKO POLO** (Cro) ex-*Peter Wessel*

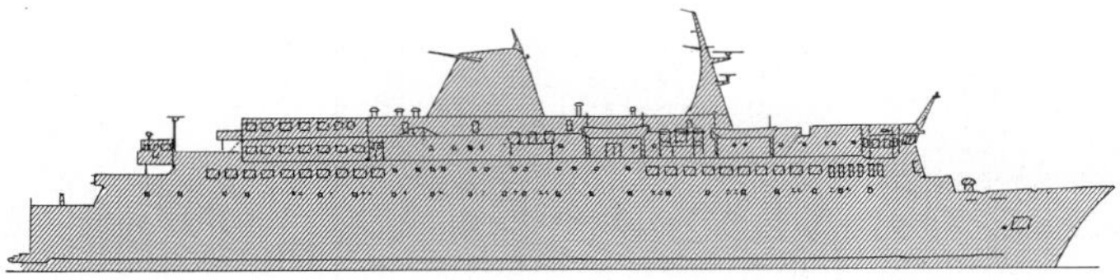

45 *MF H*
BENCHIJGUA II Sp/FRG (Schichau-U) 1974; RoPF; 8,531 grt; 118.01 × 5.02 m *(387 × 16.47 ft)*; TSM (MAN); 17 kts; ex-*Djursland II*; Bow and stern doors
Similar: **PEDER OLSEN** (De) ex-*Kalle III* (superstructure built-up aft)

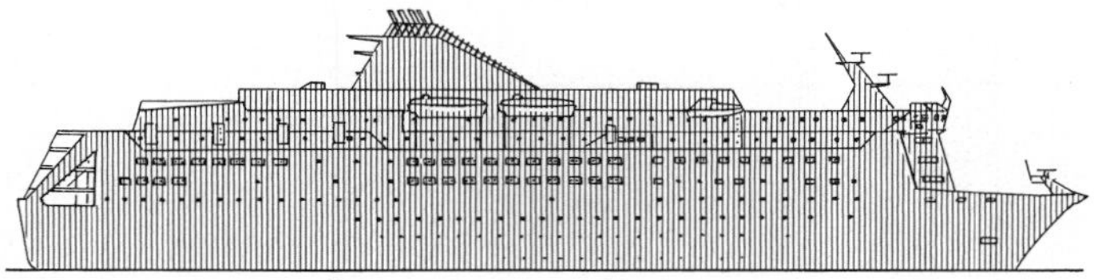

46 *MF H*
BIRKA PRINCESS Fi/Fi (Valmet) 1986; RoPCF; 21,484 grt; 141.03 × 5.6 m *(462.7 × 18.37 ft)*; TSM (Wärtsilä); 18 kts; Side door/ramp (port)

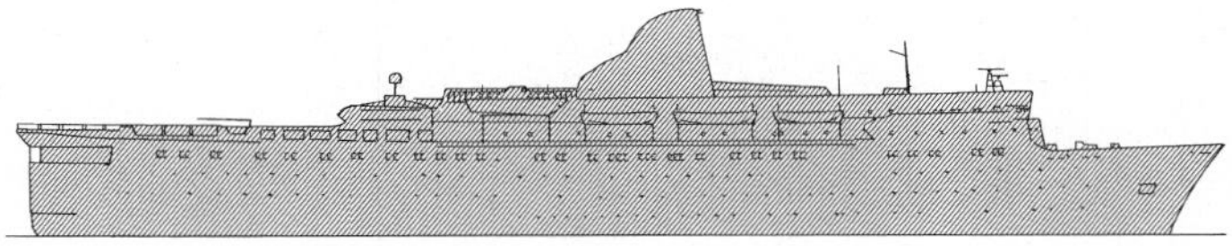

47 *MF H*
BLACK PRINCE NIS/FRG (LF-W) 1966/87; P; 11,209 grt; 141.64 × 6.42 m *(464.7 × 21.06 ft)*; TSM (Pielstick); 22.5 kts; Portable marina aft; Converted from Ro-Ro ferry 1987

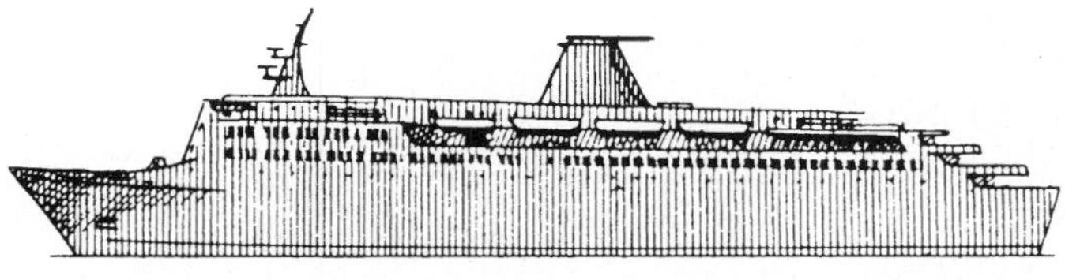

48 *MF H*
BLUENOSE Bs/Ys ('Jozo Lozovina-Mosor') 1973; RoPF; 13,179 grt; 124.9 × 5.3 m *(410 × 17.38 ft)*; TSM (Pielstick); 19.5 kts; ex-*Stena Jutlandica*; Bow and stern doors; Deepened and widened 1977
Sister: **STENA LONDONER** (Bs) ex-*Stena Danica* (lengthened, widened and deepened 1977); Similar: **SCOTIA PRINCE** (Pa) ex-*Stena Olympica* (lengthened 1987 to 143 m)

49 *MF H*
CIUDAD DE SANTA CRUZ LA PALMA Sp/Sp (UN de Levante) 1972; RoPF; 7,500 grt; 137.8 × 5.7 m *(452 × 18.7 ft)*; TSM (MAN); 22.5 kts; ex-*Canguro Cabo San Sebastian*; Stern door
Sisters: **CIUDAD DE PALMA** (Sp) ex-*Canguro Cabo San Jorge*; **CIUDAD DE BADAJOZ** (Sp); **CIUDAD DE SEVILLA** (Sp); **CIUDAD DE SALAMANCA** (Sp); **CIUDAD DE VALENCIA** (Sp)

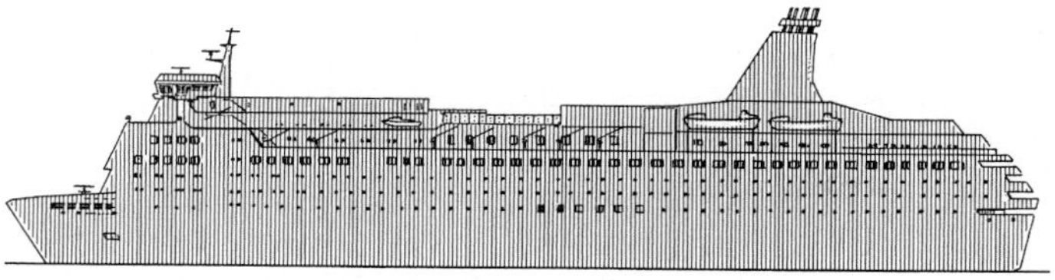

50 *MF H*
COLOR FESTIVAL No/Fr (Wärtsilä) 1985; RoPCF; 34,417 grt; 168.03 × 6.3 m *(551.28 × 20.67 ft)*; TSM (Pielstick); 21 kts; ex-*Svea*; Bow door/ramp; Two stern door/ramps
Sister: **SILJA FESTIVAL** (Fi) ex-*Wellamo*

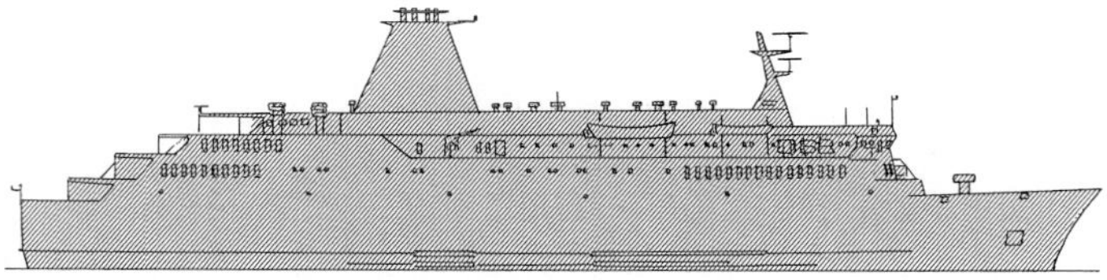

51 *MF H*
CORSICA SERENA II Pa/FRG (Nobiskrug) 1974; RoPF; 8,798 grt; 118.7 × 5 m *(390 × 16.4 ft)*; TSM (Atlas-MaK); 20.75 kts; ex-*Europafarjan III*

52 *MF H*
CROWN M Cy/FRG (LF-W) 1966; RoPF; 11,497 grt; 141.6 × 6.5 m *(466 × 21.32 ft)*; TSM (Pielstick); 22 kts; ex-*Black Watch/Jupiter*

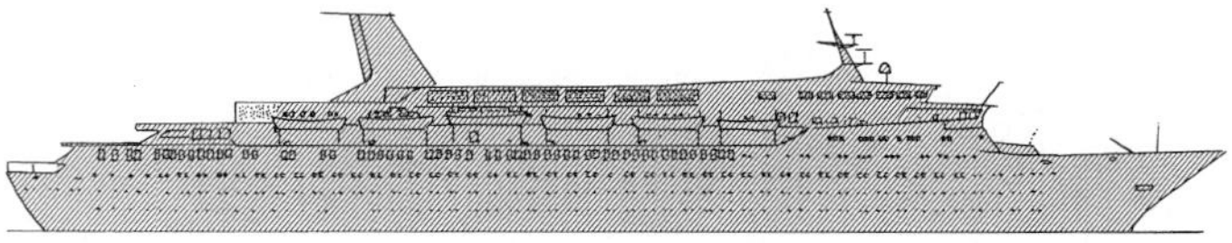

53 *MF H*
CUNARD COUNTESS Bs/De (B&W) 1976; P; 16,795 grt; 164 × 5.8 m *(538 × 19 ft)*; TSM (B&W); 21.5 kts
Sister: **CUNARD PRINCESS** (Bs) ex-*Cunard Conquest*

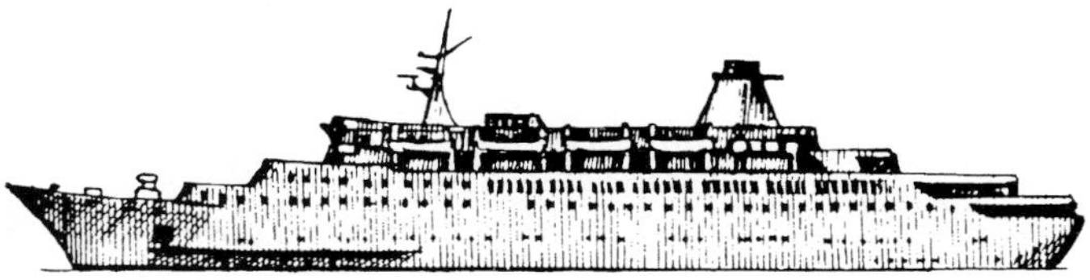

54 *MF H*
DISCOVERY SUN Pa/FRG (O & K) 1968; RoPCF; 11,979 grt; 134.5 × 5.5 m *(441.6 × 18 ft)*; TSM (Pielstick); 18 kts; ex-*Freeport*

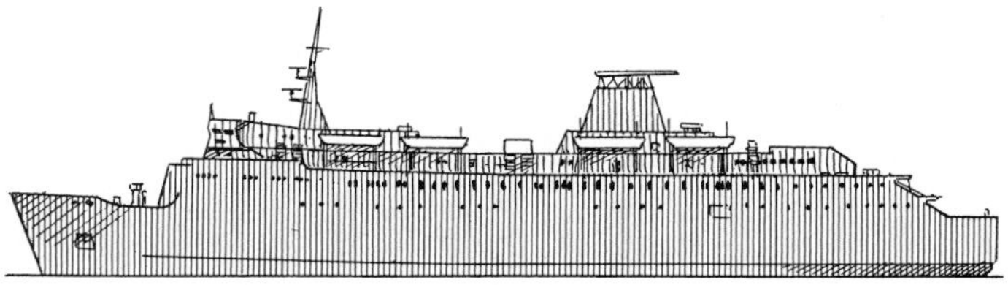

55 *MF H*
DUCHESSE ANNE Fr/Ih (Verolme Cork) 1978; RoPCF; 6,812 grt; 122.03 × 4.82 m *(400.36 × 15.81 ft)*; TSM (Atlas-MaK); 20 kts; ex-*Connacht*; Bow and stern doors/ramps
Sister: **ISLE OF INISHMORE** (Ih) ex-*Leinster*

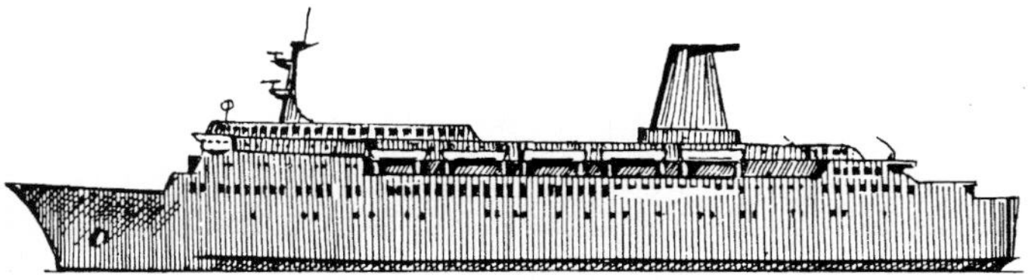

56 *MF H*
FEDRA Gr/FRG (Nobiskrug) 1974; RoPCF; 12,500 grt; 148.9 × 5.5 m *(488 × 18 ft)*; TSM (Pielstick); 22 kts; ex-*Peter Pan*; Bow and stern doors

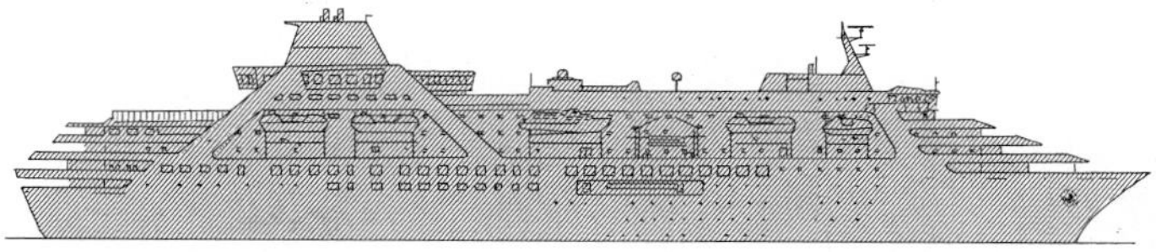

57 *MF H*
FUJI MARU Ja/Ja (Mitsubishi HI) 1989; P; 23,340 grt; 167 × 6.55 m *(547.9 × 21.49 ft)*; TSM (Mitsubishi); 20 kts

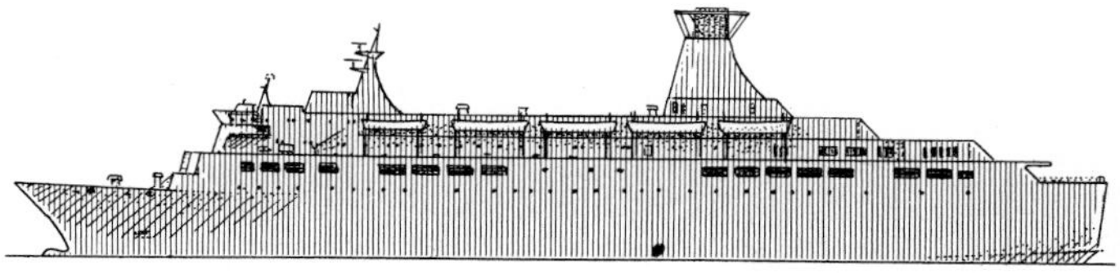

58 *MF H*
HABIB Tn/FRG (Nobiskrug) 1978; P/RoC; 16,168 grt; 145.73 × 6.16 m *(478 × 20.21 ft)*; TSM (Atlas-MaK); 22 kts; Bow door/ramp, stern ramp

See photo number 20/401
59 *MF H*
HAMBURG Bs/FRG (Nobiskrug) 1976; RoPCF; 18,888 grt; 156.4 × 5.4 m *(513.6 × 17.7 ft)*; TSM (Stork-Werkspoor); 22 kts; ex-*Kronprins Harald*; Bow door/ramp, side doors

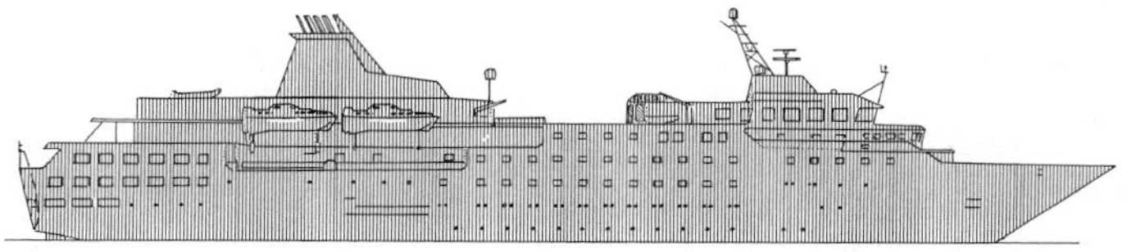

60 *MF H*
HANSEATIC Bs/Fi (Rauma Yards) 1991; P; 8,378 grt; 122.73 × 4.7 m *(402.66 × 15.42 ft)*; TSM (MaK); 14 kts; ex-*Society Adventurer*

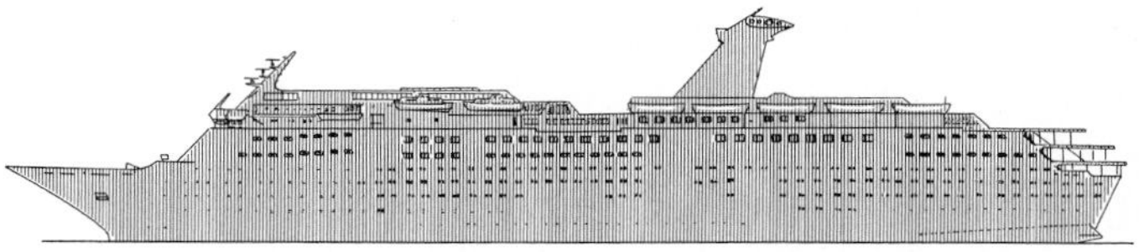

61 *MF H*
HOLIDAY Bs/De (Aalborg) 1985; P; 46,050 grt; 221.57 × 7.77 m *(726.94 × 25.49 ft)*; TSM (Sulzer); 22 kts
Sisters (Sw built—Kockums): **CELEBRATION** (Li); **JUBILEE** (Li)

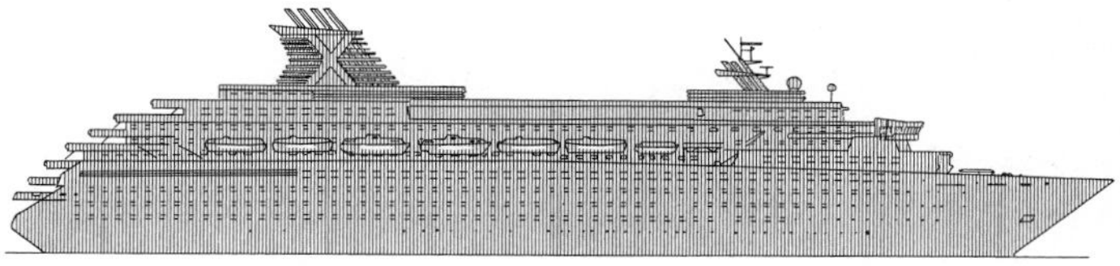

62 *MF H*
HORIZON Li/FRG (Meyer) 1990; P; 46,811 grt; 208 × 7.42 m *(682.41 × 24.34 ft)*; TSM (MAN); 21.4 kts
Sister: **ZENITH** (Li)

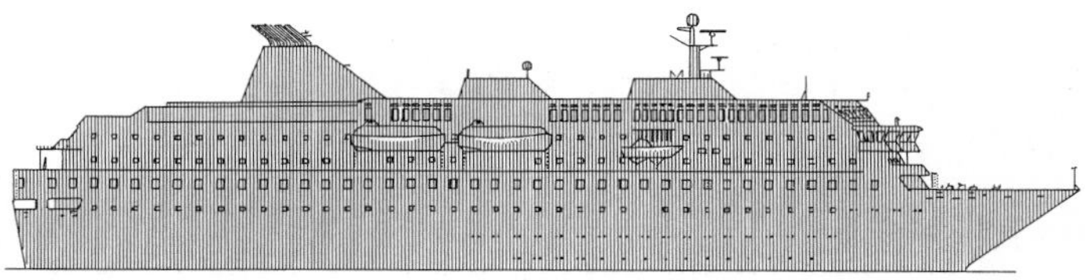

63 *MF H*
KONG HARALD No/Ge (Volkswerft) 1993; RoPCF; 11,204 grt; 121.8 × 4.7 m *(399.61 × 15.42 ft)*; TSM (MaK); 18 kts; Side door/ramp (port)
Sisters: **NORDLYS** (No); **RICHARD WITH** (No)

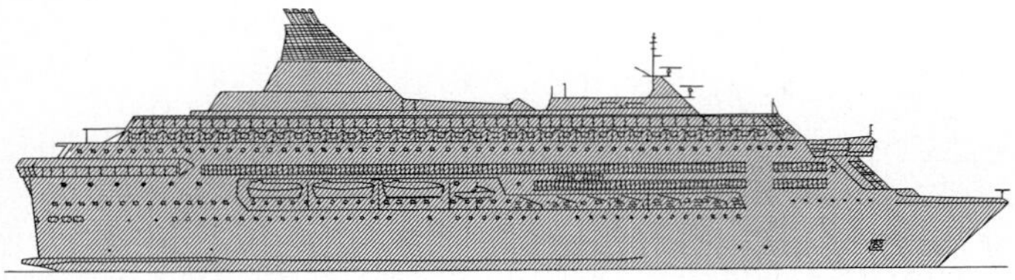

64 *MF H*
LANGKAPURI STAR AQUARIUS Pa/Fi ((Wärtsilä MI) 1989; RoPCF; 40,022 grt; 176.6 × 6.21 m *(579.4 × 20.37 ft)*; TSM (Sulzer); 21 kts; ex-*Athena*; Bow door/ramp; Two stern door/ramps

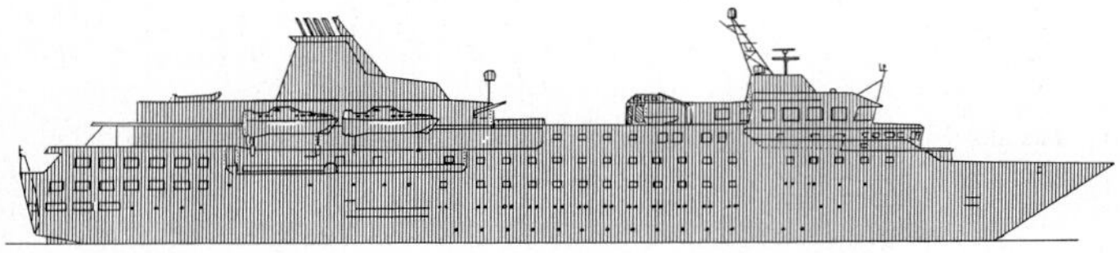

65 *MF H*
MAJESTIC It/It (Apuania) 1993; RoPCF; 32,746 grt; 188.22 × 6.72 m *(617.52 × 22.05 ft)*; TSM (Sulzer); 23 kts; Two stern door/ramps (one port/ one starboard); Upper stern door/ramp
Sister: **SPLENDID** (It); Similar: **FANTASTIC** (It)

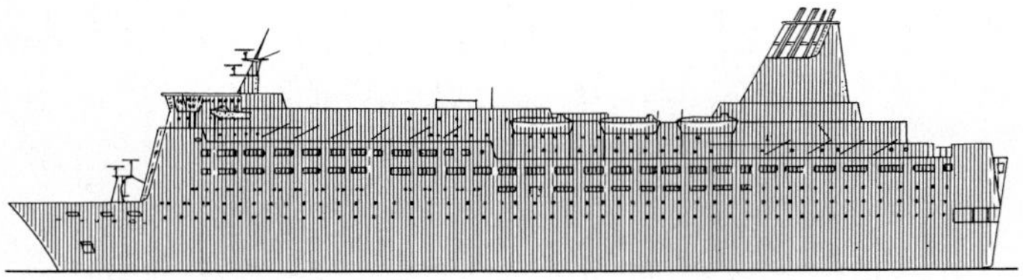

66 *MF H*
MARIELLA Fi/Fi (Wärtsilä) 1985; RoPCF; 37,799 grt; 200.01 × 6.3 m *(656.2 × 20.67 ft)*; TSM (Pielstick); 22 kts; Bow door/ramp; two stern doors/ ramps
Sister: **PRIDE OF BILBAO** (Br) ex-*Olympia*

67 *MF H*
MEDITERRANEAN SEA Pa/Br (Vickers-Armstrongs) 1953; RoPF; 13,692 grt; 164.9 × 6.4 m *(541 × 21 ft)*; TSM (Doxford); — kts; ex-*City of Exeter*; Converted from a Passenger Cargo Ship 1972
Similar: **MEDITERRANEAN SKY** (Gr) ex-*City of York*

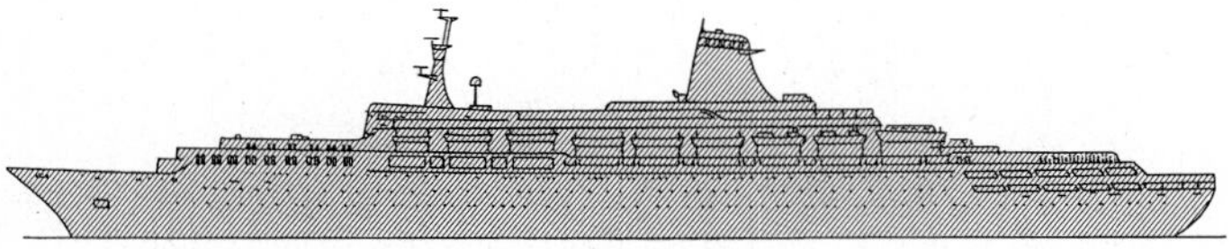

68 *MF H*
MERIDIAN Bs/It (Adriatico) 1963/84; P; 30,440 grt; 213.65 × 8.65 m *(700.95 × 28.38 ft)*; TST (De Laval); 25.5 kts; ex-*Galileo Galilei*; Rebuilt 1984

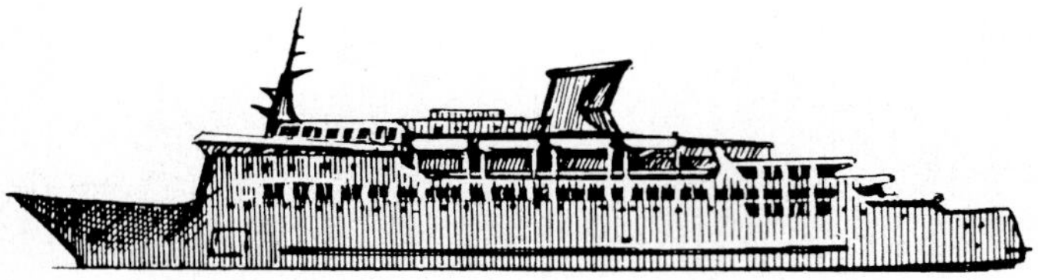

69 *MF H*
MOBY FANTASY It/Sp (UN de Levante) 1976; RoPF; 9,441 grt; 140.8 × 6.4 m *(462 × 21 ft)*; TSM (MAN); 23.5 kts; ex-*Manuel Soto*
Sister: **J J SISTER** (Pa)

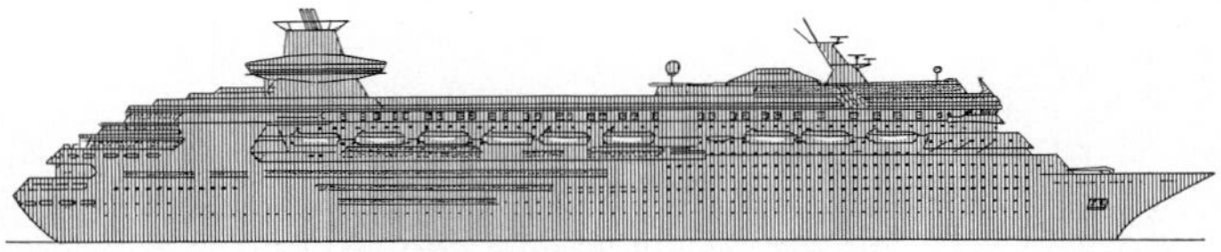

70 *MF H*
MONARCH OF THE SEAS NIS/Fr (L'Atlantique) 1991; P; 73,937 grt; 268.32 × 7.55 m *(880.31 × 24.77 ft)*; TSM (Pielstick); 20 kts
Sister: **MAJESTY OF THE SEAS** (NIS); Sister (small superstructure differences): **SOVEREIGN OF THE SEAS** (NIS)

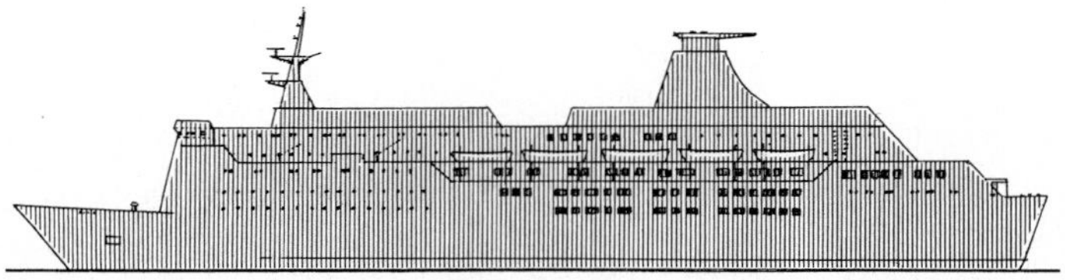

71 *MF H*
NORD GOTLANDIA Sw/FRG (A G 'Weser') 1981; RoPCF; 21,473 grt; 153.4 × 5.82 m *(503 × 19.09 ft)*; TSM (Pielstick); 21 kts; ex-*Olau Hollandia*; Bow and two stern doors
Sister: **CHRISTIAN IV** (No) ex-*Olau Britannia*

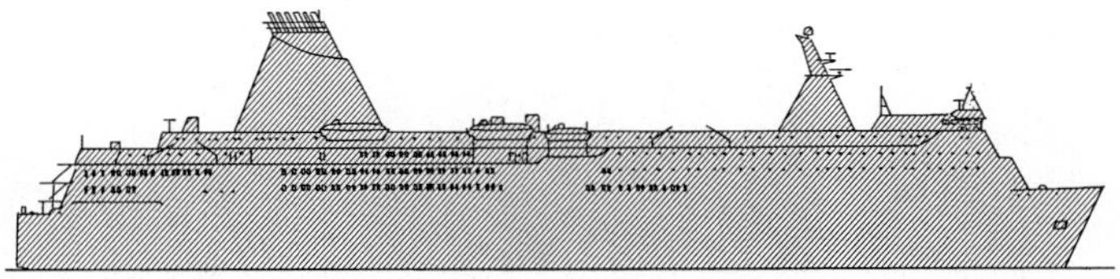

72 *MF H*
NORSEA Br/Br (Govan) 1987; RoPCF; 31,785 grt; 179.2 × 6.13 m *(587.93 × 20.11 ft)*; TSM (Sulzer); 18.5 kts; Stern door/ramp
Similar (Ja-built — NKK): **NORSUN** (Ne)

See photo number 20/406

73 *MF H*
ODESSA Uk/Br (Vickers SB) 1974; P; 13,253 grt; 136.3 × 5.8 m *(447.6 × 19 ft)*; TSM (Pielstick); 19 kts; ex-*Copenhagen*

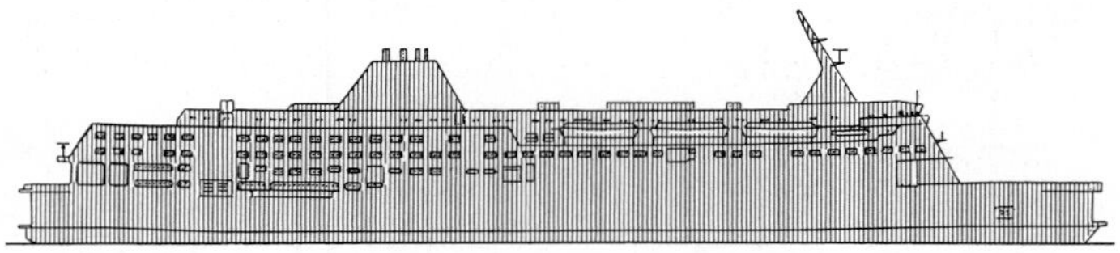

74 *MF H*
PRIDE OF DOVER Br/FRG (Schichau-U) 1987; RoPCF; 26,433 grt; 169.6 × 6.12 m *(556.43 × 20.08 ft)*; TrSM (Sulzer); 22 kts; Bow door; Stern door
Sister: **PRIDE OF CALAIS** (Br)

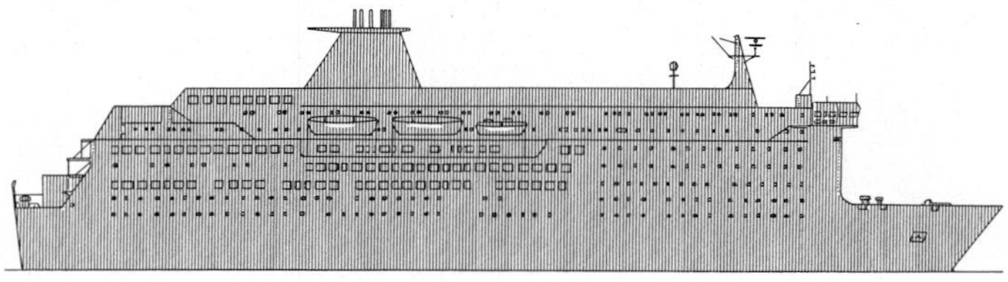

75 *MF H*
PRIDE OF LE HAVRE Br/FRG (Schichau See) 1989; RoPCF; 33,336 grt; 165 × 6.53 m *(541.34 × 21.42 ft)*; TSM (Sulzer); 21.3 kts; ex-*Olau Hollandia*; Bow door and ramp; Two stern door/ramps
Sister: **PRIDE OF PORTSMOUTH** (Br) ex-*Olau Britannia*

76 *MF H*
PRINCE OF SCANDINAVIA DIS/FRG (Flender) 1975; RoPCF; 21,545 grt; 182.4 × 6.3 m *(598.6 × 20.66 ft)*; TSM (Pielstick); 26 kts; ex-*Tor Britannia*
Sister: **PRINCESS OF SCANDINAVIA** (DIS) ex-*Tor Scandinavia*

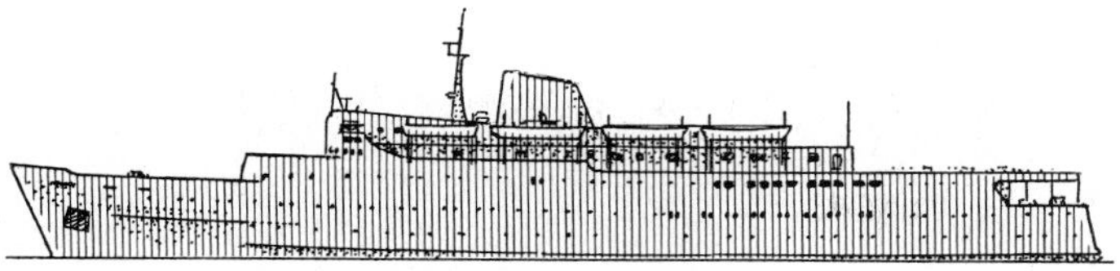

77 *MF H*
PRINCESA AMOROSA Cy/Br (H&W) 1957; P; 5,026 grt; 104.32 × 4.81 m *(342.26 × 15.78 ft)*; TSM (H&W); 17.5 kts; ex-*Scottish Coast*; Converted from ferry

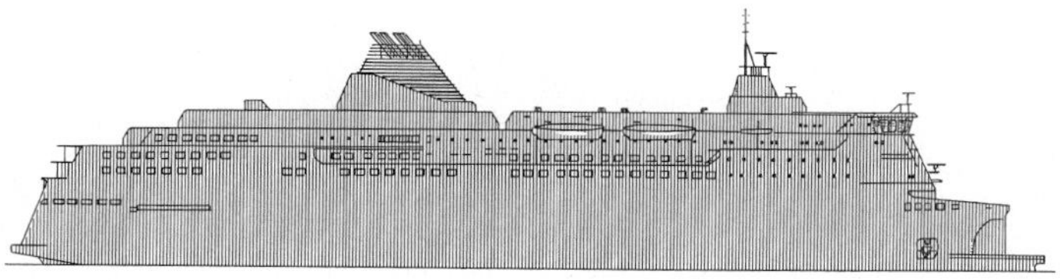

78 *MF H*
PRINS FILIP Be/Be (Boelwerf) 1992; RoPCF; 28,833 grt; 163.4 × 6.5 m *(536.09 × 21.33 ft)*; TSM (Sulzer); 21 kts; Bow door and stern door

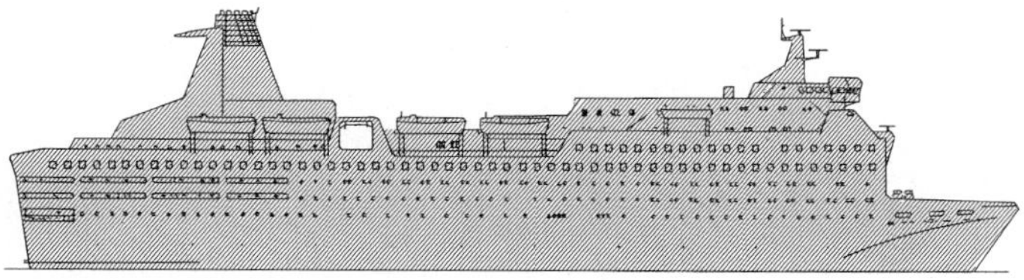

79 *MF H*
QUEEN OF SCANDINAVIA DIS/Fi (Wärtsilä) 1981; RoPF; 33,575 grt; 166.02 × 6.72 m *(544.69 × 22.05 ft)*; TSM (Pielstick); 22 kts; ex-*Finlandia*; Bow door/ramp and two stern door/ramps
Sister: **STENA SAGA** (Sw) ex-*Silvia Regina*

80 *MF H*
QUEEN OF SIDNEY Ca/Ca (Victoria Mach) 1960; RoPF; 3,100 grt; 102.4 × 3.8 m *(336 × 12.46 ft)*; TSM (Mirrlees, Bickerton & Day); 8 kts; ex-*Sidney*

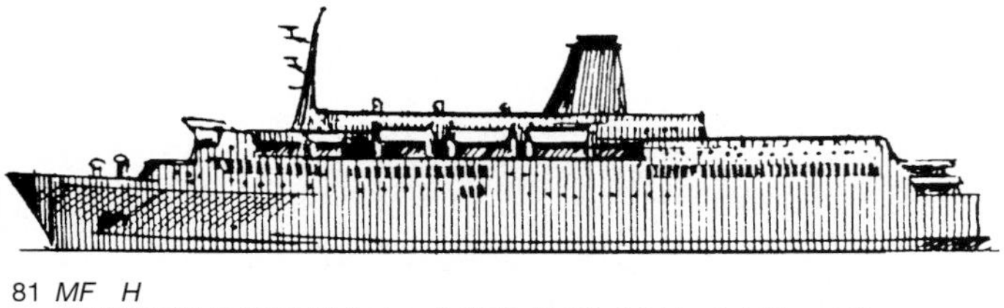

81 *MF H*
QUIBERON Fr/FRG (Nobiskrug) 1975; RoPF; 8,314 grt; 129 × 4.9 m *(424 × 16.07 ft)*; TSM (Stork-Werkspoor); 22 kts; ex-*Nils Dacke*; Bow door/ramp; Stern door/ramp

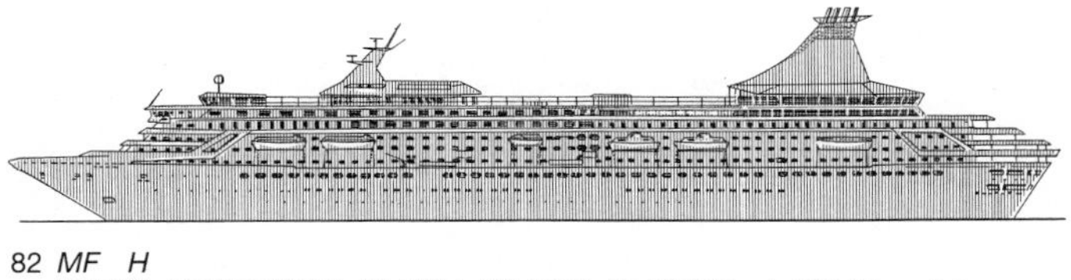

82 *MF H*
ROYAL PRINCESS Br/Fi (Wärtsilä) 1984; P; 44,348 grt; 230.61 × 7.8 m *(756.59 × 25.59 ft)*; TSM (Pielstick); 21.5 kts

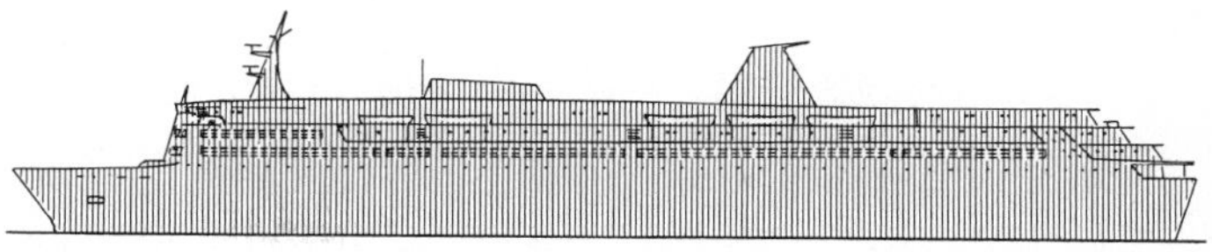

83 *MF H*
SAINT KILLIAN II Ih/Ys ('Titovo') 1973/81; RoPCF; 13,638 grt; 156.85 × 5.22 m *(514.6 × 17.13 ft)*; TSM (Pielstick); 21.5 kts; ex-*Stena Scandinavica*; Bow door and ramp; Stern door/ramp; Lengthened 1981

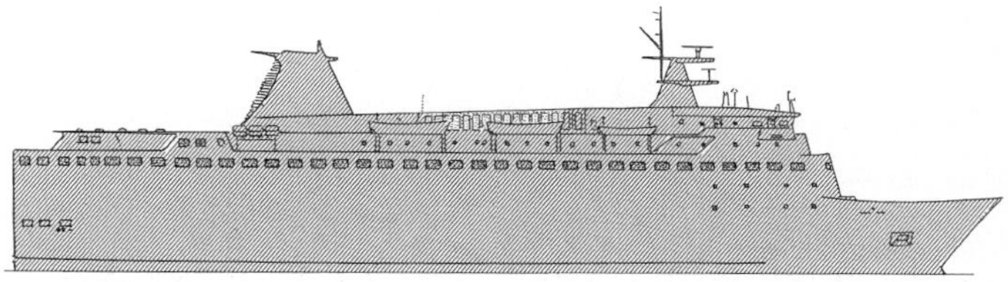

84 *MF H*
SARDINIA VERA It/FRG (Rickmers) 1975; RoPF; 11,637 grt; 120 × 5.9 m *(394 × 19.3 ft)*; TSM (Atlas-MaK); 20.25 kts; ex-*Marine Atlantica*; Bow door/ramp, stern door/ramp
Sisters: **CORSICA MARINA II** (Pa) ex-*Stena Nautica*; **REINE ASTRID** (Be) ex-*Stena Nordica*; **MOBY VINCENT** (It) ex-*Stena Normandica*

85 *MF H*
SCANDINAVIAN DAWN Bs/Br (Swan Hunter & T) 1968; P; 9,337 grt; 128 × 5 m *(420 × 16.5 ft)*; TSM (Ruston & Hornsby); 21 kts; ex-*St George*

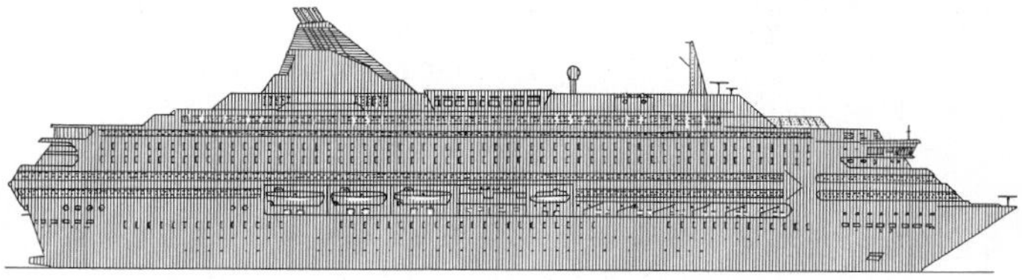

86 *MF H*
SILJA EUROPA Fi/Ge (Meyer/'Neptun' GmbH) 1993; RoPCF; 59,914 grt; 201.78 × 6.8 m *(662.01 × 22.31 ft)*; TSM (MAN); 21.5 kts; ex-*Europa*; Bow door/ramp; Two stern door/ramps; Forward and aft sections built by Meyer and mid-section built by 'Neptun' GmbH

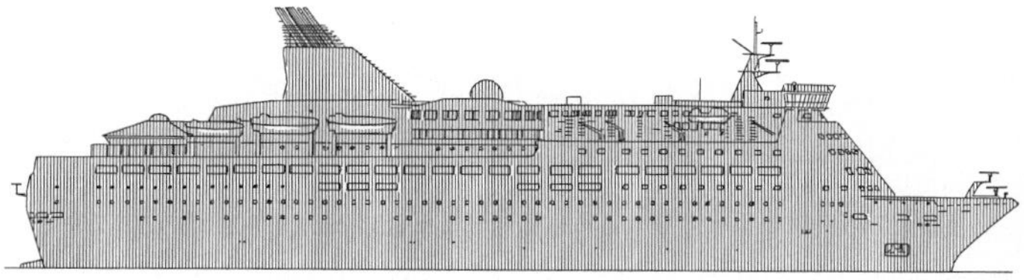

87 *MF H*
SILJA SCANDINAVIA Sw/Cro ("Split") 1992; RoPCF; 35,492 grt; 169.4 × 6.25 m *(555.77 × 20.51 ft)*; TSM (Pielstick); 21 kts; ex-*Frans Suell*; Bow door and ramp; Stern door/ramp
Sister: **CROWN OF SCANDINAVIA** (DIS)

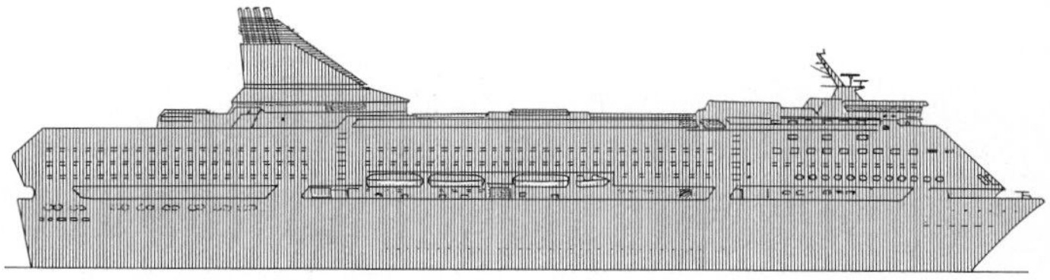

88 *MF H*
SILJA SERENADE Fi/Fi (Masa) 1990; RoPCF; 58,376 grt; 203.03 × 7.12 m *(666.11 × 23.36 ft)*; TSM (Wärtsilä); 21 kts; Bow/door ramp; Stern door/ramp
Sister: **SILJA SYMPHONY** (Sw)

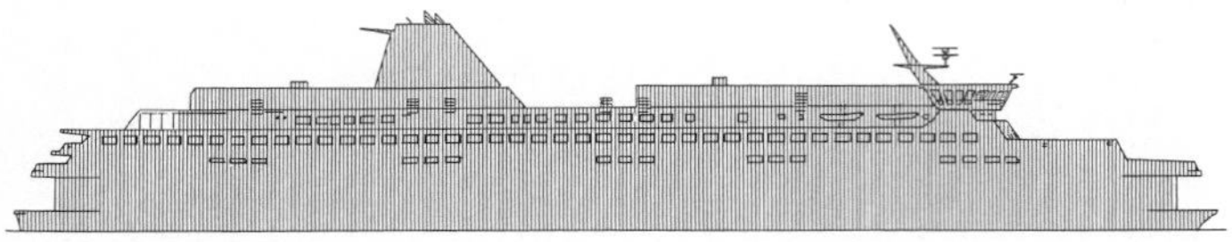

89 *MF H*
SPIRIT OF BRITISH COLUMBIA Ca/Ca (IFC/Allied) 1993; RoC/F; 18,747 grt; 167.5 × 5 m *(549.54 × 16.4 ft)*; TSM (MAN); 19 kts; Bow and stern doors; Aft section buit by IFC and forward section built by Allied
Sister: **SPIRIT OF VANCOUVER ISLAND** (Ca)

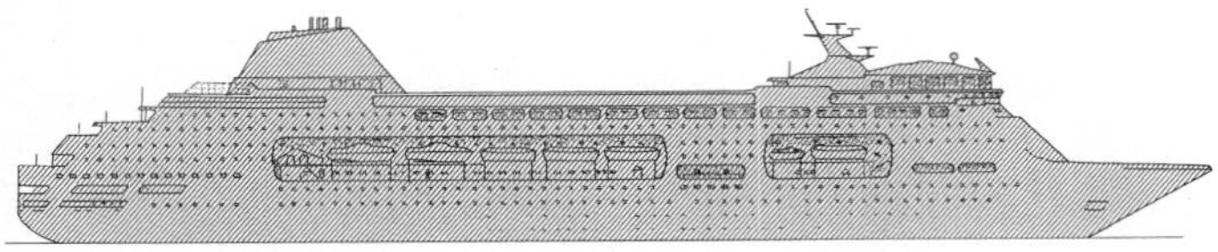

90 *MF H*
STAR PRINCESS Li/Fr (L'Atlantique) 1989; P; 63,524 grt; 245.6 × 8.15 m *(805.77 × 26.74 ft)*; TSD-E (MAN); 19.5 kts; ex-*Sitmar FairMajesty*

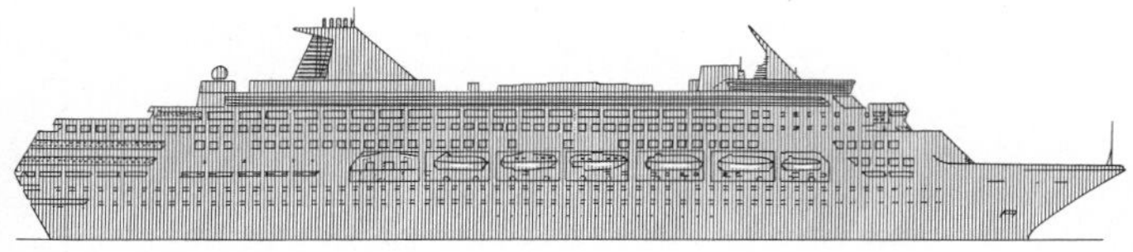

91 *MF H*
STATENDAM Bs/It (FCNI) 1993; P; 55,451 grt; 219.21 × 7.72 m *(719.19 × 25.33 ft)*; TSD-E (Sulzer); 20 kts; (see photo number 20/444
Sisters: **MAASDAM** (Bs); **RYNDAM** (Bs)

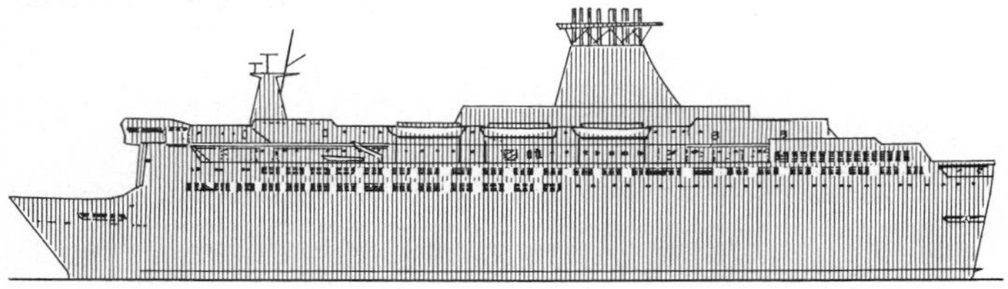

92 *MF H*
STENA DANICA Sw/Fr (Dunkerque-Normandie) 1983; RoPCF; 28,727 grt; 154.9 × 6.32 m *(508.2 × 20.73 ft)*; TSM (Sulzer); 21 kts; Bow door/two stern doors/two side doors
Sister: **STENA JUTLANDICA** (Sw)

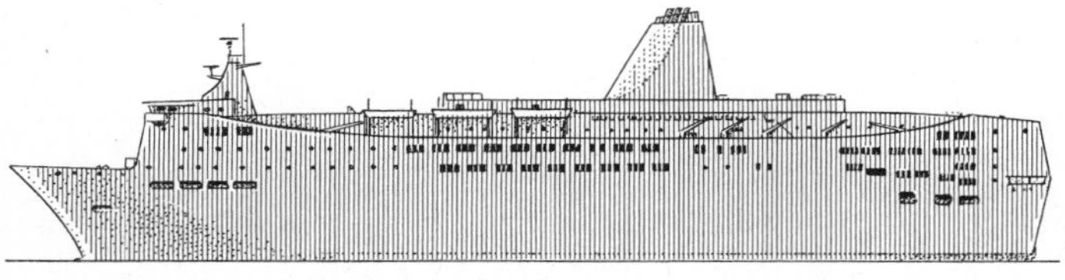

93 *MF H*
STENA EUROPE Sw/Sw (Gotav) 1981; RoPCF; 24,828 grt; 150 × 6 m *(492.13 × 19.69 ft)*; TSM (Wärtsilä); — kts; ex-*Kronprinsessan Victoria*; Three stern ramps; Bow door/ramp; Helicopter pad aft; (see photo number 20/451)
Sister: **STENA NORMANDY** (Bs) ex-*Prinsessan Birgitta*

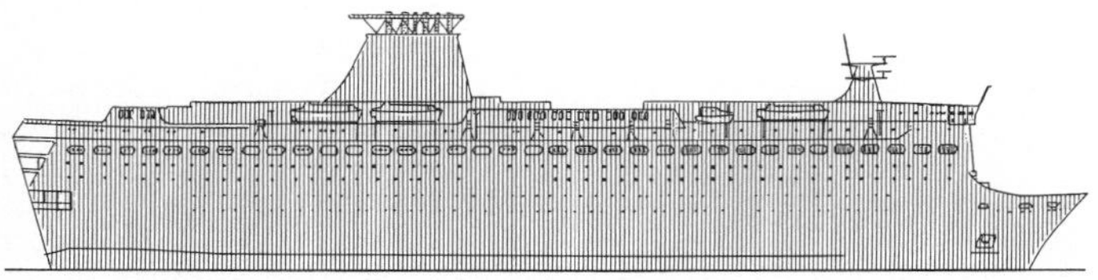

94 *MF H*
STENA SCANDINAVICA Sw/Pd (Gdanska) 1983/88; RoPCF; 38,756 grt; 175.39 × 6.7 m *(575.43 × 21.98 ft)*; TSM (Sulzer); 18.5 kts; ex-*Stena Germanica*; Two side doors (one port/one starboard); Bow door and ramp; Two stern door/ramps; 'B494' type
Sister: **STENA GERMANICA** (Sw) ex-*Stena Scandinavica*; Possible sister: **ELEFTHERIOS VENIZELOS** (Gr)

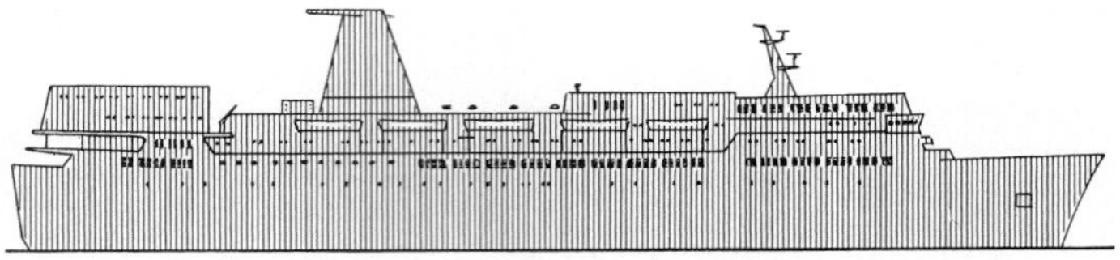

95 *MF H*
THEOFILOS Gr/FRG (Nobiskrug) 1975; RoPCF; 19,212 grt; 148.88 × 6.1 m *(488.45 × 20.01 ft)*; TSM (Pielstick); 19.5 kts; ex-*Nils Holgersson*; Bow door and ramp; Two stern door/ramps

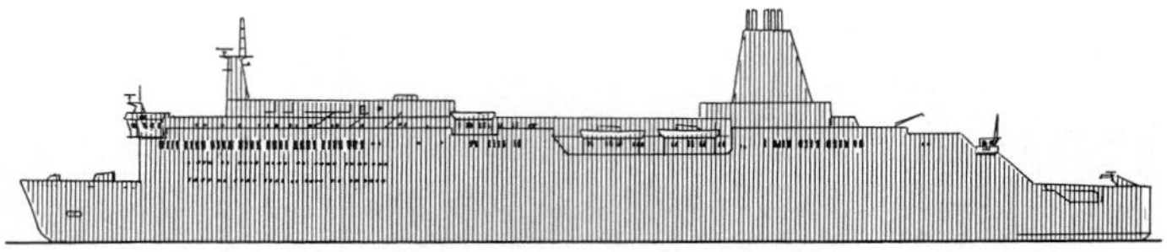

96 *MF H*
TRELLEBORG Sw/Sw (Oresunds) 1982; RoPF/TF; 20,028 grt; 170.19 × 5.82 m *(558 × 19.09 ft)*; TSM (MAN); 18.25 kts; Side door/stern door

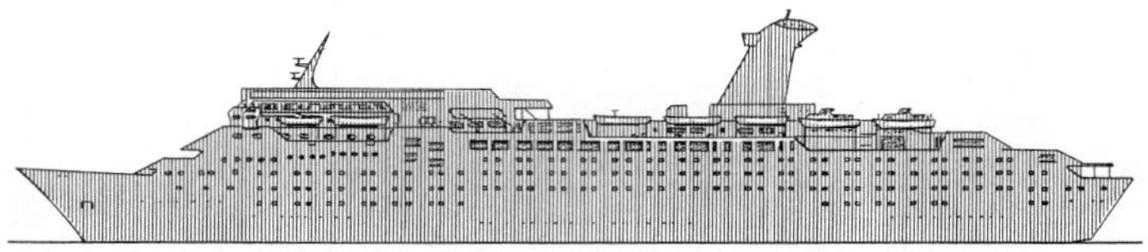

97 *MF H*
TROPICALE Li/De (Aalborg) 1981; P; 35,190 grt; 204.76 × 7.12 m *(672 × 23.36 ft)*; TSM (Sulzer); 19.5 kts

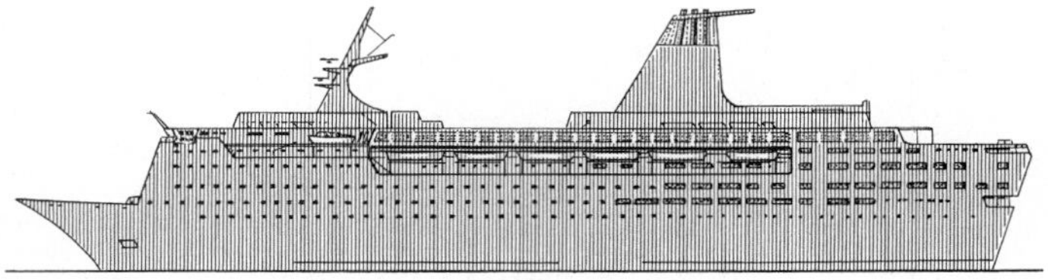

98 *MF H*
VIKING SERENADE Bs/Fr (Dubigeon-Normandie) 1982; P/RoC; 40,132 grt; 185.25 × 6.85 m *(608 × 22.47 ft)*; TSM (B&W); 18 kts; ex-*Scandinavia*; Two stern doors

99 *MF H1*
MARMARI I Gr/Ne (Schiedamsche) 1961; RoPF; 1,492 grt; 78.9 × 2.9 m *(251 × 9.5 ft)*; TSM (KHD); 15 kts; ex-*Linda Scarlett*

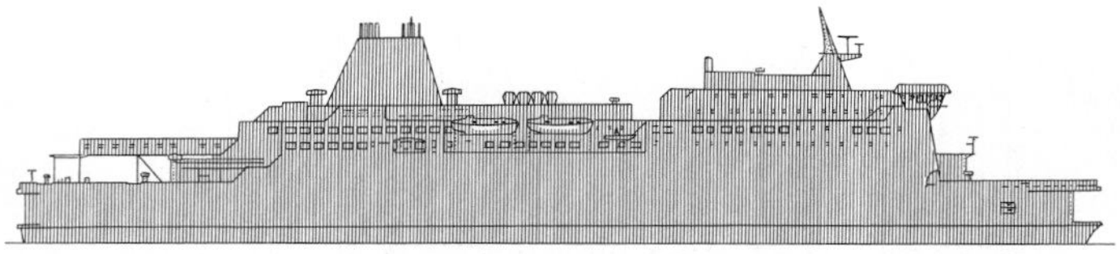

100 *MF H2*
PRIDE OF BURGUNDY Br/Ge (Schichau See) 1993; RoPCF; 28,138 grt; 179.4 × 6.27 m *(588.58 × 20.57 ft)*; TSM (Sulzer); 21 kts; Bow door; Stern door

101 *MFA H*
XIN JIAN ZHEN RC/Ja (Onomichi) 1994; RoPCF; 14,543 grt; 156.67 × 6.25 m *(514.01 × 20.51 ft)*; TSM (Pielstick); 21 kts; 218 TEU; Stern quarter ramp (starboard)

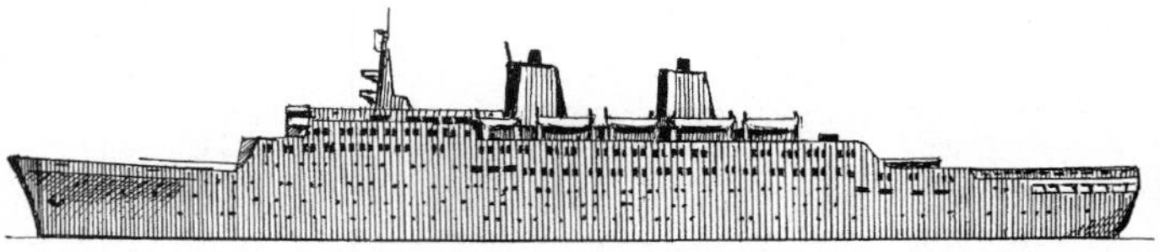

102 *MF² H*
SAPPHIRE SEAS Li/US (Federal SB & DD) 1944; P; 18,297 grt; 184 × 8 m *(604 × 26.24 ft)*; TST (De Laval); 19 kts; ex-*General W P Richardson*

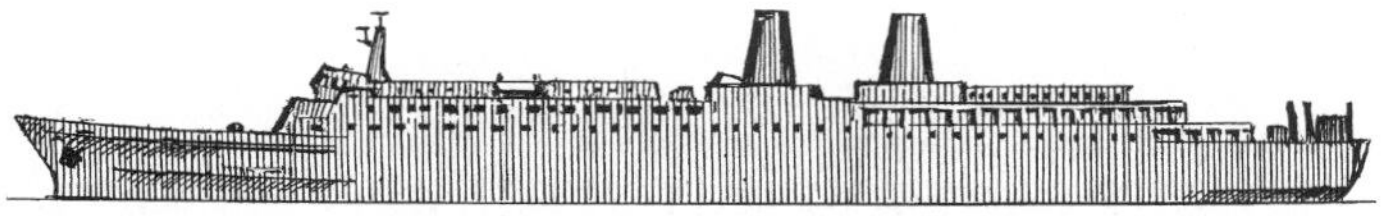

103 *MF²B H*
PRINCESS OF THE ORIENT Pi/Ja (Kurushima) 1974; P/RoPF; 13,600 grt; 196 × 6.6 m *(643 × 21.65 ft)*; TSM (MAN); 25 kts; ex-*Sun Flower 11*; Two quarter stern door/ramps (P&S)

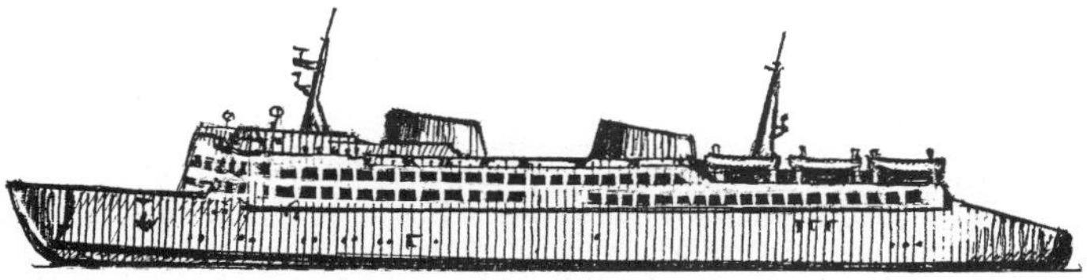

104 *MF²M H*
WARNEMUNDE Ge/DDR ('Neptun') 1963; RoPF/TF; 8,970 grt; 136 × 4.7 m *(499 × 15.41 ft)*; TSM (Halberstadt); 18 kts; Bow door and side doors

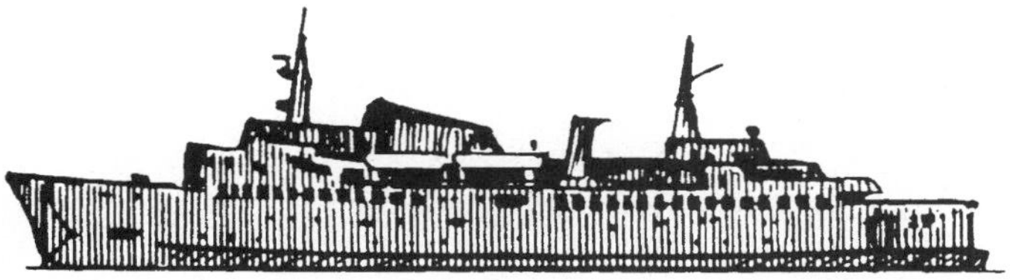

105 *MFGM H*
GHAWDEX Ma/FRG (Adler) 1962; RoPF; 2,300 grt; 88 × 4 m *(289 × 13.12 ft)*; TSM (MAN); 15 kts; ex-*Kalle*
Sister: **AL RASHEED** (Si) ex-*Julle*

106 *MFGM H*
HAMLET Sw/FRG (Lürssen) 1968; RoPF; 3,638 grt; 74.38 × 3.82 m *(244 × 12.53 ft)*; TSM (Atlas-MaK); 14.5 kts; Bow and stern doors
Sister: **OFELIA** (Sw)

107 *MFGM H*
LUCY MAUD MONTGOMERY Ca/Fr (La Seine) 1965; RoPF; 4,200 grt; 86 × 3.9 m *(262 × 12.8 ft)*; TSM (KHD); 17.5 kts; ex-*Stena Danica*; Bow and stern doors

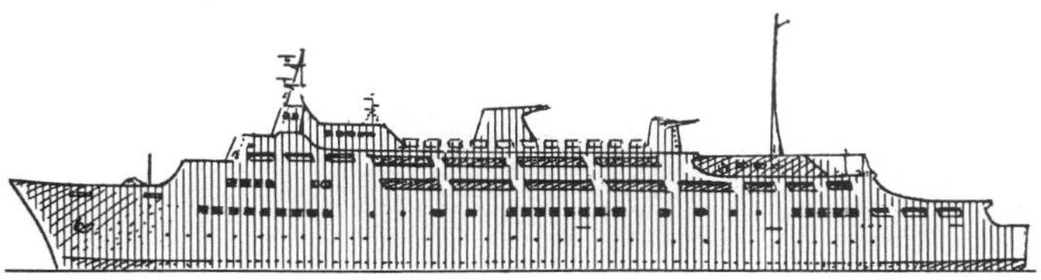

108 *MFGM H*
OTOME MARU —/Ja (Kanda) 1973; RoPF; 3,186 grt; 100.03 × 4.47 m *(328 × 14.67 ft)*; M (Niigata); 19.5 kts

109 *MFGM H*
SKOPELOS Gr/Sw (Langesunds) 1965; RoPF; 1,672 grt; 71 × 3.8 m *(233 × 12.4 ft)*; TSM (MWM); 15 kts; ex-*Gotlandia*; Bow and stern doors
Sister: **BENITO JUAREZ** (Me) ex-*Olanningen*

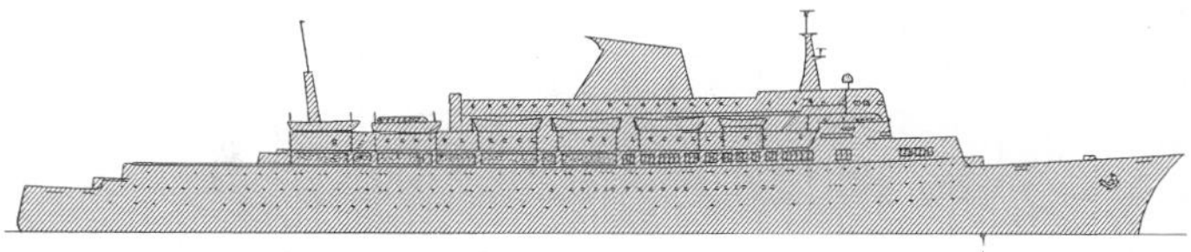

110 *MFH H2*
ENCHANTED SEAS Pa/US (Ingalls SB) 1958; P; 13,680 grt; 188.2 × 8.4 m *(617.6 × 27.5 ft)*; TST (GEC); 23 kts; ex-*Brasil*
Sister (funnel shape differs): **ENCHANTED ISLE** (Pa) ex-*Argentina*

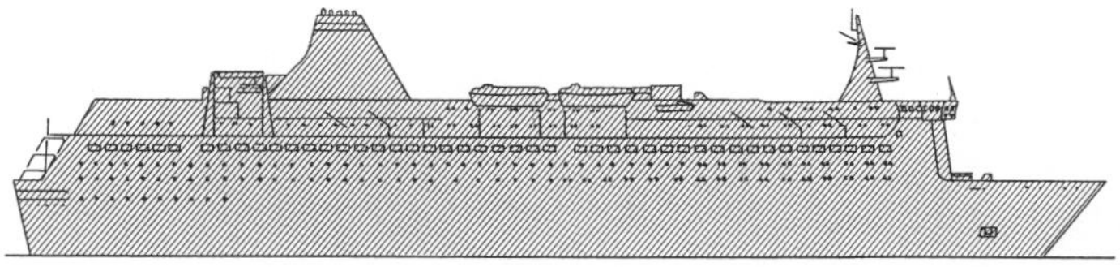

111 *MFK H*
KRONPRINS HARALD No/Fi (Wärtsilä Ml) 1987; RoPCF; 31,914 grt; 166.3 × 6.5 m *(545.6 × 21.33 ft)*; TSM (Sulzer); 22 kts; Bow door and ramp; Two stern door/ramps

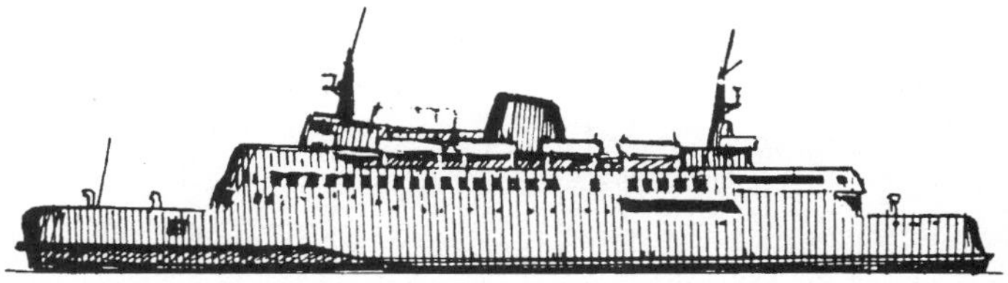

112 *MFM H*
AL FAHAD Si/Ne (Gusto) 1966; RoPF; 6,889 grt; 117.5 × 4 m *(385 × 13.12 ft)*; TSM (MAN); 20 kts; ex-*Free Enterprise III*; Bow door/ramp; Stern door/ramp

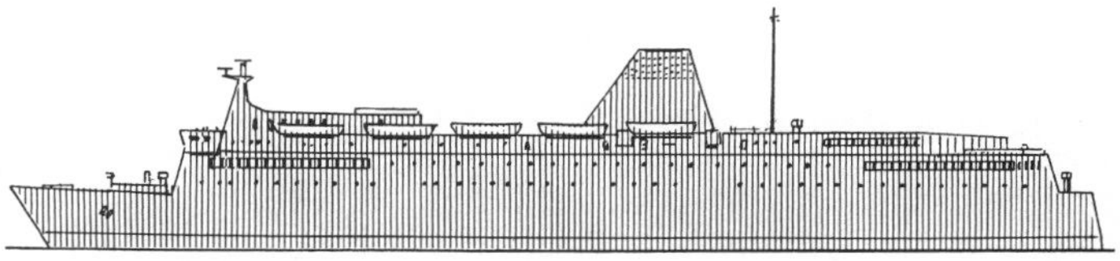

113 *MFM H*
ANKARA Tu/Pd (Szczecinska) 1983; RoPCF; 10,552 grt; 127.44 × 5.42 m *(418 × 17.78 ft)*; TSM (Sulzer); 20.25 kts; ex-*Mazowia*; Bow door and ramp; Stern door/ramp; two side doors/ramps
Sister: **SAMSUN** (Tu)

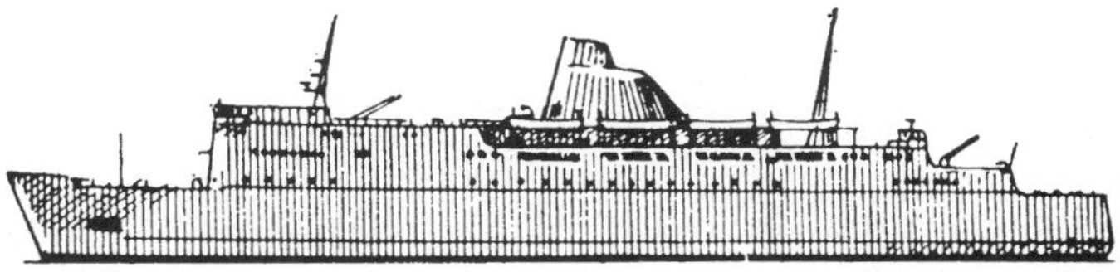

114 *MFM H*
APOLLON EXPRESS 2 Gr/Fr (DCAN) 1972; RoPF; 5,122 grt; 118.1 × 4.1 m *(387 × 13.4 ft)*; TSM (Pielstick); 19.5 kts; ex-*Hengist*; Bow and stern doors; Now has extension to after superstructure—not on drawing
Sisters (may not be modified): **PENELOPE A** (Gr) ex-*Horsa*; **APOLLON EXPRESS 1** (Gr) ex-*Senlac*

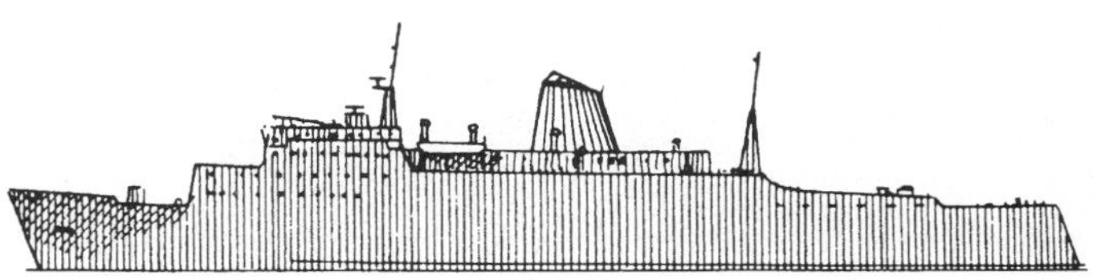

115 *MFM H*
ARAHANGA NZ/Br (Upper Clyde) 1972; RoPF/TF; 3,962 grt; 127.5 × 4.9 m *(418 × 16 ft)*; TSM (Pielstick); 17 kts; Stern door/side door

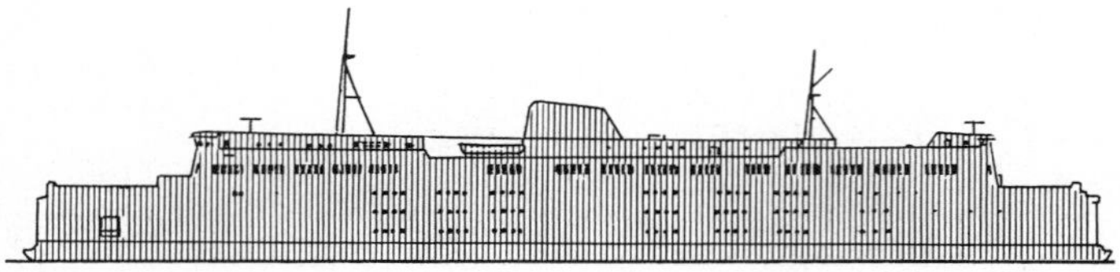

116 *MFM H*
ARVEPRINS KNUD De/De (Helsingor) 1963; RoPF; 8,548 grt; 129.9 × 4.6 m *(426 × 15.1 ft)*; TSM (B&W); 19 kts; Bow and stern doors

See photo number 20/456
117 *MFM H*
ASTRA II Bs/De (Helsingor) 1974; P; 9,848 grt; 130.2 × 5.2 m *(427 × 17.06 ft)*; TSM (MaK); 21 kts; ex-*Golden Odyssey*

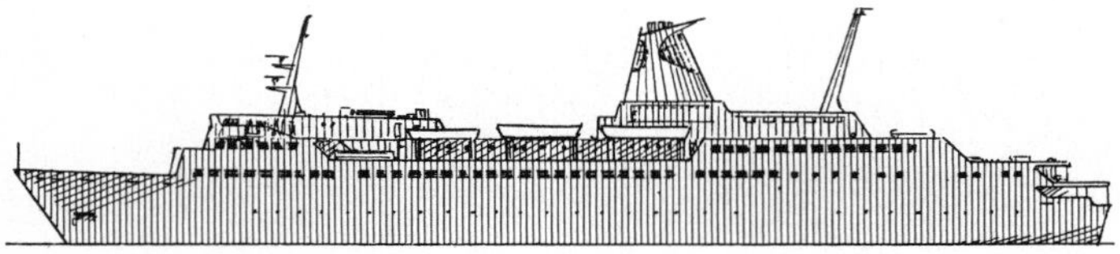

118 *MFM H*
AYVAZOVSKIY Uk/Fr (Dubigeon-Normandie) 1977; P; 7,100 grt; 121.49 × 4.4 m *(398.59 × 14.44 ft)*; TSM (Pielstick); 18.25 kts; (see photo number 20/402

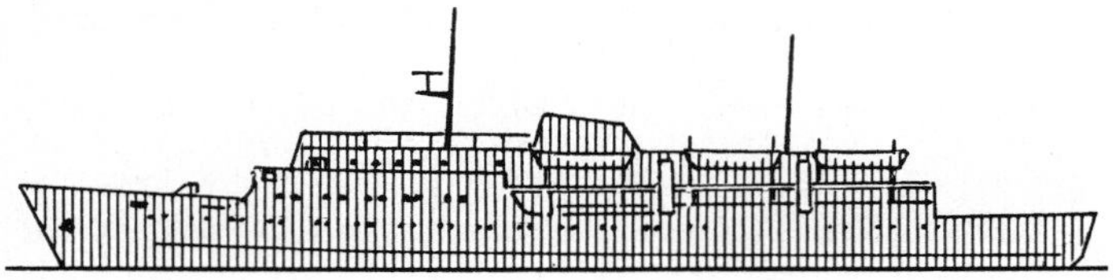

119 *MFM H*
B K BABA ZADE Az/Ru (Volgograd) 1962; F; 2,300 grt; 82.4 × 3.56 m *(270.34 × 11.68 ft)*; TS D-E (—); 16 kts; May be called **K BABA ZADE**
Sister: **VOLGOGRAD** (Az)

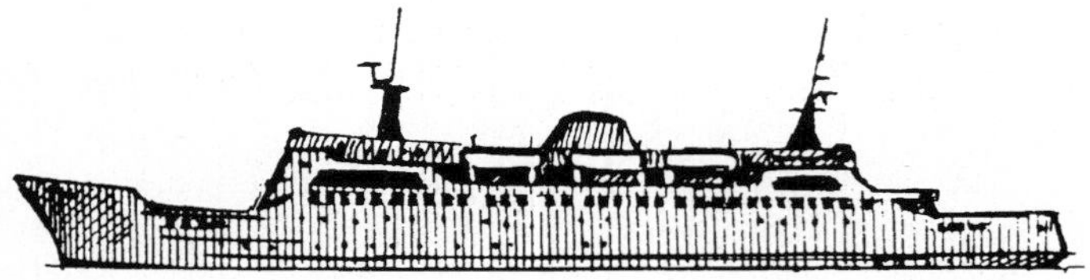

120 *MFM H*
BALTAVIA Bs/Fr (Dubigeon-Normandie) 1965; RoPF; 3,255 grt; 109.9 × 4 m *(361 × 13 ft)*; TSM (Pielstick); 20 kts; ex-*Chantilly*; Bow door/ramp; Stern door

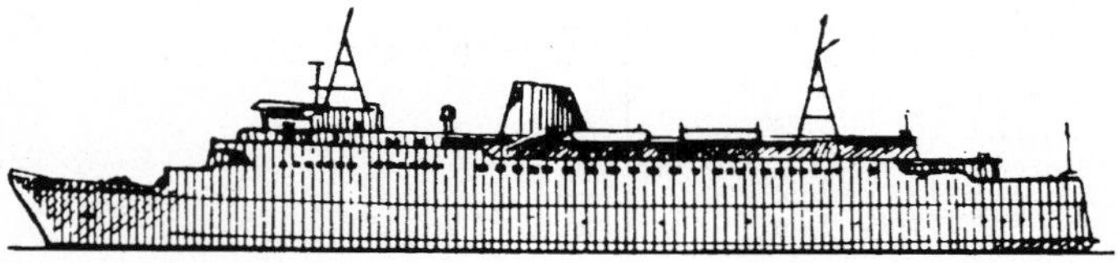

121 *MFM H*
BARI EXPRESS Gr/Be (Boelwerf) 1968; RoPF; 3,397 grt; 118 × 3.8 m *(387.4 × 12.4 ft)*; TSM (Sulzer); 22 kts; ex-*Princesse Astrid*; Stern door/ramp

122 *MFM H*
BOHUS No/De (Aalborg) 1971; RoPF; 8,772 grt; 123.4 × 5.2 m *(405 × 17 ft)*; TSM (Polar); 20.5 kts; ex-*Prinsessan Desiree*; Bow door and stern door

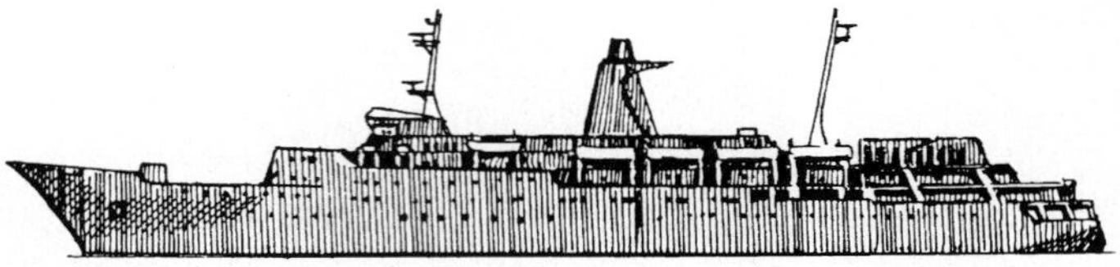

123 *MFM H*
CARLO R Ma/Br (Swan Hunter) 1972; RoPF; 13,102 grt; 152.6 × 5.3 m *(500 × 17.3 ft)*; TS T-E (Associated Electric); 21 kts; ex-*Rangatira*; Stern door

124 *MFM H*
CHANG LI RC/RC (—) 1976; P/C; 5,900 grt; 138 × 7 m *(453 × 22.97 ft)*; TSM (—); 18 kts
Sisters: **CHANG ZHENG** (RC); **CHANG SHAN** (RC). Possible sisters: **CHANG XIU** (RC); **CHANG JIN** (RC); **CHANG KEN** (RC); **CHANG SHEN** (RC); **CHANG GENG** (RC); **CHANG BENG** (RC); **CHANG HE** (RC); **CHANG HU** (RC); **CHANG LIU** (RC); **CHANG SONG** (RC); **CHANG ZI** (RC)

See photo number20/399

125 *MFM H*
DANMARK De/De (Helsingor) 1968; RoPF/TF; 10,350 grt; 144.5 × 5.5 m *(474 × 18 ft)*; TSM (B&W); 17 kts; Bow and stern doors

126 *MFM H*
DELOS Gr/Fr (Dubigeon-Normandie) 1964; RoPF; 2,286 grt; 104.9 × 4 m *(344 × 13 ft)*; TSM (Pielstick); 21 kts; ex-*Villandry*; Bow and stern doors
Sister: **EPTANISOS** (Gr) ex-*Valencay*

See photo number 20/455

127 *MFM H*
DELPHIN Ma/Fi (Wärtsilä) 1975; RoPF/P; 16,214 grt; 157 × 6.2 m *(516 × 20.4 ft)*; TSM (Pielstick); 21.25 kts; ex-*Byelorussiya*; Bow, stern and side doors
Sisters: **GRUZIYA** (Uk); **AZERBAYDZHAN** (Li); **KARELIYA** (Li) (extra deck forward of bridge front); **UKRAINA** (Li) ex-*Kazakhstan* (no bow door)

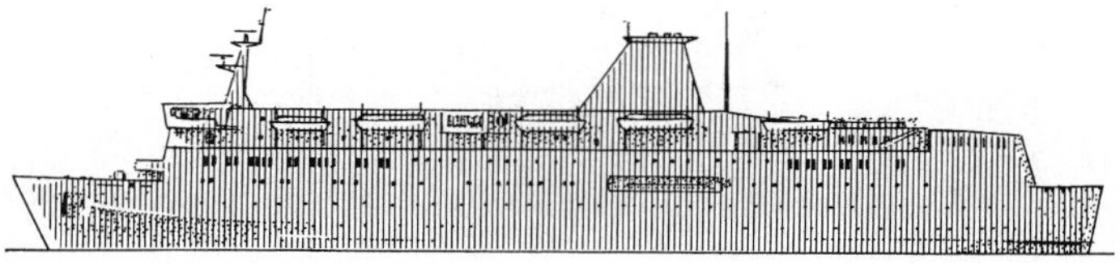

128 *MFM H*
DMITRIY SHOSTAKOVICH Li/Pd (Szczecinska) 1980; RoPF; 9,878 grt; 133.51 × 5.28 m *(438.02 × 17.32 ft)*; TSM (Sulzer); 20 kts; 'B 492' type (see photo number 20/407
Sisters: **LEV TOLSTOY** (Li); **KONSTANTIN SIMONOV** (Ru); **PYOTR PERVYY** (Uk) ex-*Vasiliy Solovyev Sedoy* (converted to passenger and hospital ship); **MIKHAIL SHOLOKHOV** (Ru); **RUSS** (Ru) ex-*Konstantin Chernenko*. Similar ('B 493' type. Not a ro-ro ship): **GEORG OTS** (Ea)

129 *MFM H*
EUROPEAN GLORY Ma/No (Marinens) 1961; F; 2,125 grt; 87.4 × 4.4 m *(287 × 14.4 ft)*; TSM (B&W); 17 kts; ex-*Kattegat*; Bow door and ramp; Stern door/ramp

130 *MFM H*
EUROPEAN PRIDE Ma/FRG (LF-W) 1967; RoPF; 4,390 grt; 123.3 × 4.8 m *(404 × 15.7 ft)*; TSM (Pielstick); 17 kts; ex-*Nils Holgersson*

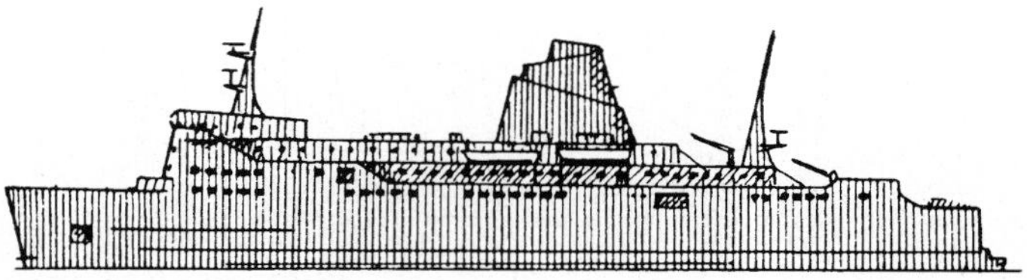

131 *MFM H*
EXPRESS SANTORINI Gr/Fr (Dubigeon-Normandie) 1974; RoPF/TF; 4,600 grt; 115.4 × 4.2 m *(379 × 13.8 ft)*; TSM (Pielstick); 20.5 kts; ex-*Chartres*; Stern door/ramp

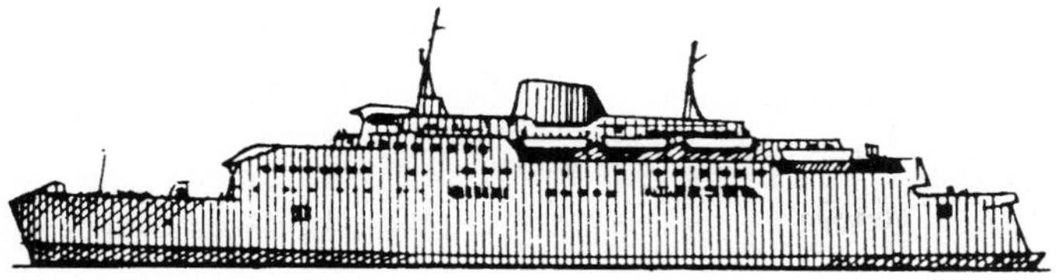

132 *MFM H*
FALSTER LINK Bs/Ne (Gusto) 1969; RoPF; 8,319 grt; 117.5 × 4.3 m *(385.6 × 14.1 ft)*; TrS M (MAN/MaK); 19 kts; ex-*Free Enterprise IV*; Bow door and ramp; Stern door/ramp
Sister: **LABURNUM** (Cy) ex-*Free Enterprise V*; Similar (longer (123.6 m; 405 ft) and mainmast further aft): **ROMILDA** (Gr) ex-*Free Enterprise VIII* (boat deck extended aft)

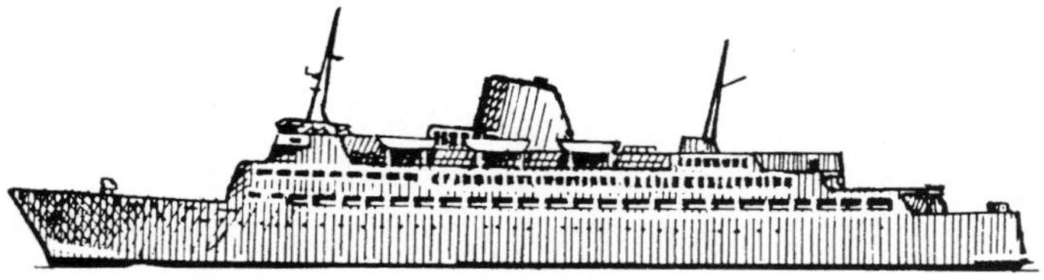

133 *MFM H*
FESTOS Gr/Sw (Lindholmens) 1966; RoPF; 12,374 grt; 141.2 × 5.5 m *(463 × 18 ft)*; TSM (Lindholmens); 18 kts; ex-*Saga*; Stern door; Side door

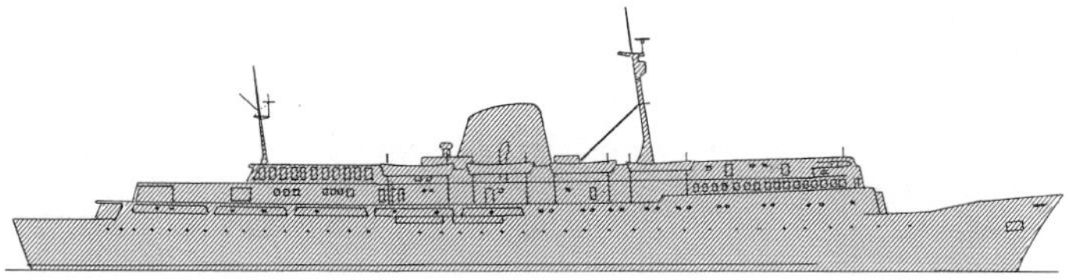

134 *MFM H*
FIBI Pa/It (Breda) 1961; F; 7,820 grt; 122.5 × 5.5 m *(402 × 18.04 ft)*; TSM (Fiat); 17 kts; ex-*Appia*; Stern door/ramp

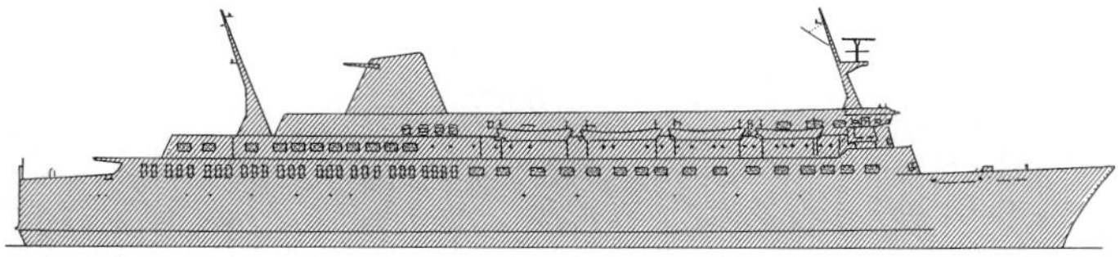

135 *MFM H*
GELTING SYD De/FRG (Meyer) 1974; RoPF; 6,672 grt; 115.2 × 4.5 m *(378 × 14.7 ft)*; TSM (Ruston Paxman); 17 kts; ex-*Stella Scarlett*; Bow door/ramp; Stern door/ramp

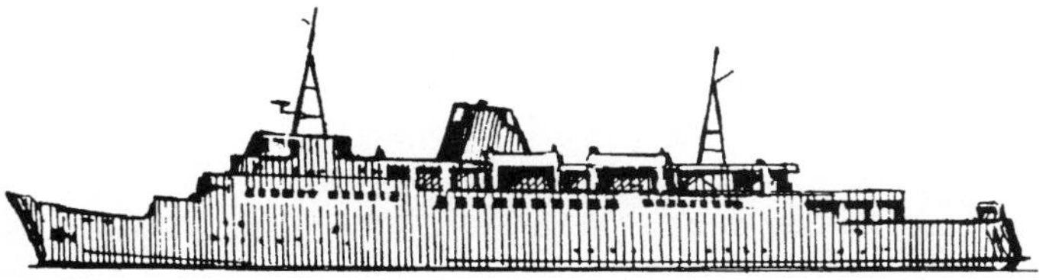

136 *MFM H*
GEORGIOS EXPRESS Gr/Be (Cockerill) 1965; RoPF; 3,023 grt; 117.8 × 3.8 m *(387 × 12.5 ft)*; TSM (Sulzer); 21 kts; ex-*Roi Baudouin*; Stern door/ramp

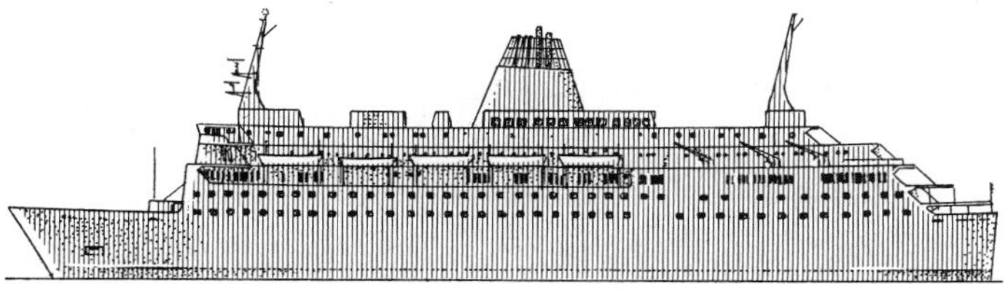

137 *MFM H*
ILE DE BEAUTE Fr/Fr (Dubigeon-Normandie) 1979; RoPF; 11,800 grt; 138.65 × 6.16 m *(454.89 × 20.21 ft)*; TSM (Pielstick); 21 kts; ex-*Cyrnos*; Bow and stern ramps/doors; Lengthened 1990; Now 159 m (521 ft); Drawing shows vessel to original appearance

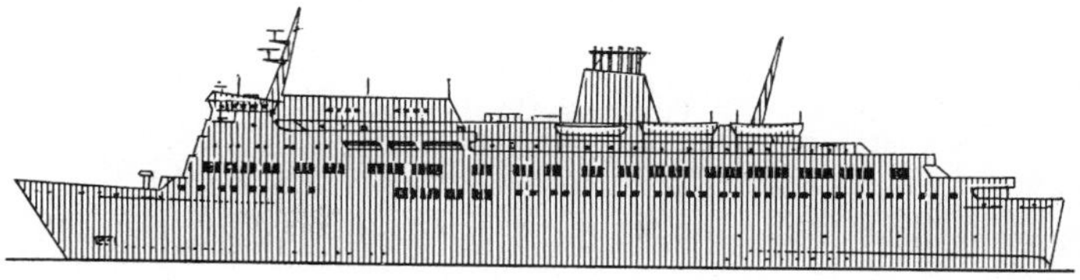

138 *MFM H*
ILYCH Ru/Fi (Wärtsilä) 1973; RoPCF; 12,281 grt; 128.02 × 5.92 m *(420.01 × 19.42 ft)*; TSM (Sulzer); 22 kts; ex-*Bore 1*; Bow and stern doors

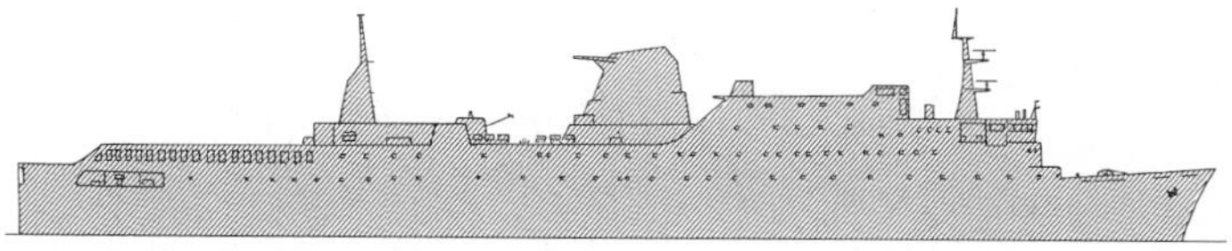

139 *MFM H*
JAPANESE DREAM Ja/Ja (Uraga HI) 1966/89; P; 9,318 grt; 132 × 5.49 m *(433.07 × 18.01 ft)*; TSM (MAN); 18 kts; ex-*Towada Maru*; Converted from Ro-Ro ferry/train ferry 1989

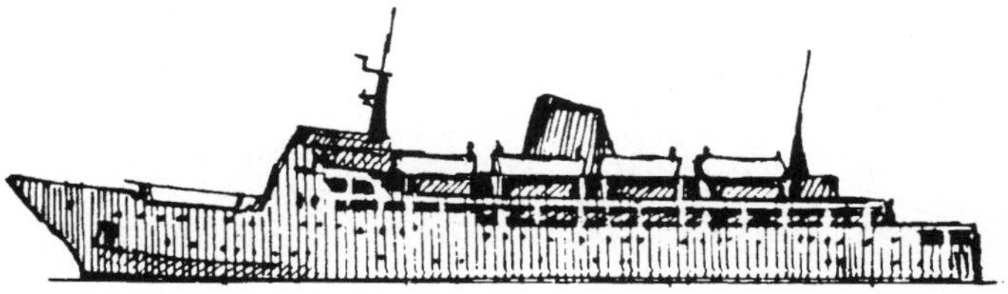

140 *MFM H*
JASON Gr/It (Adriatico) 1965; P; 3,700 grt; 97.16 × 4.51 m *(318.8 × 14.8 ft)*; TSM (Sulzer); 15 kts; ex-*Eros*; Converted from ro-ro ferry 1967

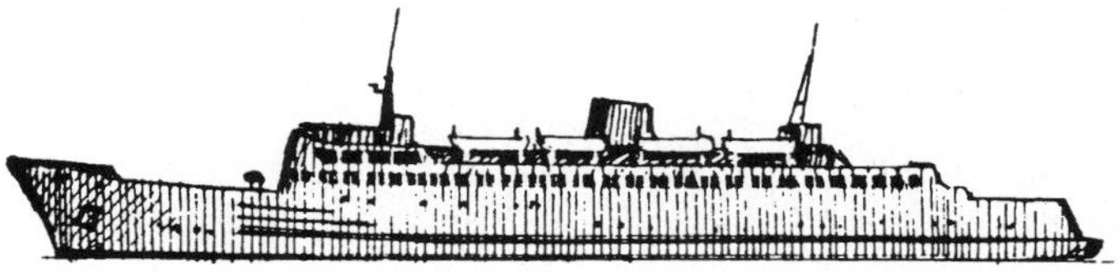

141 *MFM H*
KATARINA Sw/Fr (Loire-Normandie) 1958; RoPF; 3,670 grt; 115 × 4 m *(377 × 13.1 ft)*; TSM (Pielstick); 17 kts; ex-*Compiegne*; Stern door; Superstructure now built-up aft—not shown on drawing

See photo number 20/414

142 *MFM H*
KING OF SCANDINAVIA DIS/Fr (Wärtsilä) 1974; RoPF; 13,336 grt; 152.4 × 5.6 m *(500 × 18.3 ft)*; TSM (Pielstick); 18.5 kts; ex-*Prinsessan Birgitta*; Bow door/ramp; Stern door/ramp

143 *MFM H*
KNUDSHOVED De/De (Helsingor) 1961; RoC/TF/F; 6,811 grt; 109.2 × 4.6 m *(358 × 15.1 ft)*; TSM (B&W); 16 kts
Sister: **SPROGO** (De); Similar: **EUROPEAN SPIRIT** (Ma) ex-*Halsskov*

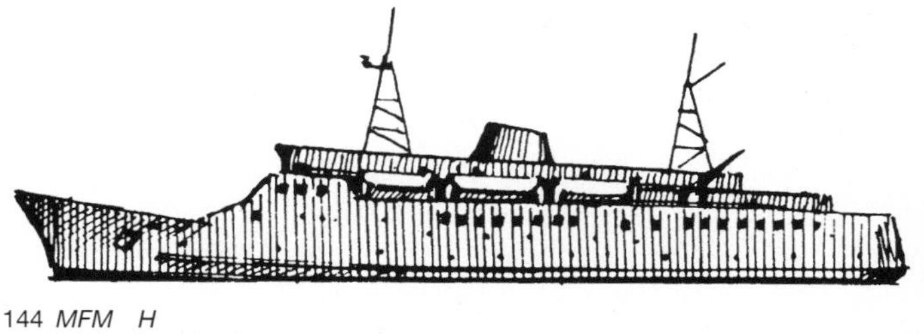

144 *MFM H*
LA PAZ Me/Ja (Kure) 1964; RoPF; 2,500 grt; 109 × 4.3 m *(358 × 14.2 ft)*; TSM (B&W); 17.5 kts; Bow door

145 *MFM H*
LECONTE US/US (Peterson) 1974; RoPF; 1,300 grt; 71.9 × 3.9 m *(236 × 12.7 ft)*; TSM (General Motors); 15.5 kts

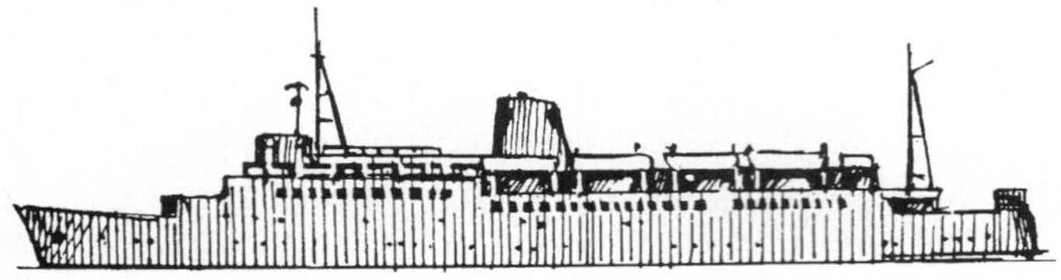

146 *MFM H*
LYDIA Ma/Be (Boel) 1962; RoPF; 3,057 grt; 117.3 × 3.8 m *(385 × 12.4 ft)*; TSM (Sulzer); 20 kts; ex-*Koningin Fabiola*; Stern door/ramp

147 *MFM H*
MALASPINA US/US (Puget Sound) 1963; RoPF; 2,900 grt; 124.2 × 4.9 m *(407.8 × 16 ft)*; TSM (General Metals); — kts; Lengthened 1972; Stern door

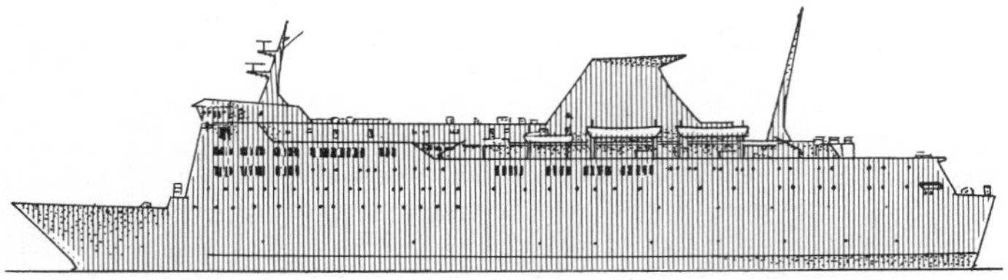

148 *MFM H*
MARE BALTICUM Ea/FRG (Meyer) 1979; RoPF; 17,955 grt; 137.2 × 5.65 m *(450.13 × 18.24 ft)*; TSM (MAN); 21.5 kts; ex-*Diana II*; Bow door/ramp; Two stern doors/ramps

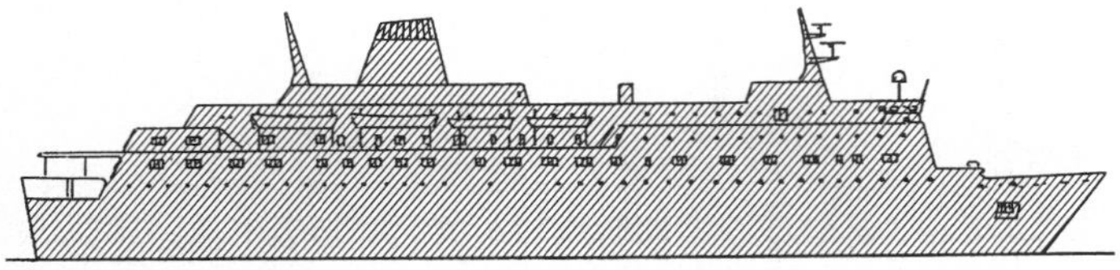

149 *MFM H*
MARRAKECH Mo/Fr (L'Atlantique) 1986; P/RoC; 11,515 grt; 126.78 × 5.07 m *(415.94 × 16.63 ft)*; TSM (B&W); 19 kts; Stern door/ramp

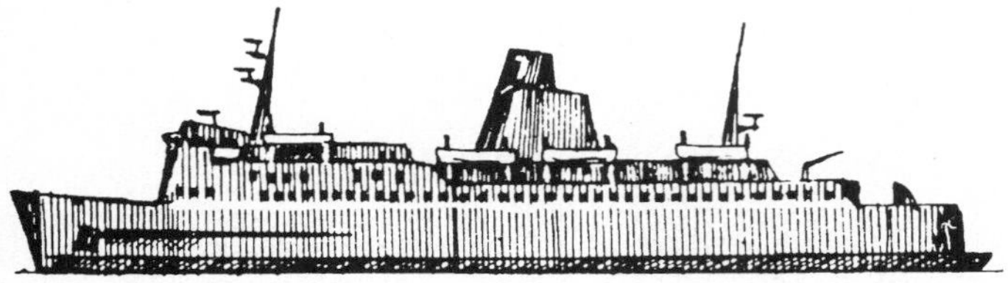

150 *MFM H*
MILOS EXPRESS Gr/Br (Swan Hunter) 1969; RoPF; 4,697 grt; 114.6 × 4.1 m *(376 × 13.4 ft)*; TSM (Pielstick); 19.5 kts; ex-*Vortigern*; Bow door/ramp; Stern door

151 *MFM H*
MOBY BLU It/Ne (Gusto) 1965; RoPF; 5,956 grt; 108.1 × 4 m *(355 × 13.1 ft)*; TSM (MAN); 19 kts; ex-*Free Enterprise II*; Bow door/ramp; Stern door/ramp

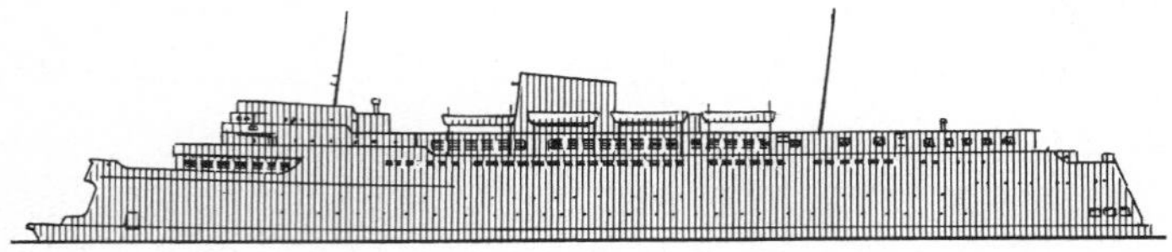

152 *MFM H*
NAN HAI MING ZHU RC/Br (Stephen) 1955/82; RoPF; 8,836 grt; 126.8 × 4.5 m *(416 × 14.7 ft)*; TSM (General Motors); 15.5 kts; ex-*Princess of Vancouver*; Modified 1982—bow door and new stern door fitted (Burrard Y)

153 *MFM H*
NEPTUNE Gr/De (Aalborg) 1955; P; 2,972 grt; 90.2 × 5.4 m *(296 × 18 ft)*; M (B&W); 18 kts; ex-*Meteor*

154 *MFM H*
PANAGIA Ma/FRG (Kieler H) 1961; RoPF; 7,034 grt; 138.3 × 5.5 m *(454 × 18 ft)*; TSM (MAN); 19.5 kts; ex-*Kronprins Harald*; Side doors

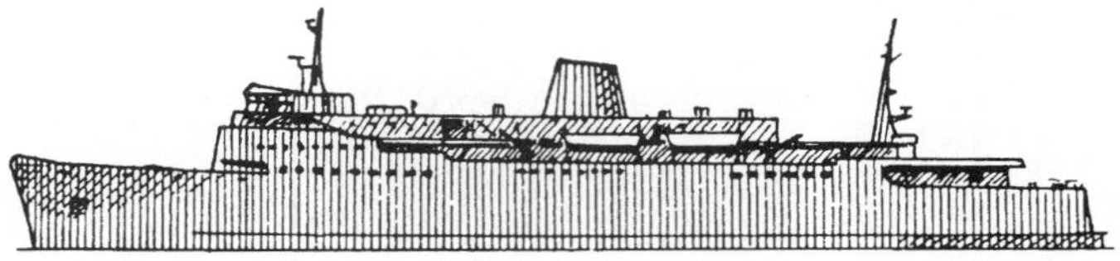

155 *MFM H*
PANAGIA TINOU II Gr/Be (Boelwerf) 1973; RoPF; 5,643 grt; 118 × 4.2 m *(387 × 13.8 ft)*; TSM (Pielstick); 22 kts; ex-*Prins Philippe*; Bow and stern doors
Sister: **SUPERFERRY II** (Gr) ex-*Prince Laurent*

156 *MFM H*
POLARIS Bs/Sw (Solvesborgs) 1960; P; 2,214 dwt; 72.1 × 4.1 m *(236 × 13.4 ft)*; TSM (Nydqvist & Holm); 16.5 kts; ex-*Oresund*; Converted from ro-ro cargo ferry 1982

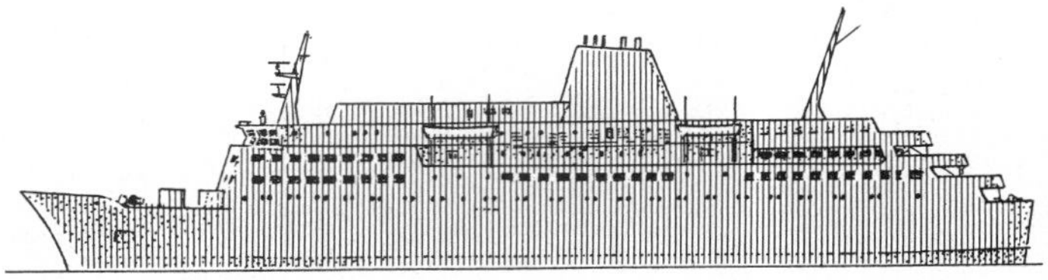

157 *MFM H*
POVL ANKER De/De (Aalborg) 1978; RoPF; 12,131 grt; 121.19 × 5.15 m *(397.6 × 16.9 ft)*; TSM (Alpha-Diesel); 17 kts; Bow door/ramp; Two stern doors/ramps; Side doors
Sister: **JENS KOFOED** (De)

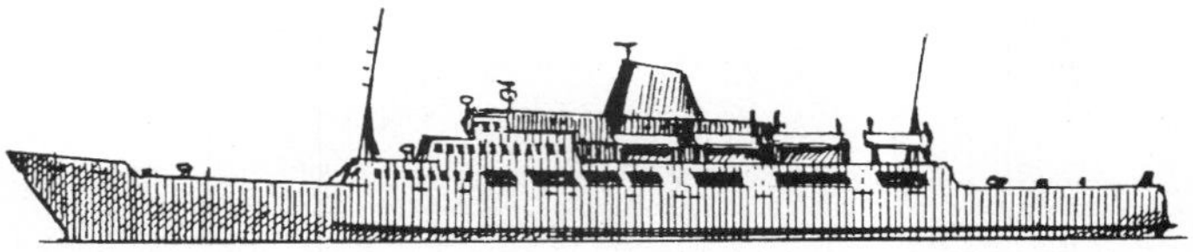

158 *MFM H*
PRINCESS OF ACADIA Ca/Ca (Saint John SB) 1971; RoPF; 10,051 grt; 146.3 × 4.6 m *(480 × 15.09 ft)*; TSM (General Motors); 15.5 kts; ex-*Princess of Nova*; Bow door/ramp; Stern door/ramp

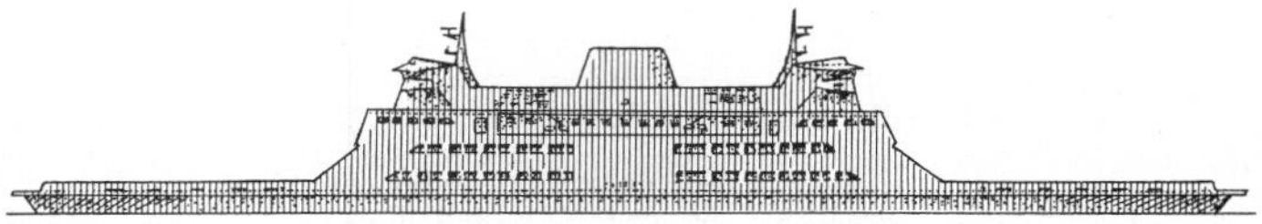

159 *MFM H*
QUEEN OF ALBERNI Ca/Ca (Vancouver) 1976; RoPF/TF; 5,863 grt; 139.3 × 5.49 m *(457.02 × 18.01 ft)*; TSM (MaK); 22 kts; Heightened by addition of new deck 1984; Drawing shows vessel before this modification; Bow and stern doors

160 *MFM H*
QUEEN OF COQUITLAM Ca/Ca (Burrard DD) 1976; RoPF; 6,600 grt; 139.3 × 5.3 m *(457 × 17.8 ft)*; M (MaK); 20 kts
Sister: **QUEEN OF COWICHAN** (Ca)

161 *MFM H*
QUEEN OF TSAWWASSEN Ca/Ca (Burrard DD) 1960; RoPF; 3,127 grt; 102.4 × 3.8 m *(336 × 12.4 ft)*; TSM (Mirrlees, Bickerton & Day); 18 kts; ex-*Tsawwassen*; Bow and stern doors

162 *MFM H*
QUEEN VERGINA Ma/Ca (Marine Indust) 1967; RoPF; 9,934 grt; 120.6 × 6.3 m *(396 × 20.6 ft)*; TS D-E (Cooper-Bessemer); 16.5 kts; ex-*Ambrose Shea*; Stern door/ramp; Four side doors

163 *MFM H*
ROYAL WING Ja/Ja (Mitsubishi HI) 1960; F; 2,743 grt; 86.7 × 3.9 m *(285 × 12.9 ft)*; TSM (Sulzer); 8 kts; ex-*Kurenai Maru*

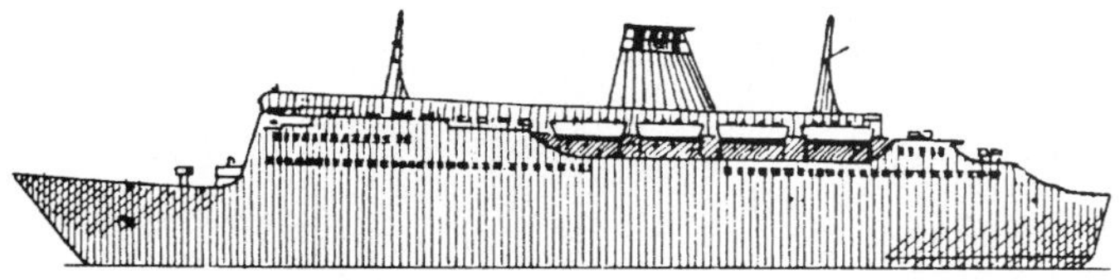

164 *MFM H*
SAINT PATRICK II Ih/FRG (Sietas) 1973; RoPF; 11,481 grt; 125.6 × 5.3 m *(412 × 17.3 ft)*; TSM (Stork-Werkspoor); 21 kts; ex-*Aurella*; Bow door/ramp; Stern door/ramp

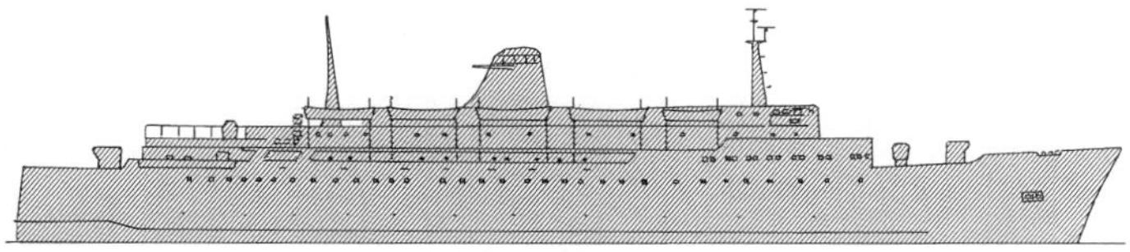

165 *MFM H*
SALEM FLOWER Pa/It (Italcantieri) 1968; RoPF; 5,340 grt; 126.3 × 5.47 m *(414.4 × 17.95 ft)*; TSM (Fiat); 18.5 kts; ex-*Canguro Bianco*
Sisters: **DIMITRA** (Gr) ex-*Canguro Bruno*; **CALYPSO** (Bs) ex-*Canguro Verde* (upper deck of superstructure extended aft of mainmast. Small cranes added forward); **SINDIBAD I** (Mo) ex-*Canguro Rosso*

166 *MFM H*
SAMAINA Gr/FRG (Hanseatische) 1962; RoPF; 3,783 grt; 110 × 4.5 m *(361 × 14.8 ft)*; TSM (Pielstick); 19 kts; ex-*Nils Holgersson*

167 *MFM H*
SCANIA Sw/De (Aalborg) 1972; RoPF; 3,474 grt; 74.2 × 3.8 m *(243 × 12.4 ft)*; TSM (Polar); 14.5 kts; Bow, stern and side doors

168 *MFM H*
SKIPPER It/De (Svendborg) 1960; RoPF/TF; 998 grt; 80.9 × 3.6 m *(265 × 11.8 ft)*; D-E (Frichs); 11 kts; ex-*Halsingborg*

169 *MFM H*
SOVIETSKIY TURKMENISTAN Az/Ru ('Krasnoye S') 1963; RoPF/TF; 8,800 grt; 133.6 × 4.5 m *(438 × 14.7 ft)*; TrS D-E (Fairbanks, Morse); 14 kts; Stern door
Sisters: **SOVIETSKIY UZBEKISTAN** (Az); **GAMID SULTANOV** (Az)

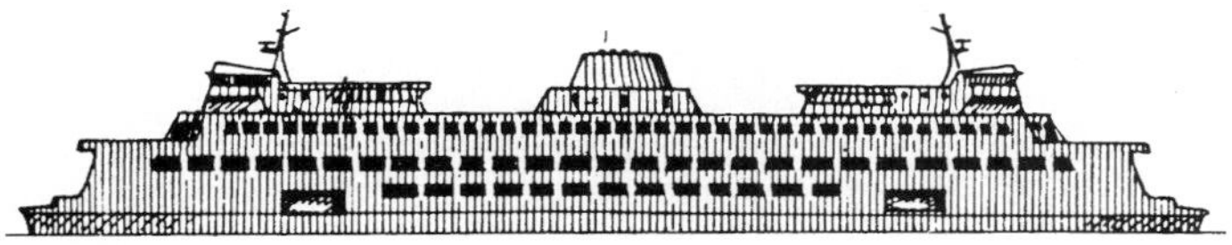

170 *MFM H*
SPOKANE US/US (Todd) 1972; RoPF; 3,200 grt; 134.1 × 5.2 m *(440 × 17.06 ft)*; D-E (General Motors); 20 kts
Sister: **WALLA-WALLA** (US)

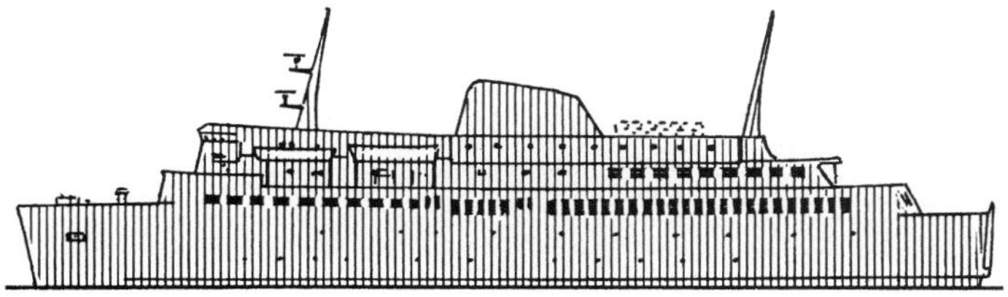

171 *MFM H*
ST OLA Br/FRG (Meyer) 1971; RoC/F; 4,833 grt; 86.3 × 4 m *(283 × 13.1 ft)*; TSM (Wärtsilä); 17 kts; ex-*Svea Scarlett*; Bow door/ramp; Stern door/ramp

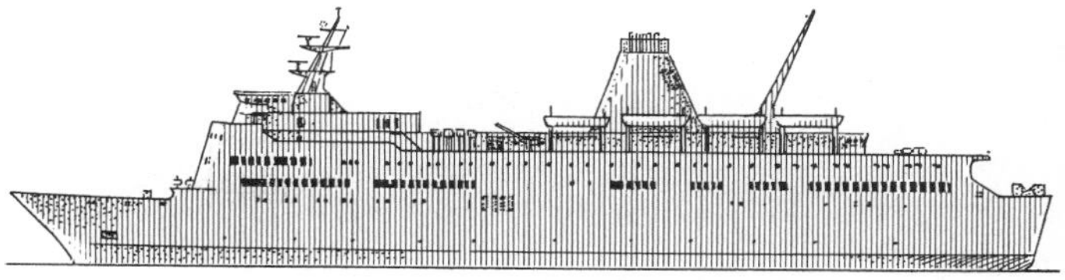

172 *MFM H*
STENA NORDICA Sw/Fi (Wärtsilä) 1979; RoPF; 10,500 grt; 136.11 × 5.5 m *(446.56 × 18.04 ft)*; TSM (Wärtsilä); 21.3 kts; ex-*Turella*; Bow door/ramp and three stern doors/ramps
Sister (extra superstructure forward of funnel): **ROSELLA** (Fi) (Two stern doors/ramps)

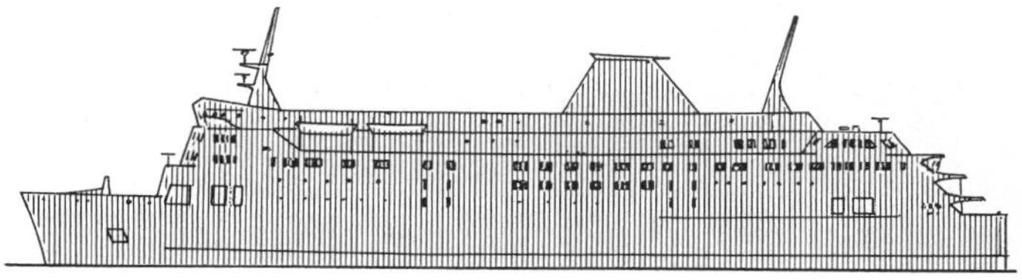

173 *MFM H*
STENA PARISIEN Fr/Fr (Dubigeon) 1984; RoPCF; 15,100 grt; 130.21 × 5.02 m *(427.2 × 16.47 ft)*; TSM (Pielstick); 20.9 kts; ex-*Champs Elysees*; Bow door and ramp; Stern door/ramp

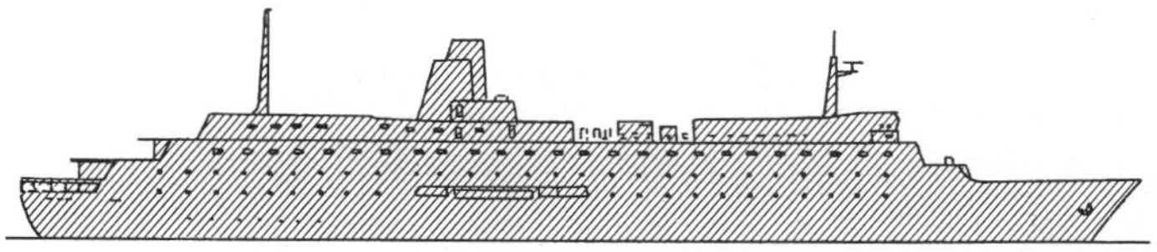

174 *MFM H*
SUNSHINE FUJI Ja/Ja (Mitsubishi HI) 1983; P; 7,262 grt; 127.01 × 4.92 m *(416.7 × 16.14 ft)*; TSM (Pielstick); 19.5 kts

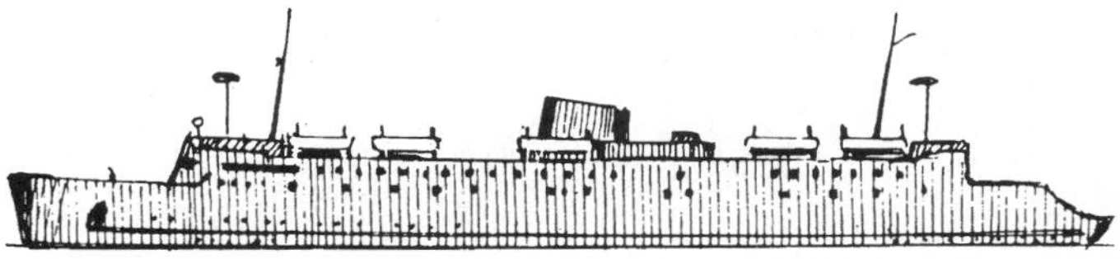

175 *MFM H*
THEODOR HEUSS Ge/FRG (Kieler H) 1957; TF; 8,505 grt; 136 × 4.9 m *(446 × 16 ft)*; TS D-E (Maybach); 17 kts

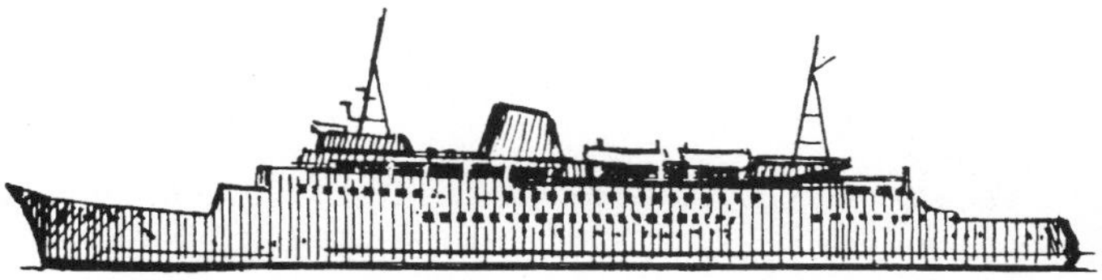

176 *MFM H*
TROPICANA Bs/Be (Cockerill) 1966; F; 4,772 grt; 117.1 × 3.8 m *(385 × 12.4 ft)*; TSM (Sulzer); 24 kts; ex-*Prinses Paola*

177 *MFM H*
TRUVA Tu/Fr (Dubigeon-Normandie) 1966; RoPF; 4,332 grt; 91.6 × 4.2 m *(300.6 × 13.7 ft)*; TSM (MWM); 19 kts

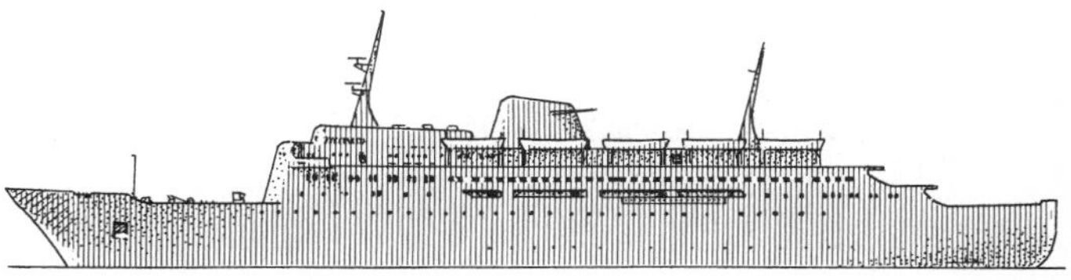

178 *MFM H*
WINSTON CHURCHILL DIS/It (Tirreno) 1967; RoPF; 10,513 grt; 140.7 × 5.5 m *(460 × 18 ft)*; TSM (B&W); 21 kts; Bow door and ramp; Stern door and ramp

179 *MFM H1*
ASA-THOR De/De (Nakskov) 1965; RoC/TF; 5,550 grt; 131.7 × 4.5 m *(452 × 15 ft)*; TSM (B&W); 17.25 kts

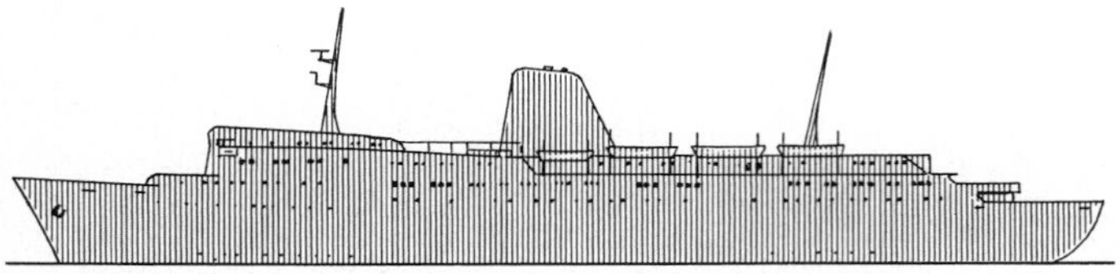

180 *MFM H1*
JI MEI RC/FRG (Kieler H) 1966; RoPF; 5,990 grt; 140.8 × 5.8 m *(463 × 19.02 ft)*; TSM (MAN); 21.5 kts; ex-*Prinsesse Ragnhild*; Side doors

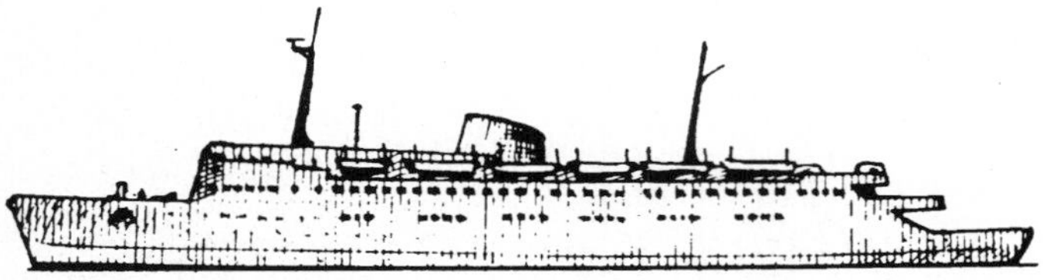

181 *MFM H1*
KONG FREDERIK IX De/De (Helsingor) 1954; RoPF; 6,592 grt; 114.3 × 4.5 m *(375 × 14.7 ft)*; TSM (B&W); 18 kts
Similar: **PHOENICIAN SEA** (Pa) ex-*Prinsesse Benedikte*

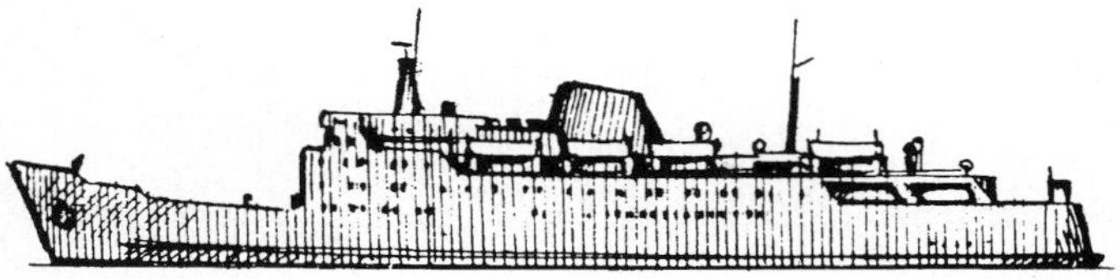

182 *MFM H1*
POSEIDONIA Cy/Br (H&W) 1967; RoPF; 4,270 grt; 115 × 4.1 m *(378 × 13.6 ft)*; TSM (Pielstick); 17 kts; ex-*Ulster Queen*; Stern door
Sister (with superstructure alterations aft—boat deck extended to stern, heavier stanchions and so on): **NEPTUNIA** (Pa) ex-*Ulster Prince*

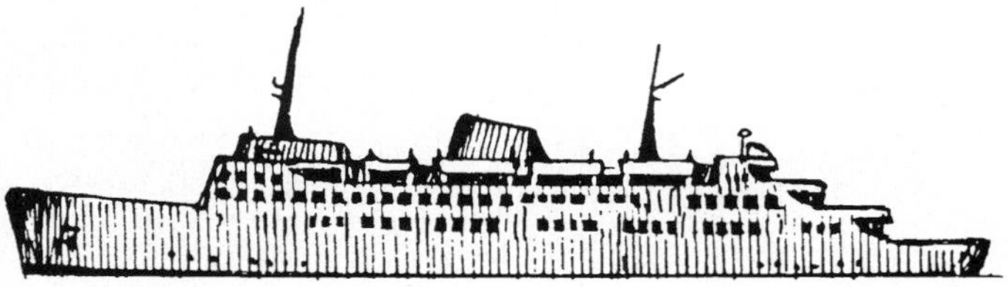

183 *MFM H1*
PRINSESSE ANNE-MARIE De/De (Aalborg) 1960; RoPF; 3,486 grt; 103.4 × 4.6 m *(339 × 15 ft)*; TSM (B&W); 18 kts

184 *MFM H1*
PRINSESSE ELISABETH De/De (Aalborg) 1964; RoPF; 5,148 grt; 103.4 × 4.6 m *(339 × 15.1 ft)*; TSM (B&W); 18 kts

185 *MFM H2*
NORDIK PASSEUR Ca/Ca (Halifax) 1962; RoPF; 2,400 grt; 86.5 × 4.2 m *(284 × 13.7 ft)*; TS D-E (Davey, Paxman); 13 kts; ex-*Confederation*

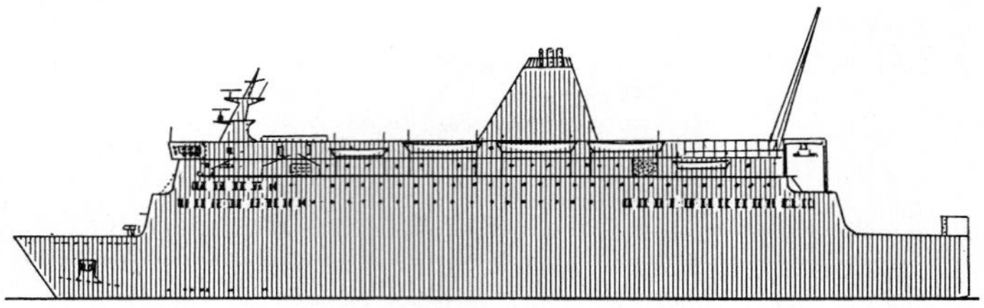

186 *MFM H2*
SALLY STAR Bs/Fi (Wärtsilä) 1981; P/RoC; 16,829 grt; 137.42 × 5.75 m *(450.85 × 18.86 ft)*; TSM (Wärtsilä); 18.5 kts; ex-*Travemunde*; Bow door/ramp; Stern door/ramp; Side doors (one port/one starboard)

187 *MFM H2*
TRANS ST LAURENT Ca/Ca (Davie & Sons) 1963; RoPF; 2,200 grt; 79.8 × 4.27 m *(262 × 14.01 ft)*; TSM (MAN); — kts; New engines 1991

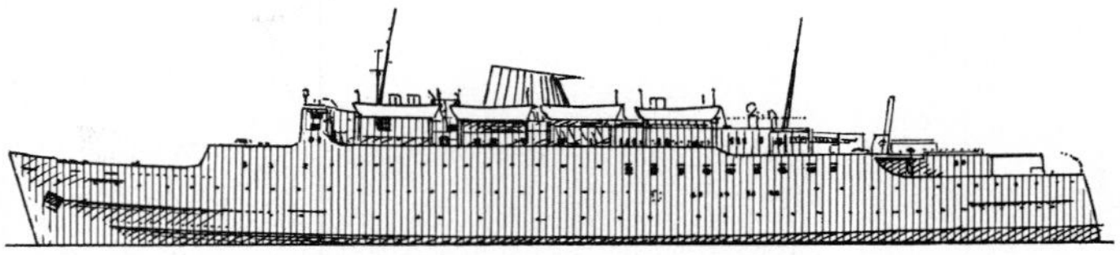

188 *MFM*^{2} *H*
ORPHEUS Gr/Br (H&W) 1948/70; P; 4,890 grt; 111.82 × 4.88 m *(366.86 × 16.01 ft)*; TSM (H&W); 14.5 kts; ex-*Munster*; Converted from ferry 1970

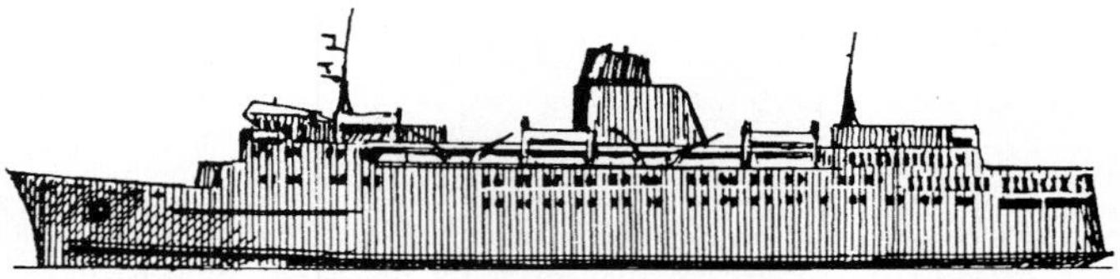

189 *MFMR H*
STENA HIBERNIA Br/De (Aalborg) 1977; RoPF; 11,690 grt; 128.6 × 4.7 m *(425 × 15.4 ft)*; TSM (Stork-Werkspoor); 19.5 kts; ex-*St Columba*; Bow door/ramp; Stern door/ramp

190 *MFMS H*
ARATIKA NZ/Fr (Dubigeon-Normandie) 1974; RoPF/TF; 5,591 grt; 127.7 × 4.9 m *(419 × 16 ft)*; TSM (Pielstick); 17.25 kts; Stern door; Converted 1977 (Hong Kong U)

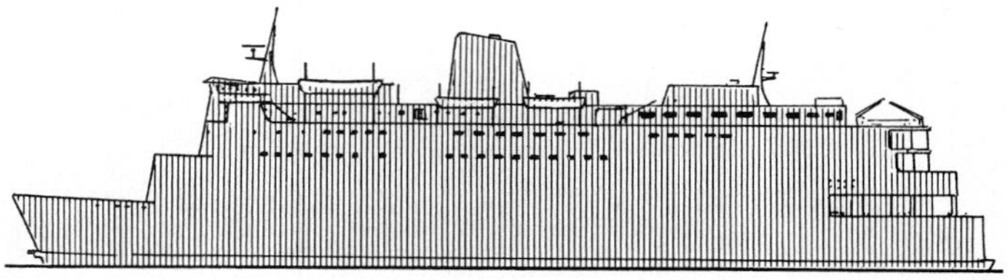

191 *MFMS*^{2} *H*
PRINCESSE MARIE CHRISTINE Be/Be (Cockerill) 1975; RoPF; 6,276 grt; 118.4 × 4.5 m *(387 × 14.7 ft)*; TSM (Pielstick); 22 kts; Bow and stern doors; Heightened by addition of new vehicle deck 1985/86
Sisters: **PRINSES MARIA ESMERALDA** (Be); **PRINS ALBERT** (Be) (after end of superstructure differs)

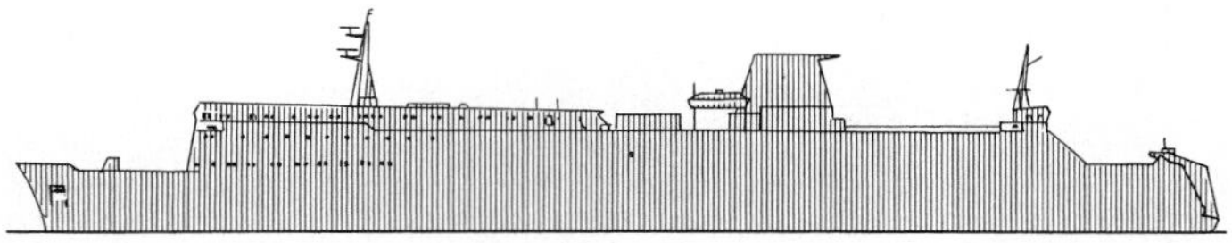

192 *MFMY H*
ROSTOCK Ge/No (Bergens) 1977; RoPF/TF; 13,788 grt; 158.35 × 5.55 m *(520 × 18.21 ft)*; TSM (MAN); 20.5 kts; Stern door and two side doors (starboard)

193 *MFM-F H*
APOLLO Fi/FRG (Meyer) 1970; RoPCF; 6,480 grt; 109 × 4.6 m *(357 × 15 ft)*; TSM (MAN); 20 kts
Similar: **MECCA 1** (Pa) ex-*Viking 1*; **EXPRESS OLYMPIA** (Gr) ex-*Viking 4*; **ROSLAGEN** (Fi) ex-*Viking 3*; **ALANDIA** (Fi) ex-*Diana*; **COROMUEL** (Me); **PUERTO VALLARTA** (Me); **AZTECA** (Me)

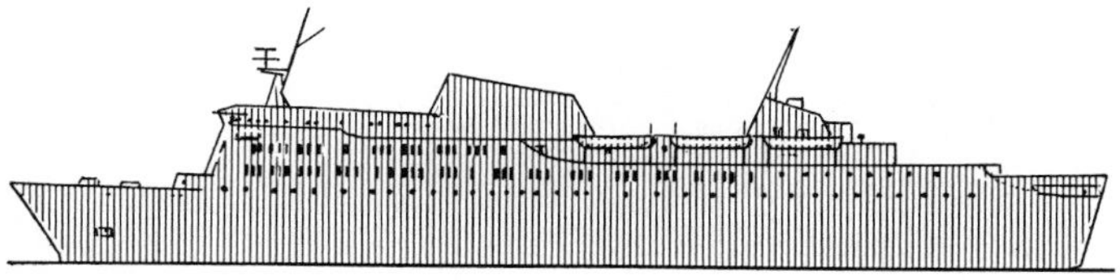

194 *MFM-F H*
BOUGHAZ Mo/FRG (Meyer) 1974; RoPCF; 8,257 grt; 117.79 × 4.7 m *(386.45 × 15.42 ft)*; TSM (KHD); 17 kts; ex-*Viking 5*; Bow door/ramp; Stern door/ramp; Ice strengthened; New engines 1982

195 *MFM-F H*
BRINDISI Ma/Ja (Hayashikane) 1968; RoCF; 3,726 grt; 127 × 4.5 m *(416 × 14.7 ft)*; TSM (MAN); 18 kts; ex-*Ferry Hankyu*; Bow door/ramp; Stern door/ramp

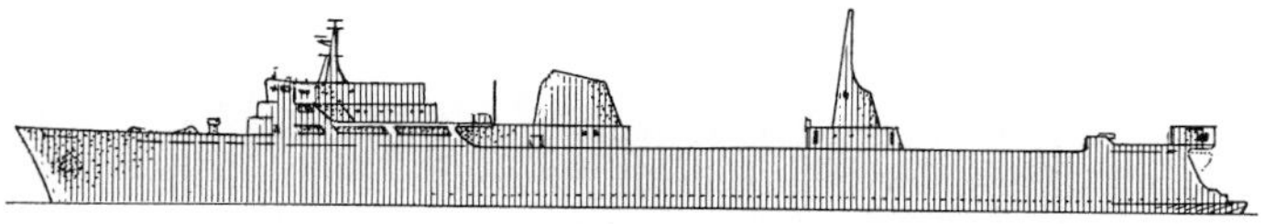

196 *MFM-F H*
HITAKA MARU —/Ja (Mitsubishi HI) 1969; RoPF; 4,100 grt; 144.5 × 5.2 m *(474 × 17 ft)*; M (MAN); 18 kts
Sister (probably rebuilt): **SEA SERENADE** (Cy) ex-*Sorachi Maru*

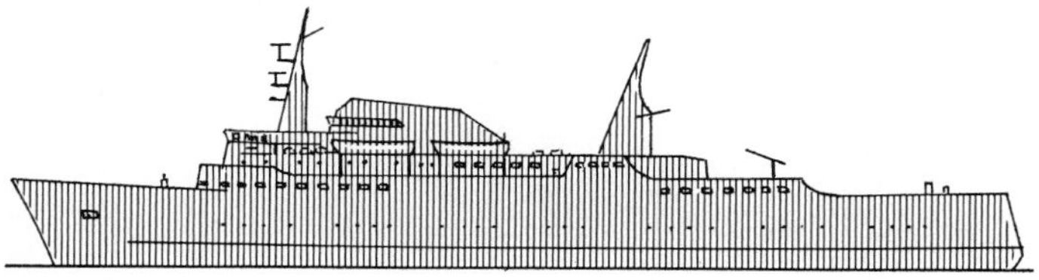

197 *MFM-F H*
LUCINDA Ma/FRG (Nobiskrug) 1965; RoPF; 3,800 grt; 110.2 × 4.4 m *(362 × 14.4 ft)*; TSM (MAN); 20 kts; ex-*Gustav Vasa*; Bow and stern doors/ramps
Similar (boat deck extended aft and extra boat added. Other small differences): **TIAN KUN** (RC) ex-*Prins Bertil*

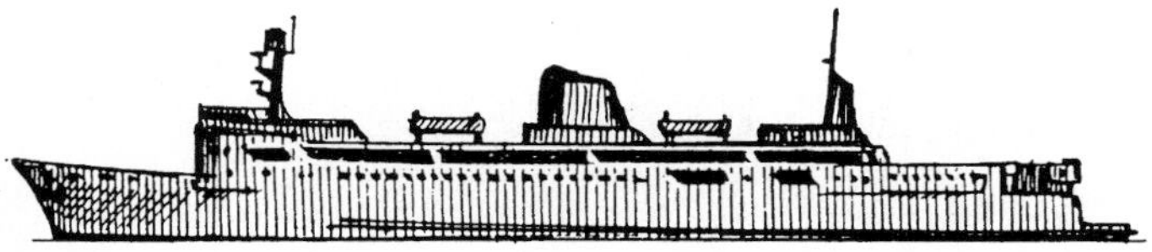

198 *MFM-F H*
MATSUMAE MARU Ja/Ja (Hakodate) 1964; RoCF; 5,376 grt; 132.04 × 5.21 m *(433 × 17.09 ft)*; TSM (MAN); 18 kts; Stern door
Sister: **AL JAWAHER** (Pa) ex-*Tsugaru Maru*

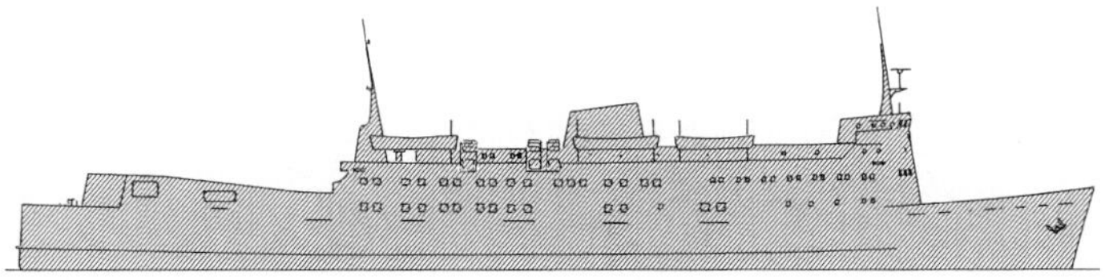

199 *MFM-F H*
MONA'S QUEEN Br/Br (Ailsa) 1972; RoPF; 4,400 grt; 104.5 × 3.6 m *(343 × 12 ft)*; TSM (Pielstick); 18 kts
Sister: **LADY OF MANN** (Br)

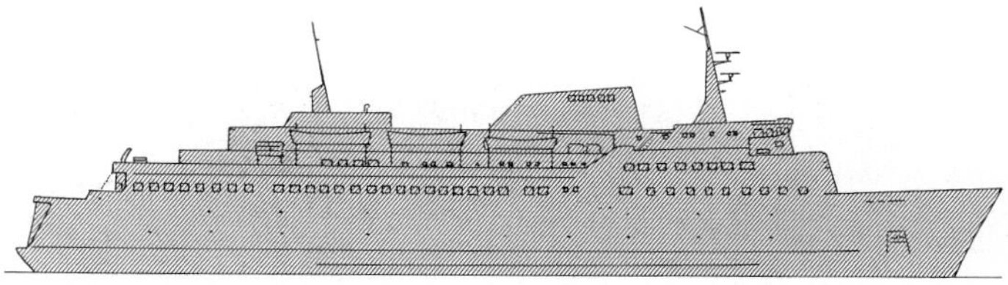

200 *MFM-G H*
CIUDAD DE LA LAGUNA Sp/Fi (Wärtsilä) 1967; RoPCF; 4,291 grt; 101.6 × 4.9 m *(334 × 16.0 ft)*; TSM (Wärtsilä); 19 kts; ex-*Botnia*; Bow door/ramp; Stern door/ramp

201 *MFM-G H*
OURANOS Cy/FRG (Meyer) 1969; RoPF; 3,800 grt; 108.1 × 4.6 m *(355 × 15.1 ft)*; TSM (MAN); 20 kts; ex-*Vikingfjord*; Bow door/ramp; Stern door/ramp and side door/ramp

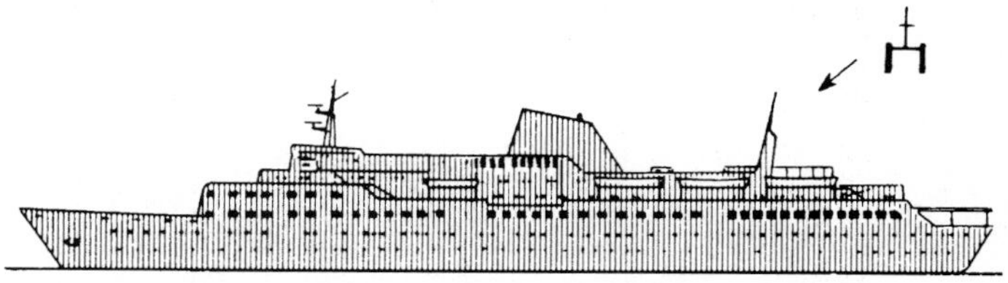

202 *MFM-G H*
VIKING PRINCESS Pa/Fi (Sandvikens) 1964; P; 6,659 grt; 128.3 × 4.4 m *(421 × 14.4 ft)*; TrS M (Sulzer); 19 kts; ex-*Ilmatar*; Side doors; Lengthened 1973 (Howaldts DW); Extensively modified in 1978/79 (Wärtsilä)

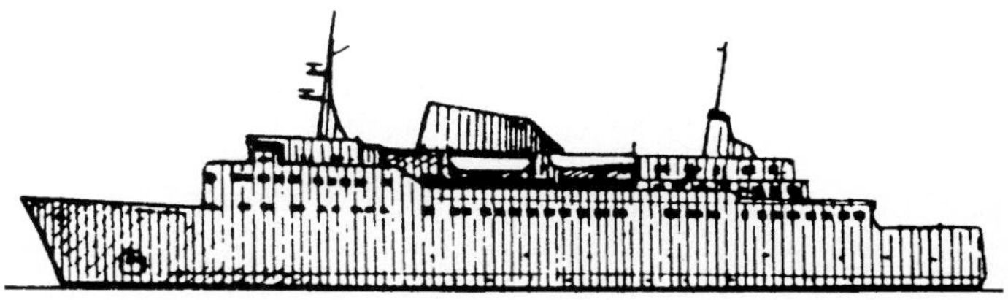

203 *MFM-G H*
VILLA DE AGAETE Sp/Fi (Wärtsilä) 1970; RoPF; 4,274 grt; 101.6 × 5 m *(334 × 16.4 ft)*; TSM (Wärtsilä); 13 kts; ex-*Floria*; Bow and stern doors

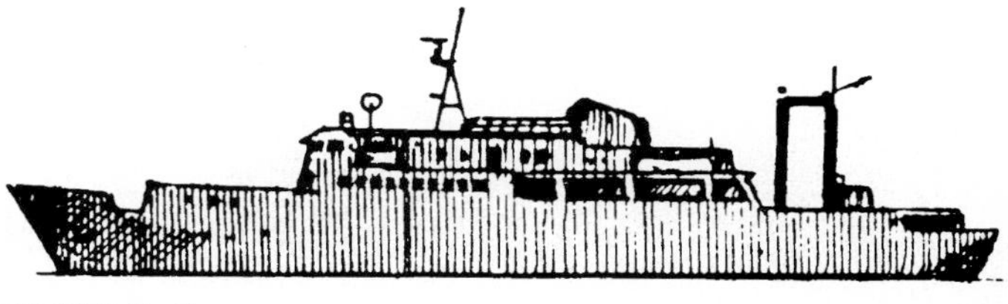

204 *MFM-K H*
TUSTUMENA US/US (Christy) 1964; RoPF; 4,593 grt; 90 × 4.4 m *(295 × 14.4 ft)*; TSM (Fairbanks, Morse); — kts; Lengthened 1969 (Bethlehem Steel); Stern door/ramp

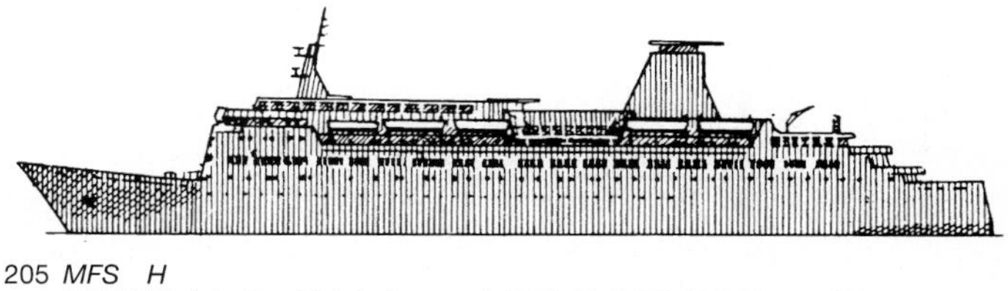

205 *MFS H*
TOLETELA Ly/Sp (UN de Levante) 1974; RoPCF; 13,868 grt; 151.5 × 6.5 m *(500.6 × 21.32 ft)*; TSM (MAN); 22 kts; ex-*Monte Toledo*; Stern and side doors
Sister: **GARNATA** (Ly) ex-*Monte Granada*

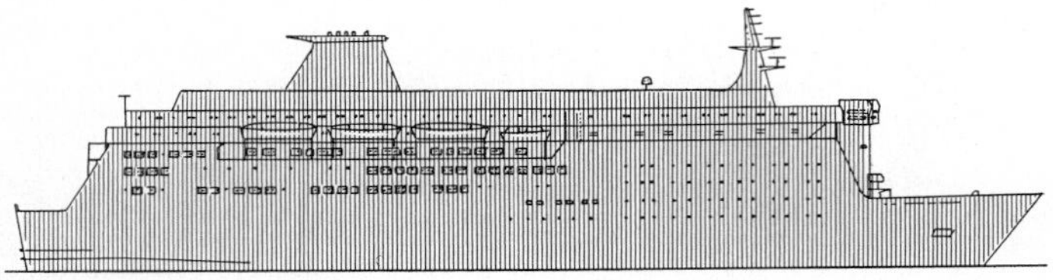

206 *MFZ H*
KONINGIN BEATRIX Ne/Ne (Giessen-De Noord) 1986; RoPCF; 31,189 grt; 161.8 × 6.2 m *(530.84 × 20.34 ft)*; TSM (MAN); 21 kts; Bow door and ramp; Two stern door/ramps

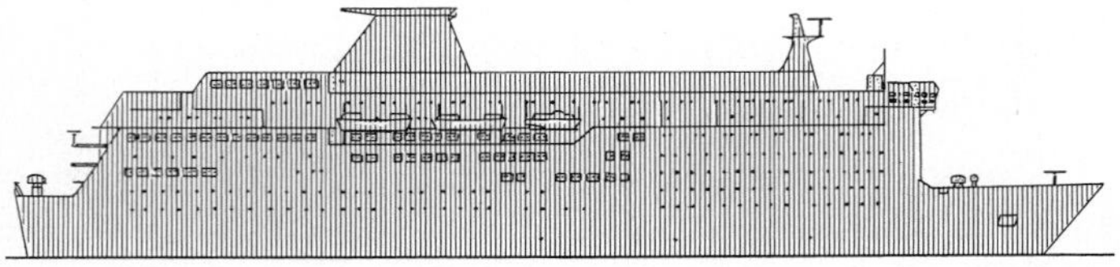

207 *MFZ H*
VAL DE LOIRE Fr/FRG (Seebeck) 1987; RoPCF; 31,395 grt; 161 × 6.22 m *(528.22 × 20.41 ft)*; TSM (MaK); 20 kts; ex-*Nils Holgersson*; Bow door and ramp; Two stern door/ramps
Sister: **SPIRIT OF TASMANIA** (Au) ex-*Peter Pan*

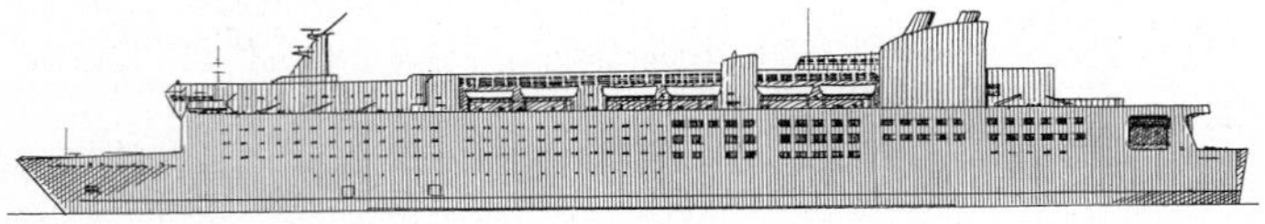

208 *MG H*
FINNJET Fi/Fi (Wärtsilä) 1977; RoPCF; 32,940 grt; 212.81 × 7.2 m *(698.2 × 23.62 ft)*; TS GT (Pratt & Whitney)/D-E (Wärtsilä); 30.5/18.5 kts; Bow door and ramp; Stern door and ramp; Can operate with gas turbine or diesel-electric machinery

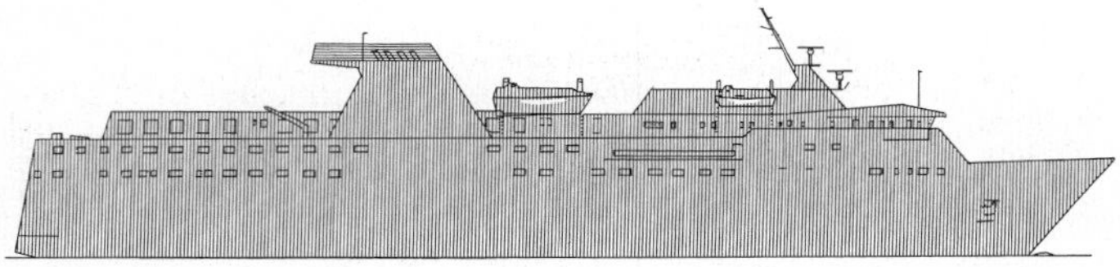

209 *MG H*
LAS PALMAS DE GRAN CANARIA Sp/Sp (UN de Levante) 1993; RoPCF; 10,473 grt; 116.79 × 5.4 m *(383.17 × 17.72 ft)*; TSM (MAN); 16 kts; Bow door/ramp; Stern door/ramp
Sister: **SANTA CRUZ DE TENERIFE** (Sp)

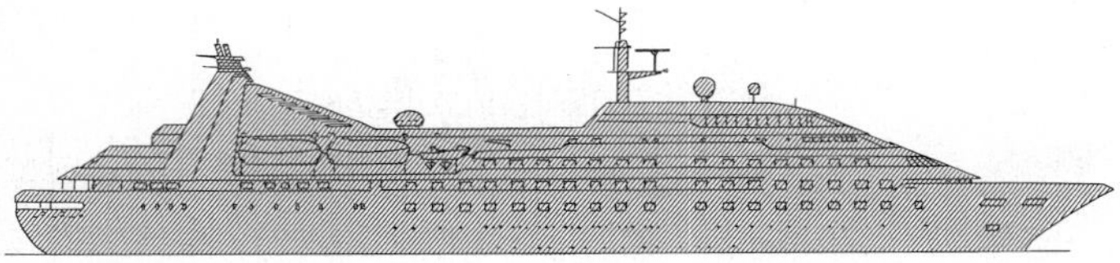

210 *MG H*
SEABOURN SPIRIT NIS/FRG (Schichau See) 1989; P; 9,975 grt; 133.8 × 5.17 m *(438.98 × 16.96 ft)*; TSM (Normo); 16 kts; Portable marina aft
Sister: **SEABOURN PRIDE** (NIS); Similar: **SEABOURN LEGEND** (NIS) ex-*Royal Viking Queen* (see photo number 20/443)

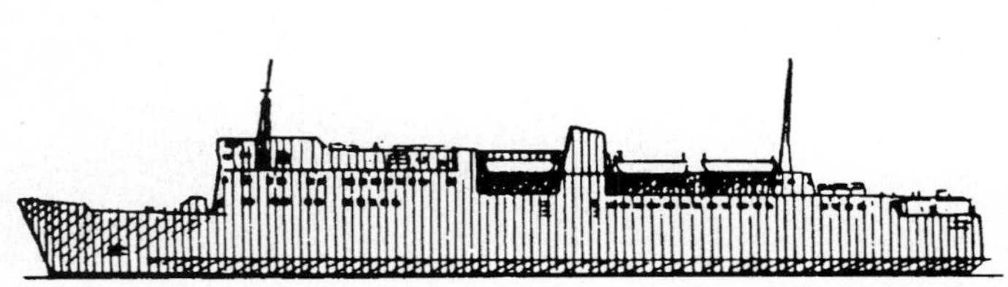

211 *MGM H*
BARONESS M Cy/Br (Cammell Laird) 1967; RoPF; 6,280 grt; 111 × 4.58 m *(365 × 15.03 ft)*; TSM (Pielstick); 18 kts; ex-*Lion*; Bow and stern doors/ramps

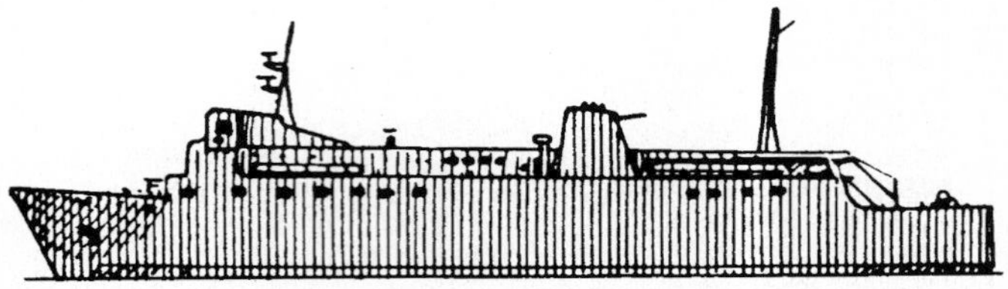

212 *MGM H*
DONG YANG EXPRESS FERRY NO 2 Ko/Ja (Naikai) 1975; RoPF; 3,007 grt; 90.5 × 4 m *(297 × 13.2 ft)*; TSM (Niigata); 17.5 kts; ex-*Kamome*; Bow door and ramp; Stern door/ramp

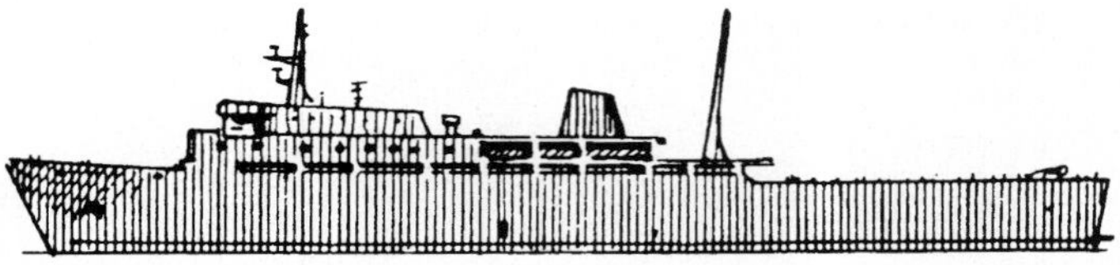

213 *MGM H*
HAYATOMO MARU Ja/Ja (Shikoku) 1971; RoPF; 6,496 grt; 105 × 4.4 m *(344 × 14.4 ft)*; TSM (Mitsubishi); 18.25 kts; ex-*Tosa*

214 *MGM H*
MEDIA II Cy/No (Kaldnes) 1964; RoPF; 5,440 grt; 99.5 × 4.4 m *(326 × 14.4 ft)*; TSM (Pielstick); 20 kts; ex-*Carferry Viking I*; Bow and stern doors
Sisters: **SANDEFJORD** (No) ex-*Viking III*; **PEARL WILLIAM** (Ma) ex-*Viking II*

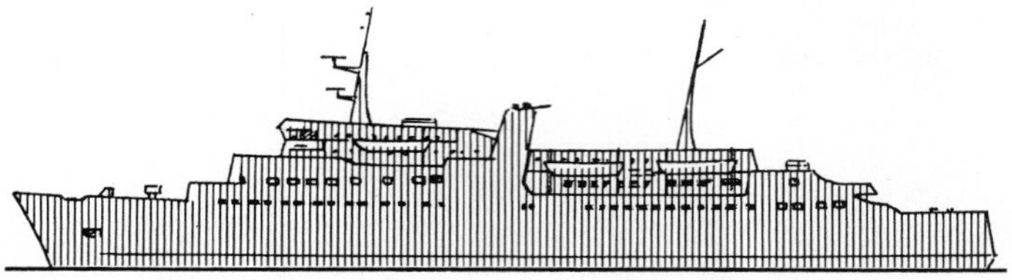

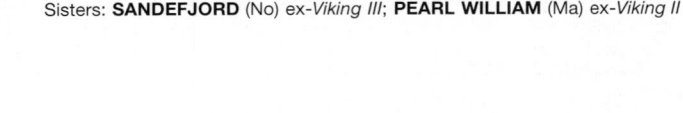

215 *MGM H*
MOBY BABY It/Sw (Oresunds) 1966; RoPF; 5,667 grt; 99.2 × 4.4 m *(325 × 14.4 ft)*; TSM (KHD); 19 kts; ex-*Svea Drott*; Bow and stern doors/ramps

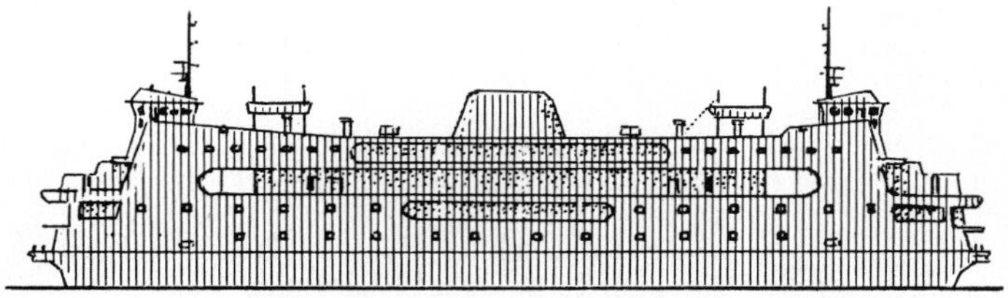

216 *MGM H*
MOLENGAT Ne/Ne (Verolme SH) 1980; RoPF; 6,170 grt; 88.42 × 3.8 m *(291 × 12.47 ft)*; TS D-E (MaK); 13.5 kts

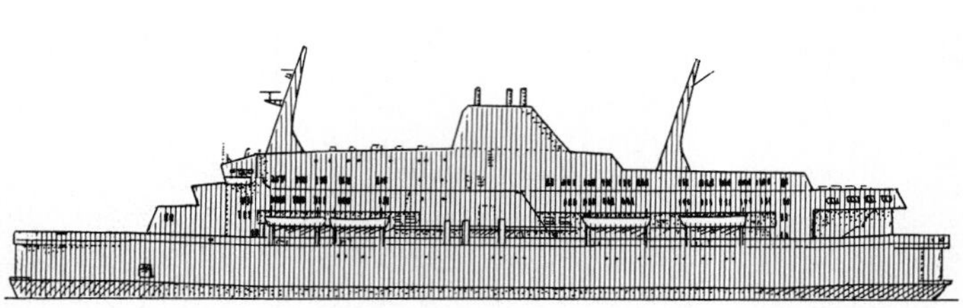

217 *MGM H*
PRIDE OF BRUGES Br/FRG (Schichau-U) 1979; RoPF; 13,061 grt; 131.96 × 5.71 m *(432.94 × 18.73 ft)*; TrS M (Sulzer); 22 kts; ex-*Pride of Free Enterprise*; Bow and stern doors

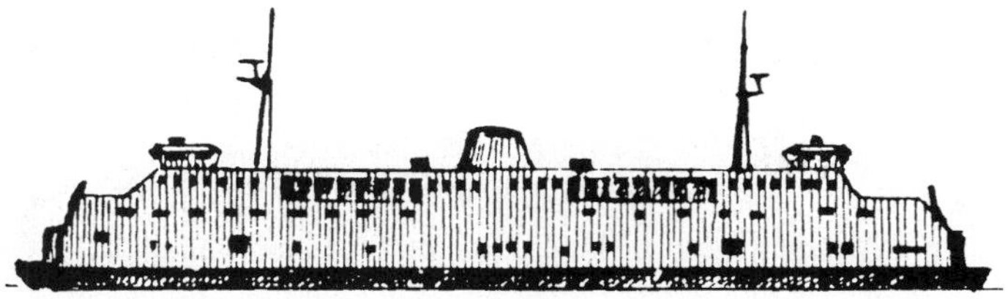

218 *MGM H*
PRINSES CHRISTINA Ne/Ne ('De Merwede') 1968; RoPF; 6,831 grt; 113.59 × 4.6 m *(373 × 15.2 ft)*; D-E (MAN); 18.5 kts; Bow and stern doors

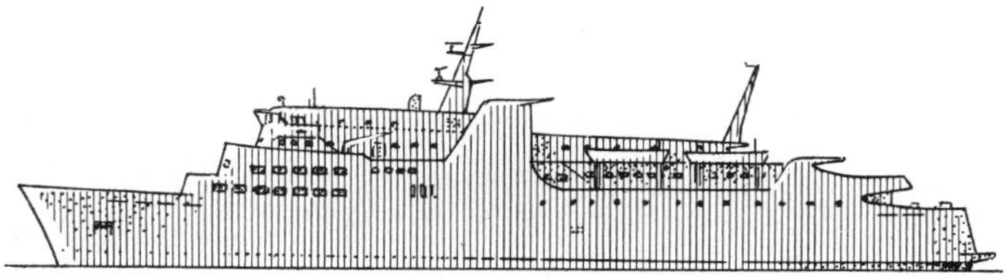

219 *MGM H*
QUEEN OF PRINCE RUPERT Ca/Ca (Victoria Mach) 1966; RoPF; 5,864 grt; 101.12 × 4.64 m *(331.76 × 15.22 ft)*; TSM (Mirrlees); 18 kts; Bow and stern doors

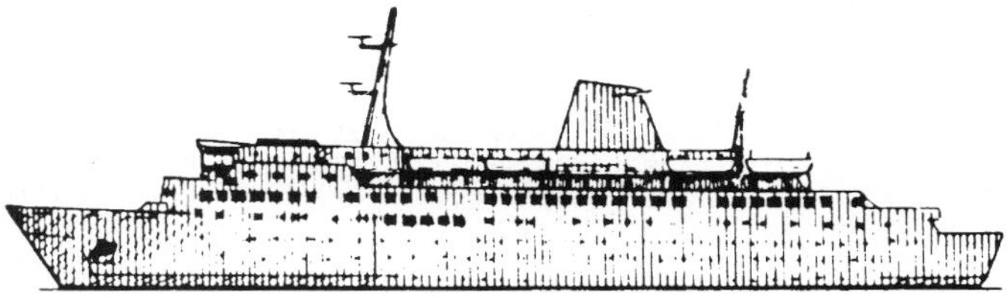

220 *MGM H*
ROGALIN Pd/Fr (Dubigeon-Normandie) 1972; RoPF; 10,241 grt; 126.9 × 5.2 m *(416 × 17.06 ft)*; TSM (Pielstick); 21 kts; ex-*Aallotar*; Bow and stern doors/ramps

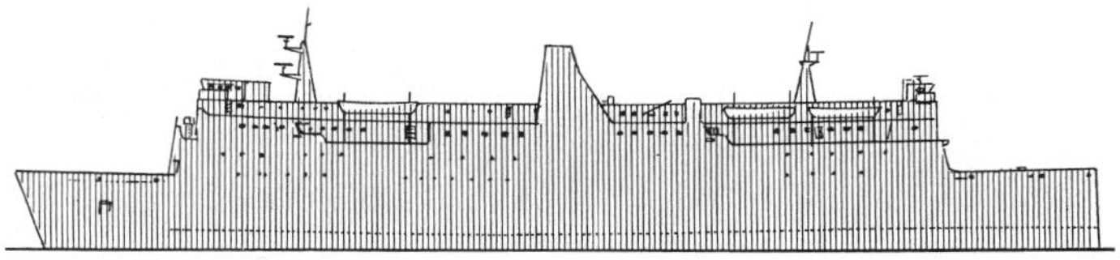

221 *MGM H*
STENA CALEDONIA Br/Br (H&W) 1981; RoPCF; 12,619 grt; 129.65 × 4.84 m *(425 × 15.88 ft)*; TSM (Pielstick); 19.5 kts; ex-*St David*; Bow and stern doors
Similar: **STENA GALLOWAY** (Br) ex-*Galloway Princess*

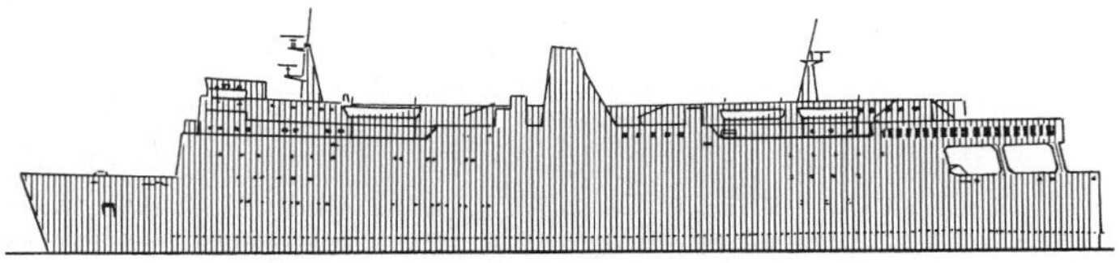

222 *MGM H*
STENA CAMBRIA Br/Br (H&W) 1980; RoPCF; 12,705 grt; 129.4 × 4.72 m *(424.54 × 15.49 ft)*; TSM (Pielstick); 19.5 kts; ex-*St Anselm*; Bow and stern doors; Modified 1982/83
Sister: **STENA ANTRIM** (Br) ex-*St Christopher*

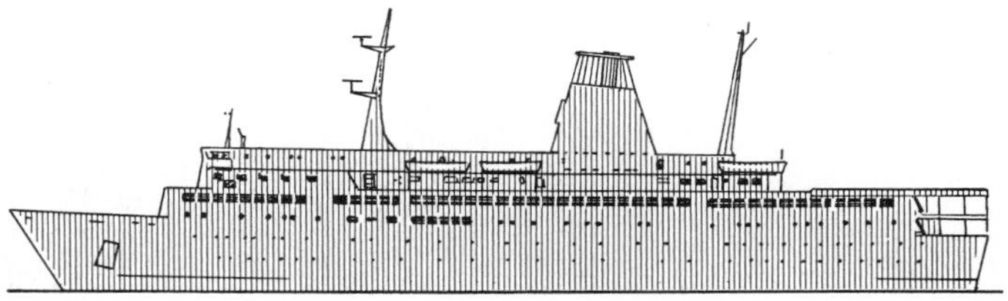

223 *MGM H*
TALLINK Ea/Fr (Dubigeon-Normandie) 1972; RoPCF; 10,341 grt; 126.93 × 5.17 m *(416.44 × 16.96 ft)*; TSM (Pielstick); 18.5 kts; ex-*Svea Regina*; Bow and stern doors

224 *MGM H*
VITSENTZOS KORNAROS Gr/De (Aalborg) 1976; RoPF; 9,735 grt; 128.81 × 4.53 m *(422.6 × 14.86 ft)*; TrS M (Stork-Werkspoor); 21 kts; ex-*Viking Viscount*; Bow door and ramp; Stern door/ramp
Sister: **BANADEROS** (Sp) ex-*Viking Voyager*

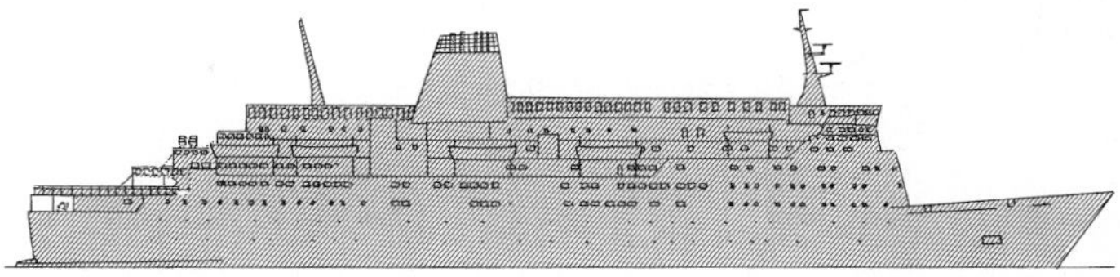

225 *MGM H*
WASA QUEEN Fi/Fr (Dubigeon-Normandie) 1975; RoPF; 16,546 grt; 153.1 × 5.1 m *(500.6 × 16.7 ft)*; TSM (Pielstick); 23 kts; ex-*Bore Star*; Bow door and ramp; Stern door and ramp
Sister (lengthened to 175 m (574 ft) and rebuilt aft): **COLOR VIKING** (No) ex-*Wellamo*. Similar (originally a sister but now rebuilt): **IONIAN EXPRESS** (—) ex-*Svea Corona*

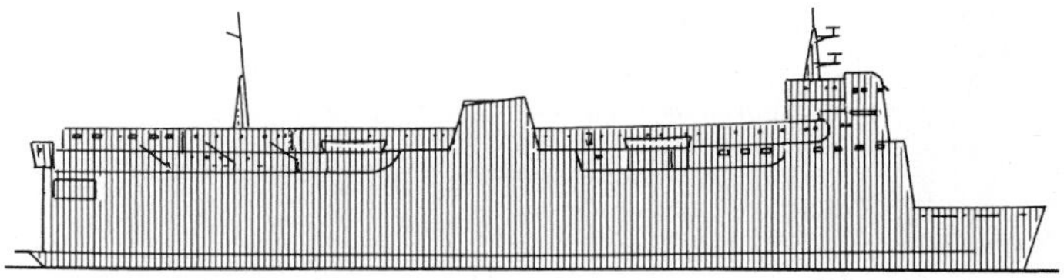

226 *MGM H2*
JOHN HAMILTON GRAY Ca/Ca (Marine Indust) 1968; RoC/F; 11,259 grt/ 3,087 dwt; 122.1 × 6.19 m *(400.59 × 20.31 ft)*; TSD-E (Fairbanks, Morse); 18 kts; Icebreaking

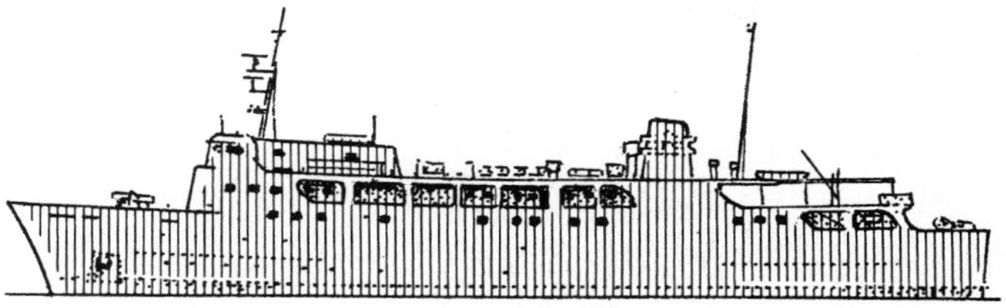

227 *MGMC H*
FERRY FUKUE Ja/Ja (Naikai) 1978; RoPF; 1,867 grt; 79.66 × 3.7 m *(261.35 × 12.14 ft)*; TSM (Daihatsu); 17.25 kts; Bow door and ramp; Stern door/ramp

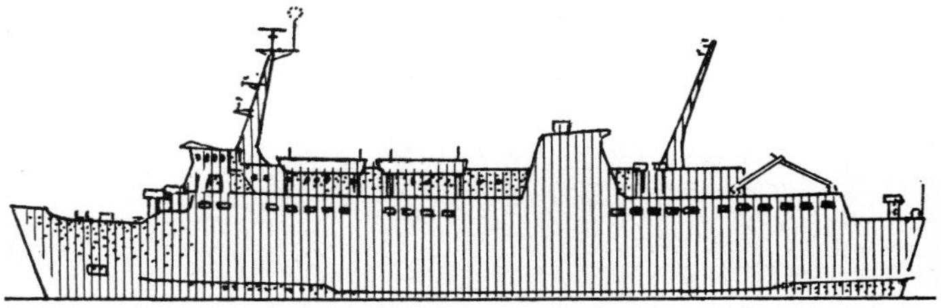

228 *MGMRS H*
ELBA NOVA It/Ja (Usuki) 1977; RoPF; 3,134 grt; 78.52 × 3.35 m *(257.61 × 10.99 ft)*; TSM (Niigata); 15.5 kts; ex-*Emsland*; Bow door/ramp; Stern door/ramp

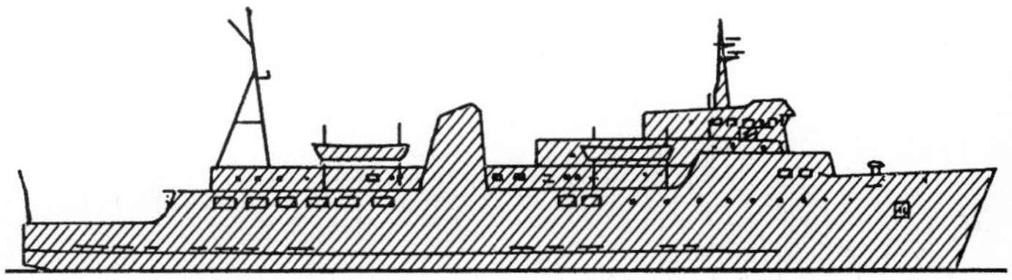

229 *MGMY H1*
ISLE OF ARRAN Br/Br (Ferguson-Ailsa) 1984; RoC/F; 3,296 grt; 84.92 × 3.19 m *(278.61 × 10.47 ft)*; TSM (Mirrlees); 15 kts; Bow door and ramp; Two stern ramps

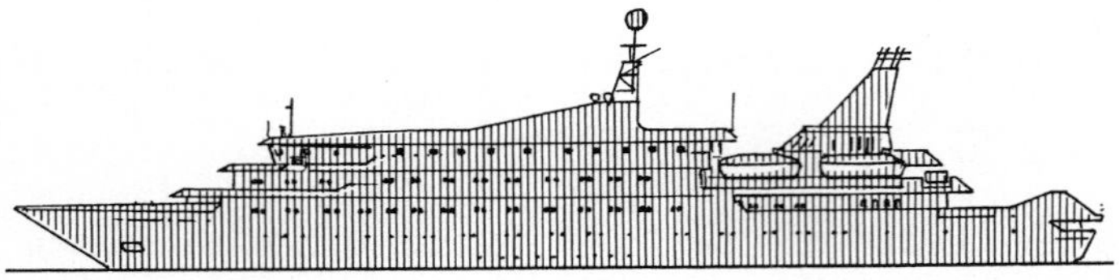

230 *MHF H*
SEA GODDESS 1 Br/Fi (Wärtsilä) 1984; P; 4,253 grt; 105 × 3.99 m *(344 × 13.09)*; TSM (Wärtsilä); 17.5 kts
Sister: **SEA GODDESS II** (Br)

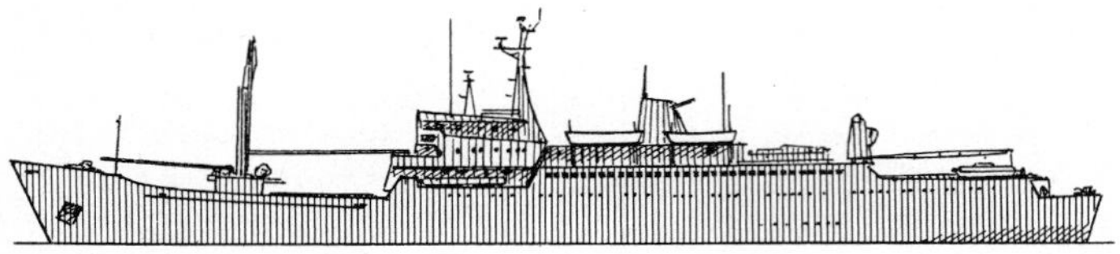

231 *MHMFC H12*
PROFESSOR SHCHYOGOLEV Ru/Pd (Szczecinska) 1970; C/TS; 6,036 grt/ 5,505 dwt; 122 × 7.3 m *(402 × 23.9 ft)*; M (Sulzer); 15.5 kts; 'B 80' type
Sisters: **PROFESSOR KUDREVICH** (Uk); **PROFESSOR ANICHKOV** (Ru); **PROFESSOR PAVLENKO** (Uk); **PROFESSOR RYBALTOVSKIY** (Ru); **PROFESSOR KHLYUSTIN** (Ru); **PROFESSOR YUSHCHENKO** (Ru). Similar (light mast from funnel): **PROFESSOR UKHOV** (Ru); **PROFESSOR MINYAYEV** (Uk)

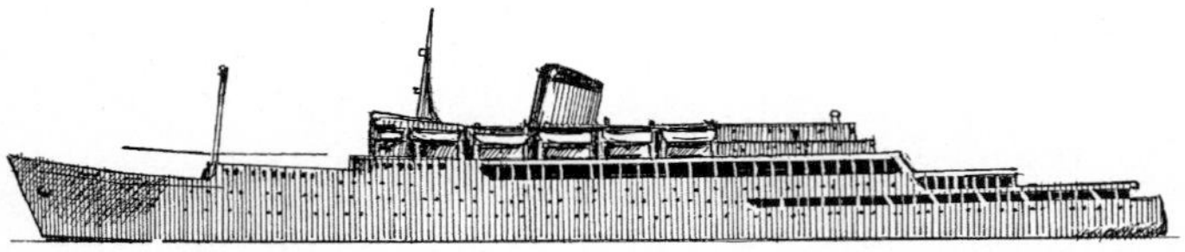

232 *M^2F H*
AMERIKANIS Pa/Br (H&W) 1952; P; 18,458 grt; 176 × 8.13 m *(577.4 × 26.67 ft)*; TST (Parsons); 19.5 kts; ex-*Kenya Castle*; Rebuilt 1968

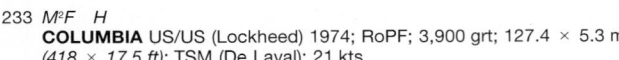

233 *M^2F H*
COLUMBIA US/US (Lockheed) 1974; RoPF; 3,900 grt; 127.4 × 5.3 m *(418 × 17.5 ft)*; TSM (De Laval); 21 kts

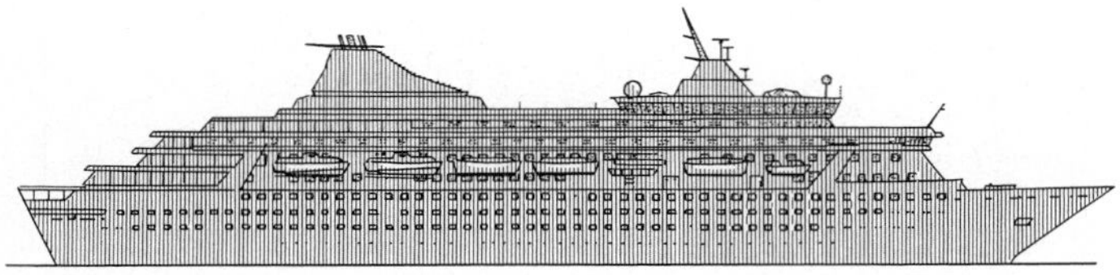

234 *M^2F H*
CROWN ODYSSEY Bs/FRG (Meyer) 1988; P; 34,242 grt; 187.71 × 7.25 m *(615.85 × 23.79 ft)*; TSM (MaK); 22.5 kts

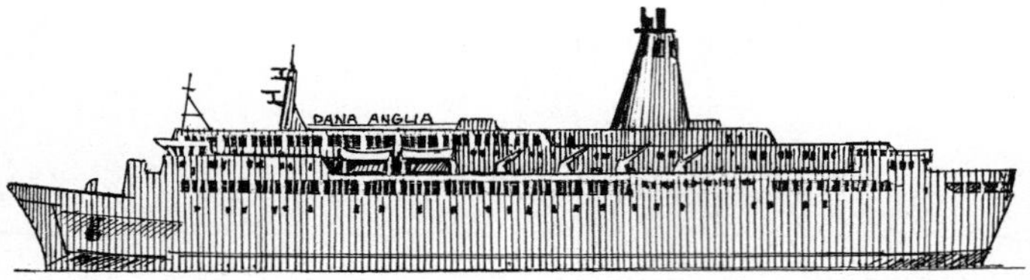

235 *M^2F H*
DANA ANGLIA De/De (Aalborg) 1978; RoPCF; 19,321 grt; 152.91 × 5.71 m *(501.67 × 18.73 ft)*; TSM (Pielstick); 21 kts; Bow and stern doors

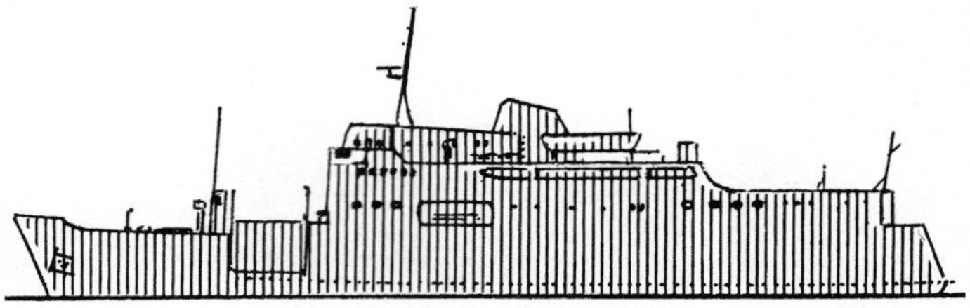

236 *M^2F H*
ILLYRIA SV/Br (Hall, Russell) 1964; RoPCF; 1,921 grt; 71.63 × 2.74 m *(235 × 8.99 ft)*; TSM (Crossley); 14.5 kts; ex-*Hebrides*
Similar (rebuilt as cruise ship, heavy mast forward, new funnel top with deflector, extra superstructure and so on): **HEBRIDEAN EXPRESS** (Br) ex-*Columba*

237 *M^2F H*
ISCHIA It/Br (Denny) 1948; RoPCF; 996 grt; 87.9 × 2.6 m *(288 × 8.6 ft)*; TSM (KHD); 19 kts; ex-*Royal Sovereign*; Converted from passenger ship

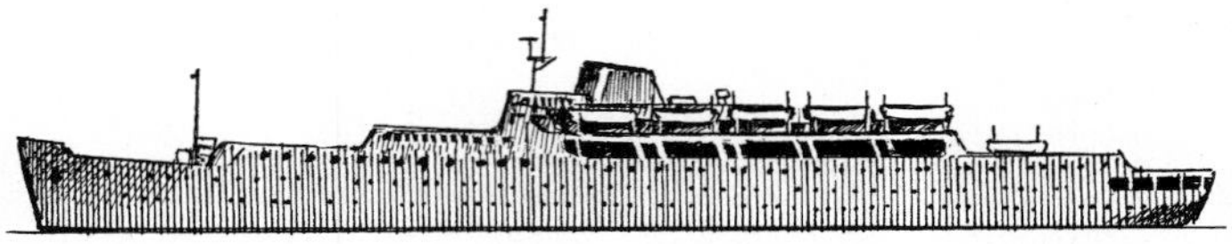

238 *M^2F H*
LA PALMA Gr/Fr (Gironde) 1952; P; 11,951 grt; 150 × 7.4 m *(493 × 24.2 ft)*; TSM (B&W); 17 kts; ex-*Ferdinand De Lesseps*

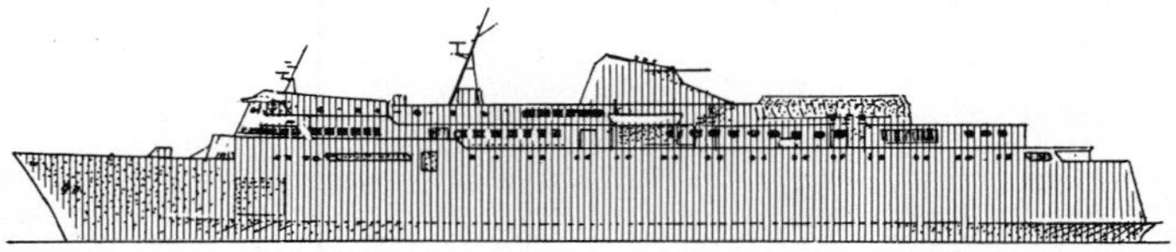

239 *M^2F H*
MATANUSKA US/US (Puget Sound) 1963/78; RoPF; 3,029 grt; 124.36 × 4.98 m *(408 × 16.34 ft)*; TSM (MaK); 16.5 kts; Lengthened 1978 (Willamette)

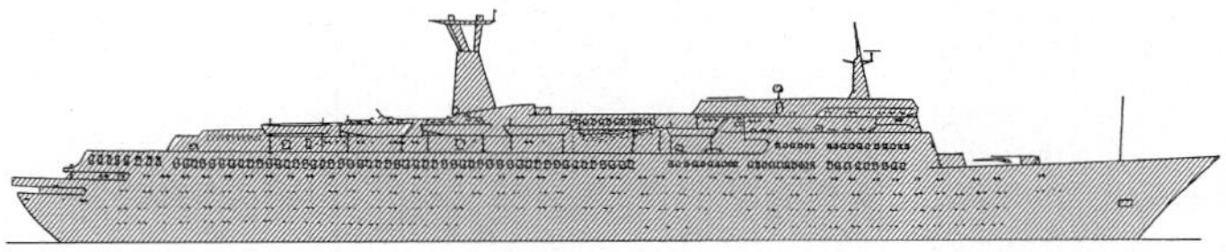

240 *M^2F H*
MAXIM GORKIY Bs/FRG (Howaldts DW) 1969; P; 24,220 grt; 194.6 × 8.3 m *(627 × 27.23 ft)*; TST (Allgemeine); 23 kts; ex-*Hamburg*

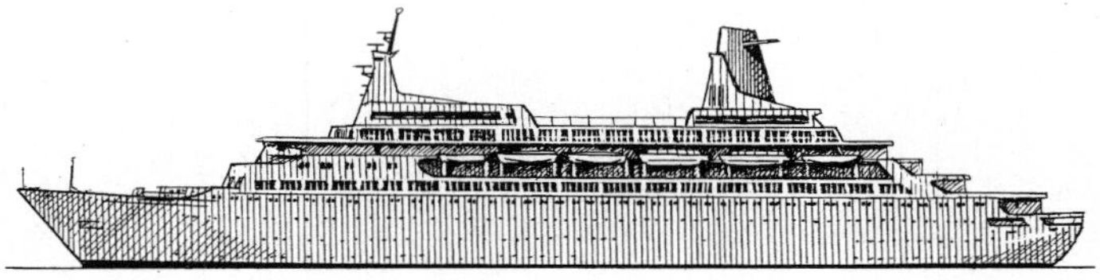

241 *M^2F H*
PACIFIC PRINCESS Br/FRG (Rhein Nordseew) 1971; P; 20,186 grt; 168.7 × 7.7 m *(553.6 × 25.3 ft)*; TSM (Fiat); 21.5 kts; ex-*Sea Venture*
Sister: **ISLAND PRINCESS** (Br) ex-*Island Venture*

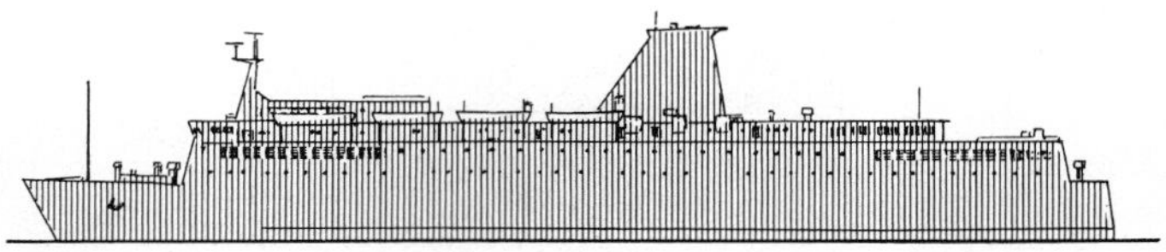

242 *M^2F H*
POMERANIA Pd/Pd (Szczecinska) 1978; RoPCF; 7,400 grt; 127.25 × 5.42 m *(417.49 × 17.78 ft)*; M (Sulzer); 20.4 kts; 'B 490' type
Sister: **SILESIA** (Pd)

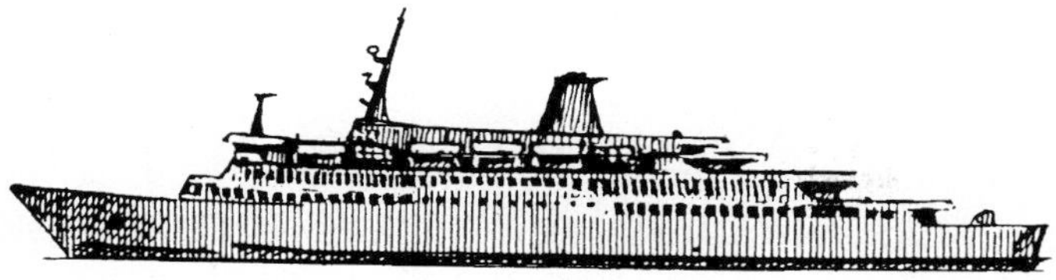

243 M^2F *H*
QUEEN OF THE NORTH Ca/FRG (A G 'Weser') 1969; RoPF; 8,800 grt; 125 × 4.87 m *(410.1 × 15.98 ft)*; TSM (MAN); 22.5 kts; ex-*Stena Danica*; Bow and stern doors

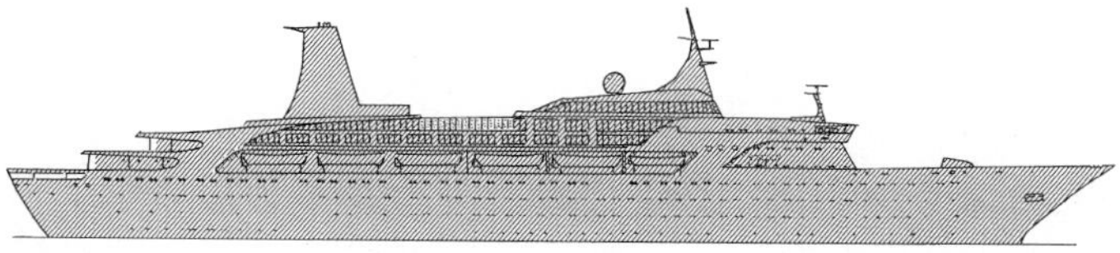

244 M^2F *H*
SOUTHERN CROSS Bs/It (Tirreno) 1972; P; 17,042 grt; 163.3 × 6.5 m *(536 × 21.32 ft)*; TSM (Fiat); 15.5 kts; ex-*Spirit of London*

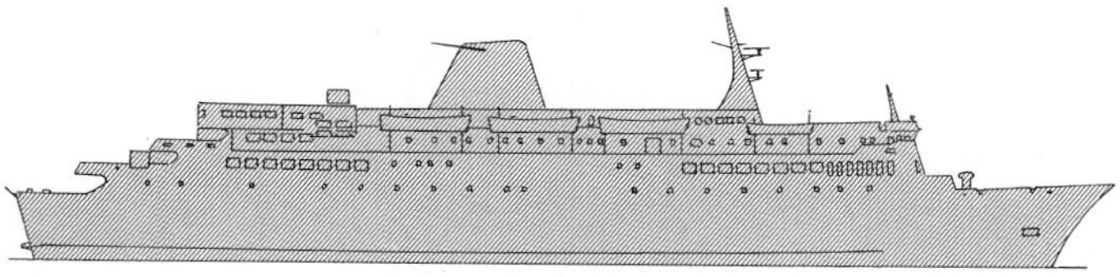

245 M^2F *H*
ST CLAIR Br/FRG (Unterweser) 1971; RoPF; 8,499 grt; 118 × 5 m *(387 × 16.5 ft)*; TSM (MAN); 21 kts; ex-*Travemunde*; Bow, stern and side doors

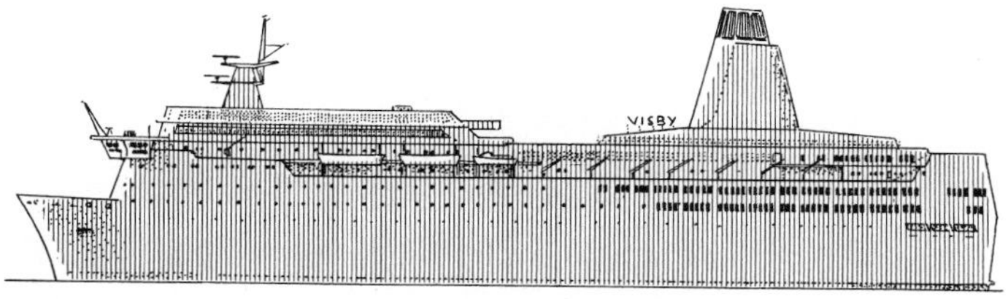

246 M^2F *H*
STENA FELICITY Sw/Sw (Oresunds) 1980; RoPCF; 23,775 grt; 142.33 × 5.5 m *(466.96 × 18.04 ft)*; TSM (B&W); 21 kts; ex-*Visby*; Three stern door/ramps; Bow door/ramp
Sister (lengthened by 22 m (72 ft)): **PETER WESSEL** (No) ex-*Wasa Star*

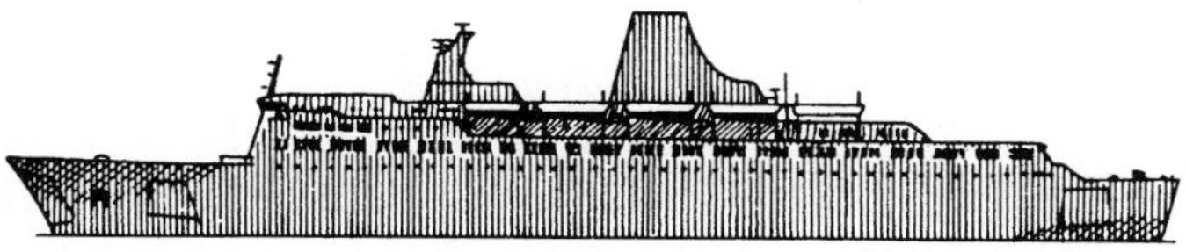

247 M^2F *H*
VANA TALLINN Ea/De (Aalborg) 1974; RoPCF; 10,002 grt; 153.7 × 6 m *(504 × 20 ft)*; TSM (B&W); 21.9 kts; ex-*Dana Regina*; Bow door; Stern door; Side door (port)

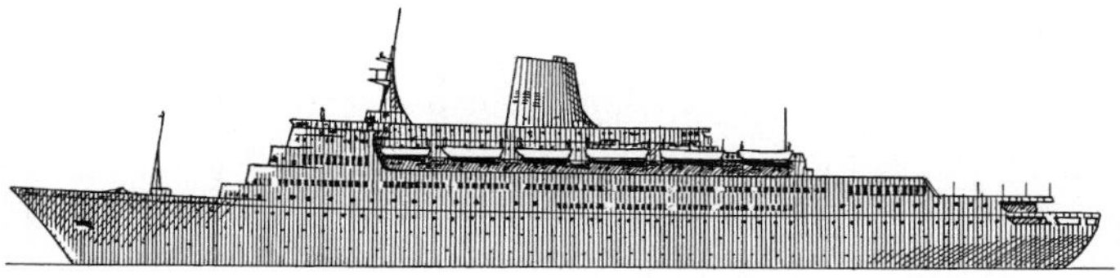

248 M^2F *H*
VISTAFJORD Bs/Br (Swan Hunter) 1973; P; 24,492 grt; 191 × 8.2 m *(627 × 27 ft)*; TSM (Sulzer); 20 kts

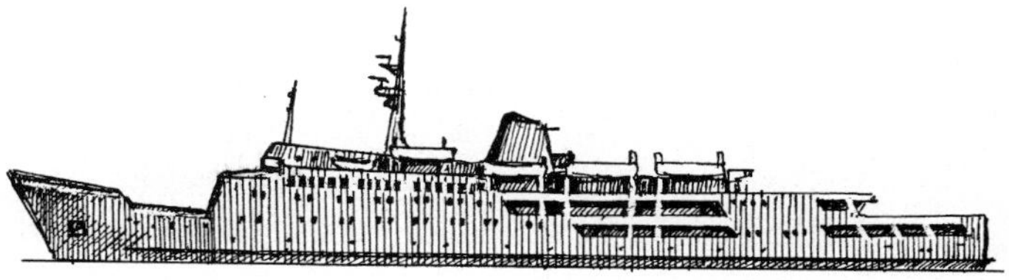

249 M^2F *H1*
GALLURA It/It (Tirreno) 1968; F; 4,938 grt; 123 × 5.5 m *(404 × 18 ft)*; TSM (Fiat); 15 kts

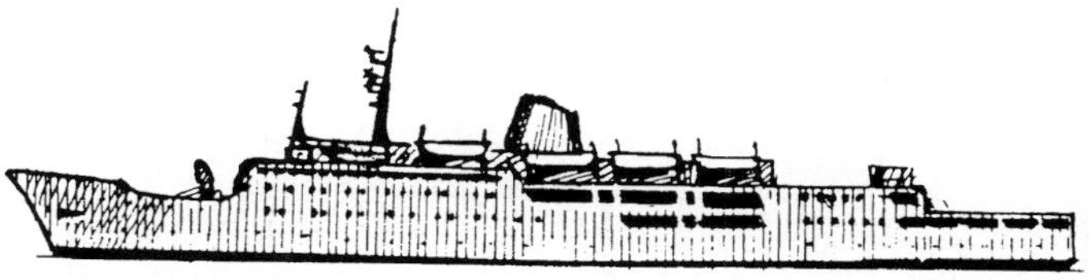

250 M^2F *H1*
GENNARGENTU It/It (Riuniti) 1965; RoPF; 4,900 grt; 122 × 5.5 m *(411 × 18.04 ft)*; TSM (Fiat); 16 kts

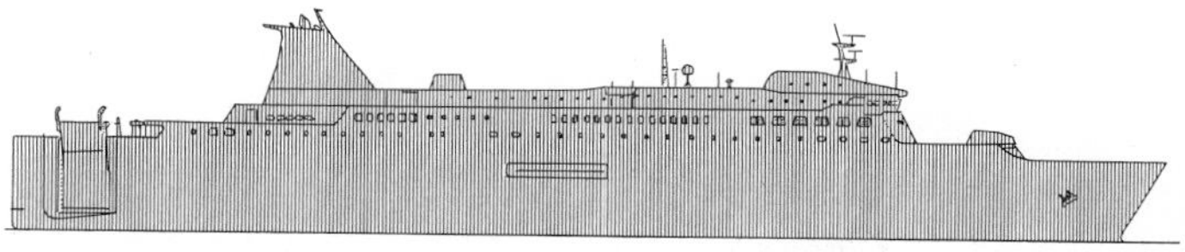

251 M^2FA *H2*
PACIFIC EXPRESS Ja/Ja (Mitsubishi HI) 1992; RoPCF; 11,580 grt; 170 × 6.72 m *(557.74 × 22.05 ft)*; TSM (Pielstick); 26.2 kts; Bow door/ramp; Angled side door/ramp (starboard aft)
Probable sister: **PHOENIX EXPRESS** (Ja)

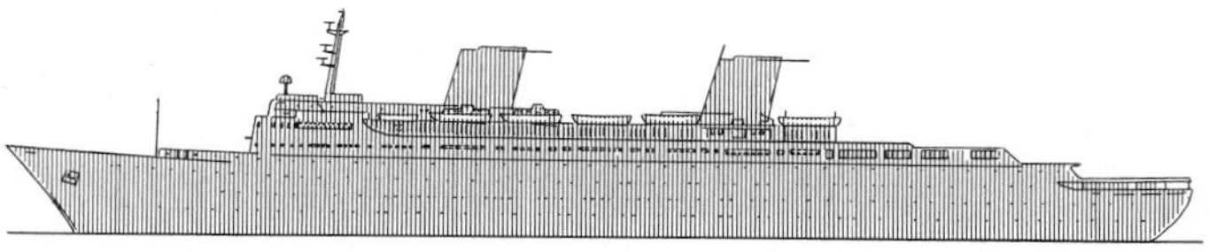

252 M^2F^2 *H*
REGENT SEA Bs/It (Ansaldo) 1957; P; 23,292 grt; 192.41 × 8.5 m *(631.27 × 27.89 ft)*; TSM (Gotaverken); 18 kts; ex-*Gripsholm*

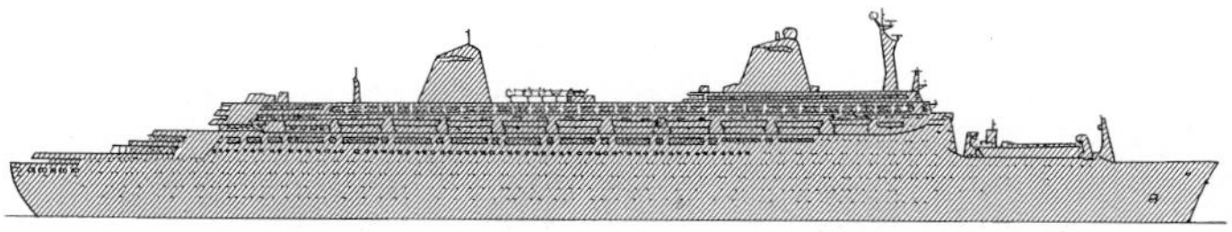

253 M^2F^2N *H*
NORWAY Bs/Fr (L'Atlantique) 1961/80; P; 76,049 grt; 315 × 10.3 m *(1,034 × 33.7 ft)*; TST (CEM-Parsons); 17 kts; ex-*France*; Modernised and rebuilt 1979/80 (Hapag-Lloyd)

254 M^2FM *H*
DIPOLOG PRINCESS Pi/Ja (Onomichi) 1969; PC; 3,501 grt; 111.2 × 5.5 m *(365 × 18 ft)*; M (Sulzer); 18.5 kts; ex-*Tokyo Maru*

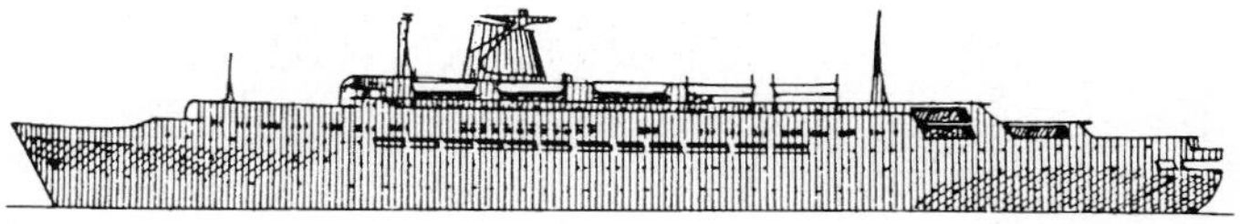

255 M^2FM *H*
DOLPHIN IV Pa/FRG (Deutsche Werft) 1956; P; 12,091 grt; 153 × 8 m *(501 × 26.7 ft)*; T (Allgemeine); 19 kts; ex-*Zion*

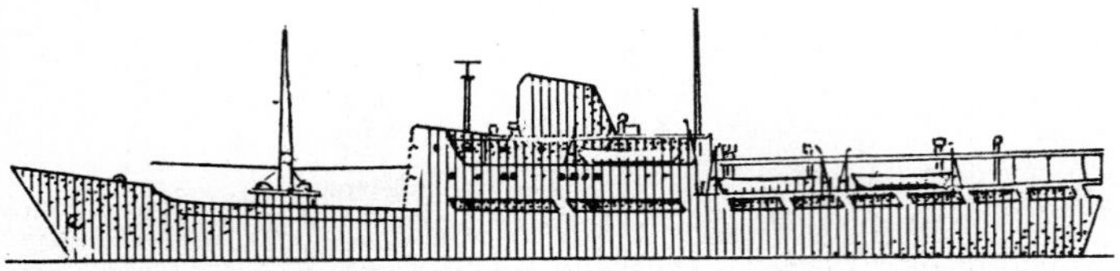

256 M^{2}FM *H*
LORENZO CONTAINER XII Pi/FRG (A G 'Weser') 1968; PC/F; 1,500 grt; 88.02 × 4.82 m *(288.78 × 15.81 ft)*; M (Atlas-MaK); 15.75 kts; ex-*Sweet Grace*

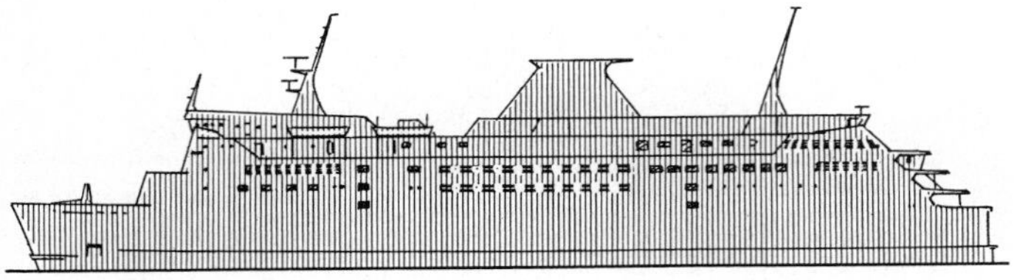

257 M^{2}FM *H*
SEAFRANCE RENOIR Fr/Fr (Havre) 1981; RoPCF; 8,478 grt; 130.03 × 5 m *(426.61 × 16.4 ft)*; TSM (Pielstick); 18 kts; Bow and stern doors

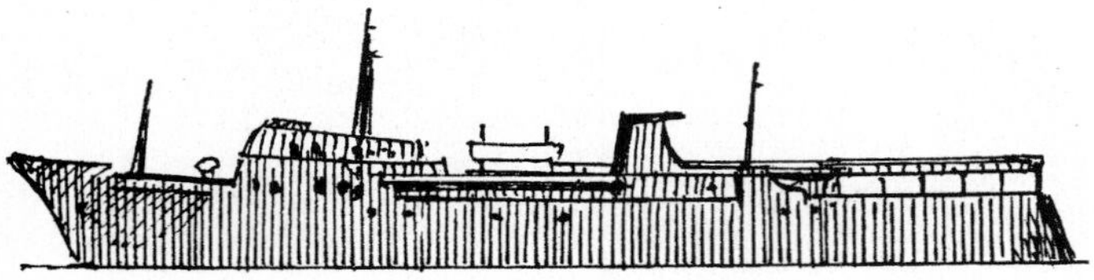

258 M^{2}FM *H*
TOBAGO Tr/Ne ('De Hoop') 1970; RoPF; 1,500 grt; 76 × 3.3 m *(250 × 11 ft)*; TSM (Alco); — kts; ex-*Santa Margarita*; Bow and stern doors

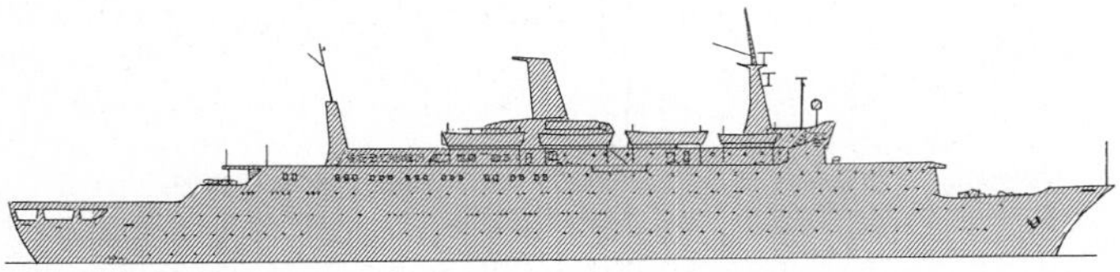

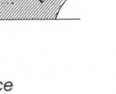

259 M^{2}FM-G *H2*
WORLD RENAISSANCE Gr/Fr (L'Atlantique) 1966; P; 8,665 grt; 150 × 6.2 m *(492 × 20.3 ft)*; TSM (B&W); 18.5 kts; ex-*Renaissance*

260 M^{2}FR *H*
QUEEN OF VICTORIA Ca/Ca (Victoria Mach) 1962; RoPF; 9,369 grt; 130 × 3.8 m *(427 × 12.46 ft)*; TSM (Atlas-MaK); 18 kts; ex-*City of Victoria*; Bow and stern doors; Lengthened 1970; Deepened by 3 m 1981; Drawing shows vessel before latter modification
Sisters: **QUEEN OF VANCOUVER** (Ca) ex-*City of Vancouver*; **QUEEN OF SAANICH** (Ca); **QUEEN OF ESQUIMALT** (Ca). Similar (not deepened): **QUEEN OF NANAIMO** (Ca); **QUEEN OF NEW WESTMINSTER** (Ca)

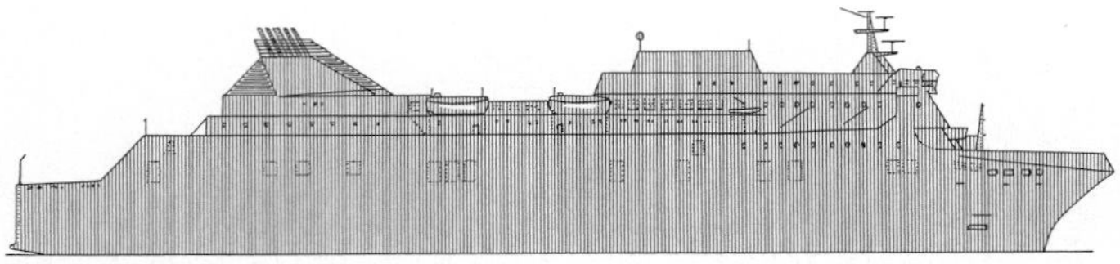

261 M^{2}FZ *H2*
JUAN J SISTER Sp/Fi (Kvaerner Masa) 1993; RoPCF; 22,409 grt; 151.1 × 6 m *(495.73 × 19.69 ft)*; TSM (Wärtsilä); 18 kts; Bow door/ramp; Two stern door/ramps

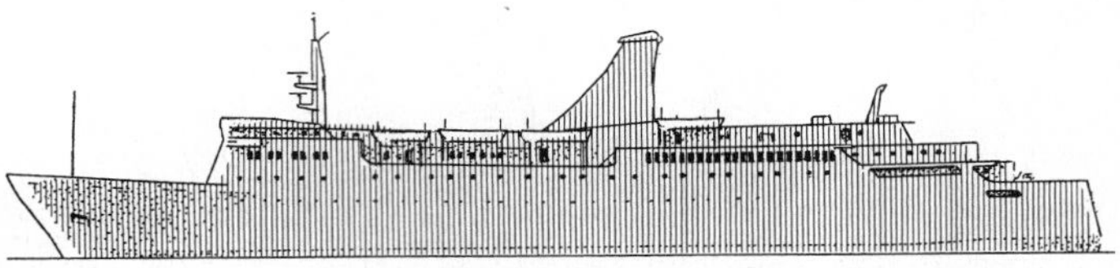

262 M^{2}G *H*
CIUDAD DE SEVILLA Sp/Sp (UN de Levante) 1980; RoPCF; 7,400 grt; 138.5 × 5.5 m *(454 × 18.04 ft)*; TSM (MAN); 21 kts; Stern door
Sisters: **CIUDAD DE SALAMANCA** (Sp); **CIUDAD DE VALENCIA** (Sp)

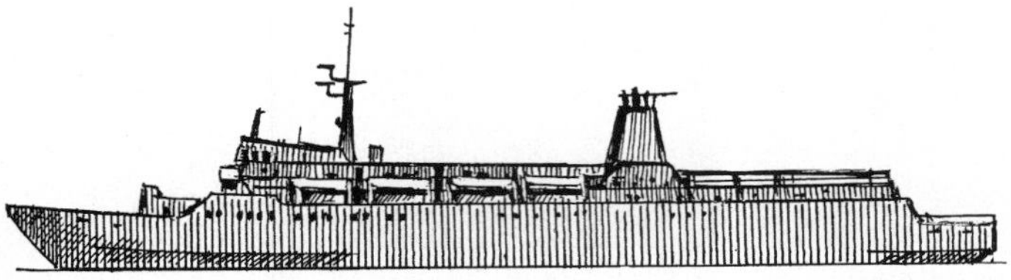

263 M^{2}G *H*
EGITTO EXPRESS It/It ('L Orlando') 1973; PoPF; 8,975 grt; 125.5 × 5.5 m *(412 × 18.04 ft)*; TSM (GMT); 21 kts; ex-*Espresso Cagliari*
Sisters: **ESPRESSO GRECIA** (It) ex-*Espresso Livorno*; **PEGASUS** (Cy) ex-*Espresso Venezia*; **ESPRESSO VENEZIA** (It) ex-*Espresso Ravenna*

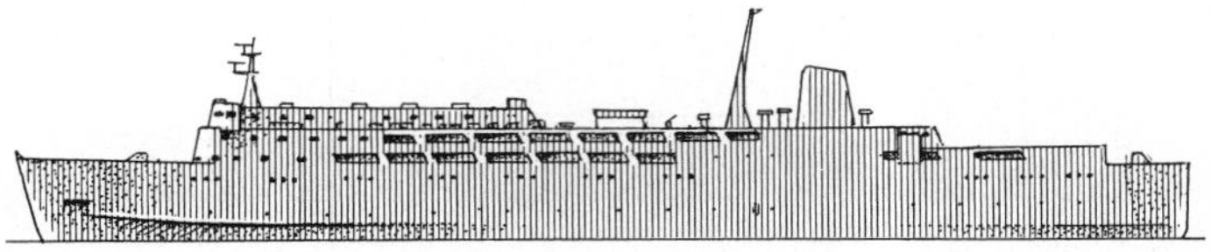

264 M^{2}G *H*
FERRY PUKWAN Ko/Ja (Kanda) 1972; RoC/F; 6,138 grt; 135.49 × 5.23 m *(444.52 × 17.16 ft)*; TSM (Pielstick); 21 kts; ex-*Tsukushi*
Sister: **FERRY KAMPU** (Ja) ex-*Hakata*

See photo number 20/411

265 M^{2}G *H*
SEAWING Bs/It (Tirreno) 1971; P; 16,710 grt; 163.4 × 6.5 m *(536.6 × 21.32 ft)*; TSM (Fiat); 21.5 kts; ex-*Southward*

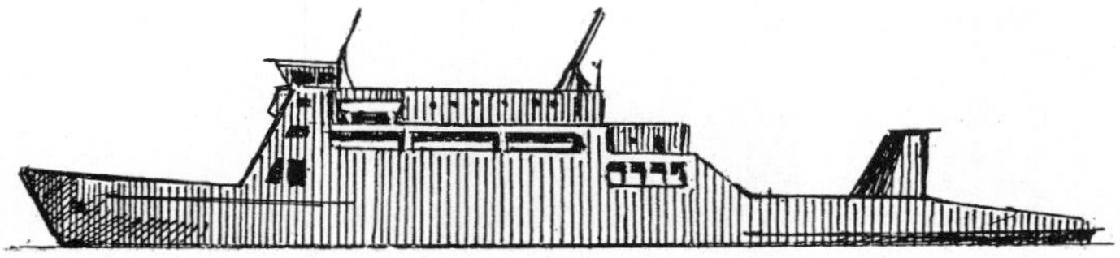

266 M^{2}G *H2*
CARRIER PRINCESS Ca/Ca (Burrard DD) 1973; RoC/TF; 5,295 grt/ 3,429 dwt; 115.83 × 4.88 m *(380.01 × 16.01 ft)*; TSM (General Motors); 18 kts

267 M^{2}G *H2*
HAVELET Bs/No (Bergens) 1977; RoPCF; 3,382 grt; 109.7 × 4.3 m *(360 × 14.11 ft)*; TSM (Pielstick); 19 kts; ex-*Cornouilles*; Bow door and ramp; Stern door/ramp

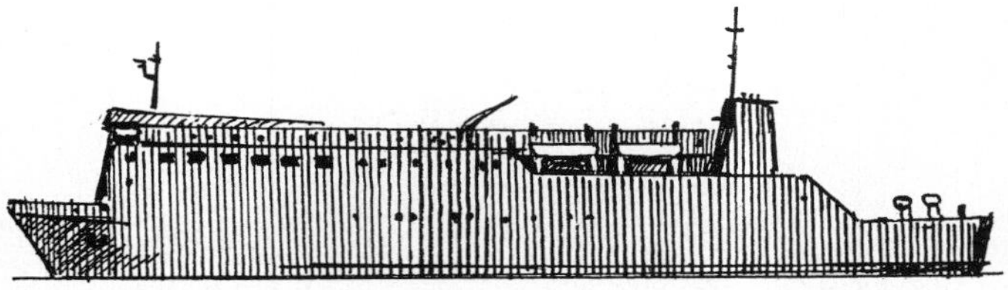

268 M^{2}G *H2*
VEGA Cy/No (Trondhjems) 1975; RoC/F; 8,881 grt; 130.26 × 4.31 m *(427.36 × 14.14 ft)*; TSM (Polar); 19 kts; ex-*Falster*; Bow door/ramp; Side door/ramp; Two stern doors/ramps; Lengthened 1977

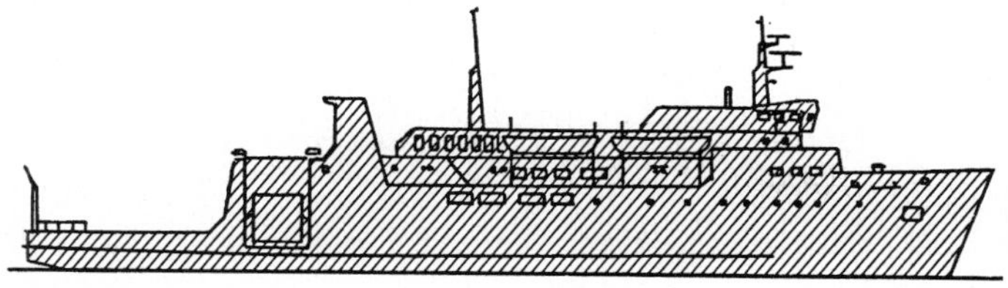

269 M^2GB *H1*
HEBRIDEAN ISLES Br/Br (Cochrane) 1985; RoC/F; 3,040 grt; 85.17 × 3.11 m *(279.43 × 10.2 ft)*; TSM (Mirrlees); 15 kts; Bow door and ramp; Two side door/ramps (one port/one starboard); Stern door/ramp

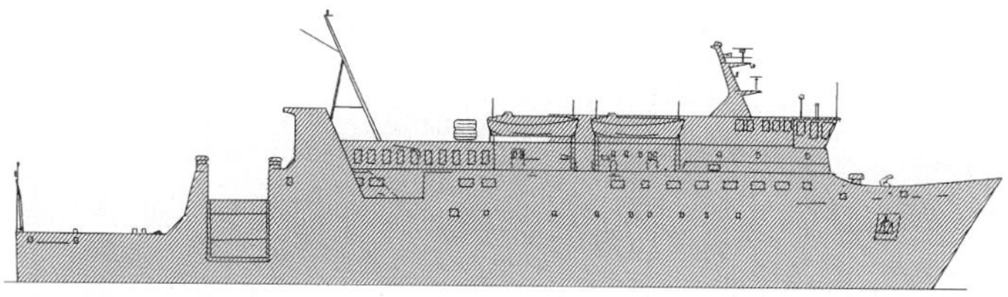

270 M^2GBY *H1*
LORD OF THE ISLES Br/Br (Appledore Ferguson) 1989; RoPCF; 3,504 grt; 84.63 × 3.13 m *(277.66 × 10.27 ft)*; TSM (Mirrlees); 16 kts; Bow door and ramp; Two side door/ramps (one port/one starboard); Stern door/ramp

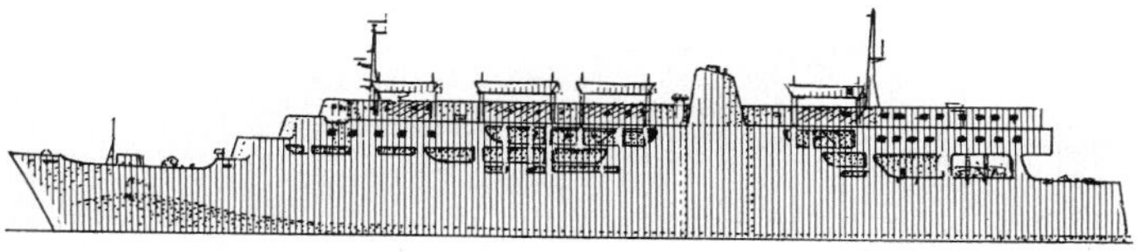

271 M^2GM *H*
TASSILI Ag/Ja (Mitsubishi HI) 1971; RoPF; 12,268 grt; 130.38 × 5.62 m *(427.76 × 18.44 ft)*; TSM (Mitsubishi); 19 kts; ex-*Central No 1*; Bow, stern and side doors

272 M^2GS *H*
MIN NAN RC/Fr (Havre) 1972; RoPCF; 5,712 grt; 116.6 × 4.3 m *(382 × 14 ft)*; TSM (Pielstick); 18.5 kts; ex-*Terje Vigen*; Bow door/ramp; Stern door/ramp

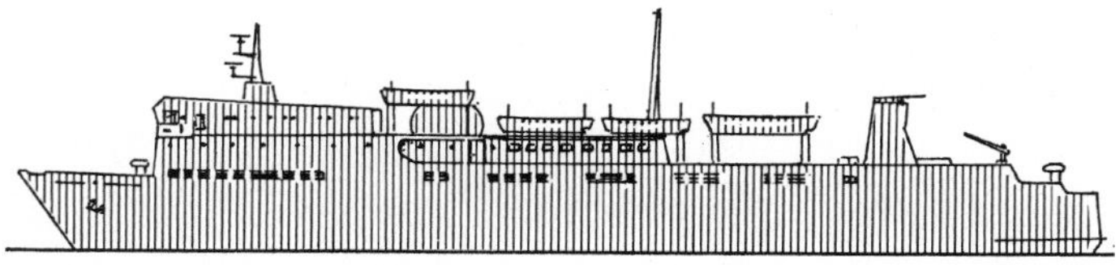

273 M^2GS *H*
NINDAWAYMA Ca/Sp (Juliana) 1976; RoC/F; 3,594 grt; 101.66 × 4.81 m *(334 × 15.78 ft)*; TSM (Pielstick); 17 kts; Launched as *Monte Cruceta*; Bow door/ramp; Stern door/ramp
Similar: **CIUDAD DE CEUTA** (Sp) ex-*Monte Contes*; **CIUDAD DE ZARAGOZA** (Sp) ex-*Monte Corona*

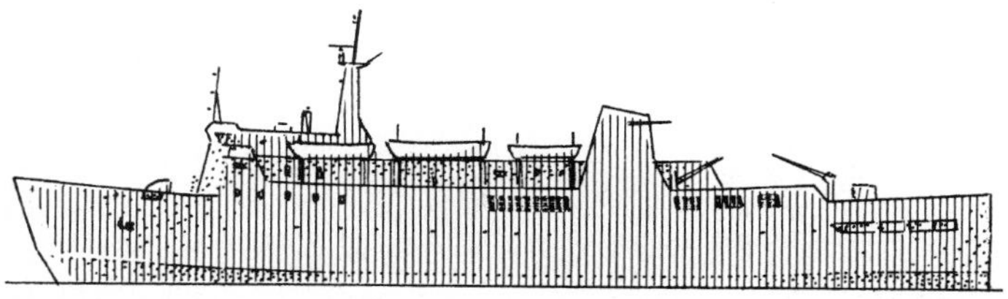

274 M^2GSS *H*
PIETRO NOVELLI It/It (Riuniti) 1979; RoPCF; 1,955 grt; 91 × 4 m *(298.56 × 13.12 ft)*; TSM (GMT); 18 kts; Bow and stern doors
Sisters: **PIERO DELLA FRANCESCA** (It); **MARMORICA** (It); Possible sister: **OGLASA** (It)

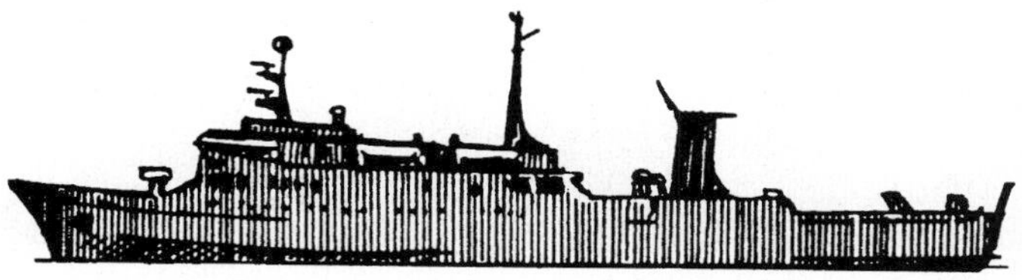

275 M^2GY *H*
LILLY R It/Fr (La Rochelle) 1974; RoPCF; 2,891 grt; 103.82 × 4.45 m *(340.6 × 14.6 ft)*; TSM (Pielstick); 18.25 kts; ex-*Penn Ar Bed*; Stern door/ramp; Now has additional superstructure aft—not shown on drawing

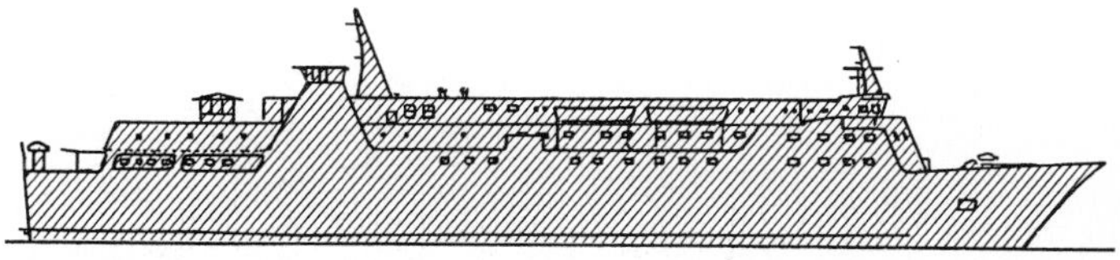

276 M^2GY *H*
PANORAMA Tr/FRG (M Jansen) 1987; RoPCF; 5,330 grt; 101.29 × 4 m *(332.32 × 13.12 ft)*; TSM (Wärtsilä); 18 kts; Bow door and ramp; Stern door/ramp; 32 TEU

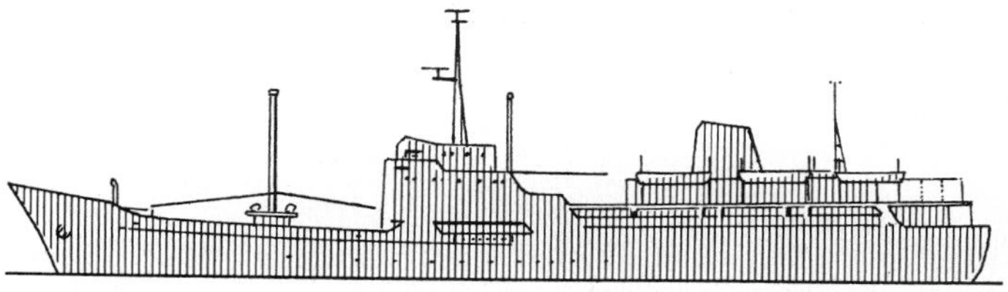

277 $\underline{M^3FM}$ *H12*
MAN GYONG BONG RK/RK (Chongjin) 1971; PC; 3,574 grt/1,727 dwt; 102 × 5 m *(334.65 × 16.4 ft)*; M (—); 13.5 kts

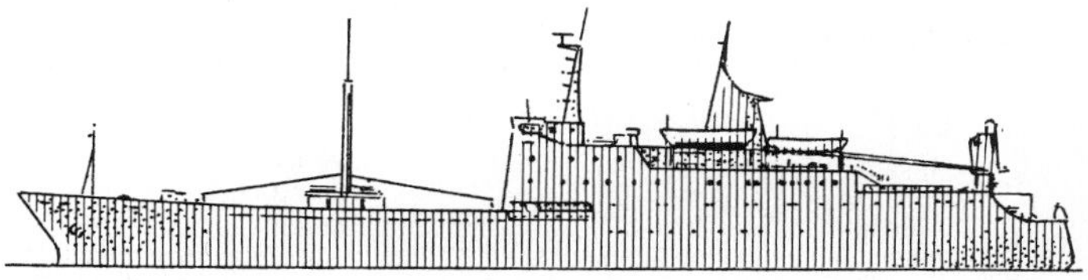

278 $\underline{M^3M\text{-}FC}$ *H2*
ACACIO MANE ELA Gn/Ja (Shikoku) 1973; PC; 3,342 grt/3,279 dwt; 100.51 × 5.68 m *(329.76 × 18.64 ft)*; M (B&W); 14 kts; ex-*Hai Ou*; Now converted to a general cargo ship so appearance may be altered

See photo number 20/408

279 $M^2M\text{-}F$ *H*
CORSICA REGINA Pa/Ys ('Jozo Lozovina-Mosor') 1972; RoPF; 12,988 grt; 146.55 × 5.02 m *(480.8 × 16.47 ft)*; TSM (Polar); 20 kts; ex-*Visby*; Lengthened by 22 m (72 ft) 1989; Extra superstructure deck between mainmast and funnel; Probably operates as a cruise ship
Similar (also lengthened): **CORSICA VICTORIA** (Pa) ex-*Gotland*

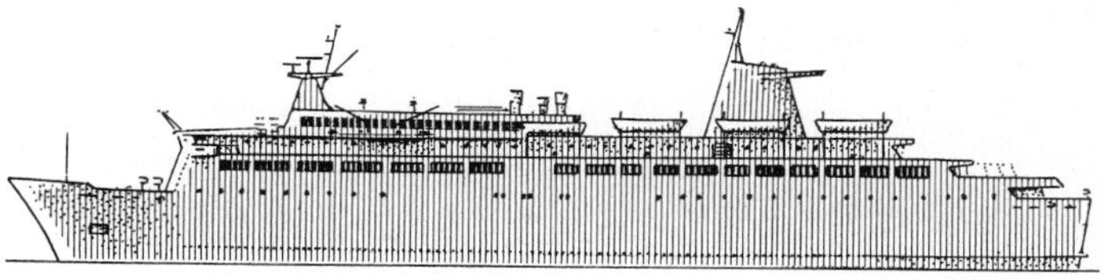

280 $M^2M\text{-}F$ *H*
DUC DE NORMANDIE Fr/Ne (Verolme SH) 1978; RoPCF; 9,677 grt; 131.02 × 5.17 m *(429.86 × 16.96 ft)*; TSM (Stork-Werkspoor); 21 kts; ex-*Prinses Beatrix*; Bow door and ramp; Stern door/ramp

See drawing number 20/40

281 $M^2M\text{-}F$ *H*
FREEWINDS Pa/Fi (Wärtsilä) 1968; P; 9,780 grt; 134.3 × 5.5 m *(440 × 18 ft)*; TSM (Sulzer); 20 kts; ex-*Boheme*

282 $M^2M\text{-}F$ *H*
WORLD DISCOVERER Li/FRG (Schichau-U) 1973; P; 3,724 grt; 71.4 × 4.2 m *(234 × 14 ft)*; M (Atlas-MaK); 16.5 kts; ex-*Bewa Discoverer*

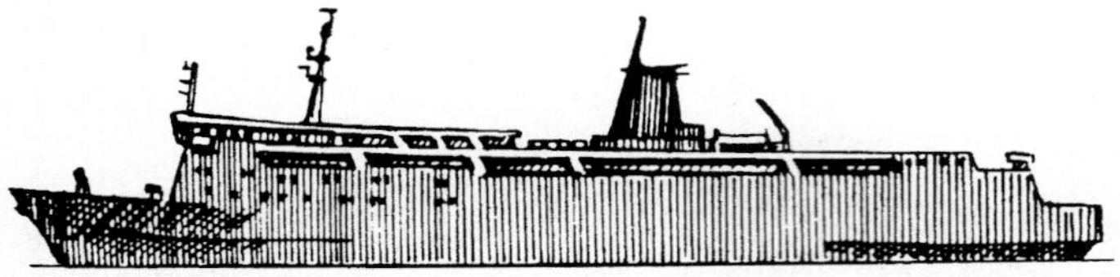

283 *M^2M-F H2*
EBINO Ja/Ja (Nipponkai) 1973; RoPF; 6,826 grt; 132 × 5.5 m *(434 × 18 ft)*; TSM (Pielstick); 19.5 kts; ex-*Al Nasl*
Similar (original sister with alterations. Lifeboats added on upper deck near bridge (Two each side). Some open decks now enclosed): **RODOS** (Gr) ex-*Argo*

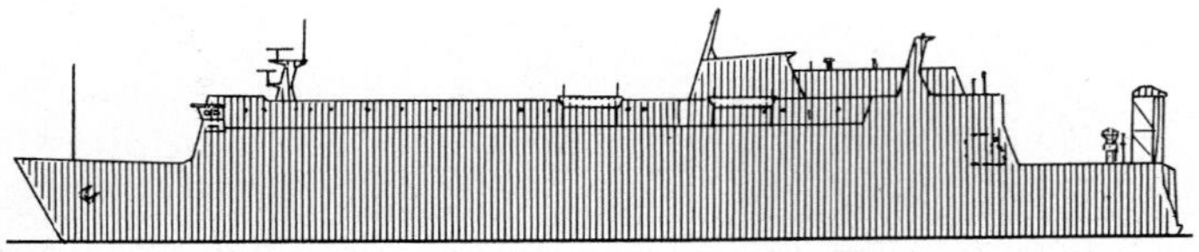

284 *M^2M-FGY H2*
MIKOLAJ KOPERNIK Pd/No (Trosvik) 1974; RoC/P/TF; 8,734 grt/2,350 dwt; 125.61 × 4.5 m *(412.11 × 14.76 ft)*; M (Sulzer); 18 kts; Stern door/ramp; Side doors

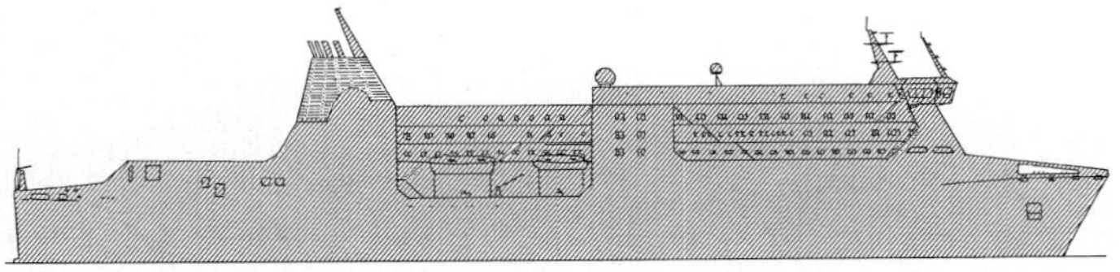

285 *M^2M-GY H12*
PAGLIA ORBA Fr/Fr (Havre) 1994; P/RoC; 29,718 grt/6,325 dwt; 165.8 × 6.63 m *(543.96 × 21.75 ft)*; TSM (Wärtsilä); 19 kts; Bow door and ramp; Two stern door/ramps (see photo number 20/395)

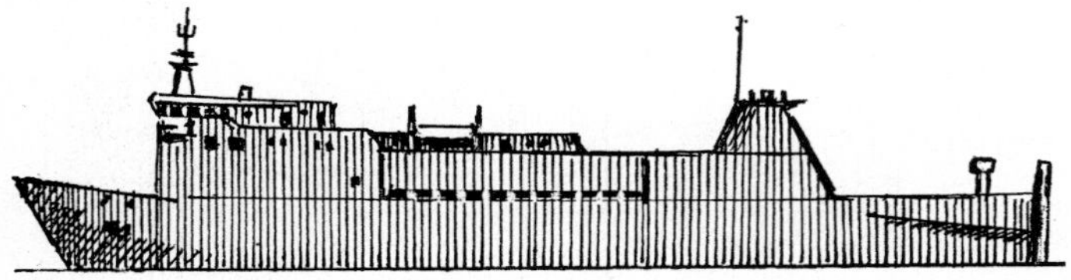

286 *M^2M-GZ H2*
SATURNUS Cy/No (Trondhjems) 1974; RoPCF; 8,739 grt; 129.88 × 4.92 m *(426.12 × 16.14 ft)*; TSM (Polar); 19 kts; ex-*Scandinavia*; Bow, side and stern doors; Lengthened 1976

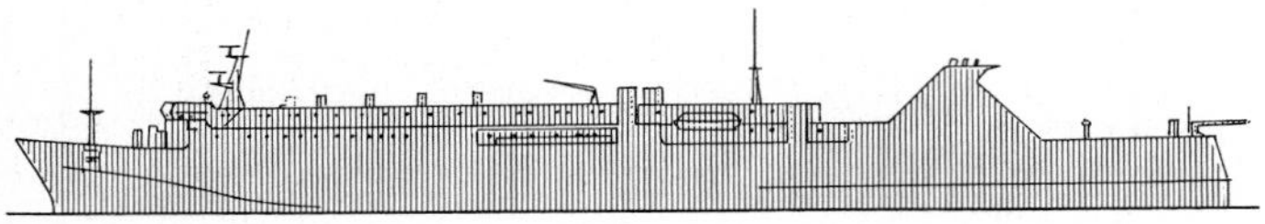

287 *M^2SMG H*
DAGISTAN Az/Ys ('Ulijanik') 1984; P/RoC/TF; 11,450 grt/3,950 dwt; 154.46 × 4.25 m *(506.76 × 13.94 ft)*; TSM (B&W); 17.25 kts; ex-*Sovietskiy Dagestan*; Stern ramp
Sisters: **MERCURI 2** (Cy) ex-*Sovietskiy Tadzhikistan*; **AZERBAIJAN** (Az) ex-*Sovietskaya Armeniya*; **MERCURI 1** (Cy) ex-*Sovietskaya Gruziya*; **AKADEMIK M TOPCHUBASHOV** (Az) ex-*Sovietskaya Kalmykiya*; **AKADEMIK HESEN ALIYEV** (Az) ex-*Sovietskaya Kirgiziya*; **PROFESSOR GUL** (Az) ex-*Sovietskaya Byelorussiya*; **NAKHCHYVAN** (Az) ex-*Sovietskiy Nakhichevan*

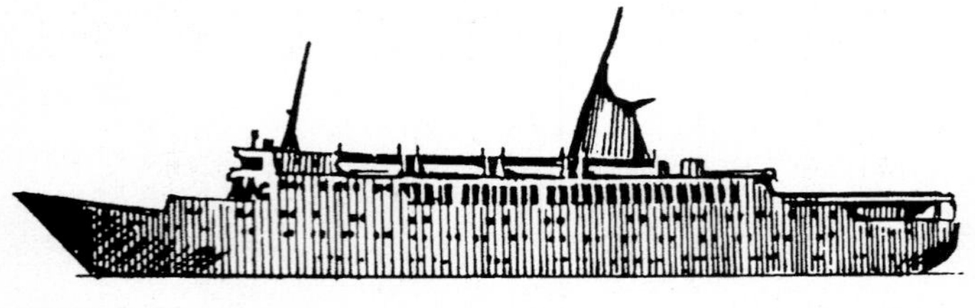

288 *MM-F H*
ADRIANA Cro/Gr (United SY) 1972; P; 4,490 grt; 103.7 × 4.7 m *(340 × 15.4 ft)*; TSM (Pielstick); 16.5 kts; ex-*Aquarius*

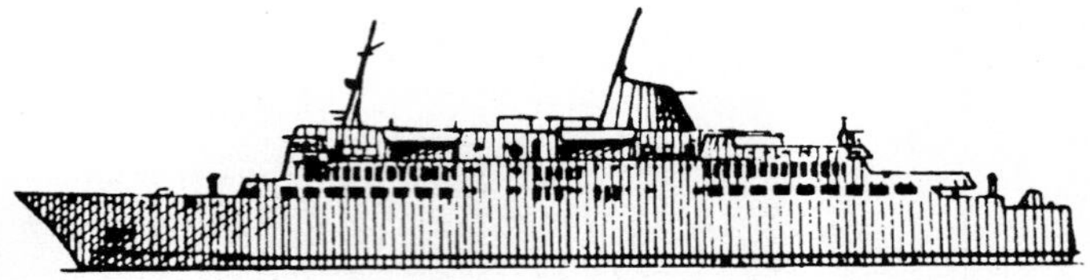

289 *MM-F H*
AL JUDI Si/FRG (Unterweser) 1968; RoPCF; 9,625 grt; 115 × 4.8 m *(377 × 15.74 ft)*; TSM (MAN); 18.5 kts; ex-*Gedser*

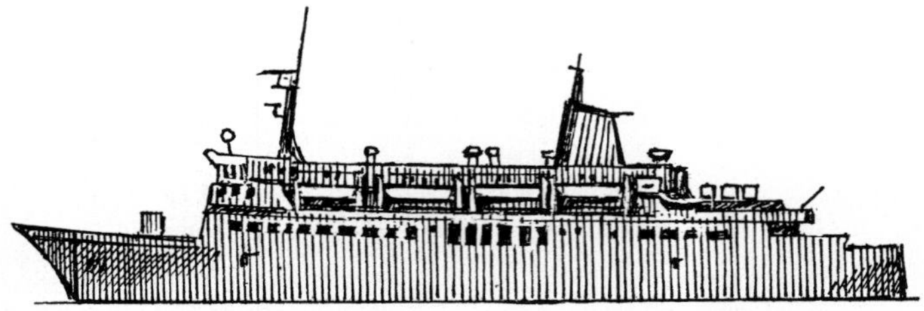

290 *MM-F H*
ALANDSFARJAN Sw/De (Helsingor) 1972; RoPCF; 6,172 grt; 104.04 × 4.37 m *(341.34 × 14.38 ft)*; TSM (B&W); 17.5 kts; ex-*Kattegat*; Bow and stern doors
Sister: **ST SUNNIVA** (Br) ex-*Djursland*

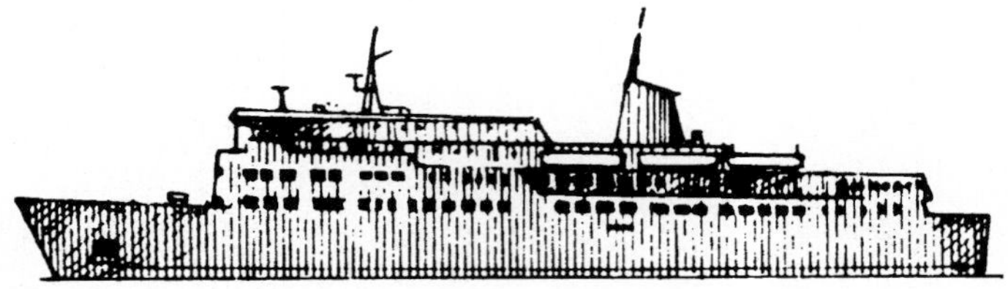

291 *MM-F H*
ALCAEOS Gr/Ys ('Titovo') 1970; RoPCF; 3,491 grt; 99.2 × 4.8 m *(325 × 16 ft)*; TSM (Sulzer); 19.75 kts; ex-*Marella*; Bow and stern doors

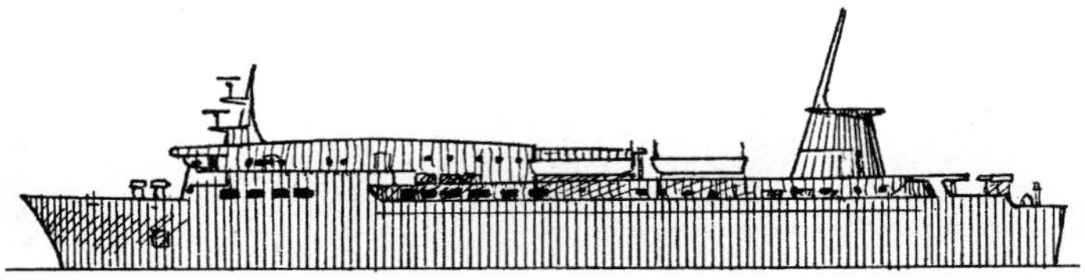

292 *MM-F H*
BHARAT SEEMA In/No (Moss V) 1973; RoPCF; 2,997 grt; 86.54 × 4.92 m *(283.92 × 16.14 ft)*; TSM (Alpha); 15 kts; ex-*Basto V*; Side door; Bow door and ramp; Stern door/ramp
Sister (converted to Ro-Ro cargo—may have alterations in appearance): **SUILVEN** (NZ)

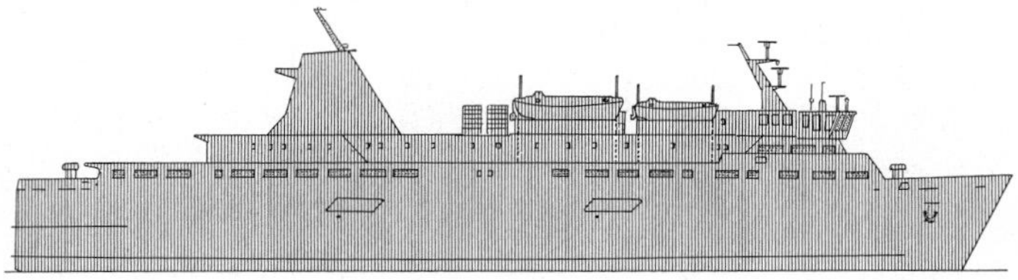

293 *MM-F H*
CALEDONIAN ISLES Br/Br (Richards) 1993; RoC/F; 5,221 grt/767 dwt; 94.25 × 3.17 m *(309.22 × 10.4 ft)*; TSM (Mirrlees); 15 kts; Bow, stern and side door

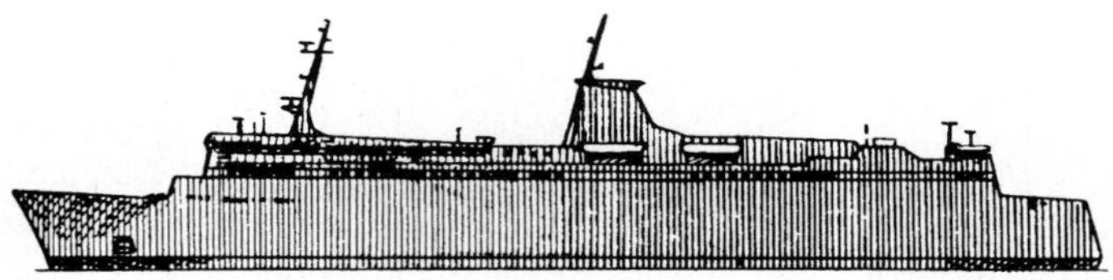

294 *MM-F H*
DEUTSCHLAND Ge/FRG (Nobiskrug) 1972; RoPCF; 11,110 grt; 144.1 × 5.9 m *(473 × 19.3 ft)*; TS D-E (MTU); 19.5 kts; Bow and stern doors

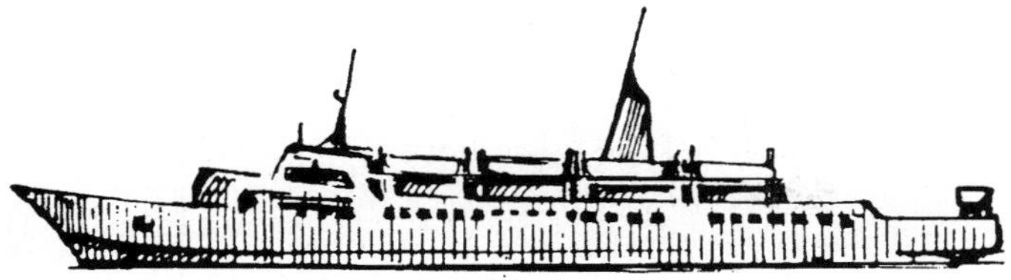

295 *MM-F H*
EL SALAM 93 Pa/It (Apuania) 1966; RoPF; 3,389 grt; 100 × 4.3 m *(328 × 14.3 ft)*; TSM (Fiat); 18 kts; ex-*Jacopo Tintoretto*

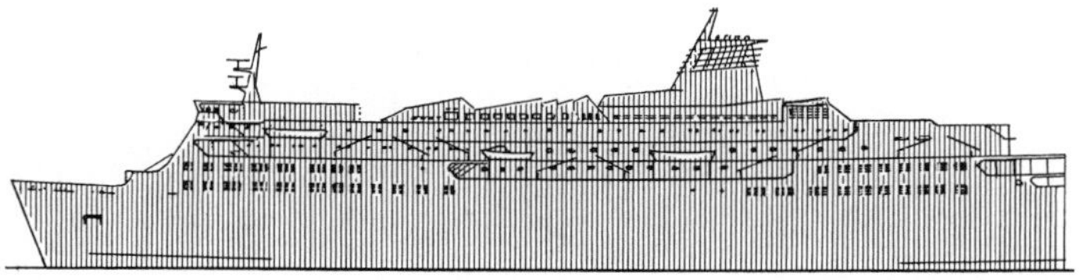

296 *MM-F H*
ESTEREL Fr/Fr (Dubigeon-Normandie) 1981; RoPCF; 12,676 grt; 145.01 × 6.34 m *(475.75 × 20.8 ft)*; TSM (Pielstick); 22.5 kts; Bow door and ramp; Two stern door/ramps
Sister: **CORSE** (Fr)

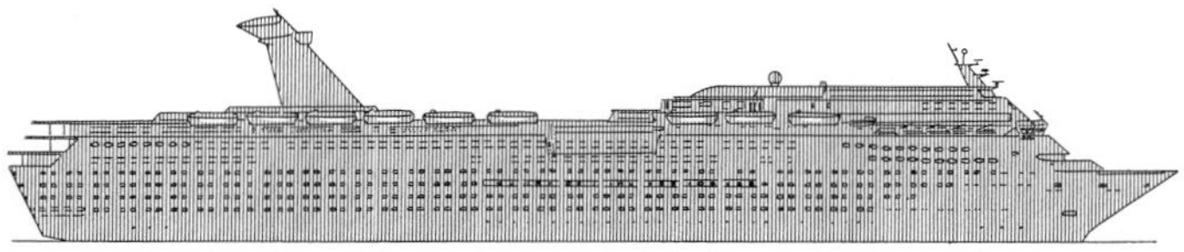

297 *MM-F H*
FANTASY Li/Fi (Masa) 1990; P; 70,367 grt; 260.6 × 7.85 m *(854.99 × 25.75 ft)*; TSD-E (Sulzer); 18 kts
Sisters: **ECSTASY** (Li); **SENSATION** (Pa); **INSPIRATION** (Pa); **IMAGINATION** (Pa)

298 *MM-F H*
IONIAN SUN Gr/Ih (Verolme Cork) 1969; RoPCF; 7,311 grt; 118.3 × 4.5 m *(388 × 14.7 ft)*; TSM (MAN); 18 kts; ex-*Leinster*; Bow and stern doors
Sister (FRG built—Nobiskrug): **SPIRIT OF INDEPENDENCE** (Fr) ex-*Innisfallen*

299 *MM-F H*
IVAN ZAJC Cro/It (Apuania) 1970; RoPCF; 3,511 grt; 101.2 × 4.3 m *(332 × 14 ft)*; TSM (Fiat); 18 kts; ex-*Tiziano*; Bow door

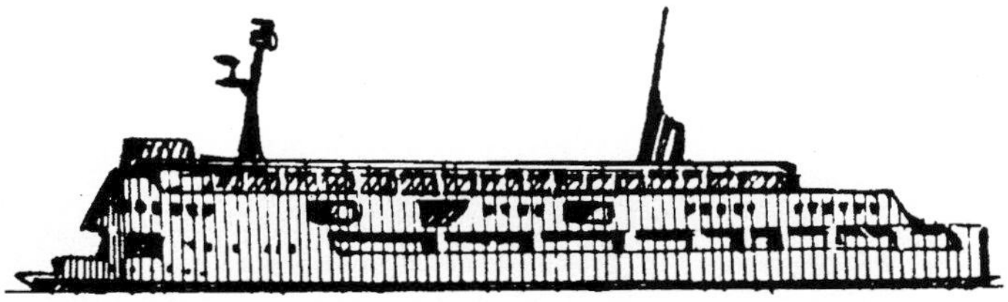

300 *MM-F H*
IYO Pa/Ja (Hitachi) 1966; RoPCF; 3,073 grt; 89.4 × 3.7 m *(276 × 12.2 ft)*; TSM (B&W); 15.25 kts; ex-*Iyo Maru*
Sister (converted to ferry): **SOUNDS OF SETO** (Ja) ex-*Tosa Maru*

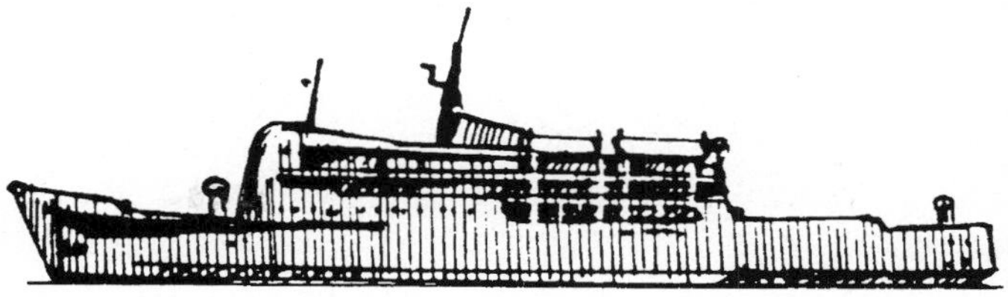

301 *MM-F H*
KARDEN Tu/Au (Evans Deakin) 1961; RoPCF; 3,614 grt; 91.4 × 3.7 m *(300 × 12.1 ft)*; TSM (British Polar); 14.5 kts; ex-*Troubridge*; Boat deck is now extended aft—not on drawing

302 *MM-F H*
LAURO EXPRESS It/Br (Hawthorn, L) 1967; RoPCF; 6,037 grt; 112.6 × 3.7 m *(369 × 12.3 ft)*; TSM (Pielstick); 19.5 kts; ex-*Antrim Princess*; Bow door/ramp; Stern door/ramp
Similar: **NAIAS EXPRESS** (Gr) ex-*Ailsa Princess*

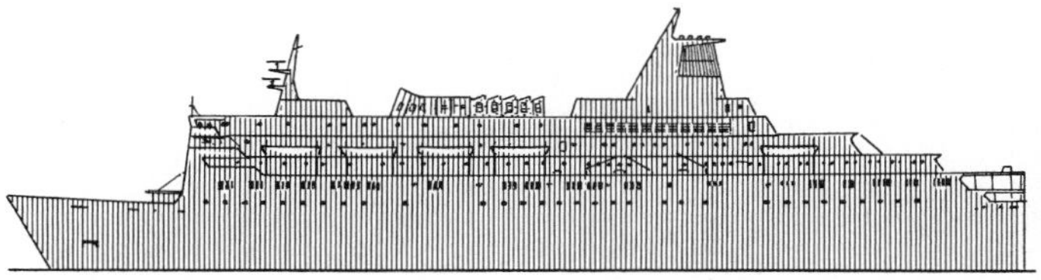

303 *MM-F H*
LIBERTE Fr/Fr (Dubigeon-Normandie) 1980; RoPCF; 18,913 grt; 141.48 × 5.5 m *(464.17 × 18.04 ft)*; TSM (Pielstick); 21.5 kts; Bow door and ramp; Stern door/ramp; Lengthened to 164 m (538 ft) 1991—drawing shows vessel as built

304 *MM-F H*
LIBURNIJA Cro/Ne ('De Merwede') 1965; RoPCF; 3,038 grt; 89.2 × 4.2 m *(292 × 14 ft)*; TSM (Sulzer); 15 kts; Bow and stern doors

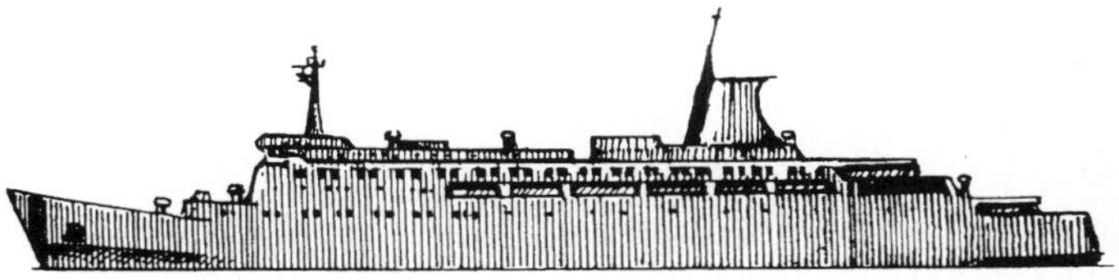

305 *MM-F H*
MIMITSU MARU Ja/Ja (Naikai) 1974; RoPCF; 9,551 grt; 160 × 6.2 m *(525 × 20.34 ft)*; TSM (MAN); 25.5 kts
Similar: **TAKACHIHO MARU** (Ja)

306 *MM-F H*
MISTRAL II Gr/It (Pellegrino) 1971; RoPCF; 3,357 grt; 89.5 × 4.3 m *(297 × 14 ft)*; TSM (Ansaldo); 16 kts; ex-*La Valletta*; Bow and stern doors

307 *MM-F H*
NISSOS CHIOS Gr/Ys ('Titovo') 1967; RoPCF; 3,118 grt; 97.5 × 4.8 m *(320 × 15.9 ft)*; TSM (Sulzer); 18 kts; ex-*Kapella*; Bow and stern doors

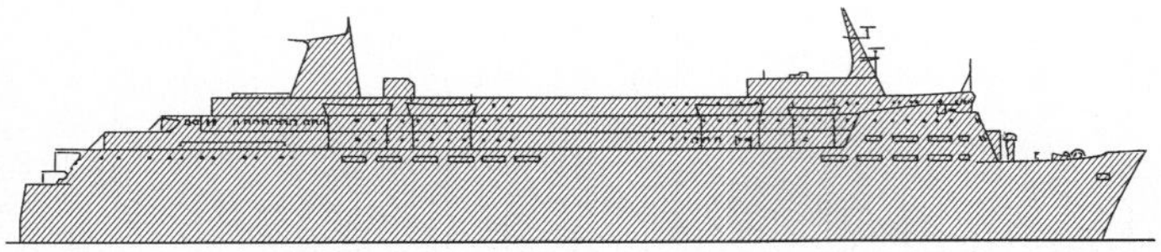

308 *MM-F H*
NORLAND Br/FRG (A G 'Weser') 1974/87; RoPCF; 26,290 grt; 173.29 × 6.02 m *(568.5 × 19.75 ft)*; TSM (Stork-Werkspoor); 19 kts; Two stern door/ramps; Side door; Lengthened 1987 (Seebeck)
Sister: **NORSTAR** (Ne)

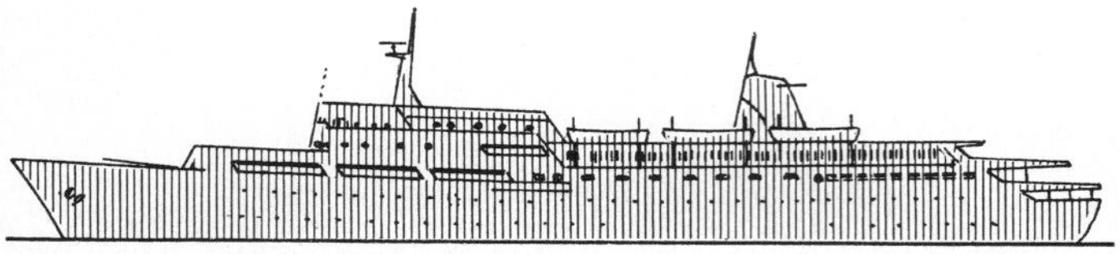

309 *MM-F H*
OSETIYA Uk/Ru (Zhdanov) 1963; P; 3,200 grt; 101.5 × 3.85 m *(333 × 12.63 ft)*; TSM (Skoda); 14.5 kts

310 *MM-F H*
RANEEM I Si/De (Aarhus) 1960; RoPCF; 3,526 grt; 88.5 × 4.6 m *(290 × 15 ft)*; TSM (Polar); 16.5 kts; ex-*Prins Bertil*; Bow door and ramp; Stern door/ramp

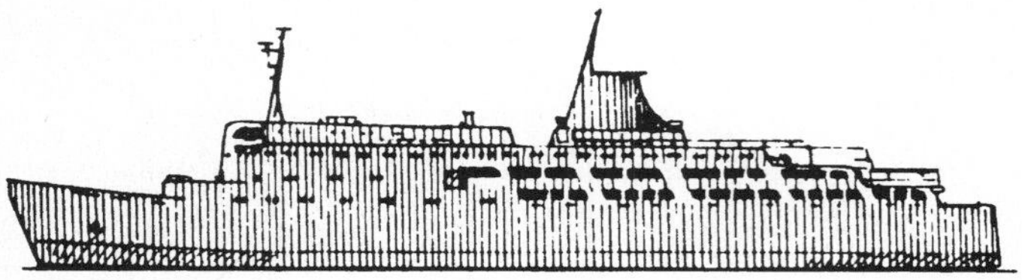

311 *MM-F H*
SAINT PAULIA Pi/Ja (NKK) 1971; RoPCF; 5,909 grt; 118 × 5.7 m *(387 × 19 ft)*; TSM (Pielstick); 19 kts
Sister: **ZERALDA** (Ag) ex-*Bougainvillea*. Similar: **HOGGAR** (Ag) ex-*Hibiscus*; **TIPAZA** (Ag) ex-*Phenix*; **ABOITIZ SUPERFERRY III** (Pi) ex-*Hamayu*

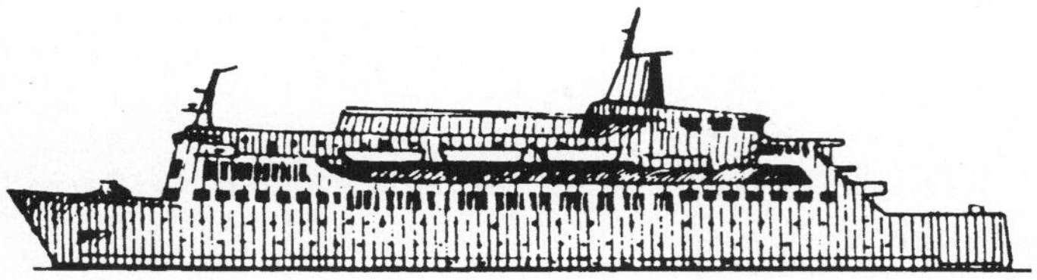

312 *MM-F H*
SARDEGNA BELLA It/Sw (Langesunds) 1967; RoPCF; 6,942 grt; 110.95 × 5.02 m *(364 × 16.47 ft)*; TSM (MAN); 17 kts; ex-*Stena Britannica*; Bow door/ramp; Two side door/ramps; Stern door/ramp

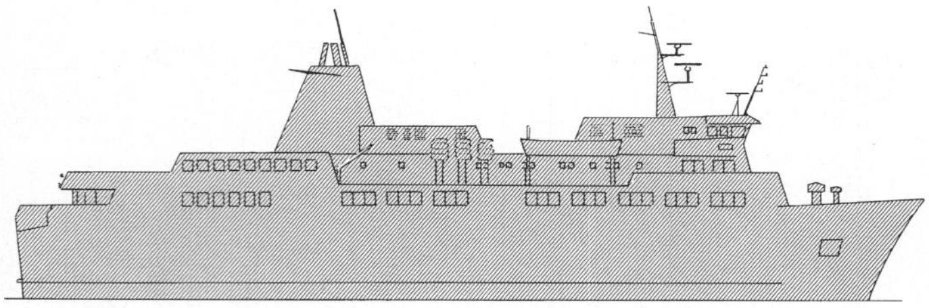

313 *MM-F H*
SOLIDOR 2 SV/Ne ('Combiship') 1977; RoPCF; 3,401 grt; 70.01 × 3.81 m *(229.69 × 12.5 ft)*; TSM (Atlas-MaK); 15.5 kts; ex-*Langeland To*; Bow door/ramp; Stern door/ramp

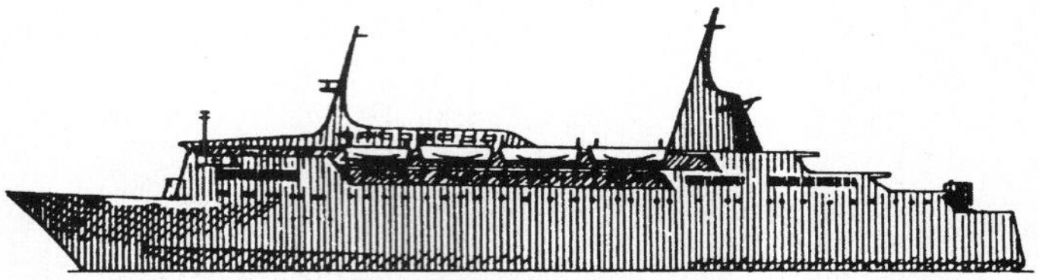

314 *MM-F H*
TROPIC STAR II Bs/Gr (Kynossura) 1974; RoPCF; 5,529 grt; 132 × 5.3 m *(433 × 17.6 ft)*; TSM (MaK); 17 kts; ex-*Castalia*

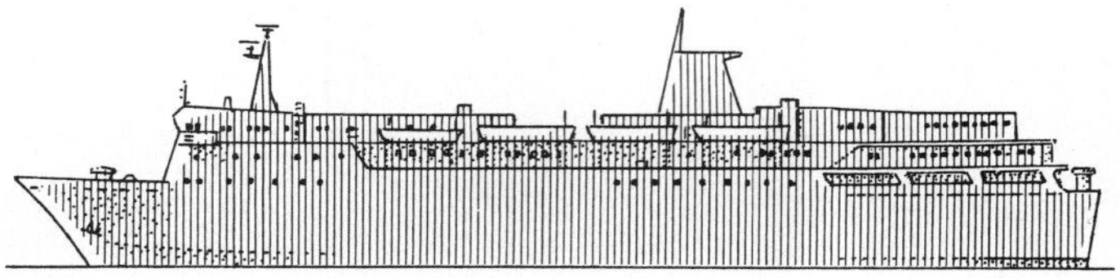

315 *MM-F H*
VITTORE CARPACCIO It/No (Bergens) 1980; RoPCF; 4,706 grt; 105 × 4.13 m *(344.5 × 13.55 ft)*; TSM (Normo); 18 kts; ex-*El Arish*; Stern door/ramp
Sister: **EL ARISH-EL TOR** (Eg) ex-*El Tor*

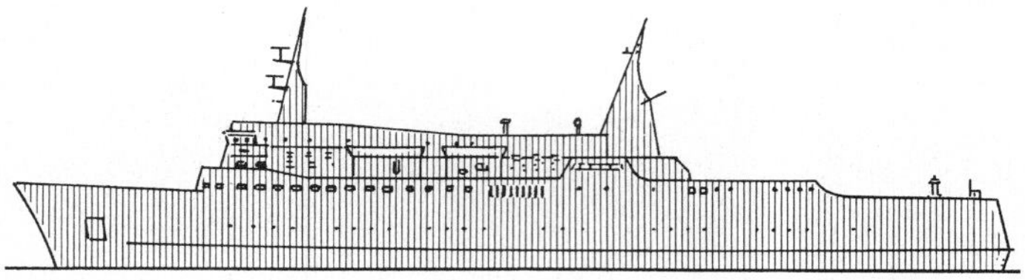

316 *MM-F H*
WILANOW Pd/FRG (Nobiskrug) 1966; RoPCF; 6,474 grt; 110.17 × 4.9 m *(361.45 × 16.08 ft)*; TSM (MAN); 20 kts; ex-*Kronprins Carl Gustav*; Bow and stern doors

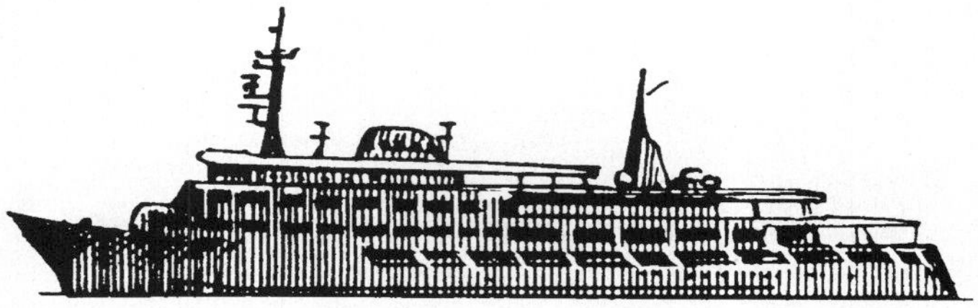

317 *MM-F H1*
VERGINA TREASURE Pa/Ja (Mitsubishi HI) 1967; F; 3,200 grt; 89.3 × 3.9 m *(293 × 13 ft)*; TSM (Mitsubishi); 19.5 kts; ex-*Cobalt Maru*

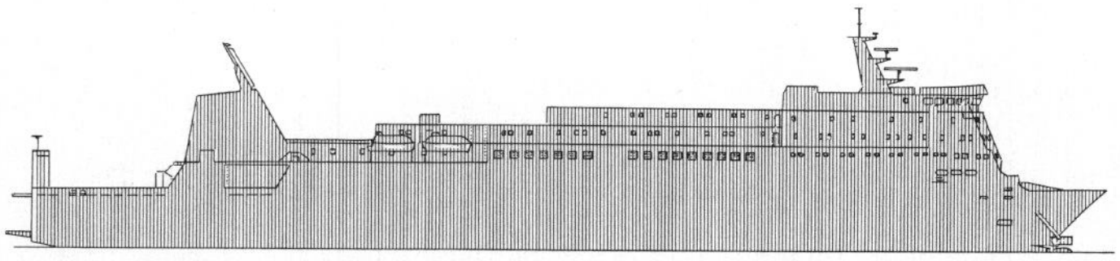

318 *MM-FH H2*
STENA CHALLENGER Br/No (Bruces) 1991; RoC/F; 18,523 grt/4,650 dwt; 157.28 × 5.52 m *(516.01 × 18.11 ft)*; TSM (Sulzer); 17.5 kts; Bow door/ramp; Stern door
Probable sisters: **KAPTAN ABIDIN DORAN** (Tu); **KAPTAN BURHANETTIN ISIM** (Tu)

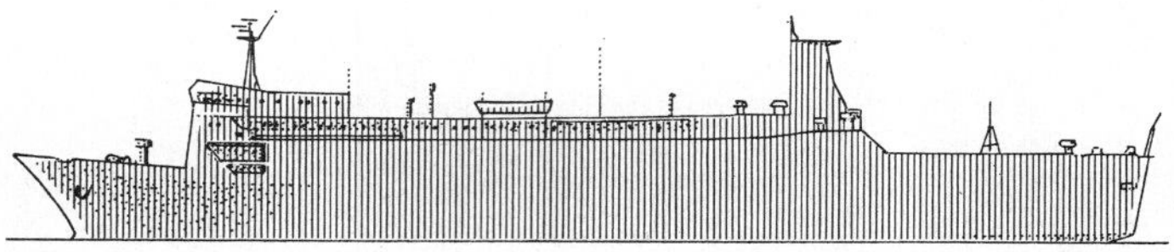

319 *MM-FR H2*
SALLY EUROWAY Cy/FRG (Kroegerw) 1976; RoPF; 9,079 grt; 127 × 5.4/6.6 m *(417 × 17.7/21.6 ft)*; TSM (KHD); 19.5 kts; ex-*Argo*; Bow door/ramp and stern door/ramp

See photo number 20/448

320 *MM-FS H*
THE AZUR Pa/Fr (Dubigeon Normandie) 1971; RoPCF; 9,159 grt; 142.1 × 5.45 m *(466 × 17.88 ft)*; TSM (Pielstick); 23 kts; ex-*Eagle*; Stern door
Similar: **CRUCERO EXPRESS** (Bs) ex-*Bolero* (Top superstructure deck now extended towards funnels and side ramps fitted foreward and aft); **REGAL VOYAGER** (Bs) ex-*Massalia* (Rebuilt after fire—appearance may be considerably altered)

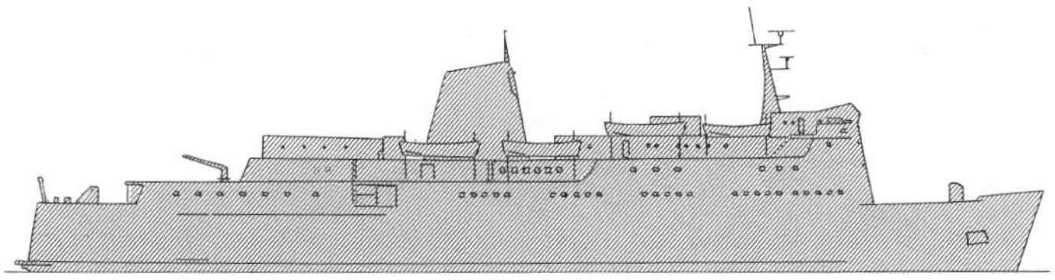

321 *MM-FS H*
KING ORRY Br/It (Pietra Ligure) 1972; RoPCF; 7,555 grt; 114.6 × 4.1 m *(376 × 13.4 ft)*; TSM (Pielstick); 21.8 kts; ex-*Saint Eloi*; Stern door/ramp

322 *MM-FS H*
TIAN PENG RC/FRG (Nobiskrug) 1968; RoPCF; 4,007 grt; 110.2 × 4.5 m *(362 × 14.7 ft)*; TSM (MAN); 17 kts; ex-*Munster*

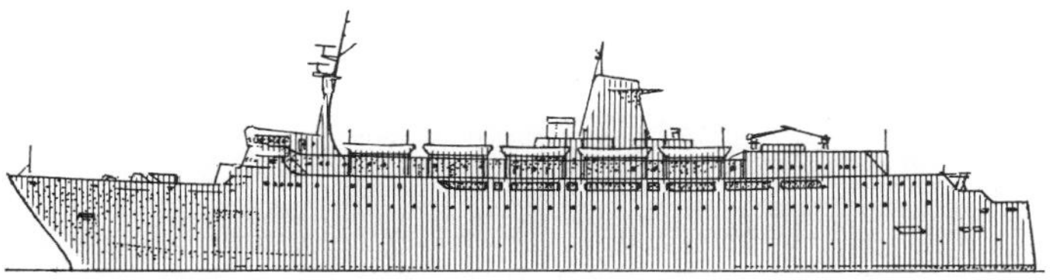

323 *MM-FS² H*
ZHONG YUAN RC/It (Italcantieri) 1978; RoPCF; 7,222 grt; 131.02 × 5.62 m *(429.86 × 18.44 ft)*; TSM (GMT); 23 kts; ex-*Deledda*; Side door/ramp; Stern door/ramp
Sisters (some or all, may have been heightened—see photograph of *Pascoli)*: **VERGA** (It); **BOCCACCIO** (It); **CARDUCCI** (It); **SANTA CATHERINE** (Pa) ex-*Leopardi*; **MANZONI** (It); **PASCOLI** (It) (see photo number 20/398); **PETRARCA** (It)

324 *MM-G H*
AGIOS VASSILOS Gr/FRG (Hanseatische) 1962; RoPCF; 4,275 grt; 96 × 4.7 m *(315 × 15.4 ft)*; TSM (Nohab); 16 kts; ex-*Hansa Express*; Bow door and ramp; Stern door/ramp
Similar (shorter, fewer lifeboats): **JIMY** (Pa) ex-*Prinsessan Desiree*

See photo number 20/446

325 *MM-G H*
BISMILLAH Mo/Mo (Ulstein) 1971/74; P/RoC; 5,213 grt/— dwt; 106.43 × 6.25 m *(349.18 × 20.51 ft)*; TSM (Stork-Werkspoor); 19 kts; ex-*Buenavista*; Side door; Stern door/ramp; Bow door and ramp; Lengthened 1974
Sister: **BAJAMAR** (Sp) ex-*Bonanza* (not lengthened)

326 *MM-G H*
CANDIA Gr/Ja (Sumitomo) 1971; RoPCF; 7,291 grt; 130 × 5.5 m *(427 × 18 ft)*; TSM (MAN); 19.5 kts; ex-*Central No 2*; Bow door and ramp; Stern door/ramp; Superstructure now extended aft—not shown on drawing
Possible sister: **RETHIMNON** (Gr) ex-*Central No 5*

327 *MM-G H*
CONCEPCION MARINO Ve/No (Trondhjems) 1978; RoPF; 2,635 grt; 105.01 × 4.01 m *(344.52 × 13.16 ft)*; TSM (KHD); 17 kts; Bow door and ramp; Stern door/ramp
Sister: **CACICA ISABEL** (Ve)

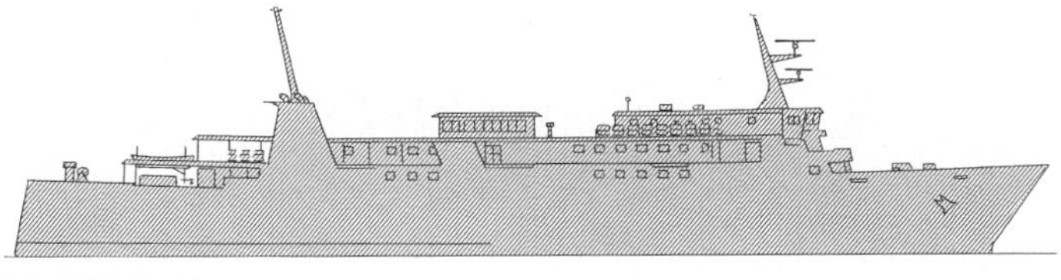

328 *MM-G H*
FERRY CHIKUSHI Ja/Ja (Naikai) 1994; RoC/F; 1,926 grt/747 dwt; 97.37 × 4.17 m *(319.46 × 13.68 ft)*; TSM (Daihatsu); 20 kts; Bow door/ramp

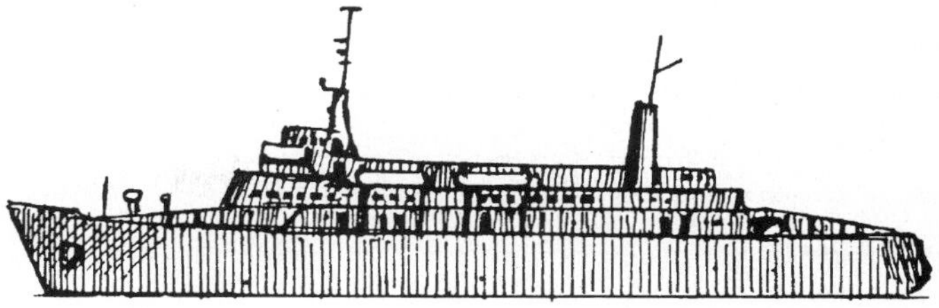

329 *MM-G H*
GRECIA EXPRESS Gr/FRG (A G 'Weser') 1965; RoPF; 4,112 grt; 108.8 × 5 m *(357 × 16.4 ft)*; TSM (Smit and Bolnes); 15 kts; ex-*Norwind*; Bow and stern doors

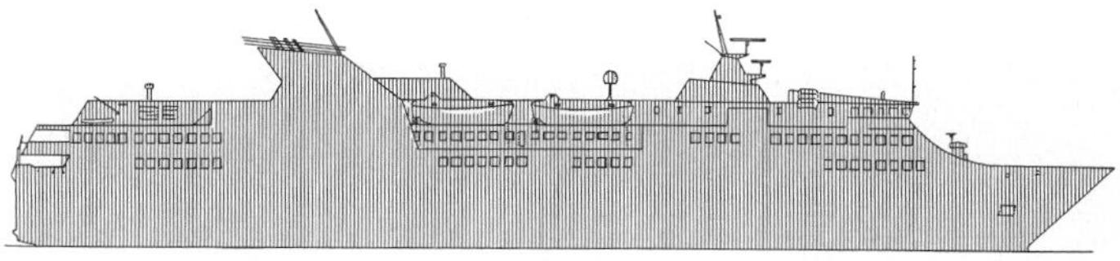

330 *MM-G H*
IBN BATTOUTA 2 Mo/Sp (Barreras) 1993; RoC/F; 9,481 grt/2,152 dwt; 116 × 5.15 m *(380.58 × 16.9 ft)*; TSM (MAN); 17.5 kts; Bow door/ramp; Stern door/ramp

331 *MM-G H*
ILIRIJA Cro/FRG (Meyer) 1963; RoPCF; 2,196 grt; 80.5 × 4.1 m *(264 × 13.4 ft)*; TSM (KHD); 15 kts; ex-*Bornholmerpilen*; Bow door and ramp; Stern door/ramp

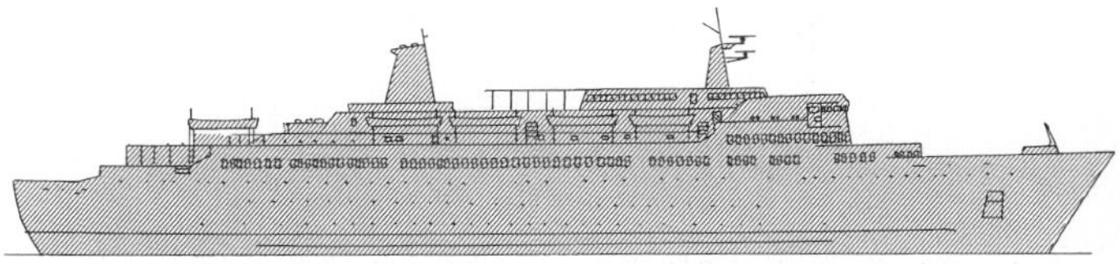

332 *MM-G H*
KAMIROS Gr/Fi (Wärtsilä) 1966; RoPCF; 7,466 grt; 134.32 × 5.72 m *(440.7 × 18.77 ft)*; TSM (Sulzer); 20 kts; ex-*Prins Hamlet*
Similar (superstructure extended aft and topmost deck also extended): **PRINCESA MARISSA** (Cy) ex-*Finnhansa*

333 *MM-G H*
MILENA Gr/Ja (Hayashikane) 1970; RoPF; 5,961 grt; 117.5 × 4.4 m *(385 × 14.4 ft)*; TSM (Wärtsilä); 18 kts; ex-*Ferry Gold*; Bow door/ramp; Stern door/ramp
Sister: **DALIANA** (Gr) ex-*Ferry Pearl*

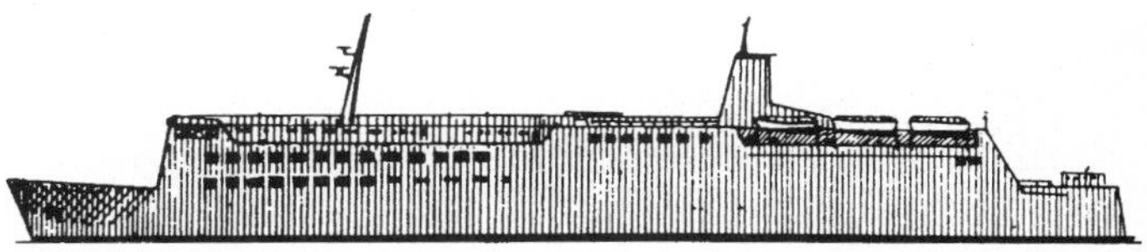

334 *MM-G H*
RUGEN Ge/DDR ('Neptun') 1972; RoPF; 12,289 grt; 152 × 5.6 m *(500 × 18.3 ft)*; TSM (MAN); 18 kts; Stern and side doors

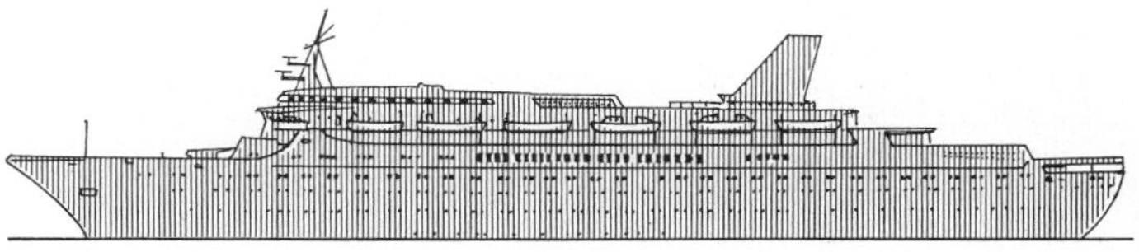

335 *MM-G H*
TRITON Gr/Ne (Rotterdamsche) 1971; P; 14,110 grt; 148.1 × 5.9 m *(486 × 19.3 ft)*; TSM (Stork-Werkspoor); 21.5 kts; ex-*Cunard Adventurer*

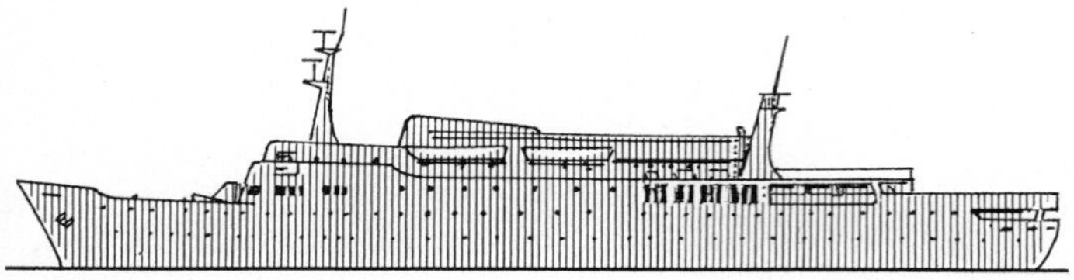

336 *MM-G H*
XING HU RC/Sp (AESA) 1967; PC; 4,338 grt; 104.9 × 4.3 m *(344 × 14.1 ft)*; TSM (B&W); 19.5 kts; ex-*Cabo Izarra*

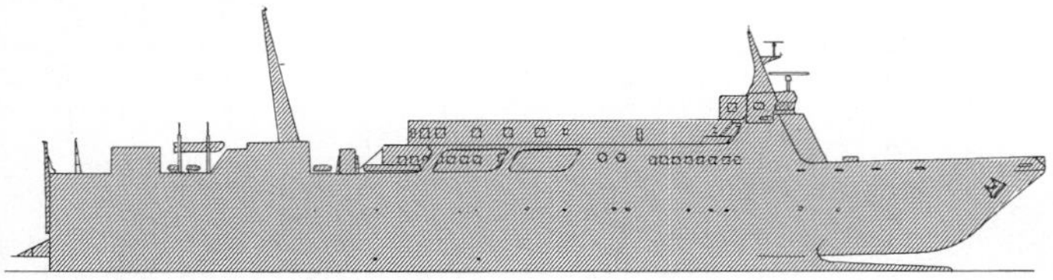

337 *MM-G H1*
HAYABUSA Ja/Ja (Kawasaki) 1994; RoC/F; 2,282 grt; 99.78 × 3.12 m *(327.36 × 10.24 ft)*; QSM (Caterpillar); 30 kts; Two bow door/ramps; Two stern door/ramps; Twin hulls

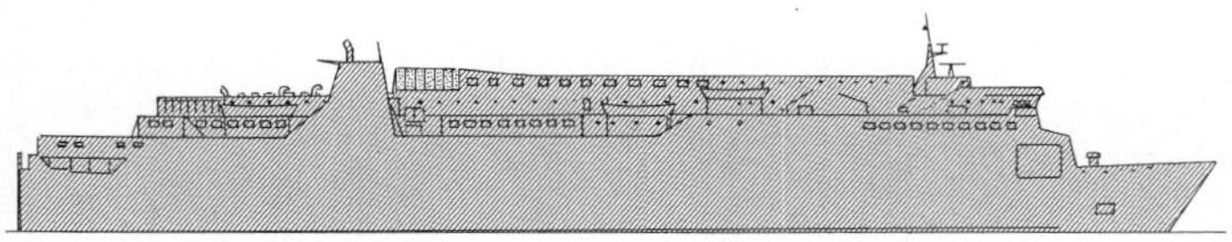

338 *MM-G H2*
SALLY SKY Bs/FRG (Schichau-U) 1976; RoPCF; 14,558 grt; 143.84 × 5.82 m *(471.9 × 19.09 ft)*; TSM (Stork-Werkspoor); 18.5 kts; ex-*Gedser*; Bow and side doors; Stern door/ramp; Lengthened 1990

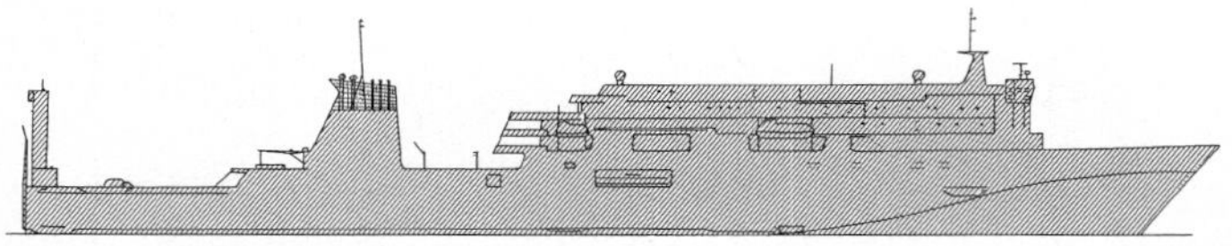

339 *MM-GHY H12*
PETERSBURG Ge/DDR (Mathias-Thesen) 1986/95; P/RoC/TF; 25,353 grt/ 12,019 dwt; 190.8 × 7.31 m *(625.98 × 23.98 ft)*; TSM (SKL); 16 kts; ex-*Mukran*; Converted from Ro-Ro cargo/train ferry 1995
Possible sister: **GREIFSWALD** (Ge)

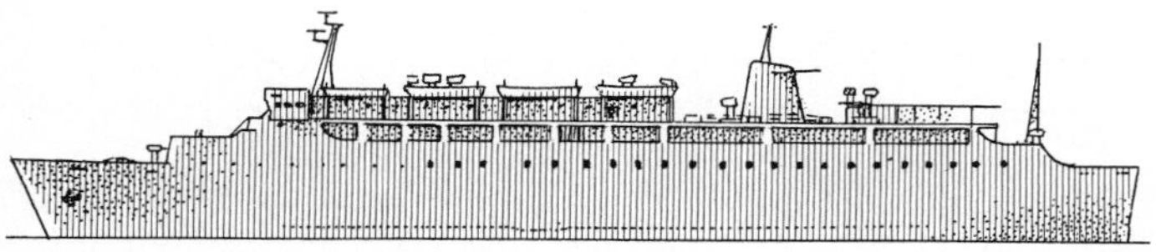

340 *MM-GM H*
EL DJAZAIR Ag/Ja (Kanasashi) 1972; RoPCF; 12,200 grt; 130.38 × 5.62 m *(427.76 × 18.44 ft)*; TSM (MAN); 19.5 kts; ex-*Central No 3*; Bow door; Side door; Stern door/ramp; Has extra superstructure aft and other alterations not shown on drawing; Mast aft is on starboard side

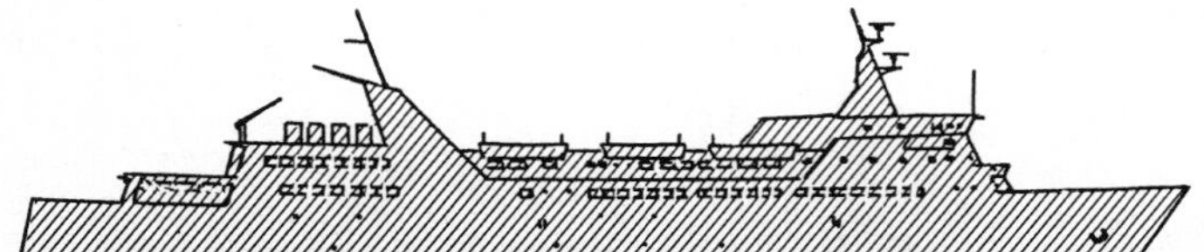

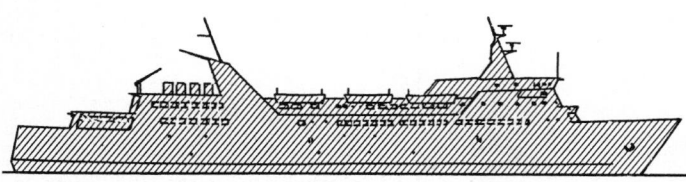

341 *MM-GS H*
BAHIA DE MALAGA Sp/Sp (Santander) 1980; RoC/F; 3,717 grt; 99.52 × 4.51 m *(326.51 × 14.8 ft)*; TSM (Deutz); 19.25 kts; Bow door/ramp; Stern door/ramp
Sisters: **BAHIA DE CEUTA** (Sp); **CIUDAD DE ALGECIRAS** (Sp) ex-*Bahia de Cadiz*; **PUNTA EUROPA** (Sp)

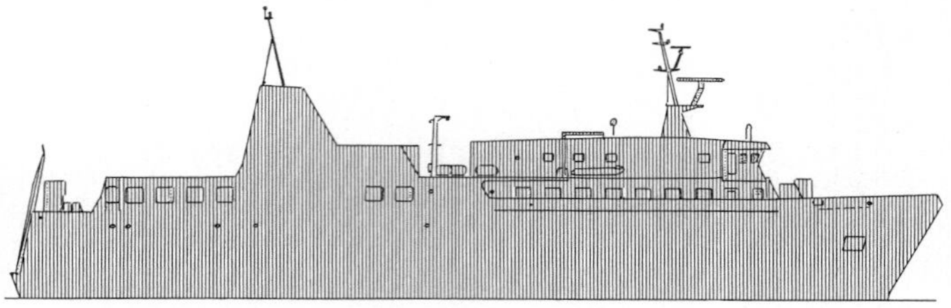

342 *MM-GY H*
GRAND MANAN V Ca/Ne ('Volharding') 1990; RoC/F; 3,833 grt; 75 × 3.6 m *(246.06 × 11.81 ft)*; TSM (Kromhout); 14.5 kts; Bow door and ramp; Stern door/ramp

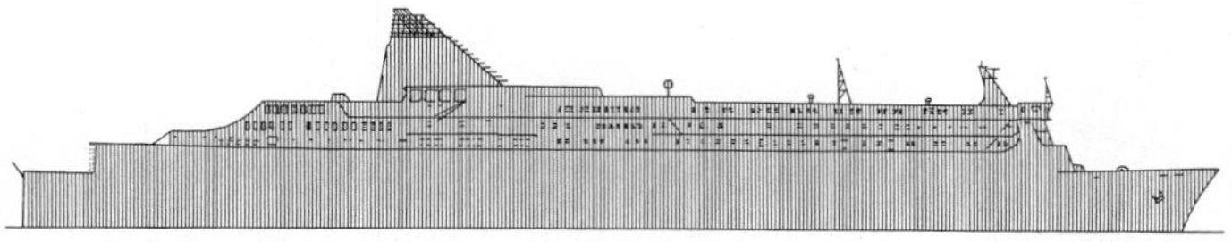

343 *MNF H*
FERRY LAVENDER Ja/Ja (IHI) 1991; RoPCF; 19,904 grt; 192.91 × 6.78 m *(632.91 × 22.24 ft)*; TSM (Pielstick); 21.8 kts; Bow door and ramp; Stern door/ramp
Sister: **NEW ACACIA** (Ja) (may be spelt **NEW AKASHIA**)

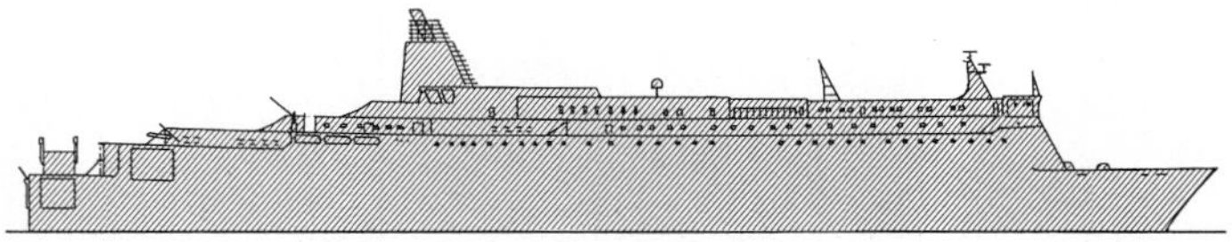

344 *MNFA H2*
NEW SHIRAYURI Ja/Ja (IHI) 1987; RoC/P; 17,305 grt/6,965 dwt; 184.51 × 6.75 m *(605.35 × 22.15 ft)*; TSM (Pielstick); 22.6 kts; Quarter stern door/ramp; Stern door/ramp
Sister: **NEW HAMANASU** (Ja)

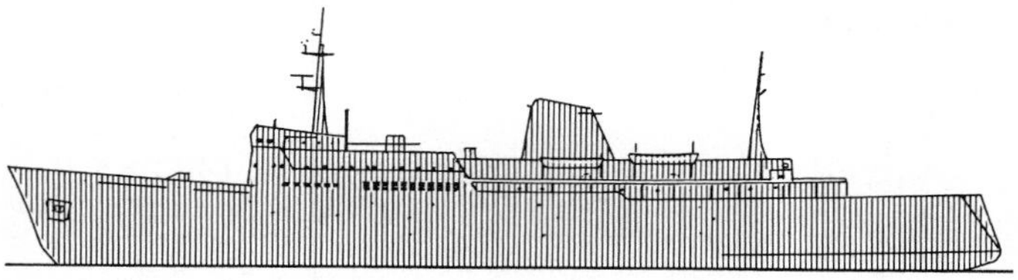

345 *MNFM H*
SAKHALIN-1 Ru/Ru ('Yantar') 1963; RoPF/TF; 9,305 grt; 127 × 6.2 m *(417 × 20.3 ft)*; D-E (Russkiy); 18 kts; Stern door
Sisters: **SAKHALIN-2** (Ru); **SAKHALIN-3** (Ru); **SAKHALIN-4** (Ru); **SAKHALIN-5** (Ru); **SAKHALIN-6** (Ru); **SAKHALIN-7** (Ru); Similar: **SAKHALIN-8** (Ru); **SAKHALIN-9** (Ru); **SAKHALIN-10** (Ru)

346 *MNMFMN H1*
OVIK SAGA De/De (Frederikshavn) 1964; PC; 2,265 grt; 74.5 × 4 m *(244 × 13.1 ft)*; M (B&W); 13 kts; ex-*Kununguak*

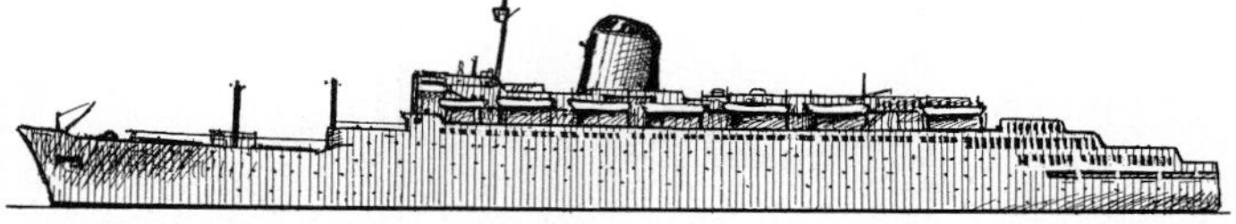

347 *MNMFN H*
LEONID SOBINOV Ma/Br (J Brown) 1954; P; 21,370 grt; 185 × 8.7 m *(608 × 28.7 ft)*; TST (J Brown); 20 kts; ex-*Saxonia*; First pair of kingposts now removed and pole added further forward
Sister: **FEDOR SHALYAPIN** (Ma) ex-*Ivernia*

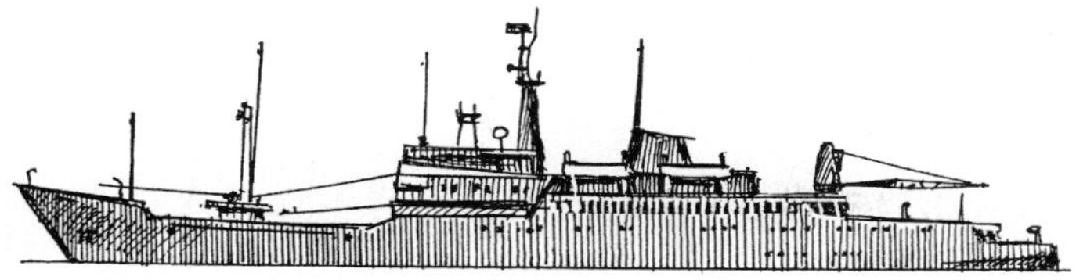

348 *MNMM-FC H12*
YU MEI RC/Pd (Szczecinska) 1974; C/TS; 5,975 grt/5,510 dwt; 122.2 × 7.4 m *(401 × 24.3 ft)*; M (Sulzer); 15.75 kts; ex-*Antoni Garnuszewski*; 'B 80' type
Sisters: **ZHENG HE** (RC) ex-*Kapitan Ledochowski*; **NEPTUN** (Rm); **NIKOLA VAPTZAROV** (Bu)

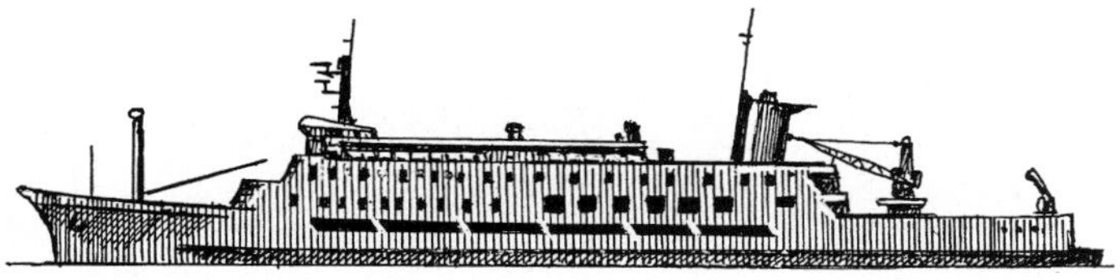

349 *MNMM-FCY H*
KURUSHIMA NO 7 —/Ja (Hayashikane) 1971; RoPCF/C; 5,216 grt/1,919 dwt; 124 × 5.5 m *(407 × 18.0 ft)*; TSM (Pielstick); 23 kts; ex-*Kuroshio Maru*

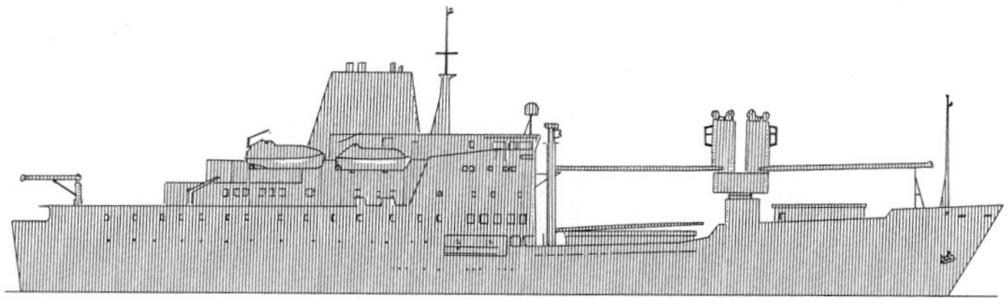

350 *MPNHFR H13*
ST HELENA Br/Br (A & P Appledore (A)) 1990; PC; 6,767 grt/3,130 dwt; 105 × 6.02 m *(344.49 × 19.75 ft)*; TSM (Mirrlees); 14.5 kts; 52 TEU

See photo number 20/397

351 *MRFRM H*
PRINS JOACHIM De/De (Nakskov) 1980; TF/RoPCF; 16,071 grt; 152 × 5.6 m *(498.69 × 18.37 ft)*; TSM (Alpha-Diesel); 18 kts; Bow and stern doors
Sisters: **DRONNING INGRID** (De); **KRONPRINS FREDERIK** (De)

352 *MSFM H2*
QUEEN OF THE ISLANDS Ca/Ca (Burrard DD) 1963; RoPF; 1,700 grt; 71.9 × — m *(263 × — ft)*; TSM (Fairbanks, Morse); 16 kts; Bow and stern doors

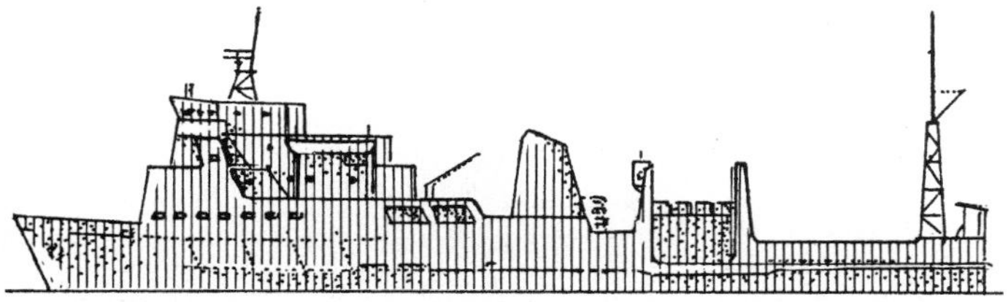

353 *MSGBH H1*
CLAYMORE Br/Br (Robb Caledon) 1978; RoPF; 1,871 grt; 77.2 × 2.9 m *(253 × 9.51 ft)*; TSM (Mirrlees Blackstone); 12.5 kts; Stern ramp and side ramps

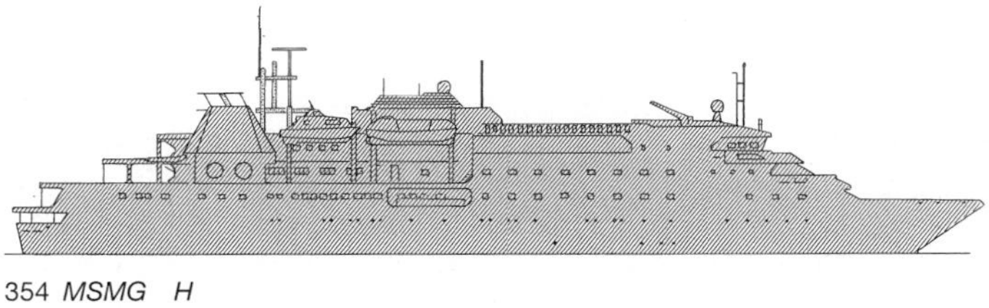

354 *MSMG H*
OCEANIC GRACE Ja/Ja (NKK) 1989; P; 5,218 grt; 102.96 × 4.31 m *(337.8 × 14.14 ft)*; TSM (Wärtsilä); 18 kts

355 *MV-F H*
LION PRINCE Sw/De (Aalborg) 1969; RoPCF; 8,909 grt; 123.5 × 5.2 m *(405 × 17 ft)*; TSM (Polar); 20.5 kts; ex-*Prinsessan Christina*; Bow and stern doors

356 *M-DFM-D H*
DING HU RC/De (B&W) 1952; P; 2,962 grt; 93 × 4.4 m *(305 × 14.5 ft)*; M (B&W); 15 kts; ex-*Kongedybet*; Lengthened 1958

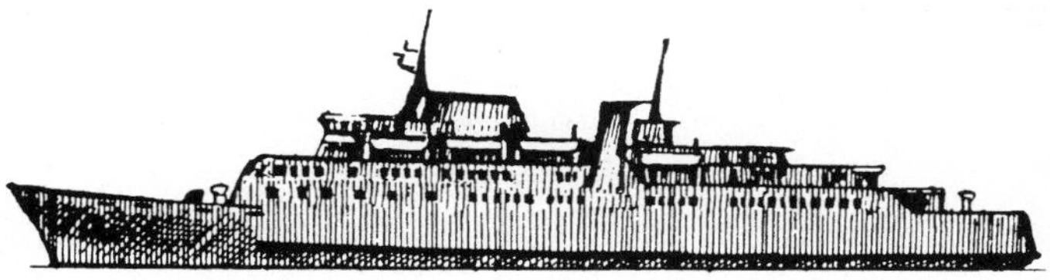

357 *M-FGM H*
ARIADNE Gr/FRG (LF-W) 1967; RoPF; 7,748 grt; 138 × 5.5 m *(453 × 18 ft)*; TSM (Pielstick); 23 kts; ex-*Tor Hollandia*; Bow and stern doors/ramps

358 *M-FGM H*
IMPERIAL EMPRESS SV/FRG (O&K) 1963; RoPF; 2,150 grt; 93.2 × 4 m *(306 × 13.12 ft)*; TSM (MWM); 19 kts; ex-*Gedser*; Bow and stern doors
Sister: **APOLLONIA II** (Pa) ex-*Travemunde*. Similar: **TIAN HU** (RC) ex-*Visby*

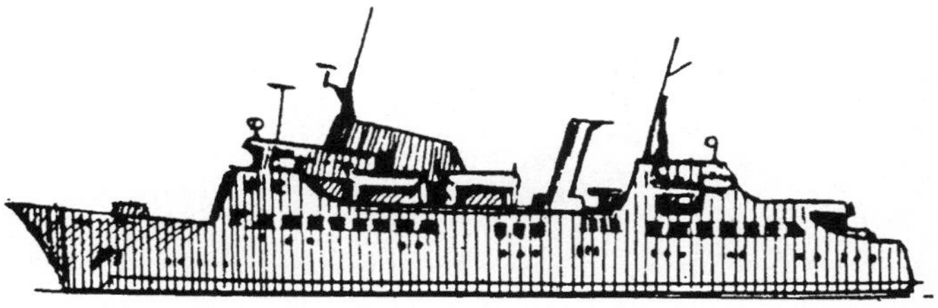

359 *M-FGM H*
ISTRA Cro/De (Aalborg) 1966; RoPF; 2,615 grt; 92.7 × 4.2 m *(304 × 13.9 ft)*; TSM (B&W); 19.5 kts; ex-*Mette Mols*; Bow door/ramp; Stern door/ramp
Sisters: **AL-ABOUD** (Si) ex-*Maren Mols*; **SMYRIL** (Fa) ex-*Morten Mols*; **TEISTIN** (Fa) ex-*Mikkel Mols*. Similar: **ALMIRANTE LUIS BRION** (Ve) ex-*Lasse*

360 *M-FGM H*
KELIBIA Ma/FRG (Unterweser) 1964; RoPF; 5,191 grt; 92.41 × 4.39 m *(303.18 × 14.4 ft)*; TSM (MAN); 19 kts; ex-*Grenaa*; Bow and stern doors

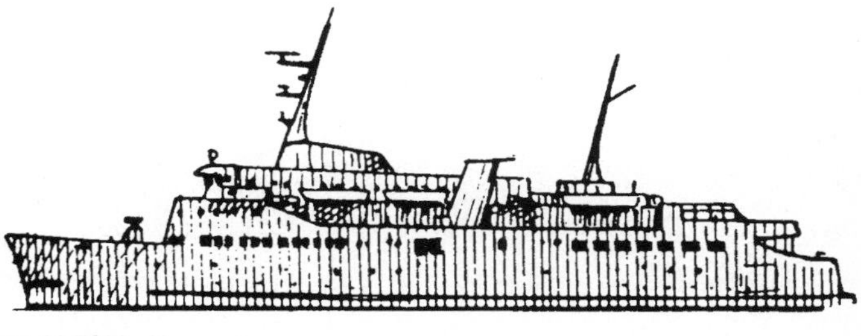

361 *M-FGM H*
SAFARI Ma/De (Aalborg) 1968; RoC/TF; 4,163 grt; 87.3 × 4.1 m *(286 × 13.4 ft)*; TSM (B&W); 19 kts; ex-*Christian IV*; Stern and side doors

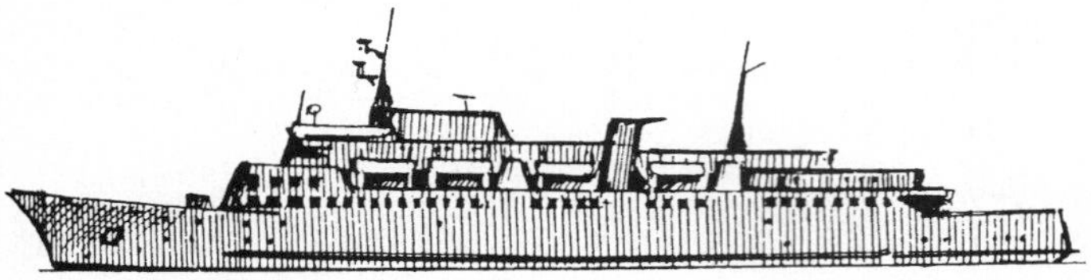

362 *M-FGM H*
SARDINIA NOVA It/FRG (LF-W) 1966; RoPF; 11,024 grt; 138 × 5.5 m *(453 × 18 ft)*; TSM (Pielstick); 23 kts; ex-*Tor Anglia*; Bow and stern doors

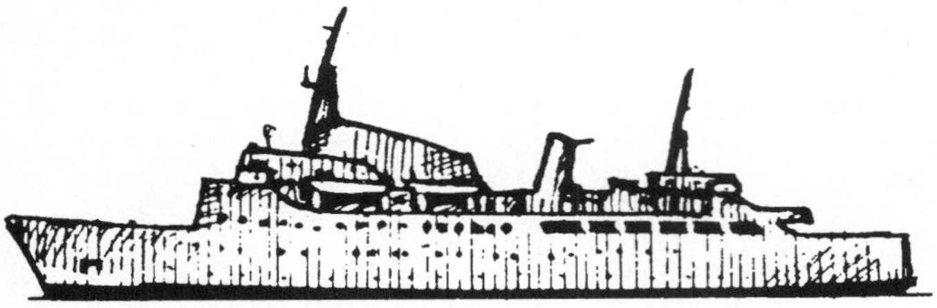

363 *M-FGM H*
SLAVIJA 1 Cro/Br (Bartram) 1963; RoPF; 3,000 grt; 88.3 × 4.2 m *(290 × 13.9 ft)*; TSM (MAN); 16 kts; ex-*Jens Kofoed*

364 *M-FGM H*
YESILADA Tu/De (Aalborg) 1968; RoPF; 3,100 grt; 87.2 × 4.2 m *(186 × 13.9 ft)*; TSM (B&W); 19.5 kts; ex-*Peter Wessel*; Bow door/ramp; Stern door/ramp and side doors

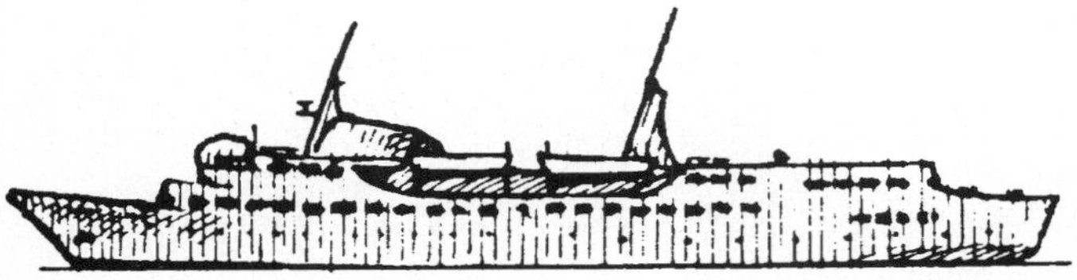

365 *M-FM-F H*
CASAMANCE EXPRESS Se/FRG (Rolandwerft) 1965; F; 1,519 grt; 77.6 × 3.4 m *(255 × 11.2 ft)*; TSM (MAN); 18 kts; ex-*Stella Marina*; Side doors

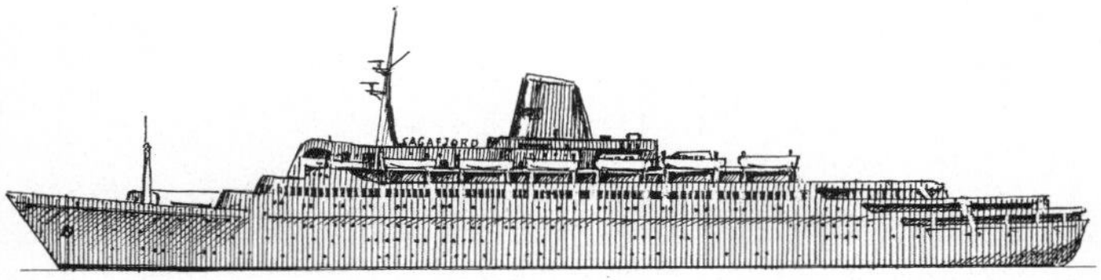

366 *M-NMF H*
SAGAFJORD Bs/Fr (Mediterranee) 1965; P; 25,147 grt; 189 × 8.2 m *(620 × 26.9 ft)*; TSM (Sulzer); 20 kts; (see photo number 20/445)

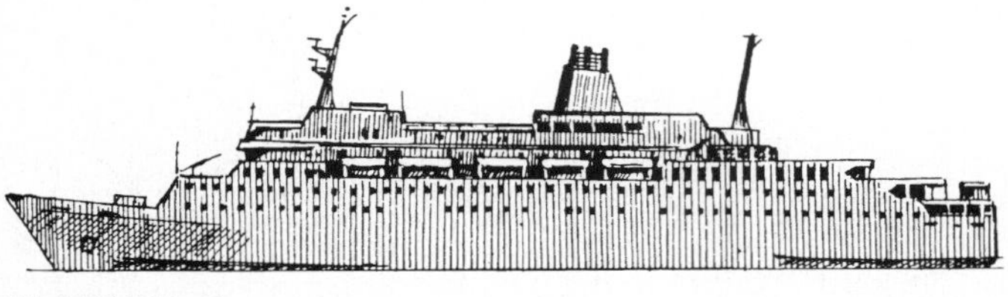

367 *M-SMFM H*
NAPOLEON Fr/Fr (Dubigeon-Normandie) 1976; RoPF; 14,900 grt; 155 × 6.4 m *(509 × 21 ft)*; TSM (Pielstick); 23.5 kts; Bow door/ramp; Side door/ramp; Stern door/ramp

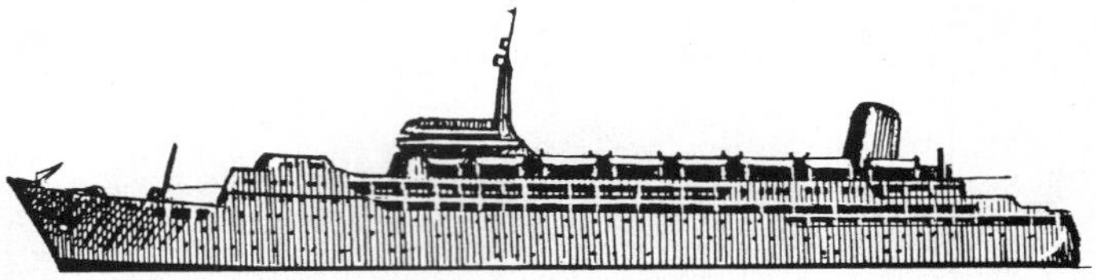

368 *NMF H*
OCEAN BREEZE Li/Br (H&W) 1955; P; 21,667 grt; 184.06 × 7.98 m *(603.87 × 26.18 ft)*; TST (H&W); 17 kts; ex-*Southern Cross*; Kingposts aft now removed

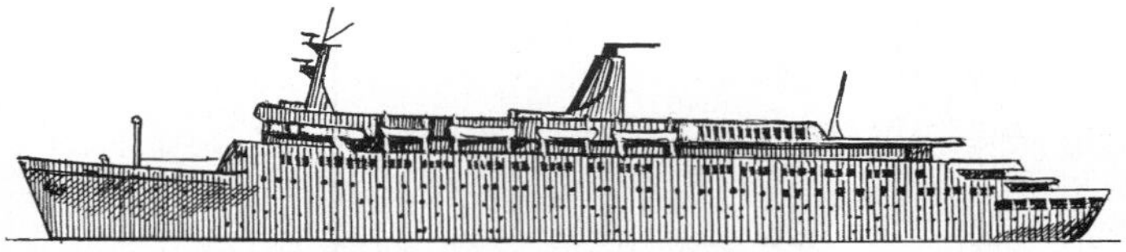

369 *NMFM H*
STELLA SOLARIS Gr/Fr (Ch de France) 1953; P; 17,490 grt; 166 × 7.9 m *(545 × 26 ft)*; TST (La Loire); 21 kts; ex-*Cambodge*

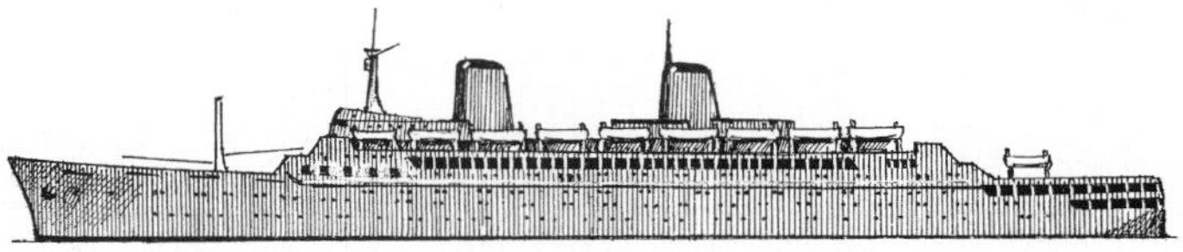

370 *NMFM-F H*
BRITANIS Pa/US (Bethlehem) 1932; P; 24,346 grt; 192 × 8.6 m *(630 × 28 ft)*; TST (Bethlehem); 21.5 kts; ex-*Monterey*

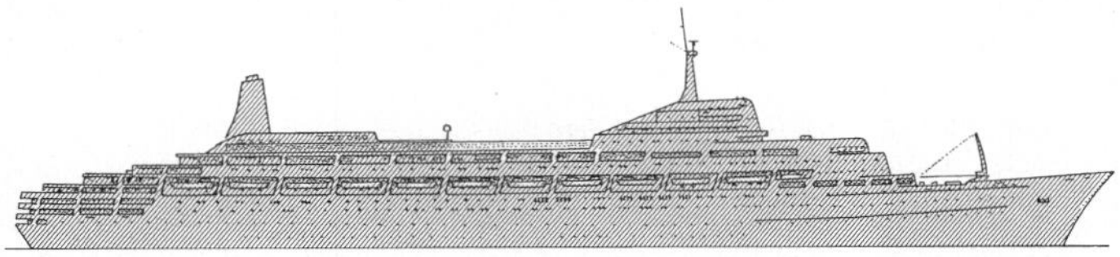

371 *NMG H*
CANBERRA Br/Br (H&W) 1961; P; 49,073 grt; 149.49 × 9.99 m *(818.54 × 32.78 ft)*; TS T-E (Associated Electric); 24 kts

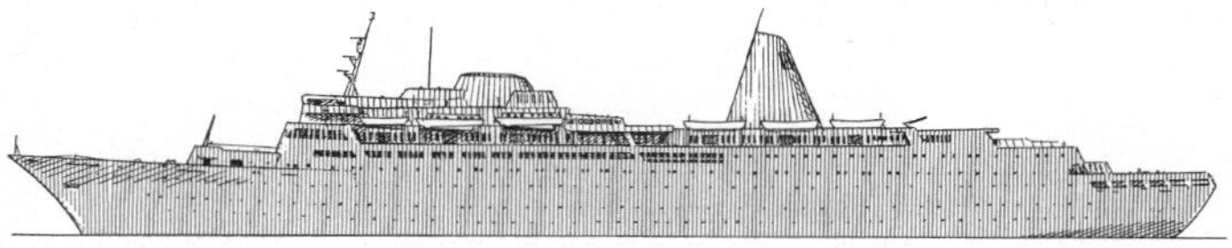

372 *NMM-F H*
VICTORIA Br/Br (J Brown) 1966/79; P; 28,891 grt; 201.23 × 8.56 m *(660.2 × 28.08 ft)*; TSM (Gotaverken); 21 kts; ex-*Sea Princess*, ex-*Kungsholm*; Rebuilt 1978/79 (Bremer V)

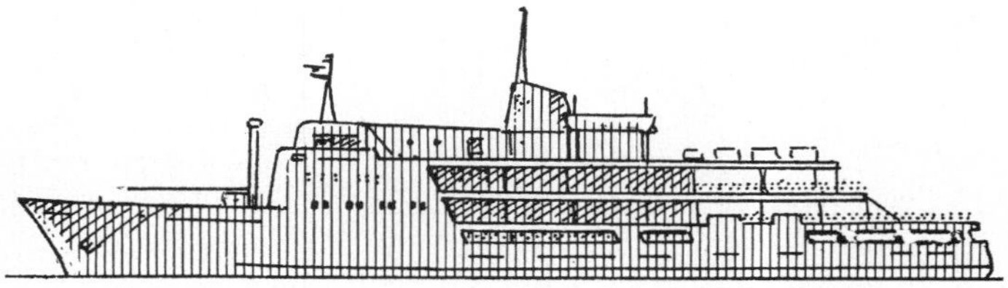

373 *NMM-F H1*
DON VICENTE Pi/Ja (Niigata) 1969; F; 1,100 grt; 77.35 × 3.77 m *(253.77 × 12.37 ft)*; TSM (Niigata); 17 kts

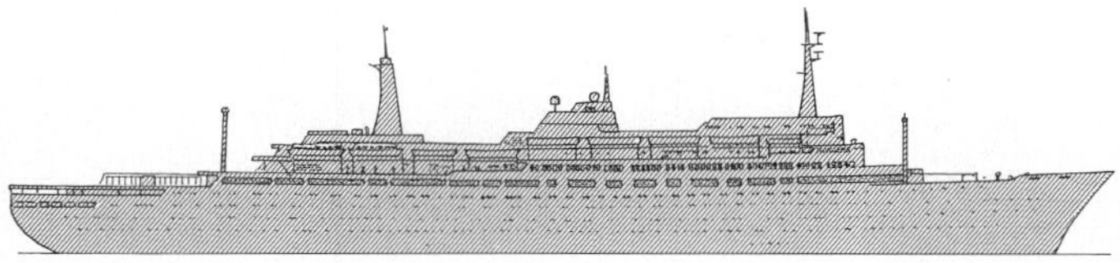

374 *NMM-GN H*
ROTTERDAM NA/Ne (Rotterdamsche) 1959; P; 37,800 grt; 228 × 9 m *(749 × 29.5 ft)*; TST ('De Schelde'); 21.5 kts

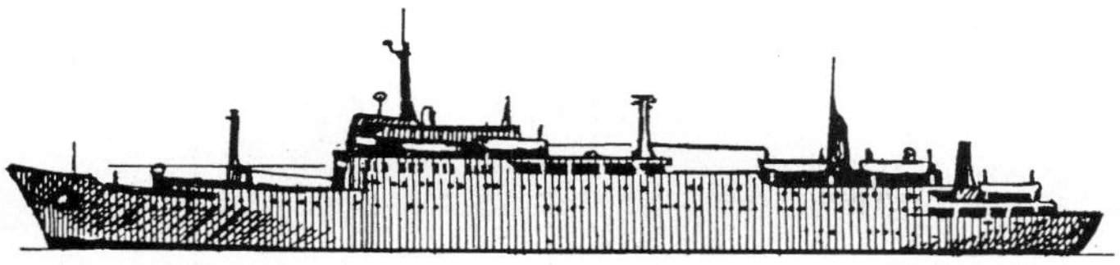

375 *NMN²M-FN H1*
ZHI LUO LAN RC/Ja (Mitsubishi HI) 1962; PC; 12,470 grt/7,743 dwt; 157 × 7.58 m *(516 × 24.87 ft)*; M (Mitsubishi); 17 kts; ex-*Sakura Maru*

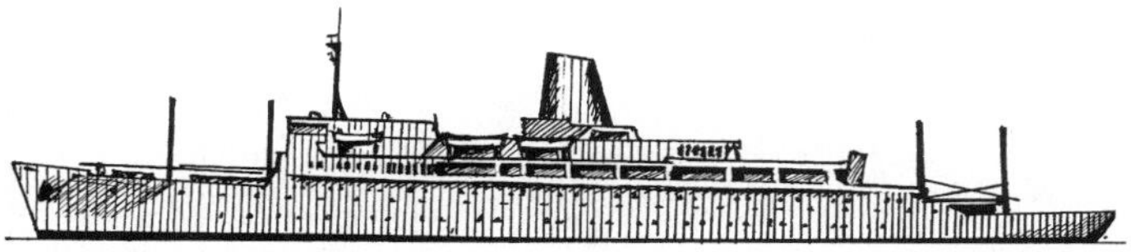

376 *N²MFN² H*
HENG LI SV/US (Bethlehem Steel) 1952/56; P; 16,653 grt; 172 × 9 m *(564 × 29.6 ft)*; M (Pielstick); 20 kts; ex-*Pine Tree Mariner*; Converted from cargo ship 1956

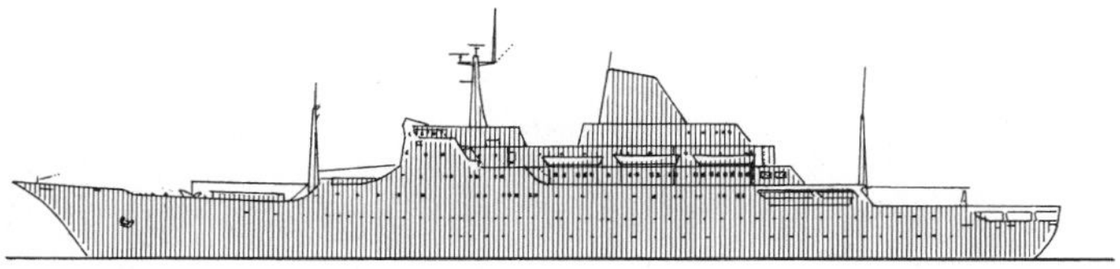

377 *NVFN H*
ORIENT PRINCESS Pa/Fr (L'Atlantique) 1967; P; 10,298 grt; 149 × 6.6 m *(489 × 21.8 ft)*; TSM (Sulzer); 21 kts; ex-*Yaohua*

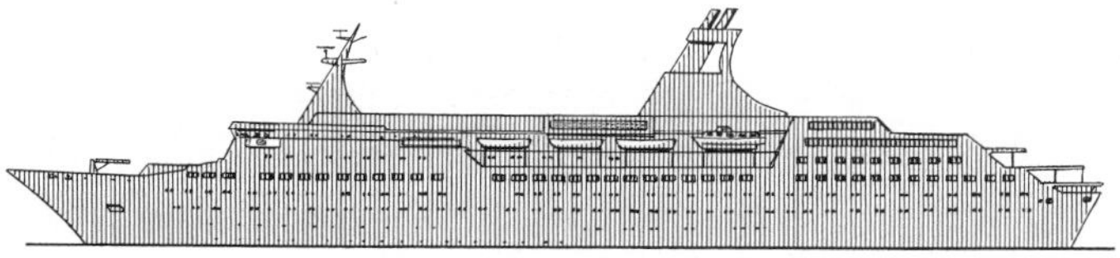

378 *RMF H*
ARKONA Ge/FRG (Howaldts DW) 1981; P; 18,591 grt; 164.34 × 6.1 m *(539 × 20.01 ft)*; TSM (MAN); 18 kts; ex-*Astor*

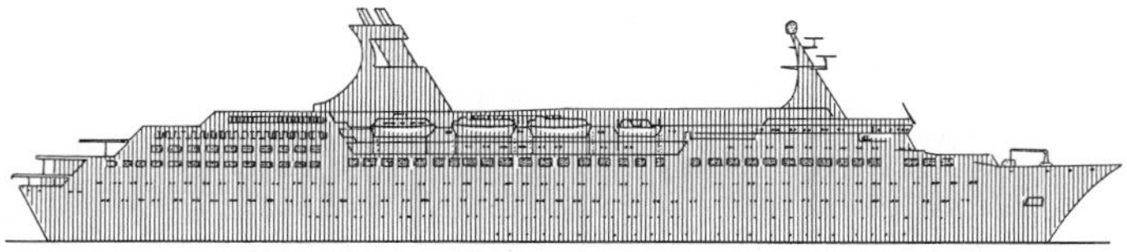

379 *RMF H*
ASTOR Bs/FRG (Howaldts DW) 1987; P; 20,606 grt; 176.26 × 6.1 m *(578.28 × 20.01 ft)*; TSM (Sulzer); 18 kts

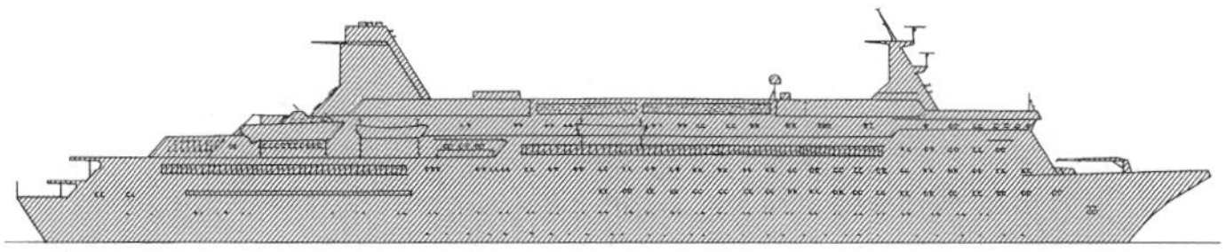

380 *RMF H*
BERLIN Ge/FRG (Howaldts DW) 1980; P; 9,570 grt; 139.3 × 4.81 m *(457 × 15.78 ft)*; TSM (MaK); 17 kts; Lengthened 1986

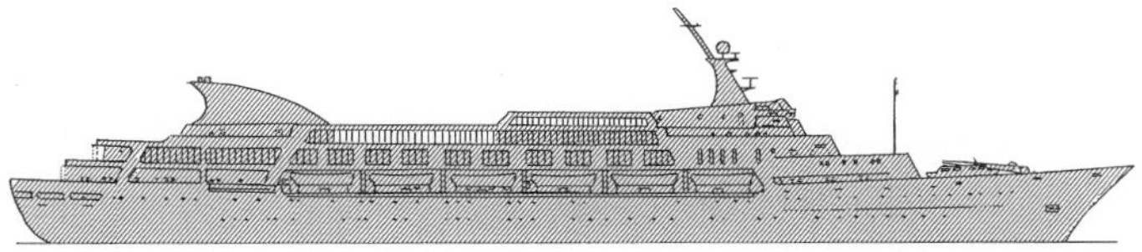

381 *RM²F H*
PRINCESA OCEANICA Cy/It (Felszegi) 1967; P; 7,186 grt; 149 × 6.4 m *(489 × 21.01 ft)*; TSM (Sulzer); 16 kts; ex-*Italia*; Now has an excursion boat stowed on foredeck and handled by single ram crane

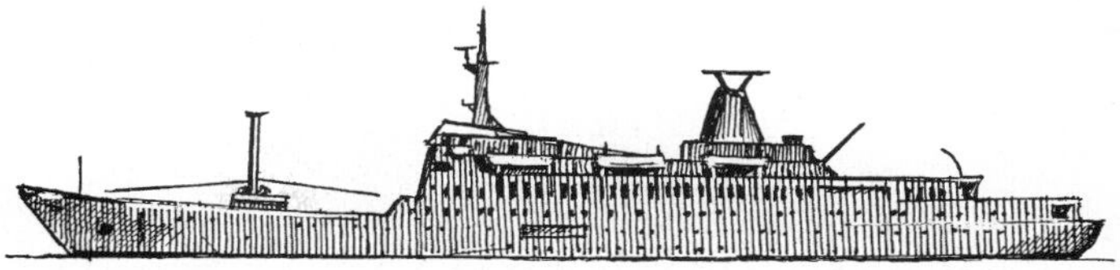

382 *RVMFR² H2*
HARSHA VARDHANA In/In (Mazagon) 1974; PC; 8,871 grt/5,271 dwt; 132.6 × 7 m *(435 × 23 ft)*; M (Sulzer); 17 kts

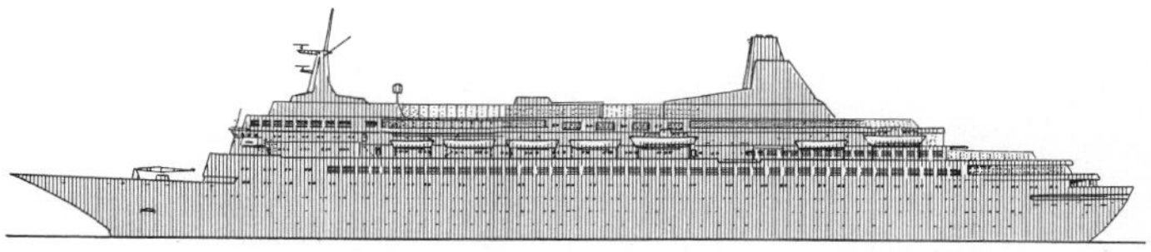

383 *SMF H*
BLACK WATCH —/Fi (Wärtsilä) 1972/81; P; 28,668 grt; 205.47 × 7.55 m *(674 × 24.77 ft)*; TSM (Wärtsilä); 21.5 kts; ex-*Royal Viking Star*; Lengthened 1981 (A G 'Weser')
Sisters: **ROYAL ODYSSEY** (Bs) ex-*Royal Viking Sea*; **GOLDEN PRINCESS** (Bs) ex-*Royal Viking Sky*

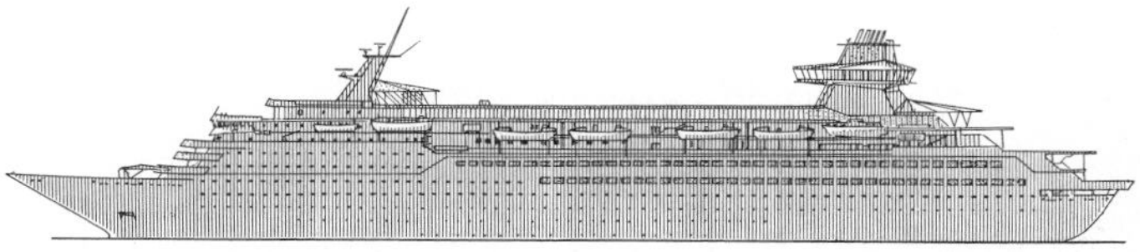

384 *SMF H*
SONG OF AMERICA NIS/Fi (Wärtsilä) 1982; P; 37,584 grt; 214.51 × 6.5 m *(704 × 21.33 ft)*; TSM (Sulzer); 20.5 kts

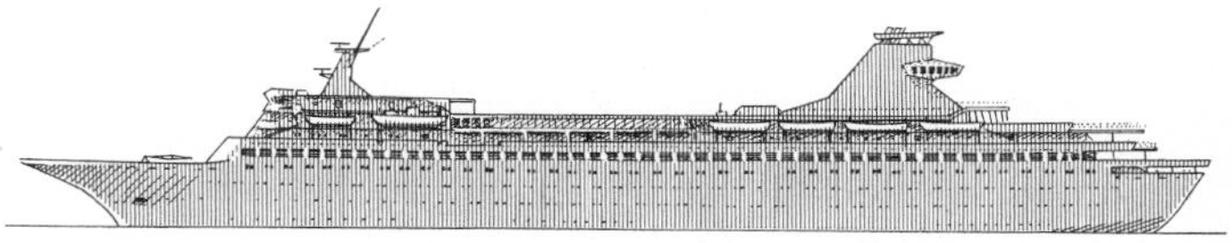

385 *SMF H*
SONG OF NORWAY NIS/Fi (Wärtsilä) 1969/78; P; 22,945 grt; 194.32 × 6.7 m *(637.47 × 21.98 ft)*; TSM (Sulzer); 20.5 kts; Lengthened 1978 (Wärtsilä)
Sister: **CAROUSEL** (Bs) ex-*Nordic Prince*; Similar (unlengthened sister): **SUN VIKING** (NIS)

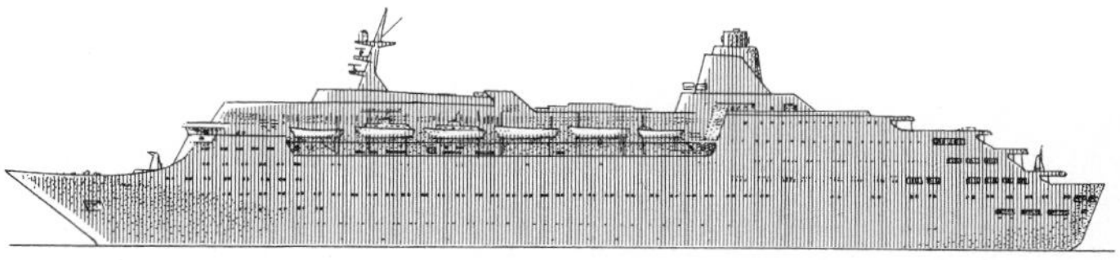

386 *SMFS H*
EUROPA Ge/FRG (Bremer V) 1981; P; 37,012 grt; 196 × 8.35 m *(643 × 27.4 ft)*; TSM (MAN); 18 kts

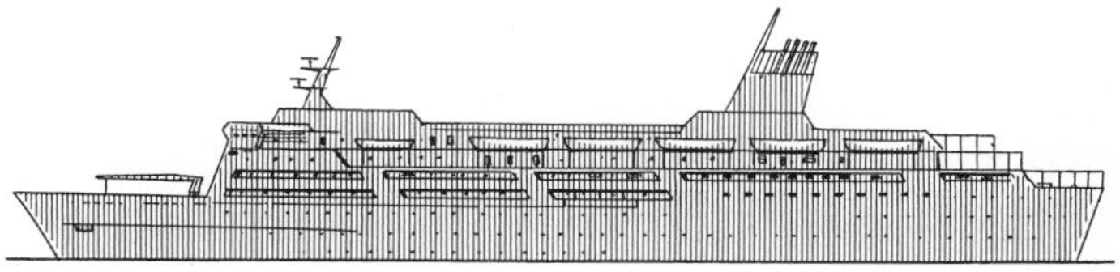

387 *SMM-F H*
KERINCI Ia/FRG (Meyer) 1983; F; 14,000 grt; 144.02 × 5.9 m *(473 × 19.36 ft)*; TSM (Krupp-MaK); 20 kts
Sisters: **KAMBUNA** (Ia); **RINJANI** (Ia); **UMSINI** (Ia); **TIDAR** (Ia) (accident boat at after end of boat deck)

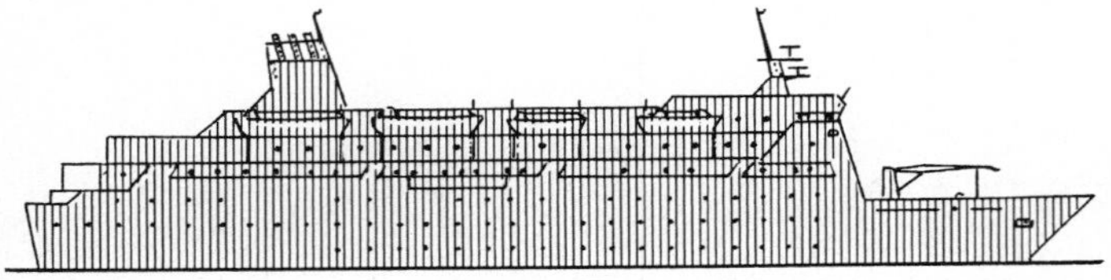

388 *SMM-F H*
LAWIT Ia/FRG (Meyer) 1986; P/F; 5,684 grt/1,413 dwt; 99.83 × 4.2 m *(327.53 × 13.78 ft)*; TSM (MaK); 14 kts
Sisters: **KELIMUTU** (Ia); **SIRIMAU** (Ia); **AWU** (Ia); **LEUSER** (Ia); **BINAIYA** (Ia); **BUKIT RAYA** (Ia); **TILONGKABILA** (Ia)

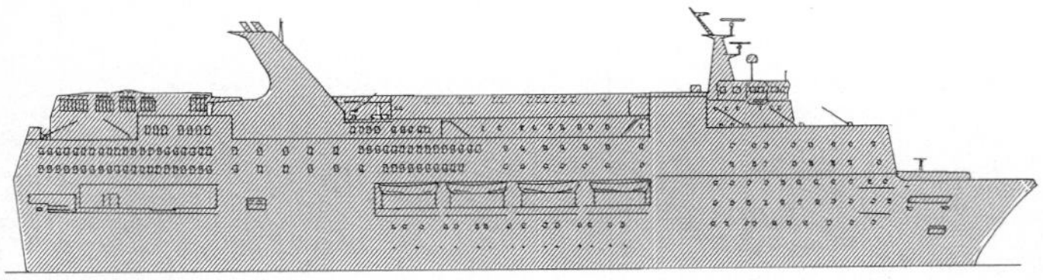

389 *SMM-GS H*
ANNA KARENINA Ru/Fi (Wärtsilä) 1980; RoPF; 14,213 grt; 145.19 × 5.52 m *(476.3 × 18.11 ft)*; TSM (Pielstick); 21.5 kts; ex-*Viking Song*; Bow door/ramp; Two stern doors/ramps

390 *TC*^{2}*TMFN H12*
HAI DA RC/Br (J Brown) 1963; P/C; 7,989 grt/4,334 dwt; 146 × 8 m *(481 × 26.4 ft)*; TSM (B&W); 20 kts; ex-*Centaur*

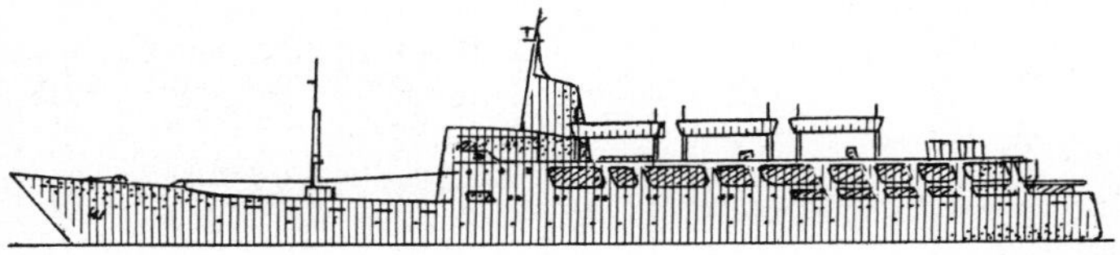

391 *TM-F H*
DON JULIO Pi/Ja (Maizuru) 1967; PC; 2,116 grt/1,424 dwt; 95.66 × 5.16 m *(313.85 × 16.93 ft)*; M (B&W); 17.5 kts

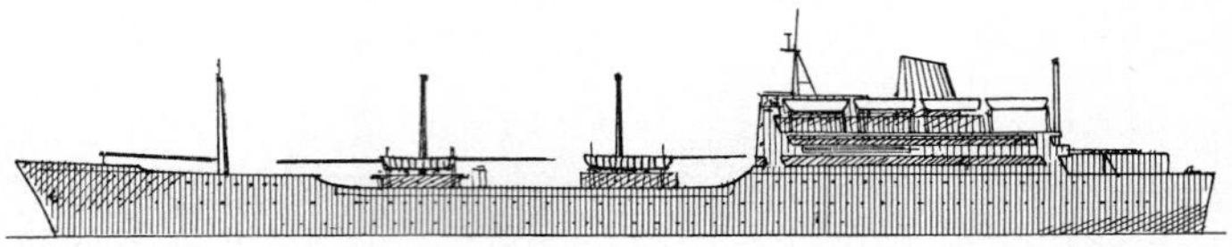

392 *T*^{3}*MFN H13*
AKBAR In/De (Helsingor) 1971; P/C; 8,279 grt/8,820 dwt; 149.51 × 7.71 m *(490.52 × 25.29 ft)*; M (B&W); 16.5 kts; Now converted to ro-ro ferry; Probably considerably altered in appearance; New engines 1995

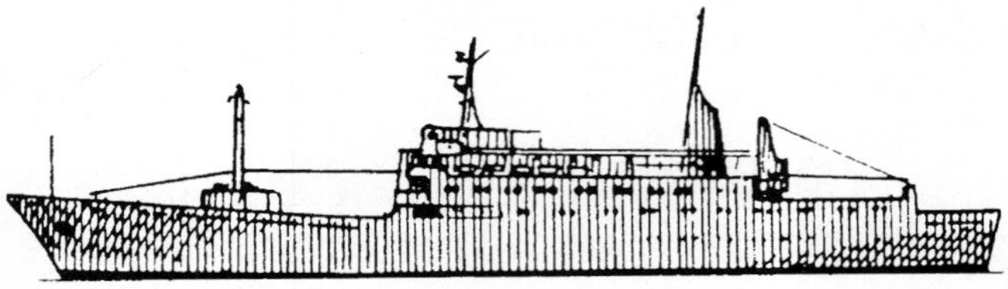

393 *VMM-FC H2*
DON CLAUDIO Pi/Ja (Sanoyasu) 1965; F; 2,700 grt; 93 × 5.4 m *(306 × 17.6 ft)*; M (B&W); 18.5 kts; ex-*Okinoshima Maru*

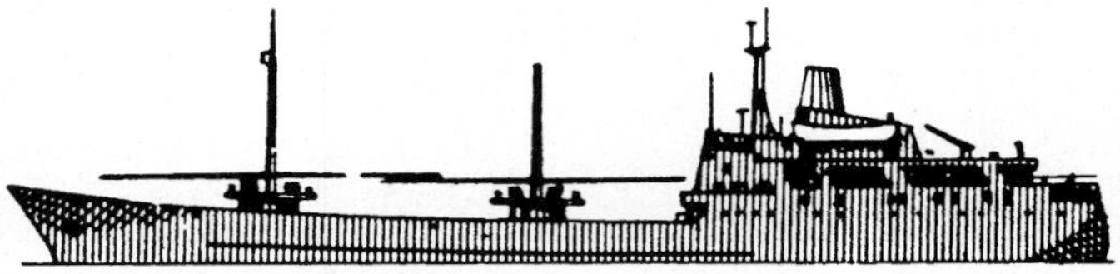

394 *V*^{2}*MFS H3*
INDOCEANIQUE Ms/Ca (Burrard DD) 1963; PC; 3,150 grt/2,264 dwt; 100.28 × 5.51 m *(329 × 18.08 ft)*; M (Stork); 14 kts; ex-*Northland Prince*

395 Paglia Orba *(Fr); 1994* *ACH/Phototechnic*

396 Century *(Li); 1995* *Foto Hero Lang*

397 Kronprins Frederik *(De); 1981* *WSPL*

398 Pascoli *(It); 1971* *WSPL*

399 Danmark *(De); 1968* *WSPL*

400 Karl Carstens *(Ge); 1986* *WSPL*

401 Hamburg *(Bs); 1976* *WSPL*

402 Ayvazovskiy *(Uk); 1977* *WSPL*

403 Albatros *(Bs); 1957/71* *WSPL*

404 Arveprins Knud *(De); 1963* *WSPL*

405 Idriss I *(No); 1974* *Norman Thomson*

406 Odessa *(Uk); 1974* *WSPL*

407 Dmitriy Shostakovich *(Li); 1980* *WSPL*

408 Corsica Victoria *(Pa); 1973* *WSPL*

409 Olympic *(Gr); 1956/76* *WSPL*

410 Meridian *(Bs); 1963/84* *FotoFlite*

411 Seawing *(Bs); 1971/77* *FotoFlite*

412 Caldeonian Star *(Bs); 1966/83* *FotoFlite*

413 Stena Invicta *(Br); 1985* *FotoFlite*

414 King of Scandinavia *(DIS); 1974* *FotoFlite*

415 Pride of Le Havre *(Br); 1989* *FotoFlite*

416 Vistamar *(Pa); 1989* *FotoFlite*

417 Westerdam *(Bs); 1986/90* *FotoFlite*

418 Splendour of the Seas *(NIS); 1996* *FotoFlite*

419 Kalliste *(Fr); 1993* *FotoFlite*

423 Royal Majesty *(Pa); 1992* *FotoFlite*

420 Radisson Diamond *(Fi); 1992* *FotoFlite*

424 Renaissance Four *(Li); 1990* *FotoFlite*

421 Barfleur *(Fr); 1992* *FotoFlite*

425 Hoverspeed Great Britain *(Bs); 1990* *FotoFlite*

422 Costa Classica *(Li); 1991* *FotoFlite*

426 Leeward *(Pa); 1980/92; (as Sally Albatross)* *FotoFlite*

427 Dreamward *(Bs); 1992* *FotoFlite*

428 Crystal Harmony *(Bs); 1990* *FotoFlite*

429 Normandie *(Fr); 1992* *FotoFlite*

430 Silver Wind *(It); 1995* *FotoFlite*

431 Oriana *(Br); 1995* *FotoFlite*

432 Stena Fantasia *(Bs); 1980/90* *FotoFlite*

433 Pride of Suffolk *(Br); 1978/82* *FotoFlite*

434 Bretagne *(Fr); 1989* *FotoFlite*

435 Pride of Hampshire *(Br); 1975/86* *FotoFlite*

436 Mermoz *(Bs); 1957/70* *FotoFlite*

437 Stena Explorer *(Br); 1996* *FotoFlite*

438 Bremen *(Bs); 1990* *FotoFlite*

439 Isle of Innisfree *(Ih); 1995* *FotoFlite*

440 Imagination *(Pa); 1995* *FotoFlite*

441 Euromantique *(Bs); 1976/94* *FotoFlite*

442 Royal Viking Sun *(Bs); 1988* *FotoFlite*

443 Seabourn Legend *(NIS); 1992; (as Royal Viking Queen)* *Ian Pakeman*

444 Statendam *(Bs); 1993* *Ian Pakeman*

445 Sagafjord *(Bs); 1965* *Ian Pakeman*

446 Bismillah *(Mo); 1971/74* *FotoFlite*

447 Ialyssos *(Gr); 1966* *WSPL*

448 Royal Star *(Bs); 1956/77; (as Ocean Islander)* *WSPL*

449 Seabourn Spirit *(NIS); 1989* *WSPL*

450 The Azur *(Pa); 1971* *WSPL*

451 Aegean Dolphin *(Gr); 1973/88* *WSPL*

452 Stena Europe *(Sw); 1981* *WSPL*

453 Pride of Kent *(Br); 1980/92* *FotoFlite*

454 Minerva *(Bs); 1996* *FotoFlite*

455 Delphin *(Ma); 1975/86; (ex-Kazakhstan II)* FotoFlite

456 Astra II *(Bs); 1974; (ex-Golden Odyssey)* FotoFlite

457 Italia Prima *(It); 1948/96* *FotoFlite*

458 Seabreeze I *(Pa); 1958/93* *WSPL*

21 Specialised Cargo Ships

21 Specialised Cargo Ships

See photo number 21/69

1 *CM²FM H1*
HAMILTON K dwt; **ALTERNATIVE SEQUENCE FOR DRAWING NUMBER 21/18** as a tall crane on the forecastle has been reported

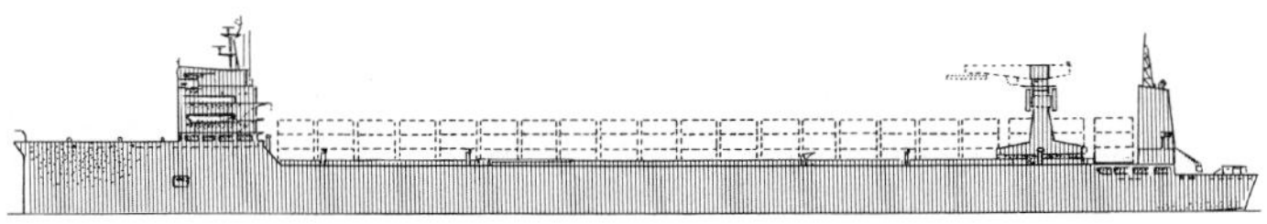

2 *DMJM–FS H1*
BACO-LINER 1 Ge/FRG (Thyssen) 1979; Bg/Con; 22,345 grt/21,801 dwt; 204.1 × 6.67 m *(669.62 × 21.88 ft)*; M (B&W); 15 kts; Bow doors; Barges float on and off; Crane is shown in stowed position—dotted lines represent it swung fore-and-aft; 501 TEU
Sister: **BACO-LINER 2** (Ge); Similar: **BACO-LINER 3** (Ge)

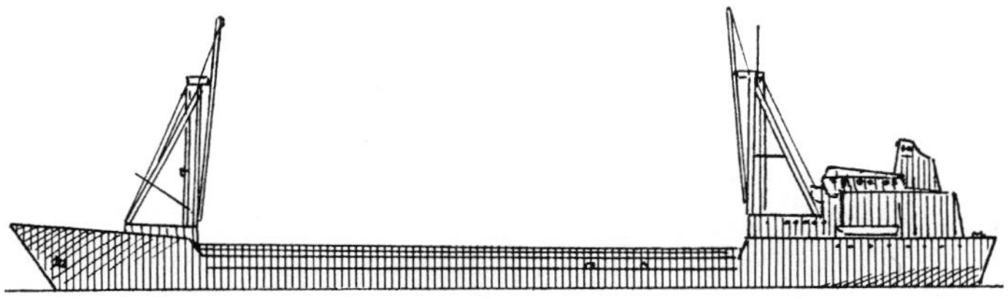

3 *H²F H13*
MEDGLORY Ma/Ne (Groot & VV) 1977; C/HL; 3,481 grt/4,415 dwt; 98.02 × 6 m *(321.59 × 19.69 ft)*; TSM (Atlas-MaK); 13 kts; ex-*Fairlane*; Heavy lift masts are quadpods and are on starboard side; Superstructure and funnels are also on starboard side
Sister: **MIRABELLA** (NA)

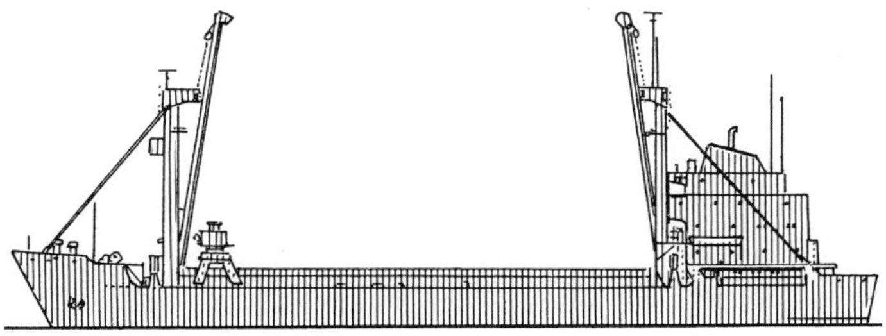

4 *HJHFM² H1*
GAJAH BORNEO My/Fr (Dubigeon-Normandie) 1978; HL/Con; 4,997 grt/ 5,076 dwt; 99.80 × 6.40 m *(327.43 × 21.00 ft)*; TSM (Pielstick); 12 kts; ex-*Internavis II*; 2 × 220 ton capacity derricks; Has a travelling crane on the foredeck which can be removed; Heavy-lift masts are quadpods

5 *HM³GN H2*
AGIA KYRIAKI Gr/Ne (Duijvendijk's) 1969/75; RoC/HL; 2,508 grt/1,087 dwt; 92 × 2.86 m *(301.83 × 9.38 ft)*; TSM (Caterpillar); 10.5 kts; ex-*Mariaeck*; Bow and stern doors; Lengthened 1975; Heavy-lift masts are on port side

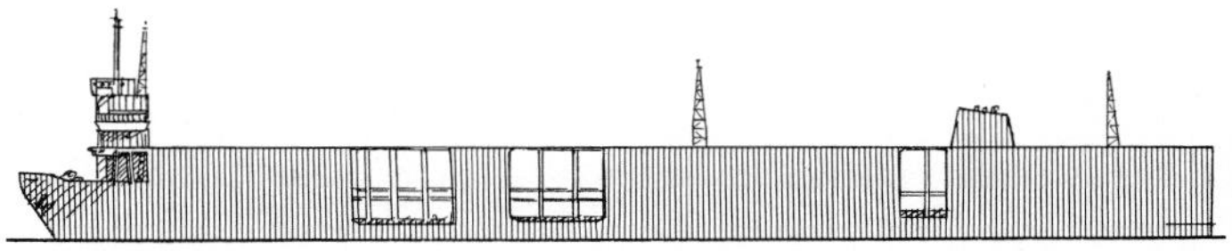

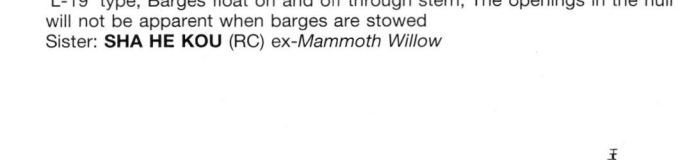

6 *HNVGN H2*
DEVELOPING ROAD Ma/Ja (Sumitomo) 1978; Bg/Dk; 1,856 grt/3,285 dwt; 134.5 × 4.8 m *(441.27 × 15.75 ft)*; TSM (Pielstick); 9 kts; ex-*Mammoth Oak*; 'L-19' type; Barges float on and off through stern; The openings in the hull will not be apparent when barges are stowed
Sister: **SHA HE KOU** (RC) ex-*Mammoth Willow*

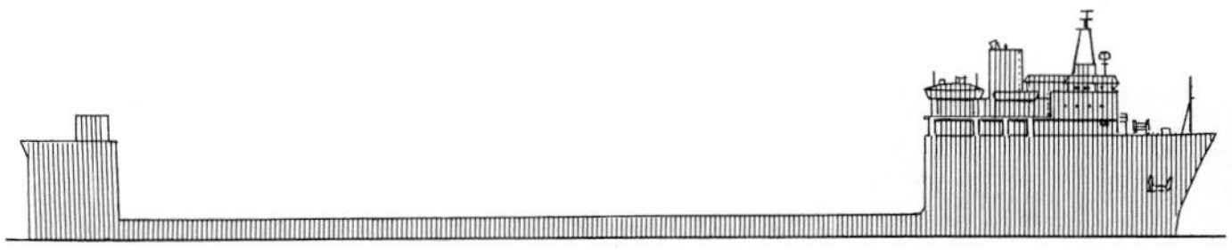

7 *HN–GC H13*
TRANSSHELF Ru/Fi (Wärtsilä MI) 1987; SSDC; 26,547 grt/34,030 dwt; 173.00 × 8.80 m *(567.59 × 28.87 ft)*; TSM (Wärtsilä); 15 kts

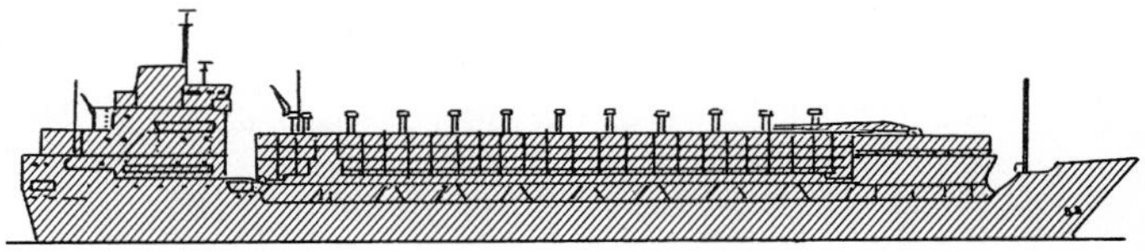

8 *HR²M–FR H13*
BENWALID Tu/Br (Appledore) 1973/85; LS; 5,395 grt/5,579 dwt; 115.30 × 6.84 m *(378.28 × 22.44 ft)*; M (Pielstick); 15.5 kts; ex-*Manchester Vigour*; Converted from container ship 1985

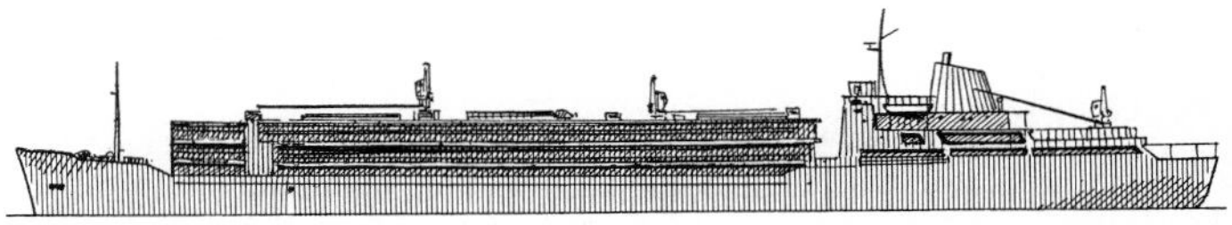

9 *MC²MFC H13*
MARINEOS UAE/No (Nakskov) 1965; LS; 14,091 grt/9,536 dwt; 164.45 × 8.15 m *(539.53 × 26.74 ft)*; M (B&W); 20.75 kts; ex-*Ancona*; Converted from cargo ship 1977 (Gotav)

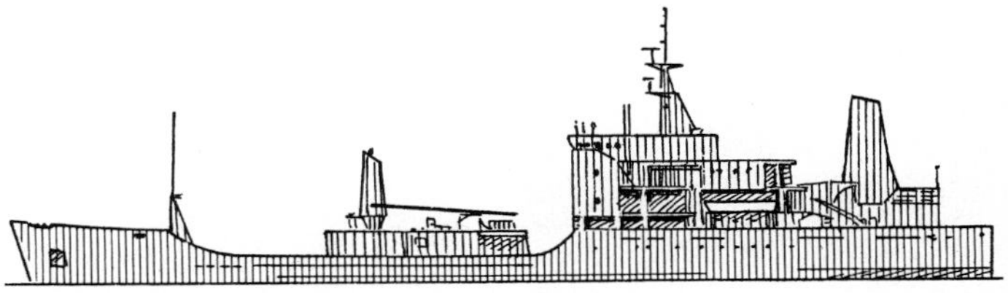

10 *MCMF H13*
GOLIATH II Sg/Au (Carrington) 1978; Cem; 3,523 grt/4,270 dwt; 97.62 × 6.01 m *(320.28 × 19.72 ft)*; M (Mitsubishi); 14 kts; ex-*Goliath*

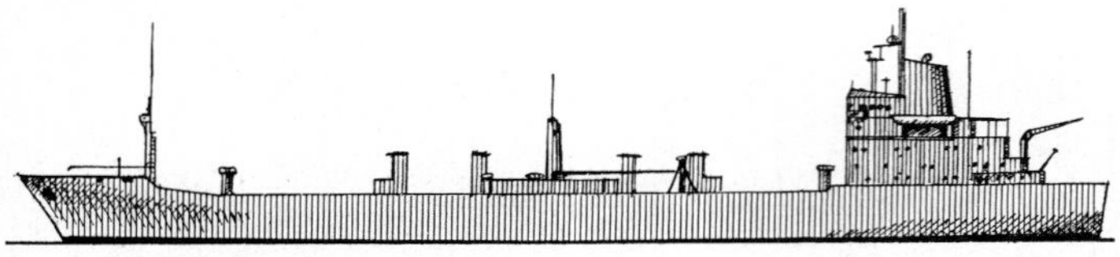

11 *MCM–FS H1*
HUMBER ARM Sw/FRG (Schichau-U) 1976; Pal/Pap; 7,587 grt/7,173 dwt; 130.03 × 6.68 m *(426.6 × 21.92 ft)*; M (Pielstick); 16.75 kts; Side doors; Crane amidships is on port side
Sister: **CORNER BROOK** (Sw)

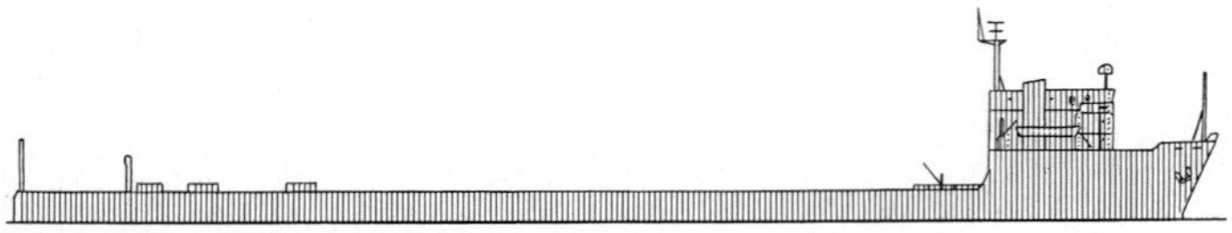

12 *MGMNY H1*
SEAHORSE I Sg/Ja (Mitsubishi HI) 1983; HL/DC/RoC; 14,215 grt/20,958 dwt; 162.01 × 6.37 m *(531.53 × 20.90 ft)*; TSM (MAN); 13.1 kts; ex-*Snimos Ace*; Stern ramp
Sister: **MAXITA** (Br) ex-*Snimos King*

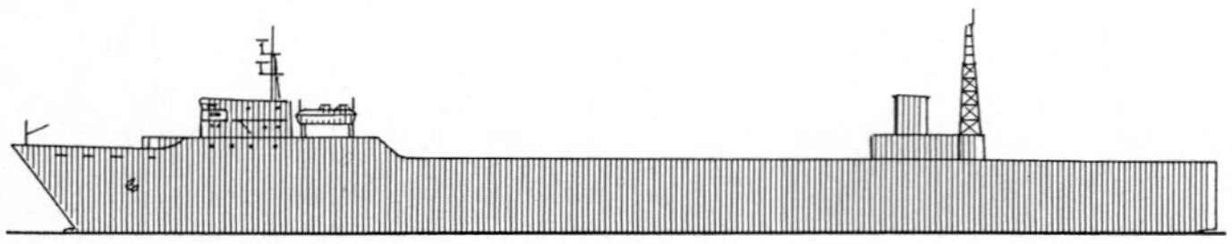

13 *MGV H2*
DANUBE SHUTTLE Ma/It (Breda) 1984; Bg; 17,395 grt/8,727 dwt; 157.77 × 4.43 m *(517.62 × 14.53 ft)*; TSM (GMT); 12.8 kts; ex-*Anatoliy Zelezhnyakov*; Semi-submersible, stern loading
Sister: **DANUBE EXPRESS** (Ma) ex-*Nikolay Markin*

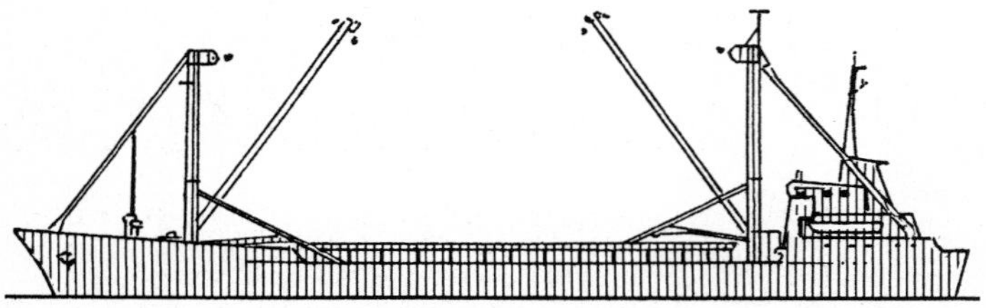

14 *MH^{2}M–F H12*
EQUATOR JADE Sg/FRG (Schlichting) 1969; C/HL; 1,765 grt/2,142 dwt; 78.52 × 4.98 m *(258 × 16.34 ft)*; M (Atlas-MaK); 11 kts; ex-*Tipperary*; Converted from cargo/container; 84 TEU; Heavy-lift masts are quadpods

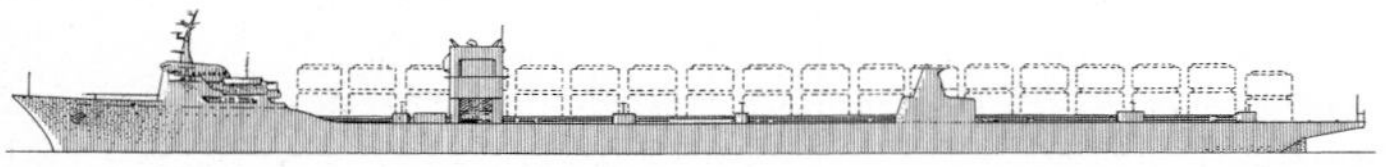

15 *MKG H1*
STONEWALL JACKSON US/US (Avondale) 1974; Bg; 28,580 grt/46,153 dwt; 272.55 × 11.62 m *(894.19 × 28.12 ft)*; T (De Laval); 22 kts; 'LASH' type
Sisters: **ROBERT E LEE** (US); **SAM HOUSTON** (US); **GREEN VALLEY** ex-*Green Valley*; **GREEN ISLAND** (US) ex-*Green Island*; **GREEN HARBOUR** (US) ex-*Green Harbour*; Similar (converted to container ships—cranes may be removed): **SEA-LAND RELIANCE** (US) ex-*Edward Rutledge*; **SEA-LAND SPIRIT** (US) ex-*Benjamin Harrison*

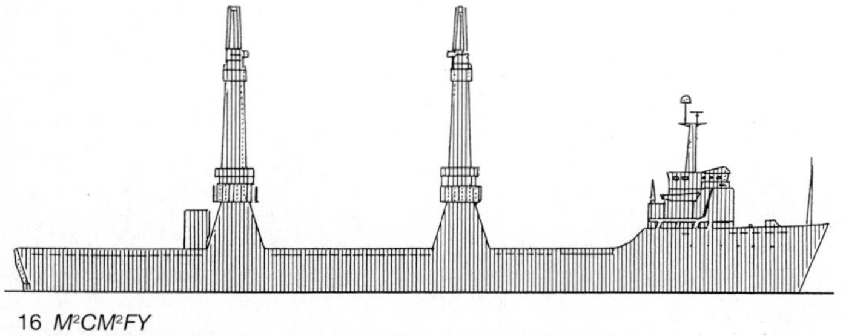

16 *M^{2}CM^{2}FY*
HAPPY BUCCANEER Ne/Ja (Hitachi) 1984; HL/RoC/Con; 16,341 grt/13,740 dwt; 145.90 × 8.25 m *(478.67 × 27.07 ft)*; TSM (Sulzer); 15.5 kts; Stern door/ramp; 1,058 TEU; Heavy lift masts and funnel are on starboard side

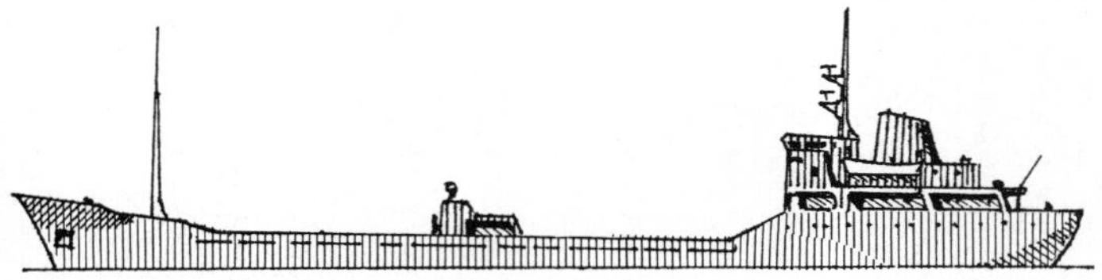

17 *M^{2}F H13*
CAMARA PESTANA Po/De (Aarhus) 1971; Cem; 2,917 grt/4,250 dwt; 98.25 × 6.27 m *(322.34 × 20.57 ft)*; M (B&W); 13.5 kts; ex-*Cimbria*; May now be fitted with an unloading system which probably alters appearance

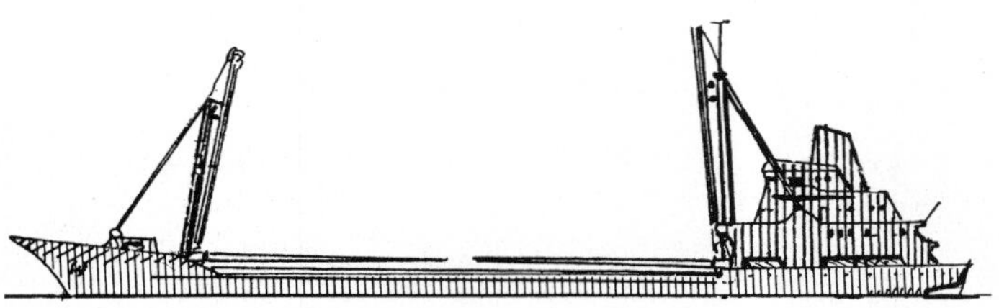

18 *M^{2}FM H1*
HAMILTON K Gy/Ne (Van Diepen) 1974; C/HL; 2,230 grt/2,558 dwt; 88.22 × 5.51 m *(289.44 × 18.08 ft)*; M (Atlas-MaK); 13.5 kts; ex-*Fairload*; Tripod heavy-lift masts; May have a tall crane on the forcastle
Similar: **SLANO** (Ma) ex-*Valkenier*

19 *M^{2}FN H1*
AL KUWAIT Ku/Ja (Mitsubishi HI) 1967/80; LS; 34,082 grt/39,266 dwt; 195.00 × 10.52 m *(639.77 × 34.51 ft)*; M (Sulzer); 16.75 kts; ex-*Erviken*; Converted from tanker and shortened 1980 (Meyer); The 'N' aft consists of a lattice tripod on the port side and a pole mast on starboard

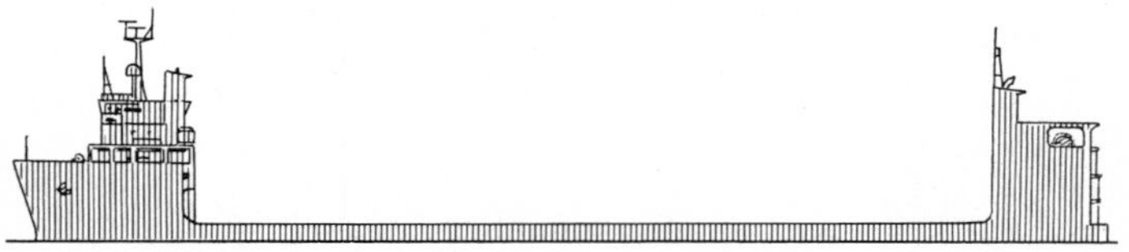

20 *M^{2}GSM–G H13*
BALI SEA Sg/Ja (Mitsubishi HI) 1982; RoC/SSDC; 29,594 grt/22,228 dwt; 138.99 × 6.02 m *(456 × 19.75 ft)*; TSM (MAN); 13 kts; ex-*Dan Lifter*; Now lengthened to 173.00m (567.59ft); Drawing shows vessel as built
Sister: **BANDA SEA** (Sg) ex-*Dan Mover*

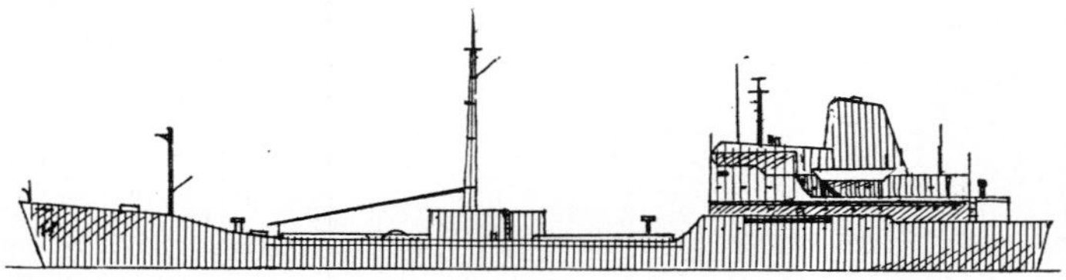

21 *M^{3}F H13*
CEMENTIA Pa/FRG (Deutsche Werft) 1967; Cem; 3,739 grt/5,335 dwt; 106.61 × 6.74 m *(349.77 × 22.11 ft)*; M (KHD); 14.75 kts
Sister: **DALIA** (Pa)

22 *M^{3}F H13*
GIBEAGLE Bl/Fi (Crichton-Vulcan) 1961; Cem; 1,729 grt/2,548 dwt; 90.84 × 4.95 m *(298.03 × 16.24 ft)*; M (Sulzer); 12.5 kts; ex-*Granvik*

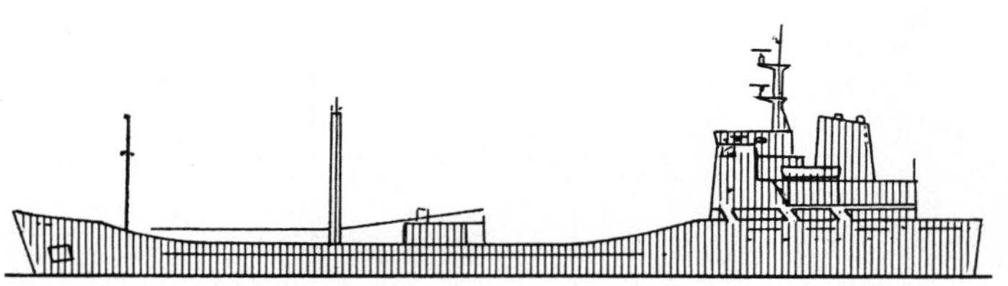

23 *M^{3}F H13*
GOLDEN BAY Pa/Br (Robb Caledon) 1979; Cem; 3,165 grt/4,493 dwt; 97.9 × 5.65 m *(321.19 × 18.54 ft)*; M (Ruston); 14 kts

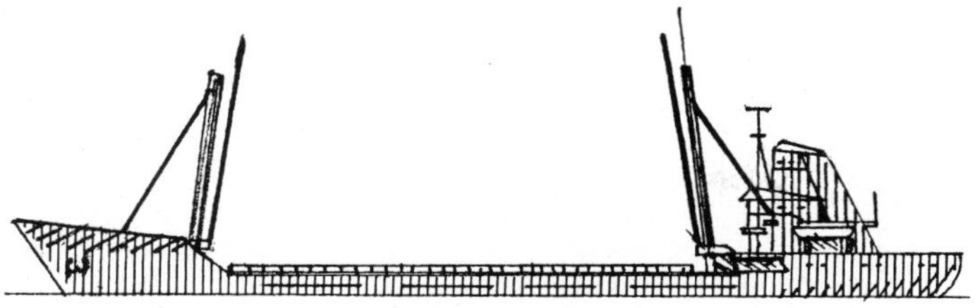

24 *M^3F H13*
NIKOS II Pa/Ne (Zaanlandsche) 1969; C/HL; 1,739 grt/3,676 dwt; 77.65 × 5.5 m *(254.76 × 18.04 ft)*; M (Atlas-MaK); 12 kts; ex-*Daniella*; Tripod heavy-lift masts

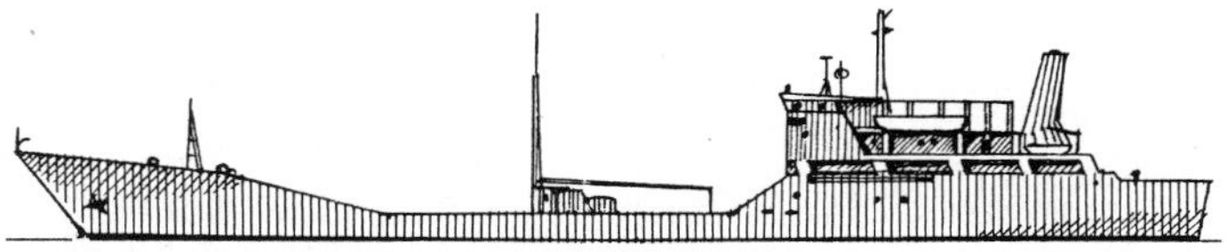

25 *M^3F H13*
TERCEIRENSE Po/No (Ankerlokken) 1973; Cem; 2,929 grt/4,156 dwt; 98.66 × 5.51 m *(323.69 × 18.08 ft)*; M (Polar); 14 kts; ex-*Cement King*

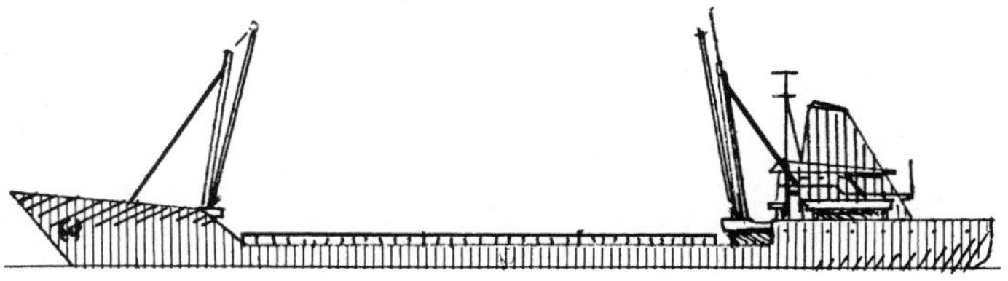

26 *M^3F H13*
YERIMU Pa/Ne (Zaanlandsche) 1969; C/HL; 1,739 grt/2,539 dwt; 78.72 × 5.5 m *(258.27 × 18.04 ft)*; M (Atlas-MaK); 12.5 kts; ex-*Fairlift*; Tripod heavy-lift masts

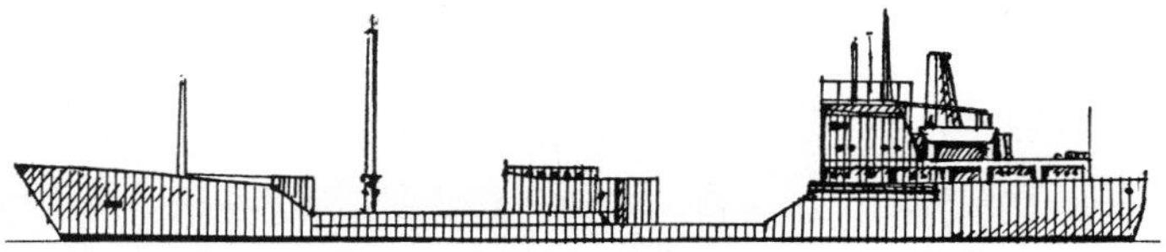

27 *M^3FR H13*
CEMBALO Bs/FRG (Sietas) 1973; Cem; 2,583 grt/3,252 dwt; 84.89 × 6.72 m *(278.51 × 22.05 ft)*; M (Normo); 14 kts; ex-*Cembulk*; Deepened 1986

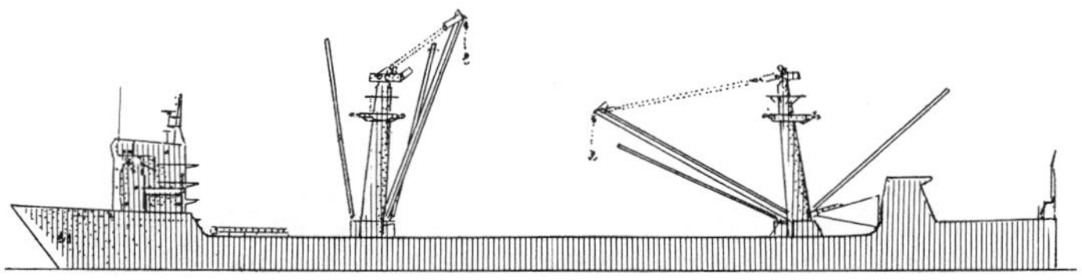

28 *M^3GY H13*
PROJECT AMERICAS NA/FRG (M Jansen) 1979; RoC/HL; 9,019 grt/12,811 dwt; 138.95 × 8.5 m *(455.87 × 27.89 ft)*; M (Atlas-MaK); 17.75 kts; Stern door/ramp; 454 TEU; Heavy-lift masts are on starboard side
Sisters: **PROJECT ORIENT** (NA); **PROJECT ARABIA** (NA)

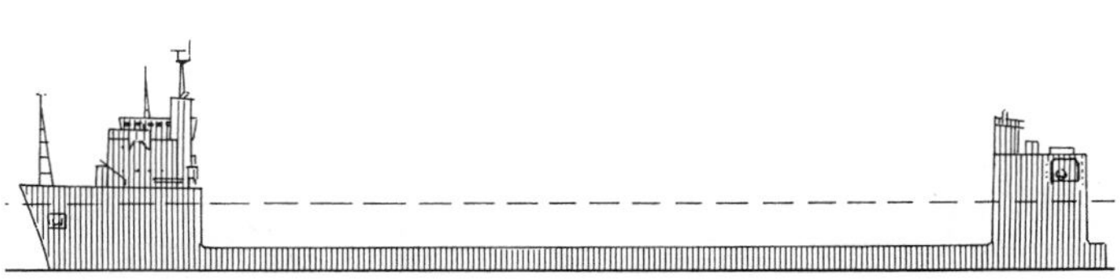

29 *M^3G–SG H13*
SUPER SERVANT 3 NA/Ja (Oshima Z) 1982; RoC/SSDC; 10,224 grt/14,138 dwt; 139.91 × 6.26 m *(459 × 20.54 ft)*; TSM (Stork-Werkspoor); 13 kts; Semi-submersible—broken line indicates maximum extent of immersion
Sister: **SUPER SERVANT 4** (NA)

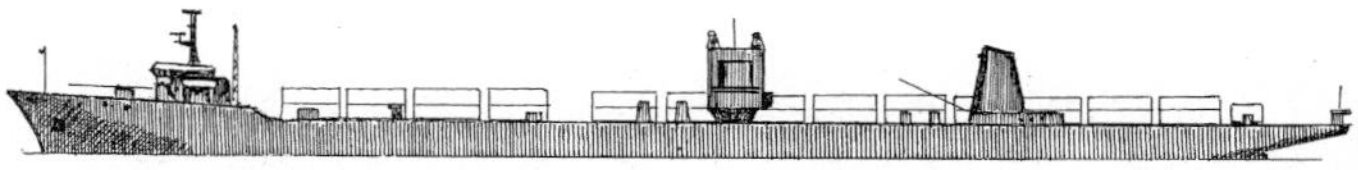

30 *M^3KG H1*
RHINE FOREST Li/Be (Cockerill) 1972; Bg/Con; 35,826 grt/35,280 dwt; 261.42 × 11.27 m *(857.68 × 36.98); M (Sulzer); 18 kts; ex-Bilderdyk*; 'Lash' type; Travelling gantry crane

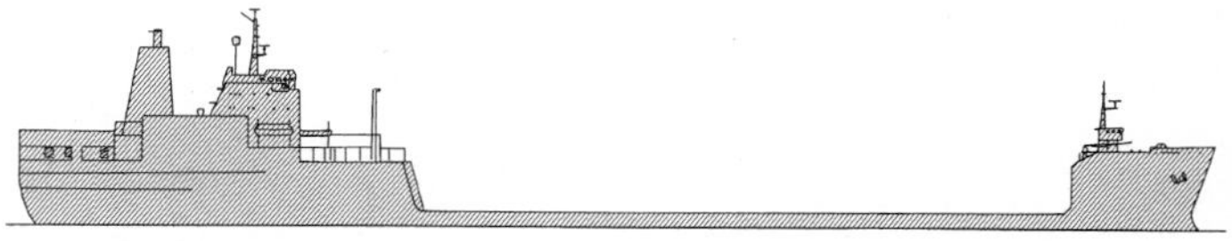

31 *M^4F H13*
AMERICAN CORMORANT US/Sw (Eriksbergs) 1975/82; SSDC; 38,571 grt/52,092 dwt; 225.08 × 10.55 m *(738.45 × 34.61 ft)*; M (B&W); 16 kts; ex-*Kollbris*; Converted from tanker and shortened 1982

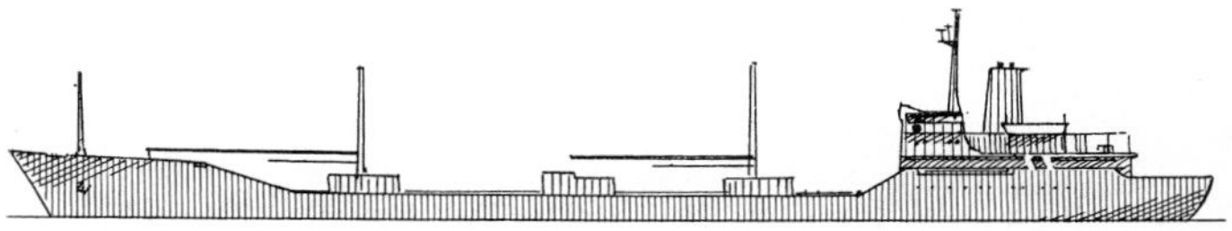

32 *M^4FR H13*
ELBIA Pa/FRG (Sietas) 1978; Cem; 8,323 grt/14,100 dwt; 135.01 × 8.02 m *(442.95 × 26.31 ft)*; M (KHD); — kts
Similar: **ASPIA** (Pa); **FLORIA** (Pa)

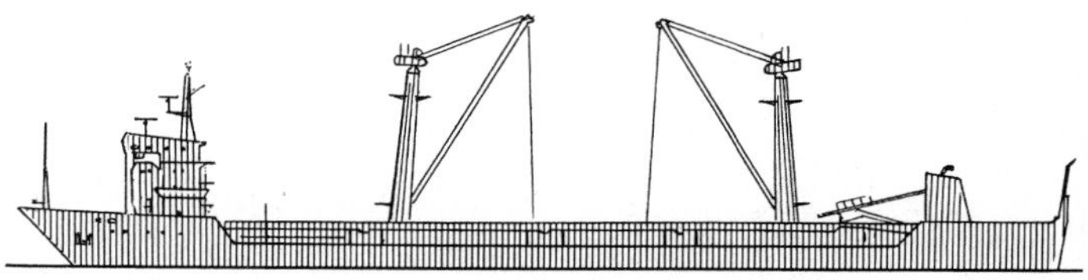

33 *M^4FY H13*
TITAN SCAN NA/FRG (Husumer) 1982; RoC/C/HL; 7,591 grt/9,864 dwt; 123.35 × 7.73 m *(404.69 × 25.36 ft)*; M (Krupp-MaK); 15 kts; Stern door/ramp; 444 TEU; Heavy-lift masts and funnel are on starboard side
Sister: **THOR SCAN** (NA)

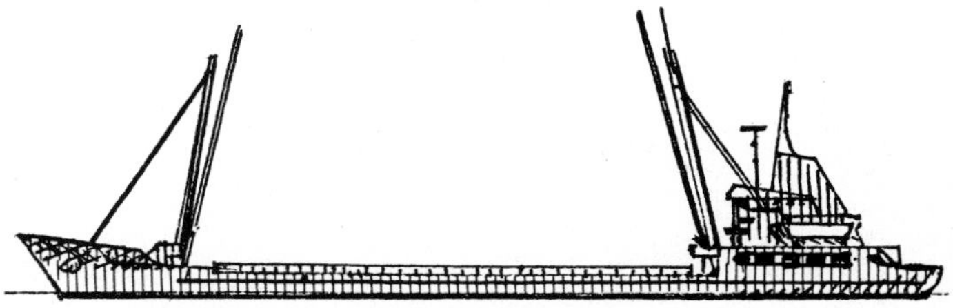

34 *M^3M–F H1*
RIBUAN JAYA My/Ne (Zaanlandsche) 1968; C/HL; 1,466 grt/2,509 dwt; 70.9 × 5.5 m *(232.61 × 18.04 ft)*; M (Atlas-MaK); 12.5 kts; ex-*Stellanova*; Heavy-lift masts are tripods

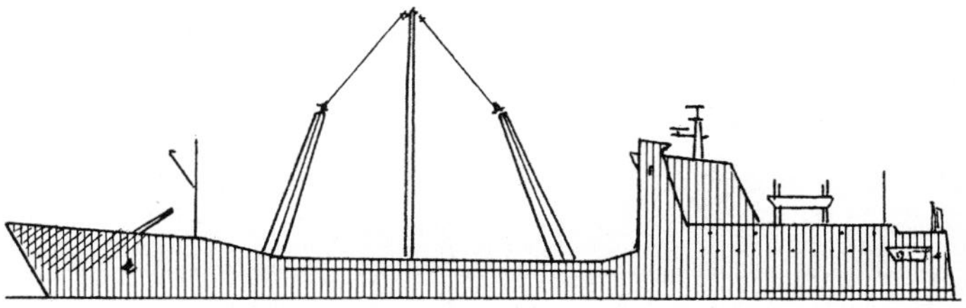

35 *M^3M–FY H13*
STAR OF AMERICA Bz/Br (Brooke) 1974; RoC/HL; 2,515 grt/2,087 dwt; 93.63 × 4.13 m *(307.19 × 13.55 ft)*; TSM (W H Allen); 12 kts; ex-*Starman*; First mast is on starboard side; Large, angled masts are on port side and funnel is on port side, adjacent to superstructure on starboard

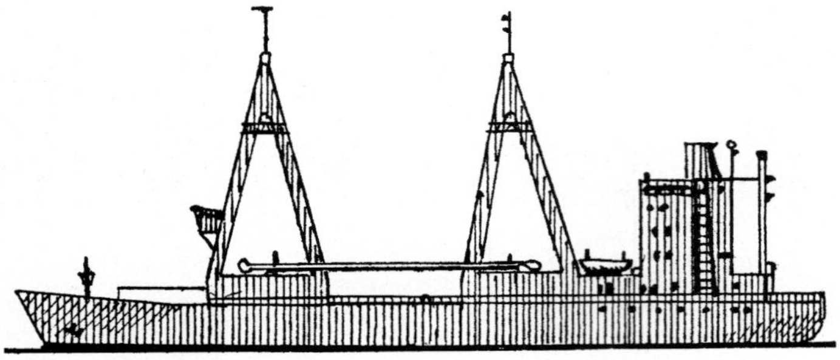

36 *M^2M–FM H*
STORMAN ASIA NA/FRG (Luehring) 1977; RoC/HL; 3,032 grt/2,487 dwt; 80.37 × 4.15 m *(263.68 × 13.62 ft)*; TSM (SKL); 10 kts; ex-*Gloria Virentium*; Stern ramp; Total lifting capacity 800 tons; Heavy-lift masts are quadpods and are on starboard side; Funnel and mast aft also on starboard side

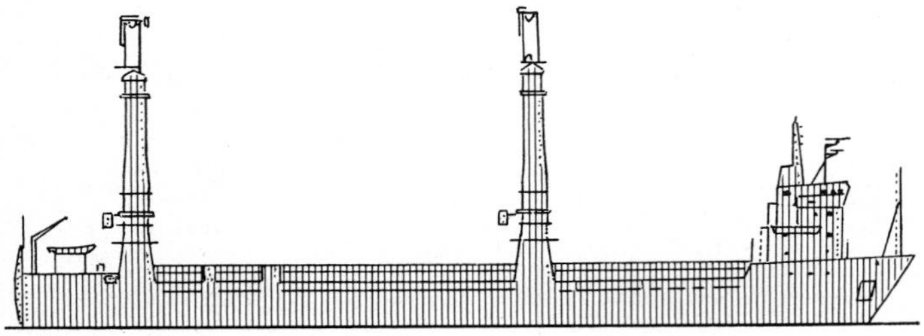

37 *M^2M–FM^2RY*
GRUZ Ma/Ne (Ysselwerf) 1986; RoC/HL/Dk; 5,952 grt/4,244 dwt; 104.02 × 4.87 m *(341.27 × 15.98 ft)*; TSM (Wärtsilä); 12 kts; Stern door/ramp; 242 TEU; Heavy-lift masts are on starboard side

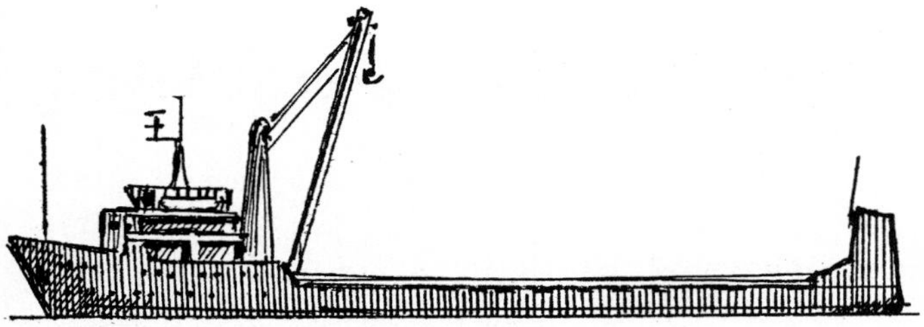

38 *M^2NG–Y H1*
STORM It/FRG (M Jansen) 1977; RoC/HL; 2,582 grt/2,015 dwt; 93.53 × 4.65 m *(306.85 × 15.25 ft)*; TSM (KHD); 12 kts; ex-*Starman Africa*; Stern door/ramp
Sister: **LAPAD** (Ma) ex-*Starman Anglia*

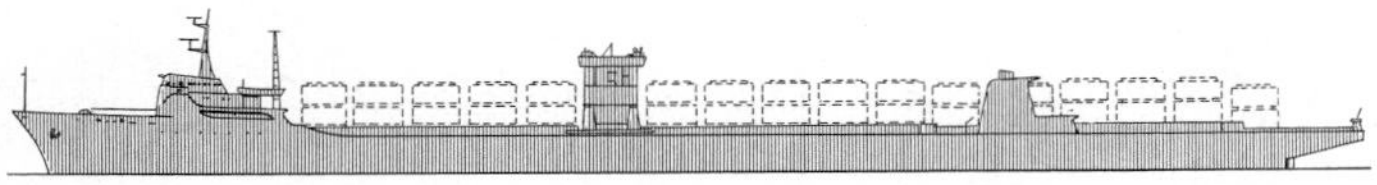

39 *M^2NKG H1*
ACADIA FOREST Li/Ja (Sumitomo) 1969; Bg; 36,021 grt/49,835 dwt; 261.42 × 12.20 m *(857.68 × 40.03 ft)*; TSM (Sulzer); 18 kts; 'LASH' type; Travelling crane
Sister: **JEB STUART** (US) ex-*Atlantic Forest*

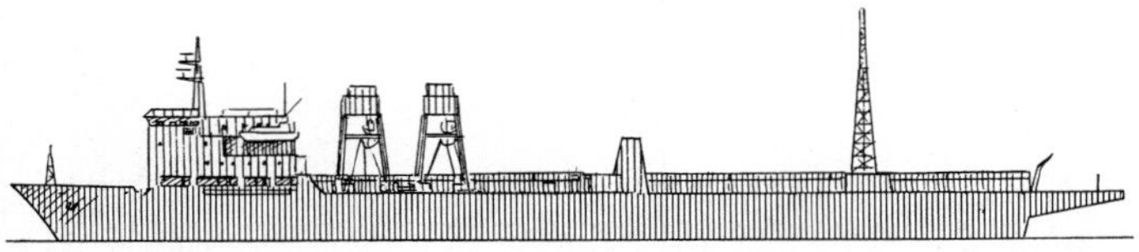

40 *M^2NK^2GH H*
STAKHANOVETSKKOTOV Ru/Fi (Hollming) 1978; RoC/Dk; 4,026 grt/5,717 dwt; 139.40 × 6.28 m *(457.35 × 20.60 ft)*; TSM (Pielstick); 14.25 kts; Stern door/ramp; 286 TEU
Sisters: **STAKHANOVETS PETRASH** (Uk); **STAKHANOVETS YERMOLENKO** (Ru)

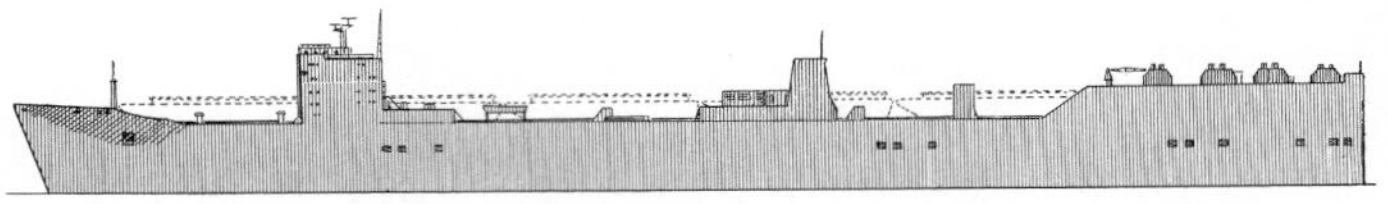

41 *M^2NM–G H13*
YULIUS FUCHIK Uk/Fi (Valmet) 1978; Bg/Con; 35,817 grt/37,850 dwt; 266.45 × 11 m *(874.18 × 36.09 ft)*; TSM (Pielstick); 20 kts; Lifting platform aft
Sister: **TIBOR SZAMUELI** (Uk)

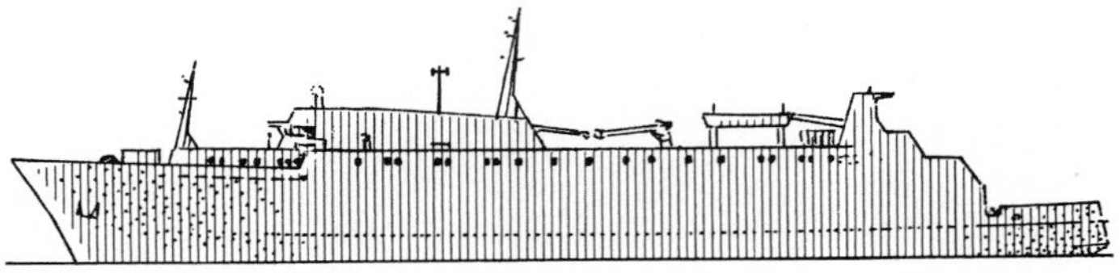

42 *M^2R^2G–R H1*
MURRAY EXPRESS Pi/No (Trosvik) 1968; LS; 4,255 grt/1,388 dwt; 92 × 4.74 m *(301.84 × 15.55 ft)*; TSM (Atlas-MaK); 15 kts; ex-*Mandeville*; Converted from RoRo cargo 1980 (Meyer)

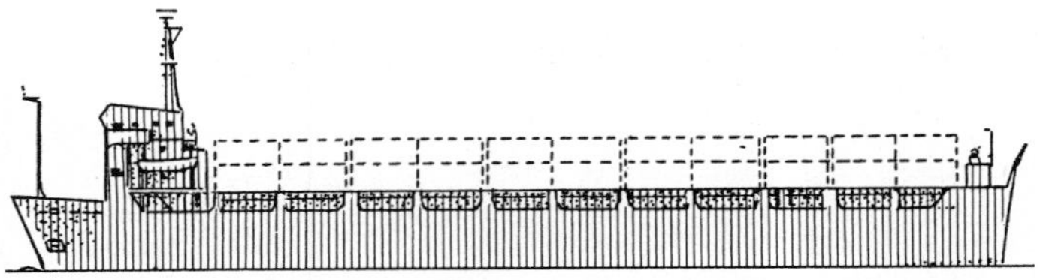

43 *M^2Y H3*
CONDOCK I NA/FRG (Nobiskrug) 1979; Dk/Con/RoC; 4,939 grt/3,603 dwt; 92.4 × 4.58 m *(303.15 × 15.03 ft)*; TSM (Atlas-MaK); 12.25 kts; Stern door/ramp; 383 TEU
Similar (longer—106m (348ft)): **CONDOCK III** (Ge)

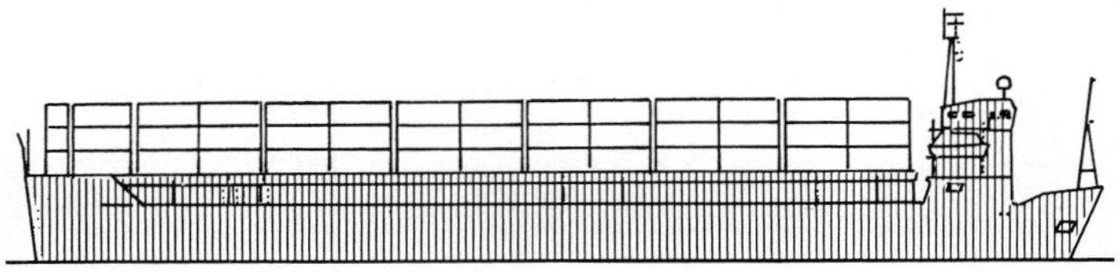

44 *M^2Y H3*
CONDOCK V Ge/FRG (Nobiskrug) 1984; Bg/Dk/RoC; 6,763 grt/4,762 dwt; 106.03 × 4.97 m *(347.87 × 16.31 ft)*; TSM (MaK); 13.25 kts; ex-*Este Submerger I*; Stern door/ramp; 478 TEU; has a low funnel level with hatch covers on port side, about three-quarters aft

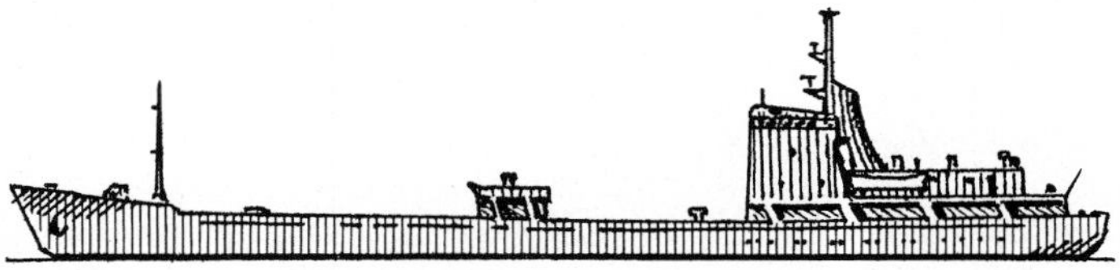

45 *MM–F H1*
CONTRADER Pa/Fi (Crichton-Vulcan) 1965; Cem; 2,233 grt/3,230 dwt; 90.33 × 5.77 m *(296.36 × 18.93 ft)*; M (Nydqvist & Holm); 13 kts; ex-*Malarvik*
Sister: **VASTANVIK** (Sw)

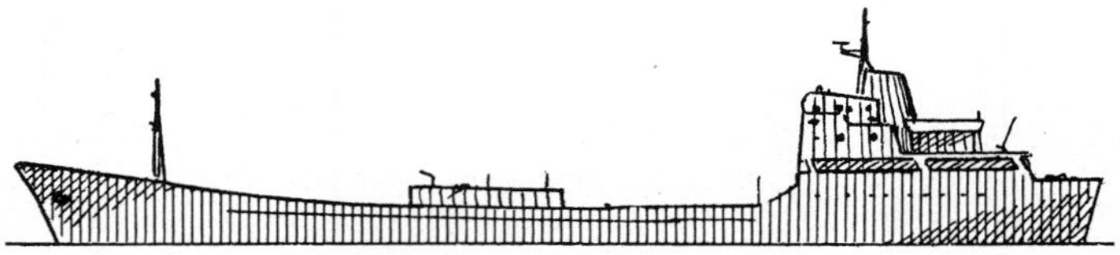

46 *MM–F H13*
VILOMAR Ms/Sp (Musel) 1977; Cem; 1,819 grt/2,558 dwt; 81.46 × 5.11 m *(267.26 × 16.77 ft)*; M (Deutz); 12 kts; ex-*Comandante Vilo Acuna*

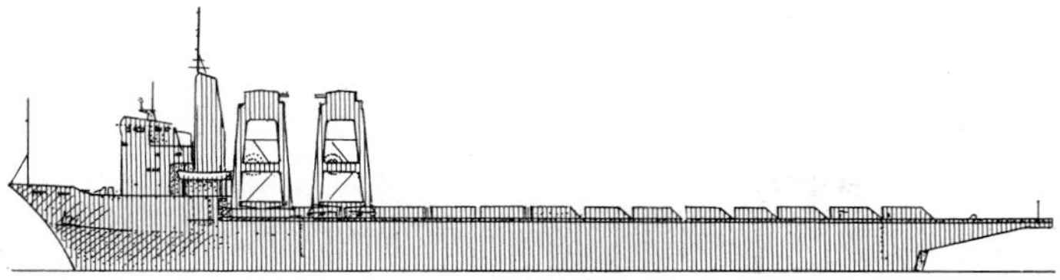

47 *MM–GK^2 H1*
DOCK EXPRESS 10 NA/Ne (Verolme S H) 1979; Dk/RoC/HL; 13,110 grt/12,928 dwt; 153.76 × 8.9 m *(504.46 × 29.2 ft)*; TSM (Stork-Werkspoor); 16 kts; Stern door
Sisters: **DOCK EXPRESS 11** (NA); **DOCK EXPRESS 12** (NA)

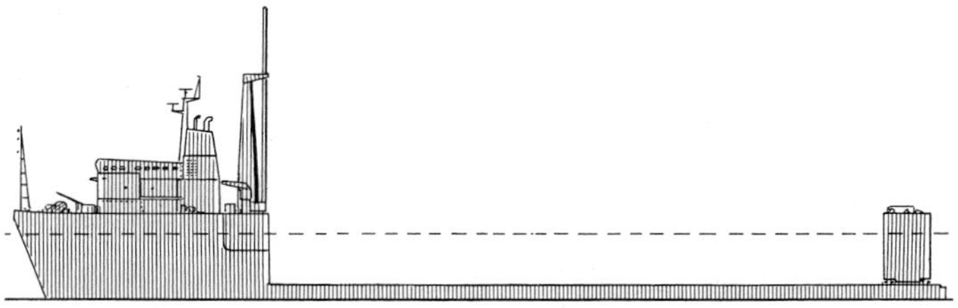

48 *MM–GT H1*
MIGHTY SERVANT 1 NA/Ja (Oshima Z) 1983; SSDC/RoC; 19,954 grt/23,473 dwt; 160.2 × 9.51 m *(525.59 × 31.2 ft)*; TS D-E (Stork-Werkspoor); 14.25 kts; Broken line shows maximum immersion
Sisters (longer): **MIGHTY SERVANT 2** (NA) (170.36m (558.92ft)); **MIGHTY SERVANT 3** (NA) (180.50m (592.19ft))

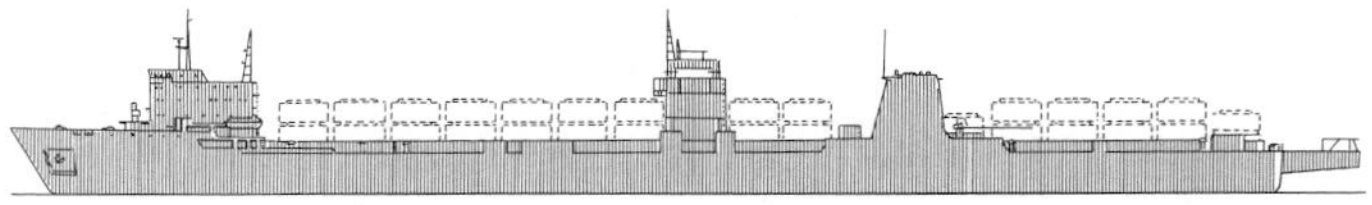

49 *MND–KG H12*
ALEKSEY KOSYGIN Ru/USSR (Kherson) 1984; Bg/IB/Con; 37,464 grt/40,881 dwt; 262.82 × 11.65 m *(862.27 × 38.22 ft)*; TSM (B&W); 18.4 kts
Sisters: **INDIRA GANDHI** (Uk); **LE DUAN** (Ru) (may be spelt **LE ZUAN**); **ERNESTO CHE GUEVARA** (Uk)

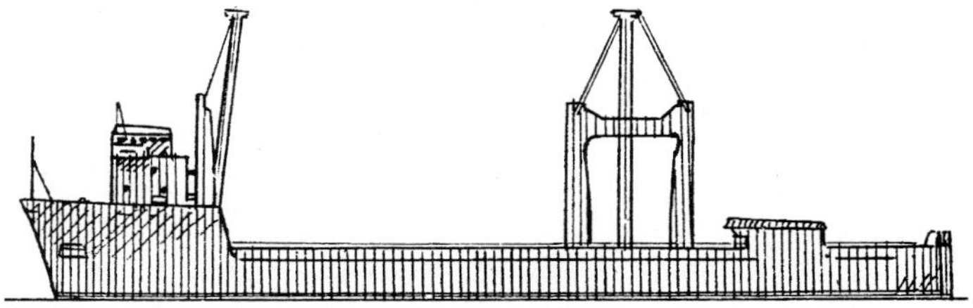

50 *MNH^{2}GY H1*
HANDY RIDER Kn/Ne (Arnhemsche/Stami) 1976; RoC/HL; 1,436 grt/2,766 dwt; 81.82 × 5.55 m *(268.43 × 18.2 ft)*; TSM (Stork-Werkspoor); 12 kts; ex-*Happy Rider*; Quarter stern door/ramp; The heavy-lift masts are goalposts, the second one being set fore-and-aft
Sister: **STRONG TEXAN** (US) ex-*Happy Runner*

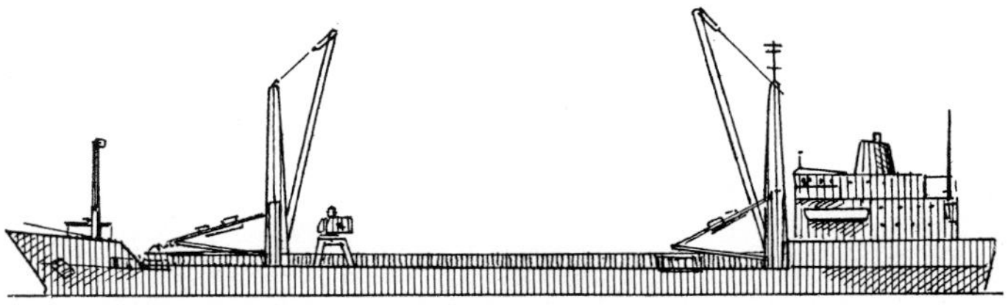

51 *MNJNFN H13*
CLIPPER CHEROKEE Fr/FRG (S&B) 1975; C/HL; 3,971 grt/5,397 dwt; 105.42 × 6.3 m *(345.87 × 20.67 ft)*; M (Atlas-MaK); 11.5 kts; ex-*Internavis 1*; 198 TEU

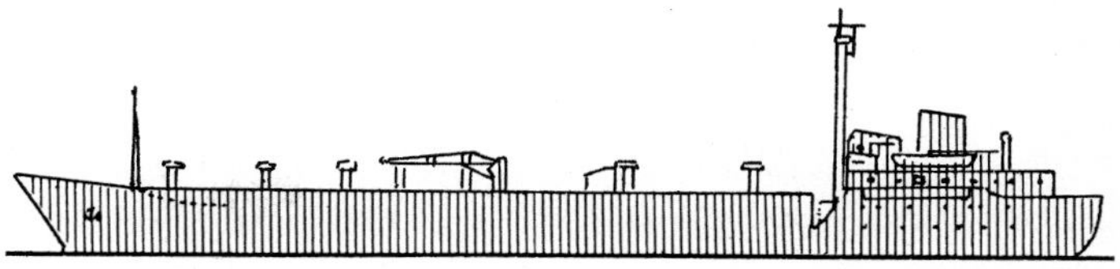

52 *MRHF H*
ADELE DIS/FRG (Sietas) 1967/81; LS; 2,471 grt/2,419 dwt; 89.26 × 5.84 m *(292.84 × 19.16 ft)*; M (MAN); 14.5 kts; ex-*Huelva*; Converted from general cargo and lengthened 1981
Sister: **ALONDRA** (DIS) ex-*Algarve*

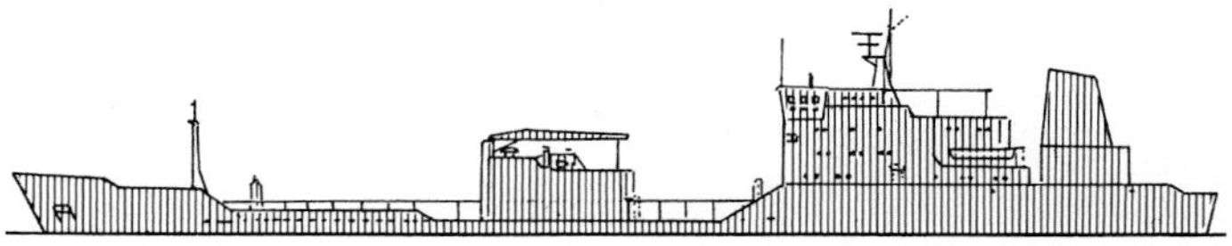

53 *MRMF H13*
FRIDA Pa/De (Dannebrog) 1985; Cem; 5,707 grt/7,682 dwt; 118.93 × 7.1 m *(390.19 × 23.29 ft)*; M (Krupp-MaK); 14 kts; ex-*Norden*; Self-unloader

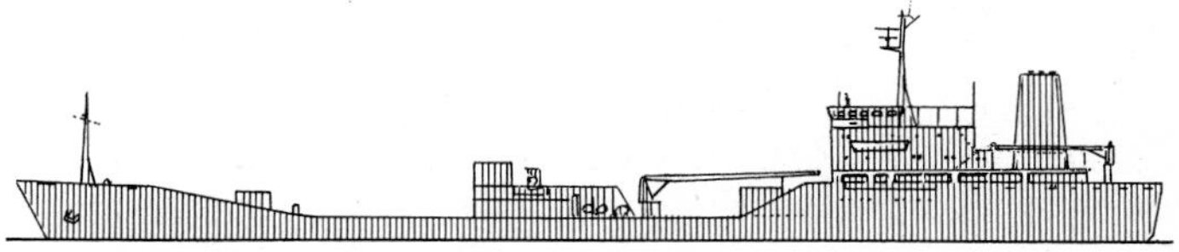

54 *MRMFR H13*
GLORIA ELENA Pa/FRG (Sietas) 1981; Cem; 7,899 grt/13,700 dwt; 136 × 8.11 m *(446 × 26.61 ft)*; M (B&W); 15 kts; Self-unloader

55 *MRMSF H13*
GOLIATH Au/Ko (Hanjin HI) 1993; Cem; 11,754 grt/15,539 dwt; 143.00 × 8.31 m *(469.16 × 27.26 ft)*; M (Sulzer); — kts; Self-unloader

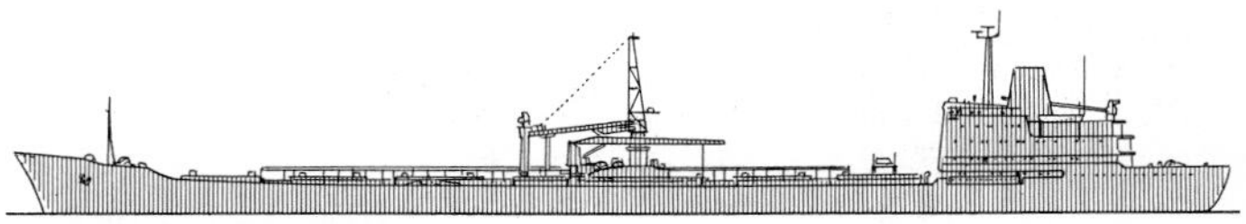

56 *MR–XMFMC H13*
HELVETIA Pa/Bu (G Dimitrov) 1980/81; B/Cem; 16,235 grt/24,000 dwt; 184.61 × 10.31 m *(606 × 33.83 ft)*; M (Sulzer); — kts; Converted from bulk carrier 1981 (Sietas); Self-unloader

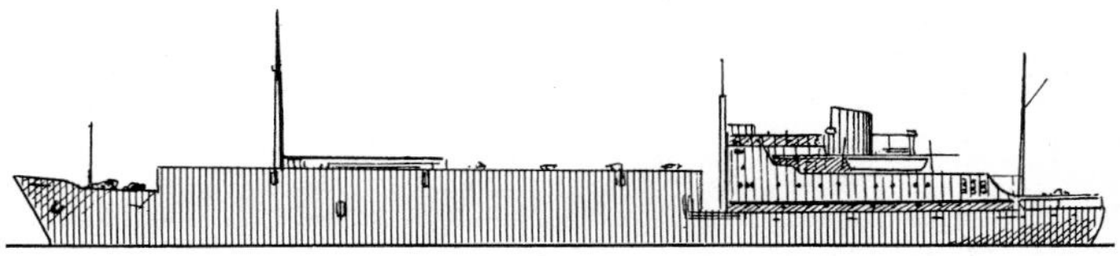

57 *MTHFM H12*
GALLOWAY EXPRESS Pi/Ne (Giessen) 1960/77; LS; 3,442 grt/3,130 dwt; 119.49 × 6.41 m *(392.03 × 21.03 ft)*; M (Stork); 15 kts; ex-*Ladon*; Converted from general cargo 1977 (Meyer)

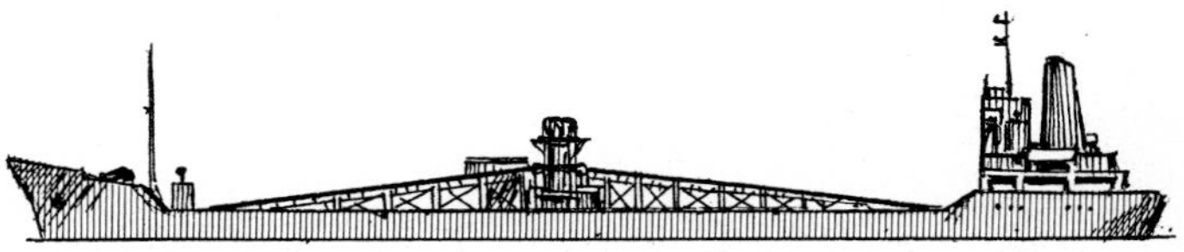

58 *MXMF H13*
DARUMASUN Pa/Ja (Setoda) 1970; Cem; 7,008 grt/10,352 dwt; 131.5 × 7.82 m *(431.43 × 25.66 ft)*; M (B&W); 12.75 kts; ex-*Chikuma Maru*; Self-unloader

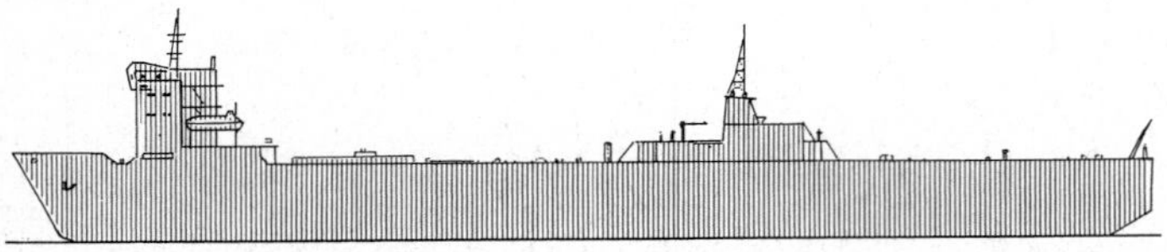

59 *M–NH–GY H*
BORIS POLEVOY Uk/Fi (Valmet) 1984; Bg/RoC/Dk; 10,684 grt/8,638 dwt; 158.91 × 4.3 m *(521.36 × 14.11 ft)*; TSM (Wärtsilä); 13.5 kts; Can carry containers (855 TEU); Stern ramp
Sister: **PAVEL ANTOKOLSKIY** (Uk)

See photo number 21/85

60 *RM^{2}FMS H13*
SEA SWAN Cy/No (Kaldnes) 1981; SSDC/Tk; 22,788 grt/30,060 dwt; 180.96 × 9.46 m *(594 × 31.04 ft)*; M (B&W); 16 kts; ex-*Dyvi Swan*
Sister: **SEA SWIFT** (Cy) ex-*Dyvi Swift* (builder—Samsung); Similar (tripod radar mast and satcom aerial on superstructure): **SEA TEAL** (Cy) ex-*Dyvi Teal* (builder—Samsung); **SEA TERN** (Cy) ex-*Dyvi Tern*

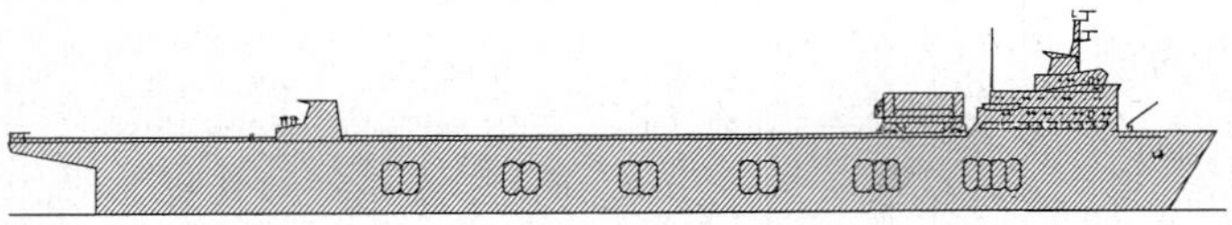

61 *RM–FKG H*
EASTGATE Li/Sp (AESA) 1983/88; Con; 19,579 grt/11,434 dwt; 193.91 × 5.00 m *(636.19 × 16.40 ft)*; TSM (Pielstick); 13.5 kts; ex-*Josefa Torres*; 616 TEU; Drawing shows vessel in its original form as a barge carrier/dock ship; Probably has alterations now

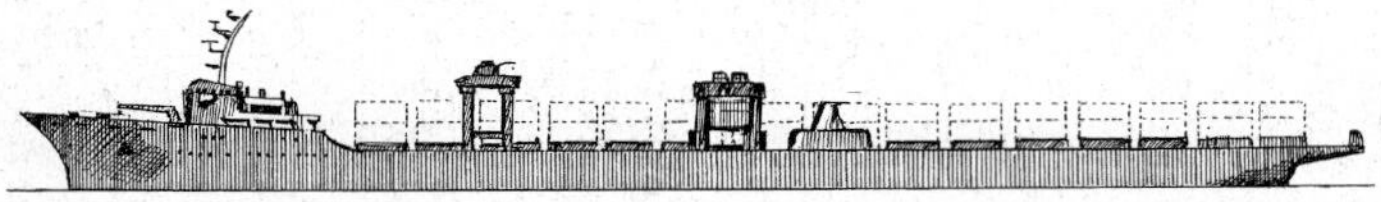

62 *SMK^{2}G H1*
LASH ATLANTICO US/US (Avondale) 1972; Bg/Con; 26,406 grt/30,298 dwt; 250 × 10.7 m *(820 × 35.5 ft)*; T (De Laval); 22.5 kts; Travelling gantry cranes
Sisters (overall lengths vary): **CAPE FEAR**(US) ex-*Lash Espana*; **AMERICAN VETERAN** (US) ex-*Philippine Bear*; **CAPE FAREWELL** (US) ex-*Delta Mar*; **CAPE FLATTERY** (US) ex-*Delta Norte*; **CAPE FLORIDA** (US) ex-*Lash Turkiye*

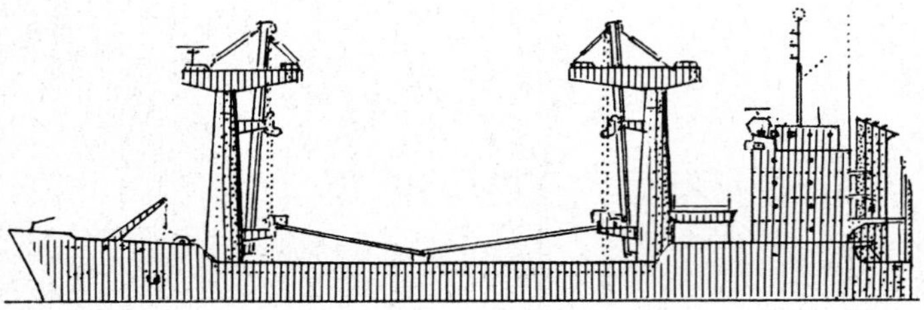

63 *ST^{2}MFY H12*
PISHVA Ir/FRG (Luerssen) 1977; RoC/HL; 3,483 grt/3,010 dwt; 91.5 × 5.17 m *(300.2 × 16.96 ft)*; TSM (MWM); 12 kts; ex-*Stahleck*; Bow door and ramp; Stern ramps
Similar (built in USA—Peterson. US Government owned): **JOHN HENRY** (US); **JAMES McHENRY** (US) ex-*Paul Bunyan*

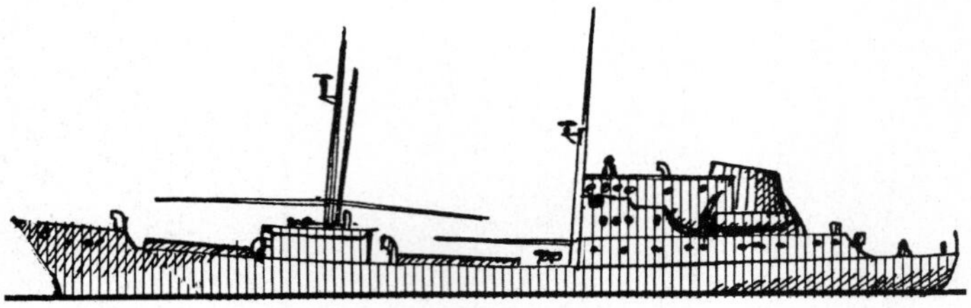

64 *THF H*
RAS-HALAGUE Pa/Br (A Hall) 1955; LS; 941 grt/1,052 dwt; 74.38 × 4.29 m *(244.03 × 14.07 ft)*; M (Sulzer); 13 kts; ex-*St Rognvald*

65 *TMFC^2 H1*
AL-KHALEEJ Ku/Sw (Oresunds) 1965/75/78; LS; 10,107 grt/10,208 dwt; 170.64 × 8.78 m *(559.8 × 28.81 ft)*; M (Gotaverken); 19.5 kts; ex-*White Ocean*; Converted from reefer 1975 (Taikoo); Lengthened 1978 (Hong Kong U)

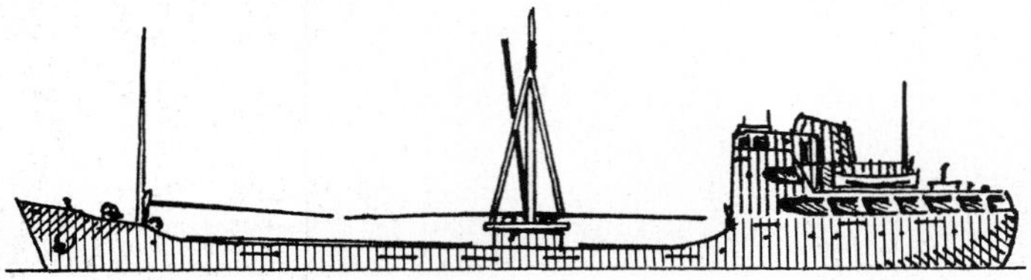

66 *TMFM H13*
MULTI SERVICE 125 UAE/Ne (Groot & VV) 1957; C/HL; 1,456 grt/2,010 dwt; 77.5 × 4.7 m *(254.27 × 15.42 ft)*; M (Werkspoor); 10.5 kts; ex-*Gloria Maris*; Heavy-lift tripod mast amidships

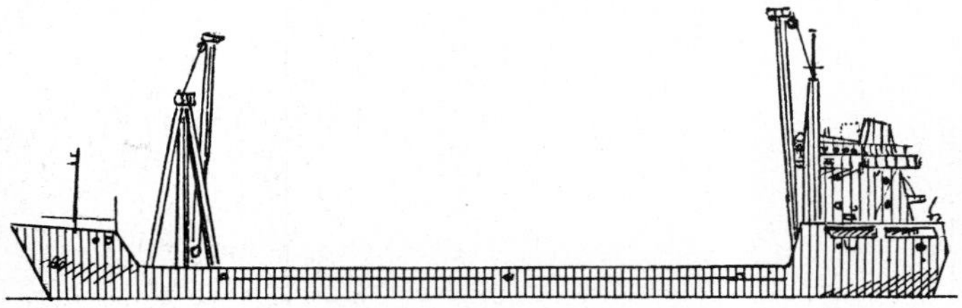

67 *VH^{2}FR H13*
KUPARI Ma/Ne ('De Waal') 1979; HL/C; 2,044 grt/2,720 dwt; 81.45 × 4.9 m *(267.22 × 16.08 ft)*; M (Bolnes); 12.75 kts; ex-*Enak*; Kingpost in well has six legs and is on a travelling gantry
Sisters: **PLITVICE** (Ma) ex-*Elger* (travelling kingpost may not be fitted); **TINA** (At) ex-*Eldir*

HEAVY-LIFT SHIPS

68 Kibi *(Pa); 1994* *"Sea Japan"—Japan Ship Exporters' Association*

69 Hamilton K *(Cy); 1974* *FotoFlite*

70 Plitvice *(Ma); 1979* *FotoFlite*

71 Carabao 1 *(Sg); 1974; (as Stril Lift)* *FotoFlite*

72 Medglory *(Ma); 1977; (as Fairlane)* *FotoFlite*

73 Pishva *(Ir); 1977; (as Starman Australia)* *FotoFlite*

74 Storman Asia *(NA); 1977* *FotoFlite*

75 Jumbo Challenger *(NA); 1983/86* *FotoFlite*

HEAVY-LIFT SHIPS (continued)

76 Happy Buccaneer *(Ne); 1984* *FotoFlite*

77 Gruz *(Ma); 1986* *FotoFlite*

78 Fairlift *(Ne); 1990* *FotoFlite*

79 Fairload *(Ne); 1995* *FotoFlite*

80 Lapad *(Ma); 1978* *FotoFlite*

81 Titan Scan *(NA); 1982* *FotoFlite*

82 Project Arabia *(NA); 1982* *FotoFlite*

83 Strong Texan *(US); 1976* *FotoFlite*

HEAVY-LIFT SHIPS (continued)

84 Clipper Cherokee *(Fr); 1975* *FotoFlite*

SEMI-SUBMERSIBLE HEAVY-LIFT

85 Sea Tern *(Cy); 1982* *FotoFlite*

86 Transshelf *(Ru); 1987* *FotoFlite*

87 Mighty Servant 3 *(NA); 1984* *FotoFlite*

88 Super Servant 4 *(NA); 1982* *FotoFlite*

89 American Cormorant *(US); 1975/82* *FotoFlite*

DOCK SHIPS

90 Spruce *(Li); 1975/78* *FotoFlite*

91 Sha He Kou *(RC); 1978; (as Mammoth Willow)* *WSPL*

DOCK SHIPS (continued)

92 Dock Express 20 *(NA); 1983; (now converted to cable ship)* *FotoFlite*

93 Condock I *(NA); 1979* *FotoFlite*

94 Condock V *(Ge); 1984* *FotoFlite*

95 Stakhanovets Kotov *(Ru); 1978* *FotoFlite*

BARGE CARRIERS

96 Green Island *(US); 1975* *WSPL*

97 Rhine Forest *(Li); 1972* *FotoFlite*

98 Acadia Forest *(Li); 1969* *FotoFlite*

99 Le Duan *(Uk); 1987* *FotoFlite*

BARGE CARRIERS (continued)

100 Yulius Fuchik *(Uk); 1978* *FotoFlite*

101 Pavel Antokolskiy *(Uk); 1984* *FotoFlite*

102 Baco-Liner 3 *(Ge); 1984* *FotoFlite*

DECK CARGO SHIPS

103 Penang Jaya *(Pi); 1978; (as Gulf Bridge)* *WSPL*

104 Seahorse 1 *(Sg); 1983; (as Snimos Ace)* *FotoFlite*

CEMENT CARRIERS

105 Kongsdal *(De); 1980* *FotoFlite*

106 Frida *(Pa); 1985; (as Norden)* *FotoFlite*

107 Invicta *(Pa); 1983* *FotoFlite*

CEMENT CARRIERS (continued)

108 Cem River *(NIS); 1972; (as Arklow River)* *FotoFlite*

109 Cemenmar Cuatro *(Sp); 1975* *FotoFlite*

110 Islas Dos *(Pa); 1975* *FotoFlite*

LIVESTOCK CARRIERS

111 Siba Brescia *(Pa); 1967/82* *FotoFlite*

112 El Novillo *(Pa); 1966/79* *FotoFlite*

113 Siba Geru *(It); 1964/80* *FotoFlite*

114 Estancia *(Ma); 1975/84; (as Siba Aprica)* *FotoFlite*

115 Alpha Livestock 19 *(Ho); 1970/83; (as Rabunion XIX)* *FotoFlite*

LIVESTOCK CARRIERS (continued)

116 Betta Livestock 17 *(Ho); 1971/79; (as Rabunion XVII)* *FotoFlite*

120 Kerry Express *(Pi); 1968/81* *FotoFlite*

117 Benwalid *(Tu); 1973/85* *FotoFlite*

121 Murray Express *(Pi); 1968/80* *FotoFlite*

118 Alondra *(DIS); 1967/80* *FotoFlite*

122 Angus Express *(Pi); 1967/88* *FotoFlite*

119 Galloway Express *(Pi); 1960/77* *FotoFlite*

123 El Cordero *(Pa); 1967/82* *FotoFlite*

Index

	SHIP TYPE	REF NO	PAGE NO
1 Congreso Del Partido	8	500	(241)
3 Maj	1	112	(10)
15 May	9	6	(263)
18 de Marzo	2	450	(59)
50 Letiye Sovietskoy Gruzii	2	469	(60)
60 Let Oktyabrya	11	102	(308)
A Alamdar	7	82	(162)
Aasland	6	42	(144)
Aastun	9	200	(279)†
Aastun	9	22	(264)
Abakan	7	14	(158)
Abant	2	464	(59)
Abava	2	414	(56)
Abbey	5	58	(111)
Abdallah Bnou Yassine	11	61	(305)
Abdelrahman	7	220	(172)
Abdul Latif-S	8	68	(208)
Abdul M	8	675	(257)†
Abdul M	8	304	(227)
Abdul Rahman S	7	60	(161)
A Bedevi	8	404	(234)
Abeer S	8	527	(243)
Ability	2	536	(64)
Abitibi Claiborne	17	104	(416)†
Abitibi Claiborne	17	18	(406)
Abitibi Concord	7	19	(158)
Abitibi Macado	7	19	(158)
Abitibi Orinoco	17	18	(406)
Able Admiral	18	76	(427)
Aboitiz Concarrier XII	8	456	(238)
Aboitiz Superferry III	20	311	(482)
Abruka	7	11	(157)
Abu Egila	17	49	(409)
Abuqir	9	162	(275)
Aburdees	17	49	(409)
Abu Zenima	17	76	(412)†
Abu Zenima	17	49	(409)
Acacia	7	271	(176)
Acacio Mane Ela	20	278	(479)
Acadia Forest	21	98	(508)†
Acadia Forest	21	39	(502)
Acapulco	11	10	(301)
Accolade II	5	311	(129)
Accord	8	527	(243)
Ace Trader	2	124	(37)
Achatina	2	344	(51)
A Cheng	8	308	(227)
Achileas P	8	134	(213)
Achileus	2	455	(59)
Achilles	8	500	(241)
Achtergracht	7	267	(176)
Acila	1	167	(14)
Acina	2	480	(60)
Acor	13	72	(354)
Acoriano	8	362	(231)
Acritas	9	45	(266)
Active	7	146	(167)
ACX Apricot	12	17	(326)
ACX Canary	12	73	(330)
ACX Clover	12	35	(327)
ACX Lotus	12	64	(329)
ACX Robin	12	73	(330)
Adabelle Lykes	12	120	(334)
Ada Eze	2	239	(45)
Adalbert Antonov	5	172	(119)
Adalya	2	454	(59)
Adamantia	7	483	(192)
Adamas	10	35	(289)
Adamastos	7	103	(164)
Addarraq	2	78	(34)
Addiriyah	12	27	(327)
Adelaide	8	401	(234)
Adele	21	52	(503)
Adelia	3	37	(78)†
Adelia	3	21	(76)
Adeline Delmas	7	368	(183)
Aden	5	163	(118)
Aden	8	582	(248)
Adhiguna Muliamarga	8	265	(224)
Adhiguna Purnamaga	8	265	(224)
Adhiguna Rayamarga	8	265	(224)
Adib	7	179	(169)
Adige	19	86	(454)†
Adigeni	2	414	(56)
Aditya Kanti	7	186	(170)
Aditya Kiran	7	78	(162)
Aditya Prabha	7	222	(172)
Aditya Prakash	7	182	(169)
Adjaria	5	317	(129)
Admas	7	400	(186)
Admiralengracht	7	267	(176)
Admiral One	9	62	(267)

	SHIP TYPE	REF NO	PAGE NO
Admiralty Bay	2	306	(49)
Admiral Ushakov	5	131	(116)
Adnan	8	68	(208)
Adonis	2	343	(51)
Adonis	7	442	(189)
Adonis	8	100	(211)
Adra	9	60	(267)
Adrian	9	196	(279)†
Adrian	9	130	(273)
Adriana	7	196	(170)
Adriana	20	288	(480)
Adriatic	10	14	(288)
Adriatico 1	6	44	(144)
Adriatic Queen	10	96	(296)†
Adriatic Queen	10	56	(291)
Adriatic Star	5	263	(125)
Advantage	9	126	(272)
Adventure	8	670	(256)†
Adventure	8	24	(205)
Adventure I	10	22	(288)
Adventurer	8	61	(208)
Adygeja	2	178	(41)
Adzhariya	20	13	(460)
Aegean Breeze	19	65	(452)†
Aegean Dolphin	20	451	(496)†
Aegean Star	5	216	(122)
Aegean V	2	345	(51)
Aegna	8	582	(248)
Aeolic Reefer	11	128	(310)
Aerosmith	5	42	(110)
Afanasiy Bogatyrev	7	340	(181)
Afko 106	11	38	(303)
Africa	2	152	(39)
Africa	2	309	(49)
Africa	5	134	(116)
African Azalea	7	341	(181)
African Begonia	7	341	(181)
African Camellia	7	341	(181)
African Dahlia	7	341	(181)
African Evergreen	7	341	(181)
African Express	2	270	(46)
African Fern	7	341	(181)
African Gardenia	7	341	(181)
African Glory	8	395	(233)
African Highway	19	60	(451)†
African Hyacinth	2	482	(61)
African Pride	2	129	(38)
African Princess	11	31	(303)
African Queen	2	99	(36)
African Queen	11	31	(303)
African Reefer	11	119	(310)
African Star	11	143	(312)
Africa Star	9	183	(277)†
Africa Star	9	15	(264)
Afric Star	11	20	(302)
Afris Pioneer	9	139	(273)
Afris Wave	9	110	(271)
Afro Asia Star	9	15	(264)
Afrodite II	18	9	(421)
Afros	5	50	(110)
Afros	8	128	(213)
Agaete	8	195	(218)
Agamemnon	8	251	(223)
Agamemnon SB	8	135	(213)
Agapi	7	452	(190)
Agdal	17	40	(408)
Agent	8	61	(208)
Aggeliki P	5	2	(107)
Aghia Markella	5	148	(117)
Aghia Markella	7	154	(168)
Aghia Sophia	7	213	(172)
Aghia Trias	5	58	(111)
Aghios Minas	7	75	(162)
Aghios Rafael	8	17	(204)
Agia Eirini	7	124	(165)
Agia Fotia	5	42	(110)
Agia Kyriaki	21	5	(499)
Agia Methodia	7	20	(158)
Agia Philothei	7	72	(162)
Agia Sofia	7	222	(172)
Agia Thalassini	2	464	(59)
Agility	1	176	(14)
Agios Andreas	7	162	(168)
Agios Dionissos S	18	85	(428)
Agios Fanourios	8	312	(228)
Agios Gerassimos	8	500	(241)
Agios Ioannis	9	92	(270)
Agios Minas	5	42	(110)
Agios Nectarios	7	41	(160)
Agios Nikolaos	2	499	(62)
Agios Nikolaos	7	162	(168)
Agios Rafael	18	99	(429)
Agios Spyridon	8	559	(246)
Agios Spyridon	9	162	(275)
Agios Spyridon I	10	1	(287)
Agios Vassilos	20	324	(483)

†Photograph

	SHIP TYPE	REF NO	PAGE NO
Agios Vissarion	8	312	(228)
Agip Gela	2	305	(49)
Agip Liguria	1	129	(11)
Agip Lombardia	1	129	(11)
Agip Piemonte	1	129	(11)
Agnita	5	248	(124)
Agostinho Neto	16	14	(392)
Agrari	5	19	(108)
Agri	8	225	(221)
Agros	6	114	(153)†
Agros	6	8	(141)
Agrotai	8	578	(247)
Agulhas	9	163	(275)
Ahlers Belgica	7	305	(178)
Ahmad Al-fateh	9	127	(272)
Ahmad J	8	199	(218)
Ahmad S	7	293	(178)
Ahmed Arab	8	389	(233)
Ahmet Uzundemir	7	91	(163)
Ahmos	9	6	(263)
Ahora	7	94	(163)
Ahrenshoop	6	77	(148)†
Ahrenshoop	6	42	(144)
Ahtela	16	80	(399)†
Ahtela	16	16	(392)
Aida	19	7	(445)
Aide	8	61	(208)
Aifanourios	5	42	(110)
Ailsa	8	16	(204)
Ainazi	2	414	(56)
Aino	4	105	(94)
Ain Temouchent	7	232	(173)
Aire	2	551	(66)†
Aire F	9	88	(269)
Ais Nikolas	8	277	(225)
Aitape	11	60	(305)
Aitodor	7	82	(162)
Aivik	17	88	(414)†
Aivik	17	56	(409)
AJ1	9	159	(275)
Ajmer	8	6	(203)
Aka	5	157	(118)
Akademik Artsimovich	16	34	(394)
Akademik Bakulev	5	17	(108)
Akademik Blagonravov	5	17	(108)
Akademik Evgeniy Paton	7	136	(166)
Akademik Glushko	7	435	(188)
Akademik Gorbunov	16	14	(392)
Akademik Guber	16	34	(394)
Akademik Hesen Aliyev	20	287	(480)
Akademik Iosif Orbeli	9	28	(265)
Akademikis Artobolevskis	11	127	(310)
Akademikis Hohlovs	11	127	(310)
Akademikis Vavilovs	11	55	(304)
Akademikis Zavarickis	11	196	(317)†
Akademikis Zavarickis	11	55	(304)
Akademik Kuprevich	16	34	(394)
Akademik Mamedaliev	2	367	(53)
Akademik Millionschikov	16	34	(394)
Akademik M Topchubashov	20	287	(480)
Akademik Pozdyunin	7	152	(167)
Akademik Pustovoy	2	317	(50)
Akademik Raspletin	7	152	(167)
Akademik Sechenov	2	92	(35)
Akademik Semenov	1	107	(10)
Akademik Shukhov	9	28	(265)
Akademik Stechkin	16	93	(401)†
Akademik Stechkin	16	34	(394)
Akademik Tupolev	16	34	(394)
Akademik Yangel	9	80	(269)
Akademis Bocvars	11	54	(304)
Akademis Celomejs	11	54	(304)
Akaroa	11	60	(305)
Akbar	20	392	(488)
Akebono	2	562	(68)†
Akebono Star	11	69	(305)
Aker	7	222	(172)
Akhaltsikhe	2	414	(56)
Aknoul	16	16	(392)
Akoli	8	450	(238)
Akova	2	454	(59)
Akradina	1	88	(8)
Akragas	8	445	(237)
Akram V	8	554	(246)
Akra Sounion	7	69	(161)
Akrogiali	8	637	(252)
Aktash	2	222	(44)
Aktea	7	131	(166)
Akti	7	450	(189)
Aktyubinsk	2	414	(56)
Alaati Alaah	7	309	(179)
Alabama	13	92	(357)†
Alabama	13	41	(352)
Al-Aboud	20	359	(485)
Alacrity	1	176	(14)
Alacrity	12	47	(328)

	SHIP TYPE	REF NO	PAGE NO
Aladdin	2	479	(60)
Aladin	15	8	(377)
Al Ahamad	18	230	(442)†
Al Ahmadiah	12	56	(329)
Al-Ain	2	318	(50)
Al Aliyu	7	82	(162)
Alam Acapulco	7	452	(190)
Alam Aman	7	53	(160)
Alam Baru	5	226	(122)
Alaminos	8	500	(241)
Alam Mexico	7	452	(190)
Alamoot	1	28	(5)
Alam Sayang	7	213	(172)
Alam Sempurna	7	145	(167)
Alam Senang	7	145	(167)
Alam Tabah	8	24	(205)
Alam Talang	8	252	(223)
Alam Tangkas	8	24	(205)
Alam Tegas	8	252	(223)
Alam Teguh	8	252	(223)
Alam Teladan	8	252	(223)
Alam Tenaga	8	24	(205)
Alam Tenggiri	8	252	(223)
Alam Tenteram	8	252	(223)
Alam United	7	145	(167)
Alam University	7	145	(167)
Alan	5	139	(117)
Alan	8	500	(241)
Al Andalus	8	193	(218)
Alandia	20	193	(473)
Alandia Bay	2	307	(49)
Alandia Breeze	2	374	(53)
Alandia Force	2	479	(60)
Alandia Nord	2	594	(72)†
Alandia Orient	2	392	(55)
Alandia Pearl	2	474	(60)
Alandia Pride	2	474	(60)
Alandia Tide	2	563	(68)†
Alandia Wave	2	393	(55)
Alandsfarjan	20	290	(480)
Alanfushi	7	439	(189)
Alanya	10	83	(294)†
Alaska	7	212	(172)
Alaska	13	36	(351)
Alatyrles	8	589	(248)
Alba	9	50	(266)
Alba	18	138	(432)
Albacora Frigo Dos	11	41	(303)
Albacore	5	185	(120)
Al Badiyah	1	198	(16)
Al Bahr Al Sabah	8	76	(209)
Al Baky	8	24	(205)
Albarka-3	9	48	(266)
Al-Bashar	9	9	(263)
Al Bashir	8	514	(242)
Alba Star	11	70	(306)
Albatros	20	403	(490)†
Albatros	20	27	(461)
Albatross	7	54	(160)
Al Battani	8	508	(242)
Albebaran	9	92	(270)
Albemarle Island	11	117	(309)
Albemarle Island	11	122	(310)
Alberni Dawn	10	103	(297)†
Al Berry	4	40	(90)
Albert J	8	194	(218)
Alberto	8	541	(244)
Al Bida	4	40	(90)
Al-Bilal	8	596	(249)
Al Biruni	8	614	(250)
Albona	5	383	(137)†
Albona	5	287	(127)
Al Bushra	8	169	(216)
Alcaeos	20	291	(480)
Alchatby	7	439	(189)
Alcudia	2	495	(62)
Alcyon	7	225	(173)
Aldabra	9	100	(270)
Aldan	8	612	(250)
Aldanles	8	589	(248)
Aldebaran	8	228	(221)
Al Deerah	1	198	(16)
Alden W Clausen	1	77	(8)
Al Dhabbiyyah	1	158	(13)
Al Dhibyaniyyah	1	246	(21)†
Aldo Cecconi	5	3	(107)
Aldrington	5	80	(112)
Aledreesi	8	173	(216)
Aleiska	1	52	(6)
Alejandra	8	579	(247)
Aleko Konstantinov	9	93	(270)
Aleksander Aberg	5	17	(108)
Aleksander Kolmpere	5	129	(116)
Aleksandra Kollontay	11	82	(306)
Aleksandr Arzhavkin	15	23	(379)
Aleksandr Fadeyev	12	126	(334)

	SHIP TYPE	REF NO	PAGE NO
Aleksandr Grin	8	630	(251)
Aleksandr Korneychuk	2	470	(60)
Aleksandr Matrosov	5	193	(120)
Aleksandr Miroshnikov	7	324	(180)
Aleksandr Nevskiy	5	131	(116)
Aleksandr Ognivtsev	9	92	(270)
Aleksandrov	7	310	(179)
Aleksandr Pankratov	7	324	(180)
Aleksandr Pashkov	15	95	(387)†
Aleksandr Pokalchuk	7	269	(176)
Aleksandr Pokryshkin	2	304	(49)
Aleksandr Popov	5	29	(109)
Aleksandr Prokofyev	12	126	(334)
Aleksandr Savelyev	7	245	(174)
Aleksandr Shotman	15	18	(378)
Aleksandr Starostenko	16	13	(392)
Aleksandr Suvorov	5	131	(116)
Aleksandr Tsulukidze	2	379	(54)
Aleksandr Tsyurupa	9	80	(269)
Aleksandr Tvardovskiy	12	126	(334)
Aleksandr Vermishev	8	630	(251)
Aleksey Danchenko	5	17	(108)
Alekseyevka	2	222	(44)
Alekseyevsk	2	222	(44)
Aleksey Kosygin	21	49	(503)
Aleksey Tolstoy	8	604	(249)
Alert	5	381	(137)†
Alert	5	82	(113)
Alessandro Volta	4	137	(97)†
Alessandro Volta	2	63	(33)
Alessia	20	19	(460)
Alex	2	410	(56)
Alex	8	232	(221)
Alexander	5	337	(131)†
Alexander	7	51	(160)
Alexander	7	81	(162)
Alexander Dimitrov	5	105	(114)
Alexandere	8	339	(229)
Alexandergracht	7	267	(176)
Alexander Perederiy	9	2	(263)
Alexandra	8	500	(241)
Alexandraki	8	24	(205)
Alexandre	8	596	(249)
Alexandria Star	14	12	(366)
Alexandros	2	406	(55)
Alexandros	7	165	(168)
Alexandros P	8	134	(213)
Alexia	5	103	(114)
Alexia	8	349	(230)
Alexis	5	9	(107)
Alexis	7	156	(168)
Alexis	8	42	(206)
Alexis II	8	446	(237)
Alfa	5	315	(129)
Alfa 1	2	484	(61)
Alfa America	2	228	(44)
Al Fahad	20	112	(467)
Alfama	14	55	(371)†
Al Fao	2	391	(55)
Al Farabi	2	78	(34)
Al Fujairah	9	127	(272)
Algarrobo	2	145	(39)
Al Gharrafah	7	356	(183)
Al Habib–II	8	597	(249)
Al Hafizu	8	500	(241)
Al Haj Ossman	8	186	(217)
Al Hamraa	9	53	(267)
Al Hijra	2	277	(47)
Al Hussein	16	28	(393)
Ali Baba	15	8	(377)
Ali Bayramov	2	504	(62)
Alibrahimiya	7	439	(189)
Alidon	10	25	(289)
Al Idrisi	8	614	(250)
Aligator Miracle	12	64	(329)
Alikrator	7	236	(173)
Ali M	9	9	(263)
Alina	5	116	(115)
Alina I	13	15	(350)
Alinda	5	315	(129)
Alinda	7	54	(160)
Aliot	2	137	(38)
Ali S	8	549	(245)
Alisgloria	5	42	(110)
Ali Zee	15	8	(377)
Al Jawaher	20	198	(473)
Al Johffa	8	500	(241)
Al Judi	20	289	(480)
Alka	9	92	(270)
Alkaid	7	305	(178)
Alkarama	7	357	(183)
Al Karnak III	2	293	(48)
Al-Khaleej	21	65	(504)
Alkhansaa	8	173	(216)
Al Khaznah	3	16	(76)
Alkmini	9	193	(278)†
	SHIP TYPE	**REF NO**	**PAGE NO**
Alkmini	8	252	(223)
Alkmini	9	33	(265)
Alkmini A	7	35	(159)
Al Kortoubi	2	78	(34)
Al Kuwait	21	19	(500)
Al Kuwaitiah	1	198	(16)
Alkyonis	7	215	(172)
Allah Kabeer	8	169	(216)
Allah Kareem	8	574	(247)
Alla Tarasova	20	23	(461)
Allegro Sea	6	42	(144)
Allesandra D'Amato	5	67	(112)
Alliance	6	108	(152)†
Allianora	11	19	(302)
Alligator Fortune	12	142	(335)
Allison Lykes	9	23	(264)
Allissa	8	17	(204)
All Round	8	520	(243)
Alma	7	82	(162)
Al Madiha	2	409	(56)
Al Mahad	2	169	(40)
Almahdy	7	114	(164)
Alma Llanera	18	179	(436)†
Alma Llanera	18	76	(427)
Almania	7	307	(179)
Almar	7	133	(166)
Almaris	7	225	(173)
Almeda Star	11	20	(302)
Almendro	8	149	(214)
Almirante Eraso	8	164	(215)
Almirante Luis Brion	20	359	(485)
Al Mohammed	9	114	(271)
Almond	8	25	(205)
Al Morgan	2	16	(30)
Al Mubarakiah	9	127	(272)
Al Mubaraq	8	560	(246)
Almustansiriyah	2	307	(49)
Al Nabila 3	2	12	(29)
Al Najwa	5	260	(125)
Alnave	7	225	(173)
Alondra	21	118	(511)†
Alondra	21	52	(503)
Alontra	11	60	(305)
Alouette Arrow	7	509	(195)†
Alouette Arrow	7	129	(166)
Alpha	15	43	(380)
Alpha Bravery	8	251	(223)
Alpha Intelligence	2	169	(40)
Alpha Jupiter	8	251	(223)
Alpha Livestock 19	21	115	(510)†
Alpheos	7	228	(173)
Alpina I	11	13	(301)
Alpine Girl	2	31	(31)
Alpine Lady	2	31	(31)
Alqadisiyah	2	307	(49)
Al Qawyyu	7	124	(165)
Alrahim	8	31	(205)
Al Rasheed	20	105	(467)
Al Rayyan	9	127	(272)
Al Sabiyah	1	198	(16)
Alsad Alaaly	2	221	(44)
Al Safaniya	2	169	(40)
Al Salam 89	18	15	(422)
Al Salam 91	18	11	(422)
Al Salimiah	9	127	(272)
Als Express	7	391	(185)
Al Shamiah	12	56	(329)
Al Shams	7	162	(168)
Al Sharifa II	1	93	(9)
Al Shaymaa	8	392	(233)
Al-Shebli Reefer	11	163	(313)
Als Strength	7	391	(185)
Alstergas	4	184	(103)†
Alstergas	4	19	(88)
Alstern	7	305	(178)
Alster Ore	2	280	(47)
Al Swamruz	8	417	(235)
Alsydon	10	25	(289)
Altaawin Alarabi	9	10	(264)
Altai	9	86	(269)
Altair	2	56	(32)
Altair	7	89	(163)
Altamonte	7	207	(171)
Altayles	8	589	(248)
Altnes	7	347	(182)
Altona	7	313	(179)
Alvic	8	521	(243)
Al Waaliyu	7	30	(159)
Al Wafic	8	169	(216)
Al Wakrah	7	11	(157)
Al Wataniah	2	375	(53)
Al Wattyah	12	27	(327)
Al Yamamah	9	127	(272)
Al Yarmouk	9	53	(267)
Alycia	7	146	(167)
Al Zaher II	18	137	(432)

†Photograph

	SHIP TYPE	REF NO	PAGE NO
Al-Zahraa	17	119	(418)†
Al Zahraa	8	392	(233)
Al Zahrah	11	17	(302)
Al Zainab	2	323	(50)
Alzawraa	8	173	(216)
Al Zohal	11	17	(302)
Amadeo	18	146	(432)
Amafhh Two	8	554	(246)
Amagisan	5	371	(135)†
Amalija	8	201	(218)
Amalthea	5	297	(128)
Amami	5	13	(108)
Amami	7	35	(159)
Aman Bintulu	4	15	(88)
Amanda 1	10	25	(289)
Amanecida	8	500	(241)
Amarynthos	8	420	(235)
Amata	11	59	(305)
Amazone	5	112	(115)
Amazon Glory	2	507	(62)
Amazonia	3	38	(79)†
Amazonia	3	21	(76)
Amazon Reefer	11	13	(301)
Ambalika	8	421	(235)
Ambar	8	445	(237)
Ambasador I	20	37	(461)
Ambassador	8	61	(208)
Ambassador	18	126	(431)
Ambassador Bridge	12	107	(333)
Ambassador I	7	146	(167)
Ambassador II	20	43	(462)
Amber	2	141	(38)
Amber	2	277	(47)
Amber	5	278	(126)
Amber	16	16	(392)
Amber Halo	7	199	(171)
Amber II	9	57	(267)
Ambroise	1	175	(14)
Amderma	17	27	(407)
Amelina	4	131	(96)
Amenity	2	536	(64)
Amer Asha	8	422	(235)
America	13	41	(352)
Americana	13	16	(350)
American Chemist	2	346	(51)
American Condor	16	91	(401)†
American Condor	16	40	(394)
American Cormorant	21	89	(507)†
American Cormorant	21	31	(501)
American Falcon	16	72	(398)†
American Falcon	16	40	(394)
American Merlin	17	7	(405)
American Pegasus	1	140	(12)
American Racer	8	93	(210)
American Ranger	8	93	(210)
American Reefer	11	119	(310)
American Reliance	8	93	(210)
American Veteran	21	62	(504)
America Star	13	48	(352)
Amerigo Vespucci	12	28	(327)
Amerikanis	20	232	(476)
Amer Prabha	8	559	(246)
Amer Shakti	9	87	(269)
Amer Shanti	9	87	(269)
Amgun	2	414	(56)
Amica	5	59	(111)
Amilla	8	445	(237)
Amin	7	179	(169)
Amina	2	394	(55)
Amina Moon	7	291	(177)
Amir A	9	102	(270)
Amir Kabir	6	48	(145)
Amisia	15	21	(379)
Amity	2	130	(38)
Amke	7	481	(192)
Amna S	8	302	(227)
Amna S	8	549	(245)
Amore	8	500	(241)
Amorgos	5	100	(114)
Amoria	2	72	(34)
Amoun	9	6	(263)
Ampilla	2	186	(42)
Ampol Sarel	1	83	(8)
Ampurias	1	183	(15)
Amro Kalkavan	7	64	(161)
A M Spiridon	8	176	(216)
Amstelborg	15	66	(384)†
Amstelgracht	7	267	(176)
Amstelwal	5	291	(127)
Amuriyah	2	307	(49)
Amur No 2	9	154	(274)
Amur No 3	9	154	(274)
Amurskiy Bereg	11	98	(308)
Amurskiy Zaliv	11	18	(302)
Amy	5	312	(129)
Anacaona	11	138	(311)
Anadyr	17	27	(407)
Anafi	5	157	(118)
Anahuac	1	158	(13)
Anakan	11	60	(305)
Ana Luisa	9	134	(273)
Anameli	7	180	(169)
Anangel Ares	8	252	(223)
Anangel Atlas	8	252	(223)
Anangel Dignity	7	213	(172)
Anangel Eagle	7	182	(169)
Anangel Endeavour	10	35	(289)
Anangel Express	7	23	(158)
Anangel Fidelity	10	35	(289)
Anangel Honour	8	445	(237)
Anangel Hope	8	445	(237)
Anangel Liberty	8	445	(237)
Anangel Might	10	111	(298)†
Anangel Might	10	35	(289)
Anangel Power	7	182	(169)
Anangel Progress	5	226	(122)
Anangel Prosperity	8	445	(237)
Anangel Prudence	8	252	(223)
Anangel Prudence	8	252	(223)
Anangel Sky	8	252	(223)
Anangel Spirit	10	35	(289)
Anangel Success	7	213	(172)
Anangel Triumph	8	445	(237)
Anangel Venture	5	226	(122)
Anangel Victory	8	252	(223)
Anangel Wisdom	8	445	(237)
Ana Raquel	14	2	(365)
Anas	8	65	(208)
Anastasia	7	146	(167)
Anastasis	2	255	(46)
Anastasis	20	35	(461)
Anatoli	8	46	(207)
Anatoliy Kolesnichenko	17	27	(407)
Anatoliy Lunacharskiy	9	56	(267)
Anatoliy Lyapidevskiy	7	273	(176)
Anatoliy Vasilyev	16	59	(397)†
Anatoliy Vasilyev	16	29	(393)
An Bao Jiang	8	252	(223)
Anchorman	1	184	(15)
Ancon	3	26	(77)
Ancora	2	245	(45)
Ancora	2	276	(47)
An Da	9	157	(275)
An Da Hai	7	60	(161)
Andaman Sea	2	256	(46)
Andaxios	7	163	(168)
Anders Maersk	12	146	(336)
Anders Rousing	15	67	(384)†
Andhika Adhitsatya	2	36	(31)
Andhika Adiparwa	2	36	(31)
Andhika Aryandhi	2	36	(31)
Andhika Ashura	2	36	(31)
Andino	8	359	(230)
Andra	7	379	(184)
Andra	7	381	(185)
Andrea	2	150	(39)
Andrea Brovig	8	124	(212)
Andrealon	10	25	(289)
Andreas M	8	177	(216)
Andre Delmas	7	234	(173)
Andrey Ivanov	7	324	(180)
Andrey Lavrov	9	80	(269)
Andrian Goncharov	8	49	(207)
Andrina F	6	9	(141)
Andriotissa	8	445	(237)
Andromache	8	396	(234)
Andromeda	1	79	(8)
Andromeda	2	367	(53)
Andromeda Star	8	396	(234)
Andronikos P	8	159	(215)
Andros	5	100	(114)
Andros Chryssi	2	262	(46)
Andros Meltemi	5	121	(115)
Andros Oceania	7	124	(165)
Andy	8	500	(241)
Anemi	8	24	(205)
Anette Theresa	2	282	(47)
An Fu	2	178	(41)
Anga	15	8	(377)
Angara	7	133	(166)
Angel	8	193	(218)
Angela	8	308	(227)
Angela Jurgens	5	112	(115)
Angel Feather	7	199	(171)
Angelia P	8	445	(237)
Angelic Grace	5	325	(130)†
Angeliki	5	147	(117)
Angeliki D.	7	6	(157)
Angeliki R.	7	146	(167)
Angelina L.	7	440	(189)
Angelique	7	446	(189)
Angel Wing	7	111	(164)

†Photograph

	SHIP TYPE	REF NO	PAGE NO
Angermanland	7	472	(191)
Anglia	5	190	(120)
Anglo	8	143	(214)
Anglo-Alliance	8	249	(223)
An Guo	7	432	(188)
Angus	6	66	(146)
Angus Express	21	122	(511)†
Angyalfold	8	582	(248)
An Hai	7	29	(159)
An He	12	110	(333)
An Hua Jiang	8	252	(223)
Ani	18	149	(433)
Ania B	5	274	(126)
Aniara	19	71	(453)†
Aniara	2	385	(54)
Anika	13	20	(350)
Anis Rose	8	555	(246)
Anita	5	382	(137)†
Anita	5	263	(125)
Anita	10	32	(289)
Anita 1	10	25	(289)
Anixis	8	500	(241)
Anja C	15	14	(378)
Anja II	5	81	(112)
Anjana D	10	1	(287)
Anjeliersgracht	7	267	(176)
An Ji Hai	7	71	(161)
Ankara	20	113	(467)
Anke Bettina	15	8	(377)
Ankergracht	7	267	(176)
Anke S	16	83	(400)†
Ankleshwar	1	201	(16)
An Li	8	217	(220)
An Lu Jiang	8	383	(232)
Anmaj	2	163	(40)
Ann	2	380	(54)
Anna	5	100	(114)
Anna	7	28	(159)
Anna	8	619	(250)
Annabella	4	154	(99)†
Anna John	8	24	(205)
Anna Karenina	20	389	(488)
Anna Kosan	4	165	(101)†
Anna L	8	427	(236)
Anna Maersk	12	146	(336)
Anna Oldendorff	7	109	(164)
Annapurna	4	104	(94)
Anna S	7	220	(172)
Anna Sierra	8	476	(239)
Anne	15	56	(383)†
Anne	6	67	(146)
Anne Catharina	7	476	(191)
Annegret	7	338	(181)
Anne-Laure	4	101	(94)
Anne M	8	3	(203)
Annette Essberger	1	55	(6)
Annika M	6	2	(141)
Annoula	8	24	(205)
Ann Sif	1	178	(14)
Annuity	1	186	(15)
Anny Austral	7	481	(192)
Anny L	8	159	(215)
Anro Australia	16	90	(400)†
Anro Gowa	13	59	(353)
Anro Jayakarta	13	59	(353)
An Sai Jiang	8	383	(232)
Antakya	8	225	(221)
Antalaha	8	202	(219)
Antalina	7	145	(167)
An Tao Jiang	9	130	(273)
Antara	18	34	(423)
Antares	2	414	(56)
Antares	6	46	(144)
Antea	2	347	(52)
Ante Banina	2	575	(69)†
Anteos	8	441	(237)
Anthenor Express	18	142	(432)
Anthia	5	19	(108)
Anthi P	5	65	(111)
Anthony	9	92	(270)
Anthos	8	252	(223)
Antigoni B	7	533	(198)†

†Photograph

	SHIP TYPE	REF NO	PAGE NO
Antigonos	8	34	(206)
Antigua	2	39	(31)
Antina	15	22	(379)
Antinea	1	127	(11)
Anting	8	561	(246)
Antje	7	338	(181)
Anton Buyukly	8	612	(250)
Antonina Nezhdanova	20	18	(460)
Antonio Gramsi	2	424	(57)
Antonis I Angelicoussis	5	216	(122)
Anton Makarenko	8	604	(249)
Antwerpen	5	106	(114)
Antwerp Express	8	400	(234)
Anund	6	2	(141)
Anuradha	8	354	(230)
Anwal	18	74	(427)
An Wu Jiang	9	130	(273)
An Yang Jiang	8	383	(232)
Anyuy	2	414	(56)
Ao Jiang	7	217	(172)
Ao Xiang	5	89	(113)
Ao Xiang	7	257	(175)
Apache	2	58	(33)
Apache	9	68	(268)
Apanemo	2	406	(55)
Ape	2	222	(44)
Apil	7	74	(162)
Apj Akhil	7	37	(159)
Apj Anjli	7	45	(160)
Apj Priti	8	141	(214)
Apj Sushma	7	45	(160)
APL Japan	12	189	(341)†
Apman II	9	232	(283)†
A P Moller	1	108	(10)
Apody	17	40	(408)
Apollo	20	193	(473)
Apollo Akama	1	128	(11)
Apollogracht	7	267	(176)
Apollon	9	33	(265)
Apollon Express 1	20	114	(467)
Apollon Express 2	20	114	(467)
Apollonia	7	434	(188)
Apollonia II	20	358	(485)
Apollonia Lion	5	149	(117)
Apollo Ohshima	1	128	(11)
Apollo Peak	7	298	(178)
Apostle Andrey	9	57	(267)
Apostolis II	8	24	(205)
Apple	14	2	(365)
Appleby	5	122	(115)
Apricity	2	119	(37)
April	11	200	(317)†
April	11	84	(307)
Apsheron	2	426	(57)
Apsheron	2	504	(62)
Apsheronsk	2	222	(44)
Aptmariner	7	65	(161)
Apuole	8	365	(231)
Aquamarine	5	135	(116)
Aqua Pioneer	15	8	(377)
Aquarius	10	63	(292)†
Aquarius	10	9	(287)
Aqua Sierra	8	80	(209)
Aquila II	11	125	(310)
Aquila II	11	127	(310)
Aquitaine Challenge	12	211	(344)†
Aquitania	7	289	(177)
Ara	6	41	(144)
Arabella	7	60	(161)
Arabella	8	251	(223)
Arab Hind	9	119	(272)
Arabia	7	425	(188)
Arabian Sea	11	134	(311)
Arabian Senator	12	102	(332)
Arab Mazin	8	609	(250)
Arab Wanderer	2	468	(60)
Arachovitika	7	388	(185)
Arachovitika Bay	9	77	(268)
Arafat	9	127	(272)
Arago	4	92	(93)
Arahanga	20	115	(467)
Arak	2	118	(37)
Aralda	2	445	(58)
Aram Khachaturyan	9	92	(270)
Arana	8	202	(219)
Ararat	2	414	(56)
Ararat	2	489	(61)
Aras	8	629	(251)
Aratika	20	190	(472)
Arawak Chief	14	44	(369)†
Arawak Chief	14	11	(366)
Arawak E	11	60	(305)
Arawak Sun	6	58	(145)
Arawak Trader	6	58	(145)
Araya	7	73	(162)
Araz	2	504	(62)

	SHIP TYPE	REF NO	PAGE NO
Arbat	1	138	(12)
Arberia	8	257	(223)
Arcade Eagle	18	198	(438)†
Arcadia	2	197	(42)
Arcadia	4	111	(94)
Arcadia	8	445	(237)
Arcadia 1	2	141	(38)
Archangelgracht	7	267	(176)
Archangelos	2	367	(53)
Archangelos	5	297	(128)
Archia	2	384	(54)
Arco Anchorage	2	319	(50)
Arco Fairbanks	2	319	(50)
Arco Juneau	2	319	(50)
Arco Prudhoe Bay	2	320	(50)
Arco Sag River	2	320	(50)
Arco Texas	2	320	(50)
Arctica	2	97	(35)
Arctic Confidence	8	656	(255)†
Arctic Goose	11	237	(322)†
Arctic Star	2	83	(35)
Arctic Sun	4	63	(91)
Arctic Trader	7	271	(176)
Arctic Trader	11	125	(310)
Arctic Trader	11	127	(310)
Arctic Universal	11	24	(302)
Arctic Viking	9	82	(269)
Areito	8	44	(206)
Arete	7	139	(166)
Arethusa	8	445	(237)
Areti	8	445	(237)
Aretusa	1	13	(4)
Argentina Star	13	96	(357)†
Argentum	1	164	(13)
Argironissos	1	104	(9)
Argoat	2	526	(64)
Argolis	7	228	(173)
Argomar	11	89	(307)
Argonaftis	2	307	(49)
Argonaut	7	326	(180)
Argonaut	12	119	(334)
Argonia	13	28	(351)
Argo Pioneer	8	312	(228)
Argosea	11	89	(307)
Argosy	5	10	(107)
Argun	8	589	(248)
Argus	2	535	(64)
Argus	8	137	(213)
Arhon	7	55	(160)
Aria	8	149	(214)
Ariadne	20	357	(485)
Ariake	12	93	(332)
Ariake Star	11	69	(305)
Arian	2	414	(56)
Ariana	17	113	(417)†
Arianta	2	72	(34)
Ariel	2	480	(60)
Ariel	7	394	(185)
Aries	5	66	(111)
Aries	8	409	(234)
Aries Gas	3	23	(76)
Ariete	2	305	(49)
Arietta	7	164	(168)
Arimao Universal	11	81	(306)
Arina Arctica	7	414	(187)
Arion	8	231	(221)
Arion	16	22	(393)
Aristarhs Belopolskis	11	127	(310)
Aristea	8	202	(219)
Aristidis	2	489	(61)
Aristogeiton	10	60	(292)†
Aristogeiton	10	7	(287)
Aristogenis	10	7	(287)
Ariston	2	283	(47)
Ariston	2	419	(56)
Aristopes	5	188	(120)
Aristoteles	9	49	(266)
Aristotelis	8	251	(223)
Aristotelis	10	7	(287)
Arizonia	11	60	(305)
Arkadia	7	157	(168)
Arkadiy Gaydar	8	630	(251)
Arkadiy Kamanin	8	621	(251)
Arkadiy Sverdlov	15	23	(379)
Arkhangelsk	17	27	(407)
Arklow Abbey	6	40	(144)
Arklow Bay	15	19	(378)
Arklow Brook	10	114	(298)†
Arklow Manor	15	19	(378)
Arklow Marsh	15	19	(378)
Arklow Meadow	15	19	(378)
Arklow Mill	15	19	(378)
Arklow Moor	15	19	(378)
Arklow Vale	15	19	(378)
Arklow Valley	15	19	(378)
Arklow Valour	15	19	(378)

†Photograph

	SHIP TYPE	REF NO	PAGE NO
Arklow Venture	15	19	(378)
Arklow View	15	19	(378)
Arklow Viking	15	19	(378)
Arklow Villa	15	19	(378)
Arkona	13	126	(361)†
Arkona	13	39	(352)
Arkona	20	378	(487)
Arktis Bay	8	374	(232)
Arktis Breeze	8	373	(232)
Arktis Carrier	8	373	(232)
Arktis Faith	7	470	(191)
Arktis Fantasy	7	470	(191)
Arktis Fighter	7	470	(191)
Arktis Grace	8	373	(232)
Arktis Ocean	8	373	(232)
Arktis Princess	8	373	(232)
Arktis River	8	373	(232)
Arktis Sea	8	374	(232)
Arktis Sirius	8	373	(232)
Arktis Sky	8	373	(232)
Arktis Sun	8	374	(232)
Arktis Trader	8	373	(232)
Arlet	2	414	(56)
Arma	2	410	(56)
Armacup Patricia	19	25	(446)
Armada Glory	8	49	(207)
Armada Permai	8	581	(248)
Armada Sprinter	5	114	(115)
Armata	2	549	(66)†
Armelle	5	125	(116)
Armenistis	6	10	(142)
Armia Krajowa	5	110	(115)
Armia Ludowa	5	304	(128)
Armin Star	8	350	(230)
Armin Star	9	123	(272)
Armour	6	27	(143)
Arnaki	5	19	(108)
Arneb	17	112	(417)†
Arno	19	81	(454)†
Arno	19	25	(446)
Arnold Schulte	12	62	(329)
Aromo	7	271	(176)
Aros	8	687	(259)†
Arosa	1	113	(10)
Arosa	5	271	(126)
Arosa	7	223	(173)
Arosette	6	58	(145)
Aros Force	7	383	(185)
Arosia	6	2	(141)
Arossel	7	367	(183)
Ar Raqib	8	24	(205)
Arrazi	2	583	(70)†
Arrow	5	82	(113)
Arrow Niki	2	478	(60)
Arroyofrio Dos	18	227	(442)†
Arseniy Moskvin	7	324	(180)
Artemis	8	513	(242)
Artemis	15	44	(381)
Artemis 1	5	274	(126)
Artemis Garofalidis	2	237	(45)
Artemis SB	7	50	(160)
Artesia	4	158	(100)†
Arthur Maersk	12	146	(336)
Artisgracht	7	267	(176)
Art Reefer	11	167	(313)
Artsiz	8	581	(248)
Arturo Michelina	8	544	(245)
Artvin	8	225	(221)
Aruba	8	408	(234)
Arun	2	45	(32)
Aruna	8	177	(216)
Arunachal Pradesh	7	406	(186)
Arunbank	17	27	(407)
Arunto	8	232	(221)
Arvagh	7	249	(174)
Arveprins Knud	20	404	(490)†
Arveprins Knud	20	116	(468)
Arwad	8	448	(238)
Arzanah	1	158	(13)
Asake Maru	3	1	(75)
Asari	1	20	(4)
Asa-Thor	20	179	(472)
Ascension	5	283	(127)
Aschberg	18	25	(423)
Ascona	5	221	(122)
Ascot	2	415	(56)
Asdrubal	2	164	(40)
Asean Enterprise	8	137	(213)
Asean Jumbo	9	137	(273)
Asean Pioneer	8	274	(225)
Asean Premier	8	521	(243)
Asean Prestige	2	376	(54)
Asean Promoter	2	82	(35)
Asean Providence	2	376	(54)
Asean Victory	7	271	(176)
Asean Winner	9	137	(273)

	SHIP TYPE	REF NO	PAGE NO
Asena 1	8	348	(230)
Asha Global	9	6	(263)
Ashakrupa	9	6	(263)
Asha Manan	9	6	(263)
Asheyra	2	321	(50)
Ashington	5	80	(112)
Ashkhabad	2	446	(58)
Ashley	7	393	(185)
Ashug Alekser	7	340	(181)
Asia Angel	2	142	(38)
Asia Express	17	57	(410)
Asian Century	18	190	(437)†
Asian Confidence	8	270	(224)
Asian Jumbo	8	393	(233)
Asian Reefer	11	133	(311)
Asian Venture	9	41	(266)
Asia Star	9	15	(264)
Asia Trader	7	92	(163)
Asia Union	5	203	(121)
A Sibiryakov	7	435	(188)
Ask	18	112	(430)
Aslinur	8	291	(226)
ASL Sanderling	16	78	(399)†
ASL Sanderling	18	160	(433)
Asma	2	3	(29)
Asmaa	9	53	(267)
Aspasia L	8	416	(235)
Asphalt Champion	2	447	(58)
Asphalt Leader	2	155	(39)
Aspia	21	32	(501)
Aspilos	2	341	(51)
Aspilos	7	69	(161)
Asprella	2	72	(34)
As Salaam	8	24	(205)
Assem	8	233	(221)
Assiduus	15	22	(379)
ASSI Euro Link	18	184	(436)†
ASSI Skan Link	18	19	(422)
Assos Bay	2	235	(44)
Assurity	2	119	(37)
Astara	2	504	(62)
Asterix I	4	156	(100)†
Astipalea	2	12	(29)
Astivi	8	537	(244)
Astor	20	379	(487)
Astoria	8	354	(230)
Astra	2	521	(63)
Astra	8	630	(251)
Astra	20	20	(460)
Astrafederico	5	357	(134)†
Astra II	20	456	(496)†
Astra II	20	117	(468)
Astra IV	3	53	(80)†
Astra IV	4	118	(95)
Astrakhan	17	82	(413)†
Astrakhan	17	51	(409)
Astral 1	6	11	(142)
Astralgas	4	13	(88)
Astra Peak	7	298	(178)
Astra Sky	9	33	(265)
Astrea	16	81	(399)†
Astro Coach	19	2	(445)
Astro Mercury	19	90	(455)†
Astron	8	500	(241)
Astro Pegasus	2	384	(54)
Astro Venus	19	12	(446)
Asturias	7	271	(176)
Asuka Reefer	11	71	(306)
Asuka Road	1	187	(15)
Atalanti	7	213	(172)
Atanur	8	100	(211)
Athena	5	65	(111)
Athenian Beauty	2	470	(60)
Athenian Charm	2	470	(60)
Athenian Fidelity	2	590	(71)†
Athenian Fidelity	2	470	(60)
Athenian Harmony	2	12	(29)
Athenian Olympics	2	470	(60)
Athenian Rex	11	194	(316)†
Athenian Rex	11	80	(306)
Athenian Theodore	2	470	(60)
Athenian Victory	2	470	(60)
Athenian Xenophon	2	470	(60)
Athens Express	18	141	(432)
Athinais P.	8	445	(237)
Athiniotissa	5	42	(110)
Athinoula	7	70	(161)
Athinoula	8	114	(212)
Athirah	20	38	(462)
Athol	8	445	(237)
Athos	2	315	(49)
Athos	2	323	(50)
Atigun Pass	2	229	(44)
Atilla K	7	174	(169)
Atlanta	8	24	(205)
Atlanta	13	26	(351)

	SHIP TYPE	REF NO	PAGE NO
Atlantica	5	42	(110)
Atlantica	17	40	(408)
Atlantic Breeze	19	80	(454)†
Atlantic Bulker	7	200	(171)
Atlantic Cartier	16	64	(397)†
Atlantic Cartier	16	10	(392)
Atlantic Coast	7	384	(185)
Atlantic Comet	6	47	(145)
Atlantic Companion	16	86	(400)†
Atlantic Companion	16	33	(394)
Atlantic Compass	16	33	(394)
Atlantic Concert	16	33	(394)
Atlantic Conveyor	16	87	(400)†
Atlantic Conveyor	16	10	(392)
Atlantic Dawn	11	226	(320)†
Atlantic Freighter	16	65	(397)†
Atlantic Freighter	16	18	(392)
Atlantic Herald	16	14	(392)
Atlantic Hope	16	14	(392)
Atlantic Ice	11	146	(312)
Atlantic Lady	12	147	(336)
Atlantic Mercado	7	11	(157)
Atlantic Moon	9	101	(270)
Atlantic Prestige	2	301	(48)
Atlantic Pride	2	301	(48)
Atlantic Reefer II	11	161	(313)
Atlantic River	8	114	(212)
Atlantic Savior	5	202	(121)
Atlantic Sea	2	395	(55)
Atlantic Splendour	5	137	(116)
Atlantic Star	4	81	(92)
Atlantic Star	11	51	(304)
Atlantic Statesman	5	307	(128)
Atlantic Trident	5	49	(110)
Atlantic Universal	11	22	(302)
Atlanticway	5	300	(128)
Atlantis	14	53	(371)†
Atlantis	7	305	(178)
Atlantis	14	22	(366)
Atlantis	18	177	(435)
Atlantis A	8	521	(243)
Atlantis Two	7	225	(173)
Atlas	17	94	(414)†
Atlas	7	225	(173)
Atlas	7	460	(190)
Atlas	9	106	(271)
Atlas	17	4	(405)
Atlasgracht	7	267	(176)
Atlasovo Sala	11	11	(301)
Atmoda	11	98	(308)
Atmoda	11	101	(308)
Atrice	4	5	(87)
Attica	7	7	(157)
Atticos	8	16	(204)
Attilio Ievoli	1	50	(6)
Auckland Express	7	305	(178)
Auckland Star	11	27	(302)
Audacious	7	159	(168)
Auersberg	18	3	(421)
Auk	5	145	(117)
Aurelia	8	351	(230)
Aures	8	505	(241)
Auriga	2	201	(42)
Aurobindo	2	477	(60)
Aurora	16	49	(395)†
Aurora	9	122	(272)
Aurora	16	23	(393)
Aurora Gold	8	420	(235)
Aurora Opal	7	155	(168)
Aurora Ruby	8	521	(243)
Aurora Topaz	7	181	(169)
Aurum	1	164	(13)
Ausma Leader	12	109	(333)
Ausma Trader	12	109	(333)
Australgas	3	52	(80)†
Australian Achiever	2	231	(44)
Australian Reefer	11	119	(310)
Australian Venture	12	134	(335)
Australia Star	1	208	(16)
Autan	1	87	(8)
Authenticity	2	536	(64)
Author	12	118	(334)
Auto Atlas	19	38	(448)†
Autobahn	18	125	(431)
Autocarrier	18	54	(425)
Autofreighter	18	168	(434)
Automobil Ace	19	35	(448)†
Autoracer	18	208	(439)†
Autoroute	18	161	(434)
Autostrada	18	51	(425)
Autotrader	18	39	(424)
Autotransporter	18	210	(439)†
Autoweg	18	167	(434)
Autumn	7	297	(178)
Au Yin Leng	7	187	(170)
Ava	8	486	(240)
Avaj 2	2	251	(45)
Avant	7	460	(190)
Avanti	8	500	(241)
Avar	2	310	(49)
Avdeevka	7	186	(170)
Aveiro	12	61	(329)
Avelona Star	11	20	(302)
Aventicum	7	241	(174)
Aventure	7	107	(164)
Averity	2	130	(38)
A Vermez	8	138	(213)
Avila Star	11	20	(302)
Avin Oil Trader	2	138	(38)
Avion	5	55	(111)
Avlis	8	252	(223)
Avocado Carmel	11	205	(318)†
Avon	7	34	(159)
Avon	8	500	(241)
Avra	8	361	(231)
Avrig	7	447	(189)
Awash	1	171	(14)
Awu	20	388	(488)
Axel Maersk	12	197	(342)†
Axel Maersk	12	146	(336)
Ayane	7	127	(165)
Ayangue	3	26	(77)
Ayatt	8	525	(243)
Ayia Marina	7	42	(160)
Ayia Markella	7	125	(165)
Aynur Kalkavan	7	221	(172)
Ayon	2	414	(56)
Ayse Ana	7	154	(168)
Ayubia	8	440	(237)
Ayvazovskiy	20	402	(489)†
Ayvazovskiy	20	118	(468)
Ayyoub	7	114	(164)
Azalea	11	150	(312)
Azapa	13	15	(350)
Azerbaijan	20	287	(480)
Azerbaydzhan	20	127	(468)
Azerot	2	526	(64)
Azija	2	465	(59)
Azilal	16	73	(398)†
Azilal	16	24	(393)
Azimuth	8	549	(245)
Azna	1	88	(8)
Azrou	16	24	(393)
Azteca	20	193	(473)
Aztek	2	58	(33)
Azuga	8	50	(207)
Baab Ullah	9	231	(283)†
Baba Gurgur	2	411	(56)
Babor	7	446	(189)
Babtai	8	404	(234)
Babur Kaptan	2	81	(34)
Babylon	9	10	(264)
Bacab	2	55	(32)
Bacesti	5	138	(117)
Baco-Liner 1	21	2	(499)
Baco-Liner 2	21	2	(499)
Baco-Liner 3	21	102	(509)†
Baco-Liner 3	21	2	(499)
Bader	18	35	(424)
Baghdad	9	10	(264)
Bago	7	444	(189)
Bahia de Ceuta	20	341	(484)
Bahia de Cochinos	8	382	(232)
Bahia de Malaga	20	341	(484)
Bahiana Reefer	11	110	(309)
Baia de Arama	5	138	(117)
Baia de Aries	5	138	(117)
Baia de Cris	5	138	(117)
Baia de Fier	5	138	(117)
Baia Noua	5	138	(117)
Bai He Kou	18	175	(435)
Baikal 1	8	575	(247)
Baikal 2	8	575	(247)
Bai Yin Shan	8	47	(207)
Bai Yu Lan	7	147	(167)
Bai Yun Hai	8	121	(212)
Bai Yun Shan	9	170	(275)
Bajamar	20	325	(483)
Bajda	8	343	(229)
Bakengracht	7	11	(157)
Bakhtemir	15	47	(381)
Bakkafoss	7	308	(179)
Bakradze	1	181	(15)
Bakri Voyager	2	56	(32)
Baky	7	340	(181)
Baladzhary	2	367	(53)
Balaji Vintage	7	69	(161)
Balashikha	9	10	(264)
Balaton	7	460	(190)
Balbao Reefer	11	97	(308)

†Photograph

	SHIP TYPE	REF NO	PAGE NO
Balder Phenix	3	83	(84)†
Balder Queen	7	271	(176)
Balduin	18	87	(428)
Baleares	2	480	(60)
Balina	4	140	(98)†
Balina	4	25	(88)
Bali Sea	21	20	(500)
Balkan	5	132	(116)
Balkan	9	130	(273)
Balkan Reefer	11	133	(311)
Ballenita	2	480	(60)
Ballerina	2	322	(50)
Balota	5	158	(118)
Balsa	7	535	(199)†
Baltavia	20	120	(468)
Baltic	10	14	(288)
Baltica	7	367	(183)
Baltic Amber	14	80	(374)†
Balticborg	7	457	(190)
Baltic Breeze	19	91	(455)†
Baltic Bulker	7	212	(172)
Baltic Courier	6	2	(141)
Baltic Eagle	18	170	(434)
Baltic Eider	16	50	(395)†
Baltic Eider	16	23	(393)
Baltic Flame	4	106	(94)
Baltic Horizon	8	643	(253)†
Baltic Ice	11	146	(312)
Baltic Link	18	16	(422)
Baltic Mermaid	5	53	(110)
Baltic Meteor	18	178	(436)†
Baltic Meteor	18	89	(428)
Baltic Prosperity	2	505	(62)
Baltic Sea	11	152	(312)
Baltic Sprinter	17	96	(415)†
Baltic Sprinter	17	40	(408)
Baltic Star	11	51	(304)
Baltic Star	20	21	(460)
Baltic Stone	7	130	(166)
Baltic Tern	12	210	(343)†
Baltic Trader	11	125	(310)
Baltic Trader	11	127	(310)
Baltic Transporter	8	274	(225)
Baltic Trident	5	297	(128)
Baltic Universal	11	24	(302)
Baltijas Cels	11	98	(308)
Baltijas Cels	11	101	(308)
Baltimore Trader	2	159	(40)
Baltiysk	17	51	(409)
'Baltiyskiy' type	15	26	(379)
Baltiyskiy type	15	35	(380)
Baltiyskiy 101	15	17	(378)
Baltiyskiy 102	15	17	(378)
Baltiyskiy 103	15	17	(378)
Baltiyskiy 105	15	17	(378)
Baltiyskiy 106	15	17	(378)
Baltiyskiy 107	15	17	(378)
Baltiyskiy 108	15	17	(378)
Baltiyskiy 109	15	17	(378)
Baltiyskiy 110	15	17	(378)
Baltiyskiy 111	15	17	(378)
Baltiyskiy Bereg	11	98	(308)
Bam	2	26	(30)
Banaderos	20	224	(475)
Bananor	11	152	(312)
Banat	2	259	(46)
Bandak	5	100	(114)
Bandama Express	17	55	(409)
Banda Sea	21	20	(500)
Baneasa	5	138	(117)
Bangbua	8	211	(219)
Banglar Baani	8	500	(241)
Banglar Jyoti	1	199	(16)
Banglar Kallol	9	222	(282)†
Banglar Mamata	9	167	(275)
Banglar Maya	9	204	(280)†
Banglar Maya	9	167	(275)
Banglar Moni	8	446	(237)
Banglar Robi	8	446	(237)
Banglar Sampad	8	360	(231)
Banglar Shourabh	1	199	(16)
Banglar Urmi	7	548	(200)†
Bangpo	8	151	(214)
Banska Bystrica	9	42	(266)
Bao An	9	13	(264)
Bao Chang	7	502	(194)†
Bao Shan	9	92	(270)
Baotrans	2	326	(50)
Bar	7	140	(166)
Barada	9	53	(267)
Baraganul	5	138	(117)
Baraka	8	532	(244)
Barba	8	619	(250)
Barbara	8	578	(247)
Barbara	8	612	(250)
Barbara E	7	461	(190)
Barbara H	7	223	(173)
Barbaros Oktay	8	420	(235)
Barbican Spirit	7	450	(189)
Barbican Star	7	450	(189)
Barbican Success	13	9	(349)
Barco	5	323	(129)
Barde Team	9	111	(271)
Bardsey	2	130	(38)
Barenbels	9	106	(271)
Barentzgracht	7	11	(157)
Barfleur	20	421	(492)†
Bari Express	20	121	(468)
Barket Allah	5	99	(114)
Barmouth	2	130	(38)
Barona	6	112	(152)†
Baroness M	20	211	(474)
Barra Head	5	168	(119)
Barrington Island	11	117	(309)
Barrister	7	9	(157)
Barry	10	8	(287)
Bartolomeu Dias	5	43	(110)
Bar'Zan	12	27	(327)
Base Wind	5	188	(120)
Basilea	11	135	(311)
Bastion	13	38	(352)
Bataafgracht	7	11	(157)
Batak	7	358	(183)
Batalion Czwartakow	5	305	(128)
Bataliony Chlopskie	5	304	(128)
Batavier	15	55	(382)†
Batis	7	199	(171)
Bauchi	10	106	(297)†
Bauchi	10	8	(287)
Baumare II	5	38	(109)
Baursberg	15	27	(379)
Bauru	2	341	(51)
Bauska	1	192	(15)
Ba VI	2	307	(49)
Bayamon	16	5	(391)
Bay Bridge	12	103	(332)
Bay Island Express	3	6	(75)
Baykal	20	14	(460)
Baykonur	8	589	(248)
Bayovar	2	371	(53)
Baystar	3	23	(76)
Bay Star	7	358	(183)
Bayway	2	174	(41)
Bazias 1	18	52	(425)
Bea 1	2	348	(52)
Bear G	2	322	(50)
Bear G	2	500	(62)
Beate	6	58	(145)
Beaulieu	7	351	(182)
Beauport	20	44	(462)
Bebatik	4	33	(89)
Bechet	5	138	(117)
Becquer	4	39	(89)
Beerberg	18	25	(423)
Bega	8	1	(203)
Behcet Canbaz	9	68	(268)
Bei An	9	79	(269)
Bei Dai He	12	55	(329)
Bei Feng Shan	8	594	(248)
Beilul	2	286	(47)
Beirut	13	86	(356)†
Beirut	13	33	(351)
Bekalang	4	33	(89)
Bekapai/Permina 56	2	377	(54)
Bekasap/Permina 54	2	377	(54)
Bekulan	4	33	(89)
Belais	4	33	(89)
Bela Kun	8	74	(209)
Belanak	4	33	(89)
Belard	18	136	(432)
Belasitza	5	154	(118)
Belatrix	17	109	(416)†
Belatrix	17	15	(406)
Bel Azur	8	443	(237)
Belchatow	5	228	(123)
Belem	5	156	(118)
Belgoroda	11	54	(304)
Belgrano	8	506	(242)
Belinda	11	118	(310)
Bell Ady	14	33	(368)†
Belle	7	50	(160)
Belle	8	353	(230)
Belli	2	286	(47)
Bellini	5	294	(127)
Bellona	2	505	(62)
Bell Pioneer	12	133	(335)
Bell Racer	14	50	(370)†
Bell Racer	14	14	(366)
Bell Ranger	14	14	(366)
Bell Ruler	14	14	(366)
Bell Swift	14	43	(369)†
Bell Swift	14	11	(366)

†Photograph

	SHIP TYPE	REF NO	PAGE NO
Belmeken	5	269	(126)
Belo Oriente	10	75	(293)†
Beloostrov	17	103	(416)†
Beloostrov	17	29	(407)
Beloyarsk	2	367	(53)
Belval	5	225	(122)
Belvaux	18	56	(425)
Belyayevka	1	153	(13)
Ben Aicha	2	78	(34)
Benakat/Permina 57	2	377	(54)
Benarita	7	135	(166)
Benceno	2	51	(32)
Benchijgua II	20	45	(462)
Bencomo	18	36	(424)
Ben Flor	4	162	(100)†
Bengalen	6	24	(143)
Benghazi	4	26	(89)
Beni Saf	18	144	(432)
Benito Juarez	2	412	(56)
Benito Juarez	20	109	(467)
Benny Queen	4	116	(95)
Bentago	18	36	(424)
Benwalid	21	117	(511)†
Benwalid	21	8	(499)
Berdsk	2	367	(53)
Berdyansk	7	454	(190)
Bereg Mechty	11	98	(308)
Bereg Nadezhdy	11	98	(308)
Berezino	1	153	(13)
Berezovneft	2	367	(53)
Berezovo	2	26	(30)
Berga	4	130	(96)
Berge Adria	2	459	(59)
Berge Arrow	4	41	(90)
Berge Big	2	257	(46)
Berge Borg	1	67	(7)
Berge Boss	1	67	(7)
Berge Bragd	2	233	(44)
Berge Broker	2	339	(51)
Berge Captain	4	50	(90)
Berge Challenger	4	50	(90)
Berge Chief	2	257	(46)
Berge Clipper	4	50	(90)
Berge Commander	4	50	(90)
Berge Duke	2	230	(44)
Berge Eagle	4	41	(90)
Berge Enterprise	2	215	(43)
Berge Fister	2	308	(49)
Berge Forest	2	308	(49)
Berge Frost	4	168	(101)†
Bergeland	5	250	(124)
Berge Lord	2	230	(44)
Berge Master	5	21	(108)
Bergen	8	527	(243)
Bergen Arrow	10	43	(290)
Bergen Malaya	7	213	(172)
Berge Pioneer	2	215	(43)
Berge Prince	2	246	(45)
Berger A	8	202	(219)
Berge Rachel	4	45	(90)
Berge Racine	4	45	(90)
Berge Ragnhild	4	45	(90)
Berger B	7	309	(179)
Berge Saga	4	76	(92)
Berge Septimus	2	230	(44)
Berge Sigval	1	130	(11)
Berge Sisar	4	138	(97)†
Berge Sisar	4	76	(92)
Berge Sisu	4	76	(92)
Berge Spirit	4	76	(92)
Berge Stadt	1	220	(18)†
Berge Stahl	5	34	(109)
Berge Stavanger	1	130	(11)
Berge Strand	4	76	(92)
Berge Sund	4	76	(92)
Berge Sword	4	78	(92)
Berge Troll	4	61	(91)
Bergina	1	150	(12)
Bergon	5	25	(109)
Beringa Sala	11	11	(301)
Bering Sea	11	26	(302)
Berjaya Dua	2	100	(36)
Berlice	8	170	(216)
Berlin	20	380	(487)
Berlin Express	12	60	(329)
Berlin Senator	12	15	(326)
Berlin Star	5	147	(117)
Bermuda Islander	14	38	(369)†
Bernadette T	5	236	(123)
Bersut	15	47	(381)
Bertina	2	179	(41)
Besitang/Permina 53	2	377	(54)
Bestekar Fikret Amirov	18	20	(422)
Bestekar Gara Garaev	18	20	(422)
Bestore	5	199	(121)
Beta	8	135	(213)

	SHIP TYPE	REF NO	PAGE NO
Beta	15	29	(379)
Betacrux	2	56	(32)
Beta Luck	7	186	(170)
Betelgeuse	17	15	(406)
Betta Livestock 17	21	116	(511)†
Bettina	6	66	(146)
Bettina K	5	66	(111)
Betung/Permina 55	2	377	(54)
Beursgracht	7	11	(157)
Bewa	9	67	(268)
Bha Express	8	329	(229)
Bharat Seema	20	292	(480)
Bhatra Bhum	12	181	(340)†
Bhoruka Vikram	8	374	(232)
Bianco Danielsen	8	206	(219)
Biba	8	312	(228)
Biban	7	446	(189)
Bibi	9	89	(269)
Bibi M	7	246	(174)
Bickersgracht	7	510	(195)†
Bickersgracht	7	11	(157)
Big Angel	5	297	(128)
Big Glory	7	241	(174)
Big Star	9	74	(268)
Bihor	7	174	(169)
Bi Jia Shan	8	519	(243)
Bilali	2	485	(61)
Bilice	8	137	(213)
Billyjeanne A	2	218	(43)
Binaiya	20	388	(488)
Bin Cheng	13	17	(350)
Binissalem	6	48	(145)
Bintang Harapan	8	683	(258)†
Bio Bio	10	43	(290)
Birgit Jurgens	7	337	(181)
Birka Princess	20	46	(462)
Birkenwald	5	256	(125)
Birlad	5	158	(118)
Birling	5	322	(129)
Birta	5	260	(125)
Biruinta	2	578	(70)†
Biryusa	8	575	(247)
Birzai	8	619	(250)
Bisanzio	14	47	(370)†
Bisanzio	14	12	(366)
Biscay	6	116	(153)†
Bishu Maru	3	29	(77)
Biskra	9	176	(276)†
Bismihita'La	8	431	(236)
Bismillah	20	446	(495)†
Bismillah	20	325	(483)
Bison	7	486	(192)
Bison	18	133	(431)
Bisotoon	2	248	(45)
Bituma	1	273	(25)†
Bituma	1	32	(5)
Bituma	2	131	(38)
Bizerte	9	128	(272)
Bjorn	10	14	(288)
B K Baba Zade	20	119	(468)
Blackbird	6	70	(146)
Black Prince	20	47	(462)
Blackrock	2	114	(37)
Black Sea	7	69	(161)
Black Sea T	8	57	(208)
Black Watch	20	383	(487)
Blagoveshchensk	8	619	(250)
Blanche	8	281	(225)
Blandine Delmas	7	368	(183)
Blankenes	5	287	(127)
Blankenese	5	319	(129)
Blas Garay	8	261	(224)
Bled	7	222	(172)
Blikur	17	6	(405)
Blissful Reefer 2	11	87	(307)
Blue Aquamarine	7	11	(157)
Bluebell Susannah	7	221	(172)
Blue Bird	7	308	(179)
Blue Cosmo	7	271	(176)
Blue Crest	11	91	(307)
Blue Crystal	11	91	(307)
Blue Frost	11	91	(307)
Blue Ice	11	87	(307)
Blue Jade	8	187	(217)
Blue Light	2	323	(50)
Blue Light	2	324	(50)
Blue Line	6	27	(143)
Blue Master	7	511	(196)†
Blue Master	7	455	(190)
Blue Nile	17	49	(409)
Bluenorth	9	33	(265)
Bluenose	20	48	(462)
Blue Ocean	4	78	(92)
Blue Ocean	7	120	(165)
Blue Ocean	8	524	(243)
Blue Ocean	9	56	(267)

†Photograph

	SHIP TYPE	REF NO	PAGE NO
Blue Pearl	7	327	(180)
Blue Reefer	11	91	(307)
Blue Sea	1	8	(3)
Blue Sky	7	300	(178)
Blue Star	2	398	(55)
Blue Stone	7	264	(175)
Bluetank Lancer	2	261	(46)
Bluewest	8	562	(246)
Blue Zephyr	20	4	(459)
Blumenau Reefer	11	49	(304)
Bobilna	5	138	(117)
Bob L	7	519	(197)†
Boccaccio	20	323	(483)
Bochnia	9	53	(267)
Bocsa	5	158	(118)
Bodrog	9	42	(266)
Bodrum	8	623	(251)
Boga 1	2	325	(50)
Bohinj	7	222	(172)
Bohus	20	122	(468)
Bokelnburg	5	254	(124)
Bol	9	92	(270)
Bolan	9	166	(275)
Bolero	20	33	(461)
Bolero Reefer	11	136	(311)
Bolshevik M Tomas	12	61	(329)
Bona Falcon	2	299	(48)
Bona Favour	2	299	(48)
Bona Fe	5	260	(125)
Bona Foam	2	301	(48)
Bona Fortuna	2	301	(48)
Bona Forum	2	301	(48)
Bona Freighter	2	480	(60)
Bona Fulmar	2	301	(48)
Bonaire	2	39	(31)
Bonaire	7	11	(157)
B Onal	8	398	(234)
Bona Sailor	1	224	(19)†
Bona Sparrow	1	135	(11)
Bona Spring	1	139	(12)
Bong Dae San	11	176	(314)
Bongo Danielsen	8	206	(219)
Bong San	5	320	(129)
Bonito	2	279	(47)
Bonn Express	12	58	(329)
Bonsai	10	24	(289)
Bontegracht	7	11	(157)
Bontrader	5	44	(110)
Borac	16	57	(396)†
Borac	16	20	(392)
Boracay	16	76	(399)†
Boracay	16	32	(394)
Bora Universal	11	96	(308)
Borc	10	73	(293)†
Borc	10	42	(290)
Borden	18	124	(431)
Boreas	5	72	(112)
Boreas	6	58	(145)
Bore Nordia	16	82	(399)†
Bore Sea	18	98	(429)
Bore Song	18	148	(433)
Boris Andreyev	8	125	(212)
Boris Babochkin	9	92	(270)
Boris Butoma	2	92	(35)
Boris Gorbatov	8	604	(249)
Boris Gordeyev	5	17	(108)
Boris Lavrenev	8	604	(249)
Boris Lavrov	7	152	(167)
Boris Livanov	5	129	(116)
Boris Livanov type	7	153	(167)
Boris Nikolaichuk	8	612	(250)
Borisoglebsk	2	367	(53)
Boris Polevoy	21	59	(504)
Boris Zhemchuzin	9	56	(267)
Borre Af Simrishamn	6	33	(143)
Borrenmill	10	43	(290)
Borsec	5	158	(118)
Borstel	14	64	(372)†
Borstel	14	8	(365)
Borsteler Berg	15	43	(380)
Borthwick	4	155	(99)†
Borya Tsarikov	8	621	(251)
Borzesti	5	138	(117)
Bosphor	20	14	(460)
Bosut	8	201	(218)
Botany Bay	12	127	(334)
Botevgrad	8	340	(229)
Bothniaborg	7	457	(190)
Bothnian Reefer	11	189	(316)†
Botic	7	146	(167)
Botosani	5	158	(118)
Botsman Moshkov	8	78	(209)
Boughaz	20	194	(473)
Bouguenais	7	351	(182)
Boundary	18	71	(426)
Bowen King	8	521	(243)

	SHIP TYPE	REF NO	PAGE NO
Bow Explorer	2	525	(64)
Bow Fighter	1	43	(6)
Bow Fortune	2	211	(43)
Bow Gerd	2	525	(64)
Bow Heron	1	231	(20)†
Bow Heron	1	43	(6)
Bow Hunter	1	35	(5)
Bow Lancer	1	43	(6)
Bow Mariner	1	34	(5)
Bow Petros	1	34	(5)
Bow Pioneer	1	272	(25)†
Bow Pioneer	1	35	(5)
Bow Sea	2	211	(43)
Bow Sky	2	211	(43)
Bow Spring	2	211	(43)
Bow Star	2	211	(43)
Bow Sun	2	211	(43)
Bow Transporter	1	34	(5)
Bow Viking	1	267	(24)†
Bow Viking	1	53	(6)
BP Jouster	2	293	(48)
B. Prus	9	91	(270)
Brabo	7	351	(182)
Brabourne	2	114	(37)
Brad	8	50	(207)
Brage Atlantic	1	59	(6)
Brage Nordic	1	250	(22)†
Brage Supplier	2	66	(33)
Brahman Express	18	24	(423)
Brahms	5	305	(128)
Brandaris	6	96	(150)†
Brandaris	6	37	(144)
Brandenburg	9	141	(273)
Brandenburg	12	115	(333)
Brasilia Reefer	11	152	(312)
Bratulesti	5	158	(118)
Bravaden	7	129	(166)
Bravo Sif	7	461	(190)
Bravur	2	521	(63)
Brazilian Venture	5	252	(124)
Brazil Star	5	280	(126)
Brazil Vitoria	2	151	(39)
Breehelle	8	598	(249)
Breeze	2	46	(32)
Breeze	7	313	(179)
Breitenburg	15	27	(379)
Breiz Klipper	11	182	(315)†
Bremen	20	438	(494)†
Bremen Senator	12	15	(326)
Bremen Star	8	527	(243)
Bremer Export	7	462	(190)
Bremer Handel	5	84	(113)
Bremer Import	17	90	(414)†
Bremer Import	17	60	(410)
Bremer Makler	7	474	(191)
Bremer Merkur	7	474	(191)
Bremer Reeder	7	376	(184)
Bremer Westen	7	474	(191)
Bremon	5	361	(134)†
Brest	11	210	(318)†
Brest	17	51	(409)
Bretagne	20	434	(493)†
Brezza	2	139	(38)
Bribir	17	32	(407)
Bridgeton	2	210	(43)
Brigantium	8	695	(260)†
Brigantium	8	578	(247)
Bright Star	8	24	(205)
Brigit Maersk	12	18	(326)
Brigitta	15	49	(382)†
Brihope	8	302	(227)
Brij	8	427	(236)
Brilliancy	2	397	(55)
Brindisi	20	195	(473)
Brinton Lykes	8	48	(207)
Brisa	9	208	(280)†
Brisa	9	88	(269)
Brisbane Star	13	82	(356)†
Britanis	20	370	(486)
Britannia	16	84	(400)†
Britannia	7	167	(168)
British Admiral	1	66	(7)
British Adventure	1	66	(7)
British Argosy	1	66	(7)
British Esk	1	88	(8)
British Ranger	2	235	(44)
British Reliance	2	235	(44)
British Resolution	2	235	(44)
British Resource	2	235	(44)
British Skill	2	231	(44)
British Spirit	2	231	(44)
British Success	2	231	(44)
British Tamar	1	88	(8)
Britta	6	58	(145)
Brocken	17	102	(415)†
Brocken	17	33	(407)

†Photograph

	SHIP TYPE	REF NO	PAGE NO
Brooklyn Bridge	12	107	(333)
Brooks Range	2	229	(44)
Broompark	7	93	(163)
Broose	2	102	(36)
Brothers	7	212	(172)
Bruce	6	38	(144)
Brussel	5	106	(114)
Bryanskiy Mashinostroitel	9	6	(263)
BT Nautilus	1	78	(8)
BT Navarin	1	78	(8)
BT Navigator	1	78	(8)
BT Neptune	1	78	(8)
BT Nestor	1	78	(8)
BT Nimrod	1	78	(8)
Budapesht	17	51	(409)
Budhi Perkasa	8	418	(235)
Budowlany	5	133	(116)
Buena Fortuna	7	170	(169)
Buffalo	8	34	(206)
Buffalo	18	133	(431)
Buffalo Soldier	17	7	(405)
Buga	8	304	(227)
Builder III	8	19	(204)
Bujoreni	5	138	(117)
Bukit Raya	20	388	(488)
Bulduri	1	257	(23)†
Bulduri	1	20	(4)
Bulgaria	5	193	(120)
Bulkazores	5	297	(128)
Bulk Challenge	6	12	(142)
Bulk Galaxy	7	213	(172)
Bulk Master	8	453	(238)
Bulk Trader	8	527	(243)
Bul Pride	18	200	(438)†
Bulunkhan	7	340	(181)
Bumbesti	5	132	(116)
Bumi Jaya	8	110	(211)
Bumi Raya	7	359	(183)
Buna	1	162	(13)
Bunga Anggerek	1	22	(4)
Bunga Dahlia	13	21	(350)
Bunga Kesumba	2	96	(35)
Bunga Penaga	13	77	(355)†
Bunga Penaga	13	21	(350)
Bunga Permai	12	23	(326)
Bunga Selasih	2	96	(35)
Bunga Semarak	1	61	(7)
Bunga Sepang	2	96	(35)
Bunga Seroja	12	72	(330)
Bunga Siantan	1	61	(7)
Bunga Suria	12	23	(326)
Bunga Teratai	12	72	(330)
Burgas	2	518	(63)
Burgas	7	345	(182)
Burgundia	7	18	(158)
Burwain Adriatic	1	156	(13)
Burwain Arctic	1	156	(13)
Burwain Torm	1	156	(13)
Bussewitz	4	147	(98)†
Bussewitz	4	77	(92)
Busteni	7	174	(169)
Butt	2	85	(35)
Buxcrown	12	102	(332)
Buxlady	12	102	(332)
Buxmaid	7	331	(181)
Buyuk Timur	2	310	(49)
Buzet	8	425	(236)
Buzias	5	158	(118)
Buzludja	7	278	(176)
Buzurgan	2	411	(56)
Bytom	5	189	(120)
Bytom	10	11	(287)
Byzantion	2	337	(51)
Cableman	2	19	(30)
Cabo Blanco	13	10	(349)
Cabo Bojador	8	219	(220)
Cabo de Hornos	1	92	(9)
Cabo Negro	2	169	(40)
Cabot	18	151	(433)
Cachimba	8	149	(214)
Cacica Isabel	20	327	(483)
Caciulata	7	174	(169)
Cadiz	13	42	(352)
Cadmus	8	632	(251)
Cady	6	49	(145)
Caecilia Schulte	13	114	(360)†
Caecilia Schulte	13	6	(349)
Cafer Ahmet	8	217	(220)
Cahokia	11	26	(302)
Cairo Sea	2	512	(63)
Cairu	2	254	(46)
Calabria	18	174	(435)
Calafia	11	88	(307)
Cala Fustam	18	136	(432)
Cala Galdana	18	89	(428)
Cala Llonga	18	12	(422)
Calamo	11	71	(306)
Calanda	8	326	(228)
Calapedra	13	11	(350)
Calarasi	8	50	(207)
Cala Salada	18	136	(432)
Caldeonian Star	20	412	(491)†
Caldiran	8	225	(221)
Caledonia	7	9	(157)
Caledonian Isles	20	293	(480)
Cali	2	202	(42)
California	7	9	(157)
California Ceres	12	111	(333)
California Current	7	443	(189)
California Star	13	8	(349)
Calimanesti	7	174	(169)
Calina	4	67	(91)
Calixto Carcia	8	500	(241)
Callian S	7	81	(162)
Calugareni	7	174	(169)
Calypso	20	165	(471)
Calypso N	7	102	(164)
Camara Pestana	21	17	(500)
Camargue	1	88	(8)
Cam Ayous Express	17	16	(406)
Cam Azobe Express	17	16	(406)
Cam Bilinga	8	430	(236)
Cam Ebene	8	430	(236)
Cam Etinde	2	102	(36)
Camilla	18	81	(427)
Cam Iroko Express	7	363	(183)
Cam Iroko Express	17	16	(406)
Campania	7	5	(157)
Campeon	2	350	(52)
Campo Duran	2	305	(49)
Campomayor	2	413	(56)
Campomino	2	349	(52)
Camponubla	2	350	(52)
Campotejar	2	220	(44)
Camuri	8	529	(244)
Canadian Ace II	19	21	(446)
Canadian Liberty	2	243	(45)
Canadian Progress	10	54	(291)
Canadian Reefer	11	133	(311)
Canan Arican	7	374	(184)
Canarias Express	16	24	(393)
Canberra	20	371	(486)
Can Deval	8	583	(248)
Candia	7	9	(157)
Candia	20	326	(483)
Cando	8	481	(240)
Canela	7	125	(165)
Canguro Fulvo	18	11	(422)
Canguro Grigio	18	11	(422)
Canmar Conquest	12	52	(328)
Canmar Enterprise	12	7	(325)
Canmar Europe	12	1	(325)
Canmar Glory	12	52	(328)
Canmar Spirit	12	71	(330)
Canmar Success	12	106	(333)
Canmar Triumph	12	52	(328)
Canmar Venture	12	71	(330)
Canmar Victory	12	52	(328)
Cannes	7	82	(162)
Canopus	12	200	(342)†
Canopus	2	599	(72)†
Canopus	1	208	(16)
Canopus	8	161	(215)
Canopus	8	259	(223)
Canopus I	15	24	(379)
Cantarell	4	150	(99)†
Canterbury Express	7	305	(178)
Canterbury Star	11	27	(302)
Cap Afrique	18	33	(423)
Cap Akritas	3	25	(76)
Capareli	2	414	(56)
Cap Bon	18	142	(432)
Cap Canaille	18	216	(440)†
Cap Canaille	18	74	(427)
Cap Changuinola	11	214	(319)†
Cape Africa	5	213	(122)
Cape Alava	8	71	(208)
Cape Alexander	8	71	(208)
Cape America	5	213	(122)
Cape Ann	8	71	(208)
Cape Archway	8	71	(208)
Cape Asia	5	213	(122)
Cape Australia	5	213	(122)
Cape Avinof	8	71	(208)
Cape Blanco	8	158	(215)
Cape Bon	8	158	(215)
Cape Borda	8	158	(215)
Cape Bover	8	158	(215)
Cape Breton	8	158	(215)
Cape Canaveral	8	60	(208)

†Photograph

	SHIP TYPE	REF NO	PAGE NO
Cape Canso	8	60	(208)
Cape Cathay	5	213	(122)
Cape Catoche	8	60	(208)
Cape Cavo	11	91	(307)
Cape Chalmers	8	60	(208)
Cape Charles	8	60	(208)
Cape Clear	8	60	(208)
Cape Cod	8	60	(208)
Cape Cod	11	91	(307)
Cape Cornwall	7	139	(166)
Cape Decision	16	15	(392)
Cape Diamond	16	15	(392)
Cape Domingo	16	15	(392)
Cape Douglas	16	15	(392)
Cape Ducato	16	15	(392)
Cape Europe	5	213	(122)
Cape Farewell	21	62	(504)
Cape Fear	21	62	(504)
Cape Finisterre	11	91	(307)
Cape Flattery	21	62	(504)
Cape Florida	21	62	(504)
Cape Gibson	8	627	(251)
Cape Girardeau	8	627	(251)
Cape Hatteras	7	164	(168)
Cape Hatteras	13	29	(351)
Cape Henry	17	21	(406)
Cape Hope	2	31	(31)
Cape Horn	17	21	(406)
Cape Hudson	17	21	(406)
Cape Jacob	8	22	(204)
Cape John	8	22	(204)
Cape Johnson	8	22	(204)
Cape Juby	8	22	(204)
Cape Kennedy	8	24	(205)
Cape Kennedy	16	7	(391)
Cape Knox	16	63	(397)†
Cape Knox	16	7	(391)
Cape Lambert	18	49	(425)
Cap Elene	3	70	(83)†
Cape Lila	5	213	(122)
Capella-1	8	553	(245)
Cape Lobos	18	49	(425)
Cape Monterey	8	24	(205)
Cape Moreton	9	131	(273)
Cape Natal	12	218	(344)†
Cape Natal	12	128	(334)
Cape Negro	12	128	(334)
Cape Nelson	8	690	(259)†
Cape Nelson	8	403	(234)
Cape Nelson	8	446	(237)
Cape Nelson	12	128	(334)
Cape Nome	17	1	(405)
Cape Norman	12	128	(334)
Cape Oceania	5	213	(122)
Cape Orlando	16	40	(394)
Cape Race	16	39	(394)
Cape Ray	7	285	(177)
Cape Ray	16	39	(394)
Cape Rise	16	39	(394)
Cape Syros	8	24	(205)
Capetan Costis	2	498	(62)
Capetan Giorgis I	5	135	(116)
Capetan Lefteris	7	165	(168)
Capetan Michalis	2	86	(35)
Capetan Michalis	7	92	(163)
Cape Taylor	18	160	(433)
Cape Texas	18	26	(423)
Cape Trinity	18	26	(423)
Cape Victory	18	199	(438)†
Cape Vincente	11	91	(307)
Cape Violet	5	372	(136)†
Cape York	8	446	(237)
Cap Finisterre	13	27	(351)
Capitaine Fearn	9	152	(274)
Capitaine Kermadec	8	446	(237)
Capital Bay	9	63	(267)
Capitan Alberto Fernandez	2	50	(32)
Capo Manuela	4	119	(95)
Capo Mele Secondo	7	491	(193)†
Capo Nord	2	375	(53)
Capo Rosso	6	2	(141)
Cap Phaistos	3	4	(75)
Cap Polonio	13	27	(351)
Capricorn	2	431	(57)
Capricorn	9	66	(268)
Capricorn	11	57	(305)
Capricorn I	7	224	(173)
Capricorn Sea	8	312	(228)
Cap Sounion	11	26	(302)
Captadimitris	7	411	(187)
Captain B. Ataman	5	13	(108)
Captain George L	5	53	(110)
Captain George Tsangaris	7	38	(159)
Captain Gurbachan Singh Salaria PVC	1	137	(12)
Captain Leon CHR. Lemos	5	103	(114)
Captain Nikolas	8	67	(208)
Captain Veniamis	5	147	(117)
Captain X Kyriakou	2	470	(60)
Captainyannis L	7	235	(173)
Capta Spyros	8	445	(237)
Capten Khaled	9	58	(267)
Cap Trafalgar	13	76	(355)†
Cap Trafalgar	13	27	(351)
Carabao 1	21	71	(505)†
Caraibe	12	118	(334)
Cara Timur Tiga	8	4	(203)
Caravos Spirit	2	396	(55)
Caravos Star	2	396	(55)
Cardigan Bay	12	153	(336)
Cardissa	1	276	(25)†
Carducci	20	323	(483)
Carena	5	188	(120)
Car Express	18	191	(437)†
Cargo Enterprise	7	121	(165)
Cargo Explorer	7	191	(170)
Cargo Trader	7	191	(170)
Cariana I	7	288	(177)
Carib Alba	7	463	(190)
Caribbean Breeze	7	377	(184)
Caribbean Mercy	20	7	(459)
Caribbean Princess	7	483	(192)
Caribbean Queen	7	483	(192)
Caribbean Trailer	18	163	(434)
Carib Dawn	10	10	(287)
Caribe	8	310	(227)
Caribe Merchant	18	138	(432)
Caribe Trader	18	84	(428)
Carib Eve	10	10	(287)
Carib Faith	17	16	(406)
Caribgas 3	3	26	(77)
Caribgas 7	4	121	(95)
Caribia Express	13	112	(359)†
Caribia Express	12	118	(334)
Caribia Express	13	67	(354)
Caribic	11	40	(303)
Carib Trader	6	19	(142)
Carigas	3	25	(76)
Carima	10	61	(292)†
Carima	10	20	(288)
Carina	11	57	(305)
Carina I	5	256	(125)
Cari Sky	5	191	(120)
Carla A Hills	1	270	(24)†
Carla A Hills	1	77	(8)
Carl Metz	7	456	(190)
Carl Metz	9	141	(273)
Carlo M	7	115	(164)
Carlo R	20	123	(468)
Carmen	19	10	(445)
Carmen Castellano	11	47	(304)
Carmencita	11	118	(310)
Carmen Dolores H	12	44	(328)
Carnia	1	88	(8)
Carnival	9	126	(272)
Carola	13	26	(351)
Carola I	7	288	(177)
Carolin	5	68	(112)
Carolina	12	131	(335)
Caroline	2	13	(29)
Caroline Delmas	7	368	(183)
Caroline Maersk	13	62	(353)
Caroline Oldendorff	7	120	(165)
Carousel	20	385	(487)
Carrier LT	2	82	(35)
Carrier Princess	20	266	(478)
Carrymar	8	425	(236)
Cartagena	17	91	(414)†
Cartagena	17	34	(407)
Carthage	7	425	(188)
Caruao	1	11	(3)
Carvik	7	188	(170)
Casablanca	14	30	(368)†
Casablanca	5	61	(111)
Casablanca	11	88	(307)
Casablanca S	9	101	(270)
Casalicchio	18	72	(427)
Casamance Express	20	365	(486)
Casandra	6	58	(145)
Caspian Trader	2	187	(42)
Caspian Trident	5	107	(114)
Caspic	6	105	(152)†
Caspic	6	24	(143)
Castillo de Almansa	5	62	(111)
Castillo de Arevalo	5	62	(111)
Castillo de Xativa	5	62	(111)
Castle Peak	5	45	(110)
Castor	13	91	(357)†
Castor	2	115	(37)
Castor	2	434	(57)
Castor	8	446	(237)
Castor Gas	3	7	(75)
Catharina	15	87	(386)†

†Photograph

	SHIP TYPE	REF NO	PAGE NO
Catharina	15	27	(379)
Catherine Desgagnes	8	234	(221)
Catherine Helen	9	143	(274)
Catherine Venture	5	208	(121)
Cathy	5	145	(117)
Catriona	8	24	(205)
Cayenne	7	308	(179)
Ccni Anakena	13	10	(349)
Ccni Atacama	13	7	(349)
Cecilia Desgagnes	7	264	(175)
Cecilia I	7	364	(183)
Cecilie Maersk	13	62	(353)
Cedar Car	18	162	(434)
Cedrela	7	125	(165)
Cedynia	5	302	(128)
Celebration	20	61	(463)
Celia	17	39	(408)
Celiksan	7	128	(165)
Celine M	6	7	(141)
Celje	8	321	(228)
Cellus	7	346	(182)
Celtic Ice	11	146	(312)
Celtic Sea	11	134	(311)
Celtic Warrior	5	91	(113)
Cembalo	21	27	(501)
Cemenmar Cuatro	21	109	(510)†
Cementia	21	21	(500)
Cemile	6	49	(145)
Cemre 2	7	36	(159)
Cem River	21	108	(510)†
Cemtex Yuan	5	292	(127)
Cengiz K	5	158	(118)
Cenk II	17	23	(407)
Cenk III	18	77	(427)
Cenk K	17	23	(407)
Centaur	2	406	(55)
Century	20	396	(489)†
Century	3	36	(78)†
Century	3	27	(77)
Century Highway No 5	19	76	(453)†
Century Star	7	528	(198)†
Cerda	2	325	(50)
Cervantes	12	45	(328)
Cervin	2	571	(69)†
Cesare	2	283	(47)
Ceti	8	291	(226)
Cetra Corona	5	291	(127)
C Express	14	18	(366)
Ceynowa	7	448	(189)
C Filyos	7	158	(168)
CGM Iguacu II	13	3	(349)
CGM la Perouse	12	113	(333)
CGM Magellan	13	60	(353)
CGM Mana II	8	446	(237)
CGM Mascareignes	7	194	(170)
CGM Racine	16	68	(398)†
CGM Racine	16	19	(392)
CGM Rimbaud	16	19	(392)
CGM St Laurent	17	42	(408)
Chac	2	55	(32)
Chacabuco	11	197	(317)†
Chaconia	4	98	(94)
Chada Naree	8	146	(214)
Chagall	2	59	(33)
Chahaya Sejati	8	235	(221)
Chainat Navee	9	136	(273)
Chaiten	11	235	(321)†
Chalka (or Chaika)	8	78	(209)
Challenger IV	7	389	(185)
Champa Star	2	35	(31)
Champion	1	57	(6)
Champion	2	502	(62)
Chang An	8	76	(209)
Chang Beng	20	124	(468)
Chang Duck No 5	8	150	(214)
Chang Geng	20	124	(468)
Chang Hai	8	344	(229)
Chang Hang	18	56	(425)
Chang He	20	124	(468)
Chang Hu	20	124	(468)
Chang Jin	20	124	(468)
Chang Ken	20	124	(468)
Chang Li	20	124	(468)
Chang Liu	20	124	(468)
Chang Long	8	207	(219)
Chang Ping	9	210	(280)†
Chang Shan	20	124	(468)
Chang Shen	20	124	(468)
Chang Song	5	11	(107)
Chang Song	20	124	(468)
Changting	8	561	(246)
Chang Wang	7	425	(188)
Chang Xiu	20	124	(468)
Chang Yi Hai	5	42	(110)
Chang Zheng	20	124	(468)
Chang Zi	20	124	(468)
Channel Enterprise	5	354	(133)†
Channel Enterprise	5	45	(110)
Chao He	12	89	(331)
Chao Yang	8	244	(222)
Chapaev	11	170	(313)
Chariot	1	57	(6)
Chariot	5	277	(126)
Charisma	2	384	(54)
Charlene	8	281	(225)
Charles Island	11	117	(309)
Charles L D	5	303	(128)
Charles Lykes	9	163	(275)
Charles Pigott	2	236	(45)
Charlotte Maersk	13	62	(353)
Charlotte Schulte	13	10	(349)
Charlotte Sif	7	461	(190)
Charme	18	66	(426)
Chartsman	1	184	(15)
Chastine Maersk	13	62	(353)
Chateaulin	11	49	(304)
Chau Long	8	589	(248)
Chaumont	2	235	(44)
Chavchavadze	1	107	(10)
Chazhma	8	619	(250)
CHC No 1	7	125	(165)
CHC No 2	7	124	(165)
Chelia	9	68	(268)
Chelm	9	53	(267)
Cheltenham	3	33	(78)†
Cheltenham	3	34	(78)†
Chelyabinsk	7	483	(192)
Chembulk Rotterdam	1	236	(20)†
Chemi Crest	2	569	(69)†
Chemsky	2	189	(42)
Chemtrans Belocean	2	480	(60)
Chem Unity	3	35	(78)†
Chem Unity	3	19	(76)
Cheng Da	8	157	(215)
Cheng Shan	8	587	(248)
Chennai Jayam	7	190	(170)
Chennai Nermai	7	133	(166)
Chennai Polivu	7	133	(166)
Chennai Sadhanai	7	190	(170)
Chennai Valarchi	7	133	(166)
Chennai Veeram	7	133	(166)
Cheremkhovo	7	483	(192)
Cherepovets	7	375	(184)
Cherkassy	7	483	(192)
Chernigov	8	612	(250)
Cherni Vrakh	5	264	(125)
Cherokee Belle	7	99	(163)
Cherry	8	81	(209)
Cherry	8	445	(237)
Cherry Flower	8	445	(237)
Cheryl C	10	13	(288)
Cheshire	4	98	(94)
Chess	2	357	(52)
Chestnut Hill	2	334	(51)
Chettinand Tradition	7	203	(171)
Chevron Arizona	1	91	(9)
Chevron Atlantic	1	89	(8)
Chevron California	2	320	(50)
Chevron Colorado	1	91	(9)
Chevron Copenhagen	2	236	(45)
Chevron Edinburgh	2	236	(45)
Chevron Feluy	2	236	(45)
Chevron Louisiana	1	91	(9)
Chevron Mississippi	2	320	(50)
Chevron Nagasaki	2	236	(45)
Chevron Oregon	1	91	(9)
Chevron Pacific	1	77	(8)
Chevron Perth	2	236	(45)
Chevron South America	2	210	(43)
Chevron Washington	1	91	(9)
Cheyenne	2	93	(35)
Chiang Mai	17	31	(407)
Chiangrai	8	319	(228)
Chi Cheng	8	618	(250)
Chickasaw	1	159	(13)
Chijin	19	12	(446)
Chikuzen Maru	5	374	(136)†
Chikuzen Maru	5	36	(109)
Chilean Reefer	11	239	(322)†
Chi Linh	2	328	(50)
China Act	5	213	(122)
China Bright	8	345	(230)
China Fortune	5	213	(122)
China Glory	5	60	(111)
China Joy	5	60	(111)
China Mountain	7	229	(173)
China Power	8	445	(237)
China Pride	5	60	(111)
China Spirit	5	60	(111)
China Steel Entrepreneur	5	204	(121)
China Steel Innovator	5	204	(121)
China Steel Realist	5	204	(121)

	SHIP TYPE	REF NO	PAGE NO
China Steel Team	5	204	(121)
China Trader	5	292	(127)
China Transport	5	213	(122)
Chios Beauty	7	452	(190)
Chios Charm	8	466	(239)
Chios Faith	8	57	(208)
Chios Fortune	7	147	(167)
Chios Glory	7	41	(160)
Chios I	2	293	(48)
Chios I	8	170	(216)
Chipmunk	8	272	(224)
Chiquita	2	240	(45)
Chiquita Baracoa	11	35	(303)
Chiquita Baru	11	35	(303)
Chiquita Belgie	11	112	(309)
Chiquita Bremen	11	198	(317)†
Chiquita Deutschland	11	112	(309)
Chiquita Italia	11	181	(315)†
Chiquita Italia	11	112	(309)
Chiquita Nederland	11	112	(309)
Chiquita Scandinavia	11	112	(309)
Chiquita Schweiz	11	112	(309)
Chiricana	11	94	(307)
Chita	8	415	(235)
Chita Maru	5	33	(109)
Chitral	9	166	(275)
Chitral	12	65	(329)
Chi Wan 301	8	448	(238)
Chkalovsk	5	196	(121)
CHL Innovator	7	163	(168)
Chocano	8	533	(244)
Choctaw	1	159	(13)
Chodziez	16	25	(393)
Chofu	7	407	(186)
Choke Reefer 1	11	131	(311)
Choke Reefer 2	11	158	(312)
Chopin	7	494	(193)†
Chopin	1	37	(5)
Chopol	8	155	(215)
Chorzow	10	62	(292)†
Chorzow	10	11	(287)
Chou Shan	5	213	(122)
Choyang Chance	12	194	(341)†
Choyang Express	12	90	(331)
Choyang Giant	12	207	(343)†
Choyang Land	12	66	(330)
Choyang Moscow	12	15	(326)
Choyang Pride	12	102	(332)
Choyang Victory	12	188	(341)†
Choyang Volga	12	15	(326)
Chrissi P	8	312	(228)
Christa Kerstin	15	27	(379)
Christian	5	256	(125)
Christiane	7	154	(168)
Christiane Schulte	5	274	(126)
Christian I	18	79	(427)
Christian IV	20	71	(464)
Christian Maersk	13	62	(353)
Christina	5	113	(115)
Christina C	7	170	(169)
Christina I	7	364	(183)
Christina J	9	85	(269)
Christina K	9	234	(283)†
Christo Botev	9	92	(270)
Christopher	15	22	(379)
Christoph Schulte	4	85	(93)
Chryssi	2	540	(65)†
Chukotskiy Bereg	11	98	(308)
Chumerna	5	264	(125)
Chungjin	5	216	(122)
Chun He	12	89	(331)
Chun Jin	8	37	(206)
Chunlin	8	547	(245)
Churruca	14	72	(373)†
Churruca	5	113	(115)
Chusovoy	5	196	(121)
Chuy	2	78	(34)
Chyornoe More	11	102	(308)
Ciboney	5	316	(129)
Cicero	18	151	(433)
Cidade de Funchal	16	96	(401)†
Cidade de Funchal	18	123	(431)
Cielo di Firenze	7	393	(185)
Cielo di Milano	2	305	(49)
Cielo di Roma	2	305	(49)
Cielo di Salerno	2	305	(49)
Cielo Esta	5	199	(121)
Cienvik	7	188	(170)
Cikolo	8	201	(218)
Cimpulung	5	248	(124)
Cinderella	3	54	(81)†
Cindya	17	97	(415)†
Cindya	17	40	(408)
Circeo	7	269	(176)
City of Akaki	9	225	(282)†
City of Alberni	9	70	(268)

	SHIP TYPE	REF NO	PAGE NO
City of Barcelona	18	209	(439)†
City of Beirut	8	284	(225)
City of Burnie	18	52	(425)
City of Durban	12	152	(336)
City of Glasgow	13	40	(352)
City of Lome	8	426	(236)
City of London	13	110	(359)†
City of London	13	51	(352)
City of Manchester	14	67	(372)†
City of Manchester	12	45	(328)
City of Nanaimo	9	70	(268)
City of New Westminster	9	205	(280)†
City of New Westminster	9	70	(268)
City of Port Melbourne	18	52	(425)
City of Salerno	12	196	(342)†
Ciudad de Algeciras	20	341	(484)
Ciudad de Alicante	18	8	(421)
Ciudad de Badajoz	20	49	(462)
Ciudad de Burgos	18	8	(421)
Ciudad de Cadiz	18	8	(421)
Ciudad de Ceuta	20	273	(479)
Ciudad de la Laguna	20	200	(473)
Ciudad de Oviedo	17	57	(410)
Ciudad de Palma	20	49	(462)
Ciudad de Salamanca	20	49	(462)
Ciudad de Salamanca	20	262	(478)
Ciudad de Santa Cruz la Palma	20	49	(462)
Ciudad de Sevilla	20	49	(462)
Ciudad de Sevilla	20	262	(478)
Ciudad de Valencia	20	49	(462)
Ciudad de Valencia	20	262	(478)
Ciudad de Zaragoza	20	273	(479)
Claes Maersk	13	62	(353)
Claire	9	9	(263)
Clara	6	2	(141)
Clara	6	43	(144)
Clara Maersk	13	62	(353)
Clary	7	545	(200)†
Claudia	15	79	(385)†
Claudia I	7	364	(183)
Claudia L	15	21	(379)
Claus	6	22	(142)
Clavigo	15	34	(380)
Claymore	20	353	(485)
Cleanthes	8	16	(204)
Clearwater Bay	8	373	(232)
Clelia HF	9	93	(270)
Clement	1	76	(8)
Clementina	11	14	(301)
Cleo D	8	159	(215)
Cleopatra	8	453	(238)
Clerville	2	284	(47)
Cleveland	8	627	(251)
Cliff	15	8	(377)
Clifford Maersk	13	121	(361)†
Clifford Maersk	13	62	(353)
Clinton K	8	427	(236)
Clio	9	179	(277)†
Clio	9	56	(267)
Clipper Alpha	8	252	(223)
Clipper Amaryllis	8	251	(223)
Clipper Amethyst	10	35	(289)
Clipper Aquamarine	10	35	(289)
Clipper Arita	8	252	(223)
Clipper Atlantic	8	527	(243)
Clipper Cherokee	21	84	(507)†
Clipper Cherokee	21	51	(503)
Clipper Dream	7	343	(182)
Clipper Fame	7	129	(166)
Clipper Fidelity	8	24	(205)
Clipper Forest	7	129	(166)
Clipper Gas	4	28	(89)
Clipper Golden Hind	10	12	(288)
Clipper Majestic	8	252	(223)
Clipper Mandarin	8	252	(223)
Clipper Pacific	8	527	(243)
Clipper Salvador	7	410	(187)
Clipper Santos	7	410	(187)
Clipper Sao Luiz	7	410	(187)
Clipper Sao Paulo	7	410	(187)
Clipper Sea	4	110	(94)
Clipper Star	5	137	(116)
Clipper Unity	8	527	(243)
Clipperventure L	2	510	(63)
Clipper Yama	10	35	(289)
Clydebank	9	149	(274)
Clyde River	4	54	(91)
C Martin	10	12	(288)
CMB Antwerp	13	3	(349)
CMB Ebony	8	118	(212)
CMB Energy	7	10	(157)
CMB Medal	13	3	(349)
CMB Melody	13	3	(349)
CMBT America	13	31	(351)
CMBT Asia	13	78	(355)†
CMBT Asia	13	5	(349)

†Photograph

	SHIP TYPE	REF NO	PAGE NO
CMBT Concord	13	122	(361)†
CMBT Concord	13	3	(349)
CMBT Corvette	5	113	(115)
CMBT Eagle	8	429	(236)
CMBT Echo	8	423	(236)
CMBT Effort	8	124	(212)
CMBT Emerald	8	125	(212)
CMBT Ensign	8	380	(232)
CMBT Equator	8	161	(215)
CMBT Equator	8	162	(215)
CMBT Equinox	8	446	(237)
CMBT Europe	13	5	(349)
CMBT Express	8	430	(236)
CMBT Tana	7	310	(179)
C Mehmet	5	217	(122)
CMS Island Express	18	83	(427)
C Nurfan	5	158	(118)
Coastal Corpus Christi	2	274	(47)
Coastal Eagle Point	2	274	(47)
Coastal Golden	2	585	(71)†
Coastal Manatee	2	269	(46)
Coburg	14	29	(368)†
Coburg	6	2	(141)
Codlea	8	50	(207)
Coimbra	15	27	(379)
Cold Express	11	160	(313)
Colditz	5	130	(116)
Coldstream Merchant	7	335	(181)
Coldstream Shipper	7	335	(181)
Coldstream Trader	7	335	(181)
Colima	7	417	(187)
Colmy	9	110	(271)
Colorado	2	260	(46)
Colorado	11	60	(305)
Color Festival	20	50	(463)
Color Viking	20	225	(475)
Columbia	1	96	(9)
Columbia	20	233	(476)
Columbia Bay	7	207	(171)
Columbialand	7	301	(178)
Columbia Neptune	2	513	(63)
Columbine	9	163	(275)
Columbus	1	76	(8)
Columbus America	12	121	(334)
Columbus Australia	12	121	(334)
Columbus California	13	65	(353)
Columbus Canada	13	65	(353)
Columbus New Zealand	12	121	(334)
Columbus Olinda	13	125	(361)†
Columbus Olivos	13	83	(356)†
Columbus Queensland	13	65	(353)
Columbus Victoria	13	65	(353)
Comandante Tomas Espora	1	19	(4)
Combi Trader	9	66	(268)
Comet	9	197	(279)†
Comet	9	45	(266)
Comet	15	27	(379)
Commencement	8	445	(237)
Commodore Clipper	18	86	(428)
Commodore Goodwill	18	43	(424)
Compaen	15	6	(377)
Companion	2	339	(51)
Company Havildar Major Piru Singh PVC	1	137	(12)
Concepcion Marino	20	327	(483)
Concord	13	10	(349)
Concord	18	11	(422)
Concorde	2	44	(32)
Concorde Spirit	5	35	(109)
Concordia	13	51	(352)
Concordia C	2	385	(54)
Concordia I	2	197	(42)
Condock I	21	93	(508)†
Condock I	21	43	(502)
Condock III	21	43	(502)
Condock IV	17	63	(411)†
Condock IV	17	36	(408)
Condock V	21	94	(508)†
Condock V	21	44	(502)
Condoleezza Rice	1	27	(5)
Condor	8	281	(225)
Condor	8	506	(242)
Condor	15	9	(377)
Condor Arrow	10	43	(290)
Conger	1	47	(6)
Conquestventure L	2	510	(63)
Conquistador	7	441	(189)
Conro Trader	5	276	(126)
Constantia V	8	524	(243)
Constantinos D	8	159	(215)
Constantinos M	8	16	(204)
Constitution	2	228	(44)
Contender	17	59	(410)
Conti Blue	8	448	(238)
Continental Partner	7	298	(178)
Contrader	21	45	(502)
Contship Asia	13	3	(349)
Contship Atlantic	13	3	(349)
Contship Barcelona	13	3	(349)
Contship Europe	13	3	(349)
Contship France	13	3	(349)
Contship Germany	13	3	(349)
Contship Italy	13	3	(349)
Contship Jork	12	102	(332)
Contship Lavagna	13	3	(349)
Contship New Zealand	13	3	(349)
Contship Pacific	13	3	(349)
Contship Singapore	13	3	(349)
Conus	1	15	(4)
Conveyor	10	51	(291)
Co-op Harvest	5	303	(128)
Co-op Partner	5	303	(128)
Co-op Sunrise	4	65	(91)
Coot	8	169	(216)
Copacabana	13	108	(359)†
Copacabana	13	34	(351)
Copernico	8	345	(230)
Copihue	8	506	(242)
Copihue	11	75	(306)
Corain 1	8	358	(230)
Corain II	8	358	(230)
Coral	2	519	(63)
Coral	7	154	(168)
Coral Antillarum	4	183	(103)†
Coral Essberger	2	1	(29)
Coral Islander	17	48	(409)
Coralli	5	84	(113)
Coral Reef	2	102	(36)
Coral Sea	11	26	(302)
Coral Star	4	119	(95)
Corato	7	154	(168)
Corco Rado	2	318	(50)
Corcovado	7	191	(170)
Corcovado	7	303	(178)
Cordiality	7	222	(172)
Cordigliera	8	434	(236)
Cordillera	8	506	(242)
Coringle Bay	7	481	(192)
Corinna	6	99	(151)†
Corinna	6	2	(141)
Corinthian Trader	7	224	(173)
Cormorant	8	500	(241)
Cornelia Maersk	13	62	(353)
Cornelis Verolme	5	63	(111)
Corner Brook	21	11	(500)
Coromuel	20	193	(473)
Corona	5	66	(111)
Corona Ace	5	101	(114)
Coronado	2	576	(69)†
Coronel	5	256	(125)
Corpus Christi	9	23	(264)
Corrientes II	7	15	(158)
Corse	20	296	(481)
Corsica	2	351	(52)
Corsica Marina II	20	84	(465)
Corsica Regina	20	279	(479)
Corsica Serena II	20	51	(463)
Corsica Victoria	20	408	(490)†
Corsica Victoria	20	279	(479)
Cortesia Duckling	7	275	(176)
Cortia	17	99	(415)†
Cortia	17	39	(408)
Corto	7	425	(188)
Corvo	14	56	(371)†
Corvo	14	3	(365)
Cosa	5	334	(131)†
Cosa	5	274	(126)
Cosman I	7	68	(161)
Cosman II	7	68	(161)
Cosmea	15	43	(380)
Cosmic	7	483	(192)
Cosmo Andromeda	2	165	(40)
Cosmo Delphinus	1	120	(10)
Cosmo Galaxy	2	373	(53)
Cosmo Maru	2	132	(38)
Cosmo Neptune	2	373	(53)
Cosmos	9	215	(281)†
Cosmo Venus	2	373	(53)
Costa Classica	20	422	(492)†
Costas S	8	143	(214)
Costinesti	7	174	(169)
Costis	7	500	(194)†
Costis	7	202	(171)
Cotinga	6	23	(142)
Cotnari	8	41	(206)
Cotswold Prince	8	180	(217)
Cottica	11	219	(319)†
Count	2	444	(58)
Courage	2	410	(56)
Courageventure L	2	510	(63)
Courier	2	503	(62)
Courtney L	13	71	(354)
Coutances	18	182	(436)†

†Photograph

	SHIP TYPE	REF NO	PAGE NO
Coutances	18	22	(422)
Covasna	8	50	(207)
Cove Endeavour	2	320	(50)
Cove Trader	2	223	(44)
C P 26	2	77	(34)
CPC Gallia	7	336	(181)
CPC Helvetia	7	307	(179)
CPC Holandia	7	307	(179)
CPC Nippon	7	336	(181)
Craigmore	6	13	(142)
Crane	7	50	(160)
Cretan Trader	7	224	(173)
Crimmitschau	8	446	(237)
Crisana	2	592	(71)†
Crisana	2	259	(46)
Crisanta	8	545	(245)
Cristallo	2	120	(37)
Cristian A	7	174	(169)
Cristian B	7	174	(169)
Cristian C	7	174	(169)
Cristoforo Colombo	12	28	(327)
Croma	1	180	(14)
Crown M	20	52	(463)
Crown Odyssey	20	234	(476)
Crown of Scandinavia	20	87	(465)
C R Tanger	18	159	(433)
Crucero Express	20	320	(483)
Crusader	7	124	(165)
Crusader Venture	5	103	(114)
Crystal Harmony	20	428	(493)†
Crystal Mermaid	4	102	(94)
Crystal Pilgrim	11	120	(310)
Crystal Pioneer	11	120	(310)
Crystal Pride	11	120	(310)
Crystal Primadonna	11	184	(315)†
Crystal Primadonna	11	120	(310)
Crystal Prince	11	120	(310)
Crystal Privilege	11	120	(310)
Crystal Reefer	11	130	(311)
Crystalventure L	2	510	(63)
CSAV Rahue	13	10	(349)
CSAV Ralun	9	51	(266)
CSAV Ranco	13	11	(350)
CSAV Rapel	9	51	(266)
CSAV Rauli	13	7	(349)
CSAV Rauten	13	40	(352)
CSAV Renaico	9	51	(266)
CSAV Roble	13	41	(352)
CSAV Rosario	13	116	(360)†
CSAV Rupanco	13	3	(349)
CSAV Teno	9	20	(264)
C S Elegant	5	303	(128)
CSK Brilliance	5	115	(115)
CSK Fortune	5	60	(111)
CSK Glory	5	60	(111)
Csokonai	8	154	(215)
CSP 1	2	494	(61)
CTE Magallanes	12	46	(328)
CTMA Voyageur	18	105	(429)
CTMA Voyageur	18	113	(430)
CT Star	1	164	(13)
Cuba	2	222	(44)
Cuenca	11	238	(322)†
Cumberland Sky	8	88	(210)
Cunard Countess	20	53	(463)
Cunard Princess	20	53	(463)
Curacao Reefer	11	97	(308)
Current	8	312	(228)
Curtea de Arges	8	132	(213)
Curtiss	17	1	(405)
Cury	2	253	(45)
Cuu Long	2	367	(53)
Cuxhaven	6	2	(141)
Cvijeta Zuzoric	7	166	(168)
C V Raman	1	21	(4)
Cyclades	7	222	(172)
Cyclades	7	453	(190)
Cyclopus K	9	16	(264)
Cygne	7	461	(190)
Cynthia	8	581	(248)
Cyrus	7	353	(182)
Czantoria	2	408	(56)
Dacca	8	581	(248)
Da Cheng	8	384	(233)
Dacia	2	259	(46)
Dadabhai Naoroji	2	477	(60)
Da de	9	146	(274)
Dades	2	77	(34)
Dae Jin	8	119	(212)
Dae Sung No 11	11	2	(301)
Da Feng	8	504	(241)
Dagistan	20	287	(480)
Dahab	16	28	(393)
Da Hong Qiao	8	501	(241)

	SHIP TYPE	REF NO	PAGE NO
Dahra	2	490	(61)
Daiana P	8	548	(245)
Da-In	20	2	(459)
Daiquiri	8	637	(252)
Daiten	5	216	(122)
Dai Yun Shan	9	170	(275)
Daizu Maru	8	304	(227)
Dakis I	8	201	(218)
Dakota	11	88	(307)
Dala Corona	1	277	(25)†
Dalaki	8	16	(204)
Dalanas	2	486	(61)
Da Li	8	504	(241)
Dalia	8	24	(205)
Dalia	8	330	(229)
Dalia	21	21	(500)
Dalian	18	30	(423)
Daliana	20	333	(483)
Dallington	5	164	(118)
Dalmacija	20	20	(460)
Dalnerechensk	1	52	(6)
Dalnerechensk	8	577	(247)
Da Long Tian	8	501	(241)
Da Luo Shan	5	42	(110)
Damodar Kaveri	5	194	(120)
Dan	2	451	(59)
Dana	6	106	(152)†
Dana	6	69	(146)
Dana Anglia	20	235	(476)
Dana Baltica	18	66	(426)
Dana Cimbria	16	74	(398)†
Dana Cimbria	18	218	(440)†
Dana Cimbria	16	30	(393)
Dana Corona	17	35	(408)
Danah	9	127	(272)
Dana Hafnia	18	219	(441)†
Dana Hafnia	16	27	(393)
Danah I	8	236	(221)
Dana Maxima	17	101	(415)†
Dana Maxima	17	44	(408)
Dana Minerva	18	90	(428)
Danat Qatar	2	326	(50)
Danau Limboto	7	220	(172)
Danau Mas	18	40	(424)
Dancing Sister	8	500	(241)
Dan Dong	7	425	(188)
Danfeeder	14	34	(368)†
Danfeeder	5	256	(125)
Dania Carina	15	8	(377)
Dania Portland	7	181	(169)
Danica Rainbow	8	652	(254)†
Danila	2	150	(39)
Danis Koper	7	369	(184)
Danita	1	258	(23)†
Danita	1	200	(16)
Danmark	20	399	(489)†
Danmark	20	125	(468)
Danube Express	21	13	(500)
Danube Shuttle	21	13	(500)
Danube Stream	8	622	(251)
Danube Trader	7	174	(169)
Danube Voyager	7	340	(181)
Danubia	15	22	(379)
Danyanne	2	74	(34)
Dany M	8	144	(214)
Da Peng	8	46	(207)
Daphne	20	9	(459)
Da Ping Shan	8	172	(216)
Da Qiang 213	2	160	(40)
Da Qing 16	2	7	(29)
Da Qing 18	2	133	(38)
Da Qing 19	2	133	(38)
Da Qing 20	2	133	(38)
Da Qing 21	2	133	(38)
Da Qing 212	2	160	(40)
Da Qing 214	2	160	(40)
Da Qing 215	2	160	(40)
Da Qing 216	1	25	(4)
Da Qing 218	1	25	(4)
Da Qing 22	2	133	(38)
Da Qing 23	2	133	(38)
Da Qing 231	2	8	(29)
Da Qing 234	2	8	(29)
Da Qing 235	2	11	(29)
Da Qing 240	2	14	(29)
Da Qing 241	2	14	(29)
Da Qing 247	2	128	(37)
Da Qing 255	2	476	(60)
Da Qing 256	2	352	(52)
Da Qing 30	2	10	(29)
Da Qing 31	2	10	(29)
Da Qing 38	2	23	(30)
Da Qing 412	2	160	(40)
Da Qing 413	2	160	(40)
Da Qing 414	2	160	(40)
Da Qing 415	2	160	(40)

†Photograph

	SHIP TYPE	REF NO	PAGE NO
Da Qing 416	2	160	(40)
Da Qing 417	2	160	(40)
Da Qing 42	2	14	(29)
Da Qing 422	1	25	(4)
Da Qing 44	2	14	(29)
Da Qing 45	2	8	(29)
Da Qing 46	2	8	(29)
Da Qing 47	2	8	(29)
Da Qing 48	2	8	(29)
Da Qing 49	2	8	(29)
Da Qing 50	2	8	(29)
Da Qing 52	2	4	(29)
Da Qing 66	2	225	(44)
Da Qing 87	1	11	(3)
Da Qing No 232	2	8	(29)
Da Qing No 29	2	10	(29)
Da Qing Shan	8	501	(241)
Darfur	9	17	(264)
Daria I	8	354	(230)
Darnitsa	2	222	(44)
Darpo Sembilan	8	634	(251)
Darpo Sepuluh	8	220	(220)
Dart 2	18	52	(425)
D'Artagnan	2	315	(49)
Darumasun	21	58	(503)
Darwin	4	61	(91)
Darya Chand	7	203	(171)
Darya Kamal	7	65	(161)
Darya Lakshmi	7	229	(173)
Darya Ma	7	65	(161)
Darya Shubh	7	102	(164)
Da Sha Ping	8	26	(205)
Da Shi Zhai	8	26	(205)
Da Tian	8	384	(233)
Daugava	1	52	(6)
David Gas	4	6	(87)
David Guramishvili	2	508	(62)
Davids Sikeiross	2	424	(57)
Davut 1	8	107	(211)
Dawn	8	71	(208)
Da Xing	8	504	(241)
Da Yao Shan	5	299	(128)
Da Ye	8	504	(241)
Da Yu Shan	5	196	(121)
Debora	9	145	(274)
Debrecenas	2	414	(56)
Deco Oldenburg	8	446	(237)
Dedovsk	7	148	(167)
Deerpool	5	137	(116)
Degero	18	16	(422)
Deike	15	27	(379)
Dekabrist	9	139	(273)
Delegat	2	380	(54)
Delfborg	7	360	(183)
Delfi	8	133	(213)
Delfini	7	179	(169)
Delight Glory	8	500	(241)
Dellach	7	387	(185)
Dellys	18	64	(426)
Delmas Kourou	8	446	(237)
Del Monte	9	147	(274)
Del Monte Consumer	11	111	(309)
Del Monte Trader	11	111	(309)
Deloris	5	64	(111)
Delos	2	227	(44)
Delos	20	126	(468)
Delphin	20	455	(496)†
Delphin	20	127	(468)
Delphine Delmas	7	368	(183)
Delta	14	4	(365)
Delta Express	7	314	(179)
Delta Freedom	8	24	(205)
Deltagas	4	108	(94)
Delta Pride	8	351	(230)
Delta Star	7	8	(157)
Delta Star	8	5	(203)
Delta Trident	5	4	(107)
Del Valle	9	147	(274)
Del Viento	9	147	(274)
Demos	2	415	(56)
Demyan Bednyy	8	630	(251)
Deneb	8	694	(259)†
Deneb	8	74	(209)
Denizati	7	81	(162)
Deniz Ay	2	353	(52)
Deo Gratias	15	6	(377)
Deo Volente	15	8	(377)
Depa Giulia	5	49	(110)
Deppe Florida	13	3	(349)
Deputat Lutskiy	5	17	(108)
Derna	18	92	(428)
Derwent	3	65	(82)†
Deryoung Star	9	154	(274)
Desafio	12	29	(327)
Descartes	4	51	(90)
Desert Falcon	7	170	(169)

	SHIP TYPE	REF NO	PAGE NO
Despina	5	8	(107)
Destino	8	95	(210)
Destiny	2	170	(40)
Dettifoss	7	308	(179)
Deutschland	20	294	(480)
Developing Road	21	6	(499)
Devo	8	427	(236)
Devon	8	251	(223)
Devotion	7	121	(165)
Dhaulagiri	7	363	(183)
Diamond	15	28	(379)
Diamond Ace	1	24	(4)
Diamond Bell	1	24	(4)
Diamond Dragon	8	291	(226)
Diamond Dream	1	114	(10)
Diamond Echo	1	114	(10)
Diamond Grace	1	221	(18)†
Diamond H	9	114	(271)
Diamond I	8	313	(228)
Diamond Land	17	30	(407)
Diamond Reefer	11	216	(319)†
Diamond Reefer	11	33	(303)
Diamond Sea	5	240	(123)
Diamond Star	1	211	(17)
Diana	2	416	(56)
Diana	9	21	(264)
Diana K	9	77	(268)
Diana-Maria	6	22	(142)
Dian Chi	2	434	(57)
Dian Laut	9	154	(274)
Diaporos	2	464	(59)
Diavolezza	5	50	(110)
Dibson 1	8	596	(249)
Dicle	8	629	(251)
Dicto	1	110	(10)
Didi	2	45	(32)
Dien Bien 3	8	682	(258)†
Dieu Si Bon	8	540	(244)
Dignity	8	304	(227)
Dikson	8	596	(249)
Dilza	7	486	(192)
Dima	8	575	(247)
Dimachk	8	20	(204)
Diman	7	50	(160)
Dimants	11	99	(308)
Dimarco	7	392	(185)
Dimitra	20	165	(471)
Dimitrakis	8	433	(236)
Dimitrakis	8	616	(250)
Dimitrios	5	147	(117)
Dimitrios Express	20	44	(462)
Dimitrios Miras	18	117	(430)
Dimitris N	2	187	(42)
Dimitris N	8	291	(226)
Dimitris P	7	421	(187)
Dimitrovsky Komsomol	5	105	(114)
Dina	14	2	(365)
Dina M	8	144	(214)
Dinara	7	166	(168)
Ding Hu	20	356	(485)
Dioli	15	8	(377)
Diomides	8	34	(206)
Dion	2	335	(51)
Dipolog Princess	20	254	(477)
Dipper Arrow	10	43	(290)
Direct Eagle	13	105	(359)†
Direct Eagle	13	54	(353)
Direct Falcon	13	54	(353)
Direct Kea	12	127	(334)
Direct Kiwi	13	54	(353)
Direct Kookaburra	12	127	(334)
Dirk Jacob	2	439	(58)
Discovery Bay	12	80	(331)
Discovery Sun	20	54	(463)
Ditas	2	417	(56)
Ditlev Lauritzen	11	121	(310)
Divnogorsk	2	418	(56)
Dixie Monarch	7	250	(174)
Djorf	8	505	(241)
Djurdjura	8	505	(241)
DK II	2	285	(47)
Dmitriy Donskoy	5	131	(116)
Dmitriy Pozharskiy	5	131	(116)
Dmitriy Shostakovich	20	407	(490)†
Dmitriy Shostakovich	20	128	(468)
Dmitriy Zhloba	2	469	(60)
Dmitry Poluyan	8	74	(209)
Dneprodzerzhinsk	7	148	(167)
Dneproges	7	206	(171)
Dneprovskiy Liman	11	154	(312)
Dobrush	7	242	(174)
Docebay	5	46	(110)
Docecape	5	46	(110)
Docefjord	1	4	(3)
Docemar	5	50	(110)
Docemarte	7	191	(170)

†Photograph

	SHIP TYPE	REF NO	PAGE NO
Doceorion	5	124	(115)
Docerio	5	47	(110)
Doceriver	5	46	(110)
Doceserra	5	47	(110)
Docetaurus	5	124	(115)
Dock Express 10	21	47	(503)
Dock Express 11	21	47	(503)
Dock Express 12	21	47	(503)
Dock Express 20	21	92	(508)†
Doctor Lykes	9	163	(275)
Doctor Rami	8	619	(250)
Dole Africa	11	174	(313)
Dole America	11	174	(313)
Dole Asia	11	174	(313)
Dole California	13	1	(349)
Dole Costarica	13	1	(349)
Dole Ecuador	13	1	(349)
Dole Europa	11	174	(313)
Doles Sala	11	11	(301)
Dolicha Bay	2	385	(54)
Dolichi	6	56	(145)
Dolichi	7	412	(187)
Dollart Gas	4	19	(88)
Dolphin 5	2	483	(61)
Dolphin IV	20	255	(477)
Dolphins 1	8	610	(250)
Dolphin V	2	483	(61)
Domar	6	2	(141)
Domar	7	354	(182)
Domiat	7	43	(160)
Domna Maria	8	184	(217)
Dona	9	11	(264)
Dona Petra M R	8	187	(217)
Donata	18	215	(440)†
Donata	18	92	(428)
Donau	2	187	(42)
Donau Ore	5	213	(122)
Dona V	7	102	(164)
Don Claudio	20	393	(488)
Donetsk	16	13	(392)
Donetskiy Shakhtyor	9	6	(263)
Dong An	9	13	(264)
Dong Fa	8	332	(229)
Dong Fang Hai	7	124	(165)
Dong Feng Shan	7	477	(191)
Dong Guang	8	631	(251)
Dong Hai	8	12	(204)
Dong He	12	30	(327)
Dong Nai	7	31	(159)
Dongnama Inchon	8	270	(224)
Dongnama Pohang	8	270	(224)
Dongola	9	17	(264)
Dong Ru	8	495	(240)
Dong Seong	8	151	(214)
Dong Shan Ling	7	151	(167)
Dong Sheng	8	552	(245)
Dong Yang Express Ferry No 2	20	212	(474)
Dong Young	8	278	(225)
Donington	18	223	(441)†
Donington	18	73	(427)
Donington	18	169	(434)
Don Jorge	10	3	(287)
Don Julio	20	391	(488)
Donnington	5	164	(118)
Don Pedro	18	197	(438)†
Don Vicente	20	373	(486)
Dooyang Brave	8	149	(214)
Dooyang Victor	7	271	(176)
Dora Baltea	18	108	(429)
Dora Oldendorff	5	157	(118)
Dora Riparia	18	108	(429)
Doria	7	331	(181)
Dori Bres	6	2	(141)
Doric Castle	5	232	(123)
Dorothea Oldendorff	7	120	(165)
Dorothea Schulte	4	135	(97)†
Dorothea Schulte	4	27	(89)
Dorsch	1	47	(6)
Dorset	2	262	(46)
Dorthe Oldendorff	7	120	(165)
Dory	7	133	(166)
Doryforos	8	452	(238)
Doua S	7	4	(157)
Doumen	8	41	(206)
Dove	8	105	(211)
Dove Arrow	10	43	(290)
Dover	8	251	(223)
Doverian	2	86	(35)
Draco	5	61	(111)
Draco No 1	8	211	(219)
Draganesti	8	50	(207)
Dragasani	8	41	(206)
Dragomiresti	8	140	(213)
Dragon	7	308	(179)
Dragon Tekong	8	304	(227)
Dragon Well	8	421	(235)

	SHIP TYPE	REF NO	PAGE NO
Dreamward	20	427	(493)†
Dresden Express	12	33	(327)
Dr Juan B Alberdi	8	117	(212)
Drnis	8	407	(234)
Drobeta 1850	8	1	(203)
Dronning Ingrid	20	351	(485)
Druzhba Narodov	15	36	(380)
DSR-Baltic	12	14	(326)
DSR Europe	12	14	(326)
DSR-Rostock	12	15	(326)
DSR Senator	12	15	(326)
DSR-Senator Ivory	7	395	(186)
DSR-Tianjin	7	413	(187)
Dubai	12	204	(343)†
Dubai Pioneer	9	10	(264)
Dubai Success	8	604	(249)
Dubai Trader	8	169	(216)
Dubai Valour	9	110	(271)
Dubai Vision	9	110	(271)
Dubhe	1	76	(8)
Dubrava	11	98	(308)
Dubrava	11	101	(308)
Dubrovnik	5	62	(111)
Dubulti	2	470	(60)
Duc de Normandie	20	280	(479)
Duchess	2	487	(61)
Duchesse Anne	20	55	(463)
Duchess M	18	120	(430)
Duden	7	236	(173)
Duesseldorf Express	12	5	(325)
Dugi Otok	8	445	(237)
Duhallow	5	279	(126)
Duke	6	2	(141)
Duke of Topsail	18	65	(426)
Dumbraveni	8	50	(207)
Duna	8	227	(221)
Dunaj	7	214	(172)
Dunany	6	72	(147)
Duncan Island	11	117	(309)
Dunkerque Express	14	70	(373)†
Dunkerque Express	6	50	(145)
Dura Bulk	8	585	(248)
Durmitor	8	161	(215)
Durnstein	14	83	(374)†
Durnstein	15	7	(377)
Durresi	8	576	(247)
Durrington	5	164	(118)
Dutch Glory	2	70	(34)
Dutch Mariner	1	278	(25)†
Dutch Master	2	70	(34)
Dvinskiy Zaliv	11	18	(302)
Dwiputra	3	85	(84)†
Dyna Caroway	5	370	(135)†
Dynamic	5	176	(119)
Dynamic Horizon	7	41	(160)
Dynamic Spirit	5	275	(126)
Dynasty	5	199	(121)
Dyvi Atlanic	10	8	(287)
Dyvi Kattegat	19	25	(446)
Dyvi Pacific	10	8	(287)
Dzerzhinsk	2	437	(58)
Dzhafer Dzhabarly	7	340	(181)
Dzhurma	8	589	(248)
Dzintari	1	181	(15)
Dzons Rids	2	424	(57)
Eagle	1	244	(21)†
Eagle	10	71	(293)†
Eagle	1	122	(11)
Eagle	10	48	(290)
Eagle Arrow	10	43	(290)
Eagle Auriga	2	232	(44)
Eagle Cloud	17	42	(408)
Eagle Dawn	13	120	(360)†
Eagle II	8	270	(224)
Eagle Moon	14	9	(365)
Eagle Nova	12	90	(331)
Eagle Prestige	13	93	(357)†
Eagle Prosperity	7	326	(180)
Eagle Respect	12	91	(331)
Eagle Sea	7	434	(188)
Eagle Wave	13	38	(352)
Eagle Wind	13	35	(351)
Early Bird	5	139	(117)
Eastcape	11	36	(303)
Eastern Bridge	10	50	(290)
Eastern Glory	7	107	(164)
Eastern Highway	19	23	(446)
Eastern Lion	2	249	(45)
Eastern Lucky	8	369	(231)
Eastern Star	8	630	(251)
Eastern Trader	9	21	(264)
Eastern Trust	8	137	(213)
Eastgate	2	460	(59)
Eastgate	21	61	(504)

†Photograph

	SHIP TYPE	REF NO	PAGE NO
East Islands	8	383	(232)
East Light	11	32	(303)
East Med	6	101	(151)†
East Shing	8	217	(220)
East Trader	7	207	(171)
Eastwind	7	138	(166)
Eastwind	14	11	(366)
Ebalina	1	10	(3)
Ebella	2	482	(61)
Ebenezer C	8	178	(216)
Eberhard	2	57	(33)
Eberstein	15	68	(384)†
Ebino	20	283	(480)
Ebn Batuta	8	370	(231)
Ebn Jubair	8	370	(231)
Ebo	8	500	(241)
Ebro	2	80	(34)
Eburna	1	10	(3)
Ecem	8	100	(211)
E Cheng	13	98	(358)†
Echoman	2	19	(30)
Echo Pioneer	8	124	(212)
Eco Africa	1	149	(12)
Eco Europa	1	149	(12)
Ecomar II	1	162	(13)
Ecowas Trader I	8	170	(216)
Ecowas Trader II	10	17	(288)
Ecstasy	20	297	(481)
Ecuadorian Reefer	11	133	(311)
Edco Star	5	53	(110)
Edel Sif	7	461	(190)
Edelweiss	7	120	(165)
Edinburgh Fruid	2	250	(45)
Edinburgh Maersk	12	155	(336)
Edip Karahsan	7	241	(174)
Edith Nielsen	8	599	(249)
Edmo	2	410	(56)
Edo	7	161	(168)
Edough	8	505	(241)
Edward R	9	134	(273)
Edyth L	13	71	(354)
Eeklo	4	146	(98)†
Eemsborg	7	457	(190)
Efdim Hope	8	252	(223)
Efdim Junior	8	252	(223)
Efessos	8	435	(236)
Efstratios G	8	630	(251)
Egasco Marina	8	418	(235)
Egasco Star	8	418	(235)
Egitto Express	20	263	(478)
Egizia	16	17	(392)
Egnazia	2	381	(54)
Egvekinot	8	612	(250)
Eider	6	28	(143)
Eiffel Star	6	104	(151)†
Eiffel Star	6	52	(145)
Eiffel Sun	6	52	(145)
Einstein	6	58	(145)
Eirini L	2	145	(39)
Eiyu Maru	2	182	(41)
Eka	8	590	(248)
Ekaterina Belashova	8	365	(231)
Eken	1	251	(22)†
Ekfjord Af Donso	1	266	(24)†
Ekfjord Af Donso	1	48	(6)
Ekowas Trader II	5	263	(125)
Ektor	5	236	(123)
Ekturus	1	192	(15)
El Arish-El Tor	20	315	(482)
Elba	2	305	(49)
Elba Nova	20	228	(475)
Elbe	12	178	(339)†
Elbe	5	61	(111)
Elbia	21	32	(501)
El Billy 1	8	619	(250)
Elblag	18	86	(428)
Elbrus	11	75	(306)
Elcano	8	108	(211)
El Cordero	21	123	(511)†
El Djazair	20	340	(484)
Eldor	15	54	(382)†
Electron	6	32	(143)
Elefsis	18	177	(435)
Eleftheria K	9	92	(270)
Eleftherios Venizelos	20	94	(466)
Elein K	8	426	(236)
Elektrostal	8	589	(248)
Elena	14	20	(366)
Elena A	7	89	(163)
Eleni	8	24	(205)
Eleni	8	140	(213)
Elenore	19	4	(445)
Eleo Maersk	1	148	(12)
Elfateh	2	65	(33)
El Flamenco	5	216	(122)
Elfwaihat	2	589	(71)†

	SHIP TYPE	REF NO	PAGE NO
Elfwaihat	2	307	(49)
Elgin	5	352	(133)†
Elgurdabia	2	307	(49)
El Hadjar	5	202	(121)
Elhani	2	307	(49)
Eliane Trader	15	10	(377)
Eliki	7	74	(162)
Elina	8	30	(205)
Elina	8	500	(241)
Elinda	8	392	(233)
Elinka	8	500	(241)
Elisabeth K	5	66	(111)
Elisabeth Maersk	1	148	(12)
Elisabeth Oldendorff	7	120	(165)
Elisabeth We	15	25	(379)
Elisa d'Alesio	2	172	(41)
Elisa F	2	187	(42)
Elisa P	5	150	(117)
Elise D	8	446	(237)
Elise Schulte	13	41	(352)
Elite	13	10	(349)
Elite B	8	137	(213)
Eliza	7	363	(183)
Eliza	8	557	(246)
Elizabeth C	5	340	(132)†
Eliza Heeren	6	80	(148)†
Eliza Heeren	6	4	(141)
Eliza PG	2	598	(72)†
El Jem	7	426	(188)
Elk	16	18	(392)
Elke	8	27	(205)
Elke	15	21	(379)
Elke K	5	66	(111)
Ella Terkol	1	186	(15)
Ellen Hudig	5	63	(111)
Elli	2	325	(50)
Elli B	5	103	(114)
Ellinis P	8	445	(237)
El Malek Khaled	18	63	(426)
Elmar Kivistik	5	17	(108)
El Moro	2	101	(36)
El Niel	8	91	(210)
El Novillo	21	112	(510)†
El Obeid	9	17	(264)
El Pampero	5	50	(110)
El Petrolero	2	98	(35)
Elpida	8	170	(216)
Elpida	8	221	(220)
Elpis	9	73	(268)
Elsa	7	303	(178)
El Salam 93	20	295	(481)
Elsborg	6	51	(145)
Else Terkol	1	186	(15)
Eltigen	2	367	(53)
Elvina	6	68	(146)
Emel 1	9	189	(278)†
Emel 1	9	57	(267)
Emelie	9	68	(268)
Emerald	5	322	(129)
Emerald	13	10	(349)
Emerald Islands	8	500	(241)
Emerald Pearl	5	268	(126)
Emerald Star	1	211	(17)
Emerald Star	8	358	(230)
Emilie K	8	374	(232)
Emil S	8	284	(225)
Emil S II	8	284	(225)
Emily Borchard	5	387	(137)†
Emily Borchard	5	23	(108)
Emja	6	49	(145)
Emma	5	113	(115)
Emma	5	323	(129)
Emma	8	228	(221)
Emma Maersk	1	148	(12)
Emmanuel	8	465	(239)
Empros	8	383	(232)
Emsgas	4	10	(87)
Enalios Ethra	2	370	(53)
Enalios Proteus	2	4	(29)
Enalios Thetis	2	588	(71)†
Enalios Triton	2	397	(55)
Enarxis	8	388	(233)
Enchanted Isle	20	110	(467)
Enchanted Seas	20	110	(467)
Encounter Bay	12	127	(334)
Encourager	9	135	(273)
Endeavor	5	184	(120)
Endeavor II	2	397	(55)
Endeavour	18	41	(424)
Endibe	8	112	(211)
Endo Star	2	307	(49)
Enerchem Asphalt	1	194	(15)
Enerchem Catalyst	2	79	(34)
Energos	2	366	(53)
Energy	13	10	(349)
Energy Pioneer	5	199	(121)

†Photograph

	SHIP TYPE	REF NO	PAGE NO
Engin Kaptanoglu	7	95	(163)
English Star	11	27	(302)
Enias	2	419	(56)
Enif	8	428	(236)
Enko	8	641	(253)†
Enlivener	9	135	(273)
Enol	6	82	(149)†
Enol	6	14	(142)
Enotria	2	381	(54)
Enterprise	5	159	(118)
Eolos	8	218	(220)
Eos	10	98	(296)†
Eos	1	157	(13)
Epic	2	542	(65)†
Epic	8	270	(224)
Epos	7	154	(168)
Epsilongas	4	35	(89)
Epta	7	225	(173)
Eptalofos	7	222	(172)
Eptanisos	20	126	(468)
Eptanissa	2	141	(38)
Equator	2	237	(45)
Equator Crystal	8	411	(235)
Equator Emerald	8	391	(233)
Equator Grand	8	188	(217)
Equator Jade	21	14	(500)
Equator Jewel	14	15	(366)
Equator Joy	8	165	(215)
Equator Pearl	8	574	(247)
Equator Pride	8	508	(242)
Equator Rise	8	508	(242)
Equator Ruby	7	137	(166)
Equator Star	7	137	(166)
Era	1	208	(16)
Ercina	6	14	(142)
Erdal	8	644	(253)†
Erebus	2	222	(44)
Eridge	5	279	(126)
Erika H	15	25	(379)
Erika Jacob	2	439	(58)
Erik Kosan	4	21	(88)
Erikousa Wave	7	156	(168)
Erikson Cooler	11	118	(310)
Erikson Crystal	11	118	(310)
Erikson Freezer	11	118	(310)
Erikson Frost	11	118	(310)
Erikson Nordic	11	118	(310)
Erikson Snow	11	118	(310)
Erikson Winter	11	118	(310)
Erissos	2	468	(60)
Erizo	14	49	(370)†
Erizo	14	14	(366)
Erka Sun	12	45	(328)
Ermioni	5	175	(119)
Erna	6	31	(143)
Erna Oldendorff	7	109	(164)
Ernesto Che Guevara	21	49	(503)
Ernst Thalmann	8	74	(209)
Ernst Thalmann	11	99	(308)
Erradale	5	108	(114)
Ervilia	1	10	(3)
Eser Kaptanoglu	7	133	(166)
Esla	5	83	(113)
Esmeralda	7	2	(157)
Esperanza	7	308	(179)
Esperanza	8	445	(237)
Esperanza C	7	36	(159)
Esperanza III	9	49	(266)
Esperos	5	175	(119)
Espresso Catania	18	118	(430)
Espresso Grecia	20	263	(478)
Espresso Ravenna	18	211	(440)†
Espresso Ravenna	18	118	(430)
Espresso Venezia	20	263	(478)
Esram	2	506	(62)
Essberger Pilot	2	32	(31)
Essberger Pioneer	2	32	(31)
Esso Bahia Blanca	2	376	(54)
Esso Normandie	2	309	(49)
Esso Parentis	2	376	(54)
Esso Picardie	2	309	(49)
Esso Port Jerome	2	242	(45)
Esso Port Jerome	2	376	(54)
Esso Santa Cruz	2	419	(56)
Estancia	21	114	(510)†
Estelle Maersk	1	148	(12)
Esterel	20	296	(481)
Esther	5	274	(126)
Estireno	2	51	(32)
Estoniya	20	15	(460)
Estoril	18	169	(434)
Estrella I	14	14	(366)
Eta	2	126	(37)
Etagas	4	124	(95)
Eternal Ace	19	61	(451)†
Eternal Glory	19	66	(452)†
Eternity	1	241	(21)†
Ethnos	9	110	(271)
Etrusco	2	106	(36)
Ettore	1	180	(14)
Etzel	5	84	(113)
Eugenie C	7	170	(169)
Eugenio Costa	20	29	(461)
Eugeniusz Kwiatkowski	8	159	(215)
Euklid	15	84	(386)†
Euplecta	1	10	(3)
Eurasian Chariot	19	18	(446)
Eurasian Dream	19	47	(450)†
Eurasian Glow	8	445	(237)
Eurobulker	7	251	(175)
Eurobulker I	7	79	(162)
Eurobulker II	7	87	(163)
Euro Clipper	6	58	(145)
Eurofreedom	7	226	(173)
Eurolady	8	144	(214)
Euroliberty	8	646	(253)†
Euromagique	16	62	(397)†
Euromagique	16	27	(393)
Euromantique	20	441	(494)†
Europa	5	156	(118)
Europa	20	31	(461)
Europa	20	386	(487)
Europe 92	9	68	(268)
European	7	499	(194)†
European 1	5	222	(122)
European Clearway	18	110	(430)
European Emerald	19	53	(450)†
European Endeavour	18	110	(430)
European Freeway	18	212	(440)†
European Glory	20	129	(468)
European Highway	18	121	(431)
European Pathway	18	121	(431)
European Pride	20	130	(468)
European Seaway	18	121	(431)
European Spirit	20	143	(469)
European Trader	18	110	(430)
Europegasus	7	252	(175)
Euro Power	12	133	(335)
Euroshipping One	16	14	(392)
Eurostar	8	16	(204)
Eurotwin	9	110	(271)
Euthymenes	2	91	(35)
Eva Maria	8	445	(237)
Evan	7	419	(187)
Evandros K	7	167	(168)
Evangelia 1	8	453	(238)
Evangelia IV	7	493	(193)†
Evangelia T	5	175	(119)
Evangeline	9	101	(270)
Evangelistas	18	172	(435)
Evangelos Ch	8	30	(205)
Evanthia	8	24	(205)
Evdokia Star	8	206	(219)
Eve	2	523	(63)
Evelyn	7	271	(176)
Evensk	2	222	(44)
Ever Access	10	45	(290)
Ever Champion	5	119	(115)
Ever Cheer	8	116	(212)
Everdina	3	42	(79)†
Everdina	3	23	(76)
Ever Fortune	8	557	(246)
Ever Gaining	12	151	(336)
Ever Gallant	12	151	(336)
Ever Garden	12	162	(337)
Ever Garland	12	151	(336)
Ever Gather	12	162	(337)
Ever General	12	151	(336)
Ever Genius	12	162	(337)
Ever Gentle	12	162	(337)
Ever Gentry	12	162	(337)
Ever Giant	12	173	(339)†
Ever Giant	12	162	(337)
Ever Gifted	12	162	(337)
Ever Given	12	151	(336)
Ever Glamour	12	151	(336)
Ever Gleamy	12	162	(337)
Ever Gleeful	12	151	(336)
Ever Globe	12	162	(337)
Ever Glory	12	162	(337)
Ever Glowing	12	151	(336)
Ever Going	12	162	(337)
Ever Golden	12	162	(337)
Ever Goods	12	151	(336)
Ever Govern	12	162	(337)
Ever Grace	12	162	(337)
Ever Grade	12	162	(337)
Ever Grand	12	162	(337)
Ever Greet	12	162	(337)
Ever Group	12	151	(336)
Ever Growth	12	162	(337)
Ever Guard	12	162	(337)

†Photograph

	SHIP TYPE	REF NO	PAGE NO
Ever Guest	12	151	(336)
Ever Guide	12	162	(337)
Ever Happy	9	126	(272)
Ever Laurel	12	154	(336)
Ever Level	12	154	(336)
Ever Linking	12	154	(336)
Ever Living	12	154	(336)
Ever Loading	12	154	(336)
Ever Lyric	12	154	(336)
Ever Racer	12	159	(337)
Ever Reach	12	159	(337)
Ever Refine	12	159	(337)
Ever Renown	12	159	(337)
Ever Repute	12	159	(337)
Ever Result	12	159	(337)
Ever Reward	12	159	(337)
Ever Right	12	159	(337)
Ever Round	12	159	(337)
Ever Royal	12	159	(337)
Ever Wise	8	146	(214)
Evgeniy Nikonov	7	324	(180)
Evgeniy Onufriev	7	324	(180)
Evgeniy Titov	1	20	(4)
Evimeria	8	445	(237)
Evita	1	275	(25)†
Evita	6	63	(146)
Evniki	5	297	(128)
Evoikos	2	307	(49)
Evpo Agnar	8	521	(243)
Evpo Agnic	8	46	(207)
Evpo Agsa	8	46	(207)
Evriali	8	16	(204)
Evrimedon	17	74	(412)†
Evrimedon	17	11	(406)
Evripos	8	185	(217)
Ew Aspen	11	77	(306)
EWL Colombia	7	363	(183)
EWL Rotterdam	7	363	(183)
EWL Suriname	7	363	(183)
EWL Venezuela	7	363	(183)
Excalibur	18	41	(424)
Excel	2	176	(41)
Excel	4	1	(87)
Excellus	8	442	(237)
Excelsior Luck	8	119	(212)
Excelsior Mercury	20	14	(460)
Expedient	8	500	(241)
Expeditioner	7	187	(170)
Explorer	7	303	(178)
Explorer LT	2	335	(51)
Exporter	13	10	(349)
Export Freedom	12	119	(334)
Export Patriot	12	119	(334)
Express Olympia	20	193	(473)
Express Santorini	20	131	(468)
Extramar Norte	6	92	(150)†
Extramar Norte	6	52	(145)
Ezz-Eldin Refaat	8	248	(222)
Faarabi	9	175	(276)†
Fadel Arab	9	83	(269)
Fadel G	7	40	(159)
Faethon	7	116	(164)
Fagaras	7	174	(169)
Fagr	18	68	(426)
Fahd	11	175	(314)
Fairbridge	12	47	(328)
Fair Cosmos	12	125	(334)
Fair Delta	2	271	(46)
Fair Hope	16	3	(391)
Fair Lady	10	68	(293)†
Fair Lady	10	22	(288)
Fairlift	21	78	(506)†
Fairload	21	79	(506)†
Fair Rainbow	8	237	(222)
Fair Sky	7	174	(169)
Fair Spirit	8	500	(241)
Fairstar	20	34	(461)
Fairway	5	91	(113)
Fairwind	5	91	(113)
Faisal Niaga	7	220	(172)
Faith	7	303	(178)
Faith	8	521	(243)
Faith IV	2	124	(37)
Fakredine	8	210	(219)
Falcon Arrow	10	43	(290)
Falcon Carrier	9	99	(270)
Falcon Eye	8	550	(245)
Falcon Sea	7	164	(168)
Falko	15	8	(377)
Falstaff	19	50	(450)†
Falster Link	20	132	(469)
Fal XVIII	1	64	(7)
Fanam	8	229	(221)
Fandango	1	146	(12)

	SHIP TYPE	REF NO	PAGE NO
Fang Cheng	8	488	(240)
Fanghai	11	63	(305)
Fang Xing	8	588	(248)
Fanling	7	348	(182)
Fannie Anne	7	224	(173)
Fantastic	20	65	(464)
Fantasy	20	297	(481)
Faramita	8	52	(207)
Farandole	1	86	(8)
Far East	8	273	(225)
Far East	8	383	(232)
Fareast Bonnie	7	378	(184)
Far Eastern Express	5	38	(109)
Fareast Fair	14	14	(366)
Fareast Trader	5	83	(113)
Farid F	11	152	(312)
Faro	13	46	(352)
Faros	5	256	(125)
Fas Colombo	7	473	(191)
Fas Gulf	13	37	(351)
Fas Istanbul	7	328	(180)
Fas Lattaquie	13	38	(352)
Fast Alexandria	18	29	(423)
Fast Filip	15	52	(382)†
Fast Lift	7	486	(192)
Fastov	8	527	(243)
Fast Trader	18	75	(427)
Fast Wal	15	81	(386)†
Fas Var	17	78	(412)†
Fatezh	8	527	(243)
Fathulkhair	9	127	(272)
Faurei	7	174	(169)
Favore	7	166	(168)
Fawaz	8	500	(241)
Fawziah	18	139	(432)
Faysal	8	9	(203)
FB Pioneer	17	58	(410)
Fearless	2	53	(32)
Feax	8	500	(241)
Federal Bergen	7	92	(163)
Federal Fraser	5	85	(113)
Federal Mackenzie	5	85	(113)
Federal Manitou	7	145	(167)
Federal Nord	7	92	(163)
Federal Pescadores	7	135	(166)
Federal Vibeke	7	65	(161)
Fedor Petrov	9	57	(267)
Fedor Shalyapin	20	347	(484)
Fedor Varaksin	8	78	(209)
Fedra	5	76	(112)
Fedra	5	186	(120)
Fedra	20	56	(463)
Feeder B	6	42	(144)
Feederchief	19	77	(453)†
Feedermaster	18	117	(430)
Feedermate	18	53	(425)
Feedersailor	18	194	(437)†
Feederteam	18	25	(423)
Feicuihai	7	66	(161)
Fei He	12	11	(325)
Fei Teng	8	632	(251)
Fei Yue	9	59	(267)
Felander	19	79	(454)†
Feldioara	7	174	(169)
Feleac	7	174	(169)
Felicita	9	38	(265)
Felipe Camarao	2	254	(46)
Feliz Duckling	5	141	(117)
Fellowship L	2	194	(42)
Fenes	8	603	(249)
Feng Cai	8	492	(240)
Feng Chang	8	352	(230)
Feng Cheng	8	123	(212)
Feng Chi	9	230	(283)†
Feng Ge	8	492	(240)
Feng Guang	9	7	(263)
Feng Hang	9	7	(263)
Feng Hua	5	158	(118)
Feng Hua	7	168	(168)
Feng Jin	9	7	(263)
Feng Mao	9	7	(263)
Feng Ming	9	7	(263)
Feng Ning	8	378	(232)
Feng Qing	8	492	(240)
Feng Sheng	8	492	(240)
Feng Tai	5	158	(118)
Fengtai	8	492	(240)
Fengtao	8	492	(240)
Feng Tian	18	104	(429)
Fengxiang	8	492	(240)
Fengyan	8	492	(240)
Fengyang	8	492	(240)
Fengyi	8	492	(240)
Fengying	8	492	(240)
Feng Yun	9	7	(263)
Feng Zhan	9	7	(263)

†Photograph

	SHIP TYPE	REF NO	PAGE NO
Fenhe	13	34	(351)
Fenicia	16	17	(392)
Fenland	11	224	(320)†
Ferara	8	24	(205)
Feras	8	7	(203)
Fereniki	8	276	(225)
Feride	5	288	(127)
Fernando Pessoa	7	100	(163)
Feroi	7	11	(157)
Ferry Chikushi	20	328	(483)
Ferry Fukue	20	227	(475)
Ferry Kampu	20	264	(478)
Ferry Lavender	20	343	(484)
Ferry Pukwan	20	264	(478)
Fes	18	142	(432)
Festos	20	133	(469)
Fetish	9	22	(264)
Feyza	7	246	(174)
Fibi	20	134	(469)
Fidelity	8	24	(205)
Fides	19	8	(445)
Fiducia	7	11	(157)
Fieni	7	174	(169)
Fierbinti	7	174	(169)
Figaro	19	10	(445)
Figaros	6	5	(141)
Figen Akat	8	225	(221)
Filaos	8	308	(227)
Fili	1	138	(12)
Filiasi	7	174	(169)
Filio	8	24	(205)
Filipos	10	45	(290)
Filipp Makharadze	5	313	(129)
Filippos	18	217	(440)†
Filippos	14	2	(365)
Filippos	18	177	(435)
Filoktitis	17	11	(406)
Findikli	7	403	(186)
Finiki	7	74	(162)
Finix	5	224	(122)
Finja	1	185	(15)
Finnfellow	18	37	(424)
Finnfighter	7	129	(166)
Finnhansa	18	107	(429)
Finnjet	20	208	(474)
Finnmaid	18	37	(424)
Finnmaster	17	35	(408)
Finnmerchant	18	221	(441)†
Finnmerchant	16	23	(393)
Finnpartner	18	107	(429)
Finnpine	18	16	(422)
Finnsnes	7	287	(177)
Finnstone	5	261	(125)
Finntrader	18	107	(429)
Fintinele	7	174	(169)
Fiord	2	367	(53)
Firas 1	9	61	(267)
Firat	8	629	(251)
First Lady	7	41	(160)
First Sun	5	43	(110)
Fischland	7	480	(192)
Fishguard Bay	12	67	(330)
Fisko	11	139	(311)
Fitzroy	11	75	(306)
Fivi	6	27	(143)
Fivi	8	34	(206)
Fizuli	7	340	(181)
Fjardvagen	18	21	(422)
Fjardvagen	18	105	(429)
Fjardvargen	18	183	(436)†
Fjodors Bredihins	11	127	(310)
Fjordshell	1	179	(14)
Flag Adrienne	7	169	(169)
Flag Emerald	5	140	(117)
Flag Karin	5	55	(111)
Flag Mersinidi	5	299	(128)
Flag Paola	8	99	(211)
Flag Rolaco	5	297	(128)
Flag Supplier	5	65	(111)
Flag Tom	7	276	(176)
Flamares	17	37	(408)
Flamenco	1	146	(12)
Flamengo	13	34	(351)
Flamingo	14	5	(365)
Flamingo Reefer	11	126	(310)
Flaminia	1	79	(8)
Flandre	2	555	(67)†
Flare	7	41	(160)
Flecha	7	508	(195)†
Flecha	7	237	(174)
Flensburger Flagge	5	265	(125)
Flensia	6	46	(144)
Fleur-De-Lys	18	8	(421)
Flevo	6	124	(154)†
Flevo	6	49	(145)
Flinders Bay	12	127	(334)

	SHIP TYPE	REF NO	PAGE NO
Flint	7	15	(158)
Flinterborg	7	457	(190)
Flinterdijk	8	111	(211)
Floating Mountain	8	500	(241)
Flora	7	271	(176)
Flora C	7	170	(169)
Flora V	8	446	(237)
Florence	2	9	(29)
Florenz	8	413	(235)
Flores Sea	2	146	(39)
Floresti	7	174	(169)
Floria	21	32	(501)
Floriana	8	155	(215)
Florida	7	306	(179)
Florida Express	2	451	(59)
Florida Star	6	63	(146)
Flourish Oriental	8	560	(246)
FLS Colombia	7	471	(191)
Flying Dragon	8	24	(205)
Flying Officer Nirmal Jit Sekhon PVC	1	137	(12)
FMG America	13	18	(350)
FMG Cartagena	7	326	(180)
Focsani	8	41	(206)
Folegandros	1	104	(9)
Folegandros	2	407	(56)
Folgoet	1	8	(3)
Fonnes	7	523	(197)†
Fontana	8	24	(205)
Force	7	60	(161)
Forest Champion	7	207	(171)
Forest Hills	2	144	(39)
Forest Link	18	82	(427)
Forest Trader	7	11	(157)
Formosa One	1	44	(6)
Formosa Two	1	44	(6)
Fort Desaix	12	203	(343)†
Forte	17	118	(417)†
Fort Fleur d'Epee	12	135	(335)
Forthbank	9	149	(274)
Fortrose	5	36	(109)
Fort Royal	12	135	(335)
Fortuna	6	85	(149)†
Fortuna	6	53	(145)
Fortuna Duckling	5	141	(117)
Fortuna I	6	35	(143)
Fortunate Star	8	383	(232)
Fortunato	3	74	(83)†
Fortuna Voyager	11	66	(305)
Fortune	8	30	(205)
'Fortune' type	8	445	(237)
Fortune Bay	7	29	(159)
Fortune Bell	8	645	(253)†
Fortune Celia	8	24	(205)
Fortune Ocean	7	425	(188)
Fortuneship L	2	194	(42)
Forum Cape	5	218	(122)
Forum Chemist	5	196	(121)
Forum Glory	5	157	(118)
Forum Product	5	196	(121)
Fosforico	2	50	(32)
Fosna	1	228	(19)†
Fotini	8	445	(237)
Four M	8	344	(229)
Four Skies	2	305	(49)
Four Winds	2	305	(49)
Framnas	2	190	(42)
Franca D'Alesio	2	376	(54)
Frances L	13	71	(354)
Francis	2	300	(48)
Francisco J Mugica	2	422	(57)
Francoli	13	20	(350)
Franconia	19	57	(451)†
Franina	7	162	(168)
Frankfurt Express	12	100	(332)
Frank M	2	297	(48)
Franky	8	204	(219)
Franz Bogush	8	74	(209)
Franz Keller	15	43	(380)
Frasinet	7	174	(169)
Fratzescos M	9	26	(265)
Fratzis M	8	559	(246)
Freccia	19	55	(451)†
Freccia Blu	18	42	(424)
Freccia Rossa	18	42	(424)
Frederick M	2	572	(69)†
'Freedom' type	8	24	(205)
'Freedom-Hispania' type	8	17	(204)
'Freedom-Hispania' type	8	43	(206)
'Freedom' Mark II type	8	252	(223)
Freedom K	7	82	(162)
Freedomship L	2	204	(43)
Freedom Star	8	220	(220)
Freedom Star 1	7	375	(184)
Freedom Star 3	7	375	(184)
Freesia	11	42	(303)
Freewinds	20	40	(462)

†Photograph

	SHIP TYPE	REF NO	PAGE NO
Freewinds	20	281	(479)
Freital	8	527	(243)
Freja	6	98	(151)†
Freja Svea	2	566	(68)†
Fremantle Star	12	74	(330)
Frenaso	11	47	(304)
Fresa	11	104	(308)
Freshwater Bay	12	147	(336)
Freya	15	28	(379)
Frida	21	106	(509)†
Frida	21	53	(503)
Fridrihs Canders	2	508	(62)
Friedrich Engels	8	74	(209)
Friendship L	2	194	(42)
Frigo Arosa	11	144	(312)
Frimaro	11	9	(301)
Frines	7	287	(177)
Frio America	11	33	(303)
Frio Arctic	11	141	(311)
Frio Argentina	11	33	(303)
Frio Bergen	11	68	(305)
Frio Brasil	11	33	(303)
Frio Canada	11	33	(303)
Frio Caribic	11	64	(305)
Frio Dolphin	11	202	(317)†
Frio Espana	11	33	(303)
Frio Galicia	11	62	(305)
Frio Ipanema	11	43	(303)
Frio Italia	11	62	(305)
Frio Japan	11	33	(303)
Frio Korea	11	33	(303)
Frio Libra	11	140	(311)
Frio Oceanic	11	64	(305)
Frisohaven	7	11	(157)
Fritz Heckert	11	99	(308)
Front Breaker	1	121	(11)
Front Climber	1	121	(11)
Front Driver	1	121	(11)
Front Guider	1	121	(11)
Front Harrier	2	180	(41)
Front Hawk	2	180	(41)
Frontier America	7	471	(191)
Frontier Express	1	229	(19)†
Frontier Spirit	1	135	(11)
Front Leader	1	121	(11)
Front Rider	1	121	(11)
Front Striver	1	121	(11)
Front Viewer	1	121	(11)
Frost 1	11	98	(308)
Frost 2	11	98	(308)
Frost 3	11	98	(308)
Frost 3	11	101	(308)
Frost 4	11	98	(308)
Frost 4	11	101	(308)
Frost 5	11	98	(308)
Frost 5	11	101	(308)
Frotabelem	13	69	(354)
Frotachile	7	191	(170)
Frotadurban	8	443	(237)
Frotamanaus	13	69	(354)
Frota Maraba	9	52	(266)
Frotamerica	7	191	(170)
Frotaoeste	5	86	(113)
Frotargentina	7	191	(170)
Frotasingapore	8	443	(237)
Frotauruguay	7	191	(170)
Fruition	7	121	(165)
Frunzanesti	7	174	(169)
Frycz Modrzewski	8	566	(246)
Fu Da	8	208	(219)
Fu Jian	20	15	(460)
Fuji Angel	7	213	(172)
Fuji Maru	20	57	(463)
Fu Jin Hai	8	13	(204)
Fuji Star	11	69	(305)
Full Beauty	5	376	(136)†
Full City	7	542	(199)†
Fullnes	7	13	(158)
Full Sources	5	216	(122)
Full Spring	5	216	(122)
Fulmar	2	498	(62)
Fulvia	8	500	(241)
Funda C	7	339	(181)
Fundeni	7	174	(169)
Fu Ping	8	23	(204)
Furetank	2	486	(61)
Furevik	1	172	(14)
Furunes	7	13	(158)
Fu Shan	9	49	(266)
Fu Shun Cheng	8	507	(242)
Futura	1	147	(12)
Futuro	8	692	(259)†
Futuro	8	95	(210)
Fu Wei	8	369	(231)
Fyodor Okhlopov	7	340	(181)
Fyodor Popov	7	340	(181)
Gabriela R	19	29	(447)
Gabriele Wehr	18	188	(437)†
Gada	7	47	(160)
Gafoor	8	589	(248)
Gagich	7	180	(169)
Gajah Borneo	21	4	(499)
Gala Del Mar	17	14	(406)
Galapagos Explorer	20	22	(460)
Galassia	5	87	(113)
Galatea	15	70	(384)†
Galaxy	8	29	(205)
Galaxy III	8	24	(205)
Galea	7	101	(163)
Galet	7	512	(196)†
Galini	16	12	(392)
Gallant II	9	172	(276)†
Gallantry	8	24	(205)
Gallant Tiger	5	291	(127)
Galloway Express	21	119	(511)†
Galloway Express	21	57	(503)
Gallura	20	249	(477)
Galp Faro	4	27	(89)
Galp Funchal	2	453	(59)
Galp Leixoes	1	253	(22)†
Galteam	8	312	(228)
Galveston Bay	8	158	(215)
Galvye	2	380	(54)
Gamal Abdel Naser	2	92	(35)
Gamid Sultanov	20	169	(471)
Gamma	8	135	(213)
Gammagas	3	10	(75)
Gamzat Tsadasa	12	75	(330)
G and C Parana	17	68	(411)†
G and C Parana	17	53	(409)
Gang Cheng	8	632	(251)
Gang Nam	9	6	(263)
Gan Jiang	9	138	(273)
Ganza	5	158	(118)
Gao Cheng	13	17	(350)
Gao He	12	30	(327)
Gao Lan Dao	8	16	(204)
Gao Ling	9	218	(281)†
Gara Djebilet	17	4	(405)
Garcilaso	8	533	(244)
Garden	18	124	(431)
Gardsea	6	41	(144)
Gardsky	10	67	(292)†
Gardsky	10	21	(288)
Gardsun	10	21	(288)
Gardway	10	113	(298)†
Gardway	10	21	(288)
Gardwind	6	41	(144)
Garnata	20	205	(473)
Garnes	5	229	(123)
Garonne	9	101	(270)
Garwolin	9	53	(267)
Gas Al Ahmadi	4	61	(91)
Gas Al Burgan	4	61	(91)
Gas Al Gurain	4	62	(91)
Gas Al Kuwait	4	61	(91)
Gas Al Minagish	4	61	(91)
Gas Al Mutlaa	4	62	(91)
Gas Diana	4	134	(97)†
Gas Gloria	4	36	(89)
Gas Leo	4	180	(103)†
Gas Rising Sun	4	76	(92)
Gastrikland	7	337	(181)
Gauss F	5	89	(113)
Gauss F	7	257	(175)
Gavrill Kirdishchev	16	13	(392)
Gaya Dua	8	33	(206)
Gazanfar Musabekov	15	15	(378)
Gaz Atlantic	4	23	(88)
Gaz Baltic	4	31	(89)
Gaz Channel	4	68	(91)
Gaz Concord	4	48	(90)
Gaz Coral	3	72	(83)†
Gaz Hudson	4	82	(92)
Gaziantep	2	386	(54)
Gaz Lion	4	117	(95)
Gaz Major	4	64	(91)
Gaz Nordsee	4	8	(87)
Gaz Pacific	4	27	(89)
Gaz Polaris	3	82	(84)†
Gaz Progress	4	23	(88)
Gaz Saint Denis	4	100	(94)
Gaz Sun	3	50	(80)†
Gaz Sun	4	128	(96)
Gaz Supplier	4	142	(98)†
Gaz Supplier	4	56	(91)
Gebang/Pertamina 8002	2	166	(40)
Gebze	2	419	(56)
Gedaref	9	17	(264)
Gediz	8	629	(251)

†Photograph

	SHIP TYPE	REF NO	PAGE NO
Geest Dominica	11	212	(319)†
Gehreman Esedov	2	171	(41)
Gehreman Guseynov	2	171	(41)
Gehreman Hadjiev	2	171	(41)
Gehreman Hesenov	2	171	(41)
Gehreman I Mamedov	2	171	(41)
Gehreman Khelilbeyli	2	171	(41)
Gehreman Osipov	2	171	(41)
Geilo	5	318	(129)
Geli P	8	500	(241)
Gelovani	1	20	(4)
Gelting Syd	20	135	(469)
Gemini	5	87	(113)
Gemini	11	81	(306)
Gemini Buri	8	211	(219)
Gemini Explorer	7	51	(160)
Geminy	8	304	(227)
Gem of Madras	7	208	(171)
Gemstar I	8	24	(205)
Genca Terzo	8	107	(211)
General Abbasov	2	171	(41)
General Ace	1	95	(9)
General A F Cebesoy	8	74	(209)
General Aslanov	1	70	(7)
General Bem	5	172	(119)
General Berling	5	105	(114)
General Blazhevich	8	527	(243)
General Delgado	9	211	(281)†
General Geydarov	2	171	(41)
General Gorbatov	12	109	(333)
General Grot-Rowecki	5	105	(114)
General Jasinski	5	172	(119)
General K Orbay	8	74	(209)
General Madalinski	5	172	(119)
General Mahmandarov	2	171	(41)
General Manuel Belgrano	8	537	(244)
General Merkviladze	2	470	(60)
General Monarch	1	95	(9)
General Pradzynski	5	172	(119)
General R Gumuspala	8	74	(209)
General Selimov	2	171	(41)
General Shikhlinskj	2	171	(41)
General Tyulenev	2	304	(49)
General Vladimir Zaimov	5	269	(126)
General Vladimir Zaimov	9	80	(269)
General Z Dogan	8	74	(209)
Geniki	9	34	(265)
Genkai Maru	4	139	(97)†
Gennargentu	20	250	(477)
Genova	12	192	(341)†
Gent	4	98	(94)
Geohart	7	146	(167)
Geolog Yuriy Bilibin	2	380	(54)
Geo Milev	9	93	(270)
George	8	343	(229)
George	8	559	(246)
George B	8	400	(234)
George H Weyerhauser	1	77	(8)
George L	7	7	(157)
Georges Alexandre Lebel	18	13	(422)
Georges Delmas	8	446	(237)
George Shultz	1	27	(5)
Georgette K	7	15	(158)
George Washington Bridge	12	103	(332)
Georgi Grigorov	5	105	(114)
Georgios	8	170	(216)
Georgios	8	567	(247)
Georgios D	7	223	(173)
Georgios Express	20	136	(469)
Georgios K	2	377	(54)
Georgios L	7	54	(160)
Georgios P	5	150	(117)
Georgiy Agafonov	15	23	(379)
Georgiy Bernachuk	7	143	(167)
Georgiy Chicherin	8	74	(209)
Georgiy Dimitrov	8	74	(209)
Georgiy Vasilyev	8	105	(211)
Georg Luhrs	15	8	(377)
Georg OTS	20	128	(468)
Geortina	8	149	(214)
Geranios Stylianos	5	218	(122)
Gerarda	15	20	(378)
Gerasimos	8	513	(242)
Gerassimos	14	39	(369)†
Gerina	6	2	(141)
Gerlin	6	2	(141)
Gerlina	6	2	(141)
Germania	7	344	(182)
Geroi Chernomorya	2	450	(59)
Geroi Novorossiyska	2	450	(59)
Geroi Panfilovtsy	9	92	(270)
Geroi Plevny	18	27	(423)
Geroi Sevastopolya	2	450	(59)
Geroi Shipki	18	27	(423)
Geroi Stalingrada	5	17	(108)
Geroite Na Odessa	18	27	(423)

	SHIP TYPE	REF NO	PAGE NO
Geroite Na Sevastopol	18	27	(423)
Gerona Star	2	370	(53)
Geroy Volkov	2	171	(41)
Gesan	8	602	(249)
Gettysburg	2	15	(30)
Gevo Express	8	50	(207)
Gevo Victory	5	263	(125)
Gevo Victory	10	17	(288)
Geyve	2	506	(62)
Ghadames	8	393	(233)
Ghardaia	16	71	(398)†
Ghardaia	16	28	(393)
Ghasha	3	16	(76)
Ghat	18	92	(428)
Ghawdex	20	105	(467)
Ghazi	2	12	(29)
Ghazvin	2	539	(65)†
Gheorghieni	8	50	(207)
Ghikas	8	252	(223)
Ghulam	8	500	(241)
Giant	8	145	(214)
Giava	10	30	(289)
Gibeagle	21	22	(500)
Gido	7	438	(189)
Gigi	8	310	(227)
Giho	5	272	(126)
Gimi	3	59	(81)†
Gimi	3	2	(75)
Gimone	2	354	(52)
Gina	14	13	(366)
Gina II	9	100	(270)
Gina Iuliano	5	282	(127)
Giorgos	7	165	(168)
Gios	8	24	(205)
Giovanna	2	431	(57)
Gisela Bartels	14	84	(374)†
Gitta Kosan	4	174	(102)†
Giurgeni	7	174	(169)
Giurgiu	7	174	(169)
Giuseppe di Vittorio	8	74	(209)
Giuseppe Lembo	5	169	(119)
Giwi II	8	527	(243)
Gjertrud Maersk	4	7	(87)
Glachau	8	446	(237)
Glaciar Ameghino	11	52	(304)
Glaciar Perito Moreno	11	52	(304)
Glacier Bay	11	75	(306)
Gladiator	7	413	(187)
Glafkos	8	30	(205)
Gleb Krzhizhanovskiy	9	57	(267)
Gleichberg	18	3	(421)
Glencora	5	132	(116)
Glenita	7	203	(171)
Glenross	2	219	(44)
Global Dream	5	281	(126)
Global Epoch	5	214	(122)
Global Express 6	7	446	(189)
Global Maceio	1	49	(6)
Global Makatcha	5	297	(128)
Global Mariner	11	76	(306)
Global Mars	2	36	(31)
Global Rio	1	49	(6)
Global Star	5	216	(122)
Globe Trader	8	500	(241)
Gloria Del Mar	17	14	(406)
Gloria Elena	21	54	(503)
Gloria Peak	7	298	(178)
Glorious Ace	19	28	(447)
Glorious Success	7	207	(171)
Glory Hope	5	38	(109)
G. Mother	5	78	(112)
Gniezno II	10	11	(287)
Gobustan	2	171	(41)
Godafoss	7	308	(179)
God Prestige	2	49	(32)
Gokcan	7	125	(165)
Gokhan Kalkavan	8	629	(251)
Gokturk	2	310	(49)
Golar Dundee	1	202	(16)
Golar Edinburgh	1	202	(16)
Golar Freeze	3	32	(78)†
Golar Freeze	3	17	(76)
Golar Glasgow	1	202	(16)
Golar Spirit	3	81	(84)†
Golar Stirling	1	202	(16)
Golar XXVIII	2	361	(52)
Gold Asia	9	118	(272)
Gold Bond Trailblazer	5	165	(118)
Gold Bridge I	8	96	(210)
Golden Alpha	7	207	(171)
Golden B	11	152	(312)
Golden Banner	8	224	(221)
Golden Bay	21	23	(500)
Golden Bear	8	549	(245)
Golden Cape	2	454	(59)
Golden Challenger	7	183	(170)

†Photograph

	SHIP TYPE	REF NO	PAGE NO
Golden Chase	8	31	(205)
Golden Condor	7	541	(199)†
Golden Crux No 8	3	45	(79)†
Golden Empire	7	62	(161)
Golden Evagelistra	7	492	(193)†
Golden Fountain	1	125	(11)
Golden Future	8	305	(227)
Golden Gate Bridge	12	103	(332)
Golden Glow	5	53	(110)
Golden Hansome	8	27	(205)
Golden Horizon	8	31	(205)
Golden Immensity	8	342	(229)
Golden Isle	7	455	(190)
Golden Lady	7	199	(171)
Golden Land	5	142	(117)
Golden Leaf	7	271	(176)
Golden Ocean	2	355	(52)
Golden Pacific	11	131	(311)
Golden Panagia	8	31	(205)
Golden Polydinamos	7	183	(170)
Golden Princess	20	383	(487)
Golden Ray	19	24	(446)
Golden Sea	5	24	(108)
Golden Shimizu	8	31	(205)
Golden Shine	7	437	(188)
Golden Sky	5	271	(126)
Golden Spear	8	31	(205)
Golden Splendour	8	493	(240)
Golden Star	8	217	(220)
Golden Star	8	284	(225)
Golden Star I	4	114	(95)
Golden Stream	1	125	(11)
Golden Sun	8	445	(237)
Golden Tennyo	8	31	(205)
Golden Trader	7	183	(170)
Golden Union	8	419	(235)
Golden Venture	7	125	(165)
Golden Victory	7	203	(171)
Golden Wing	7	199	(171)
Golden Yang	5	151	(117)
Goldobin	8	582	(248)
Goldpath	8	394	(233)
Gold Ring	8	42	(206)
Gold Sand	2	508	(62)
Gold Star I	8	221	(220)
Gole	2	479	(60)
Goleniow	5	189	(120)
Golf	15	5	(377)
Golfo de Batabano	11	10	(301)
Golfo de Guanahacabibes	11	10	(301)
Golf Star	5	92	(113)
Goliath	21	55	(503)
Goliath II	21	10	(499)
Gongora	4	39	(89)
Gonio	1	265	(24)†
Gonio	1	181	(15)
Good Carrier	2	494	(61)
Good Easy	7	14	(158)
Good Explorer	7	436	(188)
Good Faith	8	500	(241)
Good Fighter	7	392	(185)
Good Friday	7	105	(164)
Good Most	7	14	(158)
Goodrich Bay	1	100	(9)
Good Rider	7	334	(181)
Good Success	7	334	(181)
Goodwood	18	169	(434)
Goose Bay	11	236	(322)†
Gopher	8	272	(224)
Gorbeia	2	317	(50)
G Ordzhonikidze	1	107	(10)
G Ordzhonikidze	20	14	(460)
Gorgova	7	174	(169)
Gorgulho	15	6	(377)
Gorj	7	174	(169)
Gorlitz	5	13	(108)
Gorlovka	7	179	(169)
Gornopravdinsk	2	26	(30)
Gornyak	7	269	(176)
Gorun	7	174	(169)
Gospic	7	253	(175)
Gotaland	14	22	(366)
Gotlandia	8	446	(237)
Gotze Delchev	9	92	(270)
Govora	7	174	(169)
Gozde B.	7	294	(178)
Gracechurch Crown	5	113	(115)
Gracechurch Harp	5	113	(115)
Gracechurch Planet	5	113	(115)
Gracia Del Mar	17	14	(406)
Gracious Lady	5	303	(128)
Grajau	4	84	(93)
Grand Festival	7	241	(174)
Grandis	7	250	(174)
Grand Manan V	20	342	(484)
Grand Ocean 1	8	292	(226)

	SHIP TYPE	REF NO	PAGE NO
Grand River	12	130	(334)
Gran Esperanza	1	226	(19)†
Granite	1	145	(12)
Granitnyy Bereg	11	99	(308)
Grano	16	16	(392)
Gran Piedra	11	34	(303)
Gran Trader	5	373	(136)†
Gran Trader	5	199	(121)
Graz	7	121	(165)
Great Best 1	8	593	(248)
Great Cheer	7	56	(160)
Great China No 1	8	208	(219)
Great Glen	7	56	(160)
Great Lake	7	241	(174)
Great Land	16	4	(391)
Great Pearl	7	69	(161)
Great Power	8	416	(235)
Great Prize	7	56	(160)
Great Trans	7	484	(192)
Great Universe	9	174	(276)†
Grecia Express	20	329	(483)
Grecian Star	8	29	(205)
Green Arctic	11	229	(321)†
Green Bay	19	40	(449)†
Green Cape	17	83	(413)†
Green Cape	17	30	(407)
Green Freesia	11	124	(310)
Green Frio	11	45	(304)
Green Harbour	21	15	(500)
Green Ice	17	84	(413)†
Green Ice	17	52	(409)
Green Island	21	96	(508)†
Green Island	7	425	(188)
Green Island	21	15	(500)
Greenland Saga	13	102	(358)†
Green Leaf	11	156	(312)
Green Lily	11	124	(310)
Green Ridge	8	424	(236)
Green Rose	11	124	(310)
Green Star	2	398	(55)
Green Star	4	80	(92)
Green Sylvan	7	207	(171)
Green Tulip	11	124	(310)
Green Valley	1	22	(4)
Green Valley	21	15	(500)
Green Violet	11	124	(310)
Green Wave	8	424	(236)
Gregor	7	507	(195)†
Gregor	7	372	(184)
Greifswald	20	339	(484)
Greta C	5	323	(129)
Grete Terkol	1	186	(15)
Grethe	10	108	(298)†
Gretke Oldendorff	7	120	(165)
Greveno	7	369	(184)
Grietje	7	338	(181)
Griffin	7	543	(200)†
Grifo	5	188	(120)
Grigoriy Aleksandrov	5	129	(116)
Grigoriy Alekseyev	10	57	(291)
Grigoriy Kovalchuk	8	49	(207)
Grigoriy Kozintsev	8	161	(215)
Grigoriy Nesterenko	1	20	(4)
Grigoriy Petrenko	9	92	(270)
Grinna	10	23	(288)
Grisha Podobedov	8	239	(222)
Grobnik	9	110	(271)
Groners Jade	8	357	(230)
Grootsand	11	135	(311)
Grouse	6	66	(146)
Grozny	2	426	(57)
Gruia	7	174	(169)
Grumant	8	575	(247)
Grunwald	8	671	(257)†
Grunwald	8	605	(249)
Gruz	21	77	(506)†
Gruz	21	37	(502)
Gruziya	20	127	(468)
GTS Horizon	8	445	(237)
Guadalupe	8	374	(232)
Guadelupe Victoria II	1	81	(8)
Guama	8	17	(204)
Guanajuato	19	22	(446)
Guang Fu Quan	8	149	(214)
Guang Nan	8	290	(226)
Guang Shen	8	562	(246)
Guangshui	9	4	(263)
Guang Shun	7	46	(160)
Guang Yuan	7	24	(158)
Guang Yun	8	497	(241)
Guardian Angel	8	500	(241)
Guarionex	11	138	(311)
Guatemala	7	329	(180)
Guayama	12	131	(335)
Guaycura	18	85	(428)
Gu Cheng	13	17	(350)

†Photograph

	SHIP TYPE	REF NO	PAGE NO
Gudermes	2	426	(57)
Gudrun Danielsen	8	206	(219)
Gudrun II	6	118	(153)†
Gu Hai	7	26	(159)
Gui He	2	441	(58)
Gui Jiang	8	24	(205)
Guimaraes	15	57	(383)†
Gulbene	8	575	(247)
Gulf Banker	8	455	(238)
Gulf Champion	9	220	(282)†
Gulf Current	7	443	(189)
Gulf Farmer	8	455	(238)
Gulf Merchant	8	455	(238)
Gulf of Paria	1	100	(9)
Gulf Rose	15	47	(381)
Gulf Seagull	8	603	(249)
Gulf Shipper	8	455	(238)
Gulf Spirit	13	49	(352)
Gulf Splendour	8	603	(249)
Gulf Star	17	26	(407)
Gulf Trader	8	455	(238)
Gulf Trident	5	166	(118)
Gulf Venture	7	154	(168)
Gulf Wave	7	154	(168)
Gull Arrow	10	43	(290)
Gulluk	5	42	(110)
Gulsum Ana	8	34	(206)
Gumbet	5	42	(110)
Gun	2	37	(31)
Gunay A	7	65	(161)
Gunilla	18	92	(428)
Guns and Roses	8	133	(213)
Guo Cai	9	52	(266)
Guo Fa	7	73	(162)
Gur Maiden	8	26	(205)
Gur Master	8	80	(209)
Gurupa	4	84	(93)
Gurupi	4	84	(93)
Gustav Sule	5	129	(116)
Gutterman	7	527	(198)†
Guyane	16	122	(418)†
Guyane	17	55	(409)
Gu Yue	8	564	(246)
Gu Yue	8	565	(246)
Gyle	5	333	(131)†
Gyle	5	259	(125)
Gyoko	2	397	(55)
Gypsum Baron	5	14	(108)
Gypsum King	5	14	(108)
Haapsalu	16	13	(392)
Habib	20	58	(463)
Haci Arif Kaptan	8	583	(248)
Haci Sefer Kalkavan	7	32	(159)
Hadera	5	48	(110)
Hadra	1	138	(12)
Hadrian	11	123	(310)
Hae Gum Gang	8	500	(241)
Hae Nam	8	134	(213)
Hae Sung No 7	8	151	(214)
Hae Woo No 2	9	107	(271)
Hae Woo No 3	9	107	(271)
Hafnia	8	276	(225)
Hagaar	8	319	(228)
Hagieni	7	174	(169)
Hai	2	286	(47)
Hai Bao	8	448	(238)
Hai Cheng	8	308	(227)
Haida	15	47	(381)
Hai Da	20	390	(488)
Hai De Wei	5	256	(125)
Hai Feng	7	431	(188)
Hai Feng 301	11	105	(309)
Hai Feng 832	11	178	(314)
Hai Gas	4	101	(94)
Hai Hang	8	134	(213)
Hai Hing	9	5	(263)
Hai Hua	7	1	(157)
Hai Hua	9	169	(275)
Hai Huang	7	263	(175)
Hai Jiao	8	287	(226)
Hai Jing	8	149	(214)
Hai Lee	8	17	(204)
Hai Lih	8	209	(219)
Hai Mao	8	152	(214)
Hai Meng	8	24	(205)
Hainan 3	8	357	(230)
Hai Rong	8	392	(233)
Hai Sheng	9	10	(264)
Hai Shiou Shan	6	52	(145)
Hai Soong	7	1	(157)
Hai Wang Xing	10	52	(291)
Hai Xiong	8	118	(212)
Hai Yen 1	8	575	(247)
Hai Yen 2	8	589	(248)

	SHIP TYPE	REF NO	PAGE NO
Hai Yi	8	298	(226)
Hai Yu	6	17	(142)
Hajji-Khadija	8	453	(238)
Hajo	6	2	(141)
Hakki Uzunoglu	8	276	(225)
Hakufu	7	207	(171)
Hakuryu Maru	18	31	(423)
Halcon Del Mar	14	2	(365)
Halia	1	138	(12)
Halima K	8	76	(209)
Halim Topaz	9	124	(272)
Halis Kalkavan	7	133	(166)
Halki	1	160	(13)
Halla Endeavor	5	216	(122)
Hallborg	8	152	(214)
Halldis	8	24	(205)
Halldor	8	500	(241)
Hallvard	8	17	(204)
Ha Long 5	2	367	(53)
Halsingland	7	472	(191)
Halul	2	440	(58)
Hamad Allah	6	12	(142)
Hamburg	20	401	(489)†
Hamburg	20	59	(463)
Hamburg Senator	12	15	(326)
Hamburg Trader	11	98	(308)
Hamburg Trader	11	101	(308)
Hamilton K	21	69	(505)†
Hamilton K	21	1	(499)
Hamilton K	21	18	(500)
Haminea	1	138	(12)
Hamlet	20	106	(467)
Hamlet Saudia	17	57	(410)
Hammond	11	99	(308)
Hamno	16	16	(392)
Hanbonn Brother	8	383	(232)
Hanbonn Concord	8	383	(232)
Han Chuan	9	112	(271)
Handy Bonita	7	155	(168)
Handy Diamond	7	271	(176)
Handy Explorer	7	182	(169)
Handy Islander	7	207	(171)
Handy Laker	7	145	(167)
Handy Rider	21	50	(503)
Handy Success	7	182	(169)
Handy Viking	8	146	(214)
Han-Ei	1	116	(10)
Hanei Pearl	7	125	(165)
Hanei Star	7	125	(165)
Hang Cheong	8	336	(229)
Hang Shun	10	14	(288)
Hanifah	8	33	(206)
Hanjin Bangkok	12	48	(328)
Hanjin Barcelona	12	150	(336)
Hanjin Bremen	12	174	(339)†
Hanjin Bremen	12	160	(337)
Hanjin Busan	12	31	(327)
Hanjin Canberra	5	143	(117)
Hanjin Cheju	12	158	(337)
Hanjin Chungmu	12	32	(327)
Hanjin Colombo	12	150	(336)
Hanjin Dampier	5	251	(124)
Hanjin Elizabeth	12	160	(337)
Hanjin Felixstowe	12	160	(337)
Hanjin Gladstone	5	251	(124)
Hanjin Hamburg	12	160	(337)
Hanjin Hongkong	12	160	(337)
Hanjin Kaohsiung	12	160	(337)
Hanjin Keelung	12	160	(337)
Hanjin Kobe	12	160	(337)
Hanjin Kunsan	12	158	(337)
Hanjin Kwangyang	12	158	(337)
Hanjin Le Havre	12	160	(337)
Hanjin Longbeach	12	160	(337)
Hanjin Malta	12	150	(336)
Hanjin Marseilles	12	150	(336)
Hanjin Masan	12	168	(338)†
Hanjin Masan	12	32	(327)
Hanjin Newyork	12	160	(337)
Hanjin Oakland	12	160	(337)
Hanjin Osaka	12	150	(336)
Hanjin Pohang	12	31	(327)
Hanjin Portland	12	150	(336)
Hanjin Pyeong Taek	4	17	(88)
Hanjin Rotterdam	12	160	(337)
Hanjin Savannah	12	160	(337)
Hanjin Seattle	12	160	(337)
Hanjin Seoul	12	31	(327)
Hanjin Shanghai	12	150	(336)
Hanjin Singapore	12	160	(337)
Hanjin Sydney	5	201	(121)
Hanjin Tokyo	12	150	(336)
Hanjin Tonghae	12	32	(327)
Hanjin Vancouver	12	160	(337)
Hanjin Yokohama	12	160	(337)
Hanna	6	41	(144)

†Photograph

	SHIP TYPE	REF NO	PAGE NO
Hanne Bakke	13	61	(353)
Hanne Catharina	6	41	(144)
Hanni	6	2	(141)
Hannibal	7	425	(188)
Hannover Express	12	33	(327)
Hans	7	501	(194)†
Hansa Berlin	13	38	(352)
Hansa Bremen	11	108	(309)
Hansa Carrier	12	102	(332)
Hansa Carrier	13	3	(349)
Hansa Clipper	12	102	(332)
Hansa Clipper	13	3	(349)
Hansa Coral	7	331	(181)
Hansa Lubeck	11	108	(309)
Hansa Merchant	7	213	(172)
Hansa Rostock	13	38	(352)
Hansa Stockholm	11	108	(309)
Hansa Visby	11	108	(309)
Hanse	6	15	(142)
Hanseatic	20	60	(463)
Hansetor	7	304	(178)
Hans Leonhardt	8	275	(225)
Hanyang Gas	3	62	(82)†
Han Yin	8	273	(225)
Han Zhong Men	17	57	(410)
Hao Fa	7	74	(162)
Hapag Lloyd Amazonas	8	157	(215)
Hapag Lloyd Amazonas	8	472	(239)
Happy Buccaneer	21	76	(506)†
Happy Buccaneer	21	16	(500)
Happy Day	7	7	(157)
Happy Fellow	3	51	(80)†
Happy Fellow	3	10	(75)
Happy Fortune	8	615	(250)
Happy Girl	4	95	(93)
Happyman	9	121	(272)
Harald Jarl	20	8	(459)
Ha R Bin	8	273	(225)
Hardman H	7	158	(168)
Harefield	10	86	(295)†
Hari Bhum	7	363	(183)
Haris	8	2	(203)
Harmac Dawn	10	90	(295)†
Harmony Ace	19	32	(448)†
Harmony Breeze	8	500	(241)
Harmony II	9	159	(275)
Harmony Sea	8	30	(205)
Harpoon	8	33	(206)
Harrier	2	315	(49)
Harriet	5	267	(125)
Harsha Vardhana	20	382	(487)
Harta I	17	31	(407)
Harting	5	322	(129)
Harvest	8	120	(212)
Harvest	8	548	(245)
Harvest 2	8	575	(247)
Harwich Star	9	127	(272)
Hasan Atasoy	8	581	(248)
Hasan B	7	224	(173)
Hasan S	8	92	(210)
Haskerland	9	150	(274)
Haslo	5	318	(129)
Hassbat Qatar	2	326	(50)
Hasselwerder	13	6	(349)
Hassi R'Mel	4	47	(90)
Hassnaa	17	92	(414)†
Hassnaa	17	58	(410)
Hastula	1	138	(12)
Hatan	2	56	(32)
Hatasia	1	138	(12)
Hateg	7	174	(169)
Hatnyanawati	2	517	(63)
Hato Arrow	10	43	(290)
Hatzvi	8	581	(248)
Hau Giang	17	87	(414)†
Hau Giang	17	57	(410)
Hau Giang 2	8	446	(237)
Haugo	5	1	(107)
Haugvik	4	129	(96)
Havang	6	97	(151)†
Havang	6	39	(144)
Havbor	5	199	(121)
Havbris	4	110	(94)
Havdrott	4	97	(93)
Havelet	20	267	(478)
Havelland	12	63	(329)
Havfrost	4	133	(97)†
Havfrost	4	86	(93)
Havfru	3	27	(77)
Havgast	4	179	(102)†
Havgast	4	71	(92)
Havglimt	4	152	(99)†
Havik	7	188	(170)
Havildar Abdul Hamid PVC	1	137	(12)
Havis	4	132	(97)†
Havis	4	86	(93)
Havjarl	4	181	(103)†
Havjarl	4	30	(89)
Havkatt	4	101	(94)
Havkong	4	97	(93)
Havlur	4	110	(94)
Havlys	4	110	(94)
Havmann	4	37	(89)
Havpil	4	31	(89)
Havprins	4	37	(89)
Havrim	4	24	(88)
Havsol	4	110	(94)
Havtjeld	7	116	(164)
Havvind	4	110	(94)
Hawaii	2	538	(65)†
Hawaiian King	2	397	(55)
Hawaiian Monarch	2	397	(55)
Hawk	7	36	(159)
Hawk One	8	648	(254)†
Hayabusa	20	337	(484)
Hayatomo Maru	20	213	(474)
Heavy Metal	5	2	(107)
Hebe	4	32	(89)
Hebridean Express	20	236	(476)
Hebridean Isles	20	269	(479)
Hebris	4	96	(93)
Hedda	4	172	(102)†
Heemskerck	12	101	(332)
Heerengracht	7	524	(197)†
Heereplein	14	77	(374)†
He Fu	8	104	(211)
Heian	7	413	(187)
Heidberg	15	27	(379)
Heidelberg Express	12	58	(329)
Hei Hu Quan	8	149	(214)
Heike Lehmann	15	69	(384)†
Heimatland	15	29	(379)
Heimdal	16	24	(393)
Heinke	15	30	(379)
Heinlaid	16	48	(395)†
Heinlaid	16	26	(393)
Heinrich Behrmann	6	2	(141)
Heiyo	7	413	(187)
Hekabe	4	97	(93)
Hektor	4	96	(93)
Heleen C	6	45	(144)
Helen	4	32	(89)
Helen	5	64	(111)
Helen	6	67	(146)
Helena	8	619	(250)
Helena	18	55	(425)
Helena 1	15	63	(383)†
Helena 1	8	619	(250)
Helene	17	79	(413)†
Helene	17	16	(406)
Helgafell	7	315	(179)
Helgoland	20	24	(461)
Helice	4	86	(93)
Helikon	4	153	(99)†
Heliopolis Sky	9	165	(275)
Heliopolis Spring	8	331	(229)
Heliopolis Wind	8	11	(203)
Helios	4	182	(103)†
Helios	4	86	(93)
Helios II	7	146	(167)
Helje	8	581	(248)
Hella	7	352	(182)
Hellas	5	291	(127)
Hellenic Confidence	8	276	(225)
Hellespont Courage	2	468	(60)
Hellespont Embassy	2	210	(43)
Hellespont Energy	2	397	(55)
Hellespont Faith	2	399	(55)
Hellespont Grand	2	201	(42)
Hellespont Orpheum	1	67	(7)
Hellespont Paradise	1	67	(7)
Helle Stevns	7	365	(183)
Helle Stevns	7	460	(190)
Helle Terkol	1	186	(15)
Helmos	8	24	(205)
Helvetia	21	56	(503)
Hemera	4	72	(92)
Hemina	4	177	(102)†
Hemina	4	97	(93)
Hemus	5	154	(118)
Hendrik B	7	361	(183)
Heng Chun Hai	8	16	(204)
Heng Li	20	376	(487)
Heng Long	9	95	(270)
Heng Tong	8	575	(247)
Hennigsdorf	7	483	(192)
Henri Barbusse	11	82	(306)
Henrik Kosan	3	71	(83)†
Henrique Dias	2	254	(46)
Henry Hudson Bridge	12	103	(332)
Hera	4	29	(89)
Herakles	4	49	(90)

†Photograph

	SHIP TYPE	REF NO	PAGE NO
Herakles	7	149	(167)
Heraklia	5	100	(114)
Her An	8	570	(247)
Herceg Novi	9	192	(278)†
Herceg Novi	9	110	(271)
Hercegovina	7	33	(159)
Hereke 4	8	135	(213)
Herm	7	16	(158)
Herman Bodewes	8	206	(219)
Hermann	8	220	(220)
Hermann Matern	11	98	(308)
Hermann Matern	11	101	(308)
Hermann Schulte	4	27	(89)
Hermes	8	676	(257)†
Hermes	2	144	(39)
Hermes	4	72	(92)
Hermes	8	500	(241)
Hermes	20	37	(461)
Hermion	4	96	(93)
Hermion	8	152	(214)
Herm J	14	6	(365)
Hermod	4	87	(93)
Hernes	5	168	(119)
Hero	1	157	(13)
Hero A	8	227	(221)
Hero II	7	149	(167)
Heron	8	354	(230)
Heron Arrow	10	43	(290)
Hero Queen	8	581	(248)
Heros	4	29	(89)
Hesiod	4	30	(89)
Hesperia	7	268	(176)
Hesperus	4	178	(102)†
Hesperus	4	37	(89)
Hettstedt	8	527	(243)
Heung-A Grace	12	79	(331)
Heung-A Strait	12	90	(331)
He Xin	8	50	(207)
Hibat Allah	5	26	(109)
Hiddensee	7	480	(192)
Highland	14	81	(374)†
Highland	14	6	(365)
Hightide	1	234	(20)†
Hijaz	9	127	(272)
Hikawa II	12	19	(326)
Hilal II	7	171	(169)
Hilda	7	271	(176)
Hilda Knutsen	1	51	(6)
Hilli	3	2	(75)
Hilon of Sparta	5	50	(110)
Hirsova	7	174	(169)
Hispaniola	7	313	(179)
Histria Moon	2	259	(46)
Histria Star	5	158	(118)
Histria Sun	5	158	(118)
Hitachi Venture	5	230	(123)
Hitaka Maru	20	196	(473)
Hitra	1	233	(20)†
Hittin	2	307	(49)
Hoa Lu 2	9	10	(264)
Hoam	8	214	(220)
Hoa Mai	9	10	(264)
Ho Chi Min	8	74	(209)
Hockenheim	18	180	(436)†
Hockenheim	18	73	(427)
Hockenheim	18	169	(434)
Hodna	8	188	(217)
Hoe Ann	8	212	(219)
Hoechst Express	12	33	(327)
Hoegh Dene	9	1	(263)
Hoegh Drake	9	1	(263)
Hoegh Duke	9	1	(263)
Hoegh Dyke	9	1	(263)
Hoegh Gandria	3	61	(81)†
Hoegh Gandria	3	17	(76)
Hoegh Marlin	10	41	(290)
Hoegh Merchant	10	41	(290)
Hoegh Merit	10	41	(290)
Hoegh Minerva	10	41	(290)
Hoegh Miranda	10	41	(290)
Hoegh Mistral	9	71	(268)
Hoegh Musketeer	10	41	(290)
Hoggar	20	311	(482)
Hoi Cheung	8	354	(230)
Hojin	19	75	(453)†
Hoji Ya Henda	8	500	(241)
Hokkaido Star	5	200	(121)
Hokuren Maru	18	2	(421)
Holck-Larsen	7	172	(169)
Holiday	20	61	(463)
Holmon	10	9	(287)
Holmsund	10	39	(290)
Homer	8	353	(230)
Homi Bhabha	1	21	(4)
Honam Jade	2	387	(54)
Honam Pearl	2	548	(66)†

	SHIP TYPE	REF NO	PAGE NO
Honam Pearl	2	387	(54)
Hong Chang	8	210	(219)
Hong Cheng	7	11	(157)
Hong Fan	8	418	(235)
Hong Gu Cheng	9	156	(274)
Hong Ha 2	8	577	(247)
Hong Long	9	102	(270)
Hongmen	8	41	(206)
Hong Qi	8	625	(251)
Hong Qi 103	8	624	(251)
Hong Qi 116	8	325	(228)
Hong Qi 131	8	482	(240)
Hong Qi 134	8	334	(229)
Hong Qi 138	8	324	(228)
Hong Qi 150	8	76	(209)
Hong Qi 151	8	76	(209)
Hong Qi 152	8	76	(209)
Hong Qi 153	8	76	(209)
Hong Qi 160	8	76	(209)
Hong Qi 191	7	358	(183)
Hong Qi 192	7	358	(183)
Hong Qi 301	5	15	(108)
Hong Qi 302	5	167	(118)
Hong Qi 303	8	97	(210)
Hong Shou Shan	9	12	(264)
Hong Xiang	8	500	(241)
Hong Yan 3	7	463	(190)
Hong Yin	8	498	(241)
Hong Yuan	8	563	(246)
Honolulu	2	204	(43)
Honolulu	11	53	(304)
Honour	8	125	(212)
Honshu 1	19	27	(447)
Honshu 1	19	28	(447)
Honshu Spirit	2	497	(62)
Honvik	7	188	(170)
Hood	11	21	(302)
Hood Island	11	117	(309)
Hoo Falcon	6	107	(152)†
Hoop	8	299	(226)
Hope	6	91	(150)†
Hope	6	72	(147)
Hope 1	7	65	(161)
Hope Glory	8	149	(214)
Hope Sea	5	136	(116)
Horezu	7	174	(169)
Horizon	20	62	(463)
Horizon A	8	351	(230)
Horizon III	2	514	(63)
Horizon IX	2	154	(39)
Hornbay	17	50	(409)
Hornbreeze	11	123	(310)
Horncap	17	108	(416)†
Horncap	17	50	(409)
Horncliff	11	185	(315)†
Horncliff	17	50	(409)
Horncloud	11	123	(310)
Hosanna	6	12	(142)
Hose Marti	2	424	(57)
Host Country	12	50	(328)
Hotama	8	189	(217)
Hoverspeed Great Britain	20	425	(492)†
Howell Lykes	12	2	(325)
Hreljin	12	97	(332)
Hsing May	5	60	(111)
Hua Bao	8	377	(232)
Hua Bei	8	13	(204)
Hua Chang	7	187	(170)
Hua Da	8	10	(203)
Hua De	7	279	(176)
Hua Dong	7	295	(178)
Hua Fang	8	10	(203)
Hua Guang	7	69	(161)
Hua Hai	8	147	(214)
Hua Hai 2	2	155	(39)
Hua Hong	8	82	(209)
Huai An	8	76	(209)
Huai Hai	5	27	(109)
Hua Jia	8	363	(231)
Hua Jian	6	16	(142)
Hua Jie	14	14	(366)
Hua Jin	7	67	(161)
Hua Kai	5	148	(117)
Hua Kun	8	290	(226)
Hual Angelita	19	11	(446)
Hua Lian	8	30	(205)
Hualien Express	8	532	(244)
Hua Li He	12	82	(331)
Hual Ingrita	19	11	(446)
Hual Karinita	19	37	(448)†
Hual Lisita	19	11	(446)
Hual Rolita	19	11	(446)
Hual Tracer	19	9	(445)
Hual Trapper	19	9	(445)
Hual Traveller	19	49	(450)†
Hual Trinita	19	83	(454)†

†Photograph

	SHIP TYPE	REF NO	PAGE NO
Hual Trinita	19	26	(447)
Hua Lung Reefer	11	163	(313)
Hua Ming	7	411	(187)
Hua Nan	8	135	(213)
Huang Hai	5	27	(109)
Huang Jin Shan	8	245	(222)
Huang Jin Shan	8	377	(232)
Huang Long Shan	8	358	(230)
Huang Shan	5	48	(110)
Hua Ning He	12	49	(328)
Huan Jiang	8	173	(216)
Hua Peng	7	222	(172)
Hua Pu	8	15	(204)
Hua Qing He	12	82	(331)
Hua Qiong	7	429	(188)
Hua Sheng	7	402	(186)
Hua Shun	7	173	(169)
Hua Shun He	12	82	(331)
Hua Tai	8	82	(209)
Huating	8	561	(246)
Hua Tong Hai	5	102	(114)
Hua Wan	7	67	(161)
Hua Xi	8	588	(248)
Hua Xi	9	30	(265)
Hua Xing	8	588	(248)
Hua Yang	8	82	(209)
Hua Ying	7	422	(187)
Hua Yu	8	548	(245)
Hua Yuan Kou	18	175	(435)
Hua Yue	8	157	(215)
Hua Zhen	7	163	(168)
Hua Zhu 2	7	34	(159)
Hubro	10	18	(288)
Hudson Bay	5	158	(118)
Hudson Bay 1	2	501	(62)
Hui Feng	8	549	(245)
Hui Fu	5	243	(124)
Hui Yang	8	492	(240)
Huldra	7	104	(164)
Hulin	8	547	(245)
Humacao	12	131	(335)
Humber	8	84	(209)
Humber Arm	21	11	(500)
Humber Bridge	12	103	(332)
Humber Star	15	27	(379)
Humboldt Current	7	443	(189)
Humboldt Express	13	111	(359)†
Humboldt Express	13	64	(353)
Hume Highway	19	34	(448)†
Hummel	1	60	(7)
Humulesti	7	174	(169)
Hung Nam	5	11	(107)
Hung Vuong 1	8	369	(231)
Hung Yun	8	420	(235)
Hunjiang	8	383	(232)
Hunter	5	244	(124)
Hu Po Hai	7	29	(159)
Huracan	18	116	(430)
Husi	7	174	(169)
Husnes	5	168	(119)
Husum	7	363	(183)
Huta Katowice	5	102	(114)
Huta Sendzimira	5	102	(114)
Huta Zgoda	5	133	(116)
Huta Zygmunt	5	133	(116)
Hvitanes	7	353	(182)
Hwang Young	8	278	(225)
Hybur Clipper	14	2	(365)
Hybur Intrepid	14	2	(365)
Hybur Star	11	162	(313)
Hybur Trader	18	83	(427)
Hyde Park	8	206	(219)
Hyderabad	9	166	(275)
Hydra	2	388	(54)
Hydro	1	254	(22)†
Hydrogas	4	145	(98)†
Hydrogas II	4	171	(101)†
Hye Prosperity 1388	7	482	(192)
Hyok Sin	8	419	(235)
Hyphestos	2	480	(60)
Hyun Am	8	33	(206)
Hyundai Admiral	12	34	(327)
Hyundai Baron	12	34	(327)
Hyundai Commodore	12	34	(327)
Hyundai Duke	12	34	(327)
Hyundai Emperor	12	34	(327)
Hyundai Malacca	12	45	(328)
Hyundai No 17	7	133	(166)
Hyundai No 107	19	48	(450)†
Hyundai Oceania	5	385	(137)†
Hyundai Tianjin	13	18	(350)
Hyundai Utopia	3	24	(76)
Hyundai Vancouver	13	49	(352)
Ialyssos	20	447	(495)†
Iarko	8	193	(218)
Iason	8	30	(205)
Iberian Coast	15	82	(386)†
Iberian Express	8	72	(209)
Iberian Reefer	11	118	(310)
Ibn Abdoun	7	68	(161)
Ibn Al-abbar	9	127	(272)
Ibn Al-atheer	9	127	(272)
Ibn Al Haitham	7	516	(196)†
Ibn Al-Moataz	9	180	(277)†
Ibn Al-moataz	9	127	(272)
Ibn Al-nafees	9	127	(272)
Ibn Asakir	9	127	(272)
Ibn Badis	8	505	(241)
Ibn Bassam	9	127	(272)
Ibn Batouta	8	505	(241)
Ibn Battotah	9	127	(272)
Ibn Battouta 2	20	330	(483)
Ibn Hayyan	9	127	(272)
Ibn Hazm	7	68	(161)
Ibn Khaldoon	8	681	(258)†
Ibn Khaldoon	8	449	(238)
Ibn Khaldoun	8	392	(233)
Ibn Khaldoun II	8	499	(241)
Ibn Khaldoun II	8	505	(241)
Ibn Khallikan	9	127	(272)
Ibn Majid	12	136	(335)
Ibn Malik	9	127	(272)
Ibn Qutaibah	9	127	(272)
Ibn Rochd	2	84	(35)
Ibn Rochd	8	505	(241)
Ibn Rushd	9	127	(272)
Ibn Shuhaid	9	127	(272)
Ibn Sina	8	248	(222)
Ibn Sina II	8	678	(257)†
Ibn Sina II	8	499	(241)
Ibn Sina II	8	505	(241)
Ibn Siraj	8	505	(241)
Ibn Tufail	9	127	(272)
Ibn Younus	9	127	(272)
Ibrahim	8	525	(243)
Icaro	1	157	(13)
Icarus	8	500	(241)
Ice Bird	11	114	(309)
Ice Crystal	11	114	(309)
Ice Express	11	160	(313)
Ice Flake	11	116	(309)
Icepearl	10	37	(289)
Ice Star	11	114	(309)
Icha	2	367	(53)
ICL Parthiban	9	121	(272)
ICL Raja Rajan	9	121	(272)
ICL Vikraman	9	213	(281)†
ICL Vikraman	9	121	(272)
Ideal Progress	5	49	(110)
Idriss I	20	405	(490)†
Ifigenia	8	628	(251)
Igarka	17	27	(407)
Iglo Express	11	204	(318)†
Igloo Bergen	4	127	(96)
Igloo Espoo	4	9	(87)
Igloo Finn	4	9	(87)
Igloo Finn	11	140	(311)
Igloo Hav	4	7	(87)
Igloo Lion	11	139	(311)
Igloo Moon	4	7	(87)
Igloo Moss	4	9	(87)
Igloo Norse	4	9	(87)
Igloo Polar	4	9	(87)
Igloo Star	4	176	(102)†
Igloo Star	4	7	(87)
Igloo Tana	4	127	(96)
Ignacio Agramonte	8	500	(241)
Ignacy Daszynski	5	304	(128)
Ignalina	8	619	(250)
Ignatiy Sergeyev	8	74	(209)
Igor Grabar	8	365	(231)
Igor Ilyinskiy	7	14	(158)
Igoumenitsa Express	18	10	(421)
Igrim	2	26	(30)
Iguazu	5	50	(110)
Ijmuiden Maru	5	331	(130)†
Ijmuiden Maru	5	285	(127)
Ijsselland	7	361	(183)
Ikan Bilis	7	112	(164)
Ikan Selangat	7	124	(165)
Ikan Selar	8	445	(237)
Ikan Selayang	7	92	(163)
Ikan Sepat	7	244	(174)
Ikan Tamban	8	252	(223)
Ikan Tanda	8	252	(223)
Ikan Tongkol	5	144	(117)
Ikariada	8	520	(243)
Ikhnaton	9	6	(263)
Ikiztepe	17	58	(410)
Iktinos	8	16	(204)

†Photograph

	SHIP TYPE	REF NO	PAGE NO
Ile de Beaute	20	137	(469)
Ile de la Reunion	17	70	(411)†
Ile de la Reunion	17	7	(405)
Ile Maurice	17	7	(405)
Ilfov	7	174	(169)
Ilha de Komo	8	311	(228)
Ilirija	20	331	(483)
Ilka	15	27	(379)
Illyria	20	236	(476)
Ilya Erenburg	1	181	(15)
Ilya Kulik	7	136	(166)
Ilya Metchnikov	11	127	(310)
Ilya Selvinskiy	7	340	(181)
Ilya Ulyanov	9	56	(267)
Ilych	20	138	(469)
Ilyinsk	8	619	(250)
Ilze	8	107	(211)
Imagination	20	440	(494)†
Imagination	20	297	(481)
Iman	7	532	(198)†
Iman M.	6	44	(144)
Imant Sudmalis	2	367	(53)
Ima Tellina	8	214	(220)
IMG 1	11	178	(314)
IMG 2	11	179	(314)
Imilchil	11	152	(312)
Imke Wehr	13	18	(350)
Immanuel Kant	4	88	(93)
Imola	18	201	(438)†
Imperial Confidence	8	270	(224)
Imperial Empress	20	358	(485)
Imperial Skeena	1	1	(3)
Ina Lehmann	15	45	(381)
Inca	11	88	(307)
Ince 1	8	210	(219)
Ince-B	7	90	(163)
Independence	2	467	(60)
Independencia	2	422	(57)
Independencia 1	2	351	(52)
Independente	17	8	(405)
Independent Endeavor	7	331	(181)
Independent Merchant	7	331	(181)
Independent Pioneer	7	331	(181)
Independent Voyager	7	331	(181)
Indian	9	66	(268)
Indianapolis	19	73	(453)†
Indian Endurance	8	651	(254)†
Indian Express	8	72	(209)
Indian Prestige	8	126	(212)
Indian Progress	8	126	(212)
Indian Prosperity	8	126	(212)
Indian Reefer	11	241	(322)†
Indian Reefer	11	118	(310)
Indian Valour	8	463	(239)
Indira Gandhi	21	49	(503)
Indobaruna 1	8	367	(231)
Indobaruna III	8	586	(248)
Indoceanique	20	394	(488)
Indomitable	5	152	(117)
Industrial Advantage	8	161	(215)
Inessa Armand	8	74	(209)
Inga	6	36	(144)
Inger	10	36	(289)
Ingolstadt	19	56	(451)†
Ingrid	15	43	(380)
Ingrid Gorthon	17	116	(417)†
Ingrid Leonhardt	8	275	(225)
Ingrid Terkol	1	186	(15)
Inharrime	6	64	(146)
Inishark	6	86	(149)†
Inishark	6	40	(144)
Inishowen	6	14	(142)
Inkerman	2	380	(54)
Inowroclaw	18	170	(434)
Inspiration	20	297	(481)
Insulano	7	313	(179)
Inter Mare	15	50	(382)†
Intermodal Carrier	14	62	(372)†
Intermodal Carrier	14	6	(365)
Intermodal Egypt	14	6	(365)
Intermodal Levant	14	6	(365)
Intermodal Malta	14	6	(365)
Intermodal Mare	14	6	(365)
International 1	7	174	(169)
International 2	7	174	(169)
International 4	7	174	(169)
International 5	7	174	(169)
Intisar	2	479	(60)
Intra Bhum	7	363	(183)
Intrepido	17	110	(416)†
Intrepido	17	8	(405)
Invicta	21	107	(509)†
Invincible	11	99	(308)
Inzenieris Kreilis	16	35	(394)
Inzenieris Neciporenko	16	77	(399)†
Inzenieris Neciporenko	16	35	(394)

	SHIP TYPE	REF NO	PAGE NO
Inzenieris Neciporenko	16	36	(394)
Inzenieris Suhorukovs	16	35	(394)
Inzhehier Ageyev	2	377	(54)
Inzhener Bashkirov	16	98	(401)†
Inzhener Machulskiy	16	94	(401)†
Inzhener Parkhonyuk	7	245	(174)
Inzhener Plavinskiy	7	435	(188)
Inzhener Yamburenko	8	49	(207)
Inzhener Yermoshkin	16	44	(395)†
Inzhener Yermoshkin	16	21	(393)
Inzhenier Bashkirov	16	35	(394)
Inzhenier Machulskiy	16	35	(394)
Ioa	5	174	(119)
Ioanna	7	22	(158)
Ioanna	8	196	(218)
Ioannis	5	183	(120)
Ioannis H.	8	541	(244)
Ioannis I	8	500	(241)
Ioannis K.	7	15	(158)
Ioannis L	8	445	(237)
Ioannis M	5	65	(111)
Ioannis P.	5	65	(111)
Ioannis Zafirakis	5	307	(128)
Ioannitsa	5	169	(119)
Iokasti	9	28	(265)
Iolcos Flame	2	143	(39)
Iolcos Legend	8	267	(224)
Iolcos Spirit	2	400	(55)
Iona Yakir	8	74	(209)
Ionia	7	57	(160)
Ionian	11	71	(306)
Ionian Breeze	10	38	(289)
Ionian Coral	8	100	(211)
Ionian Empress	7	7	(157)
Ionian Express	8	72	(209)
Ionian Express	20	225	(475)
Ionian Fame	18	144	(432)
Ionian Jade	2	582	(70)†
Ionian King	8	16	(204)
Ionian Korti	17	58	(410)
Ionian Master	10	14	(288)
Ionian Sailor	10	38	(289)
Ionian Sea	9	24	(265)
Ionian Sky	5	298	(128)
Ionian Sprinter	11	64	(305)
Ionian Star	5	298	(128)
Ionian Sun	5	298	(128)
Ionian Sun	20	298	(481)
Ionic Reefer	11	128	(310)
Ionikos	2	167	(40)
Ionion	2	287	(47)
Ionis	7	104	(164)
Ion Soltys	5	329	(130)†
Ion Soltys	5	17	(108)
Ion Soltys	5	193	(120)
Ios	5	226	(122)
Ios	9	104	(271)
Ipanema	5	145	(117)
Ippocratis	8	197	(218)
Ira	7	97	(163)
Irafoss	9	22	(264)
Iran Abad	9	142	(273)
Iran Abozar	7	117	(165)
Iran Adalat	8	437	(237)
Iran Adl	7	69	(161)
Iran Afzal	7	69	(161)
Iran Akhavan	7	222	(172)
Iran Amanat	7	222	(172)
Iran Ashrafi	7	117	(165)
Iran Azadi	8	133	(213)
Iran Baghaei	8	386	(233)
Iran Bagheri	8	386	(233)
Iran Basheer	7	468	(191)
Iran Bayan	7	451	(189)
Iran Borhan	7	451	(189)
Iran Broojerdi	8	386	(233)
Iran Chamran	7	117	(165)
Iran Dastghayb	7	117	(165)
Iran Eghbal	7	117	(165)
Iran Ehsan	7	451	(189)
Iran Ekram	8	154	(215)
Iran Elham	8	154	(215)
Iran Entekhab	8	133	(213)
Iran Ershad	9	142	(273)
Iran Eshragi	7	117	(165)
Iran Eslami	8	133	(213)
Iran Esteghlal	8	133	(213)
Iran Fallahi	8	354	(230)
Iran Gaz	4	117	(95)
Iran Ghafari	7	117	(165)
Iran Ghazi	7	117	(165)
Iran Gheyamat	8	437	(237)
Iran Ghodousi	7	117	(165)
Iran Hamzeh	7	117	(165)
Iran Jahad	9	142	(273)
Iran Jamal	7	117	(165)

†Photograph

	SHIP TYPE	REF NO	PAGE NO
Iran Jomhouri	8	133	(213)
Iran Kashani	7	117	(165)
Iran Kolahdooz	8	386	(233)
Iran Madani	7	117	(165)
Iran Mahallati	8	386	(233)
Iran Meead	9	142	(273)
Iran Meelad	9	142	(273)
Iran Meezan	7	451	(189)
Iran Mofid	11	23	(302)
Iran Motaharai	7	222	(172)
Iran Mufateh	7	117	(165)
Iran Nabuvat	8	437	(237)
Iran Nasr	7	192	(170)
Iran Navab	7	117	(165)
Iran Rajai	2	335	(51)
Iran Sabr	7	192	(170)
Iran Sadoughi	7	117	(165)
Iran Sadr	7	117	(165)
Iran Saeidi	7	117	(165)
Iran Salam	8	591	(248)
Iran Sarbaz	7	222	(172)
Iran Seeyam	8	591	(248)
Iran Shariati	7	117	(165)
Iran Sokan	7	451	(189)
Iran Takhti	7	371	(184)
Iran Takhti	9	166	(275)
Iran Taleghani	7	117	(165)
Iran Teyfouri	7	371	(184)
Iran Torab	7	58	(161)
Iran Towheed	8	50	(207)
Iran Vahdat	8	437	(237)
Iran Vojdan	7	451	(189)
Irati	2	24	(30)
Irbenskiy Proliv	11	102	(308)
Iregua	7	349	(182)
Irene	5	60	(111)
Irene	7	70	(161)
Irene	8	45	(207)
Irene	8	559	(246)
Irene Oldendorff	5	202	(121)
Irenes Diamond	8	140	(213)
Irenes Horizon	12	35	(327)
Irenes Song	12	68	(330)
Irene V	5	19	(108)
Irene Wonsild	2	62	(33)
Irina Trader	5	256	(125)
Irishgate	2	460	(59)
Irish Sea	11	8	(301)
Irismed	17	10	(406)
Irkutsk	9	28	(265)
'Irkutsk' class	7	21	(158)
Irlo	6	58	(145)
Iro	8	647	(254)†
Iron Carpentaria	5	16	(108)
Iron Curtis	5	16	(108)
Iron Dampier	7	453	(190)
Iron Flinders	7	289	(177)
Iron Kembla	5	41	(110)
Iron Monarch	18	32	(423)
Iron Newcastle	5	41	(110)
Iron Pacific	5	273	(126)
Iruvai Hudhu	8	215	(220)
Irving Arctic	2	419	(56)
Irving Eskimo	2	419	(56)
Irving Ocean	2	419	(56)
Irving Timber	17	13	(406)
Isabel	6	76	(148)†
Isabel	6	45	(144)
Isabella	2	453	(59)
Isakogorka	8	169	(216)
Isargas	4	20	(88)
Isartal	15	7	(377)
Ischia	20	237	(476)
Iseult	2	311	(49)
Ishikari	20	1	(459)
Ishim	15	47	(381)
Isidora	8	567	(247)
Isidor Barakhov	7	340	(181)
Isis	9	6	(263)
Isis	18	116	(430)
Isis I	8	291	(226)
Isla Bolivar	8	301	(227)
Isla Bonita	11	104	(308)
Isla de la Plata	13	64	(353)
Isla de Las Volcanes	18	142	(432)
Isla Gran Malvina	13	95	(357)†
Islam Safarli	2	171	(41)
Island Commodore	18	43	(424)
Island Gem	7	145	(167)
Island King	1	26	(4)
Island Princess	20	241	(476)
Island Skipper	7	145	(167)
Island Sky	8	149	(214)
Islas Dos	21	110	(510)†
Isle Hope	4	69	(92)
Isle of Arran	20	229	(475)
Isle of Inishmore	20	55	(463)
Isle of Innisfree	20	439	(494)†
Ismailiya	9	80	(269)
Ismail M	8	402	(234)
Ismara	2	490	(61)
Ismini	7	101	(163)
Ismini	9	28	(265)
Isocardia	4	52	(90)
Isola	8	581	(248)
Isola Bianca	2	567	(68)†
Isola Delle Perle	18	87	(428)
Isola Delle Stelle	18	87	(428)
Isola Turchese	2	376	(54)
Isolde	19	10	(445)
Isomeria	4	52	(90)
Isparta	7	74	(162)
Ispaster	2	327	(50)
Ispat Gaurav	5	379	(136)†
Ist	7	506	(195)†
Ist	2	443	(58)
Ist	7	271	(176)
Istra	20	359	(485)
Istrian Exprss	8	72	(209)
Itaite	9	186	(277)†
Itaite	9	40	(266)
Italian Express	8	72	(209)
Italian Reefer	11	118	(310)
Italia Prima	20	457	(496)†
Itanage	9	40	(266)
Itapage	9	40	(266)
Itape	9	40	(266)
Itaquatia	9	40	(266)
Iter	2	253	(45)
Itfa 1	11	179	(314)
Itfa 2	11	48	(304)
Ithaki	7	159	(168)
Itororo	2	24	(30)
Iva	18	149	(433)
Ivan Bogun	5	131	(116)
Ivan Bogun	7	273	(176)
Ivan Bolotnikov	8	582	(248)
Ivan Chernykh	8	169	(216)
Ivan Derbenyev	16	52	(396)†
Ivan Derbenyev	16	13	(392)
Ivan Franko	20	30	(461)
Ivan Korobtsov	9	80	(269)
Ivan Koroteyev	8	49	(207)
Ivan Kotlyarevskiy	12	75	(330)
Ivan Kulibin	5	29	(109)
Ivan Moskalenko	9	92	(270)
Ivan Pereverzev	9	92	(270)
Ivan Polzunov	5	29	(109)
Ivan Prokhorov	15	23	(379)
Ivan Ryabov	8	51	(207)
Ivan Shadr	8	365	(231)
Ivan Shepetkov	9	92	(270)
Ivans Kulibins	11	127	(310)
Ivan Skuridin	16	13	(392)
Ivans Polzunovs	11	127	(310)
Ivan Strod	7	340	(181)
Ivan Susanin	5	131	(116)
Ivan Syrykh	8	78	(209)
Ivan Tevosyan	2	92	(35)
Ivan Vazov	8	11	(203)
Ivan Zagubanski	9	92	(270)
Ivan Zajc	20	299	(481)
Ivar Lauritzen	11	121	(310)
Ivi	7	97	(163)
Ivory Eagle	11	192	(316)†
Ivybank	9	149	(274)
Iyo	20	300	(481)
Izgutty Aytykov	5	193	(120)
Izmail	9	28	(265)
Izmaylovo	1	138	(12)
Izumrudnyy Bereg	11	99	(308)
Izvestiya	17	57	(410)
Jacaranda	1	56	(6)
Jackson Ocean	8	215	(220)
Jacmar	11	131	(311)
Jacqueline	15	25	(379)
Jacqueline	18	151	(433)
Jacui	2	519	(63)
Jad	8	144	(214)
Jade	15	25	(379)
Jade Orient	7	206	(171)
Jade Pacific	7	206	(171)
Jade Star	1	211	(17)
Jadran	5	295	(127)
Jag Laadki	1	143	(12)
Jag Leela	2	454	(59)
Jag Manek	7	228	(173)
Jag Palak	1	72	(7)
Jag Pari	1	68	(7)
Jag Prabhat	1	72	(7)

†Photograph

	SHIP TYPE	REF NO	PAGE NO
Jag Pragati	1	72	(7)
Jag Praja	2	437	(58)
Jag Prayog	2	437	(58)
Jag Preeti	1	68	(7)
Jag Rahul	7	537	(199)†
Jag Rahul	7	42	(160)
Jag Rahul	7	124	(165)
Jag Rashmi	7	95	(163)
Jag Ravi	7	57	(160)
Jag Shakti	7	224	(173)
Jag Vijay	7	183	(170)
Jag Vikas	7	78	(162)
Jag Vikram	7	53	(160)
Jag Vishnu	7	59	(161)
Jahre Pollux	2	339	(51)
Jahre Prince	1	135	(11)
Jahre Rose	2	454	(59)
Jahre Spray	2	547	(66)†
Jahre Trader	1	145	(12)
Jahre Viking	2	214	(43)
Jainarayan Vyas	2	477	(60)
Jak Kong	9	59	(267)
Jakob Maersk	4	107	(94)
Jalavijaya	5	342	(132)†
Jalavijaya	5	315	(129)
Jalisco	9	89	(269)
Jamaica Provider	18	57	(425)
Jambo	8	214	(220)
Jambo	10	47	(290)
Jambur	2	411	(56)
James Lykes	12	10	(325)
James Mchenry	21	63	(504)
James N Sullivan	1	27	(5)
Jamestown	2	15	(30)
Janana	1	134	(11)
Janbazi I	8	537	(244)
Janbaz III	8	152	(214)
Jan Becker	5	112	(115)
Jan Dlugosz	7	448	(189)
Jane Maersk	4	107	(94)
Jane Stove	2	440	(58)
Janet I	7	418	(187)
Janice Aung	7	154	(168)
Janis Sudrabkalns	2	379	(54)
Jan Kahrs	14	78	(374)†
Jan Kahrs	5	112	(115)
Jan Luiken	7	481	(192)
Jan Meeder	15	8	(377)
Jan-Rasmus	6	93	(150)†
Jan-Rasmus	6	58	(145)
Jan Ritscher	7	329	(180)
Jan Sniadecki	18	128	(431)
Jan V	15	80	(386)†
Japanese Dream	20	139	(469)
Japan Platanus	5	198	(121)
Japan Senator	12	102	(332)
Japan Tuna No 2	1	5	(3)
Japeri	4	16	(88)
Japura	2	519	(63)
Jarash	8	222	(220)
Jasmine	5	201	(121)
Jasmin Prince	8	369	(231)
Jason	20	140	(469)
Jastarnia-Bor	9	120	(272)
Ja Sunshine	4	99	(94)
Java Rainbow	4	2	(87)
Java Sea	2	489	(61)
Jay Durga	8	128	(213)
J C Phillips	2	102	(36)
Jean Alleaume	4	185	(103)†
Jeanie Brown	8	374	(232)
Jean Lykes	12	2	(325)
Jeanne Labourbe	8	74	(209)
Jeannie	7	159	(168)
Jebel Ali	12	170	(338)†
Jebel Ali	12	27	(327)
Jeb Stuart	21	39	(502)
Jehan	15	99	(388)†
Jelau	8	291	(226)
Jelsa	9	92	(270)
Jemila	4	122	(95)
Jenlil	6	58	(145)
Jennifer R	8	400	(234)
Jenolin	7	350	(182)
Jens Kofoed	20	157	(470)
Jens R	15	25	(379)
Jerba	5	89	(113)
Jerba	7	257	(175)
Jerom	2	318	(50)
Jerome H	15	21	(379)
Jervis Bay	12	215	(344)†
Jesper Maersk	4	107	(94)
Jessica	17	40	(408)
Jessie Maersk	4	107	(94)
Jet II	2	103	(36)
Jet IV	2	104	(36)
Jetty	7	16	(158)
Jevington	5	345	(132)†
Jevington	5	266	(125)
J Faster	9	103	(271)
Jhelum	8	24	(205)
Jia Fa	7	256	(175)
Jia Hai	7	76	(162)
Jian Chi	2	434	(57)
Jiang An	9	13	(264)
Jiang Cheng	8	154	(215)
Jiang Chuan	9	112	(271)
Jian Ge Hai	8	133	(213)
Jiang He	8	32	(205)
Jiang Ling Hai	8	16	(204)
Jiangmen	8	628	(251)
Jiangting	8	561	(246)
Jiang Yang	10	40	(290)
Jian Hua Ling	7	141	(166)
Jian She 51	1	177	(14)
Jian She 52	1	177	(14)
Jiao Zhou Hai	7	216	(172)
Jia Xiu Shan	6	52	(145)
Jia Yow	11	46	(304)
Jia Yu Hai	8	127	(213)
Ji Hai 10	10	15	(288)
Ji Hai 9	5	5	(107)
Ji Hao	8	574	(247)
Ji Hua	2	73	(34)
Jilfar	9	127	(272)
Ji Lin	8	152	(214)
Ji Ma	8	49	(207)
Ji Mei	20	180	(472)
Jimilta	5	195	(120)
Jimy	20	324	(483)
Jin Bi	7	182	(169)
Jin Chang	5	65	(111)
Jin Cheng	7	406	(186)
Jin Cheng Jiang	8	27	(205)
Jin Cheng Jiang	8	153	(215)
Jin Fa	12	50	(328)
Jin Fan	12	130	(334)
Jin Gang Lin	8	211	(219)
Jing Hai	8	285	(225)
Jingshun	8	664	(256)†
Jin Hai	7	29	(159)
Jin Hai Yang	8	350	(230)
Jin Hai Yang	9	123	(272)
Jin Hui	7	175	(169)
Jin Hu Quan	8	568	(247)
Jin Hu Quan	8	569	(247)
Jin Jiang	8	26	(205)
Jin Ji Shan	7	425	(188)
Jin Peng	12	130	(334)
Jin Qiao	7	422	(187)
Jin Run	9	59	(267)
Jin Shan	8	217	(220)
Jin Sheng	7	202	(171)
Jin Xiang	9	114	(271)
Jin Xian Quan	9	116	(271)
Jin Yi	7	202	(171)
Jin You 6	2	557	(67)†
Jin Zhou Hai	8	15	(204)
Jiu Jiang	8	58	(208)
Jiu Long	8	202	(219)
J J Sister	20	69	(464)
Jo Alder	1	36	(5)
Joanna Borchard	7	313	(179)
Joanna V	5	72	(112)
Joanne I	8	193	(218)
Joan Sif	7	461	(190)
Jo Aspen	1	36	(5)
Jo Birk	1	151	(12)
Jo Breid	1	41	(5)
Jo Brevik	1	53	(6)
Jobst Oldendorff	9	185	(277)†
Jobst Oldendorff	9	134	(273)
Jo Calluna	1	238	(20)†
Jo Cedar	1	62	(7)
Jo Clipper	1	235	(20)†
Jo Clipper	1	53	(6)
Jo Ebony	1	38	(5)
Jo Elm	1	41	(5)
Jo Gran	1	163	(13)
Johan Crystal	8	446	(237)
Johangela	2	348	(52)
Johan II	5	88	(113)
Johan III	5	88	(113)
Johanna	2	348	(52)
Johanna	7	326	(180)
Johanna	15	21	(379)
Johanna Trader	7	316	(179)
Johann Mahmastal	7	435	(188)
Johan Pearl	14	57	(371)†
Johan Pearl	14	21	(366)
Jo Hassel	1	38	(5)
Jo Hegg	1	38	(5)

†Photograph

	SHIP TYPE	REF NO	PAGE NO
Joh Gorthon	18	204	(439)†
John Augustus Essberger	1	55	(6)
John Hamilton Gray	20	226	(475)
John Henry	21	63	(504)
John Hope	8	201	(218)
John M	2	292	(48)
Johnny C	5	158	(118)
Johnny Two	9	90	(269)
Johs Stove	2	318	(50)
Joint Success	8	276	(225)
Joinville	2	519	(63)
Jo Lind	1	54	(6)
Jollity	8	445	(237)
Jolly Amaranto	18	48	(425)
Jolly Bianco	16	6	(391)
Jolly Blu	16	25	(393)
Jolly Grigio	18	48	(425)
Jolly Rosso	16	6	(391)
Jolly Rubino	16	55	(396)†
Jolly Rubino	16	37	(394)
Jolly Smeraldo	16	37	(394)
Jolly Turchese	16	37	(394)
Jolly Verde	16	60	(397)†
Jolly Verde	16	6	(391)
Jo Lonn	1	256	(23)†
Jo Lonn	1	151	(12)
Jonrix	6	66	(146)
Jo Oak	1	151	(12)
Jordan	8	77	(209)
Jordan II	8	500	(241)
Jordanka Nikolova	5	172	(119)
Jorgen Lauritzen	11	121	(310)
Jorita	7	143	(167)
Jo Rogn	1	163	(13)
Jorund	14	74	(373)†
Jose Dias	8	619	(250)
Jose Do Patrocinio	2	254	(46)
Jo Selje	1	62	(7)
Jose Maria Ramon	11	142	(311)
Josephina I	8	143	(214)
Joseph Lykes	12	10	(325)
Josiff I	5	270	(126)
Jo Spruce	1	62	(7)
Jostelle	5	184	(120)
Joy	8	392	(233)
Joy	15	6	(377)
Joy D	9	92	(270)
Joyful Spirit	5	205	(121)
Joy Sea	5	380	(137)†
Joy Venture	9	212	(281)†
J Sister	7	432	(188)
J Truster	9	103	(271)
Juan B Azopardo	4	112	(95)
Juan Diego	8	193	(218)
Juanita	1	213	(17)
Juan J Sister	20	261	(478)
Jubilee	20	61	(463)
Jubilee I	7	446	(189)
Jubiter	8	33	(206)
Judith Borchard	12	129	(334)
Ju Hai	5	170	(119)
Jules Verne	3	20	(76)
Julia	7	350	(182)
Julia Del Mar	17	81	(413)†
Julia Del Mar	17	14	(406)
Julie	7	2	(157)
Julie Pacific	8	256	(223)
Julpha A	7	176	(169)
Jumbo	10	47	(290)
Jumbo Challenger	21	75	(505)†
Junior	17	3	(405)
Junior M	8	552	(245)
Juniper	5	19	(108)
Juniper	18	74	(427)
Jun Liang Cheng	8	257	(223)
Juno	2	339	(51)
Jupiter	5	66	(111)
Jupiter	5	114	(115)
Jupiter	7	458	(190)
Jupiter	8	17	(204)
Jupiter 2	8	418	(235)
Jupiter I	8	24	(205)
Jurata	9	120	(272)
Jurina	7	162	(168)
Juris Avots	16	53	(396)†
Juris Avots	16	13	(392)
Jurua	2	519	(63)
Jurupema	2	519	(63)
Jussara	2	94	(35)
Justine	15	45	(381)
Justinian	11	123	(310)
Jutha Chanathip	9	108	(271)
Jutha Jessica	9	108	(271)
Jutha Kasamphan	8	388	(233)
Jutha Malee	8	388	(233)
Jutha Nattaka	7	427	(188)
Jutha Pariyanat	7	427	(188)
Jutha Phansiri	8	557	(246)
Jutha Rachavadee	8	446	(237)
Jutha Sarunpak	8	446	(237)
Jutha Suphannika	8	446	(237)
Jutha Trithip	9	113	(271)
Jytte Danielsen	8	206	(219)
Kaaksburg	15	27	(379)
Kabala	8	582	(248)
Kabanjahe	8	189	(217)
Kaberneeme	8	596	(249)
Kacharava	1	181	(15)
Kaddour I	7	114	(164)
Kadirga-5	2	455	(59)
Kadmos	1	18	(4)
Kafur Mamedov	1	70	(7)
Kaga	12	114	(333)
Kaghan	8	440	(237)
Kagoro	16	6	(391)
Kahleberg	18	3	(421)
Kahuripan	8	190	(217)
Kaiama	13	6	(349)
Kaijin	19	94	(455)†
Kailash	5	123	(115)
Kaimoku	16	5	(391)
Kainalu	16	5	(391)
Kairos	8	116	(212)
Kairouan	9	128	(272)
Kai Yuan	10	20	(288)
Kakuho	1	82	(8)
Kakushima	7	271	(176)
Kalamos	2	336	(51)
Kalba III	17	61	(410)
Kale I	7	163	(168)
Kaliningrad	8	619	(250)
'Kaliningrad' type	9	6	(263)
Kalisti	7	159	(168)
Kalkavanlar	8	228	(221)
Kallang	8	24	(205)
Kalliopi L	7	74	(162)
Kalliste	20	419	(492)†
Kalma	7	222	(172)
Kalmius	8	581	(248)
Kalo	9	92	(270)
Kalofer	7	358	(183)
Kalymnos	8	59	(208)
Kamakura	12	104	(332)
Kamandalu	8	114	(212)
Kamari I	7	223	(173)
Kamasan	8	202	(219)
Kambuna	20	387	(487)
Kamchadal	8	619	(250)
Kamchatskiy Bereg	11	98	(308)
Kamchatskiy Proliv	11	102	(308)
Kamchia	2	508	(62)
Kamenitza	5	132	(116)
Kamensk-Uralskiy	2	26	(30)
Kamikawa Maru	5	206	(121)
Kamilla	7	547	(200)†
Kamilo Sjenfuegos	11	54	(304)
Kamiros	20	332	(483)
Kamnik	8	321	(228)
Kamogawa	1	131	(11)
Kamtin	7	348	(182)
Kanchenjunga	2	462	(59)
Kandalaksha	17	27	(407)
Kandalakshskiy Zaliv	11	18	(302)
Kandilli 1	2	312	(49)
Kandilousa	1	191	(15)
Kang Da	8	304	(227)
Kang He	12	144	(336)
Kangson	8	565	(246)
Kan Su Hai	5	102	(114)
Kao Jiang	7	217	(172)
Kapall	6	111	(152)†
Kapall	6	39	(144)
Kapetan Elias	7	397	(186)
Kapetan Giannis	2	203	(43)
Kapetan Giorgis	2	262	(46)
Kapetan Hatzis	2	210	(43)
Kapetan Hiotis	2	210	(43)
Kapetan Michalis	2	203	(43)
Kapetan Panagiotis	2	262	(46)
Kapitan Alekseyev	9	36	(265)
Kapitan Anistratenko	9	36	(265)
Kapitan A Polkovskiy	9	32	(265)
Kapitan Artyukh	12	109	(333)
Kapitan Bakanov	8	78	(209)
Kapitan Betkher	7	143	(167)
Kapitan Bochek	7	273	(176)
Kapitan Boev	2	337	(51)
Kapitan Burmakin	8	78	(209)
Kapitan Byankin	13	38	(352)
Kapitan Chmutov	7	435	(188)

†Photograph

	SHIP TYPE	REF NO	PAGE NO
Kapitan Chukhchin	7	273	(176)
Kapitan Danilkin	17	27	(407)
Kapitan Dotsyenko	2	377	(54)
Kapitan Dublitskiy	8	78	(209)
Kapitan Dyachuk	2	377	(54)
Kapitan Dzhurashevich	9	36	(265)
Kapitan E Egorov	2	337	(51)
Kapitan Fomenko	7	189	(170)
Kapitan Fomin	7	452	(190)
Kapitan Georgi Georgiev	5	132	(116)
Kapitan Georgiy Baglay	9	36	(265)
Kapitan Glazachyev	8	78	(209)
Kapitan Glotov	7	435	(188)
Kapitan Goncharov	7	435	(188)
Kapitan Gribin	2	377	(54)
Kapitan Kadetskiy	9	36	(265)
Kapitan Kaminskiy	9	36	(265)
Kapitan Khabalov	7	435	(188)
Kapitan Kiriy	8	78	(209)
Kapitan Kissa	9	6	(263)
Kapitan Klunnikov	9	6	(263)
Kapitan Kobets	2	377	(54)
Kapitan Konev	12	84	(331)
Kapitan Korotayev	1	107	(10)
Kapitan Kud	12	109	(333)
Kapitan Kudlay	7	273	(176)
Kapitan Kurov	13	12	(350)
Kapitan Kushnarenko	9	36	(265)
Kapitan Leontiy Borisenko	9	36	(265)
Kapitan Lev Solovyev	9	36	(265)
Kapitan L Golubev	7	286	(177)
Kapitan Luca	4	14	(88)
Kapitan Lukhmanov	9	80	(269)
Kapitan Lyashenko	12	109	(333)
Kapitan Lyubchenko	8	78	(209)
Kapitan Man	17	27	(407)
Kapitan Medvedev	7	262	(175)
Kapitan Mezentsev	16	21	(393)
Kapitan Milovzorov	8	78	(209)
Kapitan Mochalov	8	78	(209)
Kapitan Modest Ivanov	9	36	(265)
Kapitan Nagonyuk	1	181	(15)
Kapitan Nazarev	7	273	(176)
Kapitan Nevezhkin	2	377	(54)
Kapitan Paapkov	9	6	(263)
Kapitan Penkov	7	102	(164)
Kapitan Petko Voivoda	9	92	(270)
Kapitan Petrushevskiy	15	23	(379)
Kapitan Plaushevskiy	9	80	(269)
Kapitan Polin	7	160	(168)
Kapitan Pomerants	2	337	(51)
Kapitan Ponomarev	7	435	(188)
Kapitan Ponomaryov	7	435	(188)
Kapitan Primak	7	435	(188)
Kapitan Radionov	2	54	(32)
Kapitan Rudnyev	1	107	(10)
Kapitan Samoylenko	8	78	(209)
Kapitan Serykh	13	12	(350)
Kapitan Shantsberg	9	80	(269)
Kapitan Shevchenko	8	78	(209)
Kapitan Shvetsov	2	377	(54)
Kapitan Slipko	9	36	(265)
Kapitan Smirnov	16	21	(393)
Kapitan Sokolov	2	337	(51)
Kapitan Soroka	7	189	(170)
Kapitan Sviridov	7	273	(176)
Kapitan Temkin	9	93	(270)
Kapitan Trubkin	7	56	(160)
Kapitan Tsirul	7	273	(176)
Kapitan Vakula	7	273	(176)
Kapitan V Ivanov	2	337	(51)
Kapitan Vodenko	7	273	(176)
Kapitan V Ovodovskiy	9	93	(270)
Kapitan V Trush	12	61	(329)
Kapitan Yershov	1	181	(15)
Kapitan Zamyatin	8	78	(209)
Kapitan Zuzenko	7	435	(188)
Kapitonas A. Lucka	5	128	(116)
Kapitonas Chromcov	5	128	(116)
Kapitonas Dubinin	5	128	(116)
Kapitonas Gudin	5	128	(116)
Kapitonas Izmiakov	5	128	(116)
Kapitonas Mesceriakov	5	327	(130)†
Kapitonas Mesceriakov	5	128	(116)
Kapitonas Panfilov	5	128	(116)
Kapitonas Reutov	5	128	(116)
Kapitonas Stulin	5	128	(116)
Kapitonas Stulpinas	5	128	(116)
Kapitonas Vavilov	5	128	(116)
Kapos	7	460	(190)
Kappa 1	2	97	(35)
Kappara	9	92	(270)
Kaptai	9	18	(264)
Kaptan Abidin Doran	20	318	(482)
Kaptan Burhanettin Isim	20	318	(482)
Kaptan Cebi	9	97	(270)

	SHIP TYPE	REF NO	PAGE NO
Kaptan Dursun Akbas	8	551	(245)
Kaptan Necdet Or	18	152	(433)
Kapteinis Kulinics	11	98	(308)
Kapten Konga	6	33	(143)
Kapten Voolens	6	33	(143)
Karabi	5	178	(119)
Karaga	8	612	(250)
Karakumneft	2	367	(53)
Karat II	5	84	(113)
Karawa	13	99	(358)†
Karawa	13	6	(349)
Kardamyla	7	233	(173)
Karden	20	301	(481)
Kareliya	20	127	(468)
Karema	8	294	(226)
Karen	8	399	(234)
Karen D	8	399	(234)
Karen Winther	8	205	(219)
Karibu	15	43	(380)
Karim	5	79	(112)
Karim 1	2	97	(35)
Karim M	8	92	(210)
Karin	14	48	(370)†
Karin	14	12	(366)
Karin	15	25	(379)
Karina	7	103	(164)
Karipande	8	346	(230)
Karl Carstens	20	400	(489)†
Karl Libknekht	11	100	(308)
Karl Liebknecht	8	74	(209)
Karlobag	7	514	(196)†
Karlobag	7	443	(189)
Karlovy Vary	8	445	(237)
Karlowicz	7	448	(189)
Karmsund	17	5	(405)
Karoline	2	197	(42)
Karrington	7	87	(163)
Kartal 4	5	207	(121)
Karteria	7	276	(176)
Kashima	9	137	(273)
Kasira	1	52	(6)
Kassantina	8	393	(233)
Kassiakos	9	90	(269)
Kassos	8	59	(208)
Kastelorizo	1	104	(9)
Kastilyo	7	241	(174)
Kasturba	5	278	(126)
Kasuga 1	12	165	(338)†
Kasuga I	12	22	(326)
Kasuga II	9	102	(270)
Kaszuby II	11	7	(301)
Katangli	8	612	(250)
Katarina	20	141	(469)
Kate	14	82	(374)†
Katerina L	9	110	(271)
Katerina One	8	169	(216)
Katharina Charlotte	15	21	(379)
Katharina D	5	66	(111)
Katharina S	15	27	(379)
Katherine Borchard	5	97	(114)
Kathe Sif	7	461	(190)
Katie	2	380	(54)
Katja	1	227	(19)†
Katrin	15	59	(383)†
Katya V	5	72	(112)
Katya Zelenko	16	13	(392)
Kauai	12	86	(331)
Kaunas	18	164	(434)
Kavalerovo	8	612	(250)
Kaveri	8	24	(205)
Kavo Flora	5	132	(116)
Kavo Geranos	8	500	(241)
Kavo Kaliakra	5	138	(117)
Kavo Mangalia	5	132	(116)
Kavo Midia	5	138	(117)
Kavo Yerakas	7	171	(169)
Kawa	10	35	(289)
Kawan	5	139	(117)
Kayax	7	199	(171)
Kay L	15	21	(379)
Kazatin	8	612	(250)
K-Christina	7	199	(171)
Kea	11	187	(315)†
Kea	8	452	(238)
Kea	11	52	(304)
Kedah	7	485	(192)
Kedainiai	8	619	(250)
Kedma	8	368	(231)
Kee Ann	8	212	(219)
Keitum	2	87	(35)
Keiy Kokeb	9	140	(273)
Kekova	7	71	(161)
Kekur	2	367	(53)
Kelibia	20	360	(485)
Kelimutu	20	388	(488)
Kellys Mark	8	467	(239)

†Photograph

	SHIP TYPE	REF NO	PAGE NO
Kelme	7	269	(176)
Kelme	8	619	(250)
Kels	7	387	(185)
Keltic Confidence	8	368	(231)
Kem	8	612	(250)
Kemeri	1	181	(15)
Kemerovo	17	27	(407)
Ken Ei	7	120	(165)
Kenmare	5	253	(124)
Kenmare	8	399	(234)
Kenneth T Derr	1	77	(8)
Ken Sun	9	228	(283)†
Kent Adventure	8	133	(213)
Kent Excellent	7	452	(190)
Kent Merchant	13	17	(350)
Kento	6	20	(142)
Kent Trader	13	23	(350)
Kentucky Highway	19	31	(448)†
Kerchenskiy Kommunist	2	367	(53)
Kerchenskiy Proliv	11	102	(308)
Kerem Ka	2	40	(31)
Keret	6	20	(142)
Kerinci	20	387	(487)
Kerkyra	2	247	(45)
Kernave	8	365	(231)
Kerry Express	21	120	(511)†
Kerstin	7	18	(158)
Kessulaid	16	47	(395)†
Kessulaid	16	26	(393)
Kestrel	2	441	(58)
Keta Lagoon	8	444	(237)
Keystone Canyon	2	229	(44)
K Georgios	8	232	(221)
Khaled IV	18	51	(425)
Khamza	7	152	(167)
Khan Asparukh	1	13	(4)
Khania	2	327	(50)
Khannur	3	43	(79)†
Khannur	3	2	(75)
Khariton Greku	5	17	(108)
Khark 4	2	196	(42)
Khasan	8	415	(235)
Khatanga	8	589	(248)
Khatangales	8	596	(249)
Khatulistiwa	8	684	(258)†
Kherson	2	470	(60)
Khersones	11	218	(319)†
Khersones	11	1	(301)
Khezer	2	504	(62)
Khirurg Vishnevskiy	1	107	(10)
Kholmsk	8	589	(248)
Khrustalny Bereg	11	98	(308)
Khudozhnik A Gerasimov	5	132	(116)
Khudozhnik Fedorovskiy	5	132	(116)
Khudozhnik Gabashvili	5	132	(116)
Khudozhnik Ioganson	12	68	(330)
Khudozhnik Kasiyan	5	132	(116)
Khudozhnik Kraynev	5	129	(116)
Khudozhnik Kuindzha	7	340	(181)
Khudozhnik Kustodiyev	5	132	(116)
Khudozhnik N Rerikh	12	109	(333)
Khudozhnik Plastov	7	340	(181)
Khudozhnik Toidze	5	132	(116)
Khudozhnik Vladimir Serov	5	132	(116)
Khudozhnik Zhukov	12	68	(330)
Khulna	8	581	(248)
Khyber	13	61	(353)
Kian Ann	8	211	(219)
Kibi	21	68	(505)†
Kibu	8	239	(222)
Kidira	16	14	(392)
Kiefernwald	7	367	(183)
Kifangondo	8	383	(232)
Kigilyakh	7	340	(181)
Kiho	2	388	(54)
Kihu	1	262	(23)†
Kihu	1	155	(13)
Kii Maru	5	286	(127)
Kiisla	1	31	(5)
Kika	7	36	(159)
Kikhchik	8	619	(250)
Kiku Pacific	2	397	(55)
Kilchem Baltic	2	36	(31)
Kilchem Oceania	2	65	(33)
Kildinskiy Proliv	11	98	(308)
Kildinskiy Proliv	11	101	(308)
Kilgas Discovery	4	13	(88)
Kilimanjiro	9	86	(269)
Kiliya	8	612	(250)
Killarney	6	66	(146)
Kilstraum	1	111	(10)
Kim An	8	534	(244)
Kimanis	13	29	(351)
Kimberley	1	57	(6)
Kimisis	5	103	(114)
Kimitsu Maru	5	220	(122)
Kim Lien	8	418	(235)
Kim Long	9	102	(270)
Kimolos	7	130	(166)
Kimolos II	5	139	(117)
Kimry	8	619	(250)
Kinaros V	11	10	(301)
Kindrence	5	262	(125)
King	11	53	(304)
King Alexander	2	456	(59)
Kingfisher	2	371	(53)
Kingfisher	8	567	(247)
Kingisepp	8	619	(250)
King of Scandinavia	20	414	(491)†
King of Scandinavia	20	142	(469)
King Orry	20	321	(483)
Kinokawa	5	280	(126)
Kin Ping Hai	11	15	(301)
Kinsale	8	399	(234)
Kinzan Maru	8	388	(233)
Kira	2	56	(32)
Kirby D	8	399	(234)
Kirillis Barbara	7	199	(171)
Kirishima	12	209	(343)†
Kirk Challenger	18	50	(425)
Kirk Marina	18	23	(423)
Kirkuk	2	411	(56)
Kirovskles	9	102	(270)
Kirsten	2	197	(42)
Kirsten	6	5	(141)
Kirzhach	7	498	(194)†
Kish	5	316	(129)
Kista Arctica	8	223	(220)
Kitano	12	164	(338)†
Kitano	12	114	(333)
Kithnos	2	12	(29)
Kitsa	9	182	(277)†
Kittanning	2	334	(51)
Kiwi	11	78	(306)
Klaipeda	11	79	(306)
Klaipeda	18	164	(434)
Klajpedskij Bereg	11	98	(308)
Klajpedskij Bereg	11	101	(308)
Klang Reefer	17	34	(407)
Klara Zetkin	11	82	(306)
Klavdiya Yelanskaya	20	18	(460)
Klazina C	6	117	(153)†
Klements Gotvalds	2	424	(57)
Klenoden	5	113	(115)
Kleofas	8	155	(215)
Kleon	2	325	(50)
Kleovoulos of Rhodes	2	454	(59)
Klim Voroshilov	9	80	(269)
Klisura	7	358	(183)
Kniepsand	11	135	(311)
Knight	8	291	(226)
Knock Allan	1	143	(12)
Knock Buie	2	440	(58)
Knock Clune	1	123	(11)
Knock Davie	2	479	(60)
Knock Dee	2	336	(51)
Knock Dun	1	123	(11)
Knock More	2	235	(44)
Knock Muir	1	123	(11)
Knock Stocks	1	143	(12)
Knock Taggart	2	255	(46)
Knud Jesperson	17	57	(410)
Knud Kosan	4	32	(89)
Knud Lauritzen	11	121	(310)
Knudshoved	20	143	(469)
Kobe	8	33	(206)
Kobuleti	1	181	(15)
Kocaeli 1	8	445	(237)
Kochnev	7	310	(179)
Kociewie	11	59	(305)
Kodino	8	596	(249)
Koh Jin	19	46	(449)†
Kohju	5	45	(110)
Kola	17	27	(407)
Kolandia	2	477	(60)
Kolguyev	8	596	(249)
Kolkhida	20	19	(460)
Koln Express	12	5	(325)
Kolomna	17	107	(416)†
Kolpino	17	51	(409)
Kolskiy Zaliv	11	98	(308)
Kolskiy Zaliv	11	101	(308)
Kolya Myagotin	8	621	(251)
Komandarm Fedko	2	470	(60)
Komandarm Matveyev	9	80	(269)
Komet	14	42	(369)†
Komet	14	11	(366)
Komiles	8	589	(248)
Komissar Polukhin	11	172	(313)
Kommunist	8	74	(209)
Komponists Caikovskis	18	20	(422)
Kompozitor Dargomyzhskiy	18	20	(422)

†Photograph

	SHIP TYPE	REF NO	PAGE NO
Kompozitor Musorgskiy	18	20	(422)
Kompozitor Novikov	18	20	(422)
Kompozitor Rakhmaninov	18	20	(422)
Kompozitor Rimskiy-Korsakov	18	20	(422)
Komsomolets Adzharii	9	6	(263)
Komsomolets Armenii	9	6	(263)
Komsomolets Azerbaydzhana	9	6	(263)
Komsomolets Kazakhstana	9	6	(263)
Komsomolets Litvy	9	96	(270)
Komsomolets Moldavii	9	184	(277)†
Komsomolets Moldavii	9	6	(263)
Komsomolets Primorya	11	98	(308)
Komsomolets Primorya	11	101	(308)
Komsomolets Rossii	9	6	(263)
Komsomolets Spasska	9	6	(263)
Komsomolets Turkmenii	9	6	(263)
Komsomolets Ussuriyska	9	6	(263)
Komsomolets Vladivostoka	9	6	(263)
Komsomoliya Kaliningrada	11	58	(305)
Komsomolskaya Smena	11	58	(305)
Konah	11	72	(306)
Konda	15	47	(381)
Kondratiy Bulavin	8	582	(248)
Kong Frederik IX	20	181	(472)
Kong Harald	20	63	(463)
Kongsdal	21	105	(509)†
Kong Tong Dao	9	207	(280)†
Kong Tong Dao	9	164	(275)
Konin	8	74	(209)
Koningin Beatrix	20	206	(474)
Konkar Alpin	2	313	(49)
Konkar Dinos	2	313	(49)
Konkar Intrepid	5	152	(117)
Konkar Star	5	67	(112)
Konkar Victory	5	152	(117)
Konstantina K	10	110	(298)†
Konstantin Korshunov	7	324	(180)
Konstantinos D	2	508	(62)
Konstantinovka	8	527	(243)
Konstantin Paustovskiy	12	75	(330)
Konstantin Petrovskiy	8	78	(209)
Konstantin Savelyev	7	324	(180)
Konstantins Ciolkovskis	2	508	(62)
Konstantin Shestakov	7	324	(180)
Konstantin Simonov	20	128	(468)
Konstantin Yuon	8	365	(231)
Konstantin Zaslonov	7	340	(181)
Kontula	7	118	(165)
Kookaburra	5	157	(118)
Kopalnia Jeziorko	5	171	(119)
Kopalnia Jeziorko	7	280	(177)
Kopalnia Machow	7	251	(175)
Kopalnia Piaseczno	5	171	(119)
Kopalnia Piaseczno	7	280	(177)
Kopalnia Sosnowiec	5	133	(116)
Kopalnia Szczyglowice	8	155	(215)
Kopalnia Walbrzych	5	133	(116)
Kopalnia Zofiowka	5	133	(116)
Kopersand	15	43	(380)
Koporye	8	619	(250)
Koprivstica	7	358	(183)
Korat Navee	9	127	(272)
Kordun	5	295	(127)
Korean Peace	7	144	(167)
Korean Pigeon	7	144	(167)
Korean Pioneer	7	133	(166)
Korean Trader	8	137	(213)
Korea Sunnyhill	2	398	(55)
Korea Venus	2	498	(62)
Koreiz	8	612	(250)
Koriana	1	79	(8)
Korimu	9	76	(268)
Korinthia	2	288	(48)
Korinthos	8	59	(208)
Kornat	7	373	(184)
Korni	6	46	(144)
Koros	9	42	(266)
Korsnes	5	229	(123)
Korsun-Shevchenkovskiy	17	51	(409)
Kortezubi	6	68	(146)
Kos	2	371	(53)
Koscierzyna	10	11	(287)
Kosmaj	5	295	(127)
Kostandis F	8	283	(225)
Kostrena	5	216	(122)
Kostroma	17	51	(409)
Kostromales	8	596	(249)
Kota Berani	12	132	(335)
Kota Berjaya	8	380	(232)
Kota Berkat	12	132	(335)
Kota Berlian	12	132	(335)
Kota Cahaya	13	17	(350)
Kota Indah	7	227	(173)
Kota Intan	7	227	(173)
Kota Jade	10	74	(293)†
Kota Jade	13	66	(353)
Kota Machan	7	431	(188)
Kota Maju	12	83	(331)
Kota Mawar	8	116	(212)
Kota Megah	8	116	(212)
Kota Melati	8	122	(212)
Kota Mesra	7	430	(188)
Kota Mutiara	8	446	(237)
Kota Panjang	10	6	(287)
Kota Pusaka	7	409	(186)
Kota Rakyat	8	446	(237)
Kota Ratna	8	638	(252)
Kota Ratu	8	638	(252)
Kota Ria	17	34	(407)
Kota Sabas	13	53	(353)
Kota Silat IV	8	581	(248)
Kota Suria	13	53	(353)
Kota Wijaya	12	6	(325)
Kota Wirawan	12	6	(325)
Kotel	7	358	(183)
Kothen	8	527	(243)
Kotlini	16	58	(396)†
Kotlini	16	29	(393)
Kotor	8	279	(225)
Kotovsk	8	590	(248)
Kotovskiy	11	170	(313)
Kotowaka Maru	3	29	(77)
Kotuku	1	73	(7)
Kouilou	8	657	(255)†
Kouyo Maru	2	161	(40)
Kovdor	8	575	(247)
Kovo	8	590	(248)
Kowhai	11	75	(306)
Kowloon Bay	12	166	(338)†
Kowloon Bay	12	153	(336)
Koyali	2	462	(59)
Kozelsk	7	340	(181)
Koznitsa	5	129	(116)
Kozyrevsk	8	619	(250)
Kraka	2	339	(51)
Kraka	16	24	(393)
Krakow II	7	400	(186)
Kramatorsk	8	527	(243)
Kranj	8	321	(228)
Kras	7	191	(170)
Krasica 1	7	371	(184)
Krasnoarmeysk	8	612	(250)
Krasnogorskles	9	102	(270)
Krasnogvardeyets	12	109	(333)
Krasnokamsk	9	96	(270)
Krasnopolye	8	612	(250)
Krasnoturinsk	8	612	(250)
Krasnovidovo	15	47	(381)
Krasnoyarsk	8	619	(250)
Kremenchug	17	51	(409)
Kretinga	8	619	(250)
Kreva	8	365	(231)
Krios	8	388	(233)
Kris Terasek	13	18	(350)
Kristian Palusalu	5	17	(108)
Kristin Star	9	127	(272)
Kristjan Palusalu	5	17	(108)
Kriti Champion	1	136	(11)
Kriti Color	1	136	(11)
Kriti Episkopi	2	381	(54)
Kriti Filoxenia	1	136	(11)
Kriti Gerani	2	381	(54)
Kriti Gold	2	351	(52)
Kriti Land	2	401	(55)
Kriti Palm	1	136	(11)
Kriti Star	2	401	(55)
Kriti Wave	2	401	(55)
Krk	9	110	(271)
Kronprins Frederik	20	397	(489)†
Kronprins Frederik	20	351	(485)
Kronprins Harald	20	111	(467)
Kropotkin	2	380	(54)
Krymsk	8	612	(250)
Ksar Chellala	9	198	(279)†
Ksar Chellala	9	133	(273)
Ksar El Boukhari	9	133	(273)
Ksar Ettir	9	133	(273)
Kuaka	1	73	(7)
Kuan Cheng	8	308	(227)
Kuang Hai	7	25	(158)
Kuban	2	328	(50)
Kubbar	9	127	(272)
Kudos	2	205	(43)
Kuei Wei	8	254	(223)
Kuivastu	9	57	(267)
Kula	7	544	(200)†
Kulikovo	8	339	(229)
Kuloy	11	151	(312)
Kulunda	8	612	(250)
Kumasi	17	120	(418)†
Kum Gang	8	503	(241)
Kupa	7	177	(169)

†Photograph

	SHIP TYPE	REF NO	PAGE NO
Kupari	21	67	(504)
Kupiskis	8	619	(250)
Kurama	12	176	(339)†
Kurama	12	99	(332)
Kure	10	34	(289)
Kurila	8	4	(203)
Kurpie	11	59	(305)
Kursenai	8	619	(250)
Kurska	11	54	(304)
Kurushima No 7	20	349	(485)
Kustanay	8	612	(250)
Kutai	9	229	(283)†
Kutaisi	2	420	(56)
Kuwait	8	528	(243)
Kuyvastu	8	581	(248)
Kuzbass	2	329	(50)
Kuzma Gnidash	16	13	(392)
Kuzma Minin	5	131	(116)
Kuznetsk	8	612	(250)
Kuznica	9	120	(272)
Kvarner	5	145	(117)
Kwangtung	7	490	(193)†
Kwan Siu	2	43	(31)
Kwidzyn	9	69	(268)
Kydonia	8	146	(214)
Kyknos 1	11	1	(301)
Kylemore	6	66	(146)
Kyma	11	21	(302)
Kyomi	5	35	(109)
Kyong Song	8	500	(241)
Kyrakoula	8	291	(226)
Kyrenia	5	157	(118)
Kythira	2	247	(45)
Kyushu	19	27	(447)
Kyushu	19	28	(447)
Kyzikos	8	270	(224)
Labe	7	214	(172)
la Bonita	8	369	(231)
la Briantais	8	191	(217)
Laburnum	20	132	(469)
Lacerta	1	2	(3)
Lackenby	5	122	(115)
Laconia	2	20	(30)
Laconia	2	197	(42)
Laconian Confidence	8	276	(225)
La Cordillera	5	341	(132)†
la Cordillera	5	309	(128)
Lada	8	575	(247)
'Ladoga'	15	11	(378)
Ladoga 1	15	11	(378)
Ladoga 2	15	11	(378)
Ladoga 3	15	11	(378)
Ladoga 4	15	11	(378)
Ladoga 5	15	11	(378)
Ladoga 6	15	11	(378)
Ladoga 7	15	11	(378)
Ladoga 8	15	11	(378)
Ladoga 9	15	11	(378)
Ladoga 11	15	12	(378)
Ladoga 12	15	12	(378)
Ladoga 13	15	12	(378)
Ladoga 14	15	12	(378)
Ladoga 15	15	12	(378)
Ladoga 16	15	12	(378)
Ladoga 17	15	12	(378)
Ladoga 18	15	12	(378)
Ladoga 19	15	12	(378)
Ladoga-101	15	46	(381)
Ladoga 102	15	94	(387)†
Ladoga-102	15	46	(381)
Ladoga-103	15	46	(381)
Ladoga-104	15	46	(381)
Ladoga-105	15	46	(381)
Ladoga-106	15	46	(381)
Ladoga-107	15	46	(381)
Ladoga-108	15	46	(381)
Ladoga-109	15	46	(381)
Lady Anais	9	14	(264)
Lady Anna	15	98	(388)†
Lady Bana	9	141	(273)
Lady Bella	9	14	(264)
Lady Benedikte	1	37	(5)
Lady Bos	6	5	(141)
Lady Charmain	9	14	(264)
Lady Ema	2	356	(52)
Lady Emily	9	93	(270)
Lady Fortune	8	445	(237)
Lady Franklin	17	72	(412)†
Lady Franklin	17	12	(406)
Lady Helene	1	37	(5)
Lady Ina	2	525	(64)
Lady Jannicke	1	37	(5)
Lady Juliet	9	38	(265)
Lady Kadoorie	5	45	(110)
Lady Linda	14	63	(372)†
Lady Moyne	5	121	(115)
Lady Muriel	7	446	(189)
Lady Nada	8	293	(226)
Lady Nina	8	202	(219)
Lady Noha	8	581	(248)
Lady of Lorne	8	24	(205)
Lady of Mann	20	199	(473)
Lady Rea	6	24	(143)
Lady Rebecca	8	427	(236)
Lady Rowena	4	129	(96)
Lady Sandra	6	54	(145)
Lady Sharon	9	38	(265)
Lady Sovereign	2	69	(33)
Laemthong Glory	8	24	(205)
Laemthong Pride	8	24	(205)
Lafayette	11	106	(309)
Lagard	5	254	(124)
Lagarfoss	7	346	(182)
Lagedi	2	377	(54)
la Goleta	18	137	(432)
Lai Chang	8	109	(211)
Laieta	4	74	(92)
Lai King	8	24	(205)
Laila	16	85	(400)†
Laja	13	55	(353)
Lake Avery	5	228	(123)
Lake Charles	3	5	(75)
Lake Erie	5	243	(124)
Lake George	5	301	(128)
Lake Marion	7	164	(168)
Lake Mead	5	105	(114)
Lake Michigan	5	243	(124)
Lake Oneida	5	301	(128)
Lake Ontario	5	243	(124)
Lake Placid	5	172	(119)
Lake Superior	5	243	(124)
Lake Tahoe	5	269	(126)
Lake Wales	5	313	(129)
Lakhta	8	612	(250)
Lama	2	465	(59)
Lamda	8	521	(243)
Lamone	7	317	(180)
Lampas	1	74	(7)
Lampung	18	105	(429)
Lamyra	5	100	(114)
Lan Cang Jiang	8	24	(205)
Lance Naik Albert Ekka PVC	1	137	(12)
Lance Naik Karam Singh PVC	1	137	(12)
Lancer	1	23	(4)
Lancing	6	23	(142)
Landsort	1	203	(16)
Landwind	5	192	(120)
Langkapuri Star Aquarius	20	64	(464)
Lania	15	27	(379)
Lanistes	2	233	(44)
Lanka Abhaya	13	36	(351)
Lanka Amila	13	26	(351)
Lanka Aruna	13	36	(351)
Lanka Asitha	13	36	(351)
Lanka Ruwan	13	26	(351)
Lan Qiao	18	100	(429)
Lanrick	3	46	(80)†
Laola	15	90	(387)†
Lapad	21	80	(506)†
Lapad	21	38	(502)
la Paimpolaise	9	152	(274)
La Paix	7	504	(195)†
la Paix	7	409	(186)
la Palma	20	238	(476)
la Pal San	11	176	(314)
la Pampa	5	291	(127)
la Paz	20	144	(469)
Lappland	6	2	(141)
Laptop Pioneer	8	420	(235)
Larak	8	531	(244)
Lara Mikheyenko	8	621	(251)
Larbi Ben M'Hidi	4	148	(99)†
Largs Bay	12	213	(344)†
Larina	2	141	(38)
la Rioja	9	122	(272)
Larisa Reysner	11	82	(306)
Lark	7	540	(199)†
Lark	6	66	(146)
Lark	7	33	(159)
Larkfield	10	43	(290)
Lark Lake	2	532	(64)
Larvikstone	5	261	(125)
Las Aves	14	15	(366)
Las Bolinas	7	483	(192)
la Seine	12	104	(332)
Laserbeam	7	224	(173)
Laser Pacific	13	123	(361)†
Laser Pacific	13	58	(353)
Laser Santiago	9	217	(281)†
Laser Stream	12	118	(334)

†Photograph

	SHIP TYPE	REF NO	PAGE NO
Lash Atlantico	21	62	(504)
la Sierra	5	291	(127)
Las Mercedes	11	5	(301)
Las Palmas de Gran Canaria	20	209	(474)
Las Perlas	7	424	(187)
Las Rosas	8	15	(204)
Lassia	7	103	(164)
Lass Mars	15	76	(385)†
la Tata	8	558	(246)
Latmos	16	54	(396)†
Latmos	16	1	(391)
L'Aude	18	142	(432)
Laura	8	229	(221)
Laura Helena	5	363	(134)†
Laura Helena	5	1	(107)
Laura I	14	14	(366)
Laurel Star	8	134	(213)
Lauriergracht	7	310	(179)
Laurissa	8	446	(237)
Laurits Kosan	4	32	(89)
Lauro Express	20	302	(481)
Lawit	20	388	(488)
Lazani	8	312	(228)
Lazaro Cardenas II	1	81	(8)
Lazaros L	7	72	(162)
Lazdijai	8	619	(250)
Lazurnyy Bereg	11	100	(308)
Lea	6	42	(144)
Leader	2	502	(62)
Leader	5	159	(118)
Leader	7	124	(165)
Leader	7	222	(172)
Leader A	7	224	(173)
Leader LT	2	335	(51)
Lea Terkol	1	186	(15)
Lebork	9	69	(268)
Le Castellet	18	7	(421)
Le Chene No 1	2	21	(30)
Leconte	20	145	(469)
Ledagas	4	10	(87)
Ledastern	1	211	(17)
Ledenice	17	32	(407)
Ledi	8	445	(237)
Le Duan	21	99	(508)†
Le Duan	21	49	(503)
Lee Frances	7	522	(197)†
Leerort	7	363	(183)
Leeward	20	426	(492)†
Leeward	12	79	(331)
Leila	8	192	(218)
Leira	7	124	(165)
Leisure World	20	33	(461)
Leixoes	12	61	(329)
Lei Zhou Hai	5	53	(110)
Leja	8	619	(250)
Leknes	5	1	(107)
Lembit	5	321	(129)
Lemmergracht	7	310	(179)
Lena	7	338	(181)
Lenales	8	613	(250)
Lena S	15	97	(388)†
Lena S	15	22	(379)
Leng	2	357	(52)
Leningradskiy Opolchenets	7	324	(180)
Leningradskiy Partizan	7	324	(180)
Leninsk	7	179	(169)
Leninskiy Komsomol	15	36	(380)
Lenneborg	7	361	(183)
Leo	2	358	(52)
Leo	5	260	(125)
Leo	7	101	(163)
Leon	2	143	(39)
Leon	5	317	(129)
Leon	8	452	(238)
Leona	6	36	(144)
Leona II	2	102	(36)
Leonia	1	74	(7)
Leonidas	2	248	(45)
Leonid Leonidov	8	315	(228)
Leonid Lugovoy	15	23	(379)
Leonid Smirnykh	8	612	(250)
Leonid Sobinov	20	347	(484)
Leonid Sobolyev	5	129	(116)
Leonid Utesov	1	107	(10)
Leonie	8	220	(220)
Leon Popov	9	57	(267)
Leopard	8	133	(213)
Leopardi	5	208	(121)
Lepanto Glory	7	36	(159)
Lepanto Star	5	326	(130)†
Lepeta	1	271	(25)†
Lepeta	1	74	(7)
Lepetane	5	125	(116)
Lepta Venus	7	241	(174)
Leptis Magna	1	195	(16)
Lerma	19	22	(446)
Leros Courage	8	30	(205)
Leros Spirit	7	221	(172)
Leros Star	8	34	(206)
Leros Strength	7	183	(170)
Leszek G	5	89	(113)
Leszek K	7	257	(175)
Leticia	2	559	(67)†
Leuser	20	388	(488)
Levan	5	343	(132)†
Levan	5	313	(129)
Levante	11	94	(307)
Levantgracht	7	310	(179)
Levant Neva	7	313	(179)
Levant Weser	13	124	(361)†
Levant Weser	7	313	(179)
Levent K	8	46	(207)
Leverkusen Express	12	163	(338)†
Leverkusen Express	12	33	(327)
Lev Tolstoy	20	128	(468)
Lewant	8	610	(250)
Lexington	2	15	(30)
Lex Naranjo	8	517	(242)
Leysand	15	43	(380)
Leyte Spirit	1	214	(17)
Le Yu Quan	14	3	(365)
Le Zuan	21	49	(503)
Lia M	5	145	(117)
Lian	2	241	(45)
Lian Chi	2	378	(54)
Lian Feng	7	334	(181)
Lian Feng	8	500	(241)
Liang Shan	8	438	(237)
Lian Hong	8	508	(242)
Lian Hua Feng	8	307	(227)
Lian Hua Ling	8	399	(234)
Lian Hua Shan	8	389	(233)
Lian Jiang	8	173	(216)
Lian Mao	5	68	(112)
Lian Shan	17	2	(405)
Lian Yun Shan	9	12	(264)
Liao Cheng	13	73	(355)†
Liao Hai	8	347	(230)
Liao He	13	32	(351)
Liao Yang	8	490	(240)
Lia P	8	500	(241)
Lia P	8	500	(241)
Libanus	8	559	(246)
Liberta	8	445	(237)
Libertador San Martin	1	19	(4)
Liberte	20	303	(481)
Liberty	2	178	(41)
Liberty	15	47	(381)
Liberty Sea	7	119	(165)
Liberty Spirit	7	119	(165)
Liberty Star	7	119	(165)
Liberty Star	8	220	(220)
Liberty Sun	7	119	(165)
Liberty Victory	7	202	(171)
Liberty Wave	7	119	(165)
Libexcel	10	4	(287)
Libra	6	2	(141)
Libra	7	308	(179)
Libra	11	81	(306)
Libra Chile	8	444	(237)
Libra Gas 1	4	141	(98)†
Libra Gas 1	4	120	(95)
Libra Genova	13	38	(352)
Libra II	6	66	(146)
Libre	7	241	(174)
Liburnija	20	304	(481)
Li Cheng	8	308	(227)
Lida Demesh	8	239	(222)
Lido II	2	509	(63)
Lielupe	2	424	(57)
Liepaya	2	359	(52)
Lieutenant Arun Khetarpal PVC	1	137	(12)
Lieutenant Rama Raghoba Rane PVC	1	137	(12)
Ligovo	8	619	(250)
Lijnbaansgracht	7	310	(179)
Lika	5	51	(110)
Lika 1	7	371	(184)
Lila Bhum	13	37	(351)
Lilac Islands	8	383	(232)
Liliana Dimitrova	7	513	(196)†
Liliana Dimitrova	7	164	(168)
Lillgard	6	41	(144)
Lilli Pearl	8	615	(250)
Lilly R	20	275	(479)
Li Long	8	548	(245)
Lily	8	604	(249)
Lily	9	157	(275)
Lily Pacific	4	169	(101)†
Lima	1	74	(7)
Lima	11	88	(307)
Limani	7	132	(166)
Limari	13	106	(359)†

†Photograph

	SHIP TYPE	REF NO	PAGE NO
Limari	13	43	(352)
Limbazhi	2	359	(52)
Li Ming	8	479	(240)
Limon Trader	11	136	(311)
Lina	5	139	(117)
Lina M	8	169	(216)
Lincoln	10	59	(291)
Lincoln K	8	24	(205)
Lincolnshire	4	79	(92)
Lincoln Universal	11	24	(302)
Linda	8	575	(247)
Linda	18	46	(424)
Linda K	8	369	(231)
Lindeborg	7	361	(183)
Linden	7	230	(173)
Lindengracht	7	310	(179)
Lindesay Clark	5	330	(130)†
Lindfjord	2	486	(61)
Lingegas	4	167	(101)†
Ling Feng	14	14	(366)
Ling Hu	2	421	(57)
Ling Jiang	7	217	(172)
Ling Long Hai	7	178	(169)
Ling Tong	14	24	(367)
Lin Hai 16	8	260	(224)
Lin Hai 20	8	260	(224)
Li Ning	10	45	(290)
Link Star	8	418	(235)
Link Star	18	4	(421)
Linkuva	2	380	(54)
Linz	10	49	(290)
Lion Prince	20	355	(485)
Liotina	1	28	(5)
Lipa	17	66	(411)†
Lipa	17	35	(408)
Lipetsk	2	446	(58)
Lipno	8	136	(213)
Lipno	8	320	(228)
Lircay	13	55	(353)
Lirija	8	469	(239)
Lisa	6	113	(153)†
Lisa	2	505	(62)
Lisa	6	36	(144)
Lisboa	13	79	(355)†
Lisboa	12	61	(329)
Lisboa	13	42	(352)
Liselotte Essberger	1	55	(6)
Li Shui	9	4	(263)
Litkes Sala	11	11	(301)
Litrotis	5	53	(110)
Litsa	9	25	(265)
Litsa K	7	425	(188)
Liulinhai	7	29	(159)
Liva	8	510	(242)
Livadiya	8	581	(248)
Liverpool Bay	12	153	(336)
Livezini	5	132	(116)
Livia	2	37	(31)
Livorno Bridge	16	95	(401)†
Livorno Bridge	16	13	(392)
Liwa	2	251	(45)
Li Yang	8	86	(210)
Lizrix	6	34	(143)
Llaima	7	115	(164)
Lloyd Atlantico	13	87	(356)†
Lloyd Bage	11	107	(309)
Lloyd Bahia	7	389	(185)
Lmotse	7	313	(179)
LNG Aquarius	3	56	(81)†
LNG Aquarius	3	5	(75)
LNG Aries	3	5	(75)
LNG Bonny	4	58	(91)
LNG Capricorn	3	5	(75)
LNG Finima	4	58	(91)
LNG Flora	3	30	(78)†
LNG Gemini	3	5	(75)
LNG Lagos	4	42	(90)
LNG Leo	3	5	(75)
LNG Libra	3	55	(81)†
LNG Libra	3	5	(75)
LNG Port Harcourt	4	42	(90)
LNG Taurus	3	5	(75)
LNG Virgo	3	5	(75)
Loa	7	449	(189)
Lobo	5	323	(129)
Lochness	2	219	(44)
Lodbrog	16	24	(393)
Lodz II	7	400	(186)
Lofoten	2	564	(68)†
Loire	9	101	(270)
Loka	8	224	(221)
Lok Pragati	7	150	(167)
Lok Pratima	7	150	(167)
Lola	11	129	(310)
Lomur	7	467	(191)
Lomur	17	6	(405)

	SHIP TYPE	REF NO	PAGE NO
Lomza	10	11	(287)
London	2	464	(59)
London Bridge	9	51	(266)
London Glory	1	132	(11)
London Maersk	12	155	(336)
London Pride	1	132	(11)
London Senator	12	14	(326)
London Spirit	2	560	(67)†
Lone Terkol	1	186	(15)
Long An	8	249	(223)
Longavi	7	449	(189)
Long Beach	7	120	(165)
Long Challenger	2	382	(54)
Long Chuan Jiang	8	153	(215)
Longevity	5	296	(127)
Long Hai	8	672	(257)†
Long Hai	8	14	(204)
Long Hai	8	399	(234)
Long Hai He	12	120	(334)
Long Khanh	8	468	(239)
Longmen	8	41	(206)
Long Ping	8	638	(252)
Long Teng	8	134	(213)
Long Tong	14	41	(369)†
Longva Stream	11	230	(321)†
Long Xiang	15	47	(381)
Long Xu	8	593	(248)
Lontue	13	75	(355)†
Lontue	13	13	(350)
Lootsgracht	7	310	(179)
Lorcon Luzon	8	341	(229)
Lorcon Mindanao	8	341	(229)
Lord Citrine	5	74	(112)
Lord Hinton	5	74	(112)
Lord of the Isles	20	270	(479)
Lorenzo Container XII	20	256	(478)
Loreto	18	129	(431)
Lori E	8	36	(206)
L'Orme No 1	2	102	(36)
Losinj	8	27	(205)
Lotus Islands	8	383	(232)
Loucy	8	4	(203)
Louis	8	446	(237)
Louise Trader	15	22	(379)
Louisiana	3	5	(75)
Louis Maersk	12	190	(341)†
Loulan	18	104	(429)
Loul'Wat Qatar	1	97	(9)
Lourdas	2	198	(42)
Lourdes Giralt	3	12	(76)
Loussio	5	159	(118)
Lovcen	8	161	(215)
Lovech	8	50	(207)
Lovely Lady	8	577	(247)
Loverval	16	61	(397)†
Loverval	16	27	(393)
Lovisa Gorthon	17	17	(406)
Lowlands Sunrise	5	364	(135)†
Loyal Bird	8	57	(208)
Loyalty	1	109	(10)
Lozva	15	47	(381)
L Rochette	2	102	(36)
Luan He	7	44	(160)
Luba	2	64	(33)
Luba	8	102	(211)
Lubchem	2	491	(61)
Lubeck Link	16	41	(394)
Luben Karavelov	9	92	(270)
Lublin II	7	400	(186)
Lubna S	8	92	(210)
Lucien Delmas	7	234	(173)
Lucien Paquin	7	27	(159)
Lucija	8	135	(213)
Lucille	8	193	(218)
Lucina	2	213	(43)
Lucinda	20	197	(473)
Lucingo	8	581	(248)
Lucky Fortune	7	241	(174)
Luckyman	7	49	(160)
Lucky O	8	24	(205)
Lucky Ocean	7	425	(188)
Lucky Pioneer	8	146	(214)
Lucky Raider	18	68	(426)
Lucky Runner	18	70	(426)
Lucky Sailor	5	283	(127)
Lucky Star	5	6	(107)
Lucky Trader	10	8	(287)
Lucnam	8	383	(232)
Lucy	1	142	(12)
Lucy Maud Montgomery	20	107	(467)
Lucy Oldendorff	7	120	(165)
Lucy PG	2	70	(34)
Lu Ding	8	636	(252)
Ludogoretz	7	278	(176)
Ludwig	2	265	(46)
Ludwigshafen Express	12	33	(327)

	SHIP TYPE	REF NO	PAGE NO
Lu Feng	7	430	(188)
Lufeng	8	103	(211)
Lugela	6	64	(146)
Lugoj	7	174	(169)
Lu Hai	8	286	(225)
Lu Hai 65	8	557	(246)
Luigi Lagrange	4	157	(100)†
Luise Leonhardt	8	385	(233)
Lujiang	8	509	(242)
Lukas	13	6	(349)
Lukomorye	2	380	(54)
Lula 1	2	325	(50)
Lu Long No 1	8	368	(231)
Luminence	5	262	(125)
Luna Maersk	12	182	(340)†
Lundeno	9	64	(267)
Lundoge	8	383	(232)
Lunni	1	9	(3)
Luo Fu Shan	5	153	(117)
Luo He	13	32	(351)
Luo Jiang	8	238	(222)
Luo Shan Hai	5	162	(118)
Luric	9	92	(270)
Lu Sheng	14	71	(373)†
Lu Sheng	6	2	(141)
Luso	7	363	(183)
Lutro	8	640	(253)†
Lu Yu	7	436	(188)
Luzon Spirit	1	214	(17)
Lydi	7	34	(159)
Lydia	8	619	(250)
Lydia	20	146	(470)
Lydia Flag	8	203	(219)
Lydia II	8	26	(205)
Lydra	8	662	(255)†
Lyonya Golikov	8	620	(250)
Lyonya Golykov	8	621	(251)
Lyra	7	82	(162)
Lys-Bris	5	265	(125)
Lys Coast	15	78	(385)†
Lyubov Orlova	20	23	(461)
Lyudmila Stal	9	57	(267)
Lyulin	5	154	(118)
Maasdam	20	91	(466)
Maasslot L	1	75	(8)
Maasstad L	1	268	(24)†
Maasstad L	1	75	(8)
Maasstroom L	1	75	(8)
Mabrouk	7	219	(172)
Macau Venture	17	31	(407)
Macedonia	11	167	(313)
Macedonia Hellas	5	196	(121)
Macfriendship	7	78	(162)
Maciej Rataj	5	305	(128)
Mackinac Bridge	12	103	(332)
Macle	2	410	(56)
Mactrader	5	231	(123)
Madame Butterfly	19	10	(445)
Maddalena D'Amato	2	148	(39)
Madonna Lily	5	202	(121)
Madzy	5	227	(123)
Maelifell	7	379	(184)
Maere	11	142	(311)
Maersk Anglia	18	15	(422)
Maersk Ascension	1	76	(8)
Maersk Asia Octavo	13	36	(351)
Maersk Australia	12	76	(330)
Maersk Canarias	7	313	(179)
Maersk Caracas	7	329	(180)
Maersk Constellation	17	73	(412)†
Maersk Constellation	17	9	(405)
Maersk Crest	19	58	(451)†
Maersk Euro Primo	13	89	(357)†
Maersk Euro Primo	13	24	(350)
Maersk Euro Quarto	13	24	(350)
Maersk Euro Quinto	13	24	(350)
Maersk Flanders	18	222	(441)†
Maersk Flanders	18	15	(422)
Maersk Gannet	1	11	(3)
Maersk Houston	12	146	(336)
Maersk la Paz	13	29	(351)
Maersk La Plata	7	518	(196)†
Maersk Miami	13	38	(352)
Maersk Nanhai	12	78	(330)
Maersk Nara	9	202	(279)†
Maersk Nara	9	21	(264)
Maersk Oceania	12	76	(330)
Maersk San Antonio	13	88	(356)†
Maersk Santiago	13	38	(352)
Maersk Santos	13	38	(352)
Maersk Sea	19	64	(452)†
Maersk Sembawang	7	198	(171)
Maersk Serangoon	7	198	(171)
Maersk Shetland	4	123	(95)

	SHIP TYPE	REF NO	PAGE NO
Maersk Sky	19	59	(451)†
Maersk Somerset	4	123	(95)
Maersk Stafford	4	123	(95)
Maersk Suffolk	4	123	(95)
Maersk Surrey	4	123	(95)
Maersk Sussex	4	123	(95)
Maersk Timonel	7	529	(198)†
Maersk Vancouver	12	146	(336)
Maersk Wind	19	42	(449)†
Maersk Yokohama	12	111	(333)
Magallanes	9	23	(264)
Magdalena	6	49	(145)
Magdalena	9	31	(265)
Magdalena	11	88	(307)
Magda P	8	354	(230)
Magellanic	11	152	(312)
Magellan Reefer	11	110	(309)
Magic	8	252	(223)
Magic	9	22	(264)
Magic K	9	57	(267)
Magister	8	500	(241)
Magnitogorsk	16	29	(393)
Magnolia	11	19	(302)
Magnus Challenger	7	15	(158)
Magnus E	5	70	(112)
Magnus Sincerity	9	122	(272)
Mago	6	19	(142)
Mago	8	174	(216)
Mago	8	415	(235)
Magway	7	444	(189)
Mahalene	8	214	(220)
Mahalim	8	214	(220)
Mahardi	8	214	(220)
Maharishi Dayanand	2	454	(59)
Maharishi Karve	2	454	(59)
Mahasen	8	311	(228)
Maher	8	525	(243)
Mahe Reefer	11	157	(312)
Maike	6	36	(144)
Maik Primo	8	312	(228)
Maine	7	318	(180)
Mainit	7	121	(165)
Main Ore	2	458	(59)
Maipo	13	94	(357)†
Maira	6	17	(142)
Mairangi Bay	12	134	(335)
Mairouli	8	24	(205)
Maisi	8	44	(206)
Majapahit	13	59	(353)
Maja Vestida	5	378	(136)†
Maja Vestida	5	52	(110)
Majestic	9	141	(273)
Majestic	11	132	(311)
Majestic	20	65	(464)
Majesty of the Seas	20	70	(464)
Majgard	6	2	(141)
Major Dhan Singh Thapa PVC	1	137	(12)
Major Hoshiar Singh PVC	1	137	(12)
Major Hubal	5	305	(128)
Majori	2	379	(54)
Major Shaitan Singh PVC	1	137	(12)
Major Somnath Sharma PVC	1	137	(12)
Major Sucharski	8	591	(248)
Maj Sif	7	461	(190)
Makar Mazay	5	188	(120)
Makatsaria	1	181	(15)
Makedon	16	38	(394)
Makedonia 1	18	60	(426)
Makedonia 2	18	61	(426)
Makeevka	7	242	(174)
Makhachkala	2	426	(57)
Makkia	9	9	(263)
Makran	7	371	(184)
Makron	8	24	(205)
Maksim Ammosov	7	340	(181)
Maksim Mikhaylov	12	68	(330)
Maksim Rylskiy	7	152	(167)
M Aksu	7	191	(170)
Malacca Bridge	12	171	(339)†
Malakand	9	166	(275)
Malaspina	20	147	(470)
Malbork II	5	189	(120)
Male II	7	60	(161)
Malene Sif	1	178	(14)
Malibu Reefer	11	97	(308)
Maligaya	17	20	(406)
Malik II	2	294	(48)
Malini	8	16	(204)
Malin Sea	10	19	(288)
Mallory Lykes	9	23	(264)
Malmnes	10	53	(291)
Malmo Link	16	41	(394)
Maltese Venture	6	55	(145)
Malyovitza	7	154	(168)
Mamiri	8	200	(218)
Mamry	7	265	(175)

†Photograph

	SHIP TYPE	REF NO	PAGE NO
Mana	8	262	(224)
Mana	9	121	(272)
Mana Eleni	8	302	(227)
Manaslu	7	538	(199)†
Manaslu	7	385	(185)
Manaslu	12	123	(334)
Man Cheng	8	308	(227)
Mandala	7	18	(158)
Mandalay	7	444	(189)
Mandarin	8	221	(220)
Mandarin Sea	8	146	(214)
Mandarin Star	8	392	(233)
Mandeb Bay	7	308	(179)
Mandeb Bay	7	332	(181)
Mangen	7	386	(185)
Mango	5	12	(108)
Mango Reefer	11	134	(311)
Man Gyong Bong	20	277	(479)
Man Hai	7	48	(160)
Manhattan	2	277	(47)
Manhattan Bridge	12	103	(332)
Manifest PKWN	5	247	(124)
Manilaid	16	26	(393)
Manila Progress	7	122	(165)
Manja	15	6	(377)
Manley Appledore	9	113	(271)
Manley Devon	8	573	(247)
Manley Exeter	8	573	(247)
Manley Falmouth	8	257	(223)
Manley Gosport	8	257	(223)
Manley Havant	7	162	(168)
Mannan	8	548	(245)
Manoa	12	148	(336)
Manora Bay	8	396	(234)
Mansoura 1	8	603	(249)
Mansurnave II	7	225	(173)
Manta Ray	8	217	(220)
Mantaro	17	89	(414)†
Mantaro	17	55	(409)
Mantis	8	500	(241)
Manuel Avila Comacho	2	422	(57)
Manuel Belgrano	4	109	(94)
Manuella	2	113	(37)
Manukai	12	86	(331)
Manulani	12	86	(331)
Manyas 1	7	70	(161)
Manzavik	7	188	(170)
Manzoni	20	323	(483)
Maple River	12	24	(326)
Mara	1	112	(10)
Marabu	8	270	(224)
Maraki	7	447	(189)
Maram	20	22	(460)
Maramures	5	173	(119)
Maratha Deep	7	276	(176)
Marathon	6	23	(142)
Marathon	8	447	(238)
Marat Kazey	8	621	(251)
Marbonita	7	539	(199)†
Mar Caribe	18	153	(433)
Mar Caspio	10	24	(289)
Mar Caterina	2	495	(62)
Marc Challenger	6	56	(145)
Marcel	5	66	(111)
Marcelle	3	8	(75)
Marchen Maersk	12	198	(342)†
Marc L	15	21	(379)
Marco Danielsen	8	224	(221)
Marcon	13	40	(352)
Mar Coral	9	46	(266)
Mar Courrier	8	500	(241)
Marc Spyros	18	123	(431)
Mare	7	164	(168)
Mare	8	500	(241)
Mare Adriatico	2	506	(62)
Mare Adriaticum	12	84	(331)
Mare Adriaticum	13	38	(352)
Mare Altum	2	76	(34)
Mare Argentum	2	46	(32)
Mare Asia	2	236	(45)
Mare Aurum	2	46	(32)
Mare Baltico	5	53	(110)
Mare Balticum	13	38	(352)
Mare Balticum	20	148	(470)
Mare Brazil	2	372	(53)
Mare Champion	1	67	(7)
Mare Discovery	1	67	(7)
Mare Equatoriale	1	64	(7)
Mare Hibernum	13	38	(352)
Mare Iratum	2	76	(34)
Marem	8	510	(242)
Mare Nostrum	8	453	(238)
Mare Queen	2	546	(66)†
Mare Queen	2	175	(41)
Mare Tirreno	5	19	(108)
Mare Vikingo	7	112	(164)
Marfrio	9	8	(263)
Margaret	7	266	(175)
Margareta	15	22	(379)
Margaretha	10	19	(288)
Margaretha	15	27	(379)
Margarita	11	19	(302)
Margaro R	7	29	(159)
Margherita	19	85	(454)†
Margita	2	162	(40)
Mar Grande	8	201	(218)
Maria	2	134	(38)
Maria	7	23	(158)
Maria	7	60	(161)
Maria	7	73	(162)
Maria	7	213	(172)
Maria A	8	466	(239)
Mariachris K	7	15	(158)
Maria Christina Giralt	3	12	(76)
Maria D	8	16	(204)
Maria D	15	7	(377)
Maria Diamanto	8	141	(214)
Maria Dolores	10	22	(288)
Maria G L	7	74	(162)
Maria Gorthon	18	203	(439)†
Maria H	15	21	(379)
Maria I	5	260	(125)
Maria J	17	2	(405)
Maria K	8	290	(226)
Maria K	8	445	(237)
Maria Laura	2	139	(38)
Marialena	8	310	(227)
Maria M	8	354	(230)
Marian Buczek	8	591	(248)
Marianic K	7	154	(168)
Mariann	5	65	(111)
Mariann	8	309	(227)
Marianna	7	222	(172)
Marianna VII	2	318	(50)
Marianne	6	103	(151)†
Marianne	6	28	(143)
Marianne Kosan	3	66	(82)†
Marianne Schulte	8	396	(234)
Mariano Escobedo	4	53	(90)
Mariano Moctezuma	2	422	(57)
Mariant	5	297	(128)
Maria P I	9	226	(282)†
Maria S	8	379	(232)
Maria SJ	7	261	(175)
Mariasperanza F	5	107	(114)
Maria Topic	7	115	(164)
Maria X	8	603	(249)
Maribel	1	249	(22)†
Maribor	8	321	(228)
Mari Claire	15	4	(377)
Mari Claire	15	13	(378)
Marico	19	62	(451)†
Marie	10	32	(289)
Marie H	8	559	(246)
Mariel	7	166	(168)
Mariella	20	66	(464)
Marietta C	2	448	(58)
Marif	7	207	(171)
Mari France	15	4	(377)
Mari France	15	13	(378)
Marigo	8	24	(205)
Marigola	2	63	(33)
Marigold	8	90	(210)
Marigoula K	7	270	(176)
Marijampole	8	619	(250)
Marijeannie	5	169	(119)
Marika	8	312	(228)
Marika	8	354	(230)
Marika Stravelakis	8	445	(237)
Marilia A	16	43	(395)†
Marilia A	16	38	(394)
Marilis T	7	145	(167)
Marily	7	57	(160)
Marimo	20	5	(459)
Marin	13	61	(353)
Marina	2	226	(44)
Marina	7	486	(192)
Marina	8	128	(213)
Marina	8	615	(250)
Marina	9	139	(273)
Marina Cathya	8	377	(232)
Marina Heeren	7	380	(184)
Marina I	8	201	(218)
Marinaki	5	174	(119)
Marina Lauri	8	377	(232)
Marina Pearl	5	268	(126)
Marina Raskova	11	82	(306)
Marina Star	7	488	(193)†
Marine Chemist	2	278	(47)
Marine Confidence	8	432	(236)
Marine Evangeline	18	224	(441)†
Marine Evangeline	18	88	(428)

	SHIP TYPE	REF NO	PAGE NO
Marine Express	8	661	(255)†
Marine Grace	7	232	(173)
Marine Hunter	5	309	(128)
Marineos	21	9	(499)
Mariner	8	313	(228)
Mariner	8	500	(241)
Mariner 1	7	218	(172)
Marine Ranger	5	53	(110)
Mariner C	5	145	(117)
Marine Reliance	19	18	(446)
Mariner II	8	616	(250)
Mariner LT	2	53	(32)
Marine Star	7	220	(172)
Marine World	7	203	(171)
Maringa	9	132	(273)
Marinier	15	65	(384)†
Marinor	1	46	(6)
Marios	7	20	(158)
Marios K	8	202	(219)
Mariposa	5	216	(122)
Mariscal Jose Felix Estigarribia	8	261	(224)
Maritime Bangkok	7	225	(173)
Maritime Care	7	271	(176)
Maritime Chiangmai	7	271	(176)
Maritime Diamond	7	199	(171)
Maritime Jade	7	199	(171)
Maritime Lapis	7	199	(171)
Maritime Nancy	5	369	(135)†
Maritime Pearl	7	199	(171)
Maritime Skill	7	199	(171)
Maritime Valour	7	271	(176)
Maritime Wisdom	5	377	(136)†
Maritza	2	508	(62)
Maritza Arlette	18	44	(424)
Mariupol	7	454	(190)
Marivan	10	19	(288)
Marivan	10	30	(289)
Mariya Savina	20	23	(461)
Mariya Yermolova	20	23	(461)
Marjan I	9	92	(270)
Marka L	7	7	(157)
Mark C	5	99	(114)
Markella	8	290	(226)
Marko Polo	20	44	(462)
Marlene S	13	7	(349)
Marlin	2	116	(37)
Marlin	7	50	(160)
Mar Lucia	2	565	(68)†
Marmara Princess	16	46	(395)†
Marmara Princess	16	22	(393)
Marmari I	20	99	(466)
Marmaris 1	8	623	(251)
Marmil	7	525	(197)†
Marmon	5	9	(107)
Marmorbulk	7	460	(190)
Marmorica	20	274	(479)
Marni	9	99	(270)
Maro	8	41	(206)
Maro L	7	211	(172)
Mar Patricia	2	495	(62)
Marquise	5	54	(111)
Marrakech	20	149	(470)
Marschenland	15	102	(388)†
Marschenland	15	29	(379)
Marshal Bagramyan	2	304	(49)
Marshal Budyonnyy	2	389	(54)
Marshal Chuykov	2	304	(49)
Marshal Govorov	2	533	(64)
Marshal Grechko	2	533	(64)
Marshal Konyev	2	389	(54)
Marshall	8	179	(216)
Marshal Rokossovskiy	2	389	(54)
Marshal Vasilyevskiy	2	304	(49)
Marshal Zakharov	2	533	(64)
Marshal Zhukov	2	389	(54)
Mar Sofia	2	495	(62)
Marstal Maersk	12	13	(326)
Martasatu	8	208	(219)
Martha II	5	155	(118)
Martha Russ	18	4	(421)
Martin	7	476	(191)
Martina Prima	4	130	(96)
Martin Posadillo	18	89	(428)
Martin Sif	2	36	(31)
Marulic	7	146	(167)
Marun	1	88	(8)
Marwan	8	169	(216)
Mary	8	83	(209)
Mary C	6	31	(143)
Mary D	1	16	(4)
Marygold	8	304	(227)
Mary L	7	50	(160)
Maryland	2	224	(44)
Maryli	5	148	(117)
Marylou II	5	297	(128)
Mary Stove	2	385	(54)

	SHIP TYPE	REF NO	PAGE NO
Mary Th	8	66	(208)
Maryut	9	162	(275)
Masagana	8	217	(220)
Mascarin	2	330	(50)
Mascot	10	41	(290)
Mashallah	7	371	(184)
Masovia	12	128	(334)
Mas Prosperity	8	343	(229)
Massa	2	423	(57)
Mass Enterprise	5	216	(122)
Mass Glory	5	216	(122)
Mass Merit	5	216	(122)
Mass Prosperity	5	216	(122)
Mass Success	5	216	(122)
Mass Wits	5	216	(122)
Massy Phoenix	7	213	(172)
Mastera	1	203	(16)
Master Nikos	9	33	(265)
Master Panos	7	104	(164)
Master Petros	8	83	(209)
Mastrogiorgis B	7	224	(173)
Matanuska	20	239	(476)
Mataram	8	556	(246)
Mate Zalka	2	424	(57)
Matheos	5	53	(110)
Mathias Thesen	11	99	(308)
Mathildaki	7	36	(159)
Mathilde	5	259	(125)
Mathios	7	63	(161)
Mathraki	2	12	(29)
Matrisha	6	66	(146)
Matru Kripa	7	213	(172)
Matsukaze	2	425	(57)
Matsumae Maru	20	198	(473)
Mattheos L	8	306	(227)
Mattz Altair	8	548	(245)
Mattz Deneb	8	303	(227)
Mattz Vega	8	273	(225)
Matumba	7	179	(169)
Matvey Muranov	9	57	(267)
Maui	12	86	(331)
Maullin	7	399	(186)
M A Ulusoy	11	145	(312)
Mauritius Endeavour	7	74	(162)
Mauro D'Alesio	2	573	(69)†
Maveric	11	186	(315)†
Mavi	5	55	(111)
Mawlamyine	8	679	(258)†
Mawlamyine	8	515	(242)
Maxhutte	5	104	(114)
Maxim	6	23	(142)
Maxim Gorkiy	20	240	(476)
Maximo Gomez	8	383	(232)
Maxita	21	12	(500)
Maxus Widuri	1	74	(7)
Max Victory	8	552	(245)
Maya	8	232	(221)
Maya	11	88	(307)
Mayaguez	12	131	(335)
Maya Reefer	11	165	(313)
Mayflower	8	16	(204)
Maykop	2	426	(57)
Maylin	8	224	(221)
Mayonami	2	461	(59)
Mayon Spirit	1	214	(17)
Mayor	9	94	(270)
Mayprince	9	143	(274)
Mayqueen	9	227	(283)†
Mayssaa I	8	240	(222)
May Star	7	271	(176)
Maystar	8	354	(230)
Mazal II	2	18	(30)
Mazina	8	542	(245)
Mazury	11	7	(301)
MB Clyde	6	49	(145)
MB Humber	6	49	(145)
MC Emerald	8	428	(236)
MC Pearl	7	446	(189)
Meacham	2	266	(46)
Mecca 1	20	193	(473)
Mecklenburg	12	115	(333)
Med Africa Link	7	146	(167)
Medallion	9	22	(264)
Med Barcelona	12	85	(331)
Med Carrara	7	75	(162)
Med Carrara	10	38	(289)
Medea	19	10	(445)
Med Genoa	7	180	(169)
Med Genova	12	137	(335)
Medglory	21	72	(505)†
Medglory	21	3	(499)
Med Hong Kong	12	137	(335)
Medi	5	139	(117)
Media II	20	214	(474)
Medias	8	1	(203)
Medininkai	8	365	(231)

†Photograph

	SHIP TYPE	REF NO	PAGE NO
Mediteran Frigo	11	193	(316)†
Mediterranean Sea	20	67	(464)
Mediterranean Sky	20	67	(464)
Med Keelung	12	137	(335)
Med Lerici	7	180	(169)
Med Nagoya	12	69	(330)
Med Pisa	7	483	(192)
Med Salvador	7	75	(162)
Med Singapore	12	85	(331)
Medsky	12	109	(333)
Medspirit	12	199	(342)†
Med Taipei	12	70	(330)
Med Transporter	8	567	(247)
Med Venice	7	180	(169)
Medwind	15	9	(377)
Meg	6	20	(142)
Mega Hill	5	51	(110)
Megah Jaya	8	446	(237)
Mega Point	2	479	(60)
Mega Sun	2	318	(50)
Meghna	8	445	(237)
Mehanikis Fjodorovs	16	35	(394)
Mehanikis Gerasimovs	16	56	(396)†
Mehanikis Gerasimovs	16	35	(394)
Mehedinti	7	174	(169)
Mei Gui Hai	7	29	(159)
Mei Jiang	8	500	(241)
Meiyo Maru	19	43	(449)†
Mekhaanik Krull	6	33	(143)
Mekhanik Bardetskiy	8	125	(212)
Mekhanik Brilin	7	319	(180)
Mekhanik Dren	7	262	(175)
Mekhanik Fomin	7	319	(180)
Mekhanik Garovnik	2	158	(40)
Mekhanik Gordiyenko	8	78	(209)
Mekhanik Ilchenko	2	158	(40)
Mekhanik Khmelevskiy	2	158	(40)
Mekhanik Konovalov	16	35	(394)
Mekhanik Kottsov	7	319	(180)
Mekhanik Kraskovskiy	7	319	(180)
Mekhanik Kurako	7	310	(179)
Mekhanik Makarin	7	319	(180)
Mekhanik P Kilimenchuk	5	172	(119)
Mekhanik P Kilimenchuk	7	164	(168)
Mekhanik Pustoshnyy	7	319	(180)
Mekhanik Pyatlin	7	319	(180)
Mekhanik Rybachuk	8	589	(248)
Mekhanik Semakov	7	319	(180)
Mekhanik Tyulenev	7	319	(180)
Mekhanik Vraskov	2	158	(40)
Mekhanik Yartsev	7	319	(180)
Mekhanik Yevgrafov	16	35	(394)
Mekhanik Yuryev	2	158	(40)
Mekong Fortune	7	464	(190)
Mekong Vitesse	7	461	(190)
Melaka Jaya III	7	312	(179)
Melbourne Highway	19	92	(455)†
Melbourne Star	13	48	(352)
Melbourne Trader	18	90	(428)
Melchor Ocampo	2	412	(56)
Melfi Canada	13	90	(357)†
Melgar	7	121	(165)
Melina II	9	58	(267)
Melis	2	31	(31)
Melissa	6	66	(146)
Melkki	1	167	(14)
Melodia	8	95	(210)
Meloi	7	50	(160)
Melor	2	127	(37)
Melrose	3	41	(79)†
Melrose	3	28	(77)
Melvin H Baker	5	7	(107)
Memed Abashidze	5	13	(108)
Memphis	9	6	(263)
Menado	2	554	(67)†
Menado	8	148	(214)
Meng Kiat	8	124	(212)
Meng Lee	8	515	(242)
Meng Yang	8	119	(212)
Menites	5	233	(123)
Mentor	8	445	(237)
Meonia	7	420	(187)
Merak	6	18	(142)
Meraklis	5	54	(111)
Meratus Prima	8	220	(220)
Merawi	9	17	(264)
Mercandian Arrow	18	166	(434)
Mercandian Globe	18	166	(434)
Mercandian Senator	16	24	(393)
Mercantil Araruama	7	225	(173)
Mercantil Niteroi	5	196	(121)
Mercator	6	46	(144)
Merchant Paramount	5	308	(128)
Merchant Patriot	8	118	(212)
Merchant Prelude	5	217	(122)
Merchant Premier	8	572	(247)

	SHIP TYPE	REF NO	PAGE NO
Merchant Prestige	5	308	(128)
Merchant Pride	5	375	(136)†
Merchant Pride	5	18	(108)
Merchant Principal	8	572	(247)
Merchant Valiant	18	134	(431)
Merchant Victor	18	134	(431)
Mercs Hendala	8	297	(226)
Mercs Komari	8	600	(249)
Mercs Kumana	8	600	(249)
Mercs Uhana	8	107	(211)
Mercs Wadduwa	8	626	(251)
Mercuri 1	20	287	(480)
Mercuri 2	20	287	(480)
Mercury	8	352	(230)
Mercury Ace	19	54	(450)†
Merete Wonsild	2	62	(33)
Mergui	8	381	(232)
Meric	8	629	(251)
Merida	9	89	(269)
Meridian	20	410	(490)†
Meridian	8	213	(220)
Meridian	20	68	(464)
Meridian Spica	5	39	(110)
Meridian Venus	8	276	(225)
Meriom Star	2	447	(58)
Merit	12	83	(331)
Merity	2	78	(34)
Merkine	8	365	(231)
Merkur	5	113	(115)
Merkur	7	206	(171)
Merkur Bay	12	62	(329)
Merkur Island	13	39	(352)
Merlin	7	18	(158)
Mermoz	20	436	(494)†
Merngue Express	18	147	(432)
Merrytrans	8	500	(241)
Mersin	2	267	(46)
Mersin	12	92	(332)
Merubi	9	41	(266)
Merwegas	4	166	(101)†
Meryem Ana	7	224	(173)
Meshedi Ezizbeyov	2	504	(62)
Mesta	2	206	(43)
Mete	15	25	(379)
Methane Arctic	4	46	(90)
Methane Polar	4	46	(90)
Methane Princess	4	38	(89)
Methania	4	175	(102)†
Methania	4	4	(87)
Metin Kalkavan	7	50	(160)
Metonic	11	152	(312)
Metrotank	2	197	(42)
Mets	5	84	(113)
Mette Kosan	4	161	(100)†
Metz Beirut	9	141	(273)
Metz Belgica	9	141	(273)
Mexicana	8	352	(230)
Mezhdurechensk	8	604	(249)
Mezhgorye	8	604	(249)
M G Tsangaris	5	236	(123)
Miami Express	5	256	(125)
Mian Zhu Hai	5	231	(123)
Miao Feng Shan	8	358	(230)
Micaela	17	40	(408)
Michael R	9	143	(274)
Michalakis	8	83	(209)
Michelle	9	22	(264)
Mico	7	425	(188)
Midas	7	210	(172)
Midelt	11	73	(306)
Miden Agan	12	61	(329)
Mielec	5	189	(120)
Mie Mols	18	21	(422)
Mighty Servant 1	21	48	(503)
Mighty Servant 2	21	48	(503)
Mighty Servant 3	21	87	(507)†
Mighty Servant 3	21	48	(503)
Mihails Lomonosovs	11	127	(310)
Mihalis P	5	202	(121)
Mika	6	41	(144)
Mikasa	5	368	(135)†
Mike	15	8	(377)
Mike K	8	96	(210)
Mikhail Cheremnykh	8	365	(231)
Mikhail Isakovskiy	7	152	(167)
Mikhail Kutuzov	5	131	(116)
Mikhail Lukonin	7	152	(167)
Mikhail Olminskiy	9	57	(267)
Mikhail Panfilov	7	435	(188)
Mikhail Prishvin	12	126	(334)
Mikhail Sholokhov	20	128	(468)
Mikhail Somov	8	168	(216)
Mikhail Stelmakh	7	81	(162)
Mikhail Stenko	8	49	(207)
Mikhail Strekalovskiy	7	273	(176)
Mikhail Svetlov	12	126	(334)

†Photograph

	SHIP TYPE	REF NO	PAGE NO
Mikhail Vladimirsky	9	57	(267)
Mikola Bazhan	5	17	(108)
Mikolaj Kopernik	20	284	(480)
Mikolaj Rej	8	566	(246)
Milagro	7	179	(169)
Milamores	5	216	(122)
Mildburg	13	3	(349)
Mild Ocean	12	108	(333)
Mild Sun	12	55	(329)
Mild Union	12	55	(329)
Mild Victory	5	90	(113)
Milena	20	333	(483)
Milenaki	8	452	(238)
Milin Kamak	5	132	(116)
Milos Express	20	150	(470)
Milos L	9	141	(273)
Mimer	18	98	(429)
Mimina Dormio	10	49	(290)
Mimitsu Maru	20	305	(481)
Mimosa	2	339	(51)
Mina	10	97	(296)†
Mina	8	201	(218)
Minab 2	1	88	(8)
Minab 3	1	88	(8)
Minab 4	1	88	(8)
Mina Cebi	7	172	(169)
Minamar	8	635	(252)
Mina-S	7	154	(168)
Minas Del Frio	11	34	(303)
Min Da	8	594	(248)
Mindelo	8	311	(228)
Mindful	15	25	(379)
Mineral Europe	5	225	(122)
Mineral Nippon	5	350	(133)†
Mineral Zulu	5	225	(122)
Minerva	20	454	(496)†
Minerva	5	297	(128)
Minerva	10	29	(289)
Mineva	6	57	(145)
Min Fu	8	546	(245)
Ming America	12	205	(343)†
Mingary	5	260	(125)
Ming Cheng	13	17	(350)
Ming Comfort	12	137	(335)
Ming Courage	5	292	(127)
Ming Fortune	12	137	(335)
Ming Galaxy	12	137	(335)
Ming Glory	12	137	(335)
Ming Hai	7	76	(162)
Ming Long	8	328	(228)
Ming Mercy	5	292	(127)
Ming Moon	12	137	(335)
Mingo	5	12	(108)
Ming Ocean	12	137	(335)
Ming Peace	12	70	(330)
Ming Pleasure	12	70	(330)
Ming Plenty	12	70	(330)
Ming Progress	12	70	(330)
Ming Prominence	12	70	(330)
Ming Promotion	12	70	(330)
Ming Propitious	12	70	(330)
Ming Star	12	137	(335)
Ming Sun	12	137	(335)
Ming Wisdom	5	292	(127)
Ming Zhou 8	8	527	(243)
Min He	12	30	(327)
Miniforest	6	74	(148)†
Miniforest	6	41	(144)
Mini Moon	8	674	(257)†
Mini Moon	8	197	(218)
Mini Star	18	4	(421)
Ministro Ezcurra	1	19	(4)
Min Jiang	8	500	(241)
Min Jiang	8	560	(246)
Minka C	6	60	(146)
Min Mao	7	378	(184)
Min Nan	20	272	(479)
Minoan Fame	7	300	(178)
Minos	5	54	(111)
Min Ran Gong No 7	2	12	(29)
Min Tai 88	7	27	(159)
Mint Prosperity	2	397	(55)
Minusinsk	2	380	(54)
Mira	7	400	(186)
Mirabella	21	3	(499)
Mirah	9	77	(268)
Miramar	11	129	(310)
Mira Nor	6	38	(144)
Mira Star	2	201	(42)
Mircesti	7	174	(169)
Mirnyy	8	619	(250)
Miro	2	85	(35)
Miroslawiec	5	302	(128)
Misamis Occidental	20	36	(461)
Misiones II	7	15	(158)
Mission Capistrano	2	487	(61)

	SHIP TYPE	REF NO	PAGE NO
Miss Marietta	8	83	(209)
Mister Michael	5	54	(111)
Mistral	18	30	(423)
Mistral II	20	306	(481)
Mitchell Express	8	313	(228)
Mitera Vassiliki	7	146	(167)
Mithat Vardal	1	189	(15)
Mitla	7	417	(187)
Mitrans Express	8	241	(222)
Mitro	9	43	(266)
Mitrofan Sedin	2	469	(60)
Mi Yun Hai	7	113	(164)
Mizil	7	174	(169)
Mlawa	10	11	(287)
Mljet	7	261	(175)
M Melody	8	80	(209)
MN Toucan	17	121	(418)†
Moana III	17	59	(410)
Moana Pacific	7	404	(186)
Moby Baby	20	215	(474)
Moby Blu	20	151	(470)
Moby Fantasy	20	69	(464)
Moby Vincent	20	84	(465)
Modern Supplier	2	293	(48)
Moez 2	8	313	(228)
Moges Agathis	8	217	(220)
Mohac	8	225	(221)
Mohamed S	8	92	(210)
Mohni	8	582	(248)
Moinesti	7	174	(169)
Mokran	1	88	(8)
Molat	7	253	(175)
Molengat	20	216	(474)
Molodogvardeysk	8	604	(249)
Mona	14	15	(366)
Monarch of the Seas	20	70	(464)
Monarch Queen	18	12	(422)
Mona S	7	132	(166)
Mona's Queen	20	199	(473)
Monchegorsk	17	65	(411)†
Monchegorsk	17	27	(407)
Monemvasia	2	385	(54)
Monika	7	308	(179)
Monolima	7	60	(161)
Montana	2	327	(50)
Montania	15	51	(382)†
Montauk	5	137	(116)
Mont Blanc Maru	12	184	(340)†
Mont Blanc Maru	12	116	(333)
Monte Asha	9	27	(265)
Monte Berico	2	331	(50)
Monteblanco	8	298	(226)
Monte Chiaro	2	427	(57)
Monte Pascoal	9	134	(273)
Monterey	2	144	(39)
Monte Rosa	13	113	(360)†
Monte Rosa	13	65	(353)
Monterrey	4	37	(89)
Montgomery	7	85	(162)
Montlhery	18	7	(421)
Montone	8	253	(223)
Montrose	2	153	(39)
Moon Bird	8	366	(231)
Moon Cycle	5	255	(124)
Moonlight	7	392	(185)
Moonlight 1	9	118	(272)
Moon Trader	2	97	(35)
Moon Trader	2	191	(42)
Mopa Wonsild	2	62	(33)
Moraybank	9	149	(274)
Mor Canada	12	68	(330)
Moreton Bay	12	80	(331)
Mor Europe	12	68	(330)
Morgenstond I	15	20	(378)
Morias	7	61	(161)
Morillo	11	8	(301)
Mormacdawn	8	93	(210)
Mormacglen	8	462	(239)
Mormacmoon	8	93	(210)
Mormacsun	2	558	(67)†
Mormacwave	8	22	(204)
Mornes	10	53	(291)
Morning Cloud	5	292	(127)
Morning Glory II	1	214	(17)
Morning Light	19	93	(455)†
Morning Light	19	13	(446)
Morning Prince	19	88	(455)†
Morning Queen	19	5	(445)
Mor UK	12	68	(330)
Mosa	15	21	(379)
Moscenice	9	110	(271)
Moscliff	2	507	(62)
Mosdeep	7	88	(163)
Moskovskiy Festival	1	20	(4)
Moskovskiy Komsomolets	9	6	(263)
Moslavina	8	426	(236)

†Photograph

	SHIP TYPE	REF NO	PAGE NO
Mostefa Ben Boulaid	4	3	(87)
Mostoles	2	480	(60)
Mostraum	1	164	(13)
Motovskiy Zaliv	11	98	(308)
Motovskiy Zaliv	11	101	(308)
Motovun	9	110	(271)
Motru	5	132	(116)
Moug Al Bahr	1	64	(7)
Mount	8	595	(249)
Mount Athos	2	195	(42)
Mount Olympus	5	158	(118)
Mount Parnitha	5	158	(118)
Mount Penteli	5	158	(118)
Mount Penteli	5	283	(127)
Mount Vernon	2	223	(44)
Mount Washington	2	223	(44)
Mount Ymitos	5	158	(118)
Moustafa S	9	9	(263)
Mowlavi	9	19	(264)
Moxnes	10	53	(291)
MSC Adele	13	5	(349)
MSC Alexa	12	36	(327)
MSC Alexandra	12	149	(336)
MSC Anastasia	12	145	(336)
MSC Angela	9	73	(268)
MSC Aniello	8	474	(239)
MSC Ariane	9	83	(269)
MSC Augusta	13	5	(349)
MSC Aurora	12	36	(327)
MSC Brianna	12	51	(328)
MSC Carla	7	404	(186)
MSC Carla	12	98	(332)
MSC Carmen	13	70	(354)
MSC Chiara	12	94	(332)
MSC Claudia	12	99	(332)
MSC Clorinda	12	137	(335)
MSC Daniela	12	94	(332)
MSC Deila	13	70	(354)
MSC Diego	13	45	(352)
MSC Dominique	12	117	(333)
MSC Emilia 5	9	83	(269)
MSC Federica	12	94	(332)
MSC Floriana	13	5	(349)
MSC Francesca	9	83	(269)
MSC Gina	12	195	(342)†
MSC Gina	13	68	(354)
MSC Giovanna	12	51	(328)
MSC Giulia	12	145	(336)
MSC Ilaria M	8	549	(245)
MSC Insa	12	105	(332)
MSC Jade	12	94	(332)
MSC Laura	7	450	(189)
MSC Lauren	12	137	(335)
MSC Lucy	8	160	(215)
MSC Luisa	12	94	(332)
MSC Maeva	12	117	(333)
MSC Maria Laura	12	169	(338)†
MSC Maria Laura	12	94	(332)
MSC Marina	8	557	(246)
MSC Maureen	7	10	(157)
MSC Mee May	12	145	(336)
MSC Michele	13	85	(356)†
MSC Michele	13	47	(352)
MSC Mirella	13	48	(352)
MSC Nicole	8	118	(212)
MSC Rafaela	13	68	(354)
MSC Rebecca	12	71	(330)
MSC Regina	13	104	(358)†
MSC Regina	13	45	(352)
MSC Rita	12	183	(340)†
MSC Rita	12	143	(336)
MSC Rosa M	13	103	(358)†
MSC Rosa M	13	70	(354)
MSC Rosemary	12	149	(336)
MSC Sabrina	12	94	(332)
MSC Samia	12	143	(336)
MSC Sandra 5	7	422	(187)
MSC Shaula S	8	548	(245)
MSC Targa	7	372	(184)
MSC Valeria	9	83	(269)
MSC Viviana	12	94	(332)
Mt Cabrite	2	475	(60)
Mubaraz	3	57	(81)†
Mubaraz	3	18	(76)
Mudi	11	147	(312)
Mugan	7	340	(181)
Mugla	8	623	(251)
Muhieddine I	8	202	(219)
Muhieddine V	8	511	(242)
Muhieddine VI	8	478	(240)
Muhlenberg	15	27	(379)
Muhu	7	11	(157)
Mukachevo	8	604	(249)
Mukda Naree	7	271	(176)
Mukhtar Auezov	7	152	(167)
Mulafoss	7	308	(179)
Multan	9	166	(275)
Multibulk Express	7	300	(178)
Multidiamond	9	92	(270)
Multi Service 125	21	66	(504)
Multistar	8	24	(205)
Multitank Adria	2	472	(60)
Multitank Arcadia	2	472	(60)
Multitank Armenia	2	472	(60)
Multitank Ascania	2	472	(60)
Multitank Frisia	2	33	(31)
Mundial Car	18	231	(442)†
Mundogas America	4	73	(92)
Mundogas Atlantic	4	54	(91)
Mundogas Energy	4	57	(91)
Mundogas Europe	4	54	(91)
Mundogas Orinoco	4	43	(90)
Mundogas Pioneer	3	40	(79)†
Mundogas Pioneer	3	26	(77)
Munkebo Maersk	12	13	(326)
Munksund	10	39	(290)
Mun Su Bong	8	24	(205)
Muostakh	7	269	(176)
Murachi	2	520	(63)
Murano	2	324	(50)
Murgash	7	278	(176)
Murman	8	575	(247)
Murray Express	21	121	(511)†
Murray Express	21	42	(502)
Musa Dzhalil	8	630	(251)
Musala	5	239	(123)
Musashi Spirit	1	106	(10)
Muscel	5	248	(124)
Mustansir	6	52	(145)
Muzaffar Aziz	8	537	(244)
Mykinai	8	430	(236)
Myo Hang 3	8	632	(251)
Myohyang 2	7	60	(161)
Myohyang 3	8	277	(225)
Myohyang 5	7	415	(187)
Myoma Ywa	9	115	(271)
Myrmo	6	127	(154)†
Myrtia	11	19	(302)
Myrtos Bay	2	262	(46)
Mys Kodosh	2	380	(54)
Myson	7	154	(168)
Mys Pavlovskiy	2	380	(54)
Mys Sarych	2	380	(54)
Mystic	11	132	(311)
Mytishchi	8	604	(249)
Nabil M	8	232	(221)
Nacional Rio	9	134	(273)
Nacional Santos	9	134	(273)
Nacional Vitoria	9	89	(269)
Nada	8	581	(248)
Nada II	19	67	(452)†
Nadeen	7	47	(160)
Nade Ribakovayte	8	239	(222)
Nadezhda Krupskaya	9	139	(273)
Nadine	8	144	(214)
Nadine	15	25	(379)
Nador	8	169	(216)
Nadym	2	26	(30)
Naeco	2	266	(46)
Nafis	8	181	(217)
Naftalan	2	171	(41)
Nafti	2	53	(32)
Nagatino	1	138	(12)
Nagayevo	1	52	(6)
Naias Express	20	302	(481)
Naik Jadunath Singh PVC	1	137	(12)
Naissaar	7	11	(157)
Najib	8	621	(251)
Nakhchyvan	20	287	(480)
Nakhodka	2	514	(63)
Nalon	2	483	(61)
Namsam Spirit	1	135	(11)
Nam San	8	54	(207)
Nancy G	2	496	(62)
Nand Kishore	2	579	(70)†
Nand Nakul	7	29	(159)
Nand Neeti	7	202	(171)
Nando	2	75	(34)
Nand Prakriti	2	431	(57)
Nand Rati	7	536	(199)†
Nand Shivchand	1	237	(20)†
Nand Shweta	7	213	(172)
Nand Srishti	7	106	(164)
Nand Swasti	7	213	(172)
Nandu Arrow	10	43	(290)
Nan Du Jiang	8	338	(229)
Nan Fung	7	179	(169)
Nanga Parbat	4	104	(94)
Nan Guan Ling	8	211	(219)
Nan Hai Ming Zhu	20	152	(470)

†Photograph

	SHIP TYPE	REF NO	PAGE NO
Nani	7	170	(169)
Nan Jiang	8	500	(241)
Nan Jing	8	488	(240)
Nan Ji Zhou	10	94	(296)†
Nan Kou	18	175	(435)
Nan Ping Shan	7	272	(176)
Nan Xi Jiang	7	415	(187)
Nan Yang No 18	5	256	(125)
Nan Yang No 8	2	568	(68)†
Napetco I	2	121	(37)
Napoleon	20	367	(486)
Naraval	18	89	(428)
Nariman Narimanov	2	171	(41)
Narova	1	154	(13)
Narrator	8	252	(223)
Narva	16	13	(392)
Narvos Ilanka	11	18	(302)
Narwick II	5	302	(128)
Narymneft	2	367	(53)
Nasaud	9	6	(263)
Nasos S	8	42	(206)
Natacha C	10	64	(292)†
Natacha C	10	13	(288)
Natali	8	464	(239)
Natalie	9	56	(267)
Natalie Green	7	310	(179)
Nathalie Delmas	7	194	(170)
Nathalie Green	7	310	(179)
Nathalie Sif	1	178	(14)
National Reefer	11	158	(312)
Nauru	11	199	(317)†
Nausica	8	453	(238)
Nausicaa	1	127	(11)
Nauticas Mexico	9	203	(280)†
Nauticas Mexico	9	161	(275)
Nautila	6	2	(141)
Nautilus	14	76	(373)†
Nautique	13	10	(349)
Nava Avra	7	243	(174)
Navalis	5	69	(112)
Naval Lady	8	383	(232)
Nava Maria	7	243	(174)
Navarin	8	168	(216)
Navarino	5	53	(110)
Navarino	8	24	(205)
Navicon	12	202	(342)†
Navigator	15	42	(380)
Navigator D	8	521	(243)
Navigia	6	2	(141)
Navios Bulker	5	296	(127)
Navios Mariner	5	216	(122)
Navipor	12	224	(345)†
Navira Express	8	500	(241)
Navix Adventure	1	218	(18)†
Navix Azalea	1	217	(18)†
Navix Seibu	1	24	(4)
Nawaf	17	19	(406)
Nawal	6	69	(146)
Naxos	1	207	(16)
Naxos	8	24	(205)
Naz K	8	69	(208)
Nazlican	8	213	(220)
Nazli Deniz	8	418	(235)
Nazli K	7	60	(161)
NCC Arar	1	35	(5)
NCC Asir	1	35	(5)
NCC Jizan	2	211	(43)
NCC Jouf	2	211	(43)
NCC Madinah	2	211	(43)
NCC Najran	2	211	(43)
NCC Tihamah	2	211	(43)
NCC Yamamah	2	211	(43)
Ndoni River	8	388	(233)
N Dumbadze	1	20	(4)
Nea Doxa	7	86	(163)
Neamma	11	87	(307)
Nearchos	8	24	(205)
Necat A	7	483	(192)
Necati Atasoy	8	642	(253)†
Neches	2	268	(46)
Neckar Ore	2	457	(59)
Nedal	8	232	(221)
Nedi	7	222	(172)
Nedlloyd Abidjan	7	108	(164)
Nedlloyd Africa	12	95	(332)
Nedlloyd America	12	95	(332)
Nedlloyd Antilles	7	304	(178)
Nedlloyd Asia	12	172	(339)†
Nedlloyd Asia	12	95	(332)
Nedlloyd Caldera	13	38	(352)
Nedlloyd California	7	401	(186)
Nedlloyd Catarina	13	36	(351)
Nedlloyd Cristobal	7	286	(177)
Nedlloyd Curacao	13	38	(352)
Nedlloyd Dejima	12	40	(328)
Nedlloyd Delft	12	40	(328)
Nedlloyd Europa	12	95	(332)
Nedlloyd Everest	7	286	(177)
Nedlloyd Hongkong	12	95	(332)
Nedlloyd Honshu	12	95	(332)
Nedlloyd Hoorn	12	37	(327)
Nedlloyd Houtman	12	37	(327)
Nedlloyd Inca	13	81	(356)†
Nedlloyd Inca	8	160	(215)
Nedlloyd Korrigan	12	167	(338)†
Nedlloyd Korrigan	12	156	(336)
Nedlloyd Maas	7	485	(192)
Nedlloyd Main	7	485	(192)
Nedlloyd Merwe	7	485	(192)
Nedlloyd Neerlandia	12	118	(334)
Nedlloyd Normandie	12	212	(344)†
Nedlloyd Oceania	12	95	(332)
Nedlloyd Pernambuco	13	2	(349)
Nedlloyd Recife	13	33	(351)
Nedlloyd Recife	13	38	(352)
Nedlloyd Rio	13	33	(351)
Nedlloyd River Plate	13	33	(351)
Nedlloyd Rotterdam	16	88	(400)†
Nedlloyd Santos	7	9	(157)
Nedlloyd Singapore	13	10	(349)
Nedlloyd Van Diemen	13	14	(350)
Nedlloyd Van Neck	13	57	(353)
Nedlloyd Van Noort	13	14	(350)
Nedlloyd Zaandam	12	102	(332)
Nedlloyd Zeelandia	13	101	(358)†
Nedlloyd Zeelandia	13	63	(353)
Nedroma	7	98	(163)
Neermoor	15	91	(387)†
Nefertiti	9	6	(263)
Neftegorsk	2	414	(56)
Neftekamsk	2	414	(56)
Nefterudovoz	15	37	(380)
Nefterudovoz 58M	15	37	(380)
Nefterudovoz 8M	15	37	(380)
Nego Breeze	7	271	(176)
Nego Kim	7	207	(171)
Nego Nomis	7	207	(171)
Negotiator	9	36	(265)
Nego Wes	7	155	(168)
Nei Jiang	8	26	(205)
Neil B	15	21	(379)
Nejma	4	151	(99)†
Nejmat El Petrol XXIII	2	272	(46)
Nejmat El Petrol XXV	2	527	(64)
Nela Altomare	8	544	(245)
Nelie	8	113	(211)
Nelson	8	445	(237)
Nelvana	10	95	(296)†
Nememcha	7	98	(163)
Nenufar Uno	5	91	(113)
Neo Hibiscus	7	229	(173)
Neo Pelargonium	7	122	(165)
Nephele	5	57	(111)
Neptun	20	348	(485)
'Neptun 421' type	8	405	(234)
Neptunas	11	83	(307)
Neptune	20	153	(470)
Neptune Amber	12	137	(335)
Neptune Aries	1	65	(7)
Neptune Beryl	13	19	(350)
Neptune Coral	12	137	(335)
Neptune Crux	1	118	(10)
Neptune Crystal	12	137	(335)
Neptune Diamond	12	137	(335)
Neptune Dorado	2	531	(64)
Neptune Garnet	12	185	(340)†
Neptune Iris	8	24	(205)
Neptune Jacinth	7	271	(176)
Neptune Jasper	13	107	(359)†
Neptune Jasper	13	19	(350)
Neptune Libra	1	118	(10)
Neptune Olympic	16	24	(393)
Neptune Pearl	12	137	(335)
Neptune Rhodonite	12	20	(326)
Neptune Schedar	7	124	(165)
Neptune Sky	18	130	(431)
Neptune Sun	17	58	(410)
Neptune Wind	8	543	(245)
Neptunia	20	182	(472)
Nera II	8	301	(227)
Nerd 1	12	7	(325)
Nereis P	8	445	(237)
Nereo	1	157	(13)
Nereus	7	324	(180)
Nereus	8	181	(217)
Nereus	8	531	(244)
Neringa	8	619	(250)
Nescio	15	86	(386)†
Nessie	5	324	(130)†
Nessie	5	156	(118)
Nestor	8	445	(237)
Neva	15	47	(381)

†Photograph

	SHIP TYPE	REF NO	PAGE NO
New Acacia	20	343	(484)
New Ace	2	528	(64)
New Akashia	20	343	(484)
New Amity	5	38	(109)
New Argosy	2	528	(64)
Newark Bay	12	187	(341)†
Neways	5	157	(118)
Newbury	4	128	(96)
New Crystal	7	209	(171)
New Empress	2	69	(33)
New Flora	8	453	(238)
New Fortune	8	259	(223)
New Fortuner	1	127	(11)
New Grove	8	220	(220)
New Growth	8	149	(214)
New Haihung	12	180	(340)†
New Haiteng	8	304	(227)
New Hamanasu	20	344	(484)
New Horizon	5	292	(127)
New Ideal	2	218	(43)
New Iris	8	298	(226)
New Jade	7	209	(171)
New Leading	8	33	(206)
New Light	18	83	(427)
New Louisiana	2	307	(49)
New Luck	5	348	(133)†
Newmarket	4	128	(96)
New Noble	7	210	(172)
New Providence	4	21	(88)
New Renown	2	316	(49)
New Road	8	590	(248)
New Shirayuri	20	344	(484)
New Vitality	1	106	(10)
New Wind	2	506	(62)
New York Sun	2	580	(70)†
New Zealand Pacific	12	134	(335)
New Zealand Reefer	11	74	(306)
New Zealand Star	12	74	(330)
Nezabudka	8	607	(250)
Ngowe	8	149	(214)
Niaga Energi 1	2	541	(65)†
Niaga XX	9	67	(268)
Niaga XXIV	8	194	(218)
Niaga XXXII	9	177	(276)†
Niaga XXXII	9	78	(269)
Niaxo V	7	238	(174)
Nicco	6	39	(144)
Nichigoh Maru	12	112	(333)
Nichiyo	1	95	(9)
Nicholas M.	2	297	(48)
Nicola D	8	397	(234)
Nicolaos H	8	195	(218)
Nicolas I K	7	15	(158)
Nicolas S	8	143	(214)
Nicole	7	446	(189)
Nicole Green	7	310	(179)
Nicolo Elisa	7	28	(159)
Nicoresti	7	174	(169)
Nicosia	12	157	(337)
Nida	8	239	(222)
Nidia	2	150	(39)
Nieborow	20	43	(462)
Niederelbe	15	27	(379)
Nigar Refibeyli	2	171	(41)
Niizuru	5	293	(127)
Nika	8	500	(241)
Nikaia	7	96	(163)
Nika II	8	500	(241)
Nike	2	410	(56)
Nikel	17	27	(407)
Niki	2	556	(67)†
Niki	2	324	(50)
Niki	2	336	(51)
Niki Agustina	17	45	(409)
Nikifor Rogov	1	70	(7)
Nikita Mitchenko	9	92	(270)
Nikkei Eagle	7	199	(171)
Nikko Maru	7	11	(157)
Nikko No 53	14	28	(367)
Niko K	5	313	(129)
Nikolajs Koperniks	11	127	(310)
Nikolajs Zicars	11	172	(313)
Nikolas	16	26	(393)
Nikola Vaptzarov	20	348	(485)
Nikolay Ananyev	9	92	(270)
Nikolay Bauman	8	582	(248)
Nikolay Cherkasov	16	14	(392)
Nikolay Chernyshevskiy	18	20	(422)
Nikolay Dobrolyubov	8	630	(251)
Nikolay Dolinskiy	7	152	(167)
Nikolay Emelyanov	7	324	(180)
Nikolayevsk	20	14	(460)
Nikolay Gogol	8	630	(251)
Nikolay Karamzim	8	630	(251)
Nikolay Kremlyanskiy	8	74	(209)
Nikolay Krylenko	9	56	(267)

	SHIP TYPE	REF NO	PAGE NO
Nikolay Kuznetsov	5	17	(108)
Nikolay Maksimov	9	92	(270)
Nikolay Morozov	8	49	(207)
Nikolay Nekrasov	8	604	(249)
Nikolay Novikov	8	78	(209)
Nikolay Ogarev	8	630	(251)
Nikolay Pogodin	9	56	(267)
Nikolay Przhevalskiy	16	13	(392)
Nikolay Savitskiy	15	23	(379)
Nikolay Semashko	9	57	(267)
Nikolay Shchetinin	7	269	(176)
Nikolay Shchors	11	170	(313)
Nikolay Shchukin	8	49	(207)
Nikolay Tulpin	9	56	(267)
Nikolay Zabolotskiy	7	340	(181)
Nikolay Zhukhov	8	49	(207)
Nikolis Pallis	8	313	(228)
Nikolskoye	15	47	(381)
Nikopol	2	367	(53)
Nikos II	21	24	(501)
Nikos N	7	201	(171)
Nile	1	84	(8)
Nils R	7	473	(191)
Nimet Pisak	7	210	(172)
Nimfa II	6	35	(143)
Nin	8	445	(237)
Nina	8	619	(250)
Nina Bres	6	100	(151)†
Nina Bres	6	2	(141)
Nina Kukoverova	8	621	(251)
Nina S	7	36	(159)
Nindawayma	20	273	(479)
Ning Hua 404	2	44	(32)
Nioba	7	469	(191)
Niobe 1	18	62	(426)
Nippon Reefer	11	74	(306)
Niquel	6	40	(144)
Nira Naree	7	271	(176)
Nireus	8	316	(228)
Nirja	8	562	(246)
Nirvana	7	51	(160)
Nisi	2	402	(55)
Nissei Maru	2	264	(46)
Nissos Amorgos	2	574	(69)†
Nissos Amorgos	2	528	(64)
Nissos Chios	20	307	(481)
Nissos Hydra	11	80	(306)
Nissos Kriti	11	60	(305)
Nissos Kythnos	2	397	(55)
Nissos Thera	2	586	(71)†
Nisyros	1	154	(13)
Niva	2	367	(53)
Nivaria	2	29	(30)
Nizami	7	340	(181)
Nizhnevartovsk	2	26	(30)
Nizhneyansk	17	27	(407)
Noa	8	85	(210)
Noah VI	2	11	(29)
Noble	13	38	(352)
Noble Ace	19	1	(445)
Noble Empress	7	271	(176)
Noble Fortune	5	145	(117)
Noble River	12	54	(329)
Noble Star	9	181	(277)†
Noble Star	8	24	(205)
Noble Star	9	91	(270)
Noga	2	318	(50)
NOL Amazonite	12	217	(344)†
Nolizwe	12	38	(327)
Nomadic Dixie	7	81	(162)
Nomadic Lady	7	103	(164)
Nomadic Patria	7	423	(187)
Nomadic Pollux	7	423	(187)
Nomadic Princess	7	106	(164)
Nomzi	13	31	(351)
Nong Goong Shang No 8	8	500	(241)
Noor	11	191	(316)†
Noor	9	168	(275)
Noor	11	21	(302)
Noorderling	15	6	(377)
Nooreen	2	222	(44)
Nora	5	37	(109)
Nora	6	31	(143)
Nora Heeren	6	4	(141)
Norasia Fribourg	12	39	(327)
Norasia Hong Kong	12	39	(327)
Norasia Kiel	12	39	(327)
Norasia Sharjah	12	39	(327)
Norbank	18	131	(431)
Norbay	18	131	(431)
Norbel Bulk	7	224	(173)
Norbel Oman	9	169	(275)
Norbulk Namir	8	24	(205)
Norbulk Seraya	8	669	(256)†
Norcape	10	14	(288)
Norcape	18	127	(431)

	SHIP TYPE	REF NO	PAGE NO
Norcove	18	124	(431)
Nordanhav	10	101	(297)†
Nordbay	12	130	(334)
Nordbulk	6	41	(144)
Nordcloud	13	11	(350)
Norden	5	227	(123)
Nordfarer	1	99	(9)
Nordfast	1	99	(9)
Nordfeld	6	2	(141)
Nordfrakt	6	41	(144)
Nord Gotlandia	20	71	(464)
Nordheim	8	399	(234)
Nordholm	8	399	(234)
Nordia	5	358	(134)†
Nordica	6	122	(154)†
Nordica	17	37	(408)
Nordic Bulker	7	212	(172)
Nordic Challenger	2	513	(63)
Nordic Link	18	16	(422)
Nordic Louisiana	2	95	(35)
Nordic Rainbow	4	60	(91)
Nordic Voyager	2	428	(57)
Nordik Passeur	20	185	(472)
Nord-Jahre President	1	140	(12)
Nord-Jahre Princess	1	140	(12)
Nord-Jahre Progress	1	140	(12)
Nord-Jahre Target	1	145	(12)
Nord-Jahre Transporter	1	145	(12)
Nord-Jahre Traveller	1	145	(12)
Nordjarl	11	115	(309)
Nordkap	13	17	(350)
Nordkyn	17	6	(405)
Nordlake	13	11	(350)
Nordland	7	142	(167)
Nordlight	13	36	(351)
Nordlys	20	63	(463)
Nordmark	8	399	(234)
Nord Neptunus	18	132	(431)
Nordon	7	258	(175)
Nord Pas-de-Calais	18	154	(433)
Nordscout	5	53	(110)
Nordsee	14	52	(370)†
Nordsee	14	22	(366)
Nordsino	13	109	(359)†
Nordsino	13	17	(350)
Nordstar	2	97	(35)
Nordstar	12	130	(334)
Nordstjernen	20	7	(459)
Nordstrand	15	43	(380)
Nordstraum	1	111	(10)
Nordsund	12	130	(334)
Nordtramp	1	200	(16)
Nordwelle	13	10	(349)
Nordwind	5	256	(125)
Nordwoge	13	10	(349)
Noren	7	305	(178)
Norgas Challenger	4	90	(93)
Norgas Christian	4	127	(96)
Norgas Discoverer	4	117	(95)
Norgas Energy	4	11	(87)
Norgas Mariner	4	160	(100)†
Norgas Navigator	4	115	(95)
Norgas Patricia	4	127	(96)
Norgas Pilot	3	78	(84)†
Norgas Pioneer	4	11	(87)
Norgas Trader	4	159	(100)†
Norgas Traveller	4	12	(88)
Norgas Victory	4	9	(87)
Norgas Voyager	4	117	(95)
Norient	8	193	(218)
Norilsk	17	27	(407)
Norita	1	200	(16)
Norking	18	17	(422)
Norland	20	308	(482)
Norlandia	17	37	(408)
Normandie	20	429	(493)†
Normandie Shipper	18	185	(436)†
Normandie Shipper	18	171	(434)
Norman King	2	397	(55)
Norman Lady	3	39	(79)†
Norman Lady	3	3	(75)
Normannbay	5	263	(125)
Norman Star	11	56	(305)
Normar Spirit	2	53	(32)
Nornes	5	222	(122)
Nornews Express	18	205	(439)†
Nornews Express	18	115	(430)
Nornews Leader	18	115	(430)
Nornews Supplier	18	115	(430)
Norpol Pride	10	20	(288)
Norqueen	18	17	(422)
Norquest	10	14	(288)
Norrisia	2	545	(66)†
Norrisia	2	336	(51)
Norrland	6	2	(141)
Norrona	20	43	(462)
Norsea	20	72	(464)
Norse Mersey	18	46	(424)
Norsky	18	127	(431)
Norstar	20	308	(482)
Norstone	5	261	(125)
Norsul Ipu	5	196	(121)
Norsul Sobral	7	225	(173)
Norsul Tubarao	5	197	(121)
Norsun	20	72	(464)
North Countess	5	199	(121)
North Duchess	5	53	(110)
North Emperor	5	303	(128)
Northern Dawn	9	71	(268)
Northern Enterprise	5	226	(122)
Northern Light	8	462	(239)
Northern Lights	16	5	(391)
Northern Lion	2	249	(45)
Northern Phoenix	17	40	(408)
Northern Spirit	2	33	(31)
Northgate	2	460	(59)
North Islands	8	383	(232)
North Sea	6	24	(143)
North Sea	11	169	(313)
Northsea Anvil	1	156	(13)
Northsea Trader	14	79	(374)†
North Sea Trader	15	14	(378)
Northwest Sanderling	3	13	(76)
Northwest Sandpiper	3	31	(78)†
Northwest Sandpiper	3	13	(76)
Northwest Seaeagle	3	13	(76)
Northwest Shearwater	3	13	(76)
Northwest Snipe	3	13	(76)
Northwest Stormpetrel	3	13	(76)
Northwest Swallow	3	13	(76)
Northwest Swift	3	13	(76)
North Wind	2	12	(29)
Norunn	5	10	(107)
Norviken	9	94	(270)
Nor Viking	10	105	(297)†
Nor Viking	10	26	(289)
Norway	20	253	(477)
Nosac Explorer	19	15	(446)
Nosac Express	19	15	(446)
Nosac Ranger	19	82	(454)†
Nosac Ranger	19	3	(445)
Nosac Rover	19	36	(448)†
Nosac Sun	19	74	(453)†
Nosac Takara	19	44	(449)†
Nosac Takayama	19	69	(452)†
Nostos T	5	217	(122)
Noura	2	193	(42)
Noura 1	8	230	(221)
Nour Allah	8	530	(244)
Nova	8	102	(211)
Nova 1	8	222	(220)
Novaya Ladoga	8	169	(216)
Novgorod	9	43	(266)
Novigrad	8	691	(259)†
Novigrad	8	445	(237)
Novik	2	367	(53)
Novikov Priboy	12	75	(330)
Novi T	11	147	(312)
Novoaltaysk	9	43	(266)
Novocentrol 1	2	27	(30)
Novocentrol 2	2	27	(30)
Novocentrol 3	2	524	(64)
Novocentrol 4	2	524	(64)
Novocherkassk	8	415	(235)
Novodruzhesk	9	43	(266)
Novogrudok	9	43	(266)
Novoklav 2	2	469	(60)
Novoklav 3	2	469	(60)
Novoklav 4	2	469	(60)
Novokuybyshevsk	9	43	(266)
Novokuznetsk	9	43	(266)
Novolvovsk	9	43	(266)
Novomir 1	2	469	(60)
Novomir 2	2	469	(60)
Novomir 3	2	469	(60)
Novomirgorod	9	43	(266)
Novomoskovsk	9	43	(266)
Novopolotsk	9	43	(266)
Novorzhev	8	622	(251)
Novoshakhtinsk	8	622	(251)
Novosibirsk	9	43	(266)
Novotsak 1	2	469	(60)
Novotsak 2	2	469	(60)
Novovolynsk	9	43	(266)
Novozybkov	9	43	(266)
Novy Donbass	8	622	(251)
NP Enterprise	3	79	(84)†
NP Enterprise	3	22	(76)
NP Tatina	2	397	(55)
Nuevik	7	188	(170)
Nuevo Leon	12	59	(329)
Nuevo San Juan	12	131	(335)

†Photograph

	SHIP TYPE	REF NO	PAGE NO
Nunki	5	362	(134)†
Nunki	2	415	(56)
Nuria	8	311	(228)
Nurnberg Express	12	5	(325)
Nusa Bahagia	18	172	(435)
Nusa Dharma	18	163	(434)
Nusa Mulia	18	66	(426)
Nyantic	11	223	(320)†
Nyanza	9	173	(276)†
Nyhall	4	98	(94)
Nyholm	4	94	(93)
NYK Altair	12	8	(325)
NYK Lisboa	12	225	(345)†
NYK Procyon	12	8	(325)
NYK Vega	12	8	(325)
Nyon	5	65	(111)
Nyura Kizhevatova	8	239	(222)
NZOL Contender	7	446	(189)
Oahu	12	201	(342)†
Oak	7	517	(196)†
Oakwell	1	6	(3)
Oarsman	2	71	(34)
Ob	7	143	(167)
Obbola	18	233	(442)†
Obbola	18	47	(425)
Obo Basak	2	321	(50)
Obo Deniz	2	321	(50)
Obo Elif	2	403	(55)
Obo Engin	2	144	(39)
Oborishte	7	278	(176)
Obo Selim	2	403	(55)
Obo Victory	2	337	(51)
Obroncy Poczty	5	313	(129)
Ocean A	2	377	(54)
Ocean Amber	1	12	(4)
Ocean Beauty	7	68	(161)
Ocean Bird	7	476	(191)
Ocean Breeze	20	368	(486)
Ocean Brilliancy	7	409	(186)
Ocean Centaurus	8	125	(212)
Ocean Centurion	2	332	(51)
Ocean Competence	7	409	(186)
Ocean Confidence	7	409	(186)
Ocean Conqueror	5	21	(108)
Ocean Coral	2	429	(57)
Ocean Crest	8	319	(228)
Ocean Crown	7	68	(161)
Ocean Crown	8	500	(241)
Ocean Duke	7	68	(161)
Ocean Elite	7	409	(186)
Ocean Envoy	8	500	(241)
Ocean Express	11	72	(306)
Ocean Fleet	6	19	(142)
Ocean Freeze	8	580	(247)
Oceanglory	7	405	(186)
Ocean GR	5	86	(113)
Ocean Grace	7	146	(167)
Ocean Guardian	1	219	(18)†
Ocean Hero	8	193	(218)
Ocean Ho	8	503	(241)
Ocean Hunter	8	169	(216)
Oceanic Enterprise	5	366	(135)†
Oceanic Grace	20	354	(485)
Oceanic Ice	11	164	(313)
Oceanic Mindoro	5	207	(121)
Oceanic Star	5	216	(122)
Oceanic Success	7	199	(171)
Ocean Jewel	1	12	(4)
Ocean Jewel	2	207	(43)
Ocean Jupiter	2	434	(57)
Ocean K	8	63	(208)
Ocean Kmir	19	72	(453)†
Ocean Knight	2	483	(61)
Ocean Lady	5	55	(111)
Ocean Lake	7	146	(167)
Ocean Leader	7	172	(169)
Ocean Legend	8	584	(248)
Ocean Leo	2	384	(54)
Ocean Liner	8	474	(239)
Ocean Lydia	7	207	(171)
Ocean Meg	2	36	(31)
Oceano Artico	11	10	(301)
Oceano Atlantico	11	10	(301)
Ocean Onyx	1	12	(4)
Oceano Pacifico	11	169	(313)
Ocean Opal	1	12	(4)
Ocean Orchid	7	207	(171)
Ocean Pearl	1	12	(4)
Ocean Pearl	8	575	(247)
Ocean Prize	7	203	(171)
Ocean Queen	2	395	(55)
Ocean Sapphire	1	12	(4)
Ocean Sapphire	2	433	(57)
Ocean Serene	7	120	(165)
Ocean Spirit	2	178	(41)
Ocean Spirit	7	99	(163)
Ocean Star	2	172	(41)
Ocean Swallow	2	518	(63)
Ocean Topaz	1	12	(4)
Ocean Trader	2	429	(57)
Ocean Trader	8	17	(204)
Ocean Trader	8	159	(215)
Ocean Trader I	7	478	(191)
Ocean Tramp	7	478	(191)
Ocean Tramp	8	134	(213)
Oceanus	2	277	(47)
Ocean Venture	2	376	(54)
Ocean Victor	8	310	(227)
Oceeana Kareemata	2	40	(31)
Odense Maersk	1	108	(10)
Oderstern	1	211	(17)
Odessa	20	406	(490)†
Odessa	2	367	(53)
Odessa	20	73	(464)
Odessa Song	20	16	(460)
Odessa Sun	20	19	(460)
Odet	2	47	(32)
Odet	2	60	(33)
Odin	5	70	(112)
Odyssea	2	333	(51)
Odysseas I	7	221	(172)
Odyssey	5	10	(107)
Ofelia	20	106	(467)
Offshore Master	7	294	(178)
Oglasa	20	274	(479)
Ognyan Naydov	7	340	(181)
Ogosta	2	25	(30)
Ograjden	5	154	(118)
Ohfu	7	407	(186)
Ohio	2	176	(41)
Ohminesan Maru	2	182	(41)
Ohtaka Maru	5	246	(124)
Oihonna	16	23	(393)
Oituz	8	140	(213)
Ojars Vacietis	1	181	(15)
Okapi	10	33	(289)
Okba Bnou Nafia	11	92	(307)
Okhaneft	2	380	(54)
Okinoshima Maru	1	210	(17)
Okolchitza	5	339	(131)†
Okoltchitza	5	132	(116)
Okrika Sun	2	466	(60)
Oksywie	5	306	(128)
Oktavius	1	192	(15)
Oktay Kalkavan	5	299	(128)
Ola	14	14	(366)
Olandia	13	37	(351)
Ole	5	30	(109)
Olebratt	8	500	(241)
Olenegorsk	8	575	(247)
Olga Androvskaya	20	18	(460)
Olga Androvskaya	20	23	(461)
Olga I	5	10	(107)
Olga I	9	35	(265)
Olga M	8	143	(214)
Olga Maersk	1	108	(10)
Olga Sadovskaya	20	18	(460)
Olga Ulyanova	9	56	(267)
Olive	8	264	(224)
Olive Ace	19	1	(445)
Olivebank	9	91	(270)
Olivia	6	90	(150)†
Olivia	18	202	(438)†
Olivia	5	92	(113)
Olivia Maersk	1	108	(10)
Olivier	5	384	(137)†
Olma	8	24	(205)
Oloibiri	2	462	(59)
Oluf Maersk	1	108	(10)
Olympia	1	96	(9)
Olympia	7	7	(157)
Olympian Duchess	18	181	(436)†
Olympian Duchess	18	116	(430)
Olympian Spirit	2	339	(51)
Olympic	20	409	(490)†
Olympic Armour II	1	74	(7)
Olympic Galaxy	5	245	(124)
Olympic Serenity	1	97	(9)
Olympic Sponsor	1	97	(9)
Olympic Symphony	1	97	(9)
Olyutorka	8	596	(249)
Olyutorskiy Zaliv	11	98	(308)
Olyutorskiy Zaliv	11	101	(308)
Om	15	47	(381)
Omadhoo Fortune	8	615	(250)
Omega Bay	11	1	(301)
Omegaventure L	2	529	(64)
Omer	8	291	(226)
Omikronventure L	2	529	(64)
Omiros	2	333	(51)

†Photograph

	SHIP TYPE	REF NO	PAGE NO
Omiros	8	15	(204)
Omiros	8	601	(249)
Omis	9	92	(270)
Omogy	8	581	(248)
Omolon	8	612	(250)
Omo Wonz	18	123	(431)
Once	2	235	(44)
Oncu	2	360	(52)
Onda Azzurra	1	85	(8)
Onda Bianca	2	317	(50)
Onego	6	20	(142)
Onezhskiy Zaliv	11	18	(302)
Onga Maru	5	40	(110)
Onoe Maru	5	22	(108)
Onozo Spirit	1	214	(17)
Ontario	7	60	(161)
Ontario Laker	7	7	(157)
On Yeung	7	35	(159)
OOCL Alliance	12	52	(328)
OOCL Alliance	12	91	(331)
OOCL Arrow	9	54	(267)
OOCL Assurance	12	52	(328)
OOCL Award	12	122	(334)
OOCL Beacon	12	118	(334)
OOCL Bravery	12	53	(329)
OOCL Challenge	12	1	(325)
OOCL Concord	12	149	(336)
OOCL Educator	12	117	(333)
OOCL Envoy	12	137	(335)
OOCL Executive	12	117	(333)
OOCL Explorer	12	117	(333)
OOCL Fair	12	107	(333)
OOCL Faith	12	107	(333)
OOCL Fame	12	40	(328)
OOCL Fortune	12	107	(333)
OOCL Freedom	12	107	(333)
OOCL Friendship	12	107	(333)
OOCL Frontier	12	40	(328)
Opal Naree	8	276	(225)
Opal Ray	19	20	(446)
Opatija	8	27	(205)
OPDR Tejo	5	113	(115)
Ora Bhum	12	46	(328)
Orakota	2	289	(48)
Orange Klipper	11	211	(318)†
Orange Phoenix	5	216	(122)
Orange Reefer	11	134	(311)
Orange Star	2	439	(58)
Orange Wave	1	232	(20)†
Oranienburg	7	483	(192)
Orantus	9	84	(269)
Orateca	2	93	(35)
Orava	8	136	(213)
Oravita	7	174	(169)
Ordubad	2	171	(41)
Orekhovo—Zuyevo	8	589	(248)
Orenoco Reefer	11	97	(308)
Orense	2	398	(55)
Oreo	8	42	(206)
Oresund	18	143	(432)
Orfeas	5	237	(123)
Orgullo	8	466	(239)
Orhan Ayanoglu	11	145	(312)
Orhan Ekinci	7	69	(161)
Ori A.	2	52	(32)
Oriana	20	431	(493)†
Oriana	5	199	(121)
Oriana	8	189	(217)
Oriental Dragon	15	45	(381)
Oriental Honey	7	271	(176)
Orient Challenge	8	119	(212)
Orient Cord	12	61	(329)
Orient Courier	17	34	(407)
Oriente Grace	7	120	(165)
Oriente Oceano	8	589	(248)
Orient Ganges	8	119	(212)
Orient Princess	20	377	(487)
Orient Prosperity	12	130	(334)
Orient Reefer	11	85	(307)
Orient River II	7	241	(174)
Orient Shreyas	8	425	(236)
Orient Spirit	12	72	(330)
Orient Strength	12	72	(330)
Orion Diamond	19	45	(449)†
Orion II	5	103	(114)
Orion Progress	8	399	(234)
Orion Reefer	11	10	(301)
Orion Star	10	49	(290)
Oris	9	57	(267)
Orissa	5	19	(108)
Orjen	5	295	(127)
Orlan	5	28	(109)
Orleta Lwowskie	5	110	(115)
Orlik	9	105	(271)
Orpheus	20	188	(472)
Ortos	8	582	(248)
Ortviken	18	6	(421)
Ortviken	18	47	(425)
Orweikumor	2	105	(36)
Oryu Maru	18	31	(423)
Osaka	12	21	(326)
Osaka Bay	11	43	(303)
Osaka Bay	12	153	(336)
Osam	2	206	(43)
Oscar 10	8	76	(209)
Oscar Castor	8	132	(213)
Oscar Gas	4	98	(94)
Oscar Jupiter	7	174	(169)
Oscar Saturn	8	50	(207)
Oscona	2	58	(33)
Osco Star	1	86	(8)
Osco Stripe	1	86	(8)
Osetiya	20	309	(482)
O'Shea Express	18	122	(431)
Osip Pyatnitskiy	9	57	(267)
Osiris	15	100	(388)†
Osland	7	164	(168)
Osman Bey	7	296	(178)
Osman Gazi	8	291	(226)
Osmangazi	8	291	(226)
Osman J	8	202	(219)
Osogovo	5	154	(118)
Osor	17	41	(408)
Osprey Challenger	2	530	(64)
Ossolineum	5	247	(124)
Ostankino	1	138	(12)
Ostara	17	64	(411)†
Ostara	17	36	(408)
Osterhusen	15	21	(379)
Ostfriesland	8	379	(232)
Ostrand	18	47	(425)
Ostroleka	9	53	(267)
Ostrov Shokalskogo	11	11	(301)
Ostrov Ushakova	11	11	(301)
Ostwind	6	28	(143)
Otapan	2	212	(43)
Otava	7	433	(188)
Otello	19	7	(445)
Otepya	8	581	(248)
Othoni	2	12	(29)
Otomar Oshkaln	11	82	(306)
Otome Maru	20	108	(467)
OTS Uranus	7	425	(188)
Ottaviano	2	12	(29)
Otterpool	5	238	(123)
Otto Becker	5	112	(115)
Otto Danielsen	8	227	(221)
Otto Grotewohl	11	99	(308)
Ottoman	1	39	(5)
Oualidia	5	71	(112)
Ouarzazate	5	71	(112)
Oued Guetereni	2	364	(53)
Oued Noumer	2	30	(30)
Ouezzane	5	71	(112)
Ouirgane	5	71	(112)
Oulmes	5	71	(112)
Ourania	8	17	(204)
Ourania 1	8	24	(205)
Ouranos	20	201	(473)
Ourios	7	99	(163)
Our Lady of the Sacred Heart	18	158	(433)
Ouro Do Brasil	13	84	(356)†
Ouro Do Brasil	1	173	(14)
Oversea Fruit	11	6	(301)
Overseas Alaska	2	320	(50)
Overseas Alice	2	502	(62)
Overseas Arctic	2	320	(50)
Overseas Chicago	2	334	(51)
Overseas Harriette	8	660	(255)†
Overseas Juneau	2	319	(50)
Overseas New York	2	334	(51)
Overseas Ohio	2	334	(51)
Overseas Valdez	2	502	(62)
Overseas Vivian	2	502	(62)
Overseas Washington	2	334	(51)
Ovik Saga	20	346	(484)
Oyashima Maru	5	115	(115)
Oyster Bay	9	15	(264)
Ozge S	8	5	(203)
Pablo Metz	9	141	(273)
Pablo Neruda	2	424	(57)
Pacduke	7	496	(194)†
Pacduke	7	74	(162)
Pachitea	17	55	(409)
Pacific Arrow	12	138	(335)
Pacific Brilliance	5	60	(111)
Pacific Career	7	199	(171)
Pacific Chungsam	7	103	(164)
Pacific Crystal	2	176	(41)
Pacific Diamond	2	156	(39)

†Photograph

	SHIP TYPE	REF NO	PAGE NO
Pacific Embolden	7	199	(171)
Pacific Endeavor	7	199	(171)
Pacific Envoy	5	72	(112)
Pacific Explorer	19	5	(445)
Pacific Express	20	251	(477)
Pacific Harmony	4	102	(94)
Pacific Jasmin	5	120	(115)
Pacific Lady	12	4	(325)
Pacific Link	12	21	(326)
Pacific Maru	7	408	(186)
Pacific Mercury	2	528	(64)
Pacific Nova	5	199	(121)
Pacific Ocean	7	42	(160)
Pacific Opal	2	156	(39)
Pacific Pintail	10	91	(295)†
Pacific Pride	2	596	(72)†
Pacific Princess	20	241	(476)
Pacific Prosperity	18	159	(433)
Pacific Runner	19	6	(445)
Pacific Sakti	8	217	(220)
Pacific Sandpiper	10	2	(287)
Pacific Spirit	2	66	(33)
Pacific Star	11	51	(304)
Pacific Swan	8	276	(225)
Pacific Teal	10	2	(287)
Pacific Trader	8	252	(223)
Pacific Trader	11	152	(312)
Pacific Trident	5	4	(107)
Pacific Universal	11	22	(302)
Pacific Vigorous	7	199	(171)
Pacificway	5	42	(110)
Pacifik Frigo	11	213	(319)†
Pacprince	7	534	(198)†
Padrone	13	54	(353)
Padua	15	34	(380)
Paglia Orba	20	395	(489)†
Paglia Orba	20	285	(480)
Pagoda	1	99	(9)
Pahom Makarenko	7	105	(164)
Pakrac	7	253	(175)
Pakri	8	582	(248)
Pakruojis	8	619	(250)
Palana	8	619	(250)
Palanga	7	266	(175)
Palanimalai	1	169	(14)
Palas	7	375	(184)
Palatial II	7	309	(179)
Paldiski	8	590	(248)
Paleisgracht	7	310	(179)
Pal Falcon	9	224	(282)†
Pallas	7	394	(185)
Pallas Athina	2	307	(49)
Palliser Bay	12	220	(345)†
Palliser Bay	12	134	(335)
Pal Marinos	7	180	(169)
Palmavera	8	232	(221)
Palm Beach	2	174	(41)
Palmgracht	7	310	(179)
Palmstar Cherry	1	214	(17)
Palmstar Lotus	1	214	(17)
Palmstar Orchid	1	214	(17)
Palmstar Poppy	1	214	(17)
Palmstar Rose	1	214	(17)
Palmstar Thistle	1	214	(17)
Paloma	15	8	(377)
Paltinis	18	91	(428)
Palva	1	168	(14)
Pal Vassilis	8	446	(237)
Palvia	5	107	(114)
Pal Wind	8	161	(215)
Pamela	1	57	(6)
Pamela Everard	6	25	(143)
Pampero	2	272	(46)
Pamphilos	5	65	(111)
Pamyat Ilyicha	11	98	(308)
Pamyat Ilyicha	11	101	(308)
Pamyat Kirova	11	98	(308)
Pamyat Kirova	11	101	(308)
Pamyat Lenina	2	514	(63)
Pan	8	516	(242)
Panagia	20	154	(470)
Panagia Tinou	8	247	(222)
Panagia Tinou II	20	155	(470)
Panama Flyer	14	51	(370)†
Panama Flyer	14	2	(365)
Panama Maru	7	408	(186)
Panama Senator	12	102	(332)
Panamax Pearl	7	215	(172)
Panamax Pride	5	148	(117)
Panandros	8	24	(205)
Panayiota	8	34	(206)
Pancon 3	14	59	(371)†
Pancon 3	14	27	(367)
Panda	1	117	(10)
Panda	9	110	(271)
Panda Faget	8	500	(241)

	SHIP TYPE	REF NO	PAGE NO
Pandesia	7	216	(172)
Pandias	7	213	(172)
Pandora	15	34	(380)
Pan Express	7	124	(165)
Panglima	8	305	(227)
Pan Hope	8	445	(237)
Panikos	8	18	(204)
Pan Jin Hai	8	420	(235)
Pan Journey	5	179	(119)
Pan Korea	8	137	(213)
Pannarai	8	543	(245)
Panorama	20	276	(479)
Panormitis	8	537	(244)
Panormos Bay	7	442	(189)
Panormos Wind	7	442	(189)
Pan Queen	7	124	(165)
Pan Shan	8	451	(238)
Pansy	8	294	(226)
Pantai Mas	9	78	(269)
Pantanassa	5	73	(112)
Pantazis L	7	503	(195)†
Pantazis L	7	7	(157)
Panteleymon Lepeshinskiy	9	57	(267)
Pantelleria	18	65	(426)
Pan Union	5	175	(119)
Pan Yard	5	184	(120)
Pany R	7	369	(184)
Paola	11	82	(306)
Paola D'Alesio	2	366	(53)
Para	1	64	(7)
Paradise	8	55	(207)
Paraguay Express	13	80	(355)†
Paraiso	11	6	(301)
Paramushir	7	266	(175)
Parandowski	7	448	(189)
Paraskevi M Y	7	51	(160)
Parfentiy Grechanvyy	5	193	(120)
Pargolovo	7	266	(175)
Pariata	1	11	(3)
Parila	9	57	(267)
Paris	2	339	(51)
Paris	7	60	(161)
Paris II	2	317	(50)
Paris Maersk	12	155	(336)
Parita	7	229	(173)
Parkgracht	7	310	(179)
Parkhaven	17	35	(408)
Parkhomenko	11	170	(313)
Parnar	2	150	(39)
Parnaso	1	157	(13)
Parnassus	8	632	(251)
Paromay	7	266	(175)
Parseta	18	138	(432)
Parsifal	19	39	(449)†
Partizani	8	469	(239)
Paru Meru	18	83	(427)
Pasadena Universal	11	81	(306)
Pascale Delmas	9	214	(281)†
Pascani	18	91	(428)
Pascoli	20	398	(489)†
Pascoli	20	323	(483)
Pasewalk	8	446	(237)
Passaden	5	113	(115)
Passat	6	2	(141)
Pat	8	689	(259)†
Pat	8	115	(212)
Patcharee Naree	8	146	(214)
Pathein	8	486	(240)
Pathfinder II	5	249	(124)
Patria 38	2	149	(39)
Patricia	7	77	(162)
Patricia Delmas	7	194	(170)
Patricia Star	8	193	(218)
Patrick Delmas	8	446	(237)
Patriot	2	503	(62)
Pattaya Navee	9	223	(282)†
Pattu	8	542	(245)
Paugi	8	582	(248)
Paul	2	57	(33)
Paul	8	489	(240)
Paula	7	338	(181)
Paulemose R	5	20	(108)
Paulemose R–1	11	148	(312)
Paulina	8	521	(243)
Pauline	3	67	(82)†
Pauline	3	14	(76)
Pauline Olivieri	7	146	(167)
Paulis	18	91	(428)
Paul Keres	5	17	(108)
Pauwgracht	7	310	(179)
Pavel Antokolskiy	21	101	(509)†
Pavel Antokolskiy	21	59	(504)
Pavel Mizikevich	12	109	(333)
Pavel Ponomaryev	8	168	(216)
Pavel Rybin	10	57	(291)
Pavel Shchepelev	7	152	(167)

†Photograph

	SHIP TYPE	REF NO	PAGE NO
Pavels Parenago	11	127	(310)
Pavels Sternbergs	11	127	(310)
Pavel Vavilov	7	273	(176)
Pavel Yablochkov	5	29	(109)
Pavlik Larishkin	8	621	(251)
Pavlina One	8	17	(204)
Pavlin Vinogradov	7	435	(188)
Pavlodar	9	139	(273)
Pavlograd	9	139	(273)
Pavlovo	7	266	(175)
Pawnee	1	7	(3)
Pax	15	8	(377)
Payasan	2	147	(39)
Peaceventure L	1	247	(22)†
Pearl 1	8	123	(212)
Pearl Luck	7	81	(162)
Pearl Merchant	8	161	(215)
Pearl Merchant	8	162	(215)
Pearl of Dubai	7	197	(171)
Pearl Prosperity	7	206	(171)
Pearl Reefer	11	168	(313)
Pearl Sea	7	125	(165)
Pearl Venus	7	254	(175)
Pearl William	20	214	(474)
Pechenga	7	266	(175)
Pecine	8	410	(234)
Peder Olsen	20	45	(462)
Pegasus	20	263	(478)
Pegasus Erre	2	163	(40)
Peggy	2	404	(55)
Peggy Dow	11	53	(304)
Pegy	8	240	(222)
Pelagos	11	8	(301)
Pelamber	17	42	(408)
Pelboxer	14	21	(366)
Pelchaser	6	6	(141)
Pelfisher	12	123	(334)
Pelican Arrow	10	43	(290)
Peliner	14	25	(367)
Pelita/Pertamina 1023	2	515	(63)
Pella	2	335	(51)
Pella	7	7	(157)
Pella	8	252	(223)
Pellworm	6	5	(141)
Pelmariner	12	45	(328)
Pelrider	17	13	(406)
Peltainer	14	25	(367)
Peltrader	6	81	(149)†
Peltrader	6	6	(141)
Pematang/Pertamina 1021	2	515	(63)
Penang Jaya	21	103	(509)†
Penelope A	8	128	(213)
Penelope A	20	114	(467)
Penelope II	7	453	(190)
Peng Cheng	2	489	(61)
Peng Hai	5	158	(118)
Peng Yang	5	176	(119)
Penhir	7	461	(190)
Penzhinskiy Zaliv	11	98	(308)
Penzhinskiy Zaliv	11	101	(308)
Perdana Putera	8	512	(242)
Pergamos	8	399	(234)
Periandros	7	82	(162)
Periandros of Korinthos	5	309	(128)
Pericles	8	24	(205)
Pericles G C	5	145	(117)
Peridot	7	248	(174)
Peris	18	91	(428)
Perle	11	54	(304)
Perm	7	266	(175)
Permina XXVII	2	361	(52)
Permina XXX	2	361	(52)
Permina XXXI	2	361	(52)
Pernas Arang	5	100	(114)
Pernas Suasa	8	418	(235)
Pernille	8	173	(216)
Pernille W	15	8	(377)
Pero	15	8	(377)
Perseas I	8	147	(214)
Perseus	5	19	(108)
Perseus	8	531	(244)
Perseus	11	8	(301)
Perseus	18	52	(425)
Pertamina 1020	2	515	(63)
Pertominsk	7	266	(175)
Pervomayski	9	139	(273)
Pervouralsk	8	596	(249)
Pestovo	9	139	(273)
Peter Knuppel	5	30	(109)
Peter Metz	5	97	(114)
Petersburg	2	362	(53)
Petersburg	20	339	(484)
Peter Wessel	20	246	(477)
Petimata OT RMS	5	336	(131)†
Petimata Ot RMS	5	172	(119)
Petko R Slavejnov	8	11	(203)

	SHIP TYPE	REF NO	PAGE NO
Petra	5	233	(123)
Petra F	6	94	(150)†
Petra F	6	21	(142)
Petr Aleynikov	8	161	(215)
Petralia	7	9	(157)
Petrarca	20	323	(483)
Petra Star	8	500	(241)
Petra Wave	8	383	(232)
Petr Dutov	9	92	(270)
Petrel	8	270	(224)
Petrel	11	113	(309)
Petr Gutchenko	7	269	(176)
Petro Aberdeen	2	184	(41)
Petro Avon	1	252	(22)†
Petrobulk Cougar	1	133	(11)
Petrobulk Jaguar	1	133	(11)
Petrobulk Jupiter	1	156	(13)
Petrobulk Leopard	1	133	(11)
Petrobulk Lion	1	133	(11)
Petrobulk Mars	1	156	(13)
Petrobulk Panther	1	133	(11)
Petrobulk Radiance	2	597	(72)†
Petrobulk Tiger	1	133	(11)
Petro Clyde	2	363	(53)
Petro Clyde	2	452	(59)
Petrodvorets	9	139	(273)
Petro Fawley	2	471	(60)
Petro Fife	2	307	(49)
Petrokrepost	7	266	(175)
Petrolagas 2	4	78	(92)
Petromar I	4	21	(88)
Petro Mersey	2	363	(53)
Petro Mersey	2	452	(59)
Petro Milford Haven	2	471	(60)
Petronia	7	5	(157)
Petropolis	5	65	(111)
Petro Pyla	2	129	(38)
Petros A	2	492	(61)
Petro Severn	2	363	(53)
Petro Severn	2	452	(59)
Petroship A	2	405	(55)
Petroship B	2	405	(55)
Petrotroll	1	274	(25)†
Petrotroll	1	92	(9)
Petro Tyne	2	376	(54)
Petrovskiy	7	266	(175)
Petrozavodsk	7	266	(175)
Petr Shmidt	1	20	(4)
Petr Smidovich	8	78	(209)
Petr Strelkov	8	78	(209)
Petr Velikiy	5	131	(116)
Petr Yemtsov	9	92	(270)
Petsamo	6	62	(146)
Petya Kovalyenko	8	239	(222)
Petya Shitikov	8	239	(222)
Peveril	18	92	(428)
Peyo Yavorov	9	93	(270)
Phaethon	8	500	(241)
Pha Lai	8	577	(247)
Pharos	2	480	(60)
Pharos	8	116	(212)
Pha Shwe Gyaw Ywa	7	255	(175)
Phayao Navee	9	199	(279)†
Phayao Navee	9	129	(272)
Pheasant	8	500	(241)
Phemius	2	367	(53)
Philia	8	445	(237)
Philipp	14	54	(371)†
Philipp	14	22	(366)
Philippos	8	337	(229)
Phoenicia	8	603	(249)
Phoenician Sea	20	181	(472)
Phoenix	2	295	(48)
Phoenix Express	20	251	(477)
Phoenix II	6	125	(154)†
Phoenix II	14	23	(367)
Phoenix M	7	78	(162)
Phoenix Spirit	18	68	(426)
Phonix I	15	8	(377)
Pia	15	71	(384)†
Pia Danielsen	8	220	(220)
Pia Danielsen	8	224	(221)
Pia II	8	581	(248)
Piano	15	74	(385)†
Picasso	18	18	(422)
Picasso	18	66	(426)
Pico Castelo	8	406	(234)
Pico Grande	7	354	(182)
Pic St Loup	2	296	(48)
Piero della Francesca	20	274	(479)
Pietersgracht	7	310	(179)
Pietro Novelli	20	274	(479)
Pihtla	9	57	(267)
Pijlgracht	7	310	(179)
Pilion	7	246	(174)
Pilot	5	217	(122)

†Photograph

	SHIP TYPE	REF NO	PAGE NO
Pina Prima	5	209	(121)
Pinar	8	590	(248)
Pindar	2	337	(51)
Pindos	8	197	(218)
Pine Beauty	7	135	(166)
Pinecone	8	220	(220)
Pine King	8	581	(248)
Pine Queen	8	581	(248)
Ping Ding Shan	8	548	(245)
Ping Gu	8	80	(209)
Ping Hai	8	14	(204)
Ping Jiang	8	383	(232)
Ping Quan	11	233	(321)†
Pinguin Ocean District	5	256	(125)
Ping Xiang Cheng	8	507	(242)
Pinto	18	136	(432)
Pinya	8	381	(232)
Pioneer Commander	8	89	(210)
Pioneer Contractor	8	89	(210)
Pioneer Crusader	8	89	(210)
Pioneer Elegant	8	148	(214)
Pioneer Express	11	183	(315)†
Pioneer Spirit	17	106	(416)†
Pioneer Spirit	1	135	(11)
Pioneer Star	5	176	(119)
Pioneer Sun	7	180	(169)
Pioneer Wave	9	129	(272)
Pioner	8	621	(251)
Pioner	10	28	(289)
Pioner Arkhangelska	8	51	(207)
Pioner Belorussii	8	51	(207)
Pioner Buryatii	8	51	(207)
Pioner Chukotki	8	51	(207)
Pioner Estonii	8	51	(207)
Pioner Kamchatki	8	51	(207)
Pioner Karelii	8	51	(207)
Pioner Kazakhstana	8	51	(207)
Pioner Kergizii	8	51	(207)
Pioner Kholmska	8	51	(207)
Pioner Koly	8	51	(207)
Pioner Litvy	8	51	(207)
Pioner Moldavii	8	51	(207)
Pioner Moskvy	8	51	(207)
Pioner Nakhodki	14	10	(365)
Pioner Odessy	14	10	(365)
Pioner Onegi	8	51	(207)
Pioner Primorya	14	10	(365)
Pioner Rossii	8	51	(207)
Pioner Sakhalina	8	51	(207)
Pioner Severodvinska	8	51	(207)
Pionerskaya Pravda	8	621	(251)
Pionerskaya Zorka	8	621	(251)
Pioner Slavyanki	8	51	(207)
Pioner Uzbekistana	8	51	(207)
Pioner Vladivostoka	14	10	(365)
Pioner Vyborga	14	10	(365)
Pioner Yuzhno Sakhalinska	8	51	(207)
Pionierul	5	181	(119)
Pionir	12	108	(333)
Pipob Samut	9	81	(269)
Piraeus	12	157	(337)
Piran	7	343	(182)
Pirat	15	8	(377)
Pirin	7	277	(176)
Pirol	15	8	(377)
Piryatin	2	89	(35)
Pisa	2	208	(43)
Pisang Perak	8	65	(208)
Pishgam	16	42	(394)
Pishro	5	276	(126)
Pishva	21	73	(505)†
Pishva	21	63	(504)
Pistis	8	445	(237)
Pitak Samut	9	209	(280)†
Pivot	2	473	(60)
Pkhen Hoa	8	317	(228)
Plan de Guadelupe	2	412	(56)
Planta de Betania	7	12	(158)
Planta de Mamonal	7	12	(158)
Platinum Kris	7	197	(171)
Platitera	7	124	(165)
Plato	10	47	(290)
Platon	8	24	(205)
Platon	8	276	(225)
Platon Oyunskiy	7	340	(181)
Playa Duaba	2	418	(56)
Plesetsk	7	266	(175)
Pliska	18	79	(427)
Plitvice	21	70	(505)†
Plitvice	21	67	(504)
Plopeni	8	50	(207)
Plover	7	271	(176)
Plumeria	2	176	(41)
Pluto	10	109	(298)†
Pluto	10	47	(290)
Pluto	11	90	(307)
Po	18	108	(429)
Pobyeda	2	304	(49)
Pobyedino	8	589	(248)
Podlasie	11	59	(305)
Podolsk	7	102	(164)
Podunavlje	2	494	(61)
Poel	7	480	(192)
Poiana	7	375	(184)
Pointe Clairette	1	205	(16)
Pointe de Lesven	2	117	(37)
Pointe de Morgat	2	117	(37)
Pointe Du Roc'h	2	33	(31)
Pointe Du Van	2	33	(31)
Point Lisas	15	45	(381)
Poitou	2	318	(50)
Pokkinen	7	129	(166)
Pokoj	9	126	(272)
Pol America	12	143	(336)
Polar	8	420	(235)
Polar	11	179	(314)
Polar Argentina	11	123	(310)
Polar Belgica	4	170	(101)†
Polar Bird	7	320	(180)
Polar Brasil	11	123	(310)
Polar Colombia	11	123	(310)
Polar Costa Rica	11	126	(310)
Polar Eagle	4	63	(91)
Polargas	4	101	(94)
Polar Honduras	11	126	(310)
Polaris	18	229	(442)†
Polaris	20	156	(470)
Polar Star	5	202	(121)
Policos	8	390	(233)
Polina Osipenko	11	82	(306)
Polis	8	445	(237)
Polisan 1	2	125	(37)
Polluks	2	137	(38)
Pollux	8	551	(245)
Pollux A	2	286	(47)
Pollux I	7	154	(168)
Polo	2	519	(63)
Polska Walczaca	5	110	(115)
Pols Robsons	2	424	(57)
Polterberg	15	27	(379)
Polyanka	1	138	(12)
Polycarp	5	365	(135)†
Polyclipper	1	230	(19)†
Polydefkis	7	223	(173)
Polynesia	13	50	(352)
Polytrader	2	336	(51)
Polytraveller	2	336	(51)
Pomerania	20	242	(476)
Pomorye	7	266	(175)
Pomorze Zachodnie	5	290	(127)
Ponce	16	5	(391)
Pongola	9	139	(273)
Ponor	7	174	(169)
Ponoy	7	266	(175)
Ponta de Sagres	9	63	(267)
Pontokratis	7	92	(163)
Pontoporos	7	74	(162)
Poolgracht	7	310	(179)
Poronin	8	589	(248)
Poros	7	411	(187)
Poros	8	323	(228)
Portaitissa	8	24	(205)
Port Alexandre	1	138	(12)
Port Arthur	1	138	(12)
Portoria	1	8	(3)
Port Royal	1	165	(13)
Port Said	9	80	(269)
Port Talbot	5	215	(122)
Portugal Bridge	5	360	(134)†
Poseidon	15	8	(377)
Poseidonia	20	182	(472)
Pos II	2	106	(36)
Positano	8	453	(238)
Possidonia	2	90	(35)
Poti	2	595	(72)†
Potrero del Llano	2	412	(56)
Poul Kosan	4	113	(95)
Povl Anker	20	157	(470)
Powe	1	204	(16)
Power	5	145	(117)
Powisle	11	59	(305)
Powstaniec Listopadowy	5	305	(128)
Powstaniec Slaski	5	313	(129)
Powstaniec Styczniowy	5	305	(128)
Powstaniec Wielkopolski	5	302	(128)
Prabhu Jivesh	7	125	(165)
Praca	9	126	(272)
Pragati	7	146	(167)
Prams Prakash	8	115	(212)
Pranedya Dwitya	2	515	(63)
Pranedya Pratama	2	515	(63)
Pranedya Quartya	2	515	(63)

†Photograph

	SHIP TYPE	REF NO	PAGE NO
Pranedya Tritya	2	515	(63)
Prapti	7	406	(186)
Praslin Reefer	11	141	(311)
Pravdinsk	9	139	(273)
Praxitelis	7	223	(173)
Precious River	12	54	(329)
Predeal	9	37	(265)
Premnitz	5	130	(116)
President	10	59	(291)
President Adams	12	9	(325)
Presidente Deodoro	2	6	(29)
Presidente Floriano	2	6	(29)
Presidente Frei	9	83	(269)
President Eisenhower	12	137	(335)
Presidente Kennedy	8	454	(238)
Presidente Ramon S Castillo	8	537	(244)
Presidente Rivera	2	317	(50)
Presidente Sarmiento	8	125	(212)
President F D Roosevelt	12	137	(335)
President G	5	216	(122)
President Jackson	12	9	(325)
President Jefferson	12	2	(325)
President Kennedy	12	9	(325)
President Monroe	12	148	(336)
President Polk	12	9	(325)
President Truman	12	9	(325)
President Washington	12	148	(336)
President Yeiwene	18	78	(427)
Preslav	18	79	(427)
Presnya	1	138	(12)
Prestige	2	406	(55)
Pretty Lady	5	103	(114)
Preveze	8	225	(221)
Priamos	7	271	(176)
Pride II	2	269	(46)
Pride of Bilbao	20	66	(464)
Pride of Bruges	20	217	(474)
Pride of Burgundy	20	100	(466)
Pride of Calais	20	74	(464)
Pride of Dover	20	74	(464)
Pride of Hampshire	20	435	(494)†
Pride of Kent	20	453	(496)†
Pride of Le Havre	20	415	(491)†
Pride of Le Havre	20	75	(464)
Pride of Portsmouth	20	75	(464)
Pride of Suffolk	20	433	(493)†
Pridneprovsk	9	10	(264)
Primar	2	498	(62)
Primera Peak	7	298	(178)
Prime Velvet	14	36	(368)†
Prime Velvet	14	3	(365)
Prime Venture II	14	65	(372)†
Prime Venture II	14	8	(365)
Prime View	12	226	(345)†
Prime View	14	22	(366)
Prime Vigor	5	68	(112)
Prime Vivid	7	456	(190)
Primo	1	209	(16)
Primo	5	208	(121)
Primorsk	9	139	(273)
Primosten	8	407	(234)
Prinaritis	7	36	(159)
Princefield	10	43	(290)
Prince of Scandinavia	20	76	(464)
Prince of Waves	11	180	(315)†
Princesa Amorosa	20	77	(465)
Princesa Cypria	20	11	(460)
Princesa Marissa	20	332	(483)
Princesa Oceanica	20	381	(487)
Princess Arrow	19	19	(446)
Princess Castle	7	271	(176)
Princess Clipper	5	51	(110)
Princess Danae	20	9	(459)
Princesse Marie Christine	20	191	(472)
Princess of Acadia	20	158	(470)
Princess of Scandinavia	20	76	(464)
Princess of the Orient	20	103	(467)
Princess Phaedra	2	479	(60)
Princess Superior	18	13	(422)
Prins Albert	20	191	(472)
Prins Casimir	11	116	(309)
Prinsengracht	7	310	(179)
Prinses Christina	20	218	(475)
Prinses Maria Esmeralda	20	191	(472)
Prinsesse Anne-Marie	20	183	(472)
Prinsesse Elisabeth	20	184	(472)
Prins Filip	20	78	(465)
Prins Joachim	20	351	(485)
Prins Johan Willem Friso	4	70	(92)
Prins Phillips Willem	3	69	(82)†
Prins William II	3	68	(82)†
Priozersk	9	139	(273)
Pritzwalk	8	446	(237)
Priwall	15	34	(380)
Pro Atlantica	9	149	(274)
Procyon	8	500	(241)
Prodicos	2	359	(52)
Product King	2	550	(66)†
Professor Anichkov	20	231	(476)
Professor Bubnov	7	152	(167)
Professor Buznik	9	80	(269)
Professor Gul	20	287	(480)
Professor K Bohdanowicz	1	196	(16)
Professor Khlyustin	20	231	(476)
Professor Kostiukov	7	245	(174)
Professor Kudrevich	20	231	(476)
Professor Minyayev	20	231	(476)
Professor Nebesnov	2	54	(32)
Professor Papkovich	7	152	(167)
Professor Pavlenko	20	231	(476)
Professor Popov	11	127	(310)
Professor Rybaltovskiy	20	231	(476)
Professor Shchyogolev	20	231	(476)
Professor Ukhov	20	231	(476)
Professor Viktor Vologdin	7	152	(167)
Professor Vladimir Popov	7	152	(167)
Professor Voskresenskiy	7	152	(167)
Professor Yushchenko	20	231	(476)
Progreso I	8	30	(205)
Progress	8	30	(205)
Progress Excellence	8	24	(205)
Progress Liberty	7	290	(177)
Progress Lily	8	173	(216)
Progresswind	2	383	(54)
Project Americas	21	28	(501)
Project Arabia	21	82	(506)†
Project Arabia	21	28	(501)
Project Orient	21	28	(501)
Proliv Diany	11	102	(308)
Proliv Laperuza	11	102	(308)
Proliv Longa	11	102	(308)
Proliv Nadezhdy	11	102	(308)
Proliv Sannikova	11	102	(308)
Proliv Viktoriya	11	102	(308)
Proliv Vilkitskogo	11	102	(308)
Prometheus	2	107	(36)
Prometheus	8	441	(237)
Promoter	8	252	(223)
Proof Gallant	2	88	(35)
Proso	17	7	(405)
Prospathia	7	82	(162)
Prospector II	5	249	(124)
Prosperity	2	468	(60)
Prosperity	7	286	(177)
Prosperity No 1	2	407	(56)
Prosperity Sea	7	164	(168)
Prosperity X	8	15	(204)
Protagoras	8	34	(206)
Protank Condor	2	337	(51)
Protank Medway	2	337	(51)
Protank Mersey	2	337	(51)
Protector 2	5	184	(120)
Proteo	1	157	(13)
Proteus	2	359	(52)
Proteus	8	567	(247)
Protoporos	8	272	(224)
Protsion	2	137	(38)
Providentia	5	107	(114)
Provmar Terminal II	2	108	(36)
Prudent Challenger	8	537	(244)
Prudent Voyager	8	503	(241)
Prvic	8	526	(243)
Przhevalsk	7	266	(175)
Psara	1	160	(13)
Ptolemeos	8	34	(206)
Pu An Hai	5	73	(112)
Pu Cheng	8	560	(246)
Puck	18	92	(428)
Pu Dong	10	14	(288)
Puerto Cortes	17	67	(411)†
Puerto Cortes	17	43	(408)
Puerto Eden	18	25	(423)
Puerto Vallarta	20	193	(473)
Puffin	8	79	(209)
Pu He	12	87	(331)
Pulau Kalimantan	8	220	(220)
Pulau Samutera	8	206	(219)
Pulkovo	7	266	(175)
Puma	18	133	(431)
Pumpuri	1	20	(4)
Punente	11	94	(307)
Pu Ning Hai	5	224	(122)
Punta Ala	2	41	(31)
Punta Europa	20	341	(484)
Puntland II	17	40	(408)
Puppy F	2	12	(29)
Puppy P	2	12	(29)
Pur	15	47	(381)
Purbeck	18	22	(422)
Pure	11	54	(304)
Purnima	8	24	(205)
Pushlakhta	7	266	(175)

†Photograph

	SHIP TYPE	REF NO	PAGE NO
Pustozersk	7	266	(175)
Puteri Delima	4	44	(90)
Puteri Intan	4	44	(90)
Puteri Nilam	4	44	(90)
Putivl	9	139	(273)
Putra Jaya	8	581	(248)
Pu Xing	8	81	(209)
Pyatidyesyatilyetiye Sovietskoy Gruzii	2	469	(60)
Pyatidyesyatilyetiye SSSR	11	102	(308)
Pyeng Hoa	8	317	(228)
Pylos	7	127	(165)
Pyong Chon	8	500	(241)
Pyong Won	8	589	(248)
Pyotr Aleynikov	8	161	(215)
Pyotr Anokhin	15	15	(378)
Pyotr Kakhovskiy	8	582	(248)
Pyotr Pervyy	20	128	(468)
Pyotr Shmidt	1	20	(4)
Pyotr Smorodin	7	81	(162)
Pyotr Starostin	8	49	(207)
Pyotr Tomasevich	7	160	(168)
Pyrgos	10	33	(289)
Pyrmont Bridge	16	11	(392)
Pytheas	2	91	(35)
Qamar	8	537	(244)
Qena	7	43	(160)
Qian Shan	8	26	(205)
Qian Tang Jiang	9	95	(270)
Qi Lian Shan	8	141	(214)
Qimen	8	41	(206)
Qing Ann	8	371	(231)
Qing Feng Er Hao	8	62	(208)
Qing Feng San Hao	8	491	(240)
Qing Hai	7	39	(159)
Qing He	13	34	(351)
Qing He Cheng	8	436	(236)
Qing Long 88	8	666	(256)†
Qing Long No 1	2	398	(55)
Qing Yang	8	86	(210)
Qin Hai 108	9	68	(268)
Qin Huai	8	461	(239)
Qin Ling	8	291	(226)
Qiong Xi	8	202	(219)
Qi Xia Shan	7	272	(176)
Quality I	1	26	(4)
Quality II	1	26	(4)
Quan Zhou Hai	5	53	(110)
Quarsenis	8	505	(241)
Quebec	2	442	(58)
Queen	8	120	(212)
Queen	11	53	(304)
Queen Elizabeth 2	20	26	(461)
Queen of Alberni	20	159	(470)
Queen of Coquitlam	20	160	(470)
Queen of Cowichan	20	160	(470)
Queen of Esquimalt	20	260	(478)
Queen of Heaven	11	113	(309)
Queen of Nanaimo	20	260	(478)
Queen of New Westminster	20	260	(478)
Queen of Prince Rupert	20	219	(475)
Queen of Saanich	20	260	(478)
Queen of Scandinavia	20	79	(465)
Queen of Sheeba	8	693	(259)†
Queen of Sheeba	8	553	(245)
Queen of Sidney	20	80	(465)
Queen of the Islands	20	352	(485)
Queen of the North	20	243	(477)
Queen of Tsawwassen	20	161	(470)
Queen of Vancouver	20	260	(478)
Queen of Victoria	20	260	(478)
Queensland Star	12	80	(331)
Queen Vergina	20	162	(471)
Queeny Margaret	3	44	(79)†
Quentin	4	164	(101)†
Quiberon	20	81	(465)
Quinca	1	2	(3)
Quintino	1	2	(3)
Quiriquire	2	426	(57)
Quixada	1	23	(4)
Qu Jiang	8	24	(205)
Qu Jiang	8	226	(221)
Qun Ying	11	44	(304)
Rab	8	27	(205)
Rabat	14	45	(370)†
Rabat	14	11	(366)
Rabigh Bay 1	2	53	(32)
Rabigh Bay 2	2	337	(51)
Rabigh Bay 3	2	318	(50)
Rabochaya Smena	9	6	(263)
Rachel Borchard	5	335	(131)†
Rachmanuel	8	312	(228)
Rachmanuel 1	8	193	(218)
Rachmanuel 2	8	193	(218)
Racisce	11	29	(302)
Radisson Diamond	20	420	(492)†
Radist Nesmenova	7	435	(188)
Radnes	5	222	(122)
Radnik	7	86	(163)
Radnor	8	24	(205)
Radnoti	8	154	(215)
Radomyshl	8	415	(235)
Radwah	2	430	(57)
Radzionkow	9	188	(278)†
Radzionkow	9	53	(267)
Ra Ees Ali	7	468	(191)
Rafael	7	51	(160)
Rafah	8	665	(256)†
Raffiu	8	531	(244)
Rafi Ahmed Kidwai	2	477	(60)
Rafik J	8	232	(221)
Rafio	2	257	(46)
Rafnes	5	222	(122)
Ragna Gorthon	17	98	(415)†
Ragna Gorthon	17	17	(406)
Railship 1	18	119	(430)
Rainbow	8	35	(206)
Rainbow Bridge	12	107	(333)
Rainbow Chaser	2	43	(31)
Rainbow Glory	8	199	(218)
Rainbow Hope	9	148	(274)
Rainbow Reefer	11	103	(308)
Rainbow Splendour	8	677	(257)†
Rainbow Splendour	8	250	(223)
Rainfrost	11	32	(303)
Rakhov	8	415	(235)
Rakvere	8	577	(247)
Rakvere	16	13	(392)
Rama	6	58	(145)
Rama	9	94	(270)
Rama J	2	109	(36)
Rambynas	11	220	(320)†
Ramita	8	232	(221)
Ramnes	5	229	(123)
Ranafjord	6	2	(141)
Rana M	6	69	(146)
Randi	5	265	(125)
Raneem I	20	310	(482)
Ranger	2	503	(62)
Ranger 1	8	418	(235)
Rangikura	7	379	(184)
Ranginui	7	308	(179)
Rangioara	7	321	(180)
Rangitane	7	308	(179)
Rangitata	7	330	(180)
Rangitikel	7	380	(184)
Rangitoto	7	308	(179)
Rankki	1	167	(14)
Rantum	2	87	(35)
Rapla	8	582	(248)
Rapoca	18	157	(433)
Raqefet	12	77	(330)
Rasa	8	367	(231)
Ras El Khaima	18	63	(426)
Raseltin	7	439	(189)
Ras-Halague	21	64	(504)
Rasha One	11	63	(305)
Rashidah	8	180	(217)
Ras Maersk	1	141	(12)
Rasmine Maersk	1	141	(12)
Ras Mohamed	16	28	(393)
Ratana Pailin	12	90	(331)
Rathcarra	1	3	(3)
Rathmoy	2	600	(72)†
Rathnew	2	493	(61)
Ratna Vandana	7	221	(172)
Ratno	8	415	(235)
Rattana Naree	8	649	(254)†
Rauk	6	58	(145)
Rauma	2	414	(56)
Rautz	5	323	(129)
Rava	1	3	(3)
Raven Arrow	10	43	(290)
Ravenna Bridge	18	177	(435)
Ravenscraig	5	122	(115)
Ravnanger	4	101	(94)
Ravni Kotari	8	445	(237)
Rawan I	17	40	(408)
Ray	2	323	(50)
Raya	2	325	(50)
Raychikhinsk	8	589	(248)
Razna	1	52	(6)
Rea	8	650	(254)†
Rebena	5	265	(125)
Reboucas	1	166	(13)
Recai B	7	186	(170)
Recife	7	484	(192)
Reda Allah	8	155	(215)
Red Dragon	3	49	(80)†
Redestos	8	502	(241)

	SHIP TYPE	REF NO	PAGE NO
Red Fotini	7	79	(162)
Red Ibis	2	516	(63)
Redo	2	135	(38)
Redonia	2	364	(53)
Red Rose	5	288	(127)
Red Seagull	2	577	(70)†
Red Stone	7	438	(189)
Red Teal	1	76	(8)
Redthorn	5	93	(113)
Red Tulip	5	288	(127)
Reduta Ordona	5	301	(128)
Reefer Ace	11	158	(312)
Reefer Cape	11	225	(320)†
Reefer Countess	11	86	(307)
Reefer Dolphin	11	227	(320)†
Reefer Empress	11	86	(307)
Reefer Fresh	11	201	(317)†
Reefer Jambu	11	209	(318)†
Reefer Jambu	11	119	(310)
Reefer No 1	11	64	(305)
Reefer No 2	11	65	(305)
Reefer No 3	11	65	(305)
Reefer No 5	11	188	(316)†
Reefer Penguin	11	71	(306)
Reef Island	9	100	(270)
Reef Star	8	8	(203)
Reem	11	131	(311)
Ref Lira	11	98	(308)
Ref Lira	11	101	(308)
Reforma	2	422	(57)
Ref Star	11	98	(308)
Ref Star	11	101	(308)
Ref Vega	11	98	(308)
Ref Vega	11	101	(308)
Regal Trader	5	145	(117)
Regal Voyager	20	320	(483)
Regent	8	291	(226)
Regent	9	134	(273)
Regent Isle	20	27	(461)
Regent Park	8	206	(219)
Regent Sea	20	252	(477)
Regent Spirit	20	38	(462)
Regina	15	103	(388)†
Regina	8	668	(256)†
Regina	5	147	(117)
Regina J	5	31	(109)
Regine	7	338	(181)
Rei Feng	8	341	(229)
Reifens	8	227	(221)
Reina Del Mar	8	529	(244)
Reine Astrid	20	84	(465)
Reksnes	10	104	(297)†
Reksnes	10	27	(289)
Relchem Arjun	2	298	(48)
Relchem Isha	4	66	(91)
Reliance Ocean	5	349	(133)†
Reliance Trader	7	125	(165)
Reliant	8	24	(205)
Remmer	15	28	(379)
Rena	5	351	(133)†
Renaissance Four	20	424	(492)†
Renate Schulte	13	11	(350)
Renessi	8	139	(213)
Reno	2	80	(34)
Repubblica Di Amalfi	17	117	(417)†
Repulse Bay	12	223	(345)†
Resa	7	483	(192)
Reshid Behbudov	7	340	(181)
Resolute	12	119	(334)
Resolution Bay	12	134	(335)
Rethimnon	20	326	(483)
Reunion	8	448	(238)
Reutov	8	415	(235)
Revolucion	2	422	(57)
Rex	8	271	(224)
Rex Friendship	5	297	(128)
Reykjafoss	7	304	(178)
Reynosa	4	37	(89)
Rezvaya	2	508	(62)
Rhein Feeder	14	61	(372)†
Rhein Feeder	14	6	(365)
Rheinfels	15	34	(380)
Rheingas	4	20	(88)
Rhein Merchant	14	40	(369)†
Rhein Trader	5	113	(115)
Rhenus	15	21	(379)
Rhin	2	48	(32)
Rhine Forest	21	97	(508)†
Rhine Forest	21	30	(501)
Rhine Ore	2	458	(59)
Rhine Trader	15	77	(385)†
Rhodos	2	587	(71)†
Rhodos	2	151	(39)
Rhone	2	47	(32)
Rhone	2	60	(33)
Rhone	10	43	(290)
Ribuan Jaya	21	34	(501)
Riccam	5	257	(125)
Richard C	15	21	(379)
Richard With	20	63	(463)
Rich Duchess	2	157	(39)
Rich Duke	2	157	(39)
Richfield	10	43	(290)
Rich Star	12	222	(345)†
Rich Star	14	22	(366)
Rickmers Brasil	8	412	(235)
Rickmers Dalian	9	91	(270)
Rickmers Shanghai	7	413	(187)
Rico	8	481	(240)
Rico Duckling	7	275	(176)
Rider B	9	92	(270)
Rifat	2	126	(37)
Rigel	8	255	(223)
Rigel A	2	314	(49)
Rigoletto	19	30	(447)
Riha Trader	8	522	(243)
Riha Transporter	8	522	(243)
Rijmond	7	322	(180)
Rijnborg	7	457	(190)
Rijnhaven	17	35	(408)
Rika	8	224	(221)
Rikhard Zorge	2	359	(52)
Rila	5	132	(116)
Rilos	9	92	(270)
Rima G	8	253	(223)
Rimba Empat	8	211	(219)
Rimnicu Vilcea	8	50	(207)
Rinjani	20	387	(487)
Rinos	9	110	(271)
Rio Atrato	8	387	(233)
Rio B	8	383	(232)
Rio Branco	5	186	(120)
Rio Chama	7	180	(169)
Rio Cuyamel	11	125	(310)
Rio Daule	11	152	(312)
Rio Express	9	171	(276)†
Rio Express	9	11	(264)
Rio Frio	11	53	(304)
Rio Gas	4	91	(93)
Rio Guayas	11	8	(301)
Riomar	8	663	(256)†
Rio Negro	5	186	(120)
Rio Pacuare	18	83	(427)
Rio Parana	11	10	(301)
Rio Truando	8	387	(233)
Rio Ulua	11	125	(310)
Rio Ulua	11	127	(310)
Rio Verde	5	216	(122)
Risanger	4	101	(94)
Rising Sun I	8	2	(203)
Risnes	5	222	(122)
Rita	9	110	(271)
Rita D'Amato	5	67	(112)
Rita Maersk	1	141	(12)
Riureni	8	140	(213)
Riveira	18	116	(430)
River Adada	8	439	(237)
River Andoni	8	388	(233)
River Asab	8	388	(233)
River Boyne	5	32	(109)
River Breeze	8	500	(241)
River Crystal	12	24	(326)
River Elegance	12	206	(343)†
River Embley	5	32	(109)
River Ikpan	8	388	(233)
River Lune	18	52	(425)
River Mada	8	388	(233)
River Maje	8	439	(237)
River Majidun	8	439	(237)
River Ogbese	8	439	(237)
River Oji	8	439	(237)
River Oli	8	439	(237)
River Plate	5	207	(121)
Riza	2	318	(50)
Rizcun Enterprise	8	24	(205)
Rizcun Trader	8	24	(205)
Rize K	8	17	(204)
Rizhskiy Zaliv	11	18	(302)
RMS Anglia	15	2	(377)
RMS Bavaria	15	2	(377)
RMS Francia	15	21	(379)
RMS Mercator	6	95	(150)†
RMS Mercator	6	22	(142)
RMS Scotia	15	2	(377)
RMS Westfalia	15	62	(383)†
Robela	2	65	(33)
Robert	2	58	(33)
Roberta d'Alesio	2	447	(58)
Robert E Lee	21	15	(500)
Robert M	2	365	(53)
Robert Maersk	1	141	(12)
Robin	11	82	(306)

†Photograph

	SHIP TYPE	REF NO	PAGE NO
Rocio Star	2	367	(53)
Roco	2	494	(61)
Rocon I	18	166	(434)
Rodanthi	8	16	(204)
Rodeio	1	166	(13)
Rodenbek	2	38	(31)
Rodina	5	17	(108)
Rodina	5	193	(120)
Rodlo	5	305	(128)
Rodona	18	192	(437)†
Rodopi	5	132	(116)
Rodos	20	283	(480)
Rodrigues Cabrilho	14	16	(366)
Roelof	6	115	(153)†
Roelof	6	65	(146)
Rogalin	20	220	(475)
Roger	15	8	(377)
Rognes	10	27	(289)
Rojarek Naree	7	271	(176)
Rojen	7	154	(168)
Rokiskis	8	619	(250)
Rokko San	2	338	(51)
Roland Essberger	1	55	(6)
Rolf D	6	41	(144)
Roline	18	189	(437)†
Rollcargo	18	45	(424)
Rollnes	5	9	(107)
Rolnik	5	133	(116)
Rolon Alcudia	18	156	(433)
Rolon Norte	18	145	(432)
Rolon Sur	18	145	(432)
Roma	15	31	(379)
Roman Arctic	11	99	(308)
Romanati	8	50	(207)
Roman Blizzard	11	99	(308)
Romance	8	517	(242)
Roman Cooler	11	99	(308)
Romandie	5	109	(115)
Roman Karmen	7	160	(168)
Romantica	20	10	(459)
Romashka	8	604	(249)
Rome	2	209	(43)
Romen Rollan	8	604	(249)
Romeo	6	65	(146)
Romilda	20	132	(469)
Romina	8	521	(243)
Romina G	2	327	(50)
Romios	8	181	(217)
Romito	2	174	(41)
Romny	8	415	(235)
Romo Maersk	1	141	(12)
Ron	5	159	(118)
Rong Cheng	7	406	(186)
Rong Da	6	2	(141)
Rong Hua Shan	8	496	(241)
Rong Jiang	8	383	(232)
Ronu Sala	11	11	(301)
Rook Carrier	12	55	(329)
Rook Mariner	8	308	(227)
Rook Trader	8	308	(227)
Ropazi	1	181	(15)
Rora Meru	18	83	(427)
Ro-Ro Runner	18	5	(421)
Ro-Ro Sentosa	18	166	(434)
Ros	7	265	(175)
Rosa Blanca	17	24	(407)
Rosali	5	386	(137)†
Rosali	10	33	(289)
Rosamagdalena	7	11	(157)
Rosana	8	262	(224)
Rosa Prima	9	64	(267)
Rosa Tucano	17	105	(416)†
Rosa Tucano	17	24	(407)
Rosayelena	10	20	(288)
Rose	9	49	(266)
Roseanne	18	196	(438)†
Rosebay	18	220	(441)†
Rosebay	18	58	(425)
Rosebud	1	16	(4)
Rose III	7	259	(175)
Rose Islands	8	383	(232)
Rosella	20	172	(471)
Rosellen	17	40	(408)
Rosen	7	354	(182)
Rose Stone	8	557	(246)
Rosethorn	6	40	(144)
Roshni	8	52	(207)
Rosina Topic	7	124	(165)
Rosita	7	204	(171)
Rosita Maria	6	2	(141)
Roslagen	20	193	(473)
Roslavl	8	415	(235)
Rossel Current	7	443	(189)
Rostock	20	192	(472)
Rostov	17	51	(409)
Rostov Na Donu	12	109	(333)
Rosy River	7	355	(182)
Rothnie	8	252	(223)
Rotterdam	20	374	(486)
Roubini	8	146	(214)
Rova	5	142	(117)
Rover	2	503	(62)
Rovinari	5	248	(124)
Rovno	17	51	(409)
Roxane Delmas	17	114	(417)†
Royal Arrow	1	34	(5)
Royal Clipper	5	51	(110)
Royal Klipper	11	190	(316)†
Royal Majesty	20	423	(492)†
Royal Odyssey	20	383	(487)
Royal Pilot	5	199	(121)
Royal Princess	20	82	(465)
Royal Reefer	11	31	(303)
Royal Star	20	448	(495)†
Royal Venture	7	271	(176)
Royal Viking Sun	20	442	(494)†
Royal Wing	20	163	(471)
Royksund	17	5	(405)
Roza Luksemburg	8	74	(209)
Roza Luxemburg	11	99	(308)
Roztocze	11	59	(305)
R P Cayman	11	8	(301)
R Peter M Elrick	10	14	(288)
RTC-1	2	118	(37)
Rua Ha	8	560	(246)
Ruamchai Lotus	8	217	(220)
Rubezhnoye	8	415	(235)
Rubies	8	262	(224)
Rubin Energy	5	216	(122)
Rubin Iris	7	120	(165)
Ruby	7	64	(161)
Ruby	15	28	(379)
Ruby C	7	271	(176)
Ruby Star	3	47	(80)†
Ruchi	8	27	(205)
Rudderman	1	184	(15)
Ruder Boskovic	7	166	(168)
Rudnyy	8	415	(235)
Ruen	5	239	(123)
Rufiji	2	527	(64)
Rugard	7	459	(190)
Rugen	7	480	(192)
Rugen	20	334	(483)
Ruhr Ore	2	280	(47)
Rukhulla Akhundov	1	70	(7)
Rumaila	2	411	(56)
Rumbula	2	414	(56)
Rundale	2	26	(30)
Rungholtsand	8	142	(214)
Runner B	9	92	(270)
Run Zhou	8	376	(232)
Run Zhou	8	480	(240)
Rupea	7	174	(169)
Rusalka II	6	110	(152)†
Rusalka II	6	35	(143)
Rushany	8	415	(235)
Rusne	8	239	(222)
Russ	20	128	(468)
Rusu Sala	11	11	(301)
Ruta	5	323	(129)
Ruth	5	94	(113)
Ruth Borchard	12	129	(334)
Ruthensand	7	475	(191)
Ruth M	2	385	(54)
Ruth W	15	89	(387)†
Ruvu	8	24	(205)
Ryazan	8	415	(235)
Rybinsk	8	415	(235)
Ryka	2	56	(32)
Ryndam	20	91	(466)
Ryong Gang	8	98	(210)
Ryshkany	8	415	(235)
Rystraum	2	31	(31)
Rzhev	8	415	(235)
Saaba	7	260	(175)
Saad	7	487	(193)†
Saad	7	461	(190)
Saadi	7	192	(170)
Saar Antwerp	15	30	(379)
Saar Berlin	15	34	(380)
Saar Breda	15	34	(380)
Saar Emden	15	30	(379)
Saar Genova	15	43	(380)
Saar Lisboa	15	30	(379)
Saar London	15	43	(380)
Saar Madrid	15	73	(385)†
Saar Madrid	15	30	(379)
Saar Rotterdam	15	30	(379)
Sabareni	8	50	(207)
Sabarimelai	1	169	(14)

†Photograph

	SHIP TYPE	REF NO	PAGE NO
Sabin	8	169	(216)
Sabine L	15	92	(387)†
Sabine L	15	8	(377)
Sabrina	20	4	(459)
Sacele	8	50	(207)
Sachem	2	366	(53)
Sachsen	12	115	(333)
Sac Malaga	5	271	(126)
Sadoun	8	92	(210)
Sadova	8	50	(207)
Sadriddin Ayni	7	152	(167)
Sae Byol	8	500	(241)
Saetta	2	469	(60)
Safad	6	7	(141)
Safar	8	503	(241)
Safari	20	361	(485)
Safe Star	8	383	(232)
Safi	14	46	(370)†
Safi	14	11	(366)
Safina-E-Ismail 2	8	330	(229)
Safina-E-Najjam	8	377	(232)
Saga Breeze	10	102	(297)†
Sagacity	5	323	(129)
Sagafjord	20	445	(495)†
Sagafjord	20	366	(486)
Sagaing	7	444	(189)
Saga Moon	18	106	(429)
Sagar	8	357	(230)
Sagitta	15	43	(380)
Sagittarius	5	87	(113)
Sahara	2	339	(51)
Sahara	2	340	(51)
S A Helderberg	12	25	(326)
Saida Star	8	203	(219)
Saigon 2	8	500	(241)
Saigon 3	8	383	(232)
Saigon I	8	500	(241)
Saikai Maru	5	203	(121)
Sai Kung	8	24	(205)
Saint Brevin	5	222	(122)
Saint Brice	5	222	(122)
Saint Constantinos	2	217	(43)
Saint Dimitrios	2	370	(53)
Saint John	8	276	(225)
Saint Killian II	20	83	(465)
Saint Lucia	2	475	(60)
Saint Nektarios	8	630	(251)
Saint Nicholas	2	432	(57)
Saint Patrick II	20	164	(471)
Saint Paulia	20	311	(482)
Saint Pierre	8	124	(212)
Saint Raphael II	2	488	(61)
Saint Roch	17	115	(417)†
Saint Spiridon	8	24	(205)
Saint Spiridonas	8	500	(241)
Saint Vassilios	1	259	(23)†
Saint Vassilios	1	18	(4)
Sairyu Maru No 2	2	185	(42)
Sajo	9	42	(266)
Sajo Dolphin	11	15	(301)
Sakhalin-1	20	345	(484)
Sakhalin-2	20	345	(484)
Sakhalin-3	20	345	(484)
Sakhalin-4	20	345	(484)
Sakhalin-5	20	345	(484)
Sakhalin-6	20	345	(484)
Sakhalin-7	20	345	(484)
Sakhalin-8	20	345	(484)
Sakhalin-9	20	345	(484)
Sakhalin-10	20	345	(484)
Sakhalinneft	2	414	(56)
Sakura	8	251	(223)
Sakura Reefer	11	69	(305)
Sala	1	103	(9)
Salah Aldeen	9	127	(272)
Salaj	9	6	(263)
Salam	8	115	(212)
Salama	7	130	(166)
Salama	7	388	(185)
Salama	7	420	(187)
Salamina	1	104	(9)
Salavat Yulayev	8	582	(248)
Saldus	8	596	(249)
Salem	8	232	(221)
Salem Five	9	6	(263)
Salem Flower	20	165	(471)
Salem Seven	8	586	(248)
Salem Six	8	586	(248)
Salem Ten	8	696	(260)†
Salem Two	9	75	(268)
Salif Bay	7	123	(165)
Salina	2	544	(65)†
Salina	8	196	(218)
Salindo Perdana I	8	420	(235)
Saliste	8	50	(207)
Sally Eurobridge	18	134	(431)

	SHIP TYPE	REF NO	PAGE NO
Sally Eurolink	18	52	(425)
Sally Euroroute	18	52	(425)
Sally Euroway	20	319	(482)
Sally I	2	347	(52)
Sally II	2	347	(52)
Sally Sky	20	338	(484)
Sally Star	20	186	(472)
Sally Stove	7	134	(166)
Salonta	8	50	(207)
Salta	8	537	(244)
Salva	5	132	(116)
Salvador 1	7	99	(163)
Salvador Express	7	409	(186)
Samaina	20	166	(471)
Samantha	14	1	(365)
Samargas	4	18	(88)
Samarkand	17	51	(409)
Samar Spirit	1	214	(17)
Samburga	2	26	(30)
Samco Europe	1	243	(21)†
Samed Vurgun	2	171	(41)
Samer	8	202	(219)
Samer I	8	513	(242)
Sam Hae	8	500	(241)
Sam Houston	21	15	(500)
Sami III	8	311	(228)
Samir	9	66	(268)
Samjohn Captain	5	100	(114)
Samjohn Light	5	56	(111)
Samjohn Mariner	5	169	(119)
Samjohn Spirit	5	56	(111)
Sammarina 1	7	174	(169)
Sammarina 2	7	174	(169)
Sammarina 3	7	174	(169)
Sammarina 4	7	174	(169)
Sammarina 5	7	174	(169)
Samos	7	428	(188)
Samos	8	445	(237)
Samos Reefer	11	48	(304)
Samothraki	1	160	(13)
Samotlor	2	26	(30)
Samra	8	169	(216)
Samrat Ashok	5	338	(131)†
Samrat Ashok	5	146	(117)
Samrat Rucaka	7	242	(174)
Samsara	5	328	(130)†
Samsara	5	145	(117)
Samson	5	346	(132)†
Samsun	7	425	(188)
Samsun	20	113	(467)
Samsun Atraxia	7	271	(176)
Samsun Booster	8	128	(213)
Samsun Dolphin	9	155	(274)
Samsun Earnest	7	155	(168)
Samsun Honour	8	270	(224)
Samsun Partner	8	214	(220)
Samsun Trust	8	134	(213)
Samudra Rani	9	159	(275)
Samudra Samrat	9	159	(275)
Samuel Ginn	1	225	(19)†
San Antonio	2	36	(31)
San Antonio	13	35	(351)
San Benedetto	11	177	(314)
San Carlos	1	105	(9)
San Clemente	13	35	(351)
Sandefjord	20	214	(474)
Sandgrouse	2	51	(32)
San Diego	7	247	(174)
Sand Swan	8	220	(220)
Sandvik	7	11	(157)
Sandy Pride	8	416	(235)
Sandy Pride	9	92	(270)
Sanem	8	215	(220)
San Evans	8	26	(205)
San Felice	5	297	(128)
San Giorgio	2	12	(29)
San Giovanni	1	174	(14)
Sang Thai Honor	9	68	(268)
Sang Thai Neptune	7	220	(172)
Sang Thai Power	8	214	(220)
Sang Thai Quartz	8	369	(231)
Sanguity	6	25	(143)
San Hsieh 303	11	16	(302)
San Isidro	13	35	(351)
San John I	8	149	(214)
San Juan	9	122	(272)
Sanko Emerald	7	210	(172)
Sanko Express	2	168	(40)
Sanko Heron	2	179	(41)
Sanko Hope	2	181	(41)
Sanko Humanity	7	155	(168)
Sanko Laurel	7	207	(171)
Sanko Moon	7	125	(165)
Sanko Peace	7	212	(172)
Sanko Poppy	7	207	(171)
Sanko South	7	125	(165)

†Photograph

	SHIP TYPE	REF NO	PAGE NO
Sanko Spruce	7	207	(171)
San Lorenzo	13	35	(351)
San Marcos	19	26	(447)
San Marino	1	174	(14)
San Marino	13	11	(350)
Sanmar Pioneer	7	135	(166)
San Mateo	1	174	(14)
San Miguel	13	117	(360)†
San Miguel	13	11	(350)
San Nicolas	1	180	(14)
San Pedro	1	174	(14)
San Sebastian	2	173	(41)
San Sebastian	8	24	(205)
Santa Barbara	2	431	(57)
Santa Catherine	20	323	(483)
Santa Clara	4	91	(93)
Santa Cruz de Tenerife	20	209	(474)
Santa Esmeralda	2	432	(57)
Santa Fe	7	399	(186)
Santa Helena	7	17	(158)
Santa Maria	7	17	(158)
Santa Marta	17	34	(407)
Santanita	8	637	(252)
Santa Rita	2	426	(57)
Santa Rita I	9	20	(264)
Santa Rosa de Lima	9	20	(264)
Santiago	8	307	(227)
Santiago de Cuba	9	28	(265)
Santista	11	25	(302)
Santong	3	73	(83)†
Santorini I	7	397	(186)
Santorini Rex	11	75	(306)
Santos	13	28	(351)
San Vicente	13	35	(351)
Sanwa	19	87	(455)†
Saona	8	471	(239)
Sapai	7	370	(184)
Sapanca	8	137	(213)
Sapphire	8	232	(221)
Sapphire Highway	19	41	(449)†
Sapphire Seas	20	102	(466)
Sapphire Star	8	358	(230)
'Sapphire Star'	8	322	(228)
'Sapphire Star'	8	356	(230)
Sappho	20	32	(461)
Sara 3	10	30	(289)
Saraband	2	327	(50)
Sarah	5	81	(112)
Sarah	5	295	(127)
Sarah Rousing	15	58	(383)†
Sara II	8	458	(238)
Sara Junior	8	105	(211)
Saramati	11	75	(306)
Sarata	7	375	(184)
Sara Theresa	2	521	(63)
Saratovsk	8	339	(229)
S Araz	8	276	(225)
Sardegna	18	174	(435)
Sardegna Bella	20	312	(482)
Sardinia Nova	20	362	(486)
Sardinia Vera	20	84	(465)
Sargasso	3	63	(82)†
Sari	8	204	(219)
Saribay	2	58	(33)
Sarinderjit	8	418	(235)
Sarine 2	7	348	(182)
Sarita	1	213	(17)
Sarny	7	136	(166)
Sarojini Naidu	2	508	(62)
Saronic Pride	11	208	(318)†
Sarunta 1	8	216	(220)
S A Sederberg	12	25	(326)
Sasha Borodulin	8	621	(251)
Sasha Kondratyev	8	621	(251)
Sasha Kotov	8	621	(251)
Saskatchewan Pioneer	5	85	(113)
Satsuma	1	215	(18)†
Sattam	17	19	(406)
Satucket	2	351	(52)
Satu Mare	7	174	(169)
Saturn	5	66	(111)
Saturnus	20	286	(480)
Saturn V	5	347	(132)†
Saudi Abha	16	31	(393)
Saudi Diriyah	16	66	(397)†
Saudi Diriyah	16	31	(393)
Saudi Glory	2	315	(49)
Saudi Hail	16	8	(391)
Saudi Hofuf	16	31	(393)
Saudi Makkah	16	11	(392)
Saudi Qassim	16	69	(398)†
Saudi Qassim	16	8	(391)
Saudi Riyadh	16	11	(392)
Saudi Splendour	2	315	(49)
Saudi Tabuk	16	31	(393)
Sauniere	10	55	(291)

	SHIP TYPE	REF NO	PAGE NO
Sava	7	177	(169)
Sava	8	197	(218)
Savannah	7	247	(174)
Savannah I	8	24	(205)
Saveni	8	50	(207)
Savinesti	8	50	(207)
Savonetta	4	131	(96)
Sawaminee	8	543	(245)
Sawat	7	413	(187)
S A Waterberg	12	25	(326)
S A Winterberg	12	25	(326)
Saxon Star	11	56	(305)
Saymenskiy Kanal	15	12	(378)
Scamper	11	195	(316)†
Scamper	11	23	(302)
Scandinavian Dawn	20	85	(465)
Scandinavian Express	8	383	(232)
Scania	20	167	(471)
Scarab	9	22	(264)
Scarlet Success	7	531	(198)†
Scenery Sea	5	216	(122)
SCF Vladimir	2	337	(51)
Schackenborg	17	47	(409)
Scheldeborg	7	457	(190)
Schulau	14	66	(372)†
Schulau	6	2	(141)
Schwyz	7	241	(174)
Scirocco Universal	11	96	(308)
Scorff	11	159	(312)
Scorpio	15	85	(386)†
Scorpione	2	305	(49)
Scorpius	5	66	(111)
Scotfield	6	128	(154)†
Scotfield	6	23	(142)
Scotia	6	87	(149)†
Scotia	6	24	(143)
Scotia Prince	20	48	(462)
Scotland	1	98	(9)
Scottish Star	11	27	(302)
Scot Trader	6	36	(144)
'SD14' type	8	477	(239)
'SD14' type	8	500	(241)
'SD14' type	8	538	(244)
Sea Adventure	13	56	(353)
Sea Angel	1	12	(4)
Sea Angel	7	209	(171)
Sea Arctica	13	22	(350)
Sea Atalanti I	9	151	(274)
Sea Baron	7	146	(167)
Sea Beach	18	83	(427)
Seabee I	5	169	(119)
Sea Bells	8	36	(206)
Sea Bird	7	476	(191)
Seaboard Caribe	18	166	(434)
Seaboard Express	18	95	(428)
Seaboard Express	18	101	(429)
Seaboard Florida	17	28	(407)
Seaboard Intrepid	18	95	(428)
Seaboard Intrepid	18	101	(429)
Seaboard Ocean	18	166	(434)
Seaboard Star	17	69	(411)†
Seaboard Star	17	28	(407)
Seaboard Sun	18	166	(434)
Seaboard Trader	18	69	(426)
Seaboard Universe	18	166	(434)
Seaboard Venture	18	206	(439)†
Seaboard Voyager	16	70	(398)†
Seaboard Voyager	16	9	(391)
Seabourn Legend	20	443	(495)†
Seabourn Legend	20	210	(474)
Seabourn Pride	20	210	(474)
Seabourn Spirit	20	449	(495)†
Seabourn Spirit	20	210	(474)
Sea Boyne	6	73	(148)†
Sea Boyne	6	66	(146)
Seabravery	2	427	(57)
Sea Breaker	7	225	(173)
Seabreeze I	20	458	(496)†
Seabreeze One	7	226	(173)
Sea Brilliance	7	210	(172)
Sea Bros	8	214	(220)
Seacaptain	2	431	(57)
Sea Castle	1	88	(8)
Sea Champ	8	24	(205)
Sea Clipper	5	356	(134)†
Sea Commerce	13	52	(353)
Sea Concert	7	239	(174)
Sea Container	14	60	(371)†
Sea Container	14	7	(365)
Seacross	2	553	(67)†
Seacrown	2	498	(62)
Sea Crown	7	203	(171)
Seadancer	2	385	(54)
Sea Destiny	8	149	(214)
Sea Diamond	8	36	(206)
Sea Diamond H	9	114	(271)

†Photograph

	SHIP TYPE	REF NO	PAGE NO
Sea Dominance	12	99	(332)
Sea Dragon	17	34	(407)
Seadrive	5	301	(128)
Seadrive	7	195	(170)
Seaeagle	5	103	(114)
Sea Empress	10	49	(290)
Sea Ems	15	13	(378)
Sea Energy	8	17	(204)
Seaexplorer	2	395	(55)
Sea Express	8	577	(247)
Sea Express	13	4	(349)
Seaexpress II	2	234	(44)
Sea Fan	8	36	(206)
Sea Faye	9	129	(272)
Sea Flower	8	374	(232)
Seaford	2	378	(54)
Seafortune	2	432	(57)
Sea Fortune	8	36	(206)
Seafrance Renoir	20	257	(478)
Sea Gallant	10	5	(287)
Sea Glory	10	79	(294)†
Sea Glory	10	6	(287)
Sea Goddess 1	20	230	(476)
Sea Goddess II	20	230	(476)
Seagrace II	5	138	(117)
Sea Grapes	8	536	(244)
Seaguardian	7	24	(158)
Seagull Fortune	8	34	(206)
Sea Harvest	7	440	(189)
Sea Hawk 1	8	494	(240)
Seahope II	7	41	(160)
Sea Horse	1	8	(3)
Sea Horse	7	40	(159)
Sea Horse	8	116	(212)
Seahorse 1	21	104	(509)†
Seahorse 1	21	12	(500)
Seahorse G	7	60	(161)
Sea Initiative	12	14	(326)
Sea Jade	8	36	(206)
Sea King	7	240	(174)
Seakittie	8	466	(239)
Sea Lady I	8	443	(237)
Sea-Land Anchorage	12	12	(326)
Sea-Land Challenger	12	131	(335)
Sea-Land Colombia	13	38	(352)
Sea-Land Consumer	12	86	(331)
Sea-Land Costa Rica	13	119	(360)†
Sea-Land Costa Rica	13	24	(350)
Sea-Land Crusader	12	131	(335)
Sea-Land Defender	12	16	(326)
Sea-Land Developer	12	16	(326)
Sea-Land Discovery	12	131	(335)
Sea-Land Endurance	12	16	(326)
Sea-Land Enterprise	12	3	(325)
Sea-Land Expedition	12	2	(325)
Sea-Land Explorer	12	16	(326)
Sea-Land Express	12	16	(326)
Sea-Land Freedom	12	16	(326)
Sea-Land Guatemala	13	24	(350)
Sea-Land Hawaii	12	2	(325)
Sea-Land Honduras	13	24	(350)
Sea-Land Independence	12	16	(326)
Sea-Land Innovator	12	16	(326)
Sea-Land Kodiak	12	12	(326)
Sea-Land Liberator	12	16	(326)
Sea-Land Mariner	12	16	(326)
Sea-Land Navigator	12	3	(325)
Sea-Land Pacer	13	56	(353)
Sea-Land Pacific	12	3	(325)
Sea-Land Patriot	12	16	(326)
Sea-Land Producer	12	86	(331)
Sea-Land Reliance	21	15	(500)
Sea-Land Spirit	21	15	(500)
Sea-Land Tacoma	12	12	(326)
Sea-Land Trader	12	3	(325)
Sea-Land Voyager	12	16	(326)
Sea Lantern	8	46	(207)
Sea Laurel	7	363	(183)
Seal Coral	7	125	(165)
Sea Leader	13	56	(353)
Sealift	16	24	(393)
Sealion	2	506	(62)
Sea Lion I	9	124	(272)
Seal Madagascar	7	286	(177)
Seal Mauritius	7	286	(177)
Sealord	2	537	(65)†
Sealord	2	447	(58)
Sea Lord	5	20	(108)
Seal Reunion	7	286	(177)
Sea Magula	15	60	(383)†
Sea Mariner	7	209	(171)
Seamaster	2	258	(46)
Sea Melody	8	300	(227)
Sea Merchant	13	52	(353)
Seamerit	2	253	(45)
Sea Mist	14	7	(365)
Sea Mist II	17	62	(410)
Sea Monarch	7	181	(169)
Seanav I	7	447	(189)
Sea Nordic	13	38	(352)
Sea Novia	13	10	(349)
Seaoath	2	552	(66)†
Sea Olivia	13	10	(349)
Sea Orade	15	1	(377)
Sea Pearl	10	72	(293)†
Sea Pearl	8	448	(238)
Sea Pearl	10	37	(289)
Seapearl II	7	74	(162)
Sea Phoenix	7	122	(165)
Sea Pioneer	13	56	(353)
Sea Plenty No 1	11	46	(304)
Sea Pride	19	33	(448)†
Sea Prince	1	95	(9)
Sea Princess	2	487	(61)
Sea Princess	9	34	(265)
Sea Progress	12	14	(326)
Seapromise	2	253	(45)
Seaqueen	5	95	(114)
Seaqueen III	5	55	(111)
Searadiance	5	185	(120)
Searaider	2	110	(36)
Sea Rainbow	7	210	(172)
Sea Ranger	12	139	(335)
Sea Regina	7	333	(181)
Sea Rhone	15	72	(385)†
Searider	7	24	(158)
Sea Ripple	7	202	(171)
Sea Road	18	14	(422)
Sea Rose	7	212	(172)
Sea Rover	6	69	(146)
Sea Salvia	2	497	(62)
Sea Serenade	20	196	(473)
Sea Sky	5	194	(120)
Seasong	7	54	(160)
Sea Sonnet	7	403	(186)
Sea Sparkle	7	202	(171)
Sea Spirit	7	15	(158)
Sea Star	8	24	(205)
Seastar II	7	181	(169)
Sea Swan	21	60	(504)
Sea Swift	7	202	(171)
Sea Swift	21	60	(504)
Sea Teal	21	60	(504)
Sea Tern	21	85	(507)†
Sea Tern	21	60	(504)
Sea Trade	13	52	(353)
Sea Trader	7	313	(179)
Sea Tradition	8	295	(226)
Seatra Express	8	21	(204)
Sea Tramp	5	289	(127)
Seatran Silvia	8	214	(220)
Sea Transit	19	25	(446)
Sea Tyne	15	21	(379)
Sea Union	5	149	(117)
Sea Venture	6	58	(145)
Seavenus	7	184	(170)
Sea Venus	19	12	(446)
Seavic Reefer	11	206	(318)†
Sea Wave	6	121	(154)†
Sea Wave	6	58	(145)
Sea Wave	13	30	(351)
Seaways	8	343	(229)
Sea Weed	2	508	(62)
Sea Weser	15	27	(379)
Sea Wind	1	64	(7)
Sea Wind	13	30	(351)
Sea Wind II	18	226	(441)†
Seawind II	2	140	(38)
Seawing	20	411	(491)†
Seawing	20	265	(478)
Sea Wolf	17	111	(417)†
Sebastian Lerdo de Tejada	2	450	(59)
Sebes	8	50	(207)
Sebu	1	103	(9)
Secil Angola	13	25	(351)
Secil Dinamarca	8	369	(231)
Secil Namibia	9	190	(278)†
Secil Namibia	9	118	(272)
Seda	9	9	(263)
Sedat Erkol	7	36	(159)
Sedoy	5	129	(116)
Seebrise	5	256	(125)
Seg	6	109	(152)†
Seg	6	20	(142)
Seicredit	16	1	(391)
Seiko Maru	2	581	(70)†
Seimeni	8	50	(207)
Seinehaven	5	84	(113)
Sekino V	11	93	(307)
Selat Mas	8	311	(228)
Selderi	11	102	(308)
Selectivity	6	84	(149)†

†Photograph

	SHIP TYPE	REF NO	PAGE NO
Selectivity	6	25	(143)
Selendang Baiduru	2	359	(52)
Selendang Delima	1	34	(5)
Selendang Sutera	1	34	(5)
Selenga	8	612	(250)
Selesa Maju	8	148	(214)
Selma Kosan	4	22	(88)
Selnes	5	9	(107)
Senator	18	126	(431)
Senei Maru	14	28	(367)
Senicoli Sierra	8	152	(214)
Seniority	5	344	(132)†
Senior M	8	310	(227)
Sensation	20	297	(481)
Senshu Maru	3	9	(75)
Sentinel	1	17	(4)
Sentinel II	5	234	(123)
Sentosa	8	53	(207)
Sentosa	8	466	(239)
Sentosa	9	39	(265)
Sentosa Jaya	6	2	(141)
Senya	8	401	(234)
Seorax	5	202	(121)
Serafin Topic	7	124	(165)
Seram	7	225	(173)
Seraya Jaya	16	42	(394)
Serdika	18	79	(427)
Serebryansk	7	136	(166)
Serenade	5	274	(126)
Serenade	8	221	(220)
Serenagas	4	119	(95)
Serenity	2	252	(45)
Serenity	7	286	(177)
Sereno	2	281	(47)
Sergey Buryachek	7	269	(176)
Sergey Eyzenshtein	8	105	(211)
Sergey Gritsevets	7	340	(181)
Sergey Gusev	9	57	(267)
Sergey Lazo	11	170	(313)
Sergey Smirnov	7	152	(167)
Sergey Vasilyev	8	105	(211)
Sergo Zakariadze	5	129	(116)
Sericata	1	144	(12)
Serife	7	213	(172)
Serifos	8	100	(211)
Serifos	11	4	(301)
Sernovodsk	7	375	(184)
Serov	7	136	(166)
Sersou	7	182	(169)
Sesam	15	8	(377)
Sestroretsk	14	10	(365)
Setco Gajah Mada	2	515	(63)
Setco Mammoth	2	515	(63)
Setif II	7	102	(164)
Setsuyo Maru	5	40	(110)
Sevan	7	136	(166)
Sevastaki	8	161	(215)
Seven Log Master	8	242	(222)
Seven Ocean	7	207	(171)
Seven Seas Beacon	12	26	(327)
Severn	8	500	(241)
Severodonetsk	7	136	(166)
Severyanin	2	279	(47)
Sevilla	5	61	(111)
Sevilla Wave	7	156	(168)
Sextum	12	57	(329)
Sezela	9	139	(273)
SGC Macedonia	2	388	(54)
SGC Seawind	5	134	(116)
Shabonee	2	366	(53)
Shadowdance	2	489	(61)
Shadrinsk	8	589	(248)
Shahamah	3	16	(76)
Sha He	13	74	(355)†
Sha He	13	32	(351)
Sha He Kou	21	91	(507)†
Sha He Kou	21	6	(499)
Shaher M	9	9	(263)
Shahpur	8	17	(204)
Shamhor	1	70	(7)
Shane	5	182	(120)
Shang Cheng	13	17	(350)
Shanghai Express	12	115	(333)
Shan He	12	208	(343)†
Shannon	8	24	(205)
Shantar	16	13	(392)
Shao Shan	8	452	(238)
Sharaf Alddin	8	174	(216)
Sharda	2	192	(42)
Shatura	8	589	(248)
Shawnee	1	7	(3)
Shearwater	15	61	(383)†
Sheksnales	8	596	(249)
Sheldon Lykes	12	120	(334)
Shemakha	2	504	(62)
Shen Da	8	550	(245)

	SHIP TYPE	REF NO	PAGE NO
Sheng Cai	8	393	(233)
Shengda	15	47	(381)
Sheng Kai	8	638	(252)
Sheng Mao	8	638	(252)
Sheng Rong	9	59	(267)
Sheng Yuan	8	332	(229)
Shenzhen Bay	12	221	(345)†
Shereen A	8	202	(219)
Sheryn M	12	124	(334)
Shevrell	6	40	(144)
Shibumi	2	468	(60)
Shi Hui	5	121	(115)
Shinano Reefer	11	215	(319)†
Shin-Hoh	5	223	(122)
Shinka Maru	18	102	(429)
Shinoussa	1	160	(13)
Shinrei	5	210	(121)
Shin Sakura Maru	20	39	(462)
Shinshima	7	271	(176)
Shin Yang	2	36	(31)
Shipka	5	132	(116)
Shiraz	2	89	(35)
Shirley	2	385	(54)
Shirley Lykes	8	48	(207)
Shirvan	7	340	(181)
Shiryu Maru	18	31	(423)
Shi Tang Hai	5	157	(118)
Shi Zui Shan	8	308	(227)
Shkval	11	153	(312)
Shoko	2	277	(47)
Short Sea Trader	15	14	(378)
Shotoku Maru	5	96	(114)
Shou Chang Hai	7	110	(164)
Shou Guang Hai	7	110	(164)
Shou Ning Hai	7	110	(164)
Shou Shan	8	546	(245)
Shoveller	8	372	(232)
Shui Cheng	8	667	(256)†
Shun An	8	446	(237)
Shun-Ei	8	639	(253)†
Shun Ping	7	322	(180)
Shun Yi	8	383	(232)
Shun Zhi	8	53	(207)
Shura Kober	8	621	(251)
Shushenskoye	8	619	(250)
Shuttle Ace	18	1	(421)
Shuya	2	380	(54)
Shu Yu Quan	8	606	(249)
Shyamlee	6	17	(142)
Siam	1	103	(9)
Siam Bay	7	362	(183)
Sian	6	119	(153)†
Siarkopol	1	196	(16)
Siauliai	18	20	(422)
Siba	8	330	(229)
Siba Brescia	21	111	(510)†
Siba Geru	21	113	(510)†
Sibarde	1	30	(5)
Sibirles	8	612	(250)
'Sibirles' class	8	106	(211)
Sibirskiy 2101	15	40	(380)
Sibirskiy 2102	15	40	(380)
Sibirskiy 2103	15	40	(380)
Sibirskiy 2104	15	40	(380)
Sibirskiy 2106	15	40	(380)
Sibirskiy 2108	15	40	(380)
Sibirskiy 2109	15	40	(380)
Sibirskiy 2110	15	16	(378)
Sibirskiy 2111	15	16	(378)
Sibirskiy 2112	15	16	(378)
Sibirskiy 2113	15	16	(378)
Sibirskiy 2114	15	16	(378)
Sibirskiy 2115	15	16	(378)
Sibirskiy 2116	15	16	(378)
Sibirskiy 2117	15	16	(378)
Sibirskiy 2118	15	16	(378)
Sibirskiy 2119	15	16	(378)
Sibirskiy 2123	15	40	(380)
Sibirskiy 2124	15	40	(380)
Sibirskiy 2125	15	40	(380)
Sibirskiy 2128	15	40	(380)
Sibirskiy 2129	15	40	(380)
Sibirskiy 2130	15	16	(378)
Sibirskiy 2131	15	16	(378)
Sibirskiy 2132	15	16	(378)
Sibirskiy 2133	15	16	(378)
Sibirtsyevo	8	612	(250)
Sibiu	8	76	(209)
Sicilia	18	174	(435)
Siderpollux	5	359	(134)†
Sidor Kovpak	9	80	(269)
Siegfried Lehmann	6	2	(141)
Siemiatycze	9	53	(267)
Sienna	1	242	(21)†
Sieradz	10	11	(287)
Sierra Aracena	11	41	(303)

†Photograph

	SHIP TYPE	REF NO	PAGE NO
Sierra Aralar	11	41	(303)
Sierra Express	12	118	(334)
Sierra Grana	11	50	(304)
Sierra Granera	11	50	(304)
Sierra Gredos	11	50	(304)
Sierra Guadarrama	11	50	(304)
Sierra Guadelupe	11	50	(304)
Sigal	5	97	(114)
Siggen II	6	66	(146)
Sigma	8	216	(220)
Sigmund Jahn	8	446	(237)
Sigulda	8	577	(247)
Sigyn	18	111	(430)
Silba	2	443	(58)
Silesia	20	242	(476)
Silina	2	433	(57)
Silja Europa	20	86	(465)
Silja Festival	20	50	(463)
Silja Scandinavia	20	87	(465)
Silja Serenade	20	88	(465)
Silja Symphony	20	88	(465)
Silke	6	24	(143)
Siluet	2	367	(53)
Silvera	2	433	(57)
Silver Chariot	7	446	(189)
Silver Coral	3	48	(80)†
Silver Dignity	5	72	(112)
Silver Eagle	2	337	(51)
Silver Feng	8	686	(258)†
Silverfjord	7	455	(190)
Silver Glory	7	446	(189)
Silver Hope 1	19	16	(446)
Silver Iris	2	497	(62)
Silver Kris	8	500	(241)
Silver Pride	3	84	(84)†
Silver Ray	19	5	(445)
Silver Star I	4	114	(95)
Silverthorn	6	40	(144)
Silver Wind	20	430	(493)†
Silver Ying	7	323	(180)
Silver Yu	7	505	(195)†
Silver Yu	7	141	(166)
Silvia	15	64	(384)†
Silvia	6	36	(144)
Simeon Ch	5	297	(128)
Simeon Th	8	388	(233)
Sim Forny	17	62	(410)
Simone	15	22	(379)
Sina	7	481	(192)
Sincere Apollo	7	241	(174)
Sincere Oceanus	7	241	(174)
Sincere Splendor	7	271	(176)
Sindbad	15	8	(377)
Sindibad I	20	165	(471)
Sinegorsk	7	14	(158)
Sinfa	8	500	(241)
Singa Gold	8	217	(220)
Singang	8	408	(234)
Singapore Ace	5	211	(122)
Singapore Express	16	45	(395)†
Singapore Express	16	11	(392)
Singa Saga	7	62	(161)
Singa Sky	7	60	(161)
Singa Star	2	277	(47)
Singa Sun	7	62	(161)
Singa Wilriver	2	378	(54)
Singolarita	9	65	(267)
Sin Loong	7	137	(166)
Sino Credit	10	16	(288)
Sin Tong	9	113	(271)
Sio	7	460	(190)
Sioux	2	59	(33)
Si Qi	7	422	(187)
Sir Charles Parsons	5	74	(112)
Sirena	5	175	(119)
Sirene	2	416	(56)
Sirens	9	92	(270)
Sirimau	20	388	(488)
Sirio	18	38	(424)
Sirius	8	74	(209)
Sirius	8	255	(223)
Sirius Gas	3	60	(81)†
Sirius Gas	3	23	(76)
Sir John	2	307	(49)
Sirt	8	659	(255)†
Sirt	7	460	(190)
Sitacamilla	1	156	(13)
Sitakatrine	1	200	(16)
Sitalene	1	200	(16)
Sitalouise	1	200	(16)
Sitamarie	1	156	(13)
Sitaxa	2	395	(55)
Sittwe	8	515	(242)
Skagern	7	305	(178)
Skalistyy Bereg	11	99	(308)
Skanderborg	17	47	(409)

	SHIP TYPE	REF NO	PAGE NO
Skater	11	28	(302)
Skaubay	2	531	(64)
Skaubryn	18	114	(430)
Skaufjord	2	534	(64)
Skaugran	18	114	(430)
Skenderbeg	8	317	(228)
Skier	11	28	(302)
Skikda	2	469	(60)
Skipper	20	168	(471)
S K Junior	5	158	(118)
Skodsborg	17	100	(415)†
Skodsborg	17	47	(409)
Skogafoss	7	304	(178)
Skopelos	2	290	(48)
Skopelos	7	428	(188)
Skopelos	20	109	(467)
Skradin	8	137	(213)
Skrim	2	303	(49)
Skriveri	11	102	(308)
SKS Banner	1	101	(9)
SKS Breeze	1	101	(9)
SKS Challenger	1	101	(9)
SKS Champion	1	101	(9)
SKS Endurance	1	101	(9)
SKS Horizon	1	101	(9)
SKS Spirit	1	101	(9)
SKS Star	1	101	(9)
SKS Trader	1	101	(9)
SKS Trust	1	101	(9)
Skulptor Golubkina	16	14	(392)
Skulptors Tomskis	11	55	(304)
Sky Bird	10	21	(288)
Sky Moon	8	263	(224)
Sky One	8	552	(245)
Sky River	12	41	(328)
Skyros	7	428	(188)
Sky Trader	2	461	(59)
Sky Wind	5	75	(112)
Slanic	8	50	(207)
Slano	21	18	(500)
Slapy	8	136	(213)
Slautnoye	7	375	(184)
Slavianka	5	132	(116)
Slavija 1	20	363	(486)
Slavonija	7	443	(189)
Slavyanka	11	232	(321)†
Slavyansk	7	136	(166)
Slobozia	8	148	(214)
Sloman Challenger	7	465	(190)
Sloman Champion	7	465	(190)
Sloman Commander	7	465	(190)
Sloman Ranger	17	95	(415)†
Sloman Ranger	17	40	(408)
Sloman Record	17	40	(408)
Sloman Regent	17	40	(408)
Sloman Rider	17	40	(408)
Sloman Rover	17	40	(408)
Sloman Runner	17	40	(408)
Slovenija	9	110	(271)
Slurry Express	5	219	(122)
Smaragden	5	113	(115)
Smirdan	8	50	(207)
Smolensk	16	29	(393)
S M Spiridon	2	123	(37)
S M Spiridon	5	126	(116)
Smyril	20	359	(485)
Smyrni	8	521	(243)
Snagov	8	50	(207)
SNAM Elba	4	74	(92)
SNAM Palmaria	4	74	(92)
Snezhnogorsk	7	375	(184)
Snow Bird	7	418	(187)
Snowbird	8	562	(246)
Snow Cape	11	21	(302)
Snow Crystal	11	21	(302)
Snow Delta	11	21	(302)
Snowdon	3	58	(81)†
Snow Drift	11	21	(302)
Snow Flower	11	21	(302)
Soanka	8	101	(211)
Soarer Adonis	7	241	(174)
Soarer Bellona	7	203	(171)
Soarer Zen	7	241	(174)
Sochi	7	136	(166)
Sociality	6	25	(143)
Socrates	8	500	(241)
Sofala	7	220	(172)
Sofia	8	612	(250)
Sofia	18	157	(433)
Sofiya Perovskaya	8	619	(250)
Sofiysk	7	375	(184)
Sokna	6	75	(148)†
Sokna	6	46	(144)
Sokol	9	80	(269)
Sokolica	2	408	(56)
Sokolniki	1	138	(12)

†Photograph

	SHIP TYPE	REF NO	PAGE NO
Sol	5	117	(115)
Solar	2	269	(46)
Solar	5	265	(125)
Solara	8	198	(218)
Solar Bay	6	17	(142)
Solar Glory	8	26	(205)
Solaris	1	144	(12)
Solar Wing	19	70	(452)†
Solbulk	7	82	(162)
Solca	8	50	(207)
Soldrott	7	276	(176)
Solidarnosc	5	110	(115)
Solidor 2	20	313	(482)
Solid Sun	8	308	(227)
Solin	7	483	(192)
Solnechnyy	2	367	(53)
Solnechnyy Bereg	11	100	(308)
Sologne	2	318	(50)
Solombala	8	581	(248)
Solon of Athens	5	19	(108)
Solon Turman	8	48	(207)
Solta	7	261	(175)
Sombeke	4	98	(94)
Somerset	2	262	(46)
Somers Isles	6	79	(148)†
Somers Isles	6	62	(146)
Sommen	7	305	(178)
Sompa	9	57	(267)
Sonata 1	2	489	(61)
Son Ca	8	612	(250)
Sondra	9	102	(270)
Song Cheng	13	17	(350)
Song Da 2	8	577	(247)
Song Day	8	420	(235)
Song Duong	8	383	(232)
Song He	12	89	(331)
Songlin	8	547	(245)
Song Nhue	8	327	(228)
Song of America	20	384	(487)
Song of Norway	20	385	(487)
Song Rim	8	17	(204)
Song Sai Gon	8	282	(225)
Song San	8	564	(246)
Song Shan	8	438	(237)
Song Thao	8	590	(248)
Song Thuong	8	420	(235)
Sonia	1	11	(3)
Sonia	7	373	(184)
Sonia G	8	301	(227)
Sonic Youth	7	23	(158)
Sonita	8	182	(217)
Sonja B	15	43	(380)
Sonora	12	59	(329)
Soo Geun Ho	8	243	(222)
Sopal 1	7	71	(161)
Sophie C	7	170	(169)
Soren Toubro	7	172	(169)
'Sormovskiy' type	15	38	(380)
Sormovskiy-3048	15	18	(378)
Sormovskiy-3049	15	18	(378)
Sormovskiy-3050	15	18	(378)
Sormovskiy-3051	15	18	(378)
Sormovskiy-3052	15	18	(378)
Sormovskiy-3053	15	18	(378)
Sormovskiy-3054	15	18	(378)
Sormovskiy-3055	15	18	(378)
Sormovskiy-3056	15	18	(378)
Sormovskiy-3057	15	18	(378)
Sormovskiy 3058	15	18	(378)
Sormovskiy-3058	15	18	(378)
Sormovskiy-3060	15	18	(378)
Sormovskiy-3063	15	15	(378)
Sormovskiy-3064	15	15	(378)
Sormovskiy-3066	15	15	(378)
Sormovskiy-3067	15	15	(378)
Sormovskiy-3068	15	15	(378)
Soro	1	103	(9)
Sorokaletiye Pobeda	2	304	(49)
Sosnogorsk	9	80	(269)
Sosnovets	7	375	(184)
Sosnovka	7	375	(184)
Sosva	15	47	(381)
Sotiras	7	233	(173)
Sotka	1	9	(3)
Souad M	8	460	(239)
Souha	5	79	(112)
Souillac	7	112	(164)
Soul	8	637	(252)
Sounds of Seto	20	300	(481)
Sounion	8	289	(226)
Sousa	8	50	(207)
South County	8	395	(233)
Southern Ace	19	78	(453)†
Southern Cross	7	473	(191)
Southern Cross	8	462	(239)
Southern Cross	20	244	(477)
Southern Hope	8	420	(235)
Southern Lion	2	249	(45)
Southern Opal	8	214	(220)
Southern Pearl	8	211	(219)
Southern Trader	8	210	(219)
Southgate	7	271	(176)
South Islands	8	383	(232)
South Islands	8	500	(241)
Southway	8	654	(254)†
South Wind 1	1	88	(8)
Sovcomflot Senator	12	15	(326)
Soveja	8	50	(207)
Sovereign of the Seas	20	70	(464)
Sovetskiy Moryak	7	324	(180)
Sovetskiy Pogranichnik	7	324	(180)
Sovietskaya Neft	2	329	(50)
Sovietskaya Rodina	15	36	(380)
Sovietskaya Yakutiya	7	340	(181)
Sovietskiy Moryak	7	324	(180)
Sovietskiy Pogranichnik	7	324	(180)
Sovietskiy Turkmenistan	20	169	(471)
Sovietskiy Uzbekistan	20	169	(471)
Sovietskiy Voin	7	324	(180)
Soya	8	291	(226)
Soya Queen	5	142	(117)
Sparkle Sun	8	129	(213)
Sparos	5	256	(125)
Spartian	11	125	(310)
Spartian	11	127	(310)
Speciality	5	257	(125)
Spectrum	1	144	(12)
Speedy Fortune	8	199	(218)
Spes	19	8	(445)
Spevde Vradeos	12	61	(329)
Speybank	17	27	(407)
Spheroid	18	80	(427)
Spica	7	521	(197)†
Spic Emerald	1	255	(23)†
Spic Pearl	2	84	(35)
Spiga	5	158	(118)
Spinoza	8	26	(205)
Spirit of British Columbia	20	89	(466)
Spirit of Freedom	18	123	(431)
Spirit of Free Enterprise	18	67	(426)
Spirit of Independence	20	298	(481)
Spirit of Progress	17	40	(408)
Spirit of Tasmania	20	207	(474)
Spirit of Vancouver Island	20	89	(466)
Spiros	2	341	(51)
Splendid	20	65	(464)
Splendid Fortune	17	10	(406)
Splendour	2	237	(45)
Splendour of the Seas	20	418	(491)†
Split	7	453	(190)
Spokane	20	170	(471)
Sponsalis	1	144	(12)
Sprante	6	88	(149)†
Sprante	6	26	(143)
Spray	2	269	(46)
Spring	7	297	(178)
Spring Bee	11	243	(322)†
Spring Bee	11	109	(309)
Spring Bob	11	109	(309)
Spring Breeze	8	17	(204)
Spring Delight	11	207	(318)†
Spring Drake	7	213	(172)
Spring Panda	11	109	(309)
Spring Stork	7	213	(172)
Spring Swift	7	213	(172)
Spring Tiger	11	231	(321)†
Springwood	7	125	(165)
Sprinter	11	23	(302)
Sprogo	20	143	(469)
Spruce	21	90	(507)†
Spyridon Ch	8	30	(205)
Spyridoula	9	29	(265)
Spyros	8	445	(237)
Spyros B	8	685	(258)†
Spyros B	8	42	(206)
Srakane	7	334	(181)
S/R Baton Rouge	1	90	(9)
S/R Benicia	2	229	(44)
Sredetz	18	97	(429)
Sredna Gora	7	277	(176)
Srimanee	8	391	(233)
Sri Samut	10	5	(287)
Sriwijaya	8	556	(246)
S/R North Slope	2	229	(44)
Srour	8	539	(244)
S/R Philadelphia	1	90	(9)
S/R San Francisco	1	90	(9)
Stability	5	257	(125)
Stadt Norden	7	466	(191)
Staffordshire	4	75	(92)
Stainless Duke	2	61	(33)
Stainless Duke	2	216	(43)

†Photograph

	SHIP TYPE	REF NO	PAGE NO
Stainless Queen	2	34	(31)
Stakhanovetskkotov	21	40	(502)
Stakhanovets Kotov	21	95	(508)†
Stakhanovets Petrash	21	40	(502)
Stakhanovets Yermolenko	21	40	(502)
Stamos	5	53	(110)
Standard Endeavour	5	55	(111)
Standard Valor	5	57	(111)
Standard Virtue	5	175	(119)
Stanislaw Kulczynski	5	304	(128)
Stanko Staikov	12	109	(333)
St Anton	5	310	(128)
Stapafell	1	161	(13)
Star	15	32	(380)
Star-Ace	8	392	(233)
Star Antares	7	213	(172)
Stara Planina	7	277	(176)
Star Baltic	1	105	(9)
Star Baltic	2	383	(54)
Star Bergen	1	105	(9)
Star Caribbean	2	213	(43)
Star Cebu	10	38	(289)
Star Centaurus	7	213	(172)
Star Cherry	2	397	(55)
Star Davanger	10	46	(290)
Star Derby	10	46	(290)
Star Dieppe	10	44	(290)
Star Djervanger	10	44	(290)
Star Dover	10	44	(290)
Star Drivanger	10	44	(290)
Star Drottanger	10	44	(290)
Star Eagle	10	84	(295)†
Star Europa	10	41	(290)
Star Evanger	9	206	(280)†
Star Evanger	9	72	(268)
Star Florida	10	89	(295)†
Star Geiranger	10	88	(295)†
Star Georgia	2	224	(44)
Star Grip	10	82	(294)†
Star Haven	11	36	(303)
Star Hidra	10	80	(294)†
Star Japan	2	236	(45)
Star Kansas	2	307	(49)
Star Light	13	18	(350)
Star Nitsa	7	125	(165)
Star of America	21	35	(501)
Star of Maria	5	158	(118)
Star Orchid	2	397	(55)
Starovolzhk	15	47	(381)
Star Peter	5	235	(123)
Star Princess	20	90	(466)
Star Rhode Island	2	224	(44)
Starship Oceanic	20	28	(461)
Star Skarven	10	12	(288)
Star Skoganger	10	65	(292)†
Star Skoganger	10	12	(288)
Star Stronen	10	12	(288)
Star Trader	2	111	(36)
Startramp	8	518	(243)
Star Trondanger	10	81	(294)†
Star V	2	481	(61)
Star Veraguas	2	213	(43)
Staryy Bolshevik	9	6	(263)
Stassfurt	5	104	(114)
Statendam	20	444	(495)†
Statendam	20	91	(466)
Stathis G	6	27	(143)
Statrader	2	335	(51)
Stavros G L	2	339	(51)
St Blaize	8	125	(212)
St Cergue	5	50	(110)
St Christoph	5	310	(128)
St Christopher	8	163	(215)
St Clair	20	245	(477)
Steel Flower	5	243	(124)
Steersman	1	184	(15)
Stefan	6	66	(146)
Stefan	20	17	(460)
Stefanesti	8	50	(207)
Stefania	7	222	(172)
Stefanie	6	2	(141)
Stefan Karadja	7	174	(169)
Stefanos	8	80	(209)
Steinkirchen	7	520	(197)†
Steir	11	159	(312)
Stella	8	31	(205)
Stella Arctic	6	83	(149)†
Stella Arctic	6	33	(143)
Stella Azzurra	2	148	(39)
Stella Baltic	6	33	(143)
Stella F	9	187	(278)†
Stella F	9	49	(266)
Stella Lyra	2	122	(37)
Stellaman	2	57	(33)
Stella Mar	2	520	(63)
Stella Nordic	5	127	(116)
Stella Orion	2	279	(47)
Stella Pollux	2	131	(38)
Stella Procyon	2	136	(38)
Stellar Cape	5	367	(135)†
Stellar Venus	5	216	(122)
Stella Solaris	20	369	(486)
Stellata	1	144	(12)
Stella Tingas	8	30	(205)
Stena Antrim	20	222	(475)
Stena Barbados	1	175	(14)
Stena Caledonia	20	221	(475)
Stena Cambria	20	222	(475)
Stena Carrier	16	18	(392)
Stena Challenger	20	318	(482)
Stena Clipper	18	195	(438)†
Stena Concept	2	213	(43)
Stena Concordia	2	213	(43)
Stena Conductor	2	213	(43)
Stena Congress	2	213	(43)
Stena Constellation	2	213	(43)
Stena Contender	2	213	(43)
Stena Continent	2	213	(43)
Stena Convoy	2	213	(43)
Stena Danica	20	92	(466)
Stena Europe	20	452	(496)†
Stena Europe	20	93	(466)
Stena Explorer	20	437	(494)†
Stena Fantasia	20	432	(493)†
Stena Felicity	20	246	(477)
Stena Freighter	16	18	(392)
Stena Galloway	20	221	(475)
Stena Germanica	20	94	(466)
Stena Hibernia	20	189	(472)
Stena Invicta	20	413	(491)†
Stena Jutlandica	20	92	(466)
Stena King	2	262	(46)
Stena Londoner	20	48	(462)
Stena Nordica	20	172	(471)
Stena Normandy	20	93	(466)
Stena Parisien	20	173	(471)
Stena Queen	2	262	(46)
Stena Saga	20	79	(465)
Stena Scandinavica	20	94	(466)
Stena Scanrail	18	23	(423)
Stena Searider	18	37	(424)
Stena Shipper	16	75	(399)†
Stena Shipper	16	2	(391)
Stenholm	6	2	(141)
Stepan Artemenko	7	262	(175)
Stepan Razin	5	131	(116)
Stepan Savushkin	8	612	(250)
Stepans Halturins	8	575	(247)
Stepan Vostretsov	2	469	(60)
Stepenitz	10	69	(293)†
Stepenitz	10	31	(289)
Stephanie S	15	104	(388)†
Ster Laer	11	159	(312)
Steve Glory	8	56	(207)
Steve II	9	10	(264)
Stevens	11	203	(317)†
Stevns Sea	7	367	(183)
Stevns Trader	7	367	(183)
Steyning	5	322	(129)
St Georg	14	31	(368)†
St George	7	425	(188)
St Gerasimos I	8	446	(237)
St Helena	20	350	(485)
Stig Gorthon	17	17	(406)
Stina	6	42	(144)
St Irene	13	38	(352)
St Jakob	5	310	(128)
Stjerneborg	17	47	(409)
STK-1001	15	47	(381)
STK-1002	15	47	(381)
STK-1003	15	47	(381)
STK-1004	15	47	(381)
STK-1005	15	47	(381)
STK-1007	15	47	(381)
STK-1008	15	47	(381)
STK-1009	15	47	(381)
STK-1011	15	47	(381)
STK-1012	15	47	(381)
STK-1016	15	47	(381)
STK-1017	15	47	(381)
STK-1018	15	47	(381)
STK-1019	15	47	(381)
STK-1020	15	47	(381)
STK-1021	15	47	(381)
STK-1022	15	47	(381)
STK-1023	15	47	(381)
STK-1024	15	47	(381)
STK-1025	15	47	(381)
STK-1026	15	47	(381)
STK-1028	15	47	(381)
STK-1029	15	47	(381)
STK-1031	15	47	(381)

†Photograph

	SHIP TYPE	REF NO	PAGE NO
STK-1036	15	47	(381)
STK-1037	15	47	(381)
St Malo Pearl	5	268	(126)
St Martin	7	425	(188)
St Michaelis	2	448	(58)
STN 1	8	258	(223)
St Nicolas	8	276	(225)
St Nicolas X	7	401	(186)
St Nikolai	2	448	(58)
St Ola	20	171	(471)
Stoletiye Parizhskoy Kommuny	9	80	(269)
Stolt Alliance	1	240	(21)†
Stolt Aquamarine	1	94	(9)
Stolt Australia	1	190	(15)
Stolt Colina	2	125	(37)
Stolt Condor	2	188	(42)
Stolt Eagle	2	188	(42)
Stolt Emerald	1	94	(9)
Stolt Excellence	1	33	(5)
Stolt Falcon	2	188	(42)
Stolt Guardian	1	45	(6)
Stolt Hawk	2	188	(42)
Stolt Helluland	1	40	(5)
Stolt Heron	2	188	(42)
Stolt Integrity	1	33	(5)
Stolt Jade	1	94	(9)
Stolt Kingfisher	2	570	(69)†
Stolt Llandaff	1	42	(5)
Stolt Loyalty	1	33	(5)
Stolt Maplewood	2	42	(31)
Stolt Markland	1	40	(5)
Stolt Oakwood	2	42	(31)
Stolt Osprey	2	188	(42)
Stolt Pradera	2	125	(37)
Stolt Pride	1	33	(5)
Stolt Protector	1	34	(5)
Stolt Resolute	1	245	(21)†
Stolt Sapphire	1	94	(9)
Stolt Sincerity	1	33	(5)
Stolt Span	2	298	(48)
Stolt Spirit	1	33	(5)
Stolt Spray	1	57	(6)
Stolt Stream	1	57	(6)
Stolt Surf	2	298	(48)
Stolt Tenacity	1	33	(5)
Stolt Topaz	1	94	(9)
Stolt Vestland	1	40	(5)
Stolt Vinland	1	40	(5)
Stone Gemini	5	103	(114)
Stonewall Jackson	21	15	(500)
Stor	2	68	(33)
Stork	9	29	(265)
Storm	8	459	(238)
Storm	21	38	(502)
Storman Asia	21	74	(505)†
Storman Asia	21	36	(502)
Stormy Annie	7	146	(167)
Storrington	5	164	(118)
Stoyko Peev	12	109	(333)
St Pauli	14	32	(368)†
St Petersburg Senator	12	15	(326)
Strahlhorn	5	289	(127)
Straits Star	9	41	(266)
Straits Venture	8	364	(231)
Straman	2	49	(32)
Straume	11	102	(308)
Strength	2	410	(56)
Stresa	2	316	(49)
Stridence	15	83	(386)†
Strilberg	10	12	(288)
St Rognvald	18	153	(433)
Strong Texan	21	83	(506)†
Strong Texan	21	50	(503)
Strong Virginian	17	54	(409)
St Sunniva	20	290	(480)
St Thomas	7	425	(188)
Stuben	5	323	(129)
Studzianki	5	302	(128)
Sturgeon	4	149	(99)†
Stuttgart Express	12	5	(325)
Styrso	16	16	(392)
Styval	11	159	(312)
Subedar Joginder Singh PVC	1	137	(12)
Subhan Allah	8	155	(215)
Subic Adventure	18	93	(428)
Success Bulker	5	53	(110)
Sucevita	8	50	(207)
Su Chang	8	472	(239)
Su Cheng	9	3	(263)
Sucidava	8	50	(207)
Sudak	7	375	(184)
Sudong Spirit	2	528	(64)
Sudwind	6	28	(143)
Sue Lykes	8	627	(251)
Suez	9	80	(269)
Suez Flower	8	298	(226)

	SHIP TYPE	REF NO	PAGE NO
Su Fa	8	134	(213)
Su Feng	8	358	(230)
Sugar Islander	5	160	(118)
Su He	8	266	(224)
Suijin	19	89	(455)†
Suilven	20	292	(480)
Sukhumi	2	420	(56)
Sulfurico	2	50	(32)
Su Lin	7	432	(188)
Sulina	8	50	(207)
Sulphur Enterprise	2	177	(41)
Sultan Mahmud Badaruddin II	4	93	(93)
Sulteng I	8	318	(228)
Sulu	8	108	(211)
Sulu Express	8	500	(241)
Sulu Sea	2	77	(34)
Sumidagawa	1	69	(7)
Summer	7	297	(178)
Summer Meadow	11	35	(303)
Summer Wind	11	35	(303)
Sumy	7	151	(167)
Sun Ace	19	68	(452)†
Sun Bay	7	481	(192)
Sun Bird	7	481	(192)
Suncity	8	239	(222)
Sun Flower	20	6	(459)
Sunflower 1	9	118	(272)
Sun Flower 2	20	6	(459)
Sun Flower Osaka	20	6	(459)
Sun Flower Tosa	20	6	(459)
Sun II	7	63	(161)
Sun Joy	8	617	(250)
Sun Kung No 3	8	420	(235)
Sunlight	8	96	(210)
Sunlight	8	500	(241)
Sun Long No 8	11	171	(313)
Sunluck	7	3	(157)
Sunmar	8	239	(222)
Sunmar Star	8	177	(216)
Sun Master	7	199	(171)
Sunnanhav	5	265	(125)
Sunny	7	11	(157)
Sunny Blossom	1	239	(21)†
Sunny Clipper	4	83	(92)
Sunny Clipper	4	111	(94)
Sunny Clipper	5	51	(110)
Sunny Glorious	5	137	(116)
Sunny Lady	6	69	(146)
Sunny Sarah	11	175	(314)
Sunny Success	7	199	(171)
Sunny Tina	11	140	(311)
Sun Pride	8	217	(220)
Sun Princess	11	77	(306)
Sunrana	10	1	(287)
Sunrise	5	66	(111)
Sunrise K	8	76	(209)
Sun Ritchie Two	8	291	(226)
Sun River	4	48	(90)
Sun Rose	2	323	(50)
Sunsea	8	239	(222)
Sunset	8	239	(222)
Sunshine Fuji	20	174	(471)
Sunshine II	3	77	(83)†
Sunshine Pearl	18	72	(427)
Sun Speed	8	394	(233)
Sunstar	8	239	(222)
Sun Suma	10	43	(290)
Suntis	15	53	(382)†
Sun Trader	2	111	(36)
Sun Viking	20	385	(487)
Sun Vil	8	34	(206)
Sunwave	8	239	(222)
Suomijos Ilanka	11	18	(302)
Superba	2	291	(48)
Superferry II	20	155	(470)
Superflex Beauty	7	433	(188)
Superflex Bond	7	433	(188)
Superiority	15	14	(378)
Superitas	7	276	(176)
Super Servant 3	21	29	(501)
Super Servant 4	21	88	(507)†
Super Servant 4	21	29	(501)
Supertramp	8	527	(243)
Super Vision	8	655	(255)†
Suphan Navee	17	46	(409)
Support	8	354	(230)
Suren Spandaryan	9	57	(267)
Surgut	7	375	(184)
Su Run	8	550	(245)
Surya Kripa	7	213	(172)
Surya Pacific	8	310	(227)
Susak	7	334	(181)
Susak	12	97	(332)
Susanna	5	92	(113)
Sutla	8	281	(225)
Suula	1	261	(23)†

†Photograph

	SHIP TYPE	REF NO	PAGE NO
Tirgu Trotus	5	181	(119)
Tirnaveni	8	50	(207)
Tirumalai	1	169	(14)
Titan Scan	21	81	(506)†
Titan Scan	21	33	(501)
Titian Jaya	5	217	(122)
Titika	2	367	(53)
Titovsk	8	339	(229)
Titus	5	202	(121)
Titus	19	14	(446)
Tivat	9	110	(271)
Tjoet Nya Dhien	18	109	(430)
TK-6	15	47	(381)
TK-7	15	47	(381)
TMP Aquarius	6	59	(145)
TMP Libra	9	160	(275)
TMP Taurus	6	46	(144)
T M Regulus	2	244	(45)
Toba	17	86	(413)†
Toba	1	210	(17)
Toba	17	21	(406)
Tobago	20	258	(478)
Toba Maru	2	182	(41)
Tobol	8	619	(250)
Tobruk	5	313	(129)
Tocopilla	8	31	(205)
Togo Beauty	9	127	(272)
Togo Charm	7	183	(170)
Tohzan	1	216	(18)†
Tokaryevsk	8	339	(229)
Toki Arrow	10	78	(294)†
Toki Arrow	10	43	(290)
Tokio Express	12	214	(344)†
Tokyo Bay	11	69	(305)
Tokyo Bay	12	153	(336)
Tokyo Maru	18	173	(435)
Toletela	20	205	(473)
To-Lich	8	383	(232)
Tolis	8	284	(225)
Tol Runner	2	2	(29)
Tolueno	2	51	(32)
Tolya Komar	8	621	(251)
Tolya Shumov	8	621	(251)
Tomahawk	8	34	(206)
Tom Elba	2	1	(29)
Tomfield	15	48	(382)†
Tomis Faith	5	138	(117)
Tomis Glory	5	138	(117)
Tomis Hope	5	138	(117)
Tomis Spirit	5	138	(117)
Tomiwaka	1	187	(15)
Tom Lis	2	1	(29)
Tonala	8	35	(206)
Tong An	6	2	(141)
Tong An	8	70	(208)
Tong Cheng	7	406	(186)
Tong Chuan	9	112	(271)
Tong Fu	5	243	(124)
Tong Gon Ae Huk Ho	8	280	(225)
Tong Jiang	8	268	(224)
Tongshun	8	632	(251)
Tong Yun	12	55	(329)
Tong Zhou	8	152	(214)
Tonya Bondarchuk	8	621	(251)
Toot	8	615	(250)
Topavik	7	188	(170)
Topaz	7	395	(186)
Topaz	8	500	(241)
Top Glory	7	201	(171)
Tor Anglia	18	59	(426)
Tor Belgia	18	187	(437)†
Tor Belgia	18	28	(423)
Torben Spirit	1	214	(17)
Tor Britannia	18	95	(428)
Tor Britannia	18	101	(429)
Tor Caledonia	18	19	(422)
Tor Dania	18	95	(428)
Tor Dania	18	101	(429)
Tordis Knutsen	1	212	(17)
Tor Flandria	18	28	(423)
Tor Gothia	18	96	(428)
Tor Hollandia	18	214	(440)†
Tor Hollandia	18	19	(422)
Torill Knutsen	1	51	(6)
Torino	2	591	(71)†
Torino	2	311	(49)
Torm America	9	94	(270)
Torm Birgitte	9	94	(270)
Tormes	7	349	(182)
Torm Freya	7	398	(186)
Torm Gerd	5	216	(122)
Torm Gunhild	1	108	(10)
Torm Margrethe	1	156	(13)
Torm Margrethe	1	200	(16)
Torm Marina	5	216	(122)
Torm Tekla	5	216	(122)
Torm Thyra	1	269	(24)†
Torm Thyra	1	108	(10)
Tornes	10	92	(296)†
Toro	8	688	(259)†
Toro	2	305	(49)
Tor Scandia	18	28	(423)
Tory Hill	8	18	(204)
Tosca	19	84	(454)†
Toscana	5	42	(110)
Toscana	7	24	(158)
Tourcoing	16	19	(392)
Tove Knutsen	1	110	(10)
Tower Bridge	12	103	(332)
Toxotis	5	76	(112)
Toyofuji No 2	7	426	(188)
Toyosu	4	34	(89)
Toyvo Antikaynen	8	74	(209)
Tozeur	7	426	(188)
Trade Ambassador	9	194	(278)†
Trade Ambassador	9	30	(265)
Trade Apollo	12	10	(325)
Trade Banner	9	30	(265)
Trade Bliss	10	16	(288)
Trade Carrier	9	121	(272)
Trade Eternity	12	10	(325)
Trade Fast	13	17	(350)
Trade Fortitude	2	372	(53)
Trade Greece	5	158	(118)
Trade Link	8	393	(233)
Trade Luck	12	130	(334)
Trader	5	77	(112)
Trade Rank	12	130	(334)
Trader Bulk	8	312	(228)
Trade Rich	7	5	(157)
Trade Selene	12	10	(325)
Trade Vigour	8	119	(212)
Trade Wealth	7	5	(157)
Trade Will	7	131	(166)
Tradewind	7	138	(166)
Tradewind River	2	36	(31)
Tradewind Star	2	36	(31)
Trajan	11	123	(310)
Tramco Amity	7	80	(162)
Trancisco	8	355	(230)
Tranport Schelde	17	16	(406)
Trans Arctic	1	152	(13)
Trans Argo	2	336	(51)
Transbaltica	18	207	(439)†
Trans Cargo III	9	53	(267)
Trans Comfort	7	81	(162)
Trans Dania	18	115	(430)
Transestonia	18	92	(428)
Transeuropa	18	228	(442)†
Transeuropa	18	107	(429)
Transfinlandia	18	155	(433)
Trans Hera	2	336	(51)
Transkord	12	61	(329)
Trans Minerva	2	336	(51)
Transocean	5	158	(118)
Transpace	8	492	(240)
Trans Pacific 3	19	17	(446)
Transporter LT	2	427	(57)
Trans-Port I	17	31	(407)
Trans-Port II	17	31	(407)
Transportor	5	94	(113)
Trans Scandic	1	152	(13)
Transshelf	21	86	(507)†
Transshelf	21	7	(499)
Trans St Laurent	20	187	(472)
Transvaal	12	96	(332)
Transworld Bridge	12	186	(340)†
Tranztas Trader	7	485	(192)
Traquair	4	103	(94)
Trautenbels	9	125	(272)
Traveberg	6	2	(141)
Trave Trader	13	115	(360)†
Trave Trader	13	7	(349)
Traviata	19	30	(447)
Treasure Island	8	445	(237)
Treasure Sea	5	240	(123)
Treasure Sunrise	5	115	(115)
Trekroner	18	213	(440)†
Trelleborg	20	96	(466)
Tri–an	8	575	(247)
Triana	5	161	(118)
Trias	5	243	(124)
Trias	8	28	(205)
Triatic Power	8	386	(233)
Tribels	9	125	(272)
Tribuno	7	139	(166)
Trichord Success	7	207	(171)
Tricolor Star II	7	464	(190)
Tricolor Star II	7	481	(192)
Trident	8	17	(204)
Trident Fortune	7	228	(173)
Trident Mariner	7	244	(174)

†Photograph

	SHIP TYPE	REF NO	PAGE NO
Tri Frakt	10	19	(288)
Trigger	19	25	(446)
Triglav	8	34	(206)
Trimbakeshwar	9	124	(272)
Trinacria	11	168	(313)
Trinec	5	195	(120)
Trinidad Sea	2	512	(63)
Trinity	8	274	(225)
Trinity Sierra	8	500	(241)
Trinket	6	9	(141)
Tripal	8	214	(220)
Tristan	19	10	(445)
Triton	20	335	(483)
Triton Highway	19	63	(452)†
Triumph	6	102	(151)†
Trojan	7	358	(183)
Troll	10	66	(292)†
Troll	10	14	(288)
Trollnes	10	93	(296)†
Tromaas	1	140	(12)
Troms Producer	1	34	(5)
Tropicale	20	97	(466)
Tropical Estoril	11	152	(312)
Tropical Mist	11	234	(321)†
Tropical Reefer	11	95	(308)
Tropical Sea	9	98	(270)
Tropical Sintra	11	152	(312)
Tropical Sun	11	154	(312)
Tropical Venture	7	366	(183)
Tropicana	7	184	(170)
Tropicana	20	176	(471)
Tropicana I	8	392	(233)
Tropicana Reefer	11	152	(312)
Tropic Opal	18	83	(427)
Tropic Star II	20	314	(482)
Tropic Sun	17	38	(408)
Tropic Tide	17	38	(408)
Tropiventure	8	399	(234)
Trud	2	5	(29)
Trunovsk	8	339	(229)
Truong Son	9	44	(266)
Truskavets	17	51	(409)
Truso	15	8	(377)
Trust 38	8	24	(205)
Truva	20	177	(471)
Tsakaloff	7	271	(176)
Tsang Jia	8	214	(220)
Tsesis	2	273	(46)
Tsimisaraka	2	435	(58)
TSL Bold	13	11	(350)
TSL Bravo	13	38	(352)
TSL Gallant	13	7	(349)
T S Prosperity	1	29	(5)
Tsugaru Gloria	4	173	(102)†
Tsuru Arrow	10	43	(290)
Tsuru Orient	2	199	(42)
Tuan Jie	8	171	(216)
Tuapse	2	446	(58)
Tui Cakau III	18	140	(432)
Tulip	8	141	(214)
Tuloma	11	151	(312)
Tulsk	8	339	(229)
Tuma	2	318	(50)
Tunadal	10	39	(290)
Tundra King	11	111	(309)
Tundra Princess	11	111	(309)
Tundra Queen	11	111	(309)
Tungenes	17	22	(407)
Tuo He	7	44	(160)
Tuo Jiang	9	155	(274)
Tupi Angra	5	196	(121)
Tupi Buzios	5	196	(121)
Tupi Ilha Bela	7	225	(173)
Tupi Ponta Negra	7	225	(173)
Turandot	19	14	(446)
Turchese	1	248	(22)†
Turicia	11	135	(311)
Turkay B	8	399	(234)
Turkmenistan	11	58	(305)
Turnu Severin	7	526	(197)†
Tus	2	64	(33)
Tuscania	2	436	(58)
Tushino	8	612	(250)
Tustumena	20	204	(473)
Tutova	18	3	(421)
Tuzla	18	3	(421)
Tweit IV	7	291	(177)
Tweit VI	8	470	(239)
Tycho Brahe	4	88	(93)
Tychy	16	25	(393)
Tymovsk	8	612	(250)
Tyrusland	17	39	(408)
Tyseer	10	20	(288)
Tyson Lykes	12	191	(341)†
UB Jaguar	14	37	(369)†
Ubon Navee	17	46	(409)
UB Panther	5	30	(109)
UB Parade	11	49	(304)
UB Pioneer	8	175	(216)
UB Polaris	11	97	(308)
UB Prelude	11	49	(304)
UB Premier	8	173	(216)
UB Prestige	8	175	(216)
UB Pride	11	49	(304)
UB Prince	11	155	(312)
UB Progress	17	93	(414)†
UB Progress	17	58	(410)
UB Prosper	8	173	(216)
Uco XX	5	220	(122)
Uelen	8	288	(226)
Ufuk	9	164	(275)
Ugarit	7	220	(172)
Uikku	1	9	(3)
Ukhta	2	367	(53)
Ukraina	20	127	(468)
Ukrainskiy Komsomolets	11	102	(308)
Ula	8	523	(243)
Ulan	2	410	(56)
Ulan-Bator	17	51	(409)
Ulan-Ude	8	589	(248)
Ulbanskiy Zaliv	11	98	(308)
Ulbanskiy Zaliv	11	101	(308)
Ulf Ritscher	13	118	(360)†
Ulf Ritscher	13	26	(351)
Ulla Danielsen	8	220	(220)
Ulla Danielsen	8	224	(221)
Ulla Pearl	5	268	(126)
Ullswater	5	355	(133)†
Ulsund	8	193	(218)
Ultramax	2	342	(51)
Ultrasea	2	342	(51)
Ulusoy-1	18	176	(435)
Ulyanovsk	2	437	(58)
Ulzburg	6	66	(146)
Umag Saint Malo	9	153	(274)
Uman	11	151	(312)
Umang	9	10	(264)
Umberto D'Amato	2	375	(53)
Um El Faroud	2	516	(63)
Umfolozi	7	326	(180)
Umgeni	9	178	(276)†
Umgeni	9	139	(273)
Umm Shaif	3	64	(82)†
Umsini	20	387	(487)
Una	8	291	(226)
Unan Avetisyan	5	17	(108)
Unan Avetisyan	5	193	(120)
Und Denizcilik	16	32	(394)
Unden	7	386	(185)
Und Hayri Ekinci	16	32	(394)
Und Prenses	16	97	(401)†
Und Prenses	18	109	(430)
Und Saffet Bay	18	109	(430)
Und Transfer	18	193	(437)†
Un Ha	8	134	(213)
Uniarch	7	266	(175)
Unicosta	9	110	(271)
Unije	8	418	(235)
Unika	6	41	(144)
Unilago	8	443	(237)
Unimar	9	110	(271)
Union	7	145	(167)
Union Arbo	15	88	(387)†
Union Arbo	15	8	(377)
Union Auckland	7	71	(161)
Union Glory	17	77	(412)†
Union Glory	17	2	(405)
Union Jupiter	15	14	(378)
Union Lucky	17	2	(405)
Union Pearl	15	14	(378)
Union Rotoiti	18	103	(429)
Union Rotorua	18	103	(429)
Union Venus	15	8	(377)
Unipampa	8	680	(258)†
Unipampa	9	110	(271)
Unipower	8	169	(216)
Uniprogress	9	102	(270)
Unipuna	9	109	(271)
Uniselva	7	400	(186)
Uni-Shine	12	140	(335)
Unisierra	7	400	(186)
Unisol	9	110	(271)
Unison	7	121	(165)
Unison Great	8	420	(235)
Uni-Spring	12	140	(335)
Uni-Summit	12	140	(335)
Uni-Superb	12	140	(335)
Unitank	2	84	(35)

†Photograph

	SHIP TYPE	REF NO	PAGE NO
United	9	20	(264)
United Confidence	8	276	(225)
United Fung	8	159	(215)
United Glory	8	630	(251)
United I	7	185	(170)
United Moonlight	2	449	(58)
United Pioneer	8	630	(251)
United Selma	1	209	(16)
United Sunrise	2	449	(58)
United Thule	2	522	(63)
United Tina	1	206	(16)
United Tony	1	182	(15)
United Trader	1	188	(15)
United Transporter	1	188	(15)
United Trapper	1	188	(15)
United Traveller	1	188	(15)
United Triton	2	449	(58)
United Trust	8	457	(238)
United V	5	157	(118)
United Way	7	365	(183)
Unity 1	5	118	(115)
Unity III	6	1	(141)
Unity IV	5	268	(126)
Unity V	5	268	(126)
Unity VIII	8	615	(250)
Univalle	9	110	(271)
Uni-Valor	12	158	(337)
Uni-Value	12	158	(337)
Universal	12	219	(345)†
Universe Admiral	9	67	(268)
Uni-Vigor	12	158	(337)
Uni-Vital	12	158	(337)
Uniwersytet Jagiellonski	5	178	(119)
Uniwersytet Slaski	5	301	(128)
Uniwersytet Warszawski	5	169	(119)
Uniwersytet Wroclawski	5	169	(119)
Unix Jawa	2	67	(33)
Uni Yamani	8	197	(218)
Unkas	2	59	(33)
Uno	6	41	(144)
Uppland	15	44	(381)
Uragan	11	154	(312)
Ural Mountains	11	222	(320)†
Urania	6	29	(143)
Uranus	5	66	(111)
Uranus	5	114	(115)
Uranus	11	90	(307)
Urd	18	112	(430)
Urengoy	2	26	(30)
Urfa	7	74	(162)
Urga	8	621	(251)
Uri	7	348	(182)
Uricani	5	248	(124)
Urimare	2	520	(63)
Ursa	5	66	(111)
Ursa Major	5	19	(108)
Ursula C	14	75	(373)†
Ursula Delmas	13	2	(349)
Ursus	8	73	(209)
Uruguayan Reefer	11	217	(319)†
Uruguay Express	13	100	(358)†
Uruguay Express	12	118	(334)
Urzhum	2	437	(58)
Usedom	7	480	(192)
Ushuaia	11	3	(301)
Usinsk	2	26	(30)
Ussuriysk	1	52	(6)
Ussuriyskaya Tayga	11	98	(308)
Ussuriyskaya Tayga	11	101	(308)
Ussuriyskiy Zaliv	11	18	(302)
Ust-Ilimsk	2	380	(54)
Ust-Izhma	2	380	(54)
Ust-Kan	2	380	(54)
Ust-Karsk	2	380	(54)
Ust-Kut	2	380	(54)
Ust-Labinsk	2	380	(54)
Ustrine	7	292	(177)
Utari	16	14	(392)
Uthai Navee	9	129	(272)
Utviken	7	140	(166)
Uwa Bhum	7	363	(183)
Uzbekistan	11	58	(305)
Uznadze	1	107	(10)
Vaal	12	137	(335)
Vachnadze	1	181	(15)
Vadim Glazunov	15	23	(379)
Vaeanu	8	200	(218)
Vaga	8	619	(250)
Vagay	15	47	(381)
Vagif	7	340	(181)
Vaindlo	7	11	(157)
Valbrenta	8	392	(233)
Val de Loire	20	207	(474)
Valencia Bridge	16	13	(392)

	SHIP TYPE	REF NO	PAGE NO
Valencia Star	2	370	(53)
Valentina	5	141	(117)
Valentin Khutorskoy	9	80	(269)
Valentino	18	84	(428)
Valentin Zolotaryev	8	161	(215)
Valerian Kuibyshev	9	56	(267)
Valerian Zorin	15	23	(379)
Valeriya Barsova	9	195	(279)†
Valeriya Barsova	9	92	(270)
Valeriy Chkalov	1	20	(4)
Valeriy Kuzmin	7	152	(167)
Valeriy Mezhlauk	9	80	(269)
Valeriy Volkov	8	621	(251)
Valga	16	13	(392)
Valiant	7	466	(191)
Valio	2	121	(37)
Vali P.	8	500	(241)
Valkla	9	57	(267)
Vallesina	4	125	(95)
Valmiera	2	273	(46)
Val Misa	4	163	(100)†
Valya Kotik	8	621	(251)
Vana Tallinn	20	247	(477)
Vancouver	5	42	(110)
Vanessa C	6	60	(146)
Vanguard	5	31	(109)
Vanilla	11	175	(314)
Vanino	1	52	(6)
Van K	7	222	(172)
Van Trader	7	299	(178)
Van Warrior	7	102	(164)
Varadero	8	44	(206)
Varano	2	506	(62)
Varjakka	7	129	(166)
Varkiza	2	273	(46)
Varna	7	345	(182)
Varnakova	8	567	(247)
Varuna Kachhapi	8	500	(241)
Vasilijs Fesenkovs	11	127	(310)
Vasilijs Struve	11	127	(310)
Vasilios D	2	367	(53)
Vasilios VII	2	368	(53)
Vasilios X	2	369	(53)
Vasilios XIII	2	220	(44)
Vasilios XIV	2	134	(38)
Vasilis	8	177	(216)
Vasiliy Azhayev	7	206	(171)
Vasiliy Burkhanov	17	27	(407)
Vasiliy Byelokonyenko	8	49	(207)
Vasiliy Fedoseyev	8	168	(216)
Vasiliy Kalashnikov	5	29	(109)
Vasiliy Kikvidze	2	508	(62)
Vasiliy Klochkov	9	92	(270)
Vasiliy Koval	7	245	(174)
Vasiliy Malov	15	17	(378)
Vasiliy Matuzenko	7	160	(168)
Vasiliy Musinskiy	8	78	(209)
Vasiliy Poleshchuk	11	98	(308)
Vasiliy Poleshchuk	11	101	(308)
Vasiliy Shukshin	7	152	(167)
Vasiliy Yan	7	340	(181)
Vasil Levsky	9	92	(270)
Vasily Shelgunov	9	57	(267)
Vasos	8	128	(213)
Vassilis IX	5	83	(113)
Vassilis VII	8	183	(217)
Vastanvik	21	45	(502)
Vast Jollity	9	45	(266)
Vasya Korobko	8	621	(251)
Vasya Kurka	8	239	(222)
Vatsy	8	64	(208)
Vectis Isle	15	75	(385)†
Vectis Isle	15	14	(378)
Vedette	5	332	(131)†
Veer Savarka	9	201	(279)†
Veer Savarkar	9	124	(272)
Vega	7	136	(166)
Vega	7	453	(190)
Vega	8	202	(219)
Vega	11	83	(307)
Vega	20	268	(478)
Vega II	7	269	(176)
Vegaland	17	39	(408)
Vega Star One	5	248	(124)
Veglio	2	50	(32)
Vejen	5	239	(123)
Vekua	1	107	(10)
Vela	7	382	(185)
Vela	20	3	(459)
Velebit	7	199	(171)
Velenje	8	321	(228)
Veliuona	8	365	(231)
Velma Lykes	8	48	(207)
Velos	8	351	(230)
Venedikt Andreyev	15	23	(379)
Venia	8	453	(238)

†Photograph

	SHIP TYPE	REF NO	PAGE NO
Venita	2	243	(45)
Venliza	2	281	(47)
Venlo	6	49	(145)
Venta	8	619	(250)
Ventares	2	281	(47)
Vento	14	58	(371)†
Vento	8	276	(225)
Vento	14	23	(367)
Vento di Tramontana	17	80	(413)†
Vento di Tramontana	17	16	(406)
Ventspils	1	264	(24)†
Ventspils	1	52	(6)
Ventura	1	63	(7)
Venture	1	109	(10)
Venus	9	121	(272)
Venusia	8	202	(219)
Vera	7	264	(175)
Vera	7	276	(176)
Vera Khoruzhaya	16	13	(392)
Vera Mukhina	8	365	(231)
Verano	8	444	(237)
Vera Rambow	6	30	(143)
Verazzano	2	63	(33)
Verbier	5	163	(118)
Verdi	2	432	(57)
Verdon	7	416	(187)
Vered	12	77	(330)
Verena	6	31	(143)
Verga	20	323	(483)
Vergina	17	71	(412)†
Vergina	17	7	(405)
Vergina Treasure	20	317	(482)
Verila	5	264	(125)
Vernal Star	10	14	(288)
Verner	7	125	(165)
Verona	6	89	(150)†
Verona	6	32	(143)
Verona	6	61	(146)
Verona	8	17	(204)
Veronique Delmas	13	2	(349)
Vesleo	9	57	(267)
Veslets	5	264	(125)
Vesta	20	3	(459)
Vesyegonsk	2	380	(54)
Vezira	8	581	(248)
Via Adriatico	18	118	(430)
Viangthalae	8	314	(228)
Via Tirreno	18	118	(430)
Vicky I	2	317	(50)
Victoria	5	258	(125)
Victoria	8	50	(207)
Victoria	11	12	(301)
Victoria	20	372	(486)
Victoria Bay	7	530	(198)†
Victoria Bay	7	9	(157)
Victoria de Giron	8	382	(232)
Victoria II	5	145	(117)
Victoria Reefer	11	173	(313)
Victor III	8	296	(226)
Victorius	8	283	(225)
Victory	8	575	(247)
Victory II	8	590	(248)
Vida	5	312	(129)
Vidal	8	125	(212)
Vidal de Negreiros	2	254	(46)
Viden	5	264	(125)
Vidnoye	2	380	(54)
Vien Hai I	8	589	(248)
Vienna Sky	7	221	(172)
Viento Del Siroco	16	42	(394)
Vigdis Knutsen	1	212	(17)
Vigo Express	8	532	(244)
Vigorous Luck	8	552	(245)
Vigorous Swan	8	559	(246)
Vigour	2	277	(47)
Vigsnes	7	347	(182)
Viirelaid	16	26	(393)
Vijera	8	367	(231)
Vikingland	17	39	(408)
Viking Princess	20	202	(473)
Viking Serenade	20	98	(466)
Viking Star	3	76	(83)†
Viking Star	19	2	(445)
Viking Trader	18	135	(432)
Vikla	1	260	(23)†
Vikla	1	170	(14)
Vikstraum	1	164	(13)
Viktorio Kodovilja	2	424	(57)
Viktor Khara	7	152	(167)
Viktor Kibenok	2	171	(41)
Viktor Kurnatovskiy	9	57	(267)
Viktor Talalikhin	16	13	(392)
Viktor Tkachyov	7	273	(176)
Vila Carrier	8	535	(244)
Vila Dhoadhi	8	300	(227)
Vilcea	7	174	(169)
Viljandi	16	13	(392)
Villach	8	414	(235)
Villa de Agaete	20	203	(473)
Villars	18	148	(433)
Ville de Damiete	7	461	(190)
Ville de Libra	12	81	(331)
Ville de Mina Qaboos	6	2	(141)
Ville de Sagitta	12	81	(331)
Ville de Titana	12	7	(325)
Ville de Vela	12	81	(331)
Vilm	7	480	(192)
Vilnius	18	164	(434)
Vilomar	21	46	(502)
Vilsandi	7	11	(157)
Vilyuysk	2	26	(30)
Vinca	7	229	(173)
Vince	14	69	(373)†
Vince	12	161	(337)
Vincita	1	63	(7)
Vine	1	64	(7)
Vinga	1	119	(10)
Vingasjo	2	302	(49)
Vinnitsa	17	51	(409)
Vinson	11	75	(306)
Vinta	8	141	(214)
Viola	8	195	(218)
Viola Gorthon	18	234	(442)†
Violet	2	200	(42)
Vira Bhum	9	54	(267)
Virginia	7	207	(171)
Virgo III	8	621	(251)
Visayas Victory	10	45	(290)
Viseu	5	132	(116)
Vishva Bandhan	8	484	(240)
Vishva Karuna	8	484	(240)
Vishva Kaumudi	9	110	(271)
Vishva Madhuri	8	484	(240)
Vishva Nandini	9	110	(271)
Vishva Pallav	7	390	(185)
Vishva Pankaj	7	390	(185)
Vishva Parag	7	390	(185)
Vishva Parijat	7	390	(185)
Vishva Parimal	7	390	(185)
Vishva Prafulla	7	390	(185)
Vishva Yash	8	484	(240)
Vishwadoot	2	426	(57)
Vision	8	589	(248)
Vissarion Belinskiy	8	630	(251)
Vistafjord	20	248	(477)
Vistamar	20	416	(491)†
Visvesvaraya	2	508	(62)
Vitagrain	8	100	(211)
Vitali	5	119	(115)
Vitality	7	179	(169)
Vitaliy Dyakonov	7	152	(167)
Vitaliy Kruchina	8	49	(207)
Vitocha	5	132	(116)
Vitorandis	7	80	(162)
Vitoria	2	543	(65)†
Vitorio Nemesio	7	379	(184)
Vitosha	5	132	(116)
Vitsentzos Kornaros	20	224	(475)
Vittore Carpaccio	20	315	(482)
Vitya Chalenko	8	621	(251)
Vitya Khonenko	8	621	(251)
Vitya Novitskiy	8	239	(222)
Vitya Sitnitsa	8	621	(251)
Viva	5	156	(118)
Vivaldi	1	14	(4)
Viva Treasure	8	24	(205)
Viva Victoria	8	273	(225)
Viviette	7	357	(183)
Vivita	7	202	(171)
Vladimir	17	51	(409)
Vladimir Gavrilov	7	81	(162)
Vladimir Ilich	9	56	(267)
Vladimir Kokkinaki	1	20	(4)
Vladimir Mordvinov	8	78	(209)
Vladimir Pravik	2	171	(41)
Vladimir Timfeyev	8	78	(209)
Vladimir Vaslyayev	16	21	(393)
Vladimir Vysotskiy	1	107	(10)
Vladivostok Senator	12	15	(326)
Vlas Nichkov	8	78	(209)
Vogtland	12	63	(329)
Vola	7	497	(194)†
Volans	2	339	(51)
Volchansk	11	172	(313)
Volga	1	84	(8)
Volga 4006	15	93	(387)†
Volgo-Balt	15	33	(380)
Volgo-Balt	15	39	(380)
Volgograd	20	119	(468)
Volgoneft Type	15	3	(377)
Volgoneft Type	15	41	(380)
Volgoneft Type	2	22	(30)

†Photograph

	SHIP TYPE	REF NO	PAGE NO
Volgoneft 251	15	96	(388)†
Volgorechensk	15	47	(381)
Volodya Shcherbatsevich	8	621	(251)
Volta River	8	444	(237)
Volzhsk	8	628	(251)
Vomero	18	186	(436)†
Voo Shee II	1	80	(8)
Vorios Ipiros Hellas	5	186	(120)
Vorosmarty	9	92	(270)
Vostochniy Bereg	11	98	(308)
Voyager	6	120	(153)†
Voyager	5	212	(122)
Vrissi	8	500	(241)
Vulcan	5	248	(124)
Vulcan	5	271	(126)
Vyacheslav Denisov	7	324	(180)
Vyatkales	8	612	(250)
Vyborg	17	51	(409)
Vyborgskaya Storona	7	324	(180)
Vyg	6	20	(142)
Vysokogorsk	7	14	(158)
Vzmorye	8	612	(250)
Waasland	1	126	(11)
Wabasha	2	397	(55)
Wachau	15	7	(377)
Wadag	5	187	(120)
Wadai	8	162	(215)
Wadeiaa	8	404	(234)
Wahib M	6	69	(146)
Wah Yee	8	508	(242)
Waimea	7	23	(158)
Wakaba Maru	3	9	(75)
Wakamba	9	132	(273)
Wakanatsu Okinawa	20	41	(462)
Wakenitz	8	634	(251)
Waldtraut B	15	43	(380)
Walka Mlodych	5	301	(128)
Walla-Walla	20	170	(471)
Walter F	16	42	(394)
Walter Jacob	11	39	(303)
Wan Da 1	8	264	(224)
Wanderbass	2	17	(30)
Waneta	2	463	(59)
Wan Fu	9	157	(275)
Wang Fu	20	19	(460)
Wangting	8	561	(246)
Wan Li	8	348	(230)
Wan Ling	8	46	(207)
Wan Ling	8	445	(237)
Wan Long	8	485	(240)
Wan Ning He	13	18	(350)
Wan Ping	8	487	(240)
Wan Ru	8	26	(205)
Wan Tai	2	438	(58)
Wan Xiang	7	421	(187)
Wapello	2	463	(59)
Wappen Von Hamburg	20	25	(461)
Warburg II	8	232	(221)
Warda	2	277	(47)
Warfleth	15	2	(377)
Warka	5	189	(120)
Warmia	11	59	(305)
Warnemunde	9	139	(273)
Warnemunde	20	104	(467)
Wasa Queen	20	225	(475)
Waseberg	15	27	(379)
Washington	5	180	(119)
Washington	7	318	(180)
Washington Senator	12	14	(326)
Waterford	5	213	(122)
Wawasan Megah	2	12	(29)
Wealthy River	12	118	(334)
Wealthy Star	9	93	(270)
Weasel	8	151	(214)
Wei Guang	8	552	(245)
Wei Hai	7	173	(169)
Wei He	7	44	(160)
Weining 3	8	369	(231)
Weisa	6	58	(145)
Wejherowo	9	69	(268)
Welcome	8	393	(233)
Wellington Maru	12	141	(335)
Wels	1	47	(6)
Wen Deng Hai	5	162	(118)
Wen He	13	66	(353)
Wen Zhou Hai	5	53	(110)
Werder Bremen	15	21	(379)
Werfen	14	68	(372)†
Weser	5	61	(111)
Weser Ore	2	458	(59)
Weserstern	1	211	(17)
Westerdam	20	417	(491)†
Westerhamm	7	313	(179)
Westerland	7	326	(180)
Western Bell	7	199	(171)
Western Bridge	10	100	(297)†
Western Bridge	10	50	(290)
Western Gallantry	7	231	(173)
Western Georgios	7	29	(159)
Western Greeting	7	231	(173)
Western Guardian	7	231	(173)
Western Lion	2	249	(45)
Western Lucky	8	369	(231)
Western Mariner	7	213	(172)
Westernport	4	59	(91)
Western Shore	7	203	(171)
Western Trade	5	100	(114)
Western Trader	5	199	(121)
Western Village	7	201	(171)
Western Winner	7	205	(171)
Westgard	14	35	(368)†
Westgard	6	33	(143)
Westgate	2	460	(59)
West Islands	8	383	(232)
Westman	8	427	(236)
West Sky	10	107	(297)†
West Sky	14	19	(366)
West Star	8	352	(230)
Westwood Cleo	10	87	(295)†
Westwood Fuji	7	108	(164)
Westwood Halla	7	108	(164)
Whitcrest	2	119	(37)
White Arrow	11	228	(321)†
White Castle	11	75	(306)
White Dolphin	11	221	(320)†
White Nile	17	75	(412)†
White Nile	17	49	(409)
White Opal	7	271	(176)
White Rose	2	252	(45)
White Sea	2	512	(63)
White Sea	18	82	(427)
White Star	3	75	(83)†
White Stone	7	264	(175)
White Sun	11	71	(306)
Widar	12	62	(329)
Widukind	13	26	(351)
Wieliczka	9	53	(267)
Wielun	10	11	(287)
Wigry	7	265	(175)
Wijaya Indah	8	590	(248)
Wilanow	20	316	(482)
Wilcon II	8	242	(222)
Wilcon V	14	28	(367)
Wilhelm Pieck	11	99	(308)
Willamette	2	502	(62)
William Foster	9	56	(267)
William Shakespeare	8	413	(235)
Willy	2	57	(33)
Wilomi Tanana	2	561	(68)†
Wilson Ruby	3	80	(84)†
Wind	8	531	(244)
Windfall	8	439	(237)
Windfield	10	77	(294)†
Windfrost	11	39	(303)
Windfrost	11	166	(313)
Wind Ocean	7	546	(200)†
Wind Ocean	6	71	(147)
Windsor III	9	158	(275)
Windstar	8	24	(205)
Windward	12	79	(331)
Wineta	11	7	(301)
Wine Trader	2	300	(48)
Winfast Reefer	11	78	(306)
Wing Lee No 2	9	219	(282)†
Wing Sing	14	26	(367)
Wing Son	8	124	(212)
Winner	7	82	(162)
Winner	7	82	(162)
Win Shun Shing	11	66	(305)
Winston Churchill	20	178	(471)
Winter	7	297	(178)
Winter Moon	11	30	(303)
Winter Sea	11	30	(303)
Winter Star	7	483	(192)
Winter Star	11	30	(303)
Winter Sun	11	30	(303)
Winter Water	11	30	(303)
Winter Wave	11	30	(303)
Wirek	8	155	(215)
Wittenbergen	15	34	(380)
Wittsand	11	135	(311)
Wladyslaw Jagiello	8	154	(215)
Wladyslaw Lokietek	8	154	(215)
Wladyslawowo	9	120	(272)
Wloclawek	16	25	(393)
W M Vacy Ash	2	28	(30)
Woermann Expert	8	673	(257)†
Woermann Expert	8	118	(212)
Wolfsburg	19	52	(450)†
Wolwol	9	140	(273)

†Photograph

	SHIP TYPE	REF NO	PAGE NO
Wonfu	8	475	(239)
Won San	9	36	(265)
Woodpecker	8	141	(214)
Wood Pioneers	8	521	(243)
Woodstone	5	261	(125)
Woo Yang Prince	8	217	(220)
World Achilles II	7	36	(159)
World Aegeus	7	36	(159)
World Agamemnon	7	36	(159)
World Ajax	7	36	(159)
World Amphion	7	36	(159)
World Ares	7	36	(159)
World Aretus	7	36	(159)
World Bermuda	2	209	(43)
World Bridge	2	169	(40)
World Castle	2	169	(40)
World Champion	2	390	(55)
World Creation	4	48	(90)
World Discoverer	20	282	(479)
World Lynx	13	97	(358)†
World Process	2	437	(58)
World Prodigy	2	437	(58)
World Produce	2	437	(58)
World Progress	2	202	(42)
World Prologue	2	437	(58)
World Prophet	2	437	(58)
World Renaissance	20	259	(478)
World Sea	2	530	(64)
World Sky	4	43	(90)
Worldtrend 2	8	575	(247)
World Vigour	4	48	(90)
World Wood	7	275	(176)
World Xanadu	2	208	(43)
Worthing	6	126	(154)†
Worthing	6	19	(142)
Wouri	8	423	(236)
Wu Chang	9	55	(267)
Wu Jiang	8	24	(205)
Wu Lin	7	226	(173)
Wumen	8	41	(206)
Wu Sheng Hai	7	33	(159)
Wu Tai Shan	9	12	(264)
Wu Tong Shan	8	94	(210)
Wu Yi Shan	8	501	(241)
Wyoming	2	339	(51)
Wyszkow	10	11	(287)
Xandrina	6	21	(142)
Xia Chi	2	155	(39)
Xiamen	8	41	(206)
Xiang Cheng	7	406	(186)
Xiang Hai	2	427	(57)
Xiang He	9	10	(264)
Xiang Jiang	8	560	(246)
Xiang Yang	8	244	(222)
Xiao Shi Kou	18	175	(435)
Xiao Wang II	2	24	(30)
Xifias	8	445	(237)
Xin An	8	76	(209)
Xin An Jiang	8	273	(225)
Xin Chang	9	117	(272)
Xindu	7	47	(160)
Xinfeng	8	103	(211)
Xin Feng	8	319	(228)
Xing Chang	5	2	(107)
Xing Cheng	9	110	(271)
Xing Hai	7	52	(160)
Xing Hai He	12	120	(334)
Xing Hu	20	336	(484)
Xing Li	7	74	(162)
Xing Long	8	633	(251)
Xing Long	9	47	(266)
Xing Su Hai	7	105	(164)
Xing Ye 1	8	281	(225)
Xin Hai Hua	7	422	(187)
Xin Hai Teng	8	500	(241)
Xin Ji	8	632	(251)
Xin Jian Zhen	20	101	(466)
Xin Long Jiang	8	354	(230)
Xin Tong	9	10	(264)
Xinyang	8	492	(240)
Xiong Er Shan	8	308	(227)
Xiong Yue Cheng	8	394	(233)
Xi Qiao Shan	8	286	(225)
Xi Shan	8	589	(248)
Xiu Shan	14	17	(366)
Xour Gemini	7	445	(189)
Xour Ina	7	445	(189)
Xour Singapore	10	5	(287)
Xour Tinggi	12	157	(337)
Xove	6	14	(142)
Xuan Cheng	8	24	(205)
Xue Feng Ling	7	243	(174)
Yacu Puma	9	221	(282)†
Yacu Wayo	8	497	(241)
Ya Feng	8	521	(243)
Yakob Kunder	7	324	(180)
Yakov Bondarenko	9	92	(270)
Yakov Reznichenko	7	324	(180)
Yakov Sverdlov	1	107	(10)
Yakub Kolas	7	340	(181)
Yamato	5	353	(133)†
Ya Mawlaya	5	72	(112)
Yamilah	1	158	(13)
Yana	8	612	(250)
Yan An Wu Hao	8	75	(209)
Yan Cheng	8	123	(212)
Yan Fu	8	369	(231)
Yang Cheng	8	436	(236)
Yang Cheng	8	492	(240)
Yanglin	8	547	(245)
Yang Ming Shan	5	177	(119)
Yang Yang	8	481	(240)
Yang Zi Jiang 3	9	3	(263)
Yang Zi Jiang 4	8	617	(250)
Yan Hu	2	183	(41)
Yanis Lentsmanis	11	82	(306)
Yanis Raynis	11	82	(306)
Yanka Kupala	7	340	(181)
Yanmen	8	41	(206)
Yannis	8	169	(216)
Yan Shan	9	144	(274)
Yantarnyy Bereg	11	100	(308)
Yanting	8	561	(246)
Yan Tong	12	55	(329)
Yan Xing	14	3	(365)
Ya Rab	8	149	(214)
Ya Samadu	8	24	(205)
Yasemin S	4	119	(95)
Yasena	7	282	(177)
Yasha Gordiyenko	8	239	(222)
Yassmin M	8	619	(250)
Yaya	2	474	(60)
Yayasan Dua	8	38	(206)
Yayasan Enam	8	38	(206)
Yayasan Lapan	8	38	(206)
Yayasan Lima	8	38	(206)
Yayasan Satu	8	38	(206)
Yayasan Tiga	8	38	(206)
Yayasan Tujuh	8	38	(206)
Ya Zhou Hai	5	175	(119)
Yekaterinburg	15	47	(381)
Ye Lan	7	297	(178)
Yelena Shatrova	7	14	(158)
Yellow Island	5	178	(119)
Yemaya	7	132	(166)
Yemelyan Pugachev	5	131	(116)
Yemelyan Yaroslavskiy	9	57	(267)
Yenakiyevo	5	188	(120)
Yenisei	7	133	(166)
Yenisey	15	47	(381)
Yeniseysk	2	26	(30)
Yenotayevsk	15	47	(381)
Yeoman Bank	10	76	(294)†
Yeoman Brook	10	99	(296)†
Yepifan Kovtyukh	2	469	(60)
Yerimu	21	26	(501)
Yesilada	20	364	(486)
Yesilkoy 1	2	287	(47)
Yesim 1	2	162	(40)
Yevgeniy Chaplanov	8	612	(250)
Yevgeniy Nikonov	7	324	(180)
Yevgeniy Onufriev	7	324	(180)
Yevgeniy Onufriyev	7	515	(196)†
Yevgeniy Titov	1	20	(4)
Ye Xing	8	156	(215)
Yeyskiy Liman	11	149	(312)
Ygia	8	170	(216)
Yiannis P	8	575	(247)
Yick Hua	7	145	(167)
Yick Jia	5	282	(127)
Yick Kam	5	216	(122)
Yi Hai	7	126	(165)
Yimen	8	41	(206)
Yi Ming	7	68	(161)
Yin Chuan	9	112	(271)
Yin Feng	8	446	(237)
Ying Ge Hai	7	283	(177)
Ying Kou	7	339	(181)
Ying You Shan	8	57	(208)
Ying Zhou	8	626	(251)
Yin Shan Hai	7	83	(162)
Yi Rong	7	68	(161)
Yiufa	7	284	(177)
Yi Yang	8	86	(210)
Y Lan	8	589	(248)
Yong An	7	479	(192)
Yong Feng Hai	8	452	(238)
Yong Jiang	8	560	(246)
Yong Jin	8	269	(224)

†Photograph

	SHIP TYPE	REF NO	PAGE NO
Yongmen	8	41	(206)
Yong Nian	8	519	(243)
Yong Qing	8	563	(246)
Yongshun	8	560	(246)
Yong Tong	8	305	(227)
Yon Pung Ho	9	233	(283)†
Yordan Lutibrodski	5	105	(114)
Yordan Lutibrodski	7	139	(166)
York	5	213	(122)
Yorkgate	7	139	(166)
Yorksand	11	135	(311)
You Liang	7	199	(171)
You Mei	7	199	(171)
Youming	7	197	(171)
Young Sportsman	9	97	(270)
You Sheng	7	199	(171)
Youth Strong	10	45	(290)
You Xuan	7	241	(174)
You Yi 16	7	396	(186)
You Yi 28	7	396	(186)
You Yue	7	207	(171)
Ypapadi	7	205	(171)
Ytong 1	18	150	(433)
Yuan Da	8	39	(206)
Yuan Dong I	9	159	(275)
Yuan He	12	11	(325)
Yuanjiang	8	383	(232)
Yuan Ming	8	527	(243)
Yu Cai	8	497	(241)
Yucatan	12	59	(329)
Yue Lu Shan	7	130	(166)
Yue Xiu Shan	6	17	(142)
Yue Yang	6	17	(142)
Yueyang	8	492	(240)
Yue Yang	8	500	(241)
Yugla	2	222	(44)
Yuho Maru I	2	275	(47)
Yu Hong	8	87	(210)
Yuhsei Maru	1	102	(9)
Yu Hua	8	608	(250)
Yu Liang Shan	8	333	(229)
Yulin	8	547	(245)
Yulius Fuchik	21	100	(509)†
Yulius Fuchik	21	41	(502)
Yu May	5	60	(111)
Yu Mei	20	348	(485)
Yu Men	8	518	(243)
Yu Nam No 6	8	216	(220)
Yun Cheng	7	406	(186)
Yunda	15	47	(381)
Yun Feng Ling	7	60	(161)
Yun Hai	8	571	(247)
Yun Ling	8	46	(207)
Yun Long	8	473	(239)
Yuo Xiu	7	207	(171)
Yu Qiang	8	41	(206)
Yu Qing	8	483	(240)
Yuriy Arshenenskiy	17	27	(407)
Yuriy Krimov	7	152	(167)
Yuriy Levitan	12	109	(333)
Yuriy Maksaryov	16	14	(392)
Yuriy Ostrovskiy	13	38	(352)
Yuriy Savinov	8	78	(209)
Yuriy Smirnov	16	13	(392)
Yusr	9	66	(268)
Yusuf Ziya Onis	18	156	(433)
Yusup K	1	181	(15)
Yuta Bondarovskaya	8	621	(251)
Yuting	8	561	(246)
Yutoku Maru	3	11	(75)
Yu Tsao II	1	80	(8)
Yu Ying	8	483	(240)
Yuyo Breeze	2	498	(62)
Yvette	8	453	(238)
Zabaykalsk	8	589	(248)
Zabaykalye	11	172	(313)
Zaccar	2	490	(61)
Z-Adalet	2	593	(72)†
Zadar	1	136	(11)
Zadonsk	5	314	(129)
Zaglebie Miedziowe	5	314	(129)
Zaglebie Siarkowe	1	196	(16)
Zagreb Express	12	179	(340)†
Zahari Stoianov	7	174	(169)
Zaher II	8	301	(227)
Zaher III	17	41	(408)
Zain Al-Qaws	11	97	(308)
Zakaria	6	1	(141)
Zakarpatye	5	314	(129)
Zaks Diklo	2	424	(57)
Zalco Pioneer	8	500	(241)
Zalco Shariff	8	24	(205)
Zalgiris	2	414	(56)
Zallaq	4	55	(91)

	SHIP TYPE	REF NO	PAGE NO
Zambrow	8	123	(212)
Zamet	8	410	(234)
Zaneta	1	197	(16)
Zanet II	8	26	(205)
Zangelan	2	171	(41)
Zanis Griva	1	181	(15)
Zanoobia	8	173	(216)
Zante	2	263	(46)
Zaporozhye	5	314	(129)
Zara	8	16	(204)
Zara	8	24	(205)
Zara	8	130	(213)
Zarechensk	5	314	(129)
Zarka	8	311	(228)
Zarnesti	8	50	(207)
Zarnista	15	47	(381)
Zarya	15	47	(381)
Zavyety Ilyicha	2	514	(63)
Zawichost	8	123	(212)
Zawrat	2	408	(56)
Zebbug	18	138	(432)
Zeinat	2	397	(55)
Zelenga	15	47	(381)
Zenatia	2	511	(63)
Zenith	8	500	(241)
Zenith	20	62	(463)
Zeno	7	50	(160)
Zenovia	7	489	(193)†
Zephyros	8	445	(237)
Zeralda	20	311	(482)
Zeran	16	89	(400)†
Zeran	16	25	(393)
Zeravna	7	358	(183)
Zeta	8	80	(209)
Zetagas	4	89	(93)
Zeyales	8	596	(249)
Zeynep K	7	60	(161)
Zgorzelec	10	11	(287)
Zhan Qiong No 1	7	312	(179)
Zhao Yang Hai	7	33	(159)
Zhe Hai 717	8	131	(213)
Zhemchuznyy Bereg	11	99	(308)
Zheng He	20	348	(485)
Zhen Hai	8	40	(206)
Zhenjiang	8	58	(208)
Zhen Xing	8	618	(250)
Zhe Yan	7	342	(181)
Zhe Yan	9	46	(266)
Zhi Hai	8	452	(238)
Zhi Jiang Kou	18	175	(435)
Zhi Kong	8	24	(205)
Zhi Luo Lan	20	375	(487)
Zhitomir	17	51	(409)
Zhong Fa	9	113	(271)
Zhong He	12	11	(325)
Zhong Shan	8	532	(244)
Zhong Yuan	20	323	(483)
Zhuang He	12	89	(331)
Zhu Feng Shan	7	365	(183)
Ziemia Bialostocka	5	269	(126)
Ziemia Chelminska	5	290	(127)
Ziemia Gnieznienska	5	290	(127)
Ziemia Krakowska	5	314	(129)
Ziemia Lubelska	5	314	(129)
Ziemia Olsztynska	5	269	(126)
Ziemia Suwalska	5	290	(127)
Ziemia Tarnowska	5	290	(127)
Ziemia Zamojska	5	290	(127)
Zi Jin Shan	8	531	(244)
Zilina	7	433	(188)
Zim Alexandria	12	94	(332)
Zim America	12	42	(328)
Zim Argentina	13	6	(349)
Zim Australia	13	44	(352)
Zim Brasil II	7	485	(192)
Zim Canada	12	42	(328)
Zim Colombia	15	45	(381)
Zim Constanta	5	111	(115)
Zim Elat	12	88	(331)
Zim Espana	7	302	(178)
Zim Haifa	12	94	(332)
Zim Hong Kong	12	42	(328)
Zim Iberia	12	43	(328)
Zim Israel	12	42	(328)
Zim Itajai	7	286	(177)
Zim Italia	12	42	(328)
Zim Jamaica	12	99	(332)
Zim Japan	12	42	(328)
Zim Kaohsiung	12	157	(337)
Zim Keelung	12	43	(328)
Zim Korea	12	42	(328)
Zim Livorno	12	117	(333)
Zim Manila III	12	193	(341)†
Zim Melbourne	12	82	(331)
Zim Mexico	8	396	(234)
Zim Napoli	5	98	(114)

†Photograph

	SHIP TYPE	REF NO	PAGE NO
Zim New York	7	286	(177)
Zimnicea	8	50	(207)
Zim Odessa	12	68	(330)
Zim Osaka	12	90	(331)
Zim Paraguay	13	20	(350)
Zim Pusan	12	175	(339)†
Zim Pusan	12	117	(333)
Zim Rio	7	286	(177)
Zim San Juan	13	17	(350)
Zim Santos	7	286	(177)
Zim Savannah	12	43	(328)
Zim Texas	7	434	(188)
Zim Tokyo	12	94	(332)
Zim Uruguay	13	36	(351)
Zim Valencia	12	77	(330)
Zim Venezia	12	88	(331)
Zim Yokohama	12	90	(331)
Zina	2	150	(39)
Zina Portnova	8	621	(251)
Zini	8	149	(214)
Ziya K	7	84	(162)
Zi Yu Lan	20	42	(462)
Zlarin	8	517	(242)
Zlatograd	7	358	(183)
Zlatoust	5	314	(129)
Znamya Oktyabrya	15	36	(380)
Znamya Oktyabrya	16	13	(392)
Zorinsk	5	314	(129)
Zouzou	5	142	(117)
Zoya Kosmodemyanskaya	5	193	(120)
Zugdidi	2	414	(56)
Zulawy	11	7	(301)
Zulfikar	8	24	(205)
Zuljenah	8	24	(205)
Zura Bhum	12	26	(327)
Zvenigorod	5	314	(129)
Zvyozdnyy Bereg	11	98	(308)
Zwanet	6	34	(143)
Zygmunt August	8	154	(215)
Zygmunt III Waza	8	154	(215)
Zygmunt Stary	8	154	(215)

†Photograph